PROCESSES OF CONSTITUTIONAL DECISIONMAKING

PROCESSES OF CONSTITUTIONAL DECISIONMAKING
Cases and Materials

Fifth Edition

Paul Brest
Professor, Stanford Law School
and President,
William and Flora Hewlett Foundation

Sanford Levinson
W. St. John Garwood & W. St. John Garwood, Jr.
Regents Chair in Law
University of Texas

Jack M. Balkin
Knight Professor of Constitutional Law
and the First Amendment
Yale Law School

Akhil Reed Amar
Southmayd Professor of Law
Yale Law School

Reva B. Siegel
Nicholas deB. Katzenbach Professor of Law
Yale Law School

ASPEN
PUBLISHERS

76 Ninth Avenue, New York, NY 10011
http://lawschool.aspenpublishers.com

© 2006 Aspen Publishers, Inc.
a Wolters Kluwer business
http://lawschool.aspenpublishers.com

Aspen Publishers
Attn: Permissions Department
76 Ninth Avenue, 7th Floor
New York, NY 10011-5201

Printed in the United States of America.

1 2 3 4 5 6 7 8 9 0

ISBN 0-7355-5062-X

Library of Congress Cataloging-in-Publication Data

Processes of constitutional decisionmaking : cases and materials / Paul Brest . . . [et al.]. — 5th ed.
    p. cm.
   Includes bibliographical references and index.
   ISBN 0-7355-5062-X (alk. paper)
   1. Constitutional law—United States—Cases. 2. Judicial review—United States—Cases. 3. Separation of powers—United States—Cases. I. Brest, Paul.

KF4549.B74 2006
342.73—dc22   2006003927

About Aspen Publishers

Aspen Publishers, headquartered in New York City, is a leading information provider for attorneys, business professionals, and law students. Written by preeminent authorities, our products consist of analytical and practical information covering both U.S. and international topics. We publish in the full range of formats, including updated manuals, books, periodicals, CDs, and online products.

Our proprietary content is complemented by 2,500 legal databases, containing over 11 million documents, available through our Loislaw division. Aspen Publishers also offers a wide range of topical legal and business databases linked to Loislaw's primary material. Our mission is to provide accurate, timely, and authoritative content in easily accessible formats, supported by unmatched customer care.

To order any Aspen Publishers title, go to *http://lawschool.aspenpublishers.com* or call 1-800-638-8437.

To reinstate your manual update service, call 1-800-638-8437.

For more information on Loislaw products, go to *www.loislaw.com* or call 1-800-364-2512.

For Customer Care issues, e-mail *CustomerCare@aspenpublishers.com*; call 1-800-234-1660; or fax 1-800-901-9075.

Aspen Publishers
a Wolters Kluwer business

To Iris, Hilary, and Jeremy
for the countless hours discussing
the issues in this book — P.B.

To Robert G. McCloskey,
a wonderful teacher and mentor many years ago;
to my colleagues and friends for the past two decades
at the University of Texas Law School;
and to the members of various Internet listservs
who constantly remind me
of the complexities of constitutional analysis — S.L.

To my parents,
Bernard and Bettye Balkin,
who gave me their love
and an education in the law — J.B.

To my students for their inspiration
and to my family — Vinita and Vikram, mom and dad,
mummy and poppa, brothers and sisters —
for their sustenance — A.R.A.

To Yale, my nephew and my students,
in the belief that possibility lives in memory — R.S.

Summary of Contents

Contents

Chapter 2
The Marshall Court and the Early Republic   97

Chapter 6
The Burdens of History: The Constitutional Treatment of Race 893

Chapter 7
Sex Equality 1179

Chapter 8
Implied Fundamental Rights: The Constitution, the Family,
and the Body

Chapter 9
The Constitution in the Modern Welfare State   1593

Preface

Our fifth edition brings many changes, among which the most important is the addition of a new editor, Reva Siegel. Paul Brest, the Founding Father of this particular exercise in constitutionalism, retired from active participation in the casebook after the third edition, but he deserves full credit for the remarkable innovativeness of his original 1975 edition and for helping maintain its adventurous and innovative spirit over the years. All of us acknowledge the importance of his example, and we have worked hard to preserve that spirit in what is now the casebook's fifth — quite revised and quite different — edition.

Every casebook involves the construction of a canon — a set of materials and approaches that the editors believe that every student who wishes to master the subject should know. This casebook is no exception. Indeed, we have been particularly conscious of the existing canons of constitutional thought and the kinds of choices that are involved both in the materials presented and in their editing, order, and arrangement. The history of this casebook has been a series of continuing attempts to rethink the existing canon of constitutional law and present a better one. This edition represents our latest views on the subject.

The history of this casebook

The first edition of Processes of Constitutional Decisionmaking, published in 1975, was born out of personal frustration with the existing methods of teaching constitutional law. Invariably beginning with Marbury v. Madison and introductory sections on judicial review, most casebooks proceeded to examine bodies of substantive doctrine, subject by subject. The question of *how* the courts arrived at their decisions continually arose but was not systematically examined. Nor did casebooks explore the role that legislatures, the executive, and other political institutions (for example, political parties and social movements) played in constitutional decisionmaking. The unspoken and repeated message was that the Constitution was largely what the Supreme Court said it was, and if that Court had not spoken on a particular subject, there was no constitutional law on the question at all.

The first edition, therefore, focused on the methodology of decisionmaking and constitutional interpretation that different actors in the system employed and on the different processes through which constitutional doctrine was created. Although much has changed in the book's coverage over the years, this basic focus on the methods of constitutional interpretation and on the multiple groups and institutions that participate in the creation of constitutional meaning has remained a constant.

The second edition, published in 1983, reflected the lessons learned from teaching the first edition as well as the interests of its new co-editor, Sanford Levinson. As before, the casebook continued to focus on constitutional law and constitutional interpretations made by nonjudicial institutions. However, beginning with the second edition, the opening half of the book has been explicitly organized on historical-chronological lines, so that students would confront the legal conscious-ness of a particular period in the context of several different constitutional doctrines. The third edition, published in 1992, added chapters and sections that were organized functionally (e.g., The Constitution in Time of War, Representation Within a Republican Polity, The Constitution in the Welfare State), as well as chap-ters that reflected traditional doctrinal categories (e.g., Classifications Based on Sex). The fourth edition, published in 2000, consolidated this basic approach.

The organization of the casebook

In this, the fifth edition, we have continued to benefit from classroom experi-ence. The book is divided into two parts. Part One is organized historically accord-ing to periods—The Marshall Court, the Taney Court and the Civil War, and the age of industrialization running from Reconstruction to the New Deal. Part One examines recurring constitutional issues of federalism, property rights, racial and sexual equality, governmental (and, more particularly, presidential) authority in time of war, treatment of "subversive" speech, and judicial review.

The materials within each of these periods cover different subjects and doctrines but together reflect the constitutional regimes and political realities that underlie virtually all important constitutional questions in a given era. Thus, for example, we think it is impossible to understand the *Lochner* era's substantive due process deci-sions apart from its decisions about the commerce power or the taxing and spend-ing powers. Nor can one understand the nineteenth century's treatment of women's rights apart from its understandings about race, or either apart from that era's understanding of federalism and national power.

The book's historical organization in Part One ends with the pivotal year of 1937, which marks the boundary that inaugurates the "modern" period in American constitutional law. In the chapters covering material after 1937—which constitute Part Two of the casebook — our organization is topical and doctrinal in a more conventional sense. Chapter 5 begins with an essay on the Bill of Rights and the controversies over its incorporation, including an extended discussion of the Second Amendment. Chapter 5 also features sections on modern economic regula-tion, the taxing and spending powers, Congressional power under the Civil War amendments, federalism, and separation of powers, including expanded coverage of war and executive power. Chapter 6 covers racial equality, Chapter 7 sex equality, and Chapter 8 implied fundamental rights (including abortion, sexual autonomy, sexual orientation, and medical decisionmaking).

The next chapter (Chapter 9) on The Constitution in the Welfare State retains the more functional approach of previous editions. It covers the problem of proce-dural due process, affirmative liberties (like education and the rights of the poor), and the problem of conditional subsidies, sometimes called the problem of "uncon-stitutional conditions." Chapter 9 is organized in this way because we think that it is important for students to understand the welfare state as a central constitutional structure of our own era that transcends traditional doctrinal categories. For the fifth edition we have moved the materials on alienage from Chapter 9 to the

chapter on racial equality, in part because historically the government's treatment
of aliens has often been intertwined with its treatment of race and national origin.

Our organization in this edition marks a division between pre-1937 constitutional
law, historically organized, and post-1937, or "modern," constitutional law, organized
by doctrinal topic. Nevertheless, we predict that the period we now call "modern"
will, in time, be recognized as having a similar unity to previous periods, and that
someday it too may deserve a historical treatment. Already the innovations of the
Warren Court, the Civil Rights movement, and the second wave of American feminism in the 1970s seem distant to most law students; they have become historical arti-
facts, much like the struggle over the New Deal seemed to the generation that came
of age in the 1960s and 1970s. In particular, we have noted how the legal consciousness that underlies much of the Supreme Court's work following 1937 has slowly
given way to new conceptions of federal power, race relations, and civil liberties. The
rise of conservative social movements in the 1970s and 1980s, and the dominance of
the Republican Party that they helped engender, have had multiple effects in constitutional law, perhaps in no small part because of a series of Republican appointments
to the Supreme Court and the lower federal courts. Many have speculated that the
September 11 attacks and the War on Terror they inaugurated will have far-reaching
effects on the Constitution, civil liberties, and the scope of executive power. Only
time will tell, of course; we will not understand the full ramifications of these changes
until long after this edition is published. Nevertheless, we have deliberately structured this casebook with an eye to placing contemporary events in their historical
perspective, continually asking the student to compare them to constitutional transformations and upheavals of the past. This basic strategy, we hope, will help students
take the longer view of the ebb and flow of American constitutional culture, as well as
the key role that social movements and political parties play in shaping that culture.

Our historical approach

Although we have worked to make the present edition compatible with many
different ways of organizing a basic course in constitutional law, we nevertheless
retain a strong commitment to a historical sensibility. Even in materials that are
doctrinally organized, we have tried to highlight the social and political context in
which constitutional decisionmaking occurs. A historical approach, we believe, has
virtues that are lost in a purely clause-bound approach to constitutional law.

In particular, we think it is important for students to recognize that notions of
what constitutes a good or persuasive constitutional argument have changed and
will continue to change over time. Arguments that might have seemed perfectly
reasonable for well-trained lawyers in one period can seem bizarre or "off-the-wall"
in earlier or later periods. Arguments that seem to have been written off for good
(like the compact theory of state sovereignty) uncannily reemerge in new guises a
century later. Visionary claims of social movements that would be rejected by all
right-thinking lawyers of the period become the accepted orthodoxy of later eras.
The ideological valance of arguments—as "liberal" or "conservative," moderate or
radical—also drifts as arguments are introduced or repeated in new social and
legal contexts. Finally, the popularity and persuasiveness of different styles of constitutional argument—for example, textualism or originalism—wax and wane with
historical and social change and with concomitant changes in the legal profession.

There is, in short, no transhistorical criterion for "thinking like a constitutional lawyer," other than an abiding faith in the basic constitutional enterprise. There is no better way to demonstrate this, we think, than to let students confront the actual texts produced in different periods and study closely the "common sense" and authoritative legal arguments of the past, witnessing both their strangeness and their resemblance to the constitutional common sense of our own day.

One of the reasons why constitutional argument changes as it does is that the practice of constitutional reasoning is deeply connected to changes in political and social life. Although courts play a central role in the history of constitutional law, other parties play roles equally important in shaping constitutional meaning. Our understandings of the American Constitution would have been very different without Jacksonianism, abolitionism, the Civil War, the feminist movement, the New Deal, the Civil Rights movement, and the Religious Right. For this reason, we have included constitutional arguments from the executive and legislative branches of government, as well as constitutional interpretations offered by representatives of important social movements in the country's history, and the groups that mobilized against them. And we have repeatedly tried to stress the connections between what occurs in the language of court opinions and the political and social events that surround those decisions.

Finally, we continue to emphasize a historical approach to understand our debt to the past, both in terms of our moral successes and our moral failures. From the second edition on, Processes of Constitutional Decisionmaking has contained far more sustained coverage of chattel slavery than any other casebook. We think that, as a doctrinal matter, the question of slavery haunts the whole of antebellum constitutional law and that the legacy of slavery affects the great issues of federalism and equality that came later. But we think it is equally important for law students to confront slavery precisely because everyone now recognizes it to have been a great evil. It was a great evil that was sustained and perpetuated through law and, in particular, through constitutional law as interpreted by the finest legal minds America had to offer. Law students must come to understand how well-trained lawyers acting in good faith could have participated in such a system and rationalized it according to well-accepted modes of legal argument, justifying their work in the name of America's great charter of democracy, liberty, and equality. We think that if they can recognize this use of law in America's constitutional past, they will be better equipped to ask themselves the much more difficult question of whether well-trained lawyers in our own era could be similarly engaged in the rationalization of great injustices in the name of our Constitution, even though there may be great disagreement about what these are. The goal of a historically informed approach is not merely to see the achievements and injustices of the past through our own eyes, but to remind us to consider how our present interpretations of the Constitution might look to future generations.

Constructing the constitutional canon

Our commitment to a historical approach is joined to an equally strong commitment to rethinking the canons of constitutional law—the materials, issues, and problems that law students are exposed to and that law professors write and theorize about. To this end, we have added materials on the Progressive Era amendments, the constitutional controversy surrounding the adoption of paper money, the procedural irregularities surrounding the adoption of the Fourteenth Amendment, America's constitutional treatment of Native Americans, and America's role as a colonial power. We have expanded coverage of the history of the women's movement and the constitutional treatment of women from the antebellum era to the adoption of the Nineteenth Amendment to the struggles over the Equal Rights Amendment and beyond. We think that these additions will give students a richer and fuller vision of constitutional history. They also pose genuine and interesting challenges for constitutional theorists who have neglected important aspects of constitutional interpretation and constitutional decisionmaking because traditional approaches offer much too narrow a view of the relevant materials that must be explained and justified.

If there is one theme that runs through this book, it is that the Supreme Court is not the only interpreter of the Constitution, even if it is surely the most obvious and important one for most lawyers. This view is clearly reflected in our construction of the canon. Throughout the book, we take seriously constitutional decisionmaking by nonjudicial institutions by including materials ranging from resolutions by the Kentucky and Virginia legislatures in the late eighteenth century, to constitutional interpretations by the President and Congress of the United States, to constitutional assertions by social movements, such as the Seneca Falls Declaration of 1848, to constitutional arguments by particular individuals such as senatorial candidates Abraham Lincoln and Stephen Douglas, the noted abolitionist Frederick Douglass, and civil rights pioneer Pauli Murray. Indeed, far from being the only source of constitutional law, the Supreme Court is not even the only judicial source. In this edition we have included more constitutional arguments by lower federal courts, by state supreme courts (often interpreting analogous provisions of state constitutions), and even a few references to the constitutions of other countries.

Among the most important elements of the Constitution are structural features that are rarely litigated, including, among others, bicameralism, equal voting power in the Senate, and the presidential veto. Lawyers pay little attention to them because they are rarely litigated and so little judicial doctrine has developed around them. Nevertheless, these choices are crucial features of constitutional design and the political science literature that studies their consequences is considerable. We have tried to raise a few issues of constitutional design where appropriate, but given the natural focus of a law school casebook, we can do no more than hint at some of the more important questions these provisions raise.

Just as any construction of a constitutional canon involves incorporation and inclusion of some materials, it must also include selection and exclusion of others. As constitutional law has grown in richness and complexity over the years, it has become increasingly difficult to do justice to the field within the pages of a single casebook. Fortunately, new technologies increasingly allow us to escape the limitations of traditional forms of publication. Thus, we have placed parts of our teaching materials on a special Web site, *http://www.conlaw.net*. There readers will find special topics and materials that they can download and use to supplement the materials found in the casebook. Through this combination of Web site and traditional text, we hope to create a flexible set of teaching materials that can respond better to future changes in the field.

The organization of any casebook is inevitably ideological, especially in a subject as fraught with ideology as constitutional law. No approach to the study of constitutional law is independent of the instructors' or casebook editors' more general intellectual and political interests. For example, we have already noted the amount of space devoted to the question of slavery, which reflects our view that the question of slavery pervaded American law before the Civil War and that its aftermath set the stage for epic social and constitutional struggles that show no signs of abating to this day. We have also emphasized the role of textual and structural argument in constitutional interpretation, as well as the centrality of social movements and political parties as engines of constitutional change.

The first edition of Processes of Constitutional Decisionmaking explicitly adopted the ideology of the legal process tradition identified with Albert Sacks and Henry Hart, who were especially influential teachers at the Harvard Law School following World War II (and with whom Paul Brest studied during the early 1960s). Hart and Sacks argued that there existed apolitical decisionmaking procedures, adherence to which could provide substantively acceptable and politically legitimate decisions. Although the validity of this hypothesis remains a central concern of this book — for it is a crucial matter about which every student must come to his or her own judgment — the second edition (and its successors) manifested considerable skepticism about the legitimating power of process divorced from larger substantive political values. Nothing that has happened since 1981, when the second edition was prepared, has lessened our skepticism.

The Constitution does not belong to the lawyers, to the politicians, or even to the judges. It belongs to everyone. And the Constitution matters and should matter to everyone, even if arguments about the Constitution are not always phrased in the proper constitutional grammar recognized by legal professionals. Our era, like those before it, is a time of vigorous debate about the central constitutional issues of American life. In this book we have tried to bring out the political and social assumptions of contemporary constitutional discourse and contemporary constitutional decisionmaking. We have tried to show where these assumptions originated and how they have been transformed through time. But, of course, for every assumption that is consciously illuminated, others remain hidden in the shadows. You will get the most out of a course taught from this casebook if you take its agendas seriously while keeping a sharp eye out for its unstated assumptions. For our part, the student we seek is not one who necessarily agrees with us, but one who is willing to engage critically with us and, in the process, to learn and grow.

Acknowledgments

Sanford Levinson wishes to express his continued gratitude to his University of Texas Law School colleagues, including Philip Bobbitt, Doug Laycock, Scot Powe, and Jordan Steiker. Deans Michael Sharlot and William Powers have also continued the tradition of providing the author with ample support to attend conferences and other events necessary to thinking and rethinking about what ought to be covered in a basic casebook. Levinson also wishes to emphasize the continued help given, now over many years, by his superb secretary Cheryl Harris. He also acknowledges the contributions of Mark Tushnet, not only for his stimulating scholarship but, just as importantly in this context, for his organization over a decade ago of what is affectionately known as the "Georgetown Schmooze," which has provided a principal venue for testing new ideas and receiving the wisdom of others. Similarly, Eugene Volokh deserves special mention for his indefatigable energy in organizing Internet discussion groups, the results of which are reflected in several explicit discussion notes, not to mention the far wider impact of the day-by-day discussions with a marvelously diverse group of people whom the author is especially pleased to recognize in the dedication.

Jack Balkin wishes to thank Bruce Ackerman, Lisa Cardyn, Michael Kavey, Christina Rodriguez, Bill Rubenstein, Teemu Ruskola, Reva Siegel, and Kenji Yoshino for their help and suggestions.

Akhil Amar wishes to thank Bruce Ackerman, Vikram David Amar, Neal Kumar Katyal, and Jed Rubenfeld for their comments and Lisa Berman and Josh Chafetz for their research assistance.

Reva Siegel wishes to thank Jack Balkin, Cary Franklin, Abigail Horn, Serena Mayeri, Robert Post, Alan Schoenfeld, David Tannenbaum, and Nels Ylitello for their help and suggestions

All of the authors have also benefited from the responses of a number of friends at other institutions. They include, especially, Milner Ball (who pressed the claims of Native Americans to be treated as an important part of the American constitutional narrative), Walter Dellinger (who initially suggested including material from the Lincoln-Douglas debates), Paul Finkelman, Lewis LaRue, Peter Linzer, Robert Post, and Stephen Siegel.

reserved. Reprinted by permission of the UCLA Law Review and Fred B. Rothman and Co.

Balkin, J.M., The Constitution of Status, 106 Yale L.J. 2313 (1997). Reprinted by permission of the Yale Law Review.

Balkin, J.M., Tradition, Betrayal, and the Politics of Deconstruction. This article appeared in 11 Cardozo L. Rev. 1613 (July/Aug. 1990). Reprinted by permission of the author and Cardozo Law Review.

Balkin, J.M., Roe v. Wade: An Engine of Controversy, in Jack M. Balkin, ed., What Roe v. Wade Should Have Said, N.Y.U. Press 2001. Reprinted by permission of the author.

Bell, Derrick, Introduction: Awakening after *Bakke*, 14 Harv. C.P.-C.L. L. Rev. 1 (1979). Copyright © 1979 by the President and Fellows of Harvard College. Reprinted by permission of the Harvard Civil Rights-Civil Liberties Law Review.

Bickel, Alexander, The Original Understanding and the Segregation Decision, 69 Harv. L. Rev. 1 (1995). Copyright © 1955 by the Harvard Law Review Association. Reprinted by permission.

Bickel, Alexander, The Least Dangerous Branch. Copyright © 1962 by Bobbs-Merrill Company, Inc. Reprinted by permission of the Bobbs-Merrill Co.

Black, Charles, The Lawfulness of the Segregation Decisions, 69 Yale L.J. 421 (1960). Copyright © 1959. Reprinted by permission of the Yale Law Journal Company and Fred B. Rothman and Co.

Brest, Paul, The Misconceived Quest for the Original Understanding, 60 B.U. L. Rev. 204 (1980). Copyright © 1980. Reprinted by permission of the Boston University Law Review.

Brest, Paul, Palmer v. Thompson: An Approach to the Problem of Unconstitutional Legislative Motive, 1971 Sup. Ct. Rev. 95. Copyright © 1971 by the University of Chicago. Reprinted by permission of The University of Chicago Press.

Colker, Ruth, Anti-Subordination Above All: Sex, Race, and Equal Protection, 61 N.Y.U. L. Rev. 1003 (1986). Copyright © 1986. Reprinted by permission of the New York University Law Review.

Cox, Archibald, The Role of Congress in Constitutional Determinations, 40 U. Cin. L. Rev. 199 (1971). Reprinted by permission of Archibald Cox.

Dahl, Robert, Decision-Making in a Democracy: The Supreme Court as National Policy-Maker, 6 J. Pub. L. 279 (1957). Copyright © 1957. Reprinted by permission of the Journal of Public Law of Emory University School of Law.

Ely, John, Democracy and Distrust: A Theory of Judicial Review, from Democracy and Distrust: A Theory of Judicial Review by John Hart Ely, pp. 164-170, Cambridge, Mass.: Harvard University Press. Copyright © 1980 by the President and Fellows of Harvard College. Reprinted by permission of the publisher.

Fine, Sidney, Laissez Faire and the General Welfare State (1956). Copyright © 1956. Reprinted by permission of the University of Michigan Press.

Fuchs Epstein, Cynthia, Multiple Myths and Outcomes of Sex Segregation, 14 N.Y. L. Sch. J. Hum. Rts. 185 (1997). Reprinted by permission.

Grey, Robert, Procedural Fairness and Substantive Rights, from Due Process (Nomos XVIII) (1977). Copyright © 1977 by the New York University. Reprinted by permission of New York University Press.

Gunther, Gerald, Learned Hand and the Origins of Modern First Amendment Doctrine: Some Fragments of History, 27 Stan. L. Rev. 719 (1975). Copyright © 1975 by the Board of Trustees of the Leland Stanford Junior University. Reprinted by permission of the author and Fred B. Rothman and Co.

Editorial Note

Throughout this book, additions to and deletions from quoted material are indicated by brackets and ellipses except that (without notice) citations are modified and eliminated, footnotes are eliminated, and paragraphs are modified to make edited excerpts coherent. Footnote numbers in opinions and other quoted material have been changed to consecutive letters. The authors' own footnotes, including those inserted into quoted material and cases for purposes of editorial comment, are indicated by numbers, running consecutively through each chapter.

PROCESSES OF CONSTITUTIONAL DECISIONMAKING

The Constitution of the United States

We the People of the United States, in Order to form a more perfect Union, establish Justice, insure domestic Tranquility, provide for the common defense, promote the general Welfare, and secure the Blessings of Liberty to ourselves and our Posterity, do ordain and establish this Constitution for the United States of America.

ARTICLE I

Section 1. All legislative Powers herein granted shall be vested in a Congress of the United States, which shall consist of a Senate and House of Representatives.

Section 2. [1] The House of Representatives shall be composed of Members chosen every second Year by the People of the several States, and the Electors in each State shall have the Qualifications requisite for Electors of the most numerous Branch of the State Legislature.

[2] No Person shall be a Representative who shall not have attained to the Age of twenty five Years, and been seven Years a Citizen of the United States, and who shall not, when elected, be an Inhabitant of that State in which he shall be chosen.

[3] Representatives and direct Taxes shall be apportioned among the several States which may be included within this Union, according to their respective Numbers, which shall be determined by adding to the whole Number of free Persons, including those bound to Service for a Term of Years, and excluding Indians not taxed, three fifths of all other Persons.[1] The actual Enumeration shall be made within three Years after the first Meeting of the Congress of the United States, and within every subsequent Term of ten Years, in such Manner as they shall by Law direct. The Number of Representatives shall not exceed one for every thirty Thousand, but each State shall have at Least one Representative; and until such enumeration shall be made, the State of New Hampshire shall be entitled to chuse three, Massachusetts eight, Rhode-Island and Providence Plantations one, Connecticut five, New-York six, New Jersey four, Pennsylvania eight, Delaware one, Maryland six, Virginia ten, North Carolina five, South Carolina five, and Georgia three.

[4] When vacancies happen in the Representation from any State, the Executive Authority thereof shall issue Writs of Election to fill such Vacancies.

[5] The House of Representatives shall chuse their Speaker and other Officers; and shall have the sole Power of Impeachment.

Section 3. [1] The Senate of the United States shall be composed of two Senators from each State, chosen by the Legislature thereof,[2] for six Years; and each Senator shall have one Vote.

---

1. Changed by section 2 of the Fourteenth Amendment.
2. Changed by section 2 of the Seventeenth Amendment.

[2] Immediately after they shall be assembled in Consequence of the first Election, they shall be divided as equally as may be into three Classes. The Seats of the Senators of the first Class shall be vacated at the Expiration of the second Year, of the second Class at the Expiration of the fourth Year, and of the third Class at the Expiration of the sixth Year, so that one third may be chosen every second Year; and if Vacancies happen by Resignation, or otherwise, during the Recess of the Legislature of any State, the Executive thereof may make temporary Appointments until the next Meeting of the Legislature, which shall then fill such Vacancies.[3]

[3] No Person shall be a Senator who shall not have attained to the Age of thirty Years, and been nine Years a Citizen of the United States, and who shall not, when elected, be an Inhabitant of that State for which he shall be chosen.

[4] The Vice President of the United States shall be President of the Senate, but shall have no Vote, unless they be equally divided.

[5] The Senate shall chuse their other Officers, and also a President pro tempore, in the Absence of the Vice President, or when he shall exercise the Office of President of the United States.

[6] The Senate shall have the sole Power to try all Impeachments. When sitting for that Purpose, they shall be on Oath or Affirmation. When the President of the United States is tried, the Chief Justice shall preside: And no Person shall be convicted without the Concurrence of two thirds of the Members present.

[7] Judgment in Cases of Impeachment shall not extend further than to removal from Office, and disqualification to hold and enjoy any Office of honor, Trust or Profit under the United States: but the Party convicted shall nevertheless be liable and subject to Indictment, Trial, Judgment and Punishment, according to Law.

Section 4. [1] The Times, Places and Manner of holding Elections for Senators and Representatives, shall be prescribed in each State by the Legislature thereof; but the Congress may at any time by Law make or alter such Regulations, except as to the Places of chusing Senators.

[2] The Congress shall assemble at least once in every Year, and such Meeting shall be on the first Monday in December, unless they shall by Law appoint a different Day.[4]

Section 5. [1] Each House shall be the Judge of the Elections, Returns and Qualifications of its own Members, and a Majority of each shall constitute a Quorum to do Business; but a smaller Number may adjourn from day to day, and may be authorized to compel the Attendance of absent Members, in such Manner, and under such Penalties as each House may provide.

[2] Each House may determine the Rules of its Proceedings, punish its Members for disorderly Behaviour, and, with the Concurrence of two thirds, expel a Member.

[3] Each House shall keep a Journal of its Proceedings, and from time to time publish the same, excepting such Parts as may in their Judgment require Secrecy; and the Yeas and Nays of the Members of either House on any question shall, at the Desire of one fifth of those Present, be entered on the Journal.

[4] Neither House, during the Session of Congress, shall, without the Consent of the other, adjourn for more than three days, nor to any other Place than that in which the two Houses shall be sitting.

---

3. Changed by clause 2 of the Seventeenth Amendment.
4. Changed by section 2 of the Twentieth Amendment.

Section 6. [1] The Senators and Representatives shall receive a Compensation for their Services, to be ascertained by Law, and paid out of the Treasury of the United States. They shall in all Cases, except Treason, Felony and Breach of the Peace, be privileged from Arrest during their Attendance at the Session of their respective Houses, and in going to and returning from the same; and for any Speech or Debate in either House, they shall not be questioned in any other Place.

[2] No Senator or Representative shall, during the Time for which he was elected, be appointed to any civil Office under the Authority of the United States, which shall have been created, or the Emoluments whereof shall have been increased during such time; and no Person holding any Office under the United States, shall be a Member of either House during his Continuance in Office.

Section 7. [1] All Bills for raising Revenue shall originate in the House of Representatives; but the Senate may propose or concur with Amendments as on other Bills.

[2] Every Bill which shall have passed the House of Representatives and the Senate, shall, before it become a Law, be presented to the President of the United States: If he approve he shall sign it, but if not he shall return it, with his Objections to that House in which it shall have originated, who shall enter the Objections at large on their Journal, and proceed to reconsider it. If after such Reconsideration two thirds of that House shall agree to pass the Bill, it shall be sent, together with the Objections, to the other House, by which it shall likewise be reconsidered, and if approved by two thirds of that House, it shall become a Law. But in all such Cases the Votes of both Houses shall be determined by Yeas and Nays, and the Names of the Persons voting for and against the Bill shall be entered on the Journal of each House respectively. If any Bill shall not be returned by the President within ten Days (Sundays excepted) after it shall have been presented to him, the Same shall be a Law, in like Manner as if he had signed it, unless the Congress by their Adjournment prevent its Return, in which Case it shall not be a Law.

[3] Every Order, Resolution, or Vote to which the Concurrence of the Senate and House of Representatives may be necessary (except on a question of Adjournment) shall be presented to the President of the United States; and before the Same shall take Effect, shall be approved by him, or being disapproved by him, shall be repassed by two thirds of the Senate and House of Representatives, according to the Rules and Limitations prescribed in the Case of a Bill.

Section 8. [1] The Congress shall have Power To lay and collect Taxes, Duties, Imposts and Excises, to pay the Debts and provide for the common Defence and general Welfare of the United States; but all Duties, Imposts and Excises shall be uniform throughout the United States; [2] To borrow Money on the credit of the United States; [3] To regulate Commerce with foreign Nations, and among the several States, and with the Indian Tribes; [4] To establish an uniform Rule of Naturalization, and uniform Laws on the subject of Bankruptcies throughout the United States; [5] To coin Money, regulate the Value thereof, and of foreign Coin, and fix the Standard of Weights and Measures; [6] To provide for the Punishment of counterfeiting the Securities and current Coin of the United States; [7] To establish Post Offices and post Roads; [8] To promote the Progress of Science and useful Arts, by securing for limited Times to Authors and Inventors the exclusive Right to their respective Writings and Discoveries; [9] To constitute Tribunals inferior to the supreme Court; [10] To define and punish Piracies and Felonies committed on the high Seas, and Offences against the Law of Nations; [11] To declare War, grant Letters of Marque and Reprisal, and make Rules concerning Captures on Land and Water; [12] To raise and support Armies, but no Appropriation of Money to that Use shall be for a longer Term than two Years; [13] To provide and maintain a Navy; [14] To make Rules for the Government and Regulation of the land and naval Forces; [15] To provide for calling forth the Militia to execute the Laws of the Union, suppress Insurrections and repel Invasions; [16] To provide for organizing, arming, and disciplining, the Militia, and for governing such Part of them as may be employed in the Service of the United States, reserving to the States respectively, the Appointment of the Officers, and the Authority of training the Militia according to the discipline prescribed by Congress; [17] To exercise exclusive Legislation in all Cases whatsoever, over such District (not exceeding ten Miles square) as may, by Cession of particular States, and the Acceptance of Congress, become the Seat of the Government of the United States, and to exercise like Authority over all Places purchased by the Consent of the Legislature of the State in which the Same shall be, for the Erection of Forts, Magazines, Arsenals, dock-Yards, and other needful Buildings; — And [18] To make all Laws which shall be necessary and proper for carrying into Execution the forego- ing Powers, and all other Powers vested by this Constitution in the Government of the United States, or in any Department or Officer thereof.

Section 9. [1] The Migration or Importation of such Persons as any of the States now existing shall think proper to admit, shall not be prohibited by the Congress prior to the Year one thousand eight hundred and eight, but a Tax or duty may be imposed on such Importation, not exceeding ten dollars for each Person.

[2] The Privilege of the Writ of Habeas Corpus shall not be suspended, unless when in Cases of Rebellion or Invasion the public Safety may require it.

[3] No Bill of Attainder or ex post facto Law shall be passed.

[4] No Capitation, or other direct, Tax shall be laid, unless in Proportion to the Census or enumeration herein before directed to be taken.[5]

[5] No Tax or Duty shall be laid on Articles exported from any State.

[6] No Preference shall be given by any Regulation of Commerce or Revenue to the Ports of one State over those of another; nor shall Vessels bound to, or from, one State, be obliged to enter, clear, or pay Duties in another.

[7] No Money shall be drawn from the Treasury, but in Consequence of Appropriations made by Law; and a regular Statement and Account of the Receipts and Expenditures of all public Money shall be published from time to time.

[8] No Title of Nobility shall be granted by the United States: And no Person holding any Office of Profit or Trust under them, shall, without the Consent of the Congress, accept of any present, Emolument, Office, or Title, of any kind whatever, from any King, Prince, or foreign State.

Section 10. [1] No State shall enter into any Treaty, Alliance, or Confederation; grant Letters of Marque and Reprisal; coin Money; emit Bills of Credit; make any Thing but gold and silver Coin a Tender in Payment of Debts; pass any Bill of Attainder, ex post facto Law, or Law impairing the Obligation of Contracts, or grant any Title of Nobility.

[2] No State shall, without the Consent of the Congress, lay any Imposts or Duties on Imports or Exports, except what may be absolutely necessary for executing it's inspection Laws: and the net Produce of all Duties and Imposts, laid by any State on Imports or Exports, shall be for the Use of the Treasury of the

---

5. But see the Sixteenth Amendment.

United States; and all such Laws shall be subject to the Revision and Controul of the Congress.

[3] No State shall, without the Consent of Congress, lay any Duty of Tonnage, keep Troops, or Ships of War in time of Peace, enter into any Agreement or Compact with another State, or with a foreign Power, or engage in War, unless actually invaded, or in such imminent Danger as will not admit of delay.

ARTICLE II

Section 1. [1] The executive Power shall be vested in a President of the United States of America. He shall hold his Office during the Term of four Years, and, together with the Vice President, chosen for the same Term, be elected, as follows:

[2] Each State shall appoint, in such Manner as the Legislature thereof may direct, a Number of Electors, equal to the whole Number of Senators and Representatives to which the State may be entitled in the Congress: but no Senator or Representative, or Person holding an Office of Trust or Profit under the United States, shall be appointed an Elector.

[3] The Electors shall meet in their respective States, and vote by Ballot for two Persons, of whom one at least shall not be an Inhabitant of the same State with themselves. And they shall make a List of all the Persons voted for, and of the Number of Votes for each; which List they shall sign and certify, and transmit sealed to the Seat of the Government of the United States, directed to the President of the Senate. The President of the Senate shall, in the Presence of the Senate and House of Representatives, open all the Certificates, and the Votes shall then be counted. The Person having the greatest Number of Votes shall be the President, if such Number be a Majority of the whole Number of Electors appointed; and if there be more than one who have such Majority, and have an equal Number of Votes, then the House of Representatives shall immediately chuse by Ballot one of them for President; and if no Person have a Majority, then from the five highest on the List the said House shall in like Manner chuse the President. But in chusing the President, the Votes shall be taken by States, the Representation from each State having one Vote; A quorum for this purpose shall consist of a Member or Members from two thirds of the States, and a Majority of all the States shall be necessary to a Choice. In every Case, after the Choice of the President, the Person having the greatest Number of Votes of the Electors shall be the Vice President. But if there should remain two or more who have equal Votes, the Senate shall chuse from them by Ballot the Vice President.[6]

[4] The Congress may determine the Time of chusing the Electors, and the Day on which they shall give their Votes; which Day shall be the same throughout the United States.

[5] No Person except a natural born Citizen, or a Citizen of the United States, at the time of the Adoption of this Constitution, shall be eligible to the Office of President; neither shall any Person be eligible to that Office who shall not have attained to the Age of thirty five Years, and been fourteen Years a Resident within the United States.

[6] In Case of the Removal of the President from Office, or of his Death, Resignation, or Inability to discharge the Powers and Duties of the said Office, the

6. Superseded by the Twelfth Amendment.

Same shall devolve on the Vice President, and the Congress may by Law provide for the Case of Removal, Death, Resignation or Inability, both of the President and Vice President, declaring what Officer shall then act as President, and such Officer shall act accordingly, until the Disability be removed, or a President shall be elected.[7]

[7] The President shall, at stated Times, receive for his Services, a Compensation, which shall neither be increased nor diminished during the Period for which he shall have been elected, and he shall not receive within that Period any other Emolument from the United States, or any of them.

[8] Before he enter on the Execution of his Office, he shall take the following Oath or Affirmation: "I do solemnly swear (or affirm) that I will faithfully execute the Office of President of the United States, and will to the best of my Ability, preserve, protect and defend the Constitution of the United States."

Section 2. [1] The President shall be Commander in Chief of the Army and Navy of the United States, and of the Militia of the several States, when called into the actual Service of the United States; he may require the Opinion, in writing, of the principal Officer in each of the executive Departments, upon any Subject relating to the Duties of their respective Offices, and he shall have Power to grant Reprieves and Pardons for Offences against the United States, except in Cases of Impeachment.

[2] He shall have Power, by and with the Advice and Consent of the Senate, to make Treaties, provided two thirds of the Senators present concur; and he shall nominate, and by and with the Advice and Consent of the Senate, shall appoint Ambassadors, other public Ministers and Consuls, Judges of the supreme Court, and all other Officers of the United States, whose Appointments are not herein otherwise provided for, and which shall be established by Law: but the Congress may by Law vest the Appointment of such inferior Officers, as they think proper, in the President alone, in the Courts of Law, or in the Heads of Departments.

[3] The President shall have Power to fill up all Vacancies that may happen during the Recess of the Senate, by granting Commissions which shall expire at the End of their next Session.

Section 3. He shall from time to time give to the Congress Information of the State of the Union, and recommend to their Consideration such Measures as he shall judge necessary and expedient; he may, on extraordinary Occasions, convene both Houses, or either of them, and in Case of Disagreement between them, with Respect to the Time of Adjournment, he may adjourn them to such Time as he shall think proper; he shall receive Ambassadors and other public Ministers; he shall take Care that the Laws be faithfully executed, and shall Commission all the Officers of the United States.

Section 4. The President, Vice President and all civil Officers of the United States, shall be removed from Office on Impeachment for, and Conviction of, Treason, Bribery, or other high Crimes and Misdemeanors.

ARTICLE III

Section 1. The judicial Power of the United States shall be vested in one supreme Court, and in such inferior Courts as the Congress may from time to time ordain and establish. The Judges, both of the supreme and inferior Courts, shall hold their

7. Changed by the Twenty-fifth Amendment.

Offices during good Behaviour, and shall, at stated Times, receive for their Services a Compensation, which shall not be diminished during their Continuance in Office.

Section 2. [1] The Judicial Power shall extend to all Cases, in Law and Equity, arising under this Constitution, the Laws of the United States, and Treaties made, or which shall be made, under their Authority; — to all Cases affecting Ambassadors, other public Ministers and Consuls; — to all Cases of admiralty and maritime Jurisdiction; — to Controversies to which the United States shall be a Party; — to Controversies between two or more States; — between a State and Citizens of another State; — between Citizens of different States; — between Citizens of the same State claiming Lands under Grants of different States, and between a State, or the Citizens thereof, and foreign States, Citizens or Subjects.

[2] In all Cases affecting Ambassadors, other public Ministers and Consuls, and those in which a State shall be Party, the supreme Court shall have original Jurisdiction. In all the other Cases before mentioned, the supreme Court shall have appellate Jurisdiction, both as to Law and Fact, with such Exceptions, and under such Regulations as the Congress shall make.

[3] The Trial of all Crimes, except in Cases of Impeachment, shall be by Jury; and such Trial shall be held in the State where the said Crimes shall have been committed; but when not committed within any State, the Trial shall be at such Place or Places as the Congress may by Law have directed.

Section 3. [1] Treason against the United States, shall consist only in levying War against them, or in adhering to their Enemies, giving them Aid and Comfort. No Person shall be convicted of Treason unless on the Testimony of two Witnesses to the same overt Act, or on Confession in open Court.

[2] The Congress shall have Power to declare the Punishment of Treason, but no Attainder of Treason shall work Corruption of Blood, or Forfeiture except during the Life of the Person attainted.

ARTICLE IV

Section 1. Full Faith and Credit shall be given in each State to the public Acts, Records, and judicial Proceedings of every other State. And the Congress may by general Laws prescribe the Manner in which such Acts, Records and Proceedings shall be proved, and the Effect thereof.

Section 2. [1] The Citizens of each State shall be entitled to all Privileges and Immunities of Citizens in the several States.

[2] A Person charged in any State with Treason, Felony, or other Crime, who shall flee from Justice, and be found in another State, shall on Demand of the executive Authority of the State from which he fled, be delivered up, to be removed to the State having Jurisdiction of the Crime.

[3] No Person held to Service or Labour in one State, under the Laws thereof, escaping into another, shall, in Consequence of any Law or Regulation therein, be discharged from such Service or Labour, but shall be delivered up on Claim of the Party to whom such Service or Labour may be due.[8]

Section 3. [1] New States may be admitted by the Congress into this Union; but no new State shall be formed or erected within the Jurisdiction of any other State; nor

---

8. Superseded by the Thirteenth Amendment.

any State be formed by the Junction of two or more States, or Parts of States, without the Consent of the Legislatures of the States concerned as well as of the Congress.

[2] The Congress shall have Power to dispose of and make all needful Rules and Regulations respecting the Territory or other Property belonging to the United States; and nothing in this Constitution shall be so construed as to Prejudice any Claims of the United States, or of any particular State.

Section 4. The United States shall guarantee to every State in this Union a Republican Form of Government, and shall protect each of them against Invasion; and on Application of the Legislature, or of the Executive (when the Legislature cannot be convened), against domestic Violence.

ARTICLE V

The Congress, whenever two thirds of both Houses shall deem it necessary, shall propose Amendments to this Constitution, or, on the Application of the Legislatures of two thirds of the several States, shall call a Convention for proposing Amendments, which, in either Case, shall be valid to all Intents and Purposes, as Part of this Constitution, when ratified by the Legislatures of three fourths of the several States, or by Conventions in three fourths thereof, as the one or the other Mode of Ratification may be proposed by the Congress; Provided that no Amendment which may be made prior to the Year One thousand eight hundred and eight shall in any Manner affect the first and fourth Clauses in the Ninth Section of the first Article; and that no State, without its Consent, shall be deprived of its equal Suffrage in the Senate.

ARTICLE VI

[1] All Debts contracted and Engagements entered into, before the Adoption of this Constitution, shall be as valid against the United States under this Constitution, as under the Confederation.

[2] This Constitution, and the Laws of the United States which shall be made in Pursuance thereof; and all Treaties made, or which shall be made, under the Authority of the United States, shall be the supreme Law of the Land; and the Judges in every State shall be bound thereby, any Thing in the Constitution or Laws of any State to the Contrary notwithstanding.

[3] The Senators and Representatives before mentioned, and the Members of the several State Legislatures, and all executive and judicial Officers, both of the United States and of the several States, shall be bound by Oath or Affirmation, to support this Constitution; but no religious Test shall ever be required as a Qualification to any Office or public Trust under the United States.

ARTICLE VII

The Ratification of the Conventions of nine States, shall be sufficient for the Establishment of this Constitution between the States so ratifying the Same.[9] Done

9. The ninth state ratified the Constitution on June 21, 1788. Virginia and New York ratified later in 1788, North Carolina in 1789, and Rhode Island in 1790. George Washington was inaugurated as the first President on April 30, 1789.

in Convention by the Unanimous Consent of the States present the Seventeenth Day of September in the Year of our Lord one thousand seven hundred and Eighty seven and of the Independence of the United States of America the Twelfth.

ARTICLES IN ADDITION TO, AND AMENDMENT OF THE CONSTITUTION OF THE UNITED STATES OF AMERICA, PROPOSED BY CONGRESS, AND RATIFIED BY THE LEGISLATURES OF THE SEVERAL STATES, PURSUANT TO THE FIFTH ARTICLE OF THE ORIGINAL CONSTITUTION[10]

AMENDMENT I [1791]

Congress shall make no law respecting an establishment of religion, or prohibiting the free exercise thereof; or abridging the freedom of speech, or of the press; or the right of the people peaceably to assemble, and to petition the Government for a redress of grievances.

AMENDMENT II [1791]

A well regulated Militia, being necessary to the security of a free State, the right of the people to keep and bear Arms, shall not be infringed.

AMENDMENT III [1791]

No Soldier shall, in time of peace be quartered in any house, without the consent of the Owner, nor in time of war, but in a manner to be prescribed by law.

AMENDMENT IV [1791]

The right of the people to be secure in their persons, houses, papers, and effects, against unreasonable searches and seizures, shall not be violated, and no Warrants shall issue, but upon probable cause, supported by Oath or affirmation, and particularly describing the place to be searched, and the persons or things to be seized.

AMENDMENT V [1791]

No person shall be held to answer for a capital, or otherwise infamous crime, unless on a presentment or indictment of a Grand Jury, except in cases arising in the land or naval forces, or in the Militia, when in actual service in time of War or public danger; nor shall any person be subject for the same offence to be twice put in jeopardy of life or limb; nor shall be compelled in any criminal case to be a witness against himself, nor be deprived of life, liberty, or property, without due process of law; nor shall private property be taken for public use, without just compensation.

10. The Twenty-first Amendment was ratified by state conventions.

AMENDMENT VI [1791]

In all criminal prosecutions, the accused shall enjoy the right to a speedy and public trial, by an impartial jury of the State and district wherein the crime shall have been committed, which district shall have been previously ascertained by law, and to be informed of the nature and cause of the accusation; to be confronted with the witnesses against him; to have compulsory process for obtaining witnesses in his favor, and to have the Assistance of Counsel for his defence.

AMENDMENT VII [1791]

In suits at common law, where the value in controversy shall exceed twenty dollars, the right of trial by jury shall be preserved, and no fact tried by a jury, shall be otherwise reexamined in any Court of the United States, than according to the rules of the common law.

AMENDMENT VIII [1791]

Excessive bail shall not be required, nor excessive fines imposed, nor cruel and unusual punishments inflicted.

AMENDMENT IX [1791]

The enumeration in the Constitution, of certain rights, shall not be construed to deny or disparage others retained by the people.

AMENDMENT X [1791]

The powers not delegated to the United States by the Constitution, nor prohibited by it to the States, are reserved to the States respectively, or to the people.

AMENDMENT XI [1798]

The Judicial power of the United States shall not be construed to extend to any suit in law or equity, commenced or prosecuted against one of the United States by Citizens of another State, or by Citizens or Subjects of any Foreign State.

AMENDMENT XII [1804]

The Electors shall meet in their respective states and vote by ballot for President and Vice-President, one of whom, at least, shall not be an inhabitant of the same state with themselves; they shall name in their ballots the person voted for as President, and in distinct ballots the person voted for as Vice-President, and they shall make distinct lists of all persons voted for as President, and of all persons voted for as Vice-President, and of the number of votes for each, which lists they shall sign and certify, and transmit sealed to the seat of the government of the United States, directed to the President of the Senate; — the President of the Senate shall, in the presence of the Senate and House of Representatives, open all the certificates and the votes shall then be counted; — The person having the greatest number of votes for President, shall be the President, if such number be a majority of the whole number of Electors appointed; and if no person have such majority, then from the persons having the highest numbers not exceeding three on the list of those voted for as President, the House of Representatives shall chuse immediately, by ballot, the President. But in chusing the President, the votes shall be taken by states, the representation from each state having one vote; a quorum for this purpose shall consist of a member or members from two-thirds of the states, and a majority of all the states shall be necessary to a choice. [And if the House of Representatives shall not chuse a President whenever the right of choice shall devolve upon them, before the fourth day of March next following, then the Vice-President shall act as President, as in case of the death or other constitutional disability of the President.[11] — The person having the greatest number of votes as Vice-President, shall be the Vice-President, if such number be a majority of the whole number of Electors appointed, and if no person have a majority, then from the two highest numbers on the list, the Senate shall choose the Vice-President; a quorum for the purpose shall consist of two-thirds of the whole number of Senators, and a majority of the whole number shall be necessary to a choice. But no person constitutionally ineligible to the office of President shall be eligible to that of Vice-President of the United States.

Amendment XIII [1865]

Section 1. Neither slavery nor involuntary servitude, except as a punishment for crime whereof the party shall have been duly convicted, shall exist within the United States, or any place subject to their jurisdiction.

Section 2. Congress shall have power to enforce this article by appropriate legislation.

Amendment XIV [1868]

Section 1. All persons born or naturalized in the United States, and subject to the jurisdiction thereof, are citizens of the United States and of the State wherein they reside. No State shall make or enforce any law which shall abridge the privileges or immunities of citizens of the United States; nor shall any State deprive any person of life, liberty, or property, without due process of law; nor deny to any person within its jurisdiction the equal protection of the laws.

Section 2. Representatives shall be apportioned among the several States according to their respective numbers, counting the whole number of persons in each State, excluding Indians not taxed. But when the right to vote at any election for the choice of electors for President and Vice-President of the United States, Representatives in Congress, the Executive and Judicial officers of a State, or the members of the Legislature thereof, is denied to any of the male inhabitants of such State, being twenty-one years of age, and citizens of the United States, or in any way abridged, except for participation in rebellion, or other crime, the basis of representation therein shall be reduced in the proportion which the number of such male citizens shall bear to the whole number of male citizens twenty-one years of age in such State.

---

11. Superseded by section 3 of the Twentieth Amendment.

Section 3. No person shall be a Senator or Representative in Congress, or elector of President and Vice-President, or hold any office, civil or military, under the United States, or under any State, who, having previously taken an oath, as a member of Congress, or as an officer of the United States, or as a member of any State legislature, or as an executive or judicial officer of any State, to support the Constitution of the United States, shall have engaged in insurrection or rebellion against the same, or given aid or comfort to the enemies thereof. But Congress may by a vote of two-thirds of each House, remove such disability.

Section 4. The validity of the public debt of the United States, authorized by law, including debts incurred for payment of pensions and bounties for services in suppressing insurrection or rebellion, shall not be questioned. But neither the United States nor any State shall assume or pay any debt or obligation incurred in aid of insurrection or rebellion against the United States, or any claim for the loss or emancipation of any slave; but all such debts, obligations and claims shall be held illegal and void.

Section 5. The Congress shall have the power to enforce, by appropriate legislation, the provisions of this article.

AMENDMENT XV [1870]

Section 1. The right of citizens of the United States to vote shall not be denied or abridged by the United States or by any State on account of race, color, or previous condition of servitude.

Section 2. The Congress shall have the power to enforce this article by appropriate legislation.

AMENDMENT XVI [1913]

The Congress shall have power to lay and collect taxes on incomes, from whatever source derived, without apportionment among the several States, and without regard to any census or enumeration.

AMENDMENT XVII [1913]

[1] The Senate of the United States shall be composed of two Senators from each State, elected by the people thereof, for six years; and each Senator shall have one vote. The electors in each State shall have the qualifications requisite for electors of the most numerous branch of the State legislatures.

[2] When vacancies happen in the representation of any State in the Senate, the executive authority of such State shall issue writs of election to fill such vacancies: *Provided,* That the legislature of any State may empower the executive thereof to make temporary appointments until the people fill the vacancies by election as the legislature may direct.

[3] This amendment shall not be so construed as to affect the election or term of any Senator chosen before it becomes valid as part of the Constitution.

AMENDMENT XVIII [1919]

Section 1. After one year from the ratification of this article the manufacture, sale, or transportation of intoxicating liquors within, the importation thereof into, or the exportation thereof from the United States and all territory subject to the jurisdiction thereof for beverage purposes is hereby prohibited.

Section 2. The Congress and the several States shall have concurrent power to enforce this article by appropriate legislation.

Section 3. This article shall be inoperative unless it shall have been ratified as an amendment to the Constitution by the legislatures of the several States, as provided in the Constitution, within seven years from the date of the submission hereof to the States by the Congress.[12]

AMENDMENT XIX [1920]

[1] The right of citizens of the United States to vote shall not be denied or abridged by the United States or by any State on account of sex.

[2] Congress shall have power to enforce this article by appropriate legislation.

AMENDMENT XX [1933]

Section 1. The terms of the President and the Vice President shall end at noon on the 20th day of January, and the terms of Senators and Representatives at noon on the 3d day of January, of the years in which such terms would have ended if this article had not been ratified; and the terms of their successors shall then begin.

Section 2. The Congress shall assemble at least once in every year, and such meeting shall begin at noon on the 3d day of January, unless they shall by law appoint a different day.

Section 3. If, at the time fixed for the beginning of the term of the President, the President elect shall have died, the Vice President elect shall become President. If a President shall not have been chosen before the time fixed for the beginning of his term, or if the President elect shall have failed to qualify, then the Vice President elect shall act as President until a President shall have qualified; and the Congress may by law provide for the case wherein neither a President elect nor a Vice President shall have qualified, declaring who shall then act as President, or the manner in which one who is to act shall be selected, and such person shall act accordingly until a President or Vice President shall have qualified.

Section 4. The Congress may by law provide for the case of the death of any of the persons from whom the House of Representatives may chuse a President whenever the right of choice shall have devolved upon them, and for the case of the death of any of the persons from whom the Senate may chuse a Vice President whenever the right of choice shall have devolved upon them.

Section 5. Sections 1 and 2 shall take effect on the 15th day of October following the ratification of this article.

Section 6. This article shall be inoperative unless it shall have been ratified as an amendment to the Constitution by the legislatures of three-fourths of the several States within seven years from the date of its submission.

---

12. Repealed by the Twenty-first Amendment.

AMENDMENT XXI [1933]

Section 1. The eighteenth article of amendment to the Constitution of the United States is hereby repealed.

Section 2. The transportation or importation into any State, Territory, or Possession of the United States for delivery or use therein of intoxicating liquors, in violation of the laws thereof, is hereby prohibited.

Section 3. This article shall be inoperative unless it shall have been ratified as an amendment to the Constitution by conventions in the several States, as provided in the Constitution, within seven years from the date of the submission hereof to the States by the Congress.

AMENDMENT XXII [1951]

Section 1. No person shall be elected to the office of the President more than twice, and no person who has held the office of President, or acted as President, for more than two years of a term to which some other person was elected President shall be elected to the office of President more than once. But this Article shall not apply to any person holding the office of President when this Article was proposed by Congress, and shall not prevent any person who may be holding the office of President, or acting as President, during the term within which this Article becomes operative from holding the office of President or acting as President during the remainder of such term.

Section 2. This article shall be inoperative unless it shall have been ratified as an amendment to the Constitution by the legislatures of three-fourths of the several States within seven years from the date of its submission to the States by the Congress.

AMENDMENT XXIII [1961]

Section 1. The District constituting the seat of Government of the United States shall appoint in such manner as Congress may direct: A number of electors of President and Vice President equal to the whole number of Senators and Representatives in Congress to which the District would be entitled if it were a State, but in no event more than the least populous State; they shall be in addition to those appointed by the States, but they shall be considered, for the purposes of the election of President and Vice President, to be electors appointed by a State; and they shall meet in the District and perform such duties as provided by the twelfth article of amendment.

Section 2. The Congress shall have power to enforce this article by appropriate legislation.

AMENDMENT XXIV [1964]

Section 1. The right of citizens of the United States to vote in any primary or other election for President or Vice President, for electors for President or Vice President, or for Senator or Representative in Congress, shall not be denied or abridged by the United States or any State by reason of failure to pay poll tax or other tax.

Section 2. The Congress shall have power to enforce this article by appropriate legislation.

AMENDMENT XXV [1967]

Section 1. In case of the removal of the President from office or of his death or resignation, the Vice President shall become President.

Section 2. Whenever there is a vacancy in the office of the Vice President, the President shall nominate a Vice President who shall take office upon confirmation by a majority vote of both Houses of Congress.

Section 3. Whenever the President transmits to the President pro tempore of the Senate and the Speaker of the House of Representatives his written declaration that he is unable to discharge the powers and duties of his office, and until he transmits to them a written declaration to the contrary, such powers and duties shall be discharged by the Vice President as Acting President.

Section 4. Whenever the Vice President and a majority of either the principal officers of the executive departments or of such other body as Congress may by law provide, transmit to the President pro tempore of the Senate and the Speaker of the House of Representatives their written declaration that the President is unable to discharge the powers and duties of his office, the Vice President shall immediately assume the powers and duties of the office as Acting President.

Thereafter, when the President transmits to the President pro tempore of the Senate and the Speaker of the House of Representatives his written declaration that no inability exists, he shall resume the powers and duties of his office unless the Vice President and a majority of either the principal officers of the executive department or of such other body as Congress may by law provide, transmit within four days to the President pro tempore of the Senate and the Speaker of the House of Representatives their written declaration that the President is unable to discharge the powers and duties of his office. Thereupon Congress shall decide the issue, assembling within forty-eight hours for that purpose if not in session. If the Congress, within twenty-one days after receipt of the latter written declaration, or, if Congress is not in session, within twenty-one days after Congress is required to assemble, determines by two-thirds vote of both Houses that the President is unable to discharge the powers and duties of his office, the Vice President shall continue to discharge the same as Acting President; otherwise, the President shall resume the powers and duties of his office.

AMENDMENT XXVI [1971]

Section 1. The right of citizens of the United States, who are eighteen years of age or older, to vote shall not be denied or abridged by the United States or by any State on account of age.

Section 2. The Congress shall have power to enforce this article by appropriate legislation.

AMENDMENT XXVII [1992][13]

No law, varying the compensation for the services of the Senators and Representatives, shall take effect, until an election of representatives shall have intervened.

---

13. This amendment was initially proposed in 1789. Whether a 203-year process of ratification calls its validity into question is discussed in Chapter 4, pp. 477-481.

PART ONE
INTRODUCTION

Background to the Constitution[1]

In June 1776, the Continental Congress, meeting in Philadelphia, appointed committees to draft a declaration of independence and to prepare "the form of a confederation to be entered into between these colonies."[2] The first committee was distinctly more successful than the second. Within a month, Congress approved the Declaration of Independence of which Thomas Jefferson was the principal drafter. Articles of Confederation were submitted to the states in 1777, but they did not take formal effect until 1781, when the last state, Maryland, gave its assent.

The new nation was called The United States of America, but this only generated the question whether the primary inflection should be placed on the word "United" or the word "States."[3] (What, for example, is the implication to be drawn from the fact that the United States is a member of the United Nations?) Thus one writer has suggested that the Articles of Confederation are better conceived as "a treaty among a group of small nations" than a charter for a single nation.[4] Consider in this context Article II: "Each state retains its sovereignty, freedom, and independence, and every power, jurisdiction, and right, which is not by this Confederation expressly delegated to the United States, in Congress assembled."[5] Representation in the Congress was by states (which, of course, is true today), but each state had only one vote, cast by the majority of its delegates (who could number up to seven). Moreover, the delegates were paid by the states, and they were subject to recall by their respective states should their votes be objectionable.

Congressional power was narrowly limited. There was, for example, no authority to regulate interstate or foreign commerce. Even more to the point (especially during the period in which Congress was trying to manage a war against England), Congress had no power to tax the citizenry; it was limited to "requisitioning" funds from the states themselves, which, as a practical matter, amounted to little more than a request for voluntary donations to the national treasury—what Robert Livingston described as "pompous petitions for charity."[6] Although James Madison

1. For more detailed discussion of many of the issues discussed in this Introduction, see generally Akhil Reed Amar, America's Constitution: A Biography (2005).
2. Quoted in The Formation of the Union (National Archives Pub. No. 70-13), at 34.
3. See Sebastian de Grazia, A Country with No Name: Tales from the Constitution (1997), for a fascinating discussion of the theoretical implications of the name. There were some proposals at the time to rename the new nation "Columbia," but they were resisted in part because any such name would suggest a far more united group of states than many (perhaps most) wished to acknowledge. For exposition of an argument, contrary to that set out in the text above, that the nation in fact preceded the states, see Richard B. Morris, The Forging of the Union Reconsidered: A Historical Refutation of State Sovereignty Over Seabeds, 74 Columbia L. Rev. 74 (1974).
4. The Formation of the Union, at 34.
5. This and other quotations from the Articles are taken from Sources and Documents Illustrating the American Revolution 1764-1788 (Morison ed., 2d ed. 1965), at 178-186.
6. Calvin H. Johnson, Righteous Anger at the Wicked States: The Meaning of the Founders' Constitution 15 (2005) (quoting a speech of June 27, 1788, by Robert Livingston to the New York ratifying convention).

had told his fellow members of the Congress in 1783 that requisitions were "sacred & obligatory" upon the States,[7] Hamilton accurately wrote in Federalist No. 15 that they had been treated by state legislatures as "mere recommendations"— that were simply left unpaid. Thus the "Requisition of 1786, the last before the Constitution, 'mandated' payments by the states . . . of $3.8 million, but collected only $663."[8]

Congress had the power to coin money, but states retained the power to issue paper money, which some did with abandon. The Articles established neither a national judiciary nor even a genuine executive branch. Congress was authorized to establish such "committees and civil officers as may be necessary for managing the general affairs of the united states under their direction" and to appoint a "president" of the Congress, who could serve only a single one-year term in any three-year period. In 1781, Congress established departments of Foreign Affairs, War, Marine, and Treasury, each under a single secretary.

The perceived deficiencies of the political order established by the Articles, reflected, it was felt by many, in economic turmoil following the completion of the Revolutionary War in 1783, led many to call for revisions, though an additional difficulty generated by the Articles was found in Article XIII. All state legislatures had to give their consent to any proposed amendments for them to become binding on the members of the confederation. By definition this gave a single state — Rhode Island, both the smallest and the most radical, was often selected out for particular opprobrium — a veto over any changes.

In any event, as early as 1783 Alexander Hamilton called for "a General Convention for the purpose of revising and amending the federal Government." James Madison registered his opposition, noting his fear that such a convention would excite "pernicious jealousies" among the states.[9] The situation changed rapidly, however, as more observers agreed that the system set up by the Articles was not working.[10] Congress was perceived as having both little authority and little legitimacy (not to mention little money to implement any policies, including payment of veterans of the Revolutionary War or foreign debtors). "[B]y 1785," writes Stanford historian Jack Rakove, "its reputation had fallen so low that any proposal [for amendment] Congress submitted to the states seemed tainted at the source."[11] And, of course, even if Congress had had a better reputation, amendment was still likely to be frustrated by the unanimity rule.

"With Congress clearly losing whatever influence it retained, the initiative for reform necessarily shifted to the states."[12] Thus in January 1786, the Virginia assembly adopted a resolution calling for an interstate conference that would, among

7. Id. (citing Madison, Continental Congress (February 21, 1783), in 25 Journals of the Continental Congress 908).

8. Id. at 1.

9. 9 Papers of James Madison 115-119 (Rutland & Rachal eds., 1975).

10. There is, as one might imagine, no consensus about the actual state of affairs of the United States under the Confederation. Although most historians probably agree, more or less, with the critiques of those who supported the Philadelphia convention, a dissenting view can be found in Merrill Jensen, The New Nation: A History of the United States During the Confederation, 1781-1789 (1950). See also Peter S. Onuf, The First Federal Constitution: The Articles of Confederation, in The Framing and Ratification of the Constitution 82-97 (Leonard Levy & Dennis J. Mahoney eds., 1987). This book includes a number of essays that are clearly relevant to the issues discussed in the following paragraphs.

11. Jack N. Rakove, Original Meanings: Politics and Ideas in the Making of the Constitution 32 (1996).

12. Id. at 32. A fascinating history of the move toward change can also be found in Bruce Ackerman 2 We the People: Transformations 32-68 (1998).

other things, "take into consideration the trade of the United States; to examine the relative situations and trade of the said States; [and] to consider how far a uniform system in their commercial regulations may be necessary to their common interests and their permanent harmony." Madison supported the resolution.

This led to the Annapolis Conference of September 1786; 12 delegates from 5 states met to consider the situation. Madison wrote to Jefferson, who was in Paris serving as the American ambassador to France, that "Gentlemen both within & without Congs. Wish to make this Meeting subservient to a Plenipotentiary Convention for amending the Confederation. Tho my wishes are in favor of such an event, yet I despair so much of its accomplishment at the present crisis that I do not extend my views beyond a Commercial Reform. To speak the truth I almost despair even of this."[13] The practical authority, not to mention legal mandate, of the Annapolis Convention was obviously limited. Its report therefore proposed yet another meeting "to devise such further provisions as shall appear . . . necessary to render the constitution of the Foederal Government adequate to the exigencies of the Union."[14] Congress agreed, in February 1787, to authorize a convention "for the *sole and express purpose of revising the Articles of Confederation* and reporting to Congress and the several legislatures such alterations and provisions therein as shall when agreed to in Congress and confirmed by the States render the federal constitution adequate to the exigencies of Government & the preservation of the union."[15] The Convention began meeting in Philadelphia the following May, and it ended up, of course, drafting a brand new Constitution.

The delegates had little doubt that they were exceeding the scope of their congressional authorization. Edmund Randolph, the Governor of Virginia—he would later become the first Attorney General of the United States—told the Convention, "There are great seasons when persons with limited powers are justified in exceeding them, and a person would be contemptible not to risk it."[16] His fellow Virginian, George Mason, agreed, "In certain seasons of public danger it is commendable to exceed power,"[17] as did New York's Alexander Hamilton: "To rely on & propose any plan not adequate to these exigencies, *merely because it was not clearly within our powers,* would be to sacrifice the means to the end."[18] Hamilton, of course, would, with John Jay and James Madison, go on to write the most influential tract in favor of the new Constitution, The Federalist; in the Federalist No. 40, Madison defended the Convention's action by writing that the delegates "must have borne in mind, that as the plan to be framed and proposed was to be submitted *to the people themselves* . . . its approbation [would] blot out antecedent errors and irregularities." As you read through the materials in this Casebook, you might ask yourself how often such arguments—which might be described as emphasizing the priority of exigencies (or perceived emergencies) over strict fidelity to constitutional norms—have carried the day against opponents who claim that these norms should indeed retain priority and therefore require rejection even of what are perceived as highly desirable proposals in times of emergency.

13. Madison to Jefferson, August 12, 1786, in 9 Papers, at 96.
14. The Formation of the Union, at 50.
15. Id. (emphasis added).
16. 1 Records of the Federal convention of 1787, at 362 (Farrand ed., 1937) (speech of June 16, 1787).
17. Quoted in Jon Elster, Constitutional Bootstrapping in Philadelphia and Paris, in Constitutionalism, Identity, Difference, and Legitimacy: Theoretical Perspectives 72 (Michel Rosenfeld ed., 1994).
18. 1 Records of the Federal convention of 1787, at 283 (June 18, 1787) (emphasis added). See also id. at 346 (George Mason).

The fact that the Convention went far beyond its congressional mandate was only one of the procedural problems found in the proposal and ratification of the new Constitution. The February bill assumed that Congress would play an independent role in deliberating on the Convention's recommendations and, more important, that any amendments would be subjected to the requirement of Article XIII that all state legislatures assent to any changes. Instead, Congress turned out to be nothing more than a messenger, agreeing to send on, without a single change, the handiwork of the Philadelphia convention. And Article VII of the proposed Constitution simply ignored Article XIII inasmuch as it stated that "The Ratification of the Conventions of nine States, shall be sufficient for the Establishment of this Constitution between the States so ratifying the Same." No longer could Rhode Island exercise any veto. Thus Madison wrote in the Federalist No. 40, as part of his general argument for the Convention's going well beyond the mandate given it by the Congress, that any suggestion that the Convention should simply have proposed amendments to the Articles was refuted by the "the absurdity of subjecting the fate of twelve States to the perverseness or corruption of a thirteenth." As Professor Johnson writes, "Rhode Island's opposition" to the enterprise of reforming the Articles—the state, after all, did not even send any delegates to Philadelphia—"meant that necessary changes could not operate within the framework of the Articles of Confederation."[19]

Indeed, Rhode Island rejected the Constitution on March 24, 1788; because North Carolina chose to postpone its ratification on August 2, 1788, there were only 11 states in the Union when George Washington was inaugurated as the first President of the reordered American polity on April 30, 1789. Rhode Island and North Carolina, juridically speaking, had the status of foreign countries. Bruce Ackerman describes Article VII's "assertion that nine state 'Conventions' could adequately ratify on behalf of the People [as] plainly an extra-legal assertion of democratic authority."[20] (One might, of course, conceptualize the events of 1787-88 as the secession by the ratifying states from the confederation established by the Articles and the joining of a new polity established by the Constitution, but this, too, raises obvious problems, especially given similar attempts at secession by 11 states in 1860-61.) In any event, by 1787 the first U.S. constitution, the Articles of Confederation, had become simply irrelevant.

The substantive decisions of the Philadelphia convention were of sweeping import. The delegates nearly deadlocked over the formula for state representation in the new, far more powerful, congress. The Virginia Plan, which served as a working draft for much of the document, in effect proposed that representation in

---

19. Johnson, supra n.6, at 79.

20. Ackerman, The Storrs Lectures: Discovering the Constitution, 93 Yale L.J. 1013, 1017 n.6. See also Richard Kay, The Illegality of the Constitution, 4 Constitutional Commentary 57 (1987). The most vigorous defense of the legality of the procedures by which the Constitution was adopted has been offered by Ackerman's Yale colleague Akhil Reed Amar, who relies on the notion that the articles were indeed only a "treaty" among the various sovereign states. "By 1787, the Articles had been routinely and flagrantly violated on all sides. And under well-established legal principles in 1787, these material breaches freed each compacting party—each state—to disregard the pact." See Amar, Popular Sovereignty and Constitutional Amendment, in Responding to Imperfection: The Theory and Practice of Constitutional Amendment 92-95 (Sanford Levinson ed., 1995). You might ask yourself if the extent of your esteem for the members of the founding generation depends on their fidelity to existing legal norms. If, at the end of the day, you do not really care who is correct between Ackerman and Amar, does that have implications for your views today about the importance of fidelity to the existing Constitution? Is it more important to be faithful to the law or to respond imaginatively to the "exigencies" of the moment?

both houses — there was never any serious consideration given to the possibility of a single-house Congress — would be based on the number of free inhabitants in each state. This met with vigorous opposition from less populous states as well as from Virginia's fellow Southern states. Although it was thought that the population of the South would grow more rapidly than that of the North, the South feared the possibility of Northern domination of the Congress and the concomitant threat to the institution of slavery. After more than a month of passionate controversy, the Convention agreed on a compromise: Each state would receive equal representation in the Senate — a voting distribution that required unanimity for amendment (see Article V) — and the distribution of votes in the House would be proportionate not to the numbers of free citizens, but, rather to the sum of "the whole number of free persons" and "three-fifths of all other persons" in each state, a clear reference, given the politics of the time, to slaves.[21] The debate about representation was so deep in part because Congress was getting significant new power. It would, among other things, get the ability to directly tax the citizenry. It was given the power to regulate interstate and foreign commerce. In addition to the explicit topics set out in Article I, §8, the conclusion of that section included an authorization "to make all Laws which shall be necessary and proper for carrying into Execution the foregoing Powers." The bulk of the pages that follow will be devoted to the ramifications of these (and other) grants of congressional power.

There was, of course, much discussion of these new powers granted to the national government in the ratification debates, which occurred not only at the ratification conventions required by Article VII, but also in newspaper editorials, pamphlets, and essays, the most famous of which, of course, are the *Federalist* papers written by Jay, Hamilton, and Madison to encourage the New York delegates to ratify the Constitution. As a theoretical matter, the Constitution had already come into legal existence when New Hampshire became the ninth state to ratify the Constitution on June 21, 1788. However, any look at a map of the United States will make it evident that New York's (or Virginia's) ratification was absolutely essential to the effective establishment of a new political order (in a way that North Carolina's and Rhode Island's were not). Virginia ratified on June 25, 1788, by a vote of 89-79. New York indeed followed a month later, on July 26, 1788, but the final vote was only 30-27, so a switch of two votes might well have doomed the 1787 proposal or, at the least, required a new convention. (Consider the consequences of the 2005 rejection by the French and Dutch publics of the proposed European Constitution.)

Many factors contributed to the final approval of the Constitution, of course, but one should not underestimate the importance, at least to supporters of the new Constitution, of perceived threats to the young nation. James Wilson, for example, told the members of the Pennsylvania Assembly on September 17, 1787, the very day that the Constitution was signed in Philadelphia, that war was "highly

---

21. It should be noted that it is unfair to view the South as believing that slaves were only three-fifths human beings. Southern states would have been delighted to count each slave as the equivalent of two free persons, for that would have obviously enhanced their representation immensely. Thus the South Carolina delegation at the convention demanded full representation for slaves. See Rakove, at 73. The South Carolinians were obviously not afraid to count slaves as full human beings, so long as they were disallowed any rights to participate in the polity as voting members (or, of course, in any other capacity). Concomitantly, Northern states would have wished to exclude slaves entirely from the pool of those counted for representation. The complement to the three-fifths compromise on representation was a similar three-fifths compromise in regard to taxation. See Article I, §2, cl. 2.

probable."[22] Oliver Ellsworth told his fellow delegates to the Connecticut ratifying convention that "our situation invites our enemies to make war," and he was duly appalled at the weakness of the existing political order should war break out. He asked, no doubt rhetorically, "Has [the current] government the means to enlist a man or buy an ox?"[23] A delegate to the Massachusetts ratifying convention told his colleagues that "[w]e are circumscribed with enemies from Maine to Georgia,"[24] with the primary threats being Great Britain, Spain, and American Indian tribes who were scarcely sympathetic with the territorial expansion of the United States that was already underway. Critics of the Constitution were therefore urged to put their doubts about specific parts of the Constitution aside to meet the exigencies of national security.

Political scientist and historian David Hendrickson emphasizes the importance of the view, derived both from political theorists like Thomas Hobbes and the realities of European political experience, that a fragmented group of states, perhaps divided into three separate nations comprising, respectively, the New England, mid-Atlantic, and Southern states, would inevitably end up warring with one another.[25] Alexander Hamilton made an especially vivid elaboration of such an argument in the Federalist No. 6, which summarizes a set of essays "dedicated to an enumeration of the dangers to which we should be exposed, in a state of disunion, from the arms and arts of foreign nations." Hamilton's worldview is based on his assumption

> that men are ambitious, vindictive, and rapacious. To look for a continuation of harmony between a number of independent unconnected sovereignties, situated in the same neighbourhood, would be to disregard the uniform course of human events, and to set at defiance the accumulated experience of ages.
>
> The causes of hostility among nations are innumerable. . . . [Following a review of world history from ancient Greece to contemporary Europe, he writes,] From this summary of what has taken place in other countries, whose situations have borne the nearest resemblance to our own, what reason can we have to confide in those reveries, which would seduce us into an expectation of peace and cordiality between the members of the present confederation, in a state of separation?

Hamilton concludes the essay by quoting the French author the Abbe de Mably:

> "NEIGHBOURING NATIONS (says he) are naturally ENEMIES of each other, unless their common weakness forces them to league in a CONFEDERATE REPUBLIC, and their constitution prevents the differences that neighbourhood occasions, extinguishing that secret jealousy, which disposes all States to aggrandize themselves at the expence of their neighbours. This passage, at the same time, points out the EVIL and suggests the REMEDY."[26]

An important book by Swedish political scientist and historian Max Edling describes a "revolution in favor of government" and emphasizes the overriding importance of both the taxation and standing army clauses, inasmuch as the two,

---

22. Quoted in Johnson, supra n.6, at 18.
23. Id. at 151.
24. Id.
25. See David C. Hendrickson, Peace Pact: The Lost World of the American Founding (2003).
26. Alexander Hamilton, Federalist No. 6, in 1 The Debate on the Constitution: Federalist and Antifederalist Speeches, Articles, and Letters During the Struggle over Ratification 311-316 (Bernard Bailyn ed., (1999)).

taken together, allowed the national government to finance and raise professional military defense forces.[27] Some critics of the Constitution were horrified by the prospect of a "standing army," viewed by those committed to civic-republican political theory as an inevitable threat to popular liberty. (These critics relied on citizen militias, which is one explanation for the addition of the Second Amendment to the new Constitution.) However, the exigencies of national defense ultimately prevailed and almost undoubtedly accounted for the narrow margin of victory in several states.

Nat'l Security was major factor

One basis of criticism for a few Northern ratifiers was the compromises manifested in the Constitution with slavery.[28] One of them has already been mentioned: the "three-fifths" bonus given Southern states with regard both to representation in the House of Representatives and then electing members of the Electoral College who would in turn choose the President. Slavery accounted for two other patches of constitutional text, albeit the words "slave" or "slavery" were never actually used. Article I, §9 limited Congress's right to control the "Migration or Importation of such Persons as any of the states now existing shall think proper to admit" until 1808, when Congress in fact passed a law prohibiting the importation of slaves into the United States from abroad. (The internal slave trade was not affected.) And Article IV, §2, cl. 3 establishes a duty of states to return any "Person held to Service or Labour in one State, under the Laws thereof," who attempts to escape into another state (one that presumably does not recognize the ownership of one human being by another). We have ample opportunity in this book to consider the constitutional implications of these, and other, clauses in regard to America's "peculiar institution" of race-based chattel slavery.

Far more criticism was directed at what is most obviously lacking in the original Constitution: the explicit protection of the rights of the citizenry even as the national government was being granted extensive new powers. Indeed, Virginia's George Mason, one of the most respected members of the Philadelphia delegation, refused to sign the Constitution because it lacked what the Virginia constitution included, a declaration of rights. This became one of the central arguments of those opposing ratification of the Constitution. In the 84th Federalist, Hamilton responded to such calls:

> I affirm that the bills of rights . . . are not only unnecessary in the proposed constitution, but would even be dangerous. They would contain various exceptions to powers which are not granted; and on this very account, would afford a colourable pretext to claim more than were granted. For why declare that things shall not be done which there is no power to do? Why, for instance, should it be said, that the liberty of the press shall not be restrained, when no power is given by which restrictions may be imposed? I will not contend that such a provision would confer a regulating power; but it is evident that it would furnish to men disposed to usurp, a plausible pretence for claiming that power. They might urge with a semblance of reason, that the constitution ought not to be charged with the absurdity of providing against the abuse of an authority, which was not given, and that the provision against restraining the liberty of the press afforded a clear implication, that a power to prescribe proper regulations concerning it, was intended to be vested in the national government. This may serve as

---

27. Max M. Edling, A Revolution in Favor of Government: Origins of the United States Constitution and the Making of the American State (2003).

28. For citations and discussion, see Amar, America's Constitution, supra n.1, at 87-98.

a specimen of the numerous hurdles which would be given to the doctrine of constructive powers, by the indulgence of an injudicious zeal for bills of rights.[29]

The principal anti-Federalist response to this argument emphasized the limitations contained in Article I, §9. Why, if the powers of the national government were
limited to assigned powers, was it necessary to prohibit Congress from, say, granting
titles of nobility? In any event, there was sufficient support for a bill of rights that it
became a de facto condition of ratification by many of the delegates. Madison, who
had initially agreed with his then-colleague Hamilton on the inefficacy of a formal
bill of rights, became the primary architect of the first amendments to the
Constitution during the first session of Congress in 1789. Twelve such amendments
were proposed, ten of which were ratified in 1791. (One of the two initially nonrat-
ified amendments, the original Second Amendment, was deemed to have been ratified in 1992, 203 years after its initial proposal in 1789. The legitimacy of its
ratification is considered below at pp. 477-481.) One question you might ask yourself as you confront cases dealing with the scope of congressional powers, is
whether Hamilton's and Iredell's fears have been vindicated by events.

29. Hamilton was scarcely unique in making this argument. Probably the most influential version at
the time was that of Philadelphia's James Wilson, in an address to the citizens of that city during their
consideration of the Constitution, which occurred far earlier than New York's. James Iredell of North
Carolina, who with Wilson would be appointed by George Washington to the Supreme Court, told that
state's convention that it would be "not only useless, but dangerous, to enumerate a number of rights
which are not intended to be given up, because it would be implying, in the strongest manner, that every
right not included in the exception might be impaired by the government without usurpation." Speech
of July 19, 1788, before the North Carolina ratifying convention, quoted in Dan Farber and Suzanna
Sherry, A History of the American Constitution 320 (2d ed., 2005).

Chapter 1

The Bank of the United States: A Case Study

This chapter focuses mainly on one of the first constitutional questions confronted by the new federal government: whether chartering a national bank was within the powers delegated to Congress by Article I. We move from the last decade of the eighteenth century, when the issue came before the legislative and executive branches, through the early decades of the nineteenth century, when it was faced by the Supreme Court and again by the President. Besides introducing the issue of federalism, Chapter 1 presents some themes that pervade the book, including the strategies of constitutional interpretation and the allocation of decisionmaking authority among the branches of government. The chapter concludes by examining the constitutional issues surrounding the Sedition Act of 1798, which raised many similar issues.

I. Early Background

"There is nothing in the Constitution about banks and banking, though there might well have been, for the subject was already of both economic and political importance when the Constitution was being written."[1] In 1781, the Continental Congress chartered the Bank of North America. Probably few members of that Congress disputed James Madison's assertion that this exceeded Congress's authority under the Articles of Confederation.[2] Rather, the bank was justified by its sheer necessity in helping finance the war for independence against Great Britain.

At the Philadelphia Convention in 1787, Madison himself proposed that Congress be authorized "to grant charters of incorporation where the interest of the U.S. might require & the legislative provisions of individual States may be incompetent."[3] Rufus King of Massachusetts objected to the proposal on the ground that the "States will be prejudiced and divided into parties by it"; King referred specifically to the concerns of the New York and Philadelphia banking and business communities that Congress might charter a competing banking

---

1. Bray Hammond, Banks and Politics in America from the Revolution to the Civil War 103 (1957).

2. Madison initially opposed incorporation of the bank because of "the absence within the Articles of Confederation of any authority, even that of 'inferred necessity,' to create a bank to carry on the war." 3 Papers of James Madison 175 n.16 (1963). When the ordinance of incorporation came to a vote, he cast what he later termed "an acquiescing rather than an affirmative vote." See 4 id. at 19, 21 nn.7, 23 (1965).

3. 2 Records of the Federal Convention of 1787, at 615-616 (Farrand ed., 1937) (hereinafter Farrand). No general corporation laws existed in the eighteenth and early nineteenth centuries. Corporate charters, typically giving exclusive rights to quasi-public entities, were tailor-made for the occasion. See Lawrence Friedman, A History of American Law 166-169 (1973).

institution.[4] "Other advocates of the power held back from putting the question to a vote lest it be lost and the record be definitely against it, whereas if not acted on it could be held . . . that the power existed."[5] Gouverneur Morris of Pennsylvania dissuaded his colleague, Robert Morris, from proposing a national bank lest such a provision in the Constitution jeopardize its ratification.[6] The only related proposal brought to a vote — a motion to authorize Congress to charter corporations for the construction of canals — was defeated eight to three.[7]

II.   The First Bank of the United States

In the late eighteenth and early nineteenth centuries, banks served two main functions. First, they were depositories for money. Second, they issued bank notes, on deposits or on other security, which served somewhat the same function as paper money in the absence of a national currency.[8] In December 1790, soon after ratification of the Constitution, Secretary of the Treasury Alexander Hamilton submitted a plan for a national bank to be chartered by Congress and owned jointly by private shareholders and the United States. The bank would strengthen the national government: It would aid in the collection of taxes and administration of the public finances and could provide loans to the government.[9] The Senate, half of whose 20 members had attended the Philadelphia Convention, unanimously adopted Hamilton's proposal.[10]

A.   Madison's View

[James Madison, elected to the first Congress from Virginia, opened the debate in the House of Representatives by denouncing the bank as beyond Congress's constitutionally delegated authority.][11]

Madison had entertained this opinion from the date of the Constitution. His impression might, perhaps, be the stronger, because he well recollected that a power to grant charters of incorporation had been proposed in the general convention and rejected.

---

4. 2 Farrand, supra n.3, at 615-616.
5. Hammond, supra n.1, at 104-105.
6. Id. at 105.
7. 2 Farrand, supra n.3, at 615-616.
8. Article I, §10 prohibits states from coining money or emitting bills of credit. Article I, §8 authorizes Congress to coin money (though not in terms to issue bills of credit). Not until after the Civil War did Congress authorize the issuance of paper money.
9. Hammond, supra n.1, at 114-115.
10. R.K. Moulton, Legislative and Documentary History of the Banks of the United States 13 (1834).
11. James Madison's Speech to the House of Representatives (1791), in James Madison, Writings 480-490 (Jack Rakove ed., 1999). The text of the speech refers to Madison in the third person because of stylistic practices of the House reporter whose notes are the source of our knowledge of what Madison told his colleagues.

Is the power of establishing an incorporated Bank among the powers vested by the Constitution in the Legislature of the United States? This is the question to be examined. After some general remarks on the limitations of all political power, he took notice of the peculiar manner in which the Federal Government is limited. It is not a general grant, out of which particular powers are excepted; it is a grant of particular powers only, leaving the general mass in other hands. So it has been understood by its friends and its foes, and so it was to be interpreted.

[margin note: Madison: Constitutional limitations on gov't]

As preliminaries to the right interpretation, he laid down the following rules: An interpretation that destroys the very characteristic of the Government cannot be just.

Where the meaning is clear, the consequences, whatever they may be, are to be admitted — where doubtful, it is fairly triable by its consequences.

In controverted cases, the meaning of the parties to the instrument, if to be collected by reasonable evidence, is a proper guide.

Contemporary and concurrent expositions are a reasonable evidence of the meaning of the parties.

In admitting or rejecting a constructive authority, not only the degree of its incidentality to an express authority is to be regarded, but the degree of its importance also; since on this will depend the probability or improbability of its being left to construction.

Reviewing the Constitution with an eye to these positions, it was not possible to discover in it the power to incorporate a bank. The only clauses under which such a power could be pretended, are either:

1. The power to lay and collect taxes to pay the debts, and provide for the common defence and general welfare: Or,
2. The power to borrow money on the credit of the United States: Or,
3. The power to pass all laws necessary and proper to carry into execution those powers.

The bill did not come within the first power. It laid no taxes to pay the debts, or provide for the general welfare. It laid no tax whatever. It was altogether foreign to the subject.

No argument could be drawn from the terms "common defence" and "general welfare." The power as to these general purposes was limited to acts laying taxes for them; and the general purposes themselves were limited and explained by the particular enumeration subjoined. To understand these terms in any sense, that would justify the power in question, would give the Congress an unlimited power; would render nugatory the enumeration of particular powers; would supercede all the powers reserved to the State Governments. . . .

The case of the Bank established by the former Congress has been cited as a precedent. This was known, he said, to have been the child of necessity. It never could be justified by the regular powers of the articles of Confederation. . . .

The second clause to be examined is that which empowers Congress to borrow money.

Is this bill to borrow money? It does not borrow a shilling. Is there any fair construction by which the bill can be deemed an exercise of the power to borrow money? The obvious meaning of the power to borrow money, is that of accepting it from, and stipulating payment to those who are able and willing to lend. . . .

The third clause is that which gives the power to pass all laws necessary and proper to execute the specified powers.

Whatever meaning this clause may have, none can be admitted, that would give an unlimited discretion to Congress.

Its meaning must, according to the natural and obvious force of the terms and the context, be limited to means necessary to the end, and incident to the nature of the specified powers.

The clause is in fact merely declaratory of what would have resulted by unavoidable implication, as the appropriate, and, as it were, technical means of executing those powers. In this sense it has been explained by the friends of the Constitution, and ratified by the State Conventions.

The essential characteristic of the Government, as composed of limited and enumerated powers, would be destroyed, if instead of direct and incidental means, any means could be used which, in the language of the preamble to the bill, "might be conceived to be conducive to the successful conducting of the finances, or might be conceived to tend to give facility to the obtaining of loans. . . ." If, proceeded he, Congress, by virtue of the power to borrow, can create the means of lending, and, in pursuance of these means, can incorporate a Bank, they may do any thing whatever creative of like means. . . .

If, again, Congress by virtue of the power to borrow money, can create the ability to lend, they may, by virtue of the power to levy money, create the ability to pay it. The ability to pay taxes depends on the general wealth of the society, and this, on the general prosperity of agriculture, manufactures, and commerce. Congress then may give bounties and make regulations on all these objects. . . .

Mark the reasoning on which the validity of the bill depends. To borrow money is made the end, and the accumulation of capitals implied as the means. The accumulation of money is then the end, and the Bank implied as the means. The Bank is then the end, and a charter of incorporation, a monopoly, . . . &c. implied as the means.

If implications, thus remote and thus multiplied, can be linked together, a chain may be formed that will reach every object of legislation, every object within the whole compass of political economy.

The latitude of interpretation required by the bill is condemned by the rule furnished by the Constitution itself.

Congress have power "to regulate the value of money;" yet it is expressly added, not left to be implied, that counterfeiters may be punished.

They have the power "to declare war," to which armies are more incident, than incorporated banks to borrowing; yet the power "to raise and support armies" is expressly added; and to this again, the express power "to make rules and regulations for the government of armies"; a like remark is applicable to the powers as to the navy.

The regulation and calling out of militia are more appurtenant to war than the proposed Bank to borrowing; yet the former is not left to construction.

The very power to borrow money is a less remote implication from the power of war, than an incorporated monopoly Bank from the power of borrowing; yet the power is not left to implication.

It is not pretended that every insertion or omission in the Constitution is the effect of systematic attention. This is not the character of any human work, particularly the work of a body of men. The examples cited, with others that might be added, sufficiently inculcate, nevertheless, a rule of interpretation very different from that on which the bill rests. They condemn the exercise of any power, particularly a great and important power, which is not evidently and necessarily involved in an express power.

It cannot be denied that the power proposed to be exercised is an important power. As a charter of incorporation, the bill creates an artificial person previously not existing in law. It confers important civil rights and attributes, which could not otherwise be claimed. It is, though not precisely similar, at least equivalent, to the naturalization of an alien, by which certain new civil characters are acquired by him. Would Congress have had the power to naturalize, if it had not been expressly given?

He here adverted to a distinction, which he said has not been sufficiently kept in view, between a power necessary and proper for the Government or Union, and a power necessary and proper for executing the enumerated powers.

In the latter case, the powers included in each of the enumerated powers were not expressed, but drawn from the nature of each. In the former, the powers composing the Government were expressly enumerated. This constituted the peculiar nature of the Government, no power, therefore, not enumerated could be inferred from the general nature of Government. Had the power of making treaties, for example, been omitted, however necessary it might have been, the defect could only have been lamented, or supplied by an amendment of the Constitution.

But the proposed Bank could not be called necessary to the Government; at most could be but convenient. Its uses to the Government could be supplied by keeping the taxes a little in advance; by loans from individuals; by other Banks, over which the Government would have equal command; nay greater, as it might grant or refuse to these the privilege (a free and irrevocable gift to the proposed Bank) of using their notes in the federal revenue.

He proceeded next to the contemporary expositions given to the Constitution [in various ratification conventions, which supported the conclusion] that the terms necessary and proper gave no additional powers to those enumerated. . . .

The explanatory declarations and amendment accompanying the ratifications of the several states formed a striking evidence, wearing the same complexion. He referred those who might doubt on the subject, to the several acts of ratification.

The explanatory amendments proposed by Congress themselves, at least, would be good authority with them; all these renunciations of power proceeded on a rule of construction, excluding the latitude now contended for. These explanations were the more to be respected, as they had not only been proposed by Congress, but ratified by nearly three-fourths of the states. [Virginia had not yet ratified the "Bill of Rights."] He read several of the articles proposed, remarking particularly on the [Ninth and Tenth Amendments], the former, as guarding against a latitude of interpretation — the latter, as excluding every source of power not within the constitution itself.

With all this evidence of the sense in which the Constitution was understood and adopted, will it not be said, if the bill should pass, that its adoption was brought about by one set of arguments, and that it is now administered under the influence of another set. . . . [?]

It appeared on the whole, he concluded, that the power exercised by the bill was condemned by the silence of the constitution; was condemned by the rule of interpretation arising out of the constitution; was condemned by its tendency to destroy the main characteristic of the constitution; was condemned by the expositions of the friends of the constitution, whilst depending on the before the public; was condemned by the apparent intention of the parties which ratified the constitution; was condemned by the explanatory amendments proposed by Congress themselves to the Constitution; and he hoped it would receive its final condemnation, by the vote of this house.

Most of the other participants in the House debate argued for a broader notion of congressional power, along the lines later articulated by Hamilton in his memorandum to President Washington (excerpted infra). The House adopted the bill chartering the bank by a vote of 39 to 20. Of the seven Representatives who had attended the Philadelphia Convention, four voted for the measure and three against it.

Passage of the bill did not end the debate over its constitutionality. George Washington, who had been President of the Philadelphia Convention before becoming the first President under the new Constitution, asked his cabinet to prepare memoranda on the constitutional questions. Edmund Randolph, the Attorney General, thought the bill unconstitutional, as did Secretary of State Thomas Jefferson. Hamilton, as already noted, supported the measure.

B.   The Attorney General's Opinion

Section 35 of the Judiciary Act of 1789, one of the first major pieces of legislation passed by the First Congress, created the office of Attorney General. In addition to having the duty "to prosecute and conduct all suits in the Supreme Court in which the United States shall be concerned," the Attorney General must also "give his advice and opinion upon questions of law when requested by the President of the United States, or when requested by the heads of any of the departments, touching any matters that may concern their departments."[12]

Fulfilling his duty, Randolph informed President Washington of the reasons that he found the Bank bill unconstitutional. "To be implied in the nature of the federal government would," Randolph argued, "beget a doctrine so indefinite as to grasp every power." He then moved on to a second question, "whether, upon any principle of fair construction, the specified powers of legislation involve the power of granting charters of incorporation?" Randolph noted that some proponents of the Bank "relied" on the Preamble to the Constitution. "To this, it will be here remarked, once for all, that the Preamble if it be operative is a full constitution of itself; and the body of the Constitution is useless; but that it is declarative only of the views of the convention, which they supposed would be best fulfilled by the powers delineated and that such is the legitimate nature of preambles." Randolph then moved on to specific powers listed in Article I, §8, including the taxation, borrowing, and commerce powers, as well as the Article IV authority given Congress "to dispose and make all needful Rules and Regulations respecting the Territory or

---

12. See H. Jefferson Powell, The Constitution and the Attorneys General xv (1999). Randolph's entire opinion, excerpts of which are found below, can be found at 3-9.

other Property belonging to the United States." The Attorney General finds all such arguments fruitless:

> [T]he serious alarm is in the concentered force of these sentiments. If the laying and collecting of taxes brings with it every thing which, in the opinion of Congress, may facilitate the payment of taxes; if to borrow money sets political speculation loose, to conceive what may create an ability to lend; if to regulate commerce is to range in the boundless mazes of projects for the apparently best scheme to invite from abroad, or to diffuse at home, the precious metals; if to dispose of or so to regulate property of the United States, is to incorporate a bank, that stock may be subscribed to it by them, it may without exaggeration be affirmed that a similar construction on every specified federal power, will stretch the arm of Congress into the whole circle of state legislation.
>
> The general qualities of the federal government, independent of the Constitution and the specified powers, being thus insufficient to uphold the incorporation of a bank, we come to the last inquiry, which has been already anticipated, whether it be sanctified by the power to make all laws which shall be necessary and proper for carrying into execution the powers vested by the Constitution. To be necessary is to be incidental, or in other words, may be denominated the natural means of executing a power.
>
> The phrase, "and proper," if it has any meaning, does not enlarge the power of Congress, but rather restricts them. For no power is to be assumed under the general clause, but such as is not only necessary but proper, or perhaps expedient also. But as the friends to the bill ought not to claim any advantage from this clause, so ought not the enemies to it; to quote the clause as having a restricting effect; both ought to consider it among the surplusage which as often proceeds from inattention as caution.

C. Jefferson's Critique of the Bank

Jefferson referred to the Philadelphia Convention's rejection of the congressional power to incorporate canals: "[O]ne of the reasons for rejection urged in the debate was, that then they would have a power to erect a bank, which would render the great cities, where there were prejudices and jealousies on the subject, adverse to the reception of the Constitution." Continuing in a more general vein he wrote:[13]

> I consider the foundation of the Constitution as laid on this ground: That "all powers not delegated to the United States, by the Constitution, nor prohibited by it to the States, are reserved to the States or to the people." To take a single step beyond the boundaries thus specially drawn around the powers of Congress is to take possession of a boundless field of power, no longer susceptible of any definition.
>
> The incorporation of a bank, and the powers assumed by this bill, have not, in my opinion, been delegated to the United States, by the Constitution. . . .
>
> It has been urged that a bank will give great facility or convenience in the collection of taxes. Suppose this were true: yet the Constitution allows only the means which are *"necessary"*, not those which are merely "convenient" for effecting the enumerated powers. If such a latitude of construction be allowed to this phrase as to give any non-enumerated power, it will go to every one, for there is not one which ingenuity

---

13. Opinion on the Constitutionality of the Bill for Establishing a National Bank, in 19 Papers of Thomas Jefferson 275, 279-280 (1974).

may not torture into a *convenience* in some instance *or other,* to *some one* of so long a list of enumerated powers. It would swallow up all the delegated powers, and reduce the whole to one power, as before observed. Therefore it was that the Constitution restrained them to the *necessary* means, that is to say, to those means without which the grant of power would be nugatory. . . .

The negative of the President is the shield provided by the Constitution to protect against the invasions of the legislature: 1. the right of the Executive. 2. of the Judiciary. 3. of the States and State legislatures. The present is the case of a right remaining exclusively with the States, and consequently one of those intended by the Constitution to be placed under its protection.

It must be added, however, that unless the President's mind on a view of everything which is urged for and against this bill, is tolerably clear that it is unauthorized by the Constitution; if the pro and the con hang so even as to balance his judgment, a just respect for the wisdom of the legislature would naturally decide the balance in favor of their opinion. It is chiefly for the cases where they are clearly misled by error, ambition, or interest, that the Constitution has placed a check in the negative of the President.

D. Hamilton's Defense

ALEXANDER HAMILTON, OPINION ON THE CONSTITUTIONALITY OF AN ACT TO ESTABLISH A BANK (1791)[14]

. . . [P]rinciples of construction like those espoused by the Secretary of State and the Attorney General would be fatal to the just & indispensable authority of the United States. [T]he objections of the Secretary of State and Attorney General are founded on a general denial of the authority of the United States to erect corporations. . . .

Now it appears to the Secretary of the Treasury, that this *general principle* is *inherent* in the very *definition* of *Government* and *essential* to every step of the progress to be made by that of the United States; namely — that every power vested in a Government is in its nature *sovereign,* and includes by *force* of the *term,* a right to employ all the *means* requisite, and fairly *applicable* to the attainment of the *ends* of such power; and which are not precluded by restrictions & exceptions specified in the constitution; or not immoral, or not contrary to the essential ends of political society. . . .

This general & indisputable principle puts at once an end to the *abstract* question — Whether the United States have power to *erect a corporation?* that is to say, to give a *legal* or *artificial capacity* to one or more persons, distinct from the natural. For it is unquestionably incident to *sovereign power* to erect corporations, and consequently to *that* of the United States, in *relation to the objects* intrusted to the management of the government. The difference is this: where the authority of the government is general, it can create corporations in *all cases;* where it is confined to certain branches of legislation, it can create corporations only in those cases. . . . It is not denied, that there are *implied,* as well as *express* powers, and that the former are as effectually delegated as the latter. . . .

Then it follows, that as a power of erecting a corporation may as well be *implied* as any other thing; it may as well be employed as an *instrument* or *mean* of carrying into execution any of the specified powers, as any other instrument or mean

---

14. 8 Papers of Alexander Hamilton 97 (1965).

whatever. The only question must be, in this as in every other case, whether the mean to be employed, or in this instance the corporation to be erected, has a natural relation to any of the acknowledged objects or lawful ends of the government. Thus a corporation may not be erected by congress, for superintending the police of the city of Philadelphia because they are not authorized to *regulate* the *police* of that city; but one may be erected in relation to the collection of the taxes, or to the trade with foreign countries, or to the trade between the States, or with the Indian Tribes, because it is the province of the federal government to regulate those objects & because it is incident to a general *sovereign* or *legislative power* to *regulate* a thing, to employ all the means which relate to its regulation to the *best & greatest advantage*. . . .

To this mode of reasoning respecting the right of employing all the means requisite to the execution of the specified powers of the Government, it is objected that none but *necessary* & proper means are to be employed, & the Secretary of State maintains, that no means are to be considered as *necessary*, but those without which the grant of the power would be *nugatory*. . . . All the arguments therefore against the constitutionality of the bill derived from the accidental existence of certain State-banks: institutions which *happen* to exist today, & for ought that concerns the government of the United States, may disappear tomorrow, must not only be rejected as fallacious, but must be viewed as demonstrative, that there is a *radical* source of error in the reasoning.

It is essential to the being of the National government, that so erroneous a conception of the meaning of the word *necessary*, should be exploded.

It is certain, that neither the grammatical, nor popular sense of the term requires that construction. According to both, *necessary* often means no more than *needful, requisite, incidental, useful*, or *conducive to*. It is a common mode of expression to say, that it is *necessary* for a government or a person to do this or that thing, when nothing more is intended or understood, than that the interests of the government or person require, or will be promoted, by the doing of this or that thing. The imagination can be at no loss for exemplifications of the use of the word in this sense.

. . . The whole turn of the clause containing [the word "necessary"] indicates, that it was the intent of the convention, by that clause to give a liberal latitude to the exercise of the specified powers. . . .

[The alternative] construction would beget endless uncertainty & embarrassment. The cases must be palpable & extreme in which it could be pronounced with certainty, that a measure was absolutely necessary, or one without which the exercise of a given power would be nugatory. There are few measures of any government, which would stand so severe a test. To insist upon it, would be to make the criterion of the exercise of any implied power a *case of extreme necessity*, which is rather a rule to justify the overleaping of the bounds of constitutional authority, than to govern the ordinary exercise of it. . . .

The *degree* in which a measure is necessary, can never be a test of the *legal* right to adopt it. That must ever be a matter of opinion; and can only be a test of expediency. The *relation* between the *measure* and the *end*, between the *nature* of the *mean* employed towards the execution of a power and the object of that power, must be the criterion of constitutionality not the more or less of *necessity* or *utility*.

The practice of the government is against the rule of construction advocated by the Secretary of State. Of this the act concerning light houses, beacons, buoys & public piers, is a decisive example. This doubtless must be referred to the power of regulating trade, and is fairly relative to it. But it cannot be affirmed, that the exercise of that power, in this instance, was strictly necessary; or that the power itself would be *nugatory* without that of regulating establishments of this nature.

This restrictive interpretation of the word *necessary* is also contrary to this sound maxim of construction namely, that the powers contained in a constitution of government, especially those which concern the general administration of the affairs of a country, its finances, trade, defence & ought to be construed liberally, in advancement of the public good. . . .

[T]he doctrine which is contended for . . . does not affirm that the National government is sovereign in all respects, but that it is sovereign to a certain extent: that is, to the extent of the objects of its specified powers.

It leaves therefore a criterion of what is constitutional, and of what is not so. This criterion is the *end* to which the measure relates as a *mean*. If the end be clearly comprehended within any of the specified powers, & if the measure have an obvious relation to that end, and is not forbidden by any particular provision of the constitution — it may safely be deemed to come within the compass of the national authority. . . .

To establish [the National government's power to charter a corporation,] it remains to shew the relation of such an institution to one or more of the specified powers of the government.

Accordingly it is affirmed, that it has a relation more or less direct to the power of collecting taxes; to that of borrowing money; to that of regulating trade between the states; and to those of raising, supporting & maintaining fleets & armies. To the two former, the relation may be said to be *immediate*.

And, in the last place, it will be argued, that it is, *clearly*, within the provision which authorizes the making of all *needful* rules & *regulations* concerning the *property* of the United States, as the same has been practiced upon by the Government.

A Bank relates to the collection of taxes in two ways; *indirectly*, by increasing the quantity of circulating medium & quickening circulation, which facilitates the means of paying — *directly*, by creating a *convenient species* of *medium* in which they are to be paid.

The legislative power of borrowing money, & of making all laws necessary & proper for carrying into execution that power, seems obviously competent to the appointment of the organ through which the abilities and wills of individuals may be most efficaciously exerted, for the accommodation of the government by loans. . . .

The institution of a bank has also a natural relation to the regulation of trade between the States: in so far as it is conducive to the creation of a convenient medium of *exchange* between them, and to the keeping up a full circulation by preventing the frequent displacement of the metals in reciprocal remittances, money is the very hinge on which commerce turns. And this does not mean merely gold & silver, many other things have served the purpose with different degrees of utility. Paper has been extensively employed. . . .

[A]s the bill under consideration contemplates the government in the light of a joint proprietor of the stock of the bank, it brings the case within the provision of the clause of the constitution which immediately respects the property of the United States.

Discussion

On February 25, 1791, President Washington signed the act incorporating the Bank of the United States. Note that of the three persons whose opinions he solicited, two believed it unconstitutional. Unlike Randolph, Jefferson, and Hamilton, Washington was not a lawyer. Is this relevant to assessing the legitimacy of Washington's conclusion as to the constitutionality of the Bank? Is it relevant that the Attorney General of the United States provided one of these negative opinions? Does the Judiciary Act suggest that the Chief Executive (or anyone else within the Executive Branch) is bound by the Attorney General's opinion, or is it, indeed, *merely* "advice and opinion," to be accepted or rejected only insofar as the recipient, whether or not a lawyer, finds it persuasive?

III. The Second Bank

When the bank's 20-year charter lapsed in 1811, Congress refused to renew it. Opposition to the bank came from both Jeffersonian agrarians — though Jefferson himself now publicly supported the Bank — and from the private business and banking community. Of the 39 members of Congress who spoke on the issue of renewal, 35 addressed the constitutionality of the bank. Whether because of constitutional doubts or, more likely, because of the strength of antinational forces in Congress, renewal failed by one vote.[15]

Four years later, however, Congress voted to establish the second Bank of the United States, responding in part to the economic turmoil attached to the War of 1812, as well as the perceived irresponsible fiscal practices by state banks. The federal government had been seriously inconvenienced by its need to rely on state banks to borrow money and to pay national debts. Although James Madison, now President himself, vetoed the renewal, he explicitly "waiv[ed] the question of the constitutional authority of the Legislature to establish an incorporated bank, as being precluded, in my judgment, by the repeated recognitions under varied circumstances of the validity of such an institution, in acts of the Legislative, Executive, and Judicial branches of the Government, accompanied by indications, in different modes, of a concurrence of the general will of the nation."[16] In 1816, however, his doubts about the wisdom of the Bank were stilled, and he signed the bill.

Like its predecessor, the second bank was by no means a purely governmental agency. Private investors owned 80 percent of the stock and the government the remaining 20 percent. Of its 25 directors, 20 were elected by the shareholders, and the president appointed the other 5. The bank did act as the government's primary fiscal agent: The secretary of the treasury was required to deposit all public funds in the bank; it was required to keep, transfer, and disburse all government monies given it; and its notes were made legal tender for the payment of government debts.

The constitutional dispute over the bank was not over, however. A number of states remained intensely hostile and enacted nearly annihilative taxes on the bank. It was in this context that McCulloch v. Maryland came before the Court.

15. Hammond, supra n.1, at 210-222.
16. Quoted in id. at 233. The general story of the renewal is told at 227-233.

IV. Judicial Examination of Congress' Authority to Create the Bank

Note on Reading and Editing Cases

The Supreme Court Justices' opinions in constitutional cases are often very long, and we have necessarily edited most of the cases in this book to focus the issues, to keep the book to a manageable length while covering a variety of issues, and to mitigate tedium. *McCulloch,* however, is unedited.

We suggest that you read Chief Justice Marshall's opinion through once to get a sense of its structure and arguments. Then read it again with a blue pencil (imaginary or real, depending on the projected resale value of this book), trying to omit as much superfluity as you can.

Our own experience as editors is that there is no better way to understand the substance and structure of a person's writing than to edit it. We also hope that you will gain some appreciation of the problems of editing an opinion — not, we hasten to add, so that you will appreciate our hard work, but so you will be skeptical about the relationship between any edited version and the original.

McCULLOCH v. MARYLAND
17 U.S. (4 Wheat.) 316 (1819)

[In 1818, the Maryland Assembly enacted a law imposing an annual tax of $15,000 on all banks or branches of banks in the state not chartered by the state legislature. The only bank that fit this description was the Bank of the United States, whose local cashier, J.W. McCulloch, refused to pay the tax. Maryland successfully sued McCulloch in its own courts to recover the statutory penalty for failure to comply with the statute.]

MARSHALL, C.J.

[The First Question]

[1][1] In the case now to be determined, the defendant, a sovereign State, denies the obligation of a law enacted by the legislature of the Union, and the plaintiff, on his part, contests the validity of an act which has been passed by the legislature of that State. The constitution of our country, in its most interesting and vital parts, is to be considered; the conflicting powers of the government of the Union and of its members, as marked in that constitution, are to be discussed; and an opinion given, which may essentially influence the great operation of the government. No tribunal can approach such a question without a deep sense of its importance, and of the awful responsibility involved in its decision. But it must be decided peacefully, or remain a source of hostile legislation, perhaps of hostility of a still more serious nature; and if it is to be so decided, by this tribunal alone can the decision be made.

¶1 Marshall refers to Maryland as "a sovereign state." What does this mean? *Is* Maryland a sovereign state? Wouldn't a sovereign state have the ability to tax whomever it pleased?

Marshall notes the freighted circumstances surrounding this decision, and that the controversy "must be decided peacefully" lest circumstances lead to "hostility of a still more serious nature" than merely hostile legislation. To what is he referring?

On the Supreme Court of the United States has the constitution of our country devolved this important duty.

[2] The first question made in the cause is, has Congress power to incorporate a bank? *) Issue*

[3] It has been truly said, that this can scarcely be considered as an open question, entirely unprejudiced by the former proceedings of the nation respecting it. The principle now contested was introduced at a very early period of our history, has been recognized by many successive legislatures, and has been acted upon by the judicial department, in cases of peculiar delicacy, as a law of undoubted obligation.

[4] ¶¶4-5 It will not be denied, that a bold and daring usurpation might be resisted, after an acquiescence still longer and more complete than this. But it is conceived that a doubtful question, one on which human reason may pause, and the human judgment be suspended, in the decision of which the great principles of liberty are not concerned, but the respective powers of those who are equally the representatives of the people, are to be adjusted; if not put at rest by the practice of the government, ought to receive a considerable impression from that practice. An exposition of the constitution, deliberately established by legislative acts, on the faith of which an immense property has been advanced, ought not to be lightly disregarded.

[5] The power now contested was exercised by the first Congress elected under the present constitution. The bill for incorporating the bank of the United States did not steal upon an unsuspecting legislature, and passed unobserved. Its principle was completely understood, and was opposed with equal zeal and ability. After being resisted, first in the fair and open field of debate, and afterwards in the executive cabinet, with as much persevering talent as any measure has ever experienced, and being supported by arguments which convinced minds as pure and as intelligent as this country can boast, it became a law. The original act was permitted to expire; but a short experience of the embarrassments to which the refusal to revive it exposed the government, convinced those who were most prejudiced against the measure of its necessity, and induced the passage of the present law. It would require no ordinary share of intrepidity to assert that a measure adopted under these circumstances was a bold and plain usurpation, to which the constitution gave no countenance.

[6] These observations belong to the cause; but they are not made under the impression that, were the question entirely new, the law would be found irreconcilable with the constitution.

Marshall suggests in the final sentence in this paragraph that the Constitution has "devolved" upon the Supreme Court "this important duty" to resolve the issue. Marshall supplies no evidence for this assertion. Might he have cited any relevant constitutional text? Does the text devolve any such duty on the Supreme Court "alone," as Marshall suggests? Do Congress and the President—or for that matter, "We the People"—have any role to play in construing the Constitution's meaning, and, in particular, the proper scope of national power?

¶¶4-5 One way of understanding paragraphs 4-5 of *McCulloch* is as outlining, on the one hand, those circumstances in which courts (or other constitutional adjudicators) should be *deferential* to the decisions of ordinary political actors and, on the other, those in which courts should be sufficiently *suspicious* of those actors to engage in what contemporary jargon labels as "strict scrutiny" of their decisions. Consider, then, the following sets of oppositions suggested by the argument in these two paragraphs:

[7]¶¶7-11 In discussing this question, the counsel for the State of Maryland have deemed it of some importance, in the construction of the constitution, to consider that instrument not as emanating from the people, but as the act of sovereign and independent States. The powers of the general government, it has been said, are delegated by the States, who alone are truly sovereign; and must be exercised in subordination to the States, who alone possess supreme dominion.

[8] It would be difficult to sustain this proposition. The Convention which framed the constitution was indeed electesd by the State legislatures. But the instrument, when it came from their hands, was a mere proposal, without obligation, or

"bold and daring usurpation"	scrupulous adherence to what everybody accepts as constitutional duty
clear and unequivocal language	"doubtful question[s]" upon which "human reason might pause"
presence of a "great principle of liberty"	[mere] question of "the respective powers of those who are equally the representatives of the people"
legislation "pass[ed] unobserved"	passed after full debate
political officials are stupid or corrupt	officials are "as pure and as intelligent as this country can boast"

Is it not clear that one generally would support a greater measure of judicial "intervention" in (some combination) of the first column of circumstances than in the second? Similarly, is it not equally clear that there appears to be little justification for such intervention in (some combination) of the second column? The obvious questions are twofold:

1) How does one establish criteria to identify when any given condition is met?

2) How many of the circumstances have to be met to trigger either "strict scrutiny" (and a high probability of judicial invalidation) as against a search only for what contemporary analysts call "minimum rationality" (and a high probability of judicial deference)? Less obvious, but no less important, is the question of judicial capacity to make any of the given inquiries. For example, how precisely do judges (or anyone else) decide how much debate is enough? And how formal must such a debate be? E.g., should formal "hearings" be required of controversial legislation or structured debate in the House and/or Senate, or is it enough if a lot of newspaper editorials are written and legislators with opposing views appear on various talk shows before a vote, without additional debate, in the legislature? Similarly, how does one decide whether a political leader has a "pure" or "intelligent" mind? Think only of our most recent Presidents. Even if we could agree on standards for assessing their purity or intelligence, does that have anything to do with assessing the constitutionality of actions taken under their claims of presidential powers granted by the Constitution? (Should you decide that courts ought not make such inquiries, does that entail that no one else should either?)

¶¶7-11 Why might "counsel for the State of Maryland have deemed it of some importance, in the construction of the constitution, to consider that instrument not as emanating from the people, but as the act of sovereign and independent states"? Note that eighteenth-century political theory allowed sovereignty to repose in only one entity. This, as the anti-Federalists urged during the ratification campaign, posed problems for the proposed constitution, under which two sovereignties operated simultaneously in the same jurisdiction. The Federalists responded ingeniously by denying sovereignty to both federal and state governments and placing it in "the people." See Gordon Wood, The Creation of the American Republic, 1776-1787 ch. 13 (1969). One can perhaps best understand the placement of these paragraphs early in Marshall's opinion by reference to Professor H. Jefferson Powell's point that a "maxim of political law" during the eighteenth century was that a sovereign can be deprived of any of its powers only by its express consent narrowly construed. Should the states — or the people of the states qua states — be deemed sovereign, the implication of this maxim was that the Constitution should be given "the most strict construction that the instrument will bear" in favor of the retention of power by these sovereigns. See Powell, The Original Understanding of Original Intent, 98 Harv. L. Rev. 885, 929-931 (1985) (quoting the Virginia lawyer St. George Tucker). Placement of sovereignty in the national people would still pre-

pretensions to it. It was reported to the then existing Congress of the United States, with a request that it might "be submitted to a Convention of Delegates, chosen in each State by the people thereof, under the recommendation of its Legislature, for their assent and ratification." This mode of proceeding was adopted; and by the Convention, by Congress, and by the State Legislatures, the instrument was submitted to the people. They acted upon it in the only manner in which they can act safely, effectively, and wisely, on such a subject, by assembling in Convention. It is true, they assembled in their several States — and where else should they have assembled? No political dreamer was ever wild enough to think of breaking down the lines which separate the States, and of compounding the American people into one common mass. Of consequence, when they act, they act in their States. But the measures they adopt do not, on that account, cease to be the measures of the people themselves, or become the measures of the State governments.

[9] From these Conventions the constitution derives its whole authority. The government proceeds directly from the people; is "ordained and established" in the name of the people; and is declared to be ordained, "in order to form a more perfect union, establish justice, ensure domestic tranquility, and secure the blessings of liberty to themselves and to their posterity." The assent of the States, in their sovereign capacity, is implied in calling a Convention, and thus submitting that instrument to the people. But the people were at perfect liberty to accept or reject it; and their act was final. It required not the affirmance, and could not be negatived, by the State governments. The constitution, when thus adopted, was of complete obligation, and bound the State sovereignties.

[10] It has been said, that the people had already surrendered all their powers to the State sovereignties, and had nothing more to give. But, surely, the question whether they may resume and modify the powers granted to government does not remain to be settled in this country. Much more might the legitimacy of the general

---

sumably call for "strict construction" against derogation of their rights, but the crucial point is that popular (as opposed to state) sovereignty deprives states of any special claim to having their ostensible rights privileged over the competing claims of the national government.

Marshall appears to offer three models for who was "sovereign": (1) The people of each state, organized in some meaningful way state by state; (2) the state governments; and (3) the people of an undifferentiated whole called the United States. He is surely right that the state legislatures cannot be sovereign (see Article VII), but that, of course, leaves the other two possibilities. If one opts for the first, then would it follow that one should construe the sovereignty of the national government quite narrowly, as suggested above, as against a more capacious construction that might be legitimated by the third possibility? On what basis should one choose between them? Marshall does refer to "the people" in 7-11, but is this dispositive as to choosing (3) as against (1)? How, for example, does one understand his statement, "No political dreamer was ever wild enough to think of breaking down the lines which separate the States, and of compounding the American people into one common mass. Of consequence, when they act, they act in their States." See Martin S. Flaherty, John Marshall, McCulloch v. Maryland, and "We the People": Revisions in Need of Revising, 43 William and Mary L. Rev. 1339 (2002).

Consider the August 7, 1787, draft of the Constitution, which had the following preamble:

We the people of the States of New-Hampshire, Massachusetts, Rhode-Island and Providence Plantations [and the other 13 original States] do ordain, declare and establish the following Constitution or the Government of Ourselves and our Posterity.

Does it matter that this was changed, for reasons that are wholly unclear, by the Committee on Style? What is the consequence for the "Unionist" argument of Article VII, which sets out the mode of ratification (or of Article V, which sets out the process by which the Constitution is amended)? How does Marshall respond to Maryland's invocation of Article VII? Is the response satisfactory?

government be doubted, had it been created by the States. The powers delegated to the State sovereignties were to be exercised by themselves, not by a distinct and independent sovereignty, created by themselves. To the formation of a league, such as was the confederation, the State sovereignties were certainly competent. But when, "in order to form a more perfect union," it was deemed necessary to change this alliance into an effective government, possessing great and sovereign powers, and acting directly on the people, the necessity of referring it to the people, and of deriving its powers directly from them, was felt and acknowledged by all.

[11] The government of the Union, then, (whatever may be the influence of this fact on the case,) is, emphatically, and truly, a government of the people. In form and in substance it emanates from them. Its powers are granted by them, and are to be exercised directly on them, and for their benefit.

[12] This government is acknowledged by all to be one of enumerated powers. The principle, that it can exercise only the powers granted to it, would seem too apparent to have required to be enforced by all those arguments which its enlightened friends, while it was depending before the people, found it necessary to urge. That principle is now universally admitted. But the question respecting the extent of the powers actually granted, is perpetually arising, and will probably continue to arise, as long as our system shall exist.

[13] In discussing these questions, the conflicting powers of the general and State governments must be brought into view, and the supremacy of their respective laws, when they are in opposition, must be settled.

[14] If any one proposition could command the universal assent of mankind, we might expect it would be this — that the government of the Union, though limited in its powers, is supreme within its sphere of action. This would seem to result necessarily from its nature. It is the government of all; its powers are delegated by all; it represents all, and acts for all. Though any one State may be willing to control its operations, no State is willing to allow others to control them. The nation, on those subjects on which it can act, must necessarily bind its component parts. But this question is not left to mere reason: the people have, in express terms, decided it, by saying, "this constitution, and the laws of the United States, which shall be made in pursuance thereof," "shall be the supreme law of the land," and by requiring that the members of the State legislatures, and the officers of the executive and judicial departments of the States, shall take the oath of fidelity to it.

[15] The government of the United States, then, though limited in its powers, is supreme; and its laws, when made in pursuance of the constitution, form the supreme law of the land, "any thing in the constitution or laws of any State to the contrary notwithstanding."

[16][116] Among the enumerated powers, we do not find that of establishing a bank or creating a corporation. But there is no phrase in the instrument which,

¶16 Marshall is contrasting the Tenth Amendment with Article II of the Articles of Confederation, which provided: "Each state retains its sovereignty, freedom and independence, and every power, jurisdiction, and right which is not by this confederation expressly delegated to the United States in Congress assembled." In Marbury v. Madison, 5 U.S. (1 Cranch) 137 (1803), in Chapter 2 infra, Marshall wrote: "It cannot be presumed that any clause in the constitution is intended to be without effect: and therefore, such a construction is inadmissible, unless the words require it." Does Marshall's construction of the Tenth Amendment give it any effect? Could he properly have read "expressly" into the Tenth Amendment, and, if so, what difference should it make to the outcome of the case?

How does Marshall establish that Article I marks only the "great outlines" of congressional power, and what follows from the proposition? What is the argument based on Article I, §9? Why else might its limitations have been introduced?

like the articles of confederation, excludes incidental or implied powers; and which requires that every thing granted shall be expressly and minutely described. Even the 10th amendment, which was framed for the purpose of quieting the excessive jealousies which had been excited, omits the word "expressly," and declares only that the powers "not delegated to the United States, nor prohibited to the States, are reserved to the States or to the people;" thus leaving the question, whether the particular power which may become the subject of contest has been delegated to the one government, or prohibited to the other, to depend on a fair construction of the whole instrument. The men who drew and adopted this amendment had experienced the embarrassments resulting from the insertion of this word in the articles of confederation, and probably omitted it to avoid those embarrassments. A constitution, to contain an accurate detail of all the subdivisions of which its great powers will admit, and of all the means by which they may be carried into execution, would partake of the prolixity of a legal code, and could scarcely be embraced by the human mind. It would probably never be understood by the public. Its nature, therefore, requires, that only its great outlines should be marked, its important objects designated, and the minor ingredients which compose those objects be deduced from the nature of the objects themselves. That this idea was entertained by the framers of the American constitution, is not only to be inferred from the nature of the instrument, but from the language. Why else were some of the limitations, found in the ninth section of the 1st article, introduced? It is also, in some degree, warranted by their having omitted to use any restrictive term which might prevent its receiving a fair and just interpretation. In considering this question, then, we must never forget, that it is *a constitution* we are expounding.

[17] Although, among the enumerated powers of government, we do not find the word "bank" or "incorporation," we find the great powers to lay and collect taxes; to borrow money; to regulate commerce; to declare and conduct a war; and to raise and support armies and navies. The sword and the purse, all the external relations, and no inconsiderable portion of the industry of the nation, are entrusted to its government. It can never be pretended that these vast powers draw after them others of inferior importance, merely because they are inferior. Such an idea can never be advanced. But it may with great reason be contended, that a government, entrusted with such ample powers, on the due execution of which the happiness and prosperity of the nation so vitally depends, must also be entrusted with ample means for their execution. The power being given, it is the interest of the nation to facilitate its execution. It can never be their interest, and cannot be presumed to have been their intention, to clog and embarrass its execution by withholding the most appropriate means. Throughout this vast republic, from the St. Croix to the Gulf of Mexico, from the Atlantic to the Pacific, revenue is to be collected and expended, armies are to be marched and supported. The exigencies of the nation may require that the treasure raised in the north should be transported to the south, *that* raised in the east conveyed to the west, or that this order should be reversed. Is that construction of the constitution to be preferred which would render these operations difficult, hazardous, and expensive? Can we adopt that construction, (unless the words imperiously require it,) which would impute to the framers of that instrument, when granting these powers for the public good, the intention of impeding their exercise by withholding a choice of means? If, indeed, such be the mandate of the constitution, we have only to obey; but that instrument does not profess to enumerate the means by which the powers it confers

may be executed; nor does it prohibit the creation of a corporation, if the existence of such a being be essential to the beneficial exercise of those powers. It is, then, the subject of fair inquiry, how far such means may be employed.

[18] ¶¶18-21 It is not denied, that the powers given to the government imply the ordinary means of execution. That, for example, of raising revenue, and applying it to national purposes, is admitted to imply the power of conveying money from place to place, as the exigencies of the nation may require, and of employing the usual means of conveyance. But it is denied that the government has its choice of means; or, that it may employ the most convenient means, if, to employ them, it be necessary to erect a corporation.

[19] On what foundation does this argument rest? On this alone: The power of creating a corporation, is one appertaining to sovereignty, and is not expressly conferred on Congress. This is true. But all legislative powers appertain to sovereignty. The original power of giving the law on any subject whatever, is a sovereign power; and if the government of the Union is restrained from creating a corporation, as a means for performing its functions, on the single reason that the creation of a corporation is an act of sovereignty; if the sufficiency of this reason be acknowledged, there would be some difficulty in sustaining the authority of Congress to pass other laws for the accomplishment of the same objects.

[20] The government which has a right to do an act, and has imposed on it the duty of performing that act, must, according to the dictates of reason, be allowed to select the means; and those who contend that it may not select any appropriate means, that one particular mode of effecting the object is excepted, take upon themselves the burden of establishing that exception.

[21] The creation of a corporation, it is said, appertains to sovereignty. This is admitted. But to what portion of sovereignty does it appertain? Does it belong to one more than to another? In America, the powers of sovereignty are divided between the government of the Union, and those of the States. They are each sovereign, with respect to the objects committed to it, and neither sovereign with respect to the objects committed to the other. We cannot comprehend that train of reasoning which would maintain, that the extent of power granted by the people is to be ascertained, not by the nature and terms of the grant, but by its date. Some State constitutions were formed *before,* some *since* that of the United States. We cannot believe that their relation to each other is in any degree dependent upon this circumstance. Their respective powers must, we think, be precisely the same as if they had been formed at the same time. Had they been formed at the same time, and had the people conferred on the general government the power contained in the constitution, and on the States the whole residuum of power, would it have been asserted that the government of the Union was not sovereign with respect to those objects which were entrusted to it, in relation to which its laws were declared

¶¶18-21 Counsel for Maryland conceded arguendo that "the powers given to the government imply the ordinary means of execution," but contended that chartering a corporation was extraordinary. In England, only the Crown had the power to incorporate, and in early nineteenth-century America — before the advent of general state corporation laws — charters were regarded as quite special privileges, granted by legislatures on a case-by-case basis. How does Marshall meet Maryland's argument that Congress would have the authority to issue charters only if Article I explicitly granted it? Marshall's response consists in part of the assertion that those who contend that Congress may not employ a particular means in furtherance of an enumerated power have the burden of proof. Is this self-evident? Might one not draw the opposite conclusion from the nature of the federal system and the text of the Tenth Amendment?

to be supreme? If this could not have been asserted, we cannot well comprehend the process of reasoning which maintains, that a power appertaining to sovereignty cannot be connected with that vast portion of it which is granted to the general government, so far as it is calculated to subserve the legitimate objects of that government. The power of creating a corporation, though appertaining to sovereignty, is not, like the power of making war, or levying taxes, or of regulating commerce, a great substantive and independent power, which cannot be implied as incidental to other powers, or used as a means of executing them. It is never the end for which other powers are exercised, but a means by which other objects are accomplished. No contributions are made to charity for the sake of an incorporation, but a corporation is created to administer the charity; no seminary of learning is instituted in order to be incorporated, but the corporate character is conferred to subserve the purposes of education. No city was ever built with the sole object of being incorporated, but is incorporated as affording the best means of being well governed. The power of creating a corporation is never used for its own sake, but for the purpose of effecting something else. No sufficient reason is, therefore, perceived, why it may not pass as incidental to those powers which are expressly given, if it be a direct mode of executing them.

[22]¶¶22-26 But the constitution of the United States has not left the right of Congress to employ the necessary means, for the execution of the powers conferred on the government, to general reasoning. To its enumeration of powers is added that of making "all laws which shall be necessary and proper, for carrying into execution the foregoing powers, and all other powers vested by this constitution, in the government of the United States, or in any department thereof."

[23] The counsel for the State of Maryland have urged various arguments, to prove that this clause, though in terms a grant of power, is not so in effect; but is really restrictive of the general right, which might otherwise be implied, of selecting means for executing the enumerated powers.

[24] In support of this proposition, they have found it necessary to contend, that this clause was inserted for the purpose of conferring on Congress the power of making laws. That, without it, doubts might be entertained, whether Congress could exercise its powers in the form of legislation.

[25] But could this be the object for which it was inserted? A government is created by the people, having legislative, executive, and judicial powers. Its legislative powers are vested in a Congress, which is to consist of a Senate and House of Representatives. Each house may determine the rule of its proceedings; and it is declared that every bill which shall have passed both houses, shall, before it becomes a law, be presented to the President of the United States. The 7th section describes the course of proceedings, by which a bill shall become a law; and, then, the 8th section enumerates the powers of Congress. Could it be necessary to say, that a legislature should exercise legislative powers, in the shape of legislation? After allowing each house to prescribe its own course of proceeding, after describing the manner in which a bill should become a law, would it have entered into the

---

¶¶22-26 Marshall begins by invoking the necessary and proper clause as affirmative support for the exercise of congressional power but immediately turns to defend against Maryland's contention that the clause restricts that power. Marshall deals summarily with the argument that, but for the clause, Article I would not have vested Congress with any legislative authority, and then considers the argument that "necessary" restricts Congress to the "most direct and simple" means of implementing the enumerated powers.

mind of a single member of the Convention, that an express power to make laws was necessary to enable the legislature to make them? That a legislature, endowed with legislative powers, can legislate, is a proposition too self-evident to have been questioned.

[26] But the argument on which most reliance is placed, is drawn from the peculiar language of this clause. Congress is not empowered by it to make all laws, which may have relation to the powers conferred on the government, but such only as may be *"necessary and proper"* for carrying them into execution. The word *"necessary"*, is considered as controlling the whole sentence, and as limiting the right to pass laws for the execution of the granted powers, to such as are indispensable, and without which the power would be nugatory. That it excludes the choice of means, and leaves to Congress, in each case, that only which is most direct and simple.

[27][127] Is it true, that this is the sense in which the word "necessary" is always used? Does it always import an absolute physical necessity, so strong, that one thing, to which another may be termed necessary, cannot exist without that other? We think it does not. If reference be had to its use, in the common affairs of the world, or in approved authors, we find that it frequently imports no more than that one thing is convenient, or useful, or essential to another. To employ the means necessary to an end, is generally understood as employing any means calculated to produce the end, and not as being confined to those single means, without which the end would be entirely unattainable. Such is the character of human language, that no word conveys to the mind, in all situations, one single definite idea; and nothing is more common than to use words in a figurative sense. Almost all compositions contain words, which, taken in their rigorous sense, would convey a meaning different from that which is obviously intended. It is essential to just construction, that many words which import something excessive, should be understood in a more mitigated sense — in that sense which common usage justifies. The word "necessary" is of this description. It has not a fixed character peculiar to itself. It admits of all degrees of comparison; and is often connected with other words, which increase or diminish the impression the mind receives of the urgency it imports. A thing may be necessary, very necessary, absolutely or indispensably necessary. To no mind would the same idea be conveyed, by these several phrases. This comment on the word is well illustrated, by the passage cited at the bar, from the 10th section of the 1st article of the constitution. It is, we think, impossible to compare the sentence which prohibits a State from laying "imposts, or duties on imports or exports, except what may be *absolutely* necessary for executing its inspection laws," with that which authorizes Congress "to make all laws which shall be necessary and proper for carrying into execution" the powers of the general government, without feeling a conviction that the convention understood itself to change materially the meaning of the word "necessary," by prefixing the word "absolutely." This word, then, like others, is used in various senses; and, in its construction, the subject, the context, the intention of the person using them, are all to be taken into view.

¶27 Note the sources to which Marshall alludes to support his interpretation of "necessary." What other sources were available? (Had he looked at Samuel Johnson's Dictionary of the English Language (1755) he would have found the "rigorous" definition: "needful, indispensably requisite." The first American dictionary, Noah Webster's Compendious Dictionary of the English Language (1806), included "proper.")

[28]¶¶28-32 Let this be done in the case under consideration. The subject is the execution of those great powers on which the welfare of a nation essentially depends. It must have been the intention of those who gave these powers, to insure, as far as human prudence could insure, their beneficial execution. This could not be done by confiding the choice of means to such narrow limits as not to leave it in the power of Congress to adopt any which might be appropriate, and which were conducive to the end. This provision is made in a constitution intended to endure for ages to come, and, consequently, to be adapted to the various *crises* of human affairs. To have prescribed the means by which government should, in all future time, execute its powers, would have been to change, entirely, the character of the instrument, and give it the properties of a legal code. It would have been an unwise attempt to provide, by immutable rules, for exigencies which, if foreseen at all, must have been seen dimly, and which can be best provided for as they occur. To have declared that the best means shall not be used, but those alone without which the power given would be nugatory, would have been to deprive the legislature of the capacity to avail itself of experience, to exercise its reason, and to accommodate its legislation to circumstances. If we apply this principle of construction to any of the powers of the government, we shall find it so pernicious in its operation that we shall be compelled to discard it. The powers vested in Congress may certainly be carried into execution, without prescribing an oath of office. The power to exact this security for the faithful performance of duty, is not given, nor is it indispensably necessary. The different departments may be established; taxes may be imposed and collected; armies and navies may be raised and maintained; and money may be borrowed, without requiring an oath of office. It might be argued, with as much plausibility as other incidental powers have been assailed, that the Convention was not unmindful of this subject. The oath which might be exacted — that of fidelity to the constitution — is prescribed, and no other can be required. Yet, he would be charged with insanity who should contend, that the legislature might not add to the oath as directed by the constitution, such other oath of office as its wisdom might suggest.

[29] So, with respect to the whole penal code of the United States: whence arises the power to punish in cases not prescribed by the constitution? All admit that the government may, legitimately, punish any violation of its laws; and yet, this is not among the enumerated powers of Congress. The right to enforce the observance of law, by punishing its infraction, might be denied with the more plausibility, because it is expressly given in some cases. Congress is empowered "to provide for the punishment of counterfeiting the securities and current coin of the United States," and "to define and punish piracies and felonies committed on the high seas, and offences against the law of nations." The several powers of Congress may exist, in a very imperfect state to be sure, but they may exist and be carried into execution, although no punishment should be inflicted in cases where the right to punish is not expressly given.

[30] Take, for example, the power "to establish post offices and post roads." This power is executed by the single act of making the establishment. But, from this has been inferred the power and duty of carrying the mail along the post road, from one post office to another. And, from this implied power, has again been inferred

---

¶¶28-32 To support his "figurative" reading of the word, Marshall looks to the "subject, the context, [and] the intention of the person" using it. What is the argument of 28? Does it have any force independent of the counterexamples that follow in 29-30? Is the argument by counterexample persuasive?

the right to punish those who steal letters from the post office, or rob the mail. It may be said, with some plausibility, that the right to carry the mail, and to punish those who rob it, is not indispensably necessary to the establishment of a post office and post road. This right is indeed essential to the beneficial exercise of the power, but not indispensably necessary to its existence. So, of the punishment of the crimes of stealing or falsifying a record or process of a Court of the United States, or of perjury in such Court. To punish these offences is certainly conducive to the due administration of justice. But courts may exist, and may decide the causes brought before them, though such crimes escape punishment.

[31] The baneful influence of this narrow construction on all the operations of the government, and the absolute impracticability of maintaining it without rendering the government incompetent to its great objects, might be illustrated by numerous examples drawn from the constitution, and from our laws. The good sense of the public has pronounced, without hesitation, that the power of punishment appertains to sovereignty, and may be exercised whenever the sovereign has a right to act, as incidental to his constitutional powers. It is a means for carrying into execution all sovereign powers, and may be used, although not indispensably necessary. It is a right incidental to the power, and conducive to its beneficial exercise.

[32] If this limited construction of the word "necessary" must be abandoned in order to punish, whence is derived the rule which would reinstate it, when the government would carry its powers into execution by means not vindictive in their nature? If the word "necessary" means "needful," "requisite," "essential," "conducive to," in order to let in the power of punishment for the infraction of law; why is it not equally comprehensive when required to authorize the use of means which facilitate the execution of the powers of government without the infliction of punishment?

[33] ¶33 In ascertaining the sense in which the word "necessary" is used in this clause of the constitution, we may derive some aid from that with which it is associated. Congress shall have power "to make all laws which shall be necessary and *proper* to carry into execution" the powers of the government. If the word "necessary" was used in that strict and rigorous sense for which the counsel for the State of Maryland contend, it would be an extraordinary departure from the usual course of the human mind, as exhibited in composition, to add a word, the only possible effect of which is to qualify that strict and rigorous meaning; to present to the mind the idea of some choice of means of legislation not strained and compressed within the narrow limits for which gentlemen contend.

[34] ¶¶34-37 But the argument which most conclusively demonstrates the error of the construction contended for by the counsel for the State of Maryland, is founded on the intention of the Convention, as manifested in the whole clause. To waste time and argument in proving that, without it, Congress might carry its powers into execution, would be not much less idle than to hold a lighted taper to the sun. As little can it be required to prove, that in the absence of this clause, Congress would

---

¶33 Is Marshall correct that "proper" would be superfluous if "necessary" were read in its rigorous sense? Might "proper" mean "not prohibited by Article I, §9"? Doesn't Marshall's interpretation of "necessary" make "proper" superfluous—at least unless "necessary" is given a somewhat restrictive meaning?

¶¶34-37 34 seems largely introductory to the perceptive argument of 35-36 based on the location and phraseology of the clause. But doesn't it suggest an argument in Maryland's favor that Marshall ought to meet: that if Congress would have broad ancillary powers without the clause, and a document should presumptively be read so as to make no clause superfluous, then the necessary and proper clause must be designed to restrict congressional power? Is the response implicit in 37 satisfactory?

have some choice of means. That it might employ those which, in its judgment, would most advantageously effect the object to be accomplished. That any means adapted to the end, any means which tended directly to the execution of the constitutional powers of the government, were in themselves constitutional. This clause, as construed by the State of Maryland, would abridge, and almost annihilate this useful and necessary right of the legislature to select its means. That this could not be intended, is, we should think, had it not been already controverted, too apparent for controversy. We think so for the following reasons:

[35] 1st. The clause is placed among the powers of Congress, not among the limitations on those powers.

[36] 2nd. Its terms purport to enlarge, not to diminish the powers vested in the government. It purports to be an additional power, not a restriction on those already granted. No reason has been, or can be assigned for thus concealing an intention to narrow the discretion of the national legislature under words which purport to enlarge it. The framers of the constitution wished its adoption, and well knew that it would be endangered by its strength, not by its weakness. Had they been capable of using language which would convey to the eye one idea, and, after deep reflection, impress on the mind another, they would rather have disguised the grant of power, than its limitation. If, then, their intention had been, by this clause, to restrain the free use of means which might otherwise have been implied, that intention would have been inserted in another place, and would have been expressed in terms resembling these. "In carrying into execution the foregoing powers, and all others," &c. "no laws shall be passed but such as are necessary and proper." Had the intention been to make this clause restrictive, it would unquestionably have been so in form as well as in effect.

[37] The result of the most careful and attentive consideration bestowed upon this clause is, that if it does not enlarge, it cannot be construed to restrain the powers of Congress, or to impair the right of the legislature to exercise its best judgment in the selection of measures to carry into execution the constitutional powers of the government. If no other motive for its insertion can be suggested, a sufficient one is found in the desire to remove all doubts respecting the right to legislate on that vast mass of incidental powers which must be involved in the constitution, if that instrument be not a splendid bauble.

[38]¶38 We admit, as all must admit, that the powers of the government are limited, and that its limits are not to be transcended. But we think the sound construction of the constitution must allow to the national legislature that discretion, with respect to the means by which the powers it confers are to be carried into execution, which will enable that body to perform the high duties assigned to it, in the manner most beneficial to the people. Let the end be legitimate, let it be within the scope of the constitution, and all means which are appropriate, which are plainly adapted to that end, which are not prohibited, but consist with the letter and spirit of the constitution, are constitutional.

[39] That a corporation must be considered as a means not less usual, not of higher dignity, not more requiring a particular specification than other means, has

---

¶38 This is one of the most quoted paragraphs in the American constitutional corpus. Would it be fair to paraphrase it as "Congress can do whatever it wants so long as it does not contravene an express and specific prohibition contained in this text?" How well does this culminating paragraph fit with Marshall's acknowledgment in paragraphs 15 and 16 that the national government is one of limited and enumerated powers?

been sufficiently proved. If we look to the origin of corporations, to the manner in which they have been framed in that government from which we have derived most of our legal principles and ideas, or to the uses to which they have been applied, we find no reason to suppose that a constitution, omitting, and wisely omitting, to enumerate all the means for carrying into execution the great powers vested in government, ought to have specified this. Had it been intended to grant this power as one which should be distinct and independent, to be exercised in any case whatever, it would have found a place among the enumerated powers of the government. But being considered merely as a means, to be employed only for the purpose of carrying into execution the given powers, there could be no motive for particularly mentioning it.

[40] The propriety of this remark would seem to be generally acknowledged by the universal acquiescence in the construction which has been uniformly put on the 3rd section of the 4th article of the constitution. The power to "make all needful rules and regulations respecting the territory or other property belonging to the United States," is not more comprehensive, than the power "to make all laws which shall be necessary and proper for carrying into execution" the powers of the government. Yet all admit the constitutionality of a territorial government, which is a corporate body.

Corporate body OK in another similarly worded part of Cons.

[41] If a corporation may be employed indiscriminately with other means to carry into execution the powers of the government, no particular reason can be assigned for excluding the use of a bank, if required for its fiscal operations. To use one, must be within the discretion of Congress, if it be an appropriate mode of executing the powers of government. That it is a convenient, a useful, and essential instrument in the prosecution of its fiscal operations, is not now a subject of controversy. All those who have been concerned in the administration of our finances, have concurred in representing its importance and necessity; and so strongly have they been felt, that statesmen of the first class, whose previous opinions against it had been confirmed by every circumstance which can fix the human judgment, have yielded those opinions to the exigencies of the nation. Under the confederation, Congress, justifying the measure by its necessity, transcended perhaps its power to obtain the advantage of a bank; and our own legislation attests the universal conviction of the utility of this measure. The time has passed away when it can be necessary to enter into any discussion in order to prove the importance of this instrument, as a means to effect the legitimate objects of the government.

[42]¶42 But, were its necessity less apparent, none can deny its being an appropriate measure; and if it is, the degree of its necessity, as has been very justly observed, is to be discussed in another place. Should Congress, in the execution of its powers, adopt measures which are prohibited by the constitution; or should Congress, under the pretext of executing its powers, pass laws for the accomplishment of objects not entrusted to the government; it would become the painful duty of this tribunal, should a case requiring such a decision come before it, to say that such an act was not the law of the land. But where the law is not prohibited, and is really calculated to effect any of the objects entrusted to the government, to undertake here to inquire into the degree of its necessity, would be to pass the line which circumscribes the judicial department, and to tread on legislative ground. This court disclaims all pretensions to such a power.

¶42 To some extent this paragraph is designed to reassure readers that Congress did not in fact have plenary power. What is a "pretext"? What kinds of inquiry would be necessary to demonstrate its existence?

[43] After this declaration, it can scarcely be necessary to say, that the existence of State banks can have no possible influence on the question. No trace is to be found in the constitution of an intention to create a dependence of the government of the Union on those of the States, for the execution of the great powers assigned to it. Its means are adequate to its ends; and on those means alone was it expected to rely for the accomplishment of its ends. To impose on it the necessity of resorting to means which it cannot control, which another government may furnish or withhold, would render its course precarious, the result of its measures uncertain and create a dependence on other governments, which might disappoint its most important designs, and is incompatible with the language of the constitution. But were it otherwise, the choice of means implies a right to choose a national bank in preference to State banks, and Congress alone can make the election.

[44] After the most deliberate consideration, it is the unanimous and decided opinion of this Court, that the act to incorporate the Bank of the United States is a law made in pursuance of the constitution, and is a part of the supreme law of the land.

[45] The branches, proceeding from the same stock, and being conducive to the complete accomplishment of the object, are equally constitutional. It would have been unwise to locate them in the charter, and it would be unnecessarily inconvenient to employ the legislative power in making those subordinate arrangements. The great duties of the bank are prescribed; those duties require branches; and the bank itself may, we think, be safely trusted with the selection of places where those branches shall be fixed; reserving always to the government the right to require that a branch shall be located where it may be deemed necessary.

A. The Reaction to *McCulloch*

When *McCulloch* was decided in 1819, few persons of stature in the national political community genuinely disputed the desirability or, more to the point, constitutionality of the national bank. Yet Marshall's opinion stirred great controversy, for it went far beyond the specifics of the bank, first to portray an eloquent vision of a single nation, governed by a national government possessing broad powers, coupled with a Court willing to offer what could seem like almost complete deference to the decisions reached by Congress. During the months following the decision a number of critical essays appeared in the Richmond Enquirer.[17]

One author, writing under the pseudonym of Amphictyon, criticized the breadth of Marshall's opinion, especially with respect to the source of the government's power:[18]

> If the powers of the federal government are to be viewed as the grant of the people, without regard to the distinctive features of the states, then it would follow that if a majority of the whole sovereign population of the United States had ratified the constitution, it would immediately have been binding on the minority, although that minority should consist of every individual in one or more states. But we would know

17. See John Marshall's Defense of the Constitution (Gunther ed., 1969) (hereinafter cited as Gunther).

18. Id. at 56.

that such was not the case. Each state was an independent political society. The constitution was not binding on any state, even the smallest, without its own free and voluntary consent. . . . The respective states then in their sovereign capacity did delegate the federal government its powers, and in so doing were parties to the compact.

The source of the federal government's power had been a matter of controversy at least from the time of the ratification campaigns. In the Virginia ratifying convention, Patrick Henry, a staunch opponent of the new Constitution, demanded why the Preamble to the Constitution said "*We, the people,* instead of *We the States*? States are the characteristics and the soul of a confederation. If the States be not the agents of this compact, it must be one great consolidated government of the people of all States."[19] A delegate responded that no one "but the people have a right to form government,"[20] to which Henry, referring to the fear that a "consolidated government" would ride roughshod over individual liberty, replied that "the principles of this system are extremely pernicious, impolitic, and dangerous."[21] Patrick Henry was expressing a belief, widely held in that and other times, that liberty depended on government by small political units subject to close citizen participation and control.[22] The new Constitution, by contrast, established a national government, having vastly greater powers than the Confederation and the authority over a large and expanding territory.[23]

The most important argument regarding state sovereignty and the relevance thereof to constitutional interpretation was made at the very end of the eighteenth century in the Virginia and Kentucky Resolutions, written by Madison and Jefferson, respectively, that challenged the constitutionality of the Alien and Sedition Acts of 1798.[24] Jefferson had written in the Kentucky Resolution:

> [T]he several states who formed [the Constitution], being sovereign and independent, have the unquestionable right to judge of its infraction, and . . . a nullification, by those sovereignties, of all unauthorized acts done under colour of that instrument, is the rightful remedy.[25]

19. Quoted in Sources and Documents Illustrating the American Revolution, 1764-1788 and the Formation of the Federal Constitution 309 (Morison ed., 1965).

20. Id. at 315.

21. Id. at 321-322.

22. See Hannah Arendt, On Revolution (1963); Gordon Wood, Creation of the American Republic, 1776-1787 (1969).

23. In The Federalist No. 14, Madison argued that republican liberty could survive in an area as large as the United States. Recall, though, that the United States he was explicitly referring to was the original 13 states plus the Northwest Territory and other territory that was possessed by the states and would be ceded to the new United States. By 1819, though, it had more than doubled as a result of the Louisiana Purchase, and Marshall could casually refer to a "vast republic" stretching to the Pacific. Given that the 1803 Louisiana Purchase extended only into Montana, Marshall's statement is presumably based on the Adams-Onis Treaty of 1819 with Spain, by which Spain ceded to the United States all claims on the West Coast north of the 42nd parallel. See Frederick Merk, The Oregon Question: Essays in Anglo-American Diplomacy & Politics 37 (1967). Though this might have resolved certain tensions between Spain and the United States, it did nothing to resolve far more important conflicts in the area between the United States and Great Britain. That awaited the Webster-Ashburton Treaty of 1842, which recognized U.S. claims to the Oregon Territory. Does one's view of the Constitution depend on how large the United States is (or one thinks ought to be)? Assume, for example, that one believes that westward expansion is a bad idea, for whatever reason. Would one tend to read the Constitution differently from Marshall? Insofar as a national bank facilitates expansion, that might count as a reason against its constitutionality, at least if one is seriously committed to a notion of limited congressional power, rather than an argument in its favor. We shall return to the issue of constitutional implications of expansionism in Chapter 4.

24. 1 Stat. 566, 570, 577, 696. See below, pp. 84-95, for further discussion of the Acts.

25. The Portable Jefferson 286 (Peterson ed., 1975) (hereinafter Peterson).

Amphictyon's essays on *McCulloch* reprinted much of Madison's Virginia Resolution, which similarly asserted that the states were "duty bound to interpose" their authority to arrest the evil of "deliberate, palpable, and dangerous exercise of other powers not granted by the said compact."[26]

Jefferson's response to *McCulloch* can be garnered from an 1820 letter describing the national judiciary as:

> . . . the subtle core of sappers and miners constantly working under ground to undermine the foundations of our confederated fabric. They are construing our Constitution from a coordination of general [i.e., national] and special [i.e., state] government to a general and supreme one alone. This will lay all things at their feet.[27]

Returning to the notion of the Virginia Resolution, Jefferson suggested that the people of two-thirds of the states could, through resolutions of nullification, overrule unconstitutional Supreme Court decisions. Only in this way could the principle be vindicated that the Constitution "is a compact of many independent powers, every single one of which claims an equal right to understand it, and to require its observance."[28] Writing under the name of Hampden in the Richmond Enquirer, Spencer Roane, Chief Justice of the Virginia Supreme Court, also responded to *McCulloch*. Among other arguments, he invoked Johnson's Dictionary, "which is believed to be the best in the English language" to show that "necessary" was there defined as "needful" or "indispensably requisite."[29] Roane's arguments drew an admiring letter from Madison, who noted:[30]

> It could not but happen, and was foreseen at the birth of the Constitution, that difficulties and differences of opinion might occasionally arise in expounding terms and phrases necessarily used in such a charter; more especially those which divide legislation between the general and local governments; and that it might require a regular course of practice to liquidate and settle the meaning of some of them. But it was anticipated, I believe, by few, if any, of the friends of the Constitution, that a rule of construction would be introduced as broad and pliant as what has occurred. And those who recollect, and still more, those who shared in what passed in the State conventions, through which the people ratified the Constitution, with respect to the extent of the powers vested in Congress, cannot easily be persuaded that the avowal of such a rule would not have prevented its ratification.

B. Marshall's Methods of Constitutional Interpretation

Within *McCulloch* we can find almost all of the standard forms of constitutional argument that lawyers and judges use today. Philip Bobbitt has helpfully categorized them into six modalities: (1) appeals to text (and rules for construction of

---

26. Gunther, supra n.17, at 51. These arguments were later invoked by South Carolina in its efforts to nullify federal laws and in the justification for Southern secession in 1860-1861. See The Nullification Era: A Documentary Record (Freehling ed., 1967).

27. Dumas Malone, 6 Jefferson and His Time 356 (1981) (letter to Thomas Ritchie).

28. Merrill D. Peterson, Thomas Jefferson and the New Nation 994-995 (1970).

29. Gunther, supra n.17, at 133.

30. Letter of September 2, 1819, in 3 Farrand, supra n.3, at 435.

texts), (2) constitutional structure, (3) prudence (or consequences), (4) history, (5) precedent, and (6) national (or narrative) ethos.[31]

1. *The text.* Recall the discussion of the language of the Tenth Amendment; the implications of Article I, §9; and the location of the necessary and proper clause. How would you characterize Marshall's approach to interpreting the constitutional text? Of what relevance is it that "it is *a constitution* we are expounding"? Recall the paragraph (¶16) in which the phrase appears and in which Marshall contrasts the "great outlines" of Article I with "the prolixity of a legal code." See also "Note: Uncertainties of Meaning," below.

2. *The theory and structure of the government established by the Constitution.* In Structure and Relationship in Constitutional Law (1969), Professor Charles Black, Jr., argues for a strategy of constitutional interpretation based on "inference from the structures and relationships created by the constitution." He points to *McCulloch* as an example, commenting that "Marshall does not place principal reliance on the [necessary and proper] clause as a ground of decision; . . . before he reaches it he has already decided, on the basis of far more general implications, that Congress possesses the power, not expressly named, of establishing a bank and chartering corporations; . . . he addresses himself to the necessary and proper clause only in response to counsel's arguing its *restrictive* force."[32] You will shortly see another powerful use of structural argument in the second part of *McCulloch,* which deals with Maryland's power to tax the Bank.

Does it follow from the nature of a federal constitution that the national legislative power should be construed expansively? Or, on the contrary, should one be zealous about limiting national power, lest it in effect swallow up the state autonomy that is part of what we mean by "federalism"? To be sure, our nation would be very different had arguments like those of Maryland prevailed in Congress and the Court; perhaps we would not have survived long as one nation (though, as a matter of fact, we survived only 42 years longer, until war tore the nation apart). In any event, had Marshall decided differently, would he have been proceeding on a *misconception* of the nature of a federal constitution or simply on a *different* conception — one much less nationalist than his actual opinion but more so than the Confederation or that desired by the more avid anti-Federalist opponents of ratification? Is Marshall's conception of "*a constitution*" correct, in other words, not necessarily as sound documentary interpretation but as (in our view) good government policy?

3. *Prudential argument: What are the likely consequences of a decision, and do they matter?* One might also pay attention to the predicted results of given decisions, preferring, presumably, the decision that produces, according to the analyst, the optimal set of outcomes. Thus Marshall in ¶17 refers to "[t]he exigencies of the nation" and rejects a "construction of the constitution that would render" the performance of government functions "difficult, hazardous, and expensive." Why should this matter? Should the Constitution always be interpreted to facilitate the performance of governmental functions? Recall also the paragraph (¶28) in which he makes the same comparison and notes that Article I is a provision "made in a constitution intended to endure for ages to come, and, consequently to be adapted

---

31. See generally Philip Bobbitt, Constitutional Fate (1982), an expanded version of Constitutional Fate, 58 Tex. L. Rev. 695 (1980); See also Bobbitt, Constitutional Interpretation (1991).
32. Charles Black, Structure and Relationship in Constitutional Law 7, 14 (1969).

to the various *crises* of human affairs." What do these observations contribute to the interpretation of the necessary and proper clause? (How significant is it that it is the "crises" that is italicized rather than "adapted." Do both of these words suggest that practical exigencies should take precedence over methodological purity?)

Note that there are at least two different types of prudential arguments. The broader category concerns whether an interpretation would have good consequences or bad; the narrower category concerns whether having *this particular decisionmaker* decide the question in a particular way would have good consequences or bad. Thus, judges are often concerned with how their decisions, even if otherwise justified, will play in the political arena. They may be concerned that taking up a controversial question, or offering a broad or ambitious reading of the Constitution, even if correct, will provoke a backlash from the other branches of government or from the public generally, and in the long run this will have worse consequences for the constitutional system than if courts had avoided taking up the issue directly for the moment, deferred to the political branches, or offered a narrow or limited ruling. Prudential considerations sometimes counsel not deciding a case at all, or deciding it only on technical or procedural grounds unrelated to the substantive issues at stake. As you will see in this course, these prudential considerations are never very far away from judicial practice, because constitutional questions often involve some of the most politically heated issues of their time. Are such prudential considerations consistent with the duty of courts to apply the rule of law?

4. *Appeals to history.* Recall Marshall's discussion of the purposes of the Tenth Amendment. How do you suppose he knows the purposes of the amendment?

In arguing against the first bank, Jefferson noted that the Philadelphia Convention had rejected a proposal to authorize Congress to charter certain corporations. Marshall does not mention this history. This may not be (only) because it would not have helped his argument: Judicial references to legislative history were virtually unheard of in eighteenth-century Anglo-American jurisprudence. In any event, what importance should we place on the history surrounding the adoption (or rejection) of particular texts? Is Marshall's argument regarding the (limited) scope of the Tenth Amendment enhanced by the knowledge that proposals in both the House of Representatives and the Senate to add the word "expressly" before "delegated" were rejected?[33]

Note that Marshall uses history in more than one way. He refers to the purposes of the framers of the Philadelphia Convention, but he also refers to the history of the adoption of the bank itself under the Washington Administration. That is to say, he makes historical arguments based both on preratification history and postratification history to establish the proper construction of the constitutional text. (That postratification history is also important for his precedent-based argument, discussed below.) What theory of constitutional meaning and constitutional authority justifies using preratification history? What theory justifies using postratification history? Note that one might use postratification history to discover the purposes of the adopters of the text if the events are close in time to the adoption; or one can use postratification history to demonstrate how later generations understood the constitutional commitments of the text. Still another way to use history,

[handwritten margin note: Broad 1. Consequences of interpretation 2. Consequences of this particular decision*]*

---

33. See Neil H. Cogan, ed., The Complete Bill of Rights: The Drafts, Debates, Sources, & Origins 665 (House), 667 (Senate) (1997).

as we shall see throughout this course, is to argue that mistakes or injustices that occurred in the past suggest the proper way to interpret the document in the present.

5. *Precedent.* Although Marshall cites no judicial decisions, he nonetheless invokes as precedent the incorporation by Congress in 1791 of the First Bank to support the constitutionality of the 1816 decision to incorporate the Second Bank. And we have seen that Madison justified signing the bill establishing the Second Bank by reference to "repeated recognitions, under varied circumstances, of the validity of such an institution," even though he had denounced the validity of the 1791 incorporation. Precedental argument offers the existence of previous decisions as justifying the outcome in a later case.

Judicial precedents, which constitute the lion's share of most law school casebooks, are only one type of precedent; there can also be precedents by the Congress, the President, and state and local government officials. In fact in *McCulloch* the only precedents that Marshall cites are by nonjudicial actors. Finally, courts sometimes look to traditions, which are, after all, the past actions of large numbers of Americans over a very long period of time. Within the class of judicial precedents, courts might conceivably look not only to their own decisions, but to the decisions of state courts, and, perhaps more controversially, to the decisions of courts in other countries.

Precedents from state courts and courts of other nations are not binding on the Supreme Court; at most they may provide persuasive arguments. However, the U.S. Supreme Court, like many other courts in the United States and the United Kingdom, often speaks as if it is bound by its own previous decisions, whether or not they are "persuasive." One might well wonder why previous judicial precedents should ever have *dispositive* force. As Jeremy Bentham suggested, "The deference that is due to the determination of former judgments," in a system that takes precedent with consummate seriousness, "is due not to their wisdom, but to their authority."[34] From this perspective, it matters not at all if the prior decision is decidedly unwise or even evil; it is enough that it exists to establish its authority. Is this persuasive in a system that purports to be based on reason? Consider one of Justice Holmes's most famous statements, given in a speech on "The Path of the Law" to the students and faculty of Boston University Law School in 1897: "It is revolting to have no better reason for a rule of law than that so it was laid down in the time of Henry IV. It is still more revolting if the grounds upon which it was laid down have vanished long since, and the rule simply persists from blind imitation of the past."

Even if one accepts a strong notion of precedent with regard to the common law, because, after all, a legislature can always overturn a "revolting" doctrine, should precedent be so relevant — assuming it should be relevant at all — with regard to interpreting the Constitution? Consider Justice Frankfurter's comment that "the ultimate touchstone of constitutionality is the Constitution itself and not what we have said about it."[35] One obvious response is that adherence to precedent provides a measure of stability in the law and, perhaps, serves to rein in contemporary judges. Richard Fallon, for example, has written that "a good legal system requires reasonable stability; that while decisions that are severely misguided or

34. See Gerald J. Postema, Some Roots of our Notion of Precedent, in Precedent in Law 14 (Goldstein ed., 1987).
35. Graves v. N.Y., 306 U.S. 466, 491-492 (1939).

dysfunctional surely may be overruled, continuity is presumptively desirable with respect to the rest; . . . it would overwhelm the Court and country alike to require the Justices to rethink every constitutional question in every case on the bare, unmediated authority of constitutional text, structure, and original history."[36] It is obvious, though, that Fallon is scarcely committed to a truly strong theory of precedent inasmuch as "severely misguided or dysfunctional" decisions are presumably ripe for overruling. How important, incidentally, is the word "severely"? Is it a good idea to feel bound by "misguided" decisions so long as their damage to the body politic or constitutional fabric is not "severe" or "dysfunctional"? Is there an explicitly legal metric by which to measure severity or dysfunctionality?

Justice Scalia addressed some of these questions in his dissent in South Carolina v. Gaithers, 490 U.S. 95 (1989), where he called for overruling the recently decided Booth v. Maryland, 482 U.S. 496 (1987). The particular cases involved limiting the state's right to refer to the consequences of a murder on the victim's survivors to a sentencing jury, but the considerations adduced by Scalia obviously apply to all arguments that are founded on precedent:

> It has been argued that we should not overrule so recent a decision, lest our action "appear to be . . . occasioned by nothing more than a change in the Court's personnel," and the rules we announce no more than " 'opinions of a small group of men who temporarily occupy high office.' " I doubt that overruling *Booth* will so shake the citizenry's faith in the Court. Overrulings of precedent rarely occur without a change in the Court's personnel. The only distinctive feature here is that the overruling would follow not long after the original decision. But that is hardly unprecedented. See, e.g., Daniels v. Williams, 474 U.S. 327 (1986) (overruling Parratt v. Taylor, 451 U.S. 527 (1981)); United States v. Scott, 437 U.S. 82 (1978) (overruling United States v. Jenkins, 420 U.S. 358 (1975)); West Virginia Board of Education v. Barnette, 319 U.S. 624 (1943) (overruling Minersville School District Board of Education v. Gobitis, 310 U.S. 586 (1940)).
>
> Indeed, I had thought that the respect accorded prior decisions increases, rather than decreases, with their antiquity, as the society adjusts itself to their existence, and the surrounding law becomes premised upon their validity. The freshness of error not only deprives it of the respect to which long-established practice is entitled, but also counsels that the opportunity of correction be seized at once, before state and federal laws and practices have been adjusted to embody it. . . .
>
> In any case, I would think it a violation of my oath to adhere to what I consider a plainly unjustified intrusion upon the democratic process in order that the Court might save face. With some reservation concerning decisions that have become so embedded in our system of government that return is no longer possible . . . I agree with Justice Douglas: "A judge looking at a constitutional decision may have compulsions to revere past history and accept what was once written. But he remembers above all else that it is the Constitution which he swore to support and defend, not the gloss which his predecessors may have put on it." Douglas, Stare Decisis, 49 Colum. L. Rev. 735, 736 (1949). Or as the Court itself has said: "[W]hen convinced of former error, this Court has never felt constrained to follow precedent. In constitutional questions, where correction depends upon amendment and not upon legislative action this Court throughout its history has freely exercised its power to reexamine the basis of its constitutional decisions." Smith v. Allwright, 321 U.S. 649, 665 (1944).

36. Stare Decisis and the Constitution: An Essay on Constitutional Methodology, 76 N.Y.U. L. Rev. 570, 585 (2001).

The Court did overrule both *Booth* and *Gaithers* in Payne v. Tennessee, 498 U.S. 1076 (1991). Writing for the five-member majority, Chief Justice Rehnquist stated that "[c]onsiderations in favor of *stare decisis* are at their acme in cases involving property and contract rights, where reliance interests are involved; the opposite is true in cases such as the present involving procedural and evidentiary rules." He also noted that both "*Booth* and *Gaithers* were decided by the narrowest of margins [i.e., they were both 5-4 decisions], over spirited dissents challenging the basic underpinnings of those dissents."

In his dissent, Justice Marshall castigated the majority for disregarding precedent:

> Taking into account [one of the] majority's . . . criteri[a] for overruling — that a case either was decided or reaffirmed by a 5-4 margin 'over spirited dissent' — the contin-ued vitality of literally scores of decisions must be understood to depend on nothing more than the proclivities of the individuals who *now* comprise a majority of the court. [Case citations omitted.] . . . Contrary to what the majority suggests, *stare decisis* is important not merely because individuals rely on precedent to structure their commercial activity but because fidelity to precedent is part and parcel of a concep-tion of "the judiciary as a source of impersonal and reasoned judgments."

Does "reasoned judgment" simply mean that the earlier judge gave reasons (rather than flipped a coin) or that the later reader must in fact be persuaded that the reasons given were "good reasons" that deserve to be followed in our own time? If the mere giving of reasons is sufficient, then is Marshall in effect in agreement with Bentham, at least analytically, that precedent ultimately rests on authority rather than reason?

The most extensive discussion of precedent in the Court's history occurred in Planned Parenthood of Southeastern Pennsylvania v. Casey, 505 U.S. 833 (1992), excerpted at length in Chapter Eight below, infra, although a further opportunity to discuss these questions will shortly come with Andrew Jackson's veto of the legis-lation that would have renewed the charter of the U.S. Bank, infra, pp. 74-81.

6. *National (or narrative) ethos.* A sixth and final type of constitutional argument asks whether an interpretation is faithful to the meaning or destiny of the country, its deepest commitments, or some important aspect of national character. Bobbitt calls these arguments "ethical," because they concern national ethos. Arguments about national ethos are often narrative or historical in character, and are often continuous with the other forms of constitutional argument, particularly historical arguments and arguments from tradition. Note that in ¶17 Marshall justifies the need for a flexible constitution on the grounds that "[t]hroughout this vast repub-lic, from the St. Croix to the Gulf of Mexico, from the Atlantic to the Pacific, revenue is to be collected and expended, armies are to be marched and supported. . . . Is that construction of the constitution to be preferred which would render these operations difficult, hazardous, and expensive?" This looks at first like a simple argument about good and bad consequences, but it actually rests on a deeper set of assumptions about the nature of the American nation and its eventual future:

> It is particularly telling that Marshall chooses to ascribe borders to the United States much larger than those actually existing in 1819, when *McCulloch* was written. In Marshall's narrative — one that would be retold countless times under the more familiar

name of "Manifest Destiny" — the United States was to become a great country, not only in spirit but also in resources and size; and great countries need constitutions that give them the flexibility to grow and attain their promised greatness.

As Lewis Henry LaRue has pointed out, it is this familiar narrative of America's destiny, as much as anything else, that underpins and justifies the expansive constitutional interpretation of national power in McCulloch. The narrative is not everything, but it is surely something. If we told a different story — a Jeffersonian story of a tranquil land of agrarian farmers who hoped to avoid the corruptions of ambition and avarice characteristic of European monarchies, who sought merely to live their lives in peace and harmony in small, close-knit communities — we might well imagine that it should be "difficult, hazardous, and expensive" for the national government to gather revenues, raise armies, sweep across the Continent, and conquer all in its path. If we told a story that opposed the depravity and overreaching of grasping monarchs and their prime ministers to the simple virtues of a self-reliant republican citizenry, we might well want to nip in the bud any potential mechanisms of national aggrandizement.[37]

Note: Uncertainties of Meaning

The language of a provision in a written document is often susceptible of more than one meaning; it can be ambiguous, vague, or figurative.[38]

1. Ambiguity

A word or expression is ambiguous if it admits of two or more *rather different* meanings. Ambiguity is often desirable in literature; it is essential to puns. But (as distinguished from vagueness) it is usually undesirable in legal documents.

Language is pervasively ambiguous, but even a very general understanding of the purpose of a provision resolves most serious ambiguities. As an experiment, glance at some sections of the Constitution and try to understand their meanings while consciously avoiding considering their purposes. Consider, for example, Article II, §1, cl. 5: "No person except a natural born Citizen . . . shall be eligible to the Office of President. . . ." Is the meaning of "natural born citizen" inherently clear? What might the phrase mean in a revised constitution of Scotland drafted by Macbeth (had he survived)?[39] What does the phrase mean in our Constitution, and

---

37. J.M. Balkin and Sanford Levinson, The Canons of Constitutional Law, 111 Harv. L. Rev. 963, (1998). For theories of narrative argument in constitutional law, see J.M. Balkin, The Declaration and the Promise of a Democratic Culture, 4 Widener L. Symp. J. 167 (1999); Lewis Henry LaRue, Constitutional Law as Fiction: Narrative in the Rhetoric of Authority (1995).

38. See generally William Alston, Philosophy of Language ch. 5 (1964); William Empson, Seven Types of Ambiguity (2d ed., 1947): Willard Van Orman Quine, Word and Object, ch. 4 (1960); I.A. Richards, The Philosophy of Rhetoric (1936); E. Allan Farnsworth, "Meaning" in the Law of Contracts, 76 Yale L.J. 939 (1967); Fredrich Waismann, Analytic-Synthetic V, 13 Analysis 1 (1952).

39. Recall the second apparition's assurance in Macbeth, Act IV, scene i:

Be bloody, bold, and resolute; laugh to scorn
The power of man, for none of woman born Shall harm Macbeth.

and Macbeth's ensuing confidence and his subsequent downfall (Act V, scene vii):

Macbeth: Let fall thy blade on vulnerable crests;
I bear a charmed life, which must not yield
To one of woman born.

how do you know? Consider the phrase in its full context: "No person except a natural born Citizen or a Citizen of the United States, at the time of the Adoption of this Constitution, shall be eligible to the Office of President. . . ." What does this contribute to clarifying its meaning, and how? (Was George Romney, a Michigan governor who ran for the presidency in 1968 and who was the child of U.S. citizens and hence a citizen at his birth, but born in Chihuahua, Mexico, eligible to the office?)

2. Vagueness

Whereas ambiguous meanings tend to differ discretely, vagueness involves marginal indefiniteness in the meaning and application of words.[40]

> Thus, "middle-aged" is vague, for it is not clear whether a person aged 40 or a person aged 59 is middle-aged. Of course there are uncontroversial areas of application and nonapplication. At age 5 or 80 one is clearly not middle-aged, and at age 45 one clearly is. But on either side of the area of clear application there are indefinitely bounded areas of uncertainty. . . . [T]here is no definite answer to the question, Is a person aged 40 middle-aged? . . . Our inability [to give an answer] is not the result of lack of information about such things as blood pressure and metabolic rate. No additional information would settle the matter, except indirectly by leading us to tighten up the meaning of the word. The indeterminacy is due to an aspect of the meaning of the term rather than to the current state of our knowledge.

Not only abstract concepts but ordinary (nonproper) nouns naming physical objects and intangible things are usually vague — and incurably so. For many things are defined by the confluence of a number of attributes (a, b, c, . . . n), and one can never fully describe the combinations of attributes necessary or sufficient for proper application of the noun to particular things:[41]

> Consider the term "lemon," for example. Lemons normally have certain characteristics: a yellow color when ripe, skin of a certain thickness with a waxy texture, ovoid shape, acid taste, a size and hardness that falls within a certain range, and so on. If an object has all these properties, it is definitely a lemon. It might happen that in a particular region of the world, due to atomic fallout, lemon trees started producing fruit of a pinkish color and with a sweet taste, but having all the other characteristics of ordinary lemons. These fruits would doubtless still be lemons: pink lemons or sweet pink lemons. A thing cannot lack all, or even very many, of the typical lemon properties, and still be a lemon; but there is no one property, or group of two or three properties, which an object must have to be properly called a lemon. It must simply have some combination of the cluster or properties which lemons typically have.

Macduff: Despair thy charm;
  And let the Angel, whom thou still hast serv'd
  Tell thee, Macduff was from his mother's womb
  Untimely ripp'd.
  40. William Alston, Vagueness, in 8 Encyclopedia of Philosophy 218 (Edwards ed., 1967).
  41. George Pitcher, The Philosophy of Wittgenstein 221 (1964) (borrowing an example from Michael Scriven). See also Alston, supra n.38, at 94-95 (1964); Fredrich Waismann, Verifiability, in Logic and Language-First Series (Flew ed., 1952).

Some provisions of the Constitution are quite precise: Article II, §1, cl. 5 requires that the president be at least 35 years old rather than at least "middle-aged." Many other provisions are quite vague: What is the "*Commerce . . .* among the several States" that Article I, §8, cl. 3 empowers Congress to regulate? And some provisions, such as the Fourth Amendment's prohibition of "*unreasonable* searches and seizures," seem designedly vague.

3.   Nonliteral Usage

Article I, §8, cl. 8 empowers Congress "[t]o promote the Progress of Science and useful Arts, by securing for limited Times to Authors and Inventors the exclusive Right to their respective Writings and Discoveries." Does "writings" include anything besides letters inscribed on a surface? Does it include inscriptions by means other than hand (by printing or photo process), inscriptions of things other than letters (maps, charts, drawings), three-dimensional objects (sculptures, casseroles, automobiles), things not created by humans (driftwood), things not visually perceptible (the contents of phonograph records), ideas (the one-way toll bridge), intangible creations (theater productions, television broadcasts), and systems (computer programs, accounting systems)?[42]

The word "writings" is, to be sure, vague. But the questions posed in the previous paragraph do not involve vagueness so much as they do the literalness with which the word should be read. The Oxford English Dictionary defines the "literal" meaning of a word as its "relatively primary sense . . . as distinguished from any metaphorical or merely suggested meaning." True metaphors are rare in legal documents, but other kinds of nonliteral, or figurative, usage are very common. Interpreters are frequently called upon to determine how literally or figuratively to understand a term or, to put it another way, how narrowly or broadly to define the concept that the term represents. Does the copyright clause protect only "graphic" works, does it protect only "tangible" works, or does it protect all "expressions of intellectual creation"? It seems obvious that the proper scope of the concept represented by a term depends on the context in which, and the purpose for which, the term is used.

We recur so often to the inherent indeterminacy of language that it is important to emphasize that its indeterminacy is not unlimited; the very concept of "interpretation" implies that the interpreter is not free to stipulate the meanings of the terms he is interpreting. The reason for this is suggested by Wittgenstein's insightful analogy between language and a game. As Gilbert Ryle put it:[43]

> The significance of an expression and the powers or functions in chess of a pawn, a knight or the queen have much in common. To know what the knight can and cannot do, one must know the rules of chess, as well as be familiar with various kinds of chess situations which may arise. . . . Similarly to know what an expression means is to know how it may and may not be employed.

Language is a social practice. Just as a player who stipulates that his knight may move forward one square at a time is not playing chess, someone who stipulates

---

42. See generally 1 Melville Nimmer, Copyright §8 (1973).

43. Gilbert Ryle, The Theory of Meaning, in British Philosophy in the Mid-Century 255 (Mace ed., 1957).

that a word or expression shall mean something without regard to its accepted usage is not engaging in ordinary conversation. The classic example of difficulties that emerge when linguistic conventions are ignored is Humpty Dumpty's attempt to persuade Alice that unbirthdays are better than birthdays:[44]

> "[T]here are three hundred and sixty-four days when you might get unbirthday presents."
>
> "Certainly," said Alice.
>
> "And only *one* for birthday presents, you know. There's glory for you!"
>
> "I don't know what you mean by 'glory,' " Alice said.
>
> Humpty Dumpty smiled contemptuously. "Of course you don't till I tell you. I meant 'there's a nice knock-down argument for you!' "
>
> "But 'glory' doesn't mean 'a nice knock-down argument,' " Alice objected.
>
> "When *I* use a word," Humpty Dumpty said, in rather a scornful tone, "it means just what I choose it to mean neither more nor less."
>
> "The question is," said Alice, "whether you *can* make words mean so many different things."
>
> "The question is," said Humpty Dumpty, "which is to be master that's all."

Note: "Inherent" Versus "Implied" Powers

McCulloch is the canonical example of the Court's willingness to discern *implied powers* of Congress beyond those specified in the text. The point, though, of calling them "implied" is that they are indeed linked to the textually assigned powers and serve as means to the great ends spelled out in the text. Thus, Marshall notes that "[t]his government is acknowledged by all to be one of enumerated powers" (¶12). Is it the case, though, that the national government possesses *only* assigned powers, as against *inherent* powers that do not depend on the existence of *any* textual assignment?

Consider, as a trivial example, the passage by Congress in January 1794 of an act adding two stars and two stripes to the national flag, to take account of the addition of Vermont and Kentucky to the Union. As Professor Currie notes, "The Constitution says nothing about flags. Congress must have understood the power to prescribe one to be inherent in nationhood: Every nation needs a flag, and the states were in no position to provide it."[45] Are these good enough reasons to empower Congress to pass the statute? (Do you agree, incidentally, that the authority to enact the statute cannot be plausibly be "implied" from any assignment of power in the text?)

Significantly more serious, in every way, was the passage in 1798 of the Alien and Sedition Acts. The Sedition Act is discussed below, pp. 84-95, in the context of the attack on it as violating the First Amendment's explicit prohibition of Congress's passing any law abridging freedom of speech. The Alien Act empowered the President to deport "such aliens as he shall judge dangerous to the peace and safety of the United States, or shall have reasonable grounds to suspect are concerned in any treasonable or secret machinations against the Government thereof." The attack on the Act was led by Representative Albert Gallatin, himself a naturalized

---

44. Lewis Carroll, Through the Looking Glass, ch. 6 (1865).
45. David Currie, The Constitution in Congress: The Federalist Period, 1789-1801, 204 (1997).

citizen born in Switzerland who had been excluded from the U.S. Senate, upon his selection by the New York state legislature, on the ground that he had not fulfilled the constitutional requirement of being nine years a citizen of the United States. (Upon his exclusion, he was promptly elected to the House of Representatives, where, after the retirement of James Madison, he had become the Republican floor leader. He would later gain fame as Jefferson's Secretary of the Treasury.) Gallatin, committed to Jeffersonian principles of "strict construction," argued that Congress lacked the power to pass the legislation. "The power of regulating alien friends, in every possible case, was understood to be reserved to the States at the time the Constitution was adopted."[46] He did concede, though, that Congress possessed inherent power to restrict the activities of aliens during wartime. Thus he had supported, the previous month, passage of the Alien Enemies Bill, which would apply to male citizens or subjects of a hostile nation upon declaration by the President that war had been declared or an invasion "perpetrated, attempted, or threatened."[47] Indeed, according to Gallatin, the power to pass the act rested on "a principle which existed prior to the Constitution"[48] and thus, presumably, required no specific authorization in the text. Those affected by the Alien Act, however, came from countries with whom the United States was at peace, whatever the level of tension with France that lay behind the Act. Reference was also made to the fact that Congress *is* assigned the power to provide for "an uniform Rule of Naturalization," the very specification of which, it was argued, supported the proposition that the states retained their power to control immigration per se. That is, even if states had no power to make immigrants U.S. citizens, and therefore members of the common national community, they retained their right to decide whether to welcome immigrants as guests, so to speak, and even to make them citizens of the states themselves, even if not national citizens. (This issue will be treated later in the *Dred Scott* case, infra Chapter 3.)

Note also Article 1, §9: What implications does this have for congressional power in 1798?[49] Federalist supporters of the Act responded that power to control immigration (and, therefore, to expel suspicious, even if not "enemy" aliens) was inherent in the very conception of being a sovereign state in the international system.

By its own terms, the Alien Act expired on June 25, 1800, and the constitutional arguments made by its supporters did not come before the Supreme Court for almost a century, in Chae Chan Ping v. U.S. (1889), infra, Chapter 4, which involved the prohibition of Chinese nationals from entering the United States. As you will see, the Court basically adopted the Federalist argument and relied on the "inherent" power attached to "sovereignty" rather than pointing to any textual assignment of power to Congress. Another important "inherent powers" case is United States v. Curtiss-Wright Export Corp., 299 U.S. 304 (1936). According to Justice Sutherland, "the investment of the federal government with the powers of external sovereignty did not depend upon the affirmative grants of the Constitution. The powers to declare and wage war, to conclude peace, to make treaties, to maintain

46. Quoted in Andrew Lenner, Separate Spheres: Republican Constitutionalism in the Federalist Era, 41 Am. J. Legal Hist. 250 (1997). See also Joseph M. Lynch, Negotiating the Constitution: The Earliest Debates over Original Intent, ch. 9 (1999).

47. See Currie, supra n.45, at 254-255.

48. Quoted in Lenner, op. cit.

49. For an extended discussion of the complex questions involving the sources of federal power to regulate immigration, see Thomas Alexander Aleinkoff, David A. Martin, and Hiroshi Motomura, Immigration and Citizenship: Process and Policy 178-217 (1998).

diplomatic relations with other sovereignties, if they had never been mentioned in the Constitution, would have vested in the federal government as necessary concomitants of nationality. . . ." As to treaties in particular, compare Sutherland's assertion with Madison's speech on the Bank. Justice Sutherland's history and metaphysics are open to criticism,[50] but his analysis at least suggests the spirit in which the particular grants of power to Congress and the executive have been amalgamated to create a whole greater than the sum of its parts. One might certainly note, incidentally, that both of these cases involve power of the United States as a member of the wider international system of "sovereign states."

Note: An Excursion into Louisiana

As one reflects on the importance of a "continentalist" vision of America to understanding Marshall's opinion in *McCulloch* or the presence of "inherent" powers with regard to foreign policy, it is worth considering what was arguably the single most important political and constitutional event between the ratification of the Constitution and the outbreak of civil war in 1861: the purchase of the Louisiana Territory from France in 1803.[51] Full description of the episode would require a history of the diplomatic relations of France, Great Britain, Spain, and the United States. For our purposes, one can begin with the October 1800 secret treaty by which Spain returned to France the territory of Louisiana. This created a great furor because of the implications for control of the Mississippi River and the city of New Orleans. Congress appropriated $2 million, and diplomats were sent to France to negotiate the purchase of New Orleans. Much to their surprise, Napoleon suggested his willingness to sell the Territory in its entirety, and a price of $15 million was agreed upon. Moreover, the treaty of purchase pledged that "the inhabitants of the ceded territory shall be incorporated in the Union of the United States, and admitted as soon as possible, according to the principles of the Federal Constitution, to the enjoyment of all the rights, advantages, and immunities of citizens of the United States; and in the meantime they shall be maintained and protected in the free enjoyment of their liberty, property, and the religion which they profess."

President Jefferson, a champion of states' rights and of a strict construction of national powers under the Constitution, had significant doubts about the constitutional legitimacy of adding the Territory to the United States. After all, purchase of new territory was not clearly authorized by the constitutional text; this raised problems given Jefferson's emphasis, clearly set out in his argument against the Bank, that the national government was limited to its explicitly assigned powers. Thus he wrote to John Dickinson, a fellow signer of the Declaration of Independence, that "our confederation is certainly confined to the limits established by the revolution. The general government has no powers but such as the constitution has given it; and it has not given it a power of holding foreign territory; and still less of incorporating it

---

50. See, e.g., Charles Lofgren, United States v. Curtiss-Wright Corporation: An Historical Reassessment, 83 Yale L.J. 1 (1973). See also Madison's argument against the Bank, supra.

51. See generally Everett S. Brown, The Constitutional History of the Louisiana Purchase (1920). See also Jon Kukla, A Wilderness So Immense: The Louisiana Purchase and the Destiny of America (2003); Sanford Levinson and Bartholomew H. Sparrow, eds., The Louisiana Purchase and American Expansion 1803-1898 (2005).

into this Union. An amendment of our Constitution seems necessary for this."[52] Jefferson also stressed that adding the Louisiana Territory, which stretched from the Gulf of Mexico to the interior of Montana, would double the size of the United States and fundamentally change the character of the Union. This, he argued, should require explicit ratification by "We the People" through amendment. (Some Federalists, although committed to a strong national government, opposed the purchase on the grounds, among others, that it would serve as a de facto political windfall to slave interests that could readily expand.)

Nevertheless he laid the treaty between France and the United States before Congress. Writing to Kentucky Senator Hugh Breckenridge on August 12, 1803, he said:

> This treaty must, of course, be laid before both Houses, because both have important functions to exercise respecting it. They, I presume, will see their duty to their country in ratifying and paying for it, so as to secure a good which would otherwise probably be never again in their power. But I suppose they must then appeal to the nation for an additional article to the Constitution approving and confirming an act which the nation had not previously authorized. The Constitution has made no provision for holding foreign territory, still less for incorporating foreign nations into our Union. The Executive, in seizing the fugitive occurrence which so much advances the good of our country, have done an act beyond the Constitution.[53]

Or, as he told Dickinson immediately after expressing his constitutional doubts, "In the meantime, we must ratify & pay our money, as we have treated, for a thing beyond the constitution, and rely on the nation to sanction an act done for its great good, without its previous authority."[54]

Although one of his principal allies, Secretary of the Treasury Gallatin, argued that it would be a "natural construction [of the Constitution] to say that the power of acquiring territory is delegated to the United States by the several provisions which authorize the several branches of government to make war, to make treaties, and to govern the territory of the Union,"[55] Jefferson was apparently not fully convinced. He thus prepared two amendments to the Constitution, the first of which declared that "the province of Louisiana is incorporated with the United States and made part thereof"; and the second of which was couched in somewhat different language, viz.: "Louisiana, as ceded by France to the United States, is made a part of the United States. Its white inhabitants shall be citizens, and stand, as to their rights and obligations, on the same footing as other citizens in analogous situations."

Whatever Jefferson's doubts, he did not press the constitutional point, not least, apparently, because Napoleon began giving signs of pulling back from his agreement, so that time became of the essence. Presented with this possibility, Jefferson wrote one correspondent that "whatever congress shall think it necessary to do, should be done with as little debate as possible, & particularly so far as respects the constitutional difficulty"; to another he emphasized that "the less that is said about the constitutional difficulties, the better."[56] Thus in October 1803, Jefferson sent

52. Quoted in David Meyer, The Constitutional Thought of Thomas Jefferson 246 (1994).
53. Quoted in Downes v. Bidwell, 182 U.S. 244 (1901) (discussed in Chapter 4, infra).
54. Quoted in Meyer at 247.
55. Quoted in id. at 246.
56. Quoted in id. at 230.

the treaty to the Senate, saying that "with the wisdom of Congress it will rest to take those ulterior measures which may be necessary for the immediate occupation and temporary government of the country; for its incorporation into the Union."

Several years later, writing another correspondent about the Purchase, Jefferson said that "[a] strict observance of the written law is doubtless one of the high duties of a good citizen, but it is not the highest. The laws of necessity, of self-preservation, of saving our country when in danger, are of higher obligation. To lose our country by a scrupulous adherence to the written law, would be to lose the law itself, with life, liberty, property and all those who are enjoying them with us; thus absurdly sacrificing the end to the means."

Discussion

1. Many of you have no doubt read the famous (and oft-quoted) statement by Alexis de Tocqueville, "Scarcely any political question arises in the United States that is not resolved, sooner or later, into a judicial question."[57] As Professor Graber has demonstrated, though, the statement, however much a cliché it has become about American politics, is in large measure false.[58] Had Tocqueville written that "political questions" in the United States often are turned into "legal ones," he would have been on sounder ground, but then the central inquiry would become how often "legal" questions are in fact "resolved" by courts, instead of by other institutions such as the presidency or Congress or, for that matter, by public opinion. The intense constitutional debate over the Purchase was "resolved" within the Jefferson Administration and Congress themselves; courts played no role at all. It is true that John Marshall, in American and Ocean Insurance Companies v. Canter, 26 U.S. (1 Peter) 511 (1828), laconically wrote, without further explanation, that the United States could extend its territory by treaty (or conquest), but no one would seriously regard this as "resolving" the issue rather than, a full quarter-century after the fact, accepting as dispositive the determination of 1803 that expansion was constitutionally legitimate. (Try to imagine for a moment what would have followed from a contrary holding by Marshall, i.e., that the Louisiana Purchase was unconstitutional. Would the United States have had to return the territory to France? Or would the Court have properly said that the Purchase, although unconstitutional, was so much a part of the American fabric that it simply could not be undone?)

2. Jefferson's defense of the Purchase returns us to an issue that was raised in the introductory materials (and will pervade many future discussions), which is the tension between what might be termed legal (or constitutional) fidelity and the exigent demands produced by perceived emergencies or other threats to the republic. Recall, for example, Edmund Randolph's declaration that "[t]here are great seasons when persons with limited powers are justified in exceeding them, and a person would be contemptible not to risk it." Even if one agrees with the general sentiments expressed, how, precisely does one identify the "great seasons" when ignoring ordinary legal constraints is justified? Consider Jefferson's apologia for his swallowing constitutional doubts about the Purchase. Must one agree, in order to justify Jefferson, that the Purchase involved "necessity," "self-preservation," or "saving our country when

---

57. 1 Democracy in America 280 (Vintage Edition 1945, reprinted 1990).
58. Mark A. Graber, Antebellum Perspectives on Free Speech, 10 Wm. & Mary Bill of Rts. J. 779, 804-805 (2002).

in danger"? Indeed, did it meet the criteria of "necessity" that Jefferson put forth in his criticism of chartering the Bank? Did expanding the reach of American power into Montana have anything at all to do with "self-preservation" or "saving our country when in danger," even if one is willing to use such terms with regard to the port of New Orleans itself? Historian William Freehling has suggested that we would have a better sense of what was involved with the Purchase if we called it "The Midwest Purchase," given that what we today think of as Louisiana was such a relatively small portion of the lands gained by the United States. And, he also argues, the Purchase, far from "saving our country," in fact contributed to its dissolution in 1861 inasmuch as it was the Purchase that put front and center for the next half-century the issue of the expansion of slavery into these newly purchased territories. See Chapter 3, infra.

Did, therefore, Jefferson behave consistently with his constitutional oath? Does the answer to that question fundamentally affect your view of Jefferson or of the legitimacy of the Louisiana Purchase? That is, to what extent do you really care, one way or the other, whether Jefferson serves as a model of constitutional fidelity?

V. The States' Power to Tax the Bank of the United States

McCULLOCH v. MARYLAND

[The Second Question]

[46] It being the opinion of the Court, that the act incorporating the bank is constitutional; and that the power of establishing a branch in the State of Maryland might be properly exercised by the bank itself, we proceed to inquire

[47] 2. Whether the State of Maryland may, without violating the constitution, tax that branch?

[48] That the power of taxation is one of vital importance; that it is retained by the States; that it is not abridged by the grant of a similar power to the government of the Union; that it is to be concurrently exercised by the two governments: are truths which have never been denied. But, such is the paramount character of the constitution, that its capacity to withdraw any subject from the action of even this power, is admitted. The States are expressly forbidden to lay any duties on imports or exports, except what may be absolutely necessary for executing their inspection laws. If the obligation of this prohibition must be conceded — if it may restrain a State from the exercise of its taxing power on imports and exports; the same paramount character would seem to restrain, as it certainly may restrain, a State from such other exercise of this power, as is in its nature incompatible with, and repugnant to, the constitutional laws of the Union. A law, absolutely repugnant to another, as entirely repeals that other as if express terms of repeal were used.

[49] On this ground the counsel for the bank place its claim to be exempted from the power of a State to tax its operations. There is no express provision for the case, but the claim has been sustained on a principle which so entirely pervades the constitution, is so intermixed with the materials which compose it, so interwoven with its web, so blended with its texture, as to be incapable of being separated from it, without rending it into shreds.

[50] This great principle is, that the constitution and the laws made in pursuance thereof are supreme; that they control the constitution and laws of the

respective States, and cannot be controlled by them. From this, which may be almost termed an axiom, other propositions are deduced as corollaries, on the truth or error of which, and on their application to this case, the cause has been supposed to depend. These are, 1st. That a power to create implies a power to preserve. 2nd. That a power to destroy, if wielded by a different hand, is hostile to, and incompatible with these powers to create and to preserve. 3d. That where this repugnancy exists, that authority which is supreme must control, not yield to that over which it is supreme.

[51] These propositions, as abstract truths, would, perhaps, never be controverted. Their application to this case, however, has been denied; and, both in maintaining the affirmative and the negative, a splendor of eloquence, and strength of argument, seldom, if ever, surpassed, have been displayed.

[52] The power of Congress to create, and of course to continue, the bank, was the subject of the preceding part of this opinion; and is no longer to be considered as questionable.

[53] That the power of taxing it by the States may be exercised so as to destroy it, is too obvious to be denied. But taxation is said to be an absolute power, which acknowledges no other limits than those expressly prescribed in the constitution, and like sovereign power of every other description, is trusted to the discretion of those who use it. But the very terms of this argument admit that the sovereignty of the State, in the article of taxation itself, is subordinate to, and may be controlled by the constitution of the United States. How far it has been controlled by that instrument must be a question of construction. In making this construction, no principle not declared, can be admissible, which would defeat the legitimate operations of a supreme government. It is of the very essence of supremacy to remove all obstacles to its action within its own sphere, and so to modify every power vested in subordinate governments, as to exempt its own operations from their own influence. This effect need not be stated in terms. It is so involved in the declaration of supremacy, so necessarily implied in it, that the expression of it could not make it more certain. We must, therefore, keep it in view while construing the constitution.

[54] The argument on the part of the State of Maryland, is, not that the States may directly resist a law of Congress, but that they may exercise their acknowledged powers upon it, and that the constitution leaves them this right in the confidence that they will not abuse it.

[55] Before we proceed to examine this argument, and to subject it to the test of the constitution, we must be permitted to bestow a few considerations on the nature and extent of this original right of taxation, which is acknowledged to remain with the States. It is admitted that the power of taxing the people and their property is essential to the very existence of government, and may be legitimately exercised on the objects to which it is applicable, to the utmost extent to which the government may chuse to carry it. The only security against the abuse of this power, is found in the structure of the government itself. In imposing a tax the legislature acts upon its constituents. This is in general a sufficient security against erroneous and oppressive taxation.

[56] The people of a State, therefore, give to their government a right of taxing themselves and their property, and as the exigencies of government cannot be limited, they prescribe no limits to the exercise of this right, resting confidently on the interest of the legislator, and on the influence of the constituents over their representative, to guard them against its abuse. But the means employed by the

government of the Union have no such security, nor is the right of a State to tax them sustained by the same theory. Those means are not given by the people of a particular State, not given by the constituents of the legislature, which claim the right to tax them, but by the people of all the States. They are given by all, for the benefit of all — and upon theory, should be subjected to that government only which belongs to all.

[57] It may be objected to this definition, that the power of taxation is not confined to the people and property of a State. It may be exercised upon every object brought within its jurisdiction.

[58] This is true. But to what source do we trace this right? It is obvious, that it is an incident of sovereignty, and is co-extensive with that to which it is an incident. All subjects over which the sovereign power of a State extends, are objects of taxation; but those over which it does not extend, are, upon the soundest principles, exempt from taxation. This proposition may almost be pronounced self-evident.

[59] The sovereignty of a State extends to every thing which exists by its own authority, or is introduced by its permission; but does it extend to those means which are employed by Congress to carry into execution powers conferred on that body by the people of the United States? We think it demonstrable that it does not. Those powers are not given by the people of a single State. They are given by the people of the United States, to a government whose laws, made in pursuance of the constitution, are declared to be supreme. Consequently, the people of a single State cannot confer a sovereignty which will extend over them.

[60] If we measure the power of taxation residing in a State, by the extent of sovereignty which the people of a single State possess, and can confer on its government, we have an intelligible standard, applicable to every case to which the power may be applied. We have a principle which leaves the power of taxing the people and property of a State unimpaired; which leaves to a State the command of all its resources, and which places beyond its reach, all those powers which are conferred by the people of the United States on the government of the Union, and all those means which are given for the purpose of carrying those powers into execution. We have a principle which is safe for the States, and safe for the Union. We are relieved, as we ought to be, from clashing sovereignty; from interfering powers; from a repugnancy between a right in one government to pull down what there is an acknowledged right in another to build up; from the incompatibility of a right in one government to destroy what there is a right in another to preserve. We are not driven to the perplexing inquiry, so unfit for the judicial department, what degree of taxation is the legitimate use, and what degree may amount to the abuse of the power. The attempt to use it on the means employed by the government of the Union, in pursuance of the constitution, it itself an abuse, because it is the usurpation of a power which the people of a single State cannot give.

[61] We find, then, on just theory, a total failure of this original right to tax the means employed by the government of the Union, for the execution of its powers. The right never existed, and the question whether it has been surrendered, cannot arise.

[62] But, waiving this theory for the present, let us resume the inquiry, whether this power can be exercised by the respective States, consistently with a fair construction of the constitution?

[63] That the power to tax involves the power to destroy; that the power to destroy may defeat and render useless the power to create; that there is a plain

repugnance, in conferring on one government a power to control the constitutional measures of another, which other, with respect to those very measures, is declared to be supreme over that which exerts the control, are propositions not to be denied. But all inconsistencies are to be reconciled by the magic of the word CONFIDENCE. Taxation, it is said, does not necessarily and unavoidably destroy. To carry it to the excess of destruction would be an abuse, to presume which, would banish that confidence which is essential to all government.

[64] But is this a case of confidence? Would the people of any one State trust those of another with a power to control the most insignificant operations of their State government? We know they would not. Why, then, should we suppose that the people of any one State should be willing to trust those of another with a power to control the operations of a government to which they have confided their most important and most valuable interests? In the legislature of the Union alone, are all represented. The legislature of the Union alone, therefore, can be trusted by the people with the power of controlling measures which concern all, in the confidence that it will not be abused. This, then, is not a case of confidence, and we must consider it as it really is.

[65] If we apply the principle for which the State of Maryland contends, to the constitution generally, we shall find it capable of changing totally the character of that instrument. We shall find it capable of arresting all the measures of the government, and of prostrating it at the foot of the States. The American people have declared their constitution, and the laws made in pursuance thereof, to be supreme; but this principle would transfer the supremacy, in fact, to the States.

[66] If the States may tax one instrument, employed by the government in the execution of its powers, they may tax any and every other instrument. They may tax the mail; they may tax the mint; they may tax patent rights; they may tax the papers of the custom-house; they may tax judicial process; they may tax all the means employed by the government, to an excess which would defeat all the ends of government. This was not intended by the American people. They did not design to make their government dependent on the States.

[67] Gentlemen say, they do not claim the right to extend State taxation to these objects. They limit their pretensions to property. But on what principle is this distinction made? Those who make it have furnished no reason for it, and the principle for which they contend denies it. They contend that the power of taxation has no other limit than is found in the 10th section of the 1st article of the constitution; that, with respect to every thing else, the power of the States is supreme, and admits of no control. If this be true, the distinction between property and other subjects to which the power of taxation is applicable, is merely arbitrary, and can never be sustained. This is not all. If the controlling power of the States be established; if their supremacy as to taxation be acknowledged; what is to restrain their exercising this control in any shape they may please to give it? Their sovereignty is not confined to taxation. That is not the only mode in which it might be displayed. The question is, in truth, a question of supremacy; and if the right of the States to tax the means employed by the general government be conceded the declaration that the constitution, and the laws made in pursuance thereof, shall be the supreme law of the land, is empty and unmeaning declamation.

[68] In the course of the argument, the Federalist has been quoted; and the opinions expressed by the authors of that work have been justly supposed to be entitled to great respect in expounding the constitution. No tribute can be paid to

them which exceeds their merit; but in applying their opinions to the cases which may arise in the progress of our government, a right to judge of their correctness must be retained; and, to understand the argument, we must examine the proposition it maintains, and the objections against which it is directed. The subject of those numbers, from which passages have been cited, is the unlimited power of taxation which is vested in the general government. The objection to this unlimited power, which the argument seeks to remove, is stated with fullness and clearness. It is, "that an indefinite power of taxation in the latter (the government of the Union) might, and probably would, in time, deprive the former (the government of the States) of the means of providing for their own necessities; and would subject them entirely to the mercy of the national legislature. As the laws of the Union are to become the supreme law of the land; as it is to have power to pass all laws that may be necessary for carrying into execution the authorities with which it is proposed to vest it; the national government might at any time abolish the taxes imposed for State objects, upon the pretence of an interference with its own. It might allege a necessity for doing this, in order to give efficacy to the national revenues; and thus all the resources of taxation might, by degrees, become the subjects of federal monopoly, to the entire exclusion and destruction of the State governments."

[69] The objections to the constitution which are noticed in these numbers, were to the undefined power of the government to tax, not to the incidental privilege of exempting its own measures from State taxation. The consequences apprehended from this undefined power were, that it would absorb all the objects of taxation, "to the exclusion and destruction of the State governments." The arguments of the Federalist are intended to prove the fallacy of these apprehensions; not to prove that the government was incapable of executing any of its powers, without exposing the means it employed to the embarrassments of State taxation. Arguments urged against these objections, and these apprehensions, are to be understood as relating to the points they mean to prove. Had the authors of those excellent essays been asked, whether they contended for that construction of the constitution, which would place within the reach of the States those measures which the government might adopt for the execution of its powers; no man, who has read their instructive pages, will hesitate to admit, that their answer must have been in the negative.

[70] It has also been insisted, that, as the power of taxation in the general and State governments is acknowledged to be concurrent, every argument which would sustain the right of the general government to tax banks chartered by the States, will equally sustain the right of the States to tax banks chartered by the general government.

[71] But the two cases are not on the same reason. The people of all the States have created the general government, and have conferred upon it the general power of taxation. The people of all the States, and the States themselves, are represented in Congress, and, by their representatives, exercise this power. When they tax the chartered institutions of the States, they tax their constituents; and these taxes must be uniform. But, when a State taxes the operations of the government of the United States, it acts upon institutions created, not by their own constituents, but by people over whom they claim no control. It acts upon the measures of a government created by others as well as themselves, for the benefit of others in common with themselves. The difference is that which always exists, and always must exist, between the action of the whole on a part, and the action of a part on the whole — between the laws of a government declared to be supreme, and those of a government which, when in opposition to those laws, is not supreme.

[72] But if the full application of this argument could be admitted, it might bring into question the right of Congress to tax the State banks, and could not prove the right of the States to tax the Bank of the United States.

[73] The Court has bestowed on this subject its most deliberate consideration. The result is a conviction that the States have no power, by taxation or otherwise, to retard, impede, burden, or in any manner control, the operations of the constitutional laws enacted by Congress to carry into execution the powers vested in the general government. This is, we think, the unavoidable consequence of that supremacy which the constitution has declared.

[74] We are unanimously of opinion, that the law passed by the legislature of Maryland, imposing a tax on the Bank of the United States, is unconstitutional and void.

[75] This opinion does not deprive the States of any resources which they originally possessed. It does not extend to a tax paid by the real property of the bank, in common with the other real property within the State, nor to a tax imposed on the interest which the citizens of Maryland may hold in this institution, in common with other property of the same description throughout the State. But this is a tax on the operations of the bank, and is, consequently, a tax on the operation of an instrument employed by the government of the Union to carry its powers into execution. Such a tax must be unconstitutional.

Discussion

1. *Marshall's interpretive strategy.* Outline Marshall's argument in the second part of *McCulloch.* Which of the methods of constitutional interpretation discussed does Marshall employ?

2. *Possible alternative holdings.* Under the principles announced in the first part of the opinion, Congress could surely have enacted legislation immunizing the Bank of the United States from the Maryland tax. Why does it not suffice, as a constitutional matter, to place such a decision in the hands of Congress? Are you persuaded that the Constitution, by its own force, prohibits the tax?

Is it constitutionally relevant that the Maryland tax by its terms fell only on banks not chartered by the state? Only the Bank of the United States fit that category. Could (or should) Marshall have assumed for the sake of argument that a tax on *all* banks could be upheld as applied to the national bank, but nonetheless invalidated this tax on the ground that it discriminated against the Bank of the United States? Consider in this context the final paragraph of Marshall's opinion. If some of the bank's functions and property, but not others, are constitutionally immune from state taxation, how can one determine which ones are immune?

3. *Questions of degree.* In the first part of the opinion Marshall writes that, if the Court concludes that the bank is "appropriate," then "the degree of its necessity is to be discussed in another place," apparently referring to Congress. Does the force of this statement depend on what one means by "necessity"? If Marshall were a senator or representative, how do you suppose he would approach the question of the bank's "degree of necessity" — as a constitutional question or a political issue? Compare Hamilton's argument for the first bank, supra. (What is the difference between "constitutional" and "political" in this context?) If the "degree of necessity" remains a constitutional question even after "appropriateness" has been determined, why shouldn't the Court, as well as Congress, address it?

With respect to Marshall's "rhetorical absolute"[59] in the second part of *McCulloch*, is it true that "the power to tax is the power to destroy," or is this just a "seductive cliche"?[60] Consider in this context Justice Holmes's statement, "Taxes are what we pay for civilized society," Compania General de Tabacos de Filipinas v. Collector of Internal Revenue, 275 U.S. 87, 100 (1927) (dissenting). Might not both statements be true? Might excessive taxation indeed be destructive, even as the lack of sufficient taxation would threaten the maintenance of "civilized society"? If this is the case, then who — or what institution — should be charged with deciding whether the line between sufficiency and excess has been crossed? How does Marshall's reference to "the perplexing inquiry, so unfit for the judiciary department, what degree of taxation is the legitimate use, and what degree may amount to the abuse of power" help us to answer this last question?

To the extent that Marshall might be said to base his own "rhetorical absolute" on a purely institutional consideration based on the Court's self-perceived inability to make judgments of degree, does this justify depriving the states of a legitimate power? Justice Holmes, dissenting in Panhandle Oil Co. v. Knox, 277 U.S. 218, 223 (1928), observed: "In those days it was not recognized as it is today that most of the distinctions of the law are distinctions of degree. If the States had any power it was assumed that they had all power, and that the necessary alternative was to deny it altogether." (Holmes went on to write, "The power to tax is not the power to destroy while this Court sits.") What do you think Holmes meant by this? Is it that the Court possesses a truly "legal" conception of what the limits of taxation are, or, rather, that its members will apply their own sense of basically prudential judgment when a state is going "too far" in imposing taxes?

In approaching the cases in the following chapter, consider the hypothesis that "legal" analysis for Marshall consists of *categorizing* activities and other things, whereas "political" decisionmaking consists of weighing the costs and benefits of a proposed course of action, and that, notwithstanding the emergence of an instrumental conception of law, Marshall perceived a clear distinction between law and policymaking.

4. *Federal immunities today.* Litigation continues today on the ability of states to tax or to regulate federal instrumentalities. See, e.g., Department of Employment v. United States, 385 U.S. 355 (1966), unanimously holding that the American National Red Cross is an instrumentality of the United States, immune from a state unemployment compensation tax, and that Congress has not waived its immunity. In a 1999 case, Jefferson County, Alabama v. Acker, 527 U.S. 423 (1999), the Court considered a suit brought by U.S. federal judges protesting a Jefferson County occupational tax on persons working within the county not otherwise required to pay a license fee under state law. Because the judges hold court within the county, the county attempted to collect the tax. "[T]he judges maintain that they are shielded from payment of the tax by the intergovernmental tax immunity doctrine, while the county urges that the doctrine does not apply unless the tax discriminates against an officeholder because of the source of his pay or compensation." The Court, through Justice Ginsberg, ruled in favor of the county. "The county's Ordinance lays no 'demands directly on the Federal Government,' United States v. New Mexico, 455 U.S. 720, 735 (1982); it is, and operates as, a tax on employees'

---

59. New York v. United States, 326 U.S. 572, 576 (1946) (Frankfurter, J.).
60. Graves v. O'Keefe, 306 U.S. 466, 489 (1939) (Frankfurter, J., concurring).

compensation. The Public Salary Tax Act [passed by Congress] allows a State and its taxing authorities to tax the pay federal employees receive 'if the taxation does not discriminate against the [federal] employee because of the source of the pay or compensation.' 4 U.S.C. §111. We hold that Jefferson County's tax falls within that allowance. . . . In practice, Jefferson County's license tax serves a revenue-raising, not a regulatory, purpose. Jefferson County neither issues licenses to taxpayers, nor in any way regulates them in the performance of their duties based on their status as license taxpayers." Justices Breyer and O'Connor dissented, largely on the basis of the many exceptions to paying the tax found in the Jefferson County ordinance.

As Justice Ginsberg suggests, states have far less power to *regulate* federal instrumentalities than to levy (nondiscriminatory) taxes against federal officials. A taste of the difficulties provided in regard to state regulation is provided by Johnson v. Maryland, 254 U.S. 51 (1920), which held that, in the absence of any federal regulation on the subject, a Post Office employee driving a government vehicle on official business was not required to possess a state driver's license. Citing *McCulloch*, Justice Holmes wrote:

> It seems to us that the immunity of instruments of the United States from state control in the performance of their duties extends to a requirement that they desist from performance until they satisfy a state officer upon examination that they are competent for a necessary part of them and pay a fee for permission to go on. Such a requirement does not merely touch the Government servants remotely by a general rule of conduct; it lays hold of them in their specific attempt to obey orders and requires qualifications in addition to those that the Government has pronounced sufficient. It is the duty of the Department to employ persons competent for their work and that duty it must be presumed has been performed.

Holmes cautioned, however, that "an employee of the United States does not secure a general immunity from state law while acting in the course of his employment" and suggested that "when the United States has not spoken, the subjection to local law would extend to general rules that might affect incidentally the mode of carrying out the employment — as, for instance, a statute or ordinance regulating the mode of turning at the corners of streets." What is the basis for this distinction?

VI.   The Demise of the Second Bank

The national consensus that had supported the Bank of the United States in 1816 had collapsed by the time Congress passed a bill extending its charter in 1832. President Andrew Jackson's veto of the measure was accompanied by a message to the Senate addressing not only the merits but also the question of the allocation of authority to interpret the Constitution.

ANDREW JACKSON, VETO MESSAGE, JULY 10, 1832[61]

The bill "to modify and continue" the act entitled "An act to incorporate the subscribers to the bank of the United States" was presented to me on the 4th July

___

61. 2 Messages and Papers of the Presidents 576-589 (Richardson ed., 1897).

instant. Having considered it with that solemn regard to the principles of the Constitution which the day was calculated to inspire, and come to the conclusion that it ought not to become a law, I herewith return it to the Senate, in which it originated, with my objections. . . .

It is maintained by the advocates of the bank that its constitutionality in all its features ought to be considered as settled by precedent and by the decision of the Supreme Court. To this conclusion I can not assent. Mere precedent is a dangerous source of authority, and should not be regarded as deciding questions of constitutional power except where the acquiescence of the people and the States can be considered as well settled. So far from this being the case on this subject, an argument against the bank might be based on precedent. One Congress, in 1791, decided in favor of a bank; another, in 1811, decided against it. One Congress, in 1815, decided against a bank; another, in 1816, decided in its favor. Prior to the present Congress, therefore, the precedents drawn from that source were equal. If we resort to the States, the expressions of legislative, judicial, and executive opinions against the bank have been probably to those in its favor as 4 to 1. There is nothing in precedent, therefore, which, if its authority were admitted, ought to weigh in favor of the act before me.

Overall, Congress has been against bank

States generally against bank

Precedent says no bank

If the opinion of the Supreme Court covered the whole ground of this act, it ought not to control the coordinate authorities of this Government. The Congress, the Executive, and the Court must each for itself be guided by its own opinion of the Constitution. Each public officer who takes an oath to support the Constitution swears that he will support it as he understands it, and not as it is understood by others. It is as much the duty of the House of Representatives, of the Senate, and of the President to decide upon the constitutionality of any bill or resolution which may be presented to them for passage or approval as it is of the supreme judges when it may be brought before them for judicial decision. The opinion of the judges has no more authority over Congress than the opinion of Congress has over the judges, and on that point the President is independent of both. The authority of the Supreme Court must not, therefore, be permitted to control the Congress or the Executive when acting in their legislative capacities, but to have only such influence as the force of their reasoning may deserve.

But in the case relied upon the Supreme Court have not decided that all the features of this corporation are compatible with the Constitution. It is true that the court have said that the law incorporating the bank is a constitutional exercise of power by Congress; but taking into view the whole opinion of the court and the reasoning by which they have come to that conclusion, I understand them to have decided that inasmuch as a bank is an appropriate means for carrying into effect the enumerated powers of the General Government, therefore the law incorporating it is in accordance with that provision of the Constitution which declares that Congress shall have power "to make all laws which shall be necessary and proper for carrying those powers into execution." Having satisfied themselves that the word "necessary" in the Constitution means "needful," *"requisite," "essential," "conducive to,"* and that "a bank" is a convenient, a useful, and essential instrument in the prosecution of the Government's "fiscal operations," they conclude that to "use one must be within the discretion of Congress" and that "the act to incorporate the Bank of the United States is a law made in pursuance of the Constitution"; "but," say they, *"where the law is not prohibited and is really calculated to effect any of the objects intrusted to the Government, to undertake here to inquire into the degree of its necessity would be to pass the line which circumscribes the judicial department and to tread on legislative ground."*

The principle here affirmed is that the "degree of its necessity," involving all the details of a banking institution, is a question exclusively for legislative consideration. A bank is constitutional, but it is the province of the Legislature to determine whether this or that particular power, privilege, or exemption is "necessary and proper" to enable the bank to discharge its duties to the Government, and from their decision there is no appeal to the courts of justice. Under the decision of the Supreme Court, therefore, it is the exclusive province of Congress and the President to decide whether the particular features of this act are *necessary* and *proper* in order to enable the bank to perform conveniently and efficiently the public duties assigned to it as a fiscal agent, and therefore constitutional, or *unnecessary* and *improper,* and therefore unconstitutional.

Without commenting on the general principle affirmed by the Supreme Court, let us examine the details of this act in accordance with the rule of legislative action which they have laid down. It will be found that many of the powers and privileges conferred on it can not be supposed necessary for the purpose for which it is proposed to be created, and are not, therefore, means necessary to attain the end in view, and consequently not justified by the Constitution. . . .

This act authorizes and encourages transfers of its stock to foreigners and grants them an exemption from all State and national taxation. So far from being *"necessary and proper"* that the bank should possess this power to make it a safe and efficient agent of the Government in its fiscal operations, it is calculated to convert the Bank of the United States into a foreign bank, to impoverish our people in time of peace, to disseminate a foreign influence through every section of the Republic, and in war to endanger our independence. . . .

It is maintained by some that the bank is a means of executing the constitutional power "to coin money and regulate the value thereof." Congress have established a mint to coin money and passed laws to regulate the value thereof. The money so coined, with its value so regulated, and such foreign coins as Congress may adopt are the only currency known to the Constitution. But if they have other power to regulate the currency, it was conferred to be exercised by themselves, and not to be transferred to a corporation. If the bank be established for that purpose, with a charter unalterable without its consent, Congress have parted with their power for a term of years, during which the Constitution is a dead letter. It is neither necessary nor proper to transfer its legislative power to such a bank, and therefore unconstitutional.

By its silence, considered in connection with the decision of the Supreme Court in the case of McCulloch against the State of Maryland, this act takes from the States the power to tax a portion of the banking business carried on within their limits, in subversion of one of the strongest barriers which secured them against Federal encroachments. Banking, like farming, manufacturing, or any other occupation or profession, is *a business.* . . .

Upon the formation of the Constitution the States guarded their taxing power with peculiar jealousy. They surrendered it only as it regards imports and exports. In relation to every other object within their jurisdiction, whether persons, property, business, or professions, it was secured in as ample a manner as it was before possessed. . . .

There is no more appropriate subject of taxation than banks, banking, and bank stocks, and none to which the States ought more pertinaciously to cling.

It can not be *necessary* to the character of the bank as a fiscal agent of the Government that its private business should be exempted from that taxation to which all the State banks are liable, nor can I conceive it *"proper"* that the substantive and most essential powers reserved by the States shall be thus attacked and annihilated as a means of executing the powers delegated to the General Government. . . .

If our power over means is so absolute that the Supreme Court will not call in question the constitutionality of an act of Congress the subject of which "is not prohibited, and is really calculated to effect any of the objects intrusted to the Government," although, as in the case before me, it takes away powers expressly granted to Congress and rights scrupulously reserved to the States, it becomes us to proceed in our legislation with the utmost caution. Though not directly, our own powers and the rights of the States may be indirectly legislated away in the use of means to execute substantive powers. . . . We may not pass an act prohibiting the States to tax the banking business carried on within their limits, but we may, as a means of executing our powers over other objects, place that business in the hands of our agents and then declare it exempt from State taxation in their hands. Thus may our own powers and the rights of the States, which we can not directly curtail or invade, be frittered away and extinguished in the use of means employed by us to execute other powers. That a bank of the United States, competent to all the duties which may be required by the Government, might be so organized as not to infringe on our own delegated powers or the reserved rights of the States I do not entertain a doubt. Had the Executive been called upon to furnish the project of such an institution, the duty would have been cheerfully performed. In the absence of such a call it was obviously proper that he should confine himself to pointing out those prominent features in the act presented which in his opinion make it incompatible with the Constitution and sound policy. . . .

It is to be regretted that the rich and powerful too often bend the acts of government to their selfish purposes. Distinctions in society will always exist under every just government. Equality of talents, of education, or of wealth can not be produced by human institutions. In the full enjoyment of the gifts of Heaven and the fruits of superior industry, economy, and virtue, every man is equally entitled to protection by law; but when the laws undertake to add to these natural and just advantages artificial distinctions, to grant titles, gratuities, and exclusive privileges, to make the rich richer and the potent more powerful, the humble members of society — the farmers, mechanics, and laborers — who have neither the time nor the means of securing like favors to themselves, have a right to complain of the injustice of their Government. There are no necessary evils in government. Its evils exist only in its abuses. If it would confine itself to equal protection, and, as Heaven does its rains, shower its favors alike on the high and the low, the rich and the poor, it would be an unqualified blessing. In the act before me there seems to be a wide and unnecessary departure from these just principles.

Nor is our Government to be maintained or our Union preserved by invasions of the rights and powers of the several States. In thus attempting to make our General Government strong we make it weak. Its true strength consists in leaving individuals and States as much as possible to themselves — in making itself felt, not in its power, but in its beneficence; not in its control, but in its protection; not in binding the States more closely to the center, but leaving each to move unobstructed in its proper orbit.

Discussion

1. Jackson's assertion that even "[i]f the opinion of the Supreme Court covered the whole ground of this act, it ought not to control the coordinate authorities of this Government" presents a fundamental issue of the allocation of constitutional decisionmaking authority among the branches of the national government, to which we return at length in later chapters. Jackson goes on to note that the Supreme Court in *McCulloch* had *not* "decided that all features of this corporation are compatible with the Constitution." He concludes that "it is the exclusive province of Congress and the President to decide whether the particular features of this act are *necessary* and *proper*. . . ." Is this question one of constitutional law, of politics, or both?

2. The history surrounding the adoption of the President's veto power does not shed much light on its scope. Of the early history of its use, Edward Corwin writes:[62]

> [T]he veto power did not escape the early talent of Americans for conjuring up constitutional limitations out of thin air. The veto was solely a self-defensive weapon of the President; it was the means furnished him for carrying out his oath to "preserve, protect and defend the Constitution" and was not validly usable for any other purpose; it did not extend to revenue bills, never having been so employed by the King of England; it did not extend to "insignificant and trivial" matters like private pension bills; it was never intended to give effect merely to presidential desires, but its use must rest on considerations of great weight, and so on and so forth. Although efforts of this sort to forge shackles for the power derived a certain specious plausibility from the rarity of the veto's use in English history, they met with failure from the first. Washington exercised the power twice, once on constitutional grounds, once on grounds of expediency. Neither Adams nor Jefferson exercised it at all. Of Madison's six vetoes four urged constitutional objections to the measure involved, two objections of policy. Summing the matter up for the first century under the Constitution, the leading authority on the subject says: "From Jackson's administration to the Civil War vetoes on grounds of expediency became more frequent, but they were still in a decided minority. Since the [Civil] War constitutional arguments in a veto message have been almost unknown." The latter statement applies moreover equally to more recent years, if exception be made for one or two vetoes by Presidents Taft and Coolidge, both of whom had a special penchant for constitutional niceties. . . .

3. Professor Mark Graber has suggested that the justices appointed to the Court by Jackson and his successor Martin Van Buren, who were drawn from the states-rights-oriented Democratic Party, might well have overruled the broad doctrine enunciated in *McCulloch* had the case ever presented itself.[63] The Court never had such an opportunity, however, because of Jackson's own veto, which was mirrored in later vetoes by various presidents of legislation passed by Whig-dominated Congresses that rested on an expansive view of national power. Thus, Graber suggests, *McCulloch* survived not so much because it was explicitly reaffirmed by the Court as because the procedures of the American political system, including the presidential veto, sometimes work to preclude given issues from going to the Supreme Court at a particular moment when the Court, whether by affirming or striking down the legislation, could enunciate its own view of the constitutional merits.

62. Edward Corwin, The President: Office and Powers 279 (quoting Edward Mason, The Veto Power (1891)) (4th ed. 1957).

63. Mark Graber, Naked Land Transfers and American Constitutional Development, 53 Vanderbilt L. Rev. 73 (2000).

4. President Jackson's veto was not overridden, and the Bank expired in 1836. But imagine that it *had* been overridden, or that President Jackson had reluctantly signed a bill extending the Bank's charter because, for example, it was embedded, as is often the case today, in so-called omnibus legislation treating a wide number of subjects. In the absence of line-item veto authority, the President may think it necessary to sign the bill in spite of its containing unwise or, more to the present point, even unconstitutional (from the President's perspective) aspects as well. At least since the time of Woodrow Wilson's presidency, presidents have on occasion issued "signing statements" explaining that they regard certain parts of legislation they are signing as unconstitutional and indicating their intention not to comply with the statutory language. See Statement by the State Department (Announcing President Wilson's Refusal to Carry Out the Section of the Jones Merchant Marine Act of June 5, 1920), in 17 A Compilation of the Messages and Papers of the President 8871 (Sept. 24, 1920). Such statements have become quite common since President Eisenhower's tenure in office, especially in regard to bills containing so-called legislative vetoes. The most recent consideration of this issue is contained in the following Memorandum of Walter Dellinger, Assistant Attorney General in charge of Office of Legal Counsel, United States Department of Justice, to Abner Mikva, Counsel to the President. Dellinger, who later became acting Solicitor General of the United States, had been professor of law at Duke University, where he taught constitutional law before joining the Clinton Administration.

PRESIDENTIAL AUTHORITY TO DECLINE TO EXECUTE
UNCONSTITUTIONAL STATUTES (NOVEMBER 2, 1994)

Let me start with a general proposition that I believe to be uncontroversial: there are circumstances in which the President may appropriately decline to enforce a statute that he views as unconstitutional.

First, there is significant judicial approval of this proposition. Most notable is the Court's decision in Myers v. United States, 272 U.S. 52 (1926). There the Court sustained the President's view that the statute at issue was unconstitutional without any member of the Court suggesting that the President had acted improperly in refusing to abide by the statute. More recently, in Freytag v. Commissioner, 501 U.S. 868 (1991), all four of the Justices who addressed the issue agreed that the President has "the power to veto encroaching laws . . . or even to disregard them when they are unconstitutional." Id. at 906 (Scalia, J., concurring). . . .

Second, consistent and substantial executive practice also confirms this general proposition. Opinions dating to at least 1860 assert the President's authority to decline to effectuate enactments that the President views as unconstitutional. . . . Moreover, . . . numerous Presidents have provided advance notice of their intention not to enforce specific statutory requirements that they have viewed as unconstitutional, and the Supreme Court has implicitly endorsed this practice. See INS v. Chadha, 462 U.S. 919, 942 n.13 (1983) (noting that Presidents often sign legislation containing constitutionally objectionable provisions and indicate that they will not comply with those provisions).

While the general proposition that in some situations the President may decline to enforce unconstitutional statutes is unassailable, it does not offer sufficient guidance as to the appropriate course in specific circumstances. . . . I offer the following propositions for your consideration.

1. The President's office and authority are created and bounded by the Constitution; he is required to act within its terms. Put somewhat differently, in serving as the executive created by the Constitution, the President is required to act in accordance with the laws — including the Constitution, which takes precedence over other forms of law. This obligation is reflected in the Take Care Clause and in the President's oath of office.

2. When bills are under consideration by Congress, the executive branch should promptly identify unconstitutional provisions and communicate its concerns to Congress so that the provisions can be corrected. . . .

3. The President should presume that enactments are constitutional. There will be some occasions, however, when a statute appears to conflict with the Constitution. In such cases, the President can and should exercise his independent judgment to determine whether the statute is constitutional. . . . Where possible, the President should construe provisions to avoid constitutional problems.

4. The Supreme Court plays a special role in resolving disputes about the constitutionality of enactments. As a general matter, if the President believes that the Court would sustain a particular provision as constitutional, the President should execute the statute, notwithstanding his own beliefs about the constitutional issue. If, however, the President, exercising his independent judgment, determines both that a provision would violate the Constitution and that it is probable that the Court would agree with him, the President has the authority to decline to execute the same.

5. Where the President's independent constitutional judgment and his determination of the Court's probable decision converge on a conclusion of unconstitutionality, the President must make a decision about whether or not to comply with the provision. That decision is necessarily specific to context, and it should be reached after careful weighing of the effect of compliance with the provision on the constitutional rights of affected individuals and on the executive branch's constitutional authority. Also relevant is the likelihood that compliance or non-compliance will permit judicial resolution of the issue. That is, the President may base his decision to comply (or decline to comply) in part on a desire to afford the Supreme Court an opportunity to review the constitutional judgment of the legislative branch.

6. The President has enhanced responsibility to resist unconstitutional provisions that encroach upon the constitutional powers of the Presidency. Where the President believes that an enactment unconstitutionally limits his powers, he has the authority to defend his office and decline to abide by it, unless he is convinced that the Court would disagree with his assessment. If the President does not challenge such provisions (i.e., by refusing to execute them), there often will be no occasion for judicial consideration of their constitutionality; a policy of consistent Presidential enforcement of statutes limiting his power thus would deny the Supreme Court the opportunity to review the limitations and thereby would allow for unconstitutional restrictions on the President's authority.

Some legislative encroachments on executive authority, however, will not be justiciable or are for other reasons unlikely to be resolved in court. If resolution in the courts is unlikely and the President cannot look to a judicial determination, he must shoulder the responsibility of protecting the constitutional role of the presidency. . . .

7. The fact that a [prior] sitting President signed the statute in question does not change this analysis. The text of the Constitution offers no basis for distinguishing bills based on who signed them; there is no constitutional analogue to the principles of waiver and estoppel. . . . [And it makes no difference if the incumbent President was the one who signed the bill in question.] [T]he President's signing of a bill does not affect his authority to decline to enforce constitutionally objectionable provisions thereof.

In accordance with these propositions, we do not believe that a President is limited to choosing between vetoing, for example, the Defense Appropriations Act [funding the United States armed forces] and executing an unconstitutional provision in it. In our view, the President has the authority to sign legislation containing desirable elements while refusing to execute a constitutionally defective provision. . . .

Discussion

If you accept the legitimacy of Dellinger's basic argument — that the President has the authority (and perhaps the duty) to engage in independent constitutional interpretation, do you agree with his implicit argument that the Presidents must always subordinate their own views to those of the Court? Assume that Jackson's veto had been overridden and the rechartering upheld by a Court not yet transformed by Democratic appointments. Would Dellinger have required Jackson to enforce the legislation even if he continued to believe, as argued in the Veto Message, that it was unconstitutional?

What, incidentally, if the President announces that (s)he will issue a presidential pardon, see Constitution, Article II, §2, to anyone charged with violating a given federal statute that the President believes is unconstitutional? If *that* would not be unconstitutional — can you think of any good arguments why it would be? — then why would it be unconstitutional for the President to refuse to enforce the statute in the first place, even if the Supreme Court would likely uphold it or, to take the strongest example, even if the Supreme Court had in fact already upheld it in an earlier case? Whatever your answers to these questions, you will have the opportunity to reconsider them when you come to the material, infra, concerning Abraham Lincoln's conduct as President during 1861-1865 or President Truman's seizure of the U.S. steel industry during the Korean War in 1951.

Note: Congressional Spending for the "General Welfare"

Congressional authority under the "General Welfare" clause was a recurring issue in the early republic. As one might expect from the debate over the Bank, members of the Federalist Party, heavily influenced by Hamilton, offered an expansive view of congressional power to spend for the "general welfare." As Professor Currie writes, "A fire that devastated the Georgia port city of Savannah presented a spectacular opportunity for Hamilton's disciples, for the idea of aiding the victims had

obvious emotional appeal for Southern Representatives, many of whom were ideo-
logically allergic to federal spending. . . . One has the sense that wily Federalists
were hoping to slip this one by on sympathy grounds, only to employ it mercilessly
as a precedent later on. But the Republicans refused the bait." They insisted that
the "general welfare" must be defined in terms of the specific allocations of power
in Clauses 2-17 rather than a foundation of independent power of Congress.[64] As
you will see, infra Chapter 5, the Supreme Court ultimately accepted the
Hamiltonian view and, concomitantly, rejected the more limited Madisonian
conception of congressional power.

Even if one accepts a congressional power to spend on behalf of the "general
welfare," an independent question is how it is to be defined (and *who* gets to define
it). One might wonder exactly why it was in the "general welfare" — i.e., the welfare
of Americans living in Massachusetts or Kentucky — to rebuild Savannah, in
contrast with what might be termed the "special welfare" of Georgians who might
otherwise have had to raise local taxes to pay for reconstructing their principal port
city. As Professor Currie writes elsewhere, aiding Savannah "would justify federal
relief for local disasters anywhere in the country."[65] Of course the modern
Congress, like its earliest predecessors, does indeed allocate what are often vast
amounts of money for "local disasters." Is the justification for this that whatever
happens in New Orleans, Miami, or San Diego, does in fact affect all Americans, or,
rather, is it that we accept with equanimity the ability of politically influential
groups (or cities) to make claims on the public treasury so long as Congress is
willing to declare, without more, that it is in the "general welfare" to do so?[66]

The debate over national power crystallized with regard to the passage of legislation funding "internal improvements," including roads and canals. In 1816, for
example, then-Representative John C. Calhoun of South Carolina (who would later
serve in the Senate and as Andrew Jackson's Vice President) proposed a bill that
would allocate the United States' share of dividends it received from the Bank of the
United States to a "fund for constructing roads and canals."[67] Calhoun defended his
proposal as a contribution to the "general welfare" of the entire nation:

> The first great object was to perfect the communication from Maine to Louisiana. . . .
> The next was the connexion of the Lakes with the Hudson River. . . . The next object
> of chief importance was to connect all the great commercial points on the Atlantic,
> Philadelphia, Baltimore, Washington, Richmond, Charleston, and Savannah, with the
> Western States; and finally, to perfect the intercourse between the West and New
> Orleans.

After much substantial debate, much of it made on constitutional grounds, the
House passed the bill by an 86-84 vote; the Senate, after what Professor Currie
terms only a "perfunctory" debate (although there, too, senators at least mentioned
constitutional issues), agreed with the House by a 20-15 vote. It then went to

64. See David P. Currie, supra n.45, at 224.
65. David P. Currie, 2 The Constitution in Congress: The Jeffersonians 1803-1827 292 (2001).
66. See generally Michele L. Landis, Let Me Next Time Be "Tried by Fire": Disaster Relief and the
Origins of the American Welfare State, 1789-1874, 92 Northwestern U. L. Rev. 967 (1998).
67. See Currie, supra n.65, at 260-267.

President James Madison. Madison had signed the 1816 act chartering the Second Bank of the United States, which depended on a broader view of national power than he had articulated in 1791. However, in literally his last act as President, on March 3, 1817, he vetoed the legislation:[68]

> . . . I am constrained by the insuperable difficulty I feel in reconciling the bill with the Constitution of the United States to [veto it]. . . . [I]t does not appear that the power proposed to be exercised by the bill is among the enumerated powers, or that it falls by any just interpretation within the power to make laws necessary and proper for carrying into execution those or other powers vested by the Constitution in the Government of the United States.
>
> "The power to regulate commerce among the several States" can not include such a commerce without a latitude of construction departing from the ordinary import of the terms strengthened by the known inconveniences which doubtless led to the grant of this remedial power to Congress.
>
> To refer the power in question to the clause "to provide for the common defense and general welfare" would be contrary to the established and consistent rules of interpretation, as rendering the special and careful enumeration of powers which follow the clause nugatory and improper. Such a view of the Constitution would have the effect of giving to congress a general power of legislation instead of the defined and limited one hitherto understood to belong to them, the terms "common defense and general welfare" embracing every object and act within the purview of a legislative trust. It would have the effect of subjecting both the Constitution and laws of the several States in all cases not specifically exempted to be superseded by laws of Congress. . . . Such a view of the Constitution, finally, would have the effect of excluding the judicial authority of the United States from its participation in guarding the boundary between legislative powers of the General and State Governments, inasmuch as questions relating to the general welfare, being questions of policy and expediency, are unsusceptible of judicial cognizance and decision.
>
> A restriction of the power "to provide for the common defense and general welfare" to cases which are to be provided for by the expenditure of money would still leave within legislative power of Congress all the great and most important measures of Government, money being the ordinary and necessary means of carrying them into execution.
>
> If a general power to construct roads and canals, and to improve the navigation of water courses, with the train of powers incident thereto, be not possessed by Congress, the assent of the States in the mode provided in the bill can not confer the power. The only cases in which the consent and cession of particular States can extend the power of Congress are those specified and provided for in the Constitution.
>
> I am not unaware of the great importance of roads and canals and the improved navigation of water courses, and that a power in the National Legislature to provide for them might be exercised with signal advantage to the general prosperity. But seeing that such a power is not expressly given by the Constitution, and believing that it can not be deduced from any part of it without an inadmissible latitude of construction and a reliance on insufficient precedents; believing also that the permanent success of the Constitution depends on a definite partition of powers between the General and the State Governments, and that no adequate landmarks would be left by the constructive extension of the powers of Congress as proposed in the bill, I have no option but to withhold my signature from it, and to cherishing the hope that its beneficial objects may be attained by a resort for the necessary powers to the same wisdom

68. James Richardson, ed., 1 Messages and Papers of the Presidents (1897) 584-585.

and virtue in the nation which established the Constitution in its actual form and prov-
idently marked out in the instrument itself a safe and practicable mode of improving it
as experience might suggest.

Discussion

Given Madison's reference to internal improvements as "beneficial" and his
apparent support for a constitutional amendment specifically authorizing them, it
seems plausible to interpret the veto as based on his notion of "constitutional
fidelity." Such fidelity presumably bars presidents from signing legislation they
believe to be unconstitutional, regardless of its merits. Among other things, the
veto, just like Madison's speech to the House of Representatives that begins this
chapter, exemplifies the significance of nonjudicial constitutional decisionmaking.

Do you think that Marshall would have upheld the financing of "internal
improvements" as within the power of Congress? Should the answer to that question have been determinative for President Monroe, Madison's successor, who also
vetoed, on constitutional grounds, a similar internal improvements bill in 1822,
well after, of course, the intervening opinion of the Court in *McCulloch*? If you
believe that Monroe should have responded differently from Madison, is this
because you agree, in effect, with Justice Holmes's famous statement, "The prophe-
cies of what the courts will do in fact, and nothing more pretentious, are what I
mean by the law"?[69] If "prophecy" (or prediction) is key, though, what follows for
the obligation of a President if the Court has likely changed its views? Recall
Graber's assertion that the Court of the 1840s might likely have overruled *McCulloch*
and accepted Madison's veto message as a basically accurate interpretation of the
Constitution. Would that legitimize a veto by, say, President Polk even if you believe
that Monroe was wrong in basing his own veto on constitutional grounds because
the Marshall Court would probably have upheld the legislation?

VII. Freedom of Expression and States' Rights in the Late Eighteenth Century: The Sedition Act of 1798

Late eighteenth-century debates involving issues of federalism and constitutional
interpretation were not confined to disputes over the legitimacy of a national bank.
The Bill of Rights, though adopted with relatively little fanfare, soon became the
focal point of an intense controversy regarding the scope of the First Amendment
guarantees of freedom of speech and press. In 1798, the Congress, narrowly divided
along Federalist and Republican party lines, enacted a Sedition Act that accompanied the Alien Act discussed above. Its most extreme provision made it a criminal
offense to bring into "disrepute" high political officials, including the President.
Interestingly enough, the relevant section did not mention the Vice President,
perhaps because that office was filled, in 1798, by Thomas Jefferson, whom
Federalist adherents of the Sedition Act were more than happy to bring into
disrepute.[70] In any event, the Sedition Act of 1798 was often perceived, both then

69. The Path of the Law, 10 Harv. L. Rev. 457, 460-461 (1897).

70. 1 Stat. 596 (1798) (expired 1801). Section 1 proscribes combinations or conspiracies with intent
to oppose, prevent, or intimidate government laws or operations and that "counsel, advise or attempt to

and by subsequent historians, as a Federalist measure to silence the opposition and keep themselves in power. As Professor Powe notes, "the Federalists identified opposition to their policies with support for France, and their name for the Republicans — the 'internal foe' — expressed their view that the Republican party was a threat to the republic."[71] The leading Republican papers were the targets of prosecutions, and three were forced to cease publication, two permanently. The passage of the Act, and its implementation, sparked fiery debates over the scope of the First Amendment and the proper realms of state and federal power.

A. The Meaning of the First Amendment

The history of the adoption of the First Amendment is sparse. Although there was a broad consensus that the Constitution should guarantee the freedoms of speech and press, few of the new nation's intellectual and political leaders discussed the content and extent of the First Amendment. Freedom of speech and press in 1789 England meant "freedom from prior restraint": Government could no longer censor political material prior to its publication. Once the material was in print, however, its author, printer, and publisher could still be punished for criminal libel, and truth was no defense. Indeed, as the common saying went, "the greater the truth, the greater the libel" and, presumably, the accompanying disillusionment on the part of readers with the political leaders who were the subjects of the "libels." The central question is whether this limited meaning of freedom of the press also held true in the new United States, which had been heavily influenced by its English heritage yet had rebelled against what had come to be seen as tyrannical elements of the British constitutional order.[72]

1. The Original Understanding

Did the framers of the Bill of Rights intend the First Amendment to do more than protect speech and press from prior restraint? In Freedom of Speech and Press in Early American History: Legacy of Suppression, Leonard W. Levy argues that they did not. Levy examines legislative proceedings, criminal cases in the

---

procure any insurrection, riot, unlawful assembly, or combination." Section 3 establishes that defendants can give the truth of the allegedly libelous material as evidence in their defense. In addition, the act gave the jury "a right to determine the law and the fact." Section 4 makes the Act law through March 3, 1801. Libel defendants and freedom of speech advocates had sought the two Section 3 reforms for many years. Under traditional seditious libel laws, courts would not allow the truth of the libel to be proved in court because a true libel was considered more dangerous than a false one. Furthermore, the jury had previously been allowed to decide only the question of whether the defendant had in fact published the libelous material. Judges decided the questions of law: whether the defendant made the remarks with malice and whether they were "of a bad tendency" to sedition.

71. Lucas A. Powe, Jr., The Fourth Estate and the Constitution: Freedom of the Press in America 58 (1991).

72. Seditious libel was the most repressive class of libel, according to Leonard W. Levy, Freedom of Speech and Press in Early American History: Legacy of Suppression 10 (1960). Although difficult to define, "[j]udged by actual prosecutions, the crime consisted of criticizing the government: its form, constitution, officers, laws, symbols, conduct, policies, and so on. In effect, any comment about the government which could be construed to have the bad tendency of lowering it in the public's esteem or of disturbing the peace was seditious libel, subjecting the speaker or writer to criminal prosecution."

courts and legislatures, and writings of political and intellectual leaders in America. He concludes that the evidence shows that none of them advocated any change in the common law of libel as it existed prior to 1798.[73]

> Freedom [of speech and press in the colonial period] . . . did not include a right to criticize the legislature. . . . Legislative proceedings could not be published without prior license; legislative measures were protected by parliamentary privilege from fault finders. Animadversion was regarded as subversion. Any verbal attack on government officials or policies which might be deemed an affront to the authority or honor of the legislature was subject to a power of repression from which not all the writs precious to the liberty of the subject could effect a rescue. If an exercise of parliamentary privilege was not the appropriate means of silencing an opponent, there were others of an extralegal nature. Vigilantism may be a necessary ingredient in the making of a revolution, and there may even have been occasions when its existence among the patriots was understandably provoked. But there is no denying that it did exist on a widespread scale, and it was always ugly, always a denial of due process, and always, before the outbreak of the war, directed not at an enemy but a fellow citizen whose opinions differed. There were even occasions when that citizen was a staunch patriot whose judgment in the opinion of extremists needed correction by drastic methods for the good of the cause. . . .
>
> The evidence forces the conclusion that Chief Justice Hutchinson had accurately summarized the situation when he acidly observed that the Adamses and their supporters were "contending for an unlimited Freedom of Thought and Action, which they would confine wholly to themselves."[74] Free speech for one side only is not free speech at all, or at best is an extraordinarily narrow concept of it. That, indeed, is the whole point: during the entire colonial period, from the time of the first settlements to the Revolutionary War and the framing of the first bills of rights, America had very little experience with freedom of speech or press as a meaningful condition of life. Nor did colonial America produce or inherit a broad concept of freedom of speech or press. . . .[75]

Turning to the revolutionary period, Levy writes: "No cause was more honored by rhetorical declamation and dishonored in practice than that of freedom of expression . . . from the 1760's through the cessation of hostilities."[76] The states enacted laws punishing criticism of the revolutionary government. Many post-Revolutionary state constitutions included no protection for speech or press, and, of course, neither did the Constitution of 1787. In response to criticisms by the anti-Federalists, the Federalists eventually proposed a Bill of Rights. Levy comments on the process of state ratification:[77]

> State action on the proposed Bill of Rights apparently occasioned slight comment either in or out of the legislatures, except in Virginia. Nine states perfunctorily approved the Bill of Rights by mid-June of 1790. Since records of legislative debates are nonexistent, there is no way of expressly knowing what the First Amendment freedoms were understood to mean. Private correspondence, newspapers, and tracts are unilluminating. Many may have cared about protecting freedom of speech-and-press, but no one seems

73. Id. at 68.
74. Josiah Quincy, Jr., ed., Reports of Cases Argued and Adjudged in the Superior Court of Judicature of the Province of Massachusetts Bay, Between 1761 and 1772 (Boston 1865).
75. Levy at 85-87.
76. Id. at 63.
77. Id. at 224-225, 233.

to have cared enough to clarify what he meant by the subject upon which he lavished praise. If definition were unnecessary because of the existence of a tacit and widespread understanding of "liberty of the press," only the received or traditional understanding could have been possible. To assume the existence of a general, latitudinarian understanding that veered substantially from the common-law definition is incredible, given the total absence of argumentative analysis of the meaning of the clause on speech and press. Any novel definition expanding the scope of free expression or repudiating, even altering, the concept of seditious libel would have been the subject of public debate or comment. Not even the Anti-Federalists offered the argument that the clause on speech and press was unsatisfactory because insufficiently protective. . . .

But the history of the ratification indicates no passion on the part of anyone to grind underfoot the common law of liberty of the press. Indeed the history of the framing and ratification of the First Amendment and the other nine scarcely manifests a passion on the part of anyone connected with the process. Considering its immediate background, our precious Bill of Rights was in the main the chance result of certain Federalists' having been reluctantly forced to capitalize for their own cause the propaganda that had been originated in vain by the Anti-Federalists for ulterior purposes. Thus the party that had first opposed a Bill of Rights inadvertently wound up with the responsibility for its framing and ratification, while the party that had at first professedly wanted it discovered too late that its framing and ratification were not only embarrassing but inexpedient.

Although many readers accepted Levy's view of the meaning of freedom of speech and the press in eighteenth-century America and his revisionist claim that the First Amendment was not intended to nullify the common law of criminal libel, several commentators have nevertheless chastised Levy for a crabbed reading of his evidence. For example, Merrill Jensen writes:

The impression given is that there was no freedom anywhere in America, either before or after 1763. But can we assume that the relatively few prosecutions before 1763 silenced all discussion? Did the "rude hand of the law," as Gouverneur Morris called it, touch every man who opposed governmental policies and officeholders? I doubt it. Levy goes on to assert flatly that "speech and the press were not free anywhere during the Revolution." He shows that this was correct as a matter of law but pays little attention to practice. No reader of the newspapers of the revolutionary era could accept such a statement. Of course the newspapers and people who supported Great Britain were suppressed when independence drew the line, but any nation, new or old, would do the same thing whatever its laws might be. But the debate among Americans about constitutions, governmental policies, and politicians continued with unabated fervor, and in terms that were libelous by whatever standard one applies. The prosecutions cited give one no idea of what day-to-day journalism was like. . . . Because [Levy] is concerned with seditious libel, and concentrates on the purely legal aspects, he tends to underrate the importance of practice. . . .

Another weakness of the legal approach is that it cannot explain that which is essentially political, where the law was a tool in political battles, not the guiding force. . . . [An] example is Pennsylvania during the Revolution. Levy sees no freedom of expression there because the law did not change. Yet the Pennsylvania newspapers between 1776 and 1789 contain vast amounts of some of the bitterest, most dishonest (and seditious) writing in American political history. Despite the law there was freedom of expression in fact. No governmental institution, political faction, or individual was free from attacks such as few newspapers today would dare to print.[78]

78. Merrill Jensen, 75 Harv. L. Rev. 456, 457 (1961).

Another reviewer takes issue with the conclusion Levy draws from the inconsistency between the broad popular expression of support for the freedom of speech and press and widespread public intolerance for differing views. "The serious question is whether Dean Levy is correct in saying that this broad popular spirit is meaningless because the colonists failed to demonstrate tolerance of opposing views. When our concern is with a constitutional statement of first principles, should we not be concerned with the popular ideal rather than with the gulf between principles and practice?"[79] And John Cound argues that rather than depicting a legacy of suppression, Levy's evidence actually

> shows the legacy . . . to be one of a continuing and enlarging concern for freedom. If the first amendment is a living and growing idea, as he argues, rather than a fixed statement, its growth began at least a century and a half before 1790. There were those men who, while accepting the doctrine of seditious libel (or at least not openly rejecting it) nonetheless carved out protections for free expression. . . . [I]t seems an oversimplification to say of men who had attacked prosecution after prosecution as groundless and abusive, and who by their own words courted indictment, that "they accepted in substance the Blackstone-Mansfield definition [of freedom of the press]: freedom, under law, from prior restraint," simply because they did not deny the possibility that a government can be libeled.[80]

In 1983, David Anderson, in The Origins of the Press Clause, 30 U.C.L.A. L. Rev. 455, reexamined the historical materials and vigorously attacked Levy's thesis, concluding his article as follows:

> Though scholars today may debate whether the press clause has any significance independent of the speech clause, historically there is no doubt that it did. Freedom of the press — not freedom of speech — was the primary concern of the generation that wrote the Declaration of Independence, the Constitution, and the Bill of Rights. Freedom of speech was a late addition to the pantheon of rights; freedom of the press occupied a central position from the very beginning.
>
> By the time the press clause became part of our Constitution in 1791, it had a considerable legislative history. The revolutionary state constitutions, the ratifying conventions, and the First Congress produced numerous expressions of the idea. These expressions and freedom-of-the-press literature from which they were drawn leave little doubt that press freedom was viewed as being closely related to the experiment of representative self-government. . . . The issue was born of the conflict with England, and its first expressions as a binding principle of law came in the state constitutions drafted contemporaneously with the Declaration of Independence. In these earliest expressions, the relation between freedom of the press and the idea of self-government was explicit. The press was a "bulwark of liberty," "essential to the security of freedom in a state." It had to be protected, not for its own sake, but because it provided a necessary restraint on what the patriots viewed as government's natural tendency toward tyranny and despotism.

79. 13 Stan. L. Rev. 991, 993 (1961). In 1985, Levy published Emergence of a Free Press, an updated version of Legacy of Suppression. Although he modified some of his arguments, he continued to maintain that the framers of the First Amendment cannot be shown to have intended to abolish the common law of seditious libel. For critical reviews, see David Rabban, The Ahistorical Historian: Leonard Levy on Freedom of Expression in Early American History, 37 Stan. L. Rev. 795 (1985); David Anderson, Levy vs. Levy, 84 Mich. L. Rev. 777 (1986).

80. John J. Cound, 36 N.Y.U. L. Rev. 253, 256 (1961).

In the minds of members of the First Congress, the press clause was part of the new plan of government, no less than if it had been in the original Constitution. To the Anti-Federalists, it was an essential modification of the original Constitution; to the Federalists, it expressed what was already implicit in the Constitution. Their quarrel was only over the necessity of specifically guaranteeing freedom of the press. Neither side doubted its utility. Its value lay, as Professor Blasi says, in "checking the inherent tendency of government officials to abuse the power entrusted to them." Because it plays this role, it is, in Justice Stewart's words, "a structural provision of the Constitution."

That the press clause has a distinct history does not mean, of course, that it must be given a meaning different from the speech clause today, or even that it had a different meaning in 1791. It is possible that checking government power was also the purpose of the speech clause. My own guess, however, is that the latter was more closely related to the incipient notion of individual autonomy that underlay the religion clauses. But in either event, most modern analysis, by focusing on the speech clause, gets the matter upside down. As a means of checking government power, speech was an afterthought, if it was viewed as serving that function at all; the press was expected to be the primary source of restraint.

The legislative history of the press clause has been ignored, largely because it is inconsistent with the conclusions of Leonard Levy, whose work in first amendment history has become the conventional wisdom of our generation. Levy's view is that freedom of the press meant nothing more to the Framers than freedom from prior restraint; the first amendment was not intended to enlarge that common law meaning. . . . If Levy is right, the press could hardly have been expected to occupy any significant structural role. The press would have been at the mercy (except for prior restraints) of most of those whose abuses it was supposed to check.

Levy's thesis is not unassailable. It requires us to accept several remarkable propositions. We must believe that the press clause was directed at what was in America a non-issue — prior restraint — rather than at seditious libel, which had been the primary form of restraint on the press during the colonial period. We must believe that the press clauses that were included in nine state constitutions were intended to do nothing more than preserve the English common law. We must believe that the Framers were oblivious to, or hypocritical about, their own sedition in criticizing the government under the Articles of Confederation. We must believe that they did not understand that citizens of representative democracy must be free to criticize government until the Sedition Act taught that lesson a few years later. We must believe that Madison in 1799 misrepresented (or misunderstood) his own views of ten years earlier. . . . A thesis that requires so many suspensions of disbelief ought not be preclusive.

2.   *The Kentucky and Virginia Resolutions of 1798-1799*

The Sedition Act of 1798 was important not only for its role in delineating the original understandings of the First Amendment, but also because it triggered responses that go the heart of the themes of this chapter (and casebook) about the allocation of authority to interpret the Constitution. As noted earlier, the Act was vehemently opposed by resolutions adopted by the legislatures of Kentucky and Virginia which had been written by Jefferson and Madison, respectively.[81] Madison

---

81. Both Resolutions also attacked the Alien Act of 1798, which authorized the President to order deportation of any alien he judged "dangerous to the peace and safety of the United States" or whom he

also wrote the Virginia Report of 1800, which elaborated and defended Virginia's position in the face of counter-resolutions by other states.[82] The fifth of the Virginia Resolutions asserted that the Sedition Act was an

> alarming infraction[] of the Constitution, [which] exercises . . . a power not delegated by the Constitution, but on the contrary expressly and positively forbidden by one of the amendments thereto; a power which more than any other ought to produce universal alarm, because it is leveled against that right of freely examining public characters and measures, and of free communication among the people thereon, which has ever been justly deemed the only effectual guardian of every other right.

In the Virginia Report Madison writes:

> In the attempts to vindicate the "Sedition Act," it has been contended . . . [t]hat the "freedom of the press" is to be determined by the meaning of these terms in the common law. . . . The freedom of the press under the common law, is, in the defences of the Sedition Act, made to consist in an exemption from all *previous* restraint on printed publications, by persons authorized to inspect or prohibit them. It appears to the committee, that this idea of the freedom of the press, can never be admitted to be the American idea of it: since a law inflicting penalties on printed publications would have a similar effect with a law authorizing a previous restraint on them. It would seem a mockery to say, that no law should be passed, preventing publications from being made, but that laws might be passed for punishing them in case they should be made.[83]

Madison also argues that the different natures of the British and American governments demonstrate why freedom of the press in America cannot be equated with the English common law restriction against prior restraint of seditious libel: In England, the people's rights need only be protected from the executive because Parliament has absolute power. In the United States, however, the people retain absolute sovereignty, and the power of *all* the branches of government is limited. Since the common law protects the press from the executive's prior restraint only, and not also from legislatively prescribed punishment, "[t]he state of the press, . . . under the common law, cannot . . . be the standard of its freedom in the United States."[84]

The Kentucky Resolutions also declared that the Sedition Act violated the First Amendment. Levy comments: "The reason for the sudden if belated emergence of a sharply articulated body of 'Jeffersonian' thought on freedom of speech and press was the threat that the government of the United States under the Adams administration might attempt to eliminate political criticism, create a one-party press in the country, and by controlling public opinion insure a Federalist victory in the elections of 1800."[85] In any event, Jefferson's and Madison's substantive reading of the freedoms of speech and press laid the foundation for all subsequent interpretations of the First Amendment. Opponents of the Sedition Act maintained that the Constitution granted the *federal* government no power over speech or the press.

---

had "reasonable grounds to suspect [was] concerned in any treasonable or secret machinations against the government." 1 Stat. 570 (1798) (expired 1800). See The Virginia Report 27-28, 162-167 (J.W. Randolph ed., 1850).

82. Id. at 189-237.

83. Id. at 219-220.

84. Id. at 220.

85. Levy, supra n.72, at 258.

They did not argue that the *states* were deprived of the power to control speech. As we shall see below, the First Amendment's limitations regarding speech were not deemed applicable to the states until 1925.

B. Federalism and States' Rights

The Third Kentucky Resolution provides:

That . . . no power over the freedom of religion, freedom of speech, or freedom of the press, being delegated to the United States by the Constitution, nor prohibited by it to the states, all lawful powers respecting the same did of right remain, and were reserved to the states, or to the people; that thus was manifested their determination to retain to themselves the right of judging how far the licentiousness of speech and of the press may be abridged without lessening their useful freedom, and how far those abuses which cannot be separated from their use, should be tolerated rather than destroyed; and . . . [a] special provision has been made by one of the amendments to the Constitution, which expressly declares, that "Congress shall make no law respecting an establishment of religion, or prohibiting the free exercise thereof, or abridging the freedom of speech, or of the press," . . . and that libels, falsehoods, and defamations, equally with heresy and false religion, are withheld from the cognizance of federal tribunals: that therefore the [Sedition Act] . . . , which does abridge the freedom of the press, is not law, but is altogether void and of no effect.

The fourth Virginia Resolution similarly provides:

That the General Assembly doth also express its deep regret that a spirit has in sundry instances been manifested by the Federal Government, to enlarge its powers by forced constructions of the constitutional charter which defines them; and that indications have appeared of a design to expound certain general phrases . . . , so as to destroy the meaning and effect of the particular enumeration, which necessarily explains and limits the general phrases, and so as to consolidate the States by degrees into one sovereignty, the obvious tendency and inevitable result of which would be to transform the present republican system of the United States into an absolute, or at best, a mixed monarchy.

C. The Doctrine of Nullification

Who had the authority to assess the constitutionality of the Sedition Act? Would a declaration of unconstitutionality necessarily invalidate (or "nullify") its power? Both Virginia and Kentucky claimed authority to declare the Act unconstitutional. And Kentucky seemed to suggest that its declaration would deprive the statute of legal force. Thus the Kentucky legislature resolved, in its first and ninth Resolutions:

That the several states composing the United States of America, are not united on the principle of unlimited submission to their general government; but that by compact, under the style and title of a Constitution for the United States, and of amendments thereto, they constituted a general government for special purposes, delegated to that government certain definite powers, reserving, each state to itself, the residuary mass of right to their own self government; and that whensoever the general government assumes undelegated powers, its acts are unauthoritative, void, and of no force: That to this compact each state acceded as a state, and is an integral party, its co-states forming as to itself, the other party: That the government created by this compact was not made the exclusive or final *judge* of the extent of the powers delegated to itself; since that would have made its discretion, and not the Constitution, the measure of its powers; but that, as in all other cases of compact among parties having no common judge, each party has an equal right to judge for itself, as well of infractions, as of the mode and measure of redress. . . .

That this commonwealth does, therefore, call on its co-states for an expression of their sentiments on the acts concerning aliens, and for the punishment of certain crimes herein before specified, plainly declaring whether these acts are or are not authorized by the Federal compact. And it doubts not that . . . they will view [the general government] as seizing the rights of the states, and consolidating them in the hands of the general government with a power assumed to bind the states, (not merely in cases made federal,) but in all cases whatsoever, by laws made, not with their consent, but by others against their consent . . . ; and that the co-states, recurring to their natural right in cases not made federal, will concur in declaring these acts void and of no force, and will each unite with this commonwealth, in requesting their repeal at the next session of Congress.

The final sentence is ambiguous. Can the states themselves invalidate the Sedition Act, or can they only urge Congress to repeal it? The Kentucky Resolutions of 1799 clarified Jefferson's position in asserting that "the several states who formed [the Constitution], being sovereign and independent, have the unquestionable right to judge of its infraction and that a nullification, by those sovereignties, of all unauthorized acts done under colour of that instrument, is the rightful remedy."[86] The Virginia Resolutions also address the issue of state nullification:

That this Assembly doth explicitly and peremptorily declare that it views the powers of the Federal Government as resulting from the compact, to which the States are parties, as limited by the plain sense and intention of the instrument constituting that compact; as no further valid than they are authorized by the grants enumerated in that compact; and that in case of a deliberate, palpable, and dangerous exercise of other powers not granted by the said compact, the States, who are the parties thereto, have the right, and are in duty bound, to interpose for arresting the progress of the evil, and for maintaining within their respective limits, the authorities, rights, and liberties appertaining to them.

The Virginia Report elaborates:

It appears . . . to be a plain principle, founded in common sense, illustrated by common practice, and essential to the nature of compacts, that, where resort can be had to no tribunal superior to the authority of the parties, the parties themselves must be the rightful judges, in the last resort, whether the bargain made has been pursued or violated. The Constitution of the United States was formed by the sanction of the states given by each in its sovereign capacity. It adds to the stability and dignity, as well as to the authority of the Constitution, that it rests on this legitimate and solid foundation. The states, then, being the parties to the constitutional compact, and in their sovereign capacity, it follows of necessity, that there can be no tribunal above their authority, to decide in the last resort, whether the compact made by them be violated;

86. N.E. Cunningham, Jr., ed., The Early Republic, 1789-1828, 145-146 (1968).

and, consequently, that, as the parties to it, they must themselves decide, in the last resort, such questions as may be of sufficient magnitude to require their interposition.

It does not follow, however, that because the states, as sovereign parties to their constitutional compact, must ultimately decide whether it has been violated, that such a decision ought to be interposed, either in a hasty manner, or on doubtful and inferior occasions. . . . But in the case of an intimate and constitutional union, like that of the United States, it is evident that the interposition of the parties, in their sovereign capacity, can be called for by occasions only, deeply and essentially affecting the vital principles of their political system.[87]

In the Virginia Report, Madison also responds to the objection "that the judicial authority is to be regarded as the sole expositor of the Constitution, in the last resort":

On this objection it might be observed *first*, that there may be instances of usurped power, which the forms of the Constitution would never draw within the control of the judicial department; *secondly*, that if the decisions of the judiciary be raised above the authority of the sovereign parties to the Constitution, the decision of the other departments, not carried by the forms of the Constitution before the judiciary, must be equally authoritative and final with the decisions of that department. But the proper answer to the objection is, that the resolution of the General Assembly relates to those great and extraordinary cases, in which all the forms of the Constitution may prove ineffectual against infractions dangerous to the essential rights of the parties to it. The resolution supposes that dangerous powers, not delegated, may not only be usurped and executed by the other departments, but that the judicial department also may exercise or sanction dangerous powers beyond the grant of the Constitution; and, consequently, that the ultimate right of the parties to the Constitution, to judge whether the compact has been dangerously violated, must extend to violations by one delegated authority, as well as by another; by the judiciary, as well as by the executive, or the legislature.

However true, therefore, it may be, that the judicial department, is, in all questions submitted to it by the forms of the Constitution, to decide in the last resort, this resort must necessarily be deemed the last in relation to the authorities of the other departments of the government; not in relation to the rights of the parties to the constitutional compact, from which the judicial, as well as the other departments hold their delegated trusts. On any other hypothesis, the delegation of judicial power would annul the authority delegating it; and the concurrence of this department with the others in usurped powers, might subvert for ever, and beyond the possible reach of any rightful remedy, the very Constitution which all were instituted to preserve.

The North Carolina legislature, though agreeing that the legislation was unconstitutional, refused to support the proposal that states take countermeasures against the Federal government. The Rhode Island legislature passed a resolution stating that Article III, Section 2, of the Constitution places "in the federal courts, exclusively, and in the Supreme Court of the United States, ultimately, the authority of deciding on the constitutionality of any act or law of the Congress of the United States." It further resolved that "this legislature, in their public capacity, do not feel themselves authorized to consider and decide on the constitutionality of the Sedition and Alien laws, (so called) yet they are called upon, by the exigency of this

---

87. The Virginia Report at 195-196.

occasion to declare that, in their private opinions, these laws are within the powers delegated to Congress, and promotive of the welfare of the United States."[88]

Rhode Island rejected not only the doctrine of nullification, but also the very idea that it had the authority to assess the Act's constitutionality. This may be the earliest suggestion of a strong notion of judicial supremacy regarding constitutional interpretation. Does rejection of the doctrine of nullification necessarily entail "exclusive" authority of assessment in the judiciary (or any other specific institution)? Contrast the view of the Rhode Island legislature with that of Andrew Jackson in his message vetoing the national bank. See also the discussion following Marbury v. Madison, infra.

Discussion

1. Bray Hammond once wrote that "the Constitution had not displaced rival principles or reconciled them but had become their dialectical arena."[89]

One of the fundamental principles at issue is the basis of Union itself. Return to ¶¶7-11 of McCulloch v. Maryland, in which Marshall, a Virginian who was clearly aware of the Kentucky and Virginia Resolutions, responded to what Professor H. Jefferson Powell has described as its "vision of the United States as a league of sovereign states."[90] Yet Marshall's analysis has not prevailed without opposition. For example, in his first inaugural address, President Ronald Reagan remarked that "all of us need to be reminded that the Federal Government did not create the states; the states created the Federal Government." An inaugural address, whatever its momentary importance, is not an opinion of the U.S. Supreme Court, though, and relatively little notice was taken of Reagan's implicit challenge to Marshall.

The Kentucky and Virginia Resolutions and Marshall's response have taken on new importance, however, by virtue of the opinions in Term Limits v. Thornton, 514 U.S. 779 (1995). Justice Stevens, writing for the majority, emphasized the "national" character of the United States as part of the rationale for striking down an Arkansas constitutional amendment that would have imposed term limits on candidates for the U.S. Senate and House of Representatives. He quoted, for example, Marshall's insistence that the Constitution was "not given by the people of a particular State, not given by the constituents of the legislature, . . . but by the people of all the States." And Justice Kennedy, concurring, stated, "In my view, . . . it is well settled that the *whole people of the United States* asserted their political identity and unity of purpose when they created the federal system" (emphasis added).

However, Justice Thomas, joined by Chief Justice Rehnquist and Justices O'Connor and Scalia, wrote a very sharp dissent describing "the *people of the several States* [as] the only true source of power" (emphasis added):

> The ultimate source of the Constitution's authority is the consent of the people of each individual State, not the consent of the undifferentiated people of the Nation as a whole.
>
> The ratification procedure erected by Article VII makes this point clear. The Constitution took effect once it had been ratified by the people gathered in convention in nine different States. But the Constitution went into effect only "between the

88. The responses of Rhode Island, Massachusetts, and Vermont are reprinted in Walter Murphy, James Fleming, and Will Harris, American Constitutional Interpretation 264-265 (1986).

89. Hammond, supra n.1, at 120.

90. H. Jefferson Powell, The Original Understanding of Original Intent, 98 Harv. L. Rev. 885, 927 (1985).

States so ratifying the same," Art. VII; it did not bind the people of North Carolina until they had accepted it. . . .

Is Justice Thomas thus rejecting Marshall's arguments in *McCulloch*, and, if so, does this entail adoption of Madison's and Jefferson's arguments in the Kentucky and Virginia Resolutions? In any event, which analysis do you find more persuasive, and why? What, if anything, follows from your answer?

2. One thing that might follow from adopting the state compact theory is that a state could withdraw from the Union should it believe, for example, that the terms of the compact have been breached. (Though might the Union, even if established by state compact, resemble marriage under the doctrines of the Roman Catholic Church, that is, indissoluble even though originating between separate persons without any prior obligations to one another?) Although Madison insisted that the "Doctrines of '98" offered no support for the legitimacy of secession, many advocates of secession repeatedly cited the Resolutions to justify their position. See Chapter 3, supra, for further discussion of secession.

Chapter 2
The Marshall Court and the Early Republic

I. The Supreme Court in Its Initial Years: 1789-1801[1]

The Supreme Court of the United States was a relatively insignificant institution during the first decade of the new Republic. Presidents Washington and Adams had some difficulty attracting people to serve, and the rate of turnover was high. Three men were appointed chief justice during the first 12 years. John Jay resigned after six years to serve as New York's governor, which he presumably deemed the more important office (and during his tenure he sailed to England to serve as the principal negotiator of what became known as the Jay Treaty with Great Britain, which, together with his co-authorship of the Federalist Papers, remains his primary claim to fame for most historians). His successor, John Rutledge, had been appointed as an Associate in 1789 but had resigned in 1791, without ever sitting, to go to the more prestigious South Carolina Supreme Court. He was nominated to become Chief Justice of the U.S. Supreme Court in 1795 but failed to receive Senate confirmation. Thereafter, Oliver Ellsworth was nominated and confirmed in 1796; he served until 1800, when he resigned while overseas on a diplomatic mission to France.

One source of discontent was the onerous duty of "riding circuit," which required each Justice to travel twice a year to sit in the federal circuit court districts. (There were no "circuit courts" in the modern sense; instead, they consisted of district judges sitting together with a Supreme Court justice as a "circuit court.") The trips were strenuous and time-consuming. In refusing President Adams's offer of reappointment as Chief Justice in 1801, Jay commented that "under a system so defective" the Court would never "obtain the energy, weight and dignity which were essential to its affording due support to the National Government, nor [would it] acquire the public confidence and respect which, as the last resort of the justice of the nation, it should possess."

The Court was not completely passive, though. Without much fanfare, it had simply assumed a power both to review the validity of state legislation that conflicted with federal treaties and statutes and to construe federal legislation in light of presumably binding constitutional requirements. Professor Currie, for example, writes that "in [Ware v. Hylton, 3 U.S. (3 Dall.) 199 (1796)], the Court for the first time struck down a state law under the supremacy clause, establishing for all time its power of judicial review of state laws."[2] Moreover, Justice Chase began his opinion in

---

1. See generally Julius Goebel, Jr., 1 History of the Supreme Court of the United States, Antecedents and Beginnings to 1801 (1971); 1 Charles Warren, The Supreme Court in United States History, chs. 1-3 (rev. ed. 1932); William R. Casto, The Supreme Court in the Early Republic (1995).

2. See David Currie, The Constitution in the Supreme Court: The First Hundred Years, 1789-1888, at 41 (1985).

Hylton v. United States, 3 U.S. (3 Dall.) 171 (1796), by writing that "by the case stated, only one question is submitted to the opinion of this court, whether the law of Congress [at issue] is unconstitutional and void?" Interestingly enough, after determining that the statute in question was constitutionally unproblematic, he concluded by stating that "it is unnecessary, at this time, for me to determine, whether this court, constitutionally possesses the power to declare an act of Congress void, on the ground of its being made contrary to, and in violation of, the Constitution; but if the court have such power, I am free to declare, that I will never exercise it, but in a very clear case." One might think, of course, that Chase had already answered this last question in the affirmative by his very formulation of "the one question . . . submitted to the opinion of the court." All of the other Justices who participated in the decision agreed that the statute was constitutionally legitimate; none challenged the abstract power of the Court to determine otherwise and, presumably, invalidate it. The first instance of such invalidation came with Marbury v. Madison, infra, but the basic assumption underlying *Marbury* seems to have been relatively well established by 1796. One might note, incidentally, that the opinions in these cases were "seriatim"; that is, each Justice prepared a separate opinion, as was (and remains) the custom in the United Kingdom. One of Marshall's signal achievements as Chief Justice was to establish a very different practice, by which, ideally (in his view), a single opinion joined in by all the justices would be published as the "Opinion of the Court."

The only decision of this period to attract much publicity — most of it negative — was Chisholm v. Georgia, 2 U.S. (2 Dall.) 419 (1793). This was a suit by two citizens of South Carolina, who were the executors of a British creditor, against the State of Georgia to recover on bonds confiscated by the state. Given the language of Article III, which explicitly states that "The Judicial Power shall extend to . . . Controversies . . . between a State and Citizens of another State," the Court had little trouble in holding that Georgia was indeed liable to suit by private individuals, even though it had not waived sovereign immunity. The notion of sovereign immunity developed in Great Britain, which, of course, was ruled by monarchs who claimed the mantle of sovereignty. The United States had obviously rejected any such claims, thus triggering the debate that we saw at the very heart of Marshall's opinion in *McCulloch*: who possesses "sovereignty" within the United States. If, like Marshall, one emphasizes so-called "popular sovereignty," then it is difficult to understand why any American government would be immune to suit by a member of the sovereign people. Suffice it to say that this position has never been widely accepted within U.S. law. Indeed states were sufficiently upset by *Chisholm* that they successfully pressed for the adoption of the Eleventh Amendment: "The judicial power of the United States shall not be construed to extend to any suit in law or equity, commenced or prosecuted against one of the United States by Citizens of another State, or by Citizens or Subjects of any Foreign State."

Discussion

Read the text of the Eleventh Amendment carefully. It appears clear that it was drafted as a specific response to *Chisholm*. Does this mean that it should be read to bar *only* suits against a state "by Citizens of another State, or by Citizens or Subjects of any Foreign State," because, after all, that is what the text says very clearly? Should one assume, for example, that the drafters of the Amendment were certainly capable of writing a much stronger prohibition on suits against states, and that their failure to do so is evidence of the quite limited purpose of the Amendment? Such an argument is made by John Manning.[3] In fact, though, courts have read the Eleventh Amendment far more broadly to limit a variety of other suits against states. The most important decision is Hans v. Louisiana, 134 U.S. 1 (1890), which held that the Amendment also prohibited suits against a state by one of its own citizens. Justice Bradley dismissed the appeal to the letter of the text as "an attempt to strain the Constitution and the law to a construction never imagined or dreamed of"; he denounced as basically unthinkable that the state could be brought into a federal court without its consent by any person. The scope of so-called sovereign immunity continues to be a subject of extraordinarily passionate debate within the contemporary Supreme Court and among commentators; a host of 5-4 decisions in the late 1990s and early twenty-first century offer particularly striking contrasts (and particularly bitter disagreements) concerning the doctrines of state sovereignty and federalism. Although the general subject of "federal jurisdiction" is well beyond the scope of this casebook, the debate over the Eleventh Amendment (and sovereign immunity) nevertheless emerges at various points in this course, especially in Chapter 5, infra.

II.   The Election of 1800

The members of the founding generation were generally suspicious of, and hostile to, the idea of political parties. James Madison, for example, in the Federalist No. 10, had explicitly warned against the presence of "factions" in American politics. "By a faction," Madison wrote, "I understand a number of citizens, whether amounting to a majority or minority of the whole, who are united and actuated by some common impulse or of passion, or of interest, adverse to the rights of other citizens, or to the permanent and aggregate interests of the community." The very point of Madisonian representative democracy was to select sufficiently "virtuous" citizens who would focus on only "the permanent and aggregate interests of the community" rather than, say, the strategic interests of their political party. The Electoral College as a system for electing presidents reflected a similar sensibility. The Electors would presumably pick the "best man" as president, with the "second best man," as it were, filling the office of vice president.[4] George Washington, of

3. John Manning, The Eleventh Amendment and the Reading of Precise Constitutional Texts, 113 Yale L.J. 1663 (2004).

4. This is, of course, a simplification. It does not explain the fact that the Constitution prohibits electors from voting for two persons from their own state. The reason is that it was assumed that there would be pressure to vote for local notables and favorite sons (it was inconceivable at the time that there might be "favorite daughters"). The limitation to one such vote therefore assured that the electors would be forced to transcend their parochialism and look outside their states, where they would presumably dispassionately reflect on who would indeed be the best man for the job. As one aggregated the collective votes, merely local notables would presumably fall to the bottom of the list, and the first and second choices (and, perhaps even the first five choices among whom the House of Representatives would choose if no one in fact received a majority of the electoral vote) would be truly national figures possessing the requisite civic virtue. As suggested in the text, this theory of the Electoral College did not survive, in practice, even for a decade, and by the election of 1800 it made no sense at all. See Akhil Reed Amar, America's Constitution: A Biography 167-168 (2005). As to contemporary implications of the "two-state" voting rule, which survives in the Twelfth Amendment that in effect recognized the legitimacy of the American party system, see Sanford Levinson and Ernest A. Young, Who's Afraid of the Twelfth Amendment? 29 Florida St. U. L. Rev. 925 (2001) (discussing whether Dick Cheney was in fact a Texan and therefore ineligible to receive the votes of Texas electors if they had also voted for George W. Bush).

course, was unanimously viewed as the best man to be the first president, and his initial cabinet was truly nonpartisan, consisting of Thomas Jefferson, Alexander Hamilton, and Edmund Randolph. (John Adams was the first vice president.)

By the election of 1796, Madison's initial vision was in shambles, and two parties began to emerge: the Federalists, led by John Adams and Alexander Hamilton, and the Democratic-Republicans, led by Thomas Jefferson. The debate over the Bank of the United States (and the construction of federal power generally) presaged one of the key bones of contention between the two parties. Other disputes involved such issues as the Jay Treaty, which attempted to settle outstanding disputes between the United States and the United Kingdom, and the direction of American foreign policy with respect to the great powers of the United Kingdom and France.

Because the Electoral College had been designed with the assumption that there would be no political parties, the election of 1796 concluded with the Federalist John Adams receiving 71 electoral votes and the Presidency, and his political opponent, Thomas Jefferson, receiving 68 electoral votes and becoming vice president in the new Adams Administration. Jefferson, of course, helped to draft the Kentucky Resolutions, Chapter 1, supra, that bitterly castigated the Alien and Sedition Acts, which were passed during the Adams Administration and reflected Federalist political views.

The election of 1800 turned into a bitter struggle between the two emergent political parties that threatened the political stability of the Union. Consistent with the original constitutional scheme, Democratic-Republican electors not only did not differentiate in their votes between president and vice president, but also (unlike their Federalist counterparts) did not have the wit to hold back at least one vote for Thomas Jefferson's de facto running mate, the New Yorker Aaron Burr. This resulted in a tie, with Jefferson and Burr receiving 73 votes each, whereas Adams received only 65 votes (and his running mate Charles Pinckney of South Carolina, received 64).[5] The ineptitude of the Jeffersonian electors meant that

---

5. One of the other anomalies of the election process is that under the Constitution the electoral votes are counted and announced before the Senate by the President of the Senate, whose other job, of course, is vice president of the United States. This meant that Thomas Jefferson, vice president in the Adams Administration and Adams' political opponent, got to count the electoral votes for his own election. This was no small boon; Bruce Ackerman and David Fontana have argued that Jefferson played fast and loose with the Georgia electoral votes, which appeared to contain some technical irregularities. See Ackerman and Fontana, Thomas Jefferson Counts Himself into the Presidency, 90 Virginia L. Rev. 551 (2004). Had Georgia's four electoral votes not been counted, Jefferson and Burr would have received only 69, one less than the 70 votes required to achieve a majority of the 138 total electoral votes. In that case, the House of Representatives, under the rules of the 1787 Constitution (subsequently altered by the Twelfth Amendment) would have been able to choose among the top five finishers, including John Adams and, perhaps more important, the Federalist de facto vice presidential candidate, Charles Coatesworth Pinckney, who, as a South Carolinian, might well have peeled off a sufficient number of Southern states to make a majority with the Federalist states (the House voted on a one-state/one-vote system). That would have made Pinckney president instead of Jefferson. Jefferson's willingness to overlook the technical irregularities and to count Georgia's votes foreclosed this possibility, and limited the final candidates to only himself and Burr.

Ackerman is highly critical of the 1787 Constitution inasmuch as it proved remarkably dysfunctional in handling the reality of a party system. "Only one thing is clear," he writes. "If America managed to survive its first great crisis, the written constitution wasn't going to save it — to the contrary, it was only making things worse. If there was going to be a successful transition of power, lots more would be required than following the rules laid down by the Founders. Only creative statesmanship had a chance of preventing the constitutional text from unraveling into civil war. The first act of statesmanship involved Thomas Jefferson counting his rivals out of the run-off." Bruce A. Ackerman, The Failure of the Founding Fathers: Jefferson, Marshall, and the Rise of Presidential Democracy 76 (2005).

there was no single winner, so the election was thrown, as required by the Constitution, into the House of Representatives, where each state delegation received one vote. Although Jefferson's Republicans had also won control of Congress, that new Congress would not convene until March. Thus the House of Representatives that would resolve the contested presidential election was a "lame-duck" House that was still controlled by a political party, the Federalists, that had just been repudiated in the 1800 election. (The length of the lame-duck session was shortened, and the date of the president's inaugural was moved forward by the Twentieth Amendment).

Many Federalists were outraged at the thought of Jefferson becoming president, not least because of his enthusiastic support for the French Revolution. Some so-called "irreconcilables" were particularly incensed at the fact that Jefferson's margin of victory over Adams was entirely the result of the Constitution's three-fifths clause, which gave Southern states especially an electoral bonus in the House of Representatives and the Electoral College based on their slave populations, even though these slaves had no role in the polity.[6] Many Federalists hoped to engineer an agreement by which the antislavery Burr would become president.[7] Burr explicitly disclaimed any part in such an arrangement, although, crucially, he never withdrew and therefore extended the controversy. One obstacle in Burr's path, besides the obvious political fact that he was selected to be Jefferson's vice president rather than a presidential candidate himself, was the enmity of the Federalist Alexander Hamilton (who would ultimately be killed by Burr in 1804 in the most famous duel in U.S. history). Because two state delegations were evenly divided, it took 36 ballots until, on February 17, 1801, two of the Federalist "irreconcilables" gave up the fight and allowed their states to cast their ballots for Jefferson.[8] In the meantime, the two Republican governors of Pennsylvania and Virginia had put their state militias "on alert" in case the party was denied the presidency. One result of the political crisis produced by the tie vote between the ostensible allies Jefferson and Burr was the 1803 proposal and rapid ratification in 1804 of the Twelfth Amendment, which in effect recognized the rise of political parties as part of the constitutional system by explicitly holding separate ballots for the candidates for the presidency and vice presidency, with the presumption that partisan electors would vote for the "ticket" of their party.

The fact that the Federalists acquiesced, however reluctantly, in Jefferson's election did not mean that they did not try to retain such power as they could. Having lost the presidency and Congress to Jefferson and the Republicans, this made the judiciary an especially inviting target of opportunity, and the Federalists moved to consolidate control over that branch of the national government. The Chief Justiceship was open because of Oliver Ellsworth's resignation in the autumn of

6. See Garry Wills, Negro President: President Jefferson and the Slave Power (2003); Akhil Reed Amar, America's Constitution, supra n.4. Northern states like New York, which still had some 20,000 slaves in 1800, benefitted as well. See Ira Berlin and Leslie Harris, Slavery in New York (2005).

7. Indeed, as Ackerman demonstrates, see The Failure of the Founding Fathers, supra n.5, some Federalists flirted with the idea of passing a "succession in office act" that would in effect have allowed John Marshall, then serving as both Secretary of State and Chief Justice, to become president if the House had been unable to break the tie by the Inauguration Day of March 4, 1801. He persuasively argues that any such attempt would have resulted in civil war.

8. See generally Bernard A. Weisberger, America Afire: Jefferson, Adams, and the Revolutionary Election of 1800 (2000); Joanne B. Freeman, The Election of 1800: A Study in the Logic of Political Change 108 Yale L.J. (1999).

1800. After John Jay declined to return to the Supreme Court because of advancing age and the rigors of circuit riding, Adams nominated his secretary of state, John Marshall, who was quickly confirmed by the lame-duck Federalist Congress, which remained in power until Jefferson's inauguration on March 4, 1801. On February 4, 1801, Marshall assumed the Chief Justiceship (while also retaining his position as secretary of state for the last month of Adams's term).

On February 13, 1801, just three weeks before Inauguration Day and the cessation of Federalist domination, Congress passed the Judiciary Act of 1801. It established a new set of circuit courts (and circuit judges) to complement the district and Supreme Court judges who had, prior to its passage, comprised the federal judiciary. The purported justification of the Act was to relieve Supreme Court Justices of the onerous and unpopular duty of riding circuit. (Perhaps Jay would have accepted Adams's call to return to the Supreme Court had he been offered the position *after* the passage of the Judiciary Act.) Given the timing of the legislation — and the fact that virtually all the new vacancies were filled by Federalists quickly nominated by Adams and confirmed by the lame-duck Senate — Republicans could be excused for believing that the more basic purpose was to entrench Federalist control over the judiciary. A Federalist judiciary could then be used (as Hylton v. U.S. had hinted) to declare Jeffersonian legislation unconstitutional or otherwise make life difficult for the new government. This was, after all, the first time in world history that an existing set of political leaders had been voted out of office by their opponents in a popular election. There was no precedent for a peaceful transfer of power, and such a transition was made all the harder by the fact that political parties — who held fundamentally different views about political issues — had not yet been truly accepted as legitimate.

Jeffersonians — and many subsequent historians — referred to the beneficiaries of the Federalist legislation as "midnight judges," suggesting a foul deed done in darkness. Although the circuit judges had been confirmed, taken their oaths of office, and were beginning to hear cases, the Republicans did not take things lying down. Instead, the now Republican-controlled Congress in effect purged these Federalist judges by repealing the Judiciary Act of 1801; this eliminated the new circuit courts, and thus left the circuit judges with no judicial positions to occupy. The Repeal Act was passed on March 8, 1802; seven weeks later, on April 29, Congress passed the Judiciary Act of 1802, which, among other things, reassigned the Supreme Court Justices to their previous role as circuit-riding circuit judges.

The Federalists raised at least two important constitutional issues to this course of action. The first focused on the legitimacy of eliminating the judgeships — after all, judges are presumably guaranteed their seats so long as they exhibit requisite "good behaviour," which has been interpreted as requiring life tenure.[9] The second involved the constitutional propriety of assigning members of the Supreme Court to auxiliary duty as members of "inferior" courts (and requiring them to ride circuit to reach these courts). The Republicans were fully aware that the displaced judges might try to challenge the constitutionality of the Repeal Act before the Federalist-controlled U.S. Supreme Court, so, as part of the Act, the Republicans eliminated

---

9. You might ask yourself if "life tenure" is in fact a necessary (as distinguished from a possible) inference of the "good Behaviour" clause. Could Congress, for example, have limited (or, in 2005, limit) the term of office to, say, 18 years and assert that the Good Behaviour clause stands only for the proposition that justices are protected against impeachment for ideological reasons?

the Supreme Court's 1802 term. As a result, the case attacking the Repeal Act, Stuart v. Laird, and the now-famous (and related) case of Marbury v. Madison, were not decided until 1803. The elimination of the 1802 term was a warning shot across the bow that signaled to the Federalist judiciary, including the members of the Supreme Court, that they should quickly adjust to the new political order of things. If they failed to acquiesce in what many historians have termed "the Jeffersonian Revolution," their Republican adversaries might well move to impeach and remove them from office.

Marbury v. Madison, too, can be understood only as part of the epic political struggles connected with the transition of power from the hitherto dominant Federalists to their Jeffersonian successors.[10] Thomas Jefferson ordered Secretary of State James Madison (who had succeeded John Marshall in office) not to deliver a commission of office to William Marbury, appointed by President Adams as a justice of the peace in the District of Columbia. Although Adams had signed Marbury's commission, John Marshall, who had served as both Secretary of State and Chief Justice until literally the last moment of the Adams Administration, had failed to deliver the commission to Marbury.

Marbury's actual position as justice of the peace was relatively trivial, and his term would have been limited to five years in any instance, a rather spectacular difference from the presumptive life tenure attached to being an "Article III judge." Still, he seemed to symbolize Federalist overreaching, and there was a widespread perception that Jefferson would in fact refuse to accept the legitimacy of any decision ordering Madison to deliver the commission.[11] Moreover, Republicans in Congress were already speaking of impeaching Federalist judges on the grounds that they were political partisans rather than impartial jurists. Indeed, the Republican-controlled House of Representatives would vote in 1804 to impeach the Federalist Justice Samuel Chase, although ultimately Chase's prosecutors failed to garner the necessary two-thirds majority in the Senate to convict and remove Chase from office.[12]

In hindsight, the failure to remove Chase signaled that Congress would not use the impeachment power simply to remove political adversaries; thus the episode helped establish a convention of judicial independence. In 1803, however, none of this was clear. Given the highly charged political atmosphere of the day, the central issue in both Stuart v. Laird and Marbury v. Madison was whether the Court would directly challenge the combined weight of executive and congressional authority, by carrying out the implications of earlier decisions and actually invalidating a federal statute, thereby potentially provoking a full-scale constitutional crisis. We turn now to the two cases. Although *Marbury* was decided a week earlier, we take up *Stuart* first because in political terms it was in fact the far more important of the two cases.

10. There is a copious literature on the political circumstances that generated Marbury. In addition to Ackerman, see generally Donald Dewey, Marshall Versus Jefferson: The Political Background of Marbury v. Madison (1970); Jean Edward Smith, John Marshall: Defender of a Nation 309-326 (1996); James O'Fallon, Marbury, 44 Stan. L. Rev. 219 (1992).

11. See, however, Louise Weinberg, Our Marbury, 89 Va. L. Rev. 1235 (2003) for an argument that the likelihood of Jefferson's potential disobedience is exaggerated (and that Marshall therefore assumed that Jefferson would in fact comply with such an order). Must one have a view about Jefferson's (and Marshall's) states of mind with regard to the consequences of a writ's being issued not only to understand the circumstances of the case, but also to decide whether his decision is defensible on the merits?

12. See, e.g., Keith Whittington, Constitutional Construction 20 (1999).

III.   The Cases of 1803

A.   Stuart v. Laird and the Elimination of the Intermediate Appellate Judiciary

STUART v. LAIRD 5 U.S. (1 Cranch) 299 (1803): *Stuart* involved a petition by private parties seeking to overturn a ruling by a circuit court in a land dispute. The petitioners argued that the Justices of the Supreme Court held commissions to be Supreme Court Justices, but not circuit judges. Hence they could not return to sit as circuit judges once the positions held by the Federalist circuit judges were abolished. In addition, the petitioners argued, repeal of the circuit judgeships was unconstitutional because according to Article III of the Constitution, once they had received their commissions, the circuit judges had life tenure (and the judicial independence that is the purpose of granting life tenure). Allowing Congress to abolish the courts undermined judicial independence. Finally, the petitioners argued that Congress could not require the Justices to ride circuit in courts of first instance because this would be a major burden on the Justices and would in effect hinder the Court from performing its constitutionally assigned duties.

The lower court decision in *Stuart,* written by Chief Justice Marshall himself, riding circuit, rejected the petitioner's arguments.[13] Marshall recused himself from sitting on the appeal to the Supreme Court.[14] Justice Paterson wrote the decision

---

13. Note that Marshall in fact engaged in what might be termed "behavioral acquiescence" to the Jeffersonian Repeal Act, in spite of what were privately expressed reservations about its constitutionality. Indeed, Ackerman suggests that Marshall flirted with the idea of a de facto "strike," in which the Supreme Court Justices would simply refuse to ride circuit. But perhaps a "strike" would have been unnecessary if the Republicans not also abolished the 1802 term of the Supreme Court, for it might have been the case that the Supreme Court Justices would not yet have had to decide, as a practical matter, whether to ride circuit. That possibility was foreclosed by putting off the next term until 1803. That forced Marshall and others to decide what they would do (and not merely what they thought), and they in fact followed the new law.

See Ackerman, supra, at 164-165 for correspondence expressing Marshall's doubts in 1802 about the constitutionality of the Repeal Act, doubts that apparently were never overcome. An 1823 letter from Marshall to Henry Clay suggests that Marshall continued to harbor reservations about the constitutionality of the 1802 Act. Marshall raises the possibility that Congress might "say explicitly that the courts of the union should never enter into the enquiry concerning the constitutionality of a law" or, alternatively, that courts "should dismiss for want of jurisdiction, every case depending on a law respecting such an act." Either, of course, would end the practice of judicial review. "What substantial difference is there between withdrawing a question from a court, and disabling a court from deciding that question? Those only, I should think, who were capable of drawing the memorable distinction as to tenure of office, between removing the Judge from the office [i.e., impeachment], and removing the office from the Judge [as in the 1802 Act], can take this distinction." Letter from Marshall to Clay (Dec. 22, 1823), reprinted in Ruth Wedgwood, Cousin Humphrey, 14 Const. Comment. 247, 267-268 (1997). If one assumes that Marshall believed it would be unconstitutional to order the federal judiciary in effect to ignore the Constitution, then is he not suggesting that is equally dubious to "remove the office from the Judge" as an alternative to following the quite difficult procedures of impeachment necessary to remove judges from office? Professor Powe offers this letter as evidence that "Marshall knew better" than to believe that the 1802 Act was constitutional, but that he "also knew [the justices] were in no position to successfully challenge Jefferson." See Lucas A. Powe, The Politics of American Judicial Review: Reflections on the Marshall, Warren, and Rehnquist Courts, 38 Wake Forest L. Rev. 704 (2003).

14. The reasons are unclear. There was certainly no norm that Supreme Court Justices could not sit on appeals from cases they had decided while riding circuit. (It is worth noting that members of federal

for the Supreme Court. He did not directly address the question whether the abolition of the circuit judgeships violated the life tenure provisions of Article III. Instead he merely held that the transfer of the case from a circuit court established by the now-repealed 1801 Judiciary Act to a reconstructed circuit court staffed by a Supreme Court Justice riding circuit (none other than Marshall himself) posed no constitutional problems: "Congress have constitutional authority to establish from time to time such inferior tribunals as they may think proper; and to transfer a cause from one such tribunal to another. In this last particular, there are no words in the constitution to prohibit or restrain the exercise of legislative power." Patterson then addressed the objection that the members of the Supreme Court did not have authority to ride circuit without specific commissions as circuit judges:

> Another reason for reversal is, that the judges of the supreme court have no right to sit as circuit judges, not being appointed as such, or in other words, that they ought to have distinct commissions for that purpose. To this objection, which is of recent date, it is sufficient to observe, that practice and acquiescence under it for a period of several years, commencing with the organization of the judicial system, afford an irresistible answer, and have indeed fixed the construction. It is a contemporary interpretation of the most forcible nature. This practical exposition is too strong and obstinate to be shaken or controlled. Of course, the question is at rest, and ought not now to be disturbed.

Discussion

1. *Discretion is the better part of valor.* The Court in *Stuart* in effect upheld the constitutionality of the repeal of the Judiciary Act and therefore acquiesced in the Jeffersonian purge of the Federalist circuit judges. In this respect *Stuart* is far more significant than the far more famous *Marbury:* It signifies the complete capitulation by the Supreme Court to the new political reality of Republican hegemony. Indeed, read in light of Stuart v. Laird, *Marbury* takes on a very different cast. It is often thought to symbolize the independence of the judiciary from politics and its devotion to the Rule of Law. As you will presently see, however, Marshall's opinion in *Marbury* offers several "imaginative" readings of the Judiciary Act of 1789 and Article III to avoid giving Marbury his commission and upsetting the Republicans, just as Patterson's opinion in *Stuart* dodged the most difficult constitutional questions about judicial independence to uphold the Republicans' elimination of the circuit judgeships created by the Federalist Party. What unites both decisions is that Marshall and his colleagues, however reluctant they might personally have been to resume riding circuit, backed off from a very serious confrontation and were willing to provide the Jeffersonian purge with the blessing of law.

2. Justice Patterson emphasizes the "practice and acquiescence under . . . for a period of several years" as justification for accepting the reinstatement of circuit

---

circuit courts today normally do not recuse themselves when a decision they participated in is appealed to the full court en banc.) It is perhaps even more mysterious why Marshall would recuse himself in Stuart v. Laird but not in Marbury v. Madison, given that Marshall was the Secretary of State whose failure to deliver Marbury's commission in a timely fashion in the first place gave rise to the litigation in Marbury. Moreover, as if this did not demonstrate a sufficient conflict of interest, there was a delicate evidentiary question at the heart of Marbury: Had his commission in fact been signed? The key witness would have been Marshall himself!

riding. Recall earlier discussions of precedent in Chapter 1, supra. Under what circumstances can "practice and acquiescence" be sufficient conditions for adherence to previous decisions (or practices)? Would this not in effect insulate any long-tolerated practice from later invalidation as unconstitutional?

3. How relevant, if at all, is it that the Jeffersonians did not, after abolishing the circuit courts, try to reestablish them shortly thereafter and fill them with Republican loyalists? If they had reestablished the circuit courts, would they have been required by the Constitution to fill any new positions with the Federalist judges who had already been confirmed and who had been deprived of their judicial office as a result of the Repeal Act?

Consider the following editorial that appeared in the Washington Federalist on March 3, 1802, as the Repeal Act was being debated in Congress:

> Should Mr. Breckenridge [the Republican leader in the Senate] now bring forward a resolution to repeal the law establishing the Supreme Court of the United States, we should only consider it a part of the system intended to be pursued. It can as well be done, as consistently with the constitution, as what has been done. It may seem too bold for this session, but the democrats have established the principle that there is no such thing as breaking the constitution, do what you will, we sincerely expect it will be done next session. . . . They can then repeal the law establishing [the Supreme Court], having caution not to have the repeal operate till the new law commences: then the old judges cease of course with the old law, the executive appoints new judges for the new law; & still they will comply with the constitution which says there shall be one supreme court.[15]

If one believes that the Repeal Act was constitutional, then does the logic of the Federalist follow? If not, why not?

4. *Internal and external perspectives.* One can analyze judicial decisions in one of two ways: internally, asking whether the results courts reach make sense based on the logic of the legal arguments that judges offer; or externally, attempting to explaining the results in terms of historical, political, social, economic, or other factors. The foregoing analysis of *Stuart* and *Marbury* is externalist inasmuch as it explains both *Stuart* and *Marbury* by reference to external historical and political factors. By contrast, Louise Weinberg, Our Marbury, 89 Va. L. Rev. 1235 (2003) offers the most sustained and legally sophisticated attempt to defend both opinions as motivated entirely by the duty of fidelity to law. You will encounter the alternation between internal and external perspectives repeatedly throughout this course. One possibility is that these perspectives are inherently in conflict, because the external perspective undermines the distinction between politics and law. Another possibility asserts, that, to the contrary, the external perspective is actually necessary to the rule of law. What makes judicial decisions legitimate (or illegitimate) is the particular way they respond to the social, political, and historical circumstances in which they are decided, even if judges do not always advert to these factors directly.

5. *The United States as a developing democracy.* Consider the possibility that *Stuart* and *Marbury* are best understood as examples of transitions to democracy, in which courts in fledgling republics that have only recently thrown off the yoke of colonial domination or dictatorship must accept the influence of political pressures — including threats of impeachment or refusal to comply with judicial decisions — to

---

15. Quoted in Ackerman, op. cit., at 199-200.

remain viable until respect for the rule of law and practical judicial independence can be established as an ongoing custom. One view might be that such "transitions" are exceptional and that the far more important reality, in U.S. history, is a sturdy tradition of judicial independence that has made it possible for the Supreme Court (and other courts) to invoke the impersonal commands of the law as shields against an overreaching president or Congress. On the other hand, consider the possibility that courts are only relatively independent from political struggle, even in nontransitional contexts, with the consequence that, especially in the long run, they cannot (and, more controversially, *should* not) resist the demands of a dominant national political majority.

6. *Are courts easy to push around?* Think about Alexander Hamilton's arguments for life tenure in Federalist 78 in this context:

> Whoever attentively considers the different departments of power must perceive, that, in a government in which they are separated from each other, the judiciary, from the nature of its functions, will always be the least dangerous to the political rights of the Constitution; because it will be least in a capacity to annoy or injure them. The Executive not only dispenses the honors, but holds the sword of the community. The legislature not only commands the purse, but prescribes the rules by which the duties and rights of every citizen are to be regulated. The judiciary, on the contrary, has no influence over either the sword or the purse; no direction either of the strength or of the wealth of the society; and can take no active resolution whatever. It may truly be said to have neither FORCE nor WILL, but merely judgment; and must ultimately depend upon the aid of the executive arm even for the efficacy of its judgments.
>
> This simple view of the matter suggests several important consequences. It proves incontestably, that the judiciary is beyond comparison the weakest of the three departments of power; that it can never attack with success either of the other two; and that all possible care is requisite to enable it to defend itself against their attacks. It equally proves, that though individual oppression may now and then proceed from the courts of justice, the general liberty of the people can never be endangered from that quarter; I mean so long as the judiciary remains truly distinct from both the legislature and the Executive. For I agree, that "there is no liberty, if the power of judging be not separated from the legislative and executive powers." And it proves, in the last place, that as liberty can have nothing to fear from the judiciary alone, but would have every thing to fear from its union with either of the other departments; that as all the effects of such a union must ensue from a dependence of the former on the latter, notwithstanding a nominal and apparent separation; that as, from the natural feebleness of the judiciary, it is in continual jeopardy of being overpowered, awed, or influenced by its co-ordinate branches; and that as nothing can contribute so much to its firmness and independence as permanency in office, this quality may therefore be justly regarded as an indispensable ingredient in its constitution, and, in a great measure, as the citadel of the public justice and the public security.

Do *Stuart* (and *Marbury*) help make Hamilton's case? Consider Hamilton's argument that all that have courts have working for them is "judgment," by which he means that courts make reasoned arguments about what the law is. If he is right about this, does this suggest that courts should be particularly scrupulous in paying attention only to the law and not to any "extrinsic" features of the political or social situation in deciding cases, so as to shore up their legitimacy? Or, on the contrary, does it suggest that courts must always speak publicly in terms of rule of law values and what the law requires while simultaneously paying close attention to how far they can push the political branches? Keep this possibility in mind as you read Marshall's legal arguments in *Marbury*.

7. *Just the facts, ma'am.* Imagine that you were asked to "state the facts" of Stuart v. Laird or of Marbury v. Madison, to which we turn next. Are the relevant facts, for example, found (only) within the four corners of a given case, or should an analyst of any given decision be aware of the broader context of the decision, including the general political circumstances of the time? What are the consequences of accepting one or another view of how to ascertain the facts of a case?[16]

B. Marbury and Judicial Review of Legislation

MARBURY v. MADISON[17]

5 U.S. (1 Cranch) 137 (1803)

[1] ¶1At the last term, viz. December term, 1801, William Marbury [and others] . . . moved the court for a rule to James Madison, Secretary of State of the United States, to show cause why a mandamus should not issue commanding him to cause to be delivered to them respectively their several commissions as justices of the peace in the District of Columbia. This motion was supported by affidavits of the following facts; that notice of this motion had been given to Mr. Madison; that Mr. Adams, the late president of the United States, nominated the applicants to the senate for their advice and consent to be appointed justices of the peace of the district of Columbia; that the senate advised and consented to the appointments; that commissions in due form were signed by the said president appointing them justices, &c. and that the seal of the United States was in due form affixed to the said commissions by the secretary of state; that the applicants have requested Mr. Madison to deliver them their said commissions, who has not complied with that request; and that their said commissions are withheld from them; that the applicants have made application to Mr. Madison as secretary of state of the United States at his office, for information whether the commissions were signed and sealed as aforesaid; that explicit and satisfactory information has not been given in answer to that inquiry, either by the secretary of state or any officer in the department of state; that application has been made to the secretary of the Senate for a certificate of the nomination of the applicants, and of the advice and consent of the senate, who has declined giving such a certificate; whereupon a rule was laid to show cause on the 4th day of this term. . . . Afterwards, on the 24th of February, the following opinion of the court was delivered by the Chief Justice.

---

16. See generally Sanford Levinson and Jack M. Balkin, What Are the Facts of Marbury v. Madison?, 20 Constitutional Commentary 255 (2004).

17. A useful overview of Marbury can be found in William Van Alstyne, A Critical Guide to Marbury v. Madison, 1969 Duke L.J. 1. See also Weinberg, supra; Akhil Reed Amar, Marbury, Section 13, and the Original Jurisdiction of the Supreme Court, 56 U. Chi. L. Rev. 443 (1989); William Nelson, Marbury v. Madison and the Rise of Judicial Review (2000); Mark Graber and Micahel Perhac eds., Marbury Versus Madison: Documents and Commentary (2002).

¶1. Compare Marshall's statement of the facts with those presented in our own introduction to the case.

It is, incidentally, a considerable understatement to say only that Madison did not supply "explicit and satisfactory information" to the hapless Marbury. He also failed to defend the suit before the Court, which itself may signify what Marshall called in ¶3 the "peculiar delicacy" of the case.

[2] ¶2At the last term on the affidavits then read and filed with the clerk, a rule was granted in this case, requiring the secretary of state to show cause why a mandamus should not issue, directing him to deliver to William Marbury his commission as a justice of the peace for the county of Washington, in the district of Columbia.

[3] No cause has been shown, and the present motion is for a mandamus. The peculiar delicacy of this case, the novelty of some of its circumstances, and the real difficulty attending the points which occur in it, require a complete exposition of the principles, on which the opinion to be given by the court, is founded. . . .

[4] ¶4In the order in which the court has viewed this subject, the following questions have been considered and decided.

1st. Has the applicant a right to the commission he demands?

2dly. If he has a right, and that right has been violated, do the laws of his country afford him a remedy?

3dly. If they do afford him a remedy, is it a mandamus issuing from this court?

[5] The first object of inquiry is, 1st. Has the applicant a right to the commission he demands?

¶2. A writ of mandamus is an order issued by a court to a government officer or lower court commanding the performance of a ministerial (i.e., nondiscretionary) duty pertaining to the office.

¶4. In the course of the opinion, the court holds (first) that on the facts and law Marbury is entitled to the commission; (second) that a judicial remedy will not interfere improperly with the executive's constitutional discretion; and (third) that mandamus is the appropriate remedy; that respondent Madison cannot assert sovereign immunity; that §13 of the Judiciary Act of 1789 authorizes the issuance of mandamus in this case; but that §13 is unconstitutional.

This is an extraordinary way to order the issues. Courts customarily determine initially whether they have jurisdiction to decide the case and only then, if the answer is affirmative, proceed to other issues. See, e.g., Ex parte McCardle, 74 U.S. (7 Wall.) 506, 512, 514 (1869):

> The first question necessarily is that of jurisdiction; for if the act . . . takes away the jurisdiction [of this Court], it is useless, if not improper, to enter into any discussion of other questions. . . . Without jurisdiction the court cannot proceed at all in any cause. Jurisdiction is power to declare the law, and when it ceases to exist, the only function remaining to the court is that of announcing the fact and dismissing the cause.

Professor William Van Alstyne notes that Marshall has been criticized for deciding unnecessary questions in *Marbury:* "If the Court determined that it had no jurisdiction, it would have no occasion to reach the matter of 'peculiar delicacy' [i.e., the amenability of a cabinet officer to suit]. . . . It was therefore improper for Marshall to begin as he did" (supra n.17, at 7). But Van Alstyne comes to Marshall's defense:

> Of at least equal delicacy was the question of the Court's . . . capacity to second guess the constitutionality of acts of Congress. Since the Court might avoid the necessity of confronting the constitutionality of the Judiciary Act by disposing of the case on other grounds (assuming that it were to find Marbury not entitled to his commission), it should seek to do so where possible, as here. . . . Under this view, perhaps Marshall cannot be faulted for postponing consideration of judicial review and the constitutionality of the Judiciary Act until he had first exhausted other possible bases for disposing of the case.

How valid is this defense? Granting that it is desirable to avoid unnecessary constitutional questions, Marshall did not in fact avoid *any* constitutional question. Is Van Alstyne suggesting that it was important that Marshall demonstrate that he *could not* avoid the constitutional question? Of course, Marshall nowhere says that he is striving to avoid a constitutional question, and in fact, his opinion ends up discussing a vast number of constitutional questions — and difficult ones at that, see Amar, Marbury, supra n.17.

Note Van Alstyne's suggestion that there was "clearly an 'issue' of sorts which preceded any of those touched upon in the opinion. Specifically, it would appear that Marshall should have recused himself in view of his substantial involvement in the background of this controversy" (supra n.17, at 8). See Note, Disqualification of Judges and Justices in the Federal Courts, 86 Harv. L. Rev. 736 (1973).

[6] His right originates in an act of congress passed in February 1801, concerning the district of Columbia . . . [which] enacts, "that there shall be appointed . . . such number of discreet persons to be justices of the peace as the president of the United States shall, from time to time think expedient, to continue in office for five years.

[7] It appears, from the affidavits, that in compliance with this law, a commission for William Marbury as a justice of peace for the county of Washington, was signed by John Adams, then president of the United States; after which the seal of the United States was affixed to it; but the commission has never reached the person for whom it was made out. . . .

[8] Some point of time must be taken, when the power of the executive over an officer, not removable at his will, must cease. That point of time must be, when the constitutional power of appointment has been exercised. And this power has been exercised, when the last act, required from the person possessing the power has been performed: this last act is the signature of the commission. . . .

[9] The commission being signed, the subsequent duty of the secretary of state is prescribed by law, and not to be guided by the will of the president. He is to affix the seal of the United States to the commission, and is to record it. This is not a proceeding which may be varied, if the judgment of the executive shall suggest one more eligible; but is a precise course accurately marked out by law, and is to be strictly pursued. . . .

[10] It has also occurred as possible, and barely possible, that the transmission of the commission, and the acceptance thereof, might be deemed necessary to complete the right of the plaintiff. The transmission of the commission is a practice, directed by convenience, but not by law. It cannot, therefore, be necessary to constitute the appointment. . . . The appointment is the sole act of the president; the transmission of the commission is the sole act of the officer to whom that duty is assigned, and may be accelerated or retarded by circumstances which can have no influence on the appointment. A commission is transmitted to a person already appointed; not to a person appointed or not, as the letter inclosing the commission should happen to get into the post-office and reach him in safety, or to miscarry. . . .

[11] If the transmission of a commission be not considered as necessary to give validity to an appointment, still less is its acceptance. The appointment is the sole act of the president; the acceptance is the sole act of the officer, and is, in plain common sense, posterior to the appointment. As he may resign, so may he refuse to accept: but neither the one nor the other is capable of rendering the appointment a nonentity. . . .

[12] It is, therefore, decidedly the opinion of the court, that when a commission has been signed by the president, the appointment is made; and that the commission is complete, when the seal of the United States has been affixed to it by the secretary of state.

[13] Where an officer is removable at the will of the executive, the circumstance which completes his appointment is of no concern; because the act is at any time revocable; and the commission may be arrested, if still in the office. But when the officer is not removable at the will of the executive, the appointment is not revocable, and cannot be annulled: it has conferred legal rights which cannot be resumed. The discretion of the executive is to be exercised, until the appointment has been made. But having once made the appointment, his power over the office is terminated, in all cases where, by law, the officer is not removable by him. The right to the office is then in the person appointed, and he has the absolute unconditional power of accepting or rejecting it.

Gov't argument:
Transmission to
TT must occur
to give TT
right & it
hasn't happened

Court: Not
so! Right
comes w/ Prez's
appointment

[14] ¶14Mr. Marbury, then, since his commission was signed by the President and sealed by the secretary of state, was appointed; and as the law creating the office, gave the officer a right to hold for five years, independent of the executive, the appointment was not revocable, but vested in the officer legal rights, which are protected by the laws of his country.

[15] To withhold his commission, therefore, is an act deemed by the court not warranted by law, but violative of a vested legal right.

[16] This brings us to the second inquiry; which is, 2dly. If he has a right, and that right has been violated, do the laws of his country afford him a remedy?

[17] The very essence of civil liberty certainly consists in the right of every individual to claim the protection of the laws whenever he receives an injury. One of the first duties of government is to afford that protection. . . .

[18] The government of the United States has been emphatically termed a government of laws, and not of men. It will certainly cease to deserve this high appellation, if the laws furnish no remedy for the violation of a vested legal right.

[19] If this obloquy is to be cast on the jurisprudence of our country, it must arise from the peculiar character of the case.

[20] It behooves us then to enquire whether there be in its composition any ingredient which shall exempt it from legal investigation, or exclude the injured party from legal redress . . . Is it in the nature of the transaction? Is the act of delivering or withholding a commission to be considered as a mere political act, belonging to the executive department alone, for the performance of which, entire confidence is placed by our constitution in the supreme executive; and for any misconduct respecting which, the injured individual has no remedy. That there may be such cases is not to be questioned; but that every act of duty, to be performed in any of the great departments of government, constitutes such a case is not to be admitted. [Marshall then discusses and rejects the claim that Madison is entitled to sovereign immunity merely because he is sued in his official capacity as secretary of state.] It follows then that the question, whether the legality of an act of the head of a department be examinable in a court of justice or not, must always depend on the nature of that act. If some acts be examinable, and others not, there must be some rule of law to guide the court in the exercise of its jurisdiction. In some instances there may be difficulty in applying the rule to particular cases; but there cannot, it is believed, be much difficulty in laying down the rule.

[21] By the constitution of the United States, the President is invested with certain important political powers, in the exercise of which he is to use his own discretion, and is accountable only to his country in his political character, and to his own conscience. To aid him in the performance of these duties, he is authorized to appoint certain officers, who act by his authority and in conformity with his orders. In such cases, their acts are his acts; and whatever opinion may be entertained of the manner in which executive discretion may be used, still there exists, and can exist, no power to control that discretion. The subjects are political. They respect the nation, not individual rights, and being entrusted to the executive, the decision of the executive is conclusive. The application of this remark will be perceived by adverting to the act of congress for establishing the department of foreign affairs. This office, as his duties were prescribed by that act, is to conform

¶14. Marshall's assumption that Congress generally can prevent the president from revoking executive appointments was disapproved in Myers v. United States, 272 U.S. 52 (1926).

precisely to the will of the President. He is the mere organ by whom that will is
communicated. The acts of such an officer, as an officer, can never be examinable
by the courts. But when the legislature proceeds to impose on that officer other
duties; when he is directed peremptorily to perform certain acts; when the rights of
individuals are dependent on the performance of those acts; he is so far the officer
of the law; is amenable to the laws for his conduct; and cannot at his discretion
sport away the vested rights of others. The conclusion from this reasoning is, that
where the heads of departments are the political or confidential agents of the executive, merely to execute the will of the President, or rather to act in cases in which
the executive possesses a constitutional or legal discretion, nothing can be more
perfectly clear than that their acts are only politically examinable. But where a
specific duty is assigned by law, and individual rights depend upon the performance of that duty, it seems equally clear that the individual who considers himself
injured, has a right to resort to the laws of his country for a remedy. . . .

[22] The power of nominating to the senate, and the power of appointing the
person nominated, are political powers, to be exercised by the President according
to his own discretion. When he has made an appointment, he has exercised his
whole power, and his discretion has been completely applied to the case. If, by law,
the officer be removable at the will of the President, then a new appointment may
be immediately made, and the rights of the officer are terminated. But as a fact
which has existed cannot be made never to have existed, the appointment cannot
be annihilated; and consequently if the officer is by law not removable at the will of
the President; the rights he has acquired are protected by the law, and are not
resumeable by the President. They cannot be extinguished by executive authority,
and he has the privilege of asserting them in like manner as if they had been
derived from any other source.

[23] The question whether a right has vested or not, is, in its nature, judicial,
and must be tried by the judicial authority. If, for example, Mr. Marbury had taken
the oaths of a magistrate, and proceeded to act as one; in consequence of which a
suit had been instituted against him, in which his defence had depended on his
being a magistrate; the validity of his appointment must have been determined by
judicial authority.

[24] So, if he conceives that, by virtue of his appointment, he has a legal right,
either to the commission which has been made out for him, or to a copy of that
commission, it is equally a question examinable in a court, and the decision of the
court upon it must depend on the opinion entertained of his appointment. That
question has been discussed, and the opinion is, that the latest point of time which
can be taken as that at which the appointment was complete, and evidenced, was
when, after the signature of the president, the seal of the United States was affixed
to the commission.

[25] It is then the opinion of the court, 1st. That by signing the commission of
Mr. Marbury, the president of the United States appointed him a justice of peace,
for the county of Washington, in the district of Columbia; and that the seal of the
United States, affixed thereto by the secretary of state, is conclusive testimony of
the verity of the signature, and of the completion of the appointment; and that the
appointment conferred on him a legal right to the office for the space of five years.

[26] 2dly. That, having this legal title to the office, he has a consequent right to
the commission; a refusal to deliver which, is a plain violation of that right, for
which the laws of his country afford him a remedy.

3)

[27] It remains to be inquired whether, 3dly. He is entitled to the remedy for which he applies. This depends on,

1st. The nature of the writ applied for, and,

2dly. The power of this court. . . .

[Marshall discusses the circumstances under which mandamus is appropriate at common law, to conclude:]

[28] This, then, is a plain case for a mandamus, either to deliver the commission, or a copy of it from the record; and it only remains to be inquired, Whether it can issue from this court.

[29] ¶¶29-30The act to establish the judicial courts of the United States authorizes the supreme court "to issue writs of mandamus, in cases warranted by the principles and usages of law, to any courts appointed, or persons holding office, under the authority of the United States."

[30] The secretary of state, being a person holding an office under the authority of the United States, is precisely within the letter of the description; and if this court is not authorized to issue a writ of mandamus to such an officer, it must be because the law is unconstitutional, and therefore absolutely incapable of conferring the authority, and assigning the duties which its words purport to confer and assign.

[31] ¶¶31-41The constitution vests the whole judicial power of the United States in one supreme court, and such inferior courts as congress shall, from time to time,

¶¶29-30. The relevant provision is §13 of the Judiciary Act of 1789:

[T]he Supreme Court shall have exclusive jurisdiction of all controversies of a civil nature, where a state is a party, except between a state and its citizens; and except also between a state and citizens of other states, or aliens, in which latter case it shall have original but not exclusive jurisdiction. And shall have exclusively all such jurisdiction of suits or proceedings against ambassadors, or other public ministers, or their domestics, or domestic servants, as a court of law can have or exercise consistently with the law of nations: and original, but not exclusive jurisdiction of all suits brought by ambassadors, or other public ministers, or in which a consul, or vice consul, shall be a party. And the trial of issues in fact in the Supreme Court, in all actions at law against citizens of the United States, shall be by jury. The Supreme Court shall also have appellate jurisdiction from the circuit courts and courts of the several states, in the cases herein after specially provided for; and shall have power to issue writs of prohibition to the district courts, when proceeding as courts of admiralty and maritime jurisdiction, and writs of mandamus, in cases warranted by the principles and usages of law, to any courts appointed, or persons holding office, under the authority of the United States.

Note that the first portion of §13, following Article III, §2, of the Constitution, grants the Supreme Court original jurisdiction in cases affecting, inter alia, "public ministers." Read in isolation, the term might be thought to include the secretary of state of the United States, but the context and history of Article III make quite clear that "this refers to diplomatic and consular representatives accredited to the United States by foreign powers. . . ." Ex parte Gruber, 269 U.S. 302 (1925). See also The Federalist, No. 81 (Hamilton). Why does Article III put those cases that it does within the Court's original jurisdiction? For the suggestion that the original jurisdiction clause was largely a venue provision linked to issues of geography and litigation convenience, see Amar, Marbury, supra n.17.

Marshall asserts, virtually without discussion, that §13 grants the Court jurisdiction to issue a writ of mandamus in this case. Is this the most plausible interpretation of §13? Consider the location of the "mandamus" sentence in the provision and the relevant punctuation. Cf. 28 U.S.C. §1651: "Writs: The Supreme Court and all courts established by Act of Congress may issue all writs necessary or appropriate in aid of their respective jurisdictions and agreeable to the usages and principles of law." Should Marshall have been influenced by the fact that many of the same persons who drafted Article III also drafted the Judiciary Act of 1789 and by the canon (long established in England) that ambiguous statutes should be construed, where possible, in a manner consistent with fundamental law (in this case the fundamental written law of the Constitution)?

¶¶31-41. Marbury's holding that the original jurisdiction of the Supreme Court cannot be enlarged remains the law, but the dictum that Congress cannot confer appellate jurisdiction in the enumerated cases within the Court's original jurisdiction has not been followed. See, e.g., Ames v. Kansas, 111 U.S. 449 (1884).

ordain and establish. This power is expressly extended to all cases arising under the laws of the United States; and consequently, in some form, may be exercised over the present case; because the right claimed is given by a law of the United States.

[32] In the distribution of this power it is declared that "the supreme court shall have original jurisdiction in all cases affecting ambassadors, other public ministers and consuls, and those in which a state shall be a party. In all other cases, the supreme court shall have appellate jurisdiction."

[33] It has been insisted, at the bar, that as the original grant of jurisdiction, to the supreme and inferior courts, is general, and the clause, assigning original jurisdiction to the supreme court, contains no negative or restrictive words; the power remains to the legislature, to assign original jurisdiction to that court in other cases than those specified in the article which has been recited; provided those cases belong to the judicial power of the United States.

[34] If it had been intended to leave it in the discretion of the legislature to apportion the judicial power between the supreme and inferior courts according to the will of that body, it would certainly have been useless to have proceeded further than to have defined the judicial power, and the tribunals in which it should be vested. The subsequent part of the section is mere surplusage, is entirely without meaning, if such is to be the construction. If congress remains at liberty to give this court appellate jurisdiction, where the constitution has declared their jurisdiction shall be original; and original jurisdiction where the constitution has declared it shall be appellate; the distribution of jurisdiction, made in the constitution, is form without substance.

[35] Affirmative words are often, in their operation, negative of other objects than those affirmed; and in this case, a negative or exclusive sense must be given to them or they have no operation at all.

[36] It cannot be presumed that any clause in the constitution is intended to be without effect; and therefore such a construction is inadmissible, unless the words require it.

[37] If the solicitude of the convention, respecting our peace with foreign powers, induced a provision that the supreme court should take original jurisdiction in cases which might be supposed to affect them; yet the clause would have proceeded no further than to provide for such cases, if no further restriction on the powers of congress had been intended. That they should have appellate jurisdiction in all other cases, with such exceptions as congress might make, is no restriction; unless the words be deemed exclusive of original jurisdiction.

[38] When an instrument organizing fundamentally a judicial system, divides it into one supreme, and so many inferior courts as the legislature may ordain and establish; then enumerates its powers, and proceeds so far to distribute them, as to define the jurisdiction of the supreme court by declaring the cases in which it shall take original jurisdiction, and that in others it shall take appellate jurisdiction; the plain import of the words seems to be, that in one class of cases its jurisdiction is original, and not appellate; in the other it is appellate, and not original. If any other construction would render the clause inoperative, that is an additional reason for rejecting such other construction, and for adhering to their obvious meaning.

[39] To enable this court then to issue a mandamus, it must be shown to be an exercise of appellate jurisdiction, or to be necessary to enable them to exercise appellate jurisdiction.

[40] It has been stated at the bar that the appellate jurisdiction may be exercised in a variety of forms, and that if it be the will of the legislature that a mandamus

should be used for that purpose, that will must be obeyed. This is true, yet the jurisdiction must be appellate, not original.

[41] It is the essential criterion of appellate jurisdiction, that it revises and
corrects the proceedings in a cause already instituted, and does not create that
cause. Although, therefore, a mandamus may be directed to courts, yet to issue such
a writ to an officer for the delivery of a paper, is in effect the same as to sustain an
original action for that paper, and therefore seems not to belong to appellate, but
to original jurisdiction. Neither is it necessary in such a case as this, to enable the
court to exercise its appellate jurisdiction.

[42] The authority, therefore, given to the supreme court, by the act establishing
the judicial courts of the United States, to issue writs of mandamus to public officers, appears not to be warranted by the constitution; and it becomes necessary to
inquire whether a jurisdiction, so conferred, can be exercised.

[43] The question, whether an act, repugnant to the constitution, can become
the law of the land, is a question deeply interesting to the United States; but, happily,
not of an intricacy proportioned to its interest. It seems only necessary to recognize
certain principles, supposed to have been long and well established, to decide it.

[44] That the people have an original right to establish, for their future government, such principles as, in their opinion, shall most conduce to their own happiness, is the basis, on which the whole American fabric has been erected. The
exercise of this original right is a very great exertion; nor can it, nor ought it to be
frequently repeated. The principles, therefore, so established, are deemed fundamental. And as the authority, from which they proceed, is supreme, and can seldom
act, they are designed to be permanent.

[45] This original and supreme will organizes the government, and assigns, to
different departments, their respective powers. It may either stop here; or establish
certain limits not to be transcended by those departments.

[46] The government of the United States is of the latter description. The
powers of the legislature are defined, and limited; and that those limits may not be
mistaken, or forgotten, the constitution is written. To what purpose are powers
limited, and to what purpose is that limitation committed to writing, if these limits
may, at any time, be passed by those intended to be restrained? The distinction,
between a government with limited and unlimited powers, is abolished, if those
limits do not confine the persons on whom they are imposed, and if acts prohibited
and acts allowed, are of equal obligation. It is a proposition too plain to be
contested, that the constitution controls any legislative act repugnant to it; or, that
the legislature may alter the constitution by an ordinary act.

[47] Between these alternatives there is no middle ground. The constitution is
either a superior, paramount law, unchangeable by ordinary means, or it is on a
level with ordinary legislative acts, and like other acts, is alterable when the legislature shall please to alter it.

[48] If the former part of the alternative be true, then a legislative act contrary
to the constitution is not law: if the latter part be true, then written constitutions
are absurd attempts, on the part of the people, to limit a power, in its own nature
illimitable.

[49] Certainly all those who have framed written constitutions contemplate them
as forming the fundamental and paramount law of the nation, and consequently
the theory of every such government must be, that an act of the legislature, repugnant to the constitution, is void.

[50] This theory is essentially attached to a written constitution, and is consequently to be considered, by this court, as one of the fundamental principles of our society. It is not therefore to be lost sight of in the further consideration of this subject.

[51] ¶¶51-54If an act of the legislature, repugnant to the constitution, is void, does it, notwithstanding its invalidity, bind the courts, and oblige them to give it effect? Or, in other words, though it be not law, does it constitute a rule as operative as if it was a law? This would be to overthrow in fact what was established in theory; and would seem, at first view, an absurdity too gross to be insisted on. It shall, however, receive a more attentive consideration.

[52] It is emphatically the province and duty of the judicial department to say what the law is. Those who apply the rule to particular cases, must of necessity expound and interpret that rule. If two laws conflict with each other, the courts must decide on the operation of each.

[53] So if a law be in opposition to the constitution; if both the law and the constitution apply to a particular case, so that the court must either decide that

---

¶¶51-54. What is Marshall's argument based on the "province and duty of the judicial department"? If one concedes that the Constitution is "law" and that it is paramount to legislative enactments, does it necessarily follow that the *judiciary* has authority to decide whether a congressional enactment violates the Constitution? Is the Constitution a law, just like other laws that come within a court's purview? Consider Judge Learned Hand's response:

> It is of course true that, when a court decides whether a constitution authorizes a statute, it must first decide what each means, and that, so far, is the kind of duty that courts often exercise, just as they decide conflicts between earlier and later precedents. But if a court, having concluded that a constitution did not authorize the statute, goes on to annul it, its power to do so depends upon an authority that is not involved when only statutes or precedents are involved. For a later statute will prevail over an earlier, if they conflict, because a legislature confessedly has authority to change the law as it exists. So too when a court finds two precedents in conflict, it must follow the later one, if that be a decision of a higher court, and it is free to do so if it be one of its own, because, again, confessedly it has authority to change its mind. But when a court declares that a constitution does not authorize a statute, it reviews and reverses an earlier decision of the legislature: and however well based its authority to do so may be, it does not follow from what it does in other instances in which the same question does not arise. . . .

The Bill of Rights, 9-10 (1958).

What earlier decision of the legislature does a court review and reverse when it "declares that a constitution does not authorize a statute"? Does Congress implicitly make a constitutional decision with respect to each piece of legislation it enacts?

In appraising Marshall's argument, consider that many European and South American nations have written constitutions as well as courts that perform essentially the same functions as our courts, but that their courts often do not adjudge the substantive constitutionality of legislation. Note also that, in nonconstitutional contexts, courts are sometimes required to accept as binding legal and factual determinations by other bodies, even though the courts may believe such determinations to be erroneous. See, e.g., 9 U.S.C. §10; United Steelworkers v. Enterprise Wheel & Car Corp., 363 U.S. 593 (1960).

Compare Marshall's argument with Hamilton's in The Federalist, No. 78:

> The interpretation of the laws is the proper and peculiar province of the courts. A constitution is, in fact, and must be regarded by the judges as a fundamental law. It therefore belongs to them to ascertain its meaning, as well as the meaning of any particular act proceeding from the legislative body. If there should happen to be an irreconcilable variance between the two, that which has the superior obligation and validity ought, of course, to be preferred; or, in other words, the Constitution ought to be preferred to the statute, the intention of the people of the intention of their agents. Nor does this conclusion by any means suppose a superiority of the judicial to the legislative power. It only supposes that the power of the people is superior to both; and that where the will of the legislature, declared in its statutes, stands in opposition to that of the people, declared in the Constitution, the judges ought to be governed by the latter rather than the former. They ought to regulate their decisions by the fundamental laws, rather than by those which are not fundamental.

case conformably to the law, disregarding the constitution; or conformably to the constitution, disregarding the law; the court must determine which of these conflicting rules governs the case. This is of the very essence of judicial duty.

[54] If then the courts are to regard the constitution; and the constitution is superior to any ordinary act of the legislature, the constitution, and not such ordinary act, must govern the case to which they both apply.

[55] Those then who controvert the principle that the constitution is to be considered, in court, as a paramount law, are reduced to the necessity of maintaining that courts must lose their eyes on the constitution, and see only the law.

[56] ¶56This doctrine would subvert the very foundation of all written constitutions. It would declare that an act, which, according to the principles and theory of our government, is entirely void; is yet, in practice, completely obligatory. It would declare, that if the legislature shall do what is expressly forbidden, such act, notwithstanding the express prohibition, is in reality effectual. It would be giving to the legislature a practical and real omnipotence, with the same breath which professes to restrict their powers within narrow limits. It is prescribing limits, and declaring that those limits may be passed at pleasure.

[57] ¶57That it thus reduces to nothing what we have deemed the greatest improvement on political institutions — a written constitution — would of itself be sufficient, in America, where written constitutions have been viewed with so much reverence, for rejecting the construction. But the peculiar expressions of the constitution of the United States furnish additional arguments in favour of its rejection.

[58] ¶¶58-61The judicial power of the United States is extended to all cases arising under the constitution.

¶56. This paragraph implies an argument for judicial review reminiscent of Hamilton's in The Federalist, No. 78:

> By a limited Constitution, I understand one which contains certain specified exceptions to the legislative authority; such, for instance, as that it shall pass no bills of attainder, no ex-post-facto laws, and the like. Limitations of this kind can be preserved in practice no other way than through the medium of courts of justice, whose duty it must be to declare all acts contrary to the manifest tenor of the Constitution void. Without this, all the reservations of particular rights or privileges would amount to nothing. . . .
>
> If it be said that the legislative body are themselves the constitutional judges of their own powers, and that the construction they put upon them is conclusive upon the other departments, it may be answered, . . . [i]t is far more rational to suppose, that the courts were designed to be an intermediate body between the people and the legislature, in order, among other things, to keep the latter within the limits assigned to their authority. . . .
>
> [The] independence of judges is . . . requisite to guard the Constitution and the rights of individuals from the effects of those ill humours which the arts of designing men, or the influence of particular conjunctures, sometimes disseminate among the people themselves, and which, though they speedily give place to better information, and more deliberate reflection, have a tendency in the meantime, to occasion dangerous innovations in the government, and serious oppressions of the minor party in the community.

¶57. Here, as in ¶¶49-50, Marshall seeks support for his argument in the fact that ours is a *written* constitution. Granting that the argument for judicial review would be more difficult to maintain if our constitution were not written, does the fact that it is written affirmatively support the argument? What purposes, other than providing guidance for the judiciary, can a written constitution serve? In any case, wouldn't you expect the authorization for judicial review, if there were any, to appear in the text of a written constitution?

¶¶58-61. Marshall here makes an argument based on the text of Article III, §2 — "The judicial Power shall extend to all Cases . . . arising under this Constitution. . . ." Outline the necessary steps of the argument, some of which may be only implicit in Marshall's discussion.

Note initially that Article III, §2, is in terms only a grant of jurisdiction. Some jurisdictional provisions — e.g., the Article III provisions relating to admiralty and suits between states — have been

[59] Could it be the intention of those who gave this power, to say that, in using it, the constitution should not be looked into? That a case arising under the constitution should be decided without examining the instrument under which it arises?

[60] This is too extravagant to be maintained.

[61] In some cases then, the constitution must be looked into by the judges. And if they can open it at all, what part of it are they forbidden to read, or to obey?

[62] ¶¶62-68There are many other parts of the constitution which serve to illustrate this subject.

[63] It is declared that "no tax or duty shall be laid on articles exported from any state." Suppose a duty on the export of cotton, of tobacco, or of flour; and a suit instituted to recover it. Ought judgment to be rendered in such a case? Ought the judges to close their eyes on the constitution, and only see the law?

[64] The constitution declares that "no bill of attainder of ex post facto law shall be passed."

[65] If, however, such a bill should be passed and a person should be prosecuted under it; must the court condemn to death those victims whom the constitution endeavors to preserve?

[66] "No person," says the constitution, "shall be convicted of treason unless on the testimony of two witnesses to the same overt act, or on confession in open court."

[67] Here the language of the constitution is addressed especially to the courts. It prescribes, directly for them, a rule of evidence not to be departed from. If the legislature should change that rule, and declare one witness, or a confession *out* of court, sufficient for conviction, must the constitutional principle yield to the legislative act?

[68] From these, and many other selections which might be made, it is apparent, that the framers of the constitution contemplated that instrument, as a rule for the government of *courts*, as well as of the legislature.

[69] ¶¶69-71Why otherwise does it direct the judges to take an oath to support it? This oath certainly applies, in an especial manner, to their conduct in their official

---

held to confer a general lawmaking power. See Hart & Wechsler 264-267, 809-821. But jurisdiction does not entail a general lawmaking or law-interpreting authority over all or any issues in the case. For example, in cases coming within the diversity jurisdiction, federal courts must adhere to (even erroneous) state court interpretations of state statutes and constitutions as well as to state judge-made law. See Erie R.R. v. Tompkins, 304 U.S. 64 (1938); Hart & Wechsler 667-755.

Nonetheless, wouldn't it be pointless to confer federal jurisdiction over "Cases arising under this Constitution" if no issues of constitutional interpretation were open to the courts? But if one concedes this much, does it follow that *all* issues of constitutional interpretation are open to federal judiciary, and in particular does it follow that issues of the constitutionality of acts of Congress are open? At least two other kinds of cases might arise under the Constitution. First, the argument for federal judicial review of allegedly unconstitutional acts of *state* legislatures, judges, and officials is very strong, but without the "arising under the Constitution" clause, there would be no federal jurisdiction in many such cases. Second, it might be thought that the courts should consider claims that *federal officers* have acted unconstitutionally. The colonial experience gave the framers good cause to distrust executive officials; moreover, might not one reasonably conclude that less deference is due the actions of lower-level officers than those of Congress or of the president himself?

(The question posed in the last sentence of ¶61 is the wrong one, isn't it? It is not a matter of what *parts* of the Constitution the judges may look into, but under what circumstances they may look into it.)

¶¶62-68. You will not again encounter such easy constitutional issues as these. Does the possibility that Congress might enact blatantly unconstitutional legislation entail or imply judicial authority to hold the legislation unconstitutional? To whom is each of these provisions immediately addressed? To whom is the provision involved in *Marbury* immediately addressed?

¶¶69-71. Does Marshall's "oath of office" argument prove too much? See Article VI, cl. 3, which requires all state and federal officials to swear or affirm to support the Constitution, and consider this

character. How immoral to impose it on them, if they were to be used as the instruments, and the knowing instruments, for violating what they swear to support!

[70] The oath of office, too, imposed by the legislature, is completely demonstrative of the legislative opinion on this subject. It is in these words, "I do solemnly swear that I will administer justice without respect to persons, and do equal right to the poor and to the rich; and that I will faithfully and impartially discharge all the duties incumbent on me as _____, according to the best of my abilities and understanding, agreeably to *the constitution,* and laws of the United States."

[71] Why does a judge swear to discharge his duties agreeably to the constitution of the United States, if that constitution forms no rule for his government? If it is closed upon him, and cannot be inspected by him?

[72] If such be the real state of things, this is worse than solemn mockery. To prescribe, or to take this oath, becomes equally a crime.

[73] ¶¶73-74It is also not entirely unworthy of observation, that in declaring what shall be the *supreme* law of the land, the *constitution* itself is first mentioned; and not

---

excerpt from Judge Gibson's dissent in Eakin v. Raub, 12 Serg. & Rawle 330 (Pa. 1825), which involved the authority of the Pennsylvania Supreme Court to review the constitutionality of acts of the state legislature. Judge Gibson's opinion refers to and counters almost every one of Marshall's arguments in *Marbury:*

> The oath to support the constitution is not peculiar to the judges, but is taken indiscriminately by every officer of the government and is designed rather as a test of the political principles of the man, than to bind the officer in the discharge of his duty: otherwise, it were difficult to determine, what operation it is to have in the case of a recorder of deeds, for instance, who, in the execution of his office, has nothing to do with the constitution. But granting it to relate to the official conduct of the judge, as well as every other officer, and not to his political principles, still, it must be understood in reference to supporting the constitution, *only as far as that may be involved in his official duty,* and consequently, if his official duty does not comprehend an inquiry into the authority of the legislature, neither does his oath.
>
>   . . . Granting that the object of the oath is to secure a support of the constitution in the discharge of official duty, its terms may be satisfied by restraining it to official duty in the exercise of the *ordinary* judicial powers. Thus, the constitution may furnish a rule of construction, where a particular interpretation of a law would conflict with some constitutional principle; and such interpretation, where it may, is always to be avoided. But the oath was more probably designed to secure the powers of each of the different branches from being usurped by any of the rest; for instance, to prevent the house of representatives from erecting itself into a court of judicature, or the supreme court from attempting to control the legislature: and in this view, the oath furnishes an argument equally plausible *against* the right of the judiciary. . . . The official oath, then, relates only to the official conduct of the officer, and does not prove that he ought to stray from the path of his ordinary business, to search for violations of duty in the business of others: nor does it, as supposed, define the powers of the officer.
>
>   But do not the judges do a *positive* act in violation of the constitution, when they give effect to an unconstitutional law? Not if the law has been passed according to the forms established in the constitution. The fallacy of the question is, in supposing that the judiciary adopts the acts of the legislature as its own; whereas, the enactment of a law and the interpretation of it are not concurrent acts, and as the judiciary is not required to concur in the enactment, neither is it in the breach of the constitution which may be the consequence of the enactment; the fault is imputable to the legislature, and on it the responsibility exclusively rests.

¶¶73-74. Chief Justice Marshall makes an almost offhand reference to the supremacy clause of Article VI of the Constitution. Consider the argument of Herbert Wechsler, Toward Neutral Principles of Constitutional Law, 73 Harv. L. Rev. 1 (1959):

> . . . I must make clear why I believe the power of the courts is grounded in the language of the Constitution and is not a mere interpolation. [He quotes the Supremacy Clause. Wechsler takes issue with the argument of Judge Learned Hand that the Clause means only that, in Hand's language] "state courts would at times have to decide whether state laws and constitutions, or even a federal statute, were in conflict with the federal constitution" but [Hand denies that this supports the grant of authority to *federal* courts, including the Supreme Court, to assess the constitutionality of federal legislation].

the laws of the United States generally, but those only which shall be made in *pursuance* of the constitution, have that rank.

[74] Thus, the particular phraseology of the constitution of the United States confirms and strengthens the principle, supposed to be essential to all written constitutions, that a law repugnant to the constitution is void; and that *courts*, as well as other departments, are bound by that instrument.

[75] ¶75The rule must be discharged.

Are you satisfied, however, to view the supremacy clause in this way, as a grant of jurisdiction to state courts, implying a denial of the power and the duty of all others? This certainly is not its necessary meaning; it may be construed as a mandate to all of officialdom including courts, with a special and emphatic admonition that it binds the judges of the previously independent states. That the latter is the proper reading seems to me persuasive when the other relevant provisions of the Constitution are brought into view.

Article III, section 1 declares that the federal judicial power "shall be vested in one supreme Court, and in such inferior Courts as the Congress may from time to time ordain and establish." This represented, as you know, one of the major compromises of the Constitutional Convention and relegated the establishment vel non of lower federal courts to the discretion of the Congress. None might have been established, with the consequence that, as in other federalisms, judicial work of first instance would all have been remitted to state courts. Article III, section 2 goes on, however, to delineate the scope of the federal judicial power, providing that it "shall extend [inter alia] to all Cases, in Law and Equity, arising under this Constitution . . ." and, further, that the Supreme Court "shall have appellate jurisdiction" in such cases "with such Exceptions, and under such Regulations as the Congress shall make." Surely this means, as section 25 of the Judiciary Act of 1789 took it to mean, that if a state court passes on a constitutional issue, as the supremacy clause provides that it should, its judgment is reviewable, subject to congressional exceptions, by the Supreme Court, in which event that Court must have no less authority and duty to accord priority to constitutional provisions than the court that it reviews. And such state cases might have encompassed every case in which a constitutional issue could possibly arise, since, as I have said, Congress need not and might not have exerted its authority to establish "inferior" federal courts. . . .

If Wechsler is persuasive in arguing that federal judges can properly inquire into any question under the U.S. Constitution that state judges can inquire into, does it also imply that state judges can inquire into the constitutionality of congressional legislation? (Professor Wechsler assumes that it does, but does not explain why.) Note the different way that Article VI treats "laws" and "treaties" and consider Van Alstyne's suggestion that "[t]he phrase 'in pursuance' might also mean merely that only those statutes adopted by Congress *after* the re-establishment and reconstitution of Congress pursuant to the Constitution itself shall be the supreme law of the land, whereas acts of the earlier Continental Congress constituted merely under the Articles of Confederation, would not necessarily be supreme and binding upon the several states" (supra n.17, at 21).

Assuming that you find the Marshall–Wechsler argument or, for that matter, any other textual argument for judicial review, persuasive, what are the implications with regard to the scope (and therefore, in effect, the frequency) of such review? Recall Justice Chase's conclusion in *Hylton*, that even if the power of judicial review be conceded, "I will never exercise it, but in a very clear case." Was *Marbury* itself such a "clear case"? Presumably Chase thought it was inasmuch as he joined in Marshall's opinion. What follows, however, if the Constitution is less than clear? Does *Marbury* itself support the proposition that the Court should prefer its own (by definition) debatable reading to one asserted by Congress or the president? Imagine that Marshall's opinion in *Marbury* had been accompanied by a dissenting opinion attacking his interpretation of Article III. Would that mean that Article III is in fact "unclear" or, rather, that the dissenting justice(s) were inexplicably incompetent in their understanding of the English language?

Consider the approach toward judicial review sketched in Gottfried Dietze, Judicial Review in Europe, 55 Mich. L. Rev. 539, 541 (1957): "European courts have usually tested the formal constitutionality of the laws. This consists of a review of the process of enactment. If it was discovered that the procedural requirements of the constitution had not been complied with, the law in question was declared void. On the other hand, the testing of the content of a legislative act for its 'intrinsic' constitutionality was the exception rather than the rule." Is such an emphasis on procedural requirements a plausible interpretation of the language of "congruence" in Article VI?

¶75. Consider Robert McCloskey, The American Supreme Court 25-27 (4th ed. 2005):

The decision is a masterwork of indirection, a brilliant example of Marshall's capacity to sidestep danger while seeming to court it, to advance in one direction while his opponents are looking in

Discussion

1. *Judicial interpretation: The first word or the last word?* Like Stuart v. Laird, the practical importance of *Marbury* in its own time was the Court's acquiescence (or capitulation) to the newly dominant Jeffersonians. However, its importance for most law professors (for better and worse) is that the Supreme Court was willing to invalidate a federal law on constitutional grounds. As previously noted, there was nothing particularly new about the abstract suggestion that the Court could do this; what was new was actually exerting the power. "Judicial review," after all, could still exist even if the Court never in fact found a law unconstitutional, so long as the Court claimed the authority, should the occasion ever arise, to act; although one might view this as merely a formal or ceremonial power if the Court never once said "No" to Congress. *Marbury* is the first instance of that "No," even if, in context, it involved, as McCloskey suggests, a far more important "Yes" to the practical ability of Thomas Jefferson to avoid giving Marbury the commission that was, ostensibly, rightfully his. Consider the possibility that one reason that we make *McCulloch* the first case that you read in this casebook is that the historical role of the Supreme Court has been far more to legitimize the actions of the national government than to invalidate them. (The Court's behavior toward state governments, as *McCulloch* itself suggests, has been very different.) Consider also whether the Court's ability to legitimate the work of the federal government is in fact enhanced by the theoretical (and practical) possibility that the Court might say "No" to any given federal activity.

2. *Does judicial review mean either judicial supremacy or judicial finality?* If one ignores the politics of *Marbury* and instead concentrates on the arguments presented in its text, it is still the case that Marshall's opinion scarcely submits to only one interpretation. Begin with a central question: How much power *does* it claim for the judiciary? Does it, for example, necessarily stand for the proposition that Supreme Court decisions must be accepted as authoritative by other branches of the national government? (Call this position judicial supremacy). Recall Andrew Jackson's Veto

---

another. . . . The danger of a head-on clash with the Jeffersonians was averted by the denial of jurisdiction: but, at the same time, the declaration that the commission was illegally withheld scotched any impression that the Court condoned the administration's behavior. These negative maneuvers were artful achievements in their own right. But the touch of genius is evident when Marshall, not content with having rescued a bad situation, seizes the occasion to set forth the doctrine of judicial review. It is easy for us to see in retrospect that the occasion was golden. The attention of the Republicans was focused on the question of Marbury's commission, and they cared very little how the Court went about justifying a hands-off policy so long as that policy was followed. Moreover, the Court was in a delightful position, so common in its history but so confusing to its critics, of rejecting and assuming power in a single breath, for the Congress had tried here to give the judges an authority they could not constitutionally accept and the judges were high-mindedly refusing. The moment for immortal statement was at hand all right, but only a judge of Marshall's discernment could have recognised it.

McCloskey obviously admires Marshall's political sagacity, which allowed him to avoid the dangerous confrontation with the Jefferson Administration that would have signaled the presence of a full-fledged constitutional crisis and perhaps even threatened the stability of the still very young new political order. McCloskey, a professor of government at Harvard, was not a lawyer and, perhaps, was not "thinking like a lawyer" when praising Marshall. Can (should) a lawyer accept McCloskey's terms of analysis? What if, for example, one agrees with Marshall that Marbury was in fact entitled to his commission but disagrees with him that §13 was unconstitutional? That would mean, of course, that Marbury was entitled to the remedy — the writ of mandamus — that would rectify the wrong done him. Should an honorable judge, in that instance, have failed to give him the remedy, whatever the consequences that might ensue?

Message and his discussion of the precedential force of *McCulloch*, Chapter 1, supra. Was Jackson violating the precepts of *Marbury* or, rather, adhering to them inasmuch as he could have justified what might be termed his "independent interpretation" of the Constitution on his presidential oath? Or, even if one believes that the Court is entitled to the "last word" in a "dialogue" or "colloquy" with other political institutions, does this imply that *only* the Court is authorized to proffer understandings of the Constitution? Is it possible that the result of such a "dialogue" would (and should) be the Court's concession either that it was mistaken in a previously expressed view or that the other institution's view was at least plausible enough to merit enforcement, even if the Court, in the absence of the expression of this viewpoint, would have construed the Constitution differently? (As to the difference between "judicial supremacy" and "judicial exclusivity," see Chapter 5, infra.) Recall Marshall's reference in ¶1 of *McCulloch* to the nature and quality of the debate prior to Congress's chartering of the Bank of the United States. Why bother to refer to the debate if Congress is not a worthy partner in the enterprise of constitutional interpretation?

3. *Departmentalism.* Jackson's Veto Message is an essential document for those who take a "departmentalist" view of constitutional interpretation, i.e., the proposition that each great branch of the national government — Congress, the Executive, and the Judiciary — can engage in some measure of independent constitutional interpretation. (Walter Dellinger's memorandum, Chapter 1, supra, spells out some of the complexities in determining how the "departments" sort out inevitable conflicts.) Departmentalism, however, is, in its own way, as *institutionally* oriented as is judicial supremacy; it is simply a question of to which governmental institution(s) one wishes to give priority.

4. *Constitutional protestantism.* Consider an alternative to institutionalism, however, which might be termed "popular" — or "protestant" — constitutionalism. Sanford Levinson has analogized certain tensions in American constitutionalism to those present within historical Christianity.[18] For example, Tertullian, a third-century Catholic theologian, responded to heretics who "put forward the scriptures and by their audacity make an immediate impression on some people" by asserting that only in the institutional Church could be found "the true scriptures, the true interpretations, and all the true Christian traditions." Protestantism was, among other things, a revolt against any such claims regarding the authority of the institutional Catholic Church, an authority instantiated in the office of the Papacy. "When the attempt is made," wrote Martin Luther, "to reprove [Church authorities] out of the Scriptures, they raise the objection that the interpretation of the Scriptures belongs to no one except the pope." But if this were true, asked Luther, "where would be the need or use of the Holy Scriptures?" Recall in this context Marshall's own claim that "[t]he powers of the legislature are defined, and limited; and that those limits may not be mistaken, or forgotten, the constitution is written. To what purpose are powers limited, and to what purpose is that limitation committed to writing, if these limits may, at any time, be passed by those intended to be restrained?" And then combine with Marshall's statement of the importance of a *written* Constitution Luther's assertion that "[a]n ordinary man may have true understanding: why then should we not follow him? Has not the pope erred many times? Who would help Christendom when

18. See Sanford Levinson, Constitutional Faith (1988).

the pope errs, if we were not to believe another, who had the Scriptures on his side, more than the pope?" To the traditional Catholic argument that the "keys" to the kingdom of God were given by Jesus to Peter, and, therefore, to the institutional Church, Luther responds that "it is plain enough that the keys were not given to Peter alone, but to the whole community." Indeed, Luther also makes an "oath" argument that might well be compared with Marshall's invocation of his own oath in *Marbury:* An article of the classic Christian creed is "I believe [in] one holy Christian Church." Luther interpreted this as establishing that "it is not the pope alone who is always in the right," for then the prayer "must run: 'I believe in the pope at Rome,' nothing less than a devilish error." He concluded his analysis by evoking the classic Protestant notion of the priesthood of all believers: "[I]f we are all priests . . . and all have one faith, one gospel, one sacrament, why should we not also have the power to test and judge what is correct or incorrect in matters of faith"?[19]

The constitutional analogue of such arguments is to argue that anyone inhabiting (and committed to) the "office" of citizenship in a constitutional republic has the right — even the duty — to engage in his or her own interpretation of the foundational document and to be willing in effect to resist presumably unpersuasive interpretations offered even by the Supreme Court. Consider in this context Professor Ronald Dworkin's comment that the American version of constitutionalism "does not make the decision of any court conclusive. Sometimes, even after a contrary Supreme Court decision, an individual may still reasonably believe that the law is on his side. . . . A citizen's allegiance is to the law, not to any person's view of what the law is, and he does not behave unfairly so long as he proceeds on his own considered and reasonable view of what the requires."[20]

5. *Popular constitutionalism.* Stanford Dean Larry D. Kramer has recently argued that popular constitutionalism was widely accepted at the time of the Constitution's origins.[21] Thus, he suggests, it was widely assumed that popular elections, fought in substantial part over constitutional issues, would be the forum for deliberation about constitutional meaning, and that the elections would in effect settle such controversies. To be sure, Kramer acknowledges that some courts in fact claimed powers of judicial review, but he argues that "[c]ourts exercising judicial review in the 1790s made no claims of special or exclusive responsibility for interpreting the Constitution. They justified their refusal to enforce laws as a 'political-legal' act on behalf of the people, a responsibility required by their position as the people's faithful agents. Judicial review was a substitute for popular action, a device to maintain popular sovereignty without the need for civil unrest. It was, moreover, a power to be employed cautiously, only when the unconstitutionality of a law was clear beyond doubt. . . ."[22] The ultimate guardian of the constitution, though, was not the Supreme Court (or even the judiciary in general), but rather an enlightened "public opinion" that took its constitutional duties seriously. One might be tempted to describe Kramer's position, or any other version of "popular" or "protestant" constitutionalism, as tending toward "anarchy." If you share this fear, do you believe that fixing a single determinative answer imposed by a Supreme Court is a better

---

19. Martin Luther, Three Treatises, quoted in Levinson, supra n.18, at 24.
20. Ronald Dworkin, Taking Rights Seriously 214-215 (1977).
21. See Larry D. Kramer, The People Themselves: Popular Constitutionalism and Judicial Review (2004).
22. Id. at 99.

solution than allowing constitutional meaning to be determined through the play of competing political institutions? (Recall in this context, our earlier discussion of the arguments for respecting precedents). Nevertheless, is it clear that one is faced with an either/or choice between fixed judicial interpretation and mutable popular interpretation? Throughout this course we will see how the Court's decisions, over time, have shifted in response to popular mobilizations and political pressures. That responsiveness, in turn, has helped preserve the Court's legitimacy and its acceptance by the public. Viewed over time, then, it is possible that the American constitutional order features both strong judicial review *and* robust popular constitutionalism, with the inevitable tension between them a never ending source of contention that propels the constitutional system onward into history.

C.   The Precedents for Judicial Review[23]

No provision of the Constitution explicitly authorizes the federal judiciary to review the constitutionality of acts of Congress. The extent to which those who framed and adopted the Constitution assumed or intended that the courts would exercise this power has been the subject of continuing scholarly controversy.

England provided no direct precedent for judicial review. As late as the seventeenth century, the lawmaking and law-declaring (or judicial) functions of the High Court of Parliament were not sharply differentiated, so that England lacked the concept of separation of powers that underlies the American institution of judicial review. Despite the settled notion that the common law embodied principles of natural or fundamental law (see pp. 146-147, infra) and despite Lord Coke's famous dictum in Bonham's Case,[24] the common law courts never assumed the authority to review acts of Parliament. England had no written constitution, and parliamentary supremacy was firmly established at the time of the framing of the first American constitutions. "[I]f the parliament will positively enact a thing to be done which is unreasonable," wrote Blackstone in 1765, "I know of no power in the ordinary forms of the constitution that is vested with authority to control it. . . ."[25]

Some American colonists had invoked principles of natural law to contend that the colonial courts should not enforce oppressive English legislation, and the American Revolution was justified on natural-law grounds. But if the received natural-law tradition created an atmosphere in which judicial review could flourish, that innovative American institution owed still more to John Locke's Second

23. See generally Judicial Review and the Supreme Court 1-12 (Levy ed., 1967); Alan Westin, Introduction and Historical Bibliography to Charles Beard, The Supreme Court and the Constitution 1-34, 133-146 (Westin ed., 1962). Compare Charles Beard, The Supreme Court and the Constitution (1912), Raoul Berger, Congress v. The Supreme Court (1969) and Henry Hart, Professor Crosskey and Judicial Review, 67 Harv. L. Rev. 1456 (1954) (book review) with Louis Boudin, Government by Judiciary (1932), Edward Corwin, Court over Constitution: A Study of Judicial Review as an Instrument of Popular Government (1938), and 2 William Crosskey, Politics and the Constitution in the History of the United States (1953).

24. 8 Co. Rep. 107a, 77 Eng. Rep. 638 (1610): "When an Act of Parliament is against common right and reason, or repugnant, or impossible to be performed, the common law will controul it, and adjudge such Act to be void. . . ." See Theodore Plucknett, Bonham's Case and Judicial Review, 40 Harv. L. Rev. 30 (1926); S.E. Thorne, Dr. Bonham's Case, 54 L.Q. Rev. 543 (1938).

25. Blackstone, Commentaries *91. See J.W. Gough, Fundamental Law in English Constitutional History (1955); Charles McIlwain, The High Court of Parliament and Its Supremacy (1910); Edward Corwin, The "Higher Law" Background of American Constitutional Law, 42 Harv. L. Rev. 149, 365 (1928-1929).

Treatise of Civil Government (1690). The premise of Locke's social compact was that sovereignty did not reside in any agency of government but in "the people" themselves, who (through the American invention of written constitutions) delegated limited authority to those agencies. The legislature was the direct voice of the people, and the early republicans placed a virtually unlimited, populistic faith in the representative branch. But in the years following the Revolutionary War, as state legislatures authorized the issuance of worthless paper money, enacted sweeping debtor relief legislation, and directed oppressive measures against British loyalists, the possibility of legislative abuse — of tyranny of the majority — became increasingly apparent. One remedy was bicameralism, which the states adopted in various forms. Judicial review emerged as another remedy; if the people were sovereign, and the legislature merely their agent, then (as Hamilton later put it in The Federalist, No. 78) "where the will of the legislature declared in its statutes, stands in opposition to that of the people, declared in the constitution, the judges ought to be governed by the latter, rather than the former. They ought to regulate their decisions by the fundamental laws. . . ."[26] Or consider a speech in which James Wilson, second only to Madison in importance at the Philadelphia Convention, told members of the Convention that laws "may be unjust, may be unwise, may be dangerous, may be destructive; and *yet not be so unconstitutional as to justify the judges in refusing to give them effect*" (emphasis added). One might be struck, of course, by how much would *not* be unconstitutional — i.e., "unjust," "unwise," "dangerous," and even "destructive" laws — but Wilson obviously concludes his comment by suggesting that there indeed exist a set of laws "so unconstitutional as to justify the judges in refusing to give them effect."

By 1787, several state courts had asserted the authority to nullify legislative enactments (almost always invoking the fundamental law of the written constitution rather than unwritten natural law). Most of these tentative ventures were met with criticism, however, and some even with threats of discipline and impeachment. Thus, it cannot be said that the institution of judicial review was "established" in the states by the time of the Philadelphia convention.[27] The "intent of the framers" is still the subject of dispute. For present purposes, it suffices to note that the general idea of judicial review was much in the air when the Constitution was framed and ratified. Whether there was a clear consensus that the federal judiciary should review the constitutionality of acts of Congress, there certainly was no consensus that it might not, and, as indicated earlier, several decisions of the 1790s seem to presuppose the authority to consider the constitutionality of acts of Congress (though none of these decisions invalidated any of the laws under consideration). The question was open, and though *Marbury* met with some criticism, it took no one by surprise. This being said, it is certainly the case that judicial review — and especially its scope — has been the subject of recurrent debate in American history. We turn now to some of the contemporary debate, though later parts of the casebook will treat some of the historically specific debates.

---

26. See Bernard Bailyn, The Ideological Origins of the American Revolution (1967); Carl Becker, The Declaration of Independence (1922); M.J.C. Vile, Constitutionalism and the Separation of Powers (1967); Gordon Wood, The Creation of the American Republic, 1776-1787 (1969).

27. See William Nelson, Changing Conceptions of Judicial Review: The Evolution of Constitutional Theory in the States, 1790-1860, 120 U. Pa. L. Rev. 1166 (1972). See also Jack Rakove, The Origins of Judicial Review: A Plea for New Contexts, 49 Stan. L. Rev. 1031 (1997).

D.   Judicial Review in a Democratic Polity

1.   The Countermajoritarian Difficulty

"The root difficulty," wrote Alexander Bickel in perhaps the most influential single book on the role of the Supreme Court published in the past half-century, "is that judicial review is a counter-majoritarian force in our society":

There are various ways of sliding over this ineluctable reality. Marshall did so when he spoke of enforcing, in behalf of "the people," the limits that they have ordained for the institutions of a limited government. And it has been done ever since in much the same fashion by all too many commentators. Marshall himself followed Hamilton, who in the 78th Federalist denied that judicial review implied a superiority of the judicial over the legislative power — denied, in other words, that judicial review constituted control by an unrepresentative minority of an elected majority. "It only supposes," Hamilton went on, "that the power of the people is superior to both; and that where the will of the legislature, declared in its statutes, stands in opposition to that of the people, declared in the Constitution, the judges ought to be governed by the latter rather than the former." But the word "people" so used is an abstraction . . . obscuring the reality that when the Supreme Court declares unconstitutional a legislative act or the action of an elected executive, it thwarts the will of representatives of the actual people of the here and now; it exercises control, not in behalf of the prevailing majority, but against it. That, without mystic overtones, is what actually happens. It is an altogether different kettle of fish, and it is the reason the charge can be made that judicial review is undemocratic.

Most assuredly, no democracy operates by taking continuous nose counts on the broad range of daily governmental activities. Representative democracies — that is to say, all working democracies — function by electing certain men for certain periods of time, then passing judgment periodically on their conduct of public office. . . . The elected officials, however, are expected to delegate some of their tasks to men of their own appointment, who are not directly accountable at the polls. The whole operates under public scrutiny and criticism — but not at all times or in all parts. What we mean by democracy, therefore, is much more sophisticated and complex than the making of decisions in town meeting by a show of hands. It is true also that even decisions that have been submitted to the electoral process in some fashion are not continually resubmitted, and they are certainly not continually unmade. Once run through the process, once rendered by "the people" (using the term now in its mystic sense, because the reference is to the people in the past), myriad decisions remain to govern the present and the future despite what may well be fluctuating majorities against them at any given time. A high value is put on stability, and that is also a countermajoritarian factor. Nevertheless, although democracy does not mean constant reconsideration of decisions once made, it does mean that a representative majority has the power to accomplish a reversal. This power is of the essence, and no less so because it is often merely held in reserve.

. . . [N]othing in the further complexities and perplexities of the system . . . can alter the essential reality that judicial review is a deviant institution in the American democracy.[28]

---

28. Alexander Bickel, The Least Dangerous Branch 16-18 (1962). See also Barry Friedman, The Road to Judicial Supremacy (The History of the Countermajoritarian Difficulty, Part One), 73 N.Y.U. L. Rev. 333 (1998).

Bickel's argument depends on his central assumption that "judicial review is a deviant institution in the American polity." This is, of course, an empirical question, depending for its plausibility on the complementary assumption that the American polity is generally committed to majoritarian democracy. We shall examine this assumption shortly. Nevertheless, many have agreed with Bickel's premise about its "deviant" quality, and have gone on to offer various justifications for the institution of judicial review. As we turn to them, note the extent to which they are functionalist — i.e., rooted in notions of how the Court effectively contributes to maintaining a certain kind of American polity — rather than based on analyses of the text of the Constitution or the understanding of the framing generation.

2. Justifications for Judicial Review

a. Supervising Inter- and Intra-governmental Relations

The federal judiciary has at times supervised two systems of governmental relations: (1) the federal system, involving relations between the national and state governments and relations among the states themselves;[29] and (2) the internal national system, involving the allocation of powers among the legislative, executive, and judicial branches.[30]

As a practical matter, the review (and invalidation) by federal courts of *state* legislation is almost certainly more important than their relatively infrequent invalidation of *federal* legislation. (In the federal context, especially in the modern era, the courts' most important function probably is giving meaning to federal statutes, a subject beyond the subject matter of this casebook.) Consider these two statements by eminent justices:

Oliver Wendell Holmes, Jr.:

> I do not think the United States would come to an end if we lost our power to declare an Act of Congress void. I do think the Union would be imperiled if we could not make that declaration as to the laws of the several states.[31]

Robert H. Jackson:

> [T]he power of the Supreme Court to declare acts of the *states* void under the federal Constitution presents an entirely separate issue in our history . . . [and] rests on quite different [and stronger] foundations than does the power to strike down *federal* legislation as unconstitutional.[32]

---

29. See Jenna Bednar, William N. Eskridge, Jr., and John Ferejohn, A Political Theory of Federalism, in Constitutional Culture and Democratic Rule 223 (Ferejohn, Rakove, and Riley eds., 2001) for an elegant argument that federal systems basically require a strong judicial "umpire," given that both national and state governments have strong incentives to try to renege on the federal "deal" that by definition places limits on both of these governments.

30. A third system of governmental relations, which involves the tribal governments of American Indian tribes, should at least be mentioned. See, e.g., Judith Resnik, Dependent Sovereigns: Indian Tribes, States, and Federal Courts, 56 U. Chicago L. Rev. 671 (1989).

31. Oliver Wendell Holmes, Jr., Collected Legal Papers 295-296 (1920).

32. Robert H. Jackson, The Struggle for Judicial Supremacy 15 (1941).

Justices Holmes and Jackson appear to regard review of state legislation as essential to the realization and maintenance of the federalist vision, while expressing far more skepticism about judicial monitoring of congressional legislation, especially if the purpose is to protect the states against incursions by the national government. Why should this be so? One reason might be, as Marshall suggested in *McCulloch,* that federal courts can have greater "confidence" in Congress than in state legislatures. Needless to say, such assertions are highly controversial. The Court seemed in substantial respects to accept the Holmes–Jackson position from roughly 1937 to 1995, although more recently it seems to be redefining its role as potential protector of state autonomy. See Chapter 5, infra.

In any case, the power of the federal courts to review the judgments of state courts and the constitutionality of state legislation has not been seriously questioned since Martin v. Hunter's Lessee, 14 U.S. (1 Wheat.) 304 (1816). The Virginia Court of Appeals had refused to obey the Supreme Court's mandate reversing the judgment in a case involving the preemption of state laws by federal treaties. The state court had held unanimously that section 25 of the Judiciary Act of 1789, conferring federal appellate jurisdiction, was unconstitutional. The Supreme Court again heard the case and again reversed (though to avoid another conflict, it bypassed the Virginia Court of Appeals and issued its mandate directly to the state trial court).[33] Justice Story wrote:

> [T]he constitution . . . is crowded with provisions which restrain or annul the sovereignty of the states in some of the highest branches of their prerogatives. The tenth section of the first article contains a long list of disabilities and prohibitions imposed upon the states. . . . The language of the constitution is also imperative upon the states as to the performance of many duties. It is imperative upon the state legislatures to make laws prescribing the time, places, and manner of holding elections for senators and representatives, and for electors of president and vice-president. And in these, as well as some other cases, congress have a right to revise, amend, or supercede the laws which may be passed by state legislatures. When, therefore, the states are stripped of some of the highest attributes of sovereignty, and the same are given to the United States; when the legislatures of the state are, in some respects, under the control of congress, and in every case are, under the constitution, bound by the paramount authority of the United States; it is certainly difficult to support the argument that the appellate power over the decisions of state courts is contrary to the genius of our institutions. . . .
>
> It is . . . argued, that no great public mischief can result from a construction which shall limit the appellate power of the United States to cases in their own courts . . . because state judges are bound by an oath to support the constitution of the United States, and must be presumed to be men of learning and integrity . . . [A]dmitting that the judges of the state courts are, and will be, of as much learning, integrity, and wisdom, as those of the courts of the United States, (which we very cheerfully admit,) it does not aid the argument. It is manifest that the constitution has . . . presumed (whether rightly or wrongly we do not inquire) that state attachments, state prejudices, state jealousies, and state interests, might sometimes obstruct, or control, or be supposed to obstruct or control, the regular administration of justice. . . .
>
> This is not all. A motive of another kind, perfectly compatible with the most sincere respect for state tribunals, might induce the grant of appellate power over their decisions. That motive is the importance, and even necessity of *uniformity* of decisions throughout the whole United States, upon all subjects within the purview of the

---

33. 1 Charles Warren, The Supreme Court in United States History 450 (1926).

constitution. Judges of equal learning and integrity, in different states, might differently interpret a statute, or a treaty of the United States, or even the constitution itself: If there were no revising authority to control these jarring and discordant judgments, and harmonize them into uniformity, the laws, the treaties, and the constitution of the United States would be different in different States, and might perhaps, never have precisely the same construction, obligation, or efficacy, in any two states. The public mischiefs that would attend such a state of things would be truly deplorable. . . .

The Court again addressed the constitutionality of section 25 in Cohens v. Virginia, 19 U.S. (6 Wheat.) 264 (1821), in which appellants, convicted of selling lottery tickets in violation of state law, claimed immunity under a congressional enactment permitting the District of Columbia to establish a lottery. Chief Justice Marshall rejected Virginia's argument that Article III did not confer appellate jurisdiction over state criminal cases:

With the ample powers confided to this supreme government . . . are connected many express and important limitations on the sovereignty of the States, which are made for the same purposes. The powers of the Union, on the great subjects of war, peace, and commerce, and on many others, are in themselves limitations of the sovereignty of the States. . . . [T]he judicial power of every well-constituted government must be co-extensive with the legislative, and must be capable of deciding every judicial question which grows out of the constitution and laws. . . .

In many States the judges are dependent for office and for salary on the will of the legislature. . . . When we observe the importance which [the Constitution of the United States] attaches to the independence of judges, we are the less inclined to suppose that it can have intended to leave these constitutional questions to tribunals where this independence may not exist, in all cases where a State shall prosecute an individual who claims the protection of an act of Congress. . . .

The mischievous consequences of the construction contended for on the part of Virginia, are also entitled to great consideration. It would prostrate, it has been said, the government and its laws at the feet of every State in the Union. And would not this be its effect? What power of the government could be executed by its own means, in any State disposed to resist its execution by a course of legislation? The laws must be executed by individuals acting within the several States. If these individuals may be exposed to penalties, and if the Courts of the Union cannot correct the judgments by which these penalties may be enforced, the course of the government may be, at any time, arrested by the will of one of its members. Each member will possess a *veto* on the will of the whole. . . .

Let it be admitted, that the cases which have been put are extreme and improbable, yet there are gradations of opposition to the laws, far short of those cases, which might have a baneful influence on the affairs of the nation. Different States may entertain different opinions on the true construction of the constitutional powers of Congress. We know, that at one time, the assumption of the debts contracted by the several States, during the war of our revolution, was deemed unconstitutional by some of them. We know, too, that at other times, certain taxes, imposed by Congress have been pronounced unconstitutional. Other laws have been questioned partially, while they were supported by the great majority of the American people. We have no assurance that we shall be less divided than we have been. . . .

These collisions may take place in times of no extraordinary commotion. But a constitution is framed for ages to come, and is designed to approach immortality as nearly as human institutions can approach it. Its course cannot always be tranquil. It is exposed to storms and tempests, and its framers must be unwise statesmen indeed, if they have not provided it, as far as its nature will permit, with the means of self-preservation from the perils it may be destined to encounter. No government ought to be so defective in its organization, as not to contain within itself the means of securing the execution of its own laws against other dangers than those which occur every day. Courts of justice are the means most usually employed; and it is reasonable to expect that a government should repose on its own Courts, rather than on others.

(Upon reaching the merits, the Court held that the statute did not authorize the sale of lottery tickets beyond the city limits of Washington and affirmed the judgment of the state court.) During the century and a half since these decisions — most recently in the wake of the *School Desegregation* cases — states have sometimes attempted to thwart the orders and mandates of the federal judiciary.[34] But *Martin* and *Cohens* effectively settled the Supreme Court's authority to revise the judgments of state courts and, in effect, settled the federal judicial power to determine the constitutionality of state laws.

b. Preserving Fundamental Values

Alexander Bickel argued that the protection of fundamental values was a primary justification for judicial review. Bickel recognized that the Court's justification in *Marbury*, based on judicial competence to interpret the written text of the Constitution, did not encompass many of the Court's decisions, (consider, for example, Marshall's structural argument in part 2 of *McCulloch*) but went on to argue for institutional competence of a different sort:

> [M]any actions of government have two aspects: their immediate, necessarily intended, practical effects, and their perhaps unintended or unappreciated bearing on values we hold to have more general and permanent interest. It is a premise we deduce not merely from the fact of a written constitution but from the history of the race, and ultimately as a moral judgment of the good society, that government should serve not only what we conceive from time to time to be our immediate material needs but also certain enduring values. This in part is what is meant by government under law. But such values do not present themselves ready-made. They have a past always, to be sure, but they must be continually derived, enunciated, and seen in relevant application. And it remains to ask which institution of our government — if any single one in particular — should be the pronouncer and guardian of such values.
>
> Men in all walks of public life are able occasionally to perceive this second aspect of public questions. Sometimes they are also able to base their decisions on it; that is one of the things we like to call acting on principle. Often they do not do so, however, particularly when they sit in legislative assemblies. There, when the pressure for immediate results is strong enough and emotions ride high enough, men will ordinarily prefer to act on expediency rather than take the long view. Possibly legislators — everything else being equal — are as capable as other men of following the path of principle, where the path is clear or at any rate discernible. Our system, however, like all secular systems, calls for the evolution of principle in novel circumstances, rather than only for its mechanical application. Not merely respect for the rule of established principles but the creative establishment and renewal of a coherent body of principled rules — that is what our legislatures have proven themselves ill equipped to give us. . . .
>
> [C]ourts have certain capacities for dealing with matters of principle that legislatures and executives do not possess: judges have, or should have, the leisure, the training, and

---

34. See Chapter 6, infra.

the insulation to follow the ways of the scholar in pursuing the ends of government. This is crucial in sorting out the enduring values of a society, and it is not something that institutions can do well occasionally, while operating for the most part with a different set of gears. It calls for a habit of mind, and for undeviating institutional customs. Another advantage that courts have is that questions of principle never carry the same aspect for them as they did for the legislature or the executive. Statutes, after all, deal typically with abstract or dimly foreseen problems. The courts are concerned with the flesh and blood of an actual case. This tends to modify, perhaps to lengthen everyone's view. It also provides an extremely salutary proving ground for all abstractions; it is conducive, in a phrase of Holmes, to thinking things, not words, and thus to the evolution of principle by a process that tests as it creates.

Their insulation and the marvelous mystery of time give courts the capacity to appeal to men's better natures, to call forth their aspirations, which may have been forgotten in the moment's hue and cry. This is what Justice Stone called the opportunity for "the sober second thought." Hence it is that the courts . . . are also a great and highly effective educational institution. . . . The Justices in Dean Rostow's phrase, "are inevitably teachers in a vital national seminar." No other branch of the American government is nearly so well equipped [as the judiciary] to conduct one. And such a seminar can do a great deal to keep our society from becoming so riven that no court will be able to save it. . . .[35]

The plausibility of this view of the Court is the central subject of Chapter 8. For now, simply consider what may be suggested by the metaphor of the "seminar." What, for example, is the difference between a "lecture course" and a "seminar"? (Is it simply that there are usually fewer students in a seminar, or does the metaphor of a seminar include the possibility that all the participants, including the Court as "professor," will share in a collective process of discussion and education about the meaning of the Constitution?)

c. Protecting the Integrity of Democratic Processes

In *Democracy and Distrust: A Theory of Judicial Review* (1980), John Hart Ely rejects the vindication of fundamental values as a justification for judicial review and offers instead what he calls a "participation-oriented, representation-reinforcing" model. His theory builds on Justice Stone's suggestion in footnote 4 of *United States v. Carolene Products Co.*, infra, p. 515 that the judiciary should scrutinize legislation (1) that "restricts those political processes which can ordinarily be expected to bring about repeal of undesirable legislation," or (2) that is based on "prejudice against discrete and insular minorities, which tends seriously to curtail the operation of those political processes ordinarily to be relied upon to protect minorities." Ely's thesis is that, "unlike an approach geared to the judicial imposition of 'fundamental values,' the representation reinforcing orientation . . . is not inconsistent with, but on the contrary is entirely supportive of, the American system of representative democracy. It [is devoted] to policing the mechanisms by which the system seeks to ensure that our elected representatives will actually represent." Ely argues that democratic "malfunction occurs when the *process* is undeserving of trust" — when "(1) the ins are choking off the channels of political changes to

---

35. Bickel, supra n.28, at 24-27.

ensure that they will stay in and the outs will stay out, or (2) though no one is actually denied a voice or a vote, representatives beholden to an effective majority are systematically disadvantaging some minority out of simple hostility or a prejudiced refusal to recognize commonalities of interest, and thereby denying that minority the protection afforded other groups by a representative system." Representation-reinforcing judicial review protects interests of three sorts: (1) It protects freedom of speech and freedom of the press "because they are critical to the functioning of an open and effective democratic process"; (2) it protects voting rights because the franchise is "central to a right of participation in the democratic process"; and (3) it protects minorities against defects of democratic process resulting from prejudice.[36]

3.   The Countermajoritarian Difficulty Challenged

One might wonder whether "countermajoritarianism" is all that "deviant" an institution within the American political system. Consider, for example, the Senate, where Wyoming and Vermont have equal voting power with California and Texas. (Similarly, as noted in the discussion of the election of 1800, Electoral College deadlocks are broken in the House of Representatives by a one-state/one-vote process.) Moreover, the contemporary Senate includes among its working practices the filibuster, whereby three-fifths of the Senate must vote to cut off debate on any given bill. This means that 41 senators can block legislation backed by a majority of the Senate and possibly passed by the House of the Representatives. Indeed, the Senate also operates under a rule that gives any single member the right to put a "hold" on any presidential nominations and thus prevent the full Senate from exercising its constitutional duty of giving its advice and consent to such nominations.[37] Turning to the presidency, one might ask if the presidential veto, by which a single political official gets to offset majorities of both houses of Congress, is defensible on "majoritarian" grounds. One might argue that at least the president is popularly elected, though as a technical matter this is inaccurate: The president is elected by members of the Electoral College, whose composition reflects the anti-majoritarianism of the Senate inasmuch as even the smallest state gets at least three votes. Many presidents have not in fact received a majority of the popular vote; most recently, in 2000 George W. Bush came in some 500,000 votes behind Vice President Al Gore, but won the presidency nonetheless because of a majority in the Electoral College (a victory assisted at least in part by a highly controversial decision, Bush v. Gore, 531 U.S. 98 (2000), in which five Republican Justices effectively shut down the recount of the Florida vote and guaranteed Bush the election).[38]

36. Professor Ely's thesis has hardly gone unchallenged. See, e.g., Symposium on Democracy and Distrust, 77 Va. L. Rev. 631 (1991).

37. See Philip Shenon, "In Protest of Clinton Action, Senator Blocks Nominations," N.Y. Times, June 9, 1999, A20. As Shenon writes, "Customs that permit a single lawmaker to hold up the workings of the Government might seem undemocratic. But they have a long history in the clubby confines of the Senate."

38. A good collection of essays on Bush v. Gore, from various points of view, can be found in Cass R. Sunstein and Richard A. Epstein, eds., The Vote: Bush, Gore, and the Supreme Court (2001) and Bruce Ackerman, ed., Bush v. Gore: The Question of Legitimacy (2002). See also Howard Gillman, The Votes That Counted: How the Court Decided the 2000 Presidential Election (2001); Richard A. Posner, Breaking the Deadlock: The 2000 Election, the Constitution, and the Courts (2001); Jack M. Balkin, Bush v. Gore and the Boundary Between Law and Politics, 110 Yale L.J., 1407 (2001).

Finally, consider two other distinctly "countermajoritarian" features of the constitutional text: the Treaty Clause, Article II, §2, whereby two-thirds of the Senate must concur in a treaty, and Article V, which requires first that two-thirds of each house of Congress agree to a proposed constitutional amendment and then further requires the assent of three-quarters of the states. The latter requirement means, as a practical matter, that proponents of a constitutional amendment must triumph in at least 75 state legislative houses (every state except Nebraska is bicameral, and 38 of the 50 states must agree to a proposed amendment). Opponents of an amendment can prevail simply by gaining one-third plus one of the votes in either the House or the Senate or, if unsuccessful there, by defeating the proposal in only 13 houses in separate states.[39]

The paragraph above assumes the basic legitimacy of the description of judicial review as "countermajoritarian" even as it suggests that "countermajoritarianism" is rife within the American political system. However, several political scientists have challenged the premise that judicial review presents a "countermajoritarian difficulty" at all. In a widely cited article, Decision-Making in a Democracy: The Supreme Court as a National Policy-Maker, Professor Robert Dahl attacked the very assumption that "the Court's policy decisions can be interpreted sensibly in terms of a 'majority' versus a 'minority' ":[40]

> In this respect the Court is no different from the rest of the political leadership. Generally speaking, policy at the national level is the outcome of conflicts, bargaining, and agreement among minorities; the process is neither minority rule nor majority rule but what might better be called *minorities* rule, where one aggregation of minorities achieves policies opposed by another aggregation.

Conceding that judicial review would nonetheless pose a problem if the Court systematically thwarted congressional policy, Dahl suggests that the rate of change of the Court's personnel makes this unlikely:[41]

> Over the whole history of the Court, on the average one new justice has been appointed every twenty-two months. Thus a president can expect to appoint about two new justices during one term of office; and if this were not enough to tip the balance on a normally divided Court, he is almost certain to succeed in two terms. . . . The fact is, then, that the policy views dominant on the Court are never for long out of line with the policy views dominant among the lawmaking majorities of the United States. Consequently it would be most unrealistic to suppose that the Court would, for more than a few years at most, stand against any major alternatives sought by a lawmaking majority.[42]

---

39. See Sanford Levinson, The Political Implications of Amending Clauses, 12 Constitutional Commentary 107 (1996). The Equal Rights Amendment (ERA), proposed by Congress in 1972, was ratified by two-thirds of the states, with a majority of the population. Nonetheless, it failed because it did not achieve the approval of the additional states required to bring it up to three-fourths. Assume that the Supreme Court simply interprets the Constitution as including the values instantiated in the ERA. Whatever one would think of that move, could it necessarily be described as "countermajoritarian"? See also Chapter 7.

40. 6 J. Pub. L. 279, 294 (1957).

41. Id. at 284-285.

42. From 1952 to 1975, 13 new justices were appointed (an average interval of 21 months). President Eisenhower appointed five justices during his two terms: Kennedy, two: Johnson, two; and Nixon four in one term. Ford appointed one justice in his two years in office. Since then, however, presidents have gotten fewer average appointments in large part because justices have remained on the Court for significantly longer terms than previously. Jimmy Carter became the first president since Franklin Roosevelt

Dahl goes on to examine instances in which the Court has struck down significant congressional legislation: In all but a few cases, either the Court reflected an actual or nascent consensus (e.g., the post-Reconstruction compromise of 1877 with the South that rested on shelving legislation passed by the precompromise Congress), or else its decisions were quickly reversed or overcome. The Court substantially delayed the implementation of national policy in only three areas — the income tax, child labor laws, and worker's compensation for longshoremen and harbor workers. Dahl concludes:[43]

> Except for short-lived transitional periods when the old alliance is disintegrating and the new one is struggling to take control of political institutions, the Supreme Court is inevitably part of the dominant national alliance. As an element in the political leadership of the dominant alliance, the Court of course supports the major policies of the alliance. By itself the Court is almost powerless to affect the course of national policy. . . .
>
> The Supreme Court is not, however, simply an *agent* of the alliance. It is an essential part of the political leadership and possesses some bases of power of its own, the most important of which is the unique legitimacy attributed to its interpretations of the Constitution. This legitimacy the Court jeopardizes if it flagrantly opposes the major policies of the dominant alliance; such a course of action, as we have seen, is one in which the Court will not normally be tempted to engage.
>
> It follows that within the somewhat narrow limits set by the basic policy goals of the dominant alliance, the Court *can* . . . often determine important questions of timing, effectiveness, and subordinate policy. . . .
>
> [T]he Court is least likely to be successful in blocking a determined and persistent lawmaking majority on a major policy and most likely to succeed against a "weak" majority; e.g., a dead one, a transient one, a fragile one, or one weakly united upon a policy of subordinate importance.

In Freedom of Speech: The Supreme Court and Judicial Review (1966), Martin Shapiro builds on Dahl's observations to make a different defense of judicial review. Whether or not the Court's policies generally mirror those of the "political branches" of the national government, the political branches are far from the paradigms of democracy our civics textbooks make them out to be; by compensating for defects elsewhere in the system, the Court may actually contribute to the overall representativeness of the government. Shapiro surveys the congressional committee system, the role of seniority, the power of lobbyists, the presidential nominating

---

to go through an entire term without the opportunity to make an appointment. (Roosevelt, of course, made up for that first-term deficit by making nine appointments between 1937 and his death in 1945.) In his eight years in office, Reagan appointed only three new justices to the Court, as well as raising then Associate Justice Rehnquist to the office of Chief Justice. George H.W. Bush was able to make two appointments in four years, but Bill Clinton could make only two while serving eight years, and both of those vacancies occurred relatively early in his first term. His successor, George W. Bush, was given no opportunity to make an appointment in his first term. Thus the Supreme Court had a stable membership between 1994, with the arrival of Stephen Breyer, and the 2005 death of 80-year-old Chief Justice Rehnquist after 33 years on the Court and the resignation of 75-year-old Sandra Day O'Connor after 24 years of service. This 11-year period is the longest in more than 175 years (when no appointments were made between 1811 and 1823). Does this change in the average frequency of new appointments alter the strength of Dahl's argument? Does it suggest that Congress should take steps to ensure that appointments are made more often, for example, by specifying that the president makes an appointment every other year? Would this require a constitutional amendment imposing term limits or could it be achieved by other means? See the discussion of lifetime tenure, infra.

43. Dahl at 286, 293-294 (the last paragraph is taken from earlier in the article).

conventions, the Electoral College, the myriad federal agencies, and the relations among those agencies, their parallel congressional committees, and the industries subject to agency regulation, to conclude:

> Now, the lawmaker, whom the modest [i.e., those favoring judicial restraint] so reverently endow with democracy's banner, is none other than precisely this combination of bureaucracy, President, and Congress, for quite obviously, all three are major participants in the shaping of our laws. In short, the lawmaker to whom the nasty old undemocratic Supreme Court is supposed to yield so reverently because of his greater democratic virtues is the entire mass of majoritarian-anti-majoritarian, elected-appointed, special interest-general interest, responsible-irresponsible elements that make up American national politics. If we are off on a democratic quest, the dragon begins to look better and St. George worse and worse. . . . In fact there are not three branches of government but many centers of decision-making which range from more to less "democratic" and from greater to lesser power, depending on the particular issue involved. . . .

Finally, Professor Mark Graber, in The Nonmajoritarian Difficulty: Legislative Deference to the Judiciary, 7 Studies in American Political Development 35 (1993), argues that legislators often prefer to send political hot potatoes (like abortion or affirmative action in the present, the expansion of slavery into the territories in the past) to the courts rather than pay the political costs of making inevitably politically costly decisions themselves. Like most political scientists, Graber is skeptical that the Court has often, if at all, made decisions that it perceived as strongly opposed by the political majority.

How persuasive do you find these critiques of the countermajoritarian difficulty?

Excursus on lifetime tenure. One explanation for such "countermajoritarianism" as the Court may display is the long tenure of federal judges. For example, one important explanation for John Marshall's influence is his 31-year length of service, from 1803 to 1834. This "life tenure" is thought to follow from Article III, §1, which conditions judicial tenure only on "good Behaviour." Had the United States followed the practices of many modern countries, which limit the tenure of the members of so-called "constitutional courts" (i.e., courts charged with assessing the constitutionality of parliamentary legislation) to 10, 12, or even 20 years, Marshall would not have had the opportunity to write some of his most significant decisions and to help shape the Court through the force of his considerable personality. Life tenure has not gone unchallenged by contemporary scholars. Lucas Powe, for example, writes that it

> creates the real possibility of imitating a society like China, where power is wielded by the oldest among it. Even if their minds are every bit as good as when they were appointed, there is no good reason in a democracy to vest so much power in people whose formative experiences are from an age decidedly different from that of most of the current populace. . . . It is one thing to elect such individuals to govern; it is another to have them govern because elected officials approved of them twenty or thirty years earlier.
>
> If life tenure is the problem and an independent judiciary the goal, then any number of solutions are possible, but the one that immediately suggests itself is a nonrenewable 18-year term (salary continuing on retirement), with vacancies occurring every two years. The turnover would remain roughly the previous average (2.2 years), but would be less random. A two-term president would get four appointments, and the

Court could not be packed with appointees of a single party unless that party were able to win three consecutive presidencies.[44]

Lewis H. LaRue offers a somewhat different objection to lifetime tenure.[45] "[N]one of us," he asserts, any longer shares the belief, pressed by Hamilton in the 78th Federalist, that judges are "bound down by strict rules and precedents which serve to define and point out their duty in every particular case that comes before them." Instead, says LaRue, our contemporary asumptions are that

1. We have a strong and independent judiciary;
2. our judges have the power to change the law, both common law and constitutional law;
3. our judges will exercise their power to change the law based upon their judgments about justice and utility;
4. this power to change the law is not unlimited, since there are political, institutional, and moral restraints that all judges feel;
5. this power has been used in the past sometimes for the good, sometimes for the bad.

If you grant these assumptions, then the question arises, Should we grant these judges, especially those who sit on the Supreme Court, life tenure? No.

It is, of course, too early in the course for most of you to have a considered opinion on LaRue's (as distinguished from Powe's) critique of life tenure, though, as you go through the materials of this course, you should determine how much you agree with LaRue's central argument that Hamilton's assumptions no longer are persuasive. To the extent that the Court indeed bases its decisions on factors other than "strict rules and precedents which serve to define and point out their duty in every particular case," what justifies its power to set aside as unconstitutional the decisions of presumably more politically accountable legislatures or executives?

IV. The "Marshall Court"

References to the "_____ Court," filling in the blank with the name of a Chief Justice, are sometimes simply a shorthand for periods of years and should not be taken to imply either that the Chief Justice was especially influential or that the period differed strikingly from the one that preceded or followed it. Whatever the problems of identifying a complex, multimember court with its Chief Justice, though, it is hard to resist designating the Court of 1803-1834 as the Marshall Court, for he was clearly the dominant figure of that period, particularly during the first two decades of his tenure, and under his leadership the Supreme Court asserted its own role in the federal polity.[46]

---

44. L.A. Powe, Jr., Old People and Good Behavior, in Constitutional Stupidities/Constitutional Tragedies 77-79 (William Eskridge and Sanford Levinson eds., 1998).
45. L.H. LaRue, "Neither Force Nor Will," in id. at 57-60 (1998).
46. Two volumes of the Holmes Devise History of the Supreme Court are devoted to the Marshall years. See George L. Haskins and Herbert A. Johnson, 2 History of the Supreme Court of the United States: Foundations of Power: John Marshall, 1801-15 (1981); G. Edward White, 3 History of the

As noted earlier, one aspect of this leadership involved his successful elimination of seriatim opinions and indeed, establishing at least during the first two decades or so of his tenure, a tradition — not always followed even then and now completely dissipated — of outward unanimity.[47] What Marshall tried, albeit unsuccessfully, to establish as an operating rule of the Court has in fact been accepted by several countries around the world, which explicitly prohibit dissenting (or concurring) opinions. The Irish Constitution, Article 34.5.5 directs that a decision of the Supreme Court regarding constitutional challenges to legislation "shall be pronounced by such one of the judges of that Court as that Court shall direct, and no other opinion on such question, whether assenting or dissenting, shall be pronounced, nor shall the existence of any such other opinion be disclosed." Similarly, the European Court of Justice (although not the European Court of Human Rights) operates under a rule that "the conclusions reached by the major-ity of the Judges after final discussion shall determine the decision of the Court," with these conclusions and supporting reasons to be set out in a single impersonal opinion.[48] Even under Marshall, the opinions were scarcely "impersonal," as in the European Court, but, rather, issued under the signature of a specific justice, to whom authorship of "the Opinion of the Court" may be attributed. It is precisely this latter practice that allows us to speak of "Marshall's [or Story's . . .] view of the Constitution" rather than simply "the Court" of a given era. What is the advantage, if any, of having "signed" rather than completely impersonal opinions?

In any event, there can be no doubt that John Marshall plays a special role in the saga of American constitutional development. "Marshall, according to received learning, consciously furthered the political goals of the Federalist party, first by stretching the Constitution's meaning to increase national power at the expense of state power, and second, by designing constitutional doctrines that protected the upper classes' privileges against the growing democratic onslaught that in 1829 finally placed Andrew Jackson in the White House."[49] There is little doubt that the Marshall Court provided the constitutional foundations for a strong national government and articulated a vision of an unusually powerful national judiciary that would, among other things, take special care to protect property rights against state regulation. It is important to distinguish, though, between what one might term the "high politics" of overarching political ideology and "partisanship" in the sense of specific adherence to party position or the seeking of party advantage. One might pay special attention to this distinction in assessing *Marbury* and Stuart v. Laird. In fact the Federalist Party not only lost the election of 1800; it never again seriously contended for national leadership, and it utterly collapsed following its failure adequately to support the War of 1812 (when some New England "High

Supreme Court of the United States: The Marshall Court and Cultural Change 1815-35 (1988). See also Herbert A. Johnson, The Chief Justiceship of John Marshall, 1801-1835 (1997). Marshall has been the subject of many fine biographies, the most recent and extensive of which is Jean Edward Smith, John Marshall: Defender of a Nation (1996).

47. See Laurence Baum, "Dissent," in The Oxford Companion to the Supreme Court 229-231 (1992). This does not mean there was no dissent at all during the Marshall Court. See, e.g., Donald Morgan, Justice William Johnson: The First Dissenter (1954).

48. See Sanford Levinson, Speaking in the Name of the Law: Some Reflections on Professional Responsibility and Judicial Accountability, 1 U. St. Thomas L.J. 447, 454-463 (2004).

49. William Nelson, The Eighteenth Century Background of John Marshall's Jurisprudence, 76 Mich. L. Rev. 894 (1978).

Federalists" countenanced the thought of secession as an alternative to remaining subservient to the "Virginia Dynasty" then represented by President James Madison). Yet most of the strongly nationalist decisions were issued, often unanimously, after 1811, when appointees of the Republican Presidents Jefferson and Madison constituted a majority of the Court. Whatever explains those decisions, it cannot plausibly be a desire to enhance the prospects of the Federalist Party against the Republicans.

Note: Limiting the President's Power as Commander-in-Chief

One theme of *Marbury* is that James Madison (and, inferentially, the president whose order not to deliver the commission he was presumably obeying) was subject to the rule of law as declared by the Supreme Court. Marbury, as a practical matter, might have been without a remedy because of the unconstitutionality of §13 in granting the Court the authority to issue a write of mandamus. If one rereads ¶¶13-15 of *Marbury*, there is certainly no doubt Marshall (and the Court for which he spoke) believed that Jefferson and Madison had in fact behaved illegally in refusing to deliver Marbury's commission. Thus James Madison had a legal duty (even if Marbury had no remedy that would force, at least in *this* case, compliance by Madison) to convey the commission, and Madison most certainly could not interpose an order by the president not to deliver the commission as justification for failing to give Marbury what was rightfully his.

It is no small matter, of course, to hold that even the President of the United States is not "above the law" and that federal (or even state) courts could invalidate presidential actions (in just the same way that they could invalidate congressional attempts to act beyond the legislature's assigned powers). Consider in this context Marshall's decision only a year after *Marbury* in Little v. Barreme, 6 U.S. (2 Cranch) 170 (1804), which involved the capture, on December 2, 1799, of the Danish ship Flying Fish, near Hispaniola (now the Dominican Republic) by U.S. frigates. The Flying Fish was suspected of violating the "non-intercourse act" passed by Congress on February 9, 1799, which prohibited any American ship from going "*to* any port or place within the territory of the French republic, or the dependencies thereof . . . ," including ports of French colonies in the Caribbean (emphasis added). The Act was part of the so-called "undeclared" or "imperfect" war then occurring between the United States and France, though President Adams devoted much of his own political capital to prevent it from becoming a full-scale war.[50]

As Marshall wrote, "During the hostilities between the United States and France, an act for the suspension of all intercourse between the two nations was annually passed." The Act authorized the President to "give instructions to the commanders of the public armed ships of the United States, to stop and examine any ship or vessel of the United States on the high seas" when there was suspicion that it was engaged in a violation of the Act. Should the suspicions be verified, the United States could seize the ship, take it to a port within the United States, and impose suitable penalties, including forfeiture. Presuming to act under the authority of the Act (and, presumably, defend vital American interests inasmuch as Adams supported the Non-Intercourse Acts), President Adams ordered naval officers

50. See, e.g., David McCulloch, John Adams 424 (2001).

charged with its enforcement "to be vigilant that vessels or cargoes really American, but covered by Danish or other foreign papers, and bound to *or from* French ports, do not escape you" (emphasis added). Although there was some evidence that the Flying Fish was really American in its ownership, the district judge in Boston, where the ship was taken after capture by Captain Little, held that the vessel and its cargo were indeed Danish and therefore "neutral property." However, he awarded no damages to the owners because, he held, there was in fact probable cause on the part of Captain Little to suspect that the vessel was indeed American. The circuit court reversed on the grounds that because the Flying Fish was coming from, rather than going to, a French port, it was immune from the Act, even had it been an American vessel.

The Supreme Court, in an opinion written by Marshall, upheld the circuit court and held that Captain Little was indeed liable for damages to the Danish owners:

It is by no means clear that the president of the United States whose high duty it is to "take care that the laws be faithfully executed," and who is commander in chief of the armies and navies of the United States, might not, without any special authority for that purpose, in the then existing state of things, have empowered the officers commanding the armed vessels of the United States, to seize and send into port for adjudication, American vessels which were forfeited by being engaged in this illicit commerce. But when it is observed that the general clause of the first section of the [Act] obviously contemplates a seizure within the United States; and that the 5th section gives a special authority to seize on the high seas, and limits that authority to the seizure of vessels bound or sailing to a French port, the legislature seem to have prescribed that the manner in which this law shall be carried into execution, was to exclude a seizure of any vessel not bound to a French port. Of consequence, however strong the circumstances might be, which induced captain Little to suspect the Flying-Fish to be an American vessel, they could not excuse the detention of her, since he would not have been authorized to detain her had she been really American. It was so obvious, that if only vessels sailing to a French port could be seized on the high seas, that the law would be very often evaded, that this act of congress appears to have received a different construction from the executive of the United States; a construction much better calculated to give it effect. . . .

These orders given by the executive under the construction of the act of congress made by the department to which its execution was assigned, enjoin the seizure of American vessels sailing from a French port. Is the officer who obeys them liable for damages sustained by this misconstruction of the act, or will his orders excuse him?. . .

I confess the first bias of my mind was very strong in favor of the opinion that though the instructions of the executive could not give a right, they might yet excuse from damages. I was much inclined to think that a distinction ought to be taken between acts of civil and those of military officers; and between proceedings within the body of the country and those on the high seas. That implicit obedience which military men usually pay to the orders of their superiors, which indeed is indispensably necessary to every military system, appeared to me strongly to imply the principle that those orders, if not to perform a prohibited act, ought to justify the person whose general duty it is to obey them, and who is placed by the laws of his country in a situation which in general requires that he should obey them. I was strongly inclined to think that where, in consequence of orders from the legitimate authority, a vessel is seized with pure intention, the claim of the injured party for damages would be against that government from which the orders proceeded, and would be a proper subject for negotiation. But I have been convinced that I was mistaken, and I have receded from this first opinion. I acquiesce in that of my brethren, which is, that the instructions cannot change the nature of the transaction, or legalize an act which without those instructions would have been a plain trespass.

It becomes therefore unnecessary to inquire whether the probable cause afforded by the conduct of the Flying-Fish to suspect her of being an American, would excuse Captain Little from damages for having seized and sent her into port, since had she actually been an American, the seizure would have been unlawful. . . .

Discussion

1. Would President Adams (and Captain Little) have been on stronger ground had Congress not passed the Non-Intercourse Act in the first place? Could the President have claimed some "inherent authority" in his office to protect the United States against perceived threats to its vital national interests (or "national security"), including interdiction of ships — need they necessarily be only American ships? — going to or from French ports? Or did the President have only such authority granted him by Congress, presumably acting under its "war power" (even if no formal war existed)?

2. Can Marshall be interpreted as arguing, with regard to the congressional statute, that its "meaning is clear" (recall Madison's speech) or otherwise so obvious that no good-faith argument can be made that "to" includes "from"? Does this suggest that President Adams was either incompetent as a reader of the English language or, perhaps more ominously, that he was indifferent to the statutory limitation on his own powers and chose to act as he thought necessary, confident that he, as President, possessed such powers to do what was best to preserve vital American national security interests? (Recall the arguments that would be made only a few years later by Thomas Jefferson with regard to defending the Louisiana Purchase.) In any event, is it fair to hold Captain Little, in effect, to a duty to know the precise language of the Act and to realize that the President of the United States was in effect attempting to usurp authority that he did not possess? We shall return to this question later in the context first of Abraham Lincoln's conduct as president during the events of 1861-1865 and then the contemporary "war on terrorism" with regard to the "inherent authority" of the president to use the armed forces however he wishes to protect the national interest and a concomitant exemption from potential liability of American military officers who proclaim simply that they were "following orders" of the chief executive and commander-in-chief.

3. Though *Little* concerned orders given by President John Adams, who had, of course, appointed Marshall first as Secretary of State and then Chief Justice, it was fact decided during the presidency of Thomas Jefferson, whom Marshall detested and distrusted. Is the actual timing of the Supreme Court decision a relevant "fact of the case"?

V.   The Protection of Property Rights and the Natural Law Tradition

FLETCHER v. PECK
10 U.S. (6 Cranch) 87 (1810)

[This case arose out of the notorious Yazoo land-grant scandal. In 1795, a majority of the Georgia legislature had been bribed to convey some 35 million acres of state land to private companies at the bargain price of about 1½ ¢ per acre. In 1796 the legislature rescinded the grant, but not before large parcels had been sold to northern investors. A suit on a warranty of title presented the question whether the 1796 rescission could affect the rights of bona fide purchasers not themselves part of the initially fraudulent scheme and, according to Marshall's opinion, without "notice" of it.[51]]

MARSHALL, C.J. . . .

[Subsequent purchasers] were innocent. Yet the legislature of Georgia has involved them in the fate of the first parties to the transaction, and, if the act be valid, has annihilated their rights also. The legislature of Georgia was a party to this transaction; and for a party to pronounce its own deed invalid, whatever cause may be assigned for its invalidity, must be considered as a mere act of power, which must find its vindication in a train of reasoning not often heard in courts of justice. . . .

If a suit be brought to set aside a conveyance obtained by fraud, and the fraud be clearly proved, the conveyance will be set aside, as between the parties; but the rights of third persons, who are purchasers without notice, for a valuable consideration, cannot be disregarded. . . . All titles would be insecure, and the intercourse between man and man would be very seriously obstructed, if this principle be overturned. . . . If the legislature felt itself absolved from those rules of property which are common to all the citizens of the United States, and from those principles of equity which are acknowledged in all our courts, its act is to be supported by its power alone, and the same power may divest any other individual of his lands, if it shall be the will of the legislature so to exert it. . . .

Is the power of the legislature competent to the annihilation of such title, and to a resumption of the property thus held? The principle asserted is, that one legislature is competent to repeal any act which a former legislature was competent to pass; and that one legislature cannot abridge the powers of a succeeding legislature. The correctness of this principle, so far as respects general legislation, can never be controverted. But, if an act be done under a law, a succeeding legislature

---

51. See C. Peter Magrath, Yazoo — Law and Politics in the New Republic (1966). A vivid sense of the passions underlying the recission is provided by Senator Albert Beveridge in his classic biography, 4 The Life of John Marshall 562-566(1919):

The Legislature further enacted that the "usurped act" and all "records, documents, and deeds" connected with the Yazoo fraud, "shall be expunged from the face and indexes of the books of record of the State, and the enrolled law or usurped act shall then be publicly burnt, in order that no trace of so unconstitutional, vile, and fraudulent a transaction shall remain in the public offices thereof." . . .

A committee, appointed to devise a method for destroying the records, immediately reported that this should be done by cutting out of the books the leaves containing them. As to the enrolled bill containing the "usurped act," an elaborate performance was directed to be held: "A fire shall be made in front of the State House door, and a line formed by the members of both branches around the same. The Secretary of State . . . shall then produce the enrolled bill and usurped act from among the archives of the State and deliver the same to the President of the Senate, who shall examine the same, and shall then deliver the same to the Speaker of the House of Representatives for like examination; and the Speaker shall then deliver them to the Clerk of the House of Representatives, who shall read aloud the title to the same, and shall then deliver them to Messenger of the House, who shall then pronounce — 'GOD SAVE THE STATE!! AND LONG PRESERVE HER RIGHTS!! AND MAY EVERY ATTEMPT TO INJURE THEM PERISH AS THESE CORRUPT ACTS NOW DO!!!!' " Every detail of this play was carried out with all theatrical effect. . . . Someone gifted with dramatic genius suggested that the funeral pyre of such unholy legislation should not be lighted by earthly hands, but by fire from Heaven. A sun-glass was produced; Senator Jackson held it above the fagots and the pile was kindled from 'the burning rays of the lidless eye of justice.' "

cannot undo it. The past cannot be recalled by the most absolute power. Conveyances have been made, those conveyances have vested legal estates. . . . When, then, a law is in its nature a contract, when absolute rights have vested under that contract, a repeal of the law cannot divest those rights; and the act of annulling them, if legitimate, is rendered so by a power applicable to the case of every individual in the community.

It may well be doubted, whether the nature of society and of government does not prescribe some limits to the legislative power; and if any be prescribed, where are they to be found, if the property of an individual, fairly and honestly acquired, may be seized without compensation? . . . The constitution of the United States declares that no state shall pass any . . . law impairing the obligation of contracts.

Does the case now under consideration come within this prohibitory section of the constitution? In considering this very interesting question, we immediately ask ourselves, what is a contract? Is a grant a contract? A contract is a compact between two or more parties, and is either executory or executed. . . . A contract executed, as well as one which is executory, contains obligations binding on the parties, [including an obligation] not to re-assert [rights possessed prior to the completion of the contract].

Since, then, in fact, a grant [of land] is a contract executed, the obligation of which still continues, and since the constitution uses the general term contract, without distinguishing between those which are executory and those which are executed, it must be construed to comprehend the latter as well as the former. . . .

[The next question is whether the Contract Clause should] be considered as inhibiting the state from impairing the obligation of contracts between two individuals, but as excluding from that inhibition contracts made with itself? The words themselves contain no such distinction. They are general, and are applicable to contracts of every description. If contracts made with the state are to be exempted from their operation, the exception must arise from the character of the contracting party, not from the words which are employed.

Whatever respect might have been felt for the state sovereignties, it is not to be disguised, that the framers of the constitution viewed, with some apprehension, the violent acts which might grow out of the feelings of the moment; and that the people of the United States, in adopting that instrument, have manifested a determination to shield themselves and their property from the effects of those sudden and strong passions to which men are exposed. The restrictions on the legislative power of the states are obviously founded in this sentiment; and the constitution of the United States contains what may be deemed a bill of rights for the people of each state. . . .

It is, then, the unanimous opinion of the court, that, in this case, the estate having passed into the hands of a purchaser for a valuable consideration, without notice, the state of Georgia was restrained, either by general principles which are common to our free institutions, or by the particular provisions of the constitution of the United States, from passing a law whereby the estate of the plaintiff in the premises so purchased could be constitutionally and legally impaired and rendered null and void. . . .

JOHNSON, J.

I do not hesitate to declare, that a state does not possess the power of revoking its own grants. But I do it, on a general principle, on the reason and nature of things; a principle which will impose laws even on the Deity. . . .

When the legislature have once conveyed their interest or property in any subject to the individual, they have lost all control over it; have nothing to act upon; it has passed from them; is vested in the individual; becomes intimately blended with his existence, as essentially so as the blood that circulates through his system. The government may indeed demand of him the one or the other, not because they are not his, but because whatever is his, is his country's. . . .

I have thrown out these ideas, that I may have it distinctly understood, that my opinion on this point is not founded on the provision in the constitution of the United States, relative to laws impairing the obligation of contracts. . . .

I enter with great hesitation upon this question, because it involves a subject of the greatest delicacy and much difficulty. The states and the United States are continually legislating on the subject of contracts, prescribing the mode of authentication, the time within which suits shall be prosecuted for them, in many cases, affecting existing contracts by the laws which they pass, and declaring them to cease or lose their effect for want of compliance, in the parties, with such statutory provisions. All these acts appear to be within the most correct limits of legislative powers, and most beneficially exercised, and certainly could not have been intended to be affected by this constitutional provision; yet where to draw the line, or how to define or limit the words, "obligation of contracts," will be found a subject of extreme difficulty.

Discussion

1. *Language and purpose.* During the depression following the Revolutionary War, many states enacted debtor relief laws, which modified contractual obligations or the procedures available to creditors for enforcing the obligations. The contract clause of Article I, §10, was designed to preclude a recurrence of such legislation. See Home Building & Loan Association v. Blaisdell, 290 U.S. 398 (1934) (Sutherland, J., dissenting), Chapter 5 infra. Does a purpose of preventing the state from intervening in the contractual relations between two private individuals necessarily extend to precluding the state from, in effect, rewriting its own contracts should the state legislature believe that the public interest will be served thereby? The answer may depend on the *level of generality* on which the purpose of the clause is conceived. Articulate the purpose of the contract clause narrowly enough to foreclose its application to the Georgia statute in *Fletcher.* Now articulate it broadly enough to justify Marshall's interpretation. How can one determine which is the correct level of generality on which to articulate the purpose of the provision?

2. *Judicial inquiry into legislative motivation.* The Court in *Fletcher* was also asked to invalidate the grant because of the Georgia legislature's corruption in enacting the original conveyance. Marshall resisted any such invitation to scrutinize the legislature's motivation:

> It may well be doubted how far the validity of a law depends upon the motives of its framers, and how far the particular inducements, operating on members of the supreme sovereign power of a state, to the formation of a contract by that power, are examinable in a court of justice. If the principle be conceded, that an act of the supreme sovereign power might be declared null by a court, in consequence of the means which procured it, still would there be much difficulty in saying to what extent those means must be applied to produce this effect. Must it be direct corruption, or would interest or undue influence of any kind be sufficient? Must the vitiating cause operate on a majority, or on what number of the members? Would the act be null,

whatever might be the wish of the nation, or would its obligation or nullity depend upon the public sentiment?

If the majority of the legislature be corrupted, it may well be doubted, whether it be within the province of the judiciary to control their conduct, and, if less than a majority act from impure motives, the principle by which judicial interference would be regulated, is not clearly discerned.

Marshall avoids a definite conclusion as to the propriety of looking into motivation by declaring that, in any event, "This solemn question cannot be brought . . . collaterally and incidentally before the court, as in this suit between two private parties. It would be indecent, in the extreme, upon a private contract, between two individuals, to enter into an inquiry respecting the corruption of the sovereign power of a state." What, though, of Marshall's basic qualms about looking into legislative motivation? Should a court *ever* be willing to take evidence as to the corrupt background of a bill in deciding whether or not it is constitutional?

3. *Other contract clause decisions.* Marshall's expansive interpretation of the contract clause continued in Dartmouth College v. Woodward, 17 U.S. (4 Wheat.) 518 (1819), which held that New Hampshire could not unilaterally modify a private institution's charter to place it under public control. Marshall wrote:

It is more than possible that the preservation of rights of this description was not particularly in the view of the framers of the constitution, when the clause under consideration was introduced into that instrument. It is probable, that interferences of more frequent recurrence, to which the temptation was stronger, and of which the mischief was more extensive, constituted the great motive for imposing this restriction on the State legislatures. But although a particular and a rare case may not, in itself, be of sufficient magnitude to induce a rule, yet it must be governed by the rule, when established, unless some plain and strong reason for excluding it can be given. It is not enough to say, that this particular case was not in the mind of the Convention, when the article was framed, nor of the American people, when it was adopted. It is necessary to go further, and to say that, had this particular case been suggested, the language would have been so varied, as to exclude it, or it would have been made a special exception.

In Sturges v. Crowninshield, 17 U.S. (4 Wheat.) 122 (1819), Marshall also wrote the Court's opinion, holding that a New York bankruptcy law could not operate retroactively to discharge a debt incurred before the law was enacted.

In *Fletcher,* Marshall notes that Article I, §10, besides prohibiting the impairment of the obligation of contracts, prohibits ex post facto laws and bills of attainder. An ex post facto law is a criminal law applied to conduct occurring before its enactment. A bill of attainder is a legislative act finding that specified individuals are guilty of a crime and punishing them for it. Bills of attainder were typically also ex post facto laws. Thus, these prohibited legislative measures share the feature that they apply retroactively to defeat settled expectations.

The distinction between retroactive and prospective interference with contractual obligations turned out to be of great significance in contract clause doctrine. Concurring in *Dartmouth College,* Justice Story observed that legislative grants might explicitly reserve to the state the power to amend the charters. And in Ogden v. Saunders, 25 U.S. (12 Wheat.) 213 (1827), the Court limited *Sturges* to the retroactive application of bankruptcy laws to preexisting contracts, holding that a statute in existence at the time the contract is made becomes "part of the contract."

In his only dissent in a constitutional case, the Chief Justice, joined by Justices Story and Duvall, argued from principles of natural law and social contract and from the language of the contract clause that government could not (in effect) dictate in advance the terms of private contracts to release obligors in the event of their insolvency. Marshall began by pointing to the origins of freedom of contract in natural right: "[I]ndividuals do not derive from government their right to contract, but bring that right with them into society; that obligation is not conferred upon contracts by positive law, but is intrinsic, and is conferred by the act of the parties." Society is not without any powers at all to affect the right to contract; it can control the formalities of contract formation or prohibit specific contracts as violations of public policy. Moreover, Marshall accepted the right of a state to pass laws affecting contract remedies, but he rejected the relevance of that concession by arguing that bankruptcy laws are not merely remedial, because what they do is to turn "obligatory" contracts into de facto "conditional" promises. He feared that "one of the most important features in the Constitution of the United States . . . would lie prostrate, and be construed into an inanimate, inoperative, unmeaning clause." The dissenters read the language of the clause as barring prospective as well as retrospective legislation and viewed *Ogden* as offering a method for returning to the preconstitutional era by which state legislatures felt free to pass allegedly ruinous debtor-relief legislation.

Stephen Siegel points out that a key question lurking behind the bankruptcy issue was the validity of so-called reserve clauses, whereby the legislature put into its grant of corporate charters a proviso "reserving" the right to change their terms.[52] "Until the twentieth century, property had a dual signification in Liberal thought. In one sense property denoted, as it still does, all items of wealth. In the other sense property denoted only those valuables whose acquisition was open to all individuals, typically through competition in the free market. Property, in this latter sense, stood in contrast to privilege, which signified wealth that only certain individuals could acquire, usually through designation by affirmative governmental act." Regulation of privilege was far more acceptable than regulation of ordinary property, including contract rights protected by the contract clause. It was one thing to allow reservations in charters awarded by the state because such charters were viewed as awarding a privilege to their recipients. It was quite another to allow ordinary contracts to be subject to broad reservations, and in fact no state ever enacted a general "reserve" clause governing private contracts. "[O]ver time," says Siegel, "jurists simply assumed they were unconstitutional."

4. *Appellate review and natural law.* G. Edward White emphasizes the difference in treatment between appeals to the Supreme Court from state court decisions based on Section 25 of the Judiciary Act of 1789 and appeals from lower federal courts, especially those arising under diversity jurisdiction. He suggests that only in non-Section 25 cases did the Court feel free to refer to the "general law," including norms of natural law or natural justice, whereas in Section 25 appeals the Court ostensibly limited itself to constitutional issues and to a far more positivistic, textual conception of the law it was authorized to enforce. White notes that *Fletcher* "was a diversity case, meaning that the Court could draw upon general principles of federal law as well as the Constitution for its sources." Justice Washington later

---

52. Stephen A. Siegel, Understanding the Nineteenth Century Contract Clause, The Role of the Property-Privilege Distinction and "Takings" Clause Jurisprudence, 60 So. Cal. L. Rev. 1 (1986).

wrote that "no where" in *Fletcher* is it "intimated . . . that a state statute, which divests a vested right, is repugnant to the constitution of the United States." Because *Fletcher* originated in a federal court it was appropriate to refer to general norms of justice; in a Section 25 case arising from a state court, on the other hand, the Supreme Court could only invalidate the statute where it was "repugnant to the *constitution of the United States.*"[53]

On this analysis, are only those parts of *Fletcher* relying on constitutional text rather than unenumerated norms truly "constitutional"? If so, what is the source of the Court's authority to strike down a state law on non-"constitutional" "general legal" grounds?

Note: Natural Law, Vested Rights, and the Written Constitution: Sources for Judicial Review

The reliance in *Fletcher* on "general principles" of law may sound strange, especially coming from Marshall, who seven years earlier had treated judicial review (of congressional legislation) merely as the application of the positive law of the written Constitution. This note surveys the concepts of "rights" extant in the late eighteenth and early nineteenth centuries.

1.   The Natural Law Tradition[54]

Although its influence has often been exaggerated, the concept of natural or fundamental law — a universal law superior to all man-made laws — pervaded eighteenth-century American intellectual and legal thought. Three features of the English natural law tradition influenced the development of constitutionalism in America. First, the received jurisprudence was that judges did not "make" the common law. Rather, through the "artificial reason of the law," they discovered immutable legal principles, which, together with more specific applications deduced from them, constituted the corpus of the English common law.[55] Second, centuries

53. White, The Marshall Court and Cultural Change, 1815-1835, at 611, 657-659.

54. See Bernard Bailyn, The Ideological Origins of the American Revolution (1967); Carl Becker, The Declaration of Independence, ch. 2 (1922); J.W. Gough, Fundamental Law in English Constitutional History (1955); Charles Mullett, Fundamental Law and the American Revolution (1933); Gordon Wood, The Creation of the American Republic, 1776-1787 (1969); Benjamin Wright, American Interpretations of Natural Law (1931); Edward Corwin, The "Higher Law" Background of American Constitutional Law, 42 Harv. L. Rev. 149, 365 (1928-1929); Corwin, The Basic Doctrine of American-Constitutional Law, 12 Mich. L. Rev. 247 (1914).

55. The quoted phrase is Sir Edward Coke's. James I had claimed that the king was entitled to decide cases, arguing "the law was founded upon reason, and that he and others had reason, as well as the Judges." Coke replied, "[T]rue it was that God had endowed his majesty with excellent science, and great endowments of nature; but his Majesty was not learned in the laws of his realm of England, and causes which concern the life, or inheritance, or goods, or fortunes of his subjects, are not to be decided by natural reason but by the artificial reason and judgment of the law, which law is an act which requires long study and experience, before that a man can attain the cognizance of it. . . ." The king "was greatly offended" at the notion that "he should be under the law, which was treason to affirm." Coke responded, quoting Bracton and invoking fundamental law: "Quod Rex non debet esse sub homine, sed sub Deo et lege" (the King ought to be under no man, but under God and the law). Prohibitions Del Roy, 12 Co. 63, 77 Eng. Rep. 1342 (1609). On the life of Coke, see Katherine Bowen, The Lion and the Throne (1957). See also Gough, supra n.54, ch. 3; David Little, Religion, Order and Law: A Study in Pre-Revolutionary England, ch. 6 (1969).

of revisionist history had transformed the Magna Carta (1215) from a partisan political document to a declaration of the natural rights of Englishmen, and the Petition of Right (1628) and Bill of Rights (1688-1689), as well as the Declaration of Independence (1776), were usually claimed not to establish new principles but to declare preexisting ones. The third source of natural law doctrine was John Locke's Second Treatise on Civil Government (1690). Reasoning deductively from the pregovernmental "state of nature" to the "social compact" formed to improve on that state, Locke derived both the supremacy of the legislature and limitations on its exercise of powers. Of his three basic rights of individuals — "life, liberty, and estate" — the last was most fundamental: Property was an extension of the individual, and the social compact was largely designed to protect whatever distributions of wealth came about through the varying talents and efforts of the members of society.

These elements of the natural law tradition coalesced in the eighteenth-century American view that

> the written constitution [is] . . . a species of social compact, entered into by sovereign individuals in a state of nature. . . . [G]overnmental authority . . . is a trust which, save for the grant of it effected by the written constitution, were non-existent, and private rights, since they precede the constitution, gain nothing of authoritativeness from being enumerated in it, though possibly something of security. These rights are not, in other words, fundamental because they find mention in the written instrument; they find mention there because fundamental. . . . The written constitution is, in short, but a nucleus or core of a much wider region of private rights, which though not reduced to black and white, are as fully entitled to the protection of government as if defined in the minutest detail.[56]

The natural rights of individuals were generally understood to be those that, through judicial "discovery" and the absorption of the Magna Carta, inhered in the common law. As restated in Blackstone's Commentaries 129-139 (1765), the three "absolute rights of individuals" were: "the right of personal security [which] consists in a person's legal and uninterrupted enjoyment of his life, his limbs, his body, his health, and his reputation"; the right of "personal liberty [which] consists in the power of loco-motion, of changing situation, or moving one's person to whatsoever place one's own inclination may direct, without imprisonment or restraint, unless by due course of law"; and "the absolute right, inherent in every Englishman . . . of property: which consists in the free use, enjoyment, and disposal of all his acquisitions, without any control or diminution, save only by the laws of the land."

Perhaps the most audacious invocation of natural law in our history is Justice Johnson's assertion, in his *Fletcher* concurrence, that he bases his invalidation of Georgia's statute "on a general principle, on the reason and nature of things; a principle which will impose laws even on the Deity." Johnson's suggestion that even God, in effect, has a duty to obey what might be termed "general principles of reason" goes back at least to Plato's dialogue *Euthyphro*, where he asks whether propositions of morality are true simply because God (or the gods) command them — which suggests a certain level of arbitrariness in that God presumably has the authority to propound anything at all — or whether there are preexisting principles of morality that bind even God — which paints a picture of God as a kind of "constitutional monarch" who must remain within the bounds of

---

56. Corwin, The Basic Doctrine of American Constitutional Law, supra n.54, at 247-248.

an external law. Similar questions were debated by Christian theologians of the sixteenth and seventeenth centuries. These questions all involve the nature of "sovereignty." Is it is the essence of "sovereign power" to be absolutely unlimited, or must both earthly and Divine "sovereigns" submit to "general principles"? As we saw with regard to Marshall's argument in *McCulloch,* a central proposition of American constitutionalism is "sovereignty of the people." *How* sovereign is "popular sovereignty"? One well-known assertion, going back to an eighth-century letter by Alcuin to the Emperor Charlemagne, is that "the voice of the people is the voice of God."[57] One way of interpreting this is to say that "the voice of the people" has the very same authority as "the voice of God," i.e., it is limitless in its power. If, on the other hand, one adopts Johnson's view that even the Deity is constrained, that would obviously entail that "the people" as well are similarly constrained.

2.   The Judicial Protection of Vested Rights

The substantive legal issue involved in both *Marbury* and *Fletcher* was the protection of "vested rights." The President was free to appoint or not to appoint Marbury as a justice of the peace. But once Marbury's right to the commission "vested," the Government could no more deprive him of it than a seller of real property could take it back after title had vested in the purchaser. The doctrine of vested rights did not encompass all expectations. In his well-known nineteenth-century treatise, Constitutional Limitations, Thomas Cooley explained:

> [A] right cannot be considered a vested right, unless it is something more than such a mere expectation as may be based upon an anticipated continuance of the present general laws: it must have become a title, legal or equitable, to the present or future enjoyment of property, or to the present or future enforcement of a demand, or a legal exemption from a demand, made by another.[58]

The doctrine assumed, in other words, that the basic structure of entitlements was determined by the common law as modified by legislation — that these determined the procedures by which property interests were created and transferred. But once an interest had vested in an individual — once it *belonged* to her — it was immune from government divestment. As Chancellor James Kent wrote in his comprehensive Commentaries on American Law (1826), a statute "affecting and changing vested rights is very generally considered in this country as founded on unconstitutional principles, and consequently inoperative and void."[59] When Kent characterized a law violating vested rights as *unconstitutional* he was not referring to the U.S. Constitution or even to written state constitutions, but rather to what were understood to be *general* constitutional limitations implicit in all free governments — limitations based on natural rights and the nature of the social compact.

The vested rights doctrine developed and flourished primarily in the state courts. It made its first and least equivocal Supreme Court appearance in Calder v. Bull, 3 U.S. (3 Dall.) 386 (1798).

---

57. Alexander Hamilton, speaking to the Constitutional Convention on June 18, 1787, offered the following response to this maxim: "[I]t is not true to fact. The people are turbulent and changing, they seldom judge or determine right." See 1 Records of the Federal Convention of 1787 at 299 (1937).

58. Thomas Cooley, 2 Constitutional Limitations 749 (Carrington ed., 8th ed. 1927).

59. Quoted in id. at 449.

CALDER v. BULL
3 U.S. (3 Dall.) 386 (1798)

[A Connecticut probate court had disapproved a will designating the respondents as beneficiaries, thus allowing petitioners to inherit as decedent's heirs at law. The Connecticut legislature passed a resolution setting aside the decree and granting a new hearing, at which the will was approved. To petitioners' claim that the legislative act was an ex post facto law in violation of Article I, §10, the Court responded that the clause was limited to criminal legislation. But Justice Chase, who wrote the most comprehensive of several seriatim opinions, went on to consider whether, apart from this or any other specific provision of the Constitution, a government could deprive a citizen of a vested property right.]

CHASE, J.:

I cannot subscribe to the omnipotence of a state legislature, or that it is absolute and without control; although its authority should not be expressly restrained by the Constitution, or fundamental law, of the State. The people of the United States erected their Constitutions, or forms of government, to establish justice, to promote the general welfare, to secure the blessings of liberty; and to protect their persons and property from violence. The purposes for which men enter into society will determine the nature and terms of the social compact; and as they are the foundation of the legislative power, they will decide what are the proper objects of it. The nature and ends of legislative power will limit the exercise of it. This fundamental principle flows from the very nature of our free Republican governments, that no man should be compelled to do what the laws do not require, nor to refrain from acts which the laws permit. There are acts which the Federal or State Legislature cannot do, without exceeding their authority. There are certain vital principles in our free Republican governments, which will determine and overrule an apparent and flagrant abuse of legislative power; as to authorize manifest injustice by positive law; or to take away that security for personal liberty, or private property, for the protection whereof the government was established. An ACT of the Legislature (for I cannot call it a law) contrary to the great first principles of the social compact, cannot be considered a rightful exercise of legislative authority.

The obligation of a law in governments established on express compact, and on republican principles, must be determined by the nature of the power on which it is founded. A few instances will suffice to explain what I mean. A law that punished a citizen for an innocent action, or, in other words, for an act, which, when done, was in violation of no existing law; a law that destroys, or impairs, the lawful private contracts of citizens; a law that makes a man a judge in his own cause; or a law that takes property from A. and gives it to B. It is against all reason and justice, for a people to intrust a Legislature with such powers; and, therefore, it cannot be presumed that they have done it. The genius, the nature, and the spirit of our State Governments, amount to a prohibition of such acts of legislation; and the general principles of law and reason forbid them.

The Legislature may enjoin, permit, forbid, and punish; they may declare new crimes; and establish rules of conduct for all its citizens in future cases; they may command what is right, and prohibit what is wrong; but they cannot change innocence into guilt; or punish innocence as a crime; or violate the right of an antecedent lawful private contract; or the right of private property. To maintain that our Federal or State Legislature possesses such powers, if they had not been expressly restrained; would, in my opinion, be a political heresy, altogether inadmissible in our free republican governments.

[Applying this theory to the case at bar, Justice Chase found that Connecticut's actions had not deprived the petitioners of a vested property right, since no right vested by the first decree.

Justice Iredell, in his separate opinion, challenged the basic premise of Chase's inquiry.]

IREDELL, J.:

It is true, that some speculative jurists have held, that a legislative act against natural justice must, in itself, be void; but I cannot think that, under such a government, any Court of Justice would possess a power to declare it so. Sir William Blackstone, having put the strong case of an act of Parliament which, should authorize a man to try his own cause, explicitly adds, that even in that case, "there is no court that has power to defeat the intent of the Legislature, when couched in such evident and express words, as leave no doubt whether it was the intent of the Legislature, or no." 1 Bl. Comm. 91.

In order, therefore, to guard against so great an evil, it has been the policy of all the American States, which have, individually, framed their state constitutions since the revolution, and of the people of the United States, when they framed the Federal Constitution, to define with precision the objects of the legislative power, and to restrain its exercise within marked and settled boundaries. If any act of Congress, or of the Legislature of a State, violates those constitutional provisions, it is unquestionably void; though, I admit, that as the authority to declare it void is of a delicate and awful nature, the Court will never resort to that authority, but in a clear and urgent case. If, on the other hand, the Legislature of the Union, or the Legislature of any member of the Union, shall pass a law, within the general scope of their constitutional power, the Court cannot pronounce it to be void, merely because it is, in their judgment, contrary to the principles of natural justice. The ideas of natural justice are regulated by no fixed standard; the ablest and the purest men have differed upon the subject; and all that the Court could properly say, in such an event, would be, that the Legislature, possessed of an equal right of opinion, had passed an act which, in the opinion of the judges, was inconsistent with the abstract principles of natural justice.

Discussion

1. Is Justice Chase making an appeal to what might be termed "transcendent" norms of justice, which by definition would be true in all cultures at all times, or, rather, is he arguing that it is a truth of *our* particular form of polity that the norms that he identifies are recognized? The first would count as a "natural law" argument. The latter, however, might be better described as what Professor Philip Bobbitt labels as "ethical" argument, by which he means an appeal to the particular ethos of a society, which may, of course, be quite different from that of other societies.[60]

2. Justice Iredell seems to view Justice Chase as making a "natural law" argument, about which he states that "[t]he ideas of natural justice are regulated by no fixed standard; the ablest and the purest men have differed upon the subject." He could

60. See Philip Bobbitt, Constitutional Interpretation 20-22 (1991).

be interpreted as making two quite different arguments. The first might be termed *ontological:* that is, asking whether transcendent norms of justice really exist in the universe. The second is *epistemological:* Even if one assumes that transcendent moral norms exist, one might doubt whether human beings have adequate means of discerning what they actually are; the reason, according to Iredell, is that the "ablest and the purest men have differed upon the subject." But, of course, it is also true that "the ablest and the purest" judges and scholars have "differed" about many basic issues of constitutional law. Does this prove that there is, for all intents and purposes, no real substance to the entire enterprise that we call constitutional analysis, or only that it is difficult and that very smart (and pure) people of good faith can disagree about important issues? One could, of course, ask similar questions with regard to any discipline, including heated debates among physicists with regard to the relevance of string theory or among neuropsychologists about the nature of human consciousness. In what ways are good faith disagreements about law different from good faith disagreements about scientific truths? In any event, how important is it that lawyers (and law students) work through such philosophical problems to decide the kinds of questions treated in the Chase and Iredell opinions?

3.   The Explicit Federal Constitutional Protection of Rights

The vested rights doctrine aside, judicial protection of individual rights depended mainly on the written provisions of state constitutions and the U.S. Constitution. Article I, §10 prohibited states from passing bills of attainder, ex post facto laws, and laws impairing the obligation of contracts. Article I, §9 applied the first two prohibitions to the federal government and limited the government's power to suspend the writ of habeas corpus. In 1791, the Constitution was supplemented by a Bill of Rights, which the Court held in Barron v. Baltimore, 32 U.S. (7 Pet.) 243 (1833), applied only to the federal government.[61]

4.   The Ninth Amendment[62]

The title of Bennett Patterson's 1955 book, The Forgotten Ninth Amendment, accurately captures the status of this provision of the Bill of Rights throughout most of our constitutional history.[63] Nonetheless, if any provision of the U.S. Constitution seems to embody the concept of natural rights, it is the Ninth Amendment: "The enumeration in the Constitution, of certain rights, shall not be construed to deny or disparage others retained by the people." The purpose of the amendment is ambiguous, however. Was it designed to safeguard individual liberties not enumerated in the first eight amendments or only to protect the states against the national government's assumption of powers not delegated by Articles I, II, and III?

---

61. Does anything in the language of the amendments suggest that some of them might be applicable to the states? Compare the First and Seventh Amendments with the others.

62. See generally Randy Barnett, ed., The Rights Retained by the People: The History and Meaning of the Ninth Amendment (2 vols., 1989, 1993).

63. But see Chapter 8 infra.

Much anti-Federalist opposition to the Constitution in the state conventions focused on the absence of a bill of rights. The Federalist response was that a bill of rights was unnecessary and dangerous — unnecessary because the national government, being one of delegated powers, was not authorized to infringe individual liberties; dangerous because the enumeration would imply the existence of broader powers than were delegated. Recall the critiques of the idea of a written Bill of Rights offered by Hamilton, James Wilson, and James Iredell, Introduction, supra.

James Madison had shared the concern that a Bill of Rights might imply broader federal powers than were granted. Additionally, he wrote to Jefferson,[64] "there is great reason to fear that a positive declaration of some of the most essential rights could not be obtained in the requisite latitude. I am sure that the rights of conscience, in particular, if submitted to public definition would be narrowed much more than they are likely ever to be by an assumed power." Whether because of a change of mind or, as is more likely, a submission to the political demands of his Virginia constituents, Madison became the leading architect of the amendments that would form the Bill of Rights. In presenting to the First Congress the provision that became the Ninth Amendment, Madison explained:[65]

> It has been objected also against a bill of rights, that, by enumerating particular exceptions to the grant of power, it would disparage those rights which were not placed in that enumeration; and it might follow by implication, that those rights which were not singled out, were intended to be assigned into the hands of the General Government, and were consequently insecure. This is one of the most plausible arguments I have ever heard urged against the admission of a bill of rights into this system; but, I conceive, that it may be guarded against. I have attempted it, as gentlemen may see by turning to the last clause of the fourth resolution [the Ninth Amendment]. . . .

Professor Kurt Lash has recently argued that the Ninth Amendment was originally understood as an interpretive rule requiring a narrow (perhaps what Marshall would term a "strict" construction) of national power.[66] Noting the concern expressed at many state conventions against possible abuses of national power and the extent to which the proposed Bill of Rights was a response to such fears, he emphasizes as particularly important several paragraphs toward the conclusion of Madison's speech against the constitutionality of the Bank, supra Chapter 1. There Madison refers to the "explanatory amendments proposed by Congress," including in this group the Ninth Amendment, which he describes "as guarding against a latitude of interpretation." The Tenth Amendment, Madison says, "exclude[s] every source of power not within the constitution itself."

"Madison's argument," writes Professor Lash,

> is easy to follow: The federal government is one of limited enumerated power. All nondelegated powers are reserved to the states. Unduly broad interpretations of these enumerated powers would destroy this principle by allowing the government to invade areas of law reserved to the states. Important powers like those exercised by the Bank Bill are not appropriately derived by implication but require enumeration. The state conventions that ratified the Constitution had been promised that federal power

---

64. 5 Writings of James Madison 271-272 (Hunt ed., 1904) (letter of Oct. 17, 1788).
65. 1 Annals of Cong. 439 (1789).
66. See Kurt Lash, The Lost Original Meaning of the Ninth Amendment, 83 Texas L. Rev. 331 (2004).

would not receive this kind of latitudinous interpretation, and several states made the adoption of a rule rejecting this kind of interpretation a condition of their ratifying the Constitution. Although implied in the original Constitution, an express rule against latitudinarian constructions found its ultimate expression in the Ninth Amendment.[67]

One might ask, of course, whether this is the most natural reading of the text. That is, Professor Lash is making a historical argument rather than appealing to any "obvious" meaning of the text. Moreover, he himself admits that this original understanding of the Ninth Amendment was quickly "lost" to later interpreters, to be replaced by other views as to its meaning. The very rapidity with which it was lost may suggest that, as with many other (perhaps most, or even all) of the Constitution's provisions, there were in fact different views of its purpose and meaning among those who adopted and ratified it.

Furthermore, any attempt to elucidate the amendment's purposes must deal with some enigmatic data. On the one hand, if the amendment were concerned primarily with safeguarding federalism, it seems to make surplusage of the Tenth Amendment, which speaks explicitly of powers "reserved to the States." Can one plausibly respond that the Ninth Amendment is a rule requiring narrow interpretation of those powers that *are* undoubtedly assigned to the national government, whereas the Tenth Amendment refers to powers that could not even be implied from the assigned power? On the other hand, if the amendment were concerned primarily with safeguarding individual liberties, one might expect to find similar provisions in some of the bills of rights of contemporary state constitutions. There is a further complexity here. In 1791, the Ninth Amendment was unique, but the bills of rights of many nineteenth-century state constitutions paraphrase the amendment.[68]

Note: Is Constitutional Law a Comedy or a Tragedy?

Fletcher's rhetoric, including its presentation of the Court as a "court of justice," leads the reader to believe that constitutional cases are likely to have "happy endings," in the specific sense that constitutional norms and the norms of justice, whether defined in terms of natural law or of "general principles which are common to our free institutions," will coincide. Is it possible, though, that legal norms, including constitutional ones, may have a more "tragic" dimension, so that the law and norms of justice will be in opposition rather than joined together?

Consider in this context Marshall's opinion in a non-constitutional case, The Antelope, 23 U.S. (10 Wheat.) 66 (1825), which arose in the context of the international trade in slaves. In 1808 Congress prohibited the importation of slaves into the United States. (Could it have constitutionally done so prior to 1808? See Article I, §9, cl. 1 and Article V.) A series of subsequent federal enactments punished persons engaged in the international slave trade, required forfeiture of their ships, and provided that the Negroes be returned to Africa. The ship Antelope, bearing 280 Africans, most of whom had been seized by pirates from slave ships, was apprehended in international waters off the coast of Florida by a U.S. revenue cutter for suspected violation of the slave trade acts.

67. Id. at 393.
68. See John Ely, Democracy and Distrust 202-204 (1980).

The vice consuls of Spain and Portugal claimed the Africans as the property of citizens of their countries. They denied that the slaves were ever intended to be introduced to the United States in violation of local law; instead, they claimed, the slaves were being shipped to Brazil or Cuba, where the international slave trade remained perfectly legal. The United States appealed from the circuit courts' decision for the foreign claimants. The issue before the Court was whether the federal statutes applied to forfeit slaves owned by foreign nationals.[69] As Marshall put it, the case was one "in which the sacred rights of liberty and of property come in conflict with each other."

The mood suggested by Marshall's opinion is considerably more somber than in Fletcher v. Peck, as he emphasizes that "this court must not yield to feelings which might seduce it from the path of duty, and must obey the mandate of the law." He denounces the slave trade, a traffic "abhorrent . . . to a mind whose original feelings are not blunted by familiarity with the practice," while reminding the reader that "it has[, however,] been sanctioned, in modern times, by the laws of all nations who possess distant colonies, each of whom has engaged in it as a common commercial business, which no other could rightfully interrupt."

Although "the feelings of justice and humanity" have prevailed in several of the American states and in the British parliament to abolish slavery or, at the least, to prohibit the international slave trade, these are, as yet, in effect only local practices, insufficient to change the legal reality of slavery (and the international slave trade) in states that are not so enlightened. Therefore, Marshall argues, it is ultimately irrelevant that slavery (or the slave trade) is "contrary to the law of nature" and "[t]hat every man has a natural right to the fruits of his own labor, is generally admitted," because international law has not yet adopted these principles as general legal norms.

> Throughout Christendom, . . . war is no longer considered, as giving a right to enslave captives. But this triumph of humanity has not been universal. The parties of the modern law of nations do not propagate their principles by force, and Africa has not yet adopted them. Throughout the whole extent of that immense continent, so far as we know its history, it is still the law of nations, that prisoners are slaves. Can those who have themselves renounced this law, be permitted to participate in its effects, by purchasing the beings who are its victims? Whatever might be the answer of a moralist to this question, a jurist must search for its legal solution, in those principles of action which are sanctioned by the usages, the national acts, and the general assent, of that portion of the world of which he considers himself as a part, and to whose law the appeal is made. If we resort to this standard, as the test of international law, the question, as has already been observed, is decided in favor of the legality of the trade. Both Europe and America embarked in it; and for nearly two centuries, it was carried on, without opposition, and without censure. A jurist could not say, that a practice, thus supported, was illegal, and that those engaged in it might be punished, either personally or by deprivation of property. In this commerce thus sanctioned by universal assent, every nation had an equal right to engage. How is this right to be lost? Each may renounce it for its own people; but can this renunciation effect others?
>
> No principle of general law is more universally acknowledged, than the perfect equality of nations. Russia and Geneva have equal rights. It results from this equality,

---

69. The actual facts are considerably more complex. For a rich description of the case and its contents, see John Noonan, Jr., The Antelope: The Ordeal of the Recaptured Africans in the Administrations of James Monroe and John Quincy Adams (1977).

that no one can rightfully impose a rule on another. Each legislates for itself, but its legislation can operate on itself alone. A right, then, which is vested in all, by the consent of all, can be divested only by consent; and this trade, in which all have participated, must remain lawful to those who cannot be induced to relinquish it. As no nation can prescribe a rule for others, none can make a law of nations; and this traffic remains lawful to those whose governments have not forbidden it. If it be consistent with the law of nations, it cannot in itself be piracy. It can be made so only by statute; and the obligation of the statute cannot transcend the legislative power of the state which may enact it.

Thus, said the Court, the United States must recognize the claims of the slave-owners to the return of their property that had been illegitimately seized by pirates (and then brought into American waters by the coast guard). "It follows, that a foreign vessel engaged in the African slave-trade, captured on the high seas, in time of peace, by an American cruiser, and brought in for adjudication, would be restored."

Discussion[70]

1. Although The Antelope does not arise under the Constitution, slavery presented the most divisive constitutional issue of the first 70 years of the Republic. Even if The Antelope did not directly affect domestic slavery, Marshall was well aware that anything the Court said about the matter would be critically read within the United States; he might also have been concerned not to antagonize the two foreign nations whose nationals claimed to own the slaves. Are these legitimate reasons for refusing to enforce the purported slaves' natural right to enjoy the "sacred principle" of liberty?

2. In suggesting that some courts may "have carried the principle of suppression further than a deliberate consideration of the subject would justify," Marshall may have been referring to the circuit court decision in United States v. La Jeune Eugenie, 26 F. Cas. 832 (No. 15,551) (C.C. Mass. 1822), in which Justice Story condemned the slave trade as

> repugnant to the great principles of Christian duty, the dictates of natural religion, the obligations of good faith and morality, and the eternal maxims of social justice. When any trade can be truly said to have these ingredients, it is impossible that it can be consistent with any system of law that purports to rest on the authority of reason or revelation. And it is sufficient to stamp any trade as interdicted by public law, when it can be justly affirmed, that it is repugnant to the general principles of justice and humanity.

Note, though, that Story did not dissent in The Antelope. Moreover, Marshall scarcely seems to deny the immorality of slavery. If slavery violates principles of natural law, how could the Court order the return of any of the Negroes seized on The Antelope?

One answer is found in Marshall's own description of the case as a conflict between the "sacred rights of liberty and of property." One might also turn to the distinction between natural and positive law. In 1772, in Somerset's Case, Lord Mansfield ordered discharged from service a slave who had been brought by his

---

70. See generally Robert Cover, Justice Accused: Antislavery and the Judicial Process (1975).

Virginia master to England, noting that "the state of slavery is of such a nature, that it is incapable of being introduced on any reasons . . . but only by positive law. . . . It is so odious, that nothing can be suffered to support it but positive law."[71] Marshall's decision in The Antelope is consistent with this view if, as seems likely, he regarded the unwritten but venerable "law of nations" as positive law.

3. Robert Cover writes:[72]

In a static and simplistic model of law, the judge caught between law and morality has only four choices. He may apply the law against his conscience. He may apply conscience and be faithless to the law. He may resign. Or he may cheat: He may state that the law is not what he believes it to be; and, thus preserve an appearance (to others) of conformity of law and morality. Once we assume a more realistic model of law and of the judicial process, these four positions become only poles setting limits to a complex field of action and motive. For in a dynamic model, law is always becoming. And the judge has a legitimate role in determining what it is that the law will become.

Had you read only Marshall's opinions in *McCulloch* and *Fletcher,* where would you locate him on a continuum between a "static" and "dynamic" conception of law? What if your only acquaintance with Marshall were The Antelope? Where would you wish your own "model judge" to locate herself?

4. Imagine that someone purchases a parrot abroad (say, in Brazil). This is a rare parrot that is regarded by the United States as an "endangered species." (In the alternative, imagine that the United States, influenced by animal rights activists, regards placing these birds in cages for the amusement of their owners as savage and therefore has banned it.) As a consequence, the United States has passed a law banning "bringing into the territory of the United States" any such parrot. The person purchasing the parrot has no connection with the United States. In fact, she is a citizen of a third country, which has no objection to the importation of parrots. She therefore boards an international flight, on a non-U.S. airline, from Brazil to her home country, with parrot in hand (or cage). Alas, the plane is hijacked in midair by a group who demand that it be diverted to the United States. The plane indeed lands in Miami. As the passengers disembark, waiting for the next plane, the parrot's owner is detained and ordered to give up the parrot to U.S. authorities (who will make every effort to return it to the Amazonian forests where parrots thrive). They tell her that she is lucky not to be charged with a criminal violation of the law prohibiting "bringing" parrots into U.S. territory. Needless to say, she is not impressed by this generosity and demands the return of her property. Who do you think should prevail between the United States and the ostensible "owner"? How, if at all, does your answer relate to your response to The Antelope, a case involving human beings (legally) sold into slavery for shipment to other countries where slavery is also legal?

VI.   *American Indians and the American Political Community*

American Indians — Native Americans — were recognized by European settlers as members of distinct tribal entities even as the settlers proceeded to displace them.

71. Quoted in id. at 6.
72. Id.

The U.S. government frequently negotiated with Indian tribes — although history reveals "numerous accounts of threats, coercion, bribery, and outright fraud by the negotiators for the United States."[73]

Like the issue of slavery, the treatment of Native Americans in American constitutional law also sheds interesting light on the "natural law tradition" underlying the U.S. Constitution as well as the connections (or conflict) between the notions of "courts of law" and "courts of justice" implicit in Fletcher v. Peck and The Antelope. Consider, for example, Chief Justice Marshall's decision in Johnson and Graham's Lessee v. William M'Intosh, 21 U.S. 543 (1823), in which he explained why Native Americans lost the right to lands upon their discovery (and conquest) by European states:

> Conquest gives a title which the Courts of the conqueror cannot deny, whatever the private and speculative opinions of individuals may be, respecting the original justice of the claim which has been successfully asserted. The British government, which was then our government, and whose rights have passed to the United States, asserted a title to all the lands occupied by Indians, within the chartered limits of the British colonies. It asserted also a limited sovereignty over them, and the exclusive right of extinguishing the title which occupancy gave to them. These claims have been maintained and established as far west as the river Mississippi, by the sword. The title to a vast portion of the lands we now hold, originates in them. It is not for the Courts of this country to question the validity of this title, or to sustain one which is incompatible with it.
>
> Although we do not mean to engage in the defence of those principles which Europeans have applied to Indian title, they may, we think, find some excuse, if not justification, in the character and habits of the people whose rights have been wrested from them. . . .
>
> However extravagant the pretension of converting the discovery of an inhabited country into conquest may appear; if the principle has been asserted in the first instance, and afterwards sustained; if a country has been acquired and held under it; if the property of the great mass of the community originates in it, it becomes the law of the land, and cannot be questioned. So, too, with respect to the concomitant principle, that the Indian inhabitants are to be considered merely as occupants, to be protected, indeed, while in peace, in the possession of their lands, but to be deemed incapable of transferring the absolute title to others. However this restriction may be opposed to natural right, and to the usages of civilized nations, yet, if it be indispensable to that system under which the country has been settled, and be adapted to the actual condition of the two people, it may, perhaps, be supported by reason, and certainly cannot be rejected by Courts of justice.

Is Marshall suggesting that natural justice must yield to rights established by force of arms, or is he suggesting that there is in fact no conflict? What, if anything, does this tell us about the meaning of the natural law tradition?

Indians were not deemed citizens of the new United States. Although the 1790 federal naturalization law restricting admission to free white aliens appeared to foreclose Indian naturalization, several subsequent treaties and statutes contemplated the possibility of Indian citizenship. For example, the Cherokee treaties of 1817 and 1819 included provisions granting land to heads of families "who may wish to

---

73. Wilkinson and Volkman, Judicial Review of Indian Treaty Abrogation: "As Long as Water Flows or Grass Grows upon the Earth" — How Long a Time Is That? 63 Calif. L. Rev. 601, 610 (1975).

become citizens of the United States."[74] It was clear, though, that an Indian who chose to remain a formal member of his tribe could not become a citizen. As James Kettner writes, "the tribes themselves . . . could be considered quasi-sovereign nations, enforcing their own laws and customs and requiring the immediate allegiance of their members."[75] Just as the tension between nation and states, exemplified by *McCulloch*, has remained a pervasive reality in American constitutional law up to the present, so too the relations between Indian tribes and the other units of American government have never been fully resolved. One set of questions involves the power of the national government over Indian tribes. Another concerns whether the states possess any regulatory powers over tribes and their members. One of the earliest judicial decisions involving these relations was Cherokee Nation v. Georgia, 30 U.S. (5 Pet.) 1 (1831). It provoked what Charles Warren, a leading historian of the Supreme Court, termed "the most serious crisis in the history of the Court."[76] At the height of the crisis, former President John Quincy Adams exclaimed that "the Union is in the most imminent danger of dissolution."[77]

Through various treaties with the United States the Cherokees had been allotted approximately four million acres of lands within the territory of Georgia. In 1827 gold was discovered on tribal lands, and the same year the Cherokee Nation declared itself an independent nation and adopted a constitution.[78] The Georgia legislature responded by passing "Indian laws" that, among other things, annulled all of the Cherokee "laws, usages, and customs," divided their lands into separate counties under state jurisdiction, and prohibited the Cherokee legislature and courts from meeting. As an assertion of Georgia's sovereignty over the tribe, the state tried and convicted George Tassels for an 1830 homicide he committed on the reservation against another Cherokee. Tassel appealed to the U.S. Supreme Court, which granted a writ of error directing the state to appear. In response, Georgia's governor ordered Tassel's immediate execution.

The Cherokee Nation appealed to the federal government to support their claims against Georgia's abrogation of its treaty rights. President Jackson, who was promoting a policy of Indian removal west of the Mississippi, responded that "the President of the United States has no power to protect them against the laws of Georgia."[79] The Cherokee Nation then attempted to invoke original jurisdiction of the U.S. Supreme Court by describing itself as "a foreign state, not owing allegiance to the United States, nor to any state of this union. . . ."[80] On the merits, the Cherokee Nation claimed that Georgia had violated the Contract Clause, since "treaties . . . are contracts of the highest character and of the most solemn obligation."

The Court rejected the Cherokee Nation's assertion that it was a foreign state and dismissed the claim for lack of jurisdiction. There was no majority opinion. Chief Justice Marshall wrote an opinion for himself and Justice McLean alone. Justices Johnson and Baldwin concurred in the result, but not the reasoning. Justice Thompson dissented, joined by Justice Story, arguing that the actual practice of the

74. James Kettner, The Development of American Citizenship, 1608-1870, at 292 (1978).
75. Id. at 294.
76. Charles Warren, The Supreme Court in American History 189 (1923).
77. A. Beveridge, John Marshall 544 (1919).
78. See G. Edward White, The Marshall Court and Cultural Change 715 (1987).
79. 30 U.S. (5 Pet.) 8.
80. Id. at 2.

United States — through its use of treaties, for example — confirmed that it treated the Cherokees as a separate foreign nation.

Chief Justice Marshall argued that

> Though the Indians are acknowledged to have an unquestionable, and, heretofore, unquestioned right to the lands they occupy, until that right shall be extinguished by a voluntary cession to our government; yet it may well be doubted whether those tribes which reside within the acknowledged boundaries of the United States can, with strict accuracy, be denominated foreign nations. They may, more correctly, perhaps, be denominated domestic dependent nations. They occupy a territory to which we assert a title independent of their will. . . . Meanwhile they are in a state of pupilage. Their relation to the United States resembles that of a ward to his guardian.
>
> They look to our government for protection; rely upon its kindness and its power; appeal to it for relief to their wants; and address the president as their great father. They and their country are considered by foreign nations, as well as by ourselves, as being so completely under the sovereignty and dominion of the United States, that any attempt to acquire their lands, or to form a political connexion with them, would be considered by all as an invasion of our territory, and an act of hostility.

Marshall also pointed to the fact that the commerce clause specifically distinguishes the regulation of "commerce with foreign nations, and among the several states, and with the Indian tribes." Finally, Marshall suggested that the case was inappropriate for the judiciary in any event, because it "requires us to control the legislature of Georgia, and to restrain the exertion of its physical force. . . . It savours too much of the exercise of political power to be within the proper province of the judicial department." Justice Johnson concurred:

> With the morality of the case I have no concern; I am called upon to consider it as a legal question. . . .
>
> I think it very clear that the constitution neither speaks of them as states or foreign states, but as just what they were, Indian tribes; an anomaly unknown to the books that treat of states, and which the law of nations would regard as nothing more than wandering hordes, held together only by ties of blood and habit, and having neither laws or government, beyond what is required in a savage state. The distinction is clearly made in that section which vests in Congress power to regulate commerce between the United States with foreign nations and the Indian tribes. . . .

Johnson, however, explained that had the issue been up to him alone, he would have "put my rejection of this notion upon the nature of the claim set up, exclusively."

> I cannot entertain a doubt that it is one of a political character altogether, and wholly unfit for the cognizance of a judicial tribunal. There is no possible view of the subject, that I can perceive, in which a Court of justice can take jurisdiction of the questions made in the bill. . . .
>
> What [do the Cherokee] allegations exhibit but a state of war, and the fact of invasion? . . . [T]he contest is distinctly a contest for empire. It is not a case of meum and tuum in the judicial but in the political sense. Not an appeal to laws but to force. A case in which a sovereign undertakes to assert his right upon his sovereign responsibility; to right himself, and not to appeal to any arbiter but the sword, for the justice of his cause. . . . In the exercise of sovereign right, the sovereign is sole arbiter of his own justice. The penalty or wrong is war and subjugation. . . .

What these people may have a right to claim of the executive power is one thing: whether we are to be the instruments to compel another branch of the government to make good the stipulations of treaties, is a very different question. Courts of justice are properly excluded from all considerations of policy, and therefore are very unfit instruments to control the action of that branch of government; which may often be compelled by the highest considerations of public policy to withhold even the exercise of a positive duty. . . .

Discussion

1. Although there was no majority opinion in *Cherokee Nation*, Marshall's description of Native Americans as "domestic dependent nations" greatly influenced the course of Indian law to the present day. See the discussions in Chapters 4 and 6, supra.

2. In what ways does the resolution desired by the Cherokees savor more "of the exercise of political power" than the Court's striking down Maryland's tax in *McCulloch* or invalidating Georgia's attempted rescission of the Yazoo land grants in *Fletcher*? Should the Supreme Court generally attempt to avoid accepting jurisdiction when it is foreseeable that a given decision might be met by outright defiance by those to whom it is directed? Professor White noted the widespread perception at the time that "if the Cherokees should win on the jurisdictional issue, and also on the merits, Georgia and the Jackson administration, with the tacit support of Congress, might well decline to endorse the Court's judgment, thereby isolating the Court."[81] Indeed, Georgia symbolized its view that the dispute was entirely a domestic matter by refusing even to appear before the Court to present its opposition to the Cherokees' position.

3. Describe Johnson's mode of analysis. How does it square with his concurrence in Fletcher v. Peck? Can a judge who believes that ascertainable norms of natural justice bind even the Deity, let alone states of the United States, adopt the strict separation between law and morality that is suggested in the first paragraph of opinion? Note that Johnson also suggests that "courts of justice" can say nothing about the exercise of brute force or conquest, or about the exercise of "policy" by the executive branch. How can this be reconciled with his stated views about natural justice?

4. In Worcester v. Georgia, 31 U.S. (6 Pet.) 515 (1832), the Court, with only Justice Baldwin dissenting, held that Georgia's anti-Cherokee laws were unconstitutional. The State had sentenced Worcester to four years' imprisonment for residing within Cherokee lands without procuring a license from Georgia. "The Cherokee nation," Chief Justice Marshall wrote, "is a distinct community, occupying its own territory . . . , in which the laws of Georgia can have no force. . . . The whole intercourse between the United States and this nation, is, by our constitution and laws, vested in the government of the United States." It was this decision that supposedly led to the almost certainly apocryphal remark attributed to President Jackson, "John Marshall has made his decision; now let him enforce it."[82] Even if, as many scholars believe, Jackson did not actually say this, it almost certainly described his attitude. The Supreme Court's decision, however much it seemingly protected the Cherokees from Georgia, did nothing to protect them from the national govern-

---

81. White, at 723.
82. Leonard Baker, John Marshall: A Life in Law 745 (1974).

ment of the United States. Led by Jackson, the United States embarked on the policy that forced most Cherokees to march on the "Trail of Tears" to forced relocation in Oklahoma.[83]

Note: The Property Rights of Enemy Aliens

Almost all of the cases in this chapter can be said to be united, in some sense, around the theme of what Marshall calls the "sacred right" of property. This is obvious with regard to *Fletcher*, Little v. Barreme, The Antelope, and Johnson v. McIntosh. It can even be said to be present with regard to William Marbury, who, after all, was in effect claiming a vested right to enjoy the fruits of his appointment by President Adams as a justice of the peace. Consider in this context Brown v. U.S., 12 U.S. (8 Cranch) 110 (1814), which arose in the aftermath of the War of 1812 between the United States and Great Britain. The particular case involves the seizure of an American ship following the outbreak of the war. It contained property belonging to a British subject, who was, therefore, an "enemy alien," and the United States claimed the right to confiscate the property (although not the ship).

As John Marshall wrote in his opinion for the Court, "It does not appear that the seizure was made under any instructions from the president of the United States; nor is there any evidence of its having his sanction. . . . On the contrary, it is admitted that the seizure was made by an individual, and the libel [claiming U.S. ownership of the property through confiscation] filed at his instance, by the district attorney who acted from his own impressions of what appertained to his duty." The circuit court below, reversing the district court, "condemned the pine timber as enemy property forfeited to the United States," and appeal was taken to the Supreme Court. Marshall defined "the material question" as "this. Can the pine timber . . . be condemned as prize of war?" The answer depended on what followed from Congress's "Declaration of War," under Article I of the Constitution. Marshall treated the fact that the property was on a seized ship as of no fundamental importance, and his opinion treated the larger question of whether a Declaration of War automatically served to seize the property of enemy aliens located in the United States.

> Respecting the power of government no doubt is entertained. That war gives to the sovereign full right to take the persons and confiscate the property of the enemy wherever found, is conceded. . . . [W]hen the sovereign authority shall choose to bring it into operation, the judicial department must give effect to its will. But until that will shall be expressed, no power of condemnation can exist in the Court.
>
> The questions to be decided by the Court are:
>
> 1st. May enemy's property, found on land at the commencement of hostilities, be seized and condemned as a necessary consequence of the declaration of war?
>
> 2d. Is there any legislative act which authorizes such seizure and condemnation?
>
> Since, in this country, from the structure of our government, proceedings to condemn the property of an enemy found within our territory at the declaration of war, can be sustained only upon the principle that they are instituted in execution of some existing law, we are led to ask, Is the declaration of war such a law? Does that declaration, by its own operation, so vest the property of the enemy in the government, as to

83. See John Ehle, Trail of Tears: The Rise and Fall of the Cherokee Nation (1988).

support proceedings for its seizure and confiscation, or does it vest only a right, the assertion of which depends on the will of the sovereign power? . . .

Even Bynkershoek, who maintains the broad principle, that in war every thing done against an enemy is lawful; that he may be destroyed, though unarmed and defenceless; that fraud, or even poison, may be employed against him; that a most unlimited right is acquired to his person and property; admits that war does not transfer to the sovereign a debt due to his enemy; and, therefore, if payment of such debt be not exacted, peace revives the former right of the creditor; "because," he says, "the occupation which is had by war consists more in fact than in law." . . .

[Marshall goes on to consider similar arguments from Vattel and Chitty, two eminent writers on international law.]

. . . . It may be considered as the opinion of all who have written on the jus belli, that war gives the right to confiscate, but does not itself confiscate the property of the enemy; and their rules go to the exercise of this right.

The constitution of the United States was framed at a time when this rule, introduced by commerce in favor of moderation and humanity, was received throughout the civilized world. In expounding that constitution, a construction ought not lightly to be admitted which would give to a declaration of war an effect in this country it does not possess elsewhere, and which would fetter that exercise of entire discretion respecting enemy property, which may enable the government to apply to the enemy the rule that he applies to us.

If we look to the constitution itself, we find this general reasoning much strengthened by the words of that instrument.

That the declaration of war has only the effect of placing the two nations in a state of hostility, of producing a state of war, of giving those rights which war confers; but not of operating, by its own force, any of those results, such as a transfer of property, which are usually produced by ulterior measures of government, is fairly deducible from the enumeration of powers which accompanies that of declaring war. "Congress shall have power" — "to declare war, grant letters of marque and reprisal, and make rules concerning captures on land and water." It would be restraining this clause within narrower limits than the words themselves import, to say that the power to make rules concerning captures on land and water, is to be confined to captures which are exterritorial. If it extends to rules respecting enemy property found within the territory, then we perceive an express grant to congress of the power in question as an independent substantive power, not included in that of declaring war. . . .

The proposition that a declaration of war does not, in itself, enact a confiscation of the property of the enemy within the territory of the belligerent, is believed to be entirely free from doubt. Is there in the act of congress, by which war is declared against Great Britain, any expression which would indicate such an intention?

[Marshall determines that there is no such act of Congress.]

[I]t is considered as proved that the legislature has not confiscated enemy property which was within the United States at the declaration of war, and that this sentence of condemnation cannot be sustained.

One view, however, has been taken of this subject which deserves to be further considered.

It is urged that, in executing the laws of war, the executive may seize and the Courts condemn all property which, according to the modern law of nations, is subject to confiscation, although it might require an act of the legislature to justify the condemnation of that property which, according to modern usage, ought not to be confiscated.

This argument must assume for its basis the position that modern usage constitutes a rule which acts directly upon the thing itself by its own force, and not through the sovereign power. This position is not allowed. This usage is a guide which the sovereign follows or abandons at his will. The rule, like other precepts of morality, of humanity, and even of wisdom, is addressed to the judgment of the sovereign; and although it cannot be disregarded by him without obloquy, yet it may be disregarded.

The rule is, in its nature, flexible. It is subject to infinite modification. It is not an immutable rule of law, but depends on political considerations which may continually vary.

Commercial nations, in the situation of the United States, have always a considerable quantity of property in the possession of their neighbors. When war breaks out, the question, what shall be done with enemy property in our country, is a question rather of policy than of law. The rule which we apply to the property of our enemy, will be applied by him to the property of our citizens. Like all other questions of policy, it is proper for the consideration of a department which can modify it at will; not for the consideration of a department which can pursue only the law as it is written. It is proper for the consideration of the legislature, not of the executive or judiciary.

It appears to the Court, that the power of confiscating enemy property is in the legislature, and that the legislature has not yet declared its will to confiscate property which was within our territory at the declaration of war.

[Justice Story dissented.]

Discussion

1. Given Marshall's concluding paragraphs, what is the significance of his statement that "it does not appear that the seizure was made under any instructions from the president of the United States; nor is there any evidence of its having his sanction"? Recall Little v. Barreme, where President Adams's having instructed the seizure of the ship was found irrelevant because of the lack of statutory authority. Should *Brown* have come out any differently had President Madison explicitly ordered that all locatable property of "enemy aliens" should be seized and confiscated by the United States? (Why should we care whether the seizure of enemy property, which Marshall admits is constitutionally permissible, is authorized by Congress instead of the president?)

2. Professors Curtis Bradley and Jack Goldsmith note[84] that *Brown* was decided in the era in which the presidential war power was "still in its infancy," and when Congress micromanaged wars. The Court's requirement in *Brown* of specific congressional authorization for seizure of enemy property probably did not survive the Civil War, in which President Lincoln and the Supreme Court together greatly expanded presidential war powers, including the power to seize both enemy property and neutral vessels operating in violation of a blockade, even in the absence of specific congressional authorization. See Chapter 3, infra. Does this conclusion, which is undoubtedly correct descriptively, demonstrate that either *Brown* or the

84. Curtis Bradley and Jack Goldsmith, Congressional Authorization and the War on Terrorism, 118 Harvard L. Rev. 2047, 2093-2094 (2005) (quoting Louis Henkin, Foreign Affairs and the United States Constitution 106 (2d ed. 1996)).

later cases were wrong or, rather, that the meaning of the Constitution constantly (and inevitably) changes as new contexts present themselves?

3. Professor Sarah Cleveland has cited *Brown* for the proposition that from the earliest era of constitutional decisionmaking, international law has been consulted as a means of giving meaning to the terms of the U.S. Constitution itself.[85] That is, the central issue in *Brown* is the meaning of a "declaration of war," and Marshall's answer is basically derived from the writings of foreign authorities on international law like Cornelius Bynkershoek, a Dutch author who wrote in the early eighteenth century; Emmerich de Vattel, the Swiss author of The Law of Nations (1758); and Joseph Chitty, an English author whose book, A Practical Treatise on the Law of Nations: Relative to the Legal Effect of War on the Commerce of Belligerents and Neutrals . . . was published in Boston in 1812. She also points out that Marshall's opinion in *M'Intosh,* with its emphasis on the rights attached to "conquest," also drew heavily on the law of nations. She notes as well that the "law of nations" is not necessarily "progressive" (at least in contemporary terms). That is, international law will be no better than the dominant nations that are, by and large, its de facto authors, whether through formal treaty or behavior that comes to be recognized as "customary international law." Thus in *Brown,* international law can be said to be "rights protective" with regard to private individuals (who happen to be enemy aliens) and their property, whereas in *M'Intosh* it very definitely does not protect the rights of Native Americans.

VII.   Women's Citizenship in the Antebellum Era

The preceding two sections examined the constitutional status of "outsider" or "marginalized" groups in the Early Republic: slaves and American Indians. We turn now to a third group: women. In 1776 Abigail Adams had beseeched her husband John to "[r]emember the Ladies" while drawing up "the new Code of Laws" for the nascent United States of America.[86] Although unlike slaves or Indians, women were deemed citizens of the United States at the time of the founding, they were nevertheless denied political rights, based on a theory about the relationship between the obligations of political citizenship, economic dependency, and family structure.

At the time of the founding, the franchise was generally restricted to propertied white males on the grounds that people should not be able to vote unless they possessed sufficient independence to exercise the franchise wisely. Dependent individuals included women, children, servants, slaves, apprentices, journeymen, and other propertyless men who labored for others. These individuals were thought to lack independent political judgment (and therefore the capacity to participate in

---

85. See Sarah H. Cleveland, Our International Constitution, 31 Yale J. Int'l L. 1 (2006).

86. Abigail Adams to John Adams (March 31, 1776), in The Book of Abigail and John: Selected Letters from the Adams Family, 1762-1784, at 120-121 (L.H. Butterfield et al. eds., 1975). Chiding her husband on the very grounds on which the Revolution was fought, Abigail reminded John that "[a]ll men would be tyrants if they could. If particular care and attention is not paid to the Ladies we are determined to foment a Rebelion, and will not hold ourselves bound by any laws in which we have no voice, or Representation." Id. John Adams's jocular reply presages the basic argument that would be made against women's political rights for two centuries: "We [men] dare not exert our power in its full Latitude. We are obliged to go fair, and softly and in Practice you know we are the subjects. We have only the Name of Masters." John Adams to Abigail Adams (April 14, 1776), id. at 122-123.

governance) because their vote would likely be controlled by people of property upon whom they depended.[87] This political theory of suffrage and dependency was also connected to a theory about families and family governance. Women, slaves, servants, and apprentices were dependent on, and hence governed by, the male head of a propertied household. The common law regarded relations between husband and wife, parent and child, and master and servant, slave, or apprentice as "domestic relations." The law had special doctrines for each of these status relationships. In general, these relations were hierarchical and reciprocal: The master of the household was obligated to support and represent the interests of his dependents, and they in turn were obligated to serve and obey him as head of the household. Because the master of the house represented the interests of the family as a whole, it was thought appropriate that he alone should have the right to vote.

The common law rules of coverture or marital status spelled out the legal terms of men's governance over women. Husbands had rights to a wife's paid and unpaid labor, and most property that she brought into the marriage. The wife was obligated to serve and obey her husband, and he was obligated to support and represent her in the legal system. Wives could not sue in the courts or make contracts without their husbands' consent; in turn husbands were legally responsible for many aspects of their wives' conduct.[88] The marital status rules simultaneously regulated women's legal rights, the structure of family relations, and social relations between the sexes. These rules were supported by the common law legal fiction of marital unity: the wife's legal identity was merged into the husband's, so that in the eyes of the law, husband and wife were one. As Blackstone put it: "By marriage, the husband and wife are one person in law: that is, the very being or legal existence of the woman is suspended during the marriage, or at least is incorporated and consolidated into that of the husband; under whose wing, protection and cover, she performs everything." 1 William Blackstone, Commentaries 430 (1765).

Restrictions on the franchise were status-based regulations: One's political rights were based on one's position in a larger social structure and social hierarchy. Being able to vote meant that one had a particular status in a family and thus in society; conversely, lacking the right to vote also was correlated with one's subordinate position within a family and in society.

Although these status-based rules seemed at odds with the revolutionary ideology of human liberty and equality, they were justified by a distinction between the public realm of active citizenship and public economic activity and the private realm of domestic relations. Relations between heads of households were relations between free and equal citizens in a public realm; relations between men and women, or between masters and servants, were domestic relations within a private household.[89]

---

87. Robert Steinfeld, "Property and Suffrage in the Early American Republic," 41 Stan. L. Rev. 335, 340 (1989). In short, persons who were dependent on others economically or in households were deemed unfit to govern because they were subject to the governance of others. Reva B. Siegel, Collective Memory and the Nineteenth Amendment: Reasoning about "the Woman Question" in the Discourse of Sex Discrimination, in History, Memory, and the Law 131-182 (Sarat & Kearns eds., 1999), at 144.

88. Norma Basch, In the Eyes of the Law: Women, Marriage and Property in Nineteenth-Century New York, 47-55, 70-112 (1982). Although married women could not technically own property in their own right, wealthy families could take advantage of special trust arrangements and equitable devices that gave women limited autonomy over finances. See Susanne Lebsock, Free Women of Petersburg: Status and Culture in a Southern Town, 1784-1860 (1984); Basch, at 70-112 (discussing the equitable separate estate for wives).

89. Christopher Tomlins, Subordination, Authority, Law: Subjects in Labor History, 47 International Labor and Working-Class Historian 56, 74 (1995).

Even so, the theory of coverture faced other theoretical difficulties. As Linda Kerber puts it, "If [a woman] could not make a private contract, how could she enter into the social contract" and become a citizen in the first place?[90] The Supreme Court faced the question of women's political citizenship for the first time in Shanks v. DuPont, 28 U.S. (3 Peters) 242 (1830). The heirs of Ann Shanks sued to recover lands that had been bequeathed to her. Born in the colonies, Ann Shanks had married a British officer in 1781 during the Revolutionary War, and had moved to England. If Shanks had become a British subject, her heirs could recover under the peace treaty signed with Great Britain.

Justice Story held that a married women's "political rights" to choose her country of allegiance were not affected by her loss of independent property and contractual rights under the common law rules of coverture. Thus, women did not automatically lose the right to American citizenship by marrying aliens. However, because Ann Shanks freely chose to live "voluntarily under British protection," she was deemed to have chosen British citizenship. *Shanks* was the Supreme Court's first recognition that women had any form of political rights in the face of the common law's theories of marital status.[91]

In the first decades of the nineteenth century, propertyless white males increasingly demanded and obtained suffrage rights.[92] During the same period the first movements for women's rights began, growing out of evangelical movements for temperance and the abolition of slavery.[93]

These early movements for women's rights culminated in the first women's rights convention at Seneca Falls, New York, on July 19 and 20, 1848. The convention issued a Declaration of Sentiments that demanded both suffrage for women and reform of the marital status laws. The Declaration of Sentiments was explicitly based on the language of the Declaration of Independence. It argued that "all men and women are created equal," and substituted for the Declaration's list of grievances against King George a series of examples "of repeated injuries and usurpations on the part of man toward woman, having in direct object the establishment of an absolute tyranny over her." Among these were that:

> He has never permitted her to exercise her inalienable right to the elective franchise.
> He has compelled her to submit to laws, in the formation of which she had no voice.
> He has withheld from her rights which are given to the most ignorant and degraded men — both natives and foreigners.
> Having deprived her of this first right of a citizen, the elective franchise, thereby leaving her without representation in the halls of legislation, he has oppressed her on all sides.

90. Linda K. Kerber, No Constitutional Right to Be Ladies: Women and the Obligations of Citizenship 15 (1998).

91. Shanks was not the end of the story, however. In 1907 Congress passed a statute which specifically revoked the citizenship of American women who married alien husbands. This statute was upheld in MacKenzie v. Hare, 239 U.S. 299 (1915), on the theory that Congress had the right to treat marriage to a foreigner as equivalent to voluntary expatriation. Justice McKenna explained that the "ancient principle" of the common law that "husband and wife are one" and subject to the husband's "dominance" justified Congress's decision. The Cable Act of 1922, passed in response to MacKenzie, preserved citizenship rights for married women if their husbands were from countries whose subjects were eligible for U.S. citizenship. At the time of passage this excluded persons from China and Japan. For a general discussion, see Nancy F. Cott, Marriage and Women's Citizenship in the United States, 1830-1934, 103 Am. Hist. Rev. 1440 (1998).

92. Steinfeld, at 353-360.

93. Eleanor Flexner, Century of Struggle: The Woman's Rights Movement in the United States, 41-52, 181-186 (1959); Ellen Carol Dubois, Feminism and Suffrage: The Emergence of an Independent Women's Movement in America, 1848-1869 (1978).

He has made her, if married, in the eye of the law, civilly dead.

He has taken from her all right in property, even to the wages she earns.

He has made her, morally, an irresponsible being, as she can commit many crimes, with impunity, provided they be done in the presence of her husband. In the covenant of marriage, she is compelled to promise obedience to her husband, he becoming, to all intents and purposes, her master — the law giving him power to deprive her of her liberty, and to administer chastisement.

He has so framed the laws of divorce, as to what shall be the proper causes of divorce; in case of separation, to whom the guardianship of the children shall be given, as to be wholly regardless of the happiness of women — the law, in all cases, going upon the false supposition of the supremacy of man, and giving all power into his hands.

After depriving her of all rights as a married woman, if single and the owner of property, he has taxed her to support a government which recognizes her only when her property can be made profitable to it.

He has monopolized nearly all the profitable employments, and from those she is permitted to follow, she receives but a scanty remuneration.

He closes against her all the avenues to wealth and distinction, which he considers most honorable to himself. As a teacher of theology, medicine, or law, she is not known.

He has denied her the facilities for obtaining a thorough education — all colleges being closed against her.

He allows her in Church as well as State, but a subordinate position, claiming Apostolic authority for her exclusion from the ministry, and with some exceptions, from any public participation in the affairs of the Church.

He has created a false public sentiment, by giving to the world a different code of morals for men and women, by which moral delinquencies which exclude women from society, are not only tolerated but deemed of little account in man.

He has usurped the prerogative of Jehovah himself, claiming it as his right to assign for her a sphere of action, when that belongs to her conscience and her God.

He has endeavored, in every way that he could to destroy her confidence in her own powers, to lessen her self-respect, and to make her willing to lead a dependent and abject life.

Now, in view of this entire disfranchisement of one-half the people of this country, their social and religious degradation — in view of the unjust laws above mentioned, and because women do feel themselves aggrieved, oppressed, and fraudulently deprived of their most sacred rights, we insist that they have immediate admission to all the rights and privileges which belong to them as citizens of these United States.

By the 1840s a few states had already begun to pass "married women's property acts" that allowed married women to own real property acquired before or during marriage. By the 1850s, state legislatures began to pass "earnings statutes" that allowed women to make contracts and gave them property rights in earnings for personal labor other than domestic labor they performed in their homes or labor they performed for family members. However, these statutes preserved the doctrine of marital service, by which men still owned the right to women's labor in the home.[94]

The struggle for women's suffrage was less effective. Before the Civil War, many women's rights advocates continued to work within abolitionist organizations, hoping that securing rights for blacks would also result in universal suffrage for men and women. Nevertheless, after the war the Reconstruction Republicans wrote

94. See Reva B. Siegel, Home As Work: The First Woman's Rights Claims Concerning Wives' Household Labor, 1850-1880, 103 Yale L.J. 1073 (1994).

the Fourteenth and Fifteenth Amendments to enfranchise freed men without enfranchising women.[95] They continued to justify this exclusion on the republican theory that linked the rights of political government to family structure and relations of dependence. Society was naturally organized into families whose heads were supposed to speak for them. Women were already indirectly or virtually represented by the male heads of their families — either their husbands or their fathers — who had legal control over them. Moreover, "woman suffrage would destroy the family by introducing discord into marital relations and distracting women from their primary duties as mothers."[96]

Discussion

1. The Seneca Falls Declaration of Sentiments does not invoke a single provision of the antebellum Constitution; instead its language tracks the Declaration of Independence. (Interestingly, however, the Declaration of Sentiments demands "the rights and privileges . . . [of] citizens of the United States," very similar to the language that eventually finds its way into the Fourteenth Amendment.) Note that many of the abolitionists looked to the Declaration as a justification for their ideas about equality under the Constitution, especially because there was no Equal Protection Clause in the Constitution before the Civil War. What considerations make reliance on the Declaration an appropriate or inappropriate form of constitutional argument? Is the Declaration less relevant to constitutional interpretation now because we have an Equal Protection Clause?

2. The Declaration of Sentiments models demands for reform along the lines of the egalitarian republican theory expressed in the Declaration of Independence. That republican theory, however, presumed equality only among heads of households and depended on inequality and even hierarchy within the family unit. The economic and political interests of families, in turn, were identified with the economic and political interests of the men who headed those families. If we took the demands of the early women's rights advocates seriously, what would the egalitarian principles of the Declaration mean for family life? Note that the coverture rules were abolished and suffrage was granted to women by the beginning of the twentieth century. In subsequent chapters, and especially in Chapter 7, we examine whether this has been enough to guarantee women a full measure of constitutional equality.

VIII. *Regulation of the Interstate Economy*

GIBBONS v. OGDEN
22 U.S. (9 Wheat.) 1 (1824)

[The New York State Legislature granted Robert Livingston and Robert Fulton the exclusive right to operate steamboats in New York waters for a period of years. Livingston and Fulton assigned to Ogden the exclusive right to operate steamboats between New York City and various places in New Jersey. Ogden brought this action

---

95. Ellen Carol Dubois, "Outgrowing the Compact of the Fathers: Equal Rights, Woman Suffrage, and the United States Constitution 1820-1878," 74 J. of Am. Hist. 836-852 (1987). See also the discussion of the struggle for woman suffrage in Chapter 4, infra.
96. Siegel, Collective Memory, at 149.

in New York Chancery Court to enjoin Gibbons from operating steamboats between New York and Elizabethtown, New Jersey. Gibbons responded that his boats were licensed pursuant to a 1793 Act of Congress entitled "an act for enrolling and licensing ships and vessels to be employed in the coasting trade and fisheries, and for regulating the same," and that the licenses entitled him to navigate between New York and New Jersey notwithstanding the state-granted monopoly.

The New York courts held for Ogden. The state appellate court held that the federal statute was designed solely "to establish a criterion of *national character,* with a view to enforce the laws which impose *discriminating duties* [favoring] *American* vessels [over] those of foreign countries. The term 'license' seems not be used in the sense . . . [of] a *permit to trade,*" because "it is perfectly clear that such a vessel, coasting from one state to another, would have exactly the same right to trade, and the same right of transit, whether she had the coasting license or not. . . . Whether Congress have the power to authorize the coasting trade to be carried on, in vessels propelled by steam, so as to give a *paramount right,* in opposition to the special license given by this state, is a question not yet presented to us. No such act of Congress yet exists. . . ." The Supreme Court reversed.]

MARSHALL, C.J. . . .

As preliminary to the very able discussions of the constitution, which we have heard from the bar, and as having some influence on its construction, reference has been made to the political situation of these states, anterior to its formation. It has been said, that they were sovereign, were completely independent, and were connected with each other only by a league. This is true. But when these allied sovereigns converted their league into a government, when they converted their congress of ambassadors, deputed to deliberate on their common concerns, and to recommend measures of general utility, into a legislature, empowered to enact laws on the most interesting subjects, the whole character in which the states appear, underwent a change, the extent of which must be determined by a fair consideration of the instrument by which that change was effected.

This instrument contains an enumeration of powers expressly granted by the people to their government. It has been said, that these powers ought to be construed strictly. . . . What do gentlemen mean, by a strict construction? If they contend only against that enlarged construction, which would extend words beyond their natural and obvious import, we might question the application of the term, but should not controvert the principle. If they contend for that narrow construction which, in support of some theory not to be found in the constitution, would deny to the government those powers which the words of the grant, as usually understood, import, and which are consistent with the general views and objects of the instrument — for that narrow construction, which would cripple the government, and render it unequal to the objects for which it is declared to be instituted, and to which the powers given, as fairly understood, render it competent — then we cannot perceive the propriety of this strict construction, nor adopt it as the rule by which the constitution is to be expounded. As men, whose intentions require no concealment, generally employ the words which most directly and aptly express the ideas they intend to convey, the enlightened patriots who framed our constitution, and the people who adopted it, must be understood to have employed words in their natural sense, and to have intended what they have said. If, from the imperfection of human language, there should be serious doubts respecting the extent of any given power, it is a well-settled rule, that the objects for which it was given, especially, when those objects are expressed in the instrument itself, should have great influence in the construction. . . . We know of no rule for construing the extent of such powers, other than is given by the language of the instrument which confers them, taken in connection with the purposes for which they were conferred.

The words are, "Congress shall have power to regulate commerce with foreign nations, and among the several states, and with the Indian tribes." The subject to be regulated is commerce; and our constitution being, as was aptly said at the bar, one of enumeration, and not of definition, to ascertain the extent of the power, it becomes necessary to settle the meaning of the word. The counsel for the appellee would limit it to traffic, to buying and selling, or the interchange of commodities, and do not admit that it comprehends navigation. This would restrict a general term, applicable to many objects, to one of its significations. Commerce, undoubtedly, is traffic, but it is something more — it is intercourse. It describes the commercial intercourse between nations, and parts of nations, in all its branches, and is regulated by prescribing rules for carrying on that intercourse. . . .

All America understands, and has uniformly understood, the word "commerce," to comprehend navigation. It was so understood, and must have been so understood, when the constitution was framed. The power over commerce, including navigation, was one of the primary objects for which the people of America adopted their government, and must have been contemplated in forming it. The convention must have used the word in that sense, because all have understood it in that sense; and the attempt to restrict it comes too late. . . .

The word used in the constitution, then comprehends, and has been always understood to comprehend, navigation within its meaning; and a power to regulate navigation, is as expressly granted, as if that term had been added to the word "commerce." To what commerce does this power extend? The constitution informs us, to commerce "with foreign nations, and among the several states, and with the Indian tribes." It has, we believe, been universally admitted, that these words comprehend every species of commercial intercourse between the United States and foreign nations. No sort of trade can be carried on between this country and any other, to which this power does not extend. It has been truly said, that commerce, as the word is used in the constitution, is a unit, every part of which is indicated by the term.

If this be the admitted meaning of the word, in its application to foreign nations, it must carry the same meaning throughout the sentence, and remain a unit, unless there be some plain intelligible cause which alters it. The subject to which the power is next applied, is to commerce, "among the several states." The word "among" means intermingled with. A thing which is among others, is intermingled with them. Commerce among the states, cannot stop at the external boundary line of each state, but may be introduced into the interior. It is not intended to say, that these words comprehend that commerce, which is completely internal, which is carried on between man and man in a state, or between different parts of the same state, and which does not extend to or affect other states. Such a power would be inconvenient, and is certainly unnecessary. Comprehensive as the word "among" is, it may very properly be restricted to that commerce which concerns more states than one. . . . The genius and character of the whole government seem to be, that its action is to be applied to all the external concerns of the nation, and to those internal concerns which affect the states generally; but not to those which are completely within a particular state, which do not affect other states, and with which it is not necessary to interfere, for the purpose of executing some of the general powers of the government. The completely internal commerce of a state, then may be considered as reserved for the state itself.

But in regulating commerce with foreign nations, the power of congress does not stop at the jurisdictional lines of the several states. It would be a very useless power, if it could not pass those lines. The commerce of the United States with foreign nations, is that of the whole United States; every district has a right to participate in it. The deep streams which penetrate our country in every direction, pass through the interior of almost every state in the Union, and furnish the means of exercising this right. If congress has the power to regulate it, that power must be exercised whenever the subject exists. If it exists within the states, if a foreign voyage may commence or terminate at a port within a state, then the power of congress may be exercised within a state.

This principle is, if possible, still more clear, when applied to commerce "among the several states." They either join each other, in which case they are separated by a mathematical line, or they are remote from each other, in which case other states lie between them. What is commerce "among" them; and how is it to be conducted? Can a trading expedition between two adjoining states, commence and terminate outside of each? And if the trading intercourse be between two states remote from each other, must it not commence in one, terminate in the other, and probably pass through a third? Commerce among the states must, of necessity, be commerce with the states. In the regulation of trade with the Indian tribes, the action of the law, especially, when the constitution was made, was chiefly within a state. The power of congress, then, whatever it may be, must be exercised within the territorial jurisdiction of the several states. . . .

We are now arrived at the inquiry — What is this power? It is the power to regulate; that is, to prescribe the rule by which commerce is to be governed. This power, like all others vested in congress, is complete in itself, may be exercised to its utmost extent, and acknowledges no limitations, other than are prescribed in the constitution. These are expressed in plain terms, and do not affect the questions which arise in this case, or which have been discussed at the bar. If, as has always been understood, the sovereignty of congress, though limited to specified objects, is plenary as to those objects, the power over commerce with foreign nations, and among the several states, is vested in congress as absolutely as it would be in a single government, having in its constitution the same restrictions on the exercise of the power as are found in the constitution of the United States. The wisdom and the discretion of congress, their identity with the people, and the influence which their constituents possess at elections, are, in this, as in many other instances, as that, for example, of declaring war, the sole restraints on which they have relied, to secure them from its abuse. They are the restraints on which the people must often rely solely, in all representative governments. The power of congress, then, comprehends navigation, within the limits of every state in the Union; so far as that navigation may be, in any manner, connected with "commerce with foreign nations, or among the several states, or with the Indian tribes." It may, of consequence, pass the jurisdictional line of New York, and act upon the very waters to which the prohibition now under consideration applies.

But it has been urged . . . [that] the states may severally exercise the same power, within their respective jurisdictions. In support of this argument, it is said, that they possessed it as an inseparable attribute of sovereignty, before the formation of the constitution, and still retain it, except so far as they have surrendered it by that instrument; that this principle results from the nature of the government, and is secured by the tenth amendment; that an affirmative grant of power is not exclusive, unless in its own nature it be such that the continued exercise of it by the former possessor is inconsistent with the grant, and that this is not of that description. The appellant, conceding these postulates, except the last, contends, that full power to regulate a particular subject, implies the whole power, and leaves no residuum; that a grant of the whole is incompatible with the existence of a right in another to any part of it. Both parties have appealed to the constitution, to legislative acts, and judicial decisions; and have drawn arguments from all these sources, to support and illustrate the propositions they respectively maintain.

The grant of the power to lay and collect taxes is, like the power to regulate commerce, made in general terms, and has never been understood to interfere with the exercise of the same power by the states; and hence has been drawn an argument which has been applied to the question under consideration. But the two grants are not, it is conceived, similar in their terms or their nature. Although many of the powers formerly exercised by the states, are transferred to the government of the Union, yet the state governments remain, and constitute a most important part of our system.

The power of taxation is indispensable to their existence, and is a power which, in its own nature, is capable of residing in, and being exercised by, different authorities, at the same time. We are accustomed to see it placed, for different purposes, in different hands. Taxation is the simple operation of taking small portions from a perpetually accumulating mass, susceptible of almost infinite division; and a power in one to take what is necessary for certain purposes, is not, in its nature, incompatible with a power in another to take what is necessary for other purposes. Congress is authorized to lay and collect taxes, &c., to pay the debts, and provide for the common defence and general welfare of the United States. This does not interfere with the power of the states to tax for the support of their own governments; nor is the exercise of that power by the states, an exercise of any portion of the power that is granted to the United States. In imposing taxes for state purposes, they are not doing what congress is empowered to do. Congress is not empowered to tax for those purposes which are within the exclusive province of the states. When, then, each government exercises the power of taxation, neither is exercising the power of the other. But when a state proceeds to regulate commerce with foreign nations, or among the several states, it is exercising the very power that is granted to congress, and is doing the very thing which congress is authorized to do. There is no analogy, then, between the power of taxation and the power of regulating commerce.

In discussing the question, whether this power is still in the states, in the case under consideration, we may dismiss from it the inquiry, whether it is surrendered by the mere grant to congress, or is retained until congress shall exercise the power. We may dismiss that inquiry, because it has been exercised, and the regulations which congress deemed it proper to make, are now in full operation. The sole question is, can a state regulate commerce with foreign nations and among the states, while congress is regulating it?

The counsel for the respondent answer this question in the affirmative, and rely very much on the restrictions in the 10th section, as supporting their opinion. They say, very truly, that limitations of a power furnish a strong argument in favor of the existence of that power, and that the section which prohibits the states from laying duties on imports or exports, proves that this power might have been exercised, had it not been expressly forbidden; and, consequently, that any other commercial regulation, not expressly forbidden, to which the original power of the state was competent, may still be made. That this restriction shows the opinion of the convention, that a state might impose duties on exports and imports, if not expressly forbidden, will be conceded; but that it follows, as a consequence, from this concession, that a state may regulate commerce with foreign nations and among the states, cannot be admitted.

We must first determine, whether the act of laying "duties or imposts on imports or exports," is considered in the constitution, as a branch of the taxing power, or of the power to regulate commerce. We think it very clear, that it is considered as a branch of the taxing power. It is so treated in the first clause of the 8th section: "Congress shall have power to lay and collect taxes, duties, imposts and excises"; and before commerce is mentioned, the rule by which the exercise of this power must be governed, is declared. It is, that all duties, imposts and excises shall be uniform. In a separate clause of the enumeration, the power to regulate commerce is given, as being entirely distinct from the right to levy taxes and imposts, and as being a new power, not before conferred. The constitution, then, considers these powers as substantive, and distinct from each other; and so places them in the enumeration it contains. The power of imposing duties on imports is classed with the power to levy taxes, and that seems to be its natural place. But the power to levy taxes could never be considered as abridging the right of the states on that subject; and they might, consequently, have exercised it, by levying duties on imports or exports, had the constitution contained no prohibition on this subject. This prohibition, then, is an exception from the acknowledged power of the states to levy taxes, not from the questionable power to regulate commerce.

But the inspection laws are said to be regulations of commerce, and are certainly recognised in the constitution, as being passed in the exercise of a power remaining with the states. That inspection laws may have a remote and considerable influence on commerce, will not be denied; but that a power to regulate commerce is the source from which the right to pass them is derived, cannot be admitted. The object of inspection laws, is to improve the quality of articles produced by the labor of a country; to fit them for exportation; or, it may be, for domestic use. They act upon the subject, before it becomes an article of foreign commerce, or of commerce among the states, and prepare it for that purpose. They form a portion of that immense mass of legislation, which embraces everything within the territory of a state, not surrendered to the general government; all which can be most advantageously exercised by the states themselves. Inspection laws, quarantine laws, health laws of every description, as well as laws for regulating the internal commerce of a state, and those which respect turnpike roads, ferries, etc., are component parts of this mass.

No direct general power over these objects is granted to congress; and, consequently, they remain subject to state legislation. If the legislative power of the Union can reach them, it must be for national purposes; it must be, where the power is expressly given for a special purpose, or is clearly incidental to some power which is expressly given. It is obvious, that the government of the Union, in the exercise of its express powers, that, for example, of regulating commerce with foreign nations and among the states, may use means that may also be employed by a state, in the exercise of its acknowledged powers; that, for example, of regulating commerce within the state. If congress license vessels to sail from one port to another, in the same state, the act is supposed to be, necessarily, incidental to the power expressly granted to congress, and implies no claim of a direct power to regulate the purely internal commerce of a state, or to act directly on its system of police. So, if a state, in passing laws on subjects acknowledged to be within its control, and with a view to those subjects, shall adopt a measure of the same character with one which congress may adopt, it does not derive its authority from the particular power which has been granted, but from some other, which remains with the state, and may be executed by the same means. All experience shows, that the same measures, or measures scarcely distinguishable from each other, may flow from distinct powers; but this does not prove that the powers themselves are identical. Although the means used in their execution may sometimes approach each other so nearly as to be confounded, there are other situations in which they are sufficiently distinct, to establish their individuality.

In our complex system, presenting the rare and difficult scheme of one general government, whose action extends over the whole, but which possesses only certain enumerated powers; and of numerous state governments, which retain and exercise all powers not delegated to the Union, contests respecting power must arise. Were it even otherwise, the measures taken by the respective governments to execute their acknowledged powers, would often be of the same description, and might, sometimes, interfere. This, however, does not prove that the one is exercising, or has a right to exercise, the powers of the other. . . .

It has been contended by the counsel for the appellant, that, as the word "to regulate" implies in its nature, full power over the thing to be regulated, it excludes, necessarily, the action of all others that would perform the same operation on the same thing. That regulation is designed for the entire result, applying to those parts which remain as they were, as well as to those which are altered. It produces a uniform whole, which is as much disturbed and deranged by changing what the regulating power designs to leave untouched, as that on which it has operated. There is great force in this argument, and the court is not satisfied that it has been refuted.

Since, however, in exercising the power of regulating their own purely internal affairs, whether of trading or police, the states may sometimes enact laws, the validity of which depends on their interfering with, and being contrary to, an act of congress passed in pursuance of the constitution, the court will enter upon the inquiry, whether the laws of New York, as expounded by the highest tribunal of that state, have, in their application to this case, come into collision with an act of congress, and deprived a citizen of a right to which that act entitles him. Should this collision exist, it will be immaterial, whether those laws were passed in virtue of a concurrent power "to regulate commerce with foreign nations and among the several states," or, in virtue of a power to regulate their domestic trade and police. In one case and the other, the acts of New York must yield to the law of congress. . . .

To the court, it seems very clear, that the whole act on the subject of the coasting trade, according to those principles which govern the construction of statutes, implies, unequivocally, an authority to licensed vessels to carry on the coasting trade. . . .

[Marshall goes on to conclude, contrary to the New York courts, that Gibbons's license under the 1793 federal statute entitled him to engage in interstate navigation and trade, notwithstanding Ogden's claims to the exclusive franchise granted by the New York legislature.]

JOHNSON, J.

[Justice William Johnson concurred, adopting the theory only broached by Marshall, i.e., that the power to regulate commerce was exclusively Congress's. During the colonial period, Johnson asserted, "the States had submitted, with murmurs to the commercial restrictions imposed by the parent State." Following independence, they found "themselves in the unlimited possession of those powers over their own commerce, which they had so long been deprived of, and so earnestly coveted, that selfish principle which, well controlled, is so salutary, and which, unrestricted, is so unjust and tyrannical," and consequently began passing a host of "commercial regulations, destructive to the harmony of the States, and fatal to their commercial interests abroad."]

This was the immediate cause that led to the forming of a convention.

The history of the times will, therefore, sustain the opinion, that the grant of power over commerce, if intended to be commensurate with the evils existing, and the purpose of remedying those evils, could be only commensurate with the power of the States over the subject. . . .

The "power to regulate commerce," here meant to be granted, was that power to regulate commerce which previously existed in the States. But what was that power? The States were, unquestionably, supreme; and each possessed that power over commerce, which is acknowledged to reside in every sovereign State. [The] power of a sovereign state over commerce, therefore, amounts to nothing more than a power to limit and restrain it at pleasure. And since the power to prescribe the limits to its freedom, necessarily implies the power to determine what shall remain unrestrained, it follows, that the power must be exclusive; it can reside but in one potentate; and hence, the grant of this power carries with it the whole subject, leaving nothing for the State to act upon. . . .

[With respect to the coasting license ultimately relied on by Marshall to invalidate the New York law,] I cannot overcome the conviction, that if the licensing act was repealed to-morrow, the rights of the appellant to a reversal of the decision complained of, would be as strong. . . .

But the principal objections to these opinions arise, 1st. From the unavoidable action of some of the municipal powers of the States, upon commercial subjects. 2d. From passages in the constitution, which are supposed to imply a concurrent power in the States in regulating commerce.

It is no objection to the existence of distinct, substantive powers, that, in their application, they bear upon the same subject. The same bale of goods, the same cask of provisions, or the same ship, that may be the subject of commercial regulation, may also be the vehicle of disease. And the health laws that require them to be stopped and ventilated, are no more intended as regulations on commerce, than the laws which permit their importation, are intended to inoculate the community with disease. Their different purposes mark the distinction between the powers brought into action; and while frankly exercised, they can produce no serious collision. . . . Inspection laws are of a more equivocal nature, and it is obvious that the constitution has viewed that subject with much solicitude. But so far from sustaining an inference in favour of the power of the States over commerce, I cannot but think that the guarded provisions of the 10th section, on this subject, furnish a strong argument against that inference. It was obvious, that inspection laws must combine municipal with commercial regulations; and, while the power over the subject is yielded to the States, for obvious reasons, an absolute control is given over State legislation on the subject, as far as that legislation may be exercised, so as to affect the commerce of the country. The inferences, to be correctly drawn, from this whole article, appear to me to be altogether in favour of the exclusive grants to Congress of power over commerce, and the reverse of that which the appellee contends for.

[Article 1, §10] negatives the exercise of [the commerce] power to the States, as to the only two objects which could ever tempt them to assume the exercise of that power, to wit, the collection of a revenue from imposts and duties on imports and exports; or from a tonnage duty. As to imposts on imports or exports, such a revenue might have been aimed at directly, by express legislation, or indirectly, in the form of inspection laws; and it became necessary to guard against both. Hence, first, the consent of Congress to such imposts or duties, is made necessary; and as to inspection laws, it is limited to the minimum of expenses. Then, the money so raised shall be paid in to the treasury of the United States, or may be sued for since it is declared to be for their use. And lastly, all such laws may be modified, or repealed, by an act of Congress. It is impossible for a right to be more guarded. . . .

It would be in vain to deny the possibility of a clashing and collision between the measures of the two governments. The line cannot be drawn with sufficient distinctness between the municipal powers of the one, and the commercial powers of the other. . . . Whenever the powers of the respective governments are frankly exercised, with a distinct view to the ends of such powers, they may act upon the same object, or use the same means, and yet the powers be kept perfectly distinct. A resort to the same means, therefore, is no argument to prove the identity of their respective powers. . . .

Discussion

Like *McCulloch*, decided five years earlier, *Gibbons* is an essay on federalism, presenting Marshall's solution to the novel American problem of two sovereigns occupying the same physical space. As such an essay, it has been enormously influential, especially in the post-New Deal world that has accepted an extremely wide scope for congressional regulation under the Commerce Clause (see Chapter 5, infra). It is important to realize, though, that Congress in fact passed remarkably few laws purporting to "regulate interstate commerce," prior at least to the Civil War and its aftermath. For many decades following 1826, the major practical issue before the Court would be far less the constitutional legitimacy of actual congressional enactments than the power of states to regulate matters touching on interstate commerce, as in *Gibbons*. We turn now to some questions provoked by Marshall's essay.

1. *Marshall's binary view.* In Marshall's view, on what theory does the Constitution permit both Congress and the states to levy taxes? Why may not both Congress and the states regulate interstate commerce?

What is Ogden's argument based on Article I, §10, and how does Marshall respond to it? Is it possible that the laying of "duties or imposts on imports or exports" might be a branch of both the taxing power *and* the power to regulate commerce?

How does Marshall respond to Ogden's argument that state inspection (and quarantine) laws are regulations of interstate commerce? Why is it important to Marshall that they *not* be?

Consider the relationship between Marshall's analysis of these issues and his discussions of questions of "degree" in *McCulloch*.

2. *The purposes of the commerce power.* Consider the role that the "objects" or "purposes" of constitutional provisions play in Marshall's scheme.

Toward the beginning of the opinion, in discussing interpretation of the commerce power, Marshall refers to "the well-settled rule, that the objects for which [a power] was given . . . should have great influence in the construction." For what purposes was the commerce power given? What light is shed on these by the following description of proceedings at the Philadelphia convention?

The Virginia delegation, led by Washington, Madison, and Randolph, feeling largely responsible for the calling of the Convention, had prepared a series of resolutions as a basis for discussion. The sixth of these resolutions, proposed by Governor Randolph four days after the Convention assembled, read in part as follows:

". . . that the National Legislature ought to be impowered to enjoy the Legislative Rights vested in Congress by the Confederation & moreover to legislate in all cases to which the separate States are incompetent, or in which the harmony of the United States may be interrupted by the exercise of individual Legislation."

The broad standard thus proposed for the division of power between state and nation was criticized by some of the delegates as being too indefinite, but was approved by the Convention on May 31st by a vote of nine states in favor, none against, one divided. . . .

Shortly afterwards Paterson proposed his New Jersey plan, which included in a very short enumeration of federal powers the provision that Congress could "pass Acts for the regulation of trade & commerce as well with foreign nations as with each other." In the language of James Wilson, subsequently a Supreme Court Justice, in comparing the two plans, under the Virginia Plan "the National Legislature is to make laws in all cases at which the several states are incompetent"; under the New Jersey Plan, "In place of this cong. are to have additional power in a few cases only." The New Jersey Plan was rejected and the Virginia Plan reapproved, on June 19th, by a vote of seven states to three, one being divided.

On July 17th, when Randolph's resolution on the division of powers again came up for debate, Sherman of Connecticut, who alone had opposed the resolution originally, moved that it be amended to add the expression.

"To make laws binding on the people of the United States in all cases which may concern the common interests of the Union; but not to interfere with the Government of the individual States in any matters of internal police which respect the Gov. of such States only, and wherein the general welfare of the U. States is not concerned."

". . . [This] was defeated, and a motion by [Gunning] Bedford of Delaware to clarify the wording adopted by a vote of eight to two. The resolution then read as follows: "Resolved that the national legislature ought

"1. to possess the legislative rights in Congress by the confederation; and

"2. moreover, to legislate in all cases for the general interests of the Union, and

"3. also in those to which the states are separately incompetent, or

"4. in which the harmony of the United States may be interrupted by the exercise of individual legislation."

With the other resolutions approved by the Convention, this resolution was then sent to the "Com. of detail . . . to . . . report the Constitution." This committee [of Detail] made its report on August 6th, ten days later. It had changed the indefinite language of Resolution VI into an enumeration of the powers of Congress closely resembling Article 1, Section 8 of the Constitution as it was finally adopted. . . .

[T]he Convention did not at any time challenge the radical change made by the committee in the form of the provision for the division of powers between state and nation. It accepted *without discussion* the enumeration of powers made by a committee which had been directed to prepare a constitution based upon the general propositions that the Federal Government was "to legislate in all cases for the general interests of the Union . . . and in those to which the states are separately incompetent." With a few changes and additions, the enumeration by the committee became the present Section 8 of Article I of the Constitution.[97]

Consider Jack Rakove, Original Meanings 178 (1996):

Though it has been argued that this action [turning the Bedford resolution into an enumeration of powers] marked a crucial, even subversive shift in the deliberations, the fact that it went unchallenged suggests that the committee [of Detail] was only complying with the expectations of the convention. . . . [T]he process that unfolded during its ten days of labor is better explained as an attempt to identify particular areas of governance where there were "general Interests of the Union," where the states were "separately incompetent, or where state legislation could disrupt the national "Harmony."

If Rakove is correct that the Committee of Detail was attempting to give concrete meaning to the Bedford resolution, what rule of construction might courts offer today in construing the scope of federal commerce power? One possibility is that courts should ask whether Congress is attempting to deal with a federal issue, for example, one in which Congress could reasonably conclude that actions within states will have spillover effects in other states, or an issue in which unilateral or conflicting decisions by states would undermine what Congress reasonably believes to be a federal policy.

3. *The purposes of congressional regulation.* In discussing the allocation of state and national powers under the clause, Marshall writes that inspection, quarantine, and health laws "form a portion of that immense mass of legislation, which embraces everything within the territory of a state, not surrendered to the national government." He comments that "No direct general power over these objects is granted to congress; and, consequently they remain subject to state legislation. If the legislative power of the Union can reach them, it must be for national purposes. . . ."

This suggests that the scope of national power may depend, not only on the *substance* of the regulation, but also on the *purposes* for which the regulation was adopted — on the congruence between the purposes underlying the regulation and the constitutional grant of power. Recall, in this respect, Marshall's discussion of "pretext" in ¶42 of *McCulloch:*

Should Congress, . . . under the pretext of executing its powers, pass laws for the accomplishment of objects not entrusted to the government; it would become the painful duty of this tribunal, should a case requiring such a decision come before it, to say that such an act was not the law of the land.

Think of an example of a congressional regulation of interstate commerce that might preempt a state inspection, quarantine, or health law. Think of an example of a congressional regulation of interstate commerce that is a "pretext" — i.e., that is not done to accomplish any of the objects entrusted to the national government.

97. Robert Stern, That Commerce Which Concerns More States Than One, 47 Harv. L. Rev. 1335, 1338-1340 (1934).

Can you reconcile the "pretext" language of *McCulloch* with Marshall's statements in *Gibbons* that the "[commerce] power, like all others vested in congress, is complete in itself, may be exercised to its utmost extent, and acknowledges no limitations, other than are prescribed in the constitution," and that "the sovereignty of congress, though limited to specified objects, is plenary as to those objects, [and] the power over commerce . . . among the several states, is vested in congress as absolutely as it would be in a single government"?

4. *State regulation of interstate commerce — substance and purpose.* *Gibbons* holds that a valid congressional regulation of interstate commerce (the 1793 statute) preempts inconsistent state regulations. But may a state regulate interstate commerce in the absence of congressional legislation?

Counsel for Gibbons argued that the Constitution by its own terms completely deprives the states of any powers to regulate interstate commerce: "as the word 'to regulate' implies in its nature, full power over the thing to be regulated, it excludes, necessarily, the action of all others that would perform the same operation on the same thing." Marshall found "great force in this argument," but went on to decide the case on the narrower grounds of statutory preemption.

Several years later in Willson v. Black-Bird Creek Marsh Co., 27 U.S. (2 Pet.) 245 (1829), the Court addressed the constitutionality of state law in the absence of a preemptive federal regulation. The state of Delaware had authorized the plaintiff company to build a dam across a navigable waterway. Defendants, the owners of a sloop licensed and enrolled under the federal act involved in *Gibbons*, broke the plaintiff company's dam. In an action for damages, defendants argued that a state law authorizing construction of the dam conflicted with the commerce clause. Chief Justice Marshall wrote:

[T]he question is to be considered, whether the act incorporating the Black-bird Creek Marsh company is repugnant to the constitution, so far as it authorizes a dam across the creek. The plea states the creek to be navigable, in the nature of a highway, through which the tide ebbs and flows. The act of assembly by which the plaintiffs were authorized to construct their dam, shows plainly that this is one of those many creeks, passing through a deep level marsh, adjoining the Delaware, up which the tide flows for some distance. The value of the property on its banks must be enhanced by excluding the water from the marsh, and the health of the inhabitants probably improved. Measures calculated to produce these objects, provided they do not come into collision with the powers of the general government, are undoubtedly within those which are reserved to the states. But the measure authorized by this act stops a navigable creek, and must be supposed to abridge the rights of those who have been accustomed to use it. But this abridgment, unless it comes in conflict with the constitution or a law of the United States, is an affair between the government of Delaware and its citizens, of which this court can take no cognizance.

The counsel for the plaintiffs in error insist, that it comes in conflict with the power of the United States "to regulate commerce with foreign nations, and among the several states." If congress had passed any act which bore upon the case; any act in execution of the power to regulate commerce, the object of which was to control state legislation over those small navigable creeks into which the tide flows, and which abound throughout the lower country of the middle and southern states; we should feel not much difficulty in saying, that a state law coming to conflict with such act would be void. But congress has passed no such act. The repugnancy of the law of Delaware to the constitution is placed entirely on its repugnancy to the power to regulate commerce with foreign nations and among the several states; a power which has not been so exercised as to affect the question. We do not think, that the act empowering the Black-bird Creek Marsh company to place a dam across the creek, can, under all the circumstances of the case, be considered as repugnant to the power to regulate commerce in its dormant state, or as being in conflict with any law passed on the subject.

William Wirt, counsel for the respondent company, characterized the Delaware act as a "health" measure, and described the Black-Bird Creek as "one of those sluggish reptile streams, that do not run but creep, and which, wherever it passes, spreads its venom, and destroys the health of all those who inhabit its marshes." "Can it be asserted," he asked, "that a law authorizing the erection of a dam, and the formation of banks which will draw off the pestilence, and give to those who have before suffered from disease, health and vigor, is unconstitutional?"

1. How do you suppose the case would have come out if the creek had been a major interstate waterway?

2. If the proper scope of congressional exercise of the commerce power sometimes depends on the purposes for which it is exercised, the same might be true of state law affecting interstate commerce. Might the outcome have been different had Wirt characterized the law not as a health measure, but as a regulation of navigation on the state's waterways?

Recall Marshall's attraction to the argument in *Gibbons* that the very grant of a power to one government (the United States) precludes "the action of all others that would perform the same operation on the same thing." Is *Black-Bird Creek* consistent with this view?

We have not omitted any part of Marshall's analysis in the *Black-Bird Creek* case. The opinion concludes, elliptically, that "under all the circumstances of the case" the law authorizing erection of the dam does not conflict with the commerce clause or with any federal statute. What do you suppose are the relevant "circumstances?" One possible circumstance is that this was a health law as distinguished from a commercial regulation. Do you suppose that this rationale would have sufficed to sustain damming up a major interstate waterway? If not, did the "circumstances" of the case include the perception that the benefits of damming the creek substantially outweighed any impediments to interstate navigation? Does anything in Marshall's opinion in *Black-Bird Creek* suggest this reading, and if so, is it consistent with the jurisprudence of *McCulloch* and *Gibbons*?

Note: Language, Purpose, and Meaning[98]

1. Language and Purpose

Aristotle:

All law is universal but about some things it is not possible to make a universal statement which shall be correct. In those cases then in which it is necessary to speak universally but not possible to do so correctly, the law takes the usual case, though it is

---

98. See generally Paul Brest, The Misconceived Quest for the Original Understanding, 60 B.U. L. Rev. 204 (1980); Michael Moore, The Semantics of Judging, 54 S. Cal. L. Rev. 151 (1981). See also Frederick Schauer, Playing by the Rules: A Philosophical Examination of Rule-Based Decision Making in Law and in Life (1991).

not ignorant of the possibility of error. And it is none the less correct; for the error is not in the law nor in the legislator but in the nature of the thing, since the matter of practical affairs is of this kind from the start. When the law speaks universally, then, and a case arises under it which is not covered by the universal statement, then it is right, where the legislator fails us and has erred by oversimplicity, to correct the omission — to say what the legislator himself would have put into his law, if he had known. . . . And this is the nature of the equitable, a correction of law where it is defective owing to its universality.[99]

Plowden:

A law of a certain state provides that foreigners scaling the walls of the city shall be capitally punished. But it happened that foreigners innocently passing through the city heard an outcry that enemies had suddenly attacked the city and were making inroads. The foreigners scaled the walls before the citizens, and, defending the city, they saved it. Now, therefore, what of the law? Ought they to die, as the law says? . . .

In order to form a right judgment when the letter of a statute is restrained, and when enlarged, by equity, it is a good way, when you peruse a statute, to suppose that the law-maker is present, and that you have [asked] him the question you want to know touching the equity, then you must give yourself such an answer as you may imagine he would have done, if he had been present. As for example, . . . where the strangers scale the walls, and defend the city, suppose the lawmaker to be present with you, and in your mind put this question to him, shall the strangers be put to death? Then give yourself the same answer which you imagine he, being an upright and reasonable man, would have given, and you will find that he would have said "They shall not be put to death." . . . And therefore when such cases happen which are within the letter, or out of the letter, of a statute, and yet don't directly fall within the plain and natural purport of the letter, but are in some measure to be conceived in a different idea from that in which the text seems to express, it is a good way to give questions and give answers to yourself thereupon, in the same manner as if you were actually conversing with the maker of such laws, and by this means you will easily find out what is the equity of those cases. And if the law-maker would have followed the equity, notwithstanding the words of the law . . . you may safely do the like, for while you do no more than the law-maker would have done, you do not act contrary to the law, but in conformity to it.[100]

To read a provision without regard to its context and likely purposes will yield either unresolvable indeterminacies or plain nonsense. Some judges and scholars have asserted that "[t]he whole aim of construction, as applied to a provision of the Constitution, is to discover the meaning, to ascertain and give effect to the intent, of its framers and the people who adopted it."[101] Others maintain that an interpreter should inquire into the "purpose of the provision." For example, Justice Frankfurter wrote:[102]

You may have observed that I have not yet used the word "intention." All these years I have avoided speaking of the "legislative intent." . . . Legislation has an aim; it seeks to obviate some mischief, to supply an inadequacy, to effect a change of policy, to formulate a plan of government. That aim, that policy is not drawn, like nitrogen, out of the air; it is evidenced in the language of the statute, as read in the light of other

---

99. Aristotle, Ethics, Book V., ch. 10, fol. 1137.
100. 2 Plowden 459, 466, 467, quoted in Learned Hand, The Bill of Rights 20-22 (1958).
101. Home Bldg. & Loan Assn. v. Blaisdell, 290 U.S. 398 (1934) (Sutherland, J., dissenting).
102. Felix Frankfurter, Some Reflections on the Reading of Statutes, 1947 Colum. L. Rev. 527, 538-539.

external manifestations of purpose. That is what the judge must seek and effectuate, and he ought not to be led off the trail by tests that have overtones of subjective design. We are not concerned with anything subjective. We do not delve into the minds of legislators or their draftsmen, or committee members.

Can the "purpose" of a provision be distinguished from the "intent" of those who drafted or adopted it? Taken *literally*, Justice Frankfurter's statement makes no sense. Things — including statutes and constitutional provisions — do not have "purposes" or "aims"; they do not "seek to obviate" mischiefs. These terms require animate subjects. *Figuratively* speaking, one might describe the "purpose of a provision" tautologously with its language: "the purpose of Article I, §8, cl. 3 is to permit Congress to regulate commerce . . . among the several States." But this seems a fruitless enterprise, and any other figurative reading of the term seems ultimately to refer to the purposes, aims, or seekings — in short the "intent" — of those who framed and adopted the provision.[103]

Nonetheless, Frankfurter's remarks are evocative of a real distinction. The (subjective) aims of those who drafted or adopted a provision can be described on different levels of generality. A rather general description would be: "Their purpose in adopting Article I, §8, cl. 3 was to permit Congress to legislate [in matters of commerce] where the States were separately incompetent." Much more specifically, one might describe the adopters' view of a particular fact situation: "They wanted to prevent the States from imposing tariffs." All other things being equal, a general or vague characterization is likely to describe the aims of more people than a precise or detailed characterization — the target is easier to hit. As one moves from the more specific to the less specific characterization of, or inquiry into, the aims of the framers, one moves from "intent" to "purpose." One can talk about the "purpose of the provision" simply because it must have been the purpose of (nearly) everyone who voted for the provision and, indeed, understood to be their purpose even by those who voted against it.[104]

These more and less general characterizations of the framers' objectives correlate roughly with different approaches to interpretation. One who inquires into

103. The concept of purpose incorporates an element of will. It would simply be a misuse of language to say that a thing's purpose is anything it does or can do, apart from human intention. For example, it is not a purpose of an automobile to pollute, maim, or kill, and only by using a figurative anthropomorphism is it an automobile's purpose to transport passengers.

104. On a somewhat related point, can one meaningfully talk about the purpose or intent of those who framed or adopted a provision where there is no evidence that they explicitly considered the particular application of the provision about which their views are sought? Some scholars have suggested a person has no intent whatsoever with respect to a question he did not think about. See, e.g., John Chipman Gray, The Nature and Sources of the Law 172-173 (2d ed. 1921). The contrary view is now generally accepted. See, e.g., Lon Fuller, The Morality of Law 83-87 (1964); Gerald MacCallum, Legislative Intent, 75 Yale L.J. 754 (1966); Henry Hart and Albert Sacks, The Legal Process: Basic Problems in the Making and Application of Law 98 (tent. ed. 1958):

> What is the significance of advertance or inadvertance in the concept of "intention"? Of course, one may "intend" some specific consequences to which he did not consequently advert. If a master tells a servant to "take care of the house" during his absence, he no doubt intends that the servant will do his best to extinguish a fire in the house started by lightning, even though this contingency never actually occurred to him. But does one "intend" everything within the reach of his words which he does not consciously "exclude"? [Wittgenstein writes:] "Someone says to me: 'Show the children a game.' I teach them gaming with dice, and the other says, 'I didn't mean that sort of game.' Must the exclusion of the game with dice have come before his mind when he gave me the order [to make this last statement true]?"

"purpose" may not look much beyond the language of the provision, for the language, when read in the context of the generally understood structure and values of a society, will usually indicate the society's reasons for adopting it. (This suggests why, without being tautologous, many speak anthropomorphically of the "purpose of the provision.") One who inquires into "intent," on the other hand, will examine closely the proceedings and debates that led to the provision's adoption.

[margin handwriting: language read in context of societal values structure = purpose proceedings + debate = intent]

The language and purposes of a provision enjoy a symbiotic relationship. The meaning (or application) of a provision is ascertained by examining its language and purposes. The language sets the boundaries of possible meanings and yields the initial — and often the primary — indication of its purposes. At the same time, the purposes of the provision circumscribe the range of its plausible meanings.

2. Discovering the Adopters' Purposes[105]

Four sets of proceedings bear directly on the original understanding of the constitutional provisions: the federal Constitutional Convention held in Philadelphia in 1787, the state ratification conventions, congressional proceedings in which amendments were proposed pursuant to Article V, and the state legislative proceedings in which they were ratified. Of these, the reports of the secret[106] proceedings of the Philadelphia convention are probably most often cited and are as problematic as any others. John Wofford writes:[107]

> Max Farrand, in the introduction to his compilation of all accounts of the Convention extant in 1911 [The Records of the Federal Convention of 1787], states that the official journal, apparently containing all motions and votes, was delivered to Washington, then president of the Congress of the Confederation, who in 1796 deposited the papers in the Department of State. There they remained, untouched, until Congress by joint resolution in 1818 ordered them printed. Farrand reports that President Monroe requested his Secretary of State, John Quincy Adams, to take charge of the publication: "The task proved to be a difficult one. The papers were," according to Adams, "no better than the daily minutes from which the regular journal ought to have been, but never was, made out." Adams reports that at his request William Jackson, the secretary of the Convention, called upon him and "looked over the papers, but he had no recollection of them which could remove the difficulties arising from their disorderly state, nor any papers to supply the deficiency of the missing papers." With the expenditure of considerable time and labor, and with the exercise of no little ingenuity, Adams was finally able to collate the whole to his satisfaction. General Bloomfield supplied him with several important documents from the papers of David Brearley; Charles Pinckney sent him a copy of the plan he "believed" to be

-----

105. See generally Jacobus tenBroek, Admissibility and Use by the United States Supreme Court of Extrinsic Aids in Constitutional Construction, 26 Calif. L. Rev. 287, 437, 664 (1938); 27 Calif. L. Rev. 157, 399 (1939).

106. See Max Farrand, The Framing of the Constitution of the United States 58-59 (1913).

107. Wofford, The Blinding Light: The Uses of History in Constitutional Interpretation, 31 U. Chi. L. Rev. 502, 504-506 (1964). See also Donald Dewey, James Madison Helps Clio Interpret the Constitution, 15 Am. J. Legal Hist. 38 (1971); James Hutson, The Creation of the Constitution: The Integrity of the Documentary Record, 65 Tex. L. Rev. 1 (1986).

one he presented to the Convention; Madison furnished the means of completing the records of the last four days. . . . As thus compiled, the Journal, Acts and Proceedings of the Convention . . . which formed the Constitution of the United States was printed in 1819. Adams felt that he there presented a "correct and tolerably clear view of the proceedings of the convention. . . ." Farrand's own judgment, however, is more critical: "As Adams had nothing whatever to guide him in his work of compilation and editing, mistakes were inevitable, and not a few of these were important. . . . With notes so carelessly kept, as were evidently those of the secretary, the Journal cannot be relied upon absolutely. The statement of questions is probably accurate in most cases, but the determination of those questions and in particular the votes upon them should be accepted somewhat tentatively."

Material in addition to the Journal has, of course, been discovered; this enabled Farrand to speak of "mistakes" in the Journal itself. Most important are the notes which Madison made during the proceedings. Madison himself described how he made the notes, and how he then used them to reconstruct a more complete account: "I chose a seat in front of the presiding member, with the other members, on my right and left hand. In this favorable position for hearing all that passed I noted in terms legible and in abbreviations and marks intelligible to myself what was read from the Chair or spoken by the members; and losing not a moment unnecessarily between the adjournment and reassembling of the Convention I was enabled to write out my daily notes during the session or within a few finishing days after its close." Madison's notes were not published exactly as he had transcribed them after each session. For after the publication of the official — and inaccurate — Journal, Madison went over his notes and made numerous changes in them. According to Farrand, these emendations "seriously impaired the value of his notes," since many of the Journal's errors were simply duplicated.

By 1911, when Farrand published all of the known records of the Convention, the Journal and Madison's Debates had been supplemented by other (and shorter) records made contemporaneously with the Convention and by statements made later by those who had been present. We know that other records once existed, although Farrand notes that it is "not probable . . . that any such new material would modify to any great extent our conceptions of the Convention's work." In short, we have a picture of the Philadelphia proceedings, the various parts of which are generally consistent with each other. What we do not have, and indeed will never have, is any external check upon completeness of that picture. The conceptions of what occurred at Philadelphia remain, as Farrand put it, "ours."[108]

The Court has often discovered the "intent of the framers" in their nonofficial utterances — correspondence, papers, and publications. For example, in Reynolds v. United States, 98 U.S. 145 (1879), in holding that the free exercise clause did not immunize a Mormon from a prosecution for bigamy, the Court cited Thomas Jefferson's assertion in his letter to the Danbury Baptists that the First Amendment built "a wall of separation between church and state." Chief Justice Waite explained: "Coming as this does from an acknowledged leader of the

---

108. Until relatively recently, the main source of proceedings at the state conventions, which also contains material relating to the Philadelphia convention, had been Debates in the Several State Conventions (Elliott ed., 2d ed. 1836-1845) (five volumes). It is, however, being supplanted by The Documentary History of the Ratification of the Constitution, compiled by historians at the University of Wisconsin. As of 2005, 20 volumes had been published, covering the ratification debates in Pennsylvania, Delaware, New Jersey, Georgia, Connecticut, Massachusetts, Virginia, and New York. Future volumes will cover North and South Carolina, Rhode Island, Maryland, and New Hampshire. Congressional proceedings are found in the Congressional Globe, later the Congressional Record. State legislative debates are not published in most states, although an official record of actions is kept.

advocates of the measure, it may be accepted almost as an authoritative declaration of the scope and effect of the amendment. . . ."[109]

What implicit assumptions does Waite make?

Without doubt, the most frequently cited nonofficial source is The Federalist Papers, which the Court has typically treated as an authoritative manifestation of the intent of the framers. Consider Professor Jacobus tenBroek's comment on this practice.[110]

> There can be little doubt that if the writers of The Federalist had dedicated themselves in all sincerity to the preparation of a purely impartial account of the will of the fathers, their work would have come as near to absolute historical accuracy as human limitations would permit in the circumstances. In that case, both by reason of ability and opportunity, their situation would have been unexcelled.[111] But the doctrine that they actually revealed the collective intent of the Constitution formulators, involves the assumptions that they, in framing their articles divested themselves of their former protagonistic biases and attitudes, and that The Federalist was composed in an atmosphere of calm disinterestedness. The first of these is only conjecturally possible and the second is historically false. The Federalist was composed as an argument on one side of a bitterly controverted question. It was calculated to put the Constitution in the light which would make it most acceptable to the ratifying conventions. It did not even purport to express the intention of the framers.
>
> At bottom, the Court's theory comes down to the proposition that the authors of The Federalist, having been members of the Constitutional Convention, had a first hand opportunity to know the intention of the men there assembled. Yet that identical experience has not been regarded as similarly endowing others who were not measurably less capable. Thus, Luther Martin's commentary on the Constitution appears infrequently in the reports, and then generally with disparaging comment. Likewise, the able series of articles written over the name of "Brutus" by Judge Robert Yates has never, to my knowledge, been cited by the Supreme Court. . . . We must conclude, therefore, that the difference in the position of Madison and Hamilton, on the one hand, and Martin and Yates, on the other, lies not in any difference of opportunity to know the will of the fathers, nor yet possibly in any difference of merit. It lies rather in the not altogether incidental fact that Madison and Hamilton were on the side which turned out to be victorious, and this fact, taken together with their entire careers, has made them great in the eye of posterity — a fact which has given their words a quality of persuasion which has never attached to the utterances of Martin and Yates. It is this circumstance which explains the pre-eminent popularity of The Federalist with the United States Supreme Court as against all other contemporary partisan commentators, and not the judicially asserted fact that they possessed peculiar opportunity to inform themselves on the issue of formulative intent.[112]

Is the Court justified in giving more weight to the views of the proponents than of the opponents of the Constitution?

109. See also McCollum v. Board of Educ., 333 U.S. 203, 211 (1948). For an excellent criticism of the Court's use of history in construing the religion clauses, see Mark de Wolfe Howe, The Garden and Wilderness (1965).

110. tenBroek, supra n.105, 27 Calif. L. Rev. 157, 162-164 (1939).

111. [footnote by tenBroek] This statement is substantially correct but must be modified in some degree by the fact that Hamilton attended the convention only sporadically after the first month. Moreover, John Jay, another of the authors of The Federalist, had not been a delegate to the Constitutional Convention. However, only 5 out of the 85 articles composing The Federalist are attributed to Jay, and these, curiously enough, are almost never cited by the Supreme Court, although this is probably due more to their subject matter than to their authorship.

112. The Federalist has also often been touted as a reliable gauge of opinion in the ratifying conventions, on the ground that it was widely published in the states prior to ratification and was the chief

The Court has also cited the enactments of early Congresses as indicative of the original understanding of constitutional provisions. For example, in Myers v. United States, 272 U.S. 52 (1926), in holding that a statutory provision requiring the Senate's consent for the removal of postmasters unconstitutionally usurped executive power, Chief Justice Taft relied on the debates over, and enactment of, a 1789 law that recognized the president's plenary power to remove his secretary of foreign affairs. Taft argued that the Congress had affirmed the president's exclusive constitutional authority to remove executive appointees, and explained:

> We have devoted much space to this discussion and decision of the question of the Presidential power of removal in the First Congress, not because a Congressional conclusion on a constitutional issue is conclusive, but, first, because of our agreement with the reasons upon which it was avowedly based; second, because this was the decision of the First Congress, on a question of primary importance in the organization of the Government, made within two years after the Constitutional Convention and within a much shorter time after its ratification; and, third, because that Congress numbered among its leaders those who had been members of the Convention.

Much earlier, in Martin v. Hunter's Lessee, 14 U.S. (1 Wheat.) 304 (1816), Justice Story thus concluded his argument that the Supreme Court had appellate jurisdiction over state courts.[113]

> It is an historical fact, that at the time when the Judiciary Act was submitted to the deliberations of the first congress, composed, as it was, not only of men of great learning and ability, but of men who had acted principal part in framing, supporting, or opposing that constitution, the same exposition was explicitly declared and admitted by the friends and by the opponents of that system.

What assumptions are implicit in these uses of the actions of early Congresses? With respect to the 1789 provision relied on in Myers, consider Professor Charles Miller's suggestions that "one reason why the First Congress had exerted little effort on its own behalf was that George Washington was President, and no legislator dared question his wisdom by denying him the right to remove a member of his own cabinet," and that the outcome of Congress's action was largely the result of clever parliamentary maneuvering by James Madison, who managed to divide and conquer two factions, which, for different reasons, believed that the Senate's consent *should* be necessary for presidential removals.[114] Even if he is correct on the specific point, does it hold with regard, say, to §13 of the Judiciary Act, about which there was absolutely no debate in Congress? Should Marshall have deferred to the position of the Congress in Marbury? Does his failure to do so stand as a general rejection of the relevance of the First Congress as privileged constitutional interpreter?

---

means by which the intent of the Convention was transmitted to the states. See, e.g., Legal Tender Cases, 79 U.S. (12 Wall.) 457, 585, 608 (1870). But even if the articles persuaded all who read them, "a considerable number of the conventions in the states had ratified the Constitution while a varying number of The Federalist papers were as yet unpublished. . . ." tenBroek, supra n.105, 27 Calif. L. Rev., at 171.

113. Note also that Oliver Ellsworth, who was Chief Justice of the Supreme Court from 1796 to 1800, played a major role in the framing of both Article III and the Judiciary Act of 1789. Michael Kraus, Oliver Ellsworth, in 1 The Justices of the United States Supreme Court 273 (Friedman & Israel eds., 1969).

114. Charles Miller, The Supreme Court and the Uses of History, ch. 4 (1969).

Chapter 3
The Taney Court and the Civil War, 1835-1865

The first party system of Federalists and Republicans collapsed in the aftermath of the War of 1812, not least because some prominent New England Federalists floated the idea of secession in protest against the policies of President James Madison.[1] A second party system began to emerge after the Era of Good Feelings, a period of supposed consensus under the presidency of James Monroe (who was reelected in 1820 by an electoral vote of 231-1, with the one holdout explaining that George Washington should remain unique in receiving unanimous support). John Randolph, a crusty Virginian, described this show of support as "the unanimity of indifference, and not of approbation," and by 1824 the polity was strikingly divided. One faction, which became the Whig Party, was led by John Quincy Adams, the son of John Adams and Monroe's Secretary of State and the author of the Monroe Doctrine claiming American hegemony over the fate of the Western Hemisphere. Although he received both fewer popular and electoral votes than Andrew Jackson — 114,023 and 84, respectively, against Jackson's 152,901 popular and 99 electoral votes — the election was thrown into the House of Representatives because two other candidates, Secretary of the Treasury William Crawford of Georgia and Speaker of the House Henry Clay got enough electoral votes to deprive Jackson of the majority required for election. Although Clay, the fourth-place finisher with 37 electoral votes, could not himself be elected president (because the House of Representatives, under the Twelfth Amendment, must choose among the top three finishers, on a one-state/one-vote basis), he had sufficient influence among his colleagues to be able successfully to throw his support to Adams, who promptly named Clay Secretary of State. South Carolina Representative John C. Calhoun was elected Vice President, having received a clear majority of 181 electoral votes (which, of course suggests that the new party system was still in a process of developing).

Jacksonians promptly began denouncing the "corrupt bargain" that ended the 1824 election and planning for revenge in 1828. A united Democratic Party was able to elect its ticket of Jackson and Calhoun,[2] although Calhoun would resign the vice presidency as he became increasingly distant from Jackson's nationalist policies (at least relative to South Carolina). The Democrats dominated national politics during the period covered by this chapter, electing Jackson, Martin Van Buren,

---

1. See, e.g., James Banner, To the Hartford Convention (1970).
2. See generally Morton Borden, Parties and Politics in the Early Republic, 1789-1815 (1969); Shaw Livermore, Twilight of Federalism: The Disintegration of the Federalist Party, 1815-1830 (1962); Richard McCormick, The Second American Party System: Jacksonian Era (1966).

James Polk, Franklin Pierce, and James Buchanan. The Whig victory of 1840 under the leadership of William Henry Harrison was effectively negated by his death a month after his inauguration and the succession by Vice President John Tyler, a Virginia ex-Democrat, whose principal interests appeared to be strengthening the role of slave states in the Union. (It was Tyler who successfully pressed the annexation of Texas on Congress, see p. 247 n.45, infra.) The second Whig to be elected, Zachary Taylor (1848), also died in office, to be succeeded by Millard Fillmore. Not until the triumph of the new Republican Party in 1860, through the election of Abraham Lincoln, would the Democratic hold on the presidency be broken. (No Democrat thereafter would be elected until the 1884 election of Grover Cleveland, although many historians believe that Democrat Samuel Tilden was robbed of the presidency in the disputed election of 1876.)

The period covered by this chapter is often labeled the age of Jacksonian democracy; it featured the emergence of the first mass-based political party and the relaxation on property requirements for the suffrage that took place in the states throughout the 1820s:

> Jacksonian democracy was a national movement in that it opposed disunion and knew no geographical limits. . . . But it was anti-national in rejecting Henry Clay's "American System" [under which Congress would have participated in developing systems of interstate transportation]. That is, the Democrats wanted roads, canals, and (in a few years) railroads to be chartered and aided by the states, but no Federal Government messing into the operations or sharing the expected profits. Jacksonians spoke for the men on the make who resented government grants of special privileges to rival entrepreneurs and who preferred laissez-faire to the positive state. . . . [T]he Jackson men identified themselves with the movement toward more equality. Yet they believed in equality only for white men; they were far less charitable toward the Indian and the Negro than their "aristocratic" foes. Jacksonian Democracy was not "leveling" in the European sense, having no desire to pull down men of wealth to a common plane; but it wanted a fair chance for every man to level up.[3]

Jackson also altered the face of the federal judiciary. He was able to nominate five justices by 1836, including Marshall's successor as Chief Justice, Roger B. Taney.[4] A Maryland aristocrat and former Federalist — and the first Roman Catholic to be named to the Supreme Court — Taney had aligned with the Democrats in the 1820s. Jackson first appointed him Attorney General and Secretary of the Treasury. He helped to draft Jackson's Veto Message regarding the Bank, supra Chapter 1, including the passage that denied that the constitutional interpretations of the Supreme Court necessarily bound the president. Jackson had nominated Taney to be an Associate Justice in 1835, but the strongly anti-Jackson Senate refused to bring the nomination to a vote. When John Marshall died later that year, Jackson nominated Taney once more, this time to succeed Marshall as

---

3. Samuel Eliot Morison, Henry Steele Commager, and William E. Leuchtenberg, The Growth of the American Republic 419-420 (7th ed. 1980). See also Lawrence Friedman, A History of American Law, ch. 3 (1973); Carter Goodrich, Government Promotion of American Canals and Railroads, 1800-1890 (1960).

4. Indeed, Whig presidents made only two appointments, in 1851 and 1853, during the entire period prior to Lincoln's election.

Chief Justice. After an eight-month delay, the Senate confirmed Taney as the fifth Chief Justice of the United States.[5] Carl Swisher writes:

> Taney went to the Court with a conviction as to the sanctity of rights of physical and tangible property, and the community rights connected therewith; . . . he distrusted mercantile and banking interests that were strong enough and ruthlessly selfish enough to endanger the interests of stable property and of the community; . . . he had a deep sense of local patriotism for Maryland, which easily extended to the southern states with a similar culture. . . . [A]lthough a firm believer in the Union he was also apparently in greater degree a believer in the rights of states and of what was to become the minority region of the South.[6]

Taney, like five of the seven first presidents of the United States, was a slaveholder and therefore basically accepted a view of white superiority that justified racially structured chattel slavery.

As already suggested, a major issue throughout this period concerned the constitutional implications of burgeoning economic development, much of it accompanied by a noticeable increase in the use of eminent domain by state and municipal governments and quasi-public corporations. State courts began elaborating doctrine under state constitutional provisions governing compensation for takings of property.[7] Before the Civil War, the only federal constitutional provision directly concerned with economic rights was the contract clause, which was the most recurrently litigated section of the Constitution in the nineteenth century.[8]

Two of the most noted decisions of the Taney Court were protective of state powers. Charles River Bridge v. Warren Bridge, 36 U.S. (11 Pet.) 420 (1837) established the principle that public franchises should be narrowly construed: Because the petitioner's charter to operate a toll bridge was not in terms exclusive, it would not be read to prevent the state from chartering a bridge nearby, even if, as a practical matter, this wiped out the economic value of the investment based on the original charter. (Justice Story wrote a bitter dissent.) In West River Bridge Co. v. Dix, 47 U.S. (6 How.) 507 (1848), the Court held that petitioner's franchise did not preclude the state from expropriating its bridge upon payment of compensation: All government grants are implicitly subject to the state's power of eminent domain.

One issue that frequently arose involved the authority of local municipalities within states to issue bonds as a means of attracting new business enterprises. Gelpcke v. Dubuque, 68 U.S. (1 Wall.) 175 (1864), for example, was a diversity action by the holders of municipal bonds issued as part of a railroad promotion. The city defended its nonpayment of the bonds on the ground that issuance of the bonds was beyond its authority under the Iowa Constitution. The city's interpretation of the state constitution was supported by an 1862 Iowa Supreme Court ruling, which had overruled a number of earlier decisions holding that cities must make good on such debts. In *Gelpcke*, the U.S. Supreme Court declined to follow the state supreme

---

5. At the very least, this should suggest that pitched battles over appointments to the Supreme Court are nothing new in American political life.

6. Carl Swisher, Mr. Chief Justice Taney, in Mr. Justice 38-39 (Dunham & Kurland eds., 1964).

7. See Harry Scheiber, The Road to Munn: Eminent Domain and the Concept of Public Purpose in State Courts, in Law in American History 329 (Fleming & Bailyn eds., 1971).

8. See Benjamin Wright, The Contract Clause of the Constitution (1931).

court's current interpretation, in spite of its declaration a year earlier that it would follow "the latest settled [state] adjudication" construing a state statute or constitution in Leffingwell v. Warren, 67 U.S. (2 Black) 599 (1863). The Court, however, appeared to be appalled by the substantive injustice of the Iowa court's holding:

> The late case in Iowa, and two other cases of a kindred character in another State, also overruling earlier adjudications, stand out, as far as we are advised, in unenviable solitude and notoriety. However we may regard the late case in Iowa as affecting the future, it can have no effect on the past. "The sound and true rule is, that if the contract, when made, was valid by the laws of the State as then expounded by all departments of the government, and administered in its courts of justice, its validity and obligation cannot be impaired by any subsequent action of legislation, or decision of its courts altering the construction of the law." The same principle applies where there is a change of judicial decision as to the constitutional power of the Legislature to enact the law. To this rule, thus enlarged, we adhere. It is the law of this court. It rests upon the plainest principles of justice. To hold otherwise would be as unjust as to hold that rights acquired under a statute may be lost by its repeal.
>
> We are not unmindful of the importance of uniformity in the decisions of this court, and those of the highest local courts, giving constructions to the laws and constitutions of their own States. It is the settled rule of this court in such cases, to follow the decisions of the state courts. But there have been heretofore, in the judicial history of this court, as doubtless there will be hereafter, many exceptional cases. We shall never immolate truth, justice, and the law, because a state tribunal has erected the altar and decreed the sacrifice.

Finally, one should take note, especially in light of the Taney Court's ostensible antifederalist stance, of Swift v. Tyson, 41 U.S. (16 Pet.) 1 (1842). There, the Court substantially federalized the subject of commercial law by holding that federal courts should decide commercial litigation with reference to "the general principles and doctrines of commercial jurisprudence" rather than to the "decisions of local tribunals." The substantive issue in *Swift* was whether the owner of a negotiable instrument had acquired it free of the defenses available between the original parties. The action was brought in a federal court in New York, whose state decisions arguably, and against prevailing doctrine held that, under the circumstances, the owner was not a holder in due course. In an opinion by Justice Story, the Supreme Court decided to follow the "general" commercial law, which was otherwise. The decision was based on §34 of the Judiciary Act of 1789, also known as the Rules of Decision Act, which provided "that the laws of the several states . . . shall be regarded as the rules of decision . . . in courts of the United States." Story wrote that state judicial decisions were "at most, only evidence of what the laws are, and are not, of themselves, laws."

The decision to reject a peculiar state rule in favor of widely followed commercial practice, rooted in the law merchant — that is, the body of law applying to contracts between merchants — was entirely consistent with the instrumentalist objective of facilitating negotiability (not to mention commonly helping creditors). As Story wrote, "The law respecting negotiable instruments may be truly declared in the language of Cicero . . . to be in great measure, not the law of a single country only, but of the commercial world." Although the state courts remained free to adjudicate disputes based on their own common law doctrines, *Swift* gave rise to an independent body of "federal common law," applied in the increasing number of commercial disputes coming within the federal courts' diversity jurisdiction. Grant Gilmore writes that the decision in *Swift*

> was immediately and enthusiastically accepted. No one suggested that it was an unconstitutional usurpation of power by power-crazed judges or that it was a trick played by a wily Federalist judge on his unsuspecting Jacksonian colleagues. No bumper stickers called for Justice Story's impeachment. On the contrary, the doctrine of the general commercial law was warmly welcomed and expansively construed, not only by the lower federal courts but by the state courts as well. For the next half century the Supreme Court of the United States became a great commercial law court.[9]

I.   Interstate and Foreign Commerce and Personal Mobility

Marshall declared in *Gibbons* that he was "tempted" to hold that only Congress could regulate interstate commerce. That would mean that states would be barred from regulating interstate commerce even in the absence of congressional legislation; ultimately Marshall resisted the temptation and held that the New York statute was preempted under the Supremacy Clause by federal legislation. Justice Johnson, however, adopted the more nationalist reading in his concurrence in *Gibbons*. By the end of Jackson's term, his appointees constituted a majority of the Court. At least some of the new Justices believed that the commerce clause by itself — i.e., in the absence of overt congressional legislation — imposed no constraints at all on state regulation and that the states were free to regulate interstate commerce. The attempt to find a resolution to this debate covered the entire period of Taney's Chief Justiceship.

A.   The States' "Police Powers" as a Constraint on the National Commerce Power

New York v. Miln, one of the Taney Court's earliest commerce clause decisions, arose out of the rapidly increasing flow of immigrants from Ireland and Northern Europe into the United States. Although national policy encouraged immigration, the Atlantic seaboard states were wary of indigent immigrants. There were no national, or even state, welfare systems at the time. Rather, the poor were a local problem.[10]

MAYOR OF THE CITY OF NEW YORK v. MILN
36 U.S. (11 Pet.) 102 (1837)

[An 1824 New York State law required the master of a vessel arriving in New York from another country or state to provide a detailed report on "every person brought as a passenger in the ship . . . from any country outside of the United States

---

9. Grant Gilmore, The Ages of American Law 34 (1977).

10. A 1788 New York statute explicitly enjoined that "[e]very city and town shall support and maintain their own poor." See Friedman, supra n.3, at 187-191.

or from any of the United States, into the port of New York, or into any of the United States, and of all persons landed from the ship, during the voyage at any place, or put on board, or suffered to go on board any other vessel, with intention of proceeding to the city of New York." The law further required the master to post security for the maintenance of immigrants and their children who became wards of the city and to remove any noncitizen whom the mayor deemed likely to become dependent. This was an action to recover $15,000 penalties for violation of the act.]

BARBOUR, J. . . .

It is contended by the counsel for the defendant, that the act in question is a regulation of commerce; that the power to regulate commerce is, by the constitution of the United States, granted to congress; that this power is exclusive, and that consequently, the act is a violation of the constitution of the United States.

On the part of the plaintiff, it is argued, that an affirmative grant of power previously existing in the states to congress, is not exclusive; except, 1st, where it is so expressly declared in terms, by the clause giving the power; or 2d, where a similar power is prohibited to the states; or 3d, where the power in the states would be repugnant to, and incompatible with, a similar power in congress; that this power falls within neither of these predicaments. . . . But [plaintiffs also] deny that it is a regulation of commerce; on the contrary, they assert, that it is a mere regulation of internal police, a power over which is not granted to congress; and which, therefore, as well upon the true construction of the constitution, as by force of the tenth amendment to that instrument, is reserved to, and resides in, the several states.[11]

We shall not enter into any examination of the question, whether the power to regulate commerce, be or be not exclusive of the states, because . . . we are of opinion, that the act is not a regulation of commerce, but of police; and that being thus considered, it was passed in the exercise of a power which rightfully belonged to the states.

That the state of New York possessed power to pass this law, before the adoption of the constitution of the United States, might probably be taken as a truism, without the necessity of proof. But as it may tend to present it in a clearer point of view, we will quote a few passages from a standard writer upon public law, showing the origin and character of this power. Vattel: "The sovereign may forbid the entrance of his territory, either to foreigners in general, or in particular cases, or to certain persons, or for certain particular purposes, according as he may think it advantageous to the state." . . . The power then of New York to pass this law having undeniably existed at the formation of the constitution, the simple inquiry is, whether by that instrument it was taken from the states, and granted to congress. . . .

If, as we think, it be a regulation, not of commerce, but police; then it is not taken from the states. To decide this let us examine its purpose, the end to be attained, and the means of its attainment. It is apparent, from the whole scope of the law, that the object of the legislature was, to prevent New York from being burdened by an influx of persons brought thither in ships, either from foreign countries, or from any other of the states; and for that purpose, a report was required of the names, places of birth, &c., of all passengers, that the necessary steps might be taken by the city authorities, to prevent them from becoming chargeable as paupers. Now, we

---

11. Lawyers sometimes offer "pleadings in the alternative." Here you see the plaintiff asserting first that the Commerce Clause, correctly interpreted, does not preclude New York from passing this regulation of commerce, and then that the New York legislation ought not be viewed as a regulation of commerce at all.

hold, that both the end and the means here used, are within the competency of the states, since a portion of their powers were surrendered to the federal government. Let us see, what powers are left with the states. The Federalist, No. 45, speaking of this subject, says, the powers reserved to the several states, all extend to all the objects, which in the ordinary course of affairs, concern the lives, liberties and properties of the people; and the internal order, improvement and prosperity of the state. And this court, in the case of Gibbons v. Ogden, . . . in speaking of the inspection laws of the states, say, "they form a portion of that immense mass of legislation which embraces everything within the territory of a state, not surrendered to the general government, all which can be most advantageously exercised by the states themselves. Inspection laws, quarantine laws, health laws of every description, as well as laws for regulating the internal commerce of a state, and those which respect turnpike-roads, ferries, &c., are component parts of this mass."

Now, if the act in question be tried by reference to the delineation of power laid down in the preceding quotations, it seems to us, that we are necessarily brought to the conclusion, that it falls within its limits. There is no aspect in which it can be viewed, in which it transcends them. If we look at the place of its operation, we find it to be within the territory, and therefore, within the jurisdiction of New York. If we look at the person on whom it operates, he is found within the same territory and jurisdiction. If we look at the persons for whose benefit it was passed, they are the people of New York, for whose protection and welfare the legislature of that state are authorized and in duty bound to provide. If we turn our attention to the purpose to be attained, it is to secure that very protection, and to provide for that very welfare. If we examine the means by which these ends are proposed to be accomplished, they bear a just, natural and appropriate relation to those ends.

But we are told, that it violates the constitution of the United States, and to prove this, we have been referred to two cases in this court; the first, that of Gibbons v. Ogden, 9 Wheat. 1, and the other that of Brown v. State of Maryland, 12 ibid. 419. . . .

Now, there is not, in this case, one of the circumstances which existed in that of Gibbons v. Ogden, which, in the opinion of the court, rendered it obnoxious to the charge of unconstitutionality. On the contrary, the prominent facts of this case are in striking contrast with those which characterized that. In that case, the theatre on which the law operated was navigable water, over which the court say that the power to regulate commerce extended; in this, it was the territory of New York, over which that state possesses an acknowledged, an undisputed jurisdiction for every purpose of internal regulation; in that, the subject-matter on which it operated, was a vessel claiming the right of navigation; a right which the court say is embraced in the power to regulate commerce; in this, the subjects on which it operates are persons whose rights and whose duties are rightfully prescribed and controlled by the laws of the respective states within whose territorial limits they are found; in that, say the court, the act of a state came into direct collision with an act of the United States; in this, no such collision exists.

Nor is there the least likeness between the facts of this case, and those of Brown v. State of Maryland. . . .[12] [In *Brown*] the court did indeed extend the power

---

12. Brown v. Maryland (1827) held (as Chief Justice Taney later summarized it)

that an article authorized by a law of Congress to be imported continued to be a part of the foreign commerce of the country while it remained in the hands of the importer for sale, in the original bale, package, or vessel in which it was imported; that the authority given to import

to regulate commerce, so as to protect the goods imported from a state tax, after they were landed, and were yet in bulk. . . . But how can this apply to persons? They are not the subject of commerce; and not being imported goods, cannot fall within a train of reasoning founded upon the construction of a power given to congress to regulate commerce, and the prohibition to the states from imposing a duty on imported goods. . . .

[The defendant contended that the state law conflicted with and therefore was preempted by federal statutes, enacted in 1799 and 1819, which required the masters of vessels to report on passengers and cargo transported in foreign commerce. Justice Barbour responded that the federal laws were only designed to prevent smuggling, to assure the comfort of passengers, and to "form an accurate estimate of the increase of population by emigration." In any event,] it is obvious that these laws only affect through the power over navigation, the passengers, whilst on their voyage, and until they shall have landed . . . , and can, with no propriety of language, be said to come into conflict with a law of a state, whose operation only begins when that of the laws of congress ends; whose operation is not even on the same subject. . . .

There is, then, no collision between the law in question, and the acts of congress just commented on; and therefore, if the state law were to be considered as partaking of the nature of a commercial regulation; it would stand the test of the most rigid scrutiny, if tried by the standard laid down in the reasoning of the court, quoted from the case of Gibbons v. Ogden.

But we do not place our opinion on this ground. We choose rather to plant ourselves on what we consider impregnable positions. They are these: That a state has the same undeniable and unlimited jurisdiction over all persons and things, within its territorial limits, as any foreign nation; where that jurisdiction is not surrendered or restrained by the constitution of the United States. That, by virtue of this, it is not only the right, but the bounden and solemn duty of a state, to

---

necessarily carried with it the right to sell the imported article in the form and shape in which it was imported, and that no State, either by direct assessment or by requiring a license from the importer before he was permitted to sell, could impose any burden upon him or the property imported beyond what the law of Congress had itself imposed; but that when the original package was broken up for use or for retail by the importer, and also when the commodity had passed from his hands into the hands of a purchaser, it ceased to be an import, or a part of foreign commerce, and became subject to the laws of the State, and might be taxed for State purposes, and the sale regulated by the State, like any other property.

Taney, C.J., concurring in the License Cases, 46 U.S. (5 How.) 504 (1847). Taney went on to explain:

The immense amount of foreign products used and consumed in this country are imported, landed, and offered for sale in a few commercial cities, and a very small portion of them are intended or expected to be used in the States in which they are imported. . . , And where they are in the hands of the importer . . . they may be regarded as merely in transit, on their way to the distant cities, villages, and country for which they are destined, and where they are expected to be used and consumed, and for the supply of which they were in truth imported. And a tax upon them . . . would be hardly more justifiable in principle than a transit duty upon the merchandise when passing through a State. . . . And if a State is permitted to levy it in any form, it will put in the power of a maritime importing State to raise a revenue for the support of its own government from citizens of other States, as certainly and effectively as if the tax was laid openly and without disguise as a duty on imports. Such a power in a State would defeat one of the principal objects of forming and adopting the Constitution. And as it cannot be done directly [see Article I, §10], it could hardly be a just and sound construction of the constitution which would enable a State to accomplish precisely the same thing under another name, and in a different form.

advance the safety, happiness and prosperity of its people, and to provide for its general welfare, by any and every act of legislation, which it may deem to be conducive to these ends; where the power over the particular subject, or the manner of its exercise is not surrendered or restrained, in the manner just stated. That all those powers which relate to merely municipal legislation, or what may, perhaps, more properly be called internal police, are not thus surrendered or restrained; and that, consequently, in relation to these, the authority of a state is complete, unqualified and exclusive.

We are aware, that it is at all times difficult to define any subject with proper precision and accuracy; if this be so in general, it is emphatically so, in relation to a subject so diversified and multifarious as the one which we are now considering. If we were to attempt it, we would say, that every law came within this description which concerned the welfare of the whole people of a state, or any individual within it . . . and whose operation was within the territorial limits of the state, and upon the persons and things within its jurisdiction. . . .

[T]he section in the act immediately before us [was] obviously passed with a view to prevent [New York's] citizens from being oppressed by the support of multitudes of poor persons, who come from foreign countries, without possessing the means of supporting themselves. There can be no mode in which the power to regulate internal police could be more appropriately exercised. New York, from her particular situation, is, perhaps, more than any other city in the Union, exposed to the evil of thousands of foreign emigrants arriving there, and the consequent danger of her citizens being subjected to a heavy charge in the maintenance of those who are poor. It is the duty of the state to protect its citizens from this evil; they have endeavored to do so, by passing, amongst other things, the section of the law in question. We should, upon principle, say that it had a right to do so.

Let us compare this power with a mass of power, said by this court, in Gibbons v. Ogden, not to be surrendered to the general government. They are inspection laws, quarantine laws, health laws of every description, as well as laws for regulating the internal commerce of a state, &c. . . .

We . . . think, that if the stronger powers, under the necessity of the case, by inspection laws and quarantine laws, to delay the landing of a ship and cargo, which are the subjects of commerce and navigation, and to remove or even to destroy unsound and infectious articles, also the subject of commerce, can be rightfully exercised, then, that it must follow, as a consequence, that powers less strong, such as the one in question, which operates upon no subject either of commerce or navigation, but which operates alone within the limits and jurisdiction of New York, upon a person, at the time, not even engaged in navigation, is still more clearly embraced within the general power of the states to regulate their own internal police, and to take care that no detriment come to the commonwealth. We think it as competent and as necessary for a state to provide precautionary measures against the moral pestilence of paupers, vagabonds, and possibly convicts; as it is to guard against the physical pestilence, which may arise from unsound and infectious articles imported, or from a ship, the crew of which may be laboring under an infectious disease. . . .

THOMPSON, J. . . .

It is not necessary, in this case, to fix any limits upon the legislation of congress and of the states, on this subject; or to say how far congress may, under the power to regulate commerce, control state legislation in this respect. It is enough to say, that whatever the power of congress may be, it has not been exercised so as, in any manner, to conflict with the state law; and if the mere grant of the power to congress does not necessarily imply a prohibition of the states to exercise the power, until congress assumes to exercise it, no objection, on that ground, can arise to this law. Nor is it necessary to decide, definitively, whether the provisions of this law may be considered as at all embraced within the power to regulate commerce. Under either view of the case, the law of New York, so far at least as it is drawn in question in the present suit, is entirely unobjectionable. . . .

The case of Willson v. Blackbird Creek Marsh Company, 2 Pet. 251, is a strong case to show that a power admitted to fall within the power to regulate commerce, may be exercised by the states, until congress assumes the exercise. . . . By the same rule of construction, the law of New York, not coming in conflict with any act of congress, is not void by reason of the dormant power to regulate commerce; even if it should be admitted, that the subject embraced in that law fell within such power. . . .

Whether, therefore, the law of New York, so far as it is drawn in question in this case, be considered as relating purely to the police and internal government of the state, and as part of the system of poor-laws in the city of New York, and in this view belonging exclusively to the legislation of the state; or whether the subject-matter of the law be considered as belonging concurrently to the state and to congress, but never having been exercised by the latter; no constitutional objection can be made to it. . . .

STORY, J., dissenting. . . .

I admit, in the most unhesitating manner, that the states have a right to pass health laws and quarantine laws, and other police laws, not contravening the laws of congress rightfully passed under their constitutional authority. I admit, that they have a right to pass poor-laws, and laws to prevent the introduction of paupers into the state, under the like qualifications. I go further, and admit, that in the exercise of their legitimate authority over any particular subject, the states may generally use the same means which are used by congress, if these means are suitable to the end. But I cannot admit, that the states have authority to enact laws, which act upon subjects beyond their territorial limits, or within those limits and which trench upon the authority of congress in its power to regulate commerce. . . .

It has been argued, that the act of New York is not a regulation of commerce, but is a mere police law upon the subject of paupers; and it has been likened to the cases of health laws, quarantine laws, ballast laws; gunpowder laws, and others of a similar nature. . . . I have already said, that I admit the power of the states to pass such laws, and to use the proper means to effectuate the objects of them; but it is with this reserve, that these means are not exclusively vested in congress. A state cannot make a regulation of commerce, to enforce its health laws, because it is a means withdrawn from its authority. It may be admitted, that it is a means adapted to the end; but it is quite a different question, whether it be a means within the competency of the state jurisdiction. . . .

But how can it be truly said, that the act of New York is not a regulation of commerce? No one can well doubt, that if the same act had been passed by congress, it would have been a regulation of commerce; and in that way, and in that only, would it be a constitutional act of congress. The right of congress to pass such an act has been expressly conceded at the argument. The act of New York purports, on its very face, to regulate the conduct of masters, and owners and passengers, in foreign trade; and in foreign ports and places [by requiring] a report of the passengers taken or landed [there]. . . . I listened with great attention to the argument, to ascertain upon what ground the act of New York was to be maintained not to be a regulation of commerce. I confess, that I was unable to ascertain any, from the reasoning of either of the learned counsel, who spoke for the plaintiff. Their whole argument on this point seemed to me to amount to this: that if it were a regulation of commerce, still it might also be deemed a regulation of police, and a part of the system of poor-laws; and therefore, justifiable as a means to attain the end. In my judgment, for the reasons already suggested, that is not a just consequence, or a legitimate deduction. If the act is a regulation of commerce, and that subject belongs exclusively to congress, it is a means cut off from the range of state sovereignty and state legislation.

And this leads me more distinctly to the consideration of the other point in question; and that is, whether, if the act of New York be a regulation of commerce, it is void and unconstitutional? If the power of congress to regulate commerce be an exclusive power; or if the subject-matter has been constitutionally regulated by congress, so as to exclude all additional or conflicting legislation by the states, then, and in either case, it is clear, that the act of New York is void and unconstitutional. Let us consider the question under these aspects.

It has been argued, that the power of congress to regulate commerce is not exclusive, but concurrent with that of the states. If this were a new question in this court, wholly untouched by doctrine or decision, I should not hesitate to go into a full examination of all the grounds upon which concurrent authority is attempted to be maintained. But in point of fact, the whole argument on this very question . . . was . . . deliberately examined, and deemed inadmissible by the court [in Gibbons v. Ogden]. Mr. Chief Justice Marshall, with his accustomed accuracy and fulness of illustration, reviewed at that time the whole grounds of the controversy; and from that time to the present, the question has been considered (so far as I know) to be at rest. The power given to congress to regulate commerce with foreign nations, and among the states, has been deemed exclusive, from the nature and objects of the power, and the necessary implications growing out of its exercise. Full power to regulate a particular subject, implies the whole power, and leaves no residuum; and a grant of the whole to one, is incompatible with a grant to another of a part. When a state proceeds to regulate commerce with foreign nations, or among the states, it is doing the very thing which congress is authorized to do. And it has been remarked, with great cogency and accuracy, that the regulation of a subject indicates and designates the entire result; applying to those parts which remain as they were, as well as to those parts which are altered. It produces a uniform whole, which is as much disturbed and deranged by changing what the regulating power designs to leave untouched, as that upon which it has operated.

This last suggestion is peculiarly important in the present case; for congress has, by the act of the 2d of March 1819, regulated passenger ships and vessels. Subject to the regulations therein provided, passengers may be brought into the United States from foreign ports. These regulations, being all which congress have chosen to enact, amount, upon the reasoning already stated, to a complete exercise of its power over the whole subject, as well in what is omitted as what is provided for. Unless, then, we are prepared to say, that wherever congress has legislated upon this subject, clearly within its constitutional authority, and made all such regulations, as, in its own judgment and discretion, were deemed expedient; the states may step in and supply all other regulations, which they may deem expedient, as complementary to those of congress, thus subjecting all our trade, commerce and navigation, and intercourse with foreign nations, to the double operations of distinct and independent sovereignties, it seems to me, impossible to maintain the doctrine, that the states have a concurrent jurisdiction with congress on the regulation of commerce, whether congress has or has not legislated upon the subject; a fortiori, when it has legislated.

There is another consideration, which ought not to be overlooked in discussing this subject. It is, that congress, by its legislation, has, in fact, authorized not only the transportation but the introduction of passengers into the country. The act of New York imposes restraints and burdens upon this right of transportation and introduction. It goes even further, and authorizes the removal of passengers, under certain circumstances, out of the state, and at the expense of the master and owner in whose ship they have been introduced; and this, though they are citizens of the United States, and were brought from other states. Now, if this act be constitutional to this extent, it will justify the states in regulating, controlling, and, in effect, interdicting the transportation of passengers from one state to another, in steamboats and packets. They may levy a tax upon all such passengers; they may require bonds from the master, that no such passengers shall become chargeable to the state; they may require such passengers to give bonds, that they shall not become so chargeable; they may authorize the immediate removal of such passengers back to the place from which they came. These would be most burdensome and inconvenient regulations respecting passengers, and would entirely defeat the object of congress in licensing the trade or business. And yet, if the argument which we have heard be well founded, it is a power strictly within the authority of the states, and may be exerted, at the pleasure of all or any of them, to the ruin and, perhaps, annihilation of our passenger navigation. It is no answer to the objection, to say, that the states will have too much wisdom and prudence to exercise the authority to so great an extent. Laws were actually passed, of a retaliatory nature, by the states of New York, New Jersey and Connecticut, during the steamboat controversy, which threatened the safety and security of the Union; and demonstrated the necessity, that the power to regulate commerce among the states should be exclusive in the Union, in order to prevent the most injurious restraints upon it. . . .

[Story then discusses Brown v. State of Maryland and states that its doctrine clearly applies in this case.]

Such is a brief view of the grounds upon which my judgment is, that the act of New York is unconstitutional and void. In this opinion, I have the consolation to know, that I had the entire concurrence, upon the same grounds, of that great constitutional jurist, the late Mr. Chief Justice Marshall. Having heard the former arguments, his deliberate opinion was, that the act of New York was unconstitutional; and that the present case fell directly within the principles established in the case of Gibbons v. Ogden and Brown v. State of Maryland. . . .

Discussion

1. Note well that even Justice Story grants states the right to "to prevent the introduction of paupers into the state." Indeed, in a later decision, Prigg v. Pennsylvania, infra, p. 217, Story, writing for the majority, stated that "[w]e entertain no doubt whatsoever that the states, in virtue of their general police power, possess full jurisdiction to arrest and restrain runaway slaves, and remove them from their borders,

and otherwise to secure themselves against their depredations and evil example, as they certainly may do in cases of idlers, vagabonds, and paupers." Article 4 of the Articles of Confederation, which granted to "the people of each State [a right of] free ingress and regress to and from any other State," explicitly exempted "paupers, vagabonds and fugitives from justice" from the enjoyment of any such right. As Gerald Neuman writes, "Although the 1787 Constitution omitted this qualification from its Privileges and Immunities Clause, the courts continued to assume that paupers had no right to travel." Indeed, according to Neuman,

> Perhaps the most fundamental function of immigration law has been to impede the movement of the poor. In neither the eighteenth century nor the nineteenth century did American law concede the right of the needy to geographic mobility. At the time of independence, the states took with them the heritage of the English poor laws, which made the relief of the poor the responsibility of the local community where they were legally "settled." These laws gave localities various powers to prevent the settlement of persons who might later require support and to "remove" them to the place where they were legally settled. Accordingly, some of the most important provisions of state immigration law are sprinkled through the state poor laws.[13]

Even if one believes that the Constitution's failure to adopt the language of Article IV limited New York's power to restrict the immigration of paupers who were citizens of other states of the Union, does that necessarily imply an inability to resist the entry of foreign paupers?

2. Justices Thompson and Story seem to address the constitutionality of the New York law in similar terms, though of course they reach different conclusions. Justice Barbour's opinion for the Court has a different focus altogether. After concluding that the law is not preempted by any congressional statutes, he remarks that "we do not place our opinion on this ground. We choose rather to plant ourselves on what we consider impregnable positions," referring to the powers of "internal police" that are not surrendered by the states and with respect to which "the authority of the state is complete, unqualified, and exclusive." What is Barbour's theory? How, if at all, does his concept of the role of these state powers in the federal constitutional scheme differ from Marshall's in *Gibbons*? How does Barbour differentiate the realms of national and state authority?

3. Justice Story's opinion provides the first occasion in this casebook of precedent-based argument, in which a judge analyzes a prior case by way of presenting it as the foundation for his own opinion. Reread carefully Story's discussion of Marshall's opinion in *Gibbons*. How accurate is it? Assume that Story's opinion had been the "Opinion of the Court." Would it then count as an authoritative description of *Gibbons*?

4. Extensive discussion of congressional and state authority regarding immigration occurs in The Passenger Cases, 48 U.S. (7 How.) 283 (1849). The Court invalidated New York and Massachusetts laws that imposed a landing fee on alien passengers to pay for the support or medical care of foreign paupers. There was no majority opinion; the majority was divided between those justices who viewed the regulations as an unconstitutional regulation of foreign commerce and others who struck them down as taxes on imports in violation of Article I, §10.

---

13. Gerald Neuman, Strangers to the Constitution: Immigrants, Borders, and Fundamental Law 23 (1996).

One should not overestimate the importance of The Passenger Cases. Even the majority scarcely was unsympathetic to state interests. Thus Justice Grier in his seriatim opinion acknowledged "the sacred law of self-defence" as legitimizing the exclusion by states of "lunatics, idiots, criminals, or paupers," as well as a slave state's barring the immigration of free blacks. Indeed, none of the five justices in the majority can be said to have rejected a substantial quanta of state power over immigration, see Neuman, supra, though they objected to the particular means chosen by Massachusetts and New York in the instant cases. Indeed, as Neuman writes, the Passenger Cases had only limited effect insofar as many states continued to require the posting of bonds, or the payment of a fixed fee in lieu of a bond, to replace the automatic "head tax" struck down by the Supreme Court. It would be a quarter-century before constitutional doctrine developed that placed "exclusive" control in Congress over immigration. See Henderson v. New York, 92 U.S. 259 (1876), and Chy Lung v. Freeman, 92 U.S. 275 (1876). Still, even in 1902, see Morgan's S.S. Co. v. Louisiana Board of Health, 118 U.S. 455, 465-466, the Court emphasized the legitimacy of state "quarantine laws" in regard to immigrants, which had, of course, been endorsed by Marshall in Gibbons v. Ogden, supra.

One must realize that Congress had not passed much legislation affecting immigration by the time the Passenger Cases were decided, so the discussion at that point necessarily involves many "first principles" about the allocation of authority even in the absence of full-scale confrontation between an actual law of Congress and state policy. Chief Justice Taney, perhaps concerned about legislation that Congress might be tempted to adopt, attempted to head off at the pass any notion that Congress was necessarily supreme in regard to all facets of immigration.

Thus, in his own dissent he denied the existence of any federal power at all over the immigration of persons into the states, which he viewed as a "reserved" power, impervious to limitation by federal treaty or congressional legislation. "[T]he people of the several States" retained the power to expel "from their borders any person, or class or persons, whom it might deem dangerous to its peace, or likely to produce a physical or moral evil among its citizens. . . . [T]he State has the exclusive right to determine, in its sound discretion, whether the danger does or does not exist, free from the control of the general government." The motivation behind Taney's zeal on the point is suggested by his illustration of the danger of the majority's position:

> I cannot believe that it was ever intended to vest in Congress . . . this overwhelming power over the States [of deciding who should or should not be permitted to reside among its citizens]. For [Congress could then grant] the emancipated slaves of the West Indies . . . the absolute right to reside, hire houses, and traffic and trade throughout the Southern States, in spite of any State law to the contrary; inevitably producing the most serious discontent, and ultimately leading to the most painful consequences. . . .

5. *Persons as articles of commerce.* Justice Barbour states that persons "are not the subject of commerce." As you will see later in Chapter 9, this is not an accurate statement of current doctrine. Indeed, Henderson v. New York based Congress's right to control immigration on the commerce clause. (Though recall the debate over the Alien Act, which rooted such powers in an inherent notion of sovereignty. What is the difference between these two arguments? Which is more persuasive?) As Mary Sarah Bilder points out in The Struggle over Immigration: Indentured Servants,

Slaves, and Articles of Commerce, 61 Missouri L. Rev. 743 (1996), persons were often treated as items of commerce in the eighteenth and nineteenth centuries. This is clearest, of course, in regard to slaves, who were bought and sold precisely as any other commodity, but she points out that this was true as well in regard to indentured servants, who comprised a very high percentage of the white immigrants to America before the American Revolution. Thus David Galenson writes that "between half and two-thirds of all white immigrants to the American colonies after the 1630s and before independence came under indenture."[14] "During the term of service," Bilder notes, "indentured servants constituted property: they were assignable under statutory provisions; they could be sold to satisfy a debt; and they passed by descent pursuant to testamentary laws." Indentured servitude as a system of labor basically collapsed after 1819 and had, presumably, vanished by the time that *Miln* was decided.

At the very least, isn't "commerce" any exchange of movable property between willing buyers and sellers, whether the particular "articles of commerce" be widgets, contractually bound workers (consider the modern trade in athletes), or slaves? Why, then, was Barbour so eager to deny persons the status of objects of commerce, particularly given that the "police power" rationale earlier developed in *Gibbons* would have easily offered him a way to justify the New York law even in regard to acknowledged "articles of commerce"? (After all, Marshall explicitly legitimized state quarantine laws that, by definition, block the shipment of goods between states.) One possible answer is that to concede that persons are "articles of commerce" under the commerce clause would be to concede as well congressional power to regulate the most important group of such persons, slaves. This, obviously, was a highly volatile suggestion. Thus, Bilder notes, several proslavery writers were among the most insistent that slaves were "persons" rather than "articles of commerce," whereas some anti-slavery authors were as eager to define slaves as commodities to make slavery subject to regulation by Congress. Once slavery was removed as a topic of constitutional debate by the Thirteenth Amendment, it was easy enough to accept the proposition that persons were indeed "articles of commerce," with whatever powers (for Congress) and limitations (in regard to states) that were attached to such a status.

6. *Elkison v. Deliesseline.* Consider, in the light of *Miln*, the South Carolina Negro Seaman's Act of 1822. That act, among other things, provided that "any free negroes or persons of color" brought into a South Carolina port by "any vessel" coming "from any other state or foreign port" shall "be seized and confined in gaol until such vessel shall clear out and depart from this state." The vessel's captain was liable for the payment of expenses incurred by the State for the detention; refusal to pay was itself an offense punishable by a fine of not less than $1,000 and imprisonment of not less than two months. Moreover, the persons detained "shall be deemed and taken as absolute slaves, and sold . . ." by the State.

The Act was passed at the time of the Denmark Vesey rebellion, the actual circumstances of which continue to be a highly disputed topic among American historians. Compare, e.g., David Robertson, Denmark Vesey: The Buried History of America's Largest Slave Rebellion and the Man Who Led It (1999) with Michael P. Johnson, Denmark Vesey and His Co-Conspirators, 58 William and Mary Quarterly, 3d Ser., 915-976 (2001). It is uncontroverted that Vesey, with five others, was hanged

---

14. David Galenson, White Servitude in Colonial America: An Economic Analysis 3-4 (1981).

outside Charleston on July 2, 1822, and that many white South Carolinians, who were in fact a minority of the overall population, most of which consisted of black slaves, feared that Vesey intended to bring together as many as 9,000 slaves and free blacks who were to march on Charleston, burn the city, and murder the white population.

The terms of the act were applied to a member of the crew of "the ship Homer, a British ship trading from Liverpool" to Charleston. Justice Johnson, sitting on circuit, described its purpose as "to prohibit ships coming into this port employing colored seamen." He went on to invalidate the act in Elkison v. Deliesseline, 8 F. Cas. 493 (1823), on the ground that it violated the commerce clause.

He first generalized what was at issue: "[I]f this state can prohibit Great Britain from employing her colored subjects . . . [or] her subjects of the African race, why not prohibit her from using those of Irish or Scottish nativity? . . ." After pointing out that the Act applied to domestic as well as foreign vessels, he noted that the enforcement of the Act might well encourage retaliation against South Carolina ships by the affected governments.

> [T]he commerce of this city, feeble and sickly, comparatively, as it already is, might be fatally injured. Charleston seamen, Charleston owners, Charleston vessels, might, eo nomine, be excluded from their commerce, or the United States involved in war and confusion. . . . These considerations show its utter incompatibility with the power delegated to congress to regulate commerce with foreign nations and our sister states. . . .
>
> The seaman's offense, therefore, is coming into the state in a ship or vessel; that of the captain consists in bringing him in, and not taking him out of the state, and paying all expenses. Now, according to the laws and treaties of the United States, it was both lawful for this seaman to come into this port, in this vessel, and for the captain to bring him in the capacity of a seaman; and yet these are the very acts for which the state law imposes these heavy penalties. Is there no clashing in this? It is in effect a repeal of the laws of the United States, pro tanto, converting a right into a crime.
>
> . . . [T]he right of the general government to regulate commerce with the sister states and foreign nations is a paramount and exclusive right; and this conclusion we arrive at, whether we examine it with reference to the words of the constitution, or the nature of the grant. . . . In the constitution of the United States, the most wonderful instrument ever drawn by the hand of man, there is a comprehension and precision that is unparalleled. . . . It is true that it contains no prohibition on the states to regulate foreign commerce. Nor was such a prohibition necessary, for the words of the grant sweep away the whole subject, and leave nothing for the states to act upon. Wherever this is the case, there is no prohibitory clause interposed in the constitution. Thus, the states are not prohibited from regulating the value of foreign coins or fixing a standard of weights and measures, for the very words imply a total, unlimited grant. . . .
>
> But to all this the plea of necessity is urged; and of the existence of that necessity we are told the state alone is to judge. Where is this to land us? Is it not asserting the right in each state to throw off the federal constitution at its will and pleasure? . . . But I deny that the state surrendered a single power necessary to its security, against this species of property. What is to prevent their being confined to their ships, if it is dangerous for them to go abroad? This power may be lawfully exercised. To land their cargoes, take in others, and depart, is all that is necessary to ordinary commerce.
>
> . . . But if the policy of this law was to keep foreign free persons from holding communion with our slaves, it certainly pursues a course altogether inconsistent with its object. . . . [T]he method of disposing of offenders by detaining them here presents the

finest facilities in the world for introducing themselves lawfully into the very situation in which they would enjoy the best opportunities of pursuing their designs. Now, if this plea of necessity could avail at all against the constitution and laws of the United States, certainly that law cannot be pronounced necessary which may defeat its own ends; much less when other provisions of unexceptionable legality may be resorted to, which would operate solely to the end proposed, viz., the effectual exclusion of dangerous characters.

This may help explain why Johnson wrote a concurring opinion the next year in *Gibbons* adopting the theory that Marshall was willing only to suggest — that Congress's power to regulate commerce was exclusive, even absent specific legislation.

How do you think that Justice Johnson would have voted in *Miln?* Given the result in *Miln,* how do you think the Supreme Court would have handled the South Carolina statute? Would your answer change had the majority adopted Justice Thompson's view of the concurrent power of a State? Do you think that Justice Story would agree with Justice Johnson's comments about the constitutionality of a more modest statute that simply confined black seamen to their ships?

7. Lest one believe that *Elkison* had much effect, consider Professor Neuman's observation:[15]

> The *Elkison* case was only the first of the confrontations between Britain and the Southern states over the issue of black seamen. [President John Quincy] Adams sought to calm the British by assuring them that he would try to prevent enforcement of the statute, but that in a federal system he would need time to persuade South Carolina officials. South Carolina, however, definitively rebuffed him. Incidents continued in that and other states, and so, intermittently, did British protests. The treaty issue was particularly difficult because of an ambiguous clause in the commercial treaty making reciprocal liberty of commerce "subject always to the laws and statutes of the two countries, respectively." The U.S. diplomatic stance changed after Andrew Jackson's attorney general took a more expansive view of states' rights and affirmed the states' authority to enact such laws; he also relied in part on the 1803 federal statute forbidding the bringing in of foreign blacks excluded by state laws. The Northern states also continued to protest, but Congress would not act. In 1844 Massachusetts sent agents to South Carolina and Louisiana to institute judicial proceedings to test the constitutionality of the laws, but they were forced to flee under threat of mob violence. Later in that decade, Secretary of State [James Buchanan, who would later become President] instructed the U.S. consul in Jamaica to cooperate in securing compliance with these state laws, and he informed the British that if they insisted that enforcement of the state laws violated the commercial treaty between the two nations, it would become necessary to abrogate the treaty.

B.   The *Cooley* Accommodation

Only two years after the hyperfragmented *Passenger Cases,* the Court initiated an entirely new approach to analyzing state laws affecting interstate transportation.

15. Supra n.13, at 38-39.

COOLEY v. BOARD OF WARDENS
53 U.S. (12 How.) 299 (1851)

[An 1803 Pennsylvania law required vessels entering and leaving the port of Philadelphia to engage a local pilot to guide them through the harbor. The penalty for noncompliance was one-half the regular fee (for the use of the Society for the Relief of Distressed and Decayed Pilots, their widows and children). This was an action by the Board of Wardens to recover the penalty from the consignee of noncomplying vessels engaged in the coastwise trade between New York and Philadelphia. The state courts held for the Board.[16]]

CURTIS, J. . . .

[The laws] rest upon the propriety of securing lives and property exposed to the perils of a dangerous navigation, by taking on board a person peculiarly skilled to encounter or avoid them. . . .

It remains to consider the objection, that it is repugnant to the [commerce clause]. That the power to regulate commerce includes the regulation of navigation, we consider settled. And . . . the regulation of the qualifications of pilots, of the modes and times of offering and rendering their services . . . do constitute regulations of navigation, and consequently of commerce, within the just meaning of this clause of the Constitution. . . .

[W]e are brought directly and unavoidably to the consideration of the question, whether the grant of the commercial power to Congress, did per se deprive the States of all power to regulate pilots. . . . [W]hen the nature of a power like this is spoken of, when it is said that the nature of the power requires that it should be exercised exclusively by Congress, it must be intended to refer to the subjects of that power, and to say they are of such a nature as to require exclusive legislation by Congress. Now the power to regulate commerce, embraces a vast field, containing not only many, but exceedingly various subjects, quite unlike in their nature; some imperatively demanding a single uniform rule, operating equally on the commerce of the United States in every port; and some, like the subject now in question, as imperatively demanding that diversity, which alone can meet the local necessities of navigation.

Either absolutely to affirm, or deny that the nature of this power requires exclusive legislation by Congress, is to lose sight of the nature of the subjects of this power, and to assert concerning all of them, what is really applicable but to a part. Whatever subjects of this power are in their nature national, or admit only of one uniform system, or plan of regulation, may justly be said to be of such a nature as to require exclusive legislation by Congress. That this cannot be affirmed of laws for the regulation of pilots and pilotage, is plain. The act of 1789 contains a clear and authoritative declaration by the first Congress, that the nature of this subject is such, that until Congress should find it necessary to exert its power, it should be left to the legislation of the States; that it is local and not national; that it is likely to be the best provided for,

16. In the course of their opinions, both Justices Curtis and McLean refer to a congressional act of 1789 providing: "That all pilots in the bays, inlets, rivers, harbors, and ports of the United States shall continue to be regulated in conformity with the existing laws of the States, respectively, wherein such pilots may be, or with such laws as the States may respectively hereafter enact for the purpose, until further legislative provision shall be made by Congress." For reasons not of present concern, the Justices did not hold that the challenged Pennsylvania law was authorized by this statute; they therefore treated the state law as if Congress had not legislated on the issue. However, the majority did invoke the federal statute in support of its conclusion that the regulation of pilotage was a local matter, not a national one.

not by one system, or plan of regulations, but by as many as the legislative discretion of the several States should deem applicable to the local peculiarities of the ports within their limits. . . . The practice of the States, and of the national government, has been in conformity with this declaration, from the origin of the national government to this time; and the nature of the subject when examined, is such as to leave no doubt of the superior fitness and propriety, not to say the absolute necessity, of different systems of regulation, drawn from local knowledge and experience, and conformed to local wants. How then can we say, that by the mere grant of power to regulate commerce, the States are deprived of all the power to legislate on this subject, because from the nature of the power the legislation of Congress must be exclusive? . . . It is the opinion of a majority of the court that the mere grant to Congress of the power to regulate commerce, did not deprive the States of power to regulate pilots, and that although Congress has legislated on this subject, its legislation manifests an intention . . . not to regulate this subject, but to leave its regulation to the several States. . . .

We have not adverted to the practical consequences of holding that the States possess no power to legislate for the regulation of pilots, though in our apprehension these would be of the most serious importance. For more than sixty years this subject has been acted on by the States. . . .

If the grant of commercial power in the Constitution has deprived the States of all power to legislate for the regulation of pilots, if their laws on this subject are mere usurpations upon the exclusive power of the general government, and utterly void, . . . how are the legislatures of the States to proceed in future, to watch over and amend these laws, as the progressive wants of a growing commerce will require . . . ?

We are of opinion that this State law was enacted by virtue of a power, residing in the State to legislate; that it is not in conflict with any law of Congress; that it does not interfere with any system which Congress has established by making regulations, or by intentionally leaving individuals to their own unrestricted action; that this law is therefore valid, and the judgment of the Supreme Court of Pennsylvania in each case must be affirmed.

McLean, J., dissenting. . . .

It will be found that the principle in this case, if carried out, will deeply affect the commercial prosperity of the country. . . .

Louisiana now imposes a duty upon vessels for mooring in the river opposite the city of New Orleans, which is called a levee tax, and which, on some boats performing weekly trips to that city, amounts to from $3,000 to $4,000 annually. What is there to prevent the thirteen or fourteen states bordering upon the two rivers first-named, from regulating navigation on those rivers, although Congress may have regulated the same at some prior period? I speak not of the effect of this doctrine theoretically in this matter, but practically. And if the doctrine be true, how can this court say that such regulations of commerce are invalid? . . .

From this race of legislation between Congress and the states, and between the states, if this principle be maintained, will arise a conflict similar to that which existed before the adoption of the Constitution. . . .

[A dissenting opinion by Justice Daniel is omitted.]

Discussion

1. Justice Curtis's opinion seems to break sharply with both Marshall's and Taney's view of the commerce clause. (*Cooley* is rare among commerce clause opinions of

the period in not even mentioning Gibbons v. Ogden.) Viewed in retrospect, *Cooley* presaged a functional approach to adjudicating state regulations affecting interstate transportation that would become highly influential after 1937. Curtis's approach turned out to be aberrant in its own time, however, and the opinion was widely ignored.

2. How exactly does one define a matter of "local" concern from one that demands a "national" resolution? Consider carefully Justice McLean's example of the "practical" effects of a single boat, traveling down the Mississippi River, becoming subject to a dozen different regulatory regimes, each based on "local" concerns about, say, the safety of the boats. (What if only one state bothered to pass such regulations, while the rest remained indifferent? Would that serve to validate the state regulation?)

Note on Congressional Consent

Does the Supreme Court have the "last word" in regard to state regulations affecting interstate commerce? The answer is no. The Wheeling Bridge cases presented the first situation in which Congress attempted to authorize a state law that the Court had earlier, in the absence of congressional legislation, struck down as an invalid regulation of interstate commerce.[17] The cases arose out of competition between Pennsylvania and Virginia over where the Cumberland Road, one of the major national thoroughfares of the time, would cross the Ohio River. In 1847, the Virginia legislature chartered a corporation to build a bridge across the river in Wheeling (now in West Virginia). In Pennsylvania v. Wheeling & Belmont Bridge Co., 54 U.S. (13 How.) 518 (1852), Pennsylvania sought to enjoin construction of the bridge. By the time the case was heard, the bridge had been built. Justice McLean wrote for the Court, holding that the bridge impermissibly obstructed interstate navigation and ordering it raised to a specified height. (Chief Justice Taney dissented, relying on Willson v. Black-Bird Creek Marsh Co.)

Virginia took its fight to Congress, which attached a rider to a post office appropriation bill by which the bridge was declared to be a lawful structure in its existing position and elevation and was declared to be a post road for the passage of mails. The bill was passed in the face of Pennsylvania's protest against this attempt to "reverse or render inoperative, the solemn adjudication of the Supreme Court."[18] The bridge collapsed in a storm in 1854. Invoking the judgment in the first case, plaintiffs sought to enjoin its rebuilding. In the second Wheeling Bridge case, 59 U.S. (18 How.) 421 (1855), a divided Court sustained the statute and denied the injunction. Justice Nelson wrote:

> So far . . . as this bridge created an obstruction to the free navigation of the river, in view of the previous acts of congress, they are to be regarded as modified by this subsequent legislation; and, although it still may be an obstruction in fact, it is not so in the contemplation of law. . . . The regulation of commerce includes intercourse and navigation, and, of course, the power to determine what shall or shall not be deemed in judgment of law, an obstruction to navigation.

17. The facts surrounding the case are taken from Carl Swisher, 5 History of the Supreme Court of the United States: The Taney Period, 1836-64, at 408-420 (1974).
18. Id. at 415.

Justice McLean, who had written for the majority in the first case, dissented, asserting that Congress "may . . . declare that no bridge shall be built which shall be an obstruction to the use of a navigable water. And this, it would seem, is as far as the commercial power by congress can be exercised." Since *Wheeling Bridge,* it has been established that Congress can consent to state regulation of interstate commerce which otherwise would be held to run afoul of the commerce clause,[19] though there is no theoretical account that explains exactly why this is the case. In Prudential Insurance Co. v. Benjamin, 328 U.S. 408 (1946), which sustained Congress's consent to state regulation and taxation of the interstate insurance business after the Court had struck down such regulation as beyond states' authority because of its "interstate character," Justice Rutledge noted that the Court had never invalidated a consent to state regulation of commerce:

> It is true that rationalizations have differed concerning those decisions. . . . But . . . whenever Congress' judgment has been uttered affirmatively to contradict the Court's previously expressed view that specific action taken by the states in Congress' silence was forbidden by the commerce clause, this body has accommodated its previous judgment to Congress' express approval. Some part of this readjustment may be explained in ways acceptable on any theory of the commerce clause and the relations of Congress and the courts toward its functioning. Such explanations, however, hardly go to the root of the matter. For the fact remains that, in these instances, the sustaining of Congress' overriding action has involved something beyond correction of erroneous factual judgment in deference to Congress' presumably better-informed view of the facts, and also beyond giving due deference to its conception of the scope of its powers, when it repudiates, just as when its silence is thought to support, the inference that it has forbidden state action.

"At this point," writes Professor Noel T. Dowling, "it seemed almost as if Mr. Justice Rutledge were leading to a mountain top from which he would point out the 'something beyond' which really went to the root of the matter. But after looking at this point and at that on the broad landscape of his opinion, I was still not sure that my vision had caught the 'something beyond.' "[20]

The short of it is that invalidations of state regulations under the commerce clause are less like pure "constitutional" decisions than like decisions holding state laws "preempted" by supervening congressional policy. Only the congressional policy is not — as otherwise it usually is — manifested in any enactment. In an earlier article, Professor Dowling proposed the following doctrine for this area.[21]

> [I]n the absence of affirmative consent a Congressional negative will be presumed in the courts against state action which in its effect upon interstate commerce constitutes an unreasonable interference with national interests, the presumption being rebuttable at the pleasure of Congress. Such a doctrine would free the states from any constitutional disability but at the same time would not give them license to take such action as they see fit irrespective of its effect upon interstate commerce. With respect to such commerce, the question whether the state may act upon it would depend upon

---

19. Cf. Article I, §10, cl. 2: "No State shall, without the Consent of the Congress, lay any Imposts or Duties on Imports or Exports . . ." This clause does not apply to trade within the United States. Woodruff v. Parham, 75 U.S. (8 Wall.) 123 (1869).

20. Noel Dowling, Interstate Commerce and State Power—Revised Version, 1947 Colum. L. Rev. 547.

21. Noel Dowling, Interstate Commerce and State Power, 27 Va. L. Rev. 1, 20 (1940).

the will of Congress expressed in such form as it may choose. State action falling short of such interference would prevail unless and until superseded or otherwise nullified by Congressional action.

The reach of the "dormant commerce clause" continues to be controversial. To the extent that one accepts the division of labor between Court and Congress outlined above, including the non-finality of the Court, is that because it strikes you as the best reading of the constitutional text or the likely intentions or understanding of the framing generation, on the one hand, or because it offers, on the other hand, a good functional solution to the practical issue of monitoring state legislatures who might be tempted to use their power illegitimately to prefer local as against out-of-state economic interests? Does it matter, in terms of constitutional legitimacy, whether you adopt the first rationale as against the second?

C.   The Privileges and Immunities of State Citizenship and Personal Mobility Among the States

The commerce clause is not the only part of the Constitution that addresses relationships among the states. The privileges and immunities clause of Article IV, §2, provides, "The citizens of each State shall be entitled to all privileges and immunities of citizens in the several States." Furthermore, the Court has protected individuals' rights to move and resettle among the states, based on its understanding of the structure of federalism and independent of any particular constitutional provision. This section surveys these other federalistic limitations on state action as they existed in the mid-nineteenth century. Although several of the cases mentioned were decided after the Civil War, they are consistent with the attitudes and doctrines of the Taney Court.

1.   The Privileges and Immunities Clause of Article IV

The privileges and immunities clause of Article IV is based on the fourth article of the Articles of Confederation, which provided:

> The better to secure and perpetuate mutual friendship and intercourse among the people of the different States in this Union, the free inhabitants of each of these States, paupers, vagabonds, and fugitives from justice excepted, shall be entitled to all the privileges and immunities of free citizens in the several States; and the people of each State shall have free ingress and regress to and from any other States, and shall enjoy therein all the privileges of trade and commerce, subject to the same duties, impositions, and restrictions as the inhabitants thereof respectively.

The privileges and immunities clause of Article IV does not give a citizen any rights against her own state. Rather, with qualifications, it entitles a citizen of state A, who is present in state B, to the same treatment by state B as B accords its own citizens. As the Court wrote in Paul v. Virginia, 75 U.S. (8 Wall.) 168 (1869),

> It was undoubtedly the object of the clause . . . to place the citizens of each State upon the same footing with citizens of other States, so far as the advantages resulting from citizenship in those States are concerned. It relieves them from the disabilities of

alienage in other States; it inhibits discriminating legislation against them by other States; it gives them the right of free ingress into other States, and egress from them; it insures to them in other States the same freedom possessed by the citizens of those States in the acquisition and enjoyment of property and in the pursuit of happiness; and it secures to them in other States the equal protection of their laws. It has justly been said that no provision in the Constitution has tended so strongly to constitute the citizens of the United States one people as this.

Indeed, without some provision of the kind removing from the citizens of each State the disabilities of alienage in the other States, and giving them equality of privilege with citizens of those States, the Republic would have constituted little more than a league of States. . . .

Does the privileges and immunities clause require that state B accord a citizen of state A every benefit it accords its own citizens? The answer is obviously no. Presumably a state may limit the right to vote to its own citizens.

CORFIELD v. CORYELL, F. Cas. No. 3,230 (D. Pa. 1823): [The most elaborate consideration of the reach of the privileges and immunities clause was set out in Justice Bushrod Washington's much-cited circuit court opinion in Corfield v. Coryell, which sustained a New Jersey statute forbidding anyone not "an actual inhabitant and resident" of the state to gather clams and oysters from the state's waters.]

WASHINGTON, J:

The inquiry is, what are the privileges and immunities of citizens in the several states? We feel no hesitation in confining these expressions to those privileges and immunities which are fundamental; which belong of right to the citizens of all free governments. and which have, at all times, been enjoyed by the citizens of the several states which compose this Union, from the time of their becoming free, independent, and sovereign. What these fundamental principles are, it would be more tedious than difficult to enumerate. They may all, however, be comprehended under the following general heads: protection by the government, with the right to acquire and possess property of every kind, and to pursue and obtain happiness and safety, subject, nevertheless, to such restraints as the government may prescribe for the general good of the whole. The right of a citizen of one state to pass through, or to reside in any other state, for purposes of trade, agriculture, professional pursuits, or otherwise; to claim the benefit of the writ of habeas corpus; to institute and maintain actions of any kind in the courts of the state; to take, hold and dispose of property, either real or personal; and an exemption from higher taxes or impositions than are paid by the other citizens of the state; may be mentioned as some of the particular privileges and immunities of citizens, which are clearly embraced by the general description of privileges deemed to be fundamental: to which may be added, the elective franchise, as regulated and established by the laws or constitution of the state in which it is to be exercised. These, and many others which might be mentioned, are, strictly speaking, privileges and immunities, and the enjoyment of them by the citizens of each state, in every other state, was manifestly calculated (to use the expressions of the preamble of the corresponding provision in the old articles of confederation) "the better to secure and perpetuate mutual friendship and intercourse among the people of the different states of the Union."

But we cannot accede to the proposition which was insisted on by the counsel, that, under this provision of the Constitution, the citizens of the several States are permitted to participate in all the rights which belong exclusively to the citizens of any other particular State, merely upon the ground that they are enjoyed by those citizens; much less, that in regulating the use of the common property of the citizens of such States, the legislature is bound to extend to the citizens of all the other States the same advantages secured to their own citizens.

In *Corfield*, the court held that fish within the state's waters were the common property of all of the state's citizens, and that it would be "going quite too far to construe the grant of privileges and immunities of citizens, as amounting to a grant of a co-tenancy in the common property of the States, to the citizens of all the other states." *Paul* held that a state could forbid an out-of-state corporation from doing business in the state because it was not itself a "citizen"; furthermore, incorporation was a special privilege that Virginia was not required to extend to the foreign incorporators. Both of these doctrines have been vitiated by later developments, the most important of which was the classification in 1886 of a corporation as a "person" under the Fourteenth Amendment, Santa Clara v. Southern Pacific Railroad, 118 U.S. 394.[22]

Discussion

Note carefully Justice Washington's list of fundamental rights in *Coryell*. Is it the list of fundamental liberties you would construct today? Justice Washington includes "the elective franchise" as a fundamental right, and the woman suffrage movement would later use this dictum as support for their argument that women had a constitutional right to vote. See the discussion of the New Departure in Chapter 4, infra. If Justice Washington is correct that the franchise is a privilege and immunity of citizens, does this mean that states must allow non-citizens to vote, or is the right to vote more like the right to gather clams and oysters? Why should that be?

2. Interstate Mobility

CRANDALL v. NEVADA, 73 U.S. (6 Wall.) 35 (1868): The Court struck down a Nevada statute that imposed "a capitation tax of one dollar upon every person leaving the State by any railroad, stage coach, or other vehicle engaged or employed in the business of transporting passengers for hire" and required the carrier to collect the tax from the passengers and turn it over to the state. Crandall, the agent for a stagecoach company, was prosecuted for refusing to pay the tax.

Writing for the Court, Justice Miller described the issue as "the right of a State to levy a tax upon persons residing in the State who may wish to get out of it, and upon persons not residing in it who may have occasion to pass through it." He rejected petitioner's argument that the tax violated the prohibition of Article 1, §10, against state "Imposts or Duties on Imports or Exports," holding that citizens traveling from one state to another were not imports or exports.

With respect to the claim that the tax violated the commerce clause, he first noted that Congress had passed no statute touching on the matter and then relied

---

22. See Morton Horwitz, The Transformation of American Law 1870-1960: The Crisis of Legal Orthodoxy 66-71 (1992).

on Cooley v. Board of Wardens to hold that "[i]nasmuch, therefore, as the tax does not itself institute any regulation of commerce of a national character, or which has a uniform operation over the whole country, it is not easy to maintain [that it violates the commerce clause] . . . ," though, in fact, Chief Justice Chase and Justice Clifford rested their own concurring opinions on the commerce clause. The majority based invalidation on a quite different ground.

> The people of these United States constitute one nation. They have a government in which all of them are deeply interested. This government has necessarily a capital established by law, where its principal operations are conducted. . . . That government has a right to call to this point any or all of its citizens to aid in its service, as members of the Congress, of the courts, of the executive departments, and to fill all its other offices; and this right cannot be made to depend upon the pleasure of a State over whose territory they must pass to reach the point where these services must be rendered. The government, also, has its offices of secondary importance in all other parts of the country. . . . In all these it demands the services of its citizens, and is entitled to bring them to those points from all quarters of the nation, and no power can exist in a State to obstruct this right that would not enable it to defeat the purposes for which the government was established. . . .
>
> But if the government has these rights on her own account, the citizen also has correlative rights. He has the right to come to the seat of government to assert any claim he may have upon that government, or to transact any business he may have with it. To seek its protection, to share its offices, to engage in administering its functions. He has a right to free access to its sea-ports, through which all the operations of foreign trade and commerce are conducted, to the sub-treasuries, the land offices, the revenue offices, and the courts of justice in the several States, and this right is in its nature independent of the will of any State over whose soil he must pass in the exercise of it.

Miller then cited *McCulloch* for the proposition that it was the very presence of a tax on passage through the state, rather than its actual degree of burdensomeness, that was illegitimate. Moreover, "[i]f one State can do this, so can every other State. And thus one or more States covering the only practicable routes of travel from the east to the west, or from the north to the south, may totally prevent or seriously burden all transportation of passengers from one part of the country to the other. . . ." Miller went on to quote a passage from Taney's opinion in *The Passenger Cases*, which, though a dissent, "do not relate to the matter on which the dissent was founded [and] accord with the inferences which we have already drawn from the Constitution itself, and from the decisions of this court in exposition of that instrument":

> Living as we do under a common government, charged with the great concerns of the whole Union, every citizen of the United States from the most remote States or territories, is entitled to free access, not only to the principal departments established at Washington, but also to its judicial tribunals and public offices in every State in the Union. . . . For all the great purposes for which the Federal government was formed we are one people, with one common country. We are all citizens of the United States, and as members of the same community must have the right to pass and repass through every part of it without interruption, as freely as in our own States. And a tax imposed by a State, for entering its territories or harbors, is inconsistent with the rights which belong to citizens of other States as members of the Union, and with the objects which that Union was intended to attain. Such a power in the States could produce nothing but discord and mutual irritation, and they very clearly do not possess it.

Discussion

Note that *Crandall* is an almost unique instance — another is the second part of *McCulloch* — of constitutional interpretation based exclusively on the theory and structure of the federal system without any recourse to the text of the Constitution.[23] Note also that Justice Miller makes two rather distinct "structural" arguments, which have different implications for the scope of the citizen's right of interstate mobility. One of them refers to what might be termed the "private" interests of the citizen who seeks, for example, to go to a seaport for commercial purposes; the other refers to what might be viewed as the "public" role of the citizen who seeks to participate in government (though, of course, the citizens involved might wish government to support their private interests). Does it matter whether the litigants present themselves in a "private" or "public" role? And is it crucial that the litigants be citizens? Would a resident alien, for example, be exempt from paying the *Crandall* tax?

Crandall is what might be termed a "right-of-passage" case. What if Crandall, instead of wishing to pass through Nevada on the way to some other state, had wished to settle in that state? Does Nevada have a constitutional duty to honor that desire? Imagine, for example, that Crandall was a convicted felon (in another state), a pauper, a member of a despised political or religious group, or a free person of color. Several free states, prior to the War, had prohibited settlement by blacks. Does *Crandall* stand for the proposition that this was unconstitutional? Or is the answer that the blacks involved were not citizens and thus unable to claim the rights asserted in *Crandall?* See *Dred Scott,* infra.

II. Slavery

In the years after the Louisiana Purchase many slaveholders migrated well northward of present-day Louisiana. Louisiana was uncontroversially admitted to the Union as a slave state in 1812. The next state to be carved out of the vast new territory was Missouri, whose voting inhabitants petitioned in 1819 for admission also as a slave state. This time Congress was enveloped in heated conflict. Anti-slavery Northerners pressed for conditioning Missouri's admission on freeing all slaves born in the state after admission on their 25th birthday. (This obviously would have had no effect on the existing population, the last slave of whom would presumably not die until the dawn of the twentieth century.) Ultimately, Congress agreed to the Missouri Compromise of 1820, which, among other things, admitted Missouri as a slave state but prohibited slavery in the territories north of latitude 36°30'. To preserve the balance of slave and free states in the Senate, Maine was simultaneously admitted as a new free state. "Angry passions quickly subsided, the sectional alignment dissolved, and politics resumed their delusive tranquility. But a veil had

---

23. In United States v. Guest, 383 U.S. 745 (1966), Justice Stewart wrote for the Court, sustaining a federal indictment for conspiracy to interfere with the rights of black citizens to travel interstate:

> Although the Articles of Confederation provided that "the people of each State shall have free ingress and regress to and from any other State," that right finds no explicit mention in the Constitution. The reason, it has been suggested, is that a right so elementary was conceived from the beginning to be a necessary concomitant of the stronger Union the Constitution created.

been lifted for the moment, revealing a bloody prospect ahead. 'This monumental question, like a fire bell in the night, awakened and filled me with terror,' wrote Jefferson. 'I considered it at once as the knell of the union.' And J.Q. Adams recorded in his diary: 'I take it for granted that the present question is a mere preamble — a title-page to a great, tragic volume.' "[24] The remainder of this chapter explores the role played by the Supreme Court in the tragic drama predicted by Adams.

A. The Interstate Slave Trade

GROVES v. SLAUGHTER, 40 U.S. (15 Pet.) 449 (1841): [A provision of the Mississippi Constitution of 1832, which arguably forbade importing slaves into the state for sale there, was attacked as an impermissible restriction of interstate commerce. Mississippi was, of course, a slave state, and the provision was almost certainly designed to protect its own slave trade against competition from other states. As Justice Baldwin described the provision in a concurring opinion, it "does not purport to be a regulation of police, for any defined object connected with the internal tranquility of the State, the health, or morals of the people; it is general in its terms; it is aimed at the introduction of slaves as merchandise from other States, not with the intention of excluding diseased, convicted, or insurgent slaves, or such as may be otherwise dangerous to the peace or welfare of the State. Its avowed purpose is to prevent them from being the subjects of intercourse with other States, when introduced for the purpose of sale. . . ."

Justice Thompson's opinion for the Court avoided the issue entirely by construing the state constitution to require the passage of activating legislation. Three concurring justices carried on a vigorous side debate over the issues that the majority artfully avoided.]

McLean, J., concurring.

[For Justice McLean, an Ohioan and a Marshallian nationalist, the case presented a dilemma. If slaves were an item of commerce, Congress could, if it so chose, prohibit the interstate slave trade by ordinary legislation under the commerce power. But the Marshallian view of congressional exclusivity suggested in *Gibbons* cast doubt on the validity of any state laws regulating the slave trade; it did not distinguish between Mississippi's pro-slavery, protectionist law and Ohio's ban on the slave trade as part of its prohibition of slavery in general. McLean tried to straddle the dilemma. He denied that slaves were an item of commerce: Even "if slaves are considered in some of the States as merchandise, that cannot divest them of the leading and controlling quality of persons by which they are designated in the Constitution." He went on to argue that the states were free to deal with slavery as they wished.]

. . . The power over slavery belongs to the States respectively. It is local in its character, and in its effects; and the transfer or sale of slaves cannot be separated from this power. It is, indeed, an essential part of it.

Each state has a right to protect itself against the avarice and intrusion of the slave dealer; to guard its citizens against the inconveniences and dangers of a slave population.

[handwritten margin note: States should have rights to control slave-trade in their states]

24. Quoted in Morison, Commager & Leuchtenborg, supra n.3, at 398-399.

The right to exercise this power by a State is higher and deeper than the Constitution. The evil involves the prosperity and may endanger the existence of a State. Its power to guard against, or to remedy the evil, rests upon the law of self-preservation; a law vital to every community, and especially to a sovereign State. . . .

TANEY, C.J.

[Chief Justice Taney claimed that he addressed the issue only because McLean had raised it, and came to the same conclusion.]

. . . In my judgment the power over this subject is exclusively with the several States . . . and the action of the several States upon this subject, cannot be controlled by Congress, either by virtue of its power to regulate commerce, or by virtue of any other power. . . .

BALDWIN, J.

[Justice Baldwin, who like McLean was a nationalist, argued that although a state could abolish slavery entirely, it could not allow slavery and prohibit the slave trade, for slaves were items of commerce and the regulation of interstate commerce lay within the exclusive domain of Congress. In elaborating this position, he made explicit some broader concerns of slavery and federalism.]

. . . As each state has plenary power to legislate on this subject, its laws are the test of what is property; if they recognise slaves as the property of those who hold them, they become the subjects of commerce between the states which so recognise them, and the traffic in them may be regulated by congress, as the traffic in other articles; but no further. Being property, by the law of any state, the owners are protected from any violations of the rights of property by congress, under the fifth amendment of the constitution; these rights do not consist merely in ownership; the right of disposing of property of all kinds, is incident to it, which congress cannot touch. The mode of disposition is regulated by the state of common law; and but for the first clause in the second section of the fourth article of the constitution of the United States, a state might authorize its citizens to deal in slaves, and prohibit it to all others. But that clause secures to the citizens of all the states, "all privileges and immunities of citizens" of any other state, whereby any traffic in slaves or other property, which is lawful to the citizens or settlers of Mississippi, with each other, is equally protected when carried on between them and the citizens of Virginia. Hence, it is apparent, that no state can control this traffic, so long as it may be carried on by its own citizens, within its own limits; as part of its purely internal commerce, any state may regulate it according to its own policy; but when such regulation purports to extend to other states or their citizens, it is limited by the constitution, putting the citizens of all on the same footing as their own. It follows, likewise, that any power of congress over the subject is, as has been well expressed by one of the plaintiffs' counsel, conservative in its character, for the purpose of protecting the property of the citizens of the United States, which is a lawful subject of commerce among the states, from any state law which affects to prohibit its transmission for sale from one state to another, through a third or more states.

Thus, in Ohio, and those states to which the ordinance of 1787 applies, or in those where slaves are not property, not subjects of dealing or traffic among its own citizens, they cannot become so, when brought from other states; their condition is the same as those persons of the same color already in the state; subject in all respects to the provisions of its law, if brought there for the purposes of residence or sale. If, however, the owner of slaves in Maryland, in transporting them to Kentucky or Missouri, should pass through Pennsylvania or Ohio, no law of either state could take away or affect his right of property; nor, if passing from one slave state to another, accident or distress should compel him to touch at any place within a state, where slavery did not exist. Such transit of property, whether of slaves or bales of goods is lawful commerce among the several states, which none can prohibit or regulate, which the constitution protects, and congress may, and ought, to preserve from violation. . . .

But where no object of police is discernible in a state law or constitution, nor any rule of policy, other than that which gives to its own citizens a "privilege," which is denied to citizens of other states, it is wholly different. The direct tendency of all such laws is partial, anti-national, subversive of the harmony which should exist among the states, as well as inconsistent with the most sacred principles of the constitution. . . . For these reasons, my opinion is, that had the contract in question been invalid by the constitution of Mississippi, it would be valid by the constitution of the United States. These reasons are drawn from those principles on which alone this government must be sustained: the leading one of which is, that wherever slavery exists, by the laws of a state, slaves are property in every constitutional sense, and for every purpose, whether as subjects of taxation, as the basis of representation, as articles of commerce, or fugitives from service. To consider them as persons merely, and not property, is, in my settled opinion, the first step towards a state of things to be avoided only by a firm adherence to the fundamental principles of the state and federal governments, in relation to this species of property. If the first step taken be a mistaken one, the successive ones will be fatal to the whole system. I have taken my stand on the only position which, in my judgment, is impregnable; and feel confident in its strength, however it may be assailed in public opinion, here or elsewhere.

Note: Freedom of Speech, Federalism, and Slavery

During the 1830s abolitionists began sending material detailing the iniquity of slavery through the United States mails to leaders of public opinion in the Southern states, who would presumably be persuaded to use their power to end it.[25] In response, several slave states passed laws prohibiting the circulation of anti-slavery publications. Indeed, Clement Eaton states that after 1835 there was "a virtual censorship of the mails crossing the Mason and Dixon line." Although these laws necessarily touched on the powers of federal postal officials and thus raised delicate constitutional problems, they were never litigated, primarily because the federal officials involved were altogether willing to comply with the laws.

A legal test of sorts with respect to the freedom of the mails arose in 1857. Mississippi required imprisonment and fine "if any white person circulate or put forth any book, paper, magazine, or pamphlet, containing any sentiment, doctrine, advice, or innuendoes, calculated to produce a disorderly, dangerous, or rebellious disaffection among the colored population." A deputy postmaster in Yazoo City, Mississippi, refused to deliver abolitionist material mailed from Ohio, arguing that

25. See Clement Eaton, The Freedom-of-Thought Struggle in the Old South, ch. VIII (revised ed. 1964). All of the quotations in this paragraph are taken from this chapter. See also Michael Kent Curtis, The Curious History of Attempts to Suppress Antislavery Speech, Press, and Petition in 1835-37, 89 Northwestern U. L. Rev. 785 (1995).

its delivery would violate the Mississippi statute. The publication in question, the Cincinnati Gazette, challenged the practice, and the Postmaster General turned to Attorney General Caleb Cushing for an opinion. Cushing, though from Massachusetts, was an active member of the pro-slavery wing of the Democratic Party that had elected Franklin Pierce and was soon to send James Buchanan of Pennsylvania to the presidency. Cushing issued his opinion on March 2, 1857, just before he left office upon the inauguration of the new President two days later.[26] Federal law prohibits a postmaster from "unlawfully detain[ing]" any mail. The question, therefore, is whether the Yazoo City detention was "lawful." Cushing began by noting:

> [E]ach State has, and must have, jurisdiction as regards the matter of insurrection or treason. To deny this would be to deny to the inhabitants of a State the power of self-preservation. That cannot be denied. In constitutional language, it is a right inalienable and imprescriptible. No political society can effectively cede away the power of self-preservation. If it should undertake to do so, in whatever explicitness of expression, such an act would be null and of no effect. Of course, it does not need to go into the inquiry, whether the law of the State of Mississippi be constitutionally maintainable as a provision of police. It is that, but it is much more. It is a law of self-conservation, in the category of those, which lie at the foundation of all possible forms of human society.
>
> [Given this assumption,] we have the main question very much simplified. It is this: Has a citizen of one of the United States plenary indisputable right to employ the functions and the officers of the Union as the means of enabling him to produce insurrection in another of the United States? Can the officers of the Union lawfully lend its functions to the citizens of one of the States for the purpose of promoting insurrection in another State?

It can surely be no surprise, given Cushing's assumption and statement of the question, that the postmaster's failure to deliver the Gazette was vindicated:

> [I]n regard to municipal legislation, for the most part, the several United States are foreign each to the other. And the citizens of the State of Mississippi are the only competent judges of how much they may be inconvenienced by the impeded circulation among them of this or that pamphlet or newspaper. That is a question of self-government, which it belongs to them to answer for themselves, not to the citizens of Ohio to answer for them. . . . Moreover, there is here a balance of inconveniences. Insurrections are inconvenient things. It is inconvenient to the people of one State to have their houses burned by means of incendiary missiles projected from behind the secure legal shelter of the boundary line of an adjoining State. If the non-circulation of this or that foreign newspaper in a particular State be an inconvenience to somebody, it is, in the aggregate of all public interests, a much less inconvenience than the occurrence, or even the danger, of insurrection in that State.
>
> It may be unpleasant to some person in Ohio to find that he is not free to promote insurrection in Mississippi. Nevertheless, even at the risk of not accommodating any such perverse taste, each State of the Union has the right to protect itself against domestic violence, and to invoke to that end the friendly co-operation, or at least the neutrality, of the United States.

Cushing did concede that the actual insurrectionary nature of the publication might be a disputable question, so that persons who believed that their rights to

_____

26. 8 Opinions of Attorneys General 489.

have their mail delivered had been violated could challenge the classification in State or Federal court. Note the complete absence of any discussion of the First Amendment. With respect to Mississippi's own law, the reason for the omission is doctrinally simple: In the 1833 decision of Barron v. Baltimore, 32 U.S. (7 Pet.) 243, Chief Justice Marshall held, for a unanimous Court, that the Bill of Rights applied only to the national government. Not until 1925 was the freedom of speech clause of the First Amendment made applicable to the States through incorporation in the Fourteenth Amendment. (See the Introduction to Part Two, p. 489, infra.) This, however, does not explain the absence of discussion of the First Amendment's application to the national government's refusal to deliver the mail. Might it be that Congress had not affirmatively required the limitation of delivery in question? That is, should the First Amendment be read as a limitation on Congress's powers rather than a categorical limit on the power of the national government as a whole? Or could Congress legitimately authorize postmasters to refuse to deliver mail that is legitimately deemed by local authorities to constitute an incitement to insurrection? See Chapter 4, infra, for further discussion of the First Amendment and the "clear-and-present-danger" test.

B. Fugitive Slaves

PRIGG v. PENNSYLVANIA
41 U.S. (16 Pet.) 536 (1842)

[The Fugitive Slave Act of 1793 authorized the owner to seize a fugitive slave and bring him or her before a federal judge or state magistrate, who was required to give a "certificate" to the owner or his agent upon satisfactory proof "that the person so seized or arrested doth, under the laws of the state or territory from which he or she fled, owe service or labor to the person claiming him or her. . . ."

The case arose from the capture in 1837, by Edward Prigg, Nathan Bemis, and others, of Margaret Morgan and her children in Pennsylvania and the subsequent taking of them to Maryland. Bemis had succeeded to the Maryland estate of one Ashmore, the owner of Margaret Morgan's parents, who had, says Paul Finkelman, "informally set [them] free" prior to her birth.[27] Margaret was married to Jerry Morgan, a free black, and they had, in 1832, moved just across the border to Pennsylvania, where they had several children. "These children were," according to Finkleman, "free under Pennsylvania law and were not subject to the Fugitive Slave Act; they did not fit the constitutional definition of fugitive slaves (persons 'escaping into another' state)." Moreover, inasmuch as Margaret's marriage to Jerry Morgan had occurred with the apparent acquiescence of Ashmore, Margaret might well have been considered to be free herself under either Pennsylvania or Maryland law.

Pennsylvania attorney Thomas Hambly described the circumstances of capture to the U.S. Supreme Court:[28]

[I]n February, 1837, together with Prigg the defendant and others, [Bemis] came into the State of Pennsylvania and procured a warrant from Thos. Henderson, a justice of

---

27. Paul Finkelman, Sorting Out Prigg v. Pennsylvania, 24 Rutgers L.J. 605 (1993).
28. Argument of Mr. Hambly, of York (Pa.), in the Case of Edward Prigg, Lucase & Dever (1842), reprinted in 1 Fugitive Slaves and American Courts: The Pamphlet Literature 121 (Finkelman ed., 1988).

the peace, authorising Sm McCleary, a constable of York County, to arrest and bring before him "the said Margaret and her children." They were seized before any day light, in bed; the mother, father and children put into an open wagon in a cold sleety rain, with scarcely their ordinary clothes on, and conveyed some ten or fifteen miles to Henderson's house. In the mean time Henderson had learned that he had no jurisdiction by the law of Pennsylvania, and he refused when they arrived to adjudicate. It had grown late, was dark and still raining; a consultation was had amongst the captors and it resulted in releasing Jerry Morgan the husband, who was told if he would go back they would meet him in the morning at Esq. Ross's where the mother should be disposed of. He went back, and as soon as he was out of sight, Prigg and Bemis crossed the line into Maryland, with the mother and children, and by the morning light they were sold to a negro trader and in a calaboose ready for shipment to the South.

Such a transaction, of course, aroused the public upon the Pennsylvania side of the line. Pursuit was made, the negroes found, and a complaint laid before the Governor of Pennsylvania of this violation both of territory and law. A demand was made of the executive of Maryland for the guilty parties, but after a long and tedious negociation [sic], the Governor of Maryland refused to surrender them.

Following intense negotiations between Maryland and Pennsylvania, "Maryland sent Prigg to Pennsylvania for trial after Pennsylvania officials agreed that in the event of a conviction he would not be incarcerated . . . until after the United States Supreme Court had ruled on the constitutionality of the relevant state and federal laws."[29] As Hambly informed the Supreme Court, though, "[i]n the meanwhile the mother and children were taken before Judge Archer, of Harford county, adjudged to be slaves and sold." Prigg was convicted under an 1826 Pennsylvania statute expressly designed to prevent self-help in the return of fugitive slaves. The Supreme Court reversed the conviction and held the state law unconstitutional. Justice Story wrote for the Court; six Justices wrote separate opinions, some disagreeing sharply with aspects of the opinion. We excerpt portions of Story's opinion, Taney's opinion concurring in the result, and McLean's dissent.]

STORY, J. . . .

Few questions which have ever come before this court involve more delicate and important considerations; and few upon which the public at large may be presumed to feel a more profound and pervading interest. . . .

Before, however, we proceed to the points more immediately before us, it may be well, in order to clear the case of difficulty, to say, that in the exposition of this part of the constitution, we shall limit ourselves to those considerations which appropriately and exclusively belong to it, without laying down any rules of interpretation of a more general nature. It will, indeed, probably, be found, when we look to the character of the constitution itself, the objects which it seeks to attain, the powers which it confers, the duties which it enjoins, and the rights which it secures, as well as the known historical fact, that many of its provisions were matters of compromise of opposing interests and opinions, that no uniform rule of interpretation can be applied to it, which may not allow, even if it does not positively demand, many modifications, in its actual application to particular clauses. And, perhaps, the safest rule of interpretation, after all, will be found to be to look to the nature and objects of the particular powers, duties and rights, with all the lights and aids of contemporary history; and to give to the words of each just such

29. Finkelman, at 612.

operation and force, consistent with their legitimate meaning, as may fairly secure and attain the ends proposed.

There are two clauses in the constitution upon the subject of fugitives, which stand in juxtaposition with each other, and have been thought mutually to illustrate each other. They are both contained in the second section of the fourth article, and are in the following words: "A person charged in any state with treason, felony or other crime, who shall flee from justice, and be found in another state, shall, on demand of the executive authority of the state from which he fled, be delivered up, to be removed to the state having jurisdiction of the crime." "No person held to service or labor in one state, under the laws thereof, escaping into another, shall, in consequence of any law or regulation therein, be discharged from such service or labor; but shall be delivered up, on claim of the party to whom such service or labor may be due."

The last clause is that, the true interpretation whereof is directly in judgment before us. Historically, it is well known, that the object of this clause was to secure to the citizens of the slave-holding states the complete right and title of ownership in their slaves, as property, in every state in the Union into which they might escape from the state where they were held in servitude. The full recognition of this right and title was indispensable to the security of this species of property in all the slave-holding states; and, indeed, was so vital to the preservation of their domestic interests and institutions, that it cannot be doubted, that it constituted a fundamental article, without the adoption of which the Union could not have been formed. Its true design was, to guard against the doctrines and principles prevalent in the non-slave-holding states, by preventing them from intermeddling with, or obstructing, or abolishing the rights of the owners of slaves.

By the general Law of nations, no nation is bound to recognise the state of slavery, as to foreign slaves found within its territorial dominions, when it is in opposition to its own policy and institutions, in favor of the subjects of other nations where slavery is recognised. If it does it, it is as a matter of comity, and not as a matter of international right. . . . It is manifest, from this consideration, that if the constitution had not contained this clause, every non-slave-holding state in the Union would have been at liberty to have declared free all runaway slaves coming within its limits, and to have given them entire immunity and protection against the claims of their masters; a course which would have created the most bitter animosities, and engendered perpetual strife between the different states. The clause was, therefore, of the last importance to the safety and security of the southern states, and could not have been surrendered by them, without endangering their whole property in slaves. The clause was accordingly adopted into the constitution, by the unanimous consent of the framers of it; a proof at once of its intrinsic and practical necessity.

How, then, are we to interpret the language of the clause? The true answer is, in such a manner as, consistently with the words, shall fully and completely effectuate the whole objects of it. If, by one mode of interpretation, the right must become shadowy and unsubstantial, and without any remedial power adequate to the end, and by another mode, it will attain its just end and secure its manifest purpose, it would seem, upon principles of reasoning, absolutely irresistible, that the latter ought to prevail. No court of justice can be authorized so to construe any clause of the constitution as to defeat its obvious ends, when another construction, equally accordant with the words and sense thereof, will enforce and protect them.

The clause manifestly contemplates the existence of a positive, unqualified right on the part of the owner of the slave, which no state law or regulation can in any way qualify, regulate, control or restrain. The slave is not to be discharged from service or labor, in consequence of any state law or regulation. Now, certainly, without indulging in any nicety of criticism upon words, it may fairly and reasonably be said, that any state law or state regulation, which interrupts, limits, delays or postpones the right of the owner to the immediate possession of the slave, and the immediate command of his service and labor, operates, pro tanto, a discharge of the slave therefrom. . . . The question [is one] of withholding or controlling the incidents of a positive and absolute right.

. . . Upon this ground, we have not the slightest hesitation in holding, that under and in virtue of the constitution, the owner of a slave is clothed with entire authority, in every state in the Union, to seize and recapture his slave, whenever he can do it, without any breach of the peace or any illegal violence. In this sense, and to this extent, this clause of the constitution may properly be said to execute itself, and to require no aid from legislation, state or national. But the clause of the constitution does not stop here; nor, indeed, consistently with its professed objects, could it do so. Many cases must arise, in which, if the remedy of the owner were confined to the mere right of seizure and recaption, he would be utterly without any adequate redress. He may not be able to lay his hands upon the slave. He may not be able to enforce his rights against persons, who either secrete or conceal, or withhold the slave. He may be restricted by local legislation, as to the mode of proofs of his ownership; as to the courts in which he shall sue, and as to the actions which he may bring; or the process he may use to compel the delivery of the slave. Nay! the local legislation may be utterly inadequate to furnish the appropriate redress . . . ; and this may be innocently as well as designedly done, since every state is perfectly competent, and has the exclusive right, to prescribe the remedies in its own judicial tribunals, to limit the time as well as the mode of redress, and to deny jurisdiction over cases, which its own policy and its own institutions either prohibit or discountenance. If, therefore, the clause of the constitution had stopped at the mere recognition of the right, without providing or contemplating any means by which it might be established and enforced, in cases where it did not execute itself, it is plain, that it would have been, in a great variety of cases, a delusive and empty annunciation. . . .

And this leads us to the consideration of the other part of the clause, which implies at once a guarantee and duty. It says, "but he (the slave) shall be delivered up, on claim of the party to whom such service or labor may be due." Now, we think it exceedingly difficult, if not impracticable, to read this language, and not to feel, that it contemplated some further remedial redress than that which might be administered at the hands of the owner himself. . . . If, indeed, the constitution guarantees the right, and if it requires the delivery upon the claim of the owner (as cannot well be doubted), the natural inference certainly is, that the national government is clothed with the appropriate authority and functions to enforce it. . . . The clause is found in the national constitution, and not in that of any state. It does not point out any state functionaries, or any state action, to carry its provisions into effect. The states cannot, therefore, be compelled to enforce them; and it might well be deemed an unconstitutional exercise of the power of interpretation, to insist, that the states are bound to provide means to carry into effect the duties of the national government, nowhere delegated or intrusted to them by the constitution. On the contrary, the natural, if not the necessary, conclusion is, that the national government, in the absence of all positive provisions to the contrary, is bound, through its own proper departments, legislative, judicial or executive, as the case may require, to carry into effect all the rights and duties imposed upon it by the constitution. . . .

Congress has taken this very view of the power and duty of the national government. As early as the year 1791, the attention of congress was drawn to it (as we shall hereafter more fully see), in consequence of some practical difficulties arising under the other clause, respecting fugitives from justice escaping into other states. The result of their deliberations was the passage of the act of the 12th of February 1793, which [established the right of a slaveowner or his agent to] seize or arrest such fugitive from labor and take him or her before any judge of the circuit or district courts of the United States, residing or being within the state, or before any magistrate of a county, city or town corporate, wherein such seizure or arrest shall be made; and upon proof, to the satisfaction of such judge or magistrate . . . [that the person is in fact a fugitive], to give a certificate thereof to such claimant, his agent or attorney, which shall be sufficient warrant for removing the said fugitive from labor, to the state or territory from which he or she fled. The fourth section provides a penalty against any person, who shall knowingly and willingly obstruct or hinder such claimant, his agent or attorney, in so seizing or arresting such fugitive from labor, or rescue such fugitive from the claimant, or his agent or attorney, when so arrested, or who shall harbor or conceal such fugitive, after notice that he is such; and it also saves to the person claiming such labor or service, his right of action for or on account of such injuries.

In a general sense, this act may be truly said to cover the whole ground of the constitution, . . . because it points out fully all the modes of attaining those objects, which congress, in their discretion, have as yet deemed expedient or proper to meet the exigencies of the constitution. If this be so, then it would seem, upon just principles of construction, that the legislation of congress, if constitutional, must supersede all state legislation upon the same subject; and by necessary implication prohibit it. For, if congress have a constitutional power to regulate a particular subject, and they do actually regulate it in a given manner, and in a certain form, it cannot be, that the state legislatures have a right to interfere, and as it were, by way of compliment to the legislation of congress, to prescribe additional regulations, and what they may deem auxiliary provisions for the same purpose. In such a case, the legislation of congress, in what it does prescribe, manifestly indicates, that it does not intend that there shall be any further legislation to act upon the subject-matter. Its silence as to what it does not do, is as expressive of what its intention is, as the direct provisions made by it. . . . [W]here congress have exercised a power over a particular subject given them by the constitution, it is not competent for state legislation to add to the provisions of congress upon that subject; for that the will of congress upon the whole subject is as clearly established by what it has not declared, as by what it has expressed.

But it has been argued, that the act of congress is unconstitutional, because it does not fall within the scope of any of the enumerated powers of legislation confided to that body; and therefore, it is void. Stripped of its artificial and technical structure, the argument comes to this, that although rights are exclusively secured by, or duties are exclusively imposed upon, the national government, yet, unless the power to enforce these rights or to execute these duties, can be found among the express powers of legislation enumerated in the constitution, they remain without any means of giving them effect by any act of congress; and they must operate solely proprio vigore, however defective may be their operation; nay! even although, in a practical sense, they may become a nullity, from the want of a proper remedy to enforce them, or to provide against their violation. If this be the true interpretation of the constitution, it must, in a great measure, fail to attain many of its avowed and positive objects, as a security of rights, and a recognition of duties. Such a limited construction of the constitution has never yet been adopted as correct, either in theory or practice. No one has ever supposed, that congress could, constitutionally, by its legislation, exercise powers, or enact laws, beyond the powers delegated to it by the constitution. But it has, on various occasions, exercised powers which were necessary and proper as means to carry into effect rights expressly given, and duties expressly enjoined thereby. The end being required, it has been deemed a just and necessary implication, that the means to accomplish it are given also; or, in other words, that the power flows as a necessary means to accomplish the end. . . .

[T]he nature of the provision and the objects to be attained by it, require that it should be controlled by one and the same will, and act uniformly by the same system of regulations throughout the Union. If, then, the states have a right, in the absence of legislation by congress, to act upon the subject, each state is at liberty to prescribe just such regulations as suit its own policy, local convenience and local feelings. The legislation of one state may not only be different from, but utterly repugnant to and incompatible with, that of another. . . .

It is scarcely conceivable, that the slave-holding states would have been satisfied with leaving to the legislation of the non-slave-holding states, a power of regulation, in the absence of that of congress, which would or might practically amount to a power to destroy the rights of the owner. If the argument, therefore, of a concurrent power in the states to act upon the subject-matter, in the absence of legislation by congress, be well founded; then, if congress had never acted at all, or if the act of congress should be repealed, without providing a substitute, there would be a resulting authority in each of the states to regulate the whole subject, at its pleasure, and to dole out its own remedial justice, or withhold it, at its pleasure, and according to its own views of policy and expediency. Surely, such a state of things never could have been intended, under such a solemn guarantee of right and duty. On the other hand, construe the right of legislation as exclusive in congress, and every evil and every danger vanishes. The right and the duty are then co-extensive and uniform in remedy and operation throughout the whole Union. The owner has the same security, and the same remedial justice, and the same exemption from state regulation and control, through however many states he may pass with his fugitive slave in his possession, in transit to his own domicile. . . .

These are some of the reasons, but by no means all, upon which we hold the power of legislation on this subject to be exclusive in congress. To guard, however, against any possible misconstruction of our views, it is proper to state, that we are by no means to be understood, in any manner whatsoever, to doubt or to interfere with the police power belonging to the states, in virtue of their general sovereignty. That police power extends over all subjects within territorial limits of the states, and has never been conceded to the United States. It is wholly distinguishable from the right and duty secured by the provision now under consideration; which is exclusively derived from and secured by the constitution of the United States, and owes its whole efficacy thereto. We entertain no doubt whatsoever, that the states, in virtue of their general police power, possess full jurisdiction to arrest and restrain runaway slaves, and remove them from their borders, and otherwise to secure themselves against their depredations and evil example, as they certainly may do in cases of idlers, vagabonds and paupers. The rights of the owners of fugitive slaves are in no just sense interfered with, or regulated, by such a course; and in many cases, the operations of this police power, although designed generally for other purposes, for protection, safety and peace of the state, may essentially promote and aid the interests of the owners. But such regulations can never be permitted to interfere with, or to obstruct, the just rights of the owner to reclaim his slave, derived from the constitution of the United States, or with the remedies prescribed by congress to aid and enforce the same.

Upon these grounds, we are of opinion, that the act of Pennsylvania upon which this indictment is founded, is unconstitutional and void. It purports to punish as a public offence against that state, the very act of seizing and removing a slave, by his master, which the constitution of the United States was designed to justify and uphold. . . .

TANEY, C.J., concurring. . . .

The opinion of the court maintains, that the power over this subject is so exclusively vested in congress, that no state, since the adoption of the constitution, can pass any law in relation to it. In other words, according to the opinion just delivered, the state authorities are prohibited from interfering, for the purpose of protecting the right of the master, and aiding him in the recovery of his property. I think, the states are not prohibited; and that, on the contrary, it is enjoined upon them as a duty, to protect and support the owner, when he is endeavoring to obtain possession of his property found within their respective territories. The language used in the constitution does not, in my judgment, justify the construction given to it by the court. It contains no words prohibiting the several states from passing laws to enforce this right. They are, in express terms, forbidden to make any regulation that shall impair it; but there the prohibition stops. And according to the settled rules of construction for all written instruments, the prohibition being confined to laws injurious to the right, the power to pass laws to support and enforce it, is necessarily implied. And the words of the article which direct that the fugitive "shall be delivered up," seem evidently designed to impose it as a duty upon the people of the several states, to pass laws to carry into execution, in good faith, the compact into which they thus solemnly entered with each other. . . .

[I]t is manifest, from the face of the law, that an effectual remedy was intended to be given, by the act of 1793. It never designed to compel the master to encounter the hazard and expense of taking the fugitive, in all cases, to the distant residence of one of the judges of the courts of the United States; for it authorized him also, to go before any magistrate of the county, city or town corporate wherein the seizure should be made. And congress evidently supposed, that it had provided a tribunal at the place of the arrest, capable of furnishing the master with the evidence of ownership, to protect him more effectually from unlawful interruption. So far from regarding the state authorities as prohibited from interfering in cases of this description, the congress of that day must have counted upon their cordial co-operation; they legislated with express reference to state support.

McLEAN, J., dissenting. . . .

In my judgment, there is not the least foundation in the act for the right asserted in the argument, to take the fugitive by force and remove him out of the state.

Such a proceeding can receive no sanction under the act, for it is in express violation of it. The claimant having seized the fugitive, is required by the act, to take him before a federal judge within the state, or a state magistrate within the county, city or town corporate, within which the seizure was made. Now, can there be any pretence, that after the seizure under the statute, the claimant may disregard the other express provision of it, by taking the fugitive, without claim, out of the state? But it is said, the master may seize his slave wherever he finds him, if by doing so, he does not violate the public peace; that the relation of master and slave is not affected by the laws of the state, to which the slave may have fled, and where he is found. . . .

It is admitted, that the rights of the master, so far as regards the services of the slave, are not impaired by this change; but the mode of asserting them, in my opinion, is essentially modified. In the state where the service is due, the master needs no other law than the law of force, to control the action of the slave. But can this law be applied by the master, in a state which makes the act unlawful? . . .

In a state where slavery is allowed, every colored person is presumed to be a slave; and on the same principle, in a non-slave-holding state, every person is presumed to be free, without regard to color. On this principle, the states, both slave-holding and non-slave-holding, legislate. The latter may prohibit, as Pennsylvania has done, under a certain penalty, the forcible removal of a colored person out of the state. . . .

It is very clear, that no power to seize and forcibly remove the slave, without claim, is given by the act of congress. Can it be exercised under the constitution? Congress have legislated on the constitutional power, and have directed the mode in which it shall be executed. The act, it is admitted, covers the whole ground; and that it is constitutional, there seems to be no reason to doubt. Now, under such circumstances, can the provisions of the act be disregarded, and an assumed power set up under the constitution? . . .

I cannot perceive how any one can doubt that the remedy given in the constitution, if, indeed, it give any remedy, without legislation, was designed to be a peaceful one; a remedy sanctioned by judicial authority; a remedy guarded by the forms of law. But the inquiry is reiterated, is not the master entitled to his property? I answer, that he is. His right is guarantied by the constitution, and the most summary means for its enforcement is found in the act of congress; and neither the state nor its citizens can obstruct the prosecution of this right. . . .

The presumption of the state that the colored person is free, may be erroneous in fact; and if so, there can be no difficulty in proving it. But may not the assertion of the master be erroneous also; and if so, how is his act of force to be remedied? The colored person is taken and forcibly conveyed beyond the jurisdiction of the state. This force, not being authorized by the act of congress nor by the constitution, may be prohibited by the state. As the act covers the whole power in the constitution, and carries out, by special enactments, its provisions, we are, in my judgment, bound by the act. We can no more, under such circumstances, administer a remedy under the constitution, in disregard of the act, than we can exercise a commercial or other power in disregard of an act of congress on the same subject. This view respects the rights of the master and the rights of the state; it neither jeopards nor retards the reclamation of the slave; it removes all state action prejudicial to the rights of the master; and recognises in the state a power to guard and protect its own jurisdiction, and the peace of its citizen. . . .

Discussion

1. *Prigg* held that Article IV, §2, clause 3, was self-executing (i.e., operated of its own force without the need for implementing congressional legislation) and that it authorized a slave owner to use self-help in capturing a fugitive slave. The Court held that the 1793 act was constitutional, at least insofar as it authorized federal judges to render fugitive slaves. The Court also intimated that the statute, if not the Constitution, precluded state courts from playing any role whatever in returning fugitive slaves.[30] Consider Story's analysis of these issues on the merits — especially in the light of McLean's and Taney's criticisms. Can the Court's approval of self-help be reconciled with the Fifth Amendment's requirement that no person shall be "deprived of life, liberty, or property, without due process of law?"

2. The introductory paragraphs of Justice Story's opinion indicate that he regarded the issues in *Prigg* as extraordinary. Story came from Boston, a stronghold of the abolitionist movement, and he often returned to sit as circuit judge. Judicial enforcement of the fugitive slave law was opposed by the abolitionist bar and, especially after *Prigg*, by extralegal methods as well.[31] As circuit judge, Story had condemned slavery and, in La Jeune Eugenie, 26 F. Cas. 832 (No. 15,551) (C.C.D. Mass. 1822), he had held, in effect, that the slave trade violated the law of nations. But *Prigg* involved a different issue at a different time. Story was a fervent nationalist, who feared the Union endangered by the slavery issue. As it happens, his characterization of the historical significance of the fugitive slave clause may have been more a reflection of contemporary concerns than those of the adopters of the Constitution. One leading historian, for example, has written that the "clause was not a significant issue in the Convention. Introduced late in the proceedings by a South Carolina delegate, it aroused little debate and received unanimous approval. There is little evidence to support the assertion frequently made in later years that without the clause the Constitution would have failed."[32] Even if this is true, what is its relevance to determining the weight the clause should be given in 1842?

---

30. The fugitive slave clause aside, the current doctrine is that Congress may choose to make federal jurisdiction exclusive or to grant state courts concurrent jurisdiction over any case arising under federal laws or the Constitution. The history and modern doctrine concerning the duty of state courts to entertain actions based on federal statutes is summarized in Testa v. Katt, 330 U.S. 386 (1947). Justice Black wrote:

> Enforcement of federal laws by state courts did not go unchallenged. Violent public controversies existed throughout the first part of the Nineteenth Century until the 1860's concerning the existence of the constitutional supremacy of the Federal Government. During that period there were instances in which this Court and state courts broadly questioned the power and duty of state courts to exercise their jurisdiction to enforce United States civil and penal statutes or the power of the Federal Government to require them to do so. But after the fundamental issues of federal supremacy had been resolved by war, this Court took occasion in 1876 to review the phase of the controversy concerning the relationship of state courts to the Federal Government. . . . It repudiated the assumption that federal laws can be considered by the states as though they were laws emanating from a foreign sovereign. . . . It asserted that the obligation of states to enforce these federal laws is not lessened by reason of the form in which they are cast or the remedy which they provide.

Consider carefully the implications of Justice Black's assertion that "the fundamental issues of federal supremacy [were] resolved by war." We shall have occasion later to examine in depth whether, as a descriptive matter these issues have been fully resolved even now, see Chapter 5, infra. But there is also the normative-jurisprudential point as to whether legal controversies should be considered capable of resolution by force of arms.

31. See Robert Cover, Justice Accused (1975). See also Albert J. Von Frank, The Trials of Anthony Burns: Freedom and Slavery and Emerson's Boston (1998).

32. Don Feherenbacher, The Dred Scott Case 25 (1978).

A different perspective is provided by William Story, the Justice's son, who asserted that his father had sought to sabotage enforcement of the fugitive slave law by "leaving the slaveholder to his constitutional remedy of self-help or to recourse to the federal judges — too few and far between to be of practical value."[33] Assume that he is correct is ascribing such motivation to his father. Would it be proper to choose a particular construction of the Constitution because it would sabotage effective enforcement of a legal right — the return of one's fugitive slaves — that one found repugnant?

C. Prelude to Secession

The historian William Freehling has suggested that we might better call the result of Jefferson's 1803 diplomacy the "Midwest Purchase" rather than the "Louisiana Purchase" if we are really to understand its importance for American history, including American constitutional development.[34]

> [I]n the long run, the name "Louisiana Purchase" mischaracterizes an acquisition largely unfit for Louisiana-style institutions. Before the purchase, America stood equally balanced between North and South. Each section controlled eight states. East of the Mississippi River and the purchase, the North figured to pick up five additional states and the South four. Unless slaveholders and slaves could amass in at least a couple of non-Louisiana areas west of the great river, the purchase lands would make Yankees overwhelmingly powerful in the federal government, compared to masters in Louisiana's Deep South latitudes. Or to put it another way, the diffusion of American folk to the Louisiana Purchase borderlands had the potential to pitch the republic either uncomfortably or disastrously against the slaveholders.

Antagonism between the North and South increased during the years following *Prigg*, exacerbated by the dispute over what in fact would become the most important political (and constitutional) issue of the 1850s — the status of slavery in the territories. By the so-called Compromise of 1850 — Freehling suggests that we call it instead "the Armistice of 1850"[35] — California was admitted to the union as a free state, New Mexico and Utah were organized as territories with the issue of slavery being left to future legislation, the slave trade was abolished in the District of Columbia, and a more stringent fugitive slave law was adopted. The Fugitive Slave Act of 1850 provided for the appointment of federal commissioners, who were authorized to issue certificates of removal on the ex parte testimony or affidavits of slaveholders or their agents. Testimony by the alleged slave was excluded and, as if this were not sufficient to bias the outcome, the act paid the commissioner $10 for issuing the certificate but only $5 if he denied it. Under the juryless procedure established by the Act, 90 percent of the 332 alleged fugitives tried under it were "despatched southwards."[36]

---

33. Quoted in Cover at 241. See also Paul Finkelman, *Prigg v. Pennsylvania* and Northern State Courts: Anti-Slavery Use of a Pro-Slavery Decision, 25 Civil War History 5 (1979).

34. See William W. Freehling, The Louisiana Purchase and the Coming of the Civil War, in The Louisiana Purchase and American Expansion 69-82 (Levinson & Sparrow eds., 2005).

35. See William Freehling, The Road to Disunion: Secessionists at Bay, 1776-1854, at 487 (1990).

36. Id. at 536.

" [A] prosperous black tailor who had resided in Poughkeepsie[, New York] for many years" was seized by slavecatchers and carried back to South Carolina. "In February 1851 agents arrested a black man in southern Indiana, while his horrified wife and children looked on, and returned him to an owner who claimed him as a slave who had run away nineteen years earlier."[37] In 1856, Margaret Garner, who had escaped from Kentucky to Ohio, was about to be captured by a posse; in response, she slit the throat of a daughter and attempted to kill her remaining three children rather than acquiesce in their return to slavery. When Ohio asked permission to try her for manslaughter, a federal judge ordered the Garners returned to their owners, who "promptly sold them down the river to New Orleans. On the way there one of Margaret's other children achieved the emancipation she had sought for him by drowning after a steamboat collision."[38] Such episodes sparked Northern reaction, and Southerners focused on dramatic instances of public opposition in the North, especially in Boston, where armed soldiers had to be called out to control popular demonstrations against the return of fugitives.[39] The "Battle of Christina," Pennsylvania left a slaveowner dead, and the national government indicted participants not only for violation of the Fugitive Slave Law, but also for treason![40]

Legal attacks proved unavailing: Justice McLean, sitting as a circuit court judge in Miller v. McQuerry, 17 F. Cas. 332 (No. 9,583) (C.C.D. Ohio, 1853), rejected a challenge to its constitutionality. In Ableman v. Booth, 62 U.S. (21 How.) 506 (1859), in what, for Taney, was a strikingly nationalist opinion, the Chief Justice wrote for the Court sustaining the Act and holding that a Wisconsin state court could not issue a writ of habeas corpus to free a federal prisoner convicted of violating it:

[N]o State can authorize one of its judges or courts to exercise judicial power, by habeas corpus or otherwise, within the jurisdiction of another and independent Government. And although the State of Wisconsin is sovereign within its territorial limits to a certain extent, yet that sovereignty is limited and restricted by the Constitution of the United States. . . .

The Constitution was not formed merely to guard the State against danger from foreign nations, but mainly to secure union and harmony at home; . . . and to accomplish this purpose, it was felt by the statesmen who framed the Constitution, and by the people who adopted it, that it was necessary that many of the rights of sovereignty which the States possessed should be ceded to the General Government; and that, in the sphere of action assigned to it, it should be supreme, and strong enough to execute its own laws by its own tribunals, without interruption from a State or from State authorities.

The holding concerning the relation between federal and state courts was entirely consistent with the principles of federalism developed in cases such as McCulloch v. Maryland; it remains the law today.

In 1854 the Missouri Compromise was repealed by the Kansas-Nebraska Act. The Nebraska Territory, which lay north of the 36°30′ limit on slavery, was split into two

---

37. James M. McPherson, Battle Cry of Freedom: The Civil War Era 80-81 (1988). As it happened, the tailor had his freedom purchased by black and white friends.

38. Id. at 121.

39. See id. at 119-120 for a description of the tensions in Boston generated by the return of Anthony Burns to slavery.

40. Id. at 84-85.

territories, Kansas and Nebraska. Whether slavery would be established in either territory was to be left up to the settlers themselves. The assumption was that the more northern of the two, Nebraska, would become a free state and that Kansas would, therefore, be likely to become a slave state. In fact, the conflict over Kansas settlement and whether the state would eventually become slave or free — which provoked the term "Bleeding Kansas" — was a central issue in the politics of the late 1850s.[41] The repeal of the Missouri Compromise helped to provoke the founding of the Republican Party, one of whose central policies was "free soil," i.e., no further expansion of slavery.

Together with the increasing Northern anger about the enforcement of the Fugitive Slave Act, the Kansas-Nebraska Act "may have been the most important single event pushing the nation toward civil war"[42] insofar as it led to the destruction of the Whig Party, the rise of the Republican Party, and an ultimately fatal split within the Democratic Party. Professor Graber has suggested that one explanation for the destruction of the existing party system and its replacement by largely regionally based political parties was the Constitution itself.[43] Members of Congress are elected by state constituencies, the House by popular vote and the Senate (until the Seventeenth Amendment) by state legislators. Hence there is little incentive, when campaigning for congressional office, to appear overly solicitous to "outside" interests, including the abstract interests of "the nation" when they directly conflict with local interests. Even the president is elected through a state-by-state process called the Electoral College; therefore, a candidate (both then and now) is more worried about putting together a winning coalition of states that add up to an electoral vote majority than about simply amassing a majority of popular votes. (In 1860 Abraham Lincoln, for example, would, with only 40 percent of the popular vote, receive a healthy majority of the electoral vote, though only a single electoral vote from the Southern states, many of whom denied him a place on their ballots.) These structural features of the American Constitution accelerated regional division and undermined parties without a strong regional base.

"Bleeding Kansas" got its name in part from the fact that in 1856, John Brown and five of his sons, as part of guerilla warfare against slaveowners, hacked to death five ostensibly pro-slavery settlers on Pottawottamie Creek, near Lawrence. The United States was clearly at risk, and national institutions like Congress and the presidency had become ever increasingly divided on regional lines, seemingly unable to promise any genuine solutions. Only the Supreme Court remained as a plausible "national" body, and many politicians happily turned to the Court as the last best hope for achieving yet one more compromise that would save the Union. It is against this increasingly heated political background that the *Dred Scott* case must be understood. It directly involved the status of nonfugitive slaves in free states and in the territories and the prerepeal legal consequences of the Missouri Compromise. Perhaps more to the point, it involved the legitimacy of the platform of the Republican Party, which was uncompromising in its opposition to further extension of slavery into the territories.

41. See, e.g., Kenneth Stamp, America in 1857, ch. 6 (1990); James A. Rawley, Race and Politics: "Bleeding Kansas" and the Coming of the Civil War (1979).
42. James M. McPherson, Battle Cry of Freedom 121.
43. See Mark Graber, Dred Scott and the Problem of Constitutional Evil (2006).

DRED SCOTT v. SANDFORD
60 U.S. (19 How.) 393 (1857)

[The basic facts are set out within Chief Justice Taney's opinion:

The plaintiff was a negro [sic] slave, belonging to Dr. Emerson, who was a surgeon in the army of the United States. In the year 1834, he took the plaintiff from the State of Missouri to the military post at Rock Island, in the State of Illinois, and held him there as a slave until the month of April or May, 1836. At the time last mentioned, said Dr. Emerson removed the plaintiff from said military post at Rock Island to the military post at Fort Snelling, situated on the west bank of the Mississippi river, in the Territory known as Upper Louisiana, acquired by the United States of France, and situated north of the latitude of thirty-six degrees thirty minutes north, and north of the State of Missouri. Said Dr. Emerson held the plaintiff in slavery at said Fort Snelling, from said last-mentioned date until the year 1838.

In the year 1835, Harriet, who is named in the second count of the plaintiff's declaration, was the negro slave of Major Taliaferro, who belonged to the army of the United States. In that year, 1835, said Major Taliaferro took said Harriet to said Fort Snelling, a military post, situated as hereinbefore stated, and kept her there as a slave until the year 1836, and then sold and delivered her as a slave, at said Fort Snelling, unto the said Dr. Emerson hereinbefore named. Said Dr. Emerson held said Harriet in slavery at said Fort Snelling until the year 1838.

In the year 1836, the plaintiff and Harriet intermarried, at Fort Snelling, with the consent of Dr. Emerson, who then claimed to be their master and owner. Eliza and Lizzie, named in the third count of the plaintiff's declaration, are the fruit of that marriage. Eliza is about fourteen years old, and was born on board the steamboat Gipsey, north of the north line of the State of Missouri, and upon the river Mississippi. Lizzie is about seven years old, and was born in the State of Missouri, at the military post called Jefferson Barracks.

In the year 1838, said Dr. Emerson removed the plaintiff and said Harriet, and their said daughter Eliza, from said Fort Snelling to the State of Missouri, where they have ever since resided.

Before the commencement of this suit, said Dr. Emerson sold and conveyed the plaintiff, and Harriet, Eliza, and Lizzie, to the defendant, as slaves, and the defendant has ever since claimed to hold them, and each of them, as slaves.]

Mr. Chief Justice TANEY delivered the opinion of the court.

The plaintiff in error, who was also the plaintiff in the court below, was, with his wife and children, held as slaves by the defendant, in the State of Missouri; and he brought this action in the Circuit Court of the United States for that district, to assert the title of himself and his family to freedom.

. . . The defendant pleaded in abatement to the jurisdiction of the court, that the plaintiff was not a citizen of the State of Missouri, as alleged in his declaration, being a negro of African descent, whose ancestors were of pure African blood, and who were brought into this country and sold as slaves. . . .

[A]lthough [the government of the United States] is sovereign and supreme in its appropriate sphere of action, yet it does not possess all the powers which usually belong to the sovereignty of a nation. Certain specified powers, enumerated in the Constitution, have been conferred upon it; and neither the legislative, executive, nor judicial departments of the Government can lawfully exercise any authority beyond the limits marked out by the Constitution. And in regulating the judicial department, the cases in which the courts of the United States shall have jurisdiction are particularly and specifically enumerated and defined; and they are not authorized to take cognizance of any case which does not come within the description therein specified. . . .

[T]he question to be decided is, whether the facts stated in the plea are sufficient to show that the plaintiff is not entitled to sue as a citizen in a court of the United States. . . .

The question is simply this: Can a negro, whose ancestors were imported into this country, and sold as slaves, become a member of the political community formed and brought into existence by the Constitution of the United States, and as such become entitled to all the rights, and privileges, and immunities, guarantied by that instrument to the citizen? One of which rights is the privilege of suing in a court of the United States in the cases specified in the Constitution.

It will be observed, that the plea applies to that class of persons only whose ancestors were negroes of the African race, and imported into this country, and sold and held as slaves. The only matter in issue before the court, therefore, is, whether the descendants of such slaves, when they shall be emancipated, or who are born of parents who had become free before their birth, are citizens of a State, in the sense in which the word citizen is used in the Constitution of the United States. And this being the only matter in dispute on the pleadings, the court must be understood as speaking in this opinion of that class only, that is, of those persons who are the descendants of Africans who were imported into this country, and sold as slaves.

The situation of this population was altogether unlike that of the Indian race. The latter, it is true, formed no part of the colonial communities, and never amalgamated with them in social connections or in government. But although they were uncivilized, they were yet a free and independent people, associated together in nations or tribes, and governed by their own laws. Many of these political communities were situated in territories to which the white race claimed the ultimate right of dominion. But that claim was acknowledged to be subject to the right of the Indians to occupy it as long as they thought proper, and neither the English nor colonial Governments claimed or exercised any dominion over the tribe or nation by whom it was occupied, nor claimed the right to the possession of the territory, until the tribe or nation consented to cede it. These Indian Governments were regarded and treated as foreign Governments, as much so as if an ocean had separated the red man from the white; and their freedom has constantly been acknowledged, from the time of the first emigration to the English colonies to the present day, by the different Governments which succeeded each other. Treaties have been negotiated with them, and their alliance sought for in war; and the people who compose these Indian political communities have always been treated as foreigners not living under our Government. It is true that the course of events has brought the Indian tribes within the limits of the United States under subjection to the white race; and it has been found necessary, for their sake as well as our own, to regard them as in a state of pupilage, and to legislate to a certain extent over them and the territory they occupy. But they may, without doubt, like the subjects of any other foreign Government, be naturalized by the authority of Congress, and become citizens of a State, and of the United States; and if an individual should leave his nation or tribe, and take up his abode among the white population, he would be entitled to all the rights and privileges which would belong to an emigrant from any other foreign people.

We proceed to examine the case as presented by the pleadings.

The words "people of the United States" and "citizens" are synonymous terms, and mean the same thing. They both describe the political body who, according to our republican institutions, form the sovereignty, and who hold the power and conduct the Government through their representatives. They are what we familiarly call the "sovereign people," and every citizen is one of this people, and a constituent member of this sovereignty. The question before us is, whether the class of persons described in the plea in abatement compose a portion of this people, and are constituent members of this sovereignty? We think they are not, and that they are not included, and were not intended to be included, under the word 'citizens' in the Constitution, and can therefore claim none of the rights and privileges which that instrument provides for and secures to citizens of the United States. On the contrary, they were at that time considered as a subordinate and inferior class of beings, who had been subjugated by the dominant race, and, whether emancipated or not, yet remained subject to their authority, and had no rights or privileges but such as those who held the power and the Government might choose to grant them.

It is not the province of the court to decide upon the justice or injustice, the policy or impolicy, of these laws. The decision of that question belonged to the political or law-making power; to those who formed the sovereignty and framed the Constitution. The duty of the court is, to interpret the instrument they have framed, with the best lights we can obtain on the subject, and to administer it as we find it, according to its true intent and meaning when it was adopted.

In discussing this question, we must not confound the rights of citizenship which a State may confer within its own limits, and the rights of citizenship as a member of the Union. It does not by any means follow, because he has all the rights and privileges of a citizen of a State, that he must be a citizen of the United States. He may have all of the rights and privileges of the citizen of a State, and yet not be entitled to the rights and privileges of a citizen in any other State. For, previous to the adoption of the Constitution of the United States, every State had the undoubted right to confer on whomsoever it pleased the character of citizen, and to endow him with all its rights. But this character of course was confined to the boundaries of the State, and gave him no rights or privileges in other States beyond those secured to him by the laws of nations and the comity of States. Nor have the several States surrendered the power of conferring these rights and privileges by adopting the Constitution of the United States. Each State may still confer them upon an alien, or any one it thinks proper, or upon any class or description of persons; yet he would not be a citizen in the sense in which that word is used in the Constitution of the United States, nor entitled to sue as such in one of its courts, nor to the privileges and immunities of a citizen in the other States. The rights which he would acquire would be restricted to the State which gave them. The Constitution has conferred on Congress the right to establish an uniform rule of naturalization, and this right is evidently exclusive, and has always been held by this court to be so. Consequently, no State, since the adoption of the Constitution, can by naturalizing an alien invest him with the rights and privileges secured to a citizen of a State under the Federal Government, although, so far as the State alone was concerned, he would undoubtedly be entitled to the rights of a citizen, and clothed with all the rights and immunities which the Constitution and laws of the State attached to that character.

It is very clear, therefore, that no State can, by any act or law of its own, passed since the adoption of the Constitution, introduce a new member into the political community created by the Constitution of the United States. It cannot make him a member of this community by making him a member of its own. And for the same reason it cannot introduce any person, or description of persons, who were not intended to be embraced in this new political family, which the Constitution brought into existence, but were intended to be excluded from it.

The question then arises, whether the provisions of the Constitution, in relation to the personal rights and privileges to which the citizen of a State should be entitled, embraced the negro African race, at that time in this country, or who might afterwards be imported, who had then or should afterwards be made free in any State; and to put it in the power of a single State to make him a citizen of the United States, and end[ow] him with the full rights of citizenship in every other State without their consent? Does the Constitution of the United States act upon him whenever he shall be made free under the laws of a State, and raised there to the rank of a citizen, and immediately clothe him with all the privileges of a citizen in every other State, and in its own courts?

The court think the affirmative of these propositions cannot be maintained. And if it cannot, the plaintiff in error could not be a citizen of the State of Missouri, within the meaning of the Constitution of the United States, and, consequently, was not entitled to sue in its courts.

It is true, every person, and every class and description of persons, who were at the time of the adoption of the Constitution recognized as citizens in the several States, became also citizens of this new political body; but none other; it was formed by them, and for them and their posterity, but for no one else. And the personal rights and privileges guaranteed to citizens of this new sovereignty were intended to embrace those only who were then members of the several State communities, or who should afterwards by birthright or otherwise become members, according to the provisions of the Constitution and the principles on which it was founded. It was the union of those who were at that time members of distinct and separate political communities into one political family, whose power, for certain specified purposes, was to extend over the whole territory of the United States. And it gave to each citizen rights and privileges outside of his State which he did not before possess, and placed him in every other State upon a perfect equality with its own citizens as to rights of person and rights of property; it made him a citizen of the United States.

It becomes necessary, therefore, to determine who were citizens of the several States when the Constitution was adopted. And in order to do this, we must recur to the Governments and institutions of the thirteen colonies, when they separated from Great Britain and formed new sovereignties, and took their places in the family of independent nations. We must inquire who, at that time, were recognized as the people or citizens of a State, whose rights and liberties had been outraged by the English Government; and who declared their independence, and assumed the powers of Government to defend their rights by force of arms.

In the opinion of the court, the legislation and histories of the times, and the language used in the Declaration of Independence, show, that neither the class of persons who had been imported as slaves, nor their descendants, whether they had become free or not, were then acknowledged as a part of the people, nor intended to be included in the general words used in that memorable instrument.

It is difficult at this day to realize the state of public opinion in relation to that unfortunate race, which prevailed in the civilized and enlightened portions of the world at the time of the Declaration of Independence, and when the Constitution of the United States was framed and adopted. But the public history of every European nation displays it in a manner too plain to be mistaken.

They had for more than a century before been regarded as beings of an inferior order, and altogether unfit to associate with the white race, either in social or political relations; and so far inferior, that they had no rights which the white man was bound to respect; and that the negro might justly and lawfully be reduced to slavery for his benefit. He was bought and sold, and treated as an ordinary article of merchandise and traffic, whenever a profit could be made by it. This opinion was at that time fixed and universal in the civilized portion of the white race. It was regarded as an axiom in morals as well as in politics, which no one thought of disputing, or supposed to be open to dispute; and men in every grade and position in society daily and habitually acted upon it in their private pursuits, as well as in matters of public concern, without doubting for a moment the correctness of this opinion.

And in no nation was this opinion more firmly fixed or more uniformly acted upon than by the English Government and English people. They not only seized them on the coast of Africa, and sold them or held them in slavery for their own use; but they took them as ordinary articles of merchandise to every country where they could make a profit on them, and were far more extensively engaged in this commerce than any other nation in the world.

The opinion thus entertained and acted upon in England was naturally impressed upon the colonies they founded on this side of the Atlantic. And, accordingly, a negro of the African race was regarded by them as an article of property, and held, and bought and sold as such, in every one of the thirteen colonies which united in the Declaration of Independence, and afterwards formed the Constitution of the United States. The slaves were more or less numerous in the different colonies, as slave labor was found more or less profitable. But no one seems to have doubted the correctness of the prevailing opinion of the time.

The legislation of the different colonies furnishes positive and indisputable proof of this fact.

It would be tedious, in this opinion, to enumerate the various laws they passed upon this subject. It will be sufficient, as a sample of the legislation which then generally prevailed throughout the British colonies, to give the laws of two of them; one being still a large slaveholding State, and the other the first State in which slavery ceased to exist.

The province of Maryland, in 1717, passed a law declaring "that if any free negro or mulatto intermarry with any white woman, or if any white man shall intermarry with any negro or mulatto woman, such negro or mulatto shall become a slave during life, excepting mulattoes born of white women, who, for such intermarriage, shall only become servants for seven years, to be disposed of as the justices of the county court, where such marriage so happens, shall think fit; to be applied by them towards the support of a public school within the said county. And any white man or white woman who shall intermarry as aforesaid, with any negro or mulatto, such white man or white woman shall become servants during the term of seven years, and shall be disposed of by the justices as aforesaid, and be applied to the uses aforesaid."

The other colonial law to which we refer was passed by Massachusetts in 1705. It is entitled "An act for the better preventing of a spurious and mixed issue," &c.; and it provides . . . "that none of her Majesty's English or Scottish subjects, nor of any other Christian nation, within this province, shall contract matrimony with any negro or mulatto; nor shall any person, duly authorized to solemnize marriage, presume to join any such in marriage, on pain of forfeiting the sum of fifty pounds. . . ."

We give both of these laws in the words used by the respective legislative bodies, because the language in which they are framed, as well as the provisions contained in them, show, too plainly to be misunderstood, the degraded condition of this unhappy race. They were still in force when the Revolution began, and are a faithful index to the state of feeling towards the class of persons of whom they speak, and of the position they occupied throughout the thirteen colonies, in the eyes and thoughts of the men who framed the Declaration of Independence and established the State Constitutions and Governments. They show that a perpetual and impassable barrier was intended to be erected between the white race and the one which they had reduced to slavery, and governed as subjects with absolute and despotic power, and which they then looked upon as so far below them in the scale of created beings, that intermarriages between white persons and negroes or mulattoes were regarded as unnatural and immoral, and punished as crimes, not only in the parties, but in the person who joined them in marriage. And no distinction in this respect was made between the free negro or mulatto and the slave, but this stigma, of the deepest degradation, was fixed upon the whole race. We refer to these historical facts for the purpose of showing the fixed opinions concerning that race, upon which the statesmen of that day spoke and acted. It is necessary to do this, in order to determine whether the general terms used in the Constitution of the United States, as to the rights of man and the rights of the people, was intended to include them, or to give to them or their posterity the benefit of any of its provisions.

The language of the Declaration of Independence is equally conclusive:

It begins by declaring that, "when in the course of human events it becomes necessary for one people to dissolve the political bands which have connected them with another, and to assume among the powers of the earth the separate and equal station to which the laws of nature and nature's God entitle them, a decent respect for the opinions of mankind requires that they should declare the causes which impel them to the separation."

It then proceeds to say: "We hold these truths to be self-evident: that all men are created equal; that they are endowed by their Creator with certain unalienable rights; that among them is life, liberty, and the pursuit of happiness; that to secure these rights, Governments are instituted, deriving their just powers from the consent of the governed."

The general words above quoted would seem to embrace the whole human family, and if they were used in a similar instrument at this day would be so understood. But it is too clear for dispute, that the enslaved African race were not intended to be included, and formed no part of the people who framed and adopted this declaration; for if the language, as understood in that day, would embrace them, the conduct of the distinguished men who framed the Declaration of Independence would have been utterly and flagrantly inconsistent with the principles they asserted; and instead of the sympathy of mankind, to which they so confidently appealed, they would have deserved and received universal rebuke and reprobation.

Yet the men who framed this declaration were great men — high in literary acquirements — high in their sense of honor, and incapable of asserting principles inconsistent with those on which they were acting. They perfectly understood the meaning of the language they used, and how it would be understood by others; and they knew that it would not in any part of the civilized world be supposed to embrace the negro race, which, by common consent, had been excluded from civilized Governments and the family of nations, and doomed to slavery. They spoke and acted according to the then established doctrines and principles, and in the ordinary language of the day, and no one misunderstood them. The unhappy black race were separated from the white by indelible marks, and laws long before established, and were never thought of or spoken of except as property, and when the claims of the owner or the profit of the trader were supposed to need protection.

This state of public opinion had undergone no change when the Constitution was adopted, as is equally evident from its provisions and language.

The brief preamble sets forth by whom it was formed, for what purposes, and for whose benefit and protection. It declares that it is formed by the people of the United States; that is to say, by those who were members of the different political communities in the several States; and its great object is declared to be to secure the blessings of liberty to themselves and their posterity. It speaks in general terms of the people of the United States, and of citizens of the several States, when it is providing for the exercise of the powers granted or the privileges secured to the citizen. It does not define what description of persons are intended to be included under these terms, or who shall be regarded as a citizen and one of the people. It uses them as terms so well understood, that no further description or definition was necessary.

But there are two clauses in the Constitution which point directly and specifically to the negro race as a separate class of persons, and show clearly that they were not regarded as a portion of the people or citizens of the Government then formed.

One of these clauses reserves to each of the thirteen States the right to import slaves until the year 1808, if it thinks proper. And the importation which it thus sanctions was unquestionably of persons of the race of which we are speaking, as the traffic in slaves in the United States had always been confined to them. And by the other provision the States pledge themselves to each other to maintain the right of property of the master, by delivering up to him any slave who may have escaped from his service, and be found within their respective territories. By the first above-mentioned clause, therefore, the right to purchase and hold this property is directly sanctioned and authorized for twenty years by the people who framed the Constitution. And by the second, they pledge themselves to maintain and uphold the right of the master in the manner specified, as long as the Government they then formed should endure. And these two provisions show, conclusively, that neither the description of persons therein referred to, nor their descendants, were embraced in any of the other provisions of the Constitution; for certainly these two clauses were not intended to confer on them or their posterity the blessings of liberty, or any of the personal rights so carefully provided for the citizen.

No one of that race had ever migrated to the United States voluntarily; all of them had been brought here as articles of merchandise. The number that had been emancipated at that time were but few in comparison with those held in slavery; and they were identified in the public mind with the race to which they belonged, and regarded as a part of the slave population rather than the free. It is obvious that they were not even in the minds of the framers of the Constitution when they were conferring special rights and privileges upon the citizens of a State in every other part of the Union.

Indeed, when we look to the condition of this race in the several States at the time, it is impossible to believe that these rights and privileges were intended to be extended to them.

It is very true, that in that portion of the Union where the labor of the negro race was found to be unsuited to the climate and unprofitable to the master, but few slaves were held at the time of the Declaration of Independence; and when the Constitution was adopted, it had entirely worn out in one of them, and measures had been taken for its gradual abolition in several others. But this change had not been produced by any change of opinion in relation to this race; but because it was discovered, from experience, that slave labor was unsuited to the climate and productions of these States: for some of the States, where it had ceased or nearly ceased to exist, were actively engaged in the slave trade, procuring cargoes on the coast of Africa, and transporting them for sale to those parts of the Union where their labor was found to be profitable, and suited to the climate and productions. And this traffic was openly carried on, and fortunes accumulated by it, without reproach from the people of the States where they resided. And it can hardly be supposed that, in the States where it was then countenanced in its worst form — that is, in the seizure and transportation — the people could have regarded those who were emancipated as entitled to equal rights with themselves.

And we may here again refer, in support of this proposition, to the plain and unequivocal language of the laws of the several States, some passed after the Declaration of Independence and before the Constitution was adopted, and some since the Government went into operation.

We need not refer, on this point, particularly to the laws of the present slave-holding States. Their statute books are full of provisions in relation to this class, in the same spirit with the Maryland law which we have before quoted. They have continued to treat them as an inferior class, and to subject them to strict police regulations, drawing a broad line of distinction between the citizen and the slave races, and legislating in relation to them upon the same principle which prevailed at the time of the Declaration of Independence. As relates to these States, it is too plain for argument, that they have never been regarded as a part of the people or citizens of the State, nor supposed to possess any political rights which the dominant race might not withhold or grant at their pleasure. And as long ago as 1822, the Court of Appeals of Kentucky decided that free negroes and mulattoes were not citizens within the meaning of the Constitution of the United States; and the correctness of this decision is recognized, and the same doctrine affirmed, in 1 Meigs's Tenn. Reports, 331.

And if we turn to the legislation of the States where slavery had worn out, or measures taken for its speedy abolition, we shall find the same opinions and principles equally fixed and equally acted upon.

Thus, Massachusetts, in 1786, passed a law similar to the colonial one of which we have spoken. The law of 1786, like the law of 1705, forbids the marriage of any white person with any negro, Indian, or mulatto, and inflicts a penalty of fifty pounds upon any one who shall join them in marriage; and declares all such marriage absolutely null and void, and degrades thus the unhappy issue of the marriage by fixing upon it the stain of bastardy. And this mark of degradation was renewed, and again impressed upon the race, in the careful and deliberate preparation of their revised code published in 1836. This code forbids any person from joining in marriage any white person with any Indian, negro, or mulatto, and subjects the party who shall offend in this respect, to imprisonment, not exceeding six months, in the common jail, or to hard labor, and to a fine of not less than fifty nor more than two hundred dollars; and, like the law of 1786, it declares the marriage to be absolutely null and void. It will be seen that the punishment is increased by the code upon the person who shall marry them, by adding imprisonment to a pecuniary penalty.

So, too, in Connecticut. We refer more particularly to the legislation of this State, because it was not only among the first to put an end to slavery within its own territory, but was the first to fix a mark of reprobation upon the African slave trade. . . .

[W]e find that in the same statute passed in 1774, which prohibited the further importation of slaves into the State, there is also a provision by which any negro, Indian, or mulatto servant, who was found wandering out of the town or place to which he belonged, without a written pass such as is therein described, was made liable to be seized by any one, and taken before the next authority to be examined and delivered up to his master — who was required to pay the charge which had accrued thereby. And a subsequent section of the same law provides, that if any free negro shall travel without such pass, and shall be stopped, seized, or taken up, he shall pay all charges arising thereby. And this law was in full operation when the Constitution of the United States was adopted, and was not repealed till 1797. So that up to that time free negroes and mulattoes were associated with servants and slaves in the police regulations established by the laws of the State.

And again, in 1833, Connecticut passed another law, which made it penal to set up or establish any school in that State for the instruction of persons of the African race not inhabitants of the State, or to instruct or teach in any such school or institution, or board or harbor for that purpose, any such person, without the previous consent in writing of the civil authority of the town in which such school or institution might be.

And it appears by the case of Crandall v. The State, reported in 10 Conn. Rep., 340, that upon an information filed against Prudence Crandall for a violation of this law, one of the points raised in the defence was, that the law was a violation of the Constitution of the United States; and that the persons instructed, although of the African race, were citizens of other States, and therefore entitled to the rights and privileges of citizens in the State of Connecticut. But Chief Justice Dagget, before whom the case was tried, held, that persons of that description were not citizens of a State, within the meaning of the word citizen in the Constitution of the United States, and were not therefore entitled to the privileges and immunities of citizens in other States.

The case was carried up to the Supreme Court of Errors of the State, and the question fully argued there. But the case went off upon another point, and no opinion was expressed on this question. . . .

[Discussion of the laws of New Hampshire and Rhode Island is omitted.]

It would be impossible to enumerate and compress in the space usually allotted to an opinion of a court, the various laws, marking the condition of this race, which were passed from time to time after the Revolution, and before and since the adoption of the Constitution of the United States. In addition to those already referred to, it is sufficient to say, that Chancellor Kent, whose accuracy and research no one will question, states in the sixth edition of his Commentaries (published in 1848, 2 vol., 258, note b) that in no part of the country except Maine, did the African race, in point of fact, participate equally with the whites in the exercise of civil and political rights.

The legislation of the States therefore shows, in a manner not to be mistaken, the inferior and subject condition of that race at the time the Constitution was adopted, and long afterwards, throughout the thirteen States by which that instrument was framed; and it is hardly consistent with the respect due to these States, to suppose that they regarded at that time, as fellow-citizens and members of the sovereignty, a class of beings whom they had thus stigmatized; whom, as we are bound, out of respect to the State sovereignties, to assume they had deemed it just and necessary thus to stigmatize, and upon whom they had impressed such deep and enduring marks of inferiority and degradation; or, that when they met in convention to form the Constitution, they looked upon them as a portion of their constituents, or designed to include them in the provisions so carefully inserted for the security and protection of the liberties and rights of their citizens. It cannot be supposed that they intended to secure to them rights, and privileges, and rank, in the new political body throughout the Union, which every one of them denied within the limits of its own dominion. More especially, it cannot be believed that the large slaveholding States regarded them as included in the word citizens, or would have consented to a Constitution which might compel them to receive them in that character from another State. For if they were so received, and entitled to the privileges and immunities of citizens, it would exempt them from the operation of the special laws and from the police regulations which they considered to be necessary for their own safety. It would give to persons of the negro race, who were recognized as citizens in any one State of the Union, the right to enter every other State whenever they pleased, singly or in companies, without pass or passport, and without obstruction, to sojourn there as long as they pleased, to go where they pleased at every hour of the day or night without molestation, unless they committed some violation of law for which a white man would be punished; and it would give them the full liberty of speech in public and in private upon all subjects upon which its own citizens might speak; to hold public meetings upon political affairs, and to keep and carry arms wherever they went. And all of this would be done in the face of the subject race of the same color, both free and slaves, and inevitably producing discontent and insubordination among them, and endangering the peace and safety of the State.

It is impossible, it would seem, to believe that the great men of the slaveholding States, who took so large a share in framing the Constitution of the United States, and exercised so much influence in procuring its adoption, could have been so forgetful or regardless of their own safety and the safety of those who trusted and confided in them.

Besides, this want of foresight and care would have been utterly inconsistent with the caution displayed in providing for the admission of new members into this political family. For, when they gave to the citizens of each State the privileges and immunities of citizens in the several States, they at the same time took from the several States the power of naturalization, and confined that power exclusively to the Federal Government. No State was willing to permit another State to determine who should or should not be admitted as one of its citizens, and entitled to demand equal rights and privileges with their own people, within their own territories. The right of naturalization was therefore, with one accord, surrendered by the States, and confided to the Federal Government. And this power granted to Congress to establish an uniform rule of naturalization is, by the well-understood meaning of the word, confined to persons born in a foreign country, under a foreign Government. It is not a power to raise to the rank of a citizen any one born in the United States, who, from birth or parentage, by the laws of the country, belongs to an inferior and subordinate class. And when we find the States guarding themselves from the indiscreet or improper admission by other States of emigrants from other countries, by giving the power exclusively to Congress, we cannot fail to see that they could never have left with the States a much more important power — that is, the power of transforming into citizens a numerous class of persons, who in that character would be much more dangerous to the peace and safety of a large portion of the Union, than the few foreigners one of the States might improperly naturalize. The Constitution upon its adoption obviously took from the States all power by any subsequent legislation to introduce as a citizen into the political family of the United States any one, no matter where he was born, or what might be his character or condition; and it gave to Congress the power to confer this character upon those only who were born outside of the dominions of the United States. And no law of a State, therefore, passed since the Constitution was adopted, can give any right of citizenship outside of its own territory.

A clause similar to the one in the Constitution, in relation to the rights and immunities of citizens of one State in the other States, was contained in the Articles of Confederation. But there is a difference of language, which is worthy of note. The provision in the Articles of Confederation was, "that the free inhabitants of each of the States, paupers, vagabonds, and fugitives from justice, excepted, should be entitled to all the privileges and immunities of free citizens in the several States."

It will be observed, that under this Confederation, each State had the right to decide for itself, and in its own tribunals, whom it would acknowledge as a free inhabitant of another State. The term free inhabitant, in the generality of its terms, would certainly include one of the African race who had been manumitted. But no example, we think, can be found of his admission to all the privileges of citizenship in any State of the Union after these Articles were formed, and while they continued in force. And, notwithstanding the generality of the words "free inhabitants," it is very clear that, according to their accepted meaning in that day, they did not include the African race, whether free or not: for the fifth section of the ninth article provides that Congress should have the power "to agree upon the number of land forces to be raised, and to make requisitions from each State for its quota in proportion to the number of white inhabitants in such State, which requisition should be binding."

Words could hardly have been used which more strongly mark the line of distinction between the citizen and the subject; the free and the subjugated races. The latter were not even counted when the inhabitants of a State were to be embodied in proportion to its numbers for the general defence. And it cannot for a moment be supposed, that a class of persons thus separated and rejected from those who formed the sovereignty of the States, were yet intended to be included under the words "free inhabitants," in the preceding article, to whom privileges and immunities were so carefully secured in every State.

But although this clause of the Articles of Confederation is the same in principle with that inserted in the Constitution, yet the comprehensive word inhabitant, which might be construed to include an emancipated slave, is omitted; and the privilege is confined to citizens of the State. And this alteration in words would hardly have been made, unless a different meaning was intended to be conveyed, or a possible doubt removed. The just and fair inference is, that as this privilege was about to be placed under the protection of the General Government, and the words expounded by its tribunals, and all power in relation to it taken from the State and its courts, it was deemed prudent to describe with precision and caution the persons to whom this high privilege was given — and the word citizen was on that account substituted for the words free inhabitant. The word citizen excluded, and no doubt intended to exclude, foreigners who had not become citizens of some one of the States when the Constitution was adopted; and also every description of persons who were not fully recognized as citizens in the several States. This, upon any fair construction of the instruments to which we have referred, was evidently the object and purpose of this change of words.

To all this mass of proof we have still to add, that Congress has repeatedly legislated upon the same construction of the Constitution that we have given. Three laws, two of which were passed almost immediately after the Government went into operation, will be abundantly sufficient to show this. The two first are particularly worthy of notice, because many of the men who assisted in framing the Constitution, and took an active part in procuring its adoption, were then in the halls of legislation, and certainly understood what they meant when they used the words "people of the United States" and "citizen" in that well-considered instrument.

The first of these acts is the naturalization law, which was passed at the second session of the first Congress, March 26, 1790, and confines the right of becoming citizens "to aliens being free white persons."

Now, the Constitution does not limit the power of Congress in this respect to white persons. And they may, if they think proper, authorize the naturalization of any one, of any color, who was born under allegiance to another Government. But the language of the law above quoted, shows that citizenship at that time was perfectly understood to be confined to the white race; and that they alone constituted the sovereignty in the Government.

Congress might, as we before said, have authorized the naturalization of Indians, because they were aliens and foreigners. But, in their then untutored and savage state, no one would have thought of admitting them as citizens in a civilized community. And, moreover, the atrocities they had but recently committed, when they were the allies of Great Britain in the Revolutionary war, were yet fresh in the recollection of the people of the United States, and they were even then guarding themselves against the threatened renewal of Indian hostilities. No one supposed then that any Indian would ask for, or was capable of enjoying, the privileges of an American citizen, and the word white was not used with any particular reference to them.

Neither was it used with any reference to the African race imported into or born in this country; because Congress had no power to naturalize them, and therefore there was no necessity for using particular words to exclude them.

It would seem to have been used merely because it followed out the line of division which the Constitution has drawn between the citizen race, who formed and held the Government, and the African race, which they held in subjection and slavery, and governed at their own pleasure.

Another of the early laws of which we have spoken, is the first militia law, which was passed in 1792, at the first session of the second Congress. The language of this law is equally plain and significant with the one just mentioned. It directs that every "free able-bodied white male citizen" shall be enrolled in the militia. The word white is evidently used to exclude the African race, and the word "citizen" to exclude unnaturalized foreigners; the latter forming no part of the sovereignty, owing it no allegiance, and therefore under no obligation to defend it. The African race, however, born in the country, did owe allegiance to the Government, whether they were slave or free; but it is repudiated, and rejected from the duties and obligations of citizenship in marked language.

The third act to which we have alluded is even still more decisive; it was passed as late as 1813 (2 Stat., 809) and it provides: "That from and after the termination of the war in which the United States are now engaged with Great Britain, it shall not be lawful to employ, on board of any public or private vessels of the United States, any person or persons except citizens of the United States, or persons of color, natives of the United States." Here the line of distinction is drawn in express words. Persons of color, in the judgment of Congress, were not included in the word citizens, and they are described as another and different class of persons, and authorized to be employed, if born in the United States. . . .

The conduct of the Executive Department of the Government has been in perfect harmony upon this subject with this course of legislation. The question was brought officially before the late William Wirt, when he was the Attorney General of the United States, in 1821, and he decided that the words "citizens of the United States" were used in the acts of Congress in the same sense as in the Constitution; and that free persons of color were not citizens, within the meaning of the Constitution and laws; and this opinion has been confirmed by that of the late Attorney General, Caleb Cushing, in a recent case, and acted upon by the Secretary of State, who refused to grant passports to them as "citizens of the United States." But it is said that a person may be a citizen, and entitled to that character, although he does not possess all the rights which may belong to other citizens; as, for example, the right to vote, or to hold particular offices; and that yet, when he goes into another State, he is entitled to be recognized there as a citizen, although the State may measure his rights by the rights which it allows to persons of a like character or class resident in the State, and refuse to him the full rights of citizenship.

This argument overlooks the language of the provision in the Constitution of which we are speaking.

Undoubtedly, a person may be a citizen, that is, a member of the community who form the sovereignty, although he exercises no share of the political power, and is incapacitated from holding particular offices. Women and minors, who form a part of the political family, cannot vote; and when a property qualification is required to vote or hold a particular office, those who have not the necessary qualification cannot vote or hold the office, yet they are citizens.

So, too, a person may be entitled to vote by the law of the State, who is not a citizen even of the State itself. And in some of the States of the Union foreigners not naturalized are allowed to vote. And the State may give the right to free negroes and mulattoes, but that does not make them citizens of the State, and still less of the United States. And the provision in the Constitution giving privileges and immunities in other States, does not apply to them.

Neither does it apply to a person who, being the citizen of a State, migrates to another State. For then he becomes subject to the laws of the State in which he lives, and he is no longer a citizen of the State from which he removed. And the State in which he resides may then, unquestionably, determine his status or condition, and place him among the class of persons who are not recognized as citizens, but belong to an inferior and subject race; and may deny him the privileges and immunities enjoyed by its citizens.

But so far as mere rights of person are concerned, the provision in question is confined to citizens of a State who are temporarily in another State without taking up their residence there. It gives them no political rights in the State, as to voting or holding office, or in any other respect. For a citizen of one State has no right to participate in the government of another. But if he ranks as a citizen in the State to which he belongs, within the meaning of the Constitution of the United States, then, whenever he goes into another State, the Constitution clothes him, as to the rights of person, with all the privileges and immunities which belong to citizens of the State. And if persons of the African race are citizens of a State, and of the United States, they would be entitled to all of these privileges and immunities in every State, and the State could not restrict them; for they would hold these privileges and immunities under the paramount authority of the Federal Government, and its courts would be bound to maintain and enforce them, the Constitution and laws of the State to the contrary notwithstanding. And if the States could limit or restrict them, or place the party in an inferior grade, this clause of the Constitution would be unmeaning, and could have no operation; and would give no rights to the citizen when in another State. He would have none but what the State itself chose to allow him. This is evidently not the construction or meaning of the clause in question. It guaranties rights to the citizen, and the State cannot withhold them. And these rights are of a character and would lead to consequences which make it absolutely certain that the African race were not included under the name of citizens of a State, and were not in the contemplation of the framers of the Constitution when these privileges and immunities were provided for the protection of the citizen in other States. . . .

The only two provisions which point to them and include them, treat them as property, and make it the duty of the Government to protect it; no other power, in relation to this race, is to be found in the Constitution; and as it is a Government of special, delegated, powers, no authority beyond these two provisions can be constitutionally exercised. The Government of the United States had no right to interfere for any other purpose but that of protecting the rights of the owner, leaving it altogether with the several States to deal with this race, whether emancipated or not, as each State may think justice, humanity, and the interests and safety of society, require. The States evidently intended to reserve this power exclusively to themselves.

No one, we presume, supposes that any change in public opinion or feeling, in relation to this unfortunate race, in the civilized nations of Europe or in this country, should induce the court to give to the words of the Constitution a more liberal construction in their favor than they were intended to bear when the instrument was framed and adopted. Such an argument would be altogether inadmissible in any tribunal called on to interpret it. If any of its provisions are deemed unjust, there is a mode prescribed in the instrument itself by which it may be amended; but while it remains unaltered, it must be construed now as it was understood at the time of its adoption. It is not only the same in words, but the same in meaning, and delegates the same powers to the Government, and reserves and secures the same rights and privileges to the citizen; and as long as it continues to exist in its present form, it speaks not only in the same words, but with the same meaning and intent with which it spoke when it came from the hands of its framers, and was voted on and adopted by the people of the United States. Any other rule of construction would abrogate the judicial character of this court, and make it the mere reflex of the popular opinion or passion of the day. This court was not created by the Constitution for such purposes. Higher and graver trusts have been confided to it, and it must not falter in the path of duty.

What the construction was at that time, we think can hardly admit of doubt. We have the language of the Declaration of Independence and of the Articles of Confederation, in addition to the plain words of the Constitution itself; we have the legislation of the different States, before, about the time, and since, the Constitution was adopted; we have the legislation of Congress, from the time of its adoption to a recent period; and we have the constant and uniform action of the Executive Department, all concurring together, and leading to the same result. And if anything in relation to the construction of the Constitution can be regarded as settled, it is that which we now give to the word "citizen" and the word "people."

And upon a full and careful consideration of the subject, the court is of opinion, that, upon the facts stated in the plea in abatement, Dred Scott was not a citizen of Missouri within the meaning of the Constitution of the United States, and not entitled as such to sue in its courts. . . .

CURTIS, J., dissenting. . . .

To determine whether any free persons, descended from Africans held in slavery, were citizens of the United States under the Confederation, and consequently at the time of the adoption of the Constitution of the United States, it is only necessary to know whether any such persons were citizens of either of the States under the Confederation, at the time of the adoption of the Constitution.

Of this there can be no doubt. At the time of the ratification of the Articles of Confederation, all free native-born inhabitants of the States of New Hampshire, Massachusetts, New York, New Jersey, and North Carolina, though descended from African slaves, were not only citizens of those States, but such of them as had the other necessary qualifications possessed the franchise of electors, on equal terms with other citizens. . . . [A discussion of state electoral laws is omitted.]

New York, by its Constitution of 1820, required colored persons to have some qualifications as prerequisites for voting, which white persons need not possess. And New Jersey, by its present Constitution, restricts the right to vote to white male citizens. But these changes can have no other effect upon the present inquiry, except to show, that before they were made, no such restrictions existed; and colored in common with white persons, were not only citizens of those States, but entitled to the elective franchise on the same qualifications as white persons, as they now are in New Hampshire and Massachusetts. I shall not enter into an examination of the existing opinions of that period respecting the African race, nor into any discussion concerning the meaning of those who asserted, in the Declaration of Independence, that all men are created equal; that they are endowed by their Creator with certain inalienable rights; that among these are life, liberty, and the pursuit of happiness. My own opinion is, that a calm comparison of these assertions of universal abstract truths, and of their own individual opinions and acts, would not leave these men under any reproach of inconsistency; that the great truths they asserted on that solemn occasion, they were ready and anxious to make effectual, wherever a necessary regard to circumstances, which no statesman can disregard without producing more evil than good, would allow; and that it would not be just to them, nor true in itself, to allege that they intended to say that the Creator of all men had endowed the white race, exclusively, with the great natural rights which the Declaration of Independence asserts. But this is not the place to vindicate their memory. . . .

The fourth of the fundamental articles of the Confederation was as follows: "The free inhabitants of each of these States, paupers, vagabonds, and fugitives from justice, excepted, shall be entitled to all the privileges and immunities of free citizens in the several States." The fact that free persons of color were citizens of some of the several States, and the consequence, that this fourth article of the Confederation would have the effect to confer on such persons the privileges and immunities of general citizenship, were not only known to those who framed and adopted those articles, but the evidence is decisive, that the fourth article was intended to have that effect, and that more restricted language, which would have excluded such persons, was deliberately and purposely rejected.

On the 25th of June, 1778, the Articles of Confederation being under consideration by the Congress, the delegates from South Carolina moved to amend this fourth article, by inserting after the word "free," and before the word "inhabitants," the word "white," so that the privileges and immunities of general citizenship would be secured only to white persons. Two States voted for the amendment, eight States against it, and the vote of one State was divided. The language of the article stood unchanged, and both by its terms of inclusion, "free inhabitants," and the strong implication from its terms of exclusion, "paupers, vagabonds, and fugitives from justice," who alone were excepted, it is clear, that under the Confederation, and at the time of the adoption of the Constitution, free colored persons of African descent might be, and, by reason of their citizenship in certain States, were entitled to the privileges and immunities of general citizenship of the United States.

Did the Constitution of the United States deprive them or their descendants of citizenship?

That Constitution was ordained and established by the people of the United States, through the action, in each State, of those persons who were qualified by its laws to act thereon, in behalf of themselves and all other citizens of that State. In some of the States, as we have seen, colored persons were among those qualified by law to act on this subject. . . . It would be strange, if we were to find in that instrument anything which deprived of their citizenship any part of the people of the United States who were among those by whom it was established. I can find nothing in the Constitution which proprio vigore, deprives of their citizenship any class of persons who were citizens of the United States at the time of its adoption, or who should be native-born citizens of any State after its adoption; nor any power enabling Congress to disfranchise persons born on the soil of any State, and entitled to citizenship of such State by its Constitution and laws. And my opinion is, that, under the Constitution of the United States, every free person born on the soil of a State, who is a citizen of that State by force of its Constitution or laws, is also a citizen of the United States. . . .

It has been . . . objected, that if free colored persons born within a particular State, and made citizens of that State by its Constitution and laws, are thereby made citizens of the United States, then, under the second section of the fourth article of the Constitution, such persons would be entitled to all the privileges and immunities of citizens in the several states; and if so, then colored persons could vote, and be eligible to not only Federal, but offices even in those States whose Constitutions and laws disqualify colored persons from voting or being elected to office.

But this position rests upon an assumption which I deem untenable. Its basis is, that no one can be deemed a citizen of the United States who is not entitled to enjoy all the privileges and franchises which are conferred on any citizen. That this is not true, under the Constitution of the United States, seems to be clear.

. . . So, in all the States, numerous persons, though citizens, cannot vote, or cannot hold office, either on account of their age, or sex, or that want of the necessary legal qualifications. The truth is, that citizenship, under the Constitution of the United States, is not dependent on the possession of any particular political or even of all civil rights; and any attempt so to define it must lead to error. To what citizens the elective franchise shall be confided, is a question to be determined by each State, in accordance with its own views of the necessities or expediencies of its condition. What civil rights shall be enjoyed by its citizens, and whether all shall enjoy the same, or how they may be gained or lost, are to be determined in the same way.

. . . [T]his clause of the Constitution does not confer on the citizens of one State, in all other States, specific and enumerated privileges and immunities. They are entitled to such as belong to citizenship, but not to such as belong to particular citizens attended by other qualifications. . . . It rests with the States themselves so to frame their Constitutions and laws as not to attach a particular privilege or immunity to mere naked citizenship. . . .

It has sometimes been urged that colored persons are shown not to be citizens of the United States by the fact that the naturalization laws apply only to white persons. But whether a person born in the United States be or be not a citizen, cannot depend on laws which refer only to aliens, and do not affect the *status* of persons born in the United States. The utmost effect which can be attributed to them is, to show that Congress has not deemed it expedient generally to apply the rule to colored aliens. That they might do so, if thought fit, is clear. . . .

I do not deem it necessary to review at length the legislation of Congress having more or less bearing on the citizenship of colored persons. It does not seem to me to have any considerable tendency to prove that it has been considered by the legislative department of the Government, that no such persons are citizens of the United States. Undoubtedly they have been debarred from the exercise of particular rights or privileges extended to white persons, but, I believe, always in terms which, by implication, admit they may be citizens. Thus the act of May 17, 1792, for the organization of the militia, directs the enrollment of "every free, able-bodied, white male citizen." An assumption that none but white persons are citizens, would be as inconsistent with the just import of this language, as that all citizens are able-bodied, or males. . . .

Discussion

1. Taney believed that the decision in *Dred Scott* would settle the slavery issue. Instead, the decision became the nation's symbol of the irreconcilable division between North and South.

2. *The regulation of slavery in the territories. Dred Scott* is a case of enormous complexity, involving many interlocking issues. Today its most (in)famous holding is the

claim that blacks could not be citizens. One might think that the Court, having found a lack of subject matter jurisdiction, might have ended its discussion there. Nevertheless, the majority went on to discuss other substantive issues. One of the most important at the time was the constitutionality of the Missouri Compromise of 1820. That act had declared that slavery and involuntary servitude, except as a punishment for crime, were "forever prohibited" in the Louisiana Territory north of the compromise line of 36°30' north latitude, with the exception of the state of Missouri, which entered the Union as a slave state.

Dred Scott argued that when he and his wife Harriet traveled out of Missouri into the Upper Louisiana Territory, they became free, because slavery could not exist there; hence when they returned to Missouri they became citizens of that state. Scott also argued that he was free because Emerson took him to Rock Island in Illinois, a free state. Taney did not mention a third possible claim: that Eliza, having been born "north of the north line of the State of Missouri" had a legal status different from her father.

Taney disposed of the second claim, concerning the trip to Illinois, on the authority of Strader v. Graham 51 U.S. (10 How.) 82 (1851). Applied to this case, *Strader* held that the law of Missouri, from which the plaintiffs traveled and to which they returned, and not the law of Illinois, determined Dred and Harriet's status. Under Missouri Law, a slave regained his status as soon as he returned to Missouri.

Taney's response to Scott's first argument was that the Missouri Compromise was unconstitutional. Taney and the dissenting Justices disagreed about whether the case was governed by the territory clause of Article IV, §3, cl. 2, which confers on Congress the power "to dispose of and make all needful rules and regulations respecting the territory or other property belonging to the United States." Taney argued that the clause was irrelevant to the case, because the word "territory" referred only "to the territory which at that time belonged to, or was claimed by, the United States, and was within their boundaries as settled by the treaty with Great Britain," and therefore did not apply to "a territory afterwards acquired from a foreign Government."[44]

Taney argued that although no clause of the Constitution expressly dealt with territories subsequently acquired, the powers of the United States could be inferred from "the provisions and principles of the Constitution, and its distribution of powers."

Taney then argued that when the United States acquired territories, it was bound to give the inhabitants of these territories the same Bill of Rights protections enjoyed by citizens in the states. He argued that the United States could not create colonies where less than full constitutional protections applied.

There is certainly no power given by the Constitution to the Federal Government to establish or maintain colonies bordering on the United States or at a distance, to be

---

44. This allowed Taney to explain the fact that the First Congress almost immediately repassed the Northwest Ordinance, passed initially by the Confederation Congress, which, among other things, barred slavery in the Northwest Territories. He argued that the territory clause did apply to these lands. They were claimed by various States as part of the treaty with Great Britain and were later ceded to the Federal Government after the Constitution was ratified. Moreover, Taney insisted, the Federal Government was merely ratifying the policy of those states by prohibiting slavery. Thus, Taney insisted "any argument, drawn from precedents, showing the extent of the power which the General Government exercised over slavery in this Territory . . . [was] altogether inapplicable to the case before us."

ruled and governed at its own pleasure; nor to enlarge its territorial limits in any way, except by the admission of new States. . . .[45]

The power to expand the territory of the United States by the admission of new States is plainly given; and in the construction of this power by all the departments of the Government, it has been held to authorize the acquisition of territory, not fit for admission at the time, but to be admitted as soon as its population and situation would entitle it to admission. It is acquired to become a State, and not to be held as a colony and governed by Congress with absolute authority; and as the propriety of admitting a new State is committed to the sound discretion of Congress, the power to acquire territory for that purpose, to be held by the United States until it is in a suitable condition to become a State upon an equal footing with the other States, must rest upon the same discretion. It is a question for the political department of the Government, and not the judicial; and whatever the political department of the Government shall recognize as within the limits of the United States, the judicial department is also bound to recognize, and to administer in it the laws of the United States, so far as they apply, and to maintain in the Territory the authority and rights of the Government, and also the personal rights and rights of property of individual citizens, as secured by the Constitution. . . .

[C]itizens of the United States who migrate to a Territory belonging to the people of the United States, cannot be ruled as mere colonists, dependent upon the will of the General Government, and to be governed by any laws it may think proper to impose. . . . Whatever it acquires, it acquires for the benefit of the people of the several States who created it. It is their trustee acting for them, and charged with the duty of promoting the interests of the whole people of the Union in the exercise of the powers specifically granted.

Although Congress has the power to establish territorial governments, the power of Congress over the person or property of a citizen can never be a mere discretionary power under our Constitution and form of Government. The powers of the Government and the rights and privileges of the citizen are regulated and plainly defined by the Constitution itself. And when the Territory becomes a part of the United States, the Federal Government enters into possession in the character impressed upon it by those who created it. It enters upon it with its powers over the

---

45. This sentence conceals a profound constitutional issue of its own, manifested in the admission of Texas to the Union in 1844. President Tyler had initially submitted a treaty to the Senate by which Texas, an independent country since its successful revolt against Mexico in 1837, would be annexed to the United States. The Treaty was defeated. Although some senators challenged the right of the United States to admit foreign countries to the Union, as distinguished from the purchase of territory from a foreign country, the more substantial basis of opposition was from anti-slave senators who (correctly) saw the admission of Texas as a boon to what was increasingly being termed the "slavocracy." See generally Frederick Merk, Slavery and the Annexation of Texas (1972). Faced with this defeat, Tyler and other supporters of Texas annexation simply proposed its admission under the Admissions Clause of the Constitution, which requires only a majority vote of each house of Congress, as against the two-thirds of the Senate required by the Treaty Clause. Many opponents denounced the constitutionality of this move, claiming that the Admissions Clause applied only to pre-existing territory of the United States and did not allow the direct admission to the Union of a foreign country. Thus Daniel Webster argued that "[w]hen the constitution was formed, it is not probable that either its framers or the people ever looked to the admission of any States into the Union except as they already existed, and such as should be formed out of territories then belonging to the United States." 1 Works of Daniel Webster 355 (1860), quoted in Janice Levering, The Texas Two-Step to Statehood 10 (unpublished paper). In response, proponents of the legislation referred to "the general, unrestricted, unambiguous and unlimited power to admit new States into the Union." Id., quoting Congressman Tibbatts. In March 1845, just before the inauguration of James Polk, a supporter of Texas annexation, Congress voted to admit Texas as a state. Given Taney's general political views, one can surmise that he had no constitutional qualms about the unorthodox process by which Texas came into the Union. For further treatment of the constitutional issues surrounding the Texas annexation, see Mark A. Graber, Settling the West: The Annexation of Texas, the Louisiana Purchase, and Bush v. Gore, in The Louisiana Purchase and American Expansion 1803-1898, 81-110 (Levinson and Sparrow eds., 2005); David Currie, Texas, in id. at 111-128.

citizen strictly defined, and limited by the Constitution, from which it derives its own existence, and by virtue of which alone it continues to exist and act as a Government and sovereignty. It has no power of any kind beyond it; and it cannot, when it enters a Territory of the United States, put off its character, and assume discretionary or despotic powers which the Constitution has denied to it. . . .

For example, no one, we presume, will contend that Congress can make any law in a Territory respecting the establishment of religion, or the free exercise thereof, or abridging the freedom of speech or of the press, or the right of the people of the Territory peaceably to assemble, and to petition the Government for the redress of grievances.

Nor can Congress deny to the people the right to keep and bear arms, nor the right to trial by jury, nor compel any one to be a witness against himself in a criminal proceeding.

These powers, and others, in relation to rights of person, which it is not necessary here to enumerate, are, in express and positive terms, denied to the General Government; and the rights of private property have been guarded with equal care. Thus the rights of property are united with the rights of person, and placed on the same ground by the fifth amendment to the Constitution, which provides that no person shall be deprived of life, liberty, and property, without due process of law. And an act of Congress which deprives a citizen of the United States of his liberty or property, merely because he came himself or brought his property into a particular Territory of the United States, and who had committed no offence against the laws, could hardly be dignified with the name of due process of law. . . .

Taney dismissed the argument that "there is a difference between property in a slave and other property" that would afford the former less protection. To the contrary, he argued,

The right of property in a slave is distinctly and expressly affirmed in the Constitution. The right to traffic in it, like an ordinary article of merchandise and property, was guarantied to the citizens of the United States, in every State that might desire it, for twenty years. And the Government in express terms is pledged to protect it in all future time, if the slave escapes from his owner. This is done in plain words — too plain to be misunderstood. And no word can be found in the Constitution which gives Congress a greater power over slave property, or which entitles property of that kind to less protection than property of any other description. The only power conferred is the power coupled with the duty of guarding and protecting the owner in his rights. . . .

Justice Catron concurred:

Congress cannot do indirectly what the Constitution prohibits directly. If the slave-holder is prohibited from going to the Territory with his slaves, who are parts of his family in name and in fact, it will follow that men owning lawful property in their own States, carrying with them the equality of their State to enjoy the common property, may be told, you cannot come here with your slaves, and he will be held out at the border. By this subterfuge, owners of slave property, to the amount of thousand of millions, might be almost as effectually excluded from removing into the Territory of Louisiana north of thirty-six degrees thirty minutes, as if the law declared that owners of slaves, as a class, should be excluded, even if their slaves were left behind.

Just as well might Congress have said to those of the North, you shall not introduce into the territory south of said line your cattle or horses, as the country is already over-stocked; nor can you introduce your tools of trade, or machines, as the policy of Congress is to encourage the culture of sugar and cotton south of the line, and so to provide that the Northern people shall manufacture for those of the South, and barter for the staple articles slave labor produces. And thus the Northern farmer and mechanic would be held out, as the slaveholder was for thirty years, by the Missouri restriction.

If Congress could prohibit one species of property, lawful throughout Louisiana when it was acquired, and lawful in the State from whence it was brought, so Congress might exclude any or all property. . . .

[T]he act of 1820, known as the Missouri compromise, violates the most leading feature of the Constitution — a feature on which the Union depends, and which secures to the respective States and their citizens and entire EQUALITY of rights, privileges, and immunities.

Justice McLean, dissenting, argued that the Missouri Compromise was constitutional as a regulation of federal territories prior to their eventual admission as states:

If Congress should deem slaves or free colored persons injurious to the population of a free Territory, as conducing to lessen the value of the public lands, or on any other ground connected with the public interest, they have the power to prohibit them from becoming settlers in it. This can be sustained on the ground of a sound national policy, which is so clearly shown in our history by practical results, that it would seem no considerate individual can question it. And, as regards any unfairness of such a policy to our Southern brethren, as urged in the argument, it is only necessary to say that, with one-fourth of the Federal population of the Union, they have in the slave States a larger extent of fertile territory than is included in the free States; and it is submitted, if masters of slaves be restricted from bringing them into free territory, that the restriction on the free citizens of non-slaveholding States, by bringing slaves into free territory, is four times greater than that complained of by the South. But, not only so; some three or four hundred thousand holders of slaves, by bringing them into free territory, impose a restriction on twenty millions of the free States. The repugnancy to slavery would probably prevent fifty or a hundred freemen from settling in a slave Territory, where one slaveholder would be prevented from settling in a free Territory.

This remark is made in answer to the argument urged, that a prohibition of slavery in the free Territories is inconsistent with the continuance of the Union. Where a Territorial Government is established in a slave Territory, it has uniformly remained in that condition until the people form a State Constitution; the same course where the Territory is free, both parties acting in good faith, would be attended with satisfactory results.

3. Although, as a formal matter, McLean dissented from Taney's rejection of the possibility of black citizenship — he wrote that "[t]he most general and appropriate definition of the term citizen is 'a freeman.' Being a freeman [Scott] is a citizen within the act of Congress" — he appeared to have an extremely limited notion of what rights citizenship brought within its wake. Recall his statement that "[i]f Congress should deem slaves or *free colored persons* injurious to the population of a free Territory, as conducing to lessen the value of the public lands, or on any other ground connected with the public interest, they have the power to prohibit them from becoming settlers in it" (emphasis added). Do you believe that Congress possessed a power to bar citizens of the United States from settling within a territory of the United States prior to statehood? Imagine, for example, that Congress, after determining that friction between Catholics and Protestants was a danger to the necessary political cohesion within any territory, passed a "compromise" that

limited Catholic settlement to the Minnesota Territory, although after statehood
neither the states nor the federal government presumably could have prevented
migration. Would this arrangement have been constitutional?

Moreover, what is the relevance of McLean's point that anti-slavery settlers are,
in effect, discouraged from settling far more of the actual territories than are slaveowners? Does this suggest that it would be unconstitutional to bar slavery in *all* of
the territories, i.e., that slaveowners *do* possess a constitutional right to settle, with
their slaves, in at least some of the territory, albeit not all of it?

4. As to the legal status and rights (or lack of same) enjoyed by "free blacks,"
consider the fact that the Indiana constitution of 1851 barred free blacks from
migrating into the state. Blacks already in Indiana, though allowed to remain, were
prohibited from voting, serving on juries, or participating in the militia, as well as
barred from testifying against whites in court, marrying whites, or attending schools
with whites.[46] Similar laws prohibiting black immigration were passed in Iowa,
Illinois, and Oregon, reflecting "the Negrophobia that characterized much of the
northern population."[47] At the very least, this should dispel any belief that to
condemn slavery for its threat to a regime of "free labor" necessarily implied that
one was particularly sympathetic to the black slaves themselves. In any event, return
to *Crandall* (decided in 1868, after the war) and ask if the Taney Court would have
struck down these bans on black immigration and settlement by free blacks resident in (and, perhaps, even presumptive citizens of) other states of the Union.

5. *Dred Scott and substantive due process.* Taney argues that the Missouri
Compromise violates the property rights of citizens under the Due Process Clause
of the Fifth Amendment. It is often said that *Dred Scott* is the origin of the Supreme
Court's doctrine of "substantive due process," later invoked in cases like Lochner v.
New York and Roe v. Wade. In fact, Taney seems to be invoking a much older
doctrine that was recognized at the founding: the idea that the government could
not extinguish vested rights of property. See the discussion in Chapter 2, supra, at
148-151. The roots of the idea go back to the Magna Carta, and its reference to "the
law of the land," which was generally regarded as equivalent to the formulation
"due process of law." See James W. Ely, Jr., The Oxymoron Reconsidered: Myth and
Reality in the Origins of Substantive Due Process, 16 Constitutional Commentary
315-345 (1999). The basic idea, as it developed in Blackstone and other writers, was

---

46. James M. McPherson, Ordeal by Fire: The Civil War and Reconstruction 80 (1982).
47. Battle Cry of Freedom 88. Indeed, as to Oregon, Garrett Epps writes that

> white pioneers were able to prevent black people from settling in Oregon only by the most ener-
> getic and determined recourse to legal apartheid. Even before Oregon was a United States terri-
> tory, its inhabitants formed a provisional government in 1843 and excluded black settlers. In
> 1850, Congress passed the Donation Land Claim Act, which guaranteed 320 acres to each single
> white male U.S. citizen homesteading in the Oregon Territory (married white homesteaders
> received 640 acres). These measures were not of merely theoretical import. An 1850 census noted
> the presence of at least 54 settlers of African descent, 114 Native Americans or "half-breed," and
> 38 Native Hawaiians. The total enumerated population was 13,294. The all-white proviso of the
> Act also rid Oregon of a substantial population of Native Hawaiians, who first came to Oregon
> country in 1788 as crew members of merchant vessels. Most of the Natives returned to Hawaii
> after passage of the Act. When Oregonians wrote their first statehood constitution in 1857, they
> became the first state population to include a constitutional ban on settlement by "free Negroes
> and mullatoes." Though superseded by the Fourteenth Amendment, the measure was not
> formally repealed until 1926.

Garrett Epps, To an Unknown God: The Hidden History of *Employment Division v. Smith*, 30 Ariz. St.
L.J. 983, 968-969 n.62 (1999) (citations omitted).

that when legislatures took property from A and gave it to B they violated "the law of the land" principle, and hence due process of law. (Recall Justice Chase's view, expressed in Calder v. Bull, that A to B transfers were not "a rightful exercise of authority" and "against all reason and justice.") Indeed, in 1829 in Wilkinson v. Leland, 27 US 627, 658 (1829), Justice Story suggested that principle apparently held whether or not a state had a law of the land or due process clause in its constitution: "We know of no case, in which a legislative act to transfer the property of A. to B. without his consent, has ever been held a constitutional exercise of legislative power in any state in the union."

Taney argued that when the federal government applied the Missouri Compromise to southerners bringing their slaves into free territories, it was taking their property in the slave and giving it to the slave. Hence it destroyed vested rights, which violated the Due Process Clause.

In his dissent, Justice Curtis agreed with Taney that taking vested rights of property violated the Due Process Clause: "This restriction on the legislative power is not peculiar to the Constitution of the United States; it was borrowed from Magna Charta; was brought to America by our ancestors, as part of their inherited liberties, and has existed in all the States, usually in the very words of the great charter." However, Curtis explained, people do not have vested rights in property when they voluntarily enter into jurisdictions that do not recognize that species of property: "[U]nder the power to regulate commerce, Congress could prohibit the importation of slaves; and the exercise of the power was restrained till 1808. A citizen of the United States owns slaves in Cuba, and brings them to the United States, where they are set free by the legislation of Congress. Does this legislation deprive him of his property without due process of law? If so, what becomes of the laws prohibiting the slave trade? If not, how can similar regulation respecting a Territory violate the fifth amendment of the Constitution?" The problem Curtis identifies doesn't arise with estates in land because they are not movable, so they can't cross jurisdictions, but it does apply to chattels that can be moved from place to place.

If Taney's vested rights argument is sound, why is the federal government's prohibition on slavery any more confiscatory than that of a state like Illinois through which Dr. Emerson also traveled? Does Taney's argument mean that the federal government is limited with respect to other kinds of property regulations it can enact in the territories? For example, if Congress prohibited bringing into Kansas Territory certain types of drugs (or alcohol) and Dr. Emerson wanted to set up shop as a seller of drugs or a saloon owner, would the federal government be required to permit him to do so under *Dred Scott*? Perhaps Taney meant to say that the right to own slaves was more protected than other forms of property rights subject to regulation. Why might that be so?

6. Taney's opinion included the statement that Congress "could not authorize a territorial government" to do what it itself could not do, i.e., bar slavery in the territories. This, presumably, meant that Senator Stephen Douglas's program of "popular sovereignty," which left the decision up to the settlers themselves in their territorial legislatures, was constitutionally illegitimate, that the only time slavery could be abolished was upon entry to the Union. (Everyone agreed that states had complete autonomy in regard to adoption of slavery, and the "equal footing" doctrine gave new states the same powers enjoyed by Virginia and Massachusetts to make the decision for or against slavery.) Thus, writes James M. McPherson, "It soon dawned on northern Democrats that Taney had aimed to discomfit them as

well as the Republicans."[48] Douglas responded, in June, 1857, by pointing out that even if a master's right to bring slaves into territories was absolutely protected, nonetheless it remained up to the territorial legislatures to decide, as a practical matter, how much protection to give this right by "appropriate police regulation and local legislation," the absence of which would make the master's formal right "barren and worthless."[49] Douglas's attempt to find a "centrist" position with regard to the issue was unavailing, and his articulation of what became known as the Freeport Doctrine antagonized many pro-slavery Southerners and contributed to the fragmentation within the Democratic Party in the 1860 election that would cost Douglas the presidency.

7. Consider Justice Curtis's reference to Article II and its limitation of eligibility for the presidency to "natural-born citizens." Is this enough to support an inference that anyone born within the United States is automatically a citizen of the United States (and of the state within which he or she is born)? That is, is sentence one of the Fourteenth Amendment, which is viewed as explicitly overruling *Dred Scott*, simply a reversion to a correct understanding of the 1787 Constitution, or does it in fact supply a rule of citizenship that was lacking in the original Constitution?

8. *Dred Scott*, it is safe to say, is the most reviled decision (and Taney's the most reviled opinion) in the history of the Supreme Court. If you share the distaste for them, why? Do you object to the abominable result or to the quality of the legal analysis?

It has become common to ascribe to the *Dred Scott* decision some significant share of the blame for the drift toward war, which would occur four years later. Is this plausible? Why would Southerners have been more, rather than less inclined toward secession as a result of *Dred Scott*? Republicans, of course, were extremely upset to have their party platform declared unconstitutional, but they were already committed to the prohibition of slavery in the territories. Kenneth Stampp suggests that the importance of *Dred Scott* to the onset of the Civil War has been vastly overrated; such events as the struggles in Kansas and John Brown's raids were far more important in convincing Southerners that their only hope lay in secession.[50] If one objects to Taney's opinion on the grounds that it hastened war, consider that a decision freeing Dred Scott would surely have generated intense opposition by the already secession-prone Southerners, who might not have waited until 1860-1861 to attempt secession. Consider also that the North might not have won a war begun in 1857, especially because of its lack of military preparedness and the fact that its Commander-in-Chief would have been the feckless James Buchanan rather than Abraham Lincoln. Is this a good reason to support the result in *Dred Scott* — that it bought the North valuable time? Or is your view that justice, i.e., the repudiation of slavery, should be done (and, indeed, is required by the Constitution) though the heavens (or, at least, the Union) fall?

If you revile the opinion on legal grounds, rather than the empirical (or moral) consequences of the decision, then what are the precise legal errors that you believe Taney makes? Do you, for example, believe that he makes historical errors that vitiate his analysis, or would you object even if it turned out that he was basically correct in his historical analysis (so that Taney's mistake might be believing himself

48. Battle Cry of Freedom: The Civil War Era 177.
49. Quoted in id. at 177-178.
50. See Stampp, America in 1857, at 108. The most recent biography of John Brown is David S. Reynolds, John Brown, Abolitionist: The Man Who Killed Slavery, Sparked the Civil War, and Seeded Civil Rights (2005).

confined by the original understanding)? Consider Professor Finkelman's statement that "[t]hose who revere the framers and the Constitution can find solace only in the fact that some of the founders in 1776 and 1787 (though probably a minority of both groups) did not intend the results that Taney reached."[51] Is *Dred Scott* a worse decision than *Prigg*, either in terms of its legal analysis or in terms of actual consequences for the lives of human beings? Recall that *Prigg* held, among other things, that the Constitution protected the right of a slaveowner to recapture his purportedly fugitive slaves without any legal process at all (so long as the recapture is "peaceful") and upheld the Fugitive Slave Act of 1793 in the absence of any explicit textual authorization for Congress to pass such legislation.

Professor Graber has written that most contemporary constitutional theorists today find it necessary to explain why *Dred Scott* was wrongly decided under their favorite theories of constitutional interpretation.[52] In this sense, *Dred Scott* has become an "anticanonical" case, a case that is regularly pointed to as an example of bad constitutional interpretation. Graber contests this view, arguing that the result was entirely defensible given the dominant legal understandings of Taney's day. (Note once again that the most notorious holding, that blacks could not be citizens, mustered only two dissents, and that the invalidation of the Missouri Compromise, probably more volatile as a political matter, also had the support of a healthy majority of justices.)

If *Dred Scott* was "rightly decided" as a matter of original understanding, or under the conventional standards of legal analysis of its day, what follows? A very small number of the anti-Federalists opposed ratification of the 1787 Constitution because of their opposition to slavery. Were they right? Should one endorse the noted Abolitionist William Lloyd Garrison's denunciation of the Constitution as a "Covenant with Death and Agreement with Hell," a document that no honorable person could agree to or enforce? Garrisonians essentially agreed with slaveowners as to what the Constitution, correctly interpreted, meant with respect to the protection of slavery. They simply drew a different conclusion from this interpretation, which, for Garrison, was summarized in the slogan "No Union with Slaveholders." Frederick Douglass, the leading black Abolitionist of his time, originally agreed with Garrison. Eventually, however, he rejected the conventional interpretation that the Constitution protected slavery, as illustrated in the following speech delivered in 1860, three years after *Dred Scott*. As you read it, compare its analysis, in both mode and result, with those you have read by Story and Taney (among others). Who is most convincing, and why?

FREDERICK DOUGLASS, THE CONSTITUTION OF THE UNITED STATES: IS IT PRO-SLAVERY OR ANTI-SLAVERY?
Speech Delivered in Glasgow, Scotland, March 26, 1860[53]

[F]irst let me state what is not the question. It is not whether slavery existed in the United States at the time of the adoption of the Constitution; it is not whether

51. Paul Finkelman, The Constitution and the Intentions of the Framers: The Limits of Historical Analysis, 50 U. Pitt. L. Rev. 349, 395 (1989).

52. Mark A. Graber, Desperately Ducking Slavery: Dred Scott and Contemporary Constitutional Theory, 14 Constitutional Commentary 271 (1997). Professor Graber elaborates his argument in Dred Scott and the Problem of Constitutional Evil (2006).

53. In 2 Life and Writings of Frederick Douglass 467-480 (P. Foner ed., 1950). Douglass was the son of an unknown white man and a part-Indian slave. He spent most of his life in slavery, but was taught

slaveholders took part in framing the Constitution; it is not whether those slave-holders, in their hearts, intended to secure certain advantages in that instrument for slavery; it is not whether the American Government has been wielded during seventy-two years in favour of the propagation and permanence of slavery; it is not whether a pro-slavery interpretation has been put upon the Constitution by the American Courts. . . . The real and exact question . . . may be fairly stated thus: 1st, Does the United States Constitution guarantee to any class or description of people . . . the right to enslave, or hold as property, any other class or description of people . . . ? 2nd, Is the dissolution of the union between the slave and free States required by fidelity to the slaves, or by the just demands of conscience? . . .

I . . . deny that the Constitution guarantees the right to hold property in man, and believe that the way to abolish slavery in America is to vote such men into power as will use their powers for the abolition of slavery. . . . I think we had better ascertain what the Constitution itself is . . . I will tell you. It is no vague, indefinite, floating, unsubstantial, ideal something, coloured according to any man's fancy, now a weasel, now a whale, and now nothing. On the contrary, it is a plainly written document, not in Hebrew or Greek, but in English. . . . The American Constitution is a written instrument full and complete in itself. No Court in America, no Congress, no President, can add a single word thereto, or take a single word there-from. . . . [I]t should be borne in mind that the mere text, and only the text, and not any commentaries or creeds written by those who wished to give the text a meaning apart from its plain reading, was adopted as the Constitution of the United States. It should also be borne in mind that the intentions of those who framed the Constitution, be they good or bad, for slavery or against slavery, are to be respected so far, and so far only, as will find those intentions plainly stated in the Constitution. It would be the wildest of absurdities, and lead to endless confusion and mischiefs, if, instead of looking to the written paper itself, for its meaning, it were attempted to make us search it out, in the secret motives, and dishonest intentions, of some of the men who took part in writing it. It was what they said that was adopted by the people, not what they were ashamed or afraid to say, and really omitted to say. Bear in mind, also, and the fact is an important one, that the framers of the Constitution sat with closed doors, and that this was done purposely, that nothing but the result of their labours should be seen, and that result should be judged of by the people free from any of the bias shown in the debates. It should also be borne in mind, and the fact is still more important, that the debates in the convention that framed the Constitution, and by means of which a pro-slavery inter-pretation is now attempted to be forced upon that instrument, were not published till more than a quarter of a century after the presentation and the adoption of the Constitution.

These debates were purposely kept out of view, in order that the people should adopt, not the secret motives or unexpressed intentions of any body, but the simple text of the paper itself. Those debates form no part of the original agreement. I repeat, the paper itself, and only the paper itself, with its own plainly-written purposes, is the Constitution. It must stand or fall, flourish or fade, on its own indi-vidual and self-declared character and objects. Again, where would be the advantage

---

how to read and write. Upon his escape, he became a member of the Massachusetts Anti-Slavery Society and became a significant force in the antislavery movement, publishing a paper for slaves, and counsel-ing President Lincoln during the Civil War. See William S. McFeely, Frederick Douglass (1995).

of a written Constitution, if, instead of seeking its meaning in its words, we had to seek them in the secret intentions of individuals who may have had something to do with writing the paper? What will the people of America a hundred years hence care about the intentions of the scriveners who wrote the Constitution? These men are already gone from us, and in the course of nature were expected to go from us. They were for a generation, but the Constitution is for ages. . . . Common sense, and common justice, and sound rules of interpretation all drive us to the words of the law for the meaning of the law. The practice of the Government is dwelt upon with much fervour and eloquence as conclusive to the slaveholding character of the Constitution. . . . But good as this argument is, it is not conclusive. A wise man has said that few people have been found better than their laws, but many have been found worse. To this last rule America is no exception. Her laws are one thing, her practice is another. . . . After all, the fact that men go out of the Constitution to prove it pro-slavery, whether that going out is to the practice of the Government, or to the secret intentions of the writers of the paper, the fact that they do go out is very significant. . . . It is an admission that the thing for which they are looking is not to be found where only it ought to be found, and that is in the Constitution itself. . . .

[B]ecause upon its face [the Constitution does not support a pro-slavery interpretation, my opponent] sums up what he calls the slaveholding provisions of the Constitution[: Article I, §§2, 8, and 9, and Article IV, §2.] It so happens that no such words as "African slave trade," no such words as "slave representation," no such words as "fugitive slaves," no such words as "slave insurrections," are anywhere used in that instrument. [Douglass then reads to his audience the text of these four provisions.] Let us look at them just as they stand, one by one. Let us grant, for sake of the argument, that the first of these provisions, referring to the basis of representation and taxation, does refer to slaves. . . . [G]iving the provisions the very worst construction, what does it amount to? I answer: It is a downright disability laid upon the slaveholding States; one which deprives those States of two-fifths of their natural basis of representation. A black man in a free State is worth just two-fifths more than a black man in a slave State, as a basis of political power under the Constitution. Therefore, instead of encouraging slavery, the Constitution encourages freedom by giving an increase of "two-fifths" of political power to free over slave States. So much for the three-fifths clause; taking it as its worst, it still leans to freedom, not to slavery; for, be it remembered that the Constitution nowhere forbids a coloured man to vote. I come to the next, that which is said guaranteed the continuance of the African slave trade for twenty years. I will also take that for just what my opponent alleges it to have been. . . . [W]hat follows? why, this — that this part of the Constitution, so far as the slave trade is concerned, became a dead letter more than 50 years ago, and now binds no man's conscience for the continuance of any slave trade whatever. . . . But there is still more to be said about this abolition of the slave trade. Men [in 1787], both in England and in America, looked upon the slave trade as the life of slavery. The abolition of the slave trade was supposed to be the certain death of slavery. . . .

American statesmen, in providing for the abolition of the slave trade, thought they were providing for the abolition of slavery. . . . All regarded slavery as an expiring and doomed system, destined to speedily disappear from the country. . . . [T]his very provision, if made to refer to the African slave trade at all, makes the Constitution anti-slavery rather than for slavery, for it says to the slave States, the price you will have to pay for coming into the American Union is, that the slave trade, which you would carry on indefinitely out of the Union, shall be put an end to in twenty years if you come into the Union. . . . [T]he intentions of the framers of the Constitution were good, not bad. . . . I go to the "slave insurrection" clause, though, in truth, there is no such clause. . . . But I will be generous here, as well as elsewhere, and grant that it applies to slave insurrections. Let us suppose that an anti-slavery man is President of the United States (and the day that shall see this the case is not distant) and this very power of suppressing slave insurrection would put an end to slavery. The right to put down an insurrection carries with it the right to determine the means by which it shall be put down. If it should turn out that slavery is a source of insurrection, that there is no security from insurrection while slavery lasts, why, the Constitution would be best obeyed by putting an end to slavery, and an anti-slavery Congress would do that very thing. Thus, you see, the so-called slave-holding provisions of the American Constitution, which a little while ago looked so formidable, are, after all, no defence or guarantee for slavery whatever. But there is one other provision. This is called the "Fugitive Slave Provision." It is called so by those who wish to make it subserve the interest of slavery. . . . But it may be asked — if this clause does not apply to slaves, to whom does it apply?

I answer, that when adopted, it applied to a very large class of persons — namely, redemptioners — persons who had come to America from Holland, from Ireland, and other quarters of the globe . . . and had, for a consideration duly paid, become bound to "serve and labour" for the parties to whom their service and labour was due. It applies to indentured apprentices and others who had become bound for a consideration, under contract duly made, to serve and labour. To such persons this provision applies, and only to such persons. The plain reading of this provision shows that it applies, and that it can only properly and legally apply, to persons "bound to service." Its object plainly is, to secure the fulfillment of contracts for "service and labour." . . . The legal conditions of the slave puts him beyond the operation of this provision. He is not described in it. He is a simple article of property. He does not owe and cannot owe service. He cannot even make a contract. . . . The provision, then, only respects persons who owe service, and they only can owe service who can receive an equivalent and make a bargain. The slave cannot do that, and is therefore exempted from the operation of this fugitive provision. In all matters where laws are taught to be made the means of oppression, cruelty, and wickedness, I am for strict construction. I will concede nothing. It must be shown that it is so nominated in the bond. . . . The very nature of law is opposed to all such wickedness. . . . Law is not merely an arbitrary enactment with regard to justice, reason, or humanity. . . . [Douglass's adversary] laid down some rules of legal inter-pretation. These rules send us to the history of the law for its meaning. I have no objection to such a course in ordinary cases of doubt. But where human liberty and justice are at stake, the case falls under an entirely different class of rules. There must be something more than history — something more than tradition. The Supreme Court of the United States lays down this rule, and it meets the case exactly — "Where rights are infringed — where the fundamental principles of the law are overthrown — where the general system of the law is departed from, the legislative intention must be expressed with irresistible clearness." The same court says that the language of the law must be construed strictly in favour of justice and liberty. Again, there is another rule of law. It is — Where a law is susceptible of two meanings, the one making it accomplish an innocent purpose, and the other making it accomplish a wicked purpose, we must in all cases adopt that which makes it accomplish an innocent purpose. . . . I only ask you to look at the American Constitution in the light of [these rules of interpretation], and you will see with me that no man is guaranteed a right of property in man, under the provisions of that instrument. If there are two ideas more distinct in their character and essence than another, those ideas are "persons" and "property," "men" and "things." Now, when it is proposed to transform persons into "property" and men into beasts of burden, I demand that the law that contemplates such a purpose shall be expressed with irresistible clearness. The things must not be left to inference, but must be done in plain English. . . .

[Douglass turns to the Preamble of the Constitution, which he quotes.] It has been said that Negroes are not included within the benefits sought under this declaration. This is said by the slaveholders in America . . . but it is not said by the Constitution itself. Its language is "we the people"; not we the white people, not even we the citizens, not we the privileged class, not we the high, not we the low, but we the people; . . . , we the human inhabitants; and, if Negroes are people, they are included in the benefits for which the Constitution of America was ordained and established. . . . I undertake to say, as the conclusion of the whole matter, that the constitutionality of slavery can be made out only by disregarding the plain and common-sense reading of the Constitution itself; by discrediting and casting away as worthless the most beneficent rules of legal interpretation; by ruling the Negro outside of these beneficent rules; by claiming everything for slavery; by denying everything for freedom; by assuming that the Constitution does not mean what it says, and that it says what it does not mean; by disregarding the written Constitution, and interpreting it in the light of a secret understanding. . . . The Constitution declares that no person shall be deprived of life, liberty, or property without due process of law; it secures to every man the right of trial by jury, the privilege of the writ of habeas corpus . . . it secures to every State a republican form of government. Any one of these provisions, in the hands of abolition statesmen, and backed by a right moral sentiment, would put an end to slavery in America. The Constitution forbids the passing of a bill of attainder: that is, a law entailing upon the child the disabilities and hardships imposed upon the parent. Every slave law in America might be repealed on this very ground. . . .

I am, therefore, for drawing the bond of the Union more closely, and bringing the Slave States more completely under the power of the Free States. . . . I have much confidence in the instincts of the slaveholders. They see that the Constitution will afford slavery no protection when it shall cease to be administered by slaveholders. They see, moreover, that if there is once a will in the people of America to abolish slavery, there is no word, no syllable in the Constitution to forbid that result.

D. Judicial Supremacy and *Dred Scott:* The Lincoln-Douglas Debates

Dred Scott figured centrally in the exchanges between Abraham Lincoln and Stephen Douglas during their campaign for the U.S. Senate in 1858. Lincoln, in his famous "House Divided" speech of June 16, 1858, had denounced the *Dred Scott* decision and, indeed, suggested that it was part of a conspiracy to nationalize slavery. The basis of this fear lay in the facts of a case then before the Taney Court, Lemmon v. The People, 26 Barbour 270 (1857), where Jonathan Lemmon and his wife brought eight slaves into New York as they took one boat from Virginia to New York, where they would catch another boat to New Orleans (on their way ultimately to Texas). Although warned by the ship's captain to leave their slaves on the first boat (where they could presumably be transferred to the second boat) and not to take their slaves into New York, the Lemmons did so while they all waited three days for the next boat to leave. Upon the discovery of the slaves, a New York state court issued a writ of habeas corpus freeing them; Lemmon challenged this on the basis of an alleged federal right to travel from one state to another without risking loss of his property because of the anti-slavery policies of a state through which he was traveling.[54] On July 9, Douglas attacked Lincoln's views about the validity of *Dred Scott*:

> The right and the province of expounding the Constitution, and construing the law, is vested in the judiciary established by the Constitution. As a lawyer, I feel at liberty to appear before the Court and controvert any principle of law while the question is pending before the tribunal; but when the decision is made, my private opinion, your opinion, all other opinions must yield to the majesty of that authoritative adjudication. . . . What security have you for your property, for your reputation, and for your personal rights, if the courts are not upheld, and their decisions respected when once firmly rendered by the highest tribunal known to the Constitution? . . .
>
> I am opposed to this doctrine of Mr. Lincoln, by which he proposes to take an appeal from the decision of the Supreme Court of the United States, upon this high constitutional question to a Republican caucus sitting in the country. Yes, or any other caucus or town meeting, whether it be Republican, American, or Democratic. I respect the decisions of that august tribunal; I shall always bow in deference to them.

Lincoln responded on the next day:

> I have expressed heretofore, and I now repeat, my opposition to the *Dred Scott* decision, but I should be allowed to state the nature of that opposition. . . . What is fairly implied by the term Judge Douglas has used "resistance to the decision"? I do not resist it. If I wanted to take Dred Scott from his master, I would be interfering with property. . . . But I am doing no such thing as that, but all that I am doing is refusing to obey it as a political rule. If I were in Congress, and a vote should come up on a question whether slavery should be prohibited in a new territory, in spite of that *Dred Scott* decision, I would vote that it should. [Applause; "good for you;" "we hope to see it;" "that's right."]
>
> We will try to reverse that decision. . . . Somebody has to reverse that decision, since it is made, and we mean to reverse it, and we mean to do it peaceably. . . .
>
> Judge Douglas will have it that all hands must take this extraordinary decision, made under . . . extraordinary circumstances, and give their vote in Congress in accordance with it, yield to it and obey it in every possible sense. Circumstances alter cases. Do not gentlemen here remember the case of that same Supreme Court, some twenty-five or thirty years ago, deciding that a national bank was constitutional? . . . The bank charter ran out, and a re-charter was granted by Congress. That re-charter was laid before General Jackson. It was urged upon him, when he denied the constitutionality

---

54. The facts and legal significance of *Lemmon* are spelled out in Paul Finkelman, An Imperfect Union: Slavery, Federalism, and Comity 296-312, 329-332 (1981). Recall also Justice Baldwin's opinion in *Groves v. Slaughter*, which explicitly suggested that there was a constitutional right for slaveowners to travel with their slaves through otherwise free states. *Crandall* was decided after the abolition of slavery. Ask yourself, though, how its doctrine might have applied to a slaveowner in Lemmon's position.

of the bank, that the Supreme Court had decided that it was constitutional; and that General Jackson then said that the Supreme Court had no right to lay down a rule to govern a co-ordinate branch of the government, the members of which had sworn to support the Constitution — that each member had sworn to support that Constitution as he understood it. I will venture here to say, that I have heard Judge Douglas say that he approved of General Jackson for that act. What has now become of all his tirade about "resistance to the Supreme Court?"

Douglas answered a week later, on July 17, in Springfield:

The court pronounces that law, prohibiting slavery, unconstitutional and void, and Mr. Lincoln is going to pass an act reversing that decision and making it valid. I have never heard before of an appeal being taken from the Supreme Court to the Congress of the United States to reverse its decision. . . .

Mr. Lincoln intimates that there is another mode by which he can reverse the *Dred Scott* decision. How is that? Why, he is going to appeal to the people to elect a President who will appoint judges who will reverse the *Dred Scott* decision. Well, let us see how that is going to be done. . . . [W]hy, the Republican President is to call up the candidates and catechize them, and ask them, "How will you decide this case if I appoint you judge?" [Shouts of laughter.] . . . Suppose you get a Supreme Court composed of such judges, who have been appointed by a partisan President upon their giving pledges how they would decide a case before it arise, what confidence would you have in such a court? ["None, none."] . . . It is a proposition to make that court the corrupt, unscrupulous tool of a political party. But Mr. Lincoln cannot conscientiously submit, he thinks, to the decision of a court composed of a majority of Democrats. If he cannot, how can he expect us to have confidence in a court composed of a majority of Republicans, selected for the purpose of deciding against the Democracy, and in favor of the Republicans? [Cheers.] The very proposition carries with it the demoralization and degradation destructive of the judicial department of the federal government.

Lincoln responded later that day:

I think, that in respect for judicial authority, my humble history would not suffer in a comparison with that of Judge Douglas. He would have the citizen conform his vote to that decision; the member of Congress, his; the President, his use of the veto power. He would make it a rule of political action for the people and all the departments of the government. I would not. By resisting it as a political rule, I disturb no right of property, create no disorder, excite no mobs.

Lincoln went on to read from an 1820 letter of Thomas Jefferson to a Mr. Jarvis, the author of a publication called the "Republican":

You seem . . . to consider the judges as the ultimate arbiters of all constitutional questions — a very dangerous doctrine indeed and one which would place us under the despotism of an oligarchy. Our judges see as honest as other men, and not more so. They have, with others, the same passions for party, for power, and the privilege of their corps. . . . [T]heir power is the more dangerous as they are in office for life, and not responsible, as the other functionaries are, to the elective control. The constitution has erected no such single tribunal, knowing that to whatever hands confided, with the corruptions of time and party, its members would become despots. It has more wisely made all the departments co-equal and co-sovereign within themselves.

Discussion

Douglas accuses Lincoln of wishing to "catechize" potential nominees to the Supreme Court in regard to their views about *Dred Scott.* Consider the fact that recent Republican Party platforms call for the appointment of judges "who recognize the sanctity of human life." In contrast, President Clinton repeatedly made clear his support for constitutionally protected reproductive rights and, in nominating Judges Ruth Bader Ginsburg and Stephen Breyer, picked justices who are reliable votes on behalf of maintaining *Roe.* One presumes that both Democratic and Republican presidents, whether by "catechizing" potential nominees or simply by making astute inquiries about them, have sought to determine the predispositions of their nominees on the issue of abortion. Is there anything improper about this?

When the Senate exercises its constitutional duty to "advise and consent" to appointments to the Court, what questions may it ask (and expect answers to) regarding the views of nominees on abortion (or any other issue)? In her confirmation hearings, the first Reagan appointee, Sandra Day O'Connor, refused to answer many questions on *Roe,* saying that she could not

> tell you how I might vote on a particular issue which may come before the Court, or endorse or criticize specific Supreme Court decisions presenting issues which may well come before the Court again. To do so would mean I have prejudged the matter or have morally committed myself to a certain position. Such a statement by me as to how I might resolve a particular issue or what I might do in a future Court action might make it necessary to disqualify myself on the matter.[55]

Does Justice O'Connor's statement imply that it would be equally improper for a nominee to be asked (or answer) questions about the propriety of Justice Marshall's opinions in *McCulloch* and *Gibbons,* which presented an expansive reading of Congress's powers under Article I, the core issue of many contemporary cases involving the scope of national authority under purportedly limited assignment of powers? (Justice Scalia, in his confirmation hearings, refused even to answer questions about Marbury v. Madison, saying that *Marbury* was necessarily implicated in every contemporary case involving judicial review of congressional statutes. Was he justified in doing so?)

Consider the meaning of "prejudgment." If academic appointees to the bench have published vigorous criticism of current judicial doctrines, calling for their overruling at the earliest possible time, should they be expected to answer questions about their writings? If confirmed, should they recuse themselves when those issues come up? Consider a statement by a dissenting Justice indicating hope for future reversal by the Court of its mistaken decision. Does that indicate such "prejudgment" as to require recusal when the issue next comes before the Court?[56]

---

55. Quoted in Levinson, Should Supreme Court Nominees Have Opinions, The Nation, Oct. 17, 1981, at 375.

56. See, e.g., the conclusion of Justice O'Connor's dissent in the Garcia case, p. 561 infra, where, quoting Justice Rehnquist, she indicated that the dissenters' views "will, I am confident, in time again command the support of a majority of this Court."

III. "And the War Came"[57]: The President as Commander-in-Chief and the Preservation of the Union[58]

Though defeated in his 1858 bid for the Senate, Lincoln did become President in 1861, elected in 1860 with 39 percent of the popular vote; however, the votes were concentrated such that he would have prevailed in the Electoral College "even if the popular vote of all three of his rivals had been concentrated on one candidate." The problems facing him are suggested by the fact that, while taking every northern free state except New Jersey, which split its electoral vote, Lincoln "failed to get a single [electoral] vote in any future Confederate state except Virginia."[59] By the time of his inauguration on March 4, 1861, seven states — South Carolina, Mississippi, Florida, Alabama, Georgia, Louisiana, and Texas — had announced their secession from the Union, and Lincoln was clearly worried, with good reason, that the remaining eight slave states — Maryland, Delaware, Virginia, North Carolina, Tennessee, Kentucky, Arkansas, and Missouri — would follow them into the Confederate States of America.

A. The Debate Over Secession

1. President James Buchanan Opposes Both Secession and War

One of the more peculiar features of the American political system is the long delay between an election and the inauguration of the newly elected president. Thus James Buchanan delivered his final State of the Union message on December 4, 1860, even though it was clear that his vision of the Union had been rejected by at least an Electoral College majority. He began an extensive discussion of secession by describing secessionist movements as the "natural effects" of what he termed "[t]he long-continued and intemperate interference of the Northern people with the question of slavery in the Southern States." Indeed, he placed central responsibility for "the immediate peril" on

> the incessant and violent agitation of the slavery question throughout the North for the last quarter of a century [that] has at length produced its malign influence on the slaves and inspired them with vague notions of freedom. Hence a sense of security no longer exists around the family altar. This feeling of peace at home has given place to apprehensions of servile insurrections. . . . Self-preservation is the first law of nature, and has been implanted in the heart of man by his Creator for the wisest purpose; and no political union, however fraught with blessings and benefits in all other respects,

---

57. See Abraham Lincoln, Second Inaugural Address, March 4, 1865:

On the occasion corresponding to this four years ago, all thoughts were anxiously directed to an impending civil war. All dreaded it—all sought to avert it. While the inaugural address was being delivered from this place, devoted altogether to *saving* the Union without war, insurgent agents were in the city seeking to *destroy* it without war—seeking to dissolve the Union, and divide effects, by negotiation. Both parties deprecated war; but one of them would *make* war rather than let the nation survive; and the other would *accept* war rather than let it perish. And the war came.

58. See James G. Randall, Constitutional Problems Under Lincoln (revised ed. 1964).

59. Mark Neely, The Last Best Hope of Earth: Abraham Lincoln and the Promise of America 59 (1993).

can long continue if the necessary consequence be to render the homes and the firesides of nearly half the parties to it habitually and hopelessly insecure. Sooner or later the bonds of such a union must be severed.

Yet Buchanan did not support secession; in fact, he presented powerful arguments against it. He noted, for example, that Lincoln's election "has been effected by a mere plurality, and not a majority of the people." Resort to what Buchanan called "revolutionary resistance" required, he said, "a deliberate, palpable, and dangerous exercise of powers not granted by the Constitution," and he noted that no such exercises had in fact taken place, even if one believed that Lincoln and other Republicans might support such policies. Support, though, was not equivalent to enactment. Buchanan stated that

> it is a remarkable fact in our history that, notwithstanding the repeated efforts of the antislavery party, no single act has ever passed Congress, unless we may possibly except the Missouri compromise, impairing in the slightest degree the rights of the South to their property in slaves; and it may also be observed, judging from present indications, that no probability exists of the passage of such an act by a majority of both Houses, either in the present or the next Congress. Surely under these circumstances we ought to be restrained from present action by the precept of Him who spake as man never spoke, that "sufficient unto the day is the evil thereof." The day of evil may never come unless we shall rashly bring it upon ourselves.

Dred Scott, after all, stood as a barrier against the Republican commitment to ban slavery in the territories. Buchanan was more sympathetic to complaints that free states were insufficiently willing to adhere to their constitutional obligations to enforce the Fugitive Slave Clause and, more to the point, the Fugitive Slave Laws passed by Congress, but, he argued that such complaints were scarcely of the magnitude to justify secession:

> The Southern States, standing on the basis of the Constitution, have a right to demand this act of justice from the States of the North. Should it be refused, then the Constitution, to which all the States are parties, will have been willfully violated by one portion of them in a provision essential to the domestic security and happiness of the remainder. In that event the injured States, after having first used all peaceful and constitutional means to obtain redress, would be justified in revolutionary resistance to the Government of the Union. . . . [I]t has been claimed within the last few years that any State, whenever this shall be its sovereign will and pleasure, may secede from the Union in accordance with the Constitution and without any violation of the constitutional rights of the other members of the Confederacy; that as each became parties to the Union by the vote of its own people assembled in convention, so any one of them may retire from the Union in a similar manner by the vote of such a convention.
>
> In order to justify secession as a constitutional remedy, it must be on the principle that the Federal Government is a mere voluntary association of States, to be dissolved at pleasure by any one of the contracting parties. If this be so, the Confederacy is a rope of sand, to be penetrated and dissolved by the first adverse wave of public opinion in any of the States. . . .
>
> [No] clause in the Constitution gives countenance to such a theory. It is altogether rounded upon inference; not from any language contained in the instrument itself, but from the sovereign character of the several States by which it was ratified. But is it beyond the power of a State, like an individual, to yield a portion of its sovereign rights to secure the remainder? . . .

[T]hat the Union was designed to be perpetual appears conclusively from the nature and extent of the powers conferred by the Constitution on the Federal Government. These powers embrace the very highest attributes of national sovereignty. . . .

This Government, therefore, is a great and powerful Government, invested with all the attributes of sovereignty over the special subjects to which its authority extends. Its framers never intended to implant in its bosom the seeds of its own destruction, nor were they at its creation guilty of the absurdity of providing for its own dissolution. . . .

It may be asked, then, Are the people of the States without redress against the tyranny and oppression of the Federal Government? By no means. The right of resistance on the part of the governed against the oppression of their governments can not be denied. . . . It is embodied in strong and express language in our own Declaration of Independence. But the distinction must ever be observed that this is revolution against an established government, and not a voluntary secession from it by virtue of an inherent constitutional right. . . . It may or it may not be a justifiable revolution, but still it is revolution.

What, in the meantime, is the responsibility and true position of the Executive? He is bound by solemn oath, before God and the country, "to take care that the laws be faithfully executed," and from this obligation he can not be absolved by any human power. But what if the performance of this duty, in whole or in part, has been rendered impracticable by events over which he could have exercised no control? Such at the present moment is the case throughout the State of South Carolina so far as the laws of the United States to secure the administration of justice by means of the Federal judiciary are concerned. All the Federal officers within its limits through whose agency alone these laws can be carried into execution have already resigned. We no longer have a district judge, a district attorney, or a marshal in South Carolina. In fact, the whole machinery of the Federal Government necessary for the distribution of remedial justice among the people has been demolished, and it would be difficult, if not impossible, to replace it.

The only acts of Congress on the statute book bearing upon this subject are those of February 28, 1795, and March 3, 1807. These authorize the President, after he shall have ascertained that the marshal, with his posse comitatus, is unable to execute civil or criminal process in any particular case, to call forth the militia and employ the Army and Navy to aid him in performing this service, having first by proclamation commanded the insurgents "to disperse and retire peaceably to their respective abodes within a limited time." This duty can not by possibility be performed in a State where no judicial authority exists to issue process, and where there is no marshal to execute it, and where, even if there were such an officer, the entire population would constitute one solid combination to resist him.

The bare enumeration of these provisions proves how inadequate they are without further legislation to overcome a united opposition in a single State, not to speak of other States who may place themselves in a similar attitude. Congress alone has power to decide whether the present laws can or can not be amended so as to carry out more effectually the objects of the Constitution.

The same insuperable obstacles do not lie in the way of executing the laws for the collection of the customs. The revenue still continues to be collected as heretofore at the custom-house in Charleston, and should the collector unfortunately resign a successor may be appointed to perform this duty.

[I]t is not believed that any attempt will be made to expel the United States from [its] property [including its forts and arsenals] by force; but if in this I should prove to be mistaken, the officer in command of the forts has received orders to act strictly on the defensive. In such a contingency the responsibility for consequences would rightfully rest upon the heads of the assailants.

Apart from the execution of the laws, so far as this may be practicable, the Executive has no authority to decide what shall be the relations between the Federal Government and South Carolina. He has been invested with no such discretion. He possesses no power to change the relations heretofore existing between them, much less to acknowledge the independence of that State. This would be to invest a mere executive officer with the power of recognizing the dissolution of the confederacy among our thirty-three sovereign States. . . . It is therefore my duty to submit to Congress the whole question in all its beatings. [H]as the Constitution delegated to Congress the power to coerce a State into submission which is attempting to withdraw or has actually withdrawn from the Confederacy? . . . It is manifest upon an inspection of the Constitution that this is not among the specific and enumerated powers granted to Congress, and it is equally apparent that its exercise is not "necessary and proper for carrying into execution" any one of these powers. So far from this power having been delegated to Congress, it was expressly refused by the Convention which framed the Constitution. . . .

Without descending to particulars, it may be safely asserted that the power to make war against a State is at variance with the whole spirit and intent of the Constitution. Suppose such a war should result in the conquest of a State; how are we to govern it afterwards? Shall we hold it as a province and govern it by despotic power? In the nature of things, we could not by physical force control the will of the people and compel them to elect Senators and Representatives to Congress and to perform all the other duties depending upon their own volition and required from the free citizens of a free State as a constituent member of the Confederacy.

But if we possessed this power, would it be wise to exercise it under existing circumstances? The object would doubtless be to preserve the Union. War would not only present the most effectual means of destroying it, but would vanish all hope of its peaceable reconstruction. Besides, in the fraternal conflict a vast amount of blood and treasure would be expended, rendering future reconciliation between the States impossible. In the meantime, who can foretell what would be the sufferings and privations of the people during its existence?

The fact is that our Union rests upon public opinion, and can never be cemented by the blood of its citizens shed in civil war. If it can not live in the affections of the people, it must one day perish. Congress possesses many means of preserving it by conciliation, but the sword was not placed in their hand to preserve it by force. . . .

2. Judah Benjamin Defends Secession

Louisiana Senator Judah Benjamin (who would become the Secretary of the Treasury of the Confederacy) in effect responded to Buchanan's critique of secession (and, more to the political point, issued an anticipatory response to Abraham Lincoln) in his farewell speech to the Senate on December 31, 1860:[60]

In a great crisis like this, when the right asserted by a sovereign State is questioned, a decent respect for the opinions of mankind at least requires that those who maintain that right, and mean to act upon it, should state the reasons upon which they maintain it. . . .

From the time that this people declared its independence of Great Britain, the right of the people to self-government in its fullest and broadest extent has been a cardinal principle of American liberty. None deny it. And in that right, to use the

60. The Congressional Globe, Dec. 31, 1860, at 212-217.

language of the Declaration itself, is included the right whenever a form of government becomes destructive of their interests or their safety, "to alter or to abolish it, and
to institute a new government, laying its foundation on such principles and organizing
its powers in such form as to them shall seem most likely to effect their safety and
happiness." [With one exception] to which I shall presently advert . . . the right of the
people of one generation, in convention duly assembled, to alter the institutions
bequeathed by their fathers is inherent, inalienable, not susceptible of restriction; . . .
[O]ne convention of the people duly assembled, [can] repeal the acts of a former
convention of the people duly assembled; and that [is how] South Carolina has . . .
declared her independence. She has in convention duly assembled in 1860, repealed
an ordinance passed by her people in convention duly assembled in 1788. . . . [T]he
power is inherently in [a convention of the people of a State], subject only to this
modification: that they are bound to exercise it with due regard to the obligations
imposed upon them by the compact with others.

[I]t was precisely upon this principle that this Constitution was formed. [Although]
. . . the old Articles of Confederacy provided in express terms that they should be
perpetual; that they should never be amended or altered without the consent of all the
States . . . [nonetheless] nine States of the Confederation seceded from the
Confederation, and formed a new Government. They formed it upon the express
ground that some of the States had violated their compact. Immediately after, two
other States seceded and joined them. They left two alone, Rhode Island and North
Carolina; and here is my answer to [Senator Doolittle] from Wisconsin, who asked me
the other day, if thirty-three States could expel one, inasmuch as one had the right to
leave thirty-three: I point him to the history of our country, to the acts of the fathers, as
a full answer upon that subject. After this Government had been organized . . . North
Carolina and Rhode Island were still foreign nations, and so treated. . . .

[O]ne State may allege that the compact has been broken, and others may deny it;
who is to judge? When pecuniary interests are involved, so that a case can be brought
up before courts of justice, the Constitution has provided a remedy within itself [in the
Supremacy Clause and] a supreme judiciary to determine cases arising in law or equity
which may involve the construction of the Constitution or the construction of
such laws.

But, sir, suppose infringements on the Constitution in political matters, which from
their very nature cannot be brought before the court? That was a difficulty not unforeseen; it was debated upon propositions that were made to meet it. Attempts were made
to give power to this Federal Government in all its departments, one after the other, to
meet that precise case, and the convention sternly refused to admit any. It was
proposed to enable the Federal Government, through the action of Congress, to use
force. That was refused. It was proposed to give to the President of the United States
the nomination of State Governors, and to give them a veto on State laws, so as to
preserve the supremacy of the Federal Government. That was refused. It was proposed
to make the Senate the judge of difficulties that might arise between States and the
General Government. That was refused. It was finally proposed to give Congress a
negative on State legislation interfering with the powers of the Federal Government.
That was refused. At last, at the very last moment, it was proposed to give that power to
Congress by a vote of two thirds of each branch; and that, too, was denied. . . .

Now, Mr. President, if we admit, as we must, that there are certain political rights
guarantied to the States of this Union by the terms of the Constitution itself — rights
political in their character, and not susceptible of judicial decision — if any State is
deprived of any of those rights, what is the remedy? . . . [L]et us suppose a clear, palpable case of violation of the Constitution. Let us suppose that the State of South
Carolina having sent two Senators to sit upon this floor, had been met by a resolution
of the majority here that, according to her just weight in the Confederacy, one was

enough, and that we had directed our Secretary to swear in but one, and to call but one name on our roll as the yeas and nays are called for voting. The Constitution says that each State shall be entitled to two Senators, and each Senator shall have one vote. What power is there to force the dominant majority to repair that wrong? Any court? Any tribunal? Has the Constitution provided any recourse whatever? Has it not remained designedly silent on the subject of that recourse? And yet, what man . . . will stand up in this Senate and pretend that if, under these circumstances, the State of South Carolina had declared, "I entered into a Confederacy or a compact by which I was to have my rights guarantied by the constant presence of two Senators upon your floor; you allow me but one; you refuse to repair the injustice; I withdraw"; what man would dare say that that was a violation of the Constitution on the part of South Carolina? Who would say that that was a revolutionary remedy? Who would deny the plain and palpable proposition that it was the exercise of a right inherent in her under the very principles of the Constitution, and necessarily so inherent for self-defense?

Why, sir, the North, if it has not a majority here to-day, will have it very soon. Suppose these gentlemen from the North with the majority think that it is no more than fair, inasmuch as we represent here States in which there are large numbers of slaves, that the northern States should have each three Senators: what are we to do? They swear them in. No court has the power of prohibition, of mandamus over this body in the exercise of its political powers. It is the exclusive judge of the elections, the qualifications, and the returns of its own members, a judge without appeal. Shall the whole fifteen southern States submit to that, and be told that they are guilty of revolutionary excess if they say, we will not remain with you on these terms; we never agreed to it? Is that revolution, or is it the exercise of clear constitutional rights?

Suppose this violation occurs under circumstances where it does not appear so plain to you, but where it does appear equally plain to South Carolina: then you are again brought back to the irrevocable point, who is to decide? South Carolina says, "You forced me to the expenditure of my treasure, you forced me to the shedding of the blood of my people, by a majority vote, and with my aid you acquired territory; now I have a constitutional right to go into that territory with my property, and to be there secured by your laws against its loss." You say, no, she has not. Now . . . that right is not put down in the Constitution in quite so clear terms as the right to have two Senators; but it is a right which she asserts with the concurrent opinion of the entire South. . . . Is she without a remedy under the Constitution? If not, then what tribunal? If none is provided, then natural law and the law of nations tell you that she and she alone, from the very necessity of the case, must be the judge of the infraction and of the mode and measure of redress. . . .

But, Mr. President, the President of the United States tells us that he does not admit this right to be constitutional; that it is revolutionary. . . . If I am asked how I will distinguish this from revolutionary abuse, the answer is prompt and easy. These States, parties to the compact, have a right to withdraw from it, by virtue of its own provisions, when those provisions are violated by the other parties to the compact, when either powers not granted are usurped, or rights are refused that are especially granted to the States.

But, sir, there is a large class of powers granted by this Constitution, in the exercise of which a discretion is vested in the General Government, and, in the exercise of that discretion, these admitted powers might be so perverted and abused as to give cause of complaint, and finally, to give the right to revolution; for under those circumstances there would be no other remedy. Now, taking again the supposition of a dominant northern majority in both branches, and of a sectional President and Vice President, the Congress of the United States then, in the exercise of its admitted powers, and the President to back them, could spend the entire revenue of the Confederation in the section which had control, without violating the words or the letter of the

Constitution; they could establish forts, light-houses, arsenals, magazines, and all public buildings of every character in the northern States alone, and utterly refuse any to the South. The President, with the aid of his sectional Senate, could appoint all officers of the Navy and of the Army, all the civil officers of the Government, all the judges, attorneys, and marshals, all collectors and revenue officers, all postmasters — the whole host of public officers he might, under the forms and powers vested by the Constitution, appoint exclusively from the northern States, and quarter them in the southern States, to eat out the substance of our people, and assume an insulting superiority over them. All that might be done in the exercise of admitted constitutional power; and it is just that train of evils, of outrages, of wrongs, of oppressions long continued, that the Declaration of Independence says a people preserves the inherent right of throwing off by destroying their government by revolution. I say, therefore, that I distinguish the rights of the States under the Constitution into two classes: one resulting from the nature of their bargain; if the bargain is broken by the sister States, to consider themselves freed from it on the ground of breach of compact; if the bargain be not broken, but the powers be perverted to their wrong and their oppression, then, whenever that wrong and oppression shall become sufficiently aggravated, the revolutionary right — the last inherent right of man to preserve freedom, property, and safety — arises, and must be exercised, for none other will meet the case. . . .

What may be the fate of this horrible contest, no man can tell, none pretend to foresee; but this much I will say: the fortunes of war may be adverse to our arms; you may carry desolation into our peaceful land, and with torch and fire you may set our cities in flames; you may even emulate the atrocities of those who, in the war of the Revolution, hounded on the blood-thirsty savage to attack upon the defenseless frontier; you may, under the protection of your advancing armies, give shelter to the furious fanatics who desire, and profess to desire, nothing more than to add all the horrors of a servile insurrection to the calamities of civil war; you may do all this — and more, too, if more there be — but you never can subjugate us; you never can convert the free sons of the soil into vassals, paying tribute to your power; and you never, never can degrade them to the level of an inferior and servile race. Never! Never!

3. *Jefferson Davis Takes the Helm of the Confederate States of America*

Jefferson Davis, the President of the Confederate States of America — and a former senator from Mississippi — offered yet another response in his inaugural address in Montgomery, Alabama, on February 18, 1861:

The declared purpose of the compact of Union from which we have withdrawn was "to establish justice, insure domestic tranquility, provide for the common defense, promote the general welfare, and secure the blessings of liberty to ourselves and our posterity"; and when, in the judgment of the sovereign States now composing this Confederacy, it had been perverted from the purposes for which it was ordained, and had ceased to answer the ends for which it was established, a peaceful appeal to the ballot-box declared that so far as they were concerned, the government created by that compact should cease to exist. In this they merely asserted a right which the Declaration of Independence of 1776 had defined to be inalienable; of the time and occasion for its exercise, they, as sovereigns, were the final judges, each for itself. The impartial and enlightened verdict of mankind will vindicate the rectitude of our conduct, and He who knows the hearts of men will judge of the sincerity with which we labored to preserve the Government of our fathers in its spirit. The right solemnly proclaimed at the birth of the States, and which has been affirmed and reaffirmed in the bills of rights of States subsequently admitted into the Union of 1789, undeniably recognize in the people the power to resume the authority delegated for the purposes of government. Thus the sovereign States here represented proceeded to form this Confederacy, and it is by abuse of language that their act has been denominated a revolution. . . .

4.   Lincoln Responds and Acts

March 4, 1861 at long last brought Abraham Lincoln to the White House. In his First Inaugural Address, Lincoln emphasized his devotion to the Union. He expressed his willingness to address Southern concerns by supporting the so-called Corwin Amendment, strongly supported by outgoing President Buchanan and, in the Senate, by New York's Senator William Seward (who would become Lincoln's Secretary of State). The Corwin Amendment was in fact proposed by the Congress and sent to the states for ratification. It stated that "No amendment shall ever be made to the Constitution which will authorize or give to Congress power to abolish or interfere, within any State, with the domestic institutions thereof. . . ." If ratified, ironically, it would have become the Thirteenth Amendment. Lincoln could endorse it precisely because it protected slavery in already existing states, whose legal legitimacy he never challenged. Southern states found it inadequate because it protected *only* slavery in existing states and said nothing about what both sides deemed the truly important issue: the extension of slavery into the territories. Ohio, Maryland, and Illinois ratified the Corwin Amendment, but it was obviously made moot by subsequent developments.

A key argument in Lincoln's First Inaugural Address was his complete rejection of any theory that would countenance secession:

> I hold, that in contemplation of universal law, and of the Constitution, the Union of these States is perpetual. Perpetuity is implied, if not expressed, in the fundamental law of all national governments. It is safe to assert that no government proper, ever had a provision in its organic law for its own termination. . . .
>
> Again, if the United States be not a government proper, but an association of States in the nature of contract merely, can it, as a contract, be peaceably unmade, by less than all the parties who made it? One party to a contract may violate it — break it, so to speak; but does it not require all to lawfully rescind it?
>
> Descending from these general principles, we find the proposition that, in legal contemplation, the Union is perpetual, confirmed by the history of the Union itself. The Union is much older than the Constitution. It was formed in fact, by the Articles of Association in 1774. It was matured and continued by the Declaration of Independence in 1776. It was further matured and the faith of all the then thirteen States expressly plighted and engaged that it should be perpetual, by the Articles of Confederation in 1778. And finally, in 1787, one of the declared objects for ordaining and establishing the Constitution, was "to form a more perfect union." But if destruction of the Union, by one, or by a part only, of the States, be lawfully possible, the Union is less perfect than before the Constitution, having lost the vital element of perpetuity.
>
> It follows from these views that no State, upon its own mere motion, can lawfully get out of the Union, that resolves and ordinances to that effect are legally void, and that acts of violence, within any State or States, against the authority of the United States, are insurrectionary or revolutionary, according to circumstances.

I therefore consider that, in view of the Constitution and the laws, the Union is unbroken; and, to the extent of my ability, I shall take care, as the Constitution itself expressly enjoins upon me, that the laws of the Union be faithfully executed in all the States.

Discussion

1. What kinds of arguments are presented by Buchanan, Benjamin, Davis, and Lincoln? Who persuades you, and why? What would be the consequences (for a law student or lawyer today) of being persuaded by Buchanan, Benjamin, or Davis?

2. Professor Akhil Amar presents powerful evidence that the possibility of secession was explicitly rejected by supporters of the 1787 Constitution (even though, of course, the Constitution was formally silent on the matter). He notes, for example, that New York anti-Federalists proposed to ratify the Constitution contingent on the ability of the State to withdraw from the Union if a Bill of Rights were not added to it by the first Congress. Even though ratification at the Albany convention was touch-and-go — ultimately prevailing by a 30-27 vote that would have gone the other way with the switch of only two ratifiers — Federalist supporters rejected the deal and emphasized that the Preamble's commitment to a "more perfect Union" in effect was the equivalent of the Articles of Confederation's "perpetual Union."[61] And no one at the time seriously asserted the potential dissolubility of the Union.

Even if one agrees with Amar as to the perceptions of the Constitution's ratifiers (and, for that matter, its opponents), is that dispositive as to the arguments made in 1860-1861? That is, if one is not an "originalist," committed to interpreting the Constitution as understood by its framers or ratifiers, must one accept their views on secession any more than on any other issue of constitutional meaning? Are there structural arguments beyond the text, which appears to be silent on the issue?

3. Lincoln asserts that "no government proper, ever had a provision in its organic law for its own termination." Is this an "analytic truth," as in the proposition that there are no married bachelors, or simply an empirical observation, which, however true at the time Lincoln spoke, may have been a function at least in part of the fact that very few countries at the time had written constitutions laying out their "organic law"? Indeed, one of the reasons that Lincoln was so concerned to preserve the Union was to reassure the entire world that he viewed the United States as the "last, best hope" on earth of exemplifying the very possibility of a "republican form of government," a form under relentless attack in Europe by autocratic rulers who suppressed a variety of democratic movements that arose in 1848 and afterward.[62]

Consider, though, that in the twentieth century Article 70 of the now-defunct Constitution of the Union of Soviet Socialist Republics (USSR) defined the USSR as "an integral, federal, multinational state formed on the principle of socialist federalism as a result of the free self-determination of nations and the voluntary association of equal Soviet Socialist Republics." Article 72 went on to state: "Each Union Republic shall retain the right freely to secede from the USSR." It is Article 72 that served as the basis of several secessionist movements within the republics of the Soviet Union before the dissolution of that country. Putting aside one's views about communism, did the existence of Article 72 establish that the Soviet Constitution created "no government proper" insofar as it seemingly legitimated the possibility of withdrawal? Consider as

---

61. See Amar, *America's Constitution: A Biography* 37-38 (2005).
62. See Michael Lind, *What Lincoln Believed* (2005).

well the "Draft Treaty Establishing a Constitution for Europe," submitted to the various members of the European Union on July 18, 2003, which included, as Section 60, an article concerning "Voluntary withdrawal from the Union." It provides that "Any Member State may decide to withdraw from the European Union in accordance with its own constitutional requirements." (The 2003 draft version was ultimately rejected by French and Dutch voters in May and June 2005.) Is such an article simply evidence that the contemplated "European Union" would not have been a "real" country, but merely a treaty system among "sovereign states" who can, exemplifying their sovereignty, withdraw at will from international organizations, just as the United States could, tomorrow, announce its intention to withdraw from the United Nations?

4. Many presidents of many countries, of course, make arguments similar to those presented by Lincoln when suppressing secessionist movements in their own country. Consider, for example, Yugoslav President Slobodan Milosevich's brutal suppression of secessionist movements in Kosovo and elsewhere or Russian President Vladimir Putin's equally brutal suppression of Chechen independence. (Chechnya, unlike, say, the Ukraine, was never a "Soviet Socialist Republic" with Article 72 secession rights.) Assuming that you in fact admire Lincoln's suppression of the Confederacy, is it because you share the particular views of the Constitution articulated in his inaugural speech or because you support the anti-slavery impulse undergirding Northern opposition to the South that would ultimately be vindicated in the Emancipation Proclamation and the Thirteenth Amendment?

5. As a matter of fact, several of the Southern states submitted the question of secession to the electorate. In Texas, for example, a referendum held on February 23, 1861, voted 46,129 to 14,697 in favor of the ordinance of secession. The electorate of some of the other states — Tennessee, North Carolina, Arkansas, and Missouri — in effect voted against secession, though three of these four then seceded. Is there a difference in the legitimacy of secession among these states, or did all behave equally (il)legitimately? As to Texas, consider the following inscription from the memorial to the Southern Confederacy in front of the Texas State Capitol:

DIED FOR STATE RIGHTS GUARANTEED UNDER THE CONSTITUTION

THE PEOPLE OF THE SOUTH, ANIMATED BY THE SPIRIT OF 1776, TO PRESERVE THEIR RIGHTS, WITHDREW FROM THE FEDERAL COMPACT IN 1861. THE NORTH RESORTED TO COERCION. THE SOUTH, AGAINST OVERWHELMING NUMBERS AND RESOURCES, FOUGHT UNTIL EXHAUSTED.

What is your response to this inscription? Consider these possibilities:

a. It expresses a clearly mistaken view of the 1787 Constitution, and the State of Texas should clearly indicate this.
b. Though it expresses an intellectually defensible — even if not necessarily correct — view of the 1787 Constitution, that view has not prevailed, and the State of Texas should clearly indicate this.
c. The State of Texas should do absolutely nothing and leave it up to viewers to decide for themselves what they think of the inscription.
d. The State of Texas, whatever its decision about the existing inscription, should build a monument to the Union war dead, with an inscription indicating that they fought to vindicate the Constitution of 1787.

Note that none of these possibilities directly addresses the role of slavery in triggering the Civil War. For now, consider this final possibility: The State of Texas should build a memorial to the slaves with an inscription that Lincoln's decision to resist the Confederacy, whatever the possible constitutional legitimacy of secession in the abstract, was undoubtedly justified because it overthrew an iniquitous regime of chattel slavery.

B. The Authority of the President to Repel Attacks on the Union

Lincoln's First Inaugural Address was delivered on March 4, 1861. His theoretical argument against the legitimacy of secession did not differ in any substantial respect from that of James Buchanan. What *was* different was Lincoln's conception of his own power to resist secession. Thus, when South Carolina secessionists fired on Fort Sumter on April 12, he quickly acted. On April 15, Lincoln called for a special session of Congress to meet on July 4. Prior to July 4, Lincoln made several important decisions. Some of them, such as calling out the militia, were scarcely controversial, not least because Congress had long since granted the President the authority to respond to attacks on the United States.[63] Others were much more so. On April 19 and 27, for example, he issued proclamations blockading Confederate ports and authorizing the seizure of ships caught carrying goods to them. The foreign shipowners sued, claiming that this was beyond the President's authority in the absence of a congressional recognition of a state of war, which did not occur until July 13. (Recall Brown v. U.S., 12 U.S. (8 Cranch) 110 (1814), Chapter 2, supra, which suggested that even a declaration of war did not necessarily justify the seizure of an enemy alien's property — let alone the property of "neutral" foreigners — without congressional authorization.) Nonetheless, the Supreme Court upheld the Proclamation in a 5 to 4 decision, with Justice Grier writing for the majority.

PRIZE CASES
67 U.S. (2 Black) 635 (1863)

GRIER, J:

Let us enquire whether, at the time this blockade was instituted, a state of war existed which would justify a resort to these means of subduing the hostile force. . . .

By the Constitution, Congress alone has the power to declare a national or foreign war. It cannot declare war against a State, or any number of States, by virtue of any clause in the Constitution. The Constitution confers on the President the whole Executive power. He is bound to take care that the laws be faithfully executed. He is Commander-in-Chief of the Army and Navy of the United States, and of the militia of the several States when called into the actual service of the United States. He has no power to initiate or declare a war either against a foreign nation or a domestic State. But by the Acts of Congress of February 28th, 1795, and 3d of March, 1807, he is authorized to call out the militia and use the military and naval forces of the United States in case of invasion by foreign nations, and to suppress insurrection against the government of a State or of the United States.

63. See, e.g., Stephen I. Vladeck, Note: Emergency Power and the Militia Acts, 114 Yale L. J. 149 (2004).

If a war be made by invasion of a foreign nation, the President is not only author-ized but bound to resist force by force. He does not initiate the war, but is bound to accept the challenge without waiting for any special legislative authority. And whether the hostile party be a foreign invader, or States organized in rebellion, it is none the less a war, although the declaration of it be "unilateral." . . .

The President was bound to meet [the Civil War] in the shape it presented itself, without waiting for Congress to baptize it with a name; and no name given to it by him or them could change the fact. . . .

Whether the President in fulfilling his duties, as Commander-in-Chief, in suppressing an insurrection, has met with such armed hostile resistance, and a civil war of such alarming proportions as will compel him to accord to them the charac-ter of belligerents, is a question to be decided by him, and this court must be governed by the decisions and acts of the Political Department of the government to which this power was intrusted. "He must determine what degree of force the crisis demands." The proclamation of blockade is, itself, official and conclusive evidence to the court that a state of war existed which demanded and authorized a recourse to such a measure, under the circumstances peculiar to the case.

If it were necessary to the technical existence of a war, that it should have a legislative sanction, we find it in almost every act passed at the extraordinary session of the Legislature of 1861, which was wholly employed in enacting laws to enable the Government to prosecute the war with vigor and efficiency. And finally, in 1861, we find Congress . . . passing an act "approving, legalizing, and making valid all the acts, proclamations, and orders of the President, &c., as if they had been issued and done under the previous express authority and direction of the Congress of the United States." Without admitting that such an act was necessary under the circum-stances, it is plain that if the President had in any manner assumed powers which it was necessary should have the authority or sanction of Congress, . . . this ratifica-tion has operated to perfectly cure the defect. . . .

NELSON, J., dissenting, joined by Taney, C.J., and Catron and Clifford, JJ. . . .

In the case of a rebellion or resistance of a portion of the people of a country against the established government, there is no doubt, if in its progress and enlarge-ment the government thus thought to be overthrown sees fit, it may by the compe-tent power recognize or declare the existence of a state of civil war, which will draw after it all the consequences and rights of war between the contending parties. . . . But before this insurrection against the established Government can be dealt with on the footing of a civil war, within the meaning of the law of nations and the Constitution of the United States, and which will draw after it belligerent rights, it must be recognized or declared by the war-making power of the Government. . . .

Now, in one sense, no doubt this is war, and may be a war of the most extensive and threatening dimensions and effects, but it is a statement simply of its existence in a material sense, and has no relevancy or weight when the question is what constitutes war in a legal sense, in the sense of the law of nations, and of the Constitution of the United States. For it must be a war in this sense to attach to it all the consequences that belong to belligerent rights. . . . [T]o constitute a civil war in the sense in which we are speaking, before it can exist, in contemplation of law, it must be recognized or declared by the sovereign power of the State, and which sovereign power by our Constitution is lodged in the Congress of the United States — civil war, therefore, under our system of government, can exist only by an act of Congress, which requires the assent of two of the great departments of the Government, the Executive and Legislative.

. . . But we are asked, what would become of the peace and integrity of the Union in case of an insurrection at home or invasion from abroad if this power could not be exercised by the President in the recess of Congress and until that body could be assembled?

The framers of the Constitution fully comprehended this question, and provided for the contingency. . . . The Constitution declares that Congress shall have power "to provide for calling forth the militia to execute the laws of the Union, suppress insurrections, and repel invasions." Another clause, "that the President shall be Commander-in-chief of the Army and Navy of the United States, and of the militia of the several States when called into the actual service of the United States"; and, again, "He shall take care that the laws shall be faithfully executed." Congress passed laws on this subject in 1792 and 1795.

. . . The 2d section [of the Act of 1795] provides, that when the laws of the United States shall be opposed, or the execution obstructed in any State by combinations too powerful to be suppressed by the course of judicial proceedings, it shall be lawful for the President to call forth the militia of such State, or of any other State or States as may be necessary to suppress such combinations; and by the Act 3 March, 1807 (2 U.S. Laws, 443) it is provided that in case of insurrection or obstruction of the laws, either in the United States or of any State or Territory, where it is lawful for the President to call forth the militia for the purpose of suppressing such insurrection, and causing the laws to be executed, it shall be lawful to employ for the same purpose such part of the land and naval forces of the United States as shall be judged necessary. It will be seen, therefore, that ample provision has been made under the Constitution and laws against any sudden and unexpected disturbance of the public peace from insurrection at home or invasion from abroad. The whole military and naval power of the country is put under the control of the President to meet the emergency. . . .

The Acts of 1795 and 1807 did not, and could not under the Constitution, confer on the President the power of declaring war against a State of this Union, or of deciding that war existed, and upon that ground authorized the capture and confiscation of the property of every citizen of the State whenever it was found on the waters. . . . This great power over the business and property of the citizen is reserved to the legislative department by the express words of the Constitution. It cannot be delegated or surrendered to the Executive. Congress alone can determine whether war exists or should be declared; and until they have acted, no citizen of the State can be punished in his person or property, unless he has committed some offence against a law of Congress passed before the act was committed, which made it a crime, and defined the punishment. . . .

Discussion

1. Note the delay between Lincoln's inauguration and the meeting of Congress on July 4. Why was Congress not in session on Inauguration Day, March 4? (See Article I, §4, cl. 2; Article II, §3. Compare them with the Twentieth Amendment.) Even if Lincoln violated no formal provision of the Constitution in delaying Congress's return until July 4, did he violate its democratic "spirit" by failing to call Congress back into session as soon as was reasonably possible, say May 1 to allow California's representatives sufficient time to make it to Omaha, from where they

could then take the train to Washington? (As a matter of fact, the Senate was in session on March 4 to confirm members of Lincoln's Cabinet, so presumably even the newly elected Western senators were in Washington then.) Would you think any less of Lincoln if he had called no special session at all and simply waited until Congress convened in December, the date set by the Constitution?

2. Note that Justice Grier mentions the Acts of 1795 and 1807 as providing a basis for Lincoln's actions. Thus, argues Stephen Vladeck, the basis of what is undoubtedly "a broad understanding of the President's war powers with respect to his independent authority to act during crises" is the fact that prior Congresses had delegated, as is their constitutional right, the relevant authority. Thus, he argues, "The *Prize Cases*, among the most significant" precedents with regard to presidential power "in the annals of the Supreme Court, turned not on any provision of the Constitution, but on the Militia Acts."[64] If Vladeck is correct in arguing that these early statutes were sufficient to authorize Lincoln's actions, then what precisely is the relevance of the Act of August 6, 1861, by which the members of Congress "hereby approve and in all respects legalize and make valid" the acts done by the President "as if they had been issued and done under the previous express authority and direction of the Congress of the United States"? Is this a kind of congressional "suspenders" provided on top of the "belt" of the earlier legislation, just in case anyone doubts the adequacy of the latter? But if the earlier Acts were, contra Vladeck, insufficient, then would the illegality of Lincoln's proclamation be "cured" by retroactive legitimation? Does this suggest that any violation of separation of powers can in effect be negated if its institutional "victim" acquiesces? Or do ordinary citizens have a stake in the strict maintenance of separation, whatever might be the reaction of political officials occupying the offices in question?

3. What if Congress had passed an Act (or joint resolution) specifically repudiating the President's act? (Would the President have had the right to veto any such repudiation? See Article I, §7, cl. 3.) If the earlier Acts justified Lincoln, then would Congress's ostensible withdrawal of such authority have any consequence for the actual seizure at issue in the *Prize Cases*?

Consider in this context the majority's statement that "[t]he President *was bound* to meet [the Civil War] in the shape it presented itself, without waiting for Congress to baptize it with a name; and no name given to it by him or them could change the fact" (emphasis added). Does this suggest a constitutional obligation upon the President, with concomitant constitutionally assigned power, either from the Commander-in-Chief Clause or the Oath of Office, to do whatever he thought necessary to meet the threat to the Union? Michael Stokes Paulsen[65] argues that so long as the President can plausibly be claiming to defend the overarching constitutional order, he (or in the future she) is apparently authorized by the Oath of Office itself to disregard any particular part of the Constitution if fidelity to the individual part might, according to the president, threaten the survival of the whole, the constitutional order itself. Paulsen quotes Lincoln: "I felt that measures, otherwise unconstitutional, might become lawful, by becoming indispensable to the preservation of the constitution, through the preservation of the nation."[66]

---

64. Id. at 179-180.

65. Paulsen, The Constitution of Necessity, 79 Notre Dame L. Rev. 1257 (2004).

66. Id. at 1283 (quoting from letter of April 4, 1864, from Lincoln to United States Senator Albert G. Hodges).

Paulsen fully recognizes that he is defending "dangerous principles,"[67] but, he concludes, "if I am mistaken in all this, so was President Lincoln."[68] Madison might have been cited to the same effect inasmuch as he wrote, in Federalist No. 41: "It is in vain to oppose constitutional barriers to the impulse of self-preservation. It is worse than in vain; because it plants in the Constitution itself *necessary usurpations of power,* every precedent of which is a germ of unnecessary and multiplied repetitions."[69] (Note that in this sentence, the word "oppose" means "place in opposition to," or "erect," not "argue against.")

Should one always read the Constitution as effectively legitimizing whatever a president chooses to do in responding to what the president defines as an "emergency" threatening fundamental interests of national security? Is this the practical meaning of the Court's statement that "Whether the President in fulfilling his duties, as Commander-in-Chief, in suppressing an insurrection, has met with such armed hostile resistance, and a civil war of such alarming proportions as will compel him to accord to them the character of belligerents, is a question to be decided by him, and this court must be governed by the decisions and acts of the Political Department of the government to which this power was intrusted." Does this view undermine the concept of a "limited" government, or is it simply the case that the Court has confidence that presidents will not overreach? (What is the appropriate remedy for overreaching? A suit by private parties against the president for the damage caused them? Impeachment? Loss of the next election?)

One might argue that the notion of "limits" to governmental power in general and executive power in particular rests on a background assumption of political stability, so that governmental (and executive) powers are quite different whenever these background conditions dissolve into instability or "emergency." Such emergencies are sometimes viewed as "states of exception," a term associated especially with the German legal philosopher Carl Schmitt.[70] It was Schmitt, for example, who wrote that "[t]here exists no norm that is applicable to chaos"[71] or, perhaps, even "crisis." There is in fact nothing new about the notion of the "exception" or "emergency." Indeed, political scientist Clinton Rossiter, who published in 1948 a brilliant and disturbing book, Constitutional Dictatorship, noted that the idea goes back at least to ancient Rome, which institutionalized the role of the "dictator" who could safeguard the constitutional order in a time of emergency. Rossiter writes, "No sacrifice is too great for our democracy, least of all the temporary sacrifice of democracy itself."[72]

More recently the Italian social theorist Giogio Agamben has written that "the state of exception tends increasingly to appear as the dominant paradigm of government in contemporary politics."[73] If this is true, does it threaten democracy (and the enterprise of constitutional government)?

---

67. Id. at 1296.

68. Id. at 1297.

69. Federalist No. 41 (emphasis added), available at *http://www.yale.edu/lawweb/avalon/federal/fed41.htm*

70. Who, as a matter of fact, was the chief academic apologist for Hitler's seizure of power as a means of responding to the ostensible "emergency" facing Weimar Germany.

71. Carl Schmitt, Political Theology: Four Chapters on the Theory of Sovereignty 13 (trans. George Schwab, translating the 1934 German edition) (2005).

72. Clinton Rossiter, Constitutional Dictatorship 314 (1948).

73. Giorgio Agamben, State of Exception 2 (2005).

C. Lincoln and the Suspension of Habeas Corpus[74]

On April 27, 1861, President Lincoln issued an order to Commanding General Winfield Scott authorizing him to suspend the writ of habeas corpus (by which persons deprived of liberty can challenge the legality of their detention in a court). On May 25, military troops arrested John Merryman for participating in the destruction of railroad bridges following an antiwar riot in Baltimore.

The Constitution, in §9 of Article I, specifically authorizes the suspension of habeas corpus "when in cases of rebellion or invasion the public safety may require it." The question is: Who is authorized by the Constitution to make such a determination?

1. *Chief Justice Taney on the Exclusive Authority of Congress*

Merryman was a prominent politician; his father and Chief Justice Taney had attended Dickinson College together. Merryman's lawyer filed a writ of habeas corpus before the Chief Justice, sitting as a Circuit Judge for the circuit that included Maryland. The writ was addressed to General George Cadwalader, who refused either to attend the May 27 hearing before Taney or to produce Merryman, who ignored it, refusing even to attend the May 27 hearing. Cadwalader refused to comply with a second order to be present the following day. Upon further noncompliance, Taney read a statement asserting that Merryman's detention was illegal on two grounds:

1. The President, under the Constitution and laws of the United States, cannot suspend the privilege of the writ of habeas corpus, nor authorize any military officer to do so.
2. A military officer has no right to arrest and detain a person, not subject to the rules and articles of war, for an offence against the laws of the United States, except in and of the judicial authority and subject to its control — and if the party is arrested by the military, it is the duty of the officer to deliver him over immediately to the civil authority, to be dealt with according to law.

Taney indicated his intention to write a fuller opinion elaborating his conclusions to "report them with these proceedings to the President of the United States, and call upon him to perform his constitutional duty to enforce the laws. In other words, to enforce the process of this Court." He issued his opinion the following week.

EX PARTE MERRYMAN
17 F. Cas. 144 (1861)

I understand that the President not only claims the right to suspend the writ of habeas corpus himself, at his discretion, but to delegate that discretionary power to

---

74. See Carl Swisher, 5 History of the Supreme Court of the United States: The Taney Period 1836-64, Chapter 14 (1974).

a military officer, and to leave it to him to determine whether he will or will not obey judicial process that may be served upon him. . . . I certainly listened to [the argument] with some surprise, for I had supposed it to be one of those points of constitutional law upon which there was no difference of opinion, and that it was admitted on all hands, that the privilege of the writ could not be suspended, except by act of congress. . . . [B]elieving, as I do, that the president has exercised a power which he does not possess under the constitution, a proper respect for the high office he fills, requires me to state plainly and fully the grounds of my opinion. . . .

The clause of the constitution, which authorizes the suspension of the privilege of the writ of habeas corpus, is in the 9th section of the first article. This article is devoted to the legislative department of the United States, and has not the slightest reference to the executive department. . . .

It is the second article of the constitution that provides for the organization of the executive department, enumerates the powers conferred on it, and prescribes its duties. And if the high power over the liberty of the citizen now claimed, was intended to be conferred on the president, it would undoubtedly be found in plain words in this article; but here is not a word in it that can furnish the slightest ground to justify the exercise of the power.

. . . The only power, therefore, which the president possesses, where the "life, liberty or property" of a private citizen is concerned, is the power and duty prescribed in the third section of the second article, which requires "that he shall take care that the laws shall be faithfully executed." He is not authorized to execute them himself, or through agents or officers, civil or military, appointed by himself, but he is to take care that they be faithfully carried into execution, as they are expounded and adjudged by the co-ordinate branch of the government to which that duty is assigned by the constitution. It is thus made his duty to come in aid of the judicial authority, if it shall be resisted by a force too strong to be overcome without the assistance of the executive arm; but in exercising this power he acts in subordination to judicial authority, assisting it to execute its process and enforce its judgments.

With such provisions in the constitution, expressed in language too clear to be misunderstood by any one, I can see no ground whatever for supposing that the president, in any emergency, or in any state of things, can authorize the suspension of the privileges of the writ of habeas corpus, except in aid of the judicial power. He certainly does not faithfully execute the laws, if he takes upon himself legislative power, by suspending the writ of habeas corpus, and the judicial power also, by arresting and imprisoning a person without due process of law.

Nor can any argument be drawn from the nature of sovereignty, or the necessity of government, for self-defence in times of tumult and danger. The government of the United States is one of delegated and limited power; it derives its existence and authority altogether from the constitution, and neither of its branches, executive, legislative or judicial, can exercise any of the powers of government beyond those specified and granted; for the tenth article of the amendments to the constitution, in express terms, provides that "the powers not delegated to the United States by the constitution, not prohibited by it to the states, are reserved to the states, respectively, or to the people." . . . The right of the subject to the benefit of the writ of habeas corpus, it must be recollected, was one of the great points in controversy, during the long struggle in England between arbitrary government and free institutions, and must therefore have strongly attracted the attention of the statesmen engaged in framing a new one and, as they supposed, a freer government than the one which they had thrown off by the revolution. From the earliest history of the common law, if a person were imprisoned, no matter by what authority, he had a right to the writ of habeas corpus to bring his case before the king's bench. . . .

[Blackstone writes that] "the happiness of our constitution is, that it is not left to the executive power to determine when the danger of the state is so great as to render [suspension of habeas corpus] expedient. It is the parliament only or legislative power that, whenever it sees proper, can authorize the crown by suspending the habeas corpus for a short and limited time, to imprison suspected persons without giving any reason for so doing." If the president of the United States may suspend the writ, then the constitution of the United States has conferred upon him more regal and absolute power over the liberty of the citizen, than the people of England have thought it safe to entrust to the crown; a power which the queen of England cannot exercise at this day, and which could not have been lawfully exercised by the sovereign even in the reign of Charles the First.

[Ultimately, the Administration indicted Merryman for treason by a civil grand jury. He was released on bail and never tried.]

2.   The President Asserts Executive Authority

Lincoln did not respond directly to Taney, but delivered this message to Congress on July 4:

Soon after the first call for militia, it was considered a duty to authorize the Commanding General, in proper cases, according to his discretion, to suspend the privilege of the writ of habeas corpus; or, in other words, to arrest, and detain, without resort to the ordinary processes and forms of law, such individuals as he might deem dangerous to the public safety. This authority has purposely been exercised but very sparingly. Nevertheless, the legality and propriety of what has been done under it, are questioned; and the attention of the country has been called to the proposition that one who is sworn to "take care that the laws be faithfully executed," should not himself violate them. Of course some consideration was given to the questions of power, and propriety, before this matter was acted upon. The whole of the laws which were required to be faithfully executed, were being resisted, and failing of execution, in nearly one-third of the States. Must they be allowed to finally fail of execution, even had it been perfectly clear, that by the use of the means necessary to their execution, some single law, made in such extreme tenderness of the citizen's liberty, that practically, it relieves more of the guilty, than of the innocent, should, to a very limited extent, be violated? To state the question more directly, are all the laws, but one, to go unexecuted, and the government itself go to pieces, lest that one be violated? Even in such a case, would not the official oath be broken, if the government should be overthrown, when it was believed that disregarding the single law, would tend to preserve it? But it was not believed that this question was presented. It was not believed that any law was violated. The provision of the Constitution . . . is equivalent to a provision — is a provision — that such privilege may be suspended when, in cases of rebellion, or invasion, the public safety does require it. It was decided that we have a case of rebellion, and that the public safety does require the qualified suspension of the privilege of the writ which was authorized to be made. Now it is insisted that Congress, and not the Executive, is vested with this power. But the Constitution itself, is silent as to which, or who, is to exercise the power; and as the provision was plainly made for a dangerous emergency, it cannot be believed the framers of the instrument intended, that in every case, the danger should run its course, until Congress could be called together; the very assembling of which might be prevented, as was intended in this case, by the rebellion.

Discussion

It is not clear whether Congress's retroactive approval, on August 6, 1861, of "all the acts, proclamations, and orders of the President . . . respecting the army and navy of the United States" included the suspension of the writ of habeas corpus. On March 3, 1863, Congress passed a habeas corpus act providing that "during the present rebellion the President of the United States, whenever, in his judgment, the public safety may require it, is authorized to suspend the privilege of the writ of habeas corpus in any case throughout the United States or any part thereof." Does this congressional authorization affect the power that President Lincoln held prior to its enactment? If so, was his original order suspending habeas corpus unconstitutional? (Some have argued that the suspension was legitimate only so long as Congress was not in session, but that Congress's failure specifically to enact a suspension when it reconvened invalidated further enforcement of the Presidential order.)

D. Lincoln: The Great Emancipator

As already noted, Lincoln assumed a moderate stance toward slavery in his Inaugural Address. "I have no purpose, directly or indirectly, to interfere with the institution of slavery in the States where it exists. I believe that I have no lawful right to do so, and I have no inclination to do so." He explicitly reiterated his support of the 1860 Republican platform, which endorsed "the maintenance inviolate of the rights of the States, and especially the right of each State to order and control its own domestic institutions according to its own judgment exclusively." This, of course, helps to explain his support of the Corwin Amendment. Even in the absence of the Amendment, Congress made no attempt to abolish slavery until it proposed the Thirteenth Amendment, which was ratified on December 6, 1865. However, on January 1, 1863, Lincoln issued the famous Emancipation Proclamation:

I, Abraham Lincoln, President of the United States, by virtue of the power in me vested as Commander-in-Chief, of the Army and Navy of the United States in time of actual armed rebellion against authority and government of the United States, and as a fit and necessary war measure for suppressing said rebellion, do . . . order and designate as the States and parts of States wherein the people thereof respectively, are this day in rebellion against the United States, the following, to wit: Arkansas, Texas, Louisiana, (except the Parishes of St. Bernard, Plaquemines, Jefferson, St. Johns, St. Charles, St. James[,] Ascension, Assumption, Terrebonne, Lafourche, St. Mary, St. Martin, and Orleans, including the City of New Orleans)[,] Mississippi, Alabama, Florida, Georgia, South-Carolina, North-Carolina, and Virginia, (except the forty-eight counties designated as West Virginia, and also the counties of Berkeley, Accomac, Northampton, Elizabeth-City, York, Princess Ann, and Norfolk, including the cities of Norfolk & Portsmouth[)]; and which excepted parts are, for the present, left precisely as if this proclamation were not issued.

And by virtue of the power, and for the purpose aforesaid, I do order and declare that all persons held as slaves within the designated States . . . are, and henceforward shall be free; and that the Executive government of the United States, including the military and naval authorities thereof, will recognize and maintain the freedom of said persons. . . . And upon this act, sincerely believed to be an act of justice, warranted by the Constitution, upon military necessity, I invoke the considerate judgment of mankind, and the gracious favor of Almighty God. . . .

The Emancipation Proclamation is not a general declaration of freedom. Indeed, as late as July of 1864, Lincoln reiterated that he was "unprepared . . . to declare a constitutional competency in Congress to abolish slavery in [the] States." Instead he emphasized the President's power as commander-in-chief to take actions warranted by "military necessity": "As Commander-in-Chief, I suppose I have a right to take any measure which may best subdue the enemy." Beyond this there was the President's duty to preserve the Union: "I felt that measures otherwise unconstitutional might become lawful by becoming indispensable to the preservation of the Constitution through the preservation of the nation."[75]

Note: Former Justice Curtis Dissents

The Emancipation Proclamation scarcely received universal support, even from the North. One critic, for example, was Benjamin R. Curtis, whom you earlier read vigorously dissenting in *Dred Scott,* and who resigned from the Court shortly thereafter. In October 1862 he published a pamphlet on "executive power" that expressed strong reservations about a number of Lincoln's actions, including the Proclamation, which Lincoln had, in September, announced his intention to issue should the South not return to the Union.[76] Curtis wrote:

The persons who are the subjects of this proclamation are held to service by the laws of the respective States in which they reside, enacted by State authority as clear and unquestionable, under our system of government, as any law passed by any State on any subject.

This proclamation, then, by an executive decree, proposes to repeal and annul valid State laws which regulate the domestic relations of their people. . . .

[T]his executive decree holds out this proposed repeal of State laws as a threatened penalty for the continuance of a governing majority of the people of each State, or part of a State, in rebellion against the United States. So that the President hereby assumes to himself the power to denounce it as a punishment against the entire people of a State, that the valid laws of that State which regulate the domestic condition of its inhabitants shall become null and void, at a certain future date, by reason of the criminal conduct of a governing majority of its people.

This penalty . . . is not to be inflicted on those persons who have been guilty of treason. The freedom of their slaves was already provided for by the act of Congress, recited in a subsequent part of the proclamation.[77] It is not, therefore, as a

75. See Randall, supra n.58, at 351, 358.
76. Benjamin R. Curtis, ed., 2 A Memoir of Benjamin Robbins Curtis 306-335 (1879).
77. Curtis is referring to the Second Confiscation Act, passed in July 1862, which, in the words of Professor Swisher, was "linked with provisions dealing with the punishment of treason" and

applied to the property of all civil and military officers serving under the Confederacy; to the property of any person residing in the North who should assist and give aid and comfort to the rebellion; and to the property of persons "in any state" who, being engaged in the rebellion, did not reestablish their allegiance to the United States within sixty days after a proclamation of warning by the President. Slaves were to be liberated in areas occupied by the armed forces, and the return of fugitive slaves to rebel owners was forbidden.

punishment of guilty persons that the commander-in-chief decrees the freedom of slaves. It is upon the slaves of loyal persons, or of those who, from their tender years, or other disability, cannot be either disloyal or otherwise, that the proclamation is to operate, if at all; and it is to operate to set them free, in spite of the valid laws of their States. . . .

It has never been doubted that the power to abolish slavery within the States was not delegated to the United States by the Constitution, but was reserved to the States. If the President, as commander-in-chief of the army and navy in time of war, may, by an executive decree, exercise this power to abolish slavery in the States, because he is of opinion that he may thus "best subdue the enemy," what other power, reserved to the States or to the people, may not be exercised by the President, for the same reason that he is of opinion he may thus best subdue the enemy? . . .

Besides, all the powers of the President are executive merely. He cannot make a law. He cannot repeal one. He can only execute the laws. . . .

These conclusions concerning the powers of the President cannot be shaken by the assertion that "rebels have no rights." The assertion itself is not true, in reference either to the seceding States or their people.

It is not true of those States; for the Government of the United States has never admitted, and cannot admit, that as States, they are in rebellion. . . . [T]he Constitution is as much the supreme law of the land in Tennessee to-day, as it was before the void act of secession was attempted by a part of its people. Else the act was effectual, and the State is independent of the Government of the United States, and the war is a war of conquest and subjugation.

Nor is the assertion that "rebels have no rights" applicable to the people of those States. . . . When many millions of people are involved in civil war, humanity, and that public law which in modern times is humane, forbid their treatment as outlaws. And if public law and the Constitution and laws of the United States are now their rules of duty towards us, on what ground shall we deny that public law and the Constitution, and the laws made under it, are also our rules of duty towards them? . . .

But, if [it] were conceded that "rebels have no rights," there would still be matter demanding the greatest consideration. For the inquiry which I have invited is not what are their rights, but what are our rights. . . .

It is among the rights of all of us that the executive power should be kept within its prescribed constitutional limits, and should not legislate, by its decrees, upon subjects of transcendent importance to the whole people.

Whether such decrees are wise or unwise, whether their subjects are citizens or not, if they are usurpations of power, our rights are both infringed and endangered. They are infringed, because the power to decide and to act is taken from the people without their consent. They are endangered, because, in a constitutional government, every usurpation of power dangerously disorders the whole framework of the State.

. . . Among all the causes of alarm which now distress the public mind, there are few more terrible . . . than the tendency to lawlessness which is manifesting itself in so many directions. No stronger evidence of this could be afforded than the open declaration of a respectable and widely circulated journal, that "nobody cares" whether a great public act of the President of the United States is in conformity with or is subversive of the supreme law of the land . . . ; that our public affairs have become so desperate, and our ability to retrieve them by the use of honest means is so distrusted, and our willingness to use other means so undoubted, that our great public servants may themselves break the fundamental law of the country, and become usurpers of vast powers not intrusted to them, in violation of their solemn oath of office; and "nobody cares."

Discussion

1. Mark E. Neely, Jr., points out that Lincoln's own views on his power to emancipate slaves underwent significant changes during the course of his presidency.[78] Near its beginning, for example, Lincoln wrote a letter, marked "private and confidential," to Illinois Senator Orville H. Browning, who had objected to Lincoln's prompt revocation of an August 30, 1861, order by General John C. Fremont (who had been the Republican candidate for the presidency in 1856) freeing slaves belonging to Missouri rebels. Part of the reason for overruling Fremont was Lincoln's well-merited concern about keeping other slave states, especially Kentucky, in the Union should the War so quickly take on anti-slavery (and not only anti-secession) aims. Lincoln noted as well that Fremont's order went beyond a congressional statute that had been passed on August 6 mandating the confiscation of property, including slaves "used for insurrectional purposes," which presumably did not cover all property that happened to be owned by those engaged in insurrection. But Lincoln informed Browning that he had constitutional concerns as well:[79]

> [Fremont's] proclamation . . . is simply "dictatorship." It assumes that the general may do anything he pleases — confiscate the lands and free the slaves of loyal people, as well as of disloyal ones. And going the whole figure I have no doubt would be more popular with some thoughtless people, than that which has been done. But I cannot assume this reckless position; nor allow others to assume it on my responsibility. You speak of it as being the only means of saving the government. On the contrary it is itself the surrender of the government. Can it be pretended that it is any longer the government of the U.S. — any government of Constitution and laws, — wherein a General, or a President, may make permanent rules of property by proclamation.
>
>   I do not say Congress might not with propriety pass a law, on the point. . . . I do not say I might not, as a member of Congress, vote for it. What I object to, is, that I as President, shall expressly or impliedly seize and exercise the permanent legislative functions of the government.

By the following May, when General David Hunter issued a similar proclamation in regard to federally controlled areas in South Carolina, Georgia, and Florida, Lincoln revoked it only on the ground that it went well beyond the power of a military officer. However, "I further make known that whether it be competent for me, as Commander-in-Chief of the Army and Navy, to declare the Slaves of any state or states, free, and whether at any time, in any case, it shall have become a necessity indispensable to the maintenance of the government, to exercise such supposed power, are questions which, under my responsibility, I reserve to myself. . . ."[80]

2. In his letter to Browning, Lincoln raises the question of congressional abolition of slavery. Do you agree that Congress could have abolished slavery by ordinary legislation? Could the war powers have justified its abolition in the border states, such as Maryland, Kentucky, and Missouri, with whom the United States was not at war? Lincoln presumably believed that he was without power to emancipate the slaves even in those parts of the Confederacy that had been brought back under the control of the Union. Would Congress have had any greater power? Congress, incidentally, did not repeal the Fugitive Slave Acts of 1793 and 1850 until June 28, 1864,

---

78. See Mark E. Neely Jr., The Last Best Hope on Earth, ch. 4 (1993).

79. Letter of September 22, 1861, in Lincoln: Speeches, Letters, Miscellaneous Writings, Presidential Messages and Proclamations 268-269 (Library of America 1989).

80. "Proclamation [of May 19, 1862] Revoking Hunter's Emancipation Order," in id. at 318-319.

and they were enforced to permit the recovery of fugitives by loyal slave owners in Union states until that time.

3. Does the Third Amendment — "No Soldier shall, in time of peace, be quartered in any house, without the consent of the Owner, nor in time of war, but in a manner to be prescribed by law" — throw any light on Emancipation? Imagine Union General Meade's arriving near Gettysburg on June 30, 1863, and simply ordering a loyal Pennsylvania farmer to give up her house for the quartering of Union troops while preparing for the battle that was imminent. Could she have refused, on the basis that Meade offered no documents authorizing him to do so? Would it have sufficed to show a document signed by the President — "I hereby authorize you to quarter troops in any houses that shall be convenient for the purpose" — or would it be necessary for Congress first to have authorized the President to issue such orders? Is it plausible to read the Third Amendment as applying only to the quartering of troops, so that your answer to the last question would be entirely irrelevant to the Emancipation Proclamation, or can the Amendment fairly be read as saying that even during time of war, when national existence might be at stake, constitutional norms nonetheless control and that public officials, including presidents, cannot, in the absence of certain legal formalities, simply do whatever they think advisable in order to achieve their goals?

Note: "Reverence for Law"

Speaking in 1838, Lincoln declared:[81]

Let every American, every lover of liberty, every well wisher to his posterity, swear by the blood of the Revolution, never to violate in the least particular, the laws of the country; and never to tolerate their violation by others. As the patriots of seventy-six did to the support of the Declaration of Independence, so to the support of the Constitution and Laws, let every American pledge his life, his property, and his sacred honor; let every man remember that to violate the law, is to trample on the blood of his father, and to tear the character [charter?] of his own, and his children's liberty. Let reverence for the laws, be breathed by every American mother, to the lisping babe, that prattles on her lap — let it be taught in schools, in seminaries, and in colleges; let it be written in Primers, spelling books, and in Almanacs; let it be preached from the pulpit, proclaimed in legislative halls, and enforced in courts of justice. And, in short, let it become the political religion of the nation; and let the old and the young, the rich and poor, the grave and the gay, of all sexes and tongues, and colors and conditions, sacrifice unceasingly upon its altars. . . .

When I so pressingly urge a strict observance of all the laws, let me not be understood that there are no bad laws, nor that grievances may not arise, for the redress of which, no legal provisions have been made. I mean to say no such thing. But I do mean to say, that, although bad laws, if they exist, should be repealed as soon as possible, still while they continue in force, for the sake of example, they should be religiously observed.

Lincoln concluded his impassioned speech by calling for "a reverence for the constitution and laws." As President, Lincoln wrote the following in an 1863 letter to Ohio Democrats upon their passage of a resolution denouncing his policy of military arrests and suspension of habeas corpus:[82]

81. Quoted in The Political Thought of Abraham Lincoln 16-17 (Current ed., 1967).
82. Id. at 262.

You ask, in substance, whether I really claim that I may override all the guaranteed rights of individuals, on the plea of conserving the public safety when I may choose to say the public safety requires it. This question, divested of the phraseology calculated to represent me as struggling for an arbitrary personal prerogative, is either simply a question who shall decide, or an affirmation that nobody shall decide, what the public safety does require, in cases of Rebellion of Invasion. The constitution contemplates the question as likely to occur for decision, but it does not expressly declare who is to decide it. By necessary implication, when Rebellion or Invasion comes, the decision is to be made, from time to time; and I think the man whom, for the time, the people have, under the constitution, made the commander-in-chief, of their Army and Navy, is the man who holds the power, and bears the responsibility of making it. If he uses the power justly, the same people will probably justify him; if he abuses it, he is in their hand, to be dealt with by all the modes they have reserved to themselves in the constitution.

Discussion

1. Did Lincoln display a "reverence" for the Constitution? Did he comply with the oath of office? Might the President's pledge to "preserve, protect and defend the Constitution of the United States" include the commission of acts that would be "unconstitutional" in normal times? Compare Lincoln's argument with James Madison's defense, in The Federalist No. 40, of the Philadelphia Convention's exceeding its delegated authority by drafting a new Constitution: "the plan to be framed and proposed was to be submitted to the people themselves" and their "approbation [would] blot out antecedent errors and irregularities." Recall also Thomas Jefferson's willingness to still any of his doubts concerning the constitutionality of the Louisiana Purchase. Do these precedents establish the proposition that presidents may take constitutionally debatable action on behalf of (what they perceive to be) the public good, leaving it to citizens and the Congress to decide either that the "justice" of their actions legitimates them, or, on the other hand, that they represent a sufficient threat to the constitutional order to merit impeachment?

Consider Giorgio Agamben's statement: "In the ten weeks that passed between [the outbreak of war on] April 15 and [the return of Congress on] July 4, Lincoln in fact acted as an absolute dictator," and he notes as well that Carl Schmitt referred to Lincoln as "a perfect example" of what Schmitt called the "commissarial dictatorship," that is a dictatorship entered into ostensibly to save the existing constitutional order.[83] Clinton Rossiter basically agrees: "The eleven weeks between the fall of Sumter and July 4, 1861 constitute the most interesting single episode in the history of constitutional dictatorship. The simple fact that one man was the government of the United States in the most critical period in all its 165 years; and that he acted on no precedent and under no restraint, makes this the paragon of all democratic, constitutional dictatorships." But Rossiter immediately follows this with an all important caveat: "[I]f Lincoln was a great dictator, he was a greater democrat."[84] Is this a hopelessly self-contradictory sentence, or is it in fact possible to use both "dictator" and "democrat" to describe Lincoln?

---

83. Giorgio Agamben, State of Exception 20 (2005). Schmitt contrasted a "commissarial dictator" with a "transformational" one, who, by definition, is *not* committed to the preservation of the existing constitutional order against those who threatened it. If states of emergency become normalized in contemporary societies, does this distinction start to vanish?

84. Rossiter at 224.

Drawing on the conclusion of Justice Curtis's critique of the Proclamation, Professor Levinson has asked, as the title of an article, Was the Emancipation Proclamation Constitutional? Do We/Should We Care What the Answer Is? 2001 U. of Illinois L. Rev. 1135. One might generalize the question: To what extent do you (or should you) really care about the constitutionality of Lincoln's actions that were motivated by a desire to preserve the Union? Does your answer turn on whether you believe that Lincoln acted for what we would today regard as a "good" or admirable purpose, that is, freeing the slaves? Would your answer change if a contemporary president violated the Constitution (in your opinion) for what you considered a "bad" or "ignoble" purpose?

2. How do you respond to the following excerpt from a television interview of former President Richard Nixon, forced out of office because of his complicity in the illegal conduct surrounding the so-called Watergate scandals:[85]

Mr. David Frost: So what in a sense you're saying is that there are certain situations . . . where the President can decide that it's in the best interests of the nation or something, and do something illegal.

Mr. Nixon: Well, when the President does it, that means that it is not illegal.

Mr. Frost: By definition.

Mr. Nixon: Exactly. If the President, for example, approves something, approves an action because of national security, or, in this case, because of a threat to internal peace and order, of significant magnitude, then the President's decision in that instance is one that enables those who carry it out to carry it out without violating a law. Otherwise they're in an impossible position.

Even if you disagree with Nixon's seeming assertion that the President has sweeping authority to define the law as he sees fit (though always, presumably, for the purpose of safeguarding vital national interests), what of the collateral proposition that subordinates who obey presidential orders should, in effect, be immunized against charges that they violated law? Should "I was only obeying the clear orders of the President" serve as a conclusive excuse against being criminally sanctioned? (Recall Marshall's opinion in Little v. Bareme, supra, Chapter 2.)

Note: The Gettysburg Address as Constitutional Interpretation

The Gettysburg Address, delivered by Abraham Lincoln on the occasion of the dedication of the Gettysburg national cemetery on November 19, 1863 (only 20 weeks after the decisive battle conducted there) is probably the best known speech in American history.

THE GETTYSBURG ADDRESS

Four score and seven years ago our fathers brought forth on this continent, a new nation, conceived in Liberty, and dedicated to the proposition that all men are created equal.

---

85. Transcript of Frost-Nixon Interview, N.Y. Times, May 20, 1977, at A16.

Now we are engaged in a great civil war, testing whether that nation, or any nation so conceived and so dedicated, can long endure. We are met on a great battle-field of that war. We have come to dedicate a portion of that field, as a final resting place for those who here gave their lives that that nation might live. It is altogether fitting and proper that we should do this.

But in a larger sense, we cannot dedicate — we cannot consecrate — we cannot hallow — this ground. The brave men, living and dead, who struggled here, have consecrated it, far above our poor power to add or detract. The world will little note, nor long remember what we say here, but it can never forget what they did here. It is for us the living, rather, to be dedicated here to the unfinished work which they who fought here have thus far so nobly advanced. It is rather for us to be here dedicated to the great task remaining before us — that from these honored dead we take increased devotion to that cause for which they gave the last full measure of devotion — that we here highly resolve that these dead shall not have died in vain — that this nation, under God, shall have a new birth of freedom — and that government of the people, by the people, for the people, shall not perish from the earth.

Discussion

1. What are the implications of dating the birth of the United States four score and seven years prior to 1863 (that is, in 1776) instead of three score and fifteen years (that is, 1788, the date of ratification of the Constitution)?

2. To what extent was the unamended Constitution proposed in 1787 and ratified in 1788 demonstrably "conceived in Liberty, and dedicated to the proposition that all men are created equal"? Would your answer change if one included the amendments ratified in 1791? (Recall William Lloyd Garrison's description of the Constitution as a "convenant with Death and an Agreement with Hell.")

3. Presumably the strongest evidence for Lincoln's proposition (which helps explain the reference to four score and seven years) is the Declaration of Independence. As Gary Wills explains in his book Lincoln at Gettysburg: The Words That Remade America (1992), Lincoln was one of a number of antebellum thinkers who argued that the Constitution existed to fulfill the principles of the Declaration of Independence. Referring to Proverbs 25:11, which states that "[a] word fitly spoken is like apples of gold in pictures of silver," Lincoln once wrote that the assertion of the principle of liberty for all in the Declaration "was the word, 'fitly spoken' which has proved an 'apple of gold' to us. The Union, and the Constitution, are the picture of silver, subsequently framed around it. The picture was made, not to conceal, or destroy the apple; but to adorn, and preserve it. The picture was made for the apple — not the apple for the picture."[86]

If the picture of silver — the Constitution — was made to frame the apple of gold — the Declaration — should the Declaration in effect be treated as part of the Constitution, so that those charged with interpreting the Constitution, whether presidents, members of Congress, judges, or ordinary citizens, should draw on (and quote) the Declaration as legal authority?

4. What, precisely, is the "cause" to which the Union soldiers gave their lives? Consider only three possibilities: (a) preserving the Union; (b) eradicating slavery as part of our constitutional fabric; or (c), more ambitiously, securing genuine

---

86. Abraham Lincoln, Fragment on the Constitution and the Union, in 4 The Collected Works of Abraham Lincoln 169 (Basler ed., 1953).

equality for all persons, black or white. Which is most congruent with the overall tone of the address? If you believe it is either of the latter possibilities, is this congruent with his First Inaugural Address or Lincoln's various statements concerning the constitutional propriety of emancipation?

5. Does a "new birth of freedom" necessarily translate into the fulfillment of the proposition that "all men are created equal"?

6. What is meant by government "of the people," government "by the people," and government "for the people"? Are these three different notions of government, and, if so, could they possibly conflict with one another? (If so, which should take priority?)

E. The Use of Military Tribunals as an Alternative to Trial by Jury

Lambdin P. Milligan and other prominent Democratic critics of the war were arrested by U.S. military officials in Indiana in late 1864; they were charged with planning an armed uprising to seize Union weapons, liberate Confederate prisoners of war, and kidnap the governor of Indiana. Indiana was not a theater of military operations; civil courts were open in which, for example, the defendants might have been charged with treason. However, Indiana had been quite hospitable to "Copperhead" sentiments, and there were reasonable fears that an Indiana jury might be reluctant to convict. The military therefore elected to try Milligan and his co-defendants before a military commission, which found them guilty and sentenced them to hang. They appealed the conviction to the U.S. Circuit Court in Indianapolis; the two judges disagreed and the case therefore was sent on to the Supreme Court. The Court unanimously ruled in favor of Milligan, but split 5-4 on the actual rationale. Indeed, it announced its decision in April 1866, but did not issue its opinions until December. Justice David Davis (who had been Abraham Lincoln's campaign manager in 1860) wrote the opinion for the Court, and Chief Justice Salmon P. Chase (who had been Lincoln's Secretary of the Treasury) wrote the concurring opinion.

EX PARTE MILLIGAN
71 U.S. (1 Wall.) 2 (1866)

DAVIS, J. . . .

No graver question was ever considered by this court, nor one which more nearly concerns the rights of the whole people; for it is the birthright of every American citizen when charged with crime, to be tried and punished according to law. . . . The decision of this question does not depend on argument or judicial precedents, numerous and highly illustrative as they are. These precedents inform us of the extent of the struggle to preserve liberty and to relieve those in civil life from military trials. The founders of our government were familiar with the history of that struggle; and secured in a written constitution every right which the people had wrested from power during a contest of ages. . . . These securities for personal liberty thus embodied [in the Bill of Rights and in Article II, §2, which provides that "[t]he Trial of all Crimes, except in Cases of Impeachment, shall be by Jury"], were such as wisdom and experience had demonstrated to be necessary for the protection of those accused of crime. And so strong was the sense of the country of their importance, and so jealous were the people that these rights, highly prized, might be denied them by implication, that when the original Constitution was proposed for adoption it encountered severe opposition; and, but for the belief that it would be so amended as to embrace them, it would never have been ratified. . . .

If, in foreign invasion or civil war, the courts are actually closed, and it is impossible to administer criminal justice according to law, then, on the theatre of active military operations, where war really prevails, there is a necessity to furnish a substitute for the civil authority, thus overthrown, to preserve the safety of the army and society; and as no power is left but the military, it is allowed to govern by martial rule until the laws can have their free course. As necessity creates the rule, so it limits its duration; for, if this government is continued after the courts are reinstated, it is a gross usurpation of power. Martial rule can never exist where the courts are open, and in the proper and unobstructed exercise of their jurisdiction. It is also confined to the locality of actual war. Because, during the late Rebellion it could have been enforced in Virginia, where the national authority was overturned and the courts driven out, it does not follow that it should obtain in Indiana, where that authority was never disputed, and justice was always administered. And so in the case of a foreign invasion, martial rule may become a necessity in one state, when, in another, it would be "mere lawless violence." . . .

But it is said that the jurisdiction is complete under the "laws and usages of war." It can serve no useful purpose to inquire what those laws and usages are, whence they originated, where found, and on whom they operate; they can never be applied to citizens in states which have upheld the authority of the government, and where the courts are open and their process unobstructed. This court has judicial knowledge that in Indiana the Federal authority was always unopposed, and its courts always open to hear criminal accusations and redress grievances; and no usage of war could sanction a military trial there for any offence whatever of a citizen in civil life, in nowise connected with the military service. Congress could grant no such power; and to the honor of our national legislature be it said, it has never been provoked by the state of the country even to attempt its exercise. One of the plainest constitutional provisions was, therefore, infringed when Milligan was tried by a court not ordained and established by Congress, and not composed of judges appointed during good behavior.

[Chief Justice Chase, joined by three other Justices, agreed, in a concurring opinion, that Milligan was entitled to a trial in a civilian court, but for them the central issue was Congress's failure to authorize any deviations from the presumption that Americans were entitled to trial by jury even in time of war. Indeed, the opinion suggests that they read the habeas corpus act of March 3d, 1863, which gave the president power to suspend the writ, as affirmatively barring the military trial. Thus, although "[t]he first section authorized the suspension, during the Rebellion, of the writ of habeas corpus throughout the United States by the President[, t]he two next sections *limited this authority* in important respects" (emphasis added).]

CHASE, J., concurring. . . .

We think that Congress had power, though not exercised, to authorize the military commission which was held in Indiana.

Congress has power to raise and support armies; to provide and maintain a navy; to make rules for the government and regulation of the land and naval forces; and to provide for governing such part of the militia as may be in the service of the United States. It is not denied that the power to make rules for the government of the army and navy is a power to provide for trial and punishment by military courts without a jury. It has been so understood and exercised from the adoption of the Constitution to the present time.

Nor, in our judgment, does the fifth, or any other amendment, abridge that power. "Cases arising in the land and naval forces, or in the militia in actual service in time of war or public danger," are expressly excepted from the fifth amendment, "that no person shall be held to answer for a capital or otherwise infamous crime, unless on a presentment or indictment of a grand jury," and it is admitted that the exception applies to the other amendments as well as to the fifth. . . . It is not necessary to attempt any precise definition of the boundaries of [Congress's] power. But may it not be said that government includes protection and defence as well as the regulation of internal administration? And is it impossible to imagine cases in which citizens conspiring or attempting the destruction or great injury of the national forces may be subjected by Congress to military trial and punishment in the just exercise of this undoubted constitutional power? Congress is but the agent of the nation, and does not the security of individuals against the abuse of this, as of every other power, depend on the intelligence and virtue of the people, on their zeal for public and private liberty, upon official responsibility secured by law, and upon the frequency of elections, rather than upon doubtful constructions of legislative powers? . . .

Congress has the power not only to raise and support and govern armies but to declare war. It has, therefore, the power to provide by law for carrying on war. This power necessarily extends to all legislation essential to the prosecution of war with vigor and success. . . . The power to make the necessary laws is in Congress: the power to execute in the President. Both powers imply many subordinate and auxiliary powers. Each includes all authorities essential to its due exercise. But neither can the President, in war more than in peace, intrude upon the proper authority of Congress, nor Congress upon the proper authority of the President. . . . Congress cannot direct the conduct of campaigns, nor can the President, or any commander under him, without the sanction of Congress, institute tribunals for the trial and punishment of offences, either of soldiers or civilians, unless in cases of a controlling necessity, which justifies what it compels, or at least insures acts of indemnity from the justice of the legislature.

We by no means assert that Congress can establish and apply the laws of war where no war has been declared or exists. Where peace exists the laws of peace must prevail. What we do maintain is, that when the nation is involved in war, and some portions of the country are invaded, and all are exposed to invasion, it is within the power of Congress to determine in what states or district such great and imminent public danger exists as justifies the authorization of military tribunals for the trial of crimes and offences against the discipline or security of the army or against the public safety.

In Indiana, for example, at the time of the arrest of Milligan and his co-conspirators, it is established by the papers in the record, that the state was a military district, was the theatre of military operations, had been actually invaded, and was constantly threatened with invasion. It appears, also, that a powerful secret association, composed of citizens and others, existed within the state, under military organization, conspiring against the draft, and plotting insurrection, the liberation of the prisoners of war at various depots, the seizure of the state and national arsenals, armed cooperation with the enemy, and war against the national government.

We cannot doubt that, in such a time of public danger, Congress had power, under the Constitution, to provide for the organization of a military commission, and for trial by that commission of persons engaged in this conspiracy. The fact that the Federal courts were open was regarded by Congress as a sufficient reason for not exercising the power; but that fact could not deprive Congress of the right to exercise it. Those courts might be open and undisturbed in the execution of their functions, and yet wholly incompetent to avert threatened danger, or to punish, with adequate promptitude and certainty, the guilty conspirators.

Discussion

1. Is it a central "fact of this case" that the War was actually over by the time the Supreme Court reached its decision, even if Milligan had been arrested while the War was still going on (though not, at least actively, in Indiana)? That is, are you confident that the Court would have (or *should* have) been so quick to protect Milligan's rights if the war were still ongoing?

2. *Confiscation of property.* Five years after *Milligan,* in Miller v. U.S., 78 U.S. (11 Wall.) 268 (1871), the Court upheld the constitutionality of the Confiscation Acts of 1861 and 1862, which allowed ex parte seizure of property belonging to persons believed to have supported the rebellion. Justice Strong wrote that the confiscation statutes "were not enacted under the municipal power of Congress to legislate for the punishment of crimes against the sovereignty of the United States" but were "an exercise of the war powers of the government," and so "are not affected by the restrictions imposed by the fifth and sixth amendments."

> [T]he power to declare war involves the power to prosecute it by all means and in any manner in which war may be legitimately prosecuted. It therefore includes the right to seize and confiscate all property of an enemy and to dispose of it at the will of the captor. . . . [This right] has no reference whatever to the personal guilt of the owner of confiscated property, and the act of confiscation is not a proceeding against him. The confiscation is not because of crime, but because of the relation of the property to the opposing belligerent, a relation in which it has been brought in consequence of its ownership. It is immaterial to it whether the owner be an alien or a friend, or even a citizen or subject of the power that attempts to appropriate the property. . . . The whole doctrine of confiscation is built upon the foundation that it is an instrument of coercion, which, by depriving an enemy of property within reach of his power, whether within his territory or without it, impairs his ability to resist the confiscating government, while at the same time it furnishes to that government means for carrying on the war. Hence any property which the enemy can use, either by actual appropriation or by the exercise of control over its owner, or which the adherents of the enemy have the power of devoting to the enemy's use, is a proper subject of confiscation.

Compare *Miller* with *Ex Parte Milligan.* Is there an important difference between confiscation of property during time of war and trying persons by military tribunals in places where the courts are open? (Does *Miller,* incidentally, suggest that the Emancipation Proclamation would have been an easy case had it been authorized by Congress?)

3. Does it make a difference, with regard to Chief Justice Chase's analysis, whether Congress overtly *limited* presidential authority to establish military tribunals or simply was silent as to that possibility? In his influential concurrence in Sawyer v. Youngstown Sheet and Tube Co. v. Sawyer, 343 U.S. 579 (1952), written

some 85 years later, Justice Robert Jackson distinguished (1) assertions of presidential power where Congress affirmatively authorized the action, where "his authority is at its maximum, for it includes all that he possesses in his own right plus all that Congress can delegate"; (2) assertions of presidential power where Congress had been silent on the matter in question where "he can only rely upon his own independent powers"; and (3) assertions of presidential power where Congress has attempted to limit the president's actions. In the third case, Jackson argued, the President's power "is at its lowest ebb, for then he can rely only upon his own constitutional powers minus any constitutional powers of Congress over the matter. Courts can sustain exclusive presidential control in such a case only by disabling the Congress from acting upon the subject." See the discussion of *Youngstown* in Chapter 5, infra.

4. The issues raised by the two opinions in *Milligan* are obviously of far more than historical interest. Do they entail, for example, that (at least) U.S. citizens who are detained within the United States because of suspicions that they are linked with terrorism are entitled to (prompt?) trials in civilian courts (as against military commissions) so long as these courts are "generally open" in the states in which the suspects are detained? Or does any such right depend entirely on whether Congress has authorized the president to forego such trials to more effectively carry out "the global war against terror"? See Hamdi v. Rumsfeld, 542 U.S. 507 (2004), discussed in Chapter 5, infra.

F. The Legal Tender Cases and the Constitutionality of Paper Money

The Civil War was notable for several innovations, not the least of which was the widespread introduction of paper money as legal tender. The Founders were generally hostile to the institution of paper currency. The 1787 Constitution explicitly prohibited states from emitting "bills of credit,"[87] a term generally understood at the time of the Revolution to refer to paper money.[88] During the Revolutionary War the Continental Congress had issued bills of credit

> at an accelerating rate, until by 1780 $100 in paper money was worth only $2.50 in specie. Depreciation continued until in 1781 paper money ceased to circulate as currency — whence the phrase "not worth a continental." The states, too issued, paper money, and it too, depreciated, with Virginia currency reaching 0.1 percent of its former value by December 1781.[89]

A provision in the Report on the Committee of Detail at the Philadelphia Convention would have given Congress the power to "borrow money, and emit bills on the credit of the United States." Gouverneur Morris moved to strike the power to emit bills of credit, which passed 9-2. Madison's notes suggest that most of the speakers were strongly opposed to paper money.[90] Although, as Professor Dam writes, "it

---

87. Article I, §10. The states were also prohibited from coining money.
88. Kenneth W. Dam, The Legal Tender Cases, 1981 Sup. Ct. Rev. 367, 387.
89. Id. at 383.
90. 2 Farrand, at 310. Madison explained his vote to strike based on his understanding that omitting the language "would not disable the Govt from the use of public notes as far as they could be safe & proper; & would only cut off the pretext for a paper currency and particularly for making the bills a

is difficult to escape the conclusion that the Framers intended to prohibit" paper money,[91] the Federal government soon began issuing bills of credit (though not as legal tender), beginning with the War of 1812.[92] This practice continued up to the Civil War, when the constitutionality of paper money became an important issue, in a series of three decisions collectively referred to as The Legal Tender Cases.

The Legal Tender Cases arose out of decisions by Salmon P. Chase, Lincoln's Secretary of the Treasury, about how to finance the Civil War. Chase was a strong believer in hard currency, and as Treasury Secretary he insisted that all government debts be paid in gold specie (coin). Chase had attempted to raise most of the funds through the sale of interest-bearing securities that would bring gold specie to the Treasury. However, his strategy backfired by the end of 1861 when a series of Union defeats led banks to suspend payments of specie. With Union expenses mounting, Chase reluctantly agreed to issue demand notes to pay salaries and suppliers. One could not redeem them in gold or silver but only in bonds that paid six percent interest. More important, the Act of February 25, 1862, authorizing the notes included a clause stating that the notes were to be "lawful money and a legal tender in payment of all debts, public and private, within the United States." Because the new notes were green, they became known as "greenbacks." About $431 million was issued by the end of the Civil War, although by 1864 the Treasury was able to finance the war mostly through taxes and bond sales.

By the end of the Civil War it was generally accepted that the federal government could issue bills of credit. The controversial aspect of the greenbacks was that they were also "legal tender" by law, which meant that creditors had to accept them in payment of debts. Inflationary pressures made gold dollars worth much more than their equivalents in greenbacks. Debtors naturally sought to pay contractual obligations in greenbacks instead of gold coins.

In Hepburn v. Griswold, 8 Wall. 603 (1870), the Supreme Court held that Congress lacked the power to make paper money legal tender for debts preexisting the 1862 Act. An opinion for four justices was written by Salmon P. Chase, who had been appointed Chief Justice in 1864. He argued that there was no "express grant of legislative power to make any description of credit currency a legal tender in payment of debts."[93] He therefore considered whether, under *McCulloch*, the power was implied. He rejected the argument that the power was implied from the power to carry on war. This argument proved too much, because almost all congressional powers "involve the use of money."

> The power to establish post-offices and post-roads, for example, involves the collection and disbursement of a great revenue. Is not the power to make notes a legal tender as clearly incidental to this power as to the war power? . . .

---

tender either for public and private debts." In other words, Madison believed that the Government would be able to "borrow money on the credit of the United States" through sale of interest bearing bonds and other securities; but it could not issue paper money or make it legal tender. Madison also focused particularly on the use of paper money as legal tender, a distinction that not all of the other framers made. Dam, at 384-387.

91. Dam, at 389.

92. Id. at 389-390.

93. Although the obvious candidate today would be the power "[t]o coin Money [and] regulate the Value thereof" in Art. 1, §8, cl. 5, it was generally accepted at the time that this clause referred only to coins—i.e., objects made of metal—and not to paper money. Dam, at 291. This interpretation was justified by the Counterfeiting Clause, Art. I, §8, cl. 6, which distinguishes "Securities" from "[the] current Coin of the United States."

> The argument . . . carries the doctrine of implied powers very far beyond any extent hitherto given to it. It asserts that [whatever] in any degree promotes an end within the scope of a general power, whether, in the correct sense of the word, appropriate or not, may be done in the exercise of an implied power. . . .

Chase argued that the government could have raised sufficient funds to conduct the war by issuing notes backed by government bonds without making them legal tender. Even if there was some advantage to making the notes legal tender for new debts, there was no advantage to "compelling creditors to receive them in satisfaction of pre-existing debts." Nor could the act "be upheld as such, if, while facilitating in some degree the circulation of the notes, it debases and injures the currency in its proper use to a much greater degree." Finally, Chase argued, the act was not "consistent with the spirit of the Constitution." Making the notes legal tender interfered with preexisting obligations of contract. Although the contracts clause applied to the states and not to the federal government, Chase argued,

> we think it clear that those who framed and those who adopted the Constitution, intended that the spirit of this prohibition should pervade the entire body of legislation, and that the justice which the Constitution was ordained to establish was not thought by them to be compatible with legislation of an opposite tendency. In other words, we cannot doubt that a law not made in pursuance of an express power, which necessarily and in its direct operation impairs the obligation of contracts, is inconsistent with the spirit of the Constitution.

The legal tender provision was also inconsistent with the spirit of the just compensation clause, which was applicable against the federal government. Finally, the act deprived plaintiffs of their property without due process of law contrary to the Fifth Amendment, because

> [a] very large proportion of the property of civilized men exists in the form of contracts. These contracts almost invariably stipulate for the payment of money. . . . [C]ontracts in the United States, prior to the act under consideration, for the payment of money, were contracts to pay the sums specified in gold and silver coin. And it is beyond doubt that the holders of these contracts were and are as fully entitled to the protection of this constitutional provision as the holders of any other description of property.
>
> But it may be said that the holders of no description of property are protected by it from legislation which incidentally only impairs its value. And it may be urged in illustration that the holders of stock in a turnpike, a bridge, or a manufacturing corporation, or an insurance company, or a bank, cannot invoke its protection against legislation which, by authorizing similar works or corporations, reduces its price in the market. But all this does not appear to meet the real difficulty. In the cases mentioned the injury is purely contingent and incidental. In the case we are considering it is direct and inevitable.
>
> If in the cases mentioned the holders of the stock were required by law to convey it on demand to any one who should think fit to offer half its value for it, the analogy would be more obvious. No one probably could be found to contend that an act enforcing the acceptance of fifty or seventy-five acres of land in satisfaction of a contract to convey a hundred would not come within the prohibition against arbitrary privation of property.
>
> We confess ourselves unable to perceive any solid distinction between such an act and an act compelling all citizens to accept, in satisfaction of all contracts for money,

half or three-quarters or any other proportion less than the whole of the value actually due, according to their terms. It is difficult to conceive what act would take private property without process of law if such an act would not. . . .

It is not surprising that amid the tumult of the late civil war, and under the influence of apprehensions for the safety of the Republic almost universal, different views, never before entertained by American statesmen or jurists, were adopted by many. The time was not favorable to considerate reflection upon the constitutional limits of legislative or executive authority. If power was assumed from patriotic motives, the assumption found ready justification in patriotic hearts. Many who doubted yielded their doubts; many who did not doubt were silent. Some who were strongly averse to making government notes a legal tender felt themselves constrained to acquiesce in the views of the advocates of the measure. Not a few who then insisted upon its necessity, or acquiesced in that view, have, since the return of peace, and under the influence of the calmer time, reconsidered their conclusions, and now concur in those which we have just announced. These conclusions seem to us to be fully sanctioned by the letter and spirit of the Constitution.[94]

Justice Miller dissented, joined by Justices Swayne and Davis:

The legal tender clauses of the statutes under consideration were placed emphatically by those who enacted them, upon their necessity to the further borrowing of money and maintaining the army and navy. It was done reluctantly and with hesitation, and only after the necessity had been demonstrated and had become imperative. . . .

[T]his law was a necessity in the most stringent sense in which that word can be used. But if we adopt the construction of Chief Justice Marshall . . . [c]an it be said that this provision did not conduce towards the purpose of borrowing money, of paying debts, of raising armies, of suppressing insurrection? or that it was not calculated to effect these objects? or that it was not useful and essential to that end? Can it be said that this was not among the choice of means, if not the only means, which were left to Congress to carry on this war for national existence?

Miller also rejected Chase's Fifth Amendment argument:

The argument is too vague for my perception, by which the indirect effect of a great public measure, in depreciating the value of lands, stocks, bonds, and other contracts, renders such a law invalid as taking private property for public use, or as depriving the owner of it without due course of law.

A declaration of war with a maritime power would thus be unconstitutional, because the value of every ship abroad is lessened twenty-five or thirty per cent, and those at home almost as much. The abolition of the tariff on iron or sugar would in like manner destroy the furnaces, and sink the capital employed in the manufacture of these articles. Yet no statesman, however warm an advocate of high tariff, has claimed that to abolish such duties would be unconstitutional as taking private property.

If the principle be sound, every successive issue of government bonds during the war was void, because by increasing the public debt it made those already in private hands less valuable.

This whole argument of the injustice of the law . . . and of its opposition to the spirit of the Constitution, is too abstract and intangible for application to courts of justice, and is, above all, dangerous as a ground on which to declare the legislation of Congress

---

94. Justice Grier, writing separately, held as a matter of statutory construction that the legal tender clause of the 1862 Act did not apply to preexisting debts, but agreed that if it were so construed it would be unconstitutional.

void by the decision of a court. It would authorize this court to enforce theoretical views of the genius of the government, or vague notions of the spirit of the Constitution and of abstract justice, by declaring void laws which did not square with those views. It substitutes our ideas of policy for judicial construction, an undefined code of ethics for the Constitution, and a court of justice for the National legislature. . . .

[A]re we . . . to disturb contracts, to declare the law void, because the necessity for its enactment does not appear so strong to us as it did to Congress, or so clear as it was to other courts?

Such is not my idea of the relative functions of the legislative and judicial departments of the government. Where there is a choice of means the selection is with Congress, not the court. If the act to be considered is in any sense essential to the execution of an acknowledged power, the degree of that necessity is for the legislature and not for the court to determine.

The result in *Hepburn* was short-lived. In April 1869, shortly after President Grant took office, the Republican Congress had passed a bill increasing the size of the Supreme Court from eight to nine. Justice Grier, a Democrat, resigned on December 15, 1869, effective on January 31, 1870, giving President Grant two new appointments to the Supreme Court. On February 7, 1870, the decision in *Hepburn* was announced. (The votes were taken and opinions written prior to Justice Grier's resignation. Query whether we would today count the vote of a justice in similar circumstances.) On the same day, President Grant nominated William Strong and Joseph P. Bradley to fill the two vacant Supreme Court seats.[95] In May 1871, the Court decided Knox v. Lee, 12 Wall. 457 (1871), which held that the 1862 legal tender legislation was constitutional both as to preexisting and subsequent debts. Strong and Bradley joined the three dissenters in *Hepburn* to form a new five-person majority.

Justice Strong's majority opinion argued that the legal tender provisions were justified by the utmost necessity: "The public treasury was nearly empty, and the credit of the government, if not stretched to its utmost tension, had become nearly exhausted."[96] However, Strong also offered a novel theory of federal power that seemed to go well beyond *McCulloch:*

[I]t is not indispensable to the existence of any power claimed for the Federal government that it can be found specified in the words of the Constitution, or clearly and

---

95. Strong and Bradley were actually Grant's second choices. He first tried to nominate Attorney General Ebenezer R. Hoar and former War Secretary Edwin M. Stanton. Although the Senate quickly confirmed Stanton, he died on December 24. The Senate rejected Grant's other nomination on February 3, thus guaranteeing that there would be no Justice Hoar.

96. In his dissent, Chief Justice Chase explained that while he was Secretary of the Treasury he was strongly opposed to issuing greenbacks as legal tender, but "thought it indispensably necessary that the authority to issue these notes, should be granted by Congress. The passage of the bill was delayed, if not jeoparded, by the difference of opinion which prevailed on the question of making them a legal tender." That is why, Chase argued, he had told the Ways and Means Committee that the legislation was "necessary." Chase added that

Examination and reflection under more propitious circumstances have satisfied him that this opinion was erroneous, and he does not hesitate to declare it. He would do so, just as unhesitatingly, if his favor to the legal tender clause had been at that time decided, and his opinion as to the constitutionality of the measure clear.

Given this sequence of events, should Chief Justice Chase have recused himself in *Hepburn* and *Knox?* If he had, the constitutionality of the legal tender clause would have been upheld. Should this have made any difference to his decision?

directly traceable to some one of the specified powers. Its existence may be deduced fairly from more than one of the substantive powers expressly defined, or from them all combined. It is allowable to group together any number of them and infer from them all that the power claimed has been conferred. Such a treatment of the Constitution is recognized by its own provisions. This is well illustrated in its language respecting the writ of habeas corpus. The power to suspend the privilege of that writ is not expressly given, nor can it be deduced from any one of the particularized grants of power. Yet it is provided that the privileges of the writ shall not be suspended except in certain defined contingencies. This is no express grant of power. It is a restriction. But it shows irresistibly that somewhere in the Constitution power to suspend the privilege of the writ was granted, either by some one or more of the specifications of power, or by them all combined. And, that important powers were understood by the people who adopted the Constitution to have been created by it, powers not enumerated, and not included incidentally in any one of those enumerated, is shown by the amendments [in the Bill of Rights]. . . . They tend plainly to show that, in the judgment of those who adopted the Constitution, there were powers created by it, neither expressly specified nor deducible from any one specified power, or ancillary to it alone, but which grew out of the aggregate of powers conferred upon the government, or out of the sovereignty instituted. Most of these amendments are denials of power which had not been expressly granted, and which cannot be said to have been necessary and proper for carrying into execution any other powers. Such, for example, is the prohibition of any laws respecting the establishment of religion, prohibiting the free exercise thereof, or abridging the freedom of speech or of the press.

Justice Bradley, concurring, also emphasized the broad powers of the federal government:

The doctrine so long contended for that the Federal Union was a mere compact of States, and that the States, if they chose, might annul or disregard the acts of the National legislature, or might secede from the Union at their pleasure, and that the General government had no power to coerce them into submission to the Constitution, should be regarded as definitely and forever overthrown. This has been finally effected by the National power, as it had often been before, by overwhelming argument.

   The United States is not only a government, but it is a National government, and the only government in this country that has the character of nationality. . . .

   Such being the character of the General government, it seems to be a self-evident proposition that it is invested with all those inherent and implied powers which, at the time of adopting the Constitution, were generally considered to belong to every government as such, and as being essential to the exercise of its functions.

The decision in *Knox* was grounded on the emergency situation facing the Union during the Civil War. The decision was extended a decade later in the last of the Legal Tender Cases, Julliard v. Greenman, 110 U.S. 421 (1884). After the Civil War, the government attempted to contract the money supply by retiring greenbacks from circulation, to fight the inflation caused by the Civil War and allow resumption of specie payments in gold for U.S. currency and bank notes. This policy produced an ongoing conflict over the money supply. In 1878 Congress restricted any further withdrawal of greenbacks and directed the Treasury to keep them permanently in circulation; the Treasury complied by issuing greenbacks in new denominations. When the 1878 Act was challenged in *Julliard,* The Supreme Court held, 8-1, that Congress could issue legal tender notes in peacetime whether out of necessity or convenience. Justice Gray's majority opinion argued that "the question whether . . . it is . . . wise and expedient to resort to this means, is a political question, to be determined by congress when the question of exigency arises, and not a judicial question, to be afterwards passed upon by the courts."

Justice Field, in dissent, argued that

> If there be anything in the history of the constitution which can be established with moral certainty, it is that the framers of that instrument intended to prohibit the issue of legal-tender notes both by the general government and by the states, and thus prevent interference with the contracts of private parties. . . .
>
> From the decision of the court I see only evil likely to follow. There have been times within the memory of all of us when the legal-tender notes of the United States were not exchangeable for more than one-half of their nominal value. The possibility of such depreciation will always attend paper money. This inborn infirmity no mere legislative declaration can cure. If congress has the power to make the notes a legal tender and to pass as money or its equivalent, why should not a sufficient amount be issued to pay the bonds of the United States as they mature? Why pay interest on the millions of dollars of bonds now due when congress can in one day make the money to pay the principal? And why should there be any restraint upon unlimited appropriations by the government for all imaginary schemes of public improvement, if the printing-press can furnish the money that is needed for them?

Discussion

1. Put in contemporary terms, Justice Field feared popular control over the money supply, which could not only wreck the economy, but seriously affect the market value of property and contractual rights. During the period from Reconstruction to the New Deal the struggle between advocates of "hard" and "soft" money was one of the central issues in American political life. The money supply has largely receded from day-to-day political struggle because of the delegation of monetary policy to the Federal Reserve Board. By design the Board's members are relatively isolated from political accountability; their oversight of national monetary policy is justified by their purportedly superior economic expertise.

Was Justice Field right that control over the currency is too important to be left to ordinary political processes? Was Justice Gray right that this question is inherently political and therefore should be left to whatever devices a democracy creates? In what way is the money supply more or less deserving of protection from popular will than the right to freedom of speech? The right against cruel and unusual punishments? The right to abortion? Does the subsequent creation of the Federal Reserve Board support or undercut Field's argument about the dangers of majority politics?

2. Was it appropriate under our constitutional system for President Grant to seek as new Justices persons who would be likely to vote to overturn *Hepburn,* as both Strong and Bradley did? Or should he have appointed them simply on the basis of their presumed professional stature and been content to discover only when *Knox* was issued what their views were on this central issue of the hour? Even if Grant was permitted to select them on the basis of their predicted vote, did Justices Strong and Bradley have any obligation to confound this expectation, as it were, and to respect *Hepburn* as recent precedent, perhaps to safeguard the independence of the Court or dispel any perception among the general populace that constitutional interpretation is indeed simply a function of who happens to be on the Court at a particular

time? See the discussion of precedent in Casey, infra, Chapter 8. Does your answer depend on your perception of how bad the consequences of *Hepburn* would have been (either in 1870 or in later years) if the United States had been prevented from making paper money legal tender? Note that President Grant was able to appoint two new Justices to the Supreme Court because the Reconstruction Congress manipulated the size of the Supreme Court between 1866 and 1869 to prevent Andrew Johnson from making any appointments.[97] In July 1866 Congress effectively shrank the size of the Court by providing that retirements of sitting Justices would not create a vacancy until the total number of Justices was reduced to seven. An April 1869 Act not only increased the number of Justices to nine, but also offered salary for life to any Justice who resigned having reached the age of 70 with ten years of service. This provision was specifically aimed at inducing the retirements of Justices Nelson and Grier; Grier almost immediately retired at the end of 1869, Nelson took until 1872. Were these Congressional actions appropriate under our constitutional system? Consider this question in the light of the controversy surrounding President Roosevelt's court-packing plan of 1937, discussed infra. Or consider the possibility that the current Congress might pass a law offering especially generous pensions to any justice with more than 25 years service (currently Justice Stevens) or older than 80 (also Justice Stevens) who retires by January 1, 2007, with the "deal" expiring on that date.

3. Justice Strong's and Justice Bradley's broad statements about federal power in Knox v. Lee reflect the victory of Radical Republican forces in Congress during Reconstruction, the consequences of which will pervade the next chapter. Nevertheless, if their views are taken seriously, doesn't the federal government have general power to do whatever any "sovereign" governments have traditionally done? Note that while Justice Strong engages in the rather implausible fiction that inherent powers always existed and formed the central justification for the Bill of Rights, Justice Bradley grounds his argument on the failed secession of the southern states. Under his theory, the justification for the federal government's expanded regulatory role would not be the gradual nationalization of commerce, but the reconstruction of the United States as a nation in the aftermath of the Civil War. What, exactly, is wrong with his argument? Do you agree that the correctness or incorrectness of the "compact of states theory" can be settled by war?

4. How troubling should proponents of original intention find *Knox* and *Julliard*? Is it more troublesome for courts to disobey original intention with respect to structural concerns, like the powers of the federal government, or with respect to individual rights concerns, like property rights? If you think it *does* make a difference, how does one decide which is involved in the Legal Tender Cases?

Robert Bork, who has argued that adherence to original intent is the very definition of constitutionalism, notes that *Hepburn* "may well have been correct," though he bitterly attacks Chase's opinion because of its reliance on evanescent notions of constitutional "spirit" and "justice," concepts that he believes that judges are not authorized to act upon.[98] Assuming that fidelity to original intent

---

97. Charles Fairman, Reconstruction and Reunion 1864-68, Part One (6 History of the Supreme Court of the United States) 161 (1971). By an 1863 Act of Congress, the Supreme Court had been increased from nine to ten seats, but Justice Catron died in 1865, leaving only nine Justices.

98. See Robert Bork, The Tempting of America 34-36 (1990).

would indeed compel the result in *Hepburn*, what consequences should this have for us today? Could an originalist argue when people have placed serious reliance on an incorrect decision for many years, it is immune from reversal? While emphasizing that constitutional precedents deemed incorrect have frequently been overruled (including *Hepburn*), Judge Bork also noted that a decision, albeit "clearly incorrect," might "nevertheless have become so embedded in the life of the nation, so accepted by the society, so fundamental to the private and public expectations of individuals and institutions, that the result should not be changed now. This is a judgment addressed to the prudence of a court, but it is not the less valid for that."[99] Under this theory, *Knox* and *Julliard*, though wrongly decided, should not later be reversed, at least by a "prudent" court, because people have grown accustomed to having paper money serve as legal tender for all debts, public and private. Why, precisely, would one trust judges to make appropriate judgments of "prudence" if one does not trust them to consider the "spirit" of the Constitution, to reflect on the demands of "fundamental fairness," or to make social policy?

Bork's prudential argument is based on a paradigm of incorrect cases that later become "correct" through years of reliance. But what about the opposite situation — a correct decision that remains untouched for many years? Suppose that *Hepburn* had not been overruled in *Knox* and *Julliard*, but had continued as good law up to the 1930s. Would this mean that the United States would have been powerless to leave the gold standard and let its currency float, as it did in during the Great Depression? See Norman v. Baltimore & Ohio R.R. and United States v. Bankers Trust Co., 294 U.S. 240 (1935); Nortz v. United States, 294 U.S. 317 (1935); Perry v. United States, 294 U.S. 330 (1935) (collectively referred to as the Gold Clause Cases, and upholding the federal government's economic policies against constitutional challenge). Note that the contemporary global economy depends heavily on the very sorts of currency decisions by governments and central banks that would have horrified the Framers. Does Bork's theory suggest that once original intention has been confirmed by subsequent judicial decision, it may never be abandoned short of Article V amendment? Put another way, are defenders of originalism fortunate that cases like *Hepburn* have been overturned by others not equally committed to originalism so that originalists can offer arguments for preserving the incorrect decisions based on considerations of prudence?

99. Id. at 158.

Chapter 4

From Reconstruction to the New Deal: 1866-1934

This chapter covers more years than the Marshall and Taney Courts combined and includes the Chief Justiceships of Salmon Chase (1864-1873), Morrison Waite (1874-1888), Melville Fuller (1888-1910), Edward White (1910-1921), William Taft (1921-1930), and the earlier years of Charles Evans Hughes (1930-1941). During these years, the United States underwent many changes in technology, industry, economic and social structure, and legal consciousness.

I. The Reconstruction Constitution

A. History of the Adoption of the Fourteenth Amendment[1]

On January 31, 1865, the Thirty-Eighth Congress proposed the Thirteenth Amendment — "Neither slavery nor involuntary servitude, except as a punishment for crime whereof the party shall have been duly convicted, shall exist within the United States, or any place subject to their jurisdiction" — ratification of which was completed when Georgia, on December 6, 1865, became the twenty-seventh of the 36 states to give its assent.[2] The potential unclarity of either "slavery" or "involuntary servitude" may be illustrated by the fact that many of the formerly Confederate states, eight of which had ratified the Amendment, adopted so-called Black Codes that were clearly designed to maintain, as much as possible, the subordinated status of the ostentisbly freed slaves. The codes

> perpetuated or created many discriminations in the criminal law by applying unequal penalties to Negroes for recognized offenses and by specifying offenses for Negroes only. Laws which prohibited Negroes from keeping weapons or from selling liquor were typical of the latter. Examples of discriminatory penalties were the laws which

---

1. The following materials are based primarily on a study by Alexander Bickel. See Bickel, The Original Understanding and the Segregation Decision, 69 Harv. L. Rev. 1 (1955). See also Charles Fairman, Reconstruction and Reunion, 1864-1888 (pt. 1), in 6 History of the Supreme Court of the United States (Freund ed., 1971); Michael Vorenberg, Final Freedom: The Civil War, the Abolition of Slavery, and the Thirteenth Amendment (2001); Alex Tsesis, The Thirteenth Amendment and American Freedom: A Legal History (2004).

2. This sentence is misleadingly simple. See Note: The Unusual Procedural History of the Fourteenth Amendment, infra at 310-319.

made it a capital offense for a Negro to rape a white woman, or to assault a white woman with intent to rape. . . . In addition to the discriminations of the criminal laws, post-war black codes hedged in the Negroes with a series of restraints on their business dealings of even the simplest form. Though in many states the Negro could acquire property, Mississippi put sharp limitations on that right.[3] But most restrictive were the provisions concerning contracts for personal service. Many statutes called for specific enforcement of labor contracts against freedmen, with provisions to facilitate capture should a freedman try to escape. Vagrancy laws made it a misdemeanor for a Negro to be without a long-term contract of employment; conviction was followed by a fine, payable by a white man who could then set the criminal to work for him until the benefactor had been completely reimbursed for his generosity.[4]

Section 2 of the Thirteenth Amendment declared that "Congress shall have power to enforce this article by appropriate legislation," and the Black Codes underscored for most members of Congress the necessity for federal legislation if the promise of the Amendment was to be achieved. Ultimately the Congress moved beyond legislation to the proposal of a second "Reconstruction Amendment," the Fourteenth Amendment, proposed by the Thirty-Ninth Congress in June 1866 and declared ratified two years later in July 1868.[5] Any inquiry into the intended purpose or meaning of the later Amendment must begin, however, with consideration of earlier legislation passed in the shadow of the Black Codes and the Thirteenth Amendment.

The Civil Rights Act of 1866

A key phrase in the dispute over the scope of the Thirty-Ninth Congress's concern with racial discrimination was the prohibition of discrimination in "civil rights or immunities" — the "civil rights formula" — which first appeared in the ill-fated Freedman's Bureau Bill[6] and reappeared in the Civil Rights Bill, introduced in the Senate in January 1866. Section 1 of the Civil Rights Bill provided:

---

3. As a matter of fact, the Mississippi legislature rejected the Amendment on December 4, 1865. This obviously did not prevent its being declared part of the Constitution two days later, when Georgia became the twenty-seventh of the 36 states in the Union to ratify. As a matter of fact, many states "ratified" the Amendment even after its formal addition to the Constitution, beginning with Oregon on December 8, 1865 and extending to Kentucky's March 18, 1976, ratification (after rejecting it 111 years before on February 24, 1865). Mississippi has apparently never engaged in such a symbolic ratification. See *http://www.law.emory.edu/FEDERAL/usconst/amend.html#art-13*.

4. John Frank and Robert Munro, The Original Understanding of "Equal Protection of the Laws," 1972 Wash. U. L.Q. 421, 445-446.

5. Again, see Note: The Unusual Procedural History of the Fourteenth Amendment, infra at 310-319.

6. The Freedman's Bureau Bill required the president to "extend military protection" in the rebellious states whenever Negroes were denied, inter alia, "civil rights or immunities belonging to white persons." The paucity of debate over the formula is probably explained by the bill's geographic limitation. It posed no danger to northern Democrats and conservative Republicans who, indeed, hoped that they could appease the Radical Republicans by acceding to the measure and avoiding a confrontation between President Johnson and the Congress. Their effort failed. Johnson vetoed the bill and the conservatives refused to provide the votes necessary to override the veto. As you study the materials in this section concerning Reconstruction, you should ask yourself what advantages the Constitution gave those resisting change (such as the presidential veto power) and the dilemmas the Constitution concomitantly posed to those advocating change. Recall in this context the discussion in Chapter 1 of similar questions with regard to the Articles of Confederation.

That all persons born in the United States and not subject to any foreign power, excluding Indians not taxed, are hereby declared to be citizens of the United States; that there shall be no discrimination in civil rights or immunities among the inhabitants of any State or Territory of the United States on account of race, color, or previous condition of slavery; but the inhabitants of every race and color, without regard to any previous condition of slavery or involuntary servitude, except as a punishment for crime whereof the party shall have been duly convicted, shall have the same right, in every State and Territory in the United States, to make and enforce contracts, to sue, be parties, and give evidence, to inherit, purchase, lease, sell, hold, and convey real and personal property, and to full and equal benefit of all laws and proceedings for the security of person and property, as is enjoyed by white citizens, and shall be subject to like punishment, pains, and penalties, and to none other, any law, statute, ordinance, regulation, or custom, to the contrary notwithstanding.

Almost without exception, supporters of the bill asserted that the only rights it secured were those specifically enumerated in section 1 and that a broader construction was not intended. For example, Lyman Trumbull (Republican, Illinois), the bill's Senate sponsor, explained that section 1 would ensure for blacks "the rights of citizens"[7]: "[t]he great fundamental rights set forth in this bill: the right to acquire property, the right to go and come at pleasure, the right to enforce rights in the courts, to make contracts, and to inherit and dispose of property." When James A. McDougall (Democrat, California), fearful that the phrase encompassed suffrage, pressed for a definition of "civil rights," Trumbull responded by quoting the enumeration of rights in section 1 and assuring him that there was no reference to "political" rights (i.e., the right to vote).

Still, Democrats and conservative Republicans objected vigorously that the phrase "civil rights" might well be construed much more broadly than its sponsors said they intended. Willard Saulsbury (Democrat, Delaware), also fearful of black suffrage, responded to Trumball's disclaimer of "political" rights:

> The question is not what the senator means, but what is the legitimate meaning and import of the terms employed in the bill. . . . What are civil rights? What are the rights which you, I, or any citizen of this country enjoy? . . . [H]ere you use a generic term which in its most comprehensive signification includes every species of right that man can enjoy other than those the foundation of which rests exclusively in nature and in the law of nature.

And Edward Cowan, a conservative Republican from Pennsylvania, warned about segregation:

> Now, as I understand the meaning and intent of this bill, it is that there shall be no discrimination made between the inhabitants of the several States of this Union, none in any way. In Pennsylvania, for the greater convenience of the people, and for the greater convenience, I may say, of both classes of the people, in certain districts the Legislature has provided schools for colored children, has discriminated as between the two classes of children. We put the African children in this school house, . . . and educate them there as best we can. Is this amendment to the Constitution of

---

7. Note that the first sentence of the Bill in effect overrules *Dred Scott.* Where did Congress get the power to do this? From the Thirteenth Amendment?

the United States abolishing slavery[8] to break up that system which Pennsylvania has adopted for the education of her white and colored children? Are the school directors who carry out that law and who make this distinction between classes of children to be punished for a violation of this statute of the United States? To me it is monstrous.

No one responded to Cowan's point, nor indeed was the issue of segregation ever squarely faced in the debates. And despite objections that its language was too broad, the bill passed in the Senate, 33 to 12.

James F. Wilson (Iowa), a Radical Republican, presented the bill to the House of Representatives with assurances of its limited objectives:

[Section 1] provides for the equality of citizens of the United States in the enjoyment of "civil rights and immunities." What do these terms mean? Do they mean that in all things civil, social, political, all citizens without distinction of race or color, shall be equal? By no means can they be so construed. Do they mean that all citizens shall vote in the several States? No. . . . Nor do they mean that all citizens shall sit on the juries, or that their children shall attend the same schools. These are not civil rights or immunities. Well, what is the meaning? What are civil rights? I understand civil rights to be simply the absolute rights of individuals, such as — "The right of personal security, the right of personal liberty, and the right to acquire and enjoy property." "Right itself, in civil society, is that which any man is entitled to have, or to do, or to require from others, within the limits of prescribed law." Kent's Commentaries, vol. I, p. 199. . . .

But what of the term "immunities"? . . . It merely secures to citizens of the United States equality in the exemptions of the law. A colored citizen shall not, because he is colored, be subjected to obligations, duties, pains. . . . This is the spirit and scope of the bill, and it goes not one step beyond. . . .

Laws barbaric and treatment inhuman are the rewards meted out by our white enemies to our colored friends. We should put a stop to this at once and forever.

Later he countered what he conceived as an attack on the breadth of the term "civil rights" by John Bingham of Ohio:

[Bingham] tells the House that civil rights involve all the rights that citizens have under the Government . . . , that this bill is not intended merely to enforce equality of rights, so far as they relate to citizens of the United States, but invades the States to enforce equality of rights in respect to those things which properly and rightfully depend on State regulations and laws. My friend . . . knows as every man knows, that this bill refers to those rights which belong to men as citizens of the United States and none other; and when he talks of setting aside the school laws and jury laws and franchise laws of the States by the bill . . . he steps beyond what he must know to be the rule of construction which must apply here, and as a result of which this bill can only relate to matters within the control of Congress.

The narrow scope of the bill was emphasized by other Radicals. Russell Thayer (Pennsylvania) said the bill simply declared that "all men born upon the soil of the United States shall enjoy the fundamental rights of citizenship. What rights are these? Why, sir, in order to avoid any misapprehension they are stated in the bill. The same section goes on to define with greater particularity the civil rights and

---

8. Proponents of the Civil Rights Bill argued that it implemented the Thirteenth Amendment.

immunities which are to be protected by the bill." William Windom (Minnesota) believed that the measure did not do enough because it only protected "civil" rights, not "political" rights.

Still, objections to the breadth of the language resounded in the House as they had in the Senate. Andrew Jackson Rogers (Democrat, New Jersey) declared: "As a white man is by law authorized to marry a white woman, so does this bill compel the State to grant to the negro the same right of marrying a white woman." Columbus Delano (moderate Republican, Ohio) feared that the bill would confer "upon the emancipated race the right of being jurors":

> I presume that the gentleman himself will shrink from the idea of conferring upon this race now, at this particular moment, the right of being jurors, or from so wording this bill as to leave it a serious question and render it debatable hereafter in the courts or elsewhere. . . . [W]e once had in the State of Ohio a law excluding the black population from any participation in the public schools. . . . That law did not of course, place the black population upon an equal footing with the white, and would, therefore, under the terms of this bill be void.

The objection that the bill might grant the franchise to freedmen inspired the heaviest substantive assault. George S. Shanklin (Democrat, Kentucky) requested an amendment stating explicitly that the bill did not confer suffrage. Wilson objected to the addition because "it is in the bill now." Rogers countered: "All the rights that we enjoy, except our natural rights, are derived from Government. Therefore, there are really but two kinds of rights, natural rights and civil rights. This bill, then, would prevent a State from refusing negro suffrage under the broad acceptation of the term 'civil rights and immunities.' " And Anthony Thornton (Democrat, Illinois) insisted:

> It is said that the words "civil rights" do not include the right of suffrage, because that is a political right. . . . I do not assume . . . that [they] do . . . but with the loose and liberal mode of construction adopted in this age, who can tell what rights may not be conferred by virtue of the terms as used in this bill? Where is it to end? Who can tell how it may be defined, how it may be construed? Why not, then, if it is not intended to confer the right of suffrage upon this class, accept a proviso that no such design is entertained?

The leadership finally acceded to an amendment "[t]hat nothing in this act shall be so construed as to affect the laws of any State concerning the right of suffrage," though Wilson still maintained that the amendment "will not change my construction of the bill. I do not believe the term civil rights includes the right of suffrage."

In addition to substantive objections to the breadth of the language of the Civil Rights Bill, many congressmen doubted whether the Thirteenth Amendment, which only abolished slavery, empowered Congress to enact the measure. Michael C. Kerr (Democrat, Indiana) asked:

> Is it slavery or involuntary servitude to forbid a free negro, on account of race or color, to testify against a white man? Is it either to deny to free negroes, on the same account, the privilege of engaging in certain kinds of business . . . such as retailing spiritous liquors? Is it either to deny to children of free negroes or mulattoes on the like account, the privilege of attending the common schools of a State with the children of white men?

Andrew Jackson Rogers also asserted that the bill would prohibit public school segregation and argued that Congress was without constitutional authority to do this.

This Democratic attack might have been ignored had not similar doubts about the constitutionality of the bill been expressed by some influential Republicans, including Congressman John Bingham (Ohio), a Radical Republican and principal draftsman of both the "Bingham amendment" and the Fourteenth Amendment. Bingham construed the civil rights formula broadly:

> [T]he term civil rights includes every right that pertains to the citizen under the Constitution, laws, and Government of this country. . . . [A]re not political rights all embraced in the term "civil rights," and must it not of necessity be so interpreted? . . . [T]here is scarcely a State in this Union which does not, by its constitution or by its statute laws, make some discrimination on account of race or color between citizens of the United States in respect of civil rights. . . . By the Constitution of my own State neither the right of the elective franchise nor the franchise of office can be conferred . . . save upon a white citizen of the United States.

He moved to recommit the bill to committee with instructions to strike the civil rights formula and to replace the penal provision of section 2, which made it a misdemeanor to deprive anyone of a right secured by section 1, with a civil enforcement provision:

> [A]lthough the objections which I urge against the bill must, in the very nature of the case, apply, to the proposed instructions, I venture to say no candid man, no right-minded man, will deny that by amending as proposed the bill will be less oppressive, and therefore less objectionable. Doubting, as I do, the power of Congress to pass the bill, I urge the instructions with a view to take from the bill what seems to me its oppressive and I might say its unjust provisions.

In referring to "oppressive" and "unjust" provisions, Bingham may have had section 2 chiefly in mind. In the course of his lengthy and wide-ranging speech, he objected that section 2 would "make it a penal offense for the judges of the States to obey the constitution and laws of their States. . . . I deny your power to do this. You cannot make an official act, done under color of law . . . and from a sense of public duty, a crime." But Bingham referred to "provisions" in the plural, and his motion to strike and remarks show no less a concern over the breadth of the civil rights formula.

Did Bingham object to the formula only on the ground that it was not authorized by the Thirteenth Amendment, or did he also oppose, as a matter of policy, granting the wide range of guarantees he deemed the language to comprehend? His earlier allegiance to radical antislavery ideals and the broad language he later used in drafting and defending his amendments imply that the objection was only constitutional. But the remarks quoted above also imply policy objections, and nowhere in the debates did Bingham explicitly favor the general prohibition of discrimination in "civil rights and immunities" as he favored protecting the enumerated rights, which he said "should be the law of every State, by voluntary act of every State." Moreover, Bingham made no pretense that his instructions to strike would cure the constitutional infirmity of the bill. Bingham voted against the bill even as amended, and it seems plausible that he offered the instructions in an effort to make the law conform more closely to his own racial policy, recognizing that it would be enacted despite his constitutional objection.

The bill was recommitted and the civil rights formula struck. In presenting the amended bill to the House, James Wilson stated: "Mr. Speaker, the amendment which has just been read proposes to strike out the general terms relating to civil rights. I do not think it materially changes the bill; but some gentlemen were apprehensive that the words we propose to strike out might give warrant for a latitudinarian construction not intended." Wilson also explained that the amendment made it unnecessary explicitly to exclude the franchise from the bill's coverage. The House and then the Senate passed the amended Civil Rights Act of 1866 and subsequently overrode a presidential veto.[9]

The Fourteenth Amendment

Meanwhile, the Joint Committee on Reconstruction, or Committee of Fifteen, was also addressing the problem of racial discrimination. Early in its deliberations over a possible constitutional amendment to supplement the Thirteenth, the committee rejected the civil rights formula. The committee's first product, the Bingham amendment, provided: "The Congress shall have power to make all laws which shall be necessary and proper to secure to the citizens of each State all privileges and immunities of citizens in the several States (Art. 4, Sec. 2); and to all persons in the several States equal protection in the rights of life, liberty and property (5th Amendment)." The proposal met bipartisan opposition in the House. Democrats and moderate and conservative Republicans opposed the broad delegation of power to Congress. Some Radicals were concerned that the amendment was not self-executing and left the protection of blacks to the fluctuating whims of majorities. Under this combined opposition, the amendment was tabled in the House and was never brought before the Senate.

The committee began to consider the Fourteenth Amendment after the Civil Rights Act of 1866 was on the books and the Bingham amendment had been tabled. In drafting section 1 of the Fourteenth Amendment, the committee vacillated between the civil rights formula and Bingham's language, finally reporting out the latter: "No state shall make or enforce any law which shall abridge the privileges or immunities of citizens of the United States; nor shall any state deprive any person of life, liberty or property without due process of law, nor deny to any person within its jurisdiction the equal protection of the laws."

The House and Senate debates paid little attention to the reach of section 1. Other provisions of the proposed amendment, disenfranchising much of the white southern electorate, were far more controversial.[10] Apparently, many legislators linked section 1 with the Civil Rights Act, which they had only recently enacted after lengthy debate. The old Radical Republican, Thaddeus Stevens

---

9. The text of the amended Act is as follows:

citizens of every race and color, . . . shall have the same right, in every State and Territory in the United States, to make and enforce contracts, to sue, be parties, and give evidence, to inherit, purchase, lease, sell, hold and convey real and personal property, and to full and equal benefit of all laws and proceedings for the security of person and property, as is enjoyed by white citizens.

10. These culminated in §2 of the Fourteenth Amendment.

(Pennsylvania), alluded to the connection in introducing the amendment in the House:

> This amendment . . . allows Congress to correct the unjust legislation of the States, so far that the law which operates upon one man shall operate *equally* upon all. Whatever law punishes a white man for a crime shall punish the black man precisely in the same way. . . . Whatever law protects the white man shall afford "equal" protection to the black man. Whatever means of redress is afforded to one shall be afforded to all. Whatever law allows the white man to testify in court shall allow the man of color to do the same. These are great advantages over their present codes. . . . I need not enumerate these partial and oppressive laws. Unless the Constitution should restrain them those States will . . . crush to death the hated freedmen. Some answer, "Your civil rights bill secures the same things." That is partly true, but a law is repealable by a majority. And I need hardly say that the first time that the South with their Copperhead allies obtain the command of Congress it will be repealed. . . . This Amendment once adopted cannot be amended without two-thirds of Congress. That they will hardly get.

Other Republicans asserted that section 1 constitutionalized the Civil Rights Act. "As I understand it," said M. Russell Thayer (Pennsylvania), "it is but incorporating in the Constitution . . . the principle of the civil rights bill . . . [so that it] shall be forever incorporated." John Broomall, also of Pennsylvania, referred to the amendment as the equivalent of the Civil Rights Act "in another shape." Only a few congressmen insisted that the amendment guaranteed too much. Andrew Jackson Rogers's principal concern was the privileges and immunities clause:

> What are privileges and immunities? Why, sir, all the rights we have under the laws of the country are embraced under the definition of privileges and immunities. The right to vote is a privilege. The right to marry is a privilege. The right to contract is a privilege. The right to be a juror is a privilege. The right to be a judge or President of the United States is a privilege. I hold if that ever becomes a part of the fundamental law of the land it will prevent any State from refusing to allow anything to anybody embraced under this term of privileges and immunities. . . . It will result in a revolution worse than that through which we have just passed.

Whether or not Rogers's argument was made in good faith, it was not fatuous. The vague terms of the Fourteenth Amendment had been employed by the abolitionists to encompass an undefinable variety of rights and had no settled meanings. And, during the debates on section 1 of the Fourteenth Amendment, a number of its proponents made remarks inconsistent with an assumption that its broad language was strictly limited to the enumerations of the Civil Rights Act. For example, Senator Timothy Howe, a Wisconsin Radical, though not referring to segregation, suggested that the amendment might prevent racial inequality of educational expenditures:

> The right to hold land . . . the right to collect their wages by the processes of the law . . . the right to appear in the courts as suitors . . . the right to give testimony. . . . [B]ut, sir, these are not the only rights that can be denied. . . . I have taken considerable pains to look over the actual legislation [in the South]. . . . I read not long since a statute enacted by the Legislature of Florida for the education of her colored people. . . . They make provision for the education of their white children also, and everybody who has any property there is taxed for the education of the white children. Black and white

are taxed alike for that purpose; but for the education of colored children a fund is raised only from colored men.

And Bingham himself implied that the boundaries of the amendment were amorphous.

> There . . . remains a want now, in the Constitution . . . which the proposed amendment will supply. . . . It is the power in the people . . . to protect by national law the privileges and immunities of all the citizens of the Republic and the inborn rights of every person within its jurisdiction whenever the same shall be abridged or denied by the unconstitutional acts of any State. . . .
>
> But, sir, it has been suggested . . . [that if the amendment] does not confer suffrage the need of it is not perceived. To all such I beg leave again to say, that many instances of State injustice and oppression have already occurred in the State legislation of this Union, of flagrant violations of the guaranteed privileges of citizens of the United States, for which the national Government furnished and could furnish by law no remedy whatever. Contrary to the express letter of your Constitution, "cruel and unusual punishments" have been inflicted under State laws . . . not only for crimes committed, but for sacred duty done. . . .
>
> Sir, the words of the Constitution that "the citizens of each State shall be entitled to all privileges and immunities of citizens in the several States" include, among other privileges, the right to bear true allegiance to the Constitution and laws of the United States, and to be protected in life, liberty, and property.

The Fourteenth Amendment was sent to the country on June 13, 1866, and section 1 received as little attention in the ensuing election campaign and ratification proceedings as it had in Congress.

Note: What the Fourteenth Amendment Did Not Say

Many of the cases below, and Chapters 6 through 8, concern themselves with the text of the Fourteenth Amendment, and particularly the Equal Protection and Due Process Clauses. As you read these cases and the ensuing discussions, especially as to the Equal Protection Clause, consider the fact that on July 22, 1865, Wendell Phillips, one of the most prominent abolitionists, had proposed the following constitutional amendment: "No State shall make any distinction in civil rights and privileges among the naturalized citizens of the United States residing within its limits, or among persons born on its soil of parents permanently resident there, on account of race, color, or descent." On December 5, 1865, Thaddeus Stevens, the leader of the Radical Republicans within the House of Representatives, introduced the following text as a proposed constitutional amendment: "All national and State laws shall be equally applicable to every citizen, and no discrimination shall be made on account of race and color."

Neither text, of course, was adopted, in part, says Andrew Kull, because "moderates" prevailed, and they "would allow those distinctions consistent with 'equal protection.' "[11] To what degree does the rejection of texts that arguably would have

11. Andrew Kull, The Color Blind Constitution, 62ff (1992).

required "color-blindness" throw light on the meaning to be assigned the text that *was* adopted? Is it permissible to interpret the Equal Protection Clause as mandating "color-blindness" if it was viewed by its supporters at the time as a clear rejection of such a view? Or can one legitimately say that the "moderates" were simply mistaken in believing that racial classifications could *ever* coincide with "equal protection" and that it is irrelevant that the actual drafters of the Amendment might have possessed such erroneous beliefs? (For further discussion of this problem, see Chapter 6.)

As you will see below, infra at pp. 487-490, many judges and commentators have argued that the phrase "privileges or immunities of United States citizens" was meant to "incorporate" against the states the protections against governmental overreaching that are set out in the Bill of Rights (but which were interpreted by John Marshall in 1833 as extending only to the national government). Here, too, subsequent interpretation of the Fourteenth Amendment might have been different had the Amendment contained more explicit language to this effect.

Note: The Unusual Procedural History of the Fourteenth Amendment[12]

The preceding materials treat the Fourteenth Amendment as if it were an ordinary Article V amendment, so that the only task facing the constitutional interpreter is to determine its meaning (or, if one is a political scientist, to explain the social and political forces that led to its proposal and ratification). But there is nothing at all ordinary about the procedures by which the Amendment was added to the constitutional text. Recall the requirements of Article V: two-thirds of each house must propose an amendment, which is then subject to ratification by the states, with the assent of three-quarters of the States being necessary to make it part of the Constitution. (Amendments can also be proposed by a convention, called by Congress upon petition of two-thirds of the states, but this option has in fact never occurred; congressional proposal has become, at least as an empirical matter, the exclusive path toward constitutional amendment.) What constitutes two-thirds of each house of Congress? What counts the assent of three-quarters of the states? Both of these questions are part of the tangled history of the Fourteenth Amendment.

Lee's surrender at Appomattox effectively brought the Civil War to an end, and therefore, in principle at least, restored the riven Union. Abraham Lincoln was assassinated only three days later. His successor, Andrew Johnson, a Unionist Democrat from Tennessee placed on the ticket with Lincoln as a gesture toward national unity, in effect offered to welcome back the ostensible members of the Confederate States of America if they agreed first to repudiate the legitimacy of secession and then to ratify the Thirteenth Amendment abolishing slavery. (Recall

---

12. Much of the material in this note is drawn from Bruce Ackerman's scholarship on constitutional change during Reconstruction. The initial statements of his thesis can be found in The Storrs Lectures: Discovering the Constitution, 93 Yale L.J. 1013 (1984) and Constitutional Politics/Constitutional Law, 99 Yale L.J. 453 (1989). The thesis is richly elaborated in We the People: Transformations 99-252 (1998) and extensively criticized in John Harrison, The Lawfulness of the Segregation Amendments, 68 U. Chi. L. Rev. 375 (2001) and Akhil Reed Amar, America's Constitution: A Biography 364-380 (2005).

that according to Lincoln, the Confederate States had never legally left the Union. What, then, did it mean to welcome them back? To treat them as fully functional states as distinct from, say, federal territories?) Recall that the Thirteenth Amendment had been proposed on January 31, 1865, before the termination of the War, when, for obvious reasons, none of the Confederate States was represented in Congress. However, with the end of the War, Johnson now suggested that they participate as states in the ratification of the amendment.

From Johnson's perspective, widely shared among Northern Democrats, the War had been fought principally about the issue set out in Lincoln's First Inaugural, the indivisibility of the Union. As a matter of empirical fact, the War had been transformed into a struggle to end slavery, as articulated in Lincoln's Second Inaugural, but it did not, in the view of Johnson and other Democrats, alter anything with respect to the balance of powers between state and national government. Eight of the operating governments within the states of the defeated Confederacy joined 19 other States that had never left to provide the necessary three-quarters ratification within the then 36-member Union, and on December 18, 1865, William Seward, the Secretary of State, officially proclaimed that the Amendment had become part of the Constitution.

However, on December 4, 1865, the Republican majorities in the Thirty-Ninth Congress, which was meeting for the first time since the 1864 elections,[13] exercised their constitutional power — see Article I, §5 — to judge the "Qualifications of its own Members" to exclude the men from the former Confederacy who had been elected to sit in the House and Senate. The explanation was simple: If they sat these members, then the legal consequences of the War would indeed be restricted to the addition of the Thirteenth Amendment, *and nothing more*. The Democrats would have more than enough votes to block any proposals for constitutional amendment. Moreover, the Democrats might also have the possible power to block the passage of ordinary legislation, if they could persuade Andrew Johnson to exercise his veto power. This would frustrate the will of the Republican legislative majority and require the same two-thirds majority to pass legislation as was needed to propose constitutional amendments. Beginning in the Spring of 1867 Johnson did in fact repeatedly wield his veto pen to oppose important Reconstruction legislation.

Indeed, from the Republican perspective, the future looked even bleaker politically: Before the passage of the Thirteenth Amendment, the South was allowed to count its slaves as only three-fifths of a person for purposes of computing the population base that determined how many representatives in the House each state would receive. Now, because of the Thirteenth Amendment, the Southern states would obtain a significant boost in legally recognized population: All blacks would henceforth count as whole persons, even though the Republicans were quite sure that these new persons would never be allowed to vote. As the result of losing the War, then, the former Confederate States would, if Andrew Johnson and other self-styled "moderates" prevailed, end up with enhanced power in the House of Representatives and, indirectly, in the Electoral College that elected the president.

13. Why this remarkable delay? Again, read Article I, §4, cl. 2. Why do you think that President Johnson did not call Congress into special session immediately after the assassination of his predecessor?

14. Constitutional Politics/Constitutional Law, 99 Yale L.J., at 503.

In order to prevent this perverse state of affairs — whereby the South was actually politically strengthened by losing the War — the Republican-controlled Congress refused to accept the legitimacy of the Southern representatives and senators who showed up at the Capitol to take their oaths of office. Or, perhaps more to the point, Congress rejected the legitimacy of the white-only electorate that selected the members of the House and of the white-only legislatures that named the senators.

Thus, the Fourteenth Amendment was proposed by what Bruce Ackerman calls a "rump" Congress, from which the Democratic opposition from the former Confederate States had been excluded. It did indeed receive two-thirds of the vote of each House of Congress, but only if one chooses to ignore the exclusion of potential opponents. The Fourteenth Amendment received 120 votes in the House and 33 in the Senate. With a full complement of southern representatives, it would have required 162 votes in the House and 48 in the Senate to gain a two-thirds majority. Ackerman argues that "Southern exclusion . . . was a necessary political condition for the Republicans to gain the two-thirds vote required by Article Five for the proposal of a constitutional amendment."[14] Because Ackerman regards the work of this Congress as a fundamental change in the political order, he compares it to the first constitutional convention in Philadelphia — which, as you may recall from the Introduction to Part One, he believes also acted with dubious legality. Thus, he even calls the Thirty-Ninth Congress a "Convention/Congress."

Of course, gaining two-thirds of each House — no matter how constituted — is not enough to ratify an amendment. The proposed Fourteenth Amendment still needed ratification by 27 states in order to become part of the Constitution. Although eight governments of the former Confederacy voted for the Thirteenth Amendment — presumably on the view that slavery was effectively over anyway — the Fourteenth Amendment presented a number of different issues. To begin with, it resolved any questions about Congress's powers under section 2 of the Thirteenth Amendment by explicitly granting citizenship to blacks and guaranteeing them equal civil rights. It also prohibited the assumption of Confederate War debt, imposed conditions on political officeholding by former Confederate leaders, and penalized southern states for denying black males the vote. Quite apart from all this, the Fourteenth Amendment was generally understood as changing the balance of power in the American Republic, giving the federal government new and broad powers to oversee states in the name of individual rights. The southern state legislatures sitting in 1866 were hardly likely to consent to it, and they easily had the votes under Article V to block its ratification at the state level even if Southern representatives were excluded from Congress by the radical Republicans. Indeed, by the end of 1866, North Carolina, Georgia, Texas, South Carolina, and Louisiana had voted to reject the amendment, to be followed shortly in the new year by Virginia and Mississippi. Moreover, three of the four "border states," i.e., slave states that had remained in the Union — Delaware, Maryland, and Kentucky — rejected the Amendment, though Missouri, the fourth, did ratify it.[15] These ten rejections were enough to doom the Amendment under the three-quarters rule for ratification set out by Article V. This was deemed intolerable. The War may have ended, as a formal matter, with Lee's surrender at Appomattox Courthouse in April 1865, but the terms of the de facto "peace treaty" between North and South had scarcely been resolved.

It was this legal reality generated by Article V that triggered what has come to be known as the "congressional" phase of "Reconstruction" (as distinct from "Presidential Reconstruction" under Andrew Johnson's leadership). Congress passed the First and Second Reconstruction Acts in March 1867 over President Johnson's veto.[16] The defeated states were occupied by the U.S. military, which meant, among other things, that the state governments of the former Confederacy were effectively dissolved, and the South was put under the authority of military commanders. Federal military and civilian authorities supervised new constitutional conventions that would create new state governments, which were required to accept black suffrage. The federal military was also to oversee the registration of both white and black voters. Finally representatives of the newly constituted state governments were to be allowed admission as members in good standing to the House and Senate only if the State ratified the Fourteeth Amendment, and only after the amendment had gained the support of three-fourths of the States.[17]

President Johnson opposed these policies — on constitutional as well as political grounds — and hoped to use his power as Commander-in-Chief of the military to stall the conventions that were organized to create the new state governments and ratify the Fourteenth Amendment. In order to do this, he attempted to fire Secretary of War Edwin M. Stanton, in seeming violation of the Tenure in Office Act passed by Congress that had forbidden just such an exercise of executive power by Johnson.[18] The House of Representatives responded by voting a bill of

15. The ratification history is unusually complicated, as two other states, New Jersey and Ohio, which had ratified the Amendment in 1866 and early 1867, attempted to rescind these ratifications. Although Congress and the Secretary of State chose to count these states as yes votes in mid-July 1867, the issue quickly became moot, thanks to ratifications that came in from Alabama and Georgia, who ratified in mid-July. By July 28, 1868 — the date of Seward's formal proclamation that the Fourteenth Amendment "has been adopted" — the Amendment's ratification no longer hinged on the results in New Jersey and Ohio. Note that Article V is entirely silent on whether a state, having once ratified an amendment, and before it has been ratified by enough other states to reach the three-fourths requirement, can change its mind. Given that no one would seriously argue that a state, once having voted to reject an amendment could not subsequently change its collective mind and declare its approval, then why should not a state have a prerogative to rescind a ratification that it (or, more accurately, a successor legislature within a state) deems to have been unwise? See generally, Michael S. Paulsen, A General Theory of Article V: The Constitutional Lessons of the Twenty-Seventh Amendment, 103 Yale L.J. 677 (1993).

16. Again, it should be emphasized that Johnson's veto would easily have been sustained had the Southern representatives and senators been seated in December 1865.

17. Although all of the former Confederate States did in fact comply with the conditions, it may be worth noting that the three border states did not get around to ratifying the Amendment until 1901 (Delaware); 1959 (Maryland); and 1976 (Kentucky). What may be more surprising is that California ratified the Amendment only in 1959. See *http://www.law.emory.edu/FEDERAL/usconst/amend.html#art-14.*

18. Needless to say, there is much controversy over whether Congress has the power so to limit the President's control over who shall serve in his or her cabinet. Most contemporary constitutional lawyers would probably agree with Johnson that the Act was unconstitutional. How important is it to you whether Johnson in fact had a legitimate constitutional argument with regard to the issue over which he was impeached? Consider your earlier response to a similar question with regard to Abraham Lincoln's Emancipation Proclamation. Might Congress have been right to try to remove Johnson from the presidency even if, as a formal matter, he had committed no "high crime and misdemeanor" or, indeed, no "crime" at all?

impeachment against Johnson. Johnson's impeachment trial in the Senate began in March 1868. By April, Johnson retreated, in effect recognizing Congress's power to structure the terms of the de facto "peace treaty" between North and South. He nominated a new Secretary of War acceptable to the Congress, and agreed to stop interfering with the ratification process. Johnson was eventually acquitted by one vote.[19] In June 1868, the Congress recognized the legitimacy of the governments of seven Southern states; by July all seven had ratified the Fourteenth Amendment. (An eighth defeated state, Tennessee, had ratified and been readmitted to Congress the previous year.)

Discussion

1. *The Thirteenth-Fourteenth Amendment paradox.* From the preceding discussion you can see that the Southern States (and state governments) were considered sufficiently legitimate to ratify the Thirteenth Amendment in 1866 but not the Fourteenth Amendment in 1868. (Indeed, Congress refused to seat the southern representatives two weeks before the official proclamation of the ratification of the Thirteenth Amendment!) Does this fact undermine the legitimacy of either amendment in your view? If so, which one?

Bruce Ackerman, who details the history of this period in his book We The People: Transformations (1998), claims that the Fourteenth Amendment cannot accurately be described as an "Article V" amendment, given the circumstances surrounding its proposal and ratification. He also argues that American constitutional lawyers have systematically refused to recognize the dilemmas posed by the provenance of the Fourteenth Amendment. As it happens, Ackerman offers a rich and complex theory that he believes legitimizes the Fourteenth Amendment (and the actions of the Reconstruction Congress) in spite of these procedural defects.

2. *The Guaranty Clause and black suffrage.* Professor Ackerman's colleague, Akhil Reed Amar, strongly disagrees with Ackerman's suggestion that there is anything improper, from a constitutional perspective, with the proposal and ratification of the Fourteenth Amendment.[20] Amar relies in substantial part on the Article IV duty of the United States to guarantee to each state a "republican form of government." The Civil Rights Act of 1866 had declared the newly freed slaves citizens of the United States. Because postwar Southern governments denied blacks the right to vote or otherwise participate in government, Amar argues, Congress in 1866-1868 took the position that the Southern states were not "republican" and could, therefore, legitimately be denied representation in Congress until their state

---

19. The key vote was cast by Republican Senator Ross of Kansas, and John F. Kennedy selected Ross as one of his subjects in his widely read book *Profiles in Courage* (1956), which was awarded the Pulitzer Prize in 1957 and which has remained in print since then. Assume for the moment that you believe that the Tenure in Office Act was unconstitutional, so that Johnson committed no "crime" at all in refusing to consider himself bound by it. But assume as well that he had not in effect thrown in the towel with regard to his opposition to Congressional Reconstruction. Would you still regard it as a "profile in courage" to maintain Johnson in office if it meant the death of the Fourteenth Amendment? Is it relevant to your answer that a new presidential election was coming up in November 1868 (when Ulysses S. Grant, the Union general who had won the War, would be swept into office)? But recall that prior to the Twentieth Amendment, the new president would not be inaugurated until March 4, 1869. Are any of these considerations relevant to deciding whether or not Johnson merited impeachment?

20. See Amar, *America's Constitution: A Biography*, supra n.12, at 364-380.

governments were reformed (or "reconstructed") to achieve "republican" status.[21] Amar also points out that the excluded Southern states had for years repeatedly and flagrantly violated basic rights of free political expression and had shown contempt for basic democratic principles when they took up arms against a duly elected government in 1861. All this, Amar argues, made it sensible for Congress in 1866 to exclude Southern governments from Congress until proper safeguards were in place to ensure future Southern conformity with basic republican principles of free and fair government.

Of course, Northern states also denied African-Americans the right to vote and, moreover, millions of female citizens had no participation rights. Quoting leading members of the Reconstruction Congress, Amar responds, first, that the difference in degree between North and South with reference to the actual population of African-Americans constituted a difference in kind. Ohio, for example, in disenfranchising blacks, was discriminating against only 2 percent or so of its population. This is, to be sure, regrettable, but it meant that almost all of the (male) population could in fact participate in the enterprise of republican self-government. South Carolina, on the other hand, was a majority black state, so that disenfranchisement of African-Americans in fact meant rule by a minority, the very definition of nonrepublican government.

Women, of course, might make similar arguments about the nonrepublican status of a male-dominated polity. However, Amar notes the widespread belief, however false we may now believe it to be, that women were "virtually represented" by their fathers, brothers, and husbands. To be sure, as we have already seen, strong criticism of such views had been issued at Seneca Falls and would be further amplified in the coming years, ultimately leading to the ratification of the Nineteenth Amendment. In any event, Congress did not believe that the interests of blacks (or more specifically, black males) would be virtually represented — that is, sympathetically taken into account — by the "unreconstructed" white elites who had attempted to leave the Union in order to preserve chattel slavery. Hence Congressional leaders argued that although denial of women's rights to vote did not render Southern governments unrepublican, their denial of the rights of black males to vote did, and this, Amar claims, justified Congress's decision.

3. Which of these theories do you find more persuasive? *Was* the Fourteenth Amendment properly proposed by Congress and ratified under Article V? If you believe you need more information than we have provided you in these necessarily capsule summaries, what would you like to know and why do you think it would be relevant to your answer?

If you agree with Amar that the Fourteenth Amendment is constitutionally unproblematic, then does its mode of proposal and ratification establish a precedent concerning the meaning of Article V (and Congress's ability to stipulate what counts as a "republican form of government")? Imagine, for example, that you were

---

21. Note that Amar is not content to rely simply on Congress's power, under Article I, §5, to "Judge [the] Qualifications of its own Members" except insofar as "judgment" requires presenting good and substantial reasons for the exclusion, which Amar believes were amply present. Consider whether an Article I, §5 "formalist" would have to defend the legitimacy of excluding representatives and senators simply because the majority believed that they had the wrong political views or were from an unpopular racial or ethnic group. See Powell v. McCormick, 395 U.S. 486 (1969).

in Congress in 1979, when the Equal Rights Amendment, proposed by Congress in 1972 and ratified by two-thirds of the 50 states, was languishing because of the inability to get the three further state ratifications necessary to attain the three quarters required by Article V. Consider whether it would have been legitimate to vote to refuse to seat representatives and senators from the 15 states that had not yet ratified — Alabama, Arizona, Arkansas, Florida, Georgia, Illinois, Louisiana, Mississippi, Missouri, Nevada, North Carolina, Oklahoma, South Carolina, Utah, and Virginia — on the ground that they had demonstrated themselves to be agents of "patriarchy" and therefore "nonrepublican"? They would, of course, have been allowed to take their seats upon their states' ratification of the ERA. Would this have been constitutional?[22] Could one respond that women in all these anti-ERA states were nevertheless allowed to vote, hold office, serve on juries and in legislatures, and indeed exercise all other political rights on equal terms with men? Or consider a less "extreme" possibility: Could Congress have simply withheld all highway or flood relief funding (or indeed federal funding for all programs) to these states until they ratified the Amendment?

4. If you accept neither Ackerman's or Amar's accounts of the legitimacy of the Fourteenth Amendment, what follows? Should we, for example, excise it from the text of the Constitution? If not, then what other theory best justifies its inclusion as part of the U.S. Constitution? Consider the following justifications for the legality of the Fourteenth Amendment:

a. The Southern States tried to leave the Union and therefore forfeited their right to representation in Congress until they were brought back in on proper terms. Note that this account does not explain the acceptance of the state governments for purposes of the Thirteenth Amendment. Also, is it consistent with Lincoln's theory that the Southern States had no right to leave the Union, a theory upon which the war was fought by Lincoln, at least initially? Consider the following refinement of the state-forfeiture theory. There are important differences between being "in the Union" and being a valid state government with full state's rights. For example, federal territories and the national capital were undeniably part of Lincoln's union, but were not entitled to full states' rights, standing outside both the Congress and the Article V amendment process. Could the state-forfeiture theory be sharpened by saying that states that attempted to secede in effect reverted to the status of federal territories — inside Lincoln's indivisible union but outside Congress and Article V until readmitted on proper terms?

b. The Southern states were in "the grasp of war" until they accepted the North's demands and therefore the North had the right to do whatever it wanted with them. It could count them for Thirteenth Amendment purposes and then change its mind the next day to gain whatever political advantage it thought it could obtain. Hence the Fourteenth Amendment is not an Article V amendment, but an act of raw political and military power that is justified solely on those grounds. (Thus, the justification is not, strictly speaking, a legal one but is essentially political.) Does this mean that if the U.S. Congress was willing to call out the troops, they could

---

22. Note that this is not the same thing as asking whether the Supreme Court would properly have issued an injunction requiring the seating of the (alleged) senators and representatives from Utah. Even if the Court would remain silent, it is presumably the duty of all members of Congress (see Article 6) to act in accordance with constitutional norms.

"legitimately" impose any constitutional change on any segment of the country? What does the word "legitimately" mean here?

c. The Fourteenth Amendment is so central to our Nation's sense of itself and its guarantees of justice, civil rights, and civil liberties that it must be accepted as legitimate even if there is no textual or procedural justification for it. Would this apply to any Amendment that you thought was especially important to the promotion of justice, civil rights, and civil liberties, or just to the Fourteenth Amendment?

d. By the end of the 1870s, or at least by the end of the nineteenth century, so many people accepted the Fourteenth Amendment's legitimacy that no further explanation is needed. At some point, acts of government, even if controversial at the time — and even if we believe that their opponents had the better arguments — become settled and no longer open to discussion or repudiation. Using the debate over the annexation of Texas as an example, see p. 247, supra n.45, Mark Graber has argued that whether a constitutional question remains alive or is regarded as "settled" legally depends on whether the dispute remains alive in the political process, or on the contrary, the losers in the controversy have conceded defeat. See Mark Graber, How the West Was Settled, 38 Tulsa L. Rev. 609 (2003). Consider, though, whether such settlements can ever become "unstuck," if, for example, a mass political movement revives old arguments and begins to elect officials who are committed to overturning the ostensible settlement. Suppose, as was suggested during the massive resistance to Brown v. Board of Education, Southern States should refuse to accept the legitimacy of the Fourteenth Amendment because of it was forced on them during Reconstruction. Would they be entitled to engage in interposition or nullification on behalf of their (majority white) citizenry?

Can you think of another explanation to explain why the Fourteenth Amendment is legally a part of the U.S. Constitution?

5. *Equal suffrage in the senate.* Note that Article V states that "no State, without its Consent, shall be deprived of its equal Suffrage in the Senate." This appears to suggest that a state could accept diminished representation if it consents; since, however, this would by definition generate unequal suffrage for all of the remaining states (relative to the one that agreed to lose a senator), then one might also interpret Article V as requiring unanimous consent. Is Article V merely a restriction on possible amendments, or is it also a limit on governmental action outside the amendment process? If the latter, did the exclusion of southern senators violate Article V? If it did, what would constitute an appropriate remedy? Could the affected states sue to enjoin enforcement of the Fourteenth Amendment because it was proposed without their equal representation in the Senate? Could they avoid application of any legislation passed during this period that they did not volunteer to accept diminished representation?

6. *What should the Court have done?* During the period in which the Republican Congress was reconstituting the southern state governments, the Supreme Court did not rule on the issue of the legality of this process. On April 15, 1867, the Supreme Court allowed the old government of Georgia (supported by President Johnson) to proceed with a motion against Secretary of War Edwin M. Stanton, urging an injunction against the Republicans' effort to destroy the "existing State of Georgia and to cause to be evicted and substituted in its place . . . another district and hitherto unknown State, to be called and designated the State of Georgia." By the middle of

May, the Supreme Court dismissed Georgia v. Stanton for "want of jurisdiction." The Court argued that the issue was a "political question" not susceptible to judicial review. The case involved "the rights of sovereignty, of political jurisdiction, of government, of corporate existence as a State, with all its constitutional powers and privileges," as opposed to a threatened infringement of "private rights or private property," which would presumably have been justiciable. See Georgia v. Stanton, 73 U.S. 50, 76-77 (1867). The Court added that it was irrelevant that Georgia claimed that its property (for example, its state capitol building and executive mansion) was also at stake, because the real issue was the destruction of the state's sovereignty. (Note that when the question of the legality of Reconstruction did reach the Supreme Court in Ex parte McCardle, involving a claim of individual rights affected by the Reconstruction Acts, Congress removed the Supreme Court's jurisdiction to hear the case in March 1868.) Should the Supreme Court have heard Georgia v. Stanton on its merits? If so, how should it have ruled? How do you think the Reconstruction Congress might have responded to a declaration that the Reconstruction Acts (and, presumably, the process for ratifying the Fourteenth Amendment) were unconstitutional?

7. *The Supreme Court speaks.* Finally, in 1873, in The Slaughterhouse Cases, 83 U.S. (16 Wall.) 36 (1873) (reprinted infra), the Court gave its own account of the provenance of the Thirteenth and Fourteenth Amendments:

> [T]he contests pervading the public mind for many years, between those who desired [slavery's] curtailment and ultimate extinction and those who desired additional safeguards for its security and perpetuation, culminated in the effort, on the part of most of the States in which slavery existed, to separate from the Federal government, and to resist its authority. This constituted the war of the rebellion, and whatever auxiliary causes may have contributed to bring about this war, undoubtedly the overshadowing and efficient cause was African slavery.
>
> In that struggle slavery, as a legalized social relation, perished. . . . But the war being over, those who had succeeded in re-establishing the authority of the Federal government were not content to permit this great act of emancipation to rest on the actual results of the contest or the proclamation of the Executive, both of which might have been questioned in after times, and they determined to place this main and most valuable result in the Constitution of the restored Union as one of its fundamental articles. Hence the thirteenth article of amendment of that instrument. . . .
>
> The process of restoring to their proper relations with the Federal government and with the other States those which had sided with the rebellion, undertaken under the proclamation of President Johnson in 1865, and before the assembling of Congress, developed the fact that, notwithstanding the formal recognition by those States of the abolition of slavery, the condition of the slave race would, without further protection of the Federal government, be almost as bad as it was before. Among the first acts of legislation adopted by several of the States in the legislative bodies which claimed to be in their normal relations with the Federal government, were laws which imposed upon the colored race onerous disabilities and burdens, and curtailed their rights in the pursuit of life, liberty, and property to such an extent that their freedom was of little value, while they had lost the protection which they had received from their former owners from motives both of interest and humanity. . . .
>
> These circumstances, whatever of falsehood or misconception may have been mingled with their presentation, forced upon the statesmen who had conducted the Federal government in safety through the crisis of the rebellion, and who supposed that by the thirteenth article of amendment they had secured the result of their labors, the conviction that something more was necessary in the way of constitutional protection to the unfortunate race who had suffered so much. They accordingly passed

through Congress the proposition for the fourteenth amendment, and they declined
to treat as restored to their full participation in the government of the Union the
States which had been in insurrection, until they ratified that article by a formal vote
of their legislative bodies.

What theory of the legitimacy of the Thirteenth and Fourteenth Amendments
do you think the Court is implying?

B.   The Fourteenth Amendment Limited

The central purpose of the Thirteenth (1865), Fourteenth (1868), and Fifteenth
(1870) Amendments — sometimes called the "Civil War" or "Reconstruction"
amendments — was to help provide what Lincoln might have termed "a new birth
of freedom" for the recently emancipated slaves. The central question posed to
constitutional interpreters of the Fourteenth Amendment was what comprised the
rights and freedoms presumably guaranteed. For example, did the Fourteenth
Amendment protect the former slaves by preventing only discriminatory treatment
of them (and other blacks) relative to the majority white population? Or, instead,
did it guarantee to blacks (and the general population, including non-blacks) a
substantive set of rights that were protected against governmental interference? The
Court readily decided that the Amendment did not protect the political rights of
access to the ballot, but this was a different question from what constituted the
"civil" rights that all parties to the debate conceded, at least in the abstract, were to
be protected by the new constitutional language.
    Rogers Smith argues that the Thirteenth and Fourteenth Amendments must be
understood in the context of the "free labor" ideology of the Republican Party, with
its Lockean insistence "that although the races might not be fully equal in all
respects, every human being had a natural right to pursue his trade and reap the
fruits of his labor."[23] The first case testing the meaning of "free labor" as a civil right
was the Slaughterhouse Cases, where, writes Smith, "New Orleans butchers
challenged a monopolistic slaughterhouse charter, granted by the state's North-
dominated Reconstruction legislature, which forced them to work at the Crescent
City Slaughter-House Company's facilities or give up their trade." In Smith's words,
the butchers claimed that by depriving them of the chance to practice their trade
outside of the monopoly's facilities, the law "violated the most fundamental right in
liberal 'free labor' ideology, the right to labor productively, to pursue their vocation
and reap the fruits of their efforts."[24] On behalf of the butchers, former Supreme
Court Justice John Campbell argued that the citizenship protected by the
Fourteenth Amendment "was based on the liberal commitment to securing fundamental rights against all threats, including any from the states. High among these

---

23. Rogers Smith, "One United People": Second-Class Female Citizenship and the American Quest for
Community, 1 Yale J. of L. & Humanities 229, 257 (1989). The classic scholarly treatment of this ideology is
Eric Foner, Free Soil, Free Labor, Free Men (1970). See also Eric Foner, Reconstruction: America's
Unfinished Revolution 1863-1877, at 228-280 (1988). See also Ronald M. Labbe and Jonathan Lurie, The
Slaughterhouse Cases: Regulation, Reconstruction, and the Fourteenth Amendment (2003).
    24. Smith, at 259.

rights, as 'property of a sacred kind,' was the 'right to labor . . . and to the product of one's faculties.' "[25]

THE SLAUGHTERHOUSE CASES
83 U.S. (16 Wall.) 36 (1873)

[In 1869, Louisiana enacted a statute entitled "An act to protect the health of the city of New Orleans, to locate the stock-landings and slaughter-houses, and to incorporate the Crescent City Live-Stock Landing and Slaughter-House Company." The act authorized the company to construct a large slaughterhouse, available to any butcher in the city on payment of reasonable compensation, and prohibited the maintenance of any other abattoirs. Its purpose, as described by the Court, was "to remove from the more densely populated part of the city, the noxious slaughter-houses, and large and offensive collections of animals necessarily incident to the slaughtering business of a large city, and to locate them where the convenience, health, and comfort of the people require. . . ."]

MILLER, J. . . .

It is not, and cannot be successfully controverted, that it is both the right and the duty of the legislative body — the supreme power of the State or municipality — to prescribe and determine the localities where the business of slaughtering for a great city may be conducted. To do this effectively it is indispensable that all persons who slaughter animals for food shall do it in those places *and nowhere else.*

The statute under consideration defines these localities and forbids slaughtering in any other. It does not, as has been asserted, prevent the butcher from doing his own slaughtering. On the contrary, the Slaughter-House Company is required, under a heavy penalty, to permit any person who wishes to do so, to slaughter in their houses; and they are bound to make ample provision for the convenience of all the slaughtering for the entire city. The butcher then is still permitted to slaughter, to prepare, and to sell his own meats; but he is required to slaughter at a specified place and to pay a reasonable compensation for the use of the accommodations furnished him at that place.

The wisdom of the monopoly granted by the legislature may be open to question, but it is difficult to see a justification for the assertion that the butchers are deprived of the right to labor in their occupation, or the people of their daily service in preparing food, or how this statute, with the duties and guards imposed upon the company, can be said to destroy the business of the butcher, or seriously interfere with its pursuit.

[Moreover, such regulation is traditional.] "Unwholesome trades, slaughter-houses, operations offensive to the senses, the deposit of powder, the application of steam power to propel cars, the building with combustible materials, and the burial of the dead, may all," says Chancellor Kent, "be interdicted by law, in the midst of dense masses of population, on the general and rational principle, that every person ought so to use his property as not to injure his neighbors; and that private interests must be made subservient to the general interests of the community." This is called the police power. . . .

25. Id.

This power is, and must be from its very nature, incapable of any very exact definition or limitation. Upon it depends the security of social order, the life and health of the citizen, the comfort of an existence in a thickly populated community, the enjoyment of private and social life, and the beneficial use of property. "It extends . . . to the protection of the lives, limbs, health, comfort, and quiet of all persons, and the protection of all" property within the State; . . . and persons and property are subjected to all kinds of restraints and burdens in order to secure the general comfort, health, and prosperity of the State. Of the perfect right of the legislature to do this no question ever was, or, upon acknowledged general principles, ever can be made, so far as natural persons are concerned.

The regulation of the place and manner of conducting the slaughtering of animals, and the business of butchering within a city, and the inspection of the animals to be killed for meat, and of the meat afterwards, are among the most necessary and frequent exercises of this power. It is not, therefore, needed that we should seek for a comprehensive definition, but rather look for the proper source of its exercise.

. . . The exclusive authority of State legislation over this subject is strikingly illustrated in the case of the City of New York v. Miln. . . .

It cannot be denied that the statute under consideration is aptly framed to remove from the more densely populated part of the city, the noxious slaughterhouses, and large and offensive collections of animals necessarily incident to the slaughtering business of a large city, and to locate them where the convenience, health, and comfort of the people require they shall be located. . . . But it is said that in creating a corporation for this purpose, and conferring upon it exclusive privileges — privileges which it is said constitute a monopoly — the legislature has exceeded its power. If this statute had imposed on the city of New Orleans precisely the same duties, accompanied by the same privileges, which it has on the corporation which it created, it is believed that no question would have been raised as to its constitutionality. In that case the effect on the butchers in pursuit of their occupation and on the public would have been the same as it is now. Why cannot the legislature confer the same powers on another corporation, created for a lawful and useful public object, that it can on the municipal corporation already existing? That wherever a legislature has the right to accomplish a certain result, and that result is best attained by means of a corporation, it has the right to create such a corporation, and to endow it with the powers necessary to effect the desired and lawful purpose, seems hardly to admit of debate. The proposition is ably discussed and affirmed in the case of McCulloch v. The State of Maryland, in relation to the power of Congress to organize the Bank of the United States to aid in the fiscal operations of the government. . . .

Unless, therefore, it can be maintained that the exclusive privilege granted by this charter to the corporation, is beyond the power of the legislature of Louisiana, there can be no just exception to the validity of the statute. And in this respect we are not able to see that these privileges are especially odious or objectionable. . . . It may, therefore, be considered as established, that the authority of the legislature of Louisiana to pass the present statute is ample, unless some restraint in the exercise of that power be found in the constitution of that State or in the amendments to the Constitution of the United States, adopted since the date of the decisions we have already cited. . . .

The plaintiffs in error accepting this issue, allege that the statute is a violation of the Constitution of the United States in these several particulars:

That it creates an involuntary servitude forbidden by the thirteenth article of amendment;

That it abridges the privileges and immunities of citizens of the United States;

That it denies to the plaintiffs the equal protection of the laws; and,

That it deprives them of their property without due process of law, contrary to the provisions of the first section of the fourteenth article of amendment.

This court is thus called upon for the first time to give construction to these articles. . . .

The most cursory glance at these articles discloses a unity of purpose, when taken in connection with the history of the times, which cannot fail to have an important bearing on any question of doubt concerning their true meaning. Nor can such doubts, when any reasonably exist, be safely and rationally solved without a reference to that history; for in it is found the occasion and the necessity for recurring again to the great source of power in this country, the people of the States, for additional guarantees of human rights; additional powers to the Federal government; additional restraints upon those of the States. Fortunately that history is fresh within the memory of us all, and its leading features, as they bear upon the matter before us, free from doubt. . . .

We repeat, then, in the light of this recapitulation of events, almost too recent to be called history, but which are familiar to us all; and on the most casual examination of the language of these amendments, no one can fail to be impressed with the one pervading purpose found in them all, lying at the foundation of each, and without which none of them would have been even suggested; we mean the freedom of the slave race, the security and firm establishment of that freedom, and the protection of the newly-made freeman and citizen from the oppressions of those who had formerly exercised unlimited dominion over him. It is true that only the fifteenth amendment, in terms, mentions the negro by speaking of his color and his slavery. But it is just as true that each of the other articles was addressed to the grievances of that race, and designed to remedy them as the fifteenth.

We do not say that no one else but the negro can share in this protection. Both the language and spirit of these articles are to have their fair and just weight in any question of construction. Undoubtedly while negro slavery alone was in the mind of the Congress which proposed the thirteenth article, it forbids any other kind of slavery, now or hereafter. If Mexican peonage or the Chinese coolie labor system shall develop slavery of the Mexican or Chinese race within our territory, this amendment may safely be trusted to make it void. And so if other rights are assailed by the States which properly and necessarily fall within the protection of these articles, that protection will apply, though the party interested may not be of African descent. But what we do say, and what we wish to be understood, is, that in any fair and just construction of any section or phrase of these amendments, it is necessary to look to the purpose which we have said was the pervading spirit of them all, the evil which they were designed to remedy, and the process of continued addition to the Constitution, until that purpose was supposed to be accomplished, as far as constitutional law can accomplish it. . . . [Justice Miller summarily dismisses appellants' claim based on the Thirteenth Amendment.]

The first section of the fourteenth article, to which our attention is more specially invited, opens with a definition of citizenship — not only citizenship of the United States, but citizenship of the States. No such definition was previously found in the Constitution, nor had any attempt been made to define it by act of Congress. . . . But it had been held by this court, in the celebrated *Dred Scott* case, only a few years before the outbreak of the civil war, that a man of African descent, whether a slave or not, was not and could not be a citizen of a State or of the United States. This decision, while it met the condemnation of some of the ablest statesmen and constitutional lawyers of the country, had never been overruled; and if it was to be accepted as a constitutional limitation of the right of citizenship, then all the negro race who had recently been made freemen, were still, not only not citizens, but were incapable of becoming so by anything short of an amendment to the Constitution.

To remove this difficulty primarily, and to establish a clear and comprehensive definition of citizenship which should declare what should constitute citizenship of the United States, and also citizenship of a State, the first clause of the first section was framed.

"All persons born or naturalized in the United States, and subject to the jurisdiction thereof, are citizens of the United States and of the State wherein they reside."

The first observation we have to make on this clause is, that it puts at rest both the questions which we stated to have been the subject of differences of opinion. It declares that persons may be citizens of the United States without regard to their citizenship of a particular State, and it overturns the *Dred Scott* decision by making *all persons* born within the United States and subject to its jurisdiction citizens of the United States. That its main purpose was to establish the citizenship of the negro can admit of no doubt. The phrase, "subject to its jurisdiction" was intended to exclude from its operation children of ministers, consuls, and citizens or subjects of foreign States born within the United States.

The next observation is more important in view of the arguments of counsel in the present case. It is, that the distinction between citizenship of the United States and citizenship of a State is clearly recognized and established. Not only may a man be a citizen of the United States without being a citizen of a State, but an important element is necessary to convert the former into the latter. He must reside within the State to make him a citizen of it, but it is only necessary that he should be born or naturalized in the United States to be a citizen of the Union.

It is quite clear, then, that there is a citizenship of the United States, and a citizenship of a State, which are distinct from each other, and which depend upon different characteristics or circumstances in the individual.

[*Privileges or immunities.*] We think this distinction and its explicit recognition in this amendment of great weight in this argument, because the next paragraph of this same section, which is the one mainly relied on by the plaintiffs in error, speaks only of privileges and immunities of citizens of the United States, and does not speak of those of citizens of the several States. The argument, however, in favor of the plaintiffs rests wholly on the assumption that the citizenship is the same, and the privileges and immunities guaranteed by the clause are the same.

The language is, "No State shall make or enforce any law which shall abridge the privileges or immunities of citizens of *the United States*." It is a little remarkable, if this clause was intended as a protection to the citizen of a State against the legislative power of his own State, that the word citizen of the State should be left out when it is so carefully used, and used in contradistinction to citizens of the United

States, in the very sentence which precedes it. It is too clear for argument that the change in phraseology was adopted understandingly and with a purpose.

Of the privileges and immunities of the citizen of the United States, and of the privileges and immunities of the citizen of the State, and what they respectively are, we will presently consider; but we wish to state here that it is only the former which are placed by this clause under the protection of the Federal Constitution, and that the latter, whatever they may be, are not intended to have any additional protection by this paragraph of the amendment.

If, then, there is a difference between the privileges and immunities belonging to a citizen of the United States as such, and those belonging to the citizen of the State as such the latter must rest for their security and protection where they have heretofore rested; for they are not embraced by this paragraph of the amendment. . . .

The first and the leading case on the [privileges and immunities clause of Article IV] is that of Corfield v. Coryell, decided by Mr. Justice Washington in the Circuit Court for the District of Pennsylvania in 1823. "The inquiry," he says, "is, what are the privileges and immunities of citizens of the several States? We feel no hesitation in confining these expressions to those privileges and immunities which are *fundamental*; which belong of right to the citizens of all free governments, and which have at all times been enjoyed by citizens of the several States which compose this Union, from the time of their becoming free, independent, and sovereign. What these fundamental principles are, it would be more tedious than difficult to enumerate. They may all, however, be comprehended under the following general heads: protection by the government, with the right to acquire and possess property of every kind, and to pursue and obtain happiness and safety, subject, nevertheless, to such restraints as the government may prescribe for the general good of the whole." . . .

In the case of Paul v. Virginia, the court, in expounding this clause of the Constitution, says that "the privileges and immunities secured to citizens of each State in the several States, by the provision in question, are those privileges and immunities which are common to the citizens in the latter States under their constitution and laws by virtue of their being citizens." . . .

Was it the purpose of the fourteenth amendment, by the simple declaration that no State should make or enforce any law which shall abridge the privileges and immunities of *citizens of the United States,* to transfer the security and protection of all the civil rights which we have mentioned, from the States to the Federal government? And where it is declared that Congress shall have the power to enforce that article, was it intended to bring within the power of Congress the entire domain of civil rights heretofore belonging exclusively to the States?

All this and more must follow, if the proposition of the plaintiffs in error be sound. For not only are these rights subject to the control of Congress whenever in its discretion any of them are supposed to be abridged by State legislation, but that body may also pass laws in advance, limiting and restricting the exercise of legislative power by the States, in their most ordinary and usual functions, as in its judgment it may think proper on all such subjects. And still further, such a construction followed by the reversal of the judgments of the Supreme Court of Louisiana in these cases, would constitute this court a perpetual censor upon all legislation of the States, on the civil rights of their own citizens, with authority to nullify such as it did not approve as consistent with those rights, as they existed at the time of the adoption of this amendment. The argument we admit is not always the most conclusive which is drawn from the consequences urged against the adoption of a particular construction of an instrument. But when, as in the case before us, these consequences are so serious, so far-reaching and pervading, so great a departure from the structure and spirit of our institutions; when the effect is to fetter and degrade the State governments by subjecting them to the control of Congress, in the exercise of powers heretofore universally conceded to them of the most ordinary and fundamental character; when in fact it radically changes the whole theory of the relations of the State and Federal governments to each other and of both these governments to the people; the argument has a force that is irresistible, in the absence of language which expresses such a purpose too clearly to admit of doubt.

We are convinced that no such results were intended by the Congress which proposed these amendments, nor by the legislatures of the States which ratified them.

But lest it should be said that no such privileges and immunities are to be found if those we have been considering are excluded, we venture to suggest some which owe their existence to the Federal government, its National character, its Constitution, or its laws.

One of these is well described in the case of Crandall v. Nevada, 73 U.S. (6 Wall.) 35 (1867). It is said to be the right of the citizen of this great country, protected by implied guarantees of its Constitution, "to come to the seat of government to assert any claim he may have upon that government, to transact any business he may have with it, to seek its protection, to share its offices, to engage in administering its functions. He has the right of free access to its seaports, through which all operations of foreign commerce are conducted, to the subtreasuries, land offices, and courts of justice in the several States." . . .

Another privilege of a citizen of the United States is to demand the care and protection of the Federal government over his life, liberty, and property when on the high seas or within the jurisdiction of a foreign government. Of this there can be no doubt, nor that the right depends upon his character as a citizen of the United States. The right to peaceably assemble and petition for redress of grievances, the privilege of the writ of habeas corpus, are rights of the citizen guaranteed by the Federal Constitution. The right to use the navigable waters of the United States, however they may penetrate the territory of the several States, all rights secured to our citizens by treaties with foreign nations, are dependent upon citizenship of the United States, and not citizenship of a State. One of these privileges is conferred by the very article under consideration. It is that a citizen of the United States can, of his own volition, become a citizen of any State of the Union by a bona fide residence therein, with the same rights as other citizens of that State. To these may be added the rights secured by the thirteenth and fifteenth articles of amendment, and by the other clause of the fourteenth, next to be considered. . . .

[*Due process.*] The argument has not been much pressed in these cases that the defendant's charter deprives the plaintiffs of their property without due process of law, or that it denies to them the equal protection of the law. The first of these paragraphs has been in the Constitution since the adoption of the fifth amendment, as a restraint upon the Federal power. It is also to be found in some form of expression in the constitutions of nearly all the States, as a restraint upon the power of the States. This law, then, has practically been the same as it now is during the existence of the government, except so far as the present amendment may place the restraining power over the States in this matter in the hands of the Federal government.

We are not without judicial interpretation, therefore, both State and National, of the meaning of this clause. And it is sufficient to say that under no construction of that provision that we have ever seen, or any that we deem admissible, can the restraint imposed by the State of Louisiana upon the exercise of their trade by the butchers of New Orleans be held to be a deprivation of property within the meaning of that provision....

[*Equal protection.*] In the light of the history of these amendments, and the pervading purpose of them, ... it is not difficult to give a meaning to [the equal protection] clause. The existence of laws in the States where the newly emancipated negroes resided, which discriminated with gross injustice and hardship against them as a class, was the evil to be remedied by this clause, and by it such laws are forbidden.

FIELD, J., dissenting....

It is contended in justification for the act in question that it was adopted in the interest of the city, to promote its cleanliness and protect its health, and was the legitimate exercise of what is termed the police power of the State. That power undoubtedly extends to all regulations affecting the health, good order, morals, peace, and safety of society, and is exercised on a great variety of subjects, and in almost numberless ways.... But under the pretence of prescribing a police regulation the State cannot be permitted to encroach upon any of the just rights of the citizen, which the Constitution intended to secure against abridgment.

In the law in question there are only two provisions which can properly be called police regulations — the one which requires the landing and slaughtering of animals below the city of New Orleans, and the other which requires the inspection of the animals before they are slaughtered. When these requirements are complied with, the sanitary purposes of the act are accomplished. In all other particulars the act is a mere grant to a corporation created by it of special and exclusive privileges by which the health of the city is in no way promoted. It is plain that if the corporation can, without endangering the health of the public, carry on the business of landing, keeping, and slaughtering cattle within a district below the city embracing an area of over a thousand square miles, it would not endanger the public health if other persons were also permitted to carry on the same business within the same district under similar conditions as to the inspection of the animals....

It is also sought to justify the act in question on the same principle that exclusive grants for ferries, bridges, and turnpikes are sanctioned. But it can find no support there. The grant, with exclusive privileges of a right thus appertaining to the government, is a very different thing from a grant, with exclusive privileges, of a right to pursue one of the ordinary trades or callings of life, which is a right appertaining solely to the individual....

The act of Louisiana presents the naked case, unaccompanied by any public considerations, where a right to pursue a lawful and necessary calling, previously enjoyed by every citizen, and in connection with which a thousand persons were daily employed, is taken away and vested exclusively for twenty-five years, for an extensive district and a large population, in a single corporation....

If exclusive privileges of this character can be granted to a corporation of seventeen persons, they may, in the discretion of the legislature, be equally granted to a single individual. If they may be granted for twenty-five years they may be equally granted for a century, and in perpetuity. If they may be granted for the landing and keeping of animals intended for sale or slaughter they may be equally . . . granted for any of the pursuits of human industry, even in its most simple and common forms. Indeed, upon the theory on which the exclusive privileges granted by the act in question are sustained, there is no monopoly, in the most odious form, which may not be upheld.

The question presented is, therefore, one of the gravest importance, not merely to the parties here, but to the whole country. It is nothing less than the question whether the recent amendments to the Federal Constitution protect the citizens of the United States against the deprivation of their common rights by State legislation. In my judgment the fourteenth amendment does afford such protection, and was so intended by the Congress which framed and the States which adopted it. . . .

[Under the] first clause of the fourteenth amendment . . . , [a] citizen of a State is now only a citizen of the United States residing in that State. The fundamental rights, privileges, and immunities which belong to him as a free man and a free citizen, now belong to him as a citizen of the United States, and are not dependent upon his citizenship of any State. . . .

If under the fourth article of the Constitution equality of privileges and immunities is secured between citizens of different States, under the fourteenth amendment the same equality is secured between citizens of the United States.

It will not be pretended that under the fourth article of the Constitution any State could create a monopoly in any known trade or manufacture in favor of her own citizens, or any portion of them, which would exclude an equal participation in the trade or manufacture monopolized by citizens of other States. She could not confer, for example, upon any of her citizens the sole right to manufacture shoes, or boots, or silk, or the sole right to sell those articles in the State so as to exclude non-resident citizens from engaging in a similar manufacture or sale. . . .

Now, what the clause in question does for the protection of citizens of one State against the creation of monopolies in favor of citizens of other States, the fourteenth amendment does for the protection of every citizen of the United States against the creation of any monopoly whatever. The privileges and immunities of citizens of the United States, of every one of them, is secured against abridgment in any form by any State. The fourteenth amendment places them under the guardianship of the National authority. All monopolies in any known trade or manufacture are an invasion of these privileges, for they encroach upon the liberty of citizens to acquire property and pursue happiness. . . .

That amendment was intended to give practical effect to the declaration of 1776 of inalienable rights, rights which are the gift of the Creator, which the law does not confer, but only recognizes. . . .

[The] equality of right, with exemption from all disparaging and partial enactments, in the lawful pursuits of life, throughout the whole country, is the distinguishing privilege of citizens of the United States. To them, everywhere, all pursuits, all professions, all avocations are open without other restrictions than such as are imposed equally upon all others of the same age, sex, and condition. The State may prescribe such regulations for every pursuit and calling of life as will promote the public health, secure the good order and advance the general prosperity of society, but when once prescribed, the pursuit or calling must be free to be followed by every citizen who is within the conditions designated, and will conform to the regulations. This is the fundamental idea upon which our institutions rest, and unless adhered to in the legislation of the country our government will be a republic only in name. The fourteenth amendment, in my judgment, makes it essential to the validity of the legislation of every State that this equality of right should be respected. . . .

I am authorized by the Chief Justice, Mr. Justice Swayne, and Mr. Justice Bradley, to state that they concur with me in this dissenting opinion.

BRADLEY, J., dissenting:

I concur in the opinion which has just been read by Mr. Justice Field; but desire to add a few observations for the purpose of more fully illustrating my views on the important question decided in these cases, and the special grounds on which they rest. . . .

The people of this country brought with them to its shores the rights of Englishmen; the rights which had been wrested from English sovereigns at various periods of the nation's history. One of these fundamental rights was expressed in these words, found in Magna Carta: "No freeman shall be taken or imprisoned or be dissected of his freehold or liberties or free customs, or be outlawed or exiled, or any otherwise destroyed; nor will we pass upon him or condemn him but by lawful judgment of his peers or by the law of the land." English constitutional writers expound this article as rendering life, liberty, and property inviolable, except by due process of law. This is the very right which the plaintiffs in error claim in this case. . . . Blackstone classifies these fundamental rights under three heads, as the absolute rights of individuals, to wit: the right of personal security, the right of personal liberty, and the right of private property. . . . These are the fundamental rights which can only be taken away by due process of law, and which can only be interfered with, or the enjoyment of which can only be modified, by lawful regulations necessary or proper for the mutual good of all; and these rights, I contend, belong to the citizens of every free government.

For the preservation, exercise, and enjoyment of these rights the individual citizen, as a necessity, must be left free to adopt such calling, profession, or trade as may seem to him most conducive to that end. Without this right he cannot be a freeman. This right to choose one's calling is an essential part of that liberty which it is the object of government to protect; and a calling, when chosen, is a man's property and right. Liberty and property are not protected where these rights are arbitrarily assailed. . . .

The Constitution, it is true, as it stood prior to the recent amendments, specifies, in terms, only a few of the personal privileges and immunities of citizens, but they are very comprehensive in their character. The States were merely prohibited from passing bills of attainder, ex post facto laws, laws impairing the obligation of contracts, and perhaps one or two more. But others of the greatest consequence were enumerated, although they were only secured, in express terms, from invasion by the Federal government; such as the right of habeas corpus, the right of trial by jury, of free exercise of religious worship, the right of free speech and a free press, the right peaceably to assemble for the discussion of public measures, the right to be secure against unreasonable searches and seizures, and above all, and including almost all the rest, the right of *not being deprived of life, liberty, or property, without due process of law.* These, and still others are specified in the original Constitution, or in the early amendments of it, as among the privileges and immunities of citizens of the United States, or, what is still stronger for the force of the argument, the rights of all persons, whether citizens or not. . . .

Admitting . . . that formerly the States were not prohibited from infringing any of the fundamental privileges and immunities of citizens of the United States, except in a few specified cases, that cannot be said now, since the adoption of the fourteenth amendment. In my judgment, it was the intention of the people of this country in adopting that amendment to provide National security against violation by the States of the fundamental rights of the citizen.

. . . [A]ny law which establishes a sheer monopoly, depriving a large class of citizens of the privilege of pursuing a lawful employment, does abridge the privileges of those citizens. . . . [It also deprives them] of liberty as well as property, without due process of law. Their right of choice is a portion of their liberty; their occupation is their property. Such a law also deprives those citizens of the equal protection of the laws, contrary to the last clause of the section. . . .

It is futile to argue that none but persons of the African race are intended to be benefited by this amendment. They may have been the primary cause of the amendment, but its language is general, embracing all citizens, and I think it was purposely so expressed.

The mischief to be remedied was not merely slavery and its incidents and consequences; but that spirit of insubordination and disloyalty to the National government which had troubled the country for so many years in some of the States, and that intolerance of free speech and free discussion which often rendered life and property insecure, and led to much unequal legislation. The amendment was an attempt to give voice to the strong National yearning for that time and that condition of things, in which American citizenship should be a sure guaranty of safety, and in which every citizen of the United States might stand erect on every portion of its soil, in the full enjoyment of every right and privilege belonging to a freeman, without fear of violence or molestation. . . .

SWAYNE, J., dissenting:

I concur in the dissent in these cases and in the views expressed by my brethren, Mr. Justice Field and Mr. Justice Bradley. I desire, however, to submit a few additional remarks.

The first eleven amendments to the Constitution were intended to be checks and limitations upon the government which that instrument called into existence. They had their origin in a spirit of jealousy on the part of the States, which existed when the Constitution was adopted. The first ten were proposed in 1789 by the first Congress at its first session after the organization of the government. The eleventh was proposed in 1794, and the twelfth in 1803. The one last mentioned regulates the mode of electing the President and Vice-President. It neither increased nor diminished the power of the General Government, and may be said in that respect to occupy neutral ground. No further amendments were made until 1865, a period of more than sixty years. The thirteenth amendment was proposed by Congress on the 1st of February, 1865, the fourteenth on the 16th of June, 1866, and the fifteenth on the 27th of February, 1869. These amendments are a new departure, and mark an important epoch in the constitutional history of the country. They trench directly upon the power of the States, and deeply affect those bodies. They are, in this respect, at the opposite pole from the first eleven.

Fairly construed these amendments may be said to rise to the dignity of a new Magna Charta. . . .

. . .Life, liberty, and property are forbidden to be taken "without due process of law," and "equal protection of the laws" is guaranteed to all. Life is the gift of God, and the right to preserve it is the most sacred of the rights of man. Liberty is freedom from all restraints but such as are justly imposed by law. Beyond that line lies the domain of usurpation and tyranny. Property is everything which has an exchangeable value, and the right of property includes the power to dispose of it according to the will of the owner. Labor is property, and as such merits protection. . . .

These amendments are all consequences of the late civil war. The prejudices and apprehension as to the central government which prevailed when the Constitution was adopted were dispelled by the light of experience. The public mind became satisfied that there was less danger of tyranny in the head than of anarchy and tyranny in the members. The provisions of this section are all eminently conservative in their character. They are a bulwark of defence, and can never be made an engine of oppression. The language employed is unqualified in its scope. There is no exception in its terms, and there can be properly none in their application. By the language "citizens of the United States" was meant all such citizens; and by "any person" was meant all persons within the jurisdiction of the State. No distinction is intimated on account of race or color. This court has no authority to interpolate a limitation that is neither expressed nor implied. Our duty is to execute the law, not to make it. The protection provided was not intended to be confined to those of any particular race or class, but to embrace equally all races, classes, and conditions of men. It is objected that the power conferred is novel and large. The answer is that the novelty was known and the measure deliberately adopted. The power is beneficent in its nature, and cannot be abused. It is such and should exist in every well-ordered system of polity. Where could it be more appropriately lodged than in the hands to which it is confided? It is necessary to enable the government of the nation to secure to every one within its jurisdiction the rights and privileges enumerated, which, according to the plainest considerations of reason and justice and the fundamental principles of the social compact, all are entitled to enjoy. Without such authority any government claiming to be national is glaringly defective. The construction adopted by the majority of my brethren is, in my judgment, much too narrow. It defeats, by a limitation not anticipated, the intent of those by whom the instrument was framed and of those by whom it was adopted. To the extent of that limitation it turns, as it were, what was meant for bread into a stone. By the Constitution, as it stood before the war, ample protection was given against oppression by the Union, but little was given against wrong and oppression by the States. That want was intended to be supplied by this amendment. Against the former this court has been called upon more than once to interpose. Authority of the same amplitude was intended to be conferred as to the latter. But this arm of our jurisdiction is, in these cases, stricken down by the judgment just given. Nowhere, than in this court, ought the will of the nation, as thus expressed, to be more liberally construed or more cordially executed. This determination of the majority seems to me to lie far in the other direction.

Discussion

1. *General constitutional law.* Before Justice Miller comes to the Reconstruction amendments, he discusses whether the Louisiana statute is within the state's police power. This may have been gratuitous, especially because the Slaughterhouse Cases

came before the Court on writ of error to the Louisiana Supreme Court. But, especially taken together with Justice Miller's opinion a year later in Loan Association v. Topeka, 87 U.S. (20 Wall.) 655 (1874), it indicates that the notion of a "general constitutional law" remained alive and well after the Civil War. *Loan Association* invalidated municipal bonds, issued for the benefit of a private ironworks, on the ground that their issuance lay beyond the state's taxing power:

> It must be conceded that there are such rights in every free government beyond the control of the State. A government which recognized no such rights, which held the lives, the liberty, and the property of its citizens subject at all times to the absolute disposition and unlimited control of even the most democratic depository of power, is after all but a despotism. . . .
>
> The theory of our governments, State and National, is opposed to the deposit of unlimited power anywhere. The executive, the legislative, and the judicial branches of these governments are all of limited and defined powers.
>
> There are limitations on such power which grow out of the essential nature of all free governments. Implied reservations of individual rights, without which the social compact could not exist, and which are respected by all governments entitled to the name. No court, for instance, would hesitate to declare void a statute which enacted that *A.* and *B.* who were husband and wife to each other should be so no longer, but that *A.* should thereafter be the husband of *C.*, and *B.* the wife of *D.* Or which should enact that the homestead now owned by *A.* should no longer be his, but should henceforth be the property of *B.*
>
> Of all the powers conferred upon government that of taxation is most liable to abuse. . . . The power to tax is . . . the strongest, the most pervading of all the powers of government, reaching directly or indirectly to all classes of the people. It was said by Chief Justice Marshall, in the case of McCulloch v. The State of Maryland, that the power to tax is the power to destroy. . . .
>
> To lay with one hand the power of the government on the property of the citizen, and with the other to bestow it upon favored individuals to aid private enterprises and build up private fortunes, is none the less a robbery because it is done under the forms of law and is called taxation. This is not legislation. It is a decree under legislative forms. . . .[26]

Several years later, in Davidson v. Louisiana, 96 U.S. 97 (1878), the Court drew a sharp jurisdictional boundary between general constitutional law and the clauses of the Fourteenth Amendment. On appeal from the Louisiana Supreme Court, the

---

26. Only Justice Clifford dissented, writing:

State constitutions may undoubtedly restrict the power of the legislature to pass laws, and it is plain that any law passed in violation of such a prohibition is void, but the better opinion is that where the constitution of the State contains no prohibition upon the subject, express or implied, neither the State nor Federal courts can declare a statute of the State void as unwise, unjust, or inexpedient, nor for any other cause, unless it be repugnant to the Federal Constitution. Except where the Constitution has imposed limits upon the legislative power the role of law appears to be that the power of legislation must be considered as practically absolute, whether the law operates according to natural justice or not in any particular case. . . .

Courts cannot nullify an act of the State legislature on the vague ground that they think it opposed to a general latent spirit supposed to pervade or underlie the constitution, where neither the terms nor the implications of the instrument disclose any such restriction. Such a power is denied to the courts, because to concede it would be to make the courts sovereign over both the constitution and the people, and convert the government into a judicial despotism.

owners of real estate in New Orleans claimed that a certain property tax deprived them of property without due process of law. Justice Miller noted that the due process clause was increasingly being invoked to bring before the Supreme Court "the abstract opinions of every unsuccessful litigant in a State court of the justice of the decision against him, and of the merits of the legislation on which such a decision may be founded." Miller wrote that the city tax "may violate some provision of the State Constitution against unequal taxation; but the Federal Constitution imposes no restraints on the States in that regard. . . . It may possibly violate some of those principles of general constitutional law, of which we could take jurisdiction if we were sitting in review of a Circuit Court of the United States, as we were in Loan Association v. Topeka. . . ."

2. *"Privileges or immunities."* Justice Miller reaffirmed the Court's earlier holding that the privileges and immunities clause of Article IV, Section 2, had no substantive content: The clause did not require a state to grant any particular right to any person, but only prevented a state from conferring certain benefits on its own citizens while denying them to citizens of other states. The Court acknowledged that the Fourteenth Amendment's "privileges or immunities" clause, by contrast, protected certain rights of citizens against infringement even by their own state. What are these rights?

3. *Rights arising out of a citizen's relationship with the national government.* Justice Miller wrote for the Court that the Fourteenth Amendment clause protects rights "which owe their existence to the Federal government, its National character, its Constitution, or its laws." His hodgepodge of illustrations does not illuminate. Some of the examples simply incorporate the privileges or immunities clause of Article IV and other provisions of the Civil War amendments. Others, such as the right to federal protection "on the high seas or within the jurisdiction of a foreign country," seem beyond a state's ability to infringe. But certain interests that might be thought to arise out of a citizen's relationship with the national government are susceptible to infringement by the states, for example, the rights to assemble to discuss matters pertaining to the government and to petition the government and the right of access to federal courts and to other federal agencies. See Hague v. CIO, 307 U.S. 496 (1939). To be sure, even without the privileges or immunities clause, Congress could enact legislation under its Article I powers to secure these rights — indeed, to secure them for noncitizens as well as citizens and against infringement by private persons as well as by states. But the privileges or immunities clause provides an explicit guarantee of the rights of citizens against state invasion that is self-executing — i.e., binding on the states and enforceable by the judiciary even in the absence of congressional implementing legislation.

4. *Fundamental or natural rights.* Justice Field asserted broadly that the clause "was intended to give practical effect to the declaration of 1776 of inalienable rights, rights which are gifts of the Creator, which the law does not confer but only recognizes." And Justice Bradley asserted that among the rights of citizens are Blackstone's "three absolute rights of individuals," which encompass the "privilege of engaging in any lawful employment for a livelihood." Field and Bradley were, at the least, trying to read the privileges or immunities clause of the Fourteenth Amendment to incorporate "general constitutional principles" — though it is hardly clear that the Louisiana monopoly ran afoul of those principles.

5. *The provisions of the Bill of Rights.* Justice Bradley also suggested that the privileges and immunities of citizens of the United States include the guarantees of

the first eight amendments to the Constitution. Although the Court never held that any clause of the Fourteenth Amendment fully incorporates the Bill of Rights, almost all of the provisions have been made binding on the states through "selective incorporation" into the due process clause. See the Introduction to Part Two, infra.

6. *"Due process."* The due process clause of the Fourteenth Amendment is identical to the due process clause of the Fifth Amendment. The Fifth Amendment clause, as its language implies, was generally understood to address the procedures by which individuals' rights and liabilities were adjudicated, although there is also some evidence that it was intended to include some substantive limitations as well, particularly the protection of vested rights.[27] Shortly before the Civil War, in Murray v. Hoboken Land & Improvement Co., 59 U.S. (18 How.) 272 (1855), Justice Curtis thus described the origin and scope of the due process clause of the Fifth Amendment:

> The words, "due process of law," were undoubtedly intended to convey the same meaning as the words, "by the law of the land," in Magna Carta. Lord Coke, in his commentary on those words says they mean due process of law. The constitutions which had been adopted by the several States before the formation of the federal constitution, following the language of the great charter more closely, generally contained the words, "but by the judgment of his peers, or the law of the land." . . .
>
> The constitution contains no description of those processes which it was intended to allow or forbid. It does not even declare what principles are to be applied to ascertain whether it be due process. It is manifest that it was not left to the legislative power to enact any process which might be devised. The article is a restraint on the legislative as well as on the executive and judicial powers of the government, and cannot be so construed as to leave congress free to make any process "due process of law," by its mere will. To what principles, then, are we to resort to ascertain whether this process, enacted by congress, is due process? To this the answer must be twofold. We must examine the constitution itself, to see whether this process be in conflict with any of its provisions. If not found to be so, we must look to those settled usages and modes of proceeding existing in the common and statute law of England, before the emigration of our ancestors, and which are shown not to have been unsuited to their civil and political condition by having been acted on by them after the settlement of this country.[28]

Plaintiffs in the Slaughterhouse Cases were not attacking an adjudicatory procedure but rather the substantive appropriateness or fairness of the slaughterhouse monopoly. Recall that, in Dred Scott v. Sandford, 60 U.S. (19 How.) 393 (1857), Chapter 3, supra, Taney had attacked the Missouri Compromise on the ground that it deprived slaveholders of vested rights in their property without due process of law. The plaintiffs in the Slaughterhouse Cases were concerned, not with the fairness of procedures by which rights and obligations are adjudicated, but with substantive limits on how the legislature would restrict those rights. Justice Miller's

---

27. See James W. Ely Jr., The Oxymoron Reconsidered: Myth and Reality in the Origins of Substantive Due Process, 16 Const. Commentary 315 (1999); John Harrison, Substantive Due Process and the Constitutional Text, 83 Va. L. Rev. 493 (1997).

28. The Court has not adhered to this static view of procedural due process and has developed an extensive doctrine concerning the procedures — e.g., notice, opportunity to be heard, opportunity to confront adverse witnesses, the impartiality of the tribunal-in various circumstances. See Chapter 9, infra.

29. Lewis LaRue, The Continuing Presence of *Dred Scott*, 42 Wash. & Lee L. Rev. 57, 60-61 (1985).

quick dismissal of the *substantive due process* claim may have reflected its aversion to the *Dred Scott* decision, from which the Court was still smarting, but it may also have reflected the view that plaintiff's claim was simply without merit on any constitutional (large or small "c") theory. For only a year later, in Bartemeyer v. Louisiana, 85 U.S. (18 Wall.) 129 (1874), Miller commented that the application of a state prohibition law to liquor held for sale before the law's enactment would present the "very grave question . . . [w]hether this would be a statute depriving [the owner] of his property without due process of law."

7. *Slaughterhouse and bifurcated citizenship.* Professor LaRue sees "a clear continuity, on a question of citizenship, between *Dred Scott* and the Slaughter-house Cases." By stating that "the distinction between citizenship of the United States and citizenship of a State is clearly recognized" by the Fourteenth Amendment, Justice Miller "preserved one of the most important features" of the earlier case. He holds "that the privileges and immunities of the two types of citizenship are different, and that the United States Constitution protects only the national privileges," which are in fact of limited import.

> [T]he true import of the bifurcation is that all of the important rights are left to the protection of the state governments. . . .
>
> At this point the Slaughter-house Cases begin to look like the deep mirror image of *Dred Scott*. Taney declared that blacks could not be citizens; . . . the fundamental purpose behind this move was to prevent blacks from claiming the privileges and immunities of citizenship. With the adoption of the fourteenth amendment, blacks become citizens, but Miller gutted the meaning of that by stripping citizenship of any important legal consequences. So long as blacks cannot be citizens, enormous importance is attached to the concept; as soon as blacks can become citizens, the concept is drained of all meaning. (It is this sort of thing that gives paranoia a good name.)[29]

In United States v. Cruikshank, 92 U.S. 542 (1875), the Supreme Court relied on the logic of *Slaughterhouse* to dismiss indictments under the 1870 Enforcement Act, which made it a crime to conspire to deny citizens of rights secured by the federal Constitution or laws. Cruikshank arose out of the infamous April 1873 Colfax Massacre, one of the most violent episodes of Reconstruction. Following disputed state elections in Louisiana in 1872 that produced parallel governments, whites supporting the Democratic candidate seized the village of Colfax and slaughtered hundreds of innocent blacks who included supporters of the Republican candidate. The Supreme Court, in an opinion by Chief Justice Waite, held that indictments charging conspiracy to violate blacks' rights to assemble peacefully, petition, and bear arms were insufficient because the Bill of Rights protected citizens only against violations by the federal government, not by the States or by private parties. "The right [of assembly] was not created by the [First] amendment; neither was its continuance guaranteed, except as against congressional interference. For their protection in its enjoyment, therefore, the people must look to the States. The power for that purpose was originally placed there, and it has never been surrendered to the United States." Indictments charging conspiracy to violate rights to life and liberty failed because these were natural rights properly protected by the States, not rights protected by the federal government: "It is no more the duty of the United States to punish for a conspiracy to falsely imprison or murder within a State, than it would be to punish for false imprisonment or murder itself." Indictments charging conspiracy to violate the right to vote failed because the right to vote was a state right and not a federal right: "[T]he right of suffrage is not a necessary attribute of national citizenship; but that exemption from discrimination in the exercise of that right on account of race, &c., is. The right to vote in the States comes from the States; but the right of exemption from the prohibited discrimination comes from the United States." Finally, the Court, reading the indictments narrowly, concluded that most of them did not expressly allege racial discrimination and the two counts which did mention racial animus did not sufficiently specify the rights claimed to be violated.

In United States v. Reese, 92 U.S. 214 (1875), the Court struck down sections 3 and 4 of the 1870 Enforcement Act, which prohibited interference with the right to vote. The case involved Louisiana officials who allegedly refused to register black voters in state elections. The Court noted once again that the right to vote was not a right guaranteed by the Federal Constitution but only by the states; hence the Court reasoned that sections 3 and 4 were beyond Congress's powers because they did not specifically require a showing of racial discrimination. Justice Hunt, dissenting, disagreed, arguing that "the intention of Congress on this subject is too plain to be discussed. The Fifteenth Amendment had just been adopted, the object of which was to secure to a lately enslaved population protection against violations of their right to vote on account of their color or previous condition."

8. *The original understanding of the Fourteenth Amendment.* Compare Justice Miller's characterization of the "one pervading purpose" of the Reconstruction amendments with Justice Bradley's broader description of "the mischief to be remedied." Bradley is correct that, in reaction to threats to the institution of slavery, Confederate states had egregiously infringed civil liberties and that this had been a source of national concern.[30] Although the congressional debate over the Fourteenth Amendment scarcely is unequivocal about its purpose and scope,[31] the clear focus was on racial discrimination, not on civil liberties as such. On the other hand, the language of the Fourteenth Amendment was not limited to racial concerns, and some of its phrases had been used expansively in the debates over slavery preceding the Civil War. Abolitionists indiscriminately invoked natural law, the Bill of Rights, "the inherent rights of citizens," the rights to "protection of the laws," and against the "deprivation of liberty without due process of law" to urge that slavery violated the Constitution.[32] As *Dred Scott* indicates, apologists for slavery countered in similar terms.

9. *Understanding the war.* It should be obvious that the meaning assigned the Fourteenth Amendment was (and remains, see Chapter 5, infra) linked with the

---

30. See, e.g., Clement Eaton, Freedom of Thought in the Old South (1940) and the materials in Chapter 3, supra, on suppression of the freedom of speech of critics of slavery.

31. See, e.g., Charles Fairman, Reconstruction and Reunion 1864-88 (Part One), in 6 History of the Supreme Court of the United States chs. 20-21 (1971); Fairman, Does the Fourteenth Amendment Incorporate the Bill of Rights? The Original Understanding, 2 Stan. L. Rev. 5 (1949); Alexander Bickel, The Original Understanding and the Segregation Decision, 69 Harv. L. Rev. 1 (1955).

32. See Jacobus tenBroek, Equal Under Law (1965), an expanded version of his Antislavery Origins of the Fourteenth Amendment (1951); Howard Graham, The Early Antislavery Backgrounds of the Fourteenth Amendment, 1950 Wis. L. Rev. 479, 610; Graham, Our "Declaratory" Fourteenth Amendment, 7 Stan. L. Rev. 3 (1954). These articles are reprinted in Graham, Everyman's Constitution, 152, 295 (1968).

meaning assigned the events that brought it into being, i.e., the Civil War and Reconstruction. We have seen an earlier version of the debate with regard to the struggle between Andrew Johnson and his congressional opponents. The *Slaughterhouse* opinions present similarly different narratives of the meaning of the War and its general implications for American federalism.[33] Consider especially the closing paragraphs of both Justice Bradley's and Justice Swayne's dissenting opinions. How does one decide (and, of course, *who* gets to decide) what is the "real meaning" of such a complex event as the Civil War?

10. *Justice Field and Jacksonian egalitarianism.* In his message vetoing the rechartering of the Bank of the United States, Andrew Jackson cautioned that "[t]here are no necessary evils in government. Its evils exist only in its abuses. If it would confine itself to equal protection, and, as Heaven does its rains, shower its favors alike on the high and the low, the rich and the poor, it would be an unqualified blessing." Recall the distinction, relevant to the scope of the contract clause, between ordinary property, which is presumed to be the result of the "natural," prepolitical market process, and "privilege." Justice Field opposed the state-mandated monopoly in the *Slaughterhouse Cases* precisely because it represented a use of state power to establish privileges that were in direct opposition to the kind of "equal protection" sought by Jacksonian ideology. Consider Michael Les Benedict's comment:

> [O]ne must recognize that there were two related but distinct justifications for the laissez-faire principle in the later nineteenth century. The first was based directly upon classical economists' conception of the "laws" of economics. It suggested that almost any government effort to overcome or channel those laws was doomed to failure. The second was based on a concept of human liberty implicit in the principles of classical economics. It militated only against certain kinds of government interferences in the economy, not against all interference. That concept was that the power of government could not legitimately be exercised to benefit one person or group at the expense of others. It was this conviction — not the notion that all government economic activity violated "immutable" economic laws — that lay at the heart of laissez-faire constitutionalism. . . . [It] received wide support in late nineteenth-century America not because it was based on widely adhered to economic principles and certainly not because it protected entrenched economic privilege, but rather because it was congruent with a well-established and accepted principle of American liberty.[34]

Field came out of a tradition that bitterly opposed "class legislation." William Leggett, a Jacksonian writer, commented that "[p]ower and wealth are continually stealing from the many to the few." The rich and powerful are constantly seeking "to monopolize the advantages of the Government, to hedge themselves around with exclusive privileges, and elevate themselves at the expense of the great body of the people."[35] Although the great fear concerned the rich and the wellborn, Benedict notes that Jacksonians did not accept "class legislation" that benefited the poor. Instead, the watchword was an abstract notion of "equal rights," with individuals free to make whatever use of such rights they wished within the economic marketplace.

33. See especially Pamela Brandwein, Reconstructing Reconstruction: The Supreme Court and the Production of Historical Truth (1999), which analyzes the dramatically different histories of the Fourteenth Amendment.

34. Michael Les Benedict, Laissez-Faire and Liberty: A Re-Evaluation of the Meaning and Origins of Laissez-Faire Constitutionalism, 3 L. & Hist. Rev. 293, 298 (1985).

35. Theodore Sedgewick, ed., Political Writings of William Leggett, i, 66-67 (1840), quoted in id. at 319.

Consider also Washington University v. Rouse, 75 U.S. (8 Wall.) 439 (1869), which concerned the validity of a Missouri charter that guaranteed the University permanent immunity from state taxation. Such tax exemptions were quite common and oft-litigated. The Supreme Court, in two 1854 decisions, Ohio Life Ins. & Trust Co. v. Debolt, 57 U.S. 416, and Piqua Branch Bank v. Knoup, 57 U.S. 369, held that an explicit grant of a tax exemption could not be rescinded without violating the contract clause. Critics argued that the legislature retained an "inalienable power" to tax in behalf of the public welfare and that one legislature could not bind its successor. Thus many jurists "began distinguishing between police power regulations promoting the public health, safety, and morals from those promoting the public convenience. The former were, and the latter were not, sufficiently crucial to social welfare to justify the revocation of express charter provisions."[36] The majority in *Rouse* easily upheld the exemption. Justice Miller dissented, joined by Chief Justice Chase and Justice Field: "[N]o hindrance can be seen, in the principle adopted by the court, to rich corporations, as railroads and express companies or rich men, making contracts with the Legislatures, as they best may, and with appliances as it is known they do use, for perpetual exemption from all the burdens of supporting the government. The result of such a principle, under the growing tendency to special and partial legislation, would be, to exempt the rich from taxation, and cast all the burden of the support of government, and the payment of its debts, on those who are too poor or too honest to purchase such immunity." Although Justice Field and other laissez-faire constitutionalists have been criticized for being too insensitive to the opportunities for abuse allowed the well-off within a market featuring dramatic inequalities of wealth, it may well oversimplify to describe them merely as apologists for the uses of political power that wealth often brings in its wake.

BRADWELL v. ILLINOIS, 83 U.S. 130 (1873): [This case was decided the same day as *Slaughterhouse*, on April 14, 1873. It also raised a conflict between a free labor interpretation of the Fourteenth Amendment and states' rights views. The Illinois Supreme Court refused Myra Bradwell a license to practice law solely because she was a woman; no one doubted that she otherwise qualified. Her attorney, Republican Senator Matthew Hale Carpenter, cited the rights of the Declaration of Independence as among the "privileges and immunities" protected by the new amendment; among the specific rights protected was that of laboring in one's chosen vocation. "[I]n the pursuit of happiness," said Carpenter, "all avocations, all honors, all positions, are alike open to every one[;] in the protection of these rights all are equal before the law." As Rogers Smith notes, "[b]y resting his case on the liberal right to labor and drawing an analogy between the discrimination against women and the racial oppressions the amendment was universally acknowledged to oppose, Carpenter made a very strong argument. He also faced no opposing counsel."[37] Nonetheless, the Court rebuffed Bradwell's claim, noting the limited scope of the Privileges or Immunities clause.]

MILLER, J.: [T]he right to admission to practice in the courts of a State . . . in no sense depends on citizenship of the United States. It has not, as far as we know, ever been made in any State, or in any case, to depend on citizenship at all. Certainly many prominent and distinguished lawyers have been admitted to practice . . . who were not citizens of the United States or of any State. But, on whatever basis this

36. Stephen A. Siegel, Understanding the Nineteenth Century Contract Clause, The Role of the Property-Privilege Distinction and "Takings" Clause Jurisprudence, 60 S. Cal. L. Rev. 1, 52 (1986).
37. Smith, supra n.23, at 260.

right may be placed, so far as it can have any relation to citizenship at all, it would seem that, as to the courts of a State, it would relate to citizenship of the State, and as to Federal courts, it would relate to citizenship of the United States.

The opinion just delivered in the Slaughter-House Cases renders elaborate argument in the present case unnecessary; for, unless we are wholly and radically mistaken in the principles on which those cases are decided, the right to control and regulate the granting of licenses to practice law in the courts of a State is one of those powers which are not transferred for its protection to the Federal government, and its exercise is in no manner governed or controlled by citizenship of the United States in the party seeking such licensure.

BRADLEY, J., joined by Swayne and Field JJ, concurring: [All three of these Justices had dissented in the *SlaughterHouse Cases*.]: The claim that, under the fourteenth amendment of the Constitution, which declares that no State shall make or enforce any law which shall abridge the privileges and immunities of citizens of the United States, the statute law of Illinois, or the common law prevailing in that State, can no longer be set up as a barrier against the right of females to pursue any lawful employment for a livelihood (the practice of law included), assumes that it is one of the privileges and immunities of women as citizens to engage in any and every profession, occupation, or employment in civil life.

It certainly cannot be affirmed, as an historical fact, that this has ever been established as one of the fundamental privileges and immunities of the sex. On the contrary, the civil law, as well as nature herself, has always recognized a wide difference in the respective spheres and destinies of man and woman. Man is, or should be, woman's protector and defender. The natural and proper timidity and delicacy which belongs to the female sex evidently unfits it for many of the occupations of civil life. The constitution of the family organization, which is founded in the divine ordinance, as well as in the nature of things, indicates the domestic sphere as that which properly belongs to the domain and functions of womanhood. The harmony, not to say identity, of interests and views which belong, or should belong, to the family institution is repugnant to the idea of a woman adopting a distinct and independent career from that of her husband. So firmly fixed was this sentiment in the founders of the common law that it became a maxim of that system of jurisprudence that a woman had no legal existence separate from her husband, who was regarded as her head and representative in the social state; and, notwithstanding some recent modifications of this civil status, many of the special rules of law flowing from and dependent upon this cardinal principle still exist in full force in most States. One of these is, that a married woman is incapable, without her husband's consent, of making contracts which shall be binding on her or him. This very incapacity was one circumstance which the Supreme Court of Illinois deemed important in rendering a married woman incompetent fully to perform the duties and trusts that belong to the office of an attorney and counsellor.

It is true that many women are unmarried and not affected by any of the duties, complications, and incapacities arising out of the married state, but these are exceptions to the general rule. The paramount destiny and mission of woman are to fulfil the noble and benign offices of wife and mother. This is the law of the Creator. And the rules of civil society must be adapted to the general constitution of things, and cannot be based upon exceptional cases.

The humane movements of modern society, which have for their object the multiplication of avenues for woman's advancement, and of occupations adapted to her condition and sex, have my heartiest concurrence. But I am not prepared to say that it is one of her fundamental rights and privileges to be admitted into every office and position, including those which require highly special qualifications and demanding special responsibilities. In the nature of things it is not every citizen of every age, sex, and condition that is qualified for every calling and position. It is the prerogative of the legislator to prescribe regulations founded on nature, reason, and experience for the due admission of qualified persons to professions and callings demanding special skill and confidence. This fairly belongs to the police power of the State; and, in my opinion, in view of the peculiar characteristics, destiny, and mission of woman, it is within the province of the legislature to ordain what offices, positions, and callings shall be filled and discharged by men, and shall receive the benefit of those energies and responsibilities, and that decision and firmness which are presumed to predominate in the sterner sex.

[Chief Justice Chase, who had been one of the leading abolitionist lawyers during the 1850s, dissented without opinion.]

Discussion

1. *Coverture and equal protection.* Bradwell did not consider the equal protection clause as a possible source of vindication of Bradwell's claims. As Justice Miller suggests in the *Slaughterhouse Cases,* the Justices believed that the clause was primarily designed to respond to "class legislation" like that directed against blacks; they did not think that the many restrictions on women's right to work outside the home violated this principle. Moreover, the framers of the Fourteenth Amendment did not expect that the equal protection clause, or indeed, the Fourteenth Amendment generally, would alter the common law rules of coverture, under which a woman surrendered almost all of her rights to her husband upon marriage. Thus, Myra Bradwell, as a married woman, might not be able to represent her clients effectively if she could not make binding contracts. But wouldn't this logic suggest that the state could not prevent unmarried women from becoming members of the state bar? Do you find Justice Bradley's response persuasive?

2. *Separate spheres.* Bradley's opinion in *Bradwell* exemplifies the "separate spheres" ideology of the late nineteenth century, under which social life was divided into two spheres or domains with special gender competences for men and women. According to this ideology, men were self-interested, self-seeking productive breadwinners who competed in the market, while women were nurturing caretakers centered in the home, who gave men relief from the vicissitudes of market life. The separate spheres ideology reflected changes in economy and society in the nineteenth century that produced new ways of conceptualizing gender relations. The authority-based conception of the household and marriage — in which a husband exercised dominion over his wife — gradually gave way to an affect-based conception, which featured a cult of domesticity that imagined wives willingly submitting to their husbands out of love and altruism. Thus, Bradley's opinion explains the exclusion of women from the legal profession not in terms of her husband's authority over her but, rather, her obligations to home and hearth.[38]

38. On the development of the separate spheres ideology, see, e.g., Linda K. Kerber, Separate Spheres, Female Worlds, Woman's Place: The Rhetoric of Women's History, 75 J. Am. Hist. 9, 21 (1988); Nancy F. Cott, The Bonds of Womanhood: Woman's Sphere in New England, 1780-1835, at 63-100 (1977); see also Reva B. Siegel, The Rule of Love, Wife Beating as Prerogative and Privacy, 105 Yale. L.J. 2117, 2142-2150 (1996).

Note: The "New Departure" and Women's Place in the Constitutional Order

The litigation in *Bradwell* was only one aspect of a far larger debate over women's rights contemporaneous with the passage and early interpretation of the Reconstruction Amendments. Woman suffragists, who had worked hard for the passage of the Thirteenth Amendment and for the extension of new rights to blacks, were bitterly disappointed by section 2 of the Fourteenth Amendment. Susan B. Anthony, Elizabeth Cady Stanton, and other leaders of the woman suffrage movement opposed ratification of the Fourteenth Amendment because, as Eric Foner writes, "the second clause for the first time introduced the word 'male' into the Constitution. Alone among suffrage restrictions, those founded on sex would not reduce a state's representation."[39] The movement had hoped that the Constitution would be amended to guarantee the vote to both black men and to all women. But the National Republican Party opposed woman suffrage, and the abolitionists withdrew their support, fearing an intense struggle over black voting rights. Consequently, Stanton and Anthony opposed passage of the Fifteenth Amendment because of its "humiliat[ing] rejection of extending suffrage to women."[40] Another 50 years would pass before the Nineteenth Amendment would explicitly bar denial of the suffrage on account of gender.

Whatever their disappointment regarding the language of section 2 of the Fourteenth Amendment, shortly after the ratification of the Fourteenth Amendment supporters of the franchise for women embarked on a "new departure" in suffragist constitutional interpretation and argument, based on section 1 of the Amendment. Francis and Virginia Minor developed the argument that

39. Eric Foner, Reconstruction: America's Unfinished Revolution 255 (1988).

40. Id. at 447. Stanton and Anthony were upset not only because of the rejection of their efforts at an amendment that included blacks and women but also because they regarded white women as social and cultural superiors of black men; they were concerned that black men would be elevated in status and power over them. "While the dominant party have with one hand lifted up TWO MILLION BLACK MEN and crowned them with the honor and dignity of citizenship," Anthony wrote, "with the other they have dethroned FIFTEEN MILLION WHITE WOMEN — their own mothers and sisters, their own wives and daughters — and cast them under the heel of the lowest orders of manhood." Paula Giddings, When and Where I Enter: The Impact of Black Women on Race and Sex in America 66 (1984). The woman suffrage movement split over this issue in 1869, with Stanton and Anthony founding the National Woman Suffrage Association and other suffragists, including Lucy Stone and Antoinette Brown Blackwell founding the American Woman Suffrage Association (which supported the Republican Party and passage of the Fifteenth Amendment). The NWSA pushed for a national amendment on woman suffrage, while the AWSA pushed for reform at the state and local level. See Ellen C. Dubois, Feminism and Suffrage: The Emergence of an Independent Women's Movement in American 1848-1869, at 92-161, 164-171, 180-198 (1978).

Note that black women were often ignored by both supporters and opponents of the Fifteenth Amendment, and found themselves caught between conflicting political goals: On the one hand they feared that without the ballot for black men, blacks would be increasingly oppressed by whites; on the other hand they feared that if black men gained the vote they would dominate black women even more. (For modern analogues to the political dilemmas experienced by black women in this era, see the discussion of intersectionality in Chapter 7.) Finally, although black women may have supported the vote for all women, they resented the racism of the white suffragists which made it difficult to work with them on dignified terms. Despite this, black women who did participate in the suffrage movement tended to ally themselves with Stanton and Anthony's wing.

woman suffrage was guaranteed because the right to vote was inextricably tied to the citizenship guaranteed by Section 1. According to their theory, outlined in resolutions at a St. Louis suffrage convention in October 1869, the Fourteenth Amendment made the privileges and immunities of American citizens "National in character and paramount to all State authority."[41] The St. Louis resolutions cited Corfield v. Coryell for the proposition that the right to vote was a fundamental right.[42] Although Article I §2 of the Constitution gave the states power to regulate the qualifications of electors, the states could not violate the principle of equal citizenship by denying the franchise to U.S. citizens.

The Minors' argument also drew on the federal power to naturalize citizens: A naturalized citizen's equal right to vote was guaranteed by federal authority; otherwise a state could make a naturalized citizen a second-class citizen. A fortiori a state could not do this to a natural born citizen. Moreover, if states could deny the franchise to citizens, they could also extend the franchise to noncitizens. This would give noncitizens a higher political status than citizens.[43] Repeatedly the argument for suffrage claimed that to be disenfranchised was to be lowered in status vis-à-vis other citizens, including black men.

The National Woman Suffrage Association adopted the Minors' theory in its political rhetoric. In 1871 and 1872 women attempted to vote in ten states and the District of Columbia. In the most famous demonstration, Susan B. Anthony and 13 other women voted in Rochester, New York in November 1872. The women and the election inspectors who registered them were indicted under provisions of the Ku Klux Klan Act, which had been designed to prevent voting abuses directed against freedmen. The statute made it a crime for any "person to vote without a lawful right to vote or to do any unlawful act to secure a right or opportunity to vote, for himself or any other person."[44]

Anthony argued that she had not violated the statute. In her view, the Fourteenth Amendment automatically gave all citizens, including women and blacks, an equal right to vote. Otherwise, she claimed, the Fourteenth Amendment would have been superfluous, because civil equality was automatically guaranteed by the Thirteenth Amendment and by Article IV §2.

Moreover, Anthony argued, the Fifteenth Amendment also guaranteed woman suffrage, because it prevented states from denying the vote on account of previous condition of servitude. The marital status laws reduced women to a condition of servitude because they placed women under the dominance of their husbands and denied them the right to own their own labor. Even after married women's property

---

41. Elizabeth Cady Stanton, Susan B. Anthony, and Matilda Joslyn Gage, eds., 2 History of Woman Suffrage 408 (1882).

42. Or as Susan B. Anthony put it:

> Is the right to vote one of the privileges and immunities of citizens? I think the disenfranchised ex-rebels . . . will all agree with me that it is not only one of them, but the one without which all *the others are nothing.*

Id. at 638.

43. Id. at 408-409. Note that some states and territories did, in fact, permit noncitizens to vote, in the expectation that they would eventually apply for citizenship.

44. Act of May 31, 1870, §19, 41 Stat. 140, 144-145 (1870). The act was designed to prevent southern whites from casting multiple ballots, thus nullifying the effect of black votes.

acts, Anthony argued, women were not civil equals without joint ownership of all income produced by the marriage:

> In many of the states there has been special legislation, giving to married women the right to property inherited, or received by bequest, or earned by the pursuit of any avocation outside the home; also, giving her the right to sue and be sued in matters pertaining to such separate property; *but not a single State of this Union has ever secured the wife in the enjoyment of her right to the joint ownership of the joint earnings of the marriage copartnership.* And since, in the nature of things, the vast majority of married women never earn a dollar by work outside their families, nor inherit a dollar from their fathers, it follows that from the day of their marriage to the day of the death of their husbands, not one of them ever has a dollar, except it shall please her husband to let her have it.[45]

In effect, Anthony argued that women still lived under a condition of servitude in violation of the Thirteenth Amendment.

Anthony was tried before Justice Ward Hunt of the U.S. Supreme Court, then sitting on circuit in New York. Justice Hunt, relying on Bradwell v. Illinois, rejected Anthony's constitutional arguments. United States v. Anthony, 24 F. Cas. 829 (N.D.N.Y. 1873) (No. 14,459). Hunt found Anthony guilty as a matter of law, arguing that even if she was mistaken about her right to vote the mistake of law was no defense. He directed the jurors to return a verdict of guilty against her, and refused to allow individual jurors to be polled.

The next day, Anthony was asked if she had anything to say before sentence was passed. She gave a long speech, continually interrupted by Justice Hunt, who had not expected Anthony to say anything and repeatedly demanded that she sit down and be silent, which she refused to do:

> Your denial of my citizen's right to vote is my denial of my right of consent as one of the governed, my right of representation as one of the taxed, the denial of my right to a jury of my peers as an offender against law, therefore the denial of my sacred rights to life, liberty and property. . . . [S]ince the day of my arrest last November, this is the first time that either myself or any person of my disfranchised class has been allowed a word of defense before judge or jury.
>
>   . . . [H]ad your honor submitted my case to the jury, as was clearly your duty, even then I should have had just cause for protest, for not one of those men was my peer. . . .
>
>   Even my counsel . . . is my political sovereign. Precisely as no disfranchised person is entitled to sit upon a jury, and no woman is entitled to the franchise, so none but a regularly admitted lawyer is allowed to practice in the courts, and no woman can gain admission to the bar — hence jury, judge, counsel, must all be of the superior class.[46]

The Supreme Court's decision in the *Slaughterhouse Cases* significantly undermined the suffragist arguments, because it suggested that the Privileges or

---

45. 2 History of Woman Suffrage, 642-644 (emphasis in original).

46. Justice Hunt sentenced Anthony to a fine of $100 plus the costs of the prosecution. Anthony stated that she would refuse to pay the fine. Hunt responded that Anthony would not be placed in jail to enforce his order until the fine was paid, in effect freeing her but making an appeal impossible. The other women voters pleaded nolle prosequi. The judge found the election inspectors guilty by directed verdict and put them in jail, but they were subsequently pardoned by President Grant. Id. at 689, 691, 695, 715.

47. Quoted in Linda Kerber, No Constitutional Right to Be Ladies 89 (1998).

Immunities Clause had virtually no content. The Supreme Court rejected the suffragist theory of the Fourteenth Amendment a year later.

MINOR v. HAPPERSETT
82 U.S. 162 (1874)

[In October 1872, Virginia Minor attempted to register to vote in St. Louis. After being refused, she sued for relief, arguing that women possessed a constitutional right to vote. Her case came before the U.S. Supreme Court in May 1873; the State of Missouri, thinking her arguments frivolous, did not even bother to present opposing counsel. The Supreme Court unanimously rejected Minor's arguments in an opinion by Chief Justice Waite, who had replaced Chief Justice Chase, the lone dissenter in Bradwell v. Illinois.]

WAITE, C.J.

There is no doubt that women may be citizens. . . . [I]t did not need [the Fourteenth Amendment] to give them that position. . . .

Whoever . . . was one of the people of [one of the] States when the Constitution of the United States was adopted, became ipso facto a citizen — a member of the nation created by its adoption. He was one of the persons associating together to form the nation, and was, consequently, one of its original citizens. . . .

[S]ex has never been made one of the elements of citizenship in the United States. In this respect men have never had an advantage over women. The same laws precisely apply to both. The fourteenth amendment did not affect the citizenship of women any more than it did of men. In this particular, therefore, the rights of Mrs. Minor do not depend upon the amendment. . . .

If the right of suffrage is one of the necessary privileges of a citizen of the United States, then the constitution and laws of Missouri confining it to men are in violation of the Constitution of the United States. . . . The direct question is, therefore, presented whether all citizens are necessarily voters.

The Constitution does not define the privileges and immunities of citizens. For that definition we must look elsewhere. In this case we need not determine what they are, but only whether suffrage is necessarily one of them.

It certainly is nowhere made so in express terms. . . . The amendment did not add to the privileges and immunities of a citizen. It simply furnished an additional guaranty for the protection of such as he already had. No new voters were necessarily made by it. . . .

[Was] suffrage coextensive with the citizenship of the States at the time of its adoption[?] If it was, then it may with force be argued that suffrage was one of the rights which belonged to citizenship. . . .

When the Federal Constitution was adopted, all the States, with the exception of Rhode Island and Connecticut [which operated under charters from the Crown], had constitutions of their own. . . . Upon an examination of those constitutions we find that in no State were all citizens permitted to vote. . . . [The limitation of suffrage to males was explicit in New Hampshire, Massachusetts, New York, and South Carolina. Pennsylvania, Maryland, and North Carolina referred to "freeman" or "freemen," while New Jersey spoke of "all inhabitants" and Georgia of "citizens and inhabitants of the State." All had property qualifications for the vote.]

In this condition of the law in respect to suffrage in the several States it cannot for a moment be doubted that if it had been intended to make all citizens of the United States voters, the framers of the Constitution would not have left it to implication. So important a change in the condition of citizenship as it actually existed, if intended, would have been expressly declared.

But if further proof is necessary to show that no such change was intended, it can easily be found both in and out of the Constitution. [Waite quotes the "privileges and immunities" clause of Article 4, §2.] If suffrage is necessarily a part of citizenship, then the citizens of each State must be entitled to vote in the several States precisely as their citizens are. This is more than asserting that they may change their residence and become citizens of the State and thus be voters. It goes to the extent of insisting that while retaining their original citizenship they may vote in any State. This, we think, has never been claimed. [Waite then quotes §2 of the Fourteenth Amendment.] Why this [language], if it was not in the power of the legislature to deny the right of suffrage to some male inhabitants? And if suffrage was necessarily one of the absolute rights of citizenship, why confine the operations of the limitation to male inhabitants? Women and children are, as we have seen, "persons." They are counted in the enumeration upon which the apportionment is to be made, but if they were necessarily voters because of their citizenship unless clearly excluded, why inflict the penalty for the exclusion of males alone? Clearly, no such form of words would have been selected to express the idea here indicated if suffrage was the absolute right of all citizens.

And still again, after the adoption of the fourteenth amendment, it was deemed necessary to adopt the fifteenth. . . . If suffrage was one of [the] privileges and immunities [protected by the fourteenth amendment], why amend the Constitution to prevent its being denied on account of race? . . .

It is true that the United States guarantees to every State a republican form of government. . . . No particular government is designated as republican. . . . All the States had governments when the Constitution was adopted. . . . In all, save perhaps New Jersey, [the right of suffrage] was only bestowed upon men and not upon all of them. Under these circumstances it is certainly now too late to contend that a government is not republican, within the meaning of this guaranty in the Constitution, because women are not made voters. . . .

[W]e have already sufficiently considered the proof found upon the inside of the Constitution. That upon the outside is equally effective. . . .

No new State has ever been admitted to the Union which has conferred the right of suffrage upon women, and this has never been considered a valid objection to her admission. On the contrary, . . . the right of suffrage was withdrawn from women as early as 1807 in the State of New Jersey. . . . Since then the governments of the insurgent States have been reorganized under a requirement that before their representatives could be admitted to seats in Congress they must have adopted new constitutions, republican in form. In no one of these constitutions was suffrage conferred upon women, and yet the States have all been restored to their original position as States in the Union.

Besides this, citizenship has not in all cases been made a condition precedent to the enjoyment of the right of suffrage. Thus, in Missouri, persons of foreign birth, who have declared their intention to become citizens of the United States, may under certain circumstances vote. The same provision is to be found in the constitutions of Alabama, Arkansas, Florida, Georgia, Indiana, Kansas, Minnesota, and Texas.

Certainly, if the courts can consider any question settled, this is one. For nearly ninety years the people have acted upon the idea that the Constitution, when it conferred citizenship, did not necessarily confer the right of suffrage. If uniform practices long continued can settle the construction of so important an instrument as the Constitution of the United States confessedly is, most certainly it has been done here.

No argument as to women's need of suffrage can be considered. We can only act upon her rights as they exist. It is not for us to look at the hardship of withholding. Our duty is at an end if we find it is within the power of a State to withhold.

Discussion

1. Compare Chief Justice Waite's style of constitutional interpretation in *Minor* with Chief Justice Taney's in *Dred Scott.*

2. Note that the Court offers no normative justification for the exclusion of women. For example, *Minor* does not reiterate the antebellum argument about women's necessarily being represented by their husbands. Even as to this argument, which continued to have currency in the general culture, what about those women who chose to remain unmarried? Consider, for example, Abby and Julia Smith, Connecticut sisters who in 1869 refused to pay their taxes because, being denied the right to vote, they were taxed without their representation (one of the principal ideological underpinnings, of course, of the American Revolution in 1776). As Abby Smith asked the Glastonbury, Connecticut town meeting in 1873, "Is it any more just to take a woman's property without her consent, than it is to take a man's property without his consent?" Indeed, she concluded by noting that "the robber would have the whole community against him, and he would not be apt to come but once; but from the men of our town we are never safe."[47]

3. Would a contrary ruling necessarily have entailed the grant of suffrage to other disfranchised citizens, such as minors? (Every state had an age requirement of 21.) If so, does that imply that Minor properly lost her suit, at least if predicated on the privileges and immunities clause? Or might the right to vote be a "presumptive" privilege, to be restricted only if the state has a very good reason? What constitute good reasons for denying persons the right to vote?

4. Why didn't Minor claim a violation of the equal protection clause? What do the *Slaughterhouse Cases* have to say about this?

5. As a matter of fact, the modern Supreme Court treats voting as embraced by the Fourteenth Amendment, and Congress has used its legislative powers under the Amendment to bar states from depriving persons over 18 years old of the right to vote in federal elections.[48] This development did not occur without dissent: A century after Minor v. Happersett was decided, a second Justice Harlan, the grandson of the Justice Harlan who appears frequently in this chapter, argued vigorously that the history of the Fourteenth Amendment foreclosed its application to voting and that any suffrage complaints arising only under that Amendment should be

48. See Oregon v. Mitchell, 400 U.S. 112 (1970).
49. Carrington v. Rash, 380 U.S. 89, 99 (1965).

dismissed "for failure to state a claim of federal right."[49] Professor Van Alstyne responded to Justice Harlan's analysis as follows:

[T]he case can safely be made that there was an original understanding that §1 of the proposed Fourteenth Amendment would not itself immediately invalidate state suffrage laws severely restricting the right to vote. With all of it, however, we cannot safely declare that there was also a clear, uniform understanding that the open-ended phrases of §1 — "privileges or immunities of citizens of the United States . . . life, liberty, or property . . . the equal protection of the laws" — would foreclose a different application in the future. . . . The question whether the original understanding was itself intended equally to bind the indefinite future becomes more lively when we note that the Thirty-ninth Congress did not adopt a second alternative: to accomplish specific, narrowly defined ends by producing an equally specific and narrowly defined amendment that, by clear language, could never be applied to suffrage. The failure to pursue that alternative, moreover, could scarcely have been inadvertent.[50]

Note: The Fourteenth Amendment, Birthright Citizenship, and American Indians

As noted earlier, the first sentence of section 1 has primarily been viewed as over-ruling *Dred Scott* and establishing a clear rule determining who is a "natural-born" citizen of the United States. Consider, though, the status of American Indians. As late as United States v. Sandoval, 231 U.S. 28 (1913), the Court noted that it was "an open question" whether Pueblo Indians in New Mexico were American citizens. An early decision, McKay v. Campbell, 16 F. Cas. 161 (D.Or. 1871), had held that Indians did not fall within sentence one because "the Indian tribes within the limits of the United States have always been held to be distinct and independent political communities, retaining the right of self-government, though subject to the protect-ing power of the United States." Thus, the argument ran, Indians were not "subject to the jurisdiction" of the United States, even though interpretations of the scope of "the protecting power" left Indians with very few, if any rights, that Congress was required to respect. That is, as a practical matter, whatever Congress deemed "protective" was readily acquiesced in by the judiciary, regardless of Indian views on the matter. The most dramatic evidence of this point was provided by United States v. Kagama, 118 U.S. 375 (1886), which held that Congress possessed plenary power over the Indian tribes:

[The] Indians are within the geographical limits of the United States. The soil and the people within these limits are under the political control of the Government of the United States, or of the States of the Union. There exist within the broad domain of sovereignty but these two. . . . [The] power of the Congress to organize territorial governments, and make laws for their inhabitants, arise not so much from the clause in the Constitution in regard to disposing of and making rules and regulations concern-ing the Territory and other property of the United States, as from the ownership of the

___

50. William. W. Van Alstyne, The Fourteenth Amendment, the "Right" to Vote, and the Understanding of the Thirty-Ninth Congress, 1965 Sup. Ct. Rev. 52 at 72-73. Professor Van Alstyne's argument is based on one earlier articulated by Alexander Bickel in regard to school segregation, supra n.1.

51. The material in this Note is drawn from Richard Primus, Constitutional Interpretation and the Civil War, Chapter Two (unpublished manuscript, 2005).

country in which the Territories are, and the rights of exclusive sovereignty which must exist in the National Government, and be found nowhere else. . . .

Indian tribes *are* the wards of the nation. They are communities *dependent* on the United States. Dependent largely for their daily food. Dependent for their political rights. They owe no allegiance to the States, and receive from them no protection. Because of the local ill feeling, the people of the States where they are found are often their deadliest enemies. . . .

The power of the General Government over these remnants of a race once powerful, now weak and diminished in numbers, is necessary to their protection, as well as to the safety of those among whom they dwell. It must exist in that government, because it never has existed anywhere else, because the theatre of its exercise is within the geographical limits of the United States, because it has never been denied, and because it alone can enforce its laws on all the tribe.

The Supreme Court had addressed the specific question of Indian citizenship in Elk v. Wilkins, 112 U.S. 94 (1884), in which John Elk, an American Indian, protested the refusal by the voting registrar of Omaha, Nebraska, to accept his claim for registration. Nebraska's constitution granted the right to vote to all males over 21 who were citizens of the United States or "persons of foreign birth who shall have declared their intention to become citizens, conformably to the laws of the United States on the subject of naturalization, at least thirty days prior to an election." Although he brought his suit under the Fifteenth Amendment, the predicate for his suit was the claim that he was a citizen and, as such, the victim of precisely the racial discrimination in regard to the suffrage that is prohibited by the Fifteenth Amendment.

Justice Grey's majority opinion rejected this argument:

> Though the plaintiff alleges that he "had fully and completely surrendered himself to the jurisdiction of the United States," he does not allege that the United States accepted his surrender, or that he has ever been naturalized, or taxed, or in any way recognized or treated as a citizen by the state or by the United States. Nor is it contended by his counsel that there is any statute or treaty that makes him a citizen. The question then is, whether an Indian, born a member of one of the Indian tribes within the United States, is, merely by reason of his birth within the United States, and of his afterwards voluntarily separating himself from his tribe and taking up his residence among white citizens, a citizen of the United States, within the meaning of the first section of the fourteenth amendment of the constitution.

The Court noted that the conventional legal understanding had been that members of Indian tribes "owed immediate allegiance to their several tribes, and were not part of the people of the United States. . . . The alien and dependent condition of the members of the Indian tribes could not be put off at their own will without the action or assent of the United States;" for example, "explicit provisions of [a] treaty or statute . . . declaring a certain tribe, or . . . members [who] chose to remain behind on the removal of the tribe westward, to be citizens, or authorizing individuals of particular tribes to become citizens on application to a court of the United States for naturalization and satisfactory proof of fitness for civilized life."

According to Justice Grey, "[t]he main object" of the citizenship clause of the Fourteenth Amendment "was to settle the question . . . as to the citizenship of free negroes" born in the United States. By contrast, he argued,

Indians born within the territorial limits of the United States, members of, and owing immediate allegiance to, one of the Indian tribes (an alien though dependent power) although in a geographical sense born in the United States, are no more "born in the United States and subject to the jurisdiction thereof," within the meaning of the first section of the fourteenth amendment, than the children of subjects of any foreign government born within the domain of that government, or the children born within the United States, of ambassadors or other public ministers of foreign nations. This view is confirmed by the second section of the fourteenth amendment, which provides that "representatives shall be apportioned among the several states according to their respective numbers, counting the whole number of persons in each state, excluding Indians not taxed." Slavery having been abolished, and the persons formerly held as slaves made citizens, this clause fixing the apportionment of representatives has abrogated so much of the corresponding clause of the original constitution as counted only three-fifths of such persons. But Indians not taxed are still excluded from the count, for the reason that they are not citizens. Their absolute exclusion from the basis of representation, in which all other persons are now included, is wholly inconsistent with their being considered citizens.

Such Indians, then, not being citizens by birth, can only become citizens in the second way mentioned in the fourteenth amendment, by being "naturalized in the United States," by or under some treaty or statute. . . .

Because Elk was not formally naturalized or made a citizen by treaty or statute, the Court concluded, he was therefore not a citizen and, therefore, was not eligible to vote.

Justice Harlan, joined by Justice Wood, dissented. He pointed to the language of article 1, §3, "which requires, in the apportionment of representatives and direct taxes among the several states 'according to their respective numbers,' the exclusion of 'Indians not taxed.'"

This implies that there were, at that time, in the United States, Indians who were taxed; that is, were subject to taxation by the laws of the state of which they were residents. Indians not taxed were those who held tribal relations, and therefore were not subject to the authority of any state, and were subject only to the authority of the United States. . . . The same provision is retained in the fourteenth amendment . . . Indians in the several states, who are taxed by their laws, are counted in establishing the basis of representation in congress. By the act of April 9, 1866, entitled "An act to protect all persons in the United States in their civil rights, and furnish means for their vindication," it is provided that "all persons born in the United States, and not subject to any foreign power, excluding Indians not taxed, are hereby declared to be citizens of the United States." This, so far as we are aware, is the first general enactment making persons of the Indian race citizens of the United States. Numerous statutes and treaties previously provided for all the individual members of particular Indian tribes becoming, in certain contingencies, citizens of the United States. But the act of 1866 reached Indians not in tribal relations. Beyond question, by that act, national citizenship was conferred directly upon all persons in this country, of whatever race, (excluding only "Indians not taxed,") who were born within the territorial limits of the United States, and were not subject to any foreign power. Surely every one must admit that an Indian residing in one of the states, and subject to taxation there, became, by force alone of the act of 1866, a citizen of the United States, although he may have been, when born, a member of a tribe. The exclusion of Indians not taxed evinced a purpose to include those subject to taxation in the state of their residence. . . .

Harlan pointed out that the 1866 bill originally did not contain the words "Indians not taxed." But that this was added later to avoid "mak[ing] citizens of those who were in tribal relations, with governments of their own."

> It would seem manifest, from this brief review of the history of the act of 1866, that one purpose of that legislation was to confer national citizenship upon a part of the Indian race in this country — such of them, at least, as resided in one of the states or territories, and were subject to taxation and other public burdens. . . . At the same session of the congress which passed the act of 1866, the fourteenth amendment was approved and submitted to the states for adoption. Those who sustained the former urged the adoption of the latter, [and there is no evidence in the debates that the framers of the Fourteenth Amendment wished] to abandon the policy inaugurated by the act of 1866, of admitting to national citizenship such Indians as were separated from their tribes and were residents of one of the states or territories outside of any reservation set apart for the exclusive use and occupancy of Indian tribes. [After the adoption of the Fourteenth Amendment Congress] enacted statutes providing for the citizenship of Indians [but did so by granting citizenship to whole tribes, because members] could not, while they continued in tribal relations, acquire the citizenship granted by the fourteenth amendment. . . .
>
> A careful examination of all that was said by senators and representatives, pending the consideration by congress of the fourteenth amendment, justifies us in saying that every one who participated in the debates, whether for or against the amendment, believed that, in the form in which it was approved by congress, it granted, and was intended to grant, national citizenship to every person of the Indian race in this country who was unconnected with any tribe, and who resided, in good faith, outside of Indian reservations and within one of the states or territories of the Union. This fact is, we think, entitled to great weight in determining the meaning and scope of the amendment. . . .
>
> There were, in some of our states and territories at the time the amendment was submitted by congress, many Indians who had finally left their tribes and come within the complete jurisdiction of the United States. They were as fully prepared for citizenship as were or are vast numbers of the white and colored races in the same localities. Is it conceivable that the statesmen who framed, the congress which submitted, and the people who adopted that amendment intended to confer citizenship, national and state, upon the entire population in this country of African descent (the larger part of which was shortly before held in slavery) and, by the same constitutional provision, to exclude from such citizenship Indians who had never been in slavery, and who, by becoming bona fide residents of states and territories within the complete jurisdiction of the United States, had evinced a purpose to abandon their former mode of life, and become a part of the people of the United States?

Only in 1924 did Congress pass legislation naturalizing all "Indians born within the territorial limits of the United States" (8 U.S.C. §140(a)(s)). Consider the implications of this history for the debate that arose in the 1980s and 1990s about the birthright citizenship of children of illegal aliens (i.e., those whose presence in the territory of the United States was without the permission of the United States). Yale professors Peter Shuck and Rogers Smith argued, in Citizenship Without Consent: Illegal Aliens in the American Polity (1985), that the Fourteenth Amendment need not be read "literally" to convey citizenship to such children, any more than it need necessarily be interpreted to have granted citizenship to children born within Indian tribal structures. As a matter of fact, immigration was barely regulated in

1868, and no one at the time thought in terms of "legal" and "illegal" immigrants. Is this relevant to how one should interpret the Citizenship Clause today?

Note: "The Riddle of Hiram Revels"[51]

Hiram Revels was the first African-American to serve in the U.S. Senate, having been selected by the (reconstructed) Mississippi legislature to represent that State in 1870. The "riddle" surrounding his status as senator is deceptively simple: Article I, §3 of the Constitution, states, "No person shall be a Senator who shall not have attained to the Age of thirty Years, and been nine Years a Citizen of the United States." *Had* Senator Revels been "a Citizen of the United States" since 1861? After all, *Dred Scott* had clearly stated that no slave or descendant of slaves could be a member of the American political community, and it was surely the case that Revels had not been a citizen of Mississippi in 1861 (when the State in fact had attempted to secede from the Union precisely to maintain slavery and the abject domination of blacks). On the other hand, the Fourteenth Amendment states that "[a]ll persons born or naturalized in the United States, and subject to the jurisdiction thereof, are citizens of the United States and of the State wherein they reside." However, the Fourteenth Amendment, designed to overrule *Dred Scott,* was not ratified until 1868. Did it retroactively grant Revels (and all other African-Americans born in United States territory) birth citizenship?

Not surprisingly, several Democratic senators challenged Revels's eligibility for the Senate and prevented his taking the oath of office at the same time as the other newly elected senators. (Recall that Albert Gallatin, a Swiss émigré, had been prevented from taking his seat as New York's senator because his naturalization had occurred within the relevant nine years. He was quickly elected to the House of Representatives, which has only a seven-year requirement.)

Some of the Democrats attacked the Fourteenth Amendment directly and refused to acknowledge its legitimacy, which would, among other things, leave *Dred Scott* in place. Others accepted the validity of the Amendment and the fact that §1 of the Amendment was designed to invalidate *Dred Scott,* but denied that it granted Revels citizenship before 1868. Some Republican Senators simply denounced *Dred Scott,* in the vivid words of Massachusetts Senator Charles Sumner, as a "putrid corpse . . . a stench in the nostrils . . . to be remembered only as a warning and a shame," suggesting that for them it was *never* legally valid and therefore, presumably, that because Revels would have been recognized as a citizen of the United States had the Court followed the correct understanding of the Constitution, then the Senate should do likewise.

After a three-day debate in the Senate, 48 Republican senators voted to seat him, while 8 Democrats voted against, with 12 Republican senators choosing to be absent from the vote. Thus Revels took the oath of office and served for a year until his term expired in March 1871. Another African-American Senator, Blanche Kelso Bruce, also represented Mississippi from 1875 to 1881. In the decades that followed, African-Americans were gradually disenfranchised throughout the South. The next African-American Senator was Edward Brooke of Massachusetts, who served from

---

52. See 28 U.S.C. §1443: "Any of the following civil actions or criminal prosecutions, commenced in a State court may be removed by the defendant to the district court of the United States for the district and

1967 to 1979, followed by Carol Moseley Brown, who represented Illinois from 1993 to 1999. Barack Obama was elected to the Senate from Illinois in 2004.

Discussion

How would you decide the question of Revels's eligibility to serve in the Senate, given the words of Article I? Note, incidentally, that some members of Congress objected to Texas's joining the Union in 1845 on the grounds that there would be no one eligible to represent the state in the House or the Senate because, after all, Texas had been a Mexican colony or an independent republic prior to joining the Union. One response was that many of Texas's leaders had in fact been American citizens who moved to Texas from other states. (Presumably, they did not lose their American citizenship upon pledging allegiance and serving as public officials in what was, after all, a foreign nation between 1837-1845.) Imagine that Canada fragments and the United States offers admission to British Columbia. Would anyone other than an expatriate U.S. citizen be eligible to represent the new state in the House and Senate for the first seven to nine years? Would all British Columbians born before statehood be ineligible to run for the presidency? Do the decisions to admit Texas (and seat their leaders in the House and Senate) and then to seat Revels serve as precedents for allowing British Columbians to run for office immediately on the province's joining the United States?

C. Early Application of the Fourteenth Amendment to Race Discrimination

STRAUDER v. WEST VIRGINIA
100 U.S. 303 (1880)

[Petitioner, a black, was convicted of murder in state court by a jury from which blacks were excluded by a statute providing: "All white male persons who are twenty-one years of age and who are citizens of this State shall be liable to serve as jurors. . . ." Before the trial, he unsuccessfully sought to remove the case to a federal court[52] and was thereafter unsuccessful in quashing in jury venire and challenging the jury panel. The state supreme court affirmed his conviction. The U.S. Supreme Court reversed.]

STRONG, J. . . .

[The controlling question is whether] by the Constitution and laws of the United States, every citizen of the United States has a right to a trial of an indictment against him by a jury selected and impaneled without discrimination against his race or color, because of race or color. . . .

It is to be observed that the [question] is not whether a colored man, when an indictment has been preferred against him, has a right to a grand or a petit jury composed in whole or in part of persons of his own race or color, but it is whether,

---

division embracing the place wherein it is pending: (1) Against any person who is denied or cannot enforce in the courts of such State a right under any law providing for the equal civil rights of citizens of the United States, or all persons within the jurisdiction thereof. . . ."

53. Justice Field and Justice Clifford dissented without opinion.

in the composition or selection of jurors by whom he is to be indicted or tried, all persons of his race or color may be excluded by law, solely because of their race or color, so that by no possibility can any colored man sit upon the jury. . . .

[The Fourteenth Amendment] is one of a series of constitutional provisions having a common purpose; namely, securing to a race recently emancipated, a race that through many generations had been held in slavery, all the civil rights that the superior race enjoy. The true spirit and meaning of the amendments, as we said in the SlaughterHouse Cases (16 Wall. 36), cannot be understood without keeping in view the history of the times when they were adopted, and the general objects they plainly sought to accomplish. At the time when they were incorporated into the Constitution, it required little knowledge of human nature to anticipate that those who had long been regarded as an inferior and subject race would, when suddenly raised to the rank of citizenship, be looked upon with jealousy and positive dislike, and that State laws might be enacted or enforced to perpetuate the distinctions that had before existed.

Discriminations against them had been habitual. It was well known that in some States laws making such discriminations then existed, and others might well be expected. The colored race, as a race, was abject and ignorant, and in that condition was unfitted to command the respect of those who had superior intelligence. Their training had left them mere children, and as such they needed the protection which a wise government extends to those who are unable to protect themselves. They especially needed protection against unfriendly action in the States where they were resident. It was in view of these considerations the Fourteenth Amendment was framed and adopted. It was designed to assure to the colored race the enjoyment of all the civil rights that under the law are enjoyed by white persons, and to give to that race the protection of the general government, in that enjoyment, whenever it should be denied by the States. . . .

If this is the spirit and meaning of the amendment, whether it means more or not, it is to be construed liberally, to carry out the purposes of its framers. It ordains . . . that the law in the States shall be the same for the black as for the white; that all persons, whether colored or white, shall stand equal before the laws of the States, and, in regard to the colored race, for whose protection the amendment was primarily designed, that no discrimination shall be made against them by law because of their color. . . . [The amendment guarantees] the right to exemption from unfriendly legislation against them distinctively as colored — exemption from legal discriminations, implying inferiority in civil society, lessening the security of their enjoyment of the rights which others enjoy, and discriminations which are steps towards reducing them to the condition of a subject race.

That the West Virginia statute respecting juries — the statute that controlled the selection of the grand and petit jury in the case of the plaintiff in error — is such a discrimination ought not to be doubted. Nor would it be if the persons excluded by it were white men. If in those States where the colored people constitute a majority of the entire population a law should be enacted excluding all white men from jury service, thus denying to them the privilege of participating equally with the blacks in the administration of justice, we apprehend no one would be heard to claim that it would not be a denial to white men of the equal protection of the laws. Nor if a law should be passed excluding all naturalized Celtic Irishmen, would there be any doubt of its inconsistency with the spirit of the amendment. The very fact that colored people are singled out and expressly denied by a statute all right to participate in the administration of the law, as jurors, because of their color, though they are citizens, and may be in other respects fully qualified, is practically a brand upon them, affixed by the law, an assertion of their inferiority, and a stimulant to that race prejudice which is an impediment to securing to individuals of the race that equal justice which the law aims to secure to all others.

The right to a trial by jury is guaranteed to every citizen of West Virginia by the Constitution of that State, and the constitution of juries is a very essential part of the protection such a mode of trial is intended to secure. The very idea of a jury is a body of men composed of the peers or equals of the person whose rights it is selected or summoned to determine; that is, of his neighbors, fellows, associates, persons having the same legal status in society as that which he holds. . . . It is well known that prejudices often exist against particular classes in the community, which sway the judgment of jurors, and which, therefore, operate in some cases to deny to persons of those classes the full enjoyment of that protection which others enjoy. . . . The framers of the constitutional amendment must have known full well the existence of such prejudice and its likelihood to continue against the manumitted slaves and their race, and that knowledge was doubtless a motive that led to the amendment. . . .

In view of these considerations, . . . how can it be maintained that compelling a colored man to submit to a trial for his life by a jury drawn from a panel from which the State has expressly excluded every man of his race, because of color alone, however well qualified in other respects, is not a denial to him of equal legal protection?

We do not say that within the limits from which it is not excluded by the amendment a State may not prescribe the qualifications of its jurors, and in so doing make discriminations. It may confine the selection to males, to freeholders, to citizens, to persons within certain ages, or to persons having educational qualifications. We do not believe the Fourteenth Amendment was ever intended to prohibit this. Looking at its history, it is clear it had no such purpose. Its aim was against discrimination because of race or color. As we have said more than once, its design was to protect an emancipated race, and to strike down all possible legal discriminations against those who belong to it. . . [53]

[Justice Field, joined by Justice Clifford, dissented, though their objections were set out in a dissent to a companion case, Ex parte Virginia, 100 U.S. 339 (1880), in which the majority found the Fourteenth Amendment violated by the exclusion by a Virginia judge of African-Americans from service on juries. The portion of the dissent most relevant to *Strauder* was as follows:]

The fourth clause in the first section of the amendment declares that no State shall "deny to any person within its jurisdiction the equal protection of the laws." . . . [T]he universality of the protection secured necessarily renders . . . untenable [the argument that exclusion from jury service is prohibited]. All persons within the jurisdiction of the State, whether permanent residents or temporary sojourners, whether old or young, male or female, are to be equally protected. Yet no one will contend that equal protection to women, to children, to the aged, to aliens, can only be secured by allowing persons of the class to which they belong to act as jurors in cases affecting their interests. The equality of protection intended does not require that all persons shall be permitted to participate in the government of the State and the administration of its laws, to hold its offices, or be clothed with any public trusts. As already said, the universality of the protection assured repels any such conclusion.

The equality of the protection secured extends only to civil rights as distinguished from those which are political, or arise from the form of the government and its mode of administration. And yet the reach and influence of the amendment are immense. It opens the courts of the country to every one, on the same terms, for the security of his person and property, the prevention and redress of wrongs, and the enforcement of contracts; it assures to every one the same rules of evidence and modes of procedure; it allows no impediments to the acquisition of property and the pursuit of happiness, to which all are not subjected; it suffers no other or greater burdens or charges to be laid upon one than such as are equally borne by others; and in the administration of criminal justice it permits no different or greater punishment to be imposed upon one than such as is prescribed to all for like offences. It secures to all persons their civil rights upon the same terms; but it leaves political rights, or such as arise from the form of government and its administration, as they stood previous to its adoption. It has no more reference to them than it has to social rights and duties, which do not rest upon any positive law, though they are more potential in controlling the intercourse of individuals. In the consideration of questions growing out of these amendments much confusion has arisen from a failure to distinguish between the civil and the political rights of citizens. Civil rights are absolute and personal. Political rights, on the other hand, are conditioned and dependent upon the discretion of the elective or appointing power, whether that be the people acting through the ballot, or one of the departments of their government. The civil rights of the individual are never to be withheld, and may be always judicially enforced. The political rights which he may enjoy, such as holding office and discharging a public trust, are qualified because their possession depends on his fitness, to be adjudged by those whom society has clothed with the elective authority. The Thirteenth and Fourteenth Amendments were designed to secure the civil rights of all persons, of every race, color, and condition; but they left to the States to determine to whom the possession of political powers should be intrusted. This is manifest from the fact that when it was desired to confer political power upon the newly made citizens of the States, as was done by inhibiting the denial to them of the suffrage on account of race, color, or previous condition of servitude, a new amendment was required. . . .

The position that in cases where the rights of colored persons are concerned, justice will not be done to them unless they have a mixed jury, is founded upon the notion that in such cases white persons will not be fair and honest jurors. If this position be correct, there ought not to be any white persons on the jury where the interests of colored persons only are involved. That jury would not be an honest or fair one, of which any of its members should be governed in his judgment by other considerations than the law and the evidence; and that decision would hardly be considered just which should be reached by a sort of compromise, in which the prejudices of one race were set off against the prejudices of the other. To be consistent, those who hold this notion should contend that in cases affecting members of the colored race only, the juries should be composed entirely of colored persons, and that the presiding judge should be of the same race. . . . The jury *de medietate linguoe,* anciently allowed in England for the trial of an alien,[54] was expressly authorized by statute, probably as much because of the difference of language and customs between him and Englishmen, and the greater probability of his defence being more fully understood, as because it would be heard in a more friendly spirit by jurors of his own country and language.

. . . [*Ex parte Virginia* concerned, among other things, the power of Congress, under section 5 of the Fourteenth Amendment, to criminalize the racially discriminatory conduct of the Virginia judge. According to Justice Field, if Congress] can make the exclusion of persons from jury service on account of race or color a criminal offence, it can make their exclusion from office on that account also criminal; and, adopting the doctrine of the district judge in this case [which had found the Virginia judge to have acted in violation of the law], the failure to appoint them to office will be presumptive evidence of their exclusion on that ground. To such a result are we logically led. The legislation of Congress is founded, and is sustained by this court, as it seems to me, upon a theory as to what constitutes the equal protection of the laws, which is purely speculative, not warranted by any experience of the country, and not in accordance with the understanding of the people as to the meaning of those terms since the organization of the government.

Discussion

1. *The reasoning in* Strauder. How does the Court justify its conclusion that the Fourteenth Amendment prohibits the systematic exclusion of Negroes from juries? To what extent does the conclusion flow from the text of the Amendment? Is the Court's interpretation compatible with the "intentions" or "purposes" of the Amendment's framers?

Note that the Court speaks of a concern with preventing "unfriendly" legislation against blacks. Does this mean that "friendly" legislation — i.e., legislation designed to remedy past mistreatment of blacks — is permissible under the Fourteenth Amendment? In the same paragraph the Court says that the purpose of the Amendment was to ensure that "the law in the States shall be the same for the black as for the white." Are these two formulas consistent? Finally, the Court also argues that the Fourteenth Amendment is designed to exempt blacks from "legal discriminations, implying inferiority in civil society . . . [or] which are steps towards reducing them to the condition of a subject race." Is this "antisubordination" rationale importantly different from the other formulations? What consequences would it have for classifications that do not imply inferiority and that seek to prevent or counteract racial subordination?

2. *The harm resulting from jury exclusion.* Had Strauder been a Negro excluded from serving on a jury, his legal claim would have been straightforward: The State denied him an opportunity (serving on a jury) purely on the ground of race. This claim rests on the premise that there is no legally cognizable reason to believe that blacks are different from whites for the purposes of jury service.[55] Indeed, the

---

54. This refers to an English trial procedure that ended only in the nineteenth century by which civil trials involving disputes between, say, English and foreign merchants took place before juries that included foreign members. See Marianne Constable, The Law of the Other: The Mixed Jury and Changing Conceptions of Citizenship, Law and Knowledge (1994).

55. As we shall see in Part Two, this is a standard Equal Protection argument: *A,* who is denied a benefit that *B* enjoys, claims that she is identical in all relevant respects to *B* and is therefore entitled to equal treatment.

majority condemns the statute for denying to blacks "the privilege of participating equally . . . in the administration of justice" and putting "a brand upon them, affixed by the law, an assertion of their inferiority." The Court has since recognized the standing of potential jurors to sue on their own behalf. See, e.g., Carter v. Jury Commission of Greene County, 396 U.S. 320 (1970).

Strauder, however, was not an excluded juror, but the defendant. Did his claim depend on the implicit argument that blacks and whites are *dissimilar* in relevant respects — that they are likely to perceive the world differently in ways that have legal consequences? If not, how was Strauder harmed by being tried by an all-white jury? Can one denounce racial classifications because they rest on irrelevant or nonexistent distinctions and simultaneously assert that outcomes would be different if the perspectives of the excluded group were recognized? Consider in this context Peters v. Kiff, 407 U.S. 493 (1972), which held that a white civil rights worker could challenge the exclusion of blacks from the grand jury that indicted him.[56]

3. Note carefully how many separate classifications were used by West Virginia in constituting its juries. Which of them do you find objectionable as a matter of political philosophy? Is this synonymous with believing that they are barred by the Fourteenth Amendment? Why or why not?

4. Justice Strong writes that, "[i]f *in those States where the colored people constitute a majority of the entire population* a law should be enacted excluding all white men from jury service," the Fourteenth Amendment would operate to strike it down. How important are the emphasized words to his analysis? Would the sentence have the same meaning if these words were eliminated?

5. *Civil and political rights.* Justice Strong makes no real effort to respond to Justice Field's contention that the Fourteenth Amendment is limited to *civil* rights and, therefore, does not cover *political* rights. As Mark Tushnet notes, The Politics of Equality in Constitutional Law, 74 Journal of American History 884 (1987):

> The lawmakers who discussed equality during Reconstruction accepted midcentury conceptions that distinguished equality with respect to civil rights, to social rights, and to political rights. The core of each conception was also well defined: The core of civil rights included the rights to sue and testify; social rights included the right to select one's associates; voting was the central political right.

The precise contours of these categories were contested, and as Richard Primus explains, "[t]he many political and legal actors who spoke and wrote about rights using these terms did not always employ the categories in the same way." See Primus, The American Language of Rights 154-156 (1999). Nevertheless they provided a general framework for thinking and arguing about the meaning of equality before the law. Consider in this light the following comments by Professor Kaczorowski:[57]

---

56. Justice Marshall, joined by Justices Douglas and Stewart, would have based the holding in *Peters* in part on petitioner's standing to assert the rights of potential jurors and in part on the possible prejudice to petitioner himself: "When any large and identifiable segment of the community is excluded from jury service, the effect is to remove from the jury room qualities of human nature and varieties of human experience, the range of which is unknown and perhaps unknowable. . . ." Justice White, joined by Justices Brennan and Powell, found petitioner's standing supported by a federal statute forbidding jury exclusion based on race. Chief Justice Burger and Justices Blackmun and Rehnquist dissented.

57. Robert Kaczorowski, Revolutionary Constitutionalism in the Era of the Civil War and Reconstruction, 61 N.Y.U. L. Rev. 863, 881-883 (1986). See also Michael Kent Curtis, No State Shall Abridge: The Fourteenth Amendment and the Bill of Rights (1986); Eric Foner, Reconstruction: America's Unfinished Revolution 239-261 (1988).

[A]lthough Republicans were virtually unanimous in their support for the protection of the civil rights of blacks, they divided over the question of securing blacks' voting rights. Ultimately, suffrage was intentionally excluded from the rights that the fourteenth amendment and Civil Rights Act of 1866 were to guarantee. The exclusion of suffrage thus helped to reduce political opposition to the measures by neutralizing racist opposition within the Republican party. . . .

The exclusion of suffrage from the framers' definition of civil rights was also dictated by prevailing legal opinion. Legal thinkers defined suffrage as a political privilege to be exercised by competent individuals, not as a natural right of free men. Thus principles of law buttressed political expediency.

States were not given carte blanche regarding suffrage. Indeed, perhaps the most vigorously debated part of the Amendment was its now forgotten section 2, which declared that a state's representation in the House of Representatives would be reduced should the right to vote be "denied to any of the male inhabitants of such State, being twenty-one years of age, and citizens of the United States, or in any way abridged, except for participation in rebellion, or other crime." Many of the framers argued that section 2 represented an implicit acceptance of a state's right to exclude blacks from voting, so long as it was willing to pay the price of reduced representation in Congress. Others argued that it served only as a specific penalty to be imposed on a state if it violated its presumed constitutional duty to be fair in enfranchising its citizens.[58] Professor Kaczorowski further notes that "the primary reason that the fourteenth amendment was criticized by Radical Republicans as too moderate or conservative was that it did not provide the same protection for voting rights that it did for civil rights." Thus the radical abolitionist Wendell Phillips denounced the Fourteenth Amendment as a "fatal and total surrender." Black enfranchisement awaited the passage two years later of the Fifteenth Amendment.

Assume that *Strauder* had involved the deprivation of the ballot rather than of the right to jury service. Are you confident that Strong would have written the same opinion? Vikram David Amar, in Jury Service as Political Participation, 80 Cornell L. Rev. 203 (1995), argues that *Strauder* should have been decided as a Fifteenth Amendment case, with jury service analogized to the right to vote that that Amendment protects. Do you agree (a) that *Strauder* is in fact problematic as a Fourteenth Amendment case and (b) that the Fifteenth Amendment covers juries?

D.   Establishment of the "Separate but Equal" Doctrine

Strauder contains language that, read for all it is worth, promises full racial equality. But Justice Strong also refers to the Negroes' "abject and ignorant" condition, "unfitted to command the respect of those who had superior intelligence." Although the Court did not retreat from the specific holding in *Strauder*, some of its decisions during the ensuing several decades appear more responsive to this assumption of Negro inferiority than to the goal of racial equality. The Court was not alone in this, and its decisions of the period are illuminated by

---

58. Thus Representative Bingham described section 2 as "a penalty, and nothing but a penalty, inflicted on the State if its ruling class disregard and violate the guarantees of the Constitution of the political right of all the free people therein, being male citizens of the United States of full age, to participate in the choice of electors. . . ." Quoted in Van Alstyne, supra n.50.

C. Vann Woodward's description of their social and political context. The year 1877 is generally regarded as the watershed. Under the so-called Compromise of 1877, southern Democrats abandoned their support for Democrat Samuel J. Tilden, who they claimed had been legally elected president, and supported the seating of Republican Rutherford B. Hayes in exchange, essentially, for the end of Reconstruction. Woodward writes:[59]

> The phase that began in 1877 was inaugurated by the withdrawal of federal troops from the South, the abandonment of the Negro as a ward of the nation, the giving up of the attempt to guarantee the freedman his civil and political equality, and the acquiescence of the rest of the country in the South's demand that the whole problem be left to the disposition of the dominant Southern white people. What the new status of the Negro would be was not at once apparent, nor were the Southern white people themselves so united on that subject at first as has been generally assumed. The determination of the Negro's "place" took shape gradually under the influence of economic and political conflicts among divided white people — conflicts that were eventually resolved in part at the expense of the Negro. . . .
>
> The South's adoption of extreme racism was due not so much to a conversion as it was to a relaxation of the opposition. All the elements of fear, jealousy, proscription, hatred, and fanaticism had long been present, as they are present in various degrees of intensity in any society. What enabled them to rise to dominance was not so much cleverness or ingenuity as it was a general weakening and discrediting of the numerous forces that had hitherto kept them in check. The restraining forces included not only Northern liberal opinion in the press, the courts, and the government, but also internal checks imposed by the prestige and influence of the Southern conservatives, as well as by the idealism and zeal of the Southern radicals. What happened toward the end of the century was an almost simultaneous — and sometimes not unrelated — decline in the effectiveness of restraint that had been exercised by all three forces: Northern liberalism, Southern conservatism, and Southern radicalism.
>
> The acquiescence of Northern liberalism in the Compromise of 1877 defined the beginning, but not the ultimate extent, of the liberal retreat on the race issue. The Compromise merely left the freedman to the custody of the conservative Redeemers upon their pledge that they would protect him in his constitutional rights. But as these pledges were forgotten or violated and the South veered toward proscription and extremism, Northern opinion shifted to the right, keeping pace with the South, conceding point after point, so that at no time were the sections very far apart on race policy. The failure of the liberals to resist this trend was due in part to political factors. Since reactionary politicians and their cause were identified with the bloody-shirt issue and the demagogic exploitation of sectional animosities, the liberals naturally felt themselves strongly drawn toward the cause of sectional reconciliation. And since the Negro was the symbol of sectional strife, the liberals joined in deprecating further agitation of his cause and in defending the Southern view of race in its less extreme forms. It was quite common in the eighties and nineties to find in the Nation, Harper's Weekly, the North American Review, or the Atlantic Monthly, Northern liberals and former abolitionists mouthing the shibboleths of white supremacy regarding the Negro's innate inferiority, shiftlessness, and hopeless unfitness for full participation in the white man's civilization. Such expressions doubtless did much to add to the reconciliation of North and South, but they did so at the expense of the Negro. Just as the Negro gained his emancipation and new rights through a falling out between white men, he now stood to lose his rights through the reconciliation of white men.

59. C. Vann Woodward, The Strange Career of Jim Crow 6, 69-70 (3d rev. ed. 1974).

PLESSY v. FERGUSON
163 U.S. 537 (1896)

[A Louisiana statute required railroads carrying passengers within the state to "provide equal but separate accommodations for the white and colored races" and made it a misdemeanor for a passenger to insist on "going into a coach or compartment to which by race he does not belong." The statute gave "officers of . . . passenger trains" the power and the legal obligation "to assign each passenger to the coach or compartment used for the race to which such passenger belongs."

Railroad officers who "insist[ed] on assigning a passenger to a coach or compartment other than the one set aside for the race to which said passenger belongs" were subject to fines and imprisonment. If a passenger refused assignment to any coach or compartment, "said officer shall have power to refuse to carry such passenger on his train, and for such refusal neither he nor the railway company which he represents shall be liable for damages in any of the courts of this State." Finally, the act contained a proviso that exempted racial assignment to "nurses attending children of the other race."

Homer Plessy was an "octoroon," i.e., a person of mixed race "seven eighths Caucasian and one eighth African blood." He appeared to be white; "the mixture of colored blood was not discernible in him." Plessy attempted to sit in a coach reserved for whites and was forcibly ejected and imprisoned. The information charging Plessy with violating the statute did not mention whether he was black or white, and in his own defense "the said Plessy declined and refused, either by pleading or otherwise, to admit that he was in any sense or in any proportion a colored man." After hearing Plessy's challenge to the constitutionality of Louisiana's separate accommodations law, the Supreme Court held that the statute did not violate either the Thirteenth or the Fourteenth Amendments.]

BROWN, J. . . .

The constitutionality of this act is attacked upon the ground that it conflicts both with the Thirteenth Amendment of the Constitution, abolishing slavery, and the Fourteenth Amendment, which prohibits certain restrictive legislation on the part of the States.

That it does not conflict with the Thirteenth Amendment . . . is too clear for argument. Slavery implies involuntary servitude — a state of bondage; the ownership of mankind as a chattel, or at least the control of the labor and services of one man for the benefit of another, and the absence of a legal right to the disposal of his own person, property and services. . . . A statute which implies merely a legal distinction between the white and colored races — a distinction which is founded in the color of the two races, and which must always exist so long as white men are distinguished from the other race by color — has no tendency to destroy the legal equality of the two races, or reestablish a state of involuntary servitude. . . .

The object of the [Fourteenth] [A]mendment was undoubtedly to enforce the absolute equality of the two races before the law, but in the nature of things it could not have been intended to abolish distinctions based upon color, or to enforce social, as distinguished from political equality, or a commingling of the two races upon terms unsatisfactory to either. Laws permitting, and even requiring, their separation in places where they are liable to be brought into contact do not necessarily imply the inferiority of either race to the other, and have been generally, if not universally, recognized as within the competency of the state legislatures in the exercise of their police power. The most common instance of this is connected with the establishment of separate schools for white and colored children, which has been held to be a valid exercise of the legislative power even by courts of States where the political rights of the colored race have been longest and most earnestly enforced. . . . [The Court here cites decisions in states including Massachusetts, New York, Ohio, and California.]

Laws forbidding the intermarriage of the two races may be said in a technical sense to interfere with the freedom of contract, and yet have been universally recognized as within the police power of the State.

The distinction between laws interfering with the political equality of the negro and those requiring the separation of the two races in schools, theatres and railway carriages has been frequently drawn by this court. Thus in Strauder v. West Virginia, 100 U.S. 303, it was held that a law of West Virginia limiting to white male persons, 21 years of age and citizens of the State, the right to sit upon juries, was a discrimination which implied a legal inferiority in civil society, which lessened the security of the right of the colored race, and was a step toward reducing them to a condition of servility. . . .

While we think the enforced separation of the races, as applied to the internal commerce of the State, neither abridges the privileges or immunities of the colored man, deprives him of his property without due process of law, nor denies him the equal protection of the laws, within the meaning of the Fourteenth Amendment, we are not prepared to say that the conductor, in assigning passengers to the coaches according to their race, does not act at his peril, or that the provision of the second section of the act, that denies to the passenger compensation in damages for a refusal to receive him into the coach in which he properly belongs, is a valid exercise of the legislative power. Indeed, we understand it to be conceded by the State's attorney, that such part of the act as exempts from liability the railway company and its officers is unconstitutional. The power to assign to a particular coach obviously implies the power to determine to which race the passenger belongs, as well as the power to determine who, under the laws of the particular State, is to be deemed a white, and who a colored person. This question, though indicated in the brief of the plaintiff in error, does not properly arise upon the record in this case, since the only issue made is as to the unconstitutionality of the act, so far as it requires the railway to provide separate accommodations, and the conductor to assign passengers according to their race.

It is claimed by the plaintiff in error that, in any mixed community, the reputation of belonging to the dominant race, in this instance the white race, is property, in the same sense that a right of action, or of inheritance, is property. Conceding this to be so, for the purposes of this case, we are unable to see how this statute deprives him of, or in any way affects his right to, such property. If he be a white man and assigned to a colored coach, he may have his action for damages against the company for being deprived of his so called property. Upon the other hand, if he be a colored man and be so assigned, he has been deprived of no property, since he is not lawfully entitled to the reputation of being a white man.

In this connection, it is also suggested by the learned counsel for the plaintiff in error that the same argument that will justify the state legislature in requiring railways to provide separate accommodations for the two races will also authorize them to require separate cars to be provided for people whose hair is of a certain color, or who are aliens, or who belong to certain nationalities, or to enact laws requiring colored people to walk upon one side of the street, and white people upon the other, or requiring white men's houses to be painted white, and colored men's black, or their vehicles or business signs to be of different colors, upon the theory that one side of the street is as good as the other, or that a house or vehicle of one color is as good as one of another color. The reply to all this is that every exercise of the police power must be reasonable, and extend only to such laws as are enacted in good faith for the promotion for the public good, and not for the annoyance or oppression of a particular class. Thus in Yick Wo v. Hopkins, 118 U.S. 356, it was held by this court that a municipal ordinance of the city of San Francisco [that gave municipal authorities arbitrary discretion to permit or refuse to permit the operation of] public laundries . . . without regard to the competency of the persons applying, or the propriety of the places selected for the carrying on the business [was] a covert attempt on the part of the municipality to make an arbitrary and unjust discrimination against the Chinese race.

So far, then, as a conflict with the Fourteenth Amendment is concerned, the case reduces itself to the question whether the statute of Louisiana is a reasonable regulation, and with respect to this there must necessarily be a large discretion on the part of the legislature. In determining the question of reasonableness it is at liberty to act with reference to the established usages, customs and traditions of the people, and with a view to the promotion of their comfort, and the preservation of the public peace and good order. Gauged by this standard, we cannot say that a law which authorizes or even requires the separation of the two races in public conveyances is unreasonable, or . . . obnoxious to the Fourteenth Amendment. . . .

We consider the underlying fallacy of the plaintiff's argument to consist in the assumption that the enforced separation of the two races stamps the colored race with a badge of inferiority. If this be so, it is not by reason of anything found in the act, but solely because the colored race chooses to put that construction upon it. The argument necessarily assumes that if, as has been more than once the case, and is not unlikely to be so again, the colored race should become the dominant power in the state legislature, and should enact a law in precisely similar terms, it would thereby relegate the white race to an inferior position. We imagine that the white race, at least, would not acquiesce in this assumption. The argument also assumes that social prejudices may be overcome by legislation, and that equal rights cannot be secured to the negro except by an enforced commingling of the two races. We cannot accept this proposition. If the two races are to meet upon terms of social equality, it must be the result of natural affinities, a mutual appreciation of each other's merits and a voluntary consent of individuals. As was said by the Court of Appeals of New York in People v. Gallagher, 93 N.Y. 438, 448, "this end can neither be accomplished nor promoted by laws which conflict with the general sentiment of the community upon whom they are designed to operate. When the government, therefore, has secured to each of its citizens equal rights before the law and equal opportunities for improvement and progress, it has accomplished the end for which it was organized and performed all of the functions respecting social advantages with which it is endowed." Legislation is powerless to eradicate racial instincts or to abolish distinctions based upon physical differences, and the attempt to do so can only result in accentuating the difficulties of the present situation. If the civil and political rights of both races be equal one cannot be inferior to the other civilly or politically. If one race be inferior to the other socially, the Constitution of the United States cannot put them upon the same plane.

It is true that the question of the proportion of colored blood necessary to constitute a colored person, as distinguished from a white person, is one upon which there is a difference of opinion in the different States, some holding that any visible admixture of black blood stamps the person as belonging to the colored race (State v. Chavers, 5 Jones, [N.C.] 1, p. 11); others that it depends upon the preponderance of blood (Gray v. State, 4 Ohio, 354; Monroe v. Collins, 17 Ohio St. 665); and still others that the predominance of white blood must only be in the proportion of three fourths. (People v. Dean, 14 Michigan, 406; Jones v. Commonwealth, 80 Virginia, 538.) But these are questions to be determined under the laws of each State and are not properly put in issue in this case. Under the allegations of his petition it may undoubtedly become a question of importance whether, under the laws of Louisiana, the petitioner belongs to the white or colored race.

HARLAN J., dissenting. . . .

By the Louisiana statute . . . [t]he managers of the railroad are not allowed to exercise any discretion in the premises, but are required to assign each passenger to some coach or compartment set apart for the exclusive use of his race. . . . Only "nurses attending children of the other race" are excepted from the operation of the statute. No exception is made of colored attendants travelling with adults. A white man is not permitted to have his colored servant with him in the same coach, even if his condition of health requires the constant, personal assistance of such servant. If a colored maid insists upon riding in the same coach with a white woman whom she has been employed to serve, and who may need her personal attention while travelling, she is subject to be fined or imprisoned for such an exhibition of zeal in the discharge of duty.

[The] State regulates the use of a public highway by citizens of the United States solely upon the basis of race. . . .

In respect of civil rights, common to all citizens, the Constitution of the United States does not, I think, permit any public authority to know the race of those entitled to be protected in the enjoyment of such rights. Every true man has pride of race, and under appropriate circumstances when the rights of others, his equals before the law, are not to be affected, it is his privilege to express such pride and to take such action based upon it as to him seems proper. But I deny that any legislative body or judicial tribunal may have regard to the race of citizens when the civil rights of those citizens are involved. Indeed, such legislation, as that here in question, is inconsistent not only with that equality of rights which pertains to citizenship, National and State, but with the personal liberty enjoyed by every one within the United States.

The Thirteenth Amendment . . . not only struck down the institution of slavery as previously existing in the United States, but it prevents the imposition of any burdens or disabilities that constitute badges of slavery or servitude. It decreed universal civil freedom in this country. This court has so adjudged. [The Thirteenth and Fourteenth Amendments,] if enforced according to their true intent and meaning, will protect all the civil rights that pertain to freedom and citizenship. [The Fifteenth Amendment guaranteed] that no citizen should be denied, on account of his race, the privilege of participating in the political control of his country. . . . These notable additions to the fundamental law were welcomed by the friends of liberty throughout the world. They removed the race line from our governmental systems. At the present term, referring to the previous adjudications [interpreting these amendments], this court declared that "underlying all of those decisions is the principle that the Constitution of the United States, in its present form, forbids, so far as civil and political rights are concerned, discrimination by the General Government or the States against any citizen because of his race. All citizens are equal before the law." Gibson v. Mississippi, 162 U.S. 565.

It was said in argument that the statute of Louisiana does not discriminate against either race, but prescribes a rule applicable alike to white and colored citizens. But this argument does not meet the difficulty. Every one knows that the statute in question had its origin in the purpose, not so much to exclude white persons from railroad cars occupied by blacks, as to exclude colored people from coaches occupied by or assigned to white persons. Railroad corporations of Louisiana did not make discrimination among whites in the matter of accommodation for travellers. The thing to accomplish was, under the guise of giving equal accommodation for whites and blacks, to compel the latter to keep to themselves while travelling in railroad passenger coaches. No one would be so wanting in candor as to assert the contrary. The fundamental objection, therefore, to the statute is that it interferes with the personal freedom of citizens. . . . If a white man and a black man choose to occupy the same public conveyance on a public highway, it is their right to do so, and no government, proceeding alone on grounds of race, can prevent it without infringing the personal liberty of each.

. . . If a State can prescribe, as a rule of civil conduct, that whites and blacks shall not travel as passengers in the same railroad coach, why may it not so regulate the use of the streets of its cities and towns as to compel white citizens to keep on one side of a street and black citizens to keep on the other? Why may it not, upon like grounds, punish whites and blacks who ride together in street cars or in open vehicles on a public road or street? Why may it not require sheriffs to assign whites to one side of a court-room and blacks to the other? And why may it not also prohibit the commingling of the two races in the galleries of legislative halls or in public assemblages convened for the considerations of the political questions of the day? Further, if this statute of Louisiana is consistent with the personal liberty of citizens, why may not the State require the separation in railroad coaches of native and naturalized citizens of the United States, or of Protestants and Roman Catholics?

The answer given at the argument to these questions was that regulations of the kind they suggest would be unreasonable, and could not, therefore, stand before the law. Is it meant that the determination of questions of legislative power depends upon the inquiry whether the statute whose validity is questioned is, in the judgment of the courts, a reasonable one, taking all the circumstances into consideration? A statute may be unreasonable merely because a sound public policy forbade its enactment. But I do not understand that the courts have anything to do with the policy or expediency of legislation. . . .

The white race deems itself to be the dominant race in this country. And so it is, in prestige, in achievements, in education, in wealth and in power. So, I doubt not, it will continue to be for all time, if it remains true to its great heritage and holds fast to the principles of constitutional liberty. But in view of the Constitution, in the eye of the law, there is in this country no superior, dominant, ruling class of citizens. There is no caste here. Our Constitution is color-blind, and neither knows nor tolerates classes among citizens. In respect of civil rights, all citizens are equal before the law. The humblest is the peer of the most powerful. The law regards man as man, and takes no account of his surroundings or of his color when his civil rights as guaranteed by the supreme law of the land are involved.

In my opinion, the judgment this day rendered will, in time, prove to be quite as pernicious as the decision made by this tribunal in the *Dred Scott* case. It was adjudged in that case that the descendants of Africans who were imported into this country and sold as slaves were not included nor intended to be included under the word "citizens" in the Constitution, and could not claim any of the rights and privileges which that instrument provided for and secured to citizens of the United States; that at the time of the adoption of the Constitution they were "considered as a subordinate and inferior class of beings, who had been subjugated by the dominant race, and, whether emancipated or not, yet remained subject to their authority, and had no rights or privileges but such as those who held the power and the government might choose to grant them." 19 How. 393, 404. The recent amendments of the Constitution, it was supposed, had eradicated these principles from our institutions. But it seems that we have yet, in some of the States, a dominant race — a superior class of citizens, which assumes to regulate the enjoyment of civil rights, common to all citizens, upon the basis of race. The present decision, it may well be apprehended, will not only stimulate aggressions, more or less brutal and irritating, upon the admitted rights of colored citizens, but will encourage the belief that it is possible, by means of state enactments, to defeat the beneficent purposes which the people of the United States had in view when they adopted the recent amendments of the Constitution, by one of which the blacks of this country were made citizens of the United States and of the States in which they respectively reside, and whose privileges and immunities, as citizens, the States are forbidden to abridge. Sixty millions of whites are in no danger from the presence here of eight millions of blacks. The destinies of the two races, in this country, are indissolubly linked together, and the interests of both require that the common government of all shall not permit the seeds of race hate to be planted under the sanction of law. What can more certainly arouse race hate, what can more certainly create and perpetuate a feeling of distrust between these races, than state enactments, which, in fact, proceed on the ground that colored citizens are so inferior and degraded that they cannot be allowed to sit in public coaches occupied by white citizens? That, as all will admit, is the real meaning of such legislation as was enacted in Louisiana.

The sure guarantee of the peace and security of each race is the clear, distinct, unconditional recognition by our governments, National and State, of every right that inheres in civil freedom, and of the equality before the law of all citizens of the United States without regard to race. State enactments, regulating the enjoyment of civil rights, upon the basis of race, and cunningly devised to defeat legitimate results of the war, under the pretence of recognizing equality of rights, can have no other result than to render permanent peace impossible, and to keep alive a conflict of races, the continuance of which must do harm to all concerned. This question is not met by the suggestion that social equality cannot exist between the white and black races in this country. That argument, if it can be properly regarded as one, is scarcely worthy of consideration; for social equality no more exists between two races when travelling in a passenger coach or a public highway than when members of the same races sit by each other in a street car or in the jury box, or stand or sit with each other in a political assembly, or when they use in common the streets of a city or town, or when they are in the same room for the purpose of having their names placed on the registry of voters, or when they approach the ballot-box in order to exercise the high privilege of voting.

There is a race so different from our own that we do not permit those belonging to it to become citizens of the United States. Persons belonging to it are, with few exceptions, absolutely excluded from our country. I allude to the Chinese race. But by the statute in question, a Chinaman can ride in the same passenger coach with white citizens of the United States, while citizens of the black race in Louisiana, many of whom, perhaps, risked their lives for the preservation of the Union, who are entitled, by law, to participate in the political control of the State and nation, who are not excluded, by law or by reason of their race, from public stations of any kind, and who have all the legal rights that belong to white citizens, are yet declared to be criminals, liable to imprisonment, if they ride in a public coach occupied by citizens of the white race. It is scarcely just to say that a colored citizen should not object to occupying a public coach assigned to his own race. He does not object, nor, perhaps, would he object to separate coaches for his race, if his rights under the law were recognized. But he objects, and ought never to cease objecting to the proposition, that citizens of the white and black races can be adjudged criminals because they sit, or claim the right to sit, in the same public coach on a public highway.

The arbitrary separation of citizens, on the basis of race, while they are on a public highway, is a badge of servitude wholly inconsistent with the civil freedom and the equality before the law established by the Constitution. It cannot be justified upon any legal grounds.

If evils will result from the commingling of the two races upon public highways established for the benefit of all, they will be infinitely less than those that will surely come from state legislation regulating the enjoyment of civil rights upon the basis of race. We boast of the freedom enjoyed by our people above all other peoples. But it is difficult to reconcile that boast with a state of the law which, practically, puts the brand of servitude and degradation upon a large class of our fellow-citizens, our equals before the law. The thin disguise of "equal" accommodations for passengers in railroad coaches will not mislead any one, nor atone for the wrong this day done.

Discussion

1. Justice Brown indicates that the equal protection clause was designed to assure "political" though not "social" equality. Is he correct as to its assuring "political" equality? (Do you believe that Brown considered the Fifteenth Amendment merely redundant?) As to the distinction between social and other forms of equality, Professor Tushnet in The Politics of Equality in Constitutional Law, 74 Journal of American History 884 (1987) writes:

> Equality in political and civil rights did not mean, as a legal matter, that blacks could insist on equal treatment in the ordinary course of social life. Whites could refuse to have social contacts with blacks and could exclude blacks from their homes. More significant, the rejection of [social] equality [as a command of the Fourteenth Amendment] was widely believed to imply that segregated education was permissible, as were laws prohibiting racial intermarriage.

2. Justice Brown argues that "[l]egislation is powerless to eradicate racial instincts or to abolish distinctions based upon physical differences." One wonders what "physical differences" Brown is referring to, since he almost certainly had

never laid eyes on Plessy, who was, in the racial language of New Orleans, an "octoroon," meaning that he was one-eighth black and seven-eighths white.[60] That was enough to make him "black," because by Louisiana law a "single drop" of "black blood" was enough to earn the label of "blackness." Had Louisiana, for example, adopted a "quarter-blood" rule, requiring at least one black grandparent, Plessy would have been deemed white. What was the purpose of this statute? The Court refused to inquire into the constitutionality of that definition, considering it a matter of local law. See Chapter 6, infra, for further discussion of the legal construction of racial identity, and ask if even today states are constrained in any way as to how they assign racial identity.

3. The Court implicitly contrasts "discrimination" with mere "segregation" and holds that the Constitution prohibits only the former. This view was elaborated by Professor Herbert Wechsler, a distinguished constitutional scholar, in criticizing the Court's 1954 decision in Brown v. Board of Education, Chapter 6, infra:

> For me, assuming equal facilities, the question posed by state-enforced segregation is not one of discrimination at all. Its human and its constitutional dimensions lie entirely elsewhere, in the denial by the state of freedom to associate, a denial that impinges in the same way on any groups or races that may be involved. I think, and I hope not without foundation, that the Southern white also pays heavily for segregation, not only in the sense of guilt that he must carry but also in the benefits he is denied. . . .
>
> But if the freedom of association is denied by segregation, integration forces an association upon those for whom it is unpleasant or repugnant. Is this not the heart of the issue involved, a conflict in human claims of high dimension, not unlike many others that involve the highest freedoms. . . . Given a situation where the state must practically choose between denying the association to those individuals who wish it or imposing it on those who would avoid it, is there a basis in neutral principles for holding that the Constitution demands that the claims for association should prevail?[61]

How would you answer Professor Wechsler's question?

4. The Court states that "every exercise of the police power must be reasonable, and extend only to such laws as are enacted in good faith for the promotion for the public good, and not for the annoyance or oppression of a particular class." Presumably, if a race-based law were enacted with an improper motive or were simply a pretext for "annoyance and oppression," the Court would strike it down. Note the similarity to the "pretext" qualification in paragraph 42 of *McCulloch*, supra. Would you trust the Supreme Court in 1896 to determine accurately when racial classifications meet the standard of "annoyance and suppression"? What about today?

5. Justice Harlan's dissent is famous for its statement that "[o]ur Constitution is colorblind." But for Harlan, colorblindness clearly did not mean social equality. Note that Harlan insisted that whites and blacks were not socially equal even if they sat in the same railway carriage. Thus, Harlan suggested that whites could still be socially superior to blacks even if they were equal before the law. What is the source of social inequality for Harlan — private decisionmaking, class position, social meanings, or

---

60. See Lofgren, The Plessy Case: A Legal-Historical Interpretation 54-55 (1987). Lofgren's is the standard history of this extremely fascinating and complex case.

61. Herbert Wechsler, Toward Neutral Principles of Constitutional Law, 73 Harv. L. Rev. 1, 34 (1959). Wechsler's famous use of the term "neutral principles" to describe the goals of constitutional adjudication has become the source of an endless debate as to whether it is possible to interpret the Constitution without enforcing politically contestable substantive values.

some combination of the three? What did Harlan mean when he suggested that "the white race" would continue to be "the superior race for all time"? Note that in the same paragraph Harlan also insists that "there is no caste" in the United States. What does Harlan mean by "caste," then? Does the law have to directly recognize or classify on the basis of race in order to be complicit in perpetuating a caste system?

6. Justice Harlan has won justified plaudits for his refusal to join his colleagues in upholding racial segregation. Consider, however, his comments about the Chinese. Indeed, Justice Harlan in 1898 joined Chief Justice Fuller in dissenting from the majority in United States v. Wong Kim Ark, 169 U.S. 649 (1898), which held that persons of Chinese descent born in the United States were birthright citizens under the Fourteenth Amendment. Fuller and Harlan vigorously objected, denouncing "the presence within our territory of large numbers of Chinese laborers, of a distinct race and religion, remaining strangers in the land, residing apart by themselves, tenaciously adhering to the customs and usage of their own country, unfamiliar with our institutions and religion, and apparently incapable of assimilating with our people." See generally, Gabriel J. Chin, The Plessy Myth: Justice Harlan and the Chinese Cases, 82 Iowa L. Rev. 151 (1996). For more extended treatment of anti-Chinese sentiment and resultant legislation, see the Chinese Exclusion Case, infra, pp. 398-405.

You may also recall Taney's reminder in *Dred Scott* that naturalization was limited to "white persons" by the Naturalization Act of 1795; "aliens of African nativity and . . . persons of African descent" were made eligible for citizenship in 1870, but persons of Asian origin remained ineligible to become citizens until 1952. Indeed, the Supreme Court in two cases during the 1920s construed the meaning of "white" as not including one of Japanese descent or of a "high-caste Hindu of full Indian blood." See Takao Ozawa v. United States, 260 U.S. 178 (1922); United States v. Bhagat Singh Thind, 261 U.S. 204 (1923). The Court, however, scarcely came up with a coherent theory of how one determined who was "white" and, therefore, eligible for membership in the American political community. Although *Ozawa* included the passage that "the words 'white persons' are synonymous with the words 'a person of the Caucasian race,'" the Court rejected Thind's claim of eligibility, which had prevailed in the courts below, because of his presentation of evidence that he was the member of a "Caucasian race." Justice Sutherland responded for a unanimous Court:

> The words of familiar speech, which were used by the original framers of the law, were intended to include only the type of man whom they knew as white. The immigration of that day was almost exclusively from the British Isles and Northwestern Europe, whence they and their forebears had come. When they extended the privilege of American citizenship to "any alien being a free white person" it was these immigrants — bone of their bone and flesh of their flesh — and their kind whom they must have had affirmatively in mind. The succeeding years brought immigrants from Eastern, Southern and Middle Europe, among them the Slavs and the dark-eyed, swarthy people of Alpine and Mediterranean stock, and these were received as unquestionably akin to those already here and readily amalgamated with them. It was the descendants of these, and other immigrants of like origin, who constituted the white population of the country when [the relevant legislation] was adopted.[62]

62. See generally Ian F. Haney Lopez, White by Law: The Legal Construction of Race (1996). And, as to the assignment of "swarthy" groups to the category of whites, see Matthew Frye Jacobson, Whiteness of a Different Color: European Immigrants and the Alchemy of Race (1998). For further discussion of the complexities of defining racial (and gender) identity, see Chapters 6 and 7, infra.

7. The Court asserts that nothing intrinsic to the segregation law "stamps the colored race with a badge of inferiority." Might the distinction between segregation and discrimination rest in part on the social meaning of the separation? Compare, for example, the contemporary social meaning of restrooms segregated by race and by gender. The modern Court would immediately strike down the former; the latter would certainly be upheld (even, one strongly suspects, had the ERA been ratified). What accounts for the distinction?

Note that the law in *Plessy* was not an isolated enactment but part of a pervasive scheme of Jim Crow laws, in every Southern and border state, "that extended to churches and schools, to housing and jobs, to eating and drinking . . . to virtually all forms of public transportation, to sports and recreations, to hospitals, orphanages, prisons, and asylums, and ultimately to funeral homes, morgues, and cemeteries."[63] Did the Court in *Plessy* wrongly ignore the cultural meaning of state-imposed segregation? If so, what does this imply for the "process" rationale of judicial review, by which the Court takes care to make sure that even losers within the legislative process have been treated fairly? Consider in this context the following defense of the Court's 1954 decision in Brown v. Board of Education, Chapter 6, infra, which held "separate but equal" schooling unconstitutional.

CHARLES BLACK, THE LAWFULNESS OF THE SEGREGATION DECISIONS
69 Yale L.J. 421, 424-427 (1960)

. . . I was raised in the south, in a Texas city where the pattern of segregation was firmly fixed. I am sure it never occurred to anyone, white or colored, to question its meaning. The fiction of "equality" is just about on a level with the fiction of "finding" in the action of trover. I think few candid southerners deny this. Northern people may be misled by the entirely sincere protestations of many southerners that segregation is "better" for the Negroes, is not intended to hurt them. But I think a little probing would demonstrate that what is meant is that it is better for the Negroes to accept a position of inferiority, at least for the indefinite future. . . .

Segregation in the South comes down in apostolic succession from slavery and the *Dred Scott* case. The South fought to keep slavery, and lost. Then it tried the Black Codes, and lost. Then it looked around for something else and found segregation. The movement for segregation was an integral part of the movement to maintain and further "white supremacy." . . . Segregation in the South grew up and is kept going because and only because the white race has wanted it that way. . . . [T]he life of a southern community [is not one] of mutual separation of whites and Negroes, but of one in-group enjoying full normal communal life and one out-group that is barred from this life and forced into an inferior life of its own. . . . When you are in Leeville and hear someone say "Leeville High," you know he has reference to the white high school; the Negro school will be called something else — Carver High, perhaps, or Lincoln High to our shame. . . .

Segregation is historically and contemporaneously associated in a functioning complex with practices which are indisputably and grossly discriminatory. I have in

---

63. Woodward, supra n.57, at 8.

mind especially the long-continued and still largely effective exclusion of Negroes from voting. . . . [S]egregation is the pattern of law in communities where the extralegal patterns of discrimination against Negroes are the tightest, where Negroes are subjected to the strictest codes of "unwritten law" as to job opportunities, social intercourse, patterns of housing, going to the back door, being called by the first name, saying "Sir," and all the rest of the whole sorry business. . . .

"Separate but equal" facilities are almost never really equal. Sometimes this concerns small things — if the "white" men's room has mixing hot and cold taps, the "colored" men's room will likely have separate taps; it is always the back of the bus for the Negroes; "Lincoln Beach" will rarely if ever be as good as the regular beach. Sometimes it concerns the most vital matter — through the whole history of segregation, colored schools have been so disgracefully inferior to white schools. . . .

Attention is usually focused on these inequalities as things in themselves, correctible by detailed decrees. I am more interested in their very clear character as *evidence* of what segregation means to the people who impose it and to the people who are subjected to it. . . . Further arguments could be piled on top of one another, for we have here to do with the most conspicuous characteristic of a whole regional culture. It is actionable defamation in the South to call a white man a Negro. A small proportion of Negro "blood" puts one in the inferior race for segregation purposes; this is the way in which one deals with a taint, such as a carcinogen in cranberries.

The various items I have mentioned differ in weight; not every one would suffice in itself to establish the character of segregation. Taken together they are of irrefragable strength. The society that has just lost the Negro as a slave, that has just lost out in an attempt to put him under quasi-servile "Codes," the society that views his blood as a contamination and his name as an insult, the society that extralegally imposes on him every humiliating mark of low caste and that until yesterday kept him in line by lynching — this society, careless of his consent, moves by law, first to exclude him from voting, and secondly to cut him off from mixing in the general public life of the community. The Court that refused to see inequality in this cutting off would be making the only kind of law that can be warranted outrageous in advance — law based on selfinduced blindness, on flagrant contradiction of known fact.

I have stated all these points shortly because they are matters of common notoriety, matters not so much for judicial notice as for the background knowledge of educated men who live in the world. A court may advise itself of them as it advises itself of the facts that we are a "religious people," that the country is more industrialized than in Jefferson's day, that children are the natural objects of fathers' bounty, that criminal sanctions are commonly thought to deter, that steel is a basic commodity in our economy, that the imputation of unchastity is harmful to a woman. Such judgments, made on such a basis, are in the foundations of all law, decisional as well as statutory; it would be the most unneutral of principles, improvised ad hoc, to require that a court faced with the present problem refuse to note a plain fact about the society of the United States — the fact that the social meaning of segregation is the putting of the Negro in a position of walled-off inferiority — or the other equally plain fact that such treatment is hurtful to human beings. Southern courts, on the basis of just such a judgment, have held that the placing of a white person in a Negro railroad car is an actionable humiliation; must a court pretend not to know that the Negro's situation there is humiliating?

Note: The Spirit of Plessy

Viewed in terms of the Compromise of 1877, *Strauder* and *Plessy* are not inconsistent with one another. Central to most political compromises is the saving of face. The law struck down in *Strauder,* by its very terms, treated Negroes unequally by excluding them from juries. The law upheld in *Plessy* was neutral in appearance, favoring neither blacks nor whites. The inequality appeared only when one looked behind the words of the statute, and this — though it hardly required much scrutiny — the Court refused to do. Indeed, one might well believe that *Plessy* had been presaged 13 years before in Pace v. Alabama, 106 U.S. 583 (1883), which upheld the prohibition of interracial marriage and enhanced punishment for interracial adultery or fornication. Justice Field wrote a short, almost perfunctory, opinion for a unanimous Court (which included Justice Harlan) holding that the law was not discriminatory:

> [T]he offense against which [the Alabama law] is aimed cannot be committed without involving the persons of both races in the same punishment. Whatever discrimination is made in the punishment prescribed in the two sections is directed against the offense designated and not against the person of any particular color or race. The punishment of each offending person, whether white or black, is the same.

Given *Pace,* what is surprising about *Plessy?*

Many of the Court's other decisions from about 1880 to 1930 support C. Vann Woodward's suggestion that "[t]he [C]ourt, like the liberals, was engaged in a bit of reconciliation . . . achieved at the Negro's expense."[64] *Plessy* was reaffirmed in several cases,[65] and in Gong Lum v. Rice, 275 U.S. 78 (1927), it was extended to school segregation. See also Cumming v. Richmond Co. Bd. of Educ., 175 U.S. 528 (1899); Berea College v. Kentucky, 211 U.S. 45 (1908).

The only major exception to this line of decisions is Buchanan v. Warley, 245 U.S. 60 (1917), in which a unanimous Court held invalid under the due process clause a Louisville ordinance prohibiting black persons from residing in a block in which a majority of houses were occupied by whites, and white persons from residing in a block in which a majority of the houses were occupied by blacks. *Buchanan* was a collusive suit by a white seller to compel specific performance of a contract for the purchase of a house by a black buyer, who ostensibly defended on the ground that the ordinance made the contract illegal. Justice Day was not impressed with arguments that the ordinance prevented miscegenation and preserved property values. Although he did take seriously the argument that the ordinance "will promote the public peace by preventing race conflicts," this was held not to outweigh the seller's right to dispose of his property. *Plessy* was distinguished with the cryptic explanation that "in that case there was no attempt to deprive persons

---

64. Id. at 71. For detailed and extensive surveys of the law during this period, see Charles Mangum, The Legal Status of the Negro (1940); Edward Waite, The Negro in the Supreme Court, 30 Minn. L. Rev. 219 (1946).

65. E.g., Chesapeake & O. Ry. v. Kentucky, 179 U.S. 388 (1900); Chiles v. Chesapeake & O. Ry., 218 U.S. 71 (1910); McCabe v. Atchison, T. & S.F.R., 235 U.S. 151 (1914) (in which the Court held, however, that a state could not permit carriers to provide sleeping and dining facilities only for whites). See Hall v. DeCuir, 95 U.S. 485 (1877) (commerce clause); Louisville, N.O. & T. Ry. v. Mississippi, 133 U.S. 587 (1890).

of color of transportation in the coaches of the public carrier, and the express requirements were for equal though separate accommodations." *Buchanan* probably is best explained in terms of the supposed uniqueness of real property and the then-prevailing doctrine of economic due process.[66]

It is difficult to assess the extent to which the spirit of compromise affected the Court's handling of some other areas of constitutional doctrine. Although *Strauder* had forbidden the statutory exclusion of Negroes from juries, exclusion brought about by the discriminatory action of state officials remained pervasive. The Court did intervene in some egregious instances,[67] and its failure to intervene more readily and significantly may have been due to difficulties of proof and to a tenable, though narrow, construction of jurisdictional provisions.[68]

In the area of voting rights, the Court struck down several blatant statutory attempts to circumvent the requirements of the Fifteenth Amendment,[69] but the gradual disfranchisement of southern blacks was achieved by a variety of other means, which the Court would not or could not deal with. Richard Pildes describes the process that eventually swept through the South:

> Black (male) political participation remained extraordinarily high long after federal military forces were withdrawn from the South in 1877. In 1880, two-thirds of adult black men voted in the Presidential election; even in the 1890s, half of black men still voted in key governor's races in Southern states. Black officials also held political offices (around 2,000 in number) at every level in the South, from state Supreme Courts, to the U.S. Senate, down to the county and local level. . . . [and] though black officeholding declined sharply by 1880, even that much-reduced number was not again reached until 1972, seven years after the Voting Rights Act. Yet the forces of elite, conservative, white political control, through the organized vehicle of the Democratic Party, slowly recovered political power through a series of increasingly effective tactics: outright violence and intimidation, . . . fraudulent manipulation of ballots; racial gerrymandering of election districts and other dilutive structural devices; and statutory suffrage restrictions that greatly reduced the black and poor-white electorate. . . . This step-by-step process eventually culminated in sufficient white control to produce new constitutional conventions, or suffrage-restricting constitutional amendments through referenda, in every former Confederate state, starting with Mississippi in 1890 and ending with Georgia in 1908. The avowed purpose of these new constitutions was to restore white supremacy, but that was not their only aim. For the Framers of disfranchisement were typically the most conservative, large landowning, wealthy faction of the Democratic Party, who were also seeking to entrench their partisan power and fend off challenges from Republicans, Populists, and other third parties, as well as

66. See, however, Benno C. Schmidt, Principle and Prejudice: The Supreme Court and Race in the Progressive Era. Part 1: The Heyday of Jim Crow, 82 Colum. L. Rev. 444, 498, 523 (1982), for a more generous interpretation of the Supreme Court's motivation in *Buchanan*. David Bernstein places the case within a more general libertarian framework in Philip Sober Controlling Philip Drunk: *Buchanan v. Warley* in Historical Perspective, 51 Vanderbilt L. Rev. 797 (1998). How much actual impact *Buchanan* had is open to dispute. See, e.g., Michael Klarman, From Jim Crow to Civil Rights: The Supreme Court and the Struggle for Racial Equality 142-146 (2004).

67. E.g., Neal v. Delaware, 103 U.S. 370 (1881); Carter v. Texas, 177 U.S. 442 (1900); Rogers v. Alabama, 192 U.S. 226 (1904). Cf. Yick Wo v. Hopkins, 118 U.S. 356 (1886).

68. See, e.g., Virginia v. Rives, 100 U.S. 313 (1880), holding that absent a discriminatory statute, a defendant could not remove his trial to federal court by alleging and offering to prove racial exclusion; In re Wood, 140 U.S. 278 (1891), holding that jury exclusion cannot be challenged on habeas corpus; Thomas v. Texas, 212 U.S. 278 (1909), deferring to state court's finding of no discrimination.

69. E.g., Guinn v. United States, 238 U.S. 347 (1915), striking down Oklahoma's "grandfather clause," which exempted from a literacy test all those entitled to vote in 1866 and their lineal descendants.

from the more populist wings of the Democratic Party. While pledging not to disfranchise any whites, they advocated provisions that would remove the less educated, less organized, more impoverished whites from the electorate as well — and that would ensure one-party, Democratic rule, which is precisely what happened from this moment forward through most of the 20th century in the South.

The white-supremacy purposes of these new constitutions were not disguised (though the concomitant aim of reducing populist white political influence was). As expressed by the President of the Alabama Convention whose handiwork Jackson Giles would soon challenge, "what is it that we want to do? Why it is within the limits imposed by the Federal Constitution, to establish white supremacy in this State." . . .

The effect of these disenfranchising constitutions throughout the South, combined with statutory suffrage restrictions, was immediate and devastating. In Louisiana, in 1896 there had been 130,334 black voters on the registration rolls and around the same number of white voters (the state's population was about 50 percent white and black); by 1900, two years after the new constitution, registered black voters numbered a mere 5,320. By 1910, 730 registered black voters were left (less than 0.5 percent of eligible black men). In 27 of the state's 60 parishes, not a single black voter was registered any longer; in 9 more parishes, only one black voter was. In South Carolina, black legislators had been the majority in the lower house during Reconstruction; by 1896, the entire state had only 5,500 black voters registered. In Alabama, in 1900 there were 181,471 eligible black voters, but only 3,000 were registered after the new constitutional provisions took effect. In Virginia, there was a 100% drop — in other words, to zero — in estimated black voter turnout between the Presidential elections of 1900 and 1904. North Carolina managed the same complete elimination of black voter turnout over an eight-year period, between the Presidential elections of 1896 and 1904. This was the legal situation Giles sought to challenge in the only way left, through constitutional litigation.[70]

GILES v. HARRIS, 189 U.S. 475 (1903): [Jackson Giles was a Republican-Party activist and President of the Colored Men's Suffrage Association; he held a federal patronage job as the janitor in Montgomery, Alabama's federal courthouse. He had registered and voted in Montgomery, Alabama from 1871 to 1901. Giles challenged the systematic denial of African-Americans' right to vote to in Alabama. The Court, speaking through Justice Holmes, did not dispute the facts, but refused to grant an injunction on the grounds, among others, that even if the facts were true, the Supreme Court had little practical power to address the problem.]

HOLMES, J.:

The bill imports that the great mass of the white population intends to keep the blacks from voting. To meet such an intent something more than ordering the plaintiff's name to be inscribed upon the lists of 1902 will be needed. If the conspiracy and the intent exist, a name on a piece of paper will not defeat them. Unless we are prepared to supervise the voting in that state by officers of the court, it seems to us that all that the plaintiff could get from equity would be an empty form. Apart from damages to the individual, relief from a great political wrong, if done, as alleged, by the people of a state and the state itself, must be given by them or by the legislative and political department of the government of the United States.

[Justices Brewer, Harlan, and Brown (the author of *Plessy*) dissented.[71]]

70. Richard H. Pildes, Democracy, Anti-Democracy, and the Canon, 17 Constitutional Commentary 295, 299-304 (2000).

71. See also Giles v. Teasley, 193 U.S. 146 (1904), denying legal relief arising out of the same disfranchisement scheme.

Discussion

There can be little doubt that the Court averted its eyes from the systematic disenfranchisement of African-Americans that was occurring throughout the South around the turn of the century. Should the Court have attempted vigorously to enforce the Fifteenth Amendment even if open defiance of any such efforts might well have been predicted? Is it relevant that such defiance would not likely have evoked strong responses from Congress or the President? We will have occasion later to consider the practical power (and constitutional duty) of the Court to enforce potentially unpopular doctrines in our discussion of Brown v. Board of Education in Chapter 6, infra.

E. Creation of the State Action Doctrine

THE CIVIL RIGHTS CASES
109 U.S. 3 (1883)

[Section 1 of the Civil Rights Act of 1875 provides: "That all persons within the jurisdiction of the United States shall be entitled to the full and equal enjoyment of the accommodations, advantages, facilities, and privileges of inns, public conveyances on land or water, theatres, and other places of public amusement; subject only to the conditions and limitations established by law, and applicable alike to citizens of every race and color, regardless of any previous condition of servitude." Section 2 makes violation of section 1 a misdemeanor and also permits an aggrieved party to recover a civil fine.

These consolidated cases, from California, Kansas, Missouri, New York, and Tennessee, arose out of the exclusion of Negroes from inns, theaters, and a railroad on account of their race.]

BRADLEY, J. . . .

[T]he primary and important question in all the cases is the constitutionality of the law . . . [the essence of which is to declare that] . . . colored citizens, whether formerly slaves or not, and citizens of other races, shall have the same accommodations and privileges in all inns, public conveyances, and places of amusement as are enjoyed by white citizens; and vice versa. . . .

Has Congress constitutional power to make such a law? Of course, no one will contend that the power to pass it was contained in the Constitution before the adoption of the last three amendments. The power is sought, first, in the Fourteenth Amendment. . . .

It is State action of a particular character that is prohibited. Individual invasion of individual rights is not the subject-matter of the amendment. It has a deeper and broader scope. It nullifies and makes void all State legislation, and State action of every kind, which impairs the privileges and immunities of citizens of the United States, or which injures them in life, liberty or property without due process of law, or which denies to any of them the equal protection of the laws. [T]he last section of the amendment invests Congress with power to enforce it by appropriate legislation. To enforce what? To enforce the prohibition. To adopt appropriate legislation for correcting the effects of such prohibited State laws and State acts, and thus to render them effectually null, void, and innocuous. This is the legislative power conferred upon Congress, and this is the whole of it. It does not invest Congress

with power to legislate upon subjects which are within the domain of State legislation; but to provide modes of relief against State legislation, or State action, of the
kind referred to. It does not authorize Congress to create a code of municipal law
for the regulation of private rights; but to provide modes of redress against the
operation of State laws, and the action of State officers executive or judicial, when
these are subversive of the fundamental rights specified in the amendment. Positive
rights and privileges are undoubtedly secured by the Fourteenth Amendment; but
they are secured by way of prohibition against State laws and State proceedings
affecting those rights and privileges, and by power given to Congress to legislate for
the purpose of carrying such prohibition into effect: and such legislation must
necessarily be predicated upon such supposed State laws or State proceedings, and
be directed to the correction of their operation and effect. . . .

An apt illustration of this distinction may be found in some of the provisions of
the original Constitution. Take the subject of contracts, for example. The
Constitution prohibited the States from passing any law impairing the obligation of
contracts. This did not give to Congress power to provide laws for the general
enforcement of contracts; nor power to invest the courts of the United States with
jurisdiction over contracts, so as to enable parties to sue upon them in those courts.
It did, however, give the power to provide remedies by which the impairment of
contracts by State legislation might be counteracted and corrected. . . .

And so in the present case, until some State law has been passed, or some State
action through its officers or agents has been taken, adverse to the rights of citizens
sought to be protected by the Fourteenth Amendment, no legislation of the United
States under said amendment, nor any proceeding under such legislation, can be
called into activity: for the prohibitions of the amendment are against State laws
and acts done under State authority. Of course, legislation may, and should be,
provided in advance to meet the exigency when it arises; but it should be adapted
to the mischief and wrong which the amendment was intended to provide against;
and that is, State laws, or State action of some kind, adverse to the rights of the
citizen secured by the amendment. Such legislation cannot properly cover the
whole domain of rights appertaining to life, liberty and property, defining them
and providing for their vindication. That would be to establish a code of municipal
law regulative of all private rights between man and man in society. It would be to
make Congress take the place of the State legislatures and to supersede them. It is
absurd to affirm that, because the rights of life, liberty and property (which include
all civil rights that men have), are by the amendment sought to be protected against
invasion on the part of the State without due process of law, Congress may therefore provide due process of law for their vindication in every case; and that, because
the denial by a State to any persons, of the equal protection of the laws, is prohibited by the amendment, therefore Congress may establish laws for their equal
protection. In fine, the legislation which Congress is authorized to adopt in this
behalf is not general legislation upon the rights of the citizen, but corrective legislation, that is, such as may be necessary and proper for counteracting such laws as
the States may adopt or enforce, and which, by the amendment, they are prohibited from making or enforcing, or such acts and proceedings as the States may
commit or take, and which, by the amendment, they are prohibited from committing or taking. It is not necessary for us to state, if we could, what legislation would
be proper for Congress to adopt. It is sufficient for us to examine whether the law
in question is of that character.

An inspection of the [1875 Act] shows that it makes no reference whatever to any supposed or apprehended violation of the Fourteenth Amendment on the part of the States. It is not predicated on any such view. It proceeds ex directo to declare that certain acts committed by individuals shall be deemed offenses, and shall be prosecuted and punished by proceedings in the courts of the United States. It does not profess to be corrective of any constitutional wrong committed by the States; it does not make its operation to depend upon any such wrong committed. It applies equally to cases arising in States which have the justest laws respecting the personal rights of citizens, and whose authorities are ever ready to enforce such laws, as to those which arise in States that may have violated the prohibition of the amendment. In other words, it steps into the domain of local jurisprudence, and lays down rules for the conduct of individuals in society towards each other, and imposes sanctions for the enforcement of those rules, without referring in any manner to any supposed action of the State or its authorities.

If this legislation is appropriate for enforcing the prohibitions of the amendment, it is difficult to see where it is to stop. Why may not Congress with equal show of authority enact a code of laws for the enforcement and vindication of all rights of life, liberty, and property? . . . The truth is, that the implication of a power to legislate in this manner is based upon the assumption that if the States are forbidden to legislate or act in a particular way on a particular subject, and power is conferred upon Congress to enforce the prohibition, this gives Congress power to legislate generally upon that subject, and not merely power to provide modes of redress against such State legislation or action. The assumption is certainly unsound. It is repugnant to the Tenth Amendment of the Constitution, which declares that powers not delegated to the United States by the Constitution, nor prohibited by it to the States, are reserved to the States respectively or to the people.

We have not overlooked the fact that the fourth section of the act now under consideration has been held by this court to be constitutional. That section declares "that no citizen, possessing all other qualifications which are or may be prescribed by law, shall be disqualified for service as grand or petit juror in any court of the United States, or of any State, on account of race, color, or previous condition of servitude; and any officer or other person charged with any duty in the selection or summoning of jurors who shall exclude or fail to summon any citizen for the cause aforesaid, shall, on conviction thereof, be deemed guilty of a misdemeanor, and be fined not more than five thousand dollars."

In Ex parte Virginia, 100 U.S. 339, it was held that an indictment against a State officer under this section for excluding persons of color from the jury list is sustainable. But a moment's attention to its terms will show that the section is entirely corrective in its character. Disqualifications for service on juries are only created by the law, and the first part of the section is aimed at certain disqualifying laws, namely, those which make mere race or color a disqualification; and the second clause is directed against those who, assuming to use the authority of the State government, carry into effect such a rule of disqualification. In the Virginia case, the State, through its officer, enforced a rule of disqualification which the law was intended to abrogate and counteract. Whether the statute book of the State actually laid down any such rule of disqualification, or not, the State, through its officer, enforced such a rule: and it is against such State action, through its officers and agents, that the last clause of the section is directed. This aspect of the law was deemed sufficient to divest it of any unconstitutional character, and makes it differ widely from the first and second sections of the same act which we are now considering.

These sections, in the objectionable features before referred to, are different also from the [Civil Rights Act of 1866] re-enacted with some modifications in . . . the Enforcement Act [of 1870, which] declar[es] that all persons within the jurisdiction of the United States shall have the same right in every State and Territory to make and enforce contracts, to sue, be parties, give evidence, and to the full and equal benefit of all laws and proceedings for the security of persons and property as is enjoyed by white citizens, and shall be subject to like punishment, pains, penalties, taxes, licenses and exactions of every kind, and none other, any law, statute, ordinance, regulation or custom to the contrary notwithstanding. [The Civil Rights Act then] proceeds to enact, that any person who, under color of any law, statute, ordinance, regulation or custom, shall subject, or cause to be subjected, any inhabitant of any State or Territory to the deprivation of any rights secured or protected by the preceding section (above quoted), or to different punishment, pains, or penalties, on account of such person being an alien, or by reason of his color or race, than is prescribed for the punishment of citizens, shall be deemed guilty of a misdemeanor, and subject to fine and imprisonment as specified in the act. This law is clearly corrective in its character, intended to counteract and furnish redress against State laws and proceedings, and customs having the force of law, which sanction the wrongful acts specified. . . . The Civil Rights Bill here referred to is analogous in its character to what a law would have been under the original Constitution, declaring that the validity of contracts should not be impaired, and that if any person bound by a contract should refuse to comply with it, under color or pretence that it had been rendered void or invalid by a State law, he should be liable to an action upon it in the courts of the United States, with the addition of a penalty for setting up such an unjust and unconstitutional defence.

. . . [C]ivil rights, such as are guaranteed by the Constitution against State aggression, cannot be impaired by the wrongful acts of individuals, unsupported by State authority in the shape of laws, customs, or judicial or executive proceedings. The wrongful act of an individual, unsupported by any such authority, is simply a private wrong, or a crime of that individual; an invasion of the rights of the injured party, it is true, whether they affect his person, his property, or his reputation; but if not sanctioned in some way by the State, or not done under State authority, his rights remain in full force, and may presumably be vindicated by resort to the laws of the State for redress. An individual cannot deprive a man of his right to vote, to hold property, to buy and sell, to sue in the courts, or to be a witness or a juror; he may, by force or fraud, interfere with the enjoyment of the right in a particular case; he may commit an assault against the person, or commit murder, or use ruffian violence at the polls, or slander the good name of a fellow citizen; but, unless protected in these wrongful acts by some shield of State law or State authority, he cannot destroy or injure the right; he will only render himself amenable to satisfaction or punishment; and amenable therefor to the laws of the State where the wrongful acts are committed. . . .

The law in question without any reference to adverse State legislation on the subject, declares that all persons shall be entitled to equal accommodations and privileges of inns, public conveyances, and places of public amusement, and imposes a penalty upon any individual who shall deny to any citizen such equal accommodations and privileges. This is not corrective legislation; it is primary and direct; it takes immediate and absolute possession of the subject of the right of admission to inns, public conveyances, and places of amusement. It supersedes and displaces State legislation on the same subject, or only allows it permissive force. It ignores such legislation, and assumes that the matter is one that belongs to the domain of national regulation. Whether it would not have been a more effective protection of the rights of citizens to have clothed Congress with plenary power over the whole subject, is not now the question. What we have to decide is, whether such plenary power has been conferred upon Congress by the Fourteenth Amendment; and, in our judgment, it has not.

We have discussed the question presented by the law on the assumption that a right to enjoy equal accommodations and privileges in all inns, public conveyances, and places of public amusement, is one of the essential rights of the citizens which no State can abridge or interfere with. Whether it is such a right, or not, is a different question which, in the view we have taken of the validity of the law on the ground already stated, it is not necessary to examine. . . .

But the power of Congress to adopt direct and primary, as distinguished from corrective legislation, on the subject in hand, is sought, in the second place, from the Thirteenth Amendment, which abolishes slavery. This amendment declares "that neither slavery, nor involuntary servitude, except as a punishment for crime, whereof the party shall have been duly convicted, shall exist within the United States, or any place subject to their jurisdiction"; and it gives Congress power to enforce the amendment by appropriate legislation. . . . [S]uch legislation may be primary and direct in its character; for the amendment is not a mere prohibition of State laws establishing or upholding slavery, but an absolute declaration that slavery or involuntary servitude shall not exist in any part of the United States.

. . . [I]t is assumed, that the power vested in Congress to enforce the article by appropriate legislation, clothes Congress with power to pass all laws necessary and proper for abolishing all badges and incidents of slavery in the United States: and upon this assumption it is claimed, that this is sufficient authority for declaring by law that all persons shall have equal accommodations and privileges in all inns, public conveyances, and places of amusement; the argument being, that the denial of such equal accommodations and privileges is, in itself, a subjection to a species of servitude within the meaning of the amendment. Conceding the major proposition to be true, that Congress has a right to enact all necessary and proper laws for the obliteration and prevention of slavery with all its badges and incidents, is the minor proposition also true, that the denial to any person of admission to the accommodations and privileges of an inn, a public conveyance, or a theatre, does subject that person to any form of servitude, or tend to fasten upon him any badge of slavery? . . .

It may be that by the Black Code (as it was called), in the times when slavery prevailed, the proprietors of inns and public conveyances were forbidden to receive persons of the African race, because it might assist slaves to escape from the control of their masters. This was merely a means of preventing such escapes, and was no part of the servitude itself. A law of that kind could not have any such object now, however justly it might be deemed an invasion of the party's legal right as a citizen, and amenable to the prohibitions of the Fourteenth Amendment.

The long existence of African slavery in this country gave us very distinct notions of what it was, and what were its necessary incidents. Compulsory service of the slave for the benefit of the master, restraint of his movements except by the master's will, disability to hold property, to make contracts, to have a standing in court, to be a witness against a white person, and such like burdens and incapacities, were the inseparable incidents of the institution. Severer punishments for crimes were imposed on the slave than on free persons guilty of the same offences. Congress, as we have seen, by the Civil Rights Bill of 1866, passed in view of the Thirteenth Amendment, before the Fourteenth was adopted, undertook to wipe out these burdens and disabilities, the necessary incidents of slavery, constituting its substance and visible form; and to secure to all citizens of every race and color, and without regard to previous servitude, those fundamental rights which are the essence of civil freedom, namely, the same right to make and enforce contracts, to sue, be parties, give evidence, and to inherit, purchase, lease, sell and convey property, as is enjoyed by white citizens. Whether this legislation was fully authorized by the Thirteenth Amendment alone, without the support which it afterward received from the Fourteenth Amendment, after the adoption of which it was re-enacted with some additions, it is not necessary to inquire. It is referred to for the purpose of showing that at that time (in 1866) Congress did not assume, under the authority given by the Thirteenth Amendment, to adjust what may be called the social rights of men and races in the community; but only to declare and vindicate those fundamental rights which appertain to the essence of citizenship, and the enjoyment or deprivation of which constitutes the essential distinction between freedom and slavery.

We must not forget that the province and scope of the Thirteenth and Fourteenth amendments are different: the former simply abolished slavery; the latter prohibited the States from abridging the privileges or immunities of citizens of the United States; from depriving them of life, liberty, or property without due process of law, and from denying to any the equal protection of the laws. The amendments are different, and the powers of Congress under them are different. What Congress has power to do under one, it may not have power to do under the other. Under the Thirteenth Amendment, it has only to do with slavery and its incidents. Under the Fourteenth Amendment, it has power to counteract and render nugatory all State laws and proceedings which have the effect to abridge any of the privileges or immunities of citizens of the United States, or to deprive them of life, liberty or property without due process of law, or to deny to any of them the equal protection of the laws. Under the Thirteenth Amendment, the legislation, so far as necessary or proper to eradicate all forms and incidents of slavery and involuntary servitude, may be direct and primary, operating upon the acts of individuals, whether sanctioned by State legislation or not; under the Fourteenth, as we have already shown, it must necessarily be, and can only be, corrective in its character, addressed to counteract and afford relief against State regulations or proceedings.

The only question under the present head, therefore, is, whether the refusal to any persons of the accommodations of an inn, or a public conveyance, or a place of public amusement, by an individual, and without any sanction or support from any State law or regulation, does inflict upon such persons any manner of servitude, or form of slavery, as those terms are understood in this country? Many wrongs may be obnoxious to the prohibitions of the Fourteenth Amendment which are not, in any just sense, incidents or elements of slavery. Such, for example, would be the taking of private property without due process of law; or allowing persons who have committed certain crimes (horse stealing, for example) to be seized and hung by the posse comitatus without regular trial; or denying to any person, or class of persons, the right to pursue any peaceful avocations allowed to others. What is called class legislation would belong to this category, and would be obnoxious to the prohibitions of the Fourteenth Amendment, but would not necessarily be so to the Thirteenth, when not involving the idea of any subjection of one man to another. The Thirteenth Amendment has respect, not to distinctions of race, or class, or color, but to slavery. The Fourteenth Amendment extends its protection to races and classes, and prohibits any State legislation which has the effect of denying to any race or class, or to any individual, the equal protection of the laws.

Now, conceding, for the sake of the argument, that the admission to an inn, a public conveyance, or a place of public amusement, on equal terms with all other citizens, is the right of every man and all classes of men, is it any more than one of those rights which the states by the Fourteenth Amendment are forbidden to deny to any person? And is the Constitution violated until the denial of the right has some State sanction or authority? Can the act of a mere individual, the owner of the inn, the public conveyance or place of amusement, refusing the accommodation, be justly regarded as imposing any badge of slavery or servitude upon the applicant, or only as inflicting an ordinary civil injury, properly cognizable by the laws of the State, and presumably subject to redress by those laws until the contrary appears?

After giving to these questions all the consideration which their importance demands, we are forced to the conclusion that such an act of refusal has nothing to do with slavery or involuntary servitude, and that if it is violative of any right of the party, his redress is to be sought under the laws of the State; or if those laws are adverse to his rights and do not protect him, his remedy will be found in the corrective legislation which Congress has adopted, or may adopt, for counteracting the effect of State laws, or State action, prohibited by the Fourteenth Amendment. It would be running the slavery argument into the ground to make it apply to every act of discrimination which a person may see fit to make as to the guests he will entertain, or as to the people he will take into his coach or cab or car, or admit to his concert or theatre, or deal with in other matters of intercourse or business. Innkeepers and public carriers, by the laws of all the States, so far as we are aware, are bound, to the extent of their facilities, to furnish proper accommodation to all unobjectionable persons who in good faith apply for them. If the laws themselves make any unjust discrimination, amenable to the prohibitions of the Fourteenth Amendment, Congress has full power to afford a remedy under that amendment and in accordance with it.

When a man has emerged from slavery, and by the aid of beneficent legislation has shaken off the inseparable concomitants of that state, there must be some stage in the progress of his elevation when he takes the rank of a mere citizen, and ceases to be the special favorite of the laws, and when his rights as a citizen, or a man, are to be protected in the ordinary modes by which other men's rights are protected. There were thousands of free colored people in this country before the abolition of slavery, enjoying all the essential rights of life, liberty and property the same as white citizens; yet no one, at that time, thought that it was any invasion of his personal status as a freeman because he was not admitted to all the privileges enjoyed by white citizens, or because he was subjected to discriminations in the enjoyment of accommodations in inns, public conveyances and places of amusement. Mere discriminations on account of race or color were not regarded as badges of slavery. . . .

[T]he first and second sections of the act of Congress of March 1st, 1875, entitled "An Act to protect all citizens in their civil and legal rights," are unconstitutional and void. . . .

HARLAN, J., dissenting. . . .

I cannot resist the conclusion that the substance and spirit of the recent amendments of the Constitution have been sacrificed by a subtle and ingenious verbal criticism. . . .

The Thirteenth Amendment, it is conceded, did something more than to prohibit slavery as an *institution*, resting upon distinctions of race, and upheld by positive law. . . . Was it the purpose of the nation simply to destroy the institution, and then remit the race, theretofore held in bondage, to the several States for such protection, in their civil rights, necessarily growing out of freedom, as those States, in their discretion, might choose to provide? Were the States against whose protest the institution was destroyed, to be left free, so far as national interference was concerned, to make or allow discriminations against that race, as such, in the enjoyment of those fundamental rights which by universal concession, inhere in a state of freedom?

That there are burdens and disabilities which constitute badges of slavery and servitude, and that the power to enforce by appropriate legislation the Thirteenth Amendment may be exerted by legislation of a direct and primary character, for the eradication, not simply of the institution, but of its badges and incidents, are propositions which ought to be deemed indisputable. They lie at the foundation of the Civil Rights Act of 1866. . . .

Congress, by the act of 1866, passed in view of the Thirteenth Amendment, before the Fourteenth was adopted, undertook to remove certain burdens and disabilities, the necessary incidents of slavery, and to secure to all citizens of every race and color, and without regard to previous servitude, those fundamental rights which are the essence of civil freedom, namely, the same right to make and enforce contracts, to sue, be parties, give evidence, and to inherit, purchase, lease, sell, and convey property as is enjoyed by white citizens. . . .

I do not contend that the Thirteenth Amendment invests Congress with authority, by legislation, to define and regulate the entire body of the civil rights which citizens enjoy, or may enjoy, in the several States. But I hold that since slavery . . . was the moving or principal cause of the adoption of that amendment, and since that institution rested wholly upon the inferiority, as a race, of those held in bondage, their freedom necessarily involved immunity from, and protection against, all discrimination against them, because of their race, in respect of such civil rights as belong to freemen of other races. Congress, therefore, under its express power to enforce that amendment, by appropriate legislation, may enact laws to protect that people against the deprivation, *because of their race*, of any civil rights granted to other freemen in the same State; and such legislation may be of a direct and primary character, operating upon States, their officers and agents, and, also, upon, at least, such individuals and corporations as exercise public functions and wield power and authority under the State. . . .

It remains now to inquire what are the legal rights of colored persons in respect of the accommodations, privileges and facilities of public conveyances, inns and places of public amusement?

First, as to public conveyances on land and water. . . . In Olcott v. Supervisors, 16 Wall. 678, it was ruled that railroads are public highways, established by authority of the State for the public use; that they are none the less public highways, because controlled and owned by private corporations; that it is a part of the function of government to make and maintain highways for the convenience of the public; that no matter who is the agent, or what is the agency, the function performed is *that of the State;* that although the owners may be private companies, they may be compelled to permit the public to use these works in the manner in which they can be used; that, upon these grounds alone, have the courts sustained the investiture of railroad corporations with the State's right of eminent domain, or the right of municipal corporations, under legislative authority, to assess, levy and collect taxes to aid in the construction of railroads. . . .

Such being the relations these corporations hold to the public, it would seem that the right of a colored person to use an improved public highway, upon the terms accorded to freemen of other races, is as fundamental, in the state of freedom established in this country, as are any of the rights which my brethren concede to be so far fundamental as to be deemed the essence of civil freedom. "Personal liberty consists," says Blackstone, "in the power of locomotion, of changing situation, or removing one's person to whatever places one's own inclination may direct, without restraint, unless by due course of law." But of what value is this right of locomotion, if it may be clogged by such burdens as Congress intended by the act of 1875 to remove? They are burdens which lay at the very foundation of the institution of slavery as it once existed. . . .

Second, as to inns. The same general observations which have been made as to railroads are applicable to inns. . . . In Rex v. Ivens, 7 Carrington & Payne, 213, 32 E.C.L. 495, the court, speaking by Mr. Justice Coleridge, said:

> An indictment lies against an innkeeper who refuses to receive a guest, he having at the time room in his house; and either the price of the guest's entertainment being tendered to him, or such circumstances occurring as will dispense with that tender. This law is founded in good sense. The innkeeper is not to select his guests. He has no right to say to one, you shall come to my inn, and to another you shall not, as every one coming and conducting himself in a proper manner has a right to be received; and for this purpose innkeepers are a sort of public servants, they having in return a kind of privilege of entertaining travellers and supplying them with what they want.

 . . . [A] keeper of an inn is in the exercise of a quasi-public employment. The law gives him special privileges and he is charged with certain duties and responsibilities to the public. The public nature of his employment forbids him from discriminating against any person asking admission as a guest on account of the race or color of that person.

Third, as to places of public amusement. . . . [P]laces of public amusement, within the meaning of the act of 1875, are such as are established and maintained under direct license of the law. The authority to establish and maintain them comes from the public. The colored race is a part of that public. The local government granting the license represents them as well as all other races within its jurisdiction. A license from the public to establish a place of public amusement, imports, in law, equality of right, at such places, among all the members of that public. . . .

I am of the opinion that such discrimination practised by corporations and individuals in the exercise of their public or quasi-public functions is a badge of servitude the imposition of which Congress may prevent under its power, by appropriate legislation, to enforce the Thirteenth Amendment; and consequently, without reference to its enlarged power under the Fourteenth Amendment, the act of March 1, 1875, is not, in my judgment, repugnant to the Constitution.

It remains now to consider these cases with reference to the power Congress has possessed since the adoption of the Fourteenth Amendment. Much that has been said as to the power of Congress under the Thirteenth Amendment is applicable to this branch of the discussion, and will not be repeated. . . .

The assumption that this amendment consists wholly of prohibitions upon State laws and State proceedings in hostility to its provisions, is unauthorized by its language. The first clause of the first section — "All persons born or naturalized in the United States, and subject to the jurisdiction thereof, are citizens of the United States, and of the State wherein they reside" — is of a distinctly affirmative character. . . .

The citizenship thus acquired, by [the colored] race, in virtue of an affirmative grant from the nation, may be protected, not alone by the judicial branch of the government, but by congressional legislation of a primary direct character; this, because the power of Congress is not restricted to the enforcement of prohibitions upon State laws or State action. It is, in terms distinct and positive, to enforce "the *provisions* of *this article*" of amendment; not simply those of a prohibitive character, but the provisions — *all* of the provisions — affirmative and prohibitive, of the amendment. . . .

It is, therefore, an essential inquiry what, if any, right, privilege or immunity was given, by the nation, to colored persons when they were made citizens of the State in which they reside. . . . That they became entitled, upon the adoption of the Fourteenth Amendment, "to all privileges and immunities of citizens in the several States," within the meaning of section 2 of article 4 of the Constitution, no one, I suppose, will for a moment question. What are the privileges and immunities to which, by that clause of the Constitution, they became entitled? To this it may be answered, generally, upon the authority of the adjudged cases, that they are those which are fundamental in citizenship in a free republican government, such as are "common to the citizens in the latter States under their constitutions and laws by virtue of their being citizens." . . .

But what was secured to colored citizens of the United States — as between them and their respective States — by the national grant to them of State citizenship? With what rights, privileges, or immunities did this grant invest them? There is one, if there be no other — exemption from race discrimination in respect of any civil right belonging to citizens of the white race in the same State. That, surely, is their constitutional privilege when within the jurisdiction of other States. And such must be their constitutional right, in their own State, unless the recent amendments be splendid baubles, thrown out to delude those who deserved fair and generous treatment at the hands of the nation. Citizenship in this country necessarily imports at least equality of civil rights among citizens of every race in the same State. . . . If the grant to colored citizens of the United States of citizenship in their respective States, imports exemption from race discrimination, in their States, in respect of such civil rights as belong to citizenship, then, to hold that the amendment remits that right to the States for their protection, primarily, and stays the hands of the nation, until it is assailed by State laws or State proceedings, is to adjudge that the amendment, so far from enlarging the powers of Congress — as we have heretofore said it did — not only curtails them, but reverses the policy which the general government has pursued from its very organization. . . .

But if it were conceded that the power of Congress could not be brought into activity until the rights specified in the act of 1875 had been abridged or denied by some State law or State action, I maintain that . . . [t]here has been adverse State Action within the Fourteenth Amendment. . . .

In every material sense applicable to the practical enforcement of the Fourteenth Amendment, railroad corporations, keepers of inns, and managers of places of public amusement are agents or instrumentalities of the State, because they are charged with duties to the public, and are amenable, in respect of their duties and functions, to governmental regulation. It seems to me that . . . a denial, by these instrumentalities of the State, to the citizen, because of his race, of that equality of civil rights secured to him by law, is a denial by the State, within the meaning of the Fourteenth Amendment. If it be not, then that race is left, in respect of the civil rights in question, practically at the mercy of corporations and individuals wielding power under the States. . . .

Discussion

1. The Civil Rights Cases established three distinct propositions:

a. The Thirteenth Amendment, though it addresses private persons as well as governments, does not prohibit, or empower Congress to prohibit, most racially discriminatory practices other than involuntary servitude (which it prohibits regardless of race). This holding was substantially undercut by Jones v. Alfred H. Mayer Co., 392 U.S. 409 (1968), Chapter 5, infra.

b. The Fourteenth Amendment does not empower Congress to forbid discrimination by private persons. This holding was partly questioned by a majority of the justices participating in United States v. Guest, 383 U.S. 745 (1966), where six members of the Court took the view that private conspiracies to violate civil rights were within Congress's §5 powers. Whatever precedental value *Guest* had on this question before, it is was undermined by *United States v. Morrison*, 529 U.S. 598 (2000), discussed in Chapter 5. Nevertheless, *Guest* still appears to be good authority for the proposition that Congress may regulate private parties who conspire or "connive" with state officials to abridge constitutional rights. See 383 U.S. at 756-757. And presumably Congress may still reach private conspiracies to interfere with the right to travel, which the Constitution protects from public as well as private interference. Id. at 760. See also Bray v. Alexandria Women's Health Clinic, 506 U.S. 263, 278 (1993).

c. A fortiori from b, the Fourteenth Amendment does not of its own force prevent private discrimination, as distinguished from discrimination imposed or supported by the state. This remains the articulated doctrine today: The Fourteenth Amendment reaches "only such action as may fairly be said to be that of the States." Yet Shelley v. Kraemer, 334 U.S. 1 (1948), the very case in which that statement was made, is generally thought to undermine the "state action" doctrine significantly because the "state action" involved simply the judicial enforcement of a private contract mandating that the property in question not be sold to non-whites. The notion of what is "fairly" attributable to the states has expanded to an extent not readily inferred from this formulation; indeed, Professor Charles Black in 1966 described the "state action doctrine" as a "conceptual disaster area." For a summary of the current doctrine in the context of the Welfare State, see pp. 1664-1667.

Consider, nevertheless, whether courts might take a narrower view of state action for purposes of judicial enforcement of §1 that might be different than what Congress might appropriately consider state action for purposes of exercising its powers under §5. We discuss some of the various theories of Congress's §5 powers in Chapter 5.

2. *Harris and the Ku Klux Klan Act.* The Court also gave a narrow construction to Congressional power under the Reconstruction Amendments in United States v. Harris, 106 U.S. 629 (1883). *Harris* involved prosecutions of a lynch mob in Tennessee under the Ku Klux Klan Act, which formed §2 of the Civil Rights Act of 1871. As its name implies, the Ku Klux Klan Act was designed to combat the Klan and other mobs that attempted to frighten or harass blacks and keep them from exercising or enjoying equal civil rights. It created criminal and civil liability "where two or more persons conspire or go in disguise on a highway or on the premises of another for the purpose of depriving any person or class of persons of the equal protection of the laws or of equal privileges and immunities under the laws." In *Harris,* the Court overturned criminal convictions against members of the lynching party on the ground that Congress had no power to reach private conspiracies under §5 of the Fourteenth Amendment.

Harris only struck down the criminal provisions of the Klan Act. The provisions creating a civil cause of action for private conspiracies — now codified as 42 U.S.C. 1985(3) — were identical in all other respects. They were upheld by the Court in Griffin v. Breckenridge, 403 U.S. 88, 104-105 (1971). Justice Stewart's opinion distinguished *Harris* by arguing that Congress's authority for the Ku Klux Klan Act stemmed from its powers under §2 of the Thirteenth Amendment.

In Ex parte Yarbrough, 110 U.S. 651 (1884), the Supreme Court upheld Congress's right to reach purely private conspiracies to interfere with the right to vote in federal elections. Justice Miller distinguished *Harris* and other cases construing Congress's §5 powers: "It is quite a different matter when Congress undertakes to protect the citizen in the exercise of rights conferred by the Constitution of the United States essential to the healthy organization of the government itself." Miller's argument was structural: if Congress could not protect citizens from private violence and corruption in exercising their right to vote, the integrity of the government would be threatened. Justice Miller did not identify the specific source of Congressional power: He argued that it "is a waste of time to seek for specific sources of the power to pass these laws." Id. at 665-666.

3. Focusing on the Thirteenth Amendment as a possible source of congressional power forces us to confront what precisely constitute the evils of chattel slavery. Does slavery consist in only one human being formally possessing the legal right to own another? Or does it apply more broadly to (a) the system of racial oppression — consider the example of the Black Codes; (b) systematic oppression of other groups like Latinos, Asian-Americans, religious minorities, and women, who were never subjected to "officially recognized" forms of chattel slavery; (c) extremely coercive and unfair labor conditions like those experienced in sweatshops or by oppressed agricultural workers; or (d) severe abuses of power or position by private parties, such as child abuse or domestic violence? Can one make a distinction between the forms of slavery that courts may directly hold illegal under the Thirteenth Amendment and the forms of slavery, or the "badges or incidents of slavery" that Congress may define and reach under its powers under §2 of the Thirteenth Amendment? What reasons might there be for giving Congress wider latitude to define and punish slavery (or the badges and incidents of slavery) than the courts?

4. Recall Justice Bradley's sweeping description of an empowered national government in his concurrence in the second of The Legal Tender Cases, Knox v. Lee, supra, p. 296. Is his opinion in the Civil Rights Cases consistent with the earlier opinion?

5. As part of his attack on the majority's limited reading of Congress's power to implement the Thirteenth and Fourteenth Amendments, Justice Harlan notes the

quite different approach to analyzing congressional power in Prigg v. Pennsylvania, Chapter 3, supra, which upheld the Fugitive Slave Law of 1793. Justice Harlan described *Prigg* as resting on the propositions

> That a clause of the Constitution conferring a right [in that instance the Fugitive Slave Clause of Article IV] should not be so construed as to make it shadowy, or unsubstantial, or leave the citizen without a remedial power adequate for its protection, when another construction equally accordant with the words and the sense in which they were used, would enforce and protect the right granted;
>
> That Congress is not restricted to legislation for the execution of its expressly granted powers; but, for the protection of rights guaranteed by the Constitution, may employ such means, not prohibited, as are necessary and proper; or such as are appropriate, to attain the ends proposed;
>
> That the Constitution recognized the master's right of property in his fugitive slave, and, as incidental thereto, the right of seizing and recovering him, regardless of any State law, or regulation, or local custom whatsoever; and
>
> That the right of the master to have his slave, thus escaping, delivered up on claim, being guaranteed by the Constitution, the fair implication was that the national government was clothed with appropriate authority and functions to enforce it.

Harlan appears to be arguing that, whereas the pre-War Constitution protected the rights of the slaveowner (and thus implicitly authorized Congress to pass legislation assuring the practical enforcement of his rights), the newly amended post-War Constitution, through the Thirteenth and Fourteenth Amendments, now protects the rights of Americans to be free from racial discrimination (and thus should be interpreted as authorizing Congress to pass whatever legislation it deems necessary to assure the practical enforcement of *those* rights). The majority does not suggest that the hotel owners and other purveyors of public accommodations have a right to engage in the discriminatory conduct; it appears to assume that such conduct is barred by the common law and that states will indeed enforce the right of nondiscriminatory access to public accommodations. It holds only that Congress is without the power to offer federal protection to the victims of such discrimination, thus leaving them to whatever procedures the states wish to adopt.

Pennsylvania had not formally resisted its obligations to return fugitive slaves; it merely insisted that slaveowners submit themselves to Pennsylvania procedures designed to assure that those asserted to be fugitive slaves were actually so. Yet those laws were struck down, and Congress was deemed to have power to supplant them by passing national legislation. Is it fair to describe the Court as more imaginative, in regard to its interpretation of federal power, regarding the rights of slaveowners than those of the new African-American citizens of the United States?

II.   *Creating an "American" Nation*

A.   American Expansionism, Race, Ethnicity, and the Constitution

One should not forget that the United States, which began as a country of 13 states — actually, only 11 had ratified the Constitution at the time of Washington's inauguration on April 30, 1789 — expanded westward to reach, eventually, Hawaii. This expansion was scarcely without constitutional import. The following case, Downes v. Bidwell, is one of the "Insular Cases" litigated following the conquest of Puerto Rico and the Philippines in the Spanish-American War of 1898. Prior expansion had been into territories that, upon settlement, were presumed to be eligible for admission as a state to the United States. There was also the peculiar situation of Texas, which was never a "territory" but was an independent country prior to its admission to the Union by a majority of each House of Congress in 1844. Recall that it had initially been thought that such annexation required a treaty between the United States and Texas, which in turn would have required an (unattainable) support by two-thirds of the senators. Still, both Presidents Tyler and Polk, plus a majority of Congress, badly wanted Texas in the Union, which was achieved, however irregularly. Such a welcoming attitude was most definitely not present with regard to Puerto Rico and the Philippines. *Downes* addresses not only what was at issue in regard to these new territories, but also some aspects of our past history that have been treated earlier in somewhat different contexts.

DOWNES v. BIDWELL, 182 U.S. 244 (1901): [Downes sued the collector of the port of New York to recover duties he had paid under protest for oranges that had been delivered to New York from San Juan in November 1900. The duties were collected under the authority of the Foraker Act of April 12, 1900, which temporarily provided a civil government and sources of revenue for administration of the island of Puerto Rico. Downes argued that because Puerto Rico became part of the United States after the ratification of the treaty with Spain that ended the Spanish-American War, the duty violated Article 1, §8, clause 1, of the Constitution, which provides that "the Congress shall have power to lay and collect taxes, duties, imposts, and excises, to pay the debts and provide for the common defense and general welfare of the United States; but all duties, imposts, and excises shall be uniform throughout the United States."]

Mr. Justice BROWN announced the conclusion and judgment of the Court:
 . . . In the case of De Lima v. Bidwell just decided, we held that, upon the ratification of the treaty of peace with Spain, Porto Rico ceased to be a foreign country, and became a territory of the United States. . . . We are now asked to hold that it became a part of the United States within that provision of the Constitution which declares that "all duties, imposts, and excises shall be uniform throughout the United States." Art. 1, §8. . . .
 . . . [I]t can nowhere be inferred that the territories were considered a part of the United States. The Constitution was created by the people of the United States, as a union of states, to be governed solely by representatives of the states; and even the provision relied upon here, that all duties, imposts, and excises shall be uniform "throughout the United States," is explained by subsequent provisions of the Constitution, that "no tax or duty shall be laid on articles exported from any state," and "no preference shall be given by any regulation of commerce or revenue to the ports of one state over those of another; nor shall vessels bound to or from one state be obliged to enter, clear, or pay duties in another." In short, the Constitution deals with states, their people, and their representatives.
 The 13th Amendment to the Constitution, prohibiting slavery and involuntary servitude "within the United States, or in any place subject to their jurisdiction," is

also significant as showing that there may be places within the jurisdiction of the United States that are no part of the Union. . . .

Upon the other hand, the 14th Amendment, upon the subject of citizenship, declares only that "all persons born or naturalized in the United States, and subject to the jurisdiction thereof, are citizens of the United States, and of the state wherein they reside." Here there is a limitation to persons born or naturalized in the United States, which is not extended to persons born in any place "subject to their jurisdiction."

[Justice Brown discusses the terms of the Louisiana Purchase of 1803, which provided that white citizens of the Territory would become citizens of the United States. The treaty also provided that for twelve years French and Spanish ships would be admitted into the port of New Orleans and other ports within the Louisiana territory on the same terms and paying the same duties as American ships bringing goods from French and Spanish territories. He notes that this was challenged as "an unlawful discrimination in favor of those ports and an infringement upon art. 1, §9, of the Constitution, that no preference shall be given by any regulation of commerce or revenue to the ports of one state over those of another."]

[Congress's treatment of the Louisiana Territory presumed] that a discrimination in favor of certain foreign vessels trading with the ports of a newly acquired territory is no violation of art. 1, §9. It is evident that the constitutionality of this discrimination can only be supported upon the theory that ports of territories are not ports of state within the meaning of the Constitution.

The same construction was adhered to in the treaty with Spain for the purchase of Florida. . . . .

So, too, in the act annexing the Republic of Hawaii, there was a provision continuing in effect the customs relations of the Hawaiian islands with the United States and other countries, the effect of which was to compel the collection in those islands of a duty upon certain articles, whether coming from the United States or other countries, much greater than the duty provided by the general tariff law then in force. This was a discrimination against the Hawaiian ports wholly inconsistent with the revenue clauses of the Constitution, if such clauses were there operative.

The very treaty with Spain under discussion in this case contains similar discriminative provisions. . . . By article 4 the United States agree, for the term of ten years from the date of the exchange of the ratifications of the present treaty, to admit Spanish ships and merchandise to the ports of the Philippine islands on the same terms as ships and merchandise of the United States, — a privilege not extending to any other ports. It was a clear breach of the uniformity clause in question, and a manifest excess of authority on the part of the commissioners, if ports of the Philippine islands be ports of the United States.

[I]n organizing the territory of Louisiana by act of March 26, 1804, [and] all other territories carved out of this vast inheritance, [Congress] has assumed that the Constitution did not extend to them of its own force, and has in each case made special provision, either that their legislatures shall pass no law inconsistent with the Constitution of the United States, or that the Constitution or laws of the United States shall be the supreme law of such territories. Finally, in Rev. Stat. §1891, a general provision was enacted that "the Constitution and all laws of the United States which are not locally inapplicable shall have the same force and effect within all the organized territories, and in every territory hereafter organized, as elsewhere within the United States." So, too, on March 6, 1820, in an act authorizing the people of Missouri to form a state government, after a heated debate, Congress declared that in the territory of Louisiana north of 36°30′ slavery should be forever prohibited. It is true that, for reasons which have become historical, this act was declared to be unconstitutional in Scott v. Sandford, but it is none the less a distinct annunciation by Congress of power over property in the territories, which it obviously did not possess in the several states.

. . . The decisions of this court upon this subject have not been altogether harmonious. Some of them are based upon the theory that the Constitution does not apply to the territories without legislation. Other cases, arising from territories where such legislation has been had, contain language which would justify the inference that such legislation was unnecessary, and that the Constitution took effect immediately upon the cession of the territory to the United States. . . . It may be added in this connection, that to put at rest all doubts regarding the applicability of the Constitution to the District of Columbia, Congress by the act of February 21, specifically extended the Constitution and laws of the United States to this District. . . .

[Justice Brown then distinguishes *Dred Scott*, which seemed to reject the power of the United States to establish colonies in which the Constitution did not apply.] Chief Justice [Taney] had already disposed of the case adversely to the plaintiff upon the question of [Dred Scott's right to sue under diversity] jurisdiction. [I]n view of the excited political condition of the country at the time, it is unfortunate that he felt compelled to discuss the question upon the merits, particularly so in view of the fact that it involved a ruling that an act of Congress which had been acquiesced in for thirty years was declared unconstitutional. . . . If the assumption be true that slaves are indistinguishable from other property, the inference from the Dred Scott Case is irresistible that Congress had no power to prohibit their introduction into a territory. . . . The difficulty with the Dred Scott Case was that the court refused to make a distinction between property in general and a wholly exceptional class of property. . . .

. . . The doctrine that the Constitution extended to territories as well as to states first made its appearance in the Senate in the session of 1848-1849, by an attempt to amend a bill giving territorial government to California, New Mexico, and Utah (itself "hitched on" to a general appropriation bill), by adding the words "that the Constitution of the United States and all and singular the several acts of Congress (describing them) be and the same hereby are extended and given full force and efficacy in said territories." [Justice Brown notes that Senators Daniel Webster and Henry Clay opposed the measure as absurd and unprecedented, while Senator John C. Calhoun, who "boldly avowed his intent to carry slavery into [the territories] under the wing of the Constitution," supported the measure "and denounced as enemies of the south all who opposed it." The amendment to the bill ultimately failed.]

To sustain the judgment in the case under consideration, it by no means becomes necessary to show that none of the articles of the Constitution apply to the island of Porto Rico. There is a clear distinction between such prohibitions as go to the very root of the power of Congress to act at all, irrespective of time of place, and such as are operative only "throughout the United States" or among the several states.

Thus, when the Constitution declares that "no bill of attainder or ex post facto law shall be passed," and that "no title of nobility shall be granted by the United States," it goes to the competency of Congress to pass a bill of that description.

Perhaps the same remark may apply to the 1st Amendment, that "Congress shall make no law respecting an establishment of religion, or prohibiting the free exercise thereof; or abridging the freedom of speech, or of the press; or the right of the people to peacefully assemble and to petition the government for a redress of grievances." We do not wish, however, to be understood as expressing an opinion how far the bill of rights contained in the first eight amendments is of general and how far of local application.

Upon the other hand, when the Constitution declares that all duties shall be uniform "throughout the United States," it becomes necessary to inquire whether there be any territory over which Congress has jurisdiction which is not a part of the "United States," by which term we understand the states whose people united to form the Constitution, and such as have since been admitted to the Union upon an equality with them. [Congress has recognized in the 13th amendment and in other legislation that] there may be territories subject to the jurisdiction of the United States, which are not of the United States.

In determining the meaning of the words of article 1, section 8, "uniform throughout the United States," we are bound to consider, not only the provisions forbidding preference being given to the ports of one state over those of another (to which attention has already been called), but the other clauses declaring that no tax or duty shall be laid on articles exported from any state, and that no state shall, without the consent of Congress, lay any imposts or duties upon imports or exports, nor any duty on tonnage. The object of all of these was to protect the states which united in forming the Constitution from discriminations by Congress, which would operate unfairly or injuriously upon some states and not equally upon others. . . . Indeed, the practical interpretation put by Congress upon the Constitution has been long continued and uniform to the effect that the Constitution is applicable to territories acquired by purchase or conquest, only when and so far as Congress shall so direct. Notwithstanding its duty to "guarantee to every state in this Union a republican form of government" (art. 4, §4), by which we understand, according to the definition of Webster, "a government in which the supreme power resides in the whole body of the people, and is exercised by representatives elected by them," Congress did not hesitate, in the original organization of the territories of Louisiana, Florida, the Northwest Territory, and its subdivisions of Ohio, Indiana, Michigan, Illinois, and Wisconsin and still more recently in the case of Alaska, to establish a form of government bearing a much greater analogy to a British Crown colony than a republican state of America, and to vest the legislative power either in a governor and council, or a governor and judges, to be appointed by the President. It was not until they had attained a certain population that power was given them to organize a legislature by vote of the people. In all these cases, as well as in territories subsequently organized west of the Mississippi, Congress thought it necessary either to extend to Constitution and laws of the United States over them, or to declare that the inhabitants should be entitled to enjoy the right of trial by jury, of bail, and of the privilege of the writ of habeas corpus, as well as other privileges of the bill of rights.

We are also of opinion that the power to acquire territory by treaty implies, not only the power to govern such territory, but to prescribe upon what terms the United States will receive its inhabitants, and what their status shall be in what Chief Justice Marshall termed the "American empire." There seems to be no middle ground between this position and the doctrine that if their inhabitants do not become, immediately upon annexation, citizens of the United States, their children thereafter born, whether savages or civilized, are such, and entitled to all the rights, privileges and immunities of citizens. If such be their status, the consequences will be extremely serious. Indeed, it is doubtful if Congress would ever assent to the annexation of territory upon the condition that its inhabitants, however foreign they may be to our habits, traditions, and modes of life, shall become at once citizens of the United States. In all its treaties hitherto the treaty-making power has made special provision for this subject; in the cases of Louisiana and Florida, by stipulating that "the inhabitants shall be incorporated into the Union of the United States and admitted as soon as possible . . . to the enjoyment of all the rights, advantages, and immunities of citizens of the United States;" in the case of Mexico, that they should "be incorporated into the Union, and be admitted at the proper time (to be judged of by the Congress of the United States) to the enjoyment of all the rights of citizens of the United States;" in the case of Alaska, that the inhabitants who remained three years, "with the exception of uncivilized native tribes, shall be admitted to the enjoyment of all the rights," etc; and in the case of Porto Rico and the Philippines, "that the civil rights and political status of the native inhabitants . . . shall be determined by Congress." In all these cases there is an implied denial of the right of the inhabitants to American citizenship until Congress by further action shall signify its assent thereto.

Grave apprehensions of danger are felt by many eminent men — a fear lest an unrestrained possession of power on the part of Congress may lead to unjust and oppressive legislation in which the natural rights of territories, or their inhabitants, may be engulfed in a centralized despotism. These fears, however, find no justification in the action of Congress in the past century, nor in the conduct of the British Parliament towards its outlying possessions since the American Revolution. . . .

It is obvious that in the annexation of outlying and distant possessions grave questions will arise from differences of race, habits, laws, and customs of the people, and from differences of soil, climate, and production, which may require action on the part of Congress that would be quite unnecessary in the annexation of contiguous territory inhabited only by people of the same race, or by scattered bodies of native Indians.

We suggest, without intending to decide, that there may be a distinction between certain natural rights enforced in the Constitution by prohibitions against interference with them, and what may be termed artificial or remedial rights which are peculiar to our own system of jurisprudence. Of the former class are the rights to one's own religious opinions and to a public expression of them, or, as sometimes said, to worship God according to the dictates of one's own conscience; the right to personal liberty and individual property; to freedom of speech and of the press; to free access to courts of justice, to due process of law, and to an equal protection of the laws; to immunities from unreasonable searches and seizures, as well as cruel and unusual punishments; and to such other immunities as are indispensable to a free government. Of the latter class are the rights to citizenship, to suffrage, and to the particular methods of procedure pointed out in the Constitution, which are peculiar to Anglo-Saxon jurisprudence, and some of which have already been held by the states to be unnecessary to the proper protection of individuals.

Whatever may be finally decided by the American people as to the status of these islands and their inhabitants — whether they shall be introduced into the sisterhood of states or be permitted to form independent governments — it does not follow that in the meantime, awaiting that decision, the people are in the matter of personal rights unprotected by the provisions of our Constitution and subject to the merely arbitrary control of Congress. Even if regarded as aliens, they are entitled under the principles of the Constitution to be protected in life, liberty, and property. This has been frequently held by this court in respect to the Chinese, even when aliens, not possessed of the political rights of citizens of the United States. Yick Wo v. Hopkins, 118 U.S. 356. We do not desire, however, to anticipate the difficulties which would naturally arise in this connection, but merely to disclaim any intention to hold that the inhabitants of these territories are subject to an unrestrained power on the part of Congress to deal with them upon the theory that they have no rights which it is bound to respect.

Large powers must necessarily be intrusted to Congress in dealing with these problems, and we are bound to assume that they will be judiciously exercised. That these powers may be abused is possible. But the same may be said of its powers under the Constitution as well as outside of it. Human wisdom has never devised a form of government so perfect that it may not be perverted to bad purposes. It is never conclusive to argue against the possession of certain powers from possible abuses of them. It is safe to say that if Congress should venture upon legislation manifestly dictated by selfish interests, it would receive quick rebuke at the hands of the people. . . .

[T]he Senate committee in charge of the Foraker bill . . . found, after an examination of the facts, that . . . our internal revenue laws, if applied in that island, would prove oppressive and ruinous to many people and interests; that to undertake to collect our heavy internal revenue tax, far heavier than Spain ever imposed upon their products and vocations, would be to invite violations of the law so innumerable as to make prosecutions impossible, and to almost certainly alienate and destroy the friendship and good will of that people for the United States.

[W]e ought not to overlook the fact that, while the Constitution was intended to establish a permanent form of government for the states which should elect to take advantage of its conditions, and continue for an indefinite future, the vast possibilities of that future could never have entered the minds of its framers. . . . Had the acquisition of other territories been contemplated as a possibility, could it have been foreseen that, within little more than one hundred years, we were destined to acquire, not only the whole vast region between the Atlantic and Pacific Oceans, but the Russian possessions in America and distant islands in the Pacific, it is incredible that no provision should have been made for them, and the question whether the Constitution should or should not extend to them have been definitely settled. If it be once conceded that we are at liberty to acquire foreign territory, a presumption arises that our power with respect to such territories is the same power which other nations have been accustomed to exercise with respect to territories acquired by them. If, in limiting the power which Congress was to exercise within the United States, it was also intended to limit it with regard to such territories as the people of the United States should thereafter acquire, such limitations should have been expressed. Instead of that, we find the Constitution speaking only to states, except in the territorial clause, which is absolute in its terms, and suggestive of no limitations upon the power of Congress in dealing with them. The states could only delegate to Congress such powers as they themselves possessed, and as they had no power to acquire new territory they had none to delegate in that connection. The logical inference from this is that if Congress had power to acquire new territory, which is conceded, that power was not hampered by the constitutional provisions. If, upon the other hand, we assume that the territorial clause of the Constitution was not intended to be restricted to such territory as the United States then possessed, there is nothing in the Constitution to indicate that the power of Congress in dealing with them was intended to be restricted by any of the other provisions. . . .

Patriotic and intelligent men may differ widely as to the desireableness of this or that acquisition, but this is solely a political question. [N]o construction of the Constitution should be adopted which would prevent Congress from considering each case upon its merits, unless the language of the instrument imperatively demand it. A false step at this time might be fatal to the development of what Chief Justice Marshall called the American empire. Choice in some cases, the natural gravitation of small bodies towards large ones in others, the result of a successful war in still others, may bring about conditions which would render the annexation of distant possessions desirable. If those possessions are inhabited by alien races, differing from us in religion, customs, laws, methods of taxation, and modes of thought, the administration of government and justice, according to Anglo-Saxon principles, may for a time be impossible; and the question at once arises whether large concessions ought not to be made for a time, that ultimately our own theories may be carried out, and the blessings of a free government under the Constitution extended to them. We decline to hold that there is anything in the Constitution to forbid such action.

We are therefore of opinion that the island of Porto Rico is a territory appurtenant and belonging to the United States, but not a part of the United States within the revenue clauses of the Constitution.

Mr. Justice WHITE, with whom concurred Mr. Justice Shiras and Mr. Justice McKenna, uniting in the judgment of affirmance: . . .

[White agrees that the United States "was endowed with those general powers to acquire territory which all independent governments in virtue of their sovereignty enjoyed."] Undoubtedly there are general prohibitions in the Constitution in favor of the liberty and property of the citizen, which are not mere regulations as to the form and manner in which a conceded power may be exercised, but which are an absolute denial of all authority under any circumstances or conditions to do particular acts. In the nature of things, limitations of this character cannot be under any circumstances transcended, because of the complete absence of power.

. . . There is in reason, then, no room in this case to contend that Congress can destroy the liberties of the people of Porto Rico by exercising in their regard powers against freedom and justice which the Constitution has absolutely denied. There can also be no controversy as to the right of Congress to locally govern the island of Porto Rico as its wisdom may decide, and in so doing to accord only such degree of representative government as may be determined on by that body. . . .

The sole and only issue, then, is not whether Congress has taxed Porto Rico without representation, — for, whether the tax was local or national, it could have been imposed although Porto Rico had no representative local government and was not represented in Congress, — but is whether the particular tax in question was levied in such form as to cause it to be repugnant to the Constitution. This is to be resolved by answering the inquiry, Had Porto Rico, at the time of the passage of the act in question, been incorporated into and become an integral part of the United States? [White argues that Puerto Rico was not incorporated, and offers a distinction between "incorporated" and "unincorporated" territory that became dispositive in later cases. White argues that the distinction must exist because of the nature and effect of the treaty power:]

. . . [I]t seems to me impossible to conceive that the treaty-making power by a mere cession can incorporate an alien people into the United States without the express or implied approval of Congress. . . . If the treaty-making power can absolutely, without the consent of Congress, incorporate territory, and if that power may not insert conditions against incorporation, it must follow that the treaty-making power is endowed by the Constitution with the most unlimited right, susceptible of destroying every other provision of the Constitution; that is, it may wreck our institutions. If the proposition be true, then millions of inhabitants of alien territory, if acquired by treaty, can, without the desire or consent of the people of the United States speaking through Congress, be immediately and irrevocably incorporated into the United States, and the whole structure of the government be overthrown. . . .

[Turning to a discussion of the specific terms of the Treaty between Spain and the United States relating to Puerto Rico, Justice White concludes that its relevant provisions] do not stipulate for incorporation, but, on the contrary, expressly provide that the "civil rights and political status of the native inhabitants of the territories hereby ceded" shall be determined by Congress. . . . I cannot doubt that the express purpose of the treaty was not only to leave the status of the territory to be determined by Congress, but to prevent the treaty from operating to the contrary. . . . [T]he provisions of the [Foraker Act] by which the duty here in question was imposed, taken as a whole, seem to me plainly to manifest the intention of Congress that, for the present at least, Porto Rico is not to be incorporated into the United States. . . .

The result of what has been said is that while in an international sense Porto Rico was not a foreign country, since it was subject to the sovereignty of and was owned by the United States, it was foreign to the United States in a domestic sense, because the island had not been incorporated into the United States, but was merely appurtenant thereto as a possession. As a necessary consequence, the impost in question assessed on coming from Porto Rico into the United States after the cession was within the power of Congress, and that body was not, moreover, as to such impost, controlled by the clause requiring that imposts should be uniform throughout the United States; in other words, the provision of the Constitution just referred to was not applicable to Congress in legislating for Porto Rico.

[A concurring opinion by Justice Gray is omitted.]

Mr. Chief Justice FULLER, with whom concurred Mr. Justice Harlan, Mr. Justice Brewer, and Mr. Justice Peckham, dissenting:

The 14th Amendment provides that "all persons born or naturalized in the United States, and subject to the jurisdiction thereof, are citizens of the United States and of the state wherein they reside"; and this court naturally held, in the Slaughter-House Cases, that the United States included the District and the territories. . . .

No person is eligible to the office of President unless he has "attained the age of thirty-five years, and been fourteen years a resident within the United States." Clause 5, §1, art. 2.

Would a native-born citizen of Massachusetts be ineligible if he had taken up his residence and resided in one of the territories for so many years that he had not resided altogether fourteen years in the states? When voted for he must be a citizen of one of the states (clause 3, §1, art. 2; art. 12), but as to length of time must residence in the territories be counted against him?

The 15th Amendment declares that "the right of citizens of the United States to vote shall not be denied or abridged by the United States or by any state on account of race, color, or previous condition of servitude." Where does that prohibition on the United States especially apply if not in the territories?

The 13th Amendment says that neither slavery nor involuntary servitude "shall exist within the United States or any place subject to their jurisdiction." Clearly this prohibition would have operated in the territories if the concluding words had not been added. The history of the times shows that the addition was made in view of the then condition of the country — the amendment passed the house January 31, 1865 — and it is, moreover, otherwise applicable than to the territories. Besides, generally speaking, when words are used simply out of abundant caution, the fact carries little weight.

[N]o satisfactory ground has been suggested for restricting the words "throughout the United States," as qualifying the power to impose duties, to the states, and that conclusion is the more to be avoided when we reflect that it rests, in the last analysis, on the assertion of the possession by Congress of unlimited power over the territories.

. . . [N]o utterance of this court has [ever] intimated a doubt that in its operation on the people, by whom and for whom it was established, the national government is a government of enumerated powers, the exercise of which is restricted to the use of means appropriate and plainly adapted to constitutional ends, and which are "not prohibited, but consist with the letter and spirit of the Constitution." The powers delegated by the people to their agents are not enlarged by the expansion of the domain within which they are exercised. When the restriction on the exercise of a particular power by a particular agent is ascertained, that is an end of the question.

To hold otherwise is to overthrow the basis of our constitutional law, and moreover, in effect, to reassert the proposition that the states, and not the people, created the government. . . .

. . . Much discussion was had at the bar in respect of the citizenship of the inhabitants of Porto Rico, but we are not required to consider that subject at large in these cases. It will be time enough to seek a ford when, if ever, we are brought to the stream. . . .

. . . [T]he contention seems to be that, if an organized and settled province of another sovereignty is acquired by the United States, Congress has the power to keep it, like a disembodied shade, in an intermediate state of ambiguous existence for an indefinite period; and, more than that, that after it has been called from that limbo, commerce with it is absolutely subject to the will of Congress, irrespective of constitutional provisions.

. . . Great stress is thrown upon the word "incorporation," as if possessed of some occult meaning, but I take it that the act under consideration made Porto Rico, whatever its situation before, an organized territory of the United States. Being such, and the act undertaking to impose duties by virtue of clause 1 of §8, how is it that the rule which qualifies the power does not apply to its exercise in respect of commerce with that territory? . . .

The concurring opinion recognizes the fact that Congress, in dealing with the people of new territories or possessions, is bound to respect the fundamental guaranties of life, liberty, and property, but assumes that Congress is not bound, in those territories or possessions, to follow the rules of taxation prescribed by the Constitution. And yet the power to tax involves the power to destroy, and the levy of duties touches all our people in all places under the jurisdiction of the government.

The logical result is that Congress may prohibit commerce altogether between the states and territories, and may prescribe one rule of taxation in one territory, and a different rule in another.

That theory assumes that the Constitution created a government empowered to acquire countries throughout the world, to be governed by different rules than those obtaining in the original states and territories, and substitutes for the present system of republican government a system of domination over distant provinces in the exercise of unrestricted power. . . .

[I]t is objected on behalf of the government that the possession of absolute power is essential to the acquisition of vast and distant territories, and that we should regard the situation as it is today, rather than as it was a century ago. "We must look at the situation as comprehending a possibility — I do not say a probability, but a possibility — that the question might be as to the powers of this government in the acquisition of Egypt and the Soudan, or a section of Central Africa, or a spot in the Antarctic Circle, or a section of the Chinese Empire." But it must be remembered that, as Marshall and Story declared, the Constitution was framed for ages to come, and that the sagacious men who framed it were well aware that a mighty future waited on their work. . . .

In our judgment, so much of the Porto Rican act as authorized the imposition of these duties is invalid, and plaintiffs were entitled to recover. . . .

Mr. Justice HARLAN, dissenting: . . .

Whether a particular race will or will not assimilate with our people, and whether they can or cannot with safety to our institutions be brought within the operation of the Constitution, is a matter to be thought of when it is proposed to acquire their territory by treaty. A mistake in the acquisition of territory, although such acquisition seemed at the time to be necessary, cannot be made the ground for violating the Constitution or refusing to give full effect to its provisions. The Constitution is not to be obeyed or disobeyed as the circumstances of a particular crisis in our history may suggest the one or the other course to be pursued. The People have decreed that it shall be the supreme law of the land at all times. When the acquisition of territory becomes complete, by cession, the Constitution necessarily becomes the supreme law of such new territory, and no power exists in any department of the government to make "concessions" that are inconsistent with its provisions. The authority to make such concessions implies the existence in Congress of power to declare that constitutional provisions may be ignored under special or embarrassing circumstances. No such dispensing power exists in any branch of our government. The Constitution is supreme over every foot of territory, wherever situated, under the jurisdiction of the United States, and its full operation cannot be stayed by any branch of the government in order to meet what some may suppose to be extraordinary emergencies. . . .

We heard much in argument about the "expanding future of our country." It was said that the United States is to become what is called a "world power;" and that if this government intends to keep abreast of the times and be equal to the great destiny that awaits the American people, it must be allowed to exert all the power that other nations are accustomed to exercise. My answer is, that the fathers never

intended that the authority and influence of this nation should be exerted otherwise than in accordance with the Constitution. If our government needs more
power than is conferred upon it by the Constitution, that instrument provides the
mode in which it may be amended and additional power thereby obtained. The
People of the United States who ordained the Constitution never supposed that a
change could be made in our system of government by mere judicial interpretation. They never contemplated any such juggling with the words of the Constitution
as would authorize the courts to hold that the words "throughout the United
States," in the taxing clause of the Constitution, do not embrace a domestic "territory of the United States" having a civil government established by the authority of
the United States. This is a distinction which I am unable to make, and which I do
not think ought to be made when we are endeavoring to ascertain the meaning of a
great instrument of government. . . .

[I]t is . . . said that a new territory, acquired by treaty or conquest, cannot
become incorporated into the United States without the consent of Congress. What
is meant by such incorporation we are not fully informed, nor are we instructed as
to the precise mode in which it is to be accomplished. Of course, no territory can
become a state in virtue of a treaty or without the consent of the legislative branch
of the government; for only Congress is given power by the Constitution to admit
new states. But it is an entirely different question whether a domestic "territory of
the United States," having an organized civil government established by Congress,
is not, for all purposes of government by the nation, under the complete jurisdiction of the United States, and therefore a part of, and incorporated into, the
United States, subject to all the authority which the national government may exert
over any territory or people. If Porto Rico, although a territory of the United States,
may be treated as if it were not a part of the United States, then New Mexico and
Arizona may be treated as not parts of the United States, and subject to such legislation as Congress may choose to enact without any reference to the restrictions
imposed by the Constitution. The admission that no power can be exercised under
and by authority of the United States except in accordance with the Constitution is
of no practical value whatever to constitutional liberty, if, as soon as the admission
is made — as quickly as the words expressing the thought can be uttered — the
Constitution is so liberally interpreted as to produce the same results as those which
flow from the theory that Congress may go outside of the Constitution in dealing
with newly acquired territories, and give them the benefit of that instrument only
when and as it shall direct. . . .

In my opinion Porto Rico became, at least after the ratification of the treaty with
Spain, a part of and subject to the jurisdiction of the United States in respect of all
its territory and people, and that Congress could not thereafter impose any duty,
impost, or excise with respect to that island and its inhabitants, which departed
from the rule of uniformity established by the Constitution.

Discussion

1. How would you describe the modalities of analysis found within the various
opinions? That is, to what extent do the particular opinions seem to rely on the
various interpretive modalities of text, history, structure, precedent, general ethos
of the American community, natural justice, or consequences? Which of these
approaches do you find most satisfying in regard to deciding the various issues
considered by the Court?

2. Puerto Ricans were granted statutory citizenship by Congress in 1917. Residents of the Philippines, also captured in the 1898 war, never received citizenship. Indeed, given that 1790 naturalization law prohibited the naturalization of non-whites (modified in 1870 to allow the naturalization of "aliens of African nativity and to persons of African descent"), Filipinos were held ineligible to become American citizens. See In re Lampitoe, 232 F. 382 (S.D.N.Y. 1916). Persons of Chinese descent were made eligible for citizenship in 1943 (when the United States was allied with China during World War II). Only with the passage of the Immigration and Nationality Act of 1952 did Congress adopt as policy that "[t]he right of a person to become a naturalized citizen of the United States shall not be denied or abridged because of race or sex." Note, though, that this does not necessarily apply to discrimination based on "national origin."

3. Did the grant of citizenship to Puerto Ricans automatically serve to "incorporate" Puerto Rico within the United States, as was the case for Alaska when inhabitants of that territory were accorded citizenship, see Rassmussen v. United States, 197 U.S. 516 (1905)? The Court held otherwise in Balzac v. People of Puerto Rico, 258 U.S. 298 (1922), involving the right of Puerto Rican criminal defendants to receive trial by jury. The Court, through Chief Justice Taft, held that there was no such right. The Court should not be quick "to infer, from acts thus easily explained on other grounds, an intention to incorporate in the Union those distant ocean communities of a different origin and language from those of our continental people."

4. To this day, Puerto Rico has no vote in the House or Senate, nor does Puerto Rico possess any votes in the Electoral College (unlike the District of Columbia, see the Twenty-Third Amendment). Almost 50 percent of the Puerto Rican population have voted for statehood in nonbinding referenda. Assume that a majority of the population petitions for statehood. Does Congress have a constitutional duty to grant such a petition (even if no Court would order Congress to act thusly in the matter)? What would count as proper reasons for denying it? The fact that most Puerto Ricans speak Spanish? That most are Catholic? That most are non-white? That it is significantly less economically developed than even Mississippi or Arkansas? That admission would "dilute" the voting power now held in the Senate by the 50 states and by the states in the House of Representatives? Is any of these a legitimate reason to deny statehood to Puerto Rico (assuming that a majority of the population of Puerto Rico wish it)? If none of these reasons suffice, can you imagine any others that would?

5. Almost 50 percent of the Puerto Rican population have voted to retain their "commonwealth" status vis-à-vis the United States. Does "commonwealth" represent a genuine constitutional status, or is it simply a label signifying a decision by Congress, exercising its constitutional discretion, to allow Puerto Rico such autonomy and grant Puerto Ricans such "constitutional rights" as it sees fit, subject to reversal whenever Congress and the President (or two-thirds of each house of Congress) believe the American interest demands otherwise? See generally Arnold H. Leibowitz, Defining Status: A Comprehensive Analysis of United States Territorial Relations, ch. 6 (1989); Juan R. Torruella, The Supreme Court and Puerto Rico: The Doctrine of Separate and Unequal (1988).

6. A small percentage of Puerto Ricans favor independence. Assume that the sentiment in favor of independence grows because of the refusal of the United States either to admit Puerto Rico as a state or to grant (perhaps by constitutional

amendment) a suitably "entrenched" commonwealth status to Puerto Rico. Would the United States be under any constitutional duty to honor this wish for independence, or is it entirely a matter of discretion whether the United States continues to possess Puerto Rico as a colony? Or consider a final possibility, however unlikely it is in practice: Could the United States decide to sell Puerto Rico to another country, in just the way, for example, that Russia sold Alaska to the United States — for $7,200,000, about 2.5 cents per acre, in 1867 — and Denmark sold what are now the American Virgin Islands in 1917? Would Puerto Ricans have any constitutional right to object to "deannexation" from the United States by, for example, being sold to, say, Mexico, Brazil, or Spain (which controlled the island for some 400 years prior to 1898)? See Christina Burnett, The Constitution and Deconstitution of the United States, in The Louisiana Purchase and American Expansion 181 (Levinson and Sparrow eds., 2005).

7. One of the most famous aphorisms in American history is that of "Mr. Dooley" (Finley Peter Dunne): "[N]o matter whether th' Constitution follows th' flag, th' Supreme Court follows th' iliction returns." Quoted in Owen Fiss, 8 History of the Supreme Court of the United States: Troubled Beginnings of the Modern State, 1888-1910, p. 239 (1993). Dunne, an anti-imperialist, was writing of the Insular Cases and registering his belief that McKinley's smashing victory over Williams Jennings Bryan in the 1900 presidential election, in which an important issue was the legitimacy of American empire-building, was the primary explanation for the Court's 5-4 decision. Assume for the moment that Dunne was correct. What precisely is wrong with "following the election returns" if the Constitution is indeed unclear and if the people (relatively) clearly endorse one possible interpretation of the Constitution, even if one disagrees with it, over another that one might prefer?

B. Ethnic Diversity and the Constitution: The Case of Chinese Immigration

The opinions in the Insular Cases are quite candid with regard to their views about the (in)ability of any and all ethnic groups to become part of the American community. Such discussions were certainly not limited to the context of American expansion into the Pacific or the Caribbean. Recall the discussion earlier in this chapter of the citizenship status of American Indians or Justice Harlan's distinction between African-Americans and Chinese immigrants in his famous dissenting opinion in Plessy v. Ferguson. It is, therefore, quite significant that the Court did, in United States v. Wong Kim Ark, 169 U.S. 649 (1898), read sentence one of the Fourteenth Amendment to provide birthright citizenship to children of Chinese immigrants (even though the parents themselves were ineligible for citizenship as a matter of statutory law). However, Chief Justice Fuller dissented, joined by Justice Harlan:

> [T]he fourteenth amendment does not exclude from citizenship by birth children born in the United States of parents permanently located therein, and who might themselves become citizens; nor, on the other hand, does it arbitrarily make citizens of children born in the United States of parents who, according to the will of their native government and of this government, are and must remain aliens.

Perhaps the most notable demonstration of anti-Chinese animus was the passage of so-called Chinese Exclusion Acts that barred the entry of Chinese laborers into the United States.[72] The acts were challenged and upheld in Chae Chan Ping v. U.S., 130 U.S. 581 (1889) (The Chinese Exclusion Case):

CHAE CHAN PING v. UNITED STATES, 130 U.S. 581 (1889): [Chae Chan Ping had lived in San Francisco from 1875 until June 2, 1887, when he returned to his home in China for a visit. He left, in the words of the Court, "having in his possession a certificate, in terms entitling him to return to the United States, bearing date on that day, duly issued to him by the collector of customs of the port of San Francisco. . . . ." However, on his return to San Francisco on October 8, 1888, "the collector of the port refused the permit, solely on the ground that under the act of Congress, approved October 1, 1888 [an amendment to the so-called Chinese Exclusion Act of 1882, which had prohibited Chinese laborers from entering the United States], . . . the certificate had been annulled and his right to land abrogated. . . . The captain of the steamship, therefore, detained the appellant on board the steamer." Chae Chan Ping then filed suit in federal court for a writ of habeas corpus on the ground that his detention was illegal. The court rejected his claim and "held as conclusions of law that the appellant was not entitled to enter the United States, and was not unlawfully restrained of his liberty, and ordered that he be remanded to the custody of the master of the steamship from which he had been taken under the writ." He then appealed to the Supreme Court.]

Mr. Justice FIELD delivered the opinion of the court.

The validity of the act is assailed as being in effect an expulsion from the country of Chinese laborers, in violation of existing treaties between the United States and the government of China, and of rights vested in them under the laws of Congress.

[Justice Field then reviews the history of treaties between the United States and the empire of China, beginning in 1844.] Neither the treaty of 1844 nor that of 1858 touched upon the migration and emigration of the citizens and subjects of the two nations, respectively, from one country to the other. But in 1868 a great change in the relations of the two nations was made in that respect. . . . [A key provision of a new treaty that year recognized] "the inherent and inalienable right of man to change his home and allegiance, and also the mutual advantage of the free migration and emigration of their citizens and subjects respectively from the one country to the other for purposes of curiosity, of trade, or as permanent residents." . . .

But notwithstanding these strong expressions of friendship and good will, and the desire they evince for free intercourse, events were transpiring on the Pacific coast which soon dissipated the anticipations indulged as to the benefits to follow the immigration of Chinese to this country. . . . [Subsequent modifications to the 1868 treaty] have been caused by a well-founded apprehension — from the experience of years — that a limitation to the immigration of certain classes from China was essential to the peace of the community on the Pacific coast, and possibly to the preservation of our civilization there. A few words on this point may not be deemed inappropriate here, they being confined to matters of public notoriety, which have frequently been brought to the attention of congress.

---

72. See Lucy Salyer, Laws Harsh as Tigers: Chinese Immigrants and the Shaping of Modern Immigration Law (1995); Andrew Gyory, Closing the Gate: Race, Politics, and the Chinese Exclusion Act (1998).

The discovery of gold in California in 1848, as is well known, was followed by a large immigration thither from all parts of the world, attracted not only by the hope of gain from the mines, but from the great prices paid for all kinds of labor. The news of the discovery penetrated China, and laborers came from there in great numbers, a few with their own means, but by far the greater number under contract with employers, for whose benefit they worked. These laborers readily secured employment, and, as domestic servants, and in various kinds of outdoor work, proved to be exceedingly useful. For some years little opposition was made to them, except when they sought to work in the mines, but, as their numbers increased, they began to engage in various mechanical pursuits and trades, and thus came in competition with our artisans and mechanics, as well as our laborers in the field. The competition steadily increased as the laborers came in crowds on each steamer that arrived from China, or Hong Kong, an adjacent English port. They were generally industrious and frugal. Not being accompanied by families, except in rare instances, their expenses were small; and they were content with the simplest fare, such as would not suffice for our laborers and artisans. The competition between them and our people was for this reason altogether in their favor, and the consequent irritation, proportionately deep and bitter, was followed, in many cases, by open conflicts, to the great disturbance of the public peace. The differences of race added greatly to the difficulties of the situation. . . . [T]hey remained strangers in the land, residing apart by themselves, and adhering to the customs and usages of their own country. It seemed impossible for them to assimilate with our people, or to make any change in their habits or modes of living. As they grew in numbers each year the people of the coast saw, or believed they saw, in the facility of immigration, and in the crowded millions of China, where population presses upon the means of subsistence, great danger that at no distant day that portion of our country would be overrun by them, unless prompt action was taken to restrict their immigration. The people there accordingly petitioned earnestly for protective legislation.

In December, 1878, the convention which framed the present constitution of California, being in session, took this subject up, and memorialized congress upon it, setting forth, in substance, that the presence of Chinese laborers had a baneful effect upon the material interests of the state, and upon public morals; that their immigration was in numbers approaching the character of an Oriental invasion, and was a menace to our civilization; that the discontent from this cause was not confined to any political party, or to any class or nationality, but was well nigh universal; that they retained the habits and customs of their own country, and in fact constituted a Chinese settlement within the state, without any interest in our country or its institutions; and praying congress to take measures to prevent their further immigration. This memorial was presented to congress in February, 1879. So urgent and constant were the prayers for relief against existing and anticipated evils, both from the public authorities of the Pacific coast and from private individuals, that congress was impelled to act on the subject. . . . [A new treaty was concluded with China that declared] in its first article that "Whenever, in the opinion of the government of the United States, the coming of Chinese laborers to the United States, or their residence therein, affects or threatens to affect the interests of that country, or to endanger the good order of the said country or of any locality within the territory thereof, the government of China agrees that the government of the United States may regulate, limit, or suspend such coming or residence, but may not absolutely prohibit it. The limitation or suspension shall be reasonable, and shall apply only to Chinese who may go to the United States as laborers, other classes not being included in the limitations. Legislation taken in regard to Chinese laborers will be of such a character only as is necessary to enforce the regulation, limitation, or suspension of immigration, and immigrants shall not be subject to personal maltreatment or abuse." In its second article it declares that "Chinese subjects, whether proceeding to the United States as teachers, students, merchants, or from curiosity, together with their body and household servants, and Chinese laborers who are now in the United States, shall be allowed to go and come of their own free will and accord, and shall be accorded all the rights, privileges, immunities, and exemptions which are accorded to the citizens and subjects of the most favored nation."

. . . On the 6th of May, 1882, an act of congress was approved, to carry this supplementary treaty into effect. [It suspended the immigration of Chinese laborers for 10 years, though it also stipulated that the ban] shall not apply to Chinese laborers who were in the United States November 17, 1880. . . . [The collectors of customs at American ports were given the duty of supplying such laborers with] "the proper evidence" of their right to go from and come to the United States. . . . "The certificate herein provided for," says the section, "shall entitle the Chinese laborer to whom the same is issued to return to and reenter the United States upon producing and delivering the same to the collector of customs of the district at which such Chinese laborer shall seek to re-enter."

The enforcement of this act with respect to laborers who were in the United States on November 17, 1880, was attended with great embarrassment, from the suspicious nature, in many instances, of the testimony offered to establish the residence of the parties. . . . To prevent the possibility of the policy of excluding Chinese laborers being evaded, the act of October 1, 1888, the validity of which is the subject of consideration in this case, was passed. . . . [The key provisions provided that] "from and after the passage of this act it shall be unlawful for any Chinese laborer who shall at any time heretofore have been, or who may now or hereafter be, a resident within the United States, and who shall have departed, or shall depart, therefrom, and shall not have returned before the passage of this act, to return to or remain the United States. [Moreover, any certificate of identity previously issued] is hereby declared void and of no effect, and the Chinese laborer claiming admission by virtue thereof shall not be permitted to enter the United States." . . .

Here the objection made is that the act of 1888 impairs a right vested under the treaty of 1880, as a law of the United States, and the statutes of 1882 and of 1884 passed in execution of it. It must be conceded that the act of 1888 is in contravention of express stipulations of the treaty of 1868, and of the supplemental treaty of 1880, but it is not on that account invalid, or to be restricted in its enforcement. The treaties were of no greater legal obligation than the act of congress. By the constitution, laws made in pursuance thereof, and treaties made under the authority of the United States, are both declared to be the supreme law of the land, and no paramount authority is given to one over the other. A treaty, it is true, is in its nature a contract between nations, and is often merely promissory in its character, requiring legislation to carry its stipulations into effect. Such legislation will be open to future repeal or amendment. If the treaty operates by its own force, and relates to a subject within the power of congress, it can be deemed in that particular only the equivalent of a legislative act, to be repealed or modified at the pleasure of congress. In either case the last expression of the sovereign will must control.

The effect of legislation upon conflicting treaty stipulations was elaborately considered in the Head-Money Cases, and it was there adjudged "that, so far as a treaty made by the United States with any foreign nation can become the subject of judicial cognizance in the courts of this country, it is subject to such acts as congress may pass for its enforcement, modification, or repeal." 112 U.S. 580. . . . It will not be presumed that the legislative department of the government will lightly pass laws which are in conflict with the treaties of the country; but that circumstances may arise which would not only justify the government in disregarding their stipulations, but demand in the interests of the country that it should do so, there can be no question. Unexpected events may call for a change in the policy of the country. . . .

The validity of this legislative release from the stipulations of the treaties was, of course, not a matter for judicial cognizance. The question whether our government is justified in disregarding its engagements with another nation is not one for the determination of the courts . . . [I]f the power mentioned is vested in congress, any reflection upon its motives, or the motives of any of its members in exercising it, would be entirely uncalled for. This court is not a censor of the morals of other departments of the government; it is not invested with any authority to pass judgment upon the motives of their conduct. When once it is established that congress possesses the power to pass an act, our province ends with its construction and its application to cases as they are presented for determination. Congress has the power under the constitution to declare war, and in two instances where the power has been exercised — in the war of 1812 against Great Britain, and in 1846 against Mexico — the propriety and wisdom and justice of its action were vehemently assailed by some of the ablest and best men in the country, but no one doubted the legality of the proceeding, and any imputation by this or any other court of the United States upon the motives of the members of congress who in either case voted for the declaration, would have been justly the cause of animadversion. We do not mean to intimate that the moral aspects of legislative acts may not be proper subjects of consideration. Undoubtedly they may be, at proper times and places, before the public, in the halls of congress, and in all the modes by which the public mind can be influenced. Public opinion thus enlightened, brought to bear upon legislation, will do more than all other causes to prevent abuses; but the province of the courts is to pass upon the validity of laws, not to make them, and, when their validity is established, to declare their meaning and apply their provisions. All else lies beyond their domain.

There being nothing in the treaties between China and the United States to impair the validity of the act of congress of October 1, 1888, was it on any other ground beyond the competency of congress to pass it? If so, it must be because it was not within the power of congress to prohibit Chinese laborers who had at the time departed from the United States, or should subsequently depart, from returning to the United States. Those laborers are not citizens of the United States; they are aliens. That the government of the United States, through the action of the legislative department, can exclude aliens from its territory is a proposition which we do not think open to controversy. Jurisdiction over its own territory to that extent is an incident of every independent nation. It is a part of its independence. If it could not exclude aliens it would be to that extent subject to the control of another power. As said by this court in the case of The Exchange, 7 Cranch 116, 136, speaking by Chief Justice Marshall: "The jurisdiction of the nation within its own territory is necessarily exclusive and absolute. It is susceptible of no limitation not imposed by itself. Any restriction upon it, deriving validity from an external source, would imply a diminution of its sovereignty to the extent of the restriction, and an investment of that sovereignty to the same extent in that power which could impose such restriction. All exceptions, therefore, to the full and complete power of a nation within its own territories, must be traced up to the consent of the nation itself. They can flow from no other legitimate source."

While under our constitution and form of government the great mass of local matters is controlled by local authorities, the United States, in their relation to foreign countries and their subjects or citizens, are one nation, invested with powers which belong to independent nations, the exercise of which can be invoked for the maintenance of its absolute independence and security throughout its entire territory. The powers to declare war, make treaties, suppress insurrection, repel invasion, regulate foreign commerce, secure republican governments to the states, and admit subjects of other nations to citizenship, are all sovereign powers, restricted in their exercise only by the constitution itself and considerations of public policy and justice which control, more or less, the conduct of all civilized nations. As said by this court in the case of Cohens v. Virginia, 6 Wheat. 264, 413, speaking by the same great chief justice: "That the United States form, for many, and for most important purposes, a single nation, has not yet been denied. In war, we are one people. In making peace, we are one people. In all commercial regulations, we are one and the same people. In many other respects, the American people are one; and the government which is alone capable of controlling and managing their interests in all these respects is the government of the Union. It is their government, and in that character they have no other. America has chosen to be in many respects, and to many purposes, a nation; and for all these purposes her government is complete; to all these objects, it is competent. The people have declared that in the exercise of all powers given for these objects it is supreme. It can, then, in effecting these objects, legitimately control all individuals or governments within the American territory. The constitution and laws of a state, so far as they are repugnant to the constitution and laws of the United States, are absolutely void. These states are constituent parts of the United States. They are members of one great empire, — for some purposes sovereign, for some purposes subordinate." . . . .

To preserve its independence, and give security against foreign aggression and encroachment, is the highest duty of every nation, and to attain these ends nearly all other considerations are to be subordinated. It matters not in what form such aggression and encroachment come, whether from the foreign nation acting in its national character, or from vast hordes of its people crowding in upon us. The government, possessing the powers which are to be exercised for protection and security, is clothed with authority to determine the occasion on which the powers shall be called forth; and its determinations, so far as the subjects affected are concerned, are necessarily conclusive upon all its departments and officers. If, therefore, the government of the United States, through its legislative department, considers the presence of foreigners of a different race in this country, who will not assimilate with us, to be dangerous to its peace and security, their exclusion is not to be stayed because at the time there are no actual hostilities with the nation of which the foreigners are subjects. The existence of war would render the necessity of the proceeding only more obvious and pressing. The same necessity, in a less pressing degree, may arise when war does not exist, and the same authority which adjudges the necessity in one case must also determine it in the other. In both cases its determination is conclusive upon the judiciary. If the government of the country of which the foreigners excluded are subjects is dissatisfied with this action, it can make complaint to the executive head of our government, or resort to any other measure which, in its judgment, its interests or dignity may demand; and there lies its only remedy. . . .

The power of exclusion of foreigners being an incident of sovereignty belonging to the government of the United States as a part of those sovereign powers delegated by the constitution, the right to its exercise at any time when, in the judgment of the government, the interests of the country require it, cannot be granted away or restrained on behalf of any one. The powers of government are delegated in trust to the United States, and are incapable of transfer to any other parties. They cannot be abandoned or surrendered. Nor can their exercise be hampered, when needed for the public good, by any considerations of private interest. The exercise of these public trusts is not the subject of barter or contract. Whatever license, therefore, Chinese laborers may have obtained, previous to the act of October 1, 1888, to return to the United States after their departure, is held at the will of the government, revocable at any time, at its pleasure. Whether a proper consideration by our government of its previous laws, or a proper respect for the nation whose subjects are affected by its action, ought to have qualified its inhibition, and made it applicable only to persons departing from the country after the passage of the act, are not questions for judicial determination. . . .

During the argument reference was made by counsel to the alien law of June 25, 1798, and to opinions expressed at the time by men of great ability and learning against its constitutionality. We do not attach importance to those opinions in their bearing upon this case. The act vested in the president power to order all such aliens as he should judge dangerous to the peace and safety of the United States, or should have reasonable grounds to suspect were concerned in any treasonable or secret machination against the government, to depart out of the territory of the United States within such time as should be expressed in his order. There were other provisions also distinguishing it from the act under consideration. The act was passed during a period of great political excitement, and it was attacked and defended with great zeal and ability. It is enough, however, to say that it is entirely different from the act before us, and the validity of its provisions was never brought to the test of judicial decision in the courts of the United States.

Discussion

1. Justice Field's opinion is functionally divided into two separate parts. The first concerns the power of the national government in effect to abrogate a treaty, inasmuch as there is no serious question that the legislation violated the terms of the treaty with China. The answer, of course, is that the national government (including, presumably, Congress alone, should it pass legislation over a presidential veto) does indeed have such a power, under the "last in time" rule that, in effect, bars a prior Congress from binding a future one. (The only true way to bind Congress is a constitutional amendment, which does indeed take priority over legislation in a way that a treaty does not.)

Note, though, that the Court writes that "[I]t will not be presumed that the legislative department of the government will lightly pass laws which are in conflict with the treaties of the country. . . ." He may be alluding to the so-called "*Charming Betsy* canon of interpretation," derived from John Marshall's opinion in Murray v. Schooner Charming Betsy, 6 U.S. (2 Cranch) 64 (1804). "Under the canon, courts will attempt to construe statutes, when reasonably possible, so that the statutes do not violate international law." Curtis Bradley and Jack Goldsmith, Congressional Authorization and the War on Terrorism, 118 Harvard L. Rev. 2097 (2005). But this canon does not at all challenge Congress's authority to override international law so long as the meaning of the statute is clear. We shall have occasion later in the course to read about "plain meaning" rules as ways not so much of *limiting* power as *forcing* an open acknowledgment that Congress (presumably, as a practical matter, with presidential support) is in fact intending to renounce the treaty (or, as we shall see, trench on what is a presumptively protected interest of a state within our federal system).

2. It is not enough, though, that Congress has the formal power to override a treaty. In addition, Congress must have the constitutional power to pass the legislation in question. Although Justice Field refers to "those sovereign powers delegated by the constitution" to the national government, one might note that he nowhere quotes any specific text assigning Congress a power to control immigration. He might, for example, have cited Henderson v. New York, 92 U.S. 259 (1876), which held that the Commerce Clause gave Congress exclusive control over immigration to the United States. Instead, he emphasizes control over immigration as a power deriving from the nature of sovereignty itself. Recall a similar discussion in Mayor of New York v. Miln, Chapter 3, though, ironically enough, it arose in the context of the majority's asserting New York's right, as a "sovereign state," to control its borders.

Thus Field's opinion once more raises the question whether one can properly view national government as being a necessarily "limited government with only assigned powers." Note the final paragraph of his opinion and its allusion to the debate over the constitutionality of the Alien Act in 1798, see Chapter 2, supra. He is fending off the application in the instant case of arguments made, by Albert Gallatin and others, that the Act was beyond Congress's "limited" powers. But recall that defenders of the Act were more than happy to make an argument quite similar to Field's in its reliance on the inherent power of "sovereigns" over aliens. Consider contemporary debates about the potential threat to American security presented by aliens of certain countries. Unless the Chinese Exclusion Case is overruled, do *any* aliens possess a constitutional right not to be summarily deported, upon congressional command, simply because of fears generated by their national origin?

C.   Religious Diversity and the Constitution: The Example of Mormonism

Many of the questions raised in the preceding materials involve what we today might term the issue of racial, ethnic, or cultural "diversity." They also raise the question of how a republican political order can be made consistent with such diversity. There was no doubt in the late nineteenth century that the United States was (and remains) the most diverse country in the world, and then (as now) people often expressed concerns about *how* diverse the citizenry could become, racially or culturally, and still maintain itself as a republican political order.

Social conditions in the United States have produced a variety of religious groups, whose interactions have presented fundamental questions about the limits of cultural pluralism. The particular history of one church — the Church of Jesus Christ of Latter-Day Saints, more popularly known as the Mormons—provides an illuminating example of the constitutional dimensions of the struggle over cultural diversity. The Mormon Church was founded by Joseph Smith, a then 23-year-old New York farmer who in 1827 proclaimed the discovery of a cache of golden plates to which he was directed by a vision of the angel Moroni.[73] The plates (which were later swept away by another angel) were transcribed and became the Book of Mormon, which detailed "the wanderings, vicissitudes, and battles of America's pre-Columbian inhabitants."[74] These inhabitants included the sons of Nephi, extinguished in recurrent battle with the evil sons of Laman. Two Nephites, Mormon and his son Moroni, buried their chronicles in 384 A.D., to be discovered almost 1,450 years later by Smith. As Fawn Brodie points out, Mormonism was "no mere dissenting sect" within Christianity, which featured a multiplicity of sects by the early nineteenth century, especially in America. "It was a real religious creation, one intended to be to Christianity what Christianity was to Judaism: that is, a reform and a consummation."[75]

Following the 1830 publication of the Book of Mormon, Smith gathered adherents to the new faith. These members attempted to construct new communities, first in Ohio, then later in Missouri and Illinois. (The Mormon community of Nauvoo, in Illinois, had a population in 1844 the equal of Chicago.) The hostility and violence that greeted these efforts is exemplified by Smith's lynching in Illinois in 1844, after which his successors, including Brigham Young, led his followers to new settlements in the Great Salt Lake basin of Utah. The first wagon train arrived there in July 1847. A constitutional convention in 1849 established the autonomous state of Deseret as a church-regulated community.

A provision of the Compromise of 1850 placed Deseret within the federally governed Utah Territory, and President Fillmore appointed Young the first territorial governor and superintendent of local Indian affairs. "Thus, with the temporal powers of the territorial government and the spiritual powers of the Mormon church united in his hands, Utah became a theocracy ruled by a prophet whose word was law in matters both religious and secular."[76] 1852 saw the public articulation and defense of the Mormon practice of plural marriage, which had been initiated by Smith, who reportedly had more than 30 wives. A Mormon "Reformation" in 1856-57 led to both "a new enthusiasm for their faith" and "a substantial increase in the number of polygamous families."[77] By 1856, the newly formed Republican Party emphasized in its platform Congress's "sovereign powers over the Territories"

---

73. The leading biography of Smith is Richard Bushman, Joseph Smith: Rough Stone Rolling (2005). Bushman quotes the Bostonian Josiah Quincy, who had met Smith in 1842: "It is by no means improbable that some future text-book . . . will [ask]: What historical American of the nineteenth century has exerted the most powerful influence upon the destinies of the his countrymen? And it is by no means impossible that the answer to the interrogatory may be thus written: *Joseph Smith the Mormon prophet.*" Even if one regards Quincy's prediction as hyperbolic, it is certainly true that the Church founded by Smith has indeed become a major force in the American — and increasingly the world — community, in spite of efforts, detailed in the text, to suppress it.

74. Sydney E. Ahlstrom, A Religious History of the American People 502-503 (1972). Ahlstrom provides an excellent brief overview about the history of the Mormon church at 501-507.

75. Id. at 502, quoting Fawn Brodie, No Man Knows My History: The Life of Joseph Smith, the Mormon Prophet viii (1945). As the quotation suggests, there remain serious theological questions about whether Mormonism is a genuinely "Christian" religion. See Richard John Neuhaus, "Is Mormonism Christian?" First Things, March 2000, pp. 97-115, available at *http://www.leaderu.com/ftissues/ft0003/public.html.* See also Correspondence, First Things, June-July 2000, pp. 2-12, available at *http://www.leaderu.com/ftissues/ft0006/correspondence.html.*

76. Kenneth Stampp, America in 1857, 197 (1990).

77. Id. at 198.

and the "duty" of Congress to use those powers "to prohibit in the Territories those twin relics of barbarism — Polygamy and Slavery."[78]

Mormon leaders, writes Kenneth Stampp, were increasingly viewed by the rest of America "as lawless tyrants and their followers as crazed fanatics shamelessly justifying their wicked deeds in the name of religious freedom." Indeed, "Mormonism was a political issue of a kind rarely encountered in 1857, because, with few exceptions, Northerners and Southerners, whether Democrats, Republicans, or [members of the anti-immigrant American Party], could unite wholeheartedly in condemning it." Some Democrats, such as Stephen A. Douglas, suspended their commitment to popular sovereignty and counseled federal intervention in order "to apply the knife and cut out this loathsome, disgusting ulcer."[79] In 1857 President James Buchanan replaced Young with a non-Mormon as territorial governor and sent 2,500 U.S. soldiers to Utah to enforce federal law against recalcitrant Mormons. Although the so-called Mormon War (the name given the episode by non-Mormons) featured no formal battles, "it was not one without tragedy and death. The army suffered heavy losses from sickness and the bitter cold of a mountain winter. In addition, a group of angry Mormon civilians and militiamen [and, apparently, some Indian allies] in southern Utah . . . took their revenge for past injuries on a company of 'gentile' emigrants passing through their land" in an episode remembered as the Mountain Meadows Massacre.[80]

In 1862 Congress specifically outlawed bigamy "in a Territory, or other place over which the United States have exclusive jurisdiction." Enforcement of this law provided the first formal tests of the meaning of the free exercise clause of the First Amendment and the protections, if any, that would be given to groups within American society whose behavior diverged in fundamental ways from that of the larger society.[81]

REYNOLDS v. UNITED STATES
98 U.S. 145 (1878)

[George Reynolds, a leading figure within the Mormon Church, was convicted of violating the federal antibigamy statute and sentenced to two years in prison and

78. See Sarah Barringer Gordon, The Mormon Question: Polygamy and Constitutional Conflict in Nineteenth Century America 55-58 (2002).

79. Stampp at 198-200. Other Southerners, such as South Carolina Representative Lawrence Keitt, condemned federal regulation of Utahans' marriage practices on the ground that "[t]o allow this power is to consolidate the Government" and suggest that Congress could "declare slaveholding a crime." Quoted in Gordon, at 58.

80. Stampp at 203-207. As one might predict, there is controversy about the degree of Mormon responsibility for the massacre. Although recent scholarship assigns Mormon leaders, including Brigham Young, significant responsibility for the some 120 deaths that occurred, see, e.g., Sally Denton, American Massacre: The Tragedy at Mountain Meadows, September 1857 (2003); Will Bagley, Blood of the Prophets: Brigham Young and the Massacre at Mountain Meadows (2002), the Church itself denies any such institutional responsibility. Thus Gordon B. Hinckley, then president of the LDS Church, delivered on September 11, 1999 what were meant to be words of "reconciliation" at the dedication of a monument to the victims of the massacre. "That which we have done here," he emphasized, "must never be construed as an acknowledgment on the part of the church of any complicity in the occurrences of that fateful day." Hinckley later said that "I would place blame on the local people. I've never thought for one minute — and I've read the history of that tragic episode — that Brigham Young had anything to do with it. It was a local decision and it was tragic." See *http://www.cesnur.org/testi/morm_01.htm.*

81. See generally Edwin Brown Firmage and Richard Collin Mangrum, Zion in the Courts: A Legal History of the Church of Jesus Christ of Latter-Day Saints, 1830-1900, 129-209 (1988).

a $500 fine. He appealed his conviction, invoking the Free Exercise Clause of the First Amendment. The Supreme Court unanimously rejected his claim.]

WAITE, C.J. . . .

[Reynolds] proved that at the time of his alleged second marriage he was, and for many years before had been, a member of the Church of Jesus Christ of Latter-Day Saints, commonly called the Mormon Church, and a believer in its doctrines; that it was an accepted doctrine of that church

> that it was the duty of male members of said church, circumstances permitting, to practice polygamy; . . . that this duty was enjoined by different books which the members of said church believed to be of divine origin, and among others the Holy Bible, and also that the members of the church believed that the practice of polygamy was directly enjoined upon the male members thereof by the Almighty God, in a revelation to Joseph Smith, the founder and prophet of said church; that the failing or refusing to practise polygamy . . . , when circumstances would admit, would be punished, and that the penalty for such failure and refusal would be damnation in the life to come.

[T]he question is raised, whether religious belief can be accepted as a justification of an overt act made criminal by the law of the land. . . .

Congress cannot pass a law . . . which shall prohibit the free exercise of religion. . . . The question to be determined is, whether the law now under consideration comes within this prohibition. . . . [W]hat is the religious freedom which has been guaranteed[?]

[The Court reviews some of the history of the First Amendment, ascribing particular significance to the views of Thomas Jefferson. Waite quotes from Jefferson's letter to the Danbury Baptist Association, where he used the metaphor of "a wall of separation between church and state." Jefferson wrote that "religion is a matter which lies solely between man and his God; that he owes account to none other for his faith or his worship; that the legislative powers of the government reach actions only, and not opinions. . . ."] Coming as this does from an acknowledged leader of the advocates of the measure, it may be accepted almost as an authoritative declaration of the scope and effect of the amendment thus secured. Congress was deprived of all legislative power over mere opinion, but was left free to reach actions which were in violation of social duties or subversive of good order.

Polygamy has always been odious among the northern and western nations of Europe, and, until the establishment of the Mormon Church, was almost exclusively a feature of the life of Asiatic and of African people. . . . [F]rom the earliest history of England polygamy has been treated as an offence against society. It is a significant fact that on [December 8,] 1788, after the passage of the [Virginia Act guaranteeing religious freedom] and after the convention of Virginia had recommended as an amendment to the Constitution of the United States the declaration in a bill of rights that "all men have an equal, natural, and unalienable right to the free exercise of religion, according to the dictates of conscience," the legislature of that State substantially enacted the statute of James I, death penalty included, because, as recited in the preamble, "it hath been doubted whether bigamy or poligamy be punishable by the laws of this Commonwealth." From that day to this we think it may safely be said there never has been a time in any State of the Union when polygamy has not been an offence against society, cognizable by the civil courts and punishable with more or less severity. In the face of all this evidence, it is impossible to believe that the constitutional guaranty of religious freedom was intended to prohibit legislation in respect to this most important feature of social life. Marriage, while from its very nature a sacred obligation, is nevertheless, in most civilized nations, a civil contract, and usually regulated by law. Upon it society may be said to be built, and out of its fruits spring social relations and social obligations and duties, with which government is necessarily required to deal. In fact, according as monogamous or polygamous marriages are allowed, do we find the principles on which the government of the people, to a greater or less extent, rests. Professor Lieber says, polygamy leads to the patriarchal principle, and which, when applied to large communities, fetters the people in stationary despotism, while that principle cannot long exist in connection with monogamy. Chancellor Kent observes that this remark is equally striking and profound. An exceptional colony of polygamists under an exceptional leadership may sometimes exist for a time without appearing to disturb the social condition of the people who surround it; but there cannot be a doubt that, unless restricted by some form of constitution, it is within the legitimate scope of the power of every civil government to determine whether polygamy or monogamy shall be the law of social life under its dominion.

In our opinion, the statute immediately under consideration is within the legislative power of Congress. . . . This being so, the only question which remains is, whether those who make polygamy a part of their religion are excepted from the operation of the statute. If they are, then those who do not make polygamy a part of their religious belief may be found guilty and punished, while those who do, must be acquitted and go free. This would be introducing a new element into criminal law. Laws are made for the government of actions, and while they cannot interfere with mere religious belief and opinions, they may with practices. Suppose one believed that human sacrifices were a necessary part of religious worship, would it be seriously contended that the civil government under which he lived could not interfere to prevent a sacrifice? Or if a wife religiously believed it was her duty to burn herself upon the funeral pile of her dead husband, would it be beyond the power of the civil government to prevent her carrying her belief into practice?

. . . To permit [exemption of Reynolds on grounds of his religious belief] would be to make the professed doctrines of religious belief superior to the law of the land, and in effect to permit every citizen to become a law unto himself. Government could exist only in name under such circumstances.

Subsequently, Murphy v. Ramsey, 114 U.S. 15 (1885), upheld an act of Congress excluding polygamists and bigamists from voting or holding office. Praising monogamy as "the sure foundation of all that is stable and noble in our civilization; the best guaranty of that reverent morality which is the source of all beneficent progress in social and political improvement," the Court readily supported Congress's "endeavor to withdraw all political influence from those who are practically hostile to its attainment." Similarly, Davis v. Beason, 133 U.S. 333 (1890), upheld a law of the Territory of Idaho that limited the right to vote to those persons otherwise eligible who would swear not only that they were not practicing polygamists but also that they did not support the practice or even belong to any group that "teaches, advises, counsels or encourages its members, devotees or any other person to commit the crime of bigamy or polygamy. . . ." After denouncing polygamy, Justice Field defined religion "as having reference to one's views of his relations to his Creator."

He went on to explain that "it was never intended or supposed that the [First Amendment] could be invoked as a protection against legislation for the punishment of acts inimical to the peace, good order and morals of society":

> Probably never before in the history of this country has it been seriously contended that the whole punitive power of the government for acts, recognized by the general consent of the Christian world in modern times as proper matters for prohibitory legislation, must be suspended in order that the tenets of a religious sect encouraging crime may be carried out without hindrance. . . . Crime is not the less odious because sanctioned by what any particular sect may designate as religion.

Justice Field appended a short "Note" to the end of his opinion:

> The constitutions of several states, in providing for religious freedom, have declared expressly that such freedom shall not be construed to excuse acts of licentiousness, or to justify practices inconsistent with the peace and safety of the State. Thus the constitution of New York of 1777 provided as follows: "The free exercise and enjoyment of religious profession and worship, without discrimination or preference, shall forever be allowed, within this State, to all mankind: *Provided,* That the liberty of conscience, hereby granted, shall not be so construed as to excuse acts of licentiousness, or justify practices inconsistent with the peace or safety of this State." The same declaration is repeated in the constitution of 1821 and in that of 1846, except that for the words "hereby granted," the words "hereby secured" are substituted. The constitutions of California, Colorado, Connecticut, Florida, Georgia, Illinois, Maryland, Minnesota, Mississippi, Missouri, Nevada and South Carolina contain a similar declaration.

The final Mormon case of this period was The Late Corporation of the Church of Jesus Christ of Latter-day Saints v. United States, 136 U.S. 1 (1890). Congress in 1887 passed an act repealing the corporate charter of the Mormon Church, which had initially been granted in 1851 by an assembly of the State of Deseret and thereafter confirmed by the territorial legislature of Utah. The purpose of the Church was defined as promoting charity and religion. Congress repealed the incorporation on the grounds that a major purpose of the Church was the promotion of polygamy. The act mandating disincorporation directed the court to distribute all of the Church property in accordance with the original purpose. The court below ordered the property sold and the proceeds used to operate public schools within Utah. The Act was upheld in an opinion written by Justice Bradley. He condemned as "a return to barbarism" the practice of polygamy and pronounced it "contrary to the spirit of Christianity and of the civilization which Christianity has produced in the Western world." Chief Justice Fuller, joined by Justices Field and Lamar, dissented solely on the ground that Congress had exceeded its enumerated power over the Territories.

The campaign against bigamy was successful. In 1890 the leader of the Mormon Church formally announced a revelation requiring the abandonment of the teaching and practice of polygamy. This led, among other things, to Congress's finally granting Utah's petition for statehood after numerous prior rejections predicated on antagonism to Mormon polygamy, though Congress conditioned Utah's admission on the inclusion of a prohibition of bigamy in its constitution. It may be worth noting that the 1895 constitution was one of the first to guarantee women the right to vote. With the "taming" of Mormonism and the constitutional text against bigamy, Utah entered the Union as a State on January 4, 1896, over 40 years after the first petitions for statehood by its settlers. (Query, incidentally, whether Utah is bound to follow the congressionally imposed condition after admission, given the "equal footing doctrine" that disallows discriminatory treatment of any given states. If Massachusetts, for example, can adopt same-sex marriage, then would Utah be disallowed from repealing the 1896 provision and recognizing plural marriage? Whether other states would be bound to recognize such bigamous marriages raises complex questions beyond the scope of this casebook.)

As late as 1946, in Cleveland v. United States, 329 U.S. 14, the Court interpreted the Mann Act (which prohibited the transportation across state lines of "any woman or girl for the purpose of prostitution or debauchery, or for any other immoral purpose") to extend to members of a dissenting Mormon sect that continued to practice polygamy in spite of its disavowal by the general Mormon Church. (Several communities in southern Utah and northern Arizona continue to be inhabited by adherents of "unreformed" Mormonism.) Several of those convicted had transported their plural wives across state lines. Quoting *Reynolds* and *Church of Jesus Christ of L.D.S.*, Justice Douglas commented: "The establishment or maintenance of polygamous households is a notorious example of promiscuity. . . . [P]olygamous practices have long been branded immoral in the law." As to the suggestion that marriage and divorce was a matter to be regulated by the states alone, Douglas noted simply that "[t]he power of Congress over the instrumentalities of interstate commerce is plenary; it may be used to defeat what are deemed to be immoral practices." On the development of the relevant Commerce Clause doctrine, see Champion v. Ames and Hammer v. Dagenhart, infra, this chapter.

Discussion

Professor Stephen Pepper suggests that the term "free exercise" contains a "clear connotation of at least some degree of freedom of *action*"[82] going beyond the simple right to hold abstract views of theology. Consider a revised First Amendment that guaranteed only "freedom of belief concerning religion." This general issue continues to generate extensive debate. Recent Supreme Court cases suggest that the distinction between belief and action is alive and well. See, e.g., Employment Division, Department of Human Resources of Oregon v. Smith, 494 U.S. 872 (1990), which cites *Reynolds* as operative law.

In Chapter 8, supra, you will read cases involving the criminalization of certain sexual practices, including same-sex sodomy, widely thought to be "immoral." If, as is the case, the Supreme Court has disallowed much of this regulation, then does *Reynolds* survive, at least in the absence of proof that bigamy causes what might be termed "tangible harm" — beyond the giving of moral offense — to society? *Should it survive even if the only harm is thought to be its putative immorality?*[83]

---

82. Stephen Pepper, *Reynolds, Yoder,* and Beyond: Alternatives for the Free Exercise Clause, 1981 Utah L. Rev. 309.

83. See Cheshire Calhoun, Who's Afraid of Polygamous Marriage? Lessons for Same-Sex Marriage Advocacy from the History of Polygamy, 42 San Diego L. Rev. 1023 (2005); Sanford Levinson, Thinking about Polygamy, 42 San Diego L. Rev. 1049 (2005).

III.   The Protection of Economic Rights

A.   Pressures for Intervention and the Rise of Substantive Due Process, 1874-1890[84]

As we saw in the Slaughterhouse Cases, the Supreme Court initially resisted using the Fourteenth Amendment to strike down economic regulation. By 1890, however, the Court had essentially embraced the theory of the Due Process Clause set out in Justice Bradley's dissent. The history of this transformation and the period that followed can be viewed from a variety of perspectives. After briefly describing the rise of economic regulation and the corporate bar's response to it, we reproduce Lochner v. New York, which has come to be the symbol of the era of economic substantive due process. Following *Lochner,* we raise some further questions about the social and intellectual context in which it was decided.

The decades following the Civil War were times of widespread social protest, stemming from

> the great pace of industrialization and, more particularly, from the swift concentration of economic power in the large corporation. Midwestern and Southern farmers, unable to control their marketing through organization and suffering from a long-term international price decline, complained bitterly of monopolistic rates by railroads, grain elevators, and banks. Factory workers and miners, crowded in slums with insecure status in a rapidly changing economy, periodically rebelled at low wages, long hours, and bad working conditions. Small businessmen, faced with the more efficient, and frequently more ruthless, competition of the large corporation, charged that the continued consolidation of capital was destroying individual opportunity. And many professional and white-collar people, uneasy over the accumulation of great wealth and the growing disparity of rich and poor, feared that the traditional fluidity of American society was fast disappearing. . . . Under the pressure of social discontent, legislators had begun to act in the 1870's and 1880's in regard to railroad and grain elevator rates, labor relations, and other matters affecting large business concerns. In turn, corporation lawyers had been pressing the courts to protect more vigilantly the rights of property against legislative regulation.[85]

After the Slaughterhouse Cases, corporations could not expect aid from the privileges or immunities clause of the Fourteenth Amendment. Although Justice Miller's opinion gave even shorter shrift to the due process clause, the natural law tradition clinging to that clause and its inviting references to "property" and "liberty" led corporate lawyers to seize on it.

The state courts were the first to respond. In Matter of Jacobs, 98 N.Y. 98 (1885), the New York Court of Appeals struck down a statute prohibiting the manufacture of cigars in tenement houses. The court dismissed the ostensible public health rationale of the law to hold that it "interferes with the profitable and free use of his property by the owner or lessee of a tenement house" and "arbitrarily deprives him

---

84. See generally Sidney Fine, Laissez Faire and the General Welfare State (1956); Richard Hofstadter, Social Darwinism in American Thought (rev. ed. 1955); Arnold Paul, Conservative Crisis and the Rule of Law (1960); Benjamin Twiss, Lawyers and the Constitution: How Laissez Faire Came to the Supreme Court (1942).

85. Paul, at 1-2, 5. But cf. Gabriel Kolko, Railroads and Regulation, 1877-1916 (1965).

of his property and of some portion of his personal liberty."[86] In Godcharles v. Wigeman, 113 Pa. 431, 6 A. 354 (1886), the Pennsylvania Supreme Court held "utterly unconstitutional and void" a law requiring mining and manufacturing companies to pay wages in cash (rather than in vouchers redeemable only at the company store):

> An attempt has been made by the legislature to do what, in this country, cannot be done; that is, prevent persons who are sui juris [i.e., persons who possess full legal rights and capacity] from making their own contracts. The Act is an infringement alike of the right of the employer and the employee; more than this, it is an insulting attempt to put the laborer under legislative tutelage, which is not only degrading to his manhood, but subversive of his rights as a citizen of the United States.
>
> He may sell labor for what he thinks best, whether money or goods, just as his employer may sell his iron or coal, and any and every law that proposes to prevent him from so doing is an infringement of his constitutional privileges, and consequently vicious and void.

Although not all state courts were so hostile to social legislation and some were avowedly sympathetic, decisions like these became increasingly common.

The early pressures for federal judicial intervention came mostly from regulated industries, and the Court first intervened in 1890, not against social legislation but against railroad rate regulation. The following paragraphs trace the growth of the federal doctrine of substantive due process.

The first decision, and the "bete noire of laissez faire conservatism,"[87] was Munn v. Illinois, 94 U.S. 113 (1877), which upheld a state law limiting the rates charged by Chicago grain-storage warehouses. Writing for the Court, Chief Justice Waite began by asserting that a state had inherent authority — the "police power" — to regulate "the conduct of its citizens one towards another, and the manner in which each shall use his own property, when such regulation becomes necessary for the public good." He then noted that it was the practice in England, the colonies, and the states "to regulate ferries, common carriers, hackmen, bakers, millers, wharfingers, innkeepers, &c., and in so doing to fix a maximum of charge to be made for services rendered, accommodations furnished, and articles sold," and that the practice was followed in the District of Columbia, which was subject to the Fifth Amendment due process clause. "From this it is apparent that . . . it was not supposed that statutes regulating the use, or even the price of the use, of private property necessarily deprived an owner of his property without due process of law. Under some circumstances they may, but not under all." This brought the Chief Justice "to inquire as to the principles upon which this power of regulation rests." For the answer, he turned to Lord Chief Justice Hale's seventeenth-century treatise, De Portibus Maris, to conclude that private property may be regulated when it is "affected with a public interest" and that property becomes "clothed with a public interest when used in a manner to make it of public consequence, and affects the community at large." The warehouses clearly fell within this description — indeed,

---

86. In fact, New York's contribution antedates the Civil War. In Wynehamer v. New York, 12 N.Y. 378 (1856), Judge Comstock, in one of several seriatim opinions, invoked the due process clause of the New York Constitution to invalidate a law prohibiting the sale of intoxicating liquor.

87. Paul, at 8.

the complainants had "a virtual monopoly" on the storage of grain bound from the Midwest to national markets.

Finally, the Court refused to hear an argument that the maximum permissible rates were "unreasonable."

> Undoubtedly, in mere private contracts, relating to matters in which the public has no interest, what is reasonable must be ascertained judicially. But this is because the legislature has no control over such a contract. . . . The controlling fact is the power to regulate at all. If that exists, the right to establish the maximum of charge, as one of the means of legislation, is implied. . . . We know that this is a power which may be abused; but that is no argument against its existence. For protection against abuses by legislatures the people must resort to the polls, not to the courts.

Justice Field, joined by Justice Strong, dissented.

The Court reaffirmed *Munn* in the Railroad Commission Cases, 116 U.S. 307 (1886), which upheld state regulation of railroad tariffs (notwithstanding a provision in the railroad's 1884 charter empowering it to set its own charges). Again Chief Justice Waite wrote that the reasonableness of rates was a legislative question. But he went on to caution:

> From what has thus been said, it is not to be inferred that this power of limitation or regulation is itself without limit. This power to regulate is not a power to destroy, and limitation is not the equivalent of confiscation. Under pretense of regulating fares and freights, the State cannot require a railroad corporation to carry persons or property without reward; neither can it do that which in law amounts to a taking of private property for public use without just compensation, or without due process of law.

That same year, in Santa Clara County v. Southern Pacific Railroad, 118 U.S. 394, the Court held that the word "person" in the due process clause of the Fourteenth Amendment encompassed artificial persons, i.e., corporations.[88] Viewed in retrospect, these decisions indicate a gradual weakening of the Court's rejection of substantive due process in the Slaughterhouse Cases. Waite's opinion in *Munn* implied that the Constitution might forbid state regulation of matters that were not "affected with a public interest"; the Railroad Commission Cases explicitly suggested that in extreme cases "reasonableness" might be met for judicial inquiry; and the Court's definition of "persons" opened the way for direct challenges to regulations by corporations.

Of the justices who had participated in the Slaughterhouse Cases, only Field, Bradley, and Miller remained on the Court in 1890. That year in the Minnesota Rate Cases, 134 U.S. 418, the Court struck down a statute granting a state railroad commission unreviewable authority to set rates. Justice Blatchford wrote that the reasonableness of rates "is eminently a question for judicial investigation, requiring due process of law for its determination": "If the company is deprived of the power of charging reasonable rates for the use of its property, and such deprivation takes

---

88. On the real and supposed understanding of the framers of the Fourteenth Amendment on this matter, see Graham, Everyman's Constitution, supra n.32, chs. 1-2, 10-12, which includes Graham's well-known article, The "Conspiracy Theory" of the Fourteenth Amendment, 47 Yale L.J. 371, 48 id. 171 (1938). Corporations were held not to be "citizens" under the privileges or immunities clause. See Paul v. Virginia, 75 U.S. (8 Wall.) 168 (1868); Blake v. McClung, 172 U.S. 239 (1898).

place in the absence of investigation by judicial machinery, it is deprived of the lawful use of its property, and thus, in substance and effect, of the property itself, without due process of law." Justice Bradley, joined by Justices Gray and Lamar, dissented vigorously.

At first glance, the Minnesota Rate Cases seem to build on the tradition of procedural due process to require notice and an opportunity to be heard in the courts before rates could be imposed on the railroads. Such judicializing of administrative rate-making was itself an innovation. But the opinion implied that the judiciary's role was not simply to review the application of legislative criteria to particular cases but to determine — independent of any legislative or administrative criteria — whether the rates established were "reasonable."[89] The broad implications of the decision were not lost on the corporate bar, which rejoiced in it, nor on Justice Bradley, who remarked in dissent with no joy that it "practically overrules Munn v. Illinois."[90] Within a decade, the Court expanded its inquiries beyond rate regulation to review the substantive validity of legislation of almost every sort. Economic and social theories largely abandoned in the academies and legislative chambers found their last refuge in the judiciary.

Note: Incorporation of the Eminent Domain Clause

Pumpelly v. Green Bay Company, 13 Wall. 166 (1871), presented the question whether, by authorizing the erection of a dam that flooded appellant's land, Wisconsin had "taken" Pumpelly's property and therefore had a duty to compensate him. Justice Miller wrote for the Court that "though the Constitution of the United States provides that private property shall not be taken for public use without just compensation, it is well settled that this is a limitation on the power of the Federal government, and not on the States." Pumpelly thus reaffirmed the holding of Barron v. Baltimore, 32 U.S. (7 Pet.) 243 (1833), that the Bill of Rights did not apply to the states, and, like the Slaughterhouse Cases two years later,

89. The basic formula was announced eight years later in Smyth v. Ames, 169 U.S. 466 (1898): Rates must yield a fair return upon the present value of the company's assets. For nearly 40 years, the Court was rate-maker and accountant. In FPC v. Natural Gas Pipeline Co., 315 U.S. 575 (1942), the Court noted that "[t]he Constitution does not bind rate-making bodies to the service of any single formula," and in FPC v. Hope Natural Gas Co., 320 U.S. 591 (1944), it expressly repudiated the rule of Smyth v. Ames.

90. Bradley's dissent in *Chicago, Milwaukee & St. Paul* calls for some explanation, since the Court's decision might well be viewed as adopting the position espoused in his dissent in the Slaughterhouse Cases. Bradley's earlier dissent evinces a concern for the plight of small entrepreneurs at the hands of the state-sanctioned monopoly. In a nonconstitutional decision, also written in 1873, he had rejected a railroad's attempt to disclaim common law liability, noting that the carrier and its customer do "not stand on a footing of equality." Railroad Co. v. Lockwood, 84 U.S. (17 Wall.) 357, 379 (1873). From this point of view, there was no inconsistency in upholding legislation constraining "the burdens and charges which those who own [public means of transportation] are authorized to impose upon the public." Bradley argued, moreover, that the Court should accord legislation a presumption of constitutionality:

I do not mean to say that the legislature, or . . . other legislative agency, may not so act as to deprive parties of their property without due process of law. The Constitution contemplates the possibility of such an invasion of rights. But, acting within their jurisdiction, (as in these cases they have done,) the invasion should be clear and unmistakable to bring the case within that category.

declined to hold that the Fourteenth Amendment "incorporated" any portion of the first ten amendments.

Ironically, the first clause of the Bill of Rights in effect made applicable to state legislation was the Fifth Amendment right to just compensation for property taken by the State. In Chicago, Burlington and Quincy Railroad v. Chicago, 166 U.S. 226 (1897), the Court considered Illinois's practice of delegating essentially final authority to a jury to determine the compensation due someone whose property has been taken. In the particular case, the railroads complained that the jury's award of a dollar for seizing its right of way to build a street violated the due process and equal protection clauses of the Fourteenth Amendment.

Justice Harlan wrote for the Court, rejecting the city's claim that the United States Constitution did not apply to the case:

> It is proper now to inquire whether the due process of law enjoined by the Fourteenth Amendment requires compensation to be made or adequately secured to the owner of private property taken for public use under the authority of a State.
>
> . . . Due protection of the rights of property has been regarded as a vital principle of republican institutions. . . . The requirement that the property shall not be taken for public use without just compensation is but "an affirmance of a great doctrine established by the common law for the protection of private property. It is founded in natural equity, and is laid down by jurists as a principle of universal law. Indeed, in a free government almost all rights would become worthless if the government possessed an uncontrollable power over the private fortune of every citizen."
>
> But if, as this court has adjudged [in Davidson v. Louisiana, supra 331], a legislative enactment assuming arbitrarily to take the property of one individual and give it to another individual, would not be due process of law as enjoined by the Fourteenth Amendment, it must be that the requirement of due process of law in that amendment is applicable to the direct appropriation by the State to public use and without compensation of the private property of the citizen. The legislature may prescribe a form of procedure to be observed in the taking of private property for public use, but it is not due process of law if provision be not made for compensation. . . . Due process of law as applied to judicial proceedings instituted for the taking of private property for public use means, therefore, such process as recognizes the right of the owner to be compensated if his property be wrested from him and transferred to the public. The mere form of the proceeding instituted against the owner, even if he be admitted to defend, cannot convert the process used into due process of law, if the necessary result be to deprive him of his property without compensation. . . .
>
> "It in nowise detracts from the power of the public to take whatever may be necessary for its uses; while on the other hand, it prevents the public from loading upon one individual more than his just share of the burdens of government, and says that, when he surrenders to the public something more and different from that which is exacted from other members of the public, a full and just equivalent shall be returned to him." . . .
>
> In our opinion, a judgment of a state court, even if it be authorized by statute, whereby private property is taken for the State or under its direction for public use, without compensation made or secured to the owner, is upon principle and authority, wanting in the due process of law required by the Fourteenth Amendment of the Constitution of the United States.

The Court went on to hold that the treatment accorded the railroads was in fact legitimate and not in violation of the Fourteenth Amendment. Justice Brewer dissented from this latter part of the Court's opinion.

B. The Heyday of Police Power Jurisprudence, 1890-1934

LOCHNER v. NEW YORK
198 U.S. 45 (1905)

[In April 1895, both houses of the New York legislature unanimously passed legislation stating that "[n]o employee shall be required, permitted or suffered to work in a [bakery] more than sixty hours in any one week, or more than ten hours in any one day, unless for the purpose of making a shorter work day on the last day of the week. . . ."[91] Joseph Lochner was convicted of employing a baker in excess of 60 hours in one week.]

PECKHAM, J. . . .

The statute necessarily interferes with the right of contract between the employer and employés, concerning the number of hours in which the latter may labor in the bakery of the employer. The general right to make a contract in relation to his business is part of the liberty of the individual protected by the Fourteenth Amendment of the Federal Constitution. Allgeyer v. Louisiana, 165 U.S. 578 (1897). Under that provision no State can deprive any person of life, liberty or property without due process of law. The right to purchase or to sell labor is part of the liberty protected by this amendment, unless there are circumstances which exclude the right. There are, however, certain powers, existing in the sovereignty of each State in the Union, somewhat vaguely termed police powers, the exact description and limitation of which have not been attempted by the courts. Those powers, broadly stated and without, at present, any attempt at a more specific limitation, relate to the safety, health, morals and general welfare of the public. Both property and liberty are held on such reasonable conditions as may be imposed by the governing power of the State in the exercise of those powers, and with such conditions the Fourteenth Amendment was not designed to interfere.

The State, therefore, has power to prevent the individual from making certain kinds of contracts, and in regard to them the Federal Constitution offers no protection. If the contract be one which the State, in the legitimate exercise of its police power, has the right to prohibit, it is not prevented from prohibiting it by the Fourteenth Amendment. Contracts in violation of a statute, either of the Federal or state government, or a contract to let one's property for immoral purposes, or to do any other unlawful act, could obtain no protection from the Federal Constitution, as coming under the liberty of person or of free contract. Therefore, when the State, by its legislature, in the assumed exercise of its police powers, has passed an act which seriously limits the right to labor or the right of contract in regard to their means of livelihood between persons who are sui juris (both employer and employé), it becomes of great importance to determine which shall prevail — the right of the individual to labor for such time as he may choose, or the right of the State to prevent the individual from laboring or from entering into any contract to labor beyond a certain time prescribed by the State.

---

91. See Paul Kens, Judicial Power and Reform Politics: The Anatomy of *Lochner v. New York* 58-59 (1990). Professor Kens notes that the act was amended specifically to state "employee" rather than "person" so as to avoid any inference that a self-employed baker was precluded from working in excess of the hours indicated.

This court has recognized the existence and upheld the exercise of the police powers of the States in many cases which might fairly be considered as border ones. . . . [For example, in Holden v. Hardy, 169 U.S. 336 (1898), a] provision in the act of the legislature of Utah was . . . under consideration, the act limiting the employment of workmen in all underground mines or workings . . . [and] in smelting and other institutions for the reduction or refining of ores or metals to eight hours per day. . . . The act was held to be a valid exercise of the police powers of the State. . . . It was held that the kind of employment, mining, smelting, etc., and the character of the employees in such kinds of labor, were such as to make it reasonable and proper for the State to interfere to prevent the employees from being constrained by the rules laid down by the proprietors in regard to labor. . . . There is nothing in Holden v. Hardy which covers the case now before us. . . .

It must, of course, be conceded that there is a limit to the valid exercise of the police power by the State. . . . Otherwise . . . it would be enough to say that any piece of legislation was enacted to conserve the morals, the health or the safety of the people; such legislation would be valid, no matter how absolutely without foundation the claim might be. The claim of the police power would be a mere pretext — become another and delusive name for the supreme sovereignty of the State to be exercised free from constitutional restraint. This is not contended for. In every case that comes before this court, therefore, where legislation of this character is concerned and where the protection of the Federal Constitution is sought, the question necessarily arises: Is this a fair, reasonable and appropriate exercise of the police power of the State, or is it an unreasonable, unnecessary and arbitrary interference with the right of the individual to his personal liberty or to enter into those contracts in relation to labor which may seem to him appropriate or necessary for the support of himself and his family? Of course the liberty of contract relating to labor includes both parties to it. The one has as much right to purchase as the other to sell labor.

This is not a question of substituting the judgment of the court for that of the legislature. If the act be within the power of the State it is valid, although the judgment of the court might be totally opposed to the enactment of such a law. But the question would still remain: Is it within the police power of the State? and that question must be answered by the court.

The question whether this act is valid as a labor law, pure and simple, may be dismissed in a few words. There is no reasonable ground for interfering with the liberty of person or the right of free contract, by determining the hours of labor, in the occupation of a baker. There is no contention that bakers as a class are not equal in intelligence and capacity to men in other trades or manual occupations, or that they are not able to assert their rights and care for themselves without the protecting arm of the State, interfering with their independence of judgment and of action. They are in no sense wards of the State. . . . The law must be upheld, if at all, as a law pertaining to the health of the individual engaged in the occupation of a baker. It does not affect any other portion of the public than those who are engaged in that occupation. Clean and wholesome bread does not depend upon whether the baker works but ten hours per day or only sixty hours a week. . . .

The mere assertion that the subject relates though but in a remote degree to the public health does not necessarily render the enactment valid. The act must have a more direct relation, as a means to an end, and the end itself must be appropriate and legitimate, before an act can be held to be valid which interferes with the general right of an individual to be free in his person and in his power to contract in relation to his own labor. . . .

We think the limit of the police power has been reached and passed in this case. There is, in our judgment, no reasonable foundation for holding this to be necessary or appropriate as a health law. . . .

We think that there can be no fair doubt that the trade of a baker, in and of itself, is not an unhealthy one to that degree which would authorize the legislature to interfere with the right to labor, and with the right of free contract on the part of the individual, either as employer or employé. In looking through statistics regarding all trades and occupations, it may be true that the trade of a baker does not appear to be as healthy as some other trades, and is also vastly more healthy than still others. . . . It might be safely affirmed that almost all occupations more or less affect the health. There must be more than the mere fact of the possible existence of some small amount of unhealthiness to warrant legislative interference with liberty. . . . No trade, no occupation, no mode of earning one's living, could escape this all-pervading power, and the acts of the legislature in limiting the hours of labor in all employments would be valid, although such limitation might seriously cripple the ability of the laborer to support himself and his family. . . .

It is also urged, pursuing the same line of argument, that it is to the interest of the State that its population should be strong and robust, and therefore any legislation which may be said to tend to make people healthy must be valid as health laws, enacted under the police power. If this be a valid argument and a justification for this kind of legislation, it follows that the protection of the Federal Constitution from undue interference with liberty of person and freedom of contract is visionary, wherever the law is sought to be justified as a valid exercise of the police power. Scarcely any law but might find shelter under such assumptions, and conduct, properly so called, as well as contract, would come under the restrictive sway of the legislature. Not only the hours of employés, but the hours of employers, could be regulated, and doctors, lawyers, scientists, all professional men, as well as athletes and artisans, could be forbidden to fatigue their brains and bodies by prolonged hours of exercise, lest the fighting strength of the State be impaired. . . . Statutes of the nature of that under review, limiting the hours in which grown and intelligent men may labor to earn their living, are mere meddlesome interferences with the rights of the individual, and they are not saved from condemnation by the claim that they are passed in the exercise of the police power and upon the subject of the health of the individual whose rights are interfered with, unless there be some fair ground, reasonable in and of itself, to say that there is material danger to the public health or to the health of the employés, if the hours of labor are not curtailed. . . . All that [the State] could properly do has been done by it with regard to the conduct of bakeries, as provided for in the other sections of the act. . . . These several sections provide for the inspection of the premises where the bakery is carried on, with regard to furnishing proper wash-rooms and water-closets, apart from the bake-room, also with regard to providing proper drainage, plumbing and painting. . . . These various sections . . . certainly go to the full extent of providing for the cleanliness and the healthiness, so far as possible, of the quarters in which bakeries are to be conducted. . . .

It was further urged . . . that restricting the hours of labor in the case of bakers was valid because it tended to cleanliness on the part of the workers, as a man was more apt to be cleanly when not overworked, and if cleanly then his "output" was also more likely to be so. . . . In our judgment it is not possible in fact to discover the connection between the number of hours a baker may work in the bakery and the healthful quality of the bread made by the workman. The connection, if any exists, is too shadowy and thin to build any argument for the interference of the legislature. If the man works ten hours a day it is all right, but if ten and a half or eleven his health is in danger and his bread may be unhealthful, and, therefore, he shall not be permitted to do it. This, we think, is unreasonable and entirely arbitrary. When assertions such as we have adverted to become necessary in order to give, if possible, a plausible foundation for the contention that the law is a "health law," it gives rise to at least a suspicion that there was some other motive dominating the legislature than the purpose to subserve the public health or welfare. . . .

It is impossible for us to shut our eyes to the fact that many of the laws of this character, while passed under what is claimed to be the police power for the purpose of protecting the public health or welfare, are, in reality, passed from other motives. We are justified in saying so when, from the character of the law and the subject upon which it legislates, it is apparent that the public health or welfare bears but the most remote relation to the law. The purpose of a statute must be determined from the natural and legal effect of the language employed; and whether it is or is not repugnant to the Constitution of the United States must be determined from the natural effect of such statutes when put into operation, and not from their proclaimed purpose. . . . It seems to us that the real object and purpose were simply to regulate the hours of labor between the master and his employés (all being men, sui juris), in a private business, not dangerous in any degree to morals or in any real and substantial degree, to the health of the employees. Under such circumstances the freedom of master and employés to contract with each other in relation to their employment, and in defining the same, cannot be prohibited or interfered with, without violating the Federal Constitution.

Reversed.

HARLAN, J., joined by White and Day, JJ., dissenting. . . .

Granting . . . that there is a liberty of contract which cannot be violated even under the sanction of direct legislative enactment, but assuming, as according to settled law we may assume, that such liberty of contract is subject to such regulations as the State may reasonably prescribe for the common good and the well-being of society, what are the conditions under which the judiciary may declare such regulations to be in excess of legislative authority and void? Upon this point there is no room for dispute; for, the rule is universal that . . . the power of the courts to review legislative action in respect of a matter affecting the general welfare exists *only* ". . . if a statute purporting to have been enacted to protect the public health, the public morals or the public safety, has no real or substantial relation to those objects, or is, beyond all question, a plain, palpable invasion of rights secured by the fundamental law." . . . If there be doubt as to the validity of the statute, that doubt must therefore be resolved in favor of its validity, and the courts must keep their hands off, leaving the legislature to meet the responsibility for unwise legislation. If the end which the legislature seeks to accomplish be one to which its power extends, and if the means employed to that end, although not the wisest or best, are yet not plainly and palpably unauthorized by law, then the court cannot interfere. In other words, when the validity of a statute is questioned, the burden of proof, so to speak, is upon those who assert it to be unconstitutional.

Let these principles be applied to the present case. . . .

It is plain that this statute was enacted in order to protect the physical well-being of those who work in bakery and confectionery establishments. It may be that the statute had its origin, in part, in the belief that employers and employés in such establishments were not upon an equal footing, and that the necessities of the latter often compelled them to submit to such exactions as unduly taxed their strength. Be this as it may, the statute must be taken as expressing the belief of the people of New York that, as a general rule, and in the case of the average man, labor in excess of sixty hours during a week in such establishments may endanger the health of those who thus labor. . . . I find it impossible, in view of common experience, to say that there is here no real or substantial relation between the means employed by the State and the end sought to be accomplished by its legislation. . . .

Professor Hirt in his treatise on the Diseases of the Workers has said: "The labor of the bakers is among the hardest and most laborious imaginable, because it has to be performed under conditions injurious to the health of those engaged in it. It is hard, very hard work, not only because it requires a great deal of physical exertion in an overheated workshop and during unreasonably long hours, but more so because of the erratic demands of the public, compelling the baker to perform the greater part of his work at night, thus depriving him of an opportunity to enjoy the necessary rest and sleep, a fact which is highly injurious to his health." Another writer says: "The constant inhaling of flour dust causes inflammation of the lungs and of the bronchial tubes. The eyes also suffer through this dust, which is responsible for the many cases of running eyes among the bakers. The long hours of toil to which all bakers are subjected produce rheumatism, cramps and swollen legs. The intense heat in the workshops induces the workers to resort to cooling drinks, which together with their habit of exposing the greater part of their bodies to the change in the atmosphere, is another source of a number of diseases of various organs. Nearly all bakers are pale-faced and of more delicate health than the workers of other crafts, which is chiefly due to their hard work and their irregular and unnatural mode of living, whereby the power or resistance against disease is greatly diminished. The average age of a baker is below that of other workmen; they seldom live over their fiftieth year, most of them dying between the ages of forty and fifty. . . ."

We judicially know that the question of the number of hours during which a workman should continuously labor has been, for a long period, and is yet, a subject of serious consideration among civilized peoples, and by those having special knowledge of the laws of health. . . .

I do not stop to consider whether any particular view of this economic question presents the sounder theory. What the precise facts are it may be difficult to say. It is enough for the determination of this case, and it is enough for this court to know, that the question is one about which there is room for debate and for an honest difference of opinion. There are many reasons of a weighty, substantial character, based upon the experience of mankind, in support of the theory that, all things considered, more than ten hours' steady work each day, from week to week, in a bakery or confectionery establishment, may endanger the health, and shorten the lives of the workmen, thereby diminishing their physical and mental capacity to serve the State, and to provide for those dependent upon them.

If such reasons exist that ought to be the end of this case, for the State is not amenable to the judiciary, in respect of its legislative enactments, unless such enactments are plainly, palpably, beyond all questions, inconsistent with the Constitution of the United States.

HOLMES, J., dissenting.

I regret sincerely that I am unable to agree with the judgment in this case, and that I think it my duty to express my dissent.

This case is decided upon an economic theory which a large part of the country does not entertain. If it were a question whether I agreed with that theory, I should desire to study it further and long before making up my mind. But I do not conceive that to be my duty, because I strongly believe that my agreement or disagreement has nothing to do with the right of a majority to embody their opinions in law. It is settled by various decisions of this court that state constitutions and state laws may regulate life in many ways which we as legislators might think as injudicious or if you like as tyrannical as this, and which equally with this interfere with the liberty to contract. Sunday laws and usury laws are ancient examples. A more modern one is the prohibition of lotteries. The liberty of the citizen to do as he likes so long as he does not interfere with the liberty of others to do the same, which has been a shibboleth for some well-known writers, is interfered with by school laws, by the Post Office, by every state or municipal institution which takes his money for purposes thought desirable, whether he likes it or not. The Fourteenth Amendment does not enact Mr. Herbert Spencer's Social Statics. . . .

[A] constitution is not intended to embody a particular economic theory, whether of paternalism and the organic relation of the citizen to the State or of laissez faire. It is made for people of fundamentally differing views, and the accident of our finding certain opinions natural and familiar or novel and even shocking ought not to conclude our judgment upon the question whether statutes embodying them conflict with the Constitution of the United States.

General propositions do not decide concrete cases. The decision will depend on a judgment or intuition more subtle than any articulate major premise. But I think that the proposition just stated, if it is accepted, will carry us far toward the end. Every opinion tends to become a law. I think that the word liberty in the Fourteenth Amendment is perverted when it is held to prevent the natural outcome of a dominant opinion, unless it can be said that a rational and fair man necessarily would admit that the statute proposed would infringe fundamental principles as they have been understood by the traditions of our people and our law. It does not need research to show that no such sweeping condemnation can be passed upon the statute before us. A reasonable man might think it a proper measure on the score of health. Men whom I certainly could not pronounce unreasonable would uphold it as a first instalment of a general regulation of the hours of work. Whether in the latter aspect it would be open to the charge of inequality I think it unnecessary to discuss.

1.   The Transformation and Federalization of General Constitutional Law

Lochner (which we use as a shorthand for the jurisprudence of constitutional rights of this period) expanded the scope of federal jurisdiction by, in effect, federalizing the principles of "general constitutional law," which federal courts had previously been able to invoke only in diversity cases. This might not have been of great practical consequence were it not for an accompanying change in the content of those principles. Recall that, throughout the Marshall and Taney eras, the core of general constitutional law was the vested rights doctrine, which assumed the validity of a given legal regime for the most part, but protected individuals against the *retroactive* impairment of rights acquired under the regime. Although the jurisprudence of general constitutional law also established the legitimate bounds of the legislature's police, taxing, and eminent domain powers (recall Loan Association v. Topeka, pp. 331-332, supra), the police power in particular was thought to be of broad scope. In contrast, *Lochner* signals a restricted view of the police power. As Duncan Kennedy has suggested, the Court during this era viewed individual autonomy and the government police power as two mutually exclusive, nonoverlapping domains. Within such a domain, each actor had absolute sovereignty — much as the Court, even during the Marshall and Taney eras, viewed the realms of state and federal powers. The Court conceived its own mission to be the policing of the boundaries between them.[92] Or, perhaps as much to the point, the Court was concerned that any limitations on individual autonomy in fact could be justified by reference to achieving legitimate public purposes, rather than simply representing "partial" legislation by which those political interests possessing legislative power were attempting to use the coercive power of the state only in behalf of their own "special interests."[93]

2. The Meanings of "Liberty," "Property," and "Process"

Liberty. At the beginning of the Court's opinion in *Lochner,* Justice Peckham asserts: "The general right to make a contract in relation to his business is part of the liberty of the individual protected by the Fourteenth Amendment of the Federal Constitution. Allgeyer v. Louisiana. . . . The right to purchase or to sell labor is part of the liberty protected by this amendment, unless there are circumstances which exclude the right." In Allgeyer v. Louisiana, 165 U.S. 578 (1897), Justice Peckham had written for the Court:

> The "liberty" mentioned in [the Fourteenth Amendment] means, not only the right of the citizen to be free from the mere physical restraint of his person, as by incarceration, but the term is deemed to embrace the right of the citizen to be free in the enjoyment of all his faculties; to be free to use them in all lawful ways; to live and work where he will; to earn his livelihood by any lawful calling; to pursue any livelihood or avocation, and for that purpose to enter into all contracts which may be proper, necessary and essential to his carrying out to a successful conclusion the purposes above mentioned.

The Court's adoption of this notion of "liberty" incurred considerable scholarly criticism. For example, Charles Warren wrote:[94]

> The phrase, "life, liberty or property without due process of law" came to us from the English common law; and there seems to be little question that, under the common law, the word "liberty" meant simply "liberty of the person," or, in other words, "the

---

92. Duncan Kennedy, The Rise and Fall of Classical Legal Thought, 1850-1940 (unpublished manuscript, 1975).

93. See especially the important study by Howard Gillman, The Constitution Besieged: The Rise and Demise of Lochner Era Police Powers Jurisprudence (1993).

94. Charles Warren, The New "Liberty" Under the Fourteenth Amendment, 39 Harv. L. Rev. 431, 440 (1926). See also Charles Shattuck, The True Meaning of the Term "Liberty" in Those Clauses in the Federal and State Constitutions Which Protect "Life, Liberty, and Property," 4 Harv. L. Rev. 365 (1891).

right to have one's person free from physical restraint." . . . There is no intimation . . . that this phrase in the Bill of Rights in . . . early State Constitutions meant anything more than it meant at common law. . . . It is unquestionable that when the First Congress adopted the Fifth Amendment and inserted the Due Process Clause, . . . they took it with the meaning it then bore.

The main object of Charles Warren's attack on the "new liberty" was Gitlow v. New York, 268 U.S. 652 (1925), in which the Court explicitly "assume[d] that freedom of speech and press — which are protected by the First Amendment from abridgement by Congress — are among the fundamental personal rights and liberties protected by the Fourteenth Amendment from impairment by the states."

Property. Even if the word "liberty" were construed narrowly, the due process clause also explicitly protects "property." In Coppage v. Kansas, 236 U.S. 1 (1915), in holding unconstitutional a statute prohibiting "yellow dog" contracts (contracts forbidding employees to join labor unions), the Court wrote: "Included in the right of personal liberty and the *right of private property* . . . is the right to make contracts. . . ." (emphasis added). Other substantive due process cases have similarly relied on the deprivation of property.

Of course, one might assert that the Court also construed "property" too broadly — that the term should be limited to the core common law concepts of realty and personalty.[95]

Process. Even if "liberty" and "property" may be read expansively, what about "process"? In cases like *Lochner,* what process has been inadequate — the legislative process by which the maximum hours regulation was enacted? The judicial process by which Lochner was convicted?

3. *The Scope of the Police Power: Permissible and Impermissible Objectives*

The Court notes at the outset that "the statute necessarily interferes with the rights of contract" but also asserts that "property and liberty are held on such reasonable conditions as may be imposed by the governing power of the state in the exercise of [its police] powers." What are the proper ends for which the police power may be exercised, and what objectives lie beyond them? Recall, in this respect, how Justice Peckham distinguished Holden v. Hardy in *Lochner.* Consider also Baltimore & Ohio R. Co. v. Interstate Commerce Commission, 221 U.S. 612 (1911), in which the Court upheld limitations on the hours of railroad employees. Justice Hughes wrote:

The length of hours of service has a direct relation to the efficiency of the human agencies upon which protection to life and property necessarily depends. . . . In its power suitably to provide for the safety of employees and travelers, Congress was not limited to the enactment of laws relating to mechanical appliances, but it was also competent to consider, and to endeavor to reduce, the dangers incident to the strain of excessive hours of duty on the part of engineers, conductors, train dispatchers, telegraphers, and other persons embraced within the class defined by the act. And in imposing restrictions having reasonable relation to this end there is no interference with liberty of contract as guaranteed by the Constitution.

95. See Chapter 9, infra, for further discussion of defining the "property" protected by the Due Process Clause.

What does the *Lochner* Court find wrong with the New York statute "as a labor law, pure and simple?" Consider Professor C.G. Tiedeman's assertion that the "proper limits" of the police powers are "to compel every one to so use his own property and so conduct himself as not to injure his neighbor or infringe upon his rights."[96] Consider also the following excerpt from Coppage v. Kansas, 236 U.S. 1 (1915).

As to the interest of the employed, it is said . . . to be a matter of common knowledge that "employés, as a rule, are not financially able to be as independent in making contracts for the sale of their labor as are employers in making contracts of purchase thereof." No doubt, wherever the right of private property exists, there must and will be inequalities of fortune; and thus it naturally happens that parties negotiating about a contract are not equally unhampered by circumstances. This applies to all contracts, and not merely to that between employer and employé. Indeed a little reflection will show that wherever the right of private property and the right of free contract co-exist, each party when contracting is inevitably more or less influenced by the question whether he has much property, or little, or none; for the contract is made to the very end that each may gain something that he needs or desires more urgently than that which he proposes to give in exchange. And, since it is self-evident that, unless all things are held in common, some persons must have more property than others, it is from the nature of things impossible to uphold freedom of contract and the right of private property without at the same time recognizing as legitimate those inequalities of fortune that are the necessary result of the exercise of those rights. But the Fourteenth Amendment, in declaring that a State shall not "deprive any person of life, liberty or property without due process of law," gives to each of these an equal sanction; it recognizes "liberty" and "property" as co-existent human rights, and debars the States from any unwarranted interference with either.

And since a State may not strike them down directly it is clear that it may not do so indirectly, as by declaring in effect that the public good requires the removal of those inequalities that are but the normal and inevitable result of their exercise, and then invoking the police power in order to remove the inequalities, without other object in view. The police power is broad, and not easily defined, but it cannot be given the wide scope that is here asserted for it, without in effect nullifying the constitutional guaranty.

We need not refer to the numerous and familiar cases in which this court has held that the power may properly be exercised for preserving the public health, safety, morals, or general welfare, and that such police regulations may reasonably limit the enjoyment of personal liberty, including the right of making contracts. . . . An evident and controlling distinction is this: that in those cases it has been held permissible for the States to adopt regulations fairly deemed necessary to secure some object directly affecting the public welfare, even though the enjoyment of private rights of liberty and property be thereby incidentally hampered; while in that portion of the Kansas statute which is now under consideration — that is to say, aside from coercion, etc. — there is no object or purpose, expressed or implied, that is claimed to have reference to health, safety, morals, or public welfare, beyond the supposed desirability of leveling inequalities of fortune by depriving one who has property of some part of what is characterized as his "financial independence." In short, an interference with the normal exercise of personal liberty and property rights is the primary object of the statute, and not an incident to the advancement of the general welfare.

96. Christopher Tiedeman, A Treatise on the Limitations of Police Power in the United States 8 (1886).

Can Muller v. Oregon, 208 U.S. 412 (1908), be distinguished from *Lochner* and *Coppage*? *Muller* upheld a statute limiting the workday of women in factories and laundries to ten hours. Justice Brewer wrote for the Court:

> That woman's physical structure and the performance of maternal functions place her at a disadvantage in the struggle for subsistence is obvious. This is especially true when the burdens of motherhood are upon her. Even when they are not, by abundant testimony of the medical fraternity continuance for a long time on her feet at work, repeating this from day to day, tends to injurious effects upon the body, and as healthy mothers are essential to vigorous offspring, the physical well-being of woman becomes an object of public interest and care in order to preserve the strength and vigor of the race.
>
> Still again, history discloses the fact that woman has always been dependent upon man. He established his control at the outset by superior physical strength, and this control in various forms, with diminishing intensity, has continued to the present. As minors, though not to the same extent, she has been looked upon in the courts as needing especial care that her rights may be preserved. Education was long denied her, and while now the doors of the school room are opened and her opportunities for acquiring knowledge are great, yet even with that and the consequent increase of capacity for business affairs it is still true that in the struggle for subsistence she is not an equal competitor with her brother. Though limitations upon personal and contractual rights may be removed by legislation, there is that in her disposition and habits of life which will operate against a full assertion of those rights. She will still be where some legislation to protect her seems necessary to secure a real equality of right. Doubtless there are individual exceptions, and there are many respects in which she has an advantage over him; but looking at it from the viewpoint of the effort to maintain an independent position in life, she is not upon an equality. Differentiated by these matters from the other sex, she is properly placed in a class by herself, and legislation designed for her protection may be sustained, even when like legislation is not necessary for men and could not be sustained. It is impossible to close one's eyes to the fact that she still looks to her brother and depends upon him. Even though all restrictions on political, personal and contractual rights were taken away, and she stood, so far as statutes are concerned, upon an absolutely equal plane with him, it would still be true that she is so constituted that she will rest upon and look to him for protection; that her physical structure and a proper discharge of her maternal functions — having in view not merely her own health, but the well-being of the race — justify legislation to protect her from the greed as well as the passion of man. The limitations which this statute places upon her contractual powers, upon her right to agree with her employer as to the time she shall labor, are not imposed solely for her benefit, but also largely for the benefit of all. Many words cannot make this plainer. The two sexes differ in structure of body, in the functions to be performed by each, in the amount of physical strength, in the capacity for long-continued labor, particularly when done standing, the influence of vigorous health upon the future well-being of the race, the self-reliance which enables one to assert full rights, and in the capacity to maintain the struggle for subsistence.

4.   *Burdens of Proof and Questions of Degree*

Justice Peckham considers whether the New York statute can be upheld as a regulation protecting the health of bakery employees or consumers in terms of the standard: "There [must] be some fair ground, reasonable in and of itself, to say that there is a material danger to the public health, or to the health of the employee, if the hours of labor are not curtailed." How does this differ, theoretically or in application, from Justice Harlan's criterion that the law must "have a real or substantial relation" to the promotion of health? Harlan sets out a number of facts about the health of bakers, to conclude that "there is room for debate and for an honest difference of opinion" whether long hours are injurious.[97] Peckham does not explicitly deny that there may be. On what basis, then, does the Court strike down the New York statute?

One possibility is that the majority and dissent apply essentially the same standard, but with different burdens of proof or with the burden of proof on different parties.

Another possibility, not inconsistent with the first, lies in their different concepts of the nature of permissible state regulation — of the "police power." If Peckham implicitly acknowledges that the difference between *Lochner* and the decision in Holden v. Hardy sustaining maximum hours for miners (from which he dissented) is one of degree, his opinion nevertheless has an air of categorizing occupations as intrinsically hazardous or not, rather than weighing or balancing along a continuum. Harlan's seems more pragmatically and empirically oriented.

Compare also the majority's and Justice Harlan's treatment of judicial deference to state legislation in *Lochner* with their positions in *Plessy*. What accounts for the apparent reversal of positions?

5. Laissez Faire, Lawyers, and Legal Scholarship

Opponents of nineteenth-century rate and labor regulations typically argued, in the language of traditional conservatism, that the rights of property were insecure in the hands of popularly controlled state legislatures. And they also invoked the laissez faire doctrines of the eighteenth-century economist Adam Smith and the nineteenth-century social Darwinists Herbert Spencer and William Graham Sumner.

Smith is the father of free market theory. In modern and much oversimplified terms, individuals are motivated by self-interest, which leads to competition in the marketplace, which regulates itself so as to produce just the right quantity and

---

97. In Muller v. Oregon, the Court relied on an abundance of similar data, contained in a 113-page brief filed by Louis Brandeis in support of Oregon's maximum-hour legislation for women. Justice Brewer wrote for the Court, upholding the law:

> In patent cases counsel are apt to open the argument with a discussion of the state of the art. It may not be amiss, in the present case, before examining the constitutional question, to notice the course of legislation as well as expressions of opinion from other than judicial sources. In the brief filed by Mr. Louis D. Brandeis, for the defendant in error, is a very copious collection of all these matters, an epitome of which is found in the margin.
>
> The legislation and opinions referred to in the margin may not be, technically speaking, authorities, and in them is little or no discussion of the constitutional question presented to us for determination, yet they are significant of a widespread belief that woman's physical structure, and the functions she performs in consequence thereof, justify special legislation restricting or qualifying the conditions under which she should be permitted to toil. Constitutional questions, it is true, are not settled by even a consensus of present public opinion, for it is the peculiar value of a written constitution that it places in unchanging form limitations upon legislative action, and thus gives a permanence and stability to popular government which otherwise would be lacking. At the same time, when a question of fact is debated and debatable, and the extent to which a special constitutional limitation goes is affected by the truth in respect to that fact, a widespread and long continued belief concerning it is worthy of consideration. We take cognizance of all matters of general knowledge.

Briefs of this sort have come to be called Brandeis briefs and have been submitted in a wide variety of cases.

98. "Efficiency" is, today, an economic term of art. An allocation of resources among individuals is efficient (or pareto-optimal) when no alternative distribution could make some individuals better off without

quality of goods and services demanded and to allocate them in the most efficient manner.[98] Government plays a legitimate role by providing public goods (e.g., armies and police), regulating monopolies, requiring activities to internalize the external costs they generate (e.g., by preventing or providing damage remedies for "nuisances"), and subsidizing activities (e.g., education) to the extent they produce external benefits. But government-operated enterprises and government intervention in the private sector generally are inefficient and undesirable, and government redistribution of income may subvert incentive and distort the market. Because efficient operation of the market depends on the ability of individuals and firms to transact freely with each other, government constraints on private contracting are especially destructive.

The social Darwinists provided an independent justification for government nonintervention and especially for inequalities of wealth. From the process of natural selection, Herbert Spencer, an Englishman, derived the notion that only the "fittest" ought to survive. His Social Statics (1850) argued against public education, health and safety regulations (except to prevent nuisances), medical licensing, and welfare. Those "sufficiently complete to live . . . *do* live, and it is well that they should live. If they are not sufficiently complete to live, they die, and it is best that they should die." The destitute are "unfit" and "the whole effort of nature is to get rid of such, to clear the world of them, and make room for better."[99] Sumner, a professor of sociology at Yale, brought Spencer's social theory and policy to America with a vengeance:[100] "Let it be understood that we cannot go outside of this alternative: liberty, inequality, survival of the fittest; not-liberty, equality, survival of the unfittest. The former carries society forward and favors all its best members; the latter carries society downwards and favors all its worst members." Laissez faire economics and social Darwinism were in vogue among American intellectuals in the mid-nineteenth century. But opposition to both the pure theories and their social implications began to arise among economists, sociologists, theologians, and statesmen. By the close of the nineteenth century, the notion of the purely negative state was giving way to a different view of the role of government. An advocate of the positive state writes:[101]

> Those who advocated a policy of laissez faire in the years after the Civil War seemingly were conforming to the best traditions of European and American liberalism. . . . Since liberalism originated essentially as a protest against an authoritarian order in religion, politics, and economics, it was at the outset a purely negative faith, one aimed at removing the artificial restrictions that blocked human progress. Thus, with respect to government and economics, it became associated with laissez faire and economic freedom. In a complex industrial society, however, if the liberal objectives of individual freedom and equality of opportunity are to be realized it becomes necessary to extend the sphere of social control. The result has been that liberalism, which started out as an essentially negative creed designed to do away with obstructions to individual

making at least one worse off. Conversely, an allocation is inefficient or suboptimal when some individuals could be made better off by a different allocation without making anyone worse off.

99. Herbert Spencer, Social Statics 414-15 (1850).

100. 2 Essays of William Graham Sumner 56 (Keller & Davie eds., 1934).

101. Sidney Fine, Laissez Faire and the General Welfare State 30-32 (1956).

progress, "has developed as a positive effort to better man's estate by constructive action."

Those who in the industrial order that was emerging in the United States after the Civil War continued to advocate the laissez-faire brand of liberalism tended to establish economic freedom as an end in itself rather than as a means to an end, and were out of harmony with the true spirit of liberalism. They were blind to the compelling necessity for social and economic reform and refused to recognize that some positive action on the part of the state was essential to assure the effective liberty of the individual. Laissez faire in the years after 1865 was the doctrine of the conservatives.

Classical liberalism suited the needs of the corporate bar, and a reactionary spirit pervaded the two most important constitutional law texts of the period — Thomas M. Cooley's A Treatise on the Constitutional Limitations Which Rest upon the Legislative Power of the States of the American Union (1868) and Christopher G. Tiedeman's A Treatise on the Limitations of Police Power in the United States (1886).

The central thesis of both texts was that the regulatory power of the states — the so-called police power — was narrowly circumscribed by fundamental law and written constitutions. The thesis was ahistorical. In the early Republic, when most constitutions had been adopted, the bounds of government regulation had been amorphous and broad. If Locke's theory of the state implied a narrow concept of the public good, Americans (no less than others, and no less than now) picked and chose and often ignored their philosophers. In opposition to Locke, there was Hobbes's expansive notion of the salus populi — the welfare of the people — and a tradition of government regulation going back to the colonies and England. The states had long intervened in the private sector to regulate the prices of labor and commodities and to protect consumers against unhealthy products and fraudulent merchant practices.[102] But Cooley and Tiedeman, with the characteristic dogmatism of treatise writers, asserted that their views were "the law."

Tiedeman argued that the police power could be used only to enforce the maxim "sic utere tuo ut alienum non laedas" — use your own property so as not to injure another's — and to protect public health and morality. He and Cooley agreed that "class legislation" (for example, laws aiding an employee against his employer) and legislation interfering with an individual's freedom to make contracts were plainly beyond the scope of legislative power.

6. A Survey of the Court's Work[103]

Between 1890 and 1934, the Supreme Court struck down some 200 statutory and administrative regulations, mostly under the due process clause of the Fourteenth

---

102. See Lawrence Friedman, A History of American Law 65-71, 161-163 (1973); Oscar Handlin, Commonwealth: A Study of the Role of Government in the American Economy: Massachusetts, 1774-1861 (rev. ed. 1969); Louis Hartz, Economic Policy and Democratic Thought: Pennsylvania, 1776-1860 (1948).

103. See generally William Swindler, Court and Constitution in the Twentieth Century: The Old Legality, 1889-1932 (1969); Benjamin Wright, The Growth of American Constitutional Law 153-168 (1942); The Constitution of the United States of America, Analysis and Interpretation 1602-1612, 1643-1709 (Lib. of Cong. rev. ed. 1973). For a sympathetic analysis of the economics of substantive due process, see Richard Posner, Economic Analysis of Law ch. 19 (1973); cf. Milton Friedman, Capitalism and Freedom (1962); Harold Demsetz, Minorities in the Market Place, 43 N.C. L. Rev. 271 (1965).

Amendment. The received history tends to exaggerate the Court's perverseness, however, just as it minimizes the facts that the Court sustained at least as many regulations as it invalidated, that it declined to review many others, and that Holmes and Brandeis — the progressive heroes of the period — did not invariably dissent from substantive due process invalidations or always agree with each other.[104] The Court was considerably more restrained than some of the state supreme courts, and though it certainly never "judged social legislation on the basis of any consistent pattern of ideas which can properly bear the name of an economic theory,"[105] its decisions gain some coherence if one reads them in the context of the ideologies of the times.[106] The Court let stand most laws that appeared to protect the health, safety, or morals of the general public or to prevent consumer deception. The few exceptions usually involved extraordinarily burdensome regulations where less onerous ones would have served substantially as well. E.g., Jay Burns Baking Co. v. Bryan, 264 U.S. 504 (1924) (law requiring precisely standardized weight for bread loaves), and Weaver v. Palmer Bros. Co., 270 U.S. 402 (1926) (law forbidding use of shoddy in quilts). The Court continued to permit government regulation of rates of railroads and public utilities. But it reviewed the reasonableness of these rates and narrowed the concept of "affected with a public interest" to restrict the kinds of businesses that were subject to price regulation of any sort. Legislatures could not set maximum charges for the resale of theater tickets, Tyson & Brother v. Banton, 273 U.S. 418 (1927); for services of an employment agency, Ribnik v. McBride, 277 U.S. 350 (1928); or for the sale of gasoline, Williams v. Standard Oil Co., 278 U.S. 235 (1929). These interferences with the free market were held unwarranted by monopoly power or any other compelling factor.

In the area of labor relations, the Court distinguished *Lochner* in sustaining the limitation of women's working hours in Muller v. Oregon, 208 U.S. 412 (1908), and disregarded *Lochner* in sustaining a ten-hour maximum workday for male factory employees in Bunting v. Oregon, 243 U.S. 426 (1917). But in Adair v. United States, 208 U.S. 161 (1908), and Coppage v. Kansas, 236 U.S. 1 (1915), the Court held that yellow dog contracts could not be outlawed. And in Adkins v. Children's Hospital, 261 U.S. 525 (1923), it invalidated a District of Columbia minimum wage law for women, noting, inter alia, that the Nineteenth Amendment (1920) had reduced the civil inferiority of women almost "to the vanishing point." Justice Holmes dissented in *Adkins*, stating:

> I confess that I do not understand the principle on which the power to fix a minimum for the wages of women can be denied by those who admit the power to fix a maximum for their hours of work. . . . The bargain is equally affected whichever half you regulate. . . . It will need more than the Nineteenth Amendment to convince me that there are no differences between men and women, or that legislation cannot take those differences into account.

104. Note, however, that the practice of writing dissenting opinions was much less common than it is today. Many justices dissented only if they were strongly opposed to a decision, and, having noted their disagreement in the first decision to establish a doctrine, they often acquiesced in its subsequent applications.

105. Lawrence Friedman, Freedom of Contract and Occupational Licensing, 1890-1910, 53 Calif. L. Rev. 487, 525 (1965).

106. See Howard Gillman, The Constitution Besieged: The Rise and Demise of Lochner Era Police Powers Jurisprudence (1993).

But the Court believed that there was a real difference between maximum hour and minimum wage laws. The former looked like regulations promoting health, a legitimate objective. Minimum wage laws, like laws prohibiting yellow dog contracts, seemed obviously designed to readjust the market in favor of one party to the contract — and this was entirely at odds with the underlying principle of laissez faire.

C. Freedom of Contract and the Problem of "Involuntary Servitude"

In *Nothing but Freedom*, historian Eric Foner notes that all societies that have ended slavery have struggled over the extent of actual freedom to be enjoyed by the newly emancipated slaves.[107] The title of his book is taken from the comment, by Confederate General Robert V. Richardson, that "[t]he emancipated slaves own nothing, because nothing but freedom has been given to them."[108] Suggestions by blacks and some of the so-called Radical Reconstructionists that the former slaves be given at least "40 acres and a mule" to embark on their new lives were rejected. For example, Horace Greeley, the editor of the New York Tribune who fancied himself an avid opponent of slavery, dismissed the agitation for confiscation of slaveholders' land and redistribution to former slaves as "either knavery or madness:" "People who want farms work for them. The only class we know that takes other people's property because they want it is largely represented in Sing Sing."

Thus, Southern blacks were relegated to the market with no resources besides their own labor, which white employers sought to control and exploit. The notorious Black Codes, enacted by many Southern states immediately after the Civil War, established new modes of discipline over the black labor force. For example, Mississippi required that every January all blacks be able to present written evidence of their employment for the next year, and also empowered all white persons to arrest any blacks who left the service of their employers.[109] The Civil Rights Act of 1866 formally invalidated the Black Codes, but the struggle over control of the labor force continued. Pete Daniel, the leading authority on the history of peonage, explains:

> Lacking land or capital of their own, blacks had little choice but to sign yearly contracts. . . . As military control became less strict in the South, a labor pattern emerged. Most blacks signed annual contracts. Improvident, they took advances on their expected share of the crop. When settlement time came the next fall, the laborers often discovered that their share of the crop did not cover what they owed the supply merchant or the planter. . . . [S]ome planters demanded that workers remain until they had worked out their entire debt, and when planters used indebtedness as an instrument of compulsion, the system became peonage.[110]

---

107. Eric Foner, Nothing but Freedom: Emancipation and Its Legacy (1983).
108. Id. at 55.
109. To put this in perspective, as late as 1875 English law enforced criminal penalties for breach of contract. Id. at 49, 51.
110. Pete Daniel, The Shadow of Slavery: Peonage in the South 1901-1969, 19-20 (1972). See also Daniel, The Metamorphosis of Slavery, 1865-1900, 66 J. Am. Hist. 88 (1979).

Foner and Daniel both indicate that peonage depended on the formal mechanism of contract, supplemented by the use of the criminal law to punish its breach. In 1911 this practice finally came before the Supreme Court, which struck it down, *Bailey v. Alabama*, 219 U.S. 219. Writing for the Court, Justice Hughes insisted that "[w]e at once dismiss from consideration the fact that the plaintiff in error is a black man. . . . The statute, on its face, makes no racial discrimination, and the record fails to show its existence in fact. No question of a sectional character is presented, and we may view the legislation in the same manner as if it had been enacted in New York or in Idaho." That being said, the majority condemned peonage as well within the "involuntary servitude" banned by the Thirteenth Amendment.

Justice Holmes, joined by Justice Lurton, dissented. The premise "that this case is to be considered and decided in the same way as if it arose in Idaho or New York" for them entailed "that in Alabama it mainly concerns the blacks does not matter." Holmes argued that the case concerned simply the application of an evidentiary presumption, that the failure to comply with an employment contract could be treated as evidence of an intent to defraud at the time the contract was signed.

> The Thirteenth Amendment does not outlaw contracts for labor. . . . If the contract is one that ought not to be made, prohibit it. But if it is a perfectly fair and proper contract, I can see no reason why the State should not throw its weight on the side of performance. . . . I think it a mistake to say that this statute attaches its punishment to the mere breach of a contract to labor. It does not purport to do so; what it purports to punish is fraudulently obtaining money by a false pretense of an intent to keep the written contract in consideration of which the money is advanced. . . . But the import of the statute is supposed to be changed by the provision that a refusal to perform, coupled with a failure to return the money advanced, shall be prima facie evidence of fraudulent intent. I agree that if the statute created a conclusive presumption it might be held to make a disguised change in the substantive law. But it only makes the conduct prima facie evidence, a very different matter. Is it not evidence that a man had a fraudulent intent if he receives an advance upon a contract over night and leaves in the morning? I should have thought that it very plainly was. Of course the statute is in general terms and applies to a departure at any time without excuse or repayment, but that does no harm except on a tacit assumption that this law is not administered as it would be in New York, and that juries will act with prejudice against the laboring man. For prima facie evidence is only evidence, and as such may be held by the jury insufficient to make out guilt. This being so, I take it that a fair jury would acquit, if the only evidence were a departure after eleven months' work, and if it received no color from some special well-known course of events. But the matter well may be left to a jury, because their experience as men of the world may teach them that in certain conditions it is so common for laborers to remain during a part of the season, receiving advances, and then to depart at the period of need in the hope of greater wages at a neighboring plantation, that when a laborer follows that course there is a fair inference of fact that he intended it from the beginning. The Alabama statute, as construed by the state court and as we must take it, merely says, as a court might say, that the prosecution may go to the jury. . . . The right of the State to regulate laws of evidence is admitted, and the statute does not go much beyond the common law.
>
>   . . . To sum up, I think that obtaining money by fraud may be made a crime as well as murder or theft; that a false representation, expressed or implied, at the time of making a contract of labor that one intends to perform it and thereby obtaining an advance, may be declared a case of fraudulently obtaining money as well as any other; that if made a crime it may be punished like any other crime, and that an unjustified

departure from the promised service without repayment may be declared a sufficient case to go to the jury for their judgment; all without in any way infringing the Thirteenth Amendment or the statutes of the United States.

Several years after *Bailey*, in United States v. Reynolds, 235 U.S. 133 (1914), the Court unanimously struck down Alabama's criminal surety system. The Alabama Code authorized a person to appear as a surety for a defendant convicted of a misdemeanor and pay his fine in exchange for the defendant's entering into an employment contract to repay the surety: The defendant thus avoided imprisonment, but was subject to damages and another conviction if he broke the contract. Of course, the defendant could avoid serving time for breach of the surety contract by entering into a contract with another surety. Reynolds's first labor contract was for 10 months (compared to the 2 months he would have had to spend at hard labor in prison). The second contract bound him for 20 months (compared to less than 4 months of prison labor). As Justice Day described the cycle in his opinion for the Court, "the convict is thus kept chained to an ever-turning wheel of servitude to discharge the obligation which he has incurred to his surety." The criminal surety system was part of a larger scheme designed to provide white employers with cheap black labor:

> If there is no white man to pay him out, or if his crime is too serious to be paid out, he goes to the chain-gang — and in several states he is thus hired out to private contractors. The private employer then gets him sooner or later. Some of the largest farms in the South are operated by chain-gang labor. The demand for more convicts by white employers is exceedingly strong. . . . The natural tendency . . . is to convict as many Negroes as possible, and to punish the offences charged as severely as possible.[111]

The sureties in *Reynolds* were charged with violating a federal statute, enacted pursuant to the Thirteenth Amendment, that prohibited enforcing "the voluntary or involuntary service or labor of any persons as peons, in liquidation of any debt or obligation." Striking down the Alabama criminal surety system presented a problem for the Court. Benno Schmidt explains:

> The Court was not prepared to cast doubt on the legality of convict leasing, which was also characterized by forced servitude for private masters, often under barbarous conditions. Moreover, there could be nothing wrong with contracts whereby convicts got the money to pay fines and escape imprisonment. Finally, the state's enforcement of the obligations of such contracts by its criminal law undoubtedly increased the opportunities for convicts to make such agreements. . . . But looked at as a whole, with the distorting effects of racism in the system of law enforcement and the history of black forced labor given their due, the Alabama criminal-surety system stood as a major support of involuntary servitude. The Court could not know this, however, or at least it could not claim that it did. The court had no knowledge about criminal justice system in operation; it had only the indictments . . . before it.[112]

---

111. Ray Stannard Baker, Following the Color Line 98 (1964).

112. Benno C. Schmidt, Jr., Principle and Prejudice: The Supreme Court and Race in the Progressive Era, Part 2: The *Peonage Cases*, 82 Colum. L. Rev. 646, 699 (1982).

Justice Day approached the problem by noting that the convict had not been rearrested for failing to pay the fine and costs assessed by the State — for the surety had erased that debt. Instead, he had been arrested and convicted for violating his contract with the surety. The Court concluded that forcing the convict to work to repay the debt under the constant threat of another arrest and eventual imprisonment qualified as involuntary servitude. In a brief concurring opinion, Justice Holmes wrote:

> There seems to me nothing in the Thirteenth Amendment of the Revised Statutes that prevents a State from making a breach of contract, as well a reasonable contract for labor as for other matters, a crime and punishing it as such. But impulsive people with little intelligence or foresight may be expected to lay hold of anything that affords a relief from present pain, even though it will cause greater trouble by and by. The successive contracts, each for a longer term than the last, are the inevitable, and must be taken to have been the contemplated outcome of the Alabama laws. On this ground I am inclined to agree that the statutes in question disclose the attempt to maintain service that the Revised Statutes forbid.[113]

In Principle and Prejudice, Benno Schmidt places *Bailey* and the problem of involuntary servitude within the general context of contract theory:[114]

> Does the *Bailey* decision put forward a plausible constitutional theory, indicating, as both Hughes and Holmes insisted, that the racial aspect of peonage should be ignored? Or should the decision be understood as a doctrinally disguised response to the continuing legacy of forced labor for blacks in the South? Answers to these questions are elusive, but are nonetheless of first importance in appraising the Supreme Court's work during the Progressive era. If *Bailey* is credible in its professions of race-neutrality and its attempt to ground its constitutional doctrine in "the freedom of labor," it belongs where it is virtually never placed by students of constitutional history, in the camp of decisions, such as *Lochner, Adair,* and *Coppage,* that based rights and legislative inhibitions on the labor contract, and that made freedom of contract theory the backbone of laissez-faire constitutionalism. *Bailey* is an unsettling presence among these warhorses of substantive due process, both conceptually and as a revelation of judicial attitudes. How could a Court devoted to freedom of contract find in the thirteenth amendment a freedom from strict enforcement of contract? To this day, there hovers over the freedom of contract cases the odor of class bias or, at least, benighted indifference to the cruel realities of the laborer's bargaining power in an industrial society. Yet *Bailey's* protection of workers from airtight enforcement of their labor

---

113. In two other cases, the Court declined to strike down government practices challenged under the Thirteenth Amendment. The appellant in Butler v. Perry, 240 U.S. 328 (1916), was convicted under a Florida law that required males between 21 and 45 either to work for six ten-hour days on roads and bridges each year or to avoid the task by providing an able-bodied substitute or paying $3 per day to the county road and bridge fund. Writing for a unanimous Court, Justice McReynolds wrote that the Thirteenth Amendment was not designed to end the ancient tradition of requiring residents to provide labor for road upkeep: "The great purpose in view was liberty under the protection of effective government, not the destruction of the latter by depriving it of essential powers." In the Selective Draft Law Cases, 245 U.S. 366, 390 (1918), the Court upheld the Selective Draft Law of 1917: "[W]e are unable to conceive upon what theory the exaction by government from the citizen of the performance of his supreme and noble duty of contributing to the defense of the rights and honor of the nation . . . can be said to be the imposition of involuntary servitude in violation of the prohibitions of the Thirteenth Amendment."

114. Schmidt, at 702-703. See also Schmidt's interesting discussion of the "contradiction between freedom and obligation that lies at the heart of the theory of freedom of contract." Should one's contract voluntarily placing oneself in the position of a slave be enforced?

115. Id. at 705-713.

contracts is a constitutional profession on behalf of free labor that is wholly out of sympathy with the interest of employers in having an effective legal deterrent to breach of labor contracts on farms and plantations, where constancy of labor may be critical in the planting and harvest seasons. As such, it supports the sincerity, if not the realism, of the protestations of worker-interest that mark many of the substantive due process decisions generally thought to be most damaging to the welfare of working people. On the other hand, if *Bailey* is viewed as a result-oriented response to the exploitation of black workers, it marks an instance of vigorous legal realism that sheds light both on the White Court's style of judicial statecraft and on its attitudes toward racial justice.[115]

IV. Congressional Regulation of Interstate Commerce and of the National Economy

Before the Civil War, the focus of adjudication under the commerce clause was the validity of state regulation of commerce when Congress was silent. This continued to be a staple of the Court's docket throughout the nineteenth century and much of the twentieth, and we shall return to doctrines under the "dormant" commerce clause in the next chapter. Of more interest in the post-War period, however, is adjudication over the scope of *Congress's* legislative powers — an issue scarcely confronted by the Court since *McCulloch*.[116] An early case illustrates the application to federal regulation of concepts developed in the state regulation-of-commerce cases of the Marshall and Taney eras. In United States v. DeWitt, 76 U.S. (9 Wall.) 41 (1869), Chief Justice Chase wrote for a unanimous Court, holding that a congressional safety regulation prohibiting the sale of highly combustible illuminating oils lay beyond the congressional power:

> [T]he express grant of power to regulate commerce among the States has always been understood as limited by its terms; and as a virtual denial of any power to interfere with the internal trade and business of the separate States. . . . [The illuminating oil law] is a regulation of police. . . . As a police regulation, relating exclusively to the internal trade of the States, it can only have effect where the legislative authority of Congress excludes, territorially, all State legislation, as for example, in the District of Columbia. Within State limits, it can have no constitutional operation.

The law struck down in *DeWitt* was a minor and isolated congressional attempt to use the commerce power to regulate trade. Only toward the end of the nineteenth century, with the Interstate Commerce Act of 1887 and the Sherman Antitrust Act of 1890, did Congress begin to intervene significantly in the burgeoning interstate economy. The Supreme Court's response was mixed and paralleled its reaction to state social and economic legislation in many respects. Almost anything connected with railroads was held to be within Congress's power.[117] For example, in Southern Railway v. United States, 22 U.S. 20 (1911), the Court upheld the Federal Safety

---

116. Marbury v. Madison and Dred Scott v. Sandford both invalidated congressional statutes, but neither involved the major Article I powers of commerce, taxing, and spending.

117. In Railroads and Regulation, 1877-1916 (1965), Gabriel Kolko argues that the railroads welcomed national rate regulation as a means of curbing competition.

Appliance Acts as applied to railroad cars with defective couplers moving solely within a state, noting that railroads are "highways of both interstate and intrastate commerce" and that "whatever brings delay or disaster to one [train], or results in disabling one of its operatives, is calculated to impede the progress and imperil the safety of other trains." On the same theory, the Court sustained congressional regulation of the hours of employees working on the intrastate operations of railroads that also conducted interstate operations. Baltimore & Ohio Railroad Co. v. Interstate Commerce Commission, 221 U.S. 612 (1911). And in the *Shreveport Rate* case, Houston, E. & W.T. Ry. v. United States, 234 U.S. 342 (1914), the Court held that the Interstate Commerce Commission (ICC) could prohibit railroads from charging lower rates for transportation within Texas than the rates set by the ICC for identical distances between Texas and other states.

Judicial doctrine under the Sherman Act was more complex.[118] In the first decision under the Act, United States v. E.C. Knight Co., 156 U.S. 1 (1895) (the *Sugar Trust* case), the Court dismissed an action brought under the Sherman Act to set aside the American Sugar Refining Company's acquisition of four other sugar refining companies. Chief Justice Fuller wrote: "It is vital that the independence of the commercial power and of the police power . . . should always be recognized and observed, for while the one furnishes the strongest bond of the union, the other is essential to the preservation of the autonomy of the States." American already produced 65 percent of the sugar refined in the United States, and acquisition of the companies would give it 98 percent of the market. But the power to prevent a monopoly in "manufacture," as distinguished from the "commerce" that follows manufacture, belonged exclusively to the states.

Three doctrinal issues recur throughout the cases of this period. One, suggested by the *Sugar Trust* case, is whether the particular *subject* of congressional regulation is "interstate commerce" as distinguished from some local activity.

Second, are the *purposes* of a regulation consistent with the purposes for which Congress was delegated the power to regulate interstate commerce? Recall, in this respect, Marshall's "pretext" statement in *McCulloch:* "[S]hould congress, under the pretext of executing its powers, pass laws for the accomplishment of objects not intrusted to the government, it would become the painful duty of this tribunal to say that such an act was not the law of the land." By way of elaboration on Marshall's point, consider these points: (1) General legislative authority resides in the states. (2) Lawmaking authority is delegated to the national government to achieve certain objectives. (3) There is no justification for exercising authority beyond the scope of the purposes for which it is given.

The last statement may seem to beg the question. Yet this notion is taken for granted and applied widely outside of the area of constitutional law. Consider the consequences if government officials, private trustees, and ordinary individuals — who constantly act under authorization from others — were bound only by the substantive terms of a delegation, not by the purposes for which it was made. Consider, indeed, how often an agent's pursuit of objectives beyond those underlying the delegation is a ground for criticism and even the imposition of civil and criminal penalties. For example, a trustee who administers assets in order to injure

---

118. See Lawrence Friedman, A History of American Law 407-408 (1973); Charles McCurdy, The Knight Sugar Decision of 1895 and the Modernization of American Corporation Law, 1869-1903, 53 Bus. Hist. Rev. 304 (1979).

the beneficiary or to aid a third party without regard to the beneficiary's interests may be held liable; while another trustee, whose objective conduct is no different but who acted in good faith, may not be chargeable. If the concept of ultra vires action — action outside the scope of authority — is generally concerned with purposes as well as the operative terms of the delegation, should it be different in the case of constitutional delegations of power?

The third recurring issue of the period is whether, independent of the first or second issues, a particular instance of congressional regulation of interstate commerce runs afoul of the reservation of powers to the states recognized by the Tenth Amendment. In *McCulloch*, Marshall asserted that the Tenth Amendment was a tautology. During the period considered in this section, however, the Court treated it as at least the symbol, if not the source, of what Edward Corwin called the doctrine of "dual federalism" — the view that "the coexistence of the states and their powers is itself a limitation upon national power," which restricts Congress's use of the delegated powers to purposes and results that are not reserved to the states.[119]

CHAMPION v. AMES
[The *Lottery* Case]
188 U.S. 321 (1903)

[An 1895 congressional act prohibited sending lottery tickets through the mails, or from one state to another by any means. Appellants were indicted for conspiring to transport tickets of the Pan-American Lottery Company (based in Asunción, Paraguay) from Texas to California, shipping them by railroad with Wells Fargo Express Co. They challenged the indictment on constitutional grounds.]

HARLAN, J. . . .

The appellant insists that the carrying of lottery tickets from one State to another State by an express company engaged in carrying freight and packages from State to State, although such tickets may be contained in a box or package, does not constitute, and cannot by any act of Congress be legally made to constitute, *commerce* among the States within the meaning of the clause of the Constitution. . . .

The Government insists that express companies when engaged, for hire, in the business of transportation from one State to another, are instrumentalities of commerce among the States; that the carrying of lottery tickets from one State to another is commerce which Congress may regulate; and that as a means of executing the power to regulate interstate commerce Congress may make it an offence against the United States to cause lottery tickets to be carried from one State to another.

The questions presented by these opposing contentions are of great moment, and are entitled to receive, as they have received, the most careful consideration.

What is the import of the word "commerce" as used in the Constitution? It is not defined by that instrument. Undoubtedly, the carrying from one State to another by independent carriers of things or commodities that are ordinary subjects of traffic, and which have in themselves a recognized value in money, constitutes interstate commerce. . . .

---

119. Edward Corwin, Congress' Power to Prohibit Commerce, 18 Cornell L.Q. 477, 482 (1933) (emphasis omitted).

It was said in argument that lottery tickets are not of any real or substantial value in themselves, and therefore are not subjects of commerce. If that were conceded to be the only legal test as to what are to be deemed subjects of the commerce that may be regulated by Congress, we cannot accept as accurate the broad statement that such tickets are of no value. Upon their face they showed that the lottery company offered a large capital prize, to be paid to the holder of the ticket winning the prize at the drawing advertised to be held at Asunción, Paraguay. . . .

But it is said that the statute in question does not regulate the carrying of lottery tickets from State to State, but by punishing those who cause them to be so carried Congress in effect prohibits such carrying; that in respect of the carrying from one State to another of articles or things that are, in fact, or according to usage in business, the subjects of commerce, the authority given Congress was not to *prohibit*, but only to *regulate*. This view was earnestly pressed at the bar by learned counsel, and must be examined. . . .

In determining whether regulation may not under some circumstances properly take the form or have the effect of prohibition, the nature of the interstate traffic which it was sought by the act of May 2, 1895, to suppress cannot be overlooked. When enacting that statute Congress no doubt shared the views upon the subject of lotteries heretofore expressed by this court. In Phalen v. Virginia, 8 How. 163, 168, after observing that the suppression of nuisances injurious to public health or morality is among the most important duties of Government, this court said: "Experience has shown that the common forms of gambling are comparatively innocuous when placed in contrast with the widespread pestilence of lotteries. The former are confined to a few persons and places, but the latter infests the whole community; it enters every dwelling; it reaches every class; it preys upon the hard earnings of the poor; it plunders the ignorant and simple." In other cases we have adjudged that authority given by legislative enactment to carry on a lottery, although based upon a consideration in money, was not protected by the contract clause of the Constitution; this, for the reason that no State may bargain away its power to protect the public morals, nor excuse its failure to perform a public duty by saying that it had agreed, by legislative enactment, not to do so. Stone v. Mississippi, 101 U.S. 814; Douglas v. Kentucky, 168 U.S. 488.

If a State, when considering legislation for the suppression of lotteries within its own limits, may properly take into view the evils that inhere in the raising of money, in that mode, why may not Congress, invested with the power to regulate commerce among the several States, provide that such commerce shall not be polluted by the carrying of lottery tickets from one State to another? In this connection it must not be forgotten that the power of Congress to regulate commerce among the States is plenary, is complete in itself, and is subject to no limitations except such as may be found in the Constitution. What provision in that instrument can be regarded as limiting the exercise of the power granted? . . .

If it be said that the act of 1895 is inconsistent with the Tenth Amendment, reserving to the States respectively or to the people the powers not delegated to the United States, the answer is that the power to regulate commerce among the States has been expressly delegated to Congress.

Besides, Congress, by that act, does not assume to interfere with traffic or commerce in lottery tickets carried on exclusively within the limits of any State, but has in view only commerce of that kind among the several States. It has not assumed to interfere with the completely internal affairs of any State, and has only legislated in respect of a matter which concerns the people of the United States. As a State may, for the purpose of guarding the morals of its own people, forbid all sales of lottery tickets within its limits, so Congress, for the purpose of guarding the people of the United States against the "widespread pestilence of lotteries" and to protect the commerce which concerns all the States, may prohibit the carrying of lottery tickets from one State to another. In legislating upon the subject of the traffic in lottery tickets, as carried on through interstate commerce, Congress only supplemented the action of those States — perhaps all of them — which, for the protection of the public morals, prohibit the drawing of lotteries, as well as the sale or circulation of lottery tickets, within their respective limits. It said, in effect, that it would not permit the declared policy of the States, which sought to protect their people against the mischiefs of the lottery business, to be overthrown or disregarded by the agency of interstate commerce. We should hesitate long before adjudging that an evil of such appalling character, carried on through interstate commerce, cannot be met and crushed by the only power competent to that end. We say competent to that end, because Congress alone has the power to occupy, by legislation, the whole field of interstate commerce. . . .

FULLER, C.J., joined by Brewer, Shiras, and Peckham, JJ., dissenting. . . .

The power of the State to impose restraints and burdens on persons and property in conservation and promotion of the public health, good order and prosperity is a power originally and always belonging to the States, not surrendered by them to the General Government nor directly restrained by the Constitution of the United States, and essentially exclusive, and the suppression of lotteries as a harmful business falls within this power, commonly called of police. Douglas v. Kentucky, 168 U.S. 488.

It is urged, however, that because Congress is empowered to regulate commerce between the several States, it, therefore, may suppress lotteries by prohibiting the carriage of lottery matter. Congress may indeed make all laws necessary and proper for carrying the powers granted to it into execution, and doubtless an act prohibiting the carriage of lottery matter would be necessary and proper to the execution of a power to suppress lotteries; but that power belongs to the States and not to Congress. To hold that Congress has general police power would be to hold that it may accomplish objects not entrusted to the General Government, and to defeat the operation of the Tenth Amendment. . . .

But apart from the question of bona fides, this act cannot be brought within the power to regulate commerce among the several States, unless lottery tickets are articles of commerce, and, therefore, when carried across state lines, of interstate commerce; or unless the power to regulate interstate commerce includes the absolute and exclusive power to prohibit the transportation of anything or anybody from one State to another. . . .

Is the carriage of lottery tickets from one State to another commercial intercourse? The lottery ticket purports to create contractual relations and to furnish the means of enforcing a contract right.

This is true of insurance policies, and both are contingent in their nature. Yet this court has held that the issuing of fire, marine, and life insurance policies, in one State, and sending them to another, to be there delivered to the insured on payment of premium, is not interstate commerce. Paul v. Virginia, 8 Wall. 168; Hooper v. California, 155 U.S. 648; New York Life Insurance Company v. Cravens, 178 U.S. 389.

In Paul v. Virginia, Mr. Justice Field, in delivering the unanimous opinion of the court, said: "Issuing a policy of insurance is not a transaction of commerce. The policies are simple contracts of indemnity against loss by fire, entered into between the corporations and the assured, for a consideration paid by the latter. These contracts are not articles of commerce in any proper meaning of the word. They are not subjects of trade and barter offered in the market as something having an existence and value independent of the parties to them. They are not commodities to be shipped or forwarded from one State to another, and then put up for sale. They are like other personal contracts between parties which are completed by their signature and the transfer of the consideration. Such contracts are not inter-state transactions, though the parties may be domiciled in different States. The policies do not take effect — are not executed contracts — until delivered by the agent in Virginia. They are, then, local transactions, and are governed by the local law. They do not constitute a part of the commerce between the States any more than a contract for the purchase and sale of goods in Virginia by a citizen of New York whilst in Virginia would constitute a portion of such commerce." . . .

If a lottery ticket is not an article of commerce, how can it become so when placed in an envelope or box or other covering, and transported by an express company? To say that the mere carrying of an article which is not an article of commerce in and of itself nevertheless becomes such the moment it is to be trans-ported from one State to another, is to transform a non-commercial article into a commercial one simply because it is transported. I cannot conceive that any such result can properly follow.

It would be to say that everything is an article of commerce the moment it is taken to be transported from place to place, and of interstate commerce if from State to State.

An invitation to dine, or to take a drive, or a note of introduction, all become articles of commerce under the ruling in this case, by being deposited with an express company for transportation. This in effect breaks down all the differences between that which is, and that which is not, an article of commerce, and the neces-sary consequence is to take from the States all jurisdiction over the subject so far as interstate communication is concerned. It is a long step in the direction of wiping out all traces of state lines, and the creation of a centralized Government. . . .

The Constitution gives no countenance to the theory that Congress is vested with the full powers of the British Parliament, and that, although subject to constitu-tional limitations, it is the sole judge of their extent and application; and the deci-sions of this court from the beginning have been to the contrary.

"To what purpose are powers limited, and to what purpose is that limitation committed to writing, if these limits may, at any time, be passed by those intended to be restrained?" asked Marshall, in Marbury v. Madison.

"Should Congress," said the same great magistrate in McCulloch v. Maryland, "under the pretext of executing its powers, pass laws for the accomplishment of objects not entrusted to the Government; it would become the painful duty of this tribunal, should a case requiring such a decision come before it, to say that such an act was not the law of the land."

Does the grant to Congress of the power to regulate interstate commerce impart the absolute power to prohibit it? . . .

The power to prohibit the transportation of diseased animals and infected goods over railroads or on steamboats is an entirely different thing [from the prohibition of lottery tickets], for they would be in themselves injurious to the transaction of interstate commerce, and, moreover, are essentially commercial in their nature. And the exclusion of diseased persons rests on different ground, for nobody would pretend that persons could be kept off the trains because they were going from one State to another to engage in the lottery business. However enticing that business may be, we do not understand these pieces of paper themselves can communicate bad principles by contact. . . .

Discussion

1. *The commerce power vs. the "police power."* How do Fuller's and Harlan's views of federal and state powers relate to the views of the Marshall and Taney periods? Would Fuller or Harlan permit a state to prohibit the importation of lottery tickets in the absence of congressional legislation?

How do the Justices' conceptions of the police power relate to their conceptions of the police power in *Lochner?* (Note that Justice Harlan, who dissented in *Lochner,* wrote for the majority in the *Lottery* case, and that Justice Peckham, who wrote for the Court in *Lochner,* was among the dissenters in the *Lottery* case.)

2. *"Pretext."* In the penultimate paragraph of his dissent, Fuller quotes Marshall's "pretext" statement in *McCulloch,* implying that the *purposes* underlying the act are not those for which the commerce power was granted. Why not? Would Fuller's position be stronger if, contrary to the Court's assertion, most states permitted the sale of lottery tickets?

3. *The subject of congressional regulation.* Justice Fuller distinguishes lottery tickets from diseased animals and infected goods, which he says Congress can prohibit from being transported interstate. Consider the possible analogue to his implicit distinction in *Lochner* between occupations that are inherently unhealthy and those that are not.

HAMMER v. DAGENHART
247 U.S. 251 (1918)

DAY, J. . . .

A bill was filed in the United States District Court for the Western District of North Carolina by a father in his own behalf and as next friend of his two minor sons, one under the age of fourteen years and the other between the ages of fourteen and sixteen years, employees in a cotton mill at Charlotte, North Carolina, to enjoin the enforcement of the act of Congress intended to prevent interstate commerce in the products of child labor. . . .

The District Court held the act unconstitutional and entered a decree enjoining its enforcement. This appeal brings the case here. The first section of the act is in the margin.[a]

a. That no producer, manufacturer, or dealer shall ship or deliver for shipment in interstate or foreign commerce any article or commodity the product of any mine or quarry, situated in the United States, in which within thirty days prior to the time of the removal of such product therefrom children under the age of sixteen years have been employed or permitted to work, or any article or commodity the product of any mill, cannery, workshop, factory, or manufacturing establishment, situated in the United States, in which within thirty days prior to the removal of such product therefrom children under the age of fourteen years have been employed or permitted to work, or children between the ages of fourteen years and sixteen years have been employed or permitted to work more than eight hours in any day, or more than six days in any week, or after the hour of seven o'clock postmeridian, or before the hour of six o'clock antemeridian.

The controlling question for decision is: Is it within the authority of Congress in regulating commerce among the States to prohibit the transportation in interstate commerce of manufactured goods, the product of a factory in which, within thirty days prior to their removal therefrom, children under the age of fourteen have been employed or permitted to work, or children between the ages of fourteen and sixteen years have been employed or permitted to work more than eight hours in any day, or more than six days in any week, or after the hour of 7 o'clock P.M. or before the hour of 6 o'clock A.M.?

The power essential to the passage of this act, the Government contends, is found in the commerce clause of the Constitution which authorizes Congress to regulate commerce with foreign nations and among the States. . . .

[I]t is insisted that adjudged cases in this court establish the doctrine that the power to regulate given to Congress incidentally includes the authority to prohibit the movement of ordinary commodities and therefore that the subject is not open for discussion. The cases demonstrate the contrary. They rest upon the character of the particular subjects dealt with and the fact that the scope of governmental authority, state or national, possessed over them is such that the authority to prohibit is as to them but the exertion of the power to regulate.

The first of these cases is Champion v. Ames, 188 U.S. 321 (1903), the so-called *Lottery* case, in which it was held that Congress might pass a law having the effect to keep the channels of commerce free from use in the transportation of tickets used in the promotion of lottery schemes. In Hipolite Egg Co. v. United States, 220 U.S. 45 (1911), this court sustained the power of Congress to pass the Pure Food and Drug Act which prohibited the introduction into the States by means of interstate commerce of impure foods and drugs. In Hoke v. United States, 227 U.S. 308 (1913), this court sustained the constitutionality of the so-called "White Slave Traffic Act" whereby the transportation of a woman in interstate commerce for the purpose of prostitution was forbidden. . . .

In Caminetti v. United States, 242 U.S. 470 (1917), we held that Congress might prohibit the transportation of women in interstate commerce for the purposes of debauchery and kindred purposes. In Clark Distilling Co. v. Western Maryland Ry. Co., 242 U.S. 311 (1917), the power of Congress over the transportation of intoxicating liquors was sustained. . . .

In each of these instances the use of interstate transportation was necessary to the accomplishment of harmful results. In other words, although the power over interstate transportation was to regulate, that could only be accomplished by prohibiting the use of the facilities of interstate commerce to effect the evil intended.

This element is wanting in the present case. The thing intended to be accomplished by this statute is the denial of the facilities of interstate commerce to those manufacturers in the States who employ children within the prohibited ages. The act in its effect does not regulate transportation among the States, but aims to standardize the ages at which children may be employed in mining and manufacturing within the States. The goods shipped are of themselves harmless. The act permits them to be freely shipped after thirty days from the time of their removal from the factory. When offered for shipment, and before transportation begins, the labor of their production is over, and the mere fact that they were intended for interstate commerce transportation does not make their production subject to federal control under the commerce power. . . .

It is further contended that the authority of Congress may be exerted to control interstate commerce in the shipment of child-made goods because of the effect of the circulation of such goods in other States where the evil of this class of labor has been recognized by local legislation, and the right to thus employ child labor has been more rigorously restrained than in the State of production. In other words, that the unfair competition, thus engendered, may be controlled by closing the channels of interstate commerce to manufacturers in those States where the local laws do not meet what Congress deems to be the more just standard of other States.

There is no power vested in Congress to require the States to exercise their police power so as to prevent possible unfair competition. Many causes may cooperate to give one State, by reason of local laws or conditions, an economic advantage over others. The Commerce Clause was not intended to give to Congress a general authority to equalize such conditions. In some of the States laws have been passed fixing minimum wages for women, in others the local law regulates the hours of labor of women in various employments. Business done in such States may be at an economic disadvantage when compared with States which have no such regulations; surely, this fact does not give Congress the power to deny transportation in interstate commerce to those who carry on business where the hours of labor and the rate of compensation for women have not been fixed by a standard in use in other States and approved by Congress.

The grant of power to Congress over the subject of interstate commerce was to enable it to regulate such commerce, and not to give it authority to control the States in their exercise of the police power over local trade and manufacture.

The grant of authority over a purely federal matter was not intended to destroy the local power always existing and carefully reserved to the States in the Tenth Amendment to the Constitution. . . .

The power of the States to regulate their purely internal affairs by such laws as seem wise to the local authority is inherent and has never been surrendered to the general government. To sustain this statute would not be in our judgment a recognition of the lawful exertion of congressional authority over interstate commerce, but would sanction an invasion by the federal power of the control of a matter purely local in its character, and over which no authority has been delegated to Congress in conferring the power to regulate commerce among the States. . . .

In our view the necessary effect of this act is, by means of a prohibition against the movement in interstate commerce of ordinary commercial commodities, to regulate the hours of labor of children in factories and mines within the States, a purely state authority. Thus the act in a twofold sense is repugnant to the Constitution. It not only transcends the authority delegated to Congress over commerce but also exerts a power as to a purely local matter to which the federal authority does not extend. The far reaching result of upholding the act cannot be more plainly indicated than by pointing out that if Congress can thus regulate matters entrusted to local authority by prohibition of the movement of commodities in interstate commerce, all freedom of commerce will be at an end, and the power of the States over local matters may be eliminated and thus our system of government be practically destroyed.

HOLMES, J., dissenting.

The single question in this case is whether Congress has power to prohibit the shipment [of certain goods] in interstate or foreign commerce. . . . The objection urged against the power is that the States have exclusive control over their methods of production and that Congress cannot meddle with them, and taking the proposition in the sense of direct intermeddling I agree to it and suppose that no one denies it. But if an act is within the powers specifically conferred upon Congress, it seems to me that it is not made any less constitutional because of the indirect effects that it may have, however obvious it may be that it will have those effects, and that we are not at liberty upon such grounds to hold it void.

The first step in my argument is to make plain what no one is likely to dispute — that the statute in question is within the power expressly given to Congress if considered only as to its immediate effects and that if invalid it is so only upon some collateral ground. The statute confines itself to prohibiting the carriage of certain goods in interstate or foreign commerce. Congress is given power to regulate such commerce in unqualified terms. It would not be argued today that the power to regulate does not include the power to prohibit. Regulation means the prohibition of something, and when interstate commerce is the matter to be regulated I cannot doubt that the regulation may prohibit any part of such commerce that Congress sees fit to forbid. At all events it is established by the *Lottery* case and others that have followed it that a law is not beyond the regulative power of Congress merely because it prohibits certain transportation out and out. . . . So I repeat that this statute in its immediate operation is clearly within the Congress's constitutional power.

The question then is narrowed to whether the exercise of its otherwise constitutional power by Congress can be pronounced unconstitutional because of its possible reaction upon the conduct of the States in a matter upon which I have admitted that they are free from direct control. I should have thought that matter had been disposed of so fully as to leave no room for doubt. I should have thought that the most conspicuous decisions of this Court had made it clear that the power to regulate commerce and other constitutional powers could not be cut down or qualified by the fact that it might interfere with the carrying out of the domestic policy of any State. . . .

[I]f there is any matter upon which civilized countries have agreed — far more unanimously than they have with regard to intoxicants and some other matters over which this country is now emotionally aroused — it is the evil of premature and excessive child labor. . . .

But I had thought that the propriety of the exercise of a power admitted to exist in some cases was for the consideration of Congress alone and that this Court always had disavowed the right to intrude its judgment upon questions of policy or morals. It is not for this Court to pronounce when prohibition is necessary to regulation if it ever may be necessary — to say that it is permissible as against strong drink but not as against the product of ruined lives.

The act does not meddle with anything belonging to the States. They may regulate their internal affairs and their domestic commerce as they like. But when they seek to send their products across the state line they are no longer within their rights. If there were no Constitution and no Congress their power to cross the line would depend upon their neighbors. Under the Constitution such commerce belongs not to the States but to Congress to regulate. It may carry out its views of public policy whatever indirect effect they may have upon the activities of the States. Instead of being encountered by a prohibitive tariff at her boundaries the State encounters the public policy of the United States which it is for Congress to express. The public policy of the United States is shaped with a view to the benefit of the nation as a whole. If, as has been the case within the memory of men still living, a State should take a different view of the propriety of sustaining a lottery from that which generally prevails, I cannot believe that the fact would require a different decision from that reached in Champion v. Ames. Yet in that case it would be said with quite as much force as in this that Congress was attempting to intermeddle with the State's domestic affairs. The national welfare as understood by Congress may require a different attitude within its sphere from that of some self-seeking State. It seems to me entirely constitutional for Congress to enforce its understanding by all the means at its command. . . .

Mr. Justice McKenna, Mr. Justice Brandeis and Mr. Justice Clarke concur in this opinion.

Discussion

The Child Labor Act, by its terms, operated directly upon interstate commerce. In purely formal terms, does the act differ from the prohibitions of the Federal Lottery Act, the Pure Food and Drug Act, and the White Slave Traffic Act? If not, why was it beyond the commerce power?

Were the *objectives* underlying the Child Labor Act categorically different from those underlying the other acts? In this respect, did the government overplay its hand by making the "unfair competition" argument? Recall that in the *Lottery* case the Court thought that perhaps all of the states forbade the sale of lottery tickets. The Court might have made similar assumptions about state policies concerning adulterated food and prostitution. But the very point of the "unfair competition" was that not all states prohibited child labor.[120] If, after the *Child Labor* case, in the (judicially enforced) silence of Congress, a state had attempted to exclude goods made using child labor, this trade barrier almost surely would have been deemed an impermissible state regulation of interstate commerce. (See Chapter 5, infra.) Equally surely, in the silence of Congress, a state *could* exclude diseased cattle. What is the difference, and does it provide any further insight into the Court's restriction on *Congress's* power in the *Child Labor* case?

After the *Child Labor* case, could Congress have authorized the states to exclude goods made using child labor, under the "consent" doctrines discussed at pp. 206-208?

Note: On "Prisoner's Dilemmas" and Centralized Coordination

Justice Day's opinion for the majority implicitly concedes that there is something "unfair" about state A allowing its industries a competitive advantage against the industries of state B because the former allows a wicked practice. That is, state A's toleration of child labor presumably means that its industries have lower labor costs. Thus, if state B chooses to outlaw child labor, it takes the risk of seeing its products suffer in the marketplace if the higher labor costs imposed on local industries are passed along to consumers; or, perhaps, investors will be discouraged from financing state B's industries because they will be unable to receive the same returns presumably available in the other, less protective, states. Day notes that one of the motivations for the federal Child Labor Law was "that the unfair competition, thus

---

120. For an interesting discussion of the facts, politics, and law of child labor, see Stephen Wood, Constitutional Politics in the Progressive Era (1968).

engendered, may be controlled by closing the channels of interstate commerce to manufacturers in those States where the local laws do not meet what Congress deems to be the more just standard of other States." For better or worse, though, according to the majority, the Constitution vests no power "in Congress to require the States to exercise their police power so as to prevent possible unfair competition. . . . The Commerce Clause was not intended to give to Congress a general authority to equalize such conditions." If this is an imperfection in the constitutional scheme, the solution, presumably, is to amend the Constitution.

Perhaps state A says that it will consider passing a child labor law if state B goes first. Can state B necessarily trust state A? Can one even be certain that state B, for all of its professed desire to help its children, might not be tempted to maintain child labor if state A went first, given the presumed boon to state B's products?

The situation described may be a classic "prisoner's dilemma," a concept widely used in game theory to describe certain problems of "strategic interaction."[121] The idea is that both parties would be made better off if they could cooperate, but they do not dare because they cannot be sure what the other party will do in response to their unilateral action. As a result, each engages in a strategy that maximizes his or her position on the assumption that the other person will not cooperate.

One response to these kinds of collective action problems, especially as the number of parties rises, is for a central decisionmaker — in this case the Federal Government — to intervene and force each party to engage in uniform behavior that benefits them all. Under this analysis, North Carolina, the state whose child labor law was the subject of *Hammer,* is a selfish egoist whose decision to allow child labor ends up "forcing" the other states to permit unjust labor practices. If you accept this characterization of the situation, you can perhaps understand why many people thought it so important that Congress have the power to impose a general coordinating rule. On the other hand, one could object that this is not a true prisoner's dilemma, because some states (and some interests within those states) might not agree that a uniform protection of child labor was best for their citizens. Suppose one believed, for example, that most economic regulations, even regulations on child labor, were undesirable infringements on liberty. In that case, a uniform rule would produce the worst possible outcome. If you accept *this* characterization of the situation, can you see why some people thought it important that Congress not have the power to impose a general rule on all of the states? Consider in this context the statement of Harvard political scientist Paul Pierson:[122]

> The evidence is reasonably clear that federalism constrains welfare state growth. The most important consequence of decentralized institutions is the creation of "fiscal competition" among jurisdictions. Local governments find it difficult to pursue redistributive policies for fear that high taxes will lead business and wealthy individuals to move out while attracting low-income groups who would benefit from generous social programs. Centralized authorities can make such policies uniform throughout a country, limiting the prospects that capital and labor mobility will pose such a dramatic threat to social provision.

121. See Douglas G. Baird, Robert H. Gerner and Randal C. Picker, Game Theory and the Law 31-35 (1995), from which the quoted language and examples are taken. This book is an excellent introduction to a far more complicated subject than can be adequately described in this note.

122. Dismantling the Welfare State? Reagan, Thatcher, and the Politics of Retrenchment 35 (1994).

It should be clear that a child-labor policy, from the perspective of an affected business, is the equivalent of a tax, at least so long as the movement to adult laborers would increase labor costs.

Why do you think North Carolina in 1918 and countries around the world today tolerate child labor and other labor practices barred by American law or otherwise deviate from the kinds of regulatory regimes found in all advanced industrial countries? Imagine that the United States and other developed countries today attempt to outlaw child labor or the 12-hour day in these countries. (You should assume that the prohibition is not accompanied by any financial aid directed at the welfare either of the children or of the parents who are arguably dependent on their children's income or on the marginal gains from working more than eight hours.) Might one view an international prohibition as simply a way by which rich economies protect their industries against the competition of poorer countries that are willing to engage in extraordinary efforts, including child labor, working 12 hours a day, etc., in order, presumably, to benefit future generations?

The collective action issues discussed, all too briefly in this note, arise in many different contexts. Consider for example, Steward Machine Company v. Davis, described infra at p. 565, which upheld the power of Congress under the Spending Clause to pass a federal unemployment insurance scheme created by the Social Security Act of 1935. In that opinion, Justice Cardozo described certain "state inaction" in passing unemployment insurance provisions as being generated less by "the lack of sympathetic interest" than by "alarm lest, in laying such a toll upon their industries, they would place themselves in a position of economic disadvantage as compared with neighbors or competitors." He found ample power in Congress to pass national legislation designed to overcome the "fear" that prevented each state from acting in its individual capacity. To what extent, if any, should these kinds of game theoretic analyses play a role in the best interpretation of constitutional provisions? Is this simply another example of how consequences are as important a modality of constitutional interpretation as text, history, or original intention?

Note: Binary Oppositions and Congressional Ability to Invoke Its Power Under the Commerce Clause

Hammer illustrates the importance of binary oppositions deemed crucial to ascertaining whether Congress had the power to act under the Commerce Clause. In addition to the distinction between inherently dangerous and harmless goods, the Court refers to another important opposition central to many cases of this period: "manufacture" versus "commerce." As the Court wrote in Kidd v. Pearson, 128 U.S. 1 (1888), "Manufacture is transformation — the fashioning of raw materials into a change of form for use. The functions of commerce are different." In United States v. E.C. Knight Co., 156 U.S. 1 (1895), the Court refused to apply the Sherman Act to a trust that manufactured 95 percent of the sugar sold in the United States. Chief Justice Fuller wrote: "Commerce succeeds to manufacture, and is not part of it. The fact that an article is manufactured for export to another State does not itself make it an article of interstate commerce." An important pre-1937 New Deal case, Carter v. Carter Coal Co., 298 U.S. 238 (1936), relied on the manufacture–commerce distinction to invalidate a provision of the Bituminous Coal Conservation Act of 1936 that required coal companies to engage in collective bargaining with their employees. Justice Sutherland defined "commerce" as "the equivalent of the phrase 'intercourse for the purpose of trade.'" "Plainly, the incidents leading up to and culminating in the mining of coal do not constitute such intercourse. The employment of men, the fixing of their wages, hours of labor and working conditions, the bargaining in respect of these things . . . — each and all constitute intercourse for the purposes of production, not trade. . . . Commerce in the coal mined is not brought into being by force of [the activities covered by the Act]. Mining brings the subject matter of commerce into existence. Commerce disposes of it." Linked to the distinction between "manufacture" and "commerce" was that between "direct" and "indirect" effects on commerce. Justice Sutherland in *Carter* conceded that "the production of every commodity intended for interstate sale and transportation has some effect upon interstate commerce." Moreover, "[m]uch stress is put upon the evils which come from the struggle between employers and employees," including the resulting strikes, curtailment and irregularity of production, and effect on prices; and it is insisted that interstate commerce is *greatly* affected thereby.

> But . . . the conclusive answer is that the evils are all local evils over which the federal government has no legislative control. . . . Working conditions are obviously local conditions. The employees are not engaged in or about commerce, but exclusively in producing a commodity. . . . Such effect as they may have upon commerce, however extensive it may be, is secondary and indirect. An increase in the greatness of the effect adds to its importance. It does not alter its character.

Sutherland suggested that "[t]he word 'direct' implies that the activity or condition invoked or blamed shall operate proximately — not mediately, remotely, or collaterally — to produce the effect. It connotes the absence of an efficient intervening agency or condition." The dichotomy was categorical rather than one of degree: "The matter of degree has no bearing upon the question here, since that question is not — What is the *extent* of the local activity or condition, or the *extent* of the effect produced upon interstate commerce? but — What is the *relation* between the activity or condition and the effect?" Sutherland did not deny that labor disputes about the conditions of coal mining might have "extensive" consequences for the availability of coal to be shipped in interstate commerce. But any such effects were "secondary and indirect. An increase in the greatness of the effect adds to its importance. It does not alter its character." In trying to make sense of this distinction, recall discussions about causation in your torts or criminal law classes. Consider the difference involved, for example, in finding that a particular injury was "proximately caused" by the actions of the defendant and a determination that it was merely "caused in fact" by those actions.

The Court also distinguished on occasion between items in the "flow" of commerce and those not in the flow either because they had not yet entered it or because the flow had come to an end. For example, Swift & Co. v. U.S., 196 U.S. 375 (1905), upheld the application of the Sherman Act to the price-fixing practices of stockyard owners. As Justice Sutherland later described this case, "livestock was consigned and delivered to stockyards — not as a place of final destination, but, as . . . 'a throat through which the current flows.'" The pre-1937 Court refused to extend *Swift* beyond its facts.

Thus, Schecter Poultry Corp. v. United States, 295 U.S. 495 (1935), struck down federal regulation of the live poultry industry in New York because "the commodity in question [i.e., chickens], although shipped from another state, had come to rest in the state of its destination, and, as the court pointed out, was no longer in a current or flow of interstate commerce." As you will soon see, all of these categorical distinctions disappeared in the maelstrom of the post-1937 transformations of the Commerce Clause.

Note on the Taxing Power

Shortly after the decision in Hammer v. Dagenhart, Congress enacted the Child Labor Tax Law of 1919, which imposed a 10 percent tax on the net income of any manufacturer employing children below specified ages. In the *Child Labor Tax* case, Bailey v. Drexel Furniture Co., 259 U.S. 20 (1922), the Court struck it down, with only Justice Clarke dissenting. Chief Justice Taft observed that "a court must be blind not to see that the so-called tax is imposed to stop the employment of children. . . . Its prohibitory and regulatory effect and purpose are palpable." He continued:

> Grant the validity of this law, and all that Congress would need to do, hereafter, in seeking to take over to its control any one of the great number of subjects of public interest, jurisdiction of which the States have never parted with, and which are reserved to them by the Tenth Amendment, would be to enact a detailed measure of complete regulation of the subject and enforce it by a so-called tax upon departures from it. To give such magic to the word "tax" would be to break down all constitutional limitation of the powers of Congress and completely wipe out the sovereignty of the States.
>
> The difference between a tax and a penalty is sometimes difficult to define and yet the consequences of the distinction in the required method of their collection often are important. Where the sovereign enacting the law has power to impose both tax and penalty the difference between revenue production and mere regulation may be immaterial,[123] but not so when one sovereign can impose a tax only, and the power of regulation rests in another. Taxes are occasionally imposed in the discretion of the legislature on proper subjects with the primary motive of obtaining revenue from them and with the incidental motive of discouraging them by making their continuance onerous. They do not lose their character as taxes because of the incidental motive. But there comes a time in the extension of the penalizing features of the so-called tax when it loses it character as such and becomes a mere penalty with the characteristics of regulation and punishment. Such is the case in the law before us. . . .
>
> The analogy of the *Dagenhart* case is clear. The congressional power over interstate commerce is, within its proper scope, just as complete and unlimited as the congressional

---

123. Veazie Bank v. Fenno, 75 U.S. (8 Wall.) 533 (1869), is an example. The Court sustained a 10 percent federal tax on personal and state bank notes, apparently designed to deter the use of such notes, commenting:

> Having . . . , in the exercise of undisputed constitutional powers, undertaken to provide a currency for the whole country, it cannot be questioned that Congress may, constitutionally, secure the benefit of it to the people by appropriate legislation. To this end, Congress has denied the quality of legal tender to foreign coins, and has provided by law against the imposition of counterfeit and base coin on the community. To the same end, Congress may restrain, by suitable enactments, the circulation as money of any notes not issued under its own authority. Without this power, indeed, its attempts to secure a sound and uniform currency for the country must be futile.

124. Michelle Dauber Landis, e-mail to Jack M. Balkin, August 31, 2005.

power to tax, and the legislative motive in its exercise is just as free from judicial suspicion and inquiry. Yet when Congress threatened to stop interstate commerce in ordinary and necessary commodities, unobjectionable as subjects of transportation, and to deny the same to the people of a State in order to coerce them into compliance with Congress's regulation of state concerns, the court said this was not in fact regulation of interstate commerce, but rather that of State concerns and was invalid. So here the so-called tax is a penalty to coerce people of a State to act as Congress wishes them to act in respect of a matter completely the business of the state government under the Federal Constitution. This case requires as did the *Dagenhart* case the application of the principle announced by Chief Justice Marshall in McCulloch v. Maryland, in [the "pretext" passage, p. 50, supra].

Hill v. Wallace, 259 U.S. 44 (1922), decided on the same day as the *Child Labor Tax* case, held invalid as a regulation of the (local) business of grain trading a tax of 20 cents per bushel on grain future contracts except those made through "boards of trade" designated by the secretary of agriculture upon their compliance with detailed regulations specified in the statute. United States v. Constantine, 296 U.S. 287 (1935), struck down a federal excise tax of $1,000 imposed on liquor dealers carrying on business in violation of state or local law; the Court held that the exaction was a penalty rather than a revenue-raising measure.

During the same period, the Court also upheld some federal taxes that appeared to regulate what it viewed as "local" matters. McCray v. United States, 195 U.S. 27 (1904), sustained a law, designed to discourage the sale of margarine that looked like butter, that taxed yellow margarine at 10 cents per pound and white margarine at only 0.25 cents. United States v. Doremus, 249 U.S. 86 (1919), sustained burdensome federal record-keeping requirements on sellers of narcotics, ostensibly designed to enforce a tax on the drugs. In the *Child Labor Tax* case, Chief Justice Taft distinguished these laws on the ground that, on their face, they were tax rather than regulatory measures.

Note on the Spending Power

Recall Madison's veto of an "internal improvements" measure in 1817, Chapter 1, supra. Many Democratic presidents throughout the nineteenth century emulated Madison by vetoing similar legislation and thus keeping the issue off the judicial agenda. In 1888, the Court upheld legislation that provided partial federal financing for interstate railroads, California Railroad Cases, 127 U.S. 1 (1888), but Justice Bradley relied on the commerce power rather than the spending clause:

> It cannot at the present day be doubted that Congress, under the power to regulate commerce among the several States, as well as to provide for postal accommodations and military exigencies, had authority to pass these laws. . . . Without authority in Congress to establish and maintain such highways and bridges, it would be without authority to regulate one of the most important adjuncts of commerce. [In former times, the] exertion [of this power] was but little called for, as commerce was then mostly conducted by water, and many of our statesman entertained doubts as to the existence of the power to establish ways of communication by land. But since, in consequence of the expansion of the country, the multiplication of its products, and the invention of railroads and locomotion by steam, land transportation has so vastly increased, a sounder consideration of the subject has prevailed and led to the conclusion that Congress has plenary power over the whole subject.

Bradley's argument about Congressional power to spend to promote interstate transportation was not perceived as reaching the question of "disaster relief," the constitutionality of which continued to be a recurrent issue before Congress. Precisely because of earlier legislation providing such relief, perhaps most members of Congress believed that the question of constitutionality had essentially been settled. Indeed, Michelle Landis Dauber writes that "so clearly constitutional was disaster relief that it actually played a role (a decisive role, it turns out) in the internal improvement debates" that took place in Congress following President Monroe's veto of the internal improvement bill. "A House committee headed by Henry St. George Tucker investigated and came out in favor of the broad interpretation of the general welfare power based on the precedent of disaster relief."[124] As the Republican Speaker of the House, Joseph Kiefer, put it in 1884, "The General Government has throughout its history selected extraordinary cases for granting relief. Where we shall stop, where the boundary line is, must always rest within the discretion of Congress."[125] Or, as Texas Senator John Reagan told his colleagues during an 1884 debate about relief for the victims of a Mississippi River flood, "we have a long line of precedents which have met the approbation of the most illustrious minds of the past and we know that if we shall do what we are now asked to do we do not violate the Constitution."[126]

There was, however, no unanimity on this point. Democratic presidents following Monroe continued to question internal improvement legislation on constitutional grounds, and Dauber's own illuminating scholarship reveals at least some evidence suggesting that the debate had not been definitively settled. Consider, for example, the following comments in 1884 from Democratic representatives who supported a proposal to allocate $300,000 in aid for the victims of an Ohio River flood. Republicans had gleefully taunted Democratic representatives for contradicting their usual position that the limited powers assigned by the Constitution to Congress included no right to fund, under the Spending Clause, disaster-relief legislation, which was often described as having nothing to do with the "general welfare" and instead as simply a naked transfer of resources from taxpayers in one part of the country to the lucky recipients of congressional beneficence in another.

Rather than argue forthrightly, as did Senator Reagan, that there was no constitutional problem with such transfers, Ohio Democrat John Follen thundered that "necessity knows neither law nor constitution and never did in this country,"[127] while his colleague Adoniram Warner concurred: "[M]ingled with the appeals that come to us for help are the cries of children and the petitions for women homeless, shelterless, hungry, and in this presence I cannot stop to argue literal construction of the Constitution. I will take the side of mercy and risk it on that." Isaac Jordan, also of Ohio, candidly admitted that he did "not know whether this bill is constitutional or not. We have no time to enter into a discussion of this question. While we would stand here debating it the floods would not abate and the people would perish."

---

125. Michelle Dauber Landis, The Sympathetic State, 23 Law and History Rev. 387, 404 (2005), quoting the Congressional Record, 67th Cong., 1st Sess., 1884, 15, pt. 3:2294.

126. Id. at 403, quoting the Congressional Record, 48th Cong., 1st Sess., 1884, 15, pt. 2:1037.

127. All quotations in this paragraph come from Landis, The Sympathetic State, 23 Law and History Rev. 406. quoting Congressional Record, 48th Cong., 1st Sess., 1884, 15, pt. 2:1033, 1039, 1038.

128. James Richardson, ed., 11 Messages and Papers of the Presidents 5142-5143 (1897).

Added proof that the fundamental debate still awaited definitive resolution can be found in the message issued by Democratic President Grover Cleveland on February 15, 1887, explaining his veto of "An act to enable the Commissioner of Agriculture to make a special distribution of seeds in the drought-stricken counties of Texas, and making an appropriation thereof."[128] Cleveland readily conceded that "there has existed a condition calling for relief" and that the issuance of the new seeds "would serve to avert a continuance or return of an unfortunate blight." Nonetheless, the fact that Congress wished "to indulge a benevolent and charitable sentiment through the appropriation of public funds" did not justify his signing the bill, for

> I can find no warrant for such an appropriation in the Constitution, and I do not believe that the power and duty of the General Government ought to be extended to the relief of individual suffering which is in no manner properly related to the public service [as with veterans, for example] or benefit. A prevalent tendency to disregard the limited mission of [national] power and duty should, I think, be steadfastly resisted, to the end that the lesson should be constantly enforced that though the people support the Government the Government should not support the people.

Indeed, Cleveland argued, "[f]ederal aid in such cases encourages the expectation of paternal care on the part of the Government and weakens the sturdiness of our national character, while it prevents the indulgence among our people of that kindly sentiment and conduct which strengthens the bonds of a common brotherhood."

Discussion

Once again it is important to realize the frequency with which fundamental constitutional issues were debated in Congress and addressed by presidents in veto messages. The "precedents" on which pro-aid members of Congress relied were prior congressional decisions, not judicial opinions, and President Cleveland in his veto message made no reference to courts. Both President Cleveland and congressmen and senators regarded themselves as fully worthy of making the relevant constitutional determinations.

Consider, however, the possible differences among the arguments they made, particularly those made by the Democratic representatives. One might interpret Rep. Follen as making a "first-order" constitutional argument that the Constitution, correctly interpreted, always allows responses to "necessity." (We have seen earlier examples of such arguments in wartime, see Chapter 3.) Representatives Warner and Jordan, on the other hand, might be understood as making a "second-order" argument: that *their* duty as representatives is to respond to those who need help, while leaving it up to courts to decide, in due time, whether such legislation is constitutional. Is this a proper conception of the role of a "conscientious legislator"?

Do both Madison and Cleveland provide models of constitutionally "conscientious presidents"? Madison leaves the reader with little doubt that he believes that the bill represented desirable public policy but was, alas, unconstitutional. Cleveland by contrast, seems less taken by the policy of the legislation he vetoed because it might encourage victims of disaster in effect to become dependent on public welfare and it might stifle the impulses of others to help out in the belief

---

129. E-mail to Sanford Levinson, July 20, 1999.

that there was no need for private charity. Given that Cleveland signed other disaster relief legislation during his presidency, one might choose to read his veto message quite narrowly, referring to the presumptive lack of merits of the particular claims by ostensibly needy Texans, as against a more general rejection of the very idea of congressional authority to redistribute funds to victims of disasters. At the very least, though, it is hard to believe that Cleveland's veto was based on crass political considerations. Consider the fact that Texas had provided 13 electoral votes in Cleveland's narrow 219-182 electoral vote victory over James G. Blaine in 1884. Might not a more "political" president have signed the legislation that benefited his loyal supporters, regardless of constitutional scruples?

Congress (and the White House) remained the primary venues for resolving such arguments, not least because the Supreme Court did not fully address until 1936 the question of Congress's power to spend federal funds in the pursuit of ends not within the enumerated powers of Article I, §8. United States v. Butler explicitly rejected Madison's (and many of his successors') views of the spending power, even as it invalidated the Agricultural Adjustment Act of 1933. The Act authorized the secretary of agriculture to spend federal funds in return for agreements by farmers to reduce their productive acreage — and thus, presumably, raise the prices of the crops being produced. The Court held that the Act was an invasion of the "reserved power" of the states. As will be seen in Chapter 5, although the latter aspect of *Butler* did not survive, the case remains important because it confirmed the doctrinal basis for what has become a centrally important use of congressional power in the age of the modern welfare state (see Chapter 9, infra).

UNITED STATES v. BUTLER, 297 U.S. 1 (1936): ROBERTS, J. . . . There should be no misunderstanding as to the function of this court in such a case. It is sometimes said that the court assumes a power to overrule or control the action of the people's representatives. This is a misconception. The Constitution is the supreme law of the land ordained and established by the people. All legislation must conform to the principles it lays down. When an act of Congress is appropriately challenged in the courts as not conforming to the constitutional mandate the judicial branch of the Government has only one duty, — to lay the article of the Constitution which is invoked beside the statute which is challenged and to decide whether the latter squares with the former. All the court does, or can do, is to announce its considered judgment upon the question. The only power it has, if such it may be called, is the power of judgment. This court neither approves nor condemns any legislative policy. Its delicate and difficult office is to ascertain and declare whether the legislation is in accordance with, or in contravention of, the provisions of the Constitution; and, having done that, its duty ends.

. . . Since the foundation of the Nation sharp differences of opinion have persisted as to the true interpretation of the ["general welfare" clause]. Madison asserted it amounted to no more than a reference to the other powers enumerated in the subsequent clauses of the same section; that, as the United States is a government of limited and enumerated powers, the grant of power to tax and spend for the general national welfare must be confined to the enumerated legislative fields committed to the Congress. In this view the phrase is mere tautology, for taxation and appropriation are or may be necessary incidents of the exercise of any of the enumerated legislative powers. Hamilton, on the other hand, maintained the clause confers a power separate and distinct from those later enumerated, is not restricted in meaning by the grant of them, and Congress consequently has a substantive power to tax and to appropriate, limited only by the requirement that it shall be exercised to provide for the general welfare of the United States. Each contention has had the support of those whose views are entitled to weight.

This court has noticed the question, but has never found it necessary to decide which is the true construction. Mr. Justice Story, in his Commentaries, espouses the Hamiltonian position. We shall not review the writings of public men and commentators or discuss the legislative practice. Study of all these leads us to conclude that the reading advocated by Mr. Justice Story is the correct one. While, therefore, the power to tax is not unlimited, its confines are set in the clause which confers it, and not in those of §8 which bestow and define the legislative powers of the Congress. It results that the power of Congress to authorize expenditure of public moneys for public purposes is not limited by the direct grants of legislative power found in the Constitution.

But the adoption of the broader construction leaves the power to spend subject to limitations. . . . Hamilton, in his well known Report on Manufactures, states that the purpose must be "general, and not local." . . .

We are not now required to ascertain the scope of the phrase "general welfare of the United States" or to determine whether an appropriation in aid of agriculture falls within it. Wholly apart from that question, another principle embedded in our Constitution prohibits the enforcement of the Agricultural Adjustment Act. The act invades the reserved rights of the states. It is a statutory plan to regulate and control agricultural production, a matter beyond the powers delegated to the federal government. The tax, the appropriation of the funds raised, and the direction for their disbursement, are but parts of the plan. They are but means to an unconstitutional end.

From the accepted doctrine that the United States is a government of delegated powers, it follows that those not expressly granted, or reasonably to be implied from such as are conferred, are reserved to the states or to the people. To forestall any suggestion to the contrary, the Tenth Amendment was adopted. The same proposition, otherwise stated, is that powers not granted are prohibited. None to regulate agricultural production is given, and therefore legislation by Congress for that purpose is forbidden.

It is an established principle that the attainment of a prohibited end may not be accomplished under the pretext of the exertion of powers which are granted. [Quoting Marshall's "pretext" statement in *McCulloch*] . . .

[The *Child Labor Tax* case and similar] decisions demonstrate that Congress could not, under the pretext of raising revenue, lay a tax on processors who refuse to pay a certain price for cotton, and exempt those who agree so to do, with the purpose of benefiting producers.

If the taxing power may not be used as the instrument to enforce a regulation of matters of state concern with respect to which the Congress has no authority to interfere, may it, as in the present case, be employed to raise the money necessary to purchase a compliance which the Congress is powerless to command? The Government asserts that whatever might be said against the validity of the plan if compulsory, it is constitutionally sound because the end is accomplished by voluntary cooperation. There are two sufficient answers to the contention. The regulation is not in fact voluntary. The farmer, of course, may refuse to comply, but the price of such refusal is the loss of benefits. The amount offered is intended to be sufficient to exert pressure on him to agree to the proposed regulation. The power to confer or withhold unlimited benefits is the power to coerce or destroy. If the cotton grower elects not to accept the benefits, he will receive less for his crops; those who receive payments will be able to undersell him. The result may well be financial ruin. The coercive purpose and intent of the statute is not obscured by the fact that it has not been perfectly successful. . . .

But if the plan were one for purely voluntary cooperation it would stand no better so far as federal power is concerned. At best it is a scheme for purchasing with federal funds submission to federal regulation of a subject reserved to the states. . . . The Congress cannot invade state jurisdiction to compel individual action; no more can it purchase such action. . . . It does not help to declare that local conditions throughout the nation have created a situation of national concern; for this is but to say that whenever there is a widespread similarity of local conditions, Congress may ignore constitutional limitations upon its own powers and usurp those reserved to the states. If, in lieu of compulsory regulation of subjects within the states' reserved jurisdiction, which is prohibited, the Congress could invoke the taxing and spending power as a means to accomplish the same end, clause 1 of §8 of Article I would become the instrument for total subversion of the governmental powers reserved to the individual states. . . .

STONE, J., joined by Brandeis and Cardozo, JJ., dissenting.

The present stress of widely held and strongly expressed differences of opinion of the wisdom of the Agricultural Adjustment Act makes it important, in the interest of clear thinking and sound result, to emphasize at the outset certain propositions which should have controlling influence in determining the validity of the Act. They are:

1. The power of courts to declare a statute unconstitutional is subject to two guiding principles of decision which ought never to be absent from judicial consciousness. One is that courts are concerned only with the power to enact statutes, not with their wisdom. The other is that while unconstitutional exercise of power by the executive and legislative branches of the government is subject to judicial restraint, the only check upon our own exercise of power is our own sense of self-restraint. For the removal of unwise laws from the statute books appeal lies not to the courts but to the ballot and to the processes of democratic government.

2. The constitutional power of Congress to levy an excise tax upon the processing of agricultural products is not questioned. The present levy is held invalid, not for any want of power in Congress to lay such a tax to defray public expenditures, including those for the general welfare, but because the use to which its proceeds are put is disapproved. . . .

[Federal expenditures] would fail of their purpose and thus lose their constitutional sanction if the terms of payment were not such that by their influence on the action of the recipients the permitted end would be attained. The power of Congress to spend is inseparable from persuasion to action over which Congress has no legislative control. . . .

The spending power of Congress is in addition to the legislative power and not subordinate to it. This independent grant of the power of the purse, and its very nature, involving in its exercise the duty to insure expenditure within the granted power, presuppose freedom of selection among divers ends and aims, and the capacity to impose such conditions as will render the choice effective. It is a contradiction in terms to say that there is power to spend for the national welfare, while rejecting any power to impose conditions reasonably adapted to the attainment of the end which alone would justify the expenditure. . . .

A tortured construction of the Constitution is not to be justified by recourse to extreme examples of reckless congressional spending which might occur if courts could not prevent — expenditures which, even if they could be thought to effect any national purpose, would be possible only by action of a legislature lost to all sense of public responsibility. Such suppositions are addressed to the mind accustomed to believe that it is the business of courts to sit in judgment on the wisdom of legislative action. Courts are not the only agency of government that must be assumed to have capacity to govern. Congress and the courts both unhappily may falter or be mistaken in the performance of their constitutional duty. But interpretation of our great charter of government which proceeds on any assumption that the responsibility for the preservation of our institutions is the exclusive concern of any one of the three branches of government, or that it alone can save them from destruction is far more likely, in the long run, "to obliterate the constituent members" of "an indestructible union of indestructible states" than the frank recognition that language, even of a constitution, may mean what it says: that the power to tax and spend includes the power to relieve a nationwide economic maladjustment by conditional gifts of money.

Note: Does the Treaty Power Override "Reserved Powers" of the States?

MISSOURI v. HOLLAND, 252 U.S. 416 (1920): [*Holland* involved the constitutionality of the Migratory Bird Treaty Act of July 3, 1918 and subsequent regulations issued by the Secretary of Agriculture, all of which were intended to enforce a 1916 treaty that had been entered into between the United States and Great Britain (in its capacity as the sovereign over Canada, from which the birds in question migrated). Missouri asserted that the statute unconstitutionally interfered with its reserved rights under the Tenth Amendment. The Court disagreed.]

HOLMES, J.:

[The treaty] recited that many species of birds in their annual migrations traversed many parts of the United States and of Canada, that they were of great value as a source of food and in destroying insects injurious to vegetation, but were in danger of extermination through lack of adequate protection. It therefore provided for specified closed seasons and protection in other forms, and agreed that the two powers would take or propose to their lawmaking bodies the necessary measures for carrying the treaty out. The above mentioned act . . . prohibited the killing, capturing or selling any of the migratory birds included in the terms of the treaty except as permitted by regulations compatible with those terms, to be made by the Secretary of Agriculture. . . . [T]he question raised is the general one whether the treaty and statute are void as an interference with the rights reserved to the States.

To answer this question it is not enough to refer to the Tenth Amendment, reserving the powers not delegated to the United States, because by Article 2, Section 2, the power to make treaties is delegated expressly, and by Article 6 treaties made under the authority of the United States, along with the Constitution and laws of the United States made in pursuance thereof, are declared the supreme law of the land. If the treaty is valid there can be no dispute about the validity of the statute under Article 1, Section 8, as a necessary and proper means to execute the powers of the Government. The language of the Constitution as to the supremacy of treaties being general, the question before us is narrowed to an inquiry into the ground upon which the present supposed exception is placed.

It is said that a treaty cannot be valid if it infringes the Constitution, that there are limits, therefore, to the treaty-making power, and that one such limit is that what an act of Congress could not do unaided, in derogation of the powers reserved to the States, a treaty cannot do. An earlier act of Congress that attempted by itself and not in pursuance of a treaty to regulate the killing of migratory birds within the States had been held bad in the District Court. United States v. Shauver, 214 Fed. 154. United States v. McCullagh, 221 Fed. 288. Those decisions were supported by arguments that migratory birds were owned by the States in their sovereign capacity for the benefit of their people, and that under cases like Geer v. Connecticut, 161 U.S. 519, this control was one that Congress had no power to displace. The same argument is supposed to apply now with equal force.

Whether the two cases cited were decided rightly or not they cannot be accepted as a test of the treaty power. Acts of Congress are the supreme law of the land only when made in pursuance of the Constitution, while treaties are declared to be so when made under the authority of the United States. It is open to question whether the authority of the United States means more than the formal acts prescribed to make the convention. We do not mean to imply that there are no qualifications to the treaty-making power; but they must be ascertained in a different way. It is obvious that there may be matters of the sharpest exigency for the national well being that an act of Congress could not deal with but that a treaty followed by such an act could, and it is not lightly to be assumed that, in matters requiring national action, "a power which must belong to and somewhere reside in every civilized government" is not to be found. Andrews v. Andrews, 188 U.S. 14. What was said in that case with regard to the powers of the States applies with equal force to the powers of the nation in cases where the States individually are incompetent to act. We are not yet discussing the particular case before us but only are considering the validity of the test proposed. With regard to that we may add that when we are dealing with words that also are a constituent act, like the Constitution of the United States, we must realize that they have called into life a being the development of which could not have been foreseen completely by the most gifted of its begetters. It was enough for them to realize or to hope that they had created an organism; it has taken a century and has cost their successors much sweat and blood to prove that they created a nation. The case before us must be considered in the light of out whole experience and not merely in that of what was said a hundred years ago. The treaty in question does not contravene any prohibitory words to be found in the Constitution. The only question is whether it is forbidden by some invisible radiation from the general terms of the Tenth Amendment. We must consider what this country has become in deciding what that amendment has reserved.

The State as we have intimated founds its claim of exclusive authority upon an assertion of title to migratory birds, an assertion that is embodied in statute. No doubt it is true that as between a State and its inhabitants the State may regulate the killing and sale of such birds, but it does not follow that its authority is exclusive of paramount powers. To put the claim of the State upon title is to lean upon a slender reed. Wild birds are not in the possession of anyone; and possession is the beginning of ownership. The whole foundation of the State's rights is the presence within their jurisdiction of birds that yesterday had not arrived, tomorrow may be in another State and in a week a thousand miles away. If we are to be accurate we cannot put the case of the State upon higher ground than that the treaty deals with creatures that for the moment are within the state borders, that it must be carried out by officers of the United States within the same territory, and that but for the treaty the State would be free to regulate this subject itself.

As most of the laws of the United States are carried out within the States and as many of them deal with matters which in the silence of such laws the State might regulate, such general grounds are not enough to support Missouri's claim. Valid treaties of course "are as binding within the territorial limits of the States as they are elsewhere throughout the dominion of the United States." Baldwin v. Franks, 120 U.S. 678, 683. No doubt the great body of private relations usually fall within the control of the State, but a treaty may override its power. We do not have to invoke the later developments of constitutional law for this proposition; it was recognized as early as Hopkirk v. Bell, 3 Cranch, 454, with regard to statutes of limitation, and even earlier, as to confiscation, in Ware v. Hylton, 3 Dall. 199. It was assumed by Chief Justice Marshall with regard to the escheat of land to the State in Chirac v. Chirac, 2 Wheat. 259, 275 [and other cases]. So as to a limited jurisdiction of foreign consuls within a State. Wildenhus' Case, 120 U.S. 1. Further illustration seems unnecessary, and it only remains to consider the application of established rules to the present case.

Here a national interest of very nearly the first magnitude is involved. It can be protected only by national action in concert with that of another power. The subject matter is only transitorily within the State and has no permanent habitat therein. But for the treaty and the statute there soon might be no birds for any powers to deal with. We see nothing in the Constitution that compels the Government to sit by while a food supply is cut off and the protectors of our forests and our crops are destroyed. It is not sufficient to rely upon the States. The reliance is vain, and were it otherwise, the question is whether the United States is forbidden to act. We are of opinion that the treaty and statute must be upheld.

Only two justices dissented in *Holland,* without opinion. One might ask, therefore, why a Court so seemingly committed to protecting reserved rights of the states against congressional interference would find Justice Holmes's opinion unexceptionable. One possibility, of course, is that the subject matter of the treaty and congressional statute, migratory birds, is key. How deeply can one credit Missouri's reserved right to regulate geese who might well be transitory visitors to the state on their way from Canada to Texas (or beyond)? Even if one accepted the proposition that Congress could not, by exercising ordinary Article I powers, regulate migratory birds, one might also argue, as Professor Sarah Cleveland suggests, that "a possible interpretation of Holmes is not so much that the treaty power allows the national government to override powers constitutionally reserved to the states as that the treaty power creates a competing interest in the national government, bestowed by the Constitution, which doesn't exist where ordinary legislation is at issue."[129] Query whether the Court must necessarily defer to such a statement of a "competing interest" or whether, as arguably occurred in *Holland,* it can legitimately "balance" the competing weights of the national and state interests.

A second possibility, though, is that the Court accepted the general proposition that "the President and the Senate together may achieve via the treaty power what Congress and the President cannot do under Article I, section 8 of the Constitution."[130] As G. Edward White has noted, Justice Sutherland, otherwise firmly committed to a limited conception of congressional power, had articulated as early as 1910 a highly expansive notion of national powers in regard to foreign policy; indeed, he would eventually author the *Curtiss Wright* opinion, Chapter 1, supra, which adopted an "inherent power" view of the subject.[131] The capacity of the United States to enter into any international agreements deemed to serve vital national interests could, therefore, easily come under such an analysis.

There is relatively little case law directly in point, though a plurality opinion did, in 1957, state that a treaty could not "confer power on the Congress, or on any other branch of Government, which is free from the restraints of the Constitution." Reid v. Covert, 354 U.S. 1, 16 (1957). As a practical matter, the issue, though of great theoretical interest, has not spawned significant case law, perhaps because the president and the Senate have been hesitant, on either political or constitutional grounds, to test the limits of their joint power. One reason for such hesitation, no doubt, was the intense and bitter debate that took place in the early 1950s, sparked by a California court's overturning a state law on grounds that it violated the United Nations Charter, Fujii v. State, 217 P.2d 481, aff'd on other grounds, 242 P.2d 617 (1952). Led by Ohio Senator John Bricker, with the support, among others, of the American Bar Association, an attempt was made to amend the Constitution explicitly to restrict the reach of the Treaty Clause. Although the attempt failed, as a formal matter, the *Reid* dictum, coupled with dictates of political prudence, may be said to have achieved much the same result.

Imagine, though, that the statute in Missouri v. Holland had involved child labor and was based on an international treaty, duly submitted by the president and ratified by two-thirds of the Senate, that banned child labor. Could Congress then have repassed the legislation struck down in *Hammer*? Or assume, that the Senate, when ratifying the International Covenant on Civil and Political Rights, as it did in 1992, had not, as in fact it did, indicated non-acquiescence (by "reserving" the relevant article of the treaty) to the section banning imposition of the death penalty on persons who had been minors when committing the crimes for which they were sentenced and instead ratified the Covenant literally without reservation.[132] Could Congress then have passed a statute invalidating any state statutes that in fact allow the imposition of capital punishment in such cases? Or, finally, consider Article 20 of the International Covenant on Civil and Political rights, also "reserved" when ratified by the Senate: "1. Any propaganda for war shall be prohibited by law. 2. Any advocacy of national, racial, or religious hatred that constitutes incitement to discrimination, hostility or violence shall be prohibited by law." Had Article 20 not

130. Thomas M. Franck and Michael J. Glennon, Foreign Relations and National Security Law 298 (2d ed. 1993). See generally Curtis A. Bradley, The Treaty Power and American Federalism, 97 Mich. L. Rev. 390 (1998), which summarizes much of the extant literature even as he suggests that there are indeed federalism limitations to the scope of the treaty power.

131. G. Edward White, The Transformation of the Constitutional Regime of Foreign Relations, 85 Va. L. Rev. 1, 46-61 (1999).

132. U.S. Senate Resolution of Advice and Consent to Ratification of the International Covenant on Civil and Political Rights, 102d Cong., 2d Sess., 138 Cong. Rec. S 4781-4784 (Apr. 2, 1992).

been "reserved," could Congress then have passed a statute enforcing the commitment set out? If you answer no in regard to these examples, then does that indicate that you see *no* argument for treating statutes passed to enforce treaties at all differently from ordinary Article I statutes?

V.   "When a Nation Is at War": World War I and the First Amendment

The First Amendment assumed a significant place in American constitutional jurisprudence in response to governmental attempts to suppress opposition to U.S. participation in World War I.[133] The first cases immediately followed Congress's establishment of a military draft in 1917. Emma Goldman, Alexander Berkman, and other prominent radicals were indicted and convicted for conspiring to induce eligible people not to register for the draft. The Supreme Court readily upheld the convictions, responding to the defendants' protests that they had not in fact advised people to disobey the law by noting that this question was within the province of the jury.[134]

In June 1917, two months after American entry into the war against Germany, Congress passed an Espionage Act that, among other things, prohibited speech inciting insubordination in the military and naval forces of the United States or the refusal of service in the armed forces. The basic framework for future elaboration of the meaning of the First Amendment was established in four cases decided in 1919 — Schenck v. United States, 249 U.S. 47 (1919); Sugarman v. United States, 249 U.S. 182 (1919); Frohwerk v. United States, 249 U.S. 204 (1919); Debs v. United States, 249 U.S. 211 (1919).

Debs v. United States affirmed the conviction of Eugene V. Debs, the acknowledged leader of American socialism, who had gained over a million votes as the Socialist candidate for the presidency in 1912, for violating the Espionage Act. The conviction was based on a speech, delivered in 1918 in Canton, Ohio, expressing his deep opposition to the war. In an opinion that never refers to Debs by name or identifies him as a prominent dissident, Justice Holmes described the speech as follows:

> The main theme of the speech was socialism, its growth, and a prophecy of its ultimate success. With that we have nothing to do, but if a part or the manifest intent of the more general utterances was to encourage those present to obstruct the recruiting service and if in passages such encouragement was directly given, the immunity of the general theme may not be enough to protect the speech. The speaker began by saying that he had just returned from a visit to the workhouse in the neighborhood where three of their most loyal comrades were paying the penalty for their devotion to the working class — these being Wagenknecht, Baker and Ruthenberg, who had been convicted of aiding and abetting another in failing to register for the draft. He said that he had to be prudent and might not be able to say all that he thought, thus intimating to his hearers

---

133. See David M. Rabban, Free Speech in Its Forgotten Years (1997); see also Mark A. Graber, Transforming Free Speech: The Ambiguous Legacy of Civil Libertarianism (1991).

134. Goldman v. United States, 245 U.S. 474 (1918). *Goldman* and companion cases are discussed in David Rabban, The Emergence of Modern First Amendment Doctrine, 50 U. Chi. L. Rev. 1205, 1244-1246 (1984).

that they might infer that he meant more, but he did say that those persons were paying the penalty for standing erect and for seeking to pave the way to better conditions for all mankind. Later he added further eulogies and said that he was proud of them. He then expressed opposition to Prussian militarism in a way that naturally might have been thought to be intended to include the mode of proceeding in the United States.

After considerable discourse that it is unnecessary to follow, he took up the case of Kate Richards O'Hare, convicted of obstructing the enlistment service, praised her for her loyalty to socialism and otherwise, and said that she was convicted on false testimony, under a ruling that would seem incredible to him if he had not had some experience with a Federal Court. We mention this passage simply for its connection with evidence put in at the trial. The defendant spoke of other cases, and then, after dealing with Russia, said that the master class has always declared the war and the subject class has always fought the battles — that the subject class has had nothing to gain and all to lose, including their lives; that the working class, who furnish the corpses, have never yet had a voice in declaring war and have never yet had a voice in declaring peace. "You have your lives to lose; you certainly ought to have the right to declare war if you consider a war necessary." The defendant next mentioned Rose Pastor Stokes, convicted of attempting to cause insubordination and refusal of duty in the military forces of the United States and obstructing the recruiting service. He said that she went out to render her service to the cause in this day of crises, and they sent her to the penitentiary for ten years; that she had said no more than the speaker had said that afternoon; that if she was guilty so was he, and that he would not be cowardly enough to plead his innocence; but that her message that opened the eyes of the people must be suppressed, and so, after a mock trial before a packed jury and a corporation tool on the bench, she was sent to the penitentiary for ten years.

There followed personal experiences and illustrations of the growth of socialism, a glorification of minorities, and a prophecy of the success of the international socialist crusade, with the interjection that "you need to know that you are fit for something better than slavery and cannon fodder." The rest of the discourse had only the indirect though not necessarily ineffective bearing on the offences alleged that is to be found in the usual contrasts between capitalists and laboring men, sneers at the advice to cultivate war gardens, attribution to plutocrats of the high price of coal, &c., with the implication running through it all that the working men are not concerned in the war, and a final exhortation "Don't worry about the charge of treason to your masters; but be concerned about the treason that involves yourselves." The defendant addressed the jury himself, and while contending that his speech did not warrant the charges said "I have been accused of obstructing the war. I admit it. Gentlemen, I abhor war. I would oppose the war if I stood alone." The statement was not necessary to warrant the jury in finding that one purpose of the speech, whether incidental or not does not matter, was to oppose not only war in general but this war, and that the opposition was so expressed that its natural and intended effect would be to obstruct recruiting. If that was intended and if, in all the circumstances, that would be its probable effect, it would not be protected by reason of its being part of a general program and expressions of a general and conscientious belief.

Justice Holmes responded to Debs's constitutional argument by referring to Schenck v. United States, issued a week earlier, in which Holmes had written for a unanimous Court.

It well may be that the prohibition of laws abridging the freedom of speech is not confined to previous restraints, although to prevent them may have been the main purpose. . . . We admit that in many places and in ordinary times the defendants . . . would have been within their constitutional rights. But the character of every act depends upon the circumstances in which it is done. The most stringent protection of free speech would not protect a man in falsely shouting fire in a theatre and causing a panic. . . . The question in every case is whether the words used are used in such circumstances and are of such a nature as to create a clear and present danger that they will bring about the substantive evils that Congress has a right to prevent. It is a question of proximity and degree. When a nation is at war many things that might be said in time of peace are such a hindrance to its effort that their utterance will not be endured so long as men fight and that no Court could regard them as protected by any constitutional right. It seems to be admitted that if an actual obstruction of the recruiting service were proved, liability for words that produced that effect might be enforced. The statute of 1917 in §4 punishes conspiracies to obstruct as well as actual obstruction. If the act, . . . its tendency and the intent with which it is done are the same, we perceive no ground for saying that success alone warrants making the act a crime.

Holmes concluded that in *Debs* "the jury were most carefully instructed that they could not find the defendant guilty for advocacy of any of his opinions unless the words used had as their natural tendency and reasonably probable effect to obstruct the recruiting service, &c., and unless the defendant had the specific intent to do so in his mind."

The same year as *Debs*, Holmes wrote an impassioned dissent, joined by Justice Brandeis, in Abrams v. United States, 250 U.S. 616 (1919), which marks the emergence of the clear-and-present-danger test as a constitutional standard (as distinguished from construction of the Act or definition of inchoate crimes connected with it). The Court in *Abrams* affirmed conspiracy convictions under a 1918 amendment to the act that punished urging curtailment of the production of war material "with the intent . . . to cripple or hinder the United States in the prosecution of the war." Defendants had distributed leaflets that said: "Workers in the ammunition factories, you are producing bullets, bayonets, and cannon to murder not only the Germans, but also your dearest, best, who are in Russia fighting for your freedom. . . . Workers, our reply to [America's] barbaric intervention [to destroy the Bolshevik Revolution] has to be a general strike." Justice Clarke wrote for the Court:

It will not do to say . . . that the only intent of these defendants was to prevent injury to the Russian cause. Men must be held to have intended, and to be accountable for, the effects which their acts were likely to produce. Even if their primary purpose and intent was to aid the cause of the Russian Revolution, the plan of action which they adopted necessarily involved, before it could be realized, defeat of the war program of the United States, for the obvious effect of this appeal, if it should become effective, as they hoped it might, would be to persuade persons . . . not to work in ammunition factories.

In a dissent joined by Brandeis, Holmes wrote:

[A]s against dangers peculiar to war, as against others, the principle of the right to free speech is always the same. It is only the present danger of immediate evil or an intent to bring it about that warrants Congress in setting a limit to the expression of opinion where private rights are not concerned. Congress certainly cannot forbid all effort to change the mind of the country. Now nobody can suppose that the surreptitious publishing of a silly leaflet by an unknown man, without more, would present any immediate danger that its opinions would hinder the success of the government arms or have any appreciable tendency to do so. Publishing those opinions for the very purpose of obstructing however, might indicate a great danger and at any rate would have the quality of an attempt. So I assume that the . . . leaflet if published for the [purpose of hindering the prosecution of the war] might be punishable. But it seems pretty clear to me that nothing less than that would bring these papers within the scope of this law. An actual intent in the sense that I have explained is necessary, to constitute an attempt, where a further act of the same individual is required to complete the substantive crime. . . . It is necessary where the success of the attempt depends upon others because if that intent is not present the actor's aim may be accomplished without bringing about the evils sought to be checked. An intent to prevent interference with the revolution in Russia might have been satisfied without any hindrance to carrying on the war in which we were engaged. I do not see how anyone can find the intent required by the statute in any of the defendants' words.

Holmes also wrote an influential dissent in Gitlow v. New York, 268 U.S. 652 (1925), in which the Court, even as it upheld the conviction of Benjamin Gitlow, a communist (and former state legislator), for violating New York's criminal anarchy law, nonetheless for the first time agreed that the States were limited in their power by the First Amendment. The New York law in question prohibited, inter alia, publication of any material that "advocates, advises or teaches the duty, necessity or propriety of overthrowing or overturning organized government by force or violence, . . . or by any unlawful means." Justice Clarke's opinion for the Court emphasized the constitutional legitimacy of New York's determination, "through its legislative body, that utterances advocating the overthrow of organized government by force, violence and unlawful means, are so inimical to the general welfare and involve such danger of substantive evil that they may be penalized in the exercise of its police power." By contrast to *Schenck* and companion cases where the speech in question was punished only as part of the commission of a different substantive offense, i.e., obstruction of recruiting, in *Gitlow* the "legislative body ha[d] determined generally, in the constitutional exercise of its discretion, that utterances of a certain kind involve such danger of substantive evil that they be punished."

Holmes wrote in dissent:

Mr. Justice Brandeis and I are of the opinion that this judgment should be reversed. . . . I think that the criterion sanctioned by the full Court in Schenck v. United States, 249 U.S. 47, 52, applies. "The question in every case is whether the words used are in such circumstances and are of such a nature as to create a clear and present danger that they will bring about the substantive evils that [the State] has a right to prevent." . . . If what I think the correct test is applied, it is manifest that there was no present danger of an attempt to overthrow the government by force on the part of the admittedly small minority who shared the defendant's views. It is said that this manifesto was more than a theory, that it was an incitement. Every idea is an incitement. It offers itself for belief and if believed it is acted on unless some other belief outweighs it or some failure of energy stifles the movement at its birth. The only difference between the expression of an opinion and an incitement in the narrower sense is the speaker's enthusiasm for the result. Eloquence may set fire to reason. But whatever may be thought of the redundant discourse before us it had no chance of starting a present conflagration. If in the long run the beliefs expressed in proletarian dictatorship are destined to be accepted by the dominant forces of the community, the only meaning of free speech is that they should be given their chance and have their way.

   If the publication of this document had been laid as an attempt to induce an uprising against government at once and not at some indefinite time in the future it would have presented a different question. The object would have been one with which the law might deal, subject to the doubt whether there was any danger that the publication could produce any result, or in other words whether it was not futile and too remote from possible consequences. But the indictment alleges the publication and nothing more.

Discussion

Justices Holmes and Brandeis, who are major architects of the twentieth-century American theory of freedom of speech, never indicated that they had second thoughts about the convictions of Debs and others upheld in the March 1919 cases. What, then, distinguishes *Debs* from the later cases (and the speech-protective theories enunciated in them)?

1. *The status of the speaker.* In *Abrams,* Holmes derides the possibility that the country faced any danger from "the surreptitious publishing of a silly leaflet by an unknown man." Does this suggest that a jury (or a reviewing court) can properly take into account the speaker's status or the cogency of the ideas presented in deciding whether speech is punishable? Over a million Americans had demonstrated by their ballots that they did not consider Eugene Debs to be articulating "silly" ideas. Is Debs's very prominence a justification for jailing him for ten years for the crime of opposing service in the armed forces during World War I (the "War to end War")? If not, then why was Abrams to be freed, according to Justice Holmes, from the sentence visited upon Debs?

2. *Imminence of the danger presented.* How close to actuality must the threatened danger be in order to make its advocacy punishable? (It is a feature of almost all of the major freedom of speech cases that the threatened danger did not in fact occur. For example, no evidence was presented that Debs actually persuaded anyone to resist the draft or that anyone accepted Gitlow's beseeching advice to work toward overthrow of the state.) Although Holmes never elaborated the precise dimensions of "presentness" within the clear-and-present-danger test, he joined in Brandeis's opinion in Whitney v. California, 274 U.S. 652 (1925), which stated:

> There must be reasonable ground to believe that the danger apprehended is imminent. . . . Every denunciation of existing law tends in some measure to increase the probability that there will be a violation of it. . . . But even advocacy of violation, however reprehensible morally, is not a justification for denying free speech where the advocacy falls short of incitement and there is nothing to indicate that the advocacy would be immediately acted on. The wide difference between advocacy and incitement, between preparation and attempt, between assembling and conspiracy, must be borne in mind. . . .
>
> [N]o danger flowing from speech can be deemed clear and present unless the incidence of the evil apprehended is so imminent that it may befall before there is opportunity to full discussion. If there be time to expose through discussion the falsehood and fallacies, to avert the evil by the processes of education, the remedy to be applied is more speech, not enforced silence. Only an emergency can justify repression.

Could Debs possibly be convicted under this version of the clear-and-present-danger test? Does the *Whitney* opinion therefore represent a significant, albeit unacknowledged, expansion of the limitations on state regulation suggested in the earlier opinions? (Brandeis's opinion was technically a concurrence upholding Ms. Whitney's conviction, but in effect it represented a full-scale attack on the majority rationale that upheld the conviction.)

3. *Seriousness of the offense.* Justice Brandeis wrote in *Whitney:* "To justify suppression of free speech there must be reasonable ground to fear that *serious evil* will result if free speech is practiced" (emphasis added). He continued:

> [E]ven imminent danger cannot justify prohibition of [speech] . . . unless the evil apprehended is relatively serious. Prohibition of free speech and assembly is a measure so stringent that it would be inappropriate as the means for averting a relatively trivial harm to society. A policy measure may be unconstitutional merely because the remedy, though effective as means of protection, is unduly harsh or oppressive. Thus, a State might, in the exercise of its police power, make any trespass upon the land of another a crime, regardless of the results or of the intent or purpose of the trespasser. It might, also, punish an attempt, a conspiracy, or an incitement to commit the trespass. But it is hardly conceivable that this Court would hold constitutional a statute which punished as a felony the mere voluntary assembly with a society formed to teach that pedestrians had the moral right to cross unenclosed, unposted, waste lands and to advocate their doing so, even if there was imminent danger that advocacy would lead to a trespass. The fact that speech is likely to result in some violence or in destruction of property is not enough to justify its suppression. There must be the probability of serious injury to the State. Among free men, the deterrents ordinarily to be applied to prevent crime are education and punishment for violations of the law, not abridgment of the rights of free speech and assembly.

Should the degree of imminence required for conviction ever vary depending on the seriousness of the offense? That is, should the state be required to tolerate the same risk of perceived catastrophe as of, say, trespass or some other distinctly noncatastrophic event? In Dennis v. United States, 241 U.S. 404 (1951), the Supreme Court, though stating that it was operating with the ambit of Holmes's clear-and-present-danger test, adopted a formula proffered by Judge Learned Hand: "In each case [courts] must ask whether the gravity of the 'evil,' discounted by its improbability, justifies such invasion of free speech as is necessary to avoid the danger." As Robert McCloskey points out, "The requirement of a 'present' danger is subordinated to the requirement of a 'probable' one. Immediacy is still relevant but only insofar as it may affect probability."[135] Critics of *Dennis*, including Justices Black and Douglas, argued that this test was far too accepting of the suppression of speech. Moreover, it is wholly unclear what would ever authorize a court's setting aside a legislative assessment of gravity and likelihood: "[T]he judicial inquiry becomes by this formulation as broad and as conjectural as the legislative process itself." Indeed, the concurring opinions by Justices Jackson and Frankfurter, like Justice Clarke's opinion in *Gitlow,* "were pervaded with the idea that the judiciary was unqualified to second-guess Congress about such far-flung judgments and on issues of such magnitude."

Not at all coincidentally, *Dennis* arose during the midst of the Cold War and involved the jailing of top leaders of the Communist Party. No one seriously suggested that there was any immediate likelihood (i.e., "clear and present danger") of overthrowing the constituted form of government (or, indeed, that the leaders were even on the brink of fomenting an attempted revolution). This seemed irrelevant, though, once the even-minimal likelihood was multiplied by the

135. Robert McCloskey, The Modern Supreme Court 80 (1972). The quotations in this and the next paragraph are taken from pp. 80-82 of the chapter "The Vinson Court."

almost infinite gravity of a loss of American liberty. As McCloskey says, the *Dennis* test "simply provided a metaphorical way of explaining why the judiciary felt unable to challenge, on substantive grounds, the congressional will to scotch the Red Menace." For many analysts, the repression of speech permitted by *Dennis* was enough to discredit the Hand formula. But should a legislature or court completely ignore the evil threatened? Should one be as formally indifferent to an estimated 40 percent chance of a racial massacre, if that is what is being advocated, as to a 40 percent probability of peaceful trespass or even disruption of rush-hour traffic? If your answer is no, then does this inevitably lead to a reinvention of some version of the Hand formula?

What do you think that Justice Brandeis means by his reference to "injury to the State"? Can the state deter injury to the property or person of "private" individuals by criminalizing the making of speeches likely to bring them about?

Justice Holmes in *Schenck* takes note of the fact that the case arose while the nation was "at war." Abrams's violation also arose during World War I, though Gitlow's took place only afterward. In any event, what precisely is the relevance of the wartime status of the country as a whole in determining the boundaries of free speech?

4. *Institutional competence.* The constitutional standards discussed above are concerned with questions of "fact." How relevant should it be that a jury made a purportedly context-specific determination that the particular speech in question presented a threat to public order, or that the New York legislature made a blanket determination in passing its criminal anarchy law that New York would be threatened by any such exercise of subversive speech?

One of the recurrent issues in First Amendment cases concerns the relative roles of legislature, jury, and reviewing court in determining the potential threat offered by speech. You have previously seen Holmes as the resolute champion of legislative rights in such cases as *Lochner, Hammer,* and *Bailey,* where he stressed that judges were not licensed to override even "tyrannical" legislation in the absence of a specific constitutional mandate to do so. Here, on the other hand, Holmes and Brandeis, another prominent defender of legislative prerogative in the "social" realm, would limit legislative power. One might, of course, distinguish regulation of wages and hours from regulation of speech simply by reference to the language of the First Amendment. Justice Hugo Black would later argue in mid-century, the "no law" language of the First Amendment entails the invalidity of *any* law criminalizing *any* speech. But Holmes offers no such textual argument. What, then, justifies less judicial deference to the legislature in free speech cases than in wages-and-hours cases? Might one have greater mistrust for the legislative capacity to make wise decisions in the former than the latter? If so, why? And what about juries? Why should not a jury's determination that a given speech constituted a clear and present danger be dispositive in the same way that its determination of any other legal "fact" is?

5. *Context versus formal content.* The clear-and-present-danger test has been extremely influential in later development of First Amendment doctrine. Was this test, however, the only or even the best way of delimiting accountability for violation of the Espionage Act? Would an "advocacy of unlawful action" or a still narrower "criminal solicitation" approach have been preferable? In Masses Publishing Co. v. Patten, 244 F. 535 (S.D.N.Y. 1917), Judge Learned Hand held for the plaintiffs in an action to compel the postmaster to accept their magazine in the mails, which he had refused to do on the ground that it violated the Espionage Act. The magazine vehemently criticized American participation in the war and

expressed sympathy and admiration for conscientious objectors to conscription. Judge Hand conceded that it might in fact "cause" insubordination and resistance, but held that this was not sufficient to bring it within the Act:

> One may not counsel or advise others to violate the law as it stands. Words are not only the keys of persuasion, but the triggers of action, and those which have no purport but to counsel the violation of law cannot by any latitude of interpretation be a part of that public opinion which is the final source of government in a democratic state. The defendant asserts . . . that the magazine . . . counsels and advises resistance to existing law, especially to the draft . . . To counsel or advise a man to an act is to urge upon him either that it is his interest or his duty to do it. While, of course, this may be accomplished as well by indirection as expressly, since words carry the meaning that they impart, the definition is exhaustive, I think, and I shall use it. Political agitation, by the passions it arouses or the convictions it engenders, may in fact stimulate men to the violation of law. Detestation of existing policies is easily transformed into forcible resistance of the authority which puts them in execution, and it would be folly to disregard the causal relation between the two. Yet to assimilate agitation, legitimate as such, with direct incitement to violent resistance, is to disregard the tolerance of all methods of political agitation which in normal times is a safeguard of free government. The distinction is not a scholastic subterfuge, but a hard-bought acquisition in the fight for freedom. . . . If one stops short of urging upon others that it is their duty or their interest to resist the law, it seems to me one should not be held to have attempted to cause its violation. If that be not the test, I can see no escape from the conclusion that under this section every political agitation which can be shown to be apt to create a seditious temper is illegal. I am confident that by such language Congress had no such revolutionary purpose in view.

6. Does the clear-and-present-danger test, as compared to possible alternatives, adequately accommodate the competing interests at stake in the Espionage Act cases? Is it a judicially administrable test as applied to the Espionage Act? Consider Gerald Gunther's discussion of the *Masses* alternative.[136]

> [Hand] did not think that tightening the required chain of causation was an apt or effective method of protecting speech. To second-guess enforcement officials about probable consequences of subversive speech was to him a questionable judicial function: judges had no special competence to foresee the future. Moreover, even if predictions about the consequences of words were thought to be appropriate court business, the task would ordinarily fall not to the judge but to the jury, a body reflecting majoritarian sentiments unlikely to be conducive to the protection of dissent in wartime.
>
> Hand's solution to the problem of an appropriate and effective judicial role was to focus on the speaker's words, not in their probable consequences. Instead of asking in the circumstances of each case whether the words had a tendency or even a probability of producing unlawful conduct, he sought a more "absolute and objective test" focusing on "language" — "a qualitative formula, hard, conventional, difficult to evade," as he said in his letters. What he urged was essentially an incitement test, "a test based upon the nature of the utterance itself": if the words constituted solely a counsel to law violation, they could be forbidden: all other utterances were permissible. . . .
>
> Here was a strict, literal, perhaps even strained doctrine in the interest of speech protection. The approach had its problems. As contemporaries recognized, it could

---

136. Gerald Gunther, Learned Hand and the Origins of Modern First Amendment Doctrine: Some Fragments of History, 27 Stan. L. Rev. 719, 725, 729 (1975). See also David Rabban, The First Amendment in Its Forgotten Years, 90 Yale L.J. 514 (1981).

not easily deal with the indirect but purposeful incitement of Marc Anthony's oration over the body of Caesar. Although Hand recognized that advocacy could be accomplished by "indirection," he insisted on starting with the "literal meaning" of the words and never completely explained how far beyond he was willing to go.

7. *Subsequent developments.* A full elaboration of constitutional doctrine concerning "subversive" speech is beyond the scope of this casebook. However, you should be aware of what remains the Court's most recent major statement — in Brandenburg v. Ohio. 395 U.S. 444 (1969), which reversed the conviction of a leader of the Ku Klux Klan for violating the Ohio Criminal Syndicalism statute by "advocat[ing] . . . the duty, necessity, or propriety of crime, sabotage, violence, or unlawful methods of terrorism as a means of accomplishing industrial or political reform" and for "voluntarily assembl[ing]" for those purposes. Speaking before a Klan rally, Brandenburg had called for "revengence" against Jews, blacks, and three branches of the national government. In a per curiam opinion, the Court unanimously struck down the Act and Brandenburg's conviction under it, in the process formally overruling *Whitney's* upholding of the California Criminal Syndicalism Act. The Court wrote:

> [T]he constitutional guarantees of free speech and free press do not permit a State to forbid or proscribe advocacy of the use of force or of law violation except where such advocacy is directed to inciting or producing imminent lawless action and likely to incite or produce such action. . . . "[T]he mere abstract teaching . . . of the moral propriety or even moral necessity for a resort to force and violence, is not the same as preparing a group for violent action and steeling it to such action." A statute which fails to draw this distinction impermissibly . . . sweeps within its condemnation speech which our Constitution has immunized from governmental control. . . . Statutes affecting the right of assembly, like those touching on freedom of speech, must observe the established distinctions between mere advocacy and incitement to imminent lawless action. . . . [The Ohio] statute falls within the condemnation of the First and Fourteenth Amendments.

Professor Gunther comments:[137]

> In one sense, *Brandenburg* combines the most protective ingredients of the *Masses* incitement emphasis with the most useful elements of the clear and present danger heritage. . . .
>
> The incitement emphasis is Hand's; the reference to "imminent" reflects a limited influence of Holmes, combined with later experience; and the "likely to incite or produce such action" addition in the *Brandenburg* standard is the only reference to the need to guess about future consequences of speech, so central to the *Schenck* approach. Under *Brandenburg*, probability of harm is no longer the central criterion for speech limitations.
>
> The inciting language of the speaker — the Hand focus on "objective" words — is the major consideration. And punishment of the harmless inciter is prevented by the *Schenck*-derived requirement of a likelihood of dangerous consequences.
>
> And so, via Justice Harlan and the Supreme Court majority at the end of the Warren era, the language-oriented incitement criterion, so persistently urged by Hand in *Masses* and in [his] letters, has become central to the operative law of the land. *Brandenburg* is the most speech-protective standard yet evolved by the Supreme Court.

137. Gunther, at 754-755.

Note: Further Questions on the Constitution and "Emergency Power" During Time of War

Consider again Justice Holmes's statement in *Schenck:* "When a nation is at war many things that might be said in time of peace are such a hindrance to its effort that their utterance will not be endured so long as men fight and that no Court could regard them as protected by any constitutional right." Recall Madison's "first rule" of interpretation, Chapter 1, supra, *"Where the meaning is clear,* the consequences, whatever they may be, are to be admitted. . . ." (emphasis added). The text of the First Amendment states that "Congress shall make no law . . . abridging the freedom of speech." Is the First Amendment "unclear," so that the "freedom of speech," rightly understood, simply does not extend to comments like those of Schenck or Debs? Or is Holmes suggesting that because the public would not stand for the protection of speech like that of Schenck and Debs during time of war, no court would interpret the Constitution to protect them?

Is there anything special about speech that would make it more appropriate to limit the freedoms guaranteed by the First Amendment "when a nation is at war" than other provisions of the Constitution? Consider in this context other wartime cases (including nonjudicial decisions such as the Emancipation Proclamation) that you have read in the course. Or consider the Court's argument in another case involving Eugene Debs, In re Debs, 158 U.S. 564 (1895), which concerned the inherent power of federal courts, even if not specifically authorized to do so by Congress, to issue injunctions to alleviate potential "emergencies" caused by strikes disrupting the smooth flow of interstate commerce. (For more on In re Debs see our Web site, *http://www.conlaw.net.*)

Professor Harry Scheiber notes that during World War I Congress "authorized the President to nationalize or take over the operations of railroads and water-transport systems, telegraph companies, and ship-building facilities." The Lever Act, passed in August 1917, delegated yet further powers to the President, "covering a vast array of economic activities and interests." Moreover, Wilson "ordered new controls over mining, food supply and prices, mineral production, and the processing of alcoholic beverages." Congress also gave Wilson "virtually plenary power over the property of enemy governments and enemy aliens, together with authority to establish comprehensive presidential control over imports and exports. All this, of course, happened," notes Scheiber, "parallel to the harsh campaign of repression of speech and press under espionage and sedition acts."[138] Elsewhere in his article, Scheiber discusses expansions of national and, especially, executive power in both earlier wars, most notably, of course, the Civil War, and later wars, including the current "war on terror."

Consider the second clause in Madison's address on the First Bank of the United States: "Where the meaning is clear, the consequences, *whatever they may be,* are to be admitted. . . ." (emphasis added). Do the materials you have read in this course suggest that Madison's view has been decisively rejected, at least when the consequences are indeed thought to be dire? Is there *any* part of the Constitution whose "clear meaning" you would in all circumstances enforce during time of war or time of serious emergency, even if you were persuaded that the costs to the war effort (or the national

---

138. Scheiber, Property Rights Versus "Public Necessity": A Perspective on Emergency Powers and the Supreme Court, 28 J. Sup. Ct. Hist. 339, 354-355 (2003).

economy) might be considerable? (Or would you simply say that during such periods, the meaning of the constitutional text is not as clear as it might otherwise seem?)

Imagine, for example, that Presidents Lincoln or Roosevelt had asked Congress to pass a law suspending the elections of 1864 or 1944 on the ground that the confusion and uncertainty (and the threat to national unity) posed by a presidential election is inappropriate "when a nation is at war." Indeed, one of the most serious problems of a wartime election under the American Constitution is the danger of a gap in effective governance — and coordination of the war effort with military allies — if a wartime president loses an election, due to the time lag between election and inauguration. The latter is caused in part by the mechanisms of the Electoral College, and in part by the constitutional rules regarding when Congress must be in session. (The Twentieth Amendment was passed in part to alleviate some of the difficulties of transition. Does it solve the problem entirely?)

For example, Abraham Lincoln, who defeated James Buchanan in November 1860, did not take office until March 4, 1861. In effect, the United States was without a functioning government during the "secession winter" that tore the Union apart. Ask yourself whether it would not be prudent to guard against a similar scenario during a time of actual war, especially if the candidate running against the sitting president gave indication of supporting radically different policies, as in fact General George McClellan did in 1864. Despite this, Lincoln never made the slightest attempt to forestall the 1864 election, which he in fact expected to lose until Union victories, especially at Vicksburg, turned the tide. Does this speak well of Lincoln? What if he had lost? Was it a risk worth taking? How do you think Lincoln would have distinguished the need for fidelity to this aspect of the constitutional system from his willingness to suspend other elements of the constitutional scheme during the Civil War?

Compare American practices with those of the British political system during the period of World War II. Neville Chamberlain, the sitting Prime Minister, was forced to resign his office in 1940, when King George VI named Winston Churchill to replace him. The British had suspended parliamentary elections, which were supposed to be held at least every five years, so that the Parliament elected on November 14, 1935 held office until July 1945 (when the British voted Churchill out of office and placed the Labor Party in power). The British practice is that the leader of the winning political party takes over immediately from the previous prime minister. Thus Churchill, who was conducting important negotiations with President Truman and Soviet dictator Josef Stalin at the Potsdam Conference that began on July 16, 1945, was replaced on July 27 by the new Prime Minister, Clement Atlee. Do you regard the American practice of a fairly long transition in leadership following elections as superior even in time of war, or, if not superior, at least acceptable? If you find it problematic, can anything, as a practical matter, be done about it?

Next, imagine that a wartime president becomes seriously ill, as Woodrow Wilson in fact did following his return from the Versailles Conference in Europe and his unsuccessful efforts to gain Senate ratification of the Treaty of Versailles. Wilson was, as a practical matter, not able to function as president following a catastrophic stoke on October 3, 1919, though he remained in office until Warren G. Harding was inaugurated on March 4, 1921. There was at that time no Twenty-Fifth Amendment to deal with presidential succession. Would it have been proper for the House of Representatives to vote a bill of impeachment and for the Senate to convict to replace Wilson with Vice President Thomas R. Marshall (who is best known in American history for having suggested that "what America needs most is a good five-cent cigar," though he had been Governor of Indiana prior to becoming Vice President)? The Constitution requires the commission of a "high crime or misdemeanor" to impeach a President. Is suffering a disabling stroke such a "high crime or misdemeanor"? Should your answer be determinative as to whether Wilson should have been allowed to continue occupying the office to which he had been reelected in 1916? Now look at the text of the Twenty-Fifth Amendment, which was passed specifically to deal with presidential death or disability. Does it provide an adequate alternative to impeachment in time of war or national emergency? Does it prevent what is in essence a coup d'etat in emergency situations or actually facilitate it?

Note, of course, that the Twenty-Fifth Amendment is of no help if it is Congress that is incapacitated. Suppose that a devastating attack wipes out most of the membership of the House and the Senate. Would the House or Senate be able even to meet and legislate if, for example, most of its members were left debilitated (rather than dead) after an attack? Read the "quorum" provisions of Article I §5 very carefully; compare as well the Seventeenth Amendment's response to senatorial deaths or resignations with that of the unamended Constitution with regard to vacancies that emerge in the House of Representatives. Do you believe that the president should be permitted to "legislate" in such emergency situations, including, presumably, declaring that certain conduct is criminal, where, as a technical matter, neither the House nor Senate might be able to muster a constitutionally required quorum?

Compare your answers about the First Amendment in time of emergency with your views about structural provisions like separation of powers and regular elections. If the First Amendment can be "bent" or interpreted away during time of war or national crisis, why not the structural provisions as well? Should all provisions be equally malleable in times of emergency or should some continue to be strictly, even rigidly, enforced? If the latter, which provisions and why?

VI. *Constitutional Innovation During the Progressive Period*

Formal change in the Constitution — signified by the addition of new text to the Constitution via the processes of amendment — has tended to occur in spurts. Thus the first ten amendments were added in 1791, and the Thirteenth through Fifteenth Amendments were added between 1865 and 1870. Similarly, the period of the so-called Progressive Era, dating roughly from 1900 to 1920 — also saw a burst of constitutional amendment, with the addition of the four new pieces of constitutional text.

A. The Sixteenth Amendment

Although proposed by Congress in 1909, the Sixteenth Amendment was not ratified until 1913. It was designed to override Pollock v. Farmers' Loan & Trust Co., 158 U.S. 601 (1895), in which the Court, by a 5-4 vote, had declared unconstitutional the income tax law of 1894, the first such peacetime levy by Congress. The basis of the decision was Article I, §9, cl. 4: "No Capitation, or other direct, Tax shall be laid, unless in Proportion to the Census or Enumeration herein before directed to be taken." A survival of the "requisition" system of taxation that operated during the Articles of Confederation, this in effect would require that the burden of any "direct" tax fall on each state equally in terms of its population. (Recall that the Constitution also included, in Article I, §2, cl. 3, regarding enumeration, a provision that slaves would count as only three-fifths of persons for such purposes.) This meant that if New York had twice the population of North Carolina, then its citizens, in total, should pay to the treasury a sum twice that of the amount paid by North Carolinians. A tax levied on individual incomes would obviously not achieve this result. The Sixteenth Amendment explicitly authorizes Congress "to lay and collect taxes on incomes, from whatever source derived, without apportionment among the several States, and without regard to any census or enumeration." Note carefully the language of the Amendment. Would it allow Congress to impose a "value-added tax," similar to those levied in most European countries, a wealth tax, or a national sales tax, unless, of course, one determined that these were "indirect" taxes?

The Court in fact has proved quite willing to describe important taxes as non-direct. Thus, only three years after *Pollock*, the Court found that a tax on trades on the Chicago Board of Trade was an "excise" tax because it was a tax on "use of a facility and not on ownership or sale of property." Nicol v. Ames, 173 U.S. 509, 519 (1898). More striking was a description in 1900 of the estate tax as an "excise" tax because it is not concerned with the ownership of property, but, rather, with the passing of the property at death. Knowlton v. Moore, 178 U.S. 41, 78 (1900). Similarly a corporate income tax was upheld as an "excise" tax because it was not imposed on the mere ownership of property but upon the carrying on of a business in corporate form. Flint v. Stone Tracey Co, 220 U.S. 107, 150 (1906). By 1929, the Court would summarize the excise tax exemption as allowing "a tax imposed upon a particular use of property or the exercise of single power over property incident to ownership" without apportionment, Bromley v. McCaughn, 280 U.S. 124, 136 (1929) (upholding the gift tax as an excise because it was a tax on a single incident of ownership — the power of giving).

For recent discussion of the "direct tax" conundrum and the continuing vitality, if any, of the constitutional limitation, see Amar, America's Constitution: A Biography, supra n.12, at 405-409; Bruce Ackerman, Taxation and the Constitution, 99 Colum. L. Rev. 1 (1999); Calvin H. Johnson, Apportionment of Direct Taxes: The Foul-up in the Core of the Constitution, 7 William & Mary Bill of Rights J. 1 (1998). One of the major issues treated in these works is the meaning of "direct tax" at the time of the Constitution. How significant do you think such information should be in interpreting the Constitution today?

B.   The Seventeenth Amendment

The 1787 Constitution assigned the election of senators to state legislatures. Already by the Jacksonian period there were calls to change the original Constitution in this regard,[139] and, as a practical matter, popular elections played a

---

139. See the entry on the Seventeenth Amendment in John Vile, Encyclopedia of Constitutional Amendments, Proposed Amendments, and Amending Issues, 1789-1995, at 272 (1996). Further information in the text is taken from this article. See also C.H. Hoebeke, The Road to Mass Democracy: Original Intent and the Seventeenth Amendment (1995); Vikram David Amar, Indirect Effect of Direct Election: A Structural Examination of the Seventeenth Amendment, 49 Vand. L. Rev. 1346 (1996).

role in the selection process in many states. (Thus, although the Illinois legislature chose the state's senator, Abraham Lincoln and Stephen A. Douglas conducted their debates in order to influence the electorate to vote for persons of their respective political parties who would, presumably, support their appointment to the Senate.) The House of Representatives first proposed eliminating the role of state legislatures in 1894, and repeated its proposals in 1898, 1900, and 1902. Only in 1911 did the Senate even bring the matter to a vote, and it did not gain the requisite two-thirds support. In 1911, Rep. Victor Berger of Wisconsin introduced a resolution to abolish the Senate. Moreover, a number of state legislatures invoked their Article V right to petition Congress to call a new constitutional convention, which could consider the method of election to the Senate. Thus the Senate finally acquiesced in proposing the amendment in May 1912, and it gained the support of three-quarters of the states less than a year later, when, on April 8, 1913, Connecticut became the thirty-sixth state to ratify the amendment. Two commentators have pronounced the Seventeenth Amendment to be "the most direct alteration in the system of federalism since the Civil War Amendments."[140] You should keep the Seventeenth Amendment in mind when you read more recent cases dealing with federalism, which include, among other things, debates about the extent to which Congress should be trusted to give due weight to what Justice O'Connor has labeled "the legitimate interests of States as States," Garcia v. San Antonio Metropolitan Transit Authority, 469 U.S. 528, 584 (1985) (O'Connor, J., dissenting).

C.   The Eighteenth Amendment

The Eighteenth Amendment nationalized the prohibition of alcohol. It represented the culmination of a prohibitionist crusade extending at least back to the 1850s. (Maine was the first state to adopt prohibition, in 1851, and by 1917, 23 states had adopted some form of prohibition, though only 13 were completely dry.) A coalition ranging from members of the Women's Christian Temperance Union to feminists, social reformers, and business labored on behalf of the amendment; they were assisted by anti-Catholic and anti-immigrant sentiments that identified Catholics and immigrants with alcohol consumption, and by World War I-generated sentiment that identified beer with Germany. The amendment passed Congress in December 1917, and was ratified by the thirty-sixth state in January 1919. One important feature of the Eighteenth Amendment was its bold assertion of national authority. "If the federal government could be given authority over something as personal as alcohol use," Professor David Kyvig writes, "could and should it be given responsibility for other matters as well?"[141] The Eighteenth Amendment also enjoys the distinction of being the only amendment to be formally repealed — via the Twenty-First Amendment, proposed and ratified (by state conventions rather than state legislatures) in 1933 as one of the first acts of the New Deal.

---

140. See Richard Bernstein, with Jerome Agel, Amending America: If We Love the Constitution So Much, Why Do We Keep Trying to Change It? 122 (1993).
141. David Kyvig, Authentic and Explicit Acts: Amending the U.S. Constitution 1776-1995, at 217 (1996).

D.   The Nineteenth Amendment

The Nineteenth Amendment ratified in 1920 prohibited discrimination in voting on the basis of sex. Like the Eighteenth Amendment, it represented the fruition of an important social movement that had existed for at least eight decades.[142] (Recall the discussion of the Seneca Falls conference in Chapter 2 and of Minor v. Happersett in this chapter.) As we have seen, opposition to woman suffrage was justified on a number of grounds. First, opponents argued that, by human nature and divine will, women were subordinate to men and therefore unfit to exercise the franchise. Second, because women were economically and legally dependent on men, their interests were appropriately represented by men. This was a version of the republican argument that the family, not the individual, was the basic unit of political representation. Although some women did not have husbands to represent them, they were exceptional because marriage was the appropriate condition of all women. Third, granting the women the vote would weaken this system of family governance, create domestic discord, and draw women away from their duties as wives and mothers.[143]

The suffrage movement not only challenged assumptions about women's abilities, but also the assumptions about political representation, the appropriate structure of the family and the relationship between the family and the state. Suffragists argued that women's continuing subordination both in the public sphere and within the family demonstrated that men could not and would not represent women's interests fairly. The state should be based on individuals, not households; women should have a direct relationship to the state, independent of their position as wives and mothers.

Radical suffragists argued that the family, rightly conceived, was consistent with woman suffrage. They called for a reform of family structure on more egalitarian lines. Like the anti-suffragists, the radical suffragists believed that there was a deep connection between the subordinate status of women in families and their lack of political and economic rights, but they drew a different conclusion from the fact of this connection. In order to achieve political and economic emancipation for women, one had to dismantle women's inferior status in the family, a status that was

---

142. See generally Eleanor Flexner, Century of Struggle: The Woman's Rights Movement in the United States (rev. ed. 1975); Ellen Carol DuBois, Feminism and Suffrage: The Emergence of an Independent Woman's Movement in America, 1848-1869 (1978). Much of the discussion in this section is drawn from Reva B. Siegel, Collective Memory and the Nineteenth Amendment: Reasoning about "the Woman Question" in the Discourse of Sex Discrimination in History, Memory, and the Law 131-182 (Sarat & Kearns eds., 1999). See also Reva B. Siegel, She the People: The Nineteenth Amendment, Sex Equality, Federalism, and the Family, 115 Harv. L. Rev. 947 (2002).

143. Siegel, Collective Memory, at 148-149; See also Siegel, She the People, at 980-981:

> The antis' foundational argument was the argument from virtual representation: women did not need the vote because they were already represented in the government by male heads of household. It was this claim of virtual representation that women's demand to vote most directly challenged. Every time woman suffragists invoked American traditions of individualism, "self-government," and "self-representation" in defense of the right to vote — as when during the New Departure suffragists refused to pay taxes without representation — they were challenging a centuries-old conception of the household that gave men authority to represent women in public and private law. Antis answered suffragists' claims for self-government by emphasizing how changing the distribution of the franchise would threaten the unity of the family: granting women the right to vote would introduce domestic discord into the marital relation and distract women from their primary duties as wives and mothers. Like the virtual representation argument, the marital unity argument linked public and private spheres. Examining the constitutional controversy over enfranchising women reveals that it was, from surface to core, an argument about the family.

enforced and encouraged by law. They argued that the political, economic, and domestic subordination of women were necessarily intertwined:

> Suffragists protested the sex-based restrictions on employment and compensation that impoverished women and drove them into marriage. They deplored women's legally enforced dependency in marriage, particularly property rules that vested in husbands rights to their wives' earnings and to the value of their wives' household labor. They decried law's failure to protect women from physical coercion in marriage, including domestic violence, marital rape and "forced motherhood." They protested double-standards of sexual propriety that punished one sex for conduct in which both were engaged. And they challenged the exclusion of women from juries convened to judge the fate of those in the criminal justice system.[144]

The first major Supreme Court case concerning women's rights after ratification of the Nineteenth Amendment was Adkins v. Children's Hospital, 261 U.S. 525 (1923). *Adkins* involved a District of Columbia law requiring that women (but not men) receive a minimum wage. After noting the restraint on freedom of contract and the purported lack of evidence supporting differential treatment of women and men, the Court invalidated the law as a violation of the due process clause of the Fifth Amendment. Justice Sutherland, writing for the court, stated:

> [T]he ancient inequality of the sexes, otherwise than physical . . . has continued "with diminishing intensity." In view of the great — not to say revolutionary — changes which have taken place since [Muller v. Oregon], in the contractual, political and civil status of women, culminating in the Nineteenth Amendment, it is not unreasonable to say that these differences have now come almost, if not quite, to the vanishing point. In this aspect of the matter, while the physical differences must be recognized in appropriate cases, and legislation fixing hours or conditions of work may properly take them into account, we cannot accept the doctrine that women of mature age, sui juris, require or may be subjected to restrictions upon their liberty of contract which could not lawfully be imposed in the case of men under similar circumstances. To do so would be to ignore all the implications to be drawn from the present day trend of legislation, as well as that of common thought and usage, by which woman is accorded emancipation from that old doctrine that she must be given special protection or be subjected to special restraint in her contractual and civil relationships.

Chief Justice Taft's dissent argued that "[t]he Nineteenth Amendment did not change the physical strength or limitations of women upon which the decision in Muller v. Oregon rests." Justice Holmes, dissenting, quipped that he would "need more than the Nineteenth Amendment to convince me that there are no differences between men and women, or that legislation cannot take those differences into account." Moreover, he believed that Bunting v. Oregon, see p. 430, had settled the issue "and that Lochner v. New York would be allowed a deserved repose."

Adkins represents an interesting convergence of suffragist ideas about marital status law with *Lochner*-era laissez-faire ideology. Before joining the Supreme Court, Sutherland had been an advisor to Alice Paul of the National Woman's Party on legal issues concerning woman suffrage and on the drafting of a proposed Equal

---

144. Joan Zimmerman, "The Jurisprudence of Equality: The Women's Minimum Wage, the First Equal Rights Amendment, and Adkins v. Children's Hospital, 1905-1923," J. of Am. Hist. 178 (1991).

Rights Amendment.[145] Nevertheless, many supporters of women's rights, like Florence Kelley, supported the minimum wage law, and many other forms of protective legislation for women. Kelley believed that suffragists should ally themselves with the sociological jurisprudence of Roscoe Pound and other legal progressives. Indeed, Kelley was one of the authors of the original "Brandeis brief" in Muller v. Oregon. Kelley believed that emphasizing women's maternal functions gave advocates the best chance at reforming working conditions for poor women, because the courts were hostile to arguments about unequal bargaining power and economic inequality.[146]

Alice Paul and the National Woman's Party, on the other hand, argued for an Equal Rights Amendment that would end all discrimination based on sex. Paul eventually came to oppose protective legislation for women. She was attracted to the *Lochner* era's notions of formal freedom of contract as a way to eliminate marital status restrictions on women.[147] Kelley rejected this approach. She believed that it was "worse than useless to try to force all women to accept a uniform male standard. . . . Equality under the law for Kelley meant inequality in the workplace in fact."[148] (Whose view of sex equality, Kelley's or Paul's, looks more reasonable in hindsight?)

During the 1920s a few state and federal courts read the Nineteenth Amendment broadly as modifying common law marital status rules.[149] Several state supreme courts held that the Nineteenth Amendment's guarantee of political equality for women also gave women the right to hold public office and to serve on juries. (Recall the tripartite distinction between political, civil, and social equality made in debates over ratification of the Fourteenth Amendment, in which voting and jury service were both classified as political rights.) However, many other courts construed the Nineteenth Amendment strictly as affecting only the right to vote.[150] *Adkins* was overruled in 1937; by the 1930s courts had essentially forgotten the Nineteenth Amendment as a constitutional source for women's equality rights.

One of the attributes that links these Progressive Era amendments is that they have not generated much litigation. Because most lawyers, including legal academics and their students, focus only on those parts of the Constitution that are in fact litigated before courts, these amendments have produced very little in the way of imaginative thought that might use them as the basis of more general argument. Thus, when feminists challenged a variety of jury-exclusion rules in the 1960s and 1970s, the basis was the Equal Protection Clause of the Fourteenth Amendment rather than the Nineteenth Amendment. (This, of course, repeated the doctrinal history seen in *Strauder.*) Should these amendments have any continuing importance today? For example, does the Nineteenth Amendment's guarantee of political equality have anything important to tell us about women's civil and social equality?

---

145. Joan Zimmerman, The Jurisprudence of Equality: The Women's Minimum Wage, the First Equal Rights amendment, and Adkins v. Children's Hospital, 1905-1923, J. Of Am. Hist. 178 (1991).

146. Id. at 192-193, 198-199.

147. Id. at 203-204.

148. Id. at 207.

149. See Siegel, "Collective Memory," at 158-159; United States v. Hinson, 3 F. 2d 200 (1925) (wife responsible for crimes jointly committed with husband); Hollander v. Abrams, 132 A. 224 (Ct. Chancery N.J. 1926) (contract for sale of land by wife enforceable even though made without husband's consent).

150. Siegel, "Collective Memory," at 161-163; Jennifer K. Brown, Note, "The Nineteenth Amendment and Women's Equality," 102 Yale L.J. 2175 (1993).

E.   Constitutional Limits on Article V?

One final linkage between the Eighteenth and Nineteenth Amendments is that both generated attacks on the constitutionality of the amendments themselves.

1.   Time Limits

The Eighteenth Amendment was the first in American history to carry with it a time limit — seven years — imposed by a Congress that apparently (and mistakenly) believed that this would serve to hinder its ratification.[151] The constitutionality of this time limit was challenged in Dillon v. Gloss, 256 U.S. 368 (1921); it was upheld, with Justice Van Devanter stating for a unanimous court that

> We do not find anything in [Article V] which suggests that an amendment once proposed is to be open to ratification for all time, or that ratification in some of the states may be separated from that in others by many years and yet be effective. We do find that which strongly suggests the contrary. First, proposal and ratification are not treated as unrelated acts but as succeeding steps in a single endeavor, the natural inference being that they are not to be widely separated in time. Secondly, it is only when there is deemed to be a necessity therefor that amendments are to be proposed, the reasonable implications being that when proposed they are to be considered and disposed of presently. Thirdly, as ratification is but the expression of the approbation of the people and is to be effective when had in three-fourths of the States, there is a fair implication that it must be sufficiently contemporaneous in that number of States to reflect the will of the people in all sections at relatively the same period, which of course ratification scattered through a long series of years would not do. These considerations and the general spirit of the Article lead to the conclusion expressed by Judge Jameson [citing to Jameson on Constitutional Conventions, 4th ed., Sec. 585] "that an alteration of the Constitution proposed today has relation to the sentiment and the felt needs of today, and that, if not ratified early while that sentiment may fairly be supposed to exist, it ought to be regarded as waived, and not again to be voted upon, unless a second time proposed by Congress." That this is the better conclusion becomes even more manifest when what is comprehended in the other view is considered; for, according to it, four amendments proposed long ago — two in 1789, one in

---

151. Consider the following analysis:

What §3 of the Eighteenth Amendment did for time, another section of a future amendment could do along other dimensions. For instance, §3 of a hypothetical Twenty-Eighth Amendment proposed in the year 2020 could provide that the amendment would be inoperative unless ratified by four-fifths of the states, rather than a mere three-quarters. Or it could provide that the amendment would be inoperative unless endorsed by the president; or agreed to by supermajorities within individual state legislatures; or unless approved by a national referendum; or unless ratified by states totaling more than 50 percent of the national population. Of course, none of these requirements could formally lower the Article V bar or displace it — that would be pure bootstrap. But by raising the formal bar through a provision specifying when an amendment truly becomes operative, future §3 analogues could, as a practical matter, move America toward a more directly representative system of amendment. If a future §3 required a national referendum vote of approval before the Twenty-Eighth Amendment were to become operative, that fact alone might put pressure on some fence-sitting state legislators to say yes. A yes vote by such a legislature would become less a vote on the proposed Twenty-Eighth's substance, and more a vote to "let the people decide."

Amar, America's Constitution: A Biography, supra n.12, at 418.

1810, and one in 1861 — are still pending and in a situation where their ratification in some of the States many years since by representatives of generations now largely forgotten may be effectively supplemented in enough more States to make three-fourths by representatives of the present or some future generation. To that view few would be able to subscribe, and in our opinion it is quite untenable. We conclude that the fair inference or implications from Article V is that ratification must be within some reasonable time after the proposal.

Since 1918, many proposed constitutional amendments have carried with them time limits imposed by Congress. The question of the constitutional status of time limits, however, emerged in 1992, with regard to the purported Twenty-Seventh Amendment. Initially the second of 12 amendments proposed in 1789, it prohibits Congress from raising the salaries of its members to take effect before an intervening election.[152] Like the rest of the amendments we now know as the Bill of Rights, the proposal did not have a time limit. Unlike original amendments three through twelve (which today we know as the First through Tenth Amendments), it did not fare well. By 1800 it had gained the ratification of only six states; a seventh state ratified it in 1873. "Rediscovered" in the late 1970s by a student at the University of Texas, it was brought up in many state legislatures. Beginning with Wyoming's ratification on March 3, 1978, it was ratified by 32 states thereafter, with Michigan, on May 7, 1992, becoming the 38th state to ratify the 1789 proposal. A flurry of newspaper stories brought the amendment, and questions about its status, to public attention. Several major members of Congress indicated their doubts about the circumstances of "ratification," and it appeared that a legislative debate would ensue.

Some legal commentators, citing *Dillon,* suggested that the amendment had "died" in the 200 years between its first and final ratifications. Thus Yale law professor Paul Gewirtz wrote a letter to Illinois Senator Paul Simon advising that "by concurrent resolution Congress — formally decline to proclaim the amendment as a ratified part of the Constitution; but — send the amendment back out to the states for ratification with an explicit ratification period of 7 years."

Other commentators endorsed the suggestion that, at the least, Congress hold formal hearings about the provenance of the "27th Amendment" and come to some conclusion about the issue, whether it be to agree with Professor Gewirtz and formally repropose it for new ratifications or to "declare" that the 1789 proposal had been truly ratified. Indeed, Professor Gewirtz wrote Senator Simon that "Congress clearly has the power" to decide "whether ratification has occurred within a reasonable period of time," citing Coleman v. Miller, 307 U.S. 433 (1939). Justice Black, writing for a group of four Justices, stated that "Congress has sole and complete control over the amending process," including the power to determine if an amendment "must die unless ratified within a 'reasonable time.'"

Arguments like Professor Gerwirtz's were answered by Harvard professor Laurence Tribe:[153]

Article V says an amendment "shall be valid to all Intents and Purposes, as part of this Constitution" when "ratified" by three-fourths of the states — not that it might face a

---

152. See Richard B. Bernstein, The Sleeper Wakes: The History and Legacy of the Twenty-Seventh Amendment, 61 Fordham L. Rev. 497 (1992).
153. Laurence Tribe, "The 27th Amendment Joins the Constitution," Wall St. J., May 13, 1932, A15.

veto for tardiness. Despite the Supreme Court's suggestion, no speedy ratification rule may be extracted from Article V's text, structure, or history.

Among other mysteries such a rule would create, the most obvious are ones that a society profoundly divided over questions of when human life begins and ends should grasp quite readily: What would be satisfactory criteria for constitutional "life" and "death"? Does a political wildfire that sweeps the nation and then burns itself out reflect more of a consensus than a ratification trajectory spanning the centuries and representing a considered judgment across generations? Whom would we trust to decide what counts as a consensus? Surely not the National Archivist [in whom Congress has vested the duty to certify and publish ratified amendments]? Surely not the 102nd Congress, which has an ax to grind regarding midterm pay raises and which is a dubious repository of power to veto ratifications?

. . . Congress does have an ongoing role in the amendment process under Article V and the Necessary and Proper Clause of Article I: It can choose the "Mode of Ratification" for each amendment it proposes; it may include ratifications deadlines in each, as it has since 1919; and it might even be able to make midcourse adjustments by adding time limits to still pending amendments that lacked them originally. But this makes it all the less necessary to give Congress a decisive post-hoc role in evaluating constitutional ratifications. It is not Congress's role to declare Michigan's 1992 ratification of the 27th amendment too recent or Maryland's 1789 ratification too ancient.

Another ill-considered proposal, that of the New York Times, is that early, contemporaneous ratifications are suspect, while those that came this decade — two cenuries late — are valid, and that the eight states that ratified before 1980 should be required to re-ratify. But what would they be ratifying anyway? A dead amendment that Congress has not reproposed? And if the amendment is *not* "dead," why are the earlier ratifications moribund?

As it turns out, in the words of the *New York Times,* "Congress . . . rushed to bless the 27th Amendment to the Constitution with near unanimity."[154] Without holding a single day of hearings or engaging in any serious debate, both the House and the Senate on May 20, 1992, pronounced the amendment to be "valid . . . as part of the Constitution of the United States" by votes of 414-3 and 99-0, respectively.[155]

Discussion

1. Imagine yourself then-Senator Simon's legislative assistant, called upon to advise him as to the proper response to Michigan's ratification. In particular, if hearings *had* been held, presumably by the Judiciary Committee on which Senator Simon served, to what central questions should he have sought answers? Would any particular answer to a question be dispositive as to his decision to grant or withhold recognition of the amendment?

2. 1 U.S.C. §106b provides:

Whenever official notice is received at the National Archives and Records Administration that any amendment proposed to the Constitution of the United States has been adopted, according to the provisions of the Constitution, the Archivist of the

154. N.Y. Times, May 24, 1992, Section 4, 10.

155. As described by a reporter for the New York Times, "Congressional leaders' early assertion that the House and the Senate would make the final decision on the validity of the pay-raise amendment had long since faded by the time both houses voted today. The issue had simply dried up in an environment of public anger over Congressional perquisites and pay raises, and as a result today's votes were regarded as entirely political, giving members a chance to be on record as in favor of the amendment." Richard Berke, "Congress Backs 27th Amendment," N.Y. Times, May 21, 1992, 26A (late ed. — final).

United States shall forthwith cause the amendment to be published, with his certificate, specifying the States by which the same may have been adopted, and that the same has become valid, to all intents and purposes, as a part of the Constitution of the United States.

The *New York Times* article reporting congressional affirmation of the Twenty-Seventh Amendment includes the sentence that "[t]he votes today came 24 hours after the 27th Amendment to the Constitution had already been made the law of the land with its publication in the Federal Register by Don W. Wilson, Archivist of the United States." (Indeed, Mr. Wilson had announced on May 13 that he would in fact certify the adoption of the amendment.) Is there anything problematic about this sentence? Consider, for example, the possibility that 38 states, believing that the requirement that the President be at least 35 years old is ill-advised, pass resolutions purporting to repeal it; Mr. Wilson, or his successor Archivist, consequently orders published in the Federal Register a new "Twenty-Eighth Amendment" repealing this constitutional requirement. Would its publication in the Federal Register make this new amendment "the law of the land"? Why not? In any event, imagine yourself the legal advisor to the Archivist of the United States, who asks your advice about the circumstances under which he or she should certify the existence of the new Twenty-Seventh Amendment as part of the Constitution and publish it as part of all "official" texts of the Constitution. How would you answer? What, if any, materials beyond those presented so far in this note would you wish to consult?

3. Now imagine yourself a clerk to a federal judge who is called upon to assess the validity of the amendment. For example, under current law, congressional salaries will rise automatically to take account of changes in the cost of living. Assume that someone relevant (and for our purposes no further specification is necessary) refuses to add the cost-of-living adjustment (COLA) to a congressional paycheck because of the amendment and that a representative or senator sues. Although one would surely be interested in whether a COLA is covered by the amendment, the first question that must be answered is whether the amendment even exists, legally, so that one must determine what it means. What would you advise your judge on this point?[156]

4. Perhaps more difficult than imagining yourself to be a legislative assistant, the legal advisor to the National Archivist, or a law clerk, is to take on the identity of the editor of a constitutional law casebook. What decision should be made with regard to including a purported Amendment as part of the text invariably reprinted in casebooks? Should the relevant sentence about congressional salaries simply be reprinted, with no further ado, as Amendment XXVII? Or, if you agree with Professor Gewirtz (among others), should that sentence be omitted, because it is not "really" anything we should call a constitutional amendment? Or did we do the correct thing by placing an asterisk next to the text and directing your attention to these very pages of the casebook? Consider the comments of Duke law professor

---

156. Boehner v. Anderson, 809 F. Supp. 138 (D.D.C. 1992) involved a challenge to the constitutionality of pay raises provided by the Ethics Reform of Act of 1989. The district court avoided any Twenty-Seventh Amendment questions by noting that an election had in fact intervened since passage of the challenged pay raises, though it questioned whether the amendment would have retroactive application to legislation passed before its ratification. An amicus brief apparently raised the issue of the amendment's validity, but none of the parties did; in any event, the court declined to address the issue.

William Van Alstyne, who also followed the asterisk-and-discussion route in his own casebook on the First Amendment.[157] Van Alstyne prints the purported Amendment with an asterisk, followed by a discussion of its provenance. According to Van Alstyne, his placing of the asterisk

> is just a personal way of coping with the headache I've been unable to overcome in thinking about Congress and how it sometimes behaves in matters of constitutional law.
>   . . . Dillon v. Gloss provided the Supreme Court's considered view of what Article V requires in order that an alternative or addition to the Constitution be deemed to satisfy the Constitution. It is also a compelling view, and it was measuredly ventured in a wholly noninflammatory way by a unanimous Supreme Court, a Court including Holmes, Brandeis, and Edward White, the Chief Justice of the United States. One might suppose Congress would provide good reason to suggest why it is not sound if, indeed, it is not.

5. The previous paragraphs have implicitly accepted *Dillon*'s view. See, however, Mason Kalfus, Comment: Why Time Limits on the Ratification of Constitutional Amendments Violate Article V, 66 U. Chi. L. Rev. 437 (1999), which argues that congressionally imposed time limits are unconstitutional insofar as they in effect give Congress too much power to manipulate the amendment process. As to manipulation, note that in 1979 Congress, which had in 1972 proposed the Equal Rights Amendment with a seven-year time limit for ratification, extended the limit for an additional three years. Do you see any constitutional problem with such an extension? (Could a successor Congress, less enamored of a particular proposal than its predecessor, *reduce* a time limit from, say, seven years to four years?)

2.   Are There Substantive Limits to Constitutional Amendment?

In addition to these procedural attacks, opponents also attacked the two amendments on the grounds that they invaded the reserved powers of the states. The Court rejected such attacks, in regard to the prohibition amendment, in The National Prohibition Cases, 253 U.S. 350 (1920), and again in Sprague v. U.S., 282 U.S. 716 (1931). The former case was argued by Elihu Root, one of the most distinguished lawyers of the era. He told the Court, among other things, that the authors of the Constitution "undoubtedly regarded the power to amend only as authorizing the inclusion of matter of the same general character as the instrument or thing to be amended; as all the constitutions of their day were concerned solely with the distribution and limitation of the powers of government, and not with the direct exercise thereof by the constitution makers themselves, no amendment of the latter sort would have been deemed appropriate or germane by them." Moreover, according to Root, "The so-called Eighteenth Amendment *directly* invades the police powers of the States and *directly* encroaches upon their right of local self-government." To accept its legitimacy would authorize, in effect, "the complete subversion of our dual and federal system of government," at least so long as two-thirds of each House of Congress and three-quarters of the states assented. The Court unanimously rejected the argument, though, interestingly enough, there was no genuine "opinion" of the

---

157. What Do You Think About the 27th Amendment, 10 Duke L. Mag., No. 2, 13-17 (1992), reprinted in 10 Constitutional Commentary 9 (1993).

Court, only an announcement of the view that the Amendment was not constitutionally defective.

A similar rejection met the claim, in Leser v. Garnett, 258 U.S. 130 (1922), that the Nineteenth Amendment, because it fundamentally changed the nature of the electorate in states that had limited suffrage to males, was beyond the scope of Article V. Because the electorate constituted the political community of a State, opponents argued, the Nineteenth Amendment had effectively destroyed the political communities of States that limited suffrage to men and replaced them with new ones.[158] There is an obvious problem in distinguishing the Nineteenth from the Fifteenth Amendment, which eliminated (at least as a formal matter) racial restrictions on the suffrage and added blacks to the electorate in many states. Plaintiffs argued (1) that the Fifteenth Amendment had, in effect, been unanimously assented to by the States, since none had disputed its validity for 45 years; and (2) that the Reconstruction Amendments had effectively constituted a treaty necessary to end the Civil War and prevent its recurrence.

The Supreme Court, speaking through Justice Brandeis, unanimously rejected these arguments:

> This Amendment is in character and phraseology precisely similar to the Fifteenth. For each the same method of adoption was pursued. One cannot be valid and the other invalid. That the Fifteenth is valid, although rejected by six States including Maryland, has been recognized and acted on for half a century. The suggestion that the Fifteenth was incorporated in the Constitution, not in accordance with law, but practically as a war measure which has been validated by acquiescence, cannot be entertained.

Consider whether these cases stand for the proposition that *anything* can be added to (or subtracted from) the Constitution, so long as the proposals gain the assent of two-thirds of each House of Congress and three-quarters of the states, or, on the contrary, whether they should be read as holding only that, as a substantive matter, the granting to the national government of regulatory authority over alcohol or to the collective polity of the expansion, via Article V procedures, of the state electorate, is consistent with the spirit of the Constitution and, for that reason — rather than because of a "plenary power" view of Article V — presents no constitutional problems.

Suppose, for example, that instead of expanding the electorate through amendment, three-quarters of the states voted to contract the electorate by returning to the states the power to disenfranchise blacks or women (or, for that matter, persons under 21; see the Twenty-Sixth Amendment). Could one argue that this amendment would be contrary to the basic structure of constitutional government because it would unfairly cut off part of the People from rights of political governance? How is

---

158. For a related argument, see George Stewart Brown, The Nineteenth Amendment: The Amending Clause Was Provided For Changing, Limiting, Shifting, Or Delegating "Powers of Government." It Was Not Provided for Amending "the People." The 19th Amendment is Therefore Ultra Vires, 8 Va. L. Rev. 237 (1922). Brown's argument invoked the compact of states theory: "The sovereignty of the People is expressed through the states, which together formed the Union. Acting through the states, the People delegated power to the Federal government, but did not surrender their sovereignty. It follows that Article V can only delegate powers; it cannot alter sovereignty. The Nineteenth Amendment destroyed the sovereignty of the States by altering the qualifications for electors; thus it illegally altered the Sovereignty of the People."

this argument different from the one rejected in Leser v. Garnett? Is the expansion of the franchise a "one-way ratchet," so that once blacks, women, and persons over 18 have been admitted to We the People, they cannot be excluded? Are *all* expansions of the electorate unproblematic? Suppose that an amendment forced states to give corporations or resident aliens who had filed for citizenship the right to vote. Whatever one thinks of such proposals on the merits, is it clear that future generations could not change their minds and decide to reduce the electorate accordingly? Is the appropriate response to these questions that Article V recognizes no substantive limitations on amendment other than those specifically listed in the text, i.e., that the slave trade cannot be abolished before 1808 and that no state can be deprived equal suffrage in the Senate without its consent? Note that explicit limitations on amendment can be found in the constitutions of other countries. For example, Article 79(3) of the German Basic Law prohibits amendments that would violate "the dignity of man" or destroy the democratic and federal nature of the German Union.[159] Could the German constitutional court properly strike down an amendment allowing chattel slavery because slavery fundamentally violates "the dignity" of all human beings? Note that Article V contains only two explicit substantive limitations on the content of amendments. Does this mean that no others exist and that, as a theoretical matter, the only legal protection against repeal of the Thirteenth Amendment and reinstitution of chattel slavery is the inability of such a proposal to gain the assent of a sufficient number of members of Congress and state legislators?

---

159. See also Walter F. Murphy, Merlin's Memory: The Past and Future Imperfect of the Once and Future Polity, in Responding to Imperfection: The Theory and Practice of Constitutional Amendment (Levinson ed.), 163, 178-80. The Indian Supreme Court, in Golak Nath's Case [1967], A.I.R. 1643, 1670, struck down an amendment of the Indian Constitution as violative of its basic structure.

PART TWO

CONSTITUTIONAL ADJUDICATION
IN THE MODERN[1] WORLD

Having surveyed in Part One a series of interlocking constitutional questions that arose during the first 150 years of constitutional government, we turn in Part Two to the questions that have dominated modern constitutional debate, implicating economic rights and regulations, federalism, separation of powers, race, sex, speech, other fundamental rights, and much more. Some of the questions that we must confront are substantive: For example, what does, or should, "equal protection" or "privacy" mean in today's world? Other questions focus more on the constitutional allocation of power (including the power of interpretation) among competing institutions: Who should decide a given substantive issue, courts or legislatures, the states, or the federal government? Yet another set of questions implicates matters of constitutional methodology: Exactly how should faithful interpreters go about the task of interpreting an old Constitution to apply to new issues? What should be the respective roles of text, history, structure, doctrine, prudence, and so on, in the interpretive process?

---

1. The word "modern" has many meanings. It is sometimes used to mark a division between older traditional practices and newer forms of thought that are consciously posed against them. Or it can be understood as a felt loss of connection to an earlier period of "authentic" tradition, which must be regained at all costs, or which must be consciously reinterpreted or translated in order to become comprehensible and meaningful to us today. See Sanford Levinson and J.M. Balkin, Law, Music, and Other Performing Arts, 139 U. Pa. L. Rev. 1597 (1991).

In constitutional law, we might understand "modernity" as the moment in which the period of the Founding becomes so distant that it begins to seem foreign to us. This leads to at least three possible reactions: (a) we regard ourselves as no longer bound by it, (b) we try to preserve our connection to it through zealous adherence to its concrete manifestations and understandings, or (c) we reject those concrete exemplars and attempt to be true to its spirit through self-conscious historical study, analogy, and reinterpretation.

Constitutional modernity could also refer to a period in which the Supreme Court's role and its relationship to democracy become increasingly problematized. Before the Civil War, the Supreme Court sparingly exercised judicial review to strike down federal statutes. (Indeed, federal statutes were only struck down twice, in *Marbury* and in *Dred Scott*.) After the Civil War, and in the period leading up to the New Deal, the Supreme Court increasingly begins to strike down both federal and state legislation on a number of grounds. Partly as a result, the Supreme Court increasingly becomes understood as an actor in the political system, and the relatively rigid boundaries between law and politics that preserved the Court's legitimacy in earlier times are loosened. Academic critiques of the Court first by legal progressives and later by legal realists emphasize the Court's political role and the political character of its doctrinal analysis. They also question the Court's legitimacy as an anti-democratic and anti-majoritarian institution. Particularly in the period after 1937, the Supreme Court itself begins to problematize its role, and the rhetoric of judicial restraint and the need to avoid unnecessary constitutional decisions becomes ubiquitous in judicial opinions. This modernist anxiety about the practice of judicial review and its relationship to democracy is an element of constitutional modernity that is arguably distinct from the more general problem of constitutional interpretation in a world that has lost an organic connection to tradition.

I.   The Evolution of the Bill of Rights and Its "Incorporation" Against the States[2]

Perhaps the most striking feature of modern constitutional jurisprudence is the leading role that the Bill of Rights now plays both inside courtrooms and beyond. It was not always so. A separate Bill of Rights was no part of James Madison's careful plan at the Philadelphia Convention of 1787, and the document that emerged from Philadelphia omitted an explicit Bill of Rights. When anti-Federalist skeptics pounced on this omission during ratification debates, Federalists scrambled to defend the document with a jumble of counterarguments. Some Federalists claimed that the entire Constitution was a kind of Bill of Rights; others pointed to the specific rules limiting Congress in Article I, §9 as a functional Bill of Rights; and many also claimed (sometimes contradicting themselves or their allies) that a Bill of Rights would in fact prove useless or even dangerous. Madison himself promised to revisit the issue once the Constitution went into effect. Although he kept his promise, shepherding a set of amendments through the First Congress, many of his colleagues viewed the exercise as a "nauseous" distraction from more important and immediate tasks of nation-building.[3]

Once ratified, the Bill played a remarkably small role during the antebellum era — at least in court. Recall that no federal judge invalidated the Sedition Act of 1798, which in effect made it a federal crime to criticize President John Adams or his allies in Congress. Only once in the entire antebellum era did the Supreme Court use the Bill of Rights to strike down an act of the federal government — in *Dred Scott's* highly implausible and strikingly casual claim that the Fifth Amendment's Due Process Clause invalidated free-soil laws like the Northwest Ordinance and the Missouri Compromise, 60 U.S. (19 How.) 393, 450 (1857). In a review of newspapers published in 1841, Dean Robert Reinstein could not find a single 50th anniversary celebration of the Bill of Rights.[4]

Indeed, the Bill of Rights as conventionally viewed in the antebellum era looked profoundly different from the Bill of Rights as widely understood today. Born in the shadow of a Revolutionary War waged by local governments against an imperial center, the original Bill affirmed various rights against the central government, but none against the states, as the Supreme Court made clear in Barron v. Baltimore, 32 U.S. (7 Pet.) 243 (1833). And the rights that the original Bill did affirm sounded more in localism than libertarianism. (Recall that Madison drafted the Bill, in large part, to ease the anxieties of anti-Federalists.) Congress could not establish a national church, but neither could it disestablish state churches. (Several of the states had government-sponsored churches in the 1780s, and many other "nonestablishment" states favored Protestant Christianity in some way or other.) Thus, as originally understood, the First Amendment rule that "Congress shall make no law *respecting* [that is, on the topic of] an establishment of religion" was less anti-establishment than it was pro-states' rights; religious policy would be decided locally, not nationally, in the American equivalent of the European Peace of Augsburg (1555) and Treaty of Westphalia (1648). The Second

---

2. Some of the material presented below borrows from Akhil Reed Amar, The Bill of Rights: Creation and Reconstruction (1998).

3. Letter from James Madison to Richard Peters (Aug. 19, 1789) in 12 The Papers of James Madison 346 (R. Rutland et al. eds., 1979).

4. Robert J. Reinstein, Completing the Constitution: The Declaration of Independence, Bill of Rights and Fourteenth Amendment, 66 Temp. L. Rev. 361, 365 n.25 (1993).

Amendment celebrated local militias (the heroes of Lexington and Concord), and the Third Amendment likewise reflected uneasiness about a central standing army. Much of the rest of the Bill reinforced the powers of local juries. The Fifth Amendment safeguarded grand juries; the Sixth, criminal petit juries; and the Seventh, civil juries. Beyond these specific clauses, many other parts of the original Bill also championed the role of local and populist juries — who were expected to protect popular publishers in First Amendment cases, hold abusive federal officials liable for unreasonable searches in Fourth Amendment cases, and help assess just compensation against the federal government in Fifth Amendment cases. The only amendment endorsed by every state convention demanding a Bill of Rights during the ratification debates was the Tenth Amendment, which emphatically affirmed states' rights. Madison himself wanted more — a Bill championing countermajoritarian individual rights, and protecting them against states, too — but in the First Congress, he was swimming against the tide. His proposed amendment requiring states to respect speech, press, conscience, and juries passed the House (as the presciently numbered Fourteenth Amendment) but died in a Senate that championed states' rights.

Only after a Civil War dramatized the need to limit abusive states would a new Fourteenth Amendment and distinctly modern view of the Bill emerge — a view celebrating individual rights and preventing states from abridging fundamental freedoms. From the 1830s on, antislavery crusaders began to develop, contra *Barron*, a "declaratory" interpretation of the Bill of Rights that viewed the Bill not as creating new or merely federalism-based rules applicable only against federal officials, but as affirming and declaring pre-existing higher-law norms applicable to all governments, state as well as federal. On this declaratory view, for example, although the First Amendment directly regulated "Congress," it also affirmed a pre-existing right to free expression; according to *Barron* contrarians, when the Amendment referred to "*the* freedom of speech," it thereby implied a pre-existing legal freedom. Perhaps this legal freedom of speech could not be enforced against states in federal court, some contrarians conceded. But the First Amendment reference to "the freedom of speech" was itself *evidence* that a true legal right against all governments existed, a right that states were honor-bound to obey even in the absence of a federal enforcement scheme. And what was true of the freedom of speech was also true of the other rights and freedoms explicitly declared in the remainder of the Bill of Rights — the First Amendment freedom of religious exercise, the Fourth Amendment right against unreasonable searches, the Fifth Amendment entitlement to just compensation, and so on. This declaratory theory took shape in a world where many Southern states had enacted extremely repressive laws to prop up slavery — censoring abolitionist speech and press, suppressing antislavery preachers, implementing dragnet searches against suspected fugitive slaves and slave sympathizers, imposing savagely cruel punishments on runaway slaves and their allies, and indeed violating virtually every right mentioned in the federal Bill.

With the passage of the Fourteenth Amendment, contrarians sought to write their views into the Constitution itself, and to overrule *Barron,* just as they sought to overrule *Dred Scott.* By proclaiming, in Section 1 of the Fourteenth Amendment, that "No state shall make or enforce any law which shall abridge the privileges or immunities of citizens of the United States," Reconstruction Republicans tried to make clear that henceforth states would be required by the federal Constitution and by federal courts (and by Congress, too) to obey fundamental rights and freedoms — "privileges" and "immunities" of American "citizens." Where would judges find these freedoms? Among other places, in the federal Bill of Rights itself. Inclusion in the Bill of Rights was strong evidence that a given right — free speech, free exercise, or just compensation, for example — was indeed a fundamental privilege or immunity of all American citizens.[5]

Of course, by seeking to enforce these rights against state governments, Congressman John Bingham and his fellow Reconstructionists were in effect turning the Founders' Bill of Rights on its head. The original Bill had reflected the localism of the American Revolution, whereas Bingham and company were animated by the nationalism of the Civil War. Images of British imperial misbehavior and local heroism had inspired the eighteenth-century Bill of Rights, whereas images of slave state misconduct and national heroism hovered over the Thirty-ninth Congress that drafted the Fourteenth Amendment. For example, the original First Amendment was worded to emphasize that Congress simply lacked enumerated power to regulate religion or censor speech in the several states. Note how its language — "Congress *shall make no law* . . ." — echoed and inverted the language of the necessary and proper clause: "*Congress shall* have power . . . to *make all laws.* . . ." But Bingham's vision stripped away this original veneer of states' rights, stressing instead that henceforth *states* must not "abridge" (a word borrowed from the First Amendment itself) the freedom of speech or of the press or of religion. What had initially been drafted as an amendment to protect state autonomy in religious matters became, in Bingham's revision, a basis for nationalistic restrictions on states insofar as their policies violated the rights of their citizens to the free and equal exercise of religion.[6]

But as we have already seen, the Court in the 1873 *Slaughterhouse Cases* strangled the privileges or immunities clause in its crib. (Recall also that Justice Bradley's dissent in that case contained important language recognizing that this key clause was designed to overrule *Barron*.) As a result, later generations of judges often turned to the Due Process Clause, using it to accomplish many of the purposes originally intended for the privileges or immunities clause.

The first big step away from *Barron*'s regime came in the 1897 *Chicago Burlington* case, which, like *Barron* itself, involved the norm of just compensation. Using language that nicely tracked the declaratory theory, the Court now held that states were indeed bound by the principle of just compensation laid down in the Fifth Amendment: "The [Fifth Amendment] requirement that property shall not be taken for public use without just compensation is but '*an affirmance* of a great

5. At this point, an obvious question arises: If the privileges or immunities clause was designed to prevent states from abridging fundamental freedoms and rights such as those spelled out in the federal Bill, why did the Fourteenth Amendment go on to specifically ban states from depriving persons of due process of law? Wasn't due process (a right mentioned in the Fifth Amendment) a "privilege or immunity" already covered? For an answer to this puzzle, see Amar, supra n.2, at 171-174. (Hint: Note that the privileges or immunities clause speaks of the rights of "citizens" whereas the adjoining Due Process Clause sweeps more broadly, including aliens in its protections of all "persons.") Another question is why, if the framers of the Fourteenth Amendment meant to hold states to the Bill of Rights, no more and no less, they didn't say so more directly. Consider the possibility that, strictly speaking, Bingham and company meant both more and less than the first eight amendments as such. See id. at 174-180. On applying the Amendment to protect fundamental rights beyond those specified in the Bill itself, consider the views of Justices Murphy and Rutledge, discussed infra n.9. And on the ways in which the Fourteenth Amendment might incorporate something less than the Bill of Rights as such, see infra n.12 (discussing "refined incorporation").

6. For general theoretic discussions about how a given text or other sign can come to mean different things in different historical contexts, see J.M. Balkin, Deconstructive Practice and Legal Theory, 96 Yale L.J. 743 (1987); J.M. Balkin, Ideological Drift and the Struggle Over Meaning, 25 Conn. L. Rev. 869 (1993); Lawrence Lessig, Fidelity in Translation, 71 Tex. L. Rev. 1165 (1993).

doctrine established by the common law for the protection of private property. It is founded in natural equity, and is laid down by jurists as a principle of universal law.' "[7] Standing alone, this case could be dismissed as a sport — reflecting the special solicitude for property on the turn-of-the-century Court. But over the course of the twentieth century, the Justices made clear that this case did not stand alone. By the end of the century almost all of the rights and freedoms specified in the Founders' Bill had come to be applied against state and local governments.

The process began, inauspiciously, in Patterson v. Colorado, 205 U.S. 454 (1907). Writing for the Court, Justice Holmes proclaimed that "even if we were to assume that freedom of speech and freedom of the press were protected from abridgement on the part not only of the United States but also of the states," the newspaper publisher in the case would still lose. (The publisher had published material mocking the justices of the state supreme court. Unamused, the state court — sitting without a jury, proceeding without a specific statute authorizing punishment of nonlitigants, and in effect acting as judges in their own case — held the publisher in contempt and levied a fine on him.) The elder justice Harlan (who had written the Court's majority opinion in *Chicago Burlington*) dissented, reiterating his view that the privileges or immunities clause encompassed First Amendment (and other Bill of Rights) freedoms, and construing those freedoms far more robustly than had Holmes. By 1925, Holmes's arguendo assumption in *Patterson* had evolved into a stronger assertion, given voice by Justice Sanford writing for the Court in Gitlow v. New York, 268 U.S. 652:

> For present purposes we may and do assume that the freedom of speech and of the press — which are protected by the First Amendment from abridgement by Congress — are among the fundamental personal rights and "liberties" protected by the due process clause of the Fourteenth Amendment from impairment by the States.

Although Gitlow lost his case, soon thereafter this assumption hardened into a series of holdings invalidating state laws that impermissibly restricted speech, press, and assembly rights. See, e.g., Stromberg v. California, 283 U.S. 359 (1931); Near v. Minnesota, 283 U.S. 697 (1931); De Jonge v. Oregon, 299 U.S. 353 (1937). During this same period, however, the Court also held that other provisions of the federal Bill did not fully apply against states. Writing for the Court in Palko v. Connecticut, 302 U.S. 319 (1937), Justice Cardozo upheld a state law permitting the prosecutor to appeal from a legally erroneous acquittal in a criminal case. Assuming for the sake of argument that an appeal in a comparable federal case would be barred by the Fifth Amendment's double jeopardy clause,[8] Cardozo distinguished between those aspects of the federal Bill that were "of the very essence of a scheme of ordered liberty" and those that were not. Unlike rights of free expression, the right in the case at hand fell into the latter category and should not be imposed on states, Cardozo argued. Applying this framework over the next few years, the Court in Cantwell v.

---

7. Chicago, Burlington and Quincy Railroad v. Chicago, 166 U.S. 226, 236 (1897) (emphasis added).

8. Is this an attractive assumption? Why should our criminal justice system allow appellate courts to review and correct a legal error made by the trial judge if and only if that legal error leads to an erroneous conviction as opposed to an erroneous acquittal? If the defendant is entitled to appeal a legal error made against him, why should the prosecutor not have the same entitlement? Note that the issue here is arguably different from, say, rules concerning doubt about factual guilt; although reasonable doubts are to be resolved in defendant's favor, are legal errors the same as factual doubts? For further thoughts, see Akhil Reed Amar, Double Jeopardy Law Made Simple, 106 Yale L.J. 1807 (1997).

Connecticut, 310 U.S. 296 (1940), and Everson v. Board of Education, 330 U.S. 1 (1947), held that the Fourteenth Amendment made the First Amendment's free exercise and nonestablishment principles, respectively, applicable against states.

The scene was now set for a great debate on the relationship between the Founders' Bill of Rights and the Reconstructionists' Fourteenth Amendment. In Adamson v. California, 332 U.S. 46 (1947), Justice Black's dissent put forth his now famous theory of "total incorporation."[9] On this view, the Fourteenth Amendment "incorporated" all the rights and freedoms of the federal Bill and made them applicable against states in precisely the same way as against the federal government. In a separate concurring opinion, Justice Frankfurter vigorously disagreed. On his view, the Reconstruction Amendment required that states obey principles of fundamental fairness and ordered liberty, principles that sometimes might overlap with the Bill of Rights but that bore no necessary logical or evidentiary relation to the Bill as such.[10]

Black may have lost the battle but he eventually won the war. With Frankfurter's retirement in 1962, the anti-incorporation logjam broke, and most of the previously unincorporated provisions of the Bill of Rights came to be applied against the states — though not via Black's theory. Rather, the Court pursued an approach championed by Justice Brennan, called "selective incorporation," by which the Justices purported to play by Frankfurter's ground rules while reaching Black's results. Under this third approach, the Court's analysis could proceed clause by clause, fully incorporating every provision of the Bill deemed "fundamental" without deciding in advance (as Black would have it) whether each and every clause would necessarily pass the test. Methodologically, Brennan's approach seemed to avoid a radical break with existing case law rejecting total incorporation, and even paid lip service to Frankfurter's insistence on fundamental fairness as the touchstone of the Fourteenth Amendment. In practice, however, Brennan's approach held out the possibility of total incorporation through the back door. For him, once a clause in the Bill was deemed "fundamental" it had to be "incorporated" against the states in every aspect, just as Black insisted. And nothing in the logic of selective incorporation precluded the possibility that, when all was said and done, virtually every clause of the Bill would have been deemed fundamental. As things turned out, in applying this approach, the Warren Court almost always found that a given clause of the Bill did indeed set forth a fundamental right. Today, virtually all the Bill of Rights has come to apply with equal vigor against state and local governments.[11] The only

9. Justice Douglas joined Black's dissent, and two other dissenters, Justices Murphy and Rutledge, agreed with Black that the Fourteenth Amendment incorporated the Bill of Rights. Unlike Black, however, Murphy and Rutledge suggested that courts might also use the broad language of the Fourteenth Amendment to protect additional unenumerated rights beyond the Bill of Rights.

10. Note that Frankfurter's test is, in essence, the same test that the Court has often applied generally to so-called substantive due process cases. This similarity should not be surprising once we recall that incorporation of the Bill of Rights was itself viewed by many as a kind of substantive due process, in which judges used the language of the Due Process Clause to protect what were often substantive, nonprocedural rights such as freedom of expression and freedom of religion.

11. See, e.g., In re Oliver, 333 U.S. 257 (1948) (Sixth Amendment right to public trial); Wolf v. Colorado, 338 U.S. 25 (1949) (Fourth Amendment); Mapp v. Ohio, 367 U.S. 643 (1961) (exclusionary rule); Robinson v. California, 370 U.S. 660 (1962) (Eighth Amendment right against cruel and unusual punishment); Gideon v. Wainwright, 372 U.S. 335 (1963) (Sixth Amendment right to counsel); Malloy v. Hogan, 378 U.S. 1 (1964) (Fifth Amendment right against compelled self-incrimination); Pointer v. Texas, 380 U.S. 400 (1965) (Sixth Amendment right to confront opposing witnesses); Klopfer v. North Carolina, 386 U.S. 213 (1967) (Sixth Amendment right to speedy trial); Washington v. Texas, 388 U.S. 14 (1967) (Sixth Amendment right to compulsory process); Duncan v. Louisiana, 391 U.S. 145 (1968)

major exceptions are the Second Amendment (discussed below), the Third Amendment (which rarely arises in modern adjudication), the Fifth Amendment grand jury requirement, and the Seventh Amendment's rules regarding civil juries.

The Supreme Court's approach to incorporation has generated a vast amount of academic commentary, some of it quite critical.[12] This is hardly surprising, given the enormity of the stakes: the process of incorporation has utterly transformed the meaning of the Bill of Rights, and has defined modern constitutional law. Mid-twentieth-century critics of the idea of incorporation — like Justice Frankfurter and the younger Justice Harlan — argued that applying the Bill of Rights against state and local governments would ultimately weaken American liberty. If judges were to use the Bill against states, the argument went, these judges would be tempted to water the Bill down to take account of the considerable diversity of state practice; and then in turn, these judges would hold the federal government to only this watered-down version. But as Justice Black and fellow incorporationists anticipated, extension of the Bill of Rights against the states has, in general, dramatically strengthened the Bill, not weakened it, in both legal doctrine and popular consciousness. Unused muscles atrophy, while those that are regularly put to use grow strong.

In area after area, incorporation enabled judges first to invalidate state and local laws, and then, with this doctrinal base thus built up, to keep Congress in check. The First Amendment is illustrative. Before 1925, when the *Gitlow* Court began in earnest

---

(Sixth Amendment right to jury trial); Benton v. Maryland, 395 U.S. 784 (1969) (Fifth Amendment right againstdouble jeopardy); Schilb v. Kuebel, 404 U.S. 357 (1971) (Eighth Amendment right against excessive bail) (dictum).

Apodaca v. Oregon, 406 U.S. 404 (1972), offers an interesting counterpoint. In *Apodaca*, four Justices (White, Burger, Blackmun, and Rehnquist) argued that the Sixth Amendment does not require that a criminal jury be unanimous to convict, while four other Justices (Douglas, Brennan, Stewart, and Marshall) claimed that the Sixth Amendment does require unanimity. Justice Powell cast the deciding vote to uphold Oregon's law, on the theory that although the Sixth Amendment does require unanimity, this aspect of Sixth Amendment doctrine should not be incorporated against states, jot for jot. Note that in *Apodaca*, a clear (5-4) majority believed that federal criminal convictions must be unanimous, and a strong (8-1) majority also accepted jot-for-jot incorporation treating state and federal governments identically — and yet these majorities did not "add up" to a Court majority requiring that state criminal convictions be unanimous. The case thus raises interesting social choice theory questions about how votes are and should be aggregated on a multimember Court, and how the sequencing of issues — implicating concerns about "path dependence" and "agenda manipulation" — may sometimes influence outcomes. (Imagine, for example, that well before *Apodaca,* the Court had squarely held, 5-4, that federal nonunanimous juries violated the Sixth Amendment. Imagine further that prior to *Apodaca,* the jot-for-jot incorporation issue had been also been firmly settled in a series of cases involving other aspects of the Sixth Amendment, in which the Court had repeatedly held, 8-1, that states must be held to the same standards as the federal government. With these square holdings already on the books, would the *Apodaca* Court still have refused to "add up" these holdings?) For interesting discussion of these issues, see Frank H. Easterbrook, Ways of Criticizing the Court, 95 Harv. L. Rev. 802 (1982); Lewis A. Kornhauser & Lawrence G. Sager, Unpacking the Court, 96 Yale L.J. 82 (1986); Lewis A. Kornhauser & Lawrence G. Sager, The One and the Many: Adjudication in Collegial Courts, 81 Cal. L. Rev. 1 (1993); John M. Rogers, "Issue Voting" by Multimember Appellate Courts: A Response to Some Radical Proposals, 49 Vand. L. Rev. 997 (1996).

12. For famous commentary harshly critical of Justice Black's position, see Charles Fairman, Does the Fourteenth Amendment Incorporate the Bill of Rights?, 2 Stan. L. Rev. 5 (1949). Fairman's scholarship was, in turn, sharply attacked in William Winslow Crosskey, Charles Fairman, "Legislative History," and the Constitutional Limitations on State Authority, 22 U. Chi. L. Rev. 1 (1954); Michael Kent Curtis, No State Shall Abridge: The Fourteenth Amendment and the Bill of Rights (1984); and Richard L. Aynes, On Misreading John Bipgham and the Fourteenth Amendment, 103 Yale L.J. 57 (1993). Consider also the following effort to synthesize the three main positions in this modern debate:

This synthesis, which I shall call "refined incorporation," begins with Black's insight that *all* of the privileges and immunities of citizens recognized in the Bill of Rights became "incorporated" against states by dint of the Fourteenth Amendment. But not all of the provisions of the original

the process of First Amendment incorporation, free speech had *never* prevailed against a repressive statute in the U.S. Supreme Court. Within a few years of incorporation, however, freedom of expression and religion began to win in the High Court in landmark cases involving states, like *Stromberg, Near, De Jonge,* and *Cantwell.* These and other cases began to build up a First Amendment Tradition,[13] in and out of court, and that Tradition could then be used against even federal officials. Not until 1965 did the Supreme Court strike down an Act of Congress on First Amendment grounds (in Lamont v. Postmaster General, 381 U.S. 301), and when it did so, it relied squarely on doctrine built up in earlier cases involving states. Consider also the flag burning cases of Texas v. Johnson, 491 U.S. 397 (1989), and United States v. Eichman, 496 U.S. 310 (1990). In the first case, the Justices defined the basic First Amendment principles to strike down a *state* statute and then, in the second case, the Court stood its ground on this platform to strike down an act of *Congress.*

The large body of modern legal doctrine concerning the Bill of Rights has rolled out of courtrooms and into the vocabulary and vision of law students, journalists, activists, and ultimately the citizenry at large.[14] But without incorporation, and the steady flow of cases created by state and local laws, the Supreme Court would have had far fewer opportunities to be part of the ongoing American conversation about liberty. Perhaps nowhere has the importance of incorporation in shaping American jurisprudence been more evident than in the field of constitutional criminal procedure. The overwhelming majority of criminal cases are prosecuted by state governments under state law; only after the incorporation of the Fourth, Fifth, Sixth, and Eighth Amendments did federal courts develop a robust and highly elaborate — if also highly controversial — jurisprudence of constitutional criminal procedure.[15]

Bill of Rights were indeed rights of citizens. Some instead were at least in part rights of states, and as such, awkward to fully incorporate *against* states. Most obvious, of course, is the Tenth Amendment, but other provisions of the first eight amendments resembled the Tenth much more than Justice Black admitted. Thus there is deep wisdom in Justice Brennan's invitation to consider incorporation clause by clause — or more precisely still, right by right — rather than wholesale. But having identified the right unit of analysis, Brennan posed the wrong question: Is a given provision of the original Bill really a *fundamental* right? The right question is whether the provision really guarantees a privilege or immunity of *individual citizens* rather than a right of *states* or the *public* at large. And when we ask this question, clause by clause and right by right, we must be attentive to the possibility, flagged by Frankfurter, that a particular principle in the Bill of Rights may change its shape in the process of absorption into the Fourteenth Amendment. This change can occur for reasons rather different from those that Frankfurter offered. (He, more than Black and Brennan, diverted attention from the right question by his insistence on abstract conceptions of "fundamental fairness" and "ordered liberty" as the sole Fourteenth Amendment litmus tests, and by his disregard of the language and history of the privileges or immunities clause.) Certain alloyed provisions of the original Bill — part citizen right, part state right — may need to undergo refinement and filtration before their citizen-right elements can be absorbed by the Fourteenth Amendment. And other provisions may become less majoritarian and populist, and more libertarian, as they are repackaged in the Fourteenth Amendment as liberal civil rights — "privileges or immunities" of individuals — rather than republican political "right[s] of the people," as in the original Bill.

Amar, supra n.2, at xiv-xv.

13. See generally Harry Kalven, Jr., A Worthy Tradition: Freedom of Speech in America (1988).

14. For an important argument expressing skepticism about the magnitude of impact of Supreme Court decisions generally, see Gerald N. Rosenberg, The Hollow Hope: Can Courts Bring About Social Change? (1991).

15. The corpus of constitutional criminal procedure has swelled so large, as a result of incorporation, that it is now conventional to omit this vast body of material from standard casebooks and courses on constitutional law, relegating these issues to courses and texts on criminal procedure. This casebook follows that convention. For a nice review of earlier (pre-incorporation) constitutional law casebooks

The centrality of race to modern conceptions of civil rights and civil liberties further confirms the significance of Reconstruction. Sometimes the role of the Fourteenth Amendment is explicitly acknowledged — as when the Court in Bolling v. Sharpe, 347 U.S. 497 (1954), read the Founders' Fifth Amendment's Due Process Clause in light of the Reconstructionists' Equal Protection Clause. Other times, the influence of the Fourteenth Amendment on the jurisprudence of the Bill of Rights has been almost unconscious, as in the landmark 1964 case of New York Times v. Sullivan, 376 U.S. 254. The facts of this case — involving an all-White local jury from an ex-Confederate state trying to shut down the speech of a Yankee newspaper and a national civil rights movement led by a Black preacher — obviously call to mind images of Reconstruction, but the Court tried to tell a Founding story starring Madison and John Peter Zenger rather than a Reconstruction tale touting Bingham and Frederick Douglass.[16] But only the Reconstruction can explain why — contra Zenger — local juries are not always to be trusted to protect free expression.

What are we to make of the fact that our standard legal narrative has often exaggerated the Founding and diminished the Reconstruction? Perhaps many of us are guilty of a kind of curiously selective ancestor worship — one that gives too much credit to James Madison and not enough to John Bingham, that celebrates Thomas Jefferson and Patrick Henry but slights Harriet Beecher Stowe and Frederick Douglass. Great as men like James Madison and Thomas Jefferson were, they lived and died as slaveholders, and their Bill of Rights was tainted by its quiet complicity with the original sin of slavery. Even as we celebrate the Founders, we must ponder the sobering words of Charles Cotesworth Pinckney in the 1788 South Carolina ratification debates: "Another reason weighed particularly, with the members from this state, against the insertion of a bill of rights. Such bills generally begin with declaring that all men are by nature born free. Now, we should make that declaration with a very bad grace, when a large part of our property consists in men who are actually born slaves."[17]

But the Reconstruction Amendment did begin with an affirmation of the freedom — and citizenship — of all. The midwives of this new birth of freedom were women alongside men, Blacks alongside Whites. As twentieth-century judges increasingly came to realize, because of these nineteenth-century men and women, our eighteenth-century Bill of Rights has taken on new life and meaning.

---

that included brief surveys of criminal procedure case law, see Michael Stokes Paulsen, Dirty Harry and the Real Constitution, 64 U. Chi. L. Rev. 1457, 1465-1467 (1997). For general discussions of the current scholarly split between constitutional law and criminal procedure, see Howard W. Gutman, Academic Determinism: The Division of the Bill of Rights, 54 S. Cal. L. Rev. 295 (1981); J.M. Balkin and Sanford Levinson, The Canons of Constitutional Law, 111 Harv. L. Rev. 963, 1012-1013 (1998). For an effort to bridge this gap, analyzing (and sharply criticizing) current constitutional criminal procedure doctrine from the perspective of standard constitutional law, see Akhil Reed Amar, The Constitution and Criminal Procedure: First Principles (1997).

16. For important discussions of the central role that historical "paradigm cases" do and should play in constitutional adjudication, see Jed Rubenfeld, Reading the Constitution as Spoken, 104 Yale L.J. 1119 (1995); Jed Rubenfeld, Revolution by Judiciary: The Structure of American Constitutional Law (2005).

17. 4 Debates on the Adoption of the Federal Constitution 316 (Jonathan Elliot ed., 1836).

II. A Case Study in Modern Constitutional Interpretation: The Second Amendment

As discussed above, most, but not all, of the rights set out in the Bill of Rights have been "incorporated" against the States. One which has not is the Second Amendment. Indeed, an early case interpreting the Fourteenth Amendment, United States v. Cruikshank, 92 U.S. 542 (1875), explicitly held, through Chief Justice Waite, that whatever rights are protected by the Amendment sound only against Congress. "This is one of the amendments that has no other effect than to restrict the powers of the National government." One might note the assumption that it does limit the National government. Why might the supporters of the Amendment have wished to do this?

One answer surely lies in the general suspicion of national power voiced by many opponents to the Constitution, who, having lost the fight over ratification, nevertheless received as consolation the addition of amendments designed to curtail some of the most feared excesses of the new government. One function of the Second Amendment, arguably, was not only to express a somewhat romantic belief in the efficacy of citizen militias,[18] but also, and far more importantly, to leave in the hands of the people the practical possibility of attempting to discipline, by force of arms, a national government that had indeed succumbed to the temptation to behave tyrannically. James Madison wrote in the 46th Federalist of "the advantage of being armed, which the Americans possess over the people of almost every other nation." This "advantage" was not merely with regard to the defense of American borders; it also helped to protect political liberty against more general domestic threats. Consider in this regard the argument of Justice Joseph Story, in his widely read and influential 1833 Commentaries on the Constitution, that the Second Amendment (and the militia) were "the natural defence of a free country" not only "against sudden foreign invasions" or "domestic insurrections,"[19] but also against "domestic usurpation of power by rulers," including, presumably, national rulers. Indeed, said Story, "The right of the people to keep and bear arms has justly been considered as the palladium of the liberties of a republic: since it offers a strong moral check against the usurpation and arbitrary power of rulers; and will generally, even if these are successful in the first instance, enable the people to resist and triumph over them."[20] Although some might think it oxymoronic to argue that

---

18. See, e.g., Garry Wills, A Necessary Evil: A History of American Distrust of Government 25-41 (1991) for a withering critique of the what he terms the "myth" of citizen militias.

19. Some such "insurrections" were likely to be slave uprisings. See Carl T. Bogus, Race, Riots, and Guns, 66 S. Cal. L. Rev. 1365 (1993). "There is strong evidence that the Second Amendment was intended in large part at least, to serve as an instrument of slave control. The actual militia were principally used to deter and suppress America's first race riots — slave insurrections. A view from this perspective militates in favor of treating the Second Amendment as an anachronism, in much the same manner that we treat the provision that counts a slave as three-fifths of a person. . . ." Id. at 1367. Even if Bogus is correct in suggesting that this may be one impulse behind a reliance on citizen militias, how plausible is it that this is the only, or even the major, explanation, especially in those states that had abolished slavery but nonetheless recognized some right to bear arms in their state constitutions?

20. 3 Commentaries Sec. 1890 (1833), excerpted in 5 The Founders Constitution 214 (Philip B. Kurland & Ralph Lerner eds., 1987).

there is a legal right of armed revolution — even John Locke argued only that the people could make an "appeal to heaven" when they undertook revolution, which meant, among other things, that if they lost, they could expect no particular mercy from the government they tried to overthrow — it is not contradictory to argue that American constitutionalism is willing to take greater risks of political disorder by way of protecting liberty and casting a certain amount of fear into political leaders who may be tempted to abuse their power. (Consider the discussion of the First Amendment in Chapters 3 and 4 and the rationales for tolerating seditious speech or even speech that advocates violent overthrow of the state.)

The one major judicial construction of the Second Amendment, United States v. Miller, 307 U.S. 174 (1939), involved a defendant who was charged with violating the National Firearms Act of 1934 by moving a sawed-off shotgun in interstate commerce. Among other things, he had not registered the firearm as required by the Act. The court below had dismissed the charge, accepting Miller's argument that the Act violated the Second Amendment. The Supreme Court reversed unanimously. Justice McReynolds emphasized that there was no evidence showing that a sawed-off shotgun "at this time has some reasonable relationship to the preservation or efficiency of a well regulated militia. . . . Certainly it is not within judicial notice that this weapon is any part of the ordinary military equipment or that its use could contribute to the common defense." This observation was made as part of a broader argument that the Amendment was intended "to assure the continuation and render possible the effectiveness" of the militia, a mode of military organization that would, presumably, limit the import of standing armies, a matter of great concern to many within the framing generation. "The sentiment of the time strongly disfavored standing armies; the common view was that adequate defense of country and laws could be secured through the Militia — civilians primarily, soldiers on occasion." This brought up, then, the final question: Who were viewed as within "the Militia"? Justice McReynolds noted that "the debates in the Convention, the history and legislation of Colonies and States, and the writing of approved commentators" all "[s]how plainly enough that the Militia comprised all males physically capable of acting in concert for the common defense." McReynolds might have quoted George Mason, an influential member of the Philadelphia Convention (and Virginia Ratifying Convention) who opposed the Constitution because of its lack of a Bill of Rights. "Who are the Militia?" Mason asked. "They consist now of the whole people,"[21] and not merely members of the "select Militia" formed by, and under the control of, state governments. Miller has been read by most commentators as licensing sweeping national control of firearms, but in fact the language of the opinion is less than clear in its implications, and the Court has resolutely refused, since 1939, to revisit the issue.[22]

---

21. Quoted in Don B. Kates, Jr., Handgun Prohibition and the Original Meaning of the Second Amendment, 82 Mich. L. Rev. 204, 216 n.51 (1983).

22. This is not to say that the Supreme Court has not briefly alluded to the issue in later opinions. See Laurence H. Tribe, American Constitutional Law 896 n.207 (3d ed., 2000), for a canvassing of the relevant cases. In none of these cases, though, has the Court given full consideration to potential controversies involving the interpretation of the Second Amendment.

Seven of the 13 original state constitutions recognized rights to bear arms (six more than explicitly mentioned freedom of speech), though they took a variety of linguistic forms.[23] Moreover, Chief Justice Taney seemed to view a right to bear arms as an attribute of citizenship, at least insofar as he seemed to suggest twice in his *Dred Scott* opinion, supra Chapter 4, that all citizens enjoyed such a right. (Since he found it unthinkable that the framers would have recognized any such right being possessed even by free Blacks, this became part of his more general argument that no Blacks were in fact "citizens of the United States.")

By the time of Reconstruction, the central fear was less that of an overweening central government than of organized private opposition, such as the Ku Klux Klan, to the enjoyment of rights possessed by the newly freed former slaves. Carrying arms could literally be a matter of life or death for those faced with the possibility of Klan violence. Thus, by the time of the debate over what a later generation would call the "incorporation" of the Bill of Rights against the states, the meaning of the right to bear arms had, at least in part, become transformed. One recent work of legal history has argued that it might well make sense to view the Second Amendment, as incorporated, as a protection of a decidedly personal right "to protect one's homestead. . . . Reconstruction gun-toting was individualistic, accentuating not group rights of the citizenry but self-regarding 'privileges' of discrete 'citizens' to individual self-protection. The Creation [i.e., 1789] vision was public, with the militia muster on the town square. The Reconstruction vision was private, with individual freedman keeping guns at home to ward off Klansmen and other ruffians."[24] This might suggest a limitation on the right of even a state government, perhaps controlled by elements hostile to the enjoyment of rights by a vulnerable minority, to prohibit access to arms of all but a favored few of its citizenry.

As noted earlier, the Court early on refused to apply the Second Amendment against the states, but, then, during that period it refused to read the Fourteenth Amendment as applying any of the Bill of Rights against the states. "Incorporation" as we know it is, as seen above, was a relatively recent development, beginning in 1897 but really taking off only after 1925. Assuming, arguendo, that the Second Amendment limits the powers of the national government in at least some respects, should similar limitations be incorporated against state governments (especially those 7 out of 50 states that do not include some degree of state constitutional protection with regard to arms)?

On the Web site designed to complement this casebook, your editors have placed a general essay written for a nonlegal audience, discussing the possible modern meanings of the Second Amendment. See *http://www.conlaw.net*. In pondering this essay, readers are invited to keep in mind the general questions of Part Two: How should an eighteenth-century text be interpreted in light of twenty-first-century realities? How has the Founding experience been refracted

---

23. See L. A. Powe, Jr., Guns, Words, and Constitutional Interpretation, 38 Wm. & Mary L. Rev. 1311, 1350-1351 (1997). Powe also notes that 43 of the 50 states now include some form of right-to-bear-arms provisions in their state constitutions.

24. Amar, supra n.2, at 258-259.

by the prism of Reconstruction, and by more recent technological and social developments?[25] How can text, history, constitutional structure, judicial doctrine, pragmatism, and the like be woven together to form persuasive legal narratives in a modern world that differs in many ways from the world of the Founding?[26]

25. Consider, in this regard, the very important work of Professor Ackerman, which argues the modern constitutional interpretation involves a "multigenerational synthesis" of the meanings of discrete "constitutional moments" such as the Founding and the Reconstruction.

Note that one can accept this general account of modern constitutional interpretation whether or not one additionally subscribes to Ackerman's view that the New Deal era (which left little trace in the text of the Constitution) constitutes a constitutional moment akin to the Founding and the Reconstruction (which left more substantial textual residues). See generally 1 Bruce Ackerman, We the People: Foundations (1991); 2 Bruce Ackerman, We the People: Transformations (1998).

26. Finally, consider why the editors have chosen to devote space both in the casebook and on the Web to the Second Amendment. (Remember, we want you to be aware of the choices that have gone into this casebook, and the biases that these choices might reflect.) On one hand, the Amendment has received virtually no attention from the Supreme Court in the last 60 years; and other major constitutional law casebooks mention the Amendment not at all, or only briefly. See Sanford Levinson, The Embarrassing Second Amendment, 99 Yale L.J. 637, 639-640 (1989). (See, though, Laurence Tribe, American Constitutional Law 896ff (3d ed. 2000), which offers a far more extensive discussion than was found in the two prior editions of his landmark treatise.) On the other hand, recall that many important constitutional decisions are made outside the Supreme Court — by Congress and ordinary citizens, among others. Many millions of Americans know the Second Amendment by heart, and feel passionately about it — although with sharply conflicting views. While the modern Supreme Court has kept remarkably quiet, the Second Amendment's words and meaning are fiercely debated elsewhere — in the media, in town halls, in state legislatures, in Congress, and even in living rooms. What's more, perhaps no other part of the Bill of Rights highlights more vividly the general issues of Part Two; more so than, say, the First Amendment, the Second forces us to confront the social, cultural, technological, and legal differences between the Founders' world and our own.

Chapter 5

Economic Regulation, Federalism, and Separation of Powers in the Modern Era

In 1934 the nation was in the midst of an economic depression of unprecedented proportion. Both the national government and the states had adopted emergency measures, designed to palliate or cure. At first, the Supreme Court seemed to acquiesce in these measures — by a margin of one vote. In 1935 and 1936, however, the Court took up battle, striking down a half-dozen regulatory schemes on the ground that they were beyond congressional authority and reasserting its own authority to review the merits of state economic legislation. Then, in 1937, after Franklin Roosevelt's reelection and in the shadow of his proposed plan to "pack" the Court, the Justices again acquiesced, upholding New Deal legislation against both economic due process and federalism-based challenges.

This chapter begins with the judicial retreat of the 1930s and then traces a few of the ways in which the Court began to reassert itself on some economic rights, and on issues of federalism and separation of powers, in the latter half of the twentieth century.

I.   The Decline of Judicial Intervention Against Economic Regulation[1]

A.   1934

Two decisions in 1934 presaged the Court's withdrawal from intervention against economic regulation. The first rejected a conventional substantive due process

---

1. The description of, and explanation for, the decline of judicial intervention is the subject of significant scholarly debate. What might be termed the "conventional" view, emphasizing "The Constitutional Revolution of 1937," is well laid out, briefly, in Robert McCloskey, The American Supreme Court (1960, rev ed. 1994), at 117ff. See also William E. Leuchtenburg, The Supreme Court Reborn: The Constitutional Revolution in the Age of Roosevelt (1995). These views have been strongly challenged by Barry Cushman, Rethinking the New Deal Court: The Structure of a Constitutional Revolution (1998). Cushman obviously does not challenge the presence of a "constitutional revolution." Rather, unlike McCloskey and Leuchtenburg, he offers a significantly different analysis, placing it both earlier — the *Nebbia* case of 1934, see below at p. 500 and later — the *Darby* and *Wickard* cases in 1941-42, below at p. 550. Moreover, whereas other scholars emphasize a "switch" by particular Justices, particularly Owen Roberts and Chief Justice Hughes, Cushman sees considerably more consistency in their jurisprudence and emphasizes instead the consequences of shifts of membership as members of the Court retired, to be replaced by Roosevelt appointees. For a nice range of other recent interpretations, see generally Richard D. Friedman, Switching Time and Other Thought Experiments: The Hughes Court and Constitutional Transformation, 142 U. Pa. L. Rev. 1891 (1994); 2 Bruce Ackerman, We the People: Transformations 255-382 (1998); Bruce Ackerman, Revolution on a Human Scale, 108 Yale L.J. 2279 (1999); Laura Kalman, Law, Politics, and the New Deal, 108 Yale L.J. 2165 (1999).

challenge to a price regulation; the second involved not due process but the Contract Clause.

The appellant in Nebbia v. New York, 291 U.S. 502 (1934), was a storekeeper convicted for selling milk below the minimum retail price of 9¢ a quart fixed by the New York Milk Control Board, an agency established in 1933 pursuant to the recommendation of a legislative committee. The committee attributed the critically depressed state of milk farmers to price-cutting among milk distributors and suggested that this destructive competition could be mitigated by, inter alia, setting minimum retail prices. In an opinion by Justice Roberts, the Court upheld the regulation. Stating that "the guaranty of due process . . . demands only that the law shall not be unreasonable, arbitrary, or capricious, and that the means selected shall have a real and substantial relation to the object sought to be attained," he quoted at length from the legislative committee's report to conclude that the regulation "appears not to be unreasonable or arbitrary, or without relation to the purpose to prevent ruthless competition from destroying the wholesale price structure on which the farmer depends for his livelihood, and the community for an assured supply of milk." Justice Roberts then turned to the appellant's contentions, supported by prior decisions of the Court, that price fixing was per se unconstitutional except in "businesses affected with a public interest" and that these were limited to franchised public utilities and monopolies. Conceding that the milk industry did not fit this description, Justice Roberts noted that the industry was nonetheless subject to some sorts of regulation in the public interest, and he went on to write:

> [No] constitutional principle bars the state from correcting existing maladjustments by legislation touching prices. . . . The due process clause makes no mention of sales or of prices any more than it speaks of business or contracts or buildings or other incidents of property. . . . It is clear that there is no closed class or category of businesses affected with a public interest. . . . The phrase "affected with a public interest" can, in the nature of things, mean no more than that an industry, for adequate reason, is subject to control for the public good.

Justice McReynolds, joined by Justices Van Devanter, Sutherland, and Butler, dissented: The milk industry was not affected with a public interest. And although "[r]egulation to prevent recognized evils in [any] business has long been upheld as permissible legislative action . . . , fixation of the price at which A, engaged in an ordinary business, may sell, in order to enable B, a producer, to improve his condition, has not been regarded as within legislative power. This is not regulation, but . . . amounts to the deprivation of the fundamental right which one has to conduct his own affairs honestly and along customary lines." In any case, McReynolds argued, the judiciary had abdicated its responsibility to determine for itself whether the New York law is reasonably related to its goals: "Are federal rights subject to extinction by reports of committees?" Independently evaluating the committee's data, Justice McReynolds concluded that the problem lay in the reduced buying power of consumers, and that because demand was insufficient even at low prices it was unreasonable to believe that "higher charges at stores to impoverished customers when the output is excessive and sale prices by producers are unrestrained, can possibly increase receipts at the farm."

The constitutional jurisprudence of *Lochner,* while not permitting government regulation of wages in the "private" relationship between employer and employee, did allow regulation (albeit judicially supervised) of certain "businesses affected with a public interest," such as railroads. *Nebbia* took an expansive view of this category, but it did not unmistakably signal a clean break with existing doctrine. Neither did the decision in the *Minnesota Mortgage Moratorium* case, although it, too, marked a defeat for those Justices most in the grip of *Lochner*-like thinking.

HOME BUILDING & LOAN ASSOCIATION v. BLAISDELL
[The *Minnesota Mortgage Moratorium* Case]
290 U.S. 398 (1934)

[In 1933, the Minnesota legislature enacted the Mortgage Moratorium Law, an emergency measure, which expired in May 1935, granting temporary relief from mortgage foreclosures and execution sales of real estate. At the time, mortgages were not, as they are now, amortized over the length of the contract. Instead, there were usually "balloon" payments at the conclusion of the term. For example, a mortgage might require 59 payments of $100 per month, followed by a payment of $4,000 in the sixtieth month. Typically, the bank would agree to "roll over" the mortgage without requiring the balloon payment, but this obviously presumed a reasonably flourishing economy. The unwillingness of banks to engage in such rollovers during the Depression triggered the moratorium. The particular section involved here authorized a court to extend the period during which a defaulting mortgagor might redeem his property following a foreclosure execution sale. During the period of the extension, the mortgagor was required to pay all or a reasonable part of the reasonable rental value of the property as determined by the court, including taxes, insurance, and mortgage interest. The statute did not reduce mortgage indebtedness or affect the right of a mortgagee to title in fee, or his right to obtain a deficiency judgment, if the mortgagor failed to redeem within the prescribed period.

The Blaisdells' house had been mortgaged to Home Building & Loan. Upon default, the association foreclosed and then purchased the property at the execution sale for approximately two-thirds of its market value. The Blaisdells obtained an extension of the redemption period until May 1935, during which they were required to pay the judicially ascertained fair rental value of $40 per month.

The loan company challenged the Mortgage Moratorium Law on the ground, inter alia, that it violated the Contract Clause, Article I, §10, cl. 1. The Minnesota Supreme Court upheld the law, and the association appealed.]

Hughes, C.J. . . .

In determining whether the provision for this temporary and conditional relief exceeds the power of the State by reason of the clause in the Federal Constitution prohibiting impairment of the obligations of contracts, we must consider the relation of emergency to constitutional power, the historical setting of the contract clause, the development of the jurisprudence of this Court in the construction of that clause, and the principles of construction which we may consider to be established.

Emergency does not create power. Emergency does not increase granted power or remove or diminish the restrictions imposed upon power granted or reserved. The Constitution was adopted in a period of grave emergency. Its grants of power to the Federal Government and its limitations of the power of the States were determined in the light of emergency and they are not altered by emergency. . . .

The constitutional question presented in the light of an emergency is whether the power possessed embraces the particular exercise of it in response to particular conditions. . . . When the provisions of the Constitution, in grant or restriction, are specific, so particularized as not to admit of construction, no question is presented. Thus, emergency would not permit a State to have more than two Senators in the Congress, or permit the election of President by a general popular vote without regard to the number of electors to which the States are respectively entitled, or permit the States to "coin money" or to "make anything but gold and silver coin a tender in payment of debts." But where constitutional grants and limitations of power are set forth in general clauses, which afford a broad outline, the process of construction is essential to fill in the details.

That is true of the contract clause. . . . In the construction of the contract clause, the debates in the Constitutional Convention are of little aid. But the reasons which led to the adoption of that clause, and of the other prohibitions of Section 10 of Article I, are not left in doubt and have frequently been described with eloquent emphasis. The wide-spread distress following the revolutionary period, and the plight of debtors, had called forth in the States an ignoble array of legislative schemes for the defeat of creditors and the invasion of contractual obligations. Legislative interferences had been so numerous and extreme that the confidence essential to prosperous trade had been undermined and the utter destruction of credit was threatened. "The sober people of America" were convinced that some "thorough reform" was needed which would "inspire a general prudence and industry, and give a regular course to the business of society." The Federalist, No. 44. It was necessary to interpose the restraining power of a central authority in order to secure the foundations even of "private faith." . . .

But full recognition of the occasion and general purpose of the clause does not suffice to fix its precise scope. Nor does an examination of the details of prior legislation in the States yield criteria which can be considered controlling. To ascertain the scope of the constitutional prohibition we examine the course of judicial decisions in its application. These put it beyond question that the prohibition is not an absolute one and is not to be read with literal exactness like a mathematical formula. . . .

The obligation of a contract is "the law which binds the parties to perform their agreement." This Court has said that ". . . [n]othing can be more material to the obligation than the means of enforcement. . . . The ideas of validity and remedy are inseparable, and both are parts of the obligation, which is guaranteed by the Constitution against invasion." . . . [But it] "is competent for the States to change the form of the remedy, or to modify it otherwise, as they may see fit, provided no substantial right secured by the contract is thereby impaired. No attempt has been made to fix definitely the line between alterations of the remedy, which are to be deemed legitimate, and those which under the form of modifying the remedy, impair substantial rights. Every case must be determined upon its own circumstances" . . . [and] "[i]n all such cases the question becomes, therefore, one of reasonableness, and of that the legislature is primarily the judge." . . .

The policy of protecting contracts against impairment presupposes the maintenance of a government by virtue of which contractual relations are worth while, — a government which retains adequate authority to secure the peace and good order of society. This principle of harmonizing the constitutional prohibition with the necessary residuum of state power has had progressive recognition in the decisions of this Court. . . .

The legislature cannot "bargain away the public health or the public morals." Thus, the constitutional provision against the impairment of contracts was held not to be violated by an amendment of the state constitution which put an end to a lottery theretofore authorized by the legislature. . . . A similar rule has been applied to the control by the State of the sale of intoxicating liquors. The States retain adequate power to protect the public health against the maintenance of nuisances despite insistence upon existing contracts. Legislation to protect the public safety comes within the same category of reserved power. . . .

The argument is pressed that in the cases we have cited the obligation of contracts was affected only incidentally. This argument proceeds upon a misconception. The question is not whether the legislative action affects contracts incidentally, or directly or indirectly, but whether the legislation is addressed to a legitimate end and the measures taken are reasonable and appropriate to that end. Another argument, which comes more closely to the point, is that the state power may be addressed directly to the prevention of the enforcement of contracts only when these are of a sort which the legislature in its discretion may denounce as being in themselves hostile to public morals, or public health, safety or welfare, or where the prohibition is merely of injurious practices; that interference with the enforcement of other and valid contracts according to appropriate legal procedure, although the interference is temporary and for a public purpose, is not permissible. . . . Undoubtedly, whatever is reserved of state power must be consistent with the fair intent of the constitutional limitation of that power. . . . This principle precludes a construction which would permit the State to adopt as its policy the repudiation of debts or the destruction of contracts or the denial of means to enforce them. But it does not follow that conditions may not arise in which a temporary restraint of enforcement may be consistent with the spirit and purpose of the constitutional provision and thus be found to be within the range of the reserved power of the State to protect the vital interests of the community. . . .

Whatever doubt there may have been that the protective power of the State, its police power, may be exercised — without violating the true intent of the provision of the Federal Constitution — in directly preventing the immediate and literal enforcement of contractual obligations, by a temporary and conditional restraint, where vital public interests would otherwise suffer, was removed by our decisions relating to the enforcement of provisions of leases during a period of scarcity of housing. Marcus Brown Holding Co. v. Feldman, 256 U.S. 170 (1921); Edgar A. Levy Leasing Co. v. Siegel, 258 U.S. 242 (1922). . . . The statutes of New York, declaring that a public emergency existed, directly interfered with the enforcement of covenants for the surrender of the possession of premises on the expiration of leases. Within the City of New York and contiguous counties, the owners of dwellings, including apartment and tenement houses . . . , were wholly deprived until November 1, 1922, of all possessory remedies for the purpose of removing from their premises the tenants or occupants in possession when the laws took effect, . . . providing the tenants or occupants were ready, able and willing to pay a reasonable rent or price for their use and occupation. . . .

It is manifest from this review of our decisions that there has been a growing appreciation of public needs and of the necessity of finding ground for a rational compromise between individual rights and public welfare. The settlement and consequent contraction of the public domain, the pressure of a constantly increasing density of population, the interrelation of the activities of our people and the complexity of our economic interests, have inevitably led to an increased use of the organization of society in order to protect the very bases of individual opportunity. Where, in earlier days, it was thought that only the concerns of individuals or of classes were involved, and that those of the State itself were touched only remotely, it has later been found that the fundamental interests of the State are directly affected; and that the question is no longer merely that of one party to a contract as against another, but of the use of reasonable means to safeguard the economic structure upon which the good of all depends.

It is no answer to say that this public need was not apprehended a century ago, or to insist that what the provision of the Constitution meant to the vision of that day it must mean to the vision of our time. If by the statement that what the Constitution meant at the time of its adoption it means to-day, it is intended to say that the great clauses of the Constitution must be confined to the interpretation which the framers, with the conditions and outlook of their time, would have placed upon them, the statement carries its own refutation. It was to guard against such a narrow conception that Chief Justice Marshall uttered the memorable warning — "We must never forget that it is *a constitution* we are expounding" (McCulloch v. Maryland, 4 Wheat. 316, 407) — "a constitution intended to endure for ages to come, and consequently, to be adapted to the various *crises* of human affairs." When we are dealing with the words of the Constitution, said this Court in Missouri v. Holland, 252 U.S. 416, 433, "we must realize that they have called into life a being the development of which could not have been foreseen completely by the most gifted of its begetters. . . . The case before us must be considered in the light of our whole experience and not merely in that of what was said a hundred years ago."

When we consider the contract clause and the decisions which have expounded it in harmony with the essential reserved power of the States to protect the security of their peoples, we find no warrant for the conclusion that the clause has been warped by these decisions from its proper significance or that the founders of our Government would have interpreted the clause differently had they had occasion to assume that responsibility in the conditions of the later day. The vast body of law which has been developed was unknown to the fathers, but it is believed to have preserved the essential content and the spirit of the Constitution. With a growing recognition of public needs and the relation of individual right to public security, the court has sought to prevent the perversion of the clause through its use as an instrument to throttle the capacity of the States to protect their fundamental interests. This development is a growth from the seeds which the fathers planted. . . .

Applying the criteria established by our decisions we conclude:

1. An emergency existed in Minnesota which furnished a proper occasion for the exercise of the reserved power of the State to protect the vital interests of the community. . . . As the Supreme Court of Minnesota said, the economic emergency which threatened "the loss of homes and lands which furnish those in possession the necessary shelter and means of subsistence" was a "potent cause" for the enactment of the statute.
2. The legislation was addressed to a legitimate end, that is, the legislation was not for the mere advantage of particular individuals but for the protection of a basic interest of society.
3. In view of the nature of the contracts in question — mortgages of unquestionable validity — the relief afforded and justified by the emergency, in

order not to contravene the constitutional provision, could only be of a character appropriate to that emergency and could be granted only upon reasonable conditions.

4. The conditions upon which the period of redemption is extended do not appear to be unreasonable. . . . The relief afforded by the statute has regard to the interest of mortgagees as well as to the interest of mortgagors. The legislation seeks to prevent the impending ruin of both by a considerate measure of relief. . . .

5. The legislation is temporary in operation. It is limited to the exigency which called it forth. . . .

We are of the opinion that the Minnesota statute as here applied does not violate the contract clause of the Federal Constitution. Whether the legislation is wise or unwise as a matter of policy is a question with which we are not concerned. . . .

Judgment affirmed.

SUTHERLAND, J., joined by Van Devanter, McReynolds, and Butler, JJ., dissenting. . . . The whole aim of construction, as applied to a provision of the Constitution, is to discover the meaning, to ascertain and give effect to the intent, of its framers and the people who adopted it. The necessities which gave rise to the provision, the controversies which preceded, as well as the conflicts of opinion which were settled by its adoption, are matters to be considered to enable us to arrive at a correct result. The history of the times, the state of things existing when the provision was framed and adopted, should be looked to in order to ascertain the mischief and the remedy. As nearly as possible we should place ourselves in the condition of those who framed and adopted it. . . .

An application of these principles to the question under review removes any doubt, if otherwise there would be any, that the contract impairment clause denies to the several states the power to mitigate hard consequences resulting to debtors from financial or economic exigencies by an impairment of the obligation of contracts of indebtedness. A candid consideration of the history and circumstances which led up to and accompanied the framing and adoption of this clause will demonstrate conclusively that it was framed and adopted with the specific and studied purpose of preventing legislation designed to relieve debtors *especially* in time of financial distress . . . .

Following the Revolution, and prior to the adoption of the Constitution, the American people found themselves in a greatly impoverished condition. Their commerce had been well-nigh annihilated. They were not only without luxuries, but in great degree were destitute of the ordinary comforts and necessities of life. In these circumstances they incurred indebtedness in the purchase of imported goods and otherwise, far beyond their capacity to pay. . . .

In an attempt to meet the situation recourse was had to the legislatures of the several states under the Confederation; and these bodies passed, among other acts, the following: laws providing for the emission of bills of credit and making them legal tender for the payment of debts, and providing also for such payment by the delivery of specific property at a fixed valuation; instalment laws, authorizing payment of overdue obligations at future intervals of time; stay laws and laws temporarily closing access to the courts; and laws discriminating against British creditors. . . .

In the midst of this confused, gloomy, and seriously exigent condition of affairs, the Constitutional Convention of 1787 met at Philadelphia. . . . Shortly prior to the meeting of the Convention, Madison had assailed a bill pending in the Virginia Assembly, proposing the payment of private debts in three annual instalments on the ground that "no legislative principle could vindicate such an interposition of the law in private contracts." . . .

In the plan of government especially urged by Sherman and Ellsworth there was an article proposing that the legislatures of the individual states ought not to possess a right to emit bills of credit, etc., "or in any manner to obstruct or impede the recovery of debts, whereby the interests of foreigners or the citizens of any other state may be affected." And on July 13, 1787, Congress in New York, acutely conscious of the evils engendered by state laws interfering with existing contracts, passed the Northwest Territory Ordinance, which contained the clause: "And, in the just preservation of rights and property, it is understood and declared, that no law ought ever to be made or have force in the said territory, that shall, in any manner whatever, interfere with or affect private contracts, or engagements, bona fide, and without fraud previously formed." It is not surprising, therefore, that, after the Convention had adopted the clauses, no state shall "emit bills of credit," or "make any thing but gold and silver coin a tender in payment of debts," Mr. King moved to add a "prohibition on the states to interfere in private contracts." This was opposed by Gouverneur Morris and Colonel Mason. Colonel Mason thought that this would be carrying the restraint too far; that cases would happen that could not be foreseen where some kind of interference would be essential. This was on August 28. But Mason's view did not prevail, for, on September 14 following, the first clause of Art. I, §10, was altered so as to include the provision, "No state shall . . . pass any . . . law impairing the obligation of contracts," and in that form it was adopted.

Luther Martin, in an address to the Maryland House of Delegates, declared his reasons for voting against the provision. He said that he considered there might be times of such great public calamity and distress as should render it the duty of a government in some measure to interfere by passing laws totally or partially stopping courts of justice, or authorizing the debtor to pay by installments; that such regulations had been found necessary in most or all of the states "to prevent the wealthy creditor and the moneyed man from totally destroying the poor, though industrious debtor. Such times may again arrive." And he was apprehensive of any proposal which took from the respective states the power to give their debtor citizens "a moment's indulgence, however necessary it might be, and however desirous to grant them aid."

On the other hand, Sherman and Ellsworth defended the provision in a letter to the Governor of Connecticut. In the course of the Virginia debates, Randolph declared that the prohibition would be promotive of virtue and justice, and preventive of injustice and fraud; and he pointed out that the reputation of the people had suffered because of frequent interferences by the state legislatures with private contracts. . . .

The provision was strongly defended in The Federalist, both by Hamilton in No. 7 and Madison in No. 44. . . .

Contemporaneous history is replete with evidence of the sharp conflict of opinion with respect to the advisability of adopting the clause. . . .

If it be possible by resort to the testimony of history to put any question of constitutional intent beyond the domain of uncertainty, the foregoing leaves no reasonable ground upon which to base a denial that the clause of the Constitution now under consideration was meant to foreclose state action impairing the obligation of contracts *primarily and especially* in respect of such action aimed at giving relief to debtors *in time of emergency.* And if further proof be required to strengthen what already is inexpugnable, such proof will be found in the previous decisions of this court. . . .

The present exigency is nothing new. From the beginning of our existence as a nation, periods of depression, of industrial failure, of financial distress, of unpaid and unpayable indebtedness, have alternated with years of plenty. . . .

The defense of the Minnesota law is made upon grounds which were discountenanced by the makers of the Constitution and have many times been rejected by this court. That defense should not now succeed because it constitutes an effort to overthrow the constitutional provision by an appeal to facts and circumstances identical with those which brought it into existence. With due regard for the processes of logical thinking, it legitimately cannot be urged that conditions which produced the rule may now be invoked to destroy it. . . .

I quite agree with the opinion of the court that whether the legislation under review is wise or unwise is a matter with which we have nothing to do. Whether it is likely to work well or work ill presents a question entirely irrelevant to the issue. The only legitimate inquiry we can make is whether it is constitutional. If it is not, its virtues, if it have any, cannot save it; if it is, its faults cannot be invoked to accomplish its destruction. If the provisions of the Constitution be not upheld when they pinch as well as when they comfort, they may as well be abandoned. Being unable to reach any other conclusion than that the Minnesota statute infringes the constitutional restriction under review, I have no choice but to say so.

CARDOZO, J. [unpublished concurring opinion]. . . .

A hundred years ago when this court decided Bronson v. Kinzie . . . property might be taken without due process of law through the legislation of the states, and the courts of the nation were powerless to give redress, unless indeed they could find that a contract had been broken. Dartmouth College v. Woodward . . . ; Fletcher v. Peck. . . . The judges of those courts had not yet begun to speak of the police power except in an off hand way or in expounding the effect of the commerce clause upon local regulations. The License Cases. . . . Due process in the states was whatever the states ordained. In such circumstances there was jeopardy, or the threat of it, in encroachment, however slight, upon the obligation to adhere to the letter of a contract. Once reject that test, and no other was available, or so it might well have seemed. The states could not be kept within the limits of reason and fair dealing for such restraints were then unknown as curbs upon their power. It was either all or nothing.

The Fourteenth Amendment came, and with it a profound change in the relation between the federal government and the governments of the states. No longer were the states invested with arbitrary power. Their statutes affecting property or liberty were brought within supervision of independent courts and subjected to the rule of reason. The dilemma of "all or nothing" no longer stared us in the face.

Upon the basis of that amendment, a vast body of law unknown to the fathers has been built in treatise and decision. . . . The early cases dealt with the problem as one affecting the conflicting rights and interests of individuals and classes. This was the attitude of the courts up to the Fourteenth Amendment; and the tendency to some extent persisted even later. . . . The rights and interests of the state itself were involved, as it seemed, only indirectly and remotely, if they were thought to be involved at all. We know better in these days, with the passing of the frontier and of the unpeopled spaces of the west. With these and other changes, the welfare of the social organism in any of its parts is bound up more inseparably than ever with the welfare of the whole. A gospel of laissez-faire — of individual initiative — of thrift and industry and sacrifice — may be inadequate in that great society we live in to point the way to salvation, at least for economic life. The state when it acts today by statutes like the one before us is not furthering the selfish good of individuals or classes as ends of ultimate validity. It is furthering its own good by maintaining the economic structure on which the good of all depends. Such at least is its endeavor, however much it miss the mark. The attainment of that end, so august and impersonal, will not be barred and thwarted by the obstruction of a contract set up along the way.

Looking back over the century, one perceives a process of evolution too strong to be set back. The decisions brought together by the Chief Justice [Hughes] show with impressive force how the court in its interpretation of the contract clause has been feeling its way toward a rational compromise between private rights and public welfare. From the beginning it was seen that something must be subtracted from the words of the Constitution in all their literal and stark significance. This was forcefully pointed out by Johnson, J., in Ogden v. Saunders, 12 Wheat. 213, 286. At first refuge was found in the distinction between right and remedy with all its bewildering refinements. Gradually the distinction was perceived to be inadequate. The search was for a broader base, for a division that would separate the lawful and the forbidden by lines more closely in correspondence with the necessities of government. The Fourteenth Amendment was seen to point the way. Contracts were still to be preserved. There was to be no arbitrary destruction of their binding force, nor any arbitrary impairment. There was to be no impairment, even though not arbitrary, except with the limits of fairness, of moderation, and of pressing and emergent need. But a promise exchanged between individuals was not to paralyze the state in its endeavor in times of direful crisis to keep its lifeblood flowing.

To hold this may be inconsistent with things that men said in 1787 when expounding to compatriots the newly written constitution. They did not see the changes in the relation between states and nation or in the play of social forces that lay hidden in the womb of time. It may be inconsistent with things that they believed or took for granted. Their beliefs to be significant must be adjusted to the world they knew. It is not in my judgment inconsistent with what they say today nor with what today they would believe, if they were called upon to interpret "in the light of our whole experience" the constitution that they framed for the needs of an expanding future.

Discussion

1. *Modalities of constitutional interpretation.* Note the rich assortment of methodological moves in Blaisdell. The dissenters invoke what they assert to be the obvious original intent of the Contract Clause, as applied to the paradigm case that gave rise to the clause — state relief of debtors in hard times. Cf. Jed Rubenfeld, Revolution by Judiciary (2005) (discussing the importance of historical paradigm cases in constitutional interpretation).

In response, the majority argues that the relevant constitutional text should not be read in the most absolutist way possible — not all modifications of contractual remedies impermissibly "impair" contractual obligations so as to violate the clause. Precedent confirms nonabsolutism, the majority points out. (Consider, for example, a law that prohibits the sale of some new drug; suppose the law has the incidental effect of nullifying preexisting contracts for future sales of this drug. Suppose also that such a law was not purposefully designed so as to redistribute wealth as between buyers and sellers. Is such a law an impermissible "impairment" of "contractual obligation" as such? The *Blaisdell* majority suggests not, in its allusion to the case of "intoxicating liquors.") Perhaps most interesting of all, the majority suggests that the Minnesota law should not be seen as an "ignoble" governmental attempt to redistribute wealth from creditors to debtors. In the extraordinarily severe and indeed unprecedented circumstances of the Great Depression, the Court hints, creditors as a class might be *worse off* if the government were to insist on immediate repayment, which could threaten the collapse of "the economic structure upon which the good of *all* [including, presumably, creditors] depends." The legislation, argues the majority, was "not for the mere advantage of particular individuals but for the protection of a basic interest of society," with due "regard to the interest of mortgagees as well as to the interest of mortgagors. The legislation seeks to prevent the impending ruin of *both* . . . ." On this view, the very breadth of the 1930s economic crisis — implicating not a small group of debtors but the broad swath of society — renders it markedly different from the paradigm case of the 1780s. Note that concern for the general stability of the economic structure is not one that each creditor would necessarily take into account in deciding whether to foreclose — the economic structure might collapse only if all creditors try to foreclose at once, and under these circumstances no single creditor might have a sufficient incentive to exercise restraint. The structure of the problem could thus be analogized to a "race to the bottom" or a "prisoners' dilemma," in which collective action is needed to cure a problem created by the cumulative effect of individually rational actions by individual actors. Note also how this prudential argument intertwines with constitutional text and precedent: A law sincerely designed to help creditors as well as debtors is not a law designed to impermissibly "impair" contractual "obligations." Finally, note the intriguing suggestion of Justice Cardozo that, after the adoption of the Fourteenth Amendment, the language of the Contract Clause need not be read in the same way as it was before. Whereas the "multigenerational synthesis" of the Founding and the Reconstruction ultimately led to stricter limits on states in the context of the incorporation of the Bill of Rights, here Cardozo seems to be arguing that it might also appropriately lead to less strictness for states in some contexts.[2]

---

2. Consider also the following multigenerational argument: Broad-based economic redistribution, not from person A to person B, but from one broad class (the wealthy) to another broad class (the impoverished) was arguably impermissible at the Founding, in light of the spirit of the Contract Clause and the Takings Clause (if the two clauses are read expansively and in tandem). But the Sixteenth Amendment, adopted in 1913, dramatically changed things, making clear that explicitly redistributive economic policies — like an income tax imposed only on the wealthy (a prospect contemplated by many of the proponents of the Sixteenth Amendment) — no longer violated the deep structure of American constitutionalism.

2. *Law and violence.* Minnesota passed its law (and the Supreme Court considered it) not only within the general context of the Great Depression and its massive economic disruptions, but also within more particular circumstances of social disorder and violence. For example, angry farmers denounced and in some instances forcibly stopped foreclosure of their farms. In Iowa, a local judge who refused to suspend foreclosure proceedings was dragged from a courtroom and had a rope put around his neck before the crowd let him go. The governor of Iowa also declared martial law in six counties and called out the National Guard in order to forestall the perceived threat of rural violence. A New York newspaper editorially noted that instead of worrying about a merely fantasized threat of a "red revolution" in the cities, Americans should become aware "that actual revolution already exists in the farm belt," provoked by the anguish of "conservatives fighting for the right to hold their homesteads."[3] Do these facts bear on the constitutionality of Minnesota's "moratorium"? If so, why? Because people were suffering?[4] Because judges and legal officials were threatened with violence? To what extent should the social impact of, or popular reaction to, a law influence the determination of its constitutionality? Would your views of, say, Plessy v. Ferguson change if you were persuaded that racially integrated transportation or schools would have been met with a violent response from racists?

3. *Limited emergencies.* The Minnesota statute expired in May 1935, presumably because the legislature naively expected the emergency to be over by then. What if the statute instead had said, "This moratorium shall be in effect until the Governor declares that the emergency no longer exists"? Should that have made a difference in the Court's analysis?

B.   1935-1937

The Court that decided *Nebbia* and *Blaisdell* consisted of three progressives (Stone, Brandeis, and Cardozo), the ultraconservative "four horsemen" (Van Devanter, McReynolds, Sutherland, and Butler), and two swing members (Roberts and Chief Justice Hughes). Roberts wrote *Nebbia* and joined in *Blaisdell*, but "as the New Deal was revealed in all its terrifying dimensions to the conservatives of the nation, he

---

3. See Arthur Schlesinger, The Coming of the New Deal 42-44 (1959).

4. Recall Michele Landis Dauber's argument that from the earliest times of our constitutional history, legislative attempts to provide relief for "disasters" tested certain conceptions of "limited government." See Dauber, The Sympathetic State, 23 Law and History Rev. 387 (2005). In Minnesota, one state supreme court judge compared "[t]he present nationwide and worldwide business and financial crisis" to a "flood, earthquake, or disturbance," depriving "millions of persons in this nation of their employment and means of earning a living for themselves and their families" and, therefore, generating "widespread want and suffering among our people . . . ." 189 Minn. 429, 249 N.W. 336, 340. Generally speaking we do not hold persons responsible for what happens to them as the result of natural disasters; instead we view such persons as victims of outside forces that they could not realistically be expected to have protected themselves against. To be the faultless victim of such a disaster is to make oneself eligible for public sympathy and, more to the point, aid. As Dauber argues, an important part of the argument made by proponents of the mortgage moratorium and, indeed, for much other welfare legislation at the time, was that those who had lost their jobs, and were now threatened with loss of their homes, were not in fact responsible for their fate, which was the result of general structural factors within the economy and society rather than individual weaknesses of character. This dispute about how to characterize those in want continues to play an important part in debates about "welfare" expenditures by the government.

became ready for persuasion. As for the Chief Justice, he was neither clearly liberal nor stubbornly conservative, but he seemed to be much concerned for the Court's own dignity and was likely sometimes to swing with a conservative majority to avoid the criticism that might follow a 5 to 4 decision. In 1935, therefore, the majority shifted, and for two busy terms the Court waged what is surely the most ambitious dragon-fight in its long and checkered history."[5]

The most significant decisions of these terms struck down recovery measures of the New Deal.[6] For present purposes, however, the most interesting decision is Morehead v. New York ex rel. Tipaldo, 298 U.S. 587 (1936), which invalidated a New York minimum wage law for women on authority of Adkins v. Children's Hospital, 261 U.S. 525 (1923). Justice Butler wrote for the five-man majority (including Roberts but not Hughes) that "the State is without power by any form of legislation to prohibit, change or nullify contracts between employers and adult women workers as to the amount of wages to be paid."

Morehead was decided in June 1936, toward the close of the term. Roosevelt was reelected in November, and in early February 1937, "with characteristic indirection, [he] presented Congress with a judiciary plan that purported to cope with the supposed problem of overcrowded federal court dockets. It would have enabled him to appoint a new judge to supplement any judge over seventy who failed to retire (retirement could not of course be made compulsory, for the Constitution protects judicial tenure 'during good behavior'). The significant fact was that the plan would permit the President to appoint six new Supreme Court justices, and thus to insure approval of the New Deal program. It was, as it was called, a 'court-packing plan.' . . . And it was offered by a President who had just received an overwhelming popular vote of confidence and who had not yet been denied in Congress any of his important demands. Even the five or six judges who had provoked this threat must have slept rather uneasily for a few months."[7] Less than two months later, the Justices reversed field and explicitly overruled *Adkins.*

WEST COAST HOTEL CO. v. PARRISH
300 U.S. 379 (1937)

HUGHES, C.J.:

[T]he violation alleged by those attacking minimum wage regulation for women is deprivation of freedom of contract. What is this freedom? The Constitution does not speak of freedom of contract. It speaks of liberty and prohibits the deprivation of liberty without due process of law. In prohibiting that deprivation the Constitution does not recognize an absolute and uncontrollable liberty. Liberty in each of its phases has its history and connotation. But the liberty safeguarded is liberty in a social organization which requires the protection of law against the evils which menace the health, safety, morals and welfare of the people. Liberty under

---

5. Robert McCloskey, supra n.1, at 110.

6. See, e.g., Schechter Poultry Corp. v. United States, 295 U.S. 495 (1935); Carter v. Carter Coal Co., 298 U.S. 238 (1936); United States v. Butler, 297 U.S. 1 (1936).

7. McCloskey, supra n.1, at 113. See also William Leuchtenburg, The Origins of Franklin D. Roosevelt's "Court-Packing" Plan, 1966 Sup. Ct. Rev. 347.

the Constitution is thus necessarily subject to the restraints of due process, and regulation which is reasonable in relation to its subject and is adopted in the interests of the community is due process. . . .

What can be closer to the public interest than the health of women and their protection from unscrupulous and overreaching employers? And if the protection of women is a legitimate end of the exercise of state power, how can it be said that the requirement of the payment of a minimum wage fairly fixed in order to meet the very necessities of existence is not an admissible means to that end? The legislature of the State was clearly entitled to consider the situation of women in employment, the fact that they are in the class receiving the least pay, and that they are the ready victims of those who would take advantage of their necessitous circumstances. The legislature was entitled to adopt measures to reduce the evils of the "sweating system," the exploiting of workers at wages so low as to be insufficient to meet the bare cost of living, thus making their very helplessness the occasion of a most injurious competition. The legislature had the right to consider that its minimum wage requirements would be an important aid in carrying out its policy of protection. The adoption of similar requirements by many States evidences a deep-seated conviction both as to the presence of the evil and as to the means adapted to check it. Legislative response to that conviction cannot be regarded as arbitrary or capricious, and that is all we have to decide. Even if the wisdom of the policy be regarded as debatable and its effects uncertain, still the legislature is entitled to its judgment.

There is an additional and compelling consideration which recent economic experience has brought into a strong light. The exploitation of a class of workers who are in an unequal position with respect to bargaining power and are thus relatively defenseless against the denial of a living wage is not only detrimental to their health and well being but casts a direct burden for their support upon the community. What these workers lose in wages the taxpayers are called upon to pay. The bare cost of living must be met. We may take judicial notice of the unparalleled demands for relief which arose during the recent period of depression and still continue to an alarming extent despite the degree of economic recovery which has been achieved. It is unnecessary to cite official statistics to establish what is of common knowledge through the length and breadth of the land. While in the instant case no factual brief has been presented, there is no reason to doubt that the State of Washington has encountered the same social problem that is present elsewhere. The community is not bound to provide what is in effect a subsidy for unconscionable employers. The community may direct its law-making power to correct the abuse which springs from their selfish disregard of the public interest. . . .

Our conclusion is that the case of Adkins v. Children's Hospital should be, and it is, overruled.

[Justices Van Devanter, McReynolds, Sutherland, and Butler — the "four horsemen" — dissented, reaffirming their commitment to *Adkins* and *Morehead*.]

West Coast Hotel was soon followed by decisions upholding New Deal legislation under the commerce and spending powers.[8] Just what brought about this judicial acquiescence remains somewhat obscure. The central figure is Owen

---

8. E.g., NLRB v. Jones & Laughlin Steel Corp., 301 U.S. 1 (1937); Steward Machine Co. v. Davis, 301 U.S. 548 (1937); Section II of this chapter, infra.

Roberts, whose vote made the difference between *Morehead* and *West Coast Hotel*. Although there are indications that he cast his sustaining vote in the later case before Roosevelt presented Congress with the court-packing bill,[9] the received notion is that Roberts's fear of the bill caused him to make "the stitch in time that saved nine[cr2]." Whatever Roberts's motivation, Roosevelt's court-packing plan ultimately failed, and Supreme Court doctrine ultimately came to chart a new path.

C.   The Modern Doctrine of Economic Due Process

Nebbia, Blaisdell, and *West Coast Hotel* marked a transformation in thought about the nature and purposes of judicial review. The problem that now faced the Court was to figure out exactly what that transformation meant.

UNITED STATES v. CAROLENE PRODUCTS CO.
304 U.S. 144 (1938)

Mr. Justice STONE delivered the opinion of the Court.

The question for decision is whether the "Filled Milk Act" of Congress of March 4, 1923 . . . which prohibits the shipment in interstate commerce of skimmed milk compounded with any fat or oil other than milk fat, so as to resemble milk or cream, transcends the power of Congress to regulate interstate commerce or infringes the Fifth Amendment.

[The statute contained a declaration by Congress that filled milk — i.e., skimmed milk combined with nondairy fats — "is an adulterated article of food, injurious to the public health, and its sale constitutes a fraud upon the public." The Appellee was indicted for shipping "'Milnut,' a compound of condensed skimmed milk and coconut oil made in imitation or semblance of condensed milk or cream." The Supreme Court first held that Congress had the power to prohibit shipment of adulterated foods in interstate commerce, and then addressed the due process challenge.]

Second. The prohibition of shipment of appellee's product in interstate commerce does not infringe the Fifth Amendment. . . .

[W]e might rest decision wholly on the presumption of constitutionality. But affirmative evidence also sustains the statute. In twenty years evidence has steadily accumulated of the danger to the public health from the general consumption of foods which have been stripped of elements essential to the maintenance of health. The Filled Milk Act was adopted by Congress after committee hearings, in the course of which eminent scientists and health experts testified. An extensive investigation was made of the commerce in milk compounds in which vegetable oils have been substituted for natural milk fat, and of the effect upon the public health of the use of such compounds as a food substitute for milk. The conclusions drawn from evidence

9. See Felix Frankfurter, Mr. Justice Roberts, 104 U. Pa. L. Rev. 311 (1955). For a rich assortment of views concerning Roberts' apparent "switch in time," see generally the sources cited supra n.1; see also Philip Bobbitt, Constitutional Fate: Theory of the Constitution 27-31, 39-42 (1982); Michael Ariens, A Thrice-Told Tale, Or Felix the Cat, 107 Harv. L. Rev. 620 (1994).

presented at the hearings were embodied in reports of the House Committee on Agriculture and the Senate Committee on Agriculture and Forestry. Both committees concluded, as the statute itself declares, that the use of filled milk as a substitute for pure milk is generally injurious to health and facilitates fraud on the public.[a]

There is nothing in the Constitution which compels a Legislature, either national or state, to ignore such evidence, nor need it disregard the other evidence which amply supports the conclusions of the Congressional committees that the danger is greatly enhanced where an inferior product, like appellee's, is indistinguishable from a valuable food of almost universal use, thus making fraudulent distribution easy and protection of the consumer difficult.[b]

Here the prohibition of the statute is inoperative unless the product is "in imitation or semblance of milk, cream, or skimmed milk, whether or not condensed." Whether in such circumstance the public would be adequately protected by the prohibition of false labels and false branding imposed by the Pure Food and Drugs Act, or whether it was necessary to go farther and prohibit a substitute food product thought to be injurious to health if used as a substitute when the two are not distinguishable, was a matter for the legislative judgment and not that of courts. . . .

Appellee raises no valid objection to the present statute by arguing that its prohibition has not been extended to oleomargarine or other butter substitutes in which vegetable fats or oils are substituted for butter fat. The Fifth Amendment has no equal protection clause, and even that of the Fourteenth, applicable only to the states, does not compel their Legislatures to prohibit all like evils, or none. A Legislature may hit at an abuse which it has found, even though it has failed to strike at another.

Third. We may assume for present purposes that no pronouncement of a Legislature can forestall attack upon the constitutionality of the prohibition which it enacts by applying opprobrious epithets to the prohibited act, and that a statute would deny due process which precluded the disproof in judicial proceedings of all facts which would show or tend to show that a statute depriving the suitor of life, liberty, or property had a rational basis.

a. [footnote 2] The reports may be summarized as follows: There is an extensive commerce in milk compounds made of condensed milk from which the butter fat has been extracted and an equivalent amount of vegetable oil, usually coconut oil, substituted. These compounds resemble milk in taste and appearance and are distributed in packages resembling those in which pure condensed milk is distributed. By reason of the extraction of the natural milk fat the compounded product can be manufactured and sold at a lower cost than pure milk. Butter fat, which constitutes an important part of the food value of pure milk, is rich in vitamins, food elements which are essential to proper nutrition, and are wanting in vegetable oils. The use of filled milk as a dietary substitute for pure milk results, especially in the case of children, in undernourishment, and induces diseases which attend malnutrition. Despite compliance with the branding and labeling requirements of the Pure Food and Drugs Act, there is widespread use of filled milk as a food substitute for pure milk. This is aided by their identical taste and appearance, by the similarity of the containers in which they are sold, by the practice of dealers in offering the inferior product to customers as being as good as or better than pure condensed milk sold at a higher price, by customers' ignorance of the respective food values of the two products, and in many sections of the country by their inability to read the labels placed on the containers. Large amounts of filled milk, much of it shipped and sold in bulk, are purchased by hotels and boarding houses, and by manufactures of food products, such as ice cream, to whose customers labeling restrictions afford no protection.

b. [footnote 3] There is now an extensive literature indicating wide recognition by scientists and dietitians of the great importance to the public health of butter fat and whole milk as the prime source of vitamins, which are essential growth producing and disease preventing elements in the diet.

When the Filled Milk Act was passed, eleven states had rigidly controlled the exploitation of filled milk, or forbidden it altogether. Some thirty-five states have now adopted laws which in terms, or by their operation, prohibit the sale of filled milk.

But such we think is not the purpose or construction of the statutory characterization of filled milk as injurious to health and as a fraud upon the public. There is no need to consider it here as more than a declaration of the legislative findings deemed to support and justify the action taken as a constitutional exertion of the legislative power, aiding informed judicial review, as do the reports of legislative committees, by revealing the rationale of the legislation. Even in the absence of such aids, the existence of facts supporting the legislative judgment is to be presumed, for regulatory legislation affecting ordinary commercial transactions is not to be pronounced unconstitutional unless in the light of the facts made known or generally assumed it is of such a character as to preclude the assumption that it rests upon some rational basis within the knowledge and experience of the legislators.[c] The present statutory findings affect appellee no more than the reports of the Congressional committees and since in the absence of the statutory findings they would be presumed, their incorporation in the statute is no more prejudicial than surplusage.

Where the existence of a rational basis for legislation whose constitutionality is attacked depends upon facts beyond the sphere of judicial notice, such facts may properly be made the subject of judicial inquiry, and the constitutionality of a statute predicated upon the existence of a particular state of facts may be challenged by showing to the court that those facts have ceased to exist. Similarly we recognize that the constitutionality of a statute, valid on its face, may be assailed by proof of facts tending to show that the statute as applied to a particular article is without support in reason because the article, although within the prohibited class, is so different from others of the class as to be without the reason for the prohibition, though the effect of such proof depends on the relevant circumstances of each case, as for example the administrative difficulty of excluding the article from the regulated class. But by their very nature such inquiries, where the legislative judgment is drawn in question, must be restricted to the issue whether any state of facts either known or which could reasonably be assumed affords support for it. Here the demurrer challenges the validity of the statute on its face and it is evident from all the considerations presented to Congress, and those of which we may take

c. [footnote 4] There may be narrower scope for operation of the presumption of constitutionality when legislation appears on its face to be within a specific prohibition of the Constitution, such as those of the first ten Amendments, which are deemed equally specific when held to be embraced within the Fourteenth. See Stromberg v. California, 283 U.S. 359, 369, 370; Lovell v. Griffin, 303 U.S. 444.

It is unnecessary to consider now whether legislation which restricts those political processes which can ordinarily be expected to bring about repeal of undesirable legislation, is to be subjected to more exacting judicial scrutiny under the general prohibitions of the Fourteenth Amendment than are most other types of legislation. On restrictions upon the right to vote, see Nixon v. Herndon, 273 U.S. 536; Nixon v. Condon, 286 U.S. 73; on restraints upon the dissemination of information, see Near v. Minnesota, 283 U.S. 697, 713-714, 718-720, 722; Grosjean v. American Press Co., 297 U.S. 233; Lovell v. Griffin, supra; on interferences with political organizations, see Stromberg v. California, supra, 283 U.S. 359, 369; Fiske v. Kansas, 274 U.S. 380; Whitney v. California, 274 U.S. 357, 377-378; Herndon v. Lowry, 301 U.S. 242; and see Holmes, J., in Gitlow v. New York, 268 U.S. 652, 673; as to prohibition of peaceable assembly, see De Jonge v. Oregon, 299 U.S. 353, 365.

Nor need we enquire whether similar considerations enter into the review of statutes directed at particular religious, Pierce v. Society of Sisters, 268 U.S. 510, or national, Meyer v. Nebraska, 262 U.S. 390; Bartels v. Iowa, 262 U.S. 404; Farrington v. Tokushige, 273 U.S. 284, or racial minorities. Nixon v. Herndon, supra; Nixon v. Condon, supra; whether prejudice against discrete and insular minorities may be a special condition, which tends seriously to curtail the operation of those political processes ordinarily to be relied upon to protect minorities, and which may call for a correspondingly more searching judicial inquiry. Compare McCulloch v. Maryland, 4 Wheat. 316, 428; South Carolina State Highway Department v. Barnwell Bros., 303 U.S. 177, [184] n.2, and cases cited.

judicial notice, that the question is at least debatable whether commerce in filled milk should be left unregulated, or in some measure restricted, or wholly prohibited. As that decision was for Congress, neither the finding of a court arrived at by weighing the evidence, nor the verdict of a jury can be substituted for it.

Mr. Justice BLACK concurs in the result and in all of the opinion except the part marked "Third."

[Justice Butler concurred in the result, arguing that the defendant should be permitted to prove at trial that Milnut was not injurious to public health and that its sale was not a fraud on the public, as alleged in the indictment. A statute that excluded products that were demonstrably not injurious to health or calculated to deceive would violate the Fifth Amendment's Due Process Clause. Justice McReynolds dissented. Justices Cardozo and Reed took no part in the consideration or decision of the case.]

Discussion

1. *Common law baselines and economic redistribution. Carolene Products* presents the basic problem of justifying judicial review of legislation after the 1937 transformation in constitutional thought. The use of concepts like the police power or substantive limitations derived from common law categories is essentially discarded. As *West Coast Hotel* recognized, common law rules of contract formation might actually create a "subsidy for unconscionable employers." Nor could regulation of wages and hours be dismissed, as in Lochner itself, as an illicit attempt at redistribution. If common law rules themselves could be viewed as a "subsidy," then the distribution of income was partly produced by the choice of legal regime. There was no natural or prepolitical baseline to measure what was redistributional. (Also, recall that the Sixteenth Amendment rather plainly contemplated explicit governmental efforts to reduce economic inequality, see supra n.2.)

Instead, in *West Coast Hotel,* the Court holds that "regulation which is reasonable in relation to its subject and is adopted in the interests of the community is due process." How does the Court establish the criteria of reasonableness and public spiritedness here?

Note the different justifications for upholding the statute in the parts of the opinion marked "Second" and "Third." Do they establish that the legislation is reasonable and in the public interest in the same way? After the discussion in "Third" what exactly does "rational basis" mean?

2. *Interest group pluralism.* One way of justifying the virtual abdication of judicial review in *Carolene Products* is a theory of interest group pluralism. Under this theory, the "public interest" has no real substantive content. It is (and should be) determined largely by whatever majorities happen to want at a given time. The political process allows different groups to form coalitions and to lobby legislators and other government officials to promote their particular interests. The only requirement of due process is that legislators (or those charged with defending the law) be able to explain how serving these goals will also serve the general good. As a result, a court reviewing the statute will strive to put the best face on legislation that may in fact serve a particular interest group.

For example, Professor Geoffrey Miller points out that the legislation at issue in *Carolene Products* was the result of a powerful dairy industry that feared the economic challenge posed by the new purveyors of filled milk. Geoffrey P. Miller, The True Story of Carolene Products, 1987 Supreme Court Review 397. Miller describes the "scientific case against filled milk" as "bogus from the start" (at 420) and argues that the background of *Carolene Products* is best analyzed as "one discrete minority — the nation's dairy farmers and their allies — obtain[ing] legislation harmful to consumers and the public at large" by raising the price of milk (at 428).

Implicit in this interest group theory is that the democratic process is basically fair and that people aggrieved by unjust laws can employ the political process to repeal them. In other words, the pluralist model assumes that no groups persistently exercise inappropriate or unfair degrees of political power in a democracy. Even the Court understood that this assumption was (at least sometimes) unrealistic when it announced its theory of rational basis review in *Carolene Products*; hence it offered a famous caveat in a footnote.

3. *The footnote.* Given the virtual abdication of judicial review of economic legislation implied by the last part of Stone's opinion, why should the Court ever strike down any legislation? Couldn't almost any piece of legislation pass his watered-down test of rationality? Recall that at the same time, Justice Stone and his more liberal colleagues were increasingly trying to protect civil liberties like freedom of speech and religion. The problem was how to square these positions with their preference for judicial restraint elsewhere.

Footnote four of the court's opinion (footnote c in the text) offers a tentative answer to this problem. The first paragraph, inserted at Chief Justice Hughes's request, argues that judicial review is justified by textual commitments in the Constitution, including most prominently the Bill of Rights. Note the reference to incorporation in this paragraph's suggestion that certain portions of the federal Bill "are deemed equally specific [against states] when held to be embraced within the Fourteenth" Amendment (citing, e.g., *Stromberg*). Note also Hughes's effort to distinguish between "specific" provisions of the Bill of Rights and other presumably less specific provisions. Recall Hughes's efforts to draw a similar distinction in *Blaisdell*. But is the language of the Bill of Rights any more "specific" than that of, say, the Contract Clause?

The second and third paragraphs, however justify judicial review on a different basis, that of protecting democracy. According to this theory:

> The political process works effectively most of the time; representative democracy can generally be trusted to act in the public interest. Nevertheless, in a small, selected group of cases, which can be readily identified, the process malfunctions. In that marginal set of cases the judiciary properly may subject legislation to a higher level of scrutiny, not because it is authorized to impose its value choices upon the majority, but because the process itself is defective, undemocratic, impure. And in the very act of excluding these marginal situations from the norm, the judiciary demonstrates a double fidelity to democracy: First, because it avoids interfering in the normal processes of democratic institutions, and second, because it intervenes in those and only those abnormal cases in which the democratic ideals that justify judicial deference have been disserved.[10]

Hence, footnote four suggested that protecting democracy by protecting democratic civil rights and certain "discrete and insular" minorities could form a new justification

---

10. J.M. Balkin, The Footnote, 83 Nw. U. L. Rev. 275, 298-299 (1989).

for judicial review of legislation. This justification for judicial review became highly influential among legal scholars in the 1970s and 1980s. The notion that courts should exercise judicial review almost exclusively to protect democracy and guarantee the fairness of legal processes was developed into a general theory of judicial review by John Hart Ely in his influential 1980 book, Democracy and Distrust. For many legal thinkers "footnote four" became symbolic of the general post-1937 approach to judicial review, and spawned an enormous scholarly literature.[11] Nevertheless, this approach is not without its own problems. How does one tell when the democratic process is functioning correctly other than by reference to the substantive results it produces? What makes a minority "discrete and insular" and therefore deserving of protection? Shouldn't courts also protect minorities that are hidden and diffuse and thus unable to form effective lobbies and coalitions?[12] Are there any rights that cannot be justified on the basis of protecting democracy or fair legal process (for example, the right to bodily or sexual autonomy), and if so, are they without constitutional protection (at least in court)? Put another way, are constitutional rights protected only to the extent that one can show some direct connection to democratic malfunction? How thick a conception of democracy are courts entitled to protect?[13] Perhaps most importantly, the theory assumes that judicial review is exceptional because defects in the democratic process are comparatively rare. But if the democratic process is skewed because of previous injustices, inequalities of wealth, social stratification, deep-seated prejudices, gerrymandered districts, self-dealing by politicians and bureaucratic obstruction, shouldn't more and more situations fall into the world described by the footnote (judicial scrutiny) rather than the world described by the text (judicial deference)? Conversely, if courts simply accept the existing system as basically democratic, won't they indulge in the same fictions about formal liberty and formal equality that characterized the *Lochner* era (although this time to uphold rather than invalidate legislative action)?

4. *Later cases.* Between 1937 and 1941 the Court's composition changed radically. The progressive Justices were succeeded by other progressives,[14] and the old conservatives (Van Devanter, McReynolds, Butler, and Sutherland) were replaced by New Dealers.[15] It became increasingly doubtful whether economic regulations had to meet even the minimal requirements suggested by *West Coast Hotel* and *Carolene Products.*

In Olsen v. Nebraska, 313 U.S. 236 (1941), a unanimous Court overruled Ribnik v. McBride, 277 U.S. 350 (1928), to uphold a statute fixing the maximum fee that an employment agency could collect from an employee. Justice Douglas wrote:

11. In addition to Balkin, supra, see Louis Lusky, By What Right? (1975); Bruce A. Ackerman, Beyond *Carolene Products*, 98 Harv. L. Rev. 713 (1985); Milner Ball, Judicial Protection of Powerless Minorities, 59 Iowa L. Rev. 1059 (1974); Lea Brilmayer, *Carolene*, Conflicts and the Fate of the "Insider-Outsider," 134 U. Pa. L. Rev. 1291 (1986); Robert M. Cover, The Origins of Judicial Activism in the Protection of Minorities, 91 Yale L.J. 1287 (1982). The response to Ely's book created its own literature. See, e.g., Laurence Tribe, The Puzzling Persistence of Process-Based Constitutional Theories, 89 Yale L.J. 1063 (1980); Symposium: Judicial Review v. Democracy, 42 Ohio St. L.J. 1 (1981); Douglas Laycock, Taking Constitutions Seriously: A Theory of Judicial Review (Book Review), 59 Tex. L. Rev. 343 (1981).

12. Ackerman, supra n.11.

13. See, e.g., J.M. Balkin, The Constitution of Status, 106 Yale L.J. 2313 (1997) (arguing that the Constitution is ultimately concerned not only with democratic processes but also with a democratic culture, which is opposed to unjust social structures and status hierarchies).

14. Frankfurter replaced Cardozo (1939), who himself had replaced Holmes in 1932; Douglas replaced Brandeis (1939); Stone succeeded Hughes to the chief justiceship (1941); Jackson succeeded to Stone's seat as associate justice (1941).

15. Black replaced Van Devanter (1937); Reed replaced Sutherland (1938); Murphy replaced Butler (1940); and Byrnes replaced McReynolds (1941). Roberts, who had abandoned his conservative brethren, remained on the Court until 1945.

We are not concerned . . . with the wisdom, need, or appropriateness of the legislation. Differences of opinion on that score suggest a choice which "should be left where . . . it was left by the Constitution — to the States and to Congress." There is no necessity for the state to demonstrate before us that evils persist despite the competition which attends the bargaining in this field. In final analysis, the only constitutional prohibitions or restraints which respondents have suggested for the invalidation of this legislation are those notions of public policy embodied in earlier decisions of this Court but which, as Mr. Justice Holmes long admonished, should not be read into the Constitution. Since they do not find expression in the Constitution we cannot give them continuing vitality as standards by which the constitutionality of the economic and social programs of the states is to be determined.

The same year, in United States v. Darby, 312 U.S. 100 (1941), the Court — once again, unanimously — sustained the federal Fair Labor Standards Act of 1938 against a variety of constitutional challenges. With respect to the due process objection to the act's fixing of maximum hours and minimum wages for men, Justice Stone was content to write for the Court:

> Since our decision in West Coast Hotel Co. v. Parrish, it is no longer open to question that the fixing of a minimum wage is within the legislative power and that the bare fact of its exercise is not a denial of due process under the Fifth more than under the Fourteenth Amendment. Nor is it any longer open to question that it is within the legislative power to fix maximum hours. Similarly the statute is not objectionable because applied alike to both men and women.

In Lincoln Federal Labor Union v. Northwestern Iron & Metal Co., 335 U.S. 525 (1949), a unanimous Court sustained a state prohibition of closed shops. Justice Black noted that the Court had rejected "the *Allgeyer-Lochner-Adair-Coppage* constitutional doctrine" and had returned "to the earlier constitutional principle that states have power to legislate against what are found to be injurious practices in their internal commercial and business affairs, so long as their laws do not run afoul of some specific federal constitutional prohibition." In Day-Brite Lighting, Inc. v. Missouri, 342 U.S. 421 (1952), the Court sustained a law allowing employees four hours' leave with full pay on Election Day. Justice Douglas wrote that the legislature's judgment "may be a debatable one. . . . But if our recent cases mean anything, they leave debatable issues as respects business, economic, and social affairs to legislative decision." Justice Frankfurter concurred in the result without opinion, and Justice Jackson dissented, stating that "[g]etting out the vote is not the business of employers. . . . It is either the voter's own business or the State's business." In Ferguson v. Skrupa, 372 U.S. 726 (1963), which sustained a Kansas statute prohibiting anyone except lawyers from engaging in the business of "debt adjusting,"[16] Justice Black wrote for the Court:

> [T]he Kansas Legislature was free to decide for itself that legislation was needed to deal with the business of debt adjusting. Unquestionably, there are arguments showing that the business of debt adjusting has social utility, but such arguments are properly

---

16. Debt adjusting is "the making of a contract . . . with a particular debtor whereby the debtor agrees to pay a certain amount of money periodically to the person engaged in the debt adjusting business who shall for a consideration distribute the same among certain specified creditors in accordance with a plan agreed upon."

addressed to the legislature, not to us. We refuse to sit as a "super-legislature to weigh the wisdom of legislation." . . . Whether the legislature takes for its textbook Adam Smith, Herbert Spencer, Lord Keynes, or some other is no concern of ours. The Kansas debt adjusting statute may be wise or unwise. But relief, if any be needed, lies not with us but with the body constituted to pass laws for the State of Kansas.

Justice Harlan concurred in the judgment, citing Williamson v. Lee Optical Co., a case that also featured prominently in the Court's opinion.

To that case we now turn.

WILLIAMSON v. LEE OPTICAL CO.
348 U.S. 483 (1955)

DOUGLAS, J. . . .

This suit was instituted in the District Court to have an Oklahoma law declared unconstitutional and to enjoin state officials from enforcing it for the reason that it allegedly violated various provisions of the Federal Constitution. The matter was heard by a District Court of three judges, as required by 28 U.S.C. §2281. That court held certain provisions of the law unconstitutional. The case is here by appeal.

The District Court held unconstitutional portions of three sections of the Act. First, it held invalid under the Due Process Clause of the Fourteenth Amendment the portions of §2 which make it unlawful for any person not a licensed optometrist or ophthalmologist to fit lenses to a face or to duplicate or replace into frames lenses or other optical appliances, except upon written prescriptive authority of an Oklahoma licensed ophthalmologist or optometrist.

An ophthalmologist is a duly licensed physician who specializes in the care of the eyes. An optometrist examines eyes for refractive error, recognizes (but does not treat) diseases of the eye, and fills prescriptions for eyeglasses. The optician is an artisan qualified to grind lenses, fill prescriptions, and fit frames.

The effect of §2 is to forbid the optician from fitting or duplicating lenses without a prescription from an ophthalmologist or optometrist. In practical effect, it means that no optician can fit old glasses into new frames or supply a lens, whether it be a new lens or one to duplicate a lost or broken lens, without a prescription. The District Court conceded that it was in the competence of the police power of a State to regulate the examination of the eyes. But it rebelled at the notion that a State could require a prescription from an optometrist or ophthalmologist "to take old lenses and place them in new frames and then fit the completed spectacles to the *face* of the eyeglass wearer." . . . The Court found that through mechanical devices and ordinary skills the optician could take a broken lens or a fragment thereof, measure its power, and reduce it to prescriptive terms. The Court held that "Although on this precise issue of duplication, the legislature in the instant regulation was dealing with a matter of public interest, the particular means chosen are neither reasonably necessary nor reasonably related to the end sought to be achieved." It was, accordingly, the opinion of the court that this provision of the law violated the Due Process Clause by arbitrarily interfering with the optician's right to do business. . . .

The Oklahoma law may exact a needless, wasteful requirement in many cases. But it is for the legislature, not the courts, to balance the advantages and disadvantages of the new requirement. It appears that in many cases the optician can easily supply the new frames or new lenses without reference to the old written prescription. It also appears that many written prescriptions contain no directive data in regard to fitting spectacles to the face. But in some cases the directions contained in the prescription are essential, if the glasses are to be fitted so as to correct the particular defects of vision or alleviate the eye condition. The legislature might have concluded that the frequency of occasions when a prescription is necessary was sufficient to justify this regulation of the fitting of eyeglasses. Likewise, when it is necessary to duplicate a lens, a written prescription may or may not be necessary. But the legislature might have concluded that one was needed often enough to require one in every case. Or the legislature may have concluded that eye examinations were so critical, not only for correction of vision but also for detection of latent ailments or diseases, that every change in frames and every duplication of a lens should be accompanied by a prescription from a medical expert. To be sure, the present law does not require a new examination of the eyes every time the frames are changed or the lenses duplicated. For if the old prescription is on file with the optician, he can go ahead and make the new fitting or duplicate the lenses. But the law need not be in every respect logically consistent with its aims to be constitutional. It is enough that there is an evil at hand for correction, and that it might be thought that the particular legislative measure was a rational way to correct it. . . .

Secondly, the District Court held that it violated the Equal Protection Clause of the Fourteenth Amendment to subject opticians to this regulatory system and to exempt, as §3 of the Act does, all sellers of ready-to-wear glasses.

Third, the District Court held unconstitutional, as violative of the Due Process Clause of the Fourteenth Amendment, that portion of §3 which makes it unlawful "to solicit the sale of . . . frames, mountings . . . or any other optical appliances." . . . [R]egulation of the advertising of eyeglass frames was said to intrude "into a mercantile field only casually related to the visual care of the public" and restrict "an activity which in no way can detrimentally affect the people."

An eyeglass frame, considered in isolation, is only a piece of merchandise. But an eyeglass frame is not used in isolation . . . ; it is used with lenses; and lenses, pertaining as they do to the human eye, enter the field of health. Therefore, the legislature might conclude that to regulate one effectively it would have to regulate the other. Or it might conclude that both the sellers of frames and the sellers of lenses were in a business where advertising should be limited or even abolished in the public interest. . . . The advertiser of frames may be using his ads to bring in customers who will buy lenses. If the advertisement of lenses is to be abolished or controlled, the advertising of frames must come under the same restraints; or so the legislature might think. We see no constitutional reason why a State may not treat all who deal with the human eye as members of a profession who should use no merchandising methods for obtaining customers.

Fourth, the District Court held unconstitutional, as violative of the Due Process Clause of the Fourteenth Amendment, the provision of §4 of the Oklahoma Act which reads as follows: "No person, firm, or corporation engaged in the business of retailing merchandise to the general public shall rent space, sublease departments, or otherwise permit any person purporting to do eye examination or visual care to occupy space in such retail store."

It seems to us that this regulation . . . is an attempt to free the profession, to as great an extent as possible, from all taints of commercialism. It certainly might be easy for an optometrist with space in a retail store to be merely a front for the retail establishment. In any case, the opportunity for that nexus may be too great for safety, if the eye doctor is allowed inside the retail store. Moreover, it may be deemed important to effective regulation that the eye doctor be restricted to geographical locations that reduce the temptations of commercialism. Geographical location may be an important consideration in a legislative program which aims to raise the treatment of the human eye to a strictly professional level. We cannot say that the regulation has no rational relation to that objective and therefore is beyond constitutional bounds. . . .

Discussion

1. *"Rationality" analysis: Economic equal protection.* Williamson v. Lee Optical involved challenges not only under the Due Process Clause but also under the Equal Protection Clause. In contrast to the Due Process Clause, the *Lochner* Court had given the Equal Protection Clause little importance outside the context of race. In *Williamson* the Court treated both clauses as affording essentially the same degree of protection in cases of ordinary social and economic regulation. Whether plaintiffs claimed that a law violated their economic liberties or that the law made arbitrary distinctions, the Court subjected the law to the test of "minimum rationality": The infringement on liberty or the distinctions made had to be "rational." A standard case capturing the post-1937 view of "ordinary" equal protection analysis is Railway Express Agency v. New York, 336 U.S. 106 (1949), which involved a New York City regulation providing that "[n]o person shall operate . . . in or upon any street an advertising vehicle; provided that nothing herein contained shall prevent the putting of business notices upon business delivery vehicles, so long as such vehicles are engaged in the usual business or regular work of the owner and are not used merely or mainly for advertising." The ostensible purpose of this ordinance was to increase traffic safety by limiting potential distractions to drivers. What this meant, practically speaking, was that the Railway Express Agency, which owned hundreds of delivery vans, could not rent space on the side of its delivery vans to businesses wishing to advertise their products. R.E.A. was convicted for violating the ordinance after carrying advertisements for cigarettes, a radio station, and a circus. However, the New York Times Company, which also owned hundreds of delivery trucks, could freely advertise *The New York Times* on the sides of *its* trucks. Without dissent,[17] the Court upheld the ordinance against R.E.A.'s equal protection challenge.

Writing for the Court, Justice Douglas noted R.E.A.'s contention

> that unequal treatment on the basis of such a distinction is not justified by the aim and purpose of the regulation. It is said, for example, that one of appellant's trucks carrying the advertisement of a commercial house would not cause any greater distraction of pedestrians and vehicle drivers than if the commercial house carried the same advertisement on its own truck. . . . It is therefore contended that the classification which the regulation makes has no relation to the traffic problem since a violation turns not on what kind of advertisements are carried on trucks but on whose trucks they are carried.

---

17. Though Justice Rutledge acquiesced in the Court's opinion, "dubitante on the question of equal protection of the laws."

Justice Douglas, however, described this analysis as "superficial," for he declared that "local authorities may well have concluded that those who advertise their own wares on their trucks do not present the same traffic problem in view of the nature or extent of the advertising which they use. It would take a degree of omniscience which we lack to say that such is not the case." On that assumption, then, the Court "cannot say that the judgment is not an allowable one." The classification at issue relates "to the purpose for which it is made and does not contain the kind of discrimination against which the Equal Protection Clause affords protection."[18]

For a more recent illustration of the modern Court's generally deferential approach to issues of economic regulation, consider Nordlinger v. Hahn, 505 U.S. 1 (1992). The case involved an equal protection challenge to California's well-known initiative, Proposition 13, which generally pegged state property taxes to the initial purchase price, rather than the current market price, of each parcel of real estate. With steeply rising property values, the Proposition 13 regime quickly gave rise to wide property-tax differentials (often more than 10 to 1) for homes of comparable current market value. Writing for himself and seven others, Justice Blackmun upheld this regime, noting that the equal protection standard "is especially deferential in the context of classifications made by complex tax laws." Given this deference, the Court had

> no difficulty in ascertaining at least two rational or reasonable considerations of difference or policy that justify denying petitioner the benefits of her neighbors' lower assessments. [These neighbors had houses of comparable current market value, but had bought them many years earlier, at much lower prices.] First, the State has a legitimate interest in local neighborhood preservation, continuity, and stability. The State therefore legitimately can decide to structure its tax system to discourage rapid turnover in ownership of homes and businesses, for example, in order to inhibit displacement of lower income families by the forces of gentrification or of established, "mom-and-pop" businesses by newer chain operations. By permitting older owners to pay progressively less in taxes than new owners of comparable property, the . . . assessment scheme rationally furthers this interest.
>
> Second, the State legitimately can conclude that a new owner at the time of acquiring his property does not have the same reliance interest warranting protection against higher taxes as does an existing owner. The State may deny a new owner at the point of purchase the right to "lock in" to the same assessed value as is enjoyed by an existing owner of comparable property, because an existing owner rationally may be thought

18. Is *Railway Express* still good law? At the time it was decided, the Supreme Court did not treat garden-variety commercial advertising as "speech" whose regulation triggered heightened (more-than-rational-basis) scrutiny under the First Amendment. In Greater New Orleans Broadcasting Association, Inc. v. United States, 527 U.S. 173 (1999), the Court unanimously struck down a federal statute regulating casino advertising. Some casino advertisers were covered by the statute and other casino advertisers were not. The overall pattern of exclusion and inclusion struck the Court as so "pierced by exemptions and inconsistencies" so as to violate the First Amendment freedom of speech. Inexplicably, *Railway Express* went unmentioned in the opinion.

Has the Court of late begun to turn the First Amendment into a font for a new, *Lochner*-like jurisprudence protecting the rights of corporations and other propertied folk? For expressions of concern that this might be so, see J.M. Balkin, Some Realism About Pluralism: Legal Realist Approaches to the First Amendment, 1990 Duke L. J. 375. The law in *Greater New Orleans* may well have been a patchwork. But was it truly invidious? Was there any true First Amendment threat, such as incumbent-entrenchment or political debate-skewing, afoot? Consider the argument of Judge Linde, infra, that a law should not be declared unconstitutional simply because judges find it to be a crazy quilt (consider, for example, the tax code), but only if judges can find an affirmatively impermissible government purpose at work.

to have vested expectations in his property or home that are more deserving of protection than the anticipatory expectations of a new owner at the point of purchase. A new owner has full information about the scope of future tax liability before acquiring the property, and if he thinks the future tax burden is too demanding, he can decide not to complete the purchase at all. By contrast, the existing owner, already saddled with his purchase, does not have the option of deciding not to buy his home if taxes become prohibitively high. To meet his tax obligations, he might be forced to sell his home or to divert his income away from the purchase of food, clothing, and other necessities. In short, the State may decide that it is worse to have owned and lost, than never to have owned at all.[19]

Justice Stevens dissented, arguing that the law was "arbitrary and unreasonable" and "irrational" in treating new owners so differently from old owners.[20]

2. *Gunther's Foreword.* In a famous article, Gerald Gunther argued that in reviewing economic legislation for rationality, the Court should be "less willing to supply justifying rationales by exercising its imagination." Gerald Gunther, Foreword, In Search of Evolving Doctrine on a Changing Court: A Model for a Newer Equal Protection, 86 Harv. L. Rev. 1 (1972). Rather, rationality review should require a statement of the state's purposes as gleaned from some "authoritative state source," including legislative history, or even from "a state court or state attorney general's description of [the legislation's] purpose." Do you agree?

With respect to judicial use of legislative history, note that many states do not regularly publish the reports of legislative committees and debates within the legislatures. Would Gunther's proposal mean, then, that states *must* begin publishing legislative records in order to provide evidence of the purposes underlying their handiwork? With respect to statements by a state attorney general, why wouldn't a lawyer representing the state posit *all* plausible legitimate objectives that might sustain a challenged law, even if no one suggested them in a committee report or in the legislature?

3. *Legislative errors.* Contra Gunther's suggestion, existing doctrine typically treats the actual purposes behind economic legislation as largely irrelevant to its constitutionality, as long as some hypothetical purpose exists that satisfies the requirements of minimum rationality. Nevertheless, should the Court inquire into whether members of the legislature were hoodwinked by lobbyists or misunderstood the terms of legislation they were voting on? Do the arguments for judicial deference to popular will make sense when the people's representatives do not know what they are voting for? If a court discovers that legislators were misled, should it strike down the law and "remand" the statute so that the legislature can properly reconsider the matter? Or does this solution place too great a demand on busy legislators?

---

19. Is failure to get something you want but do not yet have ever different from losing something you already have? For a quick and accessible discussion of the concepts of "loss aversion" and the "endowment effect" and some of their possible implications for law, see Cass R. Sunstein, The Future of Law and Economics: Looking Forward: Behavioral Analysis of Law, 64 U. Chi. L. Rev. 1175, 1179-1181 (1997).

20. Suppose that California instead imposed no tax at all on homes as such, but simply imposed a very large tax on the purchase of a home, to be paid by the buyer upon purchase. Would Justice Stevens find this tax unconstitutional? Note that this tax in some ways treats new buyers even worse than did Proposition 13: They are forced to pay in one lump sum, rather than over the years, whereas old homeowners who simply keep their homes are not taxed at all.

In United States Railroad Retirement Board v. Fritz, 449 U.S. 166 (1980), the Court upheld a provision of the Railroad Retirement Act of 1974, which reorganized the pension system to save money. Under the Act, employees would continue to be able to receive Railroad Retirement and Social Security benefits plus an additional "windfall" or "dual" benefit if they worked at least one day, or "retained a current connection with" a railroad in 1974. The bill, in essence, guaranteed that these benefits would be preserved for current employees but not for persons who were no longer in the railroad industry, even if their length of service and employment histories were identical in all other respects. Justice Brennan, in dissent, argued that the bill was drafted by railroad management and labor representatives who did not represent the interests of former employees, and did not inform legislators that they were preserving benefits for current employees by reducing those for former employees. Indeed, Justice Brennan argued,

> the Joint Committee negotiators and Railroad Retirement Board members who testified at congressional hearings perpetuated the inaccurate impression that all retirees with earned vested dual benefits under prior law would retain their benefits unchanged. . . . Most striking is the following colloquy between Representative Dingell and Mr. Dempsey:
>
> *"Mr. Dingell:* Who is going to be adversely affected? Somebody has to get it in the neck on this. Who is going to be that lucky fellow?
> *Mr. Dempsey:* Well, I don't think so really. I think this is the situation in which everyone wins. Let me explain. . . .
> *Mr. Dingell:* Mr Dempsey, I see some sleight of hand here but I don't see how it is happening. I applaud it but I would like to understand it. My problem is that you are going to go to a realistic system that is going to cost less but pay more in benefits. Now if you have accomplished this, I suggest we should put you in charge of the social security system."

Justice Rehnquist's majority opinion responded:

> [W]e disagree with the District Court's conclusion that Congress was unaware of what it accomplished or that it was misled by the groups that appeared before it. If this test were applied literally to every member of any legislature that ever voted on a law, there would be very few laws which would survive it. The language of the statute is clear, and we have historically assumed that Congress intended what it enacted. To be sure, appellees lost a political battle in which they had a strong interest, but this is neither the first nor the last time that such a result will occur in the legislative forum.

Justice Rehnquist then added, in a footnote:

> The Constitution presumes that, absent some reason to infer antipathy, even improvident decisions will eventually be rectified by the democratic processes and that judicial intervention is generally unwarranted, no matter how unwisely we may think a political branch has acted. Vance v. Bradley, 440 U.S. 93, 97 (1979).

4. *The constitutional basis for economic due process and equal protection.* It should be obvious that the Fourteenth Amendment does not and should not prohibit all "discrimination" as such, at least if "discrimination" simply means "distinctions among individuals or classes of individuals." The major business of any legislative body is deciding who or what should receive certain benefits or bear certain burdens. (For example, murder laws impose certain "burdens" on murderers and in that sense

"discriminate" against the activity of murder.) Indeed, can you think of *any* laws that apply universally to all persons, things, or activities — that is, that do not classify at all?

If all laws in some sense discriminate, it is also true that all laws are in another sense perfectly rational and perfectly tailored. Every law tautologically accomplishes the precise result of the law itself. A regulation that limits emissions from blue cars and only blue cars might seem irrational if we focus only on the goal of emissions reduction, but the law perfectly accomplishes the objective of "reducing emissions from blue cars." To hold a law "irrational," it seems, judges must refuse to credit at least part of the law's tautological objective.[21] This refusal is easiest to defend when judges can point to something in the Constitution that renders a certain objective or purpose *itself* unconstitutional. For example, a law that limited only the emissions of cars owned by Blacks might very well fit the joint purposes of reducing pollution and of disfavoring Blacks — but the second purpose is *itself* a clear violation of the Fourteenth Amendment, read in light of its history. (Recall that the paradigm historical case of unequal protection, in the minds of the Reconstruction Congress, involved the infamous Black Codes that sought to stigmatize Blacks and treat them unequally.)

But are laws designed to favor one industry over another constitutionally similar to laws targeting Blacks for abuse? Consider how easily the laws challenged in *Railway Express Agency* and *Williamson* could have been upheld on the simple grounds that they promoted certain industries — newspapers and optometrists, respectively — favored by the regulations. Note Judge Hans Linde's comment on *Williamson:* "If Oklahoma had said that it gave independent optometrists a monopoly on fitting eyeglass frames in order to assure them the financial ability to render their other professional services at prices people could afford, there should be no need to demonstrate any health risks from having frames fitted by opticians in drug stores." On Linde's view, "[l]aws are not unconstitutional merely because they are shown to be useless" but only if they contravene "a constitutional criterion found elsewhere in the Constitution than in the due process clause itself." Hans Linde, Without "Due Process": Unconstitutional Law in Oregon, 49 Or. L. Rev. 125, 174, 177 n.154 (1970).

Linde's views, however, are in tension with Smith v. Cahoon, 283 U.S. 553 (1931), where Chief Justice Hughes, writing for a unanimous court, invalidated a Florida statute that required commercial carriers to post liability bonds to indemnify persons injured through the carriers' negligence. Exempted from this requirement were carriers engaged exclusively in transporting farm, fish, and seafood products. Note the date of *Smith*. Is the case still good law today? Should it be? The Court called the statute "wholly arbitrary" so far as it "was designed to safeguard the public with respect to the use of the highways." But why wasn't the statute wholly nonarbitrary in accomplishing the *joint* purposes of highway safety and seafood subsidy? And what, precisely, is unconstitutional about government subsidies (even indirect ones) for seafood?

5. *Lochner's legacy?* Consider the argument that judges and legislators "make" law in different ways. Whereas judges craft common law rules with an eye toward precedent and past practice, using techniques of analogic reasoning ("treating like cases alike") and detailed reason-giving, legislatures are authorized to make

---

21. See Note, Legislative Purpose, Rationality, and Equal Protection, 82 Yale L.J. 123 (1972).

new rules, with sometimes arbitrary or at least artificial boundaries. These laws are legitimated by distinctive characteristics of the *legislative* process — democratic accountability rather than judicial reasoning. When judges require that legislators must make laws with the same kind of "rationality" characteristic of judicial opinions, the judiciary in effect subordinates legislative lawmaking to judicial lawmaking. In doing so, are judges engaging in a kind of *Lochner* jurisprudence, impermissibly privileging the common law process over the legislative process?

D.   Modern Contract Clause Doctrine

The *Minnesota Mortgage Moratorium* case did not mark the end of the Contract Clause. During the two following years, the Court distinguished *Blaisdell* to strike down a number of state laws under the clause. Most of the decisions were unanimous. For example, W.B. Worthen Co. v. Thomas, 292 U.S. 426 (1934), held that an Arkansas law exempting the proceeds of insurance policies from garnishment could not be applied to a garnishment effected before its enactment. Chief Justice Hughes wrote for the Court that this law, unlike the Minnesota statute, contained "no limitations as to time, amount, circumstances, or need." Justice Cardozo invoked these same distinctions in W.B. Worthen Co. v. Kavanaugh, 295 U.S. 56 (1935), to strike down another Arkansas law for the relief of mortgagors. And Justice Brandeis in effect read the Contract Clause into the Fifth Amendment Due Process Clause in Louisville Joint Stock Land Bank v. Radford, 295 U.S. 555 (1935), to invalidate farm mortgage moratorium provisions of the federal Frazier-Lemke Act.[22]

Since 1937, the clause has seen only sporadic litigation — partly because of the paucity of offending legislation, but at least equally because of the Court's general withdrawal from review of economic legislation. Anderson v. Brand, 303 U.S. 95 (1938), struck down an Indiana law repealing teacher tenure rights, and Wood v. Lovett, 313 U.S. 362 (1941), held that land bought at a tax sale under a statute curing irregularities that might otherwise have been raised by the owner was immune from a subsequent repeal of the statute when the original owner sought to recover the property from the purchaser at the sale.

In El Paso v. Simmons, 379 U.S. 497 (1965), the state of Texas had sold large amounts of land on installment contracts under which forfeiting purchasers retained a perpetual right to redeem upon payment of back interest. The state subsequently imposed a five-year statute of limitations on the right of redemption. The Court sustained the statute against a Contract Clause attack, holding that the state's interest in the integrity of the market, title stability, and the avoidance of litigation imbroglios outweighed the burden imposed on purchasers and their assigns. Only Justice Black dissented, arguing that the Court had "balanced away the plain guarantee" of the clause and that it had assumed that *Blaisdell* "practically read the Contract Clause out of the Constitution."

For better or worse, Justice Black's observation was generally assumed to be correct — until the late 1970s, when the Court invalidated two laws on the ground that they impaired the obligations of contracts. United States Trust Co. v. New Jersey, 431 U.S. 1 (1977), held that New York and New Jersey could not repeal a

---

22. See also Treigle v. Acme Homestead Assn., 297 U.S. 189 (1936); International Steel Co. v. Surety Co., 297 U.S. 657 (1936).

1962 covenant that limited the ability of the jointly established Port Authority to subsidize rail transportation from revenues and reserves pledged as security for bonds issued by the Authority. The covenant had been enacted to promote the marketability of the bonds. Its repeal in 1974 was designed to promote mass transportation and thus energy conservation and environmental protection. Although the effect of the repeal on the value of the bonds was uncertain, the states had neither offered the bondholders any compensation nor replaced the covenant with an arguably comparable security provision. Under these circumstances, Justice Blackmun concluded for a majority of four, outright repeal of the covenant "totally eliminated an important security provision and this impaired the obligation of the States' contract." Justice Blackmun also noted that, where a state entity was seeking to modify its own contractual obligations, judges should give less than complete deference to "legislative assessment of reasonableness and necessity" because the "State's self-interest is at stake." Justice Brennan, joined by Justices White and Marshall, dissented. (Justices Stewart and Powell did not participate.)

Allied Structural Steel v. Spannaus, 438 U.S. 234 (1978), invalidated the Minnesota Private Pension Benefits Protection Act as applied retroactively to existing pension plans. Before passage of the Act in 1974, an employer could terminate a pension plan at will. Under the Act, an employer who terminated a plan or closed offices in the State was liable to a "pension funding charge" designed to supplement the existing pension funds if they were not sufficient to cover full pensions for all employees who had worked at least ten years. Justice Stewart wrote that "the first inquiry must be whether the state law has, in fact, operated as a substantial impairment of a contractual relationship. The severity of the impairment measures the height of the hurdle the state legislation must clear. Minimal alteration of contractual obligations may end the inquiry at its first stage. Severe impairment, on the other hand, will push the inquiry to a careful examination of the nature and purpose of the state legislation." Justice Stewart observed that

> this law can hardly be characterized, like the law at issue in the *Blaisdell* case, as one enacted to protect a broad societal interest rather than a narrow class. . . . This legislation, imposing a sudden, totally unanticipated, and substantial retroactive obligation upon the company to its employees, was not enacted to deal with a situation remotely approaching the broad and desperate emergency economic conditions of the early 1930's — conditions of which the Court in *Blaisdell* took judicial notice. . . . Entering a field it had never before sought to regulate, the Minnesota Legislature grossly distorted the company's existing contractual relationships with its employees by superimposing retroactive obligations upon the company substantially beyond the terms of its employment contracts.

In a dissenting opinion joined by Justices White and Marshall, Justice Brennan argued that the Contract Clause was concerned only with legislative *diminution* of existing contractual obligations and not with the imposition of additional obligations on contracting parties. "The Act does not relieve either the employer or his employees of any existing contract obligation. Rather, the Act simply creates an additional, supplemental duty of the employer, no different in kind from myriad duties created by a wide variety of legislative measures. . . . For this reason, the Minnesota Act, in my view, does not implicate the Contract Clause in any way."

United States Trust and *Allied Structural Steel* did not usher in a new era of expansionist readings of the Contract Clause. In Energy Reserves Group v. Kansas Power and Light Co., 459 U.S. 400 (1983), the Kansas legislature had passed a statute that had the effect of limiting price increases by the Energy Reserves Group that would otherwise have been allowed under a contract signed between the Group and the Kansas Power and Light Co., a public utility. The Supreme Court unanimously rejected Energy Reserves' claim that the Kansas statute violated the Contract Clause. Justice Blackmun's opinion for the Court summarized modern Contract Clause doctrine as follows:

> The severity of the impairment is said to increase the level of scrutiny to which the legislation will be subjected. . . . In determining the extent of the impairment, we are to consider whether the industry the complaining party has entered has been regulated in the past. . . .
>
> If the state regulation constitutes a substantial impairment, the State, in justification, must have a significant and legitimate public purpose behind the regulation, such as the remedying of a broad and general social or economic problem. Furthermore, since *Blaisdell*, the Court has indicated that the public purpose need not be addressed to an emergency or temporary situation. One legitimate state interest is the elimination of unforeseen windfall profits. The requirement of a legitimate public purpose guarantees that the State is exercising its police power, rather than providing a benefit to special interests.
>
> Once a legitimate public purpose has been identified, the next inquiry is whether the adjustment of "the rights and responsibilities of contracting parties [is based] upon reasonable conditions and [is] of a character appropriate to the public purpose justifying [the legislation's] adoption." Unless the State itself is a contracting party, "[as] is customary in reviewing economic and social regulation, . . . courts properly defer to legislative judgment as to the necessity and reasonableness of a particular measure."

Applying the test enunciated above, the Court unanimously held that Kansas had not "substantially" impaired ERG's contractual rights so as to trigger the Contract Clause's prohibition. Examining the particular background of the contract in question, including the "significant . . . fact that the parties are operating in a heavily regulated industry," the Court found that "ERG's reasonable expectations have not been impaired by the Kansas Act." The Court also emphasized the "significant and legitimate state interests" justifying the statute. "The State reasonably could find that higher gas prices have caused and will cause hardship among those who use gas heat but must exist on limited fixed incomes." It also pointed to Kansas's interest in coordinating the price levels of inter- and intrastate gas. Justice Powell, joined by Chief Justice Burger and Justice Rehnquist, declined to join this part of the opinion on the grounds that the case was fully disposed of once the Court had determined that no reasonable expectations had been violated by the statute.

Keystone Bituminous Coal Association v. DeBenedictis, 480 U.S. 470 (1987), involved a state law that prohibited certain underground mining operations that might cause damage to various surface buildings and other structures. The Court, per Justice Stevens, upheld the law against a Takings Clause challenge, see infra p. 535, and also rejected a Contracts Clause challenge. Although various surface owners had entered into contracts 70 years earlier in which they agreed to waive liability for surface damage caused by underground mining, the Court upheld the law on the basis of the "strong public interest in preventing this type of harm, the environmental effect of which transcends any private agreement between contracting parties." Chief Justice Rehnquist, joined by Justices Powell, O'Connor, and Scalia, dissented on Takings Clause grounds, and did not reach the Contract Clause issue.

In *General Motors Corp. v. Romein*, 503 U.S. 181 (1992), the Court once again upheld a state law against a Contract Clause challenge. The case involved a 1987 Michigan law that adjusted the compensation payments that employers were required to pay previously disabled workers. Writing for a unanimous Court, Justice O'Connor ruled that the statute did not substantially impair contractual obligations, because there was no express contractual agreement regarding the specific workers' compensation payments at issue. Although the 1987 law modified earlier legislation, the Court declined to read the terms of that earlier legislation into the employment contracts at issue in a way that would trigger the Contract Clause. This move, the Court warned, would have the undesirable effect of "severely limit[ing] the ability of state legislatures to amend their regulatory legislation. Amendments could not take effect until all existing contracts expired, and parties could evade regulation by entering into long-term contracts."

Discussion

1. *Contract clause versus takings clause: A comparison.* Note that in some ways the Contract and Takings Clauses might be seen as close cousins: Each limits governmental efforts to redistribute private wealth. But the clauses are also different in key ways. At the Founding, the Contract Clause applied against states and not the federal government, whereas just the opposite was true of the Takings Clause, as construed by *Barron v. Baltimore*, 32 U.S. (7 Pet.) 243 (1833). Another difference: the paradigm Contract Clause violation involved a governmental attempt to redistribute from private creditor A to private debtor B; whereas the paradigmatic Takings Clause violation involved a governmental effort to redistribute from property owner A to the *government itself.* Might these two differences be analytically linked? For an elegant discussion, see Michael W. McConnell, Contract Rights and Property Rights: A Case Study in the Relationship Between Individual Liberties and the Constitutional Structure, 76 Cal. L. Rev. 267 (1988).

2. *Private versus governmental contracts.* Note that after Marshall Court cases like *Fletcher v. Peck*, 10 U.S. (6 Cranch) 87 (1810), and *Dartmouth College v. Woodward*, 17 U.S. (4 Wheat.) 518 (1819), the Contract Clause came to apply against states' efforts to abrogate their own contracts. Several of the modern contract cases have involved contracts with states themselves. Should judges in these cases give less deference to the state, because of possible governmental self-dealing?

E.   Modern Takings Clause Doctrine[23]

The Fifth Amendment's Takings Clause — which, it should be remembered, has been applied against state governments ever since the turn of the twentieth century — has given rise to a complex body of judicial doctrine. Many of the issues are covered in great detail in property courses and casebooks; here we shall merely survey the terrain and identify some of the most interesting questions concerning

---

23. See generally Joseph L. Sax, Takings and the Police Power, 74 Yale L.J. 36, 37 (1964); Frank Michelman, Property, Utility and Fairness: Comments on the Ethical Foundations of "Just Compensation Law," 80 Harv. L. Rev. 1165 (1967); Bruce Ackerman, Private Property and the Constitution (1977); Richard Epstein, Takings: Private Property and the Power of Eminent Domain (1985); Jed Rubenfeld, Usings, 102 Yale L.J. 1077 (1993).

constitutional substance, structure, and interpretation. Perhaps the most central and vexing question is: What, precisely, constitutes a "taking" for which compensation must be paid? The Court's unsteady path in attempting to answer this question is described with characteristic verve by Professor Rubenfeld.

JED RUBENFELD, USINGS
102 Yale L.J. 1077, 1081-1094 (1993)

The most historically settled application of the Just Compensation Clause — indeed perhaps the *only* historically settled application — is the requirement that government must pay for property it seizes through an exercise of eminent domain. The "eminent domain" power refers to the state's prerogative to seize private property, dispossess its owner, and assume full legal right and title to it in the name of some ostensible public good. . . .

For about the first century of state and federal constitutional law, outside of formal eminent-domain proceedings initiated by the government, the compensation guarantee was applied extremely restrictively. Occasionally courts would find for the plaintiff in inverse condemnation suits,[a] but even in such cases there was, for most of the nineteenth century, a "limitation of the term 'taking' to the actual physical appropriation of property or a divesting of title." . . .

Between 1871 and 1922, the Supreme Court decided three cases that laid the foundations of modern takings doctrine. Each case presented facts outside the traditional eminent-domain context; each created a new paradigm for takings analysis that has survived in one form or another to the present day.

1. PHYSICAL INVASION: *PUMPELLY*

In Pumpelly v. Green Bay Co., 80 U.S. (13 Wall.) 166 (1871) [discussed supra Chapter 4], the building of a dam in connection with a state canal project had caused the permanent flooding of the plaintiff's land.[b] [T]he defendant answered Pumpelly's compensation claim with the assertion that his "lands had not been taken or appropriated." The Supreme Court disagreed. . . .

Although [the Justices] seemed to open the door to compensation claims based purely on destruction of economic value, the *Pumpelly* Court went on to suggest that its ruling might be limited to cases "where real estate is actually invaded by superinduced additions of water, earth, sand, or other material." And within a few years, the Court had made this limitation explicit, holding that *Pumpelly* would be applied only where there had been "a physical invasion" of the owner's property.

Thus *Pumpelly* established the physical-invasion rule in takings law, which has remained one of its dominant components ever since. For the next century, floodings of land continued to be the most common application of *Pumpelly* in Supreme

---

a. Ordinary compensation proceedings are brought by the government following a formal exercise of eminent domain; the property taken is said to have been "condemned." In an inverse condemnation case, the plaintiff is a property owner alleging that the state has taken his property for public use without acknowledging it.

b. Although *Pumpelly* arose under the Wisconsin Constitution's compensation clause, the Court specifically noted that the state provision was "almost identical" to the federal one, and the case quickly came to be relied on as precedent for construction of the federal guarantee.

Court decisions. In 1982, however, the Court boldly extended the physical-invasion rule in *Loretto v. Teleprompter Manhattan CATV Corp.*, 458 U.S. 419 (1982).

Loretto involved New York State legislation requiring landlords to permit cable-television companies to install their equipment in rental apartment buildings. In size, the intrusion onto Loretto's property was quite minor, occupying "about one-eighth of a cubic foot of space on the roof." Nonetheless, the Supreme Court held that the statute effected an uncompensated taking.

Relying on *Pumpelly* and other physical-invasion precedents, the Court ruled that "a permanent physical occupation is a government action of such a unique character that it is a taking without regard to other factors that a court might ordinarily examine." Temporary or intermittent physical invasions, the Court noted, "are subject to a more complex balancing process to determine whether they are a taking." But a "permanent physical occupation of property is a taking" per se.[c]

2. HARM: *MUGLER*

Fifteen years after *Pumpelly*, in Mugler v. Kansas, 123 U.S. 623 (1887), a brewery owner challenged a state prohibition law forbidding the manufacture or sale of alcohol. Among other claims, Mugler argued that Kansas had "taken" his factory under *Pumpelly*, on the ground that the law had entirely destroyed the beneficial use of it.[d]

The Court rejected this claim, but not because Mugler's property had suffered no physical invasion. Instead, in language of lasting importance to the subsequent development of takings doctrine, the Court held controlling the circumstance that Kansas had legislated solely to prevent individuals from acting in a manner deemed harmful:

> The power which the States have of prohibiting such use by individuals of their property as will be prejudicial to the health, the morals, or the safety of the public, is not — and, consistently with the existence and safety of organized society, cannot be — burdened with the condition that the State must compensate such individual owners for pecuniary losses they may sustain, by reason of their not being permitted, by a noxious use of their property, to inflict injury upon the community.

Private property, said the Court, is "held under an implied obligation that the owner's use of it shall not be injurious to the community." Accordingly, a regulation preventing injurious use effected no taking.

The Court adhered to this harm principle in case after case over the ensuing decades. On this basis, for example, the Court rejected compensation claims arising from a law preventing the manufacture of margarine, ordinances prohibiting the operation of a brickyard and a livery stable in residential areas, the state-ordered felling of infested cedar trees, and a regulation closing a gravel pit.

---

c. As to the amount of compensation due, the plaintiff contended that her loss should be measured as a percentage of the cable-television company's revenues from her building, whereas a state agency, measuring the injury that the equipment did to the market value of Loretto's building, assessed her damages at $1. The Court did not resolve the valuation issue. On remand, the New York courts upheld the administrative process that had yielded the $1 award.

d. The Court addressed the plaintiff's takings claim without deciding whether the Fourteenth Amendment incorporated a compensation requirement.

3. ECONOMIC IMPACT: *PENNSYLVANIA COAL*

Finally, in Pennsylvania Coal Co. v. Mahon, 260 U.S. 393 (1922) — the "Everest" of takings law, as Professor Ackerman calls it — the Court . . . struck down a regulation as an uncompensated taking. The invalidated law was the Kohler Act, under which Pennsylvania had prohibited coal mining that would cause subsidence damage to surface structures, streets, utility lines, and so on. The Pennsylvania Coal Company, like other mining concerns in the state, initially had owned the subject land in fee simple; as the Court read the relevant deeds, when the coal company conveyed the rest of its fee it reserved the right to mine the so-called "support estate" regardless of subsidence damage.

In his opinion for the Court, Justice Holmes was clear that the Kohler Act had crossed some critical line: "We regard this as going beyond any of the cases decided by this Court." He was oblique, however, about exactly why this was so. Why didn't the *Mugler* harm paradigm easily dispose of the case (as Justice Brandeis thought it did [in dissent])? At first glance one might think that the mining companies' reservation of a right to damage exempted the case from the harm rule, but Holmes did not rely solely or even primarily on this circumstance.[e] Instead, the point most strongly emphasized in his terse reasoning was the magnitude of the loss of value suffered by the owner of the mining rights:

> Some values are enjoyed under an implied limitation and must yield to the police power. But obviously the implied limitation must have its limits, or the contract and due process clauses are gone. One fact for consideration in determining such limits is the extent of the diminution. When it reaches a certain magnitude, in most if not in all cases there must be an exercise of eminent domain and compensation to sustain the act.

In the most-quoted phrase of the opinion, Holmes wrote: "While property may be regulated to a certain extent, if regulation goes too far it will be recognized as a taking." As the Court observed, the Kohler Act left the mining companies with no economic value whatsoever in the support estate, for if the coal could not be mined, nothing productive could be done with it.[f] Perhaps in this respect, then, the Act had gone too far. Such at least is the principle for which *Pennsylvania Coal* came to stand: diminution of value would be a decisive factor in determining the existence of a "taking," and where the economic impact on the regulated property was too severe, a taking would likely be found.

As Holmes adumbrated, however, no degree of impermissible diminution of value was ever specified. Subsequent cases showed that very substantial percentage losses would be tolerated. By the early 1980's, the Court had arrived at an economic-viability formulation in which the requisite diminution of value

---

e. Holmes stressed it at various points in his opinion, but he undoubtedly was aware that the Kohler Act could not have been [invalidated] on the ground that all parties whom subsidence might harm had waived their rights. There were plenty of people not party to the deeds — for example, children — whom the state could have claimed to be protecting from injury. It should be recalled, moreover, that Holmes was writing in the middle of the *Lochner* era, a period marked by his emphatic refusal to hold unconstitutional laws that "merely" protected individuals from the harm they might come to as a result of their own contracts.

f. "What makes the right to mine coal valuable is that it can be exercised with profit. To make it commercially impracticable to mine certain coal has very nearly the same effect . . . as appropriating or destroying it."

approached total loss: "A statute regulating the uses that can be made of property effects a taking if it 'denies an owner economically viable use of his land.'"

4. MODERN TAKINGS LAW: DOCTRINAL CONFLICT, AD HOC ANALYSIS

Physical invasion, harm, and diminution of value have been the principal terms in which the Court has sought to conceptualize the "takings" question since 1922. Unfortunately, the three ideas are fraught with internal conflicts. By far the most important of these conflicts is that between the harm principle and the economic-impact test. More than anything else, the basic irreconcilability of *Mugler* and *Pennsylvania Coal* (or at least of the principles for which these two cases came to stand) has led to the doctrinal confusion so widely noted in the literature.

To put it bluntly, a diminution-of-value test cannot be squared with the harm principle as espoused in the *Mugler* line of cases. *Mugler* rested on the idea that owners have no right — and never had any right — to do harm with their property; hence they are not deprived of anything when laws enforcing this implied limitation are passed. Cases adhering to *Mugler* have reiterated this thought: "Since no individual has a right to use his property so as to create a nuisance or otherwise harm others, the State has not 'taken' anything when it asserts its power to enjoin the nuisance-like activity."[g]

But if this is so, then the fact that a harm-preventing measure diminishes the value of the regulated property — no matter to what extent — ought not to convert the regulation into a taking. No property right that the owner ever possessed has been taken. For this reason, in its decisions following *Mugler,* the Court seemed singularly unconcerned with the extent of devaluation suffered. For example, in Hadacheck v. Sebastian, 239 U.S. 394 (1915) — a case decided before *Pennsylvania Coal* under the *Mugler* rationale — the Court refused to find a taking even though an ordinance barring the plaintiff from using his property for a brick factory was said to have lowered the property's value from $800,000 to $60,000. And in Miller v. Schoene, 276 U.S. 272 (1928), in which the state had ordered the plaintiff's blighted cedar trees to be felled to preserve nearby apple orchards, the Court did not hesitate to say that outright "destruction" of harm-creating property was permissible without compensation.

Thus the co-existence of *Mugler* and *Pennsylvania Coal* created a conceptual tangle around the question of when, if ever, the state's exercise of its "police powers" could effect a "taking." By the 1960's this tangle had become quite apparent to the leading scholars of compensation law. As Professor Sax put it, takings jurisprudence since 1922 had become a "welter of confusing and apparently incompatible results," in which courts could choose freely either to invoke an economic-impact rationale (and hence to find a taking) or to invoke a police-powers rationale (and hence to refuse to find a taking). The Supreme Court itself had displayed both options in shifting from *Hadacheck* to *Pennsylvania Coal* to *Miller* — with the effect that no clear rules or principles governed the scene.

This confusion only worsened in 1978 with Penn Central Transportation Co. v. New York City, 438 U.S. 104, in which the Court — acknowledging these criticisms — forswore the pursuit of general principles to resolve takings cases and held that judges must instead engage in "essentially ad hoc, factual inquiries." The

---

g. Keystone Bituminous Coal Ass'n v. DeBenedictis, 480 U.S. 470, 491 n.20 (1987).

Court's results under this "ad hoc" approach easily earned the continuing admiration of commentators for the "disarray" they produced. A law imposing a penalty on employers for withdrawing from a multi-employer pension fund did not "take" property,[h] while a law entitling a courthouse to keep the interest on deposited interpleader funds did;[i] prohibiting the sale of property was not a taking,[j] but prohibiting the bequest of property was;[k] and forcing a marina to let people "invade" its property for the purpose of crossing into navigable waters was a taking,[l] but forcing a shopping center to let people "invade" its property for the purpose of soliciting contributions was not.[m] During the same period the Court decided *Loretto,* whose per se requirement of compensation where the plaintiff's damage may have amounted to all of one dollar stood in stark contrast to cases like *Penn Central,* in which the Court found no taking despite losses in the millions.

One advantage of the ad hoc approach was to permit the Court to avoid the conceptual conflicts between the harm rule and economic-impact analysis, both of which remained factors in the *Penn Central* balancing test. The Court's movement toward a total-loss, economic-viability rule also helped suppress this conflict, because in most cases some residual value could be found in the regulated property. Nonetheless, the day of reckoning finally came, under the name of Keystone Bituminous Coal Ass'n v. DeBenedictis, 480 U.S. 470 (1987).

Keystone presented facts virtually identical to *Pennsylvania Coal.* Once again, Pennsylvania had enacted a law prohibiting coal mining that would cause subsidence damage to surface structures. Once again, mining companies had expressly reserved the right, when originally conveying the subject property, to extract the coal comprising the support estate. This time, however, the Court found no taking.

The Court, in an opinion written by Justice Stevens, insisted that it was distinguishing *Pennsylvania Coal,* not overruling it. Yet the two principal arguments invoked to sustain the new law would have been quite as applicable in 1922 as they were in 1987. First, the Court reaffirmed the harm principle, quoting liberally from *Mugler* and declaring that the new law could be enforced without compensation because "Pennsylvania has acted to arrest what it perceives to be a significant threat to the common welfare." Second, turning to the issue of diminution of value, the Court held that the law had not caused a total loss of economic viability, because the entire package of the claimants' mining rights — of which the right to mine the support estate was only a fraction — was the relevant "property" to consider, and this property had suffered only a partial devaluation as a result of the law.

Keystone was a disturbing opinion for a number of reasons. To begin with, it seemingly overturned the seminal case of regulatory-takings jurisprudence without confronting the implications of doing so. Moreover, it exposed a deep flaw in the economic-viability rule: a regulation of property use can be characterized as effecting either a total or a partial destruction of value depending upon how the property rights are parceled up. Although this parceling problem had long been observed, *Keystone* exacerbated it by treating as a package the same bundle of property rights that

h. Connolly v. Pension Benefit Guar. Corp., 475 U.S. 211 (1986). It made no difference, the Court held, that claimant joined the plan long before the law was passed and that claimant had been contractually guaranteed the right to withdraw without penalty.
   i. Webb's Fabulous Pharmacies, Inc. v. Beckwith, 449 U.S. 155 (1980).
   j. Andrus v. Allard, 444 U.S. 51 (1979).
   k. Hodel v. Irving, 481 U.S. 704 (1987).
   l. Kaiser Aetna v. United States, 444 U.S. 164 (1979).
   m. PruneYard Shopping Ctr. v. Robins, 447 U.S. 74, 84 (1980).

Pennsylvania Coal had treated as parceled. Finally, although *Keystone* began by indicating that harm-preventing laws could not be takings no matter how severe their economic impact, it later went on (through its deployment of the parceling argument) to hold that Pennsylvania had not diminished too severely the value of the claimants' property, leaving the conflict between *Mugler* and *Pennsylvania Coal* utterly unresolved.

As a result, the clash between the economic-viability rule and the harm principle was destined to surface again, and it did [in] Lucas v. South Carolina Coastal Council, 505 U.S. 1003 (1992). [P]laintiff Lucas, a land developer, had purchased two lots of unimproved beachfront property for $975,000. Subsequently, South Carolina enacted the Beachfront Management Act, prohibiting Lucas from building any permanent structures on this property. The declared purpose of the Act was to prevent the erosion of the "beach/dune system," which assertedly served as an important barrier against dangerous storms and drew considerable tourist business to the state. Unfortunately for Lucas, the Act had the effect, according to a factual finding entered by the lowest court of the state and accepted as conclusive by the Supreme Court, of rendering his property valueless.

The South Carolina Supreme Court denied compensation to Lucas on the authority of *Mugler* and *Keystone*. The United States Supreme Court reversed and remanded. Justice Scalia's opinion for the Court in *Lucas* reads like a mirror-image of Justice Stevens's opinion for the Court in *Keystone*. Just as *Keystone* opens by finding in the precedent a categorical rule that harm-preventing regulations effect no taking (regardless of whether they totally destroy property value), so *Lucas* opens by finding in the precedent a categorical rule that regulations destroying economic viability do effect takings (regardless of whether they prevent harm). Just as Stevens had to offer a strained account of *Pennsylvania Coal* to maintain the integrity of his categorical rule, so Scalia was obliged to offer a strained account of the *Mugler* line of cases to maintain the integrity of his.

Moreover, just as Stevens effectively exposed the manipulability of the economic-viability test, so Scalia ably criticized the manipulability of the harm principle:

> The distinction between "harm-preventing" and "benefit-conferring" regulation is often in the eye of the beholder. It is quite possible, for example, to describe in either fashion the ecological, economic, and aesthetic concerns that inspired the South Carolina legislature in the present case. One could say that imposing a servitude on Lucas's land is necessary in order to prevent his use of it from "harming" South Carolina's ecological resources; or, instead, in order to achieve the "benefits" of an ecological preserve.

Accordingly, the *Lucas* Court said, "it becomes self-evident that noxious-use logic cannot serve as a touchstone to distinguish regulatory 'takings' — which require compensation — from regulatory deprivations that do not require compensation."

And yet, precisely as Justice Stevens returned to the economic-viability test at the end of *Keystone* (despite his putatively categorical harm principle), so Justice Scalia returned to the nuisance paradigm at the end of *Lucas* (despite his categorical economic-viability rule). Even if the state "prohibit[s] all economically beneficial use of land," wrote Scalia, it still does not "take" property if the state's limitation on the owner's rights already "inhered in the [owner's] title itself, in the restrictions that background principles of the State's law of property and nuisance already place upon land ownership." No "taking" will be found so long as the law "does no more than duplicate the result that could have been achieved in the courts" under the common-law principles of the law of nuisance. The Court expressed doubt that the Beachfront Management Act would pass this test, but held that the matter was one of state law to be decided on remand.

Thus what began as a ringing endorsement of a per se economic-viability rule — intended to clear away at least some of the takings confusion — ended with a direction to federal judges to decide takings claims by determining how the courts of the relevant state would have decided a hypothetical injunction action against the property owner under the state's common-law nuisance precedents. This result is astonishing, not only because it makes takings analysis turn on the various common-law precedents of the fifty states, and not only because the "common-law principles" of nuisance that judges must now consult are themselves an "impenetrable jungle," but also because this appeal to nuisance law is nothing other than an appeal to the "noxious-use logic" that the *Lucas* Court began by condemning so effectively. If the harm principle is to be jettisoned because there is no "objective conception of 'noxiousness'" that permits a "distinction between 'harm-preventing' and 'benefit-conferring' regulation," how then can judges be asked to evaluate "the degree of *harm* . . . posed by the claimant's proposed activities" and "their *suitability* to the locality in question"? These formulations, which the Court lifted almost wholesale from the Restatement of Torts, are nothing other than efforts to define an "objective conception of 'noxiousness'" in order to determine when a use of property does legally cognizable "harm" to others.

Lucas begins by telling judges why traditional nuisance reasoning is unworkable in takings law, and it ends by telling them that they must apply only traditional nuisance reasoning when they decide total-loss takings cases. According to the first part of Justice Scalia's opinion, the Court had never once held that states may destroy all economic value in an individual's real property when acting "merely" to prohibit nuisances or other noxious uses; according to the last part, the true rule is that states may destroy all economic value in an individual's real property so long as they are "merely" prohibiting nuisances or other noxious uses.

The case is a fitting culmination of takings law. The best lesson we could derive from it would be that the time is ripe to reconsider the fundamentals of the Constitution's compensation guarantee.

Discussion

1. *"Usings": A better mousetrap?* In lieu of the muddled approaches of modern judges, Professor Rubenfeld offers a different test: Just compensation is owed not simply when the government "takes" a person's property, but only when the government also "uses" that property. On Rubenfeld's view, government may "take away" without compensation so long as it does not "take over." He claims his reading squares best with the text: "Nor shall private property be taken for public *use* without just compensation." Prior to Rubenfeld, the standard reading of the words "for public use" placed the accent on *public:* If government takes private property for "private" use, such a taking is, on the standard reading, simply impermissible. But Rubenfeld argues that the standard reading does violence to the grammar and syntax of the clause, which sets out conditions for *compensation,* not prerequisites for the power of eminent domain itself. (On the standard reading, government may not "take" for "private" use, even if it is willing to pay just compensation, cf. Hawaii Housing Authority v. Midkiff, 467 U.S. 229 (1984), discussed infra p. 546.)

Rubenfeld also argues that his reading best explains what judges have in general done, if not what they have always said. In *Pumpelly*, the government was in effect using a private person's land as a reservoir and floodplain to hold excess water; whereas in *Mugler*, the government may have rendered an owner's brewery and his beer worthless, but the government did not affirmatively *use* either. (It did not drink the beer, or take over the brewery to make government widgets.) *Pennsylvania Coal*, on this reading, is indeed a hard and close case, but Rubenfeld argues that the government was affirmatively *using* the physical mass of underground coal to bear weight and prop up surface structures. By contrast, Miller v. Schoene, 276 U.S. 272 (1928) — discussed in more detail below — is like *Mugler*: The government sought to destroy disease-carrying red cedar trees, but did not "use" the trees as such — the government would have been just as happy, or happier, had the trees never existed. And as for *Lucas*, Rubenfeld argues that the government was indeed trying to "press [private property] into some form of public service," as the Court itself said in passing: In effect, South Carolina was trying to use Lucas's property as a kind of storm barrier, natural park, and tourist attraction.

Do you find this approach persuasive? Note that on this view, if government soldiers feast on a farmer's corn, compensation is owed, but if they merely burn the crop in the field while retreating (so as to prevent the invading army from feasting), no "use" has occurred, and no compensation is owed. Cf. United States v. Caltex (Phillipines), Inc., 344 U.S. 149 (1952), in which the Court denied compensation for property destroyed by the army lest it fall into enemy hands, and distinguished earlier cases requiring compensation as follows: "Both [the earlier] cases involved equipment which had been impressed by the Army for subsequent use by the Army" whereas here, the claimant's property was "destroyed, not appropriated for subsequent use." Is this a sensible distinction? Is there an attractive normative vision that underlies it, or is it simply more workable (and textually faithful) than the Court's muddled approach? In this regard, consider Rubenfeld's argument that the takings clause exemplifies a more general principle of noninstrumentalization: Government should not instrumentalize its citizens, or their private possessions. On this view, are the military draft and jury duty (which "use" persons) also suspect? Are laws that "use" a person's knowledge by requiring her to testify in situations where she would prefer not?

2. *Zoning.* Zoning is the primary means by which the political community controls the use of private land, and as such it came under attack as an infringement of property rights. Note that in some ways, the *Slaughterhouse Cases*, supra Chapter 4, might be thought of as zoning cases: Slaughtering of live animals gives rise to certain smells and health concerns, and so these activities should be confined to certain (preferably nonresidential, and downwind) portions of the city. Also consider Village of Euclid v. Ambler Realty Co., 272 U.S. 365 (1926), in which a realty company challenged a comprehensive zoning ordinance passed by the Village of Euclid, Ohio, which the company alleged had reduced the value of one parcel of its real estate from $10,000 to $2,500 an acre, and another from $150 to $50 a square foot. The Supreme Court upheld the law in an opinion written by one of its most conservative members, Justice Sutherland. (Justices Van Devanter, McReynolds, and Butler dissented without filing an opinion.)

Building zone laws are of modern origin. They began in this country about twenty-five years ago. Until recent years, urban life was comparatively simple; but with the great increase and concentration of population, problems have developed, and constantly are developing, which require, and will continue to require, additional restrictions in respect of the use and occupation of private lands in urban communities. Regulations, the wisdom, necessity and validity of which, as applied to existing conditions, are so apparent that they are now uniformly sustained, a century ago, or even half a century ago, probably would have been rejected as arbitrary and oppressive. Such regulations are sustained, under the complex conditions of our day, for reasons analogous to those which justify traffic regulations, which, before the advent of automobiles and rapid transit street railways, would have been condemned as fatally arbitrary and unreasonable. And in this there is no inconsistency, for while the meaning of constitutional guaranties never varies, the scope of their application must expand or contract to meet the new and different conditions which are constantly coming within the field of their operation. In a changing world, it is impossible that it should be otherwise. But although a degree of elasticity is thus imparted, not the meaning, but the application of constitutional principles, statutes and ordinances, which, after giving due weight to the new conditions, are found clearly not to conform to the Constitution, of course, must fall.

. . . Thus the question whether the power to forbid the erection of a building of a particular kind or for a particular use, is to be determined, not by an abstract consideration of the building or of the thing considered apart, but by considering it in connection with the circumstances and the locality. A nuisance may be merely a right thing in the wrong place, like a pig in the parlor instead of the barnyard. If the validity of the legislative classification for zoning purposes be fairly debatable, the legislative judgment must be allowed to control. . . .

The matter of zoning has received much attention at the hands of commissions and experts, and the results of their investigation have been set forth in comprehensive reports. These reports, which bear every evidence of painstaking consideration, concur in the view that the segregation of residential, business, and industrial buildings will make it easier to provide fire apparatus suitable for the character and intensity of the development in each section; that it will increase the safety and security of home life; greatly tend to prevent street accidents, especially to children, by reducing the traffic and resulting confusion in residential sections; decrease noise and other conditions which produce or intensify nervous disorders; preserve a more favorable environment in which to rear children, etc. With particular reference to apartment houses, it is pointed out that the development of detached house sections is greatly retarded by the coming of apartment houses, which has sometimes resulted in destroying the entire section for private house purposes; that in such sections very often the apartment house is a mere parasite, constructed in order to take advantage of the open spaces and attractive surroundings created by the residential character of the district. Moreover, the coming of one apartment house is followed by others . . . until, finally, the residential character of the neighborhood and its desirability as a place of detached residences are utterly destroyed. Under these circumstances, apartment houses, which in a different environment would be not only entirely unobjectionable but highly desirable, come very near to being nuisances.

If these reasons, thus summarized, do not demonstrate the wisdom or sound policy in all respects of those restrictions which we have indicated as pertinent to the inquiry, at least, the reasons are sufficiently cogent to preclude us from saying, as it must be said before the ordinance can be declared unconstitutional, that such provisions are clearly arbitrary and unreasonable, having no substantial relation to the public health, safety, morals, or general welfare.

Professor Michael Wolf notes that the laws upheld in *Euclid* involved an attempt by the local community to prevent an influx of ethnic Eastern Europeans from the nearby city of Cleveland, most of whom could only afford apartments. Consider again Justice Sutherland's reference to an apartment house as "a mere parasite," and Justice Baldwin's evocation of "vicious paupers" in *Miln*, supra Chapter 3. Should the demographic consequences of zoning laws be constitutionally relevant? See Chapter 6, infra, where this issue is discussed with respect to race.

Miller v. Schoene, 276 U.S. 272 (1928), involved vicious insects rather than vicious paupers, but it, too, can be seen as a kind of "zoning" case. The Virginia state entomologist, acting under authority of the Virginia Cedar Rust Act, ordered the destruction of a large number of ornamental red cedar trees. The Act sought to protect apple orchards, an important part of Virginia's economy; although cedar rust does not affect the value of the cedar tree, it can infect apple trees and destroy their fruit and foliage. Cedar tree owners demanded compensation for their losses. The Court, through Justice Stone, unanimously ruled against them:

> The only practicable method of controlling the disease and protecting apple trees from its ravages is the destruction of all red cedar trees subject to the infection, located within 2 miles of apple orchards. . . .
>
> [T]he state was under the necessity of making a choice between the preservation of one class or property and that of the other, wherever both existed in dangerous proximity. It would have been none the less a choice if, instead of enacting the present statute, the state, by doing nothing, had permitted serious injury to the apple orchards within its border to go on unchecked. When forced to such a choice the state does not exceed its constitutional powers by deciding upon the destruction of one class of property in order to save another which, in the judgment of the legislature, is of greater value to the public. It will not do to say that the case is merely one of a conflict of two private interests and that the misfortune of apple growers may not be shifted to cedar owners by ordering the destruction of their property; for it is obvious that there may be, and that here there is, a preponderant public concern in the preservation of the one interest over the other. . . .
>
> [W]here, as here, the choice is unavoidable, we cannot say that its exercise, controlled by considerations of social policy which are not unreasonable, involves any denial of due process.

If you believe that the cedar tree owners deserved compensation, would you be equally sympathetic (and compensatory toward) apple tree owners had the state chosen to pass no act at all, resulting in huge losses to apple orchards? What if the state, committed to preserving the cedar trees as a means of attracting tourists, had *forbidden* the destruction of cedar trees without specific state authorization? (Would this cross the line into an impermissible "using" of the cedars?) Also, would the case against compensation have been easier if the state had sought only to prevent the planting of new cedar trees rather than the destruction of existing trees?

3. *The Coase theorem.* Should the costs of apple-tree blight properly be borne by apple-tree owners or cedar growers? In a famous article that would later help earn him a Nobel Prize in economics, Professor Ronald Coase argued that, under conditions of zero "transactions costs," private parties might contract around inefficient government liability rules to achieve more efficient results. See generally Ronald Coase, The Problem of Social Cost, 3 J. Law & Econ. 1 (1960). For example, assume that apple growing is much more valuable than growing cedar trees, and yet government "inefficiently" fails to give apple growers nuisance or tort remedies against infested cedar groves. Coase in effect argues that apple growers might nevertheless seek to pay their neighbors not to

grow cedar trees — in a world with no costs associated with bargaining, apple growers have an incentive to "bribe" their cedar-growing neighbors and thereby contract around the underprotective tort system. Conversely, assume that *cedar* trees are far more valuable to the economy, yet government "inefficiently" vests apple growers with tort remedies against owners of cedar groves. In a world of zero transactions costs, cedar growers could contract around this overprotective tort law by, for example, choosing to buy up neighboring apple orchards, or paying their neighbors not to grow apples.

Of course, in the real world, there are often many obstacles to contractual solutions — such as multiple parties, imperfect information, haggling costs, "loss aversion," and other psychological factors. And even in a world of zero transactions costs, note the huge *distributional* consequences of a regime that initially favors one set of growers against the other: If, say, apples are far more valuable than cedars, it does make a distributional difference whether apple growers prevail simply by invoking nuisance law, or instead prevail only after they "bribe" cedar owners to destroy the cedars.

Note a further implication of Coase's analysis: There is no "natural" party that "causes" a certain harm — rather, the harm is created merely by two mutually inconsistent uses. There is nothing inherently harmful about apple trees or cedar groves, but the two cannot costlessly coexist side by side. Pigs are fine — in their place — but not in parlors, or upwind. But if neither party can be seen as "naturally" noxious, how can government avoid the hard *distributional* choices involved in deciding who should bear the initial liability? (Recall Justice Scalia's reference in *Lucas* to the difficulty of distinguishing between "harm-preventing" and "benefit-conferring" regulation.)

4. *Takings versus taxes.* The Court has often described one of the principal goals of the Takings Clause as barring "Government from forcing some people alone to bear public burdens which, in all fairness and justice, should be borne by the public as a whole." See, e.g., *Penn Central; Lucas.* Does this mean that government impositions that are very widespread should not be seen as "takings" at all? Imagine, for example, a hypothetical California Proposition 113, which seeks to impose a five percent property surtax on all beachfront property in the state — to be paid, not in cash, but by surrender of title to a five percent strip of each beachfront parcel. Imagine further that the proposition goes on to provide, in a severability clause, that if the judiciary were to rule that such a scheme requires just compensation, the government will pay for each strip by imposing a global eight percent beachfront property surtax, to be paid in cash. (Slightly more than half the money collected will go to each Takings Clause claimant, and the rest will be swallowed up by court costs, lawyers' fees, and so on.)

Assume further that the eight percent cash surtax regime triggered by the severability clause is constitutional, under a broad reading of the real-life Proposition 13 case, *Nordlinger v. Hahn*, supra p. 523; there are rational reasons for treating beachfront property differently from other private property in the state. (Such property is generally owned by wealthier individuals with a greater ability to pay than other Californians; such property often implicates special concerns about pollution and the environment; and, due to weather and other factors, such property also gives rise to distinctive costs that the state at times must bear.) If you were an individual beachfront property owner, would you want courts to recognize the five percent in-kind surtax as a "taking" that requires individuated just compensation? Wouldn't a ruling in favor of any individual beachfront owner who brings suit (perhaps for ideological reasons, or to establish a sweeping precedent relevant to his or her other business interests) end up — by triggering the severability clause regime — costing beach-front owners as a class even more? (Note that if courts do require individuated compensation, even those owners who were previously opposed to this result will have an incentive to come forward with their individual claims: Can you see why?) In the modern world, where redistributive taxation is plainly permissible, does it still make sense to see antiredistribution as the primary justification of the Contract and Takings Clauses? Or is the primary purpose today the prevention of localized and individu-ated injustice, where the legislature has picked out too small a group to bear a cost that should be spread out more widely?

5. *Constitutional remedies.* In First English Evangelical Lutheran Church v. County of Los Angeles, 482 U.S. 304 (1987), the Church had operated a camp, which was destroyed in a 1977 flood. In 1979 Los Angeles County adopted an "interim" ordinance prohibiting building in the flood plain, arguably rendering the Church's property practically useless. The Church sued for damages, claim-ing that the ordinance was a taking that required compensation. The California courts did not determine whether the ordinance constituted a taking. Rather, they held that state law limits the victim of a "regulatory taking" to an injunction against the operation of the offending ordinance, permitting damages only for subsequent violation of the injunction, and not, as the Church claimed, for damages from the date of the ordinance. A six-Justice majority, in an opinion written by Chief Justice Rehnquist, held the California remedial rule unconstitu-tional: "'Temporary' takings which, as here, deny a landowner all use of his prop-erty, are not different in kind from permanent takings, for which the Constitution clearly requires compensation." Therefore, "where the government's activities have already worked a taking of all use of property, no subsequent action by the government can relieve it of the duty to provide compensation for the period during which the taking was effective." Justice Stevens, joined in part by Justices Blackmun and O'Connor, dissented.

Note that other constitutional clauses, such as the Fourth Amendment, have not been construed to imply a direct cause of action against the offending government itself. See generally Bivens v. Six Unknown Named Agents, 403 U.S. 388 (1971), where the Court allowed a damage suit against errant federal officers, but not against the government itself. Is the current Court according property rights greater remedial solicitude than other (more egalitarian) rights? Or is the Takings Clause, in terms of its language, different from all other constitutional rights in its explicit recognition of a right to monetary compensation? Note also that in a typical takings (and usings) case, government has been "unjustly enriched." Not only has the citizen had something taken away, but government often has possession and use of the very thing taken. Should this make a difference?

If the regulatory taking in *First English* had occurred at the hands of the state government itself rather than one of its subdivisions (Los Angeles County), would the Court still require state courts to hear the claim? Even if the state claimed "sovereign immunity"? Compare Alden v. Maine, 527 U.S. 706 (1999), discussed infra p. 705, in which the Court held that state courts could not be obliged to hear (nontakings) constitutional suits for damages against the state itself.

6. *Unconstitutional conditions.* In Nollan v. California Coastal Commission, 483 U.S. 825 (1987), the state made the issuance of a building permit for petitioners'

beachfront house conditional upon conveyance to the public of an easement across their property above the high-tide line. (The state owns the property up to that line.) The property was located between two public beaches, and the easement was intended to facilitate passage from one beach to the other. The Coastal Commission argued that the new house would block public view of the ocean and contribute to the development of "a 'wall' of residential structures" preventing public realization that "a stretch of coastline exists nearby that they have every right to visit." The California Court of Appeal upheld the Commission's claim, ruling that imposition of an access condition was permissible whenever a project contributed to a need for public access, even if the need for access was not created by the project alone and notwithstanding the indirect relation between the condition imposed and the problem sought to be remedied. The state court also pointed out that the Nollans were not deprived of all reasonable use of their property, even if its value was diminished somewhat by the easement.

In a 5-4 decision the Court reversed. Justice Scalia began by hypothesizing the imposition of a similar easement on an existing built-up beachfront property. He noted that such an easement would constitute a "permanent physical occupation" of the land involved, thus taking the case out of the realm of "regulatory takings." The question remained whether the easement could be imposed as a condition for obtaining a building permit. The majority assumed arguendo that the Commission could prevent the building entirely if necessary to preserve a public interest, including the public's ability to see the ocean. It could also condition building on meeting requirements to preserve that interest, including "the requirement that the Nollans provide a viewing spot on their property for passersby with whose sighting of the ocean their new house would interfere":

> Although such a requirement, constituting a permanent grant of continuous access to the property, would have to be considered a taking if it were not attached to a development permit, the Commission's assumed power to forbid construction of the house in order to protect the public's view of the beach must surely include the power to condition construction upon some concession by the owner, even a concession of property rights, that serves the same end. . . .
>
> The evident constitutional propriety disappears, however, if the condition substituted for the prohibition utterly fails to further the end advanced as the justification for the prohibition. When that essential nexus is eliminated, the situation becomes the same as if California law forbade shouting fire in a crowded theater, but granted dispensations to those willing to contribute $100 to the state treasury. . . . In short, unless the permit condition serves the same governmental purpose as the development ban, the building restriction is not a valid regulation of land use but "an out-and-out plan of extortion."

Justice Brennan, joined by Justice Marshall, accused the majority of applying an "unreasonably demanding standard for determining the rationality of state regulation" and of potentially hampering "innovative efforts to preserve an increasingly fragile national resource." He also argued that the effect on the Nollans' investment-backed expectations was, at most, negligible. "Appellants can make no tenable claim that either their enjoyment of their property or its value is diminished by the public's ability merely to pass and re-pass a few feet closer to the seawall beyond which appellants' house is located." Justices Blackmun and Stevens also dissented in separate opinions.

Dolan v. City of Tigard, 512 U.S. 374 (1994), further stiffened the requirements of *Nollan*. Florence Dolan owned a plumbing supply store that she wanted to expand. This expansion, the city determined, would increase both traffic and storm-water runoff from her property. To offset these harms, the city conditioned her expansion on dedicating about 10 percent of her property to the city, for a floodplain and bicycle path. The Court, by a 5-4 vote, struck down the city's actions. Chief Justice Rehnquist acknowledged that the city's conditions were indeed germane to Dolan's proposed expansion; there was a proper logical "nexus" between the harms that would be caused by the expansion and the city's proposed conditions. Nevertheless, the Chief Justice found the conditions disproportionate to the harm: The city did not need to assert title over the strip of Dolan's lot abutting a creek to satisfy concerns over added runoff, and the city had not made sufficiently rigorous findings about how the proposed bike path would offset likely increases in car traffic generated by the expansion. Four Justices dissented. Joined by Justices Blackmun and Ginsburg, Justice Stevens argued that the exactions in question were "a species of business regulation that heretofore warranted a strong presumption of constitutional validity." Judicial deference was especially appropriate, he argued, because regulatory takings issues have "an obvious kinship with the line of substantive due process cases that *Lochner* exemplified. Besides having similar ancestry, both doctrines are potentially open-ended sources of judicial power to invalidate state economic regulations that Members of this Court view as unwise or unfair." In response, the majority countered that "simply denominating a governmental measure as a 'business regulation' does not immunize it from constitutional challenge on the grounds that it violates a portion of the Bill of Rights. . . . We see no reason why the Takings Clause of the Fifth Amendment, as much a part of the Bill of Rights as the First Amendment or the Fourth Amendment, should be relegated to the status of a poor relation. . . ." Justice Souter also dissented, on the ground that the majority had misapplied the *Nollan* test.

If (as the Court assumed), the government can completely prevent house construction in *Nollan*, and business expansion in *Dolan*, why may it not take the lesser step of conditioning approval in reasonable ways? To be sure, government cannot condition expansion on a citizen's promise to vote for the Democratic party, or for all incumbent zoning commissioners. (Do you see why?) But were the conditions in *Nollan* anything like that? Why shouldn't the proposal of the California Coastal Commission be seen as a permissible Coasean contract: "It is not efficient for us to block your house altogether, but we have a right to do so, and you should compensate us — the government — for foregoing our right to block your plan." What makes this "out-and-out extortion," rather than a legitimate Coasean contract? What is the source of the Court's "nexus" requirement? (Contra Justice Scalia, is it so clear that although the government may prohibit falsely shouting fire in a crowded theater, government somehow may not take the lesser step of taxing this "nuisance" behavior? Aren't maliciously false libels in effect "taxed" by the operation of tort law?)

To see the point another way, imagine that the state had told the Nollans that they could not build their house unless they paid a "beachfront building tax" assessed at 20 percent of the value of their property. Wouldn't *Nordlinger* obviously support the constitutionality of such a tax? Assume further that the state took this tax money and paid it right back to the Nollans, as "just compensation" for the easement that the state then forceably took from them, via its unquestioned right of eminent domain. Surely, this, too, is constitutional, no? Then why is the state barred from doing in one step what it may clearly do in two? Note that where political speech is involved, the issues are different: The government has no step-two right to demand (or even request) that the Nollans vote Democratic upon rebate of their building tax.

On this view, "unconstitutional conditions" analysis must be carefully linked to the precise shape and logic of the constitutional right in question: For example, the First Amendment might have a different logic than the Takings Clause, and facile First Amendment analogies may obscure as much as they illuminate in the takings context. For general discussions of the problems of a free-floating "unconstitutional conditions" doctrine untethered to the precise scope of differing constitutional rights, see Cass R. Sunstein, Why the Unconstitutional Conditions Doctrine Is an Anachronism (With Particular Reference to Religion, Speech, and Abortion), 70 B.U. L. Rev. 593 (1990); Michael W. McConnell, The Selective Funding Problem: Abortions and Religious Schools, 104 Harv. L. Rev. 989 (1991). See also the discussion of unconstitutional conditions in Chapter 9, infra. Assuming that the Takings Clause is indeed best read as requiring a "nexus," wasn't there such a nexus in *Nollan* itself? Building the house would block the public's visual access to the ocean; isn't this blockage reasonably offset by providing a different kind of public access, via the easement? Admittedly the government is "using" this easement, but why isn't the relevant "compensation" the government's permission to allow the Nollans to build — which (the Court assumed) the government need not have granted?

Compare *Nollan* and *Dolan* with Prune Yard Shopping Center v. Robins, 447 U.S. 74 (1980), where the Court unanimously upheld a California Supreme Court decision holding that the California Constitution protects "speech and petitioning, reasonably exercised, in shopping centers even when the centers are privately owned." The owner of the shopping center claimed that requiring it to give Robins access to solicit signatures for a petition operated as a taking. Justice Rehnquist responded:

> There is nothing to suggest that preventing appellants from prohibiting this sort of activity will unreasonably impair the value or use of their property as a shopping center. . . . The decision of the California Supreme Court makes it clear that the Prune Yard may restrict expressive activity by adopting time, place, and manner regulations that will minimize any interference with its commercial functions. . . . In these circumstances, the fact that [Robins] may have "physically invaded" appellants' property cannot be viewed as determinative. . . . [A]ppellants have failed to demonstrate that the "right to exclude others" is so essential to the use or economic value of their property that the state-authorized limitation of it amounted to a "taking."

7. *Rent control.* Would *Prune Yard* have been different if the government had not only regulated shopping centers but also compelled the owners to use their property as a shopping center, forbidding all other uses? Consider the case of Yee v. Escondido, 503 U.S. 519 (1992). A local rent control ordinance limited the ability of the owners of a mobile home park to set whatever rents they chose. Petitioners argued that the result of this ordinance was in effect an involuntary physical invasion of their park, impermissibly giving renters a kind of permanent right of occupation. The Court, per Justice O'Connor, unanimously disagreed:

> Petitioners voluntarily rented their land to mobile home owners. At least on the face of the regulatory scheme, neither the City nor the State compels petitioners, once they have rented their property to tenants, to continue doing so. To the contrary, the Mobilehome Residency Law provides that a park owner who wishes to change the use of his land may evict his tenants, albeit with six or twelve months notice. Put bluntly,

no government has required any physical invasion of petitioners' property. Petitioners' tenants were invited by petitioners, not forced upon them by the government.

Is there an important constitutional difference between, on the one hand, a governmental attempt to regulate the "use" the owner herself chooses, and, on the other hand, a governmental attempt to dictate one particular "use" of a piece of property? Professor Rubenfeld thinks so.

8. *"Public" use.* The finding that a taking has occurred and compensation been offered does not conclude the constitutional inquiry; recall that, under the standard reading of the clause, the government may only take private property for a "public" use. Consider in this context Hawaii Housing Authority v. Midkiff, 467 U.S. 229 (1984). As a result of Hawaii's unique history in which property had been controlled by the Hawaiian monarchy, 47 percent of the land in the state was held by only 72 private landowners; indeed, 18 landholders, with tracts in excess of 21,000 acres, owned more than 40 percent of this land. Twenty-two landholders owned 72.5 percent of the fee simple titles on Oahu, the most urbanized of Hawaii's islands. The Hawaiian legislature, finding this concentration of ownership undesirable, enacted the Land Reform Act of 1967, which transferred the fee ownership of certain residential tracts to existing lessors and paid compensation to the original owners. In a suit brought by some property owners, the Court of Appeals struck down the Act as "a naked attempt on the part of the state of Hawaii to take the private property of *A* and transfer it to *B* solely for *B*'s private use and benefit." The Supreme Court reversed in a unanimous opinion by Justice O'Connor (Justice Marshall did not participate):

> The starting point for our analysis of the Act's constitutionality is the Court's decision in Berman v. Parker, 348 U.S. 26 (1954). In *Berman,* the Court held constitutional the District of Columbia Redevelopment Act of 1945. That Act provided both for the comprehensive use of the eminent domain power to redevelop slum areas and for the possible sale or lease of the condemned lands to private interests. In discussing whether the takings authorized by that Act were for a "public use," the Court stated:
>
> > "Subject to specific constitutional limitations, when the legislature has spoken, the public interest has been declared in terms well-nigh conclusive. In such cases the legislature, not the judiciary, is the main guardian of the public needs to be served by social legislation, whether it be Congress legislating concerning the District of Columbia . . . or the States legislating concerning local affairs." . . .
>
> There is, of course, a role for courts to play in reviewing a legislature's judgment of what constitutes a public use, even when the eminent domain power is equated with the police power. But the Court in *Berman* made clear that it is "an extremely narrow" one. . . .
>
> To be sure, the Court's cases have repeatedly stated that "one person's property may not be taken for the benefit of another private person without a justifying public purpose, even though compensation be paid." Thompson v. Consolidated Gas Corp., 300 U.S. 55, 80 (1937). But where the exercise of the eminent domain power is rationally related to a conceivable public purpose, the Court has never held a compensated taking to be proscribed by the Public Use Clause.
>
> On this basis, we have no trouble concluding that the Hawaii Act is constitutional. The people of Hawaii have attempted, much as the settlers of the original 13 Colonies did, to reduce the perceived social and economic evils of a land oligopoly traceable to their monarchs. The land oligopoly has, according to the Hawaii Legislature, created

artificial deterrents to the normal functioning of the State's residential land market and forced thousands of individual home-owners to lease, rather than buy, the land underneath their homes. Regulating oligopoly and the evils associated with it is a classic exercise of a State's police powers. We cannot disapprove of Hawaii's exercise of this power.

Nor can we condemn as irrational the Act's approach to correcting the land oligopoly problem. The Act presumes that when a sufficiently large number of persons declare that they are willing but unable to buy lots at fair prices the land market is malfunctioning. When such a malfunction is signaled, the Act authorizes HHA to condemn lots in the relevant tract. The Act limits the number of lots any one tenant can purchase and authorizes HHA to use public funds to ensure that the market dilution goals will be achieved. This is a comprehensive and rational approach to identifying and correcting market failure.

. . . When the legislature's purpose is legitimate and its means are not irrational, our cases make clear that empirical debates over the wisdom of takings — no less than debates over the wisdom of other kinds of socioeconomic legislation — are not to be carried out in the federal courts. Redistribution of fees simple to correct deficiencies in the market determined by the state legislature to be attributable to land oligopoly is a rational exercise of the eminent domain power. Therefore, the Hawaii statute must pass the scrutiny of the Public Use Clause.[24]

9. *Abstract "legal interests" versus concrete "things."* The Founding-era paradigm of the Takings Clause involved governmental appropriation of physical things — for example, the condemnation of land for roads or the impressment of horses for war. Should the word "property" in the Takings Clause be read with this physicalist paradigm centrally in mind? See generally Ackerman, supra n.23 (contrasting the typically physicalist perspective of an "ordinary observer" with more abstract economics-or-philosophy-based views of a "scientific policymaker").

In Eastern Enterprises v. Apfel, 524 U.S. 498 (1998), four Justices (O'Connor, Rehnquist, Scalia, and Thomas) voted to invalidate the Coal Industry Retiree

---

24. Would your views about *Midkiff* change if you thought the state were robbing from the poor to give to the rich? (As a matter of fact, one large landowner in Oahu was the Bishop Trust, which had as its principal beneficiaries native Hawaiians, who tend to be toward the bottom the state's class structure.) What if the state were disrupting a tight-knit neighborhood at the behest of a large corporation? Cf. Poletown Neighborhood Council v. City of Detroit, 304 N.W.2d 455 (1981), in which a divided Michigan Supreme Court upheld Detroit's exercise of eminent domain to condemn a large tract of residential property to allow General Motors to construct an assembly plant that would add "jobs and taxes to the economic base of the municipality and state." Justice Ryan, in dissent, described the plan as "sweeping away a tightly-knit residential enclave of first- and second-generation Americans, for many of whom their home was their single most valuable and cherished asset and their stable ethnic neighborhood the unchanging symbol of the security and quality of their lives," and denounced the majority for accepting the legitimacy "of condemning private property for conveyance to another private party because the use of it by the new owner promises greater public 'benefit' than the old use." *Poletown* was overruled by the Michigan Supreme Court in County of Wayne v. Hathcock, 684 N.W.2d 765 (Mich. 2004), which described the earlier decision as a "radical and unabashed departure" from the understanding of "public use" doctrine. What might account for this development? Note that the two decades following *Midkiff* and *Poletown* saw the rise of popular social and political movements devoted to safeguarding what were claimed to be traditional rights of private property owners.

See also Kelo v. City of New London, 125 S. Ct. 2655 (2005), in which a narrowly divided Supreme Court endorsed a broad reading of *Midkiff* and upheld the authority of an economically distressed city to take private dwellings by eminent domain and then turn over the acquired properties to a private development corporation, as part of a large-scale redevelopment plan designed to create needed jobs and shore up the city's shaky tax base. Led by Justice O'Connor (who authored *Midkiff*), four Justices dissented; and within days of the Court's decision, a large number of Congressmen called for a federal statute that would bar states from engaging in *Kelo*-style uses of eminent domain. Less than a month after the Court's decision, the House voted 231 to 189 to prohibit spending federal money "to enforce

Health Benefit Act of 1992, in which Congress sought to require various companies that had previously been in the coal mining business to pay medical benefit premiums for their retired coal miners — in Eastern's case, more than 1,000 retirees who had worked for the company before 1966. These Justices brushed aside objections that the regulation in question did not "take" physical property as such; instead, they stressed the ways in which the government had retroactively singled out too narrow a group to bear too large (and unanticipated) a cost. Four Justices (Breyer, Stevens, Souter, and Ginsburg) voted to uphold the law in its entirety as reasonably tailored to the responsibilities of former coal companies for their past conduct.

These Justices counseled against further expansion of the doctrinal category of "regulatory" takings, emphasizing that this expansion departed from a judicial tradition emphasizing a more physicalist understanding of the Takings Clause. Unlike, for example, *Pennsylvania Coal, Nollan, Lucas,* and *Dolan,* the case at hand had nothing to do with land use, or tangible personal property (like horses or beer bottles or trees or corn) or even intellectual property (like a patent). Rather, the government's effort to impose health-care liability implicated a rather abstract understanding of "property" rights, and should not properly be viewed as a "taking." Cf. Connolly v. Pension Benefit Guar. Corp., 475 U.S. 211 (1986) (rejecting a takings clause challenge to a liability-creating law in part because "the Government does not physically invade or permanently appropriate any . . . assets for its own use"). For similar reasons, Justice Kennedy, writing separately, also rejected the majority's Takings Clause analysis in favor of a more physicalist view and a narrower understanding of what constituted a "taking." Justice Kennedy, however, voted to invalidate the law on the basis of the Due Process Clause.[25]

Query: Why did those voting to invalidate the law not invoke Contract Clause principles, or the case of Allied Structural Steel v. Spannaus, 438 U.S. 234 (1978), supra p. 528, in which the Court struck down a legislative effort to impose retroactive pension liability on an employer? (Hint: See the discussion notes following *Allied Structural Steel,* supra p. 530.)

---

the judgment of the Supreme Court in the case of Kelo v. City of New London." In the Senate, 30 members from both sides of the aisle cosponsored the Protection of Homes, Small Businesses and Private Property Act of 2005, which purports "[t]o protect homes, small businesses, and other private property rights, by limiting the power of eminent domain." Are such congressional statements and actions evidence of serious constitutional interpretation occurring outside the judiciary? Or is all this simply political posturing? (Is there any way to tell the difference?) To what extent are the anti-*Kelo* Congressmen reflecting a constitutional as distinct from a policy-based disagreement with the *Kelo* majority? On the contested authority of Congress to hold state action to a higher standard than the one set by federal courts in the domain of individual rights, see pp. 586-591, 639-643. Note also that leading state politicians across the country quickly responded to *Kelo* with calls for additional state statutory and state constitutional protections of private property in *Kelo*-type situations. As the *Kelo* majority took pains to point out, "nothing in our opinion precludes any State from placing further restrictions on its exercise of the takings power" than the ones the Court was willing to enforce under the federal Constitution. In other words, the federal Constitution sets the floor, but not the ceiling, for various individual rights against states, and the citizens of each state are free to raise the floor.

    25. Note the interesting social-choice feature of the Court's voting lineup: (1) all nine Justices agreed that the law was valid unless it violated the Takings or Due Process Clause; (2) a clear majority (Breyer, Stevens, Souter, Ginsburg, and Kennedy) rejected the idea that the law violated the Takings Clause; (3) only one Justice (Kennedy) claimed it violated the Due Process Clause; and yet, (4) a majority (O'Connor, Rehnquist, Scalia, Thomas, and Kennedy) in the end voted to strike down the law. Compare the discussion of Apodaca v. Oregon, 406 U.S. 404 (1972), supra p. 491.

II. Relaxation of Judicial Constraints on Congressional Power

The Court's treatment of congressional powers from 1934 to 1937 differed from its treatment of state social and economic regulation under the Due Process Clause. The 1936 decision in Morehead v. Tipaldo, 298 U.S. 587, supra p. 511, reasserting the unconstitutionality of state minimum wage laws, was an isolated decision made against the background of *Nebbia* and *Blaisdell*. During this period, by contrast, the Court struck down federal laws like the National Industrial Recovery Act of 1933, the Bituminous Coal Conservation Act of 1936, the Agricultural Adjustment Act of 1933, and the Railroad Retirement Act.[26] But over the next few years, the Court relaxed judicial review of congressional power, leading many to wonder what, if any, judicially enforced limits might remain.

A. From the Hughes Court to the Burger Court: Plenary Federal Power?

1. The Commerce Power

Judicial relaxation of substantive due process was abrupt. *West Coast Hotel* flatly overruled *Adkins* (see supra, p. 512). The relaxation of judicial constraints on the exercise of congressional powers was not so clearly signaled, but it was no less significant.

NLRB v. JONES & LAUGHLIN STEEL CORP., 301 U.S. 1 (1937): [NLRB v. Jones & Laughlin, the watershed case, purported to maintain continuity with the past. At issue was the National Labor Relations Act of 1935, which prohibits employers "from engaging in any unfair labor practice affecting commerce." The act defines "commerce" as "trade, traffic, commerce, transportation, or communication among the several States," and defines "affecting commerce" as "in commerce, or burdening or obstructing commerce or the free flow of commerce, or having led or tending to lead to a labor dispute burdening or obstructing commerce or the free flow of commerce." Respondent was charged with interfering with the rights of employees to organize and bargain collectively in its Aliquippa, Pennsylvania, steel manufacturing plant. As the Court noted, the respondent corporation with its 19 subsidiaries was a "completely integrated [multistate] enterprise, owning and operating ore, coal and limestone properties, lake and river transportation facilities and terminal railroads . . . ."

---

26. Schechter Poultry Corp. v. United States, 295 U.S. 495 (1935) (N.R.A.); Carter v. Carter Coal Co., 298 U.S. 238 (1936) (Coal Conservation Act); United States v. Butler, 297 U.S. 1 (1936) (A.A.A.); Railroad Retirement Board v. Alton, 295 U.S. 330 (1935) (R.R.R.). Some historians have divided the New Deal into an earlier period of corporatism, in which legislation such as the N.R.A. delegated regulatory power to industrial organizations, and a later period of welfarism, exemplified by the Fair Labor Standards Act and the Social Security Act. See, e.g., Paul Conklin, The New Deal (1967); Ellis Hawley, The New Deal and the Problem of Monopoly (1966). Although most of the legislation struck down by the Court was from the earlier period, the breadth of the holdings does not suggest that the Court was motivated by populist sentiments.

This made especially appealing the government's argument that the manufacturing process, though not itself commerce, was in the "stream" or "flow" of commerce. Cf. Stafford v. Wallace, 258 U.S. 495 (1922). But the Court refused to restrict its analysis to this metaphor.]

HUGHES, C.J.:

Although activities may be intrastate in character when separately considered, if they have such a close and substantial relation to interstate commerce that their control is essential or appropriate to protect that commerce from burdens and obstructions, Congress cannot be denied the power to exercise that control. Undoubtedly, the scope of this power must be considered in light of our dual system of government and may not be extended so as to embrace effects upon interstate commerce so indirect and remote that to embrace them, in view of our complex society, would effectively obliterate the distinction between what is national and what is local and create a completely centralized government. The question is necessarily one of degree. . . .

It is thus apparent that the fact that the employees here concerned were engaged in production is not determinative. The question remains as to the effect upon interstate commerce of the labor practice involved. In the *Schechter* case we found that the effect there was so remote as to be beyond the federal power. To find "immediacy or directness" there was to find it "almost everywhere," a result inconsistent with the maintenance of our federal system. . . .

[T]he stoppage of [respondent's manufacturing] operations by industrial strife would have a most serious effect upon interstate commerce. In view of respondent's far-flung activities, it is idle to say that the effect would be indirect or remote. It is obvious that it would be immediate and might be catastrophic.

In NLRB v. Friedman-Harry Marks Clothing Co., 301 U.S. 58 (1937), decided on the same day as *Jones & Laughlin,* the Court upheld the NLRA as applied to a small Virginia clothing manufacturer, most of whose materials came from, and most of whose finished products were marketed in, other states. In a brief opinion, the court cited *Jones & Laughlin* and referred to the size, importance, and interstate character of the clothing industry and the interstate impact of a strike. Justice McReynolds, joined by Justices Van Devanter, Sutherland, and Butler, dissented from both Labor Relations Act decisions, arguing that any "effect on interstate commerce by the discharge of the employees shown there would be indirect and remote in the highest degree."

In 1938, Congress passed a second Agricultural Adjustment Act, premised on the commerce rather than the spending power. The act included congressional findings that excess production moving in interstate commerce caused disorderly marketing, and the act imposed penalties for marketing farm commodities in excess of quotas set by the Secretary of Agriculture. Justice Roberts, who had written the Court's opinion in *Butler* striking down the 1933 act, supra Chapter 4, wrote for the Court in Mulford v. Smith, 307 U.S. 38 (1939), sustaining the 1938 act as applied to tobacco warehousemen penalized for marketing excessive tobacco. Justices Butler and McReynolds dissented.

If it was unlikely that the old Court would have held for the government in *Mulford,* there could be no doubt that United States v. Darby, 312 U.S. 100 (1941), and Wickard v. Filburn, 317 U.S. 111 (1942), marked a new era for the Commerce Clause.

UNITED STATES v. DARBY
312 U.S. 100 (1941)

[Sections 6 and 7 of the Fair Labor Standards Act of 1938 prescribed minimum wage and maximum hours for employees engaged in the production of goods related to interstate commerce as described in the opinion below. Appellee, a Georgia lumber manufacturer, was indicted for violating the act. The government appealed from the district court's judgment quashing the indictment.]

STONE, J. . . .

THE PROHIBITION OF SHIPMENT OF THE PROSCRIBED GOODS IN INTERSTATE COMMERCE

Section 15(a)(1) prohibits, and the indictment charges, the shipment in interstate commerce, of goods produced for interstate commerce by employees whose wages and hours of employment do not conform to the requirements of the Act. Since this section is not violated unless the commodity shipped has been produced under labor conditions prohibited by §6 and §7, the only question arising under the commerce clause with respect to such shipments is whether Congress has the constitutional power to prohibit them.

While manufacture is not of itself interstate commerce, the shipment of manufactured goods interstate is such commerce and the prohibition of such shipment by Congress is indubitably a regulation of the commerce. . . .

But it is said that . . . while the prohibition is nominally a regulation of the commerce its motive or purpose is regulation of wages and hours of persons engaged in manufacture, the control of which has been reserved to the states and upon which Georgia and some of the States of destination have placed no restriction; that the effect of the present statute is not to exclude the proscribed articles from interstate commerce in aid of state regulation . . . but instead, under the guise of a regulation of interstate commerce, it undertakes to regulate wages and hours within the state contrary to the policy of the state which has elected to leave them unregulated.

The power of Congress over interstate commerce "is complete in itself, may be exercised to its utmost extent, and acknowledges no limitations other than are prescribed in the Constitution." Gibbons v. Ogden. That power can neither be enlarged nor diminished by the exercise or non-exercise of state power. . . .

Such regulation is not a forbidden invasion of state power merely because either its motive or its consequence is to restrict the use of articles of commerce within the states of destination; and is not prohibited unless by other Constitutional provisions. It is no objection to the assertion of the power to regulate interstate commerce that its exercise is attended by the same incidents which attend the exercise of the police power of the states.

The motive and purpose of the present regulation are plainly to make effective the Congressional conception of public policy that interstate commerce should not be made the instrument of competition in the distribution of goods produced under substandard labor conditions, which competition is injurious to the commerce and to the states from and to which the commerce flows. The motive and purpose of a regulation of interstate commerce are matters for the legislative judgment upon the exercise of which the Constitution places no restriction and over which the courts are given no control. . . . [W]e conclude that the prohibition of the shipment interstate of goods produced under the forbidden substandard labor conditions is within the constitutional authority of Congress. . . .

Hammer v. Dagenhart has not been followed. The distinction on which the decision was rested that Congressional power to prohibit interstate commerce is limited to articles which in themselves have some harmful or deleterious property — a distinction which was novel when made and unsupported by any provision of the Constitution — has long since been abandoned. The thesis of the opinion that the motive of the prohibition or its effect to control in some measure the use or production within the states of the article thus excluded from the commerce can operate to deprive the regulation of its constitutional authority has long since ceased to have force. And finally we have declared "The authority of the federal government over interstate commerce does not differ in extent or character from that retained by the states over intrastate commerce."

The conclusion is inescapable that Hammer v. Dagenhart was a departure from the principles which prevailed in the interpretation of the commerce clause. . . . It should be and now is overruled.

VALIDITY OF THE WAGE AND HOUR REQUIREMENTS

Section 15(a)(2) and §§6 and 7 require employers to conform to the wage and hour provisions with respect to all employees engaged in the production of goods for interstate commerce. As appellee's employees are not alleged to be "engaged in interstate commerce" the validity of the prohibition turns on the question whether the employment, under other than the prescribed labor standards, of employees engaged in the production of goods for interstate commerce is so related to the commerce and so affects it as to be within the reach of the power of Congress to regulate it.

. . . As the Government seeks to apply the statute in the indictment, and as the court below construed the phrase "produced for interstate commerce," it embraces at least the case where an employer engaged, as is appellee, in the manufacture and shipment of goods in filling orders of extrastate customers, manufactures his product with the intent or expectation that according to the normal course of his business all or some part of it will be selected for shipment to those customers.

. . . The obvious purpose of the Act was not only to prevent the interstate transportation of the proscribed product, but to stop the initial step toward transportation, production with the purpose of so transporting it. Congress was not unaware that most manufacturing businesses shipping their product in interstate commerce make it in their shops without reference to its ultimate destination and then after manufacture select some of it for shipment interstate and some intrastate according to the daily demands of their business, and that it would be practically impossible, without disrupting manufacturing businesses, to restrict the prohibited kind of production to the particular pieces of lumber, cloth, furniture or the like which later move in interstate rather than intrastate commerce. . . .

There remains the question whether such restriction on the production of goods for commerce is a permissible exercise of the commerce power. The power of Congress over interstate commerce is not confined to the regulation of commerce among the states. It extends to those activities intrastate which so affect interstate commerce or the exercise of the power of Congress over it as to make regulation of them appropriate means to the attainment of a legitimate end, the exercise of the granted power of Congress to regulate interstate commerce. . . .

Congress, having by the present Act adopted the policy of excluding from interstate commerce all goods produced for the commerce which do not conform to the specified labor standards, it may choose the means reasonably adapted to the attainment of the permitted end, even though they involve control of intrastate activities. . . .

We think also that §15(a)(2), now under consideration, is sustainable independently of §15(a)(1), which prohibits shipment or transportation of the proscribed goods. As we have said the evils aimed at by the Act are the spread of substandard labor conditions through the use of the facilities of interstate commerce for competition by the goods so produced with those produced under the prescribed or better labor conditions; and the consequent dislocation of the commerce itself caused by the impairment or destruction of local businesses by competition made effective through interstate commerce. The Act is thus directed at the suppression of a method or kind of competition in interstate commerce which it has in effect condemned as "unfair." . . .

The means adopted by §15(a)(2) for the protection of interstate commerce by the suppression of the production of the condemned goods for interstate commerce is so related to the commerce and so affects it as to be within the reach of the commerce power. . . . So far as Carter v. Carter Coal Co. is inconsistent with this conclusion, its doctrine is limited in principle by . . . decisions under the Sherman Act and the National Labor Relations Act. . . .

Our conclusion is unaffected by the Tenth Amendment which provides: "The powers not delegated to the United States by the Constitution, nor prohibited by it to the States, are reserved to the States respectively, or to the people." The amendment states but a truism that all is retained which has not been surrendered. There is nothing in the history of its adoption to suggest that it was more than declaratory of the relationship between the national and state governments as it had been established by the Constitution before the amendment or that its purpose was other than to allay fears that the new national government might seek to exercise powers not granted, and that the states might not be able to exercise fully their reserved powers. . . .

Reversed.

WICKARD v. FILBURN, 317 U.S. 111 (1942): [The secretary of agriculture sought to penalize a farmer for growing wheat in excess of his allotment under the Agricultural Adjustment Act of 1938. Although appellee's 239-bushel surplus was intended wholly for consumption on his farm and not for sale, it was deemed "available for marketing" within the act. The district court enjoined enforcement. The Supreme Court unanimously reversed.]

JACKSON, J:

Whether the subject of the regulation in question was "production," "consumption," or "marketing" is . . . not material for purposes of deciding the question of federal power before us. That an activity is of local character . . . might help in determining whether in the absence of Congressional action it would be permissible for the state to exert its power on the subject matter, even though in so doing it to some degree affected interstate commerce. But even if appellee's activity be local and though it may not be regarded as commerce, it may still, whatever its nature, be reached by Congress if it exerts a substantial economic effect on interstate commerce, and this irrespective of whether such effect is what might at some earlier time have been defined as "direct" or "indirect." . . .

The wheat industry has been a problem industry for some years. . . . The decline in the export trade has left a large surplus in production which, in connection with an abnormally large supply of wheat and other grains in recent years, caused congestion in a number of markets. . . .

The maintenance by government regulation of a price for wheat undoubtedly can be accomplished as effectively by sustaining or increasing the demand as by limiting the supply. The effect of the statute before us is to restrict the amount which may be produced for market and the extent as well to which one may forestall resort to the market by producing to meet his own needs. That appellee's own contribution to the demand for wheat may be trivial by itself is not enough to remove him from the scope of federal regulation where, as here, his contribution, taken together with that of many others similarly situated, is far from trivial.

It is well established by decision of this Court that the power to regulate commerce includes the power to regulate the prices at which commodities in that commerce are dealt in and practices affecting such prices. One of the primary purposes of the Act in question was to increase the market price of wheat, and to that end to limit the volume thereof that could affect the market. It can hardly be denied that a factor of such volume and variability as home-consumed wheat would have a substantial influence on price and market conditions. This may arise because being in marketable condition such wheat overhangs the market and, if induced by rising prices, tends to flow into the market and check price increases. But if we assume that it is never marketed, it supplies a need of the man who grew it which would otherwise be reflected by purchases in the open market. Homegrown wheat in this sense competes with wheat in commerce. The stimulation of commerce is a use of the regulatory function quite as definitely as prohibitions or restrictions thereon. This record leaves us in no doubt that Congress may properly have considered that wheat consumed on the farm where grown, if wholly outside the scheme of regulation, would have a substantial effect in defeating and obstructing its purpose to stimulate trade therein at increased prices.

Discussion

1. *Hammer's demise.* Note how, in overruling *Hammer,* the *Darby* Court moved away from a world in which Congress could prohibit from commerce only "articles" (like lottery tickets) that could be seen as noxious "in themselves." Is there an intellectual connection between *Darby* and takings clause cases from the same era? Recall cases like *Euclid* and *Miller,* supra, which began to recognize that pigs or apartment houses or cedar trees need not be deemed *inherently* noxious to be subject to regulation and prohibition — it was enough that the legislature reasonably deemed these items incompatible with the public good in light of their social and economic effects.

2. *(Almost) no constitutional limits, or (almost) no judicial review?* Does *Darby* suggest that conscientious Congress members are free to regulate commerce for a wide variety of noneconomic reasons, or does it merely suggest that courts, for institutional reasons, should not try to smoke out Congress's actual noneconomic motivation? Does *Wickard* mean that virtually any discrete action within a single state (especially when aggregated with similar actions) truly does affect interstate commerce, or does it merely mean that judges after the fact cannot fashion many

workable and principled doctrinal limits, and will therefore almost always defer to Congress? Some constitutional norms may be real — and in principle binding on political actors, who also take oaths of office to support the Constitution — but not fully enforceable in court because of various court-specific institutional constraints. For example, in implementing the Constitution, courts must follow strict rules of evidence, often aim for clear doctrinal rules capable of principled judicial exposition and easy application in lower courts, and sometimes face constraints in their practical capacity to unsettle legislative faits accompli. Where a judicial ruling upholding a governmental practice rests on particular court-specific limits, are other branches especially obliged to carefully consider the constitutional norms that judges are underenforcing? Recall that President Jackson thought so in responding to *McCulloch*. See generally Paul Brest, The Conscientious Legislator's Guide to Constitutional Interpretation, 27 Stan. L. Rev. 585 (1975); Lawrence G. Sager, Fair Measure: The Status of Underenforced Constitutional Norms, 91 Harv. L. Rev. (1978).

3. *Interstate economic competition*. Taken together, the unanimous holdings in *Darby* and *Wickard* might seem to recognize that Congress enjoyed sweeping — virtually unbounded? — power to regulate a national economy under the Commerce Clause. But recall that both cases concerned regulation that was arguably economic in purpose, aimed at influencing prices and quantities of economic goods and services. Recall also the obvious concern about interstate competition on the surface of *Darby*. The problem was that any state seeking to require minimum wages for all in-state workers risked having this policy undercut by sister states. If State A required its employers to pay X dollars an hour, sister State B could set its minimum wage at a lower level, and cost-conscious employers might flee State A and set up shop in B instead. Indeed, goods manufactured in State B could then be sold at lower prices even in State A itself. Under such conditions, State A might find it hard to maintain its desired minimum-wage policy as a practical political matter. Note that under judicial doctrine crafted under the Commerce Clause, State A could not simply ban the sale of any good manufactured by low-wage labor in sister states; nor was it clear that A could impose some kind of offsetting tariff, which could have been seen as an impermissible effort to regulate employment relations beyond its borders. See infra Part IV. Thus, it is theoretically possible that almost every state preferred to have a minimum wage law set at X dollars an hour — but only if all sister states adopted the same policy. In such a scenario, only through collective action in Congress could the great majority of states implement their preferred policies: If each state acted on its own without any coordination with other states, a kind of "race to the bottom" might ensue. If Congress were somehow barred from acting, and states individually were in effect limited in their ability to make their desired regulations stick, then the upshot would be that *no one* could effectively regulate minimum wages. The Commerce Clause — designed merely to apportion power between Congress and the states — would have had the strong substantive effect of requiring laissez faire. Consider again, in this light, *Darby*'s language that "interstate commerce should not be made the instrument of competition in the distribution of goods produced under substandard labor conditions" and that "the spread of substandard labor conditions [via] interstate commerce" created by "competition" between low-wage and high-wage products was an "evil" that Congress could properly seek to eradicate.

Consider also the history of the specification of federal powers in the Philadelphia Convention of 1787. An early draft resolution provided "that the National Legislature ought to be impowered to . . . legislate in all cases to which the separate States are incompetent, or in which the harmony of the United States may be interrupted by the exercise of individual Legislation." This general resolution later gave way to the specific enumerations of congressional power in Article I, §8, including the Interstate Commerce Clause. In the ratification debates, the influential framer James Wilson declared that "Whatever object of government is confined, in its operation and effects, within the bounds of a particular state, should be considered as belonging to the government of that state; whatever object of government extends, in its operation or effects, beyond the bounds of a particular state, should be considered as belonging to the United States." On a broad structural view, when regulations in one state could have strong "spillover" effects in other states (what economists call "positive" or "negative" "externalities"), Congress should have power to "harmonize" relations between states, which are individually "incompetent" to internalize the full effects of their respective regulations. Cf. *McCulloch*, supra Chapter 1. Wasn't *Darby* a case of true interstate externalities? How about *Wickard?*

Note: On Constitutional Revolution

Most constitutional scholars agree that something important happened to American constitutional law in the years between 1937 and 1942, because it is widely acknowledged that key doctrines changed rather quickly in a wide range of areas. Scholars disagree about whether it counts as a revolution or a return to (or deviation from) correct constitutional understandings. They also disagree about why (or whether) it was legitimate. As a result, the New Deal has become a standard example for theorizing the grounds of legitimate constitutional change.

Bruce Ackerman's theory of "constitutional moments" argues that at significant periods in history the American people amend the Constitution outside of Article V. See Bruce Ackerman, We The People: Foundations (1991); Bruce Ackerman, We the People: Transformations (1998). In Ackerman's model, one or more branches of government, led by an ascendant social movement party that claims a mandate for revolutionary change, is opposed by a branch that resists change. The conflict between the branches leads to a major constitutional crisis that is resolved when the defenders of the old order concede defeat, leading to a new constitutional regime. As we saw in Chapter 4, Ackerman argues that Reconstruction involved a constitutional moment: Congressional Republicans claimed a mandate for change, opposed by President Johnson. He eventually capitulated under threat of impeachment.

While Congress took the lead during Reconstruction (due to Lincoln's assassination), the President took the lead during the New Deal. At first, when FDR pushed for new laws inconsistent with existing judicial understandings of federal power and economic due process, the Supreme Court struck down this legislation, producing a constitutional crisis. Ackerman argues that this led to a period of special deliberation about the country's future, and set the stage for a "triggering election," in which the American people decided whether or not to support a constitutional transformation. This election, Ackerman argues, was the 1936 election, which Roosevelt and the Democrats won by a decisive margin. Although the Democrats considered amending Article V during this period, the constitutional crisis gave way in 1937 when the Supreme Court capitulated to Roosevelt's constitutional views in *West Coast Hotel* and *NLRB v. Jones & Laughlin*. Roosevelt then used a series of "transformative appointments" to produce a Court friendly to his constitutional principles. The Justices decided a series of cases (including *Darby* and *Wickard*) that, in Ackerman's view, effectively amended the Constitution. The opposition Republican Party capitulated to this transformation by 1940 and accepted the legitimacy of the New Deal, leading to a constitutional solution to the crisis and the beginning of what Ackerman calls America's "Third Republic." (The "Second Republic" begins with Reconstruction.)

Jack Balkin and Sanford Levinson argue that constitutional law changes through "partisan entrenchment" in the judiciary. See Jack M. Balkin and Sanford Levinson, Understanding the Constitutional Revolution, 87 Va. L. Rev. 1045 (2001). Because of the President's appointments power, the party that controls the White House can appoint new jurists to the federal courts who share roughly similar views on matters that are particularly important to the party. Stocking the judiciary with jurists of roughly similar ideological views can produce, over time, significant changes in constitutional doctrine:

> When enough like minded judges are appointed to the federal judiciary, they begin to change constitutional understandings and constitutional doctrine. If more people are appointed in a relatively short period of time, the changes will occur more quickly. Constitutional revolutions are the cumulative result of successful partisan entrenchment when the entrenching party has a relatively coherent political ideology or can pick up sufficient ideological allies from the appointees of other parties. Thus, the Warren Court is the culmination of years of Democratic appointments to the Supreme Court, assisted by a few key liberal Republicans.

Not all presidents have engaged in strategies of partisan entrenchment; sometimes presidents merely seek to reward political favors or curry to particular constituencies. Moreover, when the President lacks support in the Senate, he usually must appoint more moderate candidates. Nevertheless, presidents who seek deliberately to change constitutional doctrine through the appointments process often succeed. Because President Roosevelt and the Democrats kept winning elections between 1932 and 1948, they were able to stock the courts with judges who supported the New Deal. These judges believed in broad federal power and judicial restraint in social and economic legislation, and they changed constitutional doctrine accordingly. By 1942 the Democrats had made eight consecutive appointments to the Supreme Court, all committed New Dealers. It is hardly surprising that this changed constitutional doctrine as well as more basic constitutional understandings about what sorts of arguments were plausible and implausible.

Ackerman's theory and Balkin and Levinson's differ in several respects. Ackerman views constitutional moments as the epitome of democratic self-governance; they are self-conscious transformations of the grounds of constitutionalism by We the People over a relatively short period of time. Balkin and Levinson argue that constitutional change can occur slowly and may involve gradual retrenchment as well as dramatic transformation. Such change is "roughly but imperfectly democratic" because the courts respond over the long run to changes in the governing political coalition.

According to Ackerman, if the conditions for a constitutional moment are met, they establish new standards of legitimacy and correctness. By contrast, the theory of partisan entrenchment guarantees neither legitimate nor correct interpretations of the Constitution. It describes constitutional change but does not necessarily justify it. For example, the Compromise of 1877 led to a new political coalition that appointed Justices who used the Fourteenth Amendment to protect railroad and business interests rather than the interests of African-Americans. Because this coalition kept returning to power, it eventually produced *Plessy* and *Lochner,* just as the Democrats' control of the White House before the Civil War produced a Court that decided *Dred Scott.* Thus, while Ackerman argues that the New Deal is just as binding as an Article V amendment until the next constitutional moment, Balkin and Levinson argue that the continued survival of the New Deal settlement is best explained by the needs of the dominant political coalition. If that coalition changes sufficiently over time — for example, because of the influence of new social movements — the constitutional doctrines of the New Deal could be cut back or even altered substantially.

As you ponder the material in this chapter, ask yourself whether either theory, or both, captures what happened in constitutional law during the twentieth and early twenty-first centuries. Do you think the New Deal transformation in due process and federalism doctrine was a legitimate transformation? Why or why not?

Note: The 1960s Civil Rights Legislation: Commerce Power or Reconstruction Power?

The Civil Rights Movement of the late 1950s and early 1960s transformed American politics, and led to our nation's second Reconstruction. After many years of fruitless attempts, Congress produced the first new civil rights laws since Reconstruction. However, when Congress considered prohibiting race discrimination in employment, hotels, restaurants, and the like in the early 1960s, it faced a choice. Should it rely on its commerce powers, or should it rely instead on its explicit authority under §2 of the Thirteenth Amendment and §5 of the Fourteenth Amendment to "enforce" the values of these Amendments? Reliance on its Reconstruction authority would ultimately require the Supreme Court to confront and overrule (at least large chunks of) its decision in the 1883 *Civil Rights Cases,* supra Chapter 4. Recall, in particular, questions about Congress's ability under these Amendments to reach and prohibit various forms of race discrimination practiced by (arguably) *private* persons and entities. Conversely, reliance on congressional powers over interstate commerce seemed like the path of least (judicial) resistance, going with the grain of *Darby* and *Wickard* rather than against the grain of the *Civil Rights Cases.* But there were problems with this approach, too. In his June 5, 1963, letter to the Department of Justice, Professor Gerald Gunther argued that the real issues underlying the proposed civil rights law had rather little to do with economic concerns, or with interstate externalities:

> The proposed end run by way of the commerce clause seems to me ill-advised in every respect. . . . I know of course that the commerce power is a temptingly broad one. But surely responsible statutory drafting should have a firmer basis than, for example, some of the loose talk in recent newspaper articles about the widely accepted, unrestricted

availability of the commerce clause to achieve social ends. Some qualifications seem in order. Thus, most of the obviously "social" laws, as with lottery and prostitution legislation, have their immediate impact on the interstate movement and rest on the power to prohibit that movement. Most "social" laws are not directly aimed at intrastate affairs, are not attempts to regulate internal activities as such. Where immediate regulations of intrastate conduct have been imposed, a demonstrable economic effect on interstate commerce, business, trade has normally been required. That kind of showing has been made, for example, with regard to the control of "local" affairs in the labor relations and agricultural production fields. The commerce clause "hook" has been put to some rather strained uses in the past, I know; but the substantive content of the commerce clause would have to be drained beyond any point yet reached to justify the simplistic argument that all intrastate activity may be subjected to any kind of national regulation merely because some formal crossing of an interstate boundary once took place, without regard to the relationship between the aim of the regulation and interstate trade. The aim of the proposed anti-discrimination legislation, I take it, is quite unrelated to any concern with national commerce in any substantive sense. It would, I think, pervert the meaning and purpose of the commerce clause to invoke it as the basis for this legislation.

. . . I would much prefer to see the Government channel its resources of ingenuity and advocacy into the development of a viable interpretation of the Fourteenth Amendment, the provision with a natural linkage to the race problem. That would seem to me a considerably less demeaning task than the construction of an artificial commercial facade.[27]

In the Senate Committee hearings that ensued, a variety of views were expressed.[28] Senator Thurmond argued that earlier congressional legislation under the Commerce Clause involved efforts "to regulate economic affairs of life" whereas the pending civil rights bill was designed to "regulate moral and social affairs." Attorney General Kennedy countered that discrimination itself "is having a very adverse effect on our economy." Assistant Attorney General Burke Marshall elaborated:

Discrimination burdens Negro interstate travelers and therefore inhibits interstate travel. It artificially restricts the market available for interstate goods and services. . . . It inhibits the holding of conventions and meetings in segregated cities. . . . And it restricts business enterprises in their choice of location for offices and plants, thus preventing the most effective allocation of national resources.

Senator Cooper declared:

If there is a right of equal use of accommodations held out to the public, it is a right of citizenship and a constitutional right under the 14th amendment. It has nothing to do with whether a business is in interstate commerce or whether discrimination against individuals places a burden on commerce. It does not depend upon the commerce clause and cannot be limited by that clause. . . .

Senator Pastore sounded a similar theme:

I believe in this bill, because I believe in the dignity of man, not because it impedes our commerce. I don't think any man has a right to say to another man, You can't eat in my restaurant because you have dark skin; no matter how clean you are, you can't

27. Quoted in Gerald Gunther, Constitutional Law 203 (10th ed. 1980).
28. For more extended excerpts than the items quoted here, see id. at 199-203.

eat in my restaurant. That deprives a man of his full stature as an American citizen. That shocks me. That hurts me. And that is the reason why I want to vote for this law. . . . [W]hat we are talking about is a moral issue . . . [and] that morality, it seems to me, comes under the 14th amendment.

In response, Marshall cautioned that "I think it would be a mistake to rely solely on the 14th amendment . . . [because the bill then] might not be held constitutional. I think it would be a disservice to pass a bill that was later thrown out by the Supreme Court." In the end, Congress chose to place primary emphasis on the Interstate Commerce Clause in enacting Title II of the Civil Rights Act of 1964, which prohibited discrimination and segregation in various places of "public accommodation" (such as hotels, restaurants, movie theaters, and sports arenas) "if [their] operations affect commerce." The statute went on to specify the "affect commerce" trigger with greater precision — for example, hotels containing more than five rooms, and restaurants offering to serve interstate travelers or where a "substantial portion" of the food served "has moved in commerce." The statute gave rise to two test cases, decided the same day, challenging Congress's basic power to legislate. In each case, the Supreme Court unanimously upheld the statute, with Justice Clark writing for the Court.

HEART OF ATLANTA MOTEL v. UNITED STATES, 379 U.S. 241 (1964): *Heart of Atlanta* involved a challenge to Title II brought by an Atlanta, Georgia, motel with 216 rooms. The motel, the Court noted, stood readily accessible to interstate highways, advertised in various national media, and served a clientele 75 percent of which came from out of state. The Court held that the Commerce Clause gave Congress "ample power" on the facts of the case at hand, and declined to consider other possible sources of congressional power. Justice Clark pointed to testimony before Congress suggesting that "millions of people of all races travel[] from State to State; that Negroes in particular have been the subject of discrimination in transient accommodations, having to travel great distances to secure the same; that often they have been unable to obtain accommodations and have had to call upon friends to put them up overnight; and that these conditions had become so acute as to require the listing of available lodging for Negroes in a special guidebook which was itself 'dramatic testimony to the difficulties' Negroes encounter in travel."

The Court also noted a variety of prior congressional laws regulating, inter alia, White slavery, gambling, deceptive sales practices, securities fraud, drug misbranding, wages and hours, labor unions, crop control, and discrimination against shippers. In Clark's words:

> That Congress was legislating against moral wrongs in many of these areas rendered its enactments no less valid. In framing Title II of this Act Congress was also dealing with what it considered a moral problem. But that fact does not detract from the overwhelming evidence of the disruptive effect that racial discrimination has had on commercial intercourse. It was this burden which empowered Congress to enact appropriate legislation, and, given this basis for the exercise of its power, Congress was not restricted by the fact that the particular obstruction to interstate commerce with which it was dealing was also deemed a moral and social wrong.

KATZENBACH v. McCLUNG, 379 U.S. 294 (1964): [This case involved Ollie's Barbecue, a family-owned restaurant in Birmingham, Alabama, with a seating capacity of 220 customers located on a state highway 11 blocks from an interstate highway. Of the approximately $150,000 worth of food procured by the restaurant in the preceding year, almost half consisted of meat bought from a local supplier who had in turn procured it from outside the state.]

CLARK, J.:

[The testimony before Congress] is replete with . . . the burdens placed on interstate commerce by racial discrimination in restaurants. A comparison of per capita spending by Negroes in restaurants, theaters, and like establishments indicated less spending, after discounting income differences, in areas where discrimination is widely practiced. This condition, which was especially aggravated in the South, was attributed in the testimony of the Under Secretary of Commerce to racial segregation. This diminutive spending springing from a refusal to serve Negroes and their total loss as customers has, regardless of the absence of direct evidence, a close connection to interstate commerce. The fewer customers a restaurant enjoys the less food it sells and consequently the less it buys. In addition, the Attorney General testified that this type of discrimination imposed "an artificial restriction on the market" and interfered with the flow of merchandise. In addition, there were many references to discriminatory situations causing wide unrest and having a depressant effect on general business conditions in the respective communities. . . . Likewise, it was said, that discrimination deterred professional, as well as skilled, people from moving into areas where such practices occurred and thereby caused industry to be reluctant to establish there.

We believe that this testimony afforded ample basis for the conclusion that established restaurants in such areas sold less interstate goods because of the discrimination, that interstate travel was obstructed directly by it, that business in general suffered and that many new businesses refrained from establishing there as a result of it. Hence the District Court was in error in concluding that there was no connection between discrimination and the movement of interstate commerce. The court's conclusion that such a connection is outside "common experience" flies in the face of stubborn fact. It goes without saying that, viewed in isolation, the volume of food purchased by Ollie's Barbecue from sources supplied from out of state was insignificant when compared with the total foodstuffs moving in commerce. But, as our late Brother Jackson said for the Court in Wickard v. Filburn, 317 U.S. 111 (1942): "That appellee's own contribution to the demand for wheat may be trivial by itself is not enough to remove him from scope of federal regulation where, as here, his contribution, taken together with that of many other similarly situated, is far from trivial." . . .

. . . Of course, the mere fact that Congress has said when a particular activity shall be deemed to affect commerce does not preclude further examination by this Court. But where we find that the legislators, in light of the facts and testimony before them, have a rational basis for finding a chosen regulatory scheme necessary to the protection of commerce, our investigation is at an end.

Justices Black, Douglas, and Goldberg each wrote a concurring opinion applicable to both *Heart of Atlanta* and *McClung*. All agreed that Title II could be sustained under the commerce power. Justices Black and Goldberg both implied that Congress also had power to prohibit discrimination in privately owned places of public accommodation under §5 of the Fourteenth Amendment.

Justice Douglas went further:

I would prefer to rest on the assertion of legislative power contained in section 5 of the Fourteenth Amendment which states: "The Congress shall have power to enforce, by appropriate legislation, the provisions of this article" — a power which the Court concedes was exercised at least in part in this Act.

A decision based on the Fourteenth Amendment would have a more settling effect, making unnecessary litigation over whether a particular restaurant or inn is within the commerce definitions of the Act or whether a particular customer is an interstate traveler. Under my construction, the Act would apply to all customers in all the enumerated places of public accommodation. And that construction would put an end to all obstructionist strategies and finally close one door on a bitter chapter in American history.[29]

How important was unanimity in these cases? Had Congress relied squarely and solely on its power to "enforce" the Thirteenth and Fourteenth Amendments, what were the odds that the 1964 Court would have upheld a federal law regulating the behavior of arguably "private" entities such as family-owned restaurants? Would the Court likely have been unanimous? How should a constitutionally conscientious Congressperson respond if he thinks that Congress *does* have broad Reconstruction power authority, but he also believes that at least several Justices, and perhaps a majority, might disagree? For more discussion of the modern Supreme Court's understanding of Congress's Reconstruction powers, see infra sections II.A.3, II.B.3.

Discussion

1. *Later Commerce Clause cases.* Consider also Daniel v. Paul, 395 U.S. 298 (1969) and Perez v. United States, 402 U.S. 146 (1971). In *Daniel,* the Court applied Title II to the Lake Nixon Club, "a 232-acre amusement area with swimming, boating, sun bathing, picnicking, miniature golf, and dancing facilities and a snack bar," located near Little Rock, Arkansas. Under section 201(c)(4), an entire establishment is covered by the act if any covered facility "is physically located within its premises." The Court found that the snack bar was covered both because it offered to serve interstate travelers and because it served food that had moved in interstate commerce. Although the club advertised only in local media, these included a magazine distributed to guests at Little Rock hotels and restaurants. Justice Brennan wrote that "it would be unrealistic to assume that none of the 100,000 patrons actually served by the Club each season was an interstate traveler." Additionally, the snack bar served "a limited fare — hotdogs and hamburgers on buns, soft drinks, and milk. The District Court took judicial notice of the fact that the 'principal ingredients going into the bread were produced and processed in other States' and that 'certain ingredients [of the soft drinks] were probably obtained from out-of-State sources.' . . . Thus, at the very least, three of

---

29. During the years immediately preceding enactment of the Civil Rights Act of 1964, many Blacks were convicted in state courts for criminal trespass when they refused to leave places of public accommodation after discriminatorily being denied service. In Hamm v. City of Rock Hill, 379 U.S. 306 (1964), the Court construed Title II to abate all pending sit-in convictions, assuming without discussion that the commerce power authorized retroactive application of the act. In dissent, Justices Black, Harlan, Stewart, and White criticized the Court's interpretation of the act. Justices Black and Harlan also asserted that the interpretation presented constitutional difficulties, the latter noting that "the legislative record is barren of any evidence showing that giving effect to *past* state trespass convictions would result in placing any burden on *present* interstate commerce. Such evidence, at the very least, would be a prerequisite to the validity of any purported exercise of the Commerce power in this regard." Are these constitutional doubts well founded? Would there have been comparable doubts had Congress tried to rely more prominently on its Reconstruction powers?

the four food items sold at the snack bar contain ingredients originating outside of the State. There can be no serious doubt that a 'substantial portion of the food' served at the snack bar has moved in interstate commerce."

Justice Black dissented. He objected to the Court's speculative assumptions of fact and concluded that the act could not be applied to "this country people's recreation center, lying in what may be, so far as we know, a little 'sleepy hollow' between Arkansas hills miles away from any interstate highway. This would be stretching the Commerce Clause so as to give the Federal Government complete control over every little remote country place of recreation in every nook and cranny of every precinct and county in every one of the 50 states." Justice Black believed that application of the act to the Lake Nixon Club could have been sustained under §5 of the Fourteenth Amendment but noted that, with respect to establishments of this sort, Congress had "tied the Act and limited its protection" to the commerce power.

The petitioner in *Perez* lent money to one Miranda and exacted increasingly large payments from him under threats of injuring him and his family. All of the events took place within New York State. The Court affirmed petitioner's conviction under the Federal Consumer Credit Protection Act for engaging in "extortionate credit transactions." Justice Douglas noted that the testimony before congressional committees supported the Act's findings that "[o]rganized crime is interstate and international in character. . . . A substantial part of the income of organized crime is generated by extortionate credit transactions. . . . Extortionate credit transactions are carried on to a substantial extent in interstate and foreign commerce and through the means and instrumentalities of such commerce. Even where extortionate credit transactions are purely intrastate in character, they nevertheless directly affect interstate and foreign commerce." To petitioner's argument that there was no evidence that his conduct had any interstate ramifications, Justice Douglas responded (citing *Darby* and *McClung*):

> Petitioner is clearly *a member of the class* which engages in extortionate credit transactions as defined by Congress. . . . Where the *class of activities* is regulated and that *class* is within the reach of federal power, the courts have no power "to excise as trivial, individual instances" of the class.

Only Justice Stewart dissented:

> [U]nder the statute before us a man can be convicted without any proof of interstate movement, of the use of the facilities of interstate commerce, or of facts showing that his conduct affected interstate commerce. I think the Framers of the Constitution never intended that the National Government might define as a crime and prosecute such wholly local activity through the enactment of federal criminal laws.
>
> In order to sustain this law we would, in my view, have to be able at the least to say that Congress could rationally have concluded that loan sharking is an activity with interstate attributes that distinguish it in some substantial respect from other local crime. But it is not enough to say that loan sharking is a national problem, for all crime is a national problem. It is not enough to say that some loan sharking has interstate characteristics, for any crime may have an interstate setting. And the circumstance that loan sharking has an adverse impact on interstate business is not a distinguishing attribute, for interstate business suffers from almost all criminal activity, be it shoplifting or violence in the streets.

Because I am unable to discern any rational distinction between loan sharking and other local crime, I cannot escape the conclusion that this statute was beyond the power of Congress to enact. The definition and prosecution of local, intrastate crime are reserved to the States under the Ninth and Tenth Amendments.

2. *National problems versus federal (interstate) problems.* Consider the possibility that Justice Stewart's dissent in *Perez* was right in saying that Congress, before legislating, must do more than identify a "national" problem — that is, a problem that might exist everywhere. On this view, Congress should also identify a *federal* problem — a problem *between* the states, created by positive or negative "spillover effects" between states, or by the incapacity of individual states to deal with problems on their own. On one hand, imagine a crime that occurs everywhere, but whose effects are wholly localized, and felt within the state of the crime. In this situation, why shouldn't individual states be trusted to handle the problem? In other words, what reason exists for federal intervention on top (or instead) of state lawmaking? On the other hand, imagine a crime that either has important effects outside the crime state, or that has other important interstate features. Here, the argument against the permissibility of federal involvement seems much weaker. And on the facts of *Perez*, weren't there important federal (that is, interstate) features of the problem? Loansharking is typically not done by discrete local thugs, each acting alone. Rather, it often involves interstate networks of criminals — *organized* crime that is organized in part to exploit the limits of each state's power in a federal system. Acting alone, for example, no single state has plenary and unilateral authority to pursue investigations of co-conspirators hiding out in sister states. On this view, *Perez* was indeed an easy case, involving both economic harms and interstate dimensions.

2.   The Taxing and Spending Power

The post-1937 taxing and spending power cases are not different in tone or outcome from some earlier decisions, such as McCray v. United States, 195 U.S. 27 (1904), supra Chapter 4. For example, Sonzinsky v. United States, 300 U.S. 506 (1937), upheld a law requiring persons dealing in certain firearms (e.g., machine guns with silencers, sawed-off shotguns and rifles) to register with the collector of internal revenue and pay a $200 annual tax. Petitioner argued that the act — another provision of which imposed a $200 tax on each transfer of such firearms — was not designed to raise revenue but to prohibit transfer of the weapons. Justice Stone responded:

> The case is not one where the statute contains regulatory provisions related to a purported tax in such a way as has enabled this Court to say in other cases that the latter is a penalty resorted to as means of enforcing the regulation. . . . Here §2 contains no regulation other than the mere registration provisions, which are obviously supportable in aid of a revenue purpose. On its face it is only a taxing measure. . . .
>
> Every tax is in some measure regulatory. To some extent it interposes an economic impediment to the activity taxed as compared with others not taxed. But a tax is not any the less a tax because it has a regulatory effect; and it has long been established that an Act of Congress which on its face purports to be an exercise of the taxing power is not any the less so because the tax is burdensome or tends to restrict or suppress the things taxed.

Inquiry into the hidden motives which may move Congress to exercise a power constitutionally conferred upon it is beyond the competency of courts. They will not undertake by collateral inquiry as to the measure of the regulatory effect of a tax, to ascribe to Congress an attempt, under the guise of taxation, to exercise another power denied by the Federal Constitution.

The major post-1937 challenge to Congress's taxing and spending power involved the unemployment compensation scheme created by the Social Security Act of 1935, upheld in Steward Machine Co. v. Davis.

STEWARD MACHINE COMPANY v. DAVIS, 301 U.S. 548 (1937): [A tax was imposed on employers, based on their employees' wages. The proceeds went into the United States Treasury (as do internal revenue collections generally) and were not earmarked for any purpose; however, a credit of up to 90 percent of the federal tax was allowed to the extent the employer contributed to a state unemployment fund that met detailed requirements specified in the act and was approved by the Social Security Board. Some of the federal requirements, as the Court described them, "are designed to give assurance that the state unemployment compensation law shall be one in substance as well as name. Others are designed to give assurance that the contributions shall be protected against loss after payment to the state." Among the latter was the requirement that contributions to the state fund be turned over immediately to the Treasury, which would invest, administer, and disburse them.]

CARDOZO, J. . . . The excise is not void as involving the coercion of the States in contravention of the Tenth Amendment or of restrictions implicit in our federal form of government. . . .

[Petitioner argues] that the tax and the credit in combination are weapons of coercion, destroying or impairing the autonomy of the states. . . .

To draw the line intelligently between duress and inducement there is need to remind ourselves of facts as to the problem of unemployment that are now matters of common knowledge. . . . During the years 1929 to 1936, when the country was passing through a cyclical depression, the number of the unemployed mounted to unprecedented heights. . . . The fact developed quickly that the states were unable to give the requisite relief. The problem had become national in area and dimensions. There was need of help from the nation if the people were not to starve. It is too late today for the argument to be heard with tolerance that in a crisis so extreme the use of the moneys of the nation to relieve the unemployed and their dependents is a use for any purpose narrower than the promotion of the general welfare. . . .

Before Congress acted, unemployment compensation insurance was still, for the most part, a project and no more. Wisconsin was the pioneer. Her statute was adopted in 1931. At time bills for such insurance were introduced elsewhere, but they did not reach the stage of law. . . . But if states had been holding back before the passage of the federal law, inaction was not owing, for the most part, to the lack of sympathetic interest. Many held back through alarm lest, in laying such a toll upon their industries, they would place themselves in a position of economic disadvantage as compared with neighbors or competitors. Two consequences ensued. One was that the freedom of a state to contribute its fair share to the solution of a national problem was paralyzed by fear. The other was that in so far as there was failure by the states to contribute relief according to the measure of their capacity, a disproportionate burden, and a mountainous one, was laid upon the resources of the Government of the nation.

The Social Security Act is an attempt to find a method by which all these public agencies may work together to a common end. Every dollar of the new taxes will continue in all likelihood to be used and needed by the nation as long as states are unwilling, whether through timidity or for other motives, to do what can be done at home. At least the inference is permissible that Congress so believed, though retaining undiminished freedom to spend the money as it pleased. On the other hand fulfillment of the home duty will be lightened and encouraged by crediting the taxpayer upon his account with the Treasury of the nation to the extent that his contributions under the laws of the locality have simplified or diminished the problem of relief and the probable demand upon the resources of the fisc. Duplicated taxes, or burdens that approach them, are recognized hardships that government, state or national, may properly avoid. If Congress believed that the general welfare would better be promoted by relief through local units than by the system then in vogue, the cooperating localities ought not in all fairness to pay a second time.

Who then is coerced through the operation of this statute? Not the taxpayer. He pays in fulfillment of the mandate of the local legislature. Not the state. . . . For all that appears she is satisfied with her choice, and would be sorely disappointed if it were now to be annulled. . . . [E]very rebate from a tax when conditioned upon conduct is in some measure a temptation. But to hold that . . . temptation is equivalent to coercion is to plunge the law in endless difficulties. The outcome of such a doctrine is the acceptance of a philosophical determinism by which choice becomes impossible. Till now the law has been guided by a robust common sense which assumes the freedom of the will as a working hypothesis in the solution of its problems. The wisdom of the hypothesis has illustration in this case. Nothing in the case suggests the exertion of a power akin to undue influence, if we assume that such a concept can ever be applied with fitness to the relations between state and nation. . . . We cannot say that [Alabama] was acting, not of her unfettered will, but under the strain of a persuasion equivalent to undue influence, when she chose to have relief administered under laws of her own making, by agents of her own selection, instead of under federal laws, administered by federal officers, with all the ensuing evils, at least to many minds, of federal patronage and power. . . .

In ruling as we do, we leave many questions open. We do not say that a tax is valid, when imposed by act of Congress, if it is laid upon the condition that a state may escape its operation through the adoption of a statue unrelated in subject matter to activities fairly within the scope of national policy and power. No such question is before us. In the tender of this credit Congress does not intrude upon fields foreign to its function. The purpose of its intervention, as we have shown, is to safeguard its own treasury and as an incident to that protection to place the states upon a footing of equal opportunity. Drains upon its own resources are to be checked; obstructions to the freedom of the states are to be leveled. . . .

United States v. Butler is cited by petitioner as a decision to the contrary. . . . The decision was by a divided court, a minority taking the view that the objections were untenable. None of them is applicable to the situation here developed.

(a) The proceeds of the tax in controversy are not earmarked for a special group.
(b) The unemployment compensation law which is a condition of the credit has had the approval of the state and could not be a law without it.

(c) The condition is not linked to an irrevocable agreement, for the state at its pleasure may repeal its unemployment law, terminate the credit, and place itself where it was before the credit was accepted.

(d) The condition is not directed to the attainment of an unlawful end, but to an end, the relief of unemployment, for which nation and state may lawfully cooperate.

The statute does not call for a surrender by the states of powers essential to their quasi-sovereign existence. . . . A wide range of judgment is given to the several states as to the particular type of statute to be spread upon their books. . . . What they may not do, if they would earn the credit, is to depart from those standards which in the judgment of Congress are to be ranked as fundamental. . . . In determining essentials Congress must have the benefit of a fair margin of discretion. One cannot say with reason that this margin has been exceeded, or that the basic standards have been determined in any arbitrary fashion. . . .

In a companion case, Helvering v. Davis, 301 U.S. 619 (1937), with only Justices McReynolds and Butler dissenting, the Court upheld the old-age benefit provisions of the Social Security Act:

> The problem is plainly national in area and dimensions. Moreover, laws of the separate states cannot deal with it effectively. . . . State and local governments are often lacking in the resources that are necessary to finance an adequate program of security for the aged. . . . Apart from the failure of resources, states and local governments are at times reluctant to increase so heavily the burden of taxation to be borne by their residents for fear of placing themselves in a position of economic disadvantage as compared with neighbors or competitors. . . . A system of old age pensions has special dangers of its own, if put in force in one state and rejected in another. The existence of such a system is a bait to the needy and dependent elsewhere, encouraging them to migrate and seek a haven of repose. Only a power that is national can serve the interests of all.

Discussion

1. *Interstate competition and the "general welfare."* Unlike the commerce power, Congress's Article I power to tax and spend is not, by its terms, limited to distinctly interstate problems, although the Constitution does speak of taxing and spending on behalf of "the general welfare." But wasn't there an obvious interstate — that is, federal — problem that gave rise to federal legislation in *Steward* and *Helvering*? Each state on its own might hesitate to adopt strong unemployment policies, financed by taxes on employers. Such policies might cause employers to move to sister states, and might also attract unemployed workers from other states, causing the state to become an unemployment-benefit "magnet." A similar concern might prevent a state from offering a generous old-age pension. Even if virtually every state preferred high benefits, each might end up "racing to the bottom" in the absence of some mechanism of coordination. Could an interstate compact among states, under Article I, §10, have solved the problem? (Remember that such a compact would have required congressional approval.) What if a handful of states try to "hold out" in the multistate bargaining process? For an important recent plea for greater use of interstate compacts as an instrument of "intermediate federalism," see David L. Shapiro, Federalism: A Dialogue 126-137 (1995). For more recent cases raising the benefit-magnet issue, see infra, Chapter 9.

2. *Using taxes to regulate: The pretext problem.* *Sonzinsky* disclaimed a vigorous role for judges in smoking out impermissibly motivated exercises of the tax power. Are there nonetheless certain objectives that conscientious members of Congress may not properly pursue as the sole or primary objectives of exercise of the taxing power? What about pursuing these as objectives ancillary to the raising of revenue? And would judges adopt a hands-off policy in all cases of pretextual taxation? For example, if the Congress sought to penalize women's contraception by applying a prohibitively high tax on birth control pills, would judges defer? Are federal taxes aimed at regulating "local" conduct importantly different from federal taxes aimed at regulating individual rights? Consider United States v. Kahriger, 345 U.S. 22 (1953), where a divided Court upheld a federal provision requiring persons engaged in the business of accepting wagers to pay a $50 occupational tax and register with the collector of internal revenues. Appellee argued, inter alia, that the tax was only a pretext for penalizing intrastate gambling and thus infringed "the police power which is reserved to the states." Justice Reed wrote for the Court:

> It is conceded that a federal excise tax does not cease to be valid merely because it discourages or deters the activities taxed. Nor is the tax invalid because the revenue obtained is negligible. Appellee, however, argues that the sole purpose of the statute is to penalize only illegal gambling in the states through the guise of a tax measure. As with [other] excise taxes which we have held to be valid, the instant tax has a regulatory effect. But regardless of its regulatory effect, the wagering tax produces revenue. . . .
>
> It is axiomatic that the power of Congress to tax is extensive and sometimes falls with crushing effect on businesses deemed unessential or inimical to the public welfare, or where, as in dealings with narcotics, the collection of the tax also is difficult. As is well known, the constitutional restraints on taxing are few. . . .
>
> While the Court has never questioned the ["pretext" statement] of Mr. Chief Justice Marshall in the *McCulloch* case, the application of the rule has brought varying holdings on constitutionality. Where federal legislation has rested on other congressional powers, such as the Necessary and Proper Clause or the Commerce Clause, this Court has generally sustained the statutes, despite their effect on matters ordinarily considered state concern. When federal power to regulate is found, its exercise is a matter for Congress. Where Congress has employed the taxing clause a greater variation in the decisions has resulted. The division in this Court has been more acute. . . . It is hard to understand why the power to tax should raise more doubts because of indirect effects than other federal powers. . . .
>
> Unless there are provisions extraneous to any tax need, courts are without authority to limit the exercise of the taxing power. All the provisions of this excise are adapted to the collection of a valid tax.[30]

Justice Jackson concurred, "but with such doubt that if the minority agreed upon an opinion which did not impair legitimate use of the taxing power I probably would join it." Justice Black, joined by Justice Douglas, dissented solely on the ground that the act compelled self-incrimination. Justice Frankfurter also dissented, focusing mainly on the federalism problems presented by the statute:

> Constitutional issues are likely to arise whenever Congress draws on the taxing power not to raise revenue but to regulate conduct. . . .

30. The court also rejected appellee's argument that the registration provision compelled him to incriminate himself in violation of the Fifth Amendment. In Marchetti v. United States, 390 U.S. 39 (1968), the Court overruled *Kahriger* and invalidated the wagering tax scheme on this ground.

Congress may make an oblique use of the taxing power in relation to activities with which Congress may deal directly, as for instance, commerce between the States. Thus, if the dissenting views of Mr. Justice Holmes in Hammer v. Dagenhart had been the decision of the Court, as they became in United States v. Darby, the effort to deal with the problem of child labor through an assertion of the taxing power in the statute considered in *Child Labor Tax Case* would by the latter case have been sustained. However, when oblique use is made of the taxing power as to matters which substantively are not within the powers delegated to Congress, the Court cannot shut its eyes to what is obviously, because designedly, an attempt to control conduct which the Constitution left to the responsibility of the States, merely because Congress wrapped the legislation in the verbal cellophane of a revenue measure.

Concededly the constitutional questions presented by such legislation are difficult. On the one hand, courts should scrupulously abstain from hobbling congressional choice of policies, particularly when the vast reach of the taxing power is concerned. On the other hand, to allow what otherwise is excluded from congressional authority to be brought within it by casting legislation in the form of a revenue measure could, as so significantly expounded in the *Child Labor Tax Case*, offer an easy way for the legislative imagination to control "any one of the great number of subjects of public interest, jurisdiction of which the States have never parted with. . . ."

[T]he context of the circumstances which brought forth this enactment . . . emphatically supports what was revealed on the floor of Congress, namely, that what was formally a means of raising revenue for the Federal Government was essentially an effort to check if not to stamp out professional gambling. . . .

Mr. Justice Douglas, while not joining in the entire opinion, agrees with the views expressed herein that this tax is an attempt by the Congress to control conduct which the Constitution has left to the responsibility of the States.

3. *Conditional funding.* Petitioner in *Steward* argued that the Social Security Act did not merely aid or encourage the states but coerced them into establishing unemployment compensation programs; petitioner further argued that the federal eligibility requirements for such programs were so detailed and pervasive as to intrude impermissibly on state sovereignty. The Court held that the Social Security Act did not coerce and did not go too far, but Justice Cardozo's opinion did not reject the possibility that the spending power was subject to such implicit limiting principles. Direct federal aid to state and local governments — for welfare, education, health, and a variety of municipal functions — increased enormously after 1937. The proper extent of federal supervision over state use of federal monies was a continuing subject of political debate, with advocates of every position, from unrestricted block grants to closely regulated categorical programs. In Oklahoma v. United States Civil Service Commission, 330 U.S. 127 (1947), the Court held that Congress could properly condition the expenditure of highway funds on a state's compliance with a provision of the Hatch Act prohibiting state officials principally employed in federally funded programs from taking "any active part" in political activities. It sustained the Civil Service Commission's order removing a state highway commissioner who was also chairman of the state Democratic party. Justice Reed wrote for the Court (over dissents without opinion by Justices Black and Rutledge):[31]

---

31. In a companion case, United Public Workers v. Mitchell, 330 U.S. 75 (1947), the Court sustained the Hatch Act against a First Amendment challenge. In United States Civil Service Commn. v. National Assn. of Letter Carriers, 413 U.S. 548 (1973), a divided Court again rejected a First Amendment attack on the statute, and in Broadrick v. Oklahoma, 413 U.S. 601 (1973), it sustained a similar state scheme (adopted 22 years after the case discussed in the text).

> While the United States is not concerned with, and has no power to regulate, local political activities as such of state officials, it does have power to fix the terms upon which its money allotments to states shall be disbursed. . . . The end sought by Congress through the Hatch Act is better public service by requiring those who administer funds for national needs to abstain from active political partisanship. So even though the action taken by Congress does have an effect upon certain activities within the state, it has never been thought that such effect made the federal act invalid. . . . The offer of benefits to a state by the United States dependent upon cooperation by the state with federal plans, assumedly for the general welfare, is not unusual.

Suppose Congress conditions a grant of federal highway funds on a state's commitment to move its state capital to the most geographically "efficient" location. Coyle v. Smith, 221 U.S. 559 (1911), continues to be cited for the proposition that Congress cannot directly tell a state where its capital is to be. But does the Constitution prevent Congress from "encouraging" a particular location through conditional granting of funds? Can funds be conditioned on reorganizing the state government — say, by requiring that the attorney general be elected rather than appointed? Consider in this regard Hans Linde's criticism of Oklahoma v. United States Civil Service Commission:

> there must be limits on such conditions if the political values of federalism are to be preserved despite this fiscal centralization. . . .
>
> . . . If Congress chose to forbid any state officer who spends federal grants to take part in a political campaign, could Oklahoma not choose to have an elected highway commission? State officers, from governors to legislators to city councilmen and school board members, increasingly administer programs aided by federal funds; may Congress constitutionally determine which may be elected, which others politically appointed, and which must be in a nonpartisan career status? Surely a line may be perceived between such conditions and conditions that go to the substance of the federally supported project, for instance that it fit a national plan, or be soundly engineered, or meet prescribed standards of hours, wages, or nondiscrimination in employment, or be fairly and honestly administered. "Whether and where such a line is drawn could determine, as much as any tax immunity, the role of federalism as a safeguard of political democracy in a centripetal public economy."[32]

What if a state offered to give money to the federal government, subject to comparable conditions? Are the roles of the state and federal governments symmetric in the conditional funding context? Cf. *McCulloch*, supra Chapter 1.

3. The Reconstruction Power

Between 1875 and 1957, Congress passed no major civil rights measures. And as we have seen, Congress chose to rely primarily on its Interstate Commerce Clause powers in adopting the Civil Rights Act of 1964. But over the following decades, several important cases reached the Court concerning the scope of Congress's powers under the Thirteenth, Fourteenth, and Fifteenth Amendments. The issues raised by these cases are myriad and intricate; many are considered at length in casebooks on civil rights and voting rights. For present purposes, our chief focus is

---

32. Linde, Justice Douglas on Freedom in the Welfare State, 39 Wash. L. Rev. 4, 28, 30-31 (1964).

on the interplay of congressional and judicial power to interpret and enforce the provisions of the Reconstruction Amendments.

These amendments are self-executing: The first section of each amendment prohibits certain practices even in the absence of implementing legislation. But each of the amendments also provides (with minor stylistic variation) that "Congress shall have the power to enforce this article by appropriate legislation."[33] What, precisely, does this mean? When Congress seeks to outlaw a given state law or private practice as violative of Congress's understanding of the Reconstruction Amendments, what should courts do if they have not yet ruled on the law or practice in question or, indeed, have *upheld* its constitutionality?

We have already seen one instance in which Congress may overrule a judicial decision. Since the *Wheeling Bridge* decision (1855), supra Chapter 3, Congress has had the final say about whether a state regulation of interstate commerce is impermissibly burdensome. However, the logic of the Commerce Clause arguably differs sharply from that of the Reconstruction Amendments. The Commerce Clause is in terms *solely* a grant of legislative power to Congress; its self-executing aspect had to be inferred and was, indeed, disputed well into the nineteenth century (and Justices Scalia and Thomas have revived the dispute in our own time; see infra, p. 730). When Congress legislates under the Commerce Clause, it need not concern itself with the constitutionality of any state statutes that the proposed law will affect or preempt; Congress must determine only that the proposed law is within its delegated powers and does not contravene any constitutional limitations.[34] Is the same true of congressional power under the Reconstruction Amendments, or does Congress have the power to prohibit only antecedently *unconstitutional* laws and practices? Also, note that Congress enjoys authority under the Commerce Clause to bless commerce-obstructing state laws and practices that would otherwise be declared unconstitutional by federal courts. Should Congress enjoy similar authority to undo (as opposed to add to) judicial declarations of rights under the Reconstruction Amendments?

Consider also congressional power to counter a judicial decision that a given *federal* law or practice passes constitutional muster. For example, wasn't Congress free to repeal the Sedition Act of 1798 even after federal courts had upheld the law? To repeal it even if the repeal were motivated by a belief that the courts had erred and that the Act was indeed unconstitutional? (Recall that, as events actually unfolded, Congress allowed the repressive Act to expire, and President Jefferson — who thought the Act unconstitutional — pardoned those who had already been convicted.) Does Congress's power to overrule the judiciary in a Sedition Act situation suggest that Congress should likewise be allowed to overrule judicial action that underprotects individual rights against the states? Or is there a decisive difference between a Congress that limits *its own* powers beyond what the judiciary demands (as in the Sedition Act hypothetical), and a Congress that seeks to wield affirmative authority to limit *state laws or private practices* in the name of Reconstruction values of liberty, equality, and citizenship?

33. This is also true of the Nineteenth, Twenty-fourth, and Twenty-sixth Amendments.

34. A typical example is the Federal Surface Mining Control and Reclamation Act of 1977, upheld in Hodel v. Virginia Surface Mining and Reclamation Assn., Inc., 452 U.S. 264 (1981), as a valid exercise of Congress's power under the Commerce Clause. The Act displaced a number of state regulations of strip mining, but Congress had no need to find, or even to inquire into the possibility, that these laws were "unconstitutional." It was enough that Congress found them hindrances to an effective national policy regarding strip mining.

A good deal of congressional legislation under the Civil War Amendments is essentially procedural, designed narrowly to implement and enforce judicially declared rights. For example, 42 U.S.C. §1983, which is regularly invoked in civil rights litigation, does not purport to invalidate any state practices that a court has not independently held unconstitutional; rather, it is merely a device allowing aggrieved persons to come to court and present their claims. By contrast, the Voting Rights Act of 1965 invalidated state practices that no court had, or has to this day, declared per se unconstitutional. In the two cases set out below, the Court sustained provisions of the act that banned the use of various literacy tests, although only a few years earlier, in Lassiter v. Northampton Board of Elections, 360 U.S. 45 (1959), the Court itself had unanimously upheld a literacy test against constitutional attack.

SOUTH CAROLINA v. KATZENBACH
383 U.S. 301 (1966)

WARREN, C.J.

The Voting Rights Act was designed by Congress to banish the blight of racial discrimination in voting, which has infected the electoral process in part of our country for nearly a century. The Act creates stringent new remedies for voting discrimination where it persists on a pervasive scale, and in addition the statute strengthens existing remedies for pockets of voting discrimination elsewhere in the country. . . .

I.

Two points emerge vividly from the voluminous legislative history of the Act contained in the committee hearings and floor debates. First: Congress felt itself confronted by an insidious and pervasive evil which had been perpetuated in certain parts of our country through unremitting and ingenious defiance of the Constitution. Second: Congress concluded that the unsuccessful remedies which it had prescribed in the past would have to be replaced by sterner and more elabo-rate measures in order to satisfy the clear commands of the Fifteenth Amendment. . . .

[B]eginning in 1890, the States of Alabama, Georgia, Louisiana, Mississippi, North Carolina, South Carolina, and Virginia enacted tests still in use which were specifically designed to prevent Negroes from voting. Typically, they made the ability to read and write a registration qualification and also required completion of a registration form. These laws were based on the fact that as of 1890 in each of the named States, more than two-thirds of the adult Negroes were illiterate while less than one-quarter of the adult whites were unable to read or write. At the same time, alternate tests were prescribed in all of the named States to assure that white illiterates would not be deprived of the franchise. These included grandfather clauses, property qualifications, "good character" tests, and the requirement that registrants "understand" or "interpret" certain matter.

The course of subsequent Fifteenth Amendment litigation in this Court demon-strates the variety and persistence of these and similar institutions designed to deprive Negroes of the right to vote. Grandfather clauses were invalidated in Guinn v. United States, 238 U.S. 347, and Myers v. Anderson, 238 U.S. 368. Procedural hurdles were struck down in Lane v. Wilson, 307 U.S. 268. The white primary was outlawed in Smith v. Allwright, 321 U.S. 649, and Terry v. Adams, 345 U.S. 461. Improper challenges were nullified in United States v. Thomas, 362 U.S. 58. Racial gerrymandering was forbidden by Gomillion v. Lightfoot, 364 U.S. 339. Finally, discriminatory application of voting tests was condemned in Schnell v. Davis, 336 U.S. 933; Alabama v. United States, 371 U.S. 37; and Louisiana v. United States, 380 U.S. 145.

According to the evidence in recent Justice Department voting suits, the latter stratagem is now the principal method used to bar Negroes from the polls. Discriminatory administration of voting qualifications has been found in all eight Alabama cases, in all nine Louisiana cases, and in all nine Mississippi cases which have gone to final judgment. Moreover, in almost all of these cases, the courts have held that the discrimination was pursuant to a widespread "pattern or practice." White applicants for registration have often been excused altogether from the literacy and understanding tests or have been given easy versions, have received extensive help from voting officials, and have been registered despite serious errors in their answers. Negroes, on the other hand, have typically been required to pass difficult versions of all the tests, without any outside assistance and without the slightest error. The good-morals requirement is so vague and subjective that it has constituted an open invitation to abuse at the hands of voting officials. Negroes obliged to obtain vouchers from registered voters have found it virtually impossible to comply in areas where almost no Negroes are on the rolls.

In recent years, Congress has repeatedly tried to cope with the problem by facilitating case-by-case litigation against voting discrimination. . . .

Despite the earnest efforts of the Justice Department and of many federal judges, these new laws have done little to cure the problem of voting discrimination. . . .

The previous legislation has proved ineffective for a number of reasons. Voting suits are unusually onerous to prepare, sometimes requiring as many as 6,000 manhours spent combing through registration records in preparation for trial. Litigation has been exceedingly slow, in part because of the ample opportunities for delay afforded voting officials and others involved in the proceedings. Even when favorable decisions have finally been obtained, some of the States affected have merely switched to discriminatory devices not covered by the federal decrees or have enacted difficult new tests designed to prolong the existing disparity between white and Negro registration. Alternatively, certain local officials have defied and evaded court orders or have simply closed their registration offices to freeze the voting rolls. . . .

II.

The Voting Rights Act of 1965 reflects Congress' firm intention to rid the country of racial discrimination in voting. The heart of the Act is a complex scheme of stringent remedies aimed at areas where voting discrimination has been most flagrant. Section 4(a)-(d) lays down a formula defining the States and political subdivisions to which these new remedies apply. The first of the remedies . . . is the suspension of literacy tests and similar voting qualifications for a period of five years from the last occurrence of substantial voting discrimination. Section 5 prescribes a second remedy, the suspension of all new voting regulations pending review by federal authorities to determine whether their use would perpetuate voting discrimination. The third remedy . . . is the assignment of federal examiners on certification by the Attorney General to list qualified applicants who are thereafter entitled to vote in all elections. . . .

COVERAGE FORMULA

The remedial sections of the Act assailed by South Carolina automatically apply to any State, or to any separate political subdivision such as a county or parish, for which [certain specific] findings have been made [concerning low voting registration or voting participation, and the use of certain specified voting tests susceptible to discriminatory application.]

Statutory coverage of a State or political subdivision under §4(b) is terminated if the area obtains a declaratory judgment from the District Court for the District of Columbia, determining that tests and devices have not been used during the preceding five years to abridge the franchise on racial grounds. . . .

SUSPENSION OF TESTS

In a State or political subdivision covered by §4(b) of the Act, no person may be denied the right to vote in any election because of his failure to comply with a "test or device." On account of this provision, South Carolina is temporarily barred from enforcing [its literacy test]. . . .

III.

. . . [T]he basic question presented by the case [is]: Has Congress exercised its powers under the Fifteenth Amendment in an appropriate manner with relation to the States? . . .

Section 1 of the Fifteenth Amendment . . . has always been treated as self-executing and has repeatedly been construed, without further legislative specification, to invalidate state voting qualifications or procedures which are discriminatory on their face or in practice.

South Carolina contends that the cases cited above are precedents only for the authority of the judiciary to strike down state statutes and procedures — that to allow an exercise of this authority by Congress would be to rob the courts of their rightful constitutional role. On the contrary, §2 of the Fifteenth Amendment expressly declares that "Congress shall have power to enforce this article by appropriate legislation." By adding this authorization, the framers indicated that Congress was to be chiefly responsible for implementing the rights created in §1. "It is the power of Congress which has been enlarged. Congress is authorized to *enforce* the prohibitions by appropriate legislation. Some legislation is contemplated to make the [Civil War] amendments fully effective." Ex parte Virginia, 100 U.S. 339, 345. Accordingly, in addition to the courts, Congress has full remedial powers to effectuate the constitutional prohibition against racial discrimination in voting.

Congress has repeatedly exercised these powers in the past, and its enactments have repeatedly been upheld. . . . The basic test to be applied in a case involving §2 of the Fifteenth Amendment is the same as in all cases concerning the express powers of Congress with relation to the reserved powers of the States. Chief Justice Marshall laid down the classic formulation, 50 years before the Fifteenth Amendment was ratified: "Let the end be legitimate, let it be within the scope of the constitution, and all means which are appropriate, which are plainly adapted to that end, which are not prohibited, but consist with the letter and spirit of the constitution, are constitutional." *McCulloch.* The Court has subsequently echoed his language in describing each of the Civil War Amendments. . . .

We therefore reject South Carolina's argument that Congress may appropriately do no more than to forbid violations of the Fifteenth Amendment in general terms — that the task of fashioning specific remedies or of applying them to particular localities must necessarily be left entirely to the courts. Congress is not circumscribed by any such artificial rules under §2 of the Fifteenth Amendment.

IV.

Congress exercised its authority under the Fifteenth Amendment in an inventive manner when it enacted the Voting Rights Act of 1965. . . . Congress had found that case-by-case litigation was inadequate to combat widespread and persistent discrimination in voting, because of the inordinate amount of time and energy required to overcome the obstructionist tactics invariably encountered in these lawsuits. After enduring nearly a century of systematic resistance of the Fifteenth Amendment, Congress might well decide to shift the advantage of time and inertia from the perpetrators of the evil to its victims. . . .

The Act intentionally confines these remedies to a small number of States and political subdivisions which in most instances were familiar to Congress by name. This, too, was a permissible method of dealing with the problem. Congress had learned that substantial voting discrimination presently occurs in certain sections of the country, and it knew no way of accurately forecasting whether the evil might spread elsewhere in the future. In acceptable legislative fashion, Congress chose to limit its attention to the geographic areas where immediate action seemed necessary. . . .

SUSPENSION OF TESTS

We now arrive at consideration of the specific remedies prescribed by the Act for areas included within the coverage formula. South Carolina assails the temporary suspension of existing voting qualifications, reciting the rule laid down by Lassiter v. Northampton County Bd. of Elections, 360 U.S. 45 (1959), that literacy tests and related devices are not in themselves contrary to the Fifteenth Amendment. In that very case, however, the Court went on to say, "Of course a literacy test, fair on its face, may be employed to perpetuate that discrimination which the Fifteenth Amendment was designed to uproot." The record shows that in most of the States covered by the Act, including South Carolina, various tests and devices have been instituted with the purpose of disenfranchising Negroes, have been framed in such a way as to facilitate this aim, and have been administered in a discriminatory fashion for many years. Under these circumstances, the Fifteenth Amendment has clearly been violated.

BLACK, J., concurring and dissenting.

I agree with substantially all of the Court's opinion sustaining the power of Congress under §2 of the Fifteenth Amendment to suspend state literacy tests and similar voting qualifications and to authorize the Attorney General to secure the appointment of federal examiners to register qualified voters in various sections of the country. . . .

I dissent from its holding that every part of §5 of the Act is constitutional. . . . Section 5 [provides] that a State covered by §4(b) can in no way amend its constitution or laws relating to voting without first trying to persuade the Attorney General of the United States or the Federal District Court for the District of Columbia that the new proposed laws do not have the purpose and will not have the effect of denying the right to vote to citizens on account of their race or color.

. . . Section 5, by providing that some of the States cannot pass state laws or adopt state constitutional amendments without first being compelled to beg federal authorities to approve their policies, so distorts our constitutional structure of government as to render any distinction drawn in the Constitution between state and federal power almost meaningless.

KATZENBACH v. MORGAN
384 U.S. 641 (1966)

Brennan, J.

These cases concern the constitutionality of §4(e) of the Voting Rights Act of 1965. That law, in the respects pertinent in these cases, provides that no person who has successfully completed the sixth primary grade in a public school in, or a private school accredited by, the Commonwealth of Puerto Rico in which the language of instruction was other than English shall be denied the right to vote in any election because of his inability to read or write English.

Appellees, registered voters in New York City, brought this suit to challenge the constitutionality of §4(e) insofar as it pro tanto prohibits the enforcement of the election laws of New York requiring an ability to read and write English as a condition of voting. . . . [A three-judge district court held that §4(e)] usurped powers reserved to the States by the Tenth Amendment. . . . We reverse. . . .

Under the distribution of powers effected by the Constitution, the States establish qualifications for voting for state officers, and the qualifications established by the States for voting for members of the most numerous branch of the state legislature also determine who may vote for United States Representatives and Senators, Art. I, §2; Seventeenth Amendment. But, of course, the States have no power to grant or withhold the franchise on conditions that are forbidden by the Fourteenth Amendment, or any other provision of the Constitution. . . .

The Attorney General of the State of New York argues that an exercise of congressional power under §5 of the Fourteenth Amendment that prohibits the enforcement of a state law can only be sustained if the judicial branch determines that the state law is prohibited by the provisions of the Amendment that Congress sought to enforce. More specifically, he urges that §4(e) cannot be sustained as appropriate legislation to enforce the Equal Protection Clause unless the judiciary decides — even with the guidance of a congressional judgment — that the application of the English literacy requirement prohibited by §4(e) is forbidden by the Equal Protection Clause itself. We disagree. Neither the language nor history of §5 supports such a construction. As was said with regard to §5 in Ex parte Virginia, "It is the power of Congress which has been enlarged. Congress is authorized to *enforce* the prohibitions by appropriate legislation. Some legislation is contemplated to make the amendments fully effective." A construction of §5 that would require a judicial determination that the enforcement of the state law precluded by Congress violated the Amendment, as a condition of sustaining the congressional enactment, would depreciate both congressional resourcefulness and congressional responsibility for implementing the Amendment. It would confine the legislative power in this context to the insignificant role of abrogating only those state laws that the judicial branch was prepared to adjudge unconstitutional. . . .

Thus our task in this case is not to determine whether the New York English literacy requirement as applied to deny the right to vote to a person who successfully completed the sixth grade in a Puerto Rican school violates the Equal Protection Clause. Accordingly, our decision in Lassiter v. Northampton Election Bd. sustaining the North Carolina English literacy requirement as not in all circumstances prohibited by the first sections of the Fourteenth and Fifteenth Amendments, is inapposite. *Lassiter* did not present the question before us here: Without regard to whether the judiciary would find that the Equal Protection Clause itself nullifies New York's English literacy requirement as so applied, could Congress prohibit the enforcement of the state law by legislating under §5 of the Fourteenth Amendment? In answering this question, our task is limited to determining whether such legislation is, as required by §5, appropriate legislation to enforce the Equal Protection Clause.

By including §5 the draftsmen sought to grant to Congress, by a specific provision applicable to the Fourteenth Amendment, the same broad powers expressed in the Necessary and Proper Clause. . . . Correctly viewed, §5 is a positive grant of legislative power authorizing Congress to exercise its discretion in determining whether and what legislation is needed to secure the guarantees of the Fourteenth Amendment.

We therefore proceed to the consideration whether §4(e) is "appropriate legislation" to enforce the Equal Protection Clause, that is, under the *McCulloch* standard, whether §4(e) may be regarded as an enactment to enforce the Equal Protection Clause, whether it is "plainly adapted to that end" and whether it is not prohibited by but is consistent with "the letter and spirit of the constitution."[a]

There can be no doubt that §4(e) may be regarded as an enactment to enforce the Equal Protection Clause. Congress explicitly declared that it enacted §4(e) "to secure the rights under the fourteenth amendment of persons educated in American-flag schools in which the predominant classroom language was other than English." The persons referred to include those who have migrated from the Commonwealth of Puerto Rico to New York and who have been denied the right to vote because of their inability to read and write English, and the Fourteenth Amendment rights referred to include those emanating from the Equal Protection Clause. More specifically, §4(e) may be viewed as a measure to secure for the Puerto Rican community residing in New York nondiscriminatory treatment by government — both in the imposition of voting qualifications and the provision or administration of governmental services, such as public schools, public housing and law enforcement.

Section 4(e) may be readily seen as "plainly adapted" to furthering these aims of the Equal Protection Clause. The practical effect of §4(e) is to prohibit New York

a. Contrary to the suggestion of the dissent, §5 does not grant Congress power to exercise discretion in the other direction and to enact "statutes so as in effect to dilute equal protection and due process decisions of this Court." We emphasize that Congress' power under §5 is limited to adopting measures to enforce the guarantees of the Amendment: §5 grants Congress no power to restrict, abrogate, or dilute these guarantees. Thus, for example, an enactment authorizing the States to establish racially segregated systems of education would not be — as required by §5 — a measure "to enforce" the Equal Protection Clause since that clause of its own force prohibits such state laws.

from denying the right to vote to large segments of its Puerto Rican community. Congress has thus prohibited the State from denying to that community the right that is "preservative of all rights." This enhanced political power will be helpful in gaining nondiscriminatory treatment in public services for the entire Puerto Rican community.[b] Section 4(e) thereby enables the Puerto Rican minority better to obtain "perfect equality of civil rights and the equal protection of the laws." It was well within congressional authority to say that this need of the Puerto Rican minority for the vote warranted federal intrusion upon any state interests served by the English literacy requirement. It was for Congress, as the branch that made this judgment, to assess and weigh the various conflicting considerations — the risk or pervasiveness of the discrimination in governmental services, the effectiveness of eliminating the state restriction on the right to vote as a means of dealing with the evil, the adequacy or availability of alternative remedies, and the nature and significance of the state interests that would be affected by the nullification of the English literacy requirement as applied to residents who have successfully completed the sixth grade in a Puerto Rican school. It is not for us to review the congressional resolution of these factors. It is enough that we be able to perceive a basis upon which the Congress might resolve the conflict as it did. There plainly was such a basis to support §4(e) in the application in question in this case. Any contrary conclusion would require us to be blind to the realities familiar to the legislators.

The result is no different if we confine our inquiry to the question whether §4(e) was merely legislation aimed at the elimination of an invidious discrimination in establishing voter qualifications. We are told that New York's English literacy requirement originated in the desire to provide an incentive for non-English speaking immigrants to learn the English language and in order to assure the intelligent exercise of the franchise. Yet Congress might well have questioned, in light of the many exemptions provided,[c] and some evidence suggesting that prejudice played a prominent role,[d] whether these were actually the interests being served. Congress might have also questioned whether denial of a right deemed so precious and fundamental in our society was a necessary or appropriate means of encouraging persons to learn English, or of furthering the goal of an intelligent exercise of the franchise. Finally, Congress might well have concluded that as a means of furthering the intelligent exercise of the franchise, an ability to read or understand Spanish is as effective as ability to read English for those to whom Spanish-language newspapers and Spanish-language radio and television programs are available to

b. Cf. James Everard's Breweries v. Day, 265 U.S. 545 (1924), which held that, under the enforcement clause of the Eighteenth Amendment, Congress could prohibit the prescription of intoxicating malt liquor for medicinal purposes even though the Amendment itself only prohibited the manufacture and sale of intoxicating liquors for beverage purposes. Cf. also the settled principle applied in the *Shreveport Case* . . . and expressed in United States v. Darby, 312 U.S. 100, 118, that the power of Congress to regulate interstate commerce "extends to those activities intrastate which so affect interstate commerce or the exercise of the power of Congress over it as to make regulation of them appropriate means to the attainment of a legitimate end. . . ."

c. The principal exemption complained of is that for persons who had been eligible to vote before January 1, 1922.

d. This evidence consists in part of statements made in the Constitutional Convention first considering the English literacy requirement, such as the following made by the sponsor of the measure: "More precious even than the forms of government are the mental qualities of our race. While those stand unimpaired, all is safe. They are exposed to a single danger, and that is that by constantly changing our voting citizenship through the wholesale, but valuable and necessary infusion of Southern and Eastern European races. . . . The danger has begun. . . . We should check it.". . .

inform them of election issues and governmental affairs. Since Congress undertook to legislate so as to preclude the enforcement of the state law, and did so in the context of a general appraisal of literacy requirements for voting, see South Carolina v. Katzenbach, supra, to which it brought a specially informed legislative competence, it was Congress' prerogative to weigh these competing considerations. Here again, it is enough that we perceive a basis upon which Congress might predicate a judgment that the application of New York's English literacy requirement to deny the right to vote to a person with a sixth grade education in Puerto Rican schools in which the language of instruction was other than English constituted an invidious discrimination in violation of the Equal Protection Clause.

There remains the question whether the congressional remedies adopted in §4(e) constitute means which are not prohibited by, but are consistent "with the letter and spirit of the constitution." The only respect in which appellees contend that §4(e) fails in this regard is that the section itself works an invidious discrimination in violation of the Fifth Amendment by prohibiting the enforcement of the English literacy requirement only for those educated in American-flag schools (schools located within United States jurisdiction) in which the language of instruction was other than English, and not for those educated in schools beyond the territorial limits of the United States in which the language of instruction was also other than English. This is not a complaint that Congress, in enacting §4(e), has unconstitutionally denied or diluted anyone's right to vote but rather that Congress violated the Constitution by not extending the relief effected in §4(e) to those educated in non-American-flag schools. . . .

Section 4(e) does not restrict or deny the franchise but in effect extends the franchise to persons who otherwise would be denied it by state law. . . . We need only decide whether the challenged limitation on the relief effected in §4(e) was permissible. In deciding that question, that principle that calls for the closest scrutiny of distinctions in laws *denying* fundamental rights is inapplicable; for the distinction challenged by appellees is presented only as a limitation on a reform measure aimed at eliminating an existing barrier to the exercise of the franchise. Rather, in deciding the constitutional propriety of the limitations in such a reform measure we are guided by the familiar principles that . . . "reform may take one step at a time, addressing itself to the phase of the problem which seems most acute to the legislative mind," Williamson v. Lee Optical Co.

. . . In the context of the case before us, the congressional choice to limit the relief effected in §4(e) may, for example, reflect Congress' greater familiarity with the quality of instruction in American-flag schools, a recognition of the unique historic relationship between the Congress and the Commonwealth of Puerto Rico, an awareness of the Federal Government's acceptance of the desirability of the use of Spanish as the language of instruction in Commonwealth schools, and the fact that Congress has fostered policies encouraging migration from the Commonwealth to the States. . . . We hold . . . that the limitation on relief effected in §4(e) does not constitute a forbidden discrimination since these factors might well have been the basis for the decision of Congress to go "no farther than it did."

[Cardona v. Power, 384 U.S. 672 (1966), decided on the same day as *Morgan*, overturned the New York Court of Appeals, which had sustained the English literacy requirement against the challenge of appellant, a resident of New York educated in Puerto Rico, who did not, however, allege that she had completed sixth grade (as required by §4(e) of the Voting Rights Act). The Supreme Court vacated the judgment and remanded the case to allow the state court to determine whether appellant was covered by §4(e), and, alternatively, whether "in light of this federal enactment, those applications of the New York English literacy requirement not in terms prohibited by §4(e) have continuing validity." Justice Harlan's dissent from *Cardona* and *Morgan* follows.]

HARLAN, J., joined by Stewart, J., dissenting.

Worthy as its purposes may be thought by many, I do not see how §4(e) of the Voting Rights Act of 1965, can be sustained except at the sacrifice of fundamentals in the American constitutional system — the separation between the legislative and judicial function and the boundaries between federal and state political authority. By the same token I think that the validity of New York's literacy test, a question which the Court considers *only* in the context of the federal statute, must be upheld. It will conduce to analytical clarity if I discuss the second issue first.

I. THE *CARDONA* CASE

I believe the same interests recounted in *Lassiter* indubitably point toward upholding the rationality of the New York voting test. It is true that the issue here is not so simply drawn between literacy per se and illiteracy. Appellant alleges that she is literate in Spanish, and that she studied American history and government in United States Spanish-speaking schools in Puerto Rico. . . .

Although to be sure there is a difference between a totally illiterate person and one who is literate in a foreign tongue, I do not believe that this added factor vitiates the constitutionality of the New York statute. Accepting appellant's allegations as true, it is nevertheless also true that the range of material available to a resident of New York literate only in Spanish is much more limited than what is available to an English-speaking resident, that the business of national, state, and local government is conducted in English, and that propositions, amendments, and offices for which candidates are running listed on the ballot are likewise in English. It is also true that most candidates, certainly those campaigning on a national or statewide level, make their speeches in English. New York may justifiably want its voters to be able to understand candidates directly, rather than through possibly imprecise translations or summaries reported in a limited number of Spanish news media. . . . Given the State's legitimate concern with promoting and safeguarding the intelligent use of the ballot, and given also New York's long experience with the process of integrating non-English-speaking residents into the mainstream of American life, I do not see how it can be said that this qualification for suffrage is unconstitutional. I would uphold the validity of the New York statute, unless the federal statute prevents that result, the question to which I now turn.

II. THE *MORGAN* CASES . . .

The pivotal question in [these cases] is what effect the added factor of a congressional enactment has on the straight equal protection argument dealt with above. The Court declares that since §5 of the Fourteenth Amendment gives to the Congress power to "enforce" the prohibitions of the Amendment by "appropriate" legislation, the test for judicial review of any congressional determination in this area is simply one of rationality; that is, in effect, was Congress acting rationally in declaring that the New York statute is irrational? . . . I believe the Court has confused the issue of how much enforcement power Congress possesses under §5 with the distinct issue of what questions are appropriate for congressional determination and what questions are essentially judicial in nature.

When [judicially] recognized state violations of federal constitutional standards have occurred, Congress is of course empowered by §5 to take appropriate remedial measures to redress and prevent the wrongs. But it is a judicial question whether the condition with which Congress has thus sought to deal is in truth an infringement of the Constitution, something that is the necessary prerequisite to bringing the §5 power into play at all. Thus, in Ex parte Virginia, 100 U.S. 339 (1879), involving a federal statute making it a federal crime to disqualify anyone from jury service because of race, the Court first held as a matter of constitutional law that "the Fourteenth Amendment secures, among other civil rights, to colored men, when charged with criminal offences against a State, an impartial jury trial, by jurors indifferently selected or chosen without discrimination against such jurors because of their color." Only then did the Court hold that to enforce this prohibition upon state discrimination, Congress could enact a criminal statute of the type under consideration. See also . . . South Carolina v. Katzenbach. . . .

Section 4(e), however, presents a significantly different type of congressional enactment. The question here is not whether the statute is appropriate remedial legislation to cure an established violation of a constitutional command, but whether there has in fact been an infringement of that constitutional command, that is, whether a particular state practice or, as here, a statute is so arbitrary or irrational as to offend the command of the Equal Protection Clause of the Fourteenth Amendment. That question is one for the judicial branch ultimately to determine. Were the rule otherwise, Congress would be able to qualify this Court's constitutional decisions under the Fourteenth and Fifteenth Amendments, let alone those under other provisions of the Constitution, by resorting to congressional power under the Necessary and Proper Clause. In view of this Court's holding in *Lassiter*, that an English literacy test is a permissible exercise of state supervision over its franchise, I do not think it is open to Congress to limit the effect of that decision as it has undertaken to do by §4(e). In effect the Court reads §5 of the Fourteenth Amendment as giving Congress the power to define the *substantive* scope of the Amendment. If that indeed be the true reach of §5, then I do not see why Congress should not be able as well to exercise its §5 "discretion" by enacting statutes so as in effect to dilute equal protection and due process decisions of this Court. In all such cases there is room for reasonable men to differ as to whether or not a denial of equal protection or due process has occurred, and the final decision is one of judgment. Until today this judgment has always been one for the judiciary to resolve.

I do not mean to suggest in what has been said that a legislative judgment of the type incorporated in §4(e) is without any force whatsoever. Decisions on questions of equal protection and due process are based not on abstract logic, but on empirical foundations. To the extent "legislative facts" are relevant to a judicial determination, Congress is well equipped to investigate them, and such determinations are of course entitled to due respect. In South Carolina v. Katzenbach such legislative findings were made to show that racial discrimination in voting was actually occurring. Similarly, in Heart of Atlanta Motel, Inc. v. United States, 379 U.S. 241, and

Katzenbach v. McClung, 379 U.S. 294, this Court upheld Title II of the Civil Rights Act of 1964 under the Commerce Clause. There again the congressional determination that racial discrimination in a clearly defined group of public accommodations did effectively impede interstate commerce was based on "voluminous testimony," which had been put before the Congress and in the context of which it passed remedial legislation.

But no such factual data provide a legislative record supporting §4(e) by way of showing that Spanish-speaking citizens are fully as capable of making informed decisions in a New York election as are English-speaking citizens. Nor was there any showing whatever to support the Court's alternative argument that §4(e) should be viewed as but a remedial measure designed to cure or assure against unconstitutional discrimination of other varieties, e.g., in "public schools, public housing and law enforcement," to which Puerto Rican minorities might be subject in such communities as New York. There is simply no legislative record supporting such hypothesized discrimination of the sort we have hitherto insisted upon when congressional power is brought to bear on constitutionally reserved state concerns.

Thus, we have here not a matter of giving deference to a congressional estimate, based on its determination of legislative facts, bearing upon the validity vel non of a statute, but rather what can at most be called a legislative announcement that Congress believes a state law to entail an unconstitutional deprivation of equal protection. Although this kind of declaration is of course entitled to the most respectful consideration, coming as it does from a concurrent branch and one that is knowledgeable in matters of popular political participation, I do not believe it lessens our responsibility to decide the fundamental issue of whether in fact the state enactment violates federal constitutional rights.

In assessing the deference we should give to this kind of congressional expression of policy, it is relevant that the judiciary has always given to congressional enactments a presumption of validity. However, it is also a canon of judicial review that state statutes are given a similar presumption. Whichever way this case is decided, one statute will be rendered inoperative in whole or in part, and although it has been suggested that this Court should give somewhat more deference to Congress than to a state legislature, such a simple weighing of presumptions is hardly a satisfying way of resolving a matter that touches the distribution of state and federal power in an area so sensitive as that of the regulation of the franchise. Rather it should be recognized that while the Fourteenth Amendment is a "brooding omnipresence" over all state legislation, the substantive matters which it touches are all within the primary legislative competence of the States. Federal authority, legislative no less than judicial, does not intrude unless there has been a denial by state action of Fourteenth Amendment limitations, in this instance a denial of equal protection. At least in the area of primary state concern a state statute that passes constitutional muster under the judicial standard of rationality should not be permitted to be set at naught by a mere contrary congressional pronouncement unsupported by a legislative record justifying that conclusion. . . .

Discussion

1. *Later voting cases.* The Voting Rights Act Amendments of 1970 suspended for a period of five years the use of literacy tests in any federal, state, or local election anywhere in the United States. In Oregon v. Mitchell, 400 U.S. 112 (1970),

although the Court divided on all other aspects of the 1970 amendments (as discussed below), it unanimously sustained this provision. There was no majority opinion. In one opinion, Justices Brennan, White, and Marshall wrote:

> The legislative history of the 1970 Amendments contains substantial information upon which Congress could have based a finding that the use of literacy tests in Arizona and in other States where their use was not proscribed by the 1965 Act has the effect of denying the vote to racial minorities whose illiteracy is the consequence of a previous, governmentally sponsored denial of equal educational opportunity. The Attorney General of Arizona told the Senate Subcommittee on Constitutional Rights that many older Indians in the State were "never privileged to attend a formal school." Extensive testimony before both Houses indicated that racial minorities have long received inferior educational opportunities throughout the United States. And interstate migration of such persons, particularly of Negroes from the Southern States, has long been a matter of common knowledge.

Justices Black and Douglas, in separate opinions, made essentially the same point. Justice Stewart, joined by Chief Justice Burger and Justice Blackmun, wrote:

> Because the justification for extending the ban on literacy tests to the entire Nation need not turn on whether literacy tests unfairly discriminate against Negroes in every State in the Union, Congress was not required to make state-by-state findings concerning either the equality of educational opportunity or actual impact of literacy requirements on the Negro citizen's access to the ballot box. In the interests of uniformity, Congress may paint with a much broader brush than may this Court, which must confine itself to the judicial function of deciding individual cases and controversies upon individual records. The findings that Congress made when it enacted the Voting Rights Act of 1965 would have supported a nationwide ban on literacy tests. . . . Experience gained under the 1965 Act has now led Congress to conclude that it should go the whole distance. This approach to the problem is a rational one: consequently it is within the constitutional power of Congress under §2 of the Fifteenth Amendment.

Although Justice Harlan found the issue "not free from difficulty," he concluded:

> Despite the lack of evidence of specific instances of discriminatory application or effect, Congress could have determined that racial prejudice is prevalent throughout the Nation, and that literacy tests unduly lend themselves to discriminatory application, either conscious or unconscious. This danger of violation of §1 of the Fifteenth Amendment was sufficient to authorize the exercise of congressional power under §2.

In 1975, Congress further extended the Voting Rights Act by making permanent the nationwide ban of literacy and similar tests based in part on a congressional finding that voting discrimination against citizens of language minorities is "pervasive and national in scope." The Court revisited voting rights issues in City of Mobile v. Bolden, 446 U.S. 55 (1980), and City of Rome v. United States, 446 U.S. 156 (1980), decided on the same day. In *Mobile,* an action challenging the city's "commission" form of government directly under the Fourteenth and Fifteenth Amendments, the Court held that §1 of those amendments prohibited only *intentional* discrimination. Justice Stewart wrote for a plurality including Chief Justice Burger and Justices Powell and Rehnquist. Justice Stevens concurred in the judgment. Justices White, Brennan, and Marshall wrote dissenting opinions. Cf. Keyes v. Denver School District, infra, Chapter 6.[35]

Rome involved the Voting Rights Act of 1965. Because the State of Georgia is a jurisdiction covered by section 4(b) of the Act, a change in voting practices by a Georgia municipality must be approved in advance by the Attorney General or the United States District Court for the District of Columbia, on a finding that the practice "does not have the purpose and *will not have the effect* of denying or abridging the right to vote on account of race or color" (emphasis added). In *Rome*, the Attorney General and district court had not approved of some annexations and changes in the city's electoral system. The district court found that the city had no discriminatory purpose, but that the changes would have a discriminatory effect on the city's Black residents. The Supreme Court affirmed in an opinion by Justice Marshall. It held that only the state, and not a subdivision, may invoke section 4(a) of the Act, which permits a covered jurisdiction to bail out by proving that it has not used a voting test or device discriminatorily for the preceding 17 years. "[South Carolina v. Katzenbach] makes clear that Congress may, under the authority of §2 of the Fifteenth Amendment, prohibit state action that, though in itself not violative of §1, perpetuates the effects of past discrimination." These prohibitions are valid so long as they are

> "appropriate," as that term is defined in McCulloch v. Maryland . . . , [to attack racial discrimination]. In the present case, we hold that the Act's ban on electoral changes that are discriminatory in effect is an appropriate method of promoting the purposes of the Fifteenth Amendment, even if it is assumed that §1 of the Amendment prohibits only intentional discrimination in voting. Congress could rationally have concluded that, because electoral changes by jurisdictions with a demonstrable history of intentional racial discrimination in voting create the risk of purposeful discrimination, it was proper to prohibit changes that have a discriminatory impact.[36]

Justice Powell dissented, arguing that if "section 4(a) imposes the burden of preclearance on Rome, the same section must also relieve that burden when the city can demonstrate its compliance with the Act's quite strict requirements for bailout," and that a contrary interpretation could not be sustained under the Fifteenth Amendment. Justice Rehnquist, joined by Justice Stewart, also dissented:

> Neither reason nor precedent supports the conclusion that here it is "appropriate" for Congress to attempt to prevent purposeful discrimination by prohibiting conduct which a locality proves is *not* purposeful discrimination. . . .
>
> [G]iven the difficulties of proving that an electoral change or annexation has been undertaken for the purpose of discriminating against blacks, Congress could properly conclude that as a remedial matter it was necessary to place the burden of proving lack

---

35. Congress has essentially attempted to overturn *Mobile* by passing a 1982 amendment to the Voting Rights Act that eliminates the intent requirement and substitutes a "totality of circumstances" test by which the courts should measure the "opportunity" of "members of a class of citizens protected by [the Act] . . . to participate in the political process and to elect representatives of their choice." In a series of cases, the Court has enforced this statutory amendment, "assuming but never directly addressing its constitutionality." Bush v. Vera, 517 U.S. 952 (O'Connor, J., concurring) (1996). "Meanwhile, lower courts have unanimously affirmed its constitutionality." Id. Can you see why?

36. The city invoked National League of Cities v. Usery, infra, p. 650, to argue that Congress could not interfere with the structure of state institutions. Marshall responded that "principles of federalism that might otherwise be an obstacle to congressional authority are necessarily overridden by the power to enforce the Civil War Amendments 'by appropriate legislation.'"

of discriminatory purpose on the localities. South Carolina v. Katzenbach. But all of this does not support the conclusion that Congress is acting remedially when it continues the presumption of purposeful discrimination even after the locality has disproved that presumption. Absent other circumstances, it would be a topsy-turvey judicial system which held that electoral changes which have been affirmatively proved to be permissible under the Constitution nonetheless violate the Constitution. . . .

Oregon v. Mitchell . . . established that under some circumstances, a congressional remedy may be constitutionally overinclusive by prohibiting some state action which might not be purposefully discriminatory. That possibility does not justify the overinclusiveness countenanced by the Court in this case, however. *Oregon* by no means held that Congress could simply use discriminatory effect as a proxy for discriminatory purpose, as the Court seems to imply. Instead, the Court opinions identified the factors which rendered this prohibition properly remedial. The Court found the nationwide ban to be an appropriate means of effectively preventing purposeful discrimination in the application of the literacy tests as well as an appropriate means of remedying prior constitutional violations by state and local governments in the administration of education to minorities.

The presumption that the literacy tests were either being used to purposefully discriminate, or that the disparate effects of those tests were attributable to discrimination in state-administered education was not very wide of the mark. . . . Even if not adopted with a discriminatory purpose, the tests could readily be applied in a discriminatory fashion. Thus a demonstration by the State that it sought to reinstate the tests for legitimate purposes did not eliminate the substantial risk of discrimination in application. Only a ban could effectively prevent the occurrence of purposeful discrimination. The nationwide ban was also found necessary to effectively remedy past constitutional violations. Without the nationwide ban, a voter who was illiterate due to state discrimination in education could be denied the right to vote on the basis of his illiteracy when he moved into a jurisdiction retaining a literacy test for nondiscriminatory purposes. . . .

Presumptive prohibition of vote-diluting procedures is not similarly an "appropriate" means of exacting state compliance with the Civil War Amendments. First, these prohibitions are quite unlike the literacy ban, where the disparate effects were traceable to the discrimination of governmental bodies in education even if their present desire to use the tests was legitimate. Any disparate impact associated with the nondiscriminatory electoral changes in issue here results from bloc voting — private rather than governmental discrimination. It is clear therefore that these prohibitions do not implicate congressional power to devise an effective remedy for prior constitutional violations by local governments. . . .

Nor does the prohibition of all practices with a disparate impact enhance congressional prevention of purposeful discrimination. The changes in issue are not, like literacy tests, though fair on their face, subject to discriminatory application by local authorities. They are either discriminatory from the outset or not.

Finally, the advantages supporting the imposition of a nationwide ban are simply not implicated in this case. No added administrative burdens are in issue since Congress has provided the mechanism for preclearance suits in any event, and the burden of proof for this issue is on the locality. And it is certain that the only constitutional wrong implicated — purposeful dilution — can be effectively remedied by prohibiting it where it occurs. For all these reasons, I do not think that the present case is controlled by the result in *Oregon.* By prohibiting all electoral changes with a disparate impact, Congress has attempted to prevent disparate impacts — not purposeful discrimination.

2. McCulloch *and the scope of Reconstruction power.* Note the prominent allusions to *McCulloch* in the *Katzenbach* cases and their progeny. If *McCulloch* lays down the

proper test by which judges should measure congressional action under the Reconstruction Amendments, wouldn't this mean that Congress's power is broad indeed? Recall that prior to the Civil War, the Court had never once invalidated an act of Congress on *McCulloch* grounds; nor had the Court done so between 1937 and 1966, when these *Katzenbach* cases were decided. For arguments that the Reconstruction Congress drafted the language of the enforcement clauses with *McCulloch's* sweeping vision of congressional power in mind, see Steven A. Engel, Note, The *McCulloch* Theory of the Fourteenth Amendment: *City of Boerne v. Flores* and the Original Understanding of Section 5, 109 Yale L.J. 115 (1999); Akhil Reed Amar, Intratextualism, 112 Harv. L. Rev. 747, 825-826 (1999). Consider in this regard the Reconstruction Amendments' explicit textual echo of *McCulloch's* famous passage: "Let the end be legitimate . . . and all means which are *appropriate* . . . are constitutional" (emphasis added).

3. *The nature of congressional power: Remedial, or substantive, or fact-finding, or what?* Justice Brennan supports section 4(e) of the Voting Rights Act of 1965 under two alternative theories: (1) as a provision to secure nondiscriminatory treatment of Puerto Ricans in the provision of public services; and (2) as the embodiment of a congressional judgment that disfranchising the persons covered by 4(e) is itself an unconstitutional discrimination. Under the first theory, Congress does not engage in independent constitutional interpretation but only implements a judicial interpretation of the Equal Protection Clause. Established judicial doctrine holds that discrimination in the provision of public services based on the recipients' ethnic origin violates the Fourteenth Amendment. Congress has merely made the factual determinations (a) that New York is discriminating in this fashion and (b) that enfranchising Puerto Ricans will tend to ameliorate such discrimination.

Under the alternative theory, Congress makes a substantive constitutional decision not previously or subsequently made by the Court. On this view, although the Court had held in the *Lassiter* case that literacy tests were not in themselves unconstitutional, Congress was properly entitled to hold a different substantive interpretation of the constitutional right at stake. Such a determination is not simply one of fact; it encompasses a choice of values of the sort involved in most adjudication under the Fourteenth Amendment. Read expansively, the second theory authorizes Congress to create novel Fourteenth Amendment doctrine, not only in the Court's silence, but even in the face of judicial doctrine.

4. *Brennan's ratchet.* Note one important limit on Congress's power, as expounded by the Court in Katzenbach v. Morgan: In footnote 10 of the opinion (note a in the preceding excerpt), Justice Brennan insists that Congress has power only to add to the Court's bans on states, not to subtract from them. Is this "ratchet" view of the Reconstruction Power normatively attractive? What is its constitutional basis? What happens when conflicting constitutional rights and interests press up against each other? (For example, would congressionally blessed affirmative action for Blacks ever violate the constitutional rights of non-Blacks? See infra, Chapter 6.) Also, consider the argument that even if Congress enjoys "power" under the Reconstruction Amendments, it remains bound by the affirmative limits set forth in places like the Bill of Rights. (Note that the Fifth Amendment, which limits Congress, has been construed to require Congress to abide by principles of "equal protection," see, e.g., Bolling v. Sharpe, 347 U.S. 497 (1954), infra, Chapter 6.)

5. *Reconstruction power through the eyes of the conscientious Congressperson.* If Congress is authorized to determine that a state practice is intrinsically unconstitutional, what criteria should it employ? Is *McCulloch*'s description of the scope of congressional powers — "Let the end be legitimate," etc. — relevant to this question? What, if any, deference should Congress accord the supposed judgment of a state legislature that its practice promotes desirable or important objectives? If certain federal statutes are premised on the intrinsic unconstitutionality of the invalidated state practice, should Congress be as free to repeal these as any other laws, or do they have a precedential force akin to the Court's constitutional decisions?

6. *Academic theories of congressional power under Reconstruction.* Academic theories abound trying to make sense of the idea that Congress can at times use its Reconstruction power to "reverse" a Supreme Court decision. Consider the following six views.

Professor Robert Burt's View — Congress as a Less Constrained Line-Drawer.[37]

> Congress is less burdened by the principled constraints under which courts labor. . . . Congress can make distinctions among classes that the Court would itself be hard put to explain on principled grounds both because Congress is more sensitively tuned to the competing social interests that demand accommodation and because the institutional legitimacy of a legislative act depends not so much on the rational persuasiveness of its decisions as on the simple fact that a majority of "responsible" elected officials were willing to vote for the proposition. . . . Thus the *Morgan* Court could argue that it does not authorize Congress to impose its value preferences on the states, but rather that Congress "enforces" the Court's value preferences, under the Fourteenth Amendment, on the states in circumstances where the Court does not feel able to do so itself.

Professor Burt suggests, as an example, that the Court was institutionally ill suited to extend the Fourteenth Amendment to private discrimination, because it "could not independently proscribe some private discrimination without its proclaimed principle expanding to proscribe all discrimination. [And] . . . embracing such a principle would wholly sacrifice the competing values" in privacy and property. On the other hand,

> Congress, using no principle but fiat by majority vote, could act, for example, to permit Mrs. Murphy to turn away black lodgers [from her boarding house] so long as she lived with her other lodgers in a house that could accommodate no more than four families. Congress could easily conclude that in Mrs. Murphy's case, but not in others closely analogous, the values involved in free choice of companions should predominate. The Court would have much greater difficulty independently constructing an exemption for Mrs. Murphy, no matter how important some such exemption might be, in order to mediate the clashing principles and political pressures at stake. . . . In this context — devising appropriate adjustment of directly conflicting principles — the legislative mechanism is greatly superior to the courts.

In the context of *Morgan*, Congress was similarly able to draw "arbitrary" lines — sixth-grade education in an accredited Puerto Rican school — where no "principled" justification could be given for drawing the line at any particular place.

---

37. Robert Burt, *Miranda* and Title II: A Morganatic Marriage, 1969 S. Ct. Rev. 81, 112, 113-114.

Are there occasions where courts do end up drawing arbitrary lines of the sorts embodied in the Voting Rights Act? Consider, for example, Duncan v. Louisiana, 391 U.S. 145 (1968), which held that defendants subject to imprisonment for more than six months are entitled to trial by jury. Consider also the trimester framework set forth in Roe v. Wade, 410 U.S. 113 (1973), and the rule of Dunn v. Blumstein, 405 U.S. 330 (1972), suggesting that the line between permissible and impermissible residency periods for voting in state elections is 30 days.

Professor Archibald Cox's View — Congress as a Superior Factfinder:[38]

[T]he *Morgan* decision follows logically from the basic principles determining the respective functions of the legislative and judicial branches outside the field of preferred constitutional rights. Whether a State law denies equal protection depends to a large extent upon the finding and appraisal of the practical importance of relevant facts. In the case of the English literacy requirement, it turned upon such considerations as the extent to which the requirement served as an incentive to learn English and ease the process of assimilation, the availability of Spanish-language newspapers and their sufficiency to enable non-English-speaking voters to exercise the franchise intelligently, the importance of the franchise, and the relative effectiveness of other inducements to learn English. The conventional formula, unless qualified by notions of preferred rights, would call for the Court to presume the existence of facts giving validity to State legislation. But section 5 of the fourteenth amendment gives Congress a concurrent power to enforce the fourteenth amendment even though that means invalidating State legislation.

There is also a presumption that facts exist which sustain federal legislation and a principle of deference to congressional judgment upon questions of proportion and degree, as illustrated by the due process and commerce clause cases. . . . In *Morgan* the federal and State statutes appeared to rest upon inconsistent findings and legislative evaluations of the conditions determining whether the discrimination against citizens literate only in Spanish was permissible or invidious. The Court, forced to choose between conflicting presumptions, applied the rule of deference to Congress and required the State to yield to the federal enactment thus found valid.

Some commentators have suggested that there is no reason to suppose that the congressional findings reflect the truth more accurately than the findings of a State legislature. The observation seems accurate but irrelevant. When Congress and a State legislature reach different conclusions, the supremacy clause makes the federal determination paramount regardless of its intrinsic merit.

Can a court separate Congress's findings of fact from its judgments on questions of values? Recall also Justice Harlan's criticism of the first rationale of *Morgan* — that New York's supposed discrimination in providing public services was not supported by a legislative record. Should a court be free to hypothesize legislative facts to sustain a law under Professor Cox's theory? Should Congress's formal "findings" incorporated in the Voting Rights Act Amendments of 1970 be conclusive of whatever facts they purport to find? Was there an adequate "record" to support the findings?

Can a fact-finding theory explain why the Court should defer to a Congress seeking to add to judicial restrictions on states, but not to a Congress trying to subtract from those restrictions? Consider Cox's claim that

---

38. Archibald Cox, The Role of Congress in Constitutional Determinations, 40 U. Cin. L. Rev. 199, 228-229 (1971).

There is no a priori reason for linking power to expand constitutional safeguards with power to dilute them. One can assert without logical fallacy that, since the chief function of the Supreme Court is to protect human rights, it should never defer to any legislative determination which restricts those rights without making its own independent investigation and characterization of the interests affected, even though it welcomes any legislative determination that extends human rights, and is subject to challenge only as an unconstitutional extension of federal power at the expense of the states.[39]

Professor William Cohen's View — Congress as a Superior Representative of State Governments:[40]

When Congress seeks to bless a state practice that the Court has held (or would hold) violates individual liberty, or equal protection, "Congress has no institutional competence superior to that of the state legislatures in second-guessing the courts." But where Congress seeks to invalidate a state practice that courts have upheld (or would uphold) the matter is different, because the state legislature itself could have chosen to protect the claim of right that the courts have left unprotected. Because states are adequately represented in the very composition of the Congress

> [A] congressional judgment resolving at the national level an issue that could — without constitutional objection — be decided in the same way at the state level, ought normally to be binding on the courts, since Congress presumably reflects a balance between both national and state interests and hence is better able to adjust such conflicts.

On Cohen's view, should courts ever invalidate congressional action in the name of states' rights? Cf. Part III, infra.

Professor Lawrence Sager's View — Congress as the Court's Junior Partner:

When the Court interprets the Constitution's meaning, moving from the abstract document to judicial doctrine, certain things tend to get lost in the translation. The Court may "underenforce" certain constitutional ideals for judiciary-specific reasons. For example, the Court's typical interpretations may reflect a measure of deference to legislative policy; or may shy away from full enforcement of a constitutional principle that is inextricably intertwined with a series of policy questions over which judges have little competence. In these situations, Congress should be allowed to legislate to implement the Court's true vision of the Constitution, free from these court-specific constraints. But Congress should not be allowed to implement its own substantive vision of the Constitution itself, where that vision is different from the Court's. In a recent statement of this idea, Professor Sager, joined by Professor Chris Eisgruber, distinguishes between "Congress acting as the Court's partner on the one hand, and as its adversary on the other." They propose the following thought experiment: "[I]magine[] that a Justice of the Supreme Court who shared in the Court's prevailing view on the matter in question left the Court and found herself in Congress; if she could not support proposed legislation without changing her prior view of the appropriate judicial disposition of the matter, the legislation [is impermissibly] adversarial."[41]

---

39. Id. at 253.

40. William Cohen, Congressional Power to Interpret Due Process and Equal Protection, 27 Stan. L. Rev. 603, 614 (1975).

41. Lawrence G. Sager and Christopher L. Eisgruber, Congressional Power and Religious Liberty After City of Boerne v. Flores, 1997 Sup. Ct. Rev. 79. For earlier versions of Sager's views, see Lawrence G. Sager, Fair Measure: The Legal Status of Underenforced Constitutional Norms, 91 Harv. L. Rev. 1212 (1978); Lawrence G. Sager, Justice in Plain Clothes: Reflections on the Thinness of Constitutional Law, 88 Nw. U. L. Rev. 410 (1993).

Note that, on Sager's view, the partnership is not an equal one. The Court is clearly the senior partner; in the event that Congress and the Court have different understandings of what Reconstruction Amendments truly require, the Court's view prevails.

If we accept Sager's distinction between what the Constitution truly means, and the imperfect and institutionally sensitive rules that judges craft to enforce that meaning, is it ever possible that, for institutional reasons, the Court might actually *overenforce* the "true" meaning of the Constitution? For example, if the true constitutional right is hard to define with sufficient precision in courtrooms, might judges ever opt for a cleaner and easier-to-enforce — but broader — prohibition? If so, can Congress in these areas ever adopt a rule that cuts back on, rather than extends, the Court's prohibitions on states? Cf. David A. Strauss, The Ubiquity of Prophylactic Rules, 55 U. Chi. L. Rev 190 (1988).

Professor Robert Post's and Professor Reva Siegel's View — Congress as a More Politically Sensitive Barometer of Evolving Constitutional Culture and a More Comprehensive Regulator of Complex Institutional Settings.[42]

On this view, the American Constitution "is not merely a limitation on popular will, but also its deepest expression" and Congress is "especially well-situated to respond to changes in constitutional culture." Tracing the ways in which "constitutional norms can migrate" from "social movements to Congress to the Court," Post and Siegel highlight how the Court — wisely and properly, in their view — revised its own sex-equality jurisprudence in the 1970s in light of congressional affirmations of women's rights in statutes that had been enacted at the behest of a broad populist movement of American feminists. For example, in Frontiero v. Richardson, 411 U.S. 677, 687-688 (1973), the Court plurality went out of its way to remark that "over the past decade Congress has itself manifested an increasing sensitivity to sex-based classifications" in the Civil Rights Act of 1964, the Equal Pay Act of 1963, and the proposed Equal Rights Amendment of 1972. In arguing that the judiciary should henceforth offer stronger protections against gender discriminations, the *Frontiero* plurality noted that it was "not without significance" that "Congress itself" — a "coequal branch of Government" — had already concluded that "classifications based on sex are inherently invidious." Post and Siegel stress that "Section 5 statutes are . . . a precious symbolic resource for those seeking to transform constitutional culture. They are a particularly valuable object of social mobilization" by outsider groups seeking validation. Finally, echoing Sager, Post and Siegel argue that "legislative constitutionalism . . . can establish comprehensive schemes of regulation and administration" and "can also address polycentric problems of redistribution that would be quite beyond the bounds of judicial remedies."

Given Post and Siegel's strong emphasis on pre-Rehnquist Court precedents, how might they respond to a critic who simply chose instead to stand on more recent Rehnquist Court precedents (discussed infra, p. 629) that reflect a more judge-centered view of §5?

Professor Akhil Reed Amar's View — Congress as a Coequal Interpretive Partner and Reflector of Fundamental Values.[43]

---

42. Robert C. Post and Reva B. Siegel, Legislative Constitutionalism and Section Five Power: Policentric Interpretation of the Family and Medical Leave Act, 112 Yale L.J. 1943 (2003).

43. Akhil Reed Amar, Intratextualism, 112 Harv. L. Rev. 747 (1999).

[T]here is a large gap between plenary [congressional] power on one extreme and only remedial power on the other. To reject the former is not to affirm the latter — as is clear if we spend just an instant thinking about Section 2 of the Thirteenth Amendment, under which Congress has less than plenary and more than remedial power. In the Thirteenth Amendment this middle ground is captured by the concept of "badges and incidents" of slavery, which Section 1 does not abolish of its own force, but which can be abolished by Congress under Section 2.[44]

Are there comparable middle-ground possibilities for the Fourteenth Amendment? Here are a couple of obvious contenders. Congress could have power to define rights that in good faith it considers truly fundamental and basic, and these rights, once defined — "badges and incidents of freedom and citizenship" — would thereafter be enforceable, even against states, as "privileges" and "immunities" of American "citizens." A more modest position is that even if Congress does not have this broad onto-logical power to *make* something a national privilege ipso facto, surely it should have the epistemic power to make known its views about what is truly fundamental, and have those views treated as powerful evidence of fundamentality in courts. Just as the Supreme Court looks to penal laws on the books to decide what is cruel and unusual in our culture,[a] so it could look to congressional laws as evidence of what is truly funda-mental in our culture. Thus in a close case, the Court might in the absence of a congressional declaration decide that a given right was not fundamental, but if Congress were to weigh in on behalf of the right, the Court would consider the issue afresh in light of this new evidence.[b]

Amar goes on to argue that the history and overall architecture of the Fourteenth Amendment strongly support a more-than-remedial role for Congress. Congress, he claims, should ideally stand as the Court's equal interpretive partner, rather than as its subordinate, in holding states to account. (His specific arguments are presented in the discussion following City of Flores v. Boerne, infra, pp. 639-643.) He concludes as follows:

[T]he most sensible reading of the Fourteenth Amendment would involve both courts and Congress in the task of protecting truly fundamental rights against states, with states generally held to whichever standard was stricter — more protective of funda-mental freedoms — in any given instance.

History aside, is this an attractive normative position?

7. *Mapping the middle ground: Jones v. Mayer and Oregon v. Mitchell.* In a pair of cases marking the transition from the Warren Court to the Burger Court, the Justices at first reaffirmed that Congress's Reconstruction power was sweeping and then held that the power was not plenary.

JONES v. ALFRED H. MAYER CO., 392 U.S. 409 (1968): [In *Jones*, the Justices confronted a Reconstruction-era statute, 42 U.S.C. §1982, that originally derived

44. See Jones v. Alfred H. Mayer Co., 392 U.S. 409 (1968) (Supreme Court recognition of broad congressional power under the Thirteenth Amendment to define "badges and incidents of slavery"), infra, p. 503.

a. See, e.g., Stanford v. Kentucky, 492 U.S. 361, 369-371, 373 (1989) (calling "the pattern of enacted laws" the "primary and most reliable indication of consensus").

b. For a powerful and elegant argument in support of this approach, see Michael W. McConnell, Institutions and Interpretation: A Critique of *City of Boerne v. Flores*, 111 Harv. L. Rev. 153, 189-195 (1997).

from Congress's famous Civil Rights Act of 1866, see Chapter 4, supra. Over the dissent of Justice Harlan (joined by Justice White), the Court construed the statute to prohibit certain forms of private race discrimination in real estate. In perhaps its most expansive recognition of congressional Reconstruction power, the Court upheld Congress's authority to pass such a law under Section 2 of the Thirteenth Amendment (an issue the dissenters did not reach). It bears emphasis that Congress's law, as construed by the Court, went far beyond what any previous Court had said (or any future Court would likely say) about what §1 of the Thirteenth Amendment independently prohibited: Section 1 prohibits "slavery and involuntary servitude" and it would be hard to say that a private person's mere refusal to enter into economic dealings with Blacks — perhaps in a state where slavery had never existed — amounts to "slavery" or "involuntary servitude" as such. Rather, the *Jones* Court explicitly recognized that Congress's power under §2 went well beyond what judges could plausibly prohibit under §1. Justice Stewart wrote for the Court, joined by six of his colleagues.]

STEWART, J.

[T]he fact that §1982 operates upon the unofficial acts of private individuals, whether or not sanctioned by state law, presents no constitutional problem. If Congress has power under the Thirteenth Amendment to eradicate conditions that prevent Negroes from buying and renting property because of their race or color, then no federal statute calculated to achieve that objective can be thought to exceed the constitutional power of Congress simply because it reaches beyond state action to regulate the conduct of private individuals. The constitutional question in this case, therefore, comes to this: Does the authority of Congress to enforce the Thirteenth Amendment "by appropriate legislation" include the power to eliminate all racial barriers to the acquisition of real and personal property? We think the answer to that question is plainly yes.

"By its own unaided force and effect," the Thirteenth Amendment "abolished slavery, and established universal freedom." Whether or not the Amendment itself did any more than that — a question not involved in this case — it is at least clear that the Enabling Clause of that Amendment empowered Congress to do much more. For that clause clothed "Congress with power to pass all laws necessary and proper for abolishing all badges and incidents of slavery in the United States."

Those who opposed passage of the Civil Rights Act of 1866 argued in effect that the Thirteenth Amendment merely authorized Congress to dissolve the legal bond by which the Negro slave was held to his master. Yet many had earlier opposed the Thirteenth Amendment on the very ground that it would give Congress virtually unlimited power to enact laws for the protection of Negroes in every State. And the majority leaders in Congress — who were, after all, the authors of the Thirteenth Amendment — had no doubt that its Enabling Clause contemplated the sort of positive legislation that was embodied in the 1866 Civil Rights Act. Their chief spokesman, Senator Trumbull of Illinois, the Chairman of the Judiciary Committee, had brought the Thirteenth Amendment to the floor of the Senate in 1864. In defending the constitutionality of the 1866 Act, he argued that, if the narrower construction of the Enabling Clause were correct, then

> "the trumpet of freedom that we have been blowing throughout the land has given an 'uncertain sound,' and the promised freedom is a delusion. Such was not the intention of Congress, which proposed the constitutional amendment, nor is such the fair

meaning of the amendment itself. . . . I have no doubt that under this provision . . . we may destroy all these discriminations in civil rights against the black man; and if we cannot, our constitutional amendment amounts to nothing. It was for that purpose that the second clause of that amendment was adopted, which says that Congress shall have authority, by appropriate legislation, to carry into effect the article prohibiting slavery. Who is to decide what that appropriate legislation is to be? The Congress of the United States; and it is for Congress to adopt such appropriate legislation as it may think proper, so that it be a means to accomplish the end."

Surely Senator Trumbull was right. Surely Congress has the power under the Thirteenth Amendment rationally to determine what are the badges and the incidents of slavery, and the authority to translate that determination into effective legislation. Nor can we say that the determination Congress has made is an irrational one. For this Court recognized long ago that, whatever else they may have encompassed, the badges and incidents of slavery — its "burdens and disabilities" — included restraints upon "those fundamental rights which are the essence of civil freedom, namely, the same right . . . to inherit, purchase, lease, sell and convey property, as is enjoyed by white citizens."[a] Just as the Black Codes, enacted after the Civil War to restrict the free exercise of those rights, were substitutes for the slave system, so the exclusion of Negroes from white communities became a substitute for the Black Codes. And when racial discrimination herds men into ghettos and makes their ability to buy property turn on the color of their skin, then it too is a relic of slavery.

Negro citizens, North and South, who saw in the Thirteenth Amendment a promise of freedom — freedom to "go and come at pleasure" and to "buy and sell when they please" — would be left with "a mere paper guarantee" if Congress were powerless to assure that a dollar in the hands of a Negro will purchase the same thing as a dollar in the hands of a white man. At the very least, the freedom that Congress is empowered to secure under the Thirteenth Amendment includes the freedom to buy whatever a white man can buy, the right to live wherever a white man can live. If Congress cannot say that being a free man means at least this much, then the Thirteenth Amendment made a promise the Nation cannot keep.

Representative Wilson of Iowa was the floor manager in the House for the Civil Rights Act of 1866. In urging that Congress had ample authority to pass the

---

a. The Court did conclude in the Civil Rights Cases that "the act of . . . the owner of the inn, the public conveyance or place of amusement, refusing . . . accommodation" cannot be "justly regarded as imposing any badge of slavery or servitude upon the applicant." "It would be running the slavery argument into the ground," the Court thought, "to make it apply to every act of discrimination which a person may see fit to make as to the guests he will entertain, or as to the people he will take into his coach or cab or car, or admit to his concert or theatre, or deal with in other matters of intercourse or business." Mr. Justice Harlan dissented, expressing the view that "such discrimination practised by corporations and individuals in the exercise of their public or quasi-public functions is a badge of servitude the imposition of which Congress may prevent under its power, by appropriate legislation, to enforce the Thirteenth Amendment." Whatever the present validity of the position taken by the majority on that issue — a question rendered largely academic by Title II of the Civil Rights Act of 1964 (see Heart of Atlanta Motel v. United States; Katzenbach v. McClung) — we note that the entire Court agreed upon at least one proposition: The Thirteenth Amendment authorizes Congress not only to outlaw all forms of slavery and involuntary servitude but also to eradicate the last vestiges and incidents of a society half slave and half free, by securing to all citizens, of every race and color, "the same right to make and enforce contracts, to sue, be parties, give evidence, and to inherit, purchase, lease, sell and convey property, as is enjoyed by white citizens."

pending bill, he recalled the celebrated words of Chief Justice Marshall in *McCulloch v. Maryland*:

> "Let the end be legitimate, let it be within the scope of the constitution, and all means which are appropriate, which are plainly adapted to that end, which are not prohibited, but consist with the letter and spirit of the constitution, are constitutional."

"The end is legitimate," the Congressman said, "because it is defined by the Constitution itself. The end is the maintenance of freedom. . . . A man who enjoys the civil rights mentioned in this bill cannot be reduced to slavery. . . . This settles the appropriateness of this measure, and that settles its constitutionality."
We agree.

In retrospect, *Jones* marks the high tide of judicial recognition of Congress's Reconstruction power. *Jones* was decided in the shadow of the assassination of Dr. Martin Luther King, Jr., and before the election of President Richard Nixon, who waged a campaign that sought to appeal to White southern voters.[45] By 1970, two key members of the Warren Court — Chief Justice Earl Warren himself, and Justice Abe Fortas — were gone, replaced by Nixon appointees Warren Burger and Harry Blackmun, respectively.

OREGON V. MITCHELL, 400 U.S. 112 (1970): A badly splintered Court decided that Congress went too far in attempting to confer voting rights upon young adults. Under the Voting Rights Act Amendments of 1970, Congress sought to ban the denial of suffrage on account of age, to anyone eighteen years or older. The ban applied to both state and federal elections, and was accompanied by an explicit congressional finding that the rule in place in most states, setting the voting cutoff at age 21, "(1) denies and abridges the inherent constitutional rights of citizens eighteen years of age . . . to vote — a particularly unfair treatment of such citizens in view of the national defense responsibilities imposed upon such citizens; (2) has the effect of denying to citizens eighteen years of age . . . the due process and equal protection of laws . . . ; and (3) does not bear a reasonable relationship to any compelling State interest." Five Justices ruled that this law went beyond the Reconstruction powers vested in Congress, but these five failed to coalesce around a single opinion on this key point. Four Justices (Douglas, Brennan, White, and

---

45. Aren't Justice Stewart's expansive views of congressional power in *Jones* in some tension with his votes in earlier cases like *Morgan* and later cases like *Mitchell* and *Rome*? Stewart's *Jones* opinion was criticized in a June 20, 1968 editorial in *The Wall Street Journal*, and the Justice, remarkably, wrote a letter to the editor defending his opinion. In pertinent part, it read as follows:

> The Supreme Court held (1) that this law [ie, section 1982] means what it says, and (2) that Congress had constitutional power to pass it. You say this made the Court a "legislature." What would the Court have been if it had held (1) that the law does not mean what it says, or (2) that Congress did not have power to pass it?

> I add only that Congress, having enacted 42 U.S.C. 1982, remains free to amend it at any time.

> The Wall Street Journal, July 3, 1968, at 6.

For scholarly commentary critical of the Court's statutory exegesis in *Jones*, see Gerhard Casper, *Jones v. Mayer*: Clio, Bemused and Confused Muse, 1968 Sup. Ct. Rev. 89; Earl M. Maltz, Civil Rights, the Constitution, and Congress 1863-1869, at 70-78 (1990).

Marshall) voted to uphold the law in its entirety while four other Justices (Chief Justice Burger, and Justices Harlan, Stewart, and Blackmun) voted to strike down the law as applied to both state and federal elections. In the middle stood Justice Black, who ruled that Congress did have power, under Article I, §4, to give young adults the right to vote in federal elections, but lacked authority, under the Reconstruction Amendments, to mandate this rule for state elections.[46] According to Justice Black, "Above all else, the framers of the Civil War Amendments intended to deny to the States the power to discriminate against persons on account of their race." Distinguishing away the *Katzenbach* cases, Black argued that Congress's efforts to protect young adults were not designed to remedy or prevent racial discrimination. Justice Douglas countered that

> The right to "enforce" granted by §5 of that Amendment is, as noted, parallel with the Necessary and Proper Clause whose reach Chief Justice Marshall described in McCulloch v. Maryland. . . .
>
> Equality of voting by all who are deemed mature enough to vote is certainly consistent "with the letter and spirit of the constitution." . . . [E]lection inequalities created by state laws and based on factors other than race may violate the Equal Protection Clause, as we have held over and over again. The reach of §5 to "enforce" equal protection by eliminating election inequalities would seem quite broad. Certainly there is not a word of limitation in §5 which would restrict its applicability to matters of race alone.

Joined by Justices Marshall and White, Justice Brennan proclaimed that

> We believe there is serious question whether a statute granting the franchise to citizens 21 and over while denying it to those between the ages of 18 and 21 could, in any event, withstand present scrutiny under the Equal Protection Clause. Regardless of the

46. Another section of the Act abolished state durational residency requirements for voting in presidential elections and established uniform standards for registration and absentee balloting, under which persons could register within 30 days of a presidential election. The provisions were prefaced by congressional findings that existing practice

> (1) denies or abridges the inherent constitutional right of citizens to vote for their President and Vice President; (2) denies or abridges the inherent constitutional right of citizens to enjoy their free movement across State lines; (3) denies or abridges the privileges and immunities guaranteed to the citizens of each State under Article IV, section 2, clause 1, of the Constitution; (4) in some instances has the impermissible purpose or effect of denying citizens the right to vote for such officers because of the way they may vote; (5) has the effect of denying to citizens the equality of civil rights and due process and equal protection of the laws that are guaranteed to them under the fourteenth amendment; and (6) does not bear a reasonable relationship to any compelling State interest in the conduct of presidential elections.

The *Mitchell* Court upheld these rules, with only Justice Harlan dissenting. Of particular interest here are the words of Justice Stewart, joined by the Chief Justice and Justice Blackmun:

> Federal action is required if the privilege to change residence is not to be undercut by parochial local sanctions. No State could undertake to guarantee this privilege to its citizens. At most a single State could take steps to resolve that its own laws would not unreasonably discriminate against the newly arrived resident. Even this resolve might not remain firm in the face of discriminations perceived as unfair against those of its own citizens who moved to other States. Thus, the problem could not be wholly solved by a single State, or even by several States, since every State of new residence and every State of prior residence would have a necessary role to play. In the absence of a unanimous interstate compact, the problem could only be solved by Congress. Quite clearly, then, Congress has acted to protect a constitutional privilege that finds its protection in the Federal Government and is national in character.

Compare, in this regard, commerce clause discussions identifying the appropriateness of congressional solutions for truly interstate and federal problems.

answer to this question, however, it is clear to us that proper regard for the special function of Congress in making determinations of legislative fact compels this Court to respect those determinations unless they are contradicted by evidence far stronger than anything that has been adduced in these cases. We would uphold §302 as a valid exercise of congressional power under §5 of the Fourteenth Amendment. . . .

[T]here is no reason for us to decide whether, in a proper case, we would be compelled to hold [the 21 year-old cutoff] a violation of the Equal Protection Clause. For as our decisions have long made clear, the question we face today is not one of judicial power under the Equal Protection Clause. The question is the scope of congressional power under §5 of the Fourteenth Amendment. . . .

As we have often indicated, questions of constitutional power frequently turn in the last analysis on questions of fact. This is particularly the case when an assertion of state power is challenged under the Equal Protection Clause of the Fourteenth Amendment. For although equal protection requires that all persons "under like circumstances and conditions" be treated alike, such a formulation merely raises, but does not answer the question whether a legislative classification has resulted in different treatment of persons who are in fact "under like circumstances and conditions."

Legislatures, as well as courts, are bound by the provisions of the Fourteenth Amendment. When a state legislative classification is subjected to judicial challenge as violating the Equal Protection Clause, it comes before the courts cloaked by the presumption that the legislature has, as it should, acted within constitutional limitations. . . .

But, as we have consistently held, this limitation on judicial review of state legislative classifications is a limitation stemming, not from the Fourteenth Amendment itself, but from the nature of judicial review. It is simply a "salutary principle of judicial decision," one of the "self-imposed restraints intended to protect [the Court] and the state against irresponsible exercise of [the Court's] unappealable power." The nature of the judicial process makes it an inappropriate forum for the determination of complex factual questions of the kind so often involved in constitutional adjudication. Courts, therefore, will overturn a legislative determination of a factual question only if the legislature's finding is so clearly wrong that it may be characterized as "arbitrary," "irrational," or "unreasonable."

Limitations stemming from the nature of the judicial process, however, have no application to Congress. Section 5 of the Fourteenth Amendment provides that "[t]he Congress shall have power to enforce, by appropriate legislation, the provisions of this article." Should Congress, pursuant to that power, undertake an investigation in order to determine whether the factual basis necessary to support a state legislative discrimination actually exists, it need not stop once it determines that some reasonable men could believe the factual basis exists. Section 5 empowers Congress to make its own determination on the matter. See Katzenbach v. Morgan. It should hardly be necessary to add that if the asserted factual basis necessary to support a given state discrimination does not exist, §5 of the Fourteenth Amendment vests Congress with power to remove the discrimination by appropriate means.

The scope of our review in such matters has been established by a long line of consistent decisions. "It is not for the courts to re-examine the validity of these legislative findings and reject them." "[W]here we find that the legislators, in light of the facts and testimony before them, have a rational basis for finding a chosen regulatory scheme necessary . . . our investigation is at an end."[a]

---

a. As we emphasized in Katzenbach v. Morgan, supra, "§5 does not grant Congress power to . . . enact 'statutes so as in effect to dilute equal protection and due process decisions of this Court,'" 384 U.S., at 651 n.10. As indicated above, a decision of this Court striking down a state statute expresses, among other things, our conclusion that the legislative findings upon which the statute is based are so far wrong as to be unreasonable. Unless Congress were to unearth new evidence in its investigation, its identical findings on the identical issue would be no more reasonable than those of the state legislature.

This scheme is consistent with our prior decisions in related areas. The core of dispute over the constitutionality of Title III of the 1970 Amendments is a conflict between state and federal legislative determinations of the factual issues upon which depends decision of a federal constitutional question — the legitimacy, under the Equal Protection Clause, of state discrimination against persons between the ages of 18 and 21. Our cases have repeatedly emphasized that, when state and federal claims come into conflict, the primacy of federal power requires that the federal finding of fact control. The Supremacy Clause requires an identical result when the conflict is one of legislative, not judicial, findings. . . .

In sum, Congress had ample evidence upon which it could have based the conclusion that exclusion of citizens 18 to 21 years of age from the franchise is wholly unnecessary to promote any legitimate interest the States may have in assuring intelligent and responsible voting. If discrimination is unnecessary to promote any legitimate state interest, it is plainly unconstitutional under the Equal Protection Clause, and Congress has ample power to forbid it under §5 of the Fourteenth Amendment.

In an opinion joined by Chief Justice Burger and Justice Blackmun, Justice Stewart argued that

Although it was found necessary to amend the Constitution in order to confer a federal right to vote upon Negroes and upon females, the Government asserts that a federal right to vote can be conferred upon people between 18 and 21 years of age simply by this Act of Congress. Our decision in Katzenbach v. Morgan, it is said, established the power of Congress, under §5 of the Fourteenth Amendment, to nullify state laws requiring voters to be 21 years of age or older if Congress could rationally have concluded that such laws are not supported by a "compelling state interest." In my view, neither the *Morgan* case, nor any other case upon which the Government relies, establishes such congressional power, even assuming that all those cases were rightly decided. . . .

Indeed, none of the opinions filed today suggest that the States have anything but a constitutionally unimpeachable interest in establishing some age qualification as such. Yet to test the power to establish an age qualification by the "compelling interest" standard is really to deny a State any choice at all, because no State could demonstrate a "compelling interest" in drawing the line with respect to age at one point rather than another. Obviously, the power to establish an age qualification must carry with it the power to choose 21 as a reasonable voting age, as the vast majority of the States have done.[a]

Katzenbach v. Morgan does not hold that Congress has the power to determine what are and what are not "compelling state interests" for equal protection purposes. . . . The Court's opinion made clear that Congress could impose on the

a. If the Government is correct in its submission that a particular age requirement must meet the "compelling interest" standard, then, of course, a substantial question would exist whether a 21-year-old voter qualification is constitutional even in the absence of congressional action, as my Brothers point out. Yet it is inconceivable to me that this Court would ever hold that the denial of the vote to those between the ages of 18 and 21 constitutes such an invidious discrimination as to be a denial of the equal protection of the laws. The establishment of an age qualification is not state action aimed at any discrete and insular minority. Cf. United States v. Carolene Products Co., 304 U.S. 144, 152 n.4. Moreover, so long as a State does not set the voting age higher than 21, the reasonableness of its choice is confirmed by the very Fourteenth Amendment upon which the Government relies. Section 2 of that Amendment provides for sanctions when the right to vote "is denied to any of the male inhabitants of such State, *being twenty-one years of age,* and citizens of the United States . . . ." (emphasis added).

States a remedy for the denial of equal protection that elaborated upon the direct command of the Constitution, and that it could override state laws on the ground that they were in fact used as instruments of invidious discrimination even though a court in an individual lawsuit might not have reached that factual conclusion.

But it is necessary to go much further to sustain §302. The state laws that it invalidates do not invidiously discriminate against any discrete and insular minority. Unlike the statute considered in *Morgan*, §302 is valid only if Congress has the power not only to provide the means of eradicating situations that amount to a violation of the Equal Protection Clause, but also to determine as a matter of substantive constitutional law that situations fall within the ambit of the clause, and what state interests are "compelling." . . . I cannot but conclude that §302 was beyond the constitutional power of Congress to enact.

Writing only for himself, Justice Harlan attacked the very idea that the Fourteenth Amendment addressed issues of voting discrimination. Such "political rights" were intended to be untouched by Section 1 of that Amendment, he argued.

The history of the Fourteenth Amendment with respect to suffrage qualifications is remarkably free of the problems which bedevil most attempts to find a reliable guide to present decision in the pages of the past. Instead, there is virtually unanimous agreement, clearly and repeatedly expressed, that §1 of the Amendment did not reach discriminatory voter qualifications. . . .

[T]he very fact that constitutional amendments were deemed necessary to bring about federal abolition of state restrictions on voting by reason of race (Amdt. XV), sex (Amdt. XIX), and, even with respect to federal elections, the failure to pay state poll taxes (Amdt. XXIV), is itself forceful evidence of the common understanding in 1869, 1919, and 1962, respectively, that the Fourteenth Amendment did not empower Congress to legislate in these respects. . . .

As the Court is not justified in substituting its own views of wise policy for the commands of the Constitution, still less is it justified in allowing Congress to disregard those commands as the Court understands them. Although Congress' expression of the view that it does have power to alter state suffrage qualifications is entitled to the most respectful consideration by the judiciary, coming as it does from a coordinate branch of government, this cannot displace the duty of this Court to make an independent determination whether Congress has exceeded its powers. . . .

Arguing that issues concerning the political maturity of young adults implicated not merely facts, but values and visions, Justice Harlan went on to suggest that

Judicial deference is based, not on relative factfinding competence, but on due regard for the decision of the body constitutionally appointed to decide. Establishment of voting qualifications is a matter for state legislatures.

. . . In this area, to rely on Congress would make that body a judge in its own cause. The role of final arbiter belongs to this Court. . . .

The [law can be upheld only if Congress has] power to lower the voting age as a means of preventing invidious discrimination that is within the purview of that clause.

The history of the Fourteenth Amendment may well foreclose the possibility that §5 empowers Congress to enfranchise a class of citizens so that they may protect themselves against discrimination forbidden by the first section, but it is unnecessary for me to explore that question. For I think it fair to say that the suggestion that members of the age group between 18 and 21 are threatened with unconstitutional discrimination, or that any hypothetical discrimination is likely to be affected by lowering the voting age, is little short of fanciful.[47]

Before leaving *Mitchell*, it is worthwhile to note the larger political backdrop against which the case was decided. In 1970, the United States was in the middle of a long, bloody, and highly controversial war in Vietnam, sending hundreds of thousands of young adults to fight far from home. Under these conditions, there was a strong fairness argument that those who were being asked or made to fight and die should be allowed to vote on whether and how the war should continue.[48] Were some of the Justices too quick to dismiss the "fanciful" idea that in 1970, young adults subject to the draft were especially vulnerable to a certain kind of discrimination at the hands of their elders? That, if given the vote, young adults might make a decisive political difference? In the wake of *Mitchell*, Congress proposed, and the states in 1971 ratified, the Twenty-sixth Amendment, whose opening section reads as follows: "The right of citizens of the United States, who are eighteen years of age or older, to vote shall not be denied or abridged by the United States or by any State on account of age." *Mitchell* thus stands as one of only four cases — alongside Chisholm v. Georgia, 2 U.S. (2 Dall.) 419 (1793) (overruled by the Eleventh Amendment); Dred Scott v. Sandford, 60 U.S. (19 How.) 393 (1857) (overruled by the Fourteenth Amendment); and Pollock v. Farmers' Loan & Trust Co., 157 U.S.

47. Note that the logic of Justice Harlan's dissent calls into question not merely Congress's power to cure restrictive state voting rules, but also the Court's power to do the same. Under a long line of cases, epitomized by the one-person, one-vote ruling in Reynolds v. Sims, 377 U.S. 533 (1964), the Court had invoked — and indeed, continues to invoke — the Fourteenth Amendment to strike down all sorts of voting discriminations. Are all these cases wrongly decided? Or merely wrongly labeled, assuming that Harlan's history is correct, and seen as decisive? Might Congress and federal courts have justified their efforts to democratize state voting rules by appealing not to the Fourteenth Amendment, but to the Republican Guarantee Clause of Article IV — whose text and history suggest that it is centrally concerned with the allocation of political rights within states? For a general discussion, see Akhil Reed Amar, The Central Meaning of Republican Government: Popular Sovereignty, Majority Rule, and the Denominator Problem, 65 U. Colo. L. Rev. 749 (1994).

48. Cf. Amar, supra n.47, at 771-772: "[Under classical Republican Theory, roughly] speaking, those who voted equally should be equally armed, and those who bore arms militarily should vote. Over and over, and across the centuries, we can see this Republican Theory inscribed in the text of our Constitution. The Second Amendment's two clauses equated the 'well regulated militia' with 'the People' — the same people who in the Preamble 'ordain[ed] and establish[ed]' this Constitution.' . . . Section Two of the Fourteenth Amendment defined a state's presumptive electorate as 'male inhabitants of [a] State, *being twenty-one years of age*, and citizens' — roughly speaking, the same group that constituted the state's general militia. The Fifteenth Amendment entitled black men to vote long before women of all races became eligible, in part because black men had borne arms for their country and provided the Union the margin of victory. When it became clear that wars had ceased to be highly structured, ritualized competitions between armies of men, but instead pitted entire societies and economies against each other, women won the vote under the Nineteenth Amendment. Indeed, Woodrow Wilson and other politicians explicitly endorsed women's suffrage in recognition of women's role as economic soldiers in the war effort against Germany. And more recently, the Twenty-Sixth Amendment extended the vote to young adults on the theory that if they were old enough to bear arms in Vietnam, they were old enough to vote on the wisdom of that war, and on all else.

"The same Republican linkage emerges if we focus on the Constitution as an act — as an embodied ordaining and establishing — rather than as a mere text. In various states, it appears that militiamen who had borne arms for the Revolution were part of 'the People' who elected delegates to specially-called ratifying conventions, regardless of whether these militiamen met the property qualifications for voting for ordinary state legislatures." For more discussion of these linkages, see generally Akhil Reed Amar, The Bill of Rights: Creation and Reconstruction 48-49, 216-218, 258 (1998).

429, modified on rehearing, 158 U.S. 601 (1895) (overruled by the Sixteenth Amendment) — to be overruled by an explicit constitutional amendment.

B.   The Rehnquist Court: Finding Limits on Federal Power

Oregon v. Mitchell was the only authoritative Supreme Court case from 1937 to 1987 to hold an act of Congress unconstitutional based on a lack of enumerated power (as opposed to a claim of individual right, under the Bill of Rights or elsewhere). And *Mitchell* itself, as we have seen, hardly spoke with clarity — lacking a majority opinion, featuring strong objections from four Justices, and pivoting in part on Justice Harlan's sweeping theory concerning the inapplicability of the Fourteenth Amendment to voting (a theory that all other Justices rejected, and that broke sharply with precedent, see supra n.47).

In 1987, Justice William Rehnquist became Chief Justice William Rehnquist, per the nomination of President Ronald Reagan and the confirmation of the Senate. Both the President[49] and the new Chief shared a belief in the importance

49. Recall that Reagan was a state governor for eight years. In his First Inaugural Address, he declared: "It is my intention to curb the size and influence of the Federal establishment and to demand recognition of the distinction between the powers granted to the Federal Government and those reserved to the States or to the people. All of us need to be reminded that the Federal Government did not create the States; the States created the Federal Government." In 1987, President Reagan issued Executive Order No. 12,612, 3 C.F.R. 252 (1987):

Sec. 2. Fundamental Federalism Principles. In formulating and implementing policies that have federalism implications, Executive departments and agencies shall be guided by the following fundamental federalism principles

(a) Federalism is rooted in the knowledge that our political liberties are best assured by limiting the size and scope of the national government.

(b) The people of the States created the national government when they delegated to it those enumerated governmental powers relating to matters beyond the competence of the individual States. All other sovereign powers, save those expressly prohibited the States by the Constitution, are reserved to the States or to the people.

(c) The constitutional relationship among sovereign governments, State and national, is formalized in and protected by the Tenth Amendment to the Constitution.

(d) The people of the States are free, subject only to restrictions in the Constitution itself or in constitutionally authorized Acts of Congress, to define the moral, political, and legal character of their lives.

(e) In most areas of governmental concern, the States uniquely possess the constitutional authority, the resources, and the competence to discern the sentiments of the people and to govern accordingly. In Thomas Jefferson's words, the States are "the most competent administrations for our domestic concerns and the surest bulwarks against antirepublican tendencies."

(f) The nature of our constitutional system encourages a healthy diversity in the public policies adopted by the people of the several States according to their own conditions, needs, and desires. In the search for enlightened public policy, individual States and communities are free to experiment with a variety of approaches to public issues.

(g) Acts of the national government — whether legislative, executive, or judicial in nature — that exceed the enumerated powers of that government under the Constitution violate the principle of federalism established by the Framers.

(h) Policies of the national government should recognize the responsibility of — and should encourage opportunities for — individuals, families, neighborhoods, local governments, and private associations to achieve their personal, social, and economic objectives through cooperative effort.

(i) In the absence of clear constitutional or statutory authority, the presumption of sovereignty should rest with the individual States. Uncertainties regarding the legitimate authority of the national government should be resolved against regulation at the national level.

For the subsequent fate of this order under the Clinton Administration, see Exec. Order No. 13,083, 3 C.F.R. 146 (1998); Exec. Order No. 13,095, 3 C.F.R. 202 (1998).

of state governments in a federal system — a belief also shared by several other Justices appointed by President Reagan and his successor, George Bush. But can this belief in the importance of state governments and insistence that the federal government remain a government of *limited* powers be translated into workable judicial doctrine? If so, how? Keep these questions in mind as you confront the major Rehnquist Court cases on federalism and enumerated power, discussed next.

1. The Commerce Power

UNITED STATES v. LOPEZ
514 U.S. 549 (1995)

[After respondent, then a 12th-grade student, carried a concealed handgun into his high school, he was charged with violating the Gun-Free School Zones Act of 1990, which forbids "any individual knowingly to possess a firearm at a place that [he] knows . . . is a school zone," 18 U.S.C. §922(q)(1)(A). He challenged the Act as beyond the scope of congressional power under the Commerce Clause.]

REHNQUIST, C.J. . . .
We start with first principles. The Constitution creates a Federal Government of enumerated powers. See Art. I, §8. As James Madison wrote, "the powers delegated by the proposed Constitution to the federal government are few and defined. Those which are to remain in the State governments are numerous and indefinite." The Federalist No. 45. This constitutionally mandated division of authority "was adopted by the Framers to ensure protection of our fundamental liberties." Gregory v. Ashcroft, 501 U.S. 452, 458 (1991). "Just as the separation and independence of the coordinate branches of the Federal Government serve to prevent the accumulation of excessive power in any one branch, a healthy balance of power between the States and the Federal Government will reduce the risk of tyranny and abuse from either front." . . .

[Prior to the New Deal, the Court held] that certain categories of activity such as "production," "manufacturing," and "mining" were within the province of state governments, and thus were beyond the power of Congress under the Commerce Clause. . . .

Jones & Laughlin Steel, Darby, and *Wickard* ushered in an era of Commerce Clause jurisprudence that greatly expanded the previously defined authority of Congress under that Clause. In part, this was a recognition of the great changes that had occurred in the way business was carried on in this country. Enterprises that had once been local or at most regional in nature had become national in scope. But the doctrinal change also reflected a view that earlier Commerce Clause cases artificially had constrained the authority of Congress to regulate interstate commerce.

But even these modern-era precedents which have expanded congressional power under the Commerce Clause confirm that this power is subject to outer limits. . . .

[W]e have identified three broad categories of activity that Congress may regulate under its commerce power. First, Congress may regulate the use of the channels of interstate commerce. See, e.g., *Darby; Heart of Atlanta Motel.* Second,

Congress is empowered to regulate and protect the instrumentalities of interstate commerce, or persons or things in interstate commerce, even though the threat may come only from intrastate activities. Finally, Congress' commerce authority includes the power to regulate those activities having a substantial relation to interstate commerce, *Jones & Laughlin Steel,* i.e., those activities that substantially affect interstate commerce.

Within this final category, admittedly, our case law has not been clear whether an activity must "affect" or "substantially affect" interstate commerce in order to be within Congress's power to regulate it under the Commerce Clause. We conclude, consistent with the great weight of our case law, that the proper test requires an analysis of whether the regulated activity "substantially affects" interstate commerce.

We now turn to consider the power of Congress, in the light of this framework, to enact §922(q). The first two categories of authority may be quickly disposed of: §922(q) is not a regulation of the use of the channels of interstate commerce, nor is it an attempt to prohibit the interstate transportation of a commodity through the channels of commerce; nor can §922(q) be justified as a regulation by which Congress has sought to protect an instrumentality of interstate commerce or a thing in interstate commerce. Thus, if §922(q) is to be sustained, it must be under the third category as a regulation of an activity that substantially affects interstate commerce. First, we have upheld a wide variety of congressional Acts regulating intrastate economic activity where we have concluded that the activity substantially affected interstate commerce. Examples include the regulation of intrastate coal mining, intrastate extortionate credit transactions, *Perez,* restaurants utilizing substantial interstate supplies, *McClung,* inns and hotels catering to interstate guests, *Heart of Atlanta Motel,* and production and consumption of homegrown wheat, *Wickard.* These examples are by no means exhaustive, but the pattern is clear. Where economic activity substantially affects interstate commerce, legislation regulating that activity will be sustained.

Even *Wickard,* which is perhaps the most far reaching example of Commerce Clause authority over intrastate activity, involved economic activity in a way that the possession of a gun in a school zone does not. . . .

Section 922(q) is a criminal statute that by its terms has nothing to do with "commerce" or any sort of economic enterprise, however broadly one might define those terms.[a] Section 922(q) is not an essential part of a larger regulation of economic activity, in which the regulatory scheme could be undercut unless the intrastate activity were regulated. It cannot, therefore, be sustained under our cases upholding regulations of activities that arise out of or are connected with a commercial transaction, which viewed in the aggregate, substantially affects interstate commerce.

Second, §922(q) contains no jurisdictional element which would ensure, through case-by-case inquiry, that the firearm possession in question affects interstate commerce. . . . Although as part of our independent evaluation of

---

a. Under our federal system, the "'States possess primary authority for defining and enforcing the criminal law.'" When Congress criminalizes conduct already denounced as criminal by the States, it effects a "'change in the sensitive relation between federal and state criminal jurisdiction.'" . . . [S]ee also Statement of President George Bush on Signing the Crime Control Act of 1990, 26 Weekly Comp. of Pres. Doc. 1944, 1945 (Nov. 29, 1990) ("Most egregiously, section [922(q)] inappropriately overrides legitimate State firearms laws with a new and unnecessary Federal law. The policies reflected in these provisions could legitimately be adopted by the States, but they should not be imposed upon the States by the Congress").

constitutionality under the Commerce Clause we of course consider legislative findings, and indeed even congressional committee findings, regarding effect on interstate commerce, the Government concedes that "neither the statute nor its legislative history contain[s] express congressional findings regarding the effects upon interstate commerce of gun possession in a school zone." We agree with the Government that Congress normally is not required to make formal findings as to the substantial burdens that an activity has on interstate commerce. But to the extent that congressional findings would enable us to evaluate the legislative judgment that the activity in question substantially affected interstate commerce, even though no such substantial effect was visible to the naked eye, they are lacking here. . . .

The Government's essential contention, in fine, is that we may determine here that §922(q) is valid because possession of a firearm in a local school zone does indeed substantially affect interstate commerce. The Government argues that possession of a firearm in a school zone may result in violent crime and that violent crime can be expected to affect the functioning of the national economy in two ways. First, the costs of violent crime are substantial, and, through the mechanism of insurance, those costs are spread throughout the population. Second, violent crime reduces the willingness of individuals to travel to areas within the country that are perceived to be unsafe. Cf. *Heart of Atlanta Motel.* The Government also argues that the presence of guns in schools poses a substantial threat to the educational process by threatening the learning environment. A handicapped educational process, in turn, will result in a less productive citizenry. That, in turn, would have an adverse effect on the Nation's economic well-being. As a result, the Government argues that Congress could rationally have concluded that §922(q) substantially affects interstate commerce.

We pause to consider the implications of the Government's arguments. The Government admits, under its "costs of crime" reasoning, that Congress could regulate not only all violent crime, but all activities that might lead to violent crime, regardless of how tenuously they relate to interstate commerce. Similarly, under the Government's "national productivity" reasoning, Congress could regulate any activity that it found was related to the economic productivity of individual citizens: family law (including marriage, divorce, and child custody), for example. Under the theories that the Government presents in support of §922(q), it is difficult to perceive any limitation on federal power, even in areas such as criminal law enforcement or education where States historically have been sovereign. Thus, if we were to accept the Government's arguments, we are hard pressed to posit any activity by an individual that Congress is without power to regulate.

Although Justice Breyer argues that acceptance of the Government's rationales would not authorize a general federal police power, he is unable to identify any activity that the States may regulate but Congress may not. . . .

Justice Breyer focuses, for the most part, on the threat that firearm possession in and near schools poses to the educational process and the potential economic consequences flowing from that threat. Specifically, the dissent reasons that (1) gun-related violence is a serious problem; (2) that problem, in turn, has an adverse effect on classroom learning; and (3) that adverse effect on classroom learning, in turn, represents a substantial threat to trade and commerce. This analysiswould be equally applicable, if not more so, to subjects such as family law and direct regulation of education.

604 Chapter 5. Economic Regulation, Federalism, and Separation of Powers

For instance, if Congress can, pursuant to its Commerce Clause power, regulate activities that adversely affect the learning environment, then, a fortiori, it also can regulate the educational process directly. Congress could determine that a school's curriculum has a "significant" effect on the extent of classroom learning. As a result, Congress could mandate a federal curriculum for local elementary and secondary schools because what is taught in local schools has a significant "effect on classroom learning," and that, in turn, has a substantial effect on interstate commerce.

Justice Breyer rejects our reading of precedent and argues that "Congress . . . could rationally conclude that schools fall on the commercial side of the line." Again, Justice Breyer's rationale lacks any real limits because, depending on the level of generality, any activity can be looked upon as commercial. Under the dissent's rationale, Congress could just as easily look at child rearing as "falling on the commercial side of the line" because it provides a "valuable service — namely, to equip [children] with the skills they need to survive in life and, more specifically, in the workplace." We do not doubt that Congress has authority under the Commerce Clause to regulate numerous commercial activities that substantially affect interstate commerce and also affect the educational process. That authority, though broad, does not include the authority to regulate each and every aspect of local schools. . . .

These are not precise formulations, and in the nature of things they cannot be. But we think they point the way to a correct decision of this case. The possession of a gun in a local school zone is in no sense an economic activity that might, through repetition elsewhere, substantially affect any sort of interstate commerce. Respondent was a local student at a local school; there is no indication that he had recently moved in interstate commerce, and there is no requirement that his possession of the firearm have any concrete tie to interstate commerce.

To uphold the Government's contentions here, we would have to pile inference upon inference in a manner that would bid fair to convert congressional authority under the Commerce Clause to a general police power of the sort retained by the States. Admittedly, some of our prior cases have taken long steps down that road, giving great deference to congressional action. The broad language in these opinions has suggested the possibility of additional expansion, but we decline here to proceed any further. To do so would require us to conclude that the Constitution's enumeration of powers does not presuppose something not enumerated, and that there never will be a distinction between what is truly national and what is truly local, cf. *Jones & Laughlin Steel.* This we are unwilling to do.

Justice KENNEDY, with whom Justice O'Connor joins, concurring.

The history of the judicial struggle to interpret the Commerce Clause during the transition from the economic system the Founders knew to the single, national market still emergent in our own era counsels great restraint before the Court determines that the Clause is insufficient to support an exercise of the national power. That history gives me some pause about today's decision, but I join the Court's opinion with these observations on what I conceive to be its necessary though limited holding. . . .

The case that seems to mark the Court's definitive commitment to the practical conception of the commerce power is NLRB v. Jones & Laughlin Steel Corp., where the Court sustained labor laws that applied to manufacturing facilities, making no real attempt to distinguish *Carter* and *Schechter.* The deference given to Congress has since been confirmed. United States v. Darby overruled Hammer v. Dagenhart. And in Wickard v. Filburn, the Court disapproved *E.C. Knight* and the entire line of direct-indirect and manufacture-production cases, explaining that "broader interpretations of the Commerce Clause [were] destined to supersede the earlier ones," and "whatever terminology is used, the criterion is necessarily one of degree and must be so defined. This does not satisfy those who seek mathematical or rigid formulas. But such formulas are not provided by the great concepts of the Constitution." Later examples of the exercise of federal power where commercial transactions were the subject of regulation include Heart of Atlanta Motel, Inc. v. United States, Katzenbach v. McClung, and Perez v. United States. These and like authorities are within the fair ambit of the Court's practical conception of commercial regulation and are not called in question by our decision today.

. . . [T]he Court as an institution and the legal system as a whole have an immense stake in the stability of our Commerce Clause jurisprudence as it has evolved to this point. Stare decisis operates with great force in counseling us not to call in question the essential principles now in place respecting the congressional power to regulate transactions of a commercial nature. That fundamental restraint on our power forecloses us from reverting to an understanding of commerce that would serve only an 18th-century economy, dependent then upon production and trading practices that had changed but little over the preceding centuries; it also mandates against returning to the time when congressional authority to regulate undoubted commercial activities was limited by a judicial determination that those matters had an insufficient connection to an interstate system. Congress can regulate in the commercial sphere on the assumption that we have a single market and a unified purpose to build a stable national economy.

. . . It does not follow, however, that in every instance the Court lacks the authority and responsibility to review congressional attempts to alter the federal balance. This case requires us to consider our place in the design of the Government and to appreciate the significance of federalism in the whole structure of the Constitution.

Of the various structural elements in the Constitution, separation of powers, checks and balances, judicial review, and federalism, only concerning the last does there seem to be much uncertainty respecting the existence, and the content, of standards that allow the Judiciary to play a significant role in maintaining the design contemplated by the Framers. Although the resolution of specific cases has proved difficult, we have derived from the Constitution workable standards to assist in preserving separation of powers and checks and balances. These standards are by now well accepted. Judicial review is also established beyond question, and though we may differ when applying its principles, its legitimacy is undoubted. Our role in preserving the federal balance seems more tenuous.

There is irony in this, because of the four structural elements in the Constitution just mentioned, federalism was the unique contribution of the Framers to political science and political theory. See Friendly, Federalism: A Foreword, 86 Yale L.J. 1019 (1977); G. Wood, The Creation of the American Republic, 1776-1787, pp. 524-532, 564 (1969). Though on the surface the idea may seem counter-intuitive, it was the insight of the Framers that freedom was enhanced by the creation of two governments, not one. "In the compound republic of America, the power surrendered by the people is first divided between two distinct governments, and then the portion allotted to each subdivided among distinct and separate departments. Hence a double security arises to the rights of the people. The different governments will control each other, at the same time that each will be controlled by itself." The Federalist No. 51. See also Gregory v. Ashcroft, 501 U.S. 452, 458-459 (1991) ("Just as the separation and independence of the coordinate branches of the Federal Government serve to prevent the accumulation of excessive power in any one branch, a healthy balance of power between the States and the Federal Government will reduce the risk of tyranny and abuse from either front. . . . In the tension between federal and state power lies the promise of liberty"); New York v. United States, at 181 ("The Constitution divides authority between federal and state governments for the protection of individuals. State sovereignty is not just an end in itself: 'Rather, federalism secures to citizens the liberties that derive from the diffusion of sovereign power'").

The theory that two governments accord more liberty than one requires for its realization two distinct and discernable lines of political accountability: one between the citizens and the Federal Government; the second between the citizens and the States. If, as Madison expected, the Federal and State Governments are to control each other, see The Federalist No. 51, and hold each other in check by competing for the affections of the people, see The Federalist No. 46, those citizens must have some means of knowing which of the two governments to hold accountable for the failure to perform a given function. "Federalism serves to assign political responsibility, not to obscure it." Were the Federal Government to take over the regulation of entire areas of traditional state concern, areas having nothing to do with the regulation of commercial activities, the boundaries between the spheres of federal and state authority would blur and political responsibility would become illusory. Cf. New York v. United States. . . .

To be sure, one conclusion that could be drawn from The Federalist Papers is that the balance between national and state power is entrusted in its entirety to the political process. Madison's observation that "the people ought not surely to be precluded from giving most of their confidence where they may discover it to be most due," The Federalist No. 46, can be interpreted to say that the essence of responsibility for a shift in power from the State to the Federal Government rests upon a political judgment, though he added assurance that "the State governments could have little to apprehend, because it is only within a certain sphere that the federal power can, in the nature of things, be advantageously administered." Whatever the judicial role, it is axiomatic that Congress does have substantial discretion and control over the federal balance.

For these reasons, it would be mistaken and mischievous for the political branches to forget that the sworn obligation to preserve and protect the Constitution in maintaining the federal balance is their own in the first and primary instance. In the Webster-Hayne Debates, and the debates over the Civil Rights Acts, some Congresses have accepted responsibility to confront the great questions of the proper federal balance in terms of lasting consequences for the constitutional design. The political branches of the Government must fulfill this grave constitutional obligation if democratic liberty and the federalism that secures it are to endure.

At the same time, the absence of structural mechanisms to require those officials to undertake this principled task, and the momentary political convenience often attendant upon their failure to do so, argue against a complete renunciation of the judicial role. . . .

Our position in enforcing the dormant Commerce Clause is instructive. The Court's doctrinal approach in that area has likewise "taken some turns." . . . True, if we invalidate a state law, Congress can in effect overturn our judgment, whereas in a case announcing that Congress has transgressed its authority, the decision is more consequential, for it stands unless Congress can revise its law to demonstrate its commercial character. This difference no doubt informs the circumspection with which we invalidate an Act of Congress, but it does not mitigate our duty to recognize meaningful limits on the commerce power of Congress. . . .

[I]t is well established that education is a traditional concern of the States. . . . While it is doubtful that any State, or indeed any reasonable person, would argue that it is wise policy to allow students to carry guns on school premises, considerable disagreement exists about how best to accomplish that goal. In this circumstance, the theory and utility of our federalism are revealed, for the States may perform their role as laboratories for experimentation to devise various solutions where the best solution is far from clear.

If a State or municipality determines that harsh criminal sanctions are necessary and wise to deter students from carrying guns on school premises, the reserved powers of the States are sufficient to enact those measures. Indeed, over 40 States already have criminal laws outlawing the possession of firearms on or near school grounds.

Other, more practicable means to rid the schools of guns may be thought by the citizens of some States to be preferable for the safety and welfare of the schools those States are charged with maintaining. These might include inducements to inform on violators where the information leads to arrests or confiscation of the guns; programs to encourage the voluntary surrender of guns with some provision for amnesty; penalties imposed on parents or guardians for failure to supervise the child; laws providing for suspension or expulsion of gun-toting students, or programs for expulsion with assignment to special facilities.

The statute now before us forecloses the States from experimenting and exercising their own judgment in an area to which States lay claim by right of history and expertise, and it does so by regulating an activity beyond the realm of commerce in the ordinary and usual sense of that term. The tendency of this statute to displace state regulation in areas of traditional state concern is evident from its territorial operation. There are over 100,000 elementary and secondary schools in the United States. Each of these now has an invisible federal zone extending 1,000 feet beyond the (often irregular) boundaries of the school property. In some communities no doubt it would be difficult to navigate without infringing on those zones. Yet throughout these areas, school officials would find their own programs for the prohibition of guns in danger of displacement by the federal authority unless the State chooses to enact a parallel rule.

. . . Absent a stronger connection or identification with commercial concerns that are central to the Commerce Clause, that interference contradicts the federal balance the Framers designed and that this Court is obliged to enforce.

Justice THOMAS, concurring. . . .

Although I join the majority, I write separately to observe that our case law has drifted far from the original understanding of the Commerce Clause. In a future case, we ought to temper our Commerce Clause jurisprudence in a manner that both makes sense of our more recent case law and is more faithful to the original understanding of that Clause. . . .

I.

At the time the original Constitution was ratified, "commerce" consisted of selling, buying, and bartering, as well as transporting for these purposes. See 1 S. Johnson, A Dictionary of the English Language 361 (4th ed. 1773) (defining commerce as "Intercour[s]e; exchange of one thing for another; interchange of any thing; trade; traffick"); N. Bailey, An Universal Etymological English Dictionary (26th ed. 1789) ("trade or traffic"); T. Sheridan, A Complete Dictionary of the English Language (6th ed. 1796) ("Exchange of one thing for another; trade, traffick"). This understanding finds support in the etymology of the word, which literally means "with merchandise." See 3 Oxford English Dictionary 552 (2d ed. 1989) (com — "with"; merci — "merchandise"). In fact, when Federalists and Anti-Federalists discussed the Commerce Clause during the ratification period, they often used trade (in its selling/bartering sense) and commerce interchangeably. See The Federalist No. 4 (J. Jay) (asserting that countries will cultivate our friendship when our "trade" is prudently regulated by Federal Government); id., No. 7 (A. Hamilton) (discussing "competitions of commerce" between States resulting from state "regulations of trade"); id., No. 40 (J. Madison) (asserting that it was an "acknowledged object of the Convention . . . that the regulation of trade should be submitted to the general government"); Lee, Letters of a Federal Farmer No. 5, in Pamphlets on the Constitution of the United States 319 (P. Ford ed. 1888); Smith, An Address to the People of the State of New York, in id., at 107.

As one would expect, the term "commerce" was used in contradistinction to productive activities such as manufacturing and agriculture. Alexander Hamilton, for example, repeatedly treated commerce, agriculture, and manufacturing as three separate endeavors. See, e.g., The Federalist No. 36 (referring to "agriculture, commerce, manufactures"); id., No. 21 (distinguishing commerce, arts, and industry); id., No. 12 (asserting that commerce and agriculture have shared interests). The same distinctions were made in the state ratification conventions. See, e.g., 2 Debates in the Several State Conventions on the Adoption of the Federal Constitution 57 (J. Elliot ed. 1836) (T. Dawes at Massachusetts convention); id., at 336 (M. Smith at New York convention).

Moreover, interjecting a modern sense of commerce into the Constitution generates significant textual and structural problems. For example, one cannot replace "commerce" with a different type of enterprise, such as manufacturing. When a manufacturer produces a car, assembly cannot take place "with a foreign nation" or "with the Indian Tribes." Parts may come from different States or other nations and hence may have been in the flow of commerce at one time, but manufacturing takes place at a discrete site. Agriculture and manufacturing involve the production of goods; commerce encompasses traffic in such articles.

The Port Preference Clause also suggests that the term "commerce" denoted sale and/or transport rather than business generally. According to that Clause, "no Preference shall be given by any Regulation of Commerce or Revenue to the Ports of one State over those of another." U.S. Const., Art. I, §9, cl. 6. Although it is possible to conceive of regulations of manufacturing or farming that prefer one port over another, the more natural reading is that the Clause prohibits Congress from using its commerce power to channel commerce through certain favored ports.

The Constitution not only uses the word "commerce" in a narrower sense than our case law might suggest, it also does not support the proposition that Congress has authority over all activities that "substantially affect" interstate commerce. The

Commerce Clause does not state that Congress may "regulate matters that substantially affect commerce with foreign Nations, and among the several States, and with the Indian Tribes." In contrast, the Constitution itself temporarily prohibited amendments that would "affect" Congress' lack of authority to prohibit or restrict the slave trade or to enact unproportioned direct taxation. Art. V. Clearly, the Framers could have drafted a Constitution that contained a "substantially affects interstate commerce" Clause had that been their objective.

In addition to its powers under the Commerce Clause, Congress has the authority to enact such laws as are "necessary and proper" to carry into execution its power to regulate commerce among the several States. U.S. Const., Art. I, §8, cl. 18. But on this Court's understanding of congressional power under these two Clauses, many of Congress' other enumerated powers under Art. I, §8, are wholly superfluous. After all, if Congress may regulate all matters that substantially affect commerce, there is no need for the Constitution to specify that Congress may enact bankruptcy laws, cl. 4, or coin money and fix the standard of weights and measures, cl. 5, or punish counterfeiters of United States coin and securities, cl. 6. Likewise, Congress would not need the separate authority to establish post offices and post roads, cl. 7, or to grant patents and copyrights, cl. 8, or to "punish Piracies and Felonies committed on the high Seas," cl. 10. It might not even need the power to raise and support an Army and Navy, cls. 12 and 13, for fewer people would engage in commercial shipping if they thought that a foreign power could expropriate their property with ease. Indeed, if Congress could regulate matters that substantially affect interstate commerce, there would have been no need to specify that Congress can regulate international trade and commerce with the Indians. As the Framers surely understood, these other branches of trade substantially affect interstate commerce.

Put simply, much if not all of Art. I, §8 (including portions of the Commerce Clause itself), would be surplusage if Congress had been given authority over matters that substantially affect interstate commerce. An interpretation of cl. 3 that makes the rest of §8 superfluous simply cannot be correct. Yet this Court's Commerce Clause jurisprudence has endorsed just such an interpretation: The power we have accorded Congress has swallowed Art. I, §8.[a] . . .

Our construction of the scope of congressional authority has the additional problem of coming close to turning the Tenth Amendment on its head. Our case law could be read to reserve to the United States all powers not expressly prohibited by the Constitution. Taken together, these fundamental textual problems should, at the very least, convince us that the "substantial effects" test should be reexamined. . . .

III.

B

I am aware of no cases prior to the New Deal that characterized the power flowing from the Commerce Clause as sweepingly as does our substantial effects

---

a. There are other powers granted to Congress outside of Art. I, §8, that may become wholly superfluous as well due to our distortion of the Commerce Clause. For instance, Congress has plenary power over the District of Columbia and the territories. See U.S. Const., Art. I, §8, cl. 17, and Art. IV, §3, cl. 2. The grant of comprehensive legislative power over certain areas of the Nation, when read in conjunction with the rest of the Constitution, further confirms that Congress was not ceded plenary authority over the whole Nation.

test. My review of the case law indicates that the substantial effects test is but an innovation of the 20th century. . . .

These cases all establish a simple point: From the time of the ratification of the Constitution to the mid-1930s, it was widely understood that the Constitution granted Congress only limited powers, notwithstanding the Commerce Clause. Moreover, there was no question that activities wholly separated from business, such as gun possession, were beyond the reach of the commerce power. If anything, the "wrong turn" was the Court's dramatic departure in the 1930s from a century and a half of precedent. . . .

V.

This extended discussion of the original understanding and our first century and a half of case law does not necessarily require a wholesale abandonment of our more recent opinions.[b] It simply reveals that our substantial effects test is far removed from both the Constitution and from our early case law and that the Court's opinion should not be viewed as "radical" or another "wrong turn" that must be corrected in the future. The analysis also suggests that we ought to temper our Commerce Clause jurisprudence. . . .

At an appropriate juncture, I think we must modify our Commerce Clause jurisprudence. Today, it is easy enough to say that the Clause certainly does not empower Congress to ban gun possession within 1,000 feet of a school.

Justice STEVENS, dissenting.

The welfare of our future "Commerce with foreign Nations," and among the several States," U.S. Const., Art. I, §8, cl. 3, is vitally dependent on the character of the education of our children. I therefore agree entirely with Justice Breyer's explanation of why Congress has ample power to prohibit the possession of firearms in or near schools — just as it may protect the school environment from harms posed by controlled substances such as asbestos or alcohol. I also agree with Justice Souter's exposition of the radical character of the Court's holding and its kinship with the discredited, pre-Depression version of substantive due process. Cf. Dolan v. City of Tigard, 512 U.S. 374, 405-411 (1994) (Stevens, J., dissenting). I believe, however, that the Court's extraordinary decision merits this additional comment.

Guns are both articles of commerce and articles that can be used to restrain commerce. Their possession is the consequence, either directly or indirectly, of commercial activity. In my judgment, Congress' power to regulate commerce in firearms includes the power to prohibit possession of guns at any location because of their potentially harmful use; it necessarily follows that Congress may also prohibit their possession in particular markets. The market for the possession of handguns by school-age children is, distressingly, substantial. Whether or not the national interest in eliminating that market would have justified federal legislation in 1789, it surely does today.

---

b. Although I might be willing to return to the original understanding, I recognize that many believe that it is too late in the day to undertake a fundamental reexamination of the past 60 years. Consideration of stare decisis and reliance interests may convince us that we cannot wipe the slate clean.

Justice SOUTER, dissenting.

In reviewing congressional legislation under the Commerce Clause, we defer to what is often a merely implicit congressional judgment that its regulation addresses a subject substantially affecting interstate commerce "if there is any rational basis for such a finding." . . . The practice of deferring to rationally based legislative judgments "is a paradigm of judicial restraint." In judicial review under the Commerce Clause, it reflects our respect for the institutional competence of the Congress on a subject expressly assigned to it by the Constitution and our appreciation of the legitimacy that comes from Congress's political accountability in dealing with matters open to a wide range of possible choices.

It was not ever thus, however, as even a brief overview of Commerce Clause history during the past century reminds us. The modern respect for the competence and primacy of Congress in matters affecting commerce developed only after one of this Court's most chastening experiences, when it perforce repudiated an earlier and untenably expansive conception of judicial review in derogation of congressional commerce power. A look at history's sequence will serve to show how today's decision tugs the Court off course, leading it to suggest opportunities for further developments that would be at odds with the rule of restraint to which the Court still wisely states adherence.

I.

Notwithstanding the Court's recognition of a broad commerce power in Gibbons v. Ogden, Congress saw few occasions to exercise that power prior to Reconstruction, and it was really the passage of the Interstate Commerce Act of 1887 that opened a new age of congressional reliance on the Commerce Clause for authority to exercise general police powers at the national level. Although the Court upheld a fair amount of the ensuing legislation as being within the commerce power, the period from the turn of the century to 1937 is better noted for a series of cases applying highly formalistic notions of "commerce" to invalidate federal social and economic legislation, see, e.g., Carter v. Carter Coal Co. (striking Act prohibiting unfair labor practices in coal industry as regulation of "mining" and "production," not "commerce"); A.L.A. Schechter Poultry Corp. v. United States (striking congressional regulation of activities affecting interstate commerce only "indirectly"); Hammer v. Dagenhart (striking Act prohibiting shipment in interstate commerce of goods manufactured at factories using child labor because the Act regulated "manufacturing," not "commerce"); Adair v. United States (striking protection of labor union membership as outside "commerce").

These restrictive views of commerce subject to congressional power complemented the Court's activism in limiting the enforceable scope of state economic regulation. It is most familiar history that during this same period the Court routinely invalidated state social and economic legislation under an expansive conception of Fourteenth Amendment substantive due process. See, e.g., Lochner v. New York (striking state law establishing maximum working hours for bakers). The fulcrums of judicial review in these cases were the notions of liberty and property characteristic of laissez-faire economics, whereas the Commerce Clause cases turned on what was ostensibly a structural limit of federal power, but under each conception of judicial review the Court's character for the first third of the century showed itself in exacting judicial scrutiny of a legislature's choice of economic ends and of the legislative means selected to reach them.

It was not merely coincidental, then, that sea changes in the Court's conceptions of its authority under the Due Process and Commerce Clauses occurred virtually together, in 1937, with West Coast Hotel Co. v. Parrish, and NLRB v. Jones & Laughlin Steel Corp. In *West Coast Hotel,* the Court's rejection of a due process challenge to a state law fixing minimum wages for women and children marked the abandonment of its expansive protection of contractual freedom. Two weeks later, *Jones & Laughlin* affirmed congressional commerce power to authorize NLRB injunctions against unfair labor practices. The Court's finding that the regulated activity had a direct enough effect on commerce has since been seen as beginning the abandonment, for practical purposes, of the formalistic distinction between direct and indirect effects.

In the years following these decisions, deference to legislative policy judgments on commercial regulation became the powerful theme under both the Due Process and Commerce Clauses, see United States v. Carolene Products Co.; United States v. Darby, and in due course that deference became articulate in the standard of rationality review. In due process litigation, the Court's statement of a rational basis test came quickly. See United States v. Carolene Products Co.; see also Williamson v. Lee Optical Co. The parallel formulation of the Commerce Clause test came later, only because complete elimination of the direct/indirect effects dichotomy and acceptance of the cumulative effects doctrine, Wickard v. Filburn, so far settled the pressing issues of congressional power over commerce as to leave the Court for years without any need to phrase a test explicitly deferring to rational legislative judgments. The moment came, however, with the challenge to congressional Commerce Clause authority to prohibit racial discrimination in places of public accommodation, when the Court simply made explicit what the earlier cases had implied: "where we find that the legislators, in light of the facts and testimony before them, have a rational basis for finding a chosen regulatory scheme necessary to the protection of commerce, our investigation is at an end." Katzenbach v. McClung; see Heart of Atlanta Motel, Inc. v. United States. Thus, under commerce, as under due process, adoption of rational basis review expressed the recognition that the Court had no sustainable basis for subjecting economic regulation as such to judicial policy judgments, and for the past half century the Court has no more turned back in the direction of formalistic Commerce Clause review (as in deciding whether regulation of commerce was sufficiently direct) than it has inclined toward reasserting the substantive authority of *Lochner* due process (as in the inflated protection of contractual autonomy).

II.

There is today, however, a backward glance at both the old pitfalls, as the Court treats deference under the rationality rule as subject to gradation according to the commercial or noncommercial nature of the immediate subject of the challenged regulation. The distinction between what is patently commercial and what is not looks much like the old distinction between what directly affects commerce and what touches it only indirectly. And the act of calibrating the level of deference by drawing a line between what is patently commercial and what is less purely so will probably resemble the process of deciding how much interference with contractual freedom was fatal. Thus, it seems fair to ask whether the step taken by the Court today does anything but portend a return to the untenable jurisprudence from which the Court extricated itself almost 60 years ago. The answer is not reassuring. . . .

A

The Court observes that the Gun-Free School Zones Act operates in two areas traditionally subject to legislation by the States, education and enforcement of criminal law. The suggestion is either that a connection between commerce and these subjects is remote, or that the commerce power is simply weaker when it touches subjects on which the States have historically been the primary legislators. Neither suggestion is tenable. As for remoteness, it may or may not be wise for the National Government to deal with education, but Justice Breyer has surely demonstrated that the commercial prospects of an illiterate State or Nation are not rosy, and no argument should be needed to show that hijacking interstate shipments of cigarettes can affect commerce substantially, even though the States have traditionally prosecuted robbery. And as for the notion that the commerce power diminishes the closer it gets to customary state concerns, that idea has been flatly rejected, and not long ago. The commerce power, we have often observed, is plenary. . . .

Nor is there any contrary authority in the reasoning of our cases imposing clear statement rules in some instances of legislation that would significantly alter the state-national balance. . . .

B

There remain questions about legislative findings. The Court of Appeals expressed the view, that the result in this case might well have been different if Congress had made explicit findings that guns in schools have a substantial effect on interstate commerce, and the Court today does not repudiate that position. . . . Might a court aided by such findings have subjected this legislation to less exacting scrutiny (or, put another way, should a court have deferred to such findings if Congress had made them)? The answer to either question must be no, although as a general matter findings are important and to be hoped for in the difficult cases. . . . If, indeed, the Court were to make the existence of explicit congressional findings dispositive in some close or difficult cases something other than rationality review would be afoot. The resulting congressional obligation to justify its policy choices on the merits would imply either a judicial authority to review the justification (and, hence, the wisdom) of those choices, or authority to require Congress to act with some high degree of deliberateness, of which express findings would be evidence. But review for congressional wisdom would just be the old judicial pretension discredited and abandoned in 1937, and review for deliberateness would be as patently unconstitutional as an Act of Congress mandating long opinions from this Court. . . .

On the other hand, to say that courts applying the rationality standard may not defer to findings is not, of course, to say that findings are pointless. They may, in fact, have great value in telling courts what to look for, in establishing at least one frame of reference for review, and in citing to factual authority. The research underlying Justice Breyer's dissent was necessarily a major undertaking; help is welcome, and it not incidentally shrinks the risk that judicial research will miss material scattered across the public domain or buried under pounds of legislative record. Congressional findings on a more particular plane than this record illustrates would accordingly have earned judicial thanks. But thanks do not carry the day as long as rational possibility is the touchstone, and I would not allow for the possibility, as the Court's opinion may, that the addition of congressional findings could in principle have affected the fate of the statute here.

III.

Because Justice Breyer's opinion demonstrates beyond any doubt that the Act in question passes the rationality review that the Court continues to espouse, today's decision may be seen as only a misstep, its reasoning and its suggestions not quite in gear with the prevailing standard, but hardly an epochal case. I would not argue otherwise, but I would raise a caveat. Not every epochal case has come in epochal trappings. Jones & Laughlin did not reject the direct-indirect standard in so many words; it just said the relation of the regulated subject matter to commerce was direct enough. But we know what happened.

Justice BREYER, with whom Justice Stevens, Justice Souter, and Justice Ginsburg join, dissenting.

In my view, the statute falls well within the scope of the commerce power as this Court has understood that power over the last half century.

I.

In reaching this conclusion, I apply three basic principles of Commerce Clause interpretation. First, the power to "regulate Commerce . . . among the several States" encompasses the power to regulate local activities insofar as they significantly affect interstate commerce. See, e.g. Gibbons v. Ogden; Wickard v. Filburn. . . .

Second, in determining whether a local activity will likely have a significant effect upon interstate commerce, a court must consider, not the effect of an individual act (a single instance of gun possession), but rather the cumulative effect of all similar instances (i.e., the effect of all guns possessed in or near schools). See, e.g., Wickard. . . .

Third, the Constitution requires us to judge the connection between a regulated activity and interstate commerce, not directly, but at one remove. Courts must give Congress a degree of leeway in determining the existence of a significant factual connection between the regulated activity and interstate commerce — both because the Constitution delegates the commerce power directly to Congress and because the determination requires an empirical judgment of a kind that a legislature is more likely than a court to make with accuracy. The traditional words "rational basis" capture this leeway. Thus, the specific question before us, as the Court recognizes, is not whether the "regulated activity sufficiently affected interstate commerce," but, rather, whether Congress could have had "a rational basis" for so concluding.

I recognize that we must judge this matter independently. "Simply because Congress may conclude that a particular activity substantially affects interstate commerce does not necessarily make it so." And, I also recognize that Congress did not write specific "interstate commerce" findings into the law under which Lopez was convicted. Nonetheless, as I have already noted, the matter that we review independently (i.e., whether there is a "rational basis") already has considerable leeway built into it. And, the absence of findings, at most, deprives a statute of the benefit of some extra leeway. This extra deference, in principle, might change the result in a close case, though, in practice, it has not made a critical legal difference. See, e.g., Katzenbach v. McClung (noting that "no formal findings were made, which of course are not necessary"); *Perez. . . .*

II.

Applying these principles to the case at hand, we must ask whether Congress could have had a rational basis for finding a significant (or substantial) connection between gun-related school violence and interstate commerce. Or, to put the question in the language of the explicit finding that Congress made when it amended this law in 1994: Could Congress rationally have found that "violent crime in school zones," through its effect on the "quality of education," significantly (or substantially) affects "interstate" or "foreign commerce"? As long as one views the commerce connection, not as a "technical legal conception," but as "a practical one," Swift & Co. v. United States, 196 U.S. 375, 398 (1905) (Holmes, J.), the answer to this question must be yes. Numerous reports and studies — generated both inside and outside government — make clear that Congress could reasonably have found the empirical connection that its law, implicitly or explicitly, asserts. [At this point, Justice Breyer directs the reader to the Appendix to his opinion, which spans more than a dozen pages in U.S. Reports and cites more than 150 relevant articles and studies — "Congressional Materials," "Other Federal Government Materials," and "Other Readily Available Materials" — to support the connection.]

For one thing, reports, hearings, and other readily available literature make clear that the problem of guns in and around schools is widespread and extremely serious. These materials report, for example, that four percent of American high school students (and six percent of inner-city high school students) carry a gun to school at least occasionally; that 12 percent of urban high school students have had guns fired at them; that 20 percent of those students have been threatened with guns; and that, in any 6-month period, several hundred thousand schoolchildren are victims of violent crimes in or near their schools. And, they report that this widespread violence in schools throughout the Nation significantly interferes with the quality of education in those schools. Based on reports such as these, Congress obviously could have thought that guns and learning are mutually exclusive. Congress could therefore have found a substantial educational problem — teachers unable to teach, students unable to learn — and concluded that guns near schools contribute substantially to the size and scope of that problem.

Having found that guns in schools significantly undermine the quality of education in our Nation's classrooms, Congress could also have found, given the effect of education upon interstate and foreign commerce, that gun-related violence in and around schools is a commercial, as well as a human, problem. Education, although far more than a matter of economics, has long been inextricably intertwined with the Nation's economy. When this Nation began, most workers received their education in the workplace, typically (like Benjamin Franklin) as apprentices. As late as the 1920s, many workers still received general education directly from their employers — from large corporations, such as General Electric, Ford, and Goodyear, which created schools within their firms to help both the worker and the firm. (Throughout most of

the 19th century fewer than one percent of all Americans received secondary education through attending a high school.) As public school enrollment grew in the early
20th century, the need for industry to teach basic educational skills diminished. But,
the direct economic link between basic education and industrial productivity
remained. Scholars estimate that nearly a quarter of America's economic growth in
the early years of this century is traceable directly to increased schooling; that investment in "human capital" (through spending on education) exceeded investment in
"physical capital" by a ratio of almost two to one; and that the economic returns to
this investment in education exceeded the returns to conventional capital investment.

In recent years the link between secondary education and business has strengthened, becoming both more direct and more important. Scholars on the subject
report that technological changes and innovations in management techniques have
altered the nature of the workplace so that more jobs now demand greater educational skills. There is evidence that "service, manufacturing or construction jobs are
being displaced by technology that requires a better-educated worker or, more
likely, are being exported overseas," that "workers with truly few skills by the year
2000 will find that only one job out of ten will remain," and that

> "over the long haul the best way to encourage the growth of high-wage jobs is to
> upgrade the skills of the work force. . . . Better-trained workers become more produc-
> tive workers, enabling a company to become more competitive and expand."

Increasing global competition also has made primary and secondary education
economically more important. The portion of the American economy attributable
to international trade nearly tripled between 1950 and 1980, and more than 70
percent of American-made goods now compete with imports. Yet, lagging worker
productivity has contributed to negative trade balances and to real hourly compensation that has fallen below wages in 10 other industrialized nations. At least some
significant part of this serious productivity problem is attributable to students who
emerge from classrooms without the reading or mathematical skills necessary to
compete with their European or Asian counterparts, and, presumably, to high
school dropout rates of 20 to 25 percent (up to 50 percent in inner cities). Indeed,
Congress has said, when writing other statutes, that "functionally or technologically
illiterate" Americans in the work force "erode" our economic "standing in the international marketplace," and that "our Nation is . . . paying the price of scientific and
technological illiteracy, with our productivity declining, our industrial base ailing,
and our global competitiveness dwindling."

Finally, there is evidence that, today more than ever, many firms base their location decisions upon the presence, or absence, of a work force with a basic education. Scholars on the subject report, for example, that today, "high speed
communication and transportation make it possible to produce most products
and services anywhere in the world," that "modern machinery and production
methods can therefore be combined with low wage workers to drive costs down,"
that managers can perform "back office functions anywhere in the world now,"
and say that if they "can't get enough skilled workers here" they will "move the
skilled jobs out of the country," with the consequence that "rich countries need
better education and retraining, to reduce the supply of unskilled workers and to
equip them with the skills they require for tomorrow's jobs." In light of this

increased importance of education to individual firms, it is no surprise that half of the Nation's manufacturers have become involved with setting standards and shaping curricula for local schools, that 88 percent think this kind of involvement is important, that more than 20 States have recently passed educational reforms to attract new business, and that business magazines have begun to rank cities according to the quality of their schools.

The economic links I have just sketched seem fairly obvious. Why then is it not equally obvious, in light of those links, that a widespread, serious, and substantial physical threat to teaching and learning also substantially threatens the commerce to which that teaching and learning is inextricably tied? That is to say, guns in the hands of six percent of inner-city high school students and gun-related violence throughout a city's schools must threaten the trade and commerce that those schools support. The only question, then, is whether the latter threat is (to use the majority's terminology) "substantial." The evidence of (1) the extent of the gun-related violence problem, (2) the extent of the resulting negative effect on classroom learning, and (3) the extent of the consequent negative commercial effects, see supra, when taken together, indicate a threat to trade and commerce that is "substantial." At the very least, Congress could rationally have concluded that the links are "substantial."

Specifically, Congress could have found that gun-related violence near the classroom poses a serious economic threat (1) to consequently inadequately educated workers who must endure low paying jobs, and (2) to communities and businesses that might (in today's "information society") otherwise gain, from a well-educated work force, an important commercial advantage of a kind that location near a railhead or harbor provided in the past. Congress might also have found these threats to be no different in kind from other threats that this Court has found within the commerce power, such as the threat that loan sharking poses to the "funds" of "numerous localities," *Perez*, and that unfair labor practices pose to instrumentalities of commerce. As I have pointed out, Congress has written that "the occurrence of violent crime in school zones" has brought about a "decline in the quality of education" that "has an adverse impact on interstate commerce and the foreign commerce of the United States." 18 U.S.C. §922 (q)(1)(F), (G). The violence-related facts, the educational facts, and the economic facts, taken together, make this conclusion rational. And, because under our case law, the sufficiency of the constitutionally necessary Commerce Clause link between a crime of violence and interstate commerce turns simply upon size or degree, those same facts make the statute constitutional.

To hold this statute constitutional is not to "obliterate" the "distinction between what is national and what is local"; nor is it to hold that the Commerce Clause permits the Federal Government to "regulate any activity that it found was related to the economic productivity of individual citizens," to regulate "marriage, divorce, and child custody," or to regulate any and all aspects of education. First, this statute is aimed at curbing a particularly acute threat to the educational process — the possession (and use) of life-threatening firearms in, or near, the classroom. The empirical evidence that I have discussed above unmistakably documents the special way in which guns and education are incompatible. . . . [T]he immediacy of the connection between education and the national economic well-being is documented by scholars and accepted by society at large in a way and to a degree that may not hold true for other social institutions. It must surely be the rare case, then, that a statute strikes at conduct that (when considered in the abstract) seems so removed from commerce, but which (practically speaking) has so significant an impact upon commerce.

In sum, a holding that the particular statute before us falls within the commerce power would not expand the scope of that Clause. Rather, it simply would apply pre-existing law to changing economic circumstances. It would recognize that, in today's economic world, gun-related violence near the classroom makes a significant difference to our economic, as well as our social, well-being. In accordance with well-accepted precedent, such a holding would permit Congress "to act in terms of economic . . . realities," would interpret the commerce power as "an affirmative power commensurate with the national needs," and would acknowledge that the "commerce clause does not operate so as to render the nation powerless to defend itself against economic forces that Congress decrees inimical or destructive of the national economy."

III.

The majority's holding — that §922 falls outside the scope of the Commerce Clause — creates three serious legal problems. First, the majority's holding runs contrary to modern Supreme Court cases that have upheld congressional actions despite connections to interstate or foreign commerce that are less significant than the effect of school violence. . . .

The second legal problem the Court creates comes from its apparent belief that it can reconcile its holding with earlier cases by making a critical distinction between "commercial" and noncommercial "transaction[s]." That is to say, the Court believes the Constitution would distinguish between two local activities, each of which has an identical effect upon interstate commerce, if one, but not the other, is "commercial" in nature. As a general matter, this approach fails to heed this Court's earlier warning not to turn "questions of the power of Congress" upon "formula[s]" that would give "controlling force to nomenclature such as 'production' and 'indirect' and foreclose consideration of the actual effects of the activity in question upon interstate commerce." *Wickard*. See also United States v. Darby (overturning the Court's distinction between "production" and "commerce" in the child labor case, Hammer v. Dagenhart); Swift & Co. v. United States, 196 U.S. at 398 (Holmes, J.) ("Commerce among the States is not a technical legal conception, but a practical one, drawn from the course of business"). . . .

More importantly, if a distinction between commercial and noncommercial activities is to be made, this is not the case in which to make it. . . . Schools that teach reading, writing, mathematics, and related basic skills serve both social and commercial purposes, and one cannot easily separate the one from the other. American industry itself has been, and is again, involved in teaching. . . .

In 1990, the year Congress enacted the statute before us, primary and secondary schools spent $230 billion — that is, nearly a quarter of a trillion dollars — which accounts for a significant portion of our $5.5 trillion gross domestic product for that year. The business of schooling requires expenditure of these funds on student transportation, food and custodial services, books, and teachers' salaries. These expenditures enable schools to provide a valuable service — namely, to equip students with the skills they need to survive in life and, more specifically, in the workplace. Certainly, Congress has often analyzed school expenditure as if it were a commercial investment, closely analyzing whether schools are efficient, whether they justify the significant resources they spend, and whether they can be restructured to achieve greater returns. Why could Congress, for Commerce Clause purposes, not consider schools as roughly analogous to commercial investments from which the Nation derives the benefit of an educated work force?

The third legal problem created by the Court's holding is that it threatens legal uncertainty in an area of law that, until this case, seemed reasonably well settled. . . .

Discussion

1. *How broadly does* Lopez *sweep?* Does *Lopez* betoken a dramatic rollback of congressional power under the Commerce Clause, or merely a disinclination to extend expansive cases like *Wickard* and *McClung* any further? Note the differences of tone and emphasis between, for example, Justice Thomas on the one hand, and Justices Kennedy and O'Connor on the other. For a careful and comprehensive analysis of the breadth of *Lopez,* suggesting the modesty of its reach, see Deborah Jones Merritt, Commerce!, 94 Mich. L. Rev. 674 (1995). Later cases have thus far largely born out Professor Merritt's predictions, see infra discussion note 7.

2. *Judicial review as a remand to Congress?* If Congress were to revisit and reenact the identical statute in the aftermath of *Lopez,* but this time with more careful and explicit findings attempting to identify the link between the law and bona fide issues of interstate commerce (in a manner akin to Justice Breyer's dissent), might the new law pass Supreme Court muster? The majority opinion does not rule this out — and Justice Kennedy's concurrence (joined by Justice O'Connor) contains some intriguing language about the possibility that Congress might "revise its law to demonstrate its commercial character." Also, note Justice Kennedy's concluding paragraph calling for "a stronger connection *or identification* with commercial concerns" (emphasis added). Why should the same law pass muster merely because Congress chants some magic words in a "findings" section that do not change the substantive command of the statute?

One possible answer is that "findings" after a Supreme Court invalidation would represent an explicit acknowledgment by Congress that it carefully deliberated on the specific federalism implications that concerned the Court. If, for court-specific reasons — such as the difficulty of drawing workable doctrinal lines, and the felt need to defer to legislative judgments about complicated empirical realities — judges systemically underenforce the limits on Congress's Commerce Clause powers, perhaps the Court might try to enforce federalism values more indirectly, by simply encouraging Congress to pay special attention to these concerns in drafting legislation. Legislative findings thus might serve a purpose akin to the purpose served by a clear-statement rule, cf. Gregory v. Ashcroft, infra, Part III.

Of course, the Court might also believe that, were Congress to focus more closely on federalism issues, federal lawmakers would likely modify federal intervention to better accommodate state interests. The law in *Lopez* was cleverly tailored to fit "political" concerns of federalism. Congresspersons from urban districts tended to support the law more than did those from rural districts, and the law reflected this differential support by drawing a 1,000-foot wide buffer zone around each school. Such zones left wide areas of rural districts untouched, but virtually blanketed urban areas like Manhattan. But was the law equally well tailored to fit "legal" concerns of federalism? Recall Justice Kennedy's reminder that state and local laws addressing guns and/or schools exist in most jurisdictions. How did the federal act mesh with these laws? For example, how did federal law apply to a homeowner living next to a schoolyard who lawfully buys a gun under state law, and then proceeds to drive home with it? Under one section of the federal statute, such a person would apparently be exempt if his state licensed guns, and he had a license, but would (at least arguably) be a federal felon if his state did not even require gun licenses. See 18 U.S.C. §922(q)(2)(B)(ii). Does this make sense? For specific discussion, see Merritt, supra, at 693. For outstanding general analysis of the myriad ways in which state and federal law interact, see Henry Hart, The Relations Between State and Federal Law, 54 Colum. L. Rev. 489 (1954); Paul Mishkin, The Variousness of "Federal Law": Competence and Discretion in the Choice of National and State Rules for Decision, 105 U. Pa. L. Rev. 797 (1957).

As things turned out, Congress did revisit the issue of guns in schools in the wake of *Lopez*. In late 1996, Congress enacted a new version of §922, with explicit findings, and with a narrower sweep. Under the new version, the law applies only if the firearm in question "has moved in or . . . otherwise affects interstate or foreign commerce." Pub. L. No. 104-208, §657, 110 Stat. 3009 (1996). Is this change enough to satisfy the Court's concerns? Should it be enough? Note also that before the *Lopez* case was decided, but after Mr. Lopez's gun crime had occurred, Congress in a 1994 statute did make findings about the link between school gun violence and commerce. The government in *Lopez* chose not to rely on these findings. Why? (Might the ex post facto clause be relevant here?)

3. *Modalities of interpretation.* Different Justices often approach constitutional law with distinctive methodological emphases. Justice Thomas, for example, pays great attention to constitutional text and history in *Lopez*. Particularly noteworthy is his effort to construe the words of the Commerce Clause in light of a different constitutional clause using the word "commerce" (and also a clause using the word "affect"). For more discussion of this "intratextual" technique, see the discussion following City of Boerne v. Flores, infra, p. 629. By contrast, Justice Souter places primary reliance on the lessons of New Deal case law; whereas Justice Breyer sounds repeated prudential notes in his plea that Commerce Clause doctrine must be practical. Recall Professor Bobbitt's extremely insightful catalogue and analysis of various modes of constitutional interpretation; see Philip Bobbitt, Constitutional Fate: Theory of the Constitution (1980).

4. *A structural middle approach?* Consider a structural approach to *Lopez* that tries to steer a middle course between the majority and the dissenters. On this view, each state should be trusted to regulate affairs whose effects are felt within its geographic limits, but Congress may step in to deal with interstate spillovers — where actions in one state have real effects in other states. This was the view of federal power explicitly put forth by Framer (and soon-to-be Justice) James Wilson in the Pennsylvania ratifying debates of 1788, see supra, p. 556. On a Wilsonian reading, "Commerce" should be understood not merely to mean "economic" affairs, as Justice Thomas would have it, but virtually any "dealings" or "transactions."

While structurally inspired, this noneconomic reading of "commerce" also finds some important textual support in the Oxford English Dictionary (OED), and makes good sense of early federal practice. Bolingbroke's famous mid-eighteenth-century tract, *The Idea of a Patriot King,* spoke of the "free and easy commerce of social life" and other Founding-era texts cited in the OED referred to "domestic animals which have the greatest Commerce with mankind" and "our Lord's commerce with his disciples." Structurally, the broader reading would seem to make better sense of the framers' general goals by enabling Congress to regulate all interactions (and altercations) with foreign nations and Indian tribes — interactions that, if improperly handled by a single state acting on its own, might lead to needless wars or otherwise compromise the interests of sister states. Draft language at Philadelphia had in fact empowered Congress "to regulate affairs with the Indians," but the word "affairs" dropped out when the delegates opted to fold the Indian clause into the general interstate and international "commerce" provision. Without a broad reading of "commerce" in this clause, it is not entirely clear whence the federal government would derive its needed power to deal with noneconomic international incidents — or for that matter to address the entire range of vexing nonmercantile interactions and altercations that might arise among states.[50] Notably, the First Congress did in fact enact a statute regulating noneconomic interactions and altercations — "intercourse" — with Indians. See An Act To Regulate Trade and Intercourse with the Indian Tribes, July 22, 1790, 1 Stat. 137. Section 5 of this act dealt with crimes — whether economic or not — committed by Americans on Indian lands. Wasn't this early statute obviously grounded in the Commerce Clause, and doesn't it suggest the good sense of construing "commerce" in this clause to mean "intercourse" more generally?[51]

The key distinction, on this view, is between intrastate and interstate transactions — between "national" problems everywhere, and "federal" problems affecting relations between ("among," in the words of the clause) states. For example, even if burning homegrown logs in home fireplaces is not particularly "commercial" in Justice Thomas's view, Congress should be allowed to regulate the air pollution it creates if (and only if) other states are affected — say, because the wind blows the pollution into adjoining states. Similarly, if a private person hunting on his own estate seeks to kill an endangered species that regularly migrates across state lines, or that has DNA that might help scientists in other states cure human diseases, this is an easy case for federal involvement, even if our hunter is killing for sport, not profit.

But what exactly was the interstate problem in *Lopez?* Why wouldn't each state obviously have a strong interest in protecting its children from gun violence? Indeed, if, as Justice Breyer argues, high-wage employers seek to locate in areas with strong schools, wouldn't each state have a good incentive to protect kids in schools? As a "practical" matter — to use Justice Breyer's approach — wasn't the

---

50. It might be countered that federal authority to regulate all truly international issues, whether or not economic, derives not from the Commerce Clause but from general structural principles of national sovereignty. Cf. United States v. Curtiss-Wright Export Corp., 299 U.S. 304 (1936), discussed in Chapter 1, supra. But if it is permissible to range beyond strict textual enumeration in the international domain, á la *Curtiss-Wright,* why not in the interstate domain? If sound structural principles support federal power in the former, why not in the latter as well?

51. Some of the material in this paragraph is borrowed from Akhil Reed Amar, America's Constitution: A Biography (2005).

federal law largely grandstanding, given that the vast majority of local crimes are prosecuted by state governments and not the feds?

Would this middle approach lend itself to principled doctrinal exposition and enforcement in courts? If not, does it nonetheless set out a workable distinction for a constitutionally conscientious congressperson?

5. *Narrow versus broad time-framing.* Note that whether we find effects in sister states may often depend on how narrowly or broadly we frame the issue, temporally. If we consider effects over long periods of time, then we will often find them radiating out over broad stretches of space. But guns in schools seems a rather easy case for narrow time-framing — the harm is so graphic and immediate in time that the main effects are felt locally in space. Contrast the issue of school violence with the issue of school curriculum. The *Lopez* majority seemed very skeptical of the notion that Congress should have power to "mandate a federal curriculum for local elementary and secondary schools" — but consider the following broadly framed "federal" argument for a congressionally defined curriculum: Economic growth depends on the ability of workers to move easily from state to state, within a single firm, or switching firms. But moving across states is harder when each state has a different curriculum — a common set of curricular standards makes it easier for parents to relocate with minimal disruption to their children's education. Without federal coordination, no state acting individually has sufficient incentive to develop a nationwide standard. Also, each state might underinvest in its primary education, on the rational assumption that it will not fully internalize the long-term benefits of a good educational system, or suffer the long-term harms of a bad one; people move across states over the course of their lifetime, and the benefits of a good primary education in State A largely redound to sister states. On this view, Congress might indeed have a legitimate role in setting minimum standards for states, or "bribing" states, through conditional funding statutes, to spend more on education than they might otherwise. Note how these arguments for federal intervention seek to identify genuine "transactions" across state lines — movement of employee/parents, or of former students — but these interstate effects are most visible when we expand the temporal frame of analysis. Compare, in this regard, the broader time frame implicit in Justice Breyer's approach. (But does such a broad time frame intuitively work when the harm involved is so immediate and urgent — like blood in schools?) For general discussions of narrow versus broad temporal framing in other areas of law, see Mark Kelman, Interpretive Construction in the Substantive Criminal Law, 33 Stan. L. Rev. 591 (1981); J. M. Balkin, The Rhetoric of Responsibility, 76 Va. L. Rev. 197 (1990).

6. *Maintaining fidelity to the founding in a changed world.* Suppose the Founders believed two things: (1) The federal government should be allowed to regulate all truly interstate issues; and (2) state governments would nonetheless retain regulatory control over myriad and important topics. These two beliefs could coexist in a world where most transactions did not affect sister states. But suppose that as a result of dramatic improvements in communication, transportation, and scientific knowledge over the next two centuries, many more of the transactions that occur today do genuinely involve interstate effects — movement of pollution molecules across state lines, economic impacts in sister states, interstate migration of persons, interstate shipment of goods, and so on. If so, the two beliefs of the Founders cannot coexist today. But which of the two should be abandoned?

The *Lopez* majority seems more willing to sacrifice the first principle; the Breyer dissent, the second. For more discussion, see J. M. Balkin, Constitutional Interpretation and the Problem of History, 63 N.Y.U. L. Rev. 911 (1988); Lawrence Lessig, Translating Federalism: United States v. Lopez, 1995 Sup. Ct. Rev. 125.

7. *Litigating Lopez.* In the decade since *Lopez*, the Court has decided two major cases clarifying the basic commerce clause ground rules.

First, in *United States v. Morrison*, 529 U.S. 598 (2000), Chief Justice Rehnquist spoke for the same five-person majority as in *Lopez*, and once again held that a congressional statute exceeded the proper scope of the Commerce Clause. The particular provision at issue, Section 13981 of the Violence Against Women Act of 1994 (VAWA), vested victims of gender-motivated violence with a federal civil cause of action against their assailants. In the case before the Court, Christy Brzonkala, a student enrolled at Virginia Polytechnic Institute, brought a federal suit against two members of the varsity football team, who, she alleged, had pinned her down and repeatedly raped her within 30 minutes of meeting her. The Court treated the case as squarely governed by *Lopez*:

> Gender-motivated crimes of violence are not, in any sense of the phrase, economic activity. While we need not adopt a categorical rule against aggregating the effects of any noneconomic activity in order to decide these cases, thus far in our Nation's history our cases have upheld Commerce Clause regulation of intrastate activity only where that activity is economic in nature. [Moreover,] [l]ike the Gun-Free School Zones Act at issue in *Lopez*, [VAWA] contains no jurisdictional element establishing that the federal cause of action is in pursuance of Congress' power to regulate interstate commerce. . . . We accordingly reject the argument that Congress may regulate noneconomic, violent criminal conduct based solely on that conduct's aggregate effect on interstate commerce.

Violence against women, said the majority, was neither particularly *commercial* in nature (in an economic sense), nor particularly *interstate* in character. Thus, reasoned the Court, the Interstate Commerce Clause could not provide a proper constitutional foundation for congressional legislation. Putting aside the Court's narrowly economic definition of "commerce" (see supra, discussion, note 4), the majority had a point, didn't it, that the general problem of violence against women did not involve obvious interstate spillovers? To be sure, violence against women is a huge problem everywhere. But in what sense is it an *interstate* problem, a problem "among" or between the states — a "federal" as distinct from "national" problem, see supra, p. 621?[52] Perhaps the best possible grounds for distinguishing away *Lopez*

---

52. Chief Justice Rehnquist noted that:

Petitioners' reasoning, moreover, will not limit Congress to regulating violence but may, as we suggested in *Lopez*, be applied equally as well to family law and other areas of traditional state regulation since the aggregate effect of marriage, divorce, and childrearing on the national economy is undoubtedly significant.

Cf. Jill Elaine Hasday, Federalism and the Family Reconstructed, 45 U.C.L.A. L. Rev. 1297 (1998) (pointing out that the federal government has been heavily involved in regulating domestic relations since Reconstruction); Kristin A. Collins, Federalism's Fallacy: The Early Tradition of Federal Family Law and the Invention of States' Rights, 26 Cardozo L. Rev. 1761, 1767 (2005); Ann Laquer Estin, Federalism and Child Support, 5 Va. J. Soc. Pol'y & L. 541-542 (1998) (noting broad reach of federal regulation in tax, pension, and bankruptcy statutes, as well as federal rules regarding child support,

in *Morrison* was that Congress had made various legislative findings in enacting the VAWA. But these 1994 findings were made in a pre-*Lopez* world and did not, in the eyes of the *Morrison* majority, satisfactorily identify an interstate problem that called for a federal solution. VAWA supporters also tried to uphold Section 13981 as a valid exercise of congressional power to enforce the Fourteenth Amendment, but the *Morrison* majority also rejected this §5 argument, see infra pp. 643-644.

In the Court's most recent elaboration of *Lopez*, Raich v. Gonzales, 125 S. Ct. 2195 (2005), the four *Lopez* dissenters, joined by Justices Kennedy and Scalia, voted to uphold congressional laws criminalizing marijuana possession even when these federal laws prohibited local cultivation and use of marijuana for medical reasons pursuant to a valid California statute that decriminalized the matter for state law purposes. Angel Raich, who suffered from a variety of serious medical conditions and was using marijuana as prescribed by a board-certified physician to control her excruciating pain, sought a declaratory judgment that federal drug laws could not properly be applied against her. She alleged that the marijuana that she used had never been bought or sold and had never crossed a state line. In an opinion authored by Justice Stevens and joined by Justices Kennedy, Souter, Ginsburg, and Breyer, the Court reaffirmed *Lopez*, but also stood by Wickard v. Filburn, and held that Raich fell on the *Wickard* side of the line.[53] Just as the farmer's individual consumption of wheat in *Wickard*, when combined with other comparably situated farmers' consumption, could affect prices and outputs in a genuinely interstate wheat market, so Raich's use could not be hermetically sealed off from the larger — and truly interstate — issue of the marijuana market. Both wheat and marijuana were "fungible" commodities, the Court observed; and in Raich's case the federal government had legitimate reasons to fear that some marijuana earmarked for Raich and others under the California Compassionate Use Act might be diverted into illegal uses. The majority also expressed concern that some lax physicians might face market pressure to overprescribe medical marijuana. In one footnote, the majority drew attention to the fact that "patients residing in the cities of Oakland and Santa Cruz and in the counties of Sonoma and Tehama are permitted

---

custody jurisdiction, and federal welfare policy). In any case, whether an activity is traditionally regulated by states is orthogonal to whether it has spillover effects in different jurisdictions or whether a federal solution may be valuable to harmonize inconsistent approaches. See the discussion of education in a national economy in discussion n.5, supra. Note moreover, that as the economy changes, a traditional focus of state regulation like labor or manufacturing may come to have increasing varieties and degrees of interstate spillover effects. Can you think of areas of family and social welfare policy that might have such spillover effects?

53. The Court distinguished *Lopez* and *Morrison* on the grounds that they involved regulation of noneconomic activity:

Unlike those at issue in *Lopez* and *Morrison*, the activities regulated by the CSA [Controlled Substances Act] are quintessentially economic. "Economics" refers to "the production, distribution, and consumption of commodities." Webster's Third New International Dictionary 720 (1966). The CSA is a statute that regulates the production, distribution, and consumption of commodities for which there is an established, and lucrative, interstate market. Prohibiting the intrastate possession or manufacture of an article of commerce is a rational (and commonly utilized) means of regulating commerce in that product. Such prohibitions include specific decisions requiring that a drug be withdrawn from the market as a result of the failure to comply with regulatory requirements as well as decisions excluding Schedule I drugs entirely from the market. Because the CSA is a statute that directly regulates economic, commercial activity, our opinion in *Morrison* casts no doubt on its constitutionality.

Do you accept the Court's definition of "economic" activity? Note once more that defining what is "economic" and what is not becomes unnecessary if one focuses instead on what is federal and interstate.

to possess 3 pounds of processed marijuana" — an amount "yield[ing] roughly 3,000 joints or cigarettes." According to the majority, the "likelihood that all . . . production will promptly terminate when patients recover or will precisely match the patients' medical needs during their convalescence seems remote; whereas the danger that excesses will satisfy some of the admittedly enormous demand for recreational use seems obvious. . . . [N]o small number of unscrupulous people will make use of the California exemptions to serve their commercial ends whenever it is feasible to do so."

Raich argued, nevertheless, that the state's legalization of marijuana for medical use when prescribed by a licensed physician created a distinct category that included only noneconomic intrastate activity; this justified a carve-out from federal regulatory authority. The Court rejected the idea: "limiting the activity to marijuana possession and cultivation 'in accordance with state law' cannot serve to place respondents' activities beyond congressional reach. The Supremacy Clause unambiguously provides that if there is any conflict between federal and state law, federal law shall prevail. . . . Just as state acquiescence to federal regulation cannot expand the bounds of the Commerce Clause, so too state action cannot circumscribe Congress' plenary commerce power."

Concurring in the judgment, Justice Scalia seconded the majority's point that "Drugs like marijuana are fungible commodities [and] marijuana that is grown at home and possessed for personal use is never more than an instant from the interstate market — and this is so whether or not the possession is for medicinal use or lawful use under the laws of a particular State." Justice Scalia also stressed that insofar as Congress sought to regulate issues that were not themselves interstate commerce, but that were instead intrastate and noncommercial (in an economic sense), such regulation was nonetheless permissible if the regulatory overhang was a necessary (in a *McCulloch* sense) adjunct to a valid, nonpretextual interstate regulatory program:

> [W]here Congress has the authority to enact a regulation of interstate commerce, "it possesses every power needed to make that regulation effective." . . . The regulation of an intrastate activity may be essential to a comprehensive regulation of interstate commerce even though the intrastate activity does not itself "substantially affect" interstate commerce. Moreover, as . . . *Lopez* . . . suggests, Congress may regulate even noneconomic local activity if that regulation is a necessary part of a more general regulation of interstate commerce. The relevant question is simply whether the means chosen are "reasonably adapted" to the attainment of a legitimate end under the commerce power.

In advancing this idea, Justice Scalia relied not on the Commerce Clause in isolation, but on this clause in tandem with the Necessary and Proper Clause. Citing *McCulloch*, Justice Scalia argued that the latter clause "empowers Congress to enact laws in the effectuation of its enumerated powers that are not within its authority to enact in isolation." Whether or not you agree with this principle of federal power, recall from Chapter 1 that *McCulloch* did not argue that the Necessary and Proper Clause added extra authority; rather Chief Justice Marshall placed primary reliance on his expansive understandings of the various enumerated powers individually and collectively.

Dissenting on behalf of herself, the Chief Justice, and Justice Thomas, Justice O'Connor argued that no proven problem of diversion existed, and that "California's Compassionate Use Act and similar state legislation may well isolate activities relating to medical marijuana from the illicit market." But why must the federal government run the risk in the absence of proof positive either way? And if John Marshall was right to insist in *McCulloch* that Congress did not need to rely on state banks and could choose to establish its own bank, why must the modern Congress rely on state drug enforcement programs?

Justice O'Connor complained that on the majority view in *Raich,* very little was left of *Lopez* itself. For example, a future Congress might well impose special criminal penalties on guns near schools if such penalties were linked to a larger congressional ban on *all* guns. Ironically, by *expanding* the scope of federal criminal regulation of firearms — by displacing *even more* state law with a *far broader* federal gun policy — Congress apparently could do the very thing that the *Lopez* Court, in the name of states' rights, tried to prevent Congress from doing.

There is indeed an irony here, but wasn't this irony built into *Lopez* itself? Recall that in *Lopez,* the Court pointedly observed that "Section 922(q) is not an essential part of a larger regulation of economic activity, in which the regulatory scheme could be undercut unless the intrastate activity were regulated." (For those structuralists who prefer to focus less on the economic-noneconomic distinction, clarity would be improved by substituting the word "interstate" for the word "economic" in this passage.) Note also that in other federalism contexts, the Court, when limiting Congress, has at times suggested that Congress might find other ways of skinning the cat, while dissenters have stressed that these other ways might ironically be less respectful of states' rights. For example, although Congress may not *require* state legislatures to enact laws, Congress apparently may *bribe* them to do so under the Spending Clause, see New York v. United States, 505 U.S. 144 (1992), infra, p. 674. (Could Congress have bribed states into enacting and enforcing state-law versions of the Gun-Free School Zones Act or the VAWA?) And although Congress is not always allowed to impose liability on private parties in response to state misconduct, it may have broader power to hold the states themselves liable in such situations, according to the *Morrison* Court majority. (This aspect of *Morrison* is discussed infra, p. 644 n.58.) But, as Justice Breyer pointed out in his *Morrison* dissent, federal liability imposed directly on states might be seen as *less* friendly to states' rights than the cooperative federalism system of private liability embodied in VAWA, which gave state governments incentives to work with the federal government, rather than litigate against it, in combating violence against women. Also, because Congress is prevented from commandeering state executives, it may find itself obliged to create larger federal bureaucracies displacing state structures altogether, see Printz v. United States, 521 U.S. 898 (1997), infra, p. 693.

In light of various ways in which Congress may detour around the *Lopez* line, is this case largely symbolic? (If so, is *Lopez* any different from many other doctrinal lines in modern constitutional law?) Is the symbol at issue in *Lopez* — the reminder that even today, our federal system remains, in principle, a system of limited federal powers — one worthy of judicial affirmation? Is the judicial game of finding the relatively rare case in which Congress has overstepped worth the candle?[54]

54. If there is a reasonable dispute about whether Congress has acted within its commerce power, why shouldn't the Court defer to Congress's judgment? Or is the point that since *Lopez* represents such an exceptional set of circumstances, it really doesn't matter much what rules courts settle on as long as they abide by the basic terms of the New Deal settlement?

On the other hand, hasn't the Court drawn the line in a rather sensible place? In areas where there truly are interstate (indeed, international) markets or law-evading enterprises organized on an interstate (or international) scale so as to defy or evade successful regulation by individual states, congressional power has been strongly affirmed in cases such as *Perez* and *Raich*. And in situations where no real interstate spillovers or interstate organizations exist — *Lopez* and *Morrison* — congressional power has been clipped. And, thus far at least, the Court has not sought to limit Congress from regulating truly interstate but less obviously economic issues, involving endangered species, pollution molecules, and the like.

2.   *The Taxing and Spending Power*

In South Dakota v. Dole, 483 U.S. 203 (1987), Chief Justice Rehnquist wrote for the Court to uphold a congressional statute that directed the Secretary of Transportation to withhold from a state a percentage of federal highway funds it would otherwise be entitled to should the state permit the purchase or public posses-sion of alcohol by a person under 21. South Dakota, which allowed 19-year-olds to purchase beer, argued that the statute was unconstitutional under the Twenty-first Amendment, which the Court had earlier found "grants the State virtually complete control over whether to permit importation or sale of liquor and how to structure the liquor distribution system." California Retail Liquor Dealers Assn. v. Midcal Aluminum, Inc., 445 U.S. 97, 110 (1980). South Dakota asserted that it would there-fore be unconstitutional for Congress to pass a national drinking-age law and that indirect control through the withholding of federal funds was also unconstitutional.

On behalf of himself and six other Justices, Chief Justice Rehnquist wrote that "we need not decide . . . [whether the Twenty-first Amendment] would prohibit an attempt by Congress to legislate directly a national minimum drinking age. Here, Congress has acted indirectly under its spending power to encourage uniformity in the State's drinking ages. . . . [W]e find this legislative effort within constitutional bounds even if Congress may not regulate drinking ages directly." Citing a number of cases going back to United States v. Butler, 297 U.S. 1 (1936), supra Chapter 4, the Court stated that "objectives not thought to be within Article I's 'enumerated legislative fields,' may nevertheless be attained through the use of the spending power and the conditional grant of federal funds." To be sure, Congress's power under the spending power is not unlimited: "First, the exercise of the spending power must be in pursuit of 'the general welfare,'" though Congress is entitled to considerable deference in regard to judgments about what constitutes such welfare. "Second, we have required that if Congress desires to condition the States' receipt of federal funds, it 'must do so unambiguously . . . , enabl[ing] the States to exer-cise their choice knowingly, cognizant of the consequences of their participation.' Third, our cases have suggested (without significant elaboration) that conditions on federal grants might be illegitimate if they are unrelated 'to the federal interest in particular national projects or programs.' . . . Finally, we have noted that other constitutional provisions may provide an independent bar to the conditional grant of federal funds." The statute met the first three requirements:

Congress found that the differing drinking ages in the States created particular incen-tives for young persons to combine their desire to drink with their ability to drive, and that this interstate problem required a national solution. The means it chose to address this dangerous situation were reasonably calculated to advance the general welfare. The conditions upon which States receive the funds, moreover, could not be more clearly stated by Congress. . . . Indeed, the condition imposed by Congress is directly related to one of the main purposes for which highway funds are expended — safe interstate travel. This goal of the interstate highway system had been frustrated by varying drinking ages among the States. A presidential commission appointed to study alcohol-related accidents and fatalities on the Nation's highways concluded that the lack of uniformity in the States' drinking ages created "an incentive to drink and drive" because "young persons commut[e] to border States where the drinking age is lower." By enacting, Congress conditioned the receipt of federal funds in a way reasonably calculated to address this particular impediment to a purpose for which the funds are expended.

The fourth question was "whether the Twenty-first Amendment constitutes an 'independent constitutional bar' to the conditional grant of federal funds." Citing Oklahoma v. Civil Service Comm'n., and Steward Machine Co. v. Davis, the Court described "the language in our earlier opinions" as standing "for the unexceptionable proposition that the power may not be used to induce the States to engage in activities that would themselves be unconstitutional. Thus, for example, a grant of federal funds conditioned on invidiously discriminatory state action or the infliction of cruel and unusual punishment" would be unconstitutional. Here, though, the policy being pressed upon South Dakota — the raising of the minimum drinking age — would violate no one's constitutional rights. The Court also noted that South Dakota would lose only five percent of its allotted funds for its failure to follow federal policy. This "mild encouragement" by Congress did not approach the point "at which 'pressure turns into compulsion.' " Davis.

Justice O'Connor dissented, arguing that "the Court's application of the requirement that the condition imposed be reasonably related to the purpose for which the funds are expended, is cursory and unconvincing."

> The Court reasons that Congress wishes that the roads it builds may be used safely, that drunk drivers threaten highway safety, and that young people are more likely to drive while under the influence of alcohol under existing law than would be the case if there were a uniform national drinking age of 21. It hardly needs saying, however, that if the purpose is to deter drunken driving, it is far too over- and under-inclusive. It is over-inclusive because it stops teenagers from drinking even when they are not about to drive on interstate highways. It is under-inclusive because teenagers pose only a small part of the drunken driving problem in this Nation.

Thus she found too "attenuated" the linkage between the national interest and the particular conditions imposed. To allow the statute to operate in this case in effect allowed Congress to

> regulate almost any area of a State's social, political, or economic life on the theory that use of the interstate transportation system is somehow enhanced. If, for example, the United States were to condition highway moneys upon moving the state capital, I suppose it might argue that interstate transportation is facilitated by locating local governments in places easily accessible to interstate highways — or, conversely, that highways might become overburdened if they had to carry traffic to and from the state capital. In my mind, such a relationship is hardly more attenuated than the one which the Court finds supports §158.

Justice O'Connor cited *Butler* for the distinction between spending and regulation. There Justice Roberts noted "[t]here is an obvious difference between a statute stating the conditions upon which moneys shall be expended and one effective only upon assumption of a contractual obligation to submit to a regulation which otherwise could not be enforced." According to Justice O'Connor, "the *Butler* Court saw the Agricultural Adjustment Act for what it was — an exercise of regulatory, not spending, power. The error in *Butler* was not the Court's conclusion that the Act was essentially regulatory, but rather its crabbed view of the extent of Congress' regulatory power under the Commerce Clause."

Justice Brennan also dissented, on the ground "that regulation of the minimum age of purchasers of liquor falls squarely within the ambit of those powers reserved to the States by the Twenty-first Amendment. Since States possess this constitutional power, Congress can not condition a federal grant in a manner that abridges this right."

3. The Reconstruction Power

Recall that, in the half-century between 1937 and 1987, the Court had repeatedly upheld various exercises of congressional power under the Thirteenth, Fourteenth, and Fifteenth Amendments. Only once had the Justices held that Congress had exceeded its Reconstruction power — by a 5-4 vote — in a case (Oregon v. Mitchell) that failed to generate a majority opinion and that was quickly overturned by a constitutional amendment. On the other hand, the precise basis for sweeping congressional power under the Reconstruction clauses was not entirely clear. Was the power simply remedial, or dependent on superior fact-finding or line-drawing capacities of Congress, or was it something broader still? When the Court had upheld (or would uphold) a given state practice, could Congress invoke the Reconstruction Amendments to strike down the practice on the simple theory that the Court was wrong — that, properly understood, the Reconstruction Amendments condemned the practice in question? Such sweeping authority might seem to threaten both the Rehnquist Court's resurgent theory of states' rights, and a strong version of judicial supremacy. How would the Court react? The answer came in 1997.

CITY OF BOERNE v. FLORES
521 U.S. 507 (1997)

KENNEDY, J.

A decision by local zoning authorities to deny a church a building permit was challenged under the Religious Freedom Restoration Act of 1993 (RFRA), 107 Stat. 1488, 42 U.S.C. §2000bb et seq. The case calls into question the authority of Congress to enact RFRA. We conclude the statute exceeds Congress' power. . . .

II.

Congress enacted RFRA in direct response to the Court's decision in Employment Div., Dept. of Human Resources of Ore. v. Smith, 494 U.S. 872 (1990). There we considered a Free Exercise Clause claim brought by members of the Native American Church who were denied unemployment benefits when they lost their jobs because they had used peyote. Their practice was to ingest peyote for sacramental purposes, and they challenged an Oregon statute of general applicability which made use of the drug criminal. [Distinguishing away earlier cases, the *Smith* Court held that, absent special circumstances, the free exercise clause was not violated by a facially neutral and secular law, drafted without legislative animus, that had the effect (but not the intent) of interfering with a given religious practice. In particular, the *Smith* Court] declined to apply the balancing test set forth in Sherbert v. Verner, 374 U.S. 398 (1963), under which we would have asked whether Oregon's prohibition substantially burdened a religious practice and, if it did, whether the burden was justified by a compelling government interest. . . .

Four Members of the [*Smith*] Court disagreed. They argued the law placed a substantial burden on the Native American Church members so that it could be upheld only if the law served a compelling state interest and was narrowly tailored to achieve that end. Justice O'Connor concluded Oregon had satisfied the test, while Justice Blackmun, joined by Justice Brennan and Justice Marshall, could see no compelling interest justifying the law's application to the members.

These points of constitutional interpretation were debated by Members of Congress in hearings and floor debates. Many criticized the Court's reasoning, and this disagreement resulted in the passage of RFRA. Congress announced: "(1) The framers of the Constitution, recognizing free exercise of religion as an unalienable right, secured its protection in the First Amendment to the Constitution; (2) laws 'neutral' toward religion may burden religious exercise as surely as laws intended to interfere with religious exercise; (3) governments should not substantially burden religious exercise without compelling justification; (4) in Employment Division v. Smith, the Supreme Court virtually eliminated the requirement that the government justify burdens on religious exercise imposed by laws neutral toward religion; and (5) the compelling interest test as set forth in prior Federal court rulings is a workable test for striking sensible balances between religious liberty and competing prior governmental interests." 42 U.S.C. §2000bb(a).

The Act's stated purposes are:

"(1) to restore the compelling interest test as set forth in Sherbert v. Verner and Wisconsin v. Yoder, 406 U.S. 205 (1972) and to guarantee its application in all cases where free exercise of religion is substantially burdened; and

"(2) to provide a claim or defense to persons whose religious exercise is substantially burdened by government." §2000bb(b).

RFRA prohibits "government" from "substantially burdening" a person's exercise of religion even if the burden results from a rule of general applicability unless the government can demonstrate the burden "(1) is in furtherance of . . . a compelling governmental interest; and (2) is the least restrictive means of furthering that compelling governmental interest." §2000bb-1. The Act's mandate applies to any "branch, department, agency, instrumentality, and official (or other person acting under color of law) of the United States," as well as to any "State, or . . . subdivision of a State." §2000bb-2(1). . . .

III.

A

Under our Constitution, the Federal Government is one of enumerated powers. *McCulloch*; see also The Federalist No. 45. The judicial authority to determine the constitutionality of laws, in cases and controversies, is based on the premise that the "powers of the legislature are defined and limited; and that those limits may not be mistaken, or forgotten, the constitution is written." Marbury v. Madison.

Congress relied on its Fourteenth Amendment enforcement power in enacting the most far reaching and substantial of RFRA's provisions, those which impose its requirements on the States. . . .

The parties disagree over whether RFRA is a proper exercise of Congress' §5 power "to enforce" by "appropriate legislation" the constitutional guarantee that no State shall deprive any person of "life, liberty, or property, without due process of law" nor deny any person "equal protection of the laws."

In defense of the Act respondent contends, with support from the United States as amicus, that RFRA is permissible enforcement legislation. Congress, it is said, is only protecting by legislation one of the liberties guaranteed by the Fourteenth Amendment's Due Process Clause, the free exercise of religion, beyond what is necessary under *Smith*. It is said the congressional decision to dispense with proof of deliberate or overt discrimination and instead concentrate on a law's effects accords with the settled understanding that §5 includes the power to enact legislation designed to prevent as well as remedy constitutional violations. It is further contended that Congress' §5 power is not limited to remedial or preventive legislation. All must acknowledge that §5 is "a positive grant of legislative power" to Congress, Katzenbach v. Morgan. . . .

Legislation which deters or remedies constitutional violations can fall within the sweep of Congress' enforcement power even if in the process it prohibits conduct which is not itself unconstitutional and intrudes into "legislative spheres of autonomy previously reserved to the States." For example, the Court upheld a suspension of literacy tests and similar voting requirements under Congress' parallel power to enforce the provisions of the Fifteenth Amendment as a measure to combat racial discrimination in voting, South Carolina v. Katzenbach, despite the facial constitutionality of the tests under Lassiter v. Northampton County Bd. of Elections. We have also concluded that other measures protecting voting rights are within Congress' power to enforce the Fourteenth and Fifteenth Amendments, despite the burdens those measures placed on the States. South Carolina v. Katzenbach (upholding several provisions of the Voting Rights Act of 1965); Katzenbach v. Morgan (upholding ban on literacy tests that prohibited certain people schooled in Puerto Rico from voting); Oregon v. Mitchell (upholding 5-year nationwide ban on literacy tests and similar voting requirements for registering to vote); City of Rome v. United States (upholding 7-year extension of the Voting Rights Act's requirement that certain jurisdictions preclear any change to a "standard, practice, or procedure with respect to voting").

It is also true, however, that "as broad as the congressional enforcement power is, it is not unlimited." Oregon v. Mitchell (opinion of Black, J.). In assessing the breadth of §5's enforcement power, we begin with its text. Congress has been given the power "to enforce" the "provisions of this article." We agree with respondent, of course, that Congress can enact legislation under §5 enforcing the constitutional right to the free exercise of religion. The "provisions of this article," to which §5 refers, include the Due Process Clause of the Fourteenth Amendment. Congress' power to enforce the Free Exercise Clause follows from our holding in Cantwell v. Connecticut, 310 U.S. 296, 303 (1940), that the "fundamental concept of liberty embodied in [the Fourteenth Amendment's Due Process Clause] embraces the liberties guaranteed by the First Amendment."

Congress' power under §5, however, extends only to "enforcing" the provisions of the Fourteenth Amendment. The Court has described this power as "remedial." The design of the Amendment and the text of §5 are inconsistent with the suggestion that Congress has the power to decree the substance of the Fourteenth Amendment's restrictions on the States. Legislation which alters the meaning of the Free Exercise Clause cannot be said to be enforcing the Clause. Congress does not enforce a constitutional right by changing what the right is. It has been given the power "to enforce," not the power to determine what constitutes a constitutional violation. Were it not so, what Congress would be enforcing would no longer be, in any meaningful sense, the "provisions of [the Fourteenth Amendment]."

While the line between measures that remedy or prevent unconstitutional actions and measures that make a substantive change in the governing law is not easy to discern, and Congress must have wide latitude in determining where it lies, the distinction exists and must be observed. There must be a congruence and proportionality between the injury to be prevented or remedied and the means adopted to that end. Lacking such a connection, legislation may become substantive in operation and effect. History and our case law support drawing the distinction, one apparent from the text of the Amendment.

[55]

The Fourteenth Amendment's history confirms the remedial, rather than substantive, nature of the Enforcement Clause. The Joint Committee on Reconstruction of the 39th Congress began drafting what would become the Fourteenth Amendment in January 1866. The objections to the Committee's first draft of the Amendment, and the rejection of the draft, have a direct bearing on the central issue of defining Congress' enforcement power. In February, Republican Representative John Bingham of Ohio reported the following draft amendment to the House of Representatives on behalf of the Joint Committee:

> "The Congress shall have power to make all laws which shall be necessary and proper to secure to the citizens of each State all privileges and immunities of citizens in the several States, and to all persons in the several States equal protection in the rights of life, liberty, and property." Cong. Globe, 39th Cong., 1st Sess., 1034 (1866).

The proposal encountered immediate opposition, which continued through three days of debate. Members of Congress from across the political spectrum criticized the Amendment, and the criticisms had a common theme: The proposed Amendment gave Congress too much legislative power at the expense of the existing constitutional structure. Democrats and conservative Republicans argued that the proposed Amendment would give Congress a power to intrude into traditional areas of state responsibility, a power inconsistent with the federal design central to the Constitution. Typifying these views, Republican Representative Robert Hale of New York labeled the Amendment "an utter departure from every principle ever dreamed of by the men who framed our Constitution," and warned that under it "all State legislation, in its codes of civil and criminal jurisprudence and procedures . . .

55. Note that Justice Scalia, who joined the rest of the Court's opinion, did not join this section, discussing the history of the Fourteenth Amendment.

may be overridden, may be repealed or abolished, and the law of Congress established instead." Senator William Stewart of Nevada likewise stated the Amendment would permit "Congress to legislate fully upon all subjects affecting life, liberty, and property," such that "there would not be much left for the State Legislatures," and would thereby "work an entire change in our form of government." . . . Some radicals . . . also objected that giving Congress primary responsibility for enforcing legal equality would place power in the hands of changing congressional majorities.

As a result of these objections having been expressed from so many different quarters, the House voted to table the proposal until April . . . [and] the Joint Committee began drafting a new article of Amendment, which it reported to Congress on April 30, 1866.

Section 1 of the new draft Amendment imposed self-executing limits on the States. Section 5 prescribed that "the Congress shall have power to enforce, by appropriate legislation, the provisions of this article." Under the revised Amendment, Congress' power was no longer plenary but remedial. Congress was granted the power to make the substantive constitutional prohibitions against the States effective. Representative Bingham said the new draft would give Congress "the power . . . to protect by national law the privileges and immunities of all the citizens of the Republic . . . whenever the same shall be abridged or denied by the unconstitutional acts of any State." Representative Stevens described the new draft Amendment as "allowing Congress to correct the unjust legislation of the States." See also statement of Sen. Howard (§5 "enables Congress, in case the States shall enact laws in conflict with the principles of the amendment, to correct that legislation by a formal congressional enactment"). The revised Amendment proposal did not raise the concerns expressed earlier regarding broad congressional power to prescribe uniform national laws with respect to life, liberty, and property. After revisions not relevant here, the new measure passed both Houses and was ratified in July 1868 as the Fourteenth Amendment. . . .

The design of the Fourteenth Amendment has proved significant also in maintaining the traditional separation of powers between Congress and the Judiciary. The first eight Amendments to the Constitution set forth self-executing prohibitions on governmental action, and this Court has had primary authority to interpret those prohibitions. The Bingham draft, some thought, departed from that tradition by vesting in Congress primary power to interpret and elaborate on the meaning of the new Amendment through legislation. Under it, "Congress, and not the courts, was to judge whether or not any of the privileges or immunities were not secured to citizens in the several States." While this separation of powers aspect did not occasion the widespread resistance which was caused by the proposal's threat to the federal balance, it nonetheless attracted the attention of various Members. As enacted, the Fourteenth Amendment confers substantive rights against the States which, like the provisions of the Bill of Rights, are self-executing. The power to interpret the Constitution in a case or controversy remains in the Judiciary.

2

The remedial and preventive nature of Congress' enforcement power, and the limitation inherent in the power, were confirmed in our earliest cases on the Fourteenth Amendment. In the Civil Rights Cases, 109 U.S. 3 (1883), the Court invalidated sections of the Civil Rights Act of 1875 which prescribed criminal penalties for denying to any person "the full enjoyment of" public accommodations and conveyances, on the grounds that it exceeded Congress' power by seeking to regulate private conduct. The Enforcement Clause, the Court said, did not authorize Congress to pass "general legislation upon the rights of the citizen, but corrective legislation; that is, such as may be necessary and proper for counteracting such laws as the States may adopt or enforce, and which, by the amendment, they are prohibited from making or enforcing. . . ." The power to "legislate generally upon" life, liberty, and property, as opposed to the "power to provide modes of redress" against offensive state action, was "repugnant" to the Constitution. . . . Although the specific holdings of these early cases might have been superseded or modified, see, e.g., Heart of Atlanta Motel, Inc. v. United States, their treatment of Congress' §5 power as corrective or preventive, not definitional, has not been questioned. . . .

3

Any suggestion that Congress has a substantive, non-remedial power under the Fourteenth Amendment is not supported by our case law. In Oregon v. Mitchell, a majority of the Court concluded Congress had exceeded its enforcement powers by enacting legislation lowering the minimum age of voters from 21 to 18 in state and local elections. The five Members of the Court who reached this conclusion explained that the legislation intruded into an area reserved by the *Constitution to the States.* . . .

There is language in our opinion in Katzenbach v. Morgan which could be interpreted as acknowledging a power in Congress to enact legislation that expands the rights contained in §1 of the Fourteenth Amendment. This is not a necessary interpretation, however, or even the best one. . . . The Court perceived a factual basis on which Congress could have concluded that New York's literacy requirement "constituted an invidious discrimination in violation of the Equal Protection Clause." [The Court's] rationales for upholding §4(e) rested on unconstitutional discrimination by New York and Congress' reasonable attempt to combat it. As Justice Stewart explained in Oregon v. Mitchell, interpreting *Morgan* to give Congress the power to interpret the Constitution "would require an enormous extension of that decision's rationale." If Congress could define its own powers by altering the Fourteenth Amendment's meaning, no longer would the Constitution be "superior paramount law, unchangeable by ordinary means." It would be "on a level with ordinary legislative acts, and, like other acts, . . . alterable when the legislature shall please to alter it." Marbury v. Madison. Under this approach, it is difficult to conceive of a principle that would limit congressional power. Shifting legislative majorities could change the Constitution and effectively circumvent the difficult and detailed amendment process contained in Article V.

B

Respondent contends that RFRA is a proper exercise of Congress' remedial or preventive power. The Act, it is said, is a reasonable means of protecting the free exercise of religion as defined by *Smith.* It prevents and remedies laws which are enacted with the unconstitutional object of targeting religious beliefs and practices. To avoid the difficulty of proving such violations, it is said, Congress can simply invalidate any law which imposes a substantial burden on a religious practice unless it is justified by a compelling interest and is the least restrictive means of accomplishing that interest. If Congress can prohibit laws with discriminatory effects in order to prevent racial discrimination in violation of the Equal Protection Clause, then it can do the same, respondent argues, to promote religious liberty.

While preventive rules are sometimes appropriate remedial measures, there must be a congruence between the means used and the ends to be achieved. The appropriateness of remedial measures must be considered in light of the evil presented. Strong measures appropriate to address one harm may be an unwarranted response to another, lesser one. A comparison between RFRA and the Voting Rights Act is instructive. In contrast to the record which confronted Congress and the judiciary in the voting rights cases, RFRA's legislative record lacks examples of modern instances of generally applicable laws passed because of religious bigotry. The history of persecution in this country detailed in the hearings mentions no episodes occurring in the past 40 years. . . . Rather, the emphasis of the hearings was on laws of general applicability which place incidental burdens on religion. Much of the discussion centered upon anecdotal evidence of autopsies performed on Jewish individuals and Hmong immigrants in violation of their religious beliefs, and on zoning regulations and historic preservation laws (like the one at issue here), which as an incident of their normal operation, have adverse effects on churches and synagogues. It is difficult to maintain that they are examples of legislation enacted or enforced due to animus or hostility to the burdened religious practices or that they indicate some widespread pattern of religious discrimination in this country. Congress' concern was with the incidental burdens imposed, not the object or purpose of the legislation. This lack of support in the legislative record, however, is not RFRA's most serious shortcoming. . . .

Regardless of the state of the legislative record, RFRA cannot be considered remedial, preventive legislation, if those terms are to have any meaning. RFRA is so out of proportion to a supposed remedial or preventive object that it cannot be understood as responsive to, or designed to prevent, unconstitutional behavior. It appears, instead, to attempt a substantive change in constitutional protections. Preventive measures prohibiting certain types of laws may be appropriate when there is reason to believe that many of the laws affected by the congressional enactment have a significant likelihood of being unconstitutional. . . .

RFRA is not so confined. Sweeping coverage ensures its intrusion at every level of government, displacing laws and prohibiting official actions of almost every description and regardless of subject matter. RFRA's restrictions apply to every agency and official of the Federal, State, and local Governments. RFRA applies to all federal and state law, statutory or otherwise, whether adopted before or after its enactment. RFRA has no termination date or termination mechanism. Any law is subject to challenge at any time by any individual who alleges a substantial burden on his or her free exercise of religion.

The reach and scope of RFRA distinguish it from other measures passed under Congress' enforcement power, even in the area of voting rights. In South Carolina v. Katzenbach, the challenged provisions were confined to those regions of the country where voting discrimination had been most flagrant, and affected a discrete class of state laws, i.e., state voting laws. Furthermore, to ensure that the reach of the Voting Rights Act was limited to those cases in which constitutional violations were most likely (in order to reduce the possibility of overbreadth), the coverage under the Act would terminate "at the behest of States and political subdivisions in which the danger of substantial voting discrimination has not materialized during the preceding five years." The provisions restricting and banning literacy tests, upheld in Katzenbach v. Morgan, and Oregon v. Mitchell, attacked a particular type of voting qualification, one with a long history as a "notorious means to deny and abridge voting rights on racial grounds." In *City of Rome,* the Court rejected a challenge to the constitutionality of a Voting Rights Act provision which required certain jurisdictions to submit changes in electoral practices to the Department of Justice for preimplementation review. The requirement was placed only on jurisdictions with a history of intentional racial discrimination in voting. Like the provisions at issue in South Carolina v. Katzenbach, this provision permitted a covered jurisdiction to avoid preclearance requirements under certain conditions and, moreover, lapsed in seven years. This is not to say, of course, that §5 legislation requires termination dates, geographic restrictions, or egregious predicates. Where, however, a congressional enactment pervasively prohibits constitutional state action in an effort to remedy or to prevent unconstitutional state action, limitations of this kind tend to ensure Congress' means are proportionate to ends legitimate under §5.

The stringent test RFRA demands of state laws reflects a lack of proportionality or congruence between the means adopted and the legitimate end to be achieved. If an objector can show a substantial burden on his free exercise, the State must demonstrate a compelling governmental interest and show that the law is the least restrictive means of furthering its interest. Claims that a law substantially burdens someone's exercise of religion will often be difficult to contest. Requiring a State to demonstrate a compelling interest and show that it has adopted the least restrictive means of achieving that interest is the most demanding test known to constitutional law. If "'compelling interest' really means what it says . . . many laws will not meet the test. . . . [The test] would open the prospect of constitutionally required religious exemptions from civic obligations of almost every conceivable kind." Laws valid under *Smith* would fall under RFRA without regard to whether they had the object of stifling or punishing free exercise. We make these observations not to reargue the position of the majority in *Smith* but to illustrate the substantive alteration of its holding attempted by RFRA. Even assuming RFRA would be interpreted in effect to mandate some lesser test, say one equivalent to intermediate scrutiny, the statute nevertheless would require searching judicial scrutiny of state law with the attendant likelihood of invalidation. This is a considerable congressional intrusion into the States' traditional prerogatives and general authority to regulate for the health and welfare of their citizens.

The substantial costs RFRA exacts, both in practical terms of imposing a heavy litigation burden on the States and in terms of curtailing their traditional general regulatory power, far exceed any pattern or practice of unconstitutional conduct under the Free Exercise Clause as interpreted in *Smith.* Simply put, RFRA is not designed to identify and counteract state laws likely to be unconstitutional because of their treatment of religion. In most cases, the state laws to which RFRA applies are not ones which will have been motivated by religious bigotry. If a state law disproportionately burdened a particular class of religious observers, this circumstance might be evidence of an impermissible legislative motive. Cf. Washington v. Davis, 426 U.S. 229 (1976). RFRA's substantial burden test, however, is not even a discriminatory effects or disparate impact test. It is a reality of the modern regulatory state that numerous state laws, such as the zoning regulations at issue here, impose a substantial burden on a large class of individuals. When the exercise of religion has been burdened in an incidental way by a law of general application, it does not follow that the persons affected have been burdened any more than other citizens, let alone burdened because of their religious beliefs. . . .

When Congress acts within its sphere of power and responsibilities, it has not just the right but the duty to make its own informed judgment on the meaning and force of the Constitution. This has been clear from the early days of the Republic. In 1789, when a Member of the House of Representatives objected to a debate on the constitutionality of legislation based on the theory that "it would be officious" to consider the constitutionality of a measure that did not affect the House, James Madison explained that "it is incontrovertibly of as much importance to this branch of the Government as to any other, that the constitution should be preserved entire. It is our duty." Were it otherwise, we would not afford Congress the presumption of validity its enactments now enjoy.

Our national experience teaches that the Constitution is preserved best when each part of the government respects both the Constitution and the proper actions and determinations of the other branches. When the Court has interpreted the Constitution, it has acted within the province of the Judicial Branch, which embraces the duty to say what the law is. Marbury v. Madison. When the political branches of the Government act against the background of a judicial interpretation of the Constitution already issued, it must be understood that in later cases and controversies the Court will treat its precedents with the respect due them under settled principles, including stare decisis, and contrary expectations must be disappointed. RFRA was designed to control cases and controversies, such as the one before us; but as the provisions of the federal statute here invoked are beyond congressional authority, it is this Court's precedent, not RFRA, which must control. . . . Broad as the power of Congress is under the Enforcement Clause of the Fourteenth Amendment, RFRA contradicts vital principles necessary to maintain separation of powers and the federal balance.

STEVENS, J., concurring.

In my opinion, [RFRA] is a "law respecting an establishment of religion" that violates the First Amendment to the Constitution. . . .

If the historic landmark on the hill in Boerne happened to be a museum or an art gallery owned by an atheist, it would not be eligible for an exemption from the city ordinances that forbid an enlargement of the structure. Because the landmark is owned by the Catholic Church, it is claimed that RFRA gives its owner a federal statutory entitlement to an exemption from a generally applicable, neutral civil law. Whether the Church would actually prevail under the statute or not, the statute has provided the Church with a legal weapon that no atheist or agnostic can obtain. This governmental preference for religion, as opposed to irreligion, is forbidden by the First Amendment.

[The concurring opinion of Scalia, J., joined by Stevens, J., defending the correctness of *Smith*, is omitted.]

O'CONNOR, J., dissenting, joined in part by Breyer, J. . . .

I remain of the view that *Smith* was wrongly decided, and I would use this case to reexamine the Court's holding there. Therefore, I would direct the parties to brief the question whether *Smith* represents the correct understanding of the Free Exercise Clause and set the case for reargument. If the Court were to correct the misinterpretation of the Free Exercise Clause set forth in *Smith,* it would simultaneously put our First Amendment jurisprudence back on course and allay the legitimate concerns of a majority in Congress who believed that *Smith* improperly restricted religious liberty. We would then be in a position to review RFRA in light of a proper interpretation of the Free Exercise Clause.

I

I agree with much of the reasoning set forth in Part III-A of the Court's opinion. Indeed, if I agreed with the Court's standard in *Smith,* I would join the opinion. As the Court's careful and thorough historical analysis shows, Congress lacks the "power to decree the substance of the Fourteenth Amendment's restrictions on the States." Rather, its power under §5 of the Fourteenth Amendment extends only to enforcing the Amendment's provisions. In short, Congress lacks the ability independently to define or expand the scope of constitutional rights by statute. Accordingly, whether Congress has exceeded its §5 powers turns on whether there is a "congruence and proportionality between the injury to be prevented or remedied and the means adopted to that end." This recognition does not, of course, in any way diminish Congress' obligation to draw its own conclusions regarding the Constitution's meaning. Congress, no less than this Court, is called upon to consider the requirements of the Constitution and to act in accordance with its dictates. But when it enacts legislation in furtherance of its delegated powers, Congress must make its judgments consistent with this Court's exposition of the Constitution and with the limits placed on its legislative authority by provisions such as the Fourteenth Amendment.

The Court's analysis of whether RFRA is a constitutional exercise of Congress' §5 power, set forth in Part III-B of its opinion, is premised on the assumption that *Smith* correctly interprets the Free Exercise Clause. This is an assumption that I do not accept. I continue to believe that *Smith* adopted an improper standard for deciding free exercise claims. In *Smith,* five Members of this Court — without briefing or argument on the issue — interpreted the Free Exercise Clause to permit the government to prohibit, without justification, conduct mandated by an individual's religious beliefs, so long as the prohibition is generally applicable. Contrary to the Court's holding in that case, however, the Free Exercise Clause is not simply an antidiscrimination principle that protects only against those laws that single out religious practice for unfavorable treatment. Rather, the Clause is best understood as an affirmative guarantee of the right to participate in religious practices and conduct without impermissible governmental interference, even when such conduct conflicts with a neutral, generally applicable law. Before *Smith,* our free exercise cases were generally in keeping with this idea: where a law substantially burdened religiously motivated conduct — regardless whether it was specifically targeted at religion or applied generally — we required government to justify that law with a compelling state interest and to use means narrowly tailored to achieve that interest.

The Court's rejection of this principle in *Smith* is supported neither by precedent nor . . . by history. The decision has harmed religious liberty. For example, a Federal District Court, in reliance on *Smith,* ruled that the Free Exercise Clause was not implicated where Hmong natives objected on religious grounds to their son's autopsy, conducted pursuant to a generally applicable state law. The Court of Appeals for the Eighth Circuit held that application of a city's zoning laws to prevent a church from conducting services in an area zoned for commercial uses raised no free exercise concerns, even though the city permitted secular not-for-profit organizations in that area. . . .

Stare decisis concerns should not prevent us from revisiting our holding in *Smith.* "Stare decisis is a principle of policy and not a mechanical formula of adherence to the latest decision, however recent and questionable, when such adherence involves collision with a prior doctrine more embracing in its scope, intrinsically sounder, and verified by experience." This principle is particularly true in constitutional cases, where — as this case so plainly illustrates — "correction through legislative action is practically impossible." . . .

Accordingly, I believe that we should reexamine our holding in *Smith,* and do so in this very case. In its place, I would return to a rule that requires government to justify any substantial burden on religiously motivated conduct by a compelling state interest and to impose that burden only by means narrowly tailored to achieve that interest. . . .

SOUTER, J., dissenting.

To decide whether the Fourteenth Amendment gives Congress sufficient power to enact the Religious Freedom Restoration Act, the Court measures the legislation against the free-exercise standard of *Smith.* . . . I have serious doubts about the precedential value of the *Smith* rule and its entitlement to adherence. . . . [T]his case should be set down for reargument permitting plenary reexamination of the issue. Since the Court declines to follow that course, our free-exercise law remains marked by an "intolerable tension," and the constitutionality of the Act of Congress to enforce the free-exercise right cannot now be soundly decided. I would therefore dismiss the writ of certiorari as improvidently granted, and I accordingly dissent from the Court's disposition of this case.

BREYER, J., dissenting.

I agree with Justice O'Connor that the Court should direct the parties to brief the question whether *Smith* was correctly decided, and set this case for reargument. I do not, however, find it necessary to consider the question whether, assuming *Smith* is correct, §5 of the Fourteenth Amendment would authorize Congress to enact the legislation before us. . . .

Discussion

1. *Challenging the Court's account.* None of the Justices squarely took issue with the majority's analysis of congressional power under Section 5 (although Justices Breyer and Souter did not reach the question). But consider the following counterarguments.

The textual counterargument: The Court says that whenever Congress goes beyond the Court's interpretation of the substantive rights conferred by §1 of the Fourteenth Amendment, Congress thereby ceases to "enforce" §1. Congress has the power only to "enforce" the true meaning of §1, not to add to it. But a pro-Congress critic might see this assertion as perfectly circular and question-begging. Congress believes it is not *adding to* the meaning of free exercise. Rather, (on this view) *Smith* wrongly subtracted from the meaning and Congress is merely restoring it, *enforcing* its true meaning. Why — textually — does the Court's view of *Smith*'s rightness trump Congress's view of its wrongness? At this point, the question becomes in part, who decides the true meaning of §1? To a textualist, isn't it relevant that the Fourteenth Amendment explicitly speaks of *Congress* as enforcer? Perhaps Congress is not the *exclusive* enforcer; but doesn't the text signal a very important role for Congress, above and beyond the Court (which of course is not textually mentioned in §5)?

The "intratextual" and doctrinal counterargument: "Intratextualism" is a technique of parsing the words of a contested clause in light of other clauses of the Constitution that use similar or identical words. Recall, for example, Chief Justice Marshall's efforts in *McCulloch* to parse the Article I, §8 words "necessary and proper" in light of the Article I, §10 words "absolutely necessary"; and Justice Thomas's efforts in *Lopez* to construe the word "commerce" in the Commerce Clause in light of the word "commerce" in the port preference clause. Akhil Reed Amar has criticized *Boerne* for failing to pay heed to this technique:

> [T]he words of Section 5 do not stand alone. They are part of a single coherent Constitution and must be read alongside the rest of the document. And when they are, a strong — perhaps devastating — objection to Justice Kennedy's overly confident assertions arises, an objection that he does not see because he is reading with blinkers on. Here are the words of Section 2 of the Thirteenth Amendment: "Congress shall have power to enforce this article by appropriate legislation." These words are *in pari materia* with the words of Section 5 of the Fourteenth Amendment. A very powerful intratextual presumption arises that these two parallel clauses must be interpreted in parallel fashion. What's sauce for one should be sauce for the other. But Section 2 of the Thirteenth Amendment has not been read simply to allow Congress to remedy violations of Section 1 (of the Thirteenth). Acting under Section 2, Congress has passed broad substantive legislation ranging far beyond the self-executing rights under Section 1 (as defined by the Supreme Court). No court ever said, or ever would say, that when private person A refuses to deal commercially with private person B because B is black, this refusal is "slavery" or "involuntary servitude" within the meaning of Section 1 of the Thirteenth Amendment. And yet the Court in the famous case of Jones v. Alfred Mayer Co. upheld congressional laws banning this refusal under its Section 2 enforcement power.
>
> The *Boerne* Court says that once Congress goes beyond remedial enforcement of the Fourteenth Amendment Section 1, Congress would no longer be enforcing the Amendment "in any meaningful sense." If this is so for the Fourteenth, why not for the Thirteenth, too? Or to be more blunt, as this is *not* true for the Thirteenth, why is it so for the Fourteenth? The *Boerne* Court offers no answer to the obvious inconsistency here — it never even sees the issue. It is reading Section 5 of the Fourteenth and does not even see Section 2 of the Thirteenth.[56]

Amar proceeds to argue that, just as Congress has substantive power under the Thirteenth Amendment to define "badges and incidents" of slavery that go beyond judicial definitions of slavery under §1 (of the Thirteenth), so Congress under the Fourteenth Amendment should have substantive, and not merely remedial, power to define "badges and incidents" of freedom and citizenship that

---

56. Amar, supra n.43, at 822-823.

go beyond judicial interpretations of rights under §1 (of the Fourteenth). For his precise formulation, see the discussion notes following the *Katzenbach* cases, supra pp. 502-503.

The structural counterargument: To support its view that only the Court can ultimately determine the true meaning of §1 rights (which Congress may then remedially enforce under §5), the *Boerne* majority wraps itself in *Marbury.* But isn't this too quick? If more-than-remedial congressional power in *Boerne* would have violated *Marbury,* why didn't more-than-remedial congressional power in *Jones?* Even under *Marbury,* other branches of the federal government are sometimes allowed to have a broader view of a constitutional right, and to make that broader view stick. For example, courts upheld the Sedition Act of 1798, but President Jefferson deemed the Act unconstitutional and pardoned all concerned. Surely Congress could also have repealed this Act, and done so on the simple theory that the courts were wrong? Likewise, in RFRA — putting aside Establishment Clause concerns (as did the *Boerne* majority) — Congress was free to impose an effects test on *federal* practices burdening religion — and to do so simply because it thought *Smith* wrong. And individual state legislatures were likewise free to provide similar protections in their respective states. None of this threatens *Marbury,* rightly understood; judicial review sets a floor of rights-protection, not a ceiling. If so, what is wrong with saying that although Congress cannot generally bless a state practice that the Court has held unconstitutional under §1, Congress can *add to* the list of "privileges" and "immunities" that states shall not abridge? (Note that Madison at the Philadelphia Convention sought to vest Congress with a general right to veto state practices that Congress thought violated the Constitution. Madison also believed in federal judicial review over states. Is there anything contradictory about holding states to both federal judicial and federal legislative review, with states generally held to whichever standard is higher?) These arguments return us, in a way, to Brennan's ratchet, see supra p. 586. On this view, even though Congress should have very broad power under the Fourteenth Amendment to outlaw state practices that violate *Congress's* understanding of Reconstruction values of liberty, equality, and citizenship, this broad power does not exempt Congress from compliance with affirmative limits on its powers such as those set out in the first nine Amendments. Congress may not generally bless a state law that denies Fourteenth Amendment due process (as defined by the Court) in part because Congress *itself* may not violate Fifth Amendment due process (as defined by the Court). Of course, tricky issues arise when conflicting constitutional rights bump up against each other — for example, when overly broad protections of the rights of Blacks might be seen as violating the rights of non-Blacks in the context of affirmative action, or when overly broad protections of free exercise run afoul of Establishment Clause principles. But the Court opinion in *Boerne* did not rely on the Establishment clause; only Justice Stevens did.

The historical counterargument: Several scholars have sharply criticized the *Boerne* Court's historical account, including Michael McConnell, supra p. 591, note b, Mark Graber,[57] and Akhil Reed Amar. According to Amar, supra n.43:

[T]he framers of the Fourteenth Amendment itself — the Thirty-Ninth Congress — had a broad view of Section 2 of the Thirteenth Amendment. We know this because

---

57. Mark A. Graber, The Constitution as a Whole: A Partial Political Science Perspective, 33 U. Rich. L. Rev. 343 (1999).

they adopted the Civil Rights Act of 1866, which swept far beyond merely prohibiting slavery and involuntary servitude, and the basis for their action was Section 2 of the Thirteenth Amendment. At the very moment that they were proposing another "enforcement" clause in the Fourteenth Amendment, they were speaking loud and clear about what the parallel enforcement clause of the Thirteenth Amendment meant.[a] And they said it meant more than mere remedial legislation.

This noteworthy fact about the Thirty-Ninth Congress — which, again, Justice Kennedy never notices because he never sees the freight train coming — seems much stronger than the facts about that Congress that he does mention. He stresses the fact that lawmakers rejected an early draft of the Fourteenth Amendment that in effect would have given Congress plenary legislative power. But there is a large gap between plenary power on one extreme and only remedial power on the other. To reject the former is not to affirm the latter — as is clear if we spend just an instant thinking about Section 2 of the Thirteenth Amendment, under which Congress has less than plenary and more than remedial power. In the Thirteenth Amendment this middle ground is captured by the concept of "badges and incidents" of slavery, which Section 1 does not abolish of its own force, but which can be abolished by Congress under Section 2.

[There are] comparable middle-ground possibilities for the Fourteenth Amendment. . . . [For example,] Congress could have power to define rights that in good faith it considers truly fundamental and basic, and these rights, once defined — "badges and incidents of freedom and citizenship" — would thereafter be enforceable, even against states, as "privileges" and "immunities" of American "citizens." . . .

The legislative history that *Boerne* invokes supports my middle-ground positions. The early draft of the Fourteenth Amendment, which was rejected because it in effect conferred plenary power on Congress, read as follows:

> The Congress shall have power to make all laws which shall be necessary and proper to secure to the citizens of each State all privileges and immunities of citizens in the several States, and to all persons in the several States equal protection in the rights of life, liberty, and property.

The objection to this draft was twofold: Congress would have power to legislate even in the absence of any state misconduct and even on private parties (the state action issue), and would have power over virtually everything, because everything implicates life, liberty, and property. But note how the middle ground I am proposing avoids both problems. First, it accepts the state action doctrine — Congress can legislate rights against states, not private persons. Second, it further limits Congress's power by focusing on privileges and immunities of citizens, not life, liberty, and property. Life, liberty, and property encompass almost everything, but the privileges and immunities of citizens that I am highlighting include only things that are in a real and sincere sense deemed truly fundamental.

The rejected draft is also noteworthy for its intratextual echo of the Article I, Section 8, Necessary and Proper Clause. This clause was associated with broad congressional power in *McCulloch*. It might be thought that the abandonment of this language in the final version of Section 5 signaled a retreat from a broad view of congressional enforcement authority. On the contrary, the framers saw the

---

a. Admittedly, Representative John Bingham, the father of Section 1 of the Fourteenth Amendment, did not share his colleagues' broad view of Section 2 of the Thirteenth. (Or if he did, he thought that even under a broad view, encompassing substantive and not merely remedial enforcement, Section 2 was still not broad enough to support the wide-ranging Civil Rights Bill.) But on this issue Bingham was outvoted by two-thirds of his colleagues, who overrode President Johnson's veto — the same two-thirds necessary to pass the Fourteenth Amendment on to the states.

Enforcement Clause phrase "appropriate legislation" as equivalent to the Article I, Section 8 phrase "proper laws." Ordinary dictionaries confirm the obvious etymological link between "proper" and "appropriate." And in one of *McCulloch's* most famous passages, Marshall cemented this etymological linkage in words that the Thirty-Ninth Congress knew and relied on: "Let the end be legitimate, let it be within the scope of the constitution, and all means which are *appropriate*, which are plainly adapted to that end, which are not prohibited, but consist with the letter and spirit of the constitution, are constitutional."[b] Only a couple of years after the Fourteenth Amendment became part of our supreme law, the Supreme Court itself quoted this famous passage in full and then declared that "it must be taken then as finally settled, so far as judicial decisions can settle anything, that the words" of the Necessary and Proper Clause were "equivalent" to the word "appropriate." And here is what the Court said in the 1880s, in language prominently relied on in *Jones*, about the Enforcement Clause of the Thirteenth Amendment: "[It] clothes Congress with power to pass all laws necessary and proper for abolishing all badges and incidents of slavery in the United States. . . ."

Overly exuberant statements of judicial supremacy are in vogue these days, but it is ironic to read all this back into the Fourteenth Amendment, in which Congress (the good guys) drafted emphatic constitutional language to repudiate the arrogant *Dred Scott* Court (the bad guys). Congress did not insist on being the only interpreter of fundamental rights. It was aware that it might one day fall into the wrong hands, and so it created a self-executing Section 1 that courts could enforce on their own. But courts can also at times fall into the wrong hands, as the Thirty-Ninth Congress well knew. Thus the most sensible reading of the Fourteenth Amendment would involve both courts and Congress in the task of protecting truly fundamental rights against states, with states generally held to whichever standard was stricter — more protective of fundamental freedoms — in any given instance.

2. *Applying* Boerne — *The VAWA case.* Whereas the Warren Court, as we have seen, never once struck down a congressional statute that had been enacted pursuant to Congress's power to "enforce" the Reconstruction Amendments, and the Burger Court did so only once (in the splintered 1970 case of Oregon v. Mitchell), such invalidations have become a trademark of the Rehnquist Court.

Perhaps the most notable post-*Boerne* case, United States v. Morrison, 529 U.S. 598 (2000), involved Section 13981 of the Violence Against Women Act of 1994, which empowered a victim of gender-based violence to bring suit for damages in federal court against the perpetrator of this violence. On the facts of *Morrison* itself, a young woman brought suit against two young men who, she claimed, had raped and brutalized her. As we have already seen, supra p. 623, Chief Justice Rehnquist, writing for a majority of five (including Justices O'Connor, Kennedy, Scalia, and Thomas), ruled that Section 13981 exceeded the proper scope of congressional authority under the Commerce Clause. The Court then turned to Section 5 of the

---

b. Emphasis added. For clear evidence that the 39th Congress had these key words from *McCulloch* in mind when they drafted the Fourteenth Amendment, see Cong. Globe, 39th Cong., 1st Sess. 1118 (1866) (remarks of Rep. James Wilson). Wilson was the House sponsor of the Civil Rights Act of 1866, which he defended under Section 2 of the Thirteenth Amendment. Doubts about the sufficiency of this basis for congressional power eventually helped lead to congressional adoption of the Fourteenth Amendment, which was (among other things) designed to provide a rock-solid foundation for the Act. In this passage, Wilson defended the pending civil rights bill by quoting verbatim Section 2 of the Thirteenth Amendment and then explicitly linking its wording to the key words from *McCulloch* (which Wilson also quoted verbatim). [For more discussion of the importance of *McCulloch* to the Reconstruction Congress, see Steven A. Engel, Note, supra p. 586.]

Fourteenth Amendment, and rejected it, too, as a constitutional basis for the congressionally created cause of action. Invoking the "language and purpose" of the Fourteenth Amendment, Chief Justice Rehnquist embraced "the time-honored principle that the Fourteenth Amendment, by its very terms, prohibits only state action." Precedents from the period "shortly after the Fourteenth Amendment was adopted" confirm this reading, according to the *Morrison* majority. Foremost among these precedents are the 1883 Civil Rights Cases, 109 U.S. 3 in which (as we saw supra, in Chapter 4), the Court invalidated those parts of Charles Sumner's celebrated 1875 Civil Rights Act that banned racial discrimination by innkeepers, common carriers, theaters, and the like. Chief Justice Rehnquist also relied on United States v. Harris, 106 U.S. 629 (1883), which struck down the criminal provisions of the Ku Klux Klan Act of 1871 and held that Congress had no power under Section 5 to punish a lynch mob in Tennessee. (See the discussion in Chapter 4, supra). In the words of Chief Justice Rehnquist, "The force of the doctrine of *stare decisis* behind these decisions stems not only from the length of time they have been on the books, but also from the insight attributable to the Members of the Court at that time. Every Member had been appointed by President Lincoln, Grant, Hayes, Garfield, or Arthur — and each of their judicial appointees obviously had intimate knowledge and familiarity with the events surrounding the adoption of the Fourteenth Amendment."

No member of the Rehnquist Court strongly challenged the Chief Justice's account of the Fourteenth Amendment. Two of the four dissenters, Justices Souter and Ginsburg, limited themselves to the Commerce Clause; Justice Breyer, joined by Justice Stevens, expressed "doubts about the majority's section 5 reasoning"[58] but expressly declined to "answer the section 5 question, which I would leave for more thorough analysis if necessary on another occasion."

Despite the dissenters' diffidence, a strong challenge can in fact be mounted to *Morrison*'s basic premises. Or at least, so Professor Amar has argued:[59]

> The first sentence of the Fourteenth Amendment has no explicit state action requirement in its language: "All persons born or naturalized in the United States, and subject to the jurisdiction thereof, are citizens of the United States and of the State wherein they reside." This sentence was introduced to overrule Chief Justice Taney's opinion in

58. In particular, Breyer pointed out that even if one accepted a purely remedial theory of Congress's Section 5 powers, neither *Harris* nor the *Civil Rights Cases* controlled. In VAWA Congress sought "to remedy the actions of *state actors,* namely, those States which, through discriminatory design or the discriminatory conduct of their officials, failed to provide adequate (or any) state remedies for women injured by gender-motivated violence — a failure that the States, and Congress, documented in depth" (emphasis in original). *Harris* and the *Civil Rights Cases,* by contrast, involved statutes that were directed exclusively at private conduct without reference to what states were doing.

Note the larger point implicit in Breyer's comments: VAWA was specifically designed to *help* state and local governments deal with domestic violence and sexual assault. In addition to the civil rights remedy, VAWA distributed over $1.6 billion in funds to states and local governments for rape prevention and education programs, victim services programs, improved security in public transit, the construction and maintenance of battered women's shelters, and funding for additional law enforcement to assist with prosecution of cases of violence against women. If Congress had authorized a direct civil remedy for damages against states and localities, it would be draining this money from state and local coffers. Worse yet, it would be allowing private individuals to impugn state and local officials at the very moment when it was trying to work with them. On the other hand, a civil remedy against private tortfeasors would allow local officials to cooperate with victims of sexual assault and domestic violence without fear that they would be blamed for failing to protect them through the criminal justice system.

59. The excerpt that follows is adapted from Akhil Reed Amar, The Supreme Court 1999 Term — Foreword: The Document and the Doctrine, 114 Harv. L. Rev. 26 (2000).

the *Dred Scott* case, which infamously proclaimed that blacks could never be "citizens." Ordinary Americans confronting the language of the first sentence in 1866-1868, and deciding whether to support or oppose the Amendment, understood Taney's opinion as the paradigm case of what this sentence aimed to repudiate. Taney's opinion focused not merely on the governmental aspects of citizenship — state action — but on the broader sociological and public meaning of the concept. Blacks, said Taney in notorious language, could not be citizens because they were widely regarded by the white race (and not merely by the government) as "beings of an inferior order, and altogether unfit to associate with the white race," with "no rights which the white man was bound to respect." The white man, not just the white government. Thus when the Fourteenth Amendment explicitly repudiated Taney, it did so with words suggesting that Congress — which was explicitly given sweeping, *Prigg*-ish and *McCulloch*-like enforcement power in Section 5 — would have power to enact certain laws designed to affirm that blacks were equal citizens, worthy of respect and dignity. Such laws could not compel whites to invite blacks to their dinner parties — truly private consensual relations were outside the ambit of citizenship — but could regulate larger nongovernmental systems of exclusion in places such as hotels, theaters, and trains. Such laws could also seek to protect blacks from racially motivated violence, and thereby affirm that blacks did indeed have rights that white men (and not merely governments) were bound to respect.

Or so the Reconstruction Congress might reasonably have believed — and did in fact believe — when it enacted various civil rights laws that the Court later struck down. Many of the Congressmen supporting these laws had been leading architects of the Fourteenth Amendment itself. Why doesn't Chief Justice Rehnquist focus our attention on the views of *these* men — crusaders for racial justice like John Bingham and Charles Sumner? And what about the first Justice Harlan? After all, he dissented in the *Civil Rights Cases,* arguing that Congress had broad *Prigg*-ish power to address even certain private conduct,[60] and that the Citizenship Clause of the Fourteenth Amendment had no state action requirement.[61] This is the same Harlan who later dissented in *Plessy.* If he was right in *Plessy,* perhaps he was right here? Or to put the point differently, isn't Chief Justice Rehnquist's effort to rehabilitate the *Civil Rights Cases* rather like trying to revive *Plessy* itself? Indeed, many commentators in the 1960s believed that the Warren

---

60. In the words of Justice Harlan: "Prior to the amendments, Congress, with the sanction of this court, passed the most stringent laws — operating directly and primarily upon States and their officers and agents, as well as upon individuals — in vindication of slavery and the right of the master . . . [So now may Congress,] by legislation of a like primary and direct character, guard, protect, and secure the freedom established, and the most essential right of the citizenship granted, by the constitutional amendments. . . . The national legislature may, without transcending the limits of the Constitution, do for human liberty and the fundamental rights of American citizenship, what it did, with the sanction of this court, for the protection of slavery and the rights of the masters of fugitive slaves." *The Civil Rights Cases,* 109 U.S. at 53 (Harlan, J., dissenting).

61. Justice Harlan stated: "The first clause of the first section . . . is of a distinctly affirmative character. . . . The citizenship thus acquired . . . may be protected, not alone by the judicial branch of the government, but by congressional legislation of a primary direct character; this, because the power of Congress is not restricted to the enforcement of prohibitions upon State laws or State action. It is, in terms distinct and positive, to enforce 'the provisions of this article' of amendment; not simply those of a prohibitive character, but the provisions — all of the provisions — affirmative and prohibitive, of the amendment. It is, therefore, a grave misconception to suppose that the fifth section of the amendment has reference exclusively to express prohibitions upon State laws or State action. . . . Congress is not restricted to the enactment of laws adapted to counteract and redress the operation of State legislation, or the action of State officers, of the character prohibited by the amendment. It was perfectly well known that the great danger to the equal enjoyment by citizens of their rights, as citizens, was to be apprehended not altogether from unfriendly State legislation, but from the hostile action of corporations and individuals in the States. And it is to be presumed that it was intended, by that section [5], to clothe Congress with power and authority to meet that danger." Id. at 46, 54.

Court had impliedly overruled the *Civil Rights Cases* in Jones v. Alfred Mayer, much as it had earlier overruled *Plessy* itself *sub silentio* in *Brown*.[62]

Thus, rather than dwelling on commerce clause issues far removed from women's equality, the *Morrison* dissenters would have done better to begin with the Fourteenth Amendment's citizenship clause, and to explain how gender-motivated violence against women can pose a threat to equal citizenship in a manner analogous (though not identical) to the ways that other power structures have threatened the equal citizenship of blacks. The dissenters might have noted that race and sex are not isomorphic; and that in the case of equal citizenship based on sex, it is important to read the Fourteenth Amendment in light of the much later Nineteenth. But in the case of both race and sex, the dissenters could have argued, Congress may properly act to dismantle what it plausibly perceives to be large social structures creating and sustaining conditions of unequal citizenship, in which some citizens are systematically disrespected or mistreated on the basis of birth status.[63] In the context of both race and sex, government has, by its actions and inactions, helped maintain these structures. In the case of race, the Black Codes, Jim Crow, lynchings, and disfranchisement have loomed large. In the case of sex, government has created marriage laws leaving women's property and bodies largely at the mercy of men; and has erected unjustified obstacles to rape prosecution. Through such laws, government has historically invested men with an improper sense of entitlement over women's bodies.

But the past involvement of government is probably not necessary to uphold congressional action; it merely strengthens the case. Though the issues are not free from all doubt, the best reading of the Constitution as a whole is probably this: To vindicate the vision of the Fourteenth Amendment (read through the prism of the Nineteenth), Congress may pass expressive laws affirming women's equal status and citizenship so as to make clear to all that women have rights that men are bound to respect. Congressional power is not plenary — wholly plenary power is hard to reconcile with the basic structure of enumerated power that the Reconstruction Amendments accept rather than repudiate. But when Congress can honestly be understood as affirming equal citizenship for those who have historically been denied equality on the basis of birth status, judicial review of enumerated power should be no less deferential than in *Prigg* or *McCulloch,* on which the Fourteenth Amendment's supporters justifiably relied.

Note, finally, a certain democratic irony in *Morrison*. *Boerne* and *Morrison* — whether accurately or not — claim to be vindicating the judicial role set out in Marbury v. Madison. *Marbury,* in turn, justified judicial review as a profoundly democratic act — invalidating the work of the people's agents in Congress in the name of what the People themselves had agreed to more in a more direct and populist fashion in the Constitution itself. But in *Morrison,* there would appear to be an obvious democracy deficit created when a Court with only two women on it (only one of whom joins the majority) relies on old cases from an era in which no women voted, glossing even earlier constitutional texts, to strike down a post-Nineteenth Amendment law that a great many women strongly support today.

---

62. Three years after *Jones,* the Supreme Court also undermined United States v. Harris. Griffin v. Breckenridge, 403 U.S. 88, 104-105 (1971), upheld the civil provisions of the 1871 Klan Act (which were identical to the criminal provisions struck down in *Harris*) as an exercise of Congress's powers under §2 of the Thirteenth Amendment.

63. Recall that the first sentence of the Fourteenth Amendment embodies a vision in which all Americans are "born" free and equal citizens. One sensible interpretation of this sentence, then, is that no American should be treated as a second-class citizen because of his or her birth status — because, say, he was born black or she was born female.

3. *Applying* Boerne *(and* Morrison*)* — *Where Reconstruction meets sovereign immunity.* In *Boerne* and *Morrison,* the Rehnquist Court held that Congress simply lacked power to regulate certain issues. In another, more technical line of cases, the Court has upheld congressional regulatory power, but only under the Commerce Clause and not under the Reconstruction Amendments. Ordinarily, very little might turn on the precise source of congressional power once such power is conceded to exist. But in one corner of law, the precise source does matter. According to the Court's (rather convoluted) doctrine of sovereign immunity (on which, see infra, p. 708), Congress has less authority to subject states to damage suits by individual citizens when Congress is merely regulating under the Commerce Clause; congressional power to abrogate state sovereign immunity is virtually plenary when Congress is acting pursuant to its Reconstruction powers, but not otherwise.

One might wonder about the very intelligibility of this approach. After all, when a state violates a valid federal law enacted under the Commerce Clause (or any other Article I power, for that matter), the state thereby violates the Supremacy Clause. And under even the crabbed interpretation of the Fourteenth Amendment furnished by the Court in the 1873 *Slaughterhouse Cases,* supra Chapter 4, the "privileges" and "immunities" of citizenship include rights "which owe their existence to the Federal government, its National character, its Constitution, *or its laws.*" (Recall that the dissenters believed that the Fourteenth Amendment did more than reenact the Supremacy Clause, but even they thought it did at least this much.) As a matter of logic, then, it would seem that:

(1) Whenever Congress has passed a valid law creating individual rights and a state violates that valid federal law, the state has thereby abridged a "privilege or immunity" of citizenship, in violation of Section 1 of the Fourteenth Amendment.

(2) Such a violation authorizes Congress to remedy and enforce the Section 1 right via Section 5 statute.

(3) A clearly worded congressional statute expressly enacted pursuant to the Fourteenth Amendment, explicitly aimed at states, and holding them liable for their violations of valid federal law, would be a properly "congruent" and "proportional" congressional act of enforcement.

The Court, however, has not viewed the matter this way. See Florida Prepaid Postsecondary Education Expense Board v. College Savings Bank, 527 U.S. 627 (1999); College Savings Bank v. Florida Prepaid Postsecondary Expense Board, 527 U.S. 666 (1999).

Thus, when Congress extended the Age Discrimination in Employment Act (ADEA) and the employment-law section of the Americans with Disabilities Act (ADA) to state governments, the Court refused to allow money damages against states in suits under the ADEA and the ADA because these statutes were not, said the Court, valid exercises of the Reconstruction power. Prior to the enactment of the statutes, the Court had not viewed discrimination on the basis of age or disability (in contrast to, say, discrimination on the basis of race or sex) as generally constitutionally problematic under Section 1 of the Fourteenth Amendment. Hence, the Court found congressional legislation under Section 5 to be insufficiently "congruent" and "proportionate" to the Fourteenth Amendment. Kimel v. Florida Board of Regents,

528 U.S. 62 (2000); Board of Trustees of the Univ. of Alabama v. Garrett, 531 U.S. 356 (2001). Chief Justice Rehnquist concluded in *Garrett* that "to uphold the [ADA's] application to the States would allow Congress to rewrite the Fourteenth Amendment law laid down by this Court." Each of these Section 5 cases, incidentally, featured the same 5-4 line up of Justices as did *Morrison* and *Lopez*.

However, in two more recent cases, the Court has treated two other federal laws as properly founded on Section 5 power. In the first, Nevada Department of Human Resources v. Hibbs, 538 U.S. 721 (2003), the Court upheld the application of the Family and Medical Leave Act (FMLA) to state governments as a valid exercise of Section 5 power. Under the FMLA, state employees, whether male or female, were guaranteed 12 weeks of annual leave to care for seriously ill family members. The Act aimed to ease the plight of working women, via a gender-neutral statute. (If only wives, mothers, and daughters were eligible for family leave, employers might be less enthusiastic about hiring women in the first place; thus the act applied to all workers, male and female, thereby challenging previous stereotypes — stereotypes that had been reinforced by previous state action — that family care was the unique obligation of women workers.) Joined by Justice O'Connor and the four dissenters in *Morrison*, Chief Justice Rehnquist, writing for the Court, deemed this statute a valid Section 5 enactment. (For more analysis of *Hibbs*, see infra, Chapter 7.) In Tennessee v. Lane, 541 U.S. 509 (2004), the four *Morrison* dissenters, led by Justice Stevens, combined with Justice O'Connor to uphold under Section 5 a portion of the ADA that regulated access to public buildings and governmental programs. The case at hand involved a wheelchair-bound paraplegic summoned to answer criminal charges on the second floor of a county courthouse that had no elevator. At his first appearance he crawled up two flights of stairs; the next time, he refused to crawl or be carried, and was subsequently jailed for failure to appear. Justice Stevens held that as applied to public facilities like courthouses, the ADA did more than protect against disability discrimination; it also "enforce[s] a variety of other basic constitutional guarantees, infringements of which are subject to more searching judicial review," including the due process right to access to courts and to fair hearings and the Sixth Amendment's right to confront witnesses.

In both *Hibbs* and *Lane*, the Court argued that Congress could pass prophylactic measures that reached more broadly than conduct that the Court viewed as unconstitutional. There are two kinds of prophylactic measures. The first reaches a broad range of conduct in order to alleviate problems of proof. The second reaches a broad range of conduct in order to prevent constitutional violations from happening in the first place. The FMLA, for example, obviates problems of proving that a particular employer's leave policies were based on stereotypical views about men and women; in addition, by creating a uniform national right, it nips such tendencies in the bud.

Why, we might wonder, did the Court in *Hibbs* and *Lane* deem congressional action sufficiently "congruent" and "proportionate" to pass muster? Perhaps the cases at hand were seen as closer to Fourteenth Amendment values that the Court itself had recognized in previous cases — involving the rights of women to be free from gender stereotyping and discrimination, and the fundamental right of citizens to have adequate access to courts, legislatures, and other governmental operations. But of course *Morrison* also involved gender discrimination, yet the Court gave Congress much less deference in that case. Can you explain the pattern of cases? Note that only one Justice — O'Connor — was a member of the majority in each of these cases. With her departure from the Court, which path will the Court chart in the future? Which path should it chart?

For example, should Section 5 power depend on whether Congress can point to a clear pattern of state misbehavior, as most of these cases seem to suggest? The *Kimel* Court stressed that states had not generally engaged in invidious age discrimination. And in *Morrison,* Chief Justice Rehnquist argued that "the problem of discrimination against the victims of gender-motivated crimes does not exist in all States, or even most States." But which way does that cut? The very fact that most states do not practice such discrimination means that a federal law banning it does not interfere very much with states' rights. Moreover, broad state compliance with an antidiscrimination norm may in fact be evidence that such a norm is indeed fundamental in modern society.[64] Just as the Court often looks to state practice in determining fundamental rights under Section 1, why shouldn't Congress be allowed to do so in enacting laws under Section 5? And shouldn't the fact that states generally refrain from engaging in a given dubious practice be grounds for allowing Congress to proclaim a Fourteenth Amendment right — a privilege or immunity of citizenship — against the practice in question?

III.   Affirmative Limits on Congressional Regulations of State Governments

Even if enumerated congressional power exists, under the Commerce Clause, or the Reconstruction power, or elsewhere, various rights cut across these powers, and further constrain Congress. For example, even where there is a clear connection to interstate commerce, Congress may not pass laws that abridge free expression, or freedom of religion, or due process. A law barring private interstate employers from discriminating against employees on the basis of their political viewpoints might be generally permissible, but could such a law be applied to, say, a national political-opinion magazine (like The New Republic or The Weekly Standard) deciding whom to hire as a columnist? In such a case, the First Amendment cuts across the commerce power, limiting what would otherwise be permissible.

Do state governments have a similar claim to certain kinds of affirmative exemptions from federal laws otherwise within the commerce power? If so, exactly where does this claim to affirmative exemptions come from?

A.   From the Hughes Court to the Burger Court: Practically No Limits?

In the half-century between the New Deal and the Rehnquist Court, state claims for affirmative exemptions did not fare particularly well with the Justices. For example, in United States v. California, 297 U.S. 175 (1936), the Court unanimously upheld a fine against a railroad wholly owned by the state for a violation of the Federal Safety Appliance Act. In the wake of United States v. California, states were held

---

64. Indeed, as we shall see in Chapter 8, the Court sometimes justifies the creation of fundamental rights (or the expansion of existing ones) based on whether there is an emerging consensus that the right is fundamental, and it looks to the trend in state legislatures as evidence.

subject to a variety of federal labor laws enacted pursuant to the commerce power. See, e.g., California v. Taylor, 353 U.S. 553 (1957) (Railway Labor Act); Parden v. Terminal Railway, 377 U.S. 184 (1964) (Federal Employers' Liability Act), overruled on other grounds; College Savings Bank v. Florida Prepaid Postsecondary Education Expense Board, 527 U.S. 666 (1999).

In 1961, Congress extended the Fair Labor Standards Act of 1938 to every employee "employed in an enterprise engaged in commerce or in the production of goods for commerce." Such an enterprise is defined as one that "has employees engaged in commerce or in the production of goods for commerce," with the effect of covering the fellow employees of employees covered by the 1938 act. In 1966, the act was further extended to the employees of hospitals, elementary and second-ary schools, and institutions of higher education, including those owned and oper-ated by states. In Maryland v. Wirtz, 392 U.S. 183 (1968), the Court upheld the act as amended. Justice Harlan wrote that the 1961 amendment could be sustained on either of two theories, one rooted in *Darby*, the other in *Jones & Laughlin*.

The act prevented "unfair competition" with enterprises in other states, for "[w]hen a company does an interstate business, its competition with companies elsewhere is affected by all its significant labor costs, not merely by the wages and hours of those employees who have physical contact with the goods in question." The act also prevented labor strife that might disrupt the flow of goods in commerce. Justice Harlan deemed the second rationale especially applicable to the 1966 amendments: Hospitals and schools are "major users of goods imported from other States," and strikes and work stoppages by their employees "obviously inter-rupt and burden this flow of goods across state lines."

In 1974, Congress extended the minimum wage and maximum hour regulations to almost all state and municipal employees. In National League of Cities v. Usery, 426 U.S. 833 (1976), in only the second decision since the 1930s to strike down an act of Congress on federalism grounds — Oregon v. Mitchell was the first — the Court over-ruled Maryland v. Wirtz, by a 5-4 vote. Then-Justice Rehnquist wrote for the Court:

> Appellants in no way challenge [our] decisions establishing the breadth of authority granted Congress under the commerce power. Their contention, on the contrary, is that when Congress seeks to regulate directly the activities of States as public employ-ers, it transgresses an affirmative limitation on the exercise of its power akin to other commerce power affirmative limitations contained in the Constitution. Congressional enactments which may be fully within the grant of legislative authority contained in the Commerce Clause may nonetheless be invalid because found to offend against the right to trial by jury contained in the Sixth Amendment, or the Due Process Clause of the Fifth Amendment. Appellants' essential contention is that the 1974 amendments to the Act, while undoubtedly within the scope of the Commerce Clause, encounter a similar constitutional barrier because they are to be applied directly to the States and subdivisions of States as employers.
>
> This Court has never doubted that there are limits upon the power of Congress to override state sovereignty, even when exercising its otherwise plenary powers to tax or to regulate commerce which are conferred by Art. I of the Constitution. . . . In Fry v. United States, 421 U.S. 542 (1975), the Court recognized that an express decla-ration of this limitation is found in the Tenth Amendment:
>
>> While the Tenth Amendment has been characterized as a "truism," stating merely that "all is retained which has not been surrendered," United States v. Darby, it is not without significance. The Amendment expressly declares the constitutional policy that Congress

may not exercise power in a fashion that impairs the States' integrity or their ability to function effectively in a federal system.

. . . It is one thing to recognize the authority of Congress to enact laws regulating individual businesses necessarily subject to the dual sovereignty of the government of the Nation and of the State in which they reside. It is quite another to uphold a similar exercise of congressional authority directed, not to private citizens, but to the States as States. We have repeatedly recognized that there are attributes of sovereignty attaching to every state government which may not be impaired by Congress, not because Congress may lack an affirmative grant of legislative authority to reach the matter, but because the Constitution prohibits it from exercising the authority in that manner. . . . Coyle v. Oklahoma, 221 U.S. 559 (1911). . . .

One undoubted attribute of state sovereignty is the States' power to determine the wages which shall be paid to those whom they employ in order to carry out their governmental functions, what hours those persons will work, and what compensation will be provided where these employees may be called upon to work overtime. The question we must resolve here, then, is whether these determinations are "functions essential to separate and independent existence," so that Congress may not abrogate the States' otherwise plenary authority to make them. . . .

Judged solely in terms of increased costs in dollars, [the FLSA makes] a significant impact on the functioning of the governmental bodies involved. . . .

Quite apart from the substantial costs imposed upon the States and their political subdivisions, the Act displaces state policies regarding the manner in which they will structure delivery of those governmental services which their citizens require. . . . The State might wish to employ persons with little or no training, or those who wish to work on a casual basis, or those who for some other reason do not possess minimum employment requirements, and pay them less than the federally prescribed minimum wage. It may wish to offer part-time or summer employment to teenagers at a figure less than the minimum wage, and if unable to do so may decline to offer such employment at all. But the Act would forbid such choices by the States. . . .

This dilemma presented by the minimum wage restrictions may seem not immediately different from that faced by private employers, who have long been covered by the Act and who must find ways to increase their gross income if they are to pay higher wages while maintaining current earnings. The difference, however, is that a State is not merely a factor in the "shifting economic arrangements" of the private sector of the economy, but is itself a coordinate element in the system established by the Framers for governing our Federal Union. . . .

. . . Another example of congressional choices displacing those of the States in the area of what are without doubt essential governmental decisions may be found in the practice of using volunteer firemen, a source of manpower crucial to many of our smaller towns' existence. Under the regulations proposed by appellee, whether individuals are indeed "volunteers" rather than "employees" subject to the minimum wage provisions of the Act are questions to be decided in the courts. . . .

. . . [The amendments will] significantly alter or displace the States' abilities to structure employer-employee relationships in such areas as fire prevention, police protection, sanitation, public health, and parks and recreation. These activities are typical of those performed by state and local governments in discharging their dual functions of administering the public law and furnishing public services. Indeed, it is functions such as these which governments are created to provide, services such as these which the States have traditionally afforded their citizens. If Congress may withdraw from the States the authority to make those fundamental employment decisions upon which their systems for performance of these functions must rest, we think there would be little left of the States' "separate and independent existence." Thus, . . . Congress has sought to wield its power in a fashion that would impair the States' " ability to function effectively in a federal system." This exercise of congressional authority does not comport with the federal system of government embodied in the Constitution. We hold that insofar as the challenged amendments operate to directly displace the States' freedom to structure integral operations in areas of traditional governmental functions, they are not within the authority granted Congress by Art. I, §8, cl. 3.[a]

Wirtz must be overruled.

Four Justices dissented. Justice Brennan's dissent — joined by Justices Marshall and White — was particularly stinging:

My Brethren do not successfully obscure today's patent usurpation of the role reserved for the political process by their purported discovery in the Constitution of a restraint derived from sovereignty of the States on Congress' exercise of the commerce power. . . . [L]aws within the commerce power may not infringe individual liberties protected by the First Amendment, the Fifth Amendment, or the Sixth Amendment. . . . But there is no restraint based on state sovereignty requiring or permitting judicial enforcement anywhere expressed in the Constitution; our decisions over the last century and a half have explicitly rejected the existence of any such restraint on the commerce power. . . .

[N]othing in the Tenth Amendment constitutes a limitation on congressional exercise of powers delegated by the Constitution to Congress. . . .

[D]evoid of meaningful content is my Brethren's argument that the 1974 amendments "displac[e] State policies." The amendments neither impose policy objectives on the States nor deny the States complete freedom to fix their own objectives. My Brethren boldly assert that the decision as to wages and hours is an "undoubted attribute of state sovereignty," and then never say why. . . . The portent of such a sweeping holding is so ominous for our constitutional jurisprudence as to leave one incredulous.

Certainly the paradigm of sovereign action — action qua State — is in the enactment and enforcement of state laws. Is it possible that my Brethren are signaling abandonment of the heretofore unchallenged principle that Congress "can, if it chooses, entirely displace the States to the full extent of the far-reaching Commerce Clause"? . . .

My Brethren do more than turn aside longstanding constitutional jurisprudence that emphatically rejects today's conclusion. More alarming is the startling restructuring of our federal system, and the role they create therein for the federal judiciary. This Court is simply not at liberty to erect a mirror of its own conception of a desirable governmental structure. . . .

Justice Stevens also expressed perplexity:

The Court holds that the Federal Government may not interfere with a sovereign State's inherent right to pay a substandard wage to the janitor at the state capitol. The principle on which the holding rests is difficult to perceive.

---

a. We express no view as to whether different results might obtain if Congress seeks to affect integral operations of state governments by exercising authority granted it under other sections of the Constitution such as the spending power, Art. I, §8, cl. 1, or §5 of the Fourteenth Amendment. [In the almost contemporaneous case of Fitzpatrick v. Bitzer, 427 U.S. 445 (1976), the Court, per Justice Rehnquist, held that states could be sued in federal court for violating Title VII of the Civil Rights Act of 1964, which barred employment discrimination by state governments as well as by various private employers. The *Fitzpatrick* Court stressed that Congress had relied on §5 of the Fourteenth Amendment in adopting the provisions of Title VII applicable to states, and that the specific provisions of the Fourteenth Amendment, aimed at limiting states qua states, justified federal laws limiting states that would be "constitutionally impermissible in other contexts."]

The Federal Government may, I believe, require the State to act impartially when it hires or fires the janitor, to withhold taxes from his paycheck, to observe safety regulations when he is performing his job, to forbid him from burning too much soft coal in the capitol furnace, from dumping untreated refuse in an adjacent waterway, from overloading a state-owned garbage truck, or from driving either the truck or the governor's limousine over 55 miles an hour. Even though these and many other activities of the capitol janitor are activities of the State qua State, I have no doubt that they are subject to federal regulation.

. . . Since I am unable to identify a limitation on that federal power that would not also invalidate federal regulation of state activities that I consider unquestionably permissible, I am persuaded that this statute is valid. . . .

Less than a decade later, the Court revisited the issue, and overruled *National League of Cities*. Once again, the vote was 5-4. Justice Blackmun, who had voted with the majority in *National League of Cities,* now joined its four dissenters to proclaim the Court's adventure a mistake.

GARCIA v. SAN ANTONIO METROPOLITAN TRANSIT AUTHORITY
469 U.S. 528 (1985)

[The Department of Labor determined that a San Antonio mass-transit system did not fall under the rule set forth in *National League of Cities,* and thus was required to abide by federal minimum wage laws. After an oral argument in 1983 focused on the precise meaning of the tests set forth in *National League of Cities* and its progeny, the Court ordered reargument and requested the parties to brief "[w]hether or not the principles of the Tenth Amendment as set forth in *National League of Cities* . . . should be reconsidered."]

BLACKMUN, J.

[T]he attempt to draw the boundaries of state regulatory immunity in terms of "traditional governmental function" is not only unworkable but is also inconsistent with established principles of federalism and, indeed, with those very federalism principles on which *National League of Cities* purported to rest. That case, accordingly, is overruled. . . .

II.

. . . The controversy in the present cases has focused on the . . . requirement that the challenged federal statute trench on "traditional governmental functions." The District Court voiced a common concern: "Despite the abundance of adjectives, identifying which particular state functions are immune remains difficult." Just how troublesome the task has been is revealed by the results reached in other federal cases. . . . We find it difficult, if not impossible, to identify an organizing principle. . . .

The essence of our federal system is that within the realm of authority left open to them under the Constitution, the States must be equally free to engage in any activity that their citizens choose for the common weal, no matter how unorthodox or unnecessary anyone else — including the judiciary — deems state involvement to be. Any rule of state immunity that looks to the "traditional," "integral," or "necessary" nature of governmental functions inevitably invites an unelected federal judiciary to make decisions about which state policies it favors and which ones it dislikes.". . .

We therefore now reject, as unsound in principle and unworkable in practice, a rule of state immunity from federal regulation that turns on a judicial appraisal of whether a particular governmental function is "integral" or "traditional." Any such rule leads to inconsistent results at the same time that it disserves principles of democratic self-governance, and it breeds inconsistency precisely because it is divorced from those principles. . . .

III.

. . . When we look for the States' "residuary and inviolable sovereignty," The Federalist No. 39, (J. Madison), in the shape of the constitutional scheme rather than in predetermined notions of sovereign power, a different measure of state sovereignty emerges. Apart from the limitation on federal authority inherent in the delegated nature of Congress' Article I powers, the principal means chosen by the Framers to ensure the role of the States in the federal system lies in the structure of the Federal Government itself. It is no novelty to observe that the composition of the Federal Government was designed in large part to protect the States from over-reaching by Congress. The Framers thus gave the States a role in the selection both of the Executive and the Legislative Branches of the Federal Government. The States were vested with indirect influence over the House of Representatives and the Presidency by their control of electoral qualifications and their role in Presidential elections. U.S. Const., Art. I, §2, and Art. II, §1. They were given more direct influence in the Senate, where each State received equal representation and each Senator was to be selected by the legislature of his State. Art. I, §3. The significance attached to the States' equal representation in the Senate is underscored by the prohibition of any constitutional amendment divesting a State of equal representation without the State's consent. Art. V.

The extent to which the structure of the Federal Government itself was relied on to insulate the interests of the States is evident in the views of the Framers. James Madison explained that the Federal Government "will partake sufficiently of the spirit [of the States], to be disinclined to invade the rights of the individual States, or the prerogatives of their governments." The Federalist No. 46. Similarly, James Wilson observed that "it was a favorite object in the Convention" to provide for the security of the States against federal encroachment and that the structure of the Federal Government itself served that end. . . . In short, the Framers chose to rely on a federal system in which special restraints on federal power over the States inhered principally in the workings of the National Government itself, rather than in discrete limitations on the objects of federal authority. State sovereign interests, then, are more properly protected by procedural safeguards inherent in the structure of the federal system than by judicially created limitations on federal power. . . .

We realize that changes in the structure of the Federal Government have taken place since 1789, not the least of which has been the substitution of popular election of Senators by the adoption of the Seventeenth Amendment in 1913, and that these changes may work to alter the influence of the States in the federal political process. Nonetheless, against this background, we are convinced that the fundamental limitation that the constitutional scheme imposes on the Commerce Clause to protect the "States as States" is one of process rather than one of result. Any substantive restraint on the exercise of Commerce Clause powers must find its justification in the procedural nature of this basic limitation, and it must be tailored to compensate for possible failings in the national political process rather than to dictate a "sacred province of state autonomy."

Insofar as the present cases are concerned, then, we need go no further than to state that we perceive nothing in the overtime and minimum-wage requirements of the FLSA, as applied to SAMTA, that is destructive of state sovereignty or violative of any constitutional provision. SAMTA faces nothing more than the same minimum-wage and overtime obligations that hundreds of thousands of other employers, public as well as private, have to meet. . . .

IV.

. . . Of course, we continue to recognize that the States occupy a special and specific position in our constitutional system and that the scope of Congress' authority under the Commerce Clause must reflect that position. But the principal and basic limit on the federal commerce power is that inherent in all congressional action — the built-in restraints that our system provides through state participation in federal governmental action. The political process ensures that laws that unduly burden the States will not be promulgated. In the factual setting of these cases the internal safeguards of the political process have performed as intended.

These cases do not require us to identify or define what affirmative limits the constitutional structure might impose on federal action affecting the States under the Commerce Clause. See Coyle v. Oklahoma, 221 U.S. 559 (1911).

. . . *National League of Cities* . . . attempted to articulate affirmative limits on the Commerce Clause power in terms of core governmental functions and fundamental attributes of state sovereignty. But the model of democratic decisionmaking the Court there identified underestimated, in our view, the solicitude of the national political process for the continued vitality of the States. Attempts by other courts since then to draw guidance from this model have proved it both impracticable and doctrinally barren. In sum, in *National League of Cities* the Court tried to repair what did not need repair.

We do not lightly overrule recent precedent. We have not hesitated, however, when it has become apparent that a prior decision has departed from a proper understanding of congressional power under the Commerce Clause. See United States v. Darby. Due respect for the reach of congressional power within the federal system mandates that we do so now. . . .

Justice POWELL, with whom the Chief Justice, Justice Rehnquist, and Justice O'Connor join, dissenting.

I.

. . . The stability of judicial decision, and with it respect for the authority of this Court, are not served by the precipitate overruling of multiple precedents that we witness in these cases.

Whatever effect the Court's decision may have in weakening the application of stare decisis, it is likely to be less important than what the Court has done to the Constitution itself. A unique feature of the United States is the federal system of government guaranteed by the Constitution and implicit in the very name of our country. Despite some genuflecting in the Court's opinion to the concept of federalism, today's decision effectively reduces the Tenth Amendment to meaningless rhetoric when Congress acts pursuant to the Commerce Clause. . . .

II.

In concluding that efforts to define state immunity are unsound in principle, the Court radically departs from long-settled constitutional values and ignores the role of judicial review in our system of government. . . .

B

Today's opinion does not explain how the States' role in the electoral process guarantees that particular exercises of the Commerce Clause power will not infringe on residual state sovereignty.[a] Members of Congress are elected from the various States, but once in office they are Members of the Federal Government.[b] Although the States participate in the Electoral College, this is hardly a reason to view the President as a representative of the States' interest against federal encroachment. We noted recently "[the] hydraulic pressure inherent within each of the separate Branches to exceed the outer limits of its power. . . ." INS v. Chadha, 462 U.S. 919 (1983). The Court offers no reason to think that this pressure will not operate when Congress seeks to invoke its powers under the Commerce Clause, notwithstanding the electoral role of the States.[c]

The Court apparently thinks that the States' success at obtaining federal funds for various projects and exemptions from the obligations of some federal statutes is indicative of the "effectiveness of the federal political process in preserving the States' interests. . . ." The fact that Congress generally does not transgress constitutional limits on its power to reach state activities does not make judicial review any less

a. Late in its opinion, the Court suggests that after all there may be some "affirmative limits the constitutional structure might impose on federal action affecting the States under the Commerce Clause." The Court asserts that "[in] the factual setting of these cases the internal safeguards of the political process have performed as intended." The Court does not explain the basis for this judgment. Nor does it identify the circumstances in which the "political process" may fail and "affirmative limits" are to be imposed. Presumably, such limits are to be determined by the Judicial Branch even though it is "unelected." Today's opinion, however, has rejected the balancing standard and suggests no other standard that would enable a court to determine when there has been a malfunction of the "political process." The Court's failure to specify the "affirmative limits" on federal power, or when and how these limits are to be determined, may well be explained by the transparent fact that any such attempt would be subject to precisely the same objections on which it relies to overrule *National League of Cities*.

b. One can hardly imagine this Court saying that because Congress is composed of individuals, individual rights guaranteed by the Bill of Rights are amply protected by the political process. Yet, the position adopted today is indistinguishable in principle. The Tenth Amendment also is an essential part of the Bill of Rights.

c. At one time in our history, the view that the structure of the Federal Government sufficed to protect the States might have had a somewhat more practical, although not a more logical, basis. . . . Not only is the premise of this view clearly at odds with the proliferation of national legislation over the past 30 years, but "a variety of structural and political changes occurring in this century have combined to make Congress particularly insensitive to state and local values." Advisory Commission on Intergovernmental Relations (ACIR), Regulatory Federalism: Policy, Process, Impact and Reform 50 (1984). The adoption of the Seventeenth Amendment (providing for direct election of Senators), the weakening of political parties on the local level, and the rise of national media, among other things, have made Congress increasingly less representative of state and local interests, and more likely to be responsive to the demands of various national constituencies. Id., at 50-51.

necessary to rectify the cases in which it does do so.[d] The States' role in our system of government is a matter of constitutional law, not of legislative grace. . . .

More troubling than the logical infirmities in the Court's reasoning is the result of its holding, i.e., that federal political officials, invoking the Commerce Clause, are the sole judges of the limits of their own power. This result is inconsistent with the fundamental principles of our constitutional system. See, e.g., The Federalist No. 78 (Hamilton). At least since Marbury v. Madison, it has been the settled province of the federal judiciary "to say what the law is" with respect to the constitutionality of Acts of Congress. In rejecting the role of the judiciary in protecting the States from federal overreaching, the Court's opinion offers no explanation for ignoring the teaching of the most famous case in our history. . . .

III.

A

Much of the initial opposition to the Constitution was rooted in the fear that the National Government would be too powerful and eventually would eliminate the States as viable political entities. This concern was voiced repeatedly until proponents of the Constitution made assurances that a Bill of Rights, including a provision explicitly reserving powers in the States, would be among the first business of the new Congress. . . .

Antifederalists raised these concerns in almost every state ratifying convention. As a result, eight States voted for the Constitution only after proposing amendments to be adopted after ratification. All eight of these included among their recommendations some version of what later became the Tenth Amendment. So strong was the concern that the proposed Constitution was seriously defective without a specific bill of rights, including a provision reserving powers to the States, that in order to secure the votes for ratification, the Federalists eventually conceded that such provisions were necessary. It was thus generally agreed that consideration of a bill of rights would be among the first business of the new Congress. Accordingly, the 10 Amendments that we know as the Bill of Rights were proposed and adopted early in the first session of the First Congress.

This history, which the Court simply ignores, documents the integral role of the Tenth Amendment in our constitutional theory. . . .

B

The Framers had definite ideas about the nature of the Constitution's division of authority between the Federal and State Governments. . . .

---

d. This Court has never before abdicated responsibility for assessing the constitutionality of challenged action on the ground that affected parties theoretically are able to look out for their own interests through the electoral process. As the Court noted in *National League of Cities,* a much stronger argument as to inherent structural protections could have been made in either Buckley v. Valeo, 424 U.S. 1 (1976), or Myers v. United States, 272 U.S. 52 (1926), than can be made here. In these cases, the President signed legislation that limited his authority with respect to certain appointments and thus arguably "it was . . . no concern of this Court that the law violated the Constitution." The Court nevertheless held the laws unconstitutional because they infringed on Presidential authority, the President's consent notwithstanding. The Court does not address this point; nor does it cite any authority for its contrary view.

Madison elaborated on the content of these separate spheres of sovereignty in The Federalist No. 45:

"The powers delegated by the proposed Constitution to the Federal Government, are few and defined. Those which are to remain in the State Governments are numerous and indefinite. The former will be exercised principally on external objects, as war, peace, negociation, and foreign commerce. . . . The powers reserved to the several States will extend to all the objects, which, in the ordinary course of affairs, concern the lives, liberties and properties of the people; and the internal order, improvement, and prosperity of the State."

. . . The Framers believed that the separate sphere of sovereignty reserved to the States would ensure that the States would serve as an effective "counterpoise" to the power of the Federal Government. The States would serve this essential role because they would attract and retain the loyalty of their citizens. . . . Like Hamilton, Madison saw the States' involvement in the everyday concerns of the people as the source of their citizens' loyalty. See also Nagel, Federalism as a Fundamental Value: National League of Cities in Perspective, 1981 S. Ct. Rev. 81.

Thus, the harm to the States that results from federal overreaching under the Commerce Clause is not simply a matter of dollars and cents. Nor is it a matter of the wisdom or folly of certain policy choices. Rather, by usurping functions traditionally performed by the States, federal overreaching under the Commerce Clause undermines the constitutionally mandated balance of power between the States and the Federal Government, a balance designed to protect our fundamental liberties. . . .

D

. . . In *National League of Cities,* we spoke of fire prevention, police protection, sanitation, and public health as "typical of [the services] performed by state and local governments in discharging their dual functions of administering the public law and furnishing public services." Not only are these activities remote from any normal concept of interstate commerce, they are also activities that epitomize the concerns of local, democratic self-government. In emphasizing the need to protect traditional governmental functions, we identified the kinds of activities engaged in by state and local governments that affect the everyday lives of citizens. These are services that people are in a position to understand and evaluate, and in a democracy, have the right to oversee.[e] . . .

The Court maintains that the standard approved in *National League of Cities* "disserves principles of democratic self-governance." In reaching this conclusion, the Court looks myopically only to persons elected to positions in the federal government. It disregards entirely the far more effective role of democratic

---

e. The Framers recognized that the most effective democracy occurs at local levels of government, where people with firsthand knowledge of local problems have more ready access to public officials responsible for dealing with them. E.g., The Federalist No. 17; The Federalist No. 46. This is as true today as it was when the Constitution was adopted. "Participation is likely to be more frequent, and exercised at more different stages of a governmental activity at the local level, or in regional organizations, than at the state and federal levels. [Additionally,] the proportion of people actually involved from the total population tends to be greater, the lower the level of government, and this, of course, better approximates the citizen participation ideal." ACIR, Citizen Participation in the American Federal System 95 (1980).

self-government at the state and local levels. . . . [M]embers of the immense federal bureaucracy are not elected, know less about the services traditionally rendered by States and localities, and are inevitably less responsive to recipients of such services, than are state legislatures, city councils, boards of supervisors, and state and local commissions, boards, and agencies. It is at these state and local levels — not in Washington as the Court so mistakenly thinks — that "democratic self-government" is best exemplified. . . .

Justice REHNQUIST, dissenting. . . .

[Doctrinal details aside, *National League of Cities* recognized a basic] principle that will, I am confident, in time again command the support of a majority of this Court.

Justice O'CONNOR, with whom Justice Powell and Justice Rehnquist join, dissenting. . . .

The central issue of federalism, of course, is whether any realm is left open to the States by the Constitution — whether any area remains in which a State may act free of federal interference. . . . The true "essence" of federalism is that the States as States have legitimate interests which the National Government is bound to respect even though its laws are supreme. If federalism so conceived and so carefully culti-vated by the Framers of our Constitution is to remain meaningful, this Court cannot abdicate its constitutional responsibility to oversee the Federal Government's compliance with its duty to respect the legitimate interests of the States.

Due to the emergence of an integrated and industrialized national economy, this Court has been required to examine and review a breathtaking expansion of the powers of Congress. In doing so the Court correctly perceived that the Framers of our Constitution intended Congress to have sufficient power to address national problems. But the Framers were not single-minded. The Constitution is animated by an array of intentions. Just as surely as the Framers envisioned a National Government capable of solving national problems, they also envisioned a republic whose vitality was assured by the diffusion of power not only among the branches of the Federal Government, but also between the Federal Government and the States. In the 18th century these intentions did not conflict because technology had not yet converted every local problem into a national one. A conflict has now emerged, and the Court today retreats rather than reconcile the Constitution's dual concerns for federalism and an effective commerce power.

We would do well to recall the constitutional basis for federalism and the devel-opment of the commerce power which has come to displace it. . . . This division of authority, according to Madison, would produce efficient government and protect the rights of the people:

> "In a single republic, all the power surrendered by the people, is submitted to the administration of a single government; and usurpations are guarded against by a divi-sion of the government into distinct and separate departments. In the compound republic of America, the power surrendered by the people, is first divided between two distinct governments, and then the portion allotted to each, subdivided among distinct and separate departments. Hence a double security arises to the rights of the people. The different governments will controul each other; at the same time that each will be controuled by itself." The Federalist No. 51.

See Nagel, Federalism as a Fundamental Value: National League of Cities in Perspective, 1981 S. Ct. Rev. 81, 88.

Of course, one of the "few and defined" powers delegated to the National Congress was the power "To regulate Commerce with foreign Nations, and among the several States, and with the Indian Tribes." U.S. Const., Art. I, §8, cl. 3. . . . In an era when interstate commerce represented a tiny fraction of economic activity and most goods and services were produced and consumed close to home, the interstate commerce power left a broad range of activities beyond the reach of Congress.

In the decades since ratification of the Constitution, interstate economic activity has steadily expanded. Industrialization, coupled with advances in transportation and communications, has created a national economy in which virtually every activity occurring within the borders of a State plays a part. The expansion and integration of the national economy brought with it a coordinate expansion in the scope of national problems. This Court has been increasingly generous in its interpretation of the commerce power of Congress, primarily to assure that the National Government would be able to deal with national economic problems. Most significantly, the Court in NLRB v. Jones & Laughlin Steel Corp., and United States v. Darby, rejected its previous interpretations of the commerce power which had stymied New Deal legislation. . . . It is in this context that recent changes in the workings of Congress, such as the direct election of Senators and the expanded influence of national interest groups, become relevant. These changes may well have lessened the weight Congress gives to the legitimate interests of States as States. As a result, there is now a real risk that Congress will gradually erase the diffusion of power between State and Nation on which the Framers based their faith in the efficiency and vitality of our Republic. . . .

It is worth recalling the cited passage in McCulloch v. Maryland that lies at the source of the recent expansion of the commerce power. "Let the end be legitimate, let it be within the scope of the constitution," Chief Justice Marshall said, "and all means which are appropriate, which are plainly adapted to that end, which are not prohibited, but consist with the letter *and spirit* of the constitution, are constitutional" (emphasis added). The *spirit* of the Tenth Amendment, of course, is that the States will retain their integrity in a system in which the laws of the United States are nevertheless supreme.

. . . For example, Congress might rationally conclude that the location a State chooses for its capital may affect interstate commerce, but the Court has suggested that Congress would nevertheless be barred from dictating that location because such an exercise of a delegated power would undermine the state sovereignty inherent in the Tenth Amendment. Coyle v. Oklahoma, 221 U.S. 559, 565 (1911). . . .

. . . This principle requires the Court to enforce affirmative limits on federal regulation of the States to complement the judicially crafted expansion of the interstate commerce power. . . .

The last two decades have seen an unprecedented growth of federal regulatory activity, as the majority itself acknowledges. . . . For example, recently the Federal Government has, with this Court's blessing, undertaken to tell the States the age at which they can retire their law enforcement officers, and the regulatory standards, procedures, and even the agenda which their utilities commissions must consider and follow. The political process has not protected against these encroachments on state activities, even though they directly impinge on a State's ability to make and enforce its laws. With the abandonment of *National League of Cities,* all that stands between the remaining essentials of state sovereignty and Congress is the latter's underdeveloped capacity for self-restraint. . . .

I would not shirk the duty acknowledged by *National League of Cities* and its progeny, and I share Justice Rehnquist's belief that this Court will in time again assume its constitutional responsibility.

Discussion

1. *The basis of* National League of Cities: *Text or structure?* Justice Rehnquist's decision in *National League of Cities* is typically described by scholars and lawyers as based on the Tenth Amendment. But is it? The Tenth Amendment is only mentioned in a single passage, introducing and quoting a prior case. Professor H. Jefferson Powell has argued that *National League of Cities* is written as a structural, not a textual, opinion: Even the invocation of the Amendment itself avoids careful examination of its language, and instead treats it as exemplifying the broader *structural* idea that state governments play a special role in the Constitution and do not exist merely at the sufferance of Congress. According to Powell, "The Tenth Amendment is 'an express declaration' of the state sovereignty limitation, not its source." Jeff Powell, The Compleat Jeffersonian: Justice Rehnquist and Federalism, 91 Yale L.J. 1317, 1329 (1982). Can you see why Justice Rehnquist might prefer not to build his argument on the rock of the Tenth's text? Recall that he seeks to deploy the Amendment as the source of an affirmative exemption, akin to the Sixth Amendment and the Fifth Amendment Due Process Clause. But the Fifth and Sixth Amendments, by their grammar and syntax, "cut across" Congress's enumerated powers: Even where Congress is plainly regulating, say, interstate commerce, these Amendments have bite. By contrast, the grammar of the Tenth Amendment seems to define states' rights residually — these rights merely mark the absence of enumerated power, rather than cutting across it. To see the point another way, recall that *National League of Cities* does not challenge Congress's power to apply its minimum wage, as a general matter, to private employers. But if exemption from minimum wage laws is a textual right of states under the Tenth, why isn't a similar exemption a textual right of private employers? Note that the Amendment's text speaks of rights reserved to both "the states" and "the people" in its last clause.

2. *The* Coyle *problem.* Justice Blackmun's *Garcia* opinion declines to specify "what affirmative limits the constitutional structure might impose on federal action affecting the States under the Commerce Clause. See Coyle v. Oklahoma, 221 U.S. 559 (1911)." If Congress tried to dictate to a state the location of its state capital, or the length of its governor's term of office, would the *Garcia* Court uphold such a law as long as it was plausibly linked to, say, the Commerce Clause? If not, then how and where should the line be drawn between these hypotheticals and the facts of *Garcia*? For example, is it relevant that these hypothetical laws seek to single out "states qua states," regulating them in a manner very different from typical regulations of private enterprise? That these regulations seek to restructure the political organization of a state? (If you think these or other distinctions are relevant, why? What is the theory of federalism, and of its values, that makes such distinctions relevant?) As you confront the Rehnquist Court cases, infra, consider whether the laws at issue in these cases are closer to the law in *Garcia* or closer to the state-capital issue flagged by *Coyle*. For an important and influential argument that congressional laws seeking to dictate state political structures raise special concerns and call for special judicial scrutiny,

see Deborah Jones Merritt, The Guarantee Clause and State Autonomy: Federalism for a Third Century, 88 Colum. L. Rev. 1 (1988). Cf. id. at 56-57 (distinguishing between permissible federal wage regulations of state firefighters — who do not exercise "legislative, executive, or judicial" functions — and more suspect federal efforts to regulate the state's employment of police, legislators, and judges).

3. *The political safeguards of federalism and the composition of the Supreme Court.* Building on the analysis offered by James Madison in the Federalist Nos. 45 and 46, Professor Herbert Wechsler argued in a famous and influential article that:

> the national political process in the United States — and especially the role of the states in the composition and selection of the central government — is intrinsically well-adapted to retarding or restraining new intrusions by the center on the domain of the states. Far from a national authority that is expansionist by nature, the inherent tendency in our system is precisely the reverse, necessitating the widest support before intrusive measures of importance can receive significant consideration, reacting readily to opposition grounded in resistance within the states.

Herbert Wechsler, The Political Safegaurds of Federalism: The Role of the States in the Composition and Selection of the National Government, 54 Colum. L. Rev. 543, 557-558 (1954).

Some of the political safeguards invoked by Professor Wechsler, such as the equal representation of states in the Senate, remain intact. Others, including the extent of state control over the federal election process, have been limited by subsequent judicial decisions, congressional legislation, and constitutional amendments requiring the apportionment of congressional districts on a "one person, one vote" basis, the elimination of poll taxes and literacy tests, limitations on durational residency and other state-law requirements for voting, and the enfranchisement of citizens over 18.

Professor Larry Kramer argues that several of the particular safeguards invoked by Professor Wechsler, such as equal state representation in the Senate, are implausible as safeguards of state institutions, as distinguished from protecting the political interests of people who live in small states. See Larry D. Kramer, Putting the Politics Back into the Political Safeguards of Federalism, 100 Colum. L. Rev. 215 (2000). Such institutions arguably were protected prior to the Seventeenth Amendment when state legislatures chose senators, but there is no reason to believe that the mass electorate that now chooses senators would be particularly interested in safeguarding state institutions if they believed, politically, that national institutions could do a better job of achieving their political goals. Still, Kramer argues, there are political safeguards, though they rest in something not highlighted by Wechsler: the operation of the highly decentralized system of American political parties, by which figures on the national political stage must constantly forge political alliances with state and local officials. And Kramer is, if anything, even more skeptical than Wechsler about the useful role of the Court in monitoring the relationship between Congress and the states. Thus, he writes, "I think the Justices have little idea what they are doing when they intrude . . . [:] no clear picture how their decisions affect governmental operations beyond the particular statutes they invalidate, no hint whether they have made government better or worse." One reason for this bleak view may be the fact that extremely few members of the current Court have had significant experience as actual participants in either state or national government. There are, for example, no former governors, senators, cabinet officials, or, indeed, presidents, on the current court. Compare, e.g., those courts that included former governors Charles Evans Hughes or Earl Warren, former senators George Sutherland or Hugo Black, former cabinet officials John Marshall, Roger Taney, Charles Evans Hughes again, Robert Jackson, or, finally, former president William Howard Taft. Is significant political experience a desideratum in Supreme Court appointees?

4. *Federalism and separation of powers.* To what extent are federalism and separation of powers similar? For example, if you believe that the federal judiciary should generally defer to federal laws that arguably offend states rights, because states are represented in the political process, then should the same be true of federal laws that arguably offend the rights of the President or of Congress? (Both, after all, are likewise represented.) Conversely, if these separation of powers cases are generally justiciable, should the same be true of federalism cases? If not, why not?

5. *The meaning of* Marbury. Justice Powell argues that the sort of extreme deference championed by the *Garcia* majority violates the principle of Marbury v. Madison. But does *Marbury* do anything more than affirm the right and the power of federal judges to refuse to enforce a law in their own courtrooms, once they are fully persuaded that the law is unconstitutional? Does *Marbury,* for example, bar the courts from opting to indulge a strong presumption of constitutionality prior to reaching the conclusion that a given law is indeed unconstitutional? Does *Marbury* require the Court to fashion doctrinal rules imposing substantive limits on Congress even where the Court believes that (a) Congress is well structured to respect the constitutional rights in question and that (b) courts are ill structured to implement the relevant constitutional norms in a doctrinally sound way, with sufficiently manageable judicial standards and "principled" doctrinal rules? If *Marbury* really means that deference is never proper, is *Marbury* inconsistent with some of the language of McCulloch v. Maryland? Compare Justice Powell's invocation of *Marbury* with Justice Kennedy's (and other Justices') invocation of *Marbury* in Reconstruction power cases like *City of Boerne*; also, be on the lookout for citations to *Marbury* in some of the modern separation of powers cases, infra, Parts V and VI.

B. The Rehnquist Court: Finding Affirmative Limits

William Rehnquist's 1976 *National League of Cities* opinion reflected a deep belief in the importance of states' rights, and a willingness to deploy federal judicial power in support of these rights. But over the next decade, the Court never used the *National League of Cities* doctrine — or any other states' rights doctrine, for that matter — to invalidate congressional action. And as we have seen, the *Garcia* Court seemed to lay *National League of Cities* to rest in 1985. Two years later, President Reagan nominated, and the Senate confirmed, Justice Rehnquist to sit as Chief Justice. Would the new Chief be able to lead his Court back toward his vision of federalism? If so, how would issues of stare decisis affect the Court's path back? Note that *Garcia* explicitly overruled *National League of Cities,* which in turn had explicitly overruled Maryland v. Wirtz. Note also that Justices Rehnquist and O'Connor expressed their hope that *Garcia* would be overcome (if not overruled) at some later date.[65] Keep an eye on issues of stare decisis as you read the following federalism cases, handed down by the Rehnquist Court. To what extent do these cases manage to "move" the law while maintaining fidelity to cases like *Garcia?* Some related questions to keep in mind: to what extent are the movements in case law a product of (a) a different set of issues reaching the Court, (b) new facts emerging, (c) a changed political landscape, (d) gravitational pulls exerted by developments in legal doctrine outside federalism, (e) new Justices joining the Court, and (f) simple changes of heart? What other factors may also be at work?

In South Carolina v. Baker, 485 U.S. 505 (1988), South Carolina challenged the constitutionality of Section 310 (b)(1) of the Tax Equity and Fiscal Responsibility Act of 1982 (TEFRA), which eliminated the exemption from federal income tax of interest earned on nonregistered bonds issued by states and local municipalities. The exemption was maintained for registered bonds, whose ownership is recorded on a central list. Both private and public bonds were affected, because Congress determined that nonregistered "bearer bonds" lent themselves to tax avoidance and to use in illegal activities. The State claimed that the regulation of its bonds violated the Tenth Amendment.[66] As a result of TEFRA, states now issue only registered bonds, because the sale of nonregistered bonds would require the payment of substantially higher interest rates in order to overcome the loss of the tax exemption.

The Court upheld the provision. Justice Brennan, writing for the majority, treated the statute as a functional prohibition of nonregistered bonds. He found the Tenth Amendment claim foreclosed by *Garcia,* which he described as holding that the limits of Congress's authority to regulate state activities "are structural — not substantive — i.e., that States must find their protection from congressional regulation through the national political process, not through judicially defined spheres of unregulatable state activity." South Carolina claimed that §310(b)(1) was "imposed by the vote of an uninformed Congress relying on incomplete information." Justice Brennan countered that South Carolina presented no evidence of such "extraordinary defects in the national political process" as to justify judicial intervention. "Where, as here, the national political *process* did not operate in a defective manner, the Tenth Amendment is not implicated." Chief Justice Rehnquist and Justice Scalia, concurring in separate opinions, rejected Justice Brennan's reading of *Garcia.* Justice Scalia described that case "as explicitly disclaiming the proposition attributed to it," and quoted, with emphasis, the following sentence from *Garcia:* "These cases do not require us to identify or define what affirmative limits *the constitutional structure* might impose on federal action affecting the States under the Commerce Clause." He went on to say, "I agree only that that structure does not prohibit what the Federal Government has done here." Chief Justice Rehnquist argued that South Carolina would lose even under *National League of Cities* because the facts showed that the provision had no practical impact on state borrowing practices since tax exemption (and thus lower interest rates) was still available for registered bonds:

> This well-supported conclusion that Section 310(b)(1) has had a *de minimis* impact on the States should end, rather than begin, the Court's constitutional inquiry. Even the

65. What do these developments suggest about the importance of precedent in constitutional decisionmaking? Recall Justice Scalia's comments concerning stare decisis in Chapter 1, supra.

66. South Carolina also claimed that the tax violated the doctrine of intergovernmental tax immunity. See Collector v. Day, 78 U.S. (11 Wall.) 113 (1871); Pollock v. Farmers' Loan & Trust Co., 157 U.S. 429 (1895).

more expansive conception of the Tenth Amendment espoused in *National League of Cities* recognized that only congressional action that "operate[s] to directly displace the States' freedom to structure integral operations in areas of traditional governmental functions" runs afoul of the authority granted Congress. The Special Master determined that no such displacement has occurred through the implementation of the TEFRA requirements; I see no need to go further, as the majority does, to discuss the possibility of defects in the national political process that spawned TEFRA.

Justice O'Connor dissented. Three years later, however, it would be Justice O'Connor who spoke for the majority in an important federalism case.

GREGORY v. ASHCROFT
501 U.S. 452 (1991)

[The Missouri Constitution provides that "all judges other than municipal judges shall retire at the age of seventy years." Two state judges subject to this mandatory retirement rule challenged it as violative of the federal Age Discrimination in Employment Act of 1967 (ADEA or Act), 81 Stat. 602, as amended, 29 U.S.C. §§621-634, and Fourteenth Amendment's Equal Protection Clause. Subject to certain important exceptions (discussed below), the ADEA makes it unlawful for an "employer" "to discharge any individual" who is at least 40 years old "because of such individual's age." 29 U.S.C. §§623(a), 631(a). The term "employer" is defined to include "a State or political subdivision of a State." §630(b)(2)]

O'CONNOR, J.

II.

A

As every schoolchild learns, our Constitution establishes a system of dual sovereignty between the States and the Federal Government. This Court also has recognized this fundamental principle. In Tafflin v. Levitt, 493 U.S. 455 (1990), "we beg[a]n with the axiom that, under our federal system, the States possess sovereignty concurrent with that of the Federal Government, subject only to limitations imposed by the Supremacy Clause." Over 120 years ago, the Court described the constitutional scheme of dual sovereigns:

> "'The people of each State compose a State, having its own government, and endowed with all the functions essential to separate and independent existence,'.... 'Without the States in union, there could be no such political body as the United States.' Not only, therefore, can there be no loss of separate and independent autonomy to the States, through their union under the Constitution, but it may be not unreasonably said that the preservation of the States, and the maintenance of their governments, are as much within the design and care of the Constitution as the preservation of the Union and the maintenance of the National government. The Constitution, in all its provisions, looks to an indestructible Union, composed of indestructible States." Texas v. White. . . .

This federalist structure of joint sovereigns preserves to the people numerous advantages. It assures a decentralized government that will be more sensitive to the diverse needs of a heterogenous society; it increases opportunity for citizen involvement in democratic processes; it allows for more innovation and experimentation in government; and it makes government more responsive by putting the States in competition for a mobile citizenry. See generally McConnell, Federalism: Evaluating the Founders' Design, 54 U. Chi. L. Rev. 1484, 1491-1511 (1987); Merritt, The Guarantee Clause and State Autonomy: Federalism for a Third Century, 88 Colum. L. Rev. 1, 3-10 (1988).

Perhaps the principal benefit of the federalist system is a check on abuses of government power. "The 'constitutionally mandated balance of power' between the States and the Federal Government was adopted by the Framers to ensure the protection of 'our fundamental liberties.' " Just as the separation and independence of the coordinate branches of the Federal Government serve to prevent the accumulation of excessive power in any one branch, a healthy balance of power between the States and the Federal Government will reduce the risk of tyranny and abuse from either front. Alexander Hamilton explained to the people of New York, perhaps optimistically, that the new federalist system would suppress completely "the attempts of the government to establish a tyranny":

> "In a confederacy the people, without exaggeration, may be said to be entirely the masters of their own fate. Power being almost always the rival of power, the general government will at all times stand ready to check the usurpations of the state governments, and these will have the same disposition towards the general government. The people, by throwing themselves into either scale, will infallibly make it preponderate. If their rights are invaded by either, they can make use of the other as the instrument of redress." The Federalist No. 28.

James Madison made much the same point:

> "In a single republic, all the power surrendered by the people is submitted to the administration of a single government; and the usurpations are guarded against by a division of the government into distinct and separate departments. In the compound republic of America, the power surrendered by the people is first divided between two distinct governments, and then the portion allotted to each subdivided among distinct and separate departments. Hence a double security arises to the rights of the people. The different governments will control each other, at the same time that each will be controlled by itself." [The Federalist] No. 51.

One fairly can dispute whether our federalist system has been quite as successful in checking government abuse as Hamilton promised, but there is no doubt about the design. If this "double security" is to be effective, there must be a proper balance between the States and the Federal Government. These twin powers will act as mutual restraints only if both are credible. In the tension between federal and state power lies the promise of liberty.

The Federal Government holds a decided advantage in this delicate balance: the Supremacy Clause. As long as it is acting within the powers granted it under the Constitution, Congress may impose its will on the States. Congress may legislate in areas traditionally regulated by the States. This is an extraordinary power in a federalist system. It is a power that we must assume Congress does not exercise lightly.

The present case concerns a state constitutional provision through which the people of Missouri establish a qualification for those who sit as their judges. This provision goes beyond an area traditionally regulated by the States; it is a decision of the most fundamental sort for a sovereign entity. Through the structure of its government, and the character of those who exercise government authority, a State defines itself as a sovereign. "It is obviously essential to the independence of the States, and to their peace and tranquility, that their power to prescribe the qualifications of their own officers . . . should be exclusive, and free from external interference, except so far as plainly provided by the Constitution of the United States."

Congressional interference with this decision of the people of Missouri, defining their constitutional officers, would upset the usual constitutional balance of federal and state powers. For this reason, "it is incumbent upon the federal courts to be certain of Congress' intent before finding that federal law overrides" this balance. We explained recently: "If Congress intends to alter the 'usual constitutional balance between the States and the Federal Government,' it must make its intention to do so 'unmistakably clear in the language of the statute.'" . . .

In a recent line of authority, we have acknowledged the unique nature of state decisions that "go to the heart of representative government." *Sugarman v. Dougall,* 413 U.S. 634 (1973). *Sugarman* was the first in a series of cases to consider the restrictions imposed by the Equal Protection Clause of the Fourteenth Amendment on the ability of state and local governments to prohibit aliens from public employment. In that case, the Court struck down under the Equal Protection Clause a New York City law that provided a flat ban against the employment of aliens in a wide variety of city jobs.

The Court did not hold, however, that alienage could never justify exclusion from public employment. We recognized explicitly the States' constitutional power to establish the qualifications for those who would govern:

> Just as "the Framers of the Constitution intended the States to keep for themselves, as provided in the Tenth Amendment, the power to regulate elections," Oregon v. Mitchell, each State has the power to prescribe the qualifications of its officers and the manner in which they shall be chosen. Such power inheres in the State by virtue of its obligation, already noted above, "to preserve the basic conception of a political community." And this power and responsibility of the State applies, not only to the qualifications of voters, but also to persons holding state elective and important nonelective executive, legislative, and judicial positions, for officers who participate directly in the formulation, execution, or review of broad public policy perform functions that go to the heart of representative government.

. . . In several subsequent cases we have applied the "political function" exception to laws through which States exclude aliens from positions "intimately related to the process of democratic self-government." . . .

These cases stand in recognition of the authority of the people of the States to determine the qualifications of their most important government officials. It is an authority that lies at "'the heart of representative government.'" It is a power reserved to the States under the Tenth Amendment and guaranteed them by that provision of the Constitution under which the United States "guarantee[s] to every State in this Union a Republican Form of Government." U.S. Const., Art. IV, §4. See *Sugarman,* (citing the Guarantee Clause and the Tenth Amendment). See also Merritt, 88 Colum. L. Rev., at 50-55.

The authority of the people of the States to determine the qualifications of their government officials is, of course, not without limit. Other constitutional provisions, most notably the Fourteenth Amendment, proscribe certain qualifications; our review of citizenship requirements under the political function exception is less exacting, but it is not absent. Here, we must decide what Congress did in extending the ADEA to the States, pursuant to its powers under the Commerce Clause. As against Congress' powers "to regulate Commerce . . . among the several States," the authority of the people of the States to determine the qualifications of their government officials may be inviolate.

We are constrained in our ability to consider the limits that the state-federal balance places on Congress' powers under the Commerce Clause. See *Garcia* (declining to review limitations placed on Congress' Commerce Clause powers by our federal system). But there is no need to do so if we hold that the ADEA does not apply to state judges. Application of the plain statement rule thus may avoid a potential constitutional problem. Indeed, inasmuch as this Court in *Garcia* has left primarily to the political process the protection of the States against intrusive exercises of Congress' Commerce Clause powers, we must be absolutely certain that Congress intended such an exercise. "To give the state-displacing weight of federal law to mere congressional ambiguity would evade the very procedure for lawmaking on which *Garcia* relied to protect states' interests." L. Tribe, American Constitutional Law §6-25, p. 480 (2d ed. 1988).

B

In 1974, Congress extended the substantive provisions of the ADEA to include the States as employers. Pub. L. 93-259, §28(a), 88 Stat. 74, 29 U.S.C. §630(b)(2). At the same time, Congress amended the definition of "employee" to exclude all elected and most high-ranking government officials. Under the Act, as amended:

"The term 'employee' means an individual employed by any employer except that the term 'employee' shall not include any person elected to public office in any State or political subdivision of any State by the qualified voters thereof, or any person chosen by such officer to be on such officer's personal staff, or an appointee on the policy-making level or an immediate adviser with respect to the exercise of the constitutional or legal powers of the office." 29 U.S.C. §630(f).

Governor Ashcroft contends that the §630(f) exclusion of certain public officials also excludes judges, like petitioners, who are appointed to office by the Governor and are then subject to retention election. The Governor points to two passages in §630(f). First, he argues, these judges are selected by an elected official and, because they make policy, are "appointee[s] on the policymaking level."

Petitioners counter that judges merely resolve factual disputes and decide questions of law; they do not make policy. Moreover, petitioners point out that the policymaking-level exception is part of a trilogy, tied closely to the elected-official exception. Thus, the Act excepts elected officials and: (1) "any person chosen by such officer to be on such officer's personal staff"; (2) "an appointee on the policymaking level"; and (3) "an immediate advisor with respect to the exercise of the constitutional or legal powers of the office." Applying the maxim of statutory construction noscitur a sociis — that a word is known by the company it keeps — petitioners argue that since (1) and (3) refer only to those in close working relationships with elected officials, so too must (2). Even if it can be said that judges may make policy, petitioners contend, they do not do so at the behest of an elected official.

Governor Ashcroft relies on the plain language of the statute: It exempts persons appointed "at the policymaking level." The Governor argues that state judges, in fashioning and applying the common law, make policy. Missouri is a common law state. See Mo. Rev. Stat. §1.010 (1986) (adopting "the common law of England" consistent with federal and state law). The common law, unlike a constitution or statute, provides no definitive text; it is to be derived from the interstices of prior opinions and a well-considered judgment of what is best for the community. . . .

Governor Ashcroft contends that Missouri judges make policy in other ways as well. The Missouri Supreme Court and Courts of Appeals have supervisory authority over inferior courts. The Missouri Supreme Court has the constitutional duty to establish rules of practice and procedure for the Missouri court system, and inferior courts exercise policy judgment in establishing local rules of practice. The state courts have supervisory powers over the state bar, with the Missouri Supreme Court given the authority to develop disciplinary rules.

The Governor stresses judges' policymaking responsibilities, but it is far from plain that the statutory exception requires that judges actually make policy. The statute refers to appointees "on the policymaking level," not to appointees "who make policy." It may be sufficient that the appointee is in a position requiring the exercise of discretion concerning issues of public importance. This certainly describes the bench, regardless of whether judges might be considered policymakers in the same sense as the executive or legislature.

Nonetheless, "appointee at the policymaking level," particularly in the context of the other exceptions that surround it, is an odd way for Congress to exclude judges; a plain statement that judges are not "employees" would seem the most efficient phrasing. But in this case we are not looking for a plain statement that judges are excluded. We will not read the ADEA to cover state judges unless Congress has made it clear that judges are included. This does not mean that the Act must mention judges explicitly, though it does not. Rather, it must be plain to anyone reading the Act that it covers judges. In the context of a statute that plainly excludes most important state public officials, "appointee on the policymaking level" is sufficiently broad that we cannot conclude that the statute plainly covers appointed state judges. Therefore, it does not. . . .

C

The extension of the ADEA to employment by state and local governments was a valid exercise of Congress' powers under the Commerce Clause. [H]owever, . . . the principles of federalism that constrain Congress' exercise of its Commerce Clause powers are attenuated when Congress acts pursuant to its powers to enforce the Civil War Amendments. This is because those "Amendments were specifically designed as an expansion of federal power and an intrusion on state sovereignty." One might argue, therefore, that if Congress passed the ADEA extension under its §5 powers, the concerns about federal intrusion into state government that compel the result in this case might carry less weight. . . .

. . . In light of the ADEA's clear exclusion of most important public officials, it is at least ambiguous whether Congress intended that appointed judges nonetheless be included. In the face of such ambiguity, we will not attribute to Congress an intent to intrude on state governmental functions regardless of whether Congress acted pursuant to its Commerce Clause powers or §5 of the Fourteenth Amendment.

III.

Petitioners argue that, even if they are not covered by the ADEA, the Missouri Constitution's mandatory retirement provision for judges violates the Equal Protection Clause of the Fourteenth Amendment to the United States Constitution. Petitioners contend that there is no rational basis for the decision of the people of Missouri to preclude those aged 70 and over from serving as their judges. They claim that the mandatory retirement provision makes two irrational distinctions: between judges who have reached age 70 and younger judges, and between judges 70 and over and other state employees of the same age who are not subject to mandatory retirement.

Petitioners are correct to assert their challenge at the level of rational basis. This Court has said repeatedly that age is not a suspect classification under the Equal Protection Clause. . . .

The people of Missouri have a legitimate, indeed compelling, interest in maintaining a judiciary fully capable of performing the demanding tasks that judges must perform. It is an unfortunate fact of life that physical and mental capacity sometimes diminish with age. The people may therefore wish to replace some older judges. Voluntary retirement will not always be sufficient. Nor may impeachment — with its public humiliation and elaborate procedural machinery — serve acceptably the goal of a fully functioning judiciary.

The election process may also be inadequate. Whereas the electorate would be expected to discover if their governor or state legislator were not performing adequately and vote the official out of office, the same may not be true of judges. Most voters never observe state judges in action, nor read judicial opinions. State judges also serve longer terms of office than other public officials, making them — deliberately — less dependent on the will of the people. . . . The people of Missouri rationally could conclude that retention elections — in which state judges run unopposed at relatively long intervals — do not serve as an adequate check on judges whose performance is deficient. Mandatory retirement is a reasonable response to this dilemma.

This is also a rational explanation for the fact that state judges are subject to a mandatory retirement provision, while other state officials — whose performance is subject to greater public scrutiny, and who are subject to more standard elections — are not. Judges' general lack of accountability explains also the distinction between judges and other state employees, in whom a deterioration in performance is more readily discernible and who are more easily removed.

The Missouri mandatory retirement provision, like all legal classifications, is founded on a generalization. It is far from true that all judges suffer significant deterioration in performance at age 70. It is probably not true that most do. It may not be true at all. But a State "does not violate the Equal Protection Clause merely because the classifications made by its laws are imperfect.". . . .

IV.

The people of Missouri have established a qualification for those who would be their judges. It is their prerogative as citizens of a sovereign State to do so. . . .

Justice WHITE, with whom Justice Stevens joins, concurring in part, dissenting in part, and concurring in the judgment.

I agree with the majority that neither the Age Discrimination in Employment Act of 1967 (ADEA) nor the Equal Protection Clause prohibits Missouri's mandatory retirement provision as applied to petitioners, and I therefore concur in the judgment and in Parts I and III of the majority's opinion. I cannot agree, however, with the majority's reasoning in Part II of its opinion, which ignores several areas of well-established precedent and announces a rule that is likely to prove both unwise and infeasible. That the majority's analysis in Part II is completely unnecessary to the proper resolution of this case makes it all the more remarkable.

I.

The majority's plain statement rule is not only unprecedented, it directly contravenes our decisions in Garcia v. San Antonio Metropolitan Transit Authority, and South Carolina v. Baker, 485 U.S. 505 (1988). In those cases we made it clear "that States must find their protection from congressional regulation through the national political process, not through judicially defined spheres of unregulable state activity." We also rejected as "unsound in principle and unworkable in practice" any test for state immunity that requires a judicial determination of which state activities are "traditional," "integral," or "necessary." The majority disregards those decisions in its attempt to carve out areas of state activity that will receive special protection from federal legislation. . . .

The majority asserts that its plain statement rule is helpful in avoiding a "potential constitutional problem." It is far from clear, however, why there would be a constitutional problem if the ADEA applied to state judges, in light of our decisions in *Garcia* and *Baker,* discussed above. As long as "the national political process did not operate in a defective manner, the Tenth Amendment is not implicated." There is no claim in this case that the political process by which the ADEA was extended to state employees was inadequate to protect the States from being "unduly burdened" by the Federal Government. In any event, as discussed below, a straightforward analysis of the ADEA's definition of "employee" reveals that the ADEA does not apply here. Thus, even if there were potential constitutional problems in extending the ADEA to state judges, the majority's proposed plain statement rule would not be necessary to avoid them in this case. . . .

Even more disturbing is its treatment of Congress' power under §5 of the Fourteenth Amendment. Section 5 provides that "the Congress shall have power to enforce, by appropriate legislation, the provisions of this article." Despite that sweeping constitutional delegation of authority to Congress, the majority holds that its plain statement rule will apply with full force to legislation enacted to enforce the Fourteenth Amendment. . . .

The majority's failure to recognize the special status of legislation enacted pursuant to §5 ignores that, unlike Congress' Commerce Clause power, "when Congress acts pursuant to §5, not only is it exercising legislative authority that is plenary within the terms of the constitutional grant, it is exercising that authority under one section of a constitutional Amendment whose other sections by their own terms embody limitations on state authority." Fitzpatrick v. Bitzer. Indeed, we have held that "principles of federalism that might otherwise be an obstacle to congressional authority are necessarily overridden by the power to enforce the Civil War Amendments 'by appropriate legislation.' Those Amendments were specifically designed as an expansion of federal power and an intrusion on state sovereignty." . . .

The majority's departures from established precedent are even more disturbing when it is realized . . . that this case can be affirmed based on simple statutory construction. . . .

Justice BLACKMUN, with whom Justice Marshall joins, dissenting.

I agree entirely with the cogent analysis contained in Part I of Justice White's opinion. For the reasons well stated by Justice White, the question we must resolve is whether appointed Missouri state judges are excluded from the general prohibition of mandatory retirement that Congress established in the ADEA. I part company with Justice White, however, in his determination that appointed state judges fall within the narrow exclusion from ADEA coverage that Congress created for an "appointee on the policymaking level." §630(f). . . .

Discussion

1. *Garcia's legacy.* Both the majority and the dissenters claim to follow *Garcia.* According to the majority opinion, *Garcia* deferred to Congress because states' interests were well protected in the legislative process; to ensure that this premise in fact holds, the Court should require Congress to speak clearly when it limits states, so that the affected states will have clear notice in Congress, and will make themselves heard. The dissenters, by contrast, claim that *Garcia* suggests that states can take care of themselves without the Court, and that no justiciable constitutional question would be presented if the ADEA were to be construed to apply to state judges. (The majority expresses doubt on this score; is the *Garcia* Court's reference to *Coyle* possibly relevant here?) Which approach to do you think is more faithful to *Garcia*? Is it possible to side with the *Gregory* majority as more faithful even though all the remaining Justices from the *Garcia* majority now dissent from this reading of *Garcia*? In other words, is it possible that Justice O'Connor — who dissented in *Garcia* — nevertheless has a more faithful reading of it than its own author, Justice Blackmun? If so, why might that be?

2. *Clear-statement rules and constitutional doubts.* In addition to promoting the political safeguards of federalism, *Gregory*'s clear-statement rule has a second virtue, according to the Court: It enables the Justices to avoid the hard constitutional question that would be presented if the law were to be read as applicable to state judges. This use of clear-statement rules follows in the tradition of Justice Brandeis's famous concurrence in Ashwander v. T.V.A., 297 U.S. 288 (1936), cataloguing a variety of techniques for avoiding unnecessary constitutional decisions. In England, where judges have historically lacked the direct power of judicial review, clear-statement rules have long been used to ensure that certain privileged practices are not lightly overridden by Parliament. For a thoughtful discussion of the Court's use of clear-statement rules to protect certain legal interests, see William N. Eskridge, Jr. and Philip P. Frickey, Quasi-Constitutional Law: Clear Statement Rules as Constitutional Lawmaking, 45 Vand. L. Rev. 593 (1992). When such rules are announced by the Court in advance, and applied prospectively, they may make it harder to accomplish certain legislative results — it may be difficult in some instances to round up votes for "Simon Says" language in the legislature — but the rules of the game in Congress are clear. However, when rules of

construction apply to laws passed before such rules were announced, they may effect a kind of "bait and switch" in which lawmakers think that one set of words will suffice to accomplish purpose X, only to learn later that they needed to speak more clearly. On the other hand, clear-statement rules are arguably more deferential than standard judicial review: The Justices are not (or at least, not yet) saying that Congress may not do X — only that if it seeks to do so, it must speak very clearly.

3. Gregory *and Section 5.* Justice O'Connor announced that her clear-statement rule should apply regardless of whether the ADEA was adopted pursuant to Section 5 of the Fourteenth Amendment. Do you agree? If so, is this because you find the ADEA a peripheral application of Section 5 power, or because you think that all Section 5 exercises of congressional power should be construed strictly in favor of states' rights? (Note that, insofar as racial minorities and women are concerned, application of the ADEA to the state judiciary would likely delay the integration of state benches — most of the judges forced into mandatory retirement are White men, whereas women and racial minorities are apt to constitute a higher percentage of likely judicial replacements.) If you think clear-statement rules are less appropriate to core Section 5 cases, do you think that Congress must be explicit about invoking Section 5 in order to exempt itself from the clear-statement regime? (Isn't this itself a kind of clear-statement rule, at a different level?)

4. *Agreeing to disagree?* Note that four Justices thought the statutory issue was clear, and that the majority therefore had no need to resolve statutory ambiguity by recourse to constitutionally based clear-statement rules of construction. Justice Blackmun thus lavishes praise on Justice White's critique of the Court's reliance on constitutional principles. But this teamwork between Blackmun and White is rather awkward, no? For although they agree that the statute is clear, they disagree about what it says — White says it (clearly) does not apply to state judges, while Blackmun says it (clearly) does. Doesn't this very disagreement undermine their joint claim that the statute is clear?

5. *Older and wiser?* What do you make of the fact that the two Justices who voted to apply the age-discrimination law to protect old judges are themselves the two oldest on the Court? That the five members in the majority were the Court's youngest Justices? Are these facts about the personal characteristics of the Justices too "realist" to warrant mention in a legal casebook? Could they be (tactfully) mentioned in, say, a legal brief — or are they simply irrelevant to a proper legal argument? In this regard, is age any different than, say, race

6. *Federalism and liberty.* Federalism serves multiple purposes, according to the *Gregory* majority. But the Court identifies liberty-protection as "perhaps the principal benefit." Analogizing federalism to separation of powers, and quoting at length from the Federalist Nos. 28 and 51, the Court claims that "a healthy balance of power between the States and the Federal government will reduce the risk of tyranny and abuse from either front." Do you agree? Do the facts of *Gregory* implicate liberty in any direct way? (Even if not, does the *Gregory* rule, in your view, in any way impede liberty?) For prominent statements of liberty-protection as a key virtue of federalism, with emphasis on the seldom-quoted but important language of the Federalist No. 28, see Martin Diamond, The Federalist's View of Federalism, in Essays in Federalism 21 (1961); Laurence H. Tribe, American Constitutional Law 3 n.6 (1978); Akhil Reed Amar, Of Sovereignty and Federalism, 96 Yale L.J.

1425, 1492-1520 (1987). For other more general elaborations of the theme of "vertical" checks and balances between state and federal officials in order to disperse power and limit government abuse, see Robert F. Nagel, Federalism as a Fundamental Value: National League of Cities in Perspective, 1981 Sup. Ct. Rev. 81; Andrzej Rapaczynski, From Sovereignty to Process: The Jurisprudence of Federalism After *Garcia*, 1985 Sup. Ct. Rev. 341; Michael W. McConnell, Federalism: Evaluating the Founders' Design, 54 U. Chi. L. Rev. 1484 (1987); Merritt, supra p. 662.

With *Gregory* on the books — affirming the constitutional importance of states while pledging allegiance to *Garcia* — the Rehnquist Court quickly found another case pitting congressional power against states' rights. But this time, the issue went beyond clear-statement rules. In the 1992 case reprinted below, the Court — for only the second time in a half-century (putting aside the overruled *National League of Cities* case) — struck down a federal statute in the name of states' rights. As in *Gregory*, Justice O'Connor spoke for the Court, seeking to steer around *Garcia* rather than sink it. As in *Gregory*, the remaining members of the *Garcia* majority (now down to three) sharply dissented.

NEW YORK v. UNITED STATES
505 U.S. 144 (1992)

O'CONNOR, J.

I.

We live in a world full of low level radioactive waste. . . . Millions of cubic feet of low level radioactive waste must be disposed of each year.

. . . [S]ince 1979 only three disposal sites — those in Nevada, Washington, and South Carolina — have been in operation. Waste generated in the rest of the country must be shipped to one of these three sites for disposal. . . .

Faced with the possibility that the Nation would be left with no disposal sites for low level radioactive waste, Congress responded by [declaring, in a 1980 statute] a federal policy of holding each State "responsible for providing for the availability of capacity either within or outside the State for the disposal of low-level radioactive waste generated within its borders," and found that such waste could be disposed of "most safely and efficiently . . . on a regional basis." The 1980 Act authorized States to enter into regional compacts that, once ratified by Congress, would have the authority beginning in 1986 to restrict the use of their disposal facilities to waste generated within member States. The 1980 Act included no penalties for States that failed to participate in this plan.

By 1985, only three approved regional compacts had operational disposal facilities; not surprisingly, these were the compacts formed around South Carolina, Nevada, and Washington, the three sited States. The following year, the 1980 Act would have given these three compacts the ability to exclude waste from nonmembers, and the remaining 31 States would have had no assured outlet for their low level radioactive waste. With this prospect looming, Congress once again took up the issue of waste disposal. The result was the legislation challenged here, the Low-Level Radioactive Waste Policy Amendments Act of 1985.

The 1985 Act was again based largely on a proposal submitted by the National Governors' Association. In broad outline, the Act embodies a compromise among the sited and unsited States. The sited States agreed to extend for seven years the period in which they would accept low level radioactive waste from other States. In exchange, the unsited States agreed to end their reliance on the sited States by 1992.

The mechanics of this compromise are intricate. The Act directs: "Each State shall be responsible for providing, either by itself or in cooperation with other States, for the disposal of . . . low-level radioactive waste generated within the State," with the exception of certain waste generated by the Federal Government. The Act authorizes States to "enter into such [interstate] compacts as may be necessary to provide for the establishment and operation of regional disposal facilities for low-level radioactive waste." For an additional seven years beyond the period contemplated by the 1980 Act, from the beginning of 1986 through the end of 1992, the three existing disposal sites "shall make disposal capacity available for low-level radioactive waste generated by any source," with certain exceptions not relevant here. But the three States in which the disposal sites are located are permitted to exact a graduated surcharge for waste arriving from outside the regional compact. . . . After the 7-year transition period expires, approved regional compacts may exclude radioactive waste generated outside the region.

The Act provides three types of incentives to encourage the States to comply with their statutory obligation to provide for the disposal of waste generated within their borders.

1. Monetary incentives [discussed in more detail below]. . . .
2. Access incentives. The second type of incentive involves the denial of access to disposal sites [for states that fail to meet various statutory deadlines].
3. The take title provision. The third type of incentive is the most severe. The Act provides:

> If a State (or, where applicable, a compact region) in which low-level radioactive waste is generated is unable to provide for the disposal of all such waste generated within such State or compact region by January 1, 1996, each State in which such waste is generated, upon the request of the generator or owner of the waste, shall take title to the waste, be obligated to take possession of the waste, and shall be liable for all damages directly or indirectly incurred by such generator or owner as a consequence of the failure of the State to take possession of the waste as soon after January 1, 1996, as the generator or owner notifies the State that the waste is available for shipment. . . .

In the seven years since the Act took effect, Congress has approved nine regional compacts, encompassing 42 of the States. . . .

New York, a State whose residents generate a relatively large share of the Nation's low level radioactive waste, did not join a regional compact. Instead, the State complied with the Act's requirements by enacting legislation providing for the siting and financing of a disposal facility in New York. The State has identified five potential sites, three in Allegany County and two in Cortland County. Residents of the two counties oppose the State's choice of location.

Petitioners — the State of New York and the two counties — filed this suit against the United States in 1990. They sought a declaratory judgment that the Act is inconsistent with the Tenth . . . Amendment[] . . . and with the Guarantee Clause of

Article IV of the Constitution. The States of Washington, Nevada, and South Carolina intervened as defendants. . . .

II.

A

Congress exercises its conferred powers subject to the limitations contained in the Constitution. Thus, for example, under the Commerce Clause Congress may regulate publishers engaged in interstate commerce, but Congress is constrained in the exercise of that power by the First Amendment. The Tenth Amendment likewise restrains the power of Congress, but this limit is not derived from the text of the Tenth Amendment itself, which, as we have discussed, is essentially a tautology. Instead, the Tenth Amendment confirms that the power of the Federal Government is subject to limits that may, in a given instance, reserve power to the States. . . .

This framework has been sufficiently flexible over the past two centuries to allow for enormous changes in the nature of government. The Federal Government undertakes activities today that would have been unimaginable to the Framers in two senses; first, because the Framers would not have conceived that any government would conduct such activities; and second, because the Framers would not have believed that the Federal Government, rather than the States, would assume such responsibilities. Yet the powers conferred upon the Federal Government by the Constitution were phrased in language broad enough to allow for the expansion of the Federal Government's role. . . .

The volume of interstate commerce and the range of commonly accepted objects of government regulation have . . . expanded considerably in the last 200 years, and the regulatory authority of Congress has expanded along with them. As interstate commerce has become ubiquitous, activities once considered purely local have come to have effects on the national economy, and have accordingly come within the scope of Congress' commerce power. Katzenbach v. McClung; Wickard v. Filburn. . . .

As conventional notions of the proper objects of government spending have changed over the years, so has the ability of Congress to "fix the terms on which it shall disburse federal money to the States." Compare, e.g., United States v. Butler, 297 U.S. 1 (1936) (spending power does not authorize Congress to subsidize farmers), with South Dakota v. Dole, 483 U.S. 203 (1987) (spending power permits Congress to condition highway funds on States' adoption of minimum drinking age).

B

. . . Most of our recent cases interpreting the Tenth Amendment have concerned the authority of Congress to subject state governments to generally applicable laws. The Court's jurisprudence in this area has traveled an unsteady path. See *Wirtz; National League of Cities; Garcia.* This litigation presents no occasion to apply or revisit the holdings of any of these cases, as this is not a case in which Congress has subjected a State to the same legislation applicable to private parties.

This litigation instead concerns the circumstances under which Congress may use the States as implements of regulation; that is, whether Congress may direct or otherwise motivate the States to regulate in a particular field or a particular way. Our cases have established a few principles that guide our resolution of the issue.

1

As an initial matter, Congress may not simply "commandeer the legislative processes of the States by directly compelling them to enact and enforce a federal regulatory program." Hodel v. Virginia Surface Mining & Reclamation Assn., Inc., 452 U.S. 264, 288 (1981). In *Hodel*, the Court upheld the Surface Mining Control and Reclamation Act of 1977 precisely because it did not "commandeer" the States into regulating mining. The Court found that "the States are not compelled to enforce the steep-slope standards, to expend any state funds, or to participate in the federal regulatory program in any manner whatsoever. If a State does not wish to submit a proposed permanent program that complies with the Act and implementing regulations, the full regulatory burden will be borne by the Federal Government."

The Court reached the same conclusion the following year in FERC v. Mississippi. . . . We observed that "this Court never has sanctioned explicitly a federal command to the States to promulgate and enforce laws and regulations." . . .

These statements in *FERC* and *Hodel* were not innovations. While Congress has substantial powers to govern the Nation directly, including in areas of intimate concern to the States, the Constitution has never been understood to confer upon Congress the ability to require the States to govern according to Congress' instructions. See Coyle v. Smith, 221 U.S. 559 (1911). . . .

Indeed, the question whether the Constitution should permit Congress to employ state governments as regulatory agencies was a topic of lively debate among the Framers. Under the Articles of Confederation, Congress lacked the authority in most respects to govern the people directly. In practice, Congress "could not directly tax or legislate upon individuals; it had no explicit 'legislative' or 'governmental' power to make binding 'law' enforceable as such." Amar, Of Sovereignty and Federalism, 96 Yale L.J. 1425, 1447 (1987).

The inadequacy of this governmental structure was responsible in part for the Constitutional Convention. Alexander Hamilton observed: "The great and radical vice in the construction of the existing Confederation is in the principle of LEGISLATION for STATES or GOVERNMENTS, in their CORPORATE or COLLECTIVE CAPACITIES, and as contradistinguished from the INDIVIDUALS of whom they consist." The Federalist No. 15. As Hamilton saw it, "we must resolve to incorporate into our plan those ingredients which may be considered as forming the characteristic difference between a league and a government; we must extend the authority of the Union to the persons of the citizens — the only proper objects of government." The new National Government "must carry its agency to the persons of the citizens. It must stand in need of no intermediate legislations. . . . The government of the Union, like that of each State, must be able to address itself immediately to the hopes and fears of individuals." Id., No. 16.

The Convention generated a great number of proposals for the structure of the new Government, but two quickly took center stage. Under the Virginia Plan, as first introduced by Edmund Randolph, Congress would exercise legislative authority directly upon individuals, without employing the States as intermediaries. Under the New Jersey Plan, as first introduced by William Paterson, Congress would continue to require the approval of the States before legislating, as it had under the Articles of Confederation. These two plans underwent various revisions as the Convention progressed, but they remained the two primary options discussed by the delegates. One frequently expressed objection to the New Jersey Plan was that it might require the Federal Government to coerce the States into implementing legislation. As Randolph explained the distinction, "the true question is whether we shall adhere to the federal plan [i.e., the New Jersey Plan], or introduce the national plan. The insufficiency of the former has been fully displayed. . . . There are but two modes, by which the end of a General Government can be attained: the 1st is by coercion as proposed by Mr. Paterson's plan [, the 2nd] by real legislation as proposed by the other plan. Coercion [is] impracticable, expensive, cruel to individuals. . . . We must resort therefore to a national Legislation over individuals." Madison echoed this view: "The practicability of making laws, with coercive sanctions, for the States as political bodies, had been exploded on all hands." . . .

In the end, the Convention opted for a Constitution in which Congress would exercise its legislative authority directly over individuals rather than over States; for a variety of reasons, it rejected the New Jersey Plan in favor of the Virginia Plan. This choice was made clear to the subsequent state ratifying conventions. Oliver Ellsworth, a member of the Connecticut delegation in Philadelphia, explained the distinction to his State's convention: "This Constitution does not attempt to coerce sovereign bodies, states, in their political capacity. . . . But this legal coercion singles out the . . . individual." Charles Pinckney, another delegate at the Constitutional Convention, emphasized to the South Carolina House of Representatives that in Philadelphia "the necessity of having a government which should at once operate upon the people, and not upon the states, was conceived to be indispensable by every delegation present." Rufus King, one of Massachusetts' delegates, returned home to support ratification by recalling the Commonwealth's unhappy experience under the Articles of Confederation and arguing: "Laws, to be effective, therefore, must not be laid on states, but upon individuals." At New York's convention, Hamilton (another delegate in Philadelphia) exclaimed: "But can we believe that one state will ever suffer itself to be used as an instrument of coercion? The thing is a dream; it is impossible. Then we are brought to this dilemma — either a federal standing army is to enforce the requisitions, or the federal treasury is left without supplies, and the government without support. What, sir, is the cure for this great evil? Nothing, but to enable the national laws to operate on individuals, in the same manner as those of the states do." At North Carolina's convention, Samuel Spencer recognized that "all the laws of the Confederation were binding on the states in their political capacities, . . . but now the thing is entirely different. The laws of Congress will be binding on individuals." In providing for a stronger central government, therefore, the Framers explicitly chose a Constitution that confers upon Congress the power to regulate individuals, not States. . . .

2

This is not to say that Congress lacks the ability to encourage a State to regulate in a particular way, or that Congress may not hold out incentives to the States as a method of influencing a State's policy choices. Our cases have identified a variety of methods, short of outright coercion, by which Congress may urge a State to adopt a legislative program consistent with federal interests. Two of these methods are of particular relevance here.

First, under Congress' spending power, "Congress may attach conditions on the receipt of federal funds." South Dakota v. Dole. Such conditions must (among other requirements) bear some relationship to the purpose of the federal spending;

otherwise, of course, the spending power could render academic the Constitution's other grants and limits of federal authority. Where the recipient of federal funds is a State, as is not unusual today, the conditions attached to the funds by Congress may influence a State's legislative choices. . . .

Second, where Congress has the authority to regulate private activity under the Commerce Clause, we have recognized Congress' power to offer States the choice of regulating that activity according to federal standards or having state law pre-empted by federal regulation. This arrangement, which has been termed "a program of cooperative federalism," is replicated in numerous federal statutory schemes. These include the Clean Water Act, the Occupational Safety and Health Act of 1970, the Resource Conservation and Recovery Act of 1976, and the Alaska National Interest Lands Conservation Act.

By either of these methods, as by any other permissible method of encouraging a State to conform to federal policy choices, the residents of the State retain the ultimate decision as to whether or not the State will comply. If a State's citizens view federal policy as sufficiently contrary to local interests, they may elect to decline a federal grant. If state residents would prefer their government to devote its attention and resources to problems other than those deemed important by Congress, they may choose to have the Federal Government rather than the State bear the expense of a federally mandated regulatory program, and they may continue to supplement that program to the extent state law is not pre-empted. Where Congress encourages state regulation rather than compelling it, state governments remain responsive to the local electorate's preferences; state officials remain accountable to the people.

By contrast, where the Federal Government compels States to regulate, the accountability of both state and federal officials is diminished. If the citizens of New York, for example, do not consider that making provision for the disposal of radioactive waste is in their best interest, they may elect state officials who share their view. That view can always be pre-empted under the Supremacy Clause if it is contrary to the national view, but in such a case it is the Federal Government that makes the decision in full view of the public, and it will be federal officials that suffer the consequences if the decision turns out to be detrimental or unpopular. But where the Federal Government directs the States to regulate, it may be state officials who will bear the brunt of public disapproval, while the federal officials who devised the regulatory program may remain insulated from the electoral ramifications of their decision. Accountability is thus diminished when, due to federal coercion, elected state officials cannot regulate in accordance with the views of the local electorate in matters not pre-empted by federal regulation. See Merritt, 88 Colum. L. Rev at 61-62.

With these principles in mind, we turn to the three challenged provisions of the Low-Level Radioactive Waste Policy Amendments Act of 1985. . . .

III.

A

The first set of incentives works in three steps. First, Congress has authorized States with disposal sites to impose a surcharge on radioactive waste received from other States. Second, the Secretary of Energy collects a portion of this surcharge and places the money in an escrow account. Third, States achieving a series of milestones receive portions of this fund.

The first of these steps is an unexceptionable exercise of Congress' power to authorize the States to burden interstate commerce. While the Commerce Clause has long been understood to limit the States' ability to discriminate against interstate commerce, that limit may be lifted, as it has been here, by an expression of the "unambiguous intent" of Congress. Whether or not the States would be permitted to burden the interstate transport of low level radioactive waste in the absence of Congress' approval, the States can clearly do so with Congress' approval, which is what the Act gives them.

The second step, the Secretary's collection of a percentage of the surcharge, is no more than a federal tax on interstate commerce, which petitioners do not claim to be an invalid exercise of either Congress' commerce or taxing power.

The third step is a conditional exercise of Congress' authority under the Spending Clause: Congress has placed conditions — the achievement of the milestones — on the receipt of federal funds. Petitioners do not contend that Congress has exceeded its authority in any of the four respects our cases have identified. See generally South Dakota v. Dole. The expenditure is for the general welfare; the States are required to use the money they receive for the purpose of assuring the safe disposal of radioactive waste. The conditions imposed are unambiguous . . . [and] reasonably related to the purpose of the expenditure; both the conditions and the payments embody Congress' efforts to address the pressing problem of radioactive waste disposal. . . .

. . . Because the first set of incentives is supported by affirmative constitutional grants of power to Congress, it is not inconsistent with the Tenth Amendment.

B

In the second set of incentives, Congress has authorized States and regional compacts with disposal sites gradually to increase the cost of access to the sites, and then to deny access altogether, to radioactive waste generated in States that do not meet federal deadlines. As a simple regulation, this provision would be within the power of Congress to authorize the States to discriminate against interstate commerce. Where federal regulation of private activity is within the scope of the Commerce Clause, we have recognized the ability of Congress to offer States the choice of regulating that activity according to federal standards or having state law pre-empted by federal regulation.

This is the choice presented to nonsited States by the Act's second set of incentives: States may either regulate the disposal of radioactive waste according to federal standards by attaining local or regional self-sufficiency, or their residents who produce radioactive waste will be subject to federal regulation authorizing sited States and regions to deny access to their disposal sites. The affected States are not compelled by Congress to regulate, because any burden caused by a State's refusal to regulate will fall on those who generate waste and find no outlet for its disposal, rather than on the State as a sovereign. A State whose citizens do not wish it to attain the Act's milestones may devote its attention and its resources to issues its citizens deem more worthy; the choice remains at all times with the residents of the State, not with Congress. The State need not expend any funds, or participate in any federal program, if local residents do not view such expenditures or participation as worthwhile. Nor must the State abandon the field if it does not accede to federal direction; the State may continue to regulate the generation and disposal of radioactive waste in any manner its citizens see fit. . . .

[Thus,] the second set of incentives does not intrude on the sovereignty reserved to the States by the Tenth Amendment.

C

The take title provision is of a different character. This third so-called "incentive" offers States, as an alternative to regulating pursuant to Congress' direction, the option of taking title to and possession of the low level radioactive waste generated within their borders and becoming liable for all damages waste generators suffer as a result of the States' failure to do so promptly. In this provision, Congress has crossed the line distinguishing encouragement from coercion. . . .

Because an instruction to state governments to take title to waste, standing alone, would be beyond the authority of Congress, and because a direct order to regulate, standing alone, would also be beyond the authority of Congress, it follows that Congress lacks the power to offer the States a choice between the two. . . . Either way, "the Act commandeers the legislative processes of the States by directly compelling them to enact and enforce a federal regulatory program," an outcome that has never been understood to lie within the authority conferred upon Congress by the Constitution. . . .

The take title provision appears to be unique. No other federal statute has been cited which offers a state government no option other than that of implementing legislation enacted by Congress. Whether one views the take title provision as lying outside Congress' enumerated powers, or as infringing upon the core of state sovereignty reserved by the Tenth Amendment, the provision is inconsistent with the federal structure of our Government established by the Constitution.

IV.

A

[T]he United States argues that the Constitution's prohibition of congressional directives to state governments can be overcome where the federal interest is sufficiently important to justify state submission. . . . [But no] matter how powerful the federal interest involved, the Constitution simply does not give Congress the authority to require the States to regulate. The Constitution instead gives Congress the authority to regulate matters directly and to pre-empt contrary state regulation. Where a federal interest is sufficiently strong to cause Congress to legislate, it must do so directly; it may not conscript state governments as its agents.

Second, the United States argues that the Constitution does, in some circumstances, permit federal directives to state governments. . . . Federal statutes enforceable in state courts do, in a sense, direct state judges to enforce them, but this sort of federal "direction" of state judges is mandated by the text of the Supremacy Clause. No comparable constitutional provision authorizes Congress to command state legislatures to legislate. Additional cases cited by the United States discuss the power of federal courts to order state officials to comply with federal law. Again, however, the text of the Constitution plainly confers this authority on the federal courts, the "judicial Power" of which "shall extend to all Cases, in Law and Equity, arising under this Constitution, [and] the Laws of the United States . . . ; [and] to Controversies between two or more States; [and] between a State and Citizens of another State." U.S. Const., Art. III, §2. The Constitution contains no analogous grant of authority to Congress. Moreover, the Supremacy Clause makes federal law paramount over the contrary positions of state officials; the power of federal courts to enforce federal law thus presupposes some authority to order state officials to comply. . . .

As Madison and Hamilton explained, "a sovereignty over sovereigns, a government over governments, a legislation for communities, as contradistinguished from individuals, as it is a solecism in theory, so in practice it is subversive of the order and ends of civil polity."

B

The sited state respondents focus their attention on the process by which the Act was formulated. They correctly observe that public officials representing the State of New York lent their support to the Act's enactment. A Deputy Commissioner of the State's Energy Office testified in favor of the Act. Senator Moynihan of New York spoke in support of the Act on the floor of the Senate. Respondents note that the Act embodies a bargain among the sited and unsited States, a compromise to which New York was a willing participant and from which New York has reaped much benefit. Respondents then pose what appears at first to be a troubling question: How can a federal statute be found an unconstitutional infringement of state sovereignty when state officials consented to the statute's enactment?

The answer follows from an understanding of the fundamental purpose served by our Government's federal structure. The Constitution does not protect the sovereignty of States for the benefit of the States or state governments as abstract political entities, or even for the benefit of the public officials governing the States. To the contrary, the Constitution divides authority between federal and state governments for the protection of individuals. State sovereignty is not just an end in itself: "Rather, federalism secures to citizens the liberties that derive from the diffusion of sovereign power. . . . Just as the separation and independence of the coordinate branches of the Federal Government serve to prevent the accumulation of excessive power in any one branch, a healthy balance of power between the States and the Federal Government will reduce the risk of tyranny and abuse from either front." Gregory v. Ashcroft. See The Federalist No. 51.

Where Congress exceeds its authority relative to the States, therefore, the departure from the constitutional plan cannot be ratified by the "consent" of state officials. An analogy to the separation of powers among the branches of the Federal Government clarifies this point. The Constitution's division of power among the three branches is violated where one branch invades the territory of another, whether or not the encroached-upon branch approves the encroachment. In Buckley v. Valeo, 424 U.S. 1(1976), for instance, the Court held that Congress had infringed the President's appointment power, despite the fact that the President himself had manifested his consent to the statute that caused the infringement by signing it into law. . . . In INS v. Chadha, 462 U.S. 919 (1983), we held that the legislative veto violated the constitutional requirement that legislation be presented to the President, despite Presidents' approval of hundreds of statutes containing a legislative veto provision. The constitutional authority of Congress cannot be expanded by the "consent" of the governmental unit whose domain is thereby narrowed, whether that unit is the Executive Branch or the States.

State officials thus cannot consent to the enlargement of the powers of Congress beyond those enumerated in the Constitution. Indeed, the facts of these cases raise the possibility that powerful incentives might lead both federal and state officials to view departures from the federal structure to be in their personal interests. Most citizens recognize the need for radioactive waste disposal sites, but few want sites near their homes. As a result, while it would be well within the authority of either federal or state officials to choose where the disposal sites will be, it is likely to be in the political interest of each individual official to avoid being held accountable to the voters for the choice of location. If a federal official is faced with the alternatives of choosing a location or directing the States to do it, the official may well prefer the latter, as a means of shifting responsibility for the eventual decision. If a state official is faced with the same set of alternatives — choosing a location or having Congress direct the choice of a location — the state official may also prefer the latter, as it may permit the avoidance of personal responsibility. The interests of public officials thus may not coincide with the Constitution's intergovernmental allocation of authority. Where state officials purport to submit to the direction of Congress in this manner, federalism is hardly being advanced.

Nor does the State's prior support for the Act estop it from asserting the Act's unconstitutionality. While New York has received the benefit of the Act in the form of a few more years of access to disposal sites in other States, New York has never joined a regional radioactive waste compact. Any estoppel implications that might flow from membership in a compact thus do not concern us here. The fact that the Act, like much federal legislation, embodies a compromise among the States does not elevate the Act (or the antecedent discussions among representatives of the States) to the status of an interstate agreement requiring Congress' approval under the Compact Clause. That a party collaborated with others in seeking legislation has never been understood to estop the party from challenging that legislation in subsequent litigation.

V.

Petitioners also contend that the Act is inconsistent with the Constitution's Guarantee Clause, which directs the United States to "guarantee to every State in this Union a Republican Form of Government." U.S. Const., Art. IV, §4. . . .

We approach the issue with some trepidation, because the Guarantee Clause has been an infrequent basis for litigation throughout our history. In most of the cases in which the Court has been asked to apply the Clause, the Court has found the claims presented to be nonjusticiable under the "political question" doctrine.

The view that the Guarantee Clause implicates only nonjusticiable political questions has its origin in Luther v. Borden, 48 U.S. (7 How.) 1 (1849), in which the Court was asked to decide, in the wake of Dorr's Rebellion, which of two rival governments was the legitimate government of Rhode Island. The Court held that "it rests with Congress," not the judiciary, "to decide what government is the established one in a State." Over the following century, this limited holding metamorphosed into the sweeping assertion that "violation of the great guaranty of a republican form of government in States cannot be challenged in the courts." . . .

More recently, the Court has suggested that perhaps not all claims under the Guarantee Clause present nonjusticiable political questions. Contemporary commentators have likewise suggested that courts should address the merits of such claims, at least in some circumstances. See, e.g., L. Tribe, American Constitutional Law 398 (2d ed. 1988); J. Ely, Democracy and Distrust: A Theory of Judicial Review 118, n., and 122-123 (1980); W. Wiecek, The Guarantee Clause of the U.S. Constitution 287-289, 300 (1972); Merritt, 88 Colum. L. Rev., at 70-78.

We need not resolve this difficult question today. Even if we assume that petitioners' claim is justiciable, neither the monetary incentives provided by the Act nor the possibility that a State's waste producers may find themselves excluded from the disposal sites of another State can reasonably be said to deny any State a republican form of government. . . .

VI.

[T]he take title provision may be severed without doing violence to the rest of the Act. The Act is still operative and it still serves Congress' objective of encouraging the States to attain local or regional self-sufficiency in the disposal of low level radioactive waste. It still includes two incentives that coax the States along this road. A State whose radioactive waste generators are unable to gain access to disposal sites in other States may encounter considerable internal pressure to provide for the disposal of waste, even without the prospect of taking title. The sited regional compacts need not accept New York's waste after the 7-year transition period expires, so any burden caused by New York's failure to secure a disposal site will not be borne by the residents of other States. The purpose of the Act is not defeated by the invalidation of the take title provision, so we may leave the remainder of the Act in force.

VII.

Some truths are so basic that, like the air around us, they are easily overlooked. Much of the Constitution is concerned with setting forth the form of our government, and the courts have traditionally invalidated measures deviating from that form. The result may appear "formalistic" in a given case to partisans of the measure at issue, because such measures are typically the product of the era's perceived necessity. But the Constitution protects us from our own best intentions: It divides power among sovereigns and among branches of government precisely so that we may resist the temptation to concentrate power in one location as an expedient solution to the crisis of the day. The shortage of disposal sites for radioactive waste is a pressing national problem, but a judiciary that licensed extraconstitutional government with each issue of comparable gravity would, in the long run, be far worse.

States are not mere political subdivisions of the United States. State governments are neither regional offices nor administrative agencies of the Federal Government. The positions occupied by state officials appear nowhere on the Federal Government's most detailed organizational chart. The Constitution instead "leaves to the several States a residuary and inviolable sovereignty," The Federalist No. 39, reserved explicitly to the States by the Tenth Amendment.

Whatever the outer limits of that sovereignty may be, one thing is clear: The Federal Government may not compel the States to enact or administer a federal regulatory program. The Constitution permits both the Federal Government and the States to enact legislation regarding the disposal of low level radioactive waste. The Constitution enables the Federal Government to pre-empt state regulation contrary to federal interests, and it permits the Federal Government to hold out incentives to the States as a means of encouraging them to adopt suggested regulatory schemes. It does not, however, authorize Congress simply to direct the States to provide for the disposal of the radioactive waste generated within their borders. . . .

Justice WHITE, with whom Justice Blackmun and Justice Stevens join, concurring in part and dissenting in part. . . . I can only join Parts III-A and III-B, and I respectfully dissent from the rest of [the Court's] opinion. . . .

I.

. . . The Low-Level Radioactive Waste Policy Act of 1980 (1980 Act), and its amendatory 1985 Act, resulted from the efforts of state leaders to achieve a state-based set of remedies to the waste problem. They sought not federal pre-emption or intervention, but rather congressional sanction of interstate compromises they had reached. . . .

. . . In sum, the 1985 Act was very much the product of cooperative federalism, in which the States bargained among themselves to achieve compromises for Congress to sanction. . . .

II.

A

In my view, New York's actions subsequent to enactment of the 1980 and 1985 Acts fairly indicate its approval of the interstate agreement process embodied in those laws within the meaning of Art. I, §10, cl. 3, of the Constitution, which provides that "no State shall, without the Consent of Congress, . . . enter into any Agreement or Compact with another State." . . .

. . . As it was undertaking . . . initial steps to honor the interstate compromise embodied in the 1985 Act, New York continued to take full advantage of the import concession made by the sited States, by exporting its low-level radioactive waste for the full 7-year extension period provided in the 1985 Act. By gaining these benefits and complying with certain of the 1985 Act's deadlines, therefore, New York fairly evidenced its acceptance of the federal-state arrangement — including the take title provision.

Although unlike the 42 States that compose the nine existing and approved regional compacts, New York has never formalized its assent to the 1980 and 1985 statutes, our cases support the view that New York's actions signify assent to a constitutional interstate "agreement" for purposes of Art. I, §10, cl. 3. . . . In my view, New York acted in a manner to signify its assent to the 1985 Act's take title provision as part of the elaborate compromise reached among the States.

The State should be estopped from asserting the unconstitutionality of a provision that seeks merely to ensure that, after deriving substantial advantages from the 1985 Act, New York in fact must live up to its bargain by establishing an in-state low-level radioactive waste facility or assuming liability for its failure to act. . . .

B

. . . Finally, to say, as the Court does, that the incursion on state sovereignty "cannot be ratified by the 'consent' of state officials," is flatly wrong. In a case involving a congressional ratification statute to an interstate compact, the Court upheld a provision that Tennessee and Missouri had waived their immunity from suit. Over their objection, the Court held that "the States who are parties to the compact by accepting it and acting under it assume the conditions that Congress under the Constitution attached." In so holding, the Court determined that a State may be found to have waived a fundamental aspect of its sovereignty — the right to be immune from suit — in the formation of an interstate compact even when in subsequent litigation it expressly denied its waiver. . . .

III.

The Court announces that it has no occasion to revisit such decisions as *Garcia* because "this is not a case in which Congress has subjected a State to the same legislation applicable to private parties." Although this statement sends the welcome signal that the Court does not intend to cut a wide swath through our recent Tenth Amendment precedents, it nevertheless is unpersuasive. . . .

The Court's distinction between a federal statute's regulation of States and private parties for general purposes, as opposed to a regulation solely on the activities of States, is unsupported by our recent Tenth Amendment cases. In no case has the Court rested its holding on such a distinction. . . .

Even were such a distinction to be logically sound, the Court's "anticommandeering" principle cannot persuasively be read as springing from the two cases cited for the proposition, *Hodel* and *FERC*. The Court purports to draw support for its rule against Congress "commandeering" state legislative processes from a solitary statement in dictum in *Hodel*. That statement was not necessary to the decision in *Hodel*, which involved the question whether the Tenth Amendment interfered with Congress' authority to pre-empt a field of activity that could also be subject to state regulation and not whether a federal statute could dictate certain actions by States; the language about "commandeering" States was classic dicta. . . .

Rather than seek guidance from *FERC* and *Hodel*, therefore, the more appropriate analysis should flow from *Garcia*, even if these cases do not involve a congressional law generally applicable to both States and private parties. In *Garcia*, we stated the proper inquiry: "We are convinced that the fundamental limitation that the constitutional scheme imposes on the Commerce Clause to protect the 'States as States' is one of process rather than one of result. Any substantive restraint on the exercise of Commerce Clause powers must find its justification in the procedural nature of this basic limitation, and it must be tailored to compensate for possible failings in the national political process rather than to dictate a 'sacred province of state autonomy.' " Where it addresses this aspect of respondents' argument, the Court tacitly concedes that a failing of the political process cannot be shown in these cases because it refuses to rebut the unassailable arguments that the States were well able to look after themselves in the legislative process that culminated in the 1985 Act's passage. Indeed, New York acknowledges that its "congressional delegation participated in the drafting and enactment of both the 1980 and the 1985 Acts." The Court rejects this process-based argument by resorting to generalities and platitudes about the purpose of federalism being to protect individual rights.

Ultimately, I suppose, the entire structure of our federal constitutional government can be traced to an interest in establishing checks and balances to prevent the exercise of tyranny against individuals. But these fears seem extremely far distant to me in a situation such as this. We face a crisis of national proportions in the disposal of low-level radioactive waste, and Congress has acceded to the wishes of the States by permitting local decisionmaking rather than imposing a solution from Washington. New York itself participated and supported passage of this legislation at both the gubernatorial and federal representative levels, and then enacted state laws specifically to comply with the deadlines and timetables agreed upon by the States in the 1985 Act. For me, the Court's civics lecture has a decidedly hollow ring at a time when action, rather than rhetoric, is needed to solve a national problem.[a]

IV.

Though I disagree with the Court's conclusion that the take title provision is unconstitutional, I do not read its opinion to preclude Congress from adopting a similar measure through its powers under the Spending or Commerce Clauses. The Court makes clear that its objection is to the alleged "commandeering" quality of the take title provision. As its discussion of the surcharge and rebate incentives reveals, the spending power offers a means of enacting a take title provision under the Court's standards. Congress could, in other words, condition the payment of funds on the State's willingness to take title if it has not already provided a waste disposal facility. . . .

a. With selective quotations from the era in which the Constitution was adopted, the majority attempts to bolster its holding that the take title provision is tantamount to federal "commandeering" of the States. In view of the many Tenth Amendment cases decided over the past two decades in which resort to the kind of historical analysis generated in the majority opinion was not deemed necessary, I do not read the majority's many invocations of history to be anything other than elaborate window dressing. Certainly nowhere does the majority announce that its rule is compelled by an understanding of what the Framers may have thought about statutes of the type at issue here. Moreover, I would observe that, while its quotations add a certain flavor to the opinion, the majority's historical analysis has a distinctly wooden quality. One would not know from reading the majority's account, for instance, that the nature of federal-state relations changed fundamentally after the Civil War. That conflict produced in its wake a tremendous expansion in the scope of the Federal Government's law-making authority, so much so that the persons who helped to found the Republic would scarcely have recognized the many added roles the National Government assumed for itself. Moreover, the majority fails to mention the New Deal era, in which the Court recognized the enormous growth in Congress' power under the Commerce Clause. See generally F. Frankfurter & J. Landis, The Business of the Supreme Court 56-59 (1927); H. Hyman, A More Perfect Union: The Impact of the Civil War and Reconstruction on the Constitution (1973); Corwin, The Passing of Dual Federalism, 36 Va. L. Rev. 1 (1950); Wiecek, The Reconstruction of Federal Judicial Power, 1863-1875, 13 Am. J. Legal Hist. 333 (1969); Scheiber, State Law and "Industrial Policy" in American Development, 1790-1987, 75 Calif. L. Rev. 415 (1987); Ackerman, Constitutional Politics/Constitutional Law, 99 Yale L.J. 453 (1989). While I believe we should not be blind to history, neither should we read it so selectively as to restrict the proper scope of Congress' powers under Article I, especially when the history not mentioned by the majority fully supports a more expansive understanding of the legislature's authority than may have existed in the late 18th century.

Given the scanty textual support for the majority's position, it would be far more sensible to defer to a coordinate branch of government in its decision to devise a solution to a national problem of this kind. Certainly in other contexts, principles of federalism have not insulated States from mandates by the National Government. The Court has upheld congressional statutes that impose clear directives on state officials, including those enacted pursuant to the Extradition Clause, the post-Civil War Amendments, see, e.g., South Carolina v. Katzenbach, as well as congressional statutes that require state courts to hear certain actions.

Similarly, should a State fail to establish a waste disposal facility by the appointed deadline (under the statute as presently drafted, January 1, 1996), Congress has the power pursuant to the Commerce Clause to regulate directly the producers of the waste. Thus, as I read it, Congress could amend the statute to say that if a State fails to meet the January 1, 1996, deadline for achieving a means of waste disposal, and has not taken title to the waste, no low-level radioactive waste may be shipped out of the State of New York.

Justice STEVENS, concurring in part and dissenting in part.

Under the Articles of Confederation, the Federal Government had the power to issue commands to the States. Because that indirect exercise of federal power proved ineffective, the Framers of the Constitution empowered the Federal Government to exercise legislative authority directly over individuals within the States, even though that direct authority constituted a greater intrusion on state sovereignty. Nothing in that history suggests that the Federal Government may not also impose its will upon the several States as it did under the Articles. The Constitution enhanced, rather than diminished, the power of the Federal Government.

The notion that Congress does not have the power to issue "a simple command to state governments to implement legislation enacted by Congress," is incorrect and unsound. There is no such limitation in the Constitution. The Tenth Amendment surely does not impose any limit on Congress' exercise of the powers delegated to it by Article I. Nor does the structure of the constitutional order or the values of federalism mandate such a formal rule. To the contrary, the Federal Government directs state governments in many realms. The Government regulates state-operated railroads, state school systems, state prisons, state elections, and a host of other state functions. Similarly, there can be no doubt that, in time of war, Congress could either draft soldiers itself or command the States to supply their quotas of troops. I see no reason why Congress may not also command the States to enforce federal water and air quality standards or federal standards for the disposition of low-level radioactive wastes.

The Constitution gives this Court the power to resolve controversies between the States. Long before Congress enacted pollution-control legislation, this Court crafted a body of "interstate common law" to govern disputes between States involving interstate waters. In such contexts, we have not hesitated to direct States to undertake specific actions. For example, we have "imposed on States an affirmative duty to take reasonable steps to conserve and augment the water supply of an interstate stream." Thus, we unquestionably have the power to command an upstream State that is polluting the waters of a downstream State to adopt appropriate regulations to implement a federal statutory command.

With respect to the problem presented by the cases at hand, if litigation should develop between States that have joined a compact, we would surely have the power to grant relief in the form of specific enforcement of the take title provision. Indeed, even if the statute had never been passed, if one State's radioactive waste created a nuisance that harmed its neighbors, it seems clear that we would have had the power to command the offending State to take remedial action. If this Court has such authority, surely Congress has similar authority. . . .

Discussion

1. *Congress versus court as overseer of states.* Justice Stevens emphasizes the power of federal courts to issue affirmative orders to states, and suggests that Congress should enjoy comparable power. Justice White, in a footnote, also points to the Reconstruction Amendments as an important source of congressional authority over state governments. These arguments, however, do not persuade the majority in *New York.* Is there a similarity between the vision in *New York* and the vision later articulated in *City of Boerne,* supra p. 629, in which the Court claimed for itself a privileged role vis à vis Congress in overseeing states?

2. *Accountability or autonomy?* The *New York* majority claims that its rule will promote political accountability — the electorate will know which government to blame for which problem. But doesn't the nature of our constitutional system — with an elaborate separation of powers at the federal level, overlaid by federalism, and a written Constitution — inherently lend itself to certain kinds of confusion? At the federal level, the President blames Congress; Congress blames the President; and both blame the Court for ruling certain policies off the table, or for misconstruing or rewriting legislation. (Note how the Court in *New York* almost literally "rewrote" the congressional statute at issue, eliminating one clause but enforcing the rest.) What's more, actual policies as experienced by citizens are an intricate mix of state and federal action, with both sets of governments claiming credit when things go well, and pointing fingers at each other when they don't. If clear lines of political accountability were the chief goal, might we be better off with a pure parliamentary system concentrating all power in a single government which is more clearly responsible for whatever happens on its watch?

The chief problem with such a concentrated system, however, is that it fails to sufficiently disperse power and "check" a possibly abusive regime. And so perhaps a better argument for the *New York* rule is simply this: State governments are designed to be constitutionally independent from the federal government in certain ways, in part so that they may stand as competing political power centers and rallying points for opponents of the central regime. Congress may not treat state legislatures as its puppets; such legislatures are supposed to be autonomous watchdogs, not wholly subservient lapdogs. If Congress could tell a state that it must pass certain bills, then Congress could in principle control the entire agenda of a state legislature, leaving it with no independence or time to devise its own agenda as a counterweight to Congress's. No single congressional mandate is likely to occupy a state legislature's entire docket, of course, but the cleanest and most judicially manageable line is simply to prevent all affirmative commandeering. By its nature, "the power to commandeer is the power to destroy," cf. *McCulloch,* and thus should be nipped in the bud. (The power of Congress to displace or preempt state legislatures does not pose an identical threat; each legislature would remain free to define its own agenda, and could, for example, devote its entire term to laying out in detail why Congress was misguided, and what state citizens should do to demonstrate their opposition.) On this state-autonomy view, state legislatures should remain free to define their own agendas, just as should, say, the Democratic Party, the Sierra Club, the New York Times, and the Catholic Church. Note that when Congress first threatened free speech, with the infamous Sedition Act of 1798, state legislatures in Virginia and Kentucky mobilized opposition and engaged in legislative free speech, via the Virginia and Kentucky Resolves — in a manner that obviously reenacted the role that colonial governments had played a generation earlier in response to Parliamentary abuses. For more discussion of the link between "freedom of speech" and legislative "speech and debate" and more discussion of these Resolves as exemplifying how federalism can support liberty, see Akhil Reed Amar, The Bill of Rights: Creation and Reconstruction (1998); Akhil Reed Amar, Of Sovereignty and Federalism, 96 Yale L.J. 1425, 1492-1503 (1987).

3. *Bribing versus commandeering.* The *New York* Court says that states may be "bribed" into legislating, via conditional funding statutes, but not commandeered via direct coercion. If the main idea is accountability, isn't bribery more troubling because it is so indirect and insidious? In the case of outright coercion, isn't it *easier* for the state government to say, "Don't blame us — the feds *made* us do it"? Does the autonomy/competing-power-center rationale better explain why federal "bribery" is permissible?

4. *The NIMBY problem.* If there was a special accountability problem on the facts of the *New York* case, was it created by commandeering, or by something else? Consider the general accountability concern raised by certain specific siting decisions. We all need a site to dump our waste, but each of us says, "Not In My Back Yard!" As a result, politicians want to mandate that a site be found, but want to avoid personally picking the particular site; once the site is picked, neighboring residents may turn into intense single-issue voters targeting their ire at the decisionmaker who chose the site. (The rest of us are happy to be spared, but much less focused and intense; our diffuse support for the decisionmaker may not politically offset the more focused hostility.) In NIMBY situations, can you see why politicians might choose particularly intricate and opaque procedures to blur responsibility for particular siting decisions? Would governmental compensation aimed at the adversely affected neighborhood — even if not strictly dictated by Takings Clause principles — be appropriate to "spread the cost"? Note that such compensation raises hard questions about who should get how much — and also requires higher taxes for the rest of us.

5. *Serious federal impairment?* Justice White seems to claim both that the Court's actions seriously impede Congress's ability to solve a national crisis, and that Congress can evade the *New York* rule rather easily. Which is it? Can't Congress rather easily "contract around" the case by bribing states, or by directly regulating (for example, by barring any shipment of waste across state lines, thus forcing New Yorkers to find a place for their own waste) — or simply by allowing the other sanctions in the 1985 Act to kick in and put strong pressure on the state of New York? Recall that the Court does not strike down the law in toto, only one piece of it. Was this piece particularly important? Did this piece (as opposed to the other provisions of the Act) in fact reflect the specific input of state governments?

6. *To overrule or not to overrule.* Note how Justice O'Connor takes care to distinguish away *Garcia*, rather than overrule it. Do you find her distinction persuasive? Were there special factors counseling a deferential approach to precedent in *New York*? Recall that one of the important themes of this casebook is that cases must be read "bifocally" — as part of a doctrinal line (e.g., *Wirtz, National League of Cities, Garcia,* and *Gregory*), but also alongside contemporaneous cases (hence this book's periodized discussions of the Marshall Court, the Taney Court, the New Deal Court, and the Rehnquist Court). Thus it is worth noticing that, less than two weeks after handing down her opinion in *New York* (with Justices Kennedy and Souter in full

agreement), Justice O'Connor, along with Justices Kennedy and Souter, announced the main opinion in Planned Parenthood of Southeastern Pennsylvania v. Casey, 505 U.S. 833 (1992), infra, Chapter 8. In *Casey*, the three Justices placed great emphasis on the importance of precedent; wouldn't it have been extremely awkward for these Justices to sing the praises of precedent in *Casey* if they were at the same time flinging precedent aside in *New York*?

7. *The Guarantee Clause.* Justice O'Connor also treads carefully in her treatment of the Article IV republican government Guarantee Clause. To have relied on the clause would have been doctrinally abrupt, given its generally low profile in modern Supreme Court case law. In the text, history, and structure of the Constitution itself, however, the clause is anything but peripheral. And unlike the grammar of the Tenth Amendment, which seems to protect states' rights residually, the Guarantee Clause offers a plausible textual basis for protecting states' rights in an affirmative fashion, akin to the modern Bill of Rights, cutting across federal enumerated power. Note how Justice O'Connor begins the process of "rehabilitating" the clause as important and justiciable, without actually relying on it. For recent discussions of the meaning of the clause, see Merritt, supra, pp. 661-662; Amar, supra, n.48.

8. *Congress, the Court, states, and the "dormant" Commerce Clause.* In the absence of congressional legislation, a state law that generally required private trash sites to accept only trash generated within the state would face tough sledding in federal court as a highly suspect "discrimination" against sister states, see City of Philadelphia v. New Jersey, 437 U.S. 617 (1978), infra, p. 732. But as the *New York* majority makes clear, Congress can authorize this kind of state "discrimination" under its own Commerce Clause power. For a quick summary of the modern contours of, and debate about, "dormant" commerce clause doctrine, see infra, Part IV.

9. *Founding history.* The *New York* Court claims that its anticommandeering rule finds strong support in the history of the Founding. Justice Stevens disputes this, and Justice White dismisses it as "window dressing." Note that many of the historical sources relied upon by the Court suggest that it is simply impossible or impractical for the federal government to coerce a state government as such — or at least, to coerce a state government to perform an affirmative task. Is this true today? In any event, why would the matter be any different if a recalcitrant state refused to do what it had promised after receiving federal funds (or after entering into a properly blessed interstate compact)? Does the Court's history support its doctrinal rule distinguishing between permissible federal "encouragement" via conditional funding, and impermissible federal "coercion"? For a careful analysis of the history in the wake of *New York*, see Saikrishna Bangalore Prakash, Field Office Federalism, 79 Va. L. Rev. 1957 (1993). Based on constitutional text, history, and structure, Prakash argued that Congress should not be allowed to compel state legislatures to pass laws, but should be allowed to mandate that state executive and judicial officers affirmatively enforce federal laws:

[In the words of Hamilton's Federalist No. 16, the federal government] "must stand in need of no intermediate legislations; but must itself be empowered to employ the arm of the ordinary magistrate to execute its own resolutions." ...

Why the distinction between the state magistracy and state legislatures? Ellsworth's views on the question are illustrative. "I am for coercion by law — that coercion which acts only upon delinquent individuals. This Constitution does not attempt to coerce sovereign bodies, states, in their political capacity." First, as Ellsworth notes, state legislatures ("sovereign bodies") wielded whatever sovereignty the state government possessed. The legislatures represented the people of the state and acted according to their interests. Outsiders who tried to force these institutions to obey (like the Continental Congress) were simply not going to be heeded.

Second, state legislatures exercised legislative will and discretion. They determined what laws should be passed and which legislation was better left unenacted. Because they exercised will, they could not be made to comply mechanically with federal requisitions. State legislatures, then, embodied the states "in their political capacity."

Third, the multimember character of state legislatures made coercion of legislatures difficult. Who would be held accountable for failure to satisfy a requisition, the whole legislative body or only those who had opposed fulfilling the congressional requisition? Where the national government's authority was "confined to the collective bodies of the communities that compose it, every breach of the laws must involve a state of war." Hence, the Constitution abandoned coercion of multimember "sovereign bodies."

Finally, the Founding Generation relinquished requisitioning state legislatures because in practice the system simply had failed to deliver. State legislatures repeatedly ignored Articles [of Confederation] requisitions. In such a system, requisitions were really only supplications, as even opponents of the Constitution understood. Short of a civil war, state legislatures could not be forced to comply. As Ellsworth insisted, "no coercion is applicable to such legislative bodies, but that of an armed force." Better to abandon the phantom authority altogether.

The magistracy, however, were perceived differently. They did not exercise state sovereignty; they were not "sovereign bodies." Rather they were the servants of the legislature; the servants of the laws of the land. Nor did they exercise legislative will; they were not the embodiment of a state's "political capacity" that Ellsworth discussed. Instead they mechanically enforced the laws of the land. For these reasons they could not pick and choose which laws to enforce and, thus, could not discriminate against federal law. Moreover, coercion could more easily be applied against the magistracy. Execution and adjudication normally took place through the agency of a single person. Delinquent individual executive or judicial officers could be held accountable for maladministration of the laws in a manner that state legislators could not be held responsible for failure to heed congressional attempts at commandeering. Finally, the Founding Generation considered commandeering state executives and judges more efficacious under the Articles than the misguided attempts to commandeer state legislatures. State executives and courts could not defy federal authority as easily as state legislatures had. . . .

. . . New York's "commandeering" dividing line ought to be shifted. Justice O'Connor admits that the federal government may commandeer state courts. . . . [S]tate executives are really more like state judges than state legislators. State executives and judges must administer the laws of the land, even if those laws emanate from Congress. Similarly, Justice Stevens is quite correct in noting that the federal government may commandeer state executives and courts. He merely falters in not recognizing the peculiar nature of state legislatures and the failed commandeering attempts under the Articles. Whether or not we perceive state legislatures as fundamentally different from the state magistracy, the Constitution so views them.

In essence, Prakash argued that New York was right on its facts, but overbroad in its language. In 1997, however, the Court rejected Prakash's effort to split the difference between the New York majority and its dissenters; by a 5-4 vote in the Printz case, excerpted next, the Court applied the New York rule to strike down a law that "commandeered" state executive power.

PRINTZ v. UNITED STATES
521 U.S. 898 (1997)

[The 1993 Brady Handgun Violence Prevention Act, Pub. L. 103-159, 107 Stat. 1536, 18 U.S.C. 922(s)(2), required the Attorney General to establish a national system for instantly checking prospective handgun purchasers' backgrounds. As an interim measure, prior to the establishment of this national instant background check system, the Act required the "chief law enforcement officer" (CLEO) of each local jurisdiction to conduct background checks on prospective handgun purchasers. Two western sheriffs challenged these interim provisions as violative of the *New York* principle.]

SCALIA, J., . . .

II.

. . . The petitioners here object to being pressed into federal service, and contend that congressional action compelling state officers to execute federal laws is unconstitutional. Because there is no constitutional text speaking to this precise question, the answer to the CLEOs' challenge must be sought in historical understanding and practice, in the structure of the Constitution, and in the jurisprudence of this Court. . . .

Petitioners contend that compelled enlistment of state executive officers for the administration of federal programs is, until very recent years at least, unprecedented. The Government contends, to the contrary, that "the earliest Congresses enacted statutes that required the participation of state officials in the implementation of federal laws." The Government's contention demands our careful consideration, since early congressional enactments "provide 'contemporaneous and weighty evidence' of the Constitution's meaning." . . . Conversely if, as petitioners contend, earlier Congresses avoided use of this highly attractive power, we would have reason to believe that the power was thought not to exist. . . .

These early laws establish, at most, that the Constitution was originally understood to permit imposition of an obligation on state *judges* to enforce federal prescriptions, insofar as those prescriptions related to matters appropriate for the judicial power. That assumption was perhaps implicit in one of the provisions of the Constitution, and was explicit in another. In accord with the so-called Madisonian Compromise, Article III, §1, established only a Supreme Court, and made the creation of lower federal courts optional with the Congress — even though it was obvious that the Supreme Court alone could not hear all federal cases throughout the United States. And the Supremacy Clause, Art. VI, cl. 2, announced that "the Laws of the United States . . . shall be the supreme Law of the Land; and the Judges in every State shall be bound thereby." It is understandable why courts should have been viewed distinctively in this regard; unlike legislatures and executives, they applied the law of other sovereigns all the time. The principle underlying so-called "transitory" causes of action was that laws which operated elsewhere created obligations in justice that courts of the forum state would enforce. The Constitution itself, in the Full Faith and Credit Clause, Art. IV, §1, generally required such enforcement with respect to obligations arising in other States.

For these reasons, we do not think the early statutes imposing obligations on state courts imply a power of Congress to impress the state executive into its service. Indeed, it can be argued that the numerousness of these statutes, contrasted with the utter lack of statutes imposing obligations on the States' executive (notwithstanding the attractiveness of that course to Congress), suggests an assumed absence of such power. The only early federal law the Government has brought to our attention that imposed duties on state executive officers is the Extradition Act of 1793, which required the "executive authority" of a State to cause the arrest and delivery of a fugitive from justice upon the request of the executive authority of the State from which the fugitive had fled. That was in direct implementation, however, of the Extradition Clause of the Constitution itself, see Art. IV, §2. . . .

[T]he Government also appeals to other sources we have usually regarded as indicative of the original understanding of the Constitution. It points to portions of The Federalist which reply to criticisms that Congress's power to tax will produce two sets of revenue officers . . . "Publius" responded that Congress will probably "make use of the State officers and State regulations, for collecting" federal taxes, The Federalist No. 36, and predicted that "the eventual collection [of internal revenue] under the immediate authority of the Union, will generally be made by the officers, and according to the rules, appointed by the several States," id., No. 45. The Government also invokes the Federalist's more general observations that the Constitution would "enable the [national] government to employ the ordinary magistracy of each [State] in the execution of its laws," id., No. 27, and that it was "extremely probable that in other instances, particularly in the organization of the judicial power, the officers of the States will be clothed in the correspondent authority of the Union," id., No. 45. But none of these statements necessarily implies — what is the critical point here — that Congress could impose these responsibilities *without the consent of the States*. They appear to rest on the natural assumption that the States would consent to allowing their officials to assist the Federal Government. . . .

To complete the historical record, we must note that there is not only an absence of executive-commandeering statutes in the early Congresses, but there is an absence of them in our later history as well, at least until very recent years. . . .

The Government points to a number of federal statutes enacted within the past few decades that require the participation of state or local officials in implementing federal regulatory schemes. Some of these are connected to federal funding measures, and can perhaps be more accurately described as conditions upon the grant of federal funding than as mandates to the States; others, which require only the provision of information to the Federal Government, do not involve the precise issue before us here, which is the forced participation of the States' executive in the actual administration of a federal program. . . . Even assuming they represent assertion of the very same congressional power challenged here, they are of such recent vintage that they are no more probative than the statute before us of a constitutional tradition that lends meaning to the text. Their persuasive force is far outweighed by almost two centuries of apparent congressional avoidance of the practice. Compare INS v. Chadha, 462 U.S. 919 (1983), in which the legislative veto, though enshrined in perhaps hundreds of federal statutes, most of which were enacted in the 1970s and the earliest of which was enacted in 1932, was nonetheless held unconstitutional.

III.

The constitutional practice we have examined above tends to negate the existence of the congressional power asserted here, but is not conclusive. We turn next to consideration of the structure of the Constitution. . . .

A

It is incontestible that the Constitution established a system of "dual sovereignty." Gregory v. Ashcroft. Although the States surrendered many of their powers to the new Federal Government, they retained "a residuary and inviolable sovereignty," The Federalist No. 39. This is reflected throughout the Constitution's text, including (to mention only a few examples) the prohibition on any involuntary reduction or combination of a State's territory, Art. IV, §3; the Judicial Power Clause, Art. III, §2, and the Privileges and Immunities Clause, Art. IV, §2, which speak of the "Citizens" of the States; the amendment provision, Article V, which requires the votes of three-fourths of the States to amend the Constitution; and the Guarantee Clause, Art. IV, §4, which "presupposes the continued existence of the states and . . . those means and instrumentalities which are the creation of their sovereign and reserved rights." Residual state sovereignty was also implicit, of course, in the Constitution's conferral upon Congress of not all governmental powers, but only discrete, enumerated ones, which implication was rendered express by the Tenth Amendment[]. . . .[a]

. . . We have set forth the historical record in more detail elsewhere, see New York v. United States, and need not repeat it here. It suffices to repeat the conclusion: "The Framers explicitly chose a Constitution that confers upon Congress the power to regulate individuals, not States."[b] The great innovation of this design was that "our citizens would have two political capacities, one state and one federal, each protected from incursion by the other." . . .[c]

a. [The dissent] falsely presumes that the the Tenth Amendment is the exclusive textual source of protection for principles of federalism. Our system of dual sovereignty is reflected in numerous constitutional provisions, and not only those, like the Tenth Amendment, that speak to the point explicitly. It is not at all unusual for our resolution of a significant constitutional question to rest upon reasonable implications. See, e.g., Myers v. United States, 272 U.S. 52 (1926) (finding by implication from Art. II, §§1, 2, that the President has the exclusive power to remove executive officers). [Footnote relocated by editors.]

b. The dissent, reiterating Justice Stevens' dissent in *New York*, maintains that the Constitution merely augmented the pre-existing power under the Articles to issue commands to the States with the additional power to make demands directly on individuals. That argument, however, was squarely rejected by the Court in *New York*, and with good reason. Many of Congress's powers under Art. I, §8, were copied almost verbatim from the Articles of Confederation, indicating quite clearly that "where the Constitution intends that our Congress enjoy a power once vested in the Continental Congress, it specifically grants it." Prakash, Field Office Federalism, 79 Va. L. Rev. 1957, 1972 (1993).

c. Justice Breyer's dissent would have us consider the benefits that other countries, and the European Union, believe they have derived from federal systems that are different from ours. We think such comparative analysis inappropriate to the task of interpreting a constitution, though it was of course quite relevant to the task of writing one. The Framers were familiar with many federal systems, from classical antiquity down to their own time; they are discussed in Nos. 18-20 of The Federalist. Some were (for the purpose here under discussion) quite similar to the modern "federal" systems that Justice Breyer favors. Madison's and Hamilton's opinion of such systems could not be clearer. Federalist No. 20, after an extended critique of the system of government established by the Union of Utrecht for the United Netherlands, concludes:

"I make no apology for having dwelt so long on the contemplation of these federal precedents. Experience is the oracle of truth; and where its responses are unequivocal, they ought to be

This separation of the two spheres is one of the Constitution's structural protections of liberty. "Just as the separation and independence of the coordinate branches of the Federal Government serve to prevent the accumulation of excessive power in any one branch, a healthy balance of power between the States and the Federal Government will reduce the risk of tyranny and abuse from either front." *Gregory*; . . . The Federalist No. 51; See also The Federalist No. 28. The power of the Federal Government would be augmented immeasurably if it were able to impress into its service — and at no cost to itself — the police officers of the 50 States.

B

[F]ederal control of state officers would . . . also have an effect upon . . . the separation and equilibration of powers between the three branches of the Federal Government itself. The Constitution does not leave to speculation who is to administer the laws enacted by Congress; the President, it says, "shall take Care that the Laws be faithfully executed." . . . The Brady Act effectively transfers this responsibility to thousands of CLEOs in the 50 States, who are left to implement the program without meaningful Presidential control (if indeed meaningful Presidential control is possible without the power to appoint and remove). The insistence of the Framers upon unity in the Federal Executive — to insure both vigor and accountability — is well known. See The Federalist No. 70; see also Calabresi & Prakash, The President's Power to Execute the Laws, 104 Yale L.J. 541 (1994). That unity would be shattered, and the power of the President would be subject to reduction, if Congress could act as effectively without the President as with him, by simply requiring state officers to execute its laws.[d] . . .

IV.

Finally, and most conclusively in the present litigation, we turn to the prior jurisprudence of this Court. Federal commandeering of state governments is such a novel phenomenon that this Court's first experience with it did not occur until the 1970s. . . .

When we were at last confronted squarely with a federal statute that unambiguously required the States to enact or administer a federal regulatory program, our decision should have come as no surprise. . . . "The Federal Government," we held, "may not compel the States to enact or administer a federal regulatory program." *New York.*

---

conclusive and sacred. The important truth, which it unequivocally pronounces in the present case, is that a sovereignty over sovereigns, a government over governments, a legislation for communities, as contradistinguished from individuals, as it is a solecism in theory, so in practice it is subversive of the order and ends of civil polity. . . . "

Antifederalists, on the other hand, pointed specifically to Switzerland — and its then-400 years of success as a "confederate republic" — as proof that the proposed Constitution and its federal structure was unnecessary. The fact is that our federalism is not Europe's. . . .

d. [C]ontrol by the unitary Federal Executive is also sacrificed when States voluntarily administer federal programs, but the condition of voluntary state participation significantly reduces the ability of Congress to use this device as a means of reducing the power of the Presidency.

The Government contends that *New York* is distinguishable on the following ground: . . . "The constitutional line is crossed only when Congress compels the States to make law in their sovereign capacities." . . .

The Government . . . maintains that requiring state officers to perform discrete, ministerial tasks specified by Congress does not violate the principle of *New York* because it does not diminish the accountability of state or federal officials. This argument fails even on its own terms. By forcing state governments to absorb the financial burden of implementing a federal regulatory program, Members of Congress can take credit for "solving" problems without having to ask their constituents to pay for the solutions with higher federal taxes. And even when the States are not forced to absorb the costs of implementing a federal program, they are still put in the position of taking the blame for its burdensomeness and for its defects. See Merritt, Three Faces of Federalism: Finding a Formula for the Future, 47 Vand. L. Rev. 1563, 1580, n.65 (1994). Under the present law, for example, it will be the CLEO and not some federal official who stands between the gun purchaser and immediate possession of his gun. And it will likely be the CLEO, not some federal official, who will be blamed for any error (even one in the designated federal database) that causes a purchaser to be mistakenly rejected. . . .

V.

. . . We held in *New York* that Congress cannot compel the States to enact or enforce a federal regulatory program. Today we hold that Congress cannot circumvent that prohibition by conscripting the State's officers directly. The Federal Government may neither issue directives requiring the States to address particular problems, nor command the States' officers, or those of their political subdivisions, to administer or enforce a federal regulatory program. It matters not whether policymaking is involved, and no case-by-case weighing of the burdens or benefits is necessary; such commands are fundamentally incompatible with our constitutional system of dual sovereignty. . . .

O'CONNOR, J., concurring. . . .

Our holding, of course, does not spell the end of the objectives of the Brady Act. States and chief law enforcement officers may voluntarily continue to participate in the federal program. Moreover, the directives to the States are merely interim provisions scheduled to terminate November 30, 1998. Congress is also free to amend the interim program to provide for its continuance on a contractual basis with the States if it wishes, as it does with a number of other federal programs. See, e.g., 23 U.S.C. §402 (conditioning States' receipt of federal funds for highway safety program on compliance with federal requirements).

In addition, the Court appropriately refrains from deciding whether other purely ministerial reporting requirements imposed by Congress on state and local authorities pursuant to its Commerce Clause powers are similarly invalid. See, e.g., 42 U.S.C. §5779(a) (requiring state and local law enforcement agencies to report cases of missing children to the Department of Justice). . . .

THOMAS, J., concurring.

In my "revisionist" view, the Federal Government's authority under the Commerce Clause . . . does not extend to the regulation of wholly intrastate, point-of-sale transactions. See *Lopez* (concurring opinion). Absent the underlying authority to regulate the intrastate transfer of firearms, Congress surely lacks the corollary power to impress state law enforcement officers into administering and enforcing such regulations. . . .

Even if we construe Congress' authority to regulate interstate commerce to encompass those intrastate transactions that "substantially affect" interstate commerce, I question whether Congress can regulate the particular transactions at issue here. . . . The Second Amendment . . . appears to contain an express limitation on the government's authority. . . . This Court has not had recent occasion to consider the nature of the substantive right safeguarded by the Second Amendment. If, however, the Second Amendment is read to confer a personal right to "keep and bear arms," a colorable argument exists that the Federal Government's regulatory scheme, at least as it pertains to the purely intrastate sale or possession of firearms, runs afoul of that Amendment's protections.[a] As the parties did not raise this argument, however, we need not consider it here. Perhaps, at some future date, this Court will have the opportunity to determine whether Justice Story was correct when he wrote that the right to bear arms "has justly been considered, as the palladium of the liberties of a republic." . . .

Justice STEVENS, with whom Justice Souter, Justice Ginsburg, and Justice Breyer join, dissenting.

When Congress exercises the powers delegated to it by the Constitution, it may impose affirmative obligations on executive and judicial officers of state and local governments as well as ordinary citizens. . . .

These cases do not implicate the more difficult questions associated with congressional coercion of state legislatures addressed in *New York*.

I.

The text of the Constitution provides a sufficient basis for a correct disposition of this case.

Article I, §8, grants the Congress the power to regulate commerce among the States. . . . [T]hat provision adequately supports the regulation of commerce in handguns effected by the Brady Act. . . .

Unlike the First Amendment, which prohibits the enactment of a category of laws that would otherwise be authorized by Article I, the Tenth Amendment imposes no restriction on the exercise of delegated powers. . . . The Amendment confirms the principle that the powers of the Federal Government are limited to those affirmatively granted by the Constitution, but it does not purport to limit the scope or the effectiveness of the exercise of powers that are delegated to Congress. Thus, the Amendment provides no support for a rule that immunizes local officials from obligations that might be imposed on ordinary citizens.[a] Indeed, it would be more reasonable to infer

a. [Footnote by Justice White] Marshaling an impressive array of historical evidence, a growing body of scholarly commentary indicates that the "right to keep and bear arms" is, as the Amendment's text suggests, a personal right. Other scholars, however, argue that the Second Amendment does not secure a personal right to keep or to bear arms. Although somewhat overlooked in our jurisprudence, the Amendment has certainly engendered considerable academic, as well as public, debate.

a. [Footnote by Chief Justice Burger] Recognizing the force of the argument, the Court suggests that this reasoning is in error because — even if it is responsive to the submission that the Tenth Amendment roots the principle set forth by the majority today — it does not answer the possibility that the Court's holding can be rooted in a "principle of state sovereignty" mentioned nowhere in the constitutional text. As a ground for invalidating important federal legislation, this argument is remarkably weak.

that federal law may impose greater duties on state officials than on private citizens because another provision of the Constitution requires that "all executive and judicial Officers, both of the United States and of the several States, shall be bound by Oath or Affirmation, to support this Constitution." U.S. Const., Art. VI, cl. 3. . . .

The reasoning in our unanimous opinion explaining why state tribunals with ordinary jurisdiction over tort litigation can be required to hear cases arising under the Federal Employers' Liability Act applies equally to local law enforcement officers whose ordinary duties parallel the modest obligations imposed by the Brady Act:

> The suggestion that the act of Congress is not in harmony with the policy of the State, and therefore that the courts of the State are free to decline jurisdiction, is quite inadmissible, because it presupposes what in legal contemplation does not exist. When Congress, in the exertion of the power confided to it by the Constitution, adopted that act, it spoke for all the people and all the States, and thereby established a policy for all. That policy is as much the policy of Connecticut as if the act had emanated from its own legislature, and should be respected accordingly in the courts of the State. . . .

There is not a clause, sentence, or paragraph in the entire text of the Constitution of the United States that supports the proposition that a local police officer can ignore a command contained in a statute enacted by Congress pursuant to an express delegation of power enumerated in Article I.

II.

Under the Articles of Confederation the National Government had the power to issue commands to the several sovereign states, but it had no authority to govern individuals directly. Thus, it raised an army and financed its operations by issuing requisitions to the constituent members of the Confederacy, rather than by creating federal agencies to draft soldiers or to impose taxes.

That method of governing proved to be unacceptable, not because it demeaned the sovereign character of the several States, but rather because it was cumbersome and inefficient. Indeed, a confederation that allows each of its members to determine the ways and means of complying with an overriding requisition is obviously more deferential to state sovereignty concerns than a national government that uses its own agents to impose its will directly on the citizenry. The basic change in the character of the government that the Framers conceived was designed to enhance the power of the national government, not to provide some new, unmentioned immunity for state officers. . . .

Indeed, the historical materials strongly suggest that the Founders intended to enhance the capacity of the federal government by empowering it — as a part of the new authority to make demands directly on individual citizens — to act through local officials. Hamilton made clear that the new Constitution, "by extending the authority of the federal head to the individual citizens of the several States, will enable the government to employ the ordinary magistracy of each, in the execution of its laws." The Federalist No. 27. Hamilton's meaning was unambiguous; the federal government was to have the power to demand that local officials implement national policy programs. As he went on to explain: "It is easy to perceive that this will tend to destroy, in the common apprehension, all distinction between the sources from which [the state and federal governments] might proceed; and will give the federal government the same advantage for securing a due obedience to its authority which is enjoyed by the government of each State." . . .

More specifically, during the debates concerning the ratification of the Constitution, it was assumed that state agents would act as tax collectors for the federal government. Opponents of the Constitution had repeatedly expressed fears that the new federal government's ability to impose taxes directly on the citizenry would result in an overbearing presence of federal tax collectors in the States. Federalists rejoined that this problem would not arise because, as Hamilton explained, "the United States . . . will make use of the State officers and State regulations for collecting" certain taxes. Id., No. 36. Similarly, Madison made clear that the new central government's power to raise taxes directly from the citizenry would "not be resorted to, except for supplemental purposes of revenue . . . and that the eventual collection, under the immediate authority of the Union, will generally be made by the officers . . . appointed by the several States." Id., No. 45. . . .

The Court assumes that the imposition of such essentially executive duties on state judges and their clerks sheds no light on the question whether executive officials might have an immunity from federal obligations. . . . As one scholar has noted, "two centuries ago, state and local judges and associated judicial personnel performed many of the functions today performed by executive officers, including such varied tasks as laying city streets and ensuring the seaworthiness of vessels." Caminker, State Sovereignty and Subordinacy: May Congress Commandeer State Officers to Implement Federal Law?, 95 Colum. L. Rev. 1001, 1045, n.176 (1995). . . . The majority's insistence that this evidence of federal enlistment of state officials to serve executive functions is irrelevant simply because the assistance of "judges" was at issue rests on empty formalistic reasoning of the highest order.

The Court's evaluation of the historical evidence, furthermore, fails to acknowledge the important difference between policy decisions that may have been influenced by respect for state sovereignty concerns, and decisions that are compelled by the Constitution.[b]

The Court concludes its review of the historical materials with a reference to the fact that our decision in INS v. Chadha invalidated a large number of statutes enacted in the 1970s, implying that recent enactments by Congress that are similar to the Brady Act are not entitled to any presumption of validity. But in *Chadha*, unlike this case, our decision rested on the Constitution's express bicameralism and presentment requirements, not on judicial inferences drawn from a silent text and a historical record that surely favors the congressional understanding. . . .

III.

The Court's "structural" arguments are not sufficient. . . . The fact that the Framers intended to preserve the sovereignty of the several States simply does not speak to the question whether individual state employees may be required to perform federal obligations, such as registering young adults for the draft, creating state emergency response commissions designed to manage the release of hazardous

---

b. Indeed, an entirely appropriate concern for the prerogatives of state government readily explains Congress' sparing use of this otherwise "highly attractive" power. Congress' discretion, contrary to the majority's suggestion, indicates not that the power does not exist, but rather that the interests of the States are more than sufficiently protected by their participation in the National Government.

substances, collecting and reporting data on underground storage tanks that may pose an environmental hazard, and reporting traffic fatalities and missing children to a federal agency.

As we explained in *Garcia:* "The principal means chosen by the Framers to ensure the role of the States in the federal system lies in the structure of the Federal Government itself. It is no novelty to observe that the composition of the Federal Government was designed in large part to protect the States from overreaching by Congress." Given the fact that the Members of Congress are elected by the people of the several States, with each State receiving an equivalent number of Senators in order to ensure that even the smallest States have a powerful voice in the legislature, it is quite unrealistic to assume that they will ignore the sovereignty concerns of their constituents. It is far more reasonable to presume that their decisions to impose modest burdens on state officials from time to time reflect a considered judgment that the people in each of the States will benefit therefrom.[c] . . .

[U]nelected judges are better off leaving the protection of federalism to the political process in all but the most extraordinary circumstances.

Perversely, the majority's rule seems more likely to damage than to preserve the safeguards against tyranny provided by the existence of vital state governments. By limiting the ability of the Federal Government to enlist state officials in the implementation of its programs, the Court creates incentives for the National Government to aggrandize itself. In the name of State's rights, the majority would have the Federal Government create vast national bureaucracies to implement its policies. This is exactly the sort of thing that the early Federalists promised would not occur, in part as a result of the National Government's ability to rely on the magistracy of the states. See, e.g., The Federalist No. 36 (Hamilton); id., No. 45 (Madison). . . .

These cases do not involve any mandate to state legislatures to enact new rules. When legislative action, or even administrative rule-making, is at issue, it may be appropriate for Congress either to pre-empt the State's lawmaking power and fashion the federal rule itself, or to respect the State's power to fashion its own rules. But this case, unlike any precedent in which the Court has held that Congress exceeded its powers, merely involves the imposition of modest duties on individual officers. The Court seems to accept the fact that Congress could require private persons, such as hospital executives or school administrators, to provide arms merchants with relevant information about a prospective purchaser's fitness to own a weapon; indeed, the Court does not disturb the conclusion that flows directly from our prior holdings that the burden on police officers would be permissible if a similar burden were also imposed on private parties with access to relevant data. See *New York; Garcia.* A structural problem that vanishes when the statute affects private individuals as well as public officials is not much of a structural problem. . . .

---

c. The majority also makes the more general claim that requiring state officials to carry out federal policy causes states to "take the blame" for failed programs. . . . The problem is of little real consequence . . . because to the extent that a particular action proves politically unpopular, we may be confident that elected officials charged with implementing it will be quite clear to their constituents where the source of the misfortune lies. . . . Moreover, we can be sure that CLEOs will inform disgruntled constituents who have been denied permission to purchase a handgun about the origins of the Brady Act requirements. The Court's suggestion that voters will be confused over who is to "blame" for the statute reflects a gross lack of confidence in the electorate that is at war with the basic assumptions underlying any democratic government.

IV.

Finally, the Court advises us that the "prior jurisprudence of this Court" is the most conclusive support for its position. . . .

The majority relies upon dictum in *New York* to the effect that "the Federal Government may not compel the States to enact *or administer* a federal regulatory program" (emphasis added). But that language was wholly unnecessary to the decision of the case. It is, of course, beyond dispute that we are not bound by the dicta of our prior opinions. . . .

Importantly, the majority either misconstrues or ignores three cases that are more directly on point. In *FERC,* we upheld a federal statute requiring state utilities commissions, inter alia, to take the affirmative step of considering federal energy standards in a manner complying with federally specified notice and comment procedures, and to report back to Congress. . . .

Similarly, in Puerto Rico v. Branstad, 483 U.S. 219 (1987), we overruled our earlier decision in Kentucky v. Dennison, 65 U.S. 66 (1861), and held that the Extradition Act of 1793 permitted the Commonwealth of Puerto Rico to seek extradition of a fugitive from its laws without constitutional barrier. The Extradition Act, as the majority properly concedes, plainly imposes duties on state executive officers. . . . [d]

Finally, the majority provides an incomplete explanation of our decision in Testa v. Katt, 330 U.S. 386 (1947), and demeans its importance. In that case the Court unanimously held that state courts of appropriate jurisdiction must occupy themselves adjudicating claims brought by private litigants under the federal Emergency Price Control Act of 1942, regardless of how otherwise crowded their dockets might be with state law matters. . . . The notion that the Framers would have had no reluctance to "press state judges into federal service" against their will but would have regarded the imposition of a similar — indeed, far lesser — burden on town constables as an intolerable affront to principles of state sovereignty, can only be considered perverse. If such a distinction had been contemplated by the learned and articulate men who fashioned the basic structure of our government, surely some of them would have said so.

The provision of the Brady Act that crosses the Court's newly defined constitutional threshold is more comparable to a statute requiring local police officers to report the identity of missing children to the Crime Control Center of the Department of Justice than to an offensive federal command to a sovereign state. If Congress believes that such a statute will benefit the people of the Nation, and serve

---

d. Moreover, *Branstad* unequivocally rejected an important premise that resonates throughout the majority opinion: namely, that because the States retain their sovereignty in areas that are unregulated by federal law, notions of comity rather than constitutional power govern any direction by the National Government to state executive or judicial officers. That construct was the product of the ill-starred opinion of Chief Justice Taney in Kentucky v. Dennison, announced at a time when "the practical power of the Federal Government [was] at its lowest ebb," As we explained:

"If it seemed clear to the Court in 1861, facing the looming shadow of a Civil War, that 'the Federal Government, under the Constitution, has no power to impose on a State officer, as such, any duty whatever, and compel him to perform it,' basic constitutional principles now point as clearly the other way."

"Kentucky v. Dennison is the product of another time. The conception of the relation between the States and the Federal Government there announced is fundamentally incompatible with more than a century of constitutional development. Yet this decision has stood while the world of which it was a part has passed away. We conclude that it may stand no longer."

the interests of cooperative federalism better than an enlarged federal bureaucracy, we should respect both its policy judgment and its appraisal of its constitutional power.

Justice SOUTER, dissenting. . . .

In deciding these cases, which I have found closer than I had anticipated, it is The Federalist that finally determines my position. I believe that the most straightforward reading of No. 27 is authority for the Government's position here, and that this reading is both supported by No. 44 and consistent with Nos. 36 and 45. . . .

. . . To be sure, it does not follow that any conceivable requirement may be imposed on any state official. I continue to agree, for example, that Congress may not require a state legislature to enact a regulatory scheme and that *New York* was rightly decided (even though I now believe its dicta went too far toward immunizing state administration as well as state enactment of such a scheme from congressional mandate); after all, the essence of legislative power, within the limits of legislative jurisdiction, is a discretion not subject to command. . . .

. . . I recognize that my reading of The Federalist runs counter to the view of Justice Field, who stated explicitly in United States v. Jones, 109 U.S. 513, (1883), that the early examples of state execution of federal law could not have been required against a State's will. But that statement, too, was dictum, and as against dictum even from Justice Field, Madison and Hamilton prevail. [Also,] I do not read any of The Federalist material as requiring the conclusion that Congress could require administrative support without an obligation to pay fair value for it. The quotation from No. 36, for example, describes the United States as paying. If, therefore, my views were prevailing in these cases, I would remand for development and consideration of petitioners' points, that they have no budget provision for work required under the Act and are liable for unauthorized expenditures.

Justice BREYER, with whom Justice Stevens joins, dissenting.

[T]he United States is not the only nation that seeks to reconcile the practical need for a central authority with the democratic virtues of more local control. At least some other countries, facing the same basic problem, have found that local control is better maintained through application of a principle that is the direct opposite of the principle the majority derives from the silence of our Constitution. The federal systems of Switzerland, Germany, and the European Union, for example, all provide that constituent states, not federal bureaucracies, will themselves implement many of the laws, rules, regulations, or decrees enacted by the central "federal" body. They do so in part because they believe that such a system interferes less, not more, with the independent authority of the "state," member nation, or other subsidiary government, and helps to safeguard individual liberty as well.

Of course, we are interpreting our own Constitution, not those of other nations, and there may be relevant political and structural differences between their systems and our own. Cf. The Federalist No. 20 (rejecting certain aspects of European federalism). But their experience may nonetheless cast an empirical light on the consequences of different solutions to a common legal problem — in this case the problem of reconciling central authority with the need to preserve the liberty-enhancing autonomy of a smaller constituent governmental entity. And that experience here offers empirical confirmation of the implied answer to a question Justice Stevens asks: Why, or how, would what the majority sees as a constitutional alternative — the creation of a new federal gun-law bureaucracy, or the expansion of an existing federal bureaucracy — better promote either state sovereignty or individual liberty?

As comparative experience suggests, there is no need to interpret the Constitution as containing an absolute principle — forbidding the assignment of virtually any federal duty to any state official. Nor is there a need to read the Brady Act as permitting the Federal Government to overwhelm a state civil service. The statute uses the words "reasonable effort," — words that easily can encompass the considerations of, say, time or cost, necessary to avoid any such result.

Regardless, as Justice Stevens points out, the Constitution itself is silent on the matter. Precedent supports the Government's position here. . . . Thus, there is neither need nor reason to find in the Constitution an absolute principle, the inflexibility of which poses a surprising and technical obstacle to the enactment of a law that Congress believed necessary to solve an important national problem.

Discussion

1. *Methodological musical chairs?* Justice Scalia is often described as a textualist, but his *Printz* opinion candidly stresses other modes of interpretation — doctrine, structure, and history. Conversely, Justice Stevens — who, for example, has strongly supported the less-than-textual opinion in Roe v. Wade, places particular emphasis on text, and sounds eerily like critics of *Roe* when he suggests that "unelected" judges should defer to the political process. And Justice Souter, celebrated for his especially strong belief in precedent, in this case finds original intent more compelling than various judicial "dicta." What, if anything, do you make of all this?

2. Printz *and* Prigg. Note that Justice Story's opinion in Prigg v. Pennsylvania, 41 U.S. (16 Pet.) 536 (1842), supra Chapter 3, presaged the rule laid down in *Printz* when it declared that the Constitution's Fugitive Slave Clause

> does not point to any state functionaries, or any state action, to carry its provisions into effect. The states cannot, therefore be compelled to enforce them; and it might well be deemed an unconstitutional exercise of the power of interpretation [of the Fugitive Slave Act of 1793], to insist, that states are bound to provide means to carry into effect the duties of the national government.

Prigg went unmentioned in *Printz*. Why? For a fascinating historical analysis of the "nationalistic" roots of the *Printz* rule in the eighteenth and nineteenth century — with nationalists like Story using various antecedents of the rule to force the federal government to rely on its own officers — see Roderick M. Hills, Jr., The Political Economy of Cooperative Federalism: Why State Autonomy Makes Sense and "Dual Sovereignty" Doesn't, 96 Mich. L. Rev. 813 (1998).

3. *Commandeering and the Coase Theorem.* Professor Hills suggests that *Printz* might be defensible on a "Coasean" rationale. (For discussion of the Coase Theorem, see supra p. 540.) States have something unique and valuable to the

federal government: functioning administrative systems that can be used to enforce federal policies. The *Printz* rule, Hills argues, does not prevent Congress from deploying such systems — especially when it is cheaper to use an existing state apparatus than to create a new federal one. Rather, *Printz* simply requires the federal government to "bid" for state services, just as it typically acquires other useful things (employees, pencils, buildings, and so on) by paying for them. The *Printz* rule, according to Hills, merely establishes a firm baseline entitlement as a starting point for Coasean bargaining. Without this secure baseline, the feds could simply grab rather than bribe, leaving states overly vulnerable, Hills argues. But is the baseline of states very secure, even with *Printz* on the books, given all the other ways that the federal government may affect states (via preemption threats, the federal taxing power, and broad power to withhold money from uncooperative states)? Without a vast and perhaps unworkable increase in judicial monitoring of all these other federal levers, isn't it easy enough for Congress to undermine the *Printz* baseline by using all its other powers — for example, by eliminating the current block grants given to states, and then promising to restore them only to those states willing to be cooperative?

4. *Commandeering versus "using."* Note, in this connection, Justice Souter's suggestion that Congress has a kind of eminent domain right to demand state executive enforcement, so long as the feds pay "fair value" for services rendered. Is the basic idea of *Printz* and *New York* that Congress may prohibit state action, but may not affirmatively "use" state governments without compensation? (Cf. Rubenfeld, supra p. 531.) If this is indeed the basic idea, does it have a strong functional logic, or is it simply a kind of constitutional etiquette, a rule of politesse reflecting respect for the special "dignity" of states?

5. *The unitary executive.* Doesn't Justice Scalia's emphasis on the unitary federal executive prove too much? If compelling state sheriffs to enforce the Brady Act violates some right of the President to control all law enforcement, then why isn't this right equally violated when sheriffs *voluntarily choose* to enforce the Brady Act? On Scalia's theory, is the unitary executive also violated when private persons help enforce federal laws — for example, by bringing suits for damages to enforce the Sherman Act, or federal civil rights laws?

6. *Comparative constitutional law.* Consider the exchange between Justices Scalia and Breyer about European federalism. American lawyers, judges, politicians, and law professors have tended to focus much more attention on, for example, the lessons of American history than on the lessons to be drawn from the experiences of other countries around the world. Is this focus justified? Are recent developments around the world — the rise of many new democratic and federal states, the increasing availability of English-language versions of foreign legal materials, the globalization effect of the Internet, and so on — likely to make comparative analysis more important in the future?

7. *The* Alden *case.* After *Printz*, the federal government cannot oblige state legislatures or state executives to enforce federal laws, but can generally oblige state judiciaries to enforce federal laws; see Testa v. Katt, 330 U.S. 386 (1947). This differential treatment of the three branches of state government narrowed somewhat in Alden v. Maine, 527 U.S. 706 (1999). Featuring the same 5-4 lineup as *Printz* (with Justice Kennedy writing for the five and Justice Souter for the four), the Court held that a Maine state court could not be obliged to hear damage suits brought against the state of Maine itself, even if the state had indeed violated a

valid federal law. The case involved the same statute as at issue in the 1976 *National League of Cities* case, the Fair Labor Standards Act, prescribing minimum wages for state as well as private employees. Recall that *National League of Cities* invalidated the Act as applied to state employees performing traditional state functions, and that *National League of Cities* was in turn overruled in the 1985 *Garcia* case, with dissenting Justices Rehnquist and O'Connor vowing to continue the fight. In *Alden,* unlike *National League of Cities,* the majority was emphatic that the FLSA was a proper federal law that did constitutionally bind state employers. But, said the Court, if the state violated the law, it could not be obliged to entertain a private suit for damages at the behest of the wronged employee. (Suits brought by the U.S. government might be different, said the Court; and so were suits brought under laws enacted pursuant to the Reconstruction power, cf. Fitzpatrick v. Bitzer, 427 U.S. 445 (1976), supra p. 652 n.a., and injunctive suits brought to force future compliance as opposed to damage suits brought to remedy past violations; cf. Ex Parte Young, 209 U.S. 123 (1908), discussed below.) In the earlier *Seminole Tribe* case (discussed below) the Court had in effect barred private employees from bringing FLSA damage suits in federal district court. Thus, the combination of *Seminole Tribe* and *Alden* drove a wedge between right and remedy: The federal law applied to Alden and vested him with rights as a private citizen, but no court was open to provide him a full private remedy for its violation. According to the Court, "[t]he generation that designed and adopted our federal system considered immunity from private suits central to sovereign dignity." This immunity derived not from the text of the Eleventh Amendment (discussed below) "but from the structure of the original Constitution." Immunity in one's own court — even immunity to violate a necessary and proper law and get away with it, without making the rightsholder whole — was, said the Court, part of the "dignity" and "respect" owed states as "members of the federation." In language reminiscent of *New York* and *Printz,* the Court declared:

> A power to press a State's own courts into federal service to coerce the other branches of the State . . . is the power first to turn the State against itself and ultimately to commandeer the entire political machinery of the State against its will and at the behest of individuals. Such plenary federal control of state governmental processes denigrates the separate sovereignty of the States. . . .
>
> Underlying constitutional form are considerations of great substance. Private suits against nonconsenting States — especially suits for money damages — may threaten the financial integrity of the States. It is indisputable that, at the time of the founding, many of the States could have been forced into insolvency but for their immunity from private suits for money damages. Even today, an unlimited congressional power to authorize suits in state court to levy upon the treasuries of the States for compensatory damages, attorney's fees, and even punitive damages could create staggering burdens, giving Congress a power and a leverage over the States that is not contemplated by our constitutional design. The potential national power would pose a severe and notorious danger to the States and their resources. . . .
>
> When Congress legislates in matters affecting the States, it may not treat these sovereign entities as mere prefectures or corporations. Congress must accord States the esteem due to them as joint participants in a federal system, one beginning with the premise of sovereignty in both the central Government and the separate States. Congress has ample means to ensure compliance with valid federal laws, but it must respect the sovereignty of the States.

In sharp dissent, Justice Souter argued that the majority's appeals to "sovereign dignity" were "thoroughly anomalous":

It would be hard to imagine anything more inimical to the republican conception, which rests on the understanding of its citizens precisely that the government is not above them, but of them, its actions being governed by law just like their own. . . . Furthermore, the very idea of dignity ought also to imply that the State should be subject to, and not outside of, the law. . . .

It is equally puzzling to hear the Court say that "federal power to authorize private suits for money damages would place unwarranted strain on the States' ability to govern in accordance with the will of their citizens." So long as the citizens' will, expressed through state legislation, does not violate valid federal law, the strain will not be felt; and to the extent that state action does violate federal law, the will of the citizens of the United States already trumps that of the citizens of the State: the strain then is not only expected, but necessarily intended. . . .

[T]he Court abandons a principle . . . close[] to the hearts of the Framers: that where there is a right, there must be a remedy. Lord Chief Justice Holt could state this as an unquestioned proposition already in 1702. . . . Blackstone considered it "a general and indisputable rule, that where there is a legal right, there is also a legal remedy, by suit or action at law, whenever that right is invaded." The generation of the Framers thought the principle so crucial that several States put it into their constitutions. And when Chief Justice Marshall asked about *Marbury*, "If he has a right, and that right has been violated, do the laws of his country afford him a remedy?," the question was rhetorical, and the answer clear:

> "The very essence of civil liberty certainly consists in the right of every individual to claim the protection of the laws, whenever he receives an injury. One of the first duties of government is to afford that protection. In Great Britain the king himself is sued in the respectful form of a petition, and he never fails to comply with the judgment of his court."

Yet today the Court has no qualms about saying frankly that the federal right to damages afforded by Congress under the FLSA cannot create a concomitant private remedy. The right was "made for the benefit of" petitioners; they have been "hindered by another of that benefit"; but despite what has long been understood as the "necessary consequence of law," they have no action. It will not do for the Court to respond that a remedy was never available where the right in question was against the sovereign. A State is not the sovereign when a federal claim is pressed against it, and even the English sovereign opened itself to recovery and, unlike Maine, provided the remedy to complement the right. To the Americans of the founding generation it would have been clear (as it was to Chief Justice Marshall) that if the King would do right, the democratically chosen Government of the United States could do no less. The Chief Justice's contemporaries might well have reacted to the Court's decision today in the words spoken by Edmund Randolph when responding to the objection to jurisdiction in *Chisholm:* "[The Framers] must have viewed human rights in their essence, not in their mere form."

Both the majority and dissenting opinions raise deep questions. Recall that the main purpose of federalism, according to the Rehnquist Court, is to protect liberty. We might ask the majority: How is liberty protected when valid rights go unremedied? Are governments truly "sovereign" in America when they violate the law? When a state violates a federal law, doesn't it also violate due process *of law*? If so, why does Congress lack Reconstruction power to insist that states must remedy their own violations of law, and make victims whole? And we might ask the dissenters: If, in America, the people, and not governments, are truly sovereign; if the Constitution and laws limit the government, and mark the boundaries of proper governmental power and "sovereignty"; and if every right deserves a full judicial remedy, then why should the *federal* government ever be allowed to invoke sovereign immunity to defeat a valid claim for recovery when that government has violated the limits imposed on it in the Constitution by the Sovereign People? Note that the dissenters did not challenge the idea of federal sovereign immunity for constitutional torts; and the majority explicitly founded its decision on the idea that state governments were entitled to "reciprocal" dignity.

Consider the argument that sovereign immunity — state or federal — has no proper place in a Constitution based on popular sovereignty, and that each government should have reciprocity not in shielding itself when it violates the Constitution, but in empowering citizens to gain full remedies when the *other* government has violated the Constitution. On this view, the federal government should be recognized as having broad power to provide Americans with remedies — including remedies against the states themselves — when states have violated the Constitution and valid federal laws. The "reciprocal" counterpart of this federal power is not the "sovereign" immunity of states when states are lawless; but the rightful authority of states to empower citizens to pursue remedies against the federal government when the feds have violated the Constitution. (For example, state property law helps give a citizen "standing" to sue when the federal government has taken his property without due process, in violation of the Fifth Amendment; and state tort law helps provide a remedy when federal officials violate a citizen's Fourth Amendment rights through an improper search or seizure of his person or property.) Akhil Reed Amar has argued this sort of remedial competition between state and federal government enlists federalism in support of liberty, vindicating the language of the Federalist Numbers 28 and 51 that the Rehnquist Court has identified as the foundation of its federalism jurisprudence. He associates this view of federalism with Section 1983 of Title 42 of the U.S. Code — a general remedial statute adopted by Congress during Reconstruction providing for remedies against lawless state actors — and with "converse-1983" laws that he says states should adopt to help remedy constitutional torts committed by federal officials. For elaboration, see Amar, Of Sovereignty and Federalism, 96 Yale L.J. 1425 (1987); Akhil Reed Amar, Using State Law To Protect Federal Constitutional Rights: Some Questions and Answers About Converse-1983, 64 U. Colo. L. Rev. 159 (1993); Akhil Reed Amar, Five Views of Federalism: "Converse-1983" in Context, 47 Vand. L. Rev. 1229 (1994).

8. *The modern Eleventh Amendment debate.* The Rehnquist Court's treatment of the Tenth Amendment is usefully examined alongside its Eleventh Amendment case law. Recall that the Amendment was adopted in the 1790s to reverse the Court's decision in Chisholm v. Georgia, 2 U.S. (2 Dall.) 419 (1793). In *Chisholm* — perhaps the biggest case to reach the pre-Marshall Court — the Justices construed language of Article III conferring federal jurisdiction over certain categories of lawsuits based not on the legal subject matter of the suits (e.g., the presence of a federal question or an admiralty law issue), but merely on the diverse-party alignments they presented: "Controversies . . . between a State and Citizens of another State" and "Controversies . . . between a State . . . and foreign . . . Citizens or Subjects." *The Chisholm* suit was brought in assumpsit by a South Carolina citizen against the state

of Georgia, to recover for the state's breach of a war-supplies contract. Georgia claimed that federal courts could not hear the case — the relevant diversity language of Article III, it argued, applied only to lawsuits where states were plaintiffs against out-of-staters, not involuntary defendants. The Supreme Court disagreed, and went on to suggest that Georgia should be held liable for its breach — even though both Georgia and South Carolina law would have allowed the state to escape liability for mere breach of conduct. (At common law, contracts with states were not legally enforceable.) No federal law violation was alleged in *Chisholm* — it is important to note that the plaintiff did not claim that Georgia's conduct had violated the Contract Clause or any other federal norm. To modern observers, the Court's ruling in *Chisholm* thus seems to violate important federalism principles later clarified in the famous case of Erie R.R. v. Tomkins, 304 U.S. 64 (1938): In a mere diversity lawsuit raising no question of federal law, federal courts should generally apply state law rather than fashioning their own "general federal common law." The Eleventh Amendment's response to *Chisholm* was drafted in extremely narrow terms: "The judicial power of the United States shall not be construed to extend to any suit in law or equity, commenced or prosecuted against one of the United States by Citizens of another State, or by Citizens or subjects of any Foreign State." Many leading scholars today believe that this language simply repealed part of the above-quoted language of Article III, which had conferred a species of diversity jurisdiction even in cases involving no claim of federal right. But, the modern "diversity school" insists, the Amendment left untouched plenary federal jurisdiction in federal question and admiralty cases, and of course said nothing about suits brought by a citizen against his own state. On this view, even after the Amendment, federal judicial power to enforce federal law remained co-extensive with the reach of federal law itself. For representative statements of this "diversity school," see William A. Fletcher, A Historical Interpretation of the Eleventh Amendment: A Narrow Construction of an Affirmative Grant of Jurisdiction Rather than a Prohibition Against Jurisdiction, 35 Stan. L. Rev. 1033 (1983); John J. Gibbons, The Eleventh Amendment and State Sovereign Immunity: A Reinterpretation, 83 Colum. L. Rev. 1889 (1983); Akhil Reed Amar, Of Sovereignty and Federalism, 96 Yale L.J. 1425 (1987); Vicki C. Jackson, The Supreme Court, the Eleventh Amendment, and State Sovereign Immunity, 98 Yale L.J. 1 (1988).

This, however, has not been the Court's view. In Louisiana v. Jumel, 107 U.S. 711 (1883), the Court held that the Amendment barred a lower federal court from hearing a constitutional ("federal question") claim brought against Louisiana by a citizen of a sister state. Several years later, in Hans v. Louisiana, 134 U.S. 1 (1890), the Court held that federal question suits brought by Louisiana citizens against the state should likewise be barred. (Otherwise, the Court reasoned, federal courts would be discriminating against out-of-staters like Jumel.) *Hans* also contained broad language about state sovereign immunity; and this language threatened to undermine legitimate interests in enforcing federal law against lawless states. This threat was blunted to an important extent by the Court's landmark decision in Ex Parte Young, 209 U.S. 123 (1908), which in effect allowed citizens to sue states for prospective injunctive relief by suing a state official, rather than the state itself. Nevertheless, damage suits brought against states (or against state officials in their official capacity, where the recovery sought would come directly from the state treasury) continued to be ousted from federal court under the (il)logic of *Hans*. See, e.g., Edelman v. Jordan, 415 U.S. 651 (1974).

Modern Supreme Court case law concerning the Eleventh Amendment and the intertwined issue of state sovereign immunity is a tangled web of intricate and highly controversial case law. These issues are covered in painstaking detail in casebooks on federal jurisdiction, and so here we shall simply offer a quick overview of recent developments. On at least two occasions, the "diversity school" reading of the Amendment has commanded four votes, see, e.g., Atascadero State Hosp. v. Scanlon, 473 U.S. 234 (1985) (Brennan, J., dissenting, joined by Marshall, Blackmun, and Stevens, JJ.); Seminole Tribe of Florida v. Florida, 517 U.S. 44 (1996) (Souter, J., dissenting, joined by Stevens, Ginsburg, and Breyer, JJ.). The Court has permitted Congress to "abrogate" the Amendment, and subject states to damage lawsuits in federal court, if Congress is acting pursuant to its powers under the Reconstruction Amendments, see Fitzpatrick v. Bitzer, 427 U.S. 445 (1976).

In Pennsylvania v. Union Gas Co., 491 U.S. 1 (1989), the Court upheld Congress's power to similarly abrogate the Eleventh Amendment via a statute enacted under the commerce power, but *Union Gas* did not generate a single opinion for the five Justices who adhered to this result. In the 1996 *Seminole Tribe* case, a sharply divided Court overruled *Union Gas*, in an opinion authored by Chief Justice Rehnquist. *Seminole* raised many important questions, and several were answered the day that *Alden* came down. Could a citizen barred by *Seminole* from bringing his federal damages suit in federal court instead demand that state courts open their doors? No, said *Alden*. Would *Fitzpatrick* be read broadly, enabling Congress to use its Reconstruction power to pry open court doors on behalf of federal rights-holders? No, said the Court in Florida Prepaid Postsecondary Education Expense Board v. College Savings Bank, 527 U.S. 627 (1999), in an opinion per Chief Justice Rehnquist decided the same day as *Alden*, and featuring the same 5-4 vote, with Justice Stevens writing for the four in dissent. (Note the link between *Florida*, constricting Congress's Reconstruction power, and *City of Boerne*, supra p. 629.) Could states that continued to engage in interstate commercial activities after these activities had been regulated by Congress be deemed to have waived their sovereign immunity? No, said the Court in a third case decided the same day, and featuring the same line-up, with Justice Scalia writing for the five and Justice Breyer writing for the four. Note that this case — like *Seminole* — required the Court to explicitly overrule a prior precedent. See College Savings Bank v. Florida Prepaid Postsecondary Expense Board, 527 U.S. 666 (1999), overruling Parden v. Terminal Ry. of Alabama Docks Dept., 377 U.S. 184 (1964). The dissenters in these cases gave clear notice that they did not consider the matter settled. Thus Justice Souter closed his *Alden* dissent with the following words:

The Court has swung back and forth with regrettable disruption on the enforceability of the FLSA against the States, but if the present majority had a defensible position one could at least accept its decision with an expectation of stability ahead. As it is, any such expectation would be naive. The resemblance of today's state sovereign immunity to the *Lochner* era's industrial due process is striking. The Court began this century by imputing immutable constitutional status to a conception of economic self-reliance that was never true to industrial life and grew insistently fictional with the years, and the Court has chosen to close the century by conferring like status on a conception of state sovereign immunity that is true neither to history nor to the structure of the Constitution. I expect the Court's late essay into immunity doctrine will prove the equal of its earlier experiment in laissez-faire, the one being as unrealistic as the other, as indefensible, and probably as fleeting.[67]

9. *Limiting congressional power by limiting congressional terms?* Recall *Garcia*'s argument that the main constitutional protection of state governments and state interests should not come from substantive review of congressional power by federal judges, but should instead derive from the basic structure of the political branches themselves and from the influence of states in the political process itself. Recall also that the dissenters in *Garcia* found this view unpersuasive, and placed particular emphasis on post-Founding developments, like the Seventeenth Amendment, that weakened the political safeguards of federalism extolled by Madison. The movement to limit congressional terms can be seen as an important part of this debate.

The issue of congressional term limits is often framed as a debate between those who favor amateur, rotating citizen-legislators, and those who favor more seasoned professional politicians and statespersons. But this framing may miss an important federalism dynamic, in which congressional term limits might lead to both rotation *and* professionalism: Professional politicians might rotate *among* various offices, in a constitutional variant of musical chairs. Nowadays, state and local politicians often aspire to move up to House and Senate seats in Washington; but members of Congress covet state office much less. With congressional term limits, however, more Senators might dream of becoming Governor, and the roads between state capitals and Congress might feature more traffic in the reverse-commute direction. This dynamic, in turn, might lead more sitting Congresspersons to think sympathetically about the concerns of state governments and to pay more heed to messages sent by state lawmakers to their federal counterparts.

In U.S. Term Limits v. Thornton, 514 U.S. 779 (1995), the Justices confronted a popularly-ratified amendment to the Arkansas state constitution that barred those who had served two or more terms in the U.S. Senate from appearing on the general election ballot for the Senate, and those who had served three or more terms in the U.S. House of Representatives from appearing on the general election ballot for the House. The Preamble to this state amendment read as follows:

"The people of Arkansas find and declare that elected officials who remain in office too long become preoccupied with reelection and ignore their duties as representatives of the people. Entrenched incumbency has reduced voter participation and has led to an electoral system that is less free, less competitive, and less representative than the system established by the Founding Fathers. Therefore, the people of Arkansas, exercising their reserved powers, herein limit the terms of elected officials."

The Court, by a 5-4 vote, said no.

---

67. Important questions still remain to be decided. For example, may the United States government formally join a lawsuit brought by a private citizen like Alden, and thereby pry open court doors, on the theory that state sovereign immunity cannot be invoked in a lawsuit against the federal government itself? See Jonathan R. Siegel, The Hidden Source of Congress's Power to Abrogate State Sovereign Immunity, 73 Tex. L. Rev. 539 (1995) (discussing *qui tam* actions).

U.S. TERM LIMITS, INC. v. THORNTON
514 U.S. 779 (1995)

Justice STEVENS delivered the opinion of the Court.

The Constitution sets forth qualifications for membership in the Congress of the United States. Article I, §2, cl. 2, which applies to the House of Representatives, provides: "No Person shall be a Representative who shall not have attained to the Age of twenty five Years, and been seven Years a Citizen of the United States, and who shall not, when elected, be an Inhabitant of that State in which he shall be chosen." Article I, §3, cl. 3, which applies to the Senate, similarly provides: "No Person shall be a Senator who shall not have attained to the Age of thirty Years, and been nine Years a Citizen of the United States, and who shall not, when elected, be an Inhabitant of that State for which he shall be chosen."

. . . . [Arkansas's] state-imposed restriction is contrary to the "fundamental principle of our representative democracy," embodied in the Constitution, that "the people should choose whom they please to govern them." Powell v. McCormack, 395 U.S. 486 (1969). Allowing individual States to adopt their own qualifications for congressional service would be inconsistent with the Framers' vision of a uniform National Legislature representing the people of the United States. If the qualifications set forth in the text of the Constitution are to be changed, that text must be amended.

II.

. . . . Twenty-six years ago, in Powell v. McCormack, we reviewed the history and text of the Qualifications Clauses in a case involving an attempted exclusion of a duly elected Member of Congress. The principal issue was whether the power granted to each House in Art. I, §5, cl. 1, to judge the "Qualifications of its own Members" includes the power to impose qualifications other than those set forth in the text of the Constitution. In an opinion by Chief Justice Warren for eight Members of the Court, we held that it does not. . . .

. . . In reaching that conclusion, we undertook a detailed historical review to determine the intent of the Framers [and] determined that the "relevant historical materials" reveal that Congress has no power to alter the qualifications in the text of the Constitution. . . .

[W]e viewed the [Philadelphia] Convention debates as manifesting the Framers' intent that the qualifications in the Constitution be fixed and exclusive. We found particularly revealing the debate concerning a proposal made by the Committee of Detail that would have given Congress the power to add property qualifications. James Madison argued that such a power would vest " 'an improper & dangerous power in the Legislature,' " by which the Legislature " 'can by degrees subvert the Constitution.' " Madison continued: " 'A Republic may be converted into an aristocracy or oligarchy as well by limiting the number capable of being elected, as the number authorized to elect.' ". . .

The Framers further revealed their concerns about congressional abuse of power when Gouverneur Morris suggested modifying the proposal of the Committee of Detail to grant Congress unfettered power to add qualifications. We noted that Hugh Williamson "expressed concern that if a majority of the legislature should happen to be 'composed of any particular description of men, of lawyers for example, . . . the future elections might be secured to their own body.' " . . .

We also recognized in *Powell* that the post-Convention ratification debates confirmed that the Framers understood the qualifications in the Constitution to be fixed and unalterable by Congress. For example, we noted that in response to the antifederalist charge that the new Constitution favored the wealthy and well born, Alexander Hamilton wrote:

> The truth is that there is no method of securing to the rich the preference apprehended but by prescribing qualifications of property either for those who may elect or be elected. But this forms no part of the power to be conferred upon the national government. . . . The qualifications of the persons who may choose or be chosen, as has been remarked upon other occasions, are defined and fixed in the Constitution, and are unalterable by the legislature. . . .

In *Powell*, of course, we did not rely solely on an analysis of the historical evidence, but instead complemented that analysis with "an examination of the basic principles of our democratic system." We noted that allowing Congress to impose additional qualifications would violate that "fundamental principle of our representative democracy . . . 'that the people should choose whom they please to govern them.' "

Our opinion made clear that this broad principle incorporated at least two fundamental ideas.[a] First, we emphasized the egalitarian concept that the opportunity to be elected was open to all. We noted in particular Madison's statement in The Federalist that " 'under these reasonable limitations [enumerated in the Constitution], the door of this part of the federal government is open to merit of every description, whether native or adoptive, whether young or old, and without regard to poverty or wealth, or to any particular profession of religious faith.' ". . . .

Second, we recognized the critical postulate that sovereignty is vested in the people, and that sovereignty confers on the people the right to choose freely their representatives to the National Government. For example, we noted that "Robert Livingston . . . endorsed this same fundamental principle: 'The people are the best judges who ought to represent them. To dictate and control them, to tell them whom they shall not elect, is to abridge their natural rights.' " Similarly, we observed that "before the New York convention . . . , Hamilton emphasized: 'The true principle of a republic is, that the people should choose whom they please to govern them. Representation is imperfect in proportion as the current of popular favor is checked. This great source of free government, popular election, should be perfectly pure, and the most unbounded liberty allowed.' " . . .

Powell thus establishes two important propositions: first, that the "relevant historical materials" compel the conclusion that, at least with respect to qualifications imposed by Congress, the Framers intended the qualifications listed in the Constitution to be exclusive; and second, that that conclusion is equally compelled by an understanding of the "fundamental principle of our representative democracy . . . 'that the people should choose whom they please to govern them.' ". . . .

---

a. The principle also incorporated the more practical concern that reposing the power to adopt qualifications in Congress would lead to a self-perpetuating body to the detriment of the new Republic. . . .

III.

[P]etitioners argue that whatever the constitutionality of additional qualifications for membership imposed by Congress, the historical and textual materials discussed in *Powell* do not support the conclusion that the Constitution prohibits additional qualifications imposed by States. In the absence of such a constitutional prohibition, petitioners argue, the Tenth Amendment and the principle of reserved powers require that States be allowed to add such qualifications.

Before addressing these arguments, we find it appropriate to take note of the striking unanimity among the courts that have considered the issue. None of the overwhelming array of briefs submitted by the parties and amici has called to our attention even a single case in which a state court or federal court has approved of a State's addition of qualifications for a Member of Congress. To the contrary, an impressive number of courts have determined that States lack the authority to add qualifications. Courts have struck down state-imposed qualifications in the form of term limits, district residency requirements, loyalty oath requirements, and restrictions on those convicted of felonies . . .

Contrary to petitioners' assertions, the power to add qualifications is not part of the original powers of sovereignty that the Tenth Amendment reserved to the States. Petitioners' Tenth Amendment argument misconceives the nature of the right at issue because that Amendment could only "reserve" that which existed before. . . .

Even if we believed that States possessed as part of their original powers some control over congressional qualifications, the text and structure of the Constitution, the relevant historical materials, and, most importantly, the "basic principles of our democratic system" all demonstrate that the Qualifications Clauses were intended to preclude the States from exercising any such power and to fix as exclusive the qualifications in the Constitution. . . . [b]

[I]t is most striking that nowhere in the extensive ratification debates have we found any statement by either a proponent or an opponent of rotation that the draft constitution would permit States to require rotation for the representatives of their own citizens. If the participants in the debate had believed that the States retained the authority to impose term limits, it is inconceivable that the Federalists would not have made this obvious response to the arguments of the pro-rotation forces. The absence in an otherwise freewheeling debate of any suggestion that States had the power to impose additional qualifications unquestionably reflects the Framers' common understanding that States lacked that power. . . .

[T]he *Powell* Court recognized that an egalitarian ideal — that election to the National Legislature should be open to all people of merit — provided a critical foundation for the constitutional structure. This egalitarian theme echoes

---

b. The dissent attacks our holding today by arguing that the Framers' distrust of the States extended only to measures adopted by "state legislatures," and not to measures adopted by "the people themselves." The novelty and expansiveness of the dissent's attack is quite astonishing. We are aware of no case that would even suggest that the validity of a state law under the Federal Constitution would depend at all on whether the state law was passed by the state legislature or by the people directly through amendment of the state constitution. Indeed, no party has so argued. Quite simply, in our view, the dissent's distinction between state legislation passed by the state legislature and legislation passed by state constitutional amendment is untenable. The qualifications in the Constitution are fixed, and may not be altered by either States or their legislatures.

throughout the constitutional debates. In The Federalist No. 57, for example, Madison wrote:

> Who are to be the objects of popular choice? Every citizen whose merit may recommend him to the esteem and confidence of his country. No qualification of wealth, of birth, of religious faith, or of civil profession is permitted to fetter the judgment or disappoint the inclination of the people.

. . . Additional qualifications pose the same obstacle to open elections whatever their source. The egalitarian ideal, so valued by the Framers, is thus compromised to the same degree by additional qualifications imposed by States as by those imposed by Congress. Similarly, we believe that state-imposed qualifications, as much as congressionally imposed qualifications, would undermine the second critical idea recognized in *Powell:* that an aspect of sovereignty is the right of the people to vote for whom they wish. Again, the source of the qualification is of little moment in assessing the qualification's restrictive impact.

Finally, state-imposed restrictions, unlike the congressionally imposed restrictions at issue in Powell, violate a third idea central to this basic principle: that the right to choose representatives belongs not to the States, but to the people. From the start, the Framers recognized that the "great and radical vice" of the Articles of Confederation was "the principle of LEGISLATION for STATES or GOVERNMENTS, in their CORPORATE or COLLECTIVE CAPACITIES, and as contradistinguished from the INDIVIDUALS of whom they consist." The Federalist No. 15. . . . Thus the Framers, in perhaps their most important contribution, conceived of a Federal Government directly responsible to the people, possessed of direct power over the people, and chosen directly, not by States, but by the people. The Framers implemented this ideal most clearly in the provision, extant from the beginning of the Republic, that calls for the Members of the House of Representatives to be "chosen every second Year by the People of the several States." Following the adoption of the Seventeenth Amendment in 1913, this ideal was extended to elections for the Senate. The Congress of the United States, therefore, is not a confederation of nations in which separate sovereigns are represented by appointed delegates, but is instead a body composed of representatives of the people. As Chief Justice John Marshall observed: "The government of the Union, then, . . . is, emphatically, and truly, a government of the people. In form and in substance it emanates from them. Its powers are granted by them, and are to be exercised directly on them, and for their benefit." *McCulloch*[c] Ours is a "government of the people, by the people, for the people." A. Lincoln, Gettysburg Address (1863).

. . . The Constitution thus creates a uniform national body representing the interests of a single people.

Permitting individual States to formulate diverse qualifications for their representatives would result in a patchwork of state qualifications, undermining the uniformity and the national character that the Framers envisioned and sought to ensure. Such a patchwork would also sever the direct link that the Framers found

---

c. Compare U.S. Const., Preamble ("We the People"), with The Articles of Confederation, ("we the under signed Delegates of the States").

so critical between the National Government and the people of the United States.[d]

Petitioners attempt to overcome this formidable array of evidence against the States' power to impose qualifications by arguing that the practice of the States immediately after the adoption of the Constitution demonstrates their understanding that they possessed such power. One may properly question the extent to which the States' own practice is a reliable indicator of the contours of restrictions that the Constitution imposed on States, especially when no court has ever upheld a state-imposed qualification of any sort. But petitioners' argument is unpersuasive even on its own terms. At the time of the Convention, "almost all the State Constitutions required members of their Legislatures to possess considerable property." Despite this near uniformity, only one State, Virginia, placed similar restrictions on Members of Congress, requiring that a representative be, inter alia, a "freeholder." Just 15 years after imposing a property qualification, Virginia replaced that requirement with a provision requiring that representatives be only "qualified according to the constitution of the United States." Moreover, several States, including New Hampshire, Georgia, Delaware, and South Carolina, revised their Constitutions at around the time of the Federal Constitution. In the revised Constitutions, each State retained property qualifications for its own state elected officials yet placed no property qualification on its congressional representatives.

The contemporaneous state practice with respect to term limits is similar. At the time of the Convention, States widely supported term limits in at least some circumstances. The Articles of Confederation contained a provision for term limits. As we have noted, some members of the Convention had sought to impose term limits for Members of Congress. In addition, many States imposed term limits on state officers, four placed limits on delegates to the Continental Congress, and several States voiced support for term limits for Members of Congress. Despite this widespread support, no State sought to impose any term limits on its own federal representatives. Thus, a proper assessment of contemporaneous state practice provides further persuasive evidence of a general understanding that the qualifications in the Constitution were unalterable by the States.[e]

---

d. There is little significance to the fact that Amendment 73 was adopted by a popular vote, rather than as an act of the state legislature. See n.[b], supra. In fact, none of the petitioners argues that the constitutionality of a state law would depend on the method of its adoption. This is proper, because the voters of Arkansas, in adopting Amendment 73, were acting as citizens of the State of Arkansas, and not as citizens of the National Government. The people of the State of Arkansas have no more power than does the Arkansas Legislature to supplement the qualifications for service in Congress. . . .

e. Petitioners and the dissent also point out that Georgia, Maryland, Massachusetts, Virginia, and North Carolina added district residency requirements, and petitioners note that New Jersey and Connecticut established nominating processes for congressional candidates. They rely on these facts to show that the States believed they had the power to add qualifications. We again are unpersuaded. First, establishing a nominating process is no more setting a qualification for office than is creating a primary. Second, it seems to us that States may simply have viewed district residency requirements as the necessary analog to state residency requirements. Thus, state practice with respect to residency requirements does not necessarily indicate that States believed that they had a broad power to add restrictions. Finally, we consider the number of state-imposed qualifications to be remarkably small. Despite the array of property, religious, and other qualifications that were contained in state constitutions, petitioners and the dissent can point to only one instance of a state-imposed property qualification on candidates for Congress, and five instances of district residency requirements. The state practice seems to us notable for its restraint, and thus supports the conclusion that States did not believe that they generally had the power to add qualifications.

IV.

Petitioners argue that, even if States may not add qualifications, Amendment 73 is constitutional because it is not such a qualification, and because Amendment 73 is a permissible exercise of state power to regulate the "Times, Places and Manner of holding Elections." We reject these contentions.

Unlike §§1 and 2 of Amendment 73, which create absolute bars to service for long-term incumbents running for state office, §3 merely provides that certain Senators and Representatives shall not be certified as candidates and shall not have their names appear on the ballot. They may run as write-in candidates and, if elected, they may serve. Petitioners contend that only a legal bar to service creates an impermissible qualification, and that Amendment 73 is therefore consistent with the Constitution. . . .

. . . They argue that the possibility of a write-in campaign creates a real possibility for victory, especially for an entrenched incumbent. One may reasonably question the merits of that contention. . . . But even if petitioners are correct that incumbents may occasionally win reelection as write-in candidates, there is no denying that the ballot restrictions will make it significantly more difficult for the barred candidate to win the election. In our view, an amendment with the avowed purpose and obvious effect of evading the requirements of the Qualifications Clauses by handicapping a class of candidates cannot stand. . . .

[W]e find wholly unpersuasive the dissent's suggestion that Amendment 73 was designed merely to "level the playing field." As we have noted, it is obvious that the sole purpose of Amendment 73 was to limit the terms of elected officials, both state and federal . . .

V.

. . . Term limits, like any other qualification for office, unquestionably restrict the ability of voters to vote for whom they wish. On the other hand, such limits may provide for the infusion of fresh ideas and new perspectives, and may decrease the likelihood that representatives will lose touch with their constituents. It is not our province to resolve this longstanding debate.

We are, however, firmly convinced that allowing the several States to adopt term limits for congressional service would effect a fundamental change in the constitutional framework. Any such change must come not by legislation adopted either by Congress or by an individual State, but rather — as have other important changes in the electoral process — through the amendment procedures set forth in Article V. The Framers decided that the qualifications for service in the Congress of the United States be fixed in the Constitution and be uniform throughout the Nation. That decision reflects the Framers' understanding that Members of Congress are chosen by separate constituencies, but that they become, when elected, servants of the people of the United States. They are not merely delegates appointed by separate, sovereign States; they occupy offices that are integral and essential components of a single

---

Nor are we persuaded by the more recent state practice involving qualifications such as those that bar felons from being elected. As we have noted, the practice of States is a poor indicator of the effect of restraints on the States, and no court has ever upheld one of these restrictions. Moreover, as one moves away from 1789, it seems to us that state practice is even less indicative of the Framers' understanding of state power.

National Government. In the absence of a properly passed constitutional amendment, allowing individual States to craft their own qualifications for Congress would thus erode the structure envisioned by the Framers, a structure that was designed, in the words of the Preamble to our Constitution, to form a "more perfect Union."

Justice KENNEDY, concurring.

. . . Federalism was our Nation's own discovery. The Framers split the atom of sovereignty. It was the genius of their idea that our citizens would have two political capacities, one state and one federal, each protected from incursion by the other. The resulting Constitution created a legal system unprecedented in form and design, establishing two orders of government, each with its own direct relationship, its own privity, its own set of mutual rights and obligations to the people who sustain it and are governed by it. . . .

That the States may not invade the sphere of federal sovereignty is as incontestable, in my view, as the corollary proposition that the Federal Government must be held within the boundaries of its own power when it intrudes upon matters reserved to the States. See *Lopez*.

. . . . Indeed, even though the Constitution uses the qualifications for voters of the most numerous branch of the States' own legislatures to set the qualifications of federal electors, Art. I, §2, cl. 1, when these electors vote, we have recognized that they act in a federal capacity and exercise a federal right. . . .

Justice THOMAS, with whom The Chief Justice, Justice O'Connor, and Justice Scalia join, dissenting.

It is ironic that the Court bases today's decision on the right of the people to "choose whom they please to govern them." Under our Constitution, there is only one State whose people have the right to "choose whom they please" to represent Arkansas in Congress. The Court holds, however, that neither the elected legislature of that State nor the people themselves (acting by ballot initiative) may prescribe any qualifications for those representatives. The majority therefore defends the right of the people of Arkansas to "choose whom they please to govern them" by invalidating a provision that won nearly 60% of the votes cast in a direct election and that carried every congressional district in the State.

I dissent. Nothing in the Constitution deprives the people of each State of the power to prescribe eligibility requirements for the candidates who seek to represent them in Congress. The Constitution is simply silent on this question. And where the Constitution is silent, it raises no bar to action by the States or the people.

I.

Because the majority fundamentally misunderstands the notion of "reserved" powers, I start with some first principles. Contrary to the majority's suggestion, the people of the States need not point to any affirmative grant of power in the Constitution in order to prescribe qualifications for their representatives in Congress, or to authorize their elected state legislators to do so.

A

Our system of government rests on one overriding principle: All power stems from the consent of the people. To phrase the principle in this way, however, is to be imprecise about something important to the notion of "reserved" powers. The ultimate source of the Constitution's authority is the consent of the people of each individual State, not the consent of the undifferentiated people of the Nation as a whole.

The ratification procedure erected by Article VII makes this point clear. The Constitution took effect once it had been ratified by the people gathered in convention in nine different States. But the Constitution went into effect only "between the States so ratifying the same," Art. VII; it did not bind the people of North Carolina until they had accepted it. In Madison's words, the popular consent upon which the Constitution's authority rests was "given by the people, not as individuals composing one entire nation, but as composing the distinct and independent States to which they respectively belong." The Federalist No. 39.[a]

. . . The Federal Government and the States . . . face different default rules: Where the Constitution is silent about the exercise of a particular power — that is, where the Constitution does not speak either expressly or by necessary implication — the Federal Government lacks that power and the States enjoy it.

These basic principles are enshrined in the Tenth Amendment, which declares that all powers neither delegated to the Federal Government nor prohibited to the States "are reserved to the States respectively, or to the people." With this careful last phrase, the Amendment avoids taking any position on the division of power between the state governments and the people of the States: It is up to the people of each State to determine which "reserved" powers their state government may exercise. . . .

To be sure, when the Tenth Amendment uses the phrase "the people," it does not specify whether it is referring to the people of each State or the people of the Nation as a whole. But the latter interpretation would make the Amendment pointless: There would have been no reason to provide that where the Constitution is silent about whether a particular power resides at the state level, it might or might not do so. In addition, it would make no sense to speak of powers as being reserved to the undifferentiated people of the Nation as a whole, because the Constitution does not contemplate that those people will either exercise power or delegate it. The Constitution simply does not recognize any mechanism for action by the undifferentiated people of the Nation. Thus, the amendment provision of Article V calls for amendments to be ratified not by a convention of the national people, but by conventions of the people in each State or by the state legislatures elected by those people. Likewise, the Constitution calls for Members of Congress to be chosen State by State, rather than in nationwide elections. Even the selection of the President — surely the most national of national figures — is accomplished by an electoral college made up of delegates chosen by the various States, and candidates can lose a Presidential election despite winning a majority of the votes cast in the Nation as

a. The ringing initial words of the Constitution — "We the People of the United States" — convey something of the same idea. (In the Constitution, after all, "the United States" is consistently a plural noun. See Art. I, §9, cl. 8; Art. II, §1, cl. 7; Art. III, §2, cl. 1; Art. III, §3, cl. 1; cf. Amar, Of Sovereignty and Federalism, 96 Yale L.J. 1425, 1455 (1987) (noting this fact, though reaching other conclusions). The Preamble that the Philadelphia Convention approved before sending the Constitution to the Committee of Style is even clearer. It began: "We the people of the States of New-Hampshire, Massachusetts, Rhode-Island and Providence Plantations, Connecticut, New-York, New-Jersey, Pennsylvania, Delaware, Maryland, Virginia, North-Carolina, South-Carolina, and Georgia. . . ." Scholars have suggested that the Committee of Style adopted the current language because it was not clear that all the States would actually ratify the Constitution. In this instance, at least, I agree with the majority that the Committee's edits did not work a substantive change in the Constitution.

a whole. See also Art. II, §1, cl. 3 (providing that when no candidate secures a majority of electoral votes, the election of the President is thrown into the House of Representatives, where "the Votes shall be taken by States, the Representatives from each State having one Vote"); Amdt. 12 (same).

In short, the notion of popular sovereignty that undergirds the Constitution does not erase state boundaries, but rather tracks them. . . . As Chief Justice Marshall put it, "no political dreamer was ever wild enough to think of breaking down the lines which separate the States, and of compounding the American people into one common mass." *McCulloch.*

B

. . . . From the fact that the States had not previously enjoyed any powers over the particular institutions of the Federal Government established by the Constitution,[b] the majority derives a rule precisely opposite to the one that the Amendment actually prescribes: "'The states can exercise no powers whatsoever, which exclusively spring out of the existence of the national government, which the constitution does not delegate to them.'"

The majority's essential logic is that the state governments could not "reserve" any powers that they did not control at the time the Constitution was drafted. But it was not the state governments that were doing the reserving. The Constitution derives its authority instead from the consent of the people of the States. Given the fundamental principle that all governmental powers stem from the people of the States, it would simply be incoherent to assert that the people of the States could not reserve any powers that they had not previously controlled. . . .

The majority is therefore quite wrong to conclude that the people of the States cannot authorize their state governments to exercise any powers that were unknown to the States when the Federal Constitution was drafted. . . .

The majority also. . . . asserts that because Congress as a whole is an institution of the National Government, the individual Members of Congress "owe primary allegiance not to the people of a State, but to the people of the Nation," that because each Member of Congress has a nationwide constituency once he takes office, it would be inconsistent with the Framers' scheme to let a single State prescribe qualifications for him.

Political scientists can debate about who commands the "primary allegiance" of Members of Congress once they reach Washington. From the framing to the present, however, the selection of the Representatives and Senators from each State has been left entirely to the people of that State or to their state legislature. See Art. I, §2, cl. 1 (providing that Members of the House of Representatives are chosen "by the People of the several States"); Art. I, §3, cl. 1 (originally providing that the Senators from each State are "chosen by the Legislature thereof"); Amdt. 17 (amending §3 to provide that the Senators from each State are "elected by the people thereof"). The very name "congress" suggests a coming together

---

b. At the time of the framing, of course, a Federal Congress had been operating under the Articles of Confederation for some 10 years. The States unquestionably had enjoyed the power to establish qualifications for their delegates to this body, above and beyond the qualifications created by the Articles themselves.

of representatives from distinct entities.[c] In keeping with the complexity of our federal system, once the representatives chosen by the people of each State assemble in Congress, they form a national body and are beyond the control of the individual States until the next election. But the selection of representatives in Congress is indisputably an act of the people of each State, not some abstract people of the Nation as a whole.

. . . . When the people of Georgia pick their representatives in Congress, they are acting as the people of Georgia, not as the corporate agents for the undifferentiated people of the Nation as a whole. . . . The concurring opinion protests that the exercise of "reserved" powers in the area of congressional elections would constitute "state interference with the most basic relation between the National Government and its citizens, the selection of legislative representatives." But when one strips away its abstractions, the concurring opinion is simply saying that the people of Arkansas cannot be permitted to inject themselves into the process by which they themselves select Arkansas' representatives in Congress.

. . . Even at the level of national politics, then, there always remains a meaningful distinction between someone who is a citizen of the United States and of Georgia and someone who is a citizen of the United States and of Massachusetts. The Georgia citizen who is unaware of this distinction will have it pointed out to him as soon as he tries to vote in a Massachusetts congressional election.

In short, while the majority is correct that the Framers expected the selection process to create a "direct link" between Members of the House of Representatives and the people, the link was between the Representatives from each State and the people of that State; the people of Georgia have no say over whom the people of Massachusetts select to represent them in Congress. This arrangement must baffle the majority, whose understanding of Congress would surely fit more comfortably within a system of nationwide elections. . . .

II.

A

At least on their face, then, the Qualifications Clauses do nothing to prohibit the people of a State from establishing additional eligibility requirements for their own representatives. . . .

At most, the specification of certain nationwide disqualifications in the Constitution implies the negation of other nationwide disqualifications; it does not imply that individual States or their people are barred from adopting their own disqualifications on a state-by-state basis. Thus, . . . one delegate to the Philadelphia Convention . . . said only that a recital of qualifications in the Constitution would imply that *Congress* lacked any qualification-setting power.

The Qualifications Clauses do prevent the individual States from abolishing all eligibility requirements for Congress. This restriction on state power reflects the

---

c. See 1 S. Johnson, A Dictionary of the English Language 393 (4th ed. 1773) (defining "congress" as "an appointed meeting for settlement of affairs between different nations: as, the congress of Cambray"); T. Sheridan, A Complete Dictionary of the English Language (6th ed. 1796) ("an appointed meeting for settlement of affairs between different nations; the assembly which governs the United States of America").

fact that when the people of one State send immature, disloyal, or unknowledge-able representatives to Congress, they jeopardize not only their own interests but also the interests of the people of other States. Because Congress wields power over all the States, the people of each State need some guarantee that the legislators elected by the people of other States will meet minimum standards of competence. The Qualifications Clauses provide that guarantee: They list the requirements that the Framers considered essential to protect the competence of the National Legislature.

If the people of a State decide that they would like their representatives to possess additional qualifications, however, they have done nothing to frustrate the policy behind the Qualifications Clauses. Anyone who possesses all of the constitu-tional qualifications, plus some qualifications required by state law, still has all of the federal qualifications. Accordingly, the fact that the Constitution specifies certain qualifications that the Framers deemed necessary to protect the compe-tence of the National Legislature does not imply that it strips the people of the indi-vidual States of the power to protect their own interests by adding other requirements for their own representatives.

The people of other States could legitimately complain if the people of Arkansas decide, in a particular election, to send a 6-year-old to Congress. But the Constitution gives the people of other States no basis to complain if the people of Arkansas elect a freshman representative in preference to a long-term incumbent. That being the case, it is hard to see why the rights of the people of other States have been violated when the people of Arkansas decide to enact a more general disqualification of long-term incumbents. . . .

The majority responds that "a patchwork of state qualifications" would "under-mine the uniformity and the national character that the Framers envisioned and sought to ensure." Yet the Framers thought it perfectly consistent with the "national character" of Congress for the Senators and Representatives from each State to be chosen by the legislature or the people of that State. The majority never explains why Congress' fundamental character permits this state-centered system, but nonetheless prohibits the people of the States and their state legisla-tures from setting any eligibility requirements for the candidates who seek to represent them.

B

. . . [T]he majority's evidence . . . establishes only two more modest propositions: (1) the Framers did not want the Federal Constitution itself to impose a broad set of disqualifications for congressional office, and (2) the Framers did not want the Federal Congress to be able to supplement the few disqualifications that the Constitution does set forth. The logical conclusion is simply that the Framers did not want the people of the States and their state legislatures to be constrained by too many qualifications imposed at the national level. The evidence does not support the majority's more sweeping conclusion that the Framers intended to bar the people of the States and their state legislatures from adopting additional eligi-bility requirements to help narrow their own choices.

I agree with the majority that Congress has no power to prescribe qualifications for its own Members. This fact, however, does not show that the Qualifications Clauses contain a hidden exclusivity provision. The reason for Congress' incapacity is not that the Qualifications Clauses deprive Congress of the authority to set qualifications, but rather that nothing in the Constitution grants Congress this power. In the absence of such a grant, Congress may not act. But deciding whether the Constitution denies the qualification-setting power to the States and the people of the States requires a fundamentally different legal analysis. . . .

The fact that the Framers did not grant a qualification-setting power to Congress does not imply that they wanted to bar its exercise at the state level. One reason why the Framers decided not to let Congress prescribe the qualifications of its own Members was that incumbents could have used this power to perpetuate themselves or their ilk in office. As Madison pointed out at the Philadelphia Convention, Members of Congress would have an obvious conflict of interest if they could determine who may run against them. But neither the people of the States nor the state legislatures would labor under the same conflict of interest when prescribing qualifications for Members of Congress, and so the Framers would have had to use a different calculus in determining whether to deprive them of this power.

. . . . There is a world of difference between a self-imposed constraint and a constraint imposed from above.

The majority never identifies the democratic principles that would have been violated if a state legislature, in the days before the Constitution was amended to provide for the direct election of Senators, had imposed some limits of its own on the field of candidates that it would consider for appointment.[d] Likewise, the majority does not explain why democratic principles forbid the people of a State from adopting additional eligibility requirements to help narrow their choices among candidates seeking to represent them in the House of Representatives. Indeed, the invocation of democratic principles to invalidate Amendment 73 seems particularly difficult in the present case, because Amendment 73 remains fully within the control of the people of Arkansas. If they wanted to repeal it (despite the 20-point margin by which they enacted it less than three years ago), they could do so by a simple majority vote.

The majority appears to believe that restrictions on eligibility for office are inherently undemocratic. But the Qualifications Clauses themselves prove that the Framers did not share this view; eligibility requirements to which the people of the States consent are perfectly consistent with the Framers' scheme. In fact, we have described "the authority of the people of the States to determine the qualifications of their most important government officials" as "an authority that lies at the heart of representative government." *Gregory* (refusing to read federal law to preclude States from imposing a mandatory retirement age on state judges who are subject to periodic retention elections). When the people of a State themselves decide to restrict the field of candidates whom they are willing to send to Washington as their representatives, they simply have not violated the principle that "the people should choose whom they please to govern them."

At one point, the majority suggests that the principle identified by Hamilton encompasses not only the electorate's right to choose, but also "the egalitarian concept that the opportunity to be elected [is] open to all." . . . But we have never

---

d. Oregon, for instance, pioneered a system in which the state legislature bound itself to appoint the candidates chosen in a statewide vote of the people. See Hills, A Defense of State Constitutional Limits on Federal Congressional Terms, 53 U. Pitt. L. Rev. 97, 108 (1991). The majority is in the uncomfortable position of suggesting that this system violated "democratic principles."

suggested that "the opportunity to be elected" is open even to those whom the voters have decided not to elect. On that rationale, a candidate might have a right to appear on the ballot in the general election even though he lost in the primary. Thus, the majority ultimately concedes that its "egalitarian concept" derives entirely from the electorate's right to choose. If the latter is not violated, then neither is the former.

In fact, the authority to narrow the field of candidates in this way may be part and parcel of the right to elect Members of Congress. That is, the right to choose may include the right to winnow. See Hills, A Defense of State Constitutional Limits on Federal Congressional Terms, 53 U. Pitt. L. Rev. 97, 107-109 (1991). . . .

I see nothing in the Constitution that precludes the people of each State (if they so desire) from authorizing their elected state legislators to prescribe qualifications on their behalf. If the people of a State decide that they do not trust their state legislature with this power, they are free to amend their state constitution to withdraw it. . . .

But one need not agree with me that the people of each State may delegate their qualification-setting power in order to uphold Arkansas' Amendment 73. Amendment 73 is not the act of a state legislature; it is the act of the people of Arkansas, adopted at a direct election and inserted into the state constitution. The majority never explains why giving effect to the people's decision would violate the "democratic principles" that undergird the Constitution. Instead, the majority's discussion of democratic principles is directed entirely to attacking eligibility requirements imposed on the people of a State by an entity other than themselves.

C

In addition to its arguments about democratic principles, the majority asserts that more specific historical evidence supports its view that the Framers did not intend to permit supplementation of the Qualifications Clauses. But when one focuses on the distinction between congressional power to add qualifications for congressional office and the power of the people or their state legislatures to add such qualifications, one realizes that this assertion has little basis. . . .

But even if the majority's reading of its evidence were correct, the most that one could infer is that the Framers did not want state legislatures to be able to prescribe qualifications that would narrow the people's choices. However wary the Framers might have been of permitting state legislatures to exercise such power, there is absolutely no reason to believe that the Framers feared letting the people themselves exercise this power. Cf. The Federalist No. 52 (Madison) ("It cannot be feared that the people of the States will alter this [electoral-qualification] part of their constitutions in such a manner as to abridge the rights secured to them by the federal Constitution"). . . .

In discussing the ratification period, the majority stresses two principal data. One of these pieces of evidence is no evidence at all — literally. The majority devotes considerable space to the fact that the recorded ratification debates do not contain any affirmative statement that the States can supplement the constitutional qualifications. For the majority, this void is "compelling" evidence that "unquestionably reflects the Framers' common understanding that States lacked that power." The majority reasons that delegates at several of the ratifying conventions attacked the

Constitution for failing to require Members of Congress to rotate out of office.[e] If supporters of ratification had believed that the individual States could supplement the constitutional qualifications, the majority argues, they would have blunted these attacks by pointing out that rotation requirements could still be added State by State.

But the majority's argument cuts both ways. The recorded ratification debates also contain no affirmative statement that the States *cannot* supplement the constitutional qualifications. While ratification was being debated, the existing rule in America was that the States could prescribe eligibility requirements for their delegates to Congress, see n.[b], supra, even though the Articles of Confederation gave Congress itself no power to impose such qualifications. If the Federal Constitution had been understood to deprive the States of this significant power, one might well have expected its opponents to seize on this point in arguing against ratification.

The fact is that arguments based on the absence of recorded debate at the ratification conventions are suspect, because the surviving records of those debates are fragmentary. We have no records at all of the debates in several of the conventions, and only spotty records from most of the others. . . .

[S]tate practice immediately after the ratification of the Constitution refutes the majority's suggestion that the Qualifications Clauses were commonly understood as being exclusive. Five States supplemented the constitutional disqualifications in their very first election laws, and the surviving records suggest that the legislatures of these States considered and rejected the interpretation of the Constitution that the majority adopts today.

As the majority concedes, the first Virginia election law erected a property qualification for Virginia's contingent in the Federal House of Representatives. What is more, while the Constitution merely requires representatives to be inhabitants of their State, the legislatures of five of the seven States that divided themselves into districts for House elections added that representatives also had to be inhabitants of the district that elected them. . . .

III.

. . . Today's decision also means that no State may disqualify congressional candidates whom a court has found to be mentally incompetent, who are currently in prison, or who have past vote-fraud convictions. Likewise, after today's decision, the people of each State must leave open the possibility that they will trust someone with their vote in Congress even though they do not trust him with a vote in the election for Congress.

In order to invalidate §3 of Amendment 73, however, the majority must go further. The bulk of the majority's analysis — like Part II of my dissent —

---

e. . . . The majority properly does not cite the omission of this nationwide rotation requirement as evidence that the Framers meant to preclude individual States from adopting rotation requirements of their own. Just as individual States could extend the vote to women before the adoption of the Nineteenth Amendment, could prohibit poll taxes before the adoption of the Twenty-fourth Amendment, and could lower the voting age before the adoption of the Twenty-sixth Amendment, so the Framers' decision not to impose a nationwide limit on congressional terms did not itself bar States from adopting limits of their own.

addresses the issues that would be raised if Arkansas had prescribed "genuine, unadulterated, undiluted term limits." But as the parties have agreed, Amendment 73 does not actually create this kind of disqualification. It does not say that covered candidates may not serve any more terms in Congress if reelected, and it does not indirectly achieve the same result by barring those candidates from seeking reelection. It says only that if they are to win reelection, they must do so by write-in votes.

[I]n modern times only two incumbent Congressmen have ever sought reelection as write-in candidates. One of them was Dale Alford of Arkansas, who had first entered the House of Representatives by winning 51% of the vote as a write-in candidate in 1958; Alford then waged a write-in campaign for reelection in 1960, winning a landslide 83% of the vote against an opponent who enjoyed a place on the ballot. The other incumbent write-in candidate was Philip J. Philbin of Massachusetts, who — despite losing his party primary and thus his spot on the ballot — won 27% of the vote in his unsuccessful write-in candidacy. According to Professor Fay, these results — coupled with other examples of successful write-in campaigns, such as Ross Perot's victory in North Dakota's 1992 Democratic Presidential primary — "demonstrate that when a write-in candidate is well-known and well-funded, it is quite possible for him or her to win an election.". . .

One of petitioners' central arguments is that congressionally conferred advantages have artificially inflated the pre-existing electoral chances of the covered candidates, and that Amendment 73 is merely designed to level the playing field on which challengers compete with them.

. . . Current federal law (enacted, of course, by congressional incumbents) confers numerous advantages on incumbents, and these advantages are widely thought to make it "significantly more difficult" for challengers to defeat them. For instance, federal law gives incumbents enormous advantages in building name recognition and good will in their home districts. See, e.g., 39 U.S.C. §3210 (permitting Members of Congress to send "franked" mail free of charge); 2 U.S.C. §§61-1, 72a, 332 (permitting Members to have sizable taxpayer-funded staffs); 2 U.S.C. §123b (establishing the House Recording Studio and the Senate Recording and Photographic Studios). At the same time that incumbent Members of Congress enjoy these in-kind benefits, Congress imposes spending and contribution limits in congressional campaigns that "can prevent challengers from spending more . . . to overcome their disadvantage in name recognition." Many observers believe that the campaign-finance laws also give incumbents an "enormous fund-raising edge" over their challengers by giving a large financing role to entities with incentives to curry favor with incumbents. In addition, the internal rules of Congress put a substantial premium on seniority, with the result that each Member's already plentiful opportunities to distribute benefits to his constituents increase with the length of his tenure. In this manner, Congress effectively "fines" the electorate for voting against incumbents. Hills, 53 U. Pitt. L. Rev., at 144-145. . . .

At the same time that incumbents enjoy the electoral advantages that they have conferred upon themselves, they also enjoy astonishingly high reelection rates. As Lloyd Cutler reported in 1989, "over the past thirty years a weighted average of ninety percent of all House and Senate incumbents of both parties who ran for reelection were reelected, even at times when their own party lost control of the

Presidency itself." Cutler, Now Is the Time for All Good Men . . . , 30 Wm. & Mary L. Rev. 387, 395; see also Kristol, Term Limitations: Breaking Up the Iron Triangle, 16 Harv. J. L. & Pub. Policy 95, 97, and n.11 (1993) (reporting that in the 100th Congress, as many Representatives died as were defeated at the polls). Even in the November 1994 elections, which are widely considered to have effected the most sweeping change in Congress in recent memory, 90% of the incumbents who sought reelection to the House were successful, and nearly half of the losers were completing only their first terms. Only 2 of the 26 Senate incumbents seeking reelection were defeated, see ibid., and one of them had been elected for the first time in a special election only a few years earlier.

The voters of Arkansas evidently believe that incumbents would not enjoy such overwhelming success if electoral contests were truly fair — that is, if the government did not put its thumb on either side of the scale. The majority offers no reason to question the accuracy of this belief. Given this context, petitioners portray §3 of Amendment 73 as an effort at the state level to offset the electoral advantages that congressional incumbents have conferred upon themselves at the federal level. . . .

Discussion

1. *What's the difference?* Why do states' rights and the Tenth Amendment arguments win in *Lopez, New York, Printz,* and *Alden,* but lose in *Term Limits?* Consider the easy answer that a nose-counter would give: The difference, simply put, is Justice Kennedy. He is the swing voter in these cases, and the only one in all five majorities. Of course, this quick answer may be too quick — it does not tell us *why* Justice Kennedy switched sides in *Term Limits.* But one important way of reading a case involves pondering its line-up, and those who argue before the Court do well to "count to five" in their minds, designing their arguments to persuade at least five of the nine.

2. *The sounds of silence.* Note how both sides in this debate deploy arguments about historical silence — about what was *not* said in a given debate. Can mere silence ever be a compelling argument? Which way does silence cut in this case?

3. *Felons in Congress?* Under Article I, §2, and the Seventeenth Amendment, eligibility to vote for Congress depends on eligibility to vote for one's state legislature; and this in turn is defined, at least in part, by state law (typically state constitutional law, see The Federalist No. 52). Many states deny felons the vote, and these denials have been upheld by the Court. See, e.g., Richardson v. Ramirez, 418 U.S. 24 (1974). On the majority view, do felons have a right to be elected even though they do not have a right to elect?

4. *How united are the states?* The majority stresses the theme of national uniformity for congressional elections. Does this mean that different states may no longer set rules for who may vote in congressional elections? How does the "uniformity" idea fit with the fact that the voters of one state may consistently reelect congressional incumbents more often than the voters of another state?

5. *Agency costs: People versus governments.* Can you see why it would be dangerous to give Congress plenary power to add qualifications? Government officials are "agents" of the people, but at times these agents pursue their own self-serving agendas at the expense of their "principals," the people. Cf. The Federalist No. 51. Economists call this kind of self-dealing a species of "agency costs." At the extreme, wouldn't members of Congress have incentives to make incumbency itself a qualification — or

to do something as close to this as possible — if they can get away with it (in part because their busy constituents cannot perfectly monitor all of their actions)? But why wouldn't state legislatures have similarly self-dealing incentives — for example, to make membership in the state legislature a qualification for running for Congress, thereby narrowing the field of competition? Doesn't the dissent overlook the agency cost problem at the state level, insofar as it suggests that state legislatures may add qualifications?

6. *Formalism versus functionalism.* "Formalism" is a word that can mean many things; one of its pejorative connotations arises when a rule is "formalistically" followed so as to frustrate its purpose, or function. The majority points to concerns by the Founders that Congress would become a "self-perpetuating body." Suppose, in response to this concern, the Framers had explicitly said "no additional qualifications may be added" because they feared that Congress would entrench itself. But how should this rule be applied if Congress — or the electorate — seeks to add a qualification that is *disentrenching* — a qualification that aims not to favor incumbents but to disfavor them? Arguably, "literal" or "formalistic" rule following in this context might defeat the true spirit of the rule.

7. *The term limits law as itself a congressional election?* Consider the very clever argument of Professor Rick Hills, prominently relied upon by the dissent, that Amendment 73 was itself a kind of congressional election. See Roderick M. Hills, Jr., A Defense of State Constitutional Limits on Federal Congressional Terms, 53 U. Pitt. L. Rev. 97 (1991). Surely, Hills notes, Arkansas voters are free to vote against candidate A simply because he is a three-term incumbent, even though they otherwise like him and what he stands for; why, Hills asks, aren't these very same voters permitted to do the same thing — but more generally — by voting for Amendment 73 itself? What are the differences between voting for the Amendment and voting in ordinary congressional elections? Consider a couple of possible answers: (1) Amendment 73 was decided by a statewide vote, not a district by district vote; (2) Amendment 73 is a one-time election, not an election repeated every two years. Are these differences constitutionally significant?

8. *Congressional elections as a prisoner's dilemma.* Inverting Hills's argument, the majority says, in effect, that we already have congressional term limits: They are called "elections" and the people are free to choose every two years. The Arkansas Amendment "unquestionably restrict[s] the ability of voters to vote for whom they wish" and also denies equal opportunity to talented and popular candidates. The dissenters (and Hills) paint a different picture. Ordinary elections aren't really free and equal, but are stacked by incumbents for incumbents. In every district, voters might prefer the challenger to the incumbent, but if they so vote, the district loses seniority and pork-barrel spending vis à vis other districts. This is a kind of prisoner's dilemma game, in which each district might be willing to throw its bum out, but only if other districts do the same. For example, Northern Californians and Southern Californians might both prefer regular rotation, but neither region wants unilaterally to vote against its incumbents, lest the state's congressional delegation be skewed to the other region. Term limit laws are a rather clean and easily enforceable way for voters in different districts to contract around the prisoner's dilemma; every district in California must rotate every *x* years.[68] But even this egalitarian burden sharing within California may be unstable if other parts of the country always return incumbents, whose extra seniority translates into extra pork for these regions at California's expense. In the long run, any

state that imposes term limits on its congressional delegation is unilaterally disarming. And so the national strategy for the term limits movement appeared to be as follows: In the short run, get term limits adopted in enough states so that many sitting members of Congress would be obliged to leave soon under state law, and would thus be less emphatic in seeking to block a federal Term Limits Amendment. The *Term Limits* Court closes its opinion by referring to Article V as the proper solution, if the American people truly want term limits; but as a result of its decision, how likely is it that members of Congress will ever agree to propose an Article V amendment to limit their own terms? (Note that Article V in theory allows amendments to be proposed by a national constitutional convention outside Congress; but such a thing has never happened; all of the formal amendments that have been proposed and ratified under Article V have been proposed by Congress itself.)

IV.   *Interstate Federalism and the National Economy*

Federalism has at least two important dimensions — vertical and horizontal. Vertically, federalism focuses on the relation between state governments and the federal government. Horizontally, the focus is on the relationships between sister states. These two dimensions are of course importantly related, especially given that horizontal relations are often policed vertically, by Congress and federal courts. Also, recall the language in paragraph 64 of *McCulloch,* supra Chapter 1, recasting the vertical conflict between the Bank of the United States and the state of Maryland as a horizontal conflict; in taxing a federal instrumentality that all states had helped pay for, Maryland was in effect taxing her sister states, Marshall argued. (Note also how Justice White tries to make a similar argument in his dissent in New York v. United States, supra p. 674, though the majority plainly disagrees.) Having considered in detail various aspects of vertical federalism in the modern era, we now quickly survey two aspects of horizontal federalism: "dormant" Commerce Clause doctrine, and interstate privileges and immunities under Article IV. The briskness of this quick tour is not meant to suggest the unimportance of these issues, especially in a modern, mobile, interconnected economy. But judicial doctrine under the dormant Commerce Clause is often highly fact-specific; and of course subject to easy overruling by Congress, which is free both to ban what courts have blessed, and to bless what courts have banned. Also, issues under the "dormant" Commerce Clause may at times be closely connected to statutory questions of implied congressional preemption of certain state regulatory efforts; many of these issues are best studied in courses on legislation, administrative law, and regulated industries. So too, doctrine under the Article IV Privileges and Immunities Clause is covered in greater

---

68. Note that this suggests a different way in which Amendment 73 was perhaps invalid. The voters of the state as a whole were in effect making election decisions that congressional law gave to voters in individual congressional districts. Justice Thomas notes that Amendment 73 in fact won a majority in each district; but is this true of all the other popularly adopted Term Limit rules his opinion would have sanctioned in sister states? What if the people in a given district decide that they no longer support Amendment 73, but lack a statewide majority to effect its repeal?

detail in courses and casebooks on conflicts of law. Those readers looking for more extensive analysis are also directed to the third edition of this casebook, which covers these issues at considerably greater length.

A. Dormant Commerce Clause

The so-called "dormant" Commerce Clause, a term coined by Chief Justice Marshall in his opinion in Willson v. Black-Bird Creek Marsh Co., 27 U.S. (2 Pet.) 245 (1829), supra Chapter 2, was developed by the Court to restrain states from enforcing laws that burdened interstate commerce. The textual foundations of dormant Commerce Clause doctrine, however, are shaky: The Commerce Clause empowers Congress to regulate commerce "among the several states," but does not explicitly grant power to federal courts to invalidate state laws in the absence of congressional action. From this "great silence," H.P. Hood & Sons, Inc. v. Du Mond, 336 U.S. 525 (1949), the Court has inferred that absent congressional action, states have a "residuum of power" to regulate local affairs, even if their actions affect interstate commerce, provided that their regulation does not impermissibly "trespass upon national interests." Great Atl. & Pac. Tea Co. v. Cottrell, 424 U.S. 366, 373 (1976). The textual embarrassments of dormant Commerce Clause doctrine have led some — most prominently Justices Scalia and Thomas — to call for extreme judicial restraint in this domain. See, e.g., Tyler Pipe Indus. Inc. v. Washington State Dep't of Revenue, 483 U.S. 232 (1987), and Bendix Autolite Corp. v. Midwesco Enters., 486 U.S. 888 (1988) (Scalia, J., dissenting) (calling on the Court to rein in its balancing approach, and concentrate merely on state laws that facially discriminate against out-of-state interests); Camps Newfound/Owatonna, Inc., v. Town of Harrison, 520 U.S. 564 (1997) (Thomas, J., dissenting) (offering a sharp critique of existing doctrine, and pointing to the Article I, §10 imports-exports clause as the proper focus of judicial attention). On the other hand, there is an obvious structural need for some federal institution to regularly monitor parochial, protectionistic, burdensome, and/or mutually inconsistent state regulations that threaten an integrated national economy. Congress may not be well suited to be the first line of defense against the myriad and fact-specific threats to this economy posed by an almost infinite number of possible state and local laws; and so even if Justices Scalia and Thomas were to persuade their colleagues to leave the field, it seems likely that Congress would pass a broad and loosely worded framework statute inviting the courts back in to keep doing pretty much what they have been doing. Put another way, Congress today legislates against the backdrop of default rules generated by the Court's dormant Commerce Clause doctrine, and appears by its actions and inactions over many decades to have rather forcefully embraced the federal judiciary as its partner in keeping states under control in the economic domain.

1. Burdensome Laws: The Development of a Balancing Test

Early twentieth-century dormant Commerce Clause cases — many of them involving state regulations of transportation — routinely attempted to distinguish between "direct" and "indirect" burdens on commerce. But led by Justice Stone in the 1930s and 1940s, the Court began to move away from this sharp dichotomy toward a more candid and nuanced balancing of state interests against national goals. See, e.g., South Carolina State Highway Dept. v. Barnwell Brothers, 303 U.S. 177 (1938) (Stone, J.), and South Pacific Co. v. Arizona, 325 U.S. 761 (1945) (Stone, C.J.), both of which are discussed below.

The direct-indirect approach was explicitly rejected by the Court in Pike v. Bruce Church Inc., 397 U.S. 137 (1970). The case involved an Arizona statute requiring that all cantaloupes grown in Arizona and offered for sale be packed in Arizona before shipment for sale out of state. The statute was challenged by Bruce Church, which wanted to ship uncrated cantaloupes to nearby facilities in Blythe, California, for packing and processing. The stipulated facts indicated that it would cost the company about $200,000 to build a packing facility within Arizona. In his majority opinion, Justice Stewart put forth the following "general rule":

> Where the statute regulates evenhandedly to effectuate a legitimate local public interest, and its effects on interstate commerce are only incidental, it will be upheld unless the burden imposed in such commerce is clearly excessive in relation to the putative local benefits. If a legitimate local purpose is found, then the question becomes one of degree. And the extent of the burden that will be tolerated will of course depend on the nature of the local interest involved, and on whether it could be promoted as well with a lesser impact on interstate activities.

Applying this test, Justice Stewart invalidated the Arizona statute, finding Arizona's interest in protecting the reputation of its produce "minimal" when placed against the requirement that the packer "build and operate an unneeded $200,000 packing plant in the state."

The *Pike* test was refined in Hughes v. Oklahoma, 441 U.S. 322 (1979), which struck down an Oklahoma statute that prohibited minnows procured in Oklahoma waters from being transported outside the state. The *Hughes* decision developed the *Pike* rule into a three-pronged test. The Court considered (1) whether the challenged statute regulates even-handedly with only "incidental" effects on interstate commerce, or instead discriminates against interstate commerce either on its face or in practical effect; (2) whether the statute serves a legitimate local purpose; and if so, (3) whether alternative means could promote this local purpose as effectively without discriminating against interstate commerce. Thus, like the Court's analysis in *Pike*, the *Hughes* test balanced the state's interest in promulgating a statute against the burden that the statute imposes on interstate commerce.

One particularly interesting strand of balancing cases concerns state regulations of transportation — regulations of the size and specifications of trucks traveling along highways, for example. On the one hand, the Court has recognized a state's strong safety interests in controlling its own streets and thoroughfares. On the other hand, the Court has been sensitive to the need for each state to bear its share of supporting a national transportation network that can be threatened by unnecessary or conflicting local laws. Compare, e.g., South Carolina State Highway Dept. v. Barnwell Brothers, 303 U.S. 177 (1938) (upholding a state law regulating truck size in a nondiscriminatory way, whose burdens fell largely on intrastate shippers, and whose specifics plausibly served legitimate interests in safety and road conservation) with South Pacific Co. v. Arizona, 325 U.S. 761 (1945) (striking down a state law regulating train size that had dubious safety benefits, that interfered with the "national uniformity . . . practically indispensable to the operation of an efficient and economical national railway system," and whose burdens fell on train traffic that was more than 90 percent interstate) and with Bibb v. Navajo Freight Lines, Inc. 359 U.S. 520 (1959) (invalidating a state law regulating truck mudflaps differently from — and in part inconsistently with — the mudflap regulations of sister states).

2. Facially Discriminatory Laws: The "Per Se Invalidity" Test

In cases where state law overtly discriminates against out-of-state economic interests in a fashion akin to a tariff, quota, or outright embargo, the Supreme Court has routinely abandoned the balancing approach in favor of a "virtually per se rule of invalidity." For example, in City of Philadelphia v. New Jersey, 437 U.S. 617 (1978), the Court invalidated a 1973 New Jersey statute that prohibited the importation of most solid or liquid waste originating outside the borders of the state. Although New Jersey argued that it enacted the law to protect the state's environment while additional landfills and alternative disposal methods were being developed, the Court concluded that "whatever New Jersey's ultimate purpose, it may not be accomplished by discriminating against articles of commerce coming from outside the State unless there is some reason, apart from their origin, to treat them differently." The state, said Justice Stewart for the Court, could not achieve the legitimate goals of conservation of landfill facilities by "the illegitimate means of isolating the State from the national economy. . . . [T]here is no basis to distinguish out-of-state waste from domestic waste. If the one is inherently harmful, so is the other. Yet New Jersey has banned the former while leaving its landfill sites open to the latter." Thus, the mere invocation of an allegedly benign purpose did not save a facially discriminatory statute: "the evil of protectionism can reside in legislative means as well as legislative ends." For more recent cases reaffirming this approach, see Chemical Waste Management, Inc. v. Hunt, 504 U.S. 334 (1992), Fort Gratiot Sanitary Landfill, Inc. v. Michigan Department of Natural Resources, 504 U.S. 353 (1992), and Oregon Waste Systems, Inc. v. Department of Environmental Quality of the State of Oregon, 511 U.S. 93 (1994), all of which invalidated efforts to discriminate against out-of-state garbage. Recall, in this regard, that Congress remains free to bless overt state discriminations, cf. New York v. United States, supra p. 674.

3. The Market Participant Exception

In Hughes v. Alexandria Scrap Corp., 426 U.S. 794 (1976) — handed down the same day as National League of Cities — the Court addressed for the first time "the question whether, when a state enters the market as purchaser for end use of items in interstate commerce, it may [restrict] its trade to its own citizens or businesses within the state." Upholding a Maryland statute that would otherwise have been declared per se invalid under the Philadelphia test, the Court applied the market participant test to determine whether the challenged state activity was the type of action with which the Commerce Clause was concerned, or instead, merely "market participation" by the state and thus beyond the reach of the clause.

The statutes considered in *Alexandria Scrap* were designed by Maryland to remove abandoned autos from state highways by paying a bounty to licensed scrap processors for the destruction of cars formerly titled in the state. The Maryland legislature, however, imposed stricter documentation requirements for out-of-state firms, thus producing a "precipitate decline" in the number of abandoned cars delivered to out-of-state processors. In upholding Maryland's program, Justice Powell's opinion for the Court concluded that not "every action by a state that has the effect of reducing in some manner the flow of goods in interstate commerce is potentially an impermissible burden." Although the Court recognized that the effect of the program was to reduce the movement of junked cars interstate, it ruled that discriminating between in-state processors and out-of-state processors in the purchase of cars was not "the kind of action with which the Commerce Clause is concerned." Thus, in articulating this new test, the Court emphasized the form, not the effect, of the state's activity.

The Court more fully articulated the market participant test in Reeves, Inc. v. Stake, 447 U.S. 429 (1980). For 50 years, South Dakota's state-owned cement plant had sold cement to both in-state and out-of-state buyers. In 1978, however, production problems and a nationwide cement shortage led the state to supply all in-state customers first and to distribute the remaining volume on a first-come, first-served basis. The majority, per Justice Blackmun, upheld South Dakota's policy, arguing that because "the Commerce Clause responds principally to state taxes and regulatory measures," the state is exempt when acting in its proprietary capacity. For a more recent case applying and refining this exception, see White v. Massachusetts Council of Construction Employers, 460 U.S. 204 (1983), upholding an order by the Mayor of Boston requiring all construction projects paid for by the city to hire at least half of their workers from the ranks of city residents.

4.   *General Theories of Dormant Commerce*

Scholars have vigorously debated the purpose and justification for judicial intervention under the dormant Commerce Clause. Proponents of the free trade theory claim that the doctrine promotes the national interest in free trade between the states, arguing that the Commerce Clause demands that state boundaries not be used to inhibit the flow of goods. Professor Maltz, for example, claims that the United States depends upon the "free location" principle, which permits individuals to freely engage in commerce in any state. See Earl M. Maltz, How Much Regulation Is Too Much — An Examination of Commerce Clause Jurisprudence, 50 Geo. Wash. L. Rev. 47 (1981). Thus, Maltz asserts that courts may intervene when a state discriminates against out-of-state producers, and contends that the free trade model necessitates judicial balancing where state regulations affect interstate trade. Consistent with this emphasis, the Court has also referred to the free trade principle to support its dormant commerce clause decisions. See, e.g., H.P. Hood & Sons, Inc. v. Du Mond, 336 U.S. 525, 539 (1949).

On the other hand, scholars adopting a value-oriented approach have argued that the Commerce Clause protects "national unity." Professor Regan, for example, makes a structural argument on behalf of the "political viability of the union itself" to justify the invocation of the dormant Commerce Clause. On his view, the doctrine should target state laws with a "protectionist purpose" — that is, laws that "seek[] only a transfer of wealth from foreigners to their local competitors, which is an improper goal for a state in the context of federal union." Donald H. Regan, The Supreme Court and State Protectionism: Making Sense of the Dormant Commerce Clause, 84 Mich. L. Rev. 1091 (1986).

Others have offered a process-based justification for the dormant Commerce Clause. In an approach that parallels his famous footnote 4 in *Carolene Products*, Justice Stone argued against legislation that benefits individuals within the state at the expense of those outside its borders. As he stated, "when the regulation is of such a character that its burden falls principally upon those without the state, legislative action is not likely to be subjected to those political restraints which are normally exerted on legislation where it affects adversely some interests within the state." South Carolina State Highway Dep't v. Barnwell Bros., 303 U.S. 177, 185 n.2 (1938). Is this process approach attractive? If so, can it account for the doctrine — for example, the market participant exception? Or should that exception be understood as an accommodation of a competing principle, which values the expressive autonomy of states — their "consumer sovereignty," so to speak — when they act in a nonregulatory capacity? The state's ability to hoard resources for locals is a major issue in the modern welfare state, to be examined at much greater length in Chapter 9.

B.   Interstate Privileges and Immunities

Recall that Article IV requires each state to accord citizens of sister states various "privileges and immunities." The essence of this clause, which has its roots in similar language in the Articles of Confederation, is that a state may not treat fellow Americans from sister states simply as outsiders or foreigners; rather, in many important ways, each state must evenhandedly extend the benefit of its laws to all Americans within its boundaries. For example, a state may not selectively close the doors of its courtrooms to citizens from other states; and must likewise respect the right of fellow Americans to buy real property, make contracts, open businesses, worship, speak, and exercise many other civil rights, on equal terms with state citizens.

Also recall that in Minor v. Happersett, 88 U.S. 162 (1874), supra Chapter 4, the Court made clear that Article IV had important limits. It did not, said the Court, require State A to let visitors from other states vote in State A's elections, for example. "Political rights" such as voting, jury service, state officeholding, and militia service apparently fall outside the scope of the civil rights — the "privileges" and "immunities" of "citizens" — embraced by the clause. Two years later, McCready v. Virginia, 94 U.S. 391 (1876), held that the clause did not prohibit Virginia from granting its citizens the exclusive privilege of planting oysters in the state's tidal waters. Chief Justice Waite wrote that the state — and thus, its citizenry — owns these waters, and that the planting of oysters in them "is, in fact, a property right, and not a mere privilege or immunity of citizenship. . . . [T]he citizens of one State are not invested by [the Privileges and Immunities] clause of the Constitution with any interest in the common property of the citizens of another State."

In Toomer v. Witsell, 334 U.S. 385 (1948), however, Chief Justice Vinson wrote that this "whole ownership theory . . . is now generally regarded as but a fiction expressive in legal shorthand of the importance to its people that a State have power to preserve and regulate the exploitation of an important resource." His opinion went on to hold that the Privileges and Immunities Clause safeguards the right of one state to do business in another state "on terms of substantial equality with the citizens of that State" and struck down a South Carolina law that imposed a discriminatory license fee on nonresidents shrimping in the state's territorial waters. Justice Frankfurter, joined by Justice Jackson, concurred in judgment, but thought that "it is not conceivable that the framers of the Constitution meant to obliterate all special relations between a State and its citizens." Consider also Pennsylvania v. West Virginia, 262 U.S. 553 (1923), in which the Court invalidated a West Virginia requirement that all domestic needs for natural gas be satisfied before any gas could be transported outside the state. Justice Holmes, joined by Justice Brandeis, dissented, arguing "that the Constitution does not prohibit a state from securing a reasonable preference for its own inhabitants in the enjoyment of its products even when the effect of its law is to keep property within its boundaries that otherwise would have passed outside."

In Baldwin v. Montana Fish and Game Commission, 436 U.S. 371 (1978), Justice Blackmun, for a 6-3 Court, held that, "only with respect to those 'privileges' and 'immunities' bearing upon the vitality of the Nation as a single entity must the State treat all citizens, resident and nonresident, equally." The Court thus upheld a Montana hunting licensing scheme that charged nonresidents significantly more than residents, noting that "equality in access to Montana elk is not basic to the maintenance or well-being of the Union." *Toomer* was distinguished as a case involving "commercial" licenses and thus equality of business opportunities, as opposed to recreational hunting. Justice Brennan, in a dissent joined by Justices White and Marshall, argued that such a reading rendered the Privileges and Immunities Clause "impotent."

The same year, in Hicklin v. Orbeck, 437 U.S. 518 (1978), the Court unanimously struck down an Alaska statute requiring that Alaska residents be preferred to nonresidents for jobs connected with oil and gas pipelines. Assuming, arguendo, that a state could constitutionally deal with its unemployment problem by requiring private employers to discriminate against nonresidents if the nonresidents were the unique source of the problem, Justice Brennan noted that Alaska's unemployment resulted from indigenous factors such as its residents' lack of education and training, rather than from an influx of job-seekers as such. Moreover, the statutory preference extended to all Alaskans, not just the unemployed.

The 1985 case of Supreme Court of New Hampshire v. Piper, 470 U.S. 274, involved a challenge to the New Hampshire Supreme Court's Rule 42, which made residency in the state a requirement for admittance to the New Hampshire bar. Plaintiff Kathryn Piper had passed the New Hampshire state bar examination, but wanted to continue to reside in Lower Waterford, Vermont — about 400 yards from the New Hampshire border. Justice Powell, for an eight-Justice majority, held that the opportunity to practice law is a "fundamental right." According to the Court:

> The Clause does not preclude discrimination against nonresidents where: (i) there is a substantial reason for the difference in treatment; and (ii) the discrimination practiced against nonresidents bears a substantial relationship to the State's objective. In deciding whether the discrimination bears a close or substantial relationship to the State's objective, the Court has considered the availability of less restrictive means.

Noting that the state met neither of these criteria, the Court struck down the law. Justice Rehnquist dissented, writing that, "conclusory second-guessing of difficult legislative decisions, such as the Court resorts to today, is not an attractive way for federal courts to engage in judicial review." The Court later relied on *Piper* to strike down similar residency requirements in Supreme Court of Virginia v. Friedman, 487 U.S. 59 (1988), and Virgin Islands Bar Association v. Thorsten, 489 U.S. 546 (1989).

For a thoughtful general framework of analysis for assessing various issues of horizontal federalism, see Douglas Laycock, Equal Citizens of Equal and Territorial States: The Constitutional Foundations of Choice of Law, 92 Colum. L. Rev. 249 (1992). See also infra, Chapter 9, discussing related issues of interstate federalism under the "right to travel" rubric.

V.   The Executive Power of the United States

Alongside federalism, separation of powers stands as a central structural feature of the American Constitution. Much of the material we have already reviewed in this chapter can be understood as implicating both themes, involving the three-way interplay between the Court, the Congress, and states. In this interplay, the federal executive branch has often been hidden from view — although the careful reader will have glimpsed the important roles of Franklin Roosevelt, Richard Nixon, and Ronald Reagan, among others, in the story thus far.

It is now time to bring the American President center stage, and consider in more detail some of the extraordinary powers of this office, and some important limits on those powers. Although we shall consider these powers seriatim, recall that all of them are, by the first sentence of Article II, vested in a single person: the President. Try to see how these powers might interact and overlap in specific contexts. For example, note that the same person has important war powers as Commander-in-Chief, treaty negotiator, appointer and receiver of ambassadors, and more general head of state; and also important controls over domestic prosecutions, via the pardon power and the power to appoint the Attorney General. Are there synergies across these powers? Note that in this respect the President is rather different from state governors, who are not central figures in wars and foreign affairs, and who typically lack power under their respective state constitutions over their state attorneys general.[69]

A.   The (Non)Prosecution Power

One overarching theme of this casebook is that many important constitutional decisions occur outside of the judiciary. Even within the judiciary, not all major decisions are made by the Supreme Court. Recall, for example, that various lower

---

69. For important overall assessments of presidential power, see Steven G. Calabresi & Kevin H. Rhodes, The Structural Constitution: Unitary Executive, Plural Judiciary, 105 Harv. L. Rev. 1153 (1992); Steven G. Calabresi & Saikrishna B. Prakash, The President's Power to Execute the Laws, 104 Yale L.J. 541 (1994); Steven G. Calabresi, Some Normative Arguments for the Unitary Executive, 48 Ark. L. Rev. 23 (1995). For a more recent essay inspired by the impressive work of Professor Calabresi, see Akhil Reed Amar, Some Opinions on the Opinions Clause, 82 Va. L. Rev. 647 (1996).

federal courts in the 1790s addressed the constitutionality of the 1798 Sedition Act, but that the issue never reached the Supreme Court, and was eventually mooted by the victory of Jefferson and the Republicans in the election of 1800. President Jefferson pardoned all those convicted, and the new Congress allowed the Act to expire. Thus the lower courts; the President (both Adams and Jefferson); the Congress (both in 1798 and after 1800); the state legislatures (two of which issued famous Resolutions against the Act in 1798, most of which elected Senators in 1800, and all of which helped pick the President in 1800); and the electorate — all these actors played more direct roles in the constitutional drama than did the Supreme Court itself.

In the mid-1960s, many vital questions of constitutional law were being decided by the Warren Court; but Congress and the President were also in the thick of things, adopting landmark civil rights laws and pursuing important strategies of civil rights enforcement. Another lead actor in the great national drama was the U.S. Court of Appeals for the (old) Fifth Circuit, spanning the deep South from Florida to Texas. It was this court that had primary responsibility for enforcing the Second Reconstruction coming out of Washington, DC. See generally Jack Bass, Unlikely Heroes (1981). The next case comes from that court and that era. The facts of the case are gripping, but they fully appear only at the end of the last opinion, per Judge Wisdom. No peeking.

UNITED STATES v. COX
342 F.2d 167, Cert. Denied Sub Nom. Cox v. Hauberg, 381 U.S. 935 (1965)

JONES, Circuit Judge.

On October 22, 1964, an order of the United States District Court for the Southern District of Mississippi, signed by Harold Cox, a judge of that Court, was entered. The order, with caption and formal closing omitted, is as follows:

'THE GRAND JURY, duly elected, impaneled and organized, for the Southern District of Mississippi, reconvened on order of the Court at 9:00 A.M., October 21, 1964, in Court Room Number 2 in Jackson, Mississippi, for the general dispatch of its business. . . . On the morning of October 22, 1964, the grand jury, through its foreman, made known to the Court in open court that they had requested Robert E. Hauberg, United States Attorney, to prepare certain indictments which they desired to bring against some of the persons under consideration and about which they had heard testimony, and the United States Attorney refused to draft or sign any such indictments on instructions of the Acting Attorney General of the United States; whereupon the Court ordered and directed said United States Attorney to draft such true bills or no bills as the grand jury may have duly voted and desired to report and to sign such instruments as required by law under penalty of contempt. The United States Attorney was afforded one hour within which to decide as to whether or not he would abide by the instructions and order of the Court in such respect. At the end of such time, the Court re-convened and the United States Attorney was specifically asked in open court as to whether or not he intended to conform with the order and direction of the Court in said respects where-upon the United States Attorney answered that he respectfully declined to do so on instructions from Nicholas deB. Katzenbach, Acting Attorney General. He was there-upon duly adjudged by the Court to be in civil contempt of the Court. . . .

'WHEREFORE, IT IS ORDERED AND ADJUDGED by the Court that Robert E. Hauberg, United States Attorney, is guilty of civil contempt of this Court and in the presence of the Court for his said refusal to obey its said order and he is ordered into custody of the United States Marshal to be confined by him in the Hinds County, Mississippi, jail, there to remain until he purges himself of this contempt by agreeing to conform to said order by performing his official duty for the grand jury as requested. . . .

'IT IS FURTHER ORDERED by the Court that a citation issue to Nicholas deB. Katzenbach, Acting Attorney General of the United States, directing him to appear before this Court and show cause why he should not be adjudged guilty of contempt of this Court for his instructions and directions to the United States Attorney to disregard and disobey the orders of this Court in the respects stated. . . .

The United States Attorney, Robert E. Hauberg, and the Acting Attorney General, Nicholas deB. Katzenbach, have appealed from the order. . . . The facts recited in the order are uncontroverted. No further facts are essential to a decision of the issues before this Court. Although the issues here presented arose, in part at least, as an incident of a civil rights matter, no civil rights questions are involved in the rather broad inquiry which we are called upon to make.

The constitutional requirement of an indictment or presentment as a predicate to a prosecution for capital or infamous crimes has for its primary purpose the protection of the individual from jeopardy except on a finding of probable cause by a group of his fellow citizens, and is designed to afford a safeguard against oppressive actions of the prosecutor or a court. The constitutional provision is not to be read as conferring on or preserving to the grand jury, as such, any rights or prerogatives. The constitutional provision is, as has been said, for the benefit of the accused. . . .

Traditionally, the Attorney for the United States had the power to enter a nolle prosequi of a criminal charge at any time after indictment and before trial, and this he could have done without the approval of the court or the consent of the accused. . . .

It is now provided by the Federal Rules of Criminal Procedure that the Attorney General or the United States Attorney may by leave of court file a dismissal of an indictment. Rule 48(a) Fed. Rules Crim. Proc. 18 U.S.C.A. In the absence of the Rule, leave of court would not have been required. The purpose of the Rule is to prevent harassment of a defendant by charging, dismissing and re-charging without placing a defendant in jeopardy. Rule 7 . . . provides that "[the indictment] shall be signed by the attorney for the government."

The judicial power of the United States is vested in the federal courts, and extends to prosecutions for violations of the criminal laws of the United States. The executive power is vested in the President of the United States, who is required to take care that the laws be faithfully executed. The Attorney General is the hand of the President in taking care that the laws of the United States in legal proceedings and in the prosecution of offenses, be faithfully executed. The role of the grand jury is restricted to a finding as to whether or not there is probable cause to believe that an offense has been committed. The discretionary power of the attorney for the United States in determining whether a prosecution shall be commenced or maintained may well depend upon matters of policy wholly apart from any question of probable cause. Although as a member of the bar, the attorney for the United States is an officer of the court, he is nevertheless an executive official of the Government, and it is as an officer of the executive department that he exercises a discretion as to whether or not there shall be a prosecution in a particular case. It follows, as an incident of the constitutional separation of powers, that the courts are not to interfere with the free exercise of the discretionary powers of the attorneys of the United States in their control over criminal prosecutions. The provision of Rule 7, requiring the signing of the indictment by the attorney for the Government, is a recognition of the power of Government counsel to permit or not to permit the bringing of an indictment. If the attorney refuses to sign, as he has the discretionary power of doing, we conclude that there is no valid indictment. It is not to be supposed that the signature of counsel is merely an attestation of the act of the grand jury. The signature of the foreman performs that function. . . . Rather, we think, the requirement of the signature is for the purpose of evidencing the joinder of the attorney for the United States with the grand jury in instituting a criminal proceeding in the court. Without the signature there can be no criminal proceeding brought upon an indictment.

If it were not for the discretionary power given to the United States Attorney to prevent an indictment by withholding his signature, there might be doubt as to the constitutionality of the requirement of Rule 48 for leave of court for a dismissal of a pending prosecution.

Because, as we conclude, the signature of the Government attorney is necessary to the validity of the indictment and the affixing or withholding of the signature is a matter of executive discretion which cannot be coerced or reviewed by the courts, the contempt order must be reversed. . . .

Judges Tuttle, Jones, Brown and Wisdom join in the conclusion that the signature of the United States Attorney is essential to the validity of an indictment. Judge Brown, as appears in his separate opinion, is of the view that the United States Attorney is required, upon the request of the grand jury, to draft forms of indictments in accordance with its desires. The order before us for review is in the conjunctive; it requires the United States Attorney to prepare and sign. A majority of the court, having decided that the direction to sign is erroneous, the order on appeal will be reversed. . . .

RIVES, GEWIN and GRIFFIN B. BELL, Circuit Judges (concurring in part and dissenting in part):

[T]he basic issue before this Court is whether the controlling discretion as to the institution of a felony prosecution rests with the Attorney General or with the grand jury. The majority opinion would ignore the broad inquisitorial powers of the grand jury, and limit the constitutional requirement of Amendment V to the benefit of the accused.

We agree with Professor Orfield that:

‘The grand jury serves two great functions. One is to bring to trial persons accused of crime upon just grounds. The other is to protect persons against unfounded or malicious prosecutions by insuring that no criminal proceeding will be undertaken without a disinterested determination of probable guilt. The inquisitorial function has been called the more important. . . .

A federal grand jury has the unquestioned right to inquire into any matter within the jurisdiction involving violations of law and to return an indictment if it finds a reasonable probability that a crime has been committed. This it may do at the instance of the court, the District Attorney, the Attorney General or on its own initiative, from evidence it may gather or from knowledge of its members. . . .

The finding and return of the indictment are the acts of the grand jury. When United States Attorney prepares and signs an indictment, he does not adopt, approve, or vouch for the charge, nor does he institute a criminal prosecution. . . . The United States Attorney cannot, except in an advisory capacity, inquire into the merits of whether indictments should be found and returned in particular cases being considered by the grand jury. Only the grand jurors themselves have that power. It would be grossly wrong for it to be usurped. . . .

. . . The signature of the United States Attorney is a mere authentication that the indictment is the act of the grand jury. . . .

The Attorney General insists that the prosecution of offenses against the United States is an executive function of the Attorney General deraigned from the executive power vested in the President to "take care that the laws be faithfully executed." The short answer is that one of the most fundamental and important of the laws so to be faithfully executed is the clear and explicit provision of the Fifth Amendment to the Constitution that "No person shall be held to answer for a capital, or otherwise infamous crime, unless on a presentment or indictment of a Grand Jury."

Moreover, in point of law and reality, the plenary inquisitorial power of the grand jury does not impinge in the slightest upon the executive function of the Attorney General to prosecute or not to prosecute offenses against the United States, for as soon as the indictment is returned, "The Attorney General or the United States Attorney may by leave of court file a dismissal. . . ." Rule 48(a), F. R. Crim. P. . . .

The grand jury may be permitted to function in its traditional sphere, while at the same time enforcing the separation of powers doctrine as between the executive and judicial branches of the government. This can best be done, indeed, it is mandatory, by requiring the United States Attorney to assist the grand jury in preparing indictments which they wish to consider or return, and by requiring the United States Attorney to sign any indictment that is to be returned. Then, once the indictment is returned, the Attorney General or the United States Attorney can refuse to go forward. That refusal will, of course, be in open court and not in the secret confines of the grand jury room. To permit the district court to compel the United States Attorney to proceed beyond this point would invest prosecutorial power in the judiciary, power which under the Constitution is reserved to the executive branch of the government. It may be that the court, in the interest of justice, may require a showing of good faith, and a statement of some rational basis for dismissal. In the unlikely event of bad faith or irrational action, not here present, it may be that the court could appoint counsel to prosecute the case. In brief, the court may have the same inherent power to administer justice to the government as it does to the defendant. That question is not now before us and may never arise. Except for a very limited discretion, however, the court's power to withhold leave to dismiss an indictment is solely for the protection of the defendant. . . .

We agree that proper enforcement of the law does not require that indictments should be returned in every case where probable cause exists. Public policy may in some instances require that a case not be prosecuted. Such consideration of public policy may be submitted to and acted on by the grand jury. . . . In the few cases in which the United States Attorney is unable to persuade the grand jury and the Attorney General disagrees with its action, his recourse is not to prevent the grand jury from finding and returning an effective indictment, but to file a dismissal of the indictment under Rule 48(a), F. R. Crim. P. . . . [The executive decision to forego prosecution should not be made] in the shadows of secrecy, with the

Attorney General not being required to disclose his reasons. How much better is the constitutional system by which the grand jury can find and return an effective indictment upon which a prosecution for crime is instituted. At that point the power of the grand jury ceases. It is effectively checked and overbalanced by the power of the Attorney General, recognized in Rule 48(a), to move for a dismissal of the indictment. The court may then require such a motion to be heard in open court. Instead of a prevention in the shadows of secrecy, there would be a dismissal in a formal, public judicial proceeding. . . .

JOHN R. BROWN, Circuit Judge (concurring specially):

Mine is a middle course. I agree with the opinion written by Judge Jones that the District Attorney may not be compelled to sign the formal indictment which the Grand Jury has voted to return. . . . But I do not agree that the District Attorney may ignore the efforts of the Grand Jury to the point of declining to prepare in proper legal form the indictment they have voted to return. On the contrary, I am of the view that the Court may properly compel the District Attorney to act as legal scrivener to the Grand Jury. The Court may, therefore, order the District Attorney to prepare the indictment in legal form [but not to sign it.]. . .

Responsibility for determining whether a prosecution is to be commenced or maintained must be clearly fixed. The power not to initiate is indeed awesome. But it has to reside somewhere. And the more clearly pinpointed it is, the more the public interest is served through the focus of relentless publicity upon that decision. It may not, with safety, be left to a body whose great virtue is the combination of anonymity, transitory authority, and political unresponsibility.

All must be aware now that there are times when the interests of the nation require that a prosecution be foregone. These instances will most often be in the area of state secrets and national security. With stakes so high, the safety of our country, and hence the security of the world, ought not to be imperiled by leaving the important decision to a body having no definitive political responsibility. And it is hardly realistic to suggest, as do the dissenters, that these factors may be evaluated by the Grand Jury. What will be the source of their information? How extensive will it be? How close will a Grand Jury session approach a presidential cabinet meeting? How will essential government secrets be kept when disclosed to persons none of whom as Grand Jurors will have been subjected to customary security clearance checks?

And even in less sensitive areas, the practical operation of the prosecutorial function makes imperative the need for executive determination. The familiar example is the deliberate choice between those to be prosecuted and those who, often equally guilty, are named as co-conspirators but not as defendants, or others not named who are used as star government witnesses. And in other situations, of which the instant case may well be typical, the executive's purpose to effectuate specific policies thought to be of major importance would be frustrated or encumbered were a Grand Jury given the sole prerogative of determining when a prosecution is to be effectively commenced. . . .

Finally, it seems to me incongruous to assert, as do the dissenters, that the signing of the indictment is a ministerial act having no function other than one of authentication. . . . I do not see why an indictment formally signed by the foreman and reported in a solemn open court proceeding as the act of the Grand Jury needs "authentication." And I am at a complete loss to understand how the District

Attorney — excluded as he is from the Grand Jury while it is voting, — can "authenticate" from hearsay, or why his imprimatur is any better or different than that which would come from other Grand Jurors, each of whom can be polled by the Judge, not as to his vote, but whether a majority did vote to return the true bill. . . .

The fact is that the signature of the District Attorney has much more awesome consequence. Without a doubt that signature, together with that of the Grand Jury's foreman, is a formal, effective initiation of a prosecution. . . . With it, the whole prosecution has been started. And what was previously an unfettered discretionary right on the part of the executive not to initiate prosecution has now been set in motion and can be stopped only on the executive taking affirmative action for dismissal with all of the uncertainties which F. R. Crim. P. 48(a) generates.

But while I am firm that signature is a vital and significant act which reflects the exercise of an executive discretion to initiate prosecution — a thing here lacking — I am equally positive that the District Attorney has the duty to prepare the indictment when requested to do so by the Grand Jury. . . .

To me the thing seems this simple: the Grand Jury is charged to report. It determines what it is to report. It determines the form in which it reports. Once it determines that what it wants to report is to be in the form of a true bill indictment, it obviously needs legal help. . . . Although, as the Court holds, the "indictment" thus returned would be ineffective without the signature of the District Attorney, reporting its conclusion in traditional legal form would do two things. First, it would clearly reflect the conscientious conclusion of the Grand Jury itself. And, second, it would, at the same time, sharply reveal the difference of view as between the Grand Jury and the prosecuting attorney.

This leads to the second important reason. The powers of the Executive are so awesome in determining those whom it will not prosecute, that where there is a difference between the Grand Jury and the Executive, this determination and the resulting conflict of views should be revealed in open court. With great power comes great responsibility. Disclosure of this difference of view and the resulting impasse would subject this decision of the Executive to the scrutiny of an informed electorate. The issue would be clearly drawn and the responsibility, both legally and in the public mind, plainly fixed. There would not be the sort of thing reflected in this record in which only in the loosest way could the public see what it was the Grand Jury purposed to do and what the Executive declined to help it to do. . . .

By following this middle course we preserve fully the rightful independence of the Grand Jury in its inquisitorial role and the time-proved wisdom of the separation of powers which commits determination (and responsibility) to the Executive. . . .

WISDOM, Circuit Judge (concurring specially): . . .

The dissenters show judicial craftsmanship of the highest order in writing persuasively about 'the traditional sphere' of the grand jury while not turning up one case holding that a court may compel a prosecutor to prepare and sign a bill of indictment requested by a grand jury. Not one case in all the years between 1166 and 1965! I submit that the result reached in the dissent is the product of a misunderstanding of the historical meaning of "presentment and indictment," a failure to give effect to the difference between the sword and the shield of the grand jury, and an abstract approach that disregards the factual setting in which the issue is presented.

Nothing in the position of any of the judges in the majority "ignores" or tends to diminish the purely inquisitorial role of the federal grand jury. But when that role goes beyond inquiry and report and becomes accusatorial, no aura of traditional or constitutional sanctity surrounds the grand jury. The Grand Jury earned its place in the Bill of Rights by its shield, not by its sword.

I.

The Fifth Amendment requires the grand jury's "presentment or indictment" as a prerequisite to trial for a "capital, or otherwise infamous crime." This language provides no aid and comfort to the notion that either the grand jury or the court has the power to compel prosecution once the grand jury has exercised its accusatorial function. . . .

Historians usually trace the English grand jury back to the Assize of Clarendon issued by Henry II in 1166, based not on Anglo-Saxon antecedents but on Norman-French inquests. . . .

From its beginning until its abolition by Parliament in 1933, the English common law presenting jury could act on its own knowledge, or on the information of others, or on the Crown's written bill of indictment. But only when this bill was preferred to the grand jury by the Crown and endorsed as a 'true bill' was the accusation known as an indictment. This was the accepted usage when the Fifth Amendment was adopted. Blackstone explained:

> 'A presentment, generally taken, is a very comprehensive term; including not only presentments properly so called, but also inquisitions of office, and indictments by a grand jury. A presentment, properly speaking, is the notice taken by a grand jury of any offence from their own knowledge or observation, without any bill of indictment laid before them at the suit of the king. . . . An indictment is a written accusation of one or more persons of a crime or misdemeanor, preferred to, and presented upon oath by, a grand jury. . . . When the grand jury have heard the evidence, if they think it a groundless accusation, they used formerly to endorse on the back of the bill, 'ignoramus;' or, we know nothing of it; intimating, that though the facts might possibly be true, that truth did not appear to them: but now, they assert in English, more absolutely, 'not a true bill;' or (which is the better way) 'not found;' and then the party is discharged without farther answer. . . . If they are satisfied of the truth of the accusation, they then endorse upon it, 'a true bill,' antiently, 'billa vera.' The indictment is then said to be found, and the party stands indicted.'

The Fifth Amendment, therefore, does not offer a grand jury a choice between presentment or indictment. Unless there is a bill of indictment preferred to the grand jury at the instance of the Government, there can be no indictment. It is entirely in the hands of the Government whether to submit an accusation to the grand jury leading to presentment in the form of an indictment and serving as the initial pleading in a criminal prosecution. . . .

Presentment is a natural corollary to the grand jury's inquisitorial power, either for an inquisition of office or for a prosecutory purpose. Its use here would not accomplish its prosecutory purpose, because the Attorney General still could decline to submit a bill of indictment to the grand jury. On the other hand, in this case a presentment in open court with an appropriate minute entry would meet many of the objections to the government's position raised in the dissenting opinion and Judge Brown's opinion. . . . This use of presentment would be in accord with the established procedure in the common law and with the original understanding of the framers. . . .

In sum, there is nothing in my view or in that of the other judges in the majority that would, as the dissenting judges assert, authorize Government counsel to "radically reduce the powers of the grand jury." The grand jury never had a plenary power to indict. It had a limited power to indict — after accusation by the Crown or the Government in the form of a bill of indictment preferred to the grand jury. . . .

The decision of the majority does not affect the inquisitorial power of the grand jury. No one questions the jury's plenary power to inquire, to summon and interrogate witnesses, and to present either findings and a report or an accusation in open court by presentment.

Finally, the decision does not affect the power of the grand jury to shield suspected law violators. By refusing to indict, the grand jury has the unchallengeable power to defend the innocent from government oppression by unjust prosecution. And it has the equally unchallengeable power to shield the guilty, should the whims of the jurors or their conscious or subconscious response to community pressures induce twelve or more jurors to give sanctuary to the guilty.

II.

Because recognition of the grand jury's shield-like function is lodged in the Bill of Rights, the bedrock of basic rights, it is fair to say that national policy favors a liberal construction of the power of the grand jury to protect the individual against official tyranny. No such policy favors the grand jury in its accusatorial role. Accordingly, we look for and should expect to find a check on its unjust accusations similar to the grand jury's check on the government's unjust accusations.

[T]he framers wove a web of checks and balances designed to prevent abuse of power, regardless of the age, origin, and character of the institution. . . . [T]he power of the executive not to prosecute, and therefore not to take steps necessarily leading to prosecution, is the appropriate curb on a grand jury in keeping with the constitutional theory of checks and balances. Such a check is especially necessary, if there is any question of the grand jury's and the district court's being in agreement; if they differ, of course the district court may dismiss the grand jury. The need is rendered more acute if there is a possibility that community hostility against the suspected offenders, individually or as a race, may jeopardize justice before the petit jury. In short, if we give the same meaning to "presentment or indictment" that Madison and others gave to these terms when Madison introduced the Bill of Rights in the First Congress, the grand jury provision in the Bill of Rights cuts both ways: it prevents harassment and intimidation and oppression through unjust prosecution — by the Grand Jury or by the Government.

III.

The prosecution of offenses against the United States is an executive function within the exclusive prerogative of the Attorney General. . . . That official, the chief law-enforcement officer of the Federal Government is "the hand of the president in taking care that the laws of the United States in protection of the interests of the

United States in legal proceedings and in the prosecution of offenses be faithfully executed." . . .

"The district attorney has absolute control over criminal prosecutions, and can dismiss or refuse to prosecute, any of them at his discretion. The responsibility is wholly his." The determination of whether and when to prosecute "is a matter of policy for the prosecuting officer and not for the determination of the courts." As another court has stated it:

> All of these considerations point up the wisdom of vesting broad discretion in the United States Attorney. The federal courts are powerless to interfere with his discretionary power. The Court cannot compel him to prosecute a complaint, or even an indictment, whatever his reasons for not acting. The remedy for any dereliction of his duty lies, not with the courts, but, with the executive branch of our government and ultimately with the people.[a]

. . . Thus, "courts generally refuse to order the prosecutor to initiate a prosecution on the ground that it is a discretionary act which may not be compelled by mandamus." . . . Rule 7(c), requiring that the indictment be signed by the United States Attorney, preserves the prosecutor's traditional discretion as to whether to initiate prosecution.

The reason for vesting discretion to prosecute in the Executive, acting through the Attorney General is two-fold. First, in the interests of justice and the orderly, efficient administration of the law, some person or agency should be able to prevent an unjust prosecution. The freedom of the petit jury to bring in a verdict of not guilty and the progressive development of the law in the direction of making more meaningful the guarantees of an accused person's constitutional rights give considerable protection to the individual before and after trial. They do not protect against a baseless prosecution. This is a harassment to the accused and an expensive strain on the machinery of justice. The appropriate repository for authority to prevent a baseless prosecution is the chief law-enforcement officer whose duty, unlike the grand jury's duty, is to collect evidence on both sides of a case.

Second, when, within the context of law-enforcement, national policy is involved, because of national security, conduct of foreign policy, or a conflict between two branches of government, the appropriate branch to decide the matter is the executive branch. The executive is charged with carrying out national policy on law-enforcement and, generally speaking, is informed on more levels than the more specialized judicial and legislative branches. In such a situation, a decision not to prosecute is analogous to the exercise of executive privilege. The executive's absolute and exclusive discretion to prosecute may be rationalized as an illustration

---

a. In the hearing on the confirmation of Attorney General Jackson as Associate Justice of the Supreme Court, the nomination was attacked because of Jackson's failure to prosecute Drew Pearson and Robert S. Allen for criminal libel on Senator Tydings. Jackson had taken the position that it was the policy of the Department of Justice to avoid the criminal libel laws when the courts were open to the injured party in civil proceedings, and that prosecutions of this character would tend to impair freedom of the press. Republican Senator (now Mr. Justice) Burton stated:

> "The prosecuting attorney, being charged, as he is charged, with the great responsibility of deciding under the laws of the United States, the laws under which he is serving, whether a case should be prosecuted, owes a duty to himself, his community, and the Constitution to decide whether the case should be prosecuted. . . . In my judgment the Attorney General was within his rights when he declined to prosecute, and in stating the grounds as he did state them under the circumstances."

of the doctrine of separation of powers, but it would have evolved without the doctrine and exists in countries that do not purport to accept this doctrine. . . .

IV.

This brings me to the facts. They demonstrate, better than abstract principles or legal dicta, the imperative necessity that the United States, through its Attorney General, have uncontrollable discretion to prosecute.

The crucial fact here is that Goff and Kendrick, two Negroes, testified in a suit by the United States against the Registrar of Clarke County, Mississippi, and the State of Mississippi, to enforce the voting rights of Negroes under the Fourteenth Amendment and the Civil Rights Act.

Goff and Kendrick testified that some seven years earlier at Stonewall, Mississippi, the registrar had refused to register them or give them application forms. They said that they had seen white persons registering, one of whom was a B. Floyd Jones. Ramsey, the registrar, testified that Jones had not registered at that time or place, but had registered the year before in Enterprise, Mississippi. He testified also that he had never discriminated against Negro applicants for registration.[b] Jones testified that he was near the registration table in Stonewall in 1955, had talked with the registrar, and had shaken hands with him. The presiding judge, Judge W. Harold Cox, stated from the bench that Goff and Kendrick should be "bound over to await the action of the grand jury for perjury."[c]

In January 1963 attorneys of the Department of Justice requested the Federal Bureau of Investigation to investigate the possible perjury. The FBI completed a full investigation in March 1963 and referred the matter to the Department's Criminal Division. In June 1963 the Criminal Division advised the local United States Attorney, Mr. Hauberg, that the matter presented "no basis for a perjury prosecution." Mr. Hauberg informed Judge Cox of the Department's decision. Judge Cox stated that in his view the matter was clearly one for the grand jury and that he would be inclined, if necessary, to appoint an outside attorney to present the matter to the grand jury. (I find no authority for a federal judge to displace the United States Attorney by appointing a special prosecutor.) On receiving this information, the

---

b. Judge Cox found 'as a fact from the evidence that negro citizens have been discriminated against by the registrar', although he found also that there was 'no pattern or practice of discrimination.' In its original opinion in the *Ramsey* case this Court noted the 'testimony which witness by witness convicts Ramsey of palpable discrimination.' In his opinion Judge Rives noted that 'This case reveals gross and flagrant denials of the rights of Negro citizens to vote.' And on rehearing, this Court ruled that the finding that 'there was no pattern or practice in the discrimination by the Registrar' was 'clearly erroneous.' No one has suggested that Mr. Ramsey may have been guilty of perjury.

c. When counsel for the State, Mr. Riddell, completed Mr. Ramsey's direct examination, and before his cross-examination, respondent Judge W. Harold Cox, who was presiding, stated:

'I want to hear from the government about why this Court shouldn't require this Negro Reverend W.G. Goff and his companion Kendrick to show cause why they shouldn't be bound over to await the action of the grand jury for perjury. I want to hear from you on that.

'I think they ought to be put under about a $3,000.00 bond each to await the action of a grand jury. Unless I change my mind that is going to be the order.' 'BY MR. STERN (Government counsel): I will be happy to reconcile their testimony. 'BY THE COURT: I just want these Negroes to know that they can't come into this Court and swear to something as important as that was and is and get by with it. I don't care who brings them here. 'BY MR. STERN: I understand. 'BY THE COURT: Yes sir. And I mean that for whites alike, but I am talking about the case at hand. I just don't intend to put up with perjury. . . .'

Criminal Division again reviewed its files and concluded that the charge of perjury could not be sustained. General Katzenbach, then Deputy Attorney General, after reviewing the files, concurred in the Criminal Division's decision. In September 1963 General Katzenbach called on Judge Cox as a courtesy to explain why the Department had arrived at the conclusion that no perjury was involved. Judge Cox, unconvinced, requested the United States Attorney to present to the grand jury the Goff and Kendrick cases, which he regarded as cases of "palpable perjury."

In October 1963 Goff and Kendrick were arrested, jailed for two days, and placed on a $3,000 bond for violations of State law for falsely testifying in federal court. After their indictment by a state grand jury, the Department of Justice filed suit against the State District Attorney, seeking to enjoin the state prosecution on the grounds that: (1) the States have no authority to prosecute for alleged perjury committed while testifying in a federal court; (2) the purpose and effect of the State's prosecution was to threaten and intimidate Goff and Kendrick and to inhibit them and other Negroes from registering to vote. The district court (per Mize, J.) ruled in favor of the United States. . . .

Against the backdrop of Mississippi versus the Nation in the field of civil rights, we have a heated but bona fide difference of opinion between Judge Cox and the Attorney General as to whether two Negroes, Goff and Kendrick, should be prosecuted for perjury. Taking a narrow view of the case, we would be justified in holding that the Attorney General's implied powers, by analogy to the express powers of Rule 48(a), give him discretion to prosecute. Here there was a bona fide, reasonable exercise of discretion made after a full investigation and long consideration of the case — both sides of the case, not just the evidence tending to show guilt. If the grand jury is dissatisfied with that administrative decision, it may exercise its inquisitorial power and make a presentment in open court. It could be said, that is all there is to the case. But there is more to the case.

This Court, along with everyone else, knows that Goff and Kendrick, if prosecuted, run the risk of being tried in a climate of community hostility. They run the risk of a punishment that may not fit the crime. The Registrar, who provoked the original litigation, runs no risk, notwithstanding the fact that the district court, in effect, found that Ramsay did not tell the truth on the witness stand. In these circumstances, the very least demands of justice require that the discretion to prosecute be lodged with a person or agency insulated from local prejudices and parochial pressures. This is not the hard case that makes bad law. . . . This case is unusual only for the clarity with which the facts, speaking for themselves, illuminate the imperative necessity in American Federalism that the discretion to prosecute be lodged in the Attorney General of United States.

The decision not to prosecute represents the exercise of a discretion analogous to the exercise of executive privilege. As a matter of law, the Attorney General has concluded that there is not sufficient evidence to prove perjury. As a matter of fact, the Attorney General has concluded that trial for perjury would have the effect of inhibiting not only Goff and Kendrick but other Negroes in Mississippi from registering to vote. There is a conflict, therefore, between society's interest in law enforcement (diluted in this case by the Attorney General's conclusion that the evidence does not support the charge of guilt) and the national policy, set forth in the Constitution and the Civil Rights Acts, of outlawing racial discrimination. It is unthinkable that resolution of this important conflict affecting the whole Nation should lie with a majority of twenty-three members of a jury chosen from the

Southern District of Mississippi. The nature of American Federalism, looking to the differences between the Constitution and the Articles of Confederation, requires that the power to resolve this question lies in the unfettered discretion of the President of United States or his deputy for law enforcement, the Attorney General. . . .

Discussion

1. *Just the facts, ma'am.* Ordinarily, judicial opinions open with the facts. Yet Judge Jones's plurality opinion offers a rather thin rendition of the facts; and Judge Wisdom puts the facts at the end of his opinion. What accounts for this? It is important to understand that every narrative of facts in an opinion or brief or other legal document is unavoidably selective; lawyers and judges must decide which of the infinite number of real-world facts are legally relevant to the case at hand — and to do this (or at least, to do this well), they must obviously have a legal theory that explains why some facts are relevant and others are not. Which, if any, of the facts at the end of Judge Wisdom's opinion, do you think were legally relevant? (Would your legal view of the case be different if a multiracial grand jury were seeking to indict a white lynch mob, and a white supremacist Attorney General were balking?)

2. *Construing statutes in the shadow of constitutional principles.* Note the intricate interplay between issues of statutory construction under Rules 7 and 48, and issues of constitutional principle under Articles II and III and the Fifth Amendment. A good deal of American-style "judicial review" occurs not when judges wheel out the Constitution to strike down a law, but when they invoke it more subtly to inflect their readings of statutes, regulations, ordinances, rules, and the like.

3. *Jury service and voting.* Note that the grand jury in *Cox* was doubtless all white; very few blacks served on Mississippi juries in 1965 because very few blacks were permitted to vote in that state at that time. See South Carolina v. Katzenbach, supra p. 572. Of course, this vicious cycle of jury exclusion and voting was precisely what civil rights activists and the Attorney General were trying to break by proving, for example, the voting rights violations of Mississippi registrars.

4. *The Cold War imperative.* How important were issues of foreign policy in shaping the President's response to domestic issues of race policy and prosecution policy? Consider the arguments of Professors Dudziak and Bell that these issues were tightly intertwined. America in the 1950s and 1960s was locked in a global struggle against Communism, with Asia, Africa, Central America, and South America as major ideological battlegrounds. To win this war, America needed to win the hearts and minds of "colored" persons around the globe; but the mistreatment of blacks in places like Mississippi — gleefully publicized by America's enemies — threatened to undermine America's efforts abroad. Even Presidents unmoved by considerations of justice had to pay attention, Dudziak and Bell argue. See Mary L. Dudziak, Desegregation as a Cold War Imperative, 41 Stan. L. Rev. 61 (1988); Mary L. Dudziak, The Little Rock Crisis and Foreign Affairs: Race, Resistance, and the Image of American Democracy, 70 S. Cal. L. Rev. 1641 (1997); Derrick A. Bell, Jr., Brown v. Board of Education and the Interest-Convergence Dilemma, 93 Harv. L. Rev. 518 (1980); see also Michael J. Klarman, *Brown*, Racial Change, and The Civil Rights Movement, 80 Va. L. Rev. 7 (1994). See also the discussion of *Brown* and the Cold War in Chapter 6.

5. *Prosecutions, presentments, publicity, and pardons.* Although the executive is often said to have the power of "prosecutorial" discretion, the power is better described as one of "nonprosecutorial" discretion — the discretionary and plenary power *not* to prosecute. This is the power upheld by *Cox* — the courts may not compel or mandamus a prosecution, and neither may a grand jury. Conversely, the President's power to affirmatively prosecute can rather easily be thwarted by grand juries and courts; the former may simply refuse to agree to an indictment, and the latter may always throw the case out.

Of course plenary power not to prosecute is capable of great abuse. But does *Cox* persuade you of some of the reasons why the power should exist — why not all crimes can or should be prosecuted, and why complete power to say no should reside in the executive branch? Note how all the judges propose *publicity* as the main check on this power — though at different stages of the game. Judge Wisdom points to the power of publicity early on — the grand jury's power to make known that it thinks something stinks, via a public presentment or report. For historical background on this key presentment power, see Akhil Reed Amar, The Bill of Rights: Creation and Reconstruction 19, 84-87 (1998). For a fascinating discussion of a recent grand jury's efforts to publicize perceived wrongdoing in Rocky Flats, Colorado, and a more general modern-day analysis of the presentment power, see Renee B. Lettow, Note, Reviving Federal Grand Jury Presentments, 103 Yale L.J. 1333 (1994). Judge Brown picks a slightly different mechanism of publicity, in his decision that the prosecutor must help the grand jury draft the document it seeks to publicize. The dissenters opt for a later point — in open court after the (forcibly signed) indictment has been filed. And note that even if judges were to somehow invoke Rule 48 to prevent the prosecutor from dismissing the indictment at that point, the President himself always retains the power to say no — decisively — via the pardon power vested in him by Article II. The exercise of this power of course is highly visible, satisfying the functional need to focus responsibility for controversial or dubious exercises of the power of nonprosecution. Recall that a Presidential pardon may issue well before any trial or conviction, as Hamilton pointed out in the Federalist No. 69 — and as the more famous facts surrounding our next case should remind us.

UNITED STATES v. NIXON, PRESIDENT OF THE UNITED STATES
418 U.S. 683 (1974)

Burger, C.J. . . .
On March 1, 1974, a grand jury of the United States District Court for the District of Columbia returned an indictment charging seven named individuals[a] with various offenses, including conspiracy to defraud the United States and to obstruct justice. Although he was not designated as such in the indictment, the

---

a. The seven defendants were John N. Mitchell, H. R. Haldeman, John D. Ehrlichman, Charles W. Colson, Robert C. Mardian, Kenneth W. Parkinson, and Gordon Strachan. Each had occupied either a position of responsibility on the White House staff or a position with the Committee for the Re-election of the President. [John Mitchell, for example, had served as Richard Nixon's Attorney General — eds.]

grand jury named the President, among others, as an unindicted coconspirator.[b] On April 18, 1974, upon motion of the Special Prosecutor, see n. [c], infra, a subpoena duces tecum was issued . . . to the President by the United States District Court and made returnable on May 2, 1974. This subpoena required the production, in advance of the September 9 trial date, of certain tapes, memoranda, papers, transcripts, or other writings relating to certain precisely identified meetings [in the Oval Office] between the President and others. . . . On April 30, the President publicly released edited transcripts of 43 conversations; portions of 20 conversations subject to subpoena in the present case were included. On May 1, 1974, the President's counsel filed a "special appearance" and a motion to quash the subpoena [on the ground that the subpoenaed materials were within his executive privilege against disclosure of confidential communications]. . . .

II.   Justiciability

In the District Court, the President's counsel argued that the court lacked jurisdiction to issue the subpoena because the matter was an intra-branch dispute between a subordinate and superior officer of the Executive Branch and hence not subject to judicial resolution. That argument has been renewed in this Court with emphasis on the contention that the dispute does not present a "case" or "controversy" which can be adjudicated in the federal courts. The President's counsel argues that the federal courts should not intrude into areas committed to the other branches of Government. He views the present dispute as essentially a "jurisdictional" dispute within the Executive Branch which he analogizes to a dispute between two congressional committees. Since the Executive Branch has exclusive authority and absolute discretion to decide whether to prosecute a case, Confiscation Cases, 7 Wall. 454 (1869); United States v. Cox, it is contended that a President's decision is final in determining what evidence is to be used in a given criminal case. Although his counsel concedes that the President has delegated certain specific powers to the Special Prosecutor, he has not "waived nor delegated to the Special Prosecutor the President's duty to claim privilege as to all materials . . . which fall within the President's inherent authority to refuse to disclose to any executive officer." The Special Prosecutor's demand for the items therefore presents, in the view of the President's counsel, a political question under Baker v. Carr, 369 U.S. 186 (1962), since it involves a "textually demonstrable" grant of power under Art. II. . . .

Our starting point is the nature of the proceeding for which the evidence is sought — here a pending criminal prosecution. It is a judicial proceeding in a federal court alleging violation of federal laws and is brought in the name of the United States as sovereign. Under the authority of Art. II, §2, Congress has vested in the Attorney General the power to conduct the criminal litigation of the United States Government. It has also vested in him the power to appoint subordinate officers to assist him in the discharge of his duties. Acting pursuant to those statutes, the Attorney General has delegated the authority to represent the United States in

---

b. The cross-petition . . . raised the issue whether the grand jury acted within its authority in naming the President as an unindicted coconspirator. [W]e find resolution of this issue unnecessary to resolution of the question whether the claim of privilege is to prevail . . . [footnote relocated by editors].

c. The regulation issued by the Attorney General pursuant to his statutory authority, vests in the Special Prosecutor plenary authority to control the course of investigations and litigation related to "all offenses arising out of the 1972 Presidential Election . . . , allegations involving the President, members

these particular matters to a Special Prosecutor with unique authority and tenure.[c] The regulation gives the Special Prosecutor explicit power to contest the invocation of executive privilege in the process of seeking evidence deemed relevant to the performance of these specially delegated duties.[d] So long as this regulation is extant it has the force of law. In United States *ex rel.* Accardi v. Shaughnessy, 347 U.S. 260 (1954), regulations of the Attorney General delegated certain of his discretionary powers to the Board of Immigration Appeals and required that Board to exercise its own discretion on appeals in deportation cases. The Court held that so long as the Attorney General's regulations remained operative, he denied himself the authority to exercise the discretion delegated to the Board even though the original authority was his and he could reassert it by amending the regulations. . . .

Here, as in *Accardi*, it is theoretically possible for the Attorney General to amend or revoke the regulation defining the Special Prosecutor's authority. But he has not done so.[e] So long as this regulation remains in force the Executive Branch is bound by it, and indeed the United States as the sovereign composed of the three branches is bound to respect and to enforce it. Moreover, the delegation of authority to the Special Prosecutor in this case is not an ordinary delegation by the Attorney General to a subordinate officer: with the authorization of the President, the Acting Attorney General provided in the regulation that the Special Prosecutor was not to be removed without the "consensus" of eight designated leaders of Congress. n. [c], supra. . . .

IV.   THE CLAIM OF PRIVILEGE

A

[W]e turn to the claim that the subpoena should be quashed because it demands "confidential conversations between a President and his close advisors that it would be inconsistent with the public interest to produce." The first contention is a broad claim that the separation of powers doctrine precludes judicial review of a President's claim of privilege. The second contention is that if he does not prevail

[handwritten margin notes:]
1. Courts can't review exec. priv.
2. If they can, they should find that priv. prevails

---

of the White House staff, or Presidential appointees . . ." In particular, the Special Prosecutor was given full authority, inter alia, "to contest the assertion of 'Executive Privilege' . . ." The regulation then goes on to provide:

". . . In accordance with assurances given by the President to the Attorney General that the President will not exercise his Constitutional powers to effect the discharge of the Special Prosecutor or to limit the independence that he is hereby given, the Special Prosecutor will not be removed from his duties except for extraordinary improprieties on his part and without the President's first consulting the Majority and the Minority Leaders and Chairmen and ranking Minority Members of the Judiciary Committees of the Senate and House of Representatives and ascertaining that their consensus is in accord with his proposed action."

d. That this was the understanding of Acting Attorney General Robert Bork, the author of the regulation establishing the independence of the Special Prosecutor, is shown by his testimony before the Senate Judiciary Committee. . . . Acting Attorney General Bork gave similar assurances to the House Subcommittee on Criminal Justice. . . . At his confirmation hearings, Attorney General William Saxbe testified that he shared Acting Attorney General Bork's views concerning the Special Prosecutor's authority to test any claim of executive privilege in the courts.

e. At his confirmation hearings, Attorney General William Saxbe testified that he agreed with the regulation adopted by Acting Attorney General Bork and would not remove the Special Prosecutor except for "gross impropriety." There is no contention here that the Special Prosecutor is guilty of any such impropriety.

on the claim of absolute privilege, the court should hold as a matter of constitutional law that the privilege prevails over the subpoena duces tecum.

In the performance of assigned constitutional duties each branch of the Government must initially interpret the Constitution, and the interpretation of its powers by any branch is due great respect from the others. The President's counsel, as we have noted, reads the Constitution as providing an absolute privilege of confidentiality for all Presidential communications. Many decisions of this Court, however, have unequivocally reaffirmed the holding of Marbury v. Madison, that "[it] is emphatically the province and duty of the judicial department to say what the law is." No holding of the Court has defined the scope of judicial power specifically relating to the enforcement of a subpoena for confidential Presidential communications for use in a criminal prosecution, but other exercises of power by the Executive Branch and the Legislative Branch have been found invalid as in conflict with the Constitution. Powell v. McCormack, Youngstown Sheet & Tube Co. v. Sawyer. . . .

. . . "Deciding whether a matter has in any measure been committed by the Constitution to another branch of government, or whether the action of that branch exceeds whatever authority has been committed, is itself a delicate exercise in constitutional interpretation, and is a responsibility of this Court as ultimate interpreter of the Constitution."

Notwithstanding the deference each branch must accord the others, the "judicial Power of the United States" vested in the federal courts by Art. III, §1, of the Constitution can no more be shared with the Executive Branch than the Chief Executive, for example, can share with the Judiciary the veto power, or the Congress share with the Judiciary the power to override a Presidential veto. Any other conclusion would be contrary to the basic concept of separation of powers and the checks and balances that flow from the scheme of a tripartite government. We therefore reaffirm that it is the province and duty of this Court "to say what the law is" with respect to the claim of privilege presented in this case. Marbury.

B

In support of his claim of absolute privilege, the President's counsel urges two grounds, one of which is common to all governments and one of which is peculiar to our system of separation of powers. The first ground is the valid need for protection of communications between high Government officials and those who advise and assist them in the performance of their manifold duties; the importance of this confidentiality is too plain to require further discussion. Human experience teaches that those who expect public dissemination of their remarks may well temper candor with a concern for appearances and for their own interests to the detriment of the decisionmaking process.[f] Whatever the nature of the privilege of confidentiality of Presidential communications in the exercise of Art. II powers, the privilege can be said to derive from the supremacy of each branch within its own assigned area of constitutional duties. Certain powers and privileges flow from the

---

f. There is nothing novel about governmental confidentiality. The meetings of the Constitutional Convention in 1787 were conducted in complete privacy. Moreover, all records of those meetings were sealed for more than 30 years after the Convention. Most of the Framers acknowledged that without secrecy no constitution of the kind that was developed could have been written.

g. The Special Prosecutor argues that there is no provision in the Constitution for a Presidential privilege as to the President's communications corresponding to the privilege of Members of Congress

nature of enumerated powers;[g] the protection of the confidentiality of Presidential communications has similar constitutional underpinnings.

The second ground asserted by the President's counsel in support of the claim of absolute privilege rests on the doctrine of separation of powers. Here it is argued that the independence of the Executive Branch within its own sphere, insulates a President from a judicial subpoena in an ongoing criminal prosecution, and thereby protects confidential Presidential communications.

However, neither the doctrine of separation of powers, nor the need for confidentiality of high-level communications, without more, can sustain an absolute, unqualified Presidential privilege of immunity from judicial process under all circumstances. The President's need for complete candor and objectivity from advisers calls for great deference from the courts. However, when the privilege depends solely on the broad, undifferentiated claim of public interest in the confidentiality of such conversations, a confrontation with other values arises. Absent a claim of need to protect military, diplomatic, or sensitive national security secrets, we find it difficult to accept the argument that even the very important interest in confidentiality of Presidential communications is significantly diminished by production of such material for in camera inspection with all the protection that a district court will be obliged to provide.

The impediment that an absolute, unqualified privilege would place in the way of the primary constitutional duty of the Judicial Branch to do justice in criminal prosecutions would plainly conflict with the function of the courts under Art. III. . . .

C

Since we conclude that the legitimate needs of the judicial process may outweigh Presidential privilege, it is necessary to resolve those competing interests in a manner that preserves the essential functions of each branch. The right and indeed the duty to resolve that question does not free the Judiciary from according high respect to the representations made on behalf of the President. United States v. Burr, 25 F. Cas. 187, 190, 191-192 (No. 14,694) (CC Va. 1807).

The expectation of a President to the confidentiality of his conversations and correspondence, like the claim of confidentiality of judicial deliberations, for example, has all the values to which we accord deference for the privacy of all citizens and, added to those values, is the necessity for protection of the public interest in candid, objective, and even blunt or harsh opinions in Presidential decisionmaking. A President and those who assist him must be free to explore alternatives in the process of shaping policies and making decisions and to do so in a way many would be unwilling to express except privately. These are the considerations justifying a presumptive privilege for Presidential communications. The privilege is fundamental to the operation of Government and inextricably rooted in the separation of powers under the Constitution. . . . We agree with Mr. Chief Justice Marshall's observation, therefore, that "[in] no case of this kind would a court be required to proceed against the president as against an ordinary individual." United States v. Burr.

---

under the Speech or Debate Clause. But the silence of the Constitution on this score is not dispositive. "The rule of constitutional interpretation announced in *McCulloch*, that that which was reasonably appropriate and relevant to the exercise of a granted power was to be considered as accompanying the grant, has been so universally applied that it suffices merely to state it."

But this presumptive privilege must be considered in light of our historic commitment to the rule of law. This is nowhere more profoundly manifest than in our view that "the twofold aim [of criminal justice] is that guilt shall not escape or innocence suffer." . . . The ends of criminal justice would be defeated if judgments were to be founded on a partial or speculative presentation of the facts. The very integrity of the judicial system and public confidence in the system depend on full disclosure of all the facts, within the framework of the rules of evidence. To ensure that justice is done, it is imperative to the function of courts that compulsory process be available for the production of evidence needed either by the prosecution or by the defense.

Only recently the Court restated the ancient proposition of law, albeit in the context of a grand jury inquiry rather than a trial, "that 'the public . . . has a right to every man's evidence,' except for those persons protected by a constitutional, common-law, or statutory privilege." The privileges referred to by the Court are designed to protect weighty and legitimate competing interests. Thus, the Fifth Amendment to the Constitution provides that no man "shall be compelled in any criminal case to be a witness against himself." And, generally, an attorney or a priest may not be required to disclose what has been revealed in professional confidence. These and other interests are recognized in law by privileges against forced disclosure, established in the Constitution, by statute, or at common law. Whatever their origins, these exceptions to the demand for every man's evidence are not lightly created nor expansively construed, for they are in derogation of the search for truth.

In this case the President . . . does not place his claim of privilege on the ground they are military or diplomatic secrets. As to these areas of Art. II duties the courts have traditionally shown the utmost deference to Presidential responsibilities. In C. & S. Air Lines v. Waterman S. S. Corp., 333 U.S. 103, 111 (1948), dealing with Presidential authority involving foreign policy considerations, the Court said:

> "The President, both as Commander-in-Chief and as the Nation's organ for foreign affairs, has available intelligence services whose reports are not and ought not to be published to the world. It would be intolerable that courts, without the relevant information, should review and perhaps nullify actions of the Executive taken on information properly held secret."

In United States v. Reynolds, 345 U.S. 1 (1953), dealing with a claimant's demand for evidence in a Tort Claims Act case against the Government, the Court said:

> "It may be possible to satisfy the court, from all the circumstances of the case, that there is a reasonable danger that compulsion of the evidence will expose military matters which, in the interest of national security, should not be divulged. When this is the case, the occasion for the privilege is appropriate, and the court should not jeopardize the security which the privilege is meant to protect by insisting upon an examination of the evidence, even by the judge alone, in chambers."

No case of the Court, however, has extended this high degree of deference to a President's generalized interest in confidentiality. Nowhere in the Constitution, as we have noted earlier, is there any explicit reference to a privilege of confidentiality, yet to the extent this interest relates to the effective discharge of a President's powers, it is constitutionally based.

The right to the production of all evidence at a criminal trial similarly has constitutional dimensions. The Sixth Amendment explicitly confers upon every defendant in a criminal trial the right "to be confronted with the witnesses against him" and "to have compulsory process for obtaining witnesses in his favor." Moreover, the Fifth Amendment also guarantees that no person shall be deprived of liberty without due process of law. It is the manifest duty of the courts to vindicate those guarantees, and to accomplish that it is essential that all relevant and admissible evidence be produced.

In this case we must weigh the importance of the general privilege of confidentiality of Presidential communications in performance of the President's responsibilities against the inroads of such a privilege on the fair administration of criminal justice. The interest in preserving confidentiality is weighty indeed and entitled to great respect. However, we cannot conclude that advisers will be moved to temper the candor of their remarks by the infrequent occasions of disclosure because of the possibility that such conversations will be called for in the context of a criminal prosecution.

On the other hand, the allowance of the privilege to withhold evidence that is demonstrably relevant in a criminal trial would cut deeply into the guarantee of due process of law and gravely impair the basic function of the courts. . . . Without access to specific facts a criminal prosecution may be totally frustrated. The President's broad interest in confidentiality of communications will not be vitiated by disclosure of a limited number of conversations preliminarily shown to have some bearing on the pending criminal cases.

We conclude that when the ground for asserting privilege as to subpoenaed materials sought for use in a criminal trial is based only on the generalized interest in confidentiality, it cannot prevail over the fundamental demands of due process of law in the fair administration of criminal justice. The generalized assertion of privilege must yield to the demonstrated, specific need for evidence in a pending criminal trial. . . .

We now turn to the important question of the District Court's responsibilities in conducting the in camera examination of Presidential materials or communications delivered under the compulsion of the subpoena duces tecum.

E

. . . Statements that meet the test of admissibility and relevance must be isolated; all other material must be excised. . . . It is elementary that in camera inspection of evidence is always a procedure calling for scrupulous protection against any release or publication of material not found by the court, at that stage, probably admissible in evidence and relevant to the issues of the trial for which it is sought. That being true of an ordinary situation, it is obvious that the District Court has a very heavy responsibility to see to it that Presidential conversations, which are either not relevant or not admissible, are accorded that high degree of respect due the President of the United States. Mr. Chief Justice Marshall, sitting as a trial judge in the *Burr* case, supra, was extraordinarily careful to point out that "[in] no case of this kind would a court be required to proceed against the president as against an ordinary individual."

. . . The need for confidentiality even as to idle conversations with associates in which casual reference might be made concerning political leaders within the country or foreign statesmen is too obvious to call for further treatment. We have no doubt that the District Judge will at all times accord to Presidential records that high degree of deference suggested in United States v. Burr, supra, and will discharge his responsibility to see to it that until released to the Special Prosecutor no in camera material is revealed to anyone. This burden applies with even greater force to excised material; once the decision is made to excise, the material is restored to its privileged status and should be returned under seal to its lawful custodian.

Mr. Justice REHNQUIST took no part in the consideration or decision of these cases.

Discussion

1. *Article II hierarchy and justiciability.* The Court in passing analogizes the dispute between Richard Nixon and Leon Jaworski to one between two congressional committees, but wasn't it more akin to a dispute between the Senate and a staffer, or the Court and a law clerk? Constitutionally, Nixon was *Chief* Executive, and the special prosecutor was an executive-branch *inferior* officer, who had been hand-picked by the Attorney General, who in turn had been handpicked by the President. Moreover, Nixon had been elected by the nation, whereas Jaworski and his prede-cessor Archibald Cox had not even been confirmed by the Senate. Why does the Court downplay this obvious hierarchy? Given that Jaworski was nothing more than Nixon's subordinate, wouldn't a more accurate case caption have been Nixon (infe-rior) v. Nixon (real)? If so, how was this dispute justiciable? If Jaworski wanted the tapes disclosed for good executive-branch reasons (the need to prosecute criminals) and Nixon wanted the tapes kept secret for good executive-branch reasons (the need for Oval Office confidentiality), why shouldn't the *Chief* Executive ordinarily and obviously have the last word on this dispute about executive-branch policy?

2. *Presentments, publicity, politics, and prosecutions.* The Court's answer leans heavily on the fact that the Nixon Administration had lawfully delegated certain powers to the Special Prosecutor. But the Court also concedes that the Nixon Administration is free simply to rescind the regulation unilaterally — and *then,* Nixon could tell Jaworski what to do or where to go. Thus, the Court admits that at the end of the day, Nixon does legally have the last word — but only if he first (through his Attorney General) rescinds the regulation. Why are the Justices insisting that Nixon jump through two hoops? Why isn't it enough that in their very courtroom, the President was clearly saying that he disagreed with his inferior about the proper discharge of executive-branch business?

The best answer is one the Court never states forthrightly: Richard Nixon was a crook, using the Oval Office as the hub of an ongoing criminal conspiracy to obstruct justice, and the Court already had evidence under seal that proved this. If Nixon wanted to fire or countermand Jaworksi, he would not get a finger of support from the Justices; he would have to do it himself (twice) at high noon on Main Street, for all to see. There is an obvious connection here to the publicity idea of *Cox*; in effect, the Court is forcing Nixon to attempt his whitewash in broad daylight. Politically, of course, this put Nixon in an impossible position, after he and his Administration had assured the people, the press, and the Congress that he would not fire Jaworski the way he had fired Archibald Cox, in the notorious "Saturday Night Massacre." Note how the Court subtly relies on these representa-tions in its opinion. Note also how the grand jury, by naming Nixon as an "unin-dicted" coconspirator, in effect issued a kind of presentment, which (when leaked) had precisely the publicity effect predicted by Judge Wisdom in *Cox*.

3. *Pardon me?* Putting aside rescission of the regulation, are there any other ways in which Richard Nixon could, a la Coase, have somehow "contracted around" the result in the Tapes Case? (See supra, p. 540, discussing the Coase Theorem.) Note that even after the Justices' decision, Nixon in theory retained the power to pardon Mitchell, Haldeman, Erlichman, et al. Had he done so, the pending criminal lawsuits against these defendants would have evaporated, and so too would the specific subpoenas these lawsuits had generated. Of course, such high-visibility pardons would doubtless have immediately led to a complete collapse of Nixon's political base. Impeachment proceedings — already well underway when the Justices sat — would surely have accelerated, and Congress in these proceedings would have demanded the tapes, and treated any refusal to hand them over as *itself* an impeachable offense. (Note that the Constitution explicitly denies the President the power to pardon in a case of impeachment.) These theoretical possibilities remind us that the legal decision in the Supreme Court was nested in a broader political and constitutional context in which the President retained certain formal legal powers that, politically, were unavailable to him.

Instead of pardoning or rescinding, Nixon chose to comply with the Court's order, and when the tapes came out, they quickly led to Nixon's resignation. Soon thereafter, newly installed President Gerald Ford issued a full (and highly visible) pardon to Nixon; but Ford paid a heavy political price — many believe that this cost him the election against Jimmy Carter in 1976.

4. *The legislative veto problem.* Chief Justice Burger claims that the regulation vesting Jaworski with various powers has "the force of law." But as a law, it seems constitutionally suspect, vesting certain congressional barons with a legislative veto over an inherently executive decision whether to fire a wholly executive-branch official. As President Washington and Congressman Madison helped establish early on, in one of the most important constitutional settlements of the early Republic, the President alone decides whom to fire within the executive branch; Congress members can jawbone, but cannot legally obstruct any purely executive-branch removal. To be sure, later political disputes muddied the waters — Andrew Johnson in 1868 was impeached by the House and nearly convicted by the Senate when he fired the Secretary of War without Senate approval. But early in the twentieth century, the Court emphatically endorsed President Washington's view in the landmark case of Myers v. United States, 272 U.S. 52 (1926). Authored by Chief Justice (and former President and Yale Law Professor) William Howard Taft, *Myers* stood as a towering precedent in 1974, when *Nixon* was decided. If anything, *Myers*'s condemnation of legislative vetoes stands even taller today, in light of the 1983 *Chadha* case, the 1986 *Bowsher* case, and the 1988 *Morrison* case, infra pp. 661, 773, and 796, all of which reiterated its teaching on this point. Consider also what the *Nixon* Court itself says only a few pages after treating this regulation as "law":

> [T]he "judicial Power of the United States" vested in the federal courts by Art. III, §1, of the Constitution can no more be shared with the Executive Branch than the Chief Executive, for example, can share with the Judiciary the veto power, or the Congress share with the Judiciary the power to override a Presidential veto. Any other conclusion would be contrary to the basic concept of separation of powers. . . .

How, it might be asked, is it any different if the President seeks as a matter of law to share the removal power with Congress?

If the Nixon regulation could not properly count as "law" in a courtroom, what function did it serve? A political scientist would probably see this regulation as a read-my-lips political promise designed for public consumption more than judicial doctrine; through this "regulation," Nixon was precommitting himself politically, credibly guaranteeing that if he later violated this promise he would pay a huge political penalty.

5. *The meaning of* Marbury. Does *Marbury* stand for the proposition that the Supreme Court is "the ultimate interpreter of the Constitution"? If so, where does Chief Justice Marshall say that? If not, where does the modern Court get this idea? (Note that this specific phrase itself makes its first appearance in *U.S. Reports* in 1962.) Does *Marbury* mean that the Constitution should never be read as decisively committing certain issues to the political branches? Does *Marbury* mean that other branches must defer to the Court even if they have a more expansive vision of the constitutional right in question? For example, suppose that a newspaper reporter, subpoenaed to provide information given to her by a confidential source, refuses to comply, claiming that she has a reporter's privilege under the First Amendment. If the Supreme Court were to reject her argument, would *Marbury* mean that the President *must* allow his subordinates to prosecute her, even if he agrees with her position? Cf. Judge Wisdom's opinion in *Cox*, supra p. 742 at note a (discussing nonprosecution policy of Attorney General Robert Jackson). Would *Marbury* prevent the President from pardoning her? (Recall once again that President Jefferson pardoned those convicted of violating the 1798 Sedition Act.) If the President in these cases may permissibly have a broader view of the constitutional right — and make that broader view stick — why not in *Nixon*? Why, in other words, is a broader view of the confidentiality privilege under Article II any different than a broader view of the confidentiality privilege under Amendment I? Because Nixon is in effect playing two roles — privilege claimant and President — in a way that makes us especially wary of self-dealing? Because we know that Nixon was a crook, trying to use the privilege to cover up his own wrongdoing?

Is the Court's overblown rhetoric about its own role perhaps a reflection of fear that the President might try to defy a Court order, making the Justices look impotent or plunging the country into a genuine crisis? Might this also account for the Court's unanimity? For a provocative discussion, see Michael Stokes Paulsen, Nixon Now: The Courts and the Presidency After Twenty-Five Years, 83 Minn. L. Rev. 1337 (1999).

6. *The irrelevance of* Burr *and the Bill of Rights.* In United States v. Burr, an 1807 lower court case decided by John Marshall riding circuit, Marshall had subpoenaed various documents from President Jefferson. In *Nixon*, Chief Justice Burger repeatedly insists that Marshall's subpoena was indistinguishable from the one sought by Jaworski. But isn't the distinction obvious, especially to anyone who has read *Cox*? In *Burr*, a criminal defendant (former Vice President Aaron Burr) sought to subpoena evidence to prove his innocence, whereas in *Nixon*, the "government" (i.e., Jaworski) sought to subpoena evidence to prove the guilt of various criminal defendants. Fundamental issues of due process and fairness were at stake in *Burr*: The government cannot prosecute a man while suppressing evidence of his innocence. See, e.g., Brady v. Maryland, 373 U.S. 83 (1963) (discussing the general duty of prosecutors to disclose exculpatory evidence upon request). Had Jefferson resisted the subpoena — on the perfectly

legitimate ground that the evidence sought was too confidential to be disclosed — Marshall would never have tried to coerce the President to surrender the stuff. Instead, the great judge would simply have dismissed the prosecution, and released the defendant. The Constitution and laws nowhere demanded that Burr *must* be prosecuted; they merely required that *if* prosecuted, he be given exculpatory evidence. *Burr* thus respected the President's right to decide the executive-branch policy question at hand: It was left wholly up to Jefferson to choose which was more important to him — getting Burr convicted, or keeping confidential communications secret.

But in *Nixon,* Chief Justice Burger turns *Burr* upside down, insisting that due process demands that all possible evidence of the criminal defendants' guilt *must* be produced, even if both the defendants and the President prefer otherwise. This view finds no support in the text or history of the Due Process Clause, which protects a "person" from unfair government prosecution (as in *Burr*), but says nothing about any government right or duty to prosecute every possible defendant using every possible scrap of evidence. Indeed, Burger's views here reflect a reading of due process never seen before nor since in *U.S. Reports.* (Recall the *Cox* court's reminder that the Fifth Amendment is a shield of the defendant.) Burger also oddly invokes the Sixth Amendment, which pointedly speaks of the rights of "the accused" to produce exculpatory evidence but, once again, says nothing about any government right or duty to produce all inculpatory evidence. Indeed, at times Burger seems to imply that any rule limiting prosecutors' ability to procure "all relevant and admissible evidence" is constitutionally suspect. Does he really mean to cast doubt on a great range of traditional evidentiary privileges — attorney-client, priest-penitent, doctor-patient, husband-wife, and so on? Would Congress be barred, after the *Tapes Case,* from passing a statute defining a broader executive privilege than the Court was prepared to recognize? (Doubtless this broader privilege would interfere with truth-seeking in some judicial cases — but isn't that true of all privileges?)

7. *The structural basis for executive privilege. Nixon* does purport to recognize a limited privilege for confidential Oval Office conversations, but says this executive privilege should be balanced against the judicial need for evidence. In this balance, the need for confidentiality is ordinarily outweighed (absent national security concerns) if the evidence sought for a judicial proceeding is specific, admissible, and relevant. But isn't this a rather puny privilege, on balance? After all, *anyone* can resist a subpoena that is overbroad or irrelevant. Thus, on Burger's logic, essential and wholly proper (but politically sensitive) conversations in the Oval Office are entitled to less legal protection than conversations between spouses or between attorneys and clients.

For example, suppose the President is considering whether to appoint Jane Doe to some high post. This is a key part of his job, as specified by the Constitution's Article II Appointments Clause. Aides brief the President on possible dirt on Doe, her friends, and family, reporting both facts and rumors. This information might bear on Doe's fitness and also might come up in the press or in a Senate confirmation. For the President to do the job the Constitution assigns him, it is necessary and proper — indeed imperative — that he receive this confidential information. But the *Tapes Case,* if we take its due-process, truth-over-privilege logic seriously, suggests that any county prosecutor in a state criminal case, or any plaintiff in a civil case, could subpoena this conversation in a lawsuit designed to embarrass Doe and/or the President. If so, aides will hesitate to tell the President what he needs to know to do his job. Are we back to Mississippi trumping the nation, as Judge Wisdom worried?

Admittedly, the Constitution does not create executive privilege in so many words. But it does create a system of federalism and separation of powers. And so the best argument for executive privilege is structural, and runs something like this: As a matter of federalism, state and local prosecutors should not be allowed to disrupt the proper performance of national executive functions. Cf. *McCulloch*; see also Charles L. Black, Jr., Structure and Relationship in Constitutional Law (1969). As a matter of separation of powers, each branch must have some internal space — a separate house, if you will — to ponder its delicate business free from the intermeddling of other branches. Senators must be free to talk candidly and confidentially amongst themselves and with staff in cloakrooms; judges must enjoy comparable freedom in superconfidential judicial conferences, and in conversations with law clerks; jurors in the jury room ordinarily deliberate together with absolute secrecy to promote candor; and the same basic principle holds true for the Presidency and the Oval Office. This principle was explicitly affirmed by the Supreme Court in no less a case than Marbury v. Madison. When Attorney General Levi Lincoln hesitated to answer certain questions about what President Jefferson had confided to him, feeling "himself bound to maintain the rights of the executive," the *Marbury* Court reassured him that "if he thought that any thing was communicated to him in confidence he was not bound to disclose it." Why does Burger omit all mention of *this* (highly relevant, it seems) part of *Marbury*?

8. *Just the facts, ma'am (again).* If the foregoing analysis is accepted, the *Nixon Tapes Case* reached the right result, but with sloppily overbroad reasoning that failed to identify some of the important — and limiting — facts in the case at hand. Here is what the Court could have said — but did not, quite:

> "The executive power vested in the President by the sweeping words of Article II includes the general right to decide who shall be criminally prosecuted, and how, and also the right to keep confidential good-faith conversations with executive-branch aides about proper executive-branch policy. But, like other privileges in our law, executive privilege has limits and exceptions. Under the well-established crime-fraud exception, attorneys cannot invoke lawyer-client privilege when independent evidence confirms that they are trying to shield from view ongoing criminal misconduct and obstruction of justice. Likewise, the presumptive privilege shielding conversations among jurors yields when there is independent evidence that a juror has been bribed and is using the jury room itself to obstruct justice. Similarly, conversations by executive officials planning ongoing crimes are not protected by Article II. The conversations sought by Jaworski are conversations among persons designated by the grand jury as co-conspirators — including Nixon himself, though the President was not indicted (and perhaps could not be constitutionally indicted). The evidence under seal already in the Court's possession provides strong and independent confirmation of this conspiracy. And the conversations sought by Jaworski are not merely evidence of the conspiracy — they are the conspiracy itself. (The essence of a "conspiracy," of course, is an agreement among persons effected by words.) Under these unusual circumstances, executive privilege yields."

Chief Justice Burger instead wrote a sweeping opinion that had the virtue of not attacking Richard Nixon personally — and not highlighting certain indelicate facts — but, perhaps, the vice of making little sense when honestly applied to honest Presidents.

B. The Appointment Power

Although Archibald Cox and Leon Jaworski proved fiercely independent, the structure of a system in which "watchdogs" were formally picked by the very Administration they were supposed to watch rankled some sensibilities. In retrospect, we might question whether the system was indeed broken, and needed fixing. After all, the constitutional machinery had worked rather well in Watergate. Cox and Jaworski were independent because nothing less would satisfy a Congress armed with powers of oversight, appropriations, and impeachment, and a press and opposition party armed with the First Amendment. To be sure, politics rather than law framed whether an outside prosecutor would be named, who he would be, how he would operate, and when (if ever) he would be removed. But part of the genius of the Constitution was to establish competing power centers and trust their natural incentives and mutual jealousies to keep the system in balance. And if more formal institutions were necessary, perhaps they could have been built within the Congress itself, through the development of a professionalized and bipartisan staff specially charged with White House oversight. But instead, reformers in the wake of Watergate sought to bolster the power of judges and to strengthen the hand of special prosecutors by rendering them more formally independent of the White House. Under the provisions of the so-called Ethics in Government Act of 1978, the Attorney General was authorized to bring certain preliminary investigations of high governmental officials and insiders to the attention of a special panel of three federal judges picked by the Chief Justice. These judges, in turn, were supposed to appoint a special prosecutor to continue the investigation. When the Act reached the courts in the mid-1980s, critics such as Judge Silberman and Justice Scalia warned, in sharp language, that the Act flouted basic principles of separation of powers and fundamental fairness. Supporters of the Act deemed these criticisms overwrought. As you ponder the next set of materials with the benefit of hindsight, ask yourself who had more constitutional foresight.

IN RE SEALED CASE

838 F.2d 476 (1988), rev'd sub nom. Morrison v. Olson, 487 U.S. 654 (1988)

SILBERMAN, Circuit Judge, joined by Williams, Circuit Judge:

Three former government officials, [including] Theodore B. Olson, previously Assistant Attorney General, Office of Legal Counsel, . . . challenge . . . the authority of a federal prosecutor, the independent counsel, appointed under the provisions of the Ethics in Government Act of 1978, 28 U.S.C. §§49, 591-598 (1982 & Supp. III), to issue subpoenas compelling the testimony of these appellants before a grand jury concerning actions taken while they served in their governmental positions. Appellants contend that the Act on which the independent counsel's authority is based is unconstitutional. We agree . . . .

I.

The criminal investigation involved in this case arose out of a heated dispute over document production between the Executive and Legislative Branches. . . .

On April 10, 1986 the Attorney General asked the Special Court to appoint an independent counsel to investigate

> whether the conduct of former Assistant Attorney General Theodore Olson in giving testimony at a hearing of the Subcommittee on Monopolies and Commercial Law of the House Judiciary Committee on March 10, 1983, and later revising that testimony, regarding the completeness of the Office of Legal Counsel's response to the Judiciary Committee's request for OLC documents, and regarding his knowledge of EPA's willingness to turn over certain disputed documents to Congress, violated . . . any . . . provision of federal criminal law. . . .

In April of 1986 the Special Court appointed James McKay as independent counsel. Shortly thereafter, upon McKay's resignation, the Special Court appointed Alexia Morrison to replace him. . . .

II.

. . . The appointments clause provides that the President

> shall nominate, and by and with the Advice and Consent of the Senate, shall appoint Ambassadors, other public Ministers and Consuls, Judges of the Supreme Court, and all other Officers of the United States, whose Appointments are not herein otherwise provided for, and which shall be established by Law: but the Congress may by Law vest the Appointment of such inferior Officers, as they think proper, in the President alone, in the Courts of Law, or in the Heads of Departments.

[We must decide whether] the independent counsel is an inferior officer — for under the clause, only if she is an inferior officer can she be appointed without action by the President and without the advice and consent of the Senate. The answer to that question depends, it seems to us, . . . on whether the independent counsel properly can be thought subordinate to a principal officer. Is she in the exercise of her duties, in other words, a "mere aid[] and subordinate of the head of [a] department[]" or does she instead employ such independence of authority as to place her on the principal officer side of the appointments clause dichotomy? . . . See also Collins v. United States, 14 Ct. Cl. 568, 574 (1879):

> The word inferior is not here used in that vague, indefinite, and quite inaccurate sense which has been suggested — the sense of petty or unimportant; but it means subordinate or inferior to those officers in whom respectively the power of appointment may be vested — the President, the courts of law, and the heads of departments [citation relocated — eds.].

. . . As we discuss later in our opinion, the Attorney General has essentially only the authority to petition the Special Court to authorize the removal of an independent counsel. The Attorney General therefore cannot be thought of as the independent counsel's constitutional superior. Under the statute, the Attorney General has the effective power neither to appoint her, to define, circumscribe, or supervise her duties, nor to remove her or terminate her office. . . .[a]

. . . [T]he independent counsel's authority is so broad as to compel the conclusion that she is a principal officer and therefore her appointment by the Special Court is unconstitutional. After all, the independent counsel's authority is — at least with respect to any matter within her jurisdiction — broader even than the Attorney General's. [T]he independent counsel has authority unchecked by the President himself to decide that an investigation shall continue and that a prosecution shall be initiated. She must give only that consideration that she deems appropriate to all . . . factors relevant to prosecution — including the foreign relations of the United States. . . .

. . . The independent counsel's authority over the investigation is not temporary; it is coterminous with the investigation itself. Hence, the independent counsel is not analogous to an inferior officer who temporarily carries out the tasks of a superior while the superior is absent or disabled.

That the independent counsel's appointment expires when her task is completed seems to us irrelevant. Ambassadors are often appointed in accordance with the appointments clause for discrete negotiations and the Framers, experienced as they were with foreign affairs, contemplated just that eventuality. . . .

III.

. . . The appellants claim, and we agree, that even if the independent counsel were an inferior officer, and so did not have to be appointed by the President with the advice and consent of the Senate, the Act would violate the Constitution because it impermissibly interferes with the President's constitutional duty to "take Care that the Laws be faithfully executed."

Authority to prosecute an individual is that government power which most threatens personal liberty, for a prosecutor "has the power to employ the full machinery of the state in scrutinizing any given individual. Even if a defendant is ultimately acquitted, forced immersion in criminal investigation and adjudication is a wrenching disruption of everyday life." . . .

The Constitution therefore carefully distributes the various responsibilities for criminal prosecution among each of the three branches, so that citizens may not be endangered by one branch acting alone. . . . Federal criminal law can be enacted only by Congress. This innovation marks a major shift from prior practice, which countenanced a common law of crime created by the same judges who tried the cases. United States v. Hudson, 11 U.S. (7 Cranch) 32 (1812). Congress' role in the criminal law was carefully confined to this initial stage of law creation. Congress is, accordingly, explicitly forbidden to pass bills of attainder, one of the few positive prohibitions on congressional power contained in Article I. See United States v. Brown, 381 U.S. 437, 442 (1965) ("the Bill of Attainder Clause was intended not as a narrow, technical . . . prohibition, but rather as an implementation of the separation of powers, a general safeguard against legislative exercise of the judicial function, or more simply — trial by legislature"). And the power of Congress to impeach officers

a. Any claim that the Special Court is the constitutional superior of the independent counsel would undermine much of the independent counsel's defense of the statute and would place into even starker relief the constitutional anomaly of a court of law appointing and supervising an executive officer.

of the United States is also limited — the penalty "shall not extend further than to removal from Office, and disqualification to hold and enjoy any Office of honor, Trust or Profit under the United States." Even through impeachment then, Congress is powerless to deprive any individual of liberty.

Next the Constitution vests the power to initiate a criminal prosecution exclusively in the Executive Branch; this power is encompassed within the Executive's power to "take Care that the Laws be faithfully executed." The Executive has "exclusive authority and absolute discretion to decide whether to prosecute a case." *Nixon; Cox.* "The power to decide when to investigate, and when to prosecute, lies at the core of the Executive's duty to see to the faithful execution of the laws[.]"

The Framers provided for a unitary executive to ensure that the branch wielding the power to enforce the law would be accountable to the people. . . . Under the Constitution, the President, as the head of the Executive Branch, is the person ultimately responsible for a decision to initiate a criminal prosecution. See *Cox.* If that decision is contrary to the mores and customs of the community, the community has a visible target for its grievances. No anonymous directorates hold sway here, no impenetrable bureaucracies or commissions obscure the identity of the responsible official; the chain of command leads directly upward to the President. As Hamilton wrote, "it is far more safe there should be a single object for the jealousy and watchfulness of the people; and in a word that all multiplication of the executive is rather dangerous than friendly to liberty." THE FEDERALIST No. 70; see also Myers v. United States. Not merely an abstract idea of political theory, the President's accountability is a hallmark of our democracy — perhaps best put in President Truman's gritty aphorism "The buck stops here." For no federal government function is it more vital to the protection of individual liberty that ultimately the buck stop with an accountable official — the President — than in the prosecution of criminal laws.

That the government prove its case in a jury trial before a neutral and disinterested court, insulated with extraordinary tenure protection from the other two branches of government and shielded from popular pressure, is the final safeguard contained in the original Constitution upon the federal government's power to prosecute the criminal laws. The constitutional scheme is as simple as it is complete — Congress passes the criminal law in the first instance, the President enforces the law, and individual cases are tried before a neutral judiciary involved in neither the creation nor the execution of that law. The Ethics in Government Act, it seems to us, deliberately departs from this framework in both its particular provisions and in its general purpose, which is to authorize an officer not accountable to any elected official to prosecute crimes. . . .

A

The Act directs that the independent counsel be appointed not by the President, nor by the Attorney General, but rather by a court of law. Even if we assume arguendo that the independent counsel is an inferior officer, her appointment appears quite inconsistent with the Constitution's placement of the executive power in the President. A statute that vests the appointment of an officer who prosecutes the criminal law in some branch other than the executive obstructs the President's ability to execute the law — a duty the President can practically carry out only through appointed officials. See THE FEDERALIST Nos. 70, 76, 77. The concept of a responsible and accountable unitary executive would mean very little without the power to appoint, for the President's capacity to enforce the law is largely dependent upon the identity and caliber of the officers who compose the Executive Branch, and if the President is without the power to appoint, he cannot define the character of his administration. In Buckley v. Valeo, 424 U.S. 1(1976), the Supreme Court declared unconstitutional a statute that allowed Congress to appoint members of the Federal Election Commission on grounds that congressional appointment of executive officers violated the appointments clause. The Court determined that the Commissioners exercised executive power because they had, among other powers, the power to bring civil actions against violators of the election laws.

> The vesting of the executive power in the President was essentially a grant of the power to execute the laws. But the President alone and unaided could not execute the laws. He must execute them by the assistance of subordinates. . . . As he is charged specifically to take care that they be faithfully executed, the reasonable implication, even in the absence of express words, was that as part of his executive power he should select those who were to act for him under his direction in the execution of the laws.
>
> . . . Article II grants to the President the executive power of the Government, i.e., the general administrative control of those executing the laws, including the power of appointment and removal of executive officers — a conclusion confirmed by his obligation to take care that the laws be faithfully executed. . . .

Buckley (quoting *Myers*). . . .

The independent counsel nevertheless defends her appointment with the proposition that the "plain language" of the appointments clause allows Congress to vest the appointment of inferior officers, including the independent counsel, in a court of law, or in more general terms, that the appointments clause should be read to allow officers in one branch to appoint officers in another branch, i.e., to make "inter-branch" appointments. . . . In the earliest case to raise the issue the Supreme Court [said:] "The appointing power here designated, in the latter part of the section, was, no doubt, intended to be exercised by the department of the government to which the officer to be appointed most appropriately belonged. The appointment of clerks of courts properly belongs to the courts of law. . . ." In re Hennen, 38 U.S. (13 Pet.) 230 (1839). . . .

. . . The tenor of the debate [at the Philadelphia Convention] reveals a jealous guarding of the President's appointment power, even against any participation by the Senate, to the end that one man would be solely responsible for choosing government officers. . . .

Debate in the Convention on an earlier version of the appointments clause, which contained no reference at all to inferior officers, suggested that the delegates were concerned as to the practical difficulties of staffing a government of a nation whose distances were vast at a time when travel and communications were slow and often difficult. George Mason accordingly proposed that officers be appointed by a council rather than by the President with the approval of the Senate. Otherwise he worried that the Senate would have to be in continuous session in order to approve appointments. Rufus King responded, however, that "he did not suppose it was meant that all the minute officers were to be appointed by the Senate, or any other original source, but by the higher officers of the departments to which they belong."

Later in the Convention, the inferior officer provision was added with little discussion and it appears therefore that the clause was designed to meet concerns expressed in the earlier dialogue between Mason and King. . . . Madison, like King, thought the first part of the appointments clause, without the amendment, bestowed an implied power on principal officers to appoint officers subordinate to themselves — a power the amendment merely made explicit (but nonetheless in restricted form since it was given only to the President, courts of law, and department heads). The delegates to the Convention, we conclude, did not even contemplate that the appointments clause they fashioned permitted Congress to authorize superior officers like department heads to appoint inferior officers subordinate to other department heads; still less did they intend that the courts of law could be empowered to appoint officers in the Executive Branch who could not, consistent with the separation of powers, be constitutionally "inferior" to judges.

Turning from the debates of the Convention to the Federalist Papers (which are perhaps even more important as an interpretative aid because they, unlike the records of the Convention, were available to the state ratifying conventions), we note that Hamilton repeatedly and at some length discussed the immense importance of vesting the appointment power in the President. . . . See THE FEDERALIST Nos. 70, 76, 77. . . .

. . . We think it must be incongruous if an officer of one branch is authorized to appoint an officer of another branch who is assigned a duty central to the constitutional role of that other branch. . . . [Otherwise,] a court could be empowered to appoint all officers subordinate to a department head. If, for example, two-thirds of the House and Senate — a sufficient number to override a veto — disagreed strongly with the President's agricultural policy, Congress could place in a particular court, perceived as more in agreement with Congress' policy views, the authority to appoint all Department of Agriculture officers subordinate to the Secretary. That device would neatly prevent the President from implementing his own agricultural policy. Or more shocking, because of the President's Commander-in-Chief and foreign policy functions, Congress could employ the same technique to prevent the President from exercising effective control over either the State or Defense Department. It is difficult to see, if the independent counsel is correct concerning inter-branch appointments, why Congress could not delegate to a particular court — perhaps by a definition that fitted only one district judge — the appointment of all Executive Branch officers (save department heads).

Perhaps more plausible, however, is a scenario closer to the one presented by this case. Let us assume that Congress has lost confidence in the President's policy implicating only one subject matter within a department's jurisdiction — perhaps U.S. policy towards Latin America, or arms control negotiations, or the Executive Branch's presentation of cases to the Supreme Court. Under the independent counsel's view, Congress would face no constitutional impediment in requiring that a particular court appoint the officials responsible for implementing those policies. And as with the Act before us, Congress could forbid any other Executive Branch official to interfere with the special appointee's jurisdiction.

Or reversing the inter-branch appointment device, Congress, if it had the constitutional authority the independent counsel asserts and was dissatisfied with the trend of federal judicial decisions, might place authority to appoint all inferior judicial officers including Justices' and judges' clerks in one department head (perhaps the Attorney General), thereby hoping to influence opinions or at least to obstruct the perceived undesirable trend.

It seems obvious to us that all of these examples are so at odds with the doctrine of separation of powers or the President's unitary executive authority as to be plainly contrary to our Constitution. . . .

In sum, we think the Constitution generally precludes inter-branch appointments. . . .

B

The Act further trenches on the concept of a unitary executive and departs from separation of powers doctrine by substantially limiting the President's ability to remove or supervise the independent counsel. . . .

Power to remove an executive officer is important principally because it permits the President to control the performance of that officer. Even more than the appointment power perhaps, authority to remove an officer who strays from the President's desired policy direction guarantees the President the ability to channel that officer's course of action. As Madison said in the First Congress:

> If the President should possess alone the power of removal from office, those who are employed in the execution of the law will be in their proper situation, and the chain of dependence be preserved; the lowest officers, the middle grade, and the highest, will depend, as they ought, on the President, and the President on the community. . . .

We think it inevitable that under the Constitution such officers must be members of the Executive Branch subject to the control of the President. In contrast to the limited grants of legislative power made in Article I, Article II grants authority to the President in broad terms: "The executive Power shall be vested in a President," U.S. Const., art. II, §1, and does not individually list all his various duties, but it does specifically require that he shall be the Commander-in-Chief of the Armed Forces and that he may make treaties with the advice and consent of the Senate and receive ambassadors. Id., §2. It also directs the President to "take Care that the Laws be faithfully executed." Id., §3. . . . We conclude rather that the Constitution envisioned two core domains of presidential responsibility — foreign affairs and law enforcement — and it is apparent from the structure and language of the Constitution that the initiation of a criminal prosecution in our federal system is entrusted to the President. . . .

This scheme is analytically indistinguishable from one whereby the Attorney General could remove the independent counsel only by petitioning the Special Court for a termination order which the Special Court could grant or not following its own independent investigation of the facts and the law. . . . The result of this "double key" system is therefore that the Attorney General is powerless to remove the independent counsel unless he can win the consent of the Special Court. We have then almost a precise analogy to *Myers,* where, under the statute declared unconstitutional, the President could not remove the postmaster without the concurrence of the Senate.

The "good cause" limitation on removal, coupled with the Act's extraordinary judicial review provisions and the power of the Special Court to appoint an interim independent counsel and to reinstate a fired independent counsel compromise the

President's ability to oversee the execution of the law. Not content with eliminating the President's implicit power to direct or influence the independent counsel, Congress went even further to render the President impotent to affect the independent counsel's behavior. From the moment an independent counsel is appointed, the Act, which guarantees the independent counsel "independent authority" to carry out her duties, ensures that the Attorney General cannot influence any aspect of her performance, including the scope and duration of the investigation, the standards to be applied in making a decision to prosecute or not, the direction of the investigation when competing executive concerns are implicated, or, on a more mundane, but nevertheless important level, details about staffing and budgetary matters.

The independent counsel is free to ignore Department of Justice policy if it is "not possible" to follow it, and that judgment is for her alone to make. The consequence of this scheme . . . is that targets of an independent counsel may be subjected to investigations and prosecutions governed by rules different from those that apply to the investigation of any other citizen and therefore it strikes at the very heart of the unitary executive doctrine, which has as a primary purpose the "unitary and uniform administration of the laws." *Myers*. . . .

[I]mportant decisions about the scope of the investigation and the very identity of the targets are made not by the Attorney General, but by the Special Court. The absence of Executive Branch supervisory authority is perhaps most troubling when an investigation veers toward matters affecting international relations and the independent counsel adopts positions at odds with the remainder of the Executive Branch. For example, in another investigation under the Ethics in Government Act that has previously been before this court, the independent counsel attempted to subpoena the Canadian Ambassador in the face of strenuous opposition by the Department of State on this delicate diplomatic question. And in oral argument before this court regarding still another independent counsel investigation, we were advised that in the event of a dispute between the independent counsel and the President over foreign policy and its implications for a prosecution, the independent counsel would 'in principle' prevail over the President.

In sum, Congress has created an Executive Branch office to perform a core presidential function and as far as we can determine precluded the President from exercising any influence over the performance of that office even when its performance might interfere with a range of other Executive Branch responsibilities, including those national security duties directly and solemnly entrusted to the President for the protection of all Americans. . . .

IV.

The primary defense of the constitutionality of the Act presented by the independent counsel and supporting amici is one of necessity. We are told that Presidents can no longer be trusted to ensure that their senior appointees obey the criminal laws. The independent counsel claims that "the constitutional crisis which grew out of Watergate is a sufficient demonstration that without a mechanism to achieve this goal, there is grave question whether we are in fact 'a Nation capable of governing itself effectively.' " This argument is sometimes cast in terms of an institutional lack of confidence in the Justice Department. . . . But the argument is really directed at the Presidency itself, for so long as the President takes care that the laws be faithfully executed, we see no reason why he cannot ensure that his Attorney General and senior officials in the Justice Department follow his lead. A good example of such presidential action arose during the very Truman administration scandals referred to by the Special Court. After the Attorney General improperly discharged the special prosecutor he had appointed,

President Truman in turn removed the Attorney General. Of course the Attorney General might, on his own, or by direction of the President, determine that for appearances' sake or because of an actual conflict of interest a special prosecutor or independent counsel should be appointed for a particular investigation, buttressed perhaps with an independence guaranteed by regulation. That device has been employed and its legality tested and affirmed. See United States v. Nixon.[b]

The President then has a range of choices and techniques to ensure that corruption at senior levels in his administration is deterred and, if not deterred, punished. Clearly this statute is based on the premise that the President himself cannot be trusted to choose wisely among these options. . . .

. . . Why could Congress not, according to this notion, require an independent counsel whenever the target of inquiry were a political ally of the President: Senator, Congressman, Governor, campaign contributor, or in fact any person active in affairs of the President's party? Nor do we see, if political allegiance really does generate a conflict of interest, why the argument cannot just as easily be made also to support the opposite application — that the President be deprived of authority to prosecute his political adversaries. If we follow this political conflict of interest reasoning to its logical end, it points to the desirability of removing the Department of Justice entirely from presidential influence — which we think must be a constitutional reductio ad absurdum. . . .

The Framers were not oblivious to the concerns that gave rise to this legislation. By providing Congress with the impeachment power, and declining to extend the President's pardon power to cases of impeachment, the Constitution grants to Congress the power, if needed because of criminal behavior, to discipline the President and all of his appointees. The impeachment clause and the limitation on the President's pardon power not only demonstrate that the Framers did not ignore the problem of wrongdoing in high places; these provisions further suggest that the balance between the need for official accountability for criminal acts and the prerogative of the President to oversee the execution of the laws was struck in the Constitution itself. Although the power to impeach has been used only sparingly, it has been explicitly directed against two Presidents. More importantly, however, it hangs over the Executive Branch as a brooding omnipresence, often forcing Presidents to take action that they might wish to avoid. After President Nixon caused one special prosecutor to be discharged the resulting uproar — and the explicit threats of impeachment — compelled him almost at once to acquiesce in the appointment of another, who was given full authority to pursue criminal charges against the President himself.

As did the Supreme Court in *Myers*, we note that the legislation before us was passed in the midst of a period when one political party tended to control the Presidency and the other enjoyed dominance in the Legislative Branch. It is of

---

b. Or Congress might create an "independent" prosecutorial office to be filled by an officer appointed by the President (and under his supervision) with the advice and consent of the Senate. Such an office was created during the Teapot Dome scandal of the Harding administration.

course conceivable, without in the slightest degree impugning congressional motives, that this long-standing political division has subtly contributed to the inevitable tension between the political branches and thus perhaps played a role in the perceived need for this legislation. Ironically, however, the impeachment power is a good deal more credible threat when Congress is controlled by one party and the Presidency by the other. Certainly history bears out that observation. That means the Act may well have been passed at a time in American history when its need, even assuming the validity of its defenders' positions, was least.

[W]hether or not Congress can actually exercise subtle influence over, or give implicit direction to, an independent counsel, it seems simplistic to contend that Congress' political power in our system is unaffected by a diminution (or increase) in the Chief Executive's authority. If the President's authority is diminished — and we think it utterly impossible to deny that the Act accomplishes at least that result — Congress' political power must necessarily increase vis-à-vis the President. In practical terms, repeated calls for the appointment of a statutory independent counsel may, like a flicking left jab, confound the Executive Branch in dealing with Congress. An actual appointment, furthermore, surely saps the political vitality of the Presidency and thereby renders the President a less effective political force juxtaposed against Congress. In this very case, congressional calls for appointment of an independent counsel to investigate Executive Branch withholding of documents — based on executive privilege — seem to have been only a part of a broader, and not atypical, struggle between the political branches over the expenditures of appropriated funds in the shadow of an impending election. Of course those demands could occur in the absence of the statute, but the Act . . . surely alters the political equation. . . .

[A] qualitatively significant encroachment upon the executive's control over even a single case may have a drastic impact on the individual involved. The constitutional doctrines implicated by this case do not concern merely questions of governmental organization and structure, but rather involve checks and balances that were designed "to protect the people from the improvident exercise of power." *Chadha.* Separation of powers was considered by the Framers to be an "essential precaution in favor of liberty." THE FEDERALIST No. 47. "The Framers recognized that, in the long term, structural protections against abuse of power were critical to preserving liberty." . . . One of appellant's counsel well expressed the essence of this concept: "If you look from the top down, as opposed to the bottom up, the chief defense of the statute of the independent counsel is it is only a little bit of executive power that is being taken away. If you look from the bottom up, from the accused person up. . . , all that accused person's protection that he was getting through three separate branches is taken away. . . ."

That very independence from presidential and Justice Department supervision and guidance that Congress deliberately fashioned for independent counsel has troubling consequences for those who find themselves the target of the independent counsel's attention. A person occupying this statutory office has, it seems to us, unique incentives to seek an indictment. Our concern is based on the self-evident proposition that the whole raison d'etre of the independent counsel is not to administer the criminal law across a wide population, but rather to focus on one individual or group of individuals targeted at the inception of the office. In effect, an entire self-sufficient government agency is created from scratch to investigate and perhaps prosecute a single individual. The need to justify even the expense of an office dedicated solely to one goal must generate a reluctance to decide against indictment or to conclude the investigation absent near certainty that no indictment is possible or that no further leads remain. And inevitably, the success of the office itself, in the public's eyes, at least, must turn to some extent upon whether indictment and conviction are obtained. The independent counsel is thus "subject to formidable public — and perhaps self-imposed — pressure to indict in the one case he was appointed to pursue."

These incentives to prosecute might be thought also to affect a special prosecutor appointed by the Attorney General or the President. But, under the Act the independent counsel enjoys statutory immunity from supervision by anyone else in the Executive Branch and thus, unlike a special prosecutor appointed by the Attorney General and subject to his potential supervision, is free to ignore considerations normally included within the rubric of prosecutorial discretion and which may in a particular case all point to restraint. We have already mentioned powerful executive policy concerns, such as the foreign relations of the United States, that quite legitimately could influence the executive not to seek an indictment in a given case. More fundamental, perhaps, the independent counsel has no need to view a particular case in relation to similar cases, past or future. Wise exercise of prosecutorial discretion is dependent in part upon access to officials who are participants in the ongoing process of enforcing the law and who are able to take a longer view of an individual case. Yet the independent counsel is cut off from the accumulated lore and wisdom of career Department of Justice officers, who are in a unique position to evaluate "such factors as the strength of the case, the prosecution's general deterrence value, the Government's enforcement priorities, and the case's relationship to the Government's overall enforcement plan." These factors will often counsel against prosecution; a case that seems strong and important when viewed in isolation may look weak or trivial when measured against past cases or in relation to broader considerations of sound deployment of prosecutorial resources.

[I]t is inconsistent with the doctrine of a unitary executive that under the independent counsel statute the target of an investigation may be exposed to less protection than if investigated by a United States Attorney, while the President and the Attorney General or for that matter any other politically accountable officials are powerless to affect the independent counsel's choice of the standard for prosecution. The President "may properly supervise and guide [his officers'] construction of the statutes under which they act in order to secure that unitary and uniform execution of the laws which Article II of the Constitution evidently contemplated in vesting general executive power in the President alone." *Myers.*

V.

The last basis upon which the Act is challenged is that it invests an Article III court with non-Article III powers. . . . By removing a core executive officer from the control of the Executive Branch, the Act, as we have concluded, interferes with the executive's "performance of its constitutionally assigned function." Considered from a different viewpoint, though, the Act violates the separation of powers doctrine because it entrusts a court with an executive function, which a court may not constitutionally undertake. These defects are reciprocal in nature; the Act impermissibly takes a central responsibility from the Executive Branch in violation of Article II, and it impermissibly gives that executive responsibility to the Judicial Branch, thereby violating Article III. . . .

Article III of the Constitution limits the judicial power of the United States to "Cases" and "Controversies." Federal courts therefore must "carefully abstain from exercising any power that is not strictly judicial in its character, and which is not clearly confided to [them] by the Constitution." The "case or controversy" limit "defines the 'role assigned to the judiciary in a tripartite allocation of power to assure that the federal courts will not intrude into areas committed to the other branches of government.' " It also preserves an independent and neutral judiciary, relatively removed from the decisions and activities of the other two branches. Discharging tasks other than the deciding of cases and controversies would "involve the judges too intimately in the process of policy and thereby weaken confidence in the disinterestedness of their judicatory functions."

Granted, the appointments clause of Article II bestows upon the judiciary unquestioned authority that it might not otherwise enjoy, given the circumscribed nature of Article III, to appoint, pursuant to appropriate legislation, at least those who support judges in the exercise of their Article III functions — clerks, secretaries, magistrates, and the like. It seems obvious to us, however, that this clause cannot be construed so as to undermine or nullify Article III limitations.

The Special Court under the Act not only appoints the independent counsel, it defines the jurisdiction of the independent counsel, it receives reports from the independent counsel, and it is authorized to terminate the office of the independent counsel "on its own motion. . . ." Since these provisions necessarily involve the Special Court in the non-Article III task of supervising the day-to-day activities of an Executive Branch official we hold them unconstitutional. . . .

. . . In another independent counsel investigation that has been before this court, the Iran/Contra investigation, the Special Court defined the independent counsel's jurisdiction to include more events and persons than those included in the Attorney General's application. That decision had obvious political and foreign policy overtones. The Special Court's action followed receipt of a letter from the Democratic members of the Senate Judiciary Committee requesting that the jurisdiction of the independent counsel be expanded to include an investigation into the provision of support for forces fighting the government of Nicaragua. The Special Court's determination to grant this jurisdiction to the independent counsel . . . was not made in the context of a case or controversy; no public hearing or notice to the parties involved preceded the decision. Even if the parties had been before the court, the presence of adversaries with a personal stake in the matter does not . . . convert a policy dispute into an Article III case or controversy. Like many other executive decisions, the determination of jurisdiction in both the *North* and *Olson* proceedings was made in the context of swirling controversy in which various factions hoped for opposing outcomes and the decisions necessarily rested on indeterminate considerations of policy and on information brought to the decisionmaker's attention through various avenues, including ex parte communications.

Definition of a prosecutor's jurisdiction is, of course, crucial to the whole enterprise of executing the criminal law, for in practical terms, it determines who may be subject to prosecution and for what crimes. Deciding to target certain people and certain acts, and to exclude others, necessarily involves a balancing of factors and a setting of priorities that have uniformly been held to be beyond the province of the judiciary. These decisions may not generally even be reviewed by a court, and yet the Act requires the Special Court to make them in the first instance. Where there is no law to apply and where a decision necessarily involves a paradigmatic political choice to allocate societal resources one way rather than another, a court must inevitably act "under compulsions and motives that have no relation to performance of our Art. III functions."

That is not all. When independent counsel have become concerned about whether the federal conflict-of-interest laws apply to them, they have approached a member of the Special Court in his chambers and sought his advice on this issue. In response, the Special Court has issued "orders" that purport to exempt the independent counsel and the staff of the independent counsel from conflict-of-interest laws. And in another case, the Special Court ordered an independent counsel to delay an investigation of certain allegations until completion of related state criminal proceedings. Again, it is important to note that such orders were not given in the context of a case or controversy; no notice was given to interested parties and no hearing was held or briefs filed. It seems more than a bit artificial to place the issuance of such orders into the category of accepted judicial duties. For all effects and purposes these were instructions given by a superior to an executive officer under his supervision, a task which Article III does not contemplate as judicial. . . .

Intimate involvement of an Article III court in the supervision and control of a prosecutorial office undermines the status of the judiciary as a neutral forum for the resolution of disputes between citizens and their government. . . .

The Act's inattention to Article III's limitations is particularly troubling because it implicates the course of a federal criminal investigation, which, if there were an indictment, must necessarily come before the federal courts for trial and, in all likelihood, appeal. In any such trial or appeal, the defendant may wish to call the court's attention to misconduct by the independent counsel or by the independent counsel's superior, who, as we have shown, in practical terms is the Special Court. This can raise an obvious dilemma for a defendant who may be impelled to engage in subtle calculations concerning the possibility of offending the court by pointing too vigorously to alleged overreaching by fellow judges or by an officer appointed by and supervised by fellow judges. . . .

. . . This is no abstract dispute concerning the doctrine of separation of powers. The rights of individuals are at stake.

[The dissenting opinion of then Circuit Judge Ruth Bader Ginsburg, concluding that the 1978 statute "is a measure faithful to the eighteenth century blueprint, yet fitting for our time," is omitted. On appeal, sub nom Morrison v. Olson, the Supreme Court reversed Judge Silberman as follows.]

MORRISON v. OLSON
487 U.S. 654 (1988)

Chief Justice REHNQUIST delivered the opinion of the Court. . . .

III.

. . . The line between "inferior" and "principal" officers is one that is far from clear, and the Framers provided little guidance into where it should be drawn. We need not attempt here to decide exactly where the line falls between the two types of officers, because in our view appellant clearly falls on the "inferior officer" side of that line. Several factors lead to this conclusion.

First, appellant is subject to removal by a higher Executive Branch official. Although appellant may not be "subordinate" to the Attorney General (and the President) insofar as she possesses a degree of independent discretion to exercise the powers delegated to her under the Act, the fact that she can be removed by the Attorney General indicates that she is to some degree "inferior" in rank and authority. Second, appellant is empowered by the Act to perform only certain, limited duties. . . . Admittedly, the Act delegates to appellant "full power and independent authority to exercise all investigative and prosecutorial functions and powers of the Department of Justice," but this grant of authority does not include any authority to formulate policy for the Government or the Executive Branch, nor does it give appellant any administrative duties outside of those necessary to operate her office. The Act specifically provides that in policy matters appellant is to comply to the extent possible with the policies of the Department.

Third, appellant's office is limited in jurisdiction. Not only is the Act itself restricted in applicability to certain federal officials suspected of certain serious federal crimes, but an independent counsel can only act within the scope of the jurisdiction that has been granted by the Special Division pursuant to a request by the Attorney General. Finally, appellant's office is limited in tenure. There is concededly no time limit on the appointment of a particular counsel. Nonetheless, the office of independent counsel is "temporary" in the sense that an independent counsel is appointed essentially to accomplish a single task, and when that task is over the office is terminated, either by the counsel herself or by action of the Special Division. Unlike other prosecutors, appellant has no ongoing responsibilities that extend beyond the accomplishment of the mission that she was appointed for and authorized by the Special Division to undertake. In our view, these factors relating to the "ideas of tenure, duration . . . and duties" of the independent counsel, are sufficient to establish that appellant is an "inferior" officer in the constitutional sense. . . .

This does not, however, end our inquiry under the Appointments Clause. Appellees argue that even if appellant is an "inferior" officer, the Clause . . . does not contemplate congressional authorization of "interbranch appointments," in which an officer of one branch is appointed by officers of another branch. The relevant language of the Appointments Clause is worth repeating. It reads: ". . . but the Congress may by Law vest the Appointment of such inferior Officers, as they think proper, in the President alone, in the courts of Law, or in the Heads of Departments." On its face, the language of this "excepting clause" admits of no limitation on interbranch appointments. Indeed, the inclusion of "as they think proper" seems clearly to give Congress significant discretion to determine whether it is "proper" to vest the appointment of, for example, executive officials in the "courts of Law." . . .

We also note that the history of the Clause provides no support for appellees' position. . . . [In the Philadelphia Convention,] there was little or no debate on the question whether the Clause empowers Congress to provide for interbranch appointments, and there is nothing to suggest that the Framers intended to prevent Congress from having that power.

We do not mean to say that Congress' power to provide for interbranch appointments of "inferior officers" is unlimited. In addition to separation-of-powers concerns, which would arise if such provisions for appointment had the potential to impair the constitutional functions assigned to one of the branches, [Court precedent] suggests that Congress' decision to vest the appointment power in the courts would be improper if there was some "incongruity" between the functions normally performed by the courts and the performance of their duty to appoint. In this case, however, we do not think it impermissible for Congress to vest the power to appoint independent counsel in a specially created federal court. We thus disagree with the Court of Appeals' conclusion that there is an inherent incongruity about a court having the power to appoint prosecutorial officers.[a] . . . Lower courts have also upheld interim judicial appointments of United States Attorneys, and Congress itself has vested the power to make these interim appointments in the district courts.[b] Congress, of course, was concerned when it created the office of independent counsel with the conflicts of interest that could arise in situations when the Executive Branch is called upon to investigate its own high-ranking officers. If it were to remove the appointing authority from the Executive Branch, the most logical place to put it was in the Judicial Branch. In the light of the Act's provision making the judges of the Special Division ineligible to participate in any matters relating to an independent counsel they have appointed, we do not think that appointment of the independent counsel by the court runs afoul of the constitutional limitation on "incongruous" interbranch appointments.

IV.

Appellees next contend that the powers vested in the Special Division by the Act conflict with Article III of the Constitution. We have long recognized that by the express provision of Article III, the judicial power of the United States is limited to "Cases" and "Controversies." As a general rule, we have broadly stated that "executive or administrative duties of a nonjudicial nature may not be imposed on judges holding office under Art. III of the Constitution." The purpose of this limitation is to help ensure the independence of the Judicial Branch and to prevent the Judiciary from encroaching into areas reserved for the other branches. . . .

. . . In our view, Congress' power under the Clause to vest the "Appointment" of inferior officers in the courts may, in certain circumstances, allow Congress to give the courts some discretion in defining the nature and scope of the appointed official's authority. Particularly when, as here, Congress creates a temporary "office" the nature and duties of which will by necessity vary with the factual circumstances giving rise to the need for an appointment in the first place, it may vest the power to define the scope of the office in the court as an incident to the appointment of the officer pursuant to the Appointments Clause. This said, we do not think that Congress may give the Division unlimited discretion to determine the independent counsel's jurisdiction. In order for the Division's definition of the counsel's jurisdiction to be truly

a. Indeed, in light of judicial experience with prosecutors in criminal cases, it could be said that courts are especially well qualified to appoint prosecutors. This is not a case in which judges are given power to appoint an officer in an area in which they have no special knowledge or expertise, as in, for example, a statute authorizing the courts to appoint officials in the Department of Agriculture or the Federal Energy Regulatory Commission.

b. We note also the longstanding judicial practice of appointing defense attorneys for individuals who are unable to afford representation, notwithstanding the possibility that the appointed attorney may appear in court before the judge who appointed him.

"incidental" to its power to appoint, the jurisdiction that the court decides upon must be demonstrably related to the factual circumstances that gave rise to the Attorney General's investigation and request for the appointment of the independent counsel in the particular case.

The Act also vests in the Special Division various powers and duties in relation to the independent counsel that, because they do not involve appointing the counsel or defining his or her jurisdiction, cannot be said to derive from the Division's Appointments Clause authority. . . .

. . . Some of these allegedly "supervisory" powers conferred on the court are passive: the Division merely "receives" reports from the counsel or the Attorney General, it is not entitled to act on them or to specifically approve or disapprove of their contents. Other provisions of the Act do require the court to exercise some judgment and discretion, but the powers granted by these provisions are themselves essentially ministerial. The Act simply does not give the Division the power to "supervise" the independent counsel in the exercise of his or her investigative or prosecutorial authority. And, the functions that the Special Division is empowered to perform are not inherently "Executive." . . .

V.

. . . Two Terms ago we [held in] Bowsher v. Synar, 478 U.S. 714, 730 (1986), . . . that "Congress cannot reserve for itself the power of removal of an officer charged with the execution of the laws except by impeachment." A primary antecedent for this ruling was our 1926 decision in Myers v. United States, 272 U.S. 52. *Myers* had considered the propriety of a federal statute by which certain postmasters of the United States could be removed by the President only "by and with the advice and consent of the Senate." There too, Congress' attempt to involve itself in the removal of an executive official was found to be sufficient grounds to render the statute invalid. . . .

Unlike both *Bowsher* and *Myers,* this case does not involve an attempt by Congress itself to gain a role in the removal of executive officials other than its established powers of impeachment and conviction. The Act instead puts the removal power squarely in the hands of the Executive Branch; an independent counsel may be removed from office, "only by the personal action of the Attorney General, and only for good cause." There is no requirement of congressional approval of the Attorney General's removal decision, though the decision is subject to judicial review. In our view, the removal provisions of the Act make this case more analogous to Humphrey's Executor v. United States, 295 U.S. 602 (1935), and Wiener v. United States, 357 U.S. 349 (1958), than to *Myers* or *Bowsher.* . . .

Appellees contend that *Humphrey's Executor* and *Wiener* are distinguishable from this case because they did not involve officials who performed a "core executive function." They argue that our decision in *Humphrey's Executor* rests on a distinction between "purely executive" officials and officials who exercise "quasi-legislative" and "quasi-judicial" powers. In their view, when a "purely executive" official is involved, the governing precedent is *Myers,* not *Humphrey's Executor.* And, under *Myers,* the President must have absolute discretion to discharge "purely" executive officials at will.

We undoubtedly did rely on the terms "quasi-legislative" and "quasi-judicial" to distinguish the officials involved in *Humphrey's Executor* and *Wiener* from those in

Myers, but our present considered view is that the determination of whether the Constitution allows Congress to impose a "good cause"-type restriction on the President's power to remove an official cannot be made to turn on whether or not that official is classified as "purely executive." The analysis contained in our removal cases is designed not to define rigid categories of those officials who may or may not be removed at will by the President, but to ensure that Congress does not interfere with the President's exercise of the "executive power" and his constitutionally appointed duty to "take care that the laws be faithfully executed" under Article II. . . .

. . . There is no real dispute that the functions performed by the independent counsel are "executive" in the sense that they are law enforcement functions that typically have been undertaken by officials within the Executive Branch. As we noted above, however, the independent counsel is an inferior officer under the Appointments Clause, with limited jurisdiction and tenure and lacking policymaking or significant administrative authority. Although the counsel exercises no small amount of discretion and judgment in deciding how to carry out his or her duties under the Act, we simply do not see how the President's need to control the exercise of that discretion is so central to the functioning of the Executive Branch as to require as a matter of constitutional law that the counsel be terminable at will by the President.

Nor do we think that the "good cause" removal provision at issue here impermissibly burdens the President's power to control or supervise the independent counsel, as an executive official, in the execution of his or her duties under the Act. This is not a case in which the power to remove an executive official has been completely stripped from the President, thus providing no means for the President to ensure the "faithful execution" of the laws. Rather, because the independent counsel may be terminated for "good cause," the Executive, through the Attorney General, retains ample authority to assure that the counsel is competently performing his or her statutory responsibilities in a manner that comports with the provisions of the Act. . . .[c]

B

The final question to be addressed is whether the Act, taken as a whole, violates the principle of separation of powers by unduly interfering with the role of the Executive Branch. . . .

We observe first that this case does not involve an attempt by Congress to increase its own powers at the expense of the Executive Branch. Unlike some of our previous cases, most recently Bowsher v. Synar, this case simply does not pose a "dange[r] of congressional usurpation of Executive Branch functions." See also INS v. Chadha, 462 U.S. 919, 958 (1983). Indeed, with the exception of the power of impeachment — which applies to all officers of the United States — Congress retained for itself no powers of control or supervision over an independent counsel. The Act does empower certain Members of Congress to request the Attorney General to apply for the appointment of an independent counsel, but the Attorney General has no duty to comply with the request, although he must

c. Indeed, during the hearings on the 1982 amendments to the Act, [Associate Attorney General Giuliani] testified that the "good cause" standard contained in the amendments "would make the special prosecutor no more independent than officers of the many so-called independent agencies in the executive branch."

respond within a certain time limit. Other than that, Congress' role under the Act is limited to receiving reports or other information and oversight of the independent counsel's activities, functions that we have recognized generally as being incidental to the legislative function of Congress.

Similarly, we do not think that the Act works any judicial usurpation of properly executive functions. . . . [T]he Special Division has no power to appoint an independent counsel sua sponte; it may only do so upon the specific request of the Attorney General, and the courts are specifically prevented from reviewing the Attorney General's decision not to seek appointment. In addition, once the court has appointed a counsel and defined his or her jurisdiction, it has no power to supervise or control the activities of the counsel. As we pointed out in our discussion of the Special Division in relation to Article III, the various powers delegated by the statute to the Division are not supervisory or administrative, nor are they functions that the Constitution requires be performed by officials within the Executive Branch. . . . It is undeniable that the Act reduces the amount of control or supervision that the Attorney General and, through him, the President exercises over the investigation and prosecution of a certain class of alleged criminal activity. The Attorney General is not allowed to appoint the individual of his choice; he does not determine the counsel's jurisdiction; and his power to remove a counsel is limited. Nonetheless, the Act does give the Attorney General several means of supervising or controlling the prosecutorial powers that may be wielded by an independent counsel. Most importantly, the Attorney General retains the power to remove the counsel for "good cause," a power that we have already concluded provides the Executive with substantial ability to ensure that the laws are "faithfully executed" by an independent counsel. No independent counsel may be appointed without a specific request by the Attorney General, and the Attorney General's decision not to request appointment if he finds "no reasonable grounds to believe that further investigation is warranted" is committed to his unreviewable discretion. The Act thus gives the Executive a degree of control over the power to initiate an investigation by the independent counsel. In addition, the jurisdiction of the independent counsel is defined with reference to the facts submitted by the Attorney General, and once a counsel is appointed, the Act requires that the counsel abide by Justice Department policy unless it is not "possible" to do so. Notwithstanding the fact that the counsel is to some degree "independent" and free from executive supervision to a greater extent than other federal prosecutors, in our view these features of the Act give the Executive Branch sufficient control over the independent counsel to ensure that the President is able to perform his constitutionally assigned duties. . . .

Justice SCALIA, dissenting.

It is the proud boast of our democracy that we have "a government of laws and not of men." Many Americans are familiar with that phrase; not many know its derivation. It comes from Part the First, Article XXX, of the Massachusetts Constitution of 1780, which reads in full as follows:

"In the government of this Commonwealth, the legislative department shall never exercise the executive and judicial powers, or either of them: The executive shall never exercise the legislative and judicial powers, or either of them: The judicial shall never exercise the legislative and executive powers, or either of them: to the end it may be a government of laws and not of men."

The Framers of the Federal Constitution similarly viewed the principle of separation of powers as the absolutely central guarantee of a just Government. In No. 47 of The Federalist, Madison wrote that "[n]o political truth is certainly of greater intrinsic value, or is stamped with the authority of more enlightened patrons of liberty." The Federalist No. 47. Without a secure structure of separated powers, our Bill of Rights would be worthless, as are the bills of rights of many nations of the world that have adopted, or even improved upon, the mere words of ours. . . .

II.

If to describe this case is not to decide it, the concept of a government of separate and coordinate powers no longer has meaning. The Court devotes most of its attention to such relatively technical details as the Appointments Clause and the removal power, addressing briefly and only at the end of its opinion the separation of powers. As my prologue suggests, I think that has it backwards. . . . Thus, while I will subsequently discuss why our appointments and removal jurisprudence does not support today's holding, I begin with a consideration of the fountainhead of that jurisprudence, the separation and equilibration of powers. . . .

. . . Article II, §1, cl. 1, of the Constitution provides: "The executive Power shall be vested in a President of the United States."

As I described at the outset of this opinion, this does not mean *some of* the executive power, but *all of* the executive power. It seems to me, therefore, that the decision of the Court of Appeals invalidating the present statute must be upheld on fundamental separation-of-powers principles if the following two questions are answered affirmatively: (1) Is the conduct of a criminal prosecution (and of an investigation to decide whether to prosecute) the exercise of purely executive power? (2) Does the statute deprive the President of the United States of exclusive control over the exercise of that power? Surprising to say, the Court appears to concede an affirmative answer to both questions, but seeks to avoid the inevitable conclusion that since the statute vests some purely executive power in a person who is not the President of the United States it is void.

The Court concedes that "[t]here is no real dispute that the functions performed by the independent counsel are 'executive'," though it qualifies that concession by adding "in the sense that they are law enforcement functions that typically have been undertaken by officials within the Executive Branch." The qualifier adds nothing but atmosphere. . . . Governmental investigation and prosecution of crimes is a quintessentially executive function.

As for the second question, whether the statute before us deprives the President of exclusive control over that quintessentially executive activity: The Court does not, and could not possibly, assert that it does not. That is indeed the whole object of the statute. Instead, the Court points out that the President, through his Attorney General, has at least *some* control. That concession is alone enough to invalidate the statute, but I cannot refrain from pointing out that the Court greatly exaggerates the extent of that "some" Presidential control. "Most importan[t]" among these controls, the Court asserts, is the Attorney General's "power to remove the counsel for 'good cause.'" This is somewhat like referring to shackles as an effective means of locomotion. . . .

. . . Finally, the Court points out that the Act directs the independent counsel to abide by general Justice Department policy, except when not "possible." The exception alone shows this to be an empty promise. Even without that, however, one would be hard put to come up with many investigative or prosecutorial "policies" (other than those imposed by the Constitution or by Congress through law) that are absolute. Almost all investigative and prosecutorial decisions — including the ultimate decision whether, after a technical violation of the law has been found, prosecution is warranted — involve the balancing of innumerable legal and practical considerations. Indeed, even political considerations (in the nonpartisan sense) must be considered, as exemplified by the recent decision of an independent counsel to subpoena the former Ambassador of Canada, producing considerable tension in our relations with that country. Another preeminently political decision is whether getting a conviction in a particular case is worth the disclosure of national security information that would be necessary. The Justice Department and our intelligence agencies are often in disagreement on this point, and the Justice Department does not always win. The present Act even goes so far as specifically to take the resolution of that dispute away from the President and give it to the independent counsel. In sum, the balancing of various legal, practical, and political considerations, none of which is absolute, is the very essence of prosecutorial discretion. To take this away is to remove the core of the prosecutorial function, and not merely "some" Presidential control.

As I have said, however, it is ultimately irrelevant *how much* the statute reduces Presidential control. . . . It is not for us to determine, and we have never presumed to determine, how much of the purely executive powers of government must be within the full control of the President. The Constitution prescribes that they *all* are. . . .

Is it unthinkable that the President should have such exclusive power, even when alleged crimes by him or his close associates are at issue? No more so than that Congress should have the exclusive power of legislation, even when what is at issue is its own exemption from the burdens of certain laws. No more so than that this Court should have the exclusive power to pronounce the final decision on justiciable cases and controversies, even those pertaining to the constitutionality of a statute reducing the salaries of the Justices. A system of separate and coordinate powers necessarily involves an acceptance of exclusive power that can theoretically be abused. . . . While the separation of powers may prevent us from righting every wrong, it does so in order to ensure that we do not lose liberty. The checks against any branch's abuse of its exclusive powers are twofold: First, retaliation by one of the other branch's use of its exclusive powers: Congress, for example, can impeach the executive who willfully fails to enforce the laws; the executive can decline to prosecute under unconstitutional statutes; and the courts can dismiss malicious prosecutions. Second, and ultimately, there is the political check that the people will replace those in the political branches . . . who are guilty of abuse. Political pressures produced special prosecutors — for Teapot Dome and for Watergate, for example — long before this statute created the independent counsel.

The Court has, nonetheless, replaced the clear constitutional prescription that the executive power belongs to the President with a "balancing test." What are the standards to determine how the balance is to be struck, that is, how much removal of Presidential power is too much? . . .

In my view, moreover, even as an ad hoc, standardless judgment the Court's conclusion must be wrong. . . .

[I]n the 10 years since the institution of the independent counsel was established by law, there have been nine highly publicized investigations, a source of constant political damage to two administrations. That they could not remotely be described as merely the application of "normal" investigatory and prosecutory standards is demonstrated by . . . the following facts: Congress appropriates approximately $50 million annually for general legal activities, salaries, and expenses of the Criminal Division of the Department of Justice. This money is used to support "[f]ederal appellate activity," "[o]rganized crime prosecution," "[p]ublic integrity" and "[f]raud" matters, "[n]arcotic & dangerous drug prosecution," "[i]nternal security," "[g]eneral litigation and legal advice," "special investigations," "[p]rosecution support," "[o]rganized crime drug enforcement," and "[m]anagement & administration." By comparison, between May 1986 and August 1987, four independent counsel (not all of whom were operating for that entire period of time) spent almost $5 million (one-tenth of the amount annually appropriated to the entire Criminal Division), spending almost $1 million in the month of August 1987 alone. . . .

III.

As I indicated earlier, the basic separation-of-powers principles I have discussed are what give life and content to our jurisprudence concerning the President's power to appoint and remove officers. . . .

[T]he Court does not attempt to "decide exactly" what establishes the line between principal and "inferior" officers, but is confident that, whatever the line may be, appellant "clearly falls on the 'inferior officer' side" of it. The Court gives three reasons: First, she "is subject to removal by a higher Executive Branch official," namely, the Attorney General. Second, she is "empowered by the Act to perform only certain, limited duties." Third, her office is "limited in jurisdiction" and "limited in tenure."

The first of these lends no support to the view that appellant is an inferior officer. Appellant is removable only for "good cause" or physical or mental incapacity. By contrast, most (if not all) principal officers in the Executive Branch may be removed by the President at will. I fail to see how the fact that appellant is more difficult to remove than most principal officers helps to establish that she is an inferior officer. And I do not see how it could possibly make any difference to her superior or inferior status that the President's limited power to remove her must be exercised through the Attorney General. If she were removable at will by the Attorney General, then she would be subordinate to him and thus properly designated as inferior; but the Court essentially admits that she is not subordinate. If it were common usage to refer to someone as "inferior" who is subject to removal for cause by another, then one would say that the President is "inferior" to Congress.

The second reason offered by the Court — that appellant performs only certain, limited duties — may be relevant to whether she is an inferior officer, but it mischaracterizes the extent of her powers. As the Court states: "Admittedly, the Act delegates to appellant [the] 'full power and independent authority to exercise all investigative and prosecutorial functions and powers of the Department of Justice.'" Moreover, in addition to this general grant of power she is given a broad range of specifically enumerated powers, including a power not even the Attorney General possesses: to "contes[t] in court . . . any claim of privilege or attempt to withhold evidence on grounds of national security." Once all of this is "admitted," it seems to me impossible to maintain that appellant's authority is so "limited" as to render her an inferior officer. . . .

The final set of reasons given by the Court for why the independent counsel clearly is an inferior officer emphasizes the limited nature of her jurisdiction and tenure. Taking the latter first, I find nothing unusually limited about the independent counsel's tenure. To the contrary, unlike most high ranking Executive Branch officials, she continues to serve until she (or the Special Division) decides that her work is substantially completed. This particular independent prosecutor has already served more than two years, which is at least as long as many Cabinet officials. As to the scope of her jurisdiction, there can be no doubt that is small (though far from unimportant). But within it she exercises more than the full power of the Attorney General. The Ambassador to Luxembourg is not anything less than a principal officer, simply because Luxembourg is small. And the federal judge who sits in a small district is not for that reason "inferior in rank and authority." . . .

More fundamentally, however, it is not clear from the Court's opinion why the factors it discusses — even if applied correctly to the facts of this case — are determinative of the question of inferior officer status. . . . I think it preferable to look to the text of the Constitution and the division of power that it establishes. These demonstrate, I think, that the independent counsel is not an inferior officer because she is not *subordinate* to any officer in the Executive Branch (indeed, not even to the President). Dictionaries in use at the time of the Constitutional Convention gave the word "inferiour" two meanings which it still bears today: (1) "[l]ower in place, . . . station, . . . rank of life, . . . value or excellency," and (2) "[s]ubordinate." S. Johnson, Dictionary of the English Language (6th ed. 1785). In a document dealing with the structure (the constitution) of a government, one would naturally expect the word to bear the latter meaning — indeed, in such a context it would be unpardonably careless to use the word unless a relationship of subordination was intended. If what was meant was merely "lower in station or rank," one would use instead a term such as "lesser officers." At the only other point in the Constitution at which the word "inferior" appears, it plainly connotes a relationship of subordination. Article III vests the judicial power of the United States in "one supreme Court, and in such *inferior* Courts as the Congress may from time to time ordain and establish." U.S. Const., Art. III, §1 (emphasis added). In Federalist No. 81, Hamilton pauses to describe the "inferior" courts authorized by Article III as inferior in the sense that they are "subordinate" to the Supreme Court.

That "inferior" means "subordinate" is also consistent with what little we know about the evolution of the Appointments Clause. As originally reported to the Committee on Style, the Appointments Clause provided no "exception" from the standard manner of appointment (President with the advice and consent of the Senate) for inferior officers. On September 15, 1787, the last day of the Convention before the proposed Constitution was signed, in the midst of a host of minor changes that were being considered, Gouverneur Morris moved to add the exceptions clause. No great debate ensued; the only disagreement was over whether it was necessary at all. Nobody thought that it was a fundamental change, excluding from the President's appointment power and the Senate's confirmation power a category of officers who might function on their own, outside the supervision of those appointed in the more cumbersome fashion. And it is significant that in the very brief discussion Madison mentions (as in apparent contrast to the "inferior officers" covered by the provision) "Superior Officers." Of course one is not a "superior officer" without some supervisory responsibility, just as, I suggest, one is not an "inferior officer" within the meaning of the provision under discussion unless one is subject to supervision by a "superior officer." It is perfectly obvious, therefore, both from the relative brevity of the discussion this addition received, and from the content of that discussion, that it was intended merely to make clear (what Madison thought already was clear) that those officers appointed by the President with Senate approval could on their own appoint their subordinates, who would, of course, by chain of command still be under the direct control of the President.

This interpretation is, moreover, consistent with our admittedly sketchy precedent in this area. . . . [I]in United States v. Nixon, we noted that the Attorney General's appointment of the Watergate Special Prosecutor was made pursuant to the Attorney General's "power to appoint subordinate officers to assist him in the discharge of his duties." . . . We explicitly stated that the Special Prosecutor was a "subordinate office[r]," because, in the end, the President or the Attorney General could have removed him at any time, if by no other means than amending or revoking the regulation defining his authority. . . .

To be sure, it is not a *sufficient* condition for "inferior" officer status that one be subordinate to a principal officer. . . . Even an officer who is subordinate to a department head can be a principal officer. . . . But it is surely a *necessary* condition for inferior officer status that the officer be subordinate to another officer.

The independent counsel is not even subordinate to the President. The Court essentially admits as much. . . .

IV.

. . . Before the present decision it was established . . . (1) that the President's power to remove principal officers who exercise purely executive powers could not be restricted, see *Myers,* and (2) that his power to remove inferior officers who exercise purely executive powers, and whose appointment Congress had removed from the usual procedure of Presidential appointment with Senate consent, could be restricted, at least where the appointment had been made by an officer of the Executive Branch, see ibid.; United States v. Perkins, 116 U.S. 483, 485 (1886).[a]

The Court could have resolved the removal power issue in this case by simply relying upon its erroneous conclusion that the independent counsel was an inferior officer, and then extending our holding that the removal of inferior officers appointed by the Executive can be restricted, to a new holding that even the removal of inferior officers appointed by the courts can be restricted. That would in my view be a considerable and unjustified extension, giving the Executive full discretion in neither the selection nor the removal of a purely executive officer. The course the Court has chosen, however, is even worse.

Since our 1935 decision in Humphrey's Executor v. United States, 295 U.S. 602 — which was considered by many at the time the product of an activist, anti-New Deal Court bent on reducing the power of President Franklin Roosevelt — it

---

a. [T]he President must have control over all exercises of the executive power. That requires that he have plenary power to remove principal officers such as the independent counsel, but it does not require that he have plenary power to remove inferior officers. Since the latter are, as I have described, subordinate to, i.e., subject to the supervision of, principal officers who (being removable at will) have the President's complete confidence, it is enough — at least if they have been appointed by the President or by a principal officer — that they be removable for cause, which would include, of course, the failure to accept supervision. . . .

has been established that the line of permissible restriction upon removal of principal officers lies at the point at which the powers exercised by those officers are no longer purely executive. Thus, removal restrictions have been generally regarded as lawful for so-called "independent regulatory agencies," such as the Federal Trade Commission, the Interstate Commerce Commission, and the Consumer Product Safety Commission, which engage substantially in what has been called the "quasi-legislative activity" of rulemaking, and for members of Article I courts, such as the Court of Military Appeals, who engage in the "quasi-judicial" function of adjudication. . . . Today, however, *Humphrey's Executor* is swept into the dustbin of repudiated constitutional principles. "[O]ur present considered view," the Court says, "is that the determination of whether the Constitution allows Congress to impose a 'good cause'-type restriction on the President's power to remove an official cannot be made to turn on whether or not that official is classified as 'purely executive.' " . . .

. . . "[O]ur present considered view" is simply that any executive officer's removal can be restricted, so long as the President remains "able to accomplish his constitutional role." There are now no lines. If the removal of a prosecutor, the virtual embodiment of the power to "take care that the laws be faithfully executed," can be restricted, what officer's removal cannot? This is an open invitation for Congress to experiment. What about a special Assistant Secretary of State, with responsibility for one very narrow area of foreign policy, who would not only have to be confirmed by the Senate but could also be removed only pursuant to certain carefully designed restrictions? Could this possibly render the President "[un]able to accomplish his constitutional role"? Or a special Assistant Secretary of Defense for Procurement? The possibilities are endless. . . .

V.

The purpose of the separation and equilibration of powers in general, and of the unitary Executive in particular, was not merely to assure effective government but to preserve individual freedom. Those who hold or have held offices covered by the Ethics in Government Act are entitled to that protection as much as the rest of us, and I conclude my discussion by considering the effect of the Act upon the fairness of the process they receive.

Only someone who has worked in the field of law enforcement can fully appreciate the vast power and the immense discretion that are placed in the hands of a prosecutor with respect to the objects of his investigation. Justice Robert Jackson, when he was Attorney General under President Franklin Roosevelt, described it in a memorable speech to United States Attorneys, as follows:

". . . One of the greatest difficulties of the position of prosecutor is that he must pick his cases, because no prosecutor can even investigate all of the cases in which he receives complaints. If the Department of Justice were to make even a pretense of reaching every probable violation of federal law, ten times its present staff will be inadequate. We know that no local police force can strictly enforce the traffic laws, or it would arrest half the driving population on any given morning. What every prosecutor is practically required to do is to select the cases for prosecution and to select those in which the offense is the most flagrant, the public harm the greatest, and the proof the most certain.

"If the prosecutor is obliged to choose his case, it follows that he can choose his defendants. Therein is the most dangerous power of the prosecutor: that he will pick people that he thinks he should get, rather than cases that need to be prosecuted. With the law books filled with a great assortment of crimes, a prosecutor stands a fair chance of finding at least a technical violation of some act on the part of almost anyone. In such a case, it is not a question of discovering the commission of a crime and then looking for the man who has committed it, it is a question of picking the man and then searching the law books, or putting investigators to work, to pin some offense on him. It is in this realm — in which the prosecutor picks some person whom he dislikes or desires to embarrass, or selects some group of unpopular persons and then looks for an offense, that the greatest danger of abuse of prosecuting power lies. It is here that law enforcement becomes personal, and the real crime becomes that of being unpopular with the predominant or governing group, being attached to the wrong political views, or being personally obnoxious to or in the way of the prosecutor himself."

Under our system of government, the primary check against prosecutorial abuse is a political one. The prosecutors who exercise this awesome discretion are selected and can be removed by a President, whom the people have trusted enough to elect. Moreover, when crimes are not investigated and prosecuted fairly, nonselectively, with a reasonable sense of proportion, the President pays the cost in political damage to his administration. . . . That result, of course, was precisely what the Founders had in mind when they provided that all executive powers would be exercised by a single Chief Executive. As Hamilton put it, "[t]he ingredients which constitute safety in the republican sense are a due dependence on the people, and a due responsibility." Federalist No. 70. The President is directly dependent on the people, and since there is only one President, he is responsible. The people know whom to blame, whereas "one of the weightiest objections to a plurality in the executive . . . is that it tends to conceal faults and destroy responsibility."

That is the system of justice the rest of us are entitled to, but what of that select class consisting of present or former high-level Executive Branch officials? . . . An independent counsel is selected, and the scope of his or her authority prescribed, by a panel of judges. What if they are politically partisan, as judges have been known to be, and select a prosecutor antagonistic to the administration, or even to the particular individual who has been selected for this special treatment? There is no remedy for that, not even a political one. Judges, after all, have life tenure, and appointing a surefire enthusiastic prosecutor could hardly be considered an impeachable offense. So if there is anything wrong with the selection, there is effectively no one to blame. The independent counsel thus selected proceeds to assemble a staff. . . . [I]n the nature of things this has to be done by finding lawyers who are willing to lay aside their current careers for an indeterminate amount of time, to take on a job that has no prospect of permanence and little prospect for promotion. One thing is certain, however: it involves investigating and perhaps prosecuting a particular individual. Can one imagine a less equitable manner of fulfilling the executive responsibility to investigate and prosecute? What would be the reaction if, in an area not covered by this statute, the Justice Department posted a public notice inviting applicants to assist in an investigation and possible prosecution of a certain prominent person? Does this not invite what Justice Jackson described as "picking the man and then searching the law books, or putting investigators to work, to pin some offense on him"? To be sure, the investigation must relate to the area of criminal offense specified by the life-tenured judges. But that has often been (and nothing prevents it from being) very broad — and should the independent counsel or his or her staff come up with something beyond that scope, nothing prevents him or her from asking the judges to expand his or her authority or, if that does not work, referring it to the Attorney General, whereupon the whole process would recommence and, if there was "reasonable basis to believe" that further investigation was warranted, that new offense would be referred to the Special Division, which would in all likelihood assign it to the same independent counsel. It seems to me not conducive to fairness. But even if it were entirely evident that unfairness was in fact the result — the judges hostile to the administration, the independent counsel an old foe of the President, the staff refugees from the recently defeated administration — *there would be no one accountable to the public to whom the blame could be assigned.*

. . . It is true, of course, that a similar list of horribles could be attributed to an ordinary Justice Department prosecution — a vindictive prosecutor, an antagonistic staff, etc. But the difference is the difference that the Founders envisioned when they established a single Chief Executive accountable to the people: the blame can be assigned to someone who can be punished.

. . . It is . . . an additional advantage of the unitary Executive that it can achieve a more uniform application of the law. Perhaps that is not always achieved, but the mechanism to achieve it is there. The mini-Executive that is the independent counsel, however, operating in an area where so little is law and so much is discretion, is intentionally cut off from the unifying influence of the Justice Department, and from the perspective that multiple responsibilities provide. What would normally be regarded as a technical violation (there are no rules defining such things), may in his or her small world assume the proportions of an indictable offense. What would normally be regarded as an investigation that has reached the level of pursuing such picayune matters that it should be concluded, may to him or her be an investigation that ought to go on for another year. How frightening it must be to have your own independent counsel and staff appointed, with nothing else to do but to investigate you until investigation is no longer worthwhile — with whether it is worthwhile not depending upon what such judgments usually hinge on, competing responsibilities. And to have that counsel and staff decide, with no basis for comparison, whether what you have done is bad enough, willful enough, and provable enough, to warrant an indictment. How admirable the constitutional system that provides the means to avoid such a distortion. And how unfortunate the judicial decision that has permitted it. . . .

[Justice KENNEDY did not participate in this case.]

Discussion

1. *Construing statutes in the shadow of constitutional principles.* Section 592 of the independent counsel statute provided that "The Attorney General shall apply to the division of the court for the appointment of an independent counsel if . . . the Attorney General, upon completion of a preliminary investigation under this chapter, determines that there are reasonable grounds to believe that further investigation is warranted." If read with the emphasis on the word *shall,* this provision would seem to impose a strict legal duty on the Attorney General to trigger the judicial appointment of an independent counsel even in cases where the AG would prefer otherwise as a matter of policy. But the *Morrison* majority, in an oft-overlooked passage, essentially defanged this provision. Implicitly placing

the emphasis not on the word *shall* but on the notion that it is the *Attorney General* who must decide that there are truly *reasonable* grounds for deciding that further investigation is truly *warranted,* the *Morrison* Court reads this provision to give the AG "unreviewable discretion" to not trigger the appointment. This reading helps make the statute more constitutionally palatable to majority. Note the similarity to the *Cox* court's reading of Rule 7, and the *Nixon* Court's reminder that the regulation empowering the special prosecutor may be rescinded by Executive Branch; in all three contexts, the gravitational pull of constitutional principles under Article II appears to inflect the reading of nonconstitutional texts.

2. *Recasting precedents.* Precedent counts for a great deal in modern constitutional adjudications, but precedent can be read in different ways. Note the *Morrison* majority's effort to recast the *Myers* and *Humphrey's Executor* precedents. If read at face value, these cases distinguish between officials who exercise purely executive power on the one hand, and those who wield quasi-legislative or quasi-judicial power on the other. The *Morrison* majority, however reads these cases not for what they said but for what they did; the more relevant distinction, the *Morrison* Court announces (in retrospect), is that Congress tried to participate in the removal process in *Myers* (via a legislative veto on presidential removal), but not in *Humphrey's Executor.* Regardless of what you think about the use of the technique in *Morrison,* note that judicial rewriting of old precedents — explaining why earlier decisions were right on their facts but wrong in some of their language — is an important part of the modern judicial craft, allowing case law to evolve while maintaining links to the past.

3. *The meaning of "inferiority".* Did the *Morrison* majority play fast and loose with the word "inferior"? Can one truly be both "inferior" and "independent" at the same time? Note that the Court emphasizes that the special division should not be understood as the independent counsel's supervisor — lest judges become superprosecutors of sorts. But if the three judges are not Morrison's supervisor, who is? Can there be an "inferior" officer without a corresponding "superior" officer? Following Justice Scalia's lead, let us consider the possible light that "intratextualism" — construing one clause of the Constitution in light of similarly worded clauses — might shed on the meaning of the word "inferior." Note that Article I, §8 speaks of "tribunals *inferior to* the *Supreme* Court." Here, it seems, there is a clear hierarchical chain of command — "inferior" tribunals must follow the commands of their superior, the Supreme Court. (This helps explain why such tribunals are bound by High Court precedent, see Evan H. Caminker, Why Must Inferior Courts Obey Superior Court Precedents?, 46 Stan. L. Rev. 817, 828-837 (1994).) Does the same word — "inferior" — mean the same thing in the Appointments Clause context, namely, that an "inferior" officer must be subordinate to his "superior," the relevant appointing authority (whether court or department head or President)?

A considerable amount of historical evidence suggests so. The language permitting unilateral appointment of inferior officers emerged on the last day of the Philadelphia Convention, and with little debate — facts suggesting that it was viewed as a minor housekeeping measure to spare the Senate's time. (The only other recorded discussion of inferior officers occurred a week earlier and strongly supports this interpretation: Recall that Rufus King stated that he "did not suppose it was meant that all the minute officers were to be appointed by the Senate, or any other original source, but by the higher officers *of the departments to which they belong.*") Allowing major officers to pick their own assistants keeps faith with this housekeeping reading. But authorizing judges to appoint prosecutors — or diplomats or colonels, for that matter — seems very different. Had the delegates understood that the clause could be so applied, we would expect to find considerably more discussion.

In keeping with the housekeeping reading, the First Congress in one of its earliest statutes vested the Secretary of the Department of Foreign Affairs with the power to appoint and supervise *his own assistant:* "There shall be in the said department, an inferior officer, to be appointed by the said principal officer, and to be employed therein as he shall deem proper. . . ." Soon thereafter, Congress used similar language in allowing the Secretary of War to appoint and monitor his own assistant. In his landmark 1833 treatise on the Constitution, Joseph Story wrote that:

> The courts of the Union possess the narrow prerogative of appointing *their own* clerk, and reporter. . . . The heads of department are, in like manner, generally entitled to the appointment of the clerks in their *respective* offices. . . . [And] the postmaster general . . . is invested with the sole and exclusive authority to appoint, and remove all *deputy* post-masters.

Joseph Story, Commentaries on the Constitution of the United States 1530, at 387 (Boston, Hilliard, Gray & Co. 1833) (emphasis added).

Six years after the publication of Story's 1833 treatise, the Supreme Court expounded the Appointments Clause as follows in Ex Parte Hennen, 38 U.S. (13 Pet.) 230 (1839):

> The appointing power here designated . . . was no doubt intended to be exercised by the department of the government to which the officer to be appointed most appropriately belonged. The appointment of *clerks of Courts* properly belongs to the *Courts* of law; and that a clerk is one of the inferior officers contemplated by this provision in the Constitution cannot be questioned. Congress, in the exercise of the power here given, by the act of the 24th of September, 1789, establishing the judicial Courts of the United States . . . , declare that the Supreme Court, and the District Courts shall have power to appoint clerks of their *respective* Courts; and that the clerk for each District Court shall be clerk also of the Circuit Court in such district.

The basic structural idea at play in the appointments context was accountability: when an inferior officer misbehaved, the polity would know whom to blame — the appointing authority responsible for choosing and monitoring the inferior. See, e.g., The Federalist No. 70, at 428 (Alexander Hamilton) (Clinton Rossiter ed., 1961) ("Scandalous appointments to important offices have been made [in New York by a governor acting behind closed doors with his council]. . . . When inquiry has been made, the blame has been laid by the governor on the members of the council, who, on their part, have charged it upon his nomination; while the people remain altogether at a loss to determine by whose influence their interests have been committed to hands so unqualified and so manifestly improper."); see also The Federalist No. 76, at 455 (Alexander Hamilton) ("The sole and undivided [appointment] responsibility of one man will naturally beget a livelier sense of duty and a more exact regard to reputation."); The Federalist No. 77, at 461 (Alexander Hamilton) ("The blame of a bad nomination would fall upon the President singly and absolutely.").

4. *Independent agencies.* This chapter has traced, among other things, the development of the "administrative state," characterized by the ever-increasing role of administrative agencies in the modern scheme of government. The origins of the federal administrative state reach back over 100 years to the Interstate Commerce Commission (ICC), established under the Interstate Commerce Act of 1887. The five commissioners of the ICC were appointed by the President and confirmed by the Senate. Their mode of appointment thus raised no hard questions under the Appointments Clause. But these "quasi-legislative" and "quasi-judicial" officers differed from other executive appointees in two important respects. First, they held office for a fixed term (often extending beyond the administration of the appointing President). Second, whereas presidents may dismiss most high-level officials by requesting their resignations, ICC commissioners could be removed only through congressional impeachment or upon demonstration of "cause" by the executive. There have, in fact, been no such removals in the history of the major independent agencies, which today include Federal Trade Commission and the Federal Reserve Board (both established during President Wilson's tenure); New Deal agencies such the Federal Communications Commission, the Securities and Exchange Commission, and National Labor Relations Board; and the more recently established Consumer Products Safety Commission.

On Justice Scalia's view are all these "independent" agencies a violation of the unitary executive principle? If not, is it because although the President may not fire them at will, he may nevertheless tell them what to do, and they must obey, within the bounds of their lawful discretion? Can the President lawfully order the Chairman of the Federal Reserve to lower interest rates? Or is The Fed a special case, requiring a deviation from the Framers' model to accommodate the unforeseen post-Founding developments of a modern plebiscitary presidency and the discovery of Keynesian techniques that would allow unscrupulous incumbent Presidents to artificially inflate the economy in reelection years (with perhaps disastrous effects setting in only after the election)? If a special case can be made for The Fed, what about the other "independent" agencies? The myriad issues surrounding "independent" agencies and more traditional executive branch agencies are covered in great detail in administrative law casebooks, as are landmark cases like *Myers* and *Humphrey's Executor* that are treated only in passing in this casebook.

5. *The judicial role.* Recall that the independent counsel statute was criticized (especially by Judge Silberman) not only as impermissibly intruding upon the executive branch, but also for distorting the proper role of the judicial branch. Akhil Amar has argued that

> Prosecutors wield *executive* power, whereas judges should exercise only *judicial* power. Asking judges to pick prosecutors is like asking them to appoint generals or name ambassadors. . . . [C]onsider how unwise the statute is, sucking judges into partisan politics. Judges decide law in open court. But no *law* can say who should be the prosecutor in any given case — that's a question of policy, personality, and politics. To decide this question, judges will need to act like politicos, talking secretly to politicians to figure out who will be an acceptable candidate to all sides. Judges may well pick a fellow judge lacking prosecutorial experience, who in turn may well make many rookie mistakes. (Sound familiar?) And judges in the nature of things can't properly supervise prosecutors without [impermissibly turning themselves] into superprosecutors.

Akhil Reed Amar, Should We Ditch the Independent Prosecutor Law?, Slate (*http://www.slate.com*), Feb. 16-19, 1999. Consider also the argument that judges will not be good at picking prosecutors because they have limited information about past prosecutorial performance. Whereas the Attorney General has relatively complete information about the track record of federal prosecutors (including information about cases not brought because of the sound exercise of discretion), judges generally do not and should not have access to this treasure trove of intra-executive intelligence, implicating various out-of-court activities that lie beyond the proper province of judicial supervision. Finally, consider the special awkwardness of judicial involvement when independent counsels are formally involved in the impeachment process — which the Framers generally sought to take away from ordinary judges. Did the 1978 Congress and the *Morrison* Justices give these judicial-role issues enough attention?

6. *Bargaining in the shadow of the Court.* One of the main lessons of the Coase Theorem, supra p. 540, is that legal rules often establish a baseline, or default rule, against which further bargaining among interested parties may take place. Baseline starting points matter, but these starting points need not be ending points. In *Morrison*, even if Justice Scalia's view had prevailed, note that members of Congress could have used their oversight, appropriations, publicity, and impeachment powers to put a great deal of pressure on the Attorney General and President to initiate prosecutions that the Administration might prefer not to initiate. (Oversight in Congress could even be given to a "blue ribbon" commission of outside investigators who enjoyed especially strong credibility in the press and public.) Conversely, even after the *Morrison* case, recall that the President could have effectively and unilaterally "reversed" the Court simply by pardoning Mr. Olson, thus "removing" Ms. Morrison de facto by giving her no one to prosecute. Anyone who today doubts this presidential power should recall that in December 1992, President George Bush pardoned Caspar Weinberger, thereby effectively putting the Iran-Contra independent counsel Lawrence Walsh out of business. Indeed, just as Presidents nowadays deploy their veto power proactively — waving their veto pens in the air early on and announcing what bills will and will not get past their desk — a truly skillful chief executive could wield the pardon broadsword as a surgical scalpel by explaining the facts of life to an independent counsel (publicly or privately): Unless she does X and Y and refrains from Z, the President will be obliged to pardon. Granted, all this may make the President look bad politically — and so we return once again to the critical issues of publicity highlighted by the *Cox* and *Nixon* cases.

7. *Sunrise, sunset.* The 1978 Ethics in Government Act was signed into law by President Jimmy Carter, who had won the presidency, two years after Nixon's resignation and Ford's pardon, on a reformist, anti-corruption platform. Unlike most laws, however, the independent counsel statute had a built-in sunset provision under which it lapsed after five years. Over the next two decades, the act was repeatedly readopted, with new sunset clauses — most recently in a 1994 law bearing President Clinton's signature and set to expire in 1999. The sunset provision changed the game in important ways: A President cannot unilaterally repeal an existing law, but if this law is due to sunset, a President can simply veto its reenactment. At no time have congressional supporters of independent counsels had enough votes to override a presidential veto. And so Presidents who disagreed with *Morrison* could in the long run prevail over the Court through the use of their veto

pens, as well as their pardon pens, simply by refusing to accept reauthorization of the statute. This refusal occurred at the end of the Bush Administration, and again at the end of the Clinton Administration. Note also how the veto power interacts with the basic default rule of the Appointments Clause itself: Congress may vest appointments in courts only when it acts "by law" — and of course the President plays a very large role, via the veto, in deciding what that law will be.

Consider, in this regard, the testimony of Attorney General Janet Reno on March, 17, 1999, before the Senate Committee on Governmental Affairs:

> After much reflection and inquiry, we [at the Justice Department] have decided — reluctantly — to oppose reauthorization of the Independent Counsel Act. . . .
>
> In 1993, as many of you know, I testified in support of the statute. I said that the law has been a good one, helping to restore public confidence in our system's ability to investigate wrongdoing by high-level Executive Branch officials. . . .
>
> However, after working with the Act, I have come to believe — after much reflection and with great reluctance — that the Independent Counsel Act is structurally flawed and that those flaws cannot be corrected within our constitutional framework. . . .
>
> In the first place, it has failed to instill confidence among the public that politics has been removed from the process. This is so, in large part, because the Act requires the Attorney General to make key decisions at several critical stages of the process — whether to open a preliminary investigation, whether to seek appointment of an independent counsel, what subject matter to refer to the court when seeking a counsel, and whether to remove him or her. This central role for the Attorney General was not just a congressional choice, but a constitutional mandate. In Morrison v. Olson, the Court made clear that the Act was constitutional because it required the Executive Branch — through the Attorney General — to play a critical role in these key decisions. But the very thing that makes the statute constitutional is also what prevents it from accomplishing its goals. For an Attorney General, after all, is a member of the President's cabinet, and as such, his or her decisions will inevitably be second guessed and criticized no matter what decision is made. . . .
>
> . . . Instead of giving people confidence in the system, the Act creates an artificial process that divides responsibility and fragments accountability. . . .
>
> It is for these reasons that the Justice Department has concluded that the Independent Counsel Act is structurally and fundamentally flawed, and that it should not be reauthorized. But let me be clear, also, about what our position does *not* mean. It does not mean that allegations of high-level corruption should be pursued with anything less than the utmost vigor and seriousness of purpose. And it does *not* mean that the Department considers itself capable of pursuing, in the ordinary course, each and every allegation of corruption at the highest levels of our government. We know that, sometimes, a special prosecutor is in order.
>
> Yet we have come to believe that the country would be best served by a return to the system that existed before the Independent Counsel Act — when the Justice Department took responsibility for all but the most exceptional of cases against high-ranking public officials, and when the Attorney General exercised the authority to appoint a special prosecutor in exceptional situations.
>
> Our Founders set up three branches of government: a Congress that would make the laws, an Executive that would enforce them, and a judiciary that would decide when they had been broken. The Attorney General, who is appointed by the President and confirmed by the Senate, is publicly accountable for her decisions. The Attorney General must answer to the Congress — and, ultimately, to the American people. And in this day of aggressive journalism, sophisticated public advocates, and

skilled congressional investigators, we are held — I believe — more accountable than ever.

In contrast, the independent counsel is vested with the full gamut of prosecutorial powers, but with little of its accountability. He has not been confirmed by the Senate, and he is not typically subject to the same sorts of oversight or budgetary constraints that the Department faces day in and day out. Accountability is no small matter. It goes to the very heart of our constitutional scheme. Our Founders believed that the enormity of the prosecutorial power — and all the decisions about who, what, and whether to prosecute — should be vested in one who is responsible to the people. That way — and here I'm paraphrasing Justice Scalia's dissent in Morrison v. Olson — whether we're talking about over-prosecuting or under-prosecuting, "the blame can be assigned to someone who can be punished."

It was for this reason that the American republic survived for over 200 years without an Independent Counsel Act. When high-level officials have been accused of wrongdoing, the Department has not hesitated to fully investigate. Over the last two decades, the Department of Justice has obtained the convictions of 13,345 public officials and employees from both sides of the political aisle. The Department prosecuted Vice President Spiro Agnew while he held office and also Bert Lance, the Director of the Office of Management and Budget, soon after he left the Administration.

The Attorney General has also stood ready, under his or her authority, to appoint a special prosecutor when the situation demanded it. Paul Curran investigated allegations concerning a peanut warehouse owned by President Carter's family while he was still in office. Leon Jaworski investigated President Nixon, members of his Cabinet, and others. And although the President ordered the firing of Mr. Jaworski's predecessor, Archibald Cox, Jaworski showed that a non-statutory special prosecutor can do exactly what must be done: investigate high-level members of an Administration even when the President is bent on subverting the investigation. Perhaps the real lesson of our nation's experience with the Special Prosecutor during Watergate is not that the old system was broken — but that it worked. . . .

[W]e at the Department have come to believe that the Act's goals have not been well-served by the Act itself — and that we would do better without a statute. Instead, the Department would utilize the Attorney General's authority to appoint a special prosecutor when the situation demands it. . . .

8. *Is* Morrison *good law today?* Consider, finally, another important presidential power at work in the independent counsel story — the presidential power to nominate Justices, subject of course to Senate confirmation. Only three of the Justices who voted with the majority in *Morrison* were still on the Court in 1999. Does the *Morrison* vision still command the allegiance of a Court majority? What, if anything, do you make of the following case?

EDMOND v. UNITED STATES
520 U.S. 651 (1997)

Justice SCALIA delivered the opinion of the Court.

We must determine in this case whether Congress has authorized the Secretary of Transportation to appoint civilian members of the Coast Guard Court of Criminal Appeals, and if so, whether this authorization is constitutional under the Appointments Clause of Article II. . . .

III.

. . . As we recognized in Buckley v. Valeo, 424 U.S. 1 (1976), the Appointments Clause of Article II is more than a matter of "etiquette or protocol"; it is among the significant structural safeguards of the constitutional scheme. By vesting the President with the exclusive power to select the principal (noninferior) officers of the United States, the Appointments Clause prevents congressional encroachment upon the Executive and Judicial Branches. This disposition was also designed to assure a higher quality of appointments: the Framers anticipated that the President would be less vulnerable to interest-group pressure and personal favoritism than would a collective body. "The sole and undivided responsibility of one man will naturally beget a livelier sense of duty, and a more exact regard to reputation." The Federalist No. 76. The President's power to select principal officers of the United States was not left unguarded, however, as Article II further requires the "Advice and Consent of the Senate." This serves both to curb executive abuses of the appointment power, and "to promote a judicious choice of [persons] for filling the offices of the union," The Federalist No. 76. By requiring the joint participation of the President and the Senate, the Appointments Clause was designed to ensure public accountability for both the making of a bad appointment and the rejection of a good one. Hamilton observed:

> "The blame of a bad nomination would fall upon the president singly and absolutely. The censure of rejecting a good one would lie entirely at the door of the senate; aggravated by the consideration of their having counteracted the good intentions of the executive. If an ill appointment should be made, the executive for nominating, and the senate for approvin]g, would participate, though in different degrees, in the opprobrium and disgrace." Id., No. 77.

The prescribed manner of appointment for principal officers is also the default manner of appointment for inferior officers. "But," the Appointments Clause continues, "the Congress may by Law vest the Appointment of such inferior Officers, as they think proper, in the President alone, in the Courts of Law, or in the Heads of Departments." This provision, sometimes referred to as the "Excepting Clause," was added to the proposed Constitution on the last day of the Grand Convention, with little discussion. As one of our early opinions suggests, its obvious purpose is administrative convenience — but that convenience was deemed to outweigh the benefits of the more cumbersome procedure only with respect to the appointment of "inferior Officers." Section 323(a), which confers appointment power upon the Secretary of Transportation, can constitutionally be applied to the appointment of Court of Criminal Appeals judges only if those judges are "inferior Officers."

Our cases have not set forth an exclusive criterion for distinguishing between principal and inferior officers for Appointment Clause purposes. Among the offices that we have found to be inferior are that of a district court clerk, an election supervisor, a vice-consul charged temporarily with the duties of the consul, and a "United States commissioner" in district court proceedings. Most recently, in Morrison v. Olson, we held that the independent counsel created by provisions of the Ethics in Government Act of 1978, was an inferior officer. In reaching that conclusion, we relied on several factors: that the independent counsel was subject to removal by a higher officer (the Attorney General), that she performed only limited duties, that her jurisdiction was narrow, and that her tenure was limited.

Petitioners are quite correct that the last two of these conclusions do not hold with regard to the office of military judge at issue here. It is not "limited in tenure," as that phrase was used in *Morrison* to describe "appointment essentially to accomplish a single task [at the end of which] the office is terminated." Nor are military judges "limited in jurisdiction," as used in *Morrison* to refer to the fact that an independent counsel may investigate and prosecute only those individuals, and for only those crimes, that are within the scope of jurisdiction granted by the special three-judge appointing panel. However, *Morrison* did not purport to set forth a definitive test for whether an office is "inferior" under the Appointments Clause. . . .

To support principal-officer status, petitioners emphasize the importance of the responsibilities that Court of Criminal Appeals judges bear. . . . We do not dispute that military appellate judges are charged with exercising significant authority on behalf of the United States. This, however, is also true of offices that we have held were "inferior" within the meaning of the Appointments Clause. Generally speaking, the term "inferior officer" connotes a relationship with some higher ranking officer or officers below the President: whether one is an "inferior" officer depends on whether he has a superior. It is not enough that other officers may be identified who formally maintain a higher rank, or possess responsibilities of a greater magnitude. If that were the intention, the Constitution might have used the phrase "lesser officer." Rather, in the context of a clause designed to preserve political accountability relative to important government assignments, we think it evident that "inferior officers" are officers whose work is directed and supervised at some level by others who were appointed by presidential nomination with the advice and consent of the Senate.

This understanding of the Appointments Clause conforms with the views of the first Congress. On July 27, 1789, Congress established the first executive department, the Department of Foreign Affairs. In so doing, it expressly designated the Secretary of the Department as a "principal officer," and his subordinate, the Chief Clerk of the Department, as an "inferior officer". . . . Congress used similar language in establishing the Department of War, repeatedly referring to the Secretary of that department as a "principal officer," and the chief clerk, who would be "employed" within the Department as the Secretary "shall deem proper," as an "inferior officer."

Supervision of the work of Court of Criminal Appeals judges is divided between the Judge Advocate General (who in the Coast Guard is subordinate to the Secretary of Transportation) and the Court of Appeals for the Armed Forces. The Judge Advocate General exercises administrative oversight over the Court of Criminal Appeals. He is charged with the responsibility to "prescribe uniform rules of procedure" for the court, and must "meet periodically [with other Judge Advocates General] to formulate policies and procedure in regard to review of court-martial cases." It is conceded by the parties that the Judge Advocate General may also remove a Court of Criminal Appeals judge from his judicial assignment without cause. The power to remove officers, we have recognized, is a powerful tool for control. *Bowsher; Myers.*

. . . What is significant is that the judges of the Court of Criminal Appeals have no power to render a final decision on behalf of the United States unless permitted to do so by other executive officers. . . .

We conclude that 49 U.S.C. §323(a) authorizes the Secretary of Transportation to appoint judges of the Coast Guard Court of Criminal Appeals; and that such appointment is in conformity with the Appointments Clause of the Constitution, since those judges are "inferior Officers" within the meaning of that provision, by reason of the supervision over their work exercised by the General Counsel of the Department of Transportation in his capacity as Judge Advocate General and the Court of Appeals for the Armed Forces. The judicial appointments at issue in this case are therefore valid.

Justice SOUTER, concurring in part and concurring in the judgment. . . .

The Court states that "generally speaking, the term 'inferior officer' connotes a relationship [of supervision and direction] with some higher ranking officer or officers below the President; whether one is an 'inferior' officer depends on whether he has a superior." The Court goes on to show that administrative supervision of these judges by the Judge Advocate General of the Coast Guard, combined with his power to control them by removal from a case, establishes that the intermediate appellate judges here have the necessary superior. With this conclusion I agree, but unlike the Court I am not prepared to decide on that basis alone that these judges are inferior officers.

Because the term "inferior officer" implies an official superior, one who has no superior is not an inferior officer. This unexceptionable maxim will in some instances be dispositive of status. . . .

It does not follow, however, that if one is subject to some supervision and control, one is an inferior officer. Having a superior officer is necessary for inferior officer status, but not sufficient to establish it. See, e.g., *Morrison* (Scalia, J., dissenting). Accordingly, in *Morrison*, the Court's determination that the independent counsel was "to some degree 'inferior' " to the Attorney General did not end the enquiry. The Court went on to weigh the duties, jurisdiction, and tenure associated with the office before concluding that the independent counsel was an inferior officer. Thus, under *Morrison*, the Solicitor General of the United States, for example, may well be a principal officer, despite his statutory "inferiority" to the Attorney General. . . .

Discussion

1. *Further reading.* For thoughtful discussion of *Morrison*'s status after *Edmond*, see Nick Bravin, Note, Is Morrison v. Olson Still Good Law? The Court's New Appointments Clause Jurisprudence, 98 Colum. L. Rev. 1103, 1117-1120 (1998).

C. The Veto Power

As we have seen, the President has rather broad powers to execute the laws — encompassing the power to decline criminal prosecution, the power to pardon, the power to make all appointments of principal officers (and, indeed, of inferior officers unless Congress by law properly specifies otherwise), the power to remove cabinet officers and many other high-level executive officers at will, and the power to set policies for his administration. We have also seen important limits on these powers. But the President is not simply chief executive; he is also a vital part of the legislative process, via the veto power. The combination of law-execution power and veto power is a powerful one, as the next case illustrates.

IMMIGRATION AND NATURALIZATION SERVICE v. CHADHA
462 U.S. 919 (1983)

Chief Justice BURGER delivered the opinion of the Court.

I.

[The INS began deportation proceedings against Jagdish Chadha, a Kenya citizen holding a British passport whose nonimmigrant student visa had expired. In response, Chadha sought to remain in the United States under a provision allowing the Attorney General, in his discretion and acting through the Immigration and Naturalization Service, to suspend deportation in cases where an alien had been continuously resident in America for at least seven years and where "deportation would, in the opinion of the Attorney General, result in extreme hardship." §244(a)(1) of the Act, 8 U.S.C. §1254 (a)(1). After finding that such hardship existed in Chadha's case, the INS suspended his deportation, and a report of the suspension was transmitted to Congress, per §244(c)(1) of the Act. Under §244(c)(2) of the Act, 8 U.S.C. §1254(c)(2), Congress then had the power to veto the Attorney General's determination that Chadha should not be deported:

> "if . . . , prior to the close of the session of the Congress next following the session at which a case is reported, either the Senate or the House of Representatives passes a resolution stating in substance that it does not favor the suspension of such deportation, the Attorney General shall thereupon deport such alien or authorize the alien's voluntary departure at his own expense under the order of deportation in the manner provided by law. If, within the time above specified, neither the Senate nor the House of Representatives shall pass such a resolution, the Attorney General shall cancel deportation proceedings."]

. . . Representative Eilberg, Chairman of the Judiciary Subcommittee on Immigration, Citizenship, and International Law, introduced a resolution opposing "the granting of permanent residence in the United States to [six] aliens," including Chadha. . . . The resolution had not been printed and was not made available to other Members of the House prior to or at the time it was voted on. So far as the record before us shows, the House consideration of the resolution was based on Representative Eilberg's statement from the floor that

> "[it] was the feeling of the committee, after reviewing 340 cases, that the aliens contained in the resolution [Chadha and five others] did not meet these statutory requirements, particularly as it relates to hardship; and it is the opinion of the committee that their deportation should not be suspended."

The resolution was passed without debate or recorded vote. Since the House action was pursuant to §244(c)(2), the resolution was not treated as an Art. I legislative act; it was not submitted to the Senate or presented to the President for his action.

After the House veto of the Attorney General's decision to allow Chadha to remain in the United States, the Immigration Judge reopened the deportation proceedings to implement the House order deporting Chadha. Chadha moved to terminate the proceedings on the ground that §244(c)(2) is unconstitutional. The Immigration Judge held that he had no authority to rule on the constitutional validity of §244(c)(2). On November 8, 1976, Chadha was ordered deported pursuant to the House action.

Chadha appealed the deportation order to the Board of Immigration Appeals, again contending that §244(c)(2) is unconstitutional. The Board held that it had "no power to declare unconstitutional an act of Congress" and Chadha's appeal was dismissed.

. . . Chadha filed a petition for review of the deportation order in the United States Court of Appeals for the Ninth Circuit. The Immigration and Naturalization Service agreed with Chadha's position before the Court of Appeals and joined him in arguing that §244(c)(2) is unconstitutional. In light of the importance of the question, the Court of Appeals invited both the Senate and the House of Representatives to file briefs amici curiae.

After full briefing and oral argument, the Court of Appeals held that the House was without constitutional authority to order Chadha's deportation; accordingly it directed the Attorney General "to cease and desist from taking any steps to deport this alien based upon the resolution enacted by the House of Representatives." The essence of its holding was that §244(c)(2) violates the constitutional doctrine of separation of powers.

II.

Before we address the important question of the constitutionality of the one-House veto provision of §244(c)(2), we first consider several challenges to the authority of this Court to resolve the issue raised. . . .

SEVERABILITY

Congress . . . contends that the provision for the one-House veto in §244(c)(2) cannot be severed from §244. Congress argues that if the provision for the one-House veto is held unconstitutional, all of §244 must fall. If §244 in its entirety is violative of the Constitution, it follows that the Attorney General has no authority to suspend Chadha's deportation under §244(a)(1) and Chadha would be deported. From this, Congress argues that Chadha lacks standing to challenge the constitutionality of the one-House veto provision because he could receive no relief even if his constitutional challenge proves successful.

Only recently this Court reaffirmed that the invalid portions of a statute are to be severed "[unless] it is evident that the Legislature would not have enacted those provisions which are within its power, independently of that which is not." Here, however, we need not embark on that elusive inquiry since Congress itself has provided the answer to the question of severability in §406 of the Immigration and Nationality Act, note following 8 U.S.C. §1101, which provides:

> "If any particular provision of this Act, or the application thereof to any person or circumstance, is held invalid, the remainder of the Act and the application of such provision to other persons or circumstances shall not be affected thereby."

This language is unambiguous and gives rise to a presumption that Congress did not intend the validity of the Act as a whole, or of any part of the Act, to depend upon whether the veto clause of §244(c)(2) was invalid. The one-House veto provision in

§244(c)(2) is clearly a "particular provision" of the Act as that language is used in the severability clause. Congress clearly intended "the remainder of the Act" to stand if "any particular provision" were held invalid. Congress could not have more plainly authorized the presumption that the provision for a one-House veto in §244(c)(2) is severable from the remainder of §244 and the Act of which it is a part.

The presumption as to the severability of the one-House veto provision in §244(c)(2) is supported by the legislative history of §244. That section and its precursors supplanted the long-established pattern of dealing with deportations like Chadha's on a case-by-case basis through private bills. Although it may be that Congress was reluctant to delegate final authority over cancellation of deportations, such reluctance is not sufficient to overcome the presumption of severability raised by §406.

The Immigration Act of 1924 required the Secretary of Labor to deport any alien who entered or remained in the United States unlawfully. The only means by which a deportable alien could lawfully remain in the United States was to have his status altered by a private bill enacted by both Houses and presented to the President pursuant to the procedures set out in Art. I, §7, of the Constitution. These private bills were found intolerabl[y time-consuming] by Congress. . . .

The proposal to permit one House of Congress to veto the Attorney General's suspension of an alien's deportation was incorporated in the Immigration and Nationality Act of 1952. Plainly, Congress' desire to retain a veto in this area cannot be considered in isolation but must be viewed in the context of Congress' irritation with the burden of private immigration bills. This legislative history is not sufficient to rebut the presumption of severability raised by §406 because there is insufficient evidence that Congress would have continued to subject itself to the onerous burdens of private bills had it known that §244(c)(2) would be held unconstitutional.

A provision is further presumed severable if what remains after severance "is fully operative as a law." There can be no doubt that §244 is "fully operative" and work-able administrative machinery without the veto provision in §244(c)(2). Entirely independent of the one-House veto, the administrative process enacted by Congress authorizes the Attorney General to suspend an alien's deportation under §244(a). Congress' oversight of the exercise of this delegated authority is preserved since all such suspensions will continue to be reported to it under §244(c)(1). Absent the passage of a bill to the contrary,[a] deportation proceedings will be canceled when the period specified in §244(c)(2) has expired. Clearly, §244 survives as a workable administrative mechanism without the one-House veto. . . .

JURISDICTION

. . . Although the Attorney General was satisfied that the House action was invalid and that it should not have any effect on his decision to suspend deportation, he appropriately let the controversy take its course through the courts. . . .

a. Without the provision for one-House veto, Congress would presumably retain the power, during the time allotted in §244(c)(2), to enact a law, in accordance with the requirements of Art. I of the Constitution, mandating a particular alien's deportation, unless, of course, other constitutional principles place substantive limitations on such action. Cf. Attorney General Jackson's attack on H. R. 9766, 76th Cong., 3d Sess. (1940), a bill to require the Attorney General to deport an individual alien. The Attorney General called the bill "an historical departure from an unbroken American practice and tradition. It would be the first time that an act of Congress singled out a named individual for deportation." S. Rep. No. 2031, 76th Cong., 3d Sess., pt. 1, p. 9 (1940) (reprinting Jackson's letter of June 18, 1940). See n.[d] infra.

CASE OR CONTROVERSY

It is also contended that this is not a genuine controversy but "a friendly, non-adversary, proceeding," upon which the Court should not pass. This argument rests on the fact that Chadha and the INS take the same position on the constitutionality of the one-House veto. But it would be a curious result if, in the administration of justice, a person could be denied access to the courts because the Attorney General of the United States agreed with the legal arguments asserted by the individual. A case or controversy is presented by these cases. First, from the time of Congress' formal intervention, the concrete adverseness is beyond doubt. Congress is . . . a proper party to defend the constitutionality of §244(c)(2). . . . Second, . . . the INS's agreement with Chadha's position does not alter the fact that the INS would have deported Chadha absent the Court of Appeals judgment. . . .

POLITICAL QUESTION

It is also argued that these cases present a nonjusticiable political question. . . .

. . . No policy underlying the political question doctrine suggests that Congress or the Executive, or both acting in concert and in compliance with Art. I, can decide the constitutionality of a statute; that is a decision for the courts.[b] . . .

III.

A

We turn now to the question whether action of one House of Congress under §244(c)(2) violates strictures of the Constitution. . . .

Explicit and unambiguous provisions of the Constitution prescribe and define the respective functions of the Congress and of the Executive in the legislative process. Since the precise terms of those familiar provisions are critical to the resolution of these cases, we set them out verbatim. Article I provides:

"All legislative Powers herein granted shall be vested in a Congress of the United States, which shall consist of a Senate and House of Representatives." Art. I, §1.

"Every Bill which shall have passed the House of Representatives and the Senate, shall, before it becomes a law, be presented to the President of the United States. . . ." Art. I, §7, cl. 2.

"Every Order, Resolution, or Vote to which the Concurrence of the Senate and House of Representatives may be necessary (except on a question of Adjournment) shall be presented to the President of the United States; and before the Same shall take Effect, shall be approved by him, or being disapproved by him, shall be repassed

b. The suggestion is made that §244(c)(2) is somehow immunized from constitutional scrutiny because the Act containing §244(c)(2) was passed by Congress and approved by the President. *Marbury* resolved that question. The assent of the Executive to a bill which contains a provision contrary to the Constitution does not shield it from judicial review. See *National League of Cities; Buckley; Myers.* In any event, 11 Presidents, from Mr. Wilson through Mr. Reagan, who have been presented with this issue have gone on record at some point to challenge congressional vetoes as unconstitutional. . . . Furthermore, it is not uncommon for Presidents to approve legislation containing parts which are objectionable on constitutional grounds. For example, after President Roosevelt signed the Lend-Lease Act of 1941, Attorney General [and later Justice] Jackson released a memorandum explaining the President's view that the provision allowing the Act's authorization to be terminated by concurrent resolution was unconstitutional. Jackson, A Presidential Legal Opinion, 66 Harv. L. Rev. 1353 (1953).

by two thirds of the Senate and House of Representatives, according to the Rules and Limitations prescribed in the Case of a Bill." Art. I, §7, cl. 3.

These provisions of Art. I are integral parts of the constitutional design for the separation of powers. We have recently noted that "[the] principle of separation of powers was not simply an abstract generalization in the minds of the Framers: it was woven into the document that they drafted in Philadelphia in the summer of 1787." Just as we relied on the textual provision of Art. II, §2, cl. 2, to vindicate the principle of separation of powers in *Buckley*, we see that the purposes underlying the Presentment Clauses, Art. I, §7, cls. 2, 3, and the bicameral requirement of Art. I, §1, and §7, cl. 2, guide our resolution of the important question presented in these cases. The very structure of the Articles delegating and separating powers under Arts. I, II, and III exemplifies the concept of separation of powers, and we now turn to Art. I.

THE PRESENTMENT CLAUSES

The records of the Constitutional Convention reveal that the requirement that all legislation be presented to the President before becoming law was uniformly accepted by the Framers. Presentment to the President and the Presidential veto were considered so imperative that the draftsmen took special pains to assure that these requirements could not be circumvented. During the final debate on Art. I, §7, cl. 2, James Madison expressed concern that it might easily be evaded by the simple expedient of calling a proposed law a "resolution" or "vote" rather than a "bill." As a consequence, Art. I, §7, cl. 3 was added.

The decision to provide the President with a limited and qualified power to nullify proposed legislation by veto was based on the profound conviction of the Framers that the powers conferred on Congress were the powers to be most carefully circumscribed. It is beyond doubt that lawmaking was a power to be shared by both Houses and the President. In The Federalist No. 73, Hamilton focused on the President's role in making laws:

> "If even no propensity had ever discovered itself in the legislative body to invade the rights of the Executive, the rules of just reasoning and theoretic propriety would of themselves teach us that the one ought not to be left to the mercy of the other, but ought to possess a constitutional and effectual power of self-defence."

See also The Federalist No. 51. . . .

The President's role in the lawmaking process also reflects the Framers' careful efforts to check whatever propensity a particular Congress might have to enact oppressive, improvident, or ill-considered measures. The President's veto role in the legislative process was described later during public debate on ratification:

> "It establishes a salutary check upon the legislative body, calculated to guard the community against the effects of faction, precipitancy, or of any impulse unfriendly to the public good, which may happen to influence a majority of that body.
>
> ". . . The primary inducement to conferring the power in question upon the Executive is, to enable him to defend himself; the secondary one is to increase the chances in favor of the community against the passing of bad laws, through haste, inadvertence, or design." The Federalist No. 73.

See also The Pocket Veto Case, 279 U.S. 655, 678 (1929); *Myers*. The Court also has observed that the Presentment Clauses serve the important purpose of assuring that a "national" perspective is grafted on the legislative process:

> "The President is a representative of the people just as the members of the Senate and of the House are, and it may be, at some times, on some subjects, that the President elected by all the people is rather more representative of them all than are the members of either body of the Legislature whose constituencies are local and not countrywide. . . ." *Myers.*

BICAMERALISM

The bicameral requirement of Art. I, §§1, 7, was of scarcely less concern to the Framers than was the Presidential veto and indeed the two concepts are interdependent. By providing that no law could take effect without the concurrence of the prescribed majority of the Members of both Houses, the Framers reemphasized their belief, already remarked upon in connection with the Presentment Clauses, that legislation should not be enacted unless it has been carefully and fully considered by the Nation's elected officials. . . .

. . . Madison [pointed] up the need to divide and disperse power in order to protect liberty:

> "In republican government, the legislative authority necessarily predominates. The remedy for this inconveniency is to divide the legislature into different branches; and to render them, by different modes of election and different principles of action, as little connected with each other as the nature of their common functions and their common dependence on the society will admit." The Federalist No. 51. . . .

We see therefore that the Framers were acutely conscious that the bicameral requirement and the Presentment Clauses would serve essential constitutional functions. The President's participation in the legislative process was to protect the Executive Branch from Congress and to protect the whole people from improvident laws. The division of the Congress into two distinctive bodies assures that the legislative power would be exercised only after opportunity for full study and debate in separate settings. The President's unilateral veto power, in turn, was limited by the power of two-thirds of both Houses of Congress to overrule a veto thereby precluding final arbitrary action of one person. It emerges clearly that the prescription for legislative action in Art. I, §§1, 7, represents the Framers' decision that the legislative power of the Federal Government be exercised in accord with a single, finely wrought and exhaustively considered, procedure.

IV.

The Constitution sought to divide the delegated powers of the new Federal Government into three defined categories, Legislative, Executive, and Judicial, to assure, as nearly as possible, that each branch of government would confine itself to its assigned responsibility. The hydraulic pressure inherent within each of the separate Branches to exceed the outer limits of its power, even to accomplish desirable objectives, must be resisted. Although not "hermetically" sealed from one another, the powers delegated to the three Branches are functionally identifiable. When any

Branch acts, it is presumptively exercising the power the Constitution has delegated to it. When the Executive acts, he presumptively acts in an executive or administrative capacity as defined in Art. II. And when, as here, one House of Congress purports to act, it is presumptively acting within its assigned sphere. . . .

Examination of the action taken here by one House pursuant to §244(c)(2) reveals that it was essentially legislative in purpose and effect. In purporting to exercise power defined in Art. I, §8, cl. 4, to "establish an uniform Rule of Naturalization," the House took action that had the purpose and effect of altering the legal rights, duties, and relations of persons, including the Attorney General, Executive Branch officials and Chadha, all outside the Legislative Branch. Section 244(c)(2) purports to authorize one House of Congress to require the Attorney General to deport an individual alien whose deportation otherwise would be canceled under §244. The one-House veto operated in these cases to overrule the Attorney General and mandate Chadha's deportation; absent the House action, Chadha would remain in the United States. Congress has acted and its action has altered Chadha's status.

The legislative character of the one-House veto in these cases is confirmed by the character of the congressional action it supplants. Neither the House of Representatives nor the Senate contends that, absent the veto provision in §244(c)(2), either of them, or both of them acting together, could effectively require the Attorney General to deport an alien once the Attorney General, in the exercise of legislatively delegated authority,[c] had determined the alien should remain in the United States. Without the challenged provision in §244(c)(2), this could have been achieved, if at all, only by legislation requiring deportation.[d] Similarly, a veto by one House of Congress under §244(c)(2) cannot be justified as an attempt at amending the standards set out in §244(a)(1), or as a repeal of §244 as applied to Chadha. Amendment and repeal of statutes, no less than enactment, must conform with Art. I.

The nature of the decision implemented by the one-House veto in these cases further manifests its legislative character. After long experience with the clumsy, time-consuming private bill procedure, Congress made a deliberate choice to delegate to the Executive Branch, and specifically to the Attorney General, the authority to allow deportable aliens to remain in this country in certain specified circumstances. It is not disputed that this choice to delegate authority is precisely the kind of decision that can be implemented only in accordance with the procedures set out in Art. I. Disagreement with the Attorney General's decision on Chadha's deportation — that is, Congress' decision to deport Chadha — no less than Congress' original choice to delegate to the Attorney General the authority to make that decision, involves determinations of policy that Congress can implement in only one way; bicameral passage followed by presentment to the President. Congress must abide by its delegation of authority until that delegation is legislatively altered or revoked.[e]

c. Congress protests that affirming the Court of Appeals in these cases will sanction "lawmaking by the Attorney General. . . . Why is the Attorney General exempt from submitting his proposed changes in the law to the full bicameral process?" . . . When the Attorney General performs his duties pursuant to §244, he does not exercise "legislative" power. . . .

d. We express no opinion as to whether such legislation would violate any constitutional provision. See n.[a], supra.

e. This does not mean that Congress is required to capitulate to "the accretion of policy control by forces outside its chambers." The Constitution provides Congress with abundant means to oversee and

Finally, we see that when the Framers intended to authorize either House of Congress to act alone and outside of its prescribed bicameral legislative role, they narrowly and precisely defined the procedure for such action. There are four provisions in the Constitution, explicit and unambiguous, by which one House may act alone with the unreviewable force of law, not subject to the President's veto:

(a) The House of Representatives alone was given the power to initiate impeachments. Art. I, §2, cl. 5;

(b) The Senate alone was given the power to conduct trials following impeachment on charges initiated by the House and to convict following trial. Art. I, §3, cl. 6;

(c) The Senate alone was given final unreviewable power to approve or to disapprove Presidential appointments. Art. II, §2, cl. 2;

(d) The Senate alone was given unreviewable power to ratify treaties negotiated by the President. Art. II, §2, cl. 2.

Clearly, when the Draftsmen sought to confer special powers on one House, independent of the other House, or of the President, they did so in explicit, unambiguous terms.[f] These carefully defined exceptions from presentment and bicameralism underscore the difference between the legislative functions of Congress and other unilateral but important and binding one-House acts provided for in the Constitution. These exceptions are narrow, explicit, and separately justified; none of them authorize the action challenged here. On the contrary, they provide further support for the conclusion that congressional authority is not to be implied and for the conclusion that the veto provided for in §244(c)(2) is not authorized by the constitutional design of the powers of the Legislative Branch.

Since it is clear that the action by the House under §244(c)(2) was not within any of the express constitutional exceptions authorizing one House to act alone, and equally clear that it was an exercise of legislative power, that action was subject to the standards prescribed in Art. I. The bicameral requirement, the Presentment

---

control its administrative creatures. Beyond the obvious fact that Congress ultimately controls administrative agencies in the legislation that creates them, other means of control, such as durational limits on authorizations and formal reporting requirements, lie well within Congress' constitutional power.

f. An exception from the Presentment Clauses was ratified in Hollingsworth v. Virginia, 3 Dall. 378 (1798). There the Court held Presidential approval was unnecessary for a proposed constitutional amendment which had passed both Houses of Congress by the requisite two-thirds majority. See U.S. Const., Art. V. One might also include another "exception" to the rule that congressional action having the force of law be subject to the bicameral requirement and the Presentment Clauses. Each House has the power to act alone in determining specified internal matters. Art. I, §7, cls. 2, 3, and §5, cl. 2. However, this "exception" only empowers Congress to bind itself and is noteworthy only insofar as it further indicates the Framers' intent that Congress not act in any legally binding manner outside a closely circumscribed legislative arena, except in specific and enumerated instances.

Although the bicameral check was not provided for in any of these provisions for independent congressional action, precautionary alternative checks are evident. For example, Art. II, §2, requires that two-thirds of the Senators present concur in the Senate's consent to a treaty, rather than the simple majority required for passage of legislation. Similarly, the Framers adopted an alternative protection, in the stead of Presidential veto and bicameralism, by requiring the concurrence of two-thirds of the Senators present for a conviction of impeachment. Art. I, §3. We also note that the Court's holding in Hollingsworth, supra, that a resolution proposing an amendment to the Constitution need not be presented to the President, is subject to two alternative protections. First, a constitutional amendment must command the votes of two-thirds of each House. Second, three-fourths of the states must ratify any amendment.

Clauses, the President's veto, and Congress' power to override a veto were intended to erect enduring checks on each Branch and to protect the people from the improvident exercise of power by mandating certain prescribed steps. To preserve those checks, and maintain the separation of powers, the carefully defined limits on the power of each Branch must not be eroded. To accomplish what has been attempted by one House of Congress in this case requires action in conformity with the express procedures of the Constitution's prescription for legislative action: passage by a majority of both Houses and presentment to the President. . . .

Justice POWELL, concurring in the judgment.

The Court's decision, based on the Presentment Clauses, apparently will invalidate every use of the legislative veto. The breadth of this holding gives one pause. Congress has included the veto in literally hundreds of statutes, dating back to the 1930s. Congress clearly views this procedure as essential to controlling the delegation of power to administrative agencies.[a] One reasonably may disagree with Congress' assessment of the veto's utility, but the respect due its judgment as a coordinate branch of Government cautions that our holding should be no more extensive than necessary to decide these cases. In my view, the cases may be decided on a narrower ground. When Congress finds that a particular person does not satisfy the statutory criteria for permanent residence in this country it has assumed a judicial function in violation of the principle of separation of powers. Accordingly, I concur only in the judgment.

I.

A

The Framers perceived that "[the] accumulation of all powers legislative, executive and judiciary in the same hands, whether of one, a few or many, and whether hereditary, self appointed, or elective, may justly be pronounced the very definition of tyranny." The Federalist No. 47. Theirs was not a baseless fear. . . .

One abuse that was prevalent during the Confederation was the exercise of judicial power by the state legislatures. The Framers were well acquainted with the danger of subjecting the determination of the rights of one person to the "tyranny of shifting majorities." . . .

It was to prevent the recurrence of such abuses that the Framers vested the executive, legislative, and judicial powers in separate branches. Their concern that a legislature should not be able unilaterally to impose a substantial deprivation on one person was expressed not only in this general allocation of power, but also in more specific provisions, such as the Bill of Attainder Clause, Art. I, §9, cl. 3. As the Court recognized in United States v. Brown, 381 U.S. 437, 442 (1965), "the Bill of Attainder Clause was intended not as a narrow, technical . . . prohibition, but rather as an implementation of the separation of powers, a general safeguard against legislative exercise of the judicial function, or more simply — trial by legislature."

a. [T]he legislative veto has been included in a wide variety of statutes, ranging from bills for executive reorganization to the War Powers Resolution. Whether the veto complies with the Presentment Clauses may well turn on the particular context in which it is exercised, and I would be hesitant to conclude that every veto is unconstitutional on the basis of the unusual example presented by this litigation.

This Clause, and the separation-of-powers doctrine generally, reflect the Framers' concern that trial by a legislature lacks the safeguards necessary to prevent the abuse of power. . . .

II.

. . . On its face, the House's action appears clearly adjudicatory. The House did not enact a general rule; rather it made its own determination that six specific persons did not comply with certain statutory criteria. It thus undertook the type of decision that traditionally has been left to other branches. Even if the House did not make a de novo determination, but simply reviewed the Immigration and Naturalization Service's findings, it still assumed a function ordinarily entrusted to the federal courts.[b]

The impropriety of the House's assumption of this function is confirmed by the fact that its action raises the very danger the Framers sought to avoid — the exercise of unchecked power. In deciding whether Chadha deserves to be deported, Congress is not subject to any internal constraints that prevent it from arbitrarily depriving him of the right to remain in this country.[c] Unlike the judiciary or an administrative agency,[d] Congress is not bound by established substantive rules. Nor is it subject to the procedural safeguards, such as the right to counsel and a hearing before an impartial tribunal, that are present when a court or an agency adjudicates individual rights. The only effective constraint on Congress' power is political, but Congress is most accountable politically when it prescribes rules of general applicability. When it decides rights of specific persons, those rights are subject to "the tyranny of a shifting majority."

Chief Justice Marshall observed: "It is the peculiar province of the legislature to prescribe general rules for the government of society; the application of those rules to individuals in society would seem to be the duty of other departments." Fletcher v. Peck, 6 Cranch 87, 136 (1810). In my view, when Congress undertook to apply its rules to Chadha, it exceeded the scope of its constitutionally prescribed authority. I would not reach the broader question whether legislative vetoes are invalid under the Presentment Clauses.

Justice WHITE, dissenting.

Today the Court not only invalidates §244(c)(2) of the Immigration and Nationality Act, but also sounds the death knell for nearly 200 other statutory provisions in which Congress has reserved a "legislative veto." . . .

---

b. Although the parallel is not entirely complete, the effect on Chadha's personal rights would not have been different in principle had he been acquitted of a federal crime and thereafter found by one House of Congress to have been guilty.

c. When Congress grants particular individuals relief or benefits under its spending power, the danger of oppressive action that the separation of powers was designed to avoid is not implicated. Similarly, Congress may authorize the admission of individual aliens by special Acts, but it does not follow that Congress unilaterally may make a judgment that a particular alien has no legal right to remain in this country. As Attorney General [and later Justice] Robert Jackson remarked, such a practice "would be an historical departure from an unbroken American practice and tradition."

d. We have recognized that independent regulatory agencies and departments of the Executive Branch often exercise authority that is "judicial in nature." This function, however, forms part of the agencies' execution of public law and is subject to the procedural safeguards, including judicial review, provided by the Administrative Procedure Act.

The prominence of the legislative veto mechanism in our contemporary political system and its importance to Congress can hardly be overstated. It has become a central means by which Congress secures the accountability of executive and independent agencies. Without the legislative veto, Congress is faced with a Hobson's choice: either to refrain from delegating the necessary authority, leaving itself with a hopeless task of writing laws with the requisite specificity to cover endless special circumstances across the entire policy landscape, or in the alternative, to abdicate its law-making function to the Executive Branch and independent agencies. To choose the former leaves major national problems unresolved; to opt for the latter risks unaccountable policymaking by those not elected to fill that role. Accordingly, over the past five decades, the legislative veto has been placed in nearly 200 statutes. The device is known in every field of governmental concern: reorganization, budgets, foreign affairs, war powers, and regulation of trade, safety, energy, the environment, and the economy.

I.

. . . During the 1970s the legislative veto was important in resolving a series of major constitutional disputes between the President and Congress over claims of the President to broad impoundment, war, and national emergency powers. The key provision of the War Powers Resolution, 50 U.S.C. §1544(c), authorizes the termination by concurrent resolution of the use of armed forces in hostilities. A similar measure resolved the problem posed by Presidential claims of inherent power to impound appropriations. Congressional Budget and Impoundment Control Act of 1974, 31 U.S.C. §1403. . . . Although the War Powers Resolution was enacted over President Nixon's veto, the Impoundment Control Act was enacted with the President's approval. These statutes were followed by others resolving similar problems. . . .

. . . Perhaps there are other means of accommodation and accountability, but the increasing reliance of Congress upon the legislative veto suggests that the alternatives to which Congress must now turn are not entirely satisfactory. . . .

II.

[O]ur task should be to determine whether the legislative veto is consistent with the purposes of Art. I and the principles of separation of powers which are reflected in that Article and throughout the Constitution. We should not find the lack of a specific constitutional authorization for the legislative veto surprising, and I would not infer disapproval of the mechanism from its absence. From the summer of 1787 to the present the Government of the United States has become an endeavor far beyond the contemplation of the Framers. Only within the last half century has the complexity and size of the Federal Government's responsibilities grown so greatly that the Congress must rely on the legislative veto as the most effective if not the only means to insure its role as the Nation's lawmaker. But the wisdom of the Framers was to anticipate that the Nation would grow and new problems of governance would require different solutions. Accordingly, our Federal Government was intentionally chartered with the flexibility to respond to contemporary needs without losing sight of fundamental democratic principles. . . .

III.

The power to exercise a legislative veto is not the power to write new law without bicameral approval or Presidential consideration. The veto must be authorized by statute and may only negative what an Executive department or independent agency has proposed. . . .

A

[T]he historical background of the Presentment Clause itself . . . reveals only that the Framers were concerned with limiting the methods for enacting new legislation. The Framers were aware of the experience in Pennsylvania where the legislature had evaded the requirements attached to the passing of legislation by the use of "resolves," and the criticisms directed at this practice by the Council of Censors. There is no record that the Convention contemplated, let alone intended, that these Art. I requirements would someday be invoked to restrain the scope of congressional authority pursuant to duly enacted law. . . .

B

. . . The Court's holding today that all legislative-type action must be enacted through the lawmaking process ignores that legislative authority is routinely delegated to the Executive Branch, to the independent regulatory agencies, and to private individuals and groups.

> "The rise of administrative bodies probably has been the most significant legal trend of the last century. . . . They have become a veritable fourth branch of the Government, which has deranged our three-branch legal theories. . . ."

Theoretically, agencies and officials were asked only to "fill up the details," and the rule was that "Congress cannot delegate any part of its legislative power except under the limitation of a prescribed standard." Chief Justice Taft elaborated the standard in J.W. Hampton & Co. v. United States, 276 U.S. 394, 409 (1928): "If Congress shall lay down by legislative act an intelligible principle to which the person or body authorized to fix such rates is directed to conform, such legislative action is not a forbidden delegation of legislative power." In practice, however, restrictions on the scope of the power that could be delegated diminished and all but disappeared. In only two instances did the Court find an unconstitutional delegation. Panama Refining Co. v. Ryan, 293 U.S. 388 (1935); A.L.A. Schechter Poultry Corp. v. United States, 295 U.S. 495 (1935). In other cases, the "intelligible principle" through which agencies have attained enormous control over the economic affairs of the country was held to include such formulations as "just and reasonable," "public interest," "public convenience, interest, or necessity," and "unfair methods of competition."

[F]or present purposes, these cases establish that by virtue of congressional delegation, legislative power can be exercised by independent agencies and Executive departments without the passage of new legislation. For some time, the sheer amount of law — the substantive rules that regulate private conduct and direct the operation of government — made by the agencies has far outnumbered the lawmaking engaged in by Congress through the traditional process. There is no question but that agency rulemaking is lawmaking in any functional or realistic sense of the term. . . .

If Congress may delegate lawmaking power to independent and Executive agencies, it is most difficult to understand Art. I as prohibiting Congress from also reserving a check on legislative power for itself. Absent the veto, the agencies receiving delegations of legislative or quasi-legislative power may issue regulations having the force of law without bicameral approval and without the President's signature. It is thus not apparent why the reservation of a veto over the exercise of that legislative power must be subject to a more exacting test. In both cases, it is enough that the initial statutory authorizations comply with the Art. I requirements.

[T]he Court's decision today suggests that Congress may place a "veto" power over suspensions of deportation in . . . the hands of an independent agency, but is forbidden to reserve such authority for itself. Perhaps this odd result could be justified on other constitutional grounds, such as the separation of powers, but certainly it cannot be defended as consistent with the Court's view of the Art. I presentment and bicameralism commands.[a]

. . . If the effective functioning of a complex modern government requires the delegation of vast authority which, by virtue of its breadth, is legislative or "quasi-legislative" in character, I cannot accept that Art. I — which is, after all, the source of the nondelegation doctrine — should forbid Congress to qualify that grant with a legislative veto.

c

The Court also takes no account of perhaps the most relevant consideration: However resolutions of disapproval under §244(c)(2) are formally characterized, in reality, a departure from the status quo occurs only upon the concurrence of opinion among the House, Senate, and President. Reservations of legislative authority to be exercised by Congress should be upheld if the exercise of such reserved authority is consistent with the distribution of and limits upon legislative power that Art. I provides.

1

. . . The history of the Immigration and Nationality Act makes clear that §244(c)(2) did not alter the division of actual authority between Congress and the Executive. At all times, whether through private bills, or through affirmative concurrent resolutions, or through the present one-House veto, a permanent change in a deportable alien's status could be accomplished only with the agreement of the Attorney General, the House, and the Senate.

---

a. As the Court acknowledges, the "provisions of Art. I are integral parts of the constitutional design for the separation of powers." But these separation-of-powers concerns are that legislative power be exercised by Congress, executive power by the President, and judicial power by the Courts. A scheme which allows delegation of legislative power to the President and the departments under his control, but forbids a check on its exercise by Congress itself obviously denigrates the separation-of-powers concerns underlying Art. I. . . .

2

The central concern of the presentment and bicameralism requirements of Art. I is that when a departure from the legal status quo is undertaken, it is done with the approval of the President and both Houses of Congress — or, in the event of a Presidential veto, a two-thirds majority in both Houses. This interest is fully satisfied by the operation of §244(c)(2). The President's approval is found in the Attorney General's action in recommending to Congress that the deportation order for a given alien be suspended. The House and the Senate indicate their approval of the Executive's action by not passing a resolution of disapproval within the statutory period. Thus, a change in the legal status quo — the deportability of the alien — is consummated only with the approval of each of the three relevant actors. The disagreement of any one of the three maintains the alien's pre-existing status: the Executive may choose not to recommend suspension; the House and Senate may each veto the recommendation. The effect on the rights and obligations of the affected individuals and upon the legislative system is precisely the same as if a private bill were introduced but failed to receive the necessary approval. "The President and the two Houses enjoy exactly the same say in what the law is to be as would have been true for each without the presence of the one-House veto, and nothing in the law is changed absent the concurrence of the President and a majority in each House."

Thus understood, §244(c)(2) fully effectuates the purposes of the bicameralism and presentment requirements. . . .

[I]t may be asserted that Chadha's status before legislative disapproval is one of nondeportation and that the exercise of the veto, unlike the failure of a private bill, works a change in the status quo. This position plainly ignores the statutory language. At no place in §244 has Congress delegated to the Attorney General any final power to determine which aliens shall be allowed to remain in the United States. Congress has retained the ultimate power to pass on such changes in deportable status. By its own terms, §244(a) states that whatever power the Attorney General has been delegated to suspend deportation and adjust status is to be exercisable only "[as] hereinafter prescribed in this section." Subsection (c) is part of that section. A grant of "suspension" does not cancel the alien's deportation or adjust the alien's status to that of a permanent resident alien. A suspension order is merely a "deferment of deportation," which can mature into a cancellation of deportation and adjustment of status only upon the approval of Congress — by way of silence — under §244(c)(2). Only then does the statute authorize the Attorney General to "cancel deportation proceedings," and "record the alien's lawful admission for permanent residence. . . ." The Immigration and Naturalization Service's action, on behalf of the Attorney General, "cannot become effective without ratification by Congress." Until that ratification occurs, the Executive's action is simply a recommendation that Congress finalize the suspension — in itself, it works no legal change.[b]

---

b. I agree with Justice Rehnquist that Congress did not intend the one-House veto provision of §244(c)(2) to be severable. Although the general rule is that the presence of a saving clause creates a presumption of divisibility, I read the saving clause contained in §406 of the Immigration and Nationality Act as primarily pertaining to the severability of major parts of the Act from one another, not the divisibility of different provisions within a single section. Surely, Congress would want the naturalization provisions of the Act to be severable from the deportation sections. But this does not support preserving §244 without the legislative veto any more than a saving provision would justify preserving immigration authority without quota limits.

IV.

. . . The Attorney General's suspension of deportation is equivalent to a proposal for legislation. The nature of the Attorney General's role as recommendatory is not altered because §244 provides for congressional action through disapproval rather than by ratification. In comparison to private bills, which must be initiated in the Congress and which allow a Presidential veto to be overridden by a two-thirds majority in both Houses of Congress, §244 augments rather than reduces the Executive Branch's authority. So understood, congressional review does not undermine, as the Court of Appeals thought, the "weight and dignity" that attends the decisions of the Executive Branch. . . .

I do not suggest that all legislative vetoes are necessarily consistent with separation-of-powers principles. A legislative check on an inherently executive function, for example, that of initiating prosecutions, poses an entirely different question. But the legislative veto device here — and in many other settings — is far from an instance of legislative tyranny over the Executive. It is a necessary check on the unavoidably expanding power of the agencies, both Executive and independent, as they engage in exercising authority delegated by Congress.

V.

Today's decision strikes down in one fell swoop provisions in more laws enacted by Congress than the Court has cumulatively invalidated in its history. . . . I must dissent.

Justice REHNQUIST, with whom Justice White joins, dissenting.

A severability clause creates a presumption that Congress intended the valid portion of the statute to remain in force when one part is found to be invalid. A severability clause does not, however, conclusively resolve the issue. "[The] determination, in the end, is reached by" asking "[what] was the intent of the lawmakers," and "will rarely turn on the presence or absence of such a clause." Because I believe that Congress did not intend the one-House veto provision of §244(c)(2) to be severable, I dissent.

Section 244(c)(2) is an exception to the general rule that an alien's deportation shall be suspended when the Attorney General finds that statutory criteria are met. It is severable only if Congress would have intended to permit the Attorney General to suspend deportations without it. This Court has held several times over the years that exceptions such as this are not severable because

> "by rejecting the exceptions intended by the legislature . . . the statute is made to enact what confessedly the legislature never meant. It confers upon the statute a positive operation beyond the legislative intent, and beyond what anyone can say it would have enacted in view of the illegality of the exceptions."

By severing §244(c)(2), the Court permits suspension of deportation in a class of cases where Congress never stated that suspension was appropriate. I do not believe

More relevant is the fact that for 40 years Congress has insisted on retaining a voice on individual suspension cases — it has frequently rejected bills which would place final authority in the Executive Branch. It is clear that Congress believed its retention crucial. Given this history, the Court's rewriting of the Act flouts the will of Congress. [Footnote relocated — EDS.]

we should expand the statute in this way without some clear indication that Congress intended such an expansion. . . .

The Court finds that the legislative history of §244 shows that Congress intended §244(c)(2) to be severable because Congress wanted to relieve itself of the burden of private bills. But the history elucidated by the Court shows that Congress was unwilling to give the Executive Branch permission to suspend deportation on its own. Over the years, Congress consistently rejected requests from the Executive for complete discretion in this area. Congress always insisted on retaining ultimate control, whether by concurrent resolution, as in the 1948 Act, or by one-House veto, as in the present Act. Congress has never indicated that it would be willing to permit suspensions of deportation unless it could retain some sort of veto.

It is doubtless true that Congress has the power to provide for suspensions of deportation without a one-House veto. But the Court has failed to identify any evidence that Congress intended to exercise that power. On the contrary, Congress' continued insistence on retaining control of the suspension process indicates that it has never been disposed to give the Executive Branch a free hand. By severing §244(c)(2) the Court has "confounded" Congress' "intention. . . ."

Discussion

1. *Executive review.* The Constitution is law, and executive officials take an oath to uphold it. Why, then, were the executive officials in this case prepared to do something they considered both unconstitutional (and hence, illegal) and unjust unless they got a permission slip from the judiciary? Remember, the Attorney General believes that the legislative veto provision is both unconstitutional and severable. Why then does the *Chadha* Court say that the AG acted "appropriately" when he took initial steps to carry out the House's action by deporting Chadha? Wouldn't it have been more "appropriate" to simply refuse to give any effect to the House's unconstitutional action? (If the House had resolved that Chadha's head be chopped off, or had issued some other obviously unconstitutional edict or attainder, shouldn't the AG simply ignore the House?) Of course, if the AG's refusal to deport were challenged in court, he must be prepared to defend this refusal, by pointing out that his actions were indeed lawful — he was following the Constitution rather than the unconstitutional statute, just as the Supremacy Clause commands. And if the Supreme Court were to disagree with his position — and mandamus Chadha's deportation — then presumably the AG at that point would comply, having received definitive judicial guidance that he had somehow misconstrued the Constitution. But why shouldn't his default position in the absence of such a Court order be that he will follow the Constitution, not the statute, if the two conflict? Why, in other words, should the burden be on the rather helpless Chadha to come to court, rather than, say, on Congress (which is in general more able to shoulder the burdens of litigation, and in this case constitutionally culpable, under the AG's good-faith understanding of the Constitution)?

One possible answer is that if the AG were to ignore the House legislative veto, it is unclear that the House or anyone else in fact had "standing" to challenge him. But if so, is this the AG's fault, or Congress's problem? And whence the premise that all constitutional issues must reach the Court in order to be properly decided? For a rich discussion of the occasions on which the executive branch should follow its best understanding of the Constitution unless and until courts order otherwise, see Frank H. Easterbrook, Presidential Review, 40 Cas. W. Res. L. Rev. 905 (1990).

2. *Presidential waiver?* If the President signs a bill into law, why doesn't he thereby waive his right to challenge it as a violation of presidential prerogatives? Consider the following possible answers: (a) The statute may be unconstitutional in only a small and severable particular, and he should not be obliged to veto the entire bill because of one minor glitch that can be judicially excised later. (b) The President when he signs might deem the provision constitutional but later on he might in good faith and after careful reflection change his mind, as he has a right to do. (c) The unconstitutionality of a provision may become clear only after the President has in good faith tried to implement it, and has come to perceive a constitutional difficulty not visible on the face of the provision. (d) The President who signs should not be allowed to sign away the right of his successors in office to object. (e) The right at stake is not really the President's but the people's, and thus he is not allowed to give away what is not really his. Do you agree with any of these answers? Are there other answers? For a thoughtful argument that the President has a duty to veto a bill in case (a), rather than simply sign it and later challenge it, see Michael B. Rappaport, The President's Veto and the Constitution, 87 Nw. U. L. Rev. 735 (1993). Among other things, Professor Rappaport argues that vetoes give Congress a clear choice whether it prefers no statute at all instead of a statute stripped of the offensive clause. By contrast, when Presidents sign bills and then get judges to "rewrite" them by excising the unconstitutional clause, important values of bicameralism are slighted, Professor Rappaport argues.

3. *Formalism versus realism.* Compare Chief Justice Burger's style of analysis with that of Justice White. Critics of the majority opinion find it overly "formalistic" and wooden. Conversely, critics of the White dissent see it as insufficiently attentive to rules and principles laid down by the words and architecture of the Constitution itself. Does Justice Powell offer an alternative to both?

4. *Formal proofs and functional precepts.* Consider the following two "formal" proofs of *Chadha*'s rightness. Proof #1: The federal government has only three kinds of power — legislative, executive, and judicial (as laid down in the first three Articles and confirmed by the Tenth Amendment). Hence the legislative veto must fit into one of these three boxes. If it is an exercise of legislative power, it requires bicameralism and presentment. If, conversely, it is an exercise of executive or judicial power, it may not be carried out by the Congress, which is not given such powers (outside a few carefully specified contexts). Either way, the legislative veto fails. QED. Proof #2: In voting against Jagdish Chadha, Congress was doing one of two things — either applying the "hardship" standard specified in the earlier statute, or laying down a new "hardship" standard. If the first, this effort to apply a prior law to a later and specific fact situation is an impermissible effort to wield judicial power (cf. Powell). If the second, this effort to adopt a new legislative standard requires bicameralism and presentment (cf. Burger). Either way, the legislative veto fails. QED. Do you find these "formal" proofs persuasive or clarifying?

If not, perhaps it is because without more, these organizational chart arguments fail to offer up a sufficiently rich functional account of *why* the different powers of government are indeed separated — of the values and vision informing the

Framers' design. Perhaps the best structural defense of *Chadha* would go something like this: The separation of powers is designed to encourage legislators to draft standards generally and prospectively, behind a kind of veil of ignorance: All persons who henceforth do X shall be deported unless Y and Z. Once this general legislative rule is in place, the executive branch must carry it out, and if the executive has misapplied the rule, legally aggrieved persons (those with "standing") can come to court to complain. The executive and judicial powers are mighty, because they operate on named, known individuals — they decide whether Jagdish Chadha the man wins or loses. But these branches do not get to make up the general rules applicable against Chadha — these have already been specified in advance by the legislature. And although the legislative power is also mighty, the rules laid down should be general and prospective, giving all individuals clear notice of how to avoid deportation, applying evenhandedly to all persons in the future, and setting forth the principles of law to be followed by the other branches. Thus the rule of law is suitably impersonal: No group of officials can harm Chadha simply because they don't like him as a person.

But this system is frustrated when legislatures pass rules that are no rules at all. In principle, the legislature may not "delegate" lawmaking power, as such, giving the executive branch complete carte blanche to do whatever it likes. But no law can specify everything in advance, and so as a practical matter it is hard for courts after the fact to come up with clean doctrinal tests distinguishing between those laws that in effect delegate *lawmaking* power on the one hand and those laws on the other hand that simply create permissible zones of *executive* discretion, suitably bounded by statutory rules and policies established by the legislature itself. A Depression-era statute that said "anything that President Roosevelt henceforth decrees to improve the economy shall be law" would seem to go too far — and the Court in a pair of 1935 cases did indeed strike down overly broad delegations of power. (In light of contemporaneous events in Italy and Germany, the Court was doubtless concerned about government by dictators or corporate councils; and once Congress has given up sweeping power to the President, it is hard to get it back — the President may simply veto all repeal efforts, and so Congress must muster two-thirds majorities in each House to override.) But short of such extreme cases, it is hard to say when a given law gives too much discretion, and imposes too little constraint. Because this "how much" question is judicially unmanageable we are left with a genuine but judicially underenforced constitutional principle against delegated lawmaking. But the "who" question is more manageable than the "how much" question. Congress is more likely to legislate mush with no rules if it gets to control law application *itself*. It is less likely to draft overbroad laws with little guidance if *someone else other than Congress* will get to exercise all the discretion that the law creates. And so judges can enforce the nondelegation principle more cleanly by saying to Congress, "you may not delegate enforcement discretion to yourselves; whatever discretion you create will be wielded by someone else, with no formal veto on your part — so draft as carefully as you can!" If, however, this is the best structural account undergirding *Chadha,* it calls into serious question the Court's treatment of the severability issue, see discussion n.7, infra. For additional discussion of the nondelegation principle, see our casebook Web site at *http://www.conlaw.net.*

5. *Fast-track legislation and other congressional responses.* The legislative veto was designed in part as a substitute for the cumbersome private bill system. (Note also

that private bills seem in tension with the equality, impersonality, and rule-of-law vision sketched out in discussion n.4, supra; are laws singling persons out for special benefits different from laws singling persons out for special burdens?) But the cumbersome nature of the private bills is simply a function of internal House rules and practices about agendas and debates — and these can easily be changed by Congress itself. Thus, after *Chadha,* Congress could come very close to replicating the legislative veto with the following system. First, the AG is authorized by law only to postpone deportation for, say, one year — after that, she must deport in all cases, even those of hardship. Second, where the AG finds hardship, she shall propose to Congress a private waiver for the alien in question. Third, such waiver/private bill proposals must come before Congress, and must be voted on by each House within the year. Such proposals shall be unamendable and nondebatable, and must appear on a priority legislative calendar. (All of these rules can be implemented by each House under internal house rules pursuant to Article I, §5.) In such a system, deportation will occur if either branch says no — the private bill will fail. (In effect, each branch will be able to veto a permanent suspension of deportation.) But if both branches say yes, then presumably the President will sign into law the private waiver bill that his own AG has proposed, and the deportation will be permanently suspended. For a clever discussion of how such "fast-track" legislation can accomplish virtually everything that the legislative veto tried to accomplish, but without violating any constitutional rule, see the Thomas F. Ryan Lecture delivered by then Judge (now Justice) Stephen G. Breyer, The Legislative Veto After *Chadha,* 72 Geo. L.J. 785 (1984).

Consider also Louis Fisher's statement that "[n]otwithstanding the mandate in *Chadha,* Congress continued to add legislative vetoes to bills" — he says that there have been more than 200 such bills — "and Presidents Reagan and Bush [and, presumably, Clinton] continued to sign them into law," even though the accompanying signing statements included such language, as in one by President Bush, that the provisions "constitute legislative vetoes similar to those declared unconstitutional by the Supreme Court in INS v. Chadha. Accordingly, I will treat them as having no legal force or effect in this or any other legislation in which they appear." Fisher comments, though, that "[a]lthough the President may treat committee vetoes as having no legal force or effect, agencies have a different attitude" inasmuch as "[t]hey have to live with their review committees, year after year, and have a much greater incentive to make accommodations and stick by them." See Louis Fisher, The Legislative Veto: Invalidated, It Survives, 56 Law Contemp. Probs. 273, 288 (1993).

It may also be the case, in the language of economics, that the legislative veto is an easily substitutable political commodity. Consider the following analysis:

> Also surviving *Chadha* are other mechanisms for legislative influence over agency actions: (a) hearings and informal pressure by congressional oversight committees, as well as publicity generated by legislator criticisms; (b) refusal by Congress to appropriate monies to wayward agencies, or to appropriate funds subject to substantive conditions (e.g., that the money will not be spent to carry out specified rules or policies); and (c) informal pressure by appropriations subcommittees and language in their committee reports earmarking funds for certain projects or policies and not for others.

Daniel A. Farber, William N. Eskridge, Jr. & Philip P. Frickey, Constitutional Law: Themes for the Constitution's Third Century 974 (2d. ed. 1998).

See also Jessica Korn, The Power of Separation: American Constitutionalism and the Myth of the Legislative Veto (1996), which argues that these mechanisms are in fact more effective than the legislative veto in molding agency action to accord with congressional desires. Thus, Korn says, "the legislative veto shortcut was inconsequential to congressional control of the policymaking process because of the extensive set of powers in the Constitution already available to members of Congress" (p. 13). And, as Professor Tribe notes, "even a sweeping interpretation [of *Chadha*] contains nothing that would prevent Congress from enacting 'report and wait' provisions . . . mandating that rule changes proposed pursuant to delegated authority shall not take effect as law until after the legislative session in which they have been reported to Congress by the Attorney General." Such provisions give Congress "an orderly opportunity to pass regular, otherwise valid legislation [presented to the President] denying legal effect to exercises of delegated authority with which it disagrees." Laurence H. Tribe, 1 American Constitutional Law 150-151 (3d ed. 2000).

6. *White's dissent.* The easy availability of the fast-track option tends to undercut one of White's arguments in dissent, namely, that the legislative veto is an indispensable tool in the modern world. It remains to consider three other arguments he advances. First, he stresses that the law creating the legislative veto in the first place itself satisfied bicameralism and presentment. Should that be enough to sustain the legislative veto? What if the initial law said, "everything that FDR henceforth decrees shall be law, with the same force as if it had been decreed by Congress"? What if the law gave this decree power not to FDR, but to Bill Gates, or to the Speaker of the House, or to the 435 members of Congress acting without the President? White's second argument is that if Congress can lawfully delegate its legislative power, it should be allowed to condition that delegation; and that if Congress can properly delegate broad power to the executive branch, it should likewise be allowed to delegate such broad power to itself. Does discussion note 4 satisfactorily answer this argument? If not, does the Court have a better answer? White's third argument is that the statute really does respect bicameralism and presentment if we see the baseline as Chadha-out rather than Chadha-in. If the legal status quo is that Chadha is "out" and must be deported, then this baseline is altered only when both Houses (by not vetoing) and the executive (by proposing suspension via the AG) agree that he should be allowed to stay "in." It is a clever argument, but would it persuade a strict adherent to constitutional form? Note that in cases of 50-50 ties, the results are not identical; and in White's world, the executive's "signature" comes before Congress has acted and through the hand of the AG, rather than at the end and through the hand of the President, per Article I, §7. But doesn't this argument bear on severability? Isn't the statute best construed as establishing a baseline of Chadha-out rather than Chadha-in? If so, and if the legislative veto is technically and formally unconstitutional, why isn't the proper judicial response to strike down *both* the AG's suspension power and the legislative veto condition on that power, thus returning us to a Chadha-out baseline? As Justice Rehnquist argues, weren't the two provisions — suspension power and legislative veto of that power — inextricably intertwined, with the second as an indispensable condition of the first?

7. *Severability.* The Court majority argues otherwise, but its reasoning seems suspect. First, it points to a general severability clause and says that Congress "could not have more plainly authorized" severability. But the severability clause

was not specific to §244; it was a boilerplate general clause inserted in the context of a very large statute with many sections, and the Court points to no evidence whatsoever that the clause was drafted with the legislative veto provision in mind in particular. Put another way, the severability clause cannot tell us which words, phrases, and sentences should be understood as a single provision, such that if part of the provision falls, the rest should as well since the parts were designed as mutual conditions. There is strong reason to doubt that Congress intended to give the executive total control to suspend; and if the suspension clause is struck down along with the offending legislative veto, we are back to the basic "Chadha-out" baseline created by the statute; and Breyeresque fast-track schemes can easily solve the legislative time-consumption problem that had bedeviled the earlier private bill system.

So far the argument has been couched in terms of the intent of the original legislature — striking down both suspension and veto reaches, a result much closer to what the statute did than striking down the legislative veto alone. But given that what the real-life legislators actually wanted to do was unconstitutional — as the Court holds — one might wonder whether the only question is what these people actually would have wanted or did intend. A different approach, less backward-looking, would ask whether the constitutional principles that justify invalidating the legislative veto in the first place bear on the severability question. Cf. Evan H. Caminker, Note, A Norm-Based Remedial Model for Underinclusive Statutes, 95 Yale L.J. 1185 (1986). Are the constitutional values that condemn legislative vetoes indifferent on the severability question? Not really. If the best structural argument for *Chadha*'s result is the structural vision set out supra discussion note 4, then this vision encourages Congress to be as specific as possible, and indeed tries to give Congress incentives to avoid broad delegation by warning Congress *in advance* that it may not delegate to itself. Arguably, the majority undercuts all this when it rewrites the law to give the executive branch unfettered discretion to suspend — discretion which Congress never knowingly gave up.

A final approach to severability would understand that, whichever way the Court decides the severability question, that decision might be mistaken, and the political branches should be allowed to "contract around" it, a la Coase. If the Court strikes down both executive suspension and legislative veto, Congress would be free to give the executive suspension power free of strings — and with its eyes open about what it is giving up. Congress would also be free to pass a fast-track private bill allowing Chadha in. But once the Court severs the legislative veto while preserving executive suspension power, the game-theoretic dynamic is different. First, if the baseline is Chadha-in, it is far from clear that the political branches may agree to send him out — such a private bill penalizing Jagdish Chadha by name would raise serious attainder issues. And if Congress is more concerned about the more general problem of executive suspension power without strings or guidelines, any effort to add such guidelines or to remove this power will likely be vetoed by the President himself, as a diminution of his existing and unfettered power (courtesy of the Court's rewrite of the original statute). Thus, the "transactions costs" of "contracting around" a mistaken Court-defined baseline are not symmetric; in the event of any doubt at all about severability, perhaps the issue should be resolved in a way that is easier to correct. This approach, too, argues against the Court's decision to expand executive suspension power while trimming away the legislative veto.

The Court seemed to think that if the legislative veto provision were not severable, Chadha would lack standing. This is doubtful. Severability is better understood as a remedial question arising *after* a person with standing has proved
unconstitutionality. If the statute is not severable, this might mean simply that
Chadha *loses* the relief he seeks — just as a person bringing an action for damages
against a police officer might succeed in proving that the officer acted unlawfully,
but lose in the end because the officer's actions were nevertheless performed in
good faith, such that no damages lie as a matter of remedy law. It would not,
however, mean that Chadha was the wrong person to bring the suit, or that
somehow his rights were not at stake in the litigation. Nor is it likely that the Court's
severability ruling was necessary to avoid unfairness to Jagdish Chadha, the man. As
the Court noted in a passage not included in the preceding case excerpt, Chadha
was eligible to stay in America on grounds other than the AG's actions under
Section 244.

8. *The War Powers Act.* Although the severability issue might seem a minor
wrinkle in *Chadha,* in some contexts it is anything but. For example, the War
Powers Act of 1973, discussed in more detail infra, p. 839, authorizes the
President to engage in certain military actions, and then conditions this authorization upon a legislative veto. If this statute is now unconstitutional under
Chadha, it may be quite important whether the specific legislative grant of power
survives, as severable from the conditions on that power embodied in the legislative veto provision.

9. *From the legislative veto to the line item veto.* Fulfilling a promise made as part of
the "Contract with America" that helped sweep the Republican Party into the leadership of the House of Representatives in 1994 for the first time in a half-century,
Congress enacted — and the President signed into law — the Line Item Veto Act of
1996 (LIVA), regulating the budget process. The Act had many intricacies; for
simplicity, imagine a budget consisting of three separate appropriations. Line 1 says
that X shall be spent on guns; line 2 that Y shall be spent on butter; and line 3 that
Z shall be spent on pork. LIVA sought to regulate the budget process as follows:
After the President signs this budget bill into law, he has five days to trim spending.
If he decides that any single line of the budget is wasteful, he can in effect cancel
the line and spend zero instead of X, Y, or Z. If Congress disagrees, it can then pass
a "disapproval bill," which in turn must be presented to the President. If such a
disapproval bill becomes law, with the President's signature or over his veto, the
President must spend the amount specified in the bill and his earlier cancellation
in effect becomes null and void.

In Clinton v. City of New York, 524 U.S. 417 (1998), the Court, by a 6-3 vote,
struck LIVA down. The majority opinion, per Justice Stevens, argued that LIVA
was unconstitutional because the President was in effect vetoing individual lines in
a bill rather than the bill as a whole; because he was in effect repealing a duly
enacted law without securing a new law supported by majorities in both houses;
because he was in effect rewriting the law rather than enforcing it. If any of these
characterizations were in fact true, LIVA must indeed fall, so long as *Chadha*
stands. (Can you see why?) But the *Clinton* dissenters — Justices Breyer and Scalia
joined by Justice O'Connor — argued with great force and verve that the majority's characterizations precisely missed the point. They claimed that despite the
rather outlandish label of "line item veto" — a label that, they suggested, simply
confused analysis and befuddled the Court majority — LIVA was in fact quite

traditional and constitutionally benign. Suppose, they argued, that the law explicitly said the following: "The President may choose to spend X or nothing on guns, Y or nothing on butter, and Z or nothing on pork. And he must make his decisions within five days of signing the budget." Here it is plain that the President, in trimming spending, is not vetoing a line but rather exercising the discretion given him by the statute as a whole. He is not repealing the budget unilaterally but implementing the blueprint drafted by Congress. He is not rewriting the law but faithfully executing it according to its literal terms. LIVA used different words, but meant the same thing, as this hypothetical statute, which seemed clearly constitutional to the dissenters.

The dissenters admitted that their hypothetical law vested the President with considerable discretion — but, they pointed out, no more than countless statutes enacted ever since the First Congress. Many spending laws over the last two centuries have told the President that he could spend up to X on a given project. LIVA in fact was far stricter than these traditional spending bills: It said the President who wants to spend nothing rather than X, Y, or Z must decide quickly and must report his reasons. This clean and open decision made the President visibly accountable to the American electorate.

In addition to this analysis, we might add the following important points: If Congress for any reason decided that LIVA gave up too much, Congress was free to undo the damage any time it liked simply by proposing a budget that includes the words "LIVA shall not apply to this bill [or to parts A, B, and C thereof]." If Congress were to pass a law that said the President could spend whatever he wants, with no maximum, *then* we might well have a problem — quite literally a blank check that Congress could not easily retract. (Every time it tried, the President would veto, and Congress would need two-thirds in each house to override.) But the prospect that the President might spend less than the Congress has authorized does not raise symmetric dangers of a monarch run amok: Like kings of old, the President will eventually have to return to the legislature for more money to run his government, and when he does legislators can make him dance their tune (or at least compromise).

In *Clinton*'s aftermath, lawmakers who seek to reinstate LIVA's effects have two main options. First, they can explicitly write budget laws along the lines of the dissenters' hypothetical statute. Second, they can enact each budget line as a separate bill. Given that budgets now contain thousands of lines, this approach would need to be implemented by internal house rules under Article I, §5, allowing a legislator to push a button once on a megabudget and have that vote electronically counted as a vote for each line as its own bill (unless the legislator specifies otherwise). Can you see the analogy between this pushbutton rule and the fast-track device described by then-Judge Breyer as a proper response to *Chadha*?

In rejecting LIVA, the *Clinton* Court seemed to catch the whiff of an Imperial Presidency in the air, but might we also catch of a trace of congressional imperialism? According to the statute, the President was allowed to trim lines only if he signed the budget into law. If, however, he vetoed the budget and it became law via congressional override, he apparently lost his trimming power. Thus, perhaps the real problem with LIVA was that Congress was in effect bribing the President into surrendering his veto pen. In the budgetary context, the bribe made a difference because not all lines were subject to cancellation under LIVA's technical rules; and so a President could not simply sign a budget bill he actually opposed and then undo all the damage five days later. More generally, if Congress can sneak this little kicker into all other laws — formally vesting the President with extra power only if he abdicates the veto — then the careful constitutional balance between the two branches may be slyly undone.

The obvious counterargument is that legislators play tit for tat all the time. If the President vetoes bill A, Congress will refuse to pass bill B. But to a constitutional formalist — and the majority in *City of New York* was nothing if not formalist — there is a world of difference between informal political understandings and formal legal commands. Formally, shouldn't any given law mean the same thing whether or not it contains the President's signature? Similarly, a law should formally mean the same thing whether Senator X voted for it or against it. Clever pork-packers should not be allowed to draft a budget bill that explicitly authorizes federal money for a given state if and only if the senators from that state vote for the bill. Such a bill could create a situation where all senators are in effect bribed and coerced into voting yes — lest their state lose out on its fair share of the pork — even though virtually everyone thinks the overall bill is bad. By now, readers of this casebook should recognize this as a classic "prisoner's dilemma" — individual senators acting rationally end up with a collectively irrational result. (Cf. the prisoner's dilemma discussion of congressional term limits on this casebook's Web site, *http://www.conlaw.net.*) One of the main advantages of the presidential veto is that it can be used by a truly national representative — the President — to protect the whole against the parts. And so we should not lightly allow Congress to undercut the veto formally. If, indeed, this was the true danger lurking in LIVA, no one on the Court noticed. For a thoughtful discussion, see Michael B. Rappaport, Veto Burdens and the Line Item Veto Act, 91 Nw. U. L. Rev. 771 (1997).

D. The Power of the Sword

1. Emergency Power During Wartime

Less than five years after the cessation of World War II, the United States became involved in the conflict between South Korea (supported by the United Nations) and North Korea. Following President Truman's decision to cross the 38th parallel and move toward the northern border of North Korea, the People's Republic of China entered the fray. (The war thereafter bogged down, finally ended in 1953 with an armistice that maintained the division of Korea into two countries, one allied with the West, the other with the Communist bloc.) In April 1952, following months of efforts at mediation between the United Steelworkers of America and the management of the country's major steel producers, the union announced its intention to begin a nationwide strike on April 9. President Truman ordered the Secretary of the Treasury, John Sawyer, to seize the steel mills and to operate them in the name of the United States. He claimed that uninterrupted production of steel was vital to the successful prosecution of the Korean War. Truman notified Congress of his action; Congress took no action. The affected companies immediately filed suit claiming that the seizure violated the Constitution. The executive order that they challenged read as follows:

EXECUTIVE ORDER
Directing the Secretary of Commerce to Take Possession of and Operate the Plants and
Facilities of Certain Steel Companies

WHEREAS on December 16, 1950, I proclaimed the existence of a national
emergency which requires that the military, naval, air, and civilian defenses of this
country be strengthened as speedily as possible to the end that we may be able to
repel any and all threats against our national security and to fulfill our responsibilities in the efforts being made throughout the United Nations and otherwise to
bring about a lasting peace; and

WHEREAS American fighting men and fighting men of other nations of the
United Nations are now engaged in deadly combat with the forces of aggression in
Korea, and forces of the United States are stationed elsewhere overseas for the
purpose of participating in the defense of the Atlantic Community against aggression; and

WHEREAS the weapons and other materials needed by our armed forces and by
those joined with us in the defense of the free world are produced to a great extent
in this country, and steel is an indispensable component of substantially all of such
weapons and materials; and

WHEREAS steel is likewise indispensable to the carrying out of programs of the
Atomic Energy Commission of vital importance to our defense efforts; and

WHEREAS a continuing and uninterrupted supply of steel is also indispensable
to the maintenance of the economy of the United States, upon which our military
strength depends; and

WHEREAS a controversy has arisen between certain companies in the United
States producing and fabricating steel and the elements thereof and certain of their
workers represented by the United Steel Workers of America, CIO, regarding terms
and conditions of employment; and

WHEREAS the controversy has not been settled through the processes of collective bargaining or through the efforts of the Government, including those of the
Wage Stabilization Board, to which the controversy was referred on December 22,
1951, pursuant to Executive Order No. 10233, and a strike has been called for 12:01
A.M., April 9, 1952; and

WHEREAS a work stoppage would immediately jeopardize and imperil our
national defense and the defense of those joined with us in resisting aggression,
and would add to the continuing danger of our soldiers, sailors, and airmen
engaged in combat in the field; and

WHEREAS in order to assure the continued availability of steel and steel products during the existing emergency, it is necessary that the United States take
possession of and operate the plants, facilities, and other property of the said
companies as hereinafter provided:

NOW, THEREFORE, by virtue of the authority vested in me by the Constitution
and laws of the United States, and as President of the United States and Commander
in Chief of the armed forces of the United States, it is hereby ordered as follows:

1. The Secretary of Commerce is hereby authorized and directed to take possession of all or such of the plants, facilities, and other property of the companies named in the list attached hereto, or any part thereof, as he may deem
   necessary in the interests of national defense; and to operate or to arrange

for the operation thereof and to do all things necessary for, or incidental to, such operation.

2. In carrying out this order the Secretary of Commerce may act through or with the aid of such public or private instrumentalities or persons as he may designate; and all Federal agencies shall cooperate with the Secretary of Commerce to the fullest extent possible in carrying out the purposes of this order.

3. The Secretary of Commerce shall determine and prescribe terms and conditions of employment under which the plants, facilities, and other properties possession of which is taken pursuant to this order shall be operated. The Secretary of Commerce shall recognize the rights of workers to bargain collectively through representatives of their own choosing and to engage in concerted activities for the purpose of collective bargaining, adjustment of grievances, or other mutual aid or protection, provided that such activities do not interfere with the operation of such plants, facilities, and other properties.

4. Except so far as the Secretary of Commerce shall otherwise provide from time to time, the managements of the plants, facilities, and other properties possession of which is taken pursuant to this order shall continue their functions, including the collection and disbursement of funds in the usual and ordinary course of business in the names of their respective companies and by means of any instrumentalities used by such companies.

5. Except so far as the Secretary of Commerce may otherwise direct, existing rights and obligations of such companies shall remain in full force and effect, and there may be made, in due course, payments of dividends on stock, and of principal, interest, sinking funds, and all other distributions upon bonds, debentures, and other obligations, and expenditures may be made for other ordinary corporate or business purposes.

6. Whenever in the judgment of the Secretary of Commerce further possession and operation by him of any plant, facility, or other property is no longer necessary or expedient in the interest of national defense, and the Secretary has reason to believe that effective future operation is assured, he shall return the possession and operation of such plant, facility, or other property to the company in possession and control thereof at the time possession was taken under this order.

7. The Secretary of Commerce is authorized to prescribe and issue such regulations and orders not inconsistent herewith as he may deem necessary or desirable for carrying out the purposes of this order; and he may delegate and authorize subdelegation of such of his functions under this order as he may deem desirable.

Harry S. Truman. The White House, April 8, 1952.

At the trial before the District Court, Assistant Attorney General Baldridge, representing the United States, made the following claims about the power of the President:[70]

The Court: So you contend the Executive has unlimited power in time of an emergency?

---

70. For a historical overview of the case, see Maeva Marcus, *Truman and the Steel Seizure Case: The Limits of Presidential Power* (1994).

Mr. Baldridge: He has the power to take such action as is necessary to meet the emergency.

The Court: If the emergency is great, it is unlimited, is it?

Mr. Baldridge: I suppose if you carry it to its logical conclusion, that is true. But I do want to point out that there are two limitations on the Executive power. One is the ballot box and the other is impeachment. . . .

The Court: Let me put a case to you. . . . Supposing the President should declare that the public interest required the seizure of your home and directed an agent to seize it and to dispossess you: Do you think or do you contend that the court could not restrain that act because the President had declared an emergency and because he had directed an agent to carry out his will?

Mr. Baldridge: I would rather, Your Honor, not answer a case in that extremity. We are dealing here with a situation involving a grave national emergency . . . that requires the exercise of rather unusual powers in these particular circumstances. I do not believe any President would exercise such unusual power unless, in his opinion, there was a grave and an extreme national emergency existing. . . .

The Court: [I]s it not . . . your view that the powers of the Government are limited by and enumerated in the Constitution of the United States?

Mr. Baldridge: That is true, Your Honor, with respect to legislative powers.

The Court: But it is not true, you say, as to the Executive?

Mr. Baldridge: No. Section 1, of Article II of the Constitution . . . reposes all of the executive power in the Chief Executive. . . . In so far as the Executive is concerned, all executive power is vested in the President. In so far as legislative powers are concerned, the Congress has only those powers that are specifically delegated to it, plus the implied power to carry out the powers specifically enumerated.

The Court: So, when the sovereign people adopted the Constitution, it enumerated the powers set up in the Constitution but limited the powers of the Congress and limited the powers of the judiciary, but it did not limit the powers of the Executive. Is that what you say?

Mr. Baldridge: That is the way we read Article II of the Constitution. . . . It is our position that the President is accountable only to the country, and that the decisions of the President are conclusive. . . . [H]aving a broad grant of power[,] the executive, particularly in times of national emergency, can meet whatever situation endangers the national safety of the country. . . . I want to say that we had an emergency situation here. Somebody had to deal with it. The legislative [route, i.e., asking Congress for specific authority to seize the mills] was too slow. As of April 8th, midnight, the Taft-Hartley [route] was too slow. In either event, there would have been an indefinite stoppage of steel production. Are we to say, then, that there is no power in Government any place to meet as serious a situation as this, when it confronts the security of this nation? . . . I just say that as of midnight on April 8th this seizure procedure appeared to be the only effective way to avoid a strike and to avoid a cessation for an indefinite period of production of steel necessary to national security and national defense.

District Judge Pine ("the Court" in this colloquy) enjoined the seizure. The Court of Appeals for the District of Columbia stayed the order, and the Supreme Court immediately granted certiorari. Justice Black wrote for five Justices (two of whom had been appointed by President Truman) affirming issuance of the injunction; a sixth Justice (Clark) concurred in the judgment but did not join Black's opinion for the Court. Each of the Justices who did join Black's opinion also wrote separately. Chief Justice Vinson dissented, joined by Justices Reed and Minton.

YOUNGSTOWN SHEET & TUBE CO. v. SAWYER
343 U.S. 579 (1952)

Mr. Justice BLACK delivered the opinion of the Court. . . .

In the latter part of 1951, a dispute arose between the steel companies and their employees over terms and conditions that should be included in new collective bargaining agreements. Long-continued conferences failed to resolve the dispute. On December 18, 1951, the employees' representative, United Steelworkers of America, C.I.O., gave notice of an intention to strike when the existing bargaining agreements expired on December 31. The Federal Mediation and Conciliation Service then intervened in an effort to get labor and management to agree. This failing, the President on December 22, 1951, referred the dispute to the Federal Wage Stabilization Board to investigate and make recommendations for fair and equitable terms of settlement. The Board's report resulted in no settlement. On April 4, 1952, the Union gave notice of a nation-wide strike called to begin at 12:01 a.m. April 9. The indispensability of steel as a component of substantially all weapons and other war materials led the President to believe that the proposed work stoppage would immediately jeopardize our national defense and that governmental seizure of the steel mills was necessary in order to assure the continued availability of steel. Reciting these considerations for this action, the President, a few hours before the strike was to begin, issued Executive Order 10340. . . .

II.

The President's power, if any, to issue the order must stem either from an act of Congress or from the Constitution itself. There is no statute that expressly authorizes the President to take possession of property as he did here. Nor is there any act of Congress to which our attention has been directed from which such a power can fairly be implied. Indeed, we do not understand the Government to rely on statutory authorization for this seizure. . . .

Moreover, the use of the seizure technique to solve labor disputes in order to prevent work stoppages was not only unauthorized by any congressional enactment; prior to this controversy, Congress had refused to adopt that method of settling labor disputes. . . .

It is clear that if the President had authority to issue the order he did, it must be found in some provision of the Constitution. And it is not claimed that express constitutional language grants this power to the President. The contention is that presidential power should be implied from the aggregate of his powers under the Constitution. Particular reliance is placed on provisions in Article II which say that "The executive Power shall be vested in a President . . ."; that "he shall take Care that the Laws be faithfully executed"; and that he "shall be Commander in Chief of the Army and Navy of the United States."

The order cannot properly be sustained as an exercise of the President's military power as Commander in Chief of the Armed Forces. The Government attempts to do so by citing a number of cases upholding broad powers in military commanders engaged in day-to-day fighting in a theater of war. Such cases need not concern us here. Even though "theater of war" be an expanding concept, we cannot with faithfulness to our constitutional system hold that the Commander in Chief of the Armed Forces has the ultimate power as such to take possession of private property in order to keep labor disputes from stopping production. This is a job for the Nation's lawmakers, not for its military authorities.

Nor can the seizure order be sustained because of the several constitutional provisions that grant executive power to the President. In the framework of our Constitution, the President's power to see that the laws are faithfully executed refutes the idea that he is to be a lawmaker. The Constitution limits his functions in the lawmaking process to the recommending of laws he thinks wise and the vetoing of laws he thinks bad. And the Constitution is neither silent nor equivocal about who shall make laws which the President is to execute. The first section of the first article says that "All legislative Powers herein granted shall be vested in a Congress of the United States. . . ."

The President's order does not direct that a congressional policy be executed in a manner prescribed by Congress — it directs that a presidential policy be executed in a manner prescribed by the President. The preamble of the order itself, like that of many statutes, sets out reasons why the President believes certain policies should be adopted, proclaims these policies as rules of conduct to be followed, and again, like a statute, authorizes a government official to promulgate additional rules and regulations consistent with the policy proclaimed and needed to carry that policy into execution. The power of Congress to adopt such public policies as those proclaimed by the order is beyond question. It can authorize the taking of private property for public use. It can make laws regulating the relationships between employers and employees, prescribing rules designed to settle labor disputes, and fixing wages and working conditions in certain fields of our economy. The Constitution does not subject this lawmaking power of Congress to presidential or military supervision or control.

It is said that other Presidents without congressional authority have taken possession of private business enterprises in order to settle labor disputes. But even if this be true, Congress has not thereby lost its exclusive constitutional authority to make laws necessary and proper to carry out the powers vested by the Constitution "in the Government of the United States, or any Department or Officer thereof."

The Founders of this Nation entrusted the lawmaking power to the Congress alone in both good and bad times. It would do no good to recall the historical events, the fears of power and the hopes for freedom that lay behind their choice. Such a review would but confirm our holding that this seizure order cannot stand. . . .

Mr. Justice FRANKFURTER, concurring.[a]

[W]ith the utmost unwillingness, with every desire to avoid judicial inquiry into the powers and duties of the other two branches of the government, I cannot escape consideration of the legality of Executive Order No. 10340.

---

a. In an oddly located paragraph following Justice Black's opinion of the Court, and separate from his own formal concurrence, Justice Frankfurter also offered the following words:

> Although the considerations relevant to the legal enforcement of the principle of separation of powers seem to me more complicated and flexible than may appear from what Mr. Justice Black has written, I join his opinion because I thoroughly agree with the application of the principle to the circumstances of this case. Even though such differences in attitude toward this principle may be merely differences in emphasis and nuance, they can hardly be reflected by a single opinion for the Court. Individual expression of views in reaching a common result is therefore important.

. . . It is . . . incumbent upon this Court to avoid putting fetters upon the future by needless pronouncements today. . . .

The issue before us can be met, and therefore should be, without attempting to define the President's powers comprehensively. . . .

. . . We must therefore put to one side consideration of what powers the President would have had if there had been no legislation whatever bearing on the authority asserted by the seizure, or if the seizure had been only for a short, explicitly temporary period, to be terminated automatically unless Congressional approval were given. These and other questions, like or unlike, are not now here. I would exceed my authority were I to say anything about them. . . .

In adopting the provisions which it did, by the Labor Management Relations Act of 1947, for dealing with a "national emergency" arising out of a breakdown in peaceful industrial relations, Congress was very familiar with Governmental seizure as a protective measure. On a balance of considerations, Congress chose not to lodge this power in the President. It chose not to make available in advance a remedy to which both industry and labor were fiercely hostile. . . .

In any event, nothing can be plainer than that Congress made a conscious choice of policy in a field full of perplexity and peculiarly within legislative responsibility for choice. In formulating legislation for dealing with industrial conflicts, Congress could not more clearly and emphatically have withheld authority than it did in 1947. . . .

It cannot be contended that the President would have had power to issue this order had Congress explicitly negated such authority in formal legislation. Congress has expressed its will to withhold this power from the President as though it had said so in so many words. . . . It would be not merely infelicitous draftsmanship but almost offensive gaucherie to write such a restriction upon the President's power in terms into a statute rather than to have it authoritatively expounded, as it was, by controlling legislative history.

By the Labor Management Relations Act of 1947, Congress said to the President, "You may not seize. Please report to us and ask for seizure power if you think it is needed in a specific situation."

. . . Absence of authority in the President to deal with a crisis does not imply want of power in the Government. Conversely the fact that power exists in the Government does not vest it in the President. The need for new legislation does not enact it. Nor does it repeal or amend existing law. . . .

To be sure, the content of the three authorities of government is not to be derived from an abstract analysis. The areas are partly interacting, not wholly disjointed. The Constitution is a framework for government. Therefore the way the framework has consistently operated fairly establishes that it has operated according to its true nature. Deeply embedded traditional ways of conducting government cannot supplant the Constitution or legislation, but they give meaning to the words of a text or supply them. It is an inadmissibly narrow conception of American constitutional law to confine it to the words of the Constitution and to disregard the gloss which life has written upon them. In short, a systematic, unbroken, executive practice, long pursued to the knowledge of the Congress and never before questioned, engaged in by Presidents who have also sworn to uphold the Constitution, making as it were such exercise of power part of the structure of our government, may be treated as a gloss on "executive Power" vested in the President by §1 of Art. II. . . .

. . . No [firmly established] practice can be vouched for executive seizure of property at a time when this country was not at war, in the only constitutional way in which it can be at war. It would pursue the irrelevant to reopen the controversy over the constitutionality of some acts of Lincoln during the Civil War. Suffice it to say that he seized railroads in territory where armed hostilities had already interrupted the movement of troops to the beleaguered Capital, and his order was ratified by the Congress. . . .

Down to the World War II period, then, the record is barren of instances comparable to the one before us. Of twelve seizures by President Roosevelt prior to the enactment of the War Labor Disputes Act in June, 1943, three were sanctioned by existing law, and six others were effected after Congress, on December 8, 1941, had declared the existence of a state of war. In this case, reliance on the powers that flow from declared war has been commendably disclaimed by the Solicitor General. . . .

Mr. Justice DOUGLAS, concurring.

There can be no doubt that the emergency which caused the President to seize these steel plants was one that bore heavily on the country. But the emergency did not create power; it merely marked an occasion when power should be exercised. And the fact that it was necessary that measures be taken to keep steel in production does not mean that the President, rather than the Congress, had the constitutional authority to act. The Congress, as well as the President, is trustee of the national welfare. The President can act more quickly than the Congress. The President with the armed services at his disposal can move with force as well as with speed. All executive power — from the reign of ancient kings to the rule of modern dictators — has the outward appearance of efficiency.

Legislative power, by contrast, is slower to exercise. There must be delay while the ponderous machinery of committees, hearings, and debates is put into motion. That takes time; and while the Congress slowly moves into action, the emergency may take its toll in wages, consumer goods, war production, the standard of living of the people, and perhaps even lives. Legislative action may indeed often be cumbersome, time-consuming, and apparently inefficient. But as Mr. Justice Brandeis stated in his dissent in Myers v. United States:

> "The doctrine of the separation of powers was adopted by the Convention of 1787, not to promote efficiency but to preclude the exercise of arbitrary power. The purpose was, not to avoid friction, but, by means of the inevitable friction incident to the distribution of the governmental powers among three departments, to save the people from autocracy."

. . . A determination that sanctions should be applied, that the hand of the law should be placed upon the parties, and that the force of the courts should be directed against them, is an exercise of legislative power. In some nations that power is entrusted to the executive branch as a matter of course or in case of emergencies. We chose another course. We chose to place the legislative power of the Federal Government in the Congress. The language of the Constitution is not ambiguous or qualified. It places not some legislative power in the Congress; Article I, Section 1 says "All legislative Powers herein granted shall be vested in a Congress of the United States, which shall consist of a Senate and House of Representatives."

The legislative nature of the action taken by the President seems to me to be clear. . . . The command of the Fifth Amendment is that no "private property be taken for public use, without just compensation." That constitutional requirement has an important bearing on the present case.

The President has no power to raise revenues. That power is in the Congress by Article I, Section 8 of the Constitution. The President might seize and the Congress by subsequent action might ratify the seizure. But until and unless Congress acted, no condemnation would be lawful. The branch of government that has the power to pay compensation for a seizure is the only one able to authorize a seizure or make lawful one that the President has effected. That seems to me to be the necessary result of the condemnation provision in the Fifth Amendment. It squares with the theory of checks and balances expounded by Mr. Justice Black in the opinion of the Court in which I join.

If we sanctioned the present exercise of power by the President, we would be expanding Article II of the Constitution and rewriting it to suit the political conveniences of the present emergency. Article II which vests the "executive Power" in the President defines that power with particularity. Article II, Section 2 makes the Chief Executive the Commander in Chief of the Army and Navy. But our history and tradition rebel at the thought that the grant of military power carries with it authority over civilian affairs. Article II, Section 3 provides that the President shall "from time to time give to the Congress Information of the State of the Union, and recommend to their Consideration such Measures as he shall judge necessary and expedient." The power to recommend legislation, granted to the President, serves only to emphasize that it is his function to recommend and that it is the function of the Congress to legislate. Article II, Section 3 also provides that the President "shall take Care that the Laws be faithfully executed." But . . . the power to execute the laws starts and ends with the laws Congress has enacted.

The great office of President is not a weak and powerless one. The President represents the people and is their spokesman in domestic and foreign affairs. The office is respected more than any other in the land. It gives a position of leadership that is unique. . . .

Mr. Justice JACKSON, concurring in the judgment and opinion of the Court.

That comprehensive and undefined presidential powers hold both practical advantages and grave dangers for the country will impress anyone who has served as legal adviser to a President in time of transition and public anxiety. [Justice Jackson had, before being named to the Supreme Court, served as Solicitor General and Attorney General under President Roosevelt.] While an interval of detached reflection may temper teachings of that experience, they probably are a more realistic influence on my views than the conventional materials of judicial decision which seem unduly to accentuate doctrine and legal fiction. . . .

A judge, like an executive adviser, may be surprised at the poverty of really useful and unambiguous authority applicable to concrete problems of executive power as they actually present themselves. Just what our forefathers did envision, or would have envisioned had they foreseen modern conditions, must be divined from materials almost as enigmatic as the dreams Joseph was called upon to interpret for Pharaoh. A century and a half of partisan debate and scholarly speculation yields no net result but only supplies more or less apt quotations from respected sources on each side of any question. . . . And court decisions are indecisive because of the judicial practice of dealing with the largest questions in the most narrow way.

The actual art of governing under our Constitution does not and cannot conform to judicial definitions of the power of any of its branches based on isolated clauses or even single Articles torn from context. While the Constitution diffuses power the better to secure liberty, it also contemplates that practice will integrate the dispersed powers into a workable government. It enjoins upon its branches separateness but interdependence, autonomy but reciprocity. Presidential powers are not fixed but fluctuate, depending upon their disjunction or conjunction with those of Congress. We may well begin by a somewhat over-simplified grouping of practical situations in which a President may doubt, or others may challenge, his powers, and by distinguishing roughly the legal consequences of this factor of relativity.

1. When the President acts pursuant to an express or implied authorization of Congress, his authority is at its maximum, for it includes all that he possesses in his own right plus all that Congress can delegate. In these circumstances, and in these only, may he be said (for what it may be worth) to personify the federal sovereignty. If his act is held unconstitutional under these circumstances, it usually means that the Federal Government as an undivided whole lacks power. A seizure executed by the President pursuant to an Act of Congress would be supported by the strongest of presumptions and the widest latitude of judicial interpretation, and the burden of persuasion would rest heavily upon any who might attack it.

2. When the President acts in absence of either a congressional grant or denial of authority, he can only rely upon his own independent powers, but there is a zone of twilight in which he and Congress may have concurrent authority, or in which its distribution is uncertain. Therefore, congressional inertia, indifference or quiescence may sometimes, at least as a practical matter, enable, if not invite, measures on independent presidential responsibility. In this area, any actual test of power is likely to depend on the imperatives of events and contemporary imponderables rather than on abstract theories of law.

3. When the President takes measures incompatible with the expressed or implied will of Congress, his power is at its lowest ebb, for then he can rely only upon his own constitutional powers minus any constitutional powers of Congress over the matter. Courts can sustain exclusive presidential control in such a case only by disabling the Congress from acting upon the subject. Presidential claim to a power at once so conclusive and preclusive must be scrutinized with caution, for what is at stake is the equilibrium established by our constitutional system.

Into which of these classifications does this executive seizure of the steel industry fit? It is eliminated from the first by admission, for it is conceded that no congressional authorization exists for this seizure. That takes away also the support of the many precedents and declarations which were made in relation, and must be confined, to this category.

Can it then be defended under flexible tests available to the second category? It seems clearly eliminated from that class because Congress has not left seizure of private property an open field but has covered it by three statutory policies inconsistent with this seizure. . . .

This leaves the current seizure to be justified only by the severe tests under the third grouping, where it can be supported only by any remainder of executive power after subtraction of such powers as Congress may have over the subject. In short, we can sustain the President only by holding that seizure of such strike-bound industries is within his domain and beyond control by Congress. Thus, this Court's first review of such seizures occurs under circumstances which leave presidential power most vulnerable to attack and in the least favorable of possible constitutional postures.

. . . Nothing in our Constitution is plainer than that declaration of a war is entrusted only to Congress. Of course, a state of war may in fact exist without a formal declaration. But no doctrine that the Court could promulgate would seem to me more sinister and alarming than that a President whose conduct of foreign affairs is so largely uncontrolled, and often even is unknown, can vastly enlarge his mastery over the internal affairs of the country by his own commitment of the Nation's armed forces to some foreign venture. . . .

There are indications that the Constitution did not contemplate that the title Commander in Chief of the Army and Navy will constitute him also Commander in Chief of the country, its industries and its inhabitants. He has no monopoly of "war powers," whatever they are. While Congress cannot deprive the President of the command of the army and navy, only Congress can provide him an army or navy to command. It is also empowered to make rules for the "Government and Regulation of land and naval Forces," by which it may to some unknown extent impinge upon even command functions.

That military powers of the Commander in Chief were not to supersede representative government of internal affairs seems obvious from the Constitution and from elementary American history. Time out of mind, and even now in many parts of the world, a military commander can seize private housing to shelter his troops. Not so, however, in the United States, for the Third Amendment says, "No Soldier shall, in time of peace be quartered in any house, without the consent of the Owner, nor in time of war, but in a manner to be prescribed by law." Thus, even in war time, his seizure of needed military housing must be authorized by Congress. It also was expressly left to Congress to "provide for calling forth the Militia to execute the Laws of the Union, suppress Insurrections and repel Invasions. . . ." Such a limitation on the command power, written at a time when the militia rather than a standing army was contemplated as the military weapon of the Republic, underscores the Constitution's policy that Congress, not the Executive, should control utilization of the war power as an instrument of domestic policy. Congress, fulfilling that function, has authorized the President to use the army to enforce certain civil rights. On the other hand, Congress has forbidden him to use the army for the purpose of executing general laws except when expressly authorized by the Constitution or by Act of Congress. . . .

We should not use this occasion to circumscribe, much less to contract, the lawful role of the President as Commander in Chief. I should indulge the widest latitude of interpretation to sustain his exclusive function to command the instruments of national force, at least when turned against the outside world for the security of our society. But, when it is turned inward, not because of rebellion but because of a lawful economic struggle between industry and labor, it should have no such indulgence. His command power is not such an absolute as might be implied from that office in a militaristic system but is subject to limitations consistent with a constitutional Republic whose law and policy-making branch is a representative Congress. The purpose of lodging dual titles in one man was to insure that the civilian would control the military, not to enable the military to subordinate the presidential office. . . .

. . . The claim of inherent and unrestricted presidential powers has long been a persuasive dialectical weapon in political controversy. While it is not surprising that counsel should grasp support from such unadjudicated claims of power, a judge cannot accept self-serving press statements of the attorney for one of the interested parties as authority in answering a constitutional question, even if the advocate was himself. [Justice Jackson here is referring to the Government's citation of his own opinion, written while Attorney General, upholding broad executive power in behalf of President Roosevelt.] . . .

The appeal, however, that we declare the existence of inherent powers ex necessitate to meet an emergency asks us to do what many think would be wise, although it is something the forefathers omitted. They knew what emergencies were, knew the pressures they engender for authoritative action, knew, too, how they afford a ready pretext for usurpation. We may also suspect that they suspected that emergency powers would tend to kindle emergencies. Aside from suspension of the privilege of the writ of habeas corpus in time of rebellion or invasion, when the public safety may require it, they made no express provision for exercise of extraordinary authority because of a crisis. I do not think we rightfully may so amend their work, and, if we could, I am not convinced it would be wise to do so, although many modern nations have forthrightly recognized that war and economic crises may upset the normal balance between liberty and authority. Their experience with emergency powers may not be irrelevant to the argument here that we should say that the Executive, of his own volition, can invest himself with undefined emergency powers.

Germany, after the First World War, framed the Weimar Constitution, designed to secure her liberties in the Western tradition. However, the President of the Republic, without concurrence of the Reichstag, was empowered temporarily to suspend any or all individual rights if public safety and order were seriously disturbed or endangered. This proved a temptation to every government, whatever its shade of opinion, and in 13 years suspension of rights was invoked on more than 250 occasions. Finally, Hitler persuaded President Von Hindenberg to suspend all such rights, and they were never restored. . . .

Executive power has the advantage of concentration in a single head in whose choice the whole Nation has a part, making him the focus of public hopes and expectations. In drama, magnitude and finality his decisions so far overshadow any others that almost alone he fills the public eye and ear. No other personality in public life can begin to compete with him in access to the public mind through modern methods of communications. By his prestige as head of state and his influence upon public opinion he exerts a leverage upon those who are supposed to check and balance his power which often cancels their effectiveness.

Moreover, rise of the party system has made a significant extraconstitutional supplement to real executive power. No appraisal of his necessities is realistic which overlooks that he heads a political system as well as a legal system. Party loyalties and interests, sometimes more binding than law, extend his effective control into branches of government other than his own and he often may win, as a political leader, what he cannot command under the Constitution. Indeed, Woodrow Wilson, commenting on the President as leader both of his party and of the Nation, observed, "If he rightly interpret the national thought and boldly insist upon it, he is irresistible. . . . His office is anything he has the sagacity and force to make it." I cannot be brought to believe that this country will suffer if the Court refuses further to aggrandize the presidential office, already so potent and so relatively immune from judicial review, at the expense of Congress. . . .

Mr. Justice BURTON, concurring in both the opinion and judgment of the Court.

[T]his emergency [is different] from one in which Congress takes no action and outlines no governmental policy. In the case before us, Congress authorized a procedure which the President declined to follow. . . .

. . . The present situation is not comparable to that of an imminent invasion or threatened attack. We do not face the issue of what might be the President's constitutional power to meet such catastrophic situations. Nor is it claimed that the current seizure is in the nature of a military command addressed by the President, as Commander-in-Chief, to a mobilized nation waging, or imminently threatened with, total war.

The controlling fact here is that Congress, within its constitutionally delegated power, has prescribed for the President specific procedures, exclusive of seizure, for his use in meeting the present type of emergency. Congress has reserved to itself the right to determine where and when to authorize the seizure of property in meeting such an emergency. Under these circumstances, the President's order of April 8 invaded the jurisdiction of Congress. It violated the essence of the principle of the separation of governmental powers. Accordingly, the injunction against its effectiveness should be sustained.

Mr. Justice CLARK, concurring in the judgment of the Court. . . .

I conclude that where Congress has laid down specific procedures to deal with the type of crisis confronting the President, he must follow those procedures in meeting the crisis; but that in the absence of such action by Congress, the President's independent power to act depends upon the gravity of the situation confronting the nation. I cannot sustain the seizure in question because here, . . . Congress had prescribed methods to be followed by the President in meeting the emergency at hand.

. . . [T]he Government made no effort to comply with the procedures established by the Selective Service Act of 1948, a statute which expressly authorizes seizures when producers fail to supply necessary defense materiel.[a]

Mr. Chief Justice VINSON, with whom Mr. Justice Reed and Mr. Justice Minton join, dissenting. . . . Some members of the Court are of the view that the President is without power to act in time of crisis in the absence of express statutory authorization. Other members of the Court affirm on the basis of their reading of certain statutes. . . .

---

a. The Government has offered no explanation, in the record, the briefs, or the oral argument, as to why it could not have made both a literal and timely compliance with the provisions of that Act. . . .

I.

Those who suggest that this is a case involving extraordinary powers should be mindful that these are extraordinary times. A world not yet recovered from the devastation of World War II has been forced to face the threat of another and more terrifying global conflict.

Accepting in full measure its responsibility in the world community, the United States was instrumental in securing adoption of the United Nations Charter, approved by the Senate by a vote of 89 to 2. The first purpose of the United Nations is to "maintain international peace and security, and to that end: to take effective collective measures for the prevention and removal of threats to the peace, and for the suppression of acts of aggression or other breaches of the peace. . . ." In 1950, when the United Nations called upon member nations "to render every assistance" to repel aggression in Korea, the United States furnished its vigorous support. For almost two full years, our armed forces have been fighting in Korea, suffering casualties of over 108,000 men. Hostilities have not abated. The "determination of the United Nations to continue its action in Korea to meet the aggression" has been reaffirmed. Congressional support of the action in Korea has been manifested by provisions for increased military manpower and equipment and for economic stabilization, as hereinafter described.

Further efforts to protect the free world from aggression are found in the congressional enactments of the Truman Plan for assistance to Greece and Turkey and the Marshall Plan for economic aid needed to build up the strength of our friends in Western Europe. In 1949, the Senate approved the North Atlantic Treaty under which each member nation agrees that an armed attack against one is an armed attack against all. Congress immediately implemented the North Atlantic Treaty by authorizing military assistance to nations dedicated to the principles of mutual security under the United Nations Charter. The concept of mutual security recently has been extended by treaty to friends in the Pacific. . . .

Congress also directed the President to build up our own defenses. Congress, recognizing the "grim fact . . . that the United States is now engaged in a struggle for survival" and that "it is imperative that we now take those necessary steps to make our strength equal to the peril of the hour," granted authority to draft men into the armed forces. As a result, we now have over 3,500,000 men in our armed forces. . . .

The President has the duty to execute the foregoing legislative programs. Their successful execution depends upon continued production of steel and stabilized prices for steel.

II.

. . . The steel mills were seized for a public use. . . .

Admitting that the Government could seize the mills, plaintiffs claim that the implied power of eminent domain can be exercised only under an Act of Congress; under no circumstances, they say, can that power be exercised by the President unless he can point to an express provision in enabling legislation. . . .

Under this view, the President is left powerless at the very moment when the need for action may be most pressing and when no one, other than he, is immediately capable of action. Under this view, he is left powerless because a power not expressly given to Congress is nevertheless found to rest exclusively with Congress.

III.

A review of executive action demonstrates that our Presidents have on many occasions exhibited the leadership contemplated by the Framers when they made the President Commander in Chief, and imposed upon him the trust to "take Care that the Laws be faithfully executed." With or without explicit statutory authorization, Presidents have at such times dealt with national emergencies by acting promptly and resolutely to enforce legislative programs, at least to save those programs until Congress could act. Congress and the courts have responded to such executive initiative with consistent approval.

Our first President displayed at once the leadership contemplated by the Framers. . . . When international disputes engendered by the French revolution threatened to involve this country in war, and while congressional policy remained uncertain, Washington issued his Proclamation of Neutrality. Hamilton, whose defense of the Proclamation has endured the test of time, invoked the argument that the Executive has the duty to do that which will preserve peace until Congress acts and, in addition, pointed to the need for keeping the Nation informed of the requirements of existing laws and treaties as part of the faithful execution of the laws. . . .

Jefferson's initiative in the Louisiana Purchase, the Monroe Doctrine, and Jackson's removal of Government deposits from the Bank of the United States further serve to demonstrate by deed what the Framers described by word when they vested the whole of the executive power in the President. . . .

Without declaration of war, President Lincoln took energetic action with the outbreak of the War Between the States. He summoned troops and paid them out of the Treasury without appropriation therefor. He proclaimed a naval blockade of the Confederacy and seized ships violating that blockade. Congress, far from denying the validity of these acts, gave them express approval. The most striking action of President Lincoln was the Emancipation Proclamation, issued in aid of the successful prosecution of the War Between the States, but wholly without statutory authority.

In an action furnishing a most apt precedent for this case, President Lincoln without statutory authority directed the seizure of rail and telegraph lines leading to Washington. Many months later, Congress recognized and confirmed the power of the President to seize railroads and telegraph lines and provided criminal penalties for interference with Government operation. This Act did not confer on the President any additional powers of seizure. Congress plainly rejected the view that the President's acts had been without legal sanction until ratified by the legislature. Sponsors of the bill declared that its purpose was only to confirm the power which the President already possessed. Opponents insisted a statute authorizing seizure was unnecessary and might even be construed as limiting existing Presidential powers. . . .

IV.

. . . The President reported to Congress the morning after the seizure that he acted because a work stoppage in steel production would immediately imperil the safety of the Nation by preventing execution of the legislative programs for procurement of military equipment. And, while a shutdown could be averted by granting the price concessions requested by plaintiffs, granting such concessions would disrupt the price stabilization program also enacted by Congress. Rather than fail to execute either legislative program, the President acted to execute both.

Much of the argument in this case has been directed at straw men. We do not now have before us the case of a President acting solely on the basis of his own notions of the public welfare. Nor is there any question of unlimited executive power in this case. The President himself closed the door to any such claim when he sent his Message to Congress stating his purpose to abide by any action of Congress, whether approving or disapproving his seizure action. Here, the President immediately made sure that Congress was fully informed of the temporary action he had taken only to preserve the legislative programs from destruction until Congress could act.

The absence of a specific statute authorizing seizure of the steel mills as a mode of executing the laws — both the military procurement program and the anti-inflation program — has not until today been thought to prevent the President from executing the laws. Unlike an administrative commission confined to the enforcement of the statute under which it was created, or the head of a department when administering a particular statute, the President is a constitutional officer charged with taking care that a "mass of legislation" be executed. Flexibility as to mode of execution to meet critical situations is a matter of practical necessity. . . .

There is no statute prohibiting seizure as a method of enforcing legislative programs. Congress has in no wise indicated that its legislation is not to be executed by the taking of private property (subject of course to the payment of just compensation) if its legislation cannot otherwise be executed. Indeed, the Universal Military Training and Service Act authorizes the seizure of any plant that fails to fill a Government contract or the properties of any steel producer that fails to allocate steel as directed for defense production. And the Defense Production Act authorizes the President to requisition equipment and condemn real property needed without delay in the defense effort. Where Congress authorizes seizure in instances not necessarily crucial to the defense program, it can hardly be said to have disclosed an intention to prohibit seizures where essential to the execution of that legislative program.

Whatever the extent of Presidential power on more tranquil occasions, and whatever the right of the President to execute legislative programs as he sees fit without reporting the mode of execution to Congress, the single Presidential purpose disclosed on this record is to faithfully execute the laws by acting in an emergency to maintain the status quo, thereby preventing collapse of the legislative programs until Congress could act. The President's action served the same purposes as a judicial stay entered to maintain the status quo in order to preserve the jurisdiction of a court. In his Message to Congress immediately following the seizure, the President explained the necessity of his action in executing the military procurement and anti-inflation legislative programs and expressed his desire to cooperate with any legislative proposals approving, regulating or rejecting the seizure of the steel mills. Consequently, there is no evidence whatever of any Presidential purpose to defy Congress or act in any way inconsistent with the legislative will.

. . . There is no cause to fear Executive tyranny so long as the laws of Congress are being faithfully executed. Certainly there is no basis for fear of dictatorship when the Executive acts, as he did in this case, only to save the situation until Congress could act.

V.

Plaintiffs place their primary emphasis on the Labor Management Relations Act of 1947, hereinafter referred to as the Taft-Hartley Act, but do not contend that that Act contains any provision prohibiting seizure. . . .

Plaintiffs admit that the emergency procedures of Taft-Hartley are not mandatory. Nevertheless, plaintiffs apparently argue that, since Congress did provide the 80-day injunction method for dealing with emergency strikes, the President cannot claim that an emergency exists until the procedures of Taft-Hartley have been exhausted. This argument was not the basis of the District Court's opinion and, whatever merit the argument might have had following the enactment of Taft-Hartley, it loses all force when viewed in light of the statutory pattern confronting the President in this case.

. . . Faced with immediate national peril through stoppage in steel production on the one hand and faced with destruction of the wage and price legislative programs on the other, the President took temporary possession of the steel mills as the only course open to him consistent with his duty to take care that the laws be faithfully executed.

. . . The President's action has thus far been effective, not in settling the dispute, but in saving the various legislative programs at stake from destruction until Congress could act in the matter.

VI.

The diversity of views expressed in the six opinions of the majority, the lack of reference to authoritative precedent, the repeated reliance upon prior dissenting opinions, the complete disregard of the uncontroverted facts showing the gravity of the emergency and the temporary nature of the taking all serve to demonstrate how far afield one must go to affirm the order of the District Court.

. . . Faced with the duty of executing the defense programs which Congress had enacted and the disastrous effects that any stoppage in steel production would have on those programs, the President acted to preserve those programs by seizing the steel mills. There is no question that the possession was other than temporary in character and subject to congressional direction — either approving, disapproving or regulating the manner in which the mills were to be administered and returned to the owners. The President immediately informed Congress of his action and clearly stated his intention to abide by the legislative will. . . .

Discussion

1. *Just the facts, ma'am (again).* Note the different factual narratives offered in the different opinions. Those in the majority see this as a case about strikes and industrial peace — about unions and the domestic economy far from a theater of war. They stress one statute in particular — the Taft-Hartley Act, which gives the President no express power to act as he did in a domestic labor dispute. The dissenters frame a much broader narrative; there are many statutes and treaties at play, a mass of laws, and the President must do his best to carry out the spirit of all these laws. Most important this is a case about war and death — about global commitments and American soldiers at war and their need for steel. These different

accounts of the legally relevant facts should remind you that legal arguments are embedded in larger narrative frameworks and visions. See generally J.M. Balkin & Sanford Levinson, The Canons of Constitutional Law, 111 Harv. L. Rev. 963, 987-991 (1998); J.M. Balkin, Cultural Software: A Theory of Ideology, Chapter 9 (1998); J.M. Balkin, A Night in the Topics: The Reason of Legal Rhetoric and the Rhetoric of Legal Reason, in Law's Stories: Narrative and Rhetoric in the Law 211 (Peter Brooks & Paul Gewirtz eds., 1996); L.H. LaRue, Constitutional Law as Fiction: Narrative in the Rhetoric of Authority (1995).

2. *Constitutional modalities.* Professor Philip Bobbitt has characterized Justice Black's method of constitutional interpretation as paradigmatically "textual," based on the notion that the Constitution's commands can be derived directly from the plain meaning of the text. Bobbitt contrasts this to a "prudential argument," which he defines as "constitutional argument actuated by the political and economic circumstances surrounding the decision. Thus, prudentialists generally hold that in times of national emergency even the plainest of constitutional limitations can be ignored" if it is in the public interest to do so. Philip Bobbitt, Constitutional Fate: Theory of the Constitution 25, 61 (1982). Note, for example, that the majority opinion says that post-Founding historical practice is irrelevant, whereas many of the other Justices in their separate opinions devote considerable attention to such practice.

3. *Counting noses.* The methodological tension between Black's opinion for the Court, and the concurring opinions of Justices Frankfurter, Jackson, and Burton tracks an important substantive tension. If the statute books are simply silent — neither authorizing nor prohibiting a given presidential act — the Black opinion for the Court seems to say that the President loses. The seizure of the steel mills is a kind of "legislative act" and Congress has "exclusive constitutional authority" in this situation. The case at hand is one where the President has acted "without [affirmative] congressional authority." Justice Douglas seems to agree with all this, but do the three others who "join" Black's opinion? Don't they all say that if the statute books were merely silent, the issue would be importantly different than the case at hand?

Why do you suppose that these Justices signed on to an opinion where they seem to disagree in important respects both with its interpretive methodology and its substantive logic? In order to present a more united front against the Chief Executive? (Note that all five votes are essential to generate a majority opinion.) But exactly what does a majority opinion mean if separate concurrences undercut its logic? Which should a faithful lower court judge follow — what the Court says in its majority opinion, or what the individual Justices say in their concurrences? How should today's Court view the "holding" of *Youngstown*? Note that many people consider Justice Jackson's opinion to be as important as — if not more important than — Justice Black's majority opinion.

You might wonder why Justice Black was assigned to write the opinion for the Court, given that his views were apparently not those of the Court's center. Assignments are made by the Chief Justice, or, if the Chief is in dissent (as was the case in *Youngstown*), by the senior Justice voting with the majority — in this case, Justice Black.

4. *Formal versus informal wars.* Both Justice Frankfurter and Justice Jackson indicate a reluctance to define the Korean "enterprise" as a "war" despite the engagement of American troops. Assume that Congress had formally declared war on Korea. Would the seizure then have been constitutionally proper?

5. *Legal ethics: Robert Jackson's two hats.* Note Justice Robert Jackson's response to invocations of arguments made earlier by Attorney General Robert Jackson. The distinction here is the one between an advocate and a judge. What do you think of this distinction? When, if ever, should a judge or Justice recuse himself because of earlier statements he may have made as an advocate?

Professor Levinson has argued that Justice Jackson's concurrence is the greatest single opinion in the history of the Supreme Court. See Sanford Levinson, The Rhetoric of the Judicial Opinion, in Law's Stories: Narrative and Rhetoric in the Law 187, 202-204 (Peter Brooks & Paul Gewirtz eds., 1996). Yet, of course, it gained only one vote, Justice Jackson's. One explanation is that among the most powerful features of the opinion are precisely Jackson's own self-references to his service in the Roosevelt Administration and, indeed, his authorship, as Attorney General, of an opinion justifying a very expansive reading of presidential power. Had he excised these references, might other justices have been more willing to sign on to his famous delineation of the possible relationships between President and Congress? Would it have been worth it, though? Is Justice Jackson's self-reference mere self-indulgence or does it cast a powerful light on the way that Justices ought to think, so that American constitutional law would be far poorer had those paragraphs not appeared in the United States Reports?

6. *The sounds of legislative silence.* Note that the dissenters do not necessarily disagree with the *constitutional* logic of Justices Frankfurter, Jackson, Burton, and Clark. The dissenters do not argue that President Truman may lawfully ignore a congressional prohibition on the facts of this case. Rather, they deny that the Taft-Hartley law is such a prohibition. It is, on their reading, merely silent. Note how much of a difference it makes how this silence is construed — whether the default rule of interpretation is one that allows everything not explicitly prohibited, or one that prohibits everything not explicitly allowed, or something in between. The size and shape of Justice Jackson's category 2 — the "twilight zone" where statutes are silent — will depend on a prior statutory interpretation that the statute is indeed silent, rather than impliedly authorizing (category 1) or impliedly prohibiting (category 3) presidential action.

Note that given the interplay of issues, it is possible that five Justices believe that the statutes are indeed simply silent, rather than prohibitory; and that seven Justices believe that in case of mere silence, the President wins; but that nevertheless, these two Court majorities do not "add up" to a victory for the President. Imagine that Justices Black and Douglas agree with the dissenters that the statutes are merely silent. Nevertheless, Black and Douglas also think — as a matter of constitutional law rather than statutory interpretation — that the President loses in cases of mere silence. The other seven Justices may well disagree with Black and Douglas on this constitutional point, but on the statutory question, four of these seven (Frankfurter, Jackson, Clark, and Burton) read the statute as an implied prohibition, thus taking the facts of the case outside category 2 into category 3. For more discussion of the social choice complexities raised by different majorities that don't "add up," see supra p. 548, n.25.

Now turn away from what Congress did before the seizure to what it must do afterwards. Over and over, the dissenters suggest that the President has acted — in a manner like a temporary restraining order — simply to preserve the status quo so that Congress has a chance to act. This was Lincoln's theory in the Civil War — he acted unilaterally, and then asked Congress to bless his actions by passing a statute authorizing them retroactively. Had he not acted, he argued, the war would have been lost immediately, and Congress would have lost any real chance to thwart secession. Is Truman's position similar? Did he concede that he needed an affirmative law to bless his actions? Put another way, would his seizure at some point lapse or sunset, if Congress, having had time to act, chose to do nothing or stalemated? Or was he simply saying that if Congress passes a statute disagreeing with him, he will abide by such a statute?

The difference here is between needing a majority of both Houses (in order to pass a blessing enactment), or simply needing a third plus one in either House (in order to fend off a veto override, if Congress tries to pass a statute disagreeing with the President). Consider the words of the President in his message to Congress the day after the seizure: "It may be that the Congress will deem some other course to be wiser . . . that is a matter for the Congress to determine. It may be, on the other hand, that the Congress will wish to pass legislation establishing specific terms and conditions with reference to the operation of the steel mills by the Government. Sound legislation of this character might be very desirable. On the basis of the facts that are known to me at this time, I do not believe that immediate congressional action is essential; but I would, of course, be glad to cooperate in developing any legislative proposals which the Congress may wish to consider. If the Congress does not deem it necessary to act at this time, I shall continue to do all that is within my power to keep the steel industry operating and at the same time make every effort to bring about a settlement of the dispute so the mills can be returned to their private owners as soon as possible." Consider also the letter Truman sent to the President of the Senate, 12 days later (during which Congress had taken no action): "The Congress can, if it wishes, reject the course of action I have followed in this matter." See Charles L. Black, Jr., Some Thought on the Veto, 40 Law & Contemp. Probs. 87 (1976).

7. *The judicial role.* Consider the *institutional* role of the Supreme Court in adjudicating conflicts between the Congress and the President over military policy. Does, say, a judicial injunction against the commitment of troops seem less tenable than other areas involving judicial invalidation of political acts?

8. *Subsequent history: Actual practice.* Congress has not formally declared war on an enemy since 1941. Yet the United States has been involved in recurrent military hostilities since the end of World War II, including the Korean, Vietnamese, Iraqi, and Serbian conflicts. Although in none of these did Congress invoke its Article I power "to declare war," it has often purported to approve military action; consider, for example, the 1964 Gulf of Tonkin Resolution authorizing the President to engage in retaliation for alleged attacks on American military forces in Vietnam, which served as the legal underpinning for the subsequent buildup of American forces. In addition, there have been numerous "minor" military actions, in areas of the world ranging from Lebanon to the Dominican Republic and Grenada. There has been recurrent debate about the constitutional legitimacy of these military actions.

9. *Subsequent history: A controversial statute.* In the aftermath of the Vietnam War, Congress passed, over President Nixon's veto, the War Powers Resolution of 1973. Its central purpose was to increase Congress's role in decisionmaking regarding the commitment of American troops. It requires the President to submit a report to

Congress within 48 hours of the introduction of American troops, in the absence of a declaration of war,

(1) into hostilities or into situations where imminent involvement in hostilities is clearly indicated by the circumstances;

(2) into the territory, airspace or waters of a foreign nation, while equipped for combat, except for deployments which relate solely to supply, replacement, repair, or training of such forces; or

(3) in numbers which substantially enlarge United States Armed Forces equipped for combat already located in a foreign country.

Submission of such a report triggers a 60-day decisionmaking period. At the end of that period, "the President shall terminate any use of United States Armed forces" reported on "unless the Congress (1) has declared war or has enacted a specific authorization for such use of United States Armed Forces, (2) has extended by law such sixty-day period, or (3) is physically unable to meet as a result of an armed attack upon the United States." This 60-day period can also be extended by 30 additional days should the President notify Congress "that unavoidable military necessity respecting the safety of United States Armed Forces requires the continued use of such armed forces in the course of bringing about a prompt removal of such forces." However, in the absence of a declaration of war or specific congressional authorization, "such forces shall be removed by the President if the Congress so directs by concurrent resolution." The War Powers Act has been the topic of major constitutional debate, in large measure because of the specific process chosen for invocation of congressional power. Thus, presidential authority to commit troops seemingly expires unless Congress affirmatively authorizes the commitment, and the President is given no opportunity to veto a concurrent resolution directing immediate withdrawal. Every President since Nixon has argued that this aspect of the Act is unconstitutional. Congress has not yet attempted to use the War Powers Act to limit presidential action. Dramatic examples of the practical irrelevance of the Act involved President Reagan's and Bush's commitments of American military forces to the Persian Gulf. Congressional majorities self-consciously avoided invoking of the Act, over the heated protest of several legislators.

Imagine that Congress, over the President's objections, passed a law directing the removal of American troops from a particular theater of involvement. Would the statute be constitutional?

10. *Subsequent history: The Dames & Moore case.* In Dames & Moore v. Regan, 453 U.S. 654 (1981), the Court considered the constitutionality of executive orders under which President Carter, in an agreement with Iran for the release of over 400 American hostages, "nullified attachments and liens on Iranian assets in the United States, directed that these assets be transferred to Iran, and suspended claims against Iran that may be presented to an International Claims Tribunal." Following his inauguration, President Reagan "ratified" the orders.

Dames & Moore had sued the government of Iran, an Iranian agency, and several Iranian banks for services performed under a contract. A federal district court attached the property of several defendants in order to secure any judgment that might be entered against them. The Court subsequently found in favor of

Dames & Moore, which then attempted to execute the judgment by having the attached property sold. Prior to sale, however, the district court stayed execution of its judgment and "ordered that all prejudgment attachments obtained against the Iranian defendants be vacated and that further proceedings against the bank defendants be stayed in light of the Executive Orders." Dames & Moore complained that the orders were unconstitutional. The Supreme Court granted a writ of certiorari.

Justice Rehnquist, writing for a unanimous Court on the point at issue, emphasized that "we attempt to lay down no general 'guidelines' covering other situations not involved here, and attempt to confine the opinion only to the very questions necessary to decision of the case." The Court noted that "the President's action in nullifying the attachments and ordering the transfer of the assets was taken pursuant to specific congressional authorization." As to "the President's authority to suspend claims pending in American courts," there was no such statutory authorization, though statutory provisions are nonetheless "highly relevant in the looser sense of indicating congressional acceptance of a broad scope for executive action in circumstances such as those presented in this case." Justice Rehnquist also noted "a history of congressional acquiescence in conduct of the sort engaged in by the President" and went on to pronounce as "[c]rucial to our decision today . . . the conclusion that Congress has implicitly approved the practice of claim settlement by executive agreement."

11. *Subsequent history: Congressional authorizations in the War on Terror and the War in Iraq.* Congress has generally avoided declarations of war in recent years, instead relying on resolutions authorizing the use of military force. These authorizations usually contain language exempting the President from particular features of the War Powers Act by stating that in Congress's view he has satisfied the Act's requirements. The American response to the September 11, 2001 attacks and the war on Iraq are two examples of recent congressional practice.

On September 18, 2001, Congress passed a resolution authorizing "the President . . . to use all necessary and appropriate force against those nations, organizations, or persons he determines planned, authorized, committed, or aided the terrorist attacks that occurred on September 11, 2001, or harbored such organizations or persons, in order to prevent any future acts of international terrorism against the United States by such nations, organizations or persons." Authorization for Use of Military Force, Section 2(a), 115 Stat. 224 (2001). Section 2(b) of the resolution "declares that this section is intended to constitute specific statutory authorization within the meaning of section 5(b) of the War Powers Resolution," thus in effect waiving the 60-day limit for Presidential use of the Armed Forces, but added that "[n]othing in this resolution supercedes any requirement of the War Powers Resolution." Does this mean that Congress may, by a subsequent joint resolution, remove its authorization and order an end to the President's use of military force?

On October 16, 2002, Congress gave President Bush authority "to use the Armed Forces of the United States as he determines to be necessary and appropriate in order to (1) defend the national security of the United States against the continuing threat posed by Iraq; and (2) enforce all relevant United Nations Security Council resolutions regarding Iraq." Authorization for the Use of Military Force Against Iraq Resolution of 2002, 116 Stat. 1498 (2002). Like the previous resolution,

Section 3(c)(1) of the October 16 resolution "is intended to constitute specific statutory authorization within the meaning of section 5(b) of the War Powers Resolution."

2. Executive Detention

HAMDI v. RUMSFELD
542 U.S. 507 (2004)

Justice O'CONNOR announced the judgment of the Court and delivered an opinion, in which The Chief Justice, Justice Kennedy, and Justice Breyer join.

At this difficult time in our Nation's history, we are called upon to consider the legality of the Government's detention of a United States citizen on United States soil as an "enemy combatant" and to address the process that is constitutionally owed to one who seeks to challenge his classification as such. The United States Court of Appeals for the Fourth Circuit held that petitioner's detention was legally authorized and that he was entitled to no further opportunity to challenge his enemy-combatant label. We now vacate and remand. We hold that although Congress authorized the detention of combatants in the narrow circumstances alleged here, due process demands that a citizen held in the United States as an enemy combatant be given a meaningful opportunity to contest the factual basis for that detention before a neutral decisionmaker.

I.

On September 11, 2001, the al Qaeda terrorist network used hijacked commercial airliners to attack prominent targets in the United States. Approximately 3,000 people were killed in those attacks. One week later, [on September 18, 2001] in response to these "acts of treacherous violence," Congress passed a resolution authorizing the President to "use all necessary and appropriate force against those nations, organizations, or persons he determines planned, authorized, committed, or aided the terrorist attacks" or "harbored such organizations or persons, in order to prevent any future acts of international terrorism against the United States by such nations, organizations or persons." Authorization for Use of Military Force ("the AUMF"), 115 Stat. 224. Soon thereafter, the President ordered United States Armed Forces to Afghanistan, with a mission to subdue al Qaeda and quell the Taliban regime that was known to support it.

This case arises out of the detention of a man whom the Government alleges took up arms with the Taliban during this conflict. His name is Yaser Esam Hamdi. Born an American citizen in Louisiana in 1980, Hamdi moved with his family to Saudi Arabia as a child. By 2001, the parties agree, he resided in Afghanistan. At some point that year, he was seized by members of the Northern Alliance, a coalition of military groups opposed to the Taliban government, and eventually was turned over to the United States military. The Government asserts that it initially detained and interrogated Hamdi in Afghanistan before transferring him to the United States Naval Base in Guantanamo Bay in January 2002. In April 2002, upon learning that Hamdi is an American citizen, authorities transferred him to a naval brig in Norfolk, Virginia, where he remained until a recent transfer to a brig in Charleston, South Carolina. The Government contends that Hamdi is an "enemy combatant," and that this status justifies holding him in the United States indefinitely — without formal charges or proceedings — unless and until it makes the determination that access to counsel or further process is warranted.

In June 2002, Hamdi's father, Esam Fouad Hamdi, filed the present petition for a writ of habeas corpus under 28 U.S.C. §2241 in the Eastern District of Virginia, naming as petitioners his son and himself as next friend. The elder Hamdi alleges in the petition that he has had no contact with his son since the Government took custody of him in 2001, and that the Government has held his son "without access to legal counsel or notice of any charges pending against him." . . . Although his habeas petition provides no details with regard to the factual circumstances surrounding his son's capture and detention, Hamdi's father has asserted in documents found elsewhere in the record that his son went to Afghanistan to do "relief work," and that he had been in that country less than two months before September 11, 2001, and could not have received military training. The 20-year-old was traveling on his own for the first time, his father says, and "[b]ecause of his lack of experience, he was trapped in Afghanistan once that military campaign began." . . . .

[T]he Government filed a response and a motion to dismiss the petition, [attaching] a declaration from one Michael Mobbs (hereinafter "Mobbs Declaration"), who identified himself as Special Advisor to the Under Secretary of Defense for Policy. Mobbs indicated that in this position, he has been "substantially involved with matters related to the detention of enemy combatants in the current war against the al Qaeda terrorists and those who support and harbor them (including the Taliban)." He expressed his "familiar[ity]" with Department of Defense and United States military policies and procedures applicable to the detention, control, and transfer of al Qaeda and Taliban personnel, and declared that "[b]ased upon my review of relevant records and reports, I am also familiar with the facts and circumstances related to the capture of . . . Hamdi and his detention by U.S. military forces." Ibid. Mobbs then set forth what remains the sole evidentiary support that the Government has provided to the courts for Hamdi's detention. The declaration states that Hamdi "traveled to Afghanistan" in July or August 2001, and that he thereafter "affiliated with a Taliban military unit and received weapons training." It asserts that Hamdi "remained with his Taliban unit following the attacks of September 11" and that, during the time when Northern Alliance forces were "engaged in battle with the Taliban," "Hamdi's Taliban unit surrendered" to those forces, after which he "surrender[ed] his Kalishnikov assault rifle" to them. The Mobbs Declaration also states that, because al Qaeda and the Taliban "were and are hostile forces engaged in armed conflict with the armed forces of the United States," "individuals associated with" those groups "were and continue to be enemy combatants." Mobbs states that Hamdi was labeled an enemy combatant "[b]ased upon his interviews and in light of his association with the Taliban." According to the declaration, a series of "U.S. military screening team[s]" determined that Hamdi met "the criteria for enemy combatants," and "a subsequent interview of Hamdi has confirmed that he surrendered and gave his firearm to Northern Alliance forces, which supports his classification as an enemy combatant." . . .

Concluding that the factual averments in the Mobbs Declaration, "if accurate," provided a sufficient basis upon which to conclude that the President had constitutionally detained Hamdi pursuant to the President's war powers, [the Fourth Circuit Court of Appeals] ordered the habeas petition dismissed. . . . We now vacate the judgment below and remand.

II.

The threshold question before us is whether the Executive has the authority to detain citizens who qualify as "enemy combatants." There is some debate as to the proper scope of this term, and the Government has never provided any court with the full criteria that it uses in classifying individuals as such. It has made clear, however, that, for purposes of this case, the "enemy combatant" that it is seeking to detain is an individual who, it alleges, was "'part of or supporting forces hostile to the United States or coalition partners'" in Afghanistan and who "'engaged in an armed conflict against the United States'" there. We therefore answer only the narrow question before us: whether the detention of citizens falling within that definition is authorized.

The Government maintains that no explicit congressional authorization is required, because the Executive possesses plenary authority to detain pursuant to Article II of the Constitution. We do not reach the question whether Article II provides such authority, however, because we agree with the Government's alternative position, that Congress has in fact authorized Hamdi's detention, through the AUMF.

[Hamdi argues] that his detention is forbidden by [the Non-Detention Act,] 18 U.S.C. § 4001(a). Section 4001(a) states that "[n]o citizen shall be imprisoned or otherwise detained by the United States except pursuant to an Act of Congress." Congress passed §4001(a) in 1971 as part of a bill to repeal the Emergency Detention Act of 1950, 50 U.S.C. §811 et seq., which provided procedures for executive detention, during times of emergency, of individuals deemed likely to engage in espionage or sabotage. Congress was particularly concerned about the possibility that the Act could be used to reprise the Japanese internment camps of World War II. The Government . . . argues [first] that §4001(a) . . . applies only to "the control of civilian prisons and related detentions," not to military detentions. Second, it maintains that §4001(a) is satisfied, because Hamdi is being detained "pursuant to an Act of Congress" — the AUMF. [W]e conclude that the AUMF is explicit congressional authorization for the detention of individuals in the narrow category we describe (assuming, without deciding, that such authorization is required), and that the AUMF satisfied §4001(a)'s requirement that a detention be "pursuant to an Act of Congress" (assuming, without deciding, that §4001(a) applies to military detentions).

The AUMF authorizes the President to use "all necessary and appropriate force" against "nations, organizations, or persons" associated with the September 11, 2001, terrorist attacks. 115 Stat. 224. There can be no doubt that individuals who fought against the United States in Afghanistan as part of the Taliban, an organization known to have supported the al Qaeda terrorist network responsible for those attacks, are individuals Congress sought to target in passing the AUMF. We conclude that detention of individuals falling into the limited category we are considering, for the duration of the particular conflict in which they were captured, is so fundamental and accepted an incident to war as to be an exercise of the "necessary and appropriate force" Congress has authorized the President to use.

The capture and detention of lawful combatants and the capture, detention, and trial of unlawful combatants, by "universal agreement and practice," are "important incident[s] of war." The purpose of detention is to prevent captured individuals from returning to the field of battle and taking up arms once again. Naqvi, Doubtful Prisoner-of-War Status, 84 Int'l Rev. Red Cross 571, 572 (2002) ("[C]aptivity in war is 'neither revenge, nor punishment, but solely protective custody, the only purpose of which is to prevent the prisoners of war from further participation in the war' ").

There is no bar to this Nation's holding one of its own citizens as an enemy combatant. In [*Ex parte*] *Quirin,* [317 U.S. 1, 25 (1942),] one of the detainees, Haupt, alleged that he was a naturalized United States citizen. We held that "[c]itizens who associate themselves with the military arm of the enemy government, and with its aid, guidance and direction enter this country bent on hostile acts, are enemy belligerents within the meaning of . . . the law of war." While Haupt was tried for violations of the law of war, nothing in *Quirin* suggests that his citizenship would have precluded his mere detention for the duration of the relevant hostilities. Nor can we see any reason for drawing such a line here. A citizen, no less than an alien, can be "part of or supporting forces hostile to the United States or coalition partners" and "engaged in an armed conflict against the United States;" such a citizen, if released, would pose the same threat of returning to the front during the ongoing conflict.

In light of these principles, it is of no moment that the AUMF does not use specific language of detention. Because detention to prevent a combatant's return to the battlefield is a fundamental incident of waging war, in permitting the use of "necessary and appropriate force," Congress has clearly and unmistakably authorized detention in the narrow circumstances considered here.

Hamdi objects, nevertheless, that Congress has not authorized the *indefinite* detention to which he is now subject. The Government responds that "the detention of enemy combatants during World War II was just as 'indefinite' while that war was being fought." We take Hamdi's objection to be not to the lack of certainty regarding the date on which the conflict will end, but to the substantial prospect of perpetual detention. We recognize that the national security underpinnings of the "war on terror," although crucially important, are broad and malleable. As the Government concedes, "given its unconventional nature, the current conflict is unlikely to end with a formal cease-fire agreement." The prospect Hamdi raises is therefore not far-fetched. If the Government does not consider this unconventional war won for two generations, and if it maintains during that time that Hamdi might, if released, rejoin forces fighting against the United States, then the position it has taken throughout the litigation of this case suggests that Hamdi's detention could last for the rest of his life.

It is a clearly established principle of the law of war that detention may last no longer than active hostilities. See Article 118 of the Geneva Convention (III) Relative to the Treatment of Prisoners of War, Aug. 12, 1949, [1955] 6 U.S.T. 3316, 3406, T.I.A.S. No. 3364 ("Prisoners of war shall be released and repatriated without delay after the cessation of active hostilities"). See also Article 20 of the Hague Convention (II) on Laws and Customs of War on Land, July 29, 1899, 32 Stat. 1817 (as soon as possible after "conclusion of peace"); Hague Convention (IV), supra, Oct. 18, 1907, 36 Stat. 2301 ("conclusion of peace" (Art. 20)); Geneva Convention, supra, July 27, 1929, 47 Stat.2055 (repatriation should be accomplished with the least possible delay after conclusion of peace (Art. 75)).

Hamdi contends that the AUMF does not authorize indefinite or perpetual detention. Certainly, we agree that indefinite detention for the purpose of interrogation is not authorized. Further, we understand Congress' grant of authority for the use of "necessary and appropriate force" to include the authority to detain for the duration of the relevant conflict, and our understanding is based on longstanding law-of-war principles. If the practical circumstances of a given conflict are entirely unlike those of the conflicts that informed the development of the law of war, that understanding may unravel. But that is not the situation we face as of this date. Active combat operations against Taliban fighters apparently are ongoing in Afghanistan. The United States may detain, for the duration of these hostilities, individuals legitimately determined to be Taliban combatants who "engaged in an armed conflict against the United States." If the record establishes that United States troops are still involved in active combat in Afghanistan, those detentions are part of the exercise of "necessary and appropriate force," and therefore are authorized by the AUMF.

Ex parte Milligan does not undermine our holding about the Government's authority to seize enemy combatants, as we define that term today. In that case, the Court made repeated reference to the fact that its inquiry into whether the military tribunal had jurisdiction to try and punish Milligan turned in large part on the fact that Milligan was not a prisoner of war, but a resident of Indiana arrested while at home there. That fact was central to its conclusion. Had Milligan been captured while he was assisting Confederate soldiers by carrying a rifle against Union troops on a Confederate battlefield, the holding of the Court might well have been different. The Court's repeated explanations that Milligan was not a prisoner of war suggest that had these different circumstances been present he could have been detained under military authority for the duration of the conflict, whether or not he was a citizen.[a]

[T]he Court in *Ex parte Quirin* dismissed the language of *Milligan* that the petitioners had suggested prevented them from being subject to military process. . . . Justice Scalia [argues] that the military does not have authority to try an American citizen accused of spying against his country during wartime; [but] *Quirin* makes undeniably clear that this is not the law today. Haupt . . . was accused of being a spy. The Court in *Quirin* found him "subject to trial and punishment by [a] military tribunal[ ]" for those acts, and held that his citizenship did not change this result. . . .

Justice Scalia [distinguishes] *Quirin,* . . . because "[i]n *Quirin* it was uncontested that the petitioners were members of enemy forces," while Hamdi challenges his classification as an enemy combatant. But [for] Justice Scalia . . . the only options are congressional suspension of the writ of habeas corpus or prosecution for treason or some other crime. He does not explain how his historical analysis supports . . . a third option — detention under some other process after concession of enemy-combatant status — or why a concession [that one is an enemy combatant] should carry any different effect than proof of enemy-combatant status in a proceeding that comports with due process. To be clear, our opinion only finds

---

a. Here the basis asserted for detention by the military is that Hamdi was carrying a weapon against American troops on a foreign battlefield; that is, that he was an enemy combatant. The legal category of enemy combatant has not been elaborated upon in great detail. The permissible bounds of the category will be defined by the lower courts as subsequent cases are presented to them.

legislative authority to detain under the AUMF once it is sufficiently clear that the individual is, in fact, an enemy combatant; whether that is established by concession or by some other process that verifies this fact with sufficient certainty seems beside the point.

Further, Justice Scalia largely ignores the context of this case: a United States citizen captured in a *foreign* combat zone. . . . Because Justice Scalia finds the fact of battlefield capture irrelevant, his distinction based on the fact that the petitioner "conceded" enemy combatant status is beside the point. Justice Scalia can point to no case or other authority for the proposition that those captured on a foreign battlefield (whether detained there or in U.S. territory) cannot be detained outside the criminal process.

Moreover, Justice Scalia presumably would come to a different result if Hamdi had been kept in Afghanistan or even Guantanamo Bay. This creates a perverse incentive. Military authorities faced with the stark choice of submitting to the full-blown criminal process or releasing a suspected enemy combatant captured on the battlefield will simply keep citizen-detainees abroad. Indeed, the Government transferred Hamdi from Guantanamo Bay to the United States naval brig only after it learned that he might be an American citizen. It is not at all clear why that should make a determinative constitutional difference.

III.

Even in cases in which the detention of enemy combatants is legally authorized, there remains the question of what process is constitutionally due to a citizen who disputes his enemy-combatant status. . . .

A

All [parties] agree that, absent suspension, the writ of habeas corpus remains available to every individual detained within the United States. U.S. Const., Art. I, §9, cl. 2 ("The Privilege of the Writ of Habeas Corpus shall not be suspended, unless when in Cases of Rebellion or Invasion the public Safety may require it"). Only in the rarest of circumstances has Congress seen fit to suspend the writ. See, e.g., Act of Mar. 3, 1863, ch. 81, §1, 12 Stat. 755; Act of April 20, 1871, ch. 22, §4, 17 Stat. 14. At all other times, it has remained a critical check on the Executive, ensuring that it does not detain individuals except in accordance with law. All agree suspension of the writ has not occurred here. Thus, it is undisputed that Hamdi was properly before an Article III court to challenge his detention under 28 U.S.C. §2241 [the federal habeas corpus statute]. Further, all agree that §2241 and its companion provisions provide at least a skeletal outline of the procedures to be afforded a petitioner in federal habeas review. Most notably, §2243 provides that "the person detained may, under oath, deny any of the facts set forth in the return or allege any other material facts," and §2246 allows the taking of evidence in habeas proceedings by deposition, affidavit, or interrogatories.

The simple outline of §2241 makes clear both that Congress envisioned that habeas petitioners would have some opportunity to present and rebut facts and that courts in cases like this retain some ability to vary the ways in which they do so as mandated by due process. The Government [argues that] the presentation of the Mobbs Declaration to the habeas court completed the required factual development.

[B]ecause it is "undisputed" that Hamdi's seizure took place in a combat zone, the habeas determination can be made purely as a matter of law, with no further hearing or factfinding necessary. This argument is easily rejected. [T]he circumstances surrounding Hamdi's seizure cannot in any way be characterized as "undisputed," as "those circumstances are neither conceded in fact, nor susceptible to concession in law, because Hamdi has not been permitted to speak for himself or even through counsel as to those circumstances." Further, the "facts" that constitute the alleged concession are insufficient to support Hamdi's detention. Under the definition of enemy combatant that we accept today as falling within the scope of Congress' authorization, Hamdi would need to be "part of or supporting forces hostile to the United States or coalition partners" and "engaged in an armed conflict against the United States" to justify his detention in the United States for the duration of the relevant conflict. The habeas petition states only that "[w]hen seized by the United States Government, Mr. Hamdi resided in Afghanistan." An assertion that one *resided* in a country in which combat operations are taking place is not a concession that one was "*captured* in a zone of active combat operations in a foreign theater of war," and certainly is not a concession that one was "part of or supporting forces hostile to the United States or coalition partners" and "engaged in an armed conflict against the United States." Accordingly, we reject any argument that Hamdi has made concessions that eliminate any right to further process. . . . .

C

The Government's second argument [is] that further factual exploration is unwarranted and inappropriate in light of the extraordinary constitutional interests at stake. Under the Government's most extreme rendition of this argument, "[r]espect for separation of powers and the limited institutional capabilities of courts in matters of military decision-making in connection with an ongoing conflict" ought to eliminate entirely any individual process, restricting the courts to investigating only whether legal authorization exists for the broader detention scheme. At most, the Government argues, courts should review its determination that a citizen is an enemy combatant under a very deferential "some evidence" standard. Under this review, a court would assume the accuracy of the Government's articulated basis for Hamdi's detention, as set forth in the Mobbs Declaration, and assess only whether that articulated basis was a legitimate one. In response, Hamdi emphasizes that this Court consistently has recognized that an individual challenging his detention may not be held at the will of the Executive without recourse to some proceeding before a neutral tribunal to determine whether the Executive's asserted justifications for that detention have basis in fact and warrant in law. . . . The District Court, agreeing with Hamdi, apparently believed that the appropriate process would approach the process that accompanies a criminal trial. It therefore disapproved of the hearsay nature of the Mobbs Declaration and anticipated quite extensive discovery of various military affairs. Anything less, it concluded, would not be "meaningful judicial review."

Both of these positions highlight legitimate concerns. And both emphasize the tension that often exists between the autonomy that the Government asserts is necessary in order to pursue effectively a particular goal and the process that a citizen contends he is due before he is deprived of a constitutional right. The ordinary mechanism that we use for balancing such serious competing interests, and for determining the procedures that are necessary to ensure that a citizen is not "deprived of life, liberty, or property, without due process of law," is the test that we articulated in Mathews v. Eldridge, 424 U.S. 319 (1976). *Mathews* dictates that the process due in any given instance is determined by weighing "the private interest that will be affected by the official action" against the Government's asserted interest, "including the function involved" and the burdens the Government would face in providing greater process. The *Mathews* calculus then contemplates a judicious balancing of these concerns, through an analysis of "the risk of an erroneous deprivation" of the private interest if the process were reduced and the "probable value, if any, of additional or substitute safeguards." . . . It is beyond question that substantial interests lie on both sides of the scale in this case. Hamdi's "private interest . . . affected by the official action," is the most elemental of liberty interests — the interest in being free from physical detention by one's own government. . . . Nor is the weight on this side of the *Mathews* scale offset by the circumstances of war or the accusation of treasonous behavior, for "[i]t is clear that commitment for *any* purpose constitutes a significant deprivation of liberty that requires due process protection," and at this stage in the *Mathews* calculus, we consider the interest of the *erroneously* detained individual. . . . [A]s critical as the Government's interest may be in detaining those who actually pose an immediate threat to the national security of the United States during ongoing international conflict, history and common sense teach us that an unchecked system of detention carries the potential to become a means for oppression and abuse of others who do not present that sort of threat. Because we live in a society in which "[m]ere public intolerance or animosity cannot constitutionally justify the deprivation of a person's physical liberty," our starting point for the Mathews v. Eldridge analysis is unaltered by the allegations surrounding the particular detainee or the organizations with which he is alleged to have associated. . . . On the other side of the scale are the weighty and sensitive governmental interests in ensuring that those who have in fact fought with the enemy during a war do not return to battle against the United States. . . . The Government also [emphasizes] the practical difficulties that would accompany a system of trial-like process. In its view, military officers who are engaged in the serious work of waging battle would be unnecessarily and dangerously distracted by litigation half a world away, and discovery into military operations would both intrude on the sensitive secrets of national defense and result in a futile search for evidence buried under the rubble of war. To the extent that these burdens are triggered by heightened procedures, they are properly taken into account in our due process analysis.

Striking the proper constitutional balance here is of great importance to the Nation during this period of ongoing combat. But it is equally vital that our calculus not give short shrift to the values that this country holds dear or to the privilege that is American citizenship. It is during our most challenging and uncertain moments that our Nation's commitment to due process is most severely tested; and it is in those times that we must preserve our commitment at home to the principles for which we fight abroad.

With due recognition of these competing concerns, we believe that neither the process proposed by the Government nor the process apparently envisioned by the District Court below strikes the proper constitutional balance when a United States citizen is detained in the United States as an enemy combatant. . . . We therefore hold that a citizen-detainee seeking to challenge his classification as an enemy combatant must receive notice of the factual basis for his classification, and a fair opportunity to rebut the Government's factual assertions before a neutral decision-maker. . . . At the same time, the exigencies of the circumstances may demand that, aside from these core elements, enemy combatant proceedings may be tailored to alleviate their uncommon potential to burden the Executive at a time of ongoing military conflict. Hearsay, for example, may need to be accepted as the most reliable available evidence from the Government in such a proceeding. Likewise, the Constitution would not be offended by a presumption in favor of the Government's evidence, so long as that presumption remained a rebuttable one and fair opportunity for rebuttal were provided. Thus, once the Government puts forth credible evidence that the habeas petitioner meets the enemy-combatant criteria, the onus could shift to the petitioner to rebut that evidence with more persuasive evidence that he falls outside the criteria. A burden-shifting scheme of this sort would meet the goal of ensuring that the errant tourist, embedded journalist, or local aid worker has a chance to prove military error while giving due regard to the Executive once it has put forth meaningful support for its conclusion that the detainee is in fact an enemy combatant. . . .

We think it unlikely that this basic process will have the dire impact on the central functions of warmaking that the Government forecasts. The parties agree that initial captures on the battlefield need not receive the process we have discussed here; that process is due only when the determination is made to *continue* to hold those who have been seized. The Government has made clear in its briefing that documentation regarding battlefield detainees already is kept in the ordinary course of military affairs. Any factfinding imposition created by requiring a knowledgeable affiant to summarize these records to an independent tribunal is a minimal one. Likewise, arguments that military officers ought not have to wage war under the threat of litigation lose much of their steam when factual disputes at enemy-combatant hearings are limited to the alleged combatant's acts. This focus meddles little, if at all, in the strategy or conduct of war, inquiring only into the appropriateness of continuing to detain an individual claimed to have taken up arms against the United States. While we accord the greatest respect and consideration to the judgments of military authorities in matters relating to the actual prosecution of a war, and recognize that the scope of that discretion necessarily is wide, it does not infringe on the core role of the military for the courts to exercise their own time-honored and constitutionally mandated roles of reviewing and resolving claims like those presented here. . . .

D

In so holding, we necessarily reject the Government's assertion that separation of powers principles mandate a heavily circumscribed role for the courts in such circumstances. Indeed, the position that the courts must forgo any examination of the individual case and focus exclusively on the legality of the broader detention scheme cannot be mandated by any reasonable view of separation of powers, as this approach serves only to *condense* power into a single branch of government. We have long since made clear that a state of war is not a blank check for the President when it comes to the rights of the Nation's citizens. [*Youngstown*]. Whatever power the United States Constitution envisions for the Executive in its exchanges with other nations or with enemy organizations in times of conflict, it most assuredly envisions a role for all three branches when individual liberties are at stake. Likewise, we have made clear that, unless Congress acts to suspend it, the Great Writ of habeas corpus allows the Judicial Branch to play a necessary role in maintaining this delicate balance of governance, serving as an important judicial check on the Executive's discretion in the realm of detentions. Thus, while we do not question that our due process assessment must pay keen attention to the particular burdens faced by the Executive in the context of military action, it would turn our system of checks and balances on its head to suggest that a citizen could not make his way to court with a challenge to the factual basis for his detention by his government, simply because the Executive opposes making available such a challenge. Absent suspension of the writ by Congress, a citizen detained as an enemy combatant is entitled to this process.

Because we conclude that due process demands some system for a citizen detainee to refute his classification, the proposed "some evidence" standard is inadequate. Any process in which the Executive's factual assertions go wholly unchallenged or are simply presumed correct without any opportunity for the alleged combatant to demonstrate otherwise falls constitutionally short. [T]he "some evidence" standard in the past . . . primarily has been employed by courts in examining an administrative record developed after an adversarial proceeding — one with process at least of the sort that we today hold is constitutionally mandated in the citizen enemy-combatant setting. This standard therefore is ill suited to the situation in which a habeas petitioner has received no prior proceedings before any tribunal and had no prior opportunity to rebut the Executive's factual assertions before a neutral decisionmaker.

Today we are faced only with such a case. Aside from unspecified "screening" processes, and military interrogations in which the Government suggests Hamdi could have contested his classification, Hamdi has received no process. An interrogation by one's captor, however effective an intelligence-gathering tool, hardly constitutes a constitutionally adequate factfinding before a neutral decisionmaker. Compare Brief for Respondents 42-43 (discussing the "secure interrogation environment," and noting that military interrogations require a controlled "interrogation dynamic" and "a relationship of trust and dependency" and are "a critical source" of "timely and effective intelligence") with Concrete Pipe [& Products of Cal., Inc. v. Construction Laborers Pension Trust for Southern Cal.], 508 U.S. 602, 617-618 (1993) ("one is entitled as a matter of due process of law to an adjudicator who is not in a situation which would offer a possible temptation to the average man as a judge . . . which might lead him not to hold the balance nice, clear and true" that even purportedly fair adjudicators "are disqualified by their interest in the controversy to be decided is, of course, the general rule"). Plainly, the "process" Hamdi has received is not that to which he is entitled under the Due Process Clause.

There remains the possibility that the standards we have articulated could be met by an appropriately authorized and properly constituted military tribunal. Indeed, it is notable that military regulations already provide for such process in related instances, dictating that tribunals be made available to determine the status of enemy detainees who assert prisoner-of-war status under the Geneva Convention. In the absence of such process, however, a court that receives a petition for a writ of habeas corpus from an alleged enemy combatant must itself ensure that the minimum requirements of due process are achieved. . . . We anticipate that a

District Court would proceed with the caution that we have indicated is necessary in this setting, engaging in a factfinding process that is both prudent and incremental. We have no reason to doubt that courts faced with these sensitive matters will pay proper heed both to the matters of national security that might arise in an individual case and to the constitutional limitations safeguarding essential liberties that remain vibrant even in times of security concerns.

IV.

Hamdi asks us to hold that the Fourth Circuit also erred by denying him immediate access to counsel upon his detention and by disposing of the case without permitting him to meet with an attorney. Since our grant of certiorari in this case, Hamdi has been appointed counsel, with whom he has met for consultation purposes on several occasions, and with whom he is now being granted unmonitored meetings. He unquestionably has the right to access to counsel in connection with the proceedings on remand. No further consideration of this issue is necessary at this stage of the case.

The judgment of the United States Court of Appeals for the Fourth Circuit is vacated, and the case is remanded for further proceedings.

Justice SOUTER, with whom Justice Ginsburg joins, concurring in part, dissenting in part, and concurring in the judgment.

It is undisputed that the Government has not charged [Hamdi] with espionage, treason, or any other crime under domestic law. It is likewise undisputed that for one year and nine months, on the basis of an Executive designation of Hamdi as an "enemy combatant," the Government denied him the right to send or receive any communication beyond the prison where he was held and, in particular, denied him access to counsel to represent him.[a] The Government asserts a right to hold Hamdi under these conditions indefinitely, that is, until the Government determines that the United States is no longer threatened by the terrorism exemplified in the attacks of September 11, 2001. . . . [T]he Government contends that Hamdi has no basis for any challenge by petition for habeas except to his own status as an enemy combatant; and even that challenge may go no further than to enquire whether "some evidence" supports Hamdi's designation; if there is "some evidence," Hamdi should remain locked up at the discretion of the Executive. At the argument of this case, in fact, the Government went further and suggested that as long as a prisoner could challenge his enemy combatant designation when responding to interrogation during incommunicado detention he was accorded sufficient process to support his designation as an enemy combatant. See Tr. of Oral Arg. 40; id., at 42 ("[H]e has an opportunity to explain it in his own words" "[d]uring interrogation"). Since on either view judicial enquiry so limited would be virtually worthless as a way to contest detention, the Government's concession of jurisdiction to hear Hamdi's habeas claim is more theoretical than practical, leaving the assertion of Executive authority close to unconditional.

The plurality rejects any such limit on the exercise of habeas jurisdiction and so far I agree with its opinion. The plurality does, however, accept the Government's

---

a. The Government has since February 2004 permitted Hamdi to consult with counsel as a matter of policy, but does not concede that it has an obligation to allow this.

position that if Hamdi's designation as an enemy combatant is correct, his detention (at least as to some period) is authorized by an Act of Congress as required by [the Non-Detention Act, 18 U.S.C. §4001(a)], that is, by the Authorization for Use of Military Force, 115 Stat. 224 (hereinafter Force Resolution). Here, I disagree and respectfully dissent. The Government has failed to demonstrate that the Force Resolution authorizes the detention complained of here even on the facts the Government claims. If the Government raises nothing further than the record now shows, the Non-Detention Act entitles Hamdi to be released. . . .

II.

The threshold issue is how broadly or narrowly to read the Non-Detention Act [18 U.S.C. §4001(a)], the tone of which is severe: "No citizen shall be imprisoned or otherwise detained by the United States except pursuant to an Act of Congress." Should the severity of the Act be relieved when the Government's stated factual justification for incommunicado detention is a war on terrorism, so that the Government may be said to act "pursuant" to congressional terms that fall short of explicit authority to imprison individuals? With one possible though important qualification, the answer has to be no. . . . The fact that Congress intended to guard against a repetition of the World War II internments when it repealed [an earlier Cold War statute that authorized the Attorney General in emergencies to detain anyone reasonably thought likely to engage in espionage or sabotage] and gave us §4001(a) provides a powerful reason to think that §4001(a) was meant to require clear congressional authorization before any citizen can be placed in a cell. . . . [T]he internments of the 1940's were accomplished by Executive action . . . Congress . . . intended to preclude reliance on vague congressional authority . . . for detention or imprisonment at the discretion of the Executive.

[Moreover], when Congress passed §4001(a) it was acting in light of an interpretive regime that subjected enactments limiting liberty in wartime to the requirement of a clear statement and it presumably intended §4001(a) to be read accordingly. . . . *Ex parte Endo,* [323 U.S. 283 (1944)] . . . decided the same day as *Korematsu* . . . set out this principle for scrutinizing wartime statutes in derogation of customary liberty: "In interpreting a wartime measure we must assume that [its] purpose was to allow for the greatest possible accommodation between . . . liberties and the exigencies of war. We must assume, when asked to find implied powers in a grant of legislative or executive authority, that the law makers intended to place no greater restraint on the citizen than was clearly and unmistakably indicated by the language they used." . . .

[T]he defining character of American constitutional government is its constant tension between security and liberty, serving both by partial helpings of each. In a government of separated powers, deciding finally on what is a reasonable degree of guaranteed liberty whether in peace or war (or some condition in between) is not well entrusted to the Executive Branch of Government, whose particular responsibility is to maintain security. For reasons of inescapable human nature, the branch of the Government asked to counter a serious threat is not the branch on which to rest the Nation's entire reliance in striking the balance between the will to win and the cost in liberty on the way to victory; the responsibility for security will naturally amplify the claim that security legitimately raises. A reasonable balance is more likely to be reached on the judgment of a different branch, just as Madison said in remarking that "the constant aim is to divide and arrange the several offices in such a manner as that each may be a check on the other — that the private interest of every individual may be a sentinel over the public rights." The Federalist No. 51. Hence the need for an assessment by Congress before citizens are subject to lockup, and likewise the need for a clearly expressed congressional resolution of the competing claims.

III.

Under this principle of reading §4001(a) robustly to require a clear statement of authorization to detain, none of the Government's arguments suffices to justify Hamdi's detention.

[Justice Souter argues that the legislative history of §4001(a) shows that it was not limited to detentions for domestic crimes but was intended to apply to wartime military detentions justified on grounds of national security.]

[T]he Force Resolution was adopted one week after the attacks of September 11, 2001; it naturally speaks with some generality, but its focus is clear, and that is on the use of military power. . . . [I]t never so much as uses the word detention, and . . . Congress [has already provided a] well-stocked statutory arsenal of defined criminal offenses covering the gamut of actions that a citizen sympathetic to terrorists might commit. See, e.g., 18 U.S.C. §2339A (material support for various terrorist acts); §2339B (material support to a foreign terrorist organization); §2332a (use of a weapon of mass destruction, including conspiracy and attempt); §2332b(a)(1) (acts of terrorism "transcending national boundaries," including threats, conspiracy, and attempt); 18 U.S.C.A. §2339C (Supp.2004) (financing of certain terrorist acts); see also 18 U.S.C. §3142(e) (pretrial detention). . . .

C

[T]here is one argument for treating the Force Resolution as sufficiently clear to authorize detention of a citizen consistently with §4001(a), [but] the Government is in no position to claim its advantage. Because the Force Resolution authorizes the use of military force in acts of war by the United States, the argument goes, it is reasonably clear that the military and its Commander in Chief are authorized to deal with enemy belligerents according to the treaties and customs known collectively as the laws of war.

[T]he Government . . . repeatedly argues that Hamdi's detention amounts to nothing more than customary detention of a captive taken on the field of battle: if the usages of war are fairly authorized by the Force Resolution, Hamdi's detention is authorized for purposes of §4001(a). [However,] the Government's stated legal position in its campaign against the Taliban (among whom Hamdi was allegedly captured) is apparently at odds with its claim here to be acting in accordance with customary law of war and hence to be within the terms of the Force Resolution in its detention of Hamdi. In a statement of its legal position cited in its brief, the Government says that "the Geneva Convention applies to the Taliban detainees." Hamdi presumably is such a detainee, since according to the Government's own account, he was taken bearing arms on the Taliban side of a field of battle in Afghanistan. He would therefore seem to qualify for treatment as a prisoner of war under the Third Geneva Convention, to which the United States is a party.

By holding him incommunicado, however, the Government obviously has not been treating him as a prisoner of war, and in fact the Government claims that no Taliban detainee is entitled to prisoner of war status. This treatment appears to be a violation of the Geneva Convention provision that even in cases of doubt, captives are entitled to be treated as prisoners of war "until such time as their status has been determined by a competent tribunal." The Government answers that the President's determination that Taliban detainees do not qualify as prisoners of war is conclusive as to Hamdi's status and removes any doubt that would trigger application of the Convention's tribunal requirement. But reliance on this categorical pronouncement to settle doubt is apparently at odds with the military regulation, Enemy Prisoners of War, Retained Personnel, Civilian Internees and Other Detainees, Army Reg. 190-8, §§1-5, 1-6 (1997), adopted to implement the Geneva Convention, and setting out a detailed procedure for a military tribunal to determine an individual's status. . . . One of the types of doubt these tribunals are meant to settle is whether a given individual may be, as Hamdi says he is, an "[i]nnocent civilian who should be immediately returned to his home or released." Id., 1-6e (10)(c). The regulation, jointly promulgated by the Headquarters of the Departments of the Army, Navy, Air Force, and Marine Corps, provides that "[p]ersons who have been determined by a competent tribunal not to be entitled to prisoner of war status may not be executed, imprisoned, or otherwise penalized without further proceedings to determine what acts they have committed and what penalty should be imposed." Id., §1-6g. The regulation also incorporates the Geneva Convention's presumption that in cases of doubt, "persons shall enjoy the protection of the . . . Convention until such time as their status has been determined by a competent tribunal." Id., §1-6a. Thus, there is reason to question whether the United States is acting in accordance with the laws of war it claims as authority.

Whether, or to what degree, the Government is in fact violating the Geneva Convention and is thus acting outside the customary usages of war are not matters I can resolve at this point. What I can say, though, is that the Government has not made out its claim that in detaining Hamdi in the manner described, it is acting in accord with the laws of war authorized to be applied against citizens by the Force Resolution. I conclude accordingly that the Government has failed to support the position that the Force Resolution authorizes the described detention of Hamdi for purposes of §4001(a). . . .

D

[The same objections apply to] the Government's mixed claim of inherent, extrastatutory authority under a combination of Article II of the Constitution and the usages of war. . . . [I]t is instructive to recall Justice Jackson's observation that the President is not Commander in Chief of the country, only of the military. Youngstown Sheet & Tube Co. v. Sawyer, 343 U.S. 579, 643-644, (1952) (concurring opinion); see also id., at 637-638 (Presidential authority is "at its lowest ebb" where the President acts contrary to congressional will). There may be room for one qualification to Justice Jackson's statement, however: in a moment of genuine emergency, when the Government must act with no time for deliberation, the Executive may be able to detain a citizen if there is reason to fear he is an imminent threat to the safety of the Nation and its people (though I doubt there is any want of statutory authority). This case, however, does not present that question, because an emergency power of necessity must at least be limited by the emergency; Hamdi has been locked up for over two years. . . .

IV.

Because I find Hamdi's detention forbidden by §4001(a) and unauthorized by the Force Resolution, I would not reach any questions of what process he may be due in litigating disputed issues in a proceeding under the habeas statute or prior to the habeas enquiry itself. . . . Since this disposition does not command a majority of the Court, however, the need to give practical effect to the conclusions of eight members of the Court rejecting the Government's position calls for me to join with the plurality in ordering remand on terms closest to those I would impose. Although I think litigation of Hamdi's status as an enemy combatant is unnecessary, the terms of the plurality's remand will allow Hamdi to offer evidence that he is not an enemy combatant, and he should at the least have the benefit of that opportunity.

It should go without saying that in joining with the plurality to produce a judgment, I do not adopt the plurality's resolution of constitutional issues that I would not reach. It is not that I could disagree with the plurality's determinations (given the plurality's view of the Force Resolution) that someone in Hamdi's position is entitled at a minimum to notice of the Government's claimed factual basis for holding him, and to a fair chance to rebut it before a neutral decision maker; nor, of course, could I disagree with the plurality's affirmation of Hamdi's right to counsel. On the other hand, I do not mean to imply agreement that the Government could claim an evidentiary presumption casting the burden of rebuttal on Hamdi, or that an opportunity to litigate before a military tribunal might obviate or truncate enquiry by a court on habeas.

Subject to these qualifications, I join with the plurality in a judgment of the Court vacating the Fourth Circuit's judgment and remanding the case.

Justice SCALIA, with whom Justice Stevens joins, dissenting.

Where the Government accuses a citizen of waging war against it, our constitutional tradition has been to prosecute him in federal court for treason or some other crime. Where the exigencies of war prevent that, the Constitution's Suspension Clause, Art. I, §9, cl. 2, allows Congress to relax the usual protections temporarily. Absent suspension, however, the Executive's assertion of military exigency has not been thought sufficient to permit detention without charge. No one contends that the congressional Authorization for Use of Military Force, on which the Government relies to justify its actions here, is an implementation of the Suspension Clause. Accordingly, I would reverse the decision below.

The very core of liberty secured by our Anglo-Saxon system of separated powers has been freedom from indefinite imprisonment at the will of the Executive. . . . The two ideas central to Blackstone's understanding — due process as the right secured, and habeas corpus as the instrument by which due process could be insisted upon by a citizen illegally imprisoned — found expression in the Constitution's Due Process and Suspension Clauses.

The gist of the Due Process Clause, as understood at the founding and since, was to force the Government to follow those common-law procedures traditionally deemed necessary before depriving a person of life, liberty, or property. When a citizen was deprived of liberty because of alleged criminal conduct, those procedures typically required committal by a magistrate followed by indictment and trial. . . .

Justice O'Connor, writing for a plurality of this Court, asserts that captured enemy combatants (other than those suspected of war crimes) have traditionally been detained until the cessation of hostilities and then released. That is probably an accurate description of wartime practice with respect to enemy *aliens*. The tradition with respect to American citizens, however, has been quite different. Citizens aiding the enemy have been treated as traitors subject to the criminal process. . . .

The Government justifies imprisonment of Hamdi on principles of the law of war and admits that, absent the war, it would have no such authority. But if the law of war cannot be applied to citizens where courts are open, then Hamdi's imprisonment without criminal trial is no less unlawful than Milligan's trial by military tribunal [in *Ex parte Milligan*]. . . .

[*Ex parte Quirin*] was not this Court's finest hour. . . . [E]ven if *Quirin* gave a correct description of *Milligan*, or made an irrevocable revision of it, *Quirin* would still not justify denial of the writ here. In *Quirin* it was uncontested that the petitioners were members of enemy forces. They were "*admitted* enemy invaders," and it was "undisputed" that they had landed in the United States in service of German forces. The specific holding of the Court was only that, "upon the *conceded* facts," the petitioners were "plainly within [the] boundaries" of military jurisdiction, But where those jurisdictional facts are *not* conceded — where the petitioner insists that he is *not* a belligerent — *Quirin* left the pre-existing law in place: Absent suspension of the writ, a citizen held where the courts are open is entitled either to criminal trial or to a judicial decree requiring his release.[a]

. . . The plurality finds justification for Hamdi's imprisonment in the Authorization for Use of Military Force. . . . This is not remotely a congressional suspension of the writ, and no one claims that it is. Contrary to the plurality's view, I do not think this statute even authorizes detention of a citizen with the clarity necessary to satisfy the interpretive canon that statutes should be construed so as to avoid grave constitutional concerns, with the clarity necessary to comport with cases such as *Ex parte Endo*, 323 U.S. 283 (1944); or with the clarity necessary to overcome the statutory prescription that "[n]o citizen shall be imprisoned or otherwise detained by the United States except pursuant to an Act of Congress." 18 U.S.C. §4001(a). But even if it did, I would not permit it to overcome Hamdi's entitlement

a. The Government also cites Moyer v. Peabody, 212 U.S. 78 (1909), a suit for damages against the Governor of Colorado, for violation of due process in detaining the alleged ringleader of a rebellion quelled by the state militia after the Governor's declaration of a state of insurrection and (he contended) suspension of the writ "as incident thereto." But the holding of Moyer v. Peabody (even assuming it is transferable from state-militia detention after state suspension to federal standing-army detention without suspension) is simply that "[s]o long as such arrests [were] made in good faith and in the honest belief that they [were] needed in order to head the insurrection off," an action in damages could not lie. This "good-faith" analysis is a forebear of our modern doctrine of qualified immunity. Moreover, the detention at issue in *Moyer* lasted about two and a half months, roughly the length of time permissible under the 1679 Habeas Corpus Act.

In addition to Moyer v. Peabody, Justice THOMAS relies upon Luther v. Borden, 7 How. 1 (1849), a case in which the state legislature had imposed martial law — a step even more drastic than suspension of the writ. But martial law has not been imposed here, and in any case is limited to "the theatre of active military operations, where war really prevails," and where therefore the courts are closed.

to habeas corpus relief. The Suspension Clause of the Constitution, which carefully circumscribes the conditions under which the writ can be withheld, would be a sham if it could be evaded by congressional prescription of requirements *other than the common-law requirement of committal for criminal prosecution* that render the writ, though available, unavailing. If the Suspension Clause does not guarantee the citizen that he will either be tried or released, unless the conditions for suspending the writ exist and the grave action of suspending the writ has been taken; if it merely guarantees the citizen that he will not be detained unless Congress by ordinary legislation says he can be detained; it guarantees him very little indeed.

It should not be thought, however, that the plurality's evisceration of the Suspension Clause augments, principally, the power of Congress. As usual, the major effect of its constitutional improvisation is to increase the power of the Court. Having found a congressional authorization for detention of citizens where none clearly exists; and having discarded the categorical procedural protection of the Suspension Clause; the plurality then proceeds, under the guise of the Due Process Clause, to prescribe what procedural protections *it* thinks appropriate. . . . from Mathews v. Eldridge, a case involving . . . *the withdrawal of disability benefits!* . . . This judicial remediation of executive default is unheard of. The role of habeas corpus is to determine the legality of executive detention, not to supply the omitted process necessary to make it legal. It is not the habeas court's function to make illegal detention legal by supplying a process that the Government could have provided, but chose not to. If Hamdi is being imprisoned in violation of the Constitution (because without due process of law), then his habeas petition should be granted; the Executive may then hand him over to the criminal authorities, whose detention for the purpose of prosecution will be lawful, or else must release him.

There is a certain harmony of approach in the plurality's making up for Congress's failure to invoke the Suspension Clause and its making up for the Executive's failure to apply what it says are needed procedures — an approach that reflects what might be called a Mr. Fix-it Mentality. The plurality seems to view it as its mission to Make Everything Come Out Right, rather than merely to decree the consequences, as far as individual rights are concerned, of the other two branches' actions and omissions. Has the Legislature failed to suspend the writ in the current dire emergency? Well, we will remedy that failure by prescribing the reasonable conditions that a suspension should have included. And has the Executive failed to live up to those reasonable conditions? Well, we will ourselves make that failure good, so that this dangerous fellow (if he is dangerous) need not be set free. The problem with this approach is not only that it steps out of the courts' modest and limited role in a democratic society; but that by repeatedly doing what it thinks the political branches ought to do it encourages their lassitude and saps the vitality of government by the people.

Several limitations give my views in this matter a relatively narrow compass. They apply only to citizens, accused of being enemy combatants, who are detained within the territorial jurisdiction of a federal court. This is not likely to be a numerous group; currently we know of only two, Hamdi and Jose Padilla. Where the citizen is captured outside and held outside the United States, the constitutional requirements may be different. Moreover, even within the United States, the accused citizen-enemy combatant may lawfully be detained once prosecution is in progress or in contemplation. The Government has been notably successful in securing conviction, and hence long-term custody or execution, of those who have waged war against the state.

I frankly do not know whether these tools are sufficient to meet the Government's security needs, including the need to obtain intelligence through interrogation. It is far beyond my competence, or the Court's competence, to determine that. But it is not beyond Congress's. If the situation demands it, the Executive can ask Congress to authorize suspension of the writ — which can be made subject to whatever conditions Congress deems appropriate, including even the procedural novelties invented by the plurality today. To be sure, suspension is limited by the Constitution to cases of rebellion or invasion. But whether the attacks of September 11, 2001, constitute an "invasion," and whether those attacks still justify suspension several years later, are questions for Congress rather than this Court.[b] If civil rights are to be curtailed during wartime, it must be done openly and democratically, as the Constitution requires, rather than by silent erosion through an opinion of this Court.

The Founders well understood the difficult trade off between safety and freedom. "Safety from external danger," Hamilton declared,

> "is the most powerful director of national conduct. Even the ardent love of liberty will, after a time, give way to its dictates. The violent destruction of life and property incident to war; the continual effort and alarm attendant on a state of continual danger, will compel nations the most attached to liberty, to resort for repose and security to institutions which have a tendency to destroy their civil and political rights. To be more safe, they, at length, become willing to run the risk of being less free." The Federalist No. 8.

The Founders warned us about the risk, and equipped us with a Constitution designed to deal with it.

Many think it not only inevitable but entirely proper that liberty give way to security in times of national crisis — that, at the extremes of military exigency, inter arma silent leges. Whatever the general merits of the view that war silences law or modulates its voice, that view has no place in the interpretation and application of a Constitution designed precisely to confront war and, in a manner that accords with democratic principles, to accommodate it. Because the Court has proceeded to meet the current emergency in a manner the Constitution does not envision, I respectfully dissent.

Justice THOMAS, dissenting.

The Executive Branch, acting pursuant to the powers vested in the President by the Constitution and with explicit congressional approval, has determined that Yaser Hamdi is an enemy combatant and should be detained. This detention falls squarely within the Federal Government's war powers, and we lack the expertise and capacity to second-guess that decision. As such, petitioners' habeas challenge should fail, and there is no reason to remand the case. The plurality reaches a contrary conclusion by failing adequately to consider basic principles of the constitutional structure as it

---

b. Justice THOMAS worries that the constitutional conditions for suspension of the writ will not exist "during many . . . emergencies during which . . . detention authority might be necessary." It is difficult to imagine situations in which security is so seriously threatened as to justify indefinite imprisonment without trial, and yet the constitutional conditions of rebellion or invasion are not met.

relates to national security and foreign affairs and by using the balancing scheme of Mathews v. Eldridge, 424 U.S. 319 (1976). I do not think that the Federal Government's war powers can be balanced away by this Court. Arguably, Congress could provide for additional procedural protections, but until it does, we have no right to insist upon them. But even if I were to agree with the general approach the plurality takes, I could not accept the particulars. The plurality utterly fails to account for the Government's compelling interests and for our own institutional inability to weigh competing concerns correctly. I respectfully dissent.

I.

[B]ecause the Founders understood that they could not foresee the myriad potential threats to national security that might later arise, they chose to create a Federal Government that necessarily possesses sufficient power to handle any threat to the security of the Nation. . . . The Founders intended that the President have primary responsibility — along with the necessary power — to protect the national security and to conduct the Nation's foreign relations. They did so principally because the structural advantages of a unitary Executive are essential in these domains. "Energy in the executive is a leading character in the definition of good government. It is essential to the protection of the community against foreign attacks." The Federalist No. 70 (A. Hamilton). The principle "ingredien[t]" for "energy in the executive" is "unity." This is because "[d]ecision, activity, secrecy, and dispatch will generally characterise the proceedings of one man, in a much more eminent degree, than the proceedings of any greater number."

These structural advantages are most important in the national-security and foreign-affairs contexts. "Of all the cares or concerns of government, the direction of war most peculiarly demands those qualities which distinguish the exercise of power by a single hand." The Federalist No. 74 (A. Hamilton). Also for these reasons, John Marshall explained that "[t]he President is the sole organ of the nation in its external relations, and its sole representative with foreign nations." 10 Annals of Cong. 613 (1800). To this end, the Constitution vests in the President "[t]he executive Power," Art. II, §1, provides that he "shall be Commander in Chief of the" armed forces, §2, and places in him the power to recognize foreign governments, §3.

This Court has long recognized these features and has accordingly held that the President has *constitutional* authority to protect the national security and that this authority carries with it broad discretion. The Court has acknowledged that the President has the authority to "employ [the Nation's Armed Forces] in the manner he may deem most effectual to harass and conquer and subdue the enemy." Fleming v. Page, 9 How. 603, 615 (1850). With respect to foreign affairs as well, the Court has recognized the President's independent authority and need to be free from interference. See, e.g., United States v. Curtiss-Wright Export Corp., 299 U.S. 304, 320 (1936) (explaining that the President "has his confidential sources of information. He has his agents in the form of diplomatic, consular and other officials. Secrecy in respect of information gathered by them may be highly necessary, and the premature disclosure of it productive of harmful results").

Congress, to be sure, has a substantial and essential role in both foreign affairs and national security. But it is crucial to recognize that *judicial* interference in these domains destroys the purpose of vesting primary responsibility in a unitary Executive. . . . [W]ith respect to certain decisions relating to national security and foreign affairs, the courts simply lack the relevant information and expertise to second-guess determinations made by the President based on information properly withheld. [Moreover,] even if the courts could compel the Executive to produce the necessary information, such decisions are simply not amenable to judicial determination because "[t]hey are delicate, complex, and involve large elements of prophecy."

For these institutional reasons and because "Congress cannot anticipate and legislate with regard to every possible action the President may find it necessary to take or every possible situation in which he might act," it should come as no surprise that "[s]uch failure of Congress . . . does not, 'especially . . . in the areas of foreign policy and national security,' imply 'congressional disapproval' of action taken by the Executive." Dames & Moore v. Regan, 453 U.S. 654, 678 (1981). Rather, in these domains, the fact that Congress has provided the President with broad authorities does not imply — and the Judicial Branch should not infer — that Congress intended to deprive him of particular powers not specifically enumerated. As far as the courts are concerned, "the enactment of legislation closely related to the question of the President's authority in a particular case which evinces legislative intent to accord the President broad discretion may be considered to 'invite' 'measures on independent presidential responsibility.' "

Finally, and again for the same reasons, where "the President acts pursuant to an express or implied authorization from Congress, he exercises not only his powers but also those delegated by Congress[, and i]n such a case the executive action 'would be supported by the strongest of presumptions and the widest latitude of judicial interpretation, and the burden of persuasion would rest heavily upon any who might attack it.' " Dames & Moore, (quoting Youngstown, supra, (Jackson, J., concurring)). That is why the Court has explained, in a case analogous to this one, that "the detention [,] ordered by the President in the declared exercise of his powers as Commander in Chief of the Army in time of war and of grave public danger[, is] not to be set aside by the courts without the clear conviction that [it is] in conflict with the Constitution or laws of Congress constitutionally enacted." Ex parte Quirin. This deference extends to the President's determination of all the factual predicates necessary to conclude that a given action is appropriate.

. . . I acknowledge that the question whether Hamdi's executive detention is lawful is a question properly resolved by the Judicial Branch, though the question comes to the Court with the strongest presumptions in favor of the Government. The plurality agrees that Hamdi's detention is lawful if he is an enemy combatant. But the question whether Hamdi is actually an enemy combatant is "of a kind for which the Judiciary has neither aptitude, facilities nor responsibility and which has long been held to belong in the domain of political power not subject to judicial intrusion or inquiry." That is, although it is appropriate for the Court to determine the judicial question whether the President has the asserted authority, we lack the information and expertise to question whether Hamdi is actually an enemy combatant, a question the resolution of which is committed to other branches.

II.

"The war power of the national government is 'the power to wage war successfully.' " It follows that this power "is not limited to victories in the field, but carries with it the inherent power to guard against the immediate renewal of the conflict," and quite obviously includes the ability to detain those (even United States citizens) who fight against our troops or those of our allies.

Although the President very well may have inherent authority to detain those arrayed against our troops, I agree with the plurality that we need not decide that question because Congress has authorized the President to do so. The Authorization for Use of Military Force (AUMF) authorizes the President to "use all necessary and appropriate force against those nations, organizations, or persons he determines planned, authorized, committed, or aided the terrorist attacks" of September 11, 2001.

The plurality, however, qualifies its recognition of the President's authority to detain enemy combatants in the war on terrorism in ways that are at odds with our precedent. Thus, the plurality relies primarily on Article 118 of the Geneva Convention (III) Relative to the Treatment of Prisoners of War, for the proposition that "[i]t is a clearly established principle of the law of war that detention may last no longer than active hostilities." It then appears to limit the President's authority to detain by requiring that the record establis[h] that United States troops are still involved in active combat in Afghanistan because, in that case, detention would be "part of the exercise of 'necessary and appropriate force.'" But I do not believe that we may diminish the Federal Government's war powers by reference to a treaty and certainly not to a treaty that does not apply. Further, we are bound by the political branches' determination that the United States is at war. And, in any case, the power to detain does not end with the cessation of formal hostilities.

Accordingly, the President's action here is "supported by the strongest of presumptions and the widest latitude of judicial interpretation." The question becomes whether the Federal Government (rather than the President acting alone) has power to detain Hamdi as an enemy combatant. More precisely, we must determine whether the Government may detain Hamdi given the procedures that were used.

III.

I agree with the plurality that the Federal Government has power to detain those that the Executive Branch determines to be enemy combatants. But I do not think that the plurality has adequately explained the breadth of the President's authority to detain enemy combatants, an authority that includes making virtually conclusive factual findings. In my view, the structural considerations discussed above, as recognized in our precedent, demonstrate that we lack the capacity and responsibility to second-guess this determination.

This makes complete sense once the process that is due Hamdi is made clear. As an initial matter, it is possible that the Due Process Clause requires only "that our Government must proceed according to the 'law of the land' — that is, according to written constitutional and statutory provisions." *In re Winship*, 397 U.S. 358, 382 (1970) (Black, J., dissenting). I need not go this far today because the Court has already explained the nature of due process in this context.

In a case strikingly similar to this one, the Court addressed a Governor's authority to detain for an extended period a person the executive believed to be responsible, in part, for a local insurrection. Justice Holmes wrote for a unanimous Court:

"When it comes to a decision by the head of the State upon a matter involving its life, the ordinary rights of individuals must yield to what *he deems* the necessities of the moment. Public danger warrants the substitution of executive process for judicial process. This was admitted with regard to killing men in the actual clash of arms, and we think it obvious, although it was disputed, that the same is true of temporary detention to prevent apprehended harm."

Moyer v. Peabody, 212 U.S. 78, 85 (1909) (citation omitted; emphasis added).

The Court answered Moyer's claim that he had been denied due process by emphasizing that

> "it is familiar that what is due process of law depends on circumstances. It varies with the subject-matter and the necessities of the situation. Thus summary proceedings suffice for taxes, and executive decisions for exclusion from the country. . . . Such arrests are not necessarily for punishment, but are by way of precaution to prevent the exercise of hostile power."

In this context, due process requires nothing more than a good-faith executive determination.[a] To be clear: The Court has held that an executive, acting pursuant to statutory and constitutional authority may, consistent with the Due Process Clause, unilaterally decide to detain an individual if the executive deems this necessary for the public safety *even if he is mistaken.*

. . . The Government's asserted authority to detain an individual that the President has determined to be an enemy combatant, at least while hostilities continue, comports with the Due Process Clause. . . . [T]he Executive's decision that a detention is necessary to protect the public need not and should not be subjected to judicial second-guessing. Indeed, at least in the context of enemy-combatant determinations, this would defeat the unity, secrecy, and dispatch that the Founders believed to be so important to the warmaking function.

I therefore cannot agree with Justice Scalia's conclusion that the Government must choose between using standard criminal processes and suspending the writ. I admit that *Milligan* supports his position. But because the Executive Branch there, unlike here, did not follow a specific statutory mechanism provided by Congress, the Court did not need to reach the broader question of Congress' power, and its discussion on this point was arguably dicta. More importantly, the Court referred frequently and pervasively to the criminal nature of the proceedings instituted against Milligan. . . . Because the Government does not detain Hamdi in order to punish him . . . *Milligan* . . . [does] not control. . . .

Justice Scalia apparently does not disagree that the Federal Government has all power necessary to protect the Nation. If criminal processes do not suffice, however, Justice Scalia would require Congress to suspend the writ. But the fact that the writ may not be suspended "unless when in Cases of Rebellion or Invasion the public Safety may require it," Art. I, §9, cl. 2, poses two related problems. First, this condition might not obtain here or during many other emergencies during which this detention authority might be necessary. Congress would then have to choose between acting unconstitutionally and depriving the President of the tools he needs to protect the Nation. Second, I do not see how suspension would make constitutional otherwise unconstitutional detentions ordered by the President. It simply removes a remedy. Justice Scalia's position might therefore require one or

---

a. Indeed, it is not even clear that the Court required good faith. See *Moyer,* 212 U.S., at 85 ("It is not alleged that [the Governor's] judgment was not honest, if that be material, or that [Moyer] was detained after fears of the insurrection were at an end").

both of the political branches to act unconstitutionally in order to protect the Nation. But the power to protect the Nation must be the power to do so lawfully. . . .

IV.

. . . At issue here is the . . . interest of the security of the Nation. The Government seeks to further that interest by detaining an enemy soldier not only to prevent him from rejoining the ongoing fight [but also] to gather critical intelligence regarding the intentions and capabilities of our adversaries, a function that the Government avers has become all the more important in the war on terrorism.

Additional process, the Government explains, will destroy the intelligence gathering function. It also does seem quite likely that, under the process envisioned by the plurality, various military officials will have to take time to litigate this matter. And though the plurality does not say so, a meaningful ability to challenge the Government's factual allegations will probably require the Government to divulge highly classified information to the purported enemy combatant, who might then upon release return to the fight armed with our most closely held secrets.

Ultimately, the plurality's dismissive treatment of the Government's asserted interests arises from its apparent belief that enemy-combatant determinations are not part of "the actual prosecution of a war," or one of the "central functions of warmaking." This seems wrong: Taking *and holding* enemy combatants is a quintessential aspect of the prosecution of war. Moreover, this highlights serious difficulties in applying the plurality's balancing approach here. First, in the war context, we know neither the strength of the Government's interests nor the costs of imposing additional process.

Second, it is at least difficult to explain why the result should be different for other military operations that the plurality would ostensibly recognize as "central functions of warmaking." . . . Because a decision to bomb a particular target might extinguish *life* interests, the plurality's analysis seems to require notice to potential targets. To take one more example, in November 2002, a Central Intelligence Agency (CIA) Predator drone fired a Hellfire missile at a vehicle in Yemen carrying an al Qaeda leader, a citizen of the United States, and four others. It is not clear whether the CIA knew that an American was in the vehicle. But the plurality's due process would seem to require notice and opportunity to respond here as well. . . .

For these reasons, I would affirm the judgment of the Court of Appeals.

RUMSFELD v. PADILLA, 542 U.S. 426 (2004): The Court considered a habeas petition from Jose Padilla, a U.S. citizen who had converted to Islam and taken the name Abdullah al Muhajir. Padilla was arrested at O'Hare Airport on May 8, 2002, after returning from Pakistan. He was detained under a material witness warrant issued by a federal district court in New York. On June 9, 2002, he was declared an enemy combatant and placed in a military brig in South Carolina. Originally, the Justice Department claimed that Padilla was an al Qaeda operative who was planning to explode a "dirty bomb" — a conventional bomb that would spread radioactive material — in an American city. Two years later, the Justice Department stated that it believed that Padilla was planning to leak natural gas into apartment buildings and blow them up. Padilla's lawyer filed a petition for habeas corpus claiming that his detention was unconstitutional.

Without reaching the merits, the Court held 5-4, that Padilla should have filed his habeas petition in the District Court for the Southern District of South Carolina, rather than in New York, where he had originally been detained as a material witness. Chief Justice Rehnquist wrote the majority opinion.

Justice Stevens, joined by Justices Souter, Ginsburg, and Breyer, dissented, arguing that the federal court in New York had jurisdiction to hear Padilla's claims. Stevens went on to consider the merits. "There is," Stevens wrote, "only one possible answer to the question whether [Padilla] is entitled to a hearing on the justification for his detention." In a footnote, Stevens argued that "the Non-Detention Act, 18 U.S.C. §4001(a), prohibits — and the Authorization for Use of Military Force Joint Resolution, 115 Stat. 224, adopted on September 18, 2001, does not authorize — the protracted, incommunicado detention of American citizens arrested in the United States."

In a footnote he explained:

Respondent's custodian has been remarkably candid about the Government's motive in detaining respondent: "'[O]ur interest really in his case is not law enforcement, it is not punishment because he was a terrorist or working with the terrorists. Our interest at the moment is to try and find out everything he knows so that hopefully we can stop other terrorist acts.'"

Stevens continued:

At stake in this case is nothing less than the essence of a free society. Even more important than the method of selecting the people's rulers and their successors is the character of the constraints imposed on the Executive by the rule of law. Unconstrained Executive detention for the purpose of investigating and preventing subversive activity is the hallmark of the Star Chamber. Access to counsel for the purpose of protecting the citizen from official mistakes and mistreatment is the hallmark of due process.

Executive detention of subversive citizens, like detention of enemy soldiers to keep them off the battlefield, may sometimes be justified to prevent persons from launching or becoming missiles of destruction. It may not, however, be justified by the naked interest in using unlawful procedures to extract information. Incommunicado detention for months on end is such a procedure. Whether the information so procured is more or less reliable than that acquired by more extreme forms of torture is of no consequence. For if this Nation is to remain true to the ideals symbolized by its flag, it must not wield the tools of tyrants even to resist an assault by the forces of tyranny.

Discussion

1. *Construing the scope of congressional authorization.* Where deviations from normal legal procedures are justified on grounds of war and national security, the Court is more likely to defer to the President when it believes that Congress approves; conversely, it is more likely to seek to check the President only when he acts unilaterally or in the face of congressional disapproval.[71] This means that courts often play their most significant role in determining the existence and scope of congressional approval. By finding or refusing to find such approval, or

71. See Samuel Issacharoff and Richard Pildes, Between Civil Libertarianism and Executive Unilateralism: An Institutional Process Approach to Rights During Wartime, in The Constitution in Wartime: Beyond Alarmism and Complacency 161-197 (Mark Tushnet ed., 2005), for a more developed version of this argument, with abundant historical examples.

by construing the scope of congressional approval broadly or narrowly, courts can limit and channel Presidential ambitions without directly denying the existence of Executive power.

Thus, in *Hamdi*, Justice O'Connor avoids deciding whether the President may detain enemy combatants on his own authority as Commander-in-Chief; instead she argues that Congress has approved some detentions and then construes that approval narrowly. The plurality's narrow definition of "enemy combatant" limits the political and legal legitimacy of the President's actions if he seeks to detain people on the basis of a broader definition. Of course, the President can always go to Congress to seek a broader authorization. But if he does so, he will be acting many years after the September 11 attacks, when passions have cooled and Congress may provide greater oversight. Thus, by construing the terms of consent between the two branches and then deferring to that constructed agreement, the Court creates a space of power for itself.

Do you agree with the plurality's assertion that the language of the AUMF is sufficiently clear to authorize the President to detain enemy combatants, under the laws of war, for the purposes of incapacitation? Should a clearer statement be required where detention of citizens is at stake?

According to Justice Scalia, the President may only detain citizens as enemy combatants if Congress suspends the writ of habeas corpus. Otherwise the government must use the normal resources of the criminal justice system. None of the Justices believed that the AUMF suspended the writ. Why? If the AUMF is not clear enough to suspend the writ of habeas corpus, why does it provide a sufficiently clear authorization to detain citizens as enemy combatants, especially if this will also deny citizens Bill of Rights protections?

As noted previously, the Court does not decide whether the President has inherent authority as Commander-in-Chief to detain citizens as enemy combatants in the absence of the AUMF. Should the President have such authority? After *Hamdi*, do you believe that the President can suspend the writ of habeas corpus unilaterally, as Lincoln did during the Civil War?

Justice Souter argues that the President cannot avail himself of the right to detain persons under the laws of war because the Administration has not complied with the laws of war, in particular the Geneva Conventions, which require that signatory nations hold hearings to determine whether detainees are prisoners of war. Couldn't the President respond that whether or not his interpretation of particular elements of the laws of war is mistaken, he still has the authority to detain enemy combatants under the laws of war?

2. *Who is an enemy combatant?* The *Hamdi* plurality defines the term "enemy combatant" narrowly to include "an individual who . . . was part of or supporting forces hostile to the United States or coalition partners in Afghanistan and who engaged in an armed conflict against the United States there" (internal quotation marks omitted). May the President hold citizen detainees who do not fit this definition?

Consider for example, a person detained in the United States who is suspected of being an al Qaeda operative who might plan future terrorist attacks in the United States. The *Hamdi* plurality suggests that capture on the battlefield in a foreign country is an important factor in its decision. It distinguishes *Ex parte Milligan* on the grounds that "Milligan was not a prisoner of war, but a resident of Indiana arrested while at home there. . . . Had Milligan been captured while he was assisting Confederate soldiers by carrying a rifle against Union troops on a Confederate battlefield, the holding of the Court might well have been different." How does the plurality's reasoning apply to the War on Terror, in which operatives and spies may not be apprehended on anything remotely resembling a "battlefield"?

On July 7, 2004, nine days after *Hamdi*, Deputy Secretary of Defense Paul Wolfowitz issued an Order creating military tribunals to review the status of detainees at the U.S. military base at Guantanamo Bay, Cuba.[72] The order defined the term "enemy combatant" as "an individual who was part of or supporting Taliban or al Qaeda forces, or associated forces that are engaged in hostilities against the United States or its coalition partners. This includes any person who has committed a belligerent act or has directly supported hostilities in aid of enemy armed forces."

This new definition might include alleged al Qaeda operatives working in the United States. Is it authorized by the AUMF? If it is not authorized by the AUMF, is it within the President's inherent authority? Does the AUMF (as interpreted by the courts) implicitly limit the President's power to detain citizens under a broader definition? (How would *Youngstown* apply to this question?)

3. *Detention for purposes of interrogation.* The *Hamdi* plurality argues that the President is justified in detaining citizens according to the laws of war in order to prevent the captured person from returning to the battlefield. What if the purpose of detention is not incapacitation but to facilitate interrogation?

The government's admitted purpose in holding Jose Padilla, for example, was primarily to obtain information from him. In fact the government initially opposed allowing Padilla to meet with an attorney because it "could set back by months the government's efforts to bring psychological pressure to bear upon Padilla in an effort to interrogate him, and could compromise the government's interrogation techniques." Padilla ex rel. Newman v. Rumsfeld, 243 F. Supp. 2d 42, 46 (S.D.N.Y. 2003). According to a January 9, 2003 declaration of Vice Admiral Lowell E. Jacoby, Director of the Defense Intelligence Agency, successful interrogation "is largely dependent upon creating an atmosphere of dependency and trust between the subject and the interrogator." It may take "months, or even years," to "obtain valuable intelligence from a subject." "Any insertion of counsel into the subject-interrogator relationship, for example — even if only for a limited duration or for a specific purpose — can undo months of work and may permanently shut down the interrogation process." Id. at 50.

If someone like Padilla is held primarily for the purposes of interrogation, is his detention authorized under the AUMF? The plurality says that "indefinite detention for the purpose of interrogation is not authorized." What about detention for five years? Could the government insist that a citizen's detention is justified for purposes of both interrogation and incapacitation?

4. *Indefinite detention.* The *Hamdi* plurality holds that Hamdi may only be detained "for the duration of the relevant conflict," in this case the war in Afghanistan. What about a citizen, like Padilla, who is accused of being an al Qaeda

---

72. See Memorandum from Paul Wolfowitz, Deputy Secretary of Defense, to the Secretary of the Navy (July 7, 2004), available at *http://www.defenselink.mil/news/Jul2004/d20040707review.pdf* (last visited Nov. 30, 2005).

operative? The War on Terror has no definite endpoint. If the purpose for detention is incapacitation, does this mean that someone like Padilla could, in theory, be held for the rest of his life? Given that the purpose of attacking Afghanistan was to eliminate al Qaeda, why can't the government insist that Hamdi is part of the War on Terror as well?

5. *The process that is due.* The *Hamdi* plurality suggests that the government may use "an appropriately authorized and properly constituted military tribunal" with relaxed rules of evidence to determine whether persons like Hamdi, arrested on foreign battlefields, are enemy combatants.

How much help will the decision in *Hamdi* be to future detainees who are captured on the battlefield? Suppose that the government gives detainees fairly quick administrative hearings with hearsay permitted and the burden on the detainees to show that they are not enemy combatants. Because they are incarcerated, it is unlikely that many of them will be able to adduce much evidence in their defense. At that point, the government can continue to detain them until the end of the relevant conflict. Moreover, if the government finds that the detainees are unlawful combatants, it does not need to abide by the Geneva Conventions that protect prisoners of war. Does *Hamdi* contemplate judicial appeals from such determinations? If not, then *Hamdi* is not a very great setback to the Executive, because the government can do a great deal of what it is already doing by simply going through the motions of providing administrative hearings.

Does the same reasoning apply to a citizen detained in the United States? In particular, does the balance of due process factors employed by the plurality come out differently when the arrest occurs in the United States and the courts are available? Should the government be permitted to use military tribunals to determine the enemy combatant status of citizens who are captured and held in the United States? (Remember that in *Ex parte Quirin* the military tribunal did not have to determine whether Haupt was an enemy combatant.)

The plurality says that Hamdi had the right to counsel for his habeas petition going forward, without deciding whether persons captured on foreign battlefields generally have a right to counsel. Is there any reason to think that persons arrested in the United States can be denied a right to counsel?

6. *The unitary executive and judicial review.* Does Justice Thomas's position follow from his initial argument about the "unitary" executive? Why can't the executive be unitary and still be subject to judicial review? In fact, his argument is not so much about the unity of the executive as about the problems that would flow from judicial review of executive action. Thomas assumes that "Congress . . . has a substantial and essential role in both foreign affairs and national security. But it is crucial to recognize that *judicial* interference in these domains destroys the purpose of vesting primary responsibility in a unitary Executive" (emphasis in original).

Thomas argues that the courts lack the necessary expertise to determine whether citizens like Hamdi are enemy combatants. If so, then is the President's decision that a citizen is an enemy combatant effectively unreviewable? Does Thomas's logic apply equally to citizens apprehended in the United States? Would Thomas's position permit indefinite detention of citizens for purposes of interrogation, without rights to a hearing or a right to counsel?

7. *The aftermath of* Hamdi. Following the decision in *Hamdi*, the government decided not to give Hamdi a hearing to determine his status. Instead, it announced that it believed that Hamdi no longer posed a threat to the United States or had any intelligence value, and released Hamdi to Saudi Arabia in October 2004, after holding him without charges for almost three years. In return Hamdi agreed to renounce terrorism, surrender his U.S. citizenship, and not to visit Afghanistan, Iraq, Israel, Pakistan, or Syria. Finally, he agreed not to sue the United States over his captivity.[73] What reasons might the government have had to continue to hold Hamdi and litigate its right to detain him indefinitely even if it believed that Hamdi had no intelligence value and did not constitute a threat?

8. *Guantanamo Bay and the detention of noncitizens.* Following the September 11, 2001 attacks, the United States arrested persons from many different countries suspected of fighting on behalf of the Taliban in Afghanistan, working for al Qaeda, or working for various other terrorist organizations. Many of these persons were detained at the U.S. Naval Base in Guantanamo Bay, Cuba. The United States occupies Guantanamo Bay under a lease and treaty recognizing Cuba's ultimate sovereignty, but which gives the United States complete jurisdiction and control for so long as it does not abandon the leased areas. Other detainees, including those believed to be top members of al Qaeda, have been placed in secret locations around the world operated by the CIA. The Administration's acknowledged purpose for placing detainees at Guantanamo Bay and in other undisclosed locations was to avoid falling under the supervision of American courts. The detainees have been interrogated but most have not been charged with any crime. (Recently, the Administration has begun taking steps to try a small number of detainees by military tribunals and has charged those detainees. See the discussion infra.)

Two Australians and 12 Kuwaitis captured abroad during the Afghanistan war and held at Guantanamo Bay challenged the legality of their detention, alleging that they had never been combatants against the United States or engaged in terrorist acts, and that they have never been charged with wrongdoing, permitted to consult counsel, or provided access to courts or other tribunals.

In Rasul v. Bush, 542 U.S. 466 (2004), The Supreme Court, in a decision written by Justice Stevens, held that they had the right to bring a habeas petition. Stevens distinguished Johnson v. Eisentrager, 339 U.S. 763 (1950), which held that there was no constitutional or statutory right to habeas relief for German citizens captured by U.S. forces in China, tried and convicted of war crimes by an American military commission headquartered in Nanking, and incarcerated in occupied Germany. Crucial to *Eisentrager,* Stevens argued, was that the German prisoners were (a) enemy aliens who (b) had never been or resided in the United States, (c) were captured outside U.S. territory and there held in military custody, (d) were tried and convicted by the military (e) for offenses committed there, and (f) were imprisoned there at all times. By contrast, the Guantanamo detainees were not nationals of countries at war with the United States; they denied that they had engaged in or plotted acts of aggression against the United States; they had never been afforded access to any tribunal, much

---

73. USA Today, Hamdi Returns to Saudi Arabia, *http://www.usatoday.com/news/world/2004-10-11-hamdi_x.htm?POE=NEWISVA* (last visited Nov. 8, 2005); Findlaw, Yaser Esam Hamdi v. Donald Rumsfeld: Settlement Agreement, *http://news.findlaw.com/hdocs/docs/hamdi/91704stlagrmnt.html* (last visited Nov. 8, 2005).

less charged with and convicted of wrongdoing; and for more than two years they had been imprisoned in territory over which the United States exercises exclusive jurisdiction and control. Whether or not the Guantanamo detainees had a constitutional right to habeas corpus (i.e., whether or not jurisdiction to hear such cases was an inherent part of the judicial power of the United States), Stevens held that Congress had provided a statutory right to present habeas petitions to U.S. courts.

Justice Kennedy concurred, arguing that

> Guantanamo Bay is in every practical respect a United States territory, and it is one far removed from any hostilities. . . . [The Guantanamo Bay lease] is no ordinary lease. Its term is indefinite and at the discretion of the United States. What matters is the unchallenged and indefinite control that the United States has long exercised over Guantanamo Bay. From a practical perspective, the indefinite lease of Guantanamo Bay has produced a place that belongs to the United States, extending the "implied protection" of the United States to it.
> [Moreover,] the detainees at Guantanamo Bay are being held indefinitely, and without benefit of any legal proceeding to determine their status. In *Eisentrager,* the prisoners were tried and convicted by a military commission of violating the laws of war and were sentenced to prison terms. . . . Indefinite detention without trial or other proceeding presents altogether different considerations. It allows friends and foes alike to remain in detention. It suggests a weaker case of military necessity and much greater alignment with the traditional function of habeas corpus. Perhaps, where detainees are taken from a zone of hostilities, detention without proceedings or trial would be justified by military necessity for a matter of weeks; but as the period of detention stretches from months to years, the case for continued detention to meet military exigencies becomes weaker.

Justice Scalia dissented, joined by Chief Justice Rehnquist and Justice Thomas. The Court's opinion, he argued, "overrules *Eisentrager* [and] extends the habeas statute, for the first time, to aliens held beyond the sovereign territory of the United States and beyond the territorial jurisdiction of its courts. . . . [T]he Court springs a trap on the Executive, subjecting Guantanamo Bay to the oversight of the federal courts even though it has never before been thought to be within their jurisdiction — and thus making it a foolish place to have housed alien wartime detainees."

Rasul is premised on an interpretation of the scope of the federal habeas statute. In response, Congress passed Sections 1005(e) and (h) of the Detainee Treatment Act of 2005 (also known as the Graham-Levin amendment), which withdraws habeas jurisdiction for petitions filed by aliens detained "by the Department of Defense at Guantanamo Bay, Cuba" and "any other action against the United States or its agents relating to any aspect of the detention" of aliens there. Does this restriction apply retroactively to actions currently on appeal?

Sections 1005(e)(2) and (e)(3) of the Detainee Treatment Act give exclusive jurisdiction to the D.C. Circuit to review "final decisions" of military status tribunals (which determine whether a detainee is an enemy combatant) and military commissions (which are designed to try accused terrorists for serious crimes). The act bestows jurisdiction to determine whether these decisions are cosistent with "standards and procedures" set forth in applicable Defense Department regulations and military orders and, "to the extent the Constitution and laws of the United States are applicable, whether the use of such standards and procedures . . . is consistent with the Constitution and laws of the United States." Does this allow review of allegations of torture or prisoner mistreatment?

Rasul did not decide whether detention at Guantanamo Bay violates any constitutional principle. (Note that the detainees might also have claims under the Geneva Conventions.) Justice Stevens stated in a footnote that "Petitioners' allegations — that, although they have engaged neither in combat nor in acts of terrorism against the United States, they have been held in Executive detention for more than two years in territory subject to the long-term, exclusive jurisdiction and control of the United States, without access to counsel and without being charged with any wrongdoing — unquestionably describe 'custody in violation of the Constitution or laws or treaties of the United States.' 28 U.S.C. §2241(c)(3). Cf. United States v. Verdugo-Urquidez, 494 U.S. 259, 277-278 (1990) (Kennedy, J., concurring), and cases cited therein."

Consider two possible constitutional claims. The first claim is that the President lacks power to detain the persons at Guantanamo Bay unless they are enemy combatants under the limited definition offered in *Hamdi*. That might be because they were not "part of or supporting forces hostile to the United States or coalition partners" in Afghanistan or because they were not "engaged in an armed conflict against the United States." Once again consider whether the President could argue that this is far too limited a construction of the AUMF, or whether the President has inherent authority to detain persons beyond Congress's authorization.

The second claim is that the detainees have a Fifth Amendment due process right to a fair and impartial determination of whether they are enemy combatants under whatever definition applies. Recall that under the Insular Case, Downes v. Bidwell, discussed in Chapter 4, the Constitution does not fully apply to inhabitants of "unincorporated territories" controlled by the United States. Instead, inhabitants may assert only "fundamental" rights, including "the right to personal liberty . . .; to free access to courts of justice, [and] to due process of law." See also Dorr v. United States, 195 U.S. 138 (1904) (trial by jury not a fundamental constitutional right in libel case brought in the Philippines); Ocampo v. United States, 234 U.S. 91 (1914) (Fifth Amendment grand jury provision inapplicable in Philippines); Balzac v. People of Porto Rico, 258 U.S. 298 (1922) (right to jury trial in criminal cases not a fundamental constitutional right). If Guantanamo Bay is like an "incorporated territory" then the fundamental rights listed in *Downes* might apply to the detainees at Guantanamo.

Suppose, however, that this analogy is rejected, and Guantanamo is viewed as completely foreign territory. In United States v. Verdugo-Urquidez, the Court held that the Fourth Amendment did not apply to the search and seizure by United States agents of property owned by a nonresident alien and located in Mexico. It interpreted Johnson v. Eisentrager as "reject[ing] the claim that aliens are entitled to Fifth Amendment rights outside the sovereign territory of the United States." On the other hand, the Court held that the right to a jury trial applied in Reid v. Covert, 354 U.S. 1 (1957), where a U.S. civilian residing on a military base in England with her husband was convicted of killing him by a military tribunal. A plurality of four Justices rejected the "fundamental rights" limitation of the Insular Cases; Justice Harlan, concurring, agreed only that a U.S. citizen had a Sixth Amendment right to a jury trial in a capital case. (Is *Reid* distinguishable because it involves U.S. citizens?)

Concurring in United States v. Verdugo-Urquidez, Justice Kennedy rejected a categorical rule that constitutional guarantees did not apply when the U.S. government acted against aliens in foreign territory; rather, he argued that "[t]he conditions and considerations of this case would make adherence to the Fourth Amendment's warrant requirement impracticable and anomalous." Would application of due process guarantees to determine the status of detainees at Guantanamo Bay be "impracticable and anomalous?"

Finally, assume that Justice Stevens is correct and the Guantanamo detainees state a cause of action. If citizens like Hamdi may receive no more than a cursory adminstrative hearing before a military tribunal, would noncitizens be likely to get much more from the courts?

3.   *Military Tribunals*

On November 13, 2001, President Bush issued an executive order authorizing the creation of military tribunals to try persons suspected of terrorist activities arising out of the September 11 attacks on the United States. Detention, Treatment, and Trial of Certain Non-Citizens in the War Against Terrorism, 66 Fed. Reg. 57,833 (Nov. 13, 2001). The Executive Order directs the Secretary of Defense to create the tribunals, which may sit "at any time and place" — including the United States — and to take into custody anyone who is subject to them. A person is subject to a military tribunal if the President determines that there is reason to believe that the individual is or was a member of the al Qaeda terrorist organization, "has engaged in, aided or abetted, or conspired to commit, acts of international terrorism, or acts in preparation therefore, that have caused, threaten to cause, or have as their aim to cause, injury to or adverse effects on the United States, its citizens, national security, foreign policy, or economy," or has harbored such a person. The Order does not define the term "acts of international terrorism."

The Executive Order also directs that the Secretary of Defense establish procedures for the tribunals. At a minimum these require that convictions and sentencing be based on a two-thirds vote of the members of the commission present at the time of voting. A majority of the commissioners appointed to the case must be present in order to vote. (Subsequent Department of Defense regulations issued in March 2002 made clear that a unanimous verdict would be required for a death sentence but not for noncapital offenses.) Traditional rules of criminal procedure and evidence that apply in ordinary criminal courts are relaxed and evidence that would ordinarily be excluded from a criminal trial (or a military court-martial) may be admitted as long as it would "have probative value to a reasonable person." There is no requirement of grand jury presentment or indictment. The tribunals also employ as triers of both fact and law military officers who are neither Article III judges nor members of a traditional jury. Finally, the military tribunals may be held in secret.

The new military tribunals "shall have exclusive jurisdiction with respect to offenses" committed by individuals subject to them, and "the individual shall not be privileged to seek any remedy or maintain any proceeding, directly or indirectly, or to have any such remedy or proceeding sought on the individual's behalf, in (i) any court of the United States, or any State thereof, (ii) any court of any foreign nation, or (iii) any international tribunal." Instead, the President reserves for himself the right to final review of the trial, conviction, and sentence of the military tribunal. (Regulations issued in March 2002 also specify that appeals from a verdict may be made to military officers, but not to a court.)

Note that the Executive Order authorizes detention as well as trial before a military tribunal. It reaches both citizens and noncitizens. It does not distinguish between persons apprehended within the territory of the United States and persons apprehended elsewhere. Finally, it allows hearings to be held both within the territory of the United States and outside it.

An important effect of the Order is that the protections of the Bill of Rights do not apply to persons detained and tried under it. Nor does Article III, §3 ("The trial of all crimes, except in cases of impeachment, shall be by jury; and such trial shall be held in the state where the said crimes shall have been committed; but when not committed within any state, the trial shall be at such place or places as the Congress may by law have directed."). Finally, the Executive Order appears to forbid appeal to the courts for "any remedy," including, presumably, a request for a writ of habeas corpus. Note that in *Hamdi*, the Court held that Congress had not suspended the writ of habeas corpus, although the plurality held that the September 18, 2001 AUMF had authorized detention of a narrowly defined set of enemy combatants.

Consider three sets of questions:

First, does the President have independent power to create military tribunals under his authority as Commander-in-Chief, or are such tribunals permissible only if authorized by Congress? Does the September 18, 2001 AUMF, considered in *Hamdi*, authorize such tribunals?

Second, consider whether the Executive Order authorizing detention and military tribunals is constitutional as to all cases it covers, or only a subset. For example, is it constitutional only (a) with respect to noncitizens? (b) with respect to persons detained and held outside the territory of the United States? (c) with respect to acts committed outside the territory of the United States? (d) with respect to tribunals constituted outside the territory of the United States, regardless of where the acts were committed or the persons were apprehended?

Third, the language of the Executive Order seems to preclude access to the federal courts either for appeals or to seek a writ of habeas corpus to challenge the legality of the government's actions. Is this constitutional, if Congress has not otherwise suspended the writ? Does the answer to this question depend on whether the detainee is a citizen or a noncitizen and on where the military tribunal sits?

EX PARTE QUIRIN, 317 U.S. 1 (1942): [During World War II eight Nazi saboteurs were sent by submarine to the United States. They landed on American soil (at Florida and at Long Island, NY) armed with explosives, and buried the uniforms they were wearing. They were arrested after one saboteur turned himself into the FBI and helped the FBI locate the others. One of the eight, Haupt, argued that he was an American citizen because his parents were naturalized while he was a child and he never renounced his American citizenship. President Roosevelt issued an Executive Order and Proclamation authorizing military trials for the saboteurs. The defendants were charged with violating the law of war, espionage, providing information to the enemy, and conspiracy. During the trials, the saboteurs sought habeas review both in federal district court and in the U.S. Supreme Court, which upheld the military conviction and death sentence for the saboteurs based on the charge that they had violated the laws of war. Chief Justice Stone wrote for a unanimous Court.]

STONE, C.J.:

From the very beginning of its history this Court has recognized and applied the law of war as including that part of the law of nations which prescribes, for the conduct of war, the status, rights and duties of enemy nations as well as of enemy individuals. By the Articles of War, and especially Article 15, Congress has explicitly provided, so far as it may constitutionally do so, that military tribunals shall have jurisdiction to try offenders or offenses against the law of war in appropriate cases. [Article 15, now codified at 10 U.S.C. §821 (1994), provides that "The provisions of this chapter conferring jurisdiction upon courts-martial do not deprive military commissions, provost courts, or other military tribunals of concurrent jurisdiction with respect to offenders or offenses that by statute or by the law of war may be tried by military commissions, provost courts, or other military tribunals."] Congress, in addition to making rules for the government of our Armed Forces, has thus exercised its authority to define and punish offenses against the law of nations [under Article I §8, cl. 10] by sanctioning, within constitutional limitations, the jurisdiction of military commissions to try persons for offenses which, according to the rules and precepts of the law of nations, and more particularly the law of war, are cognizable by such tribunals. . . . [Therefore] [i]t is unnecessary for present purposes to determine to what extent the President as Commander in Chief has constitutional power to create military commissions without the support of Congressional legislation. . . .

We may assume that there are acts regarded in other countries, or by some writers on international law, as offenses against the law of war which would not be triable by military tribunal here, either because they are not recognized by our courts as violations of the law of war or because they are of that class of offenses constitutionally triable only by a jury. It was upon such grounds that the Court denied the right to proceed by military tribunal in *Ex parte Milligan*. . . .

It is no objection that Congress in providing for the trial of such offenses has not itself undertaken to codify that branch of international law or to mark its precise boundaries, or to enumerate or define by statute all the acts which that law condemns. . . .

By universal agreement and practice the law of war draws a distinction between the armed forces and the peaceful populations of belligerent nations and also between those who are lawful and unlawful combatants. Lawful combatants are subject to capture and detention as prisoners of war by opposing military forces. Unlawful combatants are likewise subject to capture and detention, but in addition they are subject to trial and punishment by military tribunals for acts which render their belligerency unlawful. The spy who secretly and without uniform passes the military lines of a belligerent in time of war, seeking to gather military information and communicate it to the enemy, or an enemy combatant who without uniform comes secretly through the lines for the purpose of waging war by destruction of life or property, are familiar examples of belligerents who are generally deemed not to be entitled to the status of prisoners of war, but to be offenders against the law of war subject to trial and punishment by military tribunals. . . .

Citizenship in the United States of an enemy belligerent does not relieve him from the consequences of a belligerency which is unlawful because in violation of the law of war. Citizens who associate themselves with the military arm of the enemy government, and with its aid, guidance and direction enter this country bent on hostile acts are enemy belligerents within the meaning of the Hague Convention and the law of war. . . .

[I]t was not the purpose or effect of s[ection] 2 of Article III . . . to enlarge the then existing right to a jury trial [beyond that traditionally recognized by the common law]. . . . The Fifth and Sixth Amendments [also] did not enlarge the right to jury trial. Hence petty offenses triable at common law without a jury may be tried without a jury in the federal courts, notwithstanding Article III, s[ection] 2, and the Fifth and Sixth Amendments. Trial by jury of criminal contempts may constitutionally be dispensed with in the federal courts in those cases in which they could be tried without a jury at common law. Similarly, an action for debt to enforce a penalty inflicted by Congress is not subject to the constitutional restrictions upon criminal prosecutions. . . . [Hence, section] 2 of Article III and the Fifth and Sixth

Amendments cannot be taken to have extended the right to demand a jury to trials by military commission, or to have required that offenses against the law of war not triable by jury at common law be tried only in the civil courts. . . . Since [they] do not preclude all trials of offenses against the law of war by military commission without a jury when the offenders are aliens not members of our Armed Forces, it is plain that they present no greater obstacle to the trial in like manner of citizen enemies who have violated the law of war applicable to enemies. . . .

Petitioners, and especially petitioner Haupt, stress . . . [*Ex parte*] *Milligan*['s pronouncement] that the law of war "can never be applied to citizens in states which have upheld the authority of the government, and where the courts are open and their process unobstructed." [But] Milligan, a citizen twenty years resident in Indiana, . . . had never been a resident of any of the states in rebellion, [and] was not an enemy belligerent either entitled to the status of a prisoner of war or subject to the penalties imposed upon unlawful belligerents. . . . Milligan, not being a part of or associated with the armed forces of the enemy, was a non-belligerent, not subject to the law of war save as — in circumstances found not there to be present and not involved here — martial law might be constitutionally established. . . . We have no occasion now to define with meticulous care the ultimate boundaries of the jurisdiction of military tribunals to try persons according to the law of war. It is enough that petitioners here, upon the conceded facts, were plainly within those boundaries, and were held in good faith for trial by military commission, charged with being enemies who, with the purpose of destroying war materials and utilities, entered or after entry remained in our territory without uniform — an offense against the law of war. We hold only that those particular acts constitute an offense against the law of war which the Constitution authorizes to be tried by military commission.

Discussion

1. *Who is an enemy belligerent?* *Quirin* argues that enemy belligerents who violate the laws of war may be tried by military tribunals, even if they are American citizens. It distinguishes *Ex parte Milligan* on the grounds that Milligan was not an enemy belligerent. But why wasn't Milligan, in *Quirin*'s words, a citizen "who associate[d] [himself] with the military arm of the enemy government, and with its aid, guidance and direction enter[ed] this country bent on hostile acts?" Is the answer that, as the court says earlier in the opinion, Milligan was charged with crimes that were either "not recognized by our courts as violations of the law of war or [were] of that class of offenses constitutionally triable only by a jury?" Given that the Court allows the definition of what violates the laws of war to proceed through common law elaboration, is this distinction convincing?

Consider another possibility: Whereas the saboteurs in *Quirin* were clearly or admittedly members of an enemy force, a key question in *Milligan* was whether Milligan actually was a belligerent or had been mistakenly arrested by the military forces. It is one thing to try an enemy belligerent whose identity has already been established before a military commission; it is quite another to exercise military authority over people simply on the President's say so. Under this reading, *Quirin* does not provide authority for trying persons before military tribunals when the question of jurisdiction — who may be tried by a military tribunal — cannot be separated from the merits — whether there was a violation of the laws of war. Otherwise, the President's authority could sweep too broadly to violate the rights of innocent parties. Thus an American citizen arrested on American soil may not be tried by a military tribunal without a prior determination — subject to the guarantees of the Bill of Rights — that he is an enemy belligerent.

Is this interpretation consistent with the plurality in *Hamdi?* Note that the *Hamdi* plurality does not insist that full Bill of Rights guarantees always apply in a determination of whether a citizen is an enemy combatant. Is *Hamdi* distinguishable because it applies only to battlefield captures outside the United States?[74]

2. *Presidential power to create military tribunals. Quirin* does not decide whether the president may create tribunals without congressional consent given his inherent authority as Commander-in-Chief. Instead, it holds that the President's action was supported by congressional authorization, stemming from Article 15 of the Articles of War. On its face, however, the text of Article 15 merely preserves concurrent jurisdiction if military tribunals are in fact authorized. Given this fact, one might read *Quirin* as stretching to find congressional authorization in circumstances of political necessity (the case was decided in July 1942, less than nine months after Pearl Harbor). If so, was this sound? Because Article 15's successor, 10 U.S.C. §821, is still on the books, does it follow from *Quirin* that Congress has given a continuing authorization to create military tribunals and try enemy belligerents before them whenever the President sees fit?

Is *Quirin* distinguishable because it arose after a formal declaration of war? (Compare Chief Justice Chase's concurrence in *Milligan*). Why should this matter, given that Presidents often exercise their Commander-in-Chief powers and send troops into combat situations without formal declarations of war? Why isn't the September 18 AUMF, considered in *Hamdi,* sufficient? See Hamdan v. Rumsfeld, 415 F.3d 33 (D.C. Cir. 2005), cert granted, 2005 U.S. LEXIS 8222 (November 7, 2005) (upholding President's power to try al Qaeda supporter by a military commission on the authority of the September 18, 2001 resolution, 10 U.S.C. §821 (the successor to Article 15) and 10 U.S.C. §836(a), which authorizes the President to establish procedures for military commissions).

If Congress has authorized the President to try at least some enemy combatants by military tribunals, are there any limits to this authorization? Consider two possible issues. First, President Bush's Executive Order is not limited to the narrow class of enemy combatants as defined in *Hamdi;* it applies to anyone the President deems an international terrorist. Second, the President's order is not limited to violations of the laws of war — the basis of the decision in *Quirin* — but conceivably extends to many other violations of law.

3. *The role of executive precedent in constitutional interpretation.* In a part of the *Quirin* opinion not excerpted, the Court noted a long history of military tribunals. Does

---

74. Cf. In re Yamashita, 327 U.S. 1 (1946), which upheld the use of a military commission ordered by General William D. Styer, who commanded U.S. forces in the Phillippines, to try General Yamashita, the commander of the Japanese army in the Philippines, for allowing his men to engage in atrocities. As in *Quirin,* the Court found congressional authorization in the Articles of War, and stated that a military commission may be convened even "after hostilities have ended to try violations of the law of war committed before their cessation, at least until peace has been officially recognized by treaty or proclamation of the political branch of the Government."

Consider George Fletcher's comment that "The offenses committed in the Philippines were not subject to prosecution under American law in an American courtroom. Perhaps they could have been tried in the Philippines — and, in the future, in the International Criminal Court — but there was no sense in which General Styer was trying to take a case away from the civilian courts in the United States. It was either prosecution in his tribunal or no American initiative at all." George P. Fletcher, On Justice and War: Contradictions in the Proposed Military Tribunals, 25 Harv. J.L. & Pub. Pol'y 635, 645 (2002).

the fact that military tribunals have been used consistently by the Executive, sometimes with congressional authorization, and sometimes without, determine the question of their constitutionality? Note that there are two different trends in constitutional interpretation. Where individual rights are concerned, courts often reject the claim that a practice is made constitutional by the fact that it has occurred for many years. For example, racial segregation and sex discrimination could not be justified on the ground that racism and sexism were pervasive, and the criminal procedure decisions of the Warren Court swept away many traditional state practices that violated the rights of persons accused of crime. On the other hand, in determining the scope of national power, the balance of power between Congress and the President, and particularly the President's powers in foreign policy, courts often look to the historical development of a practice. The question of military tribunals, however, implicates both separation of powers and individual rights concerns. What weight, then, should courts give to the long history of military tribunals?

4. *Pressures on the judiciary in time of war. Ex parte Milligan* occurred after the Civil War was concluded. *Ex parte Quirin* was decided during wartime. Public announcement of the capture of the saboteurs was made on June 27, 1942. On July 2, President Roosevelt appointed the military commission that tried them. The trial began six days later. After the saboteurs were convicted and six of them sentenced to death, two Army colonels appointed by the President to defend the saboteurs before the commission sought judicial review. On July 27 the Supreme Court indicated that it would hear argument on the question. According to the New York Times on the following day, "Decision to seek recourse in the Supreme Court did not meet popular approval in Washington. On the contrary, there is great dissatisfaction here with the length to which the [military] trial has already proceeded." As Alpheus Mason, the biographer of Chief Justice Harlan Stone, explained, "The Times had put it mildly." Indeed, on July 29 the Times reported the reigning congressional sentiment through the words of New York Representative Emmanuel Celler: "Our people are of the opinion that the eight Nazi saboteurs should be executed with all possible dispatch. . . . They are confident that the military tribunal will decree their death. Any interference with that trial by civil court would strike a severe blow to public morale."[75]

On July 29, when the Supreme Court convened for the hearing, Associate Justice Frank Murphy, who had been commissioned a lieutenant colonel in the Army Reserves after repeatedly lobbying for an appointment, arrived at Court wearing his military uniform. This caused such a scandal among his fellow Justices that Murphy recused himself from the case.[76]

After hearing the case on July 29, the Court announced its decision two days later, stating that it would file its opinion subsequently. However, the executions of six of the saboteurs followed within a week, well before the *Quirin* opinion was filed. Justice William O. Douglas wrote in his memoirs that Attorney General Francis Biddle had told members of the Court privately, prior to argument, that "the Executive," by which he presumably meant President Roosevelt, "would not tolerate any delay" and "that the claims of the saboteurs were so frivolous [that] the

---

75. Alpheus Thomas Mason, Harlan Fiske Stone 653-661 (1956).
76. Do you agree that Murphy should have recused himself? Why? For wearing his uniform to Court to hear *Quirin* or for having enlisted in the Armed Forces in the first place?

Army was going [to go] ahead and execute the men whatever the Court did." Douglas described this as a "blatant affront to the Court."[77] Stone's biographer indicates that the Chief Justice, who had assigned himself the task of writing the opinion, had significant doubts that FDR had in fact complied with the Articles of War. In private communications within the Court, Justice Frankfurter agreed that "[t]here can be no doubt that the President did *not* follow the scheme of review under II G of the Articles of War," though he believed that was irrelevant with regard to the disposition of the case. Frankfurter circulated a memo among his colleagues, which he called a "soliloquy":

> Some of the very best lawyers I know are now in the Solomon Islands battle, some are seeing service in Australia, some are sub-chasers in the Atlantic, and some are on the various air fronts. It requires no poet's imagination to think of their reflections if the unanimous result reached by us in these cases should be expressed in opinions which would black out the agreement in result and reveal internecine conflict about the manner of stating that result. I know some of these men very, very intimately. I think I know what they would deem to be the governing canons of constitutional adjudication in a case like this. And I almost hear their voices were they to read more than a single opinion in this case. They would say something like this, but in language hardly becoming a judge's tongue: "What in hell do you fellows think you are doing? Haven't we got enough of a job trying to lick the Japs and the Nazis without having you fellows on the Supreme Court dissipate the thoughts and feelings and energies of the folks at home by stirring up a nice row as to who has what power, when all of you are agreed that the president had the power to establish this commission and that the procedures under the Articles of War for courts-martial and military commission don't apply to this case? Haven't you got any more sense than to get people by the ear on one of the favorite American pastimes — abstract constitutional discussions? Do we have to have another Lincoln-Taney row when everybody is agreed and in this particular case the constitutional questions aren't reached? Just relax and don't be too engrossed in your own interest in verbalistic conflicts, because the inroads on energy and national unity that such conflict inevitable [sic] produces, is a pastime we had better postpone until peacetime.[78]

Because there was general agreement within the Court that a unanimous opinion was highly desirable, Stone's opinion skirted some extremely controversial issues in order to maintain unanimity. Stone himself acknowledged that the opinion in *Quirin* was "somewhat cryptic," though he explained that this "was the result of patient negotiations to get the Court to agree unanimously to rejection of the argument that access to the Court by the prisoner could be denied." To do this, he agreed to delete a stronger statement that had appeared in an earlier draft, that "even though guilty [the saboteurs] were entitled to be tried by a tribunal and by laws which the Constitution has prescribed as the means of determining their guilt."[79]

Do the events leading up to the *Quirin* opinion — including Frankfurter's "soliloquy" — suggest something about how much we can trust judges to be the

---

77. William O. Douglas, The Court Years 139 (1980).
78. The Supreme Court in Conference (1940-1985) 533 (Del Dickson ed., 2001).
79. Mason, at 664.

"detached" enforcers of constitutional rights in time of war? Is there anything wrong with Frankfurter's display of "passion," or should judges hold themselves to a different standard of conduct and thought? In any event, is this (or any of the material in this note) relevant to considering the precedential value of *Quirin* today?

5. *Commentary on the military tribunals.* The Bush Order on military tribunals has been one of the most controversial features of the Administration's response to September 11. For a sampling of the constitutional issues, see Curtis A. Bradley & Jack L. Goldsmith, Congressional Authorization and the War on Terrorism, 118 Harv. L. Rev. 2047 (2005); Neal K. Katyal & Laurence H. Tribe, Waging War, Deciding Guilt: Trying the Military Tribunals, 111 Yale L.J. 1259 (2002); Curtis A. Bradley & Jack L. Goldsmith, The Constitutional Validity of Military Commissions, 5 Green Bag 2d 249 (2002); and George P. Fletcher, On Justice and War: Contradictions in the Proposed Military Tribunals, 25 Harv. J.L. & Pub. Pol'y 635, 645 (2002).

Note: Torture and Presidential Power

In order to fulfill its treaty obligations under the U.N. Convention Against Torture and Other Cruel, Inhuman or Degrading Treatment or Punishment, Congress has prohibited torture overseas. Section 2340A makes it illegal for anyone "outside the United States [to] commit[] or attempt[] to commit torture." Section 2340 defines torture as "an act committed by a person acting under the color of law specifically intended to inflict severe physical or mental pain or suffering (other than pain or suffering incidental to lawful sanctions) upon another person within his custody or physical control." Congress created the overseas ban on torture in Section 2340A because it assumed that torture performed by public officials in the United States was already prohibited by the Due Process Clause and the Eighth Amendment's prohibition on cruel and unusual punishments.

The prisoner abuse scandals at Abu Ghraib prison in Iraq and previous reports of prisoner abuse at Guantanamo Bay, Cuba led to investigations about government policy for prisoner interrogations after September 11, and about whether government officials permitted or engaged in torture and cruel, inhuman, and degrading treatment of prisoners for intelligence-gathering purposes. These investigations revealed that the Bush administration had been deliberating about the permissible bounds of prisoner interrogation for some time.

On August 1, 2002, the Office of Legal Counsel (OLC) produced a memo entitled "Re: Standards of Conduct for Interrogation under 18 U.S.C. 2340-2340A," for Alberto R. Gonzales, counsel to President Bush.[80] The OLC memo was written at the request of the CIA, which had been conducting interrogations of top-level al Qaeda operatives held in undisclosed locations outside the United States. The CIA sought greater authority to conduct more aggressive interrogations of prisoners

---

80. See Memorandum from Jay S. Bybee, U.S. Dep't of Justice, to Alberto R. Gonzales, Counsel to the President (Aug. 1, 2002), available at *http://www.washingtonpost.com/wp-srv/nation/documents/dojinterroga-tionmemo20020801.pdf* (last visited July 2, 2004).

than had been permitted prior to the September 11, 2001 attacks on the United States.

The OLC memo discussed to what extent the Administration and members of the Armed forces were legally bound by U.S. and international law prohibiting torture and prisoner abuse. The memorandum was signed by Jay S. Bybee, then head of OLC, and was an official legal opinion on the legality of government policies on interrogations. Bybee later became a judge on the 9th U.S. Circuit Court of Appeals.

Another memorandum, dated March 6, 2003, was authored by a Department of Defense working group that had been convened by Defense Secretary Donald H. Rumsfeld to come up with new interrogation guidelines for detainees at Guantanamo Bay, Cuba. This memo incorporated significant parts of the legal theories offered in the OLC memo.[81]

The OLC and Defense Department concluded that prohibitions on what constituted "torture" under Section 2340A and the U.N. Convention could be read quite narrowly. Hence the United States could engage in "a wide array of acts that constitute cruel, inhuman, or degrading treatment or punishment [and that] do not amount to torture." OLC Memo at 31.

Second, and more important for purposes of this Note, the OLC and Defense Department memos asserted that congressional statutes and international laws against torture could not in any case constitutionally bind the President. The OLC memo explained:

> Even if an interrogation method were arguably to violate Section 2340A, the statute would be unconstitutional if it impermissibly encroached on the President's constitutional power to conduct a military campaign. As Commander-in-Chief, the President has the constitutional authority to order interrogations of enemy combatants to gain intelligence information concerning the military plans of the enemy. The commands of the Commander-in-Chief power are especially pronounced in the middle of a war when the country has already suffered a direct attack. In such a case, the information gained from interrogations may prevent future attacks by foreign enemies. Any effort to apply Section 2340A in a manner that interferes with the President's direction of such core war matters as the detention and interrogation of enemy combatants thus would be unconstitutional."
>
> . . . [T]he President enjoys complete discretion in the exercise of his Commander-in-Chief authority and in conducting operations against hostile forces. . . . That authority is at its height in the middle of a war. . . . [W]ithout a clear statement otherwise, we will not read a criminal statute as infringing on the President's authority in these areas. . . .
>
> [S]ection 2340A must be construed as not applying to interrogations undertaking pursuant to his Commander-in-Chief authority. . . . Congress lacks authority under Article I to set the terms and conditions under which the President may exercise his authority as Commander-in-Chief to control the conduct of operations during a war. . . . Congress may no more regulate the President's ability to detain and interrogate enemy combatants than it may regulate his ability to direct troop movements on the battlefield. . . .
>
> [Even if Congress enacted Section 2340A] with full knowledge and consideration of the President's Commander-in-Chief power, and . . . intended to restrict his discretion

81. See Working Group, Report on the Detainee Interrogations in the Global War on Terrorism (2003), available at *http://news.findlaw.com/wp/docs/torture/30603wgrpt.html* (last visited July 2, 2004).

in the interrogation of enemy combatants, . . . we conclude that the Department of Justice could not enforce Section 2340A against federal officials acting pursuant to the President's constitutional authority to wage a military campaign.

. . . Any effort by Congress to regulate the interrogation of enemy combatants would violate the Constitution's sole vesting of the Commander-in-Chief authority in the President. There can be little doubt that intelligence operations, such as the detention and interrogation of enemy combatants and leaders, are both necessary and proper for the effective conduct of a military campaign. Indeed, such operations may be of more importance in a war with an international terrorist organization than one with the conventional armed forces of a nation-state, due to the former's emphasis on secret operations and surprise attacks against civilians. It may be the case that only successful interrogations can provide the information necessary to prevent the success of covert terrorist attacks upon the United States and its citizens. Congress can no more interfere with the President's conduct of the interrogation of enemy combatants than it can dictate strategic or tactical decisions on the battlefield. Just as statutes that order the President to conduct warfare in a certain manner or for specific goals would be unconstitutional, so too are laws that seek to prevent a President from gaining the intelligence he believes necessary to prevent attacks on the United States.

Id. at 31, 33-36, 39.

After the OLC and Department of Defense memos became public, the Bush administration disowned them and instructed the Justice Department to prepare new legal opinions that construed the definition of torture somewhat more broadly. These new legal opinions, however, did not disavow the constitutional theory of presidential power offered in OLC and Department of Defense memos.

Discussion

1. *Maximum power, twilight zone, or lowest ebb?* According to the OLC memo, what is Congress's proper role in questions of foreign affairs and warfare? May it ever pass laws limiting what the President might seek to do as Commander-in-Chief? The OLC memo does not mention *Youngstown*. Is it consistent with it? Consider the following arguments:

   (a)   The OLC's memo is inconsistent with *Youngstown*. When the President attempts to do what Congress has specifically forbidden him to do, his power is at its lowest ebb. He lacks inherent authority to violate both congressional law and international agreements prohibiting torture.

   (b)   The OLC's memo is completely consistent with *Youngstown*. Even though Congress has attempted to limit the President's authority to authorize torture, this does not place the President's power at its lowest ebb. Congress's attempt is ineffective because Congress does not have concurrent power with the President to regulate detention and interrogation of enemy combatants.

Is it clear from the constitutional text that Congress has no authority to regulate the interrogation or detention of prisoners captured by the military and held in custody by the military or the CIA? Consider Congress's powers in Article I section 8, clause 10 ("To define and punish piracies and felonies committed on the high seas, and offences against the law of nations"), clause 11 ("To declare war, grant letters of marque and reprisal, and make rules concerning captures on land and water"), and clause 14 ("To make rules for the government and regulation of the land and naval forces"). How should those powers be reconciled with the President's power as Commander-in-Chief? Could the President argue that Congress has some power to regulate interrogations by the military but not by the CIA?

2. Is the OLC memo consistent with the plurality opinions or concurrences in *Hamdi v. Rumsfeld*? Is it consistent with Justice Thomas's dissent?

3. How does the OLC memo's vision of the Commander-in-Chief power interact with the President's Article II duty to take care that the laws be faithfully executed? Could the President respond that there is no conflict, because the President has no duty to abide by laws that cannot constitutionally be applied to him in any case?

4. *Just following orders.* The Department of Defense memo of March 6, 2003 argues that people engaged in torture at the direction of the Executive may not be prosecuted for war crimes because they were following the orders of a superior. Following orders is usually not a defense under both American and international law if the subordinate knows or has reason to know that the order is unlawful. The memo interprets this doctrine to mean that "the defense of superior orders will generally be available for U.S. Armed Forces personnel engaged in exceptional interrogations except where the conduct goes so far as to be patently unlawful." Consider the following argument: The OLC and Department of Defense memos take the position that actions ordered by the President under his authority as Commander-in-Chief are presumptively lawful, and that statutes and international laws to the contrary must be construed as inapplicable to him. If the President orders a subordinate to torture someone, the subordinate may presume that this order does not violate any existing law when the law is properly construed so as to avoid a constitutional conflict. Hence the presidential order is not "patently unlawful" and the subordinate is insulated from liability for war crimes.

5. *Nixon and Lincoln redux.* Compare the OLC memo's theory of the Presidency with the views of Lincoln and Nixon about Presidential power (see pp. 283-285). Which view does the OLC memo most resemble?

E.   Presidential Privileges and Immunities

The Constitution specifies certain courtroom immunities for members of Congress in Article I, §6: Federal lawmakers enjoy permanent immunity from any lawsuit based on their "speech or debate" in Congress, and enjoy temporary immunity from civil arrest while the legislature is in session. (At the Founding, certain civil lawsuits could be initiated by seizing or arresting the person of the defendant; without the protection of the arrest clause a single civil plaintiff — whose legal claims might ultimately prove baseless in court and who in fact might be politically motivated — might have been able to prevent a lawmaker from representing his constituents while the Congress was in session.) The Constitution, however, is silent on what if any litigation immunities are appropriate for other government officials, including the President.

This silence, however, has not meant that other officers enjoy no courtroom immunities. Rather, it has meant that such immunities are typically derived from structural considerations. For example, although the Vice President is, strictly speaking, not covered by the text of the speech or debate clause, it would be structurally anomalous to allow him to be sued for a speech he made in the Senate as its presiding officer. Likewise, it would be strange if a President could be sued for allegedly libelous statements made in the State of the Union message — or in a press conference defending his legislative agenda, for that matter. (Suppose, for example, the President were to attack cigarette companies or gun manufacturers or the HMO industry.) In 1896, the Court made clear in Spalding v. Vilas, 161 U.S. 483, that judges were likewise privileged from lawsuits for any statements that they make in their courtrooms or judicial opinions. See also note [g] in United States v. Nixon, supra p. 752, rejecting the idea that the only proper constitutional immunities are those specified in Article I, §6.

What litigation immunities are structurally sound for the President? Or to recast the point textually, what immunities are properly interpreted as being implicit in the "executive power of the United States" vested in the President by the opening sentence of Article II? In a pair of cases in the last three decades, the Supreme Court has attempted to answer these questions. In the first case, Nixon v. Fitzgerald, 457 U.S. 731 (1982), the Court held that ex-President Nixon could not be sued for allegedly having violated the plaintiff's First Amendment rights while acting as President. Nixon, said the Court, was absolutely immune for all conduct arising out of his official duties as President. In the second lawsuit, Clinton v. Jones, 520 U.S. 681 (1997), the Court held that sitting President Clinton could be sued in federal court for allegedly having violated plaintiff's civil rights while acting as the Governor of Arkansas. Clinton, said the Court, had no immunity (at least in federal court) for private actions that did not arise out of any presidential conduct.

The *Fitzgerald* case was decided by a 5-4 vote, with Justice Powell writing for the Court, joined by Chief Justice Burger and Justices Rehnquist, Stevens, and O'Connor. Justice White wrote the main dissent, joined by Justices Brennan, Marshall, and Blackmun. Ernest Fitzgerald was a whistleblower who alleged that President Nixon had fired him in retaliation for his testimony before Congress about military cost overruns. Fitzgerald claimed that the firing violated his First Amendment rights, and sought damages. The Court assumed arguendo that Nixon had indeed violated the Constitution, but said it didn't matter — such damage lawsuits might chill Presidential behavior, and so they should be barred (unless, perhaps, Congress plainly provided otherwise).

The result in *Fitzgerald* can be questioned. If the President did indeed violate the Constitution wouldn't "chilling" such violations be a good thing? If the concern is that many frivolous suits would be filed, couldn't this problem have been addressed by a rule that required losing plaintiffs to compensate the defendant? (Such a rule would help weed out weak claims without barring strong ones.) If the fear is that some unconstitutional conduct might nevertheless have been carried out in good faith, and for sound policy reasons, wouldn't this be an argument for allowing the plaintiff to get a full remedy, but indemnifying the ex-President with public funds? There is an analogy here to takings clause doctrine — if the rest of us benefit from the way the President used Fitzgerald, why shouldn't we all bear the loss rather than singling him out for an unfair burden? Shouldn't we strive for a system in which every constitutional right has a proper remedy?

With the *Fitzgerald* case on the books, Paula Corbin Jones brought suit against President Bill Clinton. She alleged that Clinton had sexually harassed her and violated her civil rights before he became President. Clinton sought a ruling that the lawsuit must be delayed until he left the presidency. Before the case was decided, many leading scholars argued that Clinton's claims were much weaker than Nixon's: Nixon, after all, sought immunity for official acts as President, whereas Clinton was seeking immunity for obviously private conduct. Other scholars, including two of the editors of this casebook, signed a brief arguing that Clinton's claims were in fact stronger than Nixon's. Nixon sought permanent immunity in a way that withheld all remedy from Fitzgerald, and denied him his day in court; Clinton, by contrast, sought merely to postpone the lawsuit, not preclude it — sought only temporary immunity, not permanent immunity. Although the *Fitzgerald* case involved underlying conduct that touched on the presidency, at the time of the lawsuit he was simply a private citizen, and so litigation would not disrupt him from doing what he was elected to do. Conversely, Clinton was being sued while in office, and — these scholars argued — litigation might well prove disruptive. Putting aside the specific facts of the case, the structural argument was that one person should not be allowed to commandeer the President's time, divert him from his agenda, and thus undo the votes of millions — or at least, should not be allowed to do this without explaining why the lawsuit could not have been brought before the Clinton presidency, or could not wait for the end of the Clinton presidency. Note that the argument here bears a self-conscious structural similarity to arrest clause immunity for legislators under Article I, §6: While "in session" an elected lawmaker should be allowed to do the people's business, and disruptive private lawsuits should be put on hold until the end of the session.

The Supreme Court, by a 9-0 vote, ruled against Clinton. Justice Stevens wrote for the Court, and Justice Breyer concurred in the judgment only. Dismissing the concern about possible disruption, the Court declared that "if properly managed by the District Court, [the case] appears to us highly unlikely to occupy any substantial amount of [the President's] time." Justice Breyer expressed doubts on this score, and also pointed out that the historical evidence from the Founding era supported the President's claim far more than the majority had admitted. In many ways, his opinion sounded more like a dissent, until its closing paragraphs. (Is it possible that, as in the Nixon Tapes Case, the symbolism of unanimity was important to the Justices?) Perhaps most important for our purposes in studying the interactive processes of constitutional decisionmaking, it should be emphasized that both *Fitzgerald* and *Jones* noted that Congress by law might well have the power to deviate from the baseline laid down by the Court. In *Fitzgerald*, the Justices noted that the plaintiff had sued directly under the Constitution, and could point to no specific congressional statute that authorized his suit against the President. Accordingly "we need not address directly the immunity question as it would arise if Congress expressly had created a damages action against the President." (Note the connection here to Justice Jackson's *Youngstown* categories, which distinguished between congressional silence and explicit congressional statutes seeking to bolster or limit the President.) In *Jones*, the Justices were blunt: "If Congress deems it appropriate to afford the President stronger protection, it may respond with appropriate legislation." If you were a constitutionally conscientious member of Congress, would you support legislation to alter the judicial baselines set by *Fitzgerald* and *Jones*? Why or why not? Are you able to take into account certain features of the problem that would have been inappropriate or difficult for judges to consider?

At least one large and interesting question about presidential immunity remains open after *Jones:* May a sitting President be criminally prosecuted outside of an impeachment court? If so, how and by whom? The *Jones* Court pointedly did not reach this question, distinguishing the case at hand from "the question whether a court may compel the attendance of the President at any specific time or place." Note that in *Jones,* the President needn't have appeared in court; indeed, he could have simply paid a default judgment. In a typical criminal case, by contrast, defendants may be physically obliged — with leg irons, if need be — to stand trial. Also, unlike a mere civil suit, a criminal conviction and imprisonment could effect a de facto removal from office. And if a President were to be incarcerated upon conviction, and later won on appeal, how could we give back to him (and those that voted for him) the lost days of his presidency? This special problem does not arise in civil suits like *Jones.* We should also note that although the *Jones* Court thought that very little historical evidence supported presidential immunity from civil suit in federal court, there is a great deal of historical evidence supporting the notion that a sitting President may not be forced to stand trial in an ordinary criminal court against his will. (For a quick summary of this historical evidence, see the discussion of Presidential Impeachment on this casebook's Web site, *http://www.conlaw.net.*) Moreover, in a civil case, there is never a "plaintiff-standing" problem. *Anyone* can bring a civil suit. But who can bring a criminal suit against a sitting President, and in whose name? For all these reasons, it would be a mistake to read *Jones* as having decided the question of whether a sitting President can be forced to stand trial in a criminal case. (Note also that the *Jones* Court pointedly avoided ruling on whether a civil plaintiff could sue the President in *state* court presided over by a *state* judge.)

Akhil Amar and Brian Kalt have argued, based on structural grounds, that a sitting president is constitutionally immune from ordinary state or federal criminal prosecution, but that he or she can be prosecuted after leaving office. Akhil Reed Amar & Brian C. Kalt, The Presidential Privilege Against Prosecution, 2 Nexus 11 (1997). In testimony before the U.S. Senate, Amar summarized their argument as follows:

> [A] sitting President claiming the full privileges of his office may only be criminally tried by this Court, the Senate, sitting in impeachment, and can be criminally tried elsewhere only after he has left office.
>
> [The] basic constitutional argument is . . . structural . . . sounding in both separation of powers and federalism. Other impeachable officers — Vice Presidents, cabinet officers, judges and justices — may be indicted while in office. *But the Presidency is constitutionally unique — in the President the entirety of the power of a branch of government is vested.* . . .
>
> [Consider] the following hypothetical, which implicates federalism as well as separation of powers: Could some clever state or county prosecutor in Charleston, South Carolina have indicted Abraham Lincoln in March 1861, and ordered him to stand trial in Charleston? If so, there might well be no United States today bringing us all together. I believe that the Constitution gave Lincoln immunity in this situation — so long as he was in office. The President is elected by the whole nation, and no one part of the nation should have the power to undo a decision of the whole.[a] This is the kind of structural argument exemplified by Marshall's classic opinion in McCulloch v. Maryland.

a. The Lincoln hypothetical helps make clear that: (1) innocent Presidents may be targeted by political opponents; (2) local decision-makers cannot always be trusted to decide the fate of a sitting

What is true of a state criminal prosecution is also true of a federal criminal prosecution. Here too, we cannot let a part undo the whole. Any one federal grand jury or federal petit jury will come from one city — be it Charleston or Little Rock or the District of Columbia. The President is elected by the entire nation, and should be judged by the entire nation. His true grand jury is the House, his true petit jury is the Senate, and the true indictment that he is subject to is called an impeachment. What's more, any effort to indict him by an independent counsel would also violate the Constitution's Article II Appointments Clause. . . . [Independent] Counsel [Kenneth] Starr is, constitutionally speaking, an "inferior" officer. He was never, as counsel, confirmed by this body, the Senate of the United States. Were he to claim the power to indict a sitting President, it would be impossible to argue with a straight face that he is simply some "inferior" officer. He would breaking with the historical and traditional approach of the Justice Department — and even if you think he would be right, you cannot say he would truly be *inferior*. He would be claiming for himself the power to imprison the Chief Executive Officer. This power is awesome — it is anything but an "inferior" power that can be vested in an "inferior" officer. This issue of course did not arise in the 1988 Supreme Court case, Morrison v. Olson, since the President in that case was not a target. (And remember, Richard Nixon was only named an *unindicted* coconspirator.) Since *Morrison*, the Court has been even more strict in insisting that the word "inferior" be taken seriously in the Appointments Clause, as evidenced by the 1997 case, Edmond v. United States. Any indictment of the President by Counsel Starr would in my view violate the teaching of *Edmond*.

[O]f course no man is above the law. Once out of office, an ex-President may be tried just like anyone else — and that day of reckoning can of course be speeded up if the House and the Senate decide to impeach and remove. Moreover, since a sitting President's immunity sounds in personal jurisdiction, it may well be waivable, and if so, political pressure may be brought upon a President to consent to be tried.[b] The question is not whether a President is accountable to law and to the country — but *how, when,* and *by whom*.

F. Presidential Selection

In light of the momentous powers and privileges of the President, the mode by which he is chosen is hugely significant. This too is a constitutional decision of sorts, with the American people deciding via constitutional processes who our constitutional president shall be. But issues of presidential selection and succession are typically slighted in casebooks written by law professors, who tend to focus more on those parts of the Constitution that are regularly litigated in the Supreme Court. And so the study of presidential selection and succession is largely today the province of political scientists more than of constitutional law professors in law schools. Perhaps the biggest question is whether the Electoral College makes sense

---

President; and (3) the cost to the nation of allowing open season on Presidents can be extraordinary. In particular, Vice Presidents are not always perfect substitutes. (Pop Quiz: Name Lincoln's Vice President in 1861. Hint: the answer is obscure, and it is not Andrew Johnson, whose efforts to replace Lincoln four years later raised serious problems in their own right.)

b. Thus, there may be a difference between indicting a sitting President against his will, and forcing him to stand trial against his will. The former may be permissible even if the latter is not (bracketing for the moment the serious appointments clause objections to independent counsels).

in modern America. Here is what the previous edition of this casebook — written before the election of 2000 — had to say about the matter:

> Admittedly, the electoral college was a brilliant 18th-century device to solve 18th-century problems. The Framers emphatically did not want a President dependent on the legislature, so they rejected a parliamentary model in which the legislature would pick its own leader as prime minister and chief executive officer. How, then, to pick the President? The visionary James Wilson proposed direct national popular election, but the scheme was deemed unworkable for three reasons. First, very few candidates would have truly continental reputations among ordinary citizens; ordinary folk across the vast continent would not have enough good information to choose intelligently among national figures. Second, a populist Presidency was seen as dangerous — inviting demagoguery and possibly dictatorship as one man claimed to embody the Voice of the American People. Third, national election would upset a careful balance of power among states. Since the South didn't let blacks vote, southern voices would count less in a direct national election. A state could increase its clout by recklessly extending its franchise — for example, if (heaven forbid!) a state let women vote, it could double its weight in a direct national election. Under the electoral college system, by contrast, a state could get a fixed number of electoral votes whether its franchise was broad or narrow — indeed, whether or not it let ordinary voters pick electors.
>
> But do these arguments work today? Improvements in communications technology, and the rise of political parties, make possible direct election and a populist Presidency — de facto, that is our scheme today. Blacks and women are no longer selectively disenfranchised, and states no longer play key roles in defining the electorate or in deciding whether to give the voters a direct voice in choosing electors. Direct national election would encourage states to encourage voters to vote on Election Day; but today, this hardly seems a strong reason to *oppose* direct election. Ingenious, indirect, sophisticated arguments made on behalf of the electoral college by clever theorists these days are legion — but almost all seem make-weight. If the scheme is so good, why doesn't any U.S. state, or any foreign nation, copy it? A low plurality winner in a three-or four-way race is possible even with the electoral college; and could be avoided in a direct national election by single transferable voting (with voters listing their 2nd and 3rd choices on the ballot, in effect combining the "first heat" and "run off" elections into a single transaction).
>
> The only two real arguments against abolition of the electoral college sound in federalism and inertia. Only federalism can explain why we should use an electoral college to pick presidents but not governors. But it's hard to see what the federalism argument is, *today*. Should the specter of the national government administering a national election give us the cold sweats? A razor-thin popular vote margin might occasion a national recount, but states now manage recounts all the time, and new technology will make counting and recounting much easier in the future. (And today, a razor-thin electoral college margin may require recounts in a number of closely contested states even if there is a clear national popular winner.) Inertial, Burkean, arguments take two forms. First, the argument goes, a change in presidential selection rules would radically change the game in ways hard to foresee: Candidates wouldn't care about winning states — only votes — and campaign strategies might change dramatically and for the worse. But it's hard to see why. Given that, historically, the electoral college leader has also tended to be the popular vote leader, the strategy for winning shouldn't change dramatically if we switch from one measure to the other. This sets up the second inertial point: The dreaded specter of a clear popular loser becoming the electoral college winner hasn't materialized since Rutherford B. Hayes (1876) and Benjamin Harrison (1888) last century — "Why worry?" But that's what someone might say after three trigger pulls in Russian Roulette. One day, we will end

up with a clear Loser President — clear beyond any quibbles about uncertain ballots.[82] And the question is, will this Loser/Winner be seen as legitimate at home and abroad? If our modern national democratic ethos, when focused on the thing, would balk at a byzantine system that defies the people's choice on election day, true Burkean theory would seem to argue against the electoral college. If We the People would amend the Constitution after the Loser President materializes, why are we now just waiting for the inevitable accident to happen?[83]

To what extent do the elections of 2000 and 2004 confirm or contradict the foregoing analysis? On the election of 2000, see also this casebook's Web site materials on the remarkable case of Bush v. Gore, 531 U.S. 98 (2000), at *http://www.conlaw.net.*

VI.   *Some Limits on the Federal Judicial Power*

As we have seen, both Congress and the President have important powers, but these powers are limited. The same is of course true of the third branch of the federal government, the federal judiciary. In this section, we briefly consider three important ways in which the federal judicial power is limited. Our treatment here is brief because each of these topics is covered at great length in casebooks and courses on federal jurisdiction.

A.   Jurisdiction Stripping

Article III vests the federal judiciary with "the judicial power of the United States," which includes the power of judicial review. But Article III also recognizes important congressional power to define the shape and scope of the federal judiciary. Lower federal courts need not exist; and in theory, Congress is free to abolish these courts (although it might be obliged to pay the salaries of existing judges). This is the so-called "Madisonian Compromise" about the federal judiciary reached at the Philadelphia Convention. Textually, note that Article III speaks of "such inferior courts as the Congress *may* from time to time ordain and establish," and that Article I, §8 speaks of the "power" (but not the duty) of Congress to "constitute Tribunals

---

82. In the 1988 election, for example, George Bush beat Michael Dukakis by more than 7 million votes. But if fewer than 600,000 voters in certain key states had switched sides, Dukakis would have won in the electoral college, though Bush would still have trounced him in the popular vote, 52 percent to 46 percent. See 19 America Votes 9 (Richard M. Scammon & Alice V. McGillivray eds., 1991).

83. Other possible constitutional accidents waiting to happen involve presidential succession. Is democratic legitimacy well served when the people vote for President A and end up, because of death or disability, with Vice President B, representing very different policies? (Examples include William Henry Harrison and John Tyler, Abraham Lincoln and Andrew Johnson, James Garfield and Chester A. Arthur, and William McKinley and Theodore Roosevelt.) Also, what kind of legitimacy would there have been if the people in 1996 elected Democrats Bill Clinton and Al Gore, but ended up (as a result of a hypothetical double death in 1997) with Republican Newt Gingrich? (The current presidential succession statute specifies the Speaker of the House as third in line.) For suggestions that the process of vice presidential selection and the laws dealing with presidential succession should be rethought, see Ruth C. Silva, Presidential Succession (1951); Richard D. Friedman, Some Modest Proposals on the Vice-Presidency, 86 Mich. L. Rev. 1703 (1988); Akhil Reed Amar & Vik Amar, President Quayle?, 78 Va. L. Rev. 913 (1992); Akhil Reed Amar & Vikram David Amar, Is the Presidential Succession Law Constitutional?, 48 Stan. L. Rev. 113 (1995).

inferior to the supreme Court." The existence of one "Supreme Court" is mandated by the Constitution, but the Constitution says nothing about the size and shape of that Court. Historically, the size of the Court has varied from between six and ten members, but has been statutorily fixed at nine for over a century. (Could Congress theoretically expand the Court to encompass 50 or 100 judges, and oblige these judges to hear most of their cases in smaller panels, with en bancs to deal with certain interpanel conflicts?) Note also that Congress has power to make "exceptions and regulations" to the Supreme Court's appellate jurisdiction.

The largest and most debated questions about congressional power over federal jurisdiction are as follows: To what extent can Congress use its powers in tandem to remove various cases entirely from all federal courts? For example, could Congress eliminate lower federal court jurisdiction over abortion cases while simultaneously "excepting" those cases from the Supreme Court's appellate jurisdiction, thereby leaving all these issues to be decided in state courts whose judges typically lack life tenure and some of the other protections enjoyed by Article III judges? Could Congress thus "strip" the jurisdiction of federal courts if its explicit purpose were to undercut the federal judiciary's abortion rulings? If the issue were left to state courts, would such courts continue to be bound by old Supreme Court precedents? Even if not, what, as a practical matter, would prevent these courts from departing from the Supreme Court's prior pronouncements? As a predictive matter, would state courts likely reach the same results as the federal courts would have?

Modern scholars have expressed a range of views, but for simplicity it is useful to consider two main schools of thought. The first school is associated with Professor Henry Hart, who taught at the Harvard Law School in the middle of the twentieth century and whose views were widely influential. (Five of the current Justices attended the Harvard Law School in Hart's heyday.) According to the Hart school of thought, Congress may indeed combine its powers over lower federal courts and over the Supreme Court's appellate jurisdiction so as to leave the last word on certain cases in state courts. But such exceptions, Hart warned, should not go so far as to intrude upon the "essential functions" of the Supreme Court, which Hart did not attempt to define comprehensively. A competing school of thought builds on the work of Justice Joseph Story. In his landmark opinion in Martin v. Hunter's Lessee, 14 U.S. (1 Wheat.) 304 (1816), and in his famous 1833 treatise, Story stressed the mandatory nature of federal jurisdiction: "The judicial power of the United States *shall* be vested in" the federal judiciary and "*shall* extend to *all* cases, in law and equity, arising under this Constitution, the laws of the United States, and Treaties made, or which shall be made, under their authority. . . ." According to Story, this mandatory language means that although Congress can restrict both lower federal court jurisdiction and the Supreme Court's appellate jurisdiction, Congress may not do both at the same time — at least, where federal question cases are concerned. As to these cases, the federal judiciary, and not the state courts, must stand as the last word on the meaning of federal law. Just as Congress may not transfer Article II power to veto federal laws or pardon federal offenses from the President to state governors, so too Congress may not transfer Article III power to resolve finally all federal question cases from the federal judiciary to state courts. Such courts may hear federal question cases in the first instance, but may not stand as the last word: They must be subject to appellate review in some federal court (though not necessarily the Supreme Court). To defend his claim that federal question cases were mandatory whereas diversity suits were not, Story highlighted the fact that in the former category, the Constitution speaks of "*all*" cases, but not in the latter. This has come to be known as the "two-tiered" theory of Article III.

For prominent statements by members of the Hart school, see Henry M. Hart, Jr., The Power of Congress to Limit the Jurisdiction of Federal Courts: An Exercise in Dialectic, 66 Harv. L. Rev. 1362 (1953); Paul M. Bator, Congressional Power Over the Jurisdiction of the Federal Courts, 27 Vill. L. Rev. 1030 (1982); Martin H. Redish, Constitutional Limitations on Congressional Power To Control Federal Jursidiction: A Reaction to Professor Sager, 77 Nw. U. L. Rev. 143 (1982); Daniel J. Meltzer, The History and Structure of Article III, 138 U. Pa. L. Rev. 1569 (1990). For scholarship in the mandatory tradition of Justice Story, see Lawrence Gene Sager, The Supreme Court, 1980 Term — Foreword: Constitutional Limitations on Congress' Authority To Regulate the Jurisdiction of the Federal Courts, 95 Harv. L. Rev. 17 (1981); Robert N. Clinton, A Mandatory View of Federal Court Jurisdiction: A Guided Quest for the Original Understanding of Article III, 132 U. Pa. L. Rev. 741 (1984); Akhil Reed Amar, A Neo-Federalist View of Article III: Separating the Two Tiers of Federal Jurisdiction, 65 B.U. L. Rev. 205 (1985); Akhil Reed Amar, The Two-Tiered Structure of the Judiciary Act of 1789, 138 U. Pa. L. Rev. 1499 (1990).

B.   Standing

In the American tradition, litigants who come to court in general must assert their own legal rights, rather than seek to adjudicate and define the rights of others. This basic idea is captured by the doctrine of "standing." As a general matter, the Supreme Court typically requires that a plaintiff seeking access to federal courts must himself be "injured in fact," must show that his injury was caused by the defendant, and must establish that this injury is capable of proper redress in the lawsuit he seeks to bring. This seemingly tidy formulation hides a rather confusing body of case law that has grown up around it. The basic problem is this: Almost anyone who comes to court feels aggrieved in some way — but not all grievances and harms count, legally speaking. The exceedingly spare words of Article III, however, cannot tell us which harms count, when, or for whom — only substantive law can do so, whether that law derives from statutes, or other parts of the Constitution, or common law principles of property, tort, contract, and so on. For example, is a third party to a contract entitled to come to court to complain that the contract has been breached? This is a question of contract law, not Article III. Are downstream purchasers entitled to come to court to complain about price fixing committed not by their immediate suppliers, but by manufacturers further upstream? This is a question of substantive law under the Sherman Act. Article III can properly demand that plaintiffs must in general assert their own rights — but only substantive law outside Article III can define what the rights are, to whom they attach, against whom they run, and when they vest. At times the Court seems to have recognized as much, and at other times the Court seems to miss this basic point. For good general discussions that nicely clarify the issues at stake, see David P. Currie, Misunderstanding Standing, 1981 Sup. Ct. Rev. 41; William A. Fletcher, The Structure of Standing, 98 Yale L.J. 221 (1988); Cass R. Sunstein, What's Standing After *Lujan?* Of Citizen Suits, "Injuries," and Article III, 91 Mich. L. Rev. 163 (1992).

C.   Political Questions

As we have seen, there is often a gap between what the Constitution platonically means, and what judges enforce in courts in the name of the Constitution. Sometimes, judges underenforce constitutional norms for judiciary-specific reasons. Other times, judges may abdicate the field altogether. There are a variety of reasons justifying abdication, and several of these are lumped together under what has become known as the "political question" doctrine. The canonical effort to give boundaries to this doctrine took place in Baker v. Carr, 369 U.S. 186 (1962), a case involving a malapportioned state legislature. The defendants claimed that the apportionment issue was unfit for judicial resolution, but the Court disagreed. Along the way it said that a political question may arise when any one of the following circumstances is present:

> a textually demonstrable constitutional commitment of the issue to a coordinate political department; or a lack of judicially discoverable and manageable standards for resolving it; or the impossibility of deciding without an initial policy determination of a kind clearly for nonjudicial discretion; or the impossibility of a court's undertaking independent resolution without expressing lack of the respect due coordinate branches of government; or an unusual need for unquestioning adherence to a political decision already made; or the potentiality of embarrassment from multifarious pronouncements by various departments on one question.

These six factors, in turn, may be conveniently grouped into three sets of reasons for judicial abdication. The first set might be called "jurisdictional" reasons for abdication. The argument here is that in a few discrete situations, the Constitution vests judicial, adjudicatory power in another branch of government. Thus, in the celebrated case of Powell v. McCormack, 395 U.S. 486 (1969), Chief Justice Warren slightly modified the first prong of the *Baker* test, by asking whether Article I, §5 amounted to a "textually demonstrable commitment of the *adjudicatory* power to determine Powell's qualifications." The Court ruled that such adjudicatory power, if it existed, extended only to the determination of whether Congressman Powell met the Constitution's specified qualifications of age, residency, and citizenship. The Constitution did not give the Congress adjudicatory power to add new qualifications of its own. (In effect, the theory of adjudicatory power is that it involves applying a preexisting standard, not making up a new one, legislatively, cf. *Chadha*.) Since there was no bona fide dispute about whether Powell did indeed meet the Constitution's specified qualifications, the Court invalidated the effort by the House of Representatives to exclude Powell. But, the Court noted, in the case of a bona fide dispute about age, for example, each House might well be the final "judge," and Article III courts might be obliged to defer, even if they disagreed with this bona fide judgment. The reason for this is that the Constitution explicitly makes each House the "judge" of the qualifications of its own members under Article I, §5. Any attempt to relitigate the issue collaterally in an Article III court might be said to offend the idea of res judicata.

Factors two and three of the *Baker* test seem to reflect a different idea. Judges deciding cases seek clear doctrinal rules capable of principled exposition. If such rules are unavailable in a given situation, this may counsel judicial abdication — not because there are no constitutional principles at stake, but because they cannot be cleanly implemented in a "judicially manageable" way with proper "legal" tests.

The remaining factors sound more in prudentialism, counseling caution not because judges need clean lines, but because they are less politically accountable, and are often asked to act after important and hard-to-reverse decisions (like the decision to wage war) have already been made by the other branches.

Two landmark political question cases — one from the beginning of the modern era, and one rather recent — may help illustrate the basic ideas at work. In Coleman v. Miller, 307 U.S. 433 (1939), the Justices faced a claim that a constitutional amendment that Congress had proposed 14 years earlier could no longer be ratified by states — too much time had already lapsed, the claim went, and so the amendment proposal should be judicially declared dead. The Justices rejected this argument, and labeled the issue a political question for Congress to decide. Writing for himself and two others, Chief Justice Hughes argued that no judicially manageable standards existed — how was a judge to say how much time was too much? For judges to say that 11 years was too long but that 10 years was not would involve awkward line-drawing problems. The obvious counterargument, of course — made by two dissenting Justices — is that judges draw lines every day. Four other Justices agreed that the issue was a nonjusticiable political question, but used more "jurisdictional" language: Article V, they insisted, committed these issues wholly to Congress. But nowhere is there any distinctively judicial language in Article V; if judges may decide whether Congress has acted beyond the scope of its commerce power, why may they not likewise decide whether Congress has acted beyond whatever implicit time limits (if any) Article V imposes? The best argument for the result in Coleman is prudential: The Amendment in question involved child labor, and grew out of a political effort to reverse the Supreme Court's prior rulings on the question of child labor. In this context, for the Court to step in to kill the Amendment would have been rather awkward for reasons of democratic legitimacy — the Court would have been cutting off the people's biggest check on the Court, and doing so in the name of a time-limits idea that was nowhere explicit in Article V. If, however, this is the best theory to explain Coleman, it suggests that only those amendments aimed at overturning the judiciary should be seen as political questions. Where other amendments are involved, the willingness of judges to adjudicate constitutional questions (as judges generally do elsewhere) would not raise the specter of judicial self-dealing and self-entrenchment. Indeed, in some cases, quite the opposite is true. Consider for example, the case of the Twenty-seventh Amendment, proposed by James Madison in 1789, and ratified by the 38th state in 1992; this was an amendment designed to restrict congressional self-dealing in setting congressional salaries; to insist that Congress be the sole judge of the constitutional issues here seems to invert the prudential vision that best explains Coleman's result.

Consider also the case of Judge Walter Nixon, who was impeached by the House of Representatives and convicted by the U.S. Senate. When Judge Nixon sought to bring certain legal objections about his Senate trial to court, the Supreme Court unanimously declared the issues involved to be political questions. See Nixon v. United States, 506 U.S. 224 (1993). The Justices diverged in their reasons, but converged in their result, and it is not hard to see why. Constitutional history makes clear that the Framers intentionally shifted impeachment from Article III courts to the Senate, so that controversial impeachment issues would be resolved by a sufficiently large and politically accountable body. As a matter of structure and prudence, it would be awkward for judges to try to reinstate, say, an already-ousted President; and where a judge had been removed, there is something constitution-ally unseemly about other judges trying to put him back in power (with full pay, of course), thereby nullifying one of the Constitution's main checks on overweening judges. Constitutional text, carefully and holistically construed, confirms all this, and illustrates again the "jurisdictional" variant of the political question doctrine. The notion that an officer who has been impeached and removed may not seek reinstatement in an Article III lawsuit is not some weird exception to judicial review. The officer is fully entitled to judicial review of all relevant issues of fact and law — *but this review occurs in the Senate itself, which sits as a court.* Note the obvious judicial language of Article I, §3 which gives the Senate the sole power to "try" all impeach-ments, with the power to "convict" and enter "judgment" in "Cases" of Impeachment. This repeated judicial language makes clear that the Senate sits as judge and jury, and its rulings of fact and law therefore stand as res judicata in all other tribunals. Intratextual analysis confirms this. When we consult the language of Article III, we see that it exempts "Trial[s]" in "Cases of Impeachment" from the ordinary rules of Article III demanding juries for all crimes. Why? Because "trials" of "cases" of impeachment are to take place and be finally decided in a different court, specified earlier in the document.

Note: Presidential Impeachment

The constitutional doctrines governing impeachment raise the separation of powers issues we have discussed in this chapter in particularly interesting ways. Article II, §4 states that "The President, Vice President and all civil officers of the United States, shall be removed from Office on Impeachment for, and Conviction of, Treason, Bribery, or other high Crimes and Misdemeanors." Article I entrusts the House of Representatives with the power to impeach, the Senate with the power to try impeachments, and the Chief Justice with the power to act as the presiding officer at Presidential impeachments. In December 1998 President Clinton was impeached by the House of Representatives and subsequently tried and ultimately acquitted by the Senate in February 1999. The Clinton impeachment raised a number of important questions about the meaning of the Constitution and its structure. However, most of these issues were questions directed not at the judicial branch, but at conscientious House and Senate members, as well as the general public. The President also had to make important constitutional decisions about how to respond to moves made by the other branches. For reference materials and discussion notes addressing some of the most important constitutional issues raised by the Clinton impeachment, see our casebook Web site at *http://www.conlaw.net.*

Chapter 6

The Burdens of History: The Constitutional
Treatment of Race

This chapter focuses on the meaning of the Equal Protection Clause of the Fourteenth Amendment — "No state shall . . . deny to any person within its jurisdiction the equal protection of the laws" — with respect to racial equality. We begin with the school desegregation case, Brown v. Board of Education, which ushers in the modern conception of the Equal Protection Clause and trace the story of the constitutional battles over school segregation that followed in the wake of *Brown*. The rest of the chapter considers contemporary issues of racial discrimination.

I. Brown v. Board of Education and the Constitutional Struggle Over Desegregation

A. Background to the School Desegregation Case

Like most previous wars, World War II was in fact good for African-Americans insofar as the pressing needs of the military and of war industry provided jobs and a new measure of economic and political independence, especially in the great cities of the North and Midwest. New waves of migration brought Southern blacks to the North, which further increased the voting power of the Northern urban areas. African-Americans had unprecedented access to jobs, higher wages, and union membership. Alfred Kelly continues the story of the years prior to *Brown*.[1]

> [In addition to the changing domestic economic and political conditions,] the equalitarian ideology of American war propaganda, which presented the United States as a champion of democracy engaged in a death struggle with the German racists, created in the minds and hearts of most white persons a new and intense awareness of the shocking contrast between the country's too comfortable image of itself and the cold realities of American racial segregation. Both pragmatic propaganda interests and the new idealism demanded certain steps for the Negro's further integration, both in society and in the war effort.
>
> Some of this crisis-imposed, wartime integration took place on an official level: in a series of executive orders, the Roosevelt administration expanded the employment of Negroes in the federal bureaucracy, wrote "no discrimination" clauses into war contracts,

---

1. Alfred Kelly, The School Desegregation Case, Quarrels That Have Shaped the Constitution 243, 247-249, 253 (John Garraty ed., 1964). See also Michael Klarman, From Jim Crow to Civil Rights: The Supreme Court and the Struggle for Racial Equality 288-289 (2004).

established in 1941 a Fair Employment Practices Commission, and even took a few hesitant steps toward racial integration in the armed forces. Meantime, in 1939, Attorney General Frank Murphy, already something of a radical idealist on the integration and Negro civil rights questions, had established a Civil Rights Division in the Department of Justice, which in turn undertook what was to prove to be a generation-long legal quest for new federal guarantees against lynching and new safeguards for Negro voting rights. Congress, also, bestirred itself. The Soldiers Vote Act of 1942 abolished the poll tax as a prerequisite for voting by members of the armed services, while the so-called La Follette Civil Liberties Committee began its own investigation into the lynching problem.

It was inevitable that the Negro's new nationalized political power, his enhanced economic position, and the vast improvement in ideological climate in the country presently would spill over into the courts, to produce a new series of decisions reflecting the altered position of the Negro in America. The dynamics of this process are hardly very mysterious. Several of the Roosevelt appointees to the Court after 1937 were practical politicians whom the exigencies of the New Deal had made intensely aware of the "political power shift" implicit in the Negro's new party role. Hugo Black, Robert Jackson, Frank Murphy, and Wiley Rutledge all fell into this category. Or, like Felix Frankfurter and William O. Douglas, the new appointees were legal academicians who reflected the equalitarian idealism of the liberal university communities of the North. . . .

It needs only to be added here that the succession of justices appointed to the Court after the war — Fred M. Vinson, Harold Burton, Sherman Minton, and Tom Clark — while they tended generally to be more conservative than New Deal era justices, nonetheless had been trained in the hard practical school of politics and shared to the full an awareness of the altered position of the Negro in American society. Earl Warren, the mild-mannered middle-of-the-road Republican who came to the chief justiceship in 1953, epitomized as no one else could have this new politico-judicial understanding. The Negro's altered role was no mere matter of New Deal radical idealism. It was a point of view which had been thoroughly absorbed by the working politicians of both parties.

It is hardly open to question, then, that this flow of Democratic and Republican appointees to the High Court after 1937 would in no great length of time have produced something of a constitutional revolution in the Negro's status. But this process, inevitable as it may well have been, was vastly accelerated by the legal assault on segregation first launched in the late 1930's by a powerful and dedicated Negro interest group, the National Association for the Advancement of Colored People. The desegregation campaign commenced about 1935 by the NAACP got under way very slowly, but it continued without interruption and with growing success for the next generation.[2] It was a campaign which would make the NAACP the "cutting edge" of all the complex social and political forces that were at work to produce a desegregated America.

[The NAACP's postwar school desegregation began with] . . . a series of suits to force the admission of Negroes to Southern graduate professional schools, above all state university law schools. Several major considerations led NAACP officials to adopt this scheme. First, most Southern states did not even attempt to maintain a facade of equality in professional educational facilities for Negroes, so that their classic "separate but equal" defense, the Association hoped, would prove to be inapplicable. Second, NAACP lawyers believed that if the Southern states countered this strategy by

---

2. Thus Missouri ex rel. Gaines v. Canada, 305 U.S. 337 (1938), held that Missouri did not provide equal protection by paying the tuition for black students at out-of-state law schools while denying them admission to the state school. Chief Justice Hughes wrote that petitioner was entitled to "facilities [within the state] substantially equal to those which the State there afforded for persons of the white race" and that in the absence of such facilities he must be admitted to the one state school. Justice McReynolds, joined by Justice Butler, dissented, arguing that the state had made a "fair effort" to solve a difficult problem and that its solution was "far from [an] unmistakable disregard of [petitioner's] rights."

trying to provide genuinely equal facilities for Negroes in graduate education, the effort would prove to be both awesomely expensive and impossible of actual achievement. . . .

The NAACP lawyers were also deliberately exploiting a peculiarity of Southern racial sentiment. The South . . . regarded racial mixing in graduate and professional education as far less invidious than in primary and secondary schools or even in collegiate education. As a consequence, they hoped, Southern officials might be expected to resist graduate school integration with less emotional conviction than would be the case for lower-level schools. As [Thurgood] Marshall, with characteristic humor, later put the matter: "Those racial supremacy boys somehow think that little kids of six or seven are going to get funny ideas about sex and marriage just from going to school together, but for some equally funny reason youngsters in law school aren't supposed to feel that way. We didn't get it but we decided that if that was what the South believed, then the best thing for the moment was to go along."

Note: Brown *and the Cold War*

As the preceding excerpt suggests, courts always operate within a larger political, social, and cultural context. Consider Michael Klarman's list of "underlying forces that made *Brown* a realistic judicial possibility in 1954": "World War II, the ideological revulsion against Nazi fascism, the Cold War imperative, the growing political empowerment of northern blacks, the increasing economic and social integration of the nation, and changing southern racial attitudes."[3] One should also not underestimate the impact of President Truman's decision to desegregate the armed forces over the marked opposition of the Joint Chiefs of Staff.[4]

Derrick Bell has argued for what he calls the "interest convergence" thesis — that black progress only occurs when the interests of whites converge with those of blacks. Derrick Bell, Brown v. Board of Education and the Interest-Convergence Dilemma, 93 Harv. L. Rev. 518 (1980). Thus Bell suggested that *Brown* was made possible by the changes in the interests of white elites following the Cold War. Mary Dudziak amply supports Bell's thesis in her study Desegregation as a Cold War Imperative, 41 Stan. L. Rev. 61 (1988), which focuses on foreign policy events leading up to the decision in *Brown*. Dudziak shows how the domestic issue of desegregation was framed in part by the larger context of international criticism. In his now-classic study, An American Dilemma: The Negro Problem and Modern Democracy (1944), Swedish sociologist Gunnar Myrdal had directed the world's attention to the divergence between

---

3. Michael J. Klarman, *Brown*, Racial Change, and the Civil Rights Movement, 80 Va. L. Rev. 7, 14 (1994).

4. Exec Order No. 9,981, 13 Fed. Reg. 4,313 (1948). Indeed, Truman's Democratic Party split over its strong civil rights platform at the 1948 convention. Truman nevertheless was able to win reelection. The Truman administration also urged the Court to overturn *Plessy* in 1950. See William Berman, The Politics of Civil Rights in the Truman Administration 55, 68, 118 (1970). What explains Truman's rather courageous record on civil rights? Alonzo Hamby writes:

> No historian can precisely define Truman's motivation on so complex and emotional an issue; it was probably not entirely clear even to Truman. It seems fair to say that he really believed in the principles of equal rights and equal opportunity. But it is also just to observe that he was well aware of the importance of the black vote. It is reasonable to assume that he acted in part out of a sense of self-interest but more important that he interpreted his self interest in a fashion both astute and morally enlightened.

Alonzo Hamby, Liberalism and its Challengers: FDR to Reagan 66-67 (1985).

America's professed democratic ideals and the second-class status of its black citizens. Myrdal issued the following challenge: "America, for all its international prestige, power, and future security, needs to demonstrate to the world that American Negroes can be satisfactorily integrated into its democracy." Not surprisingly, after the onset of the Cold War, Myrdal's generally "well-intentioned" criticisms were put to distinctly ideological uses by East Bloc governments.

This international situation provided a strategic advantage to American opponents of segregation. In 1946, the National Negro Congress petitioned the U.N. for "relief from oppression," and in 1947 the NAACP submitted A Statement on the Denial of Human Rights to Minorities in the Case of Citizens of Negro Descent in the United States of America and an Appeal to the United Nations for Redress.[5] Although the U.N. took no action on the charges, they were publicized widely overseas. In 1951, the Civil Rights Congress filed a petition under the United Nations Convention on the Prevention and Punishment of the Crime of Genocide, charging the U.S. government with black genocide.[6]

Given these significant embarrassments, desegregation became a matter of direct concern to the State Department. In its amicus brief in *Brown*, the Department of Justice emphasized how segregation interfered with the country's foreign policy: "Racial discrimination furnishes grist for the Communist propaganda mills, and it raises doubts even among friendly nations as to the intensity of our devotion to the democratic faith."[7] In support, the brief quoted Secretary of State Dean Acheson at length, including his statement that school desegregation in particular had been

> singled out for hostile foreign comment in the United Nations and elsewhere. Other peoples cannot understand how such a practice can exist in a country which professes to be a staunch supporter of freedom, justice, and democracy. . . . [R]acial discrimination in the United States remains a source of constant embarrassment to this Government in the day-to-day conduct of its foreign relations; and it jeopardizes the effective maintenance of our moral leadership of the free and democratic nations of the world.[8]

Dudziak argues that when *Brown* finally came, part of its political utility lay in the fact that it

> laundered the principles of democracy in the eyes of the world. The decision announced that racial segregation and American constitutional rights were inconsistent with each other. After *Brown*, the State Department could blame racism on the Klan and the crazies. They could argue that the American Constitution provided for effective social change. And, most importantly, they could point to the *Brown* decision as evidence that racism was at odds with the principles of American democracy. This foreign policy angle, this Cold War imperative, was one of the critical factors driving the federal government's postwar civil rights efforts.[9]

For whatever combination of international and domestic reasons, the NAACP's legal strategy in its fight against segregation was ultimately successful.[10] A unanimous

---

5. Gerald N. Rosenberg, The Hollow Hope: Can Courts Bring About Social Change? 163 (1991).
6. Dudziak, at 96. This thesis is further elaborated in Mary Dudziak, Cold War Civil Rights: Race in the Image of American Democracy (2000).
7. Id. at 110-111.
8. Id. at 111-112.
9. Id. at 118-119.
10. See Mark Tushnet, The NAACP's Legal Strategy Against Segregated Education, 1925-1950 (1987).

Court reaffirmed *Gaines* in Sipuel v. University of Oklahoma Board of Regents, 332 U.S. 631 (1948). (Justices McReynolds and Butler had resigned in the interim and been replaced by Justices Rutledge and Murphy.) The Court held that petitioner had a constitutional right to an equal education and could not be denied entrance to a state law school solely because of her race. However, on remand, a trial court gave the state the option of establishing a separate black law school, and the Supreme Court, in Fisher v. Hurst, 333 U.S. 147 (1948), refused to order the state to desegregate its law school.

Two years later, however, in Sweatt v. Painter, 339 U.S. 629 (1950), the Court held that a hastily established law school for black law students did not and probably could not provide an education equal to that offered by the University of Texas Law School. Chief Justice Vinson wrote for the Court:

> In terms of number of the faculty, variety of courses and opportunity for specialization, size of the student body, scope of the library, availability of law review and similar activities, the University of Texas Law School is superior. What is more important, the University of Texas Law School possesses to a far greater degree those qualities which are incapable of objective measurement but which make for greatness in a law school. Such qualities, to name but a few, include reputation of the faculty, experience of the administration, position and influence of the alumni, standing in the community, traditions and prestige. . . .
>
> The law school, the proving ground for legal learning and practice, cannot be effective in isolation from the individuals and institutions with which the law interacts. . . . The law school to which Texas is willing to admit petitioner excludes from its student body members of the racial groups which number 85% of the population of the State and include most of the lawyers, witnesses, jurors, judges and other officials with whom petitioner will inevitably be dealing when he becomes a member of the Texas Bar.

McLaurin v. Oklahoma State Regents, 339 U.S. 637 (1950), decided the same day as *Sweatt,* held that petitioner, having been admitted to the state university to pursue a graduate program not offered at the state's school for blacks, could not be required to sit in separate sections of the classroom, library, and cafeteria. Chief Justice Vinson again wrote for a unanimous Court, stating that the "restrictions impair and inhibit [petitioner's] ability to study, to engage in discussions and exchange views with other students, and, in general, to learn his profession." To the argument that petitioner might still be set apart by his fellow students, Vinson responded:

> [T]here is a vast difference — a Constitutional difference — between restrictions imposed by the state which prohibit the intellectual commingling of students, and the refusal of individuals to commingle where the state presents no such bar. . . . The removal of the state restrictions will not necessarily abate individual and group predilections, prejudices and choices. But at the very least, the state will not be depriving appellant of the opportunity to secure acceptance by his fellow students on his own merits.

In 1952, the NAACP presented the Court with the issue of segregation in elementary and secondary public schools. Brown v. Board of Education, 347 U.S. 483 (1954), and its four companion cases were first argued during the 1952 term of the Supreme Court. Toward the close of the term, on June 8, 1953, the Court set the cases for reargument. A principal reason, it has been suggested, is because the Court was badly split as to the outcome of the case. Before the reargument, Chief Justice Vinson died on September 8, 1953 and was replaced by the Governor of California, Earl Warren.[11] Felix Frankfurter is said to have confided to a clerk that this was "the first indication that I have ever had that there is a God."[12]

The Court requested counsel "[i]n their briefs and on oral argument . . . to discuss particularly the following questions . . .":

1. What evidence is there that the Congress which submitted and the State legislatures and conventions which ratified the Fourteenth Amendment contemplated or did not contemplate, understood or did not understand, that it would abolish segregation in the public schools?

2. If neither the Congress in submitting nor the States in ratifying the Fourteenth Amendment understood that compliance with it would require the immediate abolition of segregation in public schools, was it nevertheless the understanding of the framers of the Amendment
   (a) that future Congresses might, in the exercise of their power under Section 5 of the Amendment, abolish such segregation, or
   (b) that it would be within the judicial power, in light of future conditions, to construe the Amendment as abolishing segregation of its own force?

3. On the assumption that the answers to questions 2(a) and (b) do not dispose of the issue, is it within the judicial power, in construing the Amendment, to abolish segregation in public schools?

The parties in *Brown* responded to the Court's questions on the original understanding with lengthy historical briefs.[13] See Chapter 4 for a summary of the historical evidence.

B.   The School Desegregation Case

BROWN v. BOARD OF EDUCATION OF TOPEKA, KANSAS[14]
347 U.S. 483 (1954)

WARREN, C.J.

These cases come to us from the States of Kansas, South Carolina, Virginia, and Delaware. They are premised on different facts and different local conditions, but a common legal question justifies their consideration together in this consolidated opinion.

---

11. The Senate confirmed Warren's appointment on March 1, 1954, two months before *Brown* was decided, but President Eisenhower had given Warren a recess appointment on September 30, 1953. See Article II, §2, cl. 3. ("The President shall have the power to fill up all vacancies that may happen during the recess of the Senate, by granting commissions, which shall expire at the end of their next session.") Consider whether this sequence of events could have occurred today.

12. Bernard Schwarz, Super Chief 72 (1983).

13. The petitioners in *Brown* commissioned various historians, including Howard J. Graham, Alfred H. Kelly, C. Vann Woodward, John Hope Franklin, and Horace Bond, to prepare monographs for their use. See generally Kelly, supra n.1.

14. *Brown* is actually a joinder of four separate cases, as the Court notes it its first sentence. A fifth case, from the District of Columbia, was decided separately as Bolling v. Sharpe, 347 U.S. 497 (1954).

In each of the cases, minors of the Negro race, through their legal representatives, seek the aid of the courts in obtaining admission to the public schools of their community on a nonsegregated basis. In each instance, they had been denied admission to schools attended by white children under laws requiring or permitting segregation according to race. This segregation was alleged to deprive the plaintiffs of the equal protection of the laws under the Fourteenth Amendment. In each of the cases other than the Delaware case, a three-judge federal district court denied relief to the plaintiffs on the so-called "separate but equal" doctrine announced by this Court in Plessy v. Ferguson, 163 U.S. 537. Under the doctrine, equality of treatment is accorded when the races are provided substantially equal facilities, even though these facilities be separate. In the Delaware case, the Supreme Court of Delaware adhered to that doctrine, but ordered that the plaintiffs be admitted to the white schools because of their superiority to the Negro schools.

The plaintiffs contend that segregated public schools are not "equal" and cannot be made "equal," and that hence they are deprived of the equal protection of the laws. Because of the obvious importance of the question presented, the Court took jurisdiction. Argument was heard in the 1952 Term, and reargument was heard this Term on certain questions propounded by the Court.

Reargument was largely devoted to the circumstances surrounding the adoption of the Fourteenth Amendment in 1868. It covered exhaustively consideration of the Amendment in Congress, ratification by the states, then existing practices in racial segregation, and the views of proponents and opponents of the Amendment. This discussion and our own investigation convince us that, although these sources cast some light, it is not enough to resolve the problem with which we are faced. At best, they are inconclusive. The most avid proponents of the post-War Amendments undoubtedly intended them to remove all legal distinctions among "all persons born or naturalized in the United States." Their opponents, just as certainly, were antagonistic to both the letter and the spirit of the Amendments and wished them to have the most limited effect. What others in Congress and the state legislatures had in mind cannot be determined with any degree of certainty.

An additional reason for the inconclusive nature of the Amendment's history, with respect to segregated schools, is the status of public education at that time.[a] In the South, the movement toward free common schools, supported by general taxation, had not yet taken hold. Education of white children was largely in the hands of private groups. Education of Negroes was almost nonexistent, and practically all of the race were illiterate. In fact, any education of Negroes was forbidden by law in some states. Today, in contrast, many Negroes have achieved outstanding success in the arts and sciences as well as in the business and professional world. It is true that public school education at the time of the Amendment had advanced further in the North, but the effect of the Amendment on Northern States was generally ignored in the congressional debates. Even in the North, the conditions of public education did

a. . . . Although the demand for free public schools followed substantially the same pattern in both the North and the South, the development in the South did not begin to gain momentum until about 1850, some twenty years after that in the North. . . . In the country as a whole, but particularly in the South, the War virtually stopped all progress in public education. The low status of Negro education in all sections of the country, both before and immediately after the War, is described in Beale, A History of Freedom of Teaching in American Schools (1941). . . . Compulsory school attendance laws were not generally adopted until after the ratification of the Fourteenth Amendment, and it was not until 1918 that such laws were in force in all the states. . . .

not approximate those existing today. The curriculum was usually rudimentary; ungraded schools were common in rural areas; the school term was but three months a year in many states; and compulsory school attendance was virtually unknown. As a consequence, it is not surprising that there should be so little in the history of the Fourteenth Amendment relating to its intended effect on public education.

In the first cases in this Court construing the Fourteenth Amendment, decided shortly after its adoption, the Court interpreted it as proscribing all state-imposed discriminations against the Negro race.[b] The doctrine of "separate but equal" did not make its appearance in this Court until 1896 in the case of Plessy v. Ferguson, supra, involving not education but transportation.[c] American courts have since labored with the doctrine for over half a century. In this Court, there have been six cases involving the "separate but equal" doctrine in the field of public education. In Cumming v. County Board of Education, 175 U.S. 528, and Gong Lum v. Rice, 275 U.S. 78, the validity of the doctrine itself was not challenged.[d] In more recent cases, all on the graduate school level, inequality was found in that specific benefits enjoyed by white students were denied to Negro students of the same educational qualifications. Missouri ex rel. Gaines v. Canada, 305 U.S. 337; Sipuel v. Oklahoma, 332 U.S. 631; Sweatt v. Painter, 339 U.S. 629; McLaurin v. Oklahoma State Regents, 339 U.S. 637. In none of these cases was it necessary to re-examine the doctrine to grant relief to the Negro plaintiff. And in Sweatt v. Painter, supra, the Court expressly reserved decision on the question whether Plessy v. Ferguson should be held inapplicable to public education.

In the instant cases, that question is directly presented. Here, unlike Sweatt v. Painter, there are findings below that the Negro and white schools involved have been equalized, or are being equalized, with respect to buildings, curricula, qualifications and salaries of teachers, and other "tangible" factors. Our decision, therefore, cannot turn on merely a comparison of these tangible factors in the Negro and white schools involved in each of the cases. We must look instead to the effect of segregation itself on public education.

In approaching this problem, we cannot turn the clock back to 1868 when the Amendment was adopted, or even to 1896 when Plessy v. Ferguson was written. We must consider public education in the light of its full development and its present place in American life throughout the Nation. Only in this way can it be determined if segregation in public schools deprives these plaintiffs of the equal protection of the laws.

Today, education is perhaps the most important function of state and local governments. Compulsory school attendance laws and the great expenditures for

b. Slaughter-House Cases, 16 Wall. 36, 67-72 (1873); Strauder v. West Virginia, 100 U.S. 303, 307-08 (1880). . . .

c. The doctrine apparently originated in Roberts v. City of Boston, 59 Mass. 198, 206 (1850), upholding school segregation against attack as being violative of a state constitutional guarantee of equality. Segregation in Boston public schools was eliminated in 1855. Mass. Acts 1855, c. 256. But elsewhere in the North segregation in public education has persisted in some communities until recent years. It is apparent that such segregation has long been a nationwide problem, not merely one of sectional concern.

d. In the *Cumming* case, Negro taxpayers sought an injunction requiring the defendant school board to discontinue the operation of a high school for white children until the board resumed operation of a high school for Negro children. Similarly, in the *Gong Lum* case, the plaintiff, a child of Chinese descent contended only that state authorities had misapplied the doctrine by classifying him with Negro children and requiring him to attend a Negro school.

education both demonstrate our recognition of the importance of education to our democratic society. It is required in the performance of our most basic public responsibilities, even service in the armed forces. It is the very foundation of good citizenship. Today it is a principal instrument in awakening the child to cultural values, in preparing him for later professional training, and in helping him to adjust normally to his environment. In these days, it is doubtful that any child may reasonably be expected to succeed in life if he is denied the opportunity of an education. Such an opportunity, where the state has undertaken to provide it, is a right which must be made available to all on equal terms.

We come then to the question presented: Does segregation of children in public schools solely on the basis of race, even though the physical facilities and other "tangible" factors may be equal, deprive the children of the minority group of equal educational opportunities? We believe that it does.

In Sweatt v. Painter, supra, in finding that a segregated law school for Negroes could not provide them equal educational opportunities, this Court relied in large part on "those qualities which are incapable of objective measurement but which make for greatness in a law school." In McLaurin v. Oklahoma State Regents, supra, the Court, in requiring that a Negro admitted to a white graduate school be treated like all other students, again resorted to intangible considerations: ". . . his ability to study, to engage in discussions and exchange views with other students, and, in general, to learn his profession." Such considerations apply with added force to children in grade and high schools. To separate them from others of similar age and qualifications solely because of their race generates a feeling of inferiority as to their status in the community that may affect their hearts and minds in a way unlikely ever to be undone. The effect of this separation on their educational opportunities was well stated by a finding in the Kansas case by a court which nevertheless felt compelled to rule against the Negro plaintiffs:

> Segregation of white and colored children in public schools has a detrimental effect upon the colored children. The impact is greater when it has the sanction of the law; for the policy of separating the races is usually interpreted as denoting the inferiority of the negro group. A sense of inferiority affects the motivation of a child to learn. Segregation with the sanction of law, therefore, has a tendency to [retard] the educational and mental development of negro children and to deprive them of some of the benefits they would receive in a racial[ly] integrated school system.[e]

Whatever may have been the extent of psychological knowledge at the time of Plessy v. Ferguson, this finding is amply supported by modern authority.[f] Any language in Plessy v. Ferguson contrary to this finding is rejected.

---

e. A similar finding was made in the Delaware case: "I conclude from the testimony that in our Delaware society, State-imposed segregation in education itself results in the Negro children, as a class, receiving educational opportunities which are substantially inferior to those available to white children otherwise similarly situated."

f. K.B. Clark, Effect of Prejudice and Discrimination on Personality Development (Midcentury White House Conference on Children and Youth, 1950); Witmer and Kotinsky, Personality in the Making (1952), c. VI; Deutscher and Chein, The Psychological Effects of Enforced Segregation: A Survey of Social Science Opinion, 26 J. Psychol. 259 (1948): Chein, What Are the Psychological Effects of Segregation Under Conditions of Equal Facilities?, 3 Int. J. Opinion and Attitude Res. 299 (1949); Brameld, Educational Costs, in Discrimination and National Welfare (MacIver, ed., 1949), 44-48; Frazier, The Negro in the United States (1949), 674-81. And see generally Myrdal, An American Dilemma (1944).

We conclude that in the field of public education the doctrine of "separate but equal" has no place. Separate educational facilities are inherently unequal. Therefore, we hold that the plaintiffs and others similarly situated for whom the actions have been brought are, by reason of the segregation complained of, deprived of the equal protection of the laws guaranteed by the Fourteenth Amendment. This disposition makes unnecessary any discussion whether such segregation also violates the Due Process Clause of the Fourteenth Amendment.

Because these are class actions, because of the wide applicability of this decision, and because of the great variety of local conditions, the formulation of decrees in these cases presents problems of considerable complexity. On reargument, the consideration of appropriate relief was necessarily subordinated to the primary question — the constitutionality of segregation in public education. We have now announced that such segregation is a denial of the equal protection of the laws. In order that we may have the full assistance of the parties in formulating decrees, the cases will be restored to the docket, and the parties are requested to present further argument on Questions 4 and 5 previously propounded by the Court for the reargument this Term.[g] The Attorney General of the United States is again invited to participate. The Attorneys General of the states requiring or permitting segregation in public education will also be permitted to appear as amici curiae upon request to do so by September 15, 1954, and submission of briefs by October 1, 1954.

It is so ordered.

Note: A "Dissent" From Brown

Brown v. Board of Education has no dissenting opinion. However, in 1956, virtually all of the Senators and Congressmen in the deep South signed the "Southern Manifesto" arguing that the Court's decision was not only incorrect but an abuse of power:

DECLARATION OF CONSTITUTIONAL PRINCIPLES[15]
[The Southern Manifesto]

. . . We regard the decisions of the Supreme Court in the school cases as a clear abuse of judicial power. It climaxes a trend in the Federal Judiciary undertaking to legislate, in derogation of the authority of Congress, and to encroach upon the reserved rights of the States and the people.

---

g. "4. Assuming it is decided that segregation in public schools violates the Fourteenth Amendment (a) would a decree necessarily follow providing that, within the limits set by normal geographic school districting, Negro children should forthwith be admitted to schools of their choice, or (b) may this Court, in the exercise of its equity powers, permit an effective gradual adjustment to be brought about from existing segregated systems to a system not based on color distinctions?

"5. On the assumption on which questions 4 (a) and (b) are based, and assuming further that this Court will exercise its equity powers to the end described in question 4 (b), (a) should this Court formulate detailed decrees in these cases; (b) if so, what specific issues should the decrees reach; (c) should this Court appoint a special master to hear evidence with a view to recommending specific terms for such decrees; (d) should this Court remand to the courts of first instance with directions to frame decrees in these cases, and if so what general directions should the decrees of this Court include and what procedures should the courts of first instance follow in arriving at the specific terms of more detailed decrees?"

15. Excerpted from 102 Cong. Rec. H3948, 4004 (Mar. 12, 1956).

The original Constitution does not mention education. Neither does the 14th Amendment nor any other amendment. The debates preceding the submission of the 14th Amendment clearly show that there was no intent that it should affect the system of education maintained by the States.

The very Congress which proposed the amendment subsequently provided for segregated schools in the District of Columbia.

When the amendment was adopted in 1868, there were 37 States of the Union. . . . Every one of the 26 States that had any substantial racial differences among its people, either approved the operation of segregated schools already in existence or subsequently established such schools by action of the same law-making body which considered the 14th Amendment.

[T]he doctrine of separate but equal schools . . . began in the North, not in the South, and it was followed not only in Massachusetts, but in Connecticut, New York, Illinois, Indiana, Michigan, Minnesota, New Jersey, Ohio, Pennsylvania and other northern states. . . .

Plessy v. Ferguson . . . has been followed in many other cases. [T]he Supreme Court . . . unanimously declared in 1927 in Lum v. Rice that the "separate but equal" principle is "within the discretion of the State in regulating its public schools and does not conflict with the 14th Amendment."

This interpretation, restated time and again, became a part of the life of the people of many of the States and confirmed their habits, traditions, and way of life. It is founded on elemental humanity and commonsense, for parents should not be deprived by Government of the right to direct the lives and education of their own children.

Though there has been no constitutional amendment or act of Congress changing this established legal principle almost a century old, the Supreme Court of the United States, with no legal basis for such action, undertook to exercise their naked judicial power and substituted their personal political and social ideas for the established law of the land.

This unwarranted exercise of power by the Court, contrary to the Constitution, is creating chaos and confusion in the States principally affected. It is destroying the amicable relations between the white and Negro races that have been created through 90 years of patient effort by the good people of both races. It has planted hatred and suspicion where there has been heretofore friendship and understanding.

Without regard to the consent of the governed, outside mediators are threatening immediate and revolutionary changes in our public schools systems. If done, this is certain to destroy the system of public education in some of the States. . . .

We decry the Supreme Court's encroachment on the rights reserved to the States and to the people, contrary to established law, and to the Constitution.

We commend the motives of those States which have declared the intention to resist forced integration by any lawful means.

We appeal to the States and people who are not directly affected by these decisions to consider the constitutional principles involved against the time when they too, on issues vital to them may be the victims of judicial encroachment.

Even though we constitute a minority in the present Congress, we have full faith that a majority of the American people believe in the dual system of government which has enabled us to achieve our greatness and will in time demand that the reserved rights of the States and of the people be made secure against judicial usurpation.

We pledge ourselves to use all lawful means to bring about a reversal of this decision which is contrary to the Constitution and to prevent the use of force in its implementation.

In this trying period, as we all seek to right this wrong, we appeal to our people not to be provoked by the agitators and troublemakers invading our States and to scrupulously refrain from disorder and lawless acts.

Discussion

1. The Southern Manifesto offers a competing interpretation of the Constitution. It argues for (1) judicial restraint, (2) adherence to long existing precedents, both judicial and nonjudicial, (3) fidelity to the original understanding, and (4) respect for structural principles of federalism. All four of these factors, it claims, point in the same direction — upholding the right of individual states to decide for themselves whether or not to segregate their public schools. Hence it concludes that the Court had abandoned sound rule of law principles and substituted its own political judgment, and that its decision was illegitimate. What, precisely, is wrong with this argument?

2. The Southern Manifesto is a prime example of constitutional interpretation outside the courts, in this case by national political leaders who acted in concert with a growing countermobilization that sought to resist an unpopular Supreme Court decision.[16] Compare this example of constitutional interpretation by nonjudicial actors with others you have studied so far. Are all such examples of popular constitutionalism equally legitimate? If some are less legitimate than others, is there a way of demarcating them independent of "winner's history" or one's own sense of whether they comport with the best interpretation of the Constitution?

3. The Southern Manifesto is not the only possible way one might dissent from the decision in *Brown*. Derrick Bell argues that the Court might have reaffirmed *Plessy* but enforced it strictly to require genuine equality between black and white schools. Bell's reinterpretation of *Plessy* would also have required the courts to order that states commit sufficient resources to make all schools measure up to national norms of educational quality. Finally, he would have insisted that black parents have representation on school boards that affected their children's education. Derrick Bell, "Bell, J., Dissenting" in What Brown v. Board of Education Should Have Said 185-200 (Jack M. Balkin ed., 2001). Would such a remedy have been possible in 1954? Would the results have been better than what actually happened in the 50 years following *Brown*?

C.   *Brown* and Constitutional Interpretation

How did the Supreme Court justify its conclusion that the Equal Protection Clause of the Fourteenth Amendment does not allow segregation in public schools? Which of the interpretive modalities of constitutional text, structure, history, precedent, consequences, and narrative ethos does the Court emphasize most? Which does it deemphasize or leave out?

16. See generally, George Lewis, The White South and the Red Menace: Segregationists, Anticommunism and Massive Resistance, 1945-1965 (2004); Clive Webb, ed. Massive Resistance: Southern Opposition to the Second Reconstruction (2005).

In its order for reargument in *Brown* the Supreme Court asked the parties to address what the framers and ratifiers of the Fourteenth Amendment "contemplated or did not contemplate, understood or did not understand" about the Fourteenth Amendment's application to school segregation. The Court ultimately concluded that the historical record was inadequate to determine the proper interpretation of the Constitution. Why is the history inadequate to answer the question?

One reason might be that the understandings of the framers and ratifiers on this question are simply too sparse or "inconclusive," which would suggest that if the legislative history or the general understandings of the time had been less ambiguous, the Court would have been bound by them.

A second reason is that changed circumstances render the history inadequate to tell us how the relevant constitutional text and constitutional principles should apply. The legislative history occurred against the backdrop of a world in which the movement for general public education had not yet taken hold, and in which most blacks were illiterate; by 1954, public elementary and secondary education was compulsory for blacks and whites alike, and providing education was "perhaps the most important function of state and local governments." Hence "we cannot turn the clock back to 1868, when the Amendment was adopted, or even to 1896, when Plessy v. Ferguson was written." What assumptions about constitutional interpretation does this argument assume? What is illegitimate about "turn[ing] the clock back"? Are we concerned here only with a change in factual circumstances or also changes in social meanings and changes in values between 1868 and 1954? What theory of interpretation allows courts to take those three types of change into account?

A third reason that the history might be inconclusive is that intervening judicial precedents like Sweatt v. Painter and McLaurin v. Oklahoma State Regents have undermined the application of *Plessy* in the context of public education; these precedents have articulated the relevant constitutional text and constitutional principles so that they now require desegregation. What theory of constitutional interpretation does this argument presuppose? (Note that the Court does not advert to nonjudicial precedents like Truman's order desegregating the Armed Forces in 1948. Should it have?) What allows judicial precedents to reshape the application of the Constitution in ways at variance with original understandings?

In any case, to decide how history matters or should matter to the decision in *Brown*, one must first consider what the relevant historical understandings were. Recall Chapter 4's discussion of the history of the ratification of the Fourteenth Amendment. A key question is whether the framers (or ratifiers) of that Amendment believed that the language of "privileges or immunities" of citizenship, or "equal protection of the laws" made state segregation in public schools unconstitutional. Another way of asking the question is whether the framers and ratifiers believed that segregation in public schooling violated the principle of civil equality.

ALEXANDER BICKEL, THE ORIGINAL UNDERSTANDING AND THE SEGREGATION DECISION
69 Harv. L. Rev. 1, 56-63 (1955)

The first approach made by the 39th Congress toward dealing with racial discrimination turned on the "civil rights" formula [i.e., the inclusion of the words "civil rights or immunities," which appeared both in the Freedman's Bureau Bill and in the Civil Rights Bill which eventually became the Civil Rights Act of 1866]. The Senate Moderates, led by Trumbull and Fessenden, who sponsored this formula, assigned a limited and well-defined meaning to it. In their view it covered the right to contract, sue, give evidence in court, and inherit, hold, and dispose of real and personal property; also a right to equal protection in the literal sense of benefiting equally from laws for the security of person and property, including presumably laws permitting ownership of firearms, and to equality in the penalties and burdens provided by law. [T]he Moderates wished also to protect rights of free movement, and a right to engage in occupations of one's choice. . . . Similarly, the Moderates often argued that one of the imperative needs of the time was to educate, to "elevate," to "Christianize" the Negro; indeed, this was almost universally held doctrine, from which even Conservatives like Cowan and Democrats like Rogers did not dissent. Hence one may surmise that Moderates believed that they were guaranteeing a right to equal benefits from state educational systems supported by general tax funds. But there is no evidence whatsoever showing that for its sponsors the civil rights formula had anything to do with unsegregated public schools; Wilson, its sponsor in the House, specifically disclaimed any such notion. Similarly, it is plain that the Moderates did not intend to confer any right of intermarriage, the right to sit on juries, or the right to vote. . . .

The Joint Committee [on Reconstruction] elected not to use the civil rights formula [in its versions of the Fourteenth Amendment] and offered instead, in the Bingham amendment, equal protection "in the rights of life, liberty and property," plus a privileges and immunities clause. Given the evils represented by the Black Codes, which were foremost in the minds of all men, it must be supposed that this language was deemed to protect all the rights specifically enumerated in the Civil Rights Bill. But it is difficult to interpret the deliberate choice against using the term "civil rights" [in the new amendment] as anything but a rejection of what were deemed its wider implications. . . .

A substantial number of Republicans were troubled by . . . [the possible] unconstitutionality [of the Civil Rights Bill]. . . . The concession these Republicans wrung from the leadership was the elimination of the civil rights formula and thus the possibility of wider "latitudinarian" construction. The Moderate position that the bill dealt only with a distinct and limited set of rights was conclusively validated. . . .

In drafting section 1 [of the Fourteenth Amendment, the Joint Committee on Reconstruction] vacillated between the civil rights formula and language proposed by Bingham, finally adopting the latter. . . . [S]ection 1 became the subject of a stock generalization; it was dismissed as embodying and, in one sense for the Republicans, in another for the Democrats and Conservatives, "constitutionalizing" the Civil Rights Act [of 1866].

The obvious conclusion to which the evidence . . . easily leads is that section 1 of the fourteenth amendment, like section 1 of the Civil Rights Act of 1866, carried out the relatively narrow objectives of the Moderates, and hence, as originally understood, was meant to apply neither to jury service, nor suffrage, nor antimiscegenation statutes, nor segregation. This conclusion is supported by the blunt expression of disappointment to which Thaddeus Stevens gave vent in the House.

If the fourteenth amendment were a statute, a court might very well hold, on the basis of what has been said so far, that it was foreclosed from applying it to segregation in public schools. The evidence of congressional purpose is as clear as such evidence is likely to be, and no language barrier stands in the way of construing the section in conformity with it. But we are dealing with a constitutional amendment, not a statute. The tradition of a broadly worded organic law not frequently or lightly amended was well-established by 1866, and, despite the somewhat revolutionary fervor with which the Radicals were pressing their changes, it cannot be assumed that they or anyone else expected or wished the future role of the Constitution in the scheme of American government to differ from the past. Should not the search for congressional purpose, therefore, properly be twofold? One inquiry should be directed at the congressional understanding of the immediate effect of the enactment on conditions then present. Another should aim to discover what if any thought was given to the long-range effect, under future circumstances, of provisions necessarily intended for permanence.

That the Court saw the need for two such inquiries with respect to the original understanding on segregation is clearly indicated by the questions it propounded at the 1952 Term. The Court asked first whether Congress and the state legislatures contemplated that the fourteenth amendment would abolish segregation in public schools. It next asked whether, assuming that the immediate abolition of segregation was not contemplated, the framers nevertheless understood that Congress acting under section 5, or the Court in the exercise of the judicial function would, in light of future conditions, have power to abolish segregation.

With this double aspect of the inquiry in mind, certain other features of the legislative history — not inconsistent with the conclusion earlier stated, but complementary to it — became significant. Thus, section 1 of the fourteenth amendment, on its face, deals not only with racial discrimination, but also with discrimination whether or not based on color. This cannot have been accidental, since the alternative considered by the Joint Committee, the civil rights formula, did apply only to racial discrimination. Everyone's immediate preoccupation in the 39th Congress — insofar as it did not go to partisan questions — was, of course, with hardships being visited on the colored race. Yet the fact that the proposed constitutional amendment was couched in more general terms could not have escaped those who voted for it. . . .

[Moreover,] the Bingham amendment['s language about] equal protection in the rights of life, liberty, and property, a phrase which so aptly evoked the evils uppermost in men's minds at the time, [was changed in the final version to] equal protection of the laws, a clause which is plainly capable of being applied to all subjects of state legislation. Could the comparison have failed to leave the implication that the new phrase, while it did not necessarily, and certainly not expressly, carry greater coverage than the old, was nevertheless roomier, more receptive to "latitudinarian" construction? . . .

Finally, it is noteworthy that the shorthand argument characterizing the fourteenth amendment as the constitutional embodiment of the Civil Rights Act was often accompanied on the Republican side by generalities about the self-evident demands of justice and the natural rights of man. This was true both in Congress and in the course of the election which followed. To all this should be added the fact that while the Joint Committee's rejection of the civil rights formula is quite manifest, there is implicit also in its choice of language a rejection — presumably as inappropriate in a constitutional provision — of such a specific and exclusive enumeration of rights as appeared in section 1 of the Civil Rights Act.

. . . It remains true that an explicit provision going further than the Civil Rights Act could not have been carried in the 39th Congress; also that a plenary grant of legislative power such as the Bingham amendment would not have mustered the necessary majority. But may it not be that the Moderates and the Radicals reached a compromise permitting them to go to the country with language which they could, where necessary, defend against damaging alarms raised by the opposition, but which at the same time was sufficiently elastic to permit reasonable future advances? . . . [T]he civil rights formula . . . could not serve the purpose of such a compromise. It had been under heavy attack at this session, and among those who had expressed fears concerning its reach were Republicans who would have to go forth and stand on the platform of the fourteenth amendment. Bingham, of course, was one of these men, and he could not be required to go on the hustings and risk being made to eat his own words. If the party was to unite behind a compromise which consisted neither of an exclusive listing of a limited series of rights, nor of a formulation dangerously vulnerable to attacks pandering to the prejudices of the people, new language had to be found. Bingham himself supplied it. It had both sweep and the appearance of a careful enumeration of rights, and it had a ring to echo in the national memory of libertarian beginnings. To put it another way, the Moderates . . . consolidated the victory they had achieved in the Civil Rights Act debate. They could go forth and honestly defend themselves against charges that on the day after ratification Negroes were going to become white men's "social equals," marry their daughters, vote in their elections, sit on their juries, and attend schools with their children.

The Radicals . . . obtained what early in the session had seemed a very uncertain price indeed: a firm alliance, under Radical leadership, with the Moderates in the struggle against the President, and thus a good, clear chance at increasing and prolonging their political power. In the future, the Radicals could, in one way or another, put through such further civil rights provisions as they thought the country would take, without being subject to the sort of effective constitutional objections which haunted them when they were forced to operate under the thirteenth amendment. . . .

Whatever other support this hypothesis may have, it has behind it the very authoritative voice of [the distinguished Radical Republican] Thaddeus Stevens, who held it, and twice gave notice of it in speaking on the fourteenth amendment. It was Stevens who dutifully defined section 1 . . . in . . . narrow terms . . . ; it fell short of his wishes. And it was Stevens, his hopes fulfilled, who [upon the enactment of the Fourteenth Amendment] powerfully and candidly emphasized the political opportunities which the amendment gained for the Radicals, and who looked to the future for better things "in further legislation, in enabling acts or other provisions." . . . [T]his hypothesis cannot be disparaged as putting forth an undisclosed, conspiratorial purpose. . . . Indeed, no specific purpose going beyond the coverage of the Civil Rights Act is suggested; rather an awareness on the part of these framers that it was *a constitution* they were writing, which led to a choice of language capable of growth.

It is such a reading as this of the original understanding, in response to the second of the questions propounded by the Court, that the Chief Justice must have had in mind when he termed the materials "inconclusive." For up to this point they tell a clear story and are anything but inconclusive. From this point on the word is apt, since the interpretation of the evidence just set out comes only to this, that the question of giving greater protection than was extended by the Civil Rights Act was deferred, was left open, to be decided another day under a constitutional provision with more scope than the unserviceable thirteenth amendment.

Note: A Dissenting Opinion on the Original Understanding

In his article Originalism and the Desegregation Decisions, 81 Va. L. Rev. 947 (1995), Michael McConnell challenges Bickel's conclusion that the Fourteenth Amendment, "as originally understood, was [not] meant to apply . . . to . . . school segregation."[17] After reexamining the documentary evidence, McConnell concludes that "[w]hether segregation of schools, transportation, or places of public accommodation represented an inequality with respect to [the civil rights protected by the Amendment] was not debated or resolved in 1866." However, he maintains, "the issue arose soon *after* ratification and was debated at length. Those *later debates,* rather than the debates of 1866, hold the real answer to the segregation question." Id. at 962 (emphases added). McConnell elaborates on the significance of the later debates:

> While the Thirty-ninth Congress concentrated on passing the Amendment — a context in which avoidance or obfuscation of controversial issues is often the best strategy — later Congresses were forced to determine what it meant, in the context of the most difficult questions of the day. The actions taken by Congress from 1868 through 1875 to enforce the Fourteenth Amendment and the congressional deliberations over those measures thus present the best available evidence of the original understanding of the meaning of the Amendment as it bears on the issue of school segregation. Although this evidence might be inferior in principle to information directly bearing on the opinions and expectations of the framers and ratifiers during deliberations over the Amendment itself, there is no significant body of evidence concerning the latter.

After a detailed analysis of the post-ratification debates, McConnell offers his final conclusion:

> Between 1870 and 1875, both houses of Congress voted repeatedly, by large margins, in favor of legislation premised on the theory that de jure segregation of public schools is unconstitutional. The desegregation bills never became law because, for procedural reasons, a two-thirds majority of the House of Representatives was required for final passage. Even so, the Reconstruction Congress passed legislation prohibiting segregation of inns, theaters, railroads, and other common carriers, and rejected legislation that would have countenanced segregated education on a separate-but-equal basis.[18]

McConnell's methodological emphasis on the intentions of the framers as expressed in postratification debates — especially those that occurred between 1870 and 1875 — is noteworthy. According to McConnell, the beliefs of the congressmen he analyzes, many of whom were in the Congress that proposed the Amendment in 1866, are significant in much the same way that the views of the First Congress have been accorded special authority in the interpretation of the 1787 Constitution. It is simply not the case, he maintains, that we have derived notions of original understanding *only* from what was said *before* constitutional enactments; we have also looked at statements that important individuals, particularly supporters, have made in the years immediately following a new constitutional enactment.

17. Alexander M. Bickel, The Original Understanding and the Segregation Decision, 69 Harv. L. Rev. 1, 58 (1955).

18. McConnell, Originalism and the Desegregation Decisions, 81 Va. L. Rev. 947, 1140 (1995).

Discussion

1. Before an Article V amendment is ratified, supporters are likely to argue that its effects will be relatively modest to gain as much support as possible. Thus, before ratification, Bickel explains, moderates received assurances that the new amendment would not require that "Negroes were going to become white men's 'social equals,' marry their daughters, vote in their elections, sit on their juries, and attend schools with their children." After the amendment is ratified, however, its supporters are free to argue that its scope is more ambitious, because it is already law. McConnell points to evidence of these broader interpretations. Given the reasons why original understandings should guide interpretation, which set of representations of the original understanding should be controlling? Note, moreover, that by 1870, the Fifteenth Amendment had enfranchised black voters, creating a potentially important new constituency for Republicans, and so Congressional Republicans had additional incentives to interpret the Fourteenth Amendment broadly. If we are trying to determine the understandings of the persons who framed the Amendment before its ratification, to what extent should any of this matter?

2. Note that McConnell's argument focuses on the intentions of congressmen rather than the intentions of the ratifiers of the Fourteenth Amendment, or general public opinion or public understandings about the constitutionality of school segregation. He concedes that

> school desegregation was deeply unpopular among whites, in both North and South, and school segregation was very commonly practiced. In ordinary times, this might be dispositive, or nearly so. Constitutional amendments generally reflect, rather than contradict, popular opinion. But these were not ordinary times. This was a time when a political minority, armed with the prestige of victory in the Civil War and with military control over the political apparatus of the rebel states, imposed constitutional change on the Nation as the price of reunion, with little regard for popular opinion.[19]

McConnell points out that this result should hardly be objectionable, given that the Fifteenth Amendment was passed under similar circumstances:

> [T]he evidence of popular opinion and actual practice on this issue is virtually the same as that regarding school desegregation: enfranchisement of black citizens was wildly unpopular, had been rejected overwhelmingly by popular referenda in numerous states, was repudiated by the Republican platform in 1868, and had been adopted in actual practice only by a small handful of states. . . . It should be obvious that there were great disjunctions between legal enactments, popular opinion, and actual practice at this time. I do not pretend to have a theory explaining why the political system diverged so sharply from popular opinion, other than to suspect that in the aftermath of a Civil War, the political victors considered entrenchment of their principles more important than pleasing constituents. Whatever the explanation, constitutional interpreters would make a serious mistake if they assumed that popular opinion and actual practice during this period were an accurate indication of legal meaning. As we know from examples of unambiguous provisions of law, like the Fifteenth Amendment, this was not always the case. That is why I have focused here on the legal dimension of the debate over school segregation, the actual arguments made by opponents and proponents regarding the

---

19. Michael McConnell, The Originalist Justification for *Brown:* A Reply to Professor Klarman, 81 Va. L. Rev. 1937, 1940 (1995).

meaning of the new amendment. That, it seems to me, is a more reliable guide to legal meaning than either popular opinion or actual practice.[20]

Given the requirements of Article V, does McConnell adequately justify why the intentions of the ratifiers and the views of the general populace should be ignored? Does the analogy to the Fifteenth Amendment succeed? After all, if the Fifteenth Amendment is "unambiguous," the Fourteenth is surely not. Does the fact that Congress effectively forced the Fourteenth Amendment on unwilling states prove that only its meaning should apply, or does it prove rather that the states gave it a much less generous interpretation?

3. Even if McConnell is correct that only the views of Congress count, under Article V, two-thirds of each House must vote for a proposed amendment, and the school desegregation bill never actually passed Congress. McConnell notes that "[o]pposition to the school desegregation bill commanded somewhat more than one third of the members of each house of Congress" and because of procedural rules this effectively prevented passage of the bill.[21] However, McConnell argues, "this overstates the degree of support for the interpretation of the Fourteenth Amendment that was advocated by the segregationists, because '[s]ome part — unquantifiable but substantial — of the opposition to the schools bill was based on admittedly nonconstitutional arguments, which should not be taken into consideration in assessing the dominant understanding of the constitutional provision.'[22] Such "nonconstitutional arguments" might presumably include prudential considerations about whom the bill would most likely benefit, which party might stand to benefit most from passage or defeat, or even opposition based on outright racial prejudice. Why do these arguments play no role in determining the meaning of the Amendment, especially if they could have been offered against passage of the Amendment in the first place?

4. Even if these objections are placed to one side, does McConnell's argument successfully avoid the basic embarrassment of originalism in racial questions — that the original understanding behind the Fourteenth Amendment was consistent with racist attitudes toward blacks and permitted many different forms of racial inequality? Consider Michael Klarman's rejoinder:

> Even McConnell's originalist defense of *Brown* does not enable him to justify Court decisions such as Strauder v. West Virginia and Loving v. Virginia [which struck down laws criminalizing interracial marriage]. McConnell accepts the conventional view that the Framers of the Fourteenth Amendment distinguished civil from political and social rights, and barred racial discrimination only with regard to the former. Jury service, like voting, was plainly deemed at the time to constitute a political right and interracial marriage a social one. Must an originalist like McConnell thus believe that the Constitution even today permits the state to bar racial minorities from jury service and to forbid interracial marriage? Likewise, McConnell's originalist interpretation of the Fourteenth Amendment would apparently permit the state to draw racial distinctions in all areas of life not qualifying as civil rights — e.g., access to public golf courses, swimming pools, etc. Thus even if McConnell has saved *Brown* for originalists, much else of consequence has eluded his grasp.[23]

20. Id. at 1940-1941.
21. Id. at 1947-1948.
22. Id. at 1948.
23. Michael Klarman, *Brown*, Originalism, and Constitutional Theory: A Response to Professor McConnell, 81 Va. L. Rev. 1881, 1919-1920 (1995).

Note: Originalism in Antidiscrimination Law

1.   Original Intentions Versus Original Understanding

Judge Robert H. Bork argues that "[t]he interpretation of the Constitution according to the original understanding . . . is the only method that can preserve the Constitution, the separation of powers, and the liberties of the people."[24] Like many originalists, Bork argues that originalism should focus properly not on the *original intentions* of the adopters but on the *original understanding* of the words the adopters chose: "Though I have written of the understanding of the ratifiers of the Constitution, since they enacted it and made it law, that is actually a shorthand formulation, because what the ratifiers understood themselves to be enacting must be taken to be what the public of that time would have understood the words to mean. It is important to be clear about this. The search is not for a subjective intention. If someone found a letter from George Washington to Martha telling her that what he meant by the power to lay taxes was not what other people meant, that would not change our reading of the Constitution in the slightest. Nor would the subjective intentions of all the members of a ratifying convention alter anything. When lawmakers use words, the law that results is what those words ordinarily mean."[25] For different formulations of the idea, see Randy Barnett, Restoring the Lost Constitution: The Presumption of Liberty (2004); Keith Whittington, Constitutional Interpretation: Textual Meaning, Original Intent, and Judicial Review (1999); Antonin Scalia, et al., A Matter of Interpretation: Federal Courts and the Law (Amy Gutman ed., 1997).[26]

Compare this focus on the original public understanding of the constitutional text with McConnell's approach, which focuses on the original intentions of the framers; McConnell seeks to determine whether the persons who voted for the Fourteenth Amendment intended the Amendment to prohibit school desegregation.

Does the move to original understanding improve the case for *Brown?* Recall Congress's specific rejection of colorblindness language and the civil rights formula, and its use of the words "privileges or immunities" and "equal protection of the laws," terms that were chosen to convey guarantees of civil equality. Note also the language of §2 of the Fourteenth Amendment, which contemplates that blacks might constitutionally be denied the right to vote, and finally, the text of the Fifteenth Amendment, which would have been superfluous if the Fourteenth Amendment prohibited all classifications based on race.

During the hearings following Bork's (ultimately unsuccessful) nomination to the Supreme Court by President Ronald Reagan, Pennsylvania Senator Arlen

---

24. Bork, The Tempting of America: The Political Seduction of the Law 159 (1989).

25. Id. at 144. See also Antonin Scalia, A Matter of Interpretation: Federal Courts and the Law 17 (Amy Gutman ed., 1997) ("we look for a sort of 'objectified' intent — the intent that a reasonable person would gather from the text of the law, placed alongside the remainder of the corpus juris. . . . Government by unexpressed intent is . . . tyrannical. It is the law that governs, not the intent of the lawgiver.").

26. In The Original Understanding of Original Intent, 98 Harv. L. Rev. 885 (1985), Professor H. Jefferson Powell pointed out that the 1787 Framers of the Constitution almost certainly did not view the Constitution as embodying their specific "intentions." Although judicial decisions of the time sometimes referred to "intent," this had little or nothing to do with "the subjective purposes of the author." Rather, "The late eighteenth century common lawyer conceived an instrument's 'intent' — and therefore its meaning — not as what the drafters meant by their words but rather as what judges, employing the 'artificial reason and judgment of law,' understood 'the reasonable and legal meaning' of those words to be."

Specter asked Judge Bork about his support for *Brown,* in view of its apparent deviation from the original understanding of the framers of the Fourteenth Amendment. Bork responded:[27]

> [P]assing [some] historical evidence, which I think casts some doubt on the flat assumption that the 14th Amendment really meant separate but equal, let me say this. [The framers] wrote a clause that does not say anything about separation. They wrote a clause that says "equal protection of the laws." I think it may well be true . . . that they had an assumption . . . that equality could be achieved with separation. Over the years it became clear that that assumption would not be borne out in reality ever. Separation would never produce equality.
>
> I think when the background assumption proved false, it was entirely proper for the court to say "we will carry out the rule they wrote" and if they would have been a little surprised that it worked out this way, that is too bad. That is the rule they wrote and they assumed something that is not true.
>
> And in that way I do not think any damage is done — you can even look at it more severely. You could say suppose they had written a clause that said "we want equality and that can be achieved by separation and we want that too." By 1954 it was perfectly apparent that you could not have both equality and separation. Now the court has to violate one aspect or the other of that clause, as I have framed it hypothetically. It seems to me that the way the actual amendment was written, it was natural to choose the equality segment, and the court did so. I think it was proper constitutional law, and I think we are all better off for it.

Note that Judge Bork's hypothetical amendment subordinates the goal of maintaining separation to that of equality, so that if they come into conflict, the former should give way. Suppose, however, that the hypothetical amendment read, "We want equality, but not if it requires mixing the races in schools or other such places." Given the actual history of the ratification of the Fourteenth Amendment, and the fact that in 1868 school segregation was widely unpopular throughout the country, which hypothetical version is more plausible as a historical reconstruction of what the words of the Fourteenth Amendment were understood to mean at the time they were adopted? Does our presumed preference for Bork's version rest on something more than the more attractive contemporary outcomes that it allows?

2. Bolling v. Sharpe and the Original Understanding of the Fifth Amendment

BOLLING v. SHARPE, 347 U.S. 497 (1954): [In Bolling v. Sharpe, decided the same day as *Brown,* the Supreme Court unanimously held the segregation of the public schools in the District of Columbia unconstitutional under the Fifth Amendment's Due Process Clause.]

WARREN, C.J.:

The Fifth Amendment, which is applicable in the District of Columbia, does not contain an equal protection clause as does the Fourteenth Amendment which applies only to the states. But the concepts of equal protection and due process, both stemming from our American ideal of fairness, are not mutually exclusive.

---

27. Nomination of Robert H. Bork to be Associate Justice of the Supreme Court of the United States, Hearings Before the Committee on the Judiciary, United States Senate, Part I, 284-286 (1987).

The "equal protection of the laws" is a more explicit safeguard of prohibited unfairness than "due process of law," and, therefore, we do not imply that the two are always interchangeable phrases. But, as this Court has recognized, discrimination may be so unjustifiable as to be violative of due process. . . .

Although the Court has not assumed to define "liberty" with any great precision, that term is not confined to mere freedom from bodily restraint. Liberty under law extends to the full range of conduct which the individual is free to pursue, and it cannot be restricted except for a proper governmental objective. Segregation in public education is not reasonably related to any proper governmental objective, and thus it imposes on Negro children of the District of Columbia a burden that constitutes an arbitrary deprivation of their liberty in violation of the Due Process Clause.

In view of our decision that the Constitution prohibits the states from maintaining racially segregated public schools, it would be unthinkable that the same Constitution would impose a lesser duty on the Federal Government. We hold that racial segregation in the public schools of the District of Columbia is a denial of the due process of law guaranteed by the Fifth Amendment to the Constitution.

Discussion

1. *Equality and due process.* Whatever your conclusions about *Brown*, is Bolling v. Sharpe consistent with the original understanding of the Fifth Amendment? There is no evidence that the 1787 Constitution or the 1791 Bill of Rights prohibited the federal government from making racial distinctions per se. Recall Taney's reliance in *Dred Scott* on the 1792 federal law directing that only "white male citizens" shall be enrolled in the militia. Ironically, those who cite this passage to attack Taney's overall argument in *Dred Scott* that blacks could not be citizens are presumably forced to concede that Congress believed itself empowered to distinguish between black and white citizens. See Stephen A. Siegel, The Federal Government's Power to Enact Color-Conscious Laws: An Originalist Inquiry 92 Nw. U. L. Rev. 477 (1998). Moreover, given that large numbers of blacks were held in slavery, it is doubtful that it was generally understood to forbid discrimination on the basis of race. In this light, consider the following excerpt from the Senate confirmation hearings of Judge Bork.[28]

Senator Specter: [H]ow can you justify Bolling v. Sharpe applying the due process clause to stopping segregation?

Judge Bork: I do not know that anybody ever has. I think that has been a case that has left people puzzled, and I have been told that some Justices on the Supreme Court felt very queasy afterwards about Bolling v. Sharpe. . . . I think that constitutionally that is a troublesome case.

Now it has been suggested that if the Supreme Court had struck down segregation in all of the States under the equal protection clause, Congress most certainly would have stopped segregation in the District of Columbia. And it would have been a national scandal if they had not.

Bolling v. Sharpe seems to have been propelled by a feeling that if we are going to do this to all of the States, we cannot let the federal government do it. I understand that feeling. . . . [But] if they apply the due process clause that way, . . . [y]ou

28. Id. at 286-287.

are off and running with substantive due process which I have long thought is a pernicious constitutional idea. . . .

Senator Specter: Final question: Do you accept Bolling v. Sharpe or not?

Judge Bork: I have not thought of a rationale for it. . . .

Senator Specter: You say you have or have not?

Judge Bork: Have not. . . . [I]f you say it is due process and we will do whatever is fair or good under due process, the court's powers are unlimited. That is the problem I have with that substantive due process.[29]

Consider also Professor Hans Linde's rejoinder to *Bolling:*[30]

[T]here is nothing difficult or even surprising in the thought that the "same Constitution," in the equal protection clause of 1868, might impose upon the states congressionally enforceable standards of equal treatment beyond that imposed upon the federal government by the Fifth Amendment in 1791 — at least nothing unthinkable if the premises for this thought are to be found in the text, the history, or the political structure of the Constitution. What defied thought in *Bolling* was the suggestion that a mere doctrinal distinction between the Fifth and Fourteenth Amendments could confine the scope of a revolution in the constitutional law of race relations. . . . But the unthinkable often bears thought.

2. *Reverse incorporation.* It is possible, nevertheless, to argue that by the time of the enactment of the Fourteenth Amendment some members of Congress believed that an equality principle bound the national government. The question is whether this belief retroactively affects the interpretation of the Fifth Amendment — in a sort of "reverse incorporation" argument[31] — or whether some constraint is actually hidden in or can be implied from the language of the Fourteenth Amendment. One might argue, for example, that among the privileges or immunities of citizens of the United States is the right to equal treatment by the federal government. For contrasting views on this point, compare Mark A. Graber, A Constitutional Conspiracy Unmasked, Why "No State" Does Not Mean "No State," 10 Const. Comm. 87 (1993) (finding an implied principle in the Privileges or Immunities Clause of Section 1), with Siegel, supra (rejecting this argument on the grounds that Congress specifically bound the Federal government in other parts of the Fourteenth Amendment as well as in the Thirteenth and Fifteenth Amendments). See also the Note in Part III, infra, on Affirmative Action and the Original Understanding.

3.   The Fourteenth Amendment and Voting Rights

Since the 1964 *Reapportionment Cases,* the Court has held that the Equal Protection Clause prohibits discrimination in matters affecting the franchise. In

29. See also Judge Bork's comments written following his failed nomination in Bork, The Tempting of America: The Political Seduction of the Law 83 (1990). (*Bolling* is "a substantive due process decision in the same vein as *Dred Scott* and *Lochner*.")

30. Hans Linde, Judges, Critics, and the Realist Tradition, 82 Yale L.J. 227, 233-234 (1972). Professor Linde goes on to suggest that Congress would have prohibited segregation in the District of Columbia within a few years.

31. On the notion of "reverse incorporation," see Akhil Reed Amar, The Bill of Rights: Creation and Reconstruction 281-283 (1998); Akhil Reed Amar, Constitutional Rights in a Federal System: Rethinking Incorporation and Reverse Incorporation, in Benchmarks: Great Constitutional Controversies in the Supreme Court 71 (Terry Eastland ed., 1995).

the first reapportionment decision, Reynolds v. Sims, 377 U.S. 533 (1964), Justice Harlan argued in dissent that this contradicted the original understanding of the Fourteenth Amendment. He noted that many proponents of the Amendment expressly stated that §1 did not interfere with states' regulation of the franchise, that §2 provides the Amendment's sole remedy for a state's denial of suffrage, and that it required the Fifteenth Amendment to prohibit abridging the right to vote "on account of race, color, or previous condition of servitude" and the Nineteenth Amendment to add sex to the prohibited classifications. Although the original understanding of the Amendment is arguably more complex, there is considerable scholarly support for Justice Harlan's reading of the history.[32] Imagine a Constitution that does not include the Fifteenth and Nineteenth Amendments but *does* include the Thirteenth and Fourteenth. Even if you agree with Justice Harlan's reading of the original history of the Fourteenth Amendment, does this necessarily prevent Congress or the courts from prohibiting racial or gender discrimination in the franchise under §§1 and 5 of the Fourteenth Amendment?

4.   Translating from Past to Present

In The Misconceived Quest for the Original Understanding, 60 B.U. L. Rev. 204 (1980), Paul Brest argues that a historian interpreter trying to recover the original understanding must engage in a complicated task of historical reconstruction: "she must often 'translate' the adopters' concepts and intentions into our time and apply them to situations that the adopters did not foresee."

> The interpreter's final task is to translate the adopters' intentions into the present in order to apply them to the question at issue. Consider, for example, whether the cruel and unusual punishment clause of the eighth amendment prohibits the imposition of the death penalty today. The adopters of the clause apparently never doubted that the death penalty was constitutional. But was death the same event for inhabitants of the American colonies in the late 18th century as it is two centuries later? Death was not only a much more routine and public phenomenon then, but the fear of death was more effectively contained within a system of religious belief. Twentieth-century Americans have a more secular cast of mind and seem less willing to accept this dreadful, forbidden, solitary, and shameful event. The interpreter must therefore determine whether we view the death penalty with the same attitude — whether of disgust or ambivalence — that the adopters viewed their core examples of cruel and unusual punishment.
>
> Intentionalist interpretation frequently requires translations of this sort. For example, to determine whether the commerce clause applies to transactions taking place wholly within the boundaries of one state, or whether the first amendment protects the mass media, the interpreter must abstract the adopters' concepts of federalism and freedom of expression in order to find their analogue in our contemporary society with its different technology, economy, and systems of communication. The alternative would be to limit the application of constitutional provisions to the particular events and transactions with which the adopters were

32. See Minor v. Happersett, 88 US 162 (1874) and accompanying discussion, pp. 265-270 supra.

familiar. Even if such an approach were coherent, however, it would produce results that even a strict intentionalist could likely reject: Congress could not regulate any item of commerce or any mode of transportation that did not exist in 1789; the first amendment would not protect any means of communication not then known.

However difficult the earlier stages of her work, the interpreter was only trying to understand the past. The act of translation required here is different in kind, for it involves the counterfactual and imaginary act of projecting the adopters' concepts and attitudes into a future they probably could not have envisioned. When the interpreter engages in this sort of projection, she is in a fantasy world more of her own than of the adopters' making.

Consider Mark V. Tushnet, Following the Rules Laid Down: A Critique of Interpretivism and Neutral Principles, 96 Harv. L. Rev. 781, 793, 800-802 (1983):

[H]istorical understanding requires an imaginative transposition of former world views into the categories of our own. [But] the project of imaginative transposition can be carried through in a number of different ways, with a number of different results, none of which is more "correct" than the others.

[For example, the framers of the Fourteenth Amendment may have seen public education as] a relatively new and peripheral social institution. . . . In contrast, they thought that freedom of contract was extremely important because it was the foundation of individual achievement, and they certainly wanted to outlaw racial discrimination with respect to this freedom. [Perhaps] public education as it exists today — a central institution for the achievement of individual goals — is in fact the functional equivalent not of public education in 1868, but of freedom of contract in 1868. [But] the need to identify functional equivalents over time necessarily imports significant indeterminacy — and therefore discretion — into the interpretivist account.

Lawrence Lessig, by contrast, argues that translation is not only possible, but required by fidelity to the original understanding. Lawrence Lessig, Fidelity in Translation, 71 Tex. L. Rev. 1165, 1263 (1993). A good translator must take into account changes in the presuppositions that shaped the adopters' thinking:

Translation moves in two steps. First, [the translator] becomes familiar with both the context of writing and the context of application. . . . Second, she seeks an equivalent in the application context to the original application in the authoring context. To identify those cases where a translation must be made, she . . . identifies changes in presuppositions between the two contexts. (Again, not all changes are changes in a presupposition; only a change that would have resulted in a different text in the originating context counts as a change in a presupposition.) And if a presupposition has changed, then . . . she may be required to accommodate that change, by making the smallest change possible in the outcome or reading to preserve the most possible from the original context.

Lessig argues that at the time of the Fourteenth Amendment's adoption, racism — belief in natural racial differences — was not considered a political or moral choice, but a normal feature of reality. Lawrence Lessig, Fidelity and Constraint, 65 Fordham L. Rev. 1365, 1367, 1420-1424 (1997). However, over time people gradually challenged the consensus view about racial difference. By 1954 "scientific racism had been displaced, by the one-two punch of science and Hitler: science didn't support it, and our defeat of Hitler's racism while maintaining segregated schools threw hypocrisy into the bargain." This change in social understandings permitted the result in *Brown*. Does this argument suggest that *Plessy* was right in 1896 — because there was a consensus about racial difference — but wrong in 1954, because the consensus had evaporated? Why should the breakdown in consensus about the legitimacy of racial segregation allow judges to hold the practice unconstitutional in all parts of the country, as opposed to leaving the issue up to the political process? Can a theory of translation be concerned only with changes in factual presuppositions of the adopters, or does the example of *Brown* suggest that translation must also recognize changes in values? If the latter, in what sense is it faithful to the original understanding?

5.   Original Meaning Versus Original Application Versus Original Intention

A recurring problem with originalist approaches to equality law is that they focus on how the adopters — or persons living at the time of adoption–would have applied the constitutional text. Because many of the adopters held views that we would today consider racist or sexist, acknowledging their authority over us seems difficult if not unpalatable. Consider, however, a further distinction between the between original public meaning of a text and the original public expectation about how the text's public meaning would be applied in concrete cases, what we might call the text's "original application" for short. Focusing on the former but not the latter would produce a theory of constitutional interpretation different from either original intention or original understanding as they are commonly employed. Jack Balkin explains:

> Original public meaning asks what did the words used in the Constitution generally mean at the time they became law. Original intention asks what did the persons who had authority to create the law intend to be law (prohibited or permitted) by their use of those words. Original application asks how did people who lived at the time expect that the words of the Constitution, taken in their original meaning, would be applied to various situations.
>
> In many contexts, original meaning, original intention, and original application converge. However, where the words used in a constitution are relatively abstract, these three ideas tend to come apart. [Consider] the words "cruel and unusual punishments." Under [the] original public meaning [approach] the original meanings of the concepts used (and their meaning in combination with each other) should be preserved, but we are not necessarily bound by either the intentions of the persons who framed the words, or by the general public expectation of how those words would be applied. The concept of cruelty stays the same, but we have to figure out what that concept means in our own time.
>
> Evidence of how people used words at a certain point in time is evidence of their original public meaning, but it is not conclusive evidence, because original public use conflates both the content of a concept and its expected application. It also conflates

the nature of a concept with the particular set of issues before people at the time they considered constitutional language.[33]

It follows that if the concepts in a constitutional text call for moral and political judgment, different generations might apply them quite differently.[34] This would not prevent judges from reading fairly abstract concepts like "cruel and unusual" to reflect contemporary moral sentiments. This "original meaning" approach might well produce a form of "living constitutionalism," in which the application of the Constitution's general clauses (but not the original meaning of the concepts contained within them) evolves over different generations.

Is *Brown* consistent with the original meaning of the words of the Fourteenth Amendment, regardless of how most people would have applied the public meaning of those words in 1868? Consider the following arguments:

1. The words used in §1 — "privileges or immunities" and "equal protection of the laws" — were terms of art, deliberately chosen to mean "civil equality" and no more. The text of the Fifteenth Amendment, which would be otherwise superfluous, demonstrates this conclusively. Therefore *Brown* is inconsistent with the original meaning of the Fourteenth Amendment.
2. The words "civil equality" do not appear in §1; nor do the words "separate but equal." The words that were used — "privileges or immunities" and "equal protection of the laws" — were deliberately vague and left the issue of segregation open for future judicial construction. The result in *Brown* is a permissible construction of the words of the Fourteenth Amendment even if it is not required.
3. The words of the Fourteenth Amendment guarantee those basic privileges and immunities that all citizens enjoy by virtue of being citizens; and they guarantee equal protection of the laws. The task of judges is to decide how those concepts apply in our world, not the world of 1868. *Brown* is an easy case in our world.

How much difference is there between arguments 2 and 3 and nonoriginalist forms of constitutional argument? Under the logic of arguments 2 and 3, could discrimination against homosexuals be a violation of equal protection? Could the right to an equal education be a privilege of citizenship?

---

33. Jack M. Balkin, "Original Meaning and Original Application," *http://balkin.blogspot.com/2005/06/original-meaning-and-original.html.* Randy Barnett, in Restoring the Lost Constitution, supra, argues for interpretation based on "original public meaning." Barnett looks not only to contemporaneous dictionary definitions of words but also to how particular words were used or applied in public debates at the time of adoption. Recall also Frederick Douglass's textual theory, discussed in Chapter 3, which draws on a tradition of abolitionist constitutional interpretation. Douglass drew many of his ideas about interpretation from the abolitionist Lysander Spooner. Douglass argued that in all textual interpretations there should be a presumption in favor of justice; Barnett argues that there should be a presumption in favor of liberty. See also Akhil Reed Amar, Foreword: The Document and the Doctrine, 114 Harv. L. Rev. 26, 28-29, 31 (2000). ("[T]extual analysis dovetails with the study of enactment history and constitutional structure. The joint aim of these related approaches is to understand what the American People meant and did when We ratified and amended the document . . . [Textualists] seek to braid arguments from text, history, and structure into an interpretive rope whose strands mutually reinforce.")

34. See Ronald Dworkin, "Comment," in Scalia, A Matter of Interpretation, 116-119.

6.   Beyond Originalism?

In The Misconceived Quest for the Original Understanding, supra, Paul Brest argues that, although an interpreter should take *account* of the text and the original understanding of the Constitution, she is not *bound* by either:

> According to the political theory most deeply rooted in the American tradition, the authority of the Constitution derives from the consent of its adopters. Even if the adopters freely consented to the Constitution, however, this is not an adequate basis for continuing fidelity to the founding document, for their consent cannot bind succeeding generations. We did not adopt the Constitution, and those who did are dead and gone.
>
> Given the questionable authority of the American Constitution — indeed, of any (quasi) revolutionary constitution at the moment of its inception — it is only through a history of continuing assent or acquiescence that the document could become law. Our constitutional tradition, however, has not focused on the document alone, but on the decisions and practices of courts and other institutions. And this tradition has included major elements of nonoriginalism. . . . [T]he practice of supplementing and derogating from the text and original understanding is itself part of our constitutional tradition.
>
> The fact of this tradition undermines the exclusivity of the written document. It does not, however, establish the legitimacy of nonoriginalism. Acquiescence is not the same as "consent," which must be informed and knowingly and freely given. Those conditions have not in fact been met, and perhaps can never be met in a large industrial society.
>
> Actual consent is not, then, a practicable measure of the legitimacy of any system of government, and a fortiori not of a particular practice or institution. Owen Fiss has suggested that it is not even an appropriate measure of institutional legitimacy: "Consent goes to the system, not the particular institution; it operates on the whole rather than on each part. The legitimacy of particular institutions, such as courts, depends not on the consent — implied or otherwise — of the people, but rather on their *competence,* on the special contribution they make to the quality of our social life. Legitimacy depends on the capacity of the institution to perform a function within the political system and its willingness to respect the limitations on that function." Whether or not the practices of constitutional decisionmaking should ideally be validated by consent as well as competence, I think we must accept Professor Fiss' observation faute de mieux.

One way of understanding the debate over originalism in constitutional interpretation is by asking which modalities of interpretation should control when there is a conflict between them. What we might call "strict" originalism would insist that one modality of interpretation supersedes all others; where the original understanding can be known, it constitutes the legal meaning of the text, and thus trumps precedent, structure, tradition, postenactment history, consequences, and ethos. Thus strict originalism is a kind of unimodalism.

The alternative view is multimodalism or eclecticism: Judges should consult evidence of the original understanding, but such evidence is not controlling, and it must be weighed against other modalities of constitutional argument. The claim that America has a "living Constitution" presupposes a multimodal approach to interpretation, because the evolution of constitutional norms arises naturally from the interaction of the different modalities of constitutional interpretation.

However, many people who would ordinarily think of themselves as originalists are also multimodal interpreters, because they accept many existing precedents and doctrines that are inconsistent with the original understanding, they reason from these precedents and doctrines, and they treat them as binding law. Hence in practice, the differences between originalists and living constitutionalists might be less than one might think; often the disagreements will come down to matters of emphasis and balance in particular cases and settings. Consider Professor Henry Monaghan:[35]

> [D]ifficulties with originalism emerge once the existing constitutional order is actually examined. The Supreme Court's repeated invocations of the Framers' understanding notwithstanding, a significant portion of our constitutional order cannot reasonably be reconciled with original understanding. For example, it is now increasingly acknowledged "that those who wrote and ratified the Fourteenth Amendment believed that it would permit racial segregation in public schools." Consequently, unless they are willing to see it overruled, Brown v. Board of Education[, among many other cases,] presents deep difficulties for those who insist upon original understanding as the only legitimate canon for constitutional adjudication. . . .
>
> Even on the assumption, itself controversial, that the fourteenth amendment was intended to make the Bill of Rights applicable to the states, much of the actual judicial development of the Bill of Rights has taken very little from original understanding. . . .
>
> [S]*tare decisis plays a very large role in constitutional law.* Many constitutional issues are so far settled that they are simply off the agenda. . . . [N]o Supreme Court would now reexamine the merits [of *Knox v. Lee* and *Julliard v. Greenman* on the constitutionality of paper money] no matter how closely wedded it was to original intent theory and no matter how certain it was of its predecessor's error.
>
> [M]any of the fundamental transformations in our governmental structure legitimated by the Supreme Court in this century are unquestionably above challenge. Is it conceivable that the Court would outlaw the administrative state? . . . The constitutional law, if not the political dimensions of the New Deal, is here to stay. . . .
>
> History counts. The only significant question is how. . . .
>
> At this juncture the pertinent question is whether stare decisis should have any substantial role in cases where the issues remain contested. . . .

Compare David Strauss's common law theory of the Constitution:[36]

> Constitutional law is, it seems to me, primarily a common law system. The text plays a significant role, but most of the important principles are settled not by the text but in the same way most of the principles of the law of torts or contracts have been settled by cases that have been decided and then followed over the years, or by practices and institutions that have been accepted for so long that they have become entrenched.

Although respect for stare decisis might explain why we retain some nonoriginalist precedents, does this help legitimate *Brown?* After all, *Brown* itself overruled a precedent of long standing, Plessy v. Ferguson, in the area of public elementary

35. Henry Monaghan, Stare Decisis and Constitutional Adjudication, 88 Colum. L. Rev. 723, 728-729, 744-753, 757-758 (1988). See also J. M. Balkin, Constitutional Interpretation and the Problem of History, 63 N.Y.U. L. Rev. 911 (1988).

36. David Strauss, "Tragedies under the Common Law Constitution," in William Eskridge and Sanford Levinson, eds., Constitutional Stupidities/Constitutional Tragedies 235, 236 (1998). Strauss's argument is set out at greater length in David A. Strauss, Common Law Constitutional Interpretation, 63 U. Chi. L. Rev. 877 (1996).

and secondary education. *Plessy* had been long relied on by school boards around the country, and not just in the South. Shouldn't respect for precedent have required that the Court retain *Plessy* in 1954, particularly if the result in *Plessy* was consistent with widely held public attitudes about public education when the Fourteenth Amendment was adopted? In short, although once *Brown* is decided, interests in reliance might justify retaining it, why doesn't the stare decisis argument counsel against creating new nonoriginalist doctrines like *Brown* in the first place?

Moreover, even if reliance counsels that one should not lightly overrule nonorignalist precedents, it hardly follows that one should read them expansively. To the contrary, if the original understanding is a touchstone of constitutional legitimacy, nonoriginalist precedents should be read narrowly and not expanded to reach a wide variety of new situations. Such precedents survive as mistakes that are too costly to correct, or which can be corrected, if at all, only very slowly. Indeed, to the extent that courts can eventually chip away at them in subsequent decisions with a view to returning to the original understanding, they should be obligated to do so.

However, viewing all nonoriginalist precedents in this way captures neither our current practices of interpretation nor our current attitudes toward many of these decisions. Decisions like Brown v. Board of Education and Bolling v. Sharpe, decisions giving women equal rights, and decisions that greatly expanded civil rights and civil liberties, are widely viewed by Americans as something to be proud of rather than as errors that should be read narrowly or slowly chipped away at. These decisions are not regrettable "mistakes" that we must, unfortunately, preserve because of reliance interests, but significant achievements of American constitutionalism that should be extended into the future. Although this perspective fits uneasily with a strict version of originalism, it is broadly consistent with a multimodal or eclectic approach.[37]

Nevertheless, one might object that a multimodal or eclectic approach that is not hemmed in by the original understanding gives judges too much discretion, which they will use to write their own political preferences into constitutional doctrine. As Justice Scalia puts it, "[i]t is very difficult for a person to discern a difference between those political values that he personally thinks most important, and those political values that are 'fundamental to our society.' "[38] (Note, nevertheless, that Justice Scalia describes himself as only a "fainthearted originalist," because, for example, he is unwilling to overturn New Deal precedents that are inconsistent with the original understanding of limited national power.)

Does adherence to original understanding in fact constrain judges from imposing their political preferences? In practice even those judges who consider themselves originalists normally combine arguments from original understanding with other modalities of argument like consequences, constitutional structure, and precedent; moreover they appeal to original understandings only in some cases, invoking different kinds of reasoning — like precedent — in others. (Consider as examples the Justices' opinions in United States v. Printz and United States v. Lopez in Chapter 5. Later in this chapter we see that none of the

37. See Jack M. Balkin, Alive and Kicking: Why no one truly believes in a dead Constitution, Slate August 29, 2005, *http://www.slate.com/id/2125226/*.
38. Antonin Scalia, Originalism: The Lesser Evil, 57 U. Cin. L. Rev. 849, 862-864 (1989).

Justices pay much attention to the original understanding when it comes to the constitutionality of affirmative action.) Moreover, judges are not perfect, and they will tend to err on the side of anachronism, reading their own present-day values into the historical record.[39] Recall, for example, Justice Taney's originalist argument in *Dred Scott,* which tracked the political views of many Southern slaveholders in 1857.

Conversely, consider whether the most effective methods of constraining judges come not from the theories of interpretation they employ but from features of American constitutional structure. The appointments process, which requires collaboration by both the President and the Senate, tends to produce candidates who are not too far out of the mainstream. Moreover, the fact that the Supreme Court is a multimember body means that "swing" or moderate Justices will cast the deciding vote in the most heavily contested cases. Finally, lower federal courts, consisting of single district judges or three-member appellate panels, are hemmed in by existing precedents of higher courts, as well as their own precedents. If constitutional structure constrains constitutional interpretation in this matter, then even if constitutional doctrines change over time, they will be continually driven toward the political mainstream, and it is likely to matter far less what theories of constitutional interpretation individual judges happen to hold. Consider whether Brown v. Board of Education and American race relations law bears out this thesis.

D.   Reflections on the Opinion in *Brown*

Note: The Rhetoric of **Brown**

Few opinions of the Supreme Court have been more controversial than Chief Justice Warren's in Brown v. Board of Education. Any decision dealing with so sensitive an issue was bound to be controversial, but both the reasoning and style of *Brown* were criticized even by commentators who supported the outcome. For example, the day after the decision, May 18, 1954, James Reston wrote in the New York Times that the Court had rejected "history, philosophy, and custom" in basing its decision in "the primacy of the general welfare. . . . Relying more on the social scientists than on legal precedents — a procedure often in controversy in the past — the Court insisted on equality of the mind and heart rather than on equal school facilities. . . . The Court's opinion read more like an expert paper on sociology than a Supreme Court opinion."[40]

Warren's desire had been to write an opinion that was "short, readable by the lay public, nonrhetorical, unemotional and, above all, non-accusatory."[41] When Justice

---

39. Id. at 864 ("The inevitable tendency of judges to think that the law is what they would like it to be will, I have no doubt, cause most errors in judicial historiography to be made in the direction of projecting upon the age of 1789 current, modern values — so that as applied, even as applied in the best of faith, originalism will (as the historical record shows) end up as something of a compromise.")

40. Quoted in Richard Kluger, Simple Justice 711 (1975), a detailed and excellent study of the background of *Brown.* See also Edmund Kahn, Jurisprudence, 30 N.Y.U. L. Rev. 150 (1955) (criticizing reliance on problematic social science evidence).

41. Richard Kluger, Simple Justice 711 (1975).

Jackson asked his law clerk, Barrett Prettyman, what he thought of the draft opinion circulated by the Chief Justice, Prettyman commented:

> I wished that it had more law in it but I didn't find anything glaringly unacceptable in it. The genius of the Warren opinion was that it was so simple and unobtrusive. He had come from political life and had a keen sense of what you could say in this opinion without getting everybody's back up. His opinion took the sting off the decision, it wasn't accusatory, and it didn't pretend that the Fourteenth Amendment was more helpful than the history suggested — he didn't equivocate on that point.[42]

However well you think the opinion succeeded in its goals, the fact is that Earl Warren *had* goals — "extralegal" ones, if you like — for it. Besides those already mentioned, he strongly desired that the Court speak with one voice on this controversial question: Achieving unanimity, even among Justices who were committed to the outcome, was no small accomplishment.[43] Moreover, it was only in the last week before the decision was handed down that the Chief Justice persuaded Justice Reed not to file a dissenting opinion:

> After the Chief Justice had left, Reed asked [his law clerk, George] Mickum, who had been raised in a community with segregated schools, how he felt about the Justice's going along with the rest of the Court. Mickum, a man not notably more convinced of the natural equality of the Negro than Reed himself was, suggested that the demands of conscience seemed to require his going beyond the knowable facts in the case and asking himself, as Warren had, what was best for America. "I think he was really troubled by the possible consequences of his position," Mickum adds. "Because he was a Southerner, even a lone dissent by him would give a lot of people a lot of grist for making trouble. For the good of the country, he put aside his own basis for dissent." The only condition he extracted from Warren for going along, Mickum believes, was a pledge that the Court implementation decree would allow segregation to be dismantled gradually instead of being wrenched apart.[44]

Many constitutional theorists have argued that the Supreme Court should consciously structure the scope and style of its decisions to take account of the likely responses of the political branches. Do you think that judges are well equipped to make such calculations? Given the massive resistance that followed on the heels of *Brown*, and the continuing controversies over race that engulfed the country in succeeding years, how should Warren have written his opinion? How much does the rhetoric of *Brown* matter today?

---

42. Id. at 697.

43. See id. at 582-699.

44. Id. at 698. From the cases read so far, you have noticed that the Court has often issued judgments without being unanimous. When and why might the Justices subordinate individual differences and strive to speak with (more or less) one voice? *Brown* suggests one occasion — when the Justices believe that the decision is likely to meet with resistance and therefore wish to invoke the impersonal authority of "the Court." For example, the decision in United States v. Nixon, 418 U.S. 683 (1974), requiring President Nixon to turn over certain tapes to the Watergate special prosecutor was also unanimous. See Scott Armstrong and Robert Woodward, The Brethren 285-347 (1979), for a description of the Court's internal bargaining to achieve unanimity in that case.

Note: The Enduring Significance of Brown: "Can Courts Bring About Social Change?"

Brown occupies a unique place in American constitutional theory. Described by various commentators as a "paradigmatic event,"[45] an "icon of liberal constitutionalism,"[46] and a "myth,"[47] it has come to mean different things to different observers. However, most analyses have started from the premise that, whether constitutionally legitimate or not, *Brown* ultimately caused a social and cultural revolution in American life.

In his 1991 book, The Hollow Hope: Can Courts Bring About Social Change?, political scientist Gerald Rosenberg challenged this conventional wisdom. Reviewing statistics on segregation in the South, he concludes: "For ten years, 1954-64, virtually *nothing happened*."[48] Rosenberg argues that real change did not come until the political branches joined the desegregation effort and Congress enacted the Civil Rights Act of 1964, which sought to deprive segregated schools of federal funds. Rosenberg considers and rejects the possibility of more indirect judicial causation — that "if the Court had not taken that first giant step in 1954 . . . there would have been [no] Civil Rights Act of 1964."[49] Rosenberg is skeptical about *Brown*'s indirect impact:

> [The] claim that a major contribution of the courts in civil rights was to give the issue salience, press political elites to act, prick the consciences of whites, legitimate the grievances of blacks, and fire blacks up to act is not substantiated. . . . The evidence suggests that *Brown*'s major positive impact was limited to reinforcing the belief in a legal strategy for change of those already committed to it.[50]

Michael Klarman has seconded Rosenberg's revisionist account of *Brown*. In *Brown*, Racial Change, and the Civil Rights Movement, 80 Va. L. Rev. 7 (1994), Klarman maintains that, in the long run, *Brown* made little difference, for, in his view, "racial change in America was inevitable owing to a variety of deep-seated social, political and economic forces." As to *Brown*'s short-term effect on the civil rights movement, Klarman acknowledges that the decision made a contribution, albeit in an "indirect, almost perverse, manner":

> The crucial link between *Brown* and the mid-1960s civil rights legislation inheres . . . in the decision's crystallizing effect on southern white *resistance* to racial change. By propelling southern politics dramatically to the right on racial issues, *Brown* created a political climate conducive to the brutal suppression of civil rights demonstrations. When such violence occurred, and was vividly transmitted through the medium of television to national audiences, previously indifferent northern whites were aroused from their apathy, leading to demands for national civil rights legislation which the Kennedy and Johnson administrations no longer deemed politically expedient to resist.[51]

---

45. Robert Cover, The Origins of Judicial Activism in the Protection of Minorities, 91 Yale L.J. 1287, 1316 (1982).

46. Stephen L. Carter, Do Courts Matter?, 90 Mich. L. Rev. 1216, 1219 (1992).

47. David L. Kirp, How Now, Brown, 254 The Nation 757 (1992).

48. Gerald N. Rosenberg, The Hollow Hope: Can Courts Bring About Social Change? 52 (1991).

49. C. Herman Pritchett, Equal Protection and the Urban Majority, 58 Am. Pol. Sc. Rev. 869, 869 (1964).

50. Rosenberg, at 156.

51. Michael J. Klarman, *Brown*, Racial Change, and the Civil Rights Movement, 80 Va. L. Rev. 7, 10, 13 (1994).

The response to Rosenberg and Klarman has been voluminous and passionate,[52] as they have been charged with "hopelessly hollow history" and "revisionist devaluing of *Brown*," among other things.[53] Mark Tushnet, a relatively sympathetic critic who concedes that lawyers have probably overestimated *Brown*'s significance, nevertheless insists that both Rosenberg and Klarman have failed to appreciate fully the "cultural significance" of the decision and the extent to which "it may have provided the civil rights movement with a moral resource that played an important part in the political response to violent reactions against the movement's activities." As Tushnet explains, "We might understand *Brown* as designed not to accomplish actual integration, but to establish a fundamental principle of constitutional law." According to Tushnet, the Court's endorsement of that principle in turn allowed it "to become more firmly imbedded in the white political culture."[54] Similarly, one reviewer of *Hollow Hope* maintains that *Brown* gave "a powerful symbolic endorsement" to the desegregation forces and, because of the moral and constitutional nature of its judgment, "forced Southern segregationists to craft arguments as convoluted and unconvincing as those made by slavery's defenders a century earlier."[55] David Schultz and Stephen Gottlieb point out that merely by becoming law *Brown* changed the framework in which political and legal decisions were made, because it placed the rule of law against continued support for segregation, and because "even limited and tepid support for *Brown*" could shift the margin of victory in swing districts:

> Game theory teaches that merely altering signals to indicate that additional choices are available may suffice to induce significant change in a situation where players previously doubted the availability of alternatives. *Brown* need only have challenged the assumption that there was no option but loyalty to the segregationist status quo.
>
> Judicial decisions can change assumptions not only by opening new options for opposition, but also through their power to grant legitimacy to certain claims and to redefine norms of institutional action. Undoubtedly, by changing the constitutional rule, *Brown* opened new doors for resisting segregation through actions at law. But it did more. It invalidated arguments in favor of segregation, both by excluding them from the courtroom and by stigmatizing their use in public debate. It also opened an avenue for changing the law elsewhere, as courts and others applied the newly approved desegregationist argument in other situations.
>
> Further, since law imposes social costs and affects incentives, the decision itself, without extra-judicial assistance, raised new obstacles to segregation. What once was a nearly costless behavior suddenly entailed increased litigation costs, fines, and injunctions; the threat of executive action against segregation now was increasingly real; and it now was likely that other related behaviors also would be similarly burdened.[56]

52. See, e.g., Neal Devins, Judicial Matters, 80 Cal. L. Rev. 1027 (1992); Michael J. Klarman, Brown v. Board of Education: Facts and Political Correctness, 80 Va. L. Rev. 185 (1994); L. A. Powe, Jr., The Supreme Court, Social Change, and Legal Scholarship, 44 Stan. L. Rev. 1615 (1992); Gerald N. Rosenberg, *Brown* Is Dead! Long Live *Brown*!: The Endless Attempt to Canonize a Case, 80 Va. L. Rev. 161 (1994); Peter H. Schuck, Public Law Litigation and Social Reform, 102 Yale L.J. 1763 (1993); David Schultz & Stephen E. Gottlieb, Legal Functionalism and Social Change: A Reassessment of Rosenberg's The Hollow Hope: Can Courts Bring About Social Change? 12 J. L. & Politics 63 (1996).

53. David J. Garrow, Hopelessly Hollow History: Revisionist Devaluing of Brown v. Board of Education, 80 Va. L. Rev. 151 (1994).

54. Mark Tushnet, The Significance of Brown v. Board of Education, 80 Va. L. Rev. 173, 176-177, 182 (1994).

55. David L. Kirp, supra n.45.

56. Schultz & Gottlieb, supra n.50, at 63.

Discussion

1. According to Stephen Carter, "If, as Rosenberg insists, courts cannot bring about major social changes, then the great bulk of contemporary constitutional theory, which assumes otherwise, is a waste."[57] Do you agree that these are the only two possible alternatives? Could courts not be simply one actor in a complicated set of political and legal interactions?

2. Another way of interpreting Rosenberg's argument is that people have placed too much faith in courts to change society. Do you agree? Which people? Addressing the post-*Brown* faith in the power of law to reshape society for good, Carter argues that it is not the failure to transform society by judicial intervention that requires explanation but our naive belief that it would:

> For a brief moment of the nation's history, bounded roughly by *Brown* and *Roe*, the Supreme Court was a reliable ally of those who style themselves progressive. This period, which did not even last two decades, has changed the way America thinks about its courts, and, in consequence, has changed the way that those who want to change America think about its courts, too. But for most of the nation's history, the Justices have been indifferent to social change or have worked to prevent it. Any other mindset would be surprising. Courts, like the law they interpret, are backward-looking, which renders judges essentially conservative creatures. It other words, it is *Brown*, for all its shining glory, that was the historical accident; the more recent jurisprudence, dismal though it often is, represents business as usual.[58]

Given your understanding of the Court's work up to this point, do you agree with this assessment? Does Carter beg any important questions about which direction of political or legal movement we should regard as "progressive?"

3. If you believe that courts are powerless to assist social change, are they also equally powerless to preserve the status quo? (In which case, one assumes, we should attribute little importance to cases like *Plessy* and *Dred Scott*.) Or is constitutional doctrine much more effective at preserving the status quo than reforming it? Why should this be so?

4. Much of the discussion of *Brown* and its effects assumes that everyone agrees on what "segregation" means. As you read through the rest of this chapter, ask yourself if that is true. Is it the case, for example, that "segregationist" arguments are no longer respectable in contemporary American society (or contemporary legal analysis)? For example, at the turn of the twenty-first century many people see nothing inherently wrong with racial separation in public schools as long as it is achieved through "private choice" as opposed to government fiat. See, for example, Justice Thomas's opinion in Missouri v. Jenkins, excerpted below. (The question of what constitutes genuine "private choice" is contested, to be sure.) Still others have resigned themselves to segregated schools because it is too difficult to prevent white flight. Note, however, that in 1954 many people supported state-sponsored segregation in the South because white people overwhelmingly wanted it, while others acquiesced because they believed it would be too difficult to enforce desegregation on unwilling whites. Is the absence of state action the central difference between the positions taken at the middle of the twentieth century and the positions taken at the century's end?

57. Carter, supra, at 1221.
58. Id. at 1222-1223.

E. Four Decades of School Desegregation

1. Brown II *and "All Deliberate Speed"*

The Court's opinion in Brown v. Board of Education concluded by setting the cases for reargument on the question of appropriate relief. In *Brown II,* 349 U.S. 294 (1955), Chief Justice Warren again wrote for a unanimous Court:

> Full implementation of [the principle announced in *Brown*] may require solution of varied local school problems. School authorities have the primary responsibility for elucidating, assessing, and solving these problems; courts will have to consider whether the action of school authorities constitutes good faith implementation of the governing constitutional principles. Because of their proximity to local conditions and the possible need for further hearings, the courts which originally heard these cases can best perform this judicial appraisal. Accordingly, we believe it appropriate to remand the cases to those courts.
>
> In fashioning and effectuating the decrees, the courts will be guided by equitable principles. Traditionally, equity has been characterized by a practical flexibility in shaping its remedies and by a facility for adjusting and reconciling public and private needs. These cases call for the exercise of these traditional attributes of equity power. At stake is the personal interest of the plaintiffs in admission to public schools as soon as practicable on a nondiscriminatory basis. To effectuate this interest may call for elimination of a variety of obstacles in making the transition to school systems operated in accordance with the constitutional principles set forth in our May 17, 1954, decision. Courts of equity may properly take into account the public interest in the elimination of such obstacles in a systematic and effective manner. But it should go without saying that the vitality of these constitutional principles cannot be allowed to yield simply because of disagreement with them.
>
> While giving weight to these public and private considerations, the courts will require that the defendants make a prompt and reasonable start toward full compliance with our May 17, 1954, ruling. Once such a start has been made, the courts may find that additional time is necessary to carry out the ruling in an effective manner. The burden rests upon the defendants to establish that such time is necessary in the public interest and is consistent with good faith compliance at the earliest practicable date. To that end, the courts may consider problems related to administration, arising from the physical condition of the school plant, the school transportation system, personnel, revision of school districts and attendance areas into compact units to achieve a system of determining admission to the public schools on a nonracial basis, and revision of local laws and regulations which may be necessary in solving the foregoing problems. They will also consider the adequacy of any plans the defendants may propose to meet these problems and to effectuate a transition to a racially nondiscriminatory school system. During this period of transition, the courts will retain jurisdiction of these cases.
>
> The . . . cases are remanded to the District Courts to take such proceedings and enter such orders and decrees consistent with this opinion as are necessary and proper to admit to public schools on a racially nondiscriminatory basis with all deliberate speed the parties to these cases.

The effect of *Brown I* and *Brown II* was that the right to be free from segregation was severed from the remedy. As a result, none of the students in the Deep South benefited directly from the cases that they brought. Even if the Court properly waited before announcing its conclusion as to the scope of the remedy in *Brown II*, should it have decreed the immediate admission to "white schools" of the named plaintiffs in the four state cases that were heard together as Brown v. Board of Education?

Ironically, the separation of right from remedy in *Brown II* presaged the history of desegregation litigation, which focused on how to structure remedies in the face of open and hidden resistance, the widely varying circumstances in which segregation occurred, and the constantly changing demographics of the country. By the century's end *Brown* stood as an icon of American constitutional law, revered by all as a statement of the country's most abiding principles. Yet large numbers of schools in the United States still remained largely segregated by race.

2.   *"Massive Resistance" to School Desegregation*

Desegregation in the thousands of districts affected by *Brown* followed no single pattern but varied with the attitudes and behavior of school officials, their white constituents, and federal district and appellate judges. The Supreme Court allowed controversies to develop and occasionally to resolve themselves in the lower federal courts until the late 1960s, when it finally intervened to establish a national policy.

Although the District of Columbia and some school districts in the border states began to desegregate their schools almost immediately, the South responded to *Brown* with a barrage of measures designed to preserve and entrench segregation. This inaugurated the era of "massive resistance" to southern desegregation. As noted previously, virtually all of the Congressmen and Senators from the deep South signed a "Southern Manifesto" claiming that *Brown* was illegitimate and asserting the right of states to ignore the decision.[59] Georgia redesigned its state flag to reincorporate elements of the Confederate battle flag as a symbol of resistance to the opinion. State legislatures adopted resolutions of "nullification" and "interposition," which declared that the Court's decisions were without effect. Southern states enacted statutes mandating school segregation, ordering state and local officials to take all measures within their authority to preserve segregation, terminating state funds for racially mixed schools, placing the public schools directly under the authority of the governor or state board of education with plenary power to close them, providing tuition grants to enable pupils to attend private schools, and repealing compulsory attendance laws.[60] Most of these schemes were struck down by lower federal courts. The Supreme Court remained largely silent during this period. However, in Cooper v. Aaron, 358 U.S. 1 (1958), it ordered Little Rock, Arkansas, to proceed with school desegregation in the face of state-inspired opposition, violence, and disorder; and in Griffin v. Prince Edward County School Board, 377 U.S. 218 (1964), the Court ordered a county school system reopened after it had been closed for five years to avoid desegregation.[61] The first strategies of massive resistance were followed by adoption of "pupil placement" acts in the late 1950s and early 1960s. Under these statutes, students were

---

59. See 102 Cong. Rec. H3948, 4004 (Mar. 12, 1956).

60. See Note, Interposition vs. Judicial Power — A Study of Ultimate Authority in Constitutional Questions, 1 Race Rel. L. Rep. 465 (1956); Robert McKay; "With All Deliberate Speed" — A Study of School Desegregation, 31 N.Y.U. L. Rev. 911, 1017-1049 (1956); McKay, "With All Deliberate Speed": Legislative Reaction and Judicial Development 1956-1957, 43 Va. L. Rev. 1205, 1216-1228 (1957).

61. The Court also thwarted the attempts of several states to harass or oust the NAACP and others seeking to implement *Brown*. See NAACP v. Alabama, 357 U.S. 449 (1958); NAACP v. Button, 371 U.S. 415 (1963). For a more recent example of massive resistance, in the context of housing segregation, see Spallone v. United States, 493 U.S. 265 (1990).

initially assigned to the school maintained for their race, and school districts were then directed to assign pupils to schools based on individualized assessments of purportedly nonracial factors. By requiring time-consuming individualized determinations of all requests for transfers, pupil placement acts allowed local school boards to preserve the racial status quo.[62]

During the 1960s, the lower courts approved two types of desegregation plans — assignment on the basis of residence and "freedom of choice." Southern districts had traditionally assigned pupils to the schools nearest their homes, employing dual, overlapping attendance zones for the black and white schools. It would have been relatively simple to consolidate the dual zones into unitary ones. Because of the contiguity of black and white neighborhoods in many southern communities, this would often have produced substantial desegregation, relegating white pupils to the formerly black schools, which, apart from their social status were inferior in every traditional measure of school quality.[63] For these reasons, unitary zoning was not common, and where adopted it was implemented on a grade-a-year basis and with a provision that pupils could transfer from any school in which their race was in the minority to one in which they would be in the majority. In Goss v. Knoxville Board of Education, 373 U.S. 683 (1963), the Supreme Court unanimously held these minority-to-majority transfer provisions unconstitutional on the ground that they were "based solely on racial factors which . . . inevitably lead toward segregation of the students by race." Assignment by residence lost what little appeal it had for most districts.

The second and by far the more popular school desegregation scheme was freedom of choice, under which each child could opt to attend either a formerly white or black school. As ultimately perfected, the plan required each pupil (or his parent) to exercise a choice each year, thus precluding automatic assignment to the school formerly maintained for his race in the absence of a choice. The district was required to furnish transportation to the nearest school of the pupil's "opposite" race. No choice could be denied for any reason other than overcrowding, in which event preference was based solely on geographic proximity. Faculty and staff and all facilities, activities, and programs were to be desegregated, and the districts were required to bring inferior black schools up to the level of the white schools or else close them.

By the late 1960s freedom of choice was prevalent. It seldom yielded much desegregation. White students rarely chose to attend black identified schools, while black students were reluctant to attend white identified schools because of fears of harassment and violent retaliation from whites. Harassment, threats, and retaliatory violence were rarely prevented or punished by school or other government officials, and thus many black parents and their children were reluctant to assert their rights.[64] Ten years after Brown, less than 1 percent of black children in

---

62. See generally Note, The Federal Courts and Integration of Southern Schools: Troubled Status of the Pupil Placement Acts, 1962 Colum. L. Rev. 1448; United States Commission on Civil Rights, Education 22-31 (1961). By the mid-1960s, it was established that pupil placement schemes could not bar class actions seeking judicial relief, and the courts held that the initial assignment on the basis of race was unconstitutional.

63. Even some liberal commentators seemed to assume that whites should not be sent to such schools (see Alexander Bickel, The Decade of School Desegregation, 1964 Colum. L. Rev. 193, 212), apparently without questioning why only black pupils should bear this burden.

64. See U.S. Commission on Civil Rights, Survey of School Desegregation in the Southern and Border States, 1965-66, at 51-52 (1966). See also the commission's report, Southern School Desegregation, 1966-67, at 88 (1967).

the Deep South attended schools with whites. Not only were the court-approved desegregation plans inadequate, but school districts did not desegregate voluntarily, so that each one had to be sued in a separate action. Almost all school litigation in the South was conducted by the NAACP Legal Defense and Educational Fund, Inc., a private organization whose small central staff, aided by handfuls of local cooperating attorneys, obviously could not take on each of the thousand-odd districts.[65] Delay was on the defendants' side. Many judges were hostile to *Brown* and to the plaintiffs and attorneys seeking to implement it; many other judges were subjected to strong pressures from the communities in which they lived.[66] Moreover, school desegregation cases, unlike most other litigation, never ended. The courts retained jurisdiction of each case, and their dockets were crowded with motions to modify or supplement orders as factual circumstances and the law changed.[67]

In Watson v. City of Memphis, 373 U.S. 526 (1963), the Supreme Court began to indicate its impatience. In rejecting the city's request for delay in desegregating recreational facilities, the Court commented that "*Brown* never contemplated that the concept of 'deliberate speed' would countenance indefinite delay in elimination of racial barriers in schools."

Similarly, in 1964, in ordering the reopening of the Prince Edward County schools after they closed to avoid desegregation, Justice Black wrote that "[t]here has been entirely too much deliberation and not enough speed" and that at least for this recalcitrant district "[t]he time for mere 'deliberate speed' has run out. . . ."[68]

3.   *The Political Branches Respond: 1964-1968*

By this point, however, the political climate of the country had changed. Lyndon Johnson's ascension to the Presidency after Kennedy's assassination in 1963, and Johnson's subsequent landslide victory in the 1964 election energized the political branches to do something about civil rights. In 1964 Congress enacted the first comprehensive civil rights act since Reconstruction. Titles IV and IX of the Civil Rights Act of 1964 authorized the attorney general to initiate and intervene in school desegregation suits.[69] More important, Title VI prohibited discrimination in programs receiving federal financial assistance and required each department responsible for federally funded programs to issue regulations to achieve this end. Congress appropriated $2.4 billion under the Elementary and Secondary Education Act of 1965, much of it for school districts having "educationally disadvantaged" children. The Department of Health, Education and Welfare issued

---

65. The Legal Defense Fund began as the legal arm of the NAACP, but in 1939 it became an independent organization.

66. Southern Justice 165-227 (Friedman ed., 1965); J.W. Peltason, Fifty-Eight Lonely Men (1961); United States Commission on Civil Rights, Federal Enforcement of School Desegregation 48-54 (1969); Note, Judicial Performance in the Fifth Circuit, 73 Yale L.J. 90 (1963).

67. See, e.g., Owen Fiss, Injunctions 417-421 (1972), listing 77 docket entries between 1964 and 1969 in United States v. Montgomery County Bd. of Educ., 395 U.S. 225 (1969).

68. Griffin v. Prince Edward County School Bd., 377 U.S. 218 (1964).

69. Prior to the adoption of Title IX, the government had sometimes effectively intervened as "amicus curiae," playing a much more active role than amici traditionally do.

regulations and guidelines requiring most recipient districts to adopt freedom-of-choice plans.[70]

The year 1963 had seen some increase in the pace of school desegregation, probably due to the neutralization of pupil placement schemes, and Title VI of the Civil Rights Act of 1964 accelerated the process. Nonetheless, in 1968, more than three-quarters of all Negro children in the South still attended the "formerly" black schools — which remained all-black — and the formerly white schools were still clearly identifiable as white, though some of them were now sprinkled with handfuls of black children who had the courage and stamina to choose them. As difficult as it was to supervise and enforce court orders and the HEW guidelines, a core cause of racially identifiable schools lay in the substance of the orders and guidelines themselves, which accepted freedom-of-choice plans.

The Legal Defense Fund continually urged that the constitutional objective was the elimination of racially identifiable schools and that, measured in these terms, freedom-of-choice plans were unconstitutional. The school districts responded that, absent improper coercion, a well-designed freedom-of-choice plan succeeded by definition: The Constitution required no more than that black and white children have the option to attend schools with children of the other race. Support for this position was typically sought in the offhand remark of the district court in *Briggs v. Elliott*, 132 F. Supp. 776, 777 (E.D.S.C. 1955), one of the cases consolidated with *Brown*, that "[t]he Constitution . . . does not require integration. It merely forbids [segregation]."

By early 1966, HEW and the Court of Appeals for the Fifth Circuit began to accept the Legal Defense Fund's criticism of freedom of choice as a remedy for segregation. Two years later, freedom of choice remained virtually the sole means of desegregation within the circuit, however, and some other courts had not even accepted the principle. Finally, in 1968, the Supreme Court intervened.

4. *The Supreme Court Reasserts Itself*

GREEN v. NEW KENT COUNTY SCHOOL BOARD, 391 U.S. 430 (1968): [The Court held that a small school district, which was not residentially segregated and which had only two schools, could not employ a freedom-of-choice plan when its effect was to perpetuate the long-standing tradition of segregation. The decision was unanimous.]

BRENNAN, J. . . . The pattern of separate "white" and "Negro" schools in the New Kent County school system established under compulsion of state laws is precisely the pattern of segregation to which *Brown I* and *Brown II* were particularly addressed, and which *Brown I* declared unconstitutionally denied Negro school children equal protection of the laws. Racial identification of the system's schools

---

70. 45 C.F.R. §§80.1 et seq. (1968) (1964 regulations); 45 C.F.R. §181.1 (1968) (1966 guidelines). The HEW guidelines influenced judge-made remedial doctrine, and in some circuits they were simply adopted by the courts; but there were also conflicts between HEW and the courts. See generally James Dunn, Title VI, the Guidelines and School Desegregation in the South, 53 Va. L. Rev. 42 (1967); Note, The Courts, HEW, and Southern School Desegregation, 77 Yale L.J. 321 (1967); United States v. Jefferson County Bd. of Educ., 372 F.2d 836 (1966), aff'd en banc, 380 F.2d 385 (5th Cir. 1967).

was complete, extending not just to the composition of student bodies at the two schools but to every facet of school operations — faculty, staff, transportation, extracurricular activities and facilities. In short, the State, acting through the local school board and school officials, organized and operated a dual system, part "white" and part "Negro."

It was such dual systems that 14 years ago *Brown I* held unconstitutional and a year later *Brown II* held must be abolished; school boards operating such school systems were *required* by *Brown II* "to effectuate a transition to a racially nondiscriminatory school system." It is of course true that for the time immediately after *Brown II* the concern was with making an initial break in a long-established pattern of excluding Negro children from schools attended by white children. The principal focus was on obtaining for those Negro children courageous enough to break with tradition a place in the "white" schools. Under *Brown II* that immediate goal was only the first step, however. The transition to a unitary, nonracial system of public education was and is the ultimate end to be brought about. . . .

In the context of the state-imposed segregated pattern of long standing, the fact that in 1965 the Board opened the doors of the former "white" school to Negro children and of the "Negro" school to white children merely begins, not ends, our inquiry whether the Board has taken steps adequate to abolish its dual, segregated system. *Brown II* was a call for the dismantling of well-entrenched dual systems tempered by an awareness that complex and multifaceted problems would arise which would require time and flexibility for a successful resolution. School boards such as the respondent then operating state-compelled dual systems were nevertheless clearly charged with the affirmative duty to take whatever steps might be necessary to convert to a unitary system in which racial discrimination would be eliminated root and branch. . . .

In determining whether respondent School Board met that command by adopting its "freedom-of-choice" plan, it is relevant that this first step did not come until some 11 years after *Brown I* was decided and 10 years after *Brown II* directed the making of a "prompt and reasonable start." This deliberate perpetuation of the unconstitutional dual system can only have compounded the harm of such a system. . . . The burden on a school board today is to come forward with a plan that promises realistically to work, and promises realistically to work *now*. . . .

We do not hold that "freedom of choice" can have no place in such a plan. We do not hold that a "freedom-of-choice" plan might of itself be unconstitutional, although that argument has been urged upon us. Rather, all we decide today is that in desegregating a dual system a plan utilizing "freedom of choice" is not an end in itself. As Judge Sobeloff has put it,

"Freedom of choice" is not a sacred talisman; it is only a means to a constitutionally required end — the abolition of the system of segregation and its effects. If the means prove effective, it is acceptable, but if it fails to undo segregation, other means must be used to achieve this end. The school officials have the continuing duty to take whatever action may be necessary to create a "unitary, non-racial system."

The New Kent School Board's "freedom-of-choice" plan cannot be accepted as a sufficient step to "effectuate a transition" to a unitary system. In three years of operation not a single white child has chosen to attend Watkins school and . . . 85% of the Negro children in the system still attend the all-Negro Watkins school. . . . The

Board must be required to formulate a new plan and in light of other courses which appear open to the Board, such as zoning, fashion steps which promise realistically to convert promptly to a system without a "white" school and a "Negro" school, but just schools. . . .

Discussion

1. *The relationship between* Brown *and* Green. *Green* is, in many ways, the most important of the Supreme Court's school desegregation cases after *Brown* itself. To a large extent the history of school desegregation can be understood in terms of the acceptance or rejection of *Green's* focus on racially identifiable schools.

From one perspective, *Green* is a logical extension of *Brown*. Racially identifiable "black" and "white" schools tend to perpetuate the racial subordination of blacks. "Black" identified schools inevitably receive less money and less attention from a majority white political process, and white parents avoid them. As long as schools are racially identified, blacks will never achieve equality of opportunity. From another perspective, *Green* is an unwarranted extension of *Brown: Brown* is simply a rule about school assignment policies, which cannot be on the basis of race. If schools become racially identified as "black" or "white" through a combination of demographic shifts, economic changes, and other "private choices," the Constitution is not thereby offended. Consider the dialectic between these two positions in the cases that follow.

After some initial delay in the implementation of *Green*, most Southern districts replaced freedom of choice with geographic zoning. In many rural areas and smaller cities where large-scale residential segregation was not pervasive, this eliminated interschool segregation. But it did not end all forms of racial discrimination. Some school boards desegregated by closing even adequate Negro schools and busing only black students.[71] Many other districts replicated aspects of the dual school system within a "desegregated" school, through ability grouping or tracking; segregation of classrooms, buses, and other facilities; discrimination in the hiring and assignment of personnel; and discrimination in disciplinary treatment, athletics, and other student activities.

Moreover, implementation of *Green* resulted in some "white flight" from districts with high percentages of black students to other areas or to private schools. In Monroe v. Board of Commissioners, 391 U.S. 450 (1968), the Court alluded to the problem by quoting *Brown II:* "the vitality of these constitutional principles cannot be allowed to yield simply because of disagreement with them."[72]

---

71. See Note, Inequality in Desegregation: Black School Closings, 39 U. Chi. L. Rev. 658 (1972); American Friends Service Committee, The Status of School Desegregation in the South 1970.

72. During this same period the Court faced the problem of governmental aid to private segregated schools that arose as a result of school desegregation. In Norwood v. Harrison, 413 U.S. 455 (1973), the Court held that Mississippi could not lend textbooks to students attending private segregated schools pursuant to a longstanding program of providing free textbooks to all public and private school students. Chief Justice Burger pointed out that "[t]his Court has consistently affirmed decisions enjoining state tuition grants to students attending racially discriminatory private schools. A textbook lending program is not legally distinguishable from the forms of state assistance foreclosed by the prior cases. . . . Racial discrimination in state-operated schools is barred by the Constitution and '[i]t is also axiomatic that a state may not induce, encourage or promote private persons to accomplish what it is constitutionally forbidden to accomplish.'"

5. Southern Metropolitan Segregation

In the larger Southern cities, the assignment of pupils by residential zones often produced patterns of school segregation superficially indistinguishable from those common in Northern cities. The Court first addressed this problem in 1971 in the context of a district encompassing the city of Charlotte, North Carolina, and surrounding Mecklenburg County.

In Swann v. Charlotte-Mecklenburg Board of Education, 402 U.S. 1 (1971), the Court approved broad equitable discretion for federal district courts in fashioning school desegregation remedies. About 24,000 (29 percent) of the pupils in the Charlotte-Mecklenburg schools were black. The system had operated under a court-approved plan since 1965, and by the 1968-1969 school year, about half of the black pupils attended formerly white schools; the other half remained in virtually all-black schools. Following *Green*, the district court ordered a new plan that redrew school districts to improve racial balance. The plan also ordered school busing: black students in the first four grades were bused to the outlying schools, and white fifth- and sixth-graders were bused to the city schools. The plan was designed to ensure that no elementary school would have fewer than 9 percent or more than 38 percent black students.

The Supreme Court upheld the plan in a unanimous decision written by Chief Justice Burger. The Court held that in the face of past deliberate segregation of students by race and the failure of school authorities to live up to their "affirmative obligations" to dismantle segregation, courts had broad and flexible powers to remedy segregation and its effects. However,

> [J]udicial powers may be exercised only on the basis of a constitutional violation. Remedial judicial authority does not put judges automatically in the shoes of school authorities whose powers are plenary. Judicial authority enters only when local authority defaults. School authorities are traditionally charged with broad power to formulate and implement educational policy and might well conclude, for example, that in order to prepare students to live in a pluralistic society each school should have a prescribed ratio of Negro to white students reflecting the proportion for the district as a whole. To do this as an educational policy is within the broad discretionary powers of school authorities; absent a finding of a constitutional violation, however, that would not be within the authority of a federal court. As with any equity case, the nature of the violation determines the scope of the remedy.

The Court approved four important remedial features in the desegregation plan. First, the Court upheld the limited use of racial goals in remedial orders: "The constitutional command to desegregate schools does not mean that every school in every community must always reflect the racial composition of the school system as a whole. . . . [However] the use made of mathematical ratios was no more than a starting point rather than an inflexible requirement. . . . Awareness of the racial composition of the whole school system is likely to be a useful starting point in shaping a remedy to correct past constitutional violations."

Second, the Court acknowledged that a plan for a unitary system could retain some one-race schools: "the existence of some small number of one-race, or virtually one-race, schools within a district is not in and of itself the mark of a system that still practices segregation by law."

Third, the Court held that once a constitutional violation was shown, the district court possessed the power to order pupil reassignments on the basis of race: " 'Racially neutral' assignment plans proposed by school authorities to a district court may be inadequate; such plans may fail to counteract the continuing effects of past school segregation resulting from discriminatory location of school sites or distortion of school size in order to achieve or maintain an artificial racial separation. When school authorities present a district court with a 'loaded game board,' affirmative action in the form of remedial altering of attendance zones is proper to achieve truly nondiscriminatory arrangements."

Fourth, the Court approved the use of busing as a judicial remedy "as one tool of school desegregation."

Finally, the Court stressed the limits of judicial intervention:

> At some point, these school authorities and others like them should have achieved full compliance with this Court's decision in *Brown.* The system would then be "unitary" in the sense required by our decision in *Green.* . . .
>
> It does not follow that the communities served by such systems will remain demographically stable, for in a growing, mobile society, few will do so. Neither school authorities nor district courts are constitutionally required to make year-by-year adjustments of the racial composition of student bodies once the affirmative duty to desegregate has been accomplished and racial discrimination through official action is eliminated from the system. This does not mean that federal courts are without power to deal with future problems; but in the absence of a showing that either the school authorities or some other agency of the State has deliberately attempted to fix or alter demographic patterns to affect the racial composition of the schools, further intervention by a district court should not be necessary.

6.   *School Segregation in the North*

Swann gave the federal courts considerable discretion to combat Southern opposition to desegregation. Armed with this power, federal judges used result-oriented remedies to circumvent the constant subterfuges of politicians and school boards. However, as the South began to integrate after 1968, Northern schools still remained largely segregated, leading to charges of unfairness by Southern politicians who felt that the federal courts were singling them out. Northern segregation was often the result of what was described as "de facto" rather than "de jure" segregation. The segregation of Northern schools was usually not the result of direct state law mandates about pupil assignments. Rather, other racially discriminatory practices by Northern states, coupled with residential segregation and general societal discrimination had produced school districts with populations segregated by race. Such segregation was called "de facto" even though it might arguably have been partly the result of previous acts of public and private discrimination outside of the context of school assignment policy. Moreover, if a school board adopted a particular assignment plan — for example, a neighborhood school policy — knowing that it would result in segregated schools, the resulting segregation would still be called de facto unless it could be shown that the school board was covertly using race as a decision-making factor.

By the time the Court began to turn to Northern segregation, the political climate had also begun to change. Although the Supreme Court had supported the use of busing in *Swann,* the idea was politically unpopular, particularly in the North. Moreover, the course of Southern integration was affected by the growth of Southern cities and suburbs, as well as a decline of the percentage of whites in urban school districts, both of which made the problems of combating Southern segregation increasingly resemble those of the North. Both Richard Nixon and George Wallace played on the unpopularity of busing in the 1968 election. A key element of Nixon's "Southern strategy" to break up the old Democratic New Deal coalition of labor, minorities, Northern liberals, and Southern Democrats was his opposition to compulsory busing of students. During the Nixon administration, Congress enacted the Education Amendments of 1972, which prohibited the use of federal funds for transportation of students to achieve racial balance. (These amendments had mostly symbolic effect because courts later interpreted them to apply only to busing designed to remedy de facto segregation.)

Perhaps equally important, President Nixon was able to appoint four new justices to the Supreme Court. Until 1971, the Supreme Court's opinions on school desegregation had been unanimous, in part to show a united front against possible Southern intransigence, and the opinions had dealt for the most part with the problems of desegregation in Southern and border states. Chief Justice Burger, a Nixon appointee, continued this tradition of unanimity in his 1971 opinion in *Swann.* With the appointment of Justices Rehnquist and Powell the same year, however, that tradition ended. Rehnquist was highly critical of the Court's approach, and Powell, a former member of the Richmond school board and the Virginia State Board of Education, had his own views about the nature and methods of Northern and Southern desegregation.

KEYES v. SCHOOL DISTRICT NO. 1, DENVER, COLORADO, 413 U.S. 189 (1973): The Court's first important statement on Northern segregation came in *Keyes.* The Denver school system, with a composition of 66 percent Anglo, 20 percent Hispanic, and 14 percent black, was highly segregated. (Note that the Court here treated schools with a "combined predominance of Negroes and Hispanos [sic]" as "segregated," based on the observation that both groups had suffered economic and cultural deprivation and discrimination.) Unlike Southern school systems, however, the Denver school system had never been segregated by the mandate of any state law. Plaintiffs claimed that the schools nonetheless were de jure segregated as the result of the school board's race-conscious manipulation of attendance zones and selection of school sites. The district court found that the board had engaged in such practices in an outlying community, Park Hill, but found no evidence of discrimination with respect to the segregated inner-city schools. The district court nonetheless ordered district-wide desegregation in order to assure the inner-city students "equal educational opportunity." The Tenth Circuit Court of Appeals reversed the portion of the decree requiring desegregation of the inner-city schools. The Supreme Court reversed.

BRENNAN, J.: [Justice Brennan's majority opinion used presumptions and burdens of proof to deal with the problem of de facto segregation:] Although plaintiffs bore the burden of showing that segregated schools had resulted from intentional state action, they did not have to prove an intent to segregate with respect to every segregated school in the school system.

[A] finding of intentionally segregative school board actions in a meaningful portion of a school system, . . . creates a presumption that other segregated schooling within the system is not adventitious. It establishes, . . . a prima facie case of unlawful segregative design on the part of school authorities, and shifts to those authorities the burden of proving that other segregated schools within the system are not also the result of intentionally segregative actions. This is true even if it is determined that different areas of the school district should be viewed independently of each other because, even in that situation, there is high probability that where school authorities have effectuated an intentionally segregative policy in a meaningful portion of the school system, similar impermissible considerations have motivated their actions in other areas of the system. . . . [T]he differentiating factor between de jure segregation and so-called de facto segregation . . . is *purpose* or *intent* to segregate. Where school authorities have been found to have practiced purposeful segregation . . . in a meaningful or significant segment of a school system, . . . it is both fair and reasonable to require that the school authorities bear the burden of showing that their actions as to other segregated schools within the system were not also motivated by segregative intent.

Rehnquist, J., dissenting: The drastic extension of *Brown* which *Green* represented was barely, if at all, explicated in the latter opinion. To require that a genuinely "dual" system be disestablished, in the sense that the assignment of a child to a particular school is not made to depend on his race, is one thing. To require that school boards affirmatively undertake to achieve racial mixing in schools were such mixing is not achieved in sufficient degree by neutrally drawn boundary lines is quite obviously something else. . . .

[*Green's* conversion of] *Brown's* prohibition against discrimination . . . into an affirmative duty to integrate was made in the context of a school system which had for a number of years rigidly excluded Negroes from attending the same schools as were attended by whites. Whatever may be the soundness of that decision in the context of a genuinely "dual" school system, where segregation of the races had once been mandated by law, I can see no constitutional justification for it in a situation such as that which the record shows to have obtained in Denver.

Powell, J., concurring in part and dissenting in part:

In my view we should abandon [the de jure/de facto] distinction which long since has outlived its time, and formulate constitutional principles of national rather than merely regional application. . . . The situation confronting the Court [in *Brown*], largely confined to the southern States, was officially imposed racial segregation in the schools extending back for many years and usually embodied in constitutional and statutory provisions. . . .

But the doctrine of *Brown I,* as amplified by *Brown II,* 349 U.S. 294 (1955), did not retain its original meaning. In a series of decisions extending from 1954 to 1971 the concept of state neutrality was transformed into the present constitutional doctrine requiring affirmative state action to desegregate school systems. The keystone case was *Green.*

[By] imposing on metropolitan southern school districts an affirmative duty, entailing large-scale transportation of pupils, to eliminate segregation in the schools [in *Swann*], the Court required these districts to alleviate conditions which in large part did *not* result from historic, state-imposed de jure segregation. Rather, the familiar root cause of segregated schools in *all* the biracial metropolitan areas of our country is essentially the same: one of segregated residential and migratory patterns the impact of which on the racial composition of the schools was often perpetuated and rarely ameliorated by action of public school authorities. This is a national, not a southern, phenomenon. And it is largely unrelated to whether a particular State had or did not have segregative school laws. . . .

I would not . . . perpetuate the de jure/de facto distinction nor would I leave to petitioners the initial tortuous effort of identifying "segregative acts" and deducing "segregative intent." I would hold, quite simply, that where segregated public schools exist within a school district to a substantial degree, there is a prima facie case that the duly constituted public authorities (I will usually refer to them collectively as the "school board") are sufficiently responsible to warrant imposing upon them a nationally applicable burden to demonstrate they nevertheless are operating a genuinely integrated school system.

[I]n view of the evolution of the holding in *Brown I* into the affirmative-duty doctrine, the distinction no longer can be justified on a principled basis. . . . *Swann* dealt with a metropolitan, urbanized area in which the basic causes of segregation were generally similar to those in all sections of the country, and also largely irrelevant to the existence of historic, state-imposed segregation at the time of the *Brown* decision. Further, the extension of the affirmative-duty concept to include compulsory student transportation went well beyond the mere remedying of that portion of school segregation for which former state segregation laws were ever responsible. Moreover, as the Court's opinion today abundantly demonstrates, the facts deemed necessary to establish de jure discrimination present problems of subjective intent which the courts cannot fairly resolve. . . .

I would now define [the constitutional interest at stake] as the right, derived from the Equal Protection Clause, to expect that once the State has assumed responsibility for education, local school boards will operate *integrated school systems* within their respective districts. This means that school authorities, consistent with the generally accepted educational goal of attaining quality education for all pupils, must make and implement their customary decisions with a view toward enhancing integrated school opportunities.

The term "integrated school system" presupposes, of course, a total absence of any laws, regulations, or policies supportive of the type of "legalized" segregation condemned in *Brown*. A system would be integrated in accord with constitutional standards if the responsible authorities had taken appropriate steps to (i) integrate faculties and administration; (ii) scrupulously assure equality of facilities, instruction, and curriculum opportunities throughout the district; (iii) utilize their authority to draw attendance zones to promote integration; and (iv) locate new schools, close old ones, and determine the size and grade categories with this same objective in mind. Where school authorities decide to undertake the transportation of students, this also must be with integrative opportunities in mind.

[A]n integrated school system does not mean — and indeed could not mean in view of the residential patterns of most of our major metropolitan areas — that *every school* must in fact be an integrated unit. A school which happens to be all or predominantly white or all or predominantly black is not a "segregated" school in an unconstitutional sense if the system itself is a genuinely integrated one. . . .

Public schools are creatures of the State, and whether the segregation is state-created or state-assisted or merely state-perpetuated should be irrelevant to constitutional principle. The school board exercises pervasive and continuing responsibility over the long-range planning as well as the daily operations of the public school system. It sets policies on attendance zones, faculty employment and assignments, school construction, closings and consolidations, and myriad other matters. School board decisions obviously are not the sole cause of segregated school conditions. But if, after such detailed and complete public supervision, substantial school segregation still persists, the presumption is strong that the school board, by its acts or omissions, is in some part responsible. Where state action and supervision are so pervasive and where, after years of such action, segregated schools continue to exist within the district to a substantial degree, this Court is justified in finding a prima facie case of a constitutional violation. The burden then must fall on the school board to demonstrate it is operating an "integrated school system." . . .

Where school authorities have defaulted in their duty to operate an integrated school system, district courts must insure that affirmative desegregative steps ensue. Many of these can be taken effectively without damaging state and parental interests in having children attend schools within a reasonable vicinity of home. Where desegregative steps are possible within the framework of a system of "neighborhood education," school authorities must pursue them. For example, boundaries of neighborhood attendance zones should be drawn to integrate, to the extent practicable, the school's student body. Construction of new schools should be of such a size and at such a location as to encourage the likelihood of integration. Faculty integration should be attained throughout the school system. An optional majority-to-minority transfer program, with the State providing free transportation to desiring students, is also a helpful adjunct to a desegregated school system. It hardly need be repeated that allocation of resources within the school district must be made with scrupulous fairness among all schools. . . .

A constitutional requirement of extensive student transportation solely to achieve integration . . . is . . . likely to divert attention and resources from the foremost goal of any school system: the best quality education for all pupils. The Equal Protection Clause . . . does not require that school authorities undertake widespread student transportation solely for the sake of maximizing integration. . . .

[The correct approach would involve] no prohibition on court-ordered student transportation in furtherance of desegregation. But it would require that the legitimate community interests in neighborhood school systems be accorded far greater respect. In the balancing of interests so appropriate to a fair and just equitable decree, transportation orders should be applied with special caution to any proposal as disruptive of family life and interests — and ultimately of education itself — as extensive transportation of elementary-age children solely for desegregation purposes. . . . [73]

Discussion

Keyes is notable for the apparent "deal" that Justice Powell, the conservative Democrat from Richmond, Virginia, offered the liberal majority headed by Justice

---

73. Justice White did not participate in the case. Chief Justice Burger concurred in the result. Justice Douglas wrote a brief concurring opinion.

Brennan. Powell offered to eliminate the de jure/de facto distinction, which, as a practical matter, would make it much easier to establish that school systems were in violation of the Fourteenth Amendment by operating systems with "racially identifiable" schools. *Green,* in effect, would move from a test of remedy to a test of liability. In return, liberals would have to agree to rein in the use of busing as a remedy. Justice Brennan rejected this offer, preferring to maintain the requirement that plaintiffs must show intent to maintain a segregated school system, buttressed by various presumptions. Why do you think he did this? Was he right to do so? Whose position seems more reasonable from today's perspective?

7. The Turning Point — Interdistrict Relief

By the mid-1970s President Nixon's appointments, as well as the changing political mood of the country, began to have an effect. In 1974, Congress passed the Equal Education Opportunities Act, 20 U.S.C. §1714, which among other things, prohibited "any court, department or agency of the United States [from ordering] transportation of any student to a school other than the school closest or next closest to his place of residence which provides the appropriate grade level and type education for such student." Although because of subsequent court interpretations the legislation had no practical effect, it symbolized increasing national opposition to busing and school desegregation remedies.

An important turning point was the Detroit metropolitan school litigation, in which the Supreme Court, for the first time since *Brown I,* overturned a district court's desegregation decree for going too far in redressing segregation. President Nixon's four Supreme Court appointees, joined by Justice Stewart, formed the five-person majority.

MILLIKEN v. BRADLEY, 418 U.S. 717 (1974): [The district court, having found de jure segregation within the city of Detroit, entered a decree that included 53 surrounding suburban districts. Although the city was predominantly Black and the suburbs White, there was no substantial evidence of race-dependent action (such as manipulating boundaries) designed to segregate the city's Blacks from the suburbs' Whites. On this basis, and emphasizing the importance of local control over public schools, the Supreme Court reversed.]

BURGER, C.J. . . .

The controlling principle consistently expounded in our holdings is that the scope of the remedy is determined by the nature and extent of the constitutional violation. Before the boundaries of separate and autonomous school districts may be set aside by consolidating the separate units for remedial purposes or by imposing a cross-district remedy, it must first be shown . . . that racially discriminatory acts of the state or local school districts, or of a single school district have been a substantial cause of inter-district segregation. Thus an inter-district remedy might be in order where the racially discriminatory acts of one or more school districts caused racial segregation in an adjacent district, or where district lines have been deliberately drawn on the basis of race. In such circumstances an inter-district remedy would be appropriate to eliminate the inter-district segregation directly caused by the constitutional violation. Conversely, without an inter-district violation and inter-district effect, there is no constitutional wrong calling for an inter-district remedy.

. . . To approve the remedy ordered by the court would impose on the outlying districts, not shown to have committed any constitutional violation, a wholly impermissible remedy based on a standard not hinted at in *Brown I* and *II* or any holding of this Court.[74]

WHITE, J., joined by Douglas, Brennan, and Marshall, JJ., dissenting. . . .

I am . . . mystified how the Court can ignore the legal reality that the constitutional violations, even if occurring locally, were committed by governmental entities for which the State is responsible and that it is the State that must respond to the command of the Fourteenth Amendment. An interdistrict remedy for the infringements that occurred in this case is well within the confines and powers of the State, which is the governmental entity ultimately responsible for desegregating its schools. . . .

The result reached by the Court certainly cannot be supported by the theory that the configuration of local governmental units is immune from alteration when necessary to redress constitutional violations. . . . [T]he Court has elsewhere required the public bodies of a State to restructure the State's political subdivisions to remedy infringements of the constitutional rights of certain members of its populace, notably in the reapportionment cases. In Reynolds v. Sims, 377 U.S. 533 (1964), for example, which held that equal protection of the laws demands that the seats in both houses of a bicameral state legislature be apportioned on a population basis, thus necessitating wholesale revision of Alabama's voting districts, the Court remarked: "Political subdivisions of States — counties, cities, or whatever — never were and never have been considered as sovereign entities. Rather, they have been traditionally regarded as subordinate governmental instrumentalities created by the State to assist in the carrying out of state governmental functions." And even more pointedly, the Court declared in Gomillion v. Lightfoot, 364 U.S. 339, 344-345 (1960), that "[l]egislative control of municipalities, no less than other state power, lies within the scope of relevant limitations imposed by the United States Constitution."

MARSHALL, J., dissenting. . . .

[Justice Marshall emphasized the state's control over public education and suggested how the state's action might have contributed to the disparity between the racial makeup of Detroit and of its surrounding suburbs.] The State's creation, through de jure acts of segregation, of a growing core of all-Negro schools inevitably acted as a magnet to attract Negroes to the areas served by such schools and to deter them from settling either in other areas of the city or in the suburbs. By the same token, the growing core of all-Negro schools inevitably helped drive whites to other areas of the city or to the suburbs. . . . The rippling effects on residential patterns caused by purposeful acts of segregation do not automatically subside at the school

74. Chief Justice Burger distinguished the Court's earlier decisions in Wright v. Emporia, 407 U.S. 451 (1972), and United States v. Scotland Neck Bd. of Educ., 407 U.S. 484 (1972), where the Court forbade carving new (largely White) school districts from existing de jure segregated districts in the process of dismantling dual school systems. Although the evident purpose of the secessions was to create segregated enclaves, the Court in the 1972 decisions relied solely on the effects and characterized the lower courts' inquiry into purpose as fruitless and irrelevant.

district border. With rare exceptions, these effects naturally spread through all the residential neighborhoods within a metropolitan area.

The State must also bear part of the blame for the white flight to the suburbs which would be forthcoming from a Detroit-only decree and would render such a remedy ineffective. Having created a system where whites and Negroes were intentionally kept apart so that they could not become accustomed to learning together, the State is responsible for the fact that many whites will react to the dismantling of that segregated system by attempting to flee to the suburbs. Allowing that flight to the suburbs to succeed, the Court today allows the State to profit from its own wrong and to perpetuate for years to come the separation of the races it achieved in the past by purposeful state action.

Discussion

On remand, the district court was faced with the task of integrating a school district that was approximately 70 percent black. It decided instead on a plan of educational reform, remedial education, magnet schools, counseling, and career guidance. On appeal, the Supreme Court affirmed. Milliken v. Bradley, 433 U.S. 267 (1977) (*Milliken II*). The Court argued that remedies for segregation were not limited to pupil reassignment, and that the court might order the state to expend funds for remedial education designed to put black students roughly in the position they would have been but for the original constitutional violation. If a local government refuses to pay for remedial education on the grounds that the tax levies for education are insufficient, may the district court order an increase in taxes? In Missouri v. Jenkins, 495 U.S. 33 (1990) (*Jenkins I*), the district court, faced with remedying segregation in the largely black Kansas City, Missouri school district, ordered a plan of magnet schools and other school improvements, and, in order to fund the program, ordered an increase of the property tax levy of close to 100 percent, in spite of the fact that in previous elections the voters had refused to raise the levy. In a 5-4 decision by Justice White, the Court upheld the principle that a district court could order a local governmental body to raise taxes, but reversed the district court's order for abuse of discretion on the particular facts of the case.

8. An Era of Retrenchment

Pasadena City Board of Education v. Spangler, 427 U.S. 424 (1976), invoked the closing paragraphs of *Swann* to hold that after four years under a court-ordered plan requiring cross-district busing to assure that no school had more than 50 percent minority students, the school board need not continue to reassign students on the basis of race to compensate for demographic changes. Justice Marshall, joined by Justice Brennan, dissented, arguing that the Court should have deferred to the District Court's finding that "the Pasadena Plan has not had the cooperation from the Board that permits a realistic measure of its educational success or failure" and that the Board had not yet fulfilled its affirmative duty to desegregate.

In Board of Education of Oklahoma City v. Dowell, 498 U.S. 111 237 (1991), the district court dissolved a ten-year-old desegregation decree against the school district. The court found that the original plan was no longer workable, that the district had complied with the court's orders in good faith, and that district's Student

Reassignment Plan, which would return a number of previously desegregated schools to one-race schools for the asserted purpose of alleviating busing burdens on black pupils, was not designed with discriminatory intent. The court of appeals reversed, holding that the injunction should remain in effect unless the school district could show "grievous wrong evolved by new and unforeseen conditions."

The Court reversed, Chief Justice Rehnquist writing:

> From the very first, federal supervision of local school systems was intended as a temporary measure to remedy past discrimination. . . . The legal justification for displacement of local authority in a school desegregation case by an injunctive decree is a violation of the Constitution by local authorities. Dissolving a desegregation decree after the local authorities have operated in compliance with it for a reasonable period of time properly recognizes that "necessary concern for the important values of local control of public schools dictates that a federal court's regulatory control of such systems does not extend beyond the time required to remedy the effects of past intentional discrimination." . . . In considering whether the vestiges of *de jure* segregation have been eliminated as far as practicable, the District Court should look not only at student assignments, but to "every facet of school operation — faculty, staff, transportation, extra-curricular activities, and facilities."

Justice Marshall, joined by Justices Blackmun and Stevens, dissented:

> I believe a desegregation decree cannot be lifted so long as conditions likely to inflict the stigmatic injury condemned in *Brown I* persist and there remain feasible methods of eliminating such conditions. . . . [T]he record here shows . . . that feasible steps could have been taken to avoid one-race schools. . . . Consistent with the mandate of *Brown I* our cases have imposed on school districts an unconditional duty to eliminate *any* condition that perpetuates the message of racial inferiority inherent in the policy of state-sponsored segregation. The racial identifiability of a district's schools is such a condition. . . . In a district with a history of state-sponsored school segregation, racial separation, in my view, *remains* inherently unequal.

In Freeman v. Pitts, 503 U.S. 467 (1992), the Supreme Court considered the desegregation plan of the DeKalb County School District, which had been operating under a consent decree since 1969. The district court had found in 1981 that the district had disestablished the dual school system. Years later it found that continued segregation, with identifiably black and white schools, was caused by changing residential patterns (i.e., "white flight") and not by any actions of local government authorities. It released the school board from judicial oversight with respect to pupil assignments although it found that the board had not attained unitary status with respect to other issues like teacher assignments and quality of education. The Court of Appeals reversed and ordered reorganization of school zones and busing. The Supreme Court reversed. Justice Kennedy wrote that "federal courts have the authority to relinquish supervision and control of school districts in incremental stages, before full compliance has been achieved in every area of school operations." It remanded to the district court to determine whether the school district had shown a "good faith commitment to the entirety of a desegregation plan."

Justice Kennedy went on to emphasize the limited nature of federal relief for resegregation when there was no finding of ongoing constitutional violations by the state:

Where resegregation is a product not of state action but of private choices, it does not have constitutional implications. It is beyond the authority and beyond the practical ability of the federal courts to try to counteract these kinds of continuous and massive demographic shifts. To attempt such results would require ongoing and never-ending supervision by the courts of school districts simply because they were once *de jure* segregated. . . . As the *de jure* violation becomes more remote in time and these demographic changes intervene, it becomes less likely that a current racial imbalance in a school district is a vestige of the prior *de jure* system. The causal link between current conditions and the prior violation is even more attenuated if the school district has demonstrated its good faith.

MISSOURI v. JENKINS, 515 U.S. 70 (1995): [In 1977 the Kansas City, Missouri, School District (KCMSD) and a class of KCMSD students sued Missouri for operating segregated schools in Kansas City. In 1985, after years of litigation in the district and circuit courts, the district court ordered an extensive capital improvements program for KCMSD schools and required the state to institute a "magnet plan" providing for the establishment of several magnet schools. The dual goal of the court's remedial orders was to attract white students back into public schools and to provide minority students an educational experience of the quality they would have received absent the effects of segregation. To this end, the district judge ordered across-the-board salary increases for teachers and staff, aimed at improving educational quality and attracting white suburban students. It also ordered continued state funding for the magnet schools so long as student achievement scores remained below national norms. In a 5-4 decision by Justice Rehnquist, the Supreme Court held that the goal of attracting white students from outside the KCMSD was not permissible within an intradistrict remedy under *Milliken II*.]

REHNQUIST, C.J.:

[T]his case involved no interdistrict constitutional violation that would support interdistrict relief. Thus, the proper response by the District Court should have been to eliminate to the extent practicable the vestiges of prior de jure segregation within the KCMSD: a systemwide reduction in student achievement and the existence of 25 racially identifiable schools with a population of over 90% black students.

The District Court and Court of Appeals, however . . . felt that because the KCMSD's enrollment remained 68.3% black, a purely intradistrict remedy would be insufficient. But, as noted in *Milliken I*, we have rejected the suggestion "that schools which have a majority of Negro students are not 'desegregated' whatever the racial makeup of the school district's population and however neutrally the district lines have been drawn and administered."

Instead of seeking to remove the racial identity of the various schools within the KCMSD, the District Court has set out on a program to create a school district that was equal to or superior to the surrounding [suburban school districts]. This remedy has included an elaborate program of capital improvements, course enrichment, and extracurricular enhancement not simply in the formerly identifiable black schools, but in schools throughout the district. The District Court's remedial orders have converted every senior high school, every middle school, and one-half of the elementary schools in the KCMSD into "magnet" schools. The District Court's remedial order has all but made the KCMSD itself into a magnet district.

We previously have approved of intradistrict desegregation remedies involving magnet schools. See, e.g., *Milliken II*. . . .

The District Court's remedial plan in this case, however, is not designed solely to redistribute the students within the KCMSD in order to eliminate racially identifiable schools within the KCMSD. Instead, its purpose is to attract non-minority students from outside the KCMSD schools. But this interdistrict goal is beyond the scope of the intradistrict violation identified by the District Court. In effect, the District Court has devised a remedy to accomplish indirectly what it admittedly lacks the remedial authority to mandate directly: the interdistrict transfer of students. . . .

It is certainly theoretically possible that the greater the expenditure per pupil within the KCMSD, the more likely it is that some unknowable number of nonminority students not presently attending schools in the KCMSD will choose to enroll in those schools. Under this reasoning, however, every increased expenditure, whether it be for teachers, noninstructional employees, books, or buildings, will make the KCMSD in some way more attractive, and thereby perhaps induce nonminority students to enroll in its schools. But this rationale is not susceptible to any objective limitation. . . .

Similar considerations lead us to conclude that the District Court's order requiring the State to continue to fund the quality education programs because student achievement levels were still "at or below national norms at many grade levels" cannot be sustained. . . .

[T]his clearly is not the appropriate test to be applied in deciding whether a previously segregated district has achieved partially unitary status. The basic task of the District Court is to decide whether the reduction in achievement by minority students attributable to prior de jure segregation has been remedied to the extent practicable. Under our precedents, the State and the KCMSD are "entitled to a rather precise statement of [their] obligations under a desegregation decree." Although the District Court has determined that "segregation has caused a system wide reduction in achievement in the schools of the KCMSD," it never has identified the incremental effect that segregation has had on minority student achievement or the specific goals of the quality education programs. . . .

Just as demographic changes independent of de jure segregation will affect the racial composition of student assignments, so too will numerous external factors beyond the control of the KCMSD and the State affect minority student achievement. So long as these external factors are not the result of segregation, they do not figure in the remedial calculus.

[A concurring opinion by Justice O'Connor and a dissenting opinion by Justice Ginsberg are omitted]

Souter, J., joined by Stevens, Ginsberg, and Breyer, JJ., dissenting:

[Justice Souter criticized the majority for misreading *Milliken I* and *II*:] In the *Milliken I* litigation, the District Court had ordered 53 surrounding school districts to be consolidated with the Detroit school system, and mandatory busing to be started within the enlarged district, even though the court had not found that any of the suburban districts had acted in violation of the Constitution. It was this imposition of remedial measures on more than the one wrongdoing school district that we termed an "interdistrict remedy."

We did not hold, however, that any remedy that takes into account conditions outside of the district in which a constitutional violation has been committed is an "interdistrict remedy," and as such improper in the absence of an "interdistrict violation." To the contrary, by emphasizing that remedies in school desegregation cases are grounded in traditional equitable principles, we left open the possibility that a district court might subject a proven constitutional wrongdoer to a remedy with intended effects going beyond the district of the wrongdoer's violation, when such a remedy is necessary to redress the harms flowing from the constitutional violation.

The Court, nonetheless, reads *Milliken I* . . . as categorically forbidding imposition of a remedy on a guilty district with intended consequences in a neighboring innocent district, unless the constitutional violation yielded segregative effects in that innocent district.

[Justice Thomas concurred in an opinion that viewed the litigation as symbolic of more basic issues in the Court's desegregation jurisprudence:]

THOMAS, J., concurring:

It never ceases to amaze me that the courts are so willing to assume that anything that is predominantly black must be inferior. Instead of focusing on remedying the harm done to those black schoolchildren injured by segregation, the District Court here sought to convert the Kansas City, Missouri, School District (KCMSD) into a "magnet district" that would reverse the "white flight" caused by desegregation. . . .

Two threads in our jurisprudence have produced this unfortunate situation, in which a District Court has taken it upon itself to experiment with the education of the KCMSD's black youth. First, the court has read our cases to support the theory that black students suffer an unspecified psychological harm from segregation that retards their mental and educational development. This approach not only relies upon questionable social science research rather than constitutional principle, but it also rests on an assumption of black inferiority. Second, we have permitted the federal courts to exercise virtually unlimited equitable powers to remedy this alleged constitutional violation. The exercise of this authority has trampled upon principles of federalism and the separation of powers and has freed courts to pursue other agendas unrelated to the narrow purpose of precisely remedying a constitutional harm.

The mere fact that a school is black does not mean that it is the product of a constitutional violation. . . . Instead, in order to find unconstitutional segregation, we require that plaintiffs "prove all of the essential elements of de jure segregation — that is, stated simply, a current condition of segregation resulting from intentional state action directed specifically to the [allegedly segregated] schools." "The differentiating factor between de jure segregation and so-called de facto segregation . . . is purpose or intent to segregate." . . .

It should by now be clear that the existence of one-race schools is not by itself an indication that the State is practicing segregation. The continuing "racial isolation" of schools after de jure segregation has ended may well reflect voluntary housing choices or other private decisions. Here, for instance, the demography of the entire KCMSD has changed considerably since 1954. Though blacks accounted for only 18.9% of KCMSD's enrollment in 1954, by 1983-1984 the school district was 67.7% black. That certain schools are overwhelmingly black in a district that is now more than two-thirds black is hardly a sure sign of intentional state action. . . .

In effect, the court found that racial imbalances constituted an ongoing constitutional violation that continued to inflict harm on black students. This position appears to rest upon the idea that any school that is black is inferior, and that blacks cannot succeed without the benefit of the company of whites.

The District Court's willingness to adopt such stereotypes stemmed from a misreading of our earliest school desegregation case. In Brown v. Board of Education, 347 U.S. 483 (1954) (*Brown I*), the Court noted several psychological and sociological studies purporting to show that de jure segregation harmed black students by generating "a feeling of inferiority" in them. Seizing upon this passage in *Brown I*, the District Court asserted that "forced segregation ruins attitudes and is inherently unequal." . . . Thus, the District Court seemed to believe that black students in the KCMSD would continue to receive an "inferior education" despite the end of de jure segregation, as long as de facto segregation persisted. As the District Court later concluded, compensatory educational programs were necessary "as a means of remedying many of the educational problems which go hand in hand with racially isolated minority student populations." Such assumptions and any social science research upon which they rely certainly cannot form the basis upon which we decide matters of constitutional principle.[a]

It is clear that the District Court misunderstood the meaning of *Brown I*. *Brown I* did not say that "racially isolated" schools were inherently inferior; the harm that it identified was tied purely to de jure segregation, not de facto segregation. Indeed, *Brown I* itself did not need to rely upon any psychological or social-science research in order to announce the simple, yet fundamental, truth that the government cannot discriminate among its citizens on the basis of race. . . .

Segregation was not unconstitutional because it might have caused psychological feelings of inferiority. Public school systems that separated blacks and provided them with superior educational resources — making blacks "feel" superior to whites sent to lesser schools — would violate the Fourteenth Amendment, whether or not the white students felt stigmatized, just as do school systems in which the positions of the races are reversed. Psychological injury or benefit is irrelevant to the question whether state actors have engaged in intentional discrimination — the critical inquiry for ascertaining violations of the Equal Protection Clause. The judiciary is fully competent to make independent determinations concerning the existence of state action without the unnecessary and misleading assistance of the social sciences.

Regardless of the relative quality of the schools, segregation violated the Constitution because the State classified students based on their race. Of course,

---

a. The studies cited in *Brown I* have received harsh criticism. See, e.g., Yudof, School Desegregation: Legal Realism, Reasoned Elaboration, and Social Science Research in the Supreme Court, 42 Law & Contemp. Probs. 57, 70 (Autumn 1978); L. Graglia, Disaster by Decree: The Supreme Court Decisions on Race and the Schools 27-28 (1976). Moreover, there simply is no conclusive evidence that desegregation either has sparked a permanent jump in the achievement scores of black children, or has remedied any psychological feelings of inferiority black schoolchildren might have had. See, e.g., Bradley & Bradley, The Academic Achievement of Black Students in Desegregated Schools, 47 Rev. Educational Research 399 (1977); N. St. John, School Desegregation: Outcomes for Children (1975); Epps, The Impact of School Desegregation on Aspirations, Self-Concepts and Other Aspects of Personality, 39 Law & Contemp. Probs. 300 (Spring 1975). Contra, Crain & Mahard, Desegregation and Black Achievement: A Review of the Research, 42 Law & Contemp. Probs. 17 (Summer 1978); Crain & Mahard, The Effect of Research Methodology on Desegregation-Achievement Studies: A Meta-Analysis, 88 Am. J. of Sociology 839 (1983). Although the gap between black and white test scores has narrowed over the past two decades, it appears that this has resulted more from gains in the socioeconomic status of black families than from desegregation. See Armor, Why is Black Educational Achievement Rising?, 108 The Public Interest 65, 77-79 (Summer 1992).

segregation additionally harmed black students by relegating them to schools with substandard facilities and resources. But neutral policies, such as local school assignments, do not offend the Constitution when individual private choices concerning work or residence produce schools with high black populations. The Constitution does not prevent individuals from choosing to live together, to work together, or to send their children to school together, so long as the State does not interfere with their choices on the basis of race.

Given that desegregation has not produced the predicted leaps forward in black educational achievement, there is no reason to think that black students cannot learn as well when surrounded by members of their own race as when they are in an integrated environment. Indeed, it may very well be that what has been true for historically black colleges is true for black middle and high schools. Despite their origins in "the shameful history of state-enforced segregation," these institutions can be "both a source of pride to blacks who have attended them and a source of hope to black families who want the benefits of . . . learning for their children." Because of their "distinctive histories and traditions," black schools can function as the center and symbol of black communities, and provide examples of independent black leadership, success, and achievement.

Thus, even if the District Court had been on firmer ground in identifying a link between the KCMSD's pre-1954 de jure segregation and the present "racial isolation" of some of the district's schools, mere de facto segregation (unaccompanied by discriminatory inequalities in educational resources) does not constitute a continuing harm after the end of de jure segregation. "Racial isolation" itself is not a harm; only state-enforced segregation is. After all, if separation itself is a harm, and if integration therefore is the only way that blacks can receive a proper education, then there must be something inferior about blacks. Under this theory, segregation injures blacks because blacks, when left on their own, cannot achieve. To my way of thinking, that conclusion is the result of a jurisprudence based upon a theory of black inferiority.

This misconception has drawn the courts away from the important goal in desegregation. The point of the Equal Protection Clause is not to enforce strict race-mixing, but to ensure that blacks and whites are treated equally by the State without regard to their skin color. The lower courts should not be swayed by the easy answers of social science, nor should they accept the findings, and the assumptions, of sociology and psychology at the price of constitutional principle.

Discussion

1. What possible remedies are available to a district court judge in a case like *Jenkins*? What is accomplished, for example, by taking steps to ensure that the remaining white students in the KCMSD are spread relatively evenly among majority black schools? Wouldn't more good be done by making sure that the schools are safe and relatively effective places to learn? One way of understanding the district court's "magnet schools" remedy was to use the law of desegregation to improve the quality of education within the district in the face of white voters who had largely abandoned the public schools. However, in *Jenkins* the Court insisted that improving the quality of the schools was not the purpose of the Equal Protection Clause. Note in this context that the Court had previously held in San Antonio Independent School District v. Rodriguez, 411 U.S. 1 (1973), that education is not a fundamental right and that states are not required to guarantee equality in educational quality or

educational expenditures.[75] Is *Brown* a case about racial classification, a case about educational opportunity, or both? Note that, taken together, *Milliken I* and *Rodriguez* effectively acquiesce in white abandonment of largely black and Hispanic inner cities, because there is no right to integration that would create incentives for equal educational funding between city and suburban schools and, after *Rodriguez*, there is no federal constitutional right to equal educational opportunity.

2. Due to demographic changes over the past 30 years, many urban public school districts are "disproportionately" minority. In practical terms, does *Jenkins* signal the acceptance of "separate but equal" as long as there is no evidence of continuing segregative intent by school districts? Do you agree with Justice Thomas that this result is acceptable? Justice Thomas seems entirely comfortable with racially identifiable schools as long as these schools are the result of "private decisions" rather than intentional government segregation. If Justice Thomas is correct, should *Green* be overruled? Justice Thomas sees majority black schools as a potential source of pride for black communities. According to Justice Thomas, what constitutional remedies, if any, do black communities have if they believe that state and local governments are paying insufficient attention to their concerns and are failing to guarantee equal educational opportunity for black children?

9. *Desegregating Institutions of Higher Education*

UNITED STATES v. FORDICE
505 U.S. 717 (1992)

[Even after *Brown*, Mississippi continued its policy of de jure segregation in its public university system consisting of five white and three black universities. In the wake of a lawsuit challenging the policy, the State Board of Trustees in 1981 issued "Mission Statements," in which they classified (1) three mostly white flagship institutions as "comprehensive" universities with the greatest variety of programs and degrees up to the doctoral level, (2) one of the black colleges as an "urban" university with limited research and degree functions appropriate to an urban setting, and (3) the rest of the colleges as "regional" institutions focusing on undergraduate education. In the mid-1980s, predominantly single-race student populations persisted in both the white and black institutions, and the suit proceeded to trial. The District Court held that, in the context of higher education, the affirmative duty to desegregate does not require either restricting student choice or the achievement of any degree of racial balance. Finding that Mississippi's current state policies and practices were racially neutral, developed and implemented in good faith, and did not contribute substantially to the racial identifiability of individual institutions, the court held that the State thereby fulfilled its affirmative duty to desegregate. The Court of Appeals affirmed this conclusion.]

WHITE, J. . . .

[T]he primary issue in this case is whether the State has met its affirmative duty to dismantle its prior dual university system.

75. This doctrine is covered in more detail in Chapter 9, supra.

. . . [A] state university system is quite different in very relevant respects from primary and secondary schools. Unlike attendance at the lower level schools, a student's decision to seek higher education has been a matter of choice. The State historically has not assigned university students to a particular institution. Moreover, like public universities throughout the country, Mississippi's institutions of higher learning are not fungible — they have been designated to perform certain missions. Students who qualify for admission enjoy a range of choices of which institution to attend. . . .

We do not agree with the Court of Appeals or the District Court, however, that the adoption and implementation of race-neutral policies alone suffice to demonstrate that the State has completely abandoned its prior dual system. In a system based on choice, student attendance is determined not simply by admissions policies, but also by many other factors. Although some of these factors clearly cannot be attributed to State policies, many can be. . . .

. . . If the State perpetuates policies and practices traceable to its prior system that continue to have segregative effects — whether by influencing student enrollment decisions or by fostering segregation in other facets of the university system — and such policies are without sound educational justification and can be practicably eliminated, the State has not satisfied its burden of proving that it has dismantled its prior system.

[Justice White pointed to] four policies of the present system: admission standards, program duplication, institutional mission assignments, and continued operation of all eight public universities. . . .

The present admissions standards are not only traceable to the de jure system and were originally adopted for a discriminatory purpose, but they also have present discriminatory effects. Every Mississippi resident under 21 seeking admission to the university system must take the ACT test. Any applicant who scores at least 15 qualifies for automatic admission to [four of the] historically white institutions. . . . In 1985, 72 percent of Mississippi's white high school seniors achieved an ACT composite score of 15 or better, while less than 30 percent of black high school seniors earned that score. It is not surprising then that Mississippi's universities remain predominantly identifiable by race.

[D]ifferences in minimum automatic entrance scores among the regional universities in Mississippi's system [also] fall disproportionately on black students. . . .

[T]he disparity between black and white students' high school grade averages was much narrower than the gap between their average ACT scores, thus suggesting that an admissions formula which included grades would increase the number of black students eligible for automatic admission to all of Mississippi's public universities. . . .

[A second factor] is the widespread duplication of programs. [This was] part and parcel of the prior dual system of higher education — the whole notion of "separate but equal" required duplicative programs in two sets of schools — and . . . the present unnecessary duplication is a continuation of that practice. . . .

[A third issue] is Mississippi's scheme of [assigning] institutional mission[s] to the various schools. The District Court found that, throughout the period of de jure segregation, [three white-only institutions, the] University of Mississippi, Mississippi State University, and University of Southern Mississippi were the flagship institutions in the state system. They received the most funds, initiated the most advanced and specialized programs, and developed the widest range of curricular functions. . . . [T]he three exclusively black universities were more limited in their assigned academic missions than the five all-white institutions. . . .

[W]hen combined with the differential admission practices and unnecessary program duplication, it is likely that the mission designations interfere with student choice and tend to perpetuate the segregated system. . . .

Fourth, the State attempted to bring itself into compliance with the Constitution by continuing to maintain and operate all eight higher educational institutions [which was originally] undoubtedly occasioned by State laws forbidding the mingling of the races. [C]ontinuing to maintain all eight universities in Mississippi is wasteful and irrational. . . .

[O]n remand [the court should] determinin[e] whether retention of all eight institutions itself affects student choice and perpetuates the segregated higher education system, [and] whether maintenance of each of the universities is educationally justifiable. . . .

If we understand private petitioners to press us to order the upgrading of [the historically black institutions] solely so that they may be publicly financed, exclusively black enclaves by private choice, we reject that request. The State provides these facilities for all its citizens and it has not met its burden under *Brown* to take affirmative steps to dismantle its prior *de jure* system when it perpetuates a separate, but "more equal" one. Whether such an increase in funding is necessary to achieve a full dismantlement under the standards we have outlined, however, is a different question, and one that must be addressed on remand. . . .

THOMAS, J., concurring.[76]

"We must rally to the defense of our schools. We must repudiate this unbearable assumption of the right to kill institutions unless they conform to one narrow standard." [W.E.B.] Du Bois, Schools, 13 *The Crisis* 111, 112 (1917).

I agree with the Court that a State does not satisfy its obligation to dismantle a dual system of higher education merely by adopting race-neutral policies for the future administration of that system. . . . I write separately to emphasize that this standard is far different from the one adopted to govern the grade-school context in *Green* and its progeny. In particular, because it does not compel the elimination of all observed racial imbalance, it portends neither the destruction of historically black colleges nor the severing of those institutions from their distinctive histories and traditions.

. . . [W]e do not foreclose the possibility that there exists "sound educational justification" for maintaining historically black colleges as such. Despite the shameful history of state-enforced segregation, these institutions have survived and flourished. Indeed, they have expanded as opportunities for blacks to enter historically white institutions have expanded.

. . . I think it undisputable that these institutions have succeeded in part because of their distinctive histories and traditions; for many, historically black colleges have become "a symbol of the highest attainments of black culture." J. Preer, Lawyers v. Educators: Black Colleges and Desegregation in Public Higher Education 2 (1982). Obviously, a State cannot maintain such traditions

---

76. A concurring opinion by Justice O'Connor is omitted.

by closing particular institutions, historically white or historically black, to particular racial groups. Nonetheless, it hardly follows that a State cannot operate a diverse assortment of institutions — including historically black institutions — open to all on a race-neutral basis, but with established traditions and programs that might disproportionately appeal to one race or another. No one, I imagine, would argue that such institutional diversity is without "sound educational justification," or that it is even remotely akin to program duplication, which is designed to separate the races for the sake of separating the races. . . . Although I agree that a State is not constitutionally required to maintain its historically black institutions as such, I do not understand our opinion to hold that a State is forbidden to do so. It would be ironic, to say the least, if the institutions that sustained blacks during segregation were themselves destroyed in an effort to combat its vestiges.

SCALIA, J., concurring in the judgment in part and dissenting in part. . . .

I agree, of course, that the Constitution compels Mississippi to remove all discriminatory barriers to its state-funded universities. . . . I reject, however, the effectively unsustainable burden the Court imposes on Mississippi, and all States that formerly operated segregated universities, to demonstrate compliance with *Brown I.* That requirement, which resembles what we prescribed for primary and secondary schools in *Green,* has no proper application in the context of higher education, provides no genuine guidance to States and lower courts, and is as likely to subvert as to promote the interests of those citizens on whose behalf the present suit was brought. . . .

Ironically enough, . . . today's decision seems to prevent adoption of . . . a conscious policy [of equal funding for historically black universities]. . . . The requirement "was part and parcel of the prior dual system." Moreover, equal funding, like program duplication, facilitates continued segregation — enabling students to attend schools where their own race predominates without paying a penalty in the quality of education. Nor could such an equal-funding policy be saved on the basis that it serves what the Court calls a "sound educational justification." The only conceivable educational value it furthers is that of fostering schools in which blacks receive their education in a "majority" setting; but to acknowledge that as a "value" would contradict the compulsory-integration philosophy that underlies *Green.* Just as vulnerable, of course, would be all other programs that have the effect of facilitating the continued existence of predominantly black institutions: [for example]; offering a so-called Afrocentric curriculum, as has been done recently on an experimental basis in some secondary and primary schools; [or] preserving eight separate universities, which is perhaps Mississippi's single policy most segregative in effect.

But this predictable impairment of HBI's [historically black institutions] should come as no surprise: for incidentally facilitating — indeed, even tolerating — the continued existence of HBI's is not what the Court's test is about, and has never been what *Green* is about. ("The Board must be required to formulate a new plan and . . . fashion steps which promise realistically to convert promptly to a system without a 'white' school and a 'Negro' school"). What the Court's test is designed to achieve is the elimination of predominantly black institutions. While that may be good social policy, the present petitioners, I suspect, would not agree; and there is much to be said for the Court of Appeals' perception that "if no [state] authority exists to deny [the student] the right to attend the institution of his choice, he is done a severe disservice by remedies which, in seeking to maximize integration, minimize diversity and vitiate his choices."

Discussion

1. The *Fordice* majority acknowledges that there are real differences between primary and secondary education, on the one hand, and higher education, on the other. Yet the opinion purports to apply essentially the same constitutional standard in both contexts. Does it in fact do so? Is Scalia correct in claiming (with disapproval) that the *Fordice* standard "resembles what we prescribed for primary and secondary schools in Green v. New Kent County School Board"? Is the Court's "sound educational justification" exception for policies with continuing segregative effects consistent with *Green*?

2. Justices Thomas and Scalia both argue that the preservation (and even strengthening) of historically black colleges is perfectly consistent with the Constitution. Both Justices have also been strongly opposed to forms of race-conscious affirmative action, arguing that racial distinctions are just as unconstitutional when they disadvantage whites as when they disadvantage blacks. Are these two positions consistent? Consider substituting the word "white" for "black" in Justice Thomas's description of historically black colleges:

> Nonetheless, it hardly follows that a State cannot operate a diverse assortment of institutions — including historically [White] institutions — open to all on a race-neutral basis, but with established traditions and programs that might disproportionately appeal to [Whites]. No one, I imagine, would argue that such institutional diversity is without "sound educational justification," or that it is even remotely akin to program duplication, which is designed to separate the races for the sake of separating the races.

Is such a policy constitutional? Isn't this what Mississippi had in place before the litigation began? If Mississippi can consciously work to preserve historically black colleges but not historically white colleges, why can't it engage in race-conscious affirmative action?

3. *Bazemore and "freedom of choice."* *Green* is not the only possible precedent for applying *Brown* to the context of higher education. In Bazemore v. Friday, 478 U.S. 385 (1986), the Court held that *Green's* "affirmative duty to desegregate" had "no application" to the 4-H and Homemaker Clubs operated by the North Carolina Agricultural Extension Service. These clubs had been segregated until 1965. In response to the 1964 Civil Rights Act, the Service opened the clubs to any person otherwise eligible to join regardless of race. Nevertheless, a majority remained single race in 1980. Justice White's majority opinion argued that "[w]hile school children must go to school, there is no compulsion to join 4-H or Homemaker Clubs, and while School Boards customarily have the power to create school attendance areas and otherwise designate the school that particular students may attend, there is no statutory or regulatory authority to deny a young person the right to join any Club he or she wishes to join." Justice Brennan dissented, joined by Justices Marshall, Blackmun, and Stevens. He argued that "[n]othing in our earlier cases suggests that the State's obligation to desegregate

is confined only to those activities in which members of the public are compelled to participate."

Justice Scalia claimed that the real question in *Fordice* was whether *Green* or *Bazemore* applied to higher education. He argued that *Bazemore* represented the appropriate standard. "[D]iscontinuation of discriminatory practices and adoption of a neutral admissions policy" is all that was necessary. "Like the club attendance in *Bazemore* (and unlike the school attendance in *Green*), attending college is voluntary, not a legal obligation, and which institution particular students attend is determined by their own choice."

Justice White held that *Bazemore* did not apply, and was in any case not inconsistent with *Green:*

[In *Bazemore*] the District Court had found that the policy of segregation [in the 4-H and Homemaker Clubs] had been completely abandoned and that no evidence existed of any lingering discrimination in either services or membership; any racial imbalance resulted from the wholly voluntary and unfettered choice of private individuals. In this context, we held inapplicable the *Green* Court's judgment that a voluntary choice program was insufficient to dismantle a de jure dual system in public primary and secondary schools, but only after satisfying ourselves that the State had not fostered segregation by playing a part in the decision of which club an individual chose to join. *Bazemore* plainly does not excuse inquiry into whether Mississippi has left in place certain aspects of its prior dual system that perpetuate the racially segregated higher education system. If the State perpetuates policies and practices traceable to its prior system that continue to have segregative effects — whether by influencing student enrollment decisions or by fostering segregation in other facets of the university system — and such policies are without sound educational justification and can be practicably eliminated, the State has not satisfied its burden of proving that it has dismantled its prior system. Such policies run afoul of the Equal Protection Clause, even though the State has abolished the legal requirement that whites and blacks be educated separately and has established racially neutral policies not animated by a discriminatory purpose.

4. *What is "freedom of choice?"* The majority's analysis centers around the fact that although students in the Mississippi university system are technically "free" to choose which university to attend, their choices are nevertheless constrained by numerous factors. The majority holds unacceptable facially race-neutral policies that "substantially restrict a person's choice of which institution to enter and contribute to the racial identifiability of the [eight public] universities." Recall the Court's admonition in *Green:* " '[F]reedom of choice' is not a sacred talisman. . . . [I]f it fails to undo segregation, other means must be used to achieve this end." 391 U.S. at 441. Thus qualified, what does "freedom of choice" really mean? Doesn't every substantive and structural feature of the university system affect student choices? As Justice Scalia argues in his dissent, "Even an open-admissions policy would fall short of ensuring that student choice is unaffected by State action." Does the addition of the word "substantially" make the court's test clearer? Is there a difference between curricular features that discourage black students from attending the historically white University of Mississippi and features that attract them to Jackson State University, a historically black college? Conversely, might some of these same features alternatively attract and discourage whites to the respective universities?

Note: Toward "Separate But Truly Equal"?

Justice Thomas is not alone in his opposition to integration as an end in itself. Recall his concurring statement in Missouri v. Jenkins: "[I]f separation itself is a harm, and integration therefore is the only way that blacks can receive a proper education, then there must be something inferior about blacks. Under this theory, segregation injures blacks because blacks, when left on their own, cannot achieve. . . ."

Others have made arguments in favor of separate educational facilities for black students — or "immersion schools," as they are sometimes called — based on pedagogical, rather than constitutional considerations. Kevin Brown, for example, evaluates immersion schools by the following standard: "The benefit of any education is measured by how well it prepares students to deal with the situations that they will encounter throughout their lives." Do African-Americans Need Immersion Schools? The Paradoxes Created by Legal Conceptualization of Race and Public Education, 78 Iowa L. Rev. 813, 819 (1993). Brown argues that immersion schools have important benefits:

> [They] provide educators with the opportunity to develop teaching strategies, techniques, and materials that take into account the influence of the dominant American and the African-American cultures on the social environment and understandings of African-Americans. Educators can formulate strategies and teach techniques to African-American students to successfully overcome racial obstacles. Immersion schools also provide educators with an opportunity to reduce the cultural conflict between the dominant American culture, which is enshrined in the traditional public education program, and African-America culture. This conflict is a primary reason for the poor performance of African-American students.

Brown also argues that immersion schools will help black students cope with the stigmatizing assumptions of the dominant white culture:

> African-Americans live in a society where common "knowledge" about blacks plays a central role in the dominant American socio-historical experience. In the dominant American culture, this produces a socially constructed category for African-Americans with particularly negative connotations. Black people occupy a social category where its inhabitants are perceived as poor, lazy, lustful, ignorant, and prone to criminal behavior. African-Americans do not choose, nor can they escape from, this omnipresent social category. Assumptions made about the personality traits of African-Americans attached to their racial-social category often form the hidden backdrop for many of their social interactions in this society.

Assuming that one accepts the critique of integrationism, are immersion schools the best solution? What alternatives should public interest groups concerned with the welfare of the black community push for in the future?

II.   The Antidiscrimination Principle and the "Suspect Classification" Standard

The opinion in *Brown* emphasized the particular harms to young children caused by segregation in the classroom. But to what forms of racial segregation did *Brown* apply, and in what institutional contexts? To de jure racial segregation in public education only? To all racially segregative practices that inflicted like harm on African-Americans? To all racially segregative practices involving state action? Did *Brown* itself hold the answers to these questions, or was further consideration of the Equal Protection Clause required? In the years following *Brown*, heated debates over the justifications for the decision evolved into equally fervent disputes about the decision's reach and proper application.

A. The Origins of the Suspect Classification Doctrine

Current Supreme Court caselaw requires close scrutiny of government policies that classify on the basis of race. But the language of classification was conspicuously absent in *Brown*, which emphasized that racially segregated schools harmed children by causing powerful feelings of "inferiority as to their status in the community." *Brown* did not proscribe racial classification or declare it suspect. Rather, it addressed the harmful consequences of separating school children in a specific institutional context.

The Court soon made it clear enough that *Brown*'s holding was not so limited. The Court enjoined segregation in public transportation and recreation facilities in a series of per curiam decisions that extended *Brown* beyond the context of education, without explaining the principle on which the decisions rested.[77] These per curiams enlarged *Brown*'s prohibition on racial segregation, while deferring explosive questions about *Brown*'s reach.

At the time, some explained the per curiam decisions as demonstrating that the Court was implicitly importing doctrines prohibiting racial classification into the Fourteenth Amendment context. Yet it was clear that the Court was not acting on the assumption that all state action that classified on the basis of race was unconstitutional.

In the same period in which the Court decided the per curiam cases, it refused to decide a challenge to Virginia's antimiscegenation law. Contemporaries understood that the Court was proceeding incrementally and by indirection, so as not further to inflame resistance to its authority. The Court seems to have been especially concerned not to address questions about the constitutionality of antimiscegenation laws too soon after *Brown*, when Southerners were denouncing *Brown* itself as a dangerous first step in a "social program for amalgamation of the two races."

---

77. See New Orleans City Park Improvement Ass'n v. Detiege, 358 U.S. 54, 54 (1958) (mem.) (per curiam), aff'g 252 F. Supp. 2d 122 (5th Cir. 1958) (public parks and golf courses); Gayle v. Browder, 352 U.S. 903, 903 (1956) (mem.) (per curiam), aff'g 142 F. Supp. 707 (M.D. Ala. 1956) (intrastate buses); Holmes v. City of Atlanta, 350 U.S. 879, 879 (1955) (mem.) (per curiam), vacating and remanding 223 F.2d 93 (5th Cir. 1955) (municipal golf courses); Mayor and City Council of Baltimore City v. Dawson, 350 U.S. 877, 877 (1955) (mem.) (per curiam), aff'g 220 F.2d 386 (4th Cir. 1955) (public beaches and bathhouses); Muir v. Louisville Park Theatrical Ass'n, 347 U.S. 971, 971 (1954) (mem.) (per curiam), vacating and remanding 202 F.2d 275 (6th Cir. 1953) (municipal recreational facilities). For a more extensive list of the Court's per curiam desegregation decisions, see 2 Thomas I. Emerson et al., Political and Civil Rights in the United States 1249 (student ed. 1967).

1.   *The Court Strikes Down Antimiscegenation Statutes*

Shortly after *Brown,* plaintiffs challenged Virginia's ban on interracial marriage. The Virginia Supreme Court upheld the ban; the Supreme Court vacated and remanded for further proceedings, ostensibly to further develop the evidentiary record, at which point the Virginia Supreme Court simply reinstated its previous decision.[78] The Supreme Court, fearful of directly addressing the question of interracial marriage so soon after its decision in *Brown,* refused to decide whether *Brown* applied to Virginia's ban on interracial marriage; instead, in Naim v. Naim, 350 U.S. 985 (1956), it dismissed the appeal from Virginia's Supreme Court as improvidently granted, leaving the status quo in place.

However, by 1964, the political situation had changed considerably. The Civil Rights Act was signed on July 2, 1964; in November, Lyndon Johnson was elected by a landslide. That December, in McLaughlin v. Florida, 379 U.S. 184 (1964), the Court invalidated a statute that punished interracial cohabitation more severely than cohabitation by persons of the same race. In so doing, the Court repudiated Pace v. Alabama, 106 U.S. 583 (1883), a Reconstruction-era decision that upheld an Alabama statute that punished interracial cohabitation or fornication more severely than intraracial fornication (see Chapter 4). Justice White argued that "*Pace* represents a limited view of the Equal Protection Clause which has not withstood analysis in the subsequent decisions of this Court":

> Judicial inquiry under the Equal Protection Clause . . . does not end with a showing of equal application among the members of the class defined by the legislation. The courts must reach and determine the question whether the classifications drawn in a statute are reasonable in light of its purpose — in this case, whether there is an arbitrary or invidious discrimination between those classes covered by Florida's cohabitation law and those excluded. That question is what *Pace* ignored and what must be faced here.
>
> Normally, the widest discretion is allowed the legislative judgment in determining whether to attack some, rather than all, of the manifestations of the evil aimed at; and normally that judgment is given the benefit of every conceivable circumstance which might suffice to characterize the classification as reasonable rather than arbitrary and invidious. But we deal here with a classification based upon the race of the participants, which must be viewed in light of the historical fact that the central purpose of the Fourteenth Amendment was to eliminate racial discrimination emanating from official sources in the States. This strong policy renders racial classifications "constitutionally suspect," Bolling v. Sharpe, and subject to the "most rigid scrutiny," Korematsu v. United States, 323 U.S. 214; and "in most circumstances irrelevant" to any constitutionally acceptable legislative purpose, Hirabayashi v. United States, 320 U.S. 81. Thus it is that racial classifications have been held invalid in a variety of contexts. See, e.g., Virginia Board of Elections v. Hamm, 379 U.S. 19 (designation of race in voting and property records); Anderson v. Martin, 375 U.S. 399 (designation of race on nomination papers and ballots); Watson v. City of Memphis, 373 U.S. 526 (segregation in public parks and

---

78. See Naim v. Naim, 350 U.S. 891, 891 (1955) (mem.) (per curiam) (vacating judgment), remanded to 90 S.E.2d 849 (Va.) (reinstating judgment), motion to recall mandate denied per curiam, 350 U.S. 985 (1956) (mem.) (dismissing for want of a properly presented federal question).

playgrounds); Brown v. Board of Education, 349 U.S. 294 (segregation in public schools). . . .

There is involved here an exercise of the state police power which trenches upon the constitutionally protected freedom from invidious official discrimination based on race. Such a law, even though enacted pursuant to a valid state interest, bears a heavy burden of justification . . . and will be upheld only if it is necessary, and not merely rationally related, to the accomplishment of a permissible state policy.

Three years later, the Supreme Court finally took up the constitutionality of Virginia's law.

LOVING v. VIRGINIA
338 U.S. 1 (1967)

Mr. Chief Justice WARREN delivered the opinion of the Court.

This case presents a constitutional question never addressed by this Court: whether a statutory scheme adopted by the State of Virginia to prevent marriages between persons solely on the basis of racial classifications violates the Equal Protection and Due Process Clauses of the Fourteenth Amendment. For reasons which seem to us to reflect the central meaning of those constitutional commands, we conclude that these statutes cannot stand consistently with the Fourteenth Amendment.

In June 1958, two residents of Virginia, Mildred Jeter, a Negro woman, and Richard Loving, a white man, were married in the District of Columbia pursuant to its laws. Shortly after their marriage, the Lovings returned to Virginia and established their marital abode in Caroline County. [A] grand jury [indicted] the Lovings [for] violating Virginia's ban on interracial marriages. On January 6, 1959, the Lovings pleaded guilty to the charge and were sentenced to one year in jail; however, the trial judge suspended the sentence for a period of 25 years on the condition that the Lovings leave the State and not return to Virginia together for 25 years. He stated in an opinion that:

Almighty God created the races white, black, yellow, malay and red, and he placed them on separate continents. And but for the interference with his arrangement there would be no cause for such marriages. The fact that he separated the races shows that he did not intend for the races to mix.

[The Supreme Court of Appeals of Virginia upheld the constitutionality of the antimiscegenation statutes and affirmed the Lovings' convictions].

The two statutes under which appellants were convicted and sentenced are part of a comprehensive statutory scheme aimed at prohibiting and punishing interracial marriages. The Lovings were convicted of violating §20-58 of the Virginia Code:

Leaving State to evade law. — If any white person and colored person shall go out of this State, for the purpose of being married, and with the intention of returning, and be married out of it, and afterwards return to and reside in it, cohabiting as man and wife, they shall be punished as provided in §20-59, and the marriage shall be governed by the same law as if it had been solemnized in this State. The fact of their cohabitation here as man and wife shall be evidence of their marriage.

Section 20-59, which defines the penalty for miscegenation, provides:

> Punishment for marriage. — If any white person intermarry with a colored person, or any colored person intermarry with a white person, he shall be guilty of a felony and shall be punished by confinement in the penitentiary for not less than one nor more than five years.

Other central provisions in the Virginia statutory scheme are §20-57, which automatically voids all marriages between "a white person and a colored person" without any judicial proceeding,[a] and §§20-54 and 1-14 which, respectively, define "white persons" and "colored persons and Indians" for purposes of the statutory prohibitions.[b] The Lovings have never disputed in the course of this litigation that Mrs. Loving is a "colored person" or that Mr. Loving is a "white person" within the meanings given those terms by the Virginia statutes.

Virginia is now one of 16 States which prohibit and punish marriages on the basis of racial classifications. Penalties for miscegenation arose as an incident to slavery and have been common in Virginia since the colonial period. The present statutory scheme dates from the adoption of the Racial Integrity Act of 1924, passed during the period of extreme nativism which followed the end of the First World War. The central features of this Act, and current Virginia law, are the absolute prohibition of a "white person" marrying other than another "white person," a prohibition against issuing marriage licenses until the issuing official is satisfied that the applicants' statements as to their race are correct, certificates of "racial composition" to be kept by both local and state registrars, and the carrying forward of earlier prohibitions against racial intermarriage.

---

a. Section 20-57 of the Virginia Code provides:

'Marriages void without decree. — All marriages between a white person and a colored person shall be absolutely void without any decree of divorce or other legal process.' Va. Code Ann. §20-57 (1960 Repl. Vol.).

b. Section 20-54 of the Virginia Code provides:

'Intermarriage prohibited; meaning of term 'white persons.' — It shall hereafter be unlawful for any white person in this State to marry any save a white person, or a person with no other admixture of blood than white and American Indian. For the purpose of this chapter, the term 'white person' shall apply only to such person as has no trace whatever of any blood other than Caucasian; but persons who have one-sixteenth or less of the blood of the American Indian and have no other non-Caucasic blood shall be deemed to be white persons. All laws heretofore passed and now in effect regarding the intermarriage of white and colored persons shall apply to marriages prohibited by this chapter.' Va. Code Ann. §20-54 (1960 Repl. Vol.).

The exception for persons with less than one-sixteenth 'of the blood of the American Indian' is apparently accounted for, in the words of a tract issued by the Registrar of the State Bureau of Vital Statistics, by 'the desire of all to recognize as an integral and honored part of the white race the descendants of John Rolfe and Pocahontas. . . .' Plecker, The New Family and Race Improvement, 17 Va. Health Bull., Extra No. 12, at 25-26 (New Family Series No. 5, 1925), cited in Wadlington, The Loving Case; Virginia's Anti-Miscegenation Statute in Historical Perspective, 52 Va. L. Rev. 1189, 1202 n.93 (1966).

Section 1-14 of the Virginia Code provides:

Colored persons and Indians defined. — Every person in whom there is ascertainable any Negro blood shall be deemed and taken to be a colored person, and every person not a colored person having one fourth or more of American Indian blood shall be deemed an American Indian; except that members of Indian tribes existing in this Commonwealth having one fourth or more of Indian blood and less than one sixteenth of Negro blood shall be deemed tribal Indians.' Va. Code Ann. §1-14 (1960 Repl.Vol.).

In upholding the constitutionality of these provisions in the decision below, the Supreme Court of Appeals of Virginia referred to its 1955 decision in Naim v. Naim, 197 Va. 80, 87 S.E.2d 749, as stating the reasons supporting the validity of these laws. In *Naim,* the state court concluded that the State's legitimate purposes were "to preserve the racial integrity of its citizens," and to prevent "the corruption of blood," "a mongrel breed of citizens," and "the obliteration of racial pride," obviously an endorsement of the doctrine of White Supremacy. The court also reasoned that marriage has traditionally been subject to state regulation without federal intervention, and, consequently, the regulation of marriage should be left to exclusive state control by the Tenth Amendment.

While the state court is no doubt correct in asserting that marriage is a social relation subject to the State's police power, the State does not contend in its argument before this Court that its powers to regulate marriage are unlimited notwithstanding the commands of the Fourteenth Amendment. . . . Instead, the State argues that the meaning of the Equal Protection Clause, as illuminated by the statements of the Framers, is only that state penal laws containing an interracial element as part of the definition of the offense must apply equally to whites and Negroes in the sense that members of each race are punished to the same degree. Thus, the State contends that, because its miscegenation statutes punish equally both the white and the Negro participants in an interracial marriage, these statutes, despite their reliance on racial classifications do not constitute an invidious discrimination based upon race. The second argument advanced by the State assumes the validity of its equal application theory. The argument is that, if the Equal Protection Clause does not outlaw miscegenation statutes because of their reliance on racial classifications, the question of constitutionality would thus become whether there was any rational basis for a State to treat interracial marriages differently from other marriages. On this question, the State argues, the scientific evidence is substantially in doubt and, consequently, this Court should defer to the wisdom of the state legislature in adopting its policy of discouraging interracial marriages.

Because we reject the notion that the mere "equal application" of a statute containing racial classifications is enough to remove the classifications from the Fourteenth Amendment's proscription of all invidious racial discriminations, we do not accept the State's contention that these statutes should be upheld if there is any possible basis for concluding that they serve a rational purpose. [In] cases involving distinctions not drawn according to race, the Court has merely asked whether there is any rational foundation for the discriminations, and has deferred to the wisdom of the state legislatures. In the case at bar, however, we deal with statutes containing racial classifications, and the fact of equal application does not immunize the statute from the very heavy burden of justification which the Fourteenth Amendment has traditionally required of state statutes drawn according to race.

The State argues that statements in the Thirty-ninth Congress about the time of the passage of the Fourteenth Amendment indicate that the Framers did not intend the Amendment to make unconstitutional state miscegenation laws. Many of the statements alluded to by the State concern the debates over the Freedmen's Bureau Bill, which President Johnson vetoed, and the Civil Rights Act of 1866 enacted over his veto. While these statements have some relevance to the intention of Congress in submitting the Fourteenth Amendment, it must be understood that the pertained to the passage of specific statutes and not to the broader, organic purpose of a constitutional amendment. As for the various statements directly concerning the

Fourteenth Amendment, we have said in connection with a related problem, that although these historical sources "cast some light" they are not sufficient to resolve the problem. . . . We have rejected the proposition that the debates in the Thirty-ninth Congress or in the state legislatures which ratified the Fourteenth Amendment supported the theory advanced by the State, that the requirement of equal protection of the laws is satisfied by penal laws defining offenses based on racial classifications so long as white and Negro participants in the offense were similarly punished. McLaughlin v. State of Florida, 379 U.S. 184 (1964).

The State finds support for its "equal application" theory in the decision of the Court in Pace v. State of Alabama, 106 U.S. 583 (1883). In that case, the Court upheld a conviction under an Alabama statute forbidding adultery or fornication between a white person and a Negro which imposed a greater penalty than that of a statute proscribing similar conduct by members of the same race. The Court reasoned that the statute could not be said to discriminate against Negroes because the punishment for each participant in the offense was the same. However, as recently as the 1964 Term, in rejecting the reasoning of that case, we stated "Pace represents a limited view of the Equal Protection Clause which has not withstood analysis in the subsequent decisions of this Court." McLaughlin. As we there demonstrated, the Equal Protection Clause requires the consideration of whether the classifications drawn by any statute constitute an arbitrary and invidious discrimination. The clear and central purpose of the Fourteenth Amendment was to eliminate all official state sources of invidious racial discrimination in the States.

There can be no question but that Virginia's miscegenation statutes rest solely upon distinctions drawn according to race. The statutes proscribe generally accepted conduct if engaged in by members of different races. Over the years, this Court has consistently repudiated "(d)istinctions between citizens solely because of their ancestry" as being "odious to a free people whose institutions are founded upon the doctrine of equality." Hirabayashi v. United States, 320 U.S. 81, 100 (1943). At the very least, the Equal Protection Clause demands that racial classifications, especially suspect in criminal statutes, be subjected to the "most rigid scrutiny," Korematsu v. United States, 323 U.S. 214, 216 (1944), and, if they are ever to be upheld, they must be shown to be necessary to the accomplishment of some permissible state objective, independent of the racial discrimination which it was the object of the Fourteenth Amendment to eliminate. Indeed, two members of this Court have already stated that they "cannot conceive of a valid legislative purpose . . . which makes the color of a person's skin the test of whether his conduct is a criminal offense." (Stewart, J., joined by Douglas, J., concurring).

There is patently no legitimate overriding purpose independent of invidious racial discrimination which justifies this classification. The fact that Virginia prohibits only interracial marriages involving white persons demonstrates that the racial classifications must stand on their own justification, as measures designed to maintain White Supremacy.[c] We have consistently denied the constitutionality of

---

c. Appellants point out that the State's concern in these statutes, as expressed in the words of the 1924 Act's title, 'An Act to Preserve Racial Integrity,' extends only to the integrity of the white race. While Virginia prohibits whites from marrying any nonwhite (subject to the exception for the descendants of Pocahontas), Negroes, Orientals, and any other racial class may intermarry without statutory interference. Appellants contend that this distinction renders Virginia's miscegenation statutes arbitrary and unreasonable even assuming the constitutional validity of an official purpose to preserve "racial integrity." We need not reach this contention because we find the racial classifications in these statutes repugnant to the Fourteenth Amendment, even assuming an even-handed state purpose to protect the "integrity" of all races.

measures which restrict the rights of citizens on account of race. There can be no doubt that restricting the freedom to marry solely because of racial classifications violates the central meaning of the Equal Protection Clause.

These statutes also deprive the Lovings of liberty without due process of law in violation of the Due Process Clause of the Fourteenth Amendment. The freedom to marry has long been recognized as one of the vital personal rights essential to the orderly pursuit of happiness by free men.

Marriage is one of the "basic civil rights of man," fundamental to our very existence and survival. To deny this fundamental freedom on so unsupportable a basis as the racial classifications embodied in these statutes, classifications so directly subversive of the principle of equality at the heart of the Fourteenth Amendment, is surely to deprive all the State's citizens of liberty without due process of law. The Fourteenth Amendment requires that the freedom of choice to marry not be restricted by invidious racial discriminations. Under our Constitution, the freedom to marry or not marry, a person of another race resides with the individual and cannot be infringed by the State.

Mr. Justice STEWART, concurring.

I have previously expressed the belief that "it is simply not possible for a state law to be valid under our Constitution which makes the criminality of an act depend upon the race of the actor." *McLaughlin.* Because I adhere to that belief, I concur in the judgment of the Court.

Discussion

1. *Anticlassification vs. antisubordination.* The Court in *Loving* objected to the statute both on the grounds that it involved an invidious racial classification and on the grounds that it promoted White Supremacy. *Brown* also described the wrong of segregated public education as inflicting injuries of racial differentiation and racial subordination: "To separate [children] from others of similar age and qualifications solely because of their race generates a feeling of inferiority as to their status in the community that may affect their hearts and minds in a way unlikely ever to be undone."

This suggests two different interpretations of the Fourteenth Amendment — the first enjoining practices of racial classification and the second enjoining practices of racial subordination. An anticlassification approach prohibits certain kinds of classifications, which are assumed by their nature to be invidious. An antisubordination approach prohibits government action that helps sustain or reinforce unjust forms of social hierarchy or social subordination. While the first approach looks to whether the statute or other government action involves a facial classification (or is secretly intended to classify), the second approach looks to the impact of state action in fostering or reproducing an unjust social structure.

2. *Status enforcing legislation.* Under the antisubordination approach, the goal of equality law is to combat unjust forms of *social stratification* — that is, forms of group inequality that occur over many different areas of social life and that tend to persist over time. Consider J. M. Balkin, The Constitution of Status, 106 Yale L.J. 2313, 2323-2324 (1997):

In many societies, *status hierarchies* emerge between groups with distinctive identities or styles of life. The most obvious example of a status hierarchy is a system of social caste;

but status hierarchies can be much less rigid and even quite fluid. . . . [A] status hierarchy is sustained by a system of social meanings in which one group receives relatively positive associations and another correspondingly negative associations. As a result, their identities are not freestanding: The identity of one is defined in part by its relationship to the identity of the other, and a change in the meanings attributed to one will affect not only its own social identity, but the identity of the other group. In a hierarchy with many status groups, there can be many different ways of differentiating the various groups and their respective lifestyles, and hence the system of social meanings (and the results of changes in social meanings) can be quite complex.

There is no necessary limitation on what characteristics can serve to distinguish status groups in a status hierarchy. They can be mutable or immutable, physical or ideological, matters of behavior or matters of appearance. The most familiar ones in the United States are organized along lines of race, sex, religion, immigrant status, and ethnicity. Conversely, not every distinguishing trait or characteristic corresponds to a status group in a status hierarchy. The number of traits that might be used to distinguish human beings is limitless, but the organization of a status hierarchy is a result of a particular history of social stratification and subordination. The question is not whether identifying traits exist that might distinguish people, but whether society has organized itself into a system of super- and subordination based on those traits. The issue is social stratification based on traits, not the nature of the traits themselves.

Thus, what constitutional lawyers call "immutability" is neither a necessary nor a sufficient criterion for a status group. The question is whether the trait can be endowed with sufficient cultural meaning to support a system of social stratification. Religious identity can serve this function even though religions proselytize and gain new converts. The point is not what the trait is, but what it can be made to mean in opposition to other traits.

Obviously, a system of subordination cannot be stable if it is too easy to exit from the criteria of subordinate status. That is why biological traits can be such useful markers of cultural differentiation. The advantage of immutability lies in its guarantee of stability — it helps ensure that social hierarchy can be reproduced effectively. Yet a trait does not have to be biologically based for group membership to be relatively stable over time.

Conversely, even biological traits like skin color can allow for the exit of one's children (through miscegenation), and hence so-called immutable criteria like race may have to be buttressed or even constituted by legal or cultural rules. Thus the Jim Crow regime featured cultural and legal prohibitions on interracial marriage (if not interracial sex) and elaborate rules of hypodescent [for example, the rule that one drop of black blood makes one black] to define who was white and black given the inevitability of racial mixing.

How did the antimiscegenation legislation in *Loving* help enforce the higher racial status of whites? One important purpose, as Balkin notes, is to help maintain notions of who is black and who is white, as well as who was a member of one's family and who was not.

During slavery, slaves were often forbidden to marry. White masters had sexual access to black women, producing illegitimate children whose status was determined by that of their mother. Hence it was essential to use marriage law to separate one's family from one's slaves, and one's relations from one's property, especially given that slavery was also regarded as a "domestic" institution. See Dorothy Roberts, The Genetic Tie, 62 U. Chi. L. Rev. 209 (1995). Conversely, because under the slave system, status traveled with the mother, it was vital to keep white women from sexual access by black men. The purity of white identity (with its accompanying rights and privileges) and the degraded status of black identity were preserved through rules of marriage and descent.

Under the system of Jim Crow that replaced chattel slavery, it was still important to preserve white racial identity and distinguish it from black identity, as well as to constrain black male and white female sexuality. Although the Fourteenth Amendment granted civil equality to blacks, it did not grant "social equality," i.e., equal social status. The civil/political/social distinction transformed the status regime that had existed during slavery and granted blacks a larger degree of freedom and equality than they had enjoyed previously. However, it still preserved the status hierarchy of whites over blacks, and the social inequality of the two races. Social equality was symbolized by all forms of social intermingling, ranging from attendance at dinner parties to membership in clubs, to the schools one's children attended; however, sexual and marriage partners were perhaps the most central aspects of social equality because rules about sex, marriage, and descent were central to preserving racial identity. Thus, Emily Van Tassel notes that " 'Social Equality' became virtually synonymous with interracial marriage in the late nineteenth century, and was used as a slogan against all manner of rights-access by blacks in much the same way as the term 'white supremacy.' "[79] In State v. Scott, 39 Ga. 321, 326-327 (1869), while upholding a conviction for miscegenation, the Court explained:

> Before the laws, the Code of Georgia makes all citizens equal, without regard to race or color. But it does not create, nor does any law of the State attempt to enforce, moral or social equality between the different races or citizens of the State. Such equality does not in fact exist, and never can. The God of nature made it otherwise, and no human law can produce it, and no human tribunal can enforce it. There are gradations and classes throughout the universe. From the tallest arch angel in Heaven down to the meanest reptile on earth, moral and social inequalities exist, and must continue to exist through all eternity.
>
> . . . The fortunes of war have compelled us to yield to the freedmen the legal rights above mentioned, but we have neither authorized nor enacted the marriage relation between the races, nor have we enacted laws or placed it in the power of the Legislature hereafter to make laws, regulating the social *status,* so as to compel our people to meet the colored race on terms of social equality. . . . Indeed, the most absolute and despotic governments do not attempt to regulate social *status* by fixed laws, or to enforce social equality among races or classes without their consent.

Note that in State v. Scott the court insisted that blacks enjoyed full legal equality in the state of Georgia, but that legal equality could coexist with social inequality. In other words, the court believed that a realm of private behavior and interaction in which whites held greater social status than blacks was entirely consistent with the equality of the two races before the law. Is this combination of legal equality and social inequality merely an aspect of a Jim Crow regime that made many racial classifications, or could it still be true today, when classifications based on race are for the most part

---

79. Emily Field Van Tassel, "Only the Law Would Rule Between Us": Antimiscegenation, the Moral Economy of Dependency, and the Debate Over Rights After the Civil War, 70 Chi.-Kent L. Rev. 873 (1995).

illegal? Does a racial status hierarchy need racial classifications to reproduce itself, or can it do so through facially neutral legal rules?

These questions raise a distinction that we will return to repeatedly in this chapter — between a theory of equality that looks to the presence or absence of racial classifications (or the intent to classify by race), and a theory that looks to the social meanings of being black and white, and to the institutions and justifications that preserve social stratification and status hierarchy. As noted earlier, both of these notions of equality are present to some degree in *Loving*.

According to the first approach, which we might call the "anticlassification" principle, the goal of equality is to avoid racial classifications; law is complicit in inequality to the extent that it makes such classifications. According to the second approach, which we might call the "antisubordination" principle, the goal of equality is to dismantle social structures that can use law in many different ways besides direct racial classification; law is complicit in inequality to the extent that it contains status-enforcing rules or doctrines. Anticlassification theory asks law to eschew racial classification, so that law can exist outside the system of racial hierarchy and regulate it. Antisubordination theory sees law as inevitably caught up in the system of racial hierarchy and racial meanings, even (and especially) when it tries to regulate them; the question for antisubordination theory is how law can best help to dismantle a system of which law is inevitably a part.

3. The strict scrutiny test. Loving is the modern origin of the "strict scrutiny" doctrine for racial classifications under the Equal Protection Clause (note that Brown v. Board of Education does not use the language of scrutiny at all). In *Loving* the Court speaks of the test as whether the law in question is "necessary to the accomplishment of some permissible state objective, independent of the racial discrimination which it was the object of the Fourteenth Amendment to eliminate." Today the Court describes the strict scrutiny test as whether the law in question is "narrowly tailored to achieve a compelling governmental interest." What are the differences between these two formulations?

Strict scrutiny was not, in fact, a new development. The Court had already invoked similar formulations in First Amendment cases, see, e.g., Sherbert v. Verner, 374 U.S. 398 (1963). However, in announcing the strict scrutiny test under the Equal Protection Clause, Chief Justice Warren borrows from the language of an even earlier opinion involving the war power, which applied the ideas of "suspect" classification and "the most rigid scrutiny" in a somewhat different fashion.

2.   Race, National Origin, and "Reasonableness"

KOREMATSU v. UNITED STATES
323 U.S. 214 (1944)

[Full American participation in World War II began on December 7, 1941, after the devastating Japanese attack on Pearl Harbor, which destroyed much of the American naval fleet. In the aftermath, latent anti-Japanese prejudice burst forth, with suspicions being expressed about the loyalty of *all* persons of Japanese descent, whether resident aliens or American citizens. Calls were made for the removal of such persons from their homes in the Western states. The Attorney General of California at the time, Earl Warren, supported such proposals, stating that "[e]very alien Japanese should be considered in the light of a potential fifth column."[80] (Although Warren apparently had reservations about applying such terms to Japanese-Americans, he registered no public complaint about the blanket policies that were adopted.) Walter Lippmann, probably the leading political journalist of the time, wrote, "Nobody's constitutional rights include the right to reside and do business on a battlefield," while the far more incendiary, but also influential journalist Westbrook Pegler wrote, "The Japanese in California should be under armed guard to the last man and woman right now, and to hell with habeas corpus until the danger is over."[81] After a bitter battle within the Executive branch, President Roosevelt on February 19, 1942 signed Executive Order 9066 directing the War Department (now known as the Department of Defense) to "prescribe military areas . . . from which any and all persons may be excluded, and with respect to which the right of any person to enter, remain in, or leave shall be subject to whatever restrictions the Commander might impose." Attorney General Francis Biddle protested that the order was "ill-advised, unnecessary, and unnecessarily cruel," to which the President responded, "[T]his must be a military decision."[82] Within two weeks, General DeWitt, Military Commander of the Western Defense Command, declared that the Pacific Coast states were "particularly subject to attack, to attempted invasion . . . and, in connection therewith . . . subject to espionage and acts of sabotage." Military zones were established; all persons of Japanese, German, or Italian ancestry residing in Military Area No. 1, which comprised most of the Western United States, were ordered to deliver to authorities a Change of Residence Notice if they wished to move from their habitual residences.

On March 21, 1942, Congress passed a statute making it a criminal offense for anyone to "enter, remain in, leave, or commit any act in any military area or military zone . . . contrary to the restrictions applicable to any such area or zone." On May 3, General DeWitt issued Civilian Exclusion Order No. 34, which stated that, by noon on May 9, all persons of Japanese ancestry were to be removed from Military Area No. 1 to detention camps. The detention camps were chosen over simply requiring resettlement outside of the forbidden area in part because "many states in the nation's interior made it clear that Japanese migration eastward spelled trouble."[83] The governor of Wyoming publicly stated that "[t]here would be Japs hanging from every pine tree" if his state became their destination. Similarly, the Idaho attorney general, stating that "[w]e want to keep this a white man's country," urged that "all Japanese should be put in concentration camps."[84] It was against this background that Fred Korematsu, a native-born Fourteenth Amendment birthright citizen convicted of disobeying the Order, challenged its constitutionality.[85] By a vote of 6 to 3, the Court upheld Korematsu's conviction for violating the exclusion order.]

---

80. Quoted in Ed Cray, Chief Justice: A Biography of Earl Warren 118 (1997). Although toward the end of his life, Warren told a former law clerk that he regretted his actions, "the stiff-necked Warren resisted any public acknowledgment of responsibility." See id. at 520.

81. Quoted in David Kennedy, Freedom from Fear: The American People in Depression and War, 1929-1945, at 751 (1999).

82. Quoted in id. at 753.

83. Id.

84. Quoted in id.

85. See Peter Irons, Justice at War (1983), for a complete review of the Japanese exclusion litigation.

BLACK, J., delivered the opinion of the Court.

It should be noted, to begin with, that all legal restrictions which curtail the civil rights of a single racial group are immediately suspect. That is not to say that all such restrictions are unconstitutional. It is to say that courts must subject them to the most rigid scrutiny. Pressing public necessity may sometimes justify the existence of such restrictions; racial antagonism never can. . . .

[A previous military order] subjected all persons of Japanese ancestry in prescribed West Coast military areas to remain in their residences from 8 P.M. to 6 A.M. As is the case with the exclusion order here, that prior curfew order was designed as a "protection against espionage and against sabotage." In Hirabayashi v. United States, 320 U.S. 81, we sustained a conviction obtained for violation of the curfew order. The Hirabayashi conviction and this one thus rest on the same 1942 Congressional Act and the same basic executive and military orders, all of which orders were aimed at the twin dangers of espionage and sabotage.

The 1942 Act was attacked in the *Hirabayashi* case as an unconstitutional delegation of power; it was contended that the curfew order and other orders on which it rested were beyond the war powers of the Congress, the military authorities and of the President, as Commander in Chief of the Army; and finally that to apply the curfew order against none but citizens of Japanese ancestry amounted to a constitutionally prohibited discrimination solely on account of race. To these questions, we gave the serious consideration which their importance justified. We upheld the curfew order as an exercise of the power of the government to take steps necessary to prevent espionage and sabotage in an area threatened by Japanese attack.

In the light of the principles we announced in the *Hirabayashi* case, we are unable to conclude that it was beyond the war power of Congress and the Executive to exclude those of Japanese ancestry from the West Coast war area at the time they did. True, exclusion from the area in which one's home is located is a far greater deprivation than constant confinement to the home from 8 P.M. to 6 A.M. Nothing short of apprehension by the proper military authorities of the gravest imminent danger to the public safety can constitutionally justify either. . . . The military authorities, charged with the primary responsibility of defending our shores, concluded that curfew provided inadequate protection and ordered exclusion. They did so . . . in accordance with Congressional authority to the military to say who should, and who should not, remain in the threatened areas. In this case the petitioner challenges the assumptions upon which we rested our conclusions in the *Hirabayashi* case. He also urges that by May 1942, when Order No. 34 was promulgated, all danger of Japanese invasion of the West Coast had disappeared. After careful consideration of these contentions we are compelled to reject them.

Here, as in the *Hirabayashi* case, "we cannot reject as unfounded the judgment of the military authorities and Congress that there were disloyal members of that population, whose number and strength could not be precisely and quickly ascertained. We cannot say that the war-making branches of the Government did not have ground for believing that in a critical hour such persons could not readily be isolated and separately dealt with, and constituted a menace to the national defense and safety, which demanded that prompt and adequate measures be taken against it."

Like curfew, exclusion of those of Japanese origin was deemed necessary because of the presence of an unascertained number of disloyal members of the group, most of whom we have no doubt were loyal to this country. It was because we could not reject the finding of the military authorities that it was impossible to bring about an immediate segregation of the disloyal from the loyal that we sustained the validity of the curfew order as applying to the whole group. In the instant case, temporary exclusion of the entire group was rested by the military on the same ground. The judgment that exclusion of the whole group was for the same reason a military imperative answers the contention that the exclusion was in the nature of group punishment based on antagonism to those of Japanese origin. That there were members of the group who retained loyalties to Japan has been confirmed by investigations made subsequent to the exclusion. Approximately five thousand American citizens of Japanese ancestry refused to swear unqualified allegiance to the United States and to renounce allegiance to the Japanese Emperor, and several thousand evacuees requested repatriation to Japan.

We uphold the exclusion order as of the time it was made and when the petitioner violated it. . . . Since the petitioner has not been convicted of failing to report or to remain in an assembly or relocation center, we cannot in this case determine the validity of those separate provisions of the order. It is sufficient here for us to pass upon the order which petitioner violated. . . .

It is said that we are dealing here with the case of imprisonment of a citizen in a concentration camp solely because of his ancestry, without evidence or inquiry concerning his loyalty and good disposition towards the United States. Our task would be simple, our duty clear, were this a case involving the imprisonment of a loyal citizen in a concentration camp because of racial prejudice. Regardless of the true nature of the assembly and relocation centers — and we deem it unjustifiable to call them concentration camps with all the ugly connotations that term implies — we are dealing specifically with nothing but an exclusion order. To cast this case into outlines or racial prejudice, without reference to the real military dangers which were presented, merely confuses the issue. Korematsu was not excluded from the Military Area because of hostility to him or his race. He *was* excluded because we are at war with the Japanese Empire, because the properly constituted military authorities feared an invasion of our West Coast and felt constrained to take proper security measures, because they decided that the military urgency of the situation demanded that all citizens of Japanese ancestry be segregated from the West Coast temporarily, and finally, because Congress, reposing its confidence in this time of war in our military leaders — as inevitably it must — determined that they should have the power to do just this. There was evidence of disloyalty on the part of some, the military authorities considered that the need for action was great, and time was short. We cannot — by availing ourselves of the calm perspective of hindsight — now say that at that time these actions were unjustified.

FRANKFURTER, J., concurring.

The provisions of the Constitution which confer on the Congress and the President powers to enable this country to wage war are as much part of the Constitution as provisions looking to a nation at peace. . . . [T]he war power of the Government is "the power to wage war successfully." Therefore, the validity of action under the war power must be judged wholly in the context of war. That action is not to be stigmatized as lawless because like action in times of peace would be lawless. To talk about a military order that expresses an allowable judgment of war needs by those entrusted with the duty of conducting war as "an unconstitutional order" is to suffuse a part of the

Constitution with an atmosphere of unconstitutionality. The respective spheres of action of military authorities and of judges are of course very different. But within their sphere, military authorities are no more outside the bounds of obedience to the Constitution than are judges within theirs. . . . To recognize that military orders are "reasonably expedient military precautions" in time of war and yet to deny them constitutional legitimacy makes of the Constitution an instrument of dialectic subtleties not reasonably to be attributed to the hard-headed Framers, of whom a majority had actual participation in war. If a military order such as that under review does not transcend the means appropriate for conducting war, such action by the military is as constitutional as would be any authorized action by the Interstate Commerce Commission within the limits of the constitutional power to regulate commerce. And being an exercise of the war power explicitly granted by the Consting its violation an offense triable in the civil courts. [This] does not carry with it approval of that which Congress and the Executive did. That is their business, not ours.

ROBERTS, J., dissenting.

[This] is the case of convicting a citizen as a punishment for not submitting to imprisonment in a concentration camp, based on his ancestry, and solely because of his ancestry, without evidence or inquiry concerning his loyalty and good disposition towards the United States. . . . I need hardly labor the conclusion that Constitutional rights have been violated. . . .

MURPHY, J., dissenting.

This exclusion of "all persons of Japanese ancestry, both alien and non-alien," from the Pacific Coast area on a plea of military necessity in the absence of martial law ought not to be approved. Such exclusion goes over "the very brink of constitutional power" and falls into the ugly abyss of racism. . . .

The judicial test of whether the Government, on a plea of military necessity, can validly deprive an individual of any of his constitutional rights is whether the deprivation is reasonable.

The judicial test of whether the Government, on a plea of military necessity, can validly deprive an individual of any of his constitutional rights is whether the deprivation is reasonably related to a public danger that is so "immediate, imminent, and impending" as not to admit of delay and not to permit the intervention of ordinary constitutional processes to alleviate the danger. Civilian Exclusion Order No. 34, banishing from a prescribed area of the Pacific Coast "all persons of Japanese ancestry, both alien and non-alien," clearly does not meet that test. Being an obvious racial discrimination, the order deprives all those within its scope of the equal protection of the laws as guaranteed by the Fifth Amendment. It further deprives these individuals of their constitutional rights to live and work where they will, to establish a home where they choose and to move about freely. In excommunicating them without benefit of hearings, this order also deprives them of all their constitutional rights to procedural due process. Yet no reasonable relation to an "immediate, imminent, and impending" public danger is evident to support this racial restriction which is one of the most sweeping and complete deprivations of constitutional rights in the history of this nation in the absence of martial law.

It must be conceded that the military and naval situation in the spring of 1942 was such as to generate a very real fear of invasion of the Pacific Coast, accompanied by fears of sabotage and espionage in that area. The military command was therefore justified in adopting all reasonable means necessary to combat these dangers. In adjudging the military action taken in light of the then apparent dangers, we must not erect too high or too meticulous standards; it is necessary only that the action have some reasonable relation to the removal of the dangers of invasion, sabotage and espionage. But the exclusion, either temporarily or permanently, of all persons with Japanese blood in their veins has no such reasonable relation. And that relation is lacking because the exclusion order necessarily must rely for its reasonableness upon the assumption that all persons of Japanese ancestry may have a dangerous tendency to commit sabotage and espionage and to aid our Japanese enemy in other ways. . . .

That this forced exclusion was the result in good measure of this erroneous assumption of racial guilt rather than bona fide military necessity is evidenced by the Commanding General's Final Report on the evacuation from the Pacific Coast area. In it he refers to all individuals of Japanese descent as "subversive," as belonging to "an enemy race" whose "racial strains are undiluted," and as constituting "over 112,000 potential enemies . . . at large today" along the Pacific Coast.[a]

In support of this blanket condemnation of all persons of Japanese descent, however, no reliable evidence is cited to show that such individuals were generally disloyal, or had generally so conducted themselves in this area as to constitute a special menace to defense installations or war industries, or had otherwise by their behavior furnished reasonable ground for their exclusion as a group.

Justification for the exclusion is sought, instead, mainly upon questionable racial and sociological grounds not ordinarily within the realm of expert military judgment. . . . Individuals of Japanese ancestry are condemned because they are said to be "a large, unassimilated, tightly knit racial group, bound to an enemy nation by strong ties of race, culture, custom and religion." . . .

The main reasons relied upon by those responsible for the forced evacuation . . . appear to be largely an accumulation of much of the misinformation, half-truths and insinuations that for years have been directed against Japanese Americans by people with racial and economic prejudices — the same people who have been among the foremost advocates of the evacuation.[b] . . .

No one denies, of course, that there were some disloyal persons of Japanese descent on the Pacific Coast who did all in their power to aid their ancestral land. Similar disloyal activities have been engaged in by many persons of German, Italian

a. Further evidence of the Commanding General's attitude toward individuals of Japanese ancestry is revealed in his voluntary testimony on April 13, 1943, in San Francisco before the House Naval Affairs Subcommittee to Investigate Congested Areas, Part 3, pp. 739-40 (78th Cong., 1st Sess.):

> I don't want any of them [persons of Japanese ancestry] here. They are a dangerous element. There is no way to determine their loyalty. The west coast contains too many vital installations essential to the defense of the country to allow any Japanese on this coast. . . . The danger of the Japanese was, and is now — if they are permitted to come back — espionage and sabotage. It makes no difference whether he is an American citizen, he is still a Japanese. American citizenship does not necessarily determine loyalty. . . . But we must worry about the Japanese all the time until he is wiped off the map. Sabotage and espionage will make problems as long as he is allowed in this area. . . ."

b. Special interest groups were extremely active in applying pressure for mass evacuation. See House Report No. 2124 (77th Cong., 2d Sess.) 154-6. Mr. Austin E. Anson, managing secretary of the Salinas Vegetable Grower-Shipper Association, has frankly admitted that "We're charged with wanting to get rid of the Japs for selfish reasons. . . . We do. It's a question of whether the white man lives on the Pacific Coast or the brown men. They came into this valley to work, and they stayed to take over. . . . They undersell the white man in the markets. . . . They work their women and children while the white farmer has to pay wages for his help. If all the Japs were removed tomorrow, we'd never miss them in two weeks, because the white farmers can take over and produce everything the Jap grows. And we don't want them back when the war ends, either." Quoted by Taylor in his article "The People Nobody Wants," 214 Sat. Eve. Post 24, 66 (May 9, 1942).

and even more pioneer stock in our country. But to infer that examples of individual disloyalty prove group disloyalty and justify discriminatory action against the entire group is to deny that under our system of law individual guilt is the sole basis for deprivation of rights.

Moreover, this inference, which is at the very heart of the evacuation orders, has been used in support of the abhorrent and despicable treatment of minority groups by the dictatorial tyrannies which this nation is now pledged to destroy. To give constitutional sanction to that inference in this case, however well-intentioned may have been the military command on the Pacific Coast, is to adopt one of the cruelest of the rationales used by our enemies to destroy the dignity of the individual and to encourage and open the door to discriminatory actions against other minority groups in the passions of tomorrow.

No adequate reason is given for the failure to treat these Japanese Americans on an individual basis by holding investigations and hearings to separate the loyal from the disloyal, as was done in the case of persons of German and Italian ancestry. See House Report No. 2124 (77th Cong., 2d Sess.) 247-52. It is asserted merely that the loyalties of this group "were unknown and time was of the essence." Yet nearly four months elapsed after Pearl Harbor before the first exclusion order was issued; nearly eight months went by until the last order was issued; and the last of these "subversive" persons was not actually removed until almost eleven months had elapsed. Leisure and deliberation seem to have been more of the essence than speed. And the fact that conditions were not such as to warrant a declaration of martial law adds strength to the belief that the factors of time and military necessity were not as urgent as they have been represented to be.

Moreover, there was no adequate proof that the Federal Bureau of Investigation and the military and naval intelligence services did not have the espionage and sabotage situation well in hand during this long period. Nor is there any denial of the fact that not one person of Japanese ancestry was accused or convicted of espionage or sabotage after Pearl Harbor while they were still free,[c] a fact which is some evidence of the loyalty of the vast majority of these individuals and of the effectiveness of the established methods of combatting these evils. It seems incredible that under these circumstances it would have been impossible to hold loyalty hearings for the mere 112,000 persons involved — or at least for the 70,000 American citizens — especially when a large part of this number represented children and elderly men and women.[d] Any inconvenience that may have accompanied an attempt to conform to procedural due process cannot be said to justify violations of constitutional rights of individuals.

I dissent, therefore, from this legalization of racism. Racial discrimination in any form and in any degree has no justifiable part whatever in our democratic way of life. It is unattractive in any setting but it is utterly revolting among a free people

c. The Final Report, p. 34, makes the amazing statement that as of February 14, 1942, "The very fact that no sabotage has taken place to date is a disturbing and confirming indication that such action will be taken." Apparently, in the minds of the military leaders, there was no way that the Japanese Americans could escape the suspicion of sabotage.

d. During a period of six months, the 112 alien tribunals or hearing boards set up by the British Government shortly after the outbreak of the present war summoned and examined approximately 74,000 German and Austrian aliens. These tribunals determined whether each individual enemy alien was a real enemy of the Allies or only a "friendly enemy." About 64,000 were freed from internment and from any special restrictions, and only 2,000 were interned.

who have embraced the principles set forth in the Constitution of the United States. All residents of this nation are kin in some way by blood or culture to a foreign land. Yet they are primarily and necessarily a part of the new and distinct civilization of the United States. They must accordingly be treated at all times as the heirs of the American experiment and as entitled to all the rights and freedoms guaranteed by the Constitution.

JACKSON, J., dissenting.

Korematsu was born on our soil, of parents born in Japan. The Constitution makes him a citizen of the United States by nativity and a citizen of California by residence. No claim is made that he is not loyal to this country. There is no suggestion that apart from the matter involved here he is not law-abiding and well disposed. Korematsu, however, has been convicted of an act not commonly a crime. It consists merely of being present in the state whereof he is a citizen, near the place where he was born, and where all his life he has lived.

Even more unusual is the series of military orders which made this conduct a crime. They forbid such a one to remain, and they also forbid him to leave. They were so drawn that the only way Korematsu could avoid violation was to give himself up to the military authority. This meant submission to custody, examination, and transportation out of the territory, to be followed by indeterminate confinement in detention camps.

A citizen's presence in the locality, however, was made a crime only if his parents were of Japanese birth. . . . Now, if any fundamental assumption underlies our system, it is that guilt is personal and not inheritable. . . . [H]ere is an attempt to make an otherwise innocent act a crime merely because this prisoner is the son of parents as to whom he had no choice, and belongs to a race from which there is no way to resign. If Congress in peace-time legislation should enact such a criminal law, I should suppose this Court would refuse to enforce it.

But the "law" which this prisoner is convicted of disregarding is not found in an act of Congress, but in a military order. . . . And it is said that if the military commander had reasonable military grounds for promulgating the orders, they are constitutional and become law, and the Court is required to enforce them. There are several reasons why I cannot subscribe to this doctrine.

It would be impracticable and dangerous idealism to expect or insist that each specific military command in an area of probable operations will conform to conventional tests of constitutionality. . . . The armed forces must protect a society, not merely its Constitution. . . . No court can require . . . a commander in such circumstances to act as a reasonable man; he may be unreasonably cautious and exacting. . . .

But if we cannot confine military expedients by the Constitution, neither would I distort the Constitution to approve all that the military may deem expedient. That is what the Court appears to be doing, whether consciously or not. I cannot say, from any evidence before me, that the orders of General DeWitt were not reasonably expedient military precautions, nor could I say that they were. But even if they were permissible military procedures, I deny that it follows that they are constitutional. If, as the Court holds, it does follow, then we may as well say that any military order will be constitutional and have done with it.

The limitation under which courts always will labor in examining the necessity for a military order are illustrated by this case. How does the Court know that these orders have a reasonable basis in necessity? No evidence whatever on that subject has been taken by this or any other court. There is sharp controversy as to the credibility of the DeWitt report. So the Court, having no real evidence before it, has no choice but to accept General DeWitt's own unsworn, self-serving statement, untested by any cross-examination, that what he did was reasonable. And thus it will always be when courts try to look into the reasonableness of a military order.

In the very nature of things, military decisions are not susceptible of intelligent judicial appraisal. They do not pretend to rest on evidence, but are made on information that often would not be admissible and on assumptions that could not proved. Information in support of an order could not be disclosed to courts without danger that it would reach the enemy. Neither can courts act on communications made in confidence. Hence courts can never have any real alternative to accepting the mere declaration of the authority that issued the order that it was reasonably necessary from a military viewpoint.

Much is said of the danger to liberty from the Army program for deporting and detaining these citizens of Japanese extraction. But a judicial construction of the due process clause that will sustain this order is a far more subtle blow to liberty than the promulgation of the order itself. A military order, however unconstitutional, is not apt to last longer than the military emergency. . . . But once a judicial opinion rationalizes such an order to show that it conforms to the Constitution, or rather rationalizes the Constitution to show that the Constitution sanctions such an order, the Court for all time has validated the principle of racial discrimination in criminal procedure and of transplanting American citizens. The principle then lies about like a loaded weapon ready for the hand of any authority that can bring forward a plausible claim of an urgent need. . . . [T]he passing incident becomes the doctrine of the Constitution. There it has a generative power of its own, and all that it creates will be in its own image. Nothing better illustrates this danger than does the Court's opinion in this case.

It argues that we are bound to uphold the conviction of Korematsu because we upheld one in *Hirabayashi,* where we sustained these orders in so far as they applied a curfew requirement to a citizen of Japanese ancestry. I think we should learn something from that experience.

In that case we were urged to consider only the curfew feature. . . . We yielded, and the Chief Justice guarded the opinion as carefully as language will do. . . . However, in spite of our limiting words we did validate a discrimination on the basis of ancestry for mild and temporary deprivation of liberty. Now the principle of racial discrimination is pushed from temporary deprivations to indeterminate ones. . . . How far the principle of this case would be extended before plausible reasons would play out, I do not know.

I should hold that a civil court cannot be made to enforce an order which violates constitutional limitations even if it is a reasonable exercise of military authority. The courts can exercise only the judicial power, can apply only law, and must abide by the Constitution, or they cease to be civil courts and become instruments of military policy.

. . . I would not lead people to rely on this Court for a review that seems to me wholly delusive. . . . The chief restraint upon those who command the physical forces of the country, in the future as in the past, must be their responsibility to the political judgments of their contemporaries and to the moral judgments of history.

My duties as a justice as I see them do not require me to make a military judgment as to whether General DeWitt's evacuation and detention program was a reasonable military necessity. I do not suggest that the courts should have attempted to interfere with the Army in carrying out its task. But I do not think they may be asked to execute a military order that has no place in law under the Constitution. I would reverse the judgment and discharge the prisoner.

Discussion

1. *Strict scrutiny versus a per se rule.* Is the Court's criterion in *Korematsu* — the "suspect classification" standard — the proper one in the circumstances, or should the Court have held that racially discriminatory burdens are unconstitutional per se whatever the countervailing interests? Assuming that the Court's criterion is proper, did the Court apply it correctly? What more information, if any, is necessary to answer this?[86] Does it matter that the Court is construing the war power in this case and that, at the time, the Court had not yet held that the federal government was bound by an equal protection component located in the Fifth Amendment's Due Process Clause?[87] Note, however, Justice Murphy's opinion, which assumes that the Fifth Amendment has an equal protection component.

2. *The use of race in immigration and foreign policy.* Although critics of *Korematsu* often emphasize its blatant racism, note that because of doctrines originally developed in The Chinese Exclusion Cases, there is no constitutional difficulty with national quotas that allow more persons of some nations to immigrate to the United States and become citizens while simultaneously limiting (or even excluding) opportunities for persons of other nations.[88] Obviously, some of these national quotas (for example, those which give different treatment to citizens of Ireland and Taiwan) are strongly correlated with race, although others are not. Is this practice importantly different from what the Court upheld in *Korematsu* on the grounds that in *Korematsu* the U.S. government arrested *its own citizens* on the basis of their race or ethnicity? Does this suggest that federal action ordering the internment of resident aliens or ordering their immediate deportation on the basis of their country of origin would be constitutionally

---

86. Note that Justice Black, the author of *Korematsu*, later became famous for his "absolutist" position on the First Amendment. In a 1960 lecture criticizing the Court's willingness to balance First Amendment rights against countervailing governmental interests, Justice Black asserted:

> The great danger of the judiciary balancing process is that in times of emergency and stress it gives Government the power to do what it thinks necessary to protect itself, regardless of the rights of individuals. If the need is great, the right of Government can always be said to outweigh the rights of the individual. If "balancing" is accepted as the test, it would be hard for any conscientious judge to hold otherwise in times of dire need. And laws adopted in times of dire need are often very hasty and oppressive laws. . . . Misuse of government power, particularly in times of stress, has brought suffering to humanity in all ages about which we have authentic history.

Hugo Black, The Bill of Rights, 35 N.Y.U. L. Rev. 865, 878-79 (1960).

87. Korematsu raised challenges under the Due Process Clause of the Fifth Amendment and under the Cruel and Unusual Punishments Clause of the Eighth Amendment. The Court did not address these. See Korematsu v. United States, 140 F.2d 289, 291 (1943) (Denman, J., concurring in the result).

88. See Fong Yue Ting v. United States, 149 U.S. 698, 704 (1893) (holding that exclusion of Chinese laborers from United States was constitutional exercise of legislature's powers); Chae Chan Ping v. United States, 130 U.S. 581, 609-610 (1889) (same).

permissible under the Fifth Amendment, assuming that it were authorized by statute?

3. *Judicial review of military decisionmaking.* From the perspective of a half-century of distance and even, probably, from the perspective of 1944, when *Korematsu* was decided, it is easy enough to agree with Justice Murphy's denunciation of the policy. By that time the fears that Pearl Harbor presaged attacks on the United States itself had been left behind, and the Battle of Midway had signaled to most military analysts that a Japanese defeat was inevitable. Moreover, it was altogether clear by that time that the fears of a Japanese "fifth column" were totally and completely groundless. Indeed, not a single Japanese resident alien or Japanese-American U.S. citizen committed any espionage during the entire period of the War. In addition, "some three thousand [Japanese-Americans] were recruited into the 442nd Regimental Combat Team, an all Japanese (segregated) unit that distinguished itself fighting in Italy."[89] (Why do you think the so-called Nisei Regiment was sent to Italy rather than to the Pacific Theater of the War? Would it have been legitimate to adopt a policy by which persons with German surnames or with relatives living in Germany were sent to the Pacific Theater?) Finally, we know, because of historian Peter Irons, that the Government was aware, by the time of the argument before the Supreme Court, that General DeWitt's fear of Japanese-Americans was wholly unfounded, but failed to inform the Court of this fact.[90] Indeed, a San Francisco Federal District Court in 1984 reversed Fred Korematsu's conviction on the basis of evidence brought forth by Irons.

Imagine, though, that the case had arisen immediately after promulgation of the policy, in early 1942, seeking to enjoin its application to Korematsu and all others similarly situated. The effect of a decision on Korematsu's behalf would have been an injunction issuing from the federal courts ordering the military to change the way it conducted the war and protected the national defense. Is it still such an "easy case"? Consider first the sheer question of "reasonableness," or in Justice Black's words, whether the judgment of the military authorities was "unfounded." Did the government have "no ground" for its concerns about the loyalties of Japanese-Americans? One response is that given by Justice Jackson: "Had Korematsu been one of four — the others being, say, a German alien enemy, an Italian alien enemy, and a citizen of American-born ancestors, convicted of treason but out on parole — only Korematsu's presence would have violated the order." This objection, however, suggests that the only problem with Order 9066

---

89. David Kennedy, supra n.79, at 255 (1999).

90. See Irons, supra n.83. Korematsu v. United States, 584 F. Supp. 1406 (N.D. Cal. 1984). In 1988 Congress passed a measure formally apologizing to the Japanese-American community for the measures adopted under Executive Order 9066 and awarding each detention survivor $20,000. See generally, Peter Irons ed., Justice Delayed: The Record of the Japanese-American Internment Cases (1989), which details the relitigation in the 1980s of several of the most important cases of the 1940s.

Cf. Jacobs v. Barr, 959 F. 2d 313 (D.C. Cir. 1992), in which the D.C. Circuit denied a claim for reparations by a German-American, born in Brooklyn in 1943, who was interned, along with his German father, at Ellis Island. The court rejected an equal protection argument that Jacobs should have received reparations like Japanese-Americans received. It held that "Congress concluded that Japanese Americans were detained en masse because of racial prejudice and demagoguery, while German Americans were detained in small numbers, and only after individual hearings about their loyalty."

was its "underinclusiveness," rather than the illegitimacy of national-origin discrimination per se.[91]

But one might still ask if there was good reason, *ex ante*, to be more suspicious of Japanese-Americans (and Japanese resident aliens) than of their Italian- and German-American counterparts and Italian and German resident aliens. Ironically, one reason, perhaps, to register such suspicion is precisely the traditional prejudice visited upon all persons from Asia, and, in particular against Japanese-American citizens and Japanese resident aliens. In addition, the United States was not particularly friendly toward Japan itself, often treating it with racialized suspicion and disdain. Consider the following comment by Stanford historian David Kennedy:

> In the years that followed [American annexation of the Philippine Islands in 1898, in the aftermath of the Spanish-American War], again and again Japan watched the United States assume the spoiler's part [against Japanese national aspirations], the American role often colored with an ugly tincture of racial condescension that exacerbated Japanese resentment. The Americans shut off further immigration from Japan to the United States in the so-called Gentleman's Agreement of 1908; they declined in 1919 to accept the Japanese proposal for a declaration of racial equality in the Versailles peace treaty, forced unwanted naval limitations on Japan in the Washington Naval Disarmament Conference of 1922, [and] permanently debarred from American citizenship the tiny Japanese immigrant community in the notorious "national origins" immigration law of 1924. . . .[92]

Furthermore, California law at the time prohibited noncitizens from owning land, widely (and accurately) perceived as another manifestation of anti-Asian prejudice. (And recall the Chinese Laundry and Chinese Queue Cases from the nineteenth century as manifestations of a general anti-Asian prejudice.) It would have required almost heroic denial for all persons of Japanese descent to feel unambiguous attachment to a country that had systematically stigmatized them on racial grounds and, moreover, systematically denigrated their country of origin. Persons of Western European descent were, generally speaking, treated far better; indeed, at least some German-Americans could trace their descent back to original settlers of Pennsylvania.

One's belief that a monstrous injustice was done by Presidential Order 9066 may in part rest on the empirical fact that despite this long history of abuses and discriminations against persons of Japanese descent, not a single Japanese-American or

---

91. Governmental surveillance, ongoing since 1935, had identified some 2,000 potentially subversive persons in the Japanese community. Along with 14,000 German and Italian security risks nationwide, they were quietly rounded up in the last days of 1941. But those individual detentions stopped well short of wholesale incarcerations. "I was determined," Attorney General Francis Biddle wrote, "to avoid mass internment, and the persecution of aliens that had characterized the First World War." Kennedy, supra n.79, at 749.

"[T]he immigrants whose loyalty had been questioned" during the earlier war were relative newcomers to the United States. "But by 1941 those older European groups were settled communities, well assimilated, their patriotism as well as their political loyalty actively cultivated by Roosevelt's New Deal." If evidence is needed for this proposition, consider that the 10 percent of the Italian community in America who had remained Italian citizens — and were therefore automatically classified as "enemy aliens" after the Italian dictator Mussolini declared war on the United States — were, by order of President Roosevelt, relieved of that status in what Kennedy describes as "a joyfully received announcement" in New York's Carnegie Hall, "shrewdly delivered on Columbus Day, 1942, just weeks before the congressional elections." Id. at 750.

92. Kennedy, supra n.79, at 500-501.

Japanese resident of the United States was even charged with espionage during the entirety of World War II. But this very fact raises a disturbing question: *Would* your response to the Supreme Court's decision in *Korematsu* be affected if, say, urban bombings accurately attributed to a half-dozen Japanese-Americans or Japanese residents had occurred in Los Angeles, San Francisco, and Seattle between 1942 and 1944?

Finally, one has to look more closely at the structure of the "compelling interest" analysis that is implicit in *Korematsu*. How much should one focus only on the strength of the interest — the *value* that is asserted — as against scrutinizing the *means chosen* to effectuate that interest? Is there *any* interest more compelling than defending the existence of the United States when threatened by foreign invasion? (Recall, e.g., the debates about Abraham Lincoln's problematic actions during the events of 1861-1865.)

Of course, one might insist, especially given doctrinal developments in post-*Korematsu* cases, that the means chosen must be "carefully tailored" to achieve the objectives. How much scrutiny should the Court have given in 1942 to whether Order 9066 was carefully tailored? Why should it not have trusted the Executive Branch — the blend of military professionals and civilian leaders — to come to the appropriate conclusion as to what was necessary? Both the Supreme Court and the lower federal courts have insisted on many occasions that executive, congressional, and professional military judgments about military matters deserve special defer-ence. (We will see this doctrine invoked again in Chapter 7 in Rostker v. Goldberg, involving a constitutional challenge to a male-only draft, and in Chapter 8 in judi-cial challenges to exclusion of homosexuals from the military.) Is there anything in the training of lawyers or judges that would make them superior to Congress, the Executive, and military professionals in assessing the requirements of national defense? On the other hand, would too great a deference undermine the constitu-tional system? Might politicians and military professionals tend to confuse their prejudices with their judgments of military necessity? Recall General DeWitt's views, and the fact that the Administration knew that they were unfounded, but neverthe-less supported them in court. Why do you think politicians would defer to and defend military officials in 1942 even if they thought they were wrong? Also consider the tortured diary entry of Secretary of War Henry Stimson, who supported the evacuation measures:

> The second generation Japanese can only be evacuated either as part of a total evacua-tion given access to the area only by permits, or by frankly trying to put them out on the ground that their racial characteristics are such that we cannot understand or even trust the citizen Japanese. This latter is the fact but I am afraid it will make a tremen-dous hole in our constitutional system to apply it.[93]

Consider carefully Justice Jackson's opinion. How similar is it to Justice Taney's argument in *Ex parte Merryman*, Chapter 4, supra? Recall that Lincoln in effect refused to follow Taney's opinion, with no apparent harm to his short-run politi-cal advantage or long-term historical reputation. If a hypothetical 1942 Court had adopted Justice Murphy's reasoning, would you necessarily have expected

93. Quoted in id. at 752.

President Roosevelt to accept it?[94] Should that be relevant to the Supreme Court's decision?

4. *The "facts" of* Korematsu. This casebook often supplements legal arguments and presentations of facts in judicial opinions with historical materials. Often these historical materials offer facts at variance with what courts and legal advocates claim to be the case, or interpret the facts in different ways. *Korematsu* is no exception, and it raises a problem we have previously asked several times: What, precisely, are "the facts" that a (legal) analyst of *Korematsu* should be aware of in order to understand the case and decide it properly (from a legal standpoint)?[95] Can one glean these facts from even the most diligent perusal of the majority opinion? From Justice Murphy's opinion? Can one properly speak of a "correct" legal analysis given the set of facts described by a court — so that *Korematsu* might be rightly decided from Justice Black's recitation of the facts — or is good legal analysis inseparable from an inquiry behind those facts? Is good legal analysis inseparable from an understanding of the historical context in which doctrine is announced and applied? (But note that the historical meaning of events may not be understood, if at all, until many years later.)

This question applies, in particular, to how one describes the particular places to which Fred Korematsu and his fellow Japanese-Americans were sent. Note that what Justice Black refers to as "the assembly and relocation centers" Justice Roberts calls "concentration camps," which evoked Justice Black's response for the majority: "[W]e deem it unjustifiable to call them concentration camps with all the ugly connotations that term implies." What *should* we call these places, as historians? As legal analysts?

Note: Discrimination Against Asian-Americans and the Black/White Paradigm

In Chapters 2 and 4 we noted the variety of forms of discrimination that were visited on Asians residing in the United States (recall, for example, the Chinese Exclusion Cases). Neil Gotanda argues that *Korematsu* demonstrates one of the distinctive features of discrimination against Asian-Americans (as well as Hispanics) that tends to differentiate it from discrimination against blacks. Gotanda is among a growing number of scholars who have rejected the "black/white paradigm" for

---

94. See *Ex parte Quirin*, 317 U.S. 1 (1942), discussed more fully in Ch. 5, supra, which upheld the summary military trial (and death sentences) of eight German saboteurs sent by submarine to infiltrate the United States. In his memoirs, Justice Douglas wrote that then-Attorney General Francis Biddle had explained to the Supreme Court, prior to its judgment, that "the Executive [presumably a reference to President Roosevelt] would not tolerate any delay" and "that the claims of the saboteurs were so frivolous, [that] the Army was going [to go] ahead and execute the men whatever the Court did." Justice Douglas described this as "a blatant affront to the Court." See Howard Ball & Phillip J. Cooper, Of Power and Right: Hugo Black, William O. Douglas, and America's Constitutional Revolution 118 (1992), quoting William O. Douglas, The Court Years 139 (1980).

Chief Justice Stone wrote the opinion and worked to make it unanimous (Justice Murphy did not participate); however he privately expressed his own doubts as to whether the proceedings had accorded with the Laws of War. See Alpheus Mason, Harlan Fiske Stone: Pillar of the Law 653-666 (1956). As it happened, six of the eight Germans were secretly executed a few days after the Court's per curiam opinion upholding the trial and sentence.

95. What work, if any, is being done by the addition of the words in parentheses?

understanding race relations in the United States: "One of the critical features of legal treatment of Other non-whites has been the inclusion of a notion of 'foreign-ness' in considering their racial identity and legal status." According to Gotanda, the specific forms of discrimination that Asian-Americans, Hispanic-Americans, Arab-Americans, and other non-black minorities suffer cannot be understood without taking into account "the persistence of the view that even American-born non-whites were somehow 'foreign.' This undeserved stigma became, and may remain, an unarticulated basis for the legal treatment of these groups, leading to unfair and often shocking consequences."[96]

Gotanda argues that "any assertion or demonstration of traditional culture [by Asian-Americans] is a potential reaffirmation of foreign and therefore un-American conduct."[97] By contrast, distinctively black cultural assertions (for example, modes of dress and behavior, the use of black dialect or slang) are not generally regarded as un-American, although they may sometimes be stigmatized by whites as inferior or threatening.

Recall Justice Harlan's dissent in Plessy v. Ferguson, in which he notes that the Chinese are "a race so different from our own that we do not permit those belonging to it to become citizens of the United States." Hence Harlan decries the unfairness that "a Chinaman can ride in the same passenger coach with white citizens of the United States" while blacks, "who have all the legal rights that belong to white citizens," cannot.[98] Harlan's dissent is notable for its rhetorical strategy of playing one minority group off against another. Blacks "really are" Americans, while the Chinese, no matter how long they may have resided in the country, are foreigners.

The flip side of Harlan's rhetorical strategy of playing off Asians (in this case Chinese) against blacks is to play blacks off against Asians, i.e., to argue that blacks should not receive special advantages that Asians do not. This produces the second distinctive way in which Asian-Americans are stereotyped, not as devious and inscrutable foreigners, but as upstanding immigrant members of society, the so-called "model minority." As Frank Wu explains:[99]

This ubiquitous superminority image has suggested that Asian Americans achieve economic success and gain societal acceptance through conservative values and hard work. . . . The image is a myth because Asian Americans have not achieved economic success except in a superficial sense. Comparing equally educated individuals, whites earn more money than Asian Americans. Qualifications count less than race, in a pattern of regular discrimination, not so-called "reverse" discrimination. The discrimination which Asian Americans in fact face can be reinforced by the exaggerations of the myth. This reinforcement occurs, for example, when non-Asian Americans believe that Asian Americans should be subjected to maximum quotas in college admissions because they have done too well and represent unfair competition. Everyone should know that the model minority myth is deployed in ways that expose the insincerity of its goodwill. The myth is used to denigrate other racial minorities. It is used to ask

96. Neil Gotanda, Other Non-Whites in American Legal History: A Review of Justice at War, 85 Colum. L. Rev. 1186, 1188 (1985).
97. Neil Gotanda, Asian American Rights and the "Miss Saigon Syndrome," in Asian Americans and the Supreme Court: A Documentary History 1087, 1097 (Hyung-chan Kim ed., 1992).
98. Plessy v. Ferguson, 163 U.S. 537, 561 (1896).
99. Frank H. Wu, Changing America: Three Arguments About Asian Americans and the Law, 45 Am. U. L. Rev. 811, 814 (1996). Wu argues that the model minority myth exposes the hollowness of the color-blind Constitution: "Ironically, when Asian Americans are used to attack affirmative action, the case for evaluating the merit of individuals focuses on the supposed success of a racial group." Id. at 816.

African Americans, rhetorically, "Well, the Asian Americans succeeded; why can't you?" As the original New York Times article introducing the image put it, Asian Americans stand in contrast to "problem minorities."

Note that the "model minority" stereotype works in two directions: It reinforces the notion that blacks are responsible for their poor socio-economic status, and it makes poverty among Asian-Americans and discrimination against them relatively invisible because Asian-Americans are simply assumed to be more successful than blacks. You should consider this dual effect of stereotypes about Asian-Americans when we turn to the materials on race-conscious affirmative action.

3.   What Justifies the Suspect Classification Standard?

PAUL BREST, FOREWORD: IN DEFENSE OF THE ANTIDISCRIMINATION PRINCIPLE
90 Harv. L. Rev. 1, 6-11 (1976)

By the "antidiscrimination principle" I mean the general principle disfavoring classifications and other decisions and practices that depend on the race (or ethnic origin) of the parties affected.[a] The antidiscrimination principle guards against certain defects in the *process* by which race-dependent decisions are made and also against certain harmful *results* of race-dependent decisions. Restricting the principle to a unitary purpose vitiates its moral force and requires the use of sophisticated reasoning to explain applications that seem self-evident.

1.   DEFECTS OF PROCESS

The antidiscrimination principle is designed to prevent both irrational and unfair infliction of injury.

Race-dependent decisions are irrational insofar as they reflect the assumption that members of one race are less worthy than other people. Not all such decisions are necessarily irrational, however. For example, if black laborers tend to be absent from work more often than their white counterparts — for whatever reason — it is not irrational for an employer to prefer white applicants for the job. If Americans of Japanese ancestry were more prone to disloyalty than Caucasians during World War II, it was not irrational for the United States government to take special precautions against sabotage and espionage by them. Regulations and decisions based on statistical generalizations are commonplace in all developed societies and essential to their functioning. And it is often rational for decisionmakers to rely on weak and even dubious generalizations. Consider, for example, a fire department's or airline's policy against employing overweight personnel, based on the rather slight probability that they will suffer a heart attack while on duty.

In short, the mere fact that most blacks are industrious and most Japanese-Americans loyal does not make the employer's or the Government's decision

a. For the moment, I leave open whether the antidiscrimination principle disfavors so-called "benign" race-dependent practices — practices designed to benefit, and that seem in fact to benefit, the members of traditionally disadvantaged minorities.

irrational. Indeed, if all race-dependent decisions were irrational, there would be no need for an antidiscrimination principle, for it would suffice to apply the widely held moral, constitutional, and practical principle that forbids treating persons irrationally. The antidiscrimination principle fills a special need because — as even a glance at history indicates — race-dependent decisions that are rational and purport to be based solely on legitimate considerations are likely in fact to rest on assumptions of the differential worth of racial groups or on the related phenomenon of racially selective sympathy and indifference.

Mr. Justice Black focused on the first of these dangers in Korematsu v. United States, the case in which the Government sought to justify its policy of interning Japanese-Americans, and in which the Court first enunciated the modern "suspect classification" doctrine. He wrote for the majority:

> [A]ll legal restrictions which curtail the civil rights of a single racial group are immediately suspect. . . . [C]ourts must subject them to the most rigid scrutiny. Pressing public necessity may sometimes justify the existence of such restrictions; racial antagonism never can.

Mr. Justice Black chose the word "suspect" advisedly. For, although a court often cannot ascertain the true motives underlying a decision, our history and traditions provide strong reasons to suspect that racial classifications ultimately rest on assumptions of the differential worth of racial groups. These racial value judgments appear in forms besides "racial antagonism" — for example in paternalistic assumptions of racial inferiority.

By the phenomenon of racially selective sympathy and indifference I mean the unconscious failure to extend to a minority the same recognition of humanity, and hence the same sympathy and care, given as a matter of course to one's own group.

Although racially selective sympathy and indifference (hereafter, just indifference) is an inevitable consequence of attributing intrinsic value to membership in a racial group, it may also result from a desire to enhance our own power and esteem by enhancing the power and esteem of members of groups to which we belong. And it may also result — often unconsciously — from our tendency to sympathize most readily with those who seem most like ourselves. Whatever its cause, decisions that reflect this phenomenon, like those reflecting overt racial hostility, are unfair; for by hypothesis, they are decisions disadvantaging minority persons that would not be made under the identical circumstances if they disadvantaged members of the dominant group. The unequal treatment could be justified only if one group were in fact more worthy than the other. This justification failing, such treatment violates the cardinal rule of fairness — the Golden Rule.

2.   HARMFUL RESULTS

A second and independent rationale for the antidiscrimination principle is the prevention of the harms which may result from race-dependent decisions. Often, the most obvious harm is the denial of the opportunity to secure a desired benefit — a job, a night's lodging at a motel, a vote. But this does not completely describe the consequences of race-dependent decisionmaking. Decisions based on assumptions of intrinsic worth and selective indifference inflict psychological injury by stigmatizing their victims as inferior. Moreover, because acts of discrimination tend to occur in pervasive patterns, their victims suffer especially frustrating, cumulative and debilitating injuries.

The prevention of stigmatic harm played a major role in Strauder v. West Virginia, the first race discrimination case to reach the Supreme Court after the Civil War. On alternative grounds, the Court struck down a state law excluding blacks from juries. Although the first ground was the black defendant's right to a jury composed of a cross-section of the community, the second involved the rights of the members of the black community themselves. Mr. Justice Strong reasoned that the fourteenth amendment protects Negroes "from legal discriminations, implying their inferiority in civil society," and held that the West Virginia statute was "practically a brand upon them . . . , an assertion of their inferiority." Dissenting in Plessy v. Ferguson, Mr. Justice Harlan likewise observed that the segregation of railway passengers was a "badge of servitude" because it proceeded "on the ground that colored citizens are . . . inferior and degraded."

Similarly, the essence of Brown v. Board of Education lay in Chief Justice Warren's observation that the segregation of black public school pupils "generates a feeling of inferiority as to their status in the community that may affect their hearts and minds in a way unlikely ever to be undone." As Charles L. Black noted, the Court could not properly have ignored "a plain fact about the society of the United States — the fact that the social meaning of segregation is the putting of the Negro in a position of walled-off inferiority — or the other equally plain fact that such treatment is hurtful to human beings."

Recognition of the stigmatic injury inflicted by discrimination explains applications of the antidiscrimination principle where the material harm seems slight or problematic. For example, it fully explains the harmfulness of de jure school segregation without the need to invoke controversial social science evidence concerning the effects of segregation on achievement, interracial attitudes, and the like, and thus explains the Supreme Court's casual extension of Brown to prohibit the segregation of public beaches, parks, golf courses and buses. It also explains how present practices that are racially neutral may nonetheless perpetuate the harms of past de jure segregation.

Racial generalizations usually inflict psychic injury whether or not they are in fact premised on assumptions of differential moral worth. Although all of us recognize that institutional decisions must depend on generalizations based on objective characteristics of persons and things rather than on individualized judgments, we nonetheless tend to feel unfairly treated when disadvantaged by a generalization that is not true as applied to us. Generalizations based on immutable personal traits such as race or sex are especially frustrating because we can do nothing to escape their operation. These generalizations are still more pernicious, for they are often premised on the supposed correlation between the inherited characteristic and the undesirable voluntary behavior of those who possess the characteristic — for example, blacks are less industrious, trustworthy or clean than whites. Because the behavior is voluntary, and hence the proper object of moral condemnation, individuals as to whom the generalization is inaccurate may justifiably feel that the decisionmaker has passed moral judgment on them.

The psychological injury inflicted by generalizations based on race is compounded by the frustrating and cumulative nature of their material injuries. Racial generalizations are pervasive and have traditionally operated in the same direction — to the disadvantage of members of the minority group. A person who is denied one opportunity because he or she is short or overweight will find other opportunities, for in our society height and weight do not often serve as the bases for generalizations determining who will receive benefits. By contrast, at least until very recently, a black was not denied *an* opportunity because of his or her race, but denied virtually *all* desirable opportunities. As door after door is shut in one's face, the individual acts of discrimination combine into a systematic and grossly inequitable frustration of opportunity.

The cumulative disadvantage caused by the use of race as a proxy even for legitimate characteristics provides an independent ground for disfavoring nonbenign race-dependent decisions regardless of the integrity of the process by which they were made. To the unprejudiced employer who would prefer white applicants to blacks solely for reasons of efficiency, the antidiscrimination principle says in effect: "If you were the only one to do this, we would permit you to make efficient generalizations based on race. But so many other firms might employ similar generalizations that black individuals would suffer great cumulative harms. And, in the absence of an overriding justification, this cannot be permitted."

In Democracy and Distrust (1980), John Ely argues that the antidiscrimination principle remedies defects of legislative process. He offers two justifications for the treatment of racial classifications as "suspect." One ground for suspicion (id. at 153) is "first degree prejudice":

> If the doctrine of suspect classifications is a roundabout way of uncovering official attempts to inflict inequality for its own sake — to treat a group worse not in the service of some overriding social goal but largely for the sake of simply disadvantaging its members — it would seem to follow that one set of classifications we should treat as suspicious are those that disadvantage groups we know to be the object of widespread vilification, groups we know others (specifically those who control the legislative process) might wish to injure.

The alternative ground for suspicion is "second degree prejudice." Although legislation inevitably involves overgeneralization, we should be suspicious of "a generalization whose incidence of counterexample is significantly higher than the legislative authority appears to have thought it was" (id.):

> [T]o disadvantage — in the perceived service of some overriding social goal — a thousand persons that a more individualized (but more costly) test or procedure would exclude, under the impression that only five hundred fit that description, is to deny the five hundred to whose existence you are oblivious their right to equal concern and respect, by valuing their welfare at zero.

"The rub comes in how the Court should go about identifying" prejudice in the second degree. Building on the observation that "prejudice is a lens that distorts reality," Professor Ely continues (id. at 158-159):

> In deciding how much presumptive credit to extend a given generalization in our everyday lives, we would want to know where it came from — who came up with it and whether it is one that serves their interests. This commonsense insight . . . seems relevant to the constitutional inquiry as well. The choice between classifying on the basis

of a comparative generalization and attempting to come up with a more discriminating formula always involves balancing the increase in fairness that greater individualization will produce against the added costs it will entail. Where the generalization involved is one that serves the interests of the decision makers, however, certain dangers that are inherent in any balancing process are significantly intensified. Where it tangibly enhances their fortunes, the dangers may be most obvious. . . . But even where no tangible gain can be identified, there are psychic rewards in self-flattering generalizations. . . . "The easiest idea to sell anyone is that he is better than someone else," and it is a rare person who isn't delighted to hear and prone to accept comparative characterizations of ethnic or other groups that suggest the relative superiority of those groups to which he belongs. . . .

Thus generalizations to the effect, say, that whites in general are smarter or more industrious than blacks, men more stable emotionally than women, or native-born Americans more patriotic than Americans born elsewhere, are likely to go down pretty easily . . . with groups whose demography is that of the typical American legislature. . . . By seizing upon the positive myths about groups to which they belong and the negative myths about those to which they don't, or for that matter the realities respecting some or most members of the two classes, legislators, like the rest of us, are likely to assume too readily that not many of "them" will be unfairly deprived, nor many of "us" unfairly benefited, by a classification of this type.

Do the theories of "process" and "result" defects fully capture your aversion to discriminatory laws and practices? Consider another familiar argument: that racial classifications should be suspect because they are immutable:

Some people say: "Well, the fourteenth amendment mandates that government be color-blind (period)." This is not a theory, however; it is an assertion in need of a theory or justification. What might that be?

The Court has never addressed the question systematically, but some opinions suggest that it is unfair to burden anyone because of characteristics that are beyond his or her control. In *Bakke,* Justices Brennan et al. referred to "our deep belief that legal burdens should bear some relationship to individual responsibility or wrongdoing." . . .

I doubt that the original history of the equal protection clause provides much support for this position. Rather, its source lies in our culture, traditions, and psychology — a psychology that tells us that it is frustrating and painful, even if we are not stigmatized or the objects of prejudice, to be classified and disadvantaged based on characteristics beyond our control. Yet there are many areas besides race and sex and the traditional suspect-type classifications where this happens to us all the time and we are willing to accept it. To develop this theory, one must at least distinguish the circumstances where being disadvantaged because of an immutable characteristic is constitutionally permissible and those where it should be disfavored or forbidden.[100]

Compare Jack Balkin's analysis of the immutability argument:

Discrimination against blacks . . . is not unjust simply because race is an immutable characteristic. Focusing on immutability per se confuses biological with sociological considerations. It confuses the physical existence of the trait with what the trait means

---

100. Paul Brest, Affirmative Action and the Constitution: Three Theories, 72 Iowa L. Rev. 281 (1987). Brest is, in fact, deeply skeptical about the possibility of a satisfactory justification for a color-blind standard.

in a social system. Racial discrimination is wrong because of the historical creation of a status hierarchy organized around the meaning of skin color. The question to ask is not whether a trait is immutable, but whether there has been a history of using the trait to create a system of social meanings, or define a social hierarchy, that helps dominate and oppress people. Any conclusions about the importance of immutability already presuppose a view about background social structure.

Indeed, a focus on immutability makes sense only as long as we recognize its relationship to social structure. Social hierarchies often assign differential social meanings to immutable traits because they make exit from low status more difficult. But not all immutable characteristics are or have been the basis for unjust social hierarchies, and not all unjust social hierarchies are founded on immutable characteristics.

Religion is not an immutable trait — many religions are always looking for new converts — but status-based discrimination against religious groups is surely also unjust. Defenders of the immutability criterion can point to the Religion Clauses as an independent justification for protection of religious minorities; but this puts the cart before the horse. The Religion Clauses exist in part because the Framers recognized that religious intolerance was an evil long before they recognized that racial intolerance was.

The importance of immutability as a criterion of judgment is also sometimes defended on the grounds that immutable characteristics — for example, race — are morally irrelevant. But this argument, too, really depends on a view about the justness of a particular status hierarchy. When status distinctions are internalized in a culture, status hierarchies make traits morally relevant. They become signs of positive and negative associations. They become permissible proxies for inferences about character, honesty, ability, and judgment. Such traits are morally irrelevant only to persons not in the grip of that particular hierarchy. In the aristocracy of pre-Revolutionary America, for example, high birth was viewed as correlating with many other positive attributes — honesty, sagacity, learning, and good manners — and society was organized to make these positive associations a self-fulfilling prophecy. Generations of whites thought blacks naturally inferior; succeeding generations who learned not to make biological arguments have nevertheless continued to regard blacks as culturally inferior — as displaying negative qualities of sloth, violence, and licentiousness. A characteristic becomes "morally irrelevant" precisely when we understand the status hierarchy it is based on to be unjust. Only then do we become embarrassed to use the trait as a signifier of, or a proxy for, positive or negative associations. Our objection to the moral relevance of the characteristic is really our objection to the system of social meanings and the hierarchy of social status that uses this trait as a criterion for judgment. The real issue is whether society has created an unjust status hierarchy organized around a particular trait or set of traits, whether those traits are immutable, or — like religion — voluntarily chosen or instilled through socialization.[101]

In her article Anti-Subordination Above All: Sex, Race, and Equal Protection, 61 N.Y.U. L. Rev. 1003, 1005-14 (1986), Ruth Colker contrasts what she calls an "anti-differentiation" approach with an "anti-subordination" approach:

> . . . Under the anti-differentiation perspective, it is inappropriate to treat individuals differently on the basis of a particular normative view about race or sex. [This] perspective . . . focuses on the motivation of the individual institution that has allegedly discriminated, without attention to the larger societal context in which the institution operates. [T]he anti-differentiation perspective [also] focuses on the specific effect of

101. Balkin, The Constitution of Status, at 2365-2367.

the alleged discrimination on discrete individuals, rather than on groups. Race- and sex-specific policies or actions are invalid under this perspective because they reflect invidious motivation and result in dissimilar treatment for similarly situated individuals. It is equally invidious for white men to be treated differently from black women as for black women to be treated differently from white men under this perspective, because both situations violate the preeminent norm of equal treatment. Anti-differentiation advocates therefore argue for "color-blindness" or "sex-blindness" in the development and analysis of legislative and institutional policies, and frequently criticize affirmative action as violating that principle.

. . . I argue that courts should analyze equal protection cases from an anti-subordination perspective. Under the anti-subordination perspective, it is inappropriate for certain groups in society to have subordinated status because of their lack of power in society as a whole. This approach seeks to eliminate the power disparities between men and women, and between whites and non-whites, through the development of laws and policies that directly redress those disparities. From an anti-subordination perspective, both facially differentiating and facially neutral policies are invidious only if they perpetuate racial or sexual hierarchy.

[T]he anti-subordination perspective is a group-based perspective. [I]t focuses on society's role in creating subordination [and] it focuses on the way in which this subordination affects, or has affected groups of people. It is more invidious for women or blacks to be treated worse than white men than for men or whites to be treated worse than black women under this perspective, because of the differing histories and contexts of subordination faced by these groups. Anti-subordination proponents therefore advocate the use of race- or sex-specific policies, such as affirmative action, when those policies redress the subordination of racial minorities or women.

. . . Historically, the equal protection principle developed to remedy a history of subordination against a particular group in society, blacks. Aspirationally, it reminds us that no group should remain subordinated in our society. . . .

Discussion

1. Are Brest and Ely advocating a different role for antidiscrimination law than Colker? What is the relationship between Balkin's focus on status groups and status hierarchies and Colker's focus on the historic subordination of groups?

2. If one adopts Colker's antisubordination principle, whom would you trust to make the kinds of empirical judgments required by the principle? In particular, would you expect members of the judiciary to be especially skilled and trustworthy in making these judgments? Recall Plessy v. Ferguson, supra, and the promise that the Court would not tolerate measures designed for the "annoyance or oppression of a particular race." Are there "neutral" tests to determine what counts as an "annoyance" or "oppression" or what is invidiously "subordinating" as opposed to "reasonable"? Does one need some special training in social interpretation — e.g., training in interpretive sociology or anthropology — in order to make such judgments? Can or should law schools offer such training?

3. In explaining why a focus on subordination is the better approach, Colker argues

> We have not decided, as a nation, that all distinctions are invidious. We permit distinctions on the basis of intelligence or ability. We only prohibit distinctions that we have

good reasons to believe are biased or irrational, and it is group-based experiences that primarily inform us as to which kinds of distinctions are biased or irrational. Thus, the anti-subordination principle, by recognizing and drawing on the historical subordination of blacks and women, offers a substantive explanation for why certain distinctions are subjected to closer scrutiny. . . .

Is it clear that distinctions based on intelligence or ability are not subordinating? Consider Robert L. Hayman, Jr., The Smart Culture: Society, Intelligence, and Law (1998). Hayman points out that historically distinctions based on intelligence testing have been used to perpetuate racial subordination through the rhetoric of scientific authority and natural differences. Second, he argues that our society wrongly assumes that intelligence is a unitary and fixed trait that forms a natural basis for inequality. Third, he claims that society uses the idea of intelligence in countless ways to deny people equal opportunity and equal dignity. Finally he contends that unjustified stereotypes about people of low intelligence are rampant in our country. Do Hayman's arguments suggest that what counts as "subordination" and what counts as "natural inequality" or "meritocracy" has historically been a moving target, and that the target may still be moving even in our own era? If the target is a moving one, how do we decide what is just and unjust?

Why does Colker suggest that subordinating distinctions are those we have "good reasons" to think are "irrational?" Why isn't subordination of blacks to preserve superior white prestige, power, and holdings completely rational for whites who wish to maximize these goods? Recall that Justice Brown's opinion in *Plessy* argued that some forms of racial segregation were reasonable, and some were oppressive. Whose conception of "reason" counts in Colker's argument, and who is the "we" that holds this conception?

4. *To what extent are the anticlassification and antisubordination principles really in conflict?* Anticlassification and antisubordination understandings developed together; it was only in disputes over *Brown's* enforcement that advocates shaped anticlassification and antisubordination into distinct and competing principles with differing practical applications. In fact, in the years immediately before and after *Brown* these frameworks were understood as interconnected, and contemporaries discussed *Brown* as vindicating values that today we associate with the antisubordination approach. See Reva B. Siegel, Equality Talk: Antisubordination and Anticlassification Values in Constitutional Struggles over Brown, 117 Harv. L. Rev. 1470, 1478-1480, 1500, 1534 (2004):

[After the Court] claim[ed] that segregation harmed minority schoolchildren[,] [t]he South relentlessly attacked the social science authority arrayed to support this claim in the opinion's Footnote Eleven. . . . [I]n announcing and applying the new [strict scrutiny] framework [in *McLaughlin* and *Loving*], the Court refrained from discussing, as it had in *Brown,* the dignitary harms that Jim Crow laws inflicted on blacks. Treating racial classification as presumptively unconstitutional, as the Court did . . . , obviated the need for such discussions. . . . [Nevertheless,] in the 1950s and 1960s, many of *Brown's* prominent defenders in the legal academy justified the decision as condemning practices that enforced group inequality[, and] courts applied that presumption in accordance with an understanding, sometimes implicit and sometimes explicit, that its purpose was to dismantle segregation and other practices that enforced racial hierarchy. In this period, segregation was understood as wrongful both because it failed to treat members of a group as individuals and because it treated one group as inferior to another, and there was little felt sense that expressing segregation's harm in terms of a presumption that racial classification was unconstitutional amounted to a choice between the accounts of the harm. . . . [T]he debate about de facto school segregation raised different kinds of questions . . . [and] drew anticlassification discourse into new forms of conflict. Now [a]nticlassification discourse act[ed] both to advance and to limit antisubordination aims, with the two forms of reasoning finally assuming familiar form as agonistic principles in the affirmative action debates of the early 1970s.

The overlap and the interdependence between anticlassification and antisubordination approaches continues to this day. As we will see in the materials that follow, what counts as an impermissible racial classification is not always clear-cut. Courts must make policy decisions about whether to count a challenged practice as a "classification" that is "on the basis of" "race"; in different situations, each of these key terms can become contestable. Consider the extent to which antisubordination values play a crucial role in deciding what violates the anticlassification principle. In fact, as Jack Balkin and Reva Siegel have pointed out

> The idea of distinguishing between anticlassification and antisubordination principles arose at a critical juncture in American race history. [T]wo decades after *Brown*, . . . American law had discredited the most prominent and overtly discriminatory practices enforcing racial segregation. [T]he Court faced important questions about the constitutionality of two kinds of practices: practices [like affirmative action] that employed racial criteria to integrate formerly segregated institutions and practices [with disparate impact on racial minorities] that preserved the racial segregation of institutions through formally neutral rules that made no overt reference to race.
>
> [S]egregation under Jim Crow violated both the anticlassification and antisubordination principles. Cases like *Brown* and *Loving* contained language condemning the practice of classifying citizens by race as well as language condemning practices that enforced subordination or inflicted status harm. . . . Depending on whether one emphasized the anticlassification or antisubordination discourse in *Brown* and *Loving*, the cases seemed to resolve the disputes facing the Court quite differently.
>
> [In fact] the anticlassification principle cannot by itself decide many important issues of antidiscrimination law. A decision maker must adopt additional criteria in order to apply the principle so that it can decide concrete cases. These implementing criteria cannot be derived from the anticlassification principle itself; as a result, many different legal regimes could be consistent with the anticlassification imperative. Courts must make a variety of implementing decisions in order to apply the anticlassification principle; and . . . they do not make such implementing decisions in any consistent manner. [This] suggests that the discourse of anticlassification conceals other values that do much of the work in determining which practices antidiscrimination law enjoins. . . .
>
> Sometimes . . . courts have implemented the anticlassification principle in a fashion that preserves status relations. But often, and particularly as the civil rights agenda expands, the judiciary has applied the anticlassification principle in ways that dismantle status relations. [A]pplication of the anticlassification principle shifts over time in response to social contestation. As social protest delegitimates certain practices, courts are often moved, consciously or unconsciously, by perceptions of status harm to find violations of the anticlassification principle where they saw none before. Considered

from this historical vantage point, American civil rights jurisprudence vindicates both anticlassification and antisubordination commitments. [102]

B.   The Reach of the Suspect Classification Doctrine

Does the strict scrutiny rule of Loving v. Virginia apply to all government classifications based on race? Consider the following contexts. (We address the case of race conscious affirmative action in Section F, infra.).

1.   Racial Segregation in Prisons

In Lee v. Washington, 390 U.S. 333 (1968), the Court summarily affirmed an order directing desegregation of the Alabama prison system, noting, however, that nothing in the order precluded "allowance for the necessities of prison security and discipline." In a one-paragraph concurrence, Justices Black, Harlan, and Stewart made explicit "something that is left to be gathered only by implication from the Court's opinion. This is that prison authorities have the right, acting in good faith and in particularized circumstances, to take into account racial tensions in maintaining security, discipline, and good order in prisons and jails." (Is Justice Stewart's concurrence consistent with his concurrence in Loving v. Virginia?) Would racial segregation in prisons be a permissible response to conditions of the sort described in the following material by James Jacobs?[103]

> The inmate leaders, except one, were black, even though almost 50 percent of the inmates were white. The white prisoners were unable to organize. Consequently, they were highly vulnerable to exploitation.
> "The exploitation matrix typically consists of four groups, and the form of exploitation found in each is fairly clear cut. At the top normally is a black leader called a 'heavy.' He is followed closely by three or four black lieutenants. The third group, a mixture of eight to sixteen black and white youths, do the bidding of those at the top. This group is divided into a top half of mostly blacks, known as 'alright guys,' with the bottom half comprised mostly of whites, designated as 'chumps.' One or two white scapegoats make up the fourth group in each cottage. These scapegoats become the sexual victims of the first three groups." . . .
> Numbers will not fully explain the hegemony of black and other minority prisoners, even when the dominant group is also a majority. The key to black dominance is their greater solidarity and ability to intimidate whites. As the distinct minority in the larger society, blacks have long experienced racial discrimination. They have

---

102. Jack M. Balkin and Reva B. Siegel, The American Civil Rights Tradition: Anticlassification or Antisubordination?, 58 U. Miami L. Rev. 9, 11-14 (2003).

103. James Jacobs, Race Relations and the Prison Subculture, in 1 Crime and Justice: An Annual Review of Research (Morris & Toury eds., 1979). Jacobs adds:

> Aside from Italian cliques clothed in the Mafia mystique, white cliques are too weak to offer individuals any protection in the predatory prisoner subculture. Only in California does it appear that white prisoners have been able to achieve a strong enough organization to protect themselves. It is significant that such organization has been achieved by groups which already had some sense of group consciousness ("okies" and "bikers"), and only then by an extreme emphasis upon white racism. Neo-Nazi prisoner movements have also appeared in Illinois, especially at Menard, and may in the long run be the basis on which white prisoners achieve solidarity.

necessarily defined themselves in terms of their racial identity and have linked their opportunities in the larger society to the fate of their race. Whites, especially outside the south, have had almost no experience in grouping together on the basis of being white. Ethnicity has been a more important basis for social interaction, although even ethnicity has been a weaker basis of collective action for whites than race for blacks. "Whiteness" simply possesses no ideological or cultural significance in American society, except for racist fringe groups. Consequently, whites face imprisonment alone or in small cliques based on outside friendships, neighborhood, or ethnic background.

JOHNSON v. CALIFORNIA, 543 U.S. 499 (2005): The California Department of Corrections (CDC) had a policy of placing all new male prisoners and all male prisoners transferred from other state facilities in double cells in reception centers for up to 60 days upon their arrival. During that time they were assigned cellmates based on their race; cellmate assignments were further subdivided within each racial group. Japanese-Americans were housed separately from Chinese-Americans, and Northern California Hispanics were separated from Southern California Hispanics. The rest of the state prison facilities — including dining areas, yards, and cells — were fully integrated. After the 60-day period prisoners were allowed to choose their own cellmates. The CDC defended the policy as necessary to prevent violence by racial gangs; it argued that the Court should review its judgment, not under strict scrutiny, but a more deferential standard appropriate for judicial review of the penological judgments of prison administrators.

The Supreme Court, in an opinion by Justice O'Connor, held that the CDC policy was subject to strict scrutiny and remanded for further proceedings to determine whether the policy could satisfy that standard. The Court, Justice O'Connor argued, had held that

> *all* racial classifications . . . must be analyzed by a reviewing court under strict scrutiny. [T]he government has the burden of proving that racial classifications 'are narrowly tailored measures that further compelling governmental interests.' We have insisted on strict scrutiny in every context, even for so-called 'benign' racial classifications, such as race-conscious university admissions policies, race-based preferences in government contracts, and race-based districting intended to improve minority representation.
>
> The reasons for strict scrutiny are familiar. Racial classifications raise special fears that they are motivated by an invidious purpose. Thus, we have admonished time and again that, "[a]bsent searching judicial inquiry into the justification for such race-based measures, there is simply no way of determining . . . what classifications are in fact motivated by illegitimate notions of racial inferiority or simple racial politics." We therefore apply strict scrutiny to all racial classifications to "smoke out" illegitimate uses of race by assuring that [government] is pursuing a goal important enough to warrant use of a highly suspect tool."
>
> The CDC claims that its policy should be exempt from our categorical rule because it is "neutral" — that is, it "neither benefits nor burdens one group or individual more than any other group or individual." . . . The CDC's argument ignores our repeated command that "racial classifications receive close scrutiny even when they may be said to burden or benefit the races equally." . . .
>
> The need for strict scrutiny is no less important here, where prison officials cite racial violence as the reason for their policy. As we have recognized in the past, racial

classifications "threaten to stigmatize individuals by reason of their membership in a racial group and to *incite racial hostility*." Indeed, by insisting that inmates be housed only with other inmates of the same race, it is possible that prison officials will breed further hostility among prisoners and reinforce racial and ethnic divisions. By perpetuating the notion that race matters most, racial segregation of inmates "may exacerbate the very patterns of [violence that it is] said to counteract." [T]he "necessities of prison security and discipline," *Lee,* are a compelling government interest justifying only those uses of race that are narrowly tailored to address those necessities.

The Court stated that the deferential standard for prisoner claims announced in Turner v. Safley, 482 U.S. 78 (1987), did not apply to questions of racial segregation. *Turner* involved a challenge to restrictions on inmate marriages and correspondence between inmates under the Due Process Clause and the First Amendment. It held that where prisoners allege that prison regulations violate their fundamental rights, deference to prison administrators counsels a relaxed standard; courts should ask only whether the regulation was "reasonably related" to "legitimate penological interests," with no inquiry into less restrictive alternatives. *Turner,* the Court argued, applied only to fundamental rights whose exercise would be "inconsistent with proper incarceration." By contrast, "[t]he right not to be discriminated against based on one's race . . . is not a right that need necessarily be compromised for the sake of proper prison administration. On the contrary, compliance with the Fourteenth Amendment's ban on racial discrimination is not only consistent with proper prison administration, but also bolsters the legitimacy of the entire criminal justice system. . . . When government officials are permitted to use race as a proxy for gang membership and violence without demonstrating a compelling government interest and proving that their means are narrowly tailored, society as a whole suffers." The *Turner* standard

> would allow prison officials to use race-based policies even when there are race-neutral means to accomplish the same goal, and even when the race-based policy does not in practice advance that goal. . . . [P]rison officials could segregate visiting areas on the ground that racial mixing would cause unrest in the racially charged prison atmosphere. [And under *Turner*] there is no obvious limit to permissible segregation in prisons. It is not readily apparent why, if segregation in reception centers is justified, segregation in the dining halls, yards, and general housing areas is not also permissible. Any of these areas could be the potential site of racial violence.
>
>   The CDC protests that strict scrutiny will handcuff prison administrators and render them unable to address legitimate problems of race-based violence in prisons. Not so. Strict scrutiny is not "strict in theory, but fatal in fact." Strict scrutiny does not preclude the ability of prison officials to address the compelling interest in prison safety. Prison administrators, however, will have to demonstrate that any race-based policies are narrowly tailored to that end.

Chief Justice Rehnquist did not participate in the case.

Justice Ginsburg, joined by Justices Souter and Breyer, concurred, noting that "the same standard of review ought not control judicial inspection of every official race classification. . . . 'Actions designed to burden groups long denied full citizenship stature are not sensibly ranked with measures taken to hasten the day when entrenched discrimination and its aftereffects have been extirpated.' There is no pretense here, however, that the California Department of Corrections (CDC) installed its segregation policy to 'correct inequalities.' "

Justice Stevens dissented. He argued that the Court should not have remanded for further proceedings because the CDC policy would not pass muster under either the strict scrutiny standard or the more relaxed *Turner* standard.

> [T]he CDC has failed to explain why it could not, as an alternative to automatic segregation, rely on an individualized assessment of each inmate's risk of violence when assigning him to a cell in a reception center. The Federal Bureau of Prisons and other state systems do so without any apparent difficulty. For inmates who are being transferred from one facility to another — who represent approximately 85% of those subject to the segregation policy — the CDC can simply examine their prison records to determine if they have any known gang affiliations or if they have ever engaged in or threatened racial violence. . . . For new inmates, assignments can be based on their presentence reports, which contain information about offense conduct, criminal record, and personal history — including any available information about gang affiliations. In fact, state law requires the county probation officer to transmit a presentence report to the CDC along with an inmate's commitment papers.

The fact that the CDC did not push to obtain timely presentence reports did not excuse its segregation policy.

Justice Thomas dissented, joined by Justice Scalia. He argued that the relaxed *Turner* standard, and not strict scrutiny, should apply to racial classifications in prisons. "The Constitution has always demanded less within the prison walls." Justice Thomas emphasized that racial violence in prisons was a serious problem that prison officials and not courts were best suited to address. The need for deference justified application of the *Turner* test. He rejected the majority's attempt to limit *Turner*:

> Inquiring whether a given right is consistent with "proper prison administration" calls for precisely the sort of judgments that *Turner* said courts were ill equipped to make.
>
> [T]wo Terms ago, in upholding the University of Michigan Law School's affirmative-action program, [in *Grutter v. Bollinger*] this Court deferred to the judgment by the law school's faculty and administrators on their need for diversity in the student body. Deference would seem all the more warranted in the prison context, for whatever the Court knows of administering educational institutions, it knows much less about administering penal ones. The potential consequences of second-guessing the judgments of prison administrators are also much more severe.

Discussion

In *Johnson*, Justices Scalia and Thomas, who have been among the most adamant in their opposition to race-conscious affirmative action, and the most supportive of a general rule of colorblindness in government decisionmaking, argue that both the colorblindness principle and the strict scrutiny rule should be relaxed in the prison context. Justice Ginsburg, who has long argued that government policies designed to redress past discrimination against racial minorities should be treated differently from laws that disadvantage racial minorities, insists on strict scrutiny in this case. What explains their respective positions in this case? Does the antidiscrimination principle resolve the dispute between them? Which antidiscrimination principle?

2.   Child Placement Policies

a.   Child Custody Decisions Following Divorce

In Palmore v. Sidoti, 466 U.S. 429 (1984), the Supreme Court unanimously invalidated "a judgment of a state court divesting a natural mother of the custody of her infant child because of her remarriage to a person of a different race." When Linda and Anthony Sidoti, both white, divorced in May 1980, the Florida court awarded custody of their three-year-old daughter to the mother. In September 1981, Anthony petitioned for a modification of that judgment on the ground, among others, that Linda was living with an African-American man (whom she had married by the time of the hearing). Although the court specifically found that Linda remained a fit parent and that her husband was "respectable," it awarded custody to Anthony. The court apparently took into account a counselor's conclusion that Linda "has chosen for herself and for her child, a lifestyle unacceptable to her father *and to society* (emphasis supplied by the Supreme Court)." The Florida court added:

> [D]espite the strides that have been made in bettering relations between the races in this country, it is inevitable that Melanie will, if allowed to remain in her present situation and attain[ ] school age and thus [become] more vulnerable to peer pressures, suffer from the social stigmatization that is sure to come.

Chief Justice Burger observed that "it is clear that the outcome would have been different had petitioner married a Caucasian male of similar respectability," and that "the action of the Florida court must be tested by 'the most exacting scrutiny.'"

> [The best interest of the child is] indisputably a substantial governmental interest for purposes of the Equal Protection Clause.
> It would ignore reality to suggest that racial and ethnic prejudices do not exist. . . . There is a risk that a child living with a step-parent of a different race may be subject to a variety of pressures and stresses not present if the child were living with parents of the same racial or ethnic origin.
> The question, however, is whether the reality of private biases and the possible injury they might inflict are permissible considerations for removal of an infant child from the custody of its natural mother. We have little difficulty concluding that they are not. The Constitution cannot control such prejudices but neither can it tolerate them. Private biases may be outside the reach of the law, but the law cannot, directly or indirectly, give them effect. . . .
> This is by no means the first time that acknowledged racial prejudice has been invoked to justify racial classifications. In Buchanan v. Warley, 245 U.S. 60 (1917), for example, this Court invalidated a Kentucky law forbidding Negroes from buying homes in white neighborhoods. "It is urged that this proposed segregation will promote the public peace by preventing race conflicts. Desirable as this is, and important as is the preservation of the public peace, this aim cannot be accomplished by laws or ordinances which deny rights created or protected by the Federal Constitution." Whatever problems racially-mixed households may pose for children in 1984 can no more support a denial of constitutional rights than could the stresses that residential integration was thought to entail in 1917. The effects of racial prejudice, however real, cannot justify a racial classification removing an infant child from the custody of its natural mother found to be an appropriate person to have such custody.

b. Race Matching Policies in Adoption

Palmore v. Sidoti involved a decision about which parent in a previously existing family (divided by divorce) would receive custody of a child. Does the same reasoning apply to adoption, in which a child is placed in a new family?

Many adoption agencies seek to "match" children to their prospective adoptive parents on the basis of religion (almost always based on the biological mother), race and ethnic background (e.g., Italian, Polish, "Mediterranean"), and physical appearance (height, hair and eye color). Is a conscious attempt by a state adoption agency to achieve a racial "match" in child placement constitutional?

Professor James S. Bowen[104] strongly endorses racial matching: "A Black child must be raised as a Black child," and "[g]iven a situation of equipoise between two possible adoptive families, race may be a determinative factor in deciding the placement of a Black child in contemporary American society." Indeed, he proposes the adoption of an "Afro-American Child Welfare Act," specifically modeled after the Indian Child Welfare Act of 1978, that would codify such racial factors. One section of the proposed Act would have Congress declare "that it is the policy of this Nation to protect the best interests of Afro-American children and to promote the stability and security of Afro-American children and to promote the stability and security of Afro-American people and families by the establishment of minimum federal standards for the placement of such children in foster or adoptive homes which will reflect the unique values of Afro-American culture." Professor Bowen argues that "[r]ather than use race as a mechanism for erecting or maintaining group domination or hierarchy, the utility of race [under his plan] is as a means to facilitate redress of past racial injustice." How does a racial preference for adoption rectify "past racial injustice"?

Professor Elizabeth Bartholet, by contrast, maintains that race-matching policies harm children by significantly hindering transracial adoptions even in cases in which in-race placement is not an option. According to Bartholet, not only do these policies conflict with "the basic law of the land on race discrimination," but they are also deeply "anomalous": "In no other area do state and state-licensed decision-makers use race so systematically as the basis for action. In no other area do they promote the use of race so openly. Indeed, in most areas of our community life, race is an absolutely impermissible basis for classification." Bartholet, Where Do Black Children Belong? The Politics of Race-Matching in Adoption, 139 U. Pa. L. Rev. 1163, 1223 (1991). Although Bartholet notes that "[a]lmost no one advocates the elimination of any preference whatsoever for in-race placement," she nevertheless argues that establishing "a regime in which there is no official preference [even presumably as a tie-breaker] for same-race preference seems the wise course and the direction in which we should move." Bartholet summarizes the current political and judicial consensus as follows:

> There seems to be an extraordinary level of agreement among policy-makers that whatever the law provides with respect to race in other contexts, it is appropriate to use race as a basis for decisionmaking in the context of the adoptive family. Courts

---

104. James S. Bowen, Cultural Convergences and Divergences: The Nexus Between Putative Afro-American Family Values and the Best Interests of the Child, 26 J. Fam. L. 487 (1987-1988).

have both failed to confront the issues involved in racial matching policies, and have shown significant sympathy for those policies.

The courts have generally agreed upon a legal doctrine that race cannot be used by agencies as the sole or automatically dispositive factor in placement decisionmaking, but can be used as a significant and even determinative factor. Some courts actually require that race be considered.

Bartholet maintains that, by promoting racial separatism rather than integration, matching policies in adoption flatly contradict the traditional affirmative action rationales, nor do they fit any other "recognized exception[] to the anti-discrimination norm."

c.   Facilitative Accommodation

Professor Richard Banks argues that "race matching is not the only form of race-based state action that structures the adoption process." Adoption agencies classify children by race and ask prospective parents what race of child they would prefer. "If a prospective parent states a desire for a white child, then the only children that agency personnel will suggest for adoption will be children from the 'white' list. Even without overt steering practices, adoption agencies may be aware how important race is to an adoptive parent's decisions and 'do nothing to discourage or guard against race-based decisionmaking.'" Banks argues that these practices, which he collectively refers to as "facilitative accommodation," also raise equal protection concerns:

> As a result of facilitative accommodation policies, most black children in need of adoption are categorically denied, on the basis of race, the opportunity to be considered individually for adoption by the majority of prospective adoptive parents. This could not occur were it not for current policies of facilitative accommodation. The racial classification on which facilitative accommodation practices rely is the type of harm prohibited by the Equal Protection Clause.
>
> Worse, facilitative accommodation reinforces and legitimizes the type of race-consciousness that produces unjustified racial inequality, both in adoption and throughout American society. Adoptive parents' racial preferences dramatically diminish the pool of potential parents available to black children relative to that available to white children. The pool of parents available to black children is also of lower average quality than that available to white children, in part because many of those whites who adopt black children do so because they are considered by agencies to be among the least desirable parents for white children. The severity of the social inequality produced by adoptive parents' preferences is made starkly clear by a fact too often accepted as inevitable, albeit lamentable, rather than as a predictable outcome of our own preference-promoting policies: Black children are simply worth less than white children.[105]

Banks argues that even if furthering the best interests of the child is a compelling state interest, facilitative adoption policies do not perform this task effectively for

---

105. R. Richard Banks, The Color of Desire: Fulfilling Adoptive Parents' Racial Preferences Through Discriminatory State Action, 107 Yale L.J. 875, 881 (1998).

many minority children; at the very least, they are not necessary to achieve this goal. Even without facilitation, no parents would be forced to accept children they did not want, and at least some would pick children of a different race that they would not otherwise ever have considered. Do you agree that state adoption agencies should not be permitted to keep separate lists of white or black children, ask about racial preferences of prospective parents, or "steer" prospective parents toward children of the same race?

Discussion

1. If state actors consider the adoptive parents' preference concerning the race of a child they might adopt, does the state's policy or practice "classify on the basis of race" within the meaning of *Loving* and subsequent equal protection cases? Is it possible to decide this question without making a judgment as to the legitimacy of the challenged practice?

2. Does the state have a compelling interest in enabling same-race adoptions? Professor Bartholet observes: "Even those blacks and whites generally committed to integration often see the family as the place to draw the line." Is there something "special" about the family that makes it qualitatively different from all other social contexts? Why is racial matching in adoption so intuitively appealing and seemingly so "natural" to many? According to Bartholet, "judges have come up with little difficulty in treating the racial issue so differently in the adoption context":

> In one leading case, the majority opinion states, "It is a natural thing for children to be raised by parents of their same ethnic background." The same opinion speaks approvingly of traditional matching policies as designed to duplicate the "natural biological environment" so that the child could develop a normal family relationship."

Is this reductionist "biologism," defined by Bartholet as "the idea that what is natural in the context of the biological family is what is normal and desirable in the context of adoption"?

How do you distinguish racial matching in adoption from antimiscegenation laws such as Virginia's Racial Integrity Act (held unconstitutional in Loving v. Virginia, discussed in the previous section), which also relied on notions of racial purity in the context of the family? What is the difference between the state making it more difficult for whites to adopt black children (or giving a preference for blacks to adopt black children) and making it more difficult for whites to marry blacks (or encouraging marriages between persons of the same race)? Is the difference that marriage is consensual and adoption is not, at least for one of the parties? Why does this fact justify the state's substitution of judgment on racial grounds?

3. Recall Professor Kevin Brown's role-model argument in favor of African-American "immersion schools": These schools will help black students acquire skills which they will need in order to cope with the pervasive racism of the dominant culture. Opponents of transracial adoption have sometimes offered similar arguments: "The ability to deal with the sometimes subtle racism which abounds in almost every aspect of American life must be learned from those who have developed survival skills." Responses to "Where do Black Children Belong?" 1 Reconstruction, No. 4, 1992, at 46, 53. Do you agree? Is the argument stronger or weaker in the adoption context? Why?

4. What does Bowen mean by the claim that "[a] Black child must be raised as a Black child." Note that the first use of the adjective "Black" appears to refer to a formal or biological conception of race, whereas the second appears to refer to a cultural conception. Bartholet quotes the following statement by the president of the National Association of Black Social Workers: "The lateral transfer of our children to white families is not in our best interest. . . . It is their aim to raise Black children with white minds." The overwhelming majority of transracial adoptions consist of white families adopting minority children, rather than minority families adopting white children. To what extent should this be relevant? Should this "transfer" be characterized as a form of legally administered racial "genocide"? Note that adoption decisions are presumably governed by a "best interests of the child" test. If you think that black children belong in black families, is it because it serves the black *community's* best interests, or because it serves black *children's* best interests?

Consider Richard Banks' rejoinder:

Both proponents of race matching and proponents of transracial adoption contend that their chosen policy is best for the children involved. Yet the best-interests-of-the-child standard is of remarkably little use in defining the role of race in adoption. The meaning of the standard with respect to race is itself a matter of race politics insofar as different determinations regarding the significance of race in adoptive placement reflect divergent ideological visions of the "proper" role of racial identity in socialization. As long as ideological differences remain significant, so will varied interpretations of the best-interests-of-the-child standard.[106]

5. The controversy over transracial adoptions is reflected by the passage of 42 U.S.C. §1996b, titled "Interethnic adoption," which provides that

A person or government that is involved in adoption or foster care placements may not — (A) deny to any individual the opportunity to become an adoptive or a foster parent, on the basis of the race, color, or national origin of the individual, or of the child, involved; or (B) delay or deny the placement of a child for adoption or into foster care, on the basis of the race, color, or national origin of the adoptive or foster parent, or the child, involved.

Compare this with 25 U.S.C. §1915, dealing with "Placement of Indian children," which requires that

In any adoptive placement of an Indian child under State law, a preference shall be given, in the absence of good cause to the contrary, to a placement with (1) a member of the child's extended family; (2) other members of the Indian child's tribe; or (3) other Indian families.

We deal below, at pp. 1151-1155, with the tension between what might be called "standard-form" doctrine involving racial and ethnic classification and doctrine dealing with American Indians. For now, it is enough to ask you to compare the two federal laws and to ask yourself which you prefer and why. Note, incidentally, that the general statute does not, at least on its face, extend to prohibiting a state

106. Banks, The Color of Desire, at 881.

agency from responding to potential adopters' own preferences as to race. Should it have?

3. Government Collection and Use of Racial Data

In Anderson v. Martin, 375 U.S. 399 (1964), the Court unanimously invalidated a Louisiana statute requiring that the ballots in all elections designate the race of the candidates. The Court rejected the state's argument that the requirement was nondiscriminatory since the labeling provision applied equally to black and white candidates. Justice Clark wrote:

> [B]y directing the citizen's attention to the single consideration of race or color, the State indicates that a candidate's race or color is an important — perhaps paramount — consideration in the citizen's choice, which may decisively influence the citizens to cast his ballot along racial lines. . . . The vice lies . . . in the placing of the power of the State behind a racial classification that induces racial prejudice at the polls.

However, the same year, in Tancil v. Wools, 379 U.S. 19 (1964), the Court summarily affirmed the judgment of a three-judge district court invalidating Virginia laws that required officials to keep voting and property-owner records on a racially segregated basis, but sustaining a law that required that every divorce decree recite the race of the spouses. Why are divorce decrees different from voting and property owner records? Is *Loving* consistent with the state practice of identifying persons (or their parents) by race on birth certificates, drivers' licenses, and other official documents?

Is *Loving* consistent with federal census practices that identify or classify citizens by race or ethnicity? Consider the following case:

MORALES v. DALEY, 116 F. Supp. 2d 801 (S.D. Tex. 2000): Since 1790 the census has asked persons for their race. The 2000 Census features several questions about racial and ethnic identity. The short form of the census questionnaire asks whether a person is of Spanish, Hispanic, or Latino heritage. It asks a person's race and directs the person to check off a box with the following choices: (1) white; (2) black, African American, or Negro; (3) American Indian or Alaska native, with space to provide the name of the enrolled or principal tribe; (4) Asian Indian; (5) Chinese; (6) Filipino; (7) other Asian, with a space to print the race; (8) Japanese; (9) Korean; (10) Vietnamese; (11) Native Hawaiian; (12) Guamanian or Chamorro; (13) Samoan; (14) Other Pacific Islander, and a space to print in the race; or (15) "Some other race," with a space in which the person is to print the name of the race. Each member of a household is asked a similar question, thus allowing the government to know which members of which races are living with each other. In addition, the census also asks how each person in the household is related to the others. A question concerning the relationships that persons who live in a single household have to each other has been included in the census since 1880.

A long form of the census questionnaire, given to a selected percentage of households, asks additionally for a person's "ancestry or ethnic origin," giving as examples "Italian, Jamaican, African American, Cambodian, Cape Verdean,

Norwegian, Dominican, French Canadian, Haitian, Korean, Lebanese, Polish, Nigerian, Mexican, Taiwanese, Ukranian, etc." It asks whether a person speaks a language other than English at home, what that language is, and how well the person speaks English, giving choices from "very well" to "not at all." A question concerning the language spoken at home was on the census form from 1890 through 1940, and reappeared on the census forms from 1960 through the 1990 census. Finally, the long form asks where a person was born, when the person first entered the United States, and whether the person is a citizen of the United States.

Plaintiffs objected that asking about their racial and ethnic identities violated their right to the equal protection component of the Due Process Clause of the Fifth Amendment and enabled the government to make race-based decisions. The government defended its questions on the grounds that collecting information about race and ethnicity was "needed to assess racial disparities in health and environmental risks," was "required by states to meet legislative redistricting requirements by knowing the racial makeup of the voting age population" and was "required to enforce provisions under the Civil Rights Act which prohibits discrimination based upon race, sex, religion and national origin."

The district court rejected the plaintiff's arguments:

The government's position is that because the plaintiffs' Fifth Amendment due process challenge to the racial class and ethnic classification questions cannot be tied to disparate treatment of those answering the questions, a compelling governmental interest need not be shown. Rather, the historical use of such information recognized by the courts, coupled with the historical use of the census to obtain answers to those questions, mandate affirming the use of the Census 2000 forms. The government emphasizes that these questions have historically been answered, and that the Supreme Court and lesser courts have accepted, without question, the propriety of collecting the data on race and ethnicity. The plaintiffs . . . argue that the government's justification [for asking about] ethnicity . . . rings hollow in light of the Japanese experience during World War II. . . . The First Circuit in New Hampshire addressed a similar argument by pointing out that "Possible and purely hypothetical misuse of data does not require the banning of reasonable procedures to acquire such data. Statistical information as such is a rather neutral entity which only becomes meaningful when it is interpreted. And any positive steps which the United States might subsequently take as a result of its interpretation of the data in question remains subject to law and judicial scrutiny."

Plaintiffs' position is based upon a misunderstanding of the distinction between collecting demographic data so that the government may have the information it believes at a given time it needs in order to govern, and governmental use of suspect classifications without a compelling interest. Plaintiffs may disagree with the government's need to know such information, but Congress has delegated to the Bureau the authority to decide what is needed and to ask the appropriate questions. The plaintiffs' position, particularly on the race and ethnicity questions, is one that attempts to strike at the root of the problem of racial and ethnic classifications. Their argument is that racial and ethnic self-classification that is mandated by the government itself can do nothing to propel this country toward a society in which race and ethnicity do not matter. Many would agree with their argument, but the issue here is not social, moral, or political. The issue is whether requiring a person to self-classify racially or ethnically, knowing to what use such classifications have been put in the past, can violate the due process implications of the Fifth Amendment. This court holds that such self-classifications do not. The issue raised by the plaintiffs is one properly addressed by Congress, not by the courts. The Bureau has stated for each of the challenged questions the statutory mandate, other reasons, or both why this demographic information is needed. The Constitution requires nothing more.

Discussion

1. Why exactly does the Court in *Morales* reject the plaintiff's claims? Does government classify on the basis of race when it conducts the census? If so, why doesn't strict scrutiny apply? Is "self-classification" not racial classification within the meaning of *Loving*? Does government use of racial self-description eliminate state action, or does it simply change the government's role in generating racial identity or information? Does people's self-reporting of their race negate the fact that the government is making racial classifications? Or is the point rather that the census merely involves the government in collecting information, and this practice has no (adverse?) racial impact — at least until the information is used. (For what purposes is racial census data used? For what purposes might it be used?) Is there an inherent dignitary harm in being asked to identify yourself by race, even if you don't have to answer?Recall Justice Harlan's claim in his dissent in *Plessy:* "In respect of civil rights, common to all citizens, the constitution of the United States does not, I think, permit any public authority to know the race of those entitled to be protected in the enjoyment of such rights. . . . Our constitution is color-blind, and neither knows nor tolerates classes among citizens." Why *should* the government be permitted to "know" the race of its citizens? If you think that this sort of "knowledge" is permissible, then what is the ban on racial classification about?

Section 709(c) of the Civil Rights Act of 1964 requires that employers "make and keep" records of their employment decisions and provide reports to the Equal Employment Opportunity Commission. These records often include the race, sex, and ethnicity of employees and applicants, and are used by the government and civil rights attorneys to demonstrate violations of civil rights laws and by courts to fashion remedies. In like fashion, §402 of the Act requires a biannual survey to determine educational opportunity by race. Does collecting information necessary to comply with the Civil Rights Act violate the Equal Protection Clause?

Reva Siegel notes that "[t]he civil rights movement's stance on racial designations and data collection seems to have shifted with the uses to which such information was put. . . . The NAACP's caution was no doubt due to the ways in which Southerners were using . . . data [on crime and illegitimate births] to construct new rationalizations for racial exclusion that would survive in the post-*Brown* world." However, "as racial designation and data collection became an integral part of the enforcement of civil rights legislation, the movement's stance on the practice changed accordingly."[107]

Consider in this light the proposed (but ultimately unsuccessful) California Racial Privacy Initiative which would have prohibited the state government from collecting data that classified individuals by race, ethnicity or national origin in "the

---

107. Reva B. Siegel, Equality Talk, at 1516 n.158.

operation of public education, public contracting or public employment" and would have raised high procedural hurdles to collecting information about race, ethnicity, or national origin in other state programs. Interestingly, police officers were exempted from the prohibition against classifying individuals by race, and "[n]either the governor, the legislature nor any statewide agency shall require law enforcement officers to maintain records that track individuals on the basis of said classifications, nor shall the governor, the legislature or any statewide agency with-hold funding to law enforcement agencies on the basis of the failure to maintain such records." What was the purpose of these exemptions?

2. *Failure to count minorities.* With *Morales* compare City of New York v. United States Department of Commerce, 34 F.3d 1114 (2d Cir., 1994), holding that the Census Bureau's decision to adopt methods that systematically undercounted minorities was subject to review "under the more traditional standard applicable to an equal protection claim that a fundamental right has been denied on the basis of race or ethnicity." If the collection of racial data by itself does not raise strict scrutiny, why does systematic undercounting of minorities?

In Prieto v. Stans, 321 F. Supp. 420, 423 (N.D. Cal. 1970), plaintiffs argued that Congress's failure to include Mexican-Americans as a separate census category would lead to significant undercounting and thus fewer educational and other resources would be directed to the Mexican-American community. The Court rejected a claim of unconstitutional discrimination, noting "the patent inability of the Bureau to account with 100% accuracy for every one of the myriad groups and subgroups in America. If there is 'discrimination' here it is of the non-legal variety which must of necessity occur whenever any categorization is made which impliedly excludes other possible categories. Because we are satisfied that the plaintiffs will be counted and their rights safeguarded, we cannot say that the failure to specifically provide for a Mexican-American category on the census forms approaches discrimination considered to be invidious and hence unlawful by the courts of this land." Are *City of New York* and *Prieto* consistent?

Note: Mixed Race/Multiethnic Identity

The phenomenon of "mixed-race" identity is becoming ever more important within American society, especially if one runs together, as is commonly done, "racial" and "ethnic" or "national" categories. Indeed, historian David Hollinger has already pronounced the advent of a "postethnic America" in which one can no longer assume that everyone is "essentially" a member of one clearly definable group.[108] In "One Drop of Blood,"[109] Lawrence Wright has written about the intense arguments surrounding the Census Bureau's use of racial and ethnic categories. His title comes from a practice in some states of attributing black identity to anyone with a "single drop" of so-called "black blood." Thus someone with three white grandparents and

108. David Hollinger, Postethnic America: Beyond Multiculturalism (1995).
109. The New Yorker, July 25, 1994, pp. 46-55. See also Christopher A. Ford, Administering Identity: The Determination of "Race" in Race-Conscious Law, 82 Calif. L. Rev. 1231 (1994).

two white parents could, nonetheless, be classified as "black" by Virginia or Louisiana. Wright's essay suggests that the attribution of racial identity has little to do with "science" and more to do with socio-political decisions about the social meaning of identity. Note, for example, that some states had quite different racial ascription policies than Virginia's or Louisiana's. What do you think accounts for these differences?

The 2000 census has only increased the number of arguments about racial identity. Since 1977 the executive branch has generally divided the American population into four racial groups: American Indian or Alaskan Native, Asian or Pacific Islander, black, and white. At least two questions are raised immediately by this list: First, is it exhaustive? That is, does everyone accept the possibility of being described as existing within one (and only one) of these four categories? Consider the claim of the National Council of La Raza that "Hispanics" be considered a "racial" rather than an "ethnic" group. Wright notes that various ethnic organizations are in effect seeking official recognition of their status by the creation of a specific census classification for their groups. Thus, "The National Coalition for an Accurate Count of Asian Pacific Americans lobbied to add Cambodians and Lao to the nine different nationalities already listed on the census forms under the heading of Asian or Pacific Islander." There is, of course, no reason to believe that only 11 nationalities comprise the group "Asian Pacific Americans."

Not surprisingly, many contemporary anthropologists find the concept of race hopelessly confused (and confusing) and vigorously deny its utility as a scientific concept; many sociologists are little happier with the notion of ethnic identity as an "objective" notion that allows one to say, for example, how many "Greek-Americans" there are in the United States. How important should it be to lawyers — or judges — what professional social scientists or biologists think about such notions as race or ethnicity? Even if one believes that race continues to be a useful category for legal analysis, how, precisely, does one decide who belongs in what group? Although Wright notes the many groups seeking ever more divisions into specific racial or ethnic categories, he also emphasizes the growing number of people who actively reject the government's list of categories and who want to be able to describe themselves simply as "multiracial." "According to various estimates," Wright notes, "at least seventy-five to more than ninety percent of the people who now check the black box could check multiracial, because of their mixed genetic heritage." Many such "blacks" — the quotes are added because the very question under discussion is what counts as being black — would, Wright suggests, gladly accept a new categorization of "multiracial," if for no other reason than that they would no longer have to choose between their mothers and fathers in deciding "what" they "essentially" are.

What would it mean if, say, 20 to 30 percent of this 75 to 90 percent decided to describe themselves as other than "black"? According to Wright, "The entire civil-rights regulatory program concerning housing, employment, and education would have to be reassessed. . . . If people are to be counted as something other than completely black, . . . how will affirmative-action programs be implemented?" If a police department, for example, is ordered to hire additional black police officers as a remedy for past discrimination, will it have complied with the order if the person hired is the product of a "mixed" marriage (whatever that means)? Will it matter whether the person hired was raised "as a black" or as something else — and what in the world does this mean?

Do you think it would be a good idea to let the state ask such questions, let alone try to answer them? Should the state focus on skin color to prove who is "really" black, with darker African-Americans prevailing over their lighter skinned counterparts? Does the manner by which the state determines whether one of its citizens is deemed white or black for purposes of the census raise any constitutional problems? Would it be tolerable, either constitutionally or politically, to give private racial or ethnic organizations official authority to decide who counts as black or Hispanic or Asian for purposes of government classifications?

After some debate, the Office of Management and Budget decided to allow respondents to identify themselves as belonging to more than one race (i.e., check off more than one box) but not to create a new category called "multiracial." This rule applied to the 2000 census. What is the practical effect of this decision? How should it affect affirmative action programs or court-ordered remedies? For a discussion of the problems that multiracial identity raises for voting rights litigation, see Nathaniel Persily, Color By Numbers: Race, Redistricting and the 2000 Census, 85 Minn. L. Rev. 899 (2001).

The existing census regulations rely heavily on self-description — i.e., people are whatever they describe themselves as being. What problems does this approach entail? Even putting aside the question of good faith, so-called self-description is a function of the possibilities that census takers and administrators of other government programs present to people. For example, when the Census Bureau included "Cajun" as a possible answer to a question regarding one's ancestry, "the number of Cajuns jumped nearly two thousand percent. To remind people of the possibility is to encourage enormous change." How many "identification-opportunities" *should* the United States offer its residents?[110] To what extent should the Constitution bear on this question?

Recall that in Plessy v. Ferguson the Court refused to inquire into the constitutionality of the system of racial classification that Louisiana employed to determine that Homer Plessy was black. In light of the problems just discussed, do you agree with the Court's decision? On the other hand, suppose that a state decided to apply the old hypodescent rule (one drop of black blood makes you black) not for the purposes of segregation but for the purposes of administering state affirmative action programs. Under this rule, a person with a distant Cherokee ancestor, or whose great-great-grandmother was black, would count as a "minority" for purposes of college admissions or government contracts. Can you imagine that some self-described "real" African-Americans, Hispanics, and Native Americans might object to this decision? Would they have reason to do so? Should the Constitution have anything to say about it?

4.   Suspect Descriptions

BROWN v. CITY OF ONEONTA, 221 F.3d 329 (2d Cir. 1999): Police responded to a call from a 77-year-old woman who reported that someone broke into her house shortly before 2:00 A.M. and attacked her. She was unable to identify her assailant's face, but said that he was wielding a knife; that he was a black man, based on her view of his hand and forearm; and that he was young, because of the speed with

---

110. For a discussion of how census questions help shape racial identities, see Naomi Mezey, Erasure and Recognition: The Census, Race, and the National Imagination, 97 Nw. L. Rev. 1701 (2003).

which he crossed her room. She also told the police that, as they struggled, the suspect had cut himself on the hand with the knife. A police canine unit tracked the assailant's scent from the scene of the crime toward a nearby college campus, the State University of New York College at Oneonta (SUCO), but lost the trail after several hundred yards. Fewer than 300 blacks live in the town of Oneonta, and just 2 percent of the students at SUCO are black.

The police immediately contacted SUCO and requested a list of its black male students. An official at SUCO supplied the list, and the police attempted to locate and question every black male student at SUCO. This endeavor produced no suspects. Then, over a period of several days, the police conducted a "sweep" of Oneonta, stopping and questioning non-white persons on the streets and inspecting their hands for cuts. More than 200 persons were questioned during that period, but no suspect was apprehended. Several people whose names appeared on the SUCO list and those who were approached and questioned by the police sued the city and the local police department, arguing that the roundup was impermissible racial profiling in violation of the Equal Protection Clause.

The Second Circuit rejected this claim on a motion for summary judgment:

> [Plaintiffs] were not questioned solely on the basis of their race. They were questioned on the altogether legitimate basis of a physical description given by the victim of a crime. Defendants' policy was race-neutral on its face; their policy was to investigate crimes by interviewing the victim, getting a description of the assailant, and seeking out persons who matched that description. This description contained not only race, but also gender and age, as well as the possibility of a cut on the hand. In acting on the description provided by the victim of the assault — a description that included race as one of several elements — defendants did not engage in a suspect racial classification that would draw strict scrutiny. The description, which originated not with the state but with the victim, was a legitimate classification within which potential suspects might be found. . . .
>
> [A]ttempting to question every person fitting a general description . . . may well have a disparate impact on small minority groups in towns such as Oneonta. If there are few black residents who fit the general description, for example, it would be more useful for the police to use race to find a black suspect than a white one. It may also be practicable for law enforcement to attempt to contact every black person who was a young male, but quite impossible to contact every such white person. If a community were primarily black with very few white residents and the search were for a young white male, the impact would be reversed. The Equal Protection Clause, however, has long been interpreted to extend to governmental action that has a disparate impact on a minority group only when that action was undertaken with discriminatory intent. Without additional evidence of discriminatory animus, the disparate impact of an investigation such as the one in this case is insufficient to sustain an equal protection claim. . . . [Plaintiffs] allege that at least one woman, Sheryl Champen, was stopped by law enforcement officials during their sweep of Oneonta. This allegation is significant because it may indicate that defendants considered race more strongly than other parts of the victim's description. However, this single incident, to the extent that it was related to the investigation, is not sufficient in our view to support an equal protection claim under the circumstances of this case.

Discussion

1. When police gather information about a crime, and ask about the racial identity of a suspect, is this a racial classification? What if they merely record racial data

that witnesses supply? In *Oneonta*, the Second Circuit argued that strict scrutiny should not apply because the suspect description originated with a private party and not the state. Why should this make a difference, given that the state credited the description and decided to engage in the sweeps? Does reliance on nonstate sources eliminate state action? The risk of error or of stereotyping? The role of the state in the construction of racial categories? How, if at all, does your analysis of whether the use of race in the census is a racial classification help you answer the question of whether the use of race in a suspect description is a racial classification?

2. Suppose that the police conduct a search for a suspect relying on racial elements of a suspect description. Is the search a racial classification? What if police discard other elements of the suspect description and rely largely if not exclusively on the racial elements of the suspect description? What if they rely only on race and gender (e.g., they search only for a black man)?

3. The Second Circuit also argued that strict scrutiny should not apply because the suspect description was not solely based on race. Should the characterization of a practice as a racial classification that is subject to strict scrutiny depend on whether the state relies solely on race or uses race only as one of several factors? Note that the Supreme Court has applied strict scrutiny in affirmative action cases like *Croson* and *Adarand*, even though government contracts are awarded on the basis of a combination of factors of which race is only one. Similarly, strict scrutiny applies to affirmative action in education even though admissions committees consider many factors other than race in assessing qualifications. Why should government contractors and universities engaged in affirmative action be treated with greater scrutiny than the police in *Oneonta*?

4. What would be the consequence of holding that the police sweep was "on the basis of race" and subject to strict scrutiny? Would this unduly hamper police investigative practices? Or would it serve as an important and necessary check on police abuses? Note that in determining whether government practices are race-based state action, courts employ a binary approach rather than a continuum; practices either are, or are not, racial classifications subject to scrutiny. Consider the possibility that the characterization "racial classification" is at least in part normative rather than positive. Intuitions that race-related practices are benign or legitimate determine whether they are characterized as racial classifications subject to strict scrutiny. Thus, the legal category of what counts as "race-based" decisionmaking, like the categories of "causation" and "intent" in criminal law and tort law, is flexible and shaped by policy considerations that may or may not be overtly acknowledged. In *Oneonta*, for example, the Second Circuit probably considered the police practices involved legitimate and wished to leave police officers considerable discretion in the future. But suppose one was concerned that police practices might be illicit or racially biased. What should the proper test be? For a discussion of possible theories of the case, see the opinions in the denial of rehearing en banc, Brown v. City of Oneonta, 235 F.3d 769 (2d Cir. 2000).

5. Recall Justice O'Connor's claim in California v. Johnson, supra, that "*all* racial classifications . . . must be analyzed by a reviewing court under strict scrutiny. . . . We have insisted on strict scrutiny in every context, even for so-called 'benign' racial classifications, such as race-conscious university admissions policies, race-based preferences in government contracts, and race-based districting intended to improve minority representation." To what extent is this an accurate description of equal protection law?

6. The general problem of telling when the state has made a classification subject to heightened scrutiny is not limited to race cases; it also haunts sex discrimination doctrine. See Chapter 7 infra.

C. What Is "Race" for Purposes of the Equal Protection Clause?

Note: On the Social and Legal Construction of "Race"

1. Four Concepts of "Race": Status-Based, Formal, Historical, and Cultural

The word "race" is ubiquitous in constitutional law, but the term has many different uses. Neil Gotanda has identified at least four different senses of the word in the Supreme Court's opinions, which reflect wider cultural and political uses. According to Gotanda's analysis of the Supreme Court's "color-blind constitutionalism," the Court uses "race" to cover four distinct ideas: "status-race, formal-race, historical-race, and culture-race."[111]

"Status race is the traditional notion of race as an indicator of social status;" that is, to be white is to have higher status and to be black is to have lower status. This is the way of talking about race that justified white supremacy; this vision saw blackness as inherently inferior and whiteness as inherently superior. Formal race "refers to socially constructed formal categories . . . under which black and white are seen as neutral, apolitical descriptions, reflecting merely 'skin color' or country of ancestral origin." A person is black or white not because of what they think or how they behave but merely because of the color of their skin. Formal race can also be defined legally through other devices, for example, a person's ancestry combined with a legal rule that defines race. That is how Homer Plessy was defined as black in Plessy v. Ferguson. Formal race, Gotanda explains, "is unrelated to ability, disadvantage, or moral culpability. Moreover, formal-race categories are unconnected to social attributes such as culture, education, wealth, or language. This 'unconnectedness' is the defining characteristic of formal-race. . . . "

Formal conceptions of race became popular as a rhetorical response to the status race talk that justified white supremacy and Jim Crow. Because status race talk stereotypes blacks as having undesirable characteristics simply in virtue of being black, formal race discourse developed in part as a denial of the stereotype. It treats race as conceptually distinct from every social attribute or attitude, so that race has no necessary cultural implications, whether good or bad. One is invoking a conception of formal race when one decries stereotyping and says things like "just because a person is black (or white) doesn't mean that they are. . . . " Obviously, talking in terms of formal race is deeply connected to the discourse of colorblindness.

By contrast, historical race "does assign substance to racial categories." It refers to the history of past and continuing racial subordination; it is the meaning of race that the Court contemplates when it applies "strict scrutiny" because of the past

111. Neil Gotanda, A Critique of "Our Constitution Is Color-Blind," 44 Stan. L. Rev. 1, 3-4 (1994).

history of racially disadvantaging government conduct. When courts view race in terms of its historical uses (and abuses), "[t]he state's use of racial categories is regarded as so closely linked to illegitimate racial subordination that it is automatically judicially suspect."

Finally, race as culture (culture-race) identifies "black" with "African-American culture, community, and consciousness." African-American "[c]ulture," explains Gotanda, "refers to broadly shared beliefs and social practices; [the African-American] community refers to both the physical and spiritual senses of the term; and African-American consciousness refers to Black Nationalist and other traditions of self-awareness and to action based on that self-awareness." Culture-race is the concept used when blackness is associated with the idea of cultural diversity.

Note that while status race and formal race treat race as a category that applies equally to all (or almost all) of its members, race as culture-race refers to traits, behaviors, attitudes, and beliefs that some but not all members of the group share, and in varying degrees. Thus, one can be "black" in a formal sense (as defined by skin color or descent) but not "black" in a cultural sense.

Throughout these materials it will be important to notice when courts and other government actors shift from one use of the term "race" to the other. For example, when courts argue that it is demeaning to assume that blacks think alike because of their race, or that race is morally irrelevant to government decision-making, they are invoking a formal notion of race. However, when courts argue that it is permissible for police officers to consider race in developing drug courier profiles, or when they argue that blackness is a proxy for a distinctive life experience, they are invoking a notion of culture-race. When courts argue that racial distinctions are odious because they breed interracial hostility and stigmatize minorities, they are invoking a notion of historical-race. When people argue that the death penalty is unfair because it punishes blacks who kill whites more than whites who kill blacks, they are implicitly criticizing a notion of racial status, i.e., that white lives are worth more than black lives. When plaintiffs argue that a certain government policy or business practice is discriminatory because it disproportionately harms blacks more than whites they are probably employing a cultural (or historical) conception of race, because not all members of the group are equally affected; when defendants respond that for this very reason the policy or practice does not discriminate on the basis of race, they are probably employing a formal conception of race. Note that people can invoke more than one sense of the word simultaneously: For example, an advocate of educational affirmative action who says that colleges should try to admit more blacks because they bring distinctive life experiences to college campuses can be referring to race both as culture and as the product of a history of subordination.

In American politics, both conservatives and progressives opportunistically invoke different conceptions of race to support their views about desegregation, affirmative action, crime, welfare policy, and other issues. The same is true of courts as well. Often when a majority opinion employs one conception of race, the dissent will employ another; each may shift uses from paragraph to paragraph and from sentence to sentence. You should learn to be aware of the subtle (and not-so-subtle) shifts in the meaning of "race" in legal and policy arguments. This will help you understand what is at stake in debates over race.

2. "Race" as a Social and Legal Construction

Many scholars argue that the courts' confusion over race reflects the fact that the term "race" is conceptually incoherent. Ian Haney-López, for example, views "race" as strictly a social and historical construct: "a vast group of people loosely bound together by historically contingent, socially significant elements of their morphology and/or ancestry, . . . a *sui generis* phenomenon in which contested systems of meaning serve as the connection between physical features, races, and personal characteristics."[112] The philosopher and cultural theorist Kwame Anthony Appiah asserts the cultural constitution of "race" even more strongly: "The truth is that there are no races: there is nothing in the world that can do all that we ask race to do for us." Rather, observes Appiah, where race "works," "it works as an attempt at a metonym for culture, and it does so only at the price of biologizing what *is* culture, ideology."[113] For these critics "race" refers to a socially produced regulatory regime that constructs people as being of a certain race and as possessing racial characteristics while purporting merely to represent the world. For example, Richard Ford argues that racial segregation of public spaces produces racially identified spaces that reinforce what it means to be black and white.[114]

Perhaps the most important way in which race is socially constructed inheres in the state's considerable power to define racial identity statutorily. Neil Gotanda recounts one woman's failed attempt to challenge this power:

> While most jurisdictions had abolished mandatory classifications by the 1970s, Louisiana's birth certificate statute required a statutorily defined racial identification. A Louisiana woman, Susie Guillory Phipps, on applying for a passport, was "sick for three days" when she discovered that her birth certificate listed both her parents as colored. She challenged the statute in court. At trial and on appeal [Doe v. State Dep't of Health & Human Resources, 479 So. 2d 369 (La. Ct. App. 1985)], the Louisiana courts upheld the constitutionality of the fractional classification statute, and Phipp's birth certificate was not changed.[115]

In what sense was Phipps denied something that was hers? Doesn't her argument depend on the state of Louisiana getting her race "wrong?" What, exactly, would that mean?

Law affects racial identification in other ways. Ian Haney-López notes how "antidiscrimination laws . . . mov[e] people to frame their identities in terms of the racial categories recognized by law":

> At the level of both individuals and groups, people must conform their identities to these rigid categories if they seek legal protection from discrimination. Thus, some legal scholars have tried to frame Mexican American identity as a specifically racial, rather than ethnic or cultural, identity for the purposes of securing constitutional or

---

112. Ian F. Haney López, The Social Construction of Race: Some Observations on Illusion, Fabrication, and Choice, 29 Harv. C.R.-C.L. L. Rev. 1, 7 (1994).

113. Kwame Anthony Appiah, In My Fathers House: Africa in the Philosophy of Culture 45 (1992).

114. Richard T. Ford, Urban Space and the Color Line: The Consequences of Demarcation and Disorientation in the Postmodern Metropolis, 9 Harv. BlackLetter J. 117, 130 (1992).

115. Gotanda, supra n.109, at 35.

statutory protection against discrimination. It is not unreasonable to argue that "races may be defined in America in some significant part by their relationship to antidiscrimination law in addition to constituting an independent influence on that body of law." The necessary persistence of legal classifications of race gives law a continuing role in the construction of racial identities by legitimating the practice of categorization and by limiting the conceptions of who we are.[116]

Noting the powerful, coercive ways in which restrictive immigration laws and, until Loving v. Virginia, miscegenation laws have sought to preserve the integrity of the idea of physically distinct, biologically real races, Haney-López observes emphatically that "[t]he law constructs race." "The legal system influences what we look like, the meanings we ascribe to our looks, and the material reality that confirms the meanings of our appearances." Racialized groups, Haney-López suggests, come into being through legally and socially produced understandings, not as a result of prelegal natural categories. He offers the example of early Armenian immigrants:

> Before their immigration here, Armenians . . . had not yet been "raced," that is, assigned a racial identity. However, upon their arrival, and despite some initial confusion, they were pronounced legally White. This pronouncement allowed them a prosperous and privileged position in American society. This prosperity then confirmed the common knowledge of their Whiteness, which in turn served to justify the judicial treatment of Armenians as White. The opposite occurred with the Japanese.[117]

If law inevitably constructs race, can law construct race in a socially desirable or socially just manner? Would it do any good to pass legislation holding that African-Americans were "white by law?" Or is the problem that this is too direct an approach — that law can shape social understandings about race, but it cannot surgically alter them wholesale with a few simple commands? If law's influence is more subtle, how could law help foster racial egalitarianism? Would law help more by making racial identity more overt or salient or more ambiguous? By expanding the number of racial categorizations or limiting them?

How should the courts define race for purposes of determining whether a particular government policy is discrimination on the basis of "race?" Consider the approaches used in the following cases.

HERNANDEZ v. TEXAS, 347 U.S. 475 (1954): [Hernandez was decided on May 3, 1954, two weeks before Brown v. Board of Education.]

Warren, C.J.:

The petitioner, Pete Hernandez, was indicted for the murder of one Joe Espinosa by a grand jury in Jackson County, Texas. He was convicted and sentenced

---

116. Ian F. Haney López, White by Law: The Legal Construction of Race 125-126 (1996).

117. Id. at 131. Another example of the impact of judicial construction of racial or ethnic identity concerns the Mashpee Indians. In a suit to recover lost tribal land, the Mashpee had to prove that they were a "tribe" when the suit was filed. Since they could not "prove" their tribal purity to the court's satisfaction, their claim was thrown out. Gerald Torres and Kathryn Milun write that the Mashpee thereby became "a legally mute and invisible culture," standing in vain before a court "trying to prove they existed." Gerald Torres & Kathryn Milun, Translating *Yonnondio* by Precedent and Evidence: The Mashpee Indian Case, 1990 Duke L.J. 625, 649. See also Mashpee Tribe v. Town of Mashpee, 447 F. Supp. 940 (D. Mass. 1978).

to life imprisonment. [P]etitioner . . . alleged that persons of Mexican descent were systematically excluded from service as jury commissioners, grand jurors, and petit jurors [and] that exclusion of this class deprived him, as a member of the class, of the equal protection of the laws guaranteed by the Fourteenth Amendment of the Constitution.

In numerous decisions, this Court has held that it is a denial of the equal protection of the laws to try a defendant of a particular race or color under an indictment issued by a grand jury, or before a petit jury, from which all persons of his race or color have, solely because of that race or color, been excluded by the State. Although the Court has had little occasion to rule on the question directly, it has been recognized since *Strauder* that the exclusion of a class of persons from jury service on grounds other than race or color may also deprive a defendant who is a member of that class of the constitutional guarantee of equal protection of the laws. The State of Texas would have us hold that there are only two classes — white and Negro — within the contemplation of the Fourteenth Amendment. The decisions of this Court do not support that view. . . . Throughout our history differences in race and color have defined easily identifiable groups which have at times required the aid of the courts in securing equal treatment under the laws. But community prejudices are not static, and from time to time other differences from the community norm may define other groups which need the same protection. Whether such a group exists within a community is a question of fact. When the existence of a distinct class is demonstrated, and it is further shown that the laws, as written or as applied, single out that class for different treatment not based on some reasonable classification, the guarantees of the Constitution have been violated. The Fourteenth Amendment is not directed solely against discrimination due to a "two-class theory" — that is, based upon differences between "white" and Negro. . . . The exclusion of otherwise eligible persons from jury service solely because of their ancestry or national origin is discrimination prohibited by the Fourteenth Amendment. The Texas statute makes no such discrimination, but the petitioner alleges that those administering the law do.

The petitioner's initial burden in substantiating his charge of group discrimination was to prove that persons of Mexican descent constitute a separate class in Jackson County, distinct from "whites." One method by which this may be demonstrated is by showing the attitude of the community. Here the testimony of responsible officials and citizens contained the admission that residents of the community distinguished between "white" and "Mexican."[a] The participation of persons of Mexican descent in business and community groups was shown to be slight. Until very recent times, children of Mexican descent were required to attend a segregated school for the first four grades.[b] At least one restaurant in town prominently displayed a sign announcing "No Mexicans Served." On the courthouse grounds at the time of the hearing, there were two men's toilets, one

---

a. We do not have before us the question whether or not the Court might take judicial notice that persons of Mexican descent are there considered as a separate class.

b. The reason given by the school superintendent for this segregation was that these children needed special help in learning English. In this special school, however, each teacher taught two grades, while in the regular school each taught only one in most instances. Most of the children of Mexican descent left school by the fifth or sixth grade.

unmarked, and the other marked "Colored Men" and "Hombres Aqui" ("Men Here"). No substantial evidence was offered to rebut the logical inference to be drawn from these facts, and it must be concluded that petitioner succeeded in his proof. . . .

The petitioner established that 14% of the population of Jackson County were persons with Mexican or Latin-American surnames, and that 11% of the males over 21 bore such names. The County Tax Assessor testified that 6 or 7% of the free-holders on the tax rolls of the County were persons of Mexican descent. The State of Texas stipulated that "for the last twenty-five years there is no record of any person with a Mexican or Latin American name having served on a jury commission, grand jury or petit jury in Jackson County." The parties also stipulated that "there are some male persons of Mexican or Latin American descent in Jackson County who, by virtue of being citizens, householders, or freeholders, and having all other legal prerequisites to jury service, are eligible to serve as members of a jury commission, grand jury and/or petit jury." . . .

To rebut the strong prima facie case of the denial of the equal protection of the laws . . . the State offered the testimony of five jury commissioners that they had not discriminated against persons of Mexican or Latin-American descent in selecting jurors. They stated that their only objective had been to select those whom they thought were best qualified. This testimony is not enough to overcome the petitioner's case. As the Court said in Norris v. Alabama:

> That showing as to the long-continued exclusion of negroes [sic] from jury service, and as to the many negroes qualified for that service, could not be met by mere generalities. If, in the presence of such testimony as defendant adduced, the mere general assertions by officials of their performance of duty were to be accepted as an adequate justification for the complete exclusion of negroes from jury service, the constitutional provision . . . would be but a vain and illusory requirement.

The same reasoning is applicable to these facts.

Circumstances or chance may well dictate that no persons in a certain class will serve on a particular jury or during some particular period. But it taxes our credulity to say that mere chance resulted in there being no members of this class among the over six thousand jurors called in the past 25 years. The result bespeaks discrimination, whether or not it was a conscious decision on the part of any individual jury commissioner. The judgment of conviction must be reversed. To say that this decision revives the rejected contention that the Fourteenth Amendment requires proportional representation of all the component ethnic groups of the community on every jury ignores the facts. The petitioner did not seek proportional representation, nor did he claim a right to have persons of Mexican descent sit on the particular juries which he faced. His only claim is the right to be indicted and tried by juries from which all members of his class are not systematically excluded — juries selected from among all qualified persons regardless of national origin or descent. To this much, he is entitled by the Constitution.

Discussion

1. *Jury selection.* Today challenges to jury selection procedures under the Equal Protection Clause are governed by the test set out in Casteneda v. Partida, 430 U.S. 482 (1977):

[In] order to show that an equal protection violation has occurred [the] defendant must show that the procedure employed resulted in substantial underrepresentation of his race or of the identifiable groups to which he belongs. The first step is to establish that the group is one that is a recognizeable, distinct class, singled out for different treatment under the laws, as written or as applied. [Then] the degree of underrepresentation must be proved, by comparing the proportion of the group in the total population to the proportion called to serve as [jurors], over a significant period of time. [Finally, a] selection procedure that is susceptible of abuse or is not racially neutral supports the presumption of discrimination raised by the statistical showing. [Once] the defendant has shown substantial underrepresentation of his group, he has made out a prima facie case of discriminatory purpose, and the burden shifts to the State to rebut that case.

2. *What kind of discrimination is discrimination against Hispanics?* Note that the Court does not say that Mexican-Americans are a race like blacks. (Also note the addition, later in the opinion, of Latin Americans to the class at issue, given that not all Hispanics are Mexican-American.) Justice Warren says that the petitioner must prove that Mexican-Americans are a class distinct from "whites" in order to be protected by the Equal Protection Clause. Is this a Freudian slip? Should the Court not have said distinct from "non-Hispanic whites?" To what extent is discrimination against Mexican-Americans (or Hispanics generally) like discrimination against African-Americans and to what extent is it different? We have already adverted to one important difference that Hispanics share with Asian-Americans in contrast to blacks: Discriminatory stereotypes tend to associate Hispanics with being foreigners or not "real" Americans. Discrimination against Hispanics may also be entangled with discrimination on the basis of language.

How does the Court demonstrate that Mexican-Americans are a class deserving of "the aid of courts in securing equal treatment under the laws?" If the question depends on "community prejudices," which "are not static," does this suggest that discrimination is based on immutable characteristics or on the social recognition and the social meaning of those characteristics? Consider Ian Haney-López:

The Court propounded [the "community attitudes"] test as a measure of whether Mexican Americans exist as a distinct, though non-racial group. In fact, no more accurate test could be fashioned to establish whether Mexican Americans, or any group, constitute a race. Race is not biological or fixed by nature; it is instead a question of social belief. Thus, albeit unwittingly, the *Hernandez* opinion offered a sophisticated insight into the nature of race: whether a racial group exists is always a local question to be answered in terms of community attitudes. To be sure, race is constructed through the interactions of a range of overlapping, fragmented communities, from local to national, ensuring that divergent and conflicting conceptions of racial identity exist within and among communities. Nevertheless, understanding race as "a question of community attitude" emphasizes that race is not biological but social. Therein lies the irony of the Court's position: Avoiding a racial understanding of *Hernandez,* in part due to a biological conception of race, the Court nevertheless correctly understood that the existence of Mexican Americans as a (racial) group in Jackson County turned, as race does, not on biology but on community attitudes.[118]

118. Ian F. Haney López, Race, Ethnicity, Erasure: The Salience of Race to LatCrit Theory, 85 Calif. L. Rev. 1143, 1164 (1997).

Do you agree that Mexican-Americans (or Hispanics generally) should be understood as a racial group in racial terms? Does it make any difference for what purposes this understanding occurs (for example, for purposes of self-understanding versus understanding by others, invidious discrimination versus affirmative action)?

3. *"Race" under the Reconstruction Civil Rights Acts.* Consider Shaare Tefila Congregation v. Cobb, 481 U.S. 615 (1987) and its companion case Saint Francis College v. Al-Khazraji, 481 U.S. 604 (1987), which concerned the ability of Jews and Arabs to file suit under 42 U.S.C. §§1981 and 1982 (passed under the Thirteenth and Fourteenth Amendments), which prohibit racial discrimination. Although Justice White, writing for a unanimous Court, readily acknowledged that Jews are not today thought to be a "race," he stated that the relevant inquiry, for purposes of statutory interpretation, was whether the drafters of the 1866 and 1870 civil rights acts believed that Jews (and Arabs) were thought to be distinct races, and he answered that question in the affirmative. Thus "Jews constituted a group of people that Congress intended to protect," even if Congress's conceptualization of race was, from our contemporary perspective, altogether dubious. In *Al-Khazraji* Justice White explained that "Congress intended to protect from discrimination identifiable classes of persons who are subjected to intentional discrimination solely because of their ancestry or ethnic characteristics. Such discrimination is racial discrimination that Congress intended . . . to forbid, whether or not it would be classified as racial in terms of modern scientific theory."

HERNANDEZ v. NEW YORK, 500 U.S. 352 (1991): [The defendant, Hernandez, claimed that the prosecutor had employed peremptory challenges to exclude Latinos from his jury. (A challenge to a prospective juror is peremptory when a party does not have to give reasons for exclusion, as opposed to challenges for cause. In Batson v. Kentucky, 476 U.S. 79 (1986), discussed infra, the Court held that prosecutors could not exercise peremptory challenges on the basis of the prospective juror's race.). The prosecutor responded that the challenge was based on race-neutral reasons: The two challenged jurors were bilingual, and he believed that they would not necessarily rely on the official interpreter for English translation of testimony given by Spanish-speaking witnesses.

There was no opinion for the Court. Although all the Justices agreed that challenging a juror because he or she was Latino would violate the Equal Protection Clause, six Justices rejected Hernandez's claim that the prosecutor's challenge was a classification based on race or national origin:]

KENNEDY, J., joined by Rehnquist, C.J., and White and Souter, JJ.:
A neutral explanation [for a peremptory challenge] means an explanation based on something other than the race of the juror. . . [However] the prosecutor did not rely on language ability without more, but explained that the specific responses and the demeanor of the two individuals during *voir dire* caused him to doubt their ability to defer to the official translation of Spanish-language testimony. . . . The prosecutor's articulated basis for these challenges divided potential jurors into two classes: those whose conduct during *voir dire* would persuade him they might have difficulty in accepting the translator's rendition of Spanish language testimony and those potential jurors who gave no such reason for doubt. Each category would

include both Latinos and non-Latinos. While the prosecutor's criterion might well result in the disproportionate removal of prospective Latino jurors, that disproportionate impact does not turn the prosecutor's actions into a *per se* violation of the Equal Protection Clause. . . . Unless a government actor adopted a criterion with the intent of causing the impact asserted, that impact itself does not violate the principle of race-neutrality. . . .

[T]he prosecutor's frank admission that his ground for excusing these jurors related to their ability to speak and understand Spanish raised a plausible, though not a necessary, inference that language might be a pretext for what in fact were race-based peremptory challenges. . . . [T]his trial took place in a community with a substantial Latino population, and petitioner and other interested parties were members of that ethnic group. It would be common knowledge in the locality that a significant percentage of the Latino population speaks fluent Spanish, and that many consider it their preferred language, the one chosen for personal communication, the one selected for speaking with the most precision and power, the one used to define the self.

The trial judge can consider these and other factors when deciding whether a prosecutor intended to discriminate. For example, though petitioner did not suggest the alternative to the trial court here, Spanish-speaking jurors could be permitted to advise the judge in a discreet way of any concerns with the translation during the course of trial. A prosecutor's persistence in the desire to exclude Spanish-speaking jurors despite this measure could be taken into account in determining whether to accept a race-neutral explanation for the challenge.

The trial judge in this case chose to believe the prosecutor's race-neutral explanation for striking the two jurors in question, rejecting petitioner's assertion that the reasons were pretextual. In *Batson*, we explained that the trial court's decision on the ultimate question of discriminatory intent represents a finding of fact of the sort accorded great deference on appeal. . . . [W]e decline to overturn the state trial court's finding on the issue of discriminatory intent unless convinced that its determination was clearly erroneous. . . .

We would face a quite different case if the prosecutor had justified his peremptory challenges with the explanation that he did not want Spanish-speaking jurors. It may well be, for certain ethnic groups and in some communities, that proficiency in a particular language, like skin color, should be treated as a surrogate for race under an equal protection analysis. Cf. Yu Cong Eng v. Trinidad, 271 U.S. 500 (1926) (law prohibiting keeping business records in other than specified languages violated equal protection rights of Chinese businessmen); Meyer v. Nebraska, [262 U.S. 390 (1923)] (striking down law prohibiting grade schools from teaching languages other than English). And, as we make clear, a policy of striking all who speak a given language, without regard to the particular circumstances of the trial or the individual responses of the jurors, may be found by the trial judge to be a pretext for racial discrimination. But that case is not before us.

O'CONNOR, J., joined by Scalia, J., concurring in the judgment:

[T]he plurality opinion goes farther than it needs to in assessing the constitutionality of the prosecutor's asserted justification for his peremptory strikes. . . .

An unwavering line of cases from this Court holds that a violation of the Equal Protection Clause requires state action motivated by discriminatory intent; the disproportionate effects of state action are not sufficient to establish such a violation. . . . Washington v. Davis, 426 U.S. 229 (1976).

[In] this case, the prosecutor's asserted justification for striking certain Hispanic jurors was his uncertainty about the jurors' ability to accept the official translation of trial testimony. If this truly was the purpose of the strikes, they were not strikes because of race, and therefore did not violate the Equal Protection Clause under *Batson*. They may have acted like strikes based on race, but they were not based on race. No matter how closely tied or significantly correlated to race the explanation for a peremptory strike may be, the strike does not implicate the Equal Protection Clause unless it is based on race. That is the distinction between disproportionate effect, which is not sufficient to constitute an equal protection violation, and intentional discrimination, which is.

Disproportionate effect may, of course, constitute evidence of intentional discrimination. The trial court may, because of such effect, disbelieve the prosecutor and find that the asserted justification is merely a pretext for intentional race-based discrimination. But if, as in this case, the trial court believes the prosecutor's nonracial justification, and that finding is not clearly erroneous, that is the end of the matter. *Batson*['s] [rule against race-based peremptory challenges] does not require that the justification be unrelated to race. *Batson* requires only that the prosecutor's reason for striking a juror not be the juror's race.

STEVENS, J., joined by Marshall, J, dissenting:[119]

Even assuming the prosecutor's explanation in rebuttal was advanced in good faith, the justification was insufficient to dispel the existing inference of racial animus.

The prosecutor's explanation was insufficient for three reasons. First, the justification would inevitably result in a disproportionate disqualification of Spanish-speaking venire persons. An explanation that is "race-neutral" on its face is nonetheless unacceptable if it is merely a proxy for a discriminatory practice. Second, the prosecutor's concern could easily have been accommodated by less drastic means. As is the practice in many jurisdictions, the jury could have been instructed that the official translation alone is evidence; bilingual jurors could have been instructed to bring to the attention of the judge any disagreements they might have with the translation so that any disputes could be resolved by the court. Third, if the prosecutor's concern was valid and substantiated by the record, it would have supported a challenge for cause. The fact that the prosecutor did not make any such challenge should disqualify him from advancing the concern as a justification for a peremptory challenge.

Each of these reasons considered alone might not render insufficient the prosecutor's facially neutral explanation. In combination, however, they persuade me that his explanation should have been rejected as a matter of law.

RICE v. CAYETANO, 528 U.S. 495 (2000): [Hawaii established a state agency, the Office of Hawaiian Affairs (OHA) to administer programs and revenue for the benefit of "native Hawaiians" and "Hawaiians." "Native Hawaiians" are defined as

---

119. Justice Blackmun dissented without opinion, stating that he substantially agreed with the part of Justice Stevens's opinion quoted below.

descendants of not less than one-half part of the races inhabiting the Islands before 1778, when Captain Cook first arrived. Following Cook's arrival, many immigrants arrived from East Asia and the Pacific, as well as Great Britain and America, and intermarried with the natives. "Hawaiians" includes this group, defined any descendant of the peoples inhabiting the Hawaiian Islands in 1778.

The OHA is run by nine trustees chosen in a statewide election. The Hawaii Constitution limits the right to vote to "Hawaiians" (which includes "native Hawaiians."). Rice, whose family had lived in Hawaii for many generations, but was neither "Hawaiian" or "native Hawaiian," sued to invalidate the limitation on voting rights under the Fourteenth and Fifteenth Amendments. The Court held the limitation unconstitutional under the Fifteenth Amendment. Justice Kennedy's majority opinion held that the restriction to "Hawaiians" and "native Hawaiians" although nominally based on descent, clearly involved a proxy for race:]

KENNEDY, J.:

Ancestry can be a proxy for race. It is that proxy here. Even if the residents of Hawaii in 1778 had been of more diverse ethnic backgrounds and cultures, it is far from clear that a voting test favoring their descendants would not be a race-based qualification. But that is not this case. For centuries Hawaii was isolated from migration. The inhabitants shared common physical characteristics, and by 1778 they had a common culture. Indeed, the drafters of the statutory definition in question emphasized the "unique culture of the ancient Hawaiians" in explaining their work. The provisions before us reflect the State's effort to preserve that commonality of people to the present day. In the interpretation of the Reconstruction era civil rights laws we have observed that "racial discrimination" is that which singles out "identifiable classes of persons . . . solely because of their ancestry or ethnic characteristics." Saint Francis College v. Al-Khazraji, 481 U.S. 604 (1987). The very object of the statutory definition in question and of its earlier congressional counterpart in the Hawaiian Homes Commission Act is to treat the early Hawaiians as a distinct people, commanding their own recognition and respect. The State, in enacting the legislation before us, has used ancestry as a racial definition and for a racial purpose. . . .

As for the further argument that the restriction differentiates even among Polynesian people and is based simply on the date of an ancestor's residence in Hawaii, this too is insufficient to prove the classification is nonracial in purpose and operation. Simply because a class defined by ancestry does not include all members of the race does not suffice to make the classification race neutral. Here, the State's argument is undermined by its express racial purpose and by its actual effects.

STEVENS, J., dissenting, joined by Ginsburg, J:

The OHA voter qualification speaks in terms of ancestry and current residence, not of race or color. . . . The ability to vote is a function of the lineal *descent* of a modern-day resident of Hawaii, not the blood-based characteristics of that resident, or of the blood-based proximity of that resident to the "peoples" from whom that descendant arises. The distinction between ancestry and race is more than simply one of plain language. The ability to trace one's ancestry to a particular progenitor at a single distant point in time may convey no information about one's own apparent or acknowledged race today. Neither does it of necessity imply one's own identification with a particular race, or the exclusion of any others "*on account of race.*" . . .

Ancestry surely can be a proxy for race, or a pretext for invidious racial discrimination. But it is simply neither proxy nor pretext here. All of the persons who are eligible to vote for the trustees of OHA share two qualifications that no other person old enough to vote possesses: They are beneficiaries of the public trust created by the State and administered by OHA, and they have at least one ancestor who was a resident of Hawaii in 1778. A trust whose terms provide that the trustees shall be elected by a class including beneficiaries is hardly a novel concept. . . .

The majority [responds] that the OHA trust — which it assumes is legitimate — should be read as principally intended to benefit the smaller class of "native Hawaiians," [and] not the larger class of "Hawaiians," [although the latter] enjoys the suffrage right in OHA elections. [But] there is surely nothing racially invidious about a decision to enlarge the class of eligible voters to include "any descendant" of a 1778 resident of the Islands. [This] serves quite practically to ensure that, regardless how "dilute" the *race* of native Hawaiians becomes . . . there will remain a voting interest whose ancestors were a part of a political, cultural community, and who have inherited through participation and memory the set of traditions the trust seeks to protect. The putative mismatch only underscores the reality that it cannot be purely a racial interest that either the trust or the election provision seeks to secure; the political and cultural interests served are — unlike *racial* survival — shared by both native Hawaiians and Hawaiians.

[T]he OHA election provision *excludes* all full-blooded Polynesians currently residing in Hawaii who are not descended from a 1778 resident of Hawaii. Conversely . . . the OHA scheme excludes no descendant of a 1778 resident because he or she is also part European, Asian, or African as a matter of race. The classification here is thus both too inclusive and not inclusive enough to fall strictly along racial lines. [T]he majority . . . posits that "[o]ne of the principal reasons race is treated as a forbidden classification is that it demeans the dignity and worth of a person to be judged by ancestry instead of by his or her own merit and essential qualities." That is, of course, true when ancestry is the basis for denying or abridging one's right to vote or to share the blessings of freedom. But it is quite wrong to ignore the relevance of ancestry to claims of an interest in trust property, or to a shared interest in a proud heritage. There would be nothing demeaning in a law that established a trust to manage Monticello and provided that the descendants of Thomas Jefferson should elect the trustees. Such a law would be equally benign, regardless of whether those descendants happened to be members of the same race.

In this light, it is easy to understand why the classification here is not "demeaning" at all, for it is simply not based on the "premise that citizens of a particular race are somehow more qualified than others to vote on certain matters." It is based on the permissible assumption in this context that families with "any" ancestor who lived in Hawaii in 1778, and whose ancestors thereafter continued to live in Hawaii, have a claim to compensation and self-determination that others do not. For the multiracial majority of the citizens of the State of Hawaii to recognize that deep reality is not to demean their own interests but to honor those of others.

Discussion

1. *Race and culture.* In *Hernandez,* Justices O'Connor and Scalia view "race" as potentially distinct from cultural traits that are correlated with race. Hence they conclude that "[n]o matter how closely tied or significantly correlated to race the explanation for a peremptory strike may be, the strike does not implicate the Equal Protection Clause unless it is based on race. That is the distinction between disproportionate effect, which is not sufficient to constitute an equal protection violation, and intentional discrimination, which is." Is this account of race equally good for all of the different conceptions and uses of the word race? For example, if race is about culture, history, or social status, then government action directly aimed at correlative traits might be "about" race, and the distinction between "disproportionate effect," on the one hand, and "intentional discrimination" on the other, begins to blur. Is this blurring effect only a problem for groups like Latinos or could it also apply to African-Americans?

2. In *Hernandez,* Professor Kenji Yoshino observes:

> Justice Kennedy's discussion of race was remarkable in entertaining the possibility of a juridical definition of race as culture-race. Rather than assuming that race was an obvious, biologically predetermined concept, the opinion expressed uncertainty about "the breadth with which the concept of race should be defined for equal protection purposes." [T]his statement was subversive in its simple acknowledgement that the definition of race could differ according to the purpose to which it was put. More specifically, Justice Kennedy observed that for equal protection purposes, [a] definition of race [might] reflect a sociological nexus between race and language [because] "ridicule and scorn" of a language "all too often result from or initiate racial hostility." [Hence] "for certain ethnic groups and in some communities, . . . proficiency in a particular language, like skin color, should be treated as a surrogate for race under an equal protection analysis." His analysis was thus open to the claim that language is no less (or more) tangential to racial identity than skin color. If that claim were true, language discrimination would be race discrimination. This is why Justice Kennedy posits that the Court "would face a quite different case if the prosecutor had justified his peremptory challenges with the explanation that he did not want Spanish-speaking jurors."[120]

Yoshino distinguishes between what he calls "formation" cases and "treatment" cases about race: In "[f]ormation cases . . . determining the racial identity of the party is the issue before the court, as in the antebellum trials or in the prerequisite cases. . . . In . . . treatment cases . . . the topic of dispute is how an individual has been treated on the basis of a race that is already known or stipulated, as in the generic equal protection or Title VII case." Id. at 904-905. He continues:

> My hypothesis is that courts are much more likely to adopt a performative conception of race (culture-race) in the formation context and a classical conception of race (formal-race) in the treatment context. This is because courts have more difficulty sustaining the illusion that race is a prediscursive concept when forced to confront the issue directly, as both the antebellum cases and the naturalization cases demonstrate.

120. Kenji Yoshino, Covering, 111 Yale L.J. 729, 899 (2002).

Yet because of the convenience — both moral and administrative — of formal-race, the courts fail to internalize the lessons about race they have learned in the formation context. When the courts turn to the treatment cases, in which the definition of race can be assumed without being articulated, the courts slip, either consciously or not, into a discourse of formal-race.

3. *Race and racial proxies. Hernandez* concludes that excluding jurors for speaking Spanish under the particular facts of that case was not a proxy for being Latino, while *Rice* holds that being the descendant of people inhabiting Hawaii in 1778 is a proxy for race. Note that Justice Kennedy explains that the inhabitants of Hawaii in 1778 were a race because they "shared common physical characteristics [and] a common culture." What conception of race — formal, cultural, historical, or status-based — is Kennedy invoking in *Hernandez?* In *Rice?*

One thing to consider is that, in contested cases, whether the Court regards the classification as "about" race (or a proxy for race) or about something else (failure to follow directions in *Hernandez,* trusteeship in *Rice*) depends on whether the Court regards the practice being challenged as essentially legitimate or illegitimate. In *Hernandez,* Justice Kennedy emphasizes that the court's findings about the prosecutor were not clearly erroneous, and that if the court is to be believed, the prosecutor was trying to secure a jury that would rely on the official translation, while Justice Stevens is worried about unfairness to Latinos in the criminal justice system. In *Rice,* Justice Kennedy thinks the OHA voting requirement smacks of the Grandfather Clause in Guinn v. United States, 238 U. S. 347, 363 (1915) (see Chapter 4), and other "[m]anipulative devices and practices . . . employed to deny the vote to blacks." Justice Stevens rejects the comparison, saying that these cases "have no application to a system designed to empower politically the remaining members of a class of once sovereign, indigenous people." In other words, he thinks that the OHA rule helps ameliorate group subordination.

4. *Reparations and ancestry.* According to Justice Stevens's argument in *Rice,* would a law giving reparations to descendants of persons held in slavery in the United States be race-neutral, because those descendants might include persons who today would be considered to be of many different races? According to Justice Kennedy's argument, would it be race-based and therefore subject to strict scrutiny?

5. *Race and Native Americans.* Note that Native American tribes have been treated according to a completely different set of rules under the theory that as tribes they have quasi-sovereign authority, and so classifications based on tribal identity or Native American ancestry are not viewed as racial classifications. Morton v. Mancari, 417 U.S. 535 (1974). See "Note: Are American Indians a 'Race' for Affirmative Action Purposes?" infra.

D.   What Is a "Race-Dependent" Decision?

The most obvious form of race-dependent decision is a statute that by its very terms classifies people by race. Like the jury-exclusion law struck down in *Strauder,* such a law might impose different burdens or confer different benefits on one race than on another. Or, like the segregation, cohabitation, and marriage laws struck down in *Brown, Loving,* and *McLaughlin,* it may apply with formal equality to persons of both races but nonetheless run afoul of the antidiscrimination principle.

Race-dependent decisions are not always embodied in statutes nor always overt, however. For example, an employer may deny someone a job because of her race while explaining the decision entirely on other grounds.

Covert race-dependent decisions are frequently referred to as "racially motivated" decisions. The word "motivation" gives rise to a potential ambiguity. One might use it to mean any decision that depends on race, or only those race-dependent decisions that are based on "prejudice" or "hostility" (as distinguished from those that are "rationally" based). In this book we use the term simply to mean "race-dependent" decisions — so that a decisionmaker's taking account of race for any purposes whatever is a race-"motivated" decision.

Do different kinds of race-dependent decisions have different legal consequences? In answering this question, it is important to keep two questions conceptually separate. (1) What obligations does the antidiscrimination principle impose on the *initial decisionmaker,* e.g., an employer, an official, a legislator? (2) Under what circumstances will a *reviewing court* inquire whether that decisionmaker's decision was race-dependent? The remainder of this section takes up this first question. The second question is taken up in Section E.

1.   Discriminatory Administration of an Otherwise "Neutral" Statute

Laws that do not classify on the basis of race may nonetheless be administered in a race-dependent manner. For example, in Yick Wo v. Hopkins, 118 U.S. 356 (1886), the San Francisco Board of Supervisors, which had authority to issue permits to operate laundries in wooden buildings, had granted permits to none of 200 Chinese applicants and to all but one of about 80 Caucasian applicants. The Court reversed petitioners' convictions for operating laundries without permits, Justice Matthews writing:

> [T]he facts shown establish an administration directed so exclusively against a particular class of persons as to warrant and require the conclusion, that, whatever may have been the intent of the ordinances as adopted, they are applied by the public authorities charged with their administration, and thus representing the State itself, with a mind so unequal and oppressive as to amount to a practical denial by the State of that equal protection of the laws which is secured to the petitioners, as to all other persons, by the broad and benign provisions of the Fourteenth Amendment to the Constitution of the United States. Though the law itself be fair on its face and impartial in appearance, yet if it is applied and administered by public authority with an evil eye and an unequal hand, so as practically to make unjust and illegal discriminations between persons in similar circumstances, material to their rights, the denial of equal justice is still within the prohibition of the Constitution. . . .
>
> The present cases, as shown by the facts disclosed in the record, are within this class. It appears that both petitioners have complied with every requisite, deemed by the law or by the public officers charged with its administration, necessary for the protection of neighboring property from fire, or as a precaution against injury to the public health. No reason whatever, except the will of the supervisors, is assigned why they

should not be permitted to carry on, in the accustomed manner, their harmless and useful occupation, on which they depend for a livelihood. And while this consent of the supervisors is withheld from them and from two hundred others who have also petitioned, all of whom happen to be Chinese subjects, eighty others, not Chinese subjects, are permitted to carry on the same business under similar conditions. The fact of this discrimination is admitted. No reason for it is shown, and the conclusion cannot be resisted, that no reason for it exists except hostility to the race and nationality to which the petitioners belong, and which in the eye of the law is not justified.

Courts have frequently relied on statistical evidence of this sort to find unlawful patterns of racial discrimination in jury selection, employment, voter registration, and pupil and teacher assignment.

Does the San Francisco Board of Supervisors' unpublished rule differ, in a constitutionally relevant way, from an ordinance explicitly prohibiting Chinese from operating laundries in wooden buildings?

2. The Race-Dependent Decision to Adopt a Nonracially Specific Regulation or Law

Laws, regulations, and policies that do not classify on the basis of race and are administered without regard to race may nonetheless be adopted for race-dependent reasons. For example, in Ho Ah Kow v. Nunan, 12 F. Cas. 252 (No. 6546) (C.C.D. Cal. 1879), a San Francisco ordinance required that every male imprisoned in the county jail have his hair "cut or clipped to a uniform length of one inch from the scalp thereof." Plaintiff, a Chinese national, defaulted on a fine imposed for a housing code violation and was imprisoned and shorn. On demurrer, the Circuit Court for the District of California sustained his action against the sheriff for damages. Justice Field wrote:

The complaint avers that it is the custom of Chinamen to shave the hair from the front of the head and to wear the remainder of it braided into a queue; that the deprivation of the queue is regarded by them as a mark of disgrace, and is attended, according to their religious faith, with misfortune and suffering after death; that the defendant knew of this custom and religious faith of the Chinese, and knew also that the plaintiff venerated the custom and held the faith; yet, in disregard of his rights, inflicted the injury complained of. . . .

The cutting off the hair of every male person within an inch of his scalp, on his arrival at the jail, was not intended and cannot be maintained as a measure of discipline or as a sanitary regulation. The act by itself has no tendency to promote discipline, and can only be a measure of health in exceptional cases. Had the ordinance contemplated a mere sanitary regulation it would have been limited to such cases and made applicable to females as well as to males, and to persons awaiting trial as well as to persons under conviction. . . . It is special legislation on the part of the supervisors against a class of persons who, under the constitution and laws of the United States, are entitled to the equal protection of the laws. The ordinance was intended only for the Chinese in San Francisco. This was avowed by the supervisors on its passage, and was so understood by every one. The ordinance is known in the community as the "Queue Ordinance," being so designated from its purpose to reach the queues of the Chinese, and it is not enforced against any other persons. The reason advanced for its adoption, and now urged for its continuance, is, that only the dread of the loss of his queue will induce a Chinaman to pay his fine. . . .

The class character of this legislation is none the less manifest because of the general terms in which it is expressed. . . .

During the various periods of English history, legislation, general in its character, has often been enacted with the avowed purpose of imposing special burdens and restrictions upon Catholics; but that legislation has since been regarded as not less odious and obnoxious to animadversion than if the persons at whom it was aimed had been particularly designated. But in our country hostile and discriminating legislation by a state against persons of any class, sect, creed or nation, in whatever form it may be expressed, is forbidden by the fourteenth amendment of the constitution.

In Gomillion v. Lightfoot, 364 U.S. 339 (1960), the Alabama legislature changed the boundaries of the city of Tuskegee from a square to what Justice Frankfurter described as "an uncouth twenty-eight-sided figure"; the effect was to remove all but a handful of black voters, but not a single white voter, from the city limits. The Court struck down the law, finding these facts "tantamount for all practical purposes to a mathematical demonstration that the legislature is solely concerned with segregating white and colored voters by fencing Negro citizens out of town."

In Griffin v. Prince Edward County School Board, 377 U.S. 218 (1964), the school board closed down the school system after a court had ordered that it be desegregated. The Supreme Court ordered it reopened, stating:

[T]he record in the present case could not be clearer that Prince Edward's public schools were closed and private schools operated in their place with state and county assistance, for one reason and one reason only: to ensure . . . that white and colored children in Prince Edward County would not, under any circumstances, go to the same school. Whatever nonracial grounds might support a State's allowing a county to abandon public schools, the object must be a constitutional one, and grounds of race and opposition to desegregation do not qualify as constitutional.

3.   Transferred de Jure Discrimination

A practice that does not itself take race into account may disproportionately disadvantage a racial minority as a result of *causally related* de jure discrimination. Suppose, for example, that the residential segregation in our hypothetical school district was the result of unconstitutional discrimination. Although the Court has not addressed this precise issue,[121] it dealt with an analogous one in a statutory context in Gaston County v. United States, 395 U.S. 235 (1969). The Voting Rights Act of 1965 prohibits a state or local government from using a test "for the purpose or with the effect of denying or abridging the right to vote on account of race or color." The issue in *Gaston County* was whether the act permitted the county to use a voting literacy test that disproportionately disfranchised blacks. The Court accepted the county's claim that it administered the tests in a fair and impartial

---

121. In Swann v. Charlotte-Mecklenburg Bd. of Educ., p. 935 supra, the district court found that the local, state, and federal governments were responsible for residential segregation, which, combined with a proximity assignment plan, resulted in school segregation. The Supreme Court affirmed a judgment requiring school desegregation on other grounds, noting that "[w]e do not reach in this case the question whether a showing that school segregation [that] is a consequence of other types of state action, without any discriminatory action by the school authorities, is a constitutional violation requiring remedial action by a school desegregation decree."

manner, but noted that blacks who are now eligible to vote had been educated in the country's segregated and inferior schools. Justice Harlan wrote:

> It is only reasonable to infer that among the black children compelled to endure a segregated and inferior education, fewer will achieve any given degree of literacy than will their better-educated white contemporaries. And . . . it was certainly proper to infer that Gaston County's inferior Negro schools provide many of its Negro residents with a subliterate education, and gave many others little inducement to enter or remain in school. . . . From this record, we cannot escape the sad truth that throughout the years Gaston County systematically deprived its black citizens of the education opportunities it granted to its white citizens. "Impartial" administration of the literacy test today would serve only to perpetuate these inequalities in a different form.

There is no standard term for describing the voting registrar's action in *Gaston County*. Perhaps "transferred de jure discrimination" is as good as any. Compare *Gaston* with Personnel Administrator of Massachusetts v. Feeney, 442 U.S. 256 (1979), discussed infra and in Chapter 7. Massachusetts provided a civil service preference for veterans; the preference effectively excluded most women from the upper levels of civil service employment in the State of Massachusetts because they had been excluded from most positions in the U.S. Armed Forces. Is *Feeney* a case of transferred de jure discrimination?

E.   When Is a Decision with Disproportionate Racial Impact a Decision "Based on Race?"

In the preceding sections the causal connection between a race-dependent decision and its effects was typically direct and obvious. One could easily infer race-dependency in cases like *Yick Wo* or *Gomillion*, for example. This section examines a variety of situations in which the causal connection is attenuated or in which decisionmakers can offer plausible alternative accounts of the basis for their decisions; it also considers the constitutionality of racially disproportionate impact that (arguably) cannot be causally traced to any (particular) race-dependent decisions at all.

Inevitably, the question whether a decision is "race-dependent" or "on account of race" is not just a question of psychology, any more than the issue of mens rea or intention is in criminal or tort law. Ultimately the question is one of social theory and social policy — under what conditions and for what reasons will we say that a decision is "on account of race" or "because of race?"

GRIGGS v. DUKE POWER CO., 401 U.S. 424 (1971): [*Griggs* construed Title VII of the Civil Rights Act of 1964 to prohibit an employer from requiring high school diplomas of job applicants and subjecting them to a general intelligence test, where the effect was to disadvantage black applicants and where the criteria had not been demonstrated to predict job performance. Chief Justice Burger wrote for a unanimous Court:]

BURGER, C.J.:

The objective of Congress in the enactment of Title VII . . . was to achieve equality of employment opportunities and remove barriers that have operated in the past to favor an identifiable group of white employees over other employees. Under the Act, practices, procedures, or tests neutral on their face, and even neutral in terms of intent, cannot be maintained if they operate to "freeze" the status quo of prior discriminatory employment practices. The Court of Appeals' opinion, and the partial dissent, agreed that, on the record in the present case, "whites register far better on the Company's alternative requirements" than Negroes. This consequence would appear to be directly traceable to race. Basic intelligence must have the means of articulation to manifest itself fairly in a testing process. Because they are Negroes, petitioners have long received inferior education in segregated schools. . . . Congress did not intend by Title VII, however, to guarantee a job to every person regardless of qualifications. . . . Discriminatory preference for any group, minority or majority, is precisely and only what Congress has proscribed. What is required by Congress is the removal of artificial, arbitrary, and unnecessary barriers to employment when the barriers operate invidiously to discriminate on the basis of racial or other impermissible classification.

Congress has now provided that tests or criteria for employment or promotion may not provide equality of opportunity merely in the sense of the fabled offer of milk to the stork and the fox.[122] On the contrary, Congress has now required that the posture and condition of the job-seeker be taken into account. It has — to resort again to the fable — provided that the vessel in which the milk is proffered be one all seekers can use. The Act proscribes not only overt discrimination but also practices that are fair in form, but discriminatory in operation. The touchstone is business necessity. If an employment practice which operates to exclude Negroes cannot be shown to be related to job performance, the practice is prohibited.

On the record before us, neither the high school completion requirement nor the general intelligence test is shown to bear a demonstrable relationship to successful performance of the jobs for which it was used. Both were adopted, as the Court of Appeals noted, without meaningful study of their relationship to job-performance ability. . . . The evidence . . . shows that employees who have not completed high school or taken the tests have continued to perform satisfactorily and make progress in departments for which the high school and test criteria are now used. The promotion record of present employees who would not be able to meet the new criteria thus suggests the possibility that the requirements may not be needed for the limited purpose of preserving the avowed policy of advancement within the Company. . . .

The Court of Appeals held that the Company had adopted the diploma and test requirements without any "intention to discriminate against Negro employees." We do not suggest that either the District Court or the Court of Appeals erred in examining the employer's intent; but good intent or absence of discriminatory intent does not redeem employment procedures or testing mechanisms that operate as "built-in headwinds" for minority groups and are unrelated to measuring job capability. . . . Congress directed the thrust of the Act to the consequences of employment practices, not simply the motivation. More than that, Congress has placed on the employer the burden of showing that any given requirement must have manifest relationship to the employment in question.

---

122. The Court is referring to one of Aesop's fables, The Fox and the Stork. The fox served the stork a drink in a shallow dish, which was useless to the stork because of its long beak; the stork retaliated by serving the fox with a tall narrow jar, which was useless to the fox.

Discussion

1. The impact of *Griggs* was qualified by Wards Cove Packing Co. v. Atonio, 490 U.S. 642 (1989). Reaction to that case led to the Civil Rights Act of 1991, which requires an employer to "demonstrate that the challenged practice is job-related for the position in question and consistent with business necessity." In order to establish a prima facie case, complainants must specify the particular practices alleged to have a disparate impact. The intricacies of employment discrimination law, and in particular, the fate of *Wards Cove* in light of the 1991 Act, are beyond the scope of this book.

2. Note that the language of Title VII specifically requires that the prohibited discrimination be "because of . . . race." What story does the Court tell to explain why the testing requirement is "because of race?" *Griggs* is sometimes referred to as a "disparate impact" case. But is the explanatory story the Court tells solely one about disproportionate impact? Or is it a story about the present effects of past unequal treatment? Why does the Court mention the history of education in North Carolina? What does the Court mean by "the posture and condition of the job seeker," or by "employment procedures or testing mechanisms that operate as 'built-in headwinds' for minority groups?" Consider the antisubordination rationale for equal protection discussed above. What relationship does it have to these casual stories?

Recall Professor Gotanda's list of different conceptions of race. When the Court says that the discrimination in *Griggs* is "because of race," what conception of "race" is it using? The Court appears to be invoking a historical or cultural conception of race rather than a formal conception. It looks to how race has historically been used for purposes of subordination, rather than treating race as simply an accident of skin color. Only when understood through a formal conception of race does *Griggs* become a disparate impact case.[123]

Griggs was decided on the basis of Title VII of the Civil Rights Act of 1964. In Washington v. Davis, the Court declined to read the "disparate impact" standard into the Fourteenth Amendment.

WASHINGTON v. DAVIS
426 U.S. 229 (1976)

[Respondents were blacks whose applications to become police officers in the District of Columbia had been rejected because they had failed a written personnel test ("Test 21," developed and widely used by the Civil Service Commission). They sued to invalidate the test on the ground that it was racially discriminatory in violation of the Fifth Amendment. (At the time respondents filed suit, Title VII of the Civil Rights Act of 1964 did not cover municipal employees.) The Court of Appeals

123. Nevertheless, note that if the challenged business practice is judged to be a matter of business necessity, the decision is not "because of" race as a matter of law, even though it disproportionately burdens blacks. Is that because there could be no causal story one could offer about how blacks historically were denied certain opportunities that led to the present disproportionate impact? Or is it because at this point the law refuses to treat such effects as being "because of" race? Consider the extent to which notions like "causation" and "intention" act as gatekeepers for permitting and withholding liability in antidiscrimination law, just as they do in tort law and criminal law.

invalidated the test solely on the ground that it disproportionately excluded minorities and that petitioners had not proved that it related to job performance. In effect, the Court of Appeals incorporated into the Fifth and (by implication) the Fourteenth Amendments the Supreme Court's interpretation of Title VII in *Griggs*. The Supreme Court reversed.]

WHITE, J. . . .

Because the Court of Appeals erroneously applied the legal standards applicable to Title VII cases in resolving the constitutional issue before it, we reverse its judgment in respondents' favor. . . .

As the Court of Appeals understood Title VII, employees or applicants proceeding under it need not concern themselves with the employer's possibly discriminatory purpose but instead may focus solely on the racially differential impact of the challenged hiring or promotion practices. This is not the constitutional rule. We have never held that the constitutional standard for adjudicating claims of invidious racial discrimination is identical to the standards applicable under Title VII, and we decline to do so today.

The central purpose of the Equal Protection Clause of the Fourteenth Amendment is the prevention of official conduct discriminating on the basis of race. It is also true that the Due Process Clause of the Fifth Amendment contains an equal protection component prohibiting the United States from invidiously discriminating between individuals or groups. But our cases have not embraced the proposition that a law or other official act, without regard to whether it reflects a racially discriminatory purpose, is unconstitutional *solely* because it has a racially disproportionate impact.

Almost 100 years ago, Strauder v. West Virginia, 100 U.S. 303 (1880), established that the exclusion of Negroes from grand and petit juries in criminal proceedings violated the Equal Protection Clause, but the fact that a particular jury or a series of juries does not statistically reflect the racial composition of the community does not in itself make out an invidious discrimination forbidden by the Clause. . . .

The school desegregation cases have also adhered to the basic equal protection principle that the invidious quality of a law claimed to be racially discriminatory must ultimately be traced to a racially discriminatory purpose. That there are both predominantly black and predominantly white schools in a community is not alone violative of the Equal Protection Clause. The essential element of de jure segregation is "a current condition of segregation resulting from intentional state action." Keyes v. School Dist. No. 1, 413 U.S. 189, 205 (1973). "The differentiating factor between de jure segregation and so-called de facto segregation . . . is *purpose* or *intent* to segregate." Id. The Court has also recently rejected allegations of racial discrimination based solely on the statistically disproportionate racial impact of various provisions of the Social Security Act because "[t]he acceptance of appellants' constitutional theory would render suspect each difference in treatment among the grant classes, however lacking in racial motivation and however otherwise rational the treatment might be." Jefferson v. Hackney, 406 U.S. 535, 548 (1972). . . .

This is not to say that the necessary discriminatory racial purpose must be express or appear on the face of the statute, or that a law's disproportionate impact is irrelevant in cases involving Constitution-based claims of racial discrimination. A statute, otherwise neutral on its face, must not be applied so as invidiously to discriminate on the basis of race. Yick Wo v. Hopkins, 118 U.S. 356 (1886). It is also clear from the cases dealing with racial discrimination in the selection of juries that the systematic exclusion of Negroes is itself such an "unequal application of the law . . . as to show intentional discrimination." Akins v. Texas. A prima facie case of discriminatory purpose may be proved as well by the absence of Negroes on a particular jury combined with the failure of the jury commissioners to be informed of eligible Negro jurors in a community or with racially non-neutral selection procedures. With a prima facie case made out, "the burden of proof shifts to the State to rebut the presumption of unconstitutional action by showing that permissible racially neutral selection criteria and procedures have produced the monochromatic result."

Necessarily, an invidious discriminatory purpose may often be inferred from the totality of the relevant facts, including the fact, if it is true, that the law bears more heavily on one race than another. It is also not infrequently true that the discriminatory impact — in the jury cases for example, the total or seriously disproportionate exclusion of Negroes from jury venires — may for all practical purposes demonstrate unconstitutionality because in various circumstances the discrimination is very difficult to explain on nonracial grounds. Nevertheless, we have not held that a law, neutral on its face and serving ends otherwise within the power of government to pursue, is invalid under the Equal Protection Clause simply because it may affect a greater proportion of one race than of another. Disproportionate impact is not irrelevant, but it is not the sole touchstone of an invidious racial discrimination forbidden by the Constitution. Standing alone, it does not trigger the rule, McLaughlin v. Florida, 379 U.S. 184 (1964), that racial classifications are to be subjected to the strictest scrutiny and are justifiable only by the weightiest of considerations.

There are some indications to the contrary in our cases. In Palmer v. Thompson, 403 U.S. 217 (1971), the city of Jackson, Miss., following a court decree to this effect, desegregated all of its public facilities save five swimming pools which had been operated by the city and which, following the decree, were closed by ordinance pursuant to a determination by the city council that closure was necessary to preserve peace and order and that integrated pools could not be economically operated. Accepting the finding that the pools were closed to avoid violence and economic loss, this Court rejected the argument that the abandonment of this service was inconsistent with the outstanding desegregation decree and that the otherwise seemingly permissible ends served by the ordinance could be impeached by demonstrating that racially invidious motivations had prompted the city council's action. The holding was that the city was not overtly or covertly operating segregated pools and was extending identical treatment to both whites and Negroes. The opinion warned against grounding decision on legislative purpose or motivation, thereby lending support for the proposition that the operative effect of the law rather than its purpose is the paramount factor. But the holding of the case was that the legitimate purposes of the ordinance — to preserve peace and avoid deficits — were not open to impeachment by evidence that the councilmen were actually motivated by racial considerations. Whatever dicta the opinion may contain, the decision did not involve, much less invalidate, a statute or ordinance having neutral purposes but disproportionate racial consequences.[a]

_____

a. To the extent that *Palmer* suggests a generally applicable proposition that legislative purpose is irrelevant in constitutional adjudication, our prior cases — as indicated in the text — are to the contrary. . . .

Wright v. Council of City of Emporia, 407 U.S. 451 (1972), also indicates that in proper circumstances, the racial impact of a law, rather than its discriminatory purpose, is the critical factor. That case involved the division of a school district. The issue was whether the division was consistent with an outstanding order of a federal court to desegregate the dual school system found to have existed in the area. The constitutional predicate for the District Court's invalidation of the divided district was "the enforcement until 1969 of racial segregation in a public school system of which Emporia had always been a part." There was thus no need to find "an independent constitutional violation." Ibid. Citing Palmer v. Thompson, we agreed with the District Court that the division of the district had the effect of interfering with the federal decree and should be set aside.

That neither *Palmer* nor *Wright* was understood to have changed the prevailing rule is apparent from Keyes v. School Dist. No. 1, supra, where the principal issue in litigation was whether and to what extent there had been purposeful discrimination resulting in a partially or wholly segregated school system. . . .

Both before and after Palmer v. Thompson, however, various Courts of Appeals have held in several contexts, including public employment, that the substantially disproportionate racial impact of a statute or official practice standing alone and without regard to discriminatory purpose, suffices to prove racial discrimination violating the Equal Protection Clause absent some justification going substantially beyond what would be necessary to validate most other legislative classifications. The cases impressively demonstrate that there is another side to the issue; but, with all due respect, to the extent that those cases rested on or expressed the view that proof of discriminatory racial purpose is unnecessary in making out an equal protection violation, we are in disagreement.

As an initial matter, we have difficulty understanding how a law establishing a racially neutral qualification for employment is nevertheless racially discriminatory and denies "any person . . . equal protection of the laws" simply because a greater proportion of Negroes fail to qualify than members of other racial or ethnic groups. Had respondents, along with all others who had failed Test 21, whether white or black, brought an action claiming that the test denied each of them equal protection of the laws as compared with those who had passed with high enough scores to qualify them as police recruits, it is most unlikely that their challenge would have been sustained. Test 21, which is administered generally to prospective Government employees, concededly seeks to ascertain whether those who take it have acquired a particular level of verbal skill; and it is untenable that the Constitution prevents the Government from seeking modestly to upgrade the communicative abilities of its employees rather than to be satisfied with some lower level of competence, particularly where the job requires special ability to communicate orally and in writing. Respondents, as Negroes, could no more successfully claim that the test denied them equal protection than could white applicants who also failed. The conclusion would not be different in the face of proof that more Negroes than whites had been disqualified by Test 21. That other Negroes also failed to score well would, alone, not demonstrate that respondents individually were being denied equal protection of the laws by the application of an otherwise valid qualifying test being administered to prospective police recruits.

Nor on the facts of the case before us would the disproportionate impact of Test 21 warrant the conclusion that it is a purposeful device to discriminate against Negroes and hence an infringement of the constitutional rights of respondents as well as other black applicants. . . .

Under Title VII, Congress provided that when hiring and promotion practices disqualifying substantially disproportionate numbers of blacks are challenged, discriminatory purpose need not be proved, and that it is an insufficient response to demonstrate some rational basis for the challenged practices. It is necessary, in addition, that they be "validated" in terms of job performance in any one of several ways, perhaps by ascertaining the minimum skill, ability or potential necessary for the position at issue and determining whether the qualifying tests are appropriate for the selection of qualified applicants for the job in question. However this process proceeds, it involves a more probing judicial review of, and less deference to, the seemingly reasonable acts of administrators and executives than is appropriate under the Constitution where special racial impact, without discriminatory purpose, is claimed. We are not disposed to adopt this more rigorous standard for the purposes of applying the Fifth and the Fourteenth Amendments in cases such as this.

A rule that a statute designed to serve neutral ends is nevertheless invalid, absent compelling justification, if in practice it benefits or burdens one race more than another would be far-reaching and would raise serious questions about, and perhaps invalidate, a whole range of tax, welfare, public service, regulatory, and licensing statutes that may be more burdensome to the poor and to the average black than to more affluent whites.[b]

Given that rule, such consequences would perhaps be likely to follow. However, in our view, extension of the rule beyond those areas where it is already applicable by reason of statute, such as in the field of public employment, should await legislative prescription. . . .

STEVENS, J., concurring.

While I agree with the Court's disposition of this case, I add these comments on the constitutional issue. . . .

The requirement of purposeful discrimination is a common thread running through the cases summarized [by the Court]. . . . Frequently the most probative evidence of intent will be objective evidence of what actually happened rather than evidence describing the subjective state of mind of the actor. For normally the actor is presumed to have intended the natural consequences of his deeds. This is particularly true in the case of governmental action which is frequently the product of compromise of collective decisionmaking, and of mixed motivation. It is unrealistic, on the one hand, to require the victim of alleged discrimination to uncover the actual subjective intent of the decisionmaker or, conversely, to invalidate otherwise legitimate action simply because an improper motive affected the deliberation of a participant in the decisional process. A law conscripting clerics should not be invalidated because an atheist voted for it.

b. Goodman, De Facto School Segregation: A Constitutional and Empirical Analysis, 60 Calif. L. Rev. 275, 300 (1972), suggests that disproportionate-impact analysis might invalidate "tests and qualifications for voting, draft deferment, public employment, jury service, and other government-conferred benefits and opportunities . . . ; [s]ales taxes, bail schedules, utility rates, bridge tolls, license fees, and other state-imposed charges." It has also been argued that minimum age and usury laws as well as professional licensing requirements would require major modifications in light of the unequal-impact rule. Silverman, Equal Protection, Economic Legislation, and Racial Discrimination, 25 Vand. L. Rev. 1183 (1972). See also Demsetz, Minorities in the Market Place, 43 N.C. L. Rev. 271 (1965).

My point in making this observation is to suggest that the line between discriminatory purpose and discriminatory impact is not nearly as bright, and perhaps not quite as critical, as the reader of the Court's opinion might assume. I agree, of course, that a constitutional issue does not arise every time some disproportionate impact is shown. On the other hand, when the disproportion is as dramatic as in Gomillion v. Lightfoot, 364 U.S. 339, or Yick Wo v. Hopkins, 1 18 U.S. 356, it really does not matter whether the standard is phrased in terms of purpose or effect. Therefore, although I accept the statement of the general rule in the Court's opinion, I am not yet prepared to indicate how that standard should be applied in the many cases which have formulated the governing standard in different language. . . .

There are two reasons why I am convinced that the challenge to Test 21 is insufficient. First, the test serves the neutral and legitimate purpose of requiring all applicants to meet a uniform minimum standard of literacy. Reading ability is manifestly relevant to the police function, there is no evidence that the required passing grade was set at an arbitrarily high level, and there is sufficient disparity among high schools and high school graduates to justify the use of a separate uniform test. Second, the same test is used throughout the federal service. The applicants for employment in the District of Columbia Police Department represent such a small fraction of the total number of persons who have taken the test that their experience is of minimal probative value in assessing the neutrality of the test itself. That evidence, without more, is not sufficient to overcome the presumption that a test which is this widely used by the Federal Government is in fact neutral in its effect as well as its "purpose" as that term is used in constitutional adjudication. . . .

[Justices Brennan and Marshall dissented on grounds unrelated to the constitutional issue of racially disproportionate impact.]

Discussion

1. *The meaning of Washington v. Davis.* In Personnel Administrator of Massachusetts v. Feeney, 442 U.S. 256 (1979), supra Chapter 7, the Court elaborated the *Davis* requirement of discriminatory purpose in a case involving sex discrimination. *Feeney* involved a challenge to a Massachusetts statute that provided a civil service preference for veterans; a preference that effectively excluded most women from the upper levels of civil service employment in the State of Massachusetts. The plaintiff argued that the Massachusetts legislature could easily have foreseen this effect, given that federal law excluded most women from military service during the relevant period. The Court, however, argued that the foreseeable impact of the statute was not sufficient to prove discriminatory purpose under the Equal Protection Clause:

> "Discriminatory purpose," . . . implies more than intent as volition or intent as awareness of consequences. It implies that the decisionmaker, in this case a state legislature, selected or reaffirmed a particular course of action at least in part "because of," not merely "in spite of," its adverse effects upon an identifiable group.

Note that the term "intent" has many different meanings in different parts of the law. For example, in intentional tort, intent merely means the intention to perform the act that violates a legally protected interest. Tort law also often assumes that tortfeasors intend the foreseeable consequences of their actions; thus a person who fires a bullet at a person at close range is assumed to have intended to strike that person. The Model Penal Code notes at least five different types of intention: purposefully (with a purpose to produce a certain result), knowingly (acting knowing that a certain result will occur), recklessly (acting without concern for consequences), negligently (failing to take due care to prevent a result), and liability without fault. Model Penal Code §2.02(1) (1962). Why does the Equal Protection Clause require the most stringent test of intention, specific purpose to harm members of a group? Why shouldn't acting with full knowledge of the consequences to a disadvantaged group be sufficient? Shouldn't knowledge of consequences at least be sufficient to raise a rebuttable presumption that an act is illegal? Why should tort plaintiffs receive more protection than African-Americans or women?

2. Davis *and* Feeney *in historical context.* Reva Siegel argues that the *Davis/Feeney* approach limits the reach of the Fourteenth Amendment's equality norm just as the nineteenth-century distinction between political, civil, and social equality limited the reach of the Equal Protection Clause.[124]

> The civil-political-social rights distinction . . . offered a framework within which white Americans could disestablish slavery, guarantee the emancipated slaves equality at law, and yet continue to justify policies and practices that perpetuated the racial stratification of American society. . . .
>
> Just as the interpretation of equal protection offered in *Plessy* emerged from the Court's efforts to disestablish slavery, the interpretation of equal protection we inherit today emerged from the Court's efforts to disestablish segregation. . . .
>
> Once *Brown* and *Loving* demonstrated that the Court had definitively repudiated the old distinction between civil and social rights, there was no longer a tenable basis for defending the constitutionality of overtly race-based regulation. State regulation of matters once held to concern social rights thus assumed the facially neutral form that had generally characterized regulation of matters deemed to concern civil and political rights since the Reconstruction era.
>
> Collapse of the distinction between civil and social rights shifted the terrain of conflict. . . . Despite objections that the de facto/de jure distinction was a "legalism," the Court embraced the concept of discriminatory purpose as the touchstone for determining the constitutionality of facially neutral state action alleged to discriminate on the basis of race. . . .
>
> Because doctrines of heightened scrutiny now require legislators enacting race- or sex-based programs to articulate legitimate, nondiscriminatory reasons for their policy choices, legislators do not make a practice of justifying legislation on the grounds that it will adversely affect groups that have historically been subject to discrimination. To the contrary, doctrines of heightened scrutiny have created incentives for legislators to explain their policy choices in terms that cannot be so impugned. . . .
>
> [M]any white Americans now view overt racism as socially unacceptable and mute expression of their racially biased opinions in public settings. [T]he sociological and psychological literature [on racial attitudes] demonstrates that (1) racial bias remains the norm among white Americans; but that (2) they are strongly inhibited in expressing the racial attitudes they consciously hold, and often are wholly unaware of the extent to

124. Reva Siegel, Why Equal Protection No Longer Protects: The Evolving Forms of Status-Enforcing State Action, 49 Stan. L. Rev. 1111, 1129-1131, 1135-1137, 1140-1145 (1997).

which their conscious judgments are unconsciously race based. . . . In short, the empirical literature on racial bias suggests that, under the [*Davis/*]*Feeney* framework, most race-dependent governmental decisionmaking will elude equal protection scrutiny. . . .

[*Davis* and] *Feeney* stand as a gateway to challenges concerning residential zoning, education, and the operation of the criminal justice system. . . . State action concerning sexual assault, [domestic violence], child care, and child support is subject to the same standard of review. In all these domains, the state acts in ways that profoundly shape the life circumstances of minorities and women, but the Court has construed the Equal Protection Clause in terms that shield these forms of state action from challenge. Indeed, the Court has interpreted the Equal Protection Clause in terms that seem to invite legislators to act without regard to the foreseeable racial or gendered impact of their actions. . . .

Davis and *Feeney,* Siegel insists, cannot be read in isolation from the Court's affirmative action cases, where the Court now applies strict scrutiny:

When plaintiffs challenge facially neutral policies that have a disparate impact on minorities or women, the Court adopts a highly deferential stance towards a legislature's judgments. But when white plaintiffs challenge affirmative action policies that increase the institutional representation of minority groups, the Court . . . applies strict scrutiny to such programs, intervening in the legislative process to protect the interests of whites in ways that it will not when plaintiffs challenge legislation having a disparate impact on minorities or women. . . .

Thus, today, especially in the area of race, doctrines of heightened scrutiny are functioning primarily as a check on affirmative action programs. By their terms, doctrines of heightened scrutiny do not apply to racial neutral laws like the sentencing guidelines, decisions concerning education and zoning, or policies concerning spousal assault and child support, whose incidence falls primarily on minorities or women. The Court assumes these policies were enacted in good faith — even as it applies "skeptical scrutiny" to policies that attempt to rectify centuries of discrimination against minorities and women. . . .

The Court [has] insist[ed] that affirmative action policies could not rectify "societal discrimination" or promote proportional representation or otherwise engage in what some have called "social engineering." (Note how justifications for constitutional restrictions on affirmative action resemble the nineteenth-century claim that civil rights measures should not legislate "social equality.") . . .

Just as importantly, this body of equal protection doctrine supplies a language and a perceptual framework that shapes popular debates about race and gender equality. The governing equal protection framework identifies race- and gender-conscious remedies as pernicious "discrimination," while deflecting attention from the many ways that the state continues to regulate the social status of minorities and women, thereby constructing discrimination against minorities and women as a practice of the (distant) past. The social position of minorities and women thus appears to be a legacy of past discrimination — or the product of culture, choice, and ability — while the state's continuing role in shaping the life prospects of minorities and women disappears from view. . . . So long as affirmative action dominates debates about the meaning of equal protection, conversation about "discrimination" continues to focus on practices of race- and gender-based classification, obscuring the myriad forms of state action that contribute to the social stratification affirmative action addresses. . . .

3. *Griggs as a constitutional principle.* What would a constitutional alternative to the *Davis/Feeney* doctrine look like? *Griggs* does not make illegal all employment

decisions that have a disparate impact on women and minorities. It permits a defense of business necessity. One alternative to *Davis* would be a constitutional equivalent of the business necessity defense. If a policy had a foreseeable disparate impact on minorities, the government would be required to show why the disproportionate burden on minorities was nevertheless in the public interest. This "regulatory necessity" defense would eliminate the "parade of horribles" that Justice White worried about, and indeed, might not change many outcomes. But it would change the discourse of antidiscrimination law. Governments would have to openly confront the racial consequences of their decisions and their effect on minority communities, rather than allowing courts to defer to their judgments as "ordinary social and economic legislation" under the rational basis test. Consider Professor Siegel's defense of such a regime:

> In such a world, state actors would be required to acknowledge and justify their role in perpetuating forms of race and gender stratification. In a world where governmental actors were regularly called upon to justify the racial and gender consequences of their policy choices, the government's role in perpetuating race and gender inequality would be far more visible than it now is. In such a world, equal protection litigation might move the nation closer to disestablishing historic patterns of race and gender stratification than current constitutional doctrines now do.

Note that under federal law developers are required to prepare "environmental impact statements." Is there any reason to think that racial minorities deserve less reasoned consideration?

4. *Griggs versus Davis.* The legislative history of Title VII provides scant support for holding that disproportionate impact, as such, supports an employment discrimination claim. This makes all the more interesting the question why the Court held that disproportionate impact stated a claim in *Griggs* and not in *Davis*. One possibility lies in the fact that the statute is limited in scope to employment, while the Fourteenth Amendment covers discrimination of every possible sort. The Court may have believed that *Griggs* was good employment policy yet thought that a constitutionally compelled disproportionate impact principle was undesirable, unpredictable, or uncontainable. Could the Court have plausibly limited a Fourteenth Amendment disproportionate-impact principle to particular subject areas of discrimination?

The facts of the two cases may also have played a role. Someone reading the record in *Griggs* and similar cases brought at the time could easily conclude that the defendants were engaging in intentional discrimination — albeit discrimination that was often difficult and expensive to prove. The jobs that plaintiffs were denied had traditionally been held only by whites. By contrast, the chief of the Washington, DC, Police Department was black and the department had many black officers. (If this is a plausible explanation for the different outcomes, is it a persuasive justification?)

5. *Washington v. Davis and the antidiscrimination principle.* Does the antidiscrimination principle support or weigh against the outcome of *Davis*? Consider first two arguments drawing on the *process* rationale for the antidiscrimination principle.

(a) Justice White notes that a racially disproportionate impact may be evidence that a decision or pattern of decisionmaking was race-dependent. Recall Yick Wo v. Hopkins and Gomillion v. Lightfoot. Would this rationale have justified a different holding in *Davis*?

(b) Would a different holding have been justified by a finding that the disproportionate black failure rate on Test 21 was the result of past de jure discrimination against blacks? In "Justice" or "Just Us": Racism and the Role of Ideology, 35 Stan. L. Rev. 831, 849 n.69 (1983), Professor Charles R. Lawrence III writes:

> [T]he discriminatory impact of the test on blacks could easily be traced to the history of racial discrimination in the city's school system. In Bolling v. Sharpe, 347 U.S. 497 (1954), a companion case to *Brown*, the Supreme Court held the District of Columbia's statutorily segregated school system unconstitutional. In Hobson v. Hansen, 269 F. Supp. 401 (D.D.C. 1967), aff'd sub nom. Smuck v. Hobson, 408 F.2d 175 (D.C. Cir. 1969), the court found that the D.C. school district had perpetuated segregated classrooms through the tracking of students. Thus, police training applicants in *Davis*, which arose only five years after *Hansen*, most likely spent the greater part of their public school careers in unconstitutionally segregated schools.

If it would be appropriate for Congress, legislating under §5 of the Fourteenth Amendment, to prohibit certain tests on this rationale, are there any reasons for the Court not to do so? Does the decision turn on facts, or require determinations of policy, that seem more appropriate for legislative than judicial resolution?

Note: Commentaries on the Intent Standard

Linda Hamilton Krieger argues that the *Davis/Feeney* framework for proving discriminatory purpose does not take account of scientific theories of human cognition.[125]

> [It] is a central premise of social cognition theory . . . that cognitive structures and processes involved in categorization and information processing can in and of themselves result in stereotyping and other forms of biased intergroup judgment previously attributed to motivational processes. The social cognition approach to discrimination [makes] three claims[:]
>
> [First,] stereotyping . . . is nothing special. It is simply a form of categorization, similar in structure and function to the categorization of natural objects. According to this view, stereotypes, like other categorical structures, are cognitive mechanisms that all people, not just "prejudiced" ones, use to simplify the task of perceiving, processing, and retaining information about people in memory. They are central, and indeed essential to normal cognitive functioning.
>
> [Second,] once in place, stereotypes bias intergroup judgment and decisionmaking. According to this view, stereotypes operate as "person prototypes" or "social schemas." As such, they function as implicit theories, biasing in predictable ways the perception, interpretation, encoding, retention, and recall of information about other people. These biases are cognitive rather than motivational. They operate absent intent to favor or disfavor members of a particular social group. And, perhaps most significant for present purposes, they bias a decisionmaker's judgment long before the "moment of decision," as a decisionmaker attends to relevant data and interprets, encodes, stores, and retrieves it from memory. These

---

125. Linda Hamilton Krieger, The Content of Our Categories: A Cognitive Bias Approach to Discrimination and Equal Employment Opportunity, 47 Stan. L. Rev. 1161 (1995).

biases "sneak up on" the decisionmaker, distorting bit by bit the data upon which his decision is eventually based.

[Third,] [s]tereotypes, when they function as implicit prototypes or schemas, operate beyond the reach of decisionmaker self-awareness. Empirical evidence indicates that people's access to their own cognitive processes is in fact poor. Accordingly, cognitive bias may well be both unintentional and unconscious. . . .

Viewed through the lens of social cognition theory, [the law] construes the role of motivation in intergroup discrimination precisely backwards. [C]ognitive biases in social judgment operate automatically and must be controlled, if at all, through subsequent "mental correction." Intergroup discrimination, or at least that variant which results from cognitive sources of bias, is automatic. It does not result from a motive or intent to discriminate; it is an unwelcome byproduct of otherwise adaptive cognitive processes. But, like many unwanted byproducts, it can be controlled. . . .

[W]e should expect that a self-professed "colorblind" decisionmaker will fall prey to the various sources of cognitive bias we have examined. For even if this decision-maker's conscious inferential process is colorblind, the categorical structures through which he collects, sorts, and recalls information are not. In a culture in which race, gender, and ethnicity are salient, even the well-intentioned will inexorably categorize along racial, gender, and ethnic lines. And once these categorical structures are in place, they can be expected to distort social perception and judgment. . . .

[P]eople cannot be admonished out of categorical divisions so long as those divisions help them explain and function in their natural or social environment. And so long as people categorize along lines of race, gender, or ethnicity, we can expect the resulting categorization-related distortions in social perception and judgment to bias intergroup decisionmaking. . . .

To establish liability for . . . discrimination, a . . . plaintiff [should] simply be required to prove that his group status played a role in causing the employer's action or decision. Causation would no longer be equated with intentionality. The critical inquiry would be whether the applicant or employee's group status "made a difference" in the employer's action, not whether the decisionmaker intended that it make a difference.

Charles Lawrence, on the other hand, argues that courts should use the cultural meaning of social practices as a proxy for unconscious racism.[126]

[T]his article proposes a new test to trigger judicial recognition of race-based behavior. It posits a connection between unconscious racism and the existence of cultural symbols that have racial meaning. It suggests that the "cultural meaning" of an allegedly racially discriminatory act is the best available analogue for, and evidence of, a collective unconscious that we cannot observe directly. This test would thus evaluate governmental conduct to determine whether it conveys a symbolic message to which the culture attaches racial significance. A finding that the culture thinks of an allegedly discriminatory governmental action in racial terms would also constitute a finding regarding the beliefs and motivations of the governmental actors: The actors are themselves part of the culture and presumably could not have acted without being influenced by racial considerations, even if they are unaware of their racist beliefs. Therefore, the court would apply strict scrutiny.

126. Charles R. Lawrence III, The Id, The Ego, And Equal Protection: Reckoning With Unconscious Racism, 39 Stan. L. Rev. 317, 319-326, 357-358 (1987).

As an example, Lawrence discusses City of Memphis v. Greene, 451 U.S. 100 (1981), in which black plaintiffs unsuccessfully challenged the construction of a wall between white and black communities in Memphis. Lawrence notes that there were plenty of reasons to be suspicious of this result.

> The closing was effected by the erection of a barrier at the point of separation between the black and white neighborhoods. It was a unique step, not part of a uniform city planning effort, taken at the request of white property owners who expressed concern about excess traffic and danger to children. One person soliciting signatures for a petition in favor of the street closing had referred to the traffic as "undesirable traffic."
>
> The Court refused to probe beneath the surface of the residents' expressed purposes, asserting that, because the plaintiffs had sued the mayor and city council, it is the latter's motivation that must be ascertained. The Court similarly refused to hold that the history of resistance to desegregation in Memphis, the fact that the white neighborhood in question developed as a result of pre-World War II segregation, and evidence of present racial animus required the district court to find that the city council's action was racially motivated, since there was no showing that "the residents of Hein Park would have welcomed the heavy flow of transient traffic through their neighborhood if the drivers had been predominantly white."

Under Lawrence's preferred approach, the city's action

> would have a cultural meaning growing out of a long history of whites' need to separate themselves from blacks as a symbol of their superiority. Individual members of the city council might well have been unaware that their continuing need to maintain their superiority over blacks, or their failure to empathize with how construction of the wall would make blacks feel, influenced their decision. But if one were to ask even the most self-deluded among them what the residents of Memphis would take the existence of the wall to mean, the obvious answer would be difficult to avoid. If one told the story leading to the wall's construction while omitting one vital fact — the race of those whose vehicular traffic the barrier excluded — and then asked Memphis citizens to describe the residents of the community claiming injury, few, if any, would not guess that they were black.
>
> The current racial meanings of governmental actions are strong evidence that the process defects of group vilification and misapprehension of costs and benefits have occurred whether or not the decisionmakers were conscious that race played a part in their decisionmaking. Moreover, actions that have racial meaning within the culture are also those actions that carry a stigma for which we should have special concern. . . .
>
> [T]he intent doctrine's focus on the narrowest and most unrealistic understanding of individual fault has also engendered much of the resistance to and resentment of affirmative action programs and other race-conscious remedies for past and continuing discrimination. If there can be no discrimination without an identifiable criminal, then "innocent" individuals will resent the burden of remedying an injury for which the law says they are not responsible. Understanding the cultural source of our racism obviates the need for fault, as traditionally conceived, without denying our collective responsibility for racism's eradication. We cannot be individually blamed for unconsciously harboring attitudes that are inescapable in a culture permeated with racism. And without the necessity for blame, our resistance to accepting the need and responsibility for remedy will be lessened.

Discussion

1. Both Professors Krieger and Lawrence assume that if defendants are not charged with intentional bias against minorities, they will be less upset and defensive

about charges of discrimination. Do you think this is true? Wouldn't Professor Lawrence agree that losing a discrimination suit has a distinctive "cultural meaning" as well, especially since most people have no idea what the actual content of legal doctrines are?

Putting these questions aside, are accusations of racism the only things at stake in employment discrimination or zoning cases, or are there distributive and material consequences as well? Consider, for example, whether tort defendants are happier with a system of strict liability, which requires no showing of fault and under which plaintiffs presumably can prove liability more easily.

2. Professor Krieger argues that plaintiffs must show that their "group status played a role in causing the employer's action or decision." But if Krieger is correct that racial and gender categorizations are ubiquitous and even helpful in getting about the world, won't it always be the case that cognitive framing played some role? Can you think of ways to make Krieger's test more precise?

3. If Professors Krieger and Lawrence are correct, what kinds of expert testimony would or should be required to succeed in a discrimination lawsuit? Does Professor Kreiger's theory require the use of cognitive psychologists in Title VII and Fourteenth Amendment cases?

Under Professor Lawrence's theory, is it enough to rely on judges to take judicial notice of the cultural meaning of racially disproportionate practices? If judges are also victims of unconscious racism, won't they deny these meanings to themselves? Does this mean that courts (or the parties) should hire cultural anthropologists to explain what a practice means culturally? Suppose that whites and blacks tend to disagree about the cultural meaning of a particular practice. For example, suppose that a large majority of blacks insist that the closing of the street in Memphis is about race, while a large majority of whites insist it is about lowering crime and preserving peace and quiet, or that it is about keeping out poor people with loud and raucous habits. Whose view about social meaning should prevail?

4. Consider the fact that in American political life people often understand that certain issues are "about race" or are racially salient even though they can also be plausibly asserted not to be racial issues. Examples are debates about education, zoning, immigration, welfare, and crime. Because overt appeals to race are considered inappropriate today, particularly by whites, over the years many white politicians have learned to speak in "code" that invokes notions of race and racial salience without explicitly mentioning race, and in ways that can also be plausibly denied. To what extent should the law recognize these facts? Are there institutional reasons why courts might refuse to base equal protection doctrine on the understanding of race discrimination that Krieger and Lawrence believe the law should recognize?

5. Something like Professor Lawrence's theory has been adopted, surprisingly, in a somewhat different area of constitutional law: the Establishment Clause. Under the Establishment Clause, government is not permitted to endorse religion over nonreligion or endorse one religion over another. See County of Allegheny v. American Civil Liberties Union, 492 U.S. 573 (1989). Questions of endorsement arise in many situations ranging from state-sponsored prayers to the display of nativity scenes. Justice O'Connor has been the primary exponent of the "no-endorsement" theory over the years. Just as Lawrence argues that the government violates the Equal Protection Clause when it sends a message of cultural inferiority to racial minorities, O'Connor argues that the government violates the Establishment

Clause when its actions have the purpose or effect of endorsing religion or nonreligion to a reasonable observer. Endorsement violates the Establishment Clause because the government may not make people's religious beliefs or their membership in a particular religious group determinative of their political standing in the community. See Wallace v. Jaffree, 472 U.S. 38, 69-70 (1985) (O'Connor, J., concurring). When government action has the purpose or effect of endorsing religion, it sends a message to some members of the community that they are favored insiders; and it sends a message to others who adhere to different beliefs that they are disfavored outsiders, "not full members of the political community." Lynch v. Donnelly, 465 U.S. 668, 688 (1984) (O'Connor, J., concurring). Justice O'Connor's endorsement test is, in effect, a test of the cultural meaning of a contested government practice.

Note that Justice O'Connor refers to both the purpose and the effect of government action. Thus, it does not matter whether a large crucifix on the top of (say) a state's Supreme Court building was designed to endorse Christianity or make non-Christians feel like less than equal citizens. What matters is that it has that effect. As a result, O'Connor's test requires that the cultural meaning be "reasonable" to avoid the problem of unreasonable or hypersensitive plaintiffs. The test is what a "reasonable observer" familiar with the history of the practice would understand the practice to mean. In *Lynch* itself, Justice O'Connor held that the display of a nativity scene, featuring the baby Jesus, Mary, and Joseph, and accompanied by a Christmas tree and various seasonal characters, was not an endorsement of Christianity. Does this mean that non-Christians who disagree with her conclusion are "unreasonable?" Is the judgment of favoritism, as Justice Brown said of segregated facilities in Plessy v. Ferguson, solely "because [non-Christians] choose to put that construction upon it?"

Can you think of any reason why the Court has adopted something like a "cultural meaning test" in religion cases but has not done so in race cases? Put another way, why shouldn't Washington v. Davis apply in Establishment Clause cases, so that the government should be able to place crosses in government buildings unless plaintiffs prove that it specifically sought to endorse Christianity? Conversely, if you think that racism is a much more serious problem in the United States than endorsement of mainstream Christianity, why shouldn't it be easier to prove racial discrimination than religious endorsement?

Suppose that the courts adopted Professor Lawrence's test, and asked whether a "reasonable observer" would see a particular practice as racially motivated. Does the decision in *Lynch* give you any suggestion of how easy it would be to get the kinds of people who are appointed to the federal judiciary to see the racial and cultural meanings that Lawrence sees?

F. Judicial Review of Covert Race-Dependent Decisions: The Inquiry into Motivation

1. *The Arlington Heights Factors*

In Village of Arlington Heights v. Metropolitan Housing Development Corp., 429 U.S. 252 (1977), the Court considered a challenge to the city's refusal to rezone a 15-acre parcel from single-family to multiple-family classification. Using federal financial assistance, MHDC planned to build 190 clustered townhouse units for low- and moderate-income tenants. The Court, in an opinion by Justice Powell, reversed the Court of Appeals holding that the "ultimate effect" of the decision was racially discriminatory. The Court reaffirmed the rule of Washington v. Davis that mere showing of discriminatory effect was not sufficient; plaintiffs had to show that intent to discriminate was a "motivating factor," even if it was not the sole, dominant, or primary factor. It offered a list of factors for courts to use to determine whether governmental decisions were racially motivated. These included (1) the impact of the official action, including whether "a clear pattern, unexplainable on grounds other than race, emerges from the effect of state action even when the governing legislation appears neutral on its face" (although the Court cautioned that such situations would be "rare"); (2) "the historical background of the decision . . . particularly if it reveals a series of official actions taken for invidious purposes"; (3) "[t]he specific sequence of events leading up the challenged decision"; (4) "[d]epartures from the normal procedural sequence"; (5) "[s]ubstantive departures [where] the factors usually considered important by the decisionmaker strongly favor a decision contrary to the one reached"; and (6) "[t]he legislative or administrative history . . . especially where there are contemporary statements by members of the decisionmaking body, minutes of its meetings, or reports."

The Court explained in a footnote that even proof that a decision "was motivated in part by a racially discriminatory purpose" did not necessarily result in its invalidation. Such proof would "have shifted to the Village the burden of establishing that the same decision would have resulted even had the impermissible purpose not been considered. . . . See Mt. Healthy City School Dist. Bd. of Education v. Doyle, 429 U.S. 274 (1977)." The Court then independently reviewed the evidence and concluded that although

> [t]he impact of the Village's decision does arguably bear more heavily on racial minorities . . . there is little about the sequence of events leading up to the decision that would spark suspicion. . . . The rezoning request progressed according to the usual procedures. . . . The statements by the Plan Commission and Village Board members, as reflected in the official minutes, focused almost exclusively on the zoning aspects of the MHDC petition, and the zoning factors on which they relied are not novel criteria in the Village's rezoning decisions. . . . In sum, . . . [r]espondents simply failed to carry their burden of proving that discriminatory purpose was a motivating factor in the Village's decision.

Discussion

1. *"But-for" motivation.* In Hunter v. Underwood, 471 U.S. 222 (1985), the Court cited *Arlington Heights* in striking down a provision of the Alabama Constitution that disenfranchised persons convicted of certain enumerated felonies and misdemeanors, including "any . . . crime involving moral turpitude." Appellees, one of whom was black and the other white, were disenfranchised after being convicted of presenting worthless checks. The lower court found that, although the provision was neutral on its face, it had a racially discriminatory impact on blacks. Justice Rehnquist, writing for a unanimous Court, stated that the proper inquiry was whether the provision was adopted with a discriminatory purpose and that "[o]nce racial discrimination is shown to have been a 'substantial' or 'motivating'"

factor behind enactment of the law, the burden shifts to the law's defenders to demonstrate that the law would have been enacted without this factor." After reviewing the circumstances of its adoption in 1901, the Court found that racial animus "was a motivating factor for the provision, and that [it] would not have been adopted . . . in the absence of the racially discriminatory motivation." In response to evidence that the provision was also motivated by a desire to disenfranchise poor whites, the Court held that "an additional purpose to discriminate against poor whites would not render nugatory the purpose to discriminate against all blacks, and it is beyond peradventure that the latter was a 'but-for' motivation for the enactment of [the provision]." The Court concluded: "Without deciding whether [the provision] would be valid if enacted today without any impermissible motivation, we simply observe that its original enactment was motivated by a desire to discriminate against blacks on account of race and the section continues to this day to have that effect. As such, it violates equal protection under *Arlington Heights*."

2. *Closing municipal facilities to avoid integration.* In Palmer v. Thompson, 403 U.S. 217 (1971), plaintiffs challenged a decision by the city council of Jackson, Mississippi to close the city's public swimming pools following a federal court order to desegregate them in 1962. The District Court found that the closing was justified to preserve peace and order and because the pools could not be operated economically on an integrated basis and held that the city's action did not deny black citizens equal protection of the laws. The Supreme Court affirmed in a 5-4 decision. Responding to plaintiff's argument that the closing was racially motivated, Justice Black's opinion stated that "no case in this Court has held that a legislative act may violate equal protection solely because of the motivations of the men who voted for it." He also argued that

> it is extremely difficult for a court to ascertain the motivation, or collection of different motivations, that lie behind a legislative enactment. . . . It is difficult or impossible for any court to determine the "sole" or "dominant" motivation behind the choices of a group of legislators. Furthermore, there is an element of futility in a judicial attempt to invalidate a law because of the bad motives of its supporters. If the law is struck down for this reason, rather than because of its facial content or effect, it would presumably be valid as soon as the legislature or relevant governing body repassed it for different reasons.

Is *Palmer* effectively overruled by Washington v. Davis and *Arlington Heights*?[127] Is *Palmer* distinguishable on the ground that it involves legislative motivation rather than executive motivation? On the grounds that blacks and whites were equally harmed? (What about the status injury to blacks?)

3. *Inquiries into motivation and "respect" for the democratic process.* It has been asserted that "a finding of impure motive sufficient to void an act of a legislature impugns [its] essential integrity"[128] and that judicial review of legislative motivation manifests

---

127. In Washington v. Davis, 426 U.S. 229 (1976), Justice White wrote: "To the extent that Palmer suggests a generally applicable proposition that legislative purpose is irrelevant in constitutional adjudication, our prior cases . . . are to the contrary." Shortly after *Palmer*, in Lemon v. Kurtzman, 403 U.S. 602 (1971), a case involving the Establishment Clause, a unanimous Court reaffirmed that legislation subsidizing church-related schools requires close judicial scrutiny of the statute's purpose.

128. Note, Developments in the Law — Equal Protection, 82 Harv. L. Rev. 1065, 1093 (1969).

disrespect for "the station" of the legislature.[129] Doesn't this beg the question whether the test for unconstitutionality should be specific intent to harm a particular racial or ethnic minority? If the test was lower, would the legislature be so "insulted"? In any case, why should one assume that legislatures are places of pure motivation in the first place? Recall the virtual abdication of scrutiny involved in United States v. Carolene Products, which allowed the rational basis behind legislation to be established as a legal fiction. When discrete and insular minorities are adversely affected by legislation, are there good reasons to maintain this legal fiction as a pretense?

What does Justice Black mean in *Palmer* by the "futility" of invalidating a law because of improper motives? Is the problem that the law may be reenacted for proper reasons, or that it may be reenacted for (better concealed) illicit reasons? Consider Paul Brest's proposal that

> [the court should] presume that the decisionmaker continues to entertain the motives that led to the original decision (and to its invalidation). In operational terms, the court should enjoin an administrative decisionmaker from making the same decision again unless he comes forward with persuasive evidence that this time it will be made only for legitimate reasons. Sometimes a material change of circumstances, or the passage of time accompanied by a change of community attitudes, will be persuasive of the decisionmaker's good faith. In other circumstances the decisionmaker may be required to demonstrate that the proposed decision is in fact desirable on the merits and that no practicable alternative is less burdensome to the class at whom the original decision was adversely aimed. . . . If the court invalidates a legislative enactment, it should similarly scrutinize reenactment of the identical or a similar law if it is challenged in a properly maintained action.[130]

Note: Assessing the Motives of Legislatures and Other Decisionmakers

In Rogers v. Lodge, 458 U.S. 613 (1982), a district court found that although a Georgia county's at-large voting system was "racially neutral when adopted, [it] is being *maintained* for invidious purposes," and ordered the establishment of single-member electoral districts. The Supreme Court affirmed. Justice Powell, joined by Justice Rehnquist, dissented, arguing that the complainants had not proved discriminatory intent. Justice Stevens also dissented with a wide-ranging discussion of the problems of assessing and remedying the motivation of political acts. Justice Stevens first observed that the county's demographics could change so that Blacks would have more representation under the at-large scheme invalidated by the district court than under a single-member district system. He argued that "constitutional adjudication that is premised on a case-by-case appraisal of the subjective intent of local decisionmakers cannot possibly satisfy the requirement of impartial administration of the law that is embodied in the Equal Protection Clause of the Fourteenth Amendment."

---

129. Alexander Bickel, The Least Dangerous Branch 214 (1962).

130. Paul Brest, Palmer v. Thompson: An Approach to the Problem of Unconstitutional Legislative Motive, 1971 Sup. Ct. Rev. 95, 126-127. For discussion of the various problems raised by *Palmer* and Washington v. Davis, see, in addition to Brest, supra, Theodore Eisenberg, Disproportionate Impact and Illicit Motive: Theories of Constitutional Adjudication, 52 N.Y.U. L. Rev. 36 (1977); John Ely, Legislative and Administrative Motivation in Constitutional Law, 79 Yale L.J. 1205 (1970); Michael Perry, The Disproportionate Impact Theory of Racial Discrimination, 125 U. Pa. L. Rev. 540 (1977); Symposium, Legislative Motivation, 15 San Diego L. Rev. 925 (1978).

In the future, it is not inconceivable that the white officials who are likely to remain in power under the District Court's plan will desire to perpetuate that system and to continue to control a majority of seats on the county commission. Under this Court's standard, if some of those officials harbor such an intent or an "invidious" reason, the District Court's plan will itself become unconstitutional. It is not clear whether the invidious intent would have to be shared by all three white commissioners, by merely a majority of two, or by simply one if he were influential. It is not clear whether the issue would be affected by the intent of the two black commissioners, who might fear that a return to an at-large system would undermine the certainty of two black seats. Of course, if the subjective intent of these officials were such as to mandate a change to a governmental structure that would permit black voters to elect an all-black commission — and if black voters did so — those black officials could not harbor an intent to maintain the system to keep whites from returning to power. . . .

The costs and the doubts associated with litigating questions of motive, which are often significant in routine trials, will be especially so in cases involving the "motives" of legislative bodies. . . . Assuming that it is the intentions of the "state actors" that is critical, how will their mental processes be discovered? Must a specific proposal for change be defeated? What if different motives are held by different legislators or, indeed, by a single official? Is a selfish desire to stay in office sufficient to justify a failure to change a governmental system? . . .

Certainly governmental action should not be influenced by irrelevant considerations. I am not convinced, however, that the Constitution affords a right — and this is the *only* right the Court finds applicable in this case — to have every official decision made without the influence of considerations that are in some way "discriminatory." Is the failure of a state legislature to ratify the Equal Rights Amendment invalid if a federal judge concludes that a majority of the legislators harbored stereotypical views of the proper role of women in society? Is the establishment of a memorial for Jews slaughtered in World War II unconstitutional if civil leaders believe that their cause is more meritorious than that of victimized Palestinian refugees? Is the failure to adopt a state holiday for Martin Luther King, Jr. invalid if it is proved that state legislators believed that he does not deserve to be commemorated? Is the refusal to provide Medicaid funding for abortions unconstitutional if officials intend to discriminate against women who would abort a fetus?

A rule that would invalidate all governmental action motivated by racial, ethnic or political considerations is too broad. Moreover, in my opinion the Court is incorrect in assuming that the intent of elected officials is invidious when they are motivated by a desire to retain control of the local political machinery. For such an intent is surely characteristic of politicians throughout the country. In implementing that sort of purpose, dominant majorities have used a wide variety of techniques to limit the political strength of aggressive minorities. In this case the minority is defined by racial characteristics, but minority groups seeking an effective political voice can, of course, be identified in many other ways. The Hasidic Jews in Kings County, New York, the Puerto Ricans in Chicago, the Spanish-speaking citizens in Dallas, the Bohemians in Cedar Rapids, the Federalists in Massachusetts, the Democrats in Indiana, and the Republicans in California have all been disadvantaged by deliberate political maneuvers by the dominant majority. As I have stated, a device that serves no purpose other than to exclude minority groups from effective political participation is unlawful under objective standards. But if a political majority's intent to maintain control of a legitimate local government is sufficient to invalidate any electoral device that makes it more difficult for a minority group to elect candidates — regardless of the nature of the interest that gives the minority group cohesion — the Court is not just entering a "political thicket"; it is entering a vast wonderland of judicial review of political activity.

Justice Scalia, dissenting in Edwards v. Aguillard, 482 U.S. 578 (1987), categorically attacked the cogency of motive analysis. The case concerned the constitutionality of a Louisiana statute requiring that "creation science" be taught in classes where evolution is presented as a possible explanation for the origin of life. The Supreme Court struck down the statute under a doctrine that invalidated a law if its purpose was "to endorse or disapprove of religion." Justice Scalia suggests that:

> Our cases interpreting and applying the purpose test have made such a maze of the Establishment Clause that even the most conscientious government officials can only guess what motives will be held unconstitutional. . . .
>
> But the difficulty is knowing how or where to find it. For while it is possible to discern the objective "purpose" of a statute (i.e., the public good at which its provisions appear to be directed), or even the formal motivation for a statute where that is explicitly set forth (as it was [in the preamble] to no avail, here) discerning the subjective motivation of those enacting the statute is, to be honest, almost always an impossible task. The number of possible motivations, to begin with, is not binary, or indeed even finite. In the present case, for example, a particular legislator need not have voted for the Act either because he wanted to foster religion or because he wanted to improve education. He may have thought the bill would provide jobs for his district, or may have wanted to make amends with a faction of his party he had alienated on another vote, or he may have been a close friend of the bill's sponsor, or he may have been repaying a favor he owed the Majority Leader, or he may have hoped the Governor would appreciate his vote and make a fundraising appearance for him, or he may have been seeking favorable publicity, or he may have been reluctant to hurt the feelings of a loyal staff member who worked on the bill, or he may have been settling an old score with a legislator who opposed the bill, or he may have been mad at his wife who opposed the bill, or he may have been intoxicated and utterly unmotivated when the vote was called, or he may have accidentally voted "yes" instead of "no," or, of course, he may have had (and very likely did have) a combination of some of the above reasons and many other motivations. To look for *the sole purpose* of even a single legislator is probably to look for something that does not exist.
>
> Putting that problem aside, however, where ought we to look for the individual legislator's purpose? We cannot of course assume that every member present (if, as is unlikely, we know who or even how many they were) agreed with the motivation expressed in a particular legislator's pre-enactment floor or committee statement. Quite obviously, "[w]hat motivates one legislator to make a speech about a statute is not necessarily what motivates scores of others to enact it." United States v. O'Brien, 391 U.S. 367, 384 (1968). Can we assume, then, that they all agree with the motivation expressed in the staff-prepared committee reports they might have read — even though we are unwilling to assume that they agreed with the motivation expressed in the very statute that they voted for? Should we consider post-enactment floor statements? Or post-enactment testimony from legislators, obtained expressly for the lawsuit? Should we consider media reports on the realities of the legislative bargaining? All of these sources, of course are eminently manipulable. Legislative histories can be contrived and sanitized, favorable media coverage orchestrated, and post-enactment recollections conveniently distorted. Perhaps most valuable of all would be more objective indications — for example, evidence regarding the individual legislators' religious affiliations. And if that, why not evidence regarding the fervor or tepidity of their beliefs?
>
> Having achieved, through these simple means, an assessment of what individual legislators intended, we must still confront the question (yet to be adressed in any of our cases) how *many* of them must have the invalidating intent. If a state senate approves a bill by vote of 36 to 35, and only one of the 26 intended solely to advance

religion [or exhibit racial prejudice], is the law unconstitutional? What if 13 of the 26 had that intent? What if 3 of the 26 had the impermissible intent, but 3 of the 25 voting against the bill were motivatied by religious hostility or were simply attempting to "balance" the votes of their impermissibly motivated colleagues? Or is it possible that the intent of the bill's sponsor is alone enough to invalidate it — on a theory, perhaps that even though everyone else's intent was pure, what they produced was the fruit of a forbidden tree?

Because there are no good answers to these questions, this court has recognized . . . that determining the subjective intent of legislators is a perilous enterprise. It is perilous, I might note, not just for the judges who will very likely reach the wrong result, but also for the legislators who find that they must assess the validity of proposed legislation — and risk the condemnation of having voted for an unconstitutional measure — not on the basis of what the legislation contains, nor even on the basis of what they themselves intend, but on the basis of what *others* have in mind.

Given the many hazards in assuming the subjective intent of governmental decisionmakers, the [duty to ascertain purpose] is defensible, I think, only if the text of the Establishment Clause demands it. That is surely not the case.

Discussion

Do you agree with Justice Scalia's general argument? Can the Fourteenth Amendment be applied without demanding inquiries into motive?

2. *The War on Drugs and the Powder Cocaine/Crack Cocaine Distinction*

UNITED STATES v. CLARY, 4 F.3d 709 (8th Cir. 1994): [Defendant brought an equal protection challenge to the federal sentencing guidelines for the crime of possession of cocaine with intent to distribute. 21 U.S.C 841(b)(1)(A)(iii) provides for a ten-year minimum sentence for persons found possessing 50 grams or more of cocaine base. A similar ten-year minimum is imposed for those possessing over 5,000 grams of powder cocaine. The Sentencing Commission adopted the 100 to 1 ratio in U.S.S.G. §2D1.1. Clary argued that the 100 to 1 ratio discriminated against African-Americans.]

John R. GIBSON, Senior Circuit Judge:

The [district] court outlined the events leading up to passage of the crack statute. The court cited several news articles submitted by members of Congress for publication in the Congressional Record which portrayed crack dealers as unemployed, gang-affiliated, gun-toting, young black males. Legislators, the court reasoned, used these media accounts as informational support for the statute. The district court also pointed to perceived procedural irregularities surrounding Congress' approval of the crack sentencing provisions. For instance, few hearings were held in the House on the enhanced penalties for crack. While many Senators called for a more measured response, the Senate committee conducted a single morning hearing. Finally, although the penalties were originally set at 50 to 1, they were arbitrarily doubled.

The district court also observed that 98.2 percent of defendants convicted of crack cocaine charges in the Eastern District of Missouri between the years 1988 and 1992 were African American. Nationally, 92.6 percent of those convicted of crack cocaine charges were African American, as opposed to 4.7 percent who were white. With respect to powder cocaine, the percentages were largely reversed. The court found that this statistical evidence demonstrated both the disparate impact of the 100 to 1 ratio and the probability that "the subliminal influence of unconscious racism had permeated federal prosecution throughout the nation."

While the government directed the court to evidence that Congress considered crack to be more dangerous because of its potency, addictiveness, affordability and prevalence, the court found evidence in the record contradicting many of the legislators' beliefs. In particular, the court questioned Congress' conclusion that crack was 100 times more potent or dangerous than powder cocaine, referring to testimony that there is no reliable medical evidence that crack cocaine is more addictive than powder cocaine. In light of these factors, the court found the punishment of crack at 100 times greater than powder cocaine to be a "frenzied, irrational response." The court repeatedly stressed that "cocaine is cocaine." . . .

[In] past decisions by this court [we found] that Congress clearly had rational motives for creating the distinction between crack and powder cocaine. Among the reasons were "the potency of the drug, the ease with which drug dealers can carry and conceal it, the highly addictive nature of the drug, and the violence which often accompanies trade in it." [We also] squarely reject[ed] the argument that crack cocaine sentences disparately impact on African Americans. [Under] Personnel Administrator of Massachusetts v. Feeney, 442 U.S. 256 (1979), . . . even if a neutral law has a disproportionate adverse impact on a racial minority, it is unconstitutional only if that effect can be traced to a discriminatory purpose. Discriminatory purpose "implies that the decisionmaker, in this case [Congress], selected or reaffirmed a particular course of action at least in part 'because of' not merely 'in spite of,' its adverse effects upon an identifiable group." [T]here was no evidence that Congress or the Sentencing Commission had a racially discriminatory motive when it crafted the Guidelines with extended sentences for crack cocaine felonies.

[At congressional hearings on crack cocaine] Dr. Robert Byck, Professor of Psychiatry and Pharmacology at Yale University, . . . contrasted inhaling crack vapor to packing a nose with cocaine powder (the most common form of using cocaine powder). Byck stated that crack is more dangerous than cocaine powder because as a person breathes crack vapor, an almost unlimited amount of the drug can enter the body. "Moreover, the speed of the material going to the brain is very rapid." He also commented on the marketability of crack cocaine, stating that "here suddenly, we have cocaine available in a little package, in unit dosage, available at a price that kids can pay initially." . . .

This case undoubtedly presents the most complete record on this issue to come before this court. Nevertheless, we are satisfied that both the record before the district court and the district court's findings fall short of establishing that Congress acted with a discriminatory purpose in enacting the statute, and that Congress selected or reaffirmed a particular course of action "at least in part 'because of,' not merely 'in spite of' its adverse effects upon an identifiable group." While impact is an important starting point, *Arlington Heights* made clear that impact alone is not determinative absent a pattern as stark as that in Gomillion v. Lightfoot, 364 U.S. 339 (1960), or Yick Wo v. Hopkins, 118 U.S. 356 (1886).

We . . . question the district court's reliance on "unconscious racism." The court reasoned that a focus on purposeful discrimination will not show more subtle and deeply-buried forms of racism. The court's reasoning, however, simply does not address the question whether Congress acted with a discriminatory purpose. Similar failings affect the court's statement that although intent per se may not have entered into Congress' enactment of the crack statutes, Congress' failure to account for a substantial and foreseeable disparate impact on African Americans nonetheless violates the spirit and letter of equal protection.

We also question the court's reliance on media-created stereotypes of crack dealers and its conclusion that this information "undoubtedly served as the touchstone that influenced racial perceptions held by legislators and the public as related to the 'crack epidemic.'" Although the placement of newspaper and magazine articles in the Congressional Record indicates that this information may have affected at least some legislators, these articles hardly demonstrate that the stereotypical images "undoubtedly" influenced the legislators' racial perceptions. It is too long a leap from newspaper and magazine articles to an inference that Congress enacted the crack statute because of its adverse effect on African American males, instead of the stated purpose of responding to the serious impact of a rapidly-developing and particularly-dangerous form of drug use. Similarly, the evidence of the haste with which Congress acted and the action it took is as easily explained by the seriousness of the perceived problem as by racial animus. . . .

Other testimony before the district court demonstrates the particular lack of support for the court's conclusion about Congress' motivation in passing the statute. . . . Eric E. Sterling, [who was] Counsel to the Subcommittee of Criminal Justice of the House of Representatives at the time the statutes in question were passed . . . stated that the members of Congress did not have racial animus, but rather "racial consciousness," an awareness that the "problem in the inner cities . . . was about to explode into the white part of the country." Sterling believed that Congress wanted the penalties to be applied wherever crack was being trafficked, although Congress was aware that crack was used primarily by minorities. He further described the seriousness of the problem as reported by the popular press, and stated his view that the creation and promulgation of the law was based on "crass political interest." His opinion was that the motivating factor for the legislation was a perception that crack cocaine posed a unique and unprecedented problem for American narcotics enforcement. . . .

For the most part, the other witnesses that testified before the district court were medical witnesses, several of whom contested the medical information before the Senate that showed differences between crack and powder cocaine. Scientific disagreement with testimony in congressional hearings, offered at a later time and after additional research, simply does not establish discriminatory purpose, or for that matter, a lack of scientific support for Congress' action.

We reverse and remand to the district court for resentencing consistent with this opinion.

Discussion

1. Given that the political debate over crack cocaine was clearly racially coded, and that legislators played on this association for "crass political interest," why does it raise no problems under the Fourteenth Amendment?

2. Is it relevant that some leading African-American members of Congress, such as Charles Rangel, who represents Harlem in New York City, did not object to the powder cocaine-crack cocaine distinction, and that 11 of the 21 blacks who were then members of the House of Representatives voted for the 1986 legislation that

created the 100-1 crack-powder differential? One reason for their voting behavior, suggested by Randall Kennedy in his book Race, Crime, and the Law 370-380 (1996), is that black crack cocaine dealers have as their primary victims other members of the black community. Kennedy calls on persons interested in the health and safety of urban African-Americans to sympathize and empathize more with the potential victims of crack cocaine dealers and less with the dealers themselves.[131] While stopping short of endorsing the sentencing differential himself, Kennedy argues that it is entirely rational for non-drug-using, law-abiding blacks to support extraordinary measures of punishment against those who are perceived as special threats to their own community. A fortiori, he insists, the sentencing differential cannot be racist or a violation of equal protection: "Even if these policies are misguided," Kennedy argues, "being mistaken is different from being racist, and the difference is one that greatly matters."[132]

3. Given that the House of Representatives has 435 voting members, does the fact that 11 out of 21 black members of Congress supported the sentencing differential, or that different elements in the black community might have different views on the bill necessarily insulate the measure from equal protection scrutiny? Suppose that white Representatives voted for the bill due to racialized stereotypes and fears of black drug dealers invading white suburban neighborhoods, and that black congressmen in inner-city districts were happy to go along because they believed that getting tough on crack cocaine would help their voting constituents more than it would hurt them. Should the test be whether the bill actually works to the benefit of a minority group in the long run (always difficult to prove), or what the bill meant to the people who voted for it? Does the fact that Charles Rangel voted for the bill primarily to help his constituents, the vast majority of whom are racial and ethnic minorities, pose any problems from the standpoint of the Equal Protection Clause?

3.   Peremptory Challenges

BATSON v. KENTUCKY, 476 U.S. 79 (1986): [Peremptory challenges, by which a party to litigation can strike prospective jurors without having to give reasons, have been part of the Anglo-American system of jury trial since the earliest recorded period. In criminal cases involving black defendants, it is a common practice for prosecutors to exercise peremptory challenges to remove all blacks from the petit jury.[133]

---

131. See also Kate Stith, The Government Interest in Criminal Law: Whose Interest is it, Anyway?, in Public Values in Constitutional Law (Stephen E. Gottlieb ed.) 137, 158 (1993).

132. For a response disputing Kennedy's argument, see David Cole, The Paradox of Race and Crime: A Comment On Randall Kennedy's "Politics of Distinction," 83 Geo. L.J. 2547 (1995). Cole emphasizes the costs to the black community of large numbers of blacks being incarcerated for long sentences as a result of the crack-powder distinction coupled with existing patterns of law enforcement that operate to the disadvantage of blacks.

133. Some prosecutors also strike blacks from the juries in cases involving white defendants, apparently because prosecutors view blacks as generally less likely to credit police testimony. A study of 100 felony trials that took place in Dallas County, Texas, in 1983-1984 showed that prosecutors used their peremptory challenges to eliminate 405 out of 467 eligible black jurors. An otherwise qualified black member of the jury venire had a one-in-ten chance of becoming a member of the petit jury, compared to a 50 percent chance for a white.

In Swain v. Alabama, 380 U.S. 202 (1965), the Court held 6-3, that a defendant could not challenge the prosecutor's use of peremptory challenges in a particular case unless the defendant demonstrate[d] that exclusion of blacks from juries was part of a systematic policy of purposeful discrimination. The exclusionary result in a particular case, including Swain's, was insufficient proof of systematic "perversion" of the long-established practice of peremptory challenges.

The Court overruled this limiting condition in Batson v. Kentucky, in which the prosecutor had peremptorily removed all four blacks on the venire from the petit jury of a black man charged with burglary and receipt of stolen goods, who was convicted by the all-white jury. Justice Powell's majority opinion argued that the Court should apply the "standards that have been developed since *Swain* for asserting a prima facie case under the Equal Protection Clause":]

POWELL, J.:

[T]o establish a prima facie case of purposeful discrimination in [jury] selection . . . [t]he defendant initially must show that he is a member of a racial group capable of being singled out for differential treatment [and] that in the particular jurisdiction members of his race have not been summoned for jury service over an extended period of time. Proof of systematic exclusion from the venire raises an inference of purposeful discrimination because the "result bespeaks discrimination." . . .

[T]his Court has [also] found a prima facie case on proof that members of the defendant's race were substantially underrepresented on the venire from which his jury was drawn, and that the venire was selected under a practice providing "the opportunity for discrimination." This combination of factors raises the necessary inference of purposeful discrimination because the Court has declined to attribute to chance the absence of black citizens on a particular jury array where the selection mechanism is subject to abuse. . . .

Thus, since the decision in *Swain*, this Court has recognized that a defendant may make a prima facie showing of purposeful racial discrimination in selection of the venire by relying solely on the factors concerning its selection *in his case*. These decisions are in accordance with the proposition, articulated in *Arlington Heights*, that "a consistent pattern of official racial discrimination" is not "a necessary predicate to a violation of the Equal Protection Clause. A single invidiously discriminatory governmental" act is not "immunized by the absence of such discrimination in the making of other comparable decisions." . . .

These principles support our conclusion that a defendant may establish a prima facie case of purposeful discrimination in selection of the petit jury solely on evidence concerning the prosecutor's exercise of peremptory challenges at the defendant's trial. To establish such a case, the defendant must first establish membership in a cognizable racial group and that the prosecutor has exercised peremptory challenges to remove from the venire members of the defendant's race. Second, the defendant is entitled to rely on the fact, as to which there can be no dispute, that peremptory challenges constitute a jury selection practice that permits "those to discriminate who are of a mind to discriminate." Finally, the defendant must show that these facts and any other relevant circumstances raise an inference that the prosecutor used that practice to exclude the veniremen from the petit jury on account of their race. This combination of factors in the empanelling of the petit jury . . . raises the necessary inference of purposeful discrimination. . . .

Once the defendant makes a prima facie showing, the burden shifts to the State to come forward with a neutral explanation for challenging black jurors. . . . [T]he prosecutor's explanation need not rise to the level justifying exercise of a challenge for cause. But the prosecutor may not rebut the defendant's prima facie case of discrimination by stating merely that he challenged jurors of the defendant's race on the assumption — or his intuitive judgment — that they would be partial to the defendant because of their shared race. . . . Nor may the prosecutor rebut the defendant's case merely by denying that he had a discriminatory motive or "affirming his good faith in individual selections." . . . The prosecutor therefore must articulate a neutral explanation related to the particular case to be tried.

[Justices White, Marshall, Stevens (joined by Brennan), and O'Connor each wrote concurring opinions. Justice Marshall wrote that the "end [of] of racial discrimination that peremptories inject into the jury-selection process . . . can be accomplished only by eliminating peremptory challenges entirely," and he would apply such a ban to defense attorneys as well as prosecutors. In the absence of such a complete ban, "trial courts face the difficult burden of assessing prosecutors' motives. Any prosecutor can easily assert facially neutral reasons for striking a juror, and trial courts are ill-equipped to second-guess those reasons." "[O]utright prevarication by prosecutors" is not the only danger of the *Batson* approach. "A prosecutor's own conscious or unconscious racism may lead him easily to the conclusion that a prospective black juror is 'sullen,' or 'distant,' a characterization that would not have come to his mind if a white juror had acted identically. A judge's own conscious or unconscious racism may lead him to accept such an explanation as well supported."[134]]

BURGER, C.J., dissenting, joined by Rehnquist, J.:

[Quoting from United States v. Leslie, 783 F.2d 541 (5th Cir. 1986) (en banc), Chief Justice Burger distinguished peremptory challenges from exclusion from the jury venire; the latter "implies that the government (usually the legislative or judicial branch) . . . has made the general determination that those excluded are unfit to try *any* case." A peremptory challenge, on the other hand, "represents the discrete decision, made by one of two or more opposed *litigants* in the trial phase of our adversary system of justice, that the challenged" juror is likely to be "more unfavorable to that litigant in that *particular case* than others on the same venire. . . . To suggest that a particular race is unfit to judge in any case is racially insulting. To suggest that each race may have its own special concerns, or even may tend to favor its own, is not." The Chief Justice continued:]

[P]eremptory challenges are often lodged, of necessity, for reasons "normally thought irrelevant to legal proceedings or official action, namely, the race, religion, nationality, occupation or affiliations of people summoned for jury duty." Moreover, in making peremptory challenges, both the prosecutor and defense attorney necessarily act on limited information or hunch. . . . As a result, unadulterated equal

---

134. Justice Marshall cited a case from California, where the state constitution had been interpreted as imposing a rule similar to that articulated in *Batson*. There a prosecutor sought to rebut an inference of prejudice by offering among his reasons for striking potential jurors that they " 'never cracked a smile' and, therefore did not possess the sensitivity to realistically look at the issues and decide the facts in this case" and that a juror "had a son about the same age as defendant." People v. Hall, 35 Cal. 3d 161, 672 P.2d 854, 856 (1983).

protection analysis is simply inapplicable to peremptory challenges exercised in any particular case. A clause that requires a minimum "rationality" in government actions has no application to "an arbitrary and capricious right." . . .

[Moreover,] if conventional equal protection principles apply, then presumably defendants could object to exclusions on the basis of not only race, but also sex; religious or political affiliation; mental capacity; number of children; living arrangements; and employment in a particular industry, or profession. . . .

In short, it is quite possible that every peremptory challenge could be objected to on the basis that, because it excluded a venireman who had some characteristic not shared by the remaining members of the venire, it constituted a "classification" subject to equal protection scrutiny. . . .

Peremptory challenges have long been viewed as a means to achieve an impartial jury that will be sympathetic toward neither an accused nor witnesses for the State on the basis of some shared factor of race, religion, occupation, or other characteristic. Nearly a century ago the Court stated that the peremptory challenge is "essential to the fairness of trial by jury." Lewis v. U.S. 370, 376 (1892). Under conventional equal protection principles, a state interest of this magnitude and ancient lineage might well overcome an equal protection objection to the application of peremptory challenges. However, the Court is silent on the strength of the state's interest. . . .

To rebut a prima facie case, the Court requires a "neutral explanation" for the challenge, but is at pains to "emphasize" that the "explanation need not rise to the level justifying exercise of a challenge for cause." I am at a loss to discern the governing principles here. . . . Apparently the Court envisions permissible challenges short of a challenge for cause that are just a little bit arbitrary — but not too much. While our trial judges are "experienced in supervising *voir dire*," they have no experience in administering rules like this.

REHNQUIST, J., dissenting, joined by Burger, C.J.:

I cannot subscribe to the Court's unprecedented use of the Equal Protection Clause to restrict the historic scope of the peremptory challenge. . . . In my view, there is simply nothing "unequal" about the State using its peremptory challenges to strike blacks from the jury in cases involving black defendants, so long as such challenges are also used to exclude whites in cases involving white defendants, Hispanics in cases involving Hispanic defendants, Asians in cases involving Asian defendants, and so on. This case-specific use of peremptory challenges by the State does not single out blacks, or members of any other race for that matter, for discriminatory treatment.[a] Such use of peremptories is at best based upon seat-of-the-pants instincts, which are undoubtedly crudely stereotypical and may in many cases be hopelessly mistaken. But as long as they are applied across the board to jurors of all races and nationalities, I do not see — and the Court most certainly has not explained — how their use violates the Equal Protection Clause.

---

a. I note that the Court does not rely on the argument that, because there are fewer "minorities" in a given population than there are "majorities," the equal use of peremptory challenges against members of "majority" racial groups has an equal impact. The flaws in this argument are demonstrated in Judge Garwood's thoughtful opinion for the en banc Fifth Circuit in U.S. v. Leslie.

Note: Subsequent Cases

Although *Batson* emphasizes the racial identity of the defendant with the excluded potential jurors, the Court dropped this requirement in Holland v. Illinois, 493 U.S. 474 (1990), which was decided under the Sixth Amendment, and in Powers v. Ohio, 499 U.S. 400 (1991), where the Equal Protection Clause was held to allow any criminal defendant, regardless of race, to protest a prosecutor's race-based exclusion of persons from the petit jury. (Recall the discussion following *Strauder* above.)

In Edmonson v. Leesville Concrete Co., 500 U.S. 614 (1991), the Court, sharply divided 6-3, further extended *Batson* to apply to private civil litigation. The central issue was the presence of "state action."

The following year, in Georgia v. McCollum, 505 U.S. 42 (1992), the Court held that, in criminal trials, *Batson* applies to peremptory challenges by defendants as well as prosecutors. *McCollum* involved two white men who were charged with assaulting a black couple. The prosecution sought to prevent defendants from using peremptory challenges to remove all blacks from the jury.

What implications does *Batson's* extension have for jury trials and jury service? In her article Ending Race Discrimination in Jury Selection: Whose Right Is It Anyway?, 92 Colum. L. Rev. 725 (1992), Barbara Underwood argues that, ever since Strauder v. West Virginia, courts have been profoundly ambivalent about the *reason* for the ban on race-based jury selection. According to Underwood, the existence of different legal theories of jury discrimination reflects differing emphases on the several competing values promoted by the prohibition of race discrimination in jury selection. Underwood describes these values as (1) the defendant's right to equal protection of the laws, (2) the defendant's right to due process and to trial by jury, and (3) the excluded juror's right to equal protection of the laws. While race-based jury selection has typically been viewed as a violation of the criminal defendant's rights, in its more recent cases, the Court has shifted the focus of attention to the excluded jurors as the primary victims of jury discrimination. Underwood argues that the excluded jurors' rights in fact provide a better and sounder basis for the entire existing body of jury discrimination law, because the principal reason for the prohibition of race-based jury selection is to bring all citizens into full and equal participation in the institutions of American self-government, which include juries. Do you agree?

In *McCollum*, Justice Thomas concurred in the result, believing himself bound by previous precedent. However, he criticized the direction in which the Court was moving. "[R]estricting a criminal defendant's use of [peremptory] challenges takes us further from the reasoning and the result of Strauder v. West Virginia." Unlike Professor Underwood, and unlike the majority in *McCollum*, Thomas argued that the rationale behind *Strauder* was that "securing representation of the defendant's race on the jury may help to overcome racial bias and provide the defendant with a better chance of having a fair trial." He continued:

In *Batson*, however, this Court began to depart from *Strauder* by holding that, without some actual showing, suppositions about the possibility that jurors may harbor prejudice have no legitimacy. We said, in particular, that a prosecutor could not justify peremptory strikes "by stating merely that he challenged jurors of the defendant's race on the assumption — or his intuitive judgment — that they would be partial to the defendant because of their shared race." [H]owever, our decision in *Strauder* rested on precisely such an "assumption" or "intuition." We reasonably surmised, without direct evidence in any particular case, that all-white juries might judge black defendants unfairly . . .

In *Strauder,* we put the rights of defendants foremost. Today's decision, while protecting jurors, leaves defendants with less means of protecting themselves. Unless jurors actually admit prejudice during voir dire, defendants generally must allow them to sit and run the risk that racial animus will affect the verdict. Cf. Fed. Rule Evid. 606(b) (generally excluding juror testimony after trial to impeach the verdict). In effect, we have exalted the right of citizens to sit on juries over the rights of the criminal defendant, even though it is the defendant, not the jurors, who faces imprisonment or even death. At a minimum, I think that this inversion of priorities should give us pause. . . . [W]hatever the benefits were that this Court perceived in a criminal defendant's having members of his class on the jury they have evaporated.

Justice Thomas also endorsed this passage from Justice O'Connor's dissent:

Considered in purely pragmatic terms, moreover, the Court's holding may fail to advance nondiscriminatory criminal justice. It is by now clear that conscious and unconscious racism can affect the way white jurors perceive minority defendants and the facts presented at their trials, perhaps determining the verdict of guilt or innocence. Using peremptory challenges to secure minority representation on the jury may help to overcome such racial bias, for there is substantial reason to believe that the distorting influence of race is minimized on a racially mixed jury. As amicus NAACP Legal Defense and Educational Fund explained in this case: "The ability to use peremptory challenges to exclude majority race jurors may be crucial to empaneling a fair jury. In many cases an African American, or other minority defendant, may be faced with a jury array in which his racial group is underrepresented to some degree, but not sufficiently to permit challenge under the Fourteenth Amendment. The only possible chance the defendant may have of having any minority jurors on the jury that actually tries him will be if he uses his peremptories to strike members of the majority race." In a world where the outcome of a minority defendant's trial may turn on the misconceptions or biases of white jurors, there is cause to question the implications of this Court's good intentions.

Note that the NAACP's argument turns on the fact that blacks are a minority in the United States. Its brief suggested that "whether white defendants can use peremptory challenges to purge minority jurors presents quite different issues from whether a minority defendant can strike majority group jurors." *McCollum* itself involved peremptory challenges by white defendants. Justice Thomas, in a footnote, responded: "Although I suppose that this issue technically remains open, it is difficult to see how the result could be different if the defendants here were black."

Discussion

1. Consider the "neutrality" of the following justifications presented by prosecutors following *Batson:*[135]

---

135. See generally Alan Raphael, Discriminatory Jury Selection: Lower Court Implementation of Batson v. Kentucky, 25 Williamette L. Rev. 293 (1989), from which the following examples are taken.

(a) In a case where the prosecutor used nine of his ten peremptories to remove African-Americans from the (ultimately all-white) jury trying an African-American defendant for burglary, the reasons for exclusion included that one juror "was close to defendant's age, unmarried, moved very recently, and was very attentive to defendant's counsel during his *voir dire*," while another was "unmarried, had no children, had been at current job for only six weeks, had insufficient community ties, and put name in wrong place on jury form." See Johnson v. State, 740 S.W.2d 868 (Tex. Ct. App. 1987).

(b) A dismissed African-American was cited as being a member of the Church of Christ, described by the prosecutor as "a little bit away from the mainstream," while another was struck for being a Jehovah's Witness (a "fringe religious group") and unmarried and having no children. See Chambers v. State, 724 S.W.2d 440 (Tex. Ct. App. 1987).

2. In Miller-El v. Dretke, 125 S. Ct. 2317 (2005), the Court, in an opinion by Justice Souter, gave several examples of evidence that might demonstrate that peremptory strikes were illegally employed despite a prosecutor's attempt at a neutral explanation. First, "[t]he prosecutors used their peremptory strikes to exclude 91% of the eligible African-American venire members. . . . Happenstance is unlikely to produce this disparity." Second, "[i]f a prosecutor's proffered reason for striking a black panelist applies just as well to an otherwise-similar nonblack who is permitted to serve, that is evidence tending to prove purposeful discrimination." Third, "broader patterns of practice during jury selection" besides questioning could serve as evidence of discriminatory purpose. In this case, the prosecutor twice asked the court to "shuffle" the order of the jury venire when a number of black jurors were seated near the front; this placed them at the back of the queue and greatly reduced the chances that they would be questioned before the remaining jury slots were filled. The Court also pointed to a longstanding policy in the Dallas County prosecutor's office of systematically excluding blacks from juries. The Court explained that if a prosecutor's neutral explanation was unsatisfactory, a reviewing court should not substitute its own explanation. "[W]hen illegitimate grounds like race are in issue, a prosecutor simply has got to state his reasons as best he can and stand or fall on the plausibility of the reasons he gives. A *Batson* challenge does not call for a mere exercise in thinking up any rational basis. If the stated reason does not hold up, its pretextual significance does not fade because a trial judge, or an appeals court, can imagine a reason that might not have been shown up as false." Justice Thomas, joined by Chief Justice Rehnquist and Justice Scalia, dissented.

Justice Breyer concurred, arguing that *Batson* had failed to eliminate race-based peremptories and that the Court should consider eliminating peremptory challenges altogether:

> At *Batson*'s first step, litigants remain free to misuse peremptory challenges as long as the strikes fall *below* the prima facie threshold level. At *Batson*'s second step, prosecutors need only tender a neutral reason, not a "persuasive, or even plausible" one. And most importantly, at step three, *Batson* asks judges to engage in the awkward, sometime hopeless, task of second-guessing a prosecutor's instinctive judgment — the underlying basis for which may be invisible even to the prosecutor exercising the challenge.

Justice Breyer pointed to "studies and anecdotal reports suggesting that, despite *Batson,* the discriminatory use of peremptory challenges remains a problem." "[P]eremptory challenges seem increasingly anomalous in our judicial system. On the one hand, the Court has widened and deepened *Batson*'s basic constitutional rule. . . . On the other hand, the use of race- and gender-based stereotypes in the jury-selection process seems better organized and more systematized than ever before." Justice Breyer noted that lawyers had increasingly turned to computer technology and other new techniques to rate potential jurors based on various demographic characteristics. "[T]he law's antidiscrimination command and a peremptory jury-selection system that permits or encourages the use of stereotypes work at cross-purposes."

3. In Johnson v. California, 125 S. Ct. 2410 (2005), the Court held that the California courts could not alter the three-step *Batson* process to increase the burden of proof at the first stage. The California Supreme Court held that the petitioner must offer, as an initial matter, "strong evidence" showing that it is "more likely than not" that "the [peremptory] challenges, if unexplained, were based on impermissible group bias." Justice Stevens, writing for an eight-person majority, explained that this was too great an initial burden under *Batson*:

> [W]e assumed in *Batson* that the trial judge would have the benefit of all relevant circumstances, including the prosecutor's explanation, before deciding whether it was more likely than not that the challenge was improperly motivated. We did not intend the first step to be so onerous that a defendant would have to persuade the judge — on the basis of all the facts, some of which are impossible for the defendant to know with certainty — that the challenge was more likely than not the product of purposeful discrimination. Instead, a defendant satisfies the requirements of *Batson*'s first step by producing evidence sufficient to permit the trial judge to draw an inference that discrimination has occurred. . . . The *Batson* framework is designed to produce actual answers to suspicions and inferences [of] discrimination. The inherent uncertainty present in inquiries of discriminatory purpose counsels against engaging in needless and imperfect speculation when a direct answer can be obtained by asking a simple question.

Justice Thomas dissented.

4. Administering Death

McCLESKEY v. KEMP
481 U.S. 279 (1987)

POWELL, J. delivered the opinion of the Court.

This case presents the question whether a complex statistical study that indicates a risk that racial considerations enter into capital sentencing determinations proves that petitioner McCleskey's capital sentence is unconstitutional under the . . . Fourteenth Amendment.

I.

[Warren McCleskey, an African-American, was convicted of killing a White police officer while committing an armed robbery. The jury that convicted him also held a separate penalty hearing following conviction. Georgia law allows the imposition of the death penalty only if the jury finds beyond reasonable doubt that the murder was accompanied by "aggravating circumstances." Two such circumstances, both found by McCleskey's jury, are the commission of the murder during the course of an armed robbery and the victim's being a peace officer engaged in the performance of his duties. The jury sentenced McCleskey to death.

McCleskey challenged the sentence on the ground that the Georgia capital sentencing process was administered in a racially discriminatory manner. His principal evidence was a complex statistical study performed by three researchers, the chief of whom was David Baldus of the University of Iowa.]

The Baldus study is actually two sophisticated statistical studies that examine over 2,000 murder cases that occurred in Georgia during the 1970s. The raw numbers collected by Professor Baldus indicate that defendants charged with killing white persons received the death penalty in 11% of the cases, but defendants charged with killing blacks received the death penalty in only 1% of the cases. The raw numbers also indicate a reverse racial disparity according to the race of the defendant: 4% of the black defendants received the death penalty, as opposed to 7% of the white defendants.

Baldus also divided the cases according to the combination of the race of the defendant and the race of the victim. He found that the death penalty was assessed in:

[1] 22% of the cases involving black defendants and white victims;
[2] 8% of the cases involving white defendants and white victims;
[3] 1% of the cases involving black defendants and black victims; and
[4] 3% of the cases involving white defendants and black victims.

Similarly, Baldus found that prosecutors sought the death penalty in

[1] 70% of the cases involving black defendants and white victims;
[2] 32% of the cases involving white defendants and white victims;
[3] 15% of the cases involving black defendants and black victims; and
[4] 19% of the cases involving white defendants and black victims.

Baldus subjected his data to an extensive analysis, taking account of 230 variables that could have explained the disparities on nonracial grounds. One of his models concludes that, even after taking account of 39 nonracial variables, defendants charged with killing white victims were 4.3 times as likely to receive a death sentence as defendants charged with killing blacks. According to this model, black defendants were 1.1 times as likely to receive a death sentence as other defendants. Thus, the Baldus study indicates that black defendants, such as McCleskey, who kill white victims have the greatest likelihood of receiving the death penalty.[a] . . .

---

a. Baldus' 230-variable model divided cases into eight different ranges, according to the estimated aggravation level of the offense. Baldus argued in his testimony to the District Court that the effects of racial bias were most striking in the mid-range cases. "[W]hen the cases become tremendously aggravated so that everybody would agree that if we're going to have a death sentence, these are the cases that should get it, the race effects go away. It's only in the mid-range of cases where the decision makers have a real choice as to what to do. If there's room for the exercise of discretion, then the [racial] factors begin to play a role." Under this model, Baldus found that 14.4% of the black-victim mid-range cases received the death penalty, and 34.4% of the white-victim cases received the death penalty. According to Baldus, the facts of McCleskey's case placed it within the mid-range.

II.

McCleskey's first claim is that the Georgia capital punishment statute violates the Equal Protection Clause of the Fourteenth Amendment.[b] . . . As a black defendant who killed a white victim, McCleskey claims that the Baldus study demonstrates that he was discriminated against because of his race and because of the race of his victim. . . . We agree with the Court of Appeals, and every other court that has considered such a challenge, that this claim must fail.

A

. . . [T]o prevail under the Equal Protection Clause, McCleskey must prove that the decisionmakers in his case acted with discriminatory purpose. He offers no evidence specific to his own case that would support an inference that racial considerations played a part in his sentence. Instead, he relies wholly on the Baldus study. . . .

The Court has accepted statistics as proof of intent to discriminate in certain limited contexts. First, this Court has accepted statistical disparities as proof of an equal protection violation in the selection of the jury venire in a particular district. . . . Second, this Court has accepted statistics in the form of multiple regression analyses to prove statutory violations under Title VII.

But the nature of the capital sentencing decision, and the relationship of the statistics to that decision, are fundamentally different from the corresponding elements in the venire-selection or Title VII cases. Most importantly, each particular decision to impose the death penalty is made by a petit jury selected from a properly constituted venire. Each jury is unique in its composition, and the Constitution requires that its decision rest on consideration of innumerable factors that vary according to the characteristics of the individual defendant and the facts of the particular capital offense. Thus, the application of an inference drawn from the general statistics to a specific decision in a trial and sentencing simply is not comparable to the application of an inference drawn from general statistics to a specific venire-selection or Title VII case. In those cases, the statistics relate to fewer entities, and fewer variables are relevant to the challenged decisions.[c]

Another important difference between the cases in which we have accepted statistics as proof of discriminatory intent and this case is that, in the venire-selection and Title VII contexts, the decisionmaker has an opportunity to explain the statistical disparity. Here, the State has no practical opportunity to rebut the Baldus study. "[C]ontrolling considerations of . . . public policy" dictate that jurors "cannot be called . . . to testify to the motives and influences that led to their verdict." Similarly, the policy considerations behind a prosecutor's traditionally "wide discretion" suggest the impropriety of our requiring prosecutors to defend their decisions to seek death penalties, "often years after they were made." Moreover, absent

---

b. . . . [W]e assume the study is valid statistically. . . .

c. In venire-selection cases, the factors that may be considered are limited, usually by state statute. . . . While employment decisions may involve a number of relevant variables, these variables are to a great extent uniform for all employees because they must all have a reasonable relationship to the employee's qualifications to perform the particular job at issue. . . . In contrast, a capital sentencing jury may consider any factor relevant to the defendant's background, character, and the offense. There is no common standard by which to evaluate all defendants who have or have not received the death penalty.

far stronger proof, it is unnecessary to seek such a rebuttal, because a legitimate and unchallenged explanation for the decision is apparent from the record: McCleskey committed an act for which the United States Constitution and Georgia laws permit imposition of the death penalty.

Finally, McCleskey's statistical proffer must be viewed in the context of his challenge. McCleskey challenges decisions at the heart of the State's criminal justice system. . . . Implementation of [the criminal law] necessarily requires discretionary judgments. Because discretion is essential to the criminal justice process, we would demand exceptionally clear proof before we would infer that the discretion has been abused. . . . Accordingly, we hold that the Baldus study is clearly insufficient to support an inference that any of the decisionmakers in McCleskey's case acted with discriminatory purpose.

B

McCleskey also suggests that the Baldus study proves that the State as a whole has acted with a discriminatory purpose. He appears to argue that the State has violated the Equal Protection Clause by adopting the capital punishment statute and allowing it to remain in force despite its allegedly discriminatory application. But "'[d]iscriminatory purpose' . . . implies more than intent as volition or intent as awareness of consequences. It implies that the decisionmaker, in this case a state legislature, selected or reaffirmed a particular course of action at least in part 'because of,' not merely 'in spite of,' its adverse effects upon an identifiable group." For this claim to prevail, McCleskey would have to prove that the Georgia Legislature enacted or maintained the death penalty statute because of an anticipated racially discriminatory effect. [There is no evidence supporting such a proposition.]

Nor has McCleskey demonstrated that the legislature maintains the capital punishment statute because of the racially disproportionate impact suggested by the Baldus study. . . . Accordingly, we reject McCleskey's equal protection claims. . . .

IV.

B

. . . [McCleskey] further contends that the Georgia capital punishment system is arbitrary and capricious in application, and therefore his sentence is excessive, because racial considerations may influence capital sentencing decisions in Georgia. We now address this claim.

To evaluate McCleskey's challenge, we must examine exactly what the Baldus study may show. Even Professor Baldus does not contend that his statistics prove that race enters into any capital sentencing decisions or that race was a factor in McCleskey's particular case. Statistics at most may show only a likelihood that a particular factor entered into some decisions. There is, of course, some risk of racial prejudice influencing a jury's decision in a criminal case. . . . The question "is at what point that risk becomes constitutionally unacceptable." McCleskey asks us to accept the likelihood allegedly shown by the Baldus study as the constitutional measure of an unacceptable risk of racial prejudice influencing capital sentencing decisions. This we decline to do. . . .

The capital sentencing decision requires the individual jurors to focus their collective judgment on the unique characteristics of a particular criminal defendant. . . .

McCleskey's argument that the Constitution condemns the discretion allowed decisionmakers in the Georgia capital sentencing system is antithetical to the fundamental role of discretion in our criminal justice system. . . . [A] capital-punishment system that did not allow for discretionary acts of leniency "would be totally alien to our notions of criminal justice."

C

At most, the Baldus study indicates a discrepancy that appears to correlate with race. Apparent disparities in sentencing are an inevitable part of our criminal justice system. . . . Where the discretion that is fundamental to our criminal process is involved, we decline to assume that what is unexplained is invidious. In light of the safeguards designed to minimize racial bias in the process, the fundamental value of jury trial in our criminal justice system, and the benefits that discretion provides to criminal defendants, we hold that the Baldus study does not demonstrate a constitutionally significant risk of racial bias affecting the Georgia capital-sentencing process.

V.

. . . [I]f we accepted McCleskey's claim that racial bias has impermissibly tainted the capital sentencing decision, we could soon be faced with similar claims as to other types of penalty.[d] Moreover, the claim that his sentence rests on the irrelevant factor of race easily could be extended to apply to claims based on unexplained discrepancies that correlate to membership in other minority groups, and even to gender. . . . Also, there is no logical reason that such a claim need be limited to racial or sexual bias. If arbitrary and capricious punishment is the touchstone under the Eighth Amendment, such a claim could — at least in theory — be based upon any arbitrary variable, such as the defendant's facial characteristics, or the physical attractiveness of the defendant or the victim, that some statistical study indicates may be influential in jury decisionmaking. As these examples illustrate, there is no limiting principle to the type of challenge brought by McCleskey. The Constitution does not require that a State eliminate any demonstrable disparity that correlates with a potentially irrelevant factor in order to operate a criminal justice system that includes capital punishment. As we have stated specifically in the context of capital punishment, the Constitution does not "plac[e] totally unrealistic conditions on its use."

BRENNAN, J., joined by Marshall, Blackmun, and Stevens, JJ., dissenting. [Justice Brennan focused primarily on the Eighth Amendment. Parts of his opinion were relevant to the Equal Protection claim as well:]

II.

At some point in this case, Warren McCleskey doubtless asked his lawyer whether a jury was likely to sentence him to die. A candid reply to this question would have

_____

d. Studies already exist that allegedly demonstrate a racial disparity in the length of prison sentences.

been disturbing. First, counsel would have to tell McCleskey that few of the details of the crime or of McCleskey's past criminal conduct were more important than the fact that his victim was white. . . . The story could be told in a variety of ways, but McCleskey could not fail to grasp its essential narrative line: there was a significant chance that race would play a prominent role in determining if he lived or died. . . .

The statistical evidence in this case . . . relentlessly documents the risk that McCleskey's sentence was influenced by racial considerations. This evidence shows that there is a better than even chance in Georgia that race will influence the decision to impose the death penalty: a majority of defendants in white-victim crimes would not have been sentenced to die if their victims had been black. . . .

C

Evaluation of McCleskey's evidence cannot rest solely on the numbers themselves. We must also ask whether the conclusion suggested by those numbers is consonant with our understanding of history and human experience. Georgia's legacy of a race-conscious criminal justice system, as well as this Court's own recognition of the persistent danger that racial attitudes may affect criminal proceedings, indicate that McCleskey's claim is not a fanciful product of mere statistical artifact. . . .

The ongoing influence of history is acknowledged, as the majority observes, by our " 'unceasing efforts' to eradicate racial prejudice from our criminal justice system." These efforts, however, signify not the elimination of the problem but its persistence. Our cases reflect a realization of the myriad of opportunities for racial considerations to influence criminal proceedings: in the exercise of peremptory challenges; in the selection of the grand jury; in the selection of the petit jury; in the exercise of prosecutorial discretion; in the conduct of argument; and in the conscious or unconscious bias of jurors. . . .

V.

. . . Warren McCleskey's evidence confronts us with the subtle and persistent influence of the past. His message is a disturbing one to a society that has formally repudiated racism, and a frustrating one to a Nation accustomed to regarding its destiny as the product of its own will. Nonetheless, we ignore him at our peril, for we remain imprisoned by the past as long as we deny its influence in the present.

BLACKMUN, J., joined by Marshall, Stevens, and Brennan, JJ., dissenting.

I.

A

. . . The Court states that it will not infer a discriminatory purpose on the part of the state legislature because "there were legitimate reasons for the Georgia Legislature to adopt and maintain capital punishment."

. . . The Court on numerous occasions during the past century has recognized that an otherwise legitimate basis for a conviction does not outweigh an equal protection violation. In cases where racial discrimination in the administration of the criminal justice system is established, it has held that setting aside the conviction is the appropriate remedy. . . .

B

. . . The Court correctly points out: "In its broadest form, McCleskey's claim of discrimination extends to every actor in the Georgia capital sentencing process, from the prosecutor who sought the death penalty and the jury that imposed the sentence, to the State itself that enacted the capital punishment statute and allows it to remain in effect despite its allegedly discriminatory application." Having recognized the complexity of McCleskey's claim, however, the Court proceeds to ignore a significant element of that claim. . . . [That element is the role of the prosecutor,] the quintessential state actor in a criminal proceeding. . . . I concentrate on the decisions within the prosecutor's office through which the State decided to seek the death penalty and, in particular, the point at which the State proceeded to the penalty phase after conviction. This is the step at which the evidence of the effect of the racial factors was especially strong, but is ignored by the Court.

II.

A

A criminal defendant alleging an equal protection violation must prove the existence of purposeful discrimination. He may establish a prima facie case of purposeful discrimination "by showing that the totality of the relevant facts gives rise to an inference of discriminatory purpose." Once the defendant establishes a prima facie case, the burden shifts to the prosecution to rebut that case. . . .

McCleskey must meet a three-factor standard. First, he must establish that he is a member of a group "that is a recognizable, distinct class, singled out for different treatment." Second, he must make a showing of a substantial degree of differential treatment. Third, he must establish that the allegedly discriminatory procedure is susceptible to abuse or is not racially neutral.

B

There can be no dispute that McCleskey has made the requisite showing under the first prong of the standard. The Baldus study demonstrates that black persons are a distinct group that are singled out for different treatment in the Georgia capital-sentencing system. . . .

With respect to the second prong, McCleskey must prove that there is a substantial likelihood that his death sentence is due to racial factors. The Court of Appeals assumed the validity of the Baldus study and found that it "showed that systemic and substantial disparities existed in the penalties imposed on homicide defendants in Georgia based on the race of homicide victim, that the disparities existed at a less substantial rate in death sentencing based on race of defendants, and that the factors of race of the victim and defendant were at work in Fulton County." The question remaining therefore is at what point does that disparity become constitutionally unacceptable. . . .

McCleskey demonstrated the degree to which his death sentence was affected by racial factors by introducing multiple-regression analyses that explain how much of the statistical distribution of the cases analyzed is attributable to the racial factors. McCleskey established that because he was charged with killing a white person he was 4.3 times as likely to be sentenced to death as he would have been had he been charged with killing a black person. McCleskey also demonstrated that it was more likely than not that the fact that the victim he was charged with killing was white determined that he received a sentence of death — 20 out of every 34 defendants in McCleskey's midrange category would not have been sentenced to be executed if their victims had been black. The most persuasive evidence of the constitutionally significant effect of racial factors in the Georgia capital-sentencing system is McCleskey's proof that the race of the victim is more important in explaining the imposition of a death sentence than is the factor whether the defendant was a prime mover in the homicide.[e] Similarly, the race-of-victim factor is nearly as crucial as the statutory aggravating circumstance whether the defendant had a prior record of a conviction for a capital crime.[f]

The Court has noted elsewhere that Georgia could not attach "the 'aggravating' label to factors that are constitutionally impermissible or totally irrelevant to the sentencing process, such as for example the race, religion, or political affiliation of the defendant." What we have held to be unconstitutional if included in the language of the statute, surely cannot be constitutional because it is a de facto characteristic of the system.

McCleskey produced evidence concerning the role of racial factors at the various steps in the decisionmaking process, focusing on the prosecutor's decision as to which cases merit the death sentence. McCleskey established that the race of the victim is an especially significant factor at the point where the defendant has been convicted of murder and the prosecutor must choose whether to proceed to the penalty phase of the trial and create the possibility that a death sentence may be imposed or to accept the imposition of a sentence of life imprisonment. McCleskey demonstrated this effect at both the statewide level and in Fulton County where he was tried and sentenced. The statewide statistics indicated that black defendant/white victim cases advanced to the penalty trial at nearly five times the rate of the black defendant/black victim cases (70% vs. 15%), and over three times the rate of white defendant/black victim cases (70% vs. 19%). . . .

As to the final element of the prima facie case, McCleskey showed that the process by which the State decided to seek a death penalty in his case and to pursue that sentence throughout the prosecution was susceptible to abuse. . . .

[A]t every stage of a prosecution, the Assistant District Attorney exercised much discretion. . . . In addition to this showing that the challenged system was susceptible to abuse, McCleskey presented evidence of the history of prior discrimination in the Georgia system. . . . This historical background of the state action challenged "is one evidentiary source" in this equal protection case. . . . [McCleskey's] showing is of sufficient magnitude that, absent evidence to the contrary, one must conclude that racial factors entered into the decisionmaking process that yielded McCleskey's

---

e. A defendant's chances of receiving a death sentence increase by a factor of 4.3 if the victim is white, but only by 2.3 if the defendant was the prime mover behind the homicide.

f. A prior record of a conviction for murder, armed robbery, rape, or kidnapping with bodily injury increases the chances of a defendant's receiving a death sentence by a factor of 4.9. . . .

death sentence. . . . [The state] must demonstrate that legitimate racially neutral criteria and procedures yielded this racially skewed result. . . .

III.

The Court's explanations for its failure to apply this well-established equal protection analysis to this case are not persuasive. . . .

I disagree with the Court's assertion that there are fewer variables relevant to the decisions of jury commissioners or prosecutors in their selection of jurors, or to the decisions of employers in their selection, promotion, or discharge of employees. Such decisions involve a multitude of factors, some rational, some irrational. Second, I disagree with the comment that the venire-selection and employment decisions are "made by fewer entities." Certainly in the employment context, personnel decisions are often the product of several levels of decisionmaking within the business or government structure. The Court's statement that the decision to impose death is made by the petit jury also disregards the fact that the prosecutor screens the cases throughout the pretrial proceedings and decides to seek the death penalty and to pursue a capital case to the penalty phase where a death sentence can be imposed. McCleskey's claim in this regard lends itself to analysis under the framework we apply in assessing challenges to other prosecutorial actions. . . .

IV.

A

One of the final concerns discussed by the Court may be the most disturbing aspect of its opinion. Granting relief to McCleskey in this case, it is said, could lead to further constitutional challenges. That, of course, is no reason to deny McCleskey his rights under the Equal Protection Clause. If a grant of relief to him were to lead to a closer examination of the effects of racial considerations throughout the criminal-justice system, the system, and hence society, might benefit. . . .

[A dissenting opinion by Justice Stevens, joined by Justice Blackmun, is omitted.]

Note that even successful equal protection challenges always lend themselves to at least two formally adequate remedies. Assuming that *A* at the outset is treated better than *B,* the remedy could be either to give *B* what *A* now gets or to reduce *A*'s benefits to the level of *B*'s. What should the remedy have been if McCleskey's claim of unequal treatment had been upheld? However you might treat the case of the particular complainant, Warren McCleskey (who was ultimately executed by Georgia in 1991), what more general changes in Georgia's death penalty process might have emerged from a victory by McCleskey?

The lawyers pressing McCleskey's claim were associated with the NAACP Legal Defense Fund, which is strongly opposed to capital punishment. They would surely have sought an overall reduction in the use of the death penalty. But consider the following comment by Randall Kennedy:[136]

136. McCleskey v. Kemp: Race, Capital Punishment, and the Supreme Court, 101 Harv. L. Rev. 1388, 1394 (1988).

My critique of McCleskey v. Kemp does not proceed from abolitionist premises. Rather, it seeks to delineate a response to race-of-the-victim disparities that vindicate the claims of racial justice — with or without capital punishment. I am more concerned with the plight of black communities whose welfare is slighted by criminal justice systems that respond more forcefully to the killing of whites than the killing of blacks than I am concerned with the plight of murderers, black or white. McCleskey understandably portrayed the case in a defendant-oriented fashion. I portray the case, by contrast, in a community-oriented fashion. I conceptualize *McCleskey* as an instance of racial inequality in the provision of public goods. Whereas other cases have involved the racially unequal provision of street lights, sidewalks and sewers, *McCleskey* involves racial inequality in the provision of a peculiar sort of public good — capital sentencing.

Note: Racial Profiling and the Equal Protection Clause

Numerous statistical studies comparing the percentage of minority motorists stopped and searched in comparison to the percentage of White motorists similarly treated strongly suggest that police throughout the United States use traffic violations as a pretext for stopping and searching motor vehicles driven by minorities.[137] This phenomenon, sometimes called "racial profiling," is often colloquially referred to as the "offense" of "driving while black." In 1995 the Maryland Police Department entered into a consent decree promising to end traffic stops on Interstate 95 based on race, but the practice apparently continues.[138] Similar studies in New Jersey and other states confirm the basic trend.[139] The Fourth Amendment protects people from unreasonable searches and seizures. Nevertheless, the Supreme Court has held that the subjective motivations of a police officer who stops an automobile are irrelevant to the legality of the stop. The only question is whether the officer had probable cause to believe that a violation of law had occurred. In Whren v. United States, 517 U.S. 806 (1996), defendants argued that because police can almost always find an excuse to stop a car for a traffic violation, police will be "tempt[ed] to use traffic stops as a means of investigating other law violations, as to which no probable cause or even articulable suspicion exists," and to stop motorists based on "impermissible factors, such as the race of the car's occupants." They argued that the Fourth Amendment test for traffic

---

137. See Jennifer A. Larrabee, "DWB (Driving While Black)" and Equal Protection: The Realities of an Unconstitutional Police Practice, 6 J. L. & Pol'y 291 (1997); Angela J. Davis, Race, Cops and Traffic Stops, 51 U. Miami L. Rev. 425, 441 (1997).

138. See Paul W. Valentine, Maryland Settles Lawsuit Over Racial Profiles; Police Allegedly Targeted Minorities for Searches, Wash. Post, Jan. 5, 1995, at B1; Michael Schneider, State Police I-95 Drug Unit Found to Search Black Motorists Four Times More Often Than White: Analysis Raises Questions About Trooper Procedures, Baltimore Sun, May 23, 1996, at 2B.

139. For example

In New Jersey, 75% of drivers stopped for investigation on portions of the New Jersey Turnpike are African-Americans and Latinos, yet this group only makes up 13.5% of the annual drivers on the Turnpike. Minority drivers traveling through the suburbs of Texas' major cities are twice as likely to receive tickets for traffic violations than are white drivers. On portions of Interstate 95 in Maryland, 71% of the motorists stopped and searched in the first nine months of 1995 were African-Americans. In one Florida county, 62% of the drivers stopped were minorities, and on an interstate in Colorado, 190 of 200 stops "targeted minorities." These statistics clearly indicate that minorities are disproportionately being stopped by police. The inference to be drawn from this is that police are using race as a factor in deciding whom to stop for traffic violations.

Larrabee, at 297-298.

stops should not be "whether probable cause existed to justify the stop; but rather, whether a police officer, acting reasonably, would have made the stop for the reason given." The Court in a unanimous opinion by Justice Scalia, rejected this test.

> [Our previous] cases foreclose any argument that the constitutional reasonableness of traffic stops depends on the actual motivations of the individual officers involved. We of course agree with petitioners that the Constitution prohibits selective enforcement of the law based on considerations such as race. But the constitutional basis for objecting to intentionally discriminatory application of laws is the Equal Protection Clause, not the Fourth Amendment. Subjective intentions play no role in ordinary, probable-cause Fourth Amendment analysis.

In United States v. Armstrong, 517 U.S. 456 (1996), the Supreme Court stated that in order to prove a selective prosecution claim under the Equal Protection Clause, the claimant

> must demonstrate that the . . . prosecutorial policy "had a discriminatory effect and that it was motivated by a discriminatory purpose." To establish a discriminatory effect in a race case, the claimant must show that similarly situated individuals of a different race were not prosecuted.

To establish the right to discovery in a selective prosecution case a criminal defendant must "produce some evidence that similarly situated defendants of other races could have been prosecuted, but were not."

In the context of racial profiling, does this mean that it is not enough to show that blacks were disproportionately stopped for traffic violations, but that the plaintiff must also show that whites who violated the traffic laws were not stopped? Most statistics on traffic stops describe the racial distribution for persons who were stopped, but not the percentages for those who violated the traffic laws but were not stopped.[140] Does this mean that existing statistics alone cannot succeed in a racial profiling case under the Equal Protection Clause? Or should courts treat cases of selective prosecution differently from the case of selective traffic stops? Note that in *Armstrong* the Supreme Court specifically reserved judgment on the question "whether a defendant must satisfy the similarly situated requirement in a case 'involving direct admissions by [prosecutors] of discriminatory purpose.'" How likely are police officers to admit that they stop motorists on the basis of their race?

---

140. In *Armstrong* the Supreme Court specifically rejected the view

> that a defendant may establish a colorable basis for discriminatory effect without evidence that the Government has failed to prosecute others who are similarly situated to the defendant. . . . The Court of Appeals reached [this] decision in part because it started "with the presumption that people of all races commit all types of crimes — not with the premise that any type of crime is the exclusive province of any particular racial or ethnic group." It cited no authority for this proposition, which seems contradicted by the most recent statistics of the United States Sentencing Commission. Those statistics show: More than 90% of the persons sentenced in 1994 for crack cocaine trafficking were black; 93.4% of convicted LSD dealers were white; and 91% of those convicted for pornography or prostitution were white. Presumptions at war with presumably reliable statistics have no proper place in the analysis of this issue.

> Is there reason to believe that blacks and other minorities commit traffic offenses more often than whites?

Does racial profiling of persons of Arab or Middle Eastern descent in the wake of 9/11 present different constitutional problems than racial profiling of blacks and Latinos? Consider the following contrasting claims:

1. The events of 9/11 should have no effect on the constitutional analysis of the issues because racial profiling is unconstitutional in any case. It is not as effective a law enforcement tool as people think, it is likely to be abused, it associates group membership with criminality (or reinforces existing associations), and it helps further the subordination of social groups on the basis of their race or ethnicity. What has happened to blacks and Latinos in the past will now be visited upon on people of Middle Eastern descent and people with Muslim names. Officials and the general public will be unlikely to understand the differences between different ethnic groups and religions. For example, police officers may harass male members of the Sikh religion who wear turbans even though they are not Muslims and come from countries having no connection to the events of 9/11. Moreover, by focusing attention on people who are of Middle Eastern descent, racial profiling tends to direct attention away from whites like Timothy McVeigh or John Walker Lindh. Even though the Oklahoma City bombing was one of the most serious terrorist incidents in American history, it is unlikely that police officers will begin to profile young disaffected white veterans.

2. Racial profiling is an effective constitutional tool of law enforcement whose rationality has been confirmed by the events of 9/11. In this sense 9/11 should have no effect on the constitutional analysis of the issues, but critics of racial profiling should now think twice about their prior criticisms of it.

In this context, consider the remarks made by the political comedian and satirist Al Franken at the National Press Club in Washington, DC on February 28, 2002:[141]

> I don't understand the reluctance to profile young Arab men. . . . The way I look at it is if it had been 19 Jewish comedians on September 11th who had done that, . . . and I'm in line to get on the plane, and they go, "Mr. Franken, we need to talk to you — you are a Jewish comedian." I'd say, "Thank you — please check my butt," you know — (laughter) — "and while you're at it, will you check Mr. Seinfeld's?" . . . I have been traveling a lot, and I do meet young Arab men who say, "Yeah, you know, sure — I feel better." So I don't understand why a 30-year-old mother with two kids in a stroller [is] put through the kind of delays, and people who sort of fit — I hate to say it — the profile of a hijacker aren't necessarily randomly pulled over. And that may be controversial, but I think it's kind of common sense.

3. The case of racial profiling against blacks and Latinos differs in important respects from the post-9/11 racial profiling that might be used against persons of Arab and Middle Eastern nationality or descent, because:

(a)   The offenses and harms that racial profiling might be used for are much more serious and pose a much greater threat to the country. The use or sale of illegal drugs is simply not in the same category as acts of terrorism.

(b)   The way race is constructed is different in the two cases. Post-9/11 racial profiling constructs those profiled as a dangerous foreign other. Racial profiling

---

141. See *http://home.hawaii.rr.com/snlcn/franken/npc1.html* (last visited June 24, 2002).

robs Arab-Americans of their American identity and reinforces the idea that to be American is to be white. How is this different from the construction of Latino or Asian racial identity? Assuming that such racial profiling is importantly different from the racial profiling used against African-Americans, how should it affect the constitutional analysis?

Conversely, because foreignness is at issue, racial profiling allows (for example) Arab Americans to demonstrate their patriotism and loyalty by voluntarily submitting to inspections, which distinguishes their situation from that of African-Americans, who do not symbolically establish their law-abidingness by allowing their cars to be searched by police officers. Even if this suggested difference is plausible, how should it affect the constitutional question?

(c)   Racial profiling on the basis of Arab and Middle Eastern descent is different because it necessarily presents two different situations constitutionally: It is based on country of origin as well as race. Some people who will be adversely affected by the profiling will be American citizens, but many others will be aliens. As discussed infra, although distinctions based on alienage by state officials are often subject to strict scrutiny, distinctions based on alienage by federal officials are subject only to a test of rationality. Is this significantly different from the problem involved in the Japanese internment cases? Does this mean that racial profiling by state officials should be viewed with greater concern than profiling by federal officials?

For a discussion of some of the constitutional and policy issues of profiling, see Albert W. Alschuler, Racial Profiling and the Constitution, 2002 U. Chi. Legal F. 163 (2002); Leti Volpp, The Citizen and the Terrorist, 49 UCLA L. Rev. 1575 (2002).

5.   *Repeals or Limitations of Civil Rights Laws and Remedies*

HUNTER v. ERICKSON
393 U.S. 385 (1969)

[Most ordinances adopted by the City Council of Akron, Ohio, become effective 30 days after passage, subject to repeal by referendum initiated by 10 percent of the voters. Section 137 of the Akron City Charter provided for a special procedure for ordinances regulating the sale and leasing of real property "on the basis of race, color, religion, national origin or ancestry": They became effective only if approved by a majority of the electors voting at a general or special election. The Court held that Section 137 violated the Equal Protection Clause.]

WHITE, J. . . . .

[Section 137 makes] an explicitly racial classification treating racial housing matters differently from other racial and housing matters. . . .

Only laws to end housing discrimination based on "race, color, religion, national origin or ancestry" must run §137's gauntlet. It is true that the section draws no distinctions among racial and religious groups. Negroes and whites, Jews and Catholics are all subject to the same requirements if there is housing discrimination against them which they wish to end. But §137 nevertheless disadvantages those who would benefit from laws barring racial, religious, or ancestral discriminations as against those who would bar other discriminations or who would otherwise regulate the real estate market in their favor. The automatic referendum system does not reach housing discrimination on sexual or political grounds, or against those with children or dogs, nor does it affect tenants seeking more heat or better maintenance from landlords, nor those seeking rent control, urban renewal, public housing, or new building codes.

Moreover, although the law on its face treats Negro and white, Jew and gentile in an identical manner, the reality is that the law's impact falls on the minority. The majority needs no protection against discrimination and if it did, a referendum might be bothersome but no more than that. Like the law requiring specification of candidates' race on the ballot, Anderson v. Martin, 375 U.S 399 (1964), §137 places special burdens on racial minorities within the governmental process. This is no more permissible than denying them the vote, on an equal basis with others. . . .

Because the core of the Fourteenth Amendment is the prevention of meaningful and unjustified official distinctions based on race, racial classifications are "constitutionally suspect," and subject to the "most rigid scrutiny." They "bear a far heavier burden of justification" than other classifications.

We are unimpressed with any of Akron's justifications for its discrimination. Characterizing it simply as a public decision to move slowly in the delicate area of race relations emphasizes the impact and burden of §137, but does not justify it. The amendment was unnecessary either to implement a decision to go slowly, or to allow the people of Akron to participate in that decision. . . . Even though Akron might have proceeded by majority vote at town meeting on all its municipal legislation, it has instead chosen a more complex system. Having done so, the State may no more disadvantage any particular group by making it more difficult to enact legislation in its behalf than it may dilute any person's vote or give any group a smaller representation than another of comparable size.

We hold that §137 discriminates against minorities, and constitutes a real, substantial, and invidious denial of the equal protection of the laws.

HARLAN, J., joined by Stewart, J., concurring. . . .

Most laws which define the structure of political institutions . . . are designed with the aim of providing a just framework within which the diverse political groups in our society may fairly compete and are not enacted with the purpose of assisting one particular group in its struggle with its political opponents. Consider, for example, Akron's procedure which requires that almost any ordinance be submitted to a general referendum if 10% of the electorate signs an appropriate petition. This rule obviously does not have the purpose of protecting one particular group to the detriment of all others. It will sometimes operate in favor of one faction; sometimes in favor of another. Akron has adopted the referendum system because its citizens believe that whenever an action of the City Council raises the emotional opposition of *any* significant group in the community, the people should have a right to decide the matter directly. Statutes of this type, which are grounded upon general democratic principle, do not violate the Equal Protection Clause simply because they occasionally operate to disadvantage Negro political interests. If a governmental institution is to be fair, one group cannot always be expected to win. If the Council's fair housing legislation were defeated at a referendum, Negroes would undoubtedly lose an important political battle, but they would not thereby be denied equal protection. . . .

In the case before us, however, the city of Akron has not attempted to allocate governmental power on the basis of any general principle. Here we have a provision that has the clear purpose of making it more difficult for certain racial and religious minorities to achieve legislation that is in their interest. Since the charter amendment is discriminatory on its face, Akron must "bear a far heavier burden of justification" than is required in the normal case. McLaughlin v. Florida, 379 U.S. 184, 194 (1964). And Akron has failed to sustain this burden. The city's principal argument in support of the charter amendment relies on the undisputed fact that fair housing legislation may often be expected to raise the passions of the community to their highest pitch. It was not necessary, however, to pass this amendment in order to assure that particularly sensitive issues will ultimately be decided by the general electorate. Akron has already provided a procedure, which is grounded in neutral principle, that requires a general referendum on this issue if 10% of the voters insist. If the prospect of fair housing legislation really arouses passionate opposition, the voters will have the final say. Consequently, the charter amendment will have its real impact only when fair housing does *not* arouse extraordinary controversy. This being the case, I can perceive no legitimate state interest which in any degree vindicates the action taken by the City here.

As I read the Court's opinion to be entirely consistent with the basic principles which I believe control this case, I join in it.

[A dissenting opinion by Justice Black is omitted.]

Discussion

1. Does Section 137 classify on the basis of race? If not, should it be treated as suspect? Suppose that Section 137 applied to ordinances dealing with a number of controversial subjects besides civil rights. Would the treatment of laws regulating discrimination in the sale and leasing of property still constitute a "racial classification" in *Hunter's* sense? Formulate a general principle that justifies *Hunter* and that is otherwise consistent with relevant existing judicial doctrine.

2. The Court relied on *Hunter* in Washington v. Seattle School District No. 1, 458 U.S. 457 (1982). In 1978, after the implementation of a mandatory busing plan to reduce de facto school desegregation, 66 percent of the voters of the State of Washington approved Initiative 350, which provided that "no school board . . . shall directly or indirectly require any student to attend a school other than the school which is geographically nearest or next nearest the student's place of residence. . . ." Several school districts that had noncomplying desegregation plans challenged Initiative 350 under the Equal Protection Clause. Justice Blackmun's majority opinion held that Initiative 350 violated the Equal Protection Clause:

"[T]he political majority may generally restructure the political process to place obstacles in the path of everyone seeking to secure the benefits of governmental action. But a different analysis is required when the State allocates governmental power non-neutrally, by explicitly using *racial* nature of a decision to determine the decisionmaking process. [D]espite its facial neutrality there is little doubt that the initiative was effectively drawn for racial purposes. . . . Proponents of the initiative candidly "represented that there would be no loss of school district flexibility other than in busing for desegregation purposes." . . . Initiative 350 in fact allows school districts to bus their students "for most, if not all," of the non-integrative purposes required by their educational policies.

[T]he United States — which has changed its position during the course of this litigation, and now supports the State — maintains that busing for integration, unlike the fair housing ordinance involved in *Hunter,* is not a peculiarly "racial" issue at all. Again, we are not persuaded. It undoubtedly is true . . . that the proponents of mandatory integration cannot be classified by race: Negroes and whites may be counted among both the supporters and the opponents of Initiative 350. And it should be equally clear that white as well as Negro children benefit from exposure to "ethnic and racial diversity in the classroom." But neither of these factors serves to distinguish *Hunter,* for we may fairly assume that members of the racial majority both favored and benefited from Akron's fair housing ordinance. For present purposes, it is enough that minorities may consider busing for integration to be "legislation that is in their interest." Given the racial focus of Initiative 350, this suffices to trigger application of the *Hunter* doctrine.

[T]he practical effect of Initiative 350 is to work a reallocation of power of the kind condemned in *Hunter.* The initiative removes the authority to address a racial problem — and only a racial problem — from the existing decisionmaking body, in such a way as to burden minority interests. Those favoring the elimination of de facto school segregation now must seek relief from the state legislature, or from the statewide electorate. Yet authority over all other student assignment decisions, as well as over most other areas of educational policy, remains vested in the local school board. . . . As in *Hunter,* then, the community's political mechanisms are modified to place effective decisionmaking authority over a racial issue at a different level of government.

In response to the argument that *Hunter* was really a disparate impact case that had been overruled by Washington v. Davis, Justice Blackmun explained:

While decisions such as Washington v. Davis . . . considered classifications facially unrelated to race, the charter amendment at issue in *Hunter* dealt in explicitly racial terms with legislation designed to benefit minorities "as minorities," not legislation intended to benefit some larger group of underprivileged citizens among whom minorities were disproportionately represented. This does not mean, of course, that every attempt to address a racial issue gives rise to an impermissible racial classification. But when the political process or the decisionmaking mechanism used to *address* racially conscious legislation — and only such legislation — is singled out for peculiar and disadvantageous treatment, the governmental action plainly "rests on 'distinctions based on race.'" And when the State's allocation of power places unusual burdens on the ability of racial groups to enact legislation specifically designed to overcome the "special condition" of prejudice, the governmental action seriously "curtail[s] the operation of those political processes ordinarily to be relied upon to protect minorities." United States v. Carolene Products Co., 304 U.S. 144, 152-153, n.4 (1938). In a most direct sense, this implicates the judiciary's special role in safeguarding the interests of those groups that are "relegated to such a position of political powerlessness as to command extraordinary protection from the majoritarian political process."

Justice Powell dissented, joined by Chief Justice Burger, and Justices Rehnquist and O'Connor. He noted that Initiative 350 concerned only de facto segregation not prohibited by the Equal Protection Clause, and that the Initiative was neutral on its face, "and racially neutral as public policy," because "children of all races benefit from neighborhood schooling."

In this case, unlike in *Hunter*, the political system has *not* been redrawn or altered. The authority of the State over the public school system, acting through Initiative or the legislature, is plenary. Thus, the State's political system is not altered when it adopts for the first time a policy, concededly within the area of its authority, for the regulation of local school districts. And certainly racial minorities are not uniquely or comparatively burdened by the State's adoption of a policy that would be lawful if adopted by any School District in the State.

In Crawford v. Los Angeles Board of Education, 458 U.S. 527 (1982), decided the same day, the Court, with only Justice Marshall dissenting, upheld a California proposition, passed by referendum, that barred state courts from using busing as a remedy for school segregation that was illegal under state, but not federal, law. (The California Constitution had been interpreted to prohibit de facto segregation.) Justice Blackmun, joined by Justice Brennan, concurred in order to explain that "State courts do not create the rights they enforce; those rights originate elsewhere — in the state legislature, in the State's political subdivisions, or in the state constitution itself. When one of those rights is repealed, and therefore is rendered unenforceable by the courts, that action can hardly be said to restructure the State's decisionmaking mechanism. While the California electorate may have made it more difficult to achieve desegregation when it enacted Proposition I, [it] did so not by working a structural change in the political *process* so much as by simply repealing the right to invoke a judicial busing remedy."

G. "Preferential" Treatment for Racial Minorities

1. The Bakke Case

The "suspect classification" doctrine, treating racial classification as presumptively unconstitutional, was developed in response to discrimination against the members of minority groups that were the objects of hostility and prejudice. In Strauder v. West Virginia, 100 U.S. 303 (1880), Justice Strong suggested, "If . . . a law should be enacted excluding all white men from jury service, . . . we apprehend that no one would be heard to claim that it would not be a denial of the equal protection of the laws. Nor if a law should be passed excluding all naturalized Celtic Irishmen, would there be any doubt of its inconsistency with the spirit of the amendment." But until several decades after *Brown* the Court had no occasion to consider the permissibility of race-dependent decisions designed to benefit rather than disadvantage the members of minorities who had been subject to prior discrimination.

The Court first addressed these issues in United States v. Montgomery County Board of Education, 395 U.S. 225 (1969), and Swann v. Charlotte-Mecklenburg Board of Education, 402 U.S. 1 (1971), where it cautiously approved of the race-conscious assignment of teachers and pupils to remedy deeply entrenched patterns of state-mandated segregation. Whatever political and constitutional problems these remedies engendered, they were not generally perceived as selectively burdening the members of one race, but rather as imposing burdens and granting benefits to minorities and nonminorities alike.

In DeFunis v. Odegaard, 416 U.S. 312 (1974), petitioner, who had been denied admission to the University of Washington Law School, challenged the school's preferential admissions program, claiming a violation of equal protection, but the Court held the controversy moot because the petitioner, who had been ordered admitted by a lower court, was nearing graduation.

Four years later, in University of California Regents v. Bakke, 438 U.S. 265 (1978), the Court finally considered the constitutionality of state affirmative action programs.[142]

REGENTS OF THE UNIVERSITY OF CALIFORNIA v. BAKKE, 438 U.S. 265 (1978): The University of California at Davis Medical School instituted a special affirmative action program in 1973 and 1974 that set aside 16 seats out of 100 for "economically and/or educationally disadvantaged" applicants and members of a "minority group," which included blacks, Chicanos, Asians, and American Indians. In 1974 the special program was reserved only for minority students. Candidates whose undergraduate GPA fellow below 2.5 were automatically rejected from the regular program but not the special program. Special admissions candidates were not rated against general applicants, but could be rejected for failure to meet certain requirements. Alan Bakke, a white male whose application was considered under the general admissions program, was denied admission in 1973 and 1974. In both years, applicants were admitted under the special program with "significantly lower" scores than Bakke. Bakke sued the university, arguing that its policy violated both the Equal Protection Clause of the Fourteenth Amendment and Title VI of the Civil Rights Act of 1964, which provides that "No person in the United States shall, on the ground of race, color, or national origin, be excluded from participation in, be denied the benefits of, or be subjected to discrimination under any program or activity receiving Federal financial assistance." The Medical School admitted that it could not prove that Bakke would not have been admitted in the absence of the special program.

Justice Powell, in a judgment concurred in by Chief Justice Burger, and Justices Stewart, Rehnquist, and Stevens affirmed the Supreme Court of California's judgment that Davis's "special admissions program [is] unlawful and . . . that [Bakke] be admitted to the Medical School." In a judgment concurred in by Justices Brennan, White, Marshall, and Blackmun, Justice Powell also overturned the California Supreme Court's "judgment enjoining petitioner from according any consideration to race in its admissions process." There was no majority opinion, but Justice Powell's separate opinion was for many years widely viewed as stating the law.

---

142. Several of the cases in this section present issues under civil rights statutes (for example, Titles VI and VII of the Civil Rights Act of 1964) as well as under the Constitution. In the eyes of most of the Justices, the statutory and constitutional demands largely coincide; but for at least some of the Justices, with respect to certain issues, they may diverge. The underlying issues of justice and public policy are, in any event, identical, and we suggest that you read the cases with a defeasible presumption that the doctrines are congruent.

"Affirmative action" programs have been variously called "preferential treatment," and "reverse discrimination." Each term has strong political and emotional connotations and each entails its own set of assumptions about history, society, and political morality. The term "affirmative action," generally favored by such programs' political supporters, first emerged in a series of executive orders by Presidents Kennedy and Johnson. On the history of affirmative action, see, e.g., Carl E. Brody, Jr., A Historical Review of Affirmative Action and the Interpretation of Its Legislative Intent by the Supreme Court, 29 Akron L. Rev. 291 (1996); James E. Jones, Jr., The Origins of Affirmative Action, 21 U.C. Davis L. Rev. 383 (1988); Robert J. Weiss, "We Want Jobs": A History of Affirmative Action (1997).

Justice Powell's opinion raised three issues that would prove important in later debates over affirmative action: (1) what was the appropriate level of scrutiny, (2) what constituted a sufficiently compelling interest to justify affirmative action, and (3) how states could prove that they met the appropriate standard of scrutiny.

Powell argued that the right to equal protection was an individual right; therefore it "cannot mean one thing when applied to one individual and something else when applied to a person of another color. If both are not accorded the same protection, then it is not equal." Hence he rejected the argument that strict scrutiny did not apply to the special admissions program because "because white males, such as respondent, are not a 'discrete and insular minority' requiring extraordinary protection from the majoritarian political process." Although Powell conceded that the Fourteenth Amendment was originally concerned with the promotion of freedom and equality for blacks, "it was no longer possible to peg the guarantees of the Fourteenth Amendment to the struggle for equality of one racial minority" because "the United States had become a Nation of minorities[,] [e]ach [of which] had to struggle — and to some extent struggles still — to overcome the prejudices not of a monolithic majority, but of a 'majority' composed of various minority groups of whom it was said — perhaps unfairly in many cases — that a shared characteristic was a willingness to disadvantage other groups."

Powell rejected a "two-class theory," arguing that

> the difficulties entailed in varying the level of judicial review according to a perceived "preferred" status of a particular racial or ethnic minority are intractable [because] the concepts of "majority" and "minority" necessarily reflect temporary arrangements and political judgments. . . . [T]he white "majority" itself is composed of various minority groups, most of which can lay claim to a history of prior discrimination at the hands of the State and private individuals. Not all of these groups can receive preferential treatment and corresponding judicial tolerance of distinctions drawn in terms of race and nationality, for then the only "majority" left would be a new minority of white Anglo-Saxon Protestants. There is no principled basis for deciding which groups would merit "heightened judicial solicitude" and which would not. Courts would be asked to evaluate the extent of the prejudice and consequent harm suffered by various minority groups. Those whose societal injury is thought to exceed some arbitrary level of tolerability then would be entitled to preferential classifications at the expense of individuals belonging to other groups. Those classifications would be free from exacting judicial scrutiny. As these preferences began to have their desired effect, and the consequences of past discrimination were undone, new judicial rankings would be necessary. The kind of variable sociological and political analysis necessary to produce such rankings simply does not lie within the judicial competence — even if they otherwise were politically feasible and socially desirable.

Justice Powell argued that preferences may not always be benign, that "preferential programs may only reinforce common stereotypes holding that certain groups are unable to achieve success without special protection based on a factor having no relationship to individual worth," and that "there is a measure of inequity in forcing innocent persons in respondent's position to bear the burdens of redressing grievances not of their making."

> By hitching the meaning of the Equal Protection Clause to these transitory considerations, we would be holding, as a constitutional principle, that judicial scrutiny of classifications touching on racial and ethnic background may vary with the ebb and flow of

political forces. Disparate constitutional tolerance of such classifications well may serve
to exacerbate racial and ethnic antagonisms rather than alleviate them. Also, the muta-
bility of a constitutional principle, based upon shifting political and social judgments,
undermines the chances for consistent application of the Constitution from one
generation to the next. . . .

Hence, Powell concluded, "When [political judgments] touch upon an individual's race or ethnic background, he is entitled to a judicial determination that the
burden he is asked to bear on that basis is precisely tailored to serve a compelling
governmental interest."

Powell next asked what interests were sufficiently compelling to meet the standard of strict scrutiny. Attempting to increase the number of minority physicians
for its own sake was an illegitimate interest, and Davis had not shown that its affirmative action program would "increas[e] the number of physicians who will practice in communities currently underserved."

Davis also argued that it could engage in affirmative action to "counter[] the
effects of societal discrimination." Powell conceded that "[t]he State certainly has
a legitimate and substantial interest in ameliorating, or eliminating where feasible, the disabling effects of identified discrimination." However, Powell distinguished between "redress[ing] the wrongs worked by specific instances of racial
discrimination" and "remedying of the effects of 'societal discrimination,' an
amorphous concept of injury that may be ageless in its reach into the past." "We
have never approved a classification that aids persons perceived as members of
relatively victimized groups at the expense of other innocent individuals in the
absence of judicial, legislative, or administrative findings of constitutional or
statutory violations."

The Regents had not made findings of past discrimination, nor were they the
proper body to do so, because their "broad mission is education, not the formulation of any legislative policy or the adjudication of particular claims of illegality. . . .
[I]solated segments of our vast governmental structures are not competent to make
those decisions, at least in the absence of legislative mandates and legislatively determined criteria. Before relying upon these sorts of findings in establishing a racial
classification, a governmental body must have the authority and capability to establish, in the record, that the classification is responsive to identified discrimination."

By contrast, Justice Powell agreed that "the attainment of a diverse student body
. . . clearly is a constitutionally permissible goal for an institution of higher education. Academic freedom, though not a specifically enumerated constitutional right,
long has been viewed as a special concern of the First Amendment. The freedom of
a university to make its own judgments as to education includes the selection of its
student body." "[T]he right to select those students who will contribute the most to
the 'robust exchange of ideas,' . . . invokes a countervailing constitutional interest,
that of the First Amendment." Powell concluded that diversity is "of paramount
importance" to the University's mission; hence it is "compelling in the context of a
university's admissions program."

Even so, Powell argued that setting aside a specified number of seats was not an
appropriate means to achieve the goal of diversity. He pointed to Harvard College's
admissions program as proof that "assignment of a fixed number of places to a
minority group is not a necessary means toward [educational diversity]."
In Harvard's program "race or ethnic background may be deemed a 'plus' in a

particular applicant's file, yet it does not insulate the individual from comparison with all other candidates for the available seats." It "consider[s] all pertinent elements of diversity in light of the particular qualifications of each applicant," and "treats each applicant as an individual in the admissions process. The applicant who loses out on the last available seat to another candidate receiving a 'plus' on the basis of ethnic background will not have been foreclosed from all consideration for that seat simply because he was not the right color or had the wrong surname. It would mean only that his combined qualifications, which may have included similar nonobjective factors, did not outweigh those of the other applicant. His qualifications would have been weighed fairly and competitively, and he would have no basis to complain of unequal treatment under the Fourteenth Amendment."

The Davis program, by contrast, "tells applicants who are not Negro, Asian, or Chicano that they are totally excluded from a specific percentage of the seats in an entering class. No matter how strong their qualifications, quantitative and extracurricular, including their own potential for contribution to educational diversity, they are never afforded the chance to compete with applicants from the preferred groups for the special admissions seats. At the same time, the preferred applicants have the opportunity to compete for every seat in the class."

Because the University "conceded that it could not carry its burden of proving that, but for the existence of its unlawful special admissions program, [Bakke] still would not have been admitted," Powell concluded that Bakke should be admitted to the medical school.

Justice Brennan, joined by Justices White, Marshall, and Blackmun, dissented. They argued that the strict scrutiny normally accorded racial classifications was inappropriate. Whites as a group lacked the "traditional indicia of suspectness: the class is not saddled with such disabilities, or subjected to such a history of purposeful unequal treatment, or relegated to such a position of political powerlessness as to command extraordinary protection from the majoritarian political process." They argued that "racial classifications designed to further remedial purposes 'must serve important governmental objectives and must be substantially related to achievement of those objectives.' " Some degree of scrutiny is necessary because "the line between honest and thoughtful appraisal of the effects of past discrimination and paternalistic stereotyping is not so clear. . . . State programs designed ostensibly to ameliorate the effects of past racial discrimination obviously create the same hazard of stigma, since they may promote racial separatism and reinforce the views of those who believe that members of racial minorities are inherently incapable of succeeding on their own." Moreover, "the most 'discrete and insular' of whites [may] be called upon to bear the immediate, direct costs of benign discrimination. . . .[B]ecause of the significant risk that racial classifications established for ostensibly benign purposes can be misused, causing effects not unlike those created by invidious classifications," rational basis review is inappropriate. "Instead, to justify such a classification an important and articulated purpose for its use must be shown. In addition, any statute must be stricken that stigmatizes any group or that singles out those least well represented in the political process to bear the brunt of a benign program."

Brennan argued that "Davis' articulated purpose of remedying the effects of past societal discrimination is . . . sufficiently important to justify the use of race-conscious admissions programs where there is a sound basis for concluding that minority underrepresentation is substantial and chronic, and that the handicap of past discrimination is impeding access of minorities to the Medical School."

Requiring "a judicial determination of a constitutional or statutory violation as a predicate for race-conscious remedial actions would be self-defeating," and "would severely undermine efforts to achieve voluntary compliance with the requirements of law." Brennan criticized Powell's view that the Regents were not authorized to make findings of past discrimination: "Generally, the manner in which a State chooses to delegate governmental functions is for it to decide. California, by constitutional provision, has chosen to place authority over the operation of the University of California in the Board of Regents. Control over the University is to be found not in the legislature, but rather in the Regents who had been vested with full legislative (including policymaking), administrative, and adjudicative powers by the citizens of California."

Brennan concluded that "a state government may adopt race-conscious programs if the purpose of such programs is to remove the disparate racial impact its actions might otherwise have and if there is reason to believe that the disparate impact is itself the product of past discrimination, whether its own or that of society at large. There is no question that Davis' program is valid under this test."

Race-neutral alternatives, Brennan argued, would not be sufficient to remedy the effects of past discrimination that had produced a dearth of minority doctors. "With respect to any factor (such as poverty or family educational background) that may be used as a substitute for race as an indicator of past discrimination, whites greatly outnumber racial minorities simply because whites make up a far larger percentage of the total population and therefore far outnumber minorities in absolute terms at every socio-economic level."

Finally, Brennan argued that the Harvard plan touted by Powell was not more constitutionally palatable than Davis's set aside: One still had to decide the degree of preference, and it will result in the exclusion of some white candidates. "Furthermore, the extent of the preference inevitably depends on how many minority applicants the particular school is seeking to admit in any particular year. It may be that the Harvard plan is more acceptable to the public than is the Davis 'quota.' If it is, any State, including California, is free to adopt it in preference to a less acceptable alternative, just as it is generally free, as far as the Constitution is concerned, to abjure granting any racial preferences in its admissions program. But there is no basis for preferring a particular preference program simply because in achieving the same goals that the Davis Medical School is pursuing, it proceeds in a manner that is not immediately apparent to the public."

Justice Marshall, dissenting, argued that

> In light of the sorry history of discrimination and its devastating impact on the lives of Negroes, bringing the Negro into the mainstream of American life should be a state interest of the highest order. . . . While I applaud the judgment of the Court that a university may consider race in its admissions process, it is more than a little ironic that, after several hundred years of class-based discrimination against Negroes, the Court is unwilling to hold that a class-based remedy for that discrimination is permissible. [T]oday's judgment ignores the fact that for several hundred years Negroes have been discriminated against, not as individuals, but rather solely because of the color of their skins. It is unnecessary in 20th-century America to have individual Negroes demonstrate that they have been victims of racial discrimination; the racism of our society has been so pervasive that none, regardless of wealth or position, has managed to escape its impact. The experience of Negroes in America has been different in kind, not just in degree, from that of other ethnic groups. It is not merely the history of

slavery alone but also that a whole people were marked as inferior by the law. And that mark has endured. The dream of America as the great melting pot has not been realized for the Negro; because of his skin color he never even made it into the pot. . . .

[H]ad the Court been willing in 1896, in Plessy v. Ferguson, to hold that the Equal Protection Clause forbids differences in treatment based on race, we would not be faced with this dilemma in 1978. [F]or 58 years, from *Plessy* to *Brown v. Board of Education,* ours was a Nation where, *by law,* an individual could be given "special" treatment based on the color of his skin.

It is because of a legacy of unequal treatment that we now must permit the institutions of this society to give consideration to race in making decisions about who will hold the positions of influence, affluence, and prestige in America. For far too long, the doors to those positions have been shut to Negroes. If we are ever to become a fully integrated society, one in which the color of a person's skin will not determine the opportunities available to him or her, we must be willing to take steps to open those doors. I do not believe that anyone can truly look into America's past and still find that a remedy for the effects of that past is impermissible. . . .

I fear that we have come full circle. After the Civil War our Government started several "affirmative action" programs. This Court in the *Civil Rights Cases* and Plessy v. Ferguson destroyed the movement toward complete equality. For almost a century no action was taken, and this nonaction was with the tacit approval of the courts. Then we had Brown v. Board of Education and the Civil Rights Acts of Congress, followed by numerous affirmative-action programs. *Now,* we have this Court again stepping in, this time to stop affirmative-action programs of the type used by the University of California.

Justice Blackmun also dissented:

It is somewhat ironic to have us so deeply disturbed over [a race-conscious program when] institutions of higher learning, albeit more on the undergraduate than the graduate level, have given conceded preferences up to a point to those possessed of athletic skills, to the children of alumni, to the affluent who may bestow their largess on the institutions, and to those having connections with celebrities, the famous, and the powerful. Programs of admission to institutions of higher learning are basically a responsibility for academicians and for administrators and the specialists they employ. The judiciary, in contrast, is ill-equipped and poorly trained for this. The administration and management of educational institutions are beyond the competence of judges and are within the special competence of educators, provided always that the educators perform within legal and constitutional bounds. For me, therefore, interference by the judiciary must be the rare exception and not the rule.

Justice Stevens, joined by Chief Justice Burger and Justices Stewart and Rehnquist, concurred in the judgment in part and dissented in part. They argued that Davis's program violated Title VI and they did not reach the constitutional issues.

Note: *Affirmative Action from* Bakke *to* Croson

Between *Bakke* and Justice Powell's retirement in 1987, the Court decided a number of cases involving affirmative action. Several of these cases involved Title VII, while others involved affirmative action programs under the Equal Protection Clause.

The year after *Bakke,* in United Steelworkers v. Weber, 443 U.S. 193 (1979), a divided Court upheld a private employer's voluntary affirmative action plan under Title VII of the Civil Rights Act of 1964, without addressing any constitutional issues. In Johnson v. Transportation Agency, 480 U.S. 616 (1987), the court upheld a voluntary affirmative action program benefiting women. Five Justices agreed, using language taken from *Weber,* that preferential programs under Title VII require only showing of a "manifest imbalance" between the percentage of minorities employed and the percentage of minorities in the population, rather than the stricter equal protection standard of a "firm" basis in the evidence. See also Sheet Metal Workers v. EEOC, 478 U.S. 421 (1986) (upholding "narrowly tailored" affirmative action program imposed upon a union found to have engaged in illegal discrimination under Title VII and later found in contempt for failing to fulfill the court's earlier remedial order); Firefighters v. Cleveland, 478 U.S. 501 (1986) (holding that Title VII permitted a consent decree that benefited minorities who were not victims of defendant's previous discrimination).

In the Court's constitutional cases, the Justices continued to debate the proper level of scrutiny. In Fullilove v. Klutznick, 448 U.S. 448 (1980), the Court upheld the "minority business enterprise" (MBE) provision of the Public Works Employment Act of 1977, which required that 10 percent of federal funds granted for local public works projects must be used to procure services or supplies from businesses owned by minority group members. Congress included the MBE program because difficulties confronting minority contractors — such as lack of working capital, inability to meet bonding requirements, and unfamiliarity with bidding opportunities and procedures — were often the results of past discrimination. The regulations allowed waiver of the 10 percent requirement on a showing that it could not reasonably be met.

There was no majority opinion; Chief Justice Burger announced the judgment of the Court sustaining the statute in an opinion joined by Justices White and Powell. Chief Justice Burger found the MBE program was within Congress's powers under §5 of the Fourteenth Amendment. Although "the Act recites no preambulary 'findings' on the subject," "we are satisfied that Congress had abundant historical basis from which it could conclude that traditional procurement practices, when applied to minority businesses, could perpetuate the effects of prior discrimination." In his view, "Congress reasonably determined that the prospective elimination of these barriers to minority firm access to public contracting opportunities generated by the 1977 Act was appropriate to ensure that those businesses were not denied equal opportunity to participate in federal grants to state and local governments, which is one aspect of the equal protection of the laws." Without articulating the standard of judicial review being applied, Burger characterized the injury to the complainant as "relatively light" and wrote that "[w]hen effectuating a limited and properly tailored remedy to cure the effects of prior discrimination such a 'sharing of the burden' by innocent parties is not impermissible." "The MBE provision would survive judicial scrutiny under either 'test' articulated in the several *Bakke* opinions."

Justice Powell concurred, arguing that Congress's competence to make findings of unlawful discrimination was "beyond question," and that the legislative history "demonstrates that Congress reasonably concluded that private and governmental discrimination had contributed to the negligible percentage of public contracts awarded minority contractors." The government interest in redressing this discrimination was "compelling." "Congress' choice of remedy should be upheld . . . if the means selected are equitable and reasonably necessary to the redress of identifiable discrimination." Although the legislative history of the MBE was sparse, Powell argued that "[Congress acquires] information and expertise . . . in the consideration and enactment of earlier legislation. After Congress has legislated repeatedly in an area of national concern, its Members gain experience that may reduce the need for fresh hearings or prolonged debate when Congress again considers action in that area. . . . [W]e properly may examine the total contemporary record of congressional action dealing with the problems of racial discrimination against minority business enterprises."

Justice Marshall, joined by Justices Brennan and Blackmun, concurred in the judgment on the basis of their separate opinion (with Justice White) in *Bakke*. Justice Stewart, joined by Justice Rehnquist, dissented on the ground that "[u]nder our Constitution, the government may never act to the detriment of a person solely because of that person's race, whether or not the person is a member of a racial minority."

Justice Stevens also dissented, arguing that the statute was not narrowly tailored as a remedy for past discrimination. "Today there is a danger that awareness of past injustice will lead to automatic acceptance of new classifications that are not in fact justified by attributes characteristic of the class as a whole":

> Why were these six racial classifications, and no others, included in the preferred class? Why are aliens excluded from the preference although they are not otherwise ineligible for public contracts? What percentage of Oriental blood or what degree of Spanish-speaking skill is required for membership in the preferred class? How does the legacy of slavery and the history of discrimination against the descendants of its victims support a preference for Spanish-speaking citizens who may be directly competing with black citizens in some overpopulated communities? Why is a preference given only to owners of business enterprises and why is that preference unaccompanied by any requirement concerning the employment of disadvantaged persons? Is the preference limited to a subclass of persons who can prove that they are subject to a special disability caused by part discrimination, as the Court's opinion indicates? Or is every member of the racial class entitled to a preference as the statutory language seems plainly to indicate? Are businesses formed just to take advantage of the preference eligible?

Stevens pointed out that affirmative action programs create uncomfortable problems of defining who qualifies as a racial minority who might receive a preference:

> Indeed, the very attempt to define with precision a beneficiary's qualifying racial characteristics is repugnant to our constitutional ideals. . . . If the National Government is to make a serious effort to define racial classes by criteria that can be administered objectively, it must study precedents such as the First Regulation to the Reichs Citizenship Law of November 14, 1935: . . . "Article 5 1. A Jew is anyone who descended from at least three grandparents who were racially full Jews. . . . 2. A Jew is also one who descended from two full Jewish parents, if: (a) he belonged to the Jewish religious community at the time this law was issued, or who joined the community later; (b) he was married to a Jewish person, at the time the law was issued, or married one subsequently; (c) he is the offspring from a marriage with a Jew, in the sense of Section 1, which was contracted after the Law for the protection of German blood and German honor became effective; (d) he is the offspring of an extramarital

relationship, with a Jew, according to Section 1, and will be born out of wedlock after July 31, 1936."

In Wygant v. Jackson Board of Education, 476 U.S. 267 (1986), the Court rejected a local school district's affirmative action plan that would layoff nonminority teachers first in order to preserve "the current percentage of minority personnel employed at the time of the layoff." The minorities covered by the program were defined as "those employees who are Black, American Indian, Oriental, or of Spanish descendancy." Justice Powell's plurality opinion was joined by Chief Justice Burger, Justice Rehnquist, and by Justice O'Connor in part.

Applying strict scrutiny, Justice Powell rejected the School Board's claim that "alleviat[ing] the effects of societal discrimination" and providing "minority faculty role models" were compelling state purposes. "[T]he role model theory," Powell argued, "has no logical stopping point [and] allows the Board to engage in discriminatory hiring and layoff practices long past the point required by any legitimate remedial purpose."

Powell argued that "[t]he Court has insisted upon some showing of prior discrimination by the governmental unit involved before allowing limited use of racial classifications in order to remedy such discrimination. . . . [B]efore it embarks on an affirmative action program, [a public employer must have] convincing evidence that remedial action is warranted[,] sufficient evidence to justify the conclusion that there has been prior discrimination." The trial court had made no "factual determination that the employer had a strong basis in evidence for its conclusion that remedial action was necessary."

Even with proof of past discrimination by the school district, "the layoff provision was not a legally appropriate means of achieving even a compelling purpose" because of "the burden that a preferential layoff scheme imposes on innocent parties. In cases involving valid hiring goals, the burden to be borne by innocent individuals is diffused to a considerable extent among society generally. Though hiring goals may burden some innocent individuals, they simply do not impose the same kind of injury that layoffs impose. Denial of a future employment opportunity is not as intrusive as loss of an existing job. . . . Layoffs disrupt these settled expectations in a way that general hiring goals do not."

Justice White concurred on the ground that laying off workers was an impermissible method of integrating a workforce. Justice O'Connor, concurring in part and concurring in the judgment, argued that the layoff provision could not pass constitutional scrutiny because it "was tied to the percentage of minority students in the school district, not to the percentage of qualified minority teachers within the relevant labor pool."

Justice Marshall, joined by Justices Brennan and Blackmun, dissented. He emphasized the history of racially motivated violence at the school, and the school district's urgent need to integrate the public schools and preserve the results of previous integration. He argued that if a satisfactory record were offered substantiating these concerns, it should pass muster under any constitutional standard, including strict scrutiny. The layoff provisions were necessary to preserve integration of the public schools because seniority provisions in the Union contract meant that minority teachers, who were the last hired, would be the first fired. "[L]ack of some layoff protection would have crippled the efforts to recruit minority applicants. Adjustment of the layoff hierarchy under these circumstances was a necessary corollary of an affirmative action hiring policy."

Justice Stevens also dissented, arguing that a finding of prior discrimination against black teachers was not necessary to justify the affirmative action program:

> [A] school board may reasonably conclude that an integrated faculty will be able to provide benefits to the student body that could not be provided by an all white, or nearly all white, faculty. [T]he inclusion of minority teachers in the educational process inevitably tends to dispel th[e] illusion [that there are significant differences between people based on skin color] whereas their exclusion could only tend to foster it. . . .
>
> The Union that represents the petitioners negotiated the provision and agreed to it; the agreement was put to a vote of the membership, and overwhelmingly approved. . . . [T]he race-conscious layoff policy here was adopted with full participation of the disadvantaged individuals and with a narrowly circumscribed berth for the policy's operation.

Finally, in United States v. Paradise, 480 U.S. 149 (1987), the Court in a 5-4 decision, upheld a court order against the Alabama Department of Public Safety arising out of protracted ligitation and consistent noncompliance with previous court orders. The lower court's order required that one black be hired for every white hired for particular upper level positions if there were qualified black candidates, if the rank were less than 25 percent black, and if the Department had not developed and implemented a promotion plan without adverse impact for the relevant rank. Justice Brennan, writing for four justices, held that the plan passed even strict scrutiny because it was narrowly tailored to remedy past discrimination by the Department of Public Safety and to preserve the "societal interest in compliance with the judgments of federal courts." Justice Stevens concurred. Justice O'Connor, joined by Chief Justice Rehnquist and Justice Scalia, dissented.

2.   *Affirmative Action in the Rehnquist Court*

In 1987, Justice Powell retired. President Reagan's nomination of Judge Robert Bork to replace Justice Powell failed to win Senate confirmation, and his second nominee, Judge Douglas Ginsburg, withdrew due to allegations that he had smoked marijuana. Reagan's third nominee, Justice Anthony Kennedy, was confirmed. 1987 is in many respects a watershed year, reflecting the beginning of a new conservative majority, which was bolstered by the replacement of Justice Marshall by Justice Thomas in 1991. We have already seen the effect of this majority in cases involving federalism. Another of its most important effects was in the area of affirmative action.

CITY OF RICHMOND v. J.A. CROSON CO.
488 U.S. 469 (1989)

Justice O'CONNOR announced the judgment of the Court and delivered the opinion of the Court with respect to Parts I, III-B, and IV, an opinion with respect to Part II, in which Chief Justice Rehnquist and Justice White joined, and an opinion with respect to Parts III-A and V, in which Justice Kennedy also joined.

I.

On April 11, 1983, the Richmond City Council adopted the Minority Business Utilization Plan . . . [which] required prime contractors to whom the city awarded construction contracts to subcontract at least 30% of the dollar amount of the contract to one or more Minority Business Enterprises (MBEs). The 30% set-aside did not apply to city contracts awarded to minority-owned prime contractors.

The Plan defined an MBE as "[a] business at least fifty-one (51) percent of which is owned and controlled . . . by minority group members." "Minority group members" were defined as "[c]itizens of the United States who are Blacks, Spanish-speaking, Orientals, Indians, Eskimos, or Aleuts." There was no geographic limit to the Plan; an otherwise qualified MBE from anywhere in the United States could avail itself of the 30% set-aside. The Plan declared that it was "remedial" in nature, and enacted "for the purpose of promoting wider participation by minority business enterprises in the construction of public projects." The Plan expired on June 30, 1988, and was in effect for approximately five years.

[A provision, formulated by a city administrative agency, permitted waiver of the requirement only where it could be shown that "sufficient, relevant, qualified [MBEs] . . . are unavailable or unwilling to participate in the contract to enable meeting the 30% MBE goal." Although there was no direct administrative appeal from a denial of waiver, once a contract had been awarded to another firm, a bidder denied a contract for failure to fulfill the MBE requirements had a "general right of protest."]

The Plan was adopted by the Richmond City Council after a public hearing. Seven members of the public spoke to the merits of the ordinance: five were in opposition, two in favor. Proponents of the set-aside provision relied on a study which indicated that, while the general population of Richmond was 50% black, only .67% of the city's prime construction contracts had been awarded to minority businesses in the 5-year period from 1978 to 1983. It was also established that a variety of contractors' associations, whose representatives appeared in opposition to the ordinance, had virtually no minority businesses within their membership. . . . There was no direct evidence of race discrimination on the part of the city in letting contracts or any evidence that the city's prime contractors had discriminated against minority-owned subcontractors.

Opponents of the ordinance questioned both its wisdom and its legality. . . . Representatives of various contractors' associations questioned whether there were enough MBEs in the Richmond area to satisfy the 30% set-aside requirement. [One representative] noted that only 4.7% of all construction firms in the United States were minority owned and that 41% of these were located in California, New York, Illinois, Florida, and Hawaii. He predicted that the ordinance would thus lead to a windfall for the few minority firms in Richmond. . . . Some of the representatives of the local contractors organizations indicated that they did not discriminate on the basis of race and were in fact actively seeking out minority members. . . . [T]he ordinance was enacted by a vote of six to two. . . .

[The ordinance was challenged by a contractor whose request for a waiver of the MBE requirement had been denied. The first time the case reached the Supreme

Court, it remanded for further consideration in light of Wygant v. Jackson Board of Education. On remand, a divided panel of the Court of Appeals struck down the Richmond set-aside program.]

II.

The parties and their supporting amici fight an initial battle over the scope of the city's power to adopt legislation designed to address the effects of past discrimination. Relying on our decision in *Wygant*, appellee argues that the city must limit any race-based remedial efforts to eradicating the effects of its own prior discrimination. This is essentially the position taken by the Court of Appeals below. Appellant argues that our decision in *Fullilove* is controlling, and that as a result the city of Richmond enjoys sweeping legislative power to define and attack the effects of prior discrimination in its local construction industry. We find that neither of these two rather stark alternatives can withstand analysis. . . .

[In the principal opinion in *Fullilove*, Chief Justice Burger] stressed two factors in upholding the MBE set-aside. First was the unique remedial powers of Congress under §5 of the Fourteenth Amendment:

. . . It is fundamental that in no organ of government, state or federal, does there repose a more comprehensive remedial power than in the Congress, expressly charged by the Constitution with competence and authority to enforce equal protection guarantees.

. . . [Chief Justice Burger also] focused on the evidence before Congress that a nationwide history of past discrimination had reduced minority participation in federal construction grants. . . . The Chief Justice concluded that "Congress had abundant historical basis from which it could conclude that traditional procurement practices, when applied to minority businesses, could perpetuate the effects of prior discrimination."

The second factor emphasized by the principal opinion in *Fullilove* was the flexible nature of the 10% set-aside. . . .

[In his concurring opinion, Justice Powell] made it clear that other governmental entities might have to show more than Congress before undertaking race-conscious measures: "The degree of specificity required in the findings of discrimination and the breadth of discretion in the choice of remedies may vary with the nature and authority of the governmental body."

Appellant and its supporting amici rely heavily on *Fullilove* for the proposition that a city council, like Congress, need not make specific findings of discrimination to engage in race-conscious relief. . . .

What appellant ignores is that Congress, unlike any State or political subdivision, has a specific constitutional mandate to enforce the dictates of the Fourteenth Amendment. The power to "enforce" may at times also include the power to define situations which Congress determines threaten principles of equality and to adopt prophylactic rules to deal with those situations. See Katzenbach v. Morgan. The Civil War Amendments themselves worked a dramatic change in the balance between congressional and state power over matters of race. . . .

That Congress may identify and redress the effects of society-wide discrimination does not mean that, a fortiori, the State and their political subdivisions are free to decide that such remedies are appropriate. Section 1 of the Fourteenth Amendment is an explicit constraint on state power, and the States must undertake any remedial efforts in accordance with that provision. To hold otherwise would be to cede control over the content of the Equal Protection Clause to the 50 state legislatures and their myriad political subdivisions. The mere recitation of a benign or compensatory purpose for the use of a racial classification would essentially entitle the States to exercise the full power of Congress under §5 of the Fourteenth Amendment and insulate any racial classification from judicial scrutiny under §1. We believe that such a result would be contrary to the intentions of the Framers of the Fourteenth Amendment, who desired to place clear limits on the State's use of race as a criterion for legislative action, and to have the federal courts enforce those limitations. . . .

It would seem equally clear, however, that a state or local subdivision (if delegated the authority from the State) has the authority to eradicate the effects of private discrimination within its own legislative jurisdiction. . . . Our decision in *Wygant* is not to the contrary. . . . It was in the context of addressing the school board's power to adopt a race-based layoff program affecting its own work force that the *Wygant* plurality indicated that the Equal Protection Clause required "some showing of prior discrimination by the governmental unit involved." As a matter of state law, the city of Richmond has legislative authority over its procurement policies, and can use its spending powers to remedy private discrimination, if it identifies that discrimination with the particularity required by the Fourteenth Amendment. . . .

Thus, if the city could show that it had essentially become a "passive participant" in a system of racial exclusion practiced by elements of the local construction industry, we think it clear that the city could take affirmative steps to dismantle such a system. It is beyond dispute that any public entity, state or federal, has a compelling interest in assuring that public dollars, drawn from the tax contributions of all citizens, do not serve to finance the evil of private prejudice.

III.

A

. . . As this Court has noted in the past, the "rights created by the first section of the Fourteenth Amendment are, by its terms, guaranteed to the individual. The rights established are personal rights." The Richmond Plan denies certain citizens the opportunity to compete for a fixed percentage of public contracts based solely upon their race. To whatever racial group these citizens belong, their "personal rights" to be treated with equal dignity and respect are implicated by a rigid rule erecting race as the sole criterion in an aspect of public decisionmaking.

Absent searching judicial inquiry into the justification for such race-based measures, there is simply no way of determining what classifications are "benign" or "remedial" and what classifications are in fact motivated by illegitimate notions of racial inferiority or simple racial politics. . . .

Classifications based on race carry a danger of stigmatic harm. Unless they are strictly reserved for remedial settings, they may in fact promote notions of racial inferiority and lead to a politics of racial hostility. We thus reaffirm the view expressed by the plurality in *Wygant* that the standard of review under the Equal

Protection Clause is not dependent on the race of those burdened or benefited by a particular classification.

Our continued adherence to the standard of review employed in *Wygant*, does not, as Justice Marshall's dissent suggests, indicate that we view "racial discrimination as largely a phenomenon of the past" or that "government bodies need no longer preoccupy themselves with rectifying racial injustice." . . . Rather, our interpretation of §1 stems from our agreement with the view expressed by Justice Powell in *Bakke*, that "[t]he guarantee of equal protection cannot mean one thing when applied to one individual and something else when applied to a person of another color."

Under the standard proposed by Justice Marshall's dissent, "[r]ace-conscious classifications designed to further remedial goals," are forthwith subject to a relaxed standard of review. How the dissent arrives at the legal conclusion that a racial classification is "designed to further remedial goals," without first engaging in an examination of the factual basis for its enactment and the nexus between its scope and that factual basis we are not told. However, once the "remedial" conclusion is reached, the dissent's standard is singularly deferential, and bears little resemblance to the close examination of legislative purpose we have engaged in when reviewing classifications based either on race or gender.

Even were we to accept a reading of the guarantee of equal protection under which the level of scrutiny varies according to the ability of different groups to defend their interests in the representative process, heightened scrutiny would still be appropriate in the circumstances of this case. One of the central arguments for applying a less exacting standard to "benign" racial classifications is that such measures essentially involve a choice made by dominant racial groups to disadvantage themselves. If one aspect of the judiciary's role under the Equal Protection Clause is to protect "discrete and insular minorities" from majoritarian prejudice or indifference, some maintain that these concerns are not implicated when the "white majority" places burdens upon itself. See J. Ely, Democracy and Distrust 170 (1980).

In this case, blacks comprise approximately 50% of the population of the city of Richmond. Five of the nine seats on the City Council are held by blacks. The concern that a political majority will more easily act to the disadvantage of a minority based on unwarranted assumptions or incomplete facts would seem to militate for, not against, the application of heightened judicial scrutiny in this case. See Ely, The Constitutionality of Reverse Racial Discrimination, 41 U. Chi. L. Rev. 723, 739, n.58 (1974) ("Of course it works both ways: a law that favors Blacks over Whites would be suspect if it were enacted by a predominantly Black legislature"). . . .

B

We think it clear that the factual predicate offered in support of the Richmond Plan suffers from the same two defects identified as fatal in *Wygant*. . . . Like the "role model" theory employed in *Wygant*, a generalized assertion that there has been past discrimination in an entire industry provides no guidance for a legislative body to determine the precise scope of the injury it seeks to remedy. It "has no logical stopping point." *Wygant*. "Relief" for such an ill-defined wrong could extend until the percentage of public contracts awarded to MBEs in Richmond mirrored the percentage of minorities in the population as a whole.

Appellant argues that it is attempting to remedy various forms of past discrimination that are alleged to be responsible for the small number of minority businesses in the local contracting industry. Among these the city cites the exclusion of blacks from skilled construction trade unions and training programs. This past discrimination has prevented them "from following the traditional path from laborer to entrepreneur." The city also lists a host of nonracial factors which would seem to face a member of any racial group attempting to establish a new business enterprise, such as deficiencies in working capital, inability to meet bonding requirements, unfamiliarity with bidding procedures, and disability caused by an inadequate track record.

While there is no doubt that the sorry history of both private and public discrimination in this country has contributed to a lack of opportunities for black entrepreneurs, this observation, standing alone, cannot justify a rigid racial quota in the awarding of public contracts in Richmond, Virginia. Like the claim that discrimination in primary and secondary schooling justifies a rigid racial preference in medical school admissions, an amorphous claim that there has been past discrimination in a particular industry cannot justify the use of an unyielding racial quota. . . .

Defining these sorts of injuries as "identified discrimination" would give local governments license to create a patchwork of racial preferences based on statistical generalizations about any particular field of endeavor.

These defects are readily apparent in this case. The 30% quota cannot in any realistic sense be tied to any injury suffered by anyone. The District Court relied upon five predicate "facts" in reaching its conclusion that there was an adequate basis for the 30% quota: (1) the ordinance declares itself to be remedial; (2) several proponents of the measure stated their views that there had been past discrimination in the construction industry; (3) minority businesses received .67% of prime contracts from the city while minorities constituted 50% of the city's population; (4) there were very few minority contractors in local and state contractors' associations; and (5) in 1977, Congress made a determination that the effects of past discrimination had stifled minority participation in the construction industry nationally.

None of these "findings," singly or together, provide the city of Richmond with a "strong basis in evidence for its conclusion that remedial action was necessary." There is nothing approaching a prima facie case of a constitutional or statutory violation by anyone in the Richmond construction industry.

The District Court accorded great weight to the fact that the city council designated the Plan as "remedial." But the mere recitation of a "benign" or legitimate purpose for a racial classification, is entitled to little or no weight. . . .

The District Court also relied on the highly conclusionary statement of a proponent of the Plan that there was racial discrimination in the construction industry "in this area, and the State, and around the nation." It also noted that the city manager had related his view that racial discrimination still plagued the construction industry in his home city of Pittsburgh. These statements are of little probative value in establishing identified discrimination in the Richmond construction industry. The factfinding process of legislative bodies is generally entitled to a presumption of regulatory and deferential review by the judiciary. But when a legislative body chooses to employ a suspect classification, it cannot rest upon a generalized assertion as to the classification's relevance to its goals. . . .

Reliance on the disparity between the number of prime contracts awarded to minority firms and the minority population of the city of Richmond is similarly misplaced. . . .

In the employment context, we have recognized that for certain entry level positions or positions requiring minimal training, statistical comparisons of the racial composition of an employer's workforce to the racial composition of the relevant population may be probative of a pattern of discrimination. But where special qualifications are necessary, the relevant statistical pool for purposes of demonstrating discriminatory exclusion must be the number of minorities qualified to undertake the particular task.

In this case, the city does not even know how many MBEs in the relevant market are qualified to undertake prime or subcontracting work in public construction projects. Nor does the city know what percentage of total city construction dollars minority firms now receive as subcontractors on prime contracts let by the city.

To a large extent, the set-aside of subcontracting dollars seems to rest on the unsupported assumption that white prime contractors simply will not hire minority firms.[a] . . . Without any information on minority participation in subcontracting, it is quite simply impossible to evaluate overall minority representation in the city's construction expenditures.

The city and the District Court also relied on evidence that MBE membership in local contractors' associations was extremely low. Again, standing alone this evidence is not probative of any discrimination in the local construction industry. There are numerous explanations for this dearth of minority participation, including past societal discrimination in education and economic opportunities as well as both black and white career and entrepreneurial choices. . . . The mere fact that black membership in these trade organizations is low, standing alone, cannot establish a prima facie case of discrimination.

For low minority membership in these associations to be relevant, the city would have to link it to the number of local MBEs eligible for membership. If the statistical disparity between eligible MBEs and MBE membership were great enough, an inference of discriminatory exclusion could arise. In such a case, the city would have a compelling interest in preventing its tax dollars from assisting these organizations in maintaining a racially segregated construction market.

Finally, the city and the District Court relied on Congress' finding in connection with the set-aside approved in *Fullilove* that there had been nationwide discrimination in the construction industry. The probative value of these findings for demonstrating the existence of discrimination in Richmond is extremely limited. By its inclusion of a waiver procedure in the national program addressed in *Fullilove*, Congress explicitly recognized that the scope of the problem would vary from market area to market area.

Moreover, as noted above, Congress was exercising its powers under §5 of the Fourteenth Amendment. . . . While the States and their subdivisions may take

---

a. Since 1975 the city of Richmond has had an ordinance on the books prohibiting both discrimination in the award of public contracts and employment discrimination by public contracts. The city points to no evidence that its prime contracts have been violating the ordinance in either their employment or subcontracting practices. The complete silence of the record concerning enforcement of the city's own anti-discrimination ordinance flies in the face of the dissent's vision of a "tight-knit industry" which has prevented blacks from obtaining the experience necessary to participate in construction contracting.

remedial action when they possess evidence that their own spending practices are exacerbating a pattern of prior discrimination, they must identify that discrimination, public or private, with some specificity before they may use race-conscious relief. . . . If all a state or local government need do is find a congressional report on the subject to enact a set-aside program, the constraints of the Equal Protection Clause will, in effect, have been rendered a nullity.

. . . The "evidence" relied upon by the dissent, the history of school desegregation in Richmond and numerous congressional reports, does little to define the scope of any injury to minority contractors in Richmond or the necessary remedy. The facts relied upon by the dissent could justify a preference of any size or duration. . . .

In sum, none of the evidence presented by the city points to any identified discrimination in the Richmond construction industry. We, therefore, hold that the city has failed to demonstrate a compelling interest in apportioning public contracting opportunities on the basis of race. . . .

The foregoing analysis applies only to the inclusion of blacks within the Richmond set-aside program. There is absolutely no evidence of past discrimination against Spanish-speaking, Oriental, Indian, Eskimo, or Aleut persons in any aspect of the Richmond construction industry. . . . The random inclusion of racial groups that, as a practical matter, may never have suffered from discrimination in the construction industry in Richmond, suggests that perhaps the city's purpose was not in fact to remedy past discrimination. . . .

IV.

As noted by the court below, it is almost impossible to assess whether the Richmond Plan is narrowly tailored to remedy prior discrimination since it is not linked to identified discrimination in any way. We limit ourselves to two observations in this regard.

First, there does not appear to have been any consideration of the use of race-neutral means to increase minority business participation in city contracting. Many of the barriers to minority participation in the construction industry relied upon by the city to justify a racial classification appear to be race neutral. If MBEs disproportionately lack capital or cannot meet bonding requirements, a race-neutral program of city financing for small firms would, a fortiori, lead to greater minority participation. The principal opinion in *Fullilove* found that Congress had carefully examined and rejected race-neutral alternatives before enacting the MBE set-aside. There is no evidence in this record that the Richmond City Council has considered any alternatives to a race-based quota.

Second, the 30% quota cannot be said to be narrowly tailored to any goal, except perhaps outright racial balancing. It rests upon the "completely unrealistic" assumption that minorities will choose a particular trade in lockstep proportion to their representation in the local population. . . .

As noted above, the congressional scheme upheld in *Fullilove* allowed for a waiver of the set-aside provision where an MBE's higher price was not attributable to the effects of past discrimination. Based upon proper findings, such programs are less problematic from an equal protection standpoint because they treat all candidates individually, rather than making the color of an applicant's skin the sole relevant consideration. Unlike the program upheld in *Fullilove*, the Richmond

Plan's waiver system focuses solely on the availability of MBEs; there is no inquiry into whether or not the particular MBE seeking a racial preference has suffered from the effects of past discrimination by the city or prime contractors.

Given the existence of an individualized procedure, the city's only interest in maintaining a quota system rather than investigating the need for remedial action in particular cases would seem to be simple administrative convenience. But the interest in avoiding the bureaucratic effort necessary to tailor remedial relief to those who truly have suffered the effects of prior discrimination cannot justify a rigid line drawn on the basis of a suspect classification. Under Richmond's scheme, a successful black, Hispanic, or Oriental entrepreneur from anywhere in the country enjoys an absolute preference over other citizens based solely on their race. We think it obvious that such a program is not narrowly tailored to remedy the effects of prior discrimination.

V.

Nothing we say today precludes a state or local entity from taking action to rectify the effects of identified discrimination within its jurisdiction. If the city of Richmond had evidence before it that nonminority contractors were systematically excluding minority businesses from subcontracting opportunities it could take action to end the discriminatory exclusion. Where there is a significant statistical disparity between the number of qualified minority contractors willing and able to perform a particular service and the number of such contractors actually engaged by the locality or the locality's prime contractors, an inference of discriminatory exclusion could arise. Under such circumstances, the city could act to dismantle the closed business system by taking appropriate measures against those who discriminate on the basis of race or other illegitimate criteria. In the extreme case, some form of narrowly tailored racial preference might be necessary to break down patterns of deliberate exclusion.

Nor is local government powerless to deal with individual instances of racially motivated refusals to employ minority contractors. Where such discrimination occurs, a city would be justified in penalizing the discriminator and providing appropriate relief to the victim of such discrimination. Moreover, evidence of a pattern of individual discriminatory acts can, if supported by appropriate statistical proof, lend support to a local government's determination that broader remedial relief is justified.

Even in the absence of evidence of discrimination, the city has at its disposal a whole array of race-neutral devices to increase the accessibility of city contracting opportunities to small entrepreneurs of all races. Simplification of bidding procedures, relaxation of bonding requirements, and training and financial aid for disadvantaged entrepreneurs of all races would open the public contracting market to all those who have suffered the effects of past societal discrimination or neglect. . . . Business as usual should not mean business pursuant to the unthinking exclusion of certain members of our society from its rewards.

In the case at hand, . . . it is simply impossible to say that the city has demonstrated "a strong basis in evidence for its conclusion that remedial action was necessary." *Wygant.*

Proper findings in this regard are necessary to define both the scope of the injury and the extent of the remedy necessary to cure its effects. Such findings also serve to assure all citizens that the deviation from the norm of equal treatment of all racial and ethnic groups is a temporary matter, a measure taken in the service of the goal of equality itself. Absent such findings, there is a danger that a racial classification is merely the product of unthinking stereotypes or a form of racial politics. . . . Because the city of Richmond has failed to identify the need for remedial action in the awarding of its public construction contracts, its treatment of its citizens on a racial basis violates the dictates of the Equal Protection Clause. Accordingly, the judgment of the Court of Appeals for the Fourth Circuit is affirmed.

STEVENS, J., concurring in part and concurring in the judgment.

A central purpose of the Fourteenth Amendment is to further the national goal of equal opportunity for all our citizens. In order to achieve that goal we must learn from our past mistakes, but I believe the Constitution requires us to evaluate our policy decisions — including those that govern the relationships among different racial and ethnic groups — primarily by studying their probable impact on the future. I therefore do not agree with the premise that seems to underlie today's decision . . . that governmental decision that rests on a racial classification is never permissible except as a remedy for a past wrong.[a] I do, however, agree with the Court's explanation of why the Richmond ordinance cannot be justified as a remedy for past discrimination, and therefore join Parts I, III-B, and IV of its opinion. I write separately to emphasize three aspects of the case that are of special importance to me.

First, the city makes no claim that the public interest in the efficient performance of its construction contracts will be served by granting a preference to minority-business enterprises. This case is therefore completely unlike *Wygant*, in which I thought it quite obvious that the School Board had reasonably concluded that an integrated faculty could provide educational benefits to the entire student body that could not be provided by an all-white, or nearly all-white faculty. . . .

Second, this litigation involves an attempt by a legislative body, rather than a court, to fashion a remedy for a past wrong. Legislatures are primarily policymaking bodies that promulgate rules to govern future conduct. . . . It is the judicial system, rather than the legislative process, that is best equipped to identify past wrongdoers and to fashion remedies that will create the conditions that presumably would have existed had no wrong been committed.

Third, instead of engaging in a debate over the proper standard of review to apply in affirmative-action litigation, I believe it is more constructive to try to identify the

a. In my view the Court's approach to this case gives unwarranted deference to race-based legislative action that purports to serve a purely remedial goal, and overlooks the potential value of race-based determinations that may serve other valid purposes. With regard to the former point . . . I am not prepared to assume that even a more narrowly tailored set-aside program supported by stronger findings would be constitutionally justified. Unless the legislature can identify both the particular victims and the particular perpetrators of past discrimination, which is precisely what a court does when it makes findings of fact and conclusions of law, a remedial justification for race-based legislation will almost certainly sweep too broadly. With regard to the latter point: I think it unfortunate that the Court in neither *Wygant* nor this case seems prepared to acknowledge that some race-based policy decisions may serve a legitimate public purpose. I agree, of course, that race is so seldom relevant to legislative decisions on how best to foster the public good that legitimate justifications for race-based legislation will usually not be available. But unlike the Court, I would not totally discount the legitimacy of race-based decisions that may produce tangible and fully justified future benefits.

characteristics of the advantaged and disadvantaged classes that may justify their disparate treatment. In this case that approach convinces me that, instead of carefully identifying the characteristics of the two classes of contractors that are respectively favored and disfavored by its ordinance, the Richmond City Council has merely engaged in the type of stereotypical analysis that is a hallmark of violations of the Equal Protection Clause. Whether we look at the class of persons benefited by the ordinance or at the disadvantaged class, the same conclusion emerges.

The justification for the ordinance is the fact that in the past white contractors — and presumably other white citizens in Richmond — have discriminated against black contractors. The class of persons benefited by the ordinance is not, however, limited to victims of such discrimination — it encompasses persons who have never been in business in Richmond as well as minority contractors who may have been guilty of discriminating against members of other minority groups. Indeed, for all the record shows, all of the minority-business enterprises that have benefited from the ordinance may be firms that have prospered notwithstanding the discriminatory conduct that may have harmed other minority firms years ago. Ironically, minority firms that have survived in the competitive struggle, rather than those that have perished, are most likely to benefit from an ordinance of this kind.

The ordinance is equally vulnerable because of its failure to identify the characteristics of the disadvantaged class of white contractors that justify the disparate treatment. . . . Thus, the composition of the disadvantaged class of white contractors presumably includes some who have been guilty of unlawful discrimination, some who practiced discrimination before it was forbidden by law, and some who have never discriminated against anyone on the basis of race. Imposing a common burden on such a disparate class merely because each member of the class is of the same race stems from reliance on a stereotype rather than fact or reason.

There is a special irony in the stereotypical thinking that prompts legislation of this kind. Although it stigmatizes the disadvantaged class with the unproven charge of past racial discrimination, it actually imposes a greater stigma on its supposed beneficiaries. . . .

Accordingly, I concur in parts I, III-B, and IV of the Court's opinion, and in the judgment.

KENNEDY, J., concurring in part and concurring in the judgment.

I join all but Part II of Justice O'Connor's opinion and give this further explanation. . . .

The process by which a law that is an equal protection violation when enacted by a State becomes transformed to an equal protection guarantee when enacted by Congress poses a difficult proposition for me; but as it is not before us, any reconsideration of that issue must await some further case. For purposes of the ordinance challenged here, it suffices to say that the State has the power to eradicate racial discrimination and its effects in both the public and private sectors, and the absolute duty to do so where those wrongs were caused intentionally by the State itself. The Fourteenth Amendment ought not to be interpreted to reduce a State's authority in this regard, unless, of course, there is a conflict with federal law or a state remedy is itself a violation of equal protection. The latter is the case presented here.

The moral imperative of racial neutrality is the driving force of the Equal Protection Clause. Justice Scalia's opinion underscores this position, quite properly, in my view. The rule suggested in his opinion, which would strike down all preferences which are not necessary remedies to victims of unlawful discrimination, would eliminate the necessity for courts to pass upon each racial preference that is enacted. . . .

Nevertheless, given that a rule of automatic invalidity for racial preferences in almost every case would be a significant break with our precedents that require a case-by-case test, I am not convinced we need adopt it at this point. On the assumption that it will vindicate the principle of race neutrality found in the Equal Protection Clause, I accept the less absolute rule contained in Justice O'Connor's opinion, a rule based on the proposition that any racial preference must face the most rigorous scrutiny by the courts. My reasons for doing so are as follows. First, I am confident that, in application, the strict scrutiny standard will operate in a manner generally consistent with the imperative of race neutrality, because it forbids the use even of narrowly drawn racial classifications except as a last resort. Second, the rule against race-conscious remedies is already less than an absolute one, for that relief may be the only adequate remedy after a judicial determination that a State or its instrumentality has violated the Equal Protection Clause. I note, in this connection, that evidence which would support a judicial finding of intentional discrimination may suffice also to justify remedial legislative action, for it diminishes the constitutional responsibilities of the political branches to say they must wait to act until ordered to do so by a court. Third, the strict scrutiny rule is consistent with our precedents, as Justice O'Connor's opinion demonstrates.

The ordinance before us falls far short of the standard we adopt. [The ordinance is] open to the fair charge that is not a remedy but is itself a preference which will cause the same corrosive animosities that the Constitution forbids in the whole sphere of government and that our national policy condemns in the rest of society as well. . . .

SCALIA, J., concurring in the judgment.

I agree with much of the Court's opinion, and, in particular, with its conclusion that strict scrutiny must be applied to all governmental classification by race, whether or not its asserted purpose is "remedial" or "benign." I do not agree, however, with the Court's dicta suggesting that, despite the Fourteenth Amendment, state and local governments may in some circumstances discriminate on the basis of race in order (in a broad sense) "to ameliorate the effects of past discrimination." The benign purpose of compensating for social disadvantages, whether they have been acquired by reason of prior discrimination or otherwise, can no more be pursued by the illegitimate means of racial discrimination than can other assertedly benign purposes we have repeatedly rejected. The difficulty of overcoming the effects of past discrimination is as nothing compared with the difficulty of eradicating from our society the source of those effects, which is the tendency — fatal to a nation such as ours — to classify and judge men and women on the basis of their country of origin or the color of their skin. A solution to the first problem that aggravates the second is no solution at all. . . .

We have in some contexts approved the use of racial classifications by the Federal Government to remedy the effects of past discrimination. I do not believe that we must or should extend those holdings to the States. . . .

A sound distinction between federal and state (or local) action based on race rests not only upon the substance of the Civil War Amendments, but upon social reality and governmental theory. . . . The struggle for racial justice has historically been a struggle by the national society against oppression in the individual States. And the struggle retains that character in modern times. . . . What the record shows, in other words, is that racial discrimination against any group finds a more ready expression at the state and local than at the federal level. To the children of the Founding Fathers, this should come as no surprise. An acute awareness of the heightened danger of oppression from political factions in small, rather than large, political units dates to the very beginning of our national history. . . .

Richmond [enacted] a set-aside clearly and directly beneficial to the dominant political group, which happens also to be the dominant racial group. The same thing has no doubt happened before in other cities (though the racial basis of the preference has rarely been made textually explicit) — and blacks have often been on the receiving end of the injustice. Where injustice is the game, however, turnabout is not fair play.

In my view there is only one circumstance in which the States may act by race to "undo the effects of past discrimination": where that is necessary to eliminate their own maintenance of a system of unlawful racial classification. . . .

A State can, of course, act "to undo the effects of past discrimination" in many permissible ways that do not involve classification by race. . . . And, of course, a State may "undo the effects of past discrimination" in the sense of giving the identified victim of state discrimination that which it wrongfully denied him. . . . That is worlds apart from the system here, in which those to be disadvantaged are identified solely by race.

I agree with the Court's dictum that a fundamental distinction must be drawn between the effects of "societal" discrimination and the effects of "identified" discrimination, and that the situation would be different if Richmond's plan were "tailored" to identify those particular bidders who "suffered from the effects of past discrimination by the city or prime contractors." In my view, however, the reason that would make a difference is not, as the Court states, that it would justify race-conscious action, but rather that it would enable race-neutral remediation. . . . In other words, far from justifying racial classification, identification of actual victims of discrimination makes it less supportable than ever, because more obviously unneeded. . . .

It is plainly true that in our society blacks have suffered discrimination immeasurably greater than any directed at other racial groups. But those who believe that racial preferences can help to "even the score" display, and reinforce, a manner of thinking by race that was the source of the injustice and that will, if it endures within our society, be the source of more injustice still. . . . Racial preferences appear to "even the score" (in some small degree) only if one embraces the proposition that our society is appropriately viewed as divided into races, making it right that an injustice rendered in the past to a black man should be compensated for by discriminating against a white. Nothing is worth that embrace. Since blacks have been disproportionately disadvantaged by racial discrimination, any race-neutral remedial program aimed at the disadvantaged as such will have a disproportionately beneficial impact on blacks. Only such a program, and not one that operates on the basis of race, is in accord with the letter and the spirit of our Constitution.

Since I believe that the appellee here had a constitutional right to have its bid succeed or fail under a decisionmaking process uninfected with racial bias, I concur in the judgment of the Court.

MARSHALL, J., with whom Justice Brennan and Justice Blackmun join, dissenting.

It is a welcome symbol of racial progress when the former capital of the Confederacy acts forthrightly to confront the effects of racial discrimination in its midst. In my view, nothing in the Constitution can be construed to prevent Richmond, Virginia, from allocating a portion of its contracting dollars for businesses owned or controlled by members of minority groups. . . .

A majority of this Court holds today, however, that the Equal Protection Clause of the Fourteenth Amendment blocks Richmond's initiative. The essence of the majority's position is that Richmond has failed to catalogue adequate findings to prove that past discrimination has impeded minorities from joining or participating fully in Richmond's construction contracting industry. I find deep irony in second-guessing Richmond's judgment on this point. As much as any municipality in the United States, Richmond knows what racial discrimination is; a century of decisions by this and other federal courts has richly documented the city's disgraceful history of public and private racial discrimination. In any event, the Richmond City Council has supported its determination that minorities have been wrongly excluded from local construction contracting. Its proof includes statistics showing that minority-owned businesses have received virtually no city contracting dollars and rarely if ever belonged to area trade associations; testimony by municipal officials that discrimination has been widespread in the local construction industry; and the same exhaustive and widely publicized federal studies relied on in *Fullilove*, studies which showed that pervasive discrimination in the Nation's tight-knit construction industry had operated to exclude minorities from public contracting. These are precisely the types of statistical and testimonial evidence which, until today, this Court had credited in cases approving of race-conscious measures designed to remedy past discrimination.

More fundamentally, today's decision marks a deliberate and giant step backward in this Court's affirmative action jurisprudence. Cynical of one municipality's attempt to redress the effects of past racial discrimination in a particular industry, the majority launches a grapeshot attack on race-conscious remedies in general. The majority's unnecessary pronouncements will inevitably discourage or prevent governmental entities, particularly States and localities, from acting to rectify the scourge of past discrimination. This is the harsh reality of the majority's decision, but it is not the Constitution's command.

I.

As an initial matter . . . the majority downplays the fact that the City Council had before it a rich trove of evidence that discrimination in the Nation's construction industry had seriously impaired the competitive position of businesses owned or controlled by members of minority groups. . . . The majority's refusal to recognize that Richmond has proven itself no exception to the dismaying pattern of national exclusion which Congress so painstakingly identified infects its entire analysis of this case. . . .

The congressional program upheld in *Fullilove* was based upon an array of congressional and agency studies which documented the powerful influence of racially exclusionary practices in the business world. A 1975 report by the House Committee on Small Business concluded:

The effects of past inequities stemming from racial prejudice have not remained in the past. The Congress has recognized the reality that past discriminatory practices have, to some degree, adversely affected our present economic system.

"While minority persons comprise about 16 percent of the Nation's population, of the 13 million businesses in the United States, only 382,000, or approximately 3.0 percent, are owned by minority individuals. The most recent data from the Department of Commerce also indicates that the gross receipts of all businesses in this country totals about $2,540.8 billion, and of this amount only $16.6 billion, or about 0.65 percent was realized by minority business concerns. . . .

Currently, we more often encounter a business system which is racially neutral on its face, but because of past overt social and economic discrimination is presently operating, in effect, to perpetuate these past inequities. Minorities, until recently, have not participated to any measurable extent, in our total business system generally, or in the construction industry in particular."

Congress further found that minorities seeking initial public contracting assignments often faced immense entry barriers which did not confront experienced nonminority contractors. . . .

Thus, as of 1977, there was "abundant evidence" in the public domain "that minority businesses ha[d] been denied effective participation in public contracting opportunities by procurement practices that perpetuated the effects of prior discrimination." Significantly, this evidence demonstrated that discrimination had prevented existing or nascent minority-owned businesses from obtaining not only federal contracting assignments, but state and local ones as well.[a]

The members of the Richmond City Council were well aware of these exhaustive congressional findings, a point the majority, tellingly, elides. The transcript of the session at which the Council enacted the local set-aside initiative contains numerous references to the 6-year-old congressional set-aside program, to the evidence of nationwide discrimination barriers described above, and to the *Fullilove* decision itself.

The City Council's members also heard . . . testimony from city official as to the exclusionary history of the local construction industry. As the District Court noted, not a single person who testified before the City Council denied that discrimination in Richmond's construction industry had been widespread. So long as one views Richmond's local evidence of discrimination against the backdrop of systematic nationwide racial discrimination which Congress had so painstakingly identified in this very industry, this case is readily resolved.

II.

. . . My view has long been that race-conscious classifications designed to further remedial goals "must serve important governmental objectives and must be

---

a. Numerous congressional studies undertaken after 1977 and issued before the Richmond City Council convened in April 1983 found that the exclusion of minorities had continued virtually unabated — and that, because of this legacy of discrimination, minority businesses across the nation had still failed, as of 1983, to gain a real toehold in the business world. . . .

substantially related to achievement of those objectives" in order to withstand constitutional scrutiny. Analyzed in terms of this two-prong standard, Richmond's set-aside, like the federal program on which it was modeled, is "plainly constitutional."

A

1

Turning first to the governmental interest inquiry, Richmond has two powerful interests in setting aside a portion of public contracting funds for minority-owned enterprises. The first is the city's interest in eradicating the effects of past racial discrimination. It is far too late in the day to doubt that remedying such discrimination is a compelling, let alone an important, interest. . . .

Richmond has a second compelling interest in setting aside, where possible, a portion of its contracting dollars. That interest is the prospective one of preventing the city's own spending decisions from reinforcing and perpetuating the exclusionary effects of past discrimination. . . .

The majority is wrong to trivialize the continuing impact of government acceptance or use of private institutions or structures once wrought by discrimination. When government channels all its contracting funds to a white-dominated community of established contractors whose racial homogeneity is the product of private discrimination, it does more than place its imprimatur on the practices which forged and which continue to define that community. It also provides a measurable boost to those economic entities that have thrived within it, while denying important economic benefits to those entities which, but for prior discrimination, might well be better qualified to receive valuable government contracts. In my view, the interest in ensuring that the government does not reflect and reinforce prior private discrimination in dispensing public contracts is every bit as strong as the interest in eliminating private discrimination — an interest which this Court has repeatedly deemed compelling. . . . Cities like Richmond may not be constitutionally required to adopt set-aside plans. But there can be no doubt that when Richmond acted affirmatively to stem the perpetuation of patterns of discrimination through its own decisionmaking, it served an interest of the highest order.

2

The remaining question with respect to the "governmental interest" prong of equal protection analysis is whether Richmond has proffered satisfactory proof of past racial discrimination to support its twin interests in remediation and in governmental nonperpetuation. Although the Members of this Court have differed on the appropriate standard of review for race-conscious remedial measures, we have always regarded this factual inquiry as a practical one. Thus, the Court has eschewed rigid tests which require the provision of particular species of evidence, statistical or otherwise. At the same time we have required that government adduce evidence that, taken as a whole, is sufficient to support its claimed interest and to dispel the natural concern that it acted out of mere "paternalistic stereotyping, not on a careful consideration of modern social conditions." . . . Our unwillingness to go beyond . . . generalized standards to require specific types of proof in all circumstances reflects, in my view, an understanding that discrimination takes a myriad of "ingenious and pervasive forms." The varied body of evidence on which Richmond relied provides a "strong," "firm," and "unquestionably legitimate" basis upon which the City Council could determine that the effects of past racial discrimination warranted a remedial and prophylactic governmental response. . . . Richmond acted against a backdrop of congressional and Executive Branch studies which demonstrated with such force the nationwide pervasiveness of prior discrimination that Congress presumed that "present economic inequities" in construction contracting resulted from "past discriminatory systems." The city's local evidence confirmed that Richmond's construction industry did not deviate from this pernicious national pattern. The fact that just .67% of public construction expenditures over the previous five years had gone to minority-owned prime contractors, despite the city's racially mixed population, strongly suggest that construction contracting in the area was rife with "present economic inequities." To the extent this enormous disparity did not itself demonstrate that discrimination had occurred, the descriptive testimony of Richmond's elected and appointed leaders drew the necessary link between the pitifully small presence of minorities in construction contracting and past exclusionary practices. That no one who testified challenged this depiction of widespread racial discrimination in area construction contracting lent significant weight to these accounts. The fact that area trade associations had virtually no minority members dramatized the extent of present inequities and suggested the lasting power of past discriminatory systems. In sum, to suggest that the facts on which Richmond has relied do not provide a sound basis for its finding of past racial discrimination simply blinks credibility. . . .

[T]he majority's criticisms of individual items of Richmond's evidence rest on flimsy foundations. The majority states, for example, that reliance on the disparity between the share of city contracts awarded to minority firms (.67%) and the minority population of Richmond (approximately 50%) is "misplaced." It is true that, when the factual predicate needed to be proved is one of present discrimination, we have generally credited statistical contrasts between the racial composition of a work force and the general population as proving discrimination only where this contrast revealed "gross statistical disparities." But this principle does not impugn Richmond's statistical contrast, for two reasons. First, considering how minuscule the share of Richmond public construction contracting dollars received by minority-owned businesses is, it is hardly unreasonable to conclude that this case involves a "gross statistical disparit[y]." . . .

Second, and more fundamentally, where the issue is not present discrimination but rather whether past discrimination has resulted in the continuing exclusion of minorities from an historically tight-knit industry, a contrast between population and work force is entirely appropriate to help gauge the degree of the exclusion. . . . This contrast is especially illuminating in cases like this, where a main avenue of introduction into the work force — here, membership in the trade associations whose members presumably train apprentices and help them procure subcontracting assignments — is itself grossly dominated by nonminorities. The majority's assertion that the city "does not even know how many MBE's in the relevant market are qualified" is thus entirely beside the point. If Richmond indeed has a monochromatic contracting community — a conclusion reached by the District Court — this most likely reflects the lingering power of past exclusionary practices. Certainly this is the explanation Congress has found persuasive at the national level. The city's requirement that prime public contractors set aside 30% of their subcontracting assignments for minority-owned enterprises, subject to the ordinance's provision for waivers where minority-owned enterprises are unavailable or unwilling to participate, is designed precisely to ease minority contractors into the industry.

The majority's perfunctory dismissal of the testimony of Richmond's appointed and elected leaders is also deeply disturbing. . . . [B]y disregarding the testimony of local leaders and the judgment of local government, the majority does violence to the very principles of comity within our federal system which this Court has long championed. Local officials, by virtue of their proximity to, and their expertise with, local affairs, are exceptionally well-qualified to make determinations of public good "within their respective spheres of authority." The majority, however, leaves any traces of comity behind in its headlong rush to strike down Richmond's race-conscious measure.

Had the majority paused for a moment on the facts of the Richmond experience, it would have discovered that the city's leadership is deeply familiar with what racial discrimination is. The members of the Richmond City Council have spent long years witnessing multifarious acts of discrimination, including, but not limited to, the deliberate diminution of black residents' voting rights, resistance to school desegregation, and publicly sanctioned housing discrimination. Numerous decisions of federal courts chronicle this disgraceful recent history. . . .

When the legislatures and leaders of cities with histories of pervasive discrimination testify that past discrimination has infected one of their industries, armchair cynicism like that exercised by the majority has no place. . . . Disbelief is particularly inappropriate here in light of the fact that appellee Croson, which had the burden of proving unconstitutionality at trial, has at no point come forward with any direct evidence that the City Council's motives were anything other than sincere.

Finally, I vehemently disagree with the majority's dismissal of the congressional and Executive Branch findings noted in *Fullilove* as having "extremely limited" probative value in this case. . . . The majority, inexplicably, would forbid Richmond to "share" in this information, and permit only Congress to take note of these ample findings. In thus requiring that Richmond's local evidence be severed from the context in which it was prepared, the majority would require cities seeking to eradicate the effects of past discrimination within their borders to reinvent the evidentiary wheel and engage in unnecessarily duplicative, costly, and time-consuming factfinding.

No principle of federalism or of federal power, however, forbids a state or local government from drawing upon a nationally relevant historical record prepared by the Federal Government. Of course, Richmond could have built an even more compendious record of past discrimination, one including additional stark statistics and additional individual accounts of past discrimination. But nothing in the Fourteenth Amendment imposes such onerous documentary obligations upon States and localities once the reality of past discrimination is apparent.

B

In my judgment, Richmond's set-aside plan also comports with the second prong of the equal protection inquiry, for it is substantially related to the interests it seeks to serve in remedying past discrimination and in ensuring that municipal contract procurement does not perpetuate that discrimination. The most striking aspect of the city's ordinance is the similarity it bears to the "appropriately limited" federal set-aside provision upheld in *Fullilove*. Like the federal provision, Richmond's is limited to five years in duration and was not renewed when it came up for reconsideration in 1988. Like the federal provision, Richmond's contains a waiver provision freeing from its subcontracting requirements those nonminority firms that demonstrate that they cannot comply with its provisions. Like the federal provision, Richmond's has a minimal impact on innocent third parties. While the measure affects 30% of public contracting dollars, that translates to only 3% of overall Richmond area contracting.

Finally, like the federal provision, Richmond's does not interfere with any vested right of a contractor to a particular contract; instead it operates entirely prospectively. . . .

The majority takes issue . . . with two aspects of Richmond's tailoring: the city's refusal to explore the use of race-neutral measures to increase minority business participation in contracting and the selection of a 30% set-aside figure. The majority's first criticism is flawed in two respects. First, the majority overlooks the fact that since 1975, Richmond has barred both discrimination by the city in awarding public contracts and discrimination by public contractors. The virtual absence of minority businesses from the city's contracting rolls, indicated by the fact that such businesses have received less than 1% of public contracting dollars, strongly suggests that this ban has not succeeded in redressing the impact of past discrimination or in preventing city contract procurement from reinforcing racial homogeneity. Second, the majority's suggestion that Richmond should have first undertaken such race-neutral measures as a program of city financing for small firms ignores the fact that such measures, while theoretically appealing, have been discredited by Congress as ineffectual in eradicating the effects of past discrimination in this very industry. . . .[b]

As for Richmond's 30% target, the majority states that this figure "cannot be said to be narrowly tailored to any goal, except perhaps outright racial balancing." The majority ignores two important facts. First, the set-aside measure affects only 3% of overall city contracting; thus, any imprecision in tailoring has far less impact than the majority suggests. But more important, the majority ignores the fact that Richmond's 30% figure was patterned directly on the *Fullilove* precedent. Congress' 10% figure fell "roughly halfway between the present percentage of minority contractors and the percentage of minority group members in the Nation." The Richmond City Council's 30% figure similarly falls roughly halfway between the present percentage of Richmond-based minority contractors (almost zero) and the percentage of minorities in Richmond (50%). In faulting Richmond for not presenting a different explanation for its choice of a set-aside figure, the majority honors *Fullilove* only in the breach.

b. The majority also faults Richmond's ordinance for including within its definition of "minority group members" not only black citizens, but also citizens who are "Spanish-speaking, Oriental, Indian, Eskimo, or Aleut persons." This is, of course, precisely the same definition Congress adopted in its set-aside legislation. Even accepting the majority's view that Richmond's ordinance is overbroad because it includes groups, such as Eskimos or Aleuts, about whom no evidence of local discrimination has been proffered, it does not necessarily follow that the balance of Richmond's ordinance should be invalidated.

III.

I would ordinarily end my analysis at this point and conclude that Richmond's ordinance satisfies both the governmental interest and substantial relationship prongs of our Equal Protection Clause analysis. However, I am compelled to add more, for the majority has gone beyond the facts of this case to announce a set of principles which unnecessarily restrict the power of governmental entities to take race-conscious measures to redress the effects of prior discrimination.

A

Today, for the first time, a majority of this Court has adopted strict scrutiny as its standard of Equal Protection Clause review of race-conscious remedial measures. This is an unwelcome development. A profound difference separates governmental actions that themselves are racist, and governmental actions that seek to remedy the effects of prior racism or to prevent neutral governmental activity from perpetuating the effects of such racism.

Racial classifications "drawn on the presumption that one race is inferior to another or because they put the weight of government behind racial hatred and separatism" warrant the strictest judicial scrutiny because of the very irrelevance of these rationales. By contrast, racial classifications drawn for the purpose of remedying the effects of discrimination that itself was race-based have a highly pertinent basis: the tragic and indelible fact that discrimination against blacks and other racial minorities in this Nation has pervaded our Nation's history and continues to scar our society. . . .

In concluding that remedial classifications warrant no different standard of review under the Constitution than the most brute and repugnant forms of state-sponsored racism, a majority of this Court signals that it regards racial discrimination as largely a phenomenon of the past, and that government bodies need no longer preoccupy themselves with rectifying racial injustice. I, however, do not believe this Nation is anywhere close to eradicating racial discrimination or its vestiges. In constitutionalizing its wishful thinking, the majority today does a grave disservice not only to those victims of past and present racial discrimination in this Nation whom government has sought to assist, but also to this Court's long tradition of approaching issues of race with the utmost sensitivity.

B

I am also troubled by the majority's assertion that, even if it did not believe generally in strict scrutiny of race-based remedial measures, "the circumstances of this case" require this Court to look upon the Richmond City Council's measure with the strictest scrutiny. The sole such circumstance which the majority cites, however, is the fact that blacks in Richmond are a "dominant racial grou[p]" in the city. In support of this characterization of dominance, the majority observes that "blacks comprise approximately 50% of the population of the city of Richmond" and that "[f]ive of the nine seats on the City Council are held by blacks."

While I agree that the numerical and political supremacy of a given racial group is a factor bearing upon the level of scrutiny to be applied, this Court has never held that numerical inferiority, standing alone, makes a racial group "suspect" and thus entitled to strict scrutiny review. Rather, we have identified other "traditional indicia of suspectness": whether a group has been "saddled with such disabilities, or subjected to such a history of purposeful unequal treatment, or relegated to such a position of political powerlessness as to command extraordinary protection from the majoritarian political process."

It cannot seriously be suggested that nonminorities in Richmond have any "history of purposeful unequal treatment." Nor is there any indication that they have any of the disabilities that have characteristically afflicted those groups this Court has deemed suspect. Indeed, the numerical and political dominance of nonminorities within the State of Virginia and the Nation as a whole provide an enormous political check against the "simple racial politics" at the municipal level which the majority fears. If the majority really believes that groups like Richmond's nonminorities, which comprise approximately half the population but which are outnumbered even marginally in political fora, are deserving of suspect class status for these reasons alone, this Court's decisions denying suspect status to women and to persons with below-average incomes stand on extremely shaky ground.

In my view, the "circumstances of this case," underscore the importance of not subjecting to a strict scrutiny straitjacket the increasing number of cities which have recently come under minority leadership and are eager to rectify, or at least prevent the perpetuation of, past racial discrimination. . . . This history of "purposefully unequal treatment" forced upon minorities, not imposed by them, should raise an inference that minorities in Richmond had much to remedy — and that the 1983 set-aside was undertaken with sincere remedial goals in mind, not "simple racial politics." . . .

The majority's view that remedial measures undertaken by municipalities with black leadership must face a stiffer test of Equal Protection Clause scrutiny than remedial measures undertaken by municipalities with white leadership implies a lack of political maturity on the part of this Nation's elected minority officials that is totally unwarranted. Such insulting judgments have no place in constitutional jurisprudence.

C

Today's decision, finally, is particularly noteworthy for the daunting standard it imposes upon States and localities contemplating the use of race-conscious measures to eradicate the present effects of prior discrimination and prevent its perpetuation. The majority restricts the use of such measures to situations in which a State or locality can put forth "a prima facie case of a constitutional or statutory violation." . . .

Nothing in the Constitution or in the prior decisions of this Court supports limiting state authority to confront the effects of past discrimination to those situations in which a prima facie case of a constitutional or statutory violation can be made out. By its very terms, the majority's standard effectively cedes control of a large component of the content of that constitutional provision to Congress and to state legislatures. If an antecedent Virginia or Richmond law had defined as unlawful the award to nonminorities of an overwhelming share of a city's contracting dollars, for example, Richmond's subsequent set-aside initiative would then satisfy the majority's standard. But without such a law, the initiative might not withstand constitutional scrutiny. The meaning of "equal protection of the laws" thus turns on the happenstance of whether a State or local body has previously defined illegal discrimination. . . .

[Similarly, i]f Congress tomorrow dramatically expanded Title VII . . . or alternatively, if it repealed that legislation altogether — the meaning of equal protection would change precipitously along with it. Whatever the Framers of the Fourteenth Amendment had in mind in 1868, it certainly was not that the content of their Amendment would turn on the amendments to or the evolving interpretations of a federal statute passed nearly a century later.[c]

To the degree that this parsimonious standard is grounded on a view that either §1 or §5 of the Fourteenth Amendment substantially disempowered States and localities from remedying past racial discrimination, the majority is seriously mistaken. With respect, first, to §5, our precedents have never suggested that this provision — or, for that matter, its companion federal-empowerment provisions in the Thirteenth and Fifteenth Amendments — was meant to pre-empt or limit state police power to undertake race-conscious remedial measures. . . .

As for §1, it is too late in the day to assert seriously that the Equal Protection Clause prohibits States — or for that matter, the Federal Government, to whom the equal protection guarantee has largely been applied, from enacting race-conscious remedies. Our cases in the areas of school desegregation, voting rights, and affirmative action have demonstrated time and again that race is constitutionally germane, precisely because race remains dismayingly relevant in American life.

In adopting its prima facie standard for States and localities, the majority closes its eyes to this constitutional history and social reality. . . .

The fact is that Congress' concern in passing the Reconstruction Amendments, and particularly their congressional authorization provisions, was that States would not adequately respond to racial violence or discrimination against newly freed slaves. To interpret any aspect of these Amendments as proscribing state remedial responses to these very problems turns the Amendments on their heads. . . .

In short, there is simply no credible evidence that the Framers of the Fourteenth Amendment sought "to transfer the security and protection of all the civil rights . . . from the States to the Federal government." The three Reconstruction Amendments undeniably "worked a dramatic change in the balance between congressional and state power." . . . But nothing in the Amendments themselves, or in our long history of interpreting or applying those momentous charters, suggests that States, exercising their police power, are in any way constitutionally inhibited from working alongside the Federal Government in the fight against discrimination and its effects.

IV.

The majority today sounds a full-scale retreat from the Court's longstanding solicitude to race-conscious remedial efforts "directed toward deliverance of the century-old

---

c. Although the majority purports to "adher[e] to the standard of review employed in *Wygant*," the "prima facie case" standard it adopts marks an implicit rejection of the more generally framed "strong basis in evidence" test endorsed by the *Wygant* plurality, and the similar "firm basis" test endorsed by Justice O'Connor in her separate concurrence in that case. Under those tests, proving a prima facie violation of Title VII would appear to have been but one means of adducing sufficient proof to satisfy Equal Protection Clause analysis. . . .

promise of equality of economic opportunity." The new and restrictive tests it applies scuttle one city's effort to surmount its discriminatory past, and imperil those of dozens more localities. I, however, profoundly disagree with the cramped vision of the Equal Protection Clause which the majority offers today and with its application of that vision to Richmond, Virginia's, laudable set-aside plan. The battle against pernicious racial discrimination or its effects is nowhere near won. I must dissent.

[Justice Blackmun wrote a brief dissent supporting Justice Marshall's opinion.]

Discussion

1. The majority in *Croson* distinguishes *Fullilove* by asserting (among other things) that Congress has unique remedial powers under §5 of the Fourteenth Amendment that the states don't share. Is the underlying rationale for the distinction (as Justice Scalia suggests) that state and local political units are more susceptible to factional control than Congress, and consequently that "racial discrimination against any group finds a more ready expression at the state and local than at the federal level"? Or is redressing general, nonparticularized discrimination simply beyond state or local legislative competence? Given that the Court subsequently would hold in Adarand Constructors v. Pena that strict scrutiny applies both to the states and the federal government, how seriously should one take either Justice O'Connor's or Justice Scalia's arguments about the differences between the states and the federal government?

2. Croson *and the fate of* Carolene Products. The theory of judicial review introduced in *Carolene Products* argues that heightened scrutiny should apply to legislation that burdens "discrete and insular minorities." It follows that legislation that burdens a group that is not a discrete and insular minority, like whites, should receive the usual presumption of constitutionality (and perhaps even minimal scrutiny), because the dispreferred can rely on the ordinary processes of democracy to repeal unwise or unfair legislation. At the very least, this is the approach the Court has taken with respect to groups like the aged, who are not considered discrete and insular minorities.

Note that the Court basically rejects this democracy-based approach in *Croson*. Although Justice O'Connor points to the fact that blacks constitute a majority of the City of Richmond and control the Richmond City Council, there is no evidence that her opinion would have reached a different conclusion if whites were a majority and, indeed, had controlled all of the Council seats. Indeed, even if the white citizens of Richmond had unanimously agreed to the plan in a referendum it would have still been subjected to strict scrutiny. Note that, in any case, the other groups benefited by the affirmative action plan — in particular Hispanics — did not constitute a majority in Richmond, yet the Court did not try to sever these parts of the plan from the portion that benefited African-Americans. Should it have?

Note as well that, like Brown v. Board of Education and Roe v. Wade, *Croson* involves unelected judges striking down an act of a democratically elected body. If democracy-reinforcement does not explain this exercise of judicial power, what does? Is *Croson* based on the text of the Equal Protection Clause? On the original understanding of the Fourteenth Amendment? On the moral and political theories of the Justices? Should *Croson* give advocates of judicial restraint pause? Why do you think the Court's most passionate advocate of judicial restraint, Chief Justice Rehnquist, joined in the majority's opinion?

3. Drew S. Days III, who represented the United States before the Supreme Court in *Fullilove*, argued in a 1987 article that courts should seek to compel "principled decisionmaking" by public and private actors adopting race-conscious remedies:

> Government agencies establishing set-asides should be held to a higher standard than at present, although they should not have to satisfy the procedural and evidentiary requirements demanded of courts or administrative tribunals engaged in resolving specific discrimination claims. State and local agencies creating set-asides should, for example, be able to rely in part upon federal legislative or agency findings and judicial determinations regarding nationwide discrimination against minority business enterprises as predicates for considering the propriety of set-asides in their respective jurisdictions. But it is essential that state and local agencies also establish the presence of discrimination in their own bailiwicks, based either upon their own fact-finding processes or upon determinations made by other competent institutions, such as courts and administrative agencies.[143]

Do you agree with Justice O'Connor that Richmond had engaged in insufficient fact-finding?

4. *Societal discrimination. Croson* rejects remedying "societal discrimination" as a compelling governmental interest sufficient to pass strict scrutiny. With respect to the "societal discrimination" rationale, consider Professor Roger Wilkins's argument that the urban black poor occupy a unique historical and social position in American life and may therefore require race-based programs specially tailored to their needs:

> No matter how much more politically palatable general programs might be, the black poor need programs designed specifically for them because some of the black poor are different. . . . [T]he racially inflicted economic, cultural, and psychological damage [the black poor] suffer is unique and hideously destructive and requires specially tailored remedies.
>
> The inner city poor are poor because they have been scarred more deeply by the legacy of slavery than the rest of us. Racism has always hurt some blacks more than others. At the time of the Revolution, some blacks were free, literate and living in Boston; others were little better than beasts of burden and sexual chattel in South Carolina.
>
> Some blacks came North before Emancipation and others were slammed back into semislavery during and especially after Reconstruction. Some of their descendants remained illiterate peasants in the South in the sixth and even seventh decades of this century. They were driven off the land by the mechanization of agriculture.
>
> When they got to the major cities, millions of the unskilled jobs that the underclasses from Europe and earlier black emigres from the South had used as ladders to the middle class were disappearing. Some survived this transition while others became disoriented and redundant in the cities' hard and dirty backwaters. . . .
>
> Economically superfluous people engulfed by societal opprobrium, environmental ugliness and cultural desolation experience the same sense of futurelessness that

143. Drew S. Days, Fullilove, 96 Yale L.J. 453 (1987).

people under wartime bombardment do. They live under constant stress. Many do not play by the rules generated by people for whom society works. . . .

Children born into this chaos are victims at birth and on their way to becoming societal burdens or menaces at 15. If these children are to be saved, we must find ways to nurse health back into families in the inner cities, where family disintegration is ripping black culture apart, putting an enormous segment of the black future at risk.[144]

Does Wilkins's argument justify affirmative action that benefits middle-class blacks in employment or education? Or is his argument a justification for increased resources for primary education for inner-city black youth and jobs for working-class blacks? Would such race-conscious initiatives by the City of Richmond (or by the State of Virginia) be constitutional under *Croson?*

5. *Why are there so few black contractors in Richmond?* Contrast the narratives told by the majority and the dissent about how blacks came to have such low representation in the construction industry in Richmond. What kinds of causal assumptions do the two sides make?

Justice O'Connor argues that "the 30% quota" chosen by the Richmond City Council "cannot be said to be narrowly tailored to any goal, except perhaps outright racial balancing. It rests upon the 'completely unrealistic' assumption that minorities will choose a particular trade in lockstep proportion to their representation in the local population." Why, precisely, does O'Connor think that, absent discrimination, minorities would not choose a particular trade in roughly the same proportion as the general population?

One theory would be that some social groups simply have cultural preferences for certain types of occupations rather than others. Thus, we might find very few Jews going into the pork sausage industry. Is there any reason to think that African-Americans have a special distaste for the contracting industry? Note that similar arguments have often been offered to explain why women stay out of certain professions, like contracting. Is this "lack of interest" phenomenon based purely on private preferences that are unrelated to societal discrimination? See Vicki Schultz, Telling Stories about Women and Work: Judicial Interpretations of Sex Segregation in the Workplace in Title VII Cases Raising the Lack of Interest Argument, 103 Harv. L. Rev. 1750 (1990).

A second reason to expect disparities in representation would be that some social groups gravitate toward certain occupations in random patterns due to the effects of immigration. Thus, if one Korean family opens a grocery store, members of their family and friends who immigrate from Korea subsequently might work for them, learn skills, and eventually open their own grocery store. As a result, without any form of social discrimination at work, more Koreans will end up working in grocery stores, than say, tobacco shops or diners. Given that most African-Americans did not immigrate into this country recently, is this an adequate explanation for their lack of representation in the construction industry?

A third explanation is that some social groups are harder working and more energetic than others, adapt themselves better to majority expectations, and therefore are better represented in the most remunerative occupations. For

---

144. Wilkins, The Black Poor Are Different, N.Y. Times, Aug. 22, 1989, at A19.

example, the higher representation of Jews in professions like law and medicine is sometimes explained in this way. However, to offer this sort of explanation means that one must also believe that other social groups have, by comparison, less of these desirable traits and that explains why they do worse. Consider Morris Abram:

> Because groups — black, white, Hispanic, male, and female — do not necessarily have the same distribution of, among other characteristics, skills, interest, motivation, and age, a fair shake system may not produce proportional representation across occupations and professions, and certainly not at any given time. This uneven distribution, however, is not necessarily the result of discrimination. Thomas Sowell has shown through comparative studies of ethnic group performance that discrimination alone cannot explain these ethnic groups' varying levels of achievement. Groups such as the Japanese, Chinese and West Indian blacks have fared very well in American society despite racial bias against these groups.[145]

Consider whether this is an explanation the Court would be likely to offer for the lack of black participation in the Richmond construction industry. Is it in tension with the colorblind assumption that government agencies (in this case, federal courts) should not presume that skin color makes a difference in how people are likely to behave?

Note once again that this sort of explanation of black underrepresentation in the construction industry involves what Professor Gotanda calls a cultural conception of race rather than the formal notion of race that lies at the heart of the colorblindness principle. Opponents of affirmative action generally reject a cultural conception of race when it is argued that blacks add special diversity in education; it is said to involve invidious stereotyping to assume that the way one thinks or behaves is strongly correlated with the color of one's skin. If so, why should one accept a cultural account as an explanation of black underrepresentation here? Is it fair to invoke a formal account of race to combat arguments for affirmative action based on diversity and invoke a cultural account of race to combat arguments for affirmative action based on the need to remedy past discrimination?[146]

Even if this kind of cultural explanation could be offered to explain black underrepresentation in the Richmond construction industry, do you think that it is unrelated to societal discrimination? Do you think, in particular, that Abram's account can explain why so few contractors were black in a city that was 50 percent black,

---

145. Morris B. Abram, Affirmative Action: Fair Shakers and Social Engineers, 99 Harv. L. Rev. 1312, 1315-1316 (1986). See also Charles Murray, What It Means to Be a Libertarian: A Personal Interpretation 85-86 (1997) ("[A] system that . . . judg[ed] each case perfectly on its merits[] would produce drastically different proportions of men and women hired by police forces, blacks and whites put in jail, or Jews and gentiles admitted to elite law schools"); Nathan Glazer, Affirmative Discrimination: Ethnic Inequality and Public Policy 62-63 (1975) (distribution of jobs among minority groups is best explained by differences in educational qualifications, regional variables, and difficult to qualify factors "such as taste, or, if you will, culture").

146. See Reva B. Siegel, The Racial Rhetorics of Colorblind Affirmative Action, in Representing Affirmative Action (Robert Post ed., 1998). If you find this sort of rhetorical strategy opportunistic and unfair, ask yourself the converse question whether it is permissible to invoke cultural notions of race to justify diversity-based affirmative action and formal accounts of race to justify remedial affirmative action.

and why only .67 percent of the city's prime construction contracts were awarded to minority businesses in the five-year period from 1978 to 1983? Even if one thought that the private preferences and tastes of blacks played a significant role in steering blacks away from construction jobs in addition to the effects of private discrimination, is the 30 percent figure chosen by the Richmond City Council in a 50 percent black population entirely unreasonable?

6. *Colorblindness versus "social engineering."* Justice O'Connor's rejection of the 30 percent figure as "outright racial balancing" suggests that she believes either that racial stratification and racial segregation of labor markets will occur naturally, without much private racial discrimination, or that even if private racial discrimination plays a significant role, there is nothing that government can do to prevent such racial stratification and racial segregation. Attempting to achieve more equal representation of blacks in the construction industry would be mere "social engineering" that would not eradicate racism but merely stoke the fires of racial resentment. Compare this analysis to Justice Brown's comment in *Plessy* that "[l]egislation is powerless to eradicate racial instincts or to abolish distinctions based upon physical differences, and the attempt to do so can only result in accentuating the difficulties of the present situation." Could one fairly summarize O'Connor's argument as substituting the word "cultural" for the word "physical"? Justice Brown added that "[i]f one race be inferior to the other socially, the Constitution of the United States cannot put them upon the same plane." Is that still true today?

7. Metro Broadcasting: *Diversity as a justification for affirmative action.* In Metro Broadcasting v. FCC, 497 U.S. 547 (1990), the Court, by a 5-4 margin, upheld two of the Federal Communications Commission's minority preference policies. One policy provided that minority-owned businesses would be given a plus in competitive evaluations for new station licenses. The other policy was the so-called "distress sale" policy. It allowed broadcasters whose licenses were subject to renewal or revocation hearings to transfer them instead to minority-owned businesses.

According to Justice Brennan's majority opinion, the lesson of *Fullilove* was that "race conscious classifications adopted by Congress to address racial and ethnic discrimination are subject to a different standard than such classifications prescribed by state and local governments." Hence "benign race-conscious measures mandated by Congress — even if those measures are not 'remedial' in the sense of being designed to compensate victims of past governmental or societal discrimination — are constitutionally permissible to the extent that they serve important governmental objectives within the power of Congress and are substantially related to achievement of those objectives." Congress's interest in "enhancing broadcast diversity" was "at the very least, an important governmental objective." Analogizing the case to *Bakke*, Justice Brennan wrote that "[j]ust as a 'diverse student body' contributing to a 'robust exchange of ideas' is a 'constitutionally permissible goal' on which a race-conscious university admissions program may be predicated, the diversity of views and information on the airwaves serves important First Amendment values." Justice Brennan also concluded that the FCC policies were substantially related to the achievement of broadcast diversity, that they were not based on inappropriate stereotyping of minorities, and that they did not impose impermissible burdens on nonminorities.

Justice O'Connor's dissent argued that at most *Fullilove* held that Congress's §5 powers allowed it to pass special kinds of remedial legislation. Citing Bolling v. Sharpe, she stated that "[t]he Constitution's guarantee of equal protection binds the Federal Government as it does the States, and no lower level of scrutiny applies to the Federal Government's use of race classifications. . . . The FCC's choice to employ a racial criterion embodies the related notions that a particular and distinct viewpoint inheres in certain racial groups, and that a particular applicant, by virtue of race or ethnicity alone, is more valued than other applicants because 'likely to provide [that] distinct perspective.' . . . The policies impermissibly value individuals because they presume that persons think in a manner associated with their race."

Justice Kennedy's dissent compared the majority's opinion to the Court's use of a reasonableness standard in Plessy v. Ferguson. He questioned the Court's abandonment of purely remedial goals for affirmative action. "Although the majority is 'confident' that it can tell when racial discrimination is benign," Justice Kennedy argued, "it offers no explanation as to how it will do so." Moreover, "the FCC's policy seems based on the demeaning notion that members of the defined racial groups ascribe to certain 'minority views' that must be different from those of other citizens." Finally, Justice Kennedy argued that the Court failed to consider the interests of nonpreferred groups:

> The perceptions of the excluded class must also be weighed, with attention to the cardinal rule that our Constitution protects each citizen as an individual, not as a member of a group. There is the danger that the "stereotypical thinking" that prompts policies such as the FCC rules here "stigmatizes the disadvantaged class with the unproven charge of past racial discrimination." Whether or not such programs can be described as "remedial," the message conveyed is that it is acceptable to harm a member of the group excluded from the benefit or privilege. If this is to be considered acceptable under the Constitution, there are various possible explanations. One is that the group disadvantaged by the preference should feel no stigma at all, because racial preferences address not the evil of intentional discrimination but the continuing unconscious use of stereotypes that disadvantage minority groups. But this is not a proposition that the many citizens, who to their knowledge "have never discriminated against anyone on the basis of race," will find easy to accept.
>
> Another explanation might be that the stigma imposed upon the excluded class should be overlooked, either because past wrongs are so grievous that the disfavored class must bear collective blame, or because individual harms are simply irrelevant in the face of efforts to compensate for racial inequalities. But these are not premises that the Court even appears willing to address in its analysis. Until the Court is candid about the existence of stigma imposed by racial preferences on both affected classes, candid about the "animosity and discontent" they create, and open about defending a theory that explains why the cost of this stigma is worth bearing and why it can consist with the Constitution, no basis can be shown for today's casual abandonment of strict scrutiny.

8. *Protecting the dispreferred.* Note that Justice Kennedy's dissent in *Metro Broadcasting* expresses deep concern for groups disadvantaged by affirmative action programs. Not all minorities were covered by the FCC regulation (note, however that Asian-Americans, Hispanics, Eskimos, Aleuts, and Native Americans as well as blacks were considered minorities for this purpose). Nevertheless, it seems fairly clear from Justice Kennedy's rhetoric (for example, his reference to accusations of

"collective blame," and to the "animosity and discontent" that preferences create) that he is speaking primarily about injury to whites. Why does Justice Kennedy not mention whites by name? Is this sort of rhetoric a necessary condition of color-blindness? Is there a connection between colorblindness and the protection of white interests? Is any such effect irrelevant if colorblindness is designed to be neutral as between racial groups?

The resignation of Justices Brennan and Marshall left vulnerable the distinction drawn in *Metro Broadcasting* between the powers of the FCC (and of Congress) and those of the States, as delineated in *Croson*. Although the appointment of Justice Souter to replace Justice Brennan did not change the balance of power on the Court on this issue, Justice Marshall's replacement by Justice Thomas did.

ADARAND CONSTRUCTORS v. PENA, 515 U.S. 200 (1995): [Adarand, which had submitted the low bid for a federal highway construction project in Colorado, challenged the award of a subcontract to the Gonzales Construction Company. Section 8(a) of the Small Business Act awarded compensation to prime contractors doing business with the federal government if they hired subcontractors certified as small businesses controlled by "socially and economically disadvantaged individuals." These are presumed by law to include "Black Americans, Hispanic Americans, Native Americans, Asian Pacific Americans, and other minorities, or any other individual found to be disadvantaged by the [Small Business] Administration pursuant to Section 8(a) of the Small Business Act." Adarand challenged the presumption as unconstitutional. The Court, by a vote of 5-4 overruled *Metro Broadcasting*.]

O'CONNOR, J.:

[T]he Court's cases through *Croson* had established three general propositions with respect to governmental racial classifications. First, skepticism: "Any prefer-ence based on racial or ethnic criteria must necessarily receive a most searching examination." Second, consistency: "The standard of review under the Equal Protection Clause is not dependent on the race of those burdened or benefited by a particular classification." And third, congruence: "Equal protection analysis in the Fifth Amendment area is the same as that under the Fourteenth Amendment." Taken together, these three propositions lead to the conclusion that any person, of whatever race, has the right to demand that any governmental actor subject to the Constitution justify any racial classification subjecting that person to unequal treat-ment under the strictest judicial scrutiny. . . .

[D]espite the surface appeal of holding "benign" racial classifications to a lower standard, . . . "it may not always be clear that a so-called preference is in fact benign." . . . Under *Metro Broadcasting*, certain racial classifications ("benign" ones enacted by the Federal Government) should be treated less skeptically than others; and the race of the benefited group is critical to the determination of which stan-dard of review to apply. *Metro Broadcasting* was thus a significant departure from much of what had come before it.

The three propositions undermined by *Metro Broadcasting* all derive from the basic principle that the Fifth and Fourteenth Amendments to the Constitution protect persons, not groups. It follows from that principle that all governmental action based on race — a group classification long recognized as "in most circumstances irrelevant and therefore prohibited" — should be subjected to detailed judicial inquiry to ensure that the personal right to equal protection of the laws has not been infringed. . . . Accordingly, we hold today that all racial classifications, imposed by whatever federal, state, or local governmental actor, must be analyzed by a reviewing court under strict scrutiny. In other words, such classifications are constitutional only if they are narrowly tailored measures that further compel governmental interests. To the extent that *Metro Broadcasting* is inconsistent with that holding, it is overruled. . . .

Justice Stevens['s dissent] fails to recognize . . . that strict scrutiny does take "relevant differences" into account — indeed, that is its fundamental purpose. The point of carefully examining the interest asserted by the government in support of a racial classification, and the evidence offered to show that the classification is needed, is precisely to distinguish legitimate from illegitimate uses of race in governmental decisionmaking. . . . Strict scrutiny does not "treat dissimilar race-based decisions as though they were equally objectionable"; to the contrary, it evaluates carefully all governmental race-based decisions in order to decide which are constitutionally objectionable and which are not. By requiring strict scrutiny of racial classifications, we require courts to make sure that a governmental classification based on race, which "so seldom provide[s] a relevant basis for disparate treatment," *Fullilove* (Stevens, J., dissenting), is legitimate, before permitting unequal treatment based on race to proceed. . . .

The principle of consistency simply means that whenever the government treats any person unequally because of his or her race, that person has suffered an injury that falls squarely within the language and spirit of the Constitution's guarantee of equal protection. It says nothing about the ultimate validity of any particular law; that determination is the job of the court applying strict scrutiny. The principle of consistency explains the circumstances in which the injury requiring strict scrutiny occurs. The application of strict scrutiny, in turn, determines whether a compelling governmental interest justifies the infliction of that injury. . . .

. . . [T]o the extent (if any) that *Fullilove* held federal racial classifications to be subject to a less rigorous standard, it is no longer controlling. But we need not decide today whether the program upheld in *Fullilove* would survive strict scrutiny as our more recent cases have defined it. . . .

Finally, we wish to dispel the notion that strict scrutiny is "strict in theory, but fatal in fact." The unhappy persistence of both the practice and the lingering effects of racial discrimination against minority groups in this country is an unfortunate reality, and government is not disqualified from acting in response to it. As recently as 1987, for example, every Justice of this Court agreed that the Alabama Department of Public Safety's "pervasive, systematic, and obstinate discriminatory conduct" justified a narrowly tailored race-based remedy. When race-based action is necessary to further a compelling interest, such action is within constitutional constraints if it satisfies the "narrow tailoring" test this Court has set out in previous cases.

Because our decision today alters the playing field in some important respects, we think it best to remand the case to the lower courts for further consideration in light of the principles we have announced. . . .

SCALIA, J., concurring in part and concurring in the judgment:

I join the opinion of the Court . . . except insofar as it may be inconsistent with the following: In my view, government can never have a "compelling interest" in discriminating on the basis of race in order to "make up" for past racial discrimination in the opposite direction. Individuals who have been wronged by unlawful racial discrimination should be made whole; but under our Constitution there can be no such thing as either a creditor or a debtor race. That concept is alien to the Constitution's focus upon the individual, see Amdt. 14, §1 ("Nor shall any State . . . deny to any *person*" the equal protection of the laws) (emphasis added), and its rejection of dispositions based on race, see Amdt. 15, §1 (prohibiting abridgment of the right to vote "on account of race"), or based on blood, see Art. III, §3 ("No Attainder of Treason shall work Corruption of Blood"); Art. I, §9, cl. 8 ("No Title of Nobility shall be granted by the United States"). To pursue the concept of racial entitlement — even for the most admirable and benign of purposes — is to reinforce and preserve for future mischief the way of thinking that produced race slavery, race privilege and race hatred. In the eyes of government, we are just one race here. It is American.

THOMAS, J: concurring in part and concurring in the judgment:

I agree with the majority's conclusion that strict scrutiny applies to all government classifications based on race. I write separately, however, to express my disagreement with the premise underlying Justice Stevens' and Justice Ginsburg's dissents: that there is a racial paternalism exception to the principle of equal protection. I believe that there is a "moral [and] constitutional equivalence" between laws designed to subjugate a race and those that distribute benefits on the basis of race in order to foster some current notion of equality. Government cannot make us equal; it can only recognize, respect, and protect us as equal before the law.

That these programs may have been motivated, in part, by good intentions cannot provide refuge from the principle that under our Constitution, the government may not make distinctions on the basis of race. As far as the Constitution is concerned, it is irrelevant whether a government's racial classifications are drawn by those who wish to oppress a race or by those who have a sincere desire to help those thought to be disadvantaged. There can be no doubt that the paternalism that appears to lie at the heart of this program is at war with the principle of inherent equality that underlies and infuses our Constitution. See Declaration of Independence ("We hold these truths to be self-evident, that all men are created equal, that they are endowed by their Creator with certain unalienable Rights, that among these are Life, Liberty, and the pursuit of Happiness"). . . .

In my mind, government-sponsored racial discrimination based on benign prejudice is just as noxious as discrimination inspired by malicious prejudice. In each instance, it is racial discrimination, plain and simple.

STEVENS, J, with whom Ginsburg, J., joins, dissenting:

The Court's concept of "consistency" assumes that there is no significant difference between a decision by the majority to impose a special burden on the members of a minority race and a decision by the majority to provide a benefit to certain members of that minority notwithstanding its incidental burden on some members of the majority. In my opinion that assumption is untenable. There is no moral or constitutional equivalence between a policy that is designed to perpetuate a caste system and one that seeks to eradicate racial subordination. Invidious discrimination is an engine of oppression, subjugating a disfavored group to enhance or maintain the power of the majority. Remedial race-based preferences reflect the opposite impulse: a desire to foster equality in society. . . .

The consistency that the Court espouses would disregard the difference between a "No Trespassing" sign and a welcome mat. It would treat a Dixiecrat Senator's decision to vote against Thurgood Marshall's confirmation in order to keep African Americans off the Supreme Court as on a par with President Johnson's evaluation of his nominee's race as a positive factor. It would equate a law that made black citizens ineligible for military service with a program aimed at recruiting black soldiers. An attempt by the majority to exclude members of a minority race from a regulated market is fundamentally different from a subsidy that enables a relatively small group of newcomers to enter that market. . . .

The Court's explanation for treating dissimilar race-based decisions as though they were equally objectionable is a supposed inability to differentiate between "invidious" and "benign" discrimination. But the term "affirmative action" is common and well understood. Its presence in everyday parlance shows that people understand the difference between good intentions and bad. As with any legal concept, some cases may be difficult to classify, but our equal protection jurisprudence has identified a critical difference between state action that imposes burdens on a disfavored few and state action that benefits the few "in spite of" its adverse effects on the many.

Indeed, our jurisprudence has made the standard to be applied in cases of invidious discrimination turn on whether the discrimination is "intentional," or whether, by contrast, it merely has a discriminatory "effect." *Washington v. Davis.* Surely this distinction is at least as subtle, and at least as difficult to apply as the usually obvious distinction between a measure intended to benefit members of a particular minority race and a measure intended to burden a minority race. A state actor inclined to subvert the Constitution might easily hide bad intentions in the guise of unintended "effects"; but I should think it far more difficult to enact a law intending to preserve the majority's hegemony while casting it plausibly in the guise of affirmative action for minorities. . . .

[T]oday's lecture about "consistency" will produce the anomalous result that the Government can more easily enact affirmative-action programs to remedy discrimination against women than it can enact affirmative-action programs to remedy discrimination against African Americans — even though the primary purpose of the Equal Protection Clause was to end discrimination against the former slaves. When a court becomes preoccupied with abstract standards, it risks sacrificing common sense at the altar of formal consistency.

As a matter of constitutional and democratic principle, a decision by representatives of the majority to discriminate against the members of a minority race is fundamentally different from those same representatives' decision to impose incidental costs on the majority of their constituents in order to provide a benefit to a disadvantaged minority. Indeed, as I have previously argued, the former is virtually always repugnant to the principles of a free and democratic society, whereas the latter is, in some circumstances, entirely consistent with the ideal of equality. . . .

[I]t is one thing to say (as no one seems to dispute) that the Fifth Amendment encompasses a general guarantee of equal protection as broad as that contained within the Fourteenth Amendment. It is another thing entirely to say that Congress'

institutional competence and constitutional authority entitles it to no greater deference when it enacts a program designed to foster equality than the deference due a
state legislature. . . .

The Fourteenth Amendment directly empowers Congress [in §5] at the same
time it expressly limits the States [in §1]. This is no accident. It represents our
Nation's consensus, achieved after hard experience throughout our sorry history of
race relations, that the Federal Government must be the primary defender of racial
minorities against the States, some of which may be inclined to oppress such
minorities. A rule of "congruence" that ignores a purposeful "incongruity" so
fundamental to our system of government is unacceptable.

[Justice Souter, joined by Justices Ginsburg and Justice Breyer, and Justice
Ginsburg, joined by Justice Breyer, also dissented.]

Discussion

1. Doctrinal distinctions aside, although after *Adarand* strict scrutiny applies to
both state *and* federal legislation, does this development necessarily affect the
outcomes of future challenges to federal affirmative action programs?

2. *Hispanic invisibility.* Note that the business that received the bid that
Adarand Construction complained of was Hispanic-owned. As the Census
Bureau continually reminds us, Hispanics can be of any race. Nevertheless, the
opinions in *Adarand* almost without exception proceed as if the issue was about
affirmative action based on race, and, in particular, affirmative action on behalf
of blacks. Why are Hispanics made invisible in the Court's rhetoric? Why do the
members of the Court speak as if the issue were primarily one of black-white
relations?

3. *Protecting whites from unfairness or blacks from stigmatic harm?* In *Bakke* and to
some extent in *Wygant*, the Court's opinions emphasized the harms to innocent
members of nonpreferred groups, i.e., whites. In *Croson* and *Adarand*, however, this
justification for opposition to affirmative action has largely disappeared. (The most
notable exception to this trend is Justice Kennedy's dissent in *Metro Broadcasting*,
quoted above.) Affirmative action is now said primarily to burden blacks and other
minorities, either because it fails to treat them as individuals or because it imposes
stigmatic harms on them. Why do you think the Court does not emphasize more
strongly the unfairness to whites rather than the harm to blacks? If affirmative
action programs so seriously stigmatize blacks, what explains continued black
support for them?

4. *Racial paternalism.* Justice Thomas rejects affirmative action as a form of "racial
paternalism." Paternalism usually refers to choices made for people who cannot
decide matters appropriately for themselves. Is it clear to you that affirmative action
is being foisted on blacks and other minorities against their will or without their
consent? Rather, isn't it more likely that affirmative action programs are created by
majorities in an attempt to curry favor with minorities and in order to gain their
political support?

The Court's decisions in *Croson* and *Adarand*, on the other hand, hold that
minorities cannot have affirmative action programs (or at least that these
programs will be constitutionally suspect) even if minorities want them, because
in the long run racial preferences are bad for minorities and bad for the country.
Moreover, these decisions also second-guess majority decisionmaking: If majorities want to gain political support from racial and ethnic minorities and avoid

constitutional problems, they will have to offer them benefits that are class based or otherwise do not make distinctions based on group membership. Should either of these results be regarded as a kind of racial paternalism by the Court? Is Justice Thomas suggesting that minorities must be prevented from seeking affirmative action programs from majorities that will only create white resentment and make them worse off in the long run? Is there anything paternalistic about this view?

5. As in *Croson*, Justice O'Connor argues that strict scrutiny should apply to all racial classifications because it may be difficult to tell which racial classifications are benign and which are invidious. Even so, is it clear that the Court views all racial classifications alike? If Congress had created a preference program for whites, do you think that the Court would have remanded the issue to the lower courts for more detailed consideration?

Note: Affirmative Action and the Original Understanding

Given that Justices Scalia and Thomas have been strong supporters of a jurisprudence of original understanding, and have invoked the original understanding in cases ranging from federalism to the First Amendment, it is strange that they have not attempted to discern whether the framers of the Fourteenth Amendment would have objected to race-conscious affirmative action programs, and whether the argument for a "colorblind" Constitution has any basis in the original understanding of the Civil War amendments. Obviously, if the framers would have supported such programs, Scalia's and Thomas's objections must rest on grounds other than fidelity to the original understanding. Reviewing the history of the period suggests some of the complicated problems that arise from a serious attempt to grapple with a philosophy of originalism and the difficulties that inevitably occur in trying to discern what the present constitutional consequences should be of past justifications and practices.

1. *Was federal Reconstruction legislation race-conscious or race-neutral?* Eric Schnapper writes:

> From the closing days of the Civil War until the end of civilian Reconstruction some five years later, Congress adopted a series of social welfare programs whose benefits were expressly limited to blacks. These programs were generally open to all blacks, not only to recently freed slaves, and were adopted over repeatedly expressed objections that such racially exclusive measures were unfair to whites. The race-conscious Reconstruction programs were enacted concurrently with the fourteenth amendment and were supported by the same legislators who favored the constitutional guarantee of equal protection. This history strongly suggests that the framers of the amendment could not have intended it generally to prohibit affirmative action for blacks or other disadvantaged groups.

Eric Schnapper, Affirmative Action and the Legislative History of the Fourteenth Amendment, 71 Va. L. Rev. 753, 754, 760-761 (1985). Schnapper emphasizes in particular the 1865 and 1866 Freedmen's Bureau Acts.

Paul Moreno has responded that all "Freedmen's Bureau and civil rights acts from 1865 onwards" granted benefits and special treatment to "refugees and freedmen," a facially race-neutral classification that also included white refugees of the Civil War. Paul Moreno, Racial Classifications and Reconstruction Legislation, 61 Journal of Southern History 271, 277-278 (1995). Although Schnapper contends that the inclusion of white refugees "was not a significant impetus in the adoption of the [1865] Act," Moreno insists that "the inclusion of white refugees was crucial to the adoption of the act." Schnapper points out that in practice, the benefits of the 1865 Act went overwhelmingly to blacks, and that "[f]reedmen were the only beneficiaries of programs such as education, labor regulation, Bureau farms, land distribution, adjustments of real estate disputes, [and] supervision of the civil and criminal justice systems through the freedmen's courts." This suggests that the inclusion of white refugees was primarily a fig leaf designed to mollify Democrats and more conservative Republicans. This also tends to support both Schnapper's view that the act was race-conscious in intention and Moreno's view that the price of passage was that it be formally race-neutral.

Stephen Siegel objects to Moreno's arguments on another ground: He points out that the reference to "freedmen" and to "previous condition of servitude" in the Freedmen's Acts (and other Reconstruction era legislation) was clearly a racial category. He points out that "[i]n post-bellum America, race, color, and 'previous condition of servitude' were fully interchangeable" particularly because Southern legislatures used the category of "previous condition of servitude" as a means of subordinating blacks. Stephen A. Siegel, The Federal Government's Power to Enact Color-Conscious Laws: An Originalist Inquiry 92 Nw. U.L. Rev. 477, 560 (1998). Hence, in Siegel's view, statutes that gave benefits to "freedmen and refugees" would still be color-conscious even if some refugees were white.

Siegel points out that not only the Freedmen's Acts but many other pieces of legislation specifically granted benefits to people based on their previous condition of servitude. For example, prior to the 1865 Freedmen's Act, Congress had created a bank for "persons heretofore held in slavery in the United States, or their descendants," Act of March 3, 1865, ch. 92, 13 Stat. 510. Moreno argues that reconstruction legislation designed to benefit former slaves was not color-conscious, but was only designed to remedy actual victims of race discrimination, a form of remedial relief that modern-day opponents of affirmative action are happy to accept. To demonstrate this, Moreno points to the fact that the phrase "and other persons of African descent" was struck from the bill. How does one explain the retention of the words "or their descendants?"

Similar problems occur in discerning the meaning of the 1866 Freedmen's Bureau Act, which extended the 1865 Act. Schnapper argues that while the 1866 Act was also formally race-neutral in its application to "freedmen and refugees," much opposition was based on the grounds that its benefits went exclusively to blacks:

> Congressmen Taylor and Ritter, opposing the bill, contended that there were no longer any refugees for the Bureau to assist. Taylor explained that "the great change wrought by the termination of the war . . . leaves the name of refugee without a meaning" and therefore that [the bill] was "solely and entirely for the freedmen." Similarly, Representative Chanler reviewed the [Freedmen's] Bureau's report [on its previous activities] in detail to demonstrate the paucity of assistance to refugees: "This

present bill is to secure the protection of government to the blacks exclusively, notwithstanding the apparent liberality of the measure to all colors and classes." . . .

Most opponents of the 1866 bill complained, in the words of Senator Willey, that it made "a distinction on account of color between the two races." Congressman Taylor most forcefully expressed this argument, in language that bears an uncanny resemblance to modern objections to affirmative action programs:

> This, sir, is what I call class legislation — legislation for a particular class of the blacks to the exclusion of all whites. . . . I warn the gentlemen in their zeal to elevate and ameliorate the condition of the freedmen not to allow this bill to pass regardless of the great principle, equality before the law. . . . Many persons in our community have been proclaiming equality before the law so long, taking their text from the institution of slavery. . . it would be well to stop and consider whether or not by passing this bill in its present shape we shall not overleap the mark and land on the other side, and before we are aware of it, not have the freedmen equal before the law, but superior.[147]

Proponents of the 1866 bill responded to these arguments by insisting that the bill was race-neutral, and emphasized the Bureau's provision of goods to White refugees, but opponents insisted that this was a sham.[148] President Johnson vetoed the first version of the 1866 bill, but Congress passed a new bill that overrode his veto. This version extended the bureau for two years, for the benefit of "all loyal refugees and freedmen," but also directed the Bureau to provide educational facilities for freedmen until the states "made provision for the education of their citizens without distinction of color." Is the latter provision race conscious? Note that it was in the interests of supporters of the Freedmen's Bureau Act to insist that the Act was race-neutral even if their intention was primarily to benefit blacks, and it was in the interests of their opponents to argue that the Act was in effect special favoritism for blacks, even if some whites were actually benefited. Given this political background, what consequences should any of this have for the question of race-conscious affirmative action programs today?

2. *Was federal Reconstruction legislation at all relevant to the meaning of the Fourteenth Amendment?* A different objection to Schnapper's arguments is that congressional action is irrelevant to the meaning of the Fourteenth Amendment, because the federal government was not bound by the Fourteenth Amendment. However, this argument proves too much for originalist opponents of affirmative action, since it completely undermines *Adarand* as a matter of original understanding, not to mention Bolling v. Sharpe. Why might originalists like Justices Scalia and Thomas nevertheless accept *Bolling* and support decisions like *Adarand* without any serious inquiry into the original understanding?

In fact, one could argue that under the original understanding, the Privileges or Immunities Clause, not the Equal Protection Clause, binds the federal government as well as the states. The Privileges or Immunities Clause was designed to

---

147. Schnapper, at 763-764.

148. Despite these accusations by opponents of the Freedmen's Act of 1866, Moreno points out that assistance to White refugees in terms of food, fuel, and clothing was quite substantial, especially "in the areas that had been most loyal to the Union, especially in the border states and the high country." Moreno, at 287.

protect the civil rights of all citizens, but under the Citizenship Clause of Section 1, all citizens are equal citizens. Therefore, if the states treat white and black citizens differently with respect to their civil rights, they abridge the privileges and immunities of citizens of the United States. However, if the states cannot abridge the privileges and immunities of national citizenship, then a fortiori neither can the national government. Hence, if the states may not treat blacks and whites unequally with respect to civil rights, neither can the federal government.[149] (Note that by giving considerable substantive content to the Privileges or Immunities Clause, this interpretation is inconsistent with *The Slaughterhouse Cases*. Which way should that cut for an originalist?) Under this interpretation, what power, if any, would Congress have to pursue race-conscious affirmative action under §5 of the Fourteenth Amendment?

Stephen Siegel rejects this argument from implication: "The exclusion of the national government from the [Privileges or Immunities Clause] seems quite deliberate. Reconstruction era constitution makers knew how to bind both the states and the federal government when they thought it appropriate."[150] As a result he concludes that "nothing in the Founding era Constitution limits federal power to enact race-based classifications" and that "although the Reconstruction Amendments constrain federal power over certain subjects, such as slavery, citizenship and voting, they still leave the national government with extensive power to enact race-based laws."[151] Do you agree?

3. *Was federal Reconstruction legislation about civil equality or social equality?* Jed Rubenfeld argues that the best evidence of the original understanding is not the Freedman's Bureau Acts, but other Congressional legislation:

> In July 1866, the Thirty-Ninth Congress — the selfsame Congress that had just framed the Fourteenth Amendment — passed a statute appropriating money for . . . the relief of destitute colored women and children." In 1867, the Fortieth Congress — the same body that was driving the Fourteenth Amendment down the throat of the bloody South — passed a statute providing money for . . . the destitute "colored" persons in the nation's capital. Year after year in the Civil War period — before, during, and after ratification of the Fourteenth Amendment — Congress made special appropriations

---

149. See Akhil Reed Amar, The Bill of Rights: Creation and Reconstruction 281-283 (1998); Akhil Reed Amar, Constitutional Rights in a Federal System: Rethinking Incorporation and Reverse Incorporation, in Benchmarks: Great Constitutional Controversies in the Supreme Court 71 (Terry Eastland ed., 1995); Mark A. Graber, A Constitutional Conspiracy Unmasked, Why "No State" Does Not Mean "No State," 10 Const. Comm. 87 (1993).

150. Siegel, at 571. Siegel points to the Thirteenth and Fifteenth Amendments as examples. He also notes that the framers of the Fourteenth Amendment

> also textually bound the states and the national government in other sections of the Fourteenth Amendment: the fourth section's prohibition on payment of the Confederate debt, the third section's limitations on office holding by former Confederates, the second section's rules on legislative apportionment, and the first section's first sentence's definition of citizenship. Moreover, the text that became the Fourteenth Amendment's second sentence expressly bound both the states and the national government when originally presented to the Joint Committee on Reconstruction by Thaddeus Stevens on April 21, 1866. After a week of consideration, the Joint Committee removed the provision's express application to the federal government when on April 28 — after intense Republican party caucusing — it replaced Stevens's original proposal with John Bingham's substitute formulation just before finalizing its workproduct.

151. Id. at 481-482.

and adopted special procedures for awarding bounty and prize money to the "colored" soldiers and sailors of the Union Army.

These statutes are not like the well-known Freedmen's Bureau Acts of the same period, directing benefits to blacks but using classifications that were formally race-neutral. On the contrary, these statutes expressly refer to color in the allotment of federal benefits. Nor are these statutes buried in archives deep within the Library of Congress. They are, if not well-known, at least knowable by anyone who takes three minutes with the United States Statutes at Large (look up "colored" in the indexes for more). What do they prove? Only that those who profess fealty to the "original under-standing," who abhor judicial "activism," or who hold that the legal practices at the time of enactment "say what they say" and dictate future interpretation, cannot categorically condemn color-based distribution of governmental benefits as they do.[152]

Is this a compelling argument that race-conscious affirmative action was acceptable to the framers of the Fourteenth Amendment? Recall that the 39th Congress was wary about granting blacks full equality. They made a distinction between civil, political, and social equality.[153] Thus, one response to Rubenfeld's argument is that the framers accepted race-conscious relief that concerned social matters like education and welfare, but not questions of civil equality like the making of contracts. This distinction flowed from the fact that they expected blacks to be socially and politically unequal and only civilly equal.

How does this translate into contemporary terms? One view would be that affirmative action in education is permissible but not affirmative action in government contracting. Another view would be that education and forms of government assistance are so central to equal opportunity in today's world that the distinction between civil and social equality has completely eroded; hence no affirmative action programs are permissible. Of course, this leads back to the general problem of the appropriate way of interpreting the original understanding. One could argue in precisely the opposite direction — that the framers' repeated use of affirmative action in social matters means that affirmative action in contracting is now permissible given that the civil/social distinction has been exploded.

Whatever one's view on these questions, the historical record also tends to undermine several features of current doctrine that limit affirmative action programs. The framers of the Fourteenth Amendment offered welfare relief to indigent blacks whether or not they were the victims of discrimination, or, at the very least, without requiring any showing of previous discrimination. In almost every case the body (Congress) that created the race-conscious program was not the governmental unit that had previously discriminated against the recipients of the program. Nor did Congress make detailed findings of its previous discriminatory acts against blacks. This suggests that the current Court's rejection of programs that remedy general societal discrimination is unsupported by the original understanding. Also inconsistent with the original understanding is the current Court's requirement that only the governmental unit that previously discriminated against

152. Jed Rubenfeld, Affirmative Action, 107 Yale L.J. 427, 430-432 (1997) (citing Act of July 28, 1866, ch. 296, 14 Stat. 310, 317; Resolution of Mar. 16, 1867, No. 4, 15 Stat. 20). See also Siegel at 560-562 (offering additional examples).

153. Note that this distinction concerned the meaning of the Privileges or Immunities Clause. Recall that prior to *The Slaughterhouse Cases,* the Privileges or Immunities Clause, and not the Equal Protection Clause, was understood to be the primary guarantor of black equality.

minorities may engage in race-conscious remedies, and then only to alleviate the effects of its (well-documented) past discrimination.

4. *Did the framers of the Fourteenth Amendment subscribe to a "colorblind" theory?* One reason to argue that the framers' desire for complete civil equality between blacks and whites should be expanded into a general prohibition on any race-conscious relief is that the deepest meaning of the Fourteenth Amendment is the principle of colorblindness. However, it is not at all clear that the framers of the Fourteenth Amendment believed in a colorblindness principle, although it was repeatedly pressed on them by more radical thinkers like Thaddeus Stevens and the abolitionist Wendell Phillips.[154] Indeed, the evidence is quite to the contrary. Colorblindness was at most something accepted in the area of civil rights. Andrew Kull writes that the framers chose to speak of "privileges or immunities" and "equal protection" rather than colorblindness because they were worried that a colorblindness rule would give Blacks the vote: "[T]he evidence shows that an open-ended promise of equality was added to the Constitution because to its moderate proponents it meant less, not more, than the rule of nondiscrimination that was the rejected radical alternative."[155]

How, then, should an originalist interpret the constitutional text? If the political/civil/social distinction was paramount for the framers, why should it not be for modern-day originalists? Why should we not permit even discrimination against blacks under the Fourteenth Amendment as long as it is not a matter of civil equality as that term was generally understood in 1868? One argument is that we should respect only those parts of the framers' purposes and expectations that are just, but not those parts that are unjust. However, this is not, strictly speaking, an argument that respects the original understanding or is seriously limited by it. Rather, it is an argument about what is just and unjust. The basic difficulty of originalist arguments is that they must assume that the intentions, purposes, and understandings of the past are worthy of obedience; what is to be done when parts of them are now generally understood to be wicked or evil? We could argue that the deeper meaning of the framers' purpose was to gradually expand the notion of equality for all citizens, but an equally plausible interpretation was that their deeper meaning was to ensure that blacks be given some degree of equality as long as they were not made the full and social equals of whites.

"With Justice Harlan's dissenting opinion in *Plessy*," Kull writes, "the color-blind Constitution became one of the available meanings of the Fourteenth Amendment."[156] But even here the meaning of colorblindness is morally ambiguous. Like the framers of the Fourteenth Amendment, Justice Harlan believed that nothing in the colorblindness principle guaranteed full social equality for blacks; to Harlan colorblindness was perfectly consistent with blacks remaining social inferiors to whites "for all time."

154. Stevens's proposal for the Fourteenth Amendment (which was essentially the same as Phillips's) was introduced on December 5, 1866, and was explicitly based on the abolitionist demand for colorblindness: "All national and State laws shall be equally applicable to every citizen, and no discrimination shall be made on account of race and color." Cong. Globe, 39th Cong., 1st Sess. 10 (1865).

155. Andrew Kull, The Colorblind Constitution 69 (1992).

156. Id. at 118.

The connection between colorblindness and black social inequality leads to a final puzzle. Some critics of the Court's jurisprudence argue that its affirmative action decisions in *Croson* and *Adarand,* coupled with cases like *Davis* and *Feeney,* help guarantee that blacks will remain socially unequal even though they are formally equal with whites before the law. If the expectation of the framers of the Fourteenth Amendment was that blacks should remain social inferiors though civil equals to whites, and if the Court's doctrines achieve this practical effect, should we say that the Court is, in fact, being faithful to the original understanding?

3.   *The Court Reaffirms* Bakke

Following *Croson* and *Adarand,* a key question was whether the Court would revisit its previous decision in *Bakke.* A year after *Adarand,* in Hopwood v. State of Texas, 78 F.3d 932 (5th Cir. 1996), the Fifth Circuit held that "Justice Powell's argument in *Bakke* garnered only his own vote and has never represented the view of a majority of the Court in *Bakke* or any other case." It read *Adarand* as holding that the only compelling justification that the Supreme Court had recognized for affirmative action was remedying past discrimination and that "non-remedial state interests will never justify racial classifications." It concluded that "the use of ethnic diversity simply to achieve racial heterogeneity, even as part of the consideration of a number of factors, is unconstitutional"; and barred the University of Texas Law School from using race in its admissions decisions. The Supreme Court did not grant certiorari in *Hopwood*; instead, it considered a pair of challenges to the admissions policies at the Law School and the undergraduate program at the University of Michigan.

GRUTTER v. BOLLINGER
539 U.S. 306 (2003)

Justice O'CONNOR delivered the opinion of the Court.

This case requires us to decide whether the use of race as a factor in student admissions by the University of Michigan Law School (Law School) is unlawful.

I.

A

The Law School ranks among the Nation's top law schools. It receives more than 3,500 applications each year for a class of around 350 students. [The goal of its admissions policy is to] "admit a group of students who individually and collectively are among the most capable," . . . with "substantial promise for success in law school" and "a strong likelihood of succeeding in the practice of law and contributing in diverse ways to the well-being of others." More broadly, the Law School seeks "a mix of students with varying backgrounds and experiences who will respect and learn from each other."

The hallmark of [the Law School's admissions] policy is its focus on academic ability coupled with a flexible assessment of applicants' talents, experiences, and potential "to contribute to the learning of those around them." The policy requires admissions officials to evaluate each applicant based on all the information available in the file, including a personal statement, letters of recommendation, and an essay describing the ways in which the applicant will contribute to the life and diversity of the Law School. . . .[A]dmissions officials must consider the applicant's undergraduate grade[s] and Law School Admissions Test (LSAT) score; [however] even the highest possible score does not guarantee admission to the Law School. Nor does a low score automatically disqualify an applicant. Rather, . . . admissions officials [must] look beyond grades and test scores to . . . [s]o-called "soft variables" such as "the enthusiasm of recommenders, the quality of the undergraduate institution, the quality of the applicant's essay, and the areas and difficulty of undergraduate course selection" are all brought to bear in assessing an "applicant's likely contributions to the intellectual and social life of the institution."

The policy aspires to "achieve that diversity which has the potential to enrich everyone's education and thus make a law school class stronger than the sum of its parts." [It] . . . recognizes "many possible bases for diversity admissions" [but] reaffirm[s] the Law School's longstanding commitment to "one particular type of diversity," that is, "racial and ethnic diversity with special reference to the inclusion of students from groups which have been historically discriminated against, like African-Americans, Hispanics and Native Americans, who without this commitment might not be represented in our student body in meaningful numbers." By enrolling a " 'critical mass' of [underrepresented] minority students," the Law School seeks to "ensur[e] their ability to make unique contributions to the character of the Law School." . . .

B

[Petitioner Barbara Grutter is a white Michigan resident who applied to the Law School in 1996 with a 3.8 grade point average and 161 LSAT score. The Law School initially placed petitioner on a waiting list, but subsequently rejected her application. She sued the University of Michigan, the Law School and various university officials arguing that their admissions policy violated the Fourteenth Amendment and Title VI of the Civil Rights Act of 1964, which requires recipients of federal funds not to discriminate on the basis of race. She alleged that her application was rejected because the Law School uses race as a "predominant" factor, giving applicants who belong to certain minority groups "a significantly greater chance of admission than students with similar credentials from disfavored racial groups."]

During the 15-day bench trial, the parties introduced extensive evidence concerning the Law School's use of race in the admissions process. Dennis Shields, Director of Admissions when petitioner applied to the Law School, testified that he did not direct his staff to admit a particular percentage or number of minority students, but rather to consider an applicant's race along with all other factors. . . . [A]t the height of the admissions season, he would frequently consult the so-called "daily reports" that kept track of the racial and ethnic composition of the class (along with other information such as residency status and gender) . . . to ensure that a critical mass of underrepresented minority students would be reached. . . . Shields stressed, however, that he did not seek to admit any particular number or percentage of underrepresented minority students.

Erica Munzel, who succeeded Shields as Director of Admissions, testified that " 'critical mass' " means " 'meaningful numbers' " or " 'meaningful representation,' "

. . . a number that encourages underrepresented minority students to participate in the classroom and not feel isolated. Munzel stated there is no number, percentage, or range of numbers or percentages that constitute critical mass. . . . The current Dean of the Law School, Jeffrey Lehman . . . indicated that critical mass means numbers such that underrepresented minority students do not feel isolated or like spokespersons for their race. . . . [P]rofessor Richard Lempert, who chaired the faculty committee that drafted the 1992 policy . . . explained that [the point of the focus on historically discriminated against groups was not] to remedy past discrimination, but rather to include students who may bring to the Law School a perspective different from that of members of groups which have not been the victims of such discrimination. . . . [O]ther groups, such as Asians and Jews, have experienced discrimination, but . . . were not mentioned in the policy because individuals who are members of those groups were already being admitted to the Law School in significant numbers. Kent Syverud . . . a professor at the Law School when the 1992 admissions policy was adopted . . . [testified] that when a critical mass of underrepresented minority students is present, racial stereotypes lose their force because nonminority students learn there is no "minority viewpoint" but rather a variety of viewpoints among minority students.

[R]elying on data obtained from the Law School, petitioner's expert, Dr. Kinley Larntz, generated and analyzed "admissions grids" for the years in question (1995-2000). . . . He concluded that membership in certain minority groups "is an extremely strong factor in the decision for acceptance," and that applicants from these minority groups "are given an extremely large allowance for admission" as compared to applicants who are members of nonfavored groups. Dr. Larntz conceded, however, that race is not the predominant factor in the Law School's admissions calculus.

Dr. Stephen Raudenbush, the Law School's expert, [testified that] a race-blind admissions system would have a " 'very dramatic,' " negative effect on underrepresented minority admissions. He testified that in 2000, 35 percent of underrepresented minority applicants were admitted [and] predicted that if race were not considered, only 10 percent of those applicants would have been admitted. [U]nderrepresented minority students would have comprised 4 percent of the entering class in 2000 instead of the actual figure of 14.5 percent.

II.

A

. . . Since this Court's splintered decision in *Bakke,* Justice Powell's opinion announcing the judgment of the Court has served as the touchstone for constitutional analysis of race-conscious admissions policies. Public and private universities across the Nation have modeled their own admissions programs on Justice Powell's views on permissible race-conscious policies. . . . In Justice Powell's view, when governmental decisions "touch upon an individual's race or ethnic background, he is entitled to a judicial determination that the burden he is asked to bear on that basis is precisely tailored to serve a compelling governmental interest." . . .

[J]ustice Powell rejected [as compelling] an interest in "reducing the historic deficit of traditionally disfavored minorities in medical schools and in the medical profession" as an unlawful interest in racial balancing. . . . Justice Powell [also] rejected an interest in remedying societal discrimination because such measures would risk placing unnecessary burdens on innocent third parties "who bear no responsibility for whatever harm the beneficiaries of the special admissions program are thought to have suffered." [Finally], Justice Powell rejected an interest in "increasing the number of physicians who will practice in communities currently underserved," concluding that even if such an interest could be compelling in some circumstances the program under review was not "geared to promote that goal."

Justice Powell approved the university's use of race to further only one interest: "the attainment of a diverse student body." With the important proviso that "constitutional limitations protecting individual rights may not be disregarded," Justice Powell grounded his analysis in the academic freedom that "long has been viewed as a special concern of the First Amendment." Justice Powell emphasized that nothing less than the " 'nation's future depends upon leaders trained through wide exposure' to the ideas and mores of students as diverse as this Nation of many peoples." In seeking the "right to select those students who will contribute the most to the 'robust exchange of ideas,' " a university seeks "to achieve a goal that is of paramount importance in the fulfillment of its mission." Both "tradition and experience lend support to the view that the contribution of diversity is substantial."

Justice Powell was, however, careful to emphasize that in his view race "is only one element in a range of factors a university properly may consider in attaining the goal of a heterogeneous student body." For Justice Powell, "[i]t is not an interest in simple ethnic diversity, in which a specified percentage of the student body is in effect guaranteed to be members of selected ethnic groups," that can justify the use of race. Rather, "[t]he diversity that furthers a compelling state interest encompasses a far broader array of qualifications and characteristics of which racial or ethnic origin is but a single though important element." . . . [F]or the reasons set out below, today we endorse Justice Powell's view that student body diversity is a compelling state interest that can justify the use of race in university admissions.

B

The Equal Protection Clause provides that no State shall "deny to any person within its jurisdiction the equal protection of the laws." Because the Fourteenth Amendment "protect[s] *persons*, not *groups*," all "governmental action based on race — a *group* classification long recognized as in most circumstances irrelevant and therefore prohibited — should be subjected to detailed judicial inquiry to ensure that the *personal* right to equal protection of the laws has not been infringed." *Adarand.* . . .

We have held that all racial classifications imposed by government "must be analyzed by a reviewing court under strict scrutiny." This means that such classifications are constitutional only if they are narrowly tailored to further compelling governmental interests. "Absent searching judicial inquiry into the justification for such race-based measures," we have no way to determine what "classifications are 'benign' or 'remedial' and what classifications are in fact motivated by illegitimate notions of racial inferiority or simple racial politics." We apply strict scrutiny to all racial classifications to " 'smoke out' illegitimate uses of race by assuring that [government] is pursuing a goal important enough to warrant use of a highly suspect tool."

Strict scrutiny is not "strict in theory, but fatal in fact." *Adarand.* Although all governmental uses of race are subject to strict scrutiny, not all are invalidated by it. . . . When race-based action is necessary to further a compelling governmental interest, such action does not violate the constitutional guarantee of equal protection so long as the narrow-tailoring requirement is also satisfied.

Context matters when reviewing race-based governmental action under the Equal Protection Clause. In Adarand Constructors, Inc. v. Pena, we made clear that strict scrutiny must take "'relevant differences' into account." Indeed, as we explained, that is its "fundamental purpose." Not every decision influenced by race is equally objectionable and strict scrutiny is designed to provide a framework for carefully examining the importance and the sincerity of the reasons advanced by the governmental decisionmaker for the use of race in that particular context.

III.

A

[B]efore this Court, as they have throughout this litigation, respondents assert only one justification for their use of race in the admissions process: obtaining "the educational benefits that flow from a diverse student body." In other words, the Law School asks us to recognize, in the context of higher education, a compelling state interest in student body diversity.

We first wish to dispel the notion that the Law School's argument has been foreclosed, either expressly or implicitly, by our affirmative-action cases decided since *Bakke.* . . . [W]e have never held that the only governmental use of race that can survive strict scrutiny is remedying past discrimination. . . . Today, we hold that the Law School has a compelling interest in attaining a diverse student body.

The Law School's educational judgment that such diversity is essential to its educational mission is one to which we defer. The Law School's assessment that diversity will, in fact, yield educational benefits is substantiated by respondents and their *amici.* Our scrutiny of the interest asserted by the Law School is no less strict for taking into account complex educational judgments in an area that lies primarily within the expertise of the university. Our holding today is in keeping with our tradition of giving a degree of deference to a university's academic decisions, within constitutionally prescribed limits.

We have long recognized that, given the important purpose of public education and the expansive freedoms of speech and thought associated with the university environment, universities occupy a special niche in our constitutional tradition. In announcing the principle of student body diversity as a compelling state interest, Justice Powell invoked our cases recognizing a constitutional dimension, grounded in the First Amendment, of educational autonomy: "The freedom of a university to make its own judgments as to education includes the selection of its student body." From this premise, Justice Powell reasoned that by claiming "the right to select those students who will contribute the most to the 'robust exchange of ideas,'" a university "seek[s] to achieve a goal that is of paramount importance in the fulfillment of its mission." Our conclusion that the Law School has a compelling interest in a diverse student body is informed by our view that attaining a diverse student body is at the heart of the Law School's proper institutional mission, and that "good faith" on the part of a university is "presumed" absent "a showing to the contrary."

As part of its goal of "assembling a class that is both exceptionally academically qualified and broadly diverse," the Law School seeks to "enroll a 'critical mass' of minority students." The Law School's interest is not simply "to assure within its student body some specified percentage of a particular group merely because of its race or ethnic origin." *Bakke* (opinion of Powell, J.). That would amount to outright racial balancing, which is patently unconstitutional. Rather, the Law School's concept of critical mass is defined by reference to the educational benefits that diversity is designed to produce.

These benefits are substantial. As the District Court emphasized, the Law School's admissions policy promotes "cross-racial understanding," helps to break down racial stereotypes, and "enables [students] to better understand persons of different races." These benefits are "important and laudable," because "classroom discussion is livelier, more spirited, and simply more enlightening and interesting" when the students have "the greatest possible variety of backgrounds."

The Law School's claim of a compelling interest is further bolstered by its *amici,* who point to the educational benefits that flow from student body diversity. In addition to the expert studies and reports entered into evidence at trial, numerous studies show that student body diversity promotes learning outcomes, and "better prepares students for an increasingly diverse workforce and society, and better prepares them as professionals."

These benefits are not theoretical but real, as major American businesses have made clear that the skills needed in today's increasingly global marketplace can only be developed through exposure to widely diverse people, cultures, ideas, and viewpoints. Brief for 3M et al. as *Amici Curiae* 5; Brief for General Motors Corp. as *Amicus Curiae* 3-4. What is more, high-ranking retired officers and civilian leaders of the United States military assert that, "[b]ased on [their] decades of experience," a "highly qualified, racially diverse officer corps . . . is essential to the military's ability to fulfill its principle mission to provide national security." Brief for Julius W. Becton, Jr. et al. as *Amici Curiae* 27. The primary sources for the Nation's officer corps are the service academies and the Reserve Officers Training Corps (ROTC), the latter comprising students already admitted to participating colleges and universities. At present, "the military cannot achieve an officer corps that is *both* highly qualified *and* racially diverse unless the service academies and the ROTC used limited race-conscious recruiting and admissions policies." Ibid. (emphasis in original). To fulfill its mission, the military "must be selective in admissions for training and education for the officer corps, *and* it must train and educate a highly qualified, racially diverse officer corps in a racially diverse setting." Id., at 29 (emphasis in original). We agree that "[i]t requires only a small step from this analysis to conclude that our country's other most selective institutions must remain both diverse and selective." Ibid.

We have repeatedly acknowledged the overriding importance of preparing students for work and citizenship, describing education as pivotal to "sustaining our political and cultural heritage" with a fundamental role in maintaining the fabric of society. This Court has long recognized that "education . . . is the very foundation of good citizenship." Brown v. Board of Education. For this reason, the diffusion of knowledge and opportunity through public institutions of higher education must be accessible to all individuals regardless of race or ethnicity. The United States, as *amicus curiae,* affirms that "[e]nsuring that public institutions are open and available to all segments of American society, including people of all races and ethnicities, represents a paramount government objective." And, "[n]owhere is the importance of such openness more acute than in the context of higher education." Effective participation by members of all racial and ethnic groups in the civic life of our Nation is essential if the dream of one Nation, indivisible, is to be realized.

Moreover, universities, and in particular, law schools, represent the training ground for a large number of our Nation's leaders. Sweatt v. Painter (describing law school as a "proving ground for legal learning and practice"). Individuals with law degrees occupy roughly half the state governorships, more than half the seats in the United States Senate, and more than a third of the seats in the United States House of Representatives. The pattern is even more striking when it comes to highly selective law schools. A handful of these schools accounts for 25 of the 100 United States Senators, 74 United States Courts of Appeals judges, and nearly 200 of the more than 600 United States District Court judges.

In order to cultivate a set of leaders with legitimacy in the eyes of the citizenry, it is necessary that the path to leadership be visibly open to talented and qualified individuals of every race and ethnicity. All members of our heterogeneous society must have confidence in the openness and integrity of the educational institutions that provide this training. As we have recognized, law schools "cannot be effective in isolation from the individuals and institutions with which the law interacts." See Sweatt v. Painter. Access to legal education (and thus the legal profession) must be inclusive of talented and qualified individuals of every race and ethnicity, so that all members of our heterogeneous society may participate in the educational institutions that provide the training and education necessary to succeed in America.

The Law School does not premise its need for critical mass on "any belief that minority students always (or even consistently) express some characteristic minority viewpoint on any issue." To the contrary, diminishing the force of such stereotypes is both a crucial part of the Law School's mission, and one that it cannot accomplish with only token numbers of minority students. Just as growing up in a particular region or having particular professional experiences is likely to affect an individual's views, so too is one's own, unique experience of being a racial minority in a society, like our own, in which race unfortunately still matters. The Law School has determined, based on its experience and expertise, that a "critical mass" of underrepresented minorities is necessary to further its compelling interest in securing the educational benefits of a diverse student body.

B

. . . To be narrowly tailored, a race-conscious admissions program cannot use a quota system — it cannot "insulat[e] each category of applicants with certain desired qualifications from competition with all other applicants." Bakke (opinion of Powell, J.). Instead, a university may consider race or ethnicity only as a "'plus' in a particular applicant's file," without "insulat[ing] the individual from comparison with all other candidates for the available seats." In other words, an admissions program must be "flexible enough to consider all pertinent elements of diversity in light of the particular qualifications of each applicant, and to place them on the same footing for consideration, although not necessarily according them the same weight."

We find that the Law School's admissions program bears the hallmarks of a narrowly tailored plan. As Justice Powell made clear in Bakke, truly individualized consideration demands that race be used in a flexible, nonmechanical way. It follows from this mandate that universities cannot establish quotas for members of certain racial groups or put members of those groups on separate admissions tracks. Nor can universities insulate applicants who belong to certain racial or ethnic groups from the competition for admission. Universities can, however, consider race or ethnicity more flexibly as a "plus" factor in the context of individualized consideration of each and every applicant.

We are satisfied that the Law School's admissions program, like the Harvard plan described by Justice Powell, does not operate as a quota. Properly understood, a "quota" is a program in which a certain fixed number or proportion of opportunities are "reserved exclusively for certain minority groups." Quotas " 'impose a fixed number or percentage which must be attained, or which cannot be exceeded,' " and "insulate the individual from comparison with all other candidates for the available seats." In contrast, "a permissible goal . . . require[s] only a good-faith effort . . . to come within a range demarcated by the goal itself," and permits consideration of race as a "plus" factor in any given case while still ensuring that each candidate "compete[s] with all other qualified applicants."

Justice Powell's distinction between the medical school's rigid 16-seat quota and Harvard's flexible use of race as a "plus" factor is instructive. Harvard certainly had minimum *goals* for minority enrollment, even if it had no specific number firmly in mind. See *Bakke* (opinion of Powell, J.) ("10 or 20 black students could not begin to bring to their classmates and to each other the variety of points of view, backgrounds and experiences of blacks in the United States"). What is more, Justice Powell flatly rejected the argument that Harvard's program was "the functional equivalent of a quota" merely because it had some " 'plus' " for race, or gave greater "weight" to race than to some other factors, in order to achieve student body diversity.

The Law School's goal of attaining a critical mass of underrepresented minority students does not transform its program into a quota. As the Harvard plan described by Justice Powell recognized, there is of course "some relationship between numbers and achieving the benefits to be derived from a diverse student body, and between numbers and providing a reasonable environment for those students admitted." "[S]ome attention to numbers," without more, does not transform a flexible admissions system into a rigid quota. Nor, as Justice Kennedy posits, does the Law School's consultation of the "daily reports," which keep track of the racial and ethnic composition of the class (as well as of residency and gender), "suggest [ ] there was no further attempt at individual review save for race itself" during the final stages of the admissions process. To the contrary, the Law School's admissions officers testified without contradiction that they never gave race any more or less weight based on the information contained in these reports. Moreover, as Justice Kennedy concedes, between 1993 and 2000, the number of African-American, Latino, and Native-American students in each class at the Law School varied from 13.5 to 20.1 percent, a range inconsistent with a quota.

The Chief Justice believes that the Law School's policy conceals an attempt to achieve racial balancing, and cites admissions data to contend that the Law School discriminates among different groups within the critical mass. But, as The Chief Justice concedes, the number of underrepresented minority students who ultimately enroll in the Law School differs substantially from their representation in the applicant pool and varies considerably for each group from year to year.

That a race-conscious admissions program does not operate as a quota does not, by itself, satisfy the requirement of individualized consideration. When using race as a "plus" factor in university admissions, a university's admissions program must remain flexible enough to ensure that each applicant is evaluated as an individual and not in a way that makes an applicant's race or ethnicity the defining feature of his or her application. The importance of this individualized consideration in the context of a race-conscious admissions program is paramount. See *Bakke* (opinion of Powell, J.) (identifying the "denial . . . of th[e] right to individualized consideration" as the "principal evil" of the medical school's admissions program).

Here, the Law School engages in a highly individualized, holistic review of each applicant's file, giving serious consideration to all the ways an applicant might contribute to a diverse educational environment. The Law School affords this individualized consideration to applicants of all races. There is no policy, either *de jure* or *de facto*, of automatic acceptance or rejection based on any single "soft" variable. Unlike the program at issue in Gratz v. Bollinger, *ante,* the Law School awards no mechanical, predetermined diversity "bonuses" based on race or ethnicity. . . .

We also find that, like the Harvard plan Justice Powell referenced in *Bakke,* the Law School's race-conscious admissions program adequately ensures that all factors that may contribute to student body diversity are meaningfully considered alongside race in admissions decisions. With respect to the use of race itself, all underrepresented minority students admitted by the Law School have been deemed qualified. By virtue of our Nation's struggle with racial inequality, such students are both likely to have experiences of particular importance to the Law School's mission, and less likely to be admitted in meaningful numbers on criteria that ignore those experiences.

The Law School does not, however, limit in any way the broad range of qualities and experiences that may be considered valuable contributions to student body diversity. To the contrary, the 1992 policy makes clear "[t]here are many possible bases for diversity admissions," and provides examples of admittees who have lived or traveled widely abroad, are fluent in several languages, have overcome personal adversity and family hardship, have exceptional records of extensive community service, and have had successful careers in other fields. The Law School seriously considers each "applicant's promise of making a notable contribution to the class by way of a particular strength, attainment, or characteristic — e.g., an unusual intellectual achievement, employment experience, nonacademic performance, or personal background." All applicants have the opportunity to highlight their own potential diversity contributions through the submission of a personal statement, letters of recommendation, and an essay describing the ways in which the applicant will contribute to the life and diversity of the Law School.

What is more, the Law School actually gives substantial weight to diversity factors besides race. The Law School frequently accepts nonminority applicants with grades and test scores lower than underrepresented minority applicants (and other nonminority applicants) who are rejected. . . . Justice Kennedy speculates that "race is likely outcome determinative for many members of minority groups" who do not fall within the upper range of LSAT scores and grades. But the same could be said of the Harvard plan discussed approvingly by Justice Powell in *Bakke,* and indeed of any plan that uses race as one of many factors.

Petitioner and the United States argue that the Law School's plan is not narrowly tailored because race-neutral means exist to obtain the educational benefits of student body diversity that the Law School seeks. We disagree. Narrow tailoring does not require exhaustion of every conceivable race-neutral alternative. Nor does it require a university to choose between maintaining a reputation for excellence or fulfilling a commitment to provide educational opportunities to members of all racial groups. Narrow tailoring does, however, require serious, good faith consideration of workable race-neutral alternatives that will achieve the diversity the university seeks.

We agree with the Court of Appeals that the Law School sufficiently considered workable race-neutral alternatives. The District Court took the Law School to task for failing to consider race-neutral alternatives such as "using a lottery system" or "decreasing the emphasis for all applicants on undergraduate GPA and LSAT scores." But these alternatives would require a dramatic sacrifice of diversity, the academic quality of all admitted students, or both.

The Law School's current admissions program considers race as one factor among many, in an effort to assemble a student body that is diverse in ways broader than race. Because a lottery would make that kind of nuanced judgment impossible, it would effectively sacrifice all other educational values, not to mention every other kind of diversity. So too with the suggestion that the Law School simply lower admissions standards for all students, a drastic remedy that would require the Law School to become a much different institution and sacrifice a vital component of its educational mission. The United States advocates "percentage plans," recently adopted by public undergraduate institutions in Texas, Florida, and California to guarantee admission to all students above a certain class-rank threshold in every high school in the State. The United States does not, however, explain how such plans could work for graduate and professional schools. Moreover, even assuming such plans are race-neutral, they may preclude the university from conducting the individualized assessments necessary to assemble a student body that is not just racially diverse, but diverse along all the qualities valued by the university. . . .

We are mindful, however, that "[a] core purpose of the Fourteenth Amendment was to do away with all governmentally imposed discrimination based on race." Accordingly, race-conscious admissions policies must be limited in time. . . .

In the context of higher education, the durational requirement can be met by sunset provisions in race-conscious admissions policies and periodic reviews to determine whether racial preferences are still necessary to achieve student body diversity. Universities in California, Florida, and Washington State, where racial preferences in admissions are prohibited by state law, are currently engaged in experimenting with a wide variety of alternative approaches. Universities in other States can and should draw on the most promising aspects of these race-neutral alternatives as they develop.

The requirement that all race-conscious admissions programs have a termination point "assure[s] all citizens that the deviation from the norm of equal treatment of all racial and ethnic groups is a temporary matter, a measure taken in the service of the goal of equality itself." *Croson* (plurality opinion).

We take the Law School at its word that it would "like nothing better than to find a race-neutral admissions formula" and will terminate its race-conscious admissions program as soon as practicable. It has been 25 years since Justice Powell first approved the use of race to further an interest in student body diversity in the context of public higher education. Since that time, the number of minority applicants with high grades and test scores has indeed increased. We expect that 25 years from now, the use of racial preferences will no longer be necessary to further the interest approved today. . . .

Justice GINSBURG, with whom Justice Breyer joins, concurring. . . .

It is well documented that conscious and unconscious race bias, even rank discrimination based on race, remain alive in our land, impeding realization of our highest values and ideals. As to public education, data for the years 2000-2001 show that 71.6% of African-American children and 76.3% of Hispanic children attended a school in which minorities made up a majority of the student body. And schools in predominantly minority communities lag far behind others measured by the educational resources available to them.

However strong the public's desire for improved education systems may be, it remains the current reality that many minority students encounter markedly inadequate and unequal educational opportunities. Despite these inequalities, some minority students are able to meet the high threshold requirements set for admission to the country's finest undergraduate and graduate educational institutions. As lower school education in minority communities improves, an increase in the number of such students may be anticipated. From today's vantage point, one may hope, but not firmly forecast, that over the next generation's span, progress toward nondiscrimination and genuinely equal opportunity will make it safe to sunset affirmative action.

Chief Justice REHNQUIST, with whom Justice Scalia, Justice Kennedy, and Justice Thomas join, dissenting.

. . . I do not believe . . . that the University of Michigan Law School's (Law School) means are narrowly tailored to the interest it asserts. The Law School claims it must take the steps it does to achieve a " 'critical mass' " of underrepresented minority students. But its actual program bears no relation to this asserted goal. Stripped of its "critical mass" veil, the Law School's program is revealed as a naked effort to achieve racial balancing. . . .

In practice, the Law School's program bears little or no relation to its asserted goal of achieving "critical mass." Respondents explain that the Law School seeks to accumulate a "critical mass" of *each* underrepresented minority group. But the record demonstrates that the Law School's admissions practices with respect to these groups differ dramatically and cannot be defended under any consistent use of the term "critical mass."

From 1995 through 2000, the Law School admitted between 1,130 and 1,310 students. Of those, between 13 and 19 were Native American, between 91 and 108 were African-Americans, and between 47 and 56 were Hispanic. If the Law School is admitting between 91 and 108 African-Americans in order to achieve "critical mass," thereby preventing African-American students from feeling "isolated or like spokespersons for their race," one would think that a number of the same order of magnitude would be necessary to accomplish the same purpose for Hispanics and Native Americans. Similarly, even if all of the Native American applicants admitted in a given year matriculate, which the record demonstrates is not at all the case,[a] how can this possibly constitute a "critical mass" of Native Americans in a class of over 350 students? In order for this pattern of admission to be consistent with the Law School's explanation of "critical mass," one would have to believe that the objectives of "critical mass" offered by respondents are

---

a. Indeed, during this 5-year time period, enrollment of Native American students dropped to as low as *three* such students. Any assertion that such a small group constituted a "critical mass" of Native Americans is simply absurd.

achieved with only half the number of Hispanics and one-sixth the number of Native Americans as compared to African-Americans. [Chief Justice Rehnquist notes statistics suggesting that it was considerably easier for African-Americans with particular combinations of GPA and LSAT scores to be admitted than Hispanics]. . . . These statistics have a significant bearing on petitioner's case. Respondents have *never* offered any race-specific arguments explaining why significantly more individuals from one underrepresented minority group are needed in order to achieve "critical mass" or further student body diversity. They certainly have not explained why Hispanics, who they have said are among "the groups most isolated by racial barriers in our country," should have their admission capped out in this manner. True, petitioner is neither Hispanic nor Native American. But the Law School's disparate admissions practices with respect to these minority groups demonstrate that its alleged goal of "critical mass" is simply a sham. . . .

Only when the "critical mass" label is discarded does a likely explanation for these numbers emerge. . . . [T]he correlation between the percentage of the Law School's pool of applicants who are members of the three minority groups and the percentage of the admitted applicants who are members of these same groups is far too precise to be dismissed as merely the result of the school paying "some attention to [the] numbers." [F]rom 1995 through 2000 the percentage of admitted applicants who were members of these minority groups closely tracked the percentage of individuals in the school's applicant pool who were from the same groups. . . .

Not only do respondents fail to explain this phenomenon, they attempt to obscure it. ("The Law School's minority enrollment percentages . . . diverged from the percentages in the applicant pool by as much as 17.7% from 1995-2000"). But the divergence between the percentages of underrepresented minorities in the applicant pool and in the *enrolled* classes is not the only relevant comparison. In fact, it may not be the most relevant comparison. The Law School cannot precisely control which of its admitted applicants decide to attend the university. But it can and, as the numbers demonstrate, clearly does employ racial preferences in extending offers of admission. Indeed, the ostensibly flexible nature of the Law School's admissions program that the Court finds appealing, appears to be, in practice, a carefully managed program designed to ensure proportionate representation of applicants from selected minority groups. [T]his is precisely the type of racial balancing that the Court itself calls "patently unconstitutional."

Justice KENNEDY, dissenting.

The Court confuses deference to a university's definition of its educational objective with deference to the implementation of this goal. In the context of university admissions the objective of racial diversity can be accepted based on empirical data known to us, but deference is not to be given with respect to the methods by which it is pursued. . . .

The Court, in a review that is nothing short of perfunctory, accepts the University of Michigan Law School's assurances that its admissions process meets with constitutional requirements. The majority fails to confront the reality of how the Law School's admissions policy is implemented. The dissenting opinion by The Chief Justice, which I join in full, demonstrates beyond question why the concept of critical mass is a delusion used by the Law School to mask its attempt to make race an automatic factor in most instances and to achieve numerical goals indistinguishable from quotas. . . .

About 80 to 85 percent of the places in the entering class are given to applicants in the upper range of Law School Admissions Test scores and grades. An applicant with these credentials likely will be admitted without consideration of race or ethnicity. With respect to the remaining 15 to 20 percent of the seats, race is likely outcome determinative for many members of minority groups. That is where the competition becomes tight and where any given applicant's chance of admission is far smaller if he or she lacks minority status. At this point the numerical concept of critical mass has the real potential to compromise individual review. . . .

The Law School has the burden of proving, in conformance with the standard of strict scrutiny, that it did not utilize race in an unconstitutional way. At the very least, the constancy of admitted minority students and the close correlation between the racial breakdown of admitted minorities and the composition of the applicant pool, discussed by The Chief Justice, require the Law School either to produce a convincing explanation or to show it has taken adequate steps to ensure individual assessment. The Law School does neither.

The obvious tension between the pursuit of critical mass and the requirement of individual review increased by the end of the admissions season. Most of the decisions where race may decide the outcome are made during this period. The admissions officers consulted the daily reports which indicated the composition of the incoming class along racial lines. . . . [This] suggests there was no further attempt at individual review save for race itself. The admissions officers could use the reports to recalibrate the plus factor given to race depending on how close they were to achieving the Law School's goal of critical mass. The bonus factor of race would then become divorced from individual review; it would be premised instead on the numerical objective set by the Law School.

The Law School made no effort to guard against this danger. It provided no guidelines to its admissions personnel on how to reconcile individual assessment with the directive to admit a critical mass of minority students. The admissions program could have been structured to eliminate at least some of the risk that the promise of individual evaluation was not being kept. The daily consideration of racial breakdown of admitted students is not a feature of affirmative-action programs used by other institutions of higher learning. . . .

To be constitutional, a university's compelling interest in a diverse student body must be achieved by a system where individual assessment is safeguarded through the entire process. There is no constitutional objection to the goal of considering race as one modest factor among many others to achieve diversity, but an educational institution must ensure, through sufficient procedures, that each applicant receives individual consideration and that race does not become a predominant factor in the admissions decisionmaking. The Law School failed to comply with this requirement, and by no means has it carried its burden to show otherwise by the test of strict scrutiny.

The Court's refusal to apply meaningful strict scrutiny will lead to serious consequences. By deferring to the law schools' choice of minority admissions programs, the courts will lose the talents and resources of the faculties and administrators in devising new and fairer ways to ensure individual consideration. Constant and rigorous judicial review forces the law school faculties to undertake their responsibilities as state employees in this most sensitive of areas with utmost fidelity to the mandate of the Constitution. Dean Allan Stillwagon, who directed the Law School's Office of Admissions from 1979 to 1990, explained the difficulties he encountered in defining racial groups entitled to benefit under the School's affirmative action policy. He testified that faculty members were "breathtakingly cynical" in deciding who would qualify as a member of underrepresented minorities. An example he offered was faculty debate as to whether Cubans should be counted as Hispanics: One professor objected on the grounds that Cubans were Republicans. Many academics at other law schools who are "affirmative action's more forthright defenders readily concede that diversity is merely the current rationale of convenience for a policy that they prefer to justify on other grounds." Schuck, Affirmative Action: Past, Present, and Future, 20 Yale L. & Pol'y Rev. 1, 34 (2002) (citing Levinson, Diversity, 2 U. Pa. J. Const. L. 573, 577-578 (2000); Rubenfeld, Affirmative Action, 107 Yale L.J. 427, 471 (1997)). This is not to suggest the faculty at Michigan or other law schools do not pursue aspirations they consider laudable and consistent with our constitutional traditions. It is but further evidence of the necessity for scrutiny that is real, not feigned, where the corrosive category of race is a factor in decisionmaking. . . . Deference is antithetical to strict scrutiny, not consistent with it.

Were the courts to apply a searching standard to race-based admissions schemes, that would force educational institutions to seriously explore race-neutral alternatives. The Court, by contrast, is willing to be satisfied by the Law School's profession of its own good faith. . . .

If universities are given the latitude to administer programs that are tantamount to quotas, they will have few incentives to make the existing minority admissions schemes transparent and protective of individual review. The unhappy consequence will be to perpetuate the hostilities that proper consideration of race is designed to avoid. The perpetuation, of course, would be the worst of all outcomes. Other programs do exist which will be more effective in bringing about the harmony and mutual respect among all citizens that our constitutional tradition has always sought. They, and not the program under review here, should be the model, even if the Court defaults by not demanding it.

It is regrettable the Court's important holding allowing racial minorities to have their special circumstances considered in order to improve their educational opportunities is accompanied by a suspension of the strict scrutiny which was the predicate of allowing race to be considered in the first place. If the Court abdicates its constitutional duty to give strict scrutiny to the use of race in university admissions, it negates my authority to approve the use of race in pursuit of student diversity. The Constitution cannot confer the right to classify on the basis of race even in this special context absent searching judicial review. For these reasons, though I reiterate my approval of giving appropriate consideration to race in this one context, I must dissent in the present case.

Justice SCALIA, with whom Justice Thomas joins, concurring in part and dissenting in part.

[As] The Chief Justice . . . demonstrates, the University of Michigan Law School's mystical "critical mass" justification . . .[is] a sham to cover a scheme of racially proportionate admissions.

I also join Parts I through VII of Justice Thomas's opinion. I find particularly unanswerable his central point: that the allegedly "compelling state interest" at issue here is not the incremental "educational benefit" that emanates from the fabled "critical mass" of minority students, but rather Michigan's interest in maintaining a "prestige" law school whose normal admissions standards disproportionately exclude blacks and other minorities. If that is a compelling state interest, everything is.

I add the following: The "educational benefit" that the University of Michigan seeks to achieve by racial discrimination consists, according to the Court, of " 'cross-racial understanding,' " and " 'better prepar[ation of] students for an increasingly diverse workforce and society,' " all of which is necessary not only for work, but also for good "citizenship." This is not, of course, an "educational benefit" on which students will be graded on their Law School transcript (Works and Plays Well with Others: B+) or tested by the bar examiners (Q: Describe in 500 words or less your cross-racial understanding). For it is a lesson of life rather than law — essentially the same lesson taught to (or rather learned by, for it cannot be "taught" in the usual sense) people three feet shorter and twenty years younger than the full-grown adults at the University of Michigan Law School, in institutions ranging from Boy Scout troops to public-school kindergartens. If properly considered an "educational benefit" at all, it is surely not one that is either uniquely relevant to law school or uniquely "teachable" in a formal educational setting. *And therefore:* If it is appropriate for the University of Michigan Law School to use racial discrimination for the purpose of putting together a "critical mass" that will convey generic lessons in socialization and good citizenship, surely it is no less appropriate — indeed, *particularly* appropriate — for the civil service system of the State of Michigan to do so. There, also, those exposed to "critical masses" of certain races will presumably become better Americans, better Michiganders, better civil servants. And surely private employers cannot be criticized — indeed, should be praised — if they also "teach" good citizenship to their adult employees through a patriotic, all-American system of racial discrimination in hiring. The nonminority individuals who are deprived of a legal education, a civil service job, or any job at all by reason of their skin color will surely understand.

Unlike a clear constitutional holding that racial preferences in state educational institutions are impermissible, or even a clear anticonstitutional holding that racial preferences in state educational institutions are OK, today's *Grutter-Gratz* split double header seems perversely designed to prolong the controversy and the litigation. Some future lawsuits will presumably focus on whether the discriminatory scheme in question contains enough evaluation of the applicant "as an individual," and sufficiently avoids "separate admissions tracks" to fall under *Grutter* rather than *Gratz.* Some will focus on whether a university has gone beyond the bounds of a "good faith effort" and has so zealously pursued its "critical mass" as to make it an unconstitutional *de facto* quota system, rather than merely "a permissible goal." Other lawsuits may focus on whether, in the particular setting at issue, any educational benefits flow from racial diversity. (That issue was not contested in *Grutter;* and while the opinion accords "a degree of deference to a university's academic decisions," deference does not imply abandonment or abdication of judicial review. Still other suits may challenge the bona fides of the institution's expressed commitment to the educational benefits of diversity that immunize the discriminatory scheme in *Grutter.* (Tempting targets, one would suppose, will be those universities that talk the talk of multiculturalism and racial diversity in the courts but walk the walk of tribalism and racial segregation on their campuses — through minority-only student organizations, separate minority housing opportunities, separate minority student centers, even separate minority-only graduation ceremonies.) And still other suits may claim that the institution's racial preferences have gone below or above the mystical *Grutter*-approved "critical mass." Finally, litigation can be expected on behalf of minority groups intentionally short changed in the institution's composition of its generic minority "critical mass." I do not look forward to any of these cases. The Constitution proscribes government discrimination on the basis of race, and state-provided education is no exception.

Justice THOMAS, with whom Justice Scalia joins as to Parts I-VII, concurring in part and dissenting in part.

Frederick Douglass, speaking to a group of abolitionists almost 140 years ago, delivered a message lost on today's majority:

> "[I]n regard to the colored people, there is always more that is benevolent, I perceive, than just, manifested towards us. What I ask for the negro is not benevolence, not pity, not sympathy, but simply *justice*. The American people have always been anxious to know what they shall do with us. . . . I have had but one answer from the beginning. Do nothing with us! Your doing with us has already played the mischief with us. Do nothing with us! If the apples will not remain on the tree of their own strength, if they are worm-eaten at the core, if they are early ripe and disposed to fall, let them fall! . . . And if the negro cannot stand on his own legs, let him fall also. All I ask is, give him a chance to stand on his own legs! Let him alone! . . . [Y]our interference is doing him positive injury." What the Black Man Wants: An Address Delivered in Boston, Massachusetts, on 26 January 1865, reprinted in 4 The Frederick Douglass Papers 59, 68 (J. Blassingame & J. McKivigan eds.1991) (emphasis in original).

Like Douglass, I believe blacks can achieve in every avenue of American life without the meddling of university administrators. . . .

No one would argue that a university could set up a lower general admission standard and then impose heightened requirements only on black applicants. Similarly, a university may not maintain a high admission standard and grant exemptions to favored races. The Law School, of its own choosing, and for its own purposes, maintains an exclusionary admissions system that it knows produces racially disproportionate results. Racial discrimination is not a permissible solution to the self-inflicted wounds of this elitist admissions policy.

The majority upholds the Law School's racial discrimination not by interpreting the people's Constitution, but by responding to a faddish slogan of the cognoscenti. Nevertheless, I concur in part in the Court's opinion. First, I agree with the Court insofar as its decision, which approves of only one racial classification, confirms that further use of race in admissions remains unlawful. Second, I agree with the Court's holding that racial discrimination in higher education admissions will be illegal in 25 years. I respectfully dissent from the remainder of the Court's opinion and the judgment, however, because I believe that the Law School's current use of race violates the Equal Protection Clause and that the Constitution means the same thing today as it will in 300 months.

I.

The majority agrees that the Law School's racial discrimination should be subjected to strict scrutiny. . . . Where the Court has accepted only national security [in *Korematsu*], and rejected even the best interests of a child [in Palmore v. Sidotti], as a justification for racial discrimination, I conclude that only those measures the State must take to provide a bulwark against anarchy, or to prevent violence, will constitute a "pressing public necessity." Cf. Lee v. Washington, 390 U.S. 333 (1968) (per curiam) (Black, J., concurring) (indicating that protecting prisoners from violence might justify narrowly tailored racial discrimination); *Croson*, supra, at 521 (Scalia, J., concurring in judgment) ("At least where state or local action is at issue, only a social emergency rising to the level of imminent danger to life and limb . . . can justify [racial discrimination]").

The Constitution abhors classifications based on race, not only because those classifications can harm favored races or are based on illegitimate motives, but also because every time the government places citizens on racial registers and makes race relevant to the provision of burdens or benefits, it demeans us all. "Purchased at the price of immeasurable human suffering, the equal protection principle reflects our Nation's understanding that such classifications ultimately have a destructive impact on the individual and our society."

II.

[T]he Law School maintains that it wishes to obtain "educational benefits that flow from student body diversity."[a] . . . [T]he Law School . . . apparently believes that only a racially mixed student body can lead to the educational benefits it seeks. How, then, is the Law School's interest in these allegedly unique educational "benefits" *not* simply the forbidden interest in "racial balancing," that the majority expressly rejects? . . .

One must . . . consider the Law School's refusal to entertain changes to its current admissions system that might produce the same educational benefits. The Law School adamantly disclaims any race-neutral alternative that would reduce "academic selectivity," which would in turn "require the Law School to become a very different institution, and to sacrifice a core part of its educational mission." In other words, the Law School seeks to improve marginally the education it offers without sacrificing too much of its exclusivity and elite status. . . . Unless each constituent part of this state interest is of pressing public necessity, the Law School's use of race is unconstitutional. I find each of them to fall far short of this standard.

III. . . .

B

Under the proper standard, there is no pressing public necessity in maintaining a public law school at all and, it follows, certainly not an elite law school. Likewise, marginal improvements in legal education do not qualify as a compelling state interest.

1

While legal education at a public university may be good policy or otherwise laudable, it is obviously not a pressing public necessity when the correct legal standard is

---

a. "[D]iversity," for all of its devotees, is more a fashionable catchphrase than it is a useful term, especially when something as serious as racial discrimination is at issue. Because the Equal Protection Clause renders the color of one's skin constitutionally irrelevant to the Law School's mission, I refer to the Law School's interest as an "aesthetic." That is, the Law School wants to have a certain appearance, from the shape of the desks and tables in its classrooms to the color of the students sitting at them. I also use the term "aesthetic" because I believe it underlines the ineffectiveness of racially discriminatory admissions in actually helping those who are truly underprivileged. [T]he Law School's racial discrimination does nothing for those too poor or uneducated to participate in elite higher education and therefore presents only an illusory solution to the challenges facing our Nation. [Relocated footnote–Eds.]

applied. Additionally, circumstantial evidence as to whether a state activity is of pressing public necessity can be obtained by asking whether all States feel compelled to engage in that activity. [T]he absence of a public, American Bar Association (ABA) accredited, law school in Alaska, Delaware, Massachusetts, New Hampshire, and Rhode Island provides further evidence that Michigan's maintenance of the Law School does not constitute a compelling state interest.

2

. . . Michigan has no compelling interest in having a law school at all, much less an *elite* one. Still, even assuming that a State may, under appropriate circumstances, demonstrate a cognizable interest in having an elite law school, Michigan has failed to do so here. . . .

The only interests that can satisfy the Equal Protection Clause's demands are those found within a State's jurisdiction. The only cognizable state interests vindicated by operating a public law school are, therefore, the education of that State's citizens and the training of that State's lawyers.

The Law School today, however, does precious little training of those attorneys who will serve the citizens of Michigan. [L]ess than 16% of the Law School's graduating class elects to stay in Michigan after law school. . . . It does not take a social scientist to conclude that it is precisely the Law School's status as an elite institution that causes it to be a waystation for the rest of the country's lawyers, rather than a training ground for those who will remain in Michigan. The Law School's decision to be an elite institution does little to advance the welfare of the people of Michigan or any cognizable interest of the State of Michigan. . . .

IV.

The interest in remaining elite and exclusive that the majority thinks so obviously critical requires the use of admissions "standards" that, in turn, create the Law School's "need" to discriminate on the basis of race. . . . The Court never explicitly holds that the Law School's desire to retain the status quo in "academic selectivity" is itself a compelling state interest. Therefore, the Law School should be forced to choose between its classroom aesthetic and its exclusionary admissions system — it cannot have it both ways.

With the adoption of different admissions methods, such as accepting all students who meet minimum qualifications, the Law School could achieve its vision of the racially aesthetic student body without the use of racial discrimination. . . .

B

1

The Court's deference to the Law School's conclusion that its racial experimentation leads to educational benefits will, if adhered to, have serious collateral consequences. The Court relies heavily on social science evidence to justify its deference. The Court never acknowledges, however, the growing evidence that racial (and other sorts) of heterogeneity actually impairs learning among black students. See, e.g., Flowers & Pascarella, Cognitive Effects of College Racial

Composition on African American Students After 3 Years of College, 40 J. of College Student Development 669, 674 (1999) (concluding that black students experience superior cognitive development at Historically Black Colleges (HBCs) and that, even among blacks, "a substantial diversity moderates the cognitive effects of attending an HBC"); Allen, The Color of Success: African-American College Student Outcomes at Predominantly White and Historically Black Public Colleges and Universities, 62 Harv. Educ. Rev. 26, 35 (1992) (finding that black students attending HBCs report higher academic achievement than those attending predominantly white colleges). . . .

The majority grants deference to the Law School's "assessment that diversity will, in fact, yield educational benefits," It follows, therefore, that an HBC's assessment that racial homogeneity will yield educational benefits would similarly be given deference. An HBC's rejection of white applicants in order to maintain racial homogeneity seems permissible, therefore, under the majority's view of the Equal Protection Clause. Contained within today's majority opinion is the seed of a new constitutional justification for a concept I thought long and rightly rejected — racial segregation.

2

Moreover one would think, in light of the Court's decision in United States v. Virginia, 518 U.S. 515 (1996), that before being given license to use racial discrimination, the Law School would be required to radically reshape its admissions process, even to the point of sacrificing some elements of its character. In *Virginia,* a majority of the Court, without a word about academic freedom, accepted the all-male Virginia Military Institute's (VMI) representation that some changes in its "adversative" method of education would be required with the admission of women, but did not defer to VMI's judgment that these changes would be too great. Instead, the Court concluded that they were "manageable." That case involved sex discrimination, which is subjected to intermediate, not strict, scrutiny. So in *Virginia,* where the standard of review dictated that greater flexibility be granted to VMI's educational policies than the Law School deserves here, this Court gave no deference. Apparently where the status quo being defended is that of the elite establishment — here the Law School — rather than a less fashionable Southern military institution, the Court will defer without serious inquiry and without regard to the applicable legal standard.

c

. . . The sky has not fallen at Boalt Hall at the University of California, Berkeley, for example. Prior to Proposition 209's adoption of Cal. Const., Art. 1, §31(a), which bars the State from "grant[ing] preferential treatment . . . on the basis of race . . . in the operation of . . . public education," Boalt Hall enrolled 20 blacks and 28 Hispanics in its first-year class for 1996. In 2002, without deploying express racial discrimination in admissions, Boalt's entering class enrolled 14 blacks and 36 Hispanics. Total underrepresented minority student enrollment at Boalt Hall now exceeds 1996 levels. Apparently the Law School cannot be counted on to be as resourceful. The Court is willfully blind to the very real experience in California and elsewhere, which raises the inference that institutions with "reputation[s] for excellence," rivaling the Law School's have satisfied their sense of mission without resorting to prohibited racial discrimination.

V.

Putting aside the absence of any legal support for the majority's reflexive deference, there is much to be said for the view that the use of tests and other measures to "predict" academic performance is a poor substitute for a system that gives every applicant a chance to prove he can succeed in the study of law. The rallying cry that in the absence of racial discrimination in admissions there would be a true meritocracy ignores the fact that the entire process is poisoned by numerous exceptions to "merit." For example, in the national debate on racial discrimination in higher education admissions, much has been made of the fact that elite institutions utilize a so-called "legacy" preference to give the children of alumni an advantage in admissions. This, and other, exceptions to a "true" meritocracy give the lie to protestations that merit admissions are in fact the order of the day at the Nation's universities. The Equal Protection Clause does not, however, prohibit the use of unseemly legacy preferences or many other kinds of arbitrary admissions procedures. What the Equal Protection Clause does prohibit are classifications made on the basis of race. So while legacy preferences can stand under the Constitution, racial discrimination cannot. I will not twist the Constitution to invalidate legacy preferences or otherwise impose my vision of higher education admissions on the Nation. The majority should similarly stay its impulse to validate faddish racial discrimination the Constitution clearly forbids.

In any event, there is nothing ancient, honorable, or constitutionally protected about "selective" admissions. The University of Michigan should be well aware that alternative methods have historically been used for the admission of students, for it brought to this country the German certificate system in the late-19th century. Under this system, a secondary school was certified by a university so that any graduate who completed the course offered by the school was offered admission to the university. The certification regime supplemented, and later virtually replaced (at least in the Midwest), the prior regime of rigorous subject-matter entrance examinations. The facially race-neutral "percent plans" now used in Texas, California, and Florida, are in many ways the descendents of the certificate system.

Certification was replaced by selective admissions in the beginning of the 20th century, as universities sought to exercise more control over the composition of their student bodies. Since its inception, selective admissions has been the vehicle for racial, ethnic, and religious tinkering and experimentation by university administrators. The initial driving force for the relocation of the selective function from the high school to the universities was the same desire to select racial winners and losers that the Law School exhibits today. Columbia, Harvard, and others infamously determined that they had "too many" Jews, just as today the Law School argues it would have "too many" whites if it could not discriminate in its admissions process.

Columbia employed intelligence tests precisely because Jewish applicants, who were predominantly immigrants, scored worse on such tests. Thus, Columbia could claim (falsely) that "'[w]e have not eliminated boys because they were Jews and do not propose to do so. We have honestly attempted to eliminate the lowest grade of applicant [through the use of intelligence testing] and it turns out that a good many of the low grade men are New York City Jews.'" In other words, the tests were adopted with full knowledge of their disparate impact.

Similarly no modern law school can claim ignorance of the poor performance of blacks, relatively speaking, on the Law School Admissions Test (LSAT). Nevertheless, law schools continue to use the test and then attempt to "correct" for black underperformance by using racial discrimination in admissions so as to obtain their aesthetic student body. The Law School's continued adherence to measures it knows produce racially skewed results is not entitled to deference by this Court. The Law School itself admits that the test is imperfect, as it must, given that it regularly admits students who score at or below 150 (the national median) on the test. See App. 156-203 (showing that, between 1995 and 2000, the Law School admitted 37 students — 27 of whom were black; 31 of whom were "under-represented minorities" — with LSAT scores of 150 or lower). . . .

Having decided to use the LSAT, the Law School must accept the constitutional burdens that come with this decision. The Law School may freely continue to employ the LSAT and other allegedly merit-based standards in whatever fashion it likes. What the Equal Protection Clause forbids, but the Court today allows, is the use of these standards hand-in-hand with racial discrimination. An infinite variety of admissions methods are available to the Law School. Considering all of the radical thinking that has historically occurred at this country's universities, the Law School's intractable approach toward admissions is striking.

The Court will not even deign to make the Law School try other methods, however, preferring instead to grant a 25-year license to violate the Constitution. And the same Court that had the courage to order the desegregation of all public schools in the South now fears, on the basis of platitudes rather than principle, to force the Law School to abandon a decidedly imperfect admissions regime that provides the basis for racial discrimination.

VI.

The absence of any articulated legal principle supporting the majority's principal holding suggests another rationale. I believe what lies beneath the Court's decision today are the benighted notions that one can tell when racial discrimination bene-fits (rather than hurts) minority groups, and that racial discrimination is necessary to remedy general societal ills. This Court's precedents supposedly settled both issues, but clearly the majority still cannot commit to the principle that racial classi-fications are per se harmful and that almost no amount of benefit in the eye of the beholder can justify such classifications. . . .

I must contest the notion that the Law School's discrimination benefits those admitted as a result of it. The Court spends considerable time discussing the impressive display of *amicus* support for the Law School in this case from all corners of society. But nowhere in any of the filings in this Court is any evidence that the purported "beneficiaries" of this racial discrimination prove themselves by performing at (or even near) the same level as those students who receive no preferences. . . . The Law School seeks only a facade — it is sufficient that the class looks right, even if it does not perform right.

The Law School tantalizes unprepared students with the promise of a University of Michigan degree and all of the opportunities that it offers. These overmatched students take the bait, only to find that they cannot succeed in the cauldron of competition. And this mismatch crisis is not restricted to elite institutions. Indeed, to cover the tracks of the aestheticists, this cruel farce of racial discrimination must continue — in selection for the Michigan Law Review, and in hiring at law firms and for judicial clerkships — until the "beneficiaries" are no longer tolerated. While these students may graduate with law degrees, there is no evidence that they have received a qualitatively better legal education (or become better lawyers) than if they had gone to a less "elite" law school for which they were better prepared. And the aestheticists will never address the real problems facing "underrepresented minorities,"[b] instead continuing their social experiments on other people's children.

Beyond the harm the Law School's racial discrimination visits upon its test subjects, no social science has disproved the notion that this discrimination "engender[s] attitudes of superiority or, alternatively, provoke [s] resentment among those who believe that they have been wronged by the government's use of race." "These programs stamp minorities with a badge of inferiority and may cause them to develop dependencies or to adopt an attitude that they are 'entitled' to preferences."

It is uncontested that each year, the Law School admits a handful of blacks who would be admitted in the absence of racial discrimination. Who can differentiate between those who belong and those who do not? The majority of blacks are admitted to the Law School because of discrimination, and because of this policy all are tarred as undeserving. . . . When blacks take positions in the highest places of government, industry, or academia, it is an open question today whether their skin color played a part in their advancement. The question itself is the stigma. . . .

The Court . . . holds that racial discrimination in admissions should be given another 25 years before it is deemed no longer narrowly tailored to the Law School's fabricated compelling state interest. While I agree that in 25 years the practices of the Law School will be illegal, they are, for the reasons I have given, illegal now. The majority does not and cannot rest its time limitation on any evidence that the gap in credentials between black and white students is shrinking or will be gone in that timeframe. In recent years there has been virtually no change, for example, in the proportion of law school applicants with LSAT scores of 165 and higher who are black. In 1993 blacks constituted 1.1% of law school applicants in that score range, though they represented 11.1% of all applicants. In 2000 the comparable numbers were 1.0% and 11.3%. No one can seriously contend, and the Court does not, that the racial gap in academic credentials will disappear in 25 years. Nor is the Court's holding that racial discrimination will be unconstitutional in 25 years made contingent on the gap closing in that time.

Indeed, the very existence of racial discrimination of the type practiced by the Law School may impede the narrowing of the LSAT testing gap. An applicant's

---

b. For example, there is no recognition by the Law School in this case "that even with their racial discrimination in place, black *men* are "underrepresented" at the Law School. See ABA-LSAC Guide 426 (reporting that the Law School has 46 black women and 28 black men). Why does the Law School not also discriminate in favor of black men over black women, given this underrepresentation? The answer is, again, that all the Law School cares about is its own image among know-it-all elites, not solving real problems like the crisis of black male underperformance.

LSAT score can improve dramatically with preparation, but such preparation is a cost, and there must be sufficient benefits attached to an improved score to justify additional study. . . .

I therefore can understand the imposition of a 25-year time limit only as a holding that the deference the Court pays to the Law School's educational judgments and refusal to change its admissions policies will itself expire. At that point these policies will clearly have failed to "eliminat[e] the [perceived] need for any racial or ethnic" discrimination because the academic credentials gap will still be there. . . .

GRATZ v. BOLLINGER, 539 U.S. 244 (2003): [This was a companion case to *Grutter*; it challenged the University of Michigan's undergraduate affirmative action program. The University ranked applications according to a 150-point scale. Based on the index score, the following decisions would usually be made: 100-150 (admit); 95-99 (admit or postpone); 90-94 (postpone or admit); 75-89 (delay or postpone); 74 and below (delay or reject). The Office of Undergraduate Admissions (OUA) assigned points based on a number of factors, including high school grades, standardized test scores, high school quality, curriculum strength, geography, alumni relationships, and leadership. An applicant automatically received a bonus of 20 points of the 100 needed to guarantee admission if he or she possessed any one of the following "miscellaneous" factors: membership in an underrepresented racial or ethnic minority group (which included African-Americans, Hispanics, and Native Americans); attendance at a predominantly minority or disadvantaged high school; or recruitment for athletics. In addition, Michigan residents receive 10 points, and children of alumni receive 4. Admissions counselors may assign an outstanding essay up to 3 points and may award up to 5 points for an applicant's personal achievement, leadership, or public service.

In addition, admissions counselors could "flag" applications for further review by an Admissions Review Committee (ARC) after determining that an applicant (1) was academically prepared to succeed at the University, (2) had achieved a minimum selection index score, and (3) possessed a quality or characteristic important to the University's composition of its freshman class, such as high class rank, unique life experiences, challenges, circumstances, interests or talents, socioeconomic disadvantage, and underrepresented race, ethnicity, or geography. The ARC reviewed "flagged" applications individually and decided whether to admit, defer, or deny the applicant.

Chief Justice Rehnquist wrote the majority opinion. On the basis of *Grutter,* he rejected petitioner's claims that "racial classifications [may only be used] to remedy identified discrimination," and that "diversity [could not be a compelling interest] for employing racial preferences." However, he held that the undergraduate admissions plan was not narrowly tailored to achieve a compelling interest in diversity:]

REHNQUIST, C.J.:

Justice Powell's opinion in *Bakke* emphasized the importance of considering each particular applicant as an individual, assessing all of the qualities that individual possesses, and in turn, evaluating that individual's ability to contribute to the unique setting of higher education. . . .

The current [admissions] policy does not provide such individualized consideration. The [College's] policy automatically distributes 20 points to every single applicant from an "underrepresented minority" group, as defined by the University. The only consideration that accompanies this distribution of points is a factual review of an application to determine whether an individual is a member of one of these minority groups. Moreover, unlike Justice Powell's example, where the race of a "particular black applicant" could be considered without being decisive, the [College's] automatic distribution of 20 points has the effect of making "the factor of race . . . decisive" for virtually every minimally qualified underrepresented minority applicant. . . .

Respondents emphasize the fact that the [College] has created the possibility of an applicant's file being flagged for individualized consideration by the ARC. . . . But the fact that the "review committee can look at the applications individually and ignore the points," once an application is flagged, is of little comfort under our strict scrutiny analysis. The record does not reveal precisely how many applications are flagged for this individualized consideration, but it is undisputed that such consideration is the exception and not the rule in the . . . admissions program. Additionally, this individualized review is only provided *after* admissions counselors automatically distribute the University's version of a "plus" that makes race a decisive factor for virtually every minimally qualified underrepresented minority applicant.

Respondents contend that "[t]he volume of applications and the presentation of applicant information make it impractical for [the College] to use the . . . admissions system" upheld by the Court today in *Grutter*. But the fact that the implementation of a program capable of providing individualized consideration might present administrative challenges does not render constitutional an otherwise problematic system.

O'CONNOR, J., concurring:

[Justice Breyer joined this opinion except for the final sentence in which Justice O'Connor joined the majority opinion.]

Although the Office of Undergraduate Admissions does assign 20 points to some "soft" variables other than race, the points available for other diversity contributions, such as leadership and service, personal achievement, and geographic diversity, are capped at much lower levels. Even the most outstanding national high school leader could never receive more than five points for his or her accomplishments — a mere quarter of the points automatically assigned to an underrepresented minority solely based on the fact of his or her race. Of course, as Justice Powell made clear in *Bakke*, a university need not "necessarily accor[d]" all diversity factors "the same weight," and the "weight attributed to a particular quality may vary from year to year depending on the 'mix' both of the student body and the applicants for the incoming class." But the selection index, by setting up automatic, predetermined point allocations for the soft variables, ensures that the diversity contributions of applicants cannot be individually assessed. This policy stands in sharp contrast to the law school's admissions plan, which enables admissions officers to make nuanced judgments with respect to the contributions each applicant is likely to make to the diversity of the incoming class.

The only potential source of individualized consideration appears to be the Admissions Review Committee. [But] the committee is a kind of afterthought, rather than an integral component of a system of individualized review. . . . Review by the committee . . . represents a necessarily limited exception to the Office of

Undergraduate Admissions' general reliance on the selection index. Indeed, the record does not reveal how many applications admissions counselors send to the review committee each year, and the University has not pointed to evidence demonstrating that a meaningful percentage of applicants receives this level of discretionary review. In addition, eligibility for consideration by the committee is itself based on automatic cut-off levels determined with reference to selection index scores. And there is no evidence of how the decisions are actually made — what type of individualized consideration is or is not used. Given these circumstances, the addition of the Admissions Review Committee to the admissions process cannot offset the apparent absence of individualized consideration from the Office of Undergraduate Admissions' general practices.

THOMAS, J., concurring:

[Although] the Court's opinion . . . correctly applies our precedents, . . . I would hold that a State's use of racial discrimination in higher education admissions is categorically prohibited by the Equal Protection Clause. . . . The [College's] admissions policy . . . does not . . . "discriminat[e] among [the] groups" included within its definition of underrepresented minorities, [but] it does not sufficiently allow for the consideration of nonracial distinctions among underrepresented minority applicants." Under today's decisions, a university may not racially discriminate between the groups constituting the critical mass. An admissions policy, however, must allow for consideration of these nonracial distinctions among applicants on both sides of the single permitted racial classification.

[Justice Breyer concurred in the judgment but noted that he "agree[d] with Justice Ginsburg that, in implementing the Constitution's equality instruction, government decisionmakers may properly distinguish between policies of inclusion and exclusion, for the former are more likely to prove consistent with the basic constitutional obligation that the law respect each individual equally."

Justice Stevens, joined by Justice Souter, dissented on the ground that the plaintiffs lacked standing to raise their claims because, in contrast to plaintiff in *Grutter*, they "had already enrolled at other schools before they filed their class-action complaint in this case."

Justice Souter also dissented separately on the merits (Justice Ginsburg joined this portion of his opinion).]

SOUTER, J., dissenting:

Grutter reaffirms the permissibility of individualized consideration of race to achieve a diversity of students, at least where race is not assigned a preordained value in all cases. On the other hand, Justice Powell's opinion in [*Bakke*] rules out a racial quota or set-aside, in which race is the sole fact of eligibility for certain places in a class. [T]he freshman admissions system . . . is closer to what *Grutter* approves than to what *Bakke* condemns. . . .

The record does not describe a system with a quota like the one struck down in *Bakke*, which "insulate[d]" all nonminority candidates from competition from certain seats. The *Bakke* plan "focused *solely* on ethnic diversity" and effectively told nonminority applicants that "[n]o matter how strong their qualifications, quantitative and extracurricular, including their own potential for contribution to educational diversity, they are never afforded the chance to compete with applicants from the preferred groups for the [set-aside] special admissions seats."

The plan here, in contrast, lets all applicants compete for all places and values an applicant's offering for any place not only on grounds of race, but on grades, test scores, strength of high school, quality of course of study, residence, alumni relationships, leadership, personal character, socioeconomic disadvantage, athletic ability, and quality of a personal essay. A nonminority applicant who scores highly in these other categories can readily garner a selection index exceeding that of a minority applicant who gets the 20-point bonus. . . .

[A]ssignment of [20] points [for membership in an underrepresented minority] does not set race apart from all other weighted considerations. Nonminority students may receive 20 points for athletic ability, socioeconomic disadvantage, attendance at a socioeconomically disadvantaged or predominantly minority high school, or at the Provost's discretion; they may also receive 10 points for being residents of Michigan, 6 for residence in an underrepresented Michigan county, 5 for leadership and service, and so on. . . .

The very nature of a college's permissible practice of awarding value to racial diversity means that race must be considered in a way that increases some applicants' chances for admission. Since college admission is not left entirely to inarticulate intuition, it is hard to see what is inappropriate in assigning some stated value to a relevant characteristic, whether it be reasoning ability, writing style, running speed, or minority race. Justice Powell's plus factors necessarily are assigned some values. The college simply does by a numbered scale what the law school accomplishes in its "holistic review," *Grutter*; the distinction does not imply that applicants to the undergraduate college are denied individualized consideration or a fair chance to compete on the basis of all the various merits their applications may disclose.

Nor is it possible to say that the 20 points convert race into a decisive factor comparable to reserving minority places as in *Bakke*. . . . . The present record obviously shows that nonminority applicants may achieve higher selection point totals than minority applicants owing to characteristics other than race, and the fact that the university admits "virtually every qualified under-represented minority applicant," may reflect nothing more than the likelihood that very few qualified minority applicants apply, as well as the possibility that self-selection results in a strong minority applicant pool. It suffices for me . . . that there are no *Bakke*-like set-asides and that consideration of an applicant's whole spectrum of ability is no more ruled out by giving 20 points for race than by giving the same points for athletic ability or socioeconomic disadvantage.

Any argument that the "tailoring" amounts to a set-aside, then, boils down to the claim that a plus factor of 20 points makes some observers suspicious, where a factor of 10 points might not. But suspicion does not carry petitioners' ultimate burden of persuasion in this constitutional challenge, and it surely does not warrant condemning the college's admissions scheme on this record. . . . The point system cannot operate as a *de facto* set-aside if the greater admissions process, including review by the [ARC] committee, results in individualized review sufficient to meet the Court's standards. Since the record is quiet, if not silent, on the case-by-case work of the committee, the Court would be on more defensible ground by vacating and remanding for evidence about the committee's specific determinations.

Without knowing more about how the Admissions Review Committee actually functions, it seems especially unfair to treat the candor of the admissions plan as an Achilles' heel. In contrast to the college's forthrightness in saying just what plus factor it gives for membership in an underrepresented minority, it is worth considering the character of one alternative thrown up as preferable, because supposedly not based on race. Drawing on admissions systems used at public universities in California, Florida, and Texas, the United States contends that Michigan could get student diversity in satisfaction of its compelling interest by guaranteeing admission to a fixed percentage of the top students from each high school in Michigan.

While there is nothing unconstitutional about such a practice, it nonetheless suffers from a serious disadvantage. It is the disadvantage of deliberate obfuscation. The "percentage plans" are just as race conscious as the point scheme (and fairly so), but they get their racially diverse results without saying directly what they are doing or why they are doing it. In contrast, Michigan states its purpose directly and, if this were a doubtful case for me, I would be tempted to give Michigan an extra point of its own for its frankness. Equal protection cannot become an exercise in which the winners are the ones who hide the ball. . . .

GINSBURG, J., dissenting, joined by Souter, J.:

Educational institutions, the Court acknowledges, are not barred from any and all consideration of race when making admissions decisions. But the Court once again maintains that the same standard of review controls judicial inspection of all official race classifications. This insistence on "consistency," *Adarand,* would be fitting were our Nation free of the vestiges of rank discrimination long reinforced by law. But we are not far distant from an overtly discriminatory past, and the effects of centuries of law-sanctioned inequality remain painfully evident in our communities and schools.

In the wake "of a system of racial caste only recently ended," large disparities endure. Unemployment, poverty, and access to health care vary disproportionately by race. Neighborhoods and schools remain racially divided. African-American and Hispanic children are all too often educated in poverty-stricken and underperforming institutions. Adult African-Americans and Hispanics generally earn less than whites with equivalent levels of education. Equally credentialed job applicants receive different receptions depending on their race. Irrational prejudice is still encountered in real estate markets and consumer transactions. "Bias both conscious and unconscious, reflecting traditional and unexamined habits of thought, keeps up barriers that must come down if equal opportunity and nondiscrimination are ever genuinely to become this country's law and practice."

[G]overnment decisionmakers may properly distinguish between policies of exclusion and inclusion. Actions designed to burden groups long denied full citizenship stature are not sensibly ranked with measures taken to hasten the day when entrenched discrimination and its after effects have been extirpated. See Carter, When Victims Happen To Be Black, 97 Yale L.J. 420, 433-434 (1988) ("[T]o say that two centuries of struggle for the most basic of civil rights have been mostly about freedom from racial categorization rather than freedom from racial oppressio[n] is to trivialize the lives and deaths of those who have suffered under racism. To pretend . . . that the issue presented in [*Bakke*] was the same as the issue in [*Brown*] is to pretend that history never happened and that the present doesn't exist.").

Our jurisprudence ranks race a "suspect" category, "not because [race] is inevitably an impermissible classification, but because it is one which usually, to our national shame, has been drawn for the purpose of maintaining racial inequality." But where race is considered "for the purpose of achieving equality," no automatic proscription is in order. . . . The mere assertion of a laudable governmental purpose, of course, should not immunize a race-conscious measure from careful judicial inspection. Close review is needed "to ferret out classifications in reality malign, but masquerading as benign," and to "ensure that preferences are not so large as to trammel unduly upon the opportunities of others or interfere too harshly with legitimate expectations of persons in once-preferred groups."

[E]very applicant admitted under the current plan, petitioners do not here dispute, is qualified to attend the College. The racial and ethnic groups to which the College accords special consideration (African-Americans, Hispanics, and Native-Americans) historically have been relegated to inferior status by law and social practice; their members continue to experience class-based discrimination to this day. There is no suggestion that the College adopted its current policy in order to limit or decrease enrollment by any particular racial or ethnic group, and no seats are reserved on the basis of race. Nor has there been any demonstration that the College's program unduly constricts admissions opportunities for students who do not receive special consideration based on race. Cf. Liu, The Causation Fallacy: *Bakke* and the Basic Arithmetic of Selective Admissions, 100 Mich. L.Rev. 1045, 1049 (2002) ("In any admissions process where applicants greatly outnumber admittees, and where white applicants greatly outnumber minority applicants, substantial preferences for minority applicants will not significantly diminish the odds of admission facing white applicants.").[a]

The stain of generations of racial oppression is still visible in our society, and the determination to hasten its removal remains vital. One can reasonably anticipate, therefore, that colleges and universities will seek to maintain their minority enrollment — and the networks and opportunities thereby opened to minority graduates — whether or not they can do so in full candor through adoption of affirmative action plans of the kind here at issue. Without recourse to such plans, institutions of higher education may resort to camouflage. For example, schools may encourage applicants to write of their cultural traditions in the essays they submit, or to indicate whether English is their second language. Seeking to improve their chances for admission, applicants may highlight the minority group associations to which they belong, or the Hispanic surnames of their mothers or grandparents. In turn, teachers' recommendations may emphasize who a student is as much as what he or she has accomplished. If honesty is the best policy, surely Michigan's accurately described, fully disclosed College affirmative action program is preferable to achieving similar numbers through winks, nods, and disguises.

---

a. The United States points to the "percentage plans" used in California, Florida, and Texas as one example of a "race-neutral alternativ[e]" that would permit the College to enroll meaningful numbers of minority students [who graduated in the top 10% or 20% of their high school classes]. Calling such 10 or 20% plans "race-neutral" seems to me disingenuous, for they "unquestionably were adopted with the specific purpose of increasing representation of African-Americans and Hispanics in the public higher education system." Percentage plans depend for their effectiveness on continued racial segregation at the secondary school level: They can ensure significant minority enrollment in universities only if the majority-minority high school population is large enough to guarantee that, in many schools, most of the students in the top 10 or 20% are minorities. Moreover, because such plans link college admission to a single criterion — high school class rank — they create perverse incentives. They encourage parents to keep their children in low-performing segregated schools, and discourage students from taking challenging classes that might lower their grade point averages. And even if percentage plans could boost the sheer numbers of minority enrollees at the undergraduate level, they do not touch enrollment in graduate and professional schools.

Discussion

1. *What is "diversity?"* Since *Bakke,* the only compelling interest the Court has recognized for race-conscious affirmative action in admissions has been diversity. Remedying past societal discrimination, promoting distributive justice among competing groups in the present, and providing role models have all been held to be not compelling governmental interests. Hence all justifications universities offered for their affirmative action policies had to be phrased in terms of promoting diversity. Not surprisingly, the word has taken on multiple and occasionally conflicting connotations.

Consider four different types of diversity: The first is ideological diversity, which is concerned with ensuring a mix of students with different beliefs (including but not limited to beliefs about politics and religion). The second is experiential diversity, which is concerned with ensuring a mix of students who have had different backgrounds and experiences (applicants who are poor or rich, have gone parachuting, have worked in relief agencies in the Third World, are former soldiers, battled childhood traumas or diseases, etc.). The third is diversity of talents, which is concerned with ensuring a mix of students with different talents and abilities (athletes, cello players, actors, etc.). The fourth type of diversity is demographic diversity, which is concerned with ensuring a mix of students from different ethnic, social, and religious groups.

Note that these forms of diversity may overlap, but they may also point in quite different directions. For example, admitting a conservative pro-life white female who plays the flute may add to ideological diversity and diversity of talents, but it may not necessarily promote demographic diversity. Admitting an additional African-American student may promote demographic or experiential diversity, but it may not promote either demographic or experiential diversity as much as adding a student from Malaysia or Kazakhstan. What kinds of diversity is the University of Michigan interested in? Which types of diversity does the critical mass policy involved in *Grutter* best promote? The use of points in *Gratz*?

Now consider the reasons that Justice O'Connor gives in *Grutter* for why diversity is important. First, diversity promotes mutual understanding between students of different races. Second, it better prepares students for life in an increasingly diverse and multicultural society. Third, diversity fosters "the diffusion of knowledge and opportunity through public institutions of higher education . . . to all individuals regardless of race or ethnicity." It promotes participation in elite institutions (and thus eventual placement in elite positions) by all racial and ethnic groups in the United States, which in turn helps secure the "[e]ffective participation by members of all racial and ethnic groups in the civic life of our Nation." Fourth, diversity enhances the legitimacy of society's leaders in the eyes of the citizenry, because to ensure legitimacy "it is necessary that the path to leadership be visibly open to talented and qualified individuals of every race and ethnicity."

Given the explanations Justice O'Connor offers for why diversity is a compelling state interest, which forms of diversity — ideological, experiential, talent-based, or demographic — are most closely connected to those reasons? Which are least closely connected?

2. *Diversity and distributive justice.* Note Justice O'Connor's third argument for why diversity is a compelling state interest — diversity helps ensure a fair distribution of elite

opportunities (including opportunities within the legal profession) among racial and ethnic groups in American society. This can be a backward-looking argument for remedying past societal discrimination and existing social stratification. Or it can be a forward-looking argument for ensuring distributive justice among existing racial and ethnic groups and promoting their integration and cooperation. In either case, is this argument consistent with Justice Powell's claim that racial balancing is not a legitimate goal of affirmative action and that remedying past societal discrimination is not a compelling state interest? Does *Grutter* sneak in through the back door considerations of distributive fairness that were excluded at the beginning of the Court's affirmative action jurisprudence?

What should we make of Justice O'Connor's fourth argument, that diversity promotes legitimacy? Is the "legitimacy" she is talking about merely sociological — that in order for society to function properly America must seem to be fair, whether it is or not? Or is the argument one of moral legitimacy — that in order for its leaders to deserve the citizenry's respect, America must provide a fair share of opportunities in elite institutions to the various social, racial, and ethnic groups in American society? For an account of how the use of "diversity" shifts and expands in the transition from *Bakke* to *Grutter*, see Robert C. Post, Foreword: Fashioning the Legal Constitution: Culture, Courts, and Law, 117 Harv. L. Rev. 4, 60-64 (2003).

3. *Did the Court apply strict scrutiny in* Grutter? Note Justice O'Connor's statement that the Court will defer to "The Law School's educational judgment that . . . diversity is essential to its educational mission" because of "complex educational judgments in an area that lies primarily within the expertise of the university."

Is deference to the judgments of an institution accused of racial discrimination characteristic of strict scrutiny? If not, then perhaps the Court is not applying strict scrutiny, even though it insists that it is. Similarly, do you believe that the court would give Michigan the same degree of deference if the university announced that educational considerations made it necessary to increase enrollments of white students? If not, then perhaps the reason why the Court gives university officials the benefit of the doubt is because it thinks that Michigan's decisionmaking process is more benign than invidious. A different degree of scrutiny applies to policies designed to assist minorities as opposed to policies that discriminate against them. Both of these positions, of course, are inconsistent with the Court's opinions in *Adarand* and *Croson*, not to mention language in *Grutter* itself. Does this mean that Justice Marshall's and Justice Brennan's positions in *Bakke* have effectively won out in educational affirmative action, although the Court is unwilling to say so?

4. *Is "critical mass" a form of racial balancing?* Does Justice O'Connor have any good response to the dissenters' charge that a critical mass of African-Americans should be of the same size as a critical mass of Latinos or Native Americans, and hence Michigan cannot justify admitting different percentages of each group? If the goal of affirmative action is to give major demographic groups in American society a fair share of opportunities at elite institutions, Michigan's admissions decisions would make some sense. Michigan might wish to ensure that blacks, Latinos, and Native Americans were represented in the entering class in rough proportion to the number of applications received. On the other hand, Michigan might conclude that because Asian Americans will likely be fairly well-represented in the entering class, there is no need to give them any admissions preference. Nevertheless, what,

if anything, does this justification for affirmative action in education have to do with achieving a "critical mass" of minorities, or with the various forms of diversity described above?

5. *Diversity or elite status but not both.* Do you agree with Justice Thomas's claim that for purposes of the Equal Protection Clause, the University of Michigan Law School cannot properly assert an interest in producing elites who will practice law outside the state? Thomas points out that if Michigan wants diversity it can simply reduce entrance requirements and surrender its elite status. If the purpose of affirmative action is to provide a fair share of elite opportunities to all races and all segments of society, it would be particularly important for Michigan to remain an elite institution, for the surest path to elite positions in society is through elite educational institutions. Note however, that this response to Justice Thomas would require the Court to admit that affirmative action is about issues of distributive justice rather than simply about a question of academic freedom.

6. *The cost of "individualized determinations."* Will all schools be equally able to adhere to the rules set forth in *Grutter* and *Gratz*? Compare very selective institutions that receive 15,000 applications to fill a class of 1,500 with large state universities that receive many times that number of applications in a single year. Will the latter institutions be able to provide individualized determinations of each and every file? Do the Court's decisions in *Grutter* and *Gratz* mean that schools cannot use computer programs to weed out or sort applications based on a set of factors assigned a particular weight, like grade point average, standardized test scores, alumni relations, athletic recruitment, and the like? Do the Court's decisions mean that race cannot be one of those factors in a computer program? Or do the decisions mean that at some point in the process, every file must be read by a human being and judged according to the totality of its characteristics before a decision is made to accept or reject an applicant for admission?

7. *Racial classifications, again.* Are all race-conscious decisions by universities equally subject to strict scrutiny? Suppose that the University of Michigan does not use race in admissions, but it makes extra efforts to encourage minority students to apply to the University of Michigan and to attend if they are accepted. It does not make the same efforts for white students. Is this policy a racial classification subject to strict scrutiny?

If one believes that these recruitment practices are not subject to strict scrutiny, then the concern must not be with race consciousness or racial distinctions per se. Rather, it is with whether a scarce and valuable resource — a slot in the entering class — is being allocated on the basis of race or on the basis of "fair" competition. That is, the issue is meritocracy, not race consciousness. Race-conscious recruitment does not offend notions of fair competition because a person is either being asked to apply without a guarantee of a slot or is being asked to attend when he or she already has secured a slot based on his or her qualifications. Even so, in practice "merit" and "meritocracy" may be complicated (and highly contestable) terms; moreover universities sometimes give children of alumni preferences that cannot be justified on the grounds of merit (unless merit is defined as increased probability of alumni contributions).

8. *Alternative action.* In several of the Court's affirmative action cases, the Court has suggested race-neutral methods as alternatives to overt racial preferences. The

use of facially neutral policies designed to benefit racial minorities is sometimes called "alternative action." See Kim Forde-Mazrui, The Constitutional Implications of Race-Neutral Affirmative Action, 88 Geo. L.J. 2331, 2335 (2000). Is such alternative action consistent with the Equal Protection Clause?

Adarand suggests that strict scrutiny applies to all racial classifications, whether majorities or minorities are adversely affected. Should this rule of symmetry apply as well to covert racial classifications under Washington v. Davis and *Feeney*? If so, then are alternative action policies that deliberately use race-neutral classifications to benefit minorities constitutional?

Consider, for example, Texas's "Ten Percent Plan" passed by the Texas Legislature in response to *Hopwood,* which had prohibited any use of race in admissions. The bill provided that Texas students in the top ten percent of their graduating high school classes will be admitted automatically to any Texas state university without consideration of standardized test scores. See Tex. Educ. Code Ann. §51.803(a). Test scores may, however, be used to determine whether students need enrichment courses before enrolling. The Ten Percent Plan trades on the fact that minorities in Texas increasingly attend racially and ethnically segregated schools. Thus, the Ten Percent Plan is consistent with at least one vision of meritocracy that is also race-conscious: It is not the students' fault where they grow up or where they attend high school, but if they work hard enough to graduate at the top of a class of their peers they deserve a slot in a Texas state university. If the Ten Percent Plan was designed to increase the number of minorities in Texas universities in the face of the *Hopwood* decision, is it constitutional under Washington v. Davis? Can one say under *Feeney* that the program was enacted not "because of" but "in spite of" its presumed effect on minority enrollments? For a discussion of some of the constitutional issues raised by alternative action, see Forde-Mazrui, supra, and Richard Primus, Equal Protection and Disparate Impact: Round Three, 117 Harv. L. Rev. 493, 540-564 (2003).

Note: Are American Indians a "Race" for Affirmative Action Purposes?

Section 12 of the Indian Reorganization Act, 25 U.S.C. §472, creates positions in the Bureau of Indian Affairs (BIA) within the Department of the Interior, and provides that "qualified Indians shall hereafter have the preference to appointments to vacancies" in those positions. The Commissioner of Indian Affairs issued a directive applying this rule not only to "appointments" but also to promotions within the BIA. Non-Indian employees of the Bureau challenged these preferences as denials of their rights under the Fifth Amendment. The Court unanimously upheld the preference, in Morton v. Mancari, 417 U.S. 535 (1974). Writing for the Court, Justice Blackmun first noted that "[t]he federal policy of according some hiring preference to Indians in the Indian service dates at least as far back as 1834," the purpose being "to give Indians a greater participation in their own self-government; to further the Government's trust obligation toward the Indian tribes; and to reduce the negative effect of having non-Indians administer matters that affect Indian tribal life." Lest one think that this simply demonstrates a "compelling interest" that licenses classifications otherwise forbidden by the Constitution, though, the Court stated:

Contrary to the characterization made by appellees, this preference does not constitute "racial discrimination." Indeed, it is not even a "racial" preference. Rather, it is an employment criterion reasonably designed to further the cause of Indian self-government and to make the BIA more responsive to the needs of its constituent groups. The preference, as applied, is granted to Indians not as a discrete racial group, but, rather, as members of quasi-sovereign tribal entities whose lives and activities are governed by the BIA in a unique fashion. Furthermore, the preference applies only to employment in the Indian service. The preference does not cover any other Government agency or activity. . . . Here, the preference is reasonably and directly related to a legitimate, nonracially based goal. This is the principal characteristic that generally is absent from proscribed forms of racial discrimination.

As long as the special treatment can be tied rationally to the fulfillment of Congress' unique obligation toward the Indians, such legislative judgments will not be disturbed. Here, where the preference is reasonable and rationally designed to further Indian self-government, we cannot say that Congress' classification violates due process.

Three years later, the Court made a similar argument in United States v. Antelope, 430 U.S. 641 (1977), which involved a section of the Major Crimes Act, 18 U.S.C. §1153, that assigned to federal, rather than state, courts prosecutions when an Indian is charged with the murder of a non-Indian. As Chief Justice Burger, writing for the Court, noted, "a non-Indian charged with precisely the same offense, namely the murder of another non-Indian within Indian country, would have been subject to prosecution only under Idaho law, which, in contrast to the federal murder statute, does not contain a felony murder provision." Given that the defendants faced more onerous laws in the federal court, they complained, and the Circuit Court agreed, that they were "put at a serious racially-based disadvantage." The Court unanimously reversed, emphasizing that

[t]he decisions of this Court leave no doubt that federal legislation with respect to Indian tribes, although relating to Indians as such, is not based upon impermissible racial classifications. . . . Indeed, respondents were not subjected to federal criminal jurisdiction because they are of the Indian race but because they are enrolled members of the Coeur d'Alene Tribe. We therefore conclude that federal criminal statutes enforced here are based neither in whole nor in part upon impermissible racial classifications.

The Court does *not* say that Indians, though members of an identifiable race, have a special status under the Constitution and are subject to regulations that would be unconstitutional if applied to members of other races. Rather, the Court seems at pains to deny that racial classifications are involved at all in *Mancari* and *Antelope*. Do you find this argument persuasive? Is it consistent with *Korematsu*? With Hernandez v. Texas? If you think that those cases are distinguishable because they involved discriminations involving American citizens, note that Congress extended citizenship to Indians in 1924. If this isn't racial discrimination, why isn't it national origin discrimination? Would the Court's response be that Indians are simply members of separate political subdivisions, so that the preference for Indians on a particular government commission is more like a preference in favor of residents of Kansas, or perhaps residents of the Commonwealth of Puerto Rico? If so, does this suggest a test of minimum rationality for any classification involving Indians?

If that is in fact the case, consider whether the Court's much heralded principles of state/federal "congruence" as expressed in *Adarand* apply to affirmative action for Native Americans. Would it be unconstitutional for the University of Texas to give an admissions preference for Native Americans? A preference from those tribes based in Texas? A preference for those from any tribe? Would all of these be subject to minimum rationality?

One would not, presumably, have to jump through such logical hoops if the Court had conceded that the classifications at issue in *Mancari* and *Antelope* were "racial classifications" and then stated that Indians are simply special and the law relating to Indians truly *sui generis*, telling us nothing useful about the rest of the Constitution. Should it have followed that path?

In *Antelope* the Court emphasizes the defendants' status as enrolled members of a tribe recognized by the United States government. Does this suggest that nonenrolled members would not be eligible for the preference upheld in *Mancari*? Although full coverage of Indian law is well beyond the scope of this casebook, you should at least be aware of the fact that the United States exercises a certain discretion in deciding what constitutes a tribe at all, so that there are at least some American Indians who consider themselves members of tribes but are not so deemed by the United States. See, e.g., Mashpee Tribe v. New Seabury Corp., 592 F.2d 575 (1st Cir. 1979), cert. denied, 444 U.S. 866 (1979), in which the court, after an extensive trial, determined, in effect, that whatever tribe of Mashpee Indians had once existed in Massachusetts had ceased to exist and that litigants who claimed to be Mashpee Indians could not sue under relevant statutes.[157]

A second, crucial, question is who gets to determine who is enrolled. Enrollment can carry with it not only burdens, as in *Antelope*, but also considerable benefits as well. Consider in this context Santa Clara Pueblo v. Martinez, 436 U.S. 49 (1978), which, among other things, involved the membership rules of the Santa Clara Pueblo in New Mexico. As the result of a 1939 ordinance, children were accepted as tribal members only if their fathers were members of the Pueblo. This meant that the children of Julia Martinez, herself an enrolled member, were not members because her husband, whom she married in 1941, was Navajo. As described by the Supreme Court, "[a]lthough the children were raised on the reservation and continue to reside there now that they are adults, as a result of their exclusion from membership they may not vote in tribal elections or hold secular office in the tribe; moreover, they have no right to remain on the reservation in the event of their mother's death, or to inherit their mother's home or her possessory interests in the communal lands." Indeed, there is apparently reason to believe that the dispute "arose in part because the Martinez children were denied the services of the Indian

157. See Gerald Torres and Kathryn Milun, Translating Yonnodio by Precedent and Evidence: The Mashpee Indian Case, 1990 Duke L.J. 625. See generally Note: Tribal Recognition, in David Getches et al., Cases and Materials on Federal Indian Law 352-358 (4th ed. 1998). The emphasis on tribal organization also allows one to distinguish between preferences for American Indians and preferences, say, for Native Hawaiians. Although Native Hawaiians might well be able to claim that they have been systematically mistreated by the dominant majority, they cannot, however, claim a history of being organized into tribes that continue as recognizable, "semi-sovereign" entities. See, e.g., Stuart Benjamin, Equal Protection and the Special Relationship: The Case of Native Hawaiians, 106 Yale L.J. 537 (1996), which argues that the *Mancari* doctrine should be limited only to American Indians and should therefore not be available to uphold any preferences for Native Hawaiians. See also Rice v. Cayetano, discussed supra.

Health Service on the ground that they were not enrolled tribal members."[158] The district court, although recognizing that the tribal rule was comparatively recent, found that it reflected (in the words of the Supreme Court) "traditional values of patriarchy still significant in tribal life. The court recognized the vital importance of respondents' interests, but also determined that membership rules were 'no more or less than a mechanism of social . . . self-definition,' and as such were basic to the tribe's survival as a cultural and economic entity." The Court of Appeals for the Tenth Circuit reversed, finding the tribe's sex-based classification "invidious" and unsupported by any compelling interest.

Writing for seven Justices,[159] Justice Marshall reversed. "As separate sovereigns pre-existing the Constitution, tribes have historically been regarded as unconstrained by those constitutional provisions framed specifically as limitations on federal or state authority." Although Congress does possess "plenary authority to limit, modify or eliminate the powers of local self-government which the tribes otherwise possess," it had not done so in a way that allowed federal courts to override the tribal rule. It is important to understand that *Martinez* is in fact a procedural decision rather than a genuine decision on the merits, for the crux of the holding is that Congress, when passing in 1968 the Indian Civil Rights Act had not granted federal courts jurisdiction over such disputes even in an action against tribal officials who lacked sovereign immunity. Federal courts had jurisdiction only to grant habeas corpus, where a person claimed to be confined in violation of the Constitution. Otherwise, enforcement of the ICRA was left up to the tribal courts. "[W]e must bear in mind that providing a federal forum for issues arising under [the equal protection section of the ICRA] constitutes an interference with tribal autonomy and self-government beyond that created by the change in substantive law itself." Although tribal courts are presumably required to adhere to equal protection norms, as a practical matter there is no review of their decisions, which leaves them free to develop their own notions of equal protection.

Discussion

1. *Public or private?* Recall that the Fourteenth Amendment applies only to "state action," Civil Rights Cases, Chapter 4. Is it obvious that the Equal Protection Clause applies to the Pueblo? Should tribes be viewed as "private groups" practicing (some degree of) self-government or as quasi-states subject to constitutional limitations? Should we view the tribe as a (conquered) semi-sovereign entity — as a special kind of "state" that retains a measure of political independence from the norms of the conquerors? Just as the polygamy involved in *Reynolds* offended the dominant society, we suspect that the gender discrimination practiced by the Santa Clara Pueblo offends many readers of this book. But by what criteria should one assess government interference in so fundamental an issue as the tribe's definition of membership in its own community?

Consider the fact that for most Jews — Reformed Jews in America are an exception — birth membership in the Jewish community requires matrilineal descent. This means, among other things, that children of Jewish fathers (but not of Jewish mothers) who have been raised as Jews must undergo formal conversion ceremonies before being

---

158. Getches et al., at 514.
159. Justice Blackmun did not participate, and Justice White dissented.

accepted as members in Jewish congregations; children of Jewish mothers and non-Jewish fathers, on the other hand, need not convert. Similarly, Orthodox synagogues traditionally place men and women in separate areas of the synagogue during services (lest men be "distracted" while praying), and they limit leadership of the service to men. (It should go without saying that within the Orthodox community only men can be rabbis.) This latter rule is, of course, similar to that of the Roman Catholic Church, which also denies women the opportunity to become priests and, consequently, to fill other positions of institutional leadership. Would you allow Congress to invalidate such practices by applying antidiscrimination laws to religious institutions? If you read the Constitution (and in particular the Free Exercise Clause of the First Amendment) to prevent application of antidiscrimination laws in these cases, then what constitutional principle permits Congress to impose the public norms of the Constitution on Indian tribes, let alone requires courts to impose such norms in the absence of a congressional decision to do so?

2. *Martinez* raises a host of issues, including questions about gender equality, and the intersections between ethnic identity and gender.[160] For purposes of this chapter, however, consider whether the United States should be required to honor a Pueblo rule that held that one lost tribal membership upon marrying "a non-Indian." (Suppose, for example, that the rule affected the distribution of compensation accruing from the condemnation of tribal lands, so that Pueblos who married non-Indians would receive no profits.) Would your answer change if the rule took membership away from anyone who married "a person who is not an enrolled member of the Pueblo"?

Note: Racial Redistricting and the Equal Protection Clause

In Baker v. Carr, 389 U.S. 186 (1962), the Supreme Court held for the first time that issues involving the fairness of drawing state legislative districts were "justiciable," i.e., appropriate for judicial resolution; two years later, in Reynolds v. Sims, 377 U.S. 533 (1964), the court adopted the "one-person-one vote standard" as the test for assessing the constitutional adequacy of such districts under the Equal Protection Clause.

The attempt to draw boundary lines to maximize particular political outcomes is often called "gerrymandering." Beginning in 1993, the Supreme Court, in a series of 5-4 decisions, held that redistricting designed to increase the electoral representation of Blacks through the creation of districts where minorities constituted a majority of voters was subject to scrutiny under the Equal Protection Clause. The key case was Shaw v Reno, 509 U.S. 630 (1993), holding that "redistricting legislation that is so extremely irregular on its face that it rationally can be viewed only as an effort to segregate the races for purposes of voting, without regard for traditional districting principles and without sufficiently compelling justification" stated

---

160. See, e.g., Catharine A. MacKinnon, Whose Culture? A Case Note on Martinez v. Santa Clara Pueblo (1983), in Feminism Unmodified: Discourses on Life and Law 65-69 (1987) (pointing out that the rule upheld in *Martinez* is male supremacist, because "[it] keeps Indian women for Indian men at the price of loss of tribal rights, from a time when Native women did not have formal power in rulemaking").

a claim under the Equal Protection Clause. The rationale of *Shaw* was clarified in succeeding cases.

In Miller v. Johnson, 515 U.S. 900 (1995), Justice Kennedy explained that the plaintiff's burden is to show

> either through circumstantial evidence of a district's shape and demographics or more direct evidence going to legislative purpose, that race was the predominant factor motivating the legislature's decision to place a significant number of voters within or without a particular district. To make this showing, a plaintiff must prove that the legislature subordinated traditional race-neutral districting principles, including but not limited to compactness, contiguity, respect for political subdivisions or communities defined by actual shared interests, to racial considerations. Where these or other race-neutral considerations are the basis for redistricting legislation, and are not subordinated to race, a state can "defeat a claim that a district has been gerrymandered on racial lines."

However, in Hunt v. Cromartie, 526 U.S. 541 (1999), the Court, in an opinion by Justice Thomas, noted that

> [o]ur prior decisions have made clear that a jurisdiction may engage in constitutional political gerrymandering, even if it so happens that the most loyal Democrats happen to be black Democrats and even if the State were conscious of that fact. Evidence that blacks constitute even a supermajority in one congressional district while amounting to less than a plurality in a neighboring district will not, by itself, suffice to prove that a jurisdiction was motivated by race in drawing its district lines when the evidence also shows a high correlation between race and party preference.

The opinions in *Shaw* and its progeny raise a number of fascinating issues about the role that race plays in the American political process. For a full discussion, see the casebook Web site at *http://www.conlaw.net*.

H.   Citizenship and Alienage Under the Equal Protection Clause

A 2001 "Profile on the Foreign-Born Population in the United States" published by the U.S. Bureau of the Census reported that "[w]hile the total foreign-born population increased by 191 percent (from 9.7 million to 28.4 million) between 1970 and 2000, the numbers of naturalized citizens and noncitizens in the foreign-born population increased at very different rates. Naturalized citizens increased by 71 percent (from 6.2 million to 10.6 million), while noncitizens rose by 401 percent (from 3/5 million to 17.8 million). As a result of the more rapid growth of noncitizens, the proportion of naturalized citizens in the foreign-born population dropped from 63.6 percent in 1970 to 50.1 percent in 1980, to 40.5 percent in 1990, and to 37.4 percent in 2000." [161]

By 2003, the number of resident aliens had grown to 20,654,000, or over 7 percent of the total U.S. population. Resident aliens represented approximately

---

161. U.S. Census Bureau, Profile of the Foreign-Born Population in the United States: 2000 (December 2001), p. 20.

two-thirds of the over 33 million foreign-born population of the United States; the remainder of them, almost 13 million, had become naturalized citizens.[162]

The 2001 Profile on the Foreign-Born Population in the United States notes that there is no constant rate of naturalization among aliens coming from different countries. For example, over half of European-born aliens had become naturalized citizens, whereas the rate was only 28.3 percent for the immigrants from Latin America (and only 21.1 percent for those from Central America, which includes Mexico). Thus, overall, "the proportion of naturalized citizens [among foreign immigrants] dropped from 63.6 percent in 1970 to 37.4 percent in 2000." The number of resident aliens is, therefore, increasing in both absolute number and the proportion among the overall American population.

Moreover, among the immigrants to the United States are those who arrive illegally. For obvious reasons, there is less confidence as to the precise number of such immigrants than there is with regard to legal immigrants. The Census Bureau has opted for estimating what it terms "the residual foreign-born population," which consists of a mixture of illegal aliens and "people who are here legally but are not yet included in the official estimates of legal migrants and refugees. It also includes people in 'quasi-legal' status who are awaiting action on their legal migration requests."[163] Thus, the authors of the Census Bureau report estimated that there were approximately 4,430,000 such persons in 1990. By 2000, they suggest, the number had increased to approximately 10,250,000.[164]

1.   The Early Interplay of Race and Alienage

The 1787 Constitution gave Congress power to regulate naturalization, and, by implication, immigration, although historically there has been some debate over the precise source of Congress's powers to control immigration. In Chapter 1, for example, we noted the debates about Congressional power to pass the Alien Act of 1798. In our discussion of Mayor of the City of New York v. Miln in Chapter 3, we noted cases such as Henderson v. New York, 92 U.S. 259 (1876), that suggested that the federal authority over immigration lay in the commerce power. Finally, in the Chinese Exclusion Cases discussed in Chapter 4 we noted the rise of the modern plenary power doctrine.

Throughout the nineteenth century, issues of citizenship were intertwined with those of race, even though the two concepts were nominally distinct. Naturalization was limited to "white persons" by the Naturalization Act of 1795, although "aliens of African nativity and . . . persons of African descent" were made eligible for citizenship in 1870. (There were, however, extremely few immigrants from Africa who took advantage of this formal change in American immigration law.)

---

162. For the 2003 figures on population, see Foreign-Born Population of the United States Current Population Survey: March 2003 Detailed Tables (PPL-174), at *http://www.census.gov/population/ www/socdemo/foreign/ppl-174.html.* Of the approximately 265 million citizens, 252 million were native born and 13 million received their citizenship through naturalization.

163. U.S. Census Bureau, Evaluating Components of International Migration: The Residual Foreign Born (December 2001), p. 4.

164. Id. at 4-5.

The national reaction to Chinese immigration also mixed issues of race and alienage. Passage of the Chinese Exclusion Act in 1882, upheld in the Chinese Exclusion Case, 130 U.S. 581 (1889) and Fong Yue Ting v. United States, 149 U.S. 698 (1893), tied together issues of race and national origin. Chinese, like other Asians, could not become U.S. citizens; as Justice Harlan pointed out in his dissent in Plessy v. Ferguson, the Chinese were "a race so different from our own that we do not permit those belonging to it to become citizens of the United States. Persons belonging to it are, with few exceptions, absolutely excluded from our country." As noted in Chapter 4, during the 1920s the Supreme Court had to construe the meaning of the word "white" to decide that a person of Japanese descent or of a "high-caste Hindu of full Indian blood" could not become citizens. Takao Ozawa v. United States, 260 U.S. 178 (1922); United States v. Bhagat Singh Thind, 261 U.S. 204 (1923). Persons of Asian descent remained ineligible to become citizens until 1952 (save for immigrants from our wartime ally China, who were made eligible for citizenship in 1943).

Nevertheless, the Citizenship Clause of the Fourteenth Amendment cross cut the racial features of immigration policy, and in United States v. Wong Kim Ark, 169 U.S. 649 (1898), the Court held that persons of Chinese descent born in the United States were birthright citizens under the Fourteenth Amendment.

Moreover, despite the federal government's power to exclude aliens from the United States, even on the basis of race, the Court nonetheless did impose some limits on *state* power with regard to discrimination against aliens. In Yick Wo v. Hopkins, 118 U.S. 356 (1886), the Court struck down the patently discriminatory application of a city ordinance regulating laundry facilities operated by Chinese immigrants. The Court explained: "The Fourteenth Amendment to the Constitution is not confined to the protection of citizens. . . . [Its] provisions are universal in their application, to all persons within the territorial jurisdiction, without regard to any differences of race, of color, or of nationality; and the equal protection of the laws is a pledge of the protection of equal laws."

Despite *Yick Wo,* aliens continued to confront facially discriminatory federal and state statutes that placed varying restrictions on noncitizens. Anti-alien laws, particularly in the employment area, were commonplace and, when challenged, usually upheld by state and federal courts. See, e.g., Ohio ex rel. Clarke v. Deckebach, 274 U.S. 392 (1927) (statute prohibiting aliens from operating pool halls upheld); Crane v. New York, 239 U.S. 195 (1915) (public works contracts); Patsone v. Pennsylvania, 232 U.S. 138 (1914) (hunting); Trageser v. Gray, 73 Md. 250, 20 A. 905 (1890) (selling liquor). But see Juniata Limestone Co. v. Fagley, 187 Pa. 193, 40 A. 977 (1898) (state tax on aliens' wages invalidated). Many statutes were upheld by the courts under a "public interest" rationale that a state, in its capacity as guardian, had the exclusive authority to limit the use of its public resources and funds solely to its citizens. But many more statutes were upheld on the ground that a state could regulate aliens pursuant to its police powers in order to protect the health, safety, welfare, and morals of the citizens of the community. See, e.g., Miller v. Niagara Falls, 207 A.D. 798, 202 N.Y.S. 549 (4th Dist. 1924) (upholding ordinance prohibiting aliens from selling soft drinks because of the danger of soft drinks to the welfare of the community); Commonwealth v. Hana, 195 Mass. 262, 81 N.E. 149 (1907) (peddler's license denied to aliens because of the opportunity to cheat customers).

The public interest doctrine was limited slightly by the Supreme Court in Truax v. Raich, 239 U.S. 33 (1915), which invalidated an Arizona statute forbidding private businesses consisting of more than five persons from having work forces comprised of more than 20 percent aliens. The Court noted that "[t]he discrimination defined by the act does not pertain to the regulation or distribution of the public domain, or of the common property or resources of the people of the state, the enjoyment of which may be limited to its citizens as against both aliens and the citizens of other states." The state's police power "to promote the health, safety, morals, and welfare of those within its jurisdiction. . . . does not go so far as to make it possible for the state to deny to lawful inhabitants, because of their race or nationality, the ordinary means of earning a livelihood. It requires no argument to show that the right to work for a living in the common occupations of the community is of the very essence of the personal freedom and opportunity that it was the purpose of the Amendment to secure. If this could be refused solely upon the ground of race or nationality, the prohibition of the denial to any person of the equal protection of the laws would be a barren form of words. . . . The discrimination against aliens in the wide range of employments to which the act relates is made an end in itself."

The Court added that the law could not be viewed as a reasonable classification because it interfered with the federal government's power to control immigration: "The authority to control immigration — to admit or exclude aliens — is vested solely in the Federal Government. The assertion of an authority to deny to aliens the opportunity of earning a livelihood when lawfully admitted to the State would be tantamount to the assertion of the right to deny them entrance and abode, for in ordinary cases they cannot live where they cannot work. And, if such a policy were permissible, the practical result would be that those lawfully admitted to the country under the authority of the acts of Congress, instead of enjoying in a substantial sense and in their full scope the privileges conferred by the admission, would be segregated in such of the States as chose to offer hospitality."

The Court concluded that "No special public interest with respect to any particular business is shown that could possibly be deemed to support the enactment, for, as we have said, it relates to every sort. The discrimination is against aliens as such in competition with citizens in the described range of enterprises, and in our opinion it clearly falls under the condemnation of the fundamental law." One might, of course, analyze *Truax* within the context of the general sympathy shown by the Court of that era to a relatively unregulated private economic market. Although the case certainly protected the interests of job-seeking aliens, it just as certainly protected the interests of employers who might well have supported an expansion of the labor pool because of the pressure this would place on applicants to work for lower wages than might otherwise have been the case.

In Takahashi v. Fish & Game Commission, 334 U.S. 410 (1948), the Court considered a California law that denied fishing licenses to aliens ineligible for citizenship. The Court rejected California's contention that the statute was justified by the state's special public interest in conserving the supply of fish in its jurisdictional waters, which, it claimed, were the common property of the citizens of the state.

The Federal Government has broad constitutional powers in determining what aliens shall be admitted to the United States, the period they may remain, regulation of their conduct before naturalization, and the terms and conditions of their naturalization. Under the Constitution the states are granted no such powers; they can neither add to nor take from the conditions lawfully imposed by Congress upon admission, naturalization and residence of aliens in the United States or the several states. State laws which impose discriminatory burdens upon the entrance or residence of aliens lawfully within the United States conflict with this constitutionally derived federal power to regulate immigration, and have accordingly been held invalid. . . . The Fourteenth Amendment and the laws adopted under its authority thus embody a general policy that all persons lawfully in this country shall abide "in any state" on an equality of legal privileges with all citizens under non-discriminatory laws.

The Court rejected "the state's claim that it has power to single out and ban its lawful alien inhabitants, and particularly certain racial and color groups within this class of inhabitants, from following a vocation simply because Congress has put some such groups in special classifications in exercise of its broad and wholly distinguishable powers over immigration and naturalization."

The Court stated that it was "unnecessary to resolve the controversy concerning the underlying racial motives that prompted enactment of the legislation." However, Justice Murphy's concurrence, joined by Justice Rutledge, argued that the statute was "the direct outgrowth of antagonism toward persons of Japanese ancestry" and therefore violated the Equal Protection Clause.

Although the public interest doctrine was undermined in *Takahashi,* it was not fully rejected until 1971, four years after the Supreme Court held in *Loving* that racial classifications were subject to strict scrutiny.

2. Regulation of Aliens by State Governments

GRAHAM v. RICHARDSON[165]
403 U.S. 365 (1971)

BLACKMUN, J., delivered the opinion of the Court. . . .

The issue here is whether the Equal Protection Clause of the Fourteenth Amendment prevents a State from conditioning welfare benefits either (a) upon the beneficiary's possession of United States citizenship, or (b) if the beneficiary is an alien, upon his having resided in this country for a specified number of years.

I.

[Arizona required citizenship or 15 years of residence in the United States in order to receive welfare benefits. Appellee Richardson had emigrated from Mexico in 1956 and resided in Arizona from that time. At the time of the litigation she was "permanently and totally disabled," but was ineligible for benefits because she had retained Mexican citizenship and had not lived in Arizona the requisite length of time. A Pennsylvania statute limited welfare only to citizens.]

II.

. . . It has long been settled . . . that the term "person" [in the Fourteenth Amendment] encompasses lawfully admitted resident aliens as well as citizens of

---

165. Together with Sailer v. Leger, on appeal from the United States District Court for the Eastern District of Pennsylvania.

the United States and entitles both citizens and aliens to the equal protection of the laws of the State in which they reside. . . .

Under traditional equal protection principles, a State retains broad discretion to classify as long as its classification has a reasonable basis. . . . But the Court's decisions have established that classifications based on alienage, like those based on nationality or race, are inherently suspect and subject to close judicial scrutiny. Aliens as a class are a prime example of a "discrete and insular" minority (see U.S. v. Carolene Products Co., 304 U.S. 144, 152-53, n.4 (1938)) for whom such heightened judicial solicitude is appropriate. . . .

Arizona and Pennsylvania seek to justify their restrictions on the eligibility of aliens for public assistance solely on the basis of a State's "special public interest" in favoring its own citizens over aliens in the distribution of limited resources such as welfare benefits. It is true that this Court on occasion has upheld state statutes that treat citizens and noncitizens differently, the ground for distinction having been that such laws were necessary to protect special interests of the State or its citizens. Thus, in Truax v. Raich, 239 U.S. 33 (1915), the Court, in striking down an Arizona statute restricting the employment of aliens, emphasized that "[t]he discrimination defined by the act does not pertain to the regulation or distribution of the public domain, or of the common property or resources of the people of the State, the enjoyment of which may be limited to its citizens as against both aliens and the citizens of other States." And in Crane v. New York, 239 U.S. 195 (1915), the Court [upheld] a New York statute prohibiting the employment of aliens on public works projects. The New York court's opinion contained [then Justice of the New York Court of Appeals Cardozo's] well known observation:

> To disqualify aliens is discrimination indeed, but not arbitrary discrimination, for the principle of exclusion is the restriction of the resources of the state to the advancement and profit of the members of the state. Ungenerous and unwise such discrimination may be. It is not for that reason unlawful. . . . The state in determining what use shall be made of its own moneys, may legitimately consult the welfare of its own citizens rather than that of aliens. Whatever is a privilege rather than a right, may be made dependent on citizenship. In its war against poverty, the state is not required to dedicate its own resources to citizens and aliens alike.

Whatever may be the contemporary vitality of the special public-interest doctrine . . . , we conclude that a State's desire to preserve limited welfare benefits for its own citizens is inadequate to justify Pennsylvania's making noncitizens ineligible for public assistance, and Arizona's restricting benefits to citizens and long-time resident aliens. First, the special public interest doctrine was heavily grounded on the notion that "[w]hatever is a privilege, rather than a right, may be made dependent upon citizenship." But this Court now has rejected the concept that constitutional rights turn upon whether a governmental benefit is characterized as a "right" or as a "privilege." Second, as the Court recognized in Shapiro v. Thompson [which struck down a law withholding welfare benefits from newly arrived persons], " . . . [t]he saving of welfare costs cannot justify an otherwise invidious classification." Since an alien as well as a citizen is a "person" for equal protection purposes, a concern for fiscal integrity is [not a] compelling justification for the questioned classification in these cases. . . .

We agree with the three-judge court in the Pennsylvania case that the

> justification of limiting expenses is particularly inappropriate and unreasonable when the discriminated class consists of aliens. Aliens like citizens pay taxes and may be called into the armed forces. . . . [A]liens may live within a state for many years, work in the state and contribute to the economic growth of the state.

There can be no "special public interest" in tax revenues to which aliens have contributed on an equal basis with the residents of the State.

Accordingly, we hold that a state statute that denies welfare benefits to resident aliens and one that denies them to aliens who have not resided in the United States for a specified number of years violate the Equal Protection Clause.

III.

An additional reason why the state statutes at issue in these cases do not withstand constitutional scrutiny emerges from the area of federal-state relations. The National Government has "broad constitutional powers in determining what aliens shall be admitted to the United States, the period they may remain, regulation of their conduct before naturalization, and the terms and conditions of their naturalization." Pursuant to that power, Congress has provided . . . that "[a]liens who are paupers, professional beggars, or vagrants" or aliens who "are likely at any time to become public charges" shall be excluded from admission into the United States and that any alien lawfully admitted shall be deported who "has within five years after entry become a public charge from causes not affirmatively shown to have arisen after entry." . . . But Congress has not seen fit to impose any burden or restriction on aliens who become indigent after their entry into the United States. . . .

State laws that restrict the eligibility of aliens for welfare benefits merely because of their alienage conflict with these overriding national policies in an area constitutionally entrusted to the Federal Government. . . .

Congress has broadly declared as federal policy that lawfully admitted resident aliens who become public charges for causes arising after their entry are not subject to deportation, and that as long as they are here they are entitled to the full and equal benefit of all state laws for the security of persons and property. The state statutes at issue in the instant cases impose auxiliary burdens upon the entrance of residence of aliens who suffer the distress, after entry, of economic dependency on public assistance. . . .

[Justice Blackmun goes on to quote from a passage of *Truax* considering the consequence of allowing states to limit the opportunities of aliens for employment:]

> [I]f such a policy were permissible, the practical result would be that those lawfully admitted to the country under the authority of the acts of Congress, instead of enjoying in a substantial sense and in their full scope the privileges conferred by the admission, would be segregated in such of the States as chose to offer hospitality.

The same is true here, for in the ordinary case, an alien, becoming indigent and unable to work, will be unable to live where, because of discriminatory denial of public assistance, he cannot "secure the necessities of life, including food, clothing and shelter." State alien residency requirements that either deny welfare benefits to noncitizens or condition them on longtime residency, equate with the assertion of a right, inconsistent with federal policy, to deny entrance and abode. Since such laws encroach upon exclusive federal power, they are constitutionally impermissible.

BERNAL v. FAINTER
467 U.S. 216 (1984)

MARSHALL, J., delivered the opinion of the Court.

The question posed by this case is whether a statute of the State of Texas violates the Equal Protection Clause of the Fourteenth Amendment . . . by denying aliens the opportunity to become notaries public. . . .

I.

[Bernal], a native of Mexico, is a resident alien who has lived in the United States since 1961. He works as a paralegal for Texas Rural Legal Aid, Inc., helping migrant farmworkers on employment and civil rights matters. In order to administer oaths to these workers and to notarize their statements for use in civil litigation, [he] applied in 1978 to become a notary public. . . . The Texas Secretary of State denied [Bernal's] application because he failed to satisfy the statutory requirement that a notary public be a citizen of the United States. . . .

II.

As a general matter, a state law that discriminates on the basis of alienage can be sustained only if it can withstand strict judicial scrutiny. In order to withstand strict scrutiny, the law must advance a compelling state interest by the least restrictive means available. Applying this principle, we have invalidated an array of state statutes that denied aliens the right to pursue various occupations. In Sugarman v. Dougall, 413 U.S. 634 (1973), we struck down a state statute barring aliens from employment in permanent positions in the competitive class of the state civil service. In In re Griffith, 413 U.S. 717 (1973), we nullified a state law excluding aliens from eligibility for membership in the State Bar. And in Examining Board v. Flores de Otero, 426 U.S. 572 (1976), we voided a state law that excluded aliens from the practice of civil engineering.

We have, however, developed a narrow exception to the rule that discrimination based on alienage triggers strict scrutiny. This exception has been labeled the "political function" exception and applies to laws that exclude aliens from positions intimately related to the process of democratic self-governance. The contours of the "political function" exception are outlined by our prior decisions. In Foley v. Connelie, 435 U.S. 291 (1978), we held that a State may require police to be citizens because, in performing a fundamental obligation of government, police "are clothed with authority to exercise an almost infinite variety of discretionary powers" often involving the most sensitive areas of daily life. In Ambach v. Norwick, 441 U.S. 68 (1979), we held that a State may bar aliens who have not declared their intent to become citizens from teaching in the public schools because teachers, like police, possess a high degree of responsibility and discretion in the fulfillment of a basic governmental obligation. They have direct, day-to-day contact with students, exercise unsupervised discretion over them, act as role models, and influence their students about the government and the political process. Finally, in Cabell v. Chavez-Salido, 454 U.S. 432 (1982), we held that a State may bar aliens from positions as probation officers because they, like police and teachers, routinely exercise discretionary power, involving a basic governmental function, that places them in a position of direct authority over other individuals.

The rationale behind the political-function exception is that within broad boundaries a State may establish its own form of government and limit the right to govern to those who are full-fledged members of the political community. Some public positions are so closely bound with the formulation and implementation of self-government that the State is permitted to exclude from those positions persons outside the political community, hence, persons who have not become part of the process of democratic self-determination.

> The exclusion of aliens from basic governmental processes is not a deficiency in the democratic system but a necessary consequence of the community's process of political self-definition. Self-government, whether direct or through representatives, begins by defining the scope of the community of the governed and thus of the governors as well: Aliens are by definition those outside of this community.

We have therefore lowered our standard of review when evaluating the validity of exclusions that entrust only to citizens important elective and nonelective positions whose operations "go to the heart of representative government." . . .

To determine whether a restriction based on alienage fits within the narrow political-function exception, we devised in *Cabell* a two-part test.

> First, the specificity of the classification will be examined: a classification that is substantially overinclusive or underinclusive tends to undercut the governmental claim that the classification serves legitimate political ends. . . . Second, even if the classification is sufficiently tailored, it may be applied in the particular case only to "persons holding state elective or important nonelective executive, legislative, and judicial positions," those officials who "participate directly in the formulation, execution, or review of broad public policy" and hence "perform functions that go to the heart of representative government."

III.

[Does the Texas statute satisfy the *Cabell* test? It applies only to appointment as a Notary Public and therefore] does not indiscriminately sweep within its ambit a wide range of offices and occupations but specifies only one particular post with respect to which the State asserts a right to exclude aliens. Clearly, then, the statute is not overinclusive. . . . Less clear is whether [it] is fatally underinclusive. Texas does not require court reporters to be United States citizens even though they perform some of the same services as notaries. Nor does Texas require that its Secretary of State be a citizen, even though he holds the highest appointive position in the State and performs many important functions, including the supervision of the licensing of all notaries public. We need not decide this issue, however, because of our decision with respect to the second prong of the *Cabell* test.

. . . [T]he State emphasizes that notaries are designated as public officers by the Texas Constitution. . . . This Court, however, has never deemed the source of a position — whether it derives from a State's statute or its Constitution — as the dispositive factor in determining whether a State may entrust the position only to citizens. Rather, this Court has always looked to the actual function of the position as the dispositive factor. The focus of our inquiry has been whether a position was such that the officeholder would necessarily exercise broad discretionary power over the formulation or execution of public policies importantly affecting the citizen population — power of the sort that a self-governing community could properly entrust only to full-fledged members of that community. . . .

The State maintains that even if the actual function of a post is the touchstone of a proper analysis, Texas notaries public should still be classified among those positions from which aliens can properly be excluded because the duties of Texas notaries entail the performance of functions sufficiently consequential to be deemed "political." The Court of Appeals ably articulated this argument:

> With the power to acknowledge instruments such as wills and deeds and leases and mortgages; to take out-of-court depositions; to administer oaths; and the discretion to refuse to perform any of the foregoing acts, notaries public in Texas are involved in countless matters of importance to the day-to-day functioning of state government. The Texas political community depends upon the notary public to insure that those persons executing documents are accurately identified, to refuse to certify any identification that is false or uncertain, and to insist that oaths are properly and accurately administered. Land titles and property succession depend upon the care and integrity of the notary public, as well as the familiarity of the notary with the community, to verify the authenticity of the execution of the documents.

We recognize the critical need for a notary's duties to be carried out correctly and with integrity. But a notary's duties, important as they are, hardly implicate responsibilities that go to the heart of representative government. Rather, these duties are essentially clerical and ministerial. In contrast to state troopers, notaries do not routinely exercise the State's monopoly of legitimate coercive force. Nor do notaries routinely exercise the wide discretion typically enjoyed by public school teachers when they present materials that educate youth respecting the information and values necessary for the maintenance of a democratic political system. To be sure, considerable damage could result from the negligent or dishonest performance of a notary's duties. But the same could be said for the duties performed by cashiers, building inspectors, the janitors who clean up the offices of public officials, and numerous other categories of personnel upon whom we depend for careful, honest service. What distinguishes such personnel from those to whom the political-function exception is properly applied is that the latter are invested either with policymaking responsibility or broad discretion in the execution of public policy that requires the routine exercise of authority over individuals. Neither of these characteristics pertains to the functions performed by Texas notaries.

The inappropriateness of applying the political-function exception to Texas notaries is further underlined by our decision in In re Griffiths, in which we subjected to strict scrutiny a Connecticut statute that prohibited noncitizens from becoming members of the State Bar. Along with the usual power and privileges accorded to members of the bar, Connecticut gave to members of its Bar additional authority that encompasses the very duties performed by Texas notaries — authority to "sign writs and subpoenas, take recognizances, administer oaths and take depositions and acknowledgements of deeds." In striking down Connecticut's citizenship requirement, we concluded that "[i]t in no way denigrates a lawyer's high responsibilities to observe that [these duties] hardly involve matters of state policy or acts of such unique responsibility as to entrust them only to citizens." If it is improper to apply the political-function exception to a citizenship requirement in a state bar, it would be anomalous to apply the exception to the citizenship requirement that governs eligibility to become a Texas notary. We conclude, then, that the "political function" exception is inapplicable . . . and that the statute is therefore subject to strict judicial scrutiny.

IV.

To satisfy strict scrutiny, the State must show that [the statute] furthers a compelling state interest by the least restrictive means available. Respondents maintain that [the statute] serves "its legitimate concern that notaries be reasonably familiar with state law and institutions" and "that notaries may be called upon years later to testify to acts they have performed." However, both of these asserted justifications utterly fail to meet the stringent requirements of strict scrutiny. There is nothing in the record that indicates that resident aliens, as a class, are so incapable of familiarizing themselves with Texas law as to justify the State's absolute and classwide exclusion. . . . Furthermore, if the State's concern with ensuring a notary's familiarity with state law were truly "compelling," one would expect the State to give some sort of test actually measuring a person's familiarity with the law. The State, however, administers no such test. . . . Similarly inadequate is the State's purported interest in ensuring the later availability of notaries' testimony. This justification fails because the State fails to advance a factual showing that the unavailability of notaries' testimony presents a real, as opposed to a merely speculative, problem to the State. Without a factual underpinning, the State's asserted interest lacks the weight we have required of interests properly denominated as compelling.

REHNQUIST, J., dissenting.

I dissent for the reasons stated in my dissenting opinion in Sugarman v. Dougall, 413 U.S. 634, 649 (1973). [In *Sugarman*, which prohibited aliens from certain civil service positions, and its companion case, In re Griffiths, which involved a prohibition on aliens becoming members of the State Bar, Justice Rehnquist wrote:]

The Court . . . holds that an alien is not really different from a citizen, and that any legislative classification on the basis of alienage is "inherently suspect."[166] The Fourteenth Amendment, the Equal Protection Clause of which the Court interprets as invalidating the state legislation here involved, contains no language concerning "inherently suspect classifications," or, for that matter, merely "suspect classifications." The principal purpose of those who drafted and adopted the Amendment was to prohibit the States from invidiously discriminating by reason of race, Slaughter-House Cases, and, because of this plainly manifested intent, classifications based on race have rightly been held "suspect" under the Amendment. But there is no language used in the Amendment, or any historical evidence as to the intent of the Framers, which would suggest to the slightest degree that it was intended to render alienage a "suspect" classification, that it was designed in any

---

166. Elsewhere in the opinion, Rehnquist wrote that what "would most disturb native-born citizens and especially naturalized citizens who have worked diligently to learn about our history, mores, and political institutions and who have successfully completed the rigorous process of naturalization, is the intimation, if not statement, that they are really not any different from aliens."

way to protect "discrete and insular minorities" other than racial minorities, or that it would in any way justify the result reached by the Court. . . .

I.

The Court, by holding . . . that a citizen-alien classification is "suspect" in the eyes of our Constitution, fails to mention, let alone rationalize, the fact that the Constitution itself recognizes a basic difference between citizens and aliens. That distinction is constitutionally important in no less than 11 instances in a political document noted for its brevity. . . .

Not only do the numerous classifications on the basis of citizenship that are set forth in the Constitution cut against both the analysis used and the results reached by the Court in these cases; the very Amendment which the Court reads to prohibit classifications based on citizenship establishes the very distinction which the Court now condemns as "suspect." . . . In constitutionally defining who is a citizen of the United States, Congress [in proposing the Fourteenth Amendment] obviously thought it was doing something, and something important. Citizenship meant something, a status in and relationship with a society which is continuing and more basic than mere presence or residence. . . .

Decisions of this Court holding that an alien is a "person" within the meaning of the Fourteenth Amendment are simply irrelevant to the question of whether that Amendment prohibits legislative classifications based upon this particular status. . . .

[T]he Court now relies in part on the decisions in Truax v. Raich, 239 U.S. 33 (1915), and Takahashi v. Fish Comm's, 334 U.S. 410 (1948). In *Truax*, the Court invalidated a state statute which prohibited employers of more than five persons from employing more than 20% noncitizens. The law was applicable to all citizens. In holding that the law was invalid . . . , the Court . . . noted that "it should be added that the act is not limited to persons who are engaged in public work or receive the benefit of public moneys." . . .

Takahashi involved a statute which prohibited aliens "ineligible for citizenship" under federal law from receiving commercial fishing licenses. . . . Two features of that law should be noted. First, the statutory classification was not one involving citizens and aliens; it classified citizens and those resident aliens eligible for citizenship into one group, and resident aliens ineligible for citizenship into another. No reason for discriminating among resident aliens is apparent. Second, and most important, is the fact that, although the Court properly refused to inquire into the legislative motive, the overwhelming effect of the law was to bar resident aliens of Japanese ancestry from procuring fishing licenses. [United States law at the time prohibited persons of Japanese ancestry from becoming naturalized citizens.] The Court was not blind to this fact, or to history. The state statute that classifies aliens on the basis of country of origin is much more likely to classify on the basis of race, and thus conflict with the core purpose of the Equal Protection Clause, than a statute that, as here, merely distinguishes between alienage as such and citizenship as such. . . .

[Justice Rehnquist then turns to Graham v. Richardson, supra. He focuses on the Court's reliance on footnote 4 of United States v. Carolene Products Co.].

The mere recitation of the words "insular and discrete minority" is hardly a constitutional reason for prohibiting state legislative classifications such as are involved here. . . .

Our society, consisting of over 200 million individuals of multitudinous origins, customs, tongues, beliefs, and cultures is, to say the least, diverse. It would hardly take extraordinary ingenuity for a lawyer to find "insular and discrete" minorities at every turn in the road. Yet, unless the Court can precisely define and constitutionally justify both the terms and analysis it uses, these decisions today stand for the proposition that the Court can choose a "minority" it "feels" deserves "solicitude" and thereafter prohibit the States from classifying that "minority" differently from the "majority." I cannot find, and the Court does not cite, any constitutional authority for such a "ward of the Court" approach to equal protection.

The only other apparent rationale for the invocation of the "suspect classification" approach in these cases is that alienage is a "status," and the Court does not feel it "appropriate" to classify on that basis. This rationale would appear to be similar to that utilized in Weber v. Aetna Casualty & Surety Co., 406 U.S. 164 (1972)[, in which the Court, with Justice Rehnquist dissenting, indicated that classifications based on the "illegitimacy" of a child would be subject to special scrutiny].... But there is a marked difference between a status or condition such as illegitimacy, national origin, or race, which cannot be altered by an individual and the "status" of the appellant. There is nothing in the record indicating that their status as aliens cannot be changed by their affirmative acts.

II.

These statutes do not classify on the basis of country of origin; the distinctions are not between native Americans and "foreigners," but between citizens and aliens. The process of naturalization was specifically designed by Congress to require a foreign national to demonstrate that he or she is familiar with the history, traditions, and institutions of our society in a way that a native-born citizen would learn from formal education and basic social contact. Congress specifically provided that an alien seeking citizenship status must demonstrate "an understanding of the English language" and "a knowledge and understanding of the fundamentals of the history, and of the principles and form of government, of the United States." The purpose was to make the alien establish that he or she understood, and could be integrated into, our social system. . . .

I do not believe that it is irrational for [states to require civil servants] to be citizens, either natural born or naturalized. The proliferation of public administration that our society has witnessed in recent years, as a result of the regulation of conduct and the dispensation of services and funds, has vested a great deal of de facto decisionmaking or policymaking authority in the hands of employees who would not be considered the textbook equivalent of policymakers of the legislative or "top" administrative variety. Nevertheless, as far as the private individual who must seek approval or services is concerned, many of these "low level" civil servants are in fact policymakers. Goldberg v. Kelly implicitly recognized that those who apply facts to individual cases are as much "governors" as those who write the laws or regulations the "low-level" administrator must "apply." Since policymaking for a political community is not necessarily the exclusive preserve of the legislators, judges, and "top" administrators, it is not irrational for New York to provide that only citizens should be admitted to the competitive civil service.

But the justification of efficient government is an even more convincing rationale. Native-born citizens can be expected to be familiar with the social and political institutions of our society; with the society and political mores that affect how we react and interact with other citizens. Naturalized citizens have also demonstrated their willingness to adjust to our patterns of living and attitudes, and have demonstrated a basic understanding of our institutions, system of government, history, and traditions. It is not irrational to assume that aliens as a class are not familiar with how we as individuals treat others and how we expect "government" to treat us. An alien who grew up in a country in which political mores do not reject bribery or self-dealing to the same extent that our culture does; in which an imperious bureaucracy historically adopted a complacent or contemptuous attitude toward those it was supposed to serve; in which fewer if any checks existed on administrative abuses; in which "low-level" civil servants serve at the will of their superiors — could rationally be thought not to be able to deal with the public and with citizen civil servants with the same rapport that one familiar with our political and social mores would, or to approach his duties with the attitude that such positions exist for service, not personal sinecures of either the civil servant or his or her superior. . . .

Connecticut's requirement of citizenship [for lawyers] reflects its judgment that something more than technical skills are needed to be a lawyer under our system. I do not believe it is irrational for a State that makes that judgment to require that lawyers have an understanding of the American political and social experience, whether gained from growing up in this country, as in the case of a native-born citizen, or from the naturalization process, as in the case of a foreign-born citizen. I suppose the Connecticut Bar Examining Committee could itself administer tests in American history, government, and sociology, but the State did not choose to go this route. Instead, it chose to operate on the assumption that citizens as a class might reasonably be thought to have a significantly greater degree of understanding of our experience than would aliens. . . .

Discussion

1. *Community and alienage.* It seems clear that a state can deny the right to vote to resident aliens. But why? One assumes that what justifies the denial of the most "fundamental" of all interests in a democratic polity is that aliens are not members of the political community and are, therefore, not entitled to help shape the community's decisions even if they clearly have strong interests in the electoral outcomes.[167] But what constitutes citizens as a political "community" (rather than simply a collection of persons who happen to share the common legal category of citizenship)? What is it that joins in political fellowship a group of citizens of the United States composed of a Jehovah's Witness from Maine, a Vietnamese refugee living in Houston, and a member of the Ku Klux Klan?

In this context, examine Justice Rehnquist's assumptions about the consequences of growing up in the United States or preparing for naturalization. How plausible are they, and how would you prove or disprove their validity? (Who ought to have the burden of coming forth with relevant evidence?) Does the persuasiveness of Justice Rehnquist's dissent ultimately turn on these assumptions?

2. *Equal protection or preemption.* Note the difference between parts II and III of the Court's opinion in Graham v. Richardson. Does it matter which theory one

---

167. See Sanford Levinson, Suffrage and Community: Who Should Vote?, 1989 Fla. L. Rev. 545.

chooses to explain the state's inability to discriminate against aliens? Which of these parts proves determinative in *Bernal*, and does it matter?

In Toll v. Moreno, 458 U.S. 1 (1982), the Court, through Justice Brennan, emphasized "the preeminent role of the Federal Government with respect to the regulation of aliens within our borders" while striking down a Maryland statute imposing special costs on aliens attending the state university. The Court quoted a passage from *Takahashi* stating that "[u]nder the Constitution the states . . . can neither add to nor take from the conditions lawfully imposed by Congress upon admission, naturalization and residence of aliens in the United States or the several states." And Justice Brennan went on to acknowledge in a footnote that several "commentators have noted . . . that many of the Court's decisions concerning alien-age classifications . . . are better explained in preemption than equal protection terms."[168] If one were to adopt such a focus, the operative rule might be something like this: When Congress adopts legislation resulting in the permanent residence of an alien, a state cannot interfere with the national policy by setting up barriers to the resident alien's ability to flourish in the United States unless those barriers can survive strict scrutiny.

3. *Illegal aliens and education.* In Plyler v. Doe, 457 U.S. 202 (1982), discussed at greater length in Chapter 9, the Supreme Court held that Texas could not prohibit children of illegal aliens from enrolling in Texas public schools. Justice Brennan, writing for a 5-4 majority, rejected Texas's argument that illegal aliens were not "persons within its jurisdiction" and therefore exempt from the requirements of the Equal Protection Clause:

> The Fourteenth Amendment provides that "No State shall . . . deprive any person of life, liberty or property, without due process of law; nor deny to *any person within its jurisdiction* the equal protection of the laws." [Emphasis added.] Appellants argue at the outset that undocumented aliens, because of their immigration status, are not "persons within the jurisdiction" of the State of Texas, and that they therefore have no right to the equal protection of Texas law. We reject this argument. Whatever his status under the immigration laws, an alien is surely a "person" in any ordinary sense of that term. Aliens, even aliens whose presence in this country is unlawful, have long been recognized as "persons" guaranteed due process of law by the Fifth and Fourteenth Amendments. Shaughnessy v. Mezei, 345 U.S. 206, 212 (1953); Wong Wing v. United States, 163 U.S. 228, 238 (1986). Indeed, we have clearly held that the Fifth Amendment protects aliens whose presence in this country is unlawful from invidious discrimination by the Federal Government. Mathews v. Diaz, 426 U.S. 67, 77 (1976). . . .
>
> There is simply no support for appellants' suggestion that "due process" is somehow of greater stature than "equal protection" and therefore available to a larger class of persons. To the contrary, each aspect of the Fourteenth Amendment reflects an elementary limitation on state power. To permit a State to employ the phrase "within its jurisdiction" in order to identify subclasses of persons whom it would define as beyond its jurisdiction, thereby relieving itself of the obligation to assure that its laws are designed and applied equally to those persons, would undermine the principal purpose for which the Equal Protection Clause was incorporated in the Fourteenth Amendment. The Equal Protection Clause was intended to work nothing less than the

---

168. See Note, The Equal Treatment of Aliens: Preemption as Equal Protection, 31 Stan. L. Rev. 1069 (1979); Note, State Burdens on Resident Aliens: A New Preemption Analysis, 89 Yale L.J. 940 (1980).

abolition of all caste and invidious class based legislation. That objective is fundamentally at odds with the power the State asserts here to classify persons subject to its laws as nonetheless excepted from its protection.

Although the congressional debate concerning §1 of the Fourteenth Amendment was limited, that debate clearly confirms the understanding that the phrase "within its jurisdiction" was intended in a broad sense to offer the guarantee of equal protection to all within a State's boundaries, and to all upon whom the State would impose the obligations of its laws. Indeed, it appears from those debates that Congress, by using the phrase "person within its jurisdiction," sought expressly to ensure that the equal protection of the laws was provided to the alien population. Representative Bingham reported to the House the draft resolution of the Joint Committee of Fifteen on Reconstruction (H.R. 63) that was to become the Fourteenth Amendment. Cong. Globe, 39th Cong., 1st Sess., 1033 (1866). Two days later, Bingham posed the following question in support of the resolution: "Is it not essential to the unity of the Government and the unity of the people that all persons, whether citizens or strangers, within this land, shall have equal protection in every State in this Union in the rights of life and liberty and property?" Senator Howard, also a member of the Joint Committee of Fifteen, and the floor manager of the Amendment in the Senate, was no less explicit about the broad objectives of the Amendment, and the intention to make its provisions applicable to all who "may happen to be" within the jurisdiction of a State: "The last two clauses of the first section of the amendment disable a State from depriving not merely a citizen of the United States, but *any person, whoever he may be,* of life, liberty, or property without due process of law, or from denying to him the equal protection of the laws of the State. This abolishes all class legislation in the States, and does away with the injustice of subjecting one caste of persons to a code not applicable to another. . . . It will, if adopted by the States, forever disable every one of them from passing laws trenching upon those fundamental rights and privileges which pertain to citizens of the United States, *and to all persons who may happen to be within their jurisdiction.*" Cong. Globe, 39th Cong. 1st Sess. 2766 (1866) (emphasis added).

Use of the phrase "within its jurisdiction" thus does not detract from, but rather confirms the understanding that the protection of the Fourteenth Amendment extends to anyone, citizen or stranger, who is subject to the laws of a State, and reaches into every corner of a State's territory. That a person's initial entry into a State or into the United States, was unlawful, and that he may for that reason be expelled, cannot negate the simple fact of his presence within the State's territorial perimeter. Given such presence, he is subject to the full range of obligations imposed by the State's civil and criminal laws. And until he leaves the jurisdiction — either voluntarily or involuntarily in accordance with the Constitution and the laws of the United States — he is entitled to the equal protection of the laws that a State may choose to establish. . . .

Justice Brennan concluded that although children of illegal immigrants were not a suspect class and although education was not a fundamental right, Texas's law failed the test of rationality because the state failed to show that its policy furthered a "substantial state interest." Texas's policy, Justice Brennan argued, "imposes a lifetime hardship on a discrete class of children not accountable for their disabling status. The stigma of illiteracy will mark them for the rest of their lives. By denying these children a basic education, we deny them the ability to live within the structure of our civic institutions, and foreclose any realistic possibility that they will contribute in even the smallest way to the progress of our Nation. In determining the rationality of [Texas's policy], we may appropriately take into account its costs to the Nation and to the innocent children who are its victims."

Chief Justice Burger, joined by Justices White, Rehnquist, and O'Connor, dissented, noting that the Texas's law involved neither a suspect class nor a fundamental right, and therefore need only pass the test of "a rational relation to a legitimate state purpose." "[I]t is simply not 'irrational' for a State to conclude that it does not have the same responsibility to provide benefits for persons whose very presence in the State and this country is illegal as it does to provide for those persons lawfully present."

3.   *Regulation of Resident Aliens by the Federal Government*

The Constitution gives Congress the right to control naturalization, and gives the federal government the power to regulate foreign affairs. Thus, the preemption arguments that apply to state regulation do not apply to the federal government. Does the Equal Protection component of the Due Process Clause of the Fifth Amendment, first adverted to in Bolling v. Sharpe, restrict the federal government in the same way that the Fourteenth Amendment restricts the states?

The Court considered Congress's power over lawfully admitted aliens in Mathews v. Diaz, 426 U.S. 67 (1976), and Hampton v. Mow Sun Wong, 426 U.S. 88 (1976). In *Diaz*, a unanimous Court upheld a congressional limitation on the participation of aliens in federal Medicare programs to aliens who had both been admitted as permanent residents and had been continuously resident in the United States for five years. Writing for the Court, Justice Stevens noted that "[i]n the exercise of its broad power over naturalization and immigration, Congress regularly makes rules that would be unacceptable if applied to citizens."

Justice Stevens wrote: "It is obvious that Congress has no constitutional duty to provide all aliens with the welfare benefits provided to citizens." The only question was whether the classifications were reasonable; the Court held that they were. Distinguishing *Graham*, the Court emphasized the difference between states and Congress:

> Insofar as state welfare policy is concerned, there is little, if any, basis for treating persons who are citizens of another State differently from persons who are citizens of another country. Both groups are noncitizens as far as the State's interests in administering its welfare programs are concerned. Thus, a division by a State of the category of persons who are not citizens of that State into subcategories of United States citizens and aliens has no apparent justification, whereas, a comparable classification by the Federal Government is a routine and normally legitimate part of its business. Furthermore, whereas the Constitution inhibits every State's power to restrict travel across its own borders, Congress is explicitly empowered to exercise that type of control across the borders of the United States.
>
> . . . [I]t is not "political hypocrisy" to recognize that the Fourteenth Amendment's limits on state powers are substantially different from the constitutional provisions applicable to the federal power over immigration and naturalization.

In *Hampton*, Justice Stevens wrote for a five-Justice majority to invalidate a United States Civil Service Commission regulation that barred resident aliens from competing for positions in the federal civil service. The Court rested the decision on pure due process grounds, explicitly declining to hold that the regulation violated the equal protection component of the Fifth Amendment. Justice Stevens emphasized the far-reaching consequences of the prohibition and the facts that it had not been directly ordered by either Congress or the President nor had its merits been fully considered by the Commission. The Court acknowledged "that overriding national interests may provide a justification for a citizenship requirement in the federal service even though an identical requirement may not be enforced by a State," but denied that "the federal power over aliens is so plenary that any agent of the National Government may arbitrarily subject all resident aliens to different substantive rules from those applied to citizens."

> The rule enforced by the Commission has its impact on an identifiable class of persons who, entirely apart from the rule itself, are already subject to disadvantages not shared by the remainder of the community. Aliens are not entitled to vote and . . . are often handicapped by a lack of familiarity with our language and customs. The added disadvantage resulting from the enforcement of the rule — ineligibility for employment in a major sector of the economy, is of sufficient significance to be characterized as a deprivation of an interest in liberty. Indeed, we deal with a rule which deprives a discrete class of persons of an interest in liberty on a wholesale basis. By reason of the Fifth Amendment, such a deprivation must be accompanied by due process.

Following the decision in *Hampton,* President Ford issued an Executive Order making citizenship a condition for federal employment. The order has not subsequently been reviewed by the Supreme Court. Consider, though, Professor Tribe's suggestion that the Fifth Amendment's equal protection component "would invalidate even congressional or presidential discrimination against resident aliens as such where no substantial justification could be shown."[169]

Discussion

1. *The reach of Mathews v. Diaz.* Does *Mathews* hold that all federal discriminations against aliens are subject only to rational basis review? Consider the following arguments for a narrower theory. Which, if any, do you think would be workable?

(a)   Federal classifications that discriminate against persons who are not resident aliens, for example, immigrants who are not yet resident aliens, persons on student visas, or other visitors who have come to the country temporarily, should be treated differently from those classifications that discriminate against resident aliens. The latter discriminations should be subject to strict scrutiny. See Rosberg, The Protection of Aliens from Discriminatory Treatment by the National Government, 1977 Sup. Ct. Rev. 275, 335. Note that this rule would have afforded little protection to, for example, nonresident aliens and aliens on student visas who were rounded up on suspicion of terrorist activities following the September 11, 2001 attacks on the United States.

(b)   Application of judicial scrutiny should depend on the purposes for the classification. "When a categorical preference for American citizens cannot be justi-

---

169. See Laurence Tribe, American Constitutional Law 1546 n.12 (1988).

fied in terms of immigration and naturalization policy or as an adjunct to our international bargaining posture, the basis for relaxing the scrutiny otherwise applicable to discrimination against aliens as a class" should not apply. Neal Katyal and Laurence Tribe, Waging War, Deciding Guilt: Trying the Military Tribunals, 111 Yale L. J. 1259, 1300-1301 (2002). What sorts of restrictions on aliens could not be justified in terms of immigration and naturalization policy, or in terms of the conduct of foreign policy?

(c)   Federal classifications that are motivated by racial prejudice should not be insulated from judicial scrutiny; hence courts must inquire whether a particular federal classification against aliens is motivated by racial stereotyping or racial prejudice. Is this theory consistent with the Chinese Exclusion Case (Chae Chan Ping v. United States) that gave Congress plenary power to exclude "foreigners of a different race"? Would this rule prohibit the government from having different quotas for admission of aliens from different countries?

(d)   Federal classifications that affect fundamental rights like those in the federal Bill of Rights, as well as rights of marriage and procreation should be subject to strict scrutiny, whether they apply to immigrants, visitors, or resident aliens. Cf. David Cole, Enemy Aliens, 54 Stan. L. Rev. 953 (2002) (arguing that "distinctions between citizens and aliens do not generally justify differential application of First Amendment speech and association rights or Fifth Amendment due process protections"). Under this theory, could Congress expel aliens who advocate violence against the United States if it could not punish citizens who do so? Could it have different rules for admitting family members (including spouses) of citizens and resident aliens?

In Zadvydas v. Davis, 533 U.S. 678 (2001), the Court held that an alien ordered removed from the country because of his criminal record but whom no country was willing to accept could not be kept in custody indefinitely. The Court interpreted the relevant statute to authorize only temporary detention pending removal in order to avoid constitutional problems under the Due Process Clause. Justice Breyer wrote for a 5-4 majority:

A statute permitting indefinite detention of an alien would raise a serious constitutional problem. The Fifth Amendment's Due Process Clause forbids the Government to "deprive" any "person . . . of . . . liberty . . . without due process of law." Freedom from imprisonment — from government custody, detention, or other forms of physical restraint — lies at the heart of the liberty that Clause protects. And this Court has said that government detention violates that Clause unless the detention is ordered in a criminal proceeding with adequate procedural protections, or, in certain special and "narrow" non-punitive "circumstances," where a special justification, such as harm-threatening mental illness, outweighs the "individual's constitutionally protected interest in avoiding physical restraint." Kansas v. Hendricks, 521 U.S. 346 (1997). . . .

It is well established that certain constitutional protections available to persons inside the United States are unavailable to aliens outside of our geographic borders. But once an alien enters the country, the legal circumstance changes, for the Due Process Clause applies to all "persons" within the United States, including aliens, whether their presence here is lawful, unlawful, temporary, or permanent. Indeed, this Court has held that the Due Process Clause protects an alien subject to a final order of deportation, though the nature of that protection may vary depending upon status and circumstance.

Justices Scalia, Thomas, Kennedy, and Chief Justice Rehnquist dissented.

How much constitutional protection does *Zadvydas* offer? Note that the Court did not dispute that aliens may be subject to quite different procedures than citizens without running afoul of the Due Process Clause. Moreover, the Court noted that although preventive detention was not authorized in this case, it did not have before it a situation involving "terrorism or other special circumstances where special arguments might be made for forms of preventive detention and for heightened deference to the judgments of the political branches with respect to matters of national security."

Zadvydas, as noted, dealt with readily deportable aliens who did not, however, have a country willing to accept them. Consider, however, Auguste v. Ridge, 395 F.3d 123 (3rd Cir. 2005), involving the deportation of a felon from Haiti. The country was willing to accept Auguste, but it has a policy of placing such persons in jail for a period of time in order to discourage a return to criminal ways by those returning to Haiti under such circumstances. Although the Third Circuit found that the conditions of Haitian jails approached "slave ships" in their severity, it held, nonetheless, that since the conditions did not meet the strict definition of "torture" adopted by the Court, Auguste had no right not to be returned to his home country.

2. *Congressional authorization.* May Congress authorize states to discriminate against aliens? In Graham v. Richardson, the Court considered Arizona's suggestion that its 15-year durational residency requirement for aliens was authorized by federal law. The Court rejected Arizona's construction of the relevant federal statutes and then went on to say:

> But if [the statutes] were to be read so as to authorize discriminatory treatment of aliens at the option of the States, [that would present] serious constitutional questions. Although the Federal Government admittedly has broad constitutional power to determine what aliens shall be admitted to the United States, the period they may remain, and the terms and conditions of their naturalization, Congress does not have the power to authorize the individual States to violate the Equal Protection Clause. Under Art. I, §8, cl. 4, of the Constitution, Congress' power is to "establish a uniform Rule of Naturalization." A congressional enactment construed so as to permit state legislatures to adopt divergent laws on the subject of citizenship requirements for federally supported welfare programs would appear to contravene this explicit constitutional requirement of uniformity.

Is the Court's advisory construction of the "uniformity" provision persuasive? So long as all immigrants are equally liable to the decisions of the states wherein they happen to reside, wouldn't the "uniformity" provision be satisfied?

Consider in this context §411 of the Personal Responsibility and Work Opportunity Reconciliation Act of 1996, which explicitly made ineligible "for any State or local public benefit" anyone who is an illegal immigrant to the United States. Note well that this does not simply grant states discretion to decide whether to extend such persons welfare benefits, but appears to require that states not offer any such benefits, presumably as part of the national policy to discourage illegal immigration. Does §411 present any constitutional difficulties? There are, however, some limited exceptions, such as "[a]ssistance for health care items and service that are necessary for the treatment of an emergency medical condition of the alien involved and are not related to an organ transplant process" and "short-term, non-cash, in-kind emergency disaster relief," and "[p]ublic health assistance for immunizations with respect to immunizable diseases and for testing and treatment of symptoms of communicable diseases." Are these exceptions constitutionally required or matters of legislative grace?

Even if the 1996 law were not part of the legal horizon, one might well wonder about the status of *Plyler,* given the changes in membership on the Court since 1982. Of the justices in the majority, only Justice Stevens remains on the Court as of 2005 (and he is 85). So consider the constitutional status of Proposition 187, passed by the voters of California in 1994 via the initiative and referendum process:

SECTION 1. Findings and Declaration.

The People of California find and declare as follows:

That they have suffered and are suffering economic hardship caused by the presence of illegal aliens in this state.

That they have suffered and are suffering personal injury and damage caused by the criminal conduct of illegal aliens in this state.

That they have a right to the protection of their government from any person or persons entering this country unlawfully.

Therefore, the People of California declare their intention to . . . prevent illegal aliens in the United States from receiving benefits or public services in the State of California.

[The following sections are added to California law by Proposition 187:]

10001.5. (a) In order to carry out the intention of the People of California that only citizens of the United States and aliens lawfully admitted to the United States may receive the benefits of public social services and to ensure that all persons employed in the providing of those services shall diligently protect public funds from misuse, the provisions of this section are adopted.

(b) A person shall not receive any public social services to which he or she may be otherwise entitled until the legal status of that person has been verified as one of the following:

(1) A citizen of the United States.

(2) An alien lawfully admitted as a permanent resident.

(3) An alien lawfully admitted for a temporary period of time. . . .

SECTION 6. Exclusion of Illegal Aliens from Publicly Funded Health Care. Chapter 1.3. Publicly-Funded Health Care Services

(a) In order to carry out the intention of the People of California that, excepting emergency medical care as required by federal law, only citizens of the United States and aliens lawfully admitted to the United States may receive the benefits of publicly-funded health care, and to ensure that all persons employed in the providing of those services shall diligently protect public funds from misuse, the provisions of this section are adopted.

(b) A person shall not receive any health care services from a publicly-funded health care facility, to which he or she is otherwise entitled, until the legal status of that person has been verified as one of the following: (1) A citizen of the United States.

(2) An alien lawfully admitted as a permanent resident.

(3) An alien lawfully admitted for a temporary period of time. . . .

SECTION 7. Exclusion of Illegal Aliens from Public Elementary and Secondary Schools. 48215. (a) No public elementary or secondary school shall admit, or permit the attendance of, any child who is not a citizen of the United States, an alien lawfully admitted as a permanent resident, or a person who is otherwise authorized under federal law to be present in the United States. . . .

SECTION 8. Exclusion of Illegal Aliens from Public Postsecondary Educational Institutions. 66010.8. (a) No public institution of postsecondary education shall admit, enroll, or permit the attendance of any person who is not a citizen of the United States, an alien lawfully admitted as a permanent resident in the United States, or a person who is otherwise authorized under federal law to be present in the United States.

Is Proposition 187 constitutional, in whole or in part? Does your answer depend on whether this question is asked as of 1995, i.e., before the passage of the 1996 "welfare reform" Act, or afterward? See League of United Latin American Citizens, v. Wilson, 997 F.Supp. 1244 (C.D. Cal. 1997).

Chapter 7
Sex Equality

The previous chapter considered how the Court has interpreted the Equal Protection Clause to speak to questions of race inequality during the last half-century. Given the history of the Fourteenth Amendment, this presents perhaps the most straightforward application of the Clause. But the Equal Protection Clause is not restricted to questions of race discrimination. The Fourteenth Amendment announces its guarantees in general language, declaring that no state shall "deny to any person within its jurisdiction the equal protection of the laws." After deciding *Brown* and associated doctrines of race discrimination, in the 1970s the Court began to interpret the Clause to speak to other forms of inequality — especially to questions of sex discrimination.

This chapter examines the decisions that apply the Equal Protection Clause to questions of sex equality. The sex discrimination cases present fundamental questions concerning constitutional change. For nearly a century after ratification of the Fourteenth Amendment, the Court invalidated no law under the Equal Protection Clause on the ground that it discriminated between the sexes. Then, during the 1970s, the Court began to interpret the Clause as prohibiting certain state laws that distributed rights and obligations by sex. The chapter examines the justifications the Court offered for this new body of equal protection law, and explores its practical reach. How did the Court decide what forms of state action, in addition to race-based state action, would require extraordinary justification (more than minimum rationality) under the Equal Protection Clause? And once it decided closely to scrutinize sex-based state action, how did the Court determine which forms of sex-based regulation warranted invalidation? In what areas might this body of law still be evolving? What does this body of law teach about the dynamics of constitutional change, and how might it serve as precedent governing the claims of other groups seeking suspect class status under the Equal Protection Clause?

I. The Court's Initial Reception of Sex Equality Claims Under the Fourteenth Amendment: Early History — Social Movements and Constitutional Change

A. The Amendment's First Century

A robust woman suffrage movement lived in the ranks of the nineteenth-century abolitionist movement and the Republican Party that it shaped. As Chapter 4

recounts, woman suffrage advocates helped petition for the Reconstruction amendments. Once the amendments were ratified, the movement made claims on them,
asserting that the Fourteenth Amendment embodied a commitment to protect
human rights and the privileges and immunities of citizenship that was broad
enough to emancipate women. Yet, as we saw in Chapter 4, the Court was not receptive to equality claims that the suffrage movement advanced under the newly ratified Fourteenth Amendment. In this period — and for much of the ensuing
century — the Court viewed state action that discriminated between the sexes as
rationally reflecting differences in the social roles of men and women. It rejected
Myra Bradwell's claim that an Illinois law denying women the right to practice law
violated the Fourteenth Amendment. Justice Bradley's concurrence in Bradwell v.
Illinois, 83 U.S. (16 Wall.) 130, 141 (1873), has since become notorious:

> [T]he civil law, as well as nature herself, has always recognized a wide difference in the
> respective spheres and destinies of man and woman. . . . The constitution of the family
> organization, which is founded in the divine ordinance, as well as in the nature of
> things, indicates the domestic sphere as that which properly belongs to the domain
> and functions of womanhood. . . . The paramount destiny and mission of woman are
> to fulfill the noble and benign offices of wife and mother. This is the law of the Creator.

Justice Bradley rested his interpretation of the Fourteenth Amendment on understandings about family structure — on the common law of marital status and the ideology of "separate spheres." Given that "a married woman is incapable, without her
husband's consent, of making contracts which shall be binding on her or him," Justice
Bradley reasoned, the Illinois Supreme Court was perfectly justified in its concerns
that Mrs. Bradwell could not adequately represent her clients. This restriction on
women's participation in professional life was wholly intelligible within the prevailing
"separate spheres" ideology, which held that women were specially suited for the work
of family maintenance, while men were destined for the world of public affairs.

Women's efforts to secure protection for the right to vote on the same terms as
men fared no better under the Fourteenth Amendment than did the claim to practice law. As Chapter 4 recounts, in the aftermath of the Civil War, when leaders of
the suffrage movement failed to persuade the Thirty-Ninth Congress to enfranchise
women, Frances Minor and others called for a "New Departure under the
Fourteenth Amendment," in which hundreds of women began to assert a constitutional right to vote. The Court rejected this claim in Minor v. Happersett, 88 U.S.
(21 Wall.) 162 (1875), ruling that the Fourteenth Amendment did not guarantee
women the right to vote. The Court acknowledged that women were citizens of the
United States, but nonetheless held without dissent that the right to vote was not a
privilege or immunity of United States citizenship.

After the Court rejected women's suffrage claims under the Fourteenth
Amendment, the movement began its quest for a constitutional amendment that
would recognize that women were entitled to vote on the same terms as men. Over
the next several decades, the movement struggled to win recognition of this equal
citizenship claim and to refute opponents of woman suffrage who argued that
differences in family roles justified different citizenship roles for men and women.[1]

---

1. For an account of the debate over marriage, citizenship, and suffrage in the campaign, see Reva B.
Siegel, She the People: The Nineteenth Amendment, Sex Equality, Federalism, and the Family, 115
Harv. L. Rev. 947 (2002).

In 1920, the movement finally secured ratification of the Nineteenth Amendment, which prohibited states from limiting suffrage on grounds of sex.

Initially, at least, ratification of the woman suffrage amendment influenced the Court's interpretation of the Fourteenth Amendment. By the early twentieth century the Court had adopted a gender-differentiated framework for enforcing liberty of contract under the Fourteenth Amendment, ruling in Muller v. Oregon, 208 U.S. 412, 422-423 (1908), that states might regulate women's employment in ways *Lochner* barred the regulation of men's employment because

> [t]he two sexes differ in structure of body, in the functions to be performed by each, in the amount of physical strength, in the capacity for long continued labor, particularly when done standing, the influence of vigorous health upon the future well-being of the race, the self-reliance which enables one to assert full rights, and in the capacity to main-tain the struggle for subsistence. This difference justifies a difference in legislation. . . .

After ratification of the Nineteenth Amendment, the Court retreated from this gender-differentiated framework for determining whether protective labor legisla-tion violated liberty of contract under the Fourteenth Amendment. In Adkins v. Children's Hospital, 261 U.S. 525 (1923), the Court ruled that a minimum wage law for women violated liberty of contract.[2] Justice Sutherland's opinion in *Adkins* pointed to changes in women's status, particularly those embodied in the Nineteenth Amendment, as a reason for distinguishing *Muller:*

> [T]he ancient inequality of the sexes, otherwise than physical, as suggested in the *Muller case.* . . , has continued "with diminishing intensity." In view of the great — not to say revolutionary — changes which have taken place since that utterance, in the contractual, political and civil status of women, culminating in the Nineteenth Amendment, it is not unreasonable to say that these differences have now come almost, if not quite, to the vanishing point.

Adkins read the Nineteenth Amendment as emancipating woman "from that old doctrine that she must be given special protection or be subjected to special restraint in her contractual and civil relationships." *Adkins*, 261 U.S. at 553. The *Adkins* Court interpreted the Nineteenth Amendment as embodying a norm of equal citizenship that had implications, outside the context of voting, for the inter-pretation of the Fourteenth Amendment.[3]

However, the Court did not continue to develop this synthetic interpretation of the Fourteenth and Nineteenth Amendments. By the end of the 1920s, courts had limited the Nineteenth Amendment's importance to the question of voting, and by 1937, as Chapter 5 recounts, the Court overruled *Adkins*'s freedom-of-contract doctrine as an outmoded relic of *Lochner*-era jurisprudence.[4] Whatever promise

---

2. Many in the women's movement supported protective labor legislation, even in sex-based form, and so were wary of the Court's decision in *Adkins*. For more on the debate in the women's movement over protective labor legislation, see Joan G. Zimmerman, The Jurisprudence of Equality: The Women's Minimum Wage, the First Equal Rights Amendment, and Adkins v. Children's Hospital, 1905-1923, 78 J. Am. Hist. 188 (1991).

3. See Siegel, She the People, supra n.1, at 1012-1019, which argues that the Court in *Adkins* recog-nized the Nineteenth Amendment as embodying a sex equality norm that extended beyond the voting booth.

4. You will recall from Chapter 5 that *West Coast Hotel* (1937) employed an extremely deferential form of review to uphold a minimum wage law that treated women differently than men.

Adkins may have held for the equal treatment of women in the workplace was repudiated in Goesaert v. Cleary, 335 U.S. 464 (1948), which applied the minimum rationality standard to sustain a Michigan statute forbidding a woman to work as a bartender unless she was the "wife or daughter of the male owner" of the establishment. "Beguiling as the subject is," Justice Frankfurter's majority opinion stated, "it need not detain us long." After noting the "historic calling" of "the alewife, sprightly and ribald," Frankfurter explained that "[t]he Fourteenth Amendment did not tear history up by the roots." In his view,

> Michigan could, beyond question, forbid all women from working behind a bar. This is so despite the vast changes in the social and legal position of women. The fact that women may now have achieved the virtues that men have long claimed as their prerogatives and now indulge in vices that men have long practiced, does not preclude the States from drawing a sharp line between the sexes, certainly in such matters as the regulation of the liquor traffic. See the Twenty-First Amendment. . . . The Constitution does not require legislatures to reflect sociological insight, or shifting social standards, any more than it requires them to keep abreast of the latest scientific standards.

Noting that Michigan did allow some women to tend bar, Frankfurter wrote that "while Michigan may deny to all women opportunities for bartending, Michigan cannot play favorites among women without rhyme or reason." Sufficient rhyme and reason, however, was found in Michigan's presumed assumption that "the oversight assured through ownership of a bar by a barmaid's husband or father minimizes hazards that may confront a barmaid without such protecting oversight. This Court is certainly not in a position to gainsay such belief by the Michigan legislature." Because "the line they have drawn is not without a basis in reason, we cannot give ear to the suggestion that the real impulse behind this legislation was an unchivalrous desire of male bartenders to try to monopolize the calling."

A similar view of gender relations appears in Hoyt v. Florida, 368 U.S. 57 (1961), which upheld a law that included women on jury lists only when they requested it. Even though the law produced virtually all-male juries, the Court sustained the sex-based exemption against equal protection challenge, reasoning that "a woman is still regarded as the center of home and family life."[5] Like *Bradwell* and *Muller, Hoyt* interpreted the Fourteenth Amendment through the lens of the family, reasoning that women's citizenship was expressed in different activities and arenas than men's.[6]

B.   Movement Roots of Modern Sex Discrimination Law

For a century, the Court had looked to the family in defining women's rights under the Fourteenth Amendment. But change was in the air. A decade after *Hoyt*, the Court unanimously rejected this line of reasoning in Reed v. Reed, 404 U.S. 71, 76

5. *Hoyt* was overruled by Taylor v. Louisiana, 419 U.S. 522 (1975), which held that a criminal defendant was deprived of his Sixth Amendment right to a jury composed of a cross-section of the community by a practice of automatically exempting women from jury duty unless they had filed a declaration of their desire to serve. See also Duren v. Missouri, 439 U.S. 357 (1979).

6. For an account of *Hoyt* that analyzes the role of privileges for women in a legal order that systematically accorded women less authority than men, see Linda K. Kerber, No Constitutional Right to Be Ladies: Women and the Obligations of Citizenship 124-220 (1998).

(1971), a case in which the Court purported to apply only the minimal rationality standard, yet held that an Idaho law that preferred men over women as estate administrators made "the very kind of arbitrary legislative choice forbidden by the Equal Protection Clause of the Fourteenth Amendment." The announcement represented a startling shift in the Court's interpretation of the Amendment. For the first time in history, the Court used the Equal Protection Clause to invalidate a statute on the grounds that it discriminated against women, characterizing as "arbitrary" the kind of legislative distinction its previous cases had repeatedly characterized as reasonable. What accounts for this fundamental shift in constitutional understanding?

The Court's decision in *Reed* reflected years of concerted advocacy by "second wave" feminists, as veterans of the suffrage movement in the National Women's Party were joined by women in the labor and civil rights movements who were inspired by the civil rights revolution of the 1960s. An early and crucial site of mobilization was President Kennedy's Commission on the Status of Women, which, beginning in 1961, brought together feminists from across the country and enabled them to develop strategies for coordinated action. The seeds of constitutional change first took root in the executive branch and over the decade spread to the legislature, and then finally to the courts.

Women involved with the President's Commission assisted in the passage of two laws — the Equal Pay Act of 1963 and Title VII of the Civil Rights Act of 1964 — that committed the federal government to enforcing sex equality principles. The Equal Pay Act required employers to provide male and female employees equal pay for equal work.[7] Given the extreme sex-segregation of the labor force in the 1960s, the Act affected only a small number of women — those who were performing the same jobs as men. The Act did not address sex discrimination in hiring and promotion, the largest barriers to equal opportunity in employment. However, the hearings in the executive and legislative branches that led to passage of the Act gave visibility to the inequalities women faced in the labor force, and publicly acknowledged the value of their labor in the market, as well as the home. In this way the Equal Pay Act created foundations for the more far-reaching antidiscrimination regime that began in 1964 with the passage of Title VII of the Civil Rights Act.[8]

Debates over Title VII focused on race discrimination in employment. "Sex" was added to the list of impermissible grounds for discrimination by a Southern legislator known for his opposition to civil rights. Although some laughed, supporters of women's rights rallied behind the amendment and secured its inclusion in the 1964 Civil Rights Act.[9] Initially, the federal government did little to enforce the

---

7. Equal Pay Act of 1963, Pub. L. No. 88-38, 77 Stat. 56 (codified as amended at 29 U.S.C. §206(d) (2000)).

8. For more on the Commission and the Equal Pay Act, see Cynthia Harrison, On Account of Sex: The Politics of Women's Issues, 1945-1968, 89-105 (1988); Leila J. Rupp and Verta Taylor, Survival in the Doldrums: The American Women's Rights Movement, 1945 to the 1960s, 174-176 (1987); Mary Becker, The Sixties Shift to Formal Equality and the Courts: An Argument for Pragmatism and Politics, 40 Wm. and Mary L. Rev. 209 (1998).

9. There is considerable debate among historians concerning the motivation behind Representative Smith's proposal. For further discussion of the sex amendment to Title VII, see Jo Freeman, How "Sex" Got into Title VII: Persistent Opportunism as a Maker of Public Policy, 9 Law & Ineq. 163 (1991); see also Carl M. Brauer, Women Activists, Southern Conservatives, and the Prohibition of Sex Discrimination in Title VII of the 1964 Civil Rights Act, 49 J. S. Hist. 37 (1983). Congress expressed its commitment to enforcing the sex equality provisions of the 1964 Civil Rights Act when amending the statute in 1972. See infra p. 14.

provision. The National Organization of Women (NOW) was formed to pressure an Equal Employment Opportunity Commission (EEOC) more interested in racial justice than sex equality to enforce the prohibition on sex discrimination in the workplace. The struggle to secure enforcement of the new federal employment discrimination statute helped mobilize women around issues of workplace equality, and forged bonds of commonality between the women's movement and the civil rights movement. Inclusion of sex in the Title VII framework suggested a new approach to questions of sex equality under the Fourteenth Amendment, demonstrating similarities in the dynamics of race and sex discrimination that, to this point in time, had eluded the courts.

The race-sex analogy was not new. The woman suffrage movement often invoked it in constitutional arguments over the shape of Reconstruction — but the political salience and appeal of the analogy waned with the repudiation of the New Departure, the demise of Reconstruction, and the spread of Jim Crow. The appeal and power of the race-sex analogy depended on contexts in which it was deployed. In the 1960s, the women's movement gave the analogy new life, as the movement sought to persuade courts and legislatures that women were entitled to the kinds of rights then accorded racial minorities.[10]

A path-breaking advocate of the race-sex analogy in this period was Pauli Murray, an African-American lawyer in the civil rights and women's rights movements, who played an important role in forging modern understandings of discrimination. As a young lawyer, Murray contributed to the NAACP's litigation strategy in Brown v. Board of Education, and in 1961, she was appointed to the President's Commission on the Status of Women. While serving on the commission and studying at Yale Law School (where she was the first African-American to earn a J.S.D.), Murray authored a series of papers outlining a legal strategy for challenging sex discriminatory state action that drew on the litigation strategies and constitutional arguments of the civil rights movement. These arguments were first published in an article co-authored with Mary Eastwood after passage of Title VII entitled "Jane Crow and the Law."[11]

Murray argued that the legal victories of the civil rights movement could be replicated for the women's rights cause by persuading courts that sexism and racism were analogous and often overlapping forms of discrimination. To explain why discriminating by sex was wrong — at a time when courts viewed sex-based state action as rationally reflecting differences in the family roles of men and women — Murray employed the concept of the "stereotype" that the civil rights movement was then using to challenge the dynamics of ethnic and racial prejudice. By the 1960s, the civil rights movement had established that racial stereotyping "results in a partial blindness to the actual qualities of individuals, and consequently is a persistent and prolific breeding ground for irrational treatment of them."[12] Murray employed the stereotyping concept to challenge sex distinctions that were then

10. See Serena Mayeri, "A Common Fate of Discrimination": Race-Gender Analogies in Legal and Historical Perspective, 110 Yale L.J. 1045 (2001).

11. Pauli Murray and Mary O. Eastwood, Jane Crow and the Law: Sex Discrimination and Title VII, 34 Geo. Wash. L. Rev. 232 (1965). For more on Murray's views on the intersection of sex and race, see Alice Kessler-Harris, In Pursuit of Equity: Women, Men, and the Quest for Economic Citizenship in 20th-Century America 226-234 (2001); Serena Mayeri, Constitutional Choices: Legal Feminism and the Historical Dynamics of Change, 92 Cal. L. Rev. 755 (2004).

12. Louis Lusky, The Stereotype: Hard Core of Racism, 13 Buff. L. Rev. 450 (1963-1964).

commonly thought rationally to reflect physical differences between men and women. She argued that gender stereotypes, like racial and ethnic stereotypes, were insensitive to differences among individuals within a group, and engendered similar harms:

> Stereotypes function to rationalize discriminatory attitudes and practices toward an identifiable group. When they are ascribed to groups on the basis of observable perma-nent biological characteristics such as race and sex, they resist change stubbornly. Sexual stereotypes have undergirded laws and customs which treat *all* women as a single class and make distinctions based upon the sole factor of their sex. They disre-gard the fact that women vary as individuals in their body structure, physical strength, intellectual and emotional capacities, aspirations and expectations, just as men do.[13]

Murray had an opportunity to test arguments drawing on concepts of stereotyp-ing and the race-sex analogy during the mid-1960s in White v. Crook, a suit brought by the American Civil Liberties Union (ACLU) challenging the exclusion of blacks and women from an Alabama jury that acquitted white defendants accused of murdering two civil rights workers. The three-judge panel that heard White v. Crook accepted the ACLU's claim that the de facto exclusion of blacks from jury service violated the Fourteenth Amendment. Declaring that its function was "to apply the Constitution as a living document to the legal cases and controversies of contemporary society," the district court also ruled that the de jure exclusion of women from jury service was arbitrary and so violated equal protection, even if the legislative history of the Fourteenth Amendment and case law applying the Equal Protection Clause had never been so construed.[14] Although the court ordered different remedies for the exclusion of blacks and women from jury service, its decision in White v. Crook vindicated Murray's belief in the race-sex analogy as a basis for making sex equality claims on the Fourteenth Amendment.[15]

The race-sex analogy was constitutionally elaborated by Ruth Bader Ginsburg, a young law professor and women's rights advocate chosen by the ACLU to write the appellant's Supreme Court brief in Reed v. Reed — the 1971 case in which the Court first invalidated a statute as violating the Equal Protection Clause because it discriminated on the basis of sex. Ginsburg's brief argued that under the Fourteenth Amendment

> it is presumptively impermissible to distinguish on the basis of congenital and unalter-able biological traits of birth over which the individual has no control and for which he or she should not be penalized. Such conditions include not only race, a matter clearly within the "suspect classification" doctrine, but include as well the sex of the individual.[16]

Ginsburg's brief in *Reed* urged the Court to take the unprecedented step of inval-idating a sex-discriminatory statute by demonstrating how sex discrimination resembled the forms of race discrimination the Court had already invalidated

---

13. Pauli Murray, The Negro Woman's Stake in the Equal Rights Amendment, 6 Harv. C.R.-C.L. L. Rev. 253, 255 (1971).

14. White v. Crook, 251 F. Supp. 401, 408 (M.D. Ala. 1966).

15. For more on White v. Crook, see Kerber, supra n.6, at 197-199.

16. Brief for Appellant, Reed v. Reed, 404 U.S. 71 (1971).

under the Equal Protection Clause. The brief repeatedly emphasized the injustice of discrimination based on traits that were "immutable" and "highly visible," arguing that "American women have been stigmatized historically as an inferior class" and "lack political power to remedy the discriminatory treatment they are accorded in the law and in society generally." Because "legislators have found it easy to draw gross, stereotypical distinctions" on the basis of the sex characteristic, it was necessary for the Court to subject sex-based legislation to a particularly searching form of inquiry under the Fourteenth Amendment.[17]

Yet to persuade the Court to treat sex distinctions like race distinctions, women's advocates had to do more than assert the analogy: They had to demonstrate how laws enforcing traditional family roles injured women. The race–gender analogy was only persuasive to the extent that the movement could demonstrate that women's exclusion from certain forms of civic life was neither an inevitable nor a benign incident of their traditional roles as wives and mothers. This was the message of NOW, which was founded in 1966 at a meeting of the state commissions of the status of women.[18] Formed in an effort to pressure the EEOC to enforce Title VII's ban on sex discrimination, NOW's Statement of Purpose contained a broad declaration that women were entitled to participate in all of the core activities of citizenship on the same terms as men. Coauthored by Betty Friedan and Pauli Murray, NOW's Statement invited Americans to reimagine the social organization of the family so that it would no longer constitute an impediment to women's participation in public life:

> WE BELIEVE that this nation has a capacity at least as great as other nations, to innovate new social institutions which will enable women to enjoy true equality of opportunity and responsibility in society, without conflict with their responsibilities as mothers and homemakers. . . . We do not accept the traditional assumption that a woman has to choose between marriage and motherhood, on the one hand, and serious participation in industry or the professions on the other. We question the present expectation that all normal women will retire from job or profession for 10 or 15 years, to devote their full time to raising children, only to reenter the job market at a relatively minor level. . . . Above all, we reject the assumption that these problems are the unique responsibility of each individual women [sic], rather than a basic social dilemma which society must solve. True equality of opportunity and freedom of choice for women requires such practical, and possible innovations as a nationwide network of child-care center[s], which will make it unnecessary for women to retire completely from society until their children are grown, and national programs to provide retraining for women who have chosen to care for their own children full-time.[19]

NOW's manifesto tied a claim of right to a claim about social structure: Vindicating women's right to equality with men required transforming the social organization of the family.

17. For more on Ginsburg's legal strategy in *Reed*, see Amy Leigh Campbell, Raising the Bar: Ruth Bader Ginsburg and the ACLU Women's Rights Project, 11 Texas J. W. L. 157 (2002); Ruth Cowan, Women's Rights Through Litigation, 8 Colum. Hum. Rts. L. Rev. 373 (1976).

18. For more on the founding of NOW, see Betty Freidan, It Changed My Life 91-232 (1976); Harrison, supra n.8, at 192-209.

19. Nat'l Org. for Women, Statement of Purpose (1966), reprinted in Feminist Chronicles, 1953-1993, at 159, 161-162 (Toni Carabillo et al. eds., 1993).

The movement made the organization of the family the centerpiece of its inaugural demonstrations. On August 26, 1970, NOW staged a "Women's Strike For Equality" on the fiftieth anniversary of the ratification of the Nineteenth Amendment. The one-day strike was staged in 40 cities across the nation to publicize the movement's three core demands: free abortion on demand, free 24-hour child-care centers, and equal opportunity in jobs and education.[20] In these three demands the movement advanced the claim that equal educational and employment opportunity required for its realization transformation of the conditions in which women bore and raised children.

By staging the strike on the fiftieth anniversary of the Nineteenth Amendment's ratification, NOW located its demands in a constitutional framework. In an era when the Court had not yet recognized sex discrimination claims under the Fourteenth Amendment or accorded constitutional protections to the abortion right, the strikers invoked the Nineteenth Amendment to assert that women had a constitutional right to equal citizenship with men. Their demands called attention to the fact that a half-century after the Nineteenth Amendment's ratification, the right to vote had not proven adequate to make women equal citizens with men, and that more change was necessary.

By the late 1960s, those in the women's movement who sought constitutional change via amendment joined ranks with those who sought change through litigation and the movement adopted a "dual strategy" for constitutional reform, seeking a more expansive interpretation of the Fourteenth Amendment and the enactment of an Equal Rights Amendment.[21] The success of the dual strategy and the growing power of the women's movement in the early 1970s engaged the attention of the Ninety-Second Congress. The Congress responded to NOW's constitutional claims by enacting an unprecedented number of federal protections for women's rights. In 1972, it passed, and sent to the states for ratification, the Equal Rights Amendment, and, that same year, applied Title VII to the states, in legislation that emphasized the urgency of combating sex discrimination in employment. The Congress also enacted Title IX, which prohibited sex discrimination in all educational programs receiving federal funds, passed legislation prohibiting sex discrimination in public- and private-sector transactions, and enacted child-care legislation plainly responsive to movement demands for reforms that would alleviate conflicts between work and family.[22]

As Congress enacted legislation that recognized women as equal citizens, the Court responded. Indeed, when the Court took the first steps toward declaring sex a "suspect" classification under the Equal Protection Clause in the early 1970s, it was to this burst of lawmaking that a plurality of the Court pointed.

---

20. For more on the strike, see Shirley Bernard, The Women's Strike: August 26, 1970 (Ph.D. thesis, Union Graduate School of Experimenting Colleges and Universities-Antioch College 1975); Jo Freeman, The Politics of Women's Liberation: A Case Study of an Emerging Social Movement and Its Relation to the Policy Process 84-85 (1975); Ruth Rosen, The World Split Open: How the Modern Women's Movement Changed America 92-93 (2001); and Robert C. Post and Reva B. Siegel, Legislative Constitutionalism and Section Five Power: Policentric Interpretation of the Family and Medical Leave Act, 112 Yale L.J. 1943, 1988-2004 (2003).

21. See Mayeri, Constitutional Choices, supra n.11, at 784-792.

22. For a more detailed account of these legislative innovations, see Freeman, supra n.20, at 202-204; Post and Siegel, Legislative Constitutionalism, supra n.20, at 1995-1996.

FRONTIERO v. RICHARDSON
411 U.S. 677 (1973)

BRENNAN, J., joined by Douglas, White, and Marshall, JJ.

[In an effort to attract career personnel through reenlistment, Congress established a scheme for the provision of fringe benefits to members of the uniformed services on a competitive basis with business and industry. A member of the uniformed services with dependents was entitled to an increased "basic allowance for quarters" and a member's dependents were provided comprehensive medical and dental care, under 37 U.S.C. §§401, 403, and 10 U.S.C. §§1072, 1076.] Under these statutes, a serviceman may claim his wife as a "dependent" without regard to whether she is in fact dependent upon him for any part of her support. A servicewoman, on the other hand, may not claim her husband as a "dependent" under these programs unless he is in fact dependent upon her for over one-half of his support. . . .

I.

[A]ppellant Sharron Frontiero, a lieutenant in the United States Air Force, sought increased quarters allowances, and housing and medical benefits for her husband, appellant Joseph Frontiero, on the ground that he was her "dependent." Although such benefits would automatically have been granted with respect to the wife of a male member of the uniformed services, appellant's application was denied because she failed to demonstrate that her husband was dependent on her for more than one-half of his support. Appellants then commenced this suit, contending that, by making this distinction, the statutes unreasonably discriminate on the basis of sex in violation of the Due Process Clause of the Fifth Amendment.[a]

In essence, appellants asserted that the discriminatory impact of the statutes is twofold: first, as a procedural matter, a female member is required to demonstrate her spouse's dependency, while no such burden is imposed upon male members; and second, as a substantive matter, a male member who does not provide more than one-half of his wife's support receives benefits, while a similarly situated female member is denied such benefits. Appellants therefore sought a permanent injunction against the continued enforcement of these statutes and an order directing the appellees to provide Lieutenant Frontiero with the same housing and medical benefits that a similarly situated male member would receive.

Although the legislative history of these statutes sheds virtually no light on the purposes underlying the differential treatment accorded male and female members, a majority of the three-judge District Court surmised that Congress might reasonably have concluded that, since the husband in our society is generally the "bread-winner" in the family — and the wife typically the "dependent" partner — "it would be more economical to require married female members claiming husbands to prove actual dependency than to extend the presumption of dependency to such members." Indeed, given the fact that approximately 99% of all members of the uniformed services are male, the District Court speculated that

a. "[W]hile the Fifth Amendment contains no equal protection clause, it does forbid discrimination that is 'so unjustifiable as to be violative of due process.'" Schneider v. Rusk, 377 U.S. 163, 168 (1964).

such differential treatment might conceivably lead to a "considerable saving of administrative expense and manpower."

II.

At the outset, appellants contend that classifications based upon sex, like classifications based upon race, alienage, and national origin, are inherently suspect and must therefore be subjected to close judicial scrutiny. We agree and, indeed, find at least implicit support for such an approach in our unanimous decision only last Term in Reed v. Reed, 404 U.S. 71 (1971).

In *Reed,* the Court considered the constitutionality of an Idaho statute providing that, when two individuals are otherwise equally entitled to appointment as administrator of an estate, the male applicant must be preferred to the female. Appellant, the mother of the deceased, and appellee, the father, filed competing petitions for appointment as administrator of their son's estate. Since the parties, as parents of the deceased, were members of the same entitlement class, the statutory preference was invoked and the father's petition was therefore granted. Appellant claimed that this statute, by giving a mandatory preference to males over females without regard to their individual qualifications, violated the Equal Protection Clause of the Fourteenth Amendment.

The Court noted that the Idaho statute "provides that different treatment be accorded to the applicants on the basis of their sex; it thus establishes a classification subject to scrutiny under the Equal Protection Clause." Under "traditional" equal protection analysis, a legislative classification must be sustained unless it is "patently arbitrary" and bears no rational relationship to a legitimate governmental interest.

In an effort to meet this standard, appellee contended that the statutory scheme was a reasonable measure designed to reduce the workload on probate courts by eliminating one class of contests. Moreover, the appellee argued that the mandatory preference for male applicants was in itself reasonable since "men [are] as a rule more conversant with business affairs than . . . women." Indeed, appellee maintained that "it is a matter of common knowledge, that women still are not engaged in politics, the professions, business or industry to the extent that men are." And the Idaho Supreme Court, in upholding the constitutionality of this statute, suggested that the Idaho Legislature might reasonably have "concluded that in general men are better qualified to act as an administrator than are women."

Despite these contentions, however, the Court held the statutory preference for male applicants unconstitutional. In reaching this result, the Court implicitly rejected appellee's apparently rational explanation of the statutory scheme, and concluded that, by ignoring the individual qualifications of particular applicants, the challenged statute provided "dissimilar treatment for men and women who are . . . similarly situated."

The Court therefore held that, even though the State's interest in achieving administrative efficiency "is not without some legitimacy," "[t]o give a mandatory preference, to members of either sex over members of the other, merely to accomplish the elimination of hearings on the merits, is to make the very kind of arbitrary legislative choice forbidden by the [Constitution]. . . ." This departure from "traditional" rational-basis analysis with respect to sex-based classifications is clearly justified.

There can be no doubt that our Nation has had a long and unfortunate history of sex discrimination.[b] Traditionally, such discrimination was rationalized by an attitude of "romantic paternalism" which, in practical effect, put women, not on a pedestal, but in a cage. Indeed, this paternalistic attitude became so firmly rooted in our national consciousness that, 100 years ago, a distinguished Member of this Court was able to proclaim:

> Man is, or should be, woman's protector and defender. The natural and proper timidity and delicacy which belongs to the female sex evidently unfits it for many of the occupations of civil life. The constitution of the family organization, which is founded in the divine ordinance, as well as in the nature of things, indicates the domestic sphere as that which properly belongs to the domain and functions of womanhood. The harmony, not to say identity, of interests and views which belong, or should belong, to the family institution is repugnant to the idea of a woman adopting a distinct and independent career from that of her husband. . . .
>
> The paramount destiny and mission of woman are to fulfill the noble and benign offices of wife and mother. This is the law of the Creator. Bradwell v. [Illinois, 83 U.S. (16 Wall.)] 130, 141 (1573) (Bradley, J., concurring).

As a result of notions such as these, our statute books gradually became laden with gross, stereotyped distinctions between the sexes and, indeed, throughout much of the 19th century the position of women in our society was, in many respects, comparable to that of blacks under the pre-Civil War slave codes. Neither slaves nor women could hold office, serve on juries, or bring suit in their own names, and married women traditionally were denied the legal capacity to hold or convey property or to serve as legal guardians of their own children. And although blacks were guaranteed the right to vote in 1870, women were denied even that right — which is itself "preservative of other basic civil and political rights" — until adoption of the Nineteenth Amendment half a century later.

It is true, of course, that the position of women in America has improved markedly in recent decades. Nevertheless, it can hardly be doubted that, in part because of the high visibility of the sex characteristic, women still face pervasive although at times more subtle, discrimination in our educational institutions, in the job market and, perhaps most conspicuously, in the political arena.[c]

Moreover, since sex, like race and national origin, is an immutable characteristic determined solely by the accident of birth, the imposition of special disabilities upon the members of a particular sex because of their sex would seem to violate "the basic concept of our system that legal burdens should bear some relationship to individual responsibility. . . ." And what differentiates sex from such non-suspect statuses as intelligence or physical disability, and aligns it with the recognized suspect criteria, is that the sex characteristic frequently bears no relation to ability to perform or contribute to society. As a result, statutory distinctions between the

b. Indeed, the position of women in this country at its inception is reflected in the view expressed by Thomas Jefferson that women should be neither seen nor heard in society's decisionmaking councils.

c. It is true, of course, that when viewed in the abstract, women do not constitute a small and powerless minority. Nevertheless, in part because of past discrimination, women are vastly underrepresented in this Nation's decisionmaking councils. There has never been a female President, nor a female member of this Court. Not a single woman presently sits in the U.S. Senate, and only 14 women hold seats in the House of Representatives. And, as appellants point out, this underrepresentation is present throughout all levels of our State and Federal Government.

sexes often have the effect of invidiously relegating the entire class of females to inferior legal status without regard to the actual capabilities of its individual members.

We might also note that, over the past decade, Congress has itself manifested an increasing sensitivity to sex-based classifications. In Tit. VII of the Civil Rights Act of 1964, for example, Congress expressly declared that no employer, labor union, or other organization subject to the provisions of the Act shall discriminate against any individual on the basis of "race, color, religion, *sex*, or national origin." Similarly, the Equal Pay Act of 1963 provides that no employer covered by the Act "shall discriminate . . . between employees on the basis of *sex*," and §1 of the Equal Rights Amendment, passed by Congress on March 22, 1972, and submitted to the legislatures of the States for ratification, declares that "[e]quality of rights under the law shall not be denied or abridged by the United States or by any State on account of sex." Thus, Congress itself has concluded that classifications based upon sex are inherently invidious, and this conclusion of a coequal branch of Government is not without significance to the question presently under consideration.

With these considerations in mind, we can only conclude that classifications based upon sex, like classifications based upon race, alienage, or national origin, are inherently suspect, and must therefore be subjected to strict judicial scrutiny. Applying the analysis mandated by that stricter standard of review, it is clear that the statutory scheme now before us is constitutionally invalid.

III.

The sole basis of the classification established in the challenged statutes is the sex of the individuals involved. . . . [T]he statutes operate so as to deny benefits to a female member, such as appellant Sharron Frontiero, who provides less than one-half of her spouse's support, while at the same time granting such benefits to a male member who likewise provides less than one-half of his spouse's support. Thus, to this extent at least, it may fairly be said that these statutes command "dissimilar treatment for men and women who are . . . similarly situated." Reed v. Reed.

Moreover, the Government concedes that the differential treatment accorded men and women under these statutes serves no purpose other than mere "administrative convenience." In essence, the Government maintains that, as an empirical matter, wives in our society frequently are dependent upon their husbands, while husbands rarely are dependent upon their wives. Thus, the Government argues that Congress might reasonably have concluded that it would be both cheaper and easier simply conclusively to presume that wives of male members are financially dependent upon their husbands, while burdening female members with the task of establishing dependency in fact.[d]

The Government offers no concrete evidence, however, tending to support its view that such differential treatment in fact saves the Government any money. In order to satisfy the demands of strict judicial scrutiny, the Government must demonstrate, for example, that it is actually cheaper to grant increased benefits with respect

---

d. It should be noted that these statutes are not in any sense designed to rectify the effects of past discrimination against women. On the contrary, these statutes seize upon a group of women who have historically suffered discrimination in employment, and rely on the effects of this past discrimination as a justification for heaping on additional economic disadvantages.

to *all* male members, than it is to determine which male members are in fact enti-tled to such benefits and to grant increased benefits only to those members whose wives actually meet the dependency requirement. Here, however, there is substantial evidence that, if put to the test, many of the wives of male members would fail to qualify for benefits. And in light of the fact that the dependency determination with respect to the husbands of female members is presently made solely on the basis of affidavits, rather than through the more costly hearing process, the Government's explanation of the statutory scheme is, to say the least, questionable.

In any case, our prior decisions make clear that, although efficacious administra-tion of governmental programs is not without some importance, "the Constitution recognizes higher values than speed and efficiency." And when we enter the realm of "strict judicial scrutiny," there can be no doubt that "administrative convenience" is not a shibboleth, the mere recitation of which dictates constitutionality. On the contrary, any statutory scheme which draws a sharp line between the sexes, *solely* for the purpose of achieving administrative convenience, necessarily commands "dissimilar treatment for men and women who are . . . similarly situated," and there-fore involves the "very kind of arbitrary legislative choice forbidden by the [Constitution]. . . ." We therefore conclude that, by according differential treat-ment to male and female members of the uniformed services for the sole purpose of achieving administrative convenience, the challenged statutes violate the Due Process Clause of the Fifth Amendment insofar as they require a female member to prove the dependency of her husband.[e]

Reversed.

Mr. Justice Stewart concurs in the judgment, agreeing that the statutes before us work an invidious discrimination in violation of the Constitution. Reed v. Reed, 404 U.S. 71.

POWELL, J., joined by Burger, C.J., and Blackmun, J., concurring.

I agree that the challenged statutes constitute an unconstitutional discrimina-tion against servicewomen in violation of the Due Process Clause of the Fifth Amendment, but I cannot join the opinion of Mr. Justice Brennan, which would hold that all classifications based upon sex, "like classifications based upon race, alienage, and national origin," are "inherently suspect and must therefore be subjected to close judicial scrutiny." It is unnecessary for the Court in this case to characterize sex as a suspect classification, with all of the far-reaching implications of such a holding. Reed v. Reed, 404 U.S. 71 (1971), which abundantly supports our decision today, did not add sex to the narrowly limited group of classifications which are inherently suspect. In my view, we can and should decide this case on the authority of *Reed* and reserve for the future any expansion of its rationale. There is another, and I find compelling, reason for deferring a general categorizing of sex classifications invoking the strictest test of judicial scrutiny. The Equal Rights Amendment, which if adopted will resolve the substance of this precise question, has been approved by the Congress and submitted for ratification by the States. If this Amendment is duly adopted, it will represent the will of the people

e. As noted earlier, the basic purpose of these statutes was to provide fringe benefits to members of the uniformed services in order to establish a compensation pattern which would attract career person-nel through reenlistment. Our conclusion in no wise invalidates the statutory schemes except insofar as they require a female member to prove the dependency of her spouse.

accomplished in the manner prescribed by the Constitution. By acting prematurely and unnecessarily, as I view it, the Court has assumed a decisional responsibility at the very time when state legislatures, functioning within the traditional democratic process, are debating the proposed Amendment. It seems to me that this reaching out to preempt by judicial action a major political decision which is currently in process of resolution does not reflect appropriate respect for duly prescribed legislative processes.

There are times when this Court, under our system, cannot avoid a constitutional decision on issues which normally should be resolved by the elected representatives of the people. But democratic institutions are weakened, and confidence in the restraint of the Court is impaired, when we appear unnecessarily to decide sensitive issues of broad social and political importance at the very time they are under consideration within the prescribed constitutional processes.

REHNQUIST, J., dissents for the reasons stated by Judge Rives in his opinion for the District Court, Frontiero v. Laird, 341 F. Supp. 201 (1972).

Discussion

1. *Frontiero* is a pay discrimination case, involving a practice, prevalent before enactment of the Equal Pay Act, of paying men and women different wages for the same work. In *Frontiero*, the government justified its decision to pay valuable dependent benefits to all male soldiers, but only to some female soldiers, by invoking what was then the most commonplace rationale for such discriminatory compensation practices. The government argued that men should receive more pay than women because most men needed to support their families, whereas most women did not.

Why does the compensation scheme at issue in *Frontiero* violate the Constitution? Does it embody "gross, stereotyped distinctions between the sexes" of the sort that Justice Brennan's opinion observes were commonplace in the legislation and common law decisions of the nineteenth century? How, if at all, did the compensation scheme reflect stereotyping? Was the government reasoning on the basis of faulty generalizations? If not, were there other forms of cognitive error that made the compensation policy constitutionally offensive? Is the belief that men often support their wives, while wives generally do not support their husbands, a form of prejudice? Does it denigrate women, or men? Does the *Frontiero* opinion suggest that it is wrong for government to support traditional family roles? Only in certain contexts? If so, why in this case? How is the policy struck down in *Frontiero* like or unlike the kinds of race-based state action invalidated in the cases you read in Chapter 6?

2. Why does the government's argument that the compensation scheme was rational fail, given real and widespread differences in the role that men and women then played in supporting dependent members of their family? Is the constitutional harm of the compensation scheme its irrationality? Or is it its rationality — the ways it reflected, naturalized, reinforced, and entrenched existing beliefs and practices about the roles of men and women?

3. Is the *Frontiero* opinion concerned about governmental practices that injure individuals, or groups? Can these concerns be disentangled? What difference does it make to emphasize one or the other? How might it bear on the way the Court evaluates the sex discrimination claims of men?

4. What criteria should guide the Court in determining whether to apply heightened scrutiny to governmental policies that differently allocate benefits and burdens among groups? Consider the grounds on which Justice Brennan builds the case for heightened scrutiny of sex-based state action. Following the suggestion of lawyers in the women's movement, Justice Brennan's plurality opinion argues that case for heightened scrutiny depends on similarities between race and sex discrimination.

Does the case for heightened scrutiny depend on the extent to which challenged discrimination resembles race discrimination? If so, why? Is the race analogy relevant as a matter of original understanding? Or does it simply supply a framework for evaluating unfairness? Perhaps it offers an easily administrable heuristic to settle disputes about the interpretation of an open-ended (or implicit) guarantee such as the equality guarantee of the Fifth and Fourteenth Amendments. What other constitutional values does the analogy vindicate? Does it limit judicial decisionmaking in the service of democratic self-determination? Federalism? Might some other analytical framework better vindicate the relevant constitutional values?

5. If the race analogy constrains the meaning of equal protection, not as a matter of original understanding, but instead in order to vindicate values of democratic self-determination or federalism, should it play the same role when the representative branches of federal or state government enforce equality guarantees?

6. Just how easily administrable is the race analogy framework? How should courts decide what kinds of discrimination are "like" race discrimination? What features of race discrimination are salient for purposes of this inquiry?

For example, how much weight should the Court place on the "history of discrimination" prong of the inquiry? How would a court determine what practices should count as a "history of discrimination" for purposes of this inquiry? Does it matter whether a practice, like the jury rule in *Hoyt* or the benefits rule in *Frontiero,* was understood as legitimate when adopted?

Should courts instead place more weight on the immutability factor in determining whether forms of discrimination are sufficiently like race discrimination to warrant similar forms of heightened scrutiny? Why is immutability germane? If individuals could change their race or sex, should they be expected to conform to a polity's preferences? Should discrimination against Jews or Muslims only be subject to rational basis review? What about discrimination on the basis of sexual orientation? Does the answer to this question depend on whether sexual orientation is genetic, or otherwise immutable?[23]

Conversely, what about traits that are immutable but may be functionally relevant to people's skills and abilities? Compare the case of discrimination on the basis of eye color to discrimination on the basis of vision. Both are traits are immutable, but one is commonly relevant to performing a multitude of tasks, especially under prevailing institutional arrangements. Should the Court closely scrutinize policies that discriminate on the basis of vision — for example, a statute that conditions the award of a driver's or a pilot's license on passing an eye test? Is state action that

---

23. For recent criticism of the immutability framework, see Kenji Yoshino, Covering, 111 Yale L.J. 769 (2002); Kenji Yoshino, Assimilationist Bias in Equal Protection: The Visibility Presumption and the Case of "Don't Ask, Don't Tell," 108 Yale L.J. 485 (1998); J. M. Balkin, The Constitution of Status, 106 Yale L.J. 2313, 2366-2367 (1997).

distinguishes on the basis of sex more like policies that discriminate on the basis of eye color, vision, or race? Should it matter?

What about policies that discriminate on the basis of pregnancy? Note Justice Brennan's observation that "what differentiates sex from such non-suspect statuses as intelligence or physical disability, and aligns it with the recognized suspect criteria, is that the sex characteristic frequently bears no relation to ability to perform or contribute to society. As a result, statutory distinctions between the sexes often have the effect of invidiously relegating the entire class of females to inferior legal status without regard to the capabilities of its individual members." The year after the Court decided *Frontiero*, the Court ruled in Geduldig v. Aiello, p. 1276 infra, that, for purposes of applying heightened scrutiny under the Equal Protection Clause, state action discriminating on the basis of pregnancy does not discriminate on the basis of sex — because such regulation distinguished between pregnant and nonpregnant persons rather than between all women and all men. It was only *after* the Court's decision in *Geduldig* (and well before settlement of the debate over ratification of the Equal Rights Amendment), that a majority of the Court ruled in *Craig v. Boren*, p. 1214 infra, that sex-based state action is subject to heightened scrutiny.

Instead of focusing on factors like a history of discrimination (which presents questions of interpretation that may converge with or replicate the question of whether to apply heightened scrutiny) or the immutability factor, perhaps courts should focus instead on the factor of political powerlessness? (Recall political-process justifications for heightened judicial scrutiny in *Carolene Products*, Footnote 4, discussed in Chapter 5.) What criteria should courts use to determine whether a group is "underrepresented in the Nation's decisionmaking councils"? Is "past discrimination" the guide to this factor's application as well?

Note how the *Frontiero* plurality looked to Congress for guidance in determining whether to apply heightened scrutiny to sex-based state action, observing that "over the past decade, Congress has itself manifested an increasing sensitivity to sex-based classifications." In what sense might a group be "politically powerless," if the Court looks to legislation recently enacted in Congress for guidance on the question of whether heightened judicial scrutiny is warranted under the Constitution? Should the Court listen to Congress on a question concerning the interpretation of the Equal Protection Clause? What are the strengths and weaknesses of this method of orienting judicial inquiry relative to the other factors the plurality pointed to in building the race-analogy argument in *Frontiero*?

Note that in this respect, the plurality and the concurring opinions in *Frontiero* converge, linking judicial interpretation of the Constitution to the deliberations of the representative branches, and differing only in the features of the lawmaking process on which the opinions focus. Are the statutes to which Justice Brennan points particularly relevant to judicial judgments about questions of constitutional meaning? More relevant than the ERA ratification process itself?

Note: The Equal Rights Amendment

Between 1923 and 1972, resolutions proposing an equal rights amendment were introduced in every term of Congress. In 1972, Congress proposed the following amendment for ratification by state legislatures:

Section 1. Equality of rights under the law shall not be denied or abridged by the United States or by any State on account of sex.

Section 2. The Congress shall have the power to enforce, by appropriate legislation, the provisions of this article.

In submitting the ERA to the states for ratification, Congress was responding to the women's movement, whose arguments and activities in the 1960s and early 1970s are described in the opening pages of this chapter. At the point that Congress submitted the amendment to the states for ratification, it seemed to have broad-based social support. The House of Representatives voted 354-23 in favor of the amendment; the Senate, in turn, overwhelmingly endorsed it by a vote of 84-8 on March 22, 1972. Hawaii unanimously approved the amendment that very day, 25 minutes after learning of the Senate's vote. Delaware, Nebraska, and New Hampshire followed suit the next day, with Idaho and Iowa joining these states on March 24. By early 1973, 30 of the 38 states needed to ratify had endorsed the amendment, most of them unanimously or by lopsided votes.[24]

Thereafter, however, a vigorous anti-ERA movement successfully blocked approval in most of the remaining states, so that by 1977 only 35 states had endorsed the amendment. By the initial expiration date of the ERA, March 22, 1979, 35 states had ratified the Amendment, just three short of the requirement for passage. However, four of those states voted to rescind their ratification. After a heated debate, Congress rejected these states' desires and voted to extend the ratification period for three additional years to 1982. Despite the extension, the ERA failed to garner approval in any more states. The proposed amendment expired on June 30, 1982.[25]

The movement to block the constitutional amendment was led by Phyllis Schlafly, who founded STOP ERA in 1972. The group was the best organized and most prominent of a number of anti-ERA organizations, including American Women Already Well Endowed (AWARE), Scratch Women's Lib, and Happiness of Womenhood (HOW). Schlafly and her allies viewed claims for equal citizenship advanced by the women's movement as threatening traditional households, diminishing the status and security of those women who cared for family members while depending on male breadwinners. In an essay entitled "What's Wrong with 'Equal Rights' for Women," Schlafly denounced ERA supporters:

> They view the home as a prison, and the wife and mother as a slave. To these women's libbers, marriage means dirty dishes and dirty laundry. . . .
>
> Women's lib is a total assault on the role of the American woman as wife and mother, and on the family as the basic unit of society.
>
> Women's libbers are promoting free sex instead of the "slavery" of marriage. They are promoting Federal "day-care centers" for babies instead of homes. They are promoting abortions instead of families.[26]

Schlafly mobilized opposition to the ERA by suggesting it threatened fundamental changes in gender arrangements. She imputed to the ERA power to effectuate

24. See Jane J. Mansbridge, Why We Lost the ERA 12-13 (1986); and Janet K. Boles, The Politics of the Equal Rights Amendment 2-3, tbl.1.1 (1979)

25. Mansbridge, supra n.24, at 13. The following states failed to ratify the ERA: Alabama, Arizona, Arkansas, Florida, Georgia, Illinois, Louisiana, Mississippi, Missouri, Nevada, North Carolina, Oklahoma, South Carolina, Utah, and Virginia. Boles, supra n.24, at 3, tbl. 1.1.

26. Quoted in Mansbridge, supra n.24, at 104.

social change of a kind that ERA supporters insisted was beyond the amendment's ambit.[27] At various points Schlafly or her supporters suggested that, as a result of the ERA, private schools would have to be coed; all sports, including contact sports, would be coed; there would be government-funded abortions and homosexual school teachers; women would be forced into combat; men would refuse to support their wives; the government would take away a women's right to her home and support of her children; and the government would legalize homosexual marriages and adoption by homosexuals.[28] A cartoon of the era captures this dispute about the reach of the proposed amendment. In it, a husband discusses with his wife the meaning of the ERA:

Husband: "Mona, darned if I can see th' harm in this 'Equal Rights Amendment.'"
Wife: "You CAN'T? Why, just READ the foul thing."
Husband: "Equality of rights under the law shall not be denied or abridged by the
    United States or by any state on account of sex."
Wife: "Go on."
Husband: "Uh—that's about it."
Wife: "No! Read th' part requiring homosexual bathrooms! An' th' part outlawing
    families! Th' mandatory abortions!"
Husband: "No, that's all—"
Wife: "It's a trick! Another feminist trick! Ohhh, they're devious!"[29]

The themes Schlafly sounded were voiced by critics in positions of government authority, as well. In 1970, when William Rehnquist was Assistant Attorney General, he wrote a memo to President Nixon's special consultant Leonard Garment advising Garment of the ERA supporters' "doctrinaire insistence upon rigid equality between men and women":

I cannot help thinking that there is also present somewhere within this movement a virtually fanatical desire to obscure not only legal differentiation between men and women, but insofar as possible, physical distinctions between the sexes. I think there are overtones of dislike and distaste for the traditional difference between men and women in the family unit, and in some cases very probably a complete rejection of the woman's traditionally different role in this regard.[30]

Discussion

1. How would or should the ERA have been interpreted? Would courts interpreting the ERA have drawn upon the strict scrutiny framework developed under the

---

27. Id. at 110-115.
28. See, e.g., ERA and Homosexual "Marriages," Phyllis Schlafly Rep. (Eagle Forum, Alton, Ill.), Sept. 1974, at §2; E.R.A. Means Abortion and Population Shrinkage, Phyllis Schlafly Rep., Dec. 1974, at §2; Will E.R.A. Make Child-Care The State's Job?, Phyllis Schlafly Rep., Nov. 1975, at §2; The Family and the Future of America, Phyllis Schlafly Rep., Oct. 1978, at §2; The International Human Rights Treaties, Phyllis Schlafly Rep., Dec. 1979, at §1; Phyllis Schlafly, The Power of the Positive Woman (1977). See also Jane De Hart-Mathews and Donald Mathews, The Cultural Politics of the ERA's defeat, in Rights of Passage: The Past and Future of the ERA 44, 48-51 (Joan Hoff-Wilson ed. 1986) (discussing anxieties about the ERA undermining traditional womanhood and blurring sex roles in areas such as the military, sex crimes, abortion, integrated restrooms, homosexuality, and the family).
29. Quoted in Mansbridge, supra n.24, at 115.
30. Memorandum from William Rehnquist, Assistant Attorney General, to Leonard Garment, Special Counsel to the President, reprinted in Rehnquist, ERA Would Threaten Family Unit, Legal Times, Sept. 15, 1986, at 4.

Fourteenth Amendment's Equal Protection Clause? Would judges also have applied to the ERA doctrines that the Court developed in the 1970s to limit the reach of the Equal Protection Clause (e.g., cases on state action, facial classifications, and discriminatory purpose discussed in Chapter 6)?

As you consider these general questions of interpretation, you might consider more concretely the kinds of cases likely to have been brought under the ERA. As we have seen, opponents predicted that courts would interpret the ERA to require sweeping changes in gender relations. Proponents did not argue so much that the amendment's text was unambiguous, as that Congress could control its interpretation by specifying its intentions about the ERA's reach. How should the Court have applied the ERA to the combat exclusion for women? (As Jane Mansbridge recounts, many opponents of the ERA charged that the amendment would require the elimination of the combat exemption for women in the armed services, although proponents took conflicting positions on this.[31]) To the Navy's ban on women serving on aircraft carriers? To gender segregation in education? Sports? Prisons? Bathrooms? (Opponents also argued that the amendment would prohibit gender-segregated bathrooms, a proposition that supporters almost unanimously denied.[32]) To sex distinctions in the law of marriage concerning custody, support, and capacity to marry?[33] To laws concerning domestic violence? To laws excluding pregnant women from work, or criminalizing abortion?[34]

31. Mansbridge, supra n.24, at 67. "[W]hile most pro-ERA pamphlets suggested that the ERA would not require Congress to send women into combat, the pamphlets never explained *why* this might be so in legal terms." Id. at 83.

32. See id., at 112-115 on proponents' argument that gender-segregated bathrooms are protected by "privacy" interests. Given, however, that such a rationale would be unacceptable in the case of racially segregated bathrooms, is it self-evident why "privacy" interests would permit sex-segregated bathrooms?

33. See Brown, Emerson, Falk, and Freedman, The Equal Rights Amendment: A Constitutional Basis for Equal Rights for Women, 80 Yale L.J. 871, 936-953 (1970-1971), discussing, inter alia, the ERA's effect on laws pertaining to marriage and the marital relationship, including statutory age requirements, divorce, family support, custody, and property forms. For discussion of how the ERA did or did not affect sex-based restrictions on who could marry, see Samuel T. Perkins and Arthur J. Silverstein, The Legality of Homosexual Marriage, 82 Yale L.J. 573 (1973); Singer v. Hara, 522 P.2d 1187 (Wash. App. Ct. 1974) (holding that a statute prohibiting same-sex marriage did not violate a state ERA); see also infra, Ch. 7, Part III.

34. Proponents of the ERA endorsed what became known as the "unique physical characteristic" (UPC) qualification to the ERA. The UPC was a "subsidiary principle," asserting that legislation pertaining to physical characteristics unique to one sex would not constitute sex discrimination, but would nevertheless be subject to strict scrutiny. Brown et al, The Equal Rights Amendment, supra n.33, at 893-894. Equal Rights 1970, Hearings on S.J. Res. 61 and S.J. Res. 231 Before Senate Comm. on the Judiciary, 91st Cong., 2d Sess. 299, 303 (1970); Equal Rights for Men and Women 1971, Hearings on S.J. Res. 35, 208, and Related Bills Before Subcomm. No. 4 of the House Comm. On the Judiciary, 92d Cong., 1st Sess. 40, 402 (1971). In subsequent floor debate, Rep. Griffiths, chief sponsor of the ERA in the House, in response to a direct question, stated that the ERA will have "no effect on any abortion law of any State" under the UPC qualification. See 117 Cong. Rec. 35302 (1971) (remarks of Rep. Griffiths); see also Ruth M. Ferrell, The Equal Rights Amendment to the United States Constitution — Areas of Controversy, 6 Urb. Law. 853, 867 (1974).

Prior to 1973, the ERA was not strongly linked to abortion. But after the Supreme Court decided Roe v. Wade, 410 U.S. 113, opponents began to assert that the ERA would be construed to entrench and extend abortion rights. Political conflict highlighted "the overlaps between antiabortion activists and ERA opponents and between proabortion activists and ERA supporters." Gilbert Y. Steiner, Constitutional Inequality: The Political Fortunes of the Equal Rights Amendment 58-66 (1985). By the time a new ERA was debated in Congress in the early 1980s, abortion and the ERA were fully linked politically. "In the 1980s, many members of Congress came to see a vote to limit the ERA as a unique opportunity to register antiabortion views. . . . Everywhere, consideration of the [new] ERA will be affected by arguments from groups that insistently equate the ERA with . . . Roe v. Wade . . . and its extension to public financing of abortion." Id. at 97.

Would legislative history have played the same role in shaping the interpretation of the ERA that it has played in shaping the interpretation of the Fourteenth Amendment? Would or should answers to these questions have changed in the decades after the amendment's ratification?

2. What significance did debates over ratification of the ERA have for judicial interpretation of the Fifth and Fourteenth Amendments? Once Congress sent the ERA to the states for ratification, should Courts deciding Fifth and Fourteenth Amendment claims like Sharron Frontiero's have deferred to the political process as the concurring justices in *Frontiero* suggested? As Justice Powell argued:

> By acting prematurely and unnecessarily, as I view it, the Court has assumed a decisional responsibility at the very time when state legislatures, functioning within the traditional democratic process, are debating the proposed [Equal Rights] Amendment. It seems to me that this reaching out to pre-empt by judicial action a major political decision which is currently in process of resolution does not reflect appropriate respect for duly prescribed legislative processes.

This was plainly not the view taken by Justice Brennan and the plurality in *Frontiero* who urged the Court to apply strict scrutiny to sex-based state action under the Fifth and Fourteenth Amendments. Should the justices have ignored ongoing debate over the ERA and decided the question that Sharron Frontiero's case posed about the meaning of equal protection guarantees under the existing Constitution's text? Was it possible for the justices not to listen to the ongoing debate? Was it their duty to listen? (Should the justices' approach have varied in Fifth and Fourteenth Amendment cases?)

Drawing on *Frontiero*'s text and conference notes, Serena Mayeri offers this account of how the ERA campaign influenced the justices' deliberation in the case:

> Brennan's plurality opinion in *Frontiero* suggests that the ERA's pendency moved at least four justices to the view that, as Brennan put it in a memorandum to Powell, "the 'suspect' approach is the proper one and . . . further . . . now is the time, and this is the case, to make that clear." . . . Freely admitting that the ERA's prospects for ratification were dim, Brennan couldn't "see that we gain anything by awaiting what is at best an uncertain outcome." . . . Decisive congressional action on the subject was enough for Justice Byron White, too. He wrote to his colleagues during the *Frontiero* deliberations: "I would think that sex is a suspect classification, if for no other reason than the fact that Congress has submitted a constitutional amendment making sex discrimination unconstitutional." . . . White went on to declare that he "would remain of the same view whether the amendment is adopted or not." . . . The language of the *Frontiero* plurality opinion is likewise unambiguous on this point, making clear that the Court's newfound recognition of a "long and unfortunate history of sex discrimination" was indebted to unprecedented, tangible congressional support of an antidiscrimination principle. It also seems likely that the backdrop of legislative solicitude for women's rights influenced the justices who went along with the result in *Frontiero* without endorsing strict scrutiny. Absent the women's movement's renaissance and its legislative manifestations, it is hard to imagine Justices Burger, Blackmun, Stewart, and Powell spontaneously responding to feminist lawyers' arguments.[35]

---

35. Mayeri, Constitutional Choices, *supra* n.11 at 827-828.

Which approach to the constitutional question in *Frontiero* was correct? The position adopted by the plurality opinion Justice Brennan authored? Or the concurring opinion Justice Powell authored? Or was there yet some other approach that the Court should have adopted?

3. As you think about these questions, consider whether the Court is best understood as a countermajoritarian body, or whether instead the Court acts in response to popular social movements. If the Supreme Court and the federal courts decide to follow changing social and political trends, they may obviate the need for Article V amendments. This happened during the New Deal, for example. Considerable talk of Article V solutions to the crisis over federal power dried up as a result of the Court's post-1937 jurisprudence.[36] Because it is so difficult to pass Article V amendments, taking even a little wind out of the sails of proponents may be enough to kill an amendment, particularly when the amendment is controversial, as the ERA surely was.

If this theory about the interplay between Supreme Court decisionmaking and Article V amendment is correct, what does this say about the Court's appropriate role with respect to social movements and proposals for constitutional change? Should courts exercise considerable restraint in deference to the possibility of Article V amendment, or, on the contrary, should courts feel authorized to follow social movements with demonstrated broad and deep support from the American public, whether or not these movements garner the supermajority support required for an Article V amendment?

Judicial review is often described as countermajoritarian. Consider the fact that the ERA was in fact approved by a significant majority of the states representing a significant majority of the population. Does it make sense to criticize Brennan's position in *Frontiero* as "countermajoritarian" if its doctrine was, arguably, approved by legislative majorities at both the federal and state levels and failed to become part of the formal text only because of the strikingly countermajoritarian procedures of Article V?

4. The ERA was not ratified. But did it fail? David Strauss calls the ERA the "leading recent example of [the] . . . rejected, yet ultimately triumphant" constitutional amendment:

> Today, it is difficult to identify any respect in which constitutional law is different from what it would have been if the ERA had been adopted. For the last quarter-century, the Supreme Court has acted as if the Constitution contains a provision forbidding discrimination on the basis of gender. The Court requires an "exceedingly persuasive" justification for gender classifications, and it invalidates gender classifications that rest on what it considers " 'archaic and overbroad' generalization[s]," such as the view that women are less likely than men to work outside the home. The Court does treat gender-based classifications differently from race-based classifications — the latter being the paradigmatic form of discrimination forbidden by the Fourteenth Amendment — but it has justified the difference not on the ground that the ERA was rejected, but rather on the ground that the two forms of classification sometimes operate differently.[37]

36. Bruce Ackerman, 2 We The People: Transformations 315, 334-335 (1998).
37. David A. Strauss, The Irrelevance of Constitutional Amendments, 114 Harv. L. Rev. 1457, 1476-1477 (2001). Other commentators have offered similar interpretations of the ERA's defeat. See Robert C. Post, The Supreme Court, 2002 Term — Foreword: Fashioning the Legal Constitution: Culture, Courts, and the Law, 117 Harv. L. Rev. 4, 55-56 (2003).

Strauss argues that the Constitution is best understood on the model of the common law, a body of law elaborated by judicial interpretation in ways that do not depend on the Constitution's embodiment as text. Alternatively, some have argued that it is the Constitution's embodiment as text that makes it a transparent, publicly accessible body of law about whose meaning ordinary Americans, like the women who challenged the Court's interpretation of the Fourteenth Amendment, can speak. On this account, it is the Constitution's character as a written text, whose meaning can be debated and amended, that makes it the object of mobilization and that ensures that its interpretation by legal professionals remains informed by evolving social understandings.[38] William N. Eskridge, Jr., observes that, "The power of the women's movement was such that the Court felt impelled in the 1970s to rule unconstitutional most invidious sex discriminations."[39]

On this account, the ERA appears to have succeeded in generating constitutional reform. The possibility of an Article V amendment elicited social mobilization and countermobilization, leading to energetic debate about the constitutional implications of equal citizenship in the family, the military, and other institutions — a debate in which proponents and opponents of the ERA were ultimately obliged to reckon with each other in an effort to persuade the public. The Article V framework thus served a crucial constitutional function even if it failed to produce changes in the Constitution's text: It channeled popular debate over constitutional values and ensured that judicial interpretation of the Constitution was tutored by nonjuridical views about the Constitution's meaning.[40]

5. Attending to the interplay of interpretive and amending processes makes salient not only the ways in which the Court responded to the views of the ERA's supporters, but also the ways that the Court responded to the views of the ERA's opponents. As you read the cases in this chapter, especially cases like *Geduldig, Feeney,* and *Rostker,* infra, consider how the Court may have construed the Constitution's equal protection guarantees in response to views expressed by the ERA's opponents concerning the enduring significance of sex differentiation, in matters of family life and of war. Chapter 8 traces the influence of debates attending the ERA and *Roe* on the Court's due process jurisprudence.

As we begin to interpret the ERA campaign and the case law in Chapters 7 and 8 together, it becomes more difficult to characterize this Article V history. Can we say that the Court decisively adopted the views of groups mobilized for, or against, constitutional change — or did it speak for Americans torn between them?

6. As we have seen, in the 1960s and early 1970s, activists concerned with women's legal status pursued a dual strategy, seeking constitutional change by reinterpretation and by amendment. What are the enduring effects and costs of this dual strategy? Had feminists pursued change through Article V alone, might they have prevailed? Does it make any difference that today the Constitution contains no sex equality provision other than the Nineteenth Amendment?

---

38. See Reva B. Siegel, Text in Contest: Gender and the Constitution from a Social Movement Perspective, 150 U. Pa. L. Rev. 297 (2001).

39. William N. Eskridge, Jr., Channeling: Identity-Based Social Movements and Public Law, 150 U. Pa. L. Rev. 419, 502 (2001).

40. See Reva B. Siegel, Constitutional Culture, Social Movement Conflict and Constitutional Change: The Case of the de facto ERA, 94 Cal. L. Rev. (forthcoming October 2006).

7. Might the Court today read the Fourteenth Amendment synthetically with the later-ratified Nineteenth Amendment, as it began to do in *Adkins,* the freedom-of-contract case the Court overruled in *West Coast Hotel*? For commentators advocating such a synthetic approach within very different interpretive frameworks, see Akhil Reed Amar, The Supreme Court, 1999 Term — Foreword: The Document and the Doctrine, 114 Harv. L. Rev. 26, 51-53 (2000); Michael C. Dorf, Equal Protection Incorporation, 88 Va. L. Rev. 951, 980-981 (2002); Vicki C. Jackson, Holistic Interpretation: Fitzpatrick v. Bitzer and Our Bifurcated Constitution, 53 Stan. L. Rev. 1259, 1290-1291 (2001); Reva B. Siegel, She the People: The Nineteenth Amendment, Sex Equality, Federalism and the Family, 115 Harv. L. Rev. 947, 976-977, 1040-1044 (2002). What practical or symbolic difference would such an approach make? Is it legitimate, given the ratification history of the ERA?

As we have seen, the second-wave movement began its campaign for constitutional reform by invoking the Nineteenth Amendment, staging its inaugural strike for equality on the half-century anniversary of the Nineteenth Amendment's ratification, in this way drawing on the collective memory of the suffrage amendment to advance new claims on the Constitution's meaning. For a suggestion that the collective memory of women's disfranchisement and of its constitutional rectification through the Nineteenth Amendment bears on the interpretation of the Fourteenth Amendment, see Justice Ginsburg's opinion for the Court in United States v. Virginia, infra.

With the ERA's enactment by Congress, the second-wave movement began to focus its quest for constitutional reform on the new Article V amendment, and made fewer claims on the Nineteenth Amendment. There are deep and little-appreciated continuities between the two campaigns for constitutional reform. The debate over the suffrage amendment and the ERA campaign each focused on the family as the institution that determined whether men and women were different kinds of citizens. In what ways might commonalities in the history of these Article V debates guide constitutional interpretation today? Should it matter that one of these amendments was ratified and the other was not? Of what significance is formal change in the Constitution's text?

II.   What Justifies Special Constitutional Scrutiny for Gender Classifications or for Gender Discrimination (And Are They the Same Thing)?

Why should unequal treatment based on gender be subject to *any* special standard of review at all? Debates over the proper boundaries of sex equality law are still ongoing, years after *Frontiero* and defeat of the ERA. The same considerations that underlie one's attempt to answer the question may, moreover, provide a foundation for determining whether distinctions and discriminations based on other traits are constitutionally suspect.

A.   Is the Problem Classification at All?

Is the problem of sex equality best understood as a problem concerning government use of sex-based classifications? For example, if the government abolished all alimony, temporary spousal support, and child support payments, its decision would not involve classification based on sex, but it would surely affect women in important ways. Similarly, rape law, family law, the law of domestic violence, and many workplace regulations can be and are stated without any classifications on the basis of sex. These laws operate against the background of social relations between men and women (even as they also to some extent help constitute that background).

In this light consider Catharine A. MacKinnon, Unthinking ERA Thinking, 54 U. Chi. L. Rev. 759, 765-768 (1987):

> Although not all ERA's supporters took so limited a view of what they were fighting for, the mainline liberal interpretation of the ERA . . . reduced the problem of the subordination of women to men to a problem of gender classification by law [and] was never seriously questioned by the pro-ERA movement. . . . This is an approach to sex equality that leaves out the social institutionalization of practices through which women are violated, abused, exploited, and patronized by men socially — in collaboration with the state, but not only or even primarily by the state as such. This approach leaves out practices that have never needed to be enacted into sex classifications in law because they are plenty powerful in civil life, practices that the state is often kept out of by law in the name of individual rights. . . .
>
> [In her history of the ERA ratification process, Jane] Mansbridge describes the decision not to litigate the abortion funding case of Harris v. McRae on a sex discrimination theory as a political choice to avoid associating sex equality with abortion rights in order to help ERA's chances of ratification. . . . [But] [a]bortion is a sex equality issue. Everyone knows it. Denial of access to abortion denies women, and only women, a final act of control over the reproductive consequences of male sexuality as it largely seals women's lack of control over their time, which is what a life is made of. . . .
>
> What if, instead, issues of sexual abuse of children, denial of the abortion choice, rape, battery, prostitution, pornography, and sex-based de facto job segregation were core examples around which a critique of the denial of civil rights to women were forged? What if, when we talked ERA, we talked about state complicity in male violence against women through writing and administering rape laws from the viewpoint of the reasonable rapist; misogynist police practices in domestic violence calls that relegate assault on women to the lowest category of concern; collaboration of law enforcement and law itself in the terrorization and stigmatization of child victims of sexual abuse, many of them girls; biased enforcement of biased laws against prostitution so that prostitutes (most of them women) are harassed and violated while pimps and johns (men) are allowed to ensure that prostitution, something men made a crime, will continue to exist for their pleasure; useless and dangerous obscenity laws that cover for the pornography industry . . . ignoring documented harms to women from its production and consumption? What if we called all this "state action" in the sex equality area?

We return to this problem throughout this chapter, particularly in the discussions of pregnancy discrimination and domestic violence in Chapter 7 and in discussions of abortion and equal protection in Chapters 7 and 8.

B.   Text and History

From one standpoint, the original intention behind the Fourteenth Amendment was quite promising for women's rights.[41] As we have seen, the Fourteenth

---

41. See Akhil Amar, Women and the Constitution, 18 Harvard J.L. & Pub. Pol'y 465, 468-469 (1995); Akhil Amar, The Bill of Rights: Creation and Reconstruction 260-261 (1998).

Amendment was generally assumed to grant civil but not political equality to blacks. During the debates over the Amendment several members of Congress argued that the model of a person who possessed civil but not political equality was an unmarried white woman.[42] Moreover, although many women protested the inclusion of the word "male" in §2 of the Amendment, they did not protest §1, assuming that it applied equally to them.[43] The notion of civil rights roughly tracked the rights protected by Article IV's Privileges and Immunities clause. Persons who were citizens of one state still had the right while in other states to sue and be sued, to own real property, make contracts and wills, inherit, devise, pursue a career, move about freely, speak freely, assemble, and worship.[44] Hence, in theory at least, unmarried women had the same rights to these activities as men.[45]

At the same time, the Fourteenth Amendment was not understood by most of its framers to grant women political rights, including the right to hold public office, the right to serve on juries, and the right to vote. (Consider whether the undermining of the political–civil distinction for blacks in *Strauder* should have had any consequences for women.)

Perhaps equally important, the Fourteenth Amendment was not generally understood to make marital status rules unconstitutional, even though these rules posed strong impediments to economic and civil equality for women. Upon marriage, women lost many of their civil rights to own and convey property, make contracts, sue and be sued; women were assumed to consent to their dependent status through their consent to marriage.[46] Indeed, there is strong evidence that the framers of the Fourteenth Amendment did not wish to disturb the marital status rules and give married women the same rights to hold and use property as men and unmarried women.[47] Marital status rules were deeply tied to important notions about family life. The idea that Congress — much less the federal courts — could interfere with domestic matters and family structure was a source of

---

42. See Cong. Globe, 38th Cong., 1st Sess. 840 (1864) (remarks of Sen. James Harlan); Cong. Globe, 39th Cong. 1st Sess. 1255, 1263, 1757, 122 app. (1866) (remarks of Sen. Henry Wilson, Rep. John Broomall, and Sens. Lyman Trumbull and John Henderson). Similar understandings were present in the woman suffrage movement. In 1866 the Eleventh National Woman's Rights Convention unanimously adopted Susan B. Anthony's resolution declaring that "[b]y the act of Emancipation and the Civil Rights Bill, the negro and the woman how hold the same civil and political *status*, alike needing only the ballot; and . . . the same arguments apply equally to both classes, proving all partial legislation fatal to republican institutions." Elizabeth Cady Stanton, Susan B. Anthony, and Matilda Joslyn Gage, eds., 2 History of Woman Suffrage 171-172 (1882).

43. See Ellen DuBois, Feminism and Suffrage: The Emergence of an Independent Women's Movement in America, 1848-1869 (1978); Nina Morais, Note, Sex Discrimination and the Fourteenth Amendment: Lost History, 97 Yale L.J. 1153 (1988).

44. Note as well that the 1848 Seneca Falls Declaration also spoke in terms of the "rights and privileges which belong to [women] as citizens of these United States."

45. This argument was the basis of Senator Matthew Carpenter's argument on behalf of Myra Bradwell in Bradwell v. Illinois. The right to practice law, he argued, was a civil right and therefore the state could not discriminate on the basis of sex. Mrs. Bradwell, was, however, married and so Justice Bradley was able to respond that the marital status rules then existing in Illinois might have prevented her from entering into certain transactions without the consent of her husband; hence the State might argue that it had the right to withhold a license to practice law because of fear that she could not adequately represent her clients.

46. See Reva B. Siegel, Home as Work: The First Woman's Rights Claims Concerning Wives' Household Labor, 1850-1880, 103 Yale L.J. 1073 (1994).

47. See, e.g., Cong. Globe, 39th Cong., 1st Sess. 1063 (1866) (Remarks of Rep. Hale and Rep. Stevens).

considerable anxiety to the framers of the Fourteenth Amendment.[48] Hence, although the femme sole, the unmarried woman, was at the heart of the Fourteenth Amendment's conception of civil liberty for its framers, the practical benefits of the amendment for most women were decidedly mixed.[49]

Given this history, how should we interpret the Fourteenth Amendment today? One might argue that just as the civil–political distinction has been exploded in the area of race discrimination, it should also be eliminated in the area of sex discrimination. What then, should we make of the marital status rules and the distinction between married and unmarried women, which played so large a role in the original understandings of the Fourteenth Amendment? Does the Nineteenth Amendment — which severed the link between marital status and political equality — have anything to add here?[50]

Note that the relevant history of the Fourteenth Amendment mainly concerns the Privileges or Immunities Clause while today we understand the question of women's equality through the Equal Protection Clause, in part due to the *Slaughterhouse Cases,* and in part due to Brown v. Board of Education. What difference, if any, should this make to one's analysis?

Consider the different levels of abstraction on which one can describe the *purposes* of the Equal Protection Clause or the *principles* attributed to it. What principle or principles would one have to attribute to the Equal Protection Clause in order to encompass gender discrimination (for married and unmarried women) as well as race discrimination?

C.   Reasoning from Race

As we have seen, the modern women's movement built its case by invoking the history of women's disfranchisement and its rectification through the Nineteenth Amendment, and by framing an analogy between race and sex discrimination. The latter appeal seems especially to have captured judicial imagination. In *Frontiero* Justice Brennan wrote: "[T]hroughout much of the 19th century the position of women in our society was, in many respects, comparable to that of blacks under the pre-Civil War slave codes." How similar is the historical discrimination of women to that of racial or ethnic minorities? In what ways does the appeal to analogy help make visible the injuries of sex inequality, and in what ways might it efface them? Do we do justice to women by seeking to identify and remedy sex inequality through the lens of race discrimination?

The first instinct of many judges, commentators, and students in addressing the constitutionality of sex discrimination is to treat race discrimination as a point of

48. Ariela R. Dubler, "Her Nature and Constitution": Reasoning About Women's Rights During Reconstruction (unpublished manuscript); Jill Hasday, Federalism and the Family, 45 U.C.L.A. L. Rev. 1297 (1998); Ward Farnsworth, Women Under Reconstruction: The Congressional Understanding, 94 Nw. U. L. Rev. 1229 (2000). You should also recall the earlier discussion in Chapters 2 and 4 of the theory of republicanism and the family and the concept of virtual representation — married women's status in the family was an important reason given against granting women the right to vote.

49. Equally important, the history shows that women's rights were in fact very much on the minds of the Framers of the Fourteenth Amendment. Their need explicitly to describe the limitations of the amendment arose out of a concern that the language of the amendment might be read expansively by women's rights advocates. (In fact, this happened during the New Departure.) Recall also that the woman suffrage movement was actively lobbying during this period, and that Elizabeth Cady Stanton and Susan B. Anthony had organized a drive for ratification of the Thirteenth Amendment.

50. See Reva B. Siegel, She the People: The Nineteenth Amendment, Sex Equality, Federalism, and the Family, 115 Harv. L. Rev. 947 (2002).

comparison and to inquire to what extent gender classifications share the characteristics that call racial classifications into disfavor. There are two overlapping strategies: (a) to recall the rationales for treating racial classifications as suspect and ask whether they apply to gender classifications, and (b) to identify the features of race that make it seem special and ask whether gender shares these features. One question to face at the outset is whether this relatively mechanical comparison of rationales and traits is essentially misguided.

There are important differences between race and gender, and between the forms of racial and sexual inequality. One can enforce status hierarchy either through segregation or role differentiation, and one's attitude toward one's social inferiors can either be disdainful or paternalistic. During slavery, blacks were treated with a mixture of contempt, fear, and paternalism by their white owners, and many slaves lived in close proximity to their masters. However, after the Civil War, and with the rise of Jim Crow, the basic strategies for subordination of blacks have been separation and degradation. Some role differentiation has existed: blacks have often played distinctly subordinate roles — as servants, for example — but many whites worked at the same jobs as blacks, for example, as manual laborers and domestic servants.

Women, on the other hand, have always lived with men as wives, mothers, and sisters (to name only the most obvious social roles). Segregation of the sexes has existed, but it is largely limited to certain kinds of facilities like education. Rather, role differentiation of the sexes has been the most important way that men have historically subordinated women, and this subordination has been achieved largely through expectations about family life. (Note, by contrast, that during Jim Crow whites did everything possible to avoid recognizing family connections with blacks, including bans on miscegenation and hypodescent rules fixing who was white and who was black.) Role differentiation has also shaped women's chances for employment opportunities outside the home — for example, certain jobs like nursing and secretarial assistance have, over time, become regarded as women's occupations.

Moreover, because of romantic love and family connections, men often express paternalistic attitudes toward women rather than overt disdain and contempt. In addition, men are likely to claim that in fact women are the real masters and men are only their devoted servants, or, in the alternative, that women's lives are much more privileged than men's. (Recall John Adams's exchange with Abigail Adams in Chapter 2, for example.) This pseudo-chivalry is actually the flip side of women's economic dependence on men. Thus, recall that during Reconstruction one argument against woman's suffrage was that women were dependent on men and thus likely to be unduly influenced by them. Another argument made at the same time was that in any case men adequately represented women's interests because women influenced them.[51]

Finally, biology still plays an important role in the justifications for sex discrimination, but it is no longer as prevalent in the case of race. Although it was common

---

51. Consider in this regard the speech of Senator Timothy Howe of Wisconsin, who argued to the great amusement of the gallery that granting women the vote would allow them to vote twice:

> I am willing to deprive those who are not males of the right of suffrage, because they exercise it by proxy, as we all know. Females send their votes to the ballot-box by their husbands or other male friends. We may affect to deny it, but in legislating upon grave matters like this it is better to tell the truth about it. We go there to carry votes. We are instructed to carry them before we leave home. [Laughter] Therefore I am willing to exclude females from this privilege of going to the polls themselves. I think they ought not to vote double; and inasmuch as their husbands vote once for them they ought not vote at all.

Cong. Globe, 38th Cong., 1st Sess. 2243 (1864) (Sen. Howe).

during the Jim Crow era to argue that blacks were biologically inferior to whites, this argument has gone out of fashion and is generally understood to be invidious and racist. On the other hand, it is quite commonplace to hear biological justifications for sex-differentiated roles and for separate facilities for women. An important question you should consider in these materials is to what extent the invocation of biological differences is appropriate and to what extent it disguises or misrepresents social structures that subordinate women to men.

Put another way, if we want to understand the similarities and differences between racial and sexual inequality, we may have to look past particular traits considered in isolation, and toward the social structures, institutions, sets of social meanings, and accepted justifications that have traditionally been used to subordinate blacks on the one hand and women on the other. The relevant structures and institutions that form the sites of inequality may be very different for the two cases. The sets of social meanings about race and gender and the accepted justifications for unequal treatment of blacks and women may also be quite different. Focusing on traits isolated from social structure and social meaning may lead us to miss the different ways that blacks and women have been subordinated. And viewing black women's subordination through the lens of the race analogy may cause us to miss the distinctive ways in which sex inequality has been organized, reproduced, and justified.

D.   Views from the Academy

SYLVIA LAW, RETHINKING SEX AND THE CONSTITUTION
132 U.S. Pa. L. Rev. 955, 965 (1984)

There are . . . important points of difference between sex- and race-based discrimination. There is no reason to believe that black and white people are inherently different in any way that should ever be allowed to matter in the law. Men and women, by contrast, are different in significant sex-specific physical ways. Most differences between men and women are like differences between blacks and whites: statistical generalizations, which are more or less true in the aggregate but untrue in relation to particular individuals. Accurate statistical differences between men and women that are false in individual cases include weight, height, longevity, mathematical aptitude, aggression, capacity for nurturance, and physical strength. There are, however, other categorical differences between men and women that are not simply statistical generalizations, but rather sex-based physical differences relating to reproductive capacity. By categorical sex-based differences, what is meant, and *all that is meant*, is that most women and no men possess the capacity to reproduce the species.

RICHARD WASSERSTROM, RACISM, SEXISM, AND PREFERENTIAL TREATMENT[52]
24 UCLA L. Rev. 581, 587-592 (1977)

It is even clearer in the case of sex than in the case of race that one's sexual identity is a centrally important, crucially relevant category within our culture. I think,

52. The ideas in this piece are treated in greater detail and in somewhat different form in two essays: Racism and Sexism, and Preferential Treatment, both contained in Wasserstrom, Philosophy and Social Issues: Five Studies (1980).

in fact, that it is more important and more fundamental than one's race. It is evident that there are substantially different role expectations and role assignments to persons in accordance with their sexual physiology, and that the positions of the two sexes in the culture are distinct. We do have a patriarchal society in which it matters enormously whether one is a male or a female. By almost all important measures it is more advantageous to be a male rather than a female. . . .

As is true for race, it is also a significant social fact that to be a female is to be an entity or creature viewed as different from the standard, fully developed person who is male as well as white. But to be female, as opposed to being black, is not to be conceived of as simply a creature of less worth. That is one important thing that differentiates sexism from racism: The ideology of sex, as opposed to the ideology of race, is a good deal more complex and confusing. Women are both put on a pedestal and deemed not fully developed persons. They are idealized; their approval and admiration is sought; and they are at the same time regarded as less competent than men and less able to live fully developed, fully human lives — for that is what men do. At best, they are viewed and treated as having properties and attributes that are valuable and admirable for humans of this type. For example, they may be viewed as especially empathetic, intuitive, loving, and nurturing. At best, these qualities are viewed as good properties for women to have, and, provided they are properly muted, are sometimes valued within the more well-rounded male. Because the sexual ideology is complex, confusing, and variable, it does not unambiguously proclaim the lesser value attached to being female rather than being male, nor does it unambiguously correspond to the existing social realities. For these, among other reasons, sexism could plausibly be regarded as a deeper phenomenon than racism. It is more deeply embedded in the culture, and thus less visible. Being harder to detect, it is harder to eradicate. Moreover, it is less unequivocally regarded as unjust and unjustifiable. That is to say, there is less agreement within the dominant ideology that sexism even implies an unjustifiable practice or attitude. Hence, many persons announce, without regret or embarrassment, that they are sexists or male chauvinists; very few announce openly that they are racists. For all of these reasons sexism may be a more insidious evil than racism, but there is little merit in trying to decide between two seriously objectionable practices which one is worse. . . .

Viewed from the perspective of social reality it should be clear, too, that racism and sexism should not be thought of as phenomena that consist simply in taking a person's race or sex into account, or even simply in taking a person's race or sex into account in an arbitrary way. Instead, racism and sexism consist in taking race and sex into account in a certain way, in the context of a specific set of institutional arrangements and a specific ideology which together create and maintain a *system* of unjust institutions and unwarranted beliefs and attitudes. That system is and has been one in which political, economic, and social power and advantage are concentrated in the hands of those who are white and male.

Discussion

Wasserstrom believes that sexism "is more deeply embedded in the culture, and thus less visible" than racism. Should we conclude from this that classifications based on gender should receive more heightened scrutiny than classifications based on race? Or, should we conclude that the law itself is complicit in the very forms of social meaning and social structure that it attempts to reform?

JOHN ELY, DEMOCRACY AND DISTRUST
164-170 (1980)

The case of women is timely and complicated. Instances of first-degree prejudice are obviously rare, but just as obviously exaggerated stereotyping — typically to the effect that women are unsuited to the work of the world and therefore belong at home — has long been rampant throughout the male population and conse- quently in our almost exclusively male legislatures in particular. It may all be in apparent good humor, even perceived as protective, but it has cost women dearly. Absent a strong demonstration of mitigating factors, therefore, we would have to treat gender-based classifications that act to the disadvantage of women as suspi- cious. If the stereotyping has been clear, however, so has the noninsularity of the group affected. The degree of contact between men and women could hardly be greater, and neither, of course, are women "in the closet" as homosexuals histori- cally have been. Finally, lest you think I missed it, women have about half the votes, apparently more. As if it weren't enough that they're not discrete and insular, they're not even a minority!

Despite that seeming avalanche of rebuttal, there remains something that seems right in the claim that women have been operating at an unfair disadvantage in the political process, though it's tricky pinning down just what gives rise to that intuition. . . . [I]f women have "chosen" not to avail themselves of their opportuni- ties, either by voting or by personally influencing those men with whom they come in contact, to correct the exaggerated stereotype that many men hold and on the basis of which they have often legislated . . . [it can] plausibly be argued . . . that many women have *accepted* the overdrawn stereotype and thus have seen nothing to "correct." . . . That could, of course, imply that it wasn't so exaggerated a stereotype after all, but it could mean something else too, that our society, including the women in it, has been so pervasively dominated by men that women quite under- standably have accepted men's stereotypes, of women as well as on other subjects.

The general idea is one that in some contexts has merit. A sufficiently pervasive prejudice can block its own correction not simply by keeping its victims "in the closet" but also by convincing even them of its correctness. In Castaneda v. Partida, decided in 1977, the Court held that a prima facie case of intentional discrimina- tion against Mexican-Americans in the selection of grand jurors was not constitu- tionally affected by the fact that Mexican-Americans enjoyed "governing majority" status in the county involved. Concurring, Justice Marshall gave the reason why: "Social scientists agree that members of minority groups frequently respond to discrimination and prejudice by attempting to disassociate themselves from the group, even to the point of adopting the majority's negative attitudes towards the minority." . . .

To apply all this to the situation of women in America in 1980, however, is to strain a metaphor past the breaking point. . . .

The very stereotypes that gave rise to laws "protecting" women by barring them from various activities are under daily and publicized attack, and are the subject of equally spirited defense. . . . Given such open discussion of the traditional stereo- types, the claim that the numerical majority is being "dominated," that women are in effect "slaves" who have no realistic choice but to assimilate the stereotypes, is one it has become impossible to maintain except at the most inflated rhetorical level. . . .

[T]he date of passage seems unquestionably relevant to what our analysis has suggested is a more promising approach to the question of suspiciousness — one geared to the existence of official or unofficial blocks on the opportunities of those the law disadvantages to counter by argument or example the overdrawn stereotypes we might, from the demography of the decision-making body, otherwise suspect were operative. . . .

[Suppose that the Court struck down a gender classification enacted in an earlier era, and that a contemporary legislature] reconsidered and repassed the same or a similar law. The fact that due process of lawmaking was denied in 1908 or even in 1939 needn't imply that it was in 1982 as well and consequently the new law should be upheld as constitutional. In fact I may be wrong in supposing that because women now are in a position to protect themselves they will, that we are thus unlikely to see in the future the sort of official gender discrimination that has marked our past. But if women don't protect themselves from sex discrimination in the future, it won't be because they can't. It will rather be because for one reason or another — substantive disagreement or most likely the assignment of a low priority to the issue — they don't choose to. Many of us may condemn such a choice as benighted on the merits, but that is not a constitutional argument.

Discussion

1. Professor Ely adopts a purely process-oriented rationale for the antidiscrimination principle. Does this rationale warrant his conclusion that a gender classification adopted at the beginning of the twenty-first century should not be subject to heightened judicial scrutiny?

2. What conception of "choice" is implicit in Ely's statement that women "don't choose to" protect themselves from sex discrimination? What vision of social structure (and in particular family structure) is assumed? Are these assumptions realistic? If women's choices are structured by their social status, why does Ely say that it "is not a constitutional argument"?

3. Note that Ely's process protection rationale becomes more plausible if women formed a majority of *legislators* rather than a majority of voters. Although the number of women who have entered politics increases every year, consider the reasons why women do not currently constitute 51 percent of most state legislatures, or, for that matter of the U.S. Congress. Is this simply because women have no taste for politics? Is it because women believe that men can and will adequately represent their interests? Recall the debates over the Nineteenth Amendment, and that amendment's rejection of the concept of virtual representation, which assumed that because women were dependent on men in traditional family structure, men could and would represent their interests. If the Nineteenth Amendment is premised on the idea that men cannot adequately represent women as voters, why are men better able to represent them as legislators?

4. *The cultural memory of gender subordination.* Ely points out that cultural stereotypes about men and women are constantly being negotiated between the sexes; as a result it is "impossible to maintain" that women are in any sense "dominated" in this country. Reva Siegel has argued that this has been a standard way of imagining gender relations throughout American history — as a process of gradual consensual transformation and enlightenment. Although Americans are able to accept

that the history of race relations has been a history of struggle and conflict, they are much less comfortable imagining this about the history of gender relations.

> While the history of race relations in this country is generally understood as a story of publicly and privately inflicted injury and imposition, the history of gender relations unfolds in the more diffuse realm of customary time, involving consensually inhabited mores that are assumed slowly to have evolved over the centuries. [Robert Bork typifies this attitude when he says that] "For women, the new choices are available largely because of technology, for blacks because of the success of the civil rights movement." In short, [unlike the collective memory of race relations] law plays at best an incidental role in the social memory of gender relations, which are assumed to result from custom and consent. . . . Again and again in such narratives, the possibility that conflict or coercion has played a role on defining women's lives is repressed and women appear as figures who give of themselves selflessly and without protest. The social memory of gender relations thus elaborates a scene that is private, consensual, and naturalized, that is to say, outside the public realm where matters of law and governance are conducted. For this reason, claims about collective agency that play so prominent a role in disputes over racial justice are notably lacking in disputes over gender justice. . . .
>
> [The] social memory of gender relations is . . . one mechanism by which this society insulates the prevailing gender order from political contestation. Our propensity to explain the relations between the sexes through stories of evolving custom and consensus rather than conflict suggests that, as a society, we remain normatively invested in the naturalization of present gender arrangements and will do much to repress the normative dissonance that confrontation with their history would produce.[53]

CATHARINE A. MACKINNON, TOWARD A FEMINIST THEORY OF THE STATE

Chapter 12, Sex Equality: On Difference and Dominance (1989)

Sex discrimination law, with mainstream moral theory, sees equality and gender as issues of sameness and difference. According to this approach, which has dominated politics, law, and social perception, equality is an equivalence not a distinction, and gender is a distinction not an equivalence. The legal mandate of equal treatment — both a systemic norm and a specific legal doctrine — becomes a matter of treating likes alike and unlikes unlike, while the sexes are socially defined as such by their mutual unlikeness. That is, gender is socially constructed as difference epistemologically, and sex discrimination law bounds gender equality by difference doctrinally. Socially, one tells a woman from a man by their difference from each other, but a woman is legally recognized to be discriminated against on the basis of sex only when she can first be said to be the same as a man. A built-in tension thus exists between this concept of equality, which presupposes sameness, and this concept of sex, which presupposes difference. Difference defines the state's approach to sex equality epistemologically and doctrinally. Sex equality

---

53. Reva Siegel, Collective Memory and the Nineteenth Amendment: Reasoning about "the Woman Question" in the Discourse of Sex Discrimination, in History, Memory, and the Law 131, 137, 139, 142 (Austin Sarat & Thomas Kearns, eds., 1999).

becomes a contradiction in terms, something of an oxymoron. The deepest issues of sex inequality, in which the sexes are most constructed as socially different, are either excluded at the threshold or precluded from coverage once in. In this way, difference is inscribed on society as the meaning of gender and written into law as the limit on sex discrimination. . . .

In this mainstream epistemologically liberal approach, the sexes are by nature biologically different, therefore socially properly differentiated for some purposes. . . . As one scholar has put it, "any prohibition against sexual classifications must be flexible enough to accommodate two legitimate sources of distinctions on the basis of sex: biological differences between the sexes and the prevailing heterosexual ethic of American society." . . . Laws or practices that express or reflect sex "stereotypes," understood as inaccurate overgeneralized attitudes often termed "archaic" or "outmoded," are at the core of this definition of discrimination. Mistaken illusions about real differences are actionable, but any distinction that can be accurately traced to biology or heterosexuality is not a discrimination but a difference.[a]

From women's point of view [i.e., under the dominance analysis], gender is more an inequality of power than a differentiation that is accurate or inaccurate. To women, sex is a social status based on who is permitted to do what to whom; only derivatively is it a difference. For example, one woman reflected on her gender: "I wish I had been born a doormat, or a man." Being a doormat is definitely different from being a man. Differences between the sexes do descriptively exist. But the fact that these are a woman's realistic options, and that they are so limiting, calls into question the perspective that considers this distinction a "difference."

From this perspective, considering gender a matter of sameness and difference covers up the reality of gender as a system of social hierarchy, as an inequality. The differences attributed to sex become lines that inequality draws, not any kind of basis for it. Social and political inequality begins indifferent to sameness and difference. Differences are inequality's post hoc excuse, its conclusory artifact, its outcome presented as its origin, its sentimentalization, its damage that is pointed to as the justification for doing the damage after the damage has been done, the distinctions that perception is socially organized to notice because inequality gives them consequences for social power. . . . [A] discourse and a law of gender that center on difference serve as ideology to neutralize, rationalize, and cover disparities of power, even as they appear to criticize or problematize them. Difference is the velvet glove on the iron fist of domination. The problem then is not that differences are not valued; the problem is that they are defined by power. This is as true when difference is affirmed as when it is denied, when its substance is applauded or disparaged, when women are punished or protected in its name.

. . . If differentiation were the problem, gender neutrality would make sense as an approach to it. Since hierarchy is the problem, it is not only inadequate, it is

___

a. Doctrinally speaking, two alternative paths to sex equality for women exist within the mainstream approach to sex discrimination, paths that follow the lines of the sameness/difference tension. The leading one is: be the same as men. This path is termed "gender neutrality" doctrinally and the single standard philosophically. It is testimony to how substance becomes form in law that this rule is considered formal equality. . . . To women who want equality yet find themselves "different," the doctrine provides an alternative route: be different from men. This equal recognition of difference is termed the special benefit rule or special protection rule legally, the double standard philosophically. [These sentences actually appear elsewhere in MacKinnon's chapter. — EDS.]

perverse. In questioning the principledness of neutral principles, this analysis suggests that current law to rectify sex inequality is premised upon, and promotes, its continued existence.

. . . To the extent that the sexuality of one sex is a social stigma, target, and provocation to violation, while the sexuality of the other is socially a source of pleasure, adventure, power (indeed, the social definition of potency), and a focus for deification, entertainment, nurturance, and repression, the sexuality of each is equally different, equally heterosexual or not, but not equally socially powerful.[b]

III.   What Does Intermediate Scrutiny Prohibit?

A.   The Emergence of Intermediate Scrutiny: Pregnancy, Sex Stereotyping, and the Family

Equal protection doctrine concerning sex-based state action has its own distinctive form, whose outlines can only partly be adduced by considering constitutional law prohibiting race discrimination. In the early 1970s, advocates argued that the similarities between race and sex discrimination were sufficiently compelling that the Court should review sex-based state action in the same strict-scrutiny framework that it used to review race-based state action; they persuaded a plurality of the Court in *Frontiero,* but never secured a majority. Instead, as the remainder of this chapter explores, in 1976 the Court adopted an "intermediate scrutiny" framework of review that bars many, but not all, forms of sex-based state action.

In the years after its decisions in *Reed* and *Frontiero,* the Court did not immediately settle on a standard for reviewing sex-based classifications. Notably, in this early period, the Court decided to limit sex discrimination doctrine under the Equal Protection Clause so that it would not constrain laws regulating pregnant women. Recall the plurality's observation in *Frontiero* that "what differentiates sex from such non-suspect statuses as intelligence or physical disability, and aligns it with the recognized suspect criteria, is that the sex characteristic frequently bears no relation to ability to perform or contribute to society. As a result, statutory distinctions between the sexes often have the effect of invidiously relegating the entire class of females to inferior legal status without regard to the actual

---

b. A rule or practice is discriminatory, in the [dominance] approach, if it participates in the systemic social deprivation of one sex because of sex. The only question for litigation is whether the policy or practice in question integrally contributes to the maintenance of an underclass or a deprived position because of gender status. The disadvantage which constitutes the injury of discrimination is not the failure to be treated "without regard to" one's sex; that is the injury of arbitrary differentiation. The unfairness lies in being deprived because of being a woman or a man, a deprivation given meaning in the social context of the dominance or preference of one sex over the other. The social problem addressed is not the failure to ignore woman's essential sameness with man, but the recognition of womanhood to women's comparative disadvantage. In this approach, few reasons, not even biological ones, can justify the institutionalized disadvantage of women. Comparability of sex characteristics is not required because policies are proscribed which transform women's sex-based differences from men into social and economic deprivations. All that is required are comparatively unequal results. . . . [From Catharine A. MacKinnon, Sexual Harassment of Working Women, 102, 117-118, 126-127 (1979). — Eds.]

capabilities of its individual members." *Frontiero*, supra p. 1188. Does the race–sex analogy provide a framework for determining when regulation directed at pregnant women is suspect?

In the years before *Frontiero*, feminist lawyers such as Pauli Murray, Ruth Bader Ginsburg, and Wendy Williams sought to demonstrate how sex stereotyping might shape regulation of pregnant women. But the Court did not follow their lead. Instead, one year after protecting the abortion right in Roe v. Wade, the Court announced in Geduldig v. Aiello, infra, that discrimination on the basis of pregnancy is not discrimination on the basis of sex within the meaning of *Reed* and *Frontiero*. The Court thus separated the new body of equal protection law regulating sex-based state action from the emerging constitutional jurisprudence of abortion. (Discussion of pregnancy discrimination appears later in this chapter, and Chapter 8, infra, addresses constitutional doctrines protecting reproductive liberties.)

Shortly after excluding regulation of pregnancy from the scope of heightened scrutiny, a majority of the Justices settled on an "intermediate" standard of review in Craig v. Boren, 429 U.S. 190 (1976). *Craig* adopts a framework that makes sex-based state action presumptively unconstitutional: To regulate in a sex-discriminatory fashion, the government must demonstrate that its use of sex-based criteria is "substantially related" to the achievement of "important governmental objectives." The standard adopted in *Craig* parallels the strict scrutiny framework, which requires the government to defend race-based state action as "necessary" to achieve a "compelling government interest." The Court never explained whether the different standard of review it decided to employ in reviewing sex- and race-based state action reflects judgments about the original understanding of the Fourteenth Amendment, or concerns about intervening in then-pending debates over the ERA's ratification — or instead might reflect differences in the structure of sex and race discrimination (e.g., the numerosity of the protected class or belief in the functional significance and benign character of certain practices of sex differentiation).

In *Craig*, a young man argued that an Oklahoma law that allowed girls aged 18-21, but not boys of the same age, to purchase "near-beer" violated equal protection. (In *Craig* and many of the ensuing 1970s cases, the Court employed the same standard of review to evaluate men's and women's sex discrimination claims.) The Court upheld his claim, reasoning that that state's evidence of sex differences in drunk driving rates was insufficient to justify its sex-based regulatory scheme. *Craig* highlighted the Court's skepticism toward the application of group-based generalizations to individuals, with Justice Brennan noting that "proving broad sociological propositions by statistics is a dubious business, and one that inevitably is in tension with the normative philosophy that underlies the Equal Protection Clause."

Under rational basis review, the Court commonly allows government to allocate benefits and burdens to groups on the basis of generalizations about them. *Craig*'s claim that state action predicated on generalizations is "in tension with the normative philosophy that underlies the Equal Protection Clause" implicitly aligned intermediate scrutiny of sex-based state action with equal protection doctrines concerning race discrimination.

But, in elaborating the new intermediate scrutiny standard, the *Craig* opinion did not explicitly invoke the race analogy as the plurality opinion in *Frontiero* did. Instead, the Court discussed the dangers of a particular form of generalizing about sex difference. *Craig* warned against sex-based state action premised on "increasingly outdated misconceptions concerning the role of females in the home rather than in the 'marketplace and world of ideas,'" noting that such laws had been "rejected as loose-fitting characterizations incapable of supporting state statutory schemes that were premised on their accuracy." *Craig,* 429 U.S. at 198-199.

In the 1970s regulatory programs still commonly discriminated between men and women in allocating burdens and benefits, and such discrimination was justi- fied as rationally reflecting differences in family roles. Government programs were premised on the male breadwinner/female caregiver model: the supposition that men were wage-earners who supported their families, while women contributed to the family through nurturing and homemaking activities as dependents of male wage earners. Federal social security and welfare law and state family law reflected the same assumptions about sex-role differentiation that informed market prac- tices of explicit sex-based wage discrimination invalidated by the Equal Pay Act and Title VII.

In a series of equal protection cases decided under the Fifth and Fourteenth Amendments in the 1970s, the Court struck down sex-based laws premised on the male breadwinner/female caregiver model. For example, in Weinberger v. Wiesenfeld, 420 U.S. 636 (1975), the Court invalidated the "mother's insurance benefit" provision of the Social Security Act, 42 U.S.C. section 402(g), which provided benefits to widows (but not widowers) having minor children in their care. Writing for the majority, Justice Brennan identified the provision as reflecting an "archaic and overbroad generalization not tolerated under the Constitution . . . namely, that male workers' earnings are vital to the support of their families, while the earnings of female wage earners do not significantly contribute to their fami- lies' support." *Weinberger,* 420 U.S. 643 (citations and internal punctuation omitted). The law was unconstitutional both as it presumed women's wages were not necessary for family support and as it denied women wage-earners the ability to provide for their family's support that was granted to similarly situated male workers. In this way, the sex-based regulatory regime helped validate and entrench the very social assumptions on which it was premised. In Califano v. Goldfarb, 430 U.S. 199 (1977), the Court struck down another Social Security provision under which a widow was entitled to survivors' benefits based on her deceased husband's coverage regardless of dependency, but only a widower who received at least half of his support from his deceased wife was entitled to benefits. Justice Brennan wrote for a plurality of the Court:

> The only conceivable justification for writing the presumption of wives' dependency into the statute is the assumption, not verified by the Government . . . but based simply on "archaic and overbroad" generalizations, that it would save the Government time, money, and effort simply to pay benefits to all widows, rather than to require proof of dependency of both sexes. We held in *Frontiero,* and again in *Wiesenfeld,* and therefore hold again here, that such assumptions do not suffice to justify a gender-based discrim- ination in the distribution of employment-related benefits.

In Califano v. Westcott, 443 U.S. 76, 89 (1979), the Court invalidated yet another Social Security policy, this one granting Aid to Families and Dependent Children (AFDC) benefits to the children of unemployed fathers but not unemployed mothers. The Court reasoned that it was "part of the baggage of sexual stereotypes that presumes the father has the primary responsibility to provide a home and its essentials, while the mother is the center of home and family life." Wengler v. Druggists Mutual Insurance Company, 446 U.S. 142 (1980), struck down a Missouri law automatically entitling widows of men who died in work-related accidents to death benefits, while requiring widowers of women who perished in such accidents to prove that they were incapacitated or actually dependent on the wife's earnings. In Kirchberg v. Feenstra, 450 U.S. 455 (1981), the Justices unanimously invalidated a Louisiana statute granting a husband, as "head and master" of the family, the unilateral right to dispose of property jointly owned with his wife without her consent.

These cases represented a dramatic shift in the Court's understanding of the Equal Protection Clause. In the century before 1970, the Court understood differences in family roles as a legitimate reason for state policies that differentiated between the sexes, but, in this period, the Court was persuaded by advocates for the women's movement that such reasons for distinguishing between the sexes were a form of illegitimate stereotyping resembling race discrimination.

In invalidating laws based on the male breadwinner/female caregiver model, the Court never ruled that family dependency itself was a wrong or a harm, but it did assert repeatedly that gender-based laws that enforced generalizations about gender roles and family dependency violated the Constitution. For example, when the Court invalidated an Alabama statute requiring husbands but not wives to pay alimony upon divorce in Orr v. Orr, 440 U.S. 268, 279-280, 283 (1979), it asserted that the State could not employ gender-based rules in marriage to reinforce a traditional breadwinner-dependent model of marriage:

> Appellant views the Alabama alimony statutes as effectively announcing the State's preference for an allocation of family responsibilities under which the wife plays a dependent role, and as seeking for their objective the reinforcement of that model among the State's citizens. We agree, as he urges, that prior cases settle that this purpose cannot sustain the statutes. Stanton v. Stanton, 421 U.S. 7, 10 (1975), held that the "old notio[n]" that "generally it is the man's primary responsibility to provide a home and its essentials," can no longer justify a statute that discriminates on the basis of gender. "No longer is the female destined solely for the home and the rearing of the family, and only the male for the marketplace and the world of ideas." . . .
>
> Legislative classifications which distribute benefits and burdens on the basis of gender carry the inherent risk of reinforcing the stereotypes about the "proper place" of women and their need for special protection. . . . Thus, even statutes purportedly designed to compensate for and ameliorate the effects of past discrimination must be carefully tailored. Where, as here, the State's compensatory and ameliorative purposes are as well served by a gender-neutral classification as one that gender classifies and therefore carries with it the baggage of sexual stereotypes, the State cannot be permitted to classify on the basis of sex.

In its early sex discrimination cases, the Court repeatedly condemns "archaic and overbroad generalizations" and "stereotypes" about the "proper roles" of men and women in the family. What exactly is the harm that generalizations and stereotypes inflict?

Stereotypes, as scholars in the fields of law, sociology, and psychology have observed, reflect a common human tendency to make sense of the world through the imposition of categories.[54] Stereotyping involves both empirical generalizations

---

54. See Linda Hamilton Krieger, The Content of Our Categories: A Cognitive Bias Approach to Discrimination and Equal Opportunity, 47 Stan. L. Rev. 1161 (1995); Mahzarin Banaji and Anthony Greenwald, Implicit Stereotyping and Prejudice, in The Psychology of Prejudice: The Ontario Symposium 55 (M. P. Zanna & J. M. Olson eds., 1994); Frederick F. Schauer, Profiles, Probabilities, and Stereotypes (2003).

about how individuals behave, and normative prescriptions about how they should behave.[55]

It is useful to distinguish several distinct, though interlocking, kinds of harms that flow from stereotyping. People apprehend groups through generalizations about their members, a useful heuristic in making sense of the social world. But generalizations about groups may be inaccurate as an account of some or all group members. Thus, stereotypical reasoning, however helpful it may be in making sense of the social world, may also lead to cognitive error. These cognitive errors may be amplified by the affective dynamics of prejudice; stereotypes may express pejorative judgments about group members. And as one analyzes stereotyping from a socio-logical, and not merely a psychological standpoint, it is possible to see that stereo-typing enforces prescriptive judgments — judgments about social norms and the status roles of certain groups.[56] Law commonly reflects and enforces social norms and status roles. Legal prescriptions about norms and roles will be experienced as a harm when those norms and roles are contested, as the male breadwinner/female caregiver model of the family was in the 1960s and 1970s.

As we have seen, in this period the women's movement was challenging aspects of family structure that enforced inequalities in the social status of men and women. The movement objected to policies that stereotyped women as mothers when such policies obscured similarities in the capacities and circum-stances of the sexes, and when such policies defined family roles in such a way as to devalue the capacities and contribution of those engaged in work traditionally considered "feminine." Treating women as caregivers rather than breadwinners was wrong because (a) not all women were or aspired to be caregivers, *and* because (b) it denigrated women engaged in caregiving for performing a socially essential practice. The movement was concerned about the freedom of women to escape role conventions, and about the welfare of women who conformed to role conventions. As the opening section of this chapter recounts, the move-ment's inaugural strike for equality protested social arrangements that relegated those who performed traditionally "feminine" domestic or caregiving roles to second-class citizenship, seeking reforms that would allow those who cared for families to participate as equals in the economic and political activities of citizenship.

In its decisions of the 1970s, the Supreme Court recognized several harmful effects of stereotyping. In striking down the "near-beer" law in *Craig* and other sex-differentiating provisions, the Court objected to sex-based laws as unfairly catego-rizing individuals on the basis of perceived group characteristics[57] and as unfairly

---

55. See Susan T. Fiske, Stereotyping Prejudice, and Discrimination in The Handbook of Social Psychology 357, 378 (Daniel T. Gilbert, Susan T. Fiske, and Gardner Lindzey eds., 4th ed. 1998); Larry Alexander, What Makes Wrongful Discrimination Wrong? Biases, Preferences, Stereotypes, and Proxies, 141 U. Pa. L. Rev. 149, 157-190 (1992); David H. Gans, Note, Stereotyping and Difference: Planned Parenthood v. Casey and the Future of Sex Discrimination Law, 104 Yale. L.J. 1875, 1877 (1995).

56. Social psychologists theorizing stereotyping have tended to focus on the individual rather than group, and have been relatively inattentive to social structural accounts of stereotyping — tendencies that are now giving way to more interdisciplinary forms of analysis. See Fiske, supra n.55, at 392. For discussion of status-based hierarchies and equal protection law, see J. M. Balkin, The Constitution of Status, 106 Yale L.J. 2313 (1997).

57. For an argument that this principle primarily drove the Court's 1970s jurisprudence, see Mary Anne Case, "The Very Stereotype the Law Condemns": Constitutional Sex Discrimination Law as a Question for Perfect Proxies, 85 Cornell L. Rev. 1447 (2000).

denigrating groups. The 1970s cases emphasize that sex-based stereotypes inflict harm as they perpetuate cognitive error, express pejorative judgments, and impose confining role prescriptions. Sex-differentiating laws, the Court recognized, "operate to perpetuate mythical or stereotyped assumptions about the proper roles and the relative capabilities of men and women that are unrelated to any inherent differences."[58] The Court also highlighted the relationship between sex stereotypes and the unequal distribution of political power, recognizing that "gender-based classifications too often have been inexcusably utilized to stereotype and stigmatize politically powerless segments of society."[59]

Thus, in proscribing sex-based state action, the Court was concerned about much more than accuracy in governmental decisionmaking. The equal protection cases of the 1970s prohibited government from using sex categorization to reinforce traditional sex roles, with the aim of protecting both individuals and groups. The new doctrine of intermediate scrutiny protected individual freedom to deviate from status roles generally ascribed to a group, and eliminated forms of state action that subordinated groups by enforcing status roles on group members as a whole.

With the growth of this new body of equal protection law in the 1970s, courts began to invalidate many traditional forms of sex-based legislation. Protective labor legislation restricting women's conditions of employment had, in the first several decades of the twentieth century, survived court challenges in cases such as Muller v. Oregon and Goesaert v. Cleary, discussed supra, and remained in effect in many states as of the passage of the Civil Rights Act of 1964. However these sex-based statutes often reflected and enforced stereotypes about women's capabilities, limiting their employment opportunities by excluding them from certain jobs, restricting their hours, regulating their wages, or barring them from lifting heavy objects. Lawsuits brought under Title VII invalidated some of these laws,[60] and the EEOC eventually promulgated implementing regulations making clear that protective labor laws that applied only to women discriminated on the basis of sex in violation of Title VII.[61] The Court also found such "protective" objectives to be invalid under the Equal Protection Clause, because they reflected stereotypic assumptions about women's relative capabilities. As Justice O'Connor wrote in Mississippi University for Women v. Hogan (1982), infra, "[I]f the statutory objective is to exclude or 'protect' members of one gender because they are presumed to suffer from an inherent handicap or to be innately inferior, the objective itself is illegitimate." Hogan, 458 U.S. at 725.

And, as we have seen, the revolution in equal protection doctrine dramatically affected family law. In the years after Frontiero, courts and legislatures moved to eliminate sex distinctions in state and federal laws regulating the marriage relationship. After the Court itself struck down sex-based classifications in Social Security, welfare, alimony, and marital property laws, courts and legislatures revised laws governing custody, domestic violence, and other aspects of the marriage relationship, seeking to define rights and obligations of the spouses in formally

58. Caban v. Mohammed, 441 U.S. 380, 398 (1979).
59. Kahn v. Shevin, 416 U.S. 351, 357 (1974).
60. See, e.g., Weeks v. Southern Bell, 408 F.2d 228 (5th Cir. 1969).
61. 29 C.F.R. §1604.1(b)(1970).

gender-neutral terms.[62] Making the law of marriage, which was once hierarchical, formally gender-neutral has not secured equality in marriage, given persisting differences in the family roles of most men and women.[63] But the law of marriage no longer expressly distinguishes between husbands and wives as it did for centuries.

B.   Intermediate Scrutiny and Same-Sex Marriage

Despite dramatic changes in the law of marriage that equal protection has wrought, there is at least one important respect in which law continues to define spousal roles by sex. Today, both federal and state governments define marriage, whether implicitly or explicitly, as a union between a male husband and a female wife. Under the intermediate scrutiny regime that we have just examined, may government still define capacity to marry by sex? To date, no court has ruled that federal equal protection cases forbid the state from discriminating between the sexes in determining who is eligible marry.[64] State judges interpreting state constitutions have begun to call into question the definition of marriage as a union of a man and a woman, as Chapter 8 discusses. And opinions in some of these state constitutional cases frame the question of same-sex marriage as a question concerning the state's prerogative to discriminate on the basis of sex. In Baehr v. Lewin, 852 P.2d 44 (Haw. 1993), the Supreme Court of Hawaii found that: "[B]y its plain language [the marriage statute] restricts the marital relation to a male and a female" and held that "the state's regulation of access to the status of married persons, on the basis of the applicants' sex" contravenes the state constitution's equal rights amendment.[65] By contrast, the dissent in *Baehr* argued that such marriage laws are not sex discrimination because the laws treat males and females alike: Each is barred from marrying a person of the same sex.

In response to arguments of this type, proponents of same-sex marriage often point to Loving v. Virginia, 388 U.S. 1 (1967), discussed in Chapter 6. In *Loving,* Virginia argued that its miscegenation statutes did not amount to invidious discrimination because they punished equally white and black participants in interracial marriage. The *Loving* Court rejected this "equal application" argument, and struck down the prohibition on interracial marriage on the grounds that there was "patently no legitimate overriding purpose independent of invidious racial discrimination" to justify the classifications, which the Court characterized "as measures

---

62. See, e.g., Martha F. Davis, Male Coverture: Law and the Illegitimate Family, 56 Rutgers L. Rev. 73, 78-79 (2003); Linda McClain, The Domain of Civic Virtue in a Good Society: Families, Schools, and Sex Equality, 69 Fordham L. Rev. 617 (2001); Reva B. Siegel, "The Rule of Love": Wife Beating as Prerogative and Privacy, 105 Yale L.J. 2117, 2190 (1996).

63. See Siegel, "The Rule of Love," at 2188-2196.

64. As discussed infra, some state courts and a number of commentators now read these cases as calling into question sex-based restrictions on who can marry.

65. Because it held that the marriage ban amounted to a sex-based classification, the court evaluated the constitutionality of the law under the equal protection clause of the Hawaii Constitution, a "more elaborate" version than the federal equal protection clause. Unlike the U.S. Supreme Court, which uses a "heightened" scrutiny standard to evaluate sex-discrimination claims, the Supreme Court of Hawaii applied a strict scrutiny standard to invalidate the law in *Baehr.* Still, despite this holding, Hawaii did not legalize same-sex marriage. Rather, the state amended its constitution in 1998 to grant the legislature the "power to reserve marriage to opposite-sex couples." Haw. Const. Art. I, §23.

designed to maintain White Supremacy." Just as the equal application argument in *Loving* failed because racial restrictions on who could marry enforced values of white supremacy, critics argue that gender-based restrictions on who can marry enforce inequality as well.

But what kind of inequality? Is it only inequality on the basis of sexual preference, as the cases in Chapter 8 explore? Or do state laws defining marriage as a union of a man and a woman enforce inequality between the sexes as well? If so, how?

The relationship between sex/gender and sexual orientation is enormously complex. Still there is a simple sense in which any act of discrimination on the basis of sexual orientation can simultaneously be understood as an act of discrimination on the basis of sex. Once we define orientation with reference to the sex of those whom an individual desires or has intimate relations with, then discrimination on the basis of sexual orientation is also discrimination on the basis of sex: The individual would be accepted, but for the sex of his or her object choice.[66]

In the marriage context, these intersections are unavoidable. Barriers to "gay marriage" are legally expressed as *sex-based* restrictions on who can marry. As a California court recently explained:

> The idea that California's marriage law does not discriminate upon gender is incorrect. If a person, male or female, wishes to marry, then he or she may do so as long as the intended spouse is of a different gender. It is the gender of the intended spouse that is the sole determining factor. To say that all men and all women are treated the same in that each may not marry someone of the same gender misses the point. The marriage laws establish classifications (same gender vs. opposite gender) and discriminate based on those gender-based classifications. As such, for the purpose of an equal protection analysis, the legislative scheme creates a gender-based classification.[67]

We know that equal protection law already subjects sex-based state action to special scrutiny. Does a state law limiting marriage to a union of a man and a woman inflict the same kinds of harms that the Court's sex discrimination cases condemn?

---

66. If we define orientation with reference to gender performance, then discrimination on the basis of orientation might still be understood as an act of sex discrimination: The individual's gender performance would be acceptable, but for his or her sex.

Courts have generally resisted applying prohibitions on sex discrimination to matters that seem to concern sexual orientation — although the ways courts understand this constraint have evolved over time. Sandi Farrell argues that the legal system systematically restricts the meaning of discrimination on the basis of sex so as to reform but maintain heterosexual norms, a dynamic she understands as "preservation through transformation." See Sandi Farrell, Reconsidering the Gender-Equality Perspective for Understanding LGBT Rights, 13 Law & Sexuality 605, 699-700 (2004). A number of advocates seek an expanded interpretation of the injunction against sex discrimination; but many others question whether this is the best framework to address practices that advocates and their opponents generally understand as discrimination on the basis of sexual orientation — not sex. For more on the ways antidiscrimination law relates sex, gender, and orientation, see Susan Frelich Appleton, Missing in Action? Searching for Gender Talk in the Same-Sex Marriage Debate, 16 Stan. L. & Pol'y Rev. 98 (2005); Mary Anne Case, Disaggregating Gender from Sex and Sexual Orientation: The Effeminate Man in the Law and Feminist Jurisprudence, 105 Yale L.J. 1 (1995). Katherine Franke, The Central Mistake of Sex Discrimination Law: The Disaggregation of Sex from Gender, 144 U. Pa. L. Rev. 1, 5 (1995); Francisco Valdes, Queers, Sissies, Dykes and Tomboys: Deconstructing the Conflation of "Sex," "Gender," and "Sexual Orientation" in Euro-American Law and Culture, 83 Cal. L. Rev. 1, 16 (1995).

67. In re Coordination Proceeding, Special Title [Rule 1550(c)], 2005 WL 583129 at 9-10 (Cal. Superior Mar. 14, 2005).

In Baker v. State, 744 A.2d 864 (Vt. 1999), Judge Johnson asserted that Vermont's sex-based restriction on who could marry violated the state's constitution because it enforced sex-role stereotypes. Judge Johnson began her argument genealogically, suggesting that the state law defining marital partners by sex was a remnant of the old common law marital status regime:

> Before applying the rational-basis standard to the State's justifications, it is helpful to examine the history of the marriage laws in Vermont. There is no doubt that, historically, the marriage laws imposed sex-based roles for the partners to a marriage — male provider and female dependent — that bore no relation to their inherent abilities to contribute to society. . . .
>
> As the Legislature enacted statutes to confer rights upon married women, this Court abolished common-law doctrines arising from the common law theory that husband and wife were one person and that the wife had no independent legal existence. . . .
>
> The question now is whether the sex-based classification in the marriage law is simply a vestige of the common-law unequal marriage relationship or whether there is some valid governmental purpose for the classification today. . . .

Judge Johnson then set out to determine whether there was any legitimate reason for the state to preserve the sex-based definition of who could marry, independent of the constitutionally impermissible aim of preserving sex roles in marriage:

> [In support of the marriage statutes] the State asserts public purposes — uniting men and women to celebrate the "complementarity" (sic) of the sexes and providing male and female role models for children — based on broad and vague generalizations about the roles of men and women that reflect outdated sex-role stereotyping. The State contends that (1) marriage unites the rich physical and psychological differences between the sexes; (2) sex differences strengthen and stabilize a marriage; (3) each sex contributes differently to a family unit and to society; and (4) uniting the different male and female qualities and contributions in the same institution instructs the young of the value of such a union. The State relies on social science literature, such as Carol Gilligan's In a Different Voice: Psychological Theory and Women's Development (1982), to support its contention that there are sex differences that justify the State requiring two people to be of opposite sex to marry. . . .
>
> . . . The goal of community diversity has no place, however, as a requirement of marriage.
>
> To begin with, carried to its logical conclusion, the State's rationale could require all marriages to be between people, not just of the opposite sex, but of different races, religions, national origins, and so forth, to promote diversity. Moreover, while it may be true that the female voice or point of view is sometimes different from the male, such differences are not necessarily found in comparing any given man and any given woman. The State's implicit assertion otherwise is sex stereotyping of the most retrograde sort. Nor could the State show that the undoubted differences between any given man and woman who wish to marry are more related to their sex than to other characteristics and life experiences. In short, the "diversity" argument is based on illogical conclusions from stereotypical imaginings that would be condemned by the very case cited for its support. See United States v. Virginia, 518 U.S. at 533 (justifications for sex-based classifications "must not rely on overbroad generalizations about the different talents, capabilities, or preferences of males and females"). . . .

The State also asserts that it has an interest in furthering the link between procreation and child rearing "to ensure that couples who engage in sexual intercourse accept[ ] responsibility for the potential children they might create." But the State cannot explain how the failure of *opposite-sex* couples to accept responsibility for the children they create relates at all to the exclusion of same-sex couples from the benefits of marriage. To the extent that couples, same-sex or opposite-sex, will fail to take responsibility for the children they create, the risk is greater where the couples are not married. Therefore, denying same-sex couples the benefits of marriage on this ground is not only arbitrary but completely at odds with the stated government purpose. . . .

In sum, the State treats similarly situated people — those who wish to marry — differently, on the basis of the sex of the person they wish to marry. The State provides no legally valid rationale for the different treatment. The justifications asserted by the State for the classification are tautological, wholly arbitrary, or based on impermissible assumptions about the roles of men and women. None of the State's justifications meets the rational-basis test under the Common Benefits Clause. Finding no legally valid justification for the sex-based classification, I conclude that the classification is a vestige of the historical unequal marriage relationship that more recent legislative enactments and our own jurisprudence have unequivocally rejected. The protections conferred on Vermonters by the Common Benefits Clause cannot be restricted by the outmoded conception that marriage requires one man and one woman, creating one person — the husband. As this Court recently stated, "equal protection of the laws cannot be limited by eighteenth-century standards.". . .

Judge Johnson reasons that government's insistence on preserving sexual dimorphism in marriage reinforces, in a crucial institutional context, the sex-role differentiation on which relations of sex inequality are predicated.[68] Several other state courts have construed sex-based limitations on who can marry as presenting questions of sex discrimination under their state constitutions.[69]

Note that Judge Johnson applies Vermont state constitutional law, but cites federal equal protection precedent as well. A number of commentators read federal equal protection cases that invalidate sex classifications in marriage as prohibiting sex-based definitions of who can marry. Andrew Koppelman argues that the Court "has consistently struck down statutes whose purpose was the imposition of traditional gender roles," and observes, "[l]aws that discriminate against gays rest upon a normative stereotype: the bald conviction that certain behavior — for example, sex with women — is appropriate for members of one sex, but not for members of the other sex. Such laws therefore flatly violate the constitutional prohibition on sex discrimination as it has been interpreted by the Supreme Court."[70] Others join Koppelman in reading the Court's intermediate scrutiny

---

68. Sylvia Law reasons that legal prohibitions on same-sex relationships can best be understood as "preserving traditional concepts of masculinity and femininity" that injure "everyone who seeks freedom to experience the full range of human emotions, behavior and relationships without gender-defined constraints." Sylvia A. Law, Homosexuality and the Social Meaning of Gender, 1988 Wis. L. Rev. 187, 188, 232.

69. See the Hawaii and California state court opinions quoted supra. See also Goodridge v. Dep't of Pub. Health, 798 N.E.2d 941, 973 (Mass. 2003) (Greaney, J., concurring) ("[This] case requires that we confront ingrained assumptions with respect to historically accepted roles of men and women within the institution of marriage . . . .").

70. Andrew Koppelman, Why Discrimination Against Lesbians and Gay Men Is Sex Discrimination, 69 N.Y.U. L. Rev. 197, 217, 219 (1994).

cases as invalidating state laws that restrict access to marriage by sex[71] — an argument that Mary Anne Case extends to federal law such as the Defense of Marriage Act, as well.

The Defense of Marriage Act, Pub. L. No. 104-199, 110 Stat. 2419, 2419 (1996) provides that, "[i]n determining the meaning of any [federal statute, regulation, or administrative ruling], the word 'marriage' means only a legal union between one man and one woman as husband and wife, and the word 'spouse' refers only to a person of the opposite sex who is a husband or wife." §3(a). "This is, of course, a sex-respecting rule," Mary Anne Case observes, "hence subject to heightened scrutiny under Supreme Court precedent."[72]

To date, no court has held that laws defining marital spouses by sex are barred by the federal equal protection cases that prohibit sex classifications in marriage that enforce sex stereotypes. And there is some authority for the proposition that the Fourteenth Amendment's Equal Protection Clause does *not* invalidate sex-based restrictions on who can marry. In 1972, almost a year after its decision in Reed v. Reed, the Supreme Court dismissed, for want of a substantial federal question, a Minnesota Supreme Court decision holding that a state law defining marriage as the union of a man and a woman did not violate the Equal Protection Clause.[73] Several courts have treated the Supreme Court's ruling as precedent, including the Supreme Court of California in its decision invalidating marriage licenses the mayor of San Francisco issued to same-sex couples in violation of state law.[74] The California court reasoned that the dismissal was still binding precedent because "[t]he United States Supreme Court has not expressly overruled Baker v. Nelson . . . nor do any of its later decisions contain doctrinal developments that are necessarily incompatible with that decision."[75]

Discussion

1. When the Minnesota Supreme Court dismissed the equal protection challenge to the sex-based restriction on who could marry in 1971 just before the Court's decision in *Reed,* it explained its holding by saying only "*Loving* does indicate that not all state restrictions upon the right to marry are beyond reach of the Fourteenth Amendment. But in commonsense and in a constitutional sense, there is a clear

71. Mary Anne Case, "The Very Stereotype the Law Condemns": Constitutional Sex Discrimination Law as a Quest for Perfect Proxies, 85 Cornell L. Rev. 1447, 1486-1490 (2000); Danielle Kie Hart, Same-Sex Marriage Revisited: Taking a Critical Look at Baehr v. Lewin, 9 Geo. Mason Civ. Rts. L.J. 1, 58 & n.258 (1998) ("Like miscegenation statutes, a ban on same-sex marriage serves the constitutionally improper purpose of perpetuating unacceptable sex-based stereotypes about the proper roles of women and men."); Francisco Valdes, Queers, Sissies, Dykes and Tomboys: Deconstructing the Conflation of "Sex," "Gender" and "Sexual Orientation" in Euro-American Law and Society, 83 Cal. L. Rev. 1, 317-320 (1995); cf. Sylvia Law, Families and Federalism, 4 Wash. U. J. L. & Policy 175, 234 (2000) ("The Constitution 'sharply limits the ability of states to allocate family rights and responsibility on the basis of gender'").

72. Case, supra n.71, at 1490.

73. Baker v. Nelson, 191 N.W.2d 185, 187 (Minn. 1971), *dismissed for want of a substantial federal question,* 409 U.S. 810 (1972). For an account of the early history of litigation challenging marriage restrictions, see William N. Eskridge, Jr., The Case for Same-Sex Marriage: From Sexual Liberty to Civilized Commitment 48-59 (1996).

74. See Lockyer v. City and Cty of San Francisco, 17 Cal. Rptr. 3d 225, 278-279 (Cal. 2004); see also Wilson v. Ake, 354 F. Supp. 2d 1298, 1304 ((M.D. Fla. 2005); Morrison v. Sadler, 821 N.E.2d 15, 19-20 (Ind. App. 2005).

75. Lockyer, 17 Cal. Rptr. 3d at 279.

distinction between a marital restriction based merely upon race and one based upon the fundamental difference in sex." Baker v. Nelson, 191 N.W.2d at 187.

a. Does the race-gender analogy help guide judgment about applying intermediate scrutiny to laws that impose gender restrictions on who can marry? Why or why not?

b. Is the California Supreme Court correct when it observes that none of the Supreme Court's "later decisions contain doctrinal developments that are necessarily incompatible with [Baker v. Nelson]"? Do the intermediate scrutiny cases we have read proscribe all sex distinctions in the law defining the marriage relationship? If not, what forms of sex-role differentiation violate equal protection under this line of cases, and what kinds of sex-role differentiation remain constitutionally permissible? Has the Court proscribed only those sex classifications that enforce the breadwinner/caregiver stereotype in marriage? And does the state's insistence on defining marital spouses by sex preserve that stereotype, as Judge Johnson suggests? For an argument that equal protection law does not abolish the use of stereotypes, but rather intervenes and reshapes social understandings about race and gender identity, see Robert C. Post, Prejudicial Appearances: The Logic of American Antidiscrimination Law 40 (2002) (characterizing the dominant account as offering "an implausible story about the actual shape of antidiscrimination law" and offering instead a sociological account that "does not ask whether 'stereotypic impressions' can be eliminated tout court, but rather how the law alters and modifies such impressions").

2. Does it make any difference in evaluating the sex discrimination challenge to laws defining marital spouses by sex that most opponents and proponents of such laws understand them as discriminating on the basis of orientation? Of what relevance to analyzing claims of sex discrimination are the views of litigants, officials, social movements, or citizens? In your judgment, what connection, if any, exists between sex-discrimination and sexual-orientation-discrimination challenges to laws that define marital spouses by sex?

Note: On Sex, Gender, and Sexual Orientation

Many scholars in women's studies and related fields use the words "sex" and "gender" as terms of art. "Sex" designates biological differences between men and women — genitalia or chromosomes. "Gender" refers to the socially produced differences between the sexes in dress, grooming, speech patterns, and other forms of behavior. However, many if not most people often use the terms "sex" and "gender" interchangeably. Judges and practicing attorneys have similarly regarded them as synonyms. As a result, critics claim, we have inherited a sexual equality jurisprudence that is often ambiguous with respect to its key concepts.

Ironically, Justice Ruth Bader Ginsburg, who litigated important sex discrimination cases in the 1970s, is partly responsible for the analytic conflation of "sex" and "gender." As reported in one news account, Ginsburg

> stopped talking about sex discrimination years ago. . . . [S]he explained that a secretary once told her, "I'm typing all these briefs and articles for you and the word sex, sex, sex is on every page. Don't you know those nine men [on the Supreme Court], they hear that word and their first association is not the way you want them to be

thinking? Why don't you use the word 'gender'? It is a grammatical term and it will ward off distracting associations."[76]

Mary Anne Case, among others, has called for the disaggregation of "gender" and "sex" as legal categories. According to Case, the conflation of the two categories, combined with a common tendency to confuse gender atypicality with homosexual orientation, imports into law a simplistic vision of "sex, gender, and orientation . . . as coming packaged together such that once one is identified, all the rest are determined": Human beings of the male sex are masculine and attracted to women, whereas human beings of the female sex are feminine and attracted to men. Moreover, Case points out, although women are discriminated against, there is also discrimination against femininity and all things coded feminine.

Thus, she points out, "feminists who wish to see feminine styles more generally valued, rather than gradually eliminated as they may be in an androgynous culture slanted toward the masculine," should also work to extend the protections of antidiscrimination law to effeminate men:

> [I]t may be that certain behaviors are just like certain jobs — they will not be valued unless and until men can feel free to engage in them. So long as stereotypically feminine behavior, from wearing dresses and jewelry to speaking softly or in a high-pitched voice, to nurturing or raising children, is forced into a female ghetto, it may continue to be devalued. . . .
>
> It is my contention that, unfortunately, the world will not be safe for women in frilly pink dresses — they will not, for example, generally be as respected as either men or women in gray flannel suits — unless and until it is made safe for men in dresses as well.[77]

Katherine Franke questions the conceptual coherence of sex/gender jurisprudence in a different way: In her view, "there is no principled way to distinguish sex from gender, and, concomitantly, sexual differentiation from sexual discrimination." However, the jurisprudential justification for less-than-heightened-scrutiny of sex-based classifications is the presumption that, because of fundamental biological differences, "males and females are not similarly situated — they are in fact different kinds of beings." Yet by Franke's account, "[b]y accepting these biological differences, equality jurisprudence reifies as foundational *fact* that which is really an *effect* of normative gender ideology."

Through a series of examples, Franke argues that if it were not for gender ideology, our sexual (i.e., anatomical/physical) differences would not code as difference in the ways we currently imagine, or, in Franke's more evocative phrasing, it is "the roles, clothing, myths, and stereotypes that transform a vagina into a *she*." Therefore, Franke argues, "biology is both a wrong and dangerous place to ground antidiscrimination law because it fails to account for the manner in which every sexual biological fact is meaningful only within a gendered frame of reference." In Franke's view, the targets of antidiscrimination law "should not be limited to the 'gross, stereotyped distinctions between the sexes' but should also include the

---

76. Ernie Freda, Washington in Brief: Clinton's Old Underwear Full of Tax Holes, Atlanta J. & Constitution, Dec. 29, 1993, at A8.

77. Mary Anne Case, Disaggregating Gender from Sex and Sexual Orientation: The Effeminate Man in the Law and Feminist Jurisprudence, 105 Yale L.J. 1, 3, 7, 14 (1995).

social processes that construct and make coherent the categories male and female."[78]

Francisco Valdes argues that much confusion has been caused by the multiple conceptual linkages (and conflations) between sex, gender, and sexual orientation. Sex is conflated with gender when people assume that a person's sex (male or female) is also their gender (masculine or feminine). Gender is conflated with sexual orientation when it is assumed that "sissies" are gay and "tomboys" are lesbians, or conversely, that very masculine men and very feminine women are necessarily heterosexual. This conflation, says Valdes, is encouraged by the assumption that "sexual orientation serves as the sexual component of gender." Finally, sex is conflated with sexual orientation when people infer sexual orientation from the sex of a person's sexual partner: Same-sex coupling leads to an inference of homosexual orientation for both participants (even if the participants do not understand themselves to be homosexual), whereas different-sex coupling creates an inference of heterosexual orientation (as in the assumption that a man cannot be gay because he is married and has children).

Valdes argues that "there is no such thing as discrimination '*based*' solely or exclusively on sexual orientation." From his analysis of case law, Valdes concludes (like Mary Anne Case) that courts tend to interpret gender-inappropriate behavior as a sign of homosexuality, especially in men, which provides sex discrimination law with a "sexual orientation loophole": As long as it is generally legal to discriminate on the basis of sexual orientation, discrimination on the basis of gender atypicality is easy to justify as permissible discrimination against (suspected) homosexuals. According to Valdes, antidiscrimination law simply cannot redeem its promise so long as it conflates sex, gender, and sexual orientation.[79]

C. Intermediate Scrutiny and the Race–Gender Analogy: Juries and Education

The race–gender analogy played a crucial role in the rise of sex discrimination doctrine, supplying the core concept of stereotyping on which the permissibility of sex-based regulation under the Equal Protection Clause now depends. There are many contexts in which application of the sex stereotyping concept under intermediate scrutiny seems to follow the law of race discrimination, constraining law from recognizing differences in the position of the sexes. Consider, for example, the Court's decision to bar sex-based peremptory strikes:

J.E.B. v. Alabama ex rel. T.B., 511 U.S. 127 (1994): The Supreme Court extended the logic of Batson v. Kentucky (discussed in Chapter 6, supra) to gender discrimination, holding that the State's use of preremptory challenges based on gender was unconstitutional. The petitioner J.E.B. was the defendant in a paternity

---

78. Katherine Franke, The Central Mistake of Sex Discrimination Law: The Disaggregation of Sex from Gender, 144 U. Pa. L. Rev. 1, 5 (1995). Despite the apparent conflict between the titles of these two articles, the authors mean different things by the word "disaggregate." Case is concerned with the conflation of discrimination based on sex with that based on gender. Franke is concerned that courts and decisionmakers do not understand the role that gender ideologies play in producing sex discrimination.

79. Francisco Valdes, Queers, Sissies, Dykes and Tomboys: Deconstructing the Conflation of "Sex," "Gender," and "Sexual Orientation" in Euro-American Law and Culture, 83 Cal. L. Rev. 1, 16 (1995).

suit brought by Alabama on behalf of T.B., the mother of a minor child allegedly fathered by J.E.B. The State then used 9 of its 10 peremptory strikes to remove male jurors; petitioner used all but one of his strikes to remove female jurors. As a result, all the selected jurors were female.

The State justified its peremptory challenges "based upon the perception, supported by history, that men otherwise totally qualified to serve upon a jury might be more sympathetic and receptive to the arguments of a man alleged in a paternity action to be the father of an out-of-wedlock child, whereas women equally qualified to serve upon a jury might be more sympathetic and receptive to the arguments of the complaining witness who bore the child." Justice Blackmun's majority opinion replied:

> We shall not accept as a defense to gender-based peremptory challenges "the very stereotype the law condemns." Respondent's rationale, not unlike those regularly expressed for gender-based strikes, is reminiscent of the arguments advanced to justify the total exclusion of women from juries. Respondent offers virtually no support for the conclusion that gender alone is an accurate predictor of juror's attitudes; yet it urges this Court to condone the same stereotypes that justified the wholesale exclusion of women from juries and the ballot box. Respondent seems to assume that gross generalizations that would be deemed impermissible if made on the basis of race are somehow permissible when made on the basis of gender. . . . [A]ctive discrimination by litigants on the basis of gender during jury selection "invites cynicism respecting the jury's neutrality and its obligation to adhere to the law." . . . Striking individual jurors on the assumption that they hold particular views simply because of their gender is "practically a brand upon them, affixed by law, an assertion of their inferiority." [*Plessy*]

Justice O'Connor concurred, while expressing some misgivings that the decision would further erode the use of peremptory challenges, because such challenges may actually help preserve jury impartiality.

> We know that like race, gender matters. A plethora of studies make clear that in rape cases, for example, female jurors are somewhat more likely to vote to convict than male jurors. Moreover, though there have been no similarly definitive studies regarding, for example, sexual harassment, child custody, or spousal or child abuse, one need not be a sexist to share the intuition that in certain cases a person's gender and resulting life experience will be relevant to his or her view of the case. "Jurors are not expected to come into the jury box and leave behind all that their human experience has taught them." Individuals are not expected to ignore as jurors what they know as men — or women.
>
> Today's decision severely limits a litigant's ability to act on this intuition, for the import of our holding is that any correlation between a juror's gender and attitudes is irrelevant as a matter of constitutional law. But to say that gender makes no difference as a matter of law is not to say that gender makes no difference as a matter of fact. I previously have said with regard to *Batson:* "That the Court will not tolerate prosecutors' racially discriminatory use of the peremptory challenge, in effect, is a special rule of relevance, a statement about what this Nation stands for, rather than a statement of fact."

Justice Kennedy, concurring in the judgment, added that "an individual denied jury service because of a peremptory challenge exercised against her on account of her sex is no less injured than the individual denied jury service because of a law banning members of her sex from serving as jurors. The injury is to personal dignity and to the individual's right to participate in the political process."

Chief Justice Rehnquist dissented, arguing that "[t]he two sexes differ biologically, and to a diminishing extent, in experience. It is not merely 'stereotyping' to say that these differences may produce a difference in outlook which is brought to the jury room. Accordingly, the use of peremptory challenges on the basis of sex is generally not the sort of derogatory and invidious act which peremptory challenges directed against black jurors may be. . . ."

Justice Scalia also dissented, joined by Chief Justice Rehnquist and Justice Thomas. He pointed out that "this lawsuit involves a complaint about the use of peremptory challenges to exclude men from a petit jury" and that in any event "[s]ince all groups are subject to the peremptory challenge (and will be made the object of it, depending upon the nature of the particular case) it is hard to see how any group is denied equal protection." [Under the Court's logic] "the prosecutor presumably violates the Constitution when he selects a male or female police officer to testify because he believes one or the other sex might be more convincing in the context of the particular case, or because he believes one or the other might be more appealing to a predominantly male or female jury."

As we have seen, the race-gender analogy played a crucial role in the development of a body of equal protection law that limits government reliance on sex-based generalizations in many contexts. Equal protection law now bars most traditional gender-based regulation in the family, and prohibits gender-based regulation in most public institutions, such as the jury.

Yet, the analogy is only intermittently helpful in explaining the working of heightened scrutiny in the Court's sex discrimination cases. Does the Court's decision in *Loving* control the permissibility of sex-based restrictions on who can marry? To date, it would seem not. Does the Court's decision in *Brown* control the permissibility of de jure sex-based segregation in education? At present, equal protection doctrine substantially constrains the use of sex-based state action in education, and the analogy has played some role in the growth of this body of doctrine. However, development of this body of doctrine has been halting. Today, explicit forms of sex segregation in education are tolerated in many ways that explicit forms of race segregation are not. Yet the Court is also signaling that sex-based state action in the design of education is constitutionally suspect, and licit in a narrowing class of circumstances.

The Court addressed the permissibility of sex segregation in education in one of its most important intermediate scrutiny cases — a decision authored by Justice Ginsburg, who has played a crucial role in the development of this line of cases, first as movement lawyer and now as judge. As you read the *VMI* case, you might reflect on how the practice and law of sex and race discrimination converge and diverge. If sex segregation in education is not "inherently" wrong, under what circumstances does it inflict constitutional harm? How, if at all, does the race analogy help answer this question? How, if at all, does the intermediate scrutiny test help answer this question? Does the Court modify the intermediate scrutiny framework in the course of applying it to the sex-based admissions practices challenged in *VMI*?

UNITED STATES v. VIRGINIA
[The *VMI* Case]
518 U.S. 515 (1996)

Justice GINSBURG delivered the opinion of the Court.

[In 1990, prompted by a complaint filed with the Attorney General by a female high-school student seeking admission to the Virginia Military Institute (VMI), the United States sued the Commonwealth of Virginia and VMI, alleging that VMI's policy of admitting only men violated the Equal Protection Clause of the Fourteenth Amendment. VMI enrolls approximately 1,300 men as cadets. In the two years prior to the suit VMI had received 347 inquiries from women seeking admission.]

I.

Founded in 1839, VMI is today the sole single-sex school among Virginia's 15 public institutions of higher learning. VMI's distinctive mission is to produce "citizen-soldiers," men prepared for leadership in civilian life and in military service. VMI pursues this mission through pervasive training of a kind not available anywhere else in Virginia. Assigning prime place to character development, VMI uses an "adversative method" modeled on English public schools and once characteristic of military instruction. VMI constantly endeavors to instill physical and mental discipline in its cadets and impart to them a strong moral code. The school's graduates leave VMI with heightened comprehension of their capacity to deal with duress and stress, and a large sense of accomplishment for completing the hazardous course.

VMI has notably succeeded in its mission to produce leaders; among its alumni are military generals, Members of Congress, and business executives. The school's alumni overwhelmingly perceive that their VMI training helped them to realize their personal goals. VMI's endowment reflects the loyalty of its graduates; VMI has the largest per-student endowment of all public undergraduate institutions in the Nation.

Neither the goal of producing citizen-soldiers nor VMI's implementing methodology is inherently unsuitable to women. And the school's impressive record in producing leaders has made admission desirable to some women. Nevertheless, Virginia has elected to preserve exclusively for men the advantages and opportunities a VMI education affords.

II.

A

In contrast to the federal service academies, institutions maintained "to prepare cadets for career service in the armed forces," VMI's program "is directed at preparation for both military and civilian life"; "[o]nly about 15% of VMI cadets enter career military service."

VMI produces its "citizen-soldiers" through "an adversative, or doubting, model of education" which features "[p]hysical rigor, mental stress, absolute equality of treatment, absence of privacy, minute regulation of behavior, and indoctrination in desirable values." As one Commandant of Cadets described it, the adversative method "dissects the young student," and makes him aware of his "limits and capabilities," so that he knows "how far he can go with his anger, . . . how much he can take under stress, . . . exactly what he can do when he is physically exhausted."

VMI cadets live in spartan barracks where surveillance is constant and privacy nonexistent; they wear uniforms, eat together in the mess hall, and regularly participate in drills. Entering students are incessantly exposed to the rat line, "an extreme form of the adversative model," comparable in intensity to Marine Corps boot camp. Tormenting and punishing, the rat line bonds new cadets to their fellow sufferers and, when they have completed the 7-month experience, to their former tormentors.

VMI's "adversative model" is further characterized by a hierarchical "class system" of privileges and responsibilities, a "dyke system" for assigning a senior class mentor to each entering class "rat," and a stringently enforced "honor code," which prescribes that a cadet "does not lie, cheat, steal nor tolerate those who do." VMI attracts some applicants because of its reputation as an extraordinarily challenging military school, and "because its alumni are exceptionally close to the school." "[W]omen have no opportunity anywhere to gain the benefits of [the system of education at VMI]."

B

The [District] court . . . recognized that, with recruitment, VMI could "achieve at least 10% female enrollment" — "a sufficient 'critical mass' to provide the female cadets with a positive educational experience" [and] that "some women are capable of all of the individual activities required of VMI cadets." In addition, experts agreed that if VMI admitted women, "the VMI ROTC experience would become a better training program from the perspective of the armed forces, because it would provide training in dealing with a mixed-gender army."

[The District Court nevertheless ruled in favor of VMI, arguing that single-sex education was justified because it added diversity to Virginia's uniformly coeducational system. Moreover, "VMI's unique method of instruction" added diversity. Although women were "denied a unique educational opportunity that is available only at VMI," VMI's "single-sex status would be lost, and some aspects of the [school's] distinctive method would be altered" if women were admitted. The school would have to make allowance "for personal privacy," "[p]hysical education requirements would have to be altered, at least for the women," and the adversative environment could not survive unmodified.

The Fourth Circuit Court of Appeals reversed, arguing that "[a] policy of diversity which aims to provide an array of educational opportunities, including single-gender institutions, must do more than favor one gender" and that "neither the goal of producing citizen soldiers nor VMI's implementing methodology is inherently unsuitable to women." However, it accepted the District Court's finding that physical training, limitations on privacy, and the adversative approach "would be materially affected by coeducation." It remanded the case asking the State of Virginia to choose among three options: Admit women to VMI, establish parallel institutions or programs for women, or abandon state support and leave VMI free to pursue its policies as a private institution.]

C

In response to the Fourth Circuit's ruling, Virginia proposed a parallel program for women: Virginia Women's Institute for Leadership (VWIL). The 4-year, state-sponsored undergraduate program would be located at Mary Baldwin College, a private liberal arts school for women, and would be open, initially, to about 25 to 30 students. Although VWIL would share VMI's mission — to produce "citizen-soldiers" — the VWIL program would differ, as does Mary Baldwin College, from VMI in academic offerings, methods of education, and financial resources.

The average combined SAT score of entrants at Mary Baldwin is about 100 points lower than the score for VMI freshmen. Mary Baldwin's faculty holds "significantly fewer Ph.D.'s than the faculty at VMI," and receives significantly lower salaries. While VMI offers degrees in liberal arts, the sciences, and engineering, Mary Baldwin, at the time of trial, offered only bachelor of arts degrees. A VWIL student seeking to earn an engineering degree could gain one, without public support, by attending Washington University in St. Louis, Missouri, for two years, paying the required private tuition.

[A] Task Force charged with designing the VWIL program . . . determined that a military model would be "wholly inappropriate" for VWIL. . . . In lieu of VMI's adversative method, the VWIL Task Force favored "a cooperative method which reinforces self-esteem." [S]tudents would take courses in leadership, complete an off-campus leadership externship, participate in community service projects, and assist in arranging a speaker series. . . .

D

[The district court approved Virginia's plan, holding that the two schools would "achieve substantially similar outcomes": "If VMI marches to the beat of a drum, then Mary Baldwin marches to the melody of a fife and when the march is over, both will have arrived at the same destination." The Court of Appeals affirmed.] . . .

IV.

We note, once again, the core instruction of this Court's pathmarking decisions in J.E.B. v. Alabama ex rel. T. B., 511 U.S. 127 (1994), and Mississippi Univ. for Women, 458 U.S. [718 (1982)]: Parties who seek to defend gender-based government action must demonstrate an "exceedingly persuasive justification" for that action. . . .

Today's skeptical scrutiny of official action denying rights or opportunities based on sex responds to volumes of history. As a plurality of this Court acknowledged a generation ago, "our Nation has had a long and unfortunate history of sex discrimination." Frontiero v. Richardson, 411 U.S. 677 (1973). Through a century plus three decades and more of that history, women did not count among voters composing "We the People";[a] not until 1920 did women gain a constitutional right

---

a. As Thomas Jefferson stated the view prevailing when the Constitution was new, "Were our State a pure democracy . . . there would yet be excluded from their deliberations . . . women, who, to prevent depravation of morals and ambiguity of issue, should not mix promiscuously in the public meetings of men."

to the franchise. And for a half century thereafter, it remained the prevailing doctrine that government, both federal and state, could withhold from women opportunities accorded men so long as any "basis in reason" could be conceived for the discrimination.

In 1971, for the first time in our Nation's history, this Court ruled in favor of a woman who complained that her State had denied her the equal protection of its laws. Reed v. Reed, 404 U.S. 71 (1971). Since *Reed*, the Court has repeatedly recognized that neither federal nor state government acts compatibly with the equal protection principle when a law or official policy denies to women, simply because they are women, full citizenship stature — equal opportunity to aspire, achieve, participate in, and contribute to society based on their individual talents and capacities.

Without equating gender classifications, for all purposes, to classifications based on race or national origin, the Court, in post-*Reed* decisions, has carefully inspected official action that closes a door or denies opportunity to women (or to men). To summarize the Court's current directions for cases of official classification based on gender: Focusing on the differential treatment or denial of opportunity for which relief is sought, the reviewing court must determine whether the proffered justification is "exceedingly persuasive." The burden of justification is demanding and it rests entirely on the State. The State must show "at least that the [challenged] classification serves 'important governmental objectives and that the discriminatory means employed' are 'substantially related to the achievement of those objectives.' " The justification must be genuine, not hypothesized or invented post hoc in response to litigation. And it must not rely on overbroad generalizations about the different talents, capacities, or preferences of males and females.

The heightened review standard our precedent establishes does not make sex a proscribed classification. Supposed "inherent differences" are no longer accepted as a ground for race or national origin classifications. See Loving v. Virginia, 388 U.S. 1 (1967). Physical differences between men and women, however, are enduring: "[T]he two sexes are not fungible; a community made up exclusively of one [sex] is different from a community composed of both." Ballard v. United States, 329 U.S. 187 (1946).

"Inherent differences" between men and women, we have come to appreciate, remain cause for celebration, but not for denigration of the members of either sex or for artificial constraints on an individual's opportunity. Sex classifications may be used to compensate women "for particular economic disabilities [they have] suffered," to "promot[e] equal employment opportunity," to advance full development of the talent and capacities of our Nation's people.[b] But such classifications may not be used, as they once were, to create or perpetuate the legal, social, and economic inferiority of women.

---

b. Several amici have urged that diversity in educational opportunities is an altogether appropriate governmental pursuit and that single-sex schools can contribute importantly to such diversity. Indeed, it is the mission of some single-sex schools "to dissipate, rather than perpetuate, traditional gender classifications." We do not question the State's prerogative evenhandedly to support diverse educational opportunities. We address specifically and only an educational opportunity recognized by the District Court and the Court of Appeals as "unique," an opportunity available only at Virginia's premier military institute, the State's sole single-sex public university or college. Cf. Mississippi Univ. for Women v. Hogan ("Mississippi maintains no other single-sex public university or college. Thus, we are not faced with the question of whether States can provide 'separate but equal' undergraduate institutions for males and females.").

[W]e conclude that Virginia has shown no "exceedingly persuasive justification" for excluding all women from the citizen-soldier training afforded by VMI. . . . Because the remedy proffered by Virginia — the Mary Baldwin VWIL program — does not cure the constitutional violation, i.e., it does not provide equal opportunity, we reverse the Fourth Circuit's final judgment in this case.

V.

Virginia . . . asserts two justifications in defense of VMI's exclusion of women. First, the Commonwealth contends, "single-sex education provides important educational benefits," and the option of single-sex education contributes to "diversity in educational approaches." Second, the Commonwealth argues, "the unique VMI method of character development and leadership training," the school's adversative approach, would have to be modified were VMI to admit women. . . .

A

Single-sex education affords pedagogical benefits to at least some students, Virginia emphasizes, and that reality is uncontested in this litigation.[c] Similarly, it is not disputed that diversity among public educational institutions can serve the public good. But Virginia has not shown that VMI was established, or has been maintained, with a view to diversifying, by its categorical exclusion of women, educational opportunities within the State. In cases of this genre, our precedent instructs that "benign" justifications proffered in defense of categorical exclusions will not be accepted automatically; a tenable justification must describe actual state purposes, not rationalizations for actions in fact differently grounded. . . .

Neither recent nor distant history bears out Virginia's alleged pursuit of diversity through single-sex educational options. In 1839, when the State established VMI, a range of educational opportunities for men and women was scarcely contemplated. Higher education at the time was considered dangerous for women;[d] reflecting

---

c. On this point, the dissent sees fire where there is no flame. "Both men and women can benefit from a single-sex education," the District Court recognized, although "the beneficial effects" of such education, . . . apparently "are stronger among women than among men." The United States does not challenge that recognition. Cf. C. Jencks & D. Riesman, The Academic Revolution 297-298 (1968):

> The pluralistic argument for preserving all-male colleges is uncomfortably similar to the pluralistic argument for preserving all-white colleges. . . . The all-male college would be relatively easy to defend if it emerged from a world in which women were established as fully equal to men. But it does not. It is therefore likely to be a witting or unwitting device for preserving tacit assumptions of male superiority — assumptions for which women must eventually pay.

d. Dr. Edward H. Clarke of Harvard Medical School, whose influential book, Sex in Education, went through 17 editions, was perhaps the most well-known speaker from the medical community opposing higher education for women. He maintained that the physiological effects of hard study and academic competition with boys would interfere with the development of girls' reproductive organs. [S]ee also H. Maudsley, Sex in Mind and in Education 17 (1874) ("It is not that girls have not ambition, nor that they fail generally to run the intellectual race [in coeducational settings], but it is asserted that they do it at a cost to their strength and health which entails life-long suffering, and even incapacitates them for the adequate performance of the natural functions of their sex."); C. Meigs, Females and Their Diseases 350 (1848) (after five or six weeks of "mental and educational discipline," a healthy woman would "lose . . . the habit of menstruation" and suffer numerous ills as a result of depriving her body for the sake of her mind).

widely held views about women's proper place, the Nation's first universities and colleges — for example, Harvard in Massachusetts, William and Mary in Virginia — admitted only men. VMI was not at all novel in this respect: In admitting no women, VMI followed the lead of the State's flagship school, the University of Virginia, founded in 1819.

"[N]o struggle for the admission of women to a state university," a historian has recounted, "was longer drawn out, or developed more bitterness, than that at the University of Virginia." . . . Familiar arguments were rehearsed. If women were admitted, it was feared, they "would encroach on the rights of men; there would be new problems of government, perhaps scandals; the old honor system would have to be changed; standards would be lowered to those of other coeducational schools; and the glorious reputation of the university, as a school for men, would be trailed in the dust."

Ultimately, in 1970, "the most prestigious institution of higher education in Virginia," the University of Virginia, introduced coeducation and, in 1972, began to admit women on an equal basis with men. . . .

Virginia describes the current absence of public single-sex higher education for women as "an historical anomaly." But the historical record indicates action more deliberate than anomalous: First, protection of women against higher education; next, schools for women far from equal in resources and stature to schools for men; finally, conversion of the separate schools to coeducation. The state legislature, prior to the advent of this controversy, had repealed "[a]ll Virginia statutes requiring individual institutions to admit only men or women." And in 1990, an official commission, "legislatively established to chart the future goals of higher education in Virginia," reaffirmed the policy "of affording broad access" while maintaining "autonomy and diversity." Significantly, the Commission reported:

> Because colleges and universities provide opportunities for students to develop values and learn from role models, it is extremely important that they deal with faculty, staff, and students without regard to sex, race, or ethnic origin.

This statement, the Court of Appeals observed, "is the only explicit one that we have found in the record in which the Commonwealth has expressed itself with respect to gender distinctions."

Our 1982 decision in *Mississippi Univ. for Women* prompted VMI to reexamine its male-only admission policy. . . . A Mission Study Committee, appointed by the VMI Board of Visitors, studied the problem from October 1983 until May 1986, and in that month counseled against "change of VMI status as a single-sex college." [W]e can hardly extract from that effort any state policy evenhandedly to advance diverse educational options. As the District Court observed, the Committee's analysis "primarily focuse[d] on anticipated difficulties in attracting females to VMI," and the report, overall, supplied "very little indication of how th[e] conclusion was reached."

In sum, we find no persuasive evidence in this record that VMI's male-only admission policy "is in furtherance of a state policy of 'diversity.'" No such policy, the Fourth Circuit observed, can be discerned from the movement of all other public colleges and universities in Virginia away from single-sex education. [It] also questioned "how one institution with autonomy, but with no authority over any other state institution, can give effect to a state policy of diversity among institutions." A purpose genuinely to advance an array of educational options . . . is not served by VMI's historic and constant plan — a plan to "affor[d] a unique educational benefit only to males." However "liberally" this plan serves the State's sons, it makes no provision whatever for her daughters. That is not equal protection.

B

Virginia next argues that VMI's adversative method of training provides educational benefits that cannot be made available, unmodified, to women. Alterations to accommodate women would necessarily be "radical," so "drastic," Virginia asserts, as to transform, indeed "destroy," VMI's program. Neither sex would be favored by the transformation, Virginia maintains: Men would be deprived of the unique opportunity currently available to them; women would not gain that opportunity because their participation would "eliminat[e] the very aspects of [the] program that distinguish [VMI] from . . . other institutions of higher education in Virginia."

[I]t is uncontested that women's admission would require accommodations, primarily in arranging housing assignments and physical training programs for female cadets. It is also undisputed, however, that "the VMI methodology could be used to educate women." The District Court even allowed that some women may prefer it to the methodology a women's college might pursue. "[S]ome women, at least, would want to attend [VMI] if they had the opportunity," the District Court recognized, and "some women," the expert testimony established, "are capable of all of the individual activities required of VMI cadets." The parties, furthermore, agree that "some women can meet the physical standards [VMI] now impose[s] on men." In sum, as the Court of Appeals stated, "neither the goal of producing citizen soldiers," VMI's raison d'etre, "nor VMI's implementing methodology is inherently unsuitable to women."

In support of its initial judgment for Virginia . . . the District Court made "findings" on "gender-based developmental differences." These "findings" restate the opinions of Virginia's expert witnesses, opinions about typically male or typically female "tendencies." For example, "[m]ales tend to need an atmosphere of adversativeness," while "[f]emales tend to thrive in a cooperative atmosphere." "I'm not saying that some women don't do well under [the] adversative model," VMI's expert on educational institutions testified, "undoubtedly there are some [women] who do"; but educational experiences must be designed "around the rule," this expert maintained, and not "around the exception."

The United States does not challenge any expert witness estimation on average capacities or preferences of men and women. Instead, the United States emphasizes that time and again since this Court's turning point decision in Reed v. Reed, we have cautioned reviewing courts to take a "hard look" at generalizations or "tendencies" of the kind pressed by Virginia, and relied upon by the District Court. State actors controlling gates to opportunity, we have instructed, may not exclude qualified individuals based on "fixed notions concerning the roles and abilities of males and females." *Mississippi Univ. for Women*; see J.E.B., 511 U.S., at 139, n.11 (equal protection principles, as applied to gender classifications, mean state actors may not rely on "overbroad" generalizations to make "judgments about people that are likely to . . . perpetuate historical patterns of discrimination").

It may be assumed . . . that most women would not choose VMI's adversative method. [I]t is also probable that "many men would not want to be educated in such an environment." . . . The issue, however, is not whether "women — or men — should be forced to attend VMI"; rather, the question is whether the State can constitutionally deny to women who have the will and capacity, the training and attendant opportunities that VMI uniquely affords.

The notion that admission of women would downgrade VMI's stature, destroy the adversative system and, with it, even the school,[e] is a judgment hardly proved, a prediction hardly different from other "self-fulfilling prophec[ies]," once routinely used to deny rights or opportunities. When women first sought admission to the bar and access to legal education, concerns of the same order were expressed. For example, in 1876, the Court of Common Pleas of Hennepin County, Minnesota, explained why women were thought ineligible for the practice of law. Women train and educate the young, the court said, which

> forbids that they shall bestow that time (early and late) and labor, so essential in attaining to the eminence to which the true lawyer should ever aspire. It cannot therefore be said that the opposition of courts to the admission of females to practice . . . is to any extent the outgrowth of . . . "old fogyism[.]" . . . [I]t arises rather from a comprehension of the magnitude of the responsibilities connected with the successful practice of law, and a desire to grade up the profession.

A like fear, according to a 1925 report, accounted for Columbia Law School's resistance to women's admission, although

> [t]he faculty . . . never maintained that women could not master legal learning. . . . No, its argument has been . . . more practical. If women were admitted to the Columbia Law School, [the faculty] said, then the choicer, more manly and red-blooded graduates of our great universities would go to the Harvard Law School!

Medical faculties similarly resisted men and women as partners in the study of medicine. More recently, women seeking careers in policing encountered resistance based on fears that their presence would "undermine male solidarity," deprive male partners of adequate assistance, and lead to sexual misconduct. Field studies did not confirm these fears.

Women's successful entry into the federal military academies, and their participation in the Nation's military forces, indicate that Virginia's fears for the future of VMI may not be solidly grounded. The State's justification for excluding all women from "citizen-soldier" training for which some are qualified, in any event, cannot rank as "exceedingly persuasive," as we have explained and applied that standard.

Virginia and VMI trained their argument on "means" rather than "end," and thus misperceived our precedent. Single-sex education at VMI serves an "important governmental objective," they maintained, and exclusion of women is not only "substantially related," it is essential to that objective. By this notably circular argument, the "straightforward" test *Mississippi Univ. for Women* described was bent and bowed.

The State's misunderstanding and, in turn, the District Court's, is apparent from VMI's mission: to produce "citizen-soldiers" individuals "imbued with love of

---

e. Forecasts of the same kind were made regarding admission of women to the federal military academies.

learning, confident in the functions and attitudes of leadership, possessing a high sense of public service, advocates of the American democracy and free enterprise system, and ready . . . to defend their country in time of national peril."

Surely that goal is great enough to accommodate women, who today count as citizens in our American democracy equal in stature to men. Just as surely, the State's great goal is not substantially advanced by women's categorical exclusion, in total disregard of their individual merit, from the State's premier "citizen-soldier" corps.[f] Virginia, in sum, "has fallen far short of establishing the 'exceedingly persuasive justification,'" that must be the solid base for any gender-defined classification.

VI.

A

. . . Having violated the Constitution's equal protection requirement, Virginia was obliged to show that its remedial proposal "directly address[ed] and relate[d] to" the violation, i.e., the equal protection denied to women ready, willing, and able to benefit from educational opportunities of the kind VMI offers. . . . VWIL affords women no opportunity to experience the rigorous military training for which VMI is famed. . . . Instead, the VWIL program "deemphasize[s]" military education, and uses a "cooperative method" of education "which reinforces self-esteem."

VWIL students participate in ROTC and a "largely ceremonial" Virginia Corps of Cadets, but Virginia deliberately did not make VWIL a military institute. The VWIL House is not a military-style residence and VWIL students need not live together throughout the 4-year program, eat meals together, or wear uniforms during the school day. VWIL students thus do not experience the "barracks" life "crucial to the VMI experience," the spartan living arrangements designed to foster an "egalitarian ethic." "[T]he most important aspects of the VMI educational experience occur in the barracks," the District Court found, yet Virginia deemed that core experience nonessential, indeed inappropriate, for training its female citizen-soldiers.

VWIL students receive their "leadership training" in seminars, externships, and speaker series, episodes and encounters lacking the "[p]hysical rigor, mental stress, . . . minute regulation of behavior, and indoctrination in desirable values" made hallmarks of VMI's citizen-soldier training. Kept away from the pressures, hazards, and psychological bonding characteristic of VMI's adversative training, VWIL students will not know the "feeling of tremendous accomplishment" commonly experienced by VMI's successful cadets.

Virginia maintains that these methodological differences are "justified pedagogically," based on "important differences between men and women in learning and developmental needs," "psychological and sociological differences" Virginia describes as "real" and "not stereotypes." The Task Force charged with developing

---

f. VMI has successfully managed another notable change. The school admitted its first African-American cadets in 1968. See The VMI Story 347-349 (students no longer sing "Dixie," salute the Confederate flag or the tomb of General Robert E. Lee at ceremonies and sports events). . . . VMI established a Program on "retention of black cadets" designed to offer academic and social-cultural support to "minority members of a dominantly white and tradition-oriented student body." The school maintains a "special recruitment program for blacks" which, the District Court found, "has had little, if any, effect on VMI's method of accomplishing its mission."

the leadership program for women, drawn from the staff and faculty at Mary Baldwin College, "determined that a military model and, especially VMI's adversative method, would be wholly inappropriate for educating and training most women." . . .

[G]eneralizations about "the way women are," estimates of what is appropriate for most women, no longer justify denying opportunity to women whose talent and capacity place them outside the average description. Notably, Virginia never asserted that VMI's method of education suits most men. It is also revealing that Virginia accounted for its failure to make the VWIL experience "the entirely militaristic experience of VMI" on the ground that VWIL "is planned for women who do not necessarily expect to pursue military careers." By that reasoning, VMI's "entirely militaristic" program would be inappropriate for men in general or as a group, for "[o]nly about 15% of VMI cadets enter career military service." . . .[g]

B

In myriad respects other than military training, VWIL does not qualify as VMI's equal. VWIL's student body, faculty, course offerings, and facilities hardly match VMI's. Nor can the VWIL graduate anticipate the benefits associated with VMI's 157-year history, the school's prestige, and its influential alumni network. . . . [T]he difference between the two schools' financial reserves is pronounced. Mary Baldwin's endowment, currently about $19 million, will gain an additional $35 million based on future commitments; VMI's current endowment, $131 million — the largest per-student endowment in the Nation — will gain $220 million.

The VWIL student does not graduate with the advantage of a VMI degree. Her diploma does not unite her with the legions of VMI "graduates [who] have distinguished themselves" in military and civilian life. . . . A VWIL graduate cannot assume that the "network of business owners, corporations, VMI graduates and non-graduate employers . . . interested in hiring VMI graduates," will be equally responsive to her search for employment. . . . Virginia's VWIL solution is reminiscent of the remedy Texas proposed 50 years ago, in response to a state trial court's 1946 ruling that, given the equal protection guarantee, African Americans could not be denied a legal education at a state facility. See Sweatt v. Painter, 339 U.S. 629 (1950). Reluctant to admit African Americans to its flagship University of Texas Law School, the State set up a separate school for Herman Sweatt and other black law students. As originally opened, the new school had no independent faculty or library, and it lacked accreditation. . . .

More important than the tangible features, the Court emphasized, are "those qualities which are incapable of objective measurement but which make for

---

g. Admitting women to VMI would undoubtedly require alterations necessary to afford members of each sex privacy from the other sex in living arrangements, and to adjust aspects of the physical training programs. Cf. note following 10 U.S.C. §4342 (academic and other standards for women admitted to the Military, Naval, and Air Force Academies "shall be the same as those required for male individuals, except for those minimum essential adjustments in such standards required because of physiological differences between male and female individuals"). Experience shows such adjustments are manageable. See U.S. Military Academy, A. Vitters, N. Kinzer, and J. Adams, Report of Admission of Women (Project Athena I-IV) (1977-1980) (4-year longitudinal study of the admission of women to West Point); Defense Advisory Committee on Women in the Services, Report on the Integration and Performance of Women at West Point 17-18 (1992).

greatness" in a school, including "reputation of the faculty, experience of the administration, position and influence of the alumni, standing in the community, traditions and prestige." Facing the marked differences reported in the Sweatt opinion, the Court unanimously ruled that Texas had not shown "substantial equality in the [separate] educational opportunities" the State offered. Accordingly, the Court held, the Equal Protection Clause required Texas to admit African Americans to the University of Texas Law School. In line with Sweatt, we rule here that Virginia has not shown substantial equality in the separate educational opportunities the State supports at VWIL and VMI.

VII.

. . . . A prime part of the history of our Constitution, historian Richard Morris recounted, is the story of the extension of constitutional rights and protections to people once ignored or excluded. VMI's story continued as our comprehension of "We the People" expanded. There is no reason to believe that the admission of women capable of all the activities required of VMI cadets would destroy the Institute rather than enhance its capacity to serve the "more perfect Union." . . .

Justice THOMAS took no part in the consideration or decision of this case.

Chief Justice REHNQUIST, concurring in judgment.

I.

. . . While the majority adheres to the test [of Craig v. Boren] today, it also says that the State must demonstrate an "exceedingly persuasive justification" to support a gender-based classification. It is unfortunate that the Court thereby introduces an element of uncertainty respecting the appropriate test.

While terms like "important governmental objective" and "substantially related" are hardly models of precision, they have more content and specificity than does the phrase "exceedingly persuasive justification." That phrase is best confined, as it was first used, as an observation on the difficulty of meeting the applicable test, not as a formulation of the test itself. See, e.g., [Massachusetts v.] Feeney, at 273 ("[T]hese precedents dictate that any state law overtly or covertly designed to prefer males over females in public employment require an exceedingly persuasive justification"). . . .

Our cases dealing with gender discrimination also require that the proffered purpose for the challenged law be the actual purpose. It is on this ground that the Court rejects the first of two justifications Virginia offers for VMI's single-sex admissions policy, namely, the goal of diversity among its public educational institutions. While I ultimately agree that the State has not carried the day with this justification, I disagree with the Court's method of analyzing the issue.

VMI was founded in 1839, and, as the Court notes, admission was limited to men because under the then-prevailing view men, not women, were destined for higher education. However misguided this point of view may be by present-day standards, it surely was not unconstitutional in 1839. The adoption of the Fourteenth Amendment, with its Equal Protection Clause, was nearly 30 years in the future. The interpretation of the Equal Protection Clause to require heightened scrutiny for gender discrimination was yet another century away.

Long after the adoption of the Fourteenth Amendment, and well into this century, legal distinctions between men and women were thought to raise no question under the Equal Protection Clause. . . . Even at the time of our decision in Reed v. Reed, . . . Virginia and VMI were scarcely on notice that its holding would be extended across the constitutional board. They were entitled to believe that "one swallow doesn't make a summer" and await further developments. Those developments were 11 years in coming. In Mississippi Univ. for Women v. Hogan, a case actually involving a single-sex admissions policy in higher education, the Court held that the exclusion of men from a nursing program violated the Equal Protection Clause. This holding did place Virginia on notice that VMI's men-only admissions policy was open to serious question. . . .

I agree with the Court that there is scant evidence in the record that [educational diversity] was the real reason that Virginia decided to maintain VMI as men only. But, unlike the majority, I would consider only evidence that postdates our decision in *Hogan*, and would draw no negative inferences from the State's actions before that time. I think that after *Hogan*, the State was entitled to reconsider its policy with respect to VMI, and to not have earlier justifications, or lack thereof, held against it.

Even if diversity in educational opportunity were the State's actual objective, . . . the diversity benefited only one sex; there was single-sex public education available for men at VMI, but no corresponding single-sex public education available for women. When *Hogan* placed Virginia on notice that VMI's admissions policy possibly was unconstitutional, VMI could have dealt with the problem by admitting women; but its governing body felt strongly that the admission of women would have seriously harmed the institution's educational approach. Was there something else the State could have done to avoid an equal protection violation? Since the State did nothing, we do not have to definitively answer that question. . . .

Had the State provided the kind of support for the private women's schools that it provides for VMI, this may have been a very different case. For in so doing, the State would have demonstrated that its interest in providing a single-sex education for men was to some measure matched by an interest in providing the same opportunity for women.

Virginia offers a second justification for the single-sex admissions policy: maintenance of the adversative method. I agree with the Court that this justification does not serve an important governmental objective. A State does not have substantial interest in the adversative methodology unless it is pedagogically beneficial. While considerable evidence shows that a single-sex education is pedagogically beneficial for some students, and hence a State may have a valid interest in promoting that methodology, there is no similar evidence in the record that an adversative method is pedagogically beneficial or is any more likely to produce character traits than other methodologies.

II.

The Court defines the constitutional violation in this case as "the categorical exclusion of women from an extraordinary educational opportunity afforded to men." By defining the violation in this way, and by emphasizing that a remedy for a constitutional violation must place the victims of discrimination in "the position they would have occupied in the absence of [discrimination]," the Court necessarily implies that the only adequate remedy would be the admission of women to the all-male institution. As the foregoing discussion suggests, I would not define the violation in this way; it is not the "exclusion of women" that violates the Equal Protection Clause, but the maintenance of an all-men's school without providing any — much less a comparable — institution for women.

Accordingly, the remedy should not necessarily require either the admission of women to VMI, or the creation of a VMI clone for women. An adequate remedy in my opinion might be a demonstration by Virginia that its interest in educating men in a single-sex environment is matched by its interest in educating women in a single-sex institution. To demonstrate such, the State does not need to create two institutions with the same number of faculty PhD's, similar SAT scores, or comparable athletic fields. Nor would it necessarily require that the women's institution offer the same curriculum as the men's; one could be strong in computer science, the other could be strong in liberal arts. It would be a sufficient remedy, I think, if the two institutions offered the same quality of education and were of the same overall calibre. . . .

Justice SCALIA, dissenting.

Today the Court shuts down an institution that has served the people of the Commonwealth of Virginia with pride and distinction for over a century and a half. To achieve that desired result, it rejects (contrary to our established practice) the factual findings of two courts below, sweeps aside the precedents of this Court, and ignores the history of our people. As to facts: it explicitly rejects the finding that there exist "gender-based developmental differences" supporting Virginia's restriction of the "adversative" method to only a men's institution, and the finding that the all-male composition of the Virginia Military Institute (VMI) is essential to that institution's character. As to precedent: it drastically revises our established standards for reviewing sex-based classifications. And as to history: it counts for nothing the long tradition, enduring down to the present, of men's military colleges supported by both States and the Federal Government.

Much of the Court's opinion is devoted to deprecating the closed-mindedness of our forebears with regard to women's education, and even with regard to the treatment of women in areas that have nothing to do with education. Closed-minded they were — as every age is, including our own, with regard to matters it cannot guess, because it simply does not consider them debatable. The virtue of a democratic system with a First Amendment is that it readily enables the people, over time, to be persuaded that what they took for granted is not so, and to change their laws accordingly. That system is destroyed if the smug assurances of each age are removed from the democratic process and written into the Constitution. So to counterbalance the Court's criticism of our ancestors, let me say a word in their praise: they left us free to change. The same cannot be said of this most illiberal Court, which has embarked on a course of inscribing one after another of the current preferences of the society (and in some cases only the counter-majoritarian preferences of the society's law-trained elite) into our Basic Law. Today it enshrines the notion that no substantial educational value is to be served by an all-men's military academy — so that the decision by the people of Virginia to maintain such an institution denies equal protection to women who cannot attend that institution but can attend others. Since it is entirely clear that the Constitution of the United States — the old one — takes no sides in this educational debate, I dissent.

I.

. . . I have no problem with a system of abstract tests such as rational-basis, intermediate, and strict scrutiny (though I think we can do better than applying strict
scrutiny and intermediate scrutiny whenever we feel like it). Such formulas are
essential to evaluating whether the new restrictions that a changing society
constantly imposes upon private conduct comport with that "equal protection" our
society has always accorded in the past. But in my view the function of this Court is
to preserve our society's values regarding (among other things) equal protection,
not to revise them; to prevent backsliding from the degree of restriction the
Constitution imposed upon democratic government, not to prescribe, on our own
authority, progressively higher degrees. For that reason it is my view that, whatever
abstract tests we may choose to devise, they cannot supersede — and indeed ought
to be crafted so as to reflect — those constant and unbroken national traditions
that embody the people's understanding of ambiguous constitutional texts. More
specifically, it is my view that "when a practice not expressly prohibited by the text
of the Bill of Rights bears the endorsement of a long tradition of open, widespread,
and unchallenged use that dates back to the beginning of the Republic, we have no
proper basis for striking it down." The same applies, mutatis mutandis, to a practice
asserted to be in violation of the post-Civil War Fourteenth Amendment.

The all-male constitution of VMI comes squarely within such a governing tradition. Founded by the Commonwealth of Virginia in 1839 and continuously maintained by it since, VMI has always admitted only men. And in that regard it has
not been unusual. For almost all of VMI's more than a century and a half of existence, its single-sex status reflected the uniform practice for government-
supported military colleges. Another famous Southern institution, The Citadel,
has existed as a state-funded school of South Carolina since 1842. And all the
federal military colleges — West Point, the Naval Academy at Annapolis, and even
the Air Force Academy, which was not established until 1954 — admitted only
males for most of their history. Their admission of women in 1976 came not by
court decree, but because the people, through their elected representatives,
decreed a change. In other words, the tradition of having government-funded
military schools for men is as well rooted in the traditions of this country as the
tradition of sending only men into military combat. The people may decide to
change the one tradition, like the other, through democratic processes; but the
assertion that either tradition has been unconstitutional through the centuries is
not law, but politics-smuggled-into-law.

And the same applies, more broadly, to single-sex education in general, which,
as I shall discuss, is threatened by today's decision with the cut-off of all state and
federal support. Government-run nonmilitary educational institutions for the two
sexes have until very recently also been part of our national tradition. "[It is]
[c]oeducation, historically, [that] is a novel educational theory. From grade school
through high school, college, and graduate and professional training, much of the
Nation's population during much of our history has been educated in sexually
segregated classrooms." These traditions may of course be changed by the democratic decisions of the people, as they largely have been.

Today, however, change is forced upon Virginia, and reversion to single-sex
education is prohibited nationwide, not by democratic processes but by order of
this Court. Even while bemoaning the sorry, bygone days of "fixed notions"
concerning women's education, the Court favors current notions so fixedly that it is

willing to write them into the Constitution of the United States by application of custom-built "tests." This is not the interpretation of a Constitution, but the creation of one.

II.

[T]he United States urged us to hold in this case "that strict scrutiny is the correct constitutional standard for evaluating classifications that deny opportunities to individuals based on their sex." . . . The Court, while making no reference to the Government's argument, effectively accepts it. . . .

Only the amorphous "exceedingly persuasive justification" phrase, and not the standard elaboration of intermediate scrutiny, can be made to yield [the] conclusion that VMI's single-sex composition is unconstitutional because there exist several women (or, one would have to conclude under the Court's reasoning, a single woman) willing and able to undertake VMI's program. Intermediate scrutiny has never required a least-restrictive-means analysis, but only a "substantial relation" between the classification and the state interests that it serves [and] not a perfect fit. . . .

[I]t is perfectly clear that, if the question of the applicable standard of review for sex-based classifications were to be regarded as an appropriate subject for reconsideration, the stronger argument would be not for elevating the standard to strict scrutiny, but for reducing it to rational-basis review. The latter certainly has a firmer foundation in our past jurisprudence: Whereas no majority of the Court has ever applied strict scrutiny in a case involving sex-based classifications, we routinely applied rational-basis review until the 1970s, see, e.g., Hoyt v. Florida, 368 U.S. 57 (1961); Goesaert v. Cleary, 335 U.S. 464 (1948). And of course normal, rational-basis review of sex-based classifications would be much more in accord with the genesis of heightened standards of judicial review, the famous footnote in United States v. Carolene Products Co., 304 U.S. 144, [152-53, n.4] (1938). . . .

It is hard to consider women a "discrete and insular minorit[y]" unable to employ the "political processes ordinarily to be relied upon," when they constitute a majority of the electorate. And the suggestion that they are incapable of exerting that political power smacks of the same paternalism that the Court so roundly condemns. Moreover, a long list of legislation proves the proposition false. See, e.g., Equal Pay Act of 1963; Title VII of the Civil Rights Act of 1964; Title IX of the Education Amendments of 1972; Women's Business Ownership Act of 1988; Violence Against Women Act of 1994.

III. . . .

A

It is beyond question that Virginia has an important state interest in providing effective college education for its citizens. That single-sex instruction is an approach substantially related to that interest should be evident enough from the long and continuing history in this country of men's and women's colleges. But beyond that, as the Court of Appeals here stated: "That single-gender education at the college level is beneficial to both sexes is a fact established in this case." The evidence establishing that fact was overwhelming — indeed, "virtually uncontradicted." . . . For example, the District Court [quoted an empirical study finding that] "[s]tudents of both sexes become more academically involved, interact with faculty frequently, show larger increases in intellectual self-esteem and are more satisfied with practically all aspects of college experience (the sole exception is social life) [in single-sex colleges] compared with their counterparts in coeducational institutions. Attendance at an all-male college substantially increases the likelihood that a student will carry out career plans in law, business and college teaching, and also has a substantial positive effect on starting salaries in business. Women's colleges increase the chances that those who attend will obtain positions of leadership, complete the baccalaureate degree, and aspire to higher degrees." . . . This finding alone, which even this Court cannot dispute, should be sufficient to demonstrate the constitutionality of VMI's all-male composition. . . .

. . . As a theoretical matter, Virginia's educational interest would have been best served . . . by six different types of public colleges — an all-men's, an all-women's, and a coeducational college run in the "adversative method," and an all-men's, an all-women's, and a coeducational college run in the "traditional method." But as a practical matter, of course, Virginia's financial resources, like any State's, are not limitless, and the Commonwealth must select among the available options. Virginia thus has decided to fund, in addition to some 14 coeducational 4-year colleges, one college that is run as an all-male school on the adversative model: the Virginia Military Institute. [Moreover, while] there are "four all-female private [colleges] in Virginia," there is only "one private all-male college," which "indicates that the private sector is providing for th[e] [former] form of education to a much greater extent than it provides for all-male education." In these circumstances, Virginia's election to fund one public all-male institution and one on the adversative model — and to concentrate its resources in a single entity that serves both these interests in diversity — is substantially related to the State's important educational interests.

B

The Court argues that VMI would not have to change very much if it were to admit women. . . . [However] [t]he District Court found [that] "key elements of the adversative VMI educational system, with its focus on barracks life, would be fundamentally altered, and the distinctive ends of the system would be thwarted, if VMI were forced to admit females and to make changes necessary to accommodate their needs and interests." Changes . . . that . . . would be required include new allowances for personal privacy in the barracks, such as locked doors and coverings on windows, which would detract from VMI's approach of regulating minute details of student behavior, "contradict the principle that everyone is constantly subject to scrutiny by everyone else," and impair VMI's "total egalitarian approach" under which every student must be "treated alike"; changes in the physical training program, which would reduce "[t]he intensity and aggressiveness of the current program"; and various modifications in other respects of the adversative training program which permeates student life. . . .

Finally, the absence of a precise "all-women's analogue" to VMI is irrelevant. In Mississippi Univ. for Women v. Hogan, we attached no constitutional significance to the absence of an all-male nursing school. . . .

IV. . . .

A

Under the constitutional principles announced and applied today, single-sex public education is unconstitutional. . . . [T]he rationale of today's decision is sweeping: for sex-based classifications, a redefinition of intermediate scrutiny that makes it indistinguishable from strict scrutiny. Indeed, the Court indicates that if any program restricted to one sex is "uniqu[e]," it must be opened to members of the opposite sex "who have the will and capacity" to participate in it. I suggest that the single-sex program that will not be capable of being characterized as "unique" is not only unique but nonexistent.[a]

In any event, regardless of whether the Court's rationale leaves some small amount of room for lawyers to argue, it ensures that single-sex public education is functionally dead. The costs of litigating the constitutionality of a single-sex education program, and the risks of ultimately losing that litigation, are simply too high to be embraced by public officials. . . . No state official in his right mind will buy such a high-cost, high-risk lawsuit by commencing a single-sex program. The enemies of single-sex education have won; by persuading only seven Justices (five would have been enough) that their view of the world is enshrined in the Constitution, they have effectively imposed that view on all 50 States. . . .

B

There are few extant single-sex public educational programs. The potential of today's decision for widespread disruption of existing institutions lies in its application to private single-sex education. Government support is immensely important to private educational institutions. . . . Charitable status under the tax laws is also highly significant for private educational institutions, and it is certainly not beyond the Court that rendered today's decision to hold that a donation to a single-sex college should be deemed contrary to public policy and therefore not deductible if the college discriminates on the basis of sex. . . .

The [future] issue will be not whether government assistance turns private colleges into state actors, but whether the government itself would be violating the Constitution by providing state support to single-sex colleges. For example, in Norwood v. Harrison, 413 U.S. 455 (1973), we saw no room to distinguish between state operation of racially segregated schools and state support of privately run segregated schools. "Racial discrimination in state-operated schools is barred by the Constitution and '[i]t is also axiomatic that a state may not induce, encourage or promote private persons to accomplish what it is constitutionally forbidden to accomplish.'" The only hope for state-assisted single-sex private schools is that the Court will not apply in the future the principles of law it has applied today. . . .

In an odd sort of way, it is precisely VMI's attachment to such old-fashioned concepts as manly "honor" that has made it, and the system it represents, the target

---

a. In this regard, I note that the Court — which I concede is under no obligation to do so — provides no example of a program that would pass muster under its reasoning today: not even, for example, a football or wrestling program. On the Court's theory, any woman ready, willing, and physically able to participate in such a program would, as a constitutional matter, be entitled to do so.

of those who today succeed in abolishing public single-sex education. The record contains a booklet that all first-year VMI students (the so-called "rats") were required to keep in their possession at all times. Near the end there appears the following period-piece, entitled "The Code of a Gentleman":

> Without a strict observance of the fundamental Code of Honor, no man, no matter how "polished," can be considered a gentleman. The honor of a gentleman demands the inviolability of his word, and the incorruptibility of his principles. He is the descendant of the knight, the crusader; he is the defender of the defenseless and the champion of justice . . . or he is not a Gentleman.
>
> A Gentleman . . .
>
> Does not discuss his family affairs in public or with acquaintances.
>
> Does not speak more than casually about his girl friend.
>
> Does not go to a lady's house if he is affected by alcohol. He is temperate in the use of alcohol.
>
> Does not lose his temper; nor exhibit anger, fear, hate, embarrassment, ardor or hilarity in public.
>
> Does not hail a lady from a club window.
>
> A gentleman never discusses the merits or demerits of a lady.
>
> Does not mention names exactly as he avoids the mention of what things cost.
>
> Does not borrow money from a friend, except in dire need. Money borrowed is a debt of honor, and must be repaid as promptly as possible. Debts incurred by a deceased parent, brother, sister or grown child are assumed by honorable men as a debt of honor.
>
> Does not display his wealth, money or possessions.
>
> Does not put his manners on and off, whether in the club or in a ballroom. He treats people with courtesy, no matter what their social position may be.
>
> Does not slap strangers on the back nor so much as lay a finger on a lady.
>
> Does not "lick the boots of those above" nor "kick the face of those below him on the social ladder."
>
> Does not take advantage of another's helplessness or ignorance and assumes that no gentleman will take advantage of him.
>
> A Gentleman respects the reserves of others, but demands that others respect those which are his.
>
> A Gentleman can become what he wills to be. . . .

I do not know whether the men of VMI lived by this Code; perhaps not. But it is powerfully impressive that a public institution of higher education still in existence sought to have them do so. I do not think any of us, women included, will be better off for its destruction.

Discussion

1. *Intermediate scrutiny evolving.* Nearly two decades after its decision in Craig v. Boren, supra, announcing the intermediate scrutiny framework for sex discrimination cases, the *VMI* Court explained the standard of review in considerably more detail. Writing for the Court, Justice Ginsburg observes that a "reviewing court must determine whether the [government's] proffered justification is 'exceedingly persuasive.' The burden of justification is demanding and it rests entirely on the State." She recites the intermediate standard of review (the state must show "that the [challenged] classification serves 'important governmental objectives and that the discriminatory means employed' are 'substantially related

to the achievement of those objectives'") and then goes on to observe that the justification on which the government relies must be "genuine, not hypothesized or invented post hoc in response to litigation." Carrying forward the themes of its 1970s cases, the Court emphasizes that the government cannot justify sex-based state action in terms that "rely on overbroad generalizations about the different talents, capacities, or preferences of males and females." It then explains that the intermediate scrutiny framework will invalidate some forms of sex-based state action and not others, emphasizing that the Fourteenth Amendment proscribes sex-based state action that subordinates women:

> "Inherent differences" between men and women, we have come to appreciate, remain cause for celebration, but not for denigration of the members of either sex or for artificial constraints on an individual's opportunity. Sex classifications may be used to compensate women "for particular economic disabilities [they have] suffered," to "promot[e] equal employment opportunity," to advance full development of the talent and capacities of our Nation's people. But such classifications may not be used, as they once were, to create or perpetuate the legal, social, and economic inferiority of women.

How, if at all, does *VMI* change the intermediate scrutiny standard?

2. *Anticlassification vs. antisubordination.* The anticlassification principle holds that government may not classify people overtly or surreptitiously on the basis of a forbidden category, for example, their race. The antisubordination principle holds that law may not aggravate or perpetuate the subordinate status of a specially disadvantaged group.[80] On what principle does the *VMI* opinion base its interpretation of the Equal Protection Clause — the anticlassification principle or the antisubordination principle? Note that *VMI* proscribes state action that classifies on the basis of sex — but only proscribes those sex-based policies that "denigrat[e] members of either sex" or impose "artificial constraints on an individual's opportunity" or "create or perpetuate the legal, social, and economic inferiority of women."

Is *VMI* properly read as proscribing sex-based state action that violates the antisubordination principle? If so, what forms of sex-based state action does it proscribe?

How might one determine whether a practice subordinates?[81] Commentators observe that practices subordinate by enforcing the social understanding that "members of certain groups, like African-Americans or women, are inferior to the members of other groups, like whites or men" or the social understanding that "members of certain groups are not part of the national or local community" — an

---

80. J. M. Balkin and Reva B. Siegel, The American Antidiscrimination Tradition: Anticlassification or Antisubordination?, 58 U. Miami L. Rev. 9 (2003).

81. See id. at 14-15 (observing that "the question of what practices or utterances or institutional arrangements might be subordinating involves interpretive judgments about social meaning, status, and the like, each of which is plainly contestable" as well as "a host of contestable value judgments . . . in determining what dignitary distinctions or distributive arrangements are unjust, and how the legal system should integrate the pursuit of antisubordination commitments with other social goals").

understanding that "can injure the excluded people's sense of self and sense of belonging." In addition:

> [W]riters in the anti-subordination tradition have . . . argued that practices, institutions, and activities can promote subordination by inflicting dignitary harms on the members of targeted groups. In this case, concern centers on practices that treat the members of disfavored classes as unworthy of equal respect and dignity and instead subject them to humiliation, stigmatization, denigration, and degradation.
>
> Finally, and most concretely, anti-subordination writers argue that practices, institutions, and activities can foster subordination by inflicting a wide variety of material harms on the members of targeted populations. Speaking generally, these writers have identified two, connected categories of material harm. The first . . . focuses on classic indicators of socioeconomic status and social welfare, explaining that practices cause subordinating material harm when they systematically leave the members of targeted groups with less wealth, less political power, less protection from private or public violence, less education, less health, less life expectancy, less access to housing, and/or less leisure. The second focuses on control and autonomy, explaining that practices cause subordinating material harm when they systematically leave the members of targeted groups with less control or power over their own lives and more subject to the control and direction of another person or the state.[82]

What guidance, if any, does the antisubordination principle supply in explaining the equal protection violation in United States v. Virginia, and in demonstrating how it is to be remedied?

a. What factors does the Court emphasize in declaring Virginia's single-sex school unconstitutional?

b. After the school admits women, can it take sex into account in matters of pedagogy or otherwise? Must it house men and women together? What does it mean to subject men and women "equally" to the adversative method? Can the school require men and women to do the same number of push-ups in daily exercises? Why or why not?

c. If administrators wish to run a single-sex school, how must they design their offering to conform with the *VMI* opinion? For one account, see Denise C. Morgan, Anti-Subordination Analysis After United States v. Virginia: Evaluating the Constitutionality of K-12 Single-Sex Public Schools, 1999 U. Chi. Legal F. 381 (1999).

3. *The uses of history.* What role does historical evidence play in guiding judgments about VMI's policy? Justice Ginsburg's opinion spends a great deal of time describing the history of women's exclusion from educational institutions in the United States. Chief Justice Rehnquist thinks this discussion largely irrelevant; for him the question is what Virginia did after the Supreme Court's decision in Mississippi University for Women v. Hogan, infra, which suggested for the first time that there might be a constitutional problem with single-sex educational institutions. Until

---

82. Jill Elaine Hasday, The Principle and Practice of Women's "Full Citizenship": A Case Study of Sex-Segregated Public Education, 101 Mich. L. Rev. 755, 775-777 (2002) (footnotes omitted).

then, Rehnquist suggests, it was perfectly reasonable for Virginia to wait and see how broadly the Equal Protection Clause would be read. Rehnquist argues that until very recently, no one thought that it was a problem to exclude women from certain institutions. However, times have changed and so we must live according to today's conceptions of justice. Thus, he does not see Virginia's post-1982 decisions as necessarily related to or infected by its pre-1982 treatment of women. Justice Ginsburg disagrees.

Who has the better argument? Is the argument limited to considerations of sex discrimination, or would it extend to considerations of race discrimination as well? Would Justice Rehnquist's remark that Virginia was entitled to wait because "one swallow doesn't make a summer" sound differently if Virginia were dragging its heels (as it and other southern states in fact were) in desegregating schools, water fountains, public transportation, and public buildings following Brown v. Board of Education?

Justice Scalia offers the basic principle that "when a practice not expressly prohibited by the text of the Bill of Rights bears the endorsement of a long tradition of open, widespread, and unchallenged use that dates back to the beginning of the Republic, we have no proper basis for striking it down," a principle that also applies "to a practice asserted to be in violation of the post-Civil War Fourteenth Amendment." Is Brown v. Board of Education consistent with this theory? Loving v. Virginia? The entire corpus of the Court's sex equality jurisprudence, including, for example, the holding in Taylor v. Louisiana that women could not be excluded from juries?

For an analysis of how the history of sex segregation in education can inform application of Virginia's framework, see Hasday, supra. For an account of how the Virginia opinion critically evaluates VMI's sex-based admissions policy by demonstrating its conformity with other repudiated past practices, see Deborah Widiss, Re-viewing the Past: The Use of the Past as Negative Precedent in United States v. Virginia, 108 Yale L.J. 237 (1998).

4. *The race analogy, and the survival of single-sex schools.* As we have seen, the sex discrimination cases begin in *Frontiero* with an account of the similarities between race and sex discrimination — an analogy the Court had not appreciated in the preceding decades. *Frontiero* employs the race analogy to determine whether a group protesting discriminatory state action should receive the protections of suspect-class status. Once the court decides this threshold question and applies heightened scrutiny, does the race analogy help determine which practices survive judicial scrutiny? In what ways can an understanding of race discrimination guide judgments about sex discrimination? Are the two practices similar in social form?

Education is a good context in which to test intuitions about this question. Despite the central role that the race analogy played in the development of sex discrimination doctrine, *VMI* illustrates that in the mid-1990s lower courts and at least several Supreme Court justices thought sex segregation in education was constitutionally permissible in ways that race segregation is not. At one point in the *VMI* opinion, the majority challenges the belief that sex segregation is benign by invoking the race analogy:

> The pluralistic argument for preserving all-male colleges is uncomfortably similar to the pluralistic argument for preserving all white-colleges. . . . The all-male college

would be relatively easy to defend if it emerged from a world in which women were established as fully equal to men. But it does not. It is therefore likely to be a witting or unwitting device for preserving tacit assumptions of male superiority — assumptions for which women must eventually pay.

Under what circumstances does *VMI* allow single-sex schools? Note the Court's observation that "it is the mission of some single-sex schools 'to dissipate, rather than perpetuate, traditional gender classifications'" and its claim that "[w]e do not question the State's prerogative evenhandedly to support diverse educational opportunities. We address specifically and only an educational opportunity recognized by the District Court and the Court of Appeals as 'unique,' an opportunity available only at Virginia's premier military institute, the Commonwealth's sole single-sex public university or college . . . [t]hus, we are not faced with the question of whether States can provide 'separate but equal' undergraduate institutions for males and females." Does the majority opinion understand sex segregation in education on the model of race segregation?

As you read the following cases, see if you can identify the factors that would determine when government can segregate education by sex.

MISSISSIPPI UNIVERSITY FOR WOMEN v. HOGAN, 458 U.S. 718 (1982): [The Mississippi University for Women is a state school, located in Columbia, Mississippi. Since its establishment in 1884, its enrollment has been limited to women. (During much of its history, of course, enrollment was limited to white women, and it was originally called the Mississippi Industrial Institute and College for the Education of White Girls of the State of Mississippi.)[83] In 1971 MUW opened a School of Nursing, to which Joe Hogan, a resident of Columbia, applied in 1979. Hogan was a registered nurse but lacked a baccalaureate degree. Although he was offered the opportunity to audit certain nursing courses without receiving credit, he was denied admission because he is male. The District Court upheld the denial of admission; the Fifth Circuit reversed.]

O'CONNOR, J., delivered the opinion of the Court.

This case presents the narrow issue of whether a state statute that excludes males from enrolling in a state-supported professional nursing school violates the Equal Protection Clause of the Fourteenth Amendment.[a] . . . [T]he party seeking to uphold a statute that classifies individuals on the basis of their gender must carry the burden of showing an "exceedingly persuasive justification" for the classification. The burden is met only by showing at least that the classification serves

---

83. The charter of MUW, basically unchanged since its founding, provided that the purpose of MUW was "the moral and intellectual advancement of the girls of the state by the maintenance of a first-class institution for their education in the arts and sciences, for their training in normal school methods and kindergarten, for their instruction in bookkeeping, photography, stenography, telegraphy, and typewriting, and in designing, drawing, engraving, and painting, and their industrial application, and for their instruction in fancy, general and practical needlework, and in such industrial branches as experience, from time to time, shall suggest as necessary or proper to fit them for the practical affairs of life."

a. Mississippi maintains no other single-sex public university of college. Thus we are not faced with the question of whether states can provide "separate but equal" undergraduate institutions for males and females. Cf. Vorchheimer v. School District of Philadelphia, 532 F.2d 880 (C.A. 3 1975), aff'd by an equally divided court, 430 U.S. 703 (1977).

"important governmental objectives and that the discriminatory means employed" are "substantially related to the achievement of those objectives." [T]he test . . . must be applied free of fixed notions concerning the roles and abilities of males and females. Care must be taken in ascertaining whether the statutory objective itself reflects archaic and stereotypic notions. Thus, if the statutory objective is to exclude or "protect" members of one gender because they are presumed to suffer from an inherent handicap or to be innately inferior, the objective itself is illegitimate.

The State's primary justification for maintaining the single-sex admissions policy of MUW's School of Nursing is that it compensates for discrimination against women and, therefore, constitutes educational affirmative action. As applied to the School of Nursing, we find the State's argument unpersuasive.

In limited circumstances, a gender-based classification favoring one sex can be justified if it intentionally and directly assists members of the sex that is disproportionately burdened. However, we consistently have emphasized that "the mere recitation of a benign, compensatory purpose is not an automatic shield which protects against any inquiry into the actual purposes underlying a statutory scheme." Weinberger v. Wiesenfeld. . . . Mississippi has made no showing that women lacked opportunities to obtain training in the field of nursing or to attain positions of leadership in that field when the MUW School of Nursing opened its door or that women currently are deprived of such opportunities. In fact, in 1970, the year before the School of Nursing's first class enrolled, women earned 94 percent of the nursing baccalaureate degrees conferred in Mississippi and 98.6 percent of the degrees earned nationwide. . . . As one would expect, the labor force reflects the same predominance of women in nursing. When MUW's School of Nursing began operation, nearly 98 percent of all employed registered nurses were female.

Rather than compensate for discriminatory barriers faced by women, MUW's policy of excluding males from admission to the School of Nursing tends to perpetuate the stereotyped view of nursing as an exclusively woman's job. By assuring that Mississippi allots more openings in its state-supported nursing schools to women than it does to men, MUW's admissions policy lends credibility to the old view that women, not men, should become nurses, and makes the assumption that nursing is a field for women a self-fulfilling prophecy. [A]lthough the State recited a "benign, compensatory purpose," it failed to establish that the alleged objective is the actual purpose underlying the discriminatory classification.

[T]he State has [also] made no showing that the gender-based classification is substantially and directly related to its proposed compensatory objective. To the contrary, MUW's policy of permitting men to attend classes as auditors fatally undermines its claim that women, at least those in the School of Nursing, are adversely affected by the presence of men. . . .

POWELL, J., with whom Rehnquist, J., joins, dissenting.

The Court's opinion bows deeply to conformity. Left without honor — indeed, held unconstitutional — is an element of diversity that has characterized much of American education and enriched much of American life. The Court in effect holds today that no State now may provide even a single institution of higher learning open only to women students. . . . [W]omen enjoy complete equality of opportunity in Mississippi's public system of higher education. Of the State's eight universities and 16 junior colleges, all except MUW are coeducational. At least two other Mississippi universities would have provided respondent with the nursing curriculum that he wishes to pursue. . . .

Nor is respondent significantly disadvantaged by MUW's all-female tradition. His constitutional complaint is based upon a single asserted harm: that he must travel to attend the state-supported nursing schools that concededly are available to him. The Court characterizes this injury as one of "inconvenience."

Coeducation, historically, is a novel educational theory. From grade school through high school, college, and graduate and professional training, much of the nation's population during much of our history has been educated in sexually segregated classrooms.

The sexual segregation of students has been a reflection of, rather than an imposition upon, the preference of those subject to the policy. It cannot be disputed, for example, that the highly qualified women attending the leading women's colleges could have earned admission to virtually any college of their choice. Women attending such colleges have chosen to be there, usually expressing a preference for the special benefits of the single-sex institutions. Similar decisions were made by the colleges that elected to remain open to women only.

. . . A 10-year empirical study by the Cooperative Institutional Research Program of the American Council of Education and the University of California, Los Angeles . . . has affirmed the distinctive benefits of single-sex colleges and universities. As summarized in A. Astin, Four Critical Years 232 (1977), the data established that

> [b]oth [male and female] single-sex colleges facilitate student involvement in several areas: academic, interaction with faculty, and verbal aggressiveness. . . . Men's and women's colleges also have a positive effect on intellectual self-esteem. Students at single-sex colleges are more satisfied than students at coeducational colleges with virtually all aspects of college life. . . . The only area where students are less satisfied is social life. . . .

The issue in this case is whether a State transgresses the Constitution when — within the context of a public system that offers a diverse range of campuses, curricula, and educational alternatives — it seeks to accommodate the legitimate personal preferences of those desiring the advantages of an all-women's college. In my view, the Court errs seriously by assuming — without argument or discussion — that the equal protection standard generally applicable to sex discrimination is appropriate here. That standard was designed to free women from "archaic and overbroad generalizations. . . ." In no previous case have we applied it to invalidate state efforts to *expand* women's choices. Nor are there prior sex discrimination decisions by this Court in which a male plaintiff, as in this case, had the choice of an equal benefit. . . . By applying heightened equal protection analysis to this case,[a] the Court frustrates the liberating spirit of the Equal Protection Clause. . . .

---

a. Even the Court does not argue that the appropriate standard here is "strict scrutiny" — a standard that none of our "sex discrimination" cases ever has adopted. Sexual segregation in education differs from the tradition, by the decision in Plessy v. Ferguson, 163 U.S. 537 (1896), of "separate but equal" racial segregation. It was characteristic of racial segregation that segregated facilities were offered, not as alternatives to increase the choices available to blacks, but as the sole alternative. MUW stands in sharp contrast. Of Mississippi's eight public universities and 16 public junior colleges, only MUW considers sex as a criterion for admission. Women consequently are free to select a coeducational education environment for themselves if they so desire; their attendance of MUW is not a matter of coercion.

Discussion

1. Would "separate but equal" male-only and female-only schools satisfy the majority in *Hogan*? The majority in the *VMI* case?

2. Hogan argued that it was inconvenient for him to travel miles away to another nursing school when MUW was in Columbia, where he lived and worked, while similarly situated women working full time as nurses could attend MUW. What result if MUW were located across the street from a co-ed nursing school?

3. Chief Justice Burger, dissenting in *Hogan*, emphasized the narrowness of the majority's holding and suggested "that a State might well be justified in maintaining, for example, the option of an all-women's business school or liberal arts program." Justice Blackmun, in a separate dissent, also noted the purported narrowness of the Court's holding, but he expressed skepticism about preventing its "spillover" into the wider issue of sex-segregated education. Justice Powell could "see no principled way — in light of the Court's rationale — to reach a different result with respect to other MUW schools and departments." After the *VMI* case, what do you think the meaning of *Hogan* is?

4. To what extent can Mississippi's fate in *Hogan* be attributed to inept lawyering? Justice O'Connor ridicules the state's claim that some sort of affirmative action is needed to encourage female Mississippians to become nurses. What if the state had argued instead that it was trying to provide maximum freedom of choice to its citizenry, including women who wanted to attend a single-sex *university,* which happened also to include a single-sex school of nursing? In his dissenting opinion, Justice Powell quoted comments by the President of Wellesley College and by the Mount Holyoke College Trustees Committee on Coeducation justifying the decisions of those two institutions to remain exclusively women's colleges. Thus Wellesley President Barbara Newell stated in 1973 that "[t]he research we have clearly demonstrates that women's colleges produce a disproportionate number of women leaders and women in responsible positions in society." Wellesley and Mount Holyoke are both private colleges and, for that very reason, quite expensive to attend. Is Mississippi forbidden to provide for its nonwealthy women what they could buy through the market were they wealthy and willing to leave the state, i.e., the opportunity to attend a women's college? Assuming it may do so constitutionally, should Massachusetts prohibit gender discrimination in admissions to private institutions just as it now prohibits racial discrimination?

5. In Vorcheimer v. School District of Philadelphia, 532 F.2d 880 (3d Cir. 1975), *aff'd by an equally divided Court,* 430 U.S. 703 (1977), a high school girl argued for the right to attend Philadelphia's all-male academic high school, Central High School. *Vorcheimer* was decided after *Reed* and *Frontiero* but before Craig v. Boren. The majority held that maintaining separate facilities did not violate the Constitution:

> Academic high schools have high admission standards and offer only college preparatory courses. There are but two such schools in Philadelphia, and they accept students from the entire city rather than operating on a neighborhood basis. Central is restricted to males, and Girls High School, as the name implies, admits only females. . . . The Philadelphia school system does not have a co-ed academic school with similar scholastic requirements for admission. . . . The courses offered by the two schools are similar and of equal quality. The academic facilities are comparable, with the exception of those in the scientific field where Central's are superior. . . .

[G]iven the objective of a quality education and a controverted, but respected theory that adolescents may study more effectively in single-sex schools, the policy of the school board here does bear a substantial relationship [to an important governmental interest].[84]

Judge Gibbon's dissenting opinion compared the majority's decision to Plessy v. Ferguson:

The majority opinion may be briefly summarized as follows:

The object of the [14th] Amendment was undoubtedly to enforce the . . . equality of the two [sexes] before the law, but in the nature of things it could not have been intended to abolish distinctions based upon [sex], or to enforce social, as distinguished from political equality, or a commingling of the two [sexes] upon terms unsatisfactory to either. Laws permitting, and even requiring, their separation in places where they are liable to be brought into contact with each other do not necessarily imply the inferiority of either [sex] to the other, and have been generally, if not universally, recognized as within the competency of the state legislatures in the exercise of their police power. The most common instance of this is connected with the establishment of separate schools for [male] and [female] children, which has been held to be a valid exercise of the legislative power even by courts of States where the political rights of [women] have been longest and most earnestly enforced. . . .

[The plaintiff's] choice, like Plessy's is to submit to . . . segregation or refrain from availing herself of the service.

The Board [of Education] did not present sufficient evidence that coeducation has an adverse effect upon a student's academic achievement. Indeed the Board could not seriously assert that argument in view of its policy of assigning the vast majority of its students to coeducational schools. . . . Thus, the Board's single-sex policy reflects a choice among educational techniques but not necessarily one substantially related to its stated educational objectives. One of those objectives, in fact, is to provide "educational options to students and their parents." The implementation of the Board's policy excluding females from Central actually precludes achievement of this objective because there is no option of a coeducational academic senior high school.

Is *Vorcheimer* consistent with *Hogan?* With the *VMI* case?

In Newberg v. Board of Public Education, 26 Pa. D. & C. 3rd 682 (C.P. Phila. 1983), a second challenge to Central High's male-only policy succeeded, this time on the grounds that the all-female high school and the all-male high school were "materially unequal" in facilities and educational opportunities provided. The court pointed to differences in teacher experience and qualifications, library acquisitions, campus size and design, instructional equipment, test scores, college acceptance rates, access to advanced courses, availability of scholarships, and general sources of funding. Are there good reasons to think that publicly supported all-female institutions will inevitably get less attention, support, and financing than all-male institutions?

---

84. The Third Circuit also noted Williams v. McNair, 316 F. Supp. 134 (D.S.C. 1970), aff'd, 401 U.S. 951 (1971) (per curiam), which upheld, without opinion, a three-judge court's decision upholding the women-only admissions policy of Winthrop College in South Carolina. *Williams* was decided a year before *Reed.*

6. *The benefits of single-sex education.* As suggested by Justice Powell's dissent in *Hogan,* and by the Third Circuit's opinion in *Vorcheimer,* some studies suggest that women may do better in single-sex educational institutions. There is also evidence to the contrary.[85] The sociologist Cynthia Fuchs Epstein, a critic of single-sex education, notes that there are a wide variety of justifications for single-sex institutions:

[t]he argument in support of sex segregation is two pronged: 1) women's nature and 2) women's situation. For the first, advocates claim there are physiological and psychological differences between men and women. Females are said to be more emotional, more relational; less aggressive, and tend more to have low self evaluation. . . . [These qualities are] regarded as leading to different styles of behavior, and choices — women opting for traditional women's careers in social work rather than atomic physics, for example. Thus, reasoning goes, in order to increase female interest in fields formerly and currently defined as male, and which are regarded as more prestigious and important, they require different learning environments. The second argument rests on the idea that the symbolic segregation women face — the perception of them as inferior, and the poor treatment they get from teachers and boys in mixed environments, requires further segregation. That is, women face discriminatory treatment by men, or become unable to speak up in the presence of assertive males, or are neglected by women teachers who prefer men over women students in coeducational settings. As a result, the reasoning goes, many do worse than boys in school, and they can learn better and take on more demanding science and math programs in schools where male students are not permitted.[86]

Epstein responds:

There are overwhelming destructive consequences to women in maintaining segregation in any social institution. . . . [S]ociety and sub-groups within society invest heavily in the maintenance of distinctions between men and women. Far from relying on what comes "naturally" — what are claimed to be the simple and obvious differences between the sexes — laws, rules, and social codes create, enforce and maintain sexually divided educational, political, and social spheres — with the attendant consequences of women's subordinate status in most spheres of private and public life. Women are thought less of as a result of segregation and think less of themselves, and may not aspire to high office or a life of accomplishment. Stereotyping sometimes leads to the self-fulfilling prophecy. [Women in sex-segregated institutions] also think more of men, without the reality check of seeing men in natural surroundings. They get stereotyped and stereotype themselves and men because of the lack of visibility that comes from segregation. Stereotypes are both descriptive and prescriptive.[87]

85. For a sampling of the literature, see Nancy Levit, Separating Equals: Educational Research and the Long-Term Consequences of Sex Segregation, 67 Geo. Wash. L. Rev. 451 (1999); Cynthia Fuchs Epstein, The Myths and Justifications of Sex Segregation in Higher Education: VMI and the Citadel, 4 Duke J. Gender L. & Pol'y 101 (1997); Dianne Avery, Institutional Myths, Historical Narratives and Social Science Evidence: Reading the "Record" in the Virginia Military Institute Case, 5 S. Cal. Rev. L. & Women's Stud. 189 (1996); Karla Cooper-Boggs, The Link Between Private and Public Single-Sex Colleges: Will Wellesley Stand or Fall with the Citadel?, 29 Ind. L. Rev. 131 (1995); Kristin S. Caplice, The Case for Public Single-Sex Education, 18 Harv. J.L. & Pub. Pol'y 227 (1994); Deborah Rhode, Association and Assimilation, 81 Nw. U. L. Rev. 106 (1986).

86. Cynthia Fuchs Epstein, Multiple Myths and Outcomes of Sex Segregation, 14 N.Y. L. Sch. J. Hum. Rts. 185, 188-191 (1997).

87. Id. at 207-208.

7. *Single-sex legal education?* Recent studies seem to indicate that women face special obstacles in law schools, which have a strongly competitive and "male" atmosphere.[88] Would it be constitutional for Mississippi (or Massachusetts, for that matter) to start a state-supported women's law school? See Jennifer Gerarda Brown, "To Give Them Countenance": The Case for a Women's Law School, 22 Harv. Women's L.J. 1 (1999). What about a women-only admission policy to certain classes, for example, a class on the law of rape and domestic violence, or a more general class on women and the law? Can a state law school have official women-only student organizations?

GARRETT v. BOARD OF EDUCATION FOR THE SCHOOL DISTRICT OF THE CITY OF DETROIT
775 F. Supp. 1004 (E.D. Mich. 1991)

Woods, District Judge:

. . . Plaintiffs are girls enrolled in Detroit public schools and their parents. Plaintiff Nancy Doe is a Detroit resident with daughters aged 11, 6, and 5, all of whom will attend Detroit public schools this fall. . . .

Three male academies ("Academies") are scheduled to open on August 26, 1991. The Academies will serve approximately 250 boys in preschool through fifth grade. Grades six through eight will be phased in over the next few years. The Academies offer special programs including a class entitled "Rites of Passage," an Afrocentric (Pluralistic) curriculum, futuristic lessons in preparation for 21st century careers, an emphasis on male responsibility, mentors, Saturday classes, individualized counseling, extended classroom hours, and student uniforms.

Plaintiffs contend that these special offerings (1) do not require a uniquely male atmosphere to succeed; and (2) address issues that face all children and adolescents, including females. . . . .

In Mississippi v. Hogan, 458 U.S. 718 (1982), the Supreme Court held that exclusion of an individual from a publicly-funded school because of his or her sex violates the Equal Protection Clause of the Fourteenth Amendment, unless the defendant can show the sex-based "classification serves 'important governmental objectives and that the discriminatory means employed'" are "substantially related to the achievement of those objectives."[a] Plaintiffs maintain the Board cannot meet this standard because the Board's policy of excluding girls inappropriately relies on gender as a proxy for "at-risk" students. The Academies were developed in response to the crisis facing African-American males manifested by high homicide, unemployment, and drop-out rates. While these statistics underscore a compelling need, they fall short of demonstrating that excluding girls is substantially related to the achievement of the Board's objectives. The Board has proffered no evidence that

---

88. See American Bar Association Commission on Women in the Profession, Elusive Equality: The Experiences of Women in Legal Education (1996); Linda F. Wightman, Women in Legal Education: A Comparison of the Law School Performance and Law School Experiences of Women and Men (1996); Lani Guinier et al., Becoming Gentlemen: Women's Experiences at One Ivy League Law School, 143 U. Pa. L. Rev. 1 (1994); Deborah Rhode, Missing Questions: Feminist Perspectives on Legal Education, 45 Stan. L. Rev. 1547 (1993).

a. According to the plaintiffs, Detroit offers no schools for girls even comparable to the Male Academies; therefore, the Court is not presented with the question of whether the Board can provide separate but equal public school institutions for boys and girls.

the presence of girls in the classroom bears a substantial relationship to the difficulties facing urban males.

Accordingly, plaintiffs conclude that the male academies improperly use gender as a "proxy for other, more germane bases of classification," in this instance, for "at risk" students.[b] Specifically, the gender specific data presented in defense of the Academies ignores the fact that all children in the Detroit public schools face significant obstacles to success. In fact, in its resolution establishing the Academies, the Board acknowledged an "equally urgent and unique crisis facing . . . female students." Urban girls drop out of school, suffer loss of self esteem and become involved in criminal activity. Ignoring the plight of urban females institutionalizes inequality and perpetuates the myth that females are doing well in the current system. Accordingly, plaintiffs contend there is no adequate justification for the Academies' exclusive focus on boys.

Plaintiffs also assert that the special curriculum proposed for the Academies suggests a false dichotomy between the roles and responsibilities of boys and girls. For example, the Rites of Passage curriculum teaches that "men need a vision and a plan for living," "men master their emotions," and "men acquire skills and knowledge to overcome life's obstacles." These issues confront all adolescents and are not rites peculiarly male. Therefore, they are insufficient to justify gender-based classification.

. . . The primary rationale for the Academies is simply that co-educational programs aimed at improving male performance have failed.

The Court is wary of accepting such a rationale. Although co-educational programs have failed, there is no showing that it is the co-educational factor that results in failure. Even more dangerous is the prospect that should the male academies proceed and succeed, success would be equated with the absence of girls rather than any of the educational factors that more probably caused the outcome.

. . . There is no evidence that the educational system is failing urban males because females attend schools with males. In fact, the educational system is also failing females. Thus, the Court concludes the application of the second prong of the Hogan test to the facts at hand, makes it likely that the plaintiffs will succeed on a constitutional argument.[c] . . .

This Court views the purpose for which the Academies came into being as an important one. It acknowledges the status of urban males as an "endangered species." The purpose, however, is insufficient to override the rights of females to equal opportunities.

Discussion

1. As a result of the *Garrett* litigation, the Detroit academies accepted girls as well as boys. The *Garrett* litigation seems to have defused the movement for all-male urban public schools that was gaining in popularity across the nation; in its wake,

b. Plaintiffs assert that the Academies fail to target even those male students who are most at risk because admission requirements specify a mix of students with a wide range of achievement levels be included.

c. Plaintiffs also argue that the voluntary assignment of students to the Academies does not save the Academies from unconstitutionality. Defendant does not dispute this argument; consequently, the Court need not discuss it. In addition, plaintiffs note that experimental programs are not exempt from constitutional requirements. Again, defendant does not respond to this argument. Finally, plaintiffs contend that the male academies do not qualify as affirmative action programs. Defendant does not dispute this statement.

several proposals for all-male schools were revised to provide for coed Afrocentric curricula.[89]

2. *Intersectionality. Garrett* poses the special problem of women of color; in this case black women. Why, precisely, are black women thought to interfere with the education of black men? What assumptions about the black family and the role of black women are suggested or implicated in defendants' arguments? What conception of black manhood is suggested by the proposed school? Is *Garrett* a case where black women are being asked to submerge their interests to those of black men in the interests of the black community?

3. *Gender in admissions vs. curriculum.* Suppose that Detroit opens the academies to boys and girls, but implements an Afrocentric curriculum that emphasizes "male responsibility," the need for males to control their emotions, and the special concerns of African-American males. Does this "male-centered" curriculum violate the Equal Protection Clause? Or is it enough to say that "male-centered" institutions are permissible as long as they do not categorically exclude females, and that it is up to girls (and their parents) to decide if they want to be exposed to this particular form of education? See Hasday, supra, for an argument that even co-ed programs could incorporate gendered assumptions and practices that violate equal protection.

Note: Discrimination Against Women of Color

Individuals have multiple affiliations, simultaneously. Each individual has a race and gender; most understand themselves to belong to at least one polity; many people understand themselves through work relations and religious affiliations, and so forth. "Intersectionality" is the name sometimes given to the special problems that arise from the crosscutting nature of identity, and throughout these materials you should consider whether and how this phenomenon is at work. Much of the scholarship on intersections of race and gender has focused on the question of discrimination against black women.[90] There are at least five ways that the intersection of race and gender affects black women:

1. In promoting the interests of "blacks" as a group, the interests of black women are submerged or subordinated to those of black men.

89. Rosemary C. Salomone, Same, Different, Equal: Rethinking Single-Sex Schooling 131, 138 (2003). For a critical discussion of recent efforts to promote single-sex education in urban schools, see Verna L. Williams, Reform or Retrenchment? Single-Sex Education and the Construction of Race and Gender, 2004 Wis. L. Rev. 15.

90. See, e.g., Paulette Cauldwell, A Hair Piece: Perspectives on the Intersection of Race and Gender, 1991 Duke L.J. 365; Kimberle Crenshaw, Mapping the Margins: Intersectionality, Identity Politics, and Violence Against Women of Color, 43 Stan. L. Rev. 1241 (1991); Angela P. Harris, Race and Essentialism in Feminist Legal Theory, 42 Stan. L. Rev. 581 (1990); Kimberle Crenshaw, Demarginalizing the Intersection of Race and Sex: A Black Feminist Critique of Antidiscrimination Doctrine, Feminist Theory, and Antiracist Politics, 13 U. Chi. Legal F. 139 (1989); Judy Scales-Trent, Black Women and the Constitution: Finding Our Place, Asserting Our Rights, 24 Harv. C.R.-C.L. L. Rev. 9, 10-11 (1989).

2. In promoting the interests of "women" as a group, the interests of black women are submerged or subordinated to those of white women.

3. Black women may experience conflicting demands of loyalty. They may be expected to overlook mysogynistic or subordinating practices by black men in the interests of racial progress. Conversely, they may also be asked to put aside racial insensitivity or racial differences in the interests of gender equality.

4. The forms of discrimination that black women suffer differ because stereotypes about white femininity and black femininity diverge. This is in part due to the overlay of racial stereotypes over gender stereotypes. For example, white feminine stereotypes of daintiness, unassertiveness, and relative sexual innocence have not been applied as regularly to black women; on the contrary, stereotypes applied to black women have more often been those of aggressiveness, promiscuity, and sexual irresponsibility. Like white women, black women are often blamed for the destruction or weakening of families, and for failing to subordinate themselves appropriately to men, but the grounds of complaint tend to be different because of different stereotypes about white masculinity and black masculinity.

5. Discrimination against black women is not easily described as being solely "about race" or "about gender." This is due in part to differing stereotypes about white and black women. It is also due in part to the differing effects of discrimination on black women on the one hand, and black men and white women on the other. As a result, discrimination against black women can more easily be characterized as not being either racial discrimination (because it is not suffered in the same way by black men) or gender discrimination (because it is not suffered in the same way by white women), and therefore as not being discrimination at all.

Because stereotypes about Asian and Hispanic women differ from those about black women, and because their experiences of discrimination both within and without the family may differ, the phenomenon of intersectionality means different things for them. There is now a considerable literature on discrimination against Asian and Hispanic women. Just as the interests and experience of black women cannot be assimilated into those of white women, the interests and experience of Asian and Hispanic women cannot be assimilated into the experience of black women.[91]

D. Intermediate Scrutiny, Title IX, and Sex Segregation in Education and Sports

In the wake of *VMI* and *Garrett,* interest in single-sex education has not diminished and may still be gathering momentum, as proponents have continued to explore

---

91. See, e.g., Jenny Rivera, Domestic Violence Against Latinas by Latino Males: An Analysis of Race, National Origin and Gender Differentials, 14 B.C. Third World L.J. 231 (1994); Leti Volpp, (Mis)identifying Culture: Asian Women and the "Cultural Defense," 17 Harv. Women's L.J. 57 (1994); Virginia Wei, Note, Asian Women and Employment Discrimination: Using Intersectionality Theory to Address Title VII Claims Based on Combined Factors of Race, Gender and National Origin, 37 B.C. L. Rev. 771 (1996).

possibilities for experimenting with sex-segregated education under the Constitution and under Title IX, the statute that applies antidiscrimination law to public and private educational institutions that receive federal funds.[92]

Title IX's implementing regulations provide that local education agencies receiving federal funds "shall not, on the basis of sex, exclude any person from admission to: (a) Any institution of vocational education operated by such recipient; or (b) Any other school or educational unit operated by such recipient, unless such recipient otherwise makes available to such person, pursuant to the same policies and criteria of admission, courses, services, and facilities comparable to each course, service, and facility offered in or through such schools."[93]

Title IX also has ramifications for single-sex classrooms within coed schools. The regulations specify that a public school cannot "provide any course or otherwise carry out any of its education program or activity separately on the basis of sex, or require or refuse participation therein by any of its students on such basis. . . ."[94]; yet Title IX also has a provision that allows school districts to take "affirmative action" to "overcome the effects of conditions which resulted in limited participation . . . by persons of a particular sex."[95]

After more than two decades of approaching single-sex programs as possible Title IX violations, the Office of Civil Rights (OCR) began to ease its stance in the wake of the *VMI* case.[96] Legislators have also introduced bills supporting experimentation with single-sex education. One recent proposal would have allowed the use of federal funds for programs that provide "same gender schools and classrooms, if comparable educational opportunities are offered for students of both sexes": As enacted, the 2001 No Child Left Behind Act allows school districts to use certain federal funds for programs that provide "same gender schools and classrooms, consistent with applicable law," thereby avoiding a direct assault on Title IX.[97]

In May 2002, the OCR issued guidelines pursuant to the new law. Those guidelines provide that Title IX does not ban nonvocational single-sex elementary and secondary schools, so long as schools meet the comparability requirement, which is interpreted to mean the provision of a single-sex school for the other sex. The regulations permit school districts to offer single-sex schools "if such action constitutes remedial or affirmative action," but cautions that single-sex programs may be susceptible to constitutional challenge in court.[98]

Segregation by sex remains commonplace in school athletics; challenges seeking parity in programs for male and female athletes, as well as access to single-sex sports teams for members of the excluded sex, have been brought under both statutory

---

92. Title IX of the Education Amendments of 1972, 20 U.S.C. §§1681 et seq. provides that "no person in the United States shall, on the basis of sex, be excluded from participation in, be denied the benefits of, or be subjected to discrimination under any education program or activity receiving Federal financial assistance," 20 U.S.C.A. §1681(a).

93. 34 C.F.R. §106.35.

94. 34 C.F.R. §106.34.

95. 34 C.F.R. §106.3(b).

96. See Salomone, at 172.

97. Pub. L. No. 107-110, §1, 115 Stat. 1425 (Jan. 8, 2002) (codifying and amending 20 U.S.C.A. §§6301-7941 (West 2003)). This revision attracted the support of previously skeptical senators like Ted Kennedy, as well as Hillary Clinton, who provided an enthusiastic endorsement. Salomone, at 174.

98. Notice: Single-Sex Classes and Schools: Guidelines on Title IX Requirements, 67 Fed. Reg. 31102-01 (May 8, 2002).

and constitutional provisions. Because Title IX's implementing regulations permit single-sex sports teams in certain circumstances, many lawsuits seeking access to single-sex athletic programs are brought under the federal Equal Protection Clause and similar state constitutional provisions. In some cases, courts have found that the Equal Protection Clause requires schools to allow qualified girls to play on all-male teams where there are no equivalent female sports opportunities. See, e.g., Adams v. Baker, 919 F. Supp. 1496 (D. Kan. 1996) (enjoining school district from excluding girl from high school wrestling team).[99] On the other hand, many courts have ruled that the exclusion of boys from girls' teams is substantially related to the state's important interest in preserving athletic opportunities for girls. See, e.g., Kleczek ex rel. Kleczek v. R.I. Interscholastic League, 768 F. Supp. 951 (D.R.I. 1991) (denying preliminary injunction to allow boys access to girls' field hockey team).[100]

Note, however, that equal-protection plaintiffs have had greater success in challenging programs where one sex is completely excluded from participating in a sport offered only to members of the other sex. What of the ubiquitous practice of maintaining separate teams for each sex? Title IX regulations explicitly allow recipients of federal funds to "operate or sponsor separate teams for members of each sex where selection for such teams is based upon competitive skill or the activity involved is a contact sport."[101] Courts have held that the Equal Protection Clause does not mandate access to men's teams for women of unusual athletic ability when an all-female team is available. In O'Connor v. Board of Education, 449 U.S. 1301 (1980), Justice Stevens denied an application to vacate the stay of a preliminary injunction that ordered a school to permit a female student to try out for the boys' basketball team. Justice Stevens reasoned that "without a gender-based classification in competitive contact sports," male athletes would be likely to "dominate the girls' programs and deny them an opportunity to compete in interscholastic events."[102]

Within this context, Title IX and its associated regulations list factors to be considered in assessing whether athletic programs provide equal opportunities to both sexes. Those factors include "[w]hether the selection of sports and levels of competition effectively accommodate the interests and abilities of members of both

---

99. For examples of earlier cases with similar holdings, see, e.g., Force ex rel. Force v. Pierce City Sch. Dist., 570 F. Supp. 1020 (W.D. Mo. 1983) (granting girl right to play on junior high football team); see also, e.g., Hoover v. Meiklejohn, 430 F. Supp. 164 (D. Colo. 1977) (allowing girl to compete on boys' soccer team when no girls' soccer team existed); Morris v. Mich. State Bd. of Educ., 472 F.2d 1207 (6th Cir. 1973) (enjoining application of Michigan High School Athletic Association rule barring girls from participating on noncontact sports teams with boys).

100. For examples of earlier cases with similar holdings, see, e.g., Clark ex rel. Clark v. Ariz. Interscholastic Athletic Ass'n, 695 F.2d 1126 (10th Cir. 1982) (upholding general exclusion of boys from girls' sports teams); Petrie v. Ill. High Sch., 394 N.E.2d 855 (Ill. App. Ct. 1979) (validating exclusion of boys from girls' volleyball squad). Male students have had some limited success in gaining access to girls' teams in sports where no boys' program is offered, see, e.g., Gomes v. R.I. Interscholastic League, 469 F. Supp. 659 (D.R.I. 1979); Attorney Gen. v. Mass. Interscholastic Athletic Ass'n, 393 N.E.2d 284 (Mass. 1979) (holding that state constitution's equal rights amendment rendered invalid a rule prohibiting boys from playing on girls' teams).

101. 34 C.F.R. §106.41. For purposes of Title IX, "contact sports include boxing, wrestling, rugby, ice hockey, football, basketball and other sports the purpose or major activity of which involves bodily contact." 34 C.F.R. §106.41(b).

102. But see Yellow Springs Exempted Village Sch. Dist. Bd. of Educ. v. Ohio High Sch. Athletic Ass'n, 647 F.2d 651 (6th Cir. 1981) (Jones, J., dissenting in part) (arguing that the existence of "separate but equal" male and female basketball teams did not justify the exclusion of girls from the boys' team).

sexes" as well as how schools provide equipment, travel funds, training, and facilities, among other things. The regulations also provide that "Unequal aggregate expenditures for members of each sex or unequal expenditures for male and female teams if a recipient operates or sponsors separate teams will not constitute noncompliance with this section, but the Director may consider the failure to provide necessary funds for teams for one sex in assessing equality of opportunity for members of each sex."[103]

These regulations, which do allow for considerable sex-based differentiation in athletic programs, raise questions about the relationship between Title IX and the Equal Protection Clause: Do the implementing regulations comport with equal protection requirements?[104] Questions also remain about the possible sources of congressional power to enact Title IX, which may have consequences for the ability of states to assert a sovereign immunity defense against suits by private individuals under the statute.[105]

IV.   Gender-Salient Policies Beyond the Reach of Heightened Scrutiny: When Do Policies Classify "on the Basis of" Sex?

A.   Criteria for Distinguishing Gender-Based and Gender-Neutral Policies

1.   Veterans' Preferences

PERSONNEL ADMINISTRATOR OF MASSACHUSETTS v. FEENEY
442 U.S. 256 (1979)

[Helen Feeney (nee Buyo) attempted during World War II to enlist in the Woman's Auxiliary Army Corps. She remembered being told by a recruiting officer, "What's a nice girl like you want to go into service?" She was ultimately unable to

103. 34 C.F.R. §106.41.

104. Although the exclusion of members of one sex from sports teams has sometimes been held to violate equal protection, Title IX's implementing regulation allowing contact sports teams to remain single-sex has been upheld against equal protection challenge. See Yellow Springs Exempted Village Sch. Dist. Bd. of Educ. v. Ohio High Sch. Athletic Ass'n, 647 F.2d 651 (6th Cir. 1981). In recent years, some male athletes and universities have complained that the elimination of men's sports teams to avoid Title IX noncompliance constitutes discrimination against men in violation of the Equal Protection Clause; however, courts have rejected such claims. See, e.g., Kelley v. University of Illinois, 35 F.3d 265 (7th Cir. 1994).

105. Title IX was intended to fill gaps in existing civil rights legislation: Title VI of the Civil Rights Act of 1964, which bans discrimination based on race, color, and national origin by recipients of federal funds, contained no sex discrimination provision, while Title VII's prohibitions on employment discrimination did not fully protect women in educational institutions. In Franklin v. Gwinnett County Public Schools, the Supreme Court reserved the question whether Title IX was enacted pursuant to §5 of the Fourteenth Amendment. 503 U.S. 60, 75 n.8 (1992). In Gebser v. Lago Vista Independent School District, 524 U.S. 274 (1998), the Supreme Court held that Title IX, like Title VI, is a Spending Clause statute. Since *Gebser,* several courts have avoided reaching the question of whether Title IX might also have been enacted pursuant to §5 of the Fourteenth Amendment by holding that states knowingly waived their sovereign immunity when they accepted federal education funds. See, e.g., Litman v. George Mason University, 186 F.3d 544 (4th Cir. 1999), cert. denied, 528 U.S. 1181 (2000).

enlist, though, because parental consent had to be given for any woman under 21, and Helen's mother refused to give such consent. (Women, of course, have never been subject to conscription.) Much later, in 1963, she was hired as a senior clerk stenographer by the Massachusetts Civil Defense Agency. She subsequently passed a number of open competitive civil service examinations for better jobs, but failed in her efforts because of a Massachusetts statute that gave an absolute preference to any veteran who had also passed the relevant tests. The statutory preference is available to "any person, male or female, including a nurse," who was honorably discharged from the United States Armed Forces after at least 90 days of active service, at least one day of which was during "wartime." In 1971 she took the civil service examination to become Assistant Secretary for the Massachusetts Board of Dental Examiners. Feeney received the second-highest score, but she was ranked sixth on the hiring list, behind five male veterans. The successful applicant had received a grade eight points lower than Feeney's.[106] As a matter of empirical fact, the preference operated overwhelmingly to the advantage of males. Feeney therefore sued, arguing that the absolute-preference formula served in effect to exclude women from the most desirable civil service jobs and, therefore, violated the Fourteenth Amendment. A three-judge court agreed, finding that, although the goals of the preference were legitimate and had not been enacted in order to discriminate against women, the exclusionary impact with regard to women was so severe as to require a more carefully tailored preference scheme.]

STEWART, J. . . .

When this litigation was commenced, then, over 98% of the veterans in Massachusetts were male; only 1.8% were female. And over one-quarter of the Massachusetts population were veterans. During the decade between 1963 and 1973 when the appellee was actively participating in the State's merit selection system, 47,005 new permanent appointments were made in the classified official service. Forty-three percent of those hired were women, and 57% were men. Of the women appointed, 1.8% were veterans, while 54% of the men had veteran status. A large unspecified percentage of the female appointees were serving in lower paying positions for which males traditionally had not applied. . . .

II.

The sole question for decision on this appeal is whether Massachusetts, in granting an absolute lifetime preference to veterans, has discriminated against women in violation of the Equal Protection Clause of the Fourteenth Amendment.

A

The equal protection guarantee of the Fourteenth Amendment does not take from the States all power of classification. Most laws classify, and many affect certain groups unevenly, even though the law itself treats them no differently from all other members of the class described by the law. When the basic classification is rationally based, uneven effects upon particular groups within a class are ordinarily of no constitutional concern. The calculus of effects, the manner in which a particular law

---

106. See Linda K. Kerber, No Constitutional Right to Be Ladies: Women and the Obligations of Citizenship 220-222 (1998).

reverberates in a society, is a legislative and not a judicial responsibility. In assessing an equal protection challenge, a court is called upon only to measure the basic validity of the legislative classification. When some other independent right is not at stake, see, e.g., Shapiro v. Thompson, 394 U.S. 618, and when there is no "reason to infer antipathy," Vance v. Bradley, 440 U.S. 93, 97, it is presumed that "even improvident decisions will eventually be rectified by the democratic process. . . ." Ibid.

Certain classifications, however, in themselves supply a reason to infer antipathy. Race is the paradigm. A racial classification, regardless of purported motivation, is presumptively invalid and can be upheld only upon an extraordinary justification. This rule applies as well to a classification that is ostensibly neutral but is an obvious pretext for racial discrimination. But, as was made clear in Washington v. Davis, 426 U.S. 229, and Arlington Heights v. Metropolitan Housing Dev. Corp., 429 U.S. 252, even if a neutral law has a disproportionately adverse effect upon a racial minority, it is unconstitutional under the Equal Protection Clause only if that impact can be traced to a discriminatory purpose.

Classifications based upon gender, not unlike those based upon race, have traditionally been the touchstone for pervasive and often subtle discrimination. This Court's recent cases teach that such classifications must bear a close and substantial relationship to important governmental objectives, Craig v. Boren, 429 U.S. 190, and are in many settings unconstitutional. Although public employment is not a constitutional right, Massachusetts Bd. of Retirement v. Murgia, supra, and the States have wide discretion in framing employee qualifications, see, e. g., New York City Transit Authority v. Beazer, supra, these precedents dictate that any state law overtly or covertly designed to prefer males over females in public employment would require an exceedingly persuasive justification to withstand a constitutional challenge under the Equal Protection Clause of the Fourteenth Amendment.

B

[*Davis* and *Arlington Heights*] recognize that when a neutral law has a disparate impact upon a group that has historically been the victim of discrimination, an unconstitutional purpose may still be at work. But those cases signaled no departure from the settled rule that the Fourteenth Amendment guarantees equal laws, not equal results. . . .

When a statute gender-neutral on its face is challenged on the ground that its effects upon women are disproportionately adverse, a twofold inquiry is thus appropriate. The first question is whether the statutory classification is indeed neutral in the sense that it is not gender based. If the classification itself, covert or overt, is not based upon gender, the second question is whether the adverse effect reflects invidious gender-based discrimination. In this second inquiry, impact provides an "important starting point," but purposeful discrimination is "the condition that offends the Constitution." . . .

III.

A

The question whether ch. 31, §23, establishes a classification that is overtly or covertly based upon gender must first be considered. The appellee has conceded that ch. 31, §23, is neutral on its face. She has also acknowledged that state hiring preferences for veterans are not per se invalid, for she has limited her challenge to the absolute lifetime preference that Massachusetts provides to veterans. The District Court made two central findings that are relevant here: first, that ch. 31, §23, serves legitimate and worthy purposes; second, that the absolute preference was not established for the purpose of discriminating against women. The appellee has thus acknowledged and the District Court has thus found that the distinction between veterans and nonveterans drawn by ch. 31, §23, is not a pretext for gender discrimination. The appellee's concession and the District Court's finding are clearly correct.

If the impact of this statute could not be plausibly explained on a neutral ground, impact itself would signal that the real classification made by the law was in fact not neutral. But there can be but one answer to the question whether this veteran preference excludes significant numbers of women from preferred state jobs because they are women or because they are nonveterans. Apart from the fact that the definition of "veterans" in the statute has always been neutral as to gender and that Massachusetts has consistently defined veteran status in a way that has been inclusive of women who have served in the military, this is not a law that can plausibly be explained only as a gender-based classification. Indeed, it is not a law that can rationally be explained on that ground. . . . Too many men are [adversely] affected by ch. 31, §23, to permit the inference that the statute is but a pretext for preferring men over women.

Moreover, as the District Court implicitly found, the purposes of the statute provide the surest explanation for its impact. Just as there are cases in which impact alone can unmask an invidious classification, cf. Yick Wo v. Hopkins, 118 U.S. 356, there are others, in which — notwithstanding impact — the legitimate noninvidious purposes of a law cannot be missed. This is one. The distinction made by ch. 31, §23, is, as it seems to be, quite simply between veterans and nonveterans, not between men and women.

B

The dispositive question, then, is whether the appellee has shown that a gender-based discriminatory purpose has, at least in some measure, shaped the Massachusetts veterans' preference legislation. As did the District Court, she points to two basic factors which in her view distinguish ch. 31, §23, from the neutral rules at issue in the Washington v. Davis and *Arlington Heights* cases. The first is the nature of the preference, which is said to be demonstrably gender-biased in the sense that it favors a status reserved under federal military policy primarily to men. The second concerns the impact of the absolute lifetime preference upon the employment opportunities of women, an impact claimed to be too inevitable to have been unintended. The appellee contends that these factors, coupled with the fact that the preference itself has little if any relevance to actual job performance, more than suffice to prove the discriminatory intent required to establish a constitutional violation.

1

The contention that this veterans' preference is "inherently nonneutral" or "gender-biased" presumes that the State, by favoring veterans, intentionally incorporated into its public employment policies the panoply of sex-based and assertedly discriminatory federal laws that have prevented all but a handful of women from becoming veterans. There are two serious difficulties with this argument. First, it is wholly at odds with the District Court's central finding that Massachusetts has not offered a preference to veterans for the purpose of discriminating against women. Second, it cannot be reconciled with the assumption made by both the appellee and the District Court that a more limited hiring preference for veterans could be sustained. Taken together, these difficulties are fatal.

To the extent that the status of veteran is one that few women have been enabled to achieve, every hiring preference for veterans, however modest or extreme, is inherently gender-biased. If Massachusetts by offering such a preference can be said intentionally to have incorporated into its state employment policies the historical gender-based federal military personnel practices, the degree of the preference would or should make no constitutional difference. Invidious discrimination does not become less so because the discrimination accomplished is of a lesser magnitude. Discriminatory intent is simply not amenable to calibration. It either is a factor that has influenced the legislative choice or it is not. The District Court's conclusion that the absolute veterans' preference was not originally enacted or subsequently reaffirmed for the purpose of giving an advantage to males as such necessarily compels the conclusion that the State intended nothing more than to prefer "veterans." Given this finding, simple logic suggests that an intent to exclude women from significant public jobs was not at work in this law. To reason that it was, by describing the preference as "inherently nonneutral" or "gender-biased," is merely to restate the fact of impact, not to answer the question of intent.

To be sure, this case is unusual in that it involves a law that by design is not neutral. The law overtly prefers veterans as such. As opposed to the written test at issue in *Davis,* it does not purport to define a job-related characteristic. To the contrary, it confers upon a specifically described group — perceived to be particularly deserving — a competitive headstart. But the District Court found, and the appellee has not disputed, that this legislative choice was legitimate. The basic distinction between veterans and nonveterans, having been found not gender-based, and the goals of the preference having been found worthy, ch. 31 must be analyzed as is any other neutral law that casts a greater burden upon women as a group than upon men as a group. The enlistment policies of the Armed Services may well have discriminated on the basis of sex. See Frontiero v. Richardson, 411 U.S. 677; cf. Schlesinger v. Ballard, 419 U.S. 498. But the history of discrimination against women in the military is not on trial in this case.

2

The appellee's ultimate argument rests upon the presumption, common to the criminal and civil law, that a person intends the natural and foreseeable consequences of his voluntary actions. . . .

The decision to grant a preference to veterans was of course "intentional." So, necessarily, did an adverse impact upon nonveterans follow from that decision. And it cannot seriously be argued that the Legislature of Massachusetts could have been unaware that most veterans are men. It would thus be disingenuous to say that the adverse consequences of this legislation for women were unintended, in the sense that they were not volitional or in the sense that they were not foreseeable.

"Discriminatory purpose," however, implies more than intent as volition or intent as awareness of consequences. It implies that the decisionmaker, in this case a state legislature, selected or reaffirmed a particular course of action at least in part "because of," not merely "in spite of," its adverse effects upon an identifiable group. Yet nothing in the record demonstrates that this preference for veterans was originally devised or subsequently re-enacted because it would accomplish the collateral goal of keeping women in a stereotypic and predefined place in the Massachusetts Civil Service.

To the contrary, the statutory history shows that the benefit of the preference was consistently offered to "any person" who was a veteran. That benefit has been extended to women under a very broad statutory definition of the term veteran. . . . When the totality of legislative actions establishing and extending the Massachusetts veterans' preference are considered, the law remains what it purports to be: a preference for veterans of either sex over nonveterans of either sex, not for men over women.

STEVENS, J., joined by White, J., concurring.

While I concur in the Court's opinion, I confess that I am not at all sure that there is any difference between the two questions posed. If a classification is not overtly based on gender, I am inclined to believe the question whether it is covertly gender-based is the same as the question whether its adverse effects reflect invidious gender-based discrimination. However the question is phrased, for me the answer is largely provided by the fact that the number of males disadvantaged by Massachusetts' veterans' preference (1,867,000) is sufficiently large — and sufficiently close to the number of disadvantaged females (2,954,000) — to refute the claim that the rule was intended to benefit males as a class over females as a class.

MARSHALL, J., joined by Brennan, J., dissenting.

Although acknowledging that in some circumstances, discriminatory intent may be inferred from the inevitable or foreseeable impact of a statute, the Court concludes that no such intent has been established here. I cannot agree. In my judgment, Massachusetts' choice of an absolute veterans' preference system evinces purposeful gender-based discrimination. And because the statutory scheme bears no substantial relationship to a legitimate governmental objective, it cannot withstand scrutiny under the Equal Protection Clause.

I.

The District Court found that the "prime objective" of the Massachusetts veterans' preference statute, Mass. Gen. Laws Ann., ch. 31, §23, was to benefit individuals with prior military service. . . .

That a legislature seeks to advantage one group does not, as a matter of logic or of common sense, exclude the possibility that it also intends to disadvantage another. Individuals in general and lawmakers in particular frequently act for a variety of reasons. . . . [T]he critical constitutional inquiry is not whether an illicit consideration was the primary or but-for cause of a decision, but rather whether it had an appreciable role in shaping a given legislative enactment. Where there is "proof that a discriminatory purpose has been *a* motivating factor in the decision,

. . . judicial deference is no longer justified." Arlington Heights v. Metropolitan Housing Dev. Corp.

Moreover, since reliable evidence of subjective intentions is seldom obtainable, resorting to inference based on objective factors is generally unavoidable. To discern the purposes underlying facially neutral policies, this Court has therefore considered the degree, inevitability, and foreseeability of any disproportionate impact as well as the alternatives reasonably available. In the instant case, the impact of the Massachusetts statute on women is undisputed. . . . Because less than 2% of the women in Massachusetts are veterans, the absolute preference formula has rendered desirable state civil service employment an almost exclusively male prerogative. As the District Court recognized, this consequence follows foreseeably, indeed inexorably, from the long history of policies severely limiting women's participation in the military. Although neutral in form, the statute is anything but neutral in application. . . . Where the foreseeable impact of a facially neutral policy is so disproportionate, the burden should rest on the State to establish that sex-based considerations played no part in the choice of the particular legislative scheme.

Clearly, that burden was not sustained here. The legislative history of the statute reflects the Commonwealth's patent appreciation of the impact the preference system would have on women, and an equally evident desire to mitigate that impact only with respect to certain traditionally female occupations. Until 1971, the statute and implementing civil service regulations exempted from operation of the preference any job requisitions "especially calling for women." In practice, this exemption, coupled with the absolute preference for veterans, has created a gender-based civil service hierarchy, with women occupying low-grade clerical secretarial jobs and men holding more responsible and remunerative positions.

Thus, for over 70 years, the Commonwealth has maintained, as an integral part of its veterans' preference system, an exemption relegating female civil service applicants to occupations traditionally filled by women. Such a statutory scheme both reflects and perpetuates precisely the kind of archaic assumptions about women's roles which we have previously held invalid. Particularly when viewed against the range of less discriminatory alternatives available to assist veterans,[a] Massachusetts' choice of a formula that so severely restricts public employment opportunities for women cannot reasonably be thought gender-neutral. . . .

II.

To survive challenge under the Equal Protection Clause, statutes reflecting gender-based discrimination must be substantially related to the achievement of important governmental objectives. Appellants here advance three interests in support of the absolute preference system: (1) assisting veterans in their readjustment to civilian life; (2) encouraging military enlistment; and (3) rewarding those who have served their country. . . .

---

a. Only four States afford a preference comparable in scope to that of Massachusetts. Other States and the Federal Government grant point or tie-breaking preferences that do not foreclose opportunities for women.

With respect to the first interest, facilitating veterans' transition to civilian status, the statute is plainly overinclusive. By conferring a permanent preference, the legislation allows veterans to invoke their advantage repeatedly, without regard to their date of discharge. . . . Nor is the Commonwealth's second asserted interest, encouraging military service, a plausible justification for this legislative scheme. In its original and subsequent re-enactments, the statute extended benefits retroactively to veterans who had served during a prior speci-fied period. . . . Moreover, even if such influence could be presumed, the statute is still grossly overinclusive in that it bestows benefits on men drafted as well as those who volunteered.

Finally, the Commonwealth's third interest, rewarding veterans, does not "adequately justify the salient features" of this preference system. Where a particu-lar statutory scheme visits substantial hardship on a class long subject to discrimina-tion, the legislation cannot be sustained unless "carefully tuned to alternative considerations." Here, there are a wide variety of less discriminatory means by which Massachusetts could effect its compensatory purposes. For example, a point preference system, such as that maintained by many States and the Federal Government, or an absolute preference for a limited duration, would reward veter-ans without excluding all qualified women from upper level civil service positions. Apart from public employment, the Commonwealth can, and does, afford assis-tance to veterans in various ways, including tax abatements, educational subsidies, and special programs for needy veterans. Unlike these and similar benefits, the costs of which are distributed across the taxpaying public generally, the Massachusetts statute exacts a substantial price from a discrete group of individuals who have long been subject to employment discrimination, and who, "because of circumstances totally beyond their control, have [had] little if any chance of becom-ing members of the preferred class."

Discussion

1. *Defining a sex-based classification.* When plaintiffs challenge a facially neutral statute with a disparate impact on women (or some other constitutionally protected group), *Feeney* suggests that a court must ask two kinds of questions to determine whether the challenged action violates the Equal Protection Clause. First the court must determine whether the statute is actually facially neutral, or whether it in fact classifies on the basis of sex. If the state has not classified on the basis of sex, then the court must determine whether the state has undertaken the challenged action with a discriminatory purpose. Thus, after Washington v. Davis and *Feeney*, the ques-tion of whether state action classifies on the basis of race or sex matters tremen-dously. Presumptions of constitutionality as well as the liability rules for establishing a constitutional violation depend on whether courts characterize regulatory prac-tices as group-based or facially neutral.

Recently, commentators have suggested that courts are not employing criteria consistently across cases in determining which practices "classify" within the meaning of *Davis* and *Feeney*. Instead, these commentators suggest, normative judg-ments about the legitimacy of the challenged practices may shape the way courts characterize the challenged practices for purposes of determining what burdens of proof and liability rules apply. Judgments about constitutionality are determining the doctrinal tests courts apply, rather than arising out of the application of doctrine. These guiding intuitions about constitutionality may reflect cultural common sense about benign and suspect practices of gender differentiation — intuitions that are sometimes shaped by social movement advocacy.[107]

What criteria should a court employ to determine whether a statute classifies on the basis of sex? Did the Court in *Feeney* employ the right criteria? As you read the ensuing cases in the chapter, you might ask whether the Court in *Feeney* employed criteria used consistently in other equal protection cases — for example, in analyzing the regulation of pregnancy and affirmative action. Is it possible to derive a standard that can be used consistently across all cases? Is it a problem if the characterization of such practices as gender-based or gender-neutral depends instead on common-sense judgments about their legitimacy?

Was the *Feeney* Court correct in deciding that the veterans' preference statute was a gender-neutral classification? Given that federal law regulates military service with reference to the gender of the applicant, doesn't the classification "veteran" incorporate by reference gender-based criteria? Under the majority's analysis, could a state limit the award of a veterans' preference or other social benefit to "all members of the armed forces who served in combat positions?" Should a court then review such a statute on the presumption that it is constitutional?

2. *Defining discriminatory purpose.* As we have seen, *Feeney* articulates a two-stage test for determining whether a facially neutral statute with a disparate impact on women discriminates on the basis of sex. First the court must confirm that the statute does not in fact expressly classify on the basis of sex. If the court concludes that government has not expressly classified on the basis of sex, then the court must determine whether "the adverse effect reflects invidious gender-based discrimination" — a showing Washington v. Davis holds can only be satisfied by proof of "purposeful discrimination." *Feeney* then proceeds to define "discriminatory purpose" for the Washington v. Davis framework in terms that verge on malice: The plaintiff must show that the challenged action was undertaken "at least in part 'because of,' not merely 'in spite of' its adverse effects upon an identifiable group."

Consider the discussion of stereotyping, supra. There are many forms of conscious, quasi-conscious, and unconscious bias that may lead government actors to adopt policies with adverse effects on protected groups. Why limit equal protection violations to cases where government undertook the challenged action at least in part because of its adverse effects on a protected group? How often will plaintiffs be able to obtain evidence that government actors have adopted policies because of their adverse effects on particular groups?

Why did *Feeney* adopt such a narrow and exculpatory liability rule? Should the Court have adopted the foreseeability standard the dissent embraced? Should it have considered the social meaning of the regulation? Statistics concerning its impact? What institutional considerations might inform *Feeney*'s interpretation of the Equal Protection Clause? Are they of a kind that equally constrain legislatures? If a legislature is deciding whether facially neutral statutes (such as criminal laws

---

107. J. M. Balkin & R. B. Siegel, The American Civil Rights Tradition: Anticlassification or Antisubordination?, 58 U. Miami L. Rev. 9, 28 (2003); R. A. Primus, Equal Protection and Disparate Impact: Round Three, 117 Harv. L. Rev. 493, 509 (2003); R. B. Siegel, A Short History of Sexual Harassment, in Directions in Sexual Harassment Law 1, 11-18 (C. A. MacKinnon & R. B. Siegel eds., 2003).

regulating drugs or abortion) are constitutional, is it sufficient for legislators to check whether their decision to adopt the policy reflects discriminatory purpose as *Feeney* has defined it?

3. *Feeney as an affirmative action case.* Among other things, *Feeney* highlights the fact that the most important "affirmative action" programs in American history have almost undoubtedly been those benefiting veterans, most of whom have been male. See Melissa Murray, Whatever Happened to G.I. Jane?: Citizenship, Gender, and Social Policy in the Postwar Era, 9 Mich. J. of Gender & Law 91 (2002). Interestingly, the government's official historical statistics on veterans do not provide data by sex, though the Army Nurse Corps became a part of the permanent Army military establishment in 1901, and the WACs and WAVEs thereafter. See Bureau of the Census, 2 Historical Statistics of the United States 1790-1970, 1135 (1976). One can be extremely confident that relatively few of the 12,123,455 persons on active duty in 1945, the final year of World War II, were women. See id. at 1041 (Series Y 904-916 Military Personnel on Active Duty: 1789 to 1970). The percentages would be significantly different today, though, of course, any contemporary veterans' preference would include the millions of veterans from the years before women were welcomed into the armed forces.

2.   Domestic Violence Policies

HYNSON v. CITY OF CHESTER LEGAL DEPARTMENT, 864 F.2d 1026 (3d Cir. 1988): [Shortly after midnight on October 15, 1984, plaintiff's decedent, Alesia Hynson, was shot and killed by her former boyfriend, Jamil Gandy, the father of one of her two children. Prior to her death, Hynson had sought and obtained a number of temporary protection from abuse orders, the last of which had expired. On the night of October 14, Hynson warned police that Gandy had threatened her, but they did not arrest him. Subsequently Gandy killed Hynson at her place of employment. The plaintiffs sued the city and the police officers who were warned of the boyfriend's threats, alleging a violation of equal protection.]

MANSMANN, Circuit Judge.

The case presently before us involves a claim that the City of Chester police officers engage in a custom, policy, and practice of failing to respond to complaints made by females against males known to them. In other words, Hynson argues that the police officers treat domestic abuse cases differently than non-domestic abuse cases. By failing to consider Alesia Hynson's complaint against her former boyfriend as seriously as they would consider the complaint of a female against an unknown assailant, Hynson contends, the police officers denied her the equal protection of the law which ultimately resulted in her tragic death. . . .

Notwithstanding the allegations of the complaint it was made clear at oral argument before us that plaintiffs were not contending that a domestic complaint to the police from a male against a female would be treated differently from a domestic complaint by a female against a male. . . .

Hynson's lawsuit reflects a growing trend of plaintiffs relying upon the due process and equal protection clauses, enforceable through [42 U.S.C. Section]

1983, to force police departments to provide women with the protection from domestic violence that police agencies are allegedly reluctant to give. One recent commentator has stated:

> The police policy towards battered women can take a variety of forms, from an outright refusal to arrest batterers and to recognize domestic violence as a criminal matter, to a practice of giving domestic violence calls lower priority than non-domestic disputes. Sometimes police policy is explained in written manuals. Often it is not in writing, but is demonstrated by a pattern of police behavior that treats assaults by men against their wives less seriously than assaults by strangers. . . . The police non-arrest policy is most commonly justified by a belief in "family privacy," a doctrine dictating that the state should not intervene in domestic matters.

Note, Battered Women and the Equal Protection Clause: Will the Constitution Help Them When the Police Won't?, 95 Yale L.J. 788, 790-791 (1986).

. . . We agree with [other Courts of Appeals who have held] that if the categories used by the police in administering the law are domestic violence and nondomestic violence, this is not sufficient to raise a claim for gender-based discrimination absent a showing of an intent, purpose, or effect of discriminating against women. In order to survive summary judgment, a plaintiff must proffer sufficient evidence that would allow a reasonable jury to infer that it is the policy or custom of the police to provide less protection to victims of domestic violence than to other victims of violence, that discrimination against women was a motivating factor, and that the plaintiff was injured by the policy or custom. . . .[108]

In Ricketts v. City of Columbia, 36 F.3d 775, 781 (8th Cir. 1994), the court agreed that plaintiffs had "demonstrated a pattern of fewer arrests in cases of domestic violence," but argued that "the plaintiffs failed to produce evidence from which a reasonable jury could determine that this pattern proved a policy which was motivated by an intent to discriminate against women." The mere fact that 90% of the victims of domestic abuse are women did not raise an inference of intention to discriminate against women. "[T]he classification itself is facially neutral and includes male victims of domestic abuse. There is no evidence that male victims of

---

108. The court also noted that under existing doctrine police officers (as opposed to the city itself) have a qualified immunity from suits for damages for violations of constitutional rights under section 1983, unless a right is clearly established: "the contours of the right must be sufficiently clear that a reasonable official would understand that what he is doing violates the law."

> [A] police officer loses a qualified immunity to a claim that a facially neutral policy is executed in a discriminatory manner only if a reasonable police officer would know that the policy has a discriminatory impact on women, that bias against women was a motivating factor behind the adoption of the policy, and that there is no important public interest served by the adoption of the policy. This standard is the result of a careful balance between the plaintiff's right to pursue his or her claim that a statutorily or constitutionally protected right was violated by a public authority administering or applying an otherwise neutral policy with "an unequal hand" and the individual public official's right to perform his duties without a constant fear of harassing litigation.
>
> Thus, even if the plaintiffs are successful in proving the existence of a discriminatory policy, or a facially neutral policy applied with discriminatory intent, the individual police officers will nevertheless possess a qualified immunity if they can demonstrate that a reasonable police officer executing the policy could not have known that the conduct violated Ms. Hynson's clearly established right to equal protection.

domestic abuse are treated differently than female victims of domestic abuse." Moreover, the Court argued

> [b]ecause of the inherent differences between domestic disputes and nondomestic disputes, legitimately different factors may affect a police officer's decision to arrest or not to arrest in any given situation. . . . *McCleskey.* "Where the discretion that is fundamental to our criminal process is involved, we decline to assume that what is unexplained is invidious."

In Soto v. Flores, 103 F.3d 1056 (1st Cir. 1997), Puerto Rico had passed a comprehensive domestic violence act, Law 54. Plaintiff's decedent and her children were killed by her husband, who had scrawled on the wall where he shot the children: "Law 54, which is only a tool for women to make men do whatever they want, is not liberty." Plaintiff's decedent had complained to police officers, who refused to process her complaints properly under Law 54. Plaintiff offered evidence that many police officers were actively opposed to Law 54 and believed that it was unfair to men. Plaintiff also introduced statements by the police superintendent Betancourt-Lebron, that it was better to resolve disputes by counseling abusive spouses than by punishing them. Plaintiff also provided evidence that Bentancourt-Lebron had hindered implementation of Law 54 among rank and file police officers and had even refused to meet with the Women's Affairs Commission charged with evaluating and promoting implementation of the new law.

The Court of Appeals held that mere evidence that police officers disagreed with Law 54 and did not wish to enforce it was not sufficient to raise an inference of bias against women under the Equal Protection Clause.

> In the end, this evidence, while painting an unwholesome picture, is not enough to meet the strict standards imposed by the Supreme Court for showing discriminatory intent in equal protection claims. As *Feeney* says, the intent to be shown must be more than an "awareness of consequences." The defendant must have "selected . . . a course of action at least in part 'because of' not merely 'in spite of' its adverse effects on an identifiable group." An expression of disagreement with Law 54 and a failure to meet with the Women's Affairs Commission, while some evidence of discriminatory intent on the part of Betancourt-Lebron, is too slender a stalk on which to rest. Thus, we conclude that plaintiff has fallen short of her difficult burden of proving discriminatory intent against these defendants as required to establish a constitutional tort. In so saying, we do not of course condone the actions and failures of duties we have described. The deaths of children, which may have followed from risks arguably created by the actions of public officials, are very serious matters. Whether this deplorable scenario is actionable under Puerto Rican law we leave, as we must, to others.

Discussion

1. *Feeney* shapes litigation of the domestic violence cases, in the narrow interpretation of sex-based classification it seems to authorize and in the narrow interpretation of discriminatory purpose it embraces. Do you agree with *Hynson* that a police policy that differentiates between "domestic" and "nondomestic" violence does not classify on the basis of sex? Does it matter if 90 percent of the victims of domestic abuse are women? That at the time the policies were adopted, victims of domestic violence were commonly understood to be women and perpetrators were commonly understood to be men?

2. *Feeney* asks courts to differentiate between gender-based and facially neutral statutes. But even if domestic violence policies are facially neutral, they may still be more deeply entangled in gender relations than other facially neutral statutes — either because of the policies' social meaning or their history.[109] Until recently many domestic violence policies were couched in explicit sex-based terms (e.g., referring to wives or women). In an effort to comply with Frontiero v. Richardson and Craig v. Boren, many states rewrote their abuse policies in gender-neutral terms, characterizing "wife-beating" as "spousal assault" or "domestic violence" without significantly altering social understandings shaping the regulation.

Hoboson v. Pow, 434 F. Supp. 362 (N.D. Ala. 1977), held invalid a Reconstruction-era provision of Alabama's state constitution that disenfranchised convicted "wife-beaters." Although the original purpose of the clause was to disenfranchise blacks, the Court struck it down on the grounds that it discriminated against men. Should courts consider the genealogy or lineage of a statute in determining whether it warrants a presumption of constitutionality?

3. What kinds of reasons or beliefs might lead government actors to adopt, or to preserve, policies that treat perpetrators and victims of domestic violence differently from other perpetrators and victims of assault? Might stereotyping or gender bias inform such reasons or beliefs? Will plaintiffs be able to establish an equal protection violation if they have to demonstrate that government has adopted a domestic violence policy with adverse effects on women at least in part because of its adverse effects on women?

Do you agree with the Court in Soto v. Flores that mere opposition to domestic violence reforms by police officers coupled with attempts to hinder implementation of these reforms is not evidence of unconstitutional intention? Is this a sound conclusion because domestic violence is not "really" about women or because police officers can have good faith reasons to oppose particular reforms as misguided? What, precisely, should be sufficient to survive a motion for summary judgment?

After considering the domestic violence example, what modifications, if any, would you propose to the equal protection framework set forth in *Feeney*?

3.   *Marital Rape*

Just as *Feeney* inhibits equal protection challenges to domestic violence policies, so, too, does it inhibit challenges to policies that restrict prosecution of rape in marriage. All states have abolished the traditional rule that a man cannot be legally culpable for raping his wife. At the same time, the majority of the states still treat marital rape differently from nonmarital rape in significant ways. First, a number of states grant spousal immunity for charges that would apply in a nonmarital context. For instance, a number of marital rape statutes exempt men from rape charges when their wives are mentally incapacitated or physically helpless. Second, even where marital rape laws do apply, many states impose lesser penalties or require additional legal criteria for prosecution. These additional criteria may include higher standards to prove force, speedy reporting requirements, or proof that a couple was

---

109. See R. B. Siegel, "The Rule of Love": Wife Beating as Prerogative and Privacy, 105 Yale L.J. 2117 (1996).

separated or filing for divorce at the time of the assault.[110] Marital rape has long been regulated as a form of assault perpetrated by husbands on wives. But today such polices may be expressed in the formal neutral language of "spousal" rape. Plaintiffs seeking to demonstrate that such policies violate equal protection would have to show that they reflect discriminatory purpose within the meaning of *Feeney*.

In People v. Liberta, 64 N.Y.2d 152 (1984), cert. denied, 471 U.S. 1020 (1985), the defendant could not take advantage of New York's marital rape exemption because he was separated from his wife at the time the assault occurred. The court held that the marital rape exemption violated the rational basis test, but nevertheless upheld the defendant's conviction.[111] It noted and rejected as "irrational and absurd" the traditional justification of Lord Hale that a woman gives irrevocable consent to sexual relations with her husband when she marries. The court then went on to consider more modern justifications for treating marital and nonmarital rapes differently:

> [The People argue that] the marital exemption protects against governmental intrusion into marital privacy and promotes reconciliation of the spouses, and thus that elimination of the exemption would be disruptive to marriages. . . . The marital exemption simply does not further marital privacy because this right of privacy protects consensual acts, not violent sexual assaults. Just as a husband cannot invoke a right of marital privacy to escape liability for beating his wife, he cannot justifiably rape his wife under the guise of a right to privacy.
>
> . . . Clearly, it is the violent act of rape and not the subsequent attempt of the wife to seek protection through the criminal justice system which "disrupts" a marriage. Moreover, if the marriage has already reached the point where intercourse is accomplished by violent assault it is doubtful that there is anything left to reconcile. . . .
>
> Another rationale sometimes advanced in support of the marital exemption is that marital rape [and in particular lack of consent] would be . . . difficult . . . to prove . . . [and] that allowing such prosecutions could lead to fabricated complaints by "vindictive" wives. . . . Proving lack of consent, however, is often the most difficult part of any rape prosecution, particularly where the rapist and the victim had a prior relationship. Similarly, the possibility that married women will fabricate complaints would seem to be no greater than the possibility of unmarried women doing so.
>
> The final argument in defense of the marital exemption is that marital rape is not as serious an offense as other rape and is thus adequately dealt with by the possibility of prosecution under criminal statutes, such as assault statutes, which provide for less severe punishment. The fact that rape statutes exist, however, is a recognition that the harm caused by a forcible rape is different, and more severe, than the harm caused by an ordinary assault. . . . Moreover, there is no evidence to support the argument that marital rape has less severe consequences than other rape. On the contrary, numerous studies have shown that marital rape is frequently quite violent and generally has more severe, traumatic effects on the victim than other rape.

---

110. Michelle J. Anderson, Marital Immunity, Intimate Relationships, and Improper Inferences: A New Law on Sexual Offenses, 54 Hastings L.J. 1465 (2003); Katherine E. Volovski, Crime and Punishment Law Chapter: Domestic Violence, 5 Geo. J. Gender & L. 175, 179-180 (2004); For a general overview of state laws and a history of the marital rape exemption, see Jill Elaine Hasday, Contest and Consent, A Legal History of Marital Rape, 88 Calif. L. Rev. 1373, 1375 nn.1-3 (2000) (listing 27 states that have reformed but not fully eliminated the marital rape exemption); Emily R. Brown, Note, Changing the Marital Rape Exemption: I Am Chattel (?!); Hear Me Roar, 18 Am. J. Trial Advoc. 657 (1995). Jill Elaine Hasday, The Canon of Family Law, 57 Stan. L. Rev. 825, 837-841 (2004).

111. The court argued that it had the authority to remedy the unconstitutional statute by expanding its scope if the legislature would rather have passed a more inclusive law than have no rape law at all.

Do you agree that the New York Court of Appeals applied the traditional rational basis test of Williamson v. Lee Optical in these arguments? Do you think that lesser penalties and different proof requirements for marital rape (which still exist in many states) also fail the rational basis test?

The Court of Appeals' constitutional objections would surely have been much easier to make under the "exceedingly persuasive justification" test of United States v. Virginia. But that requires showing that the marital rape exemption is a form of sex discrimination. What is the best way to argue that the marital rape exemption is actually discrimination "on the basis of" sex? A demonstration that the exemption is secretly motivated by hatred or contempt for women? An antisubordination rationale? A "cultural meaning test" like that described by Charles Lawrence? What about the argument that the marital rape exemption preserves the lower social status of women albeit through gender-neutral terms?

Finally, consider Robin West's argument:

> The evil flaw of these exemptions is not that they irrationally treat married couples differently from cohabitants, or married women differently from unmarried women, or husbands differently from rapists unacquainted with their victims, or women differently from men. The evil is that they legalize, and hence legitimate, a form of violence that does inestimable damage to all women, not only those who are raped. In addition to the obvious violence, brutality, and terror marital rape exemptions facilitate, marital rape exemptions, like the rapes they legalize, also sever the central connection to selfhood that links a woman's pleasure with her desires, will, and actions. The will of the married woman who learns to accept routinized rape is no longer ruled by or even connected to her desires. Eventually, her desires are no longer a product of what she enjoys or what she has learned to enjoy. What the victim of routinized rape within marriage does, sexually, is a product not of what the victim wills but of what her attacker demands. As an immediate consequence, her will becomes a function not of her desires but of his desires. Eventually her desires become a function not of her pleasures but of his pleasures; she wants literally to please him rather than herself because to please herself is too dangerous. The victim of marital rape gains survival, but she sacrifices her self-sovereignty. In other words, she sacrifices the ability to control her own will and to determine her own actions, pleasures, and desires free from external influence. In short, she sacrifices selfhood.[112]

Is this an argument for women's equality or women's liberty? What is the relationship (or should be the relationship) between these two concepts in equal protection law?

4. *Pregnancy*

GEDULDIG v. AIELLO
417 U.S. 484 (1974)

[California excluded disabilities incident to normal pregnancies from a disability insurance scheme that it had established for private employers and employees. In upholding the regulation, the Court applied only a rational basis standard.]

---

112. Robin West, Equality Theory, Marital Rape, and the Promise of the Fourteenth Amendment, 42 Fla. L. Rev. 45 (1990).

STEWART, J. . . .

II. . . .

. . . The State has a legitimate interest in maintaining the self-supporting nature of its insurance program. Similarly, it has an interest in distributing the available resources in such a way as to keep benefit payments at an adequate level for disabilities that are covered, rather than to cover all disabilities inadequately. Finally, California has a legitimate concern in maintaining the contribution rate at a level that will not unduly burden participating employees, particularly low-income employees who may be most in need of the disability insurance.

These policies provide an objective and wholly noninvidious basis for the State's decision not to create a more comprehensive insurance program than it has. There is no evidence in the record that the selection of the risks insured by the program worked to discriminate against any definable group or class in terms of the aggregate risk protection derived by that group or class from the program.[a] There is no risk from which men are protected and women are not. Likewise, there is no risk from which women are protected and men are not.

BRENNAN, J., joined by Douglas, J. and Marshall, J., dissenting.

[B]y singling out for less favorable treatment a gender-linked disability peculiar to women, the State has created a double standard for disability compensation: a limitation is imposed upon the disabilities for which women workers may recover, while men receive full compensation for all disabilities suffered, including those that affect only or primarily their sex, such as prostatectomies, circumcision, hemophilia and gout. In effect, one set of rules is applied to females and another to males. Such dissimilar treatment of men and women, on the basis of physical characteristics inextricably linked to one sex, inevitably constitutes sex discrimination.

The same conclusion has been reached by the Equal Employment Opportunity Commission, the federal agency charged with enforcement of Title VII of the Civil Rights Act of 1964, as amended by the Equal Employment Opportunity Act of 1972, which prohibits employment discrimination on the basis of sex. In guidelines issued pursuant to Title VII and designed to prohibit

---

a. . . . [T]his case is thus a far cry from cases like Reed v. Reed and Frontiero v. Richardson, involving discrimination based upon gender as such. The California insurance program does not exclude anyone from benefit eligibility because of gender but merely removes one physical condition — pregnancy — from the list of compensable disabilities. While it is true that only women can become pregnant, it does not follow that every legislative classification concerning pregnancy is a sex-based classification like those considered in *Reed* and *Frontiero*. Normal pregnancy is an objectively identifiable physical condition with unique characteristics. Absent a showing that distinctions involving pregnancy are mere pretexts designed to effect an invidious discrimination against the members of one sex or the other, lawmakers are constitutionally free to include or exclude pregnancy from the coverage of legislation such as this on any reasonable basis, just as with respect to any other physical condition.

The lack of identity between the excluded disability and gender as such under this insurance program becomes clear upon the most cursory analysis. The program divides potential recipients into two groups — pregnant women and nonpregnant persons. While the first group is exclusively female, the second includes members of both sexes. The fiscal and actuarial benefits of the program thus accrue to members of both sexes.

the disparate treatment of pregnancy disabilities in the employment context, the EEOC has declared that: "Disabilities caused or contributed to by pregnancy, miscarriage, abortion, childbirth and recovery therefrom are, for all job-related purposes, temporary disabilities and should be treated as such under any health or temporary disability insurance or sick leave plan available in connection with employment. Written and unwritten employment policies and practices involving matters such as the commencement and duration of leave, the availability of extensions, the accrual of seniority and other benefits and privileges, reinstatement, and payment under any health or temporary disability insurance or sick leave plan, formal or informal, shall be applied to disability due to pregnancy or childbirth on the same terms and conditions as they are applied to other temporary disabilities."

Discussion

1. *Burdening pregnant males and females alike?* Does the law in *Geduldig* classify on the basis of gender? Or is it simply a classification whose impact is felt only by women? If a classification affects only some blacks and no whites, should it be subject to strict scrutiny? Is the case for characterizing the regulation in *Geduldig* as sex-based stronger than in *Feeney*? Why or why not?

2. *Sex-based classifications and biological difference.* Is the problem in *Geduldig* that the impact is felt only by women, not for reasons of history or culture, but instead because of biology? Is this an uncomplicated use of the term "biology?" Should courts refuse to characterize laws regulating physical characteristics unique to one sex as "sex-based classifications" because, by definition, it is not possible to discriminate between the sexes in matters respecting that characteristic? Does it matter that the insurance plan in *Geduldig* covered conditions involving physiological characteristics unique to men? Is this a necessary condition for finding the exclusion of pregnancy discriminatory? Is the decision to exclude pregnancy from an otherwise comprehensive disability insurance plan a decision based on biology? Economics? Sex-role assumptions about young mothers in the workforce?

3. *Disparate impact or status enforcement?* Is *Geduldig* "just" a disparate impact case? Recall the discussion of *Griggs,* in which it was noted that one could analyze *Griggs* as a straight "disparate impact" case or as a case that condemned practices whose disparate impact arose out of the historical subordination of blacks. *Griggs* traced the disparate impact of hiring criteria to recent and explicit race discrimination in education. Might pregnancy discrimination be traced to gender-differentiated assumptions about work and family roles for men and women? For example, might the policy in *Geduldig* reflect the belief that female employees who become pregnant do not need disability insurance because they will choose to leave the workforce to raise the child, and will be, or should be, supported by another wage earner when they do? Is it relevant that at the time of the decision many employers had formal policies requiring pregnant employees to leave work?

Consider whether all or only some classifications based on pregnancy reinforce the subordinate or dependent status of women. If only some classifications involving pregnancy are status-enforcing, what should the doctrine look like?

4. *Classifications based on genetic disposition.* By what standard should a court review a classification based on having tested positive for genes thought to contribute to developing breast or prostate cancer? Would you apply less scrutiny or the same level of scrutiny (whatever it happens to be) to classifications involving recessive sickle-cell anemia or Tay-Sachs genes, which are carried almost exclusively by blacks and Ashkenazic Jews, respectively?

Note: Differing Approaches to Pregnancy Discrimination under the Constitution and Federal Civil Rights Law

Justice Brennan's dissent in *Geduldig* points out that at the time of the decision, the EEOC, the agency charged with enforcing federal antidiscrimination law, had interpreted the prohibition on sex discrimination in Title VII of the Civil Rights Act of 1964 to include pregnancy discrimination, and directed that in places of employment governed by the statute benefits "shall be applied to disability due to pregnancy or childbirth on the same terms and conditions as they are applied to other temporary disabilities." In General Elec. Co. v. Gilbert, 429 U.S. 125 (1976), the Supreme Court rejected the EEOC's interpretation of Title VII, and instead applied *Geduldig*'s reasoning, concluding that an employer's decision to exclude pregnancy from a temporary disability benefits plan did not discriminate on the basis of sex within the meaning of Title VII.

In 1978 Congress responded to *Geduldig* and *Gilbert* by amending Title VII to prohibit discrimination "on the basis of pregnancy, childbirth, or related medical conditions." Public Law 95-555. Referring to Title VII's prohibition of discrimination "because of sex" or "on the basis of sex," the Pregnancy Discrimination Act of 1978 (PDA) provided that these terms "include, but are not limited to, because of or on the basis of pregnancy, childbirth, or related medical conditions; and women affected by pregnancy, childbirth, or related medical conditions shall be treated the same for all employment-related purposes, including receipt of benefits under fringe benefit programs, as other persons not so affected but similar in their ability or inability to work. . . ."[113]

Does Congress's decision to amend Title VII show that the Court was wrong in its decisions? Does it suggest, to the contrary, that the Court correctly left this complex social issue to the political process while protecting the core right of women to be free from discrimination? Does your answer to this question depend on (1) how likely Congress is to respond with something like the PDA, and (2) whether or not you see legal treatment of pregnancy as at the core of women's equal citizenship?

Note: Abortion and Equal Protection

In 1973, Roe v. Wade recognized a right to privacy that protected a woman's decision whether to have an abortion (discussed infra, Chapter 8). A year later, in

113. 42 U.S.C. §2000e(k) (2000).

Geduldig, the Court held that regulation of pregnant persons was not sex-based regulation within the meaning of the Equal Protection Clause. Under *Geduldig*, laws regulating abortion do not classify on the basis of sex, and so are not subject to heightened scrutiny under the Fourteenth Amendment's Equal Protection Clause. *Geduldig* thus separated constitutional protections for the abortion right from the developing law of sex discrimination.[114]

This split was not inevitable. The second-wave feminist movement understood sex equality as a question rooted in the social organization of family life,[115] and the advocates who litigated the first sex discrimination cases in the 1970s urged courts to treat the regulation of pregnancy as sex-based state action under the Fourteenth Amendment. The movement's constitutional lawyers argued that regulation of the pregnant woman was presumptively unconstitutional when it enforced stereotypes and sex role prescriptions of the separate-spheres tradition.[116] A number of federal courts began to adopt this reasoning.[117] A classic expression of this understanding is an equal-protection brief that Ruth Ginsburg filed in 1972 in a case involving a woman who faced an involuntary discharge from the Air Force because she was pregnant.[118] As Justice Ginsburg later noted, the *Struck* case was "an ideal case to argue the sex equality dimension of laws and regulations regarding pregnancy and childbirth."[119] Ginsburg's brief in the *Struck* case has been neglected because the Court disposed of the case by remanding it to the Court of Appeals on mootness grounds and soon thereafter ruled that regulation directed at pregnant women was not the kind of "sex-based" state action that would trigger heightened scrutiny under equal protection principles.

In this early period, women advanced sex-equality arguments for the abortion right in the streets and in a number of cases. Briefs tied sex-equality arguments for the abortion right to different provisions of the Constitution — in particular, the Fifth, Eighth, Thirteenth, Fourteenth, and Nineteenth Amendments.[120] In the 1980s, then-judge Ginsburg expressed her view that the abortion right might have been more firmly grounded had the court "added a distinct sex discrimination theme to its medically oriented opinion." She cited approvingly the work of Ken

---

114. In 1993, the Court decided Bray v. Alexandria Women's Health Clinic, 506 U.S. 263 (1993), a case turning on the question of whether antiabortion activism represented animus against women. Writing for the Court, Justice Scalia cited *Geduldig* for the proposition that pregnancy discrimination was not sex discrimination — underscoring this point by emphasizing that the Court's abortion funding cases had not applied heightened scrutiny.

115. R. C. Post and R. B. Siegel, Legislative Constitutionalism and Section Five Power: Policentric Interpretation of the Family and Medical Leave Act, 112 Yale L.J. 1943, 1984-2020 (2003).

116. Advocates construed the equality language of the ERA differently, however. They asserted that the Amendment had an exception for physical characteristics unique to one sex — and that regulation of such unique physical characteristics was subject to strict scrutiny. See n.34, supra. In arguing that it was constitutional to exclude pregnancy from its disability insurance program, California invoked the ERA's unique physical characteristics exception. Brief for Appellant at 22-24, Geduldig v. Aiello, 417 U.S. 484 (1974) (No. 73-640).

117. For appellate decisions in the early 1970s, see R. B. Siegel, Revised Opinion in What Roe Should Have Said: The Nation's Top Legal Experts Rewrite America's Most Controversial Decision 63, 71-73 (J.B. Balkin ed. 2005).

118. See Brief for Petitioner, Struck v. Sec'y of Def., 409 U.S. 1071 (1972) (No. 72-178).

119. Ruth Bader Ginsburg, Remarks for the Celebration of 75 Years of Women's Enrollment at Columbia Law School, 102 Colum. L. Rev. 1441, 1447 (2002).

120. What Roe Should Have Said, supra n.117, at 244-247. This volume contains three alternative versions of *Roe* (by Jack Balkin, Reva Siegel, and Robin West) that demonstrate how *Roe* could have been written as an equal protection decision.

Karst, who "linked abortion prohibitions with discrimination against women," and wrote that *Roe* "deeply touched and concerned women's position in society in relation to men." See Ruth Bader Ginsburg, Some Thoughts on Autonomy and Equality in Relation to Roe v. Wade, 63 N.C. L. Rev 375, 382-383 (1985) (citing Kenneth Karst, Foreword: Equal Citizenship Under the Fourteenth Amendment, 91 Harv. L. Rev. 1, 58 (1977) (quoted infra, Chapter 8)).

The Court has been somewhat more receptive to such arguments in recent years. In Planned Parenthood v. Casey, infra Chapter 8, the Court reaffirmed *Roe* as protecting a right of privacy — but justified the abortion right in terms that incorporated values of sex equality at numerous crucial junctures.[121] Chapter 8 discusses sex equality arguments for the abortion right in more detail, in the materials accompanying *Roe*.

Note: Fetal Abuse Prosecutions and the Problem of Intersectionality

In ruling that regulation of pregnant women is not sex-based state action under the Equal Protection Clause, *Geduldig* also shields from constitutional scrutiny regulation of pregnant women that purports to promote the welfare of the unborn — for example, sanctions to deter women from taking drugs or engaging in other conduct thought to have negative consequences for the development of the fetus. See, e.g., Dorothy E. Roberts, Punishing Drug Addicts Who Have Babies: Women of Color, Equality, and the Right of Privacy, 104 Harv. L. Rev. 1419, 1430, 1432-1433, 1436-1437, 1455-1456 (1991):

> The response of state prosecutors, legislators, and judges to the problem of drug-exposed babies has been punitive. They have punished women who use drugs during pregnancy by depriving these mothers of custody of their children, by jailing them during their pregnancy, and by prosecuting them after their babies are born.
>
> . . . Hospitals in a number of states now screen newborns for evidence of drugs in their urine and report positive results to child welfare authorities. Some child protection agencies institute neglect proceedings to obtain custody of babies with positive toxicologies based solely on these tests. More and more government authorities are also removing drug-exposed newborns from their mothers immediately after birth pending an investigation of parental fitness. In these investigations, positive neonatal toxicologies often raise a strong presumption of parental unfitness which circumvents the inquiry into the mother's ability to care for her child that is customarily necessary to deprive a parent of custody.

Do these policies violate equal protection? (You should also consider whether they violate the woman's right to bear a child, protected under the right of privacy discussed in Chapter 8.) Roberts argues that these questions should be approached through the intersection of race and gender because the policies fall particularly heavily on women of color:

---

121. See Kenneth Karst, Constitutional Equality as a Cultural Form: The Courts and the Meanings of Sex and Gender, 38 Wake Forest L. Rev. 513, 531-535 (2003); Reva B. Siegel, Abortion as a Sex Equality Right: Its Basis in Feminist Theory in Mothers in Law: Feminist Theory and the Legal Regulation of Motherhood (M. Fineman and I. Karpin eds., 1995) (surveying equality arguments for the abortion right in law review literature and in *Casey*).

Poor Black women bear the brunt of prosecutors' punitive approach. These women
are the primary targets of prosecutors, not because they are more likely to be guilty of
fetal abuse, but because they are Black and poor. Poor women, who are disproportionately Black, are in closer contact with government agencies, and their drug use is therefore more likely to be detected. Black women are also more likely to be reported to
government authorities, in part because of the racist attitudes of health care professionals. Finally, their failure to meet society's image of the ideal mother makes their
prosecution more acceptable. . . .

Hospitals administer drug tests in a manner that further discriminates against poor
Black women. One common criterion triggering an infant toxicology screen is the
mother's failure to obtain prenatal care, a factor that correlates strongly with race and
income. Worse still, many hospitals have no formal screening procedures, relying
solely on the suspicions of health care professionals. This discretion allows doctors
and hospital staff to perform tests based on their stereotyped assumptions about drug
addicts.

It is also significant that, out of the universe of maternal conduct that can injure a
fetus, prosecutors have focused on crack use. The selection of crack addiction for
punishment can be justified neither by the number of addicts nor the extent of the
harm to the fetus. Excessive alcohol consumption during pregnancy, for example,
can cause severe fetal injury, and marijuana use may also adversely affect the
unborn. . . . [P]rosecutors do not always base their claims on actual harm to the child,
but on the mere delivery of crack by the mother. . . . [S]electing crack abuse as the
primary fetal harm to be punished has a discriminatory impact that cannot be
medically justified.

Roberts argues that these policies must be read against

the systematic, institutionalized denial of reproductive freedom [that] has uniquely
marked Black women's history in America. An important part of this denial has been
the devaluation of Black women as mothers. . . . [S]everal popular images denigrating
Black mothers — the licentious Jezebel, the careless, incompetent mother, the domi-
neering matriarch, and the lazy welfare mother — have reinforced and legitimated
their devaluation. . . .

Although the state's asserted interest in ensuring the health of babies is substantial,
prosecution does not advance that interest in a sufficiently narrow fashion. First, as I
have noted, the government's punitive course of action is inimical to the goal of
healthier pregnancies because it deters women from seeking help. In addition, a
public commitment to providing adequate prenatal care for poor women and drug
treatment programs that meet the needs of pregnant addicts would be a [less restrictive alternative and a] more effective means for the state to address the problem of
drug-exposed babies.

How would this argument fare under the tests of *Geduldig, Davis,* and *Feeney*?

B.   Pregnancy as a Justification for Sex-Differentiated Treatment of Men and Women

Equal protection law proscribes many forms of gendered state action. In several
notable cases, however, equal protection law preserves gendered state action by
characterizing it as gender-neutral — as it does in the cases concerning the regulation of veterans' preferences, domestic violence, pregnancy, and abortion that we

have just examined. In another small group of cases, the Court has applied inter-mediate scrutiny to gender-based state action and concluded that government's use of group-based classifications was constitutionally justified. Interestingly enough, some of the more prominent cases upholding government use of gender classifica-tions accept justifications for gendered state action that emphasize differences in the reproductive role of the sexes. Thus while the Court refuses to treat regulation of pregnant women as gender-based state action, it nonetheless treats reproduction as the site of defining gender-based differences.

As you read the following cases, you might ask yourself whether regulation concerns differences in physiology — or differences in social role imputed to phys-iology? Under intermediate scrutiny, could the Court uphold the regulations in question on the ground that society has different sex-role expectations of men and women?

MICHAEL M. v. SUPERIOR COURT OF SONOMA COUNTY
450 U.S. 464 (1981)

REHNQUIST, J., announced the judgment of the Court and delivered an opinion, in which the Chief Justice, Justice Stewart, and Justice Powell joined.

The question presented in this case is whether California's "statutory rape" law, §261.5 of the Cal. Penal Code Ann., violates the Equal Protection Clause of the Fourteenth Amendment. Section 261.5, defines unlawful sexual intercourse as "an act of sexual intercourse accomplished with a female not the wife of the perpetra-tor, where the female is under the age of 18 years." The statute thus makes men alone criminally liable for the act of sexual intercourse.

In July 1978, a complaint was filed in the Municipal Court of Sonoma County, Cal., alleging that petitioner, then a 17-year-old male, had had unlawful sexual intercourse with a female under the age of 18, in violation of §261.5. The evidence, adduced at a preliminary hearing showed that at approximately midnight on June 3, 1978, petitioner and two friends approached Sharon, a 16-year-old female, and her sister as they waited at a bus stop. Petitioner and Sharon, who had already been drinking, moved away from the others and began to kiss. After being struck in the face for rebuffing petitioner's initial advances, Sharon submitted to sexual inter-course with petitioner. Prior to trial, petitioner sought to set aside the information on both state and federal constitutional grounds, asserting that §261.5 unlawfully discriminated on the basis of gender. The trial court and the California Court of Appeal denied petitioner's request for relief and petitioner sought review in the Supreme Court of California.

The Supreme Court [of California] held that "section 261.5 discriminates on the basis of sex because only females may be victims, and only males may violate the section." [It] then subjected the classification to "strict scrutiny," stating that it must be justified by a compelling state interest. It found that the classification was "supported not by mere social convention but by the immutable physiological fact that it is the female exclusively who can become pregnant." Canvassing "the tragic human costs of illegitimate teenage pregnancies," including the large number of teenage abortions, the increased medical risk associated with teenage pregnancies, and the social consequences of teenage childbearing, the court concluded that the State has a compelling interest in preventing such pregnancies. Because males alone can "physiologically cause the result which the law properly seeks to avoid," the court further held that the gender classification was readily justified as a means of identifying offender and victim. For the reasons stated below, we affirm the judgment of the California Supreme Court.

. . . Unlike the California Supreme Court, we have not held that gender-based classifications are "inherently suspect" and thus we do not apply so-called "strict scrutiny" to those classifications. See Stanton v. Stanton, 421 U.S. 7 (1975). Our cases have held, however, that the traditional minimum rationality test takes on a somewhat "sharper focus" when gender-based classifications are challenged. See Craig v. Boren. In Reed v. Reed, for example, the Court stated that a gender-based classification will be upheld if it bears a "fair and substantial relationship" to legitimate state ends, while in Craig v. Boren, the Court restated the test to require the classification to bear a "substantial relationship" to "important governmental objectives."

Underlying these decisions is the principle that a legislature may not "make overbroad generalizations based on sex which are entirely unrelated to any differences between men and women or which demean the ability or social status of the affected class." But because the Equal Protection Clause does not "demand that a statute necessarily apply equally to all persons" or require "things which are different in fact . . . to be treated in law as though they were the same," Rinaldi v. Yeager, 384 U.S. 305 (1966), this Court has consistently upheld statutes where the gender classification is not invidious, but rather realistically reflects the fact that the sexes are not similarly situated in certain circumstances. Parham v. Hughes; Califano v. Webster, 430 U.S. 313 (1977); Schlesinger v. Ballard, 419 U.S. 498 (1975); Kahn v. Shevin, 416 U.S. 351 (1974). As the Court has stated, a legislature may "provide for the special problems of women." Weinberger v. Wiesenfeld, 420 U.S. 636 (1975).

Applying those principles to this case, the fact that the California Legislature criminalized the act of illicit sexual intercourse with a minor female is a sure indication of its intent or purpose to discourage that conduct. Precisely why the legislature desired that result is of course somewhat less clear. This Court has long recognized that "[i]nquiries into congressional motives or purposes are a hazardous matter," and the search for the "actual" or "primary" purpose of a statute is likely to be elusive. Here, for example, the individual legislators may have voted for the statute for a variety of reasons. Some legislators may have been concerned about preventing teenage pregnancies, others about protecting young females from physical injury or from the loss of "chastity," and still others about promoting various religious and moral attitudes towards premarital sex.

The justification for the statute offered by the State, and accepted by the Supreme Court of California, is that the legislature sought to prevent illegitimate teenage pregnancies. That finding, of course, is entitled to great deference. And although our cases establish that the State's asserted reason for the enactment of a statute may be rejected, if it "could not have been a goal of the legislation," Weinberger v. Wiesenfeld, supra, this is not such a case.

We are satisfied not only that the prevention of illegitimate pregnancy is at least one of the "purposes" of the statute, but also that the State has a strong interest in preventing such pregnancy. At the risk of stating the obvious, teenage pregnancies, which have increased dramatically over the last two decades, have significant social, medical, and economic consequences for both the mother and her child, and the State. Of particular concern to the State is that approximately half of all teenage

pregnancies end in abortion. And of those children who are born, their illegitimacy makes them likely candidates to become wards of the State.[a]

We need not be medical doctors to discern that young men and young women
are not similarly situated with respect to the problems and the risks of sexual intercourse. Only women may become pregnant, and they suffer disproportionately the
profound physical, emotional, and psychological consequences of sexual activity.
The statute at issue here protects women from sexual intercourse at an age when
those consequences are particularly severe.[b]

The question thus boils down to whether a State may attack the problem of
sexual intercourse and teenage pregnancy directly by prohibiting a male from
having sexual intercourse with a minor female. We hold that such a statute is sufficiently related to the State's objectives to pass constitutional muster.

Because virtually all of the significant harmful and inescapably identifiable
consequences of teenage pregnancy fall on the young female, a legislature acts well
within its authority when it elects to punish only the participant who, by nature,
suffers few of the consequences of his conduct. It is hardly unreasonable for a legislature acting to protect minor females to exclude them from punishment.
Moreover, the risk of pregnancy itself constitutes a substantial deterrence to young
females. No similar natural sanctions deter males. A criminal sanction imposed
solely on males thus serves to roughly "equalize" the deterrents on the sexes.

We are unable to accept petitioner's contention that the statute is impermissibly
underinclusive and must, in order to pass judicial scrutiny, be *broadened* so as to
hold the female as criminally liable as the male. It is argued that this statute is not
necessary to deter teenage pregnancy because a gender-neutral statute, where both
male and female would be subject to prosecution, would serve that goal equally
well. The relevant inquiry, however, is not whether the statute is drawn as precisely
as it might have been, but whether the line chosen by the California Legislature is
within constitutional limitations. Kahn v. Shevin.

In any event, we cannot say that a gender-neutral statute would be as effective as
the statute California has chosen to enact. The State persuasively contends that a
gender-neutral statute would frustrate its interest in effective enforcement. Its view
is that a female is surely less likely to report violations of the statute if she herself

a. The policy and intent of the California Legislature evinced in other legislation buttresses our view
that the prevention of teenage pregnancy is a purpose of the statute. The preamble to the Pregnancy
Freedom of Choice Act, for example, states: "The legislature finds that pregnancy among unmarried
persons under 21 years of age constitutes an increasing social problem in the State of California."

Subsequent to the decision below, the California Legislature considered and rejected proposals to
render §261.5 gender neutral, thereby ratifying the judgment of the California Supreme Court. That is
enough to answer petitioner's contention that the statute was the "accidental by-product of a traditional
way of thinking about females." Califano v. Webster. Certainly this decision of the California Legislature
is as good a source as is this Court in deciding what is "current" and what is "outmoded" in the perception of women.

b. Although petitioner concedes that the State has a "compelling" interest in preventing teenage
pregnancy, he contends that the "true" purpose of §261.5 is to protect the virtue and chastity of young
women. As such, the statute is unjustifiable because it rests on archaic stereotypes. What we have said
above is enough to dispose of that contention. The question for us — and the only question under the
Federal Constitution — is whether the legislation violates the Equal Protection Clause of the Fourteenth
Amendment, not whether its supporters may have endorsed it for reasons no longer generally accepted.
Even if the preservation of female chastity were one of the motives of the statute, and even if that motive
be impermissible, petitioner's argument must fail because "[i]t is a familiar practice of constitutional law
that this court will not strike down an otherwise constitutional statute on the basis of an alleged illicit
legislative motive. "

would be subject to criminal prosecution.[c] In an area already fraught with prosecutorial difficulties, we decline to hold that the Equal Protection Clause requires a legislature to enact a statute so broad that it may well be incapable of enforcement.[d]

We similarly reject petitioner's argument that §261.5 is impermissibly overbroad because it makes unlawful sexual intercourse with prepubescent females, who are, by definition, incapable of becoming pregnant. Quite apart from the fact that the statute could well be justified on the grounds that very young females are particularly susceptible to physical injury from sexual intercourse, it is ludicrous to suggest that the Constitution requires the California Legislature to limit the scope of its rape statute to older teenagers and exclude young girls. There remains only petitioner's contention that the statute is unconstitutional as it is applied to him because he, like Sharon, was under 18 at the time of sexual intercourse. Petitioner argues that the statute is flawed because it presumes that as between two persons under 18, the male is the culpable aggressor. We find petitioner's contentions unpersuasive. Contrary to his assertions, the statute does not rest on the assumption that males are generally the aggressors. It is instead an attempt by a legislature to prevent illegitimate teenage pregnancy by providing an additional deterrent for men. The age of the man is irrelevant since young men are as capable as older men of inflicting the harm sought to be prevented.

In upholding the California statute we also recognize that this is not a case where a statute is being challenged on the grounds that it "invidiously discriminates" against females. To the contrary, the statute places a burden on males which is not shared by females. But we find nothing to suggest that men, because of past discrimination or peculiar disadvantages, are in need of the special solicitude of the courts. Nor is this a case where the gender classification is made "solely for . . . administrative convenience," as in Frontiero v. Richardson, or rests on "the baggage of sexual stereotypes," as in Orr v. Orr. As we have held, the statute instead reasonably reflects the fact that the consequences of sexual intercourse and pregnancy fall more heavily on the female than on the male. Accordingly, the judgment of the California Supreme Court is affirmed.

STEWART, J., concurring. . . .

B

The Constitution is violated when government, state or federal, invidiously classifies similarly situated people on the basis of the immutable characteristics with which they were born. Thus, detrimental racial classifications by government always violate the Constitution, for the simple reason that, so far as the Constitution is

---

c. Petitioner contends that a gender-neutral statute would not hinder prosecutions because the prosecutor could take into account the relative burdens on females and males and generally only prosecute males. But to concede this is to concede all. If the prosecutor, in exercising discretion, will virtually always prosecute just the man and not the woman, we do not see why it is impermissible for the legislature to enact a statute to the same effect.

d. The question whether a statute is *substantially* related to its asserted goals is at best an opaque one. . . . Where . . . differing speculations as to the effect of a statute are plausible, we think it appropriate to defer to the decision of the California Supreme Court, "armed as it was with the knowledge of the facts and circumstances concerning the passage and potential impact of [the statute], and familiar with the milieu in which that provision would operate." Reitman v. Mulkey, 387 U.S. 369 (1967).

concerned, people of different races are always similarly situated. By contrast, while detrimental gender classifications by government often violate the Constitution, they do not always do so, for the reason that there are differences between males and females that the Constitution necessarily recognizes. In this case we deal with the most basic of these differences: females can become pregnant as the result of sexual intercourse; males cannot. . . .

Applying these principles to the classification enacted by the California Legislature, it is readily apparent that §261.5 does not violate the Equal Protection Clause. Young women and men are not similarly situated with respect to the problems and risk associated with intercourse and pregnancy, and the statute is realistically related to the legitimate state purpose of reducing those problems and risks. . . .

E

In short, the Equal Protection Clause does not mean that the physiological differences between men and women must be disregarded. While those differences must never be permitted to become a pretext for invidious discrimination, no such discrimination is presented by this case. The Constitution surely does not require a State to pretend that demonstrable differences between men and women do not really exist.

BLACKMUN, J., concurring in the judgment.

It is gratifying that the plurality recognizes that "[a]t the risk of stating the obvious, teenage pregnancies . . . have increased dramatically over the last two decades" and "have significant social, medical, and economic consequences for both the mother and her child, and the State." There have been times when I have wondered whether the Court was capable of this perception, particularly when it has struggled with the different but not unrelated problems that attend abortion issues.

. . . California's statute in this case [is] addressed to . . . the control and direction of young people's sexual activities. The plurality opinion impliedly concedes as much when it notes that "approximately half of all teenage pregnancies end in abortion," and that "those children who are born" are "likely candidates to become wards of the State."

I, however, cannot vote to strike down the California statutory rape law, for I think it is a sufficiently reasoned and constitutional effort to control the problem at its inception. For me, there is an important difference between this state action and a State's adamant and rigid refusal to face, or even to recognize, the "significant . . . consequences" — to the woman — of a forced or unwanted conception. I have found it difficult to rule constitutional, for example, state efforts to block, at that later point, a woman's attempt to deal with the enormity of the problem confronting her, just as I have rejected state efforts to prevent women from rationally taking steps to prevent that problem from arising. See, e.g., Carey v. Population Services International, 431 U.S. 678 (1977). See also Griswold v. Connecticut, 381 U.S. 479 (1965). . . .

I think, too, that it is only fair, with respect to this particular petitioner, to point out that his partner, Sharon, appears not to have been an unwilling participant in at least the initial stages of the intimacies that took place the night of June 3, 1978.[a]

a. Sharon at the preliminary hearing testified as follows:

Q: [by the Deputy District Attorney] . . . Where did you first meet [the defendant]?
A: At a bus stop . . . [Sharon reports that she and her sister met three boys, Michael, Bruce, and David].

Petitioner's and Sharon's nonacquaintance with each other before the incident: their drinking; their withdrawal from the others of the group; their foreplay, in

---

Q: Now, after you met the defendant, what happened?
A: We walked down to the railroad tracks.
Q: What happened at the railroad tracks?
A: We were drinking at the railroad tracks and we walked over to this bush and he started kissing me and stuff, and I was kissing him back, too, at first. Then, I was telling him to stop . . . and I was telling him to slow down and stop. He said, 'okay, okay.' But then he just kept doing it. He just kept doing it and then my sister and two other guys came over to where we were and my sister said — told me to get up and come home. And then I didn't . . . and then my sister and . . . David, one of the boys that were there, started walking home and we stayed there and then later . . . Bruce left Michael, you know.
The Court: Michael being the defendant?
The Witness: Yeah. We was lying there and we were kissing each other, and then he asked me if I wanted to walk him over to the park; so we walked over to the park and we sat down on a bench and then he started kissing me again and we were laying on the bench. And he told me to take my pants off. I said, 'No,' and I was trying to get up and he hit me back down on the bench and then I just said to myself, 'Forget it,' and I let him do what he wanted to do and he took my pants off and he was telling me to put my legs around him and stuff —
Q: Did you have sexual intercourse with the defendant?
A: Yeah. . . .
Q: You said that he hit you?
A: Yeah.
Q: How did he hit you?
A: He slugged me in the face.
Q: With what did he slug you?
A: His fist.
Q: Where abouts in the face?
A: On my chin.
Q: As a result of that, did you have any bruises or any kind of an injury?
A: Yeah.
Q: What happened?
A: I had bruises.
The Court: Did he hit you one time or did he hit you more than once?
The Witness: He hit me about two or three times.
Q: Now, during the course of that evening, did the defendant ask you your age?
A: Yeah.
Q: And what did you tell him?
A: Sixteen. . . .
Q: Now, you said you had been drinking, is that correct?
A: Yes.
Q: Would you describe your condition as a result of the drinking?
A: I was a little drunk.

CROSS-EXAMINATION [by defense attorney]

Q: Why did you [go off with Mr. M.]?
A: I don't know. I guess I wanted to. . . .
Q: [W]hat did you do when you and Mr. M. were there in the bushes?
A: We were kissing and hugging . . . We were laying down. . . .
Q: How far away from the rest of them were you?
A: They were just bushes right next to the railroad tracks. We just walked off into the bushes; not very far.
Q: So your sister and the other two boys came over to where you . . . and Michael were. . . . What did they say to you, if you remember?
A: My sister didn't say anything. She said, 'Come on, Sharon, let's go home.' . . .
Q: Did you go home with her?
A: No.
Q: You wanted to stay with Mr. M.?
A: I don't know.
Q: Was this before or after he hit you?
A: Before.
Q: What happened in the five minutes that Bruce stayed there with you and Michael? . . . Did you have occasion at that time to kiss Bruce?

which she willingly participated and seems to have encouraged; and the closeness of their ages (a difference of only one year and 18 days) are factors that should make this case an unattractive one to prosecute at all, and especially to prosecute as a felony, rather than as a misdemeanor chargeable under §261.5. But the State has chosen to prosecute in that manner, and the facts, I reluctantly conclude, may fit the crime.

BRENNAN, J., with whom Justices White and Marshall join, dissenting.

I.

It is disturbing to find the Court so splintered on a case that presents such a straightforward issue: Whether the admittedly gender-based classification in §261.5 bears a sufficient relationship to the State's asserted goal of preventing teenage pregnancies to survive the "mid-level" constitutional scrutiny mandated by Craig v. Boren, 429 U.S. 190 (1976). Applying the analytical framework provided by our precedents, I am convinced that there is only one proper resolution of this issue: the classification must be declared unconstitutional. I fear that the plurality opinion and Justices Stewart and Blackmun reach the opposite result by placing too much emphasis on the desirability of achieving the State's asserted statutory goal — prevention of teenage pregnancy — and not enough emphasis on the fundamental question of whether the sex-based discrimination in the California statute is *substantially* related to the achievement of that goal.[a]

II.

. . . The burden is on the government to prove both the importance of its asserted objective and the substantial relationship between the classification and that

---

A: Yeah.
Q: And were you standing up at this time?
A: No, we were sitting down.
Q: Okay. So at this point in time you had left Mr. M. and you were hugging and kissing with Bruce. . . . Was your sister still there then?
A: No. Yeah, she was at first.
Q: What was she doing?
A: She was standing up with Michael and David.
Q: Yes. Was she doing anything with Michael and David?
A: No, I don't think so.
Q: Whose idea was it for you and Bruce to kiss? Did you initiate that?
A: Yes.
Q: What happened after Bruce left?
A: Michael asked me if I wanted to go walk to the park.
Q: And what did you say?
A: I said, 'Yes.'
Q: And then what happened?
A: We walked to the park.

a. None of the three opinions upholding the California statute fairly applies the equal protection analysis this Court has so carefully developed since Craig v. Boren, 429 U.S. 190 (1976). . . . They overlook the fact that the State has not met its burden of proving that the gender discrimination in §261.5 is substantially related to the achievement of the State's asserted statutory goal. My Brethren seem not to recognize that California has the burden of proving that a gender-neutral statutory rape law would be less effective than §261.5 in deterring sexual activity leading to teenage pregnancy. Because they fail to analyze the issue in these terms, I believe they reach an unsupportable result.

objective. And the State cannot meet that burden without showing that a gender-neutral statute would be a less effective means of achieving that goal.

The State of California vigorously asserts that the "important governmental objective" to be served by §261.5 is the prevention of teenage pregnancy. It claims that its statute furthers this goal by deterring sexual activity by males — the class of persons it considers more responsible for causing those pregnancies. But even assuming that prevention of teenage pregnancy is an important governmental objective and that it is in fact an objective of §261.5, California still has the burden of proving that there are fewer teenage pregnancies under its gender-based statutory rape law than there would be if the law were gender neutral. To meet this burden, the State must show that because its statutory rape law punishes only males, and not females, it more effectively deters minor females from having sexual intercourse.

The plurality assumes that a gender-neutral statute would be less effective than §261.5 in deterring sexual activity because a gender-neutral statute would create significant enforcement problems. The plurality thus accepts the State's assertion that "a female is surely less likely to report violations of the statute if she herself would be subject to criminal prosecution. . . ." However, a State's bare assertion that its gender-based statutory classification substantially furthers an important governmental interest is not enough to meet its burden of proof under Craig v. Boren. Rather, the State must produce evidence. The State has not produced such evidence in this case. Moreover, there are at least two serious flaws in the State's assertion that law enforcement problems created by a gender-neutral statutory rape law would make such a statute less effective than a gender-based statute in deterring sexual activity. First, the experience of other jurisdictions, and California itself, belies the plurality's conclusion that a gender-neutral statutory rape law "may well be incapable of enforcement." There are now at least 37 States that have enacted gender-neutral statutory rape laws. . . .

The second flaw in the State's assertion is that even assuming that a gender-neutral statute would be more difficult to enforce, the State has still not shown that those enforcement problems would make such a statute less effective than a gender-based statute in deterring minor females from engaging in sexual intercourse. Common sense, however, suggests that a gender-neutral statutory rape law is potentially a *greater* deterrent of sexual activity than a gender-based law, for the simple reason that a gender-neutral law subjects both men and women to criminal sanctions and thus arguably has a deterrent effect on twice as many potential violators. Even if fewer persons were prosecuted under the gender-neutral law, as the State suggests, it would still be true that twice as many persons would be *subject* to arrest. The State's failure to prove that a gender-neutral law would be a less effective deterrent than a gender-based law, like the State's failure to prove that a gender-neutral law would be difficult to enforce, should have led this Court to invalidate §261.5.

III.

Until very recently, no California court or commentator had suggested that the purpose of California's statutory rape law was to protect young women from the risk of pregnancy. Indeed, the historical development of §261.5 demonstrates that the law was initially enacted on the premise that young women, in contrast to young men, were to be deemed legally incapable of consenting to an act of sexual intercourse.

Because their chastity was considered particularly precious, those young women were felt to be uniquely in need of the State's protection. In contrast, young men were assumed to be capable of making such decisions for themselves; the law therefore did not offer them any special protection.

It is perhaps because the gender classification in California's statutory rape law was initially designed to further these outmoded sexual stereotypes, rather than to reduce the incidence of teenage pregnancies, that the State has been unable to demonstrate a substantial relationship between the classification and its newly asserted goal. But whatever the reason, the State has not shown that Cal. Penal Code §261.5 is any more effective than a gender-neutral law would be in deterring minor females from engaging in sexual intercourse. It has therefore not met its burden of proving that the statutory classification is substantially related to the achievement of its asserted goal. I would hold that §261.5 violates the Equal Protection Clause of the Fourteenth Amendment, and I would reverse the judgment of the California Supreme Court.

STEVENS, J., dissenting.

. . . I think the plurality is quite correct in making the assumption that the joint act that this law seeks to prohibit creates a greater risk of harm for the female than for the male. But the plurality surely cannot believe that the risk of pregnancy confronted by the female — any more than the risk of venereal disease confronted by males as well as females — has provided an effective deterrent to voluntary female participation in the risk-creating conduct. Yet the plurality's decision seems to rest on the assumption that the California Legislature acted on the basis of that rather fanciful notion.

In my judgment, the fact that a class of persons is especially vulnerable to a risk that a statute is designed to avoid is a reason for making the statute applicable to that class. The argument that a special need for protection provides a rational explanation for an exemption is one I simply do not comprehend.[a]

In this case, the fact that a female confronts a greater risk of harm than a male is a reason for applying the prohibition to her — not a reason for granting her a license to use her own judgment on whether or not to assume the risk. Surely, if we examine the problem from the point of view of society's interest in preventing the risk-creating conduct from occurring at all, it is irrational to exempt 50% of the potential violators. And, if we view the government's interest as that of a parens patriae seeking to protect its subjects from harming themselves, the discrimination is actually perverse. Would a rational parent making rules for the conduct of twin children of opposite sex simultaneously forbid the son and authorize the daughter to engage in conduct that is especially harmful to the daughter? That is the effect of this statutory classification.

If pregnancy or some other special harm is suffered by one of the two participants in the prohibited act, that special harm no doubt would constitute a legitimate mitigating factor in deciding what, if any, punishment might be appropriate

---

a. A hypothetical racial classification will illustrate my point. Assume that skin pigmentation provides some measure of protection against cancer caused by exposure to certain chemicals in the atmosphere and, therefore, that white employees confront a greater risk than black employees in certain industrial settings. Would it be rational to require black employees to wear protective clothing but to exempt whites from that requirement? It seems to me that the greater risk of harm to white workers would be a reason for including them in the requirement — not for granting them an exemption.

in a given case. But from the standpoint of fashioning a general preventive rule —
or, indeed, in determining appropriate punishment when neither party in fact has
suffered any special harm — I regard a total exemption for the members of the
more endangered class as utterly irrational.

In my opinion, the only acceptable justification for a general rule requiring
disparate treatment of the two participants in a joint act must be a legislative
judgment that one is more guilty than the other. The risk-creating conduct that
this statute is designed to prevent requires the participation of two persons —
one male and one female. In many situations it is probably true that one is the
aggressor and the other is either an unwilling, or at least a less willing, participant
in the joint act. If a statute authorized punishment of only one participant and
required the prosecutor to prove that participant had been the aggressor, I
assume that the discrimination would be valid. Although the question is less clear,
I also assume, for the purpose of deciding this case, that it would be permissible
to punish only the male participant, if one element of the offense were proof that
he had been the aggressor, or at least in some respects the more responsible
participant in the joint act. The statute at issue in this case, however, requires no
such proof. The question raised by this statute is whether the State, consistently
with the Federal Constitution, may always punish the male and never the female
when they are equally responsible or when the female is the more responsible of
the two.

It would seem to me that an impartial lawmaker could give only one answer to
that question. The fact that the California Legislature has decided to apply its
prohibition only to the male may reflect a legislative judgment that in the typical
case the male is actually the more guilty party. Any such judgment must, in turn,
assume that the decision to engage in the risk-creating conduct is always — or at
least typically — a male decision. If that assumption is valid, the statutory classification should also be valid. But what is the support for the assumption? It is not
contained in the record of this case or in any legislative history or scholarly study
that has been called to our attention. I think it is supported to some extent by traditional attitudes toward male-female relationships. But the possibility that such a
habitual attitude may reflect nothing more than an irrational prejudice makes it an
insufficient justification for discriminatory treatment that is otherwise blatantly
unfair. For, as I read this statute, it requires that one, and only one, of two equally
guilty wrongdoers be stigmatized by a criminal conviction. . . .

Nor do I find at all persuasive the suggestion that this discrimination is
adequately justified by the desire to encourage females to inform against their male
partners. . . .

Finally, even if my logic is faulty and there actually is some speculative basis for
treating equally guilty males and females differently, I still believe that any such
speculative justification would be outweighed by the paramount interest in evenhanded enforcement of the law. A rule that authorizes punishment of only one of
two equally guilty wrongdoers violates the essence of the constitutional requirement that the sovereign must govern impartially.

Discussion

1. *Intermediate scrutiny.* Note the dispute between plurality and dissent over the
proper application of *Craig*'s intermediate scrutiny test. At various points the plurality
seems to be applying a version of the rational basis test, emphasizing that men and

women are not similarly situated with respect to the purposes of the regulation. The dissent argues that this is the wrong test — that *Craig* requires the government to show that its use of a sex-discriminatory classification is substantially related to the achievement of an important government aim (e.g., preventing teen pregnancy). Does the plurality satisfy the dissent's objections? On what grounds can California argue that its important regulatory aims are better served by a sex-specific than by a sex-neutral law? Of what practical consequence is this dispute about the proper application of intermediate scrutiny?

2. *Archaic and overbroad stereotypes?* One criticism of *Michael M.* is that sex-based statutory rape laws are not based on biology, but instead on conventional stereotypes about male and female behavior. As the dissent emphasizes, the historic purpose of statutory rape laws was to preserve the chastity of young women before marriage, not to prevent teen pregnancy. Even Justice Rehnquist concedes: "Some legislators may have been concerned about preventing teenage pregnancies, others about protecting young females from physical injury or from the loss of 'chastity,' and still others about promoting various religious and moral attitudes towards premarital sex." If the purpose of the statutory rape law were to preserve the chastity of young women, rather than to prevent teen pregnancy, would that make a difference to constitutional analysis of the statute under *Craig*'s intermediate scrutiny standard? What if preserving girls' chastity were the original purpose of a statute whose aims had evolved over time? What if both purposes moved legislators? Does it matter if the legislature acted for a mixture of constitutional and unconstitutional reasons? For a history of statutory rape laws, see Rita Eidson, Comment, The Constitutionality of Statutory Rape Laws, 27 U.C.L.A. L. Rev. 757, 762 (1980).

With *Michael M.* compare Matter of Jessie C., 565 N.Y.S.2d 941 (N.Y. App. Div. 1991), which struck down a similar statute because (1) prevention of pregnancy could not be the goal of the statute, given that girls under the age of puberty could be victims, and (2) petitioner "failed to present any cogent reason why deterring only the male would further the prevention of pregnancy better" than applying the prohibition to both the underage male and the underage female.

3. Are there relevant social differences between young men and women that legislators may constitutionally consider in regulating the conduct in question? Catharine MacKinnon writes that in *Michael M.*

the fact that it is overwhelmingly girls who are sexually victimized by older males for reasons wholly unrelated to their capacity to become pregnant was completely obscured. The facts of social inequality, of sex aggravated by age, that could have supported particular legislative attention to the sexual assault of girls were not even considered. Underage girls form a credible disadvantaged group for equal protection purposes when the social facts of sexual assault are faced, facts which prominently feature one-sided sexual aggression by older males.[122]

Does this suggest that Professor MacKinnon agrees with Justice Rehnquist's decision, albeit for different reasons? How might an equal protection decision that she

122. MacKinnon, Reflections on Sex Equality Under Law, at 1305-1306.

wrote differ? Is a decision upholding the sex-based statutory rape law that empha-sized social rather than physical differences more acceptable to you — or less?

4. A statutory rape law like California's stipulates, as a matter of law, that under-age girls lack meaningful capacity to consent to sexual relations. In social fact, there may be wide differences in psychological and social development, in socialization, and in experience, that make some girls better situated to make judgments about entering sexual relations than others. Resolving questions about a young girl's capacity to consent to sexual relations does not reveal whether a young girl has consented in fact in any particular case. Why might the state prefer to prosecute under the statutory rape law rather than a general rape statute?

Why does Justice Blackmun reproduce excerpts from the trial transcript? What do these excerpts demonstrate about the underlying facts of the *Michael M.* case? Could California have prosecuted this case under a general rape statute? Should a prosecutor have relied on the statutory rape statute to secure a conviction that she might not secure under a general rape statute?

In what sense, if at all, do questions about the consent standard and its applica-tion in cases of "date rape" present questions of equal protection? Note that these questions seem to have little, if anything, to do with the use of gender classifications that the intermediate scrutiny standard regulates. What problems does removing gender classifications from a rape statute cure? What problems persist? Is there any harm in removing gender classifications from laws that regulate gender-salient practices like rape or domestic violence?

FRANCES OLSEN, STATUTORY RAPE: A FEMINIST CRITIQUE OF RIGHTS ANALYSIS
63 Tex. L. Rev. 387, 401-02, 412, 418-20, 426 (1984)

Statutory rape laws . . . pose a classic political dilemma for feminists. On one hand, they protect females; like laws against rape, incest, child molestation, and child marriage, statutory rape laws are a statement of social disapproval of certain forms of exploitation. To some extent they reduce abuse and victimization. On the other hand, statutory rape laws restrict the sexual activity of young women and rein-force the double standard of sexual morality. The laws both protect and undermine women's rights. . . .

Feminists charge that statutes such as [California's] are harmful to women on both a practical and an ideological level. First, as an effort to control the sexual activities of young women, statutory rape laws are an unwarranted governmental intrusion into their lives and an oppressive restriction upon their freedom of action. An unmarried woman under eighteen cannot legally have intercourse in California. Whether the prohibition is enforced by prosecuting her partner or by prosecuting her as an aider and abettor, the statute interferes with the sexual freedom of the underage female. In the language of rights analysis, statutory rape laws violate the female's right to privacy and her right to be as free sexually as her male counterpart.

Feminists' second common objection to statutory rape laws is ideological. Gender-based statutory rape laws reinforce the sexual stereotype of men as aggres-sors and women as passive victims. . . . For males, sex is an accomplishment; they gain something through intercourse. For women, sex entails giving something up.

Further, for the myth of male sexual accomplishment to exist, some females must give in. The double standard divides females into two classes — virgins and whores, "good girls" whose chastity should be protected and "bad girls" who may be exploited with impunity. . . . [G]ender-based statutory rape laws violate the right of all women to be treated equally to men. . . .

A commitment to establish and protect rights for women provides us with little guidance in deciding whether to support any particular statutory rape law or to oppose all statutory rape laws. Even if we artificially simplify our task by focusing only upon the rights of women, we cannot determine how to protect these rights. Rights analysis does not help us as an analytic tool because it is indeterminate. Every effort to protect young women against private oppression by individual men risks subjecting women to state oppression, and every effort to protect them against state oppression undermines their power to resist individual oppression.

Further, any acknowledgment of the actual difference between the present situation of males and females stigmatizes females and perpetuates discrimination. But if we ignore power differences and pretend that women and men are similarly situated, we perpetuate discrimination by disempowering ourselves from instituting effective change. The strategy of protecting rights runs afoul of the conflict between rights as freedom of action and rights as security; the strategy of promoting equality runs afoul of the conflict between formal equality of opportunity and substantive equality of outcome. . . .

Michael M.'s liberal-legalist approach has a related but more serious political consequence: it co-opts feminists into acquiescing to a mystification of sexual intercourse. The plurality opinion characterizes Sharon and Michael as engaging in the same conduct. In this way, they treat sexual intercourse as though it were an equal interaction, which it is not in our society. In fact, men and women rarely receive equal benefits from sexual intercourse. The pretense of equality disempowers women from taking collective action to improve the conditions of their lives.

Note: Sex-Neutrality in Rape Laws

Most states now use sex-neutral language to describe both perpetrators and victims of the act of rape. Nevertheless, there are a few cases involving equal protection challenges to statutes that define rape in terms of nonconsensual penetration of women by men. In almost all cases the statutes have been upheld. See, e.g., Country v. Parratt, 684 F.2d 588 (8th Cir.), cert. denied, 459 U.S. 1043 (1982); People v. Salinas, 551 P.2d 703 (Colo. Sup. Ct. 1976) (en banc); State v. Witt, 245 N.W.2d 612 (Minn. 1976); Stewart v. State, 534 S.W.2d 875 (Ct. Crim. App. Tenn. 1976); State v. Kelly, 526 P.2d 720 (Ariz. 1974), cert. denied, 420 U.S. 935 (1975); State v. Ewald, 216 N.W.2d 213 (Wis. 1974); Brooks v. State, 330 A.2d 670 (Md. Ct. Spec. App. 1975). Contra, People v. Liberta, 64 N.Y.2d 152; 474 N.E.2d 567 (N.Y. 1984) (holding unconstitutional exemption of females for forcible rape of males). In most cases these decisions argue that men and women are not similarly situated physically, because of differences in genitalia and body structure, because only men can penetrate, and because only women can get pregnant. Do you agree that this is the best justification for sex-differentiated rape statutes? Note that rape statutes can make sex-based differentiations both with respect to the perpetrator and with respect to the victim. Are there good reasons to preserve sex neutrality with respect to the victim as opposed to the perpetrator? Should the law focus on penetration, when there are many other forms of nonconsensual sexual contact? Do rape laws present sex equality problems because they classify perpetrator or victim by sex, or for some other reason?

Sex-based differentiation is not the only source of sex inequality in rape statutes, if it is a problem at all. Core problems of inequality arise from doctrines about what constitutes consent to intercourse and doctrines about what presumptions and standards apply to proof of rape (especially in acquaintance rape situations). These doctrines are not sex-specific and therefore are completely missed by an approach that focuses exclusively on classification by sex.

TUAN ANH NGUYEN v. INS
533 U.S. 53 (2001)

Justice KENNEDY delivered the opinion of the Court.

[8 U.S.C. §1409(a) automatically grants American citizenship upon birth to a child born out of wedlock in a foreign country if born to an American mother, but denies citizenship in the same circumstances if the only American parent was the father, unless a paternity decree is entered before the child turns 18. Nguyen was born in Vietnam to an American father, Joseph Boulais, and a Vietnamese mother. When he was six years old he came to the United States to live with Boulais and became a permanent resident. When he was 22 Nguyen pleaded guilty to sexual assault on a minor. The INS began deportation proceedings. Nguyen defended on the grounds that he was a United States citizen, and his father established his paternity through DNA testing when Nguyen was 28 years old. Nguyen and his father argued that §1409(a) violates equal protection by providing different rules for attainment of citizenship by children born abroad and out of wedlock depending upon whether the one parent with American citizenship is the mother or the father. The Court considered a challenge to §1409(a) in Miller v. Albright, 523 U.S. 420 (1998), but was unable to agree on a single rationale.]

[If a child's parents are married, 8 U.S.C. §1401(g) governs] the general requirement for acquisition of citizenship by a child born outside the United States and its outlying possessions. [T]he child is also a citizen if, before the birth, the citizen parent had been physically present in the United States for a total of five years, at least two of which were after the parent turned 14 years of age.

[If the parents are unwed §1409(a) governs. When] the father is the citizen parent and the mother is an alien [the statute requires]:

(1) a blood relationship between the person and the father is established by clear and convincing evidence,
(2) the father had the nationality of the United States at the time of the person's birth,
(3) the father (unless deceased) has agreed in writing to provide financial support for the person until the person reaches the age of 18 years, and
(4) while the person is under the age of 18 years —
    (A) the person is legitimated under the law of the person's residence or domicile,
    (B) the father acknowledges paternity of the person in writing under oath, or
    (C) the paternity of the person is established by adjudication of a competent court.

In addition [the citizen parent must satisfy] the residency requirement of §1401(g).

When the citizen parent of the child born abroad and out of wedlock is the child's mother, [§1409(c) governs]:

> (c) Notwithstanding the provision of subsection (a) of this section, a person born, after December 23, 1952, outside the United States and out of wedlock shall be held to have acquired at birth the nationality status of his mother, if the mother had the nationality of the United States at the time of such person's birth, and if the mother had previously been physically present in the United States or one of its outlying possessions for a continuous period of one year.

Section 1409(a) thus imposes a set of requirements on the children of citizen fathers born abroad and out of wedlock to a noncitizen mother that are not imposed under like circumstances when the citizen parent is the mother. [The Court held that Nguyen's father's failure to meet §1409(a)(3) did not apply because Nguyen fell under an exception for children born before 1986. This left only the question of whether the requirements of §1409(a)(4) were unconstitutional].

[Justice Kennedy noted that after United States v. Virginia, gender-based classifications must serve "important governmental objectives" that are "substantially related to the achievement of those objectives."]

. . . §1409(a)(4) requires one of three affirmative steps to be taken if the citizen parent is the father, but not if the citizen parent is the mother: legitimation; a declaration of paternity under oath by the father; or a court order of paternity. Congress' decision . . . is based on the significant difference between their respective relationships to the potential citizen at the time of birth [and] . . . is justified by two important governmental objectives. . . .

The first . . . is the importance of assuring that a biological parent–child relationship exists. In the case of the mother, the relation is verifiable from the birth itself. The mother's status is documented in most instances by the birth certificate or hospital records and the witnesses who attest to her having given birth.

In the case of the father, the uncontestable fact is that he need not be present at the birth. If he is present, furthermore, that circumstance is not incontrovertible proof of fatherhood. . . . Section 1409(a)(4)'s provision of three options for a father seeking to establish paternity — legitimation, paternity oath, and court order of paternity — is designed to ensure an acceptable documentation of paternity.

Petitioners argue that the requirement of §1409(a)(1), that a father provide clear and convincing evidence of parentage, is sufficient to achieve the end of establishing paternity, given the sophistication of modern DNA tests. Section 1409(a)(1) does not actually mandate a DNA test, however. The Constitution, moreover, does not require that Congress elect one particular mechanism from among many possible methods of establishing paternity, even if that mechanism arguably might be the most scientifically advanced method. With respect to DNA testing, the expense, reliability, and availability of such testing in various parts of the world may have been of particular concern to Congress. . . . Given the proof of motherhood that is inherent in birth itself, it is unremarkable that Congress did not require the same affirmative steps of mothers.

Finally, to require Congress to speak without reference to the gender of the parent with regard to its objective of ensuring a blood tie between parent and child would be to insist on a hollow neutrality. . . . . Congress could have required both mothers and fathers to prove parenthood within 30 days or, for that matter, 18 years, of the child's birth. Given that the mother is always present at birth, but that the father need not be, the facially neutral rule would sometimes require fathers to take additional affirmative steps which would not be required of mothers, whose names will appear on the birth certificate as a result of their presence at the birth, and who will have the benefit of witnesses to the birth to call upon. The issue is not the use of gender specific terms instead of neutral ones. Just as neutral terms can mask discrimination that is unlawful, gender specific terms can mark a permissible distinction. . . . Here, the use of gender specific terms takes into account a biological difference between the parents.

The second important governmental interest . . . is . . . ensur[ing] that the child and the citizen parent have some demonstrated opportunity or potential to develop not just a relationship that is recognized, as a formal matter, by the law, but one that consists of the real, everyday ties that provide a connection between child and citizen parent and, in turn, the United States. In the case of a citizen mother and a child born overseas, the opportunity for a meaningful relationship between citizen parent and child inheres in the very event of birth, an event so often critical to our constitutional and statutory understandings of citizenship. The mother knows that the child is in being and is hers and has an initial point of contact with him. There is at least an opportunity for mother and child to develop a real, meaningful relationship.

The same opportunity does not result from the event of birth, as a matter of biological inevitability, in the case of the unwed father. Given the 9-month interval between conception and birth, it is not always certain that a father will know that a child was conceived, nor is it always clear that even the mother will be sure of the father's identity. This fact takes on particular significance in the case of a child born overseas and out of wedlock. One concern in this context has always been with young people, men for the most part, who are on duty with the Armed Forces in foreign countries.

. . . The ease of travel and the willingness of Americans to visit foreign countries have resulted in numbers of trips abroad that must be of real concern when we contemplate the prospect of accepting petitioners' argument, which would mandate, contrary to Congress' wishes, citizenship by male parentage subject to no condition save the father's previous length of residence in this country. In 1999 alone, Americans made almost 25 million trips abroad, excluding trips to Canada and Mexico. Visits to Canada and Mexico add to this figure almost 34 million additional visits. And the average American overseas traveler spent 15.1 nights out of the United States in 1999.

Principles of equal protection do not require Congress to ignore this reality. To the contrary, these facts demonstrate the critical importance of the Government's interest in ensuring some opportunity for a tie between citizen father and foreign born child which is a reasonable substitute for the opportunity manifest between mother and child at the time of birth. Indeed, especially in light of the number of Americans who take short sojourns abroad, the prospect that a father might not even know of the conception is a realistic possibility. Even if a father knows of the fact of conception, moreover, it does not follow that he will be present at the birth of the child. Thus, unlike the case of the mother, there is no assurance that the father and his biological child will ever meet. . . .

Petitioners and their *amici* argue . . . that, rather than fulfilling an important governmental interest, §1409 merely embodies a gender-based stereotype. . . . §1409 addresses an undeniable difference in the circumstance of the parents at the time a child is born. . . . [T]he difference does not result from some stereotype, defined as a frame of mind resulting from irrational or uncritical analysis. There is nothing irrational or improper in the recognition that at the moment of birth — a critical event in the statutory scheme and in the whole tradition of citizenship law — the mother's knowledge of the child and the fact of parenthood have been established in a way not guaranteed in the case of the unwed father. This is not a stereotype.

[T]he question remains whether the means Congress chose to further its objective — the imposition of certain additional requirements upon an unwed father — substantially relate to that end. . . . [I]t should be unsurprising that Congress decided to require that an opportunity for a parent–child relationship occur during the formative years of the child's minority. In furtherance of the desire to ensure some tie between this country and one who seeks citizenship, various other statutory provisions concerning citizenship and naturalization require some act linking the child to the United States to occur before the child reaches 18 years of age. . . .

Even if [the relevant interest is] the establishment of a real, practical relationship of considerable substance between parent and child in every case . . . [I]t is almost axiomatic that a policy which seeks to foster the opportunity for meaningful parent–child bonds to develop has a close and substantial bearing on the governmental interest in the actual formation of that bond. None of our gender-based classification equal protection cases has required that the statute under consideration must be capable of achieving its ultimate objective in every instance.

To fail to acknowledge even our most basic biological differences — such as the fact that a mother must be present at birth but the father need not be — risks making the guarantee of equal protection superficial, and so disserving it. Mechanistic classification of all our differences as stereotypes would operate to obscure those misconceptions and prejudices that are real. The distinction embodied in the statutory scheme here at issue is not marked by misconception and prejudice, nor does it show disrespect for either class. The difference between men and women in relation to the birth process is a real one, and the principle of equal protection does not forbid Congress to address the problem at hand in a manner specific to each gender.

Justice SCALIA, with whom Justice Thomas joins, concurring.

I remain of the view that the Court lacks power to provide relief of the sort requested in this suit — namely, conferral of citizenship on a basis other than that prescribed by Congress. [On] the merits of petitioners' equal protection claims,] I join the opinion of the Court.

Justice O'CONNOR, with whom Justice Souter, Justice Ginsburg, and Justice Breyer join, dissenting.

Sex-based statutes, even when accurately reflecting the way most men or women behave, deny individuals opportunity. Such generalizations must be viewed not in isolation, but in the context of our Nation's "long and unfortunate history of sex discrimination." Sex-based generalizations both reflect and reinforce "fixed notions concerning the roles and abilities of males and females." . . .

[T]he existence of comparable or superior sex-neutral alternatives has been a powerful reason to reject a sex-based classification. . . . Far from being "hollow," the avoidance of gratuitous sex-based distinctions [through sex-neutral rules] is the hallmark of equal protection. . . . [F]idelity to the Constitution's pledge of equal protection demands more when a facially sex-based classification is at issue. This is not because we sit in judgment of the wisdom of laws in one instance but not the other, but rather because of the potential for "injury . . . to personal dignity," that inheres in or accompanies so many sex-based classifications.

. . . [T]he idea that a mother's presence at birth supplies adequate assurance of an opportunity to develop a relationship while a father's presence at birth does not would appear to rest only on an overbroad sex-based generalization. A mother may not have an opportunity for a relationship if the child is removed from his or her mother on account of alleged abuse or neglect, or if the child and mother are separated by tragedy, such as disaster or war, of the sort apparently present in this case. There is no reason, other than stereotype, to say that fathers who are present at birth lack an opportunity for a relationship on similar terms. The "physical differences between men and women," therefore do not justify §1409(a)(4)'s discrimination. . . .

. . . If Congress wishes to advance [the goal of "establishing . . . a real, practical relationship of considerable substance"], it could easily do so by employing a sex-neutral classification that is a far "more germane basis of classification" than sex. For example, Congress could require some degree of regular contact between the child and the citizen parent over a period of time.

The claim that §1409(a)(4) substantially relates to the achievement of the goal of a "real, practical relationship" thus finds support not in biological differences but instead in a stereotype — *i.e.,* "the generalization that mothers are significantly more likely than fathers . . . to develop caring relationships with their children." Such a claim relies on "the very stereotype the law condemns," "lends credibility" to the generalization, and helps to convert that "assumption" into "a self-fulfilling prophecy." Indeed, contrary to this stereotype, Boulais has reared Nguyen, while Nguyen apparently has lacked a relationship with his mother. . . .

In denying petitioner's claim that §1409(a)(4) rests on stereotypes, the majority . . . asserts that a "stereotype" is "defined as a frame of mind resulting from irrational or uncritical analysis." This Court has long recognized, however, that an impermissible stereotype may enjoy empirical support and thus be in a sense "rational." Indeed, the stereotypes that underlie a sex-based classification "may hold true for many, even most, individuals." But in numerous cases where a measure of truth has inhered in the generalization, "the Court has rejected official actions that classify unnecessarily and overbroadly by gender when more accurate and impartial functional lines can be drawn."

Nor do stereotypes consist only of those overbroad generalizations that the reviewing court considers to "show disrespect" for a class. Compare, e.g., *Craig.* The hallmark of a stereotypical sex-based classification under this Court's precedents is not whether the classification is insulting, but whether it "relie[s] upon the simplistic, outdated assumption that gender could be used as a 'proxy for other, more germane bases of classification.'" *Mississippi Univ. for Women.* . . .

Section 1409 was first enacted as §205 of the Nationality Act of 1940. [Its original rationale was that] "[u]nder American law the mother has a right to custody and control of such child as against the putative father, and is *bound* to maintain it as its *natural guardian*."

Section 1409(a)(4) is thus paradigmatic of a historic regime that left women with responsibility, and freed men from responsibility, for nonmarital children. . . . Unlike §1409(a)(4), our States' child custody and support laws no longer assume that mothers alone are "bound" to serve as "natural guardians" of nonmarital children. The majority, however, rather than confronting the stereotypical notion that mothers must care for these children and fathers may ignore them, quietly condones the "very stereotype the law condemns.". . .

Finally, while the recitation of statistics concerning military personnel and overseas travel highlights the opportunities for United States citizens to interact with citizens of foreign countries, it bears little on the question whether §1409(a)(4)'s *discriminatory means* are a permissible governmental response to those circumstances. Indeed, the majority's discussion may itself simply reflect the stereotype of male irresponsibility that is no more a basis for the validity of the classification than are stereotypes about the "traditional" behavior patterns of women.

Discussion

1. *Americans abroad.* The not-so-implicit concern expressed in the majority opinion is that American men traveling around the globe may father large numbers of illegitimate children, leading to what the Court describes as "the difficult context of conferring citizenship on vast numbers of persons." Are there good reasons to think that American women will, on the average, produce fewer illegitimate offspring than men? Even if so, is this an impermissible stereotype?

2. *Deadbeat dads.* The Court dodges consideration of §1409(a)(3), which requires that the father agree in writing to support the child until the age of 18. Does this give you a sense of what Congress's real motivations were? Note that women are not required to provide any promise of financial support for the illegitimate child. Is this distinction constitutional?

3. *Biological differences or sex-role expectations?* The majority argues that the biological difference that women must be present at birth while men need not makes it easier to establish who the mother is and increases the likelihood that the mother will form a lasting relationship with the child. Is this a matter of biology or a matter of cultural expectations about how most women will behave? The implicit story behind §1409(a) and §1409(c) is that other people will know who the mother is and hold her responsible for the illegitimate child, and the mother herself will feel a responsibility to raise the child. Men, on the other hand, cannot be trusted (or expected) to take care of their illegitimate children. Nevertheless, note that if a woman gives birth at home and then abandons the child on someone else's doorstep, the child is a citizen if the mother meets the residency requirements of §1409(c). Note, moreover, that in this case the father, Joseph Boulais, raised Nguyen in the United States and fought to keep him from being deported.

Why does the Court use biology as a shorthand for culture? One possibility is that the Court believes that maternal and paternal behaviors are "biological" in the sense of being hardwired. A second possibility is that the use of the language of biology is strategic, based on the way that the doctrines have developed over time. The doctrines of constitutional sex equality are suspicious of distinctions premised on traditional differences between men and women (which have their roots in cultural expectations about gender roles) but are less suspicious of distinctions based on "real" biological differences. (Compare *Geduldig*.) Doctrine assumes that regulation responsive to biological differences does not reflect stereotypes, but "real" differences. Thus, by characterizing the government's interest as predicated on biological differences (presence at the time and place of birth) the Court can justify less judicial scrutiny.

Suppose the Court acknowledged that some cultural expectations about gendered behavior — like male irresponsibility with respect to illegitimate children — are sufficiently robust and have sufficiently important consequences that Congress must take them into account. Although §1409(a) and §1409(c) may actually reinforce gender stereotypes, that is a risk worth taking. Put in those terms, is the result reasonable? How do we tell when this balance is properly struck? Note that by putting the question in terms of biological differences, the Court can avoid the objection that it is engaged in a controversial, value-laden balancing. Do you think that if courts were more forthright they would be likely to reach more just results?

4. Does the *Nguyen* case apply the version of heightened scrutiny the Court announced in *Craig*? In United States v. Virginia? The dissenting justices in *Nguyen* argued that the majority actually applied a weaker standard of review than heightened scrutiny. They claimed that the majority "hypothesizes about the interest served by the statute and fails adequately to inquire into [its] actual purposes." Do you think that the real purpose of §1409 was to "ensur[e] some opportunity for a tie between [a] citizen father and foreign born child" during the child's minority years?

5. *Women's caretaking responsibility.* Section 1409 imposes a financial obligation on men who wish to obtain citizenship for their foreign-born nonmarital children. Kristin Collins argues that this requirement actually benefits fathers, who may avoid this burden by dissociating from their nonmarital children. At the same time, Collins argues, the law burdens mothers with full responsibility for caretaking.

A historical account locates this maternal obligation in coverture and citizenship law, which served to protect fathers from claims for property or support by nonmarital children:

> [A]n expanded history of American citizenship transmission reveals that the problem with §1409 is not simply that it rests on stereotypes of caretaker mothers and uninterested ("fleeting") fathers. Rather, there is a more coercive aspect to the law: It assumes and perpetuates a legal rule that assigns full responsibility for nonmarital children to mothers, leaving similarly situated men free from the burdens of parenthood.[123]

Is this the fundamental harm in *Nguyen*? Would a sex-neutral statute burden mothers in the same way?

---

123. Kristin Collins, When Father's Rights are Mothers' Duties: The Failure of Equal Protection in Miller v. Albright, 109 Yale L.J. 1669, 1681-1682 (2000).

Note: Putative Parenthood

In Parham v. Hughes, 441 U.S. 347 (1979), the Court upheld a Georgia statute prohibiting an unwed father, but not an unwed mother, from suing for a child's wrongful death unless the father had previously legitimated the child. The Court found that avoiding the problems involving proof of paternity that are most common in cases dealing with fathers, especially after the death of the child in question, was an important state objective. Justice Stewart, joined by Chief Justice Burger and Justices Rehnquist and Stevens, argued that

> [t]he appellant, as the natural father, was responsible for conceiving an illegitimate child and had the opportunity to legitimate the child but failed to do so. Legitimation would have removed the stigma of bastardy and allowed the child to inherit from the father in the same manner as if born in wedlock. . . . Unlike the illegitimate child for whom the status of illegitimacy is involuntary and immutable, the appellant here was responsible for fostering an illegitimate child and for failing to change its status. It is thus neither illogical nor unjust for society to express its "condemnation of irresponsible liaisons beyond the bounds of marriage" by not conferring upon a biological father the statutory right to sue for the wrongful death of his illegitimate child. . . .
>
> [I]t is clear that the Georgia statute does not invidiously discriminate against the appellant simply because he is of the male sex. The fact is that mothers and fathers of illegitimate children are not similarly situated. Under Georgia law, only a father can by voluntary unilateral action make an illegitimate child legitimate. Unlike the mother of an illegitimate child whose identity will rarely be in doubt, the identity of the father will frequently be unknown.
>
> . . . [The] state interest in avoiding fraudulent claims of paternity in order to maintain a fair and orderly system of decedent's property disposition is also present in the context of actions for wrongful death. If paternity has not been established before the commencement of a wrongful-death action, a defendant may be faced with the possibility of multiple lawsuits by individuals all claiming to be the father of the deceased child. Such uncertainty would make it difficult if not impossible for a defendant to settle a wrongful death action in many cases, since there would always exist the risk of a subsequent suit by another person claiming to be the father. The State of Georgia has chosen to deal with this problem by allowing only fathers who have established paternity by legitimating their children to sue for wrongful death, and we cannot say that this solution is an irrational one.

Justice Powell concurred in the judgment.

Justice White dissented, joined by Justices Brennan, Marshall, and Blackmun. He stated that

> Appellant is the father, rather than the mother, of a deceased illegitimate child. It is conceded that for this reason alone he may not bring an action for the wrongful death of his child. Yet four Members of the Court conclude that appellant is not discriminated against "simply" because of his sex . . . because Georgia provides a means by which fathers can legitimate their children. The dispositive point is that only a father may avail himself of this process. Therefore, we are told, "[t]he fact is that mothers and fathers of illegitimate children are not similarly situated." . . . That only fathers *may* resort to the legitimizing process cannot dissolve the sex discrimination in *requiring* them to.

C.   Pregnancy and Sex Equality: Alternative Understandings

As we have seen, equal protection doctrine exhibits two apparently contradictory instincts in matters concerning pregnancy. Doctrine treats the regulation of pregnant women as a gender-neutral practice that warrants no heightened scrutiny, at the same time that it views reproductive physiology as the site of real, categorical sex differences that supply noninvidious reasons for treating men and women differently. As Justice Kennedy observed in *Nguyen*, "The difference between men and women in relation to the birth process is a real one, and the principle of equal protection does not forbid Congress to address the problem at hand in a manner specific to each gender."

The women's movement has been pointing to the regulation of women's family roles as the paradigmatic site of sex discrimination since the 1960s. Movement lawyers argued that it was stereotyping to treat all women as caregivers, where caregivers were generally understood to be nonparticipants in civic life. The movement also argued that it was wrong to organize the socially essential work of caregiving so that those who performed it would in fact be nonparticipants in civic life. The two claims were independent but linked, each a part of the movement's challenge to the system of social understandings and arrangements that transformed the family into a source of second-class citizenship for women.

The movement had greater success in persuading the Court and nation of the merits of the first claim. Equal protection cases regularly prohibit government from discriminating between the sexes on the assumption that women are in engaged in caregiving work that impairs their participation in public life. But the Court has been slow to recognize sex stereotyping in regulation directed at women who are pregnant or to ask whether conflicts between caregiving and wage work might result from the same gender stereotypes that the Court's equal protection cases condemn.

There is, however, federal law that understands conflicts between family and market labor as arising out of traditional sex-role assumptions, and that seeks to alleviate such conflicts in order to facilitate the equal participation of caregivers in public life. Efforts to enact this law began the era in which Congress adopted the ERA. In the early 1970s, the women's movement sought from Congress not only the ERA and protection against discrimination in education and employment, but also legislation that would have involved the federal government in the provision of child care for middle-class as well as poorer families. Congress responded to the women's movement with key legislation, including the Comprehensive Child Care Development Act (CCDA), passed in 1971 but vetoed by President Nixon.[124] The CCDA would have provided Head Start, day care, and supportive education for families at no cost or according to a sliding scale based on income. It was responsive to the demand of women for "universally available, publicly supported child care." For this same reason, however, opponents of the bill perceived the CCDA as an assault on the traditional family form.

After both Nixon and Ford vetoed child-care legislation, Congress altered its strategy for alleviating conflicts between the market and family obligations of

---

124. This story is told in Robert C. Post & Reva B. Siegel, Legislative Constitutionalism and Section Five Power: Policentric Interpretation of the Family and Medical Leave Act, 112 Yale L.J. 1943, 1988, 2008-2020 (2003).

caregivers. "Rather than reform the ways that families arranged to care for their dependent members, Congress sought to alleviate conflicts between work and family by reforming aspects of the employment relationship." Toward this end, in 1978 Congress amended Title VII of the 1964 Civil Rights Act to prohibit discrimination "on the basis of pregnancy, childbirth, or related medical conditions." 42 U.S.C. §2000e(k) (2000). In enacting the Pregnancy Discrimination Act (PDA), Congress made clear that Title VII's antidiscrimination protections applied to pregnant employees and affirmed an understanding of the workplace in which women were expected to combine employment and parenting.

In 1993 Congress acted again to protect job security of caregivers at work by enacting the Family and Medical Leave Act (FMLA). 29 U.S.C. §§2601 et seq. (2000). The FMLA allows male[125] and female workers of many employers to take up to 12 weeks of unpaid leave to care for newborns, newly adopted children, and seriously ill family members, or to recover from their own serious illness.

In enacting both the PDA and the FMLA, Congress drew upon its power to regulate interstate commerce, as well as its power under Section Five of the Fourteenth Amendment to enforce its provisions by "appropriate legislation." The leave provisions of the FMLA enforced the Fourteenth Amendment's Equal Protection Clause in a form that appeared to diverge from the Court's case law, inviting claims that Congress had overstepped the scope of its powers under Section Five. We considered the reach of Congress's Section Five powers in Chapter Five. The Supreme Court's decision addressing Congress's power to enact the FMLA is important, not only as a statement of Section Five law, but also as statement of equal protection law. To uphold the FMLA as a proper exercise of Congress's power to enforce the Fourteenth Amendment, the Court had to explain how a statute providing caregivers unpaid leave enforced the Equal Protection Clause. In so doing, the Court discussed ways that work–family conflict, and many employer policies purporting to address it, reflect practices of gender stereotyping of a kind that the Court's equal protection cases condemn.

NEVADA DEPARTMENT OF HUMAN RESOURCES v. HIBBS
538 U.S. 721 (2003)

Chief Justice REHNQUIST delivered the opinion of the Court.

The Family and Medical Leave Act of 1993 (FMLA or Act) entitles eligible employees to take up to 12 work weeks of unpaid leave annually for any of several reasons, including the onset of a "serious health condition" in an employee's spouse, child, or parent. . . .

. . . Congress may, in the exercise of its §5 power, do more than simply proscribe conduct that we have held unconstitutional. "Congress' power 'to enforce' the Amendment includes the authority both to remedy and to deter violation of rights guaranteed thereunder by prohibiting a somewhat broader swath of conduct, including that which is not itself forbidden by the Amendment's text." In other

---

125. The FMLA provides unpaid leave to men and women because Congress feared that a gender-specific statute might result in discrimination against women. In addition, by providing unpaid leave for men the FMLA facilitates increased parity in caregiving responsibilities.

words, Congress may enact so-called prophylactic legislation that proscribes facially constitutional conduct, in order to prevent and deter unconstitutional conduct.

. . . According to evidence that was before Congress when it enacted the FMLA, States continue to rely on invalid gender stereotypes in the employment context, specifically in the administration of leave benefits. Reliance on such stereotypes cannot justify the States' gender discrimination in this area. The long and extensive history of sex discrimination prompted us to hold that measures that differentiate on the basis of gender warrant heightened scrutiny; here, as in *Fitzpatrick*, the persistence of such unconstitutional discrimination by the States justifies Congress' passage of prophylactic §5 legislation.

As the FMLA's legislative record reflects, a 1990 Bureau of Labor Statistics (BLS) survey stated that 37 percent of surveyed private-sector employees were covered by maternity leave policies, while only 18 percent were covered by paternity leave policies. S. Rep. No. 103-3, pp. 14-15 (1993). . . . Thus, stereotype-based beliefs about the allocation of family duties remained firmly rooted, and employers' reliance on them in establishing discriminatory leave policies remained widespread.[a]

Congress also heard testimony that "[p]arental leave for fathers . . . is rare. Even . . . [w]here child-care leave policies do exist, men, *both in the public and private sectors,* receive notoriously discriminatory treatment in their requests for such leave." *Id.,* at 147 (Washington Council of Lawyers) (emphasis added). Many States offered women extended "maternity" leave that far exceeded the typical 4- to 8-week period of physical disability due to pregnancy and childbirth, but very few States granted men a parallel benefit: Fifteen States provided women up to one year of extended maternity leave, while only four provided men with the same. This and other differential leave policies were not attributable to any differential physical needs of men and women, but rather to the pervasive sex-role stereotype that caring for family members is women's work.[b] . . .

The impact of the discrimination targeted by the FMLA is significant. Congress determined:

"Historically, denial or curtailment of women's employment opportunities has been traceable directly to the pervasive presumption that women are mothers first, and workers second. This prevailing ideology about women's roles has in turn justified discrimination against women when they are mothers or mothers-to-be."

a. While this and other material described leave policies in the private sector, a 50-state survey also before Congress demonstrated that "[t]he proportion and construction of leave policies available to public sector employees differs little from those offered private sector employees."

b. For example, state employers' collective-bargaining agreements often granted extended "maternity" leave of six months to a year to women only. . . .

Evidence pertaining to parenting leave is relevant here because state discrimination in the provision of both types of benefits is based on the same gender stereotype: that women's family duties trump those of the workplace. Justice Kennedy's dissent ignores this common foundation that, as Congress found, has historically produced discrimination in the hiring and promotion of women. Consideration of such evidence does not, as the dissent contends, expand our §5 inquiry to include "*general* gender-based stereotypes in employment." To the contrary, because parenting and family leave address very similar situations in which work and family responsibilities conflict, they implicate the same stereotypes.

Stereotypes about women's domestic roles are reinforced by parallel stereotypes presuming a lack of domestic responsibilities for men. Because employers continued to regard the family as the woman's domain, they often denied men similar accommodations or discouraged them from taking leave. These mutually reinforcing stereotypes created a self-fulfilling cycle of discrimination that forced women to continue to assume the role of primary family caregiver, and fostered employers' stereotypical views about women's commitment to work and their value as employees. Those perceptions, in turn, Congress reasoned, lead to subtle discrimination that may be difficult to detect on a case-by-case basis.

We believe that Congress' chosen remedy, the family-care leave provision of the FMLA, is "congruent and proportional to the targeted violation." Congress had already tried unsuccessfully to address this problem through Title VII and the amendment of Title VII by the Pregnancy Discrimination Act, 42 U.S.C. §2000e(k). Here, as in *Katzenbach*, Congress again confronted a "difficult and intractable problem," where previous legislative attempts had failed. Such problems may justify added prophylactic measures in response.

By creating an across-the-board, routine employment benefit for all eligible employees, Congress sought to ensure that family-care leave would no longer be stigmatized as an inordinate drain on the workplace caused by female employees, and that employers could not evade leave obligations simply by hiring men. By setting a minimum standard of family leave for all eligible employees, irrespective of gender, the FMLA attacks the formerly state-sanctioned stereotype that only women are responsible for family caregiving, thereby reducing employers' incentives to engage in discrimination by basing hiring and promotion decisions on stereotypes.

The dissent characterizes the FMLA as a "substantive entitlement program" rather than a remedial statute because it establishes a floor of 12 weeks' leave. In the dissent's view, in the face of evidence of gender-based discrimination by the States in the provision of leave benefits, Congress could do no more in exercising its §5 power than simply proscribe such discrimination. But this position cannot be squared with our recognition that Congress "is not confined to the enactment of legislation that merely parrots the precise wording of the Fourteenth Amendment," but may prohibit "a somewhat broader swath of conduct, including that which is not itself forbidden by the Amendment's text." . . .

Indeed, in light of the evidence before Congress, a statute mirroring Title VII, that simply mandated gender equality in the administration of leave benefits, would not have achieved Congress' remedial object. Such a law would allow States to provide for no family leave at all. Where "[t]wo-thirds of the nonprofessional caregivers for older, chronically ill, or disabled persons are working women," and state practices continue to reinforce the stereotype of women as caregivers, such a policy would exclude far more women than men from the workplace.

Unlike the statutes at issue in *City of Boerne, Kimel,* and *Garrett,* . . . the FMLA is narrowly targeted at the fault line between work and family — precisely where sex-based overgeneralization has been and remains strongest — and affects only one aspect of the employment relationship. . . .

For the above reasons, we conclude that §2612(a)(1)(C) is congruent and proportional to its remedial object, and can "be understood as responsive to, or designed to prevent, unconstitutional behavior."

The judgment of the Court of Appeals is therefore affirmed.

Discussion

1. Was Congress enforcing the Equal Protection Clause as the Court has interpreted it when it enacted the challenged provisions of the FMLA? How does *Hibbs* address this question? Robert Post observes:

> *Hibbs* . . . offers an extraordinarily generous account of the constitutional harm of sex discrimination, which it locates in "firmly rooted" "stereotype-based beliefs about the allocation of family duties" that operate to the disadvantage of women in "situations in which work and family responsibilities conflict." *Hibbs* holds that in enacting the FMLA Congress properly sought "to adjust family leave policies in order to eliminate their reliance on and perpetuation of invalid stereotypes, and thereby dismantle persisting gender-based barriers to the hiring, retention, and promotion of women in the workplace." This conception of the relevant constitutional violation is quite distant from narrower formulations, which the Court tends to use in Section 1 litigation, and which associate the constitutional prohibition of sex discrimination either with explicit classifications based upon sex or with neutral government actions taken "'because of,' not merely 'in spite of,' [their] adverse effects upon" women.[126]

Note that the FMLA can be understood as a remedy for disparate treatment in the provision of employment benefits (employers give early parenting leave to women and not men), and disparate treatment in hiring and promotion (employers avoid women believing that they will take family leave or have family conflicts). It might also rectify the disparate impact on women of workplace policies designed for workers without caregiving obligations. Which of these harms does the *Hibbs* Court treat as an injury of constitutional magnitude? Does *Hibbs* persuasively demonstrate how the FMLA remedies injuries recognized in the Court's earlier equal protection cases? How might *Hibbs* expand the concept of sex stereotyping that appears in the Court's earlier equal protection cases? For a reading of *Hibbs* as the first Supreme Court equal protection case to find that regulation of pregnant women rests on unconstitutional sex stereotypes, see Reva B. Siegel, "You've Come a Long Way, Baby": Rehnquist's New Approach to Pregnancy Discrimination in Hibbs, 58 Stan. L. Rev. (forthcoming 2006).

2. *Discrimination and accommodation.* Many scholars distinguish laws that prohibit simple discrimination ("differential treatment despite equality along 'relevant' dimensions") and laws that require accommodation ("demanding that the [employer] take particular affirmative steps to permit them to enjoy the relevant public accommodation or to work at the relevant job").[127] Mark Kelman sees important differences between discrimination and accommodation:

> The plaintiff seeking accommodation does not claim to merit the treatment she asks for because she has the same relevant traits as the person who has received better treatment: She concedes that a business rationally differentiates workers or customers on the basis of the differential input costs associated with serving them. Instead, she

---

126. See Robert C. Post, The Supreme Court, 2002 Term — Foreword: Fashioning the Legal Constitution: Culture, Courts, and Law, 117 Harv. L. Rev. 4, 17-18 (2003).

127. Mark Kelman, Market Discrimination and Groups, 53 Stan. L. Rev. 833, 840 (2001).

argues that her "talent" is defined by her capacity to produce, and that her capacity to produce is measured by the output she can generate without using aids that benefit workers generally. . . . Because we must expend real resources to meet the demand for accommodation, we compare the value of expending the resources to meet the policy goals of accommodation with the value of expending the resources to meet other social policy aims.[128]

By contrast, Christine Jolls questions whether there is a clear distinction between laws prohibiting discrimination and requiring accommodation. She points to ways in which familiar antidiscrimination mandates require employers to ignore potentially relevant differences and so impose costs on employers, like accommodation requirements:

> [E]ven those aspects of antidiscrimination law that are not in fact accommodation requirements in the sense just described are similar to accommodation requirements in respects that have not previously been understood. The starting point for this argument — and this is a point that has been recognized previously — is the operation of antidiscrimination law when an employer's reluctance to employ members of a particular group stems from dislike of this group by customers or coworkers or from the employer's statistically accurate generalizations about group members. In these situations antidiscrimination law fairly obviously operates to require employers to incur undeniable financial costs associated with employing the disfavored group of employees — and thus in a real sense to "accommodate" these employees.[129]

In what ways is the leave requirement of the FMLA distinct from or related to the prohibition on disparate treatment at the heart of the Court's equal protection cases?

3. *Stereotypes concerning caregivers.* Joan Williams argues that many policies that disfavor caregivers in the workplace reflect bias against caregivers, rather than economically rational judgments.[130] In Back v. Hastings-on-Hudson Union Free School District, 365 F.3d 107 (2d Cir. 2004), Elena Back, a school psychologist, had received excellent employee evaluations until after she had her children, at which point her evaluations began to decline while her supervisors made occasional comments about her inability to work the number of hours required for her job when she had young children. Evaluating Back's claim that the school discriminated against her on the basis of sex, the Second Circuit held that evidence of gendered stereotyping by an employer can indicate that an employer made an impermissible adverse employment action.

> The instant case, however, foregrounds a crucial question: What constitutes a "gender-based stereotype"? *Price Waterhouse* suggested that this question must be answered in the particular context in which it arises, and without undue formulation. . . . it takes no special training to discern stereotyping in the view that a woman cannot "be a good mother" and have a job that requires long hours, or in the statement that a mother who received tenure "would not show the same level of commitment [she] had shown because [she] had little ones at home." These are not the kind of "innocuous words"

---

128. Id. at 843-844.
129. Christine Jolls, Antidiscrimination and Accommodation, 115 Harv. L. Rev. 642, 645 (2001).
130. Joan Williams and Nancy Segal, Beyond the Maternal Wall: Relief for Family Caregivers Who Are Discriminated Against on the Job, 26 Harv. Women's L.J. 77 (2003).

that we have previously held to be insufficient, as a matter of law, to provide evidence of discriminatory intent.[131]

On remand the district court found that the plaintiff lacked sufficient evidence to sustain a §1983 claim for gender discrimination in violation of the Equal Protection Clause. What might constitute sufficient evidence of gender discrimination through stereotyping?

4. *The gender gap and the family.* While women may be closer to achieving parity with men in pay at the early stages of their career, the gap widens after they have children. Although overall, women's mean wages rose between 1978 and 1994, mothers' wages not only started off lower than non-mothers' wages, but their wages also rose less (from $10.15 to $10.97) than women without children (from $11.11 to $12.15).[132]

Gender differences manifest outside the wage context, as well. The family career gap affects men's and women's choices to have children and their ability to climb the career ladder while doing so. In law firms, for example, men are more likely to be married and more likely to have more children than women.[133] In academia, among those who have "early babies" (within five years of completion of the PhD), there is a 24 percent gap between men's and women's tenure achievement in the sciences, and a 20 percent gap in the social sciences and humanities.[134]

How, if at all, are these data evidence of sex discrimination? Should society aspire to equalize the position of caregivers with others who do not engage in the work of caregiving? Is it fair to ask those who are not engaged in caring for children or other family members to subsidize the efforts of those who do?

5. *Frontiers beyond the FMLA.* The FMLA, upheld in *Hibbs*, provides unpaid family and medical leave to some employees. Yet pressures on many caregivers continue to inhibit their full participation in the workforce. For this reason, even after enactment of the FMLA, legislatures have continued to explore options to alleviate the burden on working parents. For example, in 2002, California became the first state to adopt a comprehensive *paid* family leave law. The statute provides workers with family responsibilities with up to 6 weeks of wage replacement benefits, paid for under the state's Temporary Disability Insurance (TDI) program. Cal. Unemp. Ins. Code §3301 (Deering 2004). In addition, a number of other states are experimenting with paid leave options paid for by TDI, unemployment insurance (UI), tax subsidies, or other funds. See Gillian Lester, A Defense of Paid Family Leave, 28 Harv. J.L. & Gender 1 (2005).

---

131. *Back*, 365 F.3d. at 119-120; see also Lust v. Sealy, 277 F. Supp. 2d 973, 982 (W.D. Wisc. 2003) (in a case where plaintiff's employer denied her promotion, explaining "You have kids," court ruled that "[d]enying a woman a promotion because of a stereotypical belief about her obligation to her family is discrimination because of sex.")

132. Jane Waldfogel, Understanding the Family Gap in Pay for Women with Children, 12 Journal of Economic Perspectives 137-156 (1998).

133. Joni Hersch, The New Labor Market for Lawyers: Will Female Lawyers Still Earn Less? 10 Cardozo Women's L. J. 1 (2003).

134. Mary Ann Mason and Marc Goulden, Do Babies Matter? The Effect of Family Formation on the Lifelong Careers of Academic Men and Women, available at *http://www.aaup.org/publications/Academe/ 2002/02nd/02ndmas.htm* (last accessed Oct. 8, 2004).

Many of these programs are specifically designed for low-income parents. One key federal program, the Child Care and Development Block Grant (CCDBG) provides eligible parents with assistance to pay for child care outside the home. With the CCDBG the government recognizes the importance of child care to the success of women in welfare-to-work programs. 45 C.F.R. §98.43 (2003). Some advocates, however, have argued that the state should provide parents with the option of caring for their children themselves. In response, a few states have varied their subsidy programs to provide eligible parents with child care assistance to care for their own children at home. Minnesota, for example, implemented an "at-home infant care" program in 1997. Minn. Stat. §119B.035 (2000).

Should federal or state government enact new legislation to alleviate work–family conflicts? Should the focus be on providing accessible child care, or on securing employment accommodations for those who are struggling to combine caregiving and market work? What different understandings do these two strategies reflect?

Congress drew on its power to enforce the Fourteenth Amendment when it enacted the PDA and the FMLA. Do these more recently enacted state laws vindicate constitutional equality principles as well? Or are these statutes simply good (or bad) public policy, designed to strengthen the family and the economy, rather than to vindicate women's right to participate as equals in public life? What, if anything, is at stake in the way we characterize these initiatives?

V.   Gender in the Military: Constitutional Change Outside the Courts

A.   A Brief History of Women in the Military: The Combat Exclusion, Its Creation and Erosion[135]

Although women have officially been excluded from military service throughout most of the nation's history, they have nevertheless served in combat by passing as men. Thus, women fought (unofficially) in the Revolutionary War and on both sides of the Civil War.

Women served as nurses during the Civil War and the Spanish-American War as civilian auxiliaries. Congress created an official auxiliary Army Nurse Corps in 1901 and in 1908 the Navy followed suit. During World War I, some 34,000 women served in the Nurse Corps. In March 1917, the Navy and the Marines began to accept female "yeomen" in the naval reserves who could perform clerical and related duties that freed up additional men for combat. In 1925 Congress ended this practice by prohibiting the Navy from enlisting women.

In 1942 Congress adopted a bill sponsored by Representative Edith Rogers creating the Women's Army Auxiliary Corps (later the Women's Army Corps, or WAC), which was followed the same year by the creation of the Navy Women's Reserve (WAVES), the Marine Corps Women's Reserve, and still later by the Air Force's female auxiliary, SPAR (for Semper Paratus, or "always ready").

---

135. See Helen Hogan, Mixed Company (1981); Major General Jeanne Holm, USAF, Women in the Military: An Unfinished Revolution (1982); Judith Hicks Stiehm, Arms and the Enlisted Woman (1989).

By the end of World War II there were approximately 100,000 WACS, 86,000 WAVES, 18,000 women Marines, and 11,000 members of SPAR, in addition to 18,000 nurses. Women were engaged in clerical jobs and also in repairing radio equipment, operating control towers, rigging parachutes, and serving as air navigators, aerophotographers, gunner instructors, and engine mechanics. Nurses served overseas from the beginning and other women began serving overseas in other jobs in 1943.

In 1948, Congress passed the Women's Armed Services Act, which was officially called an "Integration Act" but in fact did precisely the opposite. The Act gave the women's corps permanent military status but required that no more than 2 percent of each service could consist of women. It restricted the number of female officers, created separate promotion lists for women, severely restricted their opportunities for promotion, and set higher minimum ages for enlisted women than men. The 1948 Act also for the first time specifically excluded women from combat. It authorized the Secretaries of each of the armed services to assign women to military duties, with the proviso that women could not be assigned to flight or ship duties when aircraft and naval vessels were engaged in "combat missions." The Army's exclusion of women from combat has been based on internal regulations that are justified as implementing Congressional intention behind the statutory restrictions on the Navy and Air Force.[136]

As a result of the new regulations and increasing conservatism in the country as a whole, women's participation in the military decreased, both in absolute numbers and in degrees of responsibility, from 1948 until the middle of the 1960s. In 1967, Congress removed the promotion restrictions of the 1948 Integration Act, and removed the 2 percent ceiling. In 1970, the Army, for the first time, promoted two women to the rank of Brigadier General.

By 1967, women began to serve in Vietnam, and their response under fire impressed members of the armed services. Approximately 7,500 women served in Vietnam, and many were decorated.

In 1974, the age requirement for enlistment without parental consent became the same for men and women. In 1976, women were admitted to the Air Force Academy, the Naval Academy, and the Military Academy. In 1978, Congress amended the 1948 Integration Act to allow women to serve on additional types of noncombat ships, including repair ships, salvage ships, and rescue ships.

In February 1988, the Department of Defense (DOD) adopted a Department-wide policy called the Risk Rule. It excluded women from noncombat units or missions if the risks of exposure to direct combat, hostile fire, or capture were equal to or greater than the risk in the combat units they supported.

The Persian Gulf War gave women more opportunities to display their abilities in wartime and led to increased calls for modification of the combat exclusion rules. In 1991, Congress repealed the prohibition against women flying combat missions in the Air Force, Navy, and Marine Corps. Congress also established a new

---

136. Congress has never defined the term "combat mission" in its statutory restrictions on the Navy and Air Force. As a result, each branch of the armed forces has its own interpretations of the jobs and missions women may participate in, which have changed over time as military doctrines and technologies have changed. Although each branch attempts to shield women from the risk of enemy fire or enemy capture, each branch assesses the risks differently, sometimes preventing women from serving even in certain noncombat positions.

Commission on the Assignment of Women in the Armed Forces and authorized it to conduct tests of women in various combat positions and situations. The Commission's November 1992 report recommended retaining the direct ground combat exclusion for women. However, in November 1993, Congress repealed the naval combat ship exclusions.

In January 1994, Secretary of Defense Les Aspin rescinded the Risk Rule, based on experiences during the Persian Gulf War, where everyone in the theater of operation was at risk. The new rules, which took effect in October 1994, stated that "service members are eligible to be assigned to all positions for which they are qualified, except that women shall be excluded from assignments to units below the brigade level whose primary mission is to engage in direct combat on the ground."[137] However, the services could also close positions to women if (1) the units and positions would be required to physically remain with direct ground combat units, (2) the cost of providing appropriate living arrangements for women would be prohibitive, (3) the units would be engaged in special operations forces' missions or long-range reconnaissance, or (4) job-related physical requirements would exclude the vast majority of women.[138]

As a result of these changes, according to a 1998 GAO report, only about 15 percent of all positions across the armed forces are now legally closed to women. A larger percentage of positions are closed in the Army (29 percent) and the Marines (25 percent) than in the Navy (9 percent) and the Air Force (less than 1 percent).[139]

Women in the armed services can now fly combat aircraft; serve on combat ships and on aircraft carriers; work in support units as medics, engineers, and maintenance workers; and serve in other dangerous jobs (as military police and on convoy duty). They still cannot serve in combat units, on submarines, or as Navy Seals or Air Force Pararescue troops.[140]

The war in Iraq dramatically increased gender integration of the military:

Historically, women's involvement in the military has surged in wartime. Today, that pattern is amplified by the all-volunteer U.S. military's growing share of women, which has steadily expanded in recent years to 15 percent of the active duty force.

Moreover, in contrast to their roles in past wars, women are serving in a widening variety of Army ground units — from logistics to military police, military intelligence and civil affairs — where they routinely face the same risks as soldiers in all-male combat units such as infantry and armor. . . .

At least as often as insurgents attack all-male infantry forces, they strike targets such as military supply convoys, checkpoints and camps where U.S. servicewomen are often present. As a result, hostile fire in Iraq has taken a proportionally larger toll on servicewomen than in any prior U.S. conflict, killing 35 and wounding 279. . . .

---

137. Brigades are ground combat units of about 3,000 to 5,000 soldiers whose primary mission is to engage and destroy enemy forces. They are comprised of battalions and form part of a division or corps. Although many positions in the armed services have secondary tasks related to direct ground combat, the combat rule focuses on the primary mission of the unit.

138. For example, as of 1998, despite the lifting of the Navy combat ship exclusion, women could not serve on submarines, or on mine hunter, mine countermeasure, or coastal patrol ships. These ships were closed to women because of the cost of providing appropriate living arrangements.

139. Mark E. Gebicke, Gender Issues — Information on DOD's Assignment Policy and Direct Ground Combat Definition (GAO Report No. GAO/NSIAD-99-7 Oct. 19, 1998).

140. T. Shawn Taylor, Combat Roles Still Outside Women's Reach, Chicago Tribune, June 1, 2005, at 1.

Male and female soldiers said many women in Iraq were performing well in risky jobs that require infantry skills — from military police and civil affairs troops to female search teams that go on raids with Army and Marine infantry units. On raids, a woman is "as much infantry soldier on the ground doing the duties as anyone else," an officer of the 3rd Infantry Division [observed]. "She may not have been the person who knocked the door in, but she's with the next stack getting ready to come in."

Most soldiers and officers interviewed also agreed that women need tougher physical fitness standards to perform well in infantry jobs, but that many could meet those standards. For some, the impact of pregnancy on readiness was a concern. Commanders of mixed-sex units in Iraq said that from 5 percent to 15 percent of their women became pregnant and did not deploy to Iraq, but one said health and family issues kept a similar percentage of men home. . . .[141]

As the military manages troop shortages in Iraq, it has begun to rely upon women in ways that erode the combat exclusion. The Army is now putting women in support units at the front lines of combat. The Army's Third Infantry Division is including women in newly created "forward support companies" that provide maintenance, food service, and other support services to infantry, armor, and Special Forces units that engage in combat.[142] Army officials acknowledge that the changes will increasingly place women in combat situations. They claim they are following federal law, which prohibits women from serving in units that engage in direct combat. "But internal Army documents indicate the service is ignoring a 1994 regulation barring women from serving alongside units that conduct offensive operations," and Pentagon sources are reported to be considering repeal of the regulation.[143] These reforms have provoked "a quiet, but highly charged debate within the Army over the role of women in the military. As a practical matter, the guerrilla tactics used against US troops during the occupation have also blurred the traditional lines between combat and support functions and is expected to prompt a wholesale review of the definition of ground 'combat' within the Bush administration."[144]

Women's evolving role in the military has produced gender conflicts of different kinds. "The specter of U.S. prisoners of war on Iraqi television . . . was a reminder . . . of the new face of war — one in which women are playing an ever expanding role closer to the front lines, adding to the debate surrounding their role in the military."[145] Not all the imagery precipitates anxieties about female vulnerability. War coverage has also featured pictures of Private Lynndie England posing amidst tortured inmates at the Abu Ghraib prison — evoking fears that military service might transform women into fighters who are just as aggressive as men.[146]

141. Ann Scott Tyson, For Female GIs, Combat Is a Fact: Many Duties in Iraq Put Women at Risk Despite Restrictive Policy, The Washington Post, May 13, 2005, at A01.

142. Bryan Bender, U.S. Women Get Closer to Combat, Knight Ridder Tribune Business News, Jan. 25, 2005, at 1.

143. Id.

144. Id.

145. Kari Huus, In Iraq Conflict, Servicewomen Closer to Front Line, available at *http:// www.msnbc.com/news/890275.asp.*

146. Cf. Barbara Ehrenreich, Feminism's Assumptions Upended, L.A. Times, May 16, 2004, at M1.

B.   The Constitutionality of the Combat Exclusion

Consider the following student note, which outlines the major arguments for the combat exclusion. To what extent are these arguments supported or undermined by what the DOD has already permitted?

The combat exclusion rules have two main justifications: the need to maintain national security and the need to protect women. . . . Exclusionists . . . believe that women in combat would adversely affect national security by decreasing combat effectiveness. [They argue that] women in combat would adversely affect combat readiness [based on] three gender-related biological differences: lowered physical capabilities, pregnancy, and menstruation. First, they believe that women are weaker than men, and thus are unable to perform the rigorous duties of a conventional combat soldier. Second, . . . women's reproductive capabilities would affect their ability to perform as combat soldiers. "[P]regnancy and single parenting [are] prime sources of lost time." . . . Menstruation and pregnancy, they argue, have no place on the battlefield.

Opponents of combat exclusion rules . . . claim that, while physical strength is important, describing combat in terms of rigorous hand-to-hand combat is no longer accurate. [B]ecause contemporary weapons are more technical, soldiers utilize their mental skills more than their physical skills. [P]hysical differences between genders do not justify excluding all women from combat, especially if some women can improve their strength through physical conditioning. [A]rguments based on disparities in physical strength are less convincing when focusing on mixed crews comprised of male and female soldiers. [As to pregnancy, i]t is unfair to deny all women the opportunity to engage in combat because some women get pregnant while in service. [P]regnant female soldiers are absent for only a short period of time, and, on average, male soldiers are more apt to be absent than women. For example, the Department of the Navy reported that male soldiers were absent from duty almost twice as often as female soldiers. . . .

[Exclusionists argue] that women do not have the capacity to be aggressors. . . . Women . . . thrive on caring and nurturing; it is against their moral make-up to kill people. [B]ecause women are unable to handle pressure as well as men, they would shrink from their duty in stressful situations. [W]omen would lose their composure on the battlefield and either break down and cry or abandon their posts. Combat effectiveness would be diminished because male soldiers would have to compensate for female soldiers. . . . Brian Mitchell, a well-known exclusionist, believes that women in combat are "psychologically unfit. They are not as aggressive as men. They are less daring. They are better suited for the more tedious, routine tasks — tasks that require little imagination."

Opponents [of the combat exclusion] argue that, in modern warfare, face-to-face combat is obsolete since most soldiers are miles away from their targets when an attack begins. [S]tudies show that women perform well in mock combat battles [and] men are also susceptible to battle stress. For example, during the Vietnam War, the military reported [post-traumatic stress disorders] in record numbers.

Exclusionists argue that women would adversely affect national security by disrupting the much needed cohesion in a combat unit. Male soldiers value the "nonerotic psychological bonding" that exists between their squads or platoons. This bonding instills a measure of loyalty within combat soldiers that a woman's presence, exclusionists contend, would disrupt.

[S]exual attraction between male and female soldiers would interfere with the bonding of a unit, thereby destroying group cohesion. [M]en would no longer develop bonding relationships; instead, they would view themselves as rivals in a sexual contest. [E]xclusionists point to the Persian Gulf War media reports of incidents of prostitution by female soldiers and pregnancies aboard the mixed-crew ship Arcadia. [D]ifferences in treatment between male and female soldiers would destroy the bonding of a combat unit.

[In addition, exclusionists argue that] [W]omen "do not bond with one another or with men." [F]emale soldiers' presence in a combat unit would "destroy[] the possibility of bonding for the men and lead[] to psychic emasculation, stifling of masculinity, and even sterilization of the whole process of combat leadership."

[O]pponents of combat exclusion argue that similar occupations, such as policemen or firemen, have mixed units and still perform effectively. [Women do not lack the capacity to bond; if anything,] male soldiers' perceptions about female soldiers . . . lead to the destruction of camaraderie between men and women. Combat exclusion instills a belief that women are not equal to men[,] lead[ing] to disrespect and resentment of women that often leads to overt hostility. The recent Tailhook scandal illustrates this phenomenon. . . .

Besides national security concerns, another justification for the combat exclusion rules is the protection of women. The legislative history of the combat exclusion rules shows that Congress wanted to protect women from the harsh realities of war. Excluding women from combat decreases their risk of being captured, injured, or killed. Exclusionists believe that, instead of fighting, women should be at home. Their vital function is to maintain the homefront. The implication is that by protecting the family, women are doing their appropriate part in protecting America.

Opponents point out that the combat exclusion rules do not adequately decrease female soldiers' risks. Despite the existence of combat exclusion rules, women get captured, shot at, and killed. The real difference between male and female soldiers is that female soldiers cannot capture, shoot, or kill offensively.

Opponents to combat exclusion also argue that being a soldier and being a mother can be compatible. Family issues concern both genders. The military . . . could be the first to discredit the stereotype that women are solely responsible for childcare. [Finally,] women should be able to decide how they will handle their own personal commitments.[147]

Do these considerations justify the combat exclusion? Consider Wendy Williams, *The Equality Crisis: Some Reflections on Culture, Courts, and Feminism*, 7 Women's Rights Law Reporter 175, 182-185 (1982), in Herma Kay, Sex-Based Discrimination 115 (3d ed. 1988):

Suppose you could step outside our culture, rise above its minutiae, and look at its great contours. Having done so, speculate for a moment about where society might draw the line and refuse to proceed further with gender equality. What does our culture identify as quintessentially masculine? Where is the locus of traditional masculine pride and self-identity? What can we identify in men's cultural experience that most divides it from women's cultural experience? Surely, one rather indisputable answer to that question is "war": physical combat and its modern equivalents.

Not surprisingly, the Court in *Rostker* [v. Goldberg, discussed below] didn't come right out and say, "We've reached our cultural limits." . . . When Congress considered whether women should be drafted, it was much more forthright about its reasons and those reasons support my thesis. . . . To translate, Congress was worried that (1) sexually mixed units would not be able to function — perhaps because of sex in the foxhole; (2) if women were assigned combat, the nation might be reluctant to go to

---

147. Pamela R. Jones, Note: Women in the Crossfire: Should the Court Allow It? 78 Cornell L. Rev. 252, 260-269 (1993).

war, presumably because the specter of women fighting would deter a protective and chivalrous populace; and (3) the idea that mom could go into battle and dad keep the home fires burning is simply beyond the cultural pale. In short, current notions of acceptable limits on sex-role behavior would be surpassed by putting women into combat.

Williams wrote these words in 1982. Do you think that intervening changes in sex roles (and in women's military service) have shifted the "acceptable limits" she describes?

In your view, are the primary justifications for the combat exclusion grounded in physiological differences between the sexes, or in cultural considerations? Would making qualified women eligible for combat roles enhance the strength of the military or weaken it? Are there other reasons to preserve the combat exclusion? Which, if any, of these factors might change over time? In what respects does your analysis of gender-based restrictions on combat depend upon gender-based restrictions on the draft?

Which equality arguments for abolishing the combat exclusion do you judge the most persuasive? In allocating responsibility for combat along lines of gender, has government irrationally differentiated among the similarly situated? Or is the problem that government policy is producing, rather than merely reflecting, differences between the sexes? Does the combat exclusion reflect or reinforce gender stereotypes like those informing policies invalidated in the cases you have read in this chapter?

If the combat exclusion represents unjustified sex-based discrimination, whom does it harm — men, women, or both sexes? How could exempting women from the risks and burdens of combat inflict harm on women? What kind of harm?[148]

The injuries inflicted on women by the combat exclusion can be analyzed within a framework concerned with status, as well as similarity. How might the combat exclusion reflect or reinforce women's secondary social status? Those who are trained for combat are taught to build physical strength and master arts of violence; they are provided a wide range of educational and employment skills; and they acquire combat training and experience that is widely thought to prepare individuals for the highest positions of national political leadership. Gender segregation in military service thus reinforces patterns of gender stratification in athletics, violence, education, work, and politics.[149]

Which of any of these concerns are of constitutional magnitude? In the years since Reed v. Reed, there have been challenges to the exclusion of women from the draft (see below), but virtually no court tests of the combat exclusion itself. Instead, courts have assumed the constitutionality of the combat exclusion — and used it to justify other exclusionary practices. Is there an "exceedingly persuasive justification" for the combat exclusion, in any of its forms? Is it substantially related to an important government interest? Even if some form of the combat exclusion is constitutional, is combat exclusion as currently structured fatally over- or underinclusive?

---

148. Linda K. Kerber has argued that society regulates the social status of citizens by the ways it distributes responsibilities of citizenship (e.g., military or jury service) among them. See Linda K. Kerber, 'A Constitutional Right to Be Treated Like . . . Ladies': Women, Civic Obligation, and Military Service, 1993 U. Chi. L. Sch. Roundtable 95, 97-98, 108-109, 115-124 (1993).

149. See generally Kenneth L. Karst, The Pursuit of Manhood and the Desegregation of the Armed Forces, 38 UCLA L. Rev. 499 (1991).

C. The Draft

In United States v. St. Clair, 291 F. Supp. 122 (D.S.D. 1968), decided during the Vietnam War, plaintiff, a male, challenged the military draft on the grounds that it discriminated on the basis of sex. The district court rejected the challenge:

> In providing for involuntary service for men and voluntary service for women, Congress followed the teachings of history that if a nation is to survive, men must provide the first line of defense while women keep the home fires burning.

With *St. Clair*, compare Selective Service Draft Cases v. United States, 245 U.S. 366 (1917), where the Court unanimously held that "[T]he very conception of a just government and its duty to the citizen includes the reciprocal obligation of the citizen to render military service in case of need and the right to compel it."

Do these cases taken together suggest that women are not full citizens of the United States if they cannot be drafted? Consider Linda Kerber's invocation of "the ancient connection, still not well understood, between arms bearing and citizenship, and between citizenship and manhood."[150]

The Vietnam draft ended in 1975. In 1980, as a result of the Soviet invasion of Afghanistan, President Carter asked Congress to amend the Military Selective Service Act to permit the registration of both men and women. Congress refused, allocating only funds for the registration of men.

In Rostker v. Goldberg, 453 U.S. 57 (1981), the Court upheld the constitutionality of the Military Selective Service Act, which exempted women from registration for the draft. Justice Rehnquist's majority opinion relied heavily on the fact that women were ineligible for combat. It also noted that the Court traditionally accords Congress great deference in cases arising in "the context of Congress' authority over national defense and military affairs." He found the exemption of women to be closely related to Congress's purpose in preparing a draft "*of combat troops*." Since women were ineligible for combat, Congress concluded there was no reason to require their registration for the draft. "The Constitution requires that Congress treat similarly situated persons similarly, not that it engage in gestures of superficial equality."

The majority noted Congress's thorough floor debate and committee action concerning the place of women in the Armed Services to suggest that ". . . the decision to exempt women from registration was not the 'accidental by-product of a traditional way of thinking about women.' Califano v. Webster. . . . The issue was considered at great length, and Congress clearly expressed its purpose and intent." The majority quoted from the Senate Report:

> The principle that women should not intentionally and routinely engage in combat is fundamental, and enjoys wide support among our people. It is universally supported by military leaders who have testified before the Committee. . . . Current law and policy exclude women from being assigned to combat in our military forces, and the Committee reaffirms this policy. . . . Men and women, because of the combat restrictions on women, are simply not similarly situated for purposes of a draft or registration for a draft.

150. Kerber, supra n.148 at 119.

The Court also addressed the issue that women might serve in noncombat positions "freeing men to go to the front." There was testimony that "in the event of a draft of 650,000 the military could absorb some 80,000 female inductees" in noncombat positions. The Court reasoned that this did not necessarily compel the registration of both men and women. Justice Rehnquist granted considerable deference to Congress:

> In the first place, assuming that a small number of women could be drafted for noncombat roles, Congress simply did not consider it worth the added burdens of including women in draft and registration plans. . . .
>
> Congress also concluded that whatever the need for women for noncombat roles during mobilization, whether 80,000 or less, it could be met by volunteers. . . .
>
> Most significantly, Congress determined that . . . [m]ilitary flexibility requires that a commander be able to move units or ships quickly. Units or ships not located at the front or not previously scheduled for the front nevertheless must be able to move into action if necessary. In peace and war, significant rotation of personnel is necessary. We should not divide the military into two groups — one in permanent combat and one in permanent support. Large numbers of non-combat positions must be available to which combat troops can return for duty before being redeployed.

Justice White, joined by Justice Brennan, dissented, stating that there was "some sense" to the notion that administrative burdens might be involved in registering all women for only some noncombat positions, but he insisted that "on the record before us, the number of women who could be used in the military without sacrificing combat-readiness is not at all small or insubstantial, and administrative convenience has not been sufficient justification for the kind of outright gender-based discrimination involved in registering and conscripting men but no women at all." Justice Powell pointed to military testimony in the record asserting that in a major military mobilization, 80,000 women could be deployed in the first six months.

Justice Marshall also dissented, joined by Justice Brennan, writing "there simply is no basis for concluding in this case that excluding women from registration is substantially related to the achievement of a concededly important governmental interest in maintaining an effective defense." He argued that the majority had focused upon the wrong issue:

> The relevant inquiry under the Craig v. Boren test is not whether a *gender-neutral* classification would substantially advance important governmental interests. Rather, the question is whether the gender-based classification is itself substantially related to the achievement of the asserted governmental interest. Thus, the Government's task in this case is to demonstrate that excluding women from registration substantially furthers the goal of preparing for a draft of combat troops. Or to put it another way, the Government must show that registering women would substantially impede its efforts to prepare for such a draft. Under our precedents, the Government cannot meet this burden without showing that a gender-neutral statute would be a less effective means of attaining this end.

Justice Marshall rejected the argument that there was "*no military need to draft women*," and he cited Defense Department estimates that in the event of a draft, "there will not be enough women volunteers to fill the positions for which women would be eligible. . . ." He maintained that "since the purpose of registration is to protect against unanticipated shortages of volunteers, it is difficult to see how excluding women from registration can be justified by conjectures about the expected number of female volunteers." While he accepted the importance of "military flexibility" posited by the majority, he denied that this warranted the exclusion of women from registration and the draft. Marshall argued that there was nothing in the Senate Report to suggest that "staffing even a limited number of noncombat positions with women would impede military flexibility."

Discussion

1. *Developments since Rostker.* Women's participation in the military has changed dramatically since 1981. Given women's increasing role and numbers in the military, does the reasoning of *Rostker,* exempting women from draft registration because they were ineligible for combat, still apply with equal force? For an argument that the volunteer military's increased reliance on women undermines *Rostker*'s reasoning, see William A. Kamens, Comment, Selective Disservice: The Indefensible Discrimination of Draft Registration, 52 Am. U. L. Rev. 703 (2003); see also Linda Chavez, The First Generation of Draft Daughters?; If Women Can Fight, They Can Also Be Conscripted, The Washington Post, July 11, 1993, at C3.

A lawsuit recently filed in the U.S. District Court for the District of Massachusetts challenged the draft as violating equal protection, arguing that changed circumstances vitiated *Rostker*'s reasoning. The court held that *Rostker* was still binding precedent and that the plaintiffs had not demonstrated that its factual underpinnings had eroded sufficiently to overrule it. See Schwartz v. Brodsky, 265 F. Supp. 2d 130 (D. Mass. 2003).

2. If the combat exception were eliminated, would women participate in combat on the same terms as men? In December 1989, the 18,000 troops involved in the American incursion into Panama included 800 women, of whom 150, including helicopter pilots, were in the immediate vicinity of enemy fire. (Indeed two women were awarded Air Medals for their participation.)[151] A significant number of women were involved in the Persian Gulf War with Iraq in 1991. Writing before that conflict, Professor Charles Moskos asked:

> [W]ill allowing qualified women to enter . . . combat . . . finally mean the resolution of [the] nettlesome issue [of] women's role in the military?
>
> Unfortunately, no. The issue is not simply "opening up" combat positions to military women. The core question — the one avoided in public debate, but the one that the women soldiers I spoke with in Panama were all too aware of — is this: Should every woman soldier be made to confront exactly the same combat liabilities as every man? All male soldiers can, if need arises, be assigned to the combat arms, whatever their normal postings. True equality would mean that women soldiers would incur the same liability. To allow women but not men the option of entering or not entering the combat arms would — rightly or wrongly — cause immense resentment among male soldiers; in a single stroke it would diminish the status and respect that female soldiers have achieved. To allow both sexes to choose whether or not to go into combat would be the end of an effective military force. Honesty requires that supporters of lifting the ban on women in combat state openly that they want to put all female soldiers at the same combat risk as all male soldiers — or that they don't.

151. See Charles Moskos, Army Women, The Atlantic, Aug. 1990, at 71-78, from whom the information and quotations in this paragraph are taken.

A trial program of women in combat roles which shows that women can hold their own in battle may put one argument to rest. But it will signal the start of another.

3. *Constitutional change outside the courts?* In the last several decades, gender integration of the military has dramatically increased, even though courts have not required these changes as a matter of equal protection law. Some of the changes the military has initiated, in order to increase the pool of skilled volunteers available, especially during time of war. But the changes also reflect the efforts of advocates who are working to make the military a gender-equal institution.

Mary Fainsod Katzenstein describes how "everyday resistance and the politics of associationalism" allowed feminists to reshape institutions such as the armed forces from within. Change resulted from informal opposition to the status quo within the military by feminists and their supporters, as well as from the efforts of organizations in the military organized for the specific purpose of furthering the interests of women in the armed forces.[152]

Katzenstein describes the work of the Defense Advisory Committee on Women in the Services (DACOWITS), a committee of political appointees that provides counsel to the DOD on women's issues in the services. The Committee has been criticized by Phyllis Schlafly as the "feminist thought-control brigade of the U.S. military,"[153] and praised by historian Cynthia Enloe for persuading "the military of the connections between sexual harassment of military women and prostitution on foreign bases."[154] The Committee was a driving force in the movement to drop the cap on women's participation in the services, to appoint women to high positions in the military, including the courts of military appeals, and to provide abortions in military hospitals.[155] In the 1980s, it led efforts to combat sexual harassment against women in the armed forces. See also Linda Bird Francke, Ground Zero: The Gender Wars in the Military (1997).

Formal and informal change agents are seeking equality for women in the military, and bringing about significant changes in their status. What is the relationship between this kind "unobtrusive mobilization inside institutions" and the Constitution? In what sense is DACOWITS forging *constitutional* change? What is at stake in characterizing its efforts in these terms — or in rejecting the characterization? Does mobilization within the military obviate the need for judicial intervention, or are courts still needed to remove legal barriers to entry that segregate women and restrict their access to many facets of military service?

4. *Gender-integration and gender-conscious policy.* How far and in what ways does the integration of women into military service require the elimination of gender-conscious policies? What values are served by preserving, or eliminating, gender-conscious policies? Consider the following recommendations in the report issued by the members of the Federal Advisory Committee on Gender-Integrated Training and Related Issues to the Secretary of Defense on December 16, 1997:

---

152. Mary Fainsod Katzenstein, Feminism Within American Institutions: Unobtrusive Mobilization in the 1980s, 16 Signs: Journal of Women in Culture and Society 27-54 (1990).

153. Id. at 48.

154. Id.

155. Id.

[A] The committee observed that all of the services' recruiting programs would be strengthened by more female recruiters. It is important that the recruit's first exposure at the recruiting station to military life and military values include both male and female role models.

The committee recommends that the number of female recruiters be increased across the services.

[B] Across the services the committee observed a clear need for more female trainers. They provide important role models for the female recruits and also help male recruits realize that females are authority figures in their own right. An increase in female instructors will also allow the services to give same-sex instructors primary responsibility for discipline in the barracks, providing another safeguard against abuses of power.

The committee recommends that all four services increase the number of female trainers. . . .

Separate barracks for male and female recruits.

Under the current gender-integrated basic training structure, the Army, Navy, and Air Force all house female recruits on separate floors or separate wings of barracks occupied by male recruits. The reason for this policy is that basic training is an intense, 24-hour-a-day program of instruction. In order to achieve the goals, particularly of team-building, unit cohesion and discipline, the operational training units must remain together day and night.

The Marines, who conduct separate training for males and females, have separate barracks for male and female trainees at Parris Island. The committee observed that integrated housing is contributing to a higher rate of disciplinary problems. Both recruits and their trainers, consequently, are distracted from their training objectives, which must be accomplished in a short period of time in basic training. In the Army, for example, some drill sergeants complained about the inordinate amount of time spent investigating or disciplining male/female misconduct. The committee observed that the problem is exacerbated in mixed-gender housing units, particularly where male and female recruits live on the same floor. It is difficult for trainers in these units to know who should or should not be in the barracks.

The committee recommends that female and male recruits be housed in separate barracks. This would decrease disciplinary problems and reduce distractions from training. The committee has reviewed the layout and surge numbers at the training installations, and believes this change can be accomplished at marginal cost, if any. The initial cost of remodeling the barracks to accommodate women was low, according to the General Accounting Office. There are no physical constraints to using current infrastructure at any of the installations and no new buildings, according to the committee review, are required to implement this recommendation. . . .

Assume that you are general counsel to the DOD, asked by the Secretary whether these particular recommendations could pass constitutional muster. What is your response? What if the words "white" and "non-white" were substituted wherever the words "male" and "female" appear? Would that change your response? Why or why not?

5. *Feminist objections to military service.* Many feminists do not discuss issues of military service. The majority of those who discuss the question argue that gender differentiation in military service is unjust and harms women. But there are some feminists who are wary of compulsory military service for women, on the grounds that women should be opposed to militarism and violence. See Stephanie A. Levin, Women and Violence: Reflections on Ending the Combat Exclusion, 26 New Eng. L. Rev. 805 (1992); Ann Scales, Militarism, Male Dominance and Law: Feminist

Jurisprudence as Oxymoron?, 12 Harv. Women's L. J. 25 (1989). Should women be permitted to opt for nonviolent national service alternatives to the military in time of war? If so, should men have the same options?

VI. Affirmative Action

What is perhaps most distinctive about the Supreme Court's decisions involving gender-conscious classifications designed to benefit women is that the Court began to consider them before it had fixed on a general standard for discrimination against women. As a result, they have a considerably different flavor from the Court's affirmative action cases involving race. For some of the early pre-*Craig* cases allowing affirmative action for women, see Kahn v. Shevin, 416 U.S. 351 (1974) (upholding a state statute granting widows, but not widowers, an annual tax exemption); Schlesinger v. Ballard, 419 U.S. 496 (1975) (upholding a Navy discharge policy favoring female officers).

Califano v. Webster, 430 U.S. 313 (1977), a per curiam opinion decided the year after Craig v. Boren, upheld a Social Security provision that provided higher monthly old-age benefits for retired female wage earners than for males. Benefits were based on a wage earner's average monthly wage during the benefit computation years, but recipients could omit a certain number of low earning years in computing the average. Until 1972, women could exclude three more years than similarly situated male wage earners. The Court noted that "allowing women, who as such have been unfairly hindered from earning as much as men, to eliminate additional low-earning years from the calculation of their retirement benefits works directly to remedy some part of the effect of past discrimination." The provision therefore met the standard announced in Craig v. Boren, that "classifications by gender must serve important government objectives and must be substantially related to the achievement of those objectives." Chief Justice Burger, joined by Justices Stewart, Blackmun, and Rehnquist, concurred in the judgment for the reasons stated by Justice Rehnquist's dissent in *Goldfarb*.

In Mississippi University for Women v. Hogan, 458 U.S. 718 (1982), the Court rejected Mississippi's claim that a nursing school for women students "compensates for discrimination against women and, therefore, constitutes educational affirmative action." Justice O'Connor noted that "[i]n limited circumstances, a gender-based classification favoring one sex can be justified if it intentionally and directly assists members of the sex that is disproportionately burdened." However, "Mississippi has made no showing that women lacked opportunities to obtain training in the field of nursing or to attain positions of leadership in that field when the MUW School of Nursing opened its door or that women currently are deprived of such opportunities. . . . Rather than compensate for discriminatory barriers faced by women, MUW's policy of excluding males from admission to the School of Nursing tends to perpetuate the stereotyped view of nursing as an exclusively woman's job." Justice O'Connor also rejected Mississippi's claim that women do better in an all-female environment, given that men could audit classes in the School of Nursing.

In Johnson v. Transportation Agency, 480 U.S. 616 (1987), a male employee who was passed over for promotion in favor of a female employee brought a Title VII suit against the county transportation agency. Without reaching any constitutional issues, Justice Brennan held that the agency did not violate Title VII by taking sex into account and promoting the female employee, despite recommendations by three Agency supervisors conducting the final interviews that the male be hired, since the decision was made

> pursuant to an Agency plan that directed that sex or race be taken into account for the purpose of remedying underrepresentation. The Agency Plan acknowledged the "limited opportunities that have existed in the past" . . . for women to find employment in certain job classifications "where women have not been traditionally employed in significant numbers." . . . The plan sought to remedy these imbalances through "hiring, training and promotion of . . . women throughout the Agency in all major job classifications where they are underrepresented."
>
> . . . The plan stressed that such goals "should not be construed as 'quotas' that must be met," but as reasonable aspirations in correcting the imbalance in the Agency's work force.[156]

Chief Justice Rehnquist and Justices White and Scalia dissented. Justice Scalia argued that the decision "completes the process of converting [Title VII] from a guarantee that race or sex will *not* be the basis for employment determinations, to a guarantee that it often *will*. Ever so subtly . . . we effectively replace the goal of a discrimination-free society with the quite incompatible goal of proportionate representation by race and sex in the workplace."

Today the most important questions arising in gender-based affirmative action concern the relationship of these older cases to the Court's newer jurisprudence on affirmative action. In particular, lower courts have tried to ascertain the standard of review and the degree of evidentiary proof necessary after the Supreme Court's decisions in *Croson* and *Adarand*, which imposed strict proof requirements for racial affirmative action, and United States v. Virginia, which announced the requirement of an "exceedingly persuasive justification" for gender-based classifications.

In Contractors Association of Eastern Pennsylvania, Inc. v. City of Philadelphia, 6 F.3d 990 (3d Cir. 1993), the Third Circuit considered a City of Philadelphia ordinance creating preferences in City contracting for businesses owned by racial and ethnic minorities, women, and handicapped persons. The ordinance set goals of 15 percent participation in city contracts for minority-owned businesses, 10 percent for women-owned businesses, and 2 percent for businesses owned by handicapped persons. The court argued that "[a]pplication of intermediate scrutiny to the Ordinance's gender preference . . . follows logically from *Croson*, which held municipal affirmative action programs benefiting racial minorities merit the same standard of review as that given other race-based classifications." It thus rejected the

---

156. Although neither the District Court nor the Court of Appeals had found prior discrimination, Justice Brennan argued that the burden of proof remained with employees challenging the validity of the plan. "Once a plaintiff establishes a prima facie case that race or sex has been taken into account in an employer's employment decision, the burden shifts to the employer to articulate a nondiscriminatory rationale for its decision. The existence of an affirmative action plan provides such a rationale. If such a plan is . . . the basis for the employer's decision, the burden shifts to the plaintiff to prove that the employer's justification is pretextual. . . . [R]eliance on an affirmative action plan is [not] to be treated as an affirmative defense requiring the employer to carry the burden of proving the validity of the plan. The burden of proving its invalidity remains on the plaintiff."

view of the Sixth Circuit and the Georgia Supreme Court, which read *Croson* to mean that affirmative action for women was subject to strict scrutiny. Conlin v. Blanchard, 890 F.2d 811 (6th Cir. 1989); American Subcontractors Ass'n v. City of Atlanta, 376 S.E.2d 662 (Ga. 1989). Note that this position, taken literally, would mean that it would be easier to justify programs deliberately designed to discriminate against women than gender-conscious programs designed to combat sex discrimination against women.

In applying the intermediate standard, the Third Circuit noted:

> Few cases have considered the evidentiary burden needed to satisfy intermediate scrutiny in this context and there is no *Croson* analogue to provide a ready reference point. In particular, it is unclear whether statistical evidence as well as anecdotal evidence is required to establish the discrimination necessary to satisfy intermediate scrutiny, and if so, how much statistical evidence is necessary. The Supreme Court gender-preference cases are inconclusive. The Court has never squarely ruled on the necessity of statistical evidence of gender discrimination. And its decisions are difficult to reconcile on the point. The Court has upheld gender preferences where no statistics were offered, *Ballard* (preferential employment treatment for women military officers) struck down gender preferences despite the presence of statistics, Craig v. Boren (statute allowing 18 year old women but only 21 year old men to purchase 3.2% beer), Weinberger v. Wiesenfeld, 420 U.S. 636 (1975) (statute allowing survivors' benefits for widows but not widowers), and also decided cases both ways by relying in part on statistics, *Hogan* (striking down female-only nursing school), Califano v. Webster, 430 U.S. 313 (1977) (upholding federal statute allowing women to eliminate more low-earning years from calculation of their retirement benefits than men). . . .
>
> Logically, a city must be able to rely on less evidence in enacting a gender preference than a racial preference because applying *Croson*'s evidentiary standard to a gender preference would eviscerate the difference between strict and intermediate scrutiny. The Supreme Court has stated that an affirmative action program survives intermediate scrutiny if the proponent can show it was "a product of analysis rather than a stereotyped reaction based on habit." Metro Broadcasting, Inc. v. F.C.C. We believe this standard requires the City to present probative evidence in support of its stated rationale for the gender preference, discrimination against women-owned contractors.

The court concluded that the "[t]he City has not produced enough evidence of discrimination here" because its statistics "only reflect[ed] the participation of women in City contracting generally, rather than in the construction industry, which is the only cognizable issue here," and because its anecdotal evidence (an affidavit and one statement by a witness) was scant.

In Concrete Works of Colorado v. City & County of Denver, 321 F.3d 950 (10th Cir. 2003) the Tenth Circuit evaluated a race- and sex-based affirmative action program that set goals for the participation of racial minorities and women in city construction and professional design projects. To evaluate the sex-based provisions of the program, the court applied the intermediate scrutiny standard, which it described in the language of United States v. Virginia. The court explained:

> This court applies intermediate scrutiny to the gender-based measures contained in the ordinances. To withstand CWC's challenge, Denver must establish an "exceedingly persuasive justification" for those measures. United States v. Virginia, 518 U.S. 515,

524 (1996). Denver can meet its burden by demonstrating that the gender-based preferences "serve[] important governmental objectives" and are "substantially related to achievement of those objectives." Id. (quotation omitted). Neither this court nor the Supreme Court has developed a framework for analyzing equal protection challenges to gender-based remedial measures. Further, the parties have not provided this court with any comprehensive arguments on this issue. CWC implicitly advocates that the gender-based classifications must also survive strict judicial scrutiny. Denver argues that the statistical and anecdotal evidence it presented is sufficient to survive strict scrutiny so, *a fortiori*, the gender-based measures necessarily survive intermediate scrutiny.

To meet its burden of demonstrating an important governmental interest, Denver must show that the gender-based measures in the ordinances were based on "reasoned analysis rather than through the mechanical application of traditional, often inaccurate, assumptions." Miss. Univ. for Women v. Hogan, 458 U.S. 718, 726 (1982). Thus, the evidentiary basis necessary to demonstrate Denver's important governmental interest may be something less than the "strong basis in evidence" required to justify race-based remedial measures. See Eng'g Contractors Ass'n, 122 F.3d at 909; Contractors Ass'n of E. Pa., 6 F.3d at 1010 ("Logically, a city must be able to rely on less evidence in enacting a gender preference than a racial preference because applying *Croson*'s evidentiary standard to a gender preference would eviscerate the difference between strict and intermediate scrutiny.").

The court ruled that Denver met its burden under the intermediate scrutiny standard because it produced evidence that the city participated in gender discrimination in the local construction industry. Given this record, the court did not need to decide whether intermediate scrutiny *required* the city to produce evidence of this type. See also Western States Paving v. Washington State Dept. of Transp., 407 F.3d 983 (9th Cir. 2005).

Discussion

1. Note that the symmetry required by *Croson* and *Adarand* means that it is more difficult to justify affirmative action programs that benefit blacks than to justify such programs for women. Indeed, it is even easier to justify affirmative action programs for homosexuals and the aged, who currently are not treated as suspect classes. Moreover, under *Croson* and *Adarand*, whites receive more protection from race-conscious affirmative action programs designed to help racial minorities than women receive from programs deliberately designed to exclude women. Do these results make sense?

2. The cases agree that remedying past discrimination against women is an important government interest.

What about other interests that the Supreme Court has not held to be compelling — for example, providing role models? Can they be important governmental interests for the purposes of gender-conscious affirmative action even if they are not compelling interests for the purposes of race-conscious affirmative action?

3. One interesting feature of the Supreme Court's 1970s gender-conscious affirmative action decisions is that they do not make the fine distinctions about the kinds of statistical and anecdotal proof that one finds in *Croson*. Nor, in these cases, does the Court raise a strong objection to remedying past societal discrimination against women. Why, then, don't courts look to general societal discrimination as a justification for the affirmative action programs? Cf. Michigan Road Builders

Assoc. v. Milliken, 834 F.2d 583, 595 (6th Cir. 1988) (general allegations of societal discrimination insufficient in gender case). Do you think that the circuit court opinions were right in modeling their tests more after *Croson* than after the Court's gender decisions of the 1970s and 1980s? Does the explanation have less to do with the differences between race and gender and more with the change in political mood in the country between the 1970s and the 1990s?

VII.   *Other Suspect Bases of Classification*

The Court has treated classifications based on ethnic origin[157] identically to race and has required more than a rational justification for classifications based on alienage[158] and legitimacy.[159] There are numerous other bases of classification that, it might be argued, should be treated as "suspect," including age,[160] height, intelligence,[161] appearance, and sexual orientation. See Watkins v. United States Army, p. 1519 infra. After our analysis of race and sex, do you have a theory of the Equal Protection Clause that helps determine which, if any, of these other classifications should receive special scrutiny?

CITY OF CLEBURNE, TEXAS v. CLEBURNE LIVING CENTER
473 U.S. 432 (1985)

[In July 1980, a four-bedroom house in Cleburne, Texas, was purchased for lease to the Cleburne Living Centers, Inc. (CLC), to serve as a group home for 13 mentally retarded men and women who would live there under the supervision of CLC staff members. CLC intended to comply with all applicable state and federal regulations. The city determined that a special use permit, required for the construction of "[h]ospitals for the insane or feeble-minded, or alcoholic[s] or drug addicts, or penal or correctional institutions," was required as well, on the basis of its classification of the home as a "hospital for the feeble-minded." CLC applied for a permit, which the city council denied by a vote of three to one. CLC then filed suit in the Federal District Court, which found that "[i]f the potential residents of the . . . home were not mentally retarded, but the home was the same in all other respects, its use would be permitted under the city's zoning ordinance." It further found that the city council's decision "was motivated primarily by the fact that the residents of the home would be persons who are mentally retarded."

157. See, e.g., Korematsu v. United States, 323 U.S. 214 (1944); Hirabayashi v. United States, 320 U.S. 81 (1943) (distinctions "between citizens solely because of their ancestry are by their very nature odious"); Hernandez v. Texas, 347 U.S. 475 (1954).

158. See, e.g., Graham v. Richardson, 403 U.S. 305 (1971); Sugarman v. Dougall, 413 U.S. 634 (1973); In re Griffiths, 413 U.S. 717 (1973); Examining Bd. v. Flores de Otero, 426 U.S. 572 (1976); Nyquist v. Mauclet, 432 U.S. 1 (1977). But see Foley v. Connelie, 435 U.S. 291 (1978); Ambach v. Norwich, 441 U.S. 68 (1979).

159. See, e.g., Levy v. Louisiana, 301 U.S. 68 (1968); Glona v. American Guar. & Liab. Co., 391 U.S. 73 (1968); Weber v. Aetna Cas. & Sur. Co., 406 U.S. 164 (1972); Trimble v. Gordon, 430 U.S. 762 (1977). Cf. Labine v. Vincent, 401 U.S. 532 (1971); Mathews v. Lucas, 427 U.S. 495 (1976).

160. But see Massachusetts Bd. of Retirement v. Murgia, 427 U.S. 307 (1976); Vance v. Bradley, 440 U.S. 93 (1979).

161. See Note, Equal Protection and Intelligence Classifications, 26 Stan. L. Rev. 647 (1974).

Nevertheless, the court held the ordinance and its application constitutional under the standard of minimal rationality, for it was rationally related to the city's legitimate interests in "the legal responsibility of CLC and its residents, . . . the safety and fears of residents in the adjoining neighborhood," and the number of people to be housed in the facility.

The Court of Appeals for the Fifth Circuit reversed, holding that mental retardation was a quasi-suspect classification triggering an intermediate-level standard of review, which the city could not pass. The city appealed.]

WHITE, J., delivered the opinion of the Court. . . .

II.

The Equal Protection Clause of the Fourteenth Amendment commands that no State shall "deny to any person within its jurisdiction the equal protection of the laws," which is essentially a direction that all persons similarly situated should be treated alike. Plyler v. Doe, 457 U.S. 202. Section 5 of the Amendment empowers Congress to enforce this mandate, but absent controlling congressional direction, the courts have themselves devised standards for determining the validity of state legislation or other official action that is challenged as denying equal protection. The general rule is that legislation is presumed to be valid and will be sustained if the classification drawn by the statute is rationally related to a legitimate state interest. . . . When social or economic legislation is at issue, the Equal Protection Clause allows the states wide latitude, and the Constitution presumes that even improvident decisions will eventually be rectified by the democratic processes.

The general rule gives way, however, when a statute classifies by race, alienage, or national origin. These factors are so seldom relevant to the achievement of any legitimate state interest that laws grounded in such considerations are deemed to reflect prejudice and antipathy — a view that those in the burdened class are not as worthy or deserving as others. For these reasons and because such discrimination is unlikely to be soon rectified by legislative means, these laws are subjected to strict scrutiny and will be sustained only if they are suitably tailored to serve a compelling state interest. . . .

Legislative classifications based on gender also call for a heightened standard of review. . . . Rather than resting on meaningful considerations, statutes distributing benefits and burdens between the sexes in different ways very likely reflect outmoded notions of the relative capabilities of men and women. A gender classification fails unless it is substantially related to a sufficiently important governmental interest. Because illegitimacy is beyond the individual's control and bears "no relation to the individual's ability to participate in and contribute to society," Mathews v. Lucas, 427 U.S. 495, 505 (1976), official discriminations resting on that characteristic are also subject to somewhat heightened review. Those restrictions "will survive equal protection scrutiny to the extent they are substantially related to a legitimate state interest." Mills v. Habluetzel, 456 U.S. 91, 99 (1982).

We have declined, however, to extend heightened review to differential treatment based on age:

While the treatment of the aged in this Nation has not been wholly free of discrimination, such persons, unlike, say, those who have been discriminated against on the basis

of race or national origin, have not experienced a "history of purposeful unequal treatment" or been subjected to unique disabilities on the basis of stereotyped characteristics not truly indicative of their abilities. Massachusetts Board of Retirement v. Murgia,
427 U.S. 307, 313 (1976).

The lesson of *Murgia* is that where individuals in the group affected by a law have
distinguishing characteristics relevant to interests the state has the authority to
implement, the courts have been very reluctant, as they should be in our federal
system and with our respect for the separation of powers, to closely scrutinize
legislative choices as to whether, how and to what extent those interests should be
pursued. In such cases, the Equal Protection Clause requires only a rational means
to serve a legitimate end.

III.

Against this background, we conclude for several reasons that the Court of Appeals
erred in holding mental retardation a quasi-suspect classification calling for a more
exacting standard of judicial review than is normally accorded economic and social
legislation. First, it is undeniable, and it is not argued otherwise here, that those
who are mentally retarded have a reduced ability to cope with and function in the
everyday world. Nor are they all cut from the same pattern: as the testimony in this
record indicates, they range from those whose disability is not immediately evident
to those who must be constantly cared for. They are thus different, immutably so, in
relevant respects, and the states' interest in dealing with and providing for them is
plainly a legitimate one. How this large and diversified group is to be treated under
the law is a difficult and often technical matter, very much a task for legislators
guided by qualified professionals and not by the perhaps ill-informed opinions of
the judiciary. Heightened scrutiny inevitably involves substantive judgments about
legislative decisions, and we doubt that the predicate for such judicial oversight is
present where the classification deals with mental retardation.

Second, the distinctive legislative response, both national and state, to the plight
of those who are mentally retarded demonstrates not only that they have unique
problems, but also that the lawmakers have been addressing their difficulties in a
manner that belies a continuing antipathy or prejudice and a corresponding need
for more intrusive oversight by the judiciary. [The Court then reviewed some recent
protective legislation passed by both the federal and Texas governments.]

. . . It may be . . . that legislation designed to benefit, rather than disadvantage,
the retarded would generally withstand examination under a test of heightened
scrutiny. The relevant inquiry, however, is whether heightened scrutiny is constitutionally mandated in the first instance. Even assuming that many of these laws could
be shown to be substantially related to an important governmental purpose, merely
requiring the legislature to justify its efforts in these terms may lead it to refrain from
acting at all. Much recent legislation intended to benefit the retarded also assumes
the need for measures that might be perceived to disadvantage them. The [federal]
Education of the Handicapped Act, for example, requires an "appropriate" education, not one that is equal in all respects to the education of non-retarded children. . . . Especially given the wide variation in the abilities and needs of the retarded
themselves, governmental bodies must have a certain amount of flexibility and
freedom from judicial oversight in shaping and limiting their remedial efforts.

Third, the legislative response, which could hardly have occurred and survived without public support, negates any claim that the mentally retarded are politically powerless in the sense that they have no ability to attract the attention of the lawmakers. Any minority can be said to be powerless to assert direct control over the legislature, but if that were a criterion for higher level scrutiny by the courts, much economic and social legislation would now be suspect. Fourth, if the large and amorphous class of the mentally retarded were deemed quasi-suspect, . . . it would be difficult to find a principled way to distinguish a variety of other groups who have perhaps immutable disabilities setting them off from others, who cannot themselves mandate the desired legislative responses, and who can claim some degree of prejudice from at least part of the public at large. One need mention in this respect only the aging, the disabled, the mentally ill, and the infirm. We are reluctant to set out on that course, and we decline to do so. . . .

IV.

We turn to the issue of the validity of the zoning ordinance insofar as it requires a special use permit for homes for the mentally retarded. We inquire first whether requiring a special use permit for the Featherston [Avenue] home in the circumstances here deprives respondents of the equal protection of the laws. If it does, there will be no occasion to decide whether the special use permit provision is facially invalid where the mentally retarded are involved. . . .

The constitutional issue is clearly posed. The city does not require a special use permit in an R-3 zone for apartment houses, multiple dwellings, boarding and lodging houses, fraternity or sorority houses, dormitories, apartment hotels, hospitals, sanitariums, nursing homes for convalescents or the aged (other than for the insane or feeble-minded or alcoholics or drug addicts), private clubs or fraternal orders, and other specified uses. It does, however, insist on a special permit for the Featherston home, and it does so, as the District Court found, because it would be a facility for the mentally retarded. May the city require the permit for this facility when other care and multiple dwelling facilities are freely permitted?

. . . Because in our view the record does not reveal any rational basis for believing that the Featherston home would pose any special threat to the city's legitimate interests, we affirm the judgment below insofar as it holds the ordinance invalid as applied in this case.

The District Court found that the City Council's insistence on the permit rested on several factors. First, the Council was concerned with the negative attitude of the majority of property owners located within 200 feet of the Featherston facility, as well as with the fears of elderly residents of the neighborhood. But mere negative attitudes, or fear, unsubstantiated by factors which are properly cognizable in a zoning proceeding, are not permissible bases for treating a home for the mentally retarded differently from apartment houses, multiple dwellings, and the like. . . . "Private biases may be outside the reach of the law, but the law cannot, directly or indirectly, give them effect." Palmore v. Sidoti.

Second, the Council had two objections to the location of the facility. It was concerned that the facility was across the street from a junior high school, and it feared that the students might harass the occupants of the Featherston home. But the school itself is attended by about 30 mentally retarded students, and denying a permit based on such vague, undifferentiated fears is again permitting some portion of the community to validate what would otherwise be an equal protection violation. The other objection to the home's location was that it was located on a "five hundred year flood plain." This concern with the possibility of a flood, however, can hardly be based on a distinction between the Featherston home and, for example, nursing homes, homes for convalescents or the aged, or sanitariums or hospitals, any of which could be located on the Featherston site without obtaining a special use permit. The same may be said of another concern of the Council — doubts about the legal responsibility for actions which the mentally retarded might take. . . .

Fourth, the Council was concerned with the size of the home and the number of people that would occupy it. . . . [But] there would be no restrictions on the number of people who could occupy this home as a boarding house, nursing home, family dwelling, fraternity house, or dormitory. . . . In the words of the Court of Appeals, "The City never justifies its apparent view that other people can live under such 'crowded' conditions when mentally retarded persons cannot."

In the courts below, the city also urged that the ordinance is aimed at avoiding concentration of population and at lessening congestion of the streets. These concerns obviously fail to explain why apartment houses, fraternity and sorority houses, hospitals and the like, may freely locate in the area without a permit. So, too, the expressed worry about fire hazards, the serenity of the neighborhood, and the avoidance of danger to other residents fail rationally to justify singling out a home such as 201 Featherston for the special use permit. . . .

The short of it is that requiring the permit in this case appears to us to rest on an irrational prejudice against the mentally retarded, including those who would occupy the Featherston facility and who would live under the closely supervised and highly regulated conditions expressly provided for by state and federal law.

The judgment of the Court of Appeals is affirmed insofar as it invalidates the zoning ordinance as applied to the Featherston home. . . .

[A concurring opinion by Justice Stevens, joined by Chief Justice Burger, is omitted.]

MARSHALL, J., joined by Brennan and Blackmun, JJ., concurring in the judgment in part and dissenting in part.

. . . Cleburne's ordinance is invalidated only after being subjected to precisely the sort of probing inquiry associated with heightened scrutiny. . . . [H]owever labeled, the rational basis test invoked today is most assuredly not the rational basis test of *Williamson.* . . .

The Court, for example, concludes that legitimate concerns for fire hazards or the serenity of the neighborhood do not justify singling out respondents to bear the burdens of these concerns, for analogous permitted uses appear to pose similar threats. Yet under the traditional and most minimal version of the rational basis test, "reform may take one step at a time, addressing itself to the phase of the problem which seems most acute to the legislative mind." Williamson v. Lee Optical Co. The "record" is said not to support the ordinance's classifications, but under the traditional standard we do not sift through the record to determine whether policy decisions are squarely supported by a firm factual foundation. Finally, the Court further finds it "difficult to believe" that the retarded present different or special hazards than other groups. In normal circumstances, the burden is not on the legislature to convince the Court that the lines it has drawn are sensible. . . .

The refusal to acknowledge that something more than minimum rationality review is at work here is, in my view, unfortunate in at least two respects. The suggestion that the traditional rational basis test allows this sort of searching inquiry creates precedent for this Court and lower courts to subject economic and commercial classifications to similar and searching "ordinary" rational basis review — a small and regrettable step back toward the days of Lochner v. New York. Moreover, by failing to articulate the factors that justify today's "second order" rational basis review, the Court provides no principled foundation for determining when more searching inquiry is to be invoked.

II.

I have long believed the level of scrutiny employed in equal protection cases should vary with "the constitutional and societal importance of the interest adversely affected and the recognized invidiousness of the basis upon which the particular classification is drawn." San Antonio Independent School District v. Rodriguez, 411 U.S. 1, 99 (1973) (dissenting). When a zoning ordinance works to exclude the retarded from all residential districts in a community, these two considerations require that the ordinance be convincingly justified as substantially furthering legitimate and important purposes.

First, the interest of the retarded in establishing group homes is substantial. . . . Excluding group homes deprives the retarded of much of what makes for human freedom and fulfillment — the ability to form bonds and take part in the life of a community.

Second, the mentally retarded have been subject to a "lengthy and tragic history," *Bakke,* of segregation and discrimination that can only be called grotesque. [In the early twentieth century, a] regime of state-mandated segregation and degradation . . . emerged that in its virulence and bigotry rivaled, and indeed paralleled, the worst excesses of Jim Crow. Massive custodial institutions were built to warehouse the retarded for life; the aim was to halt reproduction of the retarded and "nearly extinguish their race." Retarded children were categorically excluded from public schools, based on the false stereotype that all were ineducable and on the purported need to protect nonretarded children from them. State laws deemed the retarded "unfit for citizenship."

Segregation was accompanied by eugenic marriage and sterilization laws that extinguished for the retarded one of the "basic civil rights of man" — the right to marry and procreate. Marriages of the retarded were made, and in some states continue to be, not only voidable but also often a criminal offense. The purpose of such limitations, which frequently applied only to women of child-bearing age, was unabashedly eugenic: to prevent the retarded from propagating. To assure this end, 29 states enacted compulsory eugenic sterilization laws between 1907 and 1931.

Prejudice, once let loose, is not easily cabined. As of 1979, most states still categorically disqualified "idiots" from voting, without regard to individual capacity and with discretion to exclude left in the hands of low-level election officials. Not until Congress enacted the Education of the Handicapped Act were the "door[s] of public education" opened wide to handicapped children. But most important, lengthy and continuing isolation of the retarded has perpetuated the ignorance, irrational fears, and stereotyping that long have plagued them.

In light of the importance of the interest at stake and the history of discrimination the retarded have suffered, the Equal Protection Clause requires us to do more than review the distinctions drawn by Cleburne's zoning ordinance as if they appeared in a taxing statute or in economic or commercial legislation. . . .

III.

In its effort to show that Cleburne's ordinance can be struck down under no "more exacting standard . . . than is normally accorded economic and social legislation," the Court offers several justifications as to why the retarded do not warrant heightened judicial solicitude. These justifications, however, find no support in our heightened scrutiny precedents and cannot withstand logical analysis.

The Court downplays the lengthy "history of purposeful unequal treatment" of the retarded by pointing to recent legislative action that is said to "beli[e] a continuing antipathy or prejudice." Building on this point, the Court similarly concludes that the retarded are not "politically powerless" and deserve no greater judicial protection than "any minority" that wins some political battles and loses others. The import of these conclusions, it seems, is that the only discrimination courts may remedy is the discrimination they alone are perspicacious enough to see. Once society begins to recognize certain practices as discriminatory, in part because previously stigmatized groups have mobilized politically to lift this stigma, the Court would refrain from approaching such practices with the added skepticism of heightened scrutiny.

Courts, however, do not sit or act in a social vacuum. Moral philosophers may debate whether certain inequalities are absolute wrongs, but history makes clear that constitutional principles of equality, like constitutional principles of liberty, property and due process, evolve over time; what once was a "natural" and "self-evident" ordering later comes to be seen as an artificial and invidious constraint on human potential and freedom. Compare Plessy v. Ferguson and Bradwell v. Illinois with Brown v. Board of Education and Reed v. Reed. Shifting cultural, political, and social patterns at times come to make past practices appear inconsistent with fundamental principles upon which American society rests, an inconsistency legally cognizable under the Equal Protection Clause. It is natural that evolving standards of equality come to be embodied in legislation. When that occurs, courts should look to the fact of such change as a source of guidance on evolving principles of equality. In [*Frontiero*], the Court reached this very conclusion when it extended heightened scrutiny to gender classifications and drew on parallel legislative developments to support that extension. . . .

Moreover, even when judicial action has catalyzed legislative change, that change certainly does not eviscerate the underlying constitutional principle. The Court, for example, has never suggested that race-based classifications became any less suspect once extensive legislation had been enacted on the subject.

For the retarded, just as for Negroes and women, much has changed in recent years, but much remains the same; out-dated statutes are still on the books, and irrational fears or ignorance, traceable to the prolonged social cultural isolation of the retarded, continue to stymie recognition of the dignity and individuality of retarded people. Heightened judicial scrutiny of action appearing to impose unnecessary barriers to the retarded is required in light of increasing recognition that such barriers are inconsistent with evolving principles of equality embedded in the Fourteenth Amendment.

The Court also offers a more general view of heightened scrutiny, a view focused primarily on when heightened scrutiny does not apply as opposed to when it does apply. Two principles appear central to the Court's theory. First, heightened scrutiny is said to be inapplicable where individuals in a group have distinguishing characteristics that legislatures properly may take into account in some circumstances. Heightened scrutiny is also purportedly inappropriate when many legislative classifications affecting the group are likely to be valid. . . . If the Court's first principle were sound, heightened scrutiny would have to await a day when people could be cut from a cookie mold. . . . Permissible distinctions between persons must bear a reasonable relationship to their relevant characteristics, and gender per se is almost never relevant. . . .

The Court's second assertion — that the standard of review must be fixed with reference to the number of classifications to which a characteristic would validly be relevant — is similarly flawed. Certainly the assertion is not a logical one; that a characteristic may be relevant under some or even many circumstances does not suggest any reason to presume it relevant under other circumstances where there is reason to suspect it is not. A sign that says "men only" looks very different on a bathroom door than a courthouse door.

Our heightened scrutiny precedents belie the claim that a characteristic must virtually always be irrelevant to warrant heightened scrutiny. . . . While *Frontiero* stated that gender "frequently" and "often" bears no relation to legitimate legislative aims, it did not deem gender an impermissible basis of state action in all circumstances. Indeed, the Court has upheld some gender-based classifications. . . . Potentially discriminatory classifications exist only where some constitutional basis can be found for presuming that equal rights are required. Discrimination, in the Fourteenth Amendment sense, connotes a substantive constitutional judgment that two individuals or groups are entitled to be treated equally with respect to some thing. With regard to economic and commercial matters, no basis for such a conclusion exists. . . . As a matter of substantive policy, therefore, government is free to move in any direction, or to change directions, in the economic and commercial sphere. . . .

But the Fourteenth Amendment does prohibit other results under virtually all circumstances, such as castes created by law along racial or ethnic lines, and significantly constrains the range of permissible government choices where gender or illegitimacy, for example, are concerned. Where such constraints, derived from the Fourteenth Amendment, are present, and where history teaches they have systemically been ignored, a "more searching judicial inquiry" is required. United States v. Carolene Products Co.

That more searching inquiry, be it called heightened scrutiny or "second order" rational basis review, is a method of approaching certain classifications skeptically, with judgment suspended until the facts are in and the evidence considered. The government must establish that the classification is substantially related to important and legitimate objectives so that valid and sufficiently weighty policies actually justify the departure from equality. Heightened scrutiny does not allow courts to second guess reasoned legislative or professional judgments tailored to the unique needs of a group like the retarded, but it does seek to assure that the hostility or thoughtlessness with which there is reason to be concerned has not carried the day. . . .

As the history of discrimination against the retarded and its continuing legacy amply attest, the mentally retarded have been, and in some areas may still be, the targets of action the Equal Protection Clause condemns. With respect to a liberty so valued as the right to establish a home in the community, and so likely to be denied on the basis of irrational fears and outright hostility, heightened scrutiny is surely appropriate.

IV.

In light of the scrutiny that should be applied here, Cleburne's ordinance sweeps too broadly to dispel the suspicion that it rests on a bare desire to treat the retarded as outsiders, pariahs who do not belong in the community. The Court, while disclaiming that special scrutiny is necessary or warranted, reaches the same conclusion. Rather than striking the ordinance down, however, the Court invalidates it merely as applied to respondents. I must dissent from the novel proposition that "the preferred course of adjudication" is to leave standing a legislative act resting on "irrational prejudice," thereby forcing individuals in the group discriminated against to continue to run the act's gauntlet.

. . . As a consequence, the Court's as applied remedy relegates future retarded applicants to the standardless discretion of low-level officials who have already shown an all too willing readiness to be captured by the "vague, undifferentiated fears" of ignorant or frightened residents.

Invalidating on its face the ordinance's special treatment of the "feeble-minded," in contrast, would place the responsibility for tailoring and updating Cleburne's unconstitutional ordinance where it belongs: with the legislative arm of the City of Cleburne. . . .

To my knowledge, the Court has never before treated an equal protection challenge to a statute on an as applied basis. When statutes rest on impermissibly overbroad generalizations, our cases have invalidated the presumption on its face. We do not instead leave to the courts the task of redrafting the statute through an ongoing and cumbersome process of "as applied" constitutional rulings. . . .

. . . When a presumption is unconstitutionally overbroad, the preferred course of adjudication is to strike it down.

Discussion

1. In defining the scope of Congress's Section Five power to enforce the Equal Protection Clause, the Court recently described its holding in *Cleburne*. In Board of Trustees of Univ. of Alabama v. Garrett, 531 U.S. 356, 367-368 (2001), the Court observes:

> Thus, the result of *Cleburne* is that States are not required by the Fourteenth Amendment to make special accommodations for the disabled, so long as their actions toward such individuals are rational. They could quite hardheadedly — and perhaps hardheartedly — hold to job-qualification requirements which do not make allowance for the disabled. If special accommodations for the disabled are to be required, they have to come from positive law and not through the Equal Protection Clause.

a. Does this strike you as a fair account of the Court's reasoning in *Cleburne?* Can this reading of *Cleburne* be squared with the Court's decision to strike down the zoning ordinance?

b. Does this strike you as a fair account of Fourteenth Amendment case law more generally? Samuel Bagenstos objects that "[t]he assumption that discrimination on the basis of race or sex is never rational, and the related normative view that discrimination should be prohibited only when it is irrational, simply misdescribe the empirical and normative bases of antidiscrimination law." Samuel R. Bagenstos, The Supreme Court, The Americans With Disabilities Act, and Rational Discrimination, 55 Ala. L. Rev. 923, 925 (2004).

For other reflections on questions of accommodation and the antidiscrimination principle, see the discussion of *Hibbs,* supra. See also Samuel R. Bagenstos, "Rational Discrimination," Accommodation, and the Politics of (Disability) Civil Rights, 89 Va. L. Rev. 825 (2003); Samuel R. Bagenstos, The Future of Disability Law, 114 Yale L.J. 1 (2004); Christine Jolls, Antidiscrimination and Accommodation, 115 Harv. L. Rev. 642 (2001); Mark Kelman, Market Discrimination and Groups, 53 Stan. L. Rev. 833 (2001); Michael Ashley Stein, The Law and Economics of Disability Accommodations, 53 Duke L.J. 79 (2003); David A. Strauss, The Law and Economics of Racial Discrimination in Employment, 79 Geo. L.J. 1619 (1991); Richard A. Epstein, Forbidden Grounds: The Case Against Employment Discrimination Laws (1992).

2. Did the Court apply rational basis scrutiny in *Cleburne?* If not, how might one characterize the standard of review applied in the case? Reviewing recent equal protection case law, Professor William Eskridge observes "that the Court has informally moved away from giving such critical importance to the level of scrutiny and has moved toward a sliding scale approach" of a kind advocated by Justice Marshall in his *Cleburne* dissent. See William N. Eskridge, Jr., Some Effects of Identity-Based Social Movements on Constitutional Law in the Twentieth Century, 100 Mich. L. Rev. 2062, 2268-2269 (2002). For discussion of these issues see the symposium, Equal Protection After the Rational Basis Era: Is It Time To Reassess the Current Standards of Review?, 4 U. Pa. J. Const. L. 225, especially Leslie Friedman Goldstein, Between the Tiers: The New[est] Equal Protection and Bush v. Gore, 4 U. Pa. J. Const. L. 372 (2002) (tracing the evolution of equal protection analysis).

3. Professor Martha Minow has argued that the majority and dissenting opinions in *Cleburne* rest on distinct visions of the status of "difference" under the Equal Protection Clause:

> [B]eneath the debates [in *Cleburne*] over the proper fit between ends and means of legislative action and the proper level of scrutiny for reviewing legislative classifications lies a sharp division about the meaning of difference. On one side is the perhaps contentiously labeled "abnormal persons" view, a conception of real differences used to treat certain people as legally different. On the other side is the perhaps ambiguously designated "social relations" view, which emphasizes how differences acquire significance through social attributions, rather than the other way around; how we each have relationships even with those we think are different; and how "we" are as different from those we call different as they are different from us. The "abnormal persons" view makes differential treatment seem natural, unavoidable, and unproblematic; the social relations view makes differential treatment a problem of social choice and meaning, a problem for which all onlookers are responsible.[162]

---

162. Martha Minow, When Difference Has Its Home: Group Homes for the Mentally Retarded, Equal Protection and Legal Treatment of Difference, 22 Harv. C.R.-C.L. L. Rev. 111, 139-140 (1987).

Where classifications of race, ethnicity, or gender are involved, the Court justifies heightened scrutiny largely on the view that such classifications *as a factual matter* are seldom relevant to legitimate state ends, and therefore are presumed to rest on prejudice and bigotry. Under Minow's analysis, is the problem with the "abnormal persons" view that as a factual matter it misperceives the nature of the difference, or rather that it unfairly ignores the perspective and feelings of the affected class?

VIII.   Accommodation as a Norm: The Americans with Disabilities Act of 1990

In the summer of 1990, President Bush proudly signed the Americans with Disabilities Act, describing it as the most important step in civil rights since the Civil Rights Act of 1964. Section 102 provides:

> (a) General Rule. No covered entity shall discriminate against a qualified individual with a disability because of the disability of such individual in regard to . . . terms, conditions, and privileges of employment.
> (b) Construction. As used in subsection (a), the term "discriminate" includes —
> (5)(A) not making reasonable accommodations to the known physical or mental limitations of an otherwise qualified individual with a disability who is an applicant or employee, unless such covered entity can demonstrate that the accommodation would impose an undue hardship on the operation of the business of such covered entity.

Section 101 provides:

> (9) The term "reasonable accommodation" may include:
>
>> (A) making existing facilities used by employees readily accessible to and useable by individuals with disabilities; and
>> (B) job restructuring, part-time or modified work schedules, reassignment to a vacant position, acquisition or modification of equipment or devices, appropriate adjustment or modifications of examinations, training materials or policies, the provision of qualified readers or interpreters, and other similar accommodations for individuals with disabilities.
>
> (10) The term "undue hardship" means an action requiring significant difficulty or expense, when considered in the light of factors [including the nature and cost of the accommodation and the overall financial resources of the covered entity and the facility involved].

Discussion

Many view the "reasonable accommodation" provision of the Americans with Disabilities Act of 1990 (ADA) as radically different from the antidiscrimination principle as it has been interpreted by courts construing the Equal Protection Clause, the Civil Rights Act of 1964, and other federal civil rights statutes. Others see closer affinities between the prohibition on discrimination and the requirement of reasonable accommodation. (See commentary following the *Hibbs* and *Cleburne* cases, supra.) In what respects are these approaches similar and different?

What values are at stake in this debate? Is there a reason for adopting a distinct approach in constitutional cases? In cases where courts are enforcing constitutional commitments?

Chapter 8

Implied Fundamental Rights: The Constitution, the Family, and the Body

In this chapter we examine a series of modern opinions in which the Court has protected rights variously described in terms of personal privacy, procreational choice, sexual autonomy, the right to choose how to live (and how to die), family integrity, and intimate association. Judges, lawyers, and scholars disagree about whether these rights are or can be grounded in the text of or the historical understandings of provisions of the U.S. Constitution. Note, however, that since at least the decision in Calder v. Bull (discussed in Chapter 2, supra) there has been a tradition of American constitutional thought that argues that constitutional rights can exist outside the text or can be implied from the basic constitutional order, the fundamental narratives of American history and American identity, the common and honored traditions of the American people, or the deepest meanings of liberty and equality in a free and democratic republic. Moreover, some scholars argue that, far from being foreign to the constitutional text, these "implied fundamental rights" can be grounded textually as among the Privileges or Immunities of national citizenship, among the "liberties" protected by the Due Process Clause of the Fourteenth Amendment, or among those rights whose existence is presumed by the language of the Ninth Amendment.

The method of discovering and articulating these implied fundamental rights is open to considerable dispute. Some argue that these rights can be discovered through the methods of judicial reasoning, the practice of moral philosophy, or in the understandings of conventional morality. Others look to tradition, still others to the ethos of the American people, and still others to underlying narratives of American history.

Critics frequently deny that such fundamental rights exist. They also deny, in any event, that judges are capable of identifying them with the precision necessary to resolve constitutional disputes, or that the courts have the political authority to bind the polity to their conclusions.

These debates are the central concern of this chapter.

I. Antecedents of Fundamental Rights Adjudication

The modern doctrine of fundamental rights adjudication is heir to three traditions. On the most general level, it continues a tradition of judicial protection of rights that goes back to the doctrines of "general constitutional law" examined in Part One. Second, it is an outgrowth of the resurgence of judicial protection of individual rights that followed World War II, which we have seen manifested in the expansion of the equal protection doctrine chronicled in Chapters 6 and 7 and in the incorporation of the Bill of Rights into the Fourteenth Amendment described in the Introduction to Part Two.

Third, notwithstanding the Court's protestations to the contrary, modern doctrine owes much to the *Lochner* era. (Recall that even Justice Holmes, dissenting in *Lochner,* conceded that the judiciary could legitimately invalidate "the natural outcome of a dominant opinion" when "a rational and fair man necessarily would admit that the statute proposed would infringe fundamental principles as they have been understood by the traditions of our people and our law.") During the heyday of economic due process, the Court intervened on several occasions to protect interests that had a significant noneconomic component. The language in two of the leading cases of the period, Meyer v. Nebraska, 262 U.S. 390 (1923), and Pierce v. Society of Sisters, 268 U.S. 510 (1925), suggests that the Court did not consider "economic" and "personal" interests discrete areas of concern.

The petitioner in *Meyer* was an instructor in a parochial school, convicted under a state law prohibiting the teaching of a foreign language to any child not yet in the eighth grade. (The law in fact reflected the animosity against German-speaking German-Americans during World War I.) Over the dissents of Justices Holmes and Sutherland, the Court struck down the law, viewing it as an incursion on Meyer's right "to teach and the right of parents to engage him so to instruct their children." Justice McReynolds, writing for the Court, argued that "[t]he problem for our determination is whether the statute . . . unreasonably infringes the liberty guaranteed . . . by the Fourteenth Amendment":

> While this Court has not attempted to define with exactness the liberty thus guaranteed, the term has received much consideration and some of the included things have been definitely stated. Without doubt, it denotes not merely freedom from bodily restraint but also the right of the individual to contract, to engage in any of the common occupations of life, to acquire useful knowledge, to marry, establish a home and bring up children, to worship God according to the dictates of his own conscience, and generally to enjoy those privileges long recognized by common law as essential to the orderly pursuit of happiness by free men. The established doctrine is that this liberty may not be interfered with, under the guise of protecting the public interest, by legislative action which is arbitrary or without reasonable relation to some purpose within the competency of the State to effect. Determination by the legislature of what constitutes proper exercise of the police power is not final or conclusive but is subject to supervision by the courts. . . .

Pierce v. Society of Sisters and the consolidated case of Pierce v. Hill Military Academy were suits brought by parochial and private schools challenging an Oregon statute that required children to attend public schools. Justice McReynolds wrote for a unanimous Court, invalidating the statute:

> [W]e think it entirely plain that the Act of 1922 unreasonably interferes with the liberty of parents and guardians to direct the upbringing and education of children under their control. As often heretofore pointed out, rights guaranteed by the Constitution may not be abridged by legislation which has no reasonable relation to some purpose within the competency of the State. The fundamental theory of liberty upon which all governments in this Union repose excludes any general power of the State to standardize its children by forcing them to accept instruction from public teachers only. The child is not the mere creature of the State; those who nurture him and direct his destiny have the right, coupled with the high duty, to recognize and prepare him for additional obligations.

Although the Court abandoned economic due process in 1937, it was far more equivocal about the protection of noneconomic rights not specifically enumerated in the Bill of Rights. In Olsen v. Nebraska, 313 U.S. 236 (1941), an economic due process case considered in Chapter 5, Justice Douglas wrote, for a unanimous Court, that "[w]e are not concerned . . . with the wisdom, need, or appropriateness of the legislation. . . . In the final analysis, the only constitutional prohibitions or restraints which respondents have suggested for the invalidation of this legislation are those notions of public policy embodied in earlier decisions of this Court but which, as Mr. Justice Holmes long admonished, should not be read into the Constitution." One year later, however, Justice Douglas also wrote for the Court in Skinner v. Oklahoma, 316 U.S. 535 (1942), invalidating Oklahoma's Habitual Criminal Sterilization Act as a violation of the Equal Protection Clause. The Act required sterilization of a criminal offender upon a third conviction of a felony "involving moral turpitude." Several felonies, including embezzlement, were specifically exempted from serving as predicate offenses triggering the sterilization penalty. Skinner had been convicted over the course of a decade of three qualifying felonies — one chicken theft and two armed robberies — and was sentenced to sterilization. Justice Douglas wrote for the Court: "If we had here only a question as to the State's classification of crimes, such as embezzlement or larceny, no substantial federal question would be raised." Instead:

> We are dealing here with legislation which involves one of the basic civil rights of man. Marriage and procreation are fundamental to the very existence and survival of the race. The power to sterilize, if exercised, may have subtle, far-reaching and devastating effects. In evil or reckless hands it can cause races or types which are inimical to the dominant group to wither and disappear. There is no redemption for the individual whom the law touches. Any experiment which the State conducts is to his irreparable injury. He is forever deprived of a basic liberty. . . . [S]trict scrutiny of the classification which a State makes in a sterilization law is essential, lest unwittingly, or otherwise, invidious discriminations are made against groups or types of individuals in violation of the constitutional guaranty of just and equal laws. . . . When the law lays an unequal hand on those who have committed intrinsically the same quality of offense and sterilizes one and not the other, it has made as invidious a discrimination as if it had selected a particular race or nationality for oppressive treatment.

Justice Douglas went on to contrast the crime of grand larceny (a felony covered by the statute) with the exempted crime of embezzlement to demonstrate that in many instances the distinctions were based on technical questions of property law. He concluded that there was no basis for believing that the "inheritability of criminal traits follows the neat legal distinctions which the law has marked between those two legal offenses." Chief Justice Stone concurred in the result on the ground that the Due Process Clause entitled petitioner to a hearing on the heritability of his criminal tendencies before he could be subjected to "so harsh a measure."[1] Justice Jackson

---

1. Cf. Buck v. Bell, 274 U.S. 200 (1927), in which the state provided for the sterilization of institutionalized mentally defective persons after a hearing at which, apparently, the issue of heritability could be contested. Petitioner challenged not the procedure but the substantive provision itself. Noting that she was feebleminded, the mother of an illegitimate feebleminded child, and the daughter of a feebleminded woman confined to the same state institution, Justice Holmes summarily dismissed the due process challenge with the comment that "three generations of imbeciles are enough." To the equal protection claim that the sterilization law applied only to persons confined in state institutions and not to the multitudes outside, Holmes responded that "it is the usual last resort of constitutional arguments to point out shortcomings of this sort."

agreed with both Douglas and Stone, adding that "[t]here are limits to the extent to which a legislatively represented majority may conduct biological experiments at the expense of the dignity and personality and natural powers of a minority — even those who have been guilty of what the majority defines as crimes." Note that no one suggested that the state could not differentiate between embezzlement and armed robbery (or even chicken theft) by, for example, making the sentences for the latter crimes considerably longer than the sentence for embezzlement.

During the 1950s, the Court also invoked the Due Process Clause to impose substantive limitations on the criteria for the admission of lawyers to state bars.[2] In Aptheker v. Secretary of State, 378 U.S. 500 (1964), the Court invalidated a law that effectively denied passports to all members of the Communist Party, holding that it "sweeps unnecessarily broadly and thereby invade[s] the area of protected freedoms," specifically the "right to travel abroad," which the Court held was a "personal liberty" implicit in the Fifth Amendment.

What is sometimes called the second era of substantive due process came into full flower in 1965 with Griswold v. Connecticut.

II.   Methods of Fundamental Rights Adjudication

A.   The Birth of the Modern Era of Substantive Due Process

GRISWOLD v. CONNECTICUT
318 U.S. 479 (1965)

DOUGLAS, J.

Appellant Griswold is Executive Director of the Planned Parenthood League of Connecticut. Appellant Buxton is a licensed physician and a professor at the Yale Medical School who served as Medical Director for the League at its Center in New Haven — a center open and operating from November 1 to November 10, 1961, when appellants were arrested.

They gave information, instruction, and medical advice to *married persons* as to the means of preventing conception. They examined the wife and prescribed the best contraceptive device or material for her use. Fees were usually charged, although some couples were serviced free.

The statutes whose constitutionality is involved in this appeal are §§53-32 and 54-196 of the General Statutes of Connecticut. The former provides: "Any person who uses any drug, medicinal article or instrument for the purpose of preventing conception shall be fined not less than fifty dollars or imprisoned not less than sixty days nor more than one year or be both fined and imprisoned."

Section 54-196 provides: "Any person who assists, abets, counsels, causes, hires or commands another to commit any offense may be prosecuted and punished as if he were the principal offender."

The appellants were found guilty as accessories and fined $100 each, against the claim that the accessory statute as so applied violated the Fourteenth Amendment.

---

2. See Schware v. Board of Bar Examiners, 353 U.S. 232 (1957). See also Konigsberg v. State Bar, 353 U.S. 252 (1957). Cf. Wieman v. Updegraff, 344 U.S. 183 (1952).

[The Court held that appellants had standing to raise the constitutional rights of the married people with whom they had a professional relationship.]

Coming to the merits, we are met with a wide range of questions that implicate the Due Process Clause of the Fourteenth Amendment. Overtones of some arguments suggest that Lochner v. New York should be our guide. But we decline that invitation as we did in West Coast Hotel v. Parrish [and] Williamson v. Lee Optical Co. We do not sit as a super-legislature to determine the wisdom, need, and propriety of laws that touch economic problems, business affairs, or social conditions. This law, however, operates directly on an intimate relation of husband and wife and their physician's role in one aspect of that relation.

The association of people is not mentioned in the Constitution nor in the Bill of Rights. The right to educate a child in a school of the parents' choice — whether public or private or parochial — is also not mentioned. Nor is the right to study any particular subject or any foreign language. Yet the First Amendment has been construed to include certain of those rights.

By Pierce v. Society of Sisters the right to educate one's children as one chooses is made applicable to the States by the force of the First and Fourteenth Amendments. By Meyer v. Nebraska the same dignity is given the right to study the German language in a private school. In other words, the State may not consistently with the spirit of the First Amendment, contract the spectrum of available knowledge. The right of freedom of speech and press includes not only the right to utter or to print, but the right to distribute, the right to receive, the right to read and freedom of inquiry, freedom of thought, and freedom to teach — indeed the freedom of the entire university community. Without those peripheral rights the specific rights would be less secure. And so we reaffirm the principle of the *Pierce* and the *Meyer* cases.

In NAACP v. Alabama, 357 U.S. 449 (1958), we protected the "freedom to associate and privacy in one's associations," noting that freedom of association was a peripheral First Amendment right. Disclosure of membership lists of a constitutionally valid association, we held, was invalid, "as entailing the likelihood of a substantial restraint upon the exercise by petitioner's members of their right to freedom of association." In other words, the First Amendment has a penumbra where privacy is protected from governmental intrusion. In like context, we have protected forms of "association" that are not political in the customary sense but pertain to the social, legal, and economic benefit of the members. NAACP v. Button 371 U.S. 415 (1963).[3] In Schware v. Board of Bar Examiners, 353 U.S. 232 (1957), we held it not permissible to bar a lawyer from practice, because he had once been a member of the Communist Party. . . .

Those cases involved more than the "right of assembly" — a right that extends to all irrespective of their race or ideology. The right of "association," like the right of belief is more than the right to attend a meeting; it includes the right to express one's attitudes or philosophies by membership in a group or by affiliation with it or by other lawful means. Association in that context is a form of expression of opinion; and while it is not expressly included in the First Amendment its existence is necessary in making the express guarantees fully meaningful.

---

3. NAACP v. Button held that Virginia's prohibition of the solicitation of legal or professional business could not be employed to prevent the legal activities of the NAACP and NAACP Legal Defense and Educational Fund.

The foregoing cases suggest that specific guarantees in the Bill of Rights have penumbras, formed by emanations from those guarantees that help give them life and substance. See Poe v. Ullman, 367 U.S. 497, 516-22 (1961) (dissenting opinion). Various guarantees create zones of privacy. The right of association contained in the penumbra of the First Amendment is one, as we have seen. The Third Amendment in its prohibition against the quartering of soldiers "in any house" in time of peace without the consent of the owner is another facet of that privacy. The Fourth Amendment explicitly affirms the "right of the people to be secure in their persons, houses, papers, and effects, against unreasonable searches and seizures." The Fifth Amendment in its Self-Incrimination Clause enables the citizen to create a zone of privacy which government may not force him to surrender to his detriment. The Ninth Amendment provides: "The enumeration in the Constitution, of certain rights, shall not be construed to deny or disparage others retained by the people." The Fourth and Fifth Amendments were described in Boyd v. United States, 116 U.S. 616 (1886), as protection against all governmental invasions "of the sanctity of a man's home and the privacies of life." We recently referred in Mapp v. Ohio, 367 U.S. 643 (1961), to the Fourth Amendment as creating a "right to privacy, no less important than any other right carefully and particularly reserved to the people." . . .

The present case, then, concerns a relationship lying within the zone of privacy created by several fundamental constitutional guarantees. And it concerns a law which, in forbidding the *use* of contraceptives rather than regulating their manufacture or sale, seeks to achieve its goals by means having a maximum destructive impact upon that relationship. Such a law cannot stand in light of the familiar principle, so often applied by this Court, that a "governmental purpose to control or prevent activities constitutionally subject to state regulation may not be achieved by means which sweep unnecessarily broadly and thereby invade the area of protected freedoms." NAACP v. Alabama. Would we allow the police to search the sacred precincts of marital bedrooms for telltale signs of the use of contraceptives? The very idea is repulsive to the notions of privacy surrounding the marriage relationship.

We deal with a right of privacy older than the Bill of Rights — older than our political parties, older than our school system. Marriage is a coming together for better or for worse, hopefully enduring, and intimate to the degree of being sacred. It is an association that promotes a way of life, not causes; a harmony in living, not political faiths; a bilateral loyalty, not commercial or social projects. Yet it is an association for as noble a purpose as any involved in our prior decisions.

Reversed.

GOLDBERG, J., joined by Warren, C.J., and Brennan, J., concurring.

I agree with the Court that Connecticut's birth-control law unconstitutionally intrudes upon the right of marital privacy, and I join in its opinion and judgment. Although I have not accepted the view that "due process" as used in the Fourteenth Amendment incorporates all of the first eight Amendments, I do agree that the concept of liberty protects those personal rights that are fundamental, and is not confined to the specific terms of the Bill of Rights. My conclusion that the concept of liberty is not so restricted and that it embraces the right of marital privacy though that right is not mentioned explicitly in the Constitution is supported . . . by the language and history of the Ninth Amendment. . . .

The Ninth Amendment . . . was proffered to quiet expressed fears that a bill of specifically enumerated rights could not be sufficiently broad to cover all essential rights and that the specific mention of certain rights would be interpreted as a denial that others were protected. . . . [T]he Framers did not intend that the first eight amendments be construed to exhaust the basic and fundamental rights which the Constitution guaranteed to the people.

. . . To hold that a right so basic and fundamental and so deep-rooted in our society as the right of privacy in marriage may be infringed because that right is not guaranteed in so many words by the first eight amendments to the Constitution is to ignore the Ninth Amendment and to give it no effect whatsoever. . . .

I do not mean to imply that the Ninth Amendment is applied against the States by the Fourteenth. Nor do I mean to state that the Ninth Amendment constitutes an independent source of rights protected from infringement by either the States or the Federal Government. Rather the Ninth Amendment simply lends strong support to the view that the "liberty" protected by the Fifth and Fourteenth Amendments from infringement by the Federal Government or the States is not restricted to rights specifically mentioned in the first eight amendments. . . .

In determining which rights are fundamental, judges are not left at large to decide cases in light of their personal and private notions. Rather, they must look to the "traditions and [collective] conscience of our people" to determine whether a principle is "so rooted [there] . . . as to be ranked as fundamental." The inquiry is whether a right involved "is of such a character that it cannot be denied without violating those 'fundamental principles of liberty and justice which lie at the base of all our civil and political institutions.'"

The entire fabric of the Constitution and the purposes that clearly underlie its specific guarantees demonstrate that the rights to marital privacy and to marry and raise a family are of similar order and magnitude as the fundamental rights specifically protected.

Although the Constitution does not speak in so many words of the right of privacy in marriage, I cannot believe that it offers these fundamental rights no protection. The fact that no particular provision of the Constitution explicitly forbids the State from disrupting the traditional relation of the family — a relation as old and as fundamental as our entire civilization — surely does not show that the Government was meant to have the power to do so. . . .

The logic of the dissents would sanction federal or state legislation that seems to me even more plainly unconstitutional than the statute before us. Surely the Government, absent a showing of a compelling subordinating state interest, could not decree that all husbands and wives must be sterilized after two children have been born to them. Yet by their reasoning such an invasion of marital privacy would not be subject to constitutional challenge because, while it might be "silly," no provision of the Constitution specifically prevents the Government from curtailing the marital right to bear children and raise a family. . . .

In a long series of cases this Court has held that where fundamental personal liberties are involved, they may not be abridged by the States simply on a showing that a regulatory statute has some rational relationship to the effectuation of a proper state purpose. "Where there is a significant encroachment upon personal liberty, the State may prevail only upon showing a subordinating interest which is compelling," Bates v. Little Rock, 361 U.S. 516 (1960). The law must be shown "necessary, and not merely rationally related, to the accomplishment of a permissible state policy." McLaughlin v. Florida, 379 U.S. 184 (1964).

Although the Connecticut birth-control law obviously encroaches upon a fundamental personal liberty, the State does not show that the law serves any "subordinating [state] interest which is compelling" or that it is "necessary . . . to the accomplishment of a permissible state policy." The State, at most, argues that there is some rational relation between this statute and what is admittedly a legitimate subject of state concern — the discouraging of extra-marital relations. It says that preventing the use of birth-control devices by married persons helps prevent the indulgence by some in such extra-marital relations. The rationality of this justification is dubious, particularly in light of the admitted widespread availability to all persons in the State of Connecticut, unmarried as well as married, of birth-control devices for the prevention of disease, as distinguished from the prevention of conception. But, in any event, it is clear that the state interest in safeguarding marital fidelity can be served by a more discriminately tailored statute, which does not, like the present one, sweep unnecessarily broadly, reaching far beyond the evil sought to be dealt with and intruding upon the privacy of all married couples. . . . The State of Connecticut does have statutes, the constitutionality of which is beyond doubt, which prohibit adultery and fornication. These statutes demonstrate that means for achieving the same basic purpose of protecting marital fidelity are available to Connecticut without the need to "invade the area of protected freedoms." . . .

In sum, I believe that the right of privacy in the marital relation is fundamental and basic — a personal right "retained by the people" within the meaning of the Ninth Amendment. Connecticut cannot constitutionally abridge this fundamental right, which is protected by the Fourteenth Amendment from infringement by the States. I agree with the Court that petitioners' convictions must therefore be reversed. . . .

[Justice Harlan concurred in the judgment in *Griswold*, stating that "the proper constitutional inquiry in this case is whether this Connecticut statute infringes the Due Process Clause of the Fourteenth Amendment because the enactment violates basic values 'implicit in the concept of ordered liberty.' . . . For reasons stated at length in my dissenting opinion in Poe v. Ullman, 367 U.S. 497 (1961), I believe that it does." *Poe* was an earlier challenge to the Connecticut anticontraception law, in which the Court dismissed the complainants' appeal on procedural grounds. In one of four dissenting opinions in *Poe*, Justice Harlan expressed his views on the merits:]

HARLAN, J., dissenting [in Poe v. Ullman]. . . .

Were due process merely a procedural safeguard it would fail to reach those situations where the deprivation of life, liberty or property was accomplished by legislation which by operating in the future could, given even the fairest possible procedure in application to individuals, nevertheless destroy the enjoyment of all three. Thus the guaranties of due process . . . have in this country "become bulwarks also against arbitrary legislation."

However, it is not the particular enumeration of rights in the first eight Amendments which spells out the reach of Fourteenth Amendment due process, but rather, as was suggested in another context long before the adoption of that Amendment, those concepts which are considered to embrace those rights "which are . . . *fundamental;* which belong . . . to the citizens of all free governments,"

Corfield v. Coryell, 4 Wash. C.C. 371, 380, for "the purposes [of securing] which men enter into society," Calder v. Bull, 3 Dall. 386, 388. . . .

Due process has not been reduced to any formula; its content cannot be determined by reference to any code. The best that can be said is that through the course of this Court's decisions it has represented the balance which our Nation, built upon postulates of respect for the liberty of the individual, has struck between that liberty and the demands of organized society. If the supplying of content to this Constitutional concept has of necessity been a rational process, it certainly has not been one where judges have felt free to roam where unguided speculation might take them. The balance of which I speak is the balance struck by this country, having regard to what history teaches are the traditions from which it developed as well as the traditions from which it broke. That tradition is a living thing. . . .

It is this outlook which has led the Court continuingly to perceive distinctions in the imperative character of Constitutional provisions, since that character must be discerned from a particular provision's larger context. And inasmuch as this context is one not of words, but of history and purposes, the full scope of the liberty guaranteed by the Due Process Clause cannot be found in or limited by the precise terms of the specific guarantees elsewhere provided in the Constitution. This "liberty" is not a series of isolated points pricked out in terms of the taking of property; the freedom of speech, press, and religion; the right to keep and bear arms; the freedom from unreasonable searches and seizures; and so on. It is a rational continuum which, broadly speaking, includes a freedom from all substantial arbitrary impositions and purposeless restraints, see Allgeyer v. Louisiana, 165 U.S. 578; Holden v. Hardy, 169 U.S. 366; Nebbia v. New York, 291 U.S. 502; Skinner v. Oklahoma, 316 U.S. 535, 544 (concurring opinion); Schware v. Board of Bar Examiners, 353 U.S. 232, and which also recognizes, what a reasonable and sensitive judgment must, that certain interests require particularly careful scrutiny of the state needs asserted to justify their abridgment. . . .

Precisely what is involved here is this: the state is asserting the right to enforce its moral judgments by intruding upon the most intimate details of the marital relation with the full power of the criminal law. Potentially, this could allow the deployment of all the incidental machinery of the criminal law, arrests, searches, and seizures; inevitably, it must mean at the very least the lodging of criminal charges, a public trial, and testimony as to the corpus delicti. Nor could any imaginable elaboration of presumptions, testimonial privileges, or other safeguards, alleviate the necessity for testimony as to the mode and manner of the married couples' sexual relations, or at least the opportunity for the accused to make denial of the charges. In sum, the statute allows the State to enquire into, prove, and punish married people for the private use of their marital intimacy.

. . . This enactment involves what, by common understanding throughout the English-speaking world, must be granted to be a most fundamental aspect of "liberty," the privacy of the home in its most basic sense, and it is this which requires that the statute be subjected to "strict scrutiny."

That aspect of liberty which embraces the concept of the privacy of the home receives explicit Constitutional protection at two places only. These are the Third Amendment, relating to the quartering of soldiers, and the Fourth Amendment, prohibiting unreasonable searches and seizures. While these Amendments reach only the Federal Government, this Court has held in the strongest terms . . . that the concept of "privacy" embodied in the Fourth Amendment is part of the "ordered liberty" assured against state action by the Fourteenth Amendment.

It is clear, of course, that this Connecticut statute does not invade the privacy of the home in the usual sense, since the invasion involved here may, and doubtless usually would, be accomplished without any physical intrusion whatever into the home. What the statute undertakes to do, however, is to create a crime which is grossly offensive to this privacy, while the Constitution refers only to methods of ferreting out substantive wrongs, and the procedure it requires presupposes that substantive offenses may be committed and sought out in the privacy of the home. But such an analysis forecloses any claim to Constitutional protection against this form of deprivation of privacy, only if due process in this respect is limited to what is explicitly provided in the Constitution, divorced from the rational purposes, historical roots, and subsequent developments of the relevant provisions. . . .

It would surely be an extreme instance of sacrificing substance to form were it to be held that the Constitutional principle of privacy against arbitrary official intrusion comprehends only physical invasions by the police. . . . [I]f the physical curtilage of the home is protected, it is surely as a result of solicitude to protect the privacies of the life within. Certainly the safeguarding of the home does not follow merely from the sanctity of property rights. The home derives its pre-eminence as the seat of family life. . . .

Of [the] whole "private realm of family life" it is difficult to imagine what is more private or more intimate than a husband and wife's marital relations. . . . [T]he intimacy of husband and wife is necessarily an essential and accepted feature of the institution of marriage, an institution which the State not only must allow, but which always and in every age it has fostered and protected. It is one thing when the State exerts its power either to forbid extramarital sexuality altogether, or to say who may marry, but it is quite another when, having acknowledged a marriage and the intimacies inherent in it, undertakes to regulate by means of the criminal law the details of that intimacy. . . .

Since, as it appears to me, the statute marks an abridgment of important fundamental liberties protected by the Fourteenth Amendment, it will not do to urge in justification of that abridgment simply that the statute is rationally related to the effectuation of a proper state purpose. A closer scrutiny and stronger justification than that are required. . . . To me the very circumstance that Connecticut has not chosen to press the enforcement of this statute against individual users, while it nevertheless persists in asserting its right to do so at any time — in effect a right to hold this statute as an imminent threat to the privacy of the households of the State — conduces to the inference either that it does not consider the policy of the statute a very important one, or that it does not regard the means it has chosen for its effectuation as appropriate or necessary.

But conclusive, in my view, is the utter novelty of this enactment. Although the Federal Government and many States have at one time or other had on their books statutes forbidding or regulating the distribution of contraceptives, none, so far as I can find, has made the *use* of contraceptives a crime. . . .

WHITE, J., concurring [in *Griswold*].

In my view this Connecticut law as applied to married couples deprives them of "liberty" without due process of law, as that concept is used in the Fourteenth

Amendment. I therefore concur in the judgment of the Court reversing these convictions under Connecticut's aiding and abetting statute. . . .

[T]his is not the first time this Court has had occasion to articulate that the liberty entitled to protection under the Fourteenth Amendment includes the right "to marry, establish a home and bring up children," Meyer v. Nebraska, and "the liberty . . . to direct the upbringing and education of children," Pierce v. Society of Sisters, and that these are among "the basic civil rights of man," Skinner v. Oklahoma. . . . These decisions affirm that there is a "realm of family life which the state cannot enter" without substantial justification. Prince v. Massachusetts, 321 U.S. 158 (1944). Surely the right invoked in this case, to be free of regulation of the intimacies of the marriage relationship, "come[s] to this Court with a momentum for respect lacking when appeal is made to liberties which derive merely from shifting economic arrangements." . . .

An examination of the justification offered, however, cannot be avoided by saying that the Connecticut anti-use statute invades a protected area of privacy and association or that it demeans the marriage relationship. The nature of the right invaded is pertinent, to be sure, for statutes regulating sensitive areas of liberty do, under the cases of this Court, require "strict scrutiny," Skinner v. Oklahoma, and "must be viewed in the light of less drastic means for achieving the same basic purpose." "Where there is a significant encroachment upon personal liberty, the State may prevail only upon showing a subordinating interest which is compelling." But such statutes, if reasonably necessary for the effectuation of a legitimate and substantial state interest, and not arbitrary or capricious in application, are not invalid under the Due Process Clause.

As I read the opinions of the Connecticut courts and the argument of Connecticut in this Court, the State claims but one justification for its anti-use statute. . . . [T]he statute is said to serve the State's policy against all forms of promiscuous or illicit sexual relationships, be they premarital or extramarital, concededly a permissible and legitimate legislative goal.

Without taking issue with the premise that the fear of conception operates as a deterrent to such relationships in addition to the criminal proscriptions Connecticut has against such conduct, I wholly fail to see how the ban on the use of contraceptives by married couples in any way reinforces the State's ban on illicit sexual relationships. Connecticut does not bar the importation or possession of contraceptive devices; they are not considered contraband material under state law, and their availability in that State is not seriously disputed. The only way Connecticut seeks to limit or control the availability of such devices is through its general aiding and abetting statute whose operation in this context has been quite obviously ineffective and whose most serious use has been against birth-control clinics rendering advice to married, rather than unmarried, persons. . . . Moreover, it would appear that the sale of contraceptives to prevent disease is plainly legal under Connecticut law.

In these circumstances one is rather hard pressed to explain how the ban on use by married persons in any way prevents use of such devices by persons engaging in illicit sexual relations and thereby contributes to the State's policy against such relationships. . . . At most the broad ban is of marginal utility to the declared objective. A statute limiting its prohibition on use to persons engaging in the prohibited relationship would serve the end posited by Connecticut in the same way, and with the same effectiveness, or ineffectiveness, as the broad anti-use statute under attack in this case. I find nothing in this record justifying the sweeping scope of this statute, with its telling effect on the freedoms of married persons, and therefore conclude that it deprives such persons of liberty without due process of law.

BLACK, J., joined by Stewart, J., dissenting. . . .

In order that there may be no room at all to doubt why I vote as I do, I feel constrained to add that the law is every bit as offensive to me as it is to my Brethren of the majority. . . . There is no single one of the graphic and eloquent strictures and criticisms fired at the policy of this Connecticut law either by the Court's opinion or by those of my concurring Brethren to which I cannot subscribe — except their conclusion that the evil qualities they see in the law make it unconstitutional. . . .

The Court talks about a constitutional "right of privacy" as though there is some constitutional provision or provisions forbidding any law ever to be passed which might abridge the "privacy" of individuals. But there is not. There are, of course, guarantees in certain specific constitutional provisions which are designed in part to protect privacy at certain times and places with respect to certain activities. Such, for example, is the Fourth Amendment's guarantee against "unreasonable searches and seizures." But I think it belittles that Amendment to talk about it as though it protects nothing but "privacy." . . .

One of the most effective ways of diluting or expanding a constitutionally guaranteed right is to substitute for the crucial word or words of a constitutional guarantee another word or words, more or less flexible and more or less restricted in meaning. . . . "Privacy" is a broad, abstract and ambiguous concept which can easily be shrunken in meaning but which can also, on the other hand, easily be interpreted as a constitutional ban against many things other than searches and seizures. . . . For these reasons I get nowhere in this case by talk about a constitutional "right of privacy" as an emanation from one or more constitutional provisions. I like my privacy as well as the next one, but I am nevertheless compelled to admit that government has a right to invade it unless prohibited by some specific constitutional provision. . . .

I discuss the due process and Ninth Amendment arguments together because on analysis they turn out to be the same thing — merely using different words to claim for this Court and the federal judiciary power to invalidate any legislative act which the judges find irrational, unreasonable or offensive. . . .

Of the cases on which my Brothers White and Goldberg rely so heavily, undoubtedly the reasoning of two of them supports their result here — as would that of a number of others which they do not bother to name, e.g., Lochner v. New York, Coppage v. Kansas, and Adkins v. Children's Hospital. The two they do cite and quote from, Meyer v. Nebraska and Pierce v. Society of Sisters, were both decided in opinions by Mr. Justice McReynolds which elaborated the same natural law due process philosophy found in Lochner v. New York, one of the cases on which he relied in *Meyer,* along with such other long-discredited decisions as, e.g., Adkins v. Children's Hospital. . . . Without expressing an opinion as to whether either of those cases reached a correct result in light of our later decisions applying the First Amendment to the States through the Fourteenth, I merely point out that the reasoning stated in *Meyer* and *Pierce* was the same natural law due process philosophy which many later opinions repudiated, and which I cannot accept. . . .

My Brother Goldberg has adopted the recent discovery that the Ninth Amendment as well as the Due Process Clause can be used by this Court as authority to strike down all state legislation which this Court thinks violates "fundamental principles of liberty and justice," or is contrary to the "traditions and [collective] conscience of our people." He also states, without proof satisfactory to me, that in making decisions on this basis judges will not consider "their personal and private notions." One may ask how they can avoid considering them. Our Court certainly has no machinery with which to take a Gallup Poll. And the scientific miracles of this age have not yet produced a gadget which the Court can use to determine what traditions are rooted in the "[collective] conscience of our people." Moreover, one would certainly have to look far beyond the language of the Ninth Amendment to find that the Framers vested in this Court any such awesome veto powers over lawmaking, either by the States or by the Congress. . . . That Amendment was passed not to broaden the powers of this Court or any other department of "the General Government," but, as every student of history knows, to assure the people that the Constitution in all its provisions was intended to limit the Federal Government to the powers granted expressly or by necessary implication. . . .

The Due Process Clause with an "arbitrary and capricious" or "shocking to the conscience" formula was liberally used by this Court to strike down economic legislation in the early decades of this century, threatening, many people thought, the tranquility and stability of the Nation. That formula, based on subjective considerations of "natural justice," is no less dangerous when used to enforce this Court's view about personal rights than those about economic rights. . . .

STEWART, J., joined by Black, J., dissenting.

Since 1879 Connecticut has had on its books a law which forbids the use of contraceptives by anyone. I think this is an uncommonly silly law. . . . But we are not asked in this case to say whether we think this law is unwise, or even asinine. We are asked to hold that it violates the United States Constitution. And that I cannot do. . . .

As to the First, Third, Fourth, and Fifth Amendments, I can find nothing in any of them to invalidate this Connecticut law, even assuming that all those Amendments are fully applicable against the States. It has not even been argued that this is a law "respecting an establishment of religion, or prohibiting the free exercise thereof." And surely, unless the solemn process of constitutional adjudication is to descend to the level of a play on words, there is not involved here any abridgment of "the freedom of speech, or of the press; or the right of the people peaceably to assemble, and to petition the Government for a redress of grievances." No soldier has been quartered in any house. There has been no search, and no seizure. Nobody has been compelled to be a witness against himself.

The Court also quotes the Ninth Amendment, and my Brother Goldberg's concurring opinion relies heavily upon it. But to say that the Ninth Amendment has anything to do with this case is to turn somersaults with history. . . .

What provision of the Constitution, then, does make this state law invalid? The Court says it is the right of privacy "created by several fundamental constitutional guarantees." With all deference, I can find no such general right of privacy in the Bill of Rights, in any other part of the Constitution, or in any case ever before decided by this Court.

At the oral argument in this case we were told that the Connecticut law does not "conform to current community standards." But it is not the function of this Court to decide cases on the basis of community standards. We are here to decide cases "agreeably to the Constitution and laws of the United States." . . .

Discussion

1. Why does Justice Douglas appeal to the text instead of adopting Justice Harlan's nontextualist approach? Does Justice Douglas's analysis of the passages he cites provide sufficient "penumbral" support for his opinion? Under the Fourth Amendment, for example, the State may invade an individual's privacy when it presents to a judge a very good reason ("probable cause") and receives a warrant authorizing the invasion. Would the police, in Douglas's view, be foreclosed from searching the "sacred precincts of marital bedrooms" for evidence of ordinary crimes, like bank robberies? Note also that the Fifth Amendment has been construed (over Justice Douglas's dissent) to allow the state to compel a person to testify about the most personal or intimate of matters — think only of Monica Lewinsky — so long as she is granted "immunity" from having her testimony used against her.

2. Does Justice Douglas's analysis in *Griswold* imply, by analogy, that vested property rights and liberty of contract are protected by the penumbras of the contract clause and the Fifth Amendment? That is, does *Griswold* provide an independent foundation for the decisions of the *Lochner* era?

3. Identify all of the *sources,* besides the "penumbras" of the Bill of Rights, from which the Court and concurring Justices establish the liberty interest of a married couple in choosing whether to use contraceptives. Identify all of the *methods* of decisionmaking explicitly or implicitly invoked by the Court and concurring Justices. How similar and different are these sources and methods from those you encountered in adjudication under the Equal Protection Clause? How do they compare with those of common law adjudication that you have encountered in other courses such as torts and contracts?

4. What is the nature of the interest in "privacy" protected by *Griswold?* The locational interest in one's home? The interest in freedom to choose when and to whom to disclose personal information? The interest in the integrity of the marital relationship (or of *any* intimate relationship)? The interest in autonomy, that is, in freedom from governmental control? Which of these interests are implicit in the various opinions?

5. How does Justice White's argument in *Griswold* differ from those of his concurring colleagues? How might Justice White respond if the law's stated purpose was to increase the Connecticut birth rate, an important State interest given that Connecticut's representation in Congress (and thus its ability to protect its interests at the national level) depends on the size of its population?

6. Why isn't the legislature the best institution to determine "what traditions are rooted in the '[collective] conscience of our people'"? How might Justice Harlan respond to this question? Although Justice Harlan rejects "unguided speculation" by judges, how might he recognize "guided speculation"?

7. *Popular ratification of fundamental rights jurisprudence.* Judge Robert Bork famously criticized Griswold v. Connecticut as "an unprincipled decision, both in the way in which it derives a new constitutional right and in the way it defines that right or rather fails to define it. We are left with no idea of the sweep of the right of privacy and hence no notion of the cases to which it may or may not be applied in the future."[4] Judge Bork's confirmation hearings in 1987 precipitated a national debate about fundamental rights jurisprudence. Bork, of course was a noted critic of Roe v. Wade. Bork's opponents, who recognized that Roe v. Wade was still controversial, focused instead on the fact that Bork even rejected the legitimacy of *Griswold.*[5] As Lackland Bloom explains:

---

4. Robert Bork, Neutral Principles and Some First Amendment Problems, 47 Indiana L.J. 1, 9 (1971).

There is no way to tell exactly how much Judge Bork's persistent attacks on Griswold contributed to his rejection by the Senate; however, it is fair to say that it was a significant factor. Griswold was a useful case for Judge Bork's opponents because its general right to privacy and its specific holding with respect to the use of contraceptives by married couples could be presented to the public at large in a comprehensible and appealing manner. The opposition portrayed Judge Bork as a threat to privacy; he could only defend himself by talking about confusing notions such as substantive due process, *Lochner*, neutral principles, and the Madisonian model. In retrospect, it became clear that Judge Bork may have spent too much of his career attacking the wrong case. . . . If the Bork hearings accomplished anything beyond the rejection of the Bork nomination itself, it was the enshrinement of Griswold v. Connecticut as "a fixed star in our constitutional" firmament, at least on its narrow facts.[6]

Consider the following questions.

(a) Do the Bork hearings confirm that the Court "got it right" in deciding *Griswold*, and accurately reflected the national ethos? Or, do the hearings instead suggest that the Court's fundamental rights jurisprudence played a role in shaping politics and the nation's understanding of its defining values? Are either of these appropriate roles for the Court?

(b) How is it possible for confirmation hearings to alter a decision's authority as constitutional law? Constitutional change often occurs through the president's appointment of new Justices, see generally Jack M. Balkin and Sanford Levinson, Understanding the Constitutional Revolution, 87 Va. L. Rev. 1045 (2001); Bruce Ackerman, Transformative Appointments, 101 Harv. L. Rev. 1164 (1988). Given increasing recognition of this fact by politicians, has the confirmation process become an important and exceptional moment in the making of constitutional law? Consider the extent to which the change in *Griswold*'s status is a special case of a more general dynamic in which the representative branches of government, the media, and the general public play a role in entrenching authoritative constitutional understandings.

Note: Subsequent Decisions Regarding Marriage and Contraception

Several of the *Griswold* opinions emphasize the unique importance of the marital relationship. Later cases both applied *Griswold* outside the marital setting and broadened the protection surrounding the marital relationship.

EISENSTADT v. BAIRD, 405 U.S. 438 (1972): [Appellee was convicted for distributing contraceptive foam to individuals, both married and unmarried, at a public meeting at Boston University. State law allowed "married persons [to] obtain

---

5. For a sample of the dialogue between Bork and Senate Judiciary Committee Chairman Joseph Biden on Bork's published criticisms of *Griswold*, see Nomination of Robert H. Bork to be Associate Justice of the Supreme Court of the United States, Hearings Before the Senate Committee on the Judiciary, 100th Cong. 1st Session (Part I), 86-93, 570-573 (1987).

6. Lackland H. Bloom, Twenty Fifth Anniversary of Griswold v. Connecticut and the Right to Privacy: The Legacy of Griswold, 16 Ohio N. U. L. Rev. 511, 542-543 (1989).

contraceptives to prevent pregnancy, but only from doctors or druggists on prescription; . . . single persons may not obtain contraceptives from anyone to prevent pregnancy; and . . . married or single persons may obtain contraceptives from anyone to prevent, not pregnancy, but the spread of disease." The Court, through Justice Brennan, held that the conviction violated the Equal Protection Clause's rational basis test because the statutory distinctions between married and unmarried individuals did not rationally further a legitimate state interest, whether it be the preservation of health or the prevention of premarital sex. After quoting the lower court's opinion that prohibiting access to contraceptive devices might violate an individual's fundamental rights, the Court stated:] "We need not and do not, however, decide that important question in this case because, whatever the rights of the individual to access to contraceptives may be, the rights must be the same for the unmarried and the married alike.

"If under *Griswold* the distribution of contraceptives to married persons cannot be prohibited, a ban on distribution to unmarried persons would be equally impermissible. It is true that in *Griswold* the right of privacy in question inhered in the marital relationship. Yet the marital couple is not an independent entity with a mind and heart of its own, but an association of two individuals each with a separate intellectual and emotional makeup. If the right of privacy means anything, it is the right of the *individual,* married or single, to be free from unwarranted governmental intrusion into matters so fundamentally affecting a person as the decision whether to bear or beget a child."

Chief Justice Burger dissented, arguing that "I do not challenge Griswold v. Connecticut . . . despite its tenuous moorings to the text of the Constitution, but . . . [t]he Court was there confronted with a statute flatly prohibiting the use of contraceptives, not one regulating their distribution." Justices Powell and Rehnquist did not participate in the decision.

Five years later, in Carey v. Population Services International, 431 U.S. 648 (1977), the Court struck down a New York law prohibiting the sale of contraceptives to minors under 16, together with an ancillary provision (most likely designed to assure enforcement of the age regulation) forbidding anyone other than a licensed pharmacist to sell even nonprescription contraceptives to persons of any age. With respect to the latter provision, Justice Brennan wrote for the Court that "*Griswold* may no longer be read as holding only that a State may not prohibit a married couple's use of contraceptives." Instead, "the teaching of *Griswold* is that the Constitution protects individual decisions in matters of childbearing from unjustified intrusion by the State. Restrictions on the distribution of contraceptives clearly burden the freedom to make such decisions." New York's limitation on the distribution of nonprescription contraceptives "clearly imposes a significant burden on the right of the individuals to use contraceptives if they choose to do so. . . ." Chief Justice Burger and Justice Rehnquist dissented.

Zablocki v. Redhail, 434 U.S. 374 (1978), struck down a Wisconsin statute conditioning marriage by a resident obligated to support a minor not in his custody upon a showing that support had been provided and that any covered children were not, nor were likely to become, public charges. Justice Marshall, citing various opinions in which the Court had found the right to marry to be fundamental, concluded that the Equal Protection Clause requires "critical examination of the state interests advanced" in support of a classification based on the exercise of that right. He rejected the state's asserted interest in counseling persons with child-support obligations before they incurred further obligations, noting that the statute neither required counseling nor automatically permitted marriage after counseling was completed. He also rejected Wisconsin's presentation of the law as a rational means of enforcing support obligations, noting that the state had other means for enforcing such obligations and that the statute was poorly suited to this goal. Justice Stewart, concurring in the judgment, would have invalidated the law under the Due Process rather than the Equal Protection Clause. Justice Powell, also concurring in the judgment, accepted the need for heightened scrutiny (a "fair and substantial relationship") under the Due Process and Equal Protection Clauses because the intrusion on the marriage decision was "contrary to deeply rooted traditions" and because it excluded indigents from a process in which the state exercised a monopoly.[7] Justice Rehnquist wrote a lone dissent.

III. Theories of Fundamental Rights Adjudication: A Basic Outline[8]

Griswold and its progeny inspired a large outpouring of scholarly literature regarding the assignment of substantive meaning to the Due Process Clause or, its functional equivalent, the determination that certain "fundamental interests" require strict scrutiny under the Equal Protection Clause. We consider seriatim a number of approaches to the debate.

A. Conventional Morality (or Ethos)

One view holds that the Court's task in cases such as *Griswold* is to ascertain and enforce society's conventional morality. The adjective is crucial, for this approach in no way implies the existence of trans-social norms of "natural law" or "natural justice." Philip Bobbitt has coined the term "ethical argument" to refer to

> constitutional argument whose force relies on a characterization of American institutions and the role within them of the American people. . . . [E]thical arguments are not *moral* arguments. Ethical constitutional arguments do not claim that a particular solution is right or wrong in any sense larger than that the solution comports with the sort of people we are and the means we have chosen to solve political and customary constitutional problems.[9]

On this view, even if individuals have no intrinsic natural rights, they are entitled to treatment consistent with whatever moral principles their society holds. The rationale for judicial intervention is that although legislation generally reflects

---

7. See also Boddie v. Connecticut, 401 U.S. 371 (1971), Chapter 9, infra.
8. Much of this section is based on Paul Brest, The Fundamental Rights Controversy: The Essential Contradictions of Normative Constitutional Law Scholarship, 90 Yale L.J. 1063 (1981).
9. Philip Bobbitt, Constitutional Fate 94-95 (1982).

conventional morality, the legislative process is subject to certain defects. Thus Harry Wellington writes:

> [T]he environment in which legislators function makes difficult a bias-free perspective. It is often hard for law-makers to resist pressure from their constituents who react to particular events . . . with a passion that conflicts with common morality. . . . Nor is it an easy matter for legislators to find conventional morality when there are well-organized interest groups insisting on moral positions of their own.[10]

Michael Perry agrees with Wellington and emphasizes that the relevant question for a court is "not whether the conduct is disapproved by conventional morality, but whether conventional morality supports state enforcement of its disapproval through criminal and civil sanctions." For example, "the issue is not whether conventional morality disfavors sodomy, but only whether it supports treating sodomy as an issue implicating the *public* morals, by criminalizing consensual sodomous conduct by adults in private."[11] Professor Wellington might be read to suggest that judicial review provides a "sober second look" at laws passed in the heat of legislative passion. In this context, consider Sanford Levinson's thesis concerning judicial explication of the inchoate rights protected by the Ninth Amendment.[12] Although conceding that "the judiciary [may not be the] better interpreter of 'our' political tradition than a legislature," he submits that judges might nevertheless "confront [legislators] with the implications of their decisions and . . . ask if they are really willing to accept the consequences." On this view, courts would inquire whether there is "good reason to believe that the legislator or any other primary decision-maker in fact considered the implications of the given piece of legislation for values that do indeed seem central to 'our' tradition . . . [and if so,] did the consideration happen recently enough in the past that we can recognize the legislators" as truly sharing our own social world? Levinson notes that, in striking down legislation, the Court would effectively remand it to the legislature for further, presumably more thoughtful, consideration.

How might a judge identify society's conventional morality? Wellington writes that judges must "become sensitive to it, experience widely, read extensively, and ruminate, reflect, and analyze situations that seem to call moral obligations into play."[13] Other commentators have supplemented intuitive methods for ascertaining conventional morality by drawing on the methods of the social sciences, including public opinion polls. Although the Court has not made much explicit use of these methods in fundamental rights cases, some Justices invoked social science data in addressing the question of whether the death penalty was inconsistent with contemporary standards of decency. See Furman v. Georgia, 408 U.S. 238 (1972).

One of the more recent debates on the proper methodology for discerning fundamental norms arose in Stanford v. Kentucky, 492 U.S. 397 (1989). The doctrinal issue was whether the execution of 16- and 17-year-olds violated the Eighth

---

10. Harry Wellington, Common Law Rules and Constitutional Double Standards: Some Notes on Adjudication, 83 Yale L.J. 221, 248-249 (1973).

11. Michael Perry, Substantive Due Process Revisited: Reflections on (and Beyond) Recent Cases, 71 Nw. U. L. Rev. 417, 477 (1977).

12. Sanford Levinson, Constitutional Rhetoric and the Ninth Amendment, 64 Chi.-Kent L. Rev. 131, 156-158 (1988).

13. Wellington, supra n.10, at 246.

Amendment prohibition of cruel and unusual punishment. Petitioners invoked Trop v. Dulles, 356 U.S. 86 (1958), which construed the Eighth Amendment to embody the "evolving standards of decency that mark the progress of a maturing society." Justice Scalia, writing for the Court, explained that:

> [T]his court has "not confined the prohibition embodied in the Eighth Amendment to 'barbarous' methods that were generally outlawed in the 18th century," but instead has interpreted the Amendment "in a flexible and dynamic manner." In determining what standards have "evolved," however, we have looked not to our own conceptions of decency, but to those of modern American society as a whole.[a] . . .
>
> "[F]irst" among the "objective indicia that reflect the public attitude toward a given sanction" are statutes passed by society's elected representatives. . . . It is not the burden of [a state] to establish a national consensus approving what their citizens have voted to do; rather, it is the "heavy burden" of petitioners to establish a national consensus *against* it. As far as the primary and most reliable indication of consensus is concerned — the pattern of enacted laws — petitioners have failed to carry that burden. . . .
>
> [Petitioners] argue, however, that even if the laws themselves do not establish a settled consensus, the application of the laws does. That contemporary society views capital punishment of 16- and 17-year-old offenders as inappropriate is demonstrated, they say, by the reluctance of juries to impose, and prosecutors to seek, such sentences. Petitioners are quite correct that a far smaller number of offenders under 18 than over 18 have been sentenced to death in this country. . . . These statistics, however, carry little significance. Given the undisputed fact that a far smaller percentage of capital crimes is committed by persons under 18 than over 18, the discrepancy is much less than might seem. Granted, however, that a substantial discrepancy exists, that does not establish the requisite proposition that the death sentence for offenders under 18 is categorically unacceptable to prosecutors and juries. To the contrary, it is not only possible but overwhelmingly probable that the very considerations which induce petitioners and their supporters to believe that death should *never* be imposed on offenders under 18 cause prosecutors and juries to believe that it should *rarely* be imposed. . . .
>
> Having failed to establish a consensus against capital punishment for 16- and 17-year-old offenders through state and federal statutes and the behavior of prosecutors and juries, petitioners seek to demonstrate it through other indicia, including public opinion polls, the views of interest groups and the positions adopted by various professional associations. We decline the invitation to rest constitutional law upon such uncertain foundations. A revised national consensus so broad, so clear and so enduring as to justify a permanent prohibition upon all units of democratic government must appear in the operative acts (laws and the application of laws) that the people have approved.[14]

Justice Brennan, joined by Justices Marshall, Blackmun, and Stevens, dissented. He agreed that the meaning of the Eighth Amendment "is informed . . . by an examination of contemporary attitudes toward the punishment, as evidenced in the actions of legislatures and of juries," but took issue with the Court's reading of

---

a. We emphasize that it is *American* conceptions of decency that are dispositive, rejecting the contention of petitioners and their various *amici* ([and] accepted by the dissent) that the sentencing practices of other countries are relevant. [Practices of other nations] cannot serve to establish the first Eighth Amendment prerequisite, that the practice is accepted among our people.

14. Justice O'Connor did not join in the final paragraph of the opinion.

the evidence.[15] His disagreement with Justice Scalia's analysis was more fundamental, however:

> Justice Scalia forthrightly states in his separate opinion that Eighth Amendment analysis
> is at an end once legislation and jury verdicts relating to the punishment in question are
> analyzed as indicators of contemporary values. . . . [His] approach would largely return
> the task of defining the contours of Eighth Amendment protection to political majori-
> ties. . . . The promise of the Bill of Rights goes unfulfilled when we leave "[c]onstitutional
> doctrine [to] be formulated by the acts of those institutions which the Constitution is
> supposed to limit," as is the case under Justice Scalia's positivist approach to the defini-
> tion of citizens' rights. This Court abandons its proven and proper role in our constitu-
> tional system when it hands back to the very majorities the Framers distrusted the power
> to define the precise scope of protection afforded by the Bill of Rights, rather than bring-
> ing its own judgment to bear on that question, after complete analysis.

Stanford was effectively overruled in Roper v. Simmons, 543 U.S. 551 (2005),
discussed infra, pp. 1366-1370.

B.   Rights-Based Theories

A rights-based theory of fundamental rights adjudication seeks to ground the practice in rights that enjoy at least some independence from conventional moral views.
For example, Professor Laurence Tribe of Harvard writes:

> References to history, tradition, evolving community standards, and civilized consen-
> sus can provide suggestive parallels and occasional insights, but it is illusion to suppose
> that they can yield answers, much less absolve judges of responsibility for developing
> and defending a theory of what rights are "preferred" or "fundamental." . . .
> For we are talking, necessarily, about rights of individuals or groups *against* the
> larger community, and against the majority. . . . Subject to all of the perils of antima-
> joritarian judgment, courts — and all who take seriously their constitutional oaths —
> must ultimately define and defend rights against government in terms independent of
> consensus or majority will.[16]

Another rights theorist, David A.J. Richards, poses the question: "What is the
constitutionally permissible content of the legal enforcement of morals?"[17] His
answer invokes a liberal theory of human rights traced from Milton, Locke,
Rousseau, and Kant, to Ronald Dworkin and John Rawls.

Richards asserts that underlying any concept of human rights are "two crucial
assumptions: first, that persons have the capacity to be autonomous in living their
life; second, that persons are entitled, as persons, to equal concern and respect in
exercising their capacities for living autonomously.[18]. . . Under the constitutional
order, certain human rights are elevated into legally enforceable rights, so that if a
law infringes on these moral rights, the law is not valid."[19]

---

15. Justice Brennan also argued that the views of experts in the relevant fields and of other governments "merit our attention as indicators whether a punishment is acceptable in a civilized society."

16. Laurence Tribe, American Constitutional Law 1311 (2d ed. 1988).

17. David Richards, Sexual Autonomy and the Constitutional Right to Privacy: A Case Study in
Human Rights and the Unwritten Constitution, 30 Hastings L.J. 957, 976 (1979).

18. Id. at 964.

19. Id. at 958.

This principle explains and justifies the sense in which the constitutional right to privacy is a *right*. The constitutional concept expresses an underlying moral principle resting on the enhancement of sexual autonomy, the self-determination of the role of sexuality in one's life which protects values foundational to the concept of human rights, equal concern and respect for autonomy. Accordingly, in the absence of countervailing moral argument, laws which determine how one will have sex and with what consequences are constitutionally invalid.[20]

Our "constitutional morality" incorporates these principles and, by contrast to conventional morality, is subject to the metaethical constraints of moral reasoning. It follows that

> not everything invoked by democratic majorities as justified by "public morality" is, in fact, morally justified. From the moral point of view, we must always assess such claims by whether they can be sustained by the underlying structure of moral reasoning. . . . In this regard, constitutional morality is at one with the moral point of view. The values of equal concern and respect for personal autonomy, that we have unearthed as the foundations of American constitutionalism, are the same values that recent moral theory . . . has identified as the fundamental values of the moral point of view.[21]

C. Justifications for Government Regulation

Of the various justifications for laws and regulations that arguably interfere with individual rights, two seem most prominent: the state's interests in promoting morality and the stability of the family.

In Poe v. Ullman, 367 U.S. 497 (1961), Justice Harlan, while dissenting from the Court's refusal to strike down Connecticut's anticontraception law, conceded the state's authority to protect the moral welfare of its citizenry:

> [S]ociety is not limited in its objects only to the physical well-being of the community, but has traditionally concerned itself with the moral soundness of its people as well. Indeed to attempt a line between public behavior and that which is purely consensual or solitary would be to withdraw from community concern a range of subjects with which every society in civilized times has found it necessary to deal. The laws regarding marriage, which provided both when the sexual powers may be used and the legal and societal context in which children are born and brought up, as well as laws forbidding adultery, fornication, and homosexual practices which express the negative of the proposition, confining sexuality to lawful marriage, form a pattern so deeply pressed into the substance of our social life that any constitutional doctrine in this area must build upon that basis.

Although few proponents of fundamental rights adjudication have argued that the Constitution incorporates John Stuart Mill's On Liberty (1859), most have disfavored the promotion-of-decency rationale. Richards, while conceding that there is "no constitutional objection to prohibiting clearly immoral acts that threaten the existence of society," argues that enforcing mere conventional morality "is incompatible with the moral theory

---

20. Id. at 1006.
21. Id. at 977.

of human rights implicit in the constitutional order."[22] J. Harvey Wilkinson and G. Edward White, who argue for the constitutional protection of "lifestyle" choices, assert:

> The privilege of living in a free and open society entails . . . some obligation to tolerate ideals and moral choices with which one disagrees. . . . Moreover, to uphold legal proscriptions on grounds of abstract morality would permit the state to ferret out and ultimately to try and punish offenders upon the assertion, not that the given behavior was socially harmful, but that it was revolting and unnatural. Such a rule of law would invite the majority to act upon its least noble and most prejudiced impulses.[23]

The interest in protecting the traditional family has found somewhat more favor among academic commentators. For example, Tribe writes:

> [T]he stereotypical "family unit" that is so much a part of our constitutional rhetoric is becoming decreasingly central to our constitutional reality. Such exercises of familial rights and responsibilities as remain prove to be *individual* powers to resist governmental determination of who shall be born, with whom one shall live, and what values shall be transmitted.
>
> This shift might well represent an irresistible corollary of changes in the structure of American family life and social and cultural existence. Whatever its cause, the issue it raises most sharply is the recurring puzzle of liberal individualism: Once the State, whether acting through its courts or otherwise, has "liberated" the child — and the adult — from the shackles of such intermediate groups as family, what is to defend the individual against the combined tyranny of the state and her own alienation?[24]

Wilkinson and White believe that "state interests of significant strength support a prohibition of homosexuality."[25] Of these, the most significant is protecting the family by preventing homosexuality from becoming a viable alternative to heterosexual intimacy:

> Family life has been a central unifying experience throughout American society. Preserving the strength of this basic, organic unit is a central and legitimate end of the police power. The state ought to be concerned that if allegiance to traditional family arrangements declines, society as a whole may suffer. . . .
>
> Mr. Wilkinson would uphold the state's interest in the preservation of the traditional family; Mr. White would desire stronger empirical proof that the state interest is truly put in jeopardy by homosexual practices among consenting adults. Both authors acknowledge the intuitive elements in their judgments.[26]

D.   Criticisms of Fundamental Rights Adjudication

Most of the criticisms of fundamental rights adjudication have focused on the problematic nature of the sources and methods available to the judiciary. The most comprehensive critique of the practice appears in John Ely's book, Democracy and

22. Id. at 991, 992.
23. J. Harvey Wilkinson & G. Edward White, Constitutional Protection for Personal Lifestyles, 62 Cornell L. Rev. 563, 618 (1977).
24. Laurence Tribe, American Constitutional Law 987-988 (1978).
25. Wilkinson & White, supra n.23, at 593.
26. Id. at 595-596.

Distrust: A Theory of Judicial Review (1980). Professor Ely believes that fundamental rights adjudication may be authorized by the text and history of the Constitution:

> [T]he most plausible interpretation of the Privileges or Immunities Clause is, as it must be, the one suggested by its language — that it was a delegation to future constitutional decision-makers to protect certain rights that the document neither lists, at least not exhaustively, nor even in any specific way gives directions for finding. . . . [T]he Ninth Amendment was intended to signal the existence of federal constitutional rights beyond those specifically enumerated in the Constitution. . . . [Id. at 38.]

But this is "[not] a question on which history can have the last word," for the absence of textual or historical *guidance* is crucial:

> If a principled approach to judicial enforcement of the Constitution's open-ended provisions cannot be developed, one that is not hopelessly inconsistent with our nation's commitment to representative democracy, responsible commentators must consider seriously the possibility that courts simply should stay away from them. [Id. at 41.]

1.   *The Critique of Consensus or Conventional Morality*

Professor Ely denies that American society shares a conventional morality:

> There is a growing literature that argues that in fact there is no consensus to be discovered (and to the extent that one may seem to exist, that is likely to reflect only the domination of some groups by others). . . . "[D]ispute concerning the legitimate role of race in governmental decision-making, whether for purposes of segregation or affirmative action, or the legitimacy of the state's allowing the cessation of the possibility of life, by abortion or euthanasia, . . . present differences of the greatest magnitude regarding conceptions of justice." [Id. at 63-64, quoting Sanford Levinson.]

Moreover, even if a conventional morality exists, it is "not reliably discoverable, at least not by courts":

> "The more concrete the allusions to this allegedly timeless moral agreement, the less convincing they become. Therefore, to make their case the proponents of objective value must restrict themselves to a few abstract ideals whose vagueness allows almost any interpretation." . . . [B]y viewing society's values through one's own spectacles . . . one can convince oneself that some invocable consensus supports almost any position a civilized person might want to see supported. [Id. at 64-67, quoting Roberto Unger.]

Ely makes a similar point about the indeterminacy and manipulability of tradition, which "can be invoked in support of almost any cause." He cites the competing American traditions regarding both malign and benign racial discrimination and quotes Garry Wills's pithy remark that "Running men out of town on a rail is at least as much an American tradition as declaring unalienable rights." (Id. at 60.)

2.   *The Critique of Rights Theories*

Ely's critique of rights theories begins with two historical points. He disputes the claim, made by some proponents, that fundamental rights adjudication is heir to a natural law tradition virtually unbroken since the eighteenth century, and he illustrates how natural law "has been summoned in support of all manner of causes in this country — some worthy, others nefarious — and often on both sides of the same issue." (Id. at 50.) Ely's main argument is a metaethical one, however: Natural law does not exist — at least not in a form useful for resolving constitutional disputes.

> [T]he only propositions with a prayer of passing themselves off as "natural law" are those so uselessly vague that no one will notice — something along the "No one should needlessly inflict suffering" line. "[A]ll the many attempts to build a moral and political doctrine upon the conception of a universal human nature have failed. Either the allegedly universal ends are too few and abstract to give content to the idea of the good, or they are too numerous and concrete to be truly universal. One has to choose between triviality and implausibility." . . . [O]ur society does not, rightly does not, accept the notion of a discoverable and objectively valid set of moral principles. [Id. at 51-52, quoting Roberto Unger.]

If few contemporary fundamental rights theorists invoke "natural law" in quite these terms, some have suggested that "judges seek values in . . . the writings of good contemporary moral philosophers." (Id. at 58.) Ely responds:

> Some moral philosophers think utilitarianism is the answer; others feel just as strongly it is not. Some regard enforced economic redistribution as a moral imperative; others find it morally censurable. What may be the two most renowned recent works of moral and political philosophy, John Rawls's A Theory of Justice and Robert Nozick's Anarchy, State and Utopia, reach very different conclusions. There simply does not exist a method of philosophy. [Id.]

Ely sardonically proposes a Supreme Court opinion that reads, "We like Rawls, you like Nozick. We win 6-3." (Id.)

Although he denies the existence of absolute ethical truths, Ely believes that "[w]e can reason about moral issues . . . [by proceeding] from ethical principles or conclusions it is felt the reader is likely already to accept other conclusions or principles he or she might not previously have perceived as related in the way the writer suggests." (Id. at 54.) But he disputes the claim that "moral judgments are sounder if made dispassionately, and that because of their comparative insulation judges are more likely so to make them." (Id. at 57.) Moreover, he argues that judicial reasoning results in a "systematic bias . . . in favor of the values of the upper-middle, professional class," which constitutes the "reasoning class." (Id. at 59.) "Thus, the list of values the Court and the commentators tended to enshrine as fundamental . . . [include] expression, association, education, academic freedom, the privacy of the home, personal autonomy . . . ." (Id. at 59.)

In any event, how well equipped are judges to engage in moral reasoning? Michael McConnell writes:[27]

> [J]udicial decisionmaking contains very little serious deliberation on moral issues. In the abortion decision, for example, the Court majority thought it "need not resolve" the moral-legal status of the unborn child (thereby deciding it by default), while the

27. Michael McConnell, The Role of Democratic Politics in Transforming Moral Convictions into Law, 98 Yale L.J. 1501, 1536-1538 (1989).

dissenters devoted their entire opinion to issues of standing to sue and the power of the states. Of course, standing and state power are important legal issues, but surely the overriding moral-political question was how the political community goes about determining to whom it will extend the protection of the law. . . . The Court's treatment of other prominent moral-constitutional questions . . . has not been much better. The Court's analysis is typically long on manipulation of precedent and low on intelligible principle.

Nor, I believe, has there been much more moral deliberation behind the curtains. The Justices are far too busy to spend much time thinking about the cases, and their conferences are largely perfunctory. Certainly they have no time to do the kind of outside reading they would need to become able to contribute to moral-political deliberation in a serious way. In contrast to the months, even years, that are devoted to major legislative deliberation, the Justices devote one hour to oral argument and somewhat less than that to discussion at conference. Amazingly, they do not even wait to see what the dissenting opinion has to say before joining the majority. The appearance of debate and deliberation created by the opinions is largely a sham.

Third, not only do Supreme Court opinions contain little serious moral reflection, but they serve as an excuse for dispensing with moral reflection at other levels of government. Supporters of a right to abortion do not have to engage in a serious discussion of their position in the state legislatures; . . . all they need to do is cite Roe v. Wade. . . .

Fourth, it is difficult to avoid the conclusion that a preference for judicial rule contains a large element of class bias. Judges, as well as most of the lawyers who appear before them and the academics who comment on their work, are members of the upper-middle-class. They come from a highly educated sector of society. This class typically has a particular predisposition toward moral issues. By contrast, legislators have to listen to, and accommodate, the opinions of a broader segment of society. The one clear effect of nonoriginalism is to give upper middle class opinions a disproportionate role in public decisionmaking. Some may contend that upper middle class values are objectively the best; I suspect this is the real reason why nonoriginalism is so popular among academics. But these arguments are rarely made in public.

Recall Professor Levinson's thesis that "fundamental values" adjudication is most appropriate where there is evidence of legislative thoughtlessness. Does Professor McConnell provide sufficient reason to reject even that role for the Court?

3.   The Levels-of-Abstraction Problem

Professor Tribe, a proponent of fundamental values adjudication, believes that private consensual homosexual conduct should be protected because sexual expression is central to the development of a person's identity. Commenting on Bowers v. Hardwick, infra, in which the Court denied constitutional protection for homosexual sodomy, Tribe concedes that there exist "instances where homosexuality has been disapproved in western history,"[28] but argues that

in asking whether an alleged right forms a part of a traditional liberty, it is crucial to define the liberty at a high enough level of generality to permit unconventional

28. Tribe, supra n.17, at 1427.

variants to claim protection along with mainstream versions of protected conduct. The proper question, as the dissent in *Hardwick* recognized, is not whether oral sex as such has long enjoyed a special place in the pantheon of constitutional rights, but whether private, consensual, adult sexual acts partake of traditionally revered liberties of intimate association and individual autonomy.[29]

Ely criticized this type of reasoning as the "understandable temptation to vary the relevant tradition's level of abstraction to make it come out right."[30] Similarly, Professor Robert Bork criticizes *Griswold* on the ground that the Court's choice of the level on which to define the protected liberty was necessarily arbitrary. He notes that the Court surely did not adopt the very broad principle that "government may not interfere with any acts done in private."[31] On the other hand, for the Court to define the principle very narrowly — "government may not prohibit the use of contraceptives by married couples" — presents problems of "neutral definition":

> Why does the principle extend only to married couples? Why, out of all forms of sexual behavior, only to the use of contraceptives? Why, out of all forms of behavior, only to sex? . . .
>
> To put the matter another way, if a neutral judge must demonstrate why principle *X* applies to cases *A* and *B* but not to case *C* . . . , he must, by the same token, also explain why the principle is defined as *X* rather than as *X minus*, which would cover *A* but not cases *B* and *C*, or as *X plus*, which would cover all cases, *A*, *B*, and *C*.[32]

4.   *Lochnering*[33]

For many years, Lochner v. New York symbolized the negative side of fundamental rights adjudication. Tribe argues that the Court's mistake was not the mode of adjudication as such but the particular values it chose. If *Lochner* was wrong,

> the reason can *only* be that in twentieth century America, minimum wage laws, as a substantive matter, are *not* intrusions upon human freedom in any meaningful sense, but are instead entirely reasonable and just ways of attempting to combat economic subjugation and human domination. . . . What was wrong was simply that, as a picture of freedom in industrial society, the one painted by the Justices badly distorted the character and needs of the human condition and the reality of the economic situation. . . . [But] there is no escape from the difficult task of painting a better — a morally and economically truer — picture.[34]

For John Ely, however, *Lochner* illustrates the Court's intrinsic perceptual limitations:

> It may be . . . that the "right to an abortion," or noneconomic rights in general, accord more closely with "this generation's idealization of America": than the "rights" asserted

29. Id. at 1428.
30. John Ely, Democracy and Distrust 61 (1980).
31. Robert Bork, Neutral Principles and Some First Amendment Problems, 47 Ind. L.J. 1, 7 (1971).
32. Id.
33. The term is John Ely's in The Wages of Crying Wolf: A Comment on Roe v. Wade, 82 Yale L.J. 920 (1973).
34. Tribe, supra n.17, at 585, 586 n.37.

in . . . *Lochner.* . . . But that attitude, of course, is *precisely* the point of the *Lochner* philos-ophy, which would grant unusual protection to those "rights" that somehow *seem* most pressing, regardless of whether the Constitution suggests any special solicitude for them.[35]

Note: The Use of Foreign and International Sources in Constitutional Interpretation

Recent Supreme Court decisions, including Lawrence v. Texas, discussed infra, have sparked a vigorous debate among the Justices about the propriety of looking to foreign sources for interpreting the United States Constitution. U.S. Courts have looked to international law almost from the country's founding;[36] indeed, much of the debate in the *Quirin* and *Hamdi* cases, discussed in Chapter 5, supra, concerned the interpretation of the international laws of war. Rather, the debate is about the propriety of interpreting the U.S. Constitution by looking to decisions by other constitutional courts (for example, Canada) and to transna-tional law (for example, international human rights agreements, or the deci-sions of the European Court of Human Rights, cited by Justice Kennedy in *Lawrence*). Some Constitutional Courts, particularly that of South Africa, self-consciously understand themselves to be, in the words of Justice Albie Sachs, "part of a global development of constitutionalism and human rights." State v. Mhlungu, 1995 (3) SALR 867, 917 (CC) (S.Afr.). As one member in this global community, Justice Sachs argues, South Africa should look to the decisions of courts around the world for the insight that they cast on the solution of common problems.[37]

The question becomes whether American courts should be part of this global conversation, or whether this is inconsistent with their obligations to faithfully interpret the *American* Constitution.

In Atkins v. Virginia, 536 U.S 304 (2002), the Court, in an opinion by Justice Stevens, held that executing mentally retarded criminals violated the Eight Amendment's prohibition on cruel and unusual punishments. Justice Stevens noted that a number of states had abolished the death penalty for mentally retarded persons since the Court's decision in Penry v. Lynaugh, 492 U.S. 302 (1989), which held that there was a lack of consensus on the issue: "The practice, therefore, has become truly unusual, and it is fair to say that a national consensus has developed against it." In a footnote, Justice Stevens noted that "within the world community, the imposition of the death penalty for crimes committed by mentally retarded offenders is overwhelmingly disapproved." Although such factors were "by no means dispositive, their consistency with the legislative evidence lends further support to our conclusion that there is a consensus among those who have addressed the issue."

---

35. Ely, supra n.33, at 939.
36. See Sarah Cleveland, Our International Constitution, 31 Yale J. Int'l L. 1 (2006).
37. For a discussion of the South African Constitutional Court's copious use of foreign materials, see Sujit Choudhry, Globalization in Search of Justification: Toward a Theory of Constitutional Interpretation, 74 Ind. L. J. 819 (1999).

Chief Justice Rehnquist, joined by Justices Scalia and Thomas, dissented:

> In my view . . . two sources — the work product of legislatures and sentencing jury determinations — ought to be the sole indicators by which courts ascertain the contemporary American conceptions of decency for purposes of the Eighth Amendment. They are the only objective indicia of contemporary values firmly supported by our precedents. More importantly, however, they can be reconciled with the undeniable precepts that the democratic branches of government and individual sentencing juries are, by design, better suited than courts to evaluating and giving effect to the complex societal and moral considerations that inform the selection of publicly acceptable criminal punishments. . . . I fail to see . . . how the views of other countries regarding the punishment of their citizens provide any support for the Court's ultimate determination. . . . [I]f it is evidence of a *national* consensus for which we are looking, then the viewpoints of other countries simply are not relevant.

Justice Scalia's dissent also emphasized the irrelevance of "the practices of the 'world community,' whose notions of justice are (thankfully) not always those of our people. 'We must never forget that it is a Constitution for the United States of America that we are expounding. . . . [W]here there is not first a settled consensus among our own people, the views of other nations, however enlightened the Justices of this Court may think them to be, cannot be imposed upon Americans through the Constitution.' "

ROPER v. SIMMONS, 543 U.S. 551 (2005): By a 5-4 vote, the Supreme Court held that executing persons who were under the age of 18 when their crimes were committed violated the Eighth Amendment's prohibition against cruel and unusual punishments. Justice Kennedy argued that "the objective indicia of consensus in this case — the rejection of the juvenile death penalty in the majority of States; the infrequency of its use even where it remains on the books; and the consistency in the trend toward abolition of the practice — provide sufficient evidence that today our society views juveniles, in the words *Atkins* used respecting the mentally retarded, as 'categorically less culpable than the average criminal.' "

Justice Kennedy also looked to international sources:

> [T]he United States is the only country in the world that continues to give official sanction to the juvenile death penalty. This reality does not become controlling, for the task of interpreting the Eighth Amendment remains our responsibility. Yet at least from the time of the Court's decision in *Trop* [*v. Dulles*], the Court has referred to the laws of other countries and to international authorities as instructive for its interpretation of the Eighth Amendment's prohibition of "cruel and unusual punishments." . . . Article 37 of the United Nations Convention on the Rights of the Child, which every country in the world has ratified save for the United States and Somalia, contains an express prohibition on capital punishment for crimes committed by juveniles under 18. [N]o ratifying country has entered a reservation to the provision prohibiting the execution of juvenile offenders. Parallel prohibitions are contained in other significant international covenants [including the International Covenant on Civil and Political Rights]. . . . [O]nly seven countries other than the United States have executed juvenile offenders since 1990: Iran, Pakistan, Saudi Arabia, Yemen, Nigeria, the Democratic Republic of Congo, and China. Since then each of these countries has either abolished capital punishment for juveniles or made public disavowal of the practice. In sum, it is fair to say that the United States now stands alone in a world that has turned its face against the juvenile death penalty. . . .

It is proper that we acknowledge the overwhelming weight of international opinion against the juvenile death penalty, resting in large part on the understanding that the instability and emotional imbalance of young people may often be a factor in the crime. The opinion of the world community, while not controlling our outcome, does provide respected and significant confirmation for our own conclusions. . . . It does not lessen our fidelity to the Constitution or our pride in its origins to acknowledge that the express affirmation of certain fundamental rights by other nations and peoples simply underscores the centrality of those same rights within our own heritage of freedom.

Justice O'Connor dissented, noting that "[b]ecause I do not believe that a genuine *national* consensus against the juvenile death penalty has yet developed . . . I can assign no such *confirmatory* role to the international consensus described by the Court." Nevertheless, "[t]he special character of the Eighth Amendment," Justice O'Connor argued, ". . . draws its meaning directly from the maturing values of civilized society." Hence "the existence of an international consensus of this nature can serve to confirm the reasonableness of a consonant and genuine American consensus."

Justice Scalia dissented:

That the Senate and the President — those actors our Constitution empowers to enter into treaties, see Art. II, §2 — have declined to join and ratify treaties prohibiting execution of under-18 offenders can only suggest that *our country* has either not reached a national consensus on the question, or has reached a consensus contrary to what the Court announces. [T]he United Nations Convention on the Rights of the Child prohibits punishing [minors] with life in prison without the possibility of release. If we are truly going to get in line with the international community, then the Court's reassurance that the death penalty is really not needed, since "the punishment of life imprisonment without the possibility of parole is itself a severe sanction," gives little comfort.

[T]he Court is quite willing to believe that every foreign nation — of whatever tyrannical political makeup and with however subservient or incompetent a court system — in fact *adheres* to a rule of no death penalty for offenders under 18. Nor does the Court inquire into how many of the countries that have the death penalty, but have forsworn (on paper at least) imposing that penalty on offenders under 18, have what no State of this country can constitutionally have: a *mandatory* death penalty for certain crimes, with no possibility of mitigation by the sentencing authority, for youth or any other reason. I suspect it is most of them. . . .

More fundamentally, however, the basic premise of the Court's argument — that American law should conform to the laws of the rest of the world — ought to be rejected out of hand. In fact the Court itself does not believe it. In many significant respects the laws of most other countries differ from our law — including not only such explicit provisions of our Constitution as the right to jury trial and grand jury indictment, but even many interpretations of the Constitution prescribed by this Court itself. The Court-pronounced exclusionary rule, for example, is distinctively American, [described] in Mapp v. Ohio [as] "unique to American Jurisprudence." Since then a categorical exclusionary rule has been "universally rejected" by other countries, including those with rules prohibiting illegal searches and police misconduct, despite the fact that none of these countries "appears to have any alternative form of discipline for police that is effective in preventing search violations." . . . The European Court of Human Rights has held that introduction of illegally seized evidence does not violate the "fair trial" requirement in Article 6, §1, of the European Convention on Human Rights.

The Court has been oblivious to the views of other countries when deciding how to interpret [the Establishment Clause]. Most other countries — including those committed to religious neutrality — do not insist on the degree of separation between church and state that this Court requires. [C]ountries such as the Netherlands, Germany, and Australia allow direct government funding of religious schools on the ground that "the state can only be truly neutral between secular and religious perspectives if it does not dominate the provision of so key a service as education, and makes it possible for people to exercise their right of religious expression within the context of public funding." England permits the teaching of religion in state schools. Even in France, which is considered "America's only rival in strictness of church–state separation," "[t]he practice of contracting for educational services provided by Catholic schools is very widespread."

And let us not forget the Court's abortion jurisprudence, which makes us one of only six countries that allow abortion on demand until the point of viability. Though the Government and *amici* in cases following Roe v. Wade, urged the Court to follow the international community's lead, these arguments fell on deaf ears. . . .

The Court should either profess its willingness to reconsider all these matters in light of the views of foreigners, or else it should cease putting forth foreigners' views as part of the *reasoned basis* of its decisions. To invoke alien law when it agrees with one's own thinking, and ignore it otherwise, is not reasoned decisionmaking, but sophistry.

[In a footnote, Justice Scalia added:] Justice O'Connor asserts that an international consensus can at least "serve to confirm the reasonableness of a consonant and genuine American consensus." Surely not unless it can also demonstrate the *un*reasonableness of such a consensus. Either America's principles are its own, or they follow the world; one cannot have it both ways.

[Justice Scalia concluded:] I do not believe that approval by "other nations and peoples" should buttress our commitment to American principles any more than (what should logically follow) disapproval by "other nations and peoples" should weaken that commitment. . . . Foreign sources are cited today, *not* to underscore our "fidelity" to the Constitution, our "pride in its origins," and "our own [American] heritage." To the contrary, they are cited *to set aside* [a] centuries-old American practice . . . What these foreign sources "affirm," rather than repudiate, is the Justices' own notion of how the world ought to be, and their diktat that it shall be so henceforth in America.

Discussion

1. *A decent respect to the opinions of mankind.* Why exactly should the views of other countries, and in particular, Western European democracies be relevant to the content of basic liberties in the United States? One reason might be that these countries, which also claim to be devoted to the protection of basic human liberties, give us some critical distance on Americans' belief that ours is basically a just and decent society. Another notion is that the Framers, who were children of the Enlightenment, believed that through the use of reason, civilized people everywhere could agree on the basic components of liberty. Indeed, the Declaration of Independence is premised on the idea that a "decent Respect to the Opinions of Mankind" was necessary to justify the American Revolution. (At the same time, it should be noted, one of the Declaration's complaints was that George III had "combined with others to subject us to a jurisdiction foreign to our Constitution and unacknowledged by our laws, giving his assent to their acts of pretended legislation.")

In our own era, America is part of a world community that seeks to respect and enforce international human rights; hence the opinions of other nations with similar commitments can act as a check on our inadequacies and a spur to fulfill our deepest values. On the role that international human rights law might play in shaping constitutional norms, see Harold Hongju Koh, Paying "Decent Respect" to World Opinion on the Death Penalty, 35 U.C. Davis L. Rev. 1087 (2002). For more on the use of international views in substantive due process decisions, see the discussion of Lawrence v. Texas, infra.

On the other hand, note that the argument of the dissenting Justices in *Atkins* is that the test of consensus is not what Americans should believe but what they actually do believe, and therefore the critical distance that world opinion might offer is simply irrelevant. In assessing what people's values are for purposes of constitutional interpretation, is it enough to look at their actual practices (mediated by the legislative process) or is it important to recognize that people often do not live up to their own ideals? (Consider, for example, American ideals concerning equality.) Should constitutional adjudication be concerned with such ideals if people have not demonstrated through legislation or jury verdicts that they wish to embrace them? Does a focus on ideals make it too easy for judges to see their own values as representing an emerging consensus?

2. *Are American judges really serious about foreign law?* In defense of Scalia's skepticism, Sanford Levinson writes

It is worth considering the argumentative practices of Scalia's presumptively more cosmopolitan opponents. To be sure, they cite foreign materials, especially when they are in accordance with what one suspects are pre-existing views. What seems strikingly lacking, though, is any real analysis of them or explanation . . . of why we should be impressed by them. Scalia notes, for example, that if Europe is tolerant of sodomy, this is not the case in Africa, where thirty-three of fifty-one countries prohibit it or the Middle East, where eleven out of fourteen countries are similarly intolerant. Perhaps it suffices to say that "our tradition" is European and not African or Middle-Eastern (or Asian), though, as a matter of fact, such assertions become ever more controversial as the United States becomes ever more truly "multi-cultural" in terms of the ethnic background of immigrants and new citizens. But even if one maintains a more "Eurocentric" view of what constitutes "our" heritage, then one must consider the fact that among the countries with less tolerant abortion laws than our own are the United Kingdom, Finland, Iceland, Ireland, Luxembourg, Germany, New Zealand, Portugal, Spain, and Switzerland. Scalia describes the use of foreign materials by their devotees as "selective," and he is surely correct.

[T]here are courts elsewhere — South Africa's apparently being the primary, but not unique, example — that not only cite foreign materials, but also, and far more importantly, actually discuss them and grapple with their arguments, especially when they chose to go in a different direction. Justice Kennedy, however, tells us nothing interesting about the European case that he cites [in Lawrence v. Texas]. The citation is mere ornamentation, like a trill in a cadenza. Should we want to know anything more, we must go ourselves to the library (or log onto the Internet) and track the case down. Justice Breyer is a bit better, but he, too, at the end of the day, does little more than provide some bibliographical help for someone interested in reading about European experience administering modern states or the European Union.[38]

38. Sanford Levinson, Looking Abroad When Interpreting the U.S. Constitution: Some Reflections, 39 Texas Int'l L. J. 355 (2004).

Are opinions like Justice Kennedy's in *Roper* anywhere close to Justice Sachs's imagined conversation among the world's constitutional courts? Consider that Israeli Justice Aharon Barak every year hires a law clerk whose special job is to stay on top of relevant comparative law materials and bring them to his attention as appropriate. Should federal judges engage in similar practices, including, perhaps, hiring clerks from abroad? And, more to the point, if we are really to take comparative constitutional materials seriously, should American law schools (and, perhaps, the authors of constitutional law casebooks like this one) make more of an effort to make sure that their graduates are competent in comparative law before awarding them degrees?

IV.   *The Family and Other Living Arrangements*

In Village of Belle Terre v. Boraas, 416 U.S. 1 (1974), six unrelated college students challenged a local ordinance restricting land use to one-family dwellings, with "family" defined so as to exclude more than two unrelated people living together. Writing for the Court, Justice Douglas sustained the ordinance, noting that it involved no "fundamental" or "privacy" rights and that the state could use its zoning authority to safeguard "family values." Only Justice Marshall dissented on the merits.

Moore v. City of East Cleveland, 431 U.S. 494 (1977), distinguished *Belle Terre* to invalidate an ordinance that limited occupancy of a dwelling unit to members of a single family, where "family" was defined in terms of a nuclear rather than an extended family. Appellant, who lived in her home with her son and two grandsons — her son's son and his nephew — was convicted for failing to remove the nephew as an "illegal occupant." Justice Powell, writing for a plurality including Justices Brennan, Marshall, and Blackmun, contrasted *Belle Terre's* impact on unrelated individuals with *East Cleveland's* "slicing deeply into the family itself": "[W]hen the government intrudes on choices concerning family living arrangements, this Court must examine carefully the importance of the governmental interests advanced and the extent to which they are served by the challenged regulation." Justice Powell held that the Court's earlier decisions "establish that the Constitution protects the sanctity of the family precisely because the institution of the family is deeply rooted in this Nation's history and tradition," a protection that reaches even to extended families composed of "uncles, aunts, cousins, and especially grandparents sharing a household along with parents and children." He added that "the choice of relatives in this degree of kinship to live together may not lightly be denied by the State. . . . [T]he Constitution prevents East Cleveland from standardizing its children — and its adults — by forcing all to live in certain narrowly defined family patterns." He concluded that the city's proffered interests in preventing overcrowding, minimizing traffic and parking congestion, and avoiding burdening the school system were marginally served by the ordinance, but were outweighed by the appellant's constitutional interests.

Justice Stevens concurred, viewing the ordinance as "a taking of property without due process and without just compensation," which cut "deeply into a fundamental right normally associated with the ownership of real property — that of an owner to decide who may reside on her property." Justice Stewart, joined by Justice Rehnquist, dissented:

> When the Court has found that the Fourteenth Amendment placed a substantive limitation on a State's power to regulate, it has been in those rare cases in which the personal interests at issue have been deemed "implicit in the concept of ordered liberty." The interest that the appellant may have in permanently sharing a single kitchen and a suite of contiguous rooms with some of her relatives simply does not rise to that level. To equate this interest with the fundamental decisions to marry and to bear and raise children is to extend the limited substantive contours of the Due Process Clause beyond recognition.

Justice White dissented in an opinion that questioned the validity of the notion of substantive due process and argued that judicial intervention "under the general rubric of the right to privacy" should be narrowly circumscribed. (Chief Justice Burger dissented on procedural grounds.)

MICHAEL H. v. GERALD D.
491 U.S. 110 (1989)

SCALIA, J., announced the judgment of the Court and delivered an opinion in which the Chief Justice joined, and in all but note [f] of which Justice O'Connor and Justice Kennedy joined.

[Carole D., while married to Gerald D., had an affair with Michael H. In September 1980, she gave birth to Victoria. Gerald was listed as father on the birth certificate and always treated Victoria as his daughter. However, a blood test indicated with near certainty (a 98% probability) that Michael was Victoria's father. Carole and Michael intermittently lived together, and he presented Victoria as his daughter. In turn, Victoria apparently referred to him as "Daddy." After Carole and Victoria permanently returned to Gerald, Michael's attempts to visit Victoria were rebuffed. He therefore filed a special "filiation action" in a California court to establish his paternity and his right to visitation. Victoria, represented by a guardian ad litem, cross-complained that she had a right to maintain a relationship with both "fathers." After a court-ordered psychologist recommended that Michael be allowed continued contact as long as Carole retained sole custody of Victoria, Gerald intervened and moved for summary judgment on the ground that there were no triable issues of fact as to Victoria's paternity. He invoked Cal. Evid. Code §621, which provides that "the issue of a wife cohabiting with her husband, . . . is conclusively presumed to be a child of the marriage," unless within two years of the birth, paternity has been established in another man.

The Superior Court rejected Michael and Victoria's constitutional challenges to §621, and denied their motions for continued visitation. On appeal, Michael and Victoria raised a due process challenge to the statute, but the California Court of Appeals affirmed the lower court judgment and upheld the statute.]

II.

The California statute that is the subject of this litigation is, in substance, more than a century old. . . .

III.

Michael was seeking to be declared the father of Victoria. The immediate benefit he evidently sought to obtain from that status was visitation rights. . . . But if Michael were successful in being declared the father, other rights would follow — most importantly, the right to be considered as the parent who should have custody, a status which "embrace(s) the sum of parental rights with respect to the rearing of a child." All parental rights, including visitation, were automatically denied by denying Michael status as the father. . . . The [California courts] held that California law denies visitation, against the wishes of the mother, to a putative father who has been prevented by §621 from establishing his paternity.

Michael raises two related challenges to the constitutionality of §621. First, he asserts that requirements of procedural due process prevent the State from terminating his liberty interest in his relationship with his child without affording him an opportunity to demonstrate his paternity in an evidentiary hearing. We believe this claim derives from a fundamental misconception of the nature of the California statute. While §621 is phrased in terms of a presumption, that rule of evidence is the implementation of a substantive rule of law. California declares it to be, except in limited circumstances, irrelevant for paternity purposes whether a child conceived during and born into an existing marriage was begotten by someone other than the husband and had a prior relationship with him. As the Court of Appeal phrased it: "The conclusive presumption is actually a substantive rule of law based upon a determination by the Legislature as a matter of overriding social policy, that given a certain relationship between the husband and wife, the husband is to be held responsible for the child, and that the integrity of the family unit should not be impugned."

Of course the conclusive presumption not only expresses the State's substantive policy but also furthers it, excluding inquiries into the child's paternity that would be destructive of family integrity and privacy.[a]

. . . A conclusive presumption does, of course, foreclose the person against whom it is invoked from demonstrating, in a particularized proceeding, that applying the presumption to him will in fact not further the lawful governmental policy the presumption is designed to effectuate. But the same can be said of any legal rule that establishes general classifications, whether framed in terms of a presumption or not. In this respect there is no difference between a rule which says that the marital husband shall be irrebuttably presumed to be the father, and a rule which says that the adulterous natural father shall not be recognized as the legal father. Both rules deny someone in Michael's situation a hearing on whether, in the particular circumstances of his case, California's policies would best be served by giving him parental rights. . . . We therefore reject Michael's procedural due process challenge and proceed to his substantive claim.

Michael contends as a matter of substantive due process that because he has established a parental relationship with Victoria, protection of Gerald's and Carole's marital union is an insufficient state interest to support termination of

---

a. In those circumstances in which California allows a natural father to rebut the presumption of legitimacy of a child born to a married woman, e.g., where the husband is impotent or sterile, or where the husband and wife have not been cohabiting, it is more likely that the husband already knows the child is not his, and thus less likely that the paternity hearing will disrupt an otherwise harmonious and apparently exclusive marital relationship.

that relationship. This argument is, of course, predicated on the assertion that Michael has a constitutionally protected liberty interest in his relationship with Victoria.

It is an established part of our constitutional jurisprudence that the term "liberty" in the Due Process Clause extends beyond freedom from physical restraint. Without that core textual meaning as a limitation, defining the scope of the Due Process Clause "has at times been a treacherous field for this Court," giving "reason for concern lest the only limits to . . . judicial intervention become the predilections of those who happen at the time to be Members of this Court." In an attempt to limit and guide interpretation of the Clause, we have insisted not merely that the interest denominated as a "liberty" be "fundamental" (a concept that, in isolation, is hard to objectify), but also that it be an interest traditionally protected by our society.[b] As we have put it, the Due Process Clause affords only those protections "so rooted in the traditions and conscience of our people as to be ranked as fundamental." Snyder v. Massachusetts, 291 U.S. 97 (1934) (Cardozo, J.). Our cases reflect "continual insistence upon respect for the teachings of history [and] solid recognition of the basic values that underlie our society. . . ." *Griswold.*

This insistence that the asserted liberty interest be rooted in history and tradition is evident, as elsewhere, in our cases according constitutional protection to certain parental rights. Michael reads the landmark case of Stanley v. Illinois, 405 U.S. 645 (1972), and the subsequent cases of Quilloin v. Walcott, 434 U.S. 246 (1978), Caban v. Mohammed, 441 U.S. 380 (1979), and Lehr v. Robertson, 463 U.S. 248 (1983), as establishing that a liberty interest is created by biological fatherhood plus an established parental relationship — factors that exist in the present case as well. We think that distorts the rationale of those cases. As we view them, they rest not upon such isolated factors but upon the historic respect — indeed, sanctity would not be too strong a term — traditionally accorded to the relationships that develop within the unitary family.[c] In *Stanley,* for example, we forbade the destruction of such a family when, upon the death of the mother, the state had sought to remove children from the custody of a father who had lived with and supported them and their mother for 18 years. . . .

Thus, the legal issue in the present case reduces to whether the relationship between persons in the situation of Michael and Victoria has been treated as a protected family unit under the historic practices of our society, or whether on any

---

b. We do not understand what Justice Brennan has in mind by an interest "that society traditionally has thought important . . . without protecting it." The protection need not take the form of an explicit constitutional provision or statutory guarantee, but it must at least exclude . . . a societal tradition of exacting laws denying the interest. Nor do we understand why our practice of limiting the Due Process Clause to traditionally protected interests turns the clause "into a redundancy." Its purpose is to prevent future generations from lightly casting aside traditional values — not to enable this Court to invent new ones.

c. Justice Brennan asserts that only "a pinched conception of 'the family'" would exclude Michael, Carole, and Victoria from protection. We disagree. The family unit accorded traditional respect in our society, which we have referred to as the "unitary family," is typified, of course, by the marital family, but also includes the household of unmarried parents and their children. Perhaps the concept can be expanded even beyond this, but it will bear no resemblance to traditionally respected relationships — and will thus cease to have any constitutional significance — if it is stretched so far as to include the relationship established between a married woman, her lover, and their child, during a three-month sojourn in St. Thomas, or during a subsequent 8-month period when, if he happened to be in Los Angeles, he stayed with her and the child.

other basis it has been accorded special protection. We think it impossible to find that it has. In fact, quite to the contrary, our traditions have protected the marital family (Gerald, Carole, and the child they acknowledge to be theirs) against the sort of claim Michael asserts.[d]

The presumption of legitimacy was a fundamental principle of the common law. Traditionally, that presumption could be rebutted only by proof that a husband was incapable of procreation or had had no access to his wife during the relevant period. . . . And, under the common law both in England and here, "neither husband nor wife [could] be a witness to prove access or nonaccess." The primary policy rationale underlying the common law's severe restrictions on rebuttal of the presumption appears to have been an aversion to declaring children illegitimate, thereby depriving them of rights of inheritance and succession, and likely making them wards of the state. A secondary policy concern was the interest in promoting the "peace and tranquility of States and families," a goal that is obviously impaired by facilitating suits against husband and wife asserting that their children are illegitimate. . . .

We have found nothing in the older sources, nor in the older cases, addressing specifically the power of the natural father to assert parental rights over a child born into a woman's existing marriage with another man. Since it is Michael's burden to establish that such a power (at least where the natural father has established a relationship with the child) is so deeply embedded within our traditions as to be a fundamental right, the lack of evidence alone might defeat his case. But the evidence shows that even in modern times — when . . . the rigid protection of the marital family has in other respects been relaxed — the ability of a person in Michael's position to claim paternity has not been generally acknowledged. . . .

Moreover, even if it were clear that one in Michael's position generally possesses, and has generally always possessed, standing to challenge the marital child's legitimacy, that would still not establish Michael's case. As noted earlier, what is at issue here is not entitlement to a state pronouncement that Victoria was begotten by Michael. It is no conceivable denial of constitutional right for a State to decline to declare facts unless some legal consequence hinges upon the requested declaration. What Michael asserts here is a right to have himself declared the natural father and thereby to obtain parental prerogatives.[e] What he must establish, therefore, is not that our society has traditionally allowed a natural father in his circumstances to establish paternity, but that it has traditionally accorded such a father parental rights, or at least has not traditionally denied them. Even if the law in all States had

d. Justice Brennan insists that in determining whether a liberty interest exists we must look at Michael's relationship with Victoria in isolation, without reference to the circumstance that Victoria's mother was married to someone else when the child was conceived, and that that woman and her husband wish to raise the child as their own. We cannot imagine what compels this strange procedure of looking at the act which is assertedly the subject of a liberty interest in isolation from its effect upon other people. . . . The logic of Justice Brennan's position leads to the conclusion that if Michael had begotten Victoria by rape, that fact would in no way affect his possession of a liberty interest in his relationship with her.

e. According to Justice Brennan, Michael does not claim — and in order to prevail here need not claim — a substantive right to maintain a parental relationship with Victoria, but merely the right to "a hearing on the issue" of his paternity. "Michael's challenge . . . does not depend," we are told, "on his ability ultimately to obtain visitation rights." To be sure it does not depend upon his ability ultimately to obtain those rights, but it surely depends upon his asserting a claim to those rights, which is precisely what Justice Brennan denies. We cannot grasp the concept of a "right to a hearing" on the part of a person who claims no substantive entitlement that the hearing will assertedly vindicate.

always been that the entire world could challenge the marital presumption and obtain a declaration as to who was the natural father, that would not advance Michael's claim. Thus, it is ultimately irrelevant, even for purposes of determining current social attitudes towards the alleged substantive right Michael asserts, that the present law in a number of States appears to allow the natural father — including the natural father who has not established a relationship with the child — the theoretical power to rebut the marital presumption. What counts is whether the States in fact award substantive parental rights to the natural father of a child conceived within and born into an extant marital union that wishes to embrace the child. We are not aware of a single case, old or new, that has done so. This is not the stuff of which fundamental rights qualifying as liberty interests are made.[f]

In Lehr v. Robertson, a case involving a natural father's attempt to block his child's adoption by the unwed mother's new husband, we observed that "[t]he significance of the biological connection is that it offers the natural father an opportunity that no other male possesses to develop a relationship with his offspring," and we assumed that the Constitution might require some protection of that opportunity. Where, however, the child is born into an extant marital family,

---

f. Justice Brennan criticizes our methodology in using historical traditions specifically relating to the rights of an adulterous natural father, rather than inquiring more generally "whether parenthood is an interest that historically has received our attention and protection." There seems to us no basis for the contention that this methodology is "nove[l]." For example, in Bowers v. Hardwick we noted that at the time the Fourteenth Amendment was ratified all but 5 of the 37 States had criminal sodomy laws, that all 50 of the States had such laws prior to 1961, and that 24 States and the District of Columbia continued to have them; and we concluded from that record, regarding that very specific aspect of sexual conduct, that "to claim that a right to engage in such conduct is 'deeply rooted in this Nation's history and tradition' or 'implicit in the concept of ordered liberty' is, at best, facetious." In *Roe* we spent about a fifth of our opinion negating the proposition that there was a longstanding tradition of laws proscribing abortion. We do not understand why, having rejected our focus upon the societal tradition regarding the natural father's rights vis-à-vis a child whose mother is married to another man, Justice Brennan would choose to focus instead upon "parenthood." Why should the relevant category not be even more general — perhaps "family relationships"; or "personal relationships"; or even "emotional attachments in general"?

Though the dissent has no basis for the level of generality it would select, we do: We refer to the most specific level at which a relevant tradition protecting, or denying protection to, the asserted right can be identified. If, for example, there were no societal tradition, either way, regarding the rights of the natural father of a child adulterously conceived, we would have to consult, and (if possible) reason from, the traditions regarding natural fathers in general. But there is such a more specific tradition, and it unqualifiedly denies protection to such a parent.

One would think that Justice Brennan would appreciate the value of consulting the most specific tradition available, since he acknowledges that "[e]ven if we can agree . . . that 'family' and 'parenthood' are part of the good life, it is absurd to assume that we can agree on the content of those terms and destructive to pretend that we do." Because such general traditions provide such imprecise guidance, they permit judges to dictate rather than discern the society's views. The need, if arbitrary decision-making is to be avoided, to adopt the most specific tradition as the point of reference — or at least to announce, as Justice Brennan declines to do, some other criterion for selecting among the innumerable relevant traditions that could be consulted — is well enough exemplified by the fact that in the present case Justice Brennan's opinion and Justice O'Connor's opinion, which disapprove this footnote, both appeal to tradition, but on the basis of the tradition they select reach opposite results. Although assuredly having the virtue (if it be that) of leaving judges free to decide as they think best when the unanticipated occurs, a rule of law that binds neither by text nor by any particular, identifiable tradition, is no rule of law at all.

Finally, we may note that this analysis is not inconsistent with the result in cases such as Griswold v. Connecticut or Eisenstadt v. Baird. None of those cases acknowledged a longstanding and still extant societal tradition withholding the very right pronounced to be the subject of a liberty interest and then rejected it. Justice Brennan must do so here. In this case, the existence of such a tradition, continuing to the present day, refutes any possible contention that the alleged right is "so rooted in the traditions and conscience of our people as to be ranked as fundamental," Snyder v. Massachusetts, or "implicit in the concept of ordered liberty," Palko v. Connecticut.

the natural father's unique opportunity conflicts with the similarly unique opportunity of the husband of the marriage; and it is not unconstitutional for the State to give categorical preference to the latter. . . . In accord with our traditions, a limit is also imposed by the circumstance that the mother is, at the time of the child's conception and birth, married to and cohabitating with another man, both of whom wish to raise the child as the offspring of their union.[g] It is a question of legislative policy and not constitutional law whether California will allow the presumed parenthood of a couple desiring to retain a child conceived within and born into their marriage to be rebutted.

We do not accept Justice Brennan's criticism that this result "squashes" the liberty that consists of "the freedom not to conform." It seems to us that reflects the erroneous view that there is only one side to this controversy — that one disposition can expand a "liberty" of sorts without contracting an equivalent "liberty" on the other side. Such a happy choice is rarely available. Here, to provide protection to an adulterous natural father is to deny protection to a marital father, and vice versa. If Michael has a "freedom not to conform" (whatever that means), Gerald must equivalently have a "freedom to conform." One of them will pay a price for asserting that "freedom" — Michael by being unable to act as father of the child he has adulterously begotten, or Gerald by being unable to preserve the integrity of the traditional family unit he and Victoria have established. Our disposition does not choose between these two "freedoms," but leaves that to the people of California. . . .

IV.

We have never had occasion to decide whether a child has a liberty interest, symmetrical with that of her parent, in maintaining her filial relationship. We need not do so here because, even assuming that such a right exists, Victoria's claim must fail. Victoria's due process challenge is, if anything, weaker than Michael's. Her basic claim is not that California has erred in preventing her from establishing that Michael, not Gerald, should stand as her legal father. Rather, she claims a due process right to maintain filial relationships with both Michael and Gerald. This assertion merits little discussion, for, whatever the merits of the guardian ad litem's belief that such an arrangement can be of great psychological benefit to a child, the claim that a State must recognize multiple fatherhood has no support in the history or traditions of this country. Moreover, even if we were to construe Victoria's argument as forwarding the lesser proposition that, whatever her status "vis-à-vis" Gerald, she has a liberty interest in maintaining a filial relationship with her natural father, Michael, we find that, at best, her claim is the obverse of Michael's and fails for the same reasons.

[A discussion of Victoria's equal protection claim is omitted.]

O'CONNOR, J., joined by Kennedy, J., concurring in part.

I concur in all but footnote [f] of Justice Scalia's opinion. This footnote sketches a mode of historical analysis to be used when identifying liberty interests protected by the Due Process Clause of the Fourteenth Amendment that may be somewhat inconsistent with our past decisions in this area. On occasion the Court has characterized

g. Justice Brennan chides us for thus limiting our holding to situations in which, as here, the husband and wife wish to raise her child jointly. . . . We limit our pronouncements to the relevant facts of this case because it is at least possible that our traditions lead to a different conclusion with regard to adulterous fathering of a child whom the marital parents do not wish to raise as their own.

relevant traditions protecting asserted rights at levels of generality that might not be "the most specific level" available. I would not foreclose the unanticipated by the prior imposition of a single mode of historical analysis.

STEVENS, J., concurring in the judgment. . . .

I think cases like Stanley v. Illinois and Caban v. Mohammed demonstrate that enduring "family" relationships may develop in unconventional settings. I therefore would not foreclose the possibility that a constitutionally protected relationship between a natural father and his child might exist in a case like this. Indeed, I am willing to assume for the purpose of deciding this case that Michael's relationship with Victoria is strong enough to give him a constitutional right to try to convince a trial judge that Victoria's best interest would be served by granting him visitation rights. I am satisfied, however, that the California statute, as applied in this case, gave him that opportunity. . . .

I therefore concur in the Court's judgment of affirmance.

BRENNAN, J., with whom Marshall and Blackmun, JJ., join, dissenting.

. . . [I]t is fruitful to begin by emphasizing the common ground shared by a majority of this Court. Five Members of the Court refuse to foreclose "the possibility that a natural father might ever have a constitutionally protected interest in his relationship with a child whose mother was married to and cohabiting with another man at the time of the child's conception and birth." Five Justices agree that the flaw inhering in a conclusive presumption that terminates a constitutionally protected interest without any hearing whatsoever is a procedural one. Four Members of the Court agree that Michael H. has a liberty interest in his relationship with Victoria, and one assumes for purposes of this case that he does.

In contrast, only two Members of the Court fully endorse Justice Scalia's view of the proper method of analyzing questions arising under the Due Process Clause. Nevertheless, because the plurality opinion's exclusively historical analysis portends a significant and unfortunate departure from our prior cases and from sound constitutional decisionmaking, I devote a substantial portion of my discussion to it.

I.

Once we recognized that the "liberty" protected by the Due Process Clause of the Fourteenth Amendment encompasses more than freedom from bodily restraint, today's plurality opinion emphasizes, the concept was cut loose from one natural limitation on its meaning. This innovation paved the way, so the plurality hints, for judges to substitute their own preferences for those of elected officials. Dissatisfied with this supposedly unbridled and uncertain state of affairs, the plurality casts about for another limitation on the concept of liberty.

It finds this limitation in "tradition." Apparently oblivious to the fact that this concept can be as malleable and as elusive as "liberty" itself, the plurality pretends that tradition places a discernible border around the Constitution. The pretense is seductive; it would be comforting to believe that a search for "tradition" involves nothing more idiosyncratic or complicated than poring through dusty volumes on American history. Yet, as Justice White observed in his dissent in Moore v. East Cleveland, 431 U.S. 494, 549 (1977): "What the deeply rooted traditions of the country are is arguable." Indeed, wherever I would begin to look for an interest "deeply rooted in the country's traditions," one thing is certain: I would not stop (as does the plurality) at Bracton, or Blackstone, or Kent, or even the American Law Reports in conducting my search. Because reasonable people can disagree about the content of particular traditions, and because they can disagree even about which traditions are relevant to the definition of "liberty," the plurality has not found the objective boundary that it seeks.

Even if we could agree, moreover, on the content and significance of particular traditions, we still would be forced to identify the point at which a tradition becomes firm enough to be relevant to our definition of liberty and the moment at which it becomes too obsolete to be relevant any longer. The plurality supplies no objective means by which we might make these determinations. Indeed, as soon as the plurality sees signs that the tradition upon which it bases its decision (the laws denying putative fathers like Michael standing to assert paternity) is crumbling, it shifts ground and says that the case has nothing to do with that tradition, after all. "What is at issue here," the plurality asserts after canvassing the law on paternity suits, "is not entitlement to a state pronouncement that Victoria was begotten by Michael." But that is precisely what is at issue here, and the plurality's last-minute denial of this fact dramatically illustrates the subjectivity of its own analysis.

It is ironic that an approach so utterly dependent on tradition is so indifferent to our precedents. Citing barely a handful of this Court's numerous decisions defining the scope of the liberty protected by the Due Process Clause to support its reliance on tradition, the plurality acts as though English legal treatises and the American Law Reports always have provided the sole source for our constitutional principles. They have not. Just as common-law notions no longer define the "property" that the Constitution protects, see Goldberg v. Kelly, 397 U.S. 254 (1970), neither do they circumscribe the "liberty" that it guarantees. . . .

It is not that tradition has been irrelevant to our prior decisions. Throughout our decisionmaking in this important area runs the theme that certain interests and practices — freedom from physical restraint, marriage, childbearing, child-rearing, and others — form the core of our definition of "liberty." Our solicitude for these interests is partly the result of the fact that the Due Process Clause would seem an empty promise if it did not protect them, and partly the result of the historical and traditional importance of these interests in our society. In deciding cases arising under the Due Process Clause, therefore, we have considered whether the concrete limitation under consideration impermissibly impinges upon one of these more generalized interests.

Today's plurality, however, does not ask whether parenthood is an interest that historically has received our attention and protection; the answer to that question is too clear for dispute. Instead, the plurality asks whether the specific variety of parenthood under consideration — a natural father's relationship with a child whose mother is married to another man — has enjoyed such protection.

If we had looked to tradition with such specificity in past cases, many a decision would have reached a different result. Surely the use of contraceptives by unmarried couples, Eisenstadt v. Baird, or even by married couples, Griswold v. Connecticut; the freedom from corporal punishment in schools, Ingraham v. Wright, 430 U.S. 651 (1977); the freedom from an arbitrary transfer from a prison to a psychiatric institution, Vitek v. Jones, 445 U.S. 480 (1980); and even the right to raise one's natural but illegitimate children, Stanley v. Illinois, were not "interest[s] traditionally protected by our society," at the time of their consideration by this Court. If we had asked, therefore, in *Eisenstadt, Griswold, Ingraham, Vitek,* or *Stanley* itself whether the specific interest under consideration had been traditionally protected, the answer would have been a resounding "no." That we did not ask this question in those cases highlights the novelty of the interpretive method that the plurality opinion employs today.

The plurality's interpretive method is more than novel; it is misguided. It ignores the good reasons for limiting the role of "tradition" in interpreting the Constitution's deliberately capacious language. In the plurality's constitutional universe, we may not take notice of the fact that the original reasons for the conclusive presumption of paternity are out of place in a world in which blood tests can prove virtually beyond a shadow of a doubt who sired a particular child and in which the fact of illegitimacy no longer plays the burdensome and stigmatizing role it once did. Nor, in the plurality's world, may we deny "tradition" its full scope by pointing out that the rationale for the conventional rule has changed over the years; . . . instead, our task is simply to identify a rule denying the asserted interest and not to ask whether the basis for that rule — which is the true reflection of the values undergirding it — has changed too often or too recently to call the rule embodying that rationale a "tradition." Moreover, by describing the decisive question as whether Michael and Victoria's interest is one that has been "traditionally *protected by* our society," rather than one that society traditionally has thought important (with or without protecting it), and by suggesting that our sole function is to "*discern* the society's views," the plurality acts as if the only purpose of the Due Process Clause is to confirm the importance of interests already protected by a majority of the States. Transforming the protection afforded by the Due Process Clause into a redundancy mocks those who, with care and purpose, wrote the Fourteenth Amendment.

In construing the Fourteenth Amendment to offer shelter only to those interests specifically protected by historical practice, moreover, the plurality ignores the kind of society in which our Constitution exists. We are not an assimilative, homogeneous society, but a facilitative, pluralistic one, in which we must be willing to abide someone else's unfamiliar or even repellant practice because the same tolerant impulse protects our own idiosyncrasies. Even if we can agree, therefore, that "family" and "parenthood" are part of the good life, it is absurd to assume that we can agree on the content of those terms and destructive to pretend that we do. In a community such as ours, "liberty" must include the freedom not to conform. The plurality today squashes this freedom by requiring specific approval from history before protecting anything in the name of liberty.

The document that the plurality construes today is unfamiliar to me. It is not the living charter that I have taken to be our Constitution; it is instead a stagnant, archaic, hidebound document steeped in the prejudices and superstitions of a time long past. This Constitution does not recognize that times change, does not see that sometimes a practice or rule outlives its foundations. I cannot accept an interpretive method that does such violence to the charter that I am bound by oath to uphold.

II.

The plurality's reworking of our interpretive approach is all the more troubling because it is unnecessary. This is not a case in which we face a "new" kind of interest, one that requires us to consider for the first time whether the Constitution protects it. On the contrary, we confront an interest — that of a parent and child in their relationship with each other — that was among the first that this Court acknowledged in its cases defining the "liberty" protected by the Constitution, and I think I am safe in saying that no one doubts the wisdom or validity of those decisions. Where the interest under consideration is a parent-child relationship, we need not ask, over and over again, whether that interest is one that society traditionally protects.

Thus, to describe the issue in this case as whether the relationship existing between Michael and Victoria "has been treated as a protected family unit under the historic practices of our society, or whether on any other basis it has been accorded special protection," is to reinvent the wheel. The better approach — indeed, the one commanded by our prior cases and by common sense — is to ask whether the specific parent-child relationship under consideration is close enough to the interests that we already have protected to be deemed an aspect of "liberty" as well. . . .

On four prior occasions, we have considered whether unwed fathers have a constitutionally protected interest in their relationships with their children. See Stanley v. Illinois; Quilloin v. Walcott; Caban v. Mohammed; and Lehr v. Robertson. Though different in factual and legal circumstances, these cases have produced a unifying theme: although an unwed father's biological link to his child does not, in and of itself, guarantee him a constitutional stake in his relationship with that child, such a link combined with a substantial parent-child relationship will do so. . . .[a]

The evidence is undisputed that Michael, Victoria, and Carole did live together as a family; that is, they shared the same household, Victoria called Michael "Daddy," Michael contributed to Victoria's support, and he is eager to continue his relationship with her. Yet they are not, in the plurality's view, a "unitary family," whereas Gerald, Carole, and Victoria do compose such a family. The only difference between these two sets of relationships, however, is the fact of marriage. . . . However, the very premise of *Stanley* and the cases following it is that marriage is not decisive in answering the question whether the Constitution protects the parental relationship under consideration. . . .

[The plurality's] pinched conception of "the family," crucial as it is in rejecting Michael and Victoria's claim of a liberty interest, is jarring in light of our many cases preventing the States from denying important interests or statuses to those whose situations do not fit the government's narrow view of the family. From Loving v. Virginia to . . . Moore v. East Cleveland, we have declined to respect a State's notion, as manifested in its allocation of privileges and burdens, of what the family should be. . . .

The plurality's focus on the "unitary family" is misdirected for another reason. It conflates the question whether a liberty interest exists with the question what procedures may be used to terminate or curtail it. It is no coincidence that we never before have looked at the relationship that the unwed father seeks to disrupt, rather than the one he seeks to preserve, in determining whether he has a liberty interest in his relationship with his child. To do otherwise is to allow the State's interest in terminating the relationship to play a role in defining the "liberty" that

---

a. The plurality's claim that "the logic of (my) position leads to the conclusion that if Michael had begotten Victoria by rape, that fact would in no way affect his possession of a liberty interest in his relationship with her," ignores my observation that a mere biological connection is insufficient to establish a liberty interest on the part of an unwed father.

is protected by the Constitution. According to our established framework under the Due Process Clause, however, we first ask whether the person claiming constitutional protection has an interest that the Constitution recognizes; if we find that she does, we next consider the State's interest in limiting the extent of the procedures that will attend the deprivation of that interest. By stressing the need to preserve the "unitary family" and by focusing not just on the relationship between Michael and Victoria but on their "situation" as well, today's plurality opinion takes both of these steps at once.

The plurality's premature consideration of California's interests is evident from its careful limitation of its holding to those cases in which "the mother is, at the time of the child's conception and birth, married to and cohabiting with another man, *both of whom wish to raise the child as the offspring of their union*." (emphasis added). . . . The highlighted language suggests that if Carole or Gerald alone wished to raise Victoria, or if both were dead and the State wished to raise her, Michael and Victoria might be found to have a liberty interest in their relationship with each other.

But that would be to say that whether Michael and Victoria have a liberty interest varies with the State's interest in recognizing that interest, for it is the State's interest in protecting the marital family — and not Michael and Victoria's interest in their relationship with each other — that varies with the status of Carole and Gerald's relationship. It is a bad day for due process when the State's interest in terminating a parent-child relationship is reason to conclude that that relationship is not part of the "liberty" protected by the Fourteenth Amendment.

The plurality has wedged itself between a rock and a hard place. If it limits its holding to those situations in which a wife and husband wish to raise the child together, then it necessarily takes the State's interest into account in defining "liberty"; yet if it extends that approach to circumstances in which the marital union already has been dissolved, then it may no longer rely on the State's asserted interest in protecting the "unitary family" in denying that Michael and Victoria have been deprived of liberty. . . .

III.

Because the plurality decides that Michael and Victoria have no liberty interest in their relationship with each other, it need consider neither the effect of §621 on their relationship nor the State's interest in bringing about that effect. It is obvious, however, that the effect of §621 is to terminate the relationship between Michael and Victoria before affording any hearing whatsoever on the issue whether Michael is Victoria's father. This refusal to hold a hearing is properly analyzed under our procedural due process cases, which instruct us to consider the State's interest in curtailing the procedures accompanying the termination of a constitutionally protected interest. [Justice Brennan's discussion of this point is omitted.] . . .

IV.

The atmosphere surrounding today's decision is one of make-believe. Beginning with the suggestion that the situation confronting us here does not repeat itself every day in every corner of the country, moving on to the claim that it is tradition alone that supplies the details of the liberty that the Constitution protects, and passing finally to the notion that the Court always has recognized a cramped vision of "the family," today's decision lets stand California's pronouncement that Michael — world very different from the one it expects.

WHITE, J., with whom Brennan, J., joins, dissenting. . . .

[T]he fact that Michael H. is the biological father of Victoria is to me highly relevant to whether he has rights, as a father or otherwise, with respect to the child. Because I believe that Michael H. has a liberty interest that cannot be denied without due process of the law, I must dissent.

I.

Like Justices Brennan, Marshall, Blackmun, and Stevens, I do not agree with the plurality opinion's conclusion that a natural father can never "have a constitutionally protected interest in his relationship with a child whose mother was married to and cohabiting with another man at the time of the child's conception and birth." . . . The basic principle enunciated in the Court's unwed father cases is that an unwed father who has demonstrated a sufficient commitment to his paternity by way of personal, financial, or custodial responsibilities has a protected liberty interest in a relationship with his child. . . .

In the case now before us, Michael H. is not a father unwilling to assume his responsibilities as a parent. To the contrary, he is a father who has asserted his interests in raising and providing for his child since the very time of the child's birth. . . . The facts in this case satisfy the *Lehr* criteria, which focused on the relationship between father and child, not on the relationship between father and mother. Under *Lehr* a "mere biological relationship" is not enough, but in light of Carole's vicissitudes, what more could Michael H. have done? It is clear enough that Michael H. more than meets the mark in establishing the constitutionally protected liberty interest. . . .

II.

[Justice White's discussion of the process due Michael H. at the hearing is omitted.] As the Court has said: "The significance of the biological connection is that it offers the natural father an opportunity that no other male possesses to develop a relationship with his offspring. If he grasps that opportunity and accepts some measure of responsibility for the child's future, he may enjoy the blessings of the parent-child relationship and make uniquely valuable contributions to the child's development." It is as if this passage was addressed to Michael H. Yet the plurality today recants. Michael H. eagerly grasped the opportunity to have a relationship with his daughter (he lived with her; he declared her to be his child; he provided financial support for her) and still, with today's opinion, his opportunity has vanished. He has been rendered a stranger to his child. . . .

J.M. BALKIN, TRADITION, BETRAYAL, AND THE POLITICS OF DECONSTRUCTION
11 Cardozo L. Rev. 1623 (1990)

Justice Scalia's test of the most specific tradition . . . assumes that constitutionally protected liberties match or do not match existing traditions in an unproblematic way. For each asserted right there either is or is not a specific tradition associated with its protection. Yet there are many different ways of describing a liberty, and many different ways of characterizing a tradition. For example, we might point out that under his test, there has been no established tradition in California for protecting Justice Scalia's own rights to visit his children, since there is no tradition of affording protection to fathers who are children of Italian immigrants and who graduated from Ivy League law schools before 1965, were appointed to the United States Supreme Court by former governors of the state of California, and have more than two children but less than thirteen. Indeed, the question has hardly ever come up. . . .

To be sure, Justice Scalia has a plausible response. When Justice Scalia claims parental rights to his children, the liberty he claims is the parental right of fathers with respect to biological children born while the father was married to the child's mother. This has been traditionally protected. The rights of adulterous fathers, however, have not been traditionally protected.

But this answer reveals that Justice Scalia's theory is not simply a preference for narrower traditions over broader traditions. It rests upon an important metaphysical set of assumptions — that traditions or (more importantly) the absences of traditions, come in discrete units with discrete boundaries. To describe a tradition accurately is to respect the preexisting boundaries of the tradition. Similarly, to describe a liberty traditionally protected is to describe its actual contours. Thus, one cannot simply divide up traditions or liberties any way one wants. Like glass bottles, traditions and liberties come in premade sizes. One cannot cut them to fit, or else one will break the glass. Thus, there is a tradition of protecting marital privacy but not a tradition of protecting the marital privacy of a narrower class — for example, middle class persons, and certainly not a tradition of protecting the privacy of a broader class of persons that would include unmarried couples. Yet, under this logic, it is also historically clear that there is a tradition of protecting the marital right of privacy, but not a historical tradition of protecting married couples' right to purchase contraceptives. Griswold v. Connecticut is thus a potential embarrassment for Justice Scalia.

Moreover, Justice Scalia's vision of tradition assumes that traditions are not only discrete, but presumptively normatively correct. What is traditional is worthy of constitutional protection, and what is not traditional is not, whether it be marital privacy, the rights of married fathers to visit their children, sexual harassment in the workplace or racial segregation. This, too, is a potential source of embarrassment. . . . [I]f sexual harassment directed toward women in the workplace and respect for marital privacy are both traditions, but only one is worth protecting, how do we tell the difference? If back alley abortions are a tradition in response to the "traditional" prohibition on abortion in America, does this make abortion (in or out of a back alley) a tradition worth protecting and sustaining? In short, what normative status should be assigned to a set of values given the fact that many people have held these values at one point or another in our nation's history?

In his dissent in Poe v. Ullman, [Justice Harlan] spoke of the need for "regard to what history teaches are the traditions from which [this country] developed as well as the traditions from which it broke." [He] thus recognized, in a way that Justice Scalia appears not to, that the existence of a tradition may be a reason for rejecting it as controlling. Just as Learned Hand rejected the defense of custom in tort law on the ground that "a whole calling may have unduly lagged," so too the existing customs of the American people may not be appropriate for constitutional perpetuation. This is especially true, one might think, when they are impositions of values by a majority on a political, cultural, ethnic, religious, or ideological minority.

In fact, what is most troubling about Justice Scalia's call for respecting the most specific tradition available is that our most specific historical traditions may often be opposed to our more general commitments to liberty or equality. Curiously, then, different parts of the American tradition may conflict with each other. And indeed, this is one of the untidy facts of historical experience. The fourteenth amendment's abstract commitment to racial equality was accompanied by simultaneous acceptance of segregated public schools in the District of Columbia and acquiescence in antimiscegenation laws. The establishment clause and the principle of separation of church and state have coexisted with presidential proclamations of national days of prayer, official congressional chaplains, and national Christmas trees. Traditions do not exist as integrated wholes. They are a motley collection of principles and counterprinciples, standing for one thing when viewed narrowly and standing for another when viewed more generally. Tradition never speaks with one voice, although, to be sure, persons of particular predilections may hear only one. . . .

Nevertheless, a more realistic approach to tradition, along the lines of Justice Harlan, is cold comfort to Justice Scalia. It undermines the very reasons he has attempted to hew to tradition — [to avoid judges' engaging in] value-laden inquir[ies]. . . . To follow tradition because it reflects the values of the many is insufficient — one must also believe that these values are justified, or not so unjustified that they must be contradicted. Inquiry into tradition leads us back, in other words, to the basic problem of constitutionalism.

Discussion

1. *Tradition and betrayal.* Balkin points out that the word "tradition" comes from the same root as the word "betrayal." The original word (*traditio*) meant to deliver or hand over.

> To respect tradition is also to betray in at least three senses. First, it is to forsake other alternatives for the future . . . to hinder and eliminate them in the name of social solidarity, propriety, order, or other goals. Tradition is always extradition. Second, to respect tradition is also to betray other existing and competing traditions, to submerge and extinguish them . . . just as in *Michael H.* Justice Scalia tried to write 1950s white middle class theories of the family into the Constitution — thus establishing the hegemony of Ozzie and Harriet, if you will. There are, of course, other traditions of family life in this country. There are traditions of extended families, of spousal separations, of common law marriage and unmarried cohabitation — but apparently they don't count, since we didn't see them on "I Love Lucy." Third, a tradition is often, in an uncanny way, a betrayal of itself. For Scalia's vision of the unitary family, as exemplified by television situation comedies of the 1950s, portrays a theory of the family that was hypocritical even in its own time since even what white middle class families in the 1950s said one should do and not do sexually was not in fact what they always did, as we all found out later on. To establish and enshrine a tradition is thus at the same time to establish a countertradition — a seamy underside consisting of what society also does and perhaps cannot help but do, but will not admit to doing. The overt, respectable tradition depends upon the forgetting of its submerged, less respectable

opposite, even as it thrives and depends on its existence in unexpected ways. For example, in the television and movies of the 1950s, one sees Rock Hudson and other homosexual or bisexual males playing the parts of monogamous heterosexual males, and implicitly endorsing a heterosexual lifestyle. These roles served to support and define the very tradition of sexual practices of which Justice Scalia speaks. They furthered and reinforced a tradition of values that the persons playing these roles owed no fealty to — a tradition that . . . required of each of them a particular form of self-betrayal.

What follows from Balkin's analysis? Consider the following alternatives:

   a. Appeals to tradition are not a check on majoritarianism, they are actually another form of majoritarianism and therefore deserve no special constitutional protection. In fact the language of tradition is just another way of legitimating disregard for unpopular practices or minority subcultures. This is particularly true if the tradition is articulated at a low level of generality. Is this an argument against appeals to tradition or an argument about the proper level of generality?
   b. Appeals to tradition do not restrain judges from inserting their own values and preferences into the law. Different judges will see different things in the same tradition, or different traditions in the same history, and, in particular, they will tend to see their own values enshrined there. Moreover, because not all traditional practices are equally worthy of preservation, they will have different views about which practices are to be preserved and which are to be abandoned and broken away from. In what way do these features of constitutional arguments from tradition differ from other forms of constitutional argument?[39]
   c. Appeals to tradition are not a value-free form of discourse or a method that discovers preexisting values in the Constitution. Rather, appeals to tradition are a way of arguing about conflicting values; they can be useful, but not if they become determinative tests. Simply toting up historical examples misses the unstable and internally conflicted nature of tradition. Is this an argument against the use of tradition or an argument against rigid and univocal assessments of tradition? Is that sort of rigidity and demand for clarity inevitable for lawyers, who want a rule that governs the case?
   d. Appeals to tradition are actually appeals to contrasting narratives about the growth and development of the country and the meaning of its deepest commitments. Because one can always tell multiple stories about our nation's history, tradition can have no stable use in constitutional discourse. Is this true? Don't constitutional arguments continuously appeal to narratives (recall Marshall's story of American growth in *McCulloch*, or Ginsburg's narrative in the VMI case). Are some narratives about the country simply more plausible than others? Plausible to whom?

---

39. On the need for judges to define which traditions one has broken from, consider Rogers M. Smith, Civil Ideals: Conflicting Visions of Citizenship in U.S. History (1997), which documents the presence within American history of three distinctive and often conflicting traditions of American thought. In particular, Smith argues that there is a long-standing nativist tradition in American thought that has been used to justify anti-black and anti-immigrant views, as well as the subordination of women.

2. *The nature of the right at stake in Michael H.* Do you agree with Justice Scalia that the fundamental right in question is that of an "[adulterous] natural father to assert parental rights over a child born into a woman's existing marriage with another man"? Or is it the right of "a parent to be heard before being deprived of any contact with his or her child" by the other parent? Is there a "neutral" or "principled" method of describing the right in question or determining the proper level of generality in construing previously recognized fundamental rights? If you agree with Justice Scalia's approach, what claim might someone like Michael H. have brought that deserved protection as a fundamental right? If you agree with Justice Brennan's approach, what sort of facts would lead you to reject a claim based on fundamental rights? For example, would you grant a hearing to a rapist father? Does Justice Brennan adequately answer Justice Scalia's charge that the rapist *would* be able to assert a "fundamental right" if Brennan's analysis were accepted?

3. *Troxel v. Granville.* The Court addressed parental rights once again in Troxel v. Granville, 530 U.S. 57 (2000). Paternal grandparents sued the mother for visitation rights under a Washington statute that allowed "[a]ny person [to] petition the court for visitation rights at any time including, but not limited to, custody proceedings" based on "the best interest of the child." The trial court ordered visitation rights greater than the mother was willing to permit. Justice O'Connor, writing for a plurality that included Chief Justice Rehnquist, Justice Ginsburg, and Justice Breyer, held that, as applied to the facts of the case, the Washington statute violated the mother's "fundamental constitutional right to make decisions concerning the rearing of her own daughters" because "a parent's decision that visitation would not be in the child's best interest is accorded no deference. . . . Instead, the Washington statute places the best-interest determination solely in the hands of the judge." Justice Souter concurred in the judgment on the grounds that the statute was unconstitutional on its face. Justice Kennedy, dissenting, disagreed with the claim that "the application of the best interests of the child standard is always unconstitutional in third-party visitation cases" and would have remanded for further proceedings. Justice Stevens, dissenting, argued that "the Due Process Clause of the Fourteenth Amendment leaves room for States to consider the impact on a child of possibly arbitrary parental decisions that neither serve nor are motivated by the best interests of the child." Justice Scalia, dissenting, argued that *Meyer, Pierce,* and Wisconsin v. Yoder, 406 U.S. 205 (1972), were wrongly decided. "While I would not now over-rule those earlier cases (that has not been urged), neither would I extend the theory upon which they rested to this new context." Justice Thomas, concurring in the judgment, stated that the case was controlled by *Pierce,* but noted "that neither party has argued that our substantive due process cases were wrongly decided and that the original understanding of the Due Process Clause precludes judicial enforcement of unenumerated rights under that constitutional provision."

Note that none of the Justices argued that the grandparents in this case — the Troxels — had *Meyer* and *Pierce* rights to have a say over the raising of their grandchildren. Why not? (Compare Moore v. City of East Cleveland.) What should be constitutionally necessary for a person to have such rights? Is it possible for more than one set of persons to have *Meyer* and *Pierce* rights? If so, how should the courts arbitrate between them?

V.   The Abortion Dilemma

A.   The Decision in Roe v. Wade

Throughout this book, we have noted the complex interaction between Supreme Court decisions and social and political change. The controversy over Roe v. Wade provides yet another example. Before *Roe* was decided, access to abortion in the United States was largely bifurcated. As the historian David J. Garrow remarks, "abortion was very widely available in many places all across the United States if you were a woman who had both good medical contacts and sufficient money. If you lacked either those contacts or the money, then abortion was either not available or available only under exceptionally unsafe circumstances." David J. Garrow, Abortion Before and After Roe v. Wade: An Historical Perspective, 62 Alb. L. Rev. 833, 834, 836-837 (1999). See also Mark A. Graber, Rethinking Abortion: Equal Choice, the Constitution, and Reproductive Politics 70 (1996).

Several different streams of social movement politics pushed for abortion rights over the course of 30 years or more.[40] The medical profession sought freedom to practice medicine and help their patients without arbitrary interference from what they regarded as religiously motivated legislatures. They sought abortion reform statutes that would leave the decision whether to abort in the hands of doctors. Public health advocates viewed abortion laws as a public health crisis. They denounced the class and race discrimination in existing abortion practices; they argued that poor women and minorities should have the same access to safe methods of abortion as the rich and well connected already did.[41] Finally, by the late 1960s, growing numbers of women had begun to join the ranks of the second wave feminist movement; and the majority of these women mobilized to claim abortion as a basic right for women and to press for the repeal of existing abortion laws.

Initially, the pro-choice movement attempted to liberalize state statutes one by one, and also pushed for the passage of model statutes in the tradition of the American Law Institute.[42] The decision in *Griswold* changed matters considerably; although legislative reform efforts continued apace after 1965, the Court's decision spurred the imagination of lawyers around the country, who brought case after case attempting to extend the decision in *Griswold* to the question of abortion. *Griswold* allowed pro-choice activists to pursue a much more powerful litigation strategy than they had previously been able to adopt. Instead of pushing for reforms one by one, they could effectively change the country's abortion laws with a single decision. Because of the sheer number of challenges in the federal courts, Garrow argues, there is no doubt that, eventually, the Court would have to hear a case like *Roe*.

---

40. The following discussion is drawn from Jack M. Balkin, Roe v. Wade: An Engine of Controversy, in What Roe v. Wade Should Have Said: America's Top Legal Experts Rewrite America's Most Controversial Decision (Jack M. Balkin ed. 2005).

41. See Mark Graber, Rethinking Abortion: Equal Choice, the Constitution, and Reproductive Politics 41-64 (1996).

42. See David J. Garrow, Liberty and Sexuality: The Right to Privacy and the Making of Roe v. Wade (1994).

ROE v. WADE
410 U.S. 113 (1973)

[An unmarried pregnant woman and others brought a class action challenging the constitutionality of the Texas criminal abortion laws, which prohibited procuring or attempting an abortion except for the purpose of saving the mother's life. A three-judge district court granted declaratory relief, holding that the statutes infringed plaintiff's rights protected by the Ninth Amendment.]

BLACKMUN, J.

This Texas federal appeal and its Georgia companion, Doe v. Bolton, present constitutional challenges to state criminal abortion legislation. The Texas statutes under attack here are typical of those that have been in effect in many States for approximately a century. The Georgia statutes, in contrast, have a modern cast and are a legislative product that, to an extent at least, obviously reflects the influences of recent attitudinal change, of advancing medical knowledge and techniques, and of new thinking about an old issue.

We forthwith acknowledge our awareness of the sensitive and emotional nature of the abortion controversy, of the vigorous opposing views, even among physicians, and of the deep and seemingly absolute convictions that the subject inspires. One's philosophy, one's experiences, one's exposure to the raw edges of human existence, one's religious training, one's attitudes toward life and family and their values, and the moral standards one establishes and seeks to observe, are all likely to influence and to color one's thinking and conclusions about abortion. In addition, population growth, pollution, poverty, and racial overtones tend to complicate and not to simplify the problem.

Our task, of course, is to resolve the issue by constitutional measurement, free of emotion and of predilection. We seek earnestly to do this, and, because we do, we have inquired into, and in this opinion place some emphasis upon, medical and medical-legal history and what that history reveals about man's attitudes toward the abortion procedure over the centuries. We bear in mind, too, Mr. Justice Holmes' admonition in his now-vindicated dissent in Lochner v. New York: "[The Constitution] is made for people of fundamentally differing views, and the accident of our finding certain opinions natural and familiar or novel and even shocking ought not to conclude our judgment upon the question whether statutes embodying them conflict with the Constitution of the United States."

I.

The Texas statutes that concern us here . . . make it a crime to "procure an abortion," . . . or to attempt one, except with respect to "an abortion procured or attempted by medical advice for the purpose of saving the life of the mother." Similar statutes are in existence in a majority of the States. . . .

V.

The principal thrust of appellant's attack on the Texas statutes is that they improperly invade a right, said to be possessed by the pregnant woman, to choose to terminate her pregnancy. Appellant would discover this right in the concept of personal "liberty" embodied in the Fourteenth Amendment's Due Process Clause; or in personal, marital, familial, and sexual privacy said to be protected by the Bill of Rights or its penumbras, see Griswold v. Connecticut, or among those rights reserved to the people by the Ninth Amendment, Griswold v. Connecticut (Goldberg, J., concurring). Before addressing this claim, we feel it desirable briefly to survey, in several aspects, the history of abortion, for such insight as that history may afford us, and then to examine the state purposes and interests behind the criminal abortion laws.

VI.

[Justice Blackmun divides his 18-page survey of abortion laws and practices into eight categories: (1) ancient attitudes, (2) the Hippocratic oath, (3) the common law, (4) the English statutory law, (5) the American law, (6) the position of the American Medical Association, (7) the position of the American Public Health Association, and (8) the position of the American Bar Association.

The Hippocratic oath, which, among other things, prohibited giving "to a woman an abortive remedy," was not widely accepted in ancient Greece and Rome, where abortions were common, but with the emergence of Christianity "[t]he Oath 'became the nucleus of all medical ethics.'. . ." "It is undisputed that at the common law, abortion performed *before* 'quickening' — the first recognizable movement of the fetus in utero, appearing usually from the 16th to the 18th week of pregnancy — was not an indictable offense." Coke and Blackstone wrote that abortion after quickening was a crime, and this view was uncritically adopted by American courts. But "[whether] abortion of a *quick* fetus was a felony at common law, or even a lesser crime" now appears "doubtful." Abortion was made a statutory crime in England in 1803. The first statute distinguished between abortion before and after quickening, with lighter penalties for the former, but later statutes dropped the distinction. The English Abortion Act of 1967 permits abortions when, inter alia, "the continuance of the pregnancy would involve risks to the . . . physical or mental health of the pregnant woman or any existing children of her family," taking account of her "actual or reasonably foreseen environment."

Justice Blackmun then turns to historical and present views of abortion in the United States:] . . . In this country, the law in effect in all but a few States until mid-19th century was the pre-existing English common law. . . . In 1828, New York enacted legislation that, in two respects, was to serve as a model for early anti-abortion statutes. First, while barring destruction of an unquickened fetus as well as a quick fetus, it made the former only a misdemeanor, but the latter second-degree manslaughter. Second, it incorporated a concept of therapeutic abortion by providing that an abortion was excused if it "shall have been necessary to preserve the life of such mother, or shall have been advised by two physicians to be necessary for such purpose." By 1840, when Texas had received the common law, only eight American States had statutes dealing with abortion. It was not until after the War Between the States that legislation began generally to replace the common law. Most of these initial statutes dealt severely with abortion after quickening but were lenient with it before quickening. . . .

Gradually, in the middle and late 19th century the quickening distinction disappeared from the statutory law of most States and the degree of the offense and the penalties were increased. By the end of the 1950s, a large majority of the jurisdictions banned abortion, however and whenever performed, unless done to save or preserve the life of the mother. . . . In the past several years, however, a trend toward liberalization of abortion statutes has resulted in adoption, by about one-third of the States, of less stringent laws, most of them patterned after the ALI Model Penal Code, §230.3.[43]

It is thus apparent that at common law, at the time of the adoption of our Constitution, and throughout the major portion of the 19th century, abortion was viewed with less disfavor than under most American statutes currently in effect. Phrasing it another way, a woman enjoyed a substantially broader right to terminate a pregnancy than she does in most States today. At least with respect to the early stage of pregnancy, and very possibly without such a limitation, the opportunity to make this choice was present in this country well into the 19th century. Even later, the law continued for some time to treat less punitively an abortion procured in early pregnancy. . . .

[Finally, Justice Blackmun discusses the views of the American Medical Association, the American Public Health Association, and the American Bar Association: "The anti-abortion mood prevalent in this country in the late 19th century was shared by the medical profession. Indeed, the attitude of the profession may have played a significant role in the enactment of stringent criminal abortion legislation during the period." By 1970, however, an AMA committee noted that the profession was polarized and that there had been a remarkable shift of views "felt to be influenced 'by the rapid changes in state law and by the judicial decisions which tend to make abortion more freely available.' . . ." The AMA House of Delegates adopted statements emphasizing " 'the best interests of the patient,' 'sound clinical judgment,' and 'informed patient consent,' in contrast to 'mere acquiescence to the patient's demand.' " In 1970 the Executive Board of the APHA adopted standards providing, inter alia, that "rapid and simple abortion referral must be readily available through state and local public health departments, medical societies, or other nonprofit organizations." And in 1972 the ABA House of Delegates approved the quite liberal Uniform Abortion Act.]

VII.

Three reasons have been advanced to explain historically the enactment of criminal abortion laws in the 19th century and to justify their continued existence.

It has been argued occasionally that these laws were the product of a Victorian social concern to discourage illicit sexual conduct. Texas, however, does not advance this justification in the present case, and it appears that no court or commentator has taken the argument seriously. . . .

---

43. Section 230.3 reads:

(1) *Unjustified Abortion.* A person who purposely and unjustifiably terminates the pregnancy of another otherwise than by a live birth commits a felony of the third degree or, where the pregnancy has continued beyond the twenty-sixth week, a felony of the second degree.

(2) *Justifiable Abortion.* A licensed physician is justified in terminating a pregnancy if he believes there is substantial risk that continuance of the pregnancy would gravely impair the physical or mental health of the mother or that the child would be born with grave physical or mental defect, or that the pregnancy resulted from rape, incest, or other felonious intercourse. All illicit intercourse with a girl below the age of 16 shall be deemed felonious for purposes of this subsection.

A second reason is concerned with abortion as a medical procedure. When most criminal abortion laws were first enacted, the procedure was a hazardous one for the woman. . . . Thus, it has been argued that a State's real concern in enacting a criminal abortion law was to protect the pregnant woman, that is, to restrain her from submitting to a procedure that placed her life in serious jeopardy.

Modern medical techniques have altered this situation. Appellants and various amici refer to medical data indicating that abortion in early pregnancy, that is, prior to the end of the first trimester, although not without its risk, is now relatively safe. Mortality rates for women undergoing early abortions, where the procedure is legal, appear to be as low as or lower than the rates for normal childbirth. Consequently, any interest of the State in protecting the woman from an inherently hazardous procedure, except when it would be equally dangerous for her to forgo it, has largely disappeared. Of course, important state interests in the area of health and medical standards do remain. The State has a legitimate interest in seeing to it that abortion, like any other medical procedure, is performed under circumstances that insure maximum safety for the patient. This interest obviously extends at least to the performing physician and his staff, to the facilities involved, to the availability of after-care, and to adequate provision for any complication or emergency that might arise. The prevalence of high mortality rates at illegal "abortion mills" strengthens, rather than weakens, the State's interest in regulating the conditions under which abortions are performed. Moreover, the risk to the woman increases as her pregnancy continues. Thus, the State retains a definite interest in protecting the woman's own health and safety when an abortion is proposed at a late stage of pregnancy.

The third reason is the State's interest — some phrase it in terms of duty — in protecting prenatal life. Some of the argument for this justification rests on the theory that a new human life is present from the moment of conception. The State's interest and general obligation to protect life then extends, it is argued, to prenatal life. Only when the life of the pregnant mother herself is at stake, balanced against the life she carries within her, should the interest of the embryo or fetus not prevail. Logically, of course, a legitimate state interest in this area need not stand or fall on acceptance or the belief that life begins at conception or at some other point prior to live birth. In assessing the State's interest, recognition may be given to the less rigid claim that as long as at least *potential* life is involved, the State may assert interests beyond the protection of the pregnant woman alone. . . .

It is with these interests, and the weight to be attached to them, that this case is concerned.

VIII.

The Constitution does not explicitly mention any right of privacy. In a [long] line of decisions, however, . . . the Court has recognized that a right of personal privacy, or a guarantee of certain areas or zones of privacy, does exist under the Constitution. In varying contexts, the Court or individual Justices have, indeed, found at least the roots of that right in the First Amendment; in the penumbras of the Bill of Rights; in the Ninth Amendment; or in the concept of liberty guaranteed by the first section of the Fourteenth Amendment. These decisions make it clear that only personal rights that can be deemed "fundamental" or "implicit in the concept of ordered liberty," Palko v. Connecticut, are included in this guarantee of personal privacy. They also make it clear that the right has some extension to activities relating to marriage, Loving v. Virginia; procreation, Skinner v. Oklahoma; contraception, Eisenstadt v. Baird; family relationships, Prince v. Massachusetts; and child rearing and education, Pierce v. Society of Sisters, Meyer v. Nebraska.

This right of privacy, whether it be founded in the Fourteenth Amendment's concept of personal liberty and restrictions upon state action, as we feel it is, or, as the District Court determined, in the Ninth Amendment's reservation of rights to the people, is broad enough to encompass a woman's decision whether or not to terminate her pregnancy. The detriment that the State would impose upon the pregnant woman by denying this choice altogether is apparent. Specific and direct harm medically diagnosable even in early pregnancy may be involved. Maternity, or additional offspring, may force upon the woman a distressful life and future. Psychological harm may be imminent. Mental and physical health may be taxed by child care. There is also the distress, for all concerned, associated with the unwanted child; and there is the problem of bringing a child into a family already unable, psychologically and otherwise, to care for it. In other cases, as in this one, the additional difficulties and continuing stigma of unwed motherhood may be involved. All these are factors the woman and her responsible physician necessarily will consider in consultation.

On the basis of elements such as these, appellant and some amici argue that the woman's right is absolute and that she is entitled to terminate her pregnancy at whatever time, in whatever way, and for whatever reason she alone chooses. With this we do not agree. Appellant's arguments that Texas either has no valid interest at all in regulating the abortion decision, or no interest strong enough to support any limitation upon the woman's sole determination, is unpersuasive. The Court's decisions recognizing a right of privacy also acknowledge that some state regulation in areas protected by that right is appropriate. As noted above, a State may properly assert important interests in safeguarding health, in maintaining medical standards, and in protecting potential life. At some point in pregnancy, these respective interests become sufficiently compelling to sustain regulation of the factors that govern the abortion decision. The privacy right involved, therefore, cannot be said to be absolute. . . .

We, therefore, conclude that the right of personal privacy includes the abortion decision, but that this right is not unqualified and must be considered against important state interests in regulation. . . .

Where certain "fundamental rights" are involved, the Court has held that regulation limiting these rights may be justified only by a "compelling state interest," . . . and that legislative enactments must be narrowly drawn to express only the legitimate state interests at stake. . . .

IX.

The District Court held that the appellee failed to meet his burden of demonstrating that the Texas statute's infringement upon Roe's rights was necessary to support a compelling state interest, and that, although the appellee presented "several compelling justifications for state presence in the area of abortions," the statutes outstripped these justifications and swept "far beyond any areas of compelling state interest." Appellant and appellee both contest that holding. . . .

The appellee and certain amici argue that the fetus is a "person" within the language and meaning of the Fourteenth Amendment. In support of this, they outline at length and in detail the well-known facts of fetal development. If this suggestion of personhood is established, the appellant's case, of course, collapses, for the fetus' right to life is then guaranteed specifically by the Amendment. . . . [However, no case] holds that a fetus is a person within the meaning of the Fourteenth Amendment.

The Constitution does not define "person" in so many words. Section 1 of the Fourteenth Amendment contains three references to "person." The first, in defining "citizens," speaks of "persons born or naturalized in the United States." The word also appears both in the Due Process Clause and in the Equal Protection Clause. "Person" is used in other places in the Constitution. . . . But in nearly all these instances, the use of the word is such that it has application only postnatally. None indicates, with any assurance, that it has any possible prenatal application.[a]

All this, together with our observation, supra, that throughout the major portion of the 19th century prevailing legal abortion practices were far freer than they are today, persuades us that the word "person," as used in the Fourteenth Amendment, does not include the unborn. . . .

This conclusion, however, does not of itself fully answer the contentions raised by Texas, and we pass on to other considerations.

The pregnant woman cannot be isolated in her privacy. She carries an embryo and, later, a fetus, if one accepts the medical definitions of the developing young in the human uterus. The situation therefore is inherently different from marital intimacy, or bedroom possession of obscene material, or marriage, or procreation, or education, with which *Eisenstadt, Griswold, Stanley, Loving, Skinner, Pierce,* and *Meyer* were respectively concerned. As we have intimated above, it is reasonable and appropriate for a State to decide that at some point in time another interest, that of health of the mother or that of potential human life, becomes significantly involved. The woman's privacy is no longer sole and any right of privacy she possesses must be measured accordingly.

Texas urges that, apart from the Fourteenth Amendment, life begins at conception and is present throughout pregnancy, and that, therefore, the State has a compelling interest in protecting that life from and after conception. We need not resolve the difficult question of when life begins. When those trained in the respective disciplines of medicine, philosophy, and theology are unable to arrive at any consensus, the judiciary, at this point in the development of man's knowledge, is not in a position to speculate as to the answer.

It should be sufficient to note briefly the wide divergence of thinking on this most sensitive and difficult question. There has always been strong support for the view that life does not begin until live birth. This was the belief of the Stoics. It appears to be the predominant, though not the unanimous, attitude of the Jewish faith. It may be taken to represent also the position of a large segment of the Protestant community, insofar as that can be ascertained; organized groups that

a. When Texas urges that a fetus is entitled to Fourteenth Amendment protection as a person, it faces a dilemma. Neither in Texas nor in any other State are all abortions prohibited. Despite broad proscription, an exception always exists. The exception . . . for an abortion procured or attempted by medical advice for the purpose of saving the life of the mother, is typical. But if the fetus is a person who is not to be deprived of life without due process of law, and if the mother's condition is the sole determinant, does not the Texas exception appear to be out of line with the Amendment's command?

have taken a formal position on the abortion issue have generally regarded abortion as a matter for the conscience of the individual and her family. As we have noted, the common law found greater significance in quickening. Physicians and their scientific colleagues have regarded that event with less interest and have tended to focus either upon conception, upon live birth, or upon the interim point at which the fetus becomes "viable," that is, potentially able to live outside the mother's womb, albeit with artificial aid. Viability is usually placed at about seven months (28 weeks) but may occur earlier, even at 24 weeks. The Aristotelian theory of "mediate animation," that held sway throughout the Middle Ages and the Renaissance in Europe, continued to be official Roman Catholic dogma until the 19th century, despite opposition to this "ensoulment" theory from those in the Church who would recognize the existence of life from the moment of conception. The latter is now, of course, the official belief of the Catholic Church. As one of the briefs amicus discloses, this is a view strongly held by many non-Catholics as well, and by many physicians. Substantial problems for precise definition of this view are posed, however, by new embryological data that purport to indicate that conception is a "process" over time; rather than an event, and by new medical techniques such as menstrual extraction, the "morning-after" pill, implantation of embryos, artificial insemination, and even artificial wombs.

In areas other than criminal abortion, the law has been reluctant to endorse any theory that life, as we recognize it, begins before live birth or to accord legal rights to the unborn except in narrowly defined situations and except when the rights are contingent upon live birth. For example, the traditional rule of tort law denied recovery for prenatal injuries even though the child was born alive. That rule has been changed in almost every jurisdiction. In most States, recovery is said to be permitted only if the fetus was viable, or at least quick, when the injuries were sustained, though few courts have squarely so held. In a recent development, generally opposed by the commentators, some States permit the parents of a stillborn child to maintain an action for wrongful death because of prenatal injuries. Such an action, however, would appear to be one to vindicate the parents' interest and is thus consistent with the view that the fetus, at most, represents only the potentiality of life. Similarly, unborn children have been recognized as acquiring rights or interests by way of inheritance or other devolution of property, and have been represented by guardians ad litem. Perfection of the interests involved, again, has generally been contingent upon live birth. In short, the unborn have never been recognized in the law as persons in the whole sense.

X.

In view of all this, we do not agree that, by adopting one theory of life, Texas may override the rights of the pregnant woman that are at stake. We repeat, however, that the State does have an important and legitimate interest in preserving and protecting the health of the pregnant woman, whether she be a resident of the State or a nonresident who seeks medical consultation and treatment there, and that it has still *another* important and legitimate interest in protecting the potentiality of human life. These interests are separate, and distinct. Each grows in substantiality as the woman approaches term and, at a point during pregnancy, each becomes "compelling."

With respect to the State's important and legitimate interest in the health of the mother, the "compelling" point, in the light of present medical knowledge, is at approximately the end of the first trimester. This is so because of the now established medical fact . . . that until the end of the first trimester mortality in abortion may be less than mortality in normal childbirth. It follows that, from and after this point, a State may regulate the abortion procedure to the extent that the regulation reasonably relates to the preservation and protection of maternal health. Examples of permissible state regulation in this area are requirements as to the qualifications of the person who is to perform the abortion; as to the licensure of that person; as to the facility in which the procedure is to be performed, that is, whether it must be a hospital or may be a clinic or some other place of less-than-hospital status; as to the licensing of the facility; and the like.

This means, on the other hand, that, for the period of pregnancy prior to this "compelling" point, the attending physician, in consultation with his patient, is free to determine, without regulation by the State, that, in his medical judgment, the patient's pregnancy should be terminated. If that decision is reached, the judgment may be effectuated by an abortion free of interference by the State.

With respect to the State's important and legitimate interest in potential life, the "compelling" point is at viability. This is so because the fetus then presumably has the capability of meaningful life outside the mother's womb. State regulation protective of fetal life after viability thus has both logical and biological justifications. If the State is interested in protecting fetal life after viability, it may go so far as to proscribe abortion during that period, except when it is necessary to preserve the life or health of the mother.

Measured against these standards, . . . the Texas Penal Code, in restricting legal abortions to those "procured or attempted by medical advice for the purpose of saving the life of the mother," sweeps too broadly. The statute makes no distinction between abortions performed early in pregnancy and those performed later, and it limits to a single reason, "saving" the mother's life, the legal justification for the procedure. The statute, therefore, cannot survive the constitutional attack made upon it here. . . .

XI.

To summarize and to repeat:

1. A state criminal abortion statute of the current Texas type, that excepts from criminality only a *lifesaving* procedure on behalf of the mother, without regard to pregnancy stage and without recognition of the other interests involved, is violative of the Due Process Clause of the Fourteenth Amendment.

(a) For the stage prior to approximately the end of the first trimester, the abortion decision and its effectuation must be left to the medical judgment of the pregnant woman's attending physician.

(b) For the stage subsequent to approximately the end of the first trimester, the State, in promoting its interest in the health of the mother, may, if it chooses, regulate the abortion procedure in ways that are reasonably related to maternal health.

(c) For the stage subsequent to viability, the State in promoting its interest in the potentiality of human life may, if it chooses, regulate, and even proscribe, abortion except where it is necessary, in appropriate medical judgment, for the preservation of the life or health of the mother.

2. The State may define the term "physician" . . . to mean only a physician currently licensed by the State, and may proscribe any abortion by a person who is not a physician as so defined.

In Doe v. Bolton, . . . procedural requirements contained in one of the modern abortion statutes are considered. That opinion and this one, of course, are to be read together.[b]

This holding, we feel, is consistent with the relative weights of the respective interests involved, with the lessons and examples of medical and legal history, with the lenity of the common law, and with the demands of the profound problems of the present day. The decision leaves the State free to place increasing restrictions on abortion as the period of pregnancy lengthens, so long as those restrictions are tailored to the recognized state interests. The decision vindicated the right of the physician to administer medical treatment according to his professional judgment up to the points where important state interests provide compelling justifications for intervention. Up to those points, the abortion decision in all its aspects is inherently, and primarily, a medical decision, and basic responsibility for it must rest with the physician. If an individual practitioner abuses the privilege of exercising proper medical judgment, the usual remedies, judicial and intra-professional, are available.

[Chief Justice Burger, concurring in the companion case of Doe v. Bolton, stated that "[p]lainly, the Court today rejects any claim that the Constitution requires abortions on demand."]

Douglas, J., concurring [in Doe v. Bolton] . . .
While I join the opinion of the Court, I add a few words.

I.

The Ninth Amendment obviously does not create federally enforceable rights.

It merely says, "The enumeration in the Constitution, of certain rights, shall not be construed to deny or disparage others retained by the people." But a catalogue of these rights includes customary, traditional, and time-honored rights, amenities, privileges, and immunities that come within the sweep of "the Blessings of Liberty" mentioned in the preamble to the Constitution. Many of them, in my view, come within the meaning of the term "liberty" as used in the Fourteenth Amendment.

First is the autonomous control over the development and expression of one's intellect, interests, tastes, and personality.

These are rights protected by the First Amendment and, in my view, they are absolute, permitting of no exceptions. . . .

Second is freedom of choice in the basic decisions of one's life respecting marriage, divorce, procreation, contraception, and the education and upbringing of children.

These rights, unlike those protected by the First Amendment, are subject to some control by the police power. . . . These rights are "fundamental" and we have

---

b. Neither in this opinion nor in Doe v. Bolton do we discuss the father's rights, if any exist in the constitutional context, in the abortion decision. No paternal right has been asserted in either of the cases, and the Texas and the Georgia statutes on their face take no cognizance of the father. We are aware that some statutes recognize the father under certain circumstances. North Carolina, for example, requires written permission for the abortion from the husband when the woman is a married minor, that is, when she is less than 18 years of age: if the woman is an unmarried minor, written permission from the parents is required. We need not now decide whether provisions of this kind are constitutional.

held that in order to support legislative action the statute must be narrowly and precisely drawn and that a "compelling state interest" must be shown in support of the limitation. . . .

Third is the freedom to care for one's health and person, freedom from bodily restraint or compulsion, freedom to walk, stroll, or loaf.

These rights, though fundamental, are likewise subject to regulation on a showing of "compelling state interest." . . .

The Georgia[44] statute is at war with the clear message . . . that a woman is free to make the basic decision whether to bear an unwanted child. Elaborate argument is hardly necessary to demonstrate that childbirth may deprive a woman of her preferred lifestyle and force upon her a radically different and undesired future. For example, rejected applicants under the Georgia statute are required to endure the discomforts of pregnancy; to incur the pain, higher mortality rate, and after-effects of childbirth; to abandon educational plans; to sustain loss of income; to forgo the satisfactions of careers; to tax further mental and physical health in providing child care; and, in some cases, to bear the lifelong stigma of unwed motherhood, a badge which may haunt, if not deter, later legitimate family relationships.

II.

The present statute has struck the balance between the woman's and the State's interests wholly in favor of the latter. I am not prepared to hold that a State may equate, as Georgia has done, all phases of maturation preceding birth. We held in *Griswold* that the States may not preclude spouses from attempting to avoid the joinder of sperm and egg. If this is true, it is difficult to perceive any overriding public necessity which might attach precisely at the moment of conception. . . .

In summary, the enactment is overbroad. It is not closely correlated to the aim of preserving prenatal life. In fact, it permits its destruction in several cases, including pregnancies resulting from sex acts in which unmarried females are below the statutory age of consent. At the same time, however, the measure broadly proscribes aborting other pregnancies which may cause severe mental disorders. Additionally, the statute is overbroad because it equates the value of embryonic life immediately after conception with the worth of life immediately before birth.

STEWART, J., concurring.

In 1963, this Court, in Ferguson v. Skrupa, 372 U.S. 726, purported to sound the death knell for the doctrine of substantive due process. . . . As Mr. Justice Black's opinion for the Court in *Skrupa* put it: "We have returned to the original constitutional proposition that courts do not substitute their social and economic beliefs for the judgment of legislative bodies, who are elected to pass laws."

Barely two years later, in Griswold v. Connecticut, the Court held a Connecticut birth control law unconstitutional. In view of what had been so recently said in *Skrupa*, the Court's opinion in *Griswold* understandably did its best to avoid reliance on the Due Process Clause of the Fourteenth Amendment as the ground for decision. Yet, the Connecticut law did not violate any provision of the Bill of Rights, nor any other specific provision of the Constitution. So it was clear to me then, and it is

44. Justice Douglas's concurrence is addressed largely to Georgia's relatively liberal abortion statute, much of which was invalidated in Doe v. Bolton. His remarks apply a fortiori to the Texas statute.

equally clear to me now, that the *Griswold* decision can be rationally understood only as a holding that the Connecticut statute substantively invaded the "liberty" that is protected by the Due Process Clause of the Fourteenth Amendment. As so understood, *Griswold* stands as one in a long line of pre-*Skrupa* cases decided under the doctrine of substantive due process, and I now accept it as such.

"In a Constitution for a free people, there can be no doubt that the meaning of 'liberty' must be broad indeed." The Constitution nowhere mentions a specific right of personal choice in matters of marriage and family life, but the "liberty" protected by the Due Process Clause of the Fourteenth Amendment covers more than those freedoms explicitly named in the Bill of Rights. . . .

Several decisions of this Court make clear that freedom of personal choice in matters of marriage and family life is one of the liberties protected by the Due Process Clause of the Fourteenth Amendment. As recently as last Term, in Eisenstadt v. Baird, we recognized "the right of the *individual,* married or single, to be free from unwarranted governmental intrusion into matters so fundamentally affecting a person as the decision whether to bear or beget a child." That right necessarily includes the right of a woman to decide whether or not to terminate her pregnancy. "Certainly the interests of a woman in giving of her physical and emotional self during pregnancy and the interests that will be affected throughout her life by the birth and raising of a child are of a far greater degree of significance and personal intimacy than the right to send a child to private school protected in Pierce v. Society of Sisters, or the right to teach a foreign language protected in Meyer v. Nebraska." Clearly, therefore, the Court today is correct in holding that the right asserted by Jane Roe is embraced within the personal liberty protected by the Due Process Clause of the Fourteenth Amendment.

It is evident that the Texas abortion statute infringes that right directly. Indeed, it is difficult to imagine a more complete abridgment of a constitutional freedom than that worked by the inflexible criminal statute now in force in Texas. The question then becomes whether the state interests advanced to justify this abridgment can survive the "particularly careful scrutiny" that the Fourteenth Amendment here requires.

The asserted state interests are protection of the health and safety of the pregnant woman, and protection of the potential future human life within her. These are legitimate objectives, amply sufficient to permit a State to regulate abortions as it does other surgical procedures, and perhaps sufficient to permit a State to regulate abortions more stringently or even to prohibit them in the late stages of pregnancy. But such legislation is not before us, and I think the Court today has thoroughly demonstrated that these state interests cannot constitutionally support the broad abridgment of personal liberty worked by the existing Texas law. Accordingly, I join the Court's opinion holding that that law is invalid under the Due Process Clause of the Fourteenth Amendment.

REHNQUIST, J., dissenting. . . .

I have difficulty in concluding, as the Court does, that the right of "privacy" is involved in this case. Texas by the statute here challenged, bars the performance of a medical abortion by a licensed physician on a plaintiff such as Roe. A transaction resulting in an operation such as this is not "private" in the ordinary usage of that word. Nor is the "privacy" that the Court finds here even a distant relative of the freedom from searches and seizures protected by the Fourth Amendment to the Constitution, which the Court has referred to as embodying a right to privacy.

If the Court means by the term "privacy" no more than that the claim of a person to be free from unwanted state regulation of consensual transactions may be a form of "liberty" protected by the Fourteenth Amendment, there is no doubt that similar claims have been upheld in our earlier decision on the basis of that liberty. I agree with the statement of Mr. Justice Stewart in his concurring opinion that the "liberty," against deprivation of which without due process the Fourteenth Amendment protects, embraces more than the rights found in the Bill of Rights. But that liberty is not guaranteed absolutely against deprivation, only against deprivation without due process of law. The test traditionally applied in the area of social and economic legislation is whether or not a law such as that challenged has a rational relation to a valid state objective. Williamson v. Lee Optical Co., 348 U.S. 483, 491 (1955). The Due Process Clause of the Fourteenth Amendment undoubtedly does place a limit, albeit a broad one, on legislative power to enact laws such as this. If the Texas statute were to prohibit an abortion even where the mother's life is in jeopardy, I have little doubt that such a statute would lack a rational relation to a valid state objective under the test stated in *Williamson,* supra. But the Court's sweeping invalidation of any restrictions on abortion during the first trimester is impossible to justify under that standard, and the conscious weighing of competing factors that the Court's opinion apparently substitutes for the established test is far more appropriate to a legislative judgment than to a judicial one. . . .

While the Court's opinion quotes from the dissent of Mr. Justice Holmes in Lochner v. New York, the result it reaches is more closely attuned to the majority opinion of Mr. Justice Peckham in that case. As in *Lochner* and similar cases applying substantive due process standards to economic and social welfare legislation, the adoption of the compelling state interest standard will inevitably require this Court to examine the legislative policies and pass on the wisdom of these policies in the very process of deciding whether a particular state interest put forward may or may not be "compelling." The decision here to break pregnancy into three distinct terms and to outline the permissible restrictions the State may impose in each one, for example, partakes more of judicial legislation than it does of a determination of the intent of the drafters of the Fourteenth Amendment.

The fact that a majority of the States reflecting, after all, the majority sentiment in those States, have had restrictions on abortions for at least a century is a strong indication, it seems to me, that the asserted right to an abortion is not "so rooted in the traditions and conscience of our people as to be ranked as fundamental." Even today, when society's views on abortion are changing, the very existence of the debate is evidence that the "right" to an abortion is not so universally accepted as the appellants would have us believe.

To reach its result the Court necessarily has had to find within the scope of the Fourteenth Amendment a right that was apparently completely unknown to the drafters of the Amendment. . . . By the time of the adoption of the Fourteenth Amendment in 1868, there were at least 36 laws enacted by state or territorial legislatures limiting abortion. While many States have amended or updated their laws, 21 of the laws on the books in 1868 remain in effect today. . . .

There apparently was no question concerning the validity of [the Texas] or of any of the other state statutes when the Fourteenth Amendment was adopted. The only conclusion possible from this history is that the drafters did not intend to have the Fourteenth Amendment withdraw from the States the power to legislate with respect to this matter. . . .

WHITE, J., joined by Rehnquist, J., dissenting [in Doe v. Bolton.]

At the heart of the controversy in these cases are those recurring pregnancies that pose no danger whatsoever to the life or health of the mother but are, nevertheless, unwanted for any one or more of a variety of reasons — convenience, family planning, economics, dislike of children, the embarrassment of illegitimacy, etc. The common claim before us is that for any one of such reasons, or for no reason at all, and without asserting or claiming any threat to life or health, any woman is entitled to an abortion at her request if she is able to find a medical advisor willing to undertake the procedure.

The Court for the most part sustains this position: During the period prior to the time the fetus becomes viable, the Constitution of the United States values the convenience, whim, or caprice of the putative mother more than the life or potential life of the fetus; the Constitution, therefore, guarantees the right to an abortion as against any state law or policy seeking to protect the fetus from an abortion not prompted by more compelling reasons of the mother.

With all due respect, I dissent. I find nothing in the language or history of the Constitution to support the Court's judgment. The Court simply fashions and announces a new constitutional right for pregnant mothers and, with scarcely any reason or authority for its action, invests that right with sufficient substance to override most existing state abortion statutes. The upshot is that the people and the legislatures of the 50 States are constitutionally disentitled to weigh the relative importance of the continued existence and development of the fetus, on the one hand, against a spectrum of possible impacts on the mother, on the other hand. As an exercise of raw judicial power, the Court perhaps has authority to do what it does today; but in my view its judgment is an improvident and extravagant exercise of the power of judicial review that the Constitution extends to this Court.

The Court apparently values the convenience of the pregnant mother more than the continued existence and development of the life or potential life that she carries. Whether or not I might agree with that marshaling of values, I can in no event join the Court's judgment because I find no constitutional warrant for imposing such an order of priorities on the people and legislatures of the States. In a sensitive area such as this, involving as it does issues over which reasonable men may easily and heatedly differ, I cannot accept the Court's exercise of its clear power of choice by interposing a constitutional barrier to state efforts to protect human life and by investing mothers and doctors with the constitutionally protected right to exterminate it. This issue, for the most part, should be left with the people and to the political processes the people have devised to govern their affairs. . . .

DOE v. BOLTON, 410 U.S. 179 (1973): *Doe*, the companion case to *Roe*, considered the constitutionality of Georgia's abortion reform statute, passed in 1968, and based on the Model Penal Code. The Court, in an opinion by Justice Blackmun, invalidated various procedural provisions of the Georgia abortion statute.

First, the Georgia statute required that all abortions, even in the earliest phases of pregnancy, be performed in hospitals as opposed to less expensive abortion clinics. The Court held this was invalid with respect to abortions performed in the first trimester.

Second, Georgia required that hospitals that performed abortions have special accreditation requirements separate from those for hospitals not specifically connected to abortion practice and not required for hospitals performing any other kind of surgery. Justice Blackmun struck this down on the grounds that "the State must show more than it has in order to prove that only the full resources of a licensed hospital, rather than those of some other appropriately licensed institution, satisfy these health interests."

Third, Georgia required prior permission of special hospital staff committees, as well as independent examinations by two other physicians; it did not apply these restrictions to any other surgical procedures. The Court rejected the staff committee requirement as "unduly restrictive of the patient's rights and needs that, at this point, have already been medically delineated and substantiated by her personal physician." It also struck down the independent examination requirement: "[N]o other voluntary medical or surgical procedure for which Georgia requires confirmation by two other physicians has been cited to us. If a physician is licensed by the State, he is recognized by the State as capable of exercising acceptable clinical judgment. If he fails in this, professional censure and deprivation of his license are available remedies. Required acquiescence by co-practitioners has no rational connection with a patient's needs and unduly infringes on the physician's right to practice."

Fourth, Georgia limited abortions to residents of the state. The Court held that this violated the Privileges and Immunities Clause, Const. Art. IV, 2. "Just as [the Clause] protects persons who enter other States to ply their trade, so must it protect persons who enter Georgia seeking the medical services that are available there. A contrary holding would mean that a State could limit to its own residents the general medical care available within its borders."

Discussion[45]

1. Parts VII-IX of Justice Blackmun's opinion for the Court contain the core of its reasoning: A woman has a (prima facie) right to abort her pregnancy, which can only be defeated by a compelling state interest. During the first two trimesters, the state's interest is limited to protecting the woman's health: During the first, the state can require that a physician approve and perform the abortion; during the second, it may require other health-related measures. During the third trimester, an interest in the "potentiality of human life" emerges and justifies restricting the decision to abort.

2. *The right of privacy.* Roe's argument is based on doctrinal extension of previous cases recognizing a right of privacy: *Meyer, Pierce, Skinner, Eisenstadt,* Loving v. Virginia (which recognized a fundamental right to marry), and Prince v. Massachusetts, 321 U.S. 158 (1944), which upheld a child labor law in the course of reaffirming the principle that there is a "private realm of family life which the state cannot enter."

Do all these cases, taken together, form a coherent conception of a right of privacy? How would you describe this right? Is it the right to be free from state interference in family life? The right to decide whether and how to raise children? Aren't these rights both subject to considerable state regulation? Is the right of

45. See generally John Ely, The Wages of Crying Wolf, 82 Yale L.J. 920 (1973); Philip Heymann & Douglas Barzelay, The Forest and the Trees, 53 B.U. L. Rev. 765 (1973); Laurence Tribe, Toward a Model of Roles in the Due Process of Life and Law, 87 Harv. L. Rev. 1 (1973). For a collection of essays that attempt to rewrite Roe v. Wade, offered by supporters and critics of the result, see What Roe v. Wade Should Have Said, supra.

privacy the right to be free from significant state interference in the decision to procreate (or not to procreate)? Note that in Carey v. Population Services International, Justice Brennan remarked that the right of privacy was in fact a "cluster of constitutionally protected choices," at the heart of which is "[t]he decision whether or not to beget or bear a child." Why does the constitutional principle that guarantees a constitutional right to avoid sterilization (*Skinner*) or to use contraceptives (*Griswold, Eisenstadt*) include the right to abortions, when in the case of abortion conception has already occurred?

Consider the possibility that the right to abortion is actually two different rights. The first is women's "right not to be forced by the state to sacrifice their lives or their health in order to bear children." The second is women's "right to decide whether or not to become parents and take on the obligations of motherhood."[46] The first right protects the woman's interest in her bodily integrity, and her right not to be used by the state for reproductive purposes. The second right protects a woman's ability to choose whether to take on the considerable social, moral, and legal expectations and obligations society imposes on parents, and particularly on mothers. These expectations and obligations are often life-altering and may place women in conditions of social and economic dependency.

The consequences of parenthood usually weigh far more heavily on women than on men, because, fairly or not, women are still expected to devote themselves to the care of their children, are expected to make considerable sacrifices of time and energy on behalf of their children, and are far more likely than men to be morally condemned if they fail to do so. When the state forces a woman to become a mother, it forces her to assume a life-changing obligation for a very long period of time, restricting both her present and future liberty, and limiting her ability to participate fully in the public world of work outside of the traditional roles assigned to women. Thus, the right to abortion is the right to refuse to be a mother and to be pressed into the obligations, restrictions, and dependencies that accompany motherhood.

Why are these rights so important to women? Are they more important to some women than to others? Are they equally or more important than the rights to contract, to own property, or to practice religion? If some women believe that traditional maternal roles of caregiving and dependency are honorable and likely to be undervalued by society, why shouldn't they oppose the right to abortion, because its widespread availability simply furthers the devaluation of traditional maternal roles?

Conversely, if "mothering children, as we presently socially construct that work, is incompatible with the basic rights and responsibilities of citizenship," why isn't the right to terminate pregnancy "a pathetically inadequate remedy" for this problem?[47] Why should courts give women rights to abortions rather than requiring the states to secure women's practical ability to control their lives as equal citizens, through, for example, greatly increased resources for child care, restructuring workplaces so that women with children can compete on a more equal footing with men, promoting widespread education about and availability of contraception, and so on? Is the answer that it is far easier for courts to strike down abortion statutes than to order massive government investments and large-scale restructuring of the workplace, and that securing a right to abortion is the best that courts can do?

46. Jack M. Balkin, Judgment of the Court, in What Roe v. Wade Should Have Said, at 45.
47. Robin West, Concurring in the Judgment, in What Roe v. Wade Should Have Said, at 141.

If the right to abortion protects women from being forced to take on the life-altering obligations of rearing children, why doesn't the availability of adoption sufficiently protect women's rights? Consider two possibilities: (1) Adoption does not adequately protect women's rights because the state still requires women, against their will, to use their bodies to bear children. (2) The possibility of giving children up for adoption does not adequately protect women's rights to decide whether to become mothers because giving up a child for adoption does not mean that women have not become mothers. Instead, the state's law subjects women to trauma, shame, and moral condemnation because they have failed as mothers, a failure demonstrated by the very fact that they have surrendered their children. Are these responses sufficient?

3. *The fetus as constitutional person. Roe* holds that fetuses are not persons within the meaning of the Fourteenth Amendment. It also holds that states do not have a compelling state interest in protection of potential human life from the moment of conception, but rather may only prevent abortions after the point of viability.

(a) Consider Justice Blackmun's textual argument that the word "person" as used in the Fourteenth Amendment does not include the unborn. Could a fetus be a "person" for some legal purposes (due process, equal protection) but not others (the census, the privilege against self-incrimination)? What would be the legal consequences if fetuses were considered persons?[48] Would the fetus have procedural due process rights to a hearing before an abortion could be performed? Would the fetus have substantive due process rights not to be aborted? Would states be required to punish mothers and doctors for performing abortions the same as other persons who committed premeditated (i.e., first-degree) murder, so that if states made murder a crime they would be constitutionally required to outlaw all abortions? Note that, even before Roe v. Wade, no state treated abortion as equivalent, in all respects, with first-degree murder. Why do you think this is?

(b) Justice Blackmun states that "[w]e need not resolve the difficult question of when life begins." Is this true? Doesn't the Court need to resolve that issue to some degree in order to hold that Texas's interest in the fetus is not compelling from the moment of conception?

In view of the fact that much of the opinion preceding Part X demonstrates the lack of a consensus regarding the medico-ethical issues of abortion, why shouldn't the first sentence of Part X have read as follows:

> In view of all this, we cannot conclude that the Constitution adopts one particular theory of life. Therefore we cannot conclude that the Ninth or Fourteenth Amendment prevents a state from determining that the unborn child's right to life attaches at any point after conception, or that the Constitution precludes a state from making whatever accommodation of the competing interests of the mother and her unborn child it believes appropriate.

48. For an argument that the fetus has due process rights not to be aborted, see David Louisell, Abortion, The Practice of Medicine and the Due Process of Law, 16 UCLA L. Rev. 233 (1969). But see Donald Regan, Rewriting Roe v. Wade, 77 Mich. L. Rev. 1569 (1979), arguing that, even if the fetus is considered a person, general common law principles of good samaritanism would justify abortion in many contexts. See also Eileen L. McDonagh, Breaking the Abortion Deadlock: From Choice to Consent (1996) (arguing that a pregnant woman can always assert rights of self-defense against a fetus/person threatening her bodily integrity).

4. *Preservation of potential life as a compelling state interest.* Even if women have a fundamental right to terminate their pregnancies, presumably that right may be limited by a compelling state interest that is narrowly tailored to achieve that interest. Why isn't a ban on abortions precisely tailored to achieve the state's compelling interest in the preservation of potential human life? A ban on abortions might not be narrowly tailored if the state makes exceptions that are unrelated to the furtherance of its asserted interest; that might suggest either that the interest is not as compelling as the state claims or that the law actually serves other, unstated purposes that may not be compelling or may even be illegitimate.

The Texas statute in *Roe* punished doctors who performed abortions but not women who procured them, and it did not punish women who self-aborted. (Thus, the statute gave incentives for women to undergo more dangerous methods of self-abortion that did not protect fetal life.) If the state has a compelling interest in the potentiality of human life, what justifies this underinclusiveness? The most likely reason is that the 1854 Texas statute was probably not passed originally to protect fetal life at all but rather to prevent unscrupulous doctors from injuring women through botched abortions.

The Georgia abortion statute in Doe v. Bolton allowed abortions in cases of statutory or forcible rape. Why does the state have a compelling interest in preserving some fetuses (those conceived through consensual sex with women over the age of consent) but not others? Are fetuses conceived through rape or through sex with underage women less human or less deserving of state protection?

Do exceptions like Georgia's suggest that the state is less interested in protecting fetal life per se than in establishing women's responsibility for their sexuality? This would be based on the notion that women should be able to end pregnancies they aren't responsible for, and they aren't responsible for their pregnancies when they are underage or have been forcibly raped. (If so, would this mean that women who have been coerced into sex by any means short of what a court would find to be rape are responsible for their pregnancies?) Consider in this respect Reva Siegel's comment that "[a]bortion laws do not treat women as murderers but as *mothers*," i.e., that the point of abortion statutes is not to protect fetal life but rather to assign responsibility for the consequences of sex and to "coerce and intimidate women into performing the work of motherhood."[49]

Do exceptions for rape, incest, fetal deformity, and risks to maternal health undermine a state's claim that it has a compelling interest in the protection of fetal life from the moment of conception that would overcome any fundamental right to abortion? Could states justify carving out exceptions from general prohibitions on abortion on the grounds that states should be permitted to balance away the compelling interest in life for a wide range of different factors? Conversely, would a statute that treated abortion exactly the same as first-degree murder pass a test of strict scrutiny?

If a state wishes to assert a compelling interest in protecting potential life before birth, must it also protect life after birth, for example, by expenditures on social welfare programs? Even if the state would otherwise have no duty to support children after birth, does it assume this duty if it intervenes to prevent an act of contraception or an abortion? (See the discussion of affirmative rights and *DeShaney* in Chapter 9, supra.)

49. Reva Siegel, Concurring, in What Roe v. Wade Should Have Said, at 80-81.

5. *Drawing lines.* Was the Court justified in holding that states do not have a sufficiently compelling interest in the protection of fetal life before viability? Would it be accurate to say that the basic question is whether and when the fetus is a being with a claim to life, i.e., a "person" for moral purposes?[50]

Unless one adopts the position that this claim of personhood attaches at conception, is there any judicially cognizable basis for choosing a time, in terms of physical development or events, when this claim attaches (or when the state's interest becomes "compelling")? Should the Court have left this question up to legislatures to decide in the first instance? If it did, what would be the boundaries of permissible state regulation of abortion?

Recall the point made earlier that we can think of the right to abortion as two rights — (1) the right not to be forced to sacrifice life or health to bear children, and (2) the right to choose whether or not to become a parent and take on the obligations of motherhood. To be effective, the first right — to protect life and health — must continue throughout a woman's pregnancy, and, indeed, in *Roe* itself, women retain a right to abortions to preserve their life and health even after the point of viability. The second right, however, requires only a reasonable amount of time to decide.

Instead of imposing the trimester framework, the Court might simply have told state legislatures to draft new abortion laws with (1) a statutorily defined period that gave women a reasonable time to decide whether they wanted to become parents, and (2) the right to obtain abortions after the statutory cutoff point if necessary (as judged by a physician) to preserve their life or health.[51] Compare this strategy with what the Court did in the death penalty context at around the same time it decided Roe v. Wade. In Furman v. Georgia, 408 US 238 (1972), the Court struck down all the states' death penalty laws and then instructed states to pass new ones according to a set of principles derived from the Eighth Amendment. Several years later, in Gregg v. Georgia, 428 U.S. 153 (1976), it began reviewing the new statutes as constitutional challenges bubbled up through the lower courts. Would this approach have been superior to what the Court actually did in *Roe* and *Doe?*

6. *The trimester framework and* Roe's *"collision course."* Roe's trimester framework has been one of its most heavily criticized features, on the grounds that the trimester framework was essentially legislative in character and gave states too little discretion to design their own abortion regulations. In City of Akron v. Akron Center for Reproductive Health, 462 U.S. 416 (1983) (Akron I), Justice O'Connor's dissent argued that the trimester framework, arguably derived from medical science and physiological features of the woman and the fetus, was inherently unstable as a basis for constitutional doctrine, because it was subject to changes in medical technology:

---

50. Consider whether the Court might have adopted Professor Michael Tooley's position that an "organism possesses a serious right to life only if it possesses the concept of a self as a continuing subject of experiences and other mental states, and believes that it is itself such a continuing entity." Abortion and Infanticide, 2 Phil. & Pub. Affairs 37, 44 (1972). Cf. Sydney Shoemaker, Self-Knowledge and Self-Identity (1963). Note that Tooley's position eliminates the moral dilemma of abortion, but in so doing strongly implies that infanticide may also raise no serious moral issues. For discussions of the philosophical issues involving abortion, see, e.g., Daniel Callahan, Abortion: Law, Choice and Morality (1970); Judith Thompson, A Defense of Abortion, 1 Phil. & Pub. Affairs 47 (1971).

51. See Balkin, Judgment of the Court, in What Roe v. Wade Should Have Said, at 53-54; Comment, id. at 234-236.

Just as improvements in medical technology inevitably will move *forward* the point at which the State may regulate for reasons of maternal health, different technological improvements will move *backward* the point of viability at which the State may proscribe abortions except when necessary to preserve the life and health of the mother. . . .

[R]ecent studies have demonstrated increasingly earlier fetal viability. It is certainly reasonable to believe that fetal viability in the first trimester of pregnancy may be possible in the not too distant future. . . .

The *Roe* framework, then, is clearly on a collision course with itself. As the medical risks of various abortion procedures decrease, the point at which the State may regulate for reasons of maternal health is moved further forward to actual childbirth. As medical science becomes better able to provide for the separate existence of the fetus, the point of viability is moved further back toward conception. Moreover, it is clear that the trimester approach violates the fundamental aspiration of judicial decision making through the application of neutral principles "sufficiently absolute to give them roots throughout the community and continuity over significant periods of time. . . ." A. Cox, The Role of the Supreme Court in American Government 114 (1976).

Justice O'Connor also argued that the Court's articulation of the State's interest was ad hoc:

> The State interest in potential human life is . . . extant throughout pregnancy. In *Roe,* the Court held that although the State had an important and legitimate interest in protecting potential life, that interest could not become compelling until the point at which the fetus was viable. The difficulty with this analysis is clear: *potential* life is no less potential in the first weeks of pregnancy than it is at viability or afterward. At any stage of pregnancy, there is the *potential* for human life. Although the Court refused to "resolve the difficult question of when life begins," the Court chose the point of viability — when the fetus is *capable* of life independent of its mother — to permit the complete proscription of abortion. The choice of viability as the point at which the State interest in *potential* life becomes compelling is no less arbitrary than choosing any point before viability or any point afterward. Accordingly, I believe that the State's interest in protecting potential human life exists throughout the pregnancy.

If you combine these two objections — the incoherence of the trimester framework with the compelling interest in the preservation of potential life from the moment of pregnancy — is there anything left of the abortion right? Based on this analysis, many people speculated that Justice O'Connor would join an opinion to overturn *Roe* as soon as four other votes appeared. However, in *Akron* itself, O'Connor argued only that the right to abortion should be judged by a lesser standard than strict scrutiny. Abortion regulations, she argued, should be upheld unless they were "unduly burdensome" or created an "undue burden" on the right.

When the chance finally came in Webster v. Reproductive Health Services, 492 U.S. 490 (1989), O'Connor declined to vote to overturn *Roe,* much to the chagrin of Justice Scalia, who eagerly sought reversal of the decision. Three years later, she finally announced her support for *Roe* in Planned Parenthood of Southeastern Pennsylvania v. Casey, 505 U.S. 833 (1992), discussed infra, which adopted a version of her "undue burden" test.

Note: Was Roe a Political Mistake?

In 1985, (then) Judge Ruth Bader Ginsburg suggested that the Court's decision in *Roe* was unfortunate for the cause of abortion rights. Ruth Bader Ginsburg, Some Thoughts on Autonomy and Equality in Relation to Roe v. Wade, 63 N.C. L. Rev. 375, 376, 381-382 (1985). Contrasting the gender discrimination decisions (many of which she argued before the Supreme Court) with *Roe,* Judge Ginsberg noted:

> The Court's gender classification decisions overturning state and federal legislation, in the main, have not provoked large controversy; . . . Roe v. Wade on the other hand, became and remains a storm center. Roe v. Wade sparked public opposition and academic criticism, in part, I believe, because the Court ventured too far in the change it ordered and presented an incomplete justification for its action. . . .
>
> The sweep and detail of the opinion stimulated the mobilization of a right-to-life movement and an attendant reaction in Congress and state legislatures. In place of the trend "toward liberalization of abortion statutes" noted in *Roe,* legislatures adopted measures aimed at minimizing the impact of the 1973 rulings, including notification and consent requirements, prescriptions for the protection of fetal life, and bans on public expenditures for poor women's abortions.

Ginsburg also criticized the medical focus of the opinion and the trimester formula, arguing that the Court should have limited itself to the question whether complete criminalization of abortion was consistent with the Due Process Clause.

> If *Roe* had left off at that point and not adopted . . . a "medical approach," physicians might have been less pleased with the decision, but the legislative trend might have continued in the direction in which it was headed in the early 1970s. . . . Academic criticism of *Roe,* charging the Court with reading its own values into the due process clause, might have been less pointed had the Court placed the woman alone, rather than the woman tied to her physician, at the center of its attention.

Ginsburg linked "abortion prohibitions with discrimination against women," suggesting that *Roe*'s medicalized account of the abortion right was incomplete:

> It is not a sufficient answer to charge it all to women's anatomy — a natural, not man-made, phenomenon. Society, not anatomy, "places a greater stigma on unmarried women who become pregnant than on the men who father their children." Society expects, but nature does not command, that "women take the major responsibility . . . for child care" and that they will stay with their children, bearing nurture and support burdens alone, when fathers deny paternity or otherwise refuse to provide care or financial support for unwanted offspring.

Nevertheless, Ginsburg added:

> I do not pretend that, if the Court had added a distinct sex discrimination theme to its medically oriented opinion, the storm *Roe* generated would have been less furious.

Speaking seven years later, shortly before she was nominated to the Supreme Court, Judge Ginsburg added:

> [T]he Justices generally follow, they do not lead, changes taking place elsewhere in society. But without taking giant strides and thereby risking a backlash too forceful to

contain, the Court, through constitutional adjudication, can reinforce or signal a green light for a social change. In most of the post-1970 gender-classification cases, unlike *Roe,* the Court functioned in just that way. It approved the direction of change through a temperate brand of decisionmaking, one that was not extravagant or divisive. *Roe,* on the other hand, halted a political process that was moving in a reform direction and thereby, I believe, prolonged divisiveness and deferred stable settlement of the issue.[52]

Justice Ginsburg's assumptions about the general trend of abortion liberalization before 1973 have been sharply criticized. David Garrow points out that the key triggering event in the creation of a significant right-to-life movement was not the Court's decision in *Roe* but the passage of legislation legalizing abortion in New York State in 1970:[53]

> Prior to the 1970 victory in New York, pro-choice forces had encountered surprisingly little well-organized or outspokenly vocal opposition. The Roman Catholic Church's hierarchy had been relatively inactive on the issue prior to 1970, but the legalization of abortion in New York led to a very rapid mobilization of right-to-life opposition.

Garrow notes that the "fictionalized but nonetheless widely-accepted version of history" is that *Roe* mobilized pro-life forces and that without *Roe* "there supposedly would have been extensive but more gradual abortion law liberalization stemming from less shrill debates in countless state legislatures" This view, he contends, "is simply and utterly wrong":

> Not only did the New York legalization energize right to life forces, [it] helped stimulate a very politically influential right to life upsurge all across the country, in state after state after state, throughout 1971 and 1972. During 1971 and 1972, pro-choice forces won no political victories, and New York activists were worried as to whether they could continue to protect their statute from legislative repeal. . . . In the two states that held 1972 popular vote referenda on abortion, pro-choice measures went down to heavy defeats, and in many others, legislators took the position that they could let the courts resolve the problem, that they did not need to go out on any political limbs by confronting the issue themselves. Thus, by November 1972, when Richard Nixon was overwhelmingly re-elected to the presidency after mounting a very explicitly anti-abortion general election campaign, prospects for making any sort of non-judicial headway with abortion law liberalization looked very bleak indeed. Pro-choice activists feared that more setbacks might be ahead.

Discussion

1. Even if Garrow is correct about the emergence of the right-to-life movement before *Roe,* would he necessarily deny that *Roe* further energized the right-to-life movement, gave it a highly visible national symbol on which to focus its energies, and allowed opposition to abortion rights to be combined with the rhetoric of majority rule and with the long rhetorical tradition of resistance to judicial oversight and judicial elitism?

52. Ruth Bader Ginsburg, Speaking in a Judicial Voice, 67 N.Y.U. L. Rev. 1185, 1208 (1992). For a more extensive version of the claim that *Roe* blunted liberalization of abortion laws, see Mary Ann Glendon, Abortion and Divorce in Western Law 42-46 (1987).

53. David J. Garrow, Abortion Before and After Roe v. Wade: An Historical Perspective, 62 Alb. L. Rev. 833, 836-837, 840-841 (1999).

Does Justice Ginsburg think that characterizing *Roe* as an equality right for women would have significantly blunted the right-to-life movement or opposition to abortion reform? If *Roe* had been grounded in equality principles, wouldn't opponents of abortion have understood it as yet another instance of "radical feminism" that would tend to undermine families?

Consider the fact that the abortion issue strongly shaped the modern Republican and Democratic Parties, facilitated the emergence of conservative Christians as a force to be reckoned with in American politics, and helped Ronald Reagan gain the Presidency and many other pro-life candidates gain political office. Would these effects have been amplified or dampened without *Roe*? Should *any* of this matter to constitutional interpretation?

2. Both the title of Justice Ginsburg's 1992 article (Speaking in a Judicial Voice), and her arguments in that article suggest that she believes that the political effects of Court decisions on legislative reform are appropriate considerations for judges who interpret the Constitution. Do you agree? Would it be permissible for a judge to state such considerations openly in an opinion?

3. *The Court as a scapegoat and a backstop.* Courts affect the political process in ways other than by energizing opposition. Consider that *Roe* allowed conservative politicians to take much stronger pro-life stands than they otherwise might have taken, on the grounds that they knew that the federal courts would surely strike down the most extreme measures. Conversely, *Roe* undermined the ability of pro-choice politicians to fight against restrictions on abortion in the legislative arena because *Roe* gave moderates a "free vote" with respect to certain legislation.

Conversely, as Republican Presidents increasingly stocked the judiciary with conservative and pro-life appointments, the possibility of overturning or drastically undercutting *Roe* became increasingly likely. As a result, some politicians tried to moderate their positions in opposition to abortion or avoid the subject altogether so as to appeal to a wider base of supporters.

More liberal or pro-choice politicians, on the other hand, could use the increased danger of restrictions on abortion to attract moderate voters, particularly moderate women. This suggests that the Supreme Court plays a key political function not merely as a guarantor of rights but as an effective political foil or political backstop for politicians of different ideological views. (Compare this with the slavery issue in the nineteenth century.)[54] If the Court is used in this way by politicians of both parties, does this tell you anything about what the Court should have done in the abortion area?

B. Abortion and the Equal Protection Clause

Roe is based on a fundamental rights analysis under the Due Process Clause, not the Equal Protection Clause. Because abortion rights so clearly affect women, why didn't the Court approach the question in equality terms?

One reason, as noted previously, is that for many years the major proponents of abortion reform were the medical profession and groups like Planned Parenthood.

---

54. For a number of historical examples of how politicians play off of judicial review of controversial legislation, see Mark A. Graber, The Non-Majoritarian Difficulty: Legislative Deference to the Judiciary, 7 Stud. Am. Pol. Dev. 35, 5361 (1993).

When the second wave of feminism emerged in the early 1960s, it was slow to coalesce around a pro-choice position. As Kristin Luker explains, the position that abortion was a woman's issue or a woman's right is largely a product of the period after 1967.[55] Indeed, until Betty Friedan argued for repeal of restrictive abortion laws at the second annual convention of the National Organization of Women in 1967, the organization had never officially spoken on the issue. Friedan obtained an official endorsement, "but only at the cost of profoundly alienating a significant number of members who, while not necessarily antiabortion, did not believe that the issue had to be addressed by a women's rights organization."[56]

Nevertheless, by the late 1960s, a number of feminist advocates asserted reproductive rights claims as equal rights claims. In this era, the women's movement argued that the social organization of family roles excluded women from participating in education, market, and politics — key sites of citizenship. As Chapter 7 recounts, in 1970, on the half-century anniversary of the Nineteenth Amendment's ratification, the movement held a Strike for Equality that sought reform of the conditions in which women bore and raised children. In addition to the ratification of the Equal Rights Amendment (ERA), strike demands included equal education and employment opportunity, abortion rights, and 24-hour child care.

Indeed, before *Roe,* feminists seeking abortion rights spoke in language of both liberty and equality. Feminist litigators challenged discrimination against pregnant women as a violation of equal protection, and some even drew on equality concepts to amplify *Griswold*-based challenges to abortion restrictions (see Chapter 7, supra). But abortion supporters tended to separate abortion rights and the ERA, suggesting that the Amendment might exempt physical characteristics unique to one sex. The Court soon embraced this analytical framework as a basis for limiting the Equal Protection Clause's significance in cases of pregnancy and abortion.

That brings us to the second reason why courts did not embrace sex equality arguments for abortion: the path of doctrinal evolution in the years following *Roe.* In Chapter 7 we noted the effect of Geduldig v. Aiello, 417 U.S. 484 (1974), and Personnel Administrator of Massachusetts v. Feeney, 442 U.S. 256 (1979), in undermining equal protection arguments for abortion rights. *Geduldig* holds that classifications based on pregnancy are not classifications based on sex. *Feeney* holds that non-sex-based classifications that have a disparate impact on women do not violate equal protection unless one can demonstrate that the decisionmaker acted because of, rather than in spite of, a desire to harm women. Together, *Geduldig* and *Feeney* undercut the most obvious ways of arguing that abortion regulations are sex-based classifications that work to the disadvantage of women.

Nevertheless, following *Roe* many scholars have repeatedly suggested that the question of abortion rights is fundamentally an issue of sexual equality and therefore might more appropriately be analyzed under equal protection doctrine.[57] By casting

55. Kristin Luker, Abortion and the Politics of Motherhood 92 (1984).

56. David J. Garrow, Liberty and Sexuality, at 343.

57. See, e.g., Kenneth Karst, Foreword: Equal Citizenship Under the Fourteenth Amendment, 91 Harv. L. Rev. 1 (1977). Professor Tribe has also recognized the equality implications of Roe: "To give society — especially a male-dominated society — the power to sentence women to childbearing against their will is to delegate to some a sweeping and unaccountable authority over the lives of others. Any such allocation of power operates to the serious detriment of women as a class . . . [and] burden[s] the participation of women as equals in society." Tribe, American Constitutional Law 1354 (2d ed. 1988). See also Jed Rubenfeld, The Right of Privacy, 102 Harv. L. Rev. 737, 782 (1989); Guido Calabresi, The Supreme Court, 1990 Term, Foreword: Antidiscrimination and Constitutional Accountability (What the Bork-Brennan Debate Ignores), 105 Harv. L. Rev. 80, 103-108 (1991); Cass R. Sunstein, The Partial Constitution 270-285 (1993).

the issue in essentially gender-neutral terms, the Court, in this view, suppresses the extent to which abortion regulations disadvantage women in society. Professor Sylvia Law writes:

> The rhetoric of privacy, as opposed to equality, blunts our ability to focus on the fact that it is *women* who are oppressed when abortion is denied. A privacy right that demands that "the abortion decision . . . be left to the medical judgment of the pregnant woman's physician," gives doctors undue power by falsely casting the abortion decision as primarily a medical question. The rhetoric of privacy also reinforces a public/private dichotomy that is at the heart of the structures that perpetuate the powerlessness of women.[58]

The equal protection argument for abortion rights is often combined with one of the antisubordination approaches we discussed in Chapters 6 and 7.[59] (These approaches, of course, have also been particularly critical of cases like *Geduldig* and *Feeney*.)[60]

The following excerpt, written by a constitutional scholar who is also a historian of abortion regulation, argues that equal protection analysis must be based on the social and historical context in which abortion regulations occur.

REVA SIEGEL, REASONING FROM THE BODY: A HISTORICAL PERSPECTIVE ON ABORTION REGULATION AND QUESTIONS OF EQUAL PROTECTION
44 Stan. L. Rev. 261, 276-77, 350, 371-79 (1992)

Because *Roe* analyzes an exercise of state power from a medical, rather than a social, point of view, it authorizes state action against the pregnant woman on the basis of physiological criteria, requiring no inquiry into the state's reasons for acting against the pregnant woman, or the impact of its actions on her. Indeed, *Roe* analyzes the state's interest in potential life as a benign exercise of state power for the protection of the unborn, and not as a coercive exercise of state power against pregnant women, often reasoning as if the state's interest in protecting potential life scarcely pertained to the pregnant woman herself.

Abortion-restrictive regulation is sex-based regulation, the use of public power to force women to bear children. Yet, the Court has never described the state's interest in protecting potential life as an interest in forcing women to bear children. *Roe*'s physiological reasoning obscures that simple social fact. "[I]f one accepts the medical definitions of the developing young in the human uterus" as a sufficient, objective, and authoritative framework for evaluating the state's regulatory interest in abortion — as *Roe* did — state action compelling women to perform

---

58. Sylvia A. Law, Rethinking Sex and the Constitution, 132 U. Pa. L. Rev. 955, 1020 (1984) (quoting Roe v. Wade).

59. See, e.g., Catharine A. MacKinnon, Toward a Feminist Theory of the State 189-194 (1989); Catharine A. MacKinnon, Reflections on Sex Equality Under the Law, 100 Yale L.J. 1281, 1308-1327 (1991).

60. See What Roe v. Wade Should Have Said, supra, containing alternative opinions in Roe v. Wade by Jack Balkin, Reva Siegel, and Robin West which argue for protecting abortion as an equality right.

the work of motherhood can be justified without ever acknowledging that the state is enforcing a gender status role. In part, this is because analyzing abortion-restrictive regulation within physiological paradigms obscures its social logic, but also, and as importantly, it is because physiological reasons for regulating women's conduct are already laden with socio-political import: Facts about women's bodies have long served to justify regulation enforcing judgments about women's roles. . . .

Abortion-restrictive regulation is state action compelling pregnancy and motherhood, and this simple fact cannot be evaded by invoking nature or a woman's choices to explain the situation in which the pregnant woman subject to abortion restrictions finds herself. A pregnant woman seeking an abortion has the practical capacity to terminate a pregnancy, which she would exercise but for the community's decision to prevent or deter her. If the community successfully effectuates its will, it is the state, and not nature, which is responsible for causing her to continue the pregnancy. . . .

Hypothetically, a woman compelled to bear a child she does not want could give it up for adoption, abandon it, or pay someone to care for the child until maturity. In this society, however, these are not options that women avail themselves of with great frequency for the simple reason that few women are able to abandon a child born of their body. [A woman] is likely to experience intense familial and social pressure to raise a child she has borne. The pressure . . . will intensify dramatically if [women] are married and/or have other children, as current adoption placements illustrate. [W]hile discussions of abortion-restrictive regulation often assume that women who are forced to bear children can simply abandon them at will, the premise is wholly at odds with the norms of the society that would compel women to bear children. . . . Legislatures that enact restrictions on abortion understand this. They both desire and expect that most women will raise the child they are forced to bear, and in the vast majority of cases, women will.

Of course, a state can deny responsibility for imposing motherhood on women simply by emphasizing that the pregnant woman has chosen to raise the child that the state forced her to bear. Arguments about women's choices offer a familiar way to rationalize state action enforcing gender status roles. But, if one considers the powerful norms governing women's choices about whether to raise their children, it is clear that such formalistic arguments do not relieve the state of responsibility for dictating the pregnant woman's social fate.

[N]otwithstanding changing norms of family life, it remains the case that it is women who perform the vast majority of the labor necessary to make infants into adults. Mothers are expected to subordinate their personal interests to children in a way that men are not; most women give themselves over to the nurturance of life in a way that men do not — and face stigmatization, unlike men, if they will not. Consequently, a woman's identity, relations, and prospects are defined by becoming a parent in a way that a man's are not.

While this society celebrates the work of childcare, it continues to view the work of raising children as "women's work." Childcare remains status work, organized and valued in ways that limit the life prospects of those who perform it. Most prominently, childcare is uncompensated labor, traditionally performed under conditions of economic dependency; consequently, it remains a form of undercompensated labor for those who are paid to assist in the work. It is not merely the uncompensated character of childcare that betrays its peculiar social valuation. Those who devote their personal energies to raising children are likely to find their freedom to participate in so-called public sphere activities impaired for years on end, for the evident reason that most activities in the realms of education, employment, and politics are defined and structured as incommensurate with that work. Thus, a woman who becomes a parent will likely find that the energy she invests in childrearing will compromise her already constrained opportunities and impair her already unequal compensation in the work force — all the more so if she raises the child alone, whether by choice, divorce, or abandonment. Considered in cold dollar terms, it is the institution of motherhood that gives a gendered structure to the economics of family life, and a gendered face to poverty in the nation's life. . . . [W]hen the state enacts restrictions on abortion, it coerces women to perform the work of motherhood without altering the conditions that continue to make such work a principal cause of their secondary social status.

[S]tate action compelling motherhood injures women in predictable ways. Both the work of childbearing and the work of childrearing compromise women's opportunities in education and employment; neither the work of childbearing nor the work of childrearing produces any material compensation for women; most often the work of childbearing and the work of childrearing entangle women in relations of emotional and economic dependency — to men, extended family, or the state. None of these consequences is inherent in the physiology of reproduction; all are socially produced, reflecting communal designation of the work of mothering as "women's work." There is no other form of socially essential labor in this society similarly organized or valued: The more effort a woman personally invests in it, the more time she devotes to it, the more inexorably economically dependent she becomes. From this perspective, it is apparent that compelled pregnancy will injure women in context-dependent ways. It may be endured by women who have ordered their lives in conformity with traditional norms of motherhood, but it will profoundly threaten the material and psychic welfare of any woman whose life deviates from this traditional norm, whether by choice or socio-economic circumstance. When the state deprives women of choice in matters of motherhood, it deprives women of the ability to lead their lives with some rudimentary control over the sex-role constraints this society imposes on those who bear and rear children. It makes the social reality of women's lives more nearly conform with social stereotypes of women's lives. Considered from this perspective, choice in matters of motherhood implicates constitutional values of equality and liberty both.

Restrictions on abortion thus offend constitutional guarantees of equal protection, not simply because of the status-based injuries they inflict on women, but also because of the status-based attitudes about women they reflect. For centuries, this society has defined women as mothers and defined the work of motherhood as women's work. These are the assumptions which make it "reasonable" to force women to become mothers. Absent these deep-rooted assumptions about women, it is impossible to explain why this society insists that restrictions on abortion are intended to protect the unborn, and yet has never even considered taking action that would alleviate the burdens forced motherhood imposes on women.

Restrictions on abortion reflect the kind of bias that is at the root of the most invidious forms of stereotyping: a failure to consider, in a society always at risk of forgetting, that women are persons, too. It is a bias that manifests itself in this society's unreflective expectation that women should assume the burdens of bearing and rearing future generations, its tendency to denigrate the work of motherhood, and its readiness to castigate women who seek to avoid maternity as lacking in humanity, proof of which consists in a woman's failure perfectly to subordinate her energies, resources, and prospects to the task of making life — to a degree that men, employers, and the community as a whole most often will not.

Discussion

1. *Abortion regulation as status enforcing state action.* Siegel argues that restrictions on abortion are based on and tend to reinforce traditional notions about women's subordinate status in society and women's traditional obligations to have children and raise them without compensation. Siegel's concern is a combination of social meanings about motherhood that are systematically linked to economic disadvantage for women. What role does liberty play in her story? If a legislature combined abortion restrictions with a general scheme of compensation to mothers, free child care, and a comprehensive system of family leave provisions designed to reduce the economic costs of motherhood to women, would this be constitutional under Siegel's account?

2. *Giving practical effect to the anti-subordination principle.* Siegel's account focuses on the subordination of women through abortion regulation. She argues that abortion-restrictive regulation is gender-biased in impetus and impact. Under Siegel's account, what, if any, kinds of abortion restrictions would be permissible? At what point, and under what circumstances, would the state be able to claim that its interest in preserving unborn life would justify the additional coercive pressure on women to bear children? Could the state ban abortions in the third trimester? Would health measures that were asserted to be in the mother's interest be constitutional?

Is the anti-subordination approach Siegel (and other anti-subordination scholars) recommend inherently ad hoc in its judgments of particular statutory schemes? Is the Court's existing fundamental rights approach any more clear cut?

3. *Physiological naturalism.* Siegel criticizes the *Roe* decision for focusing exclusively on the woman's body and the developmental status of the fetus. She argues that talking in terms of fetal development and phrasing all constitutional analysis in morphological terms makes the social and economic consequences of motherhood invisible. Can you think of other examples of constitutional doctrines or arguments in which courts talk about a problem in terms that effectively disguise its social consequences? Note, moreover, that Siegel's argument is not merely a criticism of abortion restrictions, but of the expectations society has about motherhood generally and the ways that these subordinate women. How might the opinion in *Roe* have been written to take these issues into account?

4. Geduldig *and* Feeney *(again).* To what extent does Siegel's argument depend on overruling *Geduldig*? On the other hand, would government compensation programs designed to relieve some of the burdens of motherhood that Siegel describes be constitutionally permissible if *Geduldig* were overruled? (The answer to this second question depends in part on whether the Equal Protection Clause concerns classification or subordination, doesn't it?) Siegel argues that the state interest in protecting potential life is effectively a state interest in forcing women to become mothers. Could the state respond that this is an *effect* of abortion regulation because of the fact that the fetus is lodged inside the mother's body, but that it is not the *purpose* of the regulation, citing *Feeney*? Is viewing the fetus separate from the mother (and separate from effects on the mother) constitutionally permissible?

To what extent can the state respond that the fetal presence inside the mother is due to some action to which the mother has consented or for which she is responsible? Do either of these replies to Siegel's argument rely on judgments about women forbidden by the Equal Protection Clause?

5. *Abortion and consent.* One central question raised by Siegel's argument is what it means for women to consent to raising a child. The series of cases from *Skinner* to *Griswold* to *Roe* all presume that the right to choose whether to bear or beget a child is constitutionally protected. Siegel, however, argues that women's "consent" is necessarily constructed and hemmed in by societal attitudes about the duties and obligations of motherhood and by economic structures. Does this suggest that even if abortion were unregulated that women would not have a completely free choice in the matter, since deregulation of abortion would not, by itself, alter those social norms or economic conditions? Does the same argument apply to women's choice to use contraceptives in *Griswold* and *Eisenstadt?* How free a choice does the Constitution guarantee women?

Note, moreover, that if Siegel is correct, the very notion of choice is not really separable from women's social construction by gender norms. That is, women's sense of who they are, what they want, and what they should do is partly constructed by the very gender norms and social forces that constrain them. How should courts make sense of the principle of "free choice" for women under these conditions?

6. *Abortion regulation as involuntary servitude.* Recall Susan B. Anthony's argument in Chapter 4 raising a Thirteenth Amendment objection to coverture rules and to women's uncompensated labor in the home. Does Siegel's argument suggest a Thirteenth Amendment as well as a Fourteenth Amendment objection to abortion restrictions? See Andrew Koppelman, Forced Labor: A Thirteenth Amendment Defense of Abortion, 84 Nw. U. L. Rev. 480, 486 (1990): "If citizens may not be forced to surrender control of their persons and services, then women's persons may not be invaded and their services may not be coerced for the benefit of fetuses." Do you agree? If Koppelman is correct, should women who choose to have children have any cause of action against the government for child care expenses or costs of raising the child, or does the fact that a woman chooses to keep the child mean that she consents to all of these expenses?

7. *The history of abortion regulation.* Many state statutes restricting abortion date from the nineteenth century. At common law abortion prior to "quickening" of the fetus — the point at which a pregnant woman could perceive fetal movement, typically late in the fourth month or early in the fifth month of gestation — was not considered a crime or necessarily immoral. The new prohibitions arose from two different campaigns, one an anti-vice crusade against all forms of (and discussion of) contraception, and the second a crusade by the medical profession against abortion.[61] Like feminism itself, abortion was generally viewed by the medical profession

---

61. On the history of the nineteenth century campaigns against abortion, see Siegel, supra; Linda Gordon, Woman's Body, Woman's Right: A Social History of Birth Control in America (1976); Kristin Luker, Abortion and the Politics of Motherhood (1984); James C. Mohr, Abortion in America: The Origins and Evolution of National Policy, 1800-1900 (1978); Carroll Smith-Rosenberg, Disorderly Conduct: Visions of Gender in Victorian America 217-244 (1985).

as "a threat to social order and male authority."[62] Restricting abortions, doctors argued, "was necessary not only to protect the unborn, but also to ensure that women performed their obligations as wives and mothers and to preserve the ethnic character of the nation."[63] Protestant doctors feared that allowing abortions would result in Catholic immigrants producing more children.

The medical arguments against abortion were phrased in physiological terms as statements about women's bodies. Doctors opposed to abortion argued that the embryo was a separate form of human life from the moment of conception, wholly distinct from the woman's body, and that quickening was an irrelevant event. Women, in this view, were merely the passive instrumentalities of nature's inherent purposes. Second, doctors argued that the purpose of marital sexuality was procreation and that attempts to prevent procreation were physiologically inappropriate and unhealthy for women's bodies, or, in the words of one prominent advocate, a "physiological sin." Finally, the doctors' campaign argued that wives who shirked their natural duty of bearing and rearing children were selfish and self-indulgent, neglecting their natural material duty. Doctors argued that women wanted abortions simply to avoid the inconvenience of pregnancy, the labor and expense of raising children, and interference with their pleasure, their pursuit of fashion, and other trivial feminine pursuits.

Although the doctors' campaign often associated demands for abortion with the woman's rights movement, the feminist movement during this period did not strongly support abortion rights, and, indeed, most feminists actively opposed abortion. Feminists feared that contraception would make it easier for men to force sex on their wives, and would encourage extramarital sex. The feminist concern with "voluntary motherhood" during this period was less a concern with abortion rights and more a concern with the right not to be forced into sexual relations by their husbands, have children against their will, or be enslaved by economic dependency on their husbands. Rather than blaming women's selfishness for abortion, as the medical profession did, feminists explained (and sometimes even condoned) abortion as something women were driven to by marital rape or the pressures of motherhood.[64] What relevance, if any, should this history have in assessing the due process or equal protection claims for abortion rights? Recall the discussion of tradition in Michael H. v. Gerald D. There is a common law tradition of protecting abortion prior to the middle of the nineteenth century, but it is not a continuous

---

62. Smith-Rosenberg, at 235-236 (1985).

63. Siegel, at 262.

64. The stark differences between the two groups' attitudes toward abortion is summed up in their contrasting uses of the term "legalized prostitution":

> Woman's rights advocates insisted that marriage was no better than legalized prostitution if a wife's consent to marital sex was inferred from the marital contract itself, or if marital sex was treated as a reciprocal obligation flowing from the fact of marital support. By contrast, doctors argued that marriage was a relation of legalized prostitution so long as man's natural sexual urge was allowed expression in marriage without reproductive consequence. Thus, while feminists used the critique of marriage as "legalized prostitution" to argue that wives should control decisions respecting reproduction, physicians used the same metaphor to justify depriving women of control over decisions respecting reproduction. In feminist usage, the critique of marriage as "legalized prostitution" identified a range of social reasons why a wife would seek to avoid maternity; in medical usage, the critique of marriage as "legalized prostitution" condemned the very aspiration to avoid maternity as an expression of unnatural egoism or immoral license.

Siegel, at 309-310.

tradition to the present. One might argue that if there is something deeply rooted in our nation's traditions, it is the tradition of using expectations about gender and marriage to force women to become mothers against their will, and justifying this policy through discourses about women's natural proclivities or obligations. Is this a tradition worthy of constitutional protection?

Much of the history of abortion regulation in the nineteenth century seems grounded in stereotypes and judgments that would be considered constitutionally impermissible today under the Equal Protection Clause. Does this history undermine present justifications for restrictions on abortion? Consider the following "geneaological argument": Current opposition to abortion is descended from impermissible premises about women and motherhood in the nineteenth century, just as the anti-miscegenation statute in Loving v. Virginia was descended from impermissible views about Whites and Blacks. Have you seen this sort of argument before? (Recall, e.g., Justice Ginsburg's opinion in the VMI case.) What more would be required to create a successful version of such a genealogical argument? What evidence would be necessary to rebut such an argument?

8. *Pro-choice and pro-life women.* If anti-subordination theorists are correct that restrictions on abortion perpetuate the inferior status of women, what explains the large number of women who are pro-life? In her study of pro-choice and pro-life women activists in California, sociologist Kristin Luker argued that differences over abortion are tied to differences in social class and economic opportunity, and from the different conceptions of motherhood that tend to flow from those different positions. "While on the surface it is the embryo's fate that seems to be at stake, the abortion debate is actually about the meaning of women's lives." Kristin Luker, Abortion and the Politics of Motherhood 194 (1984). Luker reports that pro-life activists are more likely to be invested heavily in "traditional" views of women's roles as wives and mothers, whereas pro-choice activists tend to be more career-oriented. Pro-life activists were more likely to come from working-class backgrounds, were less likely to work outside the home, and earned less when they did, whereas pro-choice activists were more likely to come from the middle class and work outside the home.

Luker reports that both pro-choice and pro-life activists understood that society generally devalues women and women's work but each group had different reactions to it. Pro-choice women were more likely to see abortion rights as necessary to free themselves from unwanted dependence on men. Pro-life women, who were more likely to find themselves in positions of economic dependence on men, believed that abortion helped to devalue motherhood even further and undermined the social controls that the responsibilities of family life placed on male sexual aggression. In her study of Fargo, North Dakota pro-life and pro-choice activists, Faye Ginsburg found that pro-life activists tended to identify more with the values of "domesticity," while pro-choice activists tended to see women as autonomous agents with an interest in pursuing self-development through careers as well as families. Faye D. Ginsburg, Contested Lives: The Abortion Debate in an American Community, 139-145, 169-170, 194-197 (1989).

Even so, Ginsburg reports that pro-life activists were not necessarily acquiescing in or working to support male domination or male privilege. Rather, they were trying to preserve delicate social relationships that value women and motherhood by promoting "traditionally" feminine values of nurturance and acceptance of responsibility for sexuality and motherhood. Restrictions on abortion tend to forge closer links between sex, pregnancy, and marriage and hence help preserve the dignity and security of women who have chosen traditional lives of nurturance and care of children. The very possibility of unplanned pregnancies and the obligations of parenthood that come with them may strongly shape women's lives, but they also help to constrain men's sexual aggressiveness toward women. Easy access to abortion increases men's tendencies to disassociate sex from marriage, pregnancy, and parenthood, and view women as sexual objects. It also weakens the social pressures on men to take emotional and financial responsibility for their sexual activities. Abortion rights, in short, help men exploit women more easily.

Finally, the pro-life women that Ginsburg interviewed felt that access to abortion made both men and women prone to a "heartless individualism." Abortion encourages women to end a fetus's life based on a cold calculation of costs and benefits to her. It thus devalues motherhood and nurturance by allowing women to sacrifice the fetus on behalf of their personal and financial ambition. Thus, abortion is part of a growing trend that sacrifices human values and human connection to the values of the marketplace. Because the availability of abortion encourages women to believe that they, like men, can separate ambition and sexual desire from procreation and caregiving, it denies "two essential conditions of female gender identity: pregnancy and the obligations of nurturance that should follow."[65] Do these studies support or undermine the argument that restrictions on abortion are linked to the subordination of women and the devaluing of motherhood, women, and women's work? Do they support or undermine the use of judicial review under the Equal Protection Clause? To what extent might pro-choice and pro-life women agree in their critiques of male sexuality or market individualism?[66] Compare this debate to the disagreement between African-Americans who support race-conscious affirmative action and the significant minority (symbolized by Justice Clarence Thomas) who oppose it. To what extent does this dispute within the African-American community bear on the appropriate interpretation of the Equal Protection Clause?

Should it matter to the anti-subordination analysis that many men might be in favor of abortion rights because it helps them avoid responsibility for their sexuality? Consider Mary Ann Glendon's remark that "It does not take Sherlock Holmes . . . to discern why the strongest supporters of elective abortion are young men."[67]

---

65. Ginsburg, at 215-216.
66. Compare Catharine MacKinnon's comments:

> In feminist terms, [*Roe*] translates the ideology of the private sphere into the individual woman's legal right to privacy as a means of subordinating women's collective needs to the imperatives of male supremacy. . . . [U]nder conditions of gender inequality, [*Roe*] does not free women, it frees male sexual aggression. The availability of abortion . . . removes the one remaining legitimized reason that women have had for refusing sex besides the headache.

Catharine A. MacKinnon, Roe v. Wade: A Study in Male Ideology, in Abortion: Moral and Legal Perspectives 45, 49-51 (Jay L. Garfield & Patricia Hennessey eds., 1984). Note, however, that MacKinnon's argument is that *Roe* does not go far enough in producing the radical changes in society that are necessary to guarantee true freedom and equality for women; it is not an argument that procreative freedom should be limited in the interests of women.

67. Mary Ann Glendon, Intra-Tribal Warfare, First Things 55, 57 (Aug.-Sept. 1990). See also Michael W. McConnell, How Not to Promote Serious Deliberation About Abortion, 58 U. Chi. L. Rev. 1181, 1190-1193 (1991).

What, if anything, follows from this fact? Does it suggest, for example, that restricting abortion rights is the best way to combat male subordination of women?

C. Decisions After *Roe*

Roe has proved one of the most controversial and bitterly contested Supreme Court decisions of this century. A series of fragmented decisions sometimes expanded *Roe*'s holding, while at other times allowing state regulation of at least certain aspects of the abortion decision. As is true of many subject areas raised throughout this casebook, we make no pretense of offering a full overview of this extremely complex topic.

We thus mention only some representative decisions before turning to the most extensive reconsideration of *Roe* in the 1992 *Casey* case.

1. *State funding and use of state facilities.* The Court decided a series of cases holding that states had no duty to fund abortions even if they funded childbirth, Maher v. Roe, 432 U.S. 464 (1977), Harris v. McRae, 448 U.S. 297 (1980); and that public hospitals had no duty to allow their facilities to be used for abortions. Webster v. Reproductive Health Services, 452 U.S. 450 (1989). These are considered in more detail in Chapter 9.

2. *"Informed consent" and mandatory reporting requirements.* In Thornburgh v. American College of Obstetricians and Gynecologists, 476 U.S. 747 (1986), the Court struck down a number of abortion regulations, including: (1) a requirement that a physician inform the patient of possible detrimental physical and psychological effects of abortion, medical assistance benefits for carrying the child to term, the father's liability for child support, and a list of agencies offering alternatives to abortion; (2) a requirement that literature be available describing the anatomical and physiological characteristics of the fetus at two-week gestational increments; (3) detailed reporting requirements; and (4) special postviability requirements, including the presence of a second physician. Justice Blackmun, writing for the Court, found that the "informed consent" requirements were "an outright attempt to wedge the Commonwealth's message discouraging abortion into the privacy of the . . . dialogue between the woman and her physician." He further found that the reporting requirements "raise the specter of public exposure and harassment of women who choose to exercise their personal, intensely private right, with their physician, to end a pregnancy," and concluded that "States are not free, under the guise of protecting maternal health or potential life, to intimidate women into continuing pregnancies."

3. *Spousal consent.* In Planned Parenthood of Central Missouri v. Danforth, 428 U.S. 52 (1976), the Court considered a Missouri requirement that a husband give "prior written consent" to the decision of his wife to seek an abortion during the first 12 weeks of pregnancy, unless the abortion is necessary to preserve the mother's life. The Court concluded that, "since the State cannot regulate or proscribe abortion during the first stage, . . . the State cannot delegate authority to any particular person, even the spouse, to prevent abortion during that same period." Justice Blackmun recognized "the deep and proper concern and interest that a devoted and protective husband has in his wife's pregnancy and in the growth and development of the fetus she is carrying," and thought that "ideally, the decision to terminate a pregnancy should be one concurred in by both the wife and her

husband." But he thought it unlikely that the marital relationship would be enhanced by giving the husband a veto power exercisable for any reason whatsoever or for no reason at all and concluded that "[i]nasmuch as it is the woman who physically bears the child and who is the more directly and immediately affected by the pregnancy, as between the two, the balance weighs in her favor." Dissenting on this issue, Justice White, joined by Chief Justice Burger and Justice Rehnquist, wrote:

> A father's interest in having a child — perhaps his only child — may be unmatched by any other interest in his life. . . . In describing the nature of a mother's interest in terminating a pregnancy, the Court in Roe v. Wade mentioned only the post-birth burdens of rearing a child, and rejected a rule based on her interest in controlling her own body during pregnancy. Missouri has a law which prevents a woman from putting a child up for adoption over her husband's objection. This law represents a judgment by the State that the mother's interest in avoiding the burdens of child rearing do not outweigh or snuff out the father's interest in participating in bringing up his own child. That law is plainly valid, but no more so than §3(3) of the Act now before us, resting as it does on precisely the same judgment.

4. *Parental consent.* In another portion of *Danforth,* the Court invalidated a Missouri statute prohibiting an unmarried woman under the age of 18 from obtaining an abortion without the written consent of a parent or person in loco parentis unless a licensed physician certified that the abortion was necessary to preserve the life of the mother. Subsequently, in Belotti v. Baird, 432 U.S. 622 (1979) (*Belotti II*), the Court struck down a Massachusetts statute prohibiting an unmarried minor from obtaining an abortion unless both parents consent or the minor obtains a court order "for good cause shown." Justice Powell argued that

> every minor must have the opportunity [to] go directly to a court without first consulting or notifying her parents. If she satisfies the court that she is mature and well enough informed to make intelligently the abortion decision on her own, the court must authorize her to act without parental consultation or consent. If she fails to satisfy the court that she is competent to make this decision independently, she must be permitted to show that an abortion nevertheless would be in her best interests.

Justice Powell added that a court may ask itself whether her best interests would be served by parental consultation, "[b]ut this is the full extent to which parental involvement may be required." The Court subsequently upheld a parental consent provision in Planned Parenthood Association of Kansas City v. Ashcroft, 462 U.S. 476 (1983), which contained an "alternative procedure" that was considered consistent with the test Justice Powell announced in *Bellotti II.* Justice O'Connor argued that the statute "imposes no undue burden on any right that a minor may have to undergo an abortion."

5. *Parental notification.* In Hodgson v. Minnesota, 457 U.S. 417 (1990), and Ohio v. Akron Center for Reproductive Health, 457 U.S. 502 (1990), the Court considered parental-notification requirements for a minor to gain access to an abortion. In *Hodgson,* the Court invalidated a provision of a Minnesota statute that prohibited performance of an abortion on a woman under the age of 18 unless 48 hours has elapsed since both parents were notified. The notification provision applied even if the minor's parents had never been married, were divorced, or were

otherwise not living with one another or the child. Justice Stevens, joined in part by Justices Brennan, Marshall, Blackmun, and O'Connor, held that the two-parent notification scheme by itself was unconstitutional. The Court emphasized trial testimony that parents of minors seeking abortions were often divorced or separated, and that requiring notice of both parents could provoke violence from family members, particularly fathers. The trial court also found that "many minors in Minnesota 'live in fear of violence by family members' and 'are, in fact, victims of rape, incest, neglect, and violence.'" At the same time, Justice O'Connor's opinion held that a two-parent notification rule would be constitutional if combined with a "judicial bypass procedure" — whereby a pregnant minor could obtain a court order for an abortion without notifying her parents. The Minnesota statute in *Hodgson* provided for a judicial bypass if the statute would otherwise be held unconstitutional. Because four other Justices (Kennedy, Rehnquist, White, and Scalia) believed that a two-parent notification provision was reasonable and therefore constitutional, the effect of O'Connor's position was that Minnesota's two-parent notification law was upheld with a judicial bypass.

Justice Marshall dissented from this holding. "[M]any women will carry the fetus to term rather than notify a parent. Other women may decide to inform a parent but then confront parental pressure or abuse so severe as to obstruct the abortion. For these women, the judge's refusal to authorize an abortion effectively constitutes an absolute veto." Justice Marshall noted that the trial court found that seeking a judicial order imposed "significant burdens on minors," including long delays, traveling long distances to obtain an order, absences from home and school, and "emotional trauma" for young women.

The *Akron* case involved a statute that prohibited any person from performing an abortion on an unmarried, unemancipated minor without giving notice to one parent at least 24 hours in advance. Notice would not be required if the minor obtained a court order approving the abortion, or if the minor and another relative filed an affidavit stating that the minor feared physical, sexual, or severe emotional abuse from the parent. Finally, the minor could also bypass notice by filing a complaint showing that notice was not in her best interest or that she had sufficient maturity and information to make an intelligent decision without notice, or that one of her parents had engaged in a pattern of physical, sexual, or emotional abuse. The Court upheld these provisions in an opinion by Justice Kennedy, which stated that whether or not bypass procedures were constitutionally required, the ones in this statute were adequate.

Together *Hodgson* and *Akron* created a complicated mass of contrasting positions among the Justices. In his opinion in *Hodgson*, Justice Scalia dissented "from this enterprise of devising an Abortion Code, and from the illusion that we have authority to do so." In her concurring opinion in *Hodgson*, Justice O'Connor agreed with the Court's statement that "[a] woman's decision to beget or to bear a child is a component of her liberty that is protected by the Due Process Clause of the Fourteenth Amendment to the Constitution." She also noted that, after *Roe*, minors could be treated differently from adults. She then restated her previously expressed view that "[i]f the particular regulation does not 'unduly burde[n]' the fundamental right, . . . then our evaluation of that regulation is limited to our determination that the regulation rationally relates to a legitimate state purpose." Applying this standard, she concluded that the Minnesota statute imposed an undue burden, by requiring, for example, a minor to notify even an abusive parent of her pregnancy.

6. *The constitutional politics of abortion.* Larger trends in American politics greatly affected the development of constitutional doctrine in all of these areas.[68] When *Roe* was first decided, the two major political parties were not strongly identified with the issue and Justices appointed by both Democrats and Republicans supported the decision and opposed it. In fact, in 1976, the Democratic candidate, Jimmy Carter, an evangelical Christian, was more pro-life than his opponent Gerald Ford. Nevertheless, *Roe* generated a political reaction that helped spur the development of new conservative social movements and helped precipitate an alliance between the New Right and conservative Christian groups. Ronald Reagan, who had almost won the Republican nomination in 1976, welcomed evangelical and fundamentalist Christian voters into the Republican Party and actively courted pro-life leaders. In the 1980 election, many evangelicals and fundamentalist Christians moved squarely into the Republican camp, and became an important part of the party's base of support. The Republican Party became primarily a pro-life party, with some moderates still favoring abortion rights, and the more liberal Democratic Party became largely pro-choice. In 1980 the Republican Party platform, for the first time, included a call for "a constitutional amendment to restore protection of the right to life for unborn children."[69]

Once in office Reagan set out to nominate judges who would roll back liberal judicial decisions and promote his favored constitutional values, which included opposition to abortion. (We have seen the effects of his appointment strategy in the area of federalism in Chapter 5.) Not entirely coincidentally, the 1984 Republican Party platform "applaud[ed] President Reagan's fine record of judicial appointments, and . . . reaffirm[ed] [the party's] support for the appointment of judges at all levels of the judiciary who respect traditional family values and the sanctity of innocent human life."[70] Reagan's first three Supreme Court appointments, Sandra Day O'Connor, William Rehnquist (elevated to Chief Justice to replace Warren Burger), and Antonin Scalia, were all critics of *Roe*. By the beginning of 1987, the Supreme Court was generally believed to have five strong supporters of *Roe* and four equally strong critics. When Justice Lewis Powell announced his retirement in January 1987, President Reagan nominated D.C. Circuit Judge Robert Bork, an outspoken opponent of *Roe*. Reagan seemed poised to accelerate the entrenchment of his constitutional principles in the Supreme Court and secure a crucial fifth vote to overturn *Roe v. Wade.*

The Bork nomination produced a national controversy, and ultimately the Senate failed to confirm him. Pro-choice groups, who had often relied heavily on the courts to protect abortion rights, mobilized to help defeat the nomination.[71] President Reagan had also lost some of his popularity and political power due to the Iran-Contra scandal. Perhaps most important, the Republican Party had lost control of the Senate in the midterm elections of 1986. Generally speaking, when the Senate and President are controlled by opposite parties, the President has less

---

68. This discussion note is drawn (with some minor editing) from Jack M. Balkin, Roe v. Wade: An Engine of Controversy, in What Roe v. Wade Should Have Said, supra at 12-15.
69. See Barbara Hinkson Craig and David M. O'Brien, Abortion and American Politics 166-168 (1993) (reprinting Republican and Democratic Party platform planks on abortion from 1980-1992).
70. Id.
71. For a history, see Ethan Bronner, Battle for Justice: How the Bork Nomination Shook America (1989).

leeway to push his favored candidates and must moderate his choices, particularly in the case of Supreme Court nominations. There is no reason to think that Antonin Scalia was considerably more moderate than Robert Bork, and his appointment to the Supreme Court sailed through the Senate. But in 1986 Scalia faced a Republican-controlled Senate and a Senate Judiciary Committee headed by the conservative Senator Strom Thurmond, while in 1987 Bork faced a Democratic-controlled Senate and a Judiciary Committee headed by the liberal Joseph Biden.

After Reagan's next nominee, D.C. Circuit Judge Douglas Ginsburg, withdrew his name after his marijuana use was discovered, Reagan nominated Anthony Kennedy, a conservative circuit judge from California who was nevertheless widely regarded as more moderate than Bork.

In hindsight, the failure of the Bork nomination marked an important turning point in the constitutional struggles over abortion, because pro-choice forces showed that they could mobilize effectively and demonstrated that pro-life politicians might pay more heavily than they had previously believed if they tried to overturn *Roe* through judicial appointments. Nevertheless, by 1987, President Reagan had succeeded in appointing three Justices to the Supreme Court who were widely regarded to be critics of *Roe* to join the two original dissenters in the opinion. The Supreme Court's decision in *Roe* had helped set off a political chain reaction that now seemed to threaten the decision itself.

The next test of *Roe*'s continued vitality came in 1989 in Webster v. Reproductive Health Services, 492 U.S. 490 (1989). A Missouri statute prohibited the use of public employees and facilities to perform or assist abortions that were not necessary to save the mother's life, and made it unlawful to use public funds, employees, or facilities to "encourag[e] or counsel[]" a woman to have an abortion not necessary to save her life. The statute also required that physicians determine whether a fetus is viable before performing an abortion where physicians had reason to believe the fetus is more than 20 weeks old. Finally, the preamble to the legislation declared that "[t]he life of each human being begins at conception," and that "unborn children have protectable interests in life, health, and well-being."

The Court upheld all of the statute's restrictions but was unable to agree on a rationale. Chief Justice Rehnquist's plurality opinion, joined by Justices White and Kennedy, stated that it was not necessary to overturn *Roe*'s constitutional prohibition on criminalization of abortions to decide the case but that *Roe*'s trimester framework should be jettisoned. Rehnquist stated that abortion was not a fundamental right; hence restrictions on abortion need only pass the rational basis test. Justice O'Connor, concurring in the result, argued that it was unnecessary to reject *Roe*'s trimester framework to uphold the Missouri law; the challenged provisions were consistent with her interpretation of the Court's previous decisions, and none of the provisions imposed an undue burden on the right to abortion. Justice Scalia also concurring in the judgment, argued that *Roe* should be overturned immediately, and directly criticized Justice O'Connor for failing to provide the fifth vote.

The result in *Webster* left *Roe* in legal limbo, and it was widely assumed that it was only a matter of time before it would be officially overruled. This energized pro-choice forces; they successfully supported a number of pro-choice candidates who won state and local elections. Matters were further complicated when two of the Court's most liberal Justices, William Brennan and Thurgood Marshall, left the Court due to failing health. This brought the abortion issue front and center in subsequent confirmation hearings. Brennan resigned in July 1990 and was replaced by David Souter, whose views on abortion were unknown even to President George H.W. Bush, who had nominated him. Justice Marshall announced his retirement in June 1991. He was replaced by Clarence Thomas, an African-American judge on the D.C. Circuit and former head of the Equal Employment Opportunity Commission (EEOC). Although Thomas was widely believed to be hostile to *Roe,* Thomas stated at his confirmation hearings that he had never "debated" *Roe v. Wade,* did not "recollect ever commenting on it," could not "recall saying" whether it was properly decided or not, and had no "personal opinion" about it.[72] Matters were thrown into an uproar when Thomas was accused of sexual harassment by a former employee at the EEOC, Anita Hill. After weeks of controversy, Thomas was finally confirmed by a 52-48 vote, the narrowest margin in Supreme Court history.

Once Thomas took his seat on the Supreme Court in 1991 it seemed that there were finally enough votes to overturn Roe v. Wade. Of the seven Justices who had voted with the majority in *Roe,* only Blackmun, the author of *Roe,* remained on the Court. Brennan, Marshall, Stewart, Douglas, Burger, and Powell were gone, replaced by Souter, Thomas, O'Connor, Stevens, Scalia, and Kennedy, all appointed by Republican presidents, and all but Stevens appointed after the Republican Party had become a pro-life party.

O'Connor's opinion in *Hodgson* seemed to assume that *Roe* remained good law, although she now reinterpreted the abortion right in terms of the "undue burden" test she had introduced in her dissent in *Akron.* The question was what a Court staffed with the new Justices would do once the question of overturning *Roe* was presented again. When the Court finally spoke on the issue, the views of these new Justices — and Justice O'Connor herself — proved crucial.

PLANNED PARENTHOOD OF SOUTHEASTERN PENNSYLVANIA v. CASEY
505 U.S. 833 (1992)

Justice O'CONNOR, Justice KENNEDY, and Justice SOUTER announced the judgment of the Court and delivered the opinion of the Court with respect to Parts I, II, III, V-A, V-C, and VI, an opinion with respect to Part V-E, in which Justice Stevens joins, and an opinion with respect to Parts IV, V-B, and V-D.

I.

Liberty finds no refuge in a jurisprudence of doubt. . . .

At issue in these cases are five provisions of the Pennsylvania Abortion Control Act of 1982 as amended in 1988 and 1989. . . . The Act requires that a woman seeking an abortion give her informed consent prior to the abortion procedure, and specifies that she be provided with certain information at least 24 hours before the abortion is performed. For a minor to obtain an abortion, the Act requires the informed consent of one of her parents, but provides for a judicial bypass option if the minor does not wish to or cannot obtain a parent's consent. Another provision

---

72. See Nomination of Judge Clarence Thomas to be Associate Justice of the Supreme Court of the United States: Hearings Before the Comm. on the Judiciary, United States Senate, 102d Cong., 1st Sess. pt. 1, 222-223 (1991).

of the Act requires that, unless certain exceptions apply, a married woman seeking an abortion must sign a statement indicating that she has notified her husband of her intended abortion. The Act exempts compliance with these three requirements in the event of a "medical emergency." . . . In addition to the above provisions regulating the performance of abortions, the Act imposes certain reporting requirements on facilities that provide abortion services.

. . . [W]e acknowledge that our decisions after *Roe* cast doubt upon the meaning and reach of its holding. . . . State and federal courts as well as legislatures throughout the Union must have guidance as they seek to address this subject in conformance with the Constitution. Given these premises, we find it imperative to review once more the principles that define the rights of the woman and the legitimate authority of the State respecting the termination of pregnancies by abortion procedures.

After considering the fundamental constitutional questions resolved by *Roe*, principles of institutional integrity, and the rule of stare decisis, we are led to conclude this: the essential holding of Roe v. Wade should be retained and once again reaffirmed.

It must be stated at the outset and with clarity that *Roe*'s essential holding, the holding we reaffirm, has three parts. First is a recognition of the right of the woman to choose to have an abortion before viability and to obtain it without undue interference from the State. Before viability, the State's interests are not strong enough to support a prohibition of abortion or the imposition of a substantial obstacle to the woman's effective right to elect the procedure. Second is a confirmation of the State's power to restrict abortions after fetal viability, if the law contains exceptions for pregnancies which endanger a woman's life or health. And third is the principle that the State has legitimate interests from the outset of the pregnancy in protecting the health of the woman and the life of the fetus that may become a child. These principles do not contradict one another; and we adhere to each.

II.

Constitutional protection of the woman's decision to terminate her pregnancy derives from the Due Process Clause of the Fourteenth Amendment. . . . Although a literal reading of the Clause might suggest that it governs only the procedures by which a State may deprive persons of liberty, for at least 105 years, at least since Mugler v. Kansas, 123 U.S. 623, 660-61 (1887), the Clause has been understood to contain a substantive component as well, one "barring certain government actions regardless of the fairness of the procedures used to implement them." . . .

It is tempting, as a means of curbing the discretion of federal judges, to suppose that liberty encompasses no more than those rights already guaranteed to the individual against federal interference by the express provisions of the first eight amendments to the Constitution. But of course this Court has never accepted that view.

It is also tempting, for the same reason, to suppose that the Due Process Clause protects only those practices, defined at the most specific level, that were protected against government interference by other rules of law when the Fourteenth Amendment was ratified. See Michael H. v. Gerald D., n.[f] (opinion of Scalia, J.). But such a view would be inconsistent with our law. It is a promise of the Constitution that there is a realm of personal liberty which the government may not enter. We have vindicated this principle before. Marriage is mentioned nowhere in the Bill of Rights and interracial marriage was illegal in most States in the 19th century, but the Court was no doubt correct in finding it to be an aspect of liberty protected against state interference by the substantive component of the Due Process Clause in Loving v. Virginia. [N]either the Bill of Rights nor the specific practices of States at the time of the adoption of the Fourteenth Amendment marks the outer limits of the substantive sphere of liberty which the Fourteenth Amendment protects. See U.S. Const., Amend. 9.

The inescapable fact is that adjudication of substantive due process claims may call upon the Court in interpreting the Constitution to exercise that same capacity which by tradition courts always have exercised: reasoned judgment. Its boundaries are not susceptible to expression as a simple rule. . . .

Our law affords constitutional protection to personal decisions relating to marriage, procreation, contraception, family relationships, child rearing, and education. *Carey.* Our cases recognize the right of the *individual,* married or single, to be free from unwarranted governmental intrusion into matters so fundamentally affecting a person as the decision whether to bear or beget a child. *Eisenstadt.* (emphasis in original). Our precedents "have respected the private realm of family life which the state cannot enter." Prince v. Massachusetts, 321 U.S. 158, 166 (1944). These matters, involving the most intimate and personal choices a person may make in a lifetime, choices central to personal dignity and autonomy, are central to the liberty protected by the Fourteenth Amendment. At the heart of liberty is the right to define one's own concept of existence, of meaning, of the universe, and of the mystery of human life. Beliefs about these matters could not define the attributes of personhood were they formed under compulsion of the State.

[A]bortion is a unique act. It is an act fraught with consequences for others: for the woman who must live with the implications of her decision; for the persons who perform and assist in the procedure; for the spouse, family, and society which must confront the knowledge that these procedures exist, procedures some deem nothing short of an act of violence against innocent human life; and, depending on one's beliefs, for the life or potential life that is aborted. . . . The mother who carries a child to full term is subject to anxieties, to physical constraints, to pain that only she must bear. That these sacrifices have from the beginning of the human race been endured by woman with a pride that ennobles her in the eyes of others and gives to the infant a bond of love cannot alone be grounds for the State to insist she make the sacrifice. Her suffering is too intimate and personal for the State to insist, without more, upon its own vision of the woman's role, however dominant that vision has been in the course of our history and our culture. The destiny of the woman must be shaped to a large extent on her own conception of her spiritual imperatives and her place in society.

It should be recognized, moreover, that in some critical respects the abortion decision is of the same character as the decision to use contraception, to which Griswold v. Connecticut, Eisenstadt v. Baird, and Carey v. Population Services International, afford constitutional protection. We have no doubt as to the correctness of those decisions. They support the reasoning in *Roe* relating to the woman's liberty because they involve personal decisions concerning not only the meaning of procreation but also human responsibility and respect for it. . . .

[T]he reservations any of us may have in reaffirming the central holding of *Roe* are outweighed by the explication of individual liberty we have given combined with the force of stare decisis. We turn now to that doctrine.

III.

[I]t is common wisdom that the rule of stare decisis is not an "inexorable command," and certainly it is not such in every constitutional case. Rather, when this Court reexamines a prior holding, its judgment is customarily informed by a series of prudential and pragmatic considerations designed to test the consistency of overruling a prior decision with the ideal of the rule of law, and to gauge the respective costs of reaffirming and overruling a prior case. Thus, for example, we may ask whether the rule has proved to be intolerable simply in defying practical workability; whether the rule is subject to a kind of reliance that would lend a special hardship to the consequences of overruling and add inequity to the cost of repudiation; whether related principles of law have so far developed as to have left the old rule no more than a remnant of abandoned doctrine; or whether facts have so changed or come to be seen so differently, as to have robbed the old rule of significant application or justification.

So in this case we may inquire whether *Roe*'s central rule has been found unworkable; whether the rule's limitation on state power could be removed without serious inequity to those who have relied upon it or significant damage to the stability of the society governed by the rule in question; whether the law's growth in the intervening years has left *Roe*'s central rule a doctrinal anachronism discounted by society; and whether *Roe*'s premises of fact have so far changed in the ensuing two decades as to render its central holding somehow irrelevant or unjustifiable in dealing with the issue it addressed.

1

Although *Roe* has engendered opposition, it has in no sense proven "unworkable," representing as it does a simple limitation beyond which a state law is unenforceable. While *Roe* has, of course, required judicial assessment of state laws . . . and although the need for such review will remain as a consequence of today's decision, the required determinations fall within judicial competence.

2

The inquiry into reliance counts the cost of a rule's repudiation as it would fall on those who have relied reasonably on the rule's continued application. Since the classic case for weighing reliance heavily in favor of following the earlier rule occurs in the commercial context, where advance planning of great precision is most obviously a necessity, it is no cause for surprise that some would find no reliance worthy of consideration in support of *Roe*.

While neither respondents nor their amici in so many words deny that the abortion right invites some reliance prior to its actual exercise, one can readily imagine an argument stressing the dissimilarity of this case to one involving property or contract. Abortion is customarily chosen as an unplanned response to the consequence of unplanned activity or to the failure of conventional birth control, and except on the assumption that no intercourse would have occurred but for *Roe*'s holding, such behavior may appear to justify no reliance claim. . . .

To eliminate the issue of reliance that easily, however, one would need to limit cognizable reliance to specific instances of sexual activity. But to do this would be simply to refuse to face the fact that for two decades of economic and social developments, people have organized intimate relationships and made choices that define their views of themselves and their places in society, in reliance on the availability of abortion in the event that contraception should fail. The ability of women to participate equally in the economic and social life of the Nation has been facilitated by their ability to control their reproductive lives. The Constitution serves human values, and while the effect of reliance on *Roe* cannot be exactly measured, neither can the certain cost of overruling *Roe* for people who have ordered their thinking and living around that case be dismissed.

3

No evolution of legal principle has left *Roe*'s doctrinal footings weaker than they were in 1973. No development of constitutional law since the case was decided has implicitly or explicitly left *Roe* behind as a mere survivor of obsolete constitutional thinking. . . .

Roe . . . may be seen not only as an exemplar of [the liberty protected by] *Griswold* . . . but as a rule (whether or not mistaken) of personal autonomy and bodily integrity, with doctrinal affinity to cases recognizing limits on governmental power to mandate medical treatment or to bar its rejection. If so, our cases since *Roe* accord with *Roe*'s view that a State's interest in the protection of life falls short of justifying any plenary override of individual liberty claims. Cruzan v. Director, Missouri Dept. of Health, 497 U.S. 261, 278 (1990). Finally, one could classify *Roe* as sui generis. If the case is so viewed, then there clearly has been no erosion of its central determination. . . . Nor will courts building upon *Roe* be likely to hand down erroneous decisions as a consequence. Even on the assumption that the central holding of *Roe* was in error, that error would go only to the strength of the state interest in fetal protection, not to the recognition afforded by the Constitution to the woman's liberty. . . .

The soundness of this prong of the *Roe* analysis is apparent from a consideration of the alternative. If indeed the woman's interest in deciding whether to bear and beget a child had not been recognized as in *Roe*, the State might as readily restrict a woman's right to choose to carry a pregnancy to term as to terminate it, to further asserted state interests in population control, or eugenics, for example. Yet *Roe* has been sensibly relied upon to counter any such suggestions. E.g., Arnold v. Board of Education of Escambia County, Ala., 880 F.2d 305, 311 (CA11 1989) (relying upon *Roe* and concluding that government officials violate the Constitution by coercing a minor to have an abortion); Avery v. County of Burke, 660 F.2d 111, 115 (CA4 1981) (county agency inducing teenage girl to undergo unwanted sterilization on the basis of misrepresentation that she had sickle cell trait). . . .

4

[T]ime has overtaken some of *Roe*'s factual assumptions: advances in maternal health care allow for abortions safe to the mother later in pregnancy than was true in 1973, and advances in neonatal care have advanced viability to a point somewhat earlier. But these facts go only to the scheme of time limits on the realization of competing interests, and the divergences from the factual premises of 1973 have no bearing on the validity of *Roe*'s central holding, that viability marks the earliest point at which the State's interest in fetal life is constitutionally adequate to justify a legislative ban on nontherapeutic abortions. The soundness or unsoundness of that constitutional judgment in no sense turns on whether viability occurs at approximately 28 weeks, as was usual at the time of *Roe*, at 23 to 24 weeks, as it sometimes does today, or at some moment even slightly earlier in pregnancy, as it may if fetal respiratory capacity can somehow be enhanced in the future.

5

The sum of the precedential inquiry to this point shows *Roe*'s underpinnings unweakened in any way affecting its central holding. [Within] the bounds of normal stare decisis analysis then . . . the stronger argument is for affirming *Roe*'s central holding, with whatever degree of personal reluctance any of us may have, not for overruling it.

B

In a less significant case, stare decisis analysis could, and would, stop at the point we have reached. But the sustained and widespread debate *Roe* has provoked calls for some comparison between that case and others of comparable dimension that have responded to national controversies and taken on the impress of the controversies addressed. Only two such decisional lines from the past century present themselves for examination, and in each instance the result reached by the Court accorded with the principles we apply today.

The first example is that line of cases identified with Lochner v. New York. . . . West Coast Hotel Co. v. Parrish, 300 U.S. 379 (1937), signalled the demise of *Lochner* by overruling *Adkins*. In the meantime, the Depression had come and, with it, the lesson that seemed unmistakable to most people by 1937, that the interpretation of contractual freedom protected in *Adkins* rested on fundamentally false factual assumptions about the capacity of a relatively unregulated market to satisfy minimal levels of human welfare. As Justice Jackson wrote of the constitutional crisis of 1937 shortly before he came on the bench, "The older world of laissez-faire was recognized everywhere outside the Court to be dead." R. Jackson, The Struggle for Judicial Supremacy 85 (1941). The facts upon which the earlier case had premised a constitutional resolution of social controversy had proved to be untrue, and history's demonstration of their untruth not only justified but required the new choice of constitutional principle that *West Coast Hotel* announced. Of course, it was true that the Court lost something by its misperception, or its lack of prescience, and the Court-packing crisis only magnified the loss; but the clear demonstration that the facts of economic life were different from those previously assumed warranted the repudiation of the old law.

The second comparison that 20th century history invites is with the cases employing the separate-but-equal rule for applying the Fourteenth Amendment's equal protection guarantee. They began with Plessy v. Ferguson. . . . The *Plessy* Court considered "the underlying fallacy of the plaintiff's argument to consist in the assumption that the enforced separation of the two races stamps the colored race with a badge of inferiority. If this be so, it is not by reason of anything found in the act, but solely because the colored race chooses to put that construction upon it." Whether . . . the Justices in the *Plessy* majority believed this or not, this . . . was the stated justification for the Court's opinion. But this understanding of the facts and the rule it was stated to justify were repudiated in Brown v. Board of Education (1954). . . .

The Court in *Brown* . . . observ[ed] that whatever may have been the understanding in Plessy's time of the power of segregation to stigmatize those who were segregated with a "badge of inferiority," it was clear by 1954 that legally sanctioned segregation had just such an effect, to the point that racially separate public educational facilities were deemed inherently unequal. Society's understanding of the facts upon which a constitutional ruling was sought in 1954 was thus fundamentally different from the basis claimed for the decision in 1896. While we think *Plessy* was wrong the day it was decided, we must also recognize that the *Plessy* Court's explanation for its decision was so clearly at odds with the facts apparent to the Court in 1954 that the decision to reexamine *Plessy* was on this ground alone not only justified but required.

West Coast Hotel and *Brown* each rested on facts, or an understanding of facts, changed from those which furnished the claimed justifications for the earlier constitutional resolutions. Each case was comprehensible as the Court's response to facts that the country could understand, or had come to understand already, but which the Court of an earlier day, as its own declarations disclosed, had not been able to perceive. As the decisions were thus comprehensible they were also defensible, not merely as the victories of one doctrinal school over another by dint of numbers (victories though they were), but as applications of constitutional principle to facts as they had not been seen by the Court before. In constitutional adjudication as elsewhere in life, changed circumstances may impose new obligations, and the thoughtful part of the Nation could accept each decision to overrule a prior case as a response to the Court's constitutional duty.

Because the case before us presents no such occasion, it could be seen as no such response. Because neither the factual underpinnings of *Roe*'s central holding nor our understanding of it has changed (and because no other indication of weakened precedent has been shown) the Court could not pretend to be reexamining the prior law with any justification beyond a present doctrinal disposition to come out differently from the Court of 1973. To overrule prior law for no other reason than that would run counter to the view repeated in our cases, that a decision to overrule should rest on some special reason over and above the belief that a prior case was wrongly decided. . . .

C

The examination of the conditions justifying the repudiation of *Adkins* by *West Coast Hotel* and *Plessy* by *Brown* is enough to suggest the terrible price that would have been paid if the Court had not overruled as it did. In the present case, however, as our analysis to this point makes clear, the terrible price would be paid for overruling. Our analysis would not be complete, however, without explaining why overruling *Roe*'s central holding would not only reach an unjustifiable result under principles of stare decisis, but would seriously weaken the Court's capacity to exercise the judicial power and to function as the Supreme Court of a Nation dedicated to the rule of law. . . .

The Court's power lies . . . in its legitimacy, a product of substance and perception that shows itself in the people's acceptance of the Judiciary as fit to determine what the Nation's law means and to declare what it demands.

The underlying substance of this legitimacy is of course the warrant for the Court's decisions in the Constitution and the lesser sources of legal principle on which the Court draws. That substance is expressed in the Court's opinions, and our contemporary understanding is such that a decision without principled justification would be no judicial act at all. But even when justification is furnished by apposite legal principle, something more is required. Because not every conscientious claim of principled justification will be accepted as such, the justification claimed must be beyond dispute. The Court must take care to speak and act in ways that allow people to accept its decisions on the terms the Court claims for them, as grounded truly in principle, not as compromises with social and political pressures having, as such, no bearing on the principled choices that the Court is obliged to make. Thus, the Court's legitimacy depends on making legally principled decisions under circumstances in which their principled character is sufficiently plausible to be accepted by the Nation.

The need for principled action to be perceived as such is implicated to some degree whenever this, or any other appellate court, overrules a prior case. This is not to say, of course, that this Court cannot give a perfectly satisfactory explanation in most cases. People understand that some of the Constitution's language is hard to fathom and that the Court's Justices are sometimes able to perceive significant facts or to understand principles of law that eluded their predecessors and that justify departures from existing decisions. However upsetting it may be to those most directly affected when one judicially derived rule replaces another, the country can accept some correction of error without necessarily questioning the legitimacy of the Court.

In two circumstances, however, the Court would almost certainly fail to receive the benefit of the doubt in overruling prior cases. There is, first, a point beyond which frequent overruling would overtax the country's belief in the Court's good faith. . . . There is a limit to the amount of error that can plausibly be imputed to prior courts. If that limit should be exceeded, disturbance of prior rulings would be taken as evidence that justifiable reexamination of principle had given way to drives for particular results in the short term. The legitimacy of the Court would fade with the frequency of its vacillation.

That first circumstance can be described as hypothetical; the second is to the point here and now. Where, in the performance of its judicial duties, the Court decides a case in such a way as to resolve the sort of intensely divisive controversy reflected in *Roe* and those rare, comparable cases, its decision has a dimension that the resolution of the normal case does not carry. It is the dimension present whenever the Court's interpretation of the Constitution calls the contending sides of a national controversy to end their national division by accepting a common mandate rooted in the Constitution.

The Court is not asked to do this very often, having thus addressed the Nation only twice in our lifetime, in the decisions of *Brown* and *Roe*. But when the Court does act in this way, its decision requires an equally rare precedential force to counter the inevitable efforts to overturn it and to thwart its implementation. Some of those efforts may be mere unprincipled emotional reactions; others may proceed from principles worthy of profound respect. But whatever the premises of opposition may be, only the most convincing justification under accepted standards of precedent could suffice to demonstrate that a later decision overruling the first was anything but a surrender to political pressure, and an unjustified repudiation of the principle on which the Court staked its authority in the first instance. So to overrule under fire in the absence of the most compelling reason to reexamine a watershed decision would subvert the Court's legitimacy beyond any serious question.

The country's loss of confidence in the judiciary would be underscored by an equally certain and equally reasonable condemnation for another failing in overruling unnecessarily and under pressure. Some cost will be paid by anyone who approves or implements a constitutional decision where it is unpopular, or who refuses to work to undermine the decision or to force its reversal. The price may be criticism or ostracism, or it may be violence. An extra price will be paid by those who themselves disapprove of the decision's results when viewed outside of constitutional terms, but who nevertheless struggle to accept it, because they respect the rule of law. To all those who will be so tested by following, the Court implicitly undertakes to remain steadfast, lest in the end a price be paid for nothing. The promise of constancy, once given, binds its maker for as long as the power to stand by the decision survives and the understanding of the issue has not changed so fundamentally as to render the commitment obsolete. From the obligation of this promise this Court cannot and should not assume any exemption when duty requires it to decide a case in conformance with the Constitution. A willing breach of it would be nothing less than a breach of faith, and no Court that broke its faith with the people could sensibly expect credit for principle in the decision by which it did that.

It is true that diminished legitimacy may be restored, but only slowly. Unlike the political branches, a Court thus weakened could not seek to regain its position with a new mandate from the voters, and even if the Court could somehow go to the polls, the loss of its principled character could not be retrieved by the casting of so many votes. Like the character of an individual, the legitimacy of the Court must be earned over time. So, indeed, must be the character of a Nation of people who aspire to live according to the rule of law. Their belief in themselves as such a people is not readily separable from their understanding of the Court invested with the authority to decide their constitutional cases and speak before all others for their constitutional ideals. If the Court's legitimacy should be undermined, then, so would the country be in its very ability to see itself through its constitutional ideals. The Court's concern with legitimacy is not for the sake of the Court but for the sake of the Nation to which it is responsible.

The Court's duty in the present case is clear. In 1973, it confronted the already-divisive issue of governmental power to limit personal choice to undergo abortion, for which it provided a new resolution based on the due process guaranteed by the Fourteenth Amendment. Whether or not a new social consensus is developing on that issue, its divisiveness is no less today than in 1973, and pressure to overrule the decision, like pressure to retain it, has grown only more intense. A decision to overrule *Roe*'s essential holding under the existing circumstances would address error, if error there was, at the cost of both profound and unnecessary damage to the Court's legitimacy, and to the Nation's commitment to the rule of law. It is therefore imperative to adhere to the essence of *Roe*'s original decision, and we do so today.

IV.

. . . We conclude that the basic decision in *Roe* was based on a constitutional analysis which we cannot now repudiate. The woman's liberty is not so unlimited, however, that from the outset the State cannot show its concern for the life of the unborn, and at a later point in fetal development the State's interest in life has sufficient force so that the right of the woman to terminate the pregnancy can be restricted.

That brings us, of course, to the point where much criticism has been directed at *Roe*, a criticism that always inheres when the Court draws a specific rule from what in the Constitution is but a general standard. . . . Liberty must not be extinguished for want of a line that is clear. . . .

We conclude the line should be drawn at viability, so that before that time the woman has a right to choose to terminate her pregnancy. We adhere to this principle for two reasons. First, as we have said, is the doctrine of stare decisis. . . . Although we must overrule those parts of *Thornburgh* and *Akron I* which, in our view, are inconsistent with *Roe*'s statement that the State has a legitimate interest in promoting the life or potential life of the unborn, the central premise of those cases represents an unbroken commitment by this Court to the essential holding of *Roe*. [T]he second reason is that the concept of viability, as we noted in *Roe*, is the time at which there is a realistic possibility of maintaining and nourishing a life outside the womb, so that the independent existence of the second life can in reason and all fairness be the object of state protection that now overrides the rights of the woman. Consistent with other constitutional norms, legislatures may draw lines which appear arbitrary without the necessity of offering a justification. But courts may not. We must justify the lines we draw. And there is no line other than viability which is more workable. . . . The viability line also has, as a practical matter, an element of fairness. In some broad sense it might be said that a woman who fails to act before viability has consented to the State's intervention on behalf of the developing child. The woman's right to terminate her pregnancy before viability is the most central principle of Roe v. Wade. It is a rule of law and a component of liberty we cannot renounce.

On the other side of the equation is the interest of the State in the protection of potential life. [T]he weight to be given this state interest, not the strength of the woman's interest, was the difficult question faced in *Roe*. We do not need to say whether each of us, had we been Members of the Court when the valuation of the State interest came before it as an original matter, would have concluded, as the *Roe* Court did, that its weight is insufficient to justify a ban on abortions prior to viability even when it is subject to certain exceptions. [Y]et it must be remembered that Roe v. Wade speaks with clarity in establishing not only the woman's liberty but also the State's "important and legitimate interest in potential life." That portion of the decision in *Roe* has been given too little acknowledgement and implementation by the Court in its subsequent cases. Those cases decided that any regulation touching upon the abortion decision must survive strict scrutiny, to be sustained only if drawn in narrow terms to further a compelling state interest. Not all of the cases decided under that formulation can be reconciled with the holding in *Roe* itself that the State has legitimate interests in the health of the woman and in protecting the potential life within her. In resolving this tension, we choose to rely upon *Roe*, as against the later cases.

. . . The trimester framework [established by *Roe*] no doubt was erected to ensure that the woman's right to choose not become so subordinate to the State's interest in promoting fetal life that her choice exists in theory but not in fact. We do not agree, however, that the trimester approach is necessary to accomplish this objective. . . .

Though the woman has a right to choose to terminate or continue her pregnancy before viability, it does not at all follow that the State is prohibited from taking steps to ensure that this choice is thoughtful and informed. Even in the earliest stages of pregnancy, the State may enact rules and regulations designed to encourage her to know that there are philosophic and social arguments of great weight that can be brought to bear in favor of continuing the pregnancy to full term and that there are procedures and institutions to allow adoption of unwanted children as well as a certain degree of state assistance if the mother chooses to raise the child herself.

"[T]he Constitution does not forbid a State or city, pursuant to democratic processes, from expressing a preference for normal childbirth." Webster v. Reproductive Health Services, 492 U.S., at 511. . . .

We reject the trimester framework, which we do not consider to be part of the essential holding of *Roe*. Measures aimed at ensuring that a woman's choice contemplates the consequences for the fetus do not necessarily interfere with the right recognized in *Roe*, although those measures have been found to be inconsistent with the rigid trimester framework announced in that case. A logical reading of the central holding in *Roe* itself, and a necessary reconciliation of the liberty of the woman and the interest of the State in promoting prenatal life, require, in our view, that we abandon the trimester framework as a rigid prohibition on all previability regulation aimed at the protection of fetal life. The trimester framework suffers from these basic flaws: in its formulation it misconceives the nature of the pregnant woman's interest; and in practice it undervalues the State's interest in potential life, as recognized in *Roe*.

[N]ot every law which makes a right more difficult to exercise is, ipso facto, an infringement of that right. . . . We have held that not every ballot access limitation amounts to an infringement of the right to vote. Rather, the States are granted substantial flexibility in establishing the framework within which voters choose the candidates for whom they wish to vote.

The abortion right is similar. Numerous forms of state regulation might have the incidental effect of increasing the cost or decreasing the availability of medical care, whether for abortion or any other medical procedure. The fact that a law which serves a valid purpose, one not designed to strike at the right itself, has the incidental effect of making it more difficult or more expensive to procure an abortion cannot be enough to invalidate it. Only where state regulation imposes an undue burden on a woman's ability to make this decision does the power of the State reach into the heart of the liberty protected by the Due Process Clause. . . .

[I]t is an overstatement to describe [the abortion right] as a right to decide whether to have an abortion "without interference from the State." All abortion regulations interfere to some degree with a woman's ability to decide whether to terminate her pregnancy. . . . Not all governmental intrusion is of necessity unwarranted; and that brings us to the other basic flaw in the trimester framework: even in *Roe*'s terms, in practice it undervalues the State's interest in the potential life within the woman. . . . The trimester framework . . . does not fulfill *Roe*'s own promise that the State has an interest in protecting fetal life or potential life. . . . [Because] there is a substantial state interest in potential life throughout pregnancy . . . not all regulations must be deemed unwarranted. Not all burdens on the right to decide whether to terminate a pregnancy will be undue. In our view, the undue burden standard is the appropriate means of reconciling the State's interest with the woman's constitutionally protected liberty. . . .

A finding of an undue burden is a shorthand for the conclusion that a state regulation has the purpose or effect of placing a substantial obstacle in the path of a woman seeking an abortion of a nonviable fetus. A statute with this purpose is invalid because the means chosen by the State to further the interest in potential life must be calculated to inform the woman's free choice, not hinder it. And a statute which, while furthering the interest in potential life or some other valid state interest, has the effect of placing a substantial obstacle in the path of a woman's choice cannot be considered a permissible means of serving its legitimate ends. . . .

[W]hat is at stake is the woman's right to make the ultimate decision, not a right to be insulated from all others in doing so. Regulations which do no more than create a structural mechanism by which the State, or the parent or guardian of a minor, may express profound respect for the life of the unborn are permitted, if they are not a substantial obstacle to the woman's exercise of the right to choose. Unless it has that effect on her right of choice, a state measure designed to persuade her to choose childbirth over abortion will be upheld if reasonably related to that goal. Regulations designed to foster the health of a woman seeking an abortion are valid if they do not constitute an undue burden.

[W]e give this summary:

(a) To protect the central right recognized by Roe v. Wade while at the same time accommodating the State's profound interest in potential life, we will employ the undue burden analysis as explained in this opinion. An undue burden exists, and therefore a provision of law is invalid, if its purpose or effect is to place a substantial obstacle in the path of a woman seeking an abortion before the fetus attains viability.

(b) We reject the rigid trimester framework of Roe v. Wade. To promote the State's profound interest in potential life, throughout pregnancy the State may take measures to ensure that the woman's choice is informed, and measures designed to advance this interest will not be invalidated as long as their purpose is to persuade the woman to choose childbirth over abortion. These measures must not be an undue burden on the right.

(c) As with any medical procedure, the State may enact regulations to further the health or safety of a woman seeking an abortion. Unnecessary health regulations that have the purpose or effect of presenting a substantial obstacle to a woman seeking an abortion impose an undue burden on the right.

(d) Our adoption of the undue burden analysis does not disturb the central holding of Roe v. Wade, and we reaffirm that holding. Regardless of whether exceptions are made for particular circumstances, a State may not prohibit any woman from making the ultimate decision to terminate her pregnancy before viability.

(e) We also reaffirm Roe's holding that "subsequent to viability, the State in promoting its interest in the potentiality of human life may, if it chooses, regulate, and even proscribe, abortion except where it is necessary, in appropriate medical judgment, for the preservation of the life or health of the mother."

V.

A

Because it is central to the operation of various other requirements, we begin with the [Pennsylvania] statute's definition of medical emergency. Under the statute, a medical emergency is "[t]hat condition which, on the basis of the physician's good faith clinical judgment, so complicates the medical condition of a pregnant woman as to necessitate the immediate abortion of her pregnancy to avert her death or for which a delay will create serious risk of substantial and irreversible impairment of a major bodily function."

Petitioners argue that the definition is too narrow, contending that it forecloses the possibility of an immediate abortion despite some significant health risks. If the contention were correct, we would be required to invalidate the restrictive operation of the provision, for the essential holding of *Roe* forbids a State from interfering with a woman's choice to undergo an abortion procedure if continuing her pregnancy would constitute a threat to her health.

. . . [The Court of Appeals stated that it] "read the medical emergency exception as intended by the Pennsylvania legislature to assure that compliance with its abortion regulations would not in any way pose a significant threat to the life or health of a woman." . . . We . . . conclude that, as construed by the Court of Appeals, the medical emergency definition imposes no undue burden on a woman's abortion right.

B

We next consider the informed consent requirement. Except in a medical emergency, the statute requires that at least 24 hours before performing an abortion a physician inform the woman of the nature of the procedure, the health risks of the abortion and of childbirth, and the "probable gestational age of the unborn child." The physician or a qualified nonphysician must inform the woman of the availability of printed materials published by the State describing the fetus and providing information about medical assistance for childbirth, information about child support from the father, and a list of agencies which provide adoption and other services as alternatives to abortion. An abortion may not be performed unless the woman certifies in writing that she has been informed of the availability of these printed materials and has been provided them if she chooses to view them.

To the extent *Akron I* and *Thornburgh* find a constitutional violation when the government requires, as it does here, the giving of truthful, nonmisleading information about the nature of the procedure, the attendant health risks and those of childbirth, and the "probable gestational age" of the fetus, those cases go too far, are inconsistent with *Roe*'s acknowledgment of an important interest in potential life, and are overruled. . . . In attempting to ensure that a woman apprehend the full consequences of her decision, the State furthers the legitimate purpose of reducing the risk that a woman may elect an abortion, only to discover later, with devastating psychological consequences, that her decision was not fully informed. If the information the State requires to be made available to the woman is truthful and not misleading, the requirement may be permissible.

We also see no reason why the State may not require doctors to inform a woman seeking an abortion of the availability of materials relating to the consequences to the fetus, even when those consequences have no direct relation to her health. . . . We would think it constitutional for the State to require that in order for there to be informed consent to a kidney transplant operation the recipient must be supplied with information about risks to the donor as well as risks to himself or herself. . . . Our prior cases also suggest that the "straitjacket," *Thornburgh*, of particular information which must be given in each case interferes with a constitutional right of privacy between a pregnant woman and her physician. As a preliminary matter, it is worth noting that the statute now before us does not require a physician to comply with the informed consent provisions "if he or she can demonstrate by a preponderance of the evidence, that he or she reasonably believed that furnishing the information would have resulted in a severely adverse effect on the physical or mental health of the patient." In this respect, the statute does not prevent the physician from exercising his or her medical judgment. . . .

All that is left of petitioners' argument is an asserted First Amendment right of a physician not to provide information about the risks of abortion, and childbirth, in a manner mandated by the State. To be sure, the physician's First Amendment rights not to speak are implicated, but only as part of the practice of medicine, subject to reasonable licensing and regulation by the State. We see no constitutional infirmity in the requirement that the physician provide the information mandated by the State here.

The Pennsylvania statute also requires us to reconsider the holding in *Akron I* that the State may not require that a physician, as opposed to a qualified assistant, provide information relevant to a woman's informed consent. Since there is no evidence on this record that requiring a doctor to give the information as provided by the statute would amount in practical terms to a substantial obstacle to a woman seeking an abortion, we conclude that it is not an undue burden. . . .

Our analysis of Pennsylvania's 24-hour waiting period between the provision of the information deemed necessary to informed consent and the performance of an abortion under the undue burden standard requires us to reconsider the premise behind the decision in *Akron I* invalidating a parallel requirement. . . . The idea that important decisions will be more informed and deliberate if they follow some period of reflection does not strike us as unreasonable, particularly where the statute directs that important information become part of the background of the decision. The statute, as construed by the Court of Appeals, permits avoidance of the waiting period in the event of a medical emergency and the record evidence shows that in the vast majority of cases, a 24-hour delay does not create any appreciable health risk. In theory, at least, the waiting period is a reasonable measure to implement the State's interest in protecting the life of the unborn, a measure that does not amount to an undue burden.

Whether the mandatory 24-hour waiting period is nonetheless invalid because in practice it is a substantial obstacle to a woman's choice to terminate her pregnancy is a closer question. The findings of fact by the District Court indicate that because of the distances many women must travel to reach an abortion provider, the practical effect will often be a delay of much more than a day because the waiting period requires that a woman seeking an abortion make at least two visits to the doctor. The District Court also found that in many instances this will increase the exposure of women seeking abortions to "the harassment and hostility of anti-abortion protestors demonstrating outside a clinic." As a result, the District Court found that for those women who have the fewest financial resources, those who must travel long distances, and those who have difficulty explaining their whereabouts to husbands, employers, or others, the 24-hour waiting period will be "particularly burdensome."

These findings are troubling in some respects, but they do not demonstrate that the waiting period constitutes an undue burden. . . . [U]nder the undue burden standard a State is permitted to enact persuasive measures which favor childbirth over abortion, even if those measures do not further a health interest. And while the waiting period does limit a physician's discretion, that is not, standing alone, a reason to invalidate it. In light of the construction given the statute's definition of medical emergency by the Court of Appeals, and the District Court's findings, we cannot say that the waiting period imposes a real health risk.

We also disagree with the District Court's conclusion that the "particularly burdensome" effects of the waiting period on some women require its invalidation. A particular burden is not of necessity a substantial obstacle. Whether a burden falls on a particular group is a distinct inquiry from whether it is a substantial obstacle even as to the women in that group. And the District Court did not conclude that the waiting period is such an obstacle even for the women who are most burdened by it. Hence, on the record before us, and in the context of this facial challenge, we are not convinced that the 24-hour waiting period constitutes an undue burden.

We are left with the argument that the various aspects of the informed consent requirement are unconstitutional because they place barriers in the way of abortion on demand. Even the broadest reading of *Roe*, however, has not suggested that there is a constitutional right to abortion on demand. Rather, the right protected by *Roe* is a right to decide to terminate a pregnancy free of undue interference by the State. Because the informed consent requirement facilitates the wise exercise of that right it cannot be classified as an interference with the right *Roe* protects. The informed consent requirement is not an undue burden on that right.

C

Section 3209 of Pennsylvania's abortion law provides, except in cases of medical emergency, that no physician shall perform an abortion on a married woman without receiving a signed statement from the woman that she has notified her spouse that she is about to undergo an abortion. The woman has the option of providing an alternative signed statement certifying that her husband is not the man who impregnated her; that her husband could not be located; that the pregnancy is the result of spousal sexual assault which she has reported; or that the woman believes that notifying her husband will cause him or someone else to inflict bodily injury upon her. A physician who performs an abortion on a married woman without receiving the appropriate signed statement will have his or her license revoked, and is liable to the husband for damages.

The District Court heard the testimony of numerous expert witnesses, and made detailed findings of fact regarding the effect of this statute. These included:

> 273. The vast majority of women consult their husbands prior to deciding to terminate their pregnancy. . . .
>
> . . .
>
> 279. The 'bodily injury' exception could not be invoked by a married woman whose husband, if notified, would, in her reasonable belief, threaten to (a) publicize her intent to have an abortion to family, friends or acquaintances; (b) retaliate against her in future child custody or divorce proceedings; (c) inflict psychological intimidation or emotional harm upon her, her children or other persons; (d) inflict bodily harm on other persons such as children, family members or other loved ones; or (e) use his control over finances to deprive of necessary monies for herself or her children. . . .
>
> . . .

281. Studies reveal that family violence occurs in two million families in the United States. This figure, however, is a conservative one that substantially understates (because battering is usually not reported until it reaches life-threatening proportions) the actual number of families affected by domestic violence. In fact, researchers estimate that one of every two women will be battered at some time in their life. . . .

282. A wife may not elect to notify her husband of her intention to have an abortion for a variety of reasons, including the husband's illness, concern about her own health, the imminent failure of the marriage, or the husband's absolute opposition to the abortion. . . .

283. The required filing of the spousal consent form would require plaintiff-clinics to change their counseling procedures and force women to reveal their most intimate decision-making on pain of criminal sanctions. The confidentiality of these revelations could not be guaranteed, since the woman's records are not immune from subpoena. . . .

284. Women of all class levels, educational backgrounds, and racial, ethnic and religious groups are battered. . . .

285. Wife-battering or abuse can take on many physical and psychological forms. The nature and scope of the battering can cover a broad range of actions and be gruesome and tortuous. . . .

286. Married women, victims of battering, have been killed in Pennsylvania and throughout the United States. . . .

287. Battering can often involve a substantial amount of sexual abuse, including marital rape and sexual mutilation. . . .

288. In a domestic abuse situation, it is common for the battering husband to also abuse the children in an attempt to coerce the wife. . . .

289. Mere notification of pregnancy is frequently a flashpoint for battering and violence within the family. The number of battering incidents is high during the pregnancy and often the worst abuse can be associated with pregnancy. . . . The battering husband may deny parentage and use the pregnancy as an excuse for abuse. . . .

290. Secrecy typically shrouds abusive families. Family members are instructed not to tell anyone, especially police or doctors, about the abuse and violence. Battering husbands often threaten their wives or her children with further abuse if she tells an outsider of the violence and tells her that nobody will believe her. A battered woman, therefore, is highly unlikely to disclose the violence against her for fear of retaliation by the abuser. . . .

291. Even when confronted directly by medical personnel or other helping professionals, battered women often will not admit to the battering because they have not admitted to themselves that they are battered. . . .

. . .

294. A woman in a shelter or a safe house unknown to her husband is not "reasonably likely" to have bodily harm inflicted upon her by her batterer, however her attempt to notify her husband pursuant to section 3209 could accidentally disclose her whereabouts to her husband. Her fear of future ramifications would be realistic under the circumstances.

295. Marital rape is rarely discussed with others or reported to law enforcement authorities, and of those reported only a few are prosecuted. . . .

296. It is common for battered women to have sexual intercourse with their husbands to avoid being battered. While this type of coercive sexual activity would be spousal sexual assault as defined by the Act, many women may not consider it to be so and others would fear disbelief. . . .

297. The marital rape exception to section 3209 cannot be claimed by women who are victims of coercive sexual behavior other than penetration. The 90-day reporting requirement of the spousal sexual assault statute further narrows the class of sexually abused wives who can claim the exception, since many of these women may be psychologically unable to discuss or report the rape for several years after the incident. . . .

298. Because of the nature of the battering relationship, battered women are unlikely to avail themselves of the exceptions to section 3209 of the Act, regardless of whether the section applies to them.

These findings are supported by studies of domestic violence. . . . [T]here are millions of women in this country who are the victims of regular physical and psychological abuse at the hands of their husbands. Should these women become pregnant, they may have very good reasons for not wishing to inform their husbands of their decision to obtain an abortion. . . . And many women who are pregnant as a result of sexual assaults by their husbands will be unable to avail themselves of the exception for spousal sexual assault, §3209(b)(3), because the exception requires that the woman have notified law enforcement authorities within 90 days of the assault, and her husband will be notified of her report once an investigation begins. If anything in this field is certain, it is that victims of spousal sexual assault are extremely reluctant to report the abuse to the government; hence, a great many spousal rape victims will not be exempt from the notification requirement imposed by §3209.

The spousal notification requirement is thus likely to prevent a significant number of women from obtaining an abortion. It does not merely make abortions a little more difficult or expensive to obtain; for many women, it will impose a substantial obstacle. We must not blind ourselves to the fact that the significant number of women who fear for their safety and the safety of their children are likely to be deterred from procuring an abortion as surely as if the Commonwealth had outlawed abortion in all cases.

Respondents attempt to avoid the conclusion that §3209 is invalid by pointing out that . . . the effects of §3209 are felt by only one percent of the women who obtain abortions. [However,] [t]he analysis does not end with the one percent of women upon whom the statute operates; it begins there. Legislation is measured for consistency with the Constitution by its impact on those whose conduct it affects. For example, we would not say that a law which requires a newspaper to print a candidate's reply to an unfavorable editorial is valid on its face because most newspapers would adopt the policy even absent the law. See Miami Herald Publishing Co. v. Tornillo, 418 U.S. 241 (1974). The proper focus of constitutional inquiry is the group for whom the law is a restriction, not the group for whom the law is irrelevant.

. . . The unfortunate yet persisting conditions we document above will mean that in a large fraction of the cases in which §3209 is relevant, it will operate as a substantial obstacle to a woman's choice to undergo an abortion. It is an undue burden, and therefore invalid.

This conclusion is in no way inconsistent with our decisions upholding parental notification or consent requirements. Those enactments, and our judgment that they are constitutional, are based on the quite reasonable assumption that minors will benefit from consultation with their parents and that children will often not realize that their parents have their best interests at heart. We cannot adopt a parallel assumption about adult women.

. . . It is an inescapable biological fact that state regulation with respect to the child a woman is carrying will have a far greater impact on the mother's liberty than on the father's. The effect of state regulation on a woman's protected liberty is doubly deserving of scrutiny in such a case, as the State has touched not only upon the private sphere of the family but upon the very bodily integrity of the pregnant woman. The Court has held that "when the wife and the husband disagree on this decision, the view of only one of the two marriage partners can prevail. Inasmuch as it is the woman who physically bears the child and who is the more directly and immediately affected by the pregnancy, as between the two, the balance weighs in her favor." *Danforth*. This conclusion rests upon the basic nature of marriage and the nature of our Constitution: "The marital couple is not an independent entity with a mind and heart of its own, but an association of two individuals each with a separate intellectual and emotional makeup. . . . The Constitution protects individuals, men and women alike, from unjustified state interference, even when that interference is enacted into law for the benefit of their spouses."

There was a time, not so long ago, when a different understanding of the family and of the Constitution prevailed. In Bradwell v. State, 83 U.S. (16 Wall.) 130 (1872), three Members of this Court reaffirmed the common-law principle that "a woman had no legal existence separate from her husband, who was regarded as her head and representative in the social state; and, notwithstanding some recent modifications of this civil status, many of the special rules of law flowing from and dependent upon this cardinal principle still exist in full force in most States." Id. at 141 (Bradley, J., joined by Swayne and Field, JJ., concurring in judgment). Only one generation has passed since this Court observed that "woman is still regarded as the center of home and family life," with attendant "special responsibilities" that precluded full and independent legal status under the Constitution. Hoyt v. Florida, 368 U.S. 57 (1961). These views, of course, are no longer consistent with our understanding of the family, the individual, or the Constitution.

In keeping with our rejection of the common-law understanding of a woman's role within the family, the Court held in *Danforth* that the Constitution does not permit a State to require a married woman to obtain her husband's consent before undergoing an abortion. The principles that guided the Court in *Danforth* should be our guides today. For the great many women who are victims of abuse inflicted by their husbands, or whose children are the victims of such abuse, a spousal notice requirement enables the husband to wield an effective veto over his wife's decision. Whether the prospect of notification itself deters such women from seeking abortions, or whether the husband, through physical force or psychological pressure or economic coercion, prevents his wife from obtaining an abortion until it is too late, the notice requirement will often be tantamount to the veto found unconstitutional in *Danforth*. The women most affected by this law — those who most reasonably fear the consequences of notifying their husbands that they are pregnant — are in the gravest danger.

The husband's interest in the life of the child his wife is carrying does not permit the State to empower him with this troubling degree of authority over his wife. The contrary view leads to consequences reminiscent of the common law. A husband has no enforceable right to require a wife to advise him before she exercises her personal choices. If a husband's interest in the potential life of the child outweighs a wife's liberty, the State could require a married woman to notify her husband before she uses a postfertilization contraceptive. Perhaps next in line would be a statute requiring pregnant married women to notify their husbands before engaging in conduct causing risks to the fetus. After all, if the husband's interest in the fetus' safety is a sufficient predicate for state regulation, the State could reasonably conclude that pregnant wives should notify their husbands before drinking alcohol or smoking. Perhaps married women should notify their husbands before using contraceptives or before undergoing any type of surgery that may have complications affecting the husband's interest in his wife's reproductive organs. And if a husband's interest justifies notice in any of these cases, one might reasonably argue that it justifies exactly what the *Danforth* Court held it did not justify — a requirement of the husband's consent as well. A State may not give to a man the kind of dominion over his wife that parents exercise over their children. Section 3209 embodies a view of marriage consonant with the common-law status of married women but repugnant to our present understanding of marriage and of the nature of the rights secured by the Constitution. Women do not lose their constitutionally protected liberty when they marry. The Constitution protects all individuals, male or female, married or unmarried, from the abuse of governmental power, even where that power is employed for the supposed benefit of a member of the individual's family. These considerations confirm our conclusion that §3209 is invalid.

D

We next consider the parental consent provision. Except in a medical emergency, an unemancipated young woman under 18 may not obtain an abortion unless she and one of her parents (or guardian) provides informed consent as defined above. If neither a parent nor a guardian provides consent, a court may authorize the performance of an abortion upon a determination that the young woman is mature and capable of giving informed consent and has in fact given her informed consent, or that an abortion would be in her best interests.

We have been over most of this ground before. Our cases establish, and we reaffirm today, that a State may require a minor seeking an abortion to obtain the consent of a parent or guardian, provided that there is an adequate judicial bypass procedure. . . . [I]n our view, the one-parent consent requirement and judicial bypass procedure are constitutional. . . .

E

Under the recordkeeping and reporting requirements of the statute, every facility which performs abortions is required to file a report stating its name and address as well as the name and address of any related entity, such as a controlling or subsidiary organization. In the case of state-funded institutions, the information becomes public. . . .

In *Danforth*, we held that recordkeeping and reporting provisions "that are reasonably directed to the preservation of maternal health and that properly respect a patient's confidentiality and privacy are permissible." We think that under this standard, all the provisions at issue here except that relating to spousal notice are constitutional. Although they do not relate to the State's interest in informing the woman's choice, they do relate to health. The collection of information with respect to actual patients is a vital element of medical research, and so it cannot be said that the requirements serve no purpose other than to make abortions more difficult. Nor do we find that the requirements impose a substantial obstacle to a woman's choice. At most they might increase the cost of some abortions by a slight amount. While at some point increased cost could become a substantial obstacle, there is no such showing on the record before us.

Subsection (12) of the reporting provision requires the reporting of, among other things, a married woman's "reason for failure to provide notice" to her husband. This provision in effect requires women, as a condition of obtaining an abortion, to provide the Commonwealth with the precise information we have already recognized that many women have pressing reasons not to reveal. Like the spousal notice requirement itself, this provision places an undue burden on a woman's choice, and must be invalidated for that reason.

VI.

Our Constitution is a covenant running from the first generation of Americans to us and then to future generations. It is a coherent succession. Each generation must learn anew that the Constitution's written terms embody ideas and aspirations that must survive more ages than one. We accept our responsibility not to retreat from interpreting the full meaning of the covenant in light of all of our precedents. We invoke it once again to define the freedom guaranteed by the Constitution's own promise, the promise of liberty.

Justice STEVENS, concurring in part and dissenting in part. . . .

II.

[T]he interest in protecting potential life is not grounded in the Constitution.

It is, instead, an indirect interest in . . . minimizing . . . offense [to people opposed to abortion]. The State may also have a broader interest in expanding the population. [Under] these principles, §3205(a)(2)(i)-(iii) are unconstitutional. Those sections require a physician or counselor to provide the woman with a range of materials clearly designed to persuade her to choose not to undergo the abortion. While the State is free to produce and disseminate such material, the State may not inject such information into the woman's deliberations just as she is weighing such an important choice.

Under this same analysis, §§3205(a)(1)(i) and (iii) of the Pennsylvania statute are constitutional. Those sections, which require the physician to inform a woman of the nature and risks of the abortion procedure and the medical risks of carrying to term, are neutral requirements comparable to those imposed in other medical procedures. Those sections indicate no effort by the State to influence the woman's choice in any way. If anything, such requirements enhance, rather than skew, the woman's decisionmaking.

III.

The 24-hour waiting period required by §§3205(a)(1)-(2) of the Pennsylvania statute raises even more serious concerns. Such a requirement arguably furthers the State's interests in two ways, neither of which is constitutionally permissible.

First, it may be argued that the 24-hour delay is justified by the mere fact that it is likely to reduce the number of abortions, thus furthering the State's interest in potential life. But such an argument would justify any form of coercion that placed an obstacle in the woman's path. The State cannot further its interests by simply wearing down the ability of the pregnant woman to exercise her constitutional right.

Second, it can more reasonably be argued that the 24-hour delay furthers the State's interest in ensuring that the woman's decision is informed and thoughtful. But there is no evidence that the mandated delay benefits women or that it is necessary to enable the physician to convey any relevant information to the patient. The mandatory delay thus appears to rest on outmoded and unacceptable assumptions about the decisionmaking capacity of women. While there are well-established and consistently maintained reasons for the State to view with skepticism the ability of minors to make decisions, none of those reasons applies to an adult woman's decisionmaking ability. . . .

In the alternative, the delay requirement may be premised on the belief that the decision to terminate a pregnancy is presumptively wrong. This premise is illegitimate. Those who disagree vehemently about the legality and morality of abortion agree about one thing: The decision to terminate a pregnancy is profound and difficult. No person undertakes such a decision lightly — and States may not presume that a woman has failed to reflect adequately merely because her conclusion differs from the State's preference. A woman who has, in the privacy of her thoughts and conscience, weighed the options and made her decision cannot be forced to reconsider all, simply because the State believes she has come to the wrong conclusion.

Part of the constitutional liberty to choose is the equal dignity to which each of us is entitled. A woman who decides to terminate her pregnancy is entitled to the same respect as a woman who decides to carry the fetus to term. The mandatory waiting period denies women that equal respect.

IV.

In my opinion, a correct application of the "undue burden" standard leads to the same conclusion concerning the constitutionality of these requirements. A state-imposed burden on the exercise of a constitutional right is measured both by its effects and by its character: A burden may be "undue" either because the burden is too severe or because it lacks a legitimate, rational justification.

The 24-hour delay requirement fails both parts of this test. The findings of the District Court establish the severity of the burden that the 24-hour delay imposes on many pregnant women. Yet even in those cases in which the delay is not especially onerous, it is, in my opinion, "undue" because there is no evidence that such a delay serves a useful and legitimate purpose. As indicated above, there is no legitimate reason to require a woman who has agonized over her decision to leave the clinic or hospital and return again another day. While a general requirement that a physician notify her patients about the risks of a proposed medical procedure is appropriate, a rigid requirement that all patients wait 24 hours or (what is true in practice) much longer to evaluate the significance of information that is either common knowledge or irrelevant is an irrational and, therefore, "undue" burden.

The counseling provisions are similarly infirm. Whenever government commands private citizens to speak or to listen, careful review of the justification for that command is particularly appropriate. In this case, the Pennsylvania statute directs that counselors provide women seeking abortions with information concerning alternatives to abortion, the availability of medical assistance benefits, and the possibility of child-support payments. The statute requires that this information be given to all women seeking abortions, including those for whom such information is clearly useless, such as those who are married, those who have undergone the procedure in the past and are fully aware of the options, and those who are fully convinced that abortion is their only reasonable option. Moreover, the statute requires physicians to inform all of their patients of "the probable gestational age of the unborn child." This information is of little decisional value in most cases, because 90% of all abortions are performed during the first trimester when fetal age has less relevance than when the fetus nears viability. . . . Accordingly, while I disagree with Parts IV, V-B, and V-D of the joint opinion, I join the remainder of the Court's opinion.

Justice BLACKMUN, concurring in part, concurring in the judgment in part, and dissenting in part.

I join parts I, II, III, V-A, V-C, and VI of the joint opinion of Justices O'Connor, Kennedy, and Souter, ante.

[R]estrictive abortion laws force women to endure physical invasions far more substantial than those this Court has held to violate the constitutional principle of bodily integrity in other contexts. . . . Further, [such restrictions] deprive[] a woman of the right to make her own decision about reproduction and family planning. . . . The decision to terminate or continue a pregnancy has no less an impact on a woman's life than decisions about contraception or marriage. Because motherhood has a dramatic impact on a woman's educational prospects, employment opportunities, and self-determination, restrictive abortion laws deprive her of basic control over her life. For these reasons, "the decision whether or not to beget or bear a child" lies at "the very heart of this cluster of constitutionally protected choices."

A State's restrictions on a woman's right to terminate her pregnancy also implicate constitutional guarantees of gender equality. State restrictions on abortion compel women to continue pregnancies they otherwise might terminate. By restricting the right to terminate pregnancies, the State conscripts women's bodies into its service, forcing women to continue their pregnancies, suffer the pains of childbirth, and in most instances, provide years of maternal care. The State does not compensate women for their services; instead, it assumes that they owe this duty as a matter of course. This assumption — that women can simply be forced to accept the "natural" status and incidents of motherhood — appears to rest upon a conception of women's role that has triggered the protection of the Equal Protection Clause. The joint opinion recognizes that these assumptions about women's place in society "are no longer consistent with our understanding of the family, the individual, or the Constitution." . . .

Application of the strict scrutiny standard results in the invalidation of all the challenged provisions. Indeed, as this Court has invalidated virtually identical provisions in prior cases, stare decisis requires that we again strike them down.

Chief Justice REHNQUIST, with whom Justice White, Justice Scalia, and Justice Thomas join, concurring in the judgment in part and dissenting in part.

The joint opinion, following its newly-minted variation on stare decisis, retains the outer shell of Roe v. Wade, but beats a wholesale retreat from the substance of that case. We believe that Roe was wrongly decided, and that it can and should be overruled consistently with our traditional approach to stare decisis in constitutional cases. We would . . . uphold the challenged provisions of the Pennsylvania statute in their entirety.

I.

Unlike marriage, procreation and contraception, abortion "involves the purposeful termination of potential life." The abortion decision must therefore "be recognized as sui generis, different in kind from the others that the Court has protected under the rubric of personal or family privacy and autonomy." One cannot ignore the fact that a woman is not isolated in her pregnancy, and that the decision to abort necessarily involves the destruction of a fetus. See Michael H. v. Gerald D., n. [d] (To look "at the act which is assertedly the subject of a liberty interest in isolation from its effect upon other people [is] like inquiring whether there is a liberty interest in firing a gun where the case at hand happens to involve its discharge into another person's body").

Nor do the historical traditions of the American people support the view that the right to terminate one's pregnancy is "fundamental." The common law which we inherited from England made abortion after "quickening" an offense. At the time of the adoption of the Fourteenth Amendment, statutory prohibitions or restrictions on abortion were commonplace; in 1868, at least 28 of the then-37 States and 8 Territories had statutes banning or limiting abortion. By the turn of the century virtually every State had a law prohibiting or restricting abortion on its books. By the middle of the present century, a liberalization trend had set in. But 21 of the restrictive abortion laws in effect in 1868 were still in effect in 1973 when *Roe* was decided, and an overwhelming majority of the States prohibited abortion unless necessary to preserve the life or health of the mother. On this record, it can scarcely be said that any deeply rooted tradition of relatively unrestricted abortion in our history supported the classification of the right to abortion as "fundamental" under the Due Process Clause of the Fourteenth Amendment.

We think, therefore, both in view of this history and of our decided cases dealing with substantive liberty under the Due Process Clause, that the Court was mistaken in *Roe* when it classified a woman's decision to terminate her pregnancy as a "fundamental right" that could be abridged only in a manner which withstood "strict scrutiny." . . .

II.

[The] joint opinion [cannot] bring itself to say that *Roe* was correct as an original matter. . . . Instead, . . . the opinion . . . contains an elaborate discussion of stare decisis. This discussion of the principle of stare decisis appears to be almost entirely dicta, because the joint opinion does not apply that principle in dealing with *Roe*. *Roe* decided that a woman had a fundamental right to an abortion. The joint opinion rejects that view. *Roe* decided that abortion regulations were to be subjected to "strict scrutiny" and could be justified only in the light of "compelling state interests." The joint opinion rejects that view. *Roe* analyzed abortion regulation under a rigid trimester framework, a framework which has guided this Court's decisionmaking for 19 years. The joint opinion rejects that framework. . . . Whatever the "central holding" of *Roe* that is left after the joint opinion finishes dissecting it is surely not the result of that principle.

In our view, authentic principles of stare decisis do not require that any portion of the reasoning in *Roe* be kept intact. [E]rroneous decisions in such constitutional cases are uniquely durable, because correction through legislative action, save for constitutional amendment, is impossible. [W]hen it becomes clear that a prior constitutional interpretation is unsound we are obliged to reexamine the question.

The joint opinion discusses several stare decisis factors which, it asserts, point toward retaining a portion of *Roe*. Two of these factors are that the main "factual underpinning" of *Roe* has remained the same, and that its doctrinal foundation is no weaker now than it was in 1973. Of course, what might be called the basic facts which gave rise to *Roe* have remained the same — women become pregnant, there is a point somewhere, depending on medical technology, where a fetus becomes viable, and women give birth to children. But this is only to say that the same facts which gave rise to *Roe* will continue to give rise to similar cases. It is not a reason, in and of itself, why those cases must be decided in the same incorrect manner as was the first case to deal with the question. . . .

The joint opinion also points to the reliance interests involved in this context in its effort to explain why precedent must be followed for precedent's sake. . . . But . . . any traditional notion of reliance is not applicable here. The Court today cuts back on the protection afforded by *Roe*, and no one claims that this action defeats any reliance interest in the disavowed trimester framework. . . .

The joint opinion thus turns to what can only be described as an unconventional — and unconvincing — notion of reliance, a view based on the surmise that the availability of abortion since *Roe* has led to "two decades of economic and social developments" that would be undercut if the error of *Roe* were recognized. The joint opinion's assertion of this fact is undeveloped and totally conclusory. . . . Surely it is dubious to suggest that women have reached their "places in society" in reliance upon *Roe*, rather than as a result of their determination to obtain higher education and compete with men in the job market, and of society's increasing recognition of their ability to fill positions that were previously thought to be reserved only for men.

[T]he joint opinion's argument is based solely on generalized assertions about the national psyche, on a belief that the people of this country have grown accustomed to the *Roe* decision over the last 19 years and have "ordered their thinking and living around" it. As an initial matter, one might inquire how the joint opinion can view the "central holding" of *Roe* as so deeply rooted in our constitutional culture, when it so casually uproots and disposes of that same decision's trimester framework. Furthermore, at various points in the past, the same could have been said about this Court's erroneous decisions that the Constitution allowed "separate but equal" treatment of minorities, see Plessy v. Ferguson, or that "liberty" under the Due Process Clause protected "freedom of contract." See Lochner v. New York. . . . [T]he simple fact that a generation or more had grown used to these major decisions did not prevent the Court from correcting its errors in those cases, nor should it prevent us from correctly interpreting the Constitution here.

Apparently realizing that conventional stare decisis principles do not support its position, the joint opinion advances a belief that retaining a portion of *Roe* is necessary to protect the "legitimacy" of this Court. Because the Court must take care to render decisions "grounded truly in principle," and not simply as political and social compromises, the joint opinion properly declares it to be this Court's duty to ignore the public criticism and protest that may arise as a result of a decision. . . .

But the joint opinion goes on to state that when the Court "resolve[s] the sort of intensely divisive controversy reflected in *Roe* and those rare, comparable cases," its decision is exempt from reconsideration under established principles of stare decisis in constitutional cases. This is so, the joint opinion contends, because in those "intensely divisive" cases the Court has "call[ed] the contending sides of a national controversy to end their national division by accepting a common mandate rooted in the Constitution," and must therefore take special care not to be perceived as "surrender[ing] to political pressure" and continued opposition. This is a truly novel principle, one which is contrary to both the Court's historical practice and to the Court's traditional willingness to tolerate criticism of its opinions. Under this principle, when the Court has ruled on a divisive issue, it is apparently prevented from overruling that decision for the sole reason that it was incorrect, unless opposition to the original decision has died away.

The first difficulty with this principle lies in its assumption that cases which are "intensely divisive" can be readily distinguished from those that are not. . . . In addition, because the Court's duty is to ignore public opinion and criticism on issues that come before it, its members are in perhaps the worst position to judge whether a decision divides the Nation deeply enough to justify such uncommon protection. Although many of the Court's decisions divide the populace to a large degree, we have not previously on that account shied away from applying normal rules of stare decisis when urged to reconsider earlier decisions. Over the past 21 years, for example, the Court has overruled in whole or in part 34 of its previous constitutional decisions.

The joint opinion picks out and discusses two prior Court rulings [*Plessy* and *Lochner*], that it believes are of the "intensely divisive" variety, and concludes that they are of comparable dimension to *Roe.* It appears to us very odd indeed that the joint opinion chooses as benchmarks two cases in which the Court chose not to adhere to erroneous constitutional precedent, but instead enhanced its stature by acknowledging and correcting its error, apparently in violation of the joint opinion's "legitimacy" principle. . . . There is no reason to think that either *Plessy* or *Lochner* produced the sort of public protest when they were decided that *Roe* did. There were undoubtedly large segments of the bench and bar who agreed with the dissenting views in those cases, but surely that cannot be what the Court means when it uses the term "intensely divisive," or many other cases would have to be added to the list. In terms of public protest, however, *Roe,* so far as we know, was unique. But just as the Court should not respond to that sort of protest by retreating from the decision simply to allay the concerns of the protesters, it should likewise not respond by determining to adhere to the decision at all costs lest it seem to be retreating under fire. Public protests should not alter the normal application of stare decisis, lest perfectly lawful protest activity be penalized by the Court itself.

Taking the joint opinion on its own terms, we doubt that its distinction between *Roe,* on the one hand, and *Plessy* and *Lochner,* on the other, withstands analysis. The joint opinion acknowledges that the Court improved its stature by overruling *Plessy* in *Brown* on a deeply divisive issue. And our decision in *West Coast Hotel,* which overruled Adkins v. Children's Hospital and *Lochner,* was rendered at a time when Congress was considering President Franklin Roosevelt's proposal to "reorganize" this Court and enable him to name six additional Justices in the event that any member of the Court over the age of 70 did not elect to retire. It is difficult to imagine a situation in which the Court would face more intense opposition to a prior ruling than it did at that time, and, under the general principle proclaimed in the joint opinion, the Court seemingly should have responded to this opposition by stubbornly refusing to reexamine the Lochner rationale, lest it lose legitimacy by appearing to "overrule under fire."

The joint opinion agrees that the Court's stature would have been seriously damaged if in *Brown* and *West Coast Hotel* it had dug in its heels and refused to apply normal principles of stare decisis to the earlier decisions. But the opinion contends that the Court was entitled to overrule *Plessy* and *Lochner* in those cases, despite the existence of opposition to the original decisions, only because both the Nation and the Court had learned new lessons in the interim. This is at best a feebly supported, post hoc rationalization for those decisions.

For example, the opinion asserts that the Court could justifiably overrule its decision in Lochner only because the Depression had convinced "most people" that constitutional protection of contractual freedom contributed to an economy that failed to protect the welfare of all. Surely the joint opinion does not mean to suggest that people saw this Court's failure to uphold minimum wage statutes as the cause of the Great Depression! In any event, the *Lochner* Court did not base its rule upon the policy judgment that an unregulated market was fundamental to a stable economy; it simply believed, erroneously, that "liberty" under the Due Process Clause protected the "right to make a contract." Nor is it the case that the people of this Nation only discovered the dangers of extreme laissez faire economics because of the Depression. State laws regulating maximum hours and minimum wages were in existence well before that time. . . .

When the Court finally recognized its error in *West Coast Hotel*, it did not engage in the post hoc rationalization that the joint opinion attributes to it today; it did not state that *Lochner* had been based on an economic view that had fallen into disfavor, and that it therefore should be overruled. Chief Justice Hughes in his opinion for the Court simply recognized what Justice Holmes had previously recognized in his *Lochner* dissent, that "[t]he Constitution does not speak of freedom of contract." Although the Court did acknowledge in the last paragraph of its opinion the state of affairs during the then-current Depression, the theme of the opinion is that the Court had been mistaken as a matter of constitutional law when it embraced "freedom of contract" 32 years previously.

The joint opinion also agrees that the Court acted properly in rejecting the doctrine of "separate but equal" in *Brown*. In fact, the opinion lauds *Brown* in comparing it to *Roe*. This is strange, in that under the opinion's "legitimacy" principle the Court would seemingly have been forced to adhere to its erroneous decision in *Plessy* because of its "intensely divisive" character. To us, adherence to *Roe* today under the guise of "legitimacy" would seem to resemble more closely adherence to *Plessy* on the same ground. The joint opinion concludes that . . . repudiation [of *Plessy*] was justified only because of newly discovered evidence that segregation had the effect of treating one race as inferior to another. But it can hardly be argued that this was not urged upon those who decided *Plessy*, . . . The Court in *Brown* simply recognized, as Justice Harlan had recognized beforehand, that the Fourteenth Amendment does not permit racial segregation. The rule of *Brown* is not tied to popular opinion about the evils of segregation; it is a judgment that the Equal Protection Clause does not permit racial segregation, no matter whether the public might come to believe that it is beneficial. . . .

. . . The Judicial Branch derives its legitimacy, not from following public opinion, but from deciding by its best lights whether legislative enactments of the popular branches of Government comport with the Constitution. The doctrine of stare decisis is an adjunct of this duty, and should be no more subject to the vagaries of public opinion than is the basic judicial task.

[I]n assuming that the Court is perceived as "surrender[ing] to political pressure" when it overrules a controversial decision, the joint opinion forgets that there are two sides to any controversy. The joint opinion asserts that, in order to protect its legitimacy, the Court must refrain from overruling a controversial decision lest it be viewed as favoring those who oppose the decision. But a decision to adhere to prior precedent is subject to the same criticism, for in such a case one can easily argue that the Court is responding to those who have demonstrated in favor of the original decision. The decision in *Roe* has engendered large demonstrations, including repeated marches on this Court and on Congress, both in opposition to and in support of that opinion. A decision either way on *Roe* can therefore be perceived as favoring one group or the other. But this perceived dilemma arises only if one assumes, as the joint opinion does, that the Court should make its decisions with a view toward speculative public perceptions. If one assumes instead, as the Court surely did in both *Brown* and *West Coast Hotel,* that the Court's legitimacy is enhanced by faithful interpretation of the Constitution irrespective of public opposition, such self-engendered difficulties may be put to one side. . . .

The end result of the joint opinion's paeans of praise for legitimacy is the enunciation of a brand new standard for evaluating state regulation of a woman's right to abortion — the "undue burden" standard. [T]his standard is based even more on a judge's subjective determinations than was the trimester framework, [it] will do nothing to prevent "judges from roaming at large in the constitutional field" guided only by their personal views. Because the undue burden standard is plucked from nowhere, the question of what is a "substantial obstacle" to abortion will undoubtedly engender a variety of conflicting views. For example, in the very matter before us now, the authors of the joint opinion would uphold Pennsylvania's 24-hour waiting period, concluding that a "particular burden" on some women is not a substantial obstacle. But the authors would at the same time strike down Pennsylvania's spousal notice provision, after finding that in a "large fraction" of cases the provision will be a substantial obstacle. . . .

Furthermore, while striking down the spousal notice regulation, the joint opinion would uphold a parental consent restriction that certainly places very substantial obstacles in the path of a minor's abortion choice. The joint opinion is forthright in admitting that it draws this distinction based on a policy judgment that parents will have the best interests of their children at heart, while the same is not necessarily true of husbands as to their wives. This may or may not be a correct judgment, but it is quintessentially a legislative one. . . . Despite the efforts of the joint opinion, the undue burden standard presents nothing more workable than the trimester framework which it discards today. Under the guise of the Constitution, this Court will still impart its own preferences on the States in the form of a complex abortion code. . . .

We have stated above our belief that the Constitution does not subject state abortion regulations to heightened scrutiny. . . . A woman's interest in having an abortion is a form of liberty protected by the Due Process Clause, but States may regulate abortion procedures in ways rationally related to a legitimate state interest. . . .

[Requiring physicians to provide information about] "[t]he risks associated with an abortion and the availability of assistance that might make the alternative of normal childbirth more attractive than it might otherwise appear" . . . is rationally related to the State's interest in assuring that a woman's consent to an abortion be a fully informed decision. [I]n providing time for reflection and reconsideration, the waiting period helps ensure that a woman's decision to abort is a well-considered one, and reasonably furthers the State's legitimate interest in maternal health and in the unborn life of the fetus. . . . [T]he spousal notification requirement also rationally furthers . . . legitimate state interests. First, a husband's interests in procreation within marriage and in the potential life of his unborn child are certainly substantial ones. [B]y providing that a husband will usually know of his spouse's intent to have an abortion, the provision makes it more likely that the husband will participate in deciding the fate of his unborn child, a possibility that might otherwise have been denied him. This participation might in some cases result in a decision to proceed with the pregnancy.

[The] State also has a legitimate interest in promoting "the integrity of the marital relationship." [I]n our view, the spousal notice requirement is a rational attempt by the State to improve truthful communication between spouses and encourage collaborative decisionmaking, and thereby fosters marital integrity. . . .

[W]e therefore would hold that each of the challenged provisions of the Pennsylvania statute is consistent with the Constitution. It bears emphasis that our conclusion in this regard does not carry with it any necessary approval of these regulations. Our task is, as always, to decide only whether the challenged provisions of a law comport with the United States Constitution. If, as we believe, these do, their wisdom as a matter of public policy is for the people of Pennsylvania to decide.

Justice SCALIA, with whom the Chief Justice, Justice White, and Justice Thomas join, concurring in the judgment in part and dissenting in part.

[T]he issue in this case [is] not whether the power of a woman to abort her unborn child is a "liberty" in the absolute sense; or even whether it is a liberty of great importance to many women. Of course it is both. The issue is whether it is a liberty protected by the Constitution of the United States. I am sure it is not. I reach that conclusion [for] the same reason I reach the conclusion that bigamy is not constitutionally protected — because of two simple facts: (1) the Constitution says absolutely nothing about it, and (2) the longstanding traditions of American society have permitted it to be legally proscribed.[a]

The Court destroys the proposition, evidently meant to represent my position, that "liberty" includes "only those practices, defined at the most specific level, that were protected against government interference by other rules of law when the Fourteenth Amendment was ratified." That is not, however, what *Michael H.* says; it merely observes that, in defining "liberty," we may not disregard a specific, "relevant tradition protecting, or denying protection to, the asserted right." But the Court does not wish to be fettered by any such limitations on its preferences. The

---

a. The Court's suggestion that adherence to tradition would require us to uphold laws against interracial marriage is entirely wrong. Any tradition in that case was contradicted by a text — an Equal Protection Clause that explicitly establishes racial equality as a constitutional value. The enterprise launched in *Roe,* by contrast, sought to establish — in the teeth of a clear, contrary tradition — a value found nowhere in the constitutional text. There is, of course, no comparable tradition barring recognition of a "liberty interest" in carrying one's child to term free from state efforts to kill it. . . .

Court's statement that it is "tempting" to acknowledge the authoritativeness of tradition in order to "cur[b] the discretion of federal judges," is of course rhetoric rather than reality; no government official is "tempted" to place restraints upon his own freedom of action, which is why Lord Acton did not say "Power tends to purify." The Court's temptation is in the quite opposite and more natural direction — towards systematically eliminating checks upon its own power; and it succumbs.

. . . [A]pplying the rational basis test, I would uphold the Pennsylvania statute in its entirety. I must, however, respond to a few of the more outrageous arguments in today's opinion, which it is beyond human nature to leave unanswered. . . .

[A]fter more than 19 years of effort by some of the brightest (and most determined) legal minds in the country, after more than 10 cases upholding abortion rights in this Court, and after dozens upon dozens of amicus briefs submitted in this and other cases, the best the Court can do to explain how it is that the word "liberty" must be thought to include the right to destroy human fetuses is to rattle off a collection of adjectives that simply decorate a value judgment and conceal a political choice. The right to abort, we are told, inheres in "liberty" because it is among "a person's most basic decisions"; it involves a "most intimate and personal choic[e]"; it is "central to personal dignity and autonomy"; it "originate[s]" within the zone of conscience and belief"; it is "too intimate and personal" for state interference; it reflects "intimate views" of a "deep, personal character"; it involves "intimate relationships," and notions of "personal autonomy and bodily integrity"; and it concerns a particularly "important decisio[n]." But it is obvious to anyone applying "reasoned judgment" that the same adjectives can be applied to many forms of conduct that this Court . . . has held are not entitled to constitutional protection — because, like abortion, they are forms of conduct that have long been criminalized in American society. Those adjectives might be applied, for example, to homosexual sodomy, polygamy, adult incest, and suicide, all of which are equally "intimate" and "deep[ly] personal" decisions involving "personal autonomy and bodily integrity," and all of which can constitutionally be proscribed because it is our unquestionable constitutional tradition that they are proscribable. It is not reasoned judgment that supports the Court's decision; only personal predilection. . . .

The "undue burden" standard is not at all the generally applicable principle the joint opinion pretends it to be; rather, it is a unique concept created specially for this case, to preserve some judicial foothold in this ill-gotten territory. . . . And "viability" is no longer the "arbitrary" dividing line previously decried by Justice O'Connor in *Akron I*; the Court now announces that "the attainment of viability may continue to serve as the critical fact."[b] It is difficult to maintain the illusion that we are interpreting a Constitution rather than inventing one, when we amend its provisions so breezily.

---

b. Of course Justice O'Connor was correct in her former view. The arbitrariness of the viability line is confirmed by the Court's inability to offer any justification for it beyond the conclusory assertion that it is only at that point that the unborn child's life "can in reason and all fairness" be thought to override the interests of the mother. Precisely why is it that, at the magical second when machines currently in use (though not necessarily available to the particular woman) are able to keep an unborn child alive apart from its mother, the creature is suddenly able (under our Constitution) to be protected by law, whereas before that magical second it was not? That makes no more sense than according infants legal protection only after the point when they can feed themselves.

[W]hat is remarkable about the joint opinion's fact-intensive analysis is that it does not result in any measurable clarification of the "undue burden" standard. Rather, the approach of the joint opinion is, for the most part, simply to highlight certain facts in the record that apparently strike the three Justices as particularly significant in establishing (or refuting) the existence of an undue burden; after describing these facts, the opinion then simply announces that the provision either does or does not impose a "substantial obstacle" or an "undue burden." We do not know whether the same conclusions could have been reached on a different record, or in what respects the record would have had to differ before an opposite conclusion would have been appropriate. The inherently standardless nature of this inquiry invites the district judge to give effect to his personal preferences about abortion. By finding and relying upon the right facts, he can invalidate, it would seem, almost any abortion restriction that strikes him as "undue" — subject, of course, to the possibility of being reversed by a Circuit Court or Supreme Court that is as unconstrained in reviewing his decision as he was in making it.

To the extent I can discern any meaningful content in the "undue burden" standard as applied in the joint opinion, it appears to be that a State may not regulate abortion in such a way as to reduce significantly its incidence. The joint opinion repeatedly emphasizes that an important factor in the "undue burden" analysis is whether the regulation "prevent[s] a significant number of women from obtaining an abortion"; whether a "significant number of women . . . are likely to be deterred from procuring an abortion"; and whether the regulation often "deters" women from seeking abortions. We are not told, however, what forms of "deterrence" are impermissible or what degree of success in deterrence is too much to be tolerated. . . . [D]espite flowery rhetoric about the State's "substantial" and "profound" interest in "potential human life," and criticism of *Roe* for undervaluing that interest, the joint opinion permits the State to pursue that interest only so long as it is not too successful. . . . Reason finds no refuge in this jurisprudence of confusion. . . .

The Court's description of the place of *Roe* in the social history of the United States is unrecognizable. Not only did *Roe* not, as the Court suggests, resolve the deeply divisive issue of abortion; it did more than anything else to nourish it, by elevating it to the national level where it is infinitely more difficult to resolve. National politics were not plagued by abortion protests, national abortion lobbying, or abortion marches on Congress, before Roe v. Wade was decided. Profound disagreement existed among our citizens over the issue — as it does over other issues, such as the death penalty — but that disagreement was being worked out at the state level. As with many other issues, the division of sentiment within each State was not as closely balanced as it was among the population of the Nation as a whole, meaning not only that more people would be satisfied with the results of state-by-state resolution, but also that those results would be more stable. Pre-*Roe,* moreover, political compromise was possible.

Roe's mandate for abortion-on-demand destroyed the compromises of the past, rendered compromise impossible for the future, and required the entire issue to be resolved uniformly, at the national level. At the same time, *Roe* created a vast new class of abortion consumers and abortion proponents by eliminating the moral opprobrium that had attached to the act. ("If the Constitution guarantees abortion, how can it be bad?" — not an accurate line of thought, but a natural one.) Many favor all of those developments, and it is not for me to say that they are wrong.

But to portray *Roe* as the statesmanlike "settlement" of a divisive issue, a jurispru-dential Peace of Westphalia that is worth preserving, is nothing less than Orwellian. *Roe* fanned into life an issue that has inflamed our national politics in general, and has obscured with its smoke the selection of Justices to this Court in particular, ever since. . . .

. . . I cannot agree with, indeed I am appalled by, the Court's suggestion that the decision whether to stand by an erroneous constitutional decision must be strongly influenced — against overruling, no less — by the substantial and continuing public opposition the decision has generated. The Court's judgment that any other course would "subvert the Court's legitimacy" must be another consequence of reading the error-filled history book that described the deeply divided country brought together by *Roe*. In my history book, the Court was covered with dishonor and deprived of legitimacy by Dred Scott v. Sandford, 19 How. 393 (1857), an erro-neous (and widely opposed) opinion that it did not abandon, rather than by West Coast Hotel Co. v. Parrish, which produced the famous "switch in time" from the Court's erroneous (and widely opposed) constitutional opposition to the social measures of the New Deal. . . .

In truth, I am as distressed as the Court is . . . about the "political pressure" directed to the Court: the marches, the mail, the protests aimed at inducing us to change our opinions. How upsetting it is, that so many of our citizens (good people, not lawless ones, on both sides of this abortion issue, and on various sides of other issues as well) think that we Justices should properly take into account their views, as though we were engaged not in ascertaining an objective law but in deter-mining some kind of social consensus. The Court would profit, I think, from giving less attention to the fact of this distressing phenomenon, and more attention to the cause of it. That cause permeates today's opinion: a new mode of constitutional adjudication that relies not upon text and traditional practice to determine the law, but upon what the Court calls "reasoned judgment," which turns out to be nothing but philosophical predilection and moral intuition. . . .

What makes all this relevant to the bothersome application of "political pres-sure" against the Court are the twin facts that the American people love democracy and the American people are not fools. As long as this Court thought (and the people thought) that we Justices were doing essentially lawyers' work up here — reading text and discerning our society's traditional understanding of that text — the public pretty much left us alone. Texts and traditions are facts to study, not convictions to demonstrate about. But if . . . our pronouncement of constitutional law rests primarily on value judgments, then a free and intelligent people's attitude towards us can be expected to be (ought to be) quite different. The people know that their value judgments are quite as good as those taught in any law school — maybe better. If, indeed, the "liberties" protected by the Constitution are, as the Court says, undefined and unbounded, then the people should demonstrate, to protest that we do not implement their values instead of ours. Not only that, but confirmation hearings for new Justices should deteriorate into question-and-answer sessions in which Senators go through a list of their constituents' most favored and most disfavored alleged constitutional rights, and seek the nominee's commitment to support or oppose them. Value judgments, after all, should be voted on, not dictated; and if our Constitution has somehow accidently committed them to the Supreme Court, at least we can have a sort of plebiscite each time a new nominee to that body is put forward. . . .

[T]here is a poignant aspect to today's opinion. Its length, and what might be called its epic tone, suggest that its authors believe they are bringing to an end a troublesome era in the history of our Nation and of our Court. "It is the dimension" of authority, they say, to "cal[l] the contending sides of national controversy to end their national division by accepting a common mandate rooted in the Constitution."

There comes vividly to mind a portrait by Emanuel Leutze that hangs in the Harvard Law School: Roger Brooke Taney, painted in 1859, the 82d year of his life, the 24th of his Chief Justiceship, the second after his opinion in *Dred Scott*. He is all in black, sitting in a shadowed red armchair, left hand resting upon a pad of paper in his lap, right hand hanging limply, almost lifelessly, beside the inner arm of the chair. He sits facing the viewer, and staring straight out. There seems to be on his face, and in his deep-set eyes, an expression of profound sadness and disillusionment. Perhaps he always looked that way, even when dwelling upon the happiest of thoughts. But those of us who know how the lustre of his great Chief Justiceship came to be eclipsed by *Dred Scott* cannot help believing that he had that case — its already apparent consequences for the Court, and its soon-to-be-played-out consequences for the Nation — burning on his mind. I expect that two years earlier he, too, had thought himself "call[ing] the contending sides of national controversy to end their national division by accepting a common mandate rooted in the Constitution." It is no more realistic for us in this case, than it was for him in that, to think that an issue of the sort they both involved — an issue involving life and death, freedom and subjugation — can be "speedily and finally settled" by the Supreme Court, as President James Buchanan in his inaugural address said the issue of slavery in the territories would be. Quite to the contrary, by foreclosing all democratic outlet for the deep passions this issue arouses, by banishing the issue from the political forum that gives all participants, even the losers, the satisfaction of a fair hearing and an honest fight, by continuing the imposition of a rigid national rule instead of allowing for regional differences, the Court merely prolongs and intensifies the anguish.

We should get out of this area, where we have no right to be, and where we do neither ourselves nor the country any good by remaining.

Discussion

1. Casey *and women's equality.* Note carefully how the Joint Opinion begins to emphasize the special interests of women more than the original opinion in *Roe*. For example, in the section on stare decisis the Joint Opinion states that "[t]he ability of women to participate equally in the economic and social life of the Nation has been facilitated by their ability to control their reproductive lives." The authors of the Joint Opinion argue that a pregnant woman's "suffering is too intimate and personal for the State to insist, without more, upon its own vision of the woman's role, however dominant that vision has been in the course of our history and our culture. The destiny of the woman must be shaped to a large extent on her own conception of her spiritual imperatives and her place in society." Finally, the Joint Opinion compares the spousal notice provision to the traditional gender status regulations of the law of coverture, which gave husbands absolute dominion over their wives. Note also Justice Blackmun's concurrence, which emphasizes equality concerns: He argues that the "assumption — that women can simply be forced to accept the 'natural' status and incidents of motherhood — appears to rest on a conception of women's role that has

triggered the protection of the Equal Protection Clause." Can you formulate an equal protection argument for abortion rights based on the opinions in *Casey*? How does this argument avoid the problems created by *Geduldig* and *Feeney*?

2. *Stare decisis.* If the Joint Opinion were willing to state that *Roe* was rightly decided in 1973, would the section on stare decisis have been at all necessary? After all, the arguments for stare decisis matter most in cases that the Court thinks were wrongly decided originally but that should nevertheless not be overruled for a variety of prudential reasons. Is *Roe* such a case?

Indeed, if the Court does not begin with the premise that *Roe* was correctly decided, it places *Roe* in the same position as a decision like *Plessy*, i.e., an opinion which is presumed to be wrong but whose overruling would disturb reliance interests. The question then becomes whether its evils are sufficiently great that it must be overruled or whether those evils can be tolerated. However, wouldn't the most powerful arguments against overturning *Roe* be not that *Roe*'s evils are not too great but that (as the Court itself suggests) the right to abortion has worked a positive good for women in the United States?

3. *The Court's role.* The Joint Opinion suggests that it would be inappropriate for the Court to overturn *Roe* because a consensus has not formed that it is wrong, and the Court would appear to be buckling in the face of political pressure.

(a) If a consensus did form that *Roe* was incorrectly decided, and the Court responded to it, why would this not also be buckling in the face of political pressure? Is the Court saying that overwhelming public sentiment against an opinion isn't political pressure or that when a consensus has formed it no longer feels particularly partisan to follow it? In what sense, then, is the Court a countermajoritarian institution?

(b) The Joint Opinion also argues that

> The Court must take care to speak and act in ways that allow people to accept its decisions on the terms the Court claims for them, as grounded truly in principle, not as compromises with social and political pressures having, as such, no bearing on the principled choices that the Court is obliged to make. Thus, the Court's legitimacy depends on making legally principled decisions under circumstances in which their principled character is sufficiently plausible to be accepted by the Nation.

Is this argument itself an argument from principle or an argument that strongly evidences the Court's reaction to social and political pressures?

(c) Even if *Casey* does not overrule *Roe*, it significantly revises *Roe* in ways that appear responsive to the concerns of *Roe*'s critics. For example, *Casey* abolishes the trimester framework, and it allows restrictions on abortion for the purpose of protecting unborn life in the period *before* viability, so long as the burden on exercise of the pregnant woman's right to choice is not "undue." In revising *Roe* in these ways, why isn't the Court doing what the Joint Opinion said it should not do?

Are there good reasons for the Court to interpret the Constitution in ways that are responsive to public opinion? On balance, is it a good or bad thing that the plurality's opinion in *Casey* is more in dialogue with the claims of the pro-choice and pro-life movements than *Roe* itself had been?

4. *Undue burden.* The test that emerges from the *Casey* opinion is that the states may not place an "undue burden" on the woman's right to choose to abort. It

defines this as "a state regulation [that] has the purpose or effect of placing a substantial obstacle in the path of a woman seeking an abortion of a nonviable fetus." The Court draws an opposition between statutes that are "calculated to inform the woman's free choice," and those that "hinder it." This allows abortion opponents an opportunity to persuade, but not coerce, a pregnant woman to forego exercising her right to have an abortion. Why does the Court think that the 24-hour waiting period is in the former category rather than the latter?

Is the Court's application of the undue burden test with respect to the 24-hour waiting period consistent with its application of the test with respect to the spousal notification provision? In both cases the district court found that the provisions at issue would hinder women from obtaining abortions. Why did the Court argue that only the spousal consent provision was an undue burden? Note that although only some women would be deterred by the 24-hour waiting period, the same is also true of the spousal notification provision. Is the difference that the spousal notification provision reminded the Court too much of the old model of coverture, whereby the husband exercised control over a woman's decisions, whereas the 24-hour waiting period appeared to ensure that women deliberated about their decisions? (This might suggest that sex equality values guide application of the undue burden test, even though the test makes no mention of them.)

Why is paternalism by a State less troublesome from the standpoint of the Due Process Clause than paternalism by a husband? Should it matter that the state does not impose a 24-hour waiting period on women for any other medical operation (for example, breast surgery, mastectomies, in vitro fertilization, or sterilization)? Recall the nineteenth-century arguments by the medical profession that women wanted abortions for frivolous reasons. Why would a State assume that women are more likely to make decisions about abortion without due consideration than any other decision affecting their lives and their health?

STENBERG v. CARHART, 530 U.S. 914 (2000): The Court struck down a Nebraska law that banned any "partial birth abortion" unless that procedure "is necessary to save the life of the mother." The mother's life must be "endangered by a physical disorder, physical illness, or physical injury, including a life-endangering physical condition caused by or arising from the pregnancy itself." The statute defines "partial birth abortion" as a procedure in which the doctor "partially delivers vaginally a living unborn child before killing the . . . child." It defines that to mean "intentionally delivering into the vagina a living unborn child, or a substantial portion thereof, for the purpose of performing a procedure that the [abortionist] knows will kill the . . . child and does kill the . . . child." Violation of the law is a felony, and it provides for the automatic revocation of a convicted doctor's state license to practice medicine.

Ninety percent of all abortions occur in the first trimester (up to 12 weeks), and about 10 percent of all abortions occur during the second trimester (12 to 24 weeks). The most common abortion procedure in the second trimester is dilation and evacuation (D&E), which involves dilation of the cervix and removal of at least some fetal tissue using nonvacuum surgical instruments. After the 15th week D&E procedures may require that the fetus be dismembered or that parts of the fetus be collapsed to facilitate evacuation from the uterus. When the fetus is dismembered, it typically occurs as the doctor pulls a portion of the fetus through the cervix into the birth canal. The risks of mortality and complication that accompany D&E are significantly lower than those that accompany the next safest mid-second-trimester procedures, called induced labor procedures.

A variation of D&E, known as intact D&E, is used after 16 weeks, when the fetus's head has become too big to pass through the cervix, so that vacuum aspiration is no longer an effective method for abortion. Intact D&E involves removing the fetus from the uterus through the cervix "intact," i.e., in one pass rather than several passes. The intact D&E proceeds in one of two ways, depending on whether the fetus presents head first or feet first. In the head-first method, the doctor collapses the skull of the fetus; and the doctor then extracts the entire fetus through the cervix. The feet-first method is known as dilation and extraction (D&X). D&X is ordinarily associated with the term "partial birth abortion." The plaintiff, Dr. Carhart, sees approximately 10 to 20 cases a year that require a D&X procedure. The trial court concluded that clear and convincing evidence established that the D&X procedure used by Carhart is superior to, and safer than, the D&E and other abortion procedures used during the relevant gestational period.

Eight justices wrote opinions in the case. Justice Breyer wrote the majority opinion, joined by Justices Stevens, O'Connor, Souter, and Ginsburg. He argued that the Nebraska law violated *Casey* on two grounds. First the prohibition on partial birth abortions in the second trimester "lacks any exception 'for the preservation of the . . . health of the mother.'" Breyer quoted *Casey* and *Roe* for the proposition that "'subsequent to viability, the State in promoting its interest in the potentiality of human life may, if it chooses, regulate, and even proscribe, abortion except where it is necessary, in appropriate medical judgment, for the preservation of the life or health of the mother.'" 505 U.S., at 879 (quoting *Roe*). He then noted that, under *Casey*, "[t]he State's interest in regulating abortion previability is considerably weaker than postviability." Because *Casey* "requires a health exception in order to validate even a postviability abortion regulation, it at a minimum requires the same in respect to previability regulation."

This principle Justice Breyer argued, is not limited "to situations where the pregnancy itself creates a threat to health." "[A] State cannot subject women's health to significant risks . . . where state regulations force women to use riskier methods of abortion." . . . A risk to a woman's "health is the same whether it happens to arise from regulating a particular method of abortion, or from barring abortion entirely."

Justice Breyer pointed out that the court in *Casey* had permitted regulation of postviability abortions only based on the State's interest in "the potentiality of human life." In this case, the ban on partial birth abortions did not "directly further an interest 'in the potentiality of human life' by saving the fetus in question from destruction, as it regulates only a method of performing abortion." Although "Nebraska describes its interests differently," claiming that "the law 'show[s] concern for the life of the unborn,' 'prevent[s] cruelty to partially born children,' and 'preserve[s] the integrity of the medical profession,'" these different interests did not justify omitting any exception for a woman's health.

Finally, Breyer rejected Nebraska's claim that alternatives to D&X abortion are actually safer, so that a health exception permitting D&X abortions is not necessary. He relied on the district court's factual findings and accompanying testimony that D&X may be safer in some cases. Nevertheless, he agreed with Nebraska's claim that "[t]here are no general medical studies documenting comparative safety," and acknowledged that there is "a division of opinion among some medical experts over whether D&X is generally safer."

Because *Casey* requires an exception "where it is necessary, in appropriate medical judgment for the preservation of the life or health of the mother," the issue boiled down to what was meant by "necessary." Justice Breyer argued that this phrase "cannot refer to an absolute necessity or to absolute proof. Medical treatments and procedures are often considered appropriate (or inappropriate) in light of estimated comparative health risks (and health benefits) in particular cases. Neither can that phrase require unanimity of medical opinion. Doctors often differ in their estimation of comparative health risks and appropriate treatment. . . . [T]the division of medical opinion about the matter at most means uncertainty, a factor that signals the presence of risk, not its absence. That division here involves highly qualified knowledgeable experts on both sides of the issue. Where a significant body of medical opinion believes a procedure may bring with it greater safety for some patients and explains the medical reasons supporting that view, we cannot say that the presence of a different view by itself proves the contrary. Rather, the uncertainty means a significant likelihood that those who believe that D&X is a safer abortion method in certain circumstances may turn out to be right. If so, then the absence of a health exception will place women at an unnecessary risk of tragic health consequences. If they are wrong, the exception will simply turn out to have been unnecessary."

Second, Breyer held that the Nebraska statute violated the right to abortion because the language of the statute "applies to the more commonly used D&E procedure as well as to D&X." D&E may also involve drawing a substantial portion of a living fetus through the cervix, into the vagina. By restricting the safest and most common form of second trimester abortion, the statute imposed an "undue burden" under *Casey*.

Justice O'Connor concurred, noting that Nebraska could redraft the statute to remedy its constitutional defects: "[A] ban on partial-birth abortion that only proscribed the D&X method of abortion and that included an exception to preserve the life and health of the mother would be constitutional in my view."

Justice Stevens and Justice Ginsburg joined in each other's concurrences. Justice Stevens argued that "the procedure Nebraska here claims it seeks to ban is [not] more brutal, more gruesome, or less respectful of 'potential life' than the equally gruesome procedure Nebraska claims it still allows. . . . [T]he notion that either of these two equally gruesome procedures performed at this late stage of gestation is more akin to infanticide than the other, or that the State furthers any legitimate interest by banning one but not the other, is simply irrational." He also argued that "it [is] impossible for me to understand how a State has any legitimate interest in requiring a doctor to follow any procedure other than the one that he or she reasonably believes will best protect the woman in her exercise of this constitutional liberty." Quoting a Seventh Circuit opinion by Judge Richard Posner, Justice Ginsburg argued that the real purpose of Nebraska's law was not to protect fetuses or prohibit cruelty, but to "chip away" at the right to abortion. This in itself constituted an undue burden.

Justice Kennedy dissented, joined by Justice Rehnquist: "In the D&X [procedure] . . . . The fetus' arms and legs are delivered outside the uterus while the fetus is alive; witnesses to the procedure report seeing the body of the fetus moving outside the woman's body. At this point, the abortion procedure has the appearance of a live birth. . . . With only the head of the fetus remaining in utero, the abortionist tears open the skull. According to Dr. Martin Haskell, a leading proponent of the procedure, the appropriate instrument to be used at this stage of the abortion is a pair of scissors. Witnesses report observing the portion of the fetus outside the woman react to the skull penetration. The abortionist then inserts a suction tube and vacuums out the developing brain and other matter found within the skull. The process of making the size of the fetus' head smaller is given the clinically neutral term 'reduction procedure.' Brain death does not occur until after the skull invasion, and, according to Dr. Carhart, the heart of the fetus may continue to beat for minutes after the contents of the skull are vacuumed out. The abortionist next completes the delivery of a dead fetus, intact except for the damage to the head and the missing contents of the skull. Of the two described procedures, Nebraska seeks only to ban the D&X. In light of the description of the D&X procedure, it should go without saying that Nebraska's ban on partial-birth abortion furthers purposes States are entitled to pursue. Dr. Carhart nevertheless maintains the State has no legitimate interest in forbidding the D&X. As he interprets the controlling cases in this Court, the only two interests the State may advance through regulation of abortion are in the health of the woman who is considering the procedure and in the life of the fetus she carries. The Court, as I read its opinion, accedes to his views, misunderstanding *Casey* and the authorities it confirmed."

Justice Kennedy argued that "*Casey* is premised on the States having an important constitutional role in defining their interests in the abortion debate. . . . States may take sides in the abortion debate and come down on the side of life, even life in the unborn . . . States also have an interest in forbidding medical procedures which, in the State's reasonable determination, might cause the medical profession or society as a whole to become insensitive, even disdainful, to life, including life in the human fetus. Abortion, *Casey* held, has consequences beyond the woman and her fetus. The States' interests in regulating are of concomitant extension. *Casey* recognized that abortion is, 'fraught with consequences for . . . the persons who perform and assist in the procedure [and for] society which must confront the knowledge that these procedures exist, procedures some deem nothing short of an act of violence against innocent human life.' A State may take measures to ensure the medical profession and its members are viewed as healers, sustained by a compassionate and rigorous ethic and cognizant of the dignity and value of human life, even life which cannot survive without the assistance of others. *Casey* demonstrates that the interests asserted by the State are legitimate and recognized by law. It is argued, however, that a ban on the D&X does not further these interests. This is because, the reasoning continues, the D&E method, which Nebraska claims to be beyond its intent to regulate, can still be used to abort a fetus and is no less dehumanizing than the D&X method. . . . The issue is not whether members of the judiciary can see a difference between the two procedures. It is whether Nebraska can. The Court's refusal to recognize Nebraska's right to declare a moral difference between the procedure is a dispiriting disclosure of the illogic and illegitimacy of the Court's approach to the entire case."

The State of Nebraska "was entitled to find the existence of a consequential moral difference between the procedures," Justice Kennedy argued, given "substantial medical authority that D&X perverts the natural birth process to a greater degree than D&E, commandeering the live birth process until the skull is pierced. American Medical Association (AMA) publications describe the D&X abortion method as 'ethically wrong.' The D&X differs from the D&E because in the D&X the fetus is 'killed outside of the womb' where the fetus has 'an autonomy which

separates it from the right of the woman to choose treatments for her own body.';
see also App. 639-640; Brief for Association of American Physicians and Surgeons et
al. as Amici Curiae 27 ('Intact D&X is aberrant and troubling because the technique confuses the disparate role of a physician in childbirth and abortion in such
a way as to blur the medical, legal, and ethical line between infanticide and abortion'). Witnesses to the procedure relate that the fingers and feet of the fetus are
moving prior to the piercing of the skull; when the scissors are inserted in the back
of the head, the fetus' body, wholly outside the woman's body and alive, reacts as
though startled and goes limp. D&X's stronger resemblance to infanticide means
Nebraska could conclude the procedure presents a greater risk of disrespect for life
and a consequent greater risk to the profession and society, which depend for their
sustenance upon reciprocal recognition of dignity and respect. The Court is
without authority to second-guess this conclusion."

Justice Kennedy argued that the statute's lack of an exception for the health of
the mother was irrelevant. "Nebraska . . . was entitled to conclude that its ban, while
advancing important interests regarding the sanctity of life, deprived no woman of
a safe abortion and therefore did not impose a substantial obstacle on the rights of
any woman."

"The most to be said for the D&X is it may present an unquantified lower risk of
complication for a particular patient but that other proven safe procedures remain
available even for this patient. Under these circumstances, the Court is wrong to
limit its inquiry to the relative physical safety of the two procedures, with the slightest potential difference requiring the invalidation of the law. . . . Where the difference in physical safety is, at best, marginal, the State may take into account the
grave moral issues presented by a new abortion method. Dr. Carhart does not
decide to use the D&X based on a conclusion that it is best for a particular woman.
Unsubstantiated and generalized health differences which are, at best, marginal,
do not amount to a substantial obstacle to the abortion right. It is also important to
recognize that the D&X is effective only when the fetus is close to viable or, in fact,
viable; thus the State is regulating the process at the point where its interest in life
is nearing its peak."

"[I]n deferring to the physician's judgment, the Court turns back to cases
decided in the wake of *Roe,* cases which gave a physician's treatment decisions
controlling weight. . . . The Court's decision today echoes the *Akron* Court's deference to a physician's right to practice medicine in the way he sees fit. The Court, of
course, does not wish to cite *Akron;* yet the Court's holding is indistinguishable
from the reasoning in *Akron* that *Casey* repudiated. No doubt exists that today's
holding is based on a physician-first view which finds its primary support in that
now-discredited case."

Finally, Justice Kennedy rejected Justice Breyer's interpretation of the Nebraska
statute, concluding that "[i]n light of the statutory text, the commonsense understanding must be that the statute covers only the D&X [procedure]."

Justice Thomas wrote a long dissent, joined by Justice Scalia and Chief Justice
Rehnquist, in which he agreed that the Court had misinterpreted Nebraska's
statute, which in his view banned only D&X procedures. He criticized the majority's opinion as a return to pre-*Casey* jurisprudence: "According to the majority . . .
unless a State can conclusively establish that an abortion procedure is no safer
than other procedures, the State cannot regulate that procedure without including a health exception. The rule set forth by the majority and Justice O'Connor

dramatically expands on our prior abortion cases and threatens to undo any state regulation of abortion procedures. . . .

"[*Roe* and *Casey*] addressed only the situation in which a woman must obtain an abortion because of some threat to her health from continued pregnancy. But *Roe* and *Casey* say nothing at all about cases in which a physician considers one prohibited method of abortion to be preferable to permissible methods. Today's majority and Justice O'Connor twist *Roe* and *Casey* to apply to the situation in which a woman desires — for whatever reason — an abortion and wishes to obtain the abortion by some particular method. In other words, the majority and Justice O'Connor fail to distinguish between cases in which health concerns require a woman to obtain an abortion and cases in which health concerns cause a woman who desires an abortion (for whatever reason) to prefer one method over another. . . .

"[O]ne can think of vast bodies of law regulating abortion that are valid, one would hope, despite the lack of health exceptions. For example, physicians are presumably prohibited from using abortifacients that have not been approved by the Food and Drug Administration even if some physicians reasonably believe that these abortifacients would be safer for women than existing abortifacients. . . .

"Although *Roe* and *Casey* mandated a health exception for cases in which abortion is 'necessary' for a woman's health, the majority concludes that a procedure is 'necessary' if it has any comparative health benefits. In other words, according to the majority, so long as a doctor can point to support in the profession for his (or the woman's) preferred procedure, it is 'necessary' and the physician is entitled to perform it. But such a health exception requirement eviscerates *Casey*'s undue burden standard and imposes unfettered abortion-on-demand. The exception entirely swallows the rule. In effect, no regulation of abortion procedures is permitted because there will always be some support for a procedure and there will always be some doctors who conclude that the procedure is preferable. If Nebraska reenacts its partial birth abortion ban with a health exception, the State will not be able to prevent physicians like Dr. Carhart from using partial birth abortion as a routine abortion procedure. This Court has now expressed its own conclusion that there is 'highly plausible' support for the view that partial birth abortion is safer, which, in the majority's view, means that the procedure is therefore 'necessary.' Any doctor who wishes to perform such a procedure under the new statute will be able to do so with impunity. Therefore, Justice O'Connor's assurance that the constitutional failings of Nebraska's statute can be easily fixed, is illusory. The majority's insistence on a health exception is a fig leaf barely covering its hostility to any abortion regulation by the States — a hostility that *Casey* purported to reject. . . .

"The *Casey* joint opinion makes clear that the Court should not strike down state regulations of abortion based on the fact that some women might face a marginally higher health risk from the regulation. In *Casey*, the Court upheld a 24-hour waiting period even though the Court credited evidence that for some women the delay would, in practice, be much longer than 24 hours, and even though it was undisputed that any delay in obtaining an abortion would impose additional health risks."

Chief Justice Rehnquist and Justice Scalia also dissented.

Discussion

1. Casey*'s precedental value.* *Stenberg* is the Court's first major abortion case since *Casey* and establishes that the joint opinion lays out the framework for future

doctrinal development. Chief Justice Rehnquist's brief dissent acknowledges that "[d]espite my disagreement with the opinion, under the rule laid down in Marks v. United States, 430 U.S. 188, 193 (1977), the *Casey* joint opinion represents the holding of the Court in that case" even though he "continue[s] to believe that case is wrongly decided."

Note that although Justices O'Connor, Kennedy, and Souter wrote the joint opinion in *Casey* that reaffirmed *Roe,* Justice Kennedy dissents in *Stenberg.* This suggests that the 6-3 majority in *Casey* may not prove lasting on many particular questions of abortion regulation. It also suggests that the replacement of Justices Stevens and O'Connor in the next few years may raise the question seemingly put to rest in *Casey* all over again.

2. *More healthy alternatives?* Is Justice Thomas correct that the majority has announced a general principle that no restrictions on previability abortions are permissible if the prohibited practice might be safer for some women? Or is the holding merely that specific practices cannot be banned completely unless there is an exception for situations in which they are arguably healthier as judged by some class of competent medical professionals? Is there an important difference between these two formulations?

3. *Akron redux?* Both Justices Kennedy and Thomas accuse the Court of returning to pre-*Casey* and pre-*Webster* suspicion of all abortion regulation. They argue that even regulations of abortion that they regard as eminently reasonable are subjected to intense scrutiny. Whether this characterization is true of the majority opinion, clearly Justices Stevens and Ginsburg believe that Nebraska's law was a thinly disguised attempt to undermine *Roe.*

Part of the problem stems from *Casey* itself. *Casey* imagined that states could achieve a middle ground on the abortion question. It imagined a political world of modest regulations on abortion passed by reasonable legislatures deeply concerned about the morality of abortion but still respecting the basic right recognized in Roe v. Wade. Such modest regulations of abortion would be held constitutional as long as states did not deliberately attempt to prevent women from obtaining abortions. As part of this political and legal bargain, the Court would defer to state judgments about morals, health, and respect for unborn life using the "undue burden" test.

The basic difficulty with this picture of politics is that abortion does not seem to be an issue that encourages compromise or moderation. Rather, as long as abortion remains a political flashpoint, and as long as substantial numbers of American citizens continue to believe that *Roe* was wrongly decided and that abortion is immoral, state legislators are likely to try to appeal to their constituents by pushing for new laws that restrict abortion in ever new ways. That is because abortion regulations in the United States are ideological struggles as much as they are nicely balanced decisions of public policy. Thus, the Court will always be faced with the possibility (if not the suspicion) that new abortion regulations are not carefully balanced assessments of public policy but are deliberately designed to place obstacles in the path of women seeking abortions. This is quite similar to the situation the Court faced in cases like *Thornburgh* and *Akron,* only the debate is now structured in terms of the rather amorphous "undue burden" standard. Thus, Justice Ginsburg argues that laws passed out of hostility to abortion constitute an "undue burden," whereas Justice Kennedy thinks that the Nebraska statute should be read as a good faith articulation of deep moral concern.

4. *Scalia's "I told you so."* In connection with the previous point, consider Justice Scalia's dissent, which argued that *Casey* had failed to bring controversies over abortion to a close. Rather, it had made them all the more inevitable because Casey's "undue burden" standard was simply unworkable:

> [W]hat I consider to be an "undue burden" is different from what the majority considers to be an "undue burden" — a conclusion that can not be demonstrated true or false by factual inquiry or legal reasoning. It is a value judgment, dependent upon how much one respects (or believes society ought to respect) the life of a partially delivered fetus, and how much one respects (or believes society ought to respect) the freedom of the woman who gave it life to kill it. Evidently, the five Justices in today's majority value the former less, or the latter more, (or both), than the four of us in dissent. Case closed. There is no cause for anyone who believes in *Casey* to feel betrayed by this outcome. It has been arrived at by precisely the process *Casey* promised — a democratic vote by nine lawyers, not on the question whether the text of the Constitution has anything to say about this subject (it obviously does not); nor even on the question (also appropriate for lawyers) whether the legal traditions of the American people would have sustained such a limitation upon abortion (they obviously would); but upon the pure policy question whether this limitation upon abortion is "undue" — i.e., goes too far. [T]hose who believe that a 5-to-4 vote on a policy matter by unelected lawyers should not overcome the judgment of 30 state legislatures have a problem, not with the application of *Casey*, but with its existence. *Casey* must be overruled.
>
> While I am in an I-told-you-so mood, I must recall my bemusement, in *Casey*, at the joint opinion's expressed belief that Roe v. Wade had "call[ed] the contending sides of a national controversy to end their national division by accepting a common mandate rooted in the Constitution," and that the decision in *Casey* would ratify that happy truce. . . . Today's decision, that the Constitution of the United States prevents the prohibition of a horrible mode of abortion, will be greeted by a firestorm of criticism — as well it should. I cannot understand why those who acknowledge that, in the opening words of Justice O'Connor's concurrence, "[t]he issue of abortion is one of the most contentious and controversial in contemporary American society," persist in the belief that this Court, armed with neither constitutional text nor accepted tradition, can resolve that contention and controversy rather than be consumed by it. If only for the sake of its own preservation, the Court should return this matter to the people — where the Constitution, by its silence on the subject, left it — and let them decide, State by State, whether this practice should be allowed. *Casey* must be overruled.

5. *The Partial Birth Abortion Act of 2003.* In response to *Stenberg*, Congress passed the Partial Birth Abortion Act of 2003, which banned partial birth abortions, defined as "an abortion in which the person performing the abortion . . . deliberately and intentionally vaginally delivers a living fetus until, in the case of a head-first presentation, the entire fetal head is outside the body of the mother, or, in the case of breech presentation, any part of the fetal trunk past the navel is outside the body of the mother, for the purpose of performing an overt act that the person knows will kill the partially delivered living fetus." Opponents of the bill argued that this definition literally includes not only D&X abortions, but also some common abortion procedures used in the first trimester, when the fetus's head is still small enough to pass through the cervix.

The statute makes an exception for partial birth abortions that are "necessary to save the life of a mother" but makes no exception for health. To avoid a possible conflict with *Stenberg*, the statute cites Congressional findings that "[p]artial-birth abortion poses serious risks to the health of a woman undergoing the procedure," that "[t]here is no credible medical evidence that partial-birth abortions are safe or are safer than other abortion procedures," and that "[t]here exists substantial record evidence upon which Congress has reached its conclusion that a ban on partial-birth abortion is not required to contain a 'health' exception, because the facts indicate that a partial-birth abortion is never necessary to preserve the health of a woman, poses serious risks to a woman's health, and lies outside the standard of medical care."

The statute went on to explain: "[U]nder well-settled Supreme Court jurisprudence, the United States Congress is not bound to accept the same factual findings that the Supreme Court was bound to accept in *Stenberg* under the 'clearly erroneous' standard. Rather, the United States Congress is entitled to reach its own factual findings — findings that the Supreme Court accords great deference — and to enact legislation based upon these findings so long as it seeks to pursue a legitimate interest that is within the scope of the Constitution, and draws reasonable inferences based upon substantial evidence."

The Act then cites Katzenbach v. Morgan, among other cases, for the proposition that the Court should defer to Congress's findings of fact about the comparative safety of partial birth abortion procedures.

Given these congressional statements in the legislation, is the Partial Birth Abortion Act constitutional? To what extent is the Court's recent Section 5 jurisprudence relevant? Note that in cases like *Kimel* and *Garrett*, Congress was arguing for greater Fourteenth Amendment protections than the Court currently recognized. Should Congress be able to give women less protection under the Fourteenth Amendment than the Court affords on the grounds that the Court has relied on an incorrect set of factual assumptions? Does this statute involve an independent congressional attempt at interpretation of the Fourteenth Amendment, a disagreement about facts, or both?

VI. Sexuality and Sexual Orientation

Like many constitutional debates you have read in this book, the issues in this section arise out of legal responses to a social movement. The modern gay rights movement is generally thought to have begun on June 27, 1969, when New York police raided a gay bar in Greenwich Village, the Stonewall Inn. Angered by the arrests and by the New York Police Department's history of repeatedly raiding gay clubs and harassing gay patrons, Stonewall's patrons rioted, throwing bottles and bricks at the police. The riot was followed by another round of protests the following night. The Stonewall riots led to the formation of political organizations representing gay and lesbian interests and public demonstrations affirming homosexual identity.[73]

---

73. Toby Marotta, The Politics of Homosexuality 71-99 (1981), gives a detailed account of the Stonewall Riots. See also Martin Duberman, Stonewall (1993).

Like the woman suffrage movement, abolitionism, the civil rights movement, and the second wave of feminism that began in the 1960s, the movement for gay rights has employed a combination of political and legal tactics to make its claims visible before the public, shape public debate, and change social and legal norms.[74] And, like these other social movements, the gay rights movement has had its share of defeats as well as victories. In 1977, for example, the struggle for homosexual rights gained national attention when Anita Bryant successfully led a fight to repeal a Dade County, Florida ordinance that protected gay rights. The AIDS crisis of the early 1980s heightened the visibility of gays but also stoked new forms of prejudice against them. By the middle of the 1980s the Supreme Court ruled on gay rights claims for the first time in a constitutional challenge to state sodomy laws.

A. Sexual Orientation and Privacy

BOWERS v. HARDWICK
478 U.S. 186 (1986)

Justice WHITE delivered the opinion of the Court.

[On the morning of August 3, 1982, Officer K.R. Torick entered Michael Hardwick's house in Atlanta, Georgia, to serve him with an arrest warrant for failing to appear in court for drinking in public. Torick later claimed in his official report that when he arrived to serve the arrest warrant, one of Michael's housemates answered the door and admitted the officer. 'The roommate told me [he] didn't know if Hardwick was home but said I could come in to look for him. While walking down the hallway inside the house, I saw a bedroom door partially open.'[75] Torick entered the bedroom and found Hardwick engaged in oral sex with a male companion. Torick arrested the men for violating the Georgia sodomy statute. After a preliminary hearing, the District Attorney decided not to present the matter to the grand jury unless further evidence developed.

Respondent [Hardwick] then brought suit in Federal District Court, challenging the constitutionality of the statute insofar as it criminalized consensual sodomy. A married couple, John and Mary Doe, also challenged the statute but were dismissed for lack of standing because there was no danger that they would be prosecuted. In

---

74. See William B. Rubenstein, Divided We Litigate: Addressing Disputes Among Group Members and Lawyers in Civil Rights Campaigns, 106 Yale L.J. 1623 (1997); Andrew M. Jacobs, The Rhetorical Construction of Rights: The Case of the Gay Rights Movement 1969-1991, 72 Neb. L. Rev. 723 (1993); Patricia A. Cain, Litigating for Lesbian and Gay Rights: A Legal History, 79 Va. L. Rev. 1551 (1993).

A complete discussion of the legal issues regarding sexuality and sexual orientation is beyond the scope of this book. For more comprehensive treatments, see Sexuality, Gender, and the Law (William N. Eskridge, Jr. & Nan Hunter eds., 2d. ed 2004); Cases and Materials on Sexual Orientation and the Law (William B. Rubenstein ed., 1997).

75. Peter Irons, The Courage of Their Convictions 381 (1989). The statutory provision at issue, Ga. Code Ann. §16-6-2 (1984) reads as follows:

(a) A person commits the offense of sodomy when he performs or submits to any sexual act involving the sex organs of one person and the mouth or anus of another. . . .
(b) A person convicted of the offense of sodomy shall be punished by imprisonment for not less than one nor more than 20 years. . . .

a footnote, Justice White asserted that "[t]he only claim properly before the Court, therefore, is Hardwick's challenge to the Georgia statute as applied to consensual homosexual sodomy. We express no opinion on the constitutionality of the Georgia statute as applied to other acts of sodomy."]

The issue presented is whether the Federal Constitution confers a fundamental right upon homosexuals to engage in sodomy and hence invalidates the laws of the many States that still make such conduct illegal and have done so for a very long time. . . .

We first register our disagreement with the Court of Appeals and with respondent that the Court's prior cases have construed the Constitution to confer a right of privacy that extends to homosexual sodomy and for all intents and purposes have decided this case. The reach of this line of cases was sketched in Carey v. Population Services International. Pierce v. Society of Sisters and Meyer v. Nebraska were described as dealing with child rearing and education; Prince v. Massachusetts, 321 U.S. 158 (1944), with family relationships; Skinner v. Oklahoma ex rel. Williamson, with procreation; Loving v. Virginia, with marriage; Griswold v. Connecticut and Eisenstadt v. Baird, with contraception; and Roe v. Wade, with abortion. The latter three cases were interpreted as construing the Due Process Clause of the Fourteenth Amendment to confer a fundamental individual right to decide whether or not to beget or bear a child. . . .

[W]e think it evident that none of the rights announced in those cases bears any resemblance to the claimed constitutional right of homosexuals to engage in acts of sodomy that is asserted in this case. No connection between family, marriage, or procreation on the one hand and homosexual activity on the other has been demonstrated. . . . Moreover, any claim that these cases nevertheless stand for the proposition that any kind of private sexual conduct between consenting adults is constitutionally insulated from state proscription is unsupportable. Indeed, the Court's opinion in *Carey* twice asserted that the privacy right, which the *Griswold* line of cases found to be one of the protections provided by the Due Process Clause, did not reach so far. . . .

Precedent aside, however, respondent would have us announce . . . a fundamental right to engage in homosexual sodomy. This we are quite unwilling to do. It is true that despite the language of the Due Process Clauses of the Fifth and Fourteenth Amendments, which appears to focus only on the processes by which life, liberty, or property is taken, the cases are legion in which those Clauses have been interpreted to have substantive content. . . . Among such cases are those recognizing rights that have little or no textual support in the constitutional language. . . .

Striving to assure itself and the public that announcing rights not readily identifiable in the Constitution's text involves much more than the imposition of the Justices' own choice of values on the States and the Federal Government, the Court has sought to identify the nature of the rights qualifying for heightened judicial protection. In Palko v. Connecticut, 302 U.S. 319, 325, 326 (1937), it was said that this category includes those fundamental liberties that are "implicit in the concept of ordered liberty," such that "neither liberty nor justice would exist if [they] were sacrificed." A different description of fundamental liberties appeared in Moore v. East Cleveland, 431 U.S. 494, 503 (1977) (opinion of Powell, J.), where they are characterized as those liberties that are "deeply rooted in this Nation's history and tradition."

It is obvious to us that neither of these formulations would extend a fundamental right to homosexuals to engage in acts of consensual sodomy. Proscriptions against that conduct have ancient roots. Sodomy was a criminal offense at common law and was forbidden by the laws of the original thirteen States when they ratified the Bill of Rights. In 1868, when the Fourteenth Amendment was ratified, all but 5 of the 37 States in the Union had criminal sodomy laws. In fact, until 1961, all 50 States outlawed sodomy, and today, 24 States and the District of Columbia continue to provide criminal penalties for sodomy performed in private and between consenting adults. Against this background, to claim that a right to engage in such conduct is "deeply rooted in this Nation's history and tradition" or "implicit in the concept of ordered liberty" is, at best, facetious.

Nor are we inclined to take a more expansive view of our authority to discover new fundamental rights imbedded in the Due Process Clause. The Court is most vulnerable and comes nearest to illegitimacy when it deals with judge-made constitutional law having little or no cognizable roots in the language or design of the Constitution. [T]his was painfully demonstrated by the face-off between the Executive and the Court in the 1930s which resulted in the repudiation of much of the substantive gloss that the Court had placed on the Due Process Clause of the Fifth and Fourteenth Amendments. There should be, therefore, great resistance to expand the substantive reach of those Clauses, particularly if it requires redefining the category of rights deemed to be fundamental. Otherwise, the Judiciary necessarily takes to itself further authority to govern the country without express constitutional authority. The claimed right pressed on us today falls far short of overcoming this resistance.

Respondent, however, asserts that the result should be different where the homosexual conduct occurs in the privacy of the home. He relies on Stanley v. Georgia, 394 U.S. 557, 565 (1969), where the Court held that the First Amendment prevents conviction for possessing and reading obscene material in the privacy of his home: "If the First Amendment means anything, it means that a State has no business telling a man, sitting alone in his house, what books he may read or what films he may watch."

Stanley did protect conduct that would not have been protected outside the home, and it partially prevented the enforcement of state obscenity laws; but the decision was firmly grounded in the First Amendment. The right pressed upon us here has no similar support in the text of the Constitution, and it does not qualify for recognition under the prevailing principles for construing the Fourteenth Amendment. Its limits are also difficult to discern. Plainly enough, otherwise illegal conduct is not always immunized whenever it occurs in the home. Victimless crimes, such as the possession and use of illegal drugs do not escape the law where they are committed at home. *Stanley* itself recognized that its holding offered no protection for the possession in the home of drugs, firearms, or stolen goods. And if respondent's submission is limited to the voluntary sexual conduct between consenting adults, it would be difficult, except by fiat, to limit the claimed right to homosexual conduct while leaving exposed to prosecution adultery, incest, and other sexual crimes even though they are committed in the home. We are unwilling to start down that road.

Even if the conduct at issue here is not a fundamental right, respondent asserts that there must be a rational basis for the law and that there is none in this case other than the presumed belief of a majority of the electorate in Georgia that homosexual sodomy is immoral and unacceptable. This is said to be an inadequate rationale to support the law. The law, however, is constantly based on notions of morality, and if all laws representing essentially moral choices are to be invalidated under the Due Process Clause, the courts will be very busy indeed. Even respondent makes no such claim, but insists that majority sentiments about the morality of homosexuality should be declared inadequate. We do not agree, and are unpersuaded that the sodomy laws of some 25 States should be invalidated on this basis.[a]

BURGER, C.J., concurring.

I join the Court's opinion, but I write separately to underscore my view that in constitutional terms there is no such thing as a fundamental right to commit homosexual sodomy.

As the Court notes, the proscriptions against sodomy have very "ancient roots." Decisions of individuals relating to homosexual conduct have been subject to state intervention throughout the history of Western Civilization. Condemnation of those practices is firmly rooted in Judaeo-Christian moral and ethical standards. Homosexual sodomy was a capital crime under Roman law. During the English Reformation when powers of the ecclesiastical courts were transferred to the King's Courts, the first English statute criminalizing sodomy was passed. 25 Hen. VIII, c. 6. Blackstone described "the infamous crime against nature" as an offense of "deeper malignity" than rape, a heinous act "the very mention of which is a disgrace to human nature," and "a crime not fit to be named." The common law of England, including its prohibition of sodomy, became the received law of Georgia and the other Colonies. In 1816 the Georgia Legislature passed the statute at issue here, and that statute has been continuously in force in one form or another since that time. To hold that the act of homosexual sodomy is somehow protected as a fundamental right would be to cast aside millennia of moral teaching.

This is essentially not a question of personal "preferences" but rather of the legislative authority of the State. I find nothing in the Constitution depriving a State of the power to enact the statute challenged here.

POWELL, J., concurring.

I join the opinion of the Court. I agree with the Court that there is no fundamental right — i.e., no substantive right under the Due Process Clause — such as that claimed by respondent. . . . This is not to suggest, however, that respondent may not be protected by the Eighth Amendment of the Constitution. The Georgia statute at issue in this case . . . authorizes a court to imprison a person for up to 20 years for a single private, consensual act of sodomy. In my view, a prison sentence for such conduct — certainly a sentence of long duration — would create a serious Eighth Amendment issue. . . .

In this case, however, respondent has not been tried, much less convicted and sentenced.[a] Moreover, respondent has not raised the Eighth Amendment issue below. For these reasons this constitutional argument is not before us.

---

a. Respondent does not defend the judgment below based on the Ninth Amendment, the Equal Protection Clause or the Eighth Amendment.

a. It was conceded at oral argument that, prior to the complaint against respondent Hardwick, there had been no reported decision involving prosecution for private homosexual activity under this statute for several decades. Moreover, the state has declined to present the criminal charge against Hardwick to a grand jury, and this is a suit for declaratory judgment brought by respondents challenging the validity of the statute. The history of nonenforcement suggests the moribund character today of laws criminalizing this type of private, consensual conduct. Some 26 States have repealed similar statutes. But the constitutional validity of the Georgia statute was put at issue by respondents, and for the reasons stated by the Court, I cannot say that conduct condemned for hundreds of years has now become a fundamental right.

BLACKMUN, J., joined by Brennan, Marshall, and Stevens, JJ., dissenting.

This case is no more about "a fundamental right to engage in homosexual sodomy," as the Court purports to declare, than Stanley v. Georgia was about a fundamental right to watch obscene movies, or Katz v. United States, 389 U.S. 347 (1967) [holding a warrantless wiretap of a public telephone prohibited by the Fourth Amendment], was about a fundamental right to place interstate bets from a telephone booth. Rather, this case is about "the most comprehensive of rights and the right most valued by civilized men," namely, "the right to be let alone." Olmstead v. United States, 277 U.S. 438, 478 (1928) (Brandeis, J., dissenting). The statute at issue denies individuals the right to decide for themselves whether to engage in particular forms of private, consensual sexual activity. The Court concludes that [the statute] is valid essentially because "the laws of . . . many States . . . still make such conduct illegal and have done so for a very long time.". . . Like Justice Holmes, I believe that "[i]t is revolting to have no better reason for a rule of law than that so it was laid down in the time of Henry IV. It is still more revolting if the grounds upon which it was laid down have vanished long since, and the rule simply persists from blind imitation of the past." Holmes, The Path of the Law, 10 Harv. L. Rev. 457, 469 (1897). I believe we must analyze respondent's claim in the light of the values that underlie the constitutional right to privacy. . . .

I.

A fair reading of the statute and of the complaint clearly reveals that the majority has distorted the question this case presents.

First, the Court's almost obsessive focus on homosexual activity is particularly hard to justify in light of the broad language Georgia has used. Unlike the Court, the Georgia Legislature has not proceeded on the assumption that homosexuals are so different from other citizens that their lives may be controlled in a way that would not be tolerated if it limited the choices of those other citizens. Rather, Georgia has provided that "(a) person commits the offense of sodomy when he performs or submits to any sexual act involving the sex organs of one person and the mouth or anus of another." Ga. Code Ann. §16-6-2(a). The sex or status of the persons who engage in the act is irrelevant as a matter of state law. In fact, to the extent I can discern a legislative purpose for Georgia's 1968 enactment of §16-6-2, that purpose seems to have been to broaden the coverage of the law to reach heterosexual as well as homosexual activity.[a] I therefore see no basis for the Court's decision to treat this case as an "as applied" challenge to §16-6-2 or for Georgia's attempt, both in its brief and at oral argument, to defend §16-6-2 solely on the grounds that it prohibits homosexual activity. . . . [Hardwick's] claim that §16-6-2 involves an unconstitutional intrusion into his privacy and his right of intimate association does not depend in any way on his sexual orientation. . . .

In construing the right to privacy, the Court has proceeded along two somewhat distinct, albeit complementary, lines. First, it has recognized a privacy interest with

a. Until 1968, Georgia defined sodomy as "the carnal knowledge and connection against the order of nature, by man with man, or in the same unnatural manner with woman." Ga. Crim. Code §26-5901 (1933). [After two Georgia Supreme Court decisions refusing to apply the statute, respectively, to lesbian activity and to heterosexual cunnilingus,] Georgia passed the act-specific statute currently in force "perhaps in response to the restrictive court decisions. . . ." Note, The Crimes Against Nature, 16 J. Pub. L. 159, 167, n.47 (1967).

reference to certain decisions that are properly for the individual to make. Second, it has recognized a privacy interest with reference to certain places without regard for the particular activities in which the individuals who occupy them are engaged. The case before us implicates both the decisional and the spatial aspects of the right to privacy.

A

The Court concludes today that none of our prior cases dealing with various decisions that individuals are entitled to make free of governmental interference "bears any resemblance to the claimed constitutional right of homosexuals to engage in acts of sodomy that is asserted in this case." While it is true that these cases may be characterized by their connection to protection of the family, the Court's conclusion that they extend no further than this boundary ignores the warning in Moore v. East Cleveland, 431 U.S. 494, 501 (1977) (plurality opinion), against "clos[ing] our eyes to the basic reasons why certain rights associated with the family have been accorded shelter under the Fourteenth Amendment's Due Process Clause." We protect those rights not because they contribute, in some direct and material way, to the general public welfare, but because they form so central a part of an individual's life. . . .

And so we protect the decision whether to marry precisely because marriage "is an association that promotes a way of life, not causes; a harmony in living, not political faiths; a bilateral loyalty, not commercial or social projects." Griswold v. Connecticut, 381 U.S., at 486. We protect the decision whether to have a child because parenthood alters so dramatically an individual's self-definition, not because of demographic considerations or the Bible's command to be fruitful and multiply. And we protect the family because it contributes so powerfully to the happiness of individuals, not because of a preference for stereotypical households. The Court recognized in Roberts v. United States Jaycees, 468 U.S. 609, 619 (1984), that the "ability independently to define one's identity that is central to any concept of liberty" cannot truly be exercised in a vacuum; we all depend on the "emotional enrichment of close ties with others."

Only the most willful blindness could obscure the fact that sexual intimacy is "a sensitive, key relationship of human existence, central to family life, community welfare, and the development of human personality." The fact that individuals define themselves in a significant way through their intimate sexual relationships with others suggests, in a Nation as diverse as ours, that there may be many "right" ways of conducting those relationships, and that much of the richness of a relationship will come from the freedom an individual has to choose the form and nature of these intensely personal bonds. . . .

The Court claims that its decision today merely refuses to recognize a fundamental right to engage in homosexual sodomy; what the Court really has refused to recognize is the fundamental interest all individuals have in controlling the nature of their intimate associations with others.

B

The behavior for which Hardwick faces prosecution occurred in his own home, a place to which the Fourth Amendment attaches special significance. The Court's treatment of this aspect of the case is symptomatic of its overall refusal to consider the broad principles that have informed our treatment of privacy in specific cases.

Just as the right to privacy is more than the mere aggregation of a number of entitlements to engage in specific behavior, so too, protecting the physical integrity of the home is more than merely a means of protecting specific activities that often take place there. . . . The Court's interpretation of the pivotal case of Stanley v. Georgia, 394 U.S. 557 (1969), is entirely unconvincing. Stanley held that Georgia's undoubted power to punish the public distribution of constitutionally unprotected, obscene material did not permit the State to punish the private possession of such material. According to the majority here, *Stanley* relied entirely on the First Amendment, and thus, it is claimed, sheds no light on cases not involving printed materials. But that is not what *Stanley* said. Rather, the *Stanley* Court anchored its holding in the Fourth Amendment's special protection for the individual in his home. . . . "He is asserting the right to read or observe what he pleases — the right to satisfy his intellectual and emotional needs in the privacy of his own home." . . .

"The right of the people to be secure in their . . . houses," expressly guaranteed by the Fourth Amendment, is perhaps the most "textual" of the various constitutional provisions that inform our understanding of the right to privacy, and thus I cannot agree with the Court's statement that "[t]he right pressed upon us here has no . . . support in the text of the Constitution." Indeed, the right of an individual to conduct intimate relationships in the intimacy of his or her own home seems to me to be the heart of the Constitution's protection of privacy.

III.

The Court's failure to comprehend the magnitude of the liberty interests at stake in this case leads it to slight the question whether petitioner, on behalf of the State, has justified Georgia's infringement on these interests. I believe that neither of the two general justifications for §16-6-2 that petitioner has advanced warrants dismissing respondent's challenge for failure to state a claim.

First, petitioner asserts that the acts made criminal by the statute may have serious adverse consequences for "the general public health and welfare," such as spreading communicable diseases or fostering other criminal activity. Inasmuch as this case was dismissed by the District Court on the pleadings, it is not surprising that . . . [n]othing in the record before the Court provides any justification for finding the activity forbidden by §16-6-2 to be physically dangerous, either to the persons engaged in it or to others.

The core of petitioner's defense of §16-6-2, however, is that respondent and others who engage in the conduct prohibited by §16-6-2 interfere with Georgia's exercise of the "right of the Nation and of the States to maintain a decent society" Paris Adult Theater I v. Slaton, 413 U.S. 49 (1973). . . . I cannot agree that either the length of time a majority has held its convictions or the passions with which it defends them can withdraw legislation from this Court's scrutiny. See, e.g., Loving v. Virginia, 388 U.S. 1 (1967) [invalidating state anti-miscegenation law].[b] It is

---

b. The parallel between *Loving* and this case is almost uncanny. There, too, the State relied on a religious justification for its law. There, too, defenders of the challenged statute relied heavily on the fact that when the Fourteenth Amendment was ratified, most of the States had similar prohibitions. There, too, at the time the case came before the Court, many of the States still had criminal statutes concerning the conduct at issue. Yet the Court held, not only that the invidious racism of Virginia's law violated the Equal Protection Clause, but also that the law deprived the Lovings of due process by denying them the "freedom of choice to marry" that had "long been recognized as one of the vital personal rights essential to the orderly pursuit of happiness by free men."

precisely because the issue raised by this case touches the heart of what makes individuals what they are that we should be especially sensitive to the rights of those whose choices upset the majority.

The assertion that "traditional Judaeo-Christian values proscribe" the conduct involved cannot provide an adequate justification for §16-6-2. . . . The legitimacy of secular legislation depends instead on whether the State can advance some justification for its law beyond its conformity to religious doctrine. Thus, far from buttressing his case, [Bowers's] invocation of Leviticus, Romans, St. Thomas Aquinas, and sodomy's heretical status during the Middle Ages undermines his suggestion that §16-6-2 represents a legitimate use of secular coercive power. A State can no more punish private behavior because of religious intolerance than it can punish such behavior because of racial animus. . . .

Nor can §16-6-2 be justified as a "morally neutral" exercise of Georgia's power to "protect the public environment." Certainly, some private behavior can affect the fabric of society as a whole. . . . [But petitioner] and the Court fail to see the difference between laws that protect public sensibilities and those that enforce private morality. Statutes banning public sexual activity are entirely consistent with protecting the individual's liberty interest in decisions concerning sexual relations: the same recognition that those decisions are intensely private which justifies protecting them from governmental interference can justify protecting individuals from unwilling exposure to the sexual activities of others. But the mere fact that intimate behavior may be punished when it takes place in public cannot dictate how States can regulate intimate behavior that occurs in intimate places.

This case involves no real interference with the rights of others, for the mere knowledge that other individuals do not adhere to one's value system cannot be a legally cognizable interest, let alone an interest that can justify invading the houses, hearts, and minds of citizens who choose to live their lives differently. . . .

STEVENS, J., joined by Brennan and Marshall, JJ., dissenting.

Like the statute that is challenged in this case, the rationale of the Court's opinion applies equally to the prohibited conduct regardless of whether the parties who engage in it are married or unmarried, or are of the same or different sexes. Sodomy was condemned as an odious and sinful type of behavior during the formative period of the common law. That condemnation was equally damning for heterosexual and homosexual sodomy. Moreover, it provided no special exemption for married couples. The license to cohabit and to produce legitimate offspring simply did not include any permission to engage in sexual conduct that was considered a "crime against nature."

The history of the Georgia statute before us clearly reveals this traditional prohibition of heterosexual, as well as homosexual sodomy. Indeed, at one point in the 20th century, Georgia's law was construed to permit certain sexual conduct between homosexual women even though such conduct was prohibited between heterosexuals. The history of the statutes cited by the majority as proof for the proposition that sodomy is not constitutionally protected, . . . similarly reveals a prohibition on heterosexual, as well as homosexual, sodomy.

Because the Georgia statute expresses the traditional view that sodomy is an immoral kind of conduct regardless of the identity of the persons who engage in it, I believe that a proper analysis of its constitutionality requires consideration of two questions: First, may a State totally prohibit the described conduct by means of a neutral law applying without exception to all persons subject to its jurisdiction? If not, may the State save the statute by announcing that it will only enforce the law against homosexuals? The two questions merit separate discussion.

I.

Our prior cases make two propositions abundantly clear. First, the fact that the governing majority in a State has traditionally viewed a particular practice as immoral is not a sufficient reason for upholding a law prohibiting the practice; neither history nor tradition could save a law prohibiting miscegenation from constitutional attack. Second, individual decisions by married persons, concerning the intimacies of their physical relationship, even when not intended to produce offspring, are a form of "liberty" protected by the Due Process Clause of the Fourteenth Amendment. Moreover, this protection extends to intimate choices by unmarried as well as married persons.

In consideration of claims of this kind, the Court has emphasized the individual interest in privacy, but its decisions have actually been animated by an even more fundamental concern. As I wrote some years ago:

> These cases do not deal with the individual's interest in protection from unwarranted public attention, comment, or exploitation. They deal, rather, with the individual's right to make certain unusually important decisions that will affect his own, or his family's, destiny. The Court has referred to such decisions as implicating "basic values," as being "fundamental," and as being dignified by history and tradition. The character of the Court's language in these cases brings to mind the origins of the American heritage of freedom — the abiding interest in individual liberty that makes certain state intrusions on the citizen's right to decide how he will live his own life intolerable. Guided by history, our tradition of respect for the dignity of individual choice in matters of conscience and the restraints implicit in the federal system, federal judges have accepted the responsibility for recognition and protection of these rights in appropriate cases. Fitzgerald v. Porter Memorial Hospital, 523 F.2d 716, 719-20 (7th Cir. 1975).

Society has every right to encourage its individual members to follow particular traditions in expressing affection for one another and in gratifying their personal desires. It, of course, may prohibit an individual from imposing his will on another to satisfy his own selfish interests. It also may prevent an individual from interfering with, or violating, a legally sanctioned and protected relationship, such as marriage. And it may explain the relative advantages and disadvantages of different forms of intimate expression. But when individual married couples are isolated from observation by others, the way in which they voluntarily choose to conduct their intimate relations is a matter for them — not the State — to decide. The essential "liberty" that animated the development of the law in cases like *Griswold*, *Eisenstadt*, and *Carey* surely embraces the right to engage in nonreproductive, sexual conduct that others may consider offensive or immoral.

. . . [O]ur prior cases thus establish that a State may not prohibit sodomy within "the sacred precincts of marital bedrooms," *Griswold*, or, indeed, between unmarried heterosexual adults. *Eisenstadt*. In all events, it is perfectly clear that the State of Georgia may not totally prohibit the conduct proscribed by §16-6-2 of the Georgia Criminal Code.

II.

If the Georgia statute cannot be enforced as it is written — if the conduct it seeks to prohibit is a protected form of liberty for the vast majority of Georgia's citizens — the State must assume the burden of justifying a selective application of its law. Either the persons to whom Georgia seeks to apply its statute do not have the same interest in "liberty" that others have, or there must be a reason why the State may be permitted to apply a generally applicable law to certain persons that it does not apply to others.

The first possibility is plainly unacceptable. Although the meaning of the principle that "all men are created equal" is not always clear, it surely must mean that every free citizen has the same interest in "liberty" that the members of the majority share. From the standpoint of the individual, the homosexual and the heterosexual have the same interest in deciding how he will live his own life, and, more narrowly, how he will conduct himself in his personal and voluntary associations with his companions. State intrusion into the private conduct of either is equally burdensome.

The second possibility is similarly unacceptable. A policy of selective application must be supported by a neutral and legitimate interest — something more substantial than a habitual dislike for, or ignorance about, the disfavored group. Neither the State nor the Court has identified any such interest in this case. The Court has posited as a justification for the Georgia statute "the presumed belief of a majority of the electorate in Georgia that homosexual sodomy is immoral and unacceptable." But the Georgia electorate has expressed no such belief — instead, its representatives enacted a law that presumably reflects the belief that all sodomy is immoral and unacceptable. . . . [T]he Georgia statute does not single out homosexuals as a separate class meriting special disfavored treatment. . . . Georgia's prohibition on private, consensual sodomy has not been enforced for decades. The record of nonenforcement, in this case and in the last several decades, belies the Attorney General's representations about the importance of the State's selective application of its generally applicable law. . . .

III.

The Court orders the dismissal of respondent's complaint even though the State's statute prohibits all sodomy; even though that prohibition is concededly unconstitutional with respect to heterosexuals; and even though the State's post hoc explanations for selective application are belied by the State's own actions. . . . I respectfully dissent.

Discussion

1. *The impact of sodomy laws.* At the time Bowers was decided approximately half of the states and the District of Columbia still criminalized same-sex sodomy, but the practice was rarely prosecuted. What, then, was the practical significance of the result in *Bowers*? Was the defeat for the rights of gays and lesbians primarily symbolic?

Note Justice Powell's opinion carefully. He assumes a compromise under which statutory prohibitions on sodomy will remain on the books but actual violations of the law will either not be prosecuted or will receive light sentences. Does this seem reasonable? Is it consistent with what the Court did in *Griswold?* Does Justice Powell underestimate the possibilities of police or prosecutorial abuse that occur when sodomy remains a crime, or the legitimation of violence against homosexuals that arises from deeming them to be outlaws? See Kendall Thomas, Beyond the Privacy Principle, 92 Colum. L. Rev. 1431 (1992).

Despite the infrequency of criminal prosecutions for private adult consensual sexual conduct, sodomy laws — and judicial decisions upholding them — have in fact had far-reaching effects on the law's treatment of gays and lesbians. Consider, for example, *Bowers's* effect on employment discrimination claims. In 1987, the Court of Appeals for the District of Columbia rejected a claim that discrimination by the FBI against gay job applicants violated the Equal Protection Clause. "If the [Supreme] Court was unwilling to object to state laws that criminalize the behavior that defines the class," the court explained, "it is hardly open to a lower court to conclude that state sponsored discrimination against the class is invidious. After all, there can hardly be more palpable discrimination against a class than making the conduct that defines the class criminal." Padula v. Webster, 822 F.2d 97, 103 (D.C. Cir. 1987).

Sodomy statutes have also been invoked in custody disputes. In 1998, for example, the Supreme Court of Alabama upheld a divorce judgment that granted custody to the father of the two minor children and placed severe restrictions on their lesbian mother's visitation rights. The court noted that "the conduct inherent in lesbianism [was] illegal in Alabama," and that the mother was therefore "continually engaging in conduct that violates the criminal law of this state." Ex parte D.W.W., 717 So. 2d 793, 796 (Ala. 1998). To expose her children to that "lifestyle, one that is illegal under the laws of this state and immoral in the eyes of most of its citizens, could greatly traumatize them." Id. Five years earlier, the Supreme Court of Virginia had engaged in a similar analysis, noting that "[c]onduct inherent in lesbianism is punishable as a Class 6 felony in the Commonwealth," and concluding that the conduct was therefore an "important consideration in determining custody." Bottoms v. Bottoms, 457 S.E.2d 102, 108 (Va. 1995).

The "ripple effects" of sodomy laws extended to high school education policy as well.[76] Several states, including Alabama, Mississippi, South Carolina, and Texas, have statutes requiring high school health educators to teach that homosexuality is a criminal offense. See Ala. Code §16-40a-2(c)(8) (LexisNexis 2001); Miss. Code Ann. §37-13-171(1)(e) (West 1999); Miss. Code Ann. §97-29-59 (West 1999); Tex. Health & Safety Code Ann. §85.007 (Vernon 2001). And state legislators, as well as local school boards, have attempted to block the formation of high school gay–straight alliances through policies banning student groups that condone illegal conduct. (See, e.g., James Brooke, To Be Young, Gay and Going to High School in Utah, N.Y. Times, Feb. 28, 1996, at 8.)

What is the relevance of these collateral effects of sodomy laws in a debate about their constitutionality under the Due Process Clause? If states may criminalize sodomy, is there any constitutional basis for invalidating discrimination in other areas of the law?

2. *The "ancient roots" of the prohibition against homosexual sodomy.* Many scholars have pointed out that Justice White's and Chief Justice Burger's historical claims

---

76. Joseph Landau, Ripple Effect: Sodomy Statutes as Weapons, New Republic, June 23, 2003, p. 12.

about longstanding moral condemnation of homosexual sodomy "oversimplif[y] and distort[] a complex historical record." Anne B. Goldstein, History, Homosexuality, and Political Values: Searching for the Hidden Determinants of Bowers v. Hardwick, 97 Yale L.J. 1073, 1086-89 (1988). In the ancient world, sexual acts between males were both tolerated and condemned. (Plato's *Symposium* of course, is a celebration not just of love but of same-sex love.) The Roman Empire permitted some marriages between men until at least 342 A.D.[77] During the early Middle Ages, both church and state openly tolerated same-sex practices between men.[78]

Moreover, before the 1800's sexuality and sexual practices — whether tolerated or condemned — were understood in terms of what one did, not who one was. Hence through most of history same-sex practices by men were not understood as "homosexual" practices because the category of "homosexuals" is largely a product of the mid-nineteenth century.[79] Goldstein writes that "[a]lthough both the behavior and the desires we now call homosexual existed in earlier eras, our currently common assumption that persons who make love with others of their own sex are fundamentally different from the rest of humanity is only about one hundred years old." Prohibitions on sexual conduct tended to concern which parts of the body were touched rather than the sex of the parties. "Although illicit sexual acts were seen as sinful, immoral, criminal or all three, before the 1870s illicit sexual acts between men were not seen as fundamentally different from, or necessarily worse than, illicit acts between a man or a woman."

Moreover, Goldstein asserts, the "sodomy" that Michael Hardwick was convicted of — oral sex — was not considered "sodomy" until the late nineteenth and early twentieth centuries. In 1817 English Courts held that oral sex was not sodomy under the common law and its statutory complements; by legal definition sodomy was limited to anal sex. In 1886, Parliament created a new crime of "gross indecency" to cover oral sex, and most American jurisdictions adopted similar laws between 1885 and 1930.

Assuming that the history behind White's and Burger's opinions is incorrect in the way that Goldstein states, how does this affect the result in *Bowers*? Couldn't White and Burger respond that contemporary Americans do believe in a category called homosexuality, that same-sex sodomy (including oral sex) is considered immoral by many Americans, and that legislatures should be free to enact their moral views into law, just as they do in the case of drug laws and laws against adultery, incest, and sex with minors? Is White and Burger's best argument, then, not historical but prudential: that controversial moral issues are best left to democratic political processes? Does this adequately distinguish *Roe, Griswold*, and *Eisenstadt*?

3. *Acts and identities*. Janet Halley notes that Justice White's and Chief Justice Burger's opinions in *Bowers* alternate between viewing sodomy as an act that people

---

77. See the discussion in William N. Eskridge, The Case for Same-Sex Marriage 22-27 (1996).

78. See generally John Boswell, Christianity, Social Tolerance, and Homosexuality (1980).

79. In this context one should note one of Michel Foucault's most famous claims: that the status-based, as opposed to the conduct-based, conception of homosexuality is a relatively recent development, dating only to the late nineteenth century. Before that era's "perverse implantation" of conduct into status, homosexuality was a kind of behavior, rather than a core attribute of the self. "The sodomite had been a temporary aberration; the homosexual was now a species." 1 Michel Foucault, The History of Sexuality 43 (Robert Hurley trans., Vintage Books 1990) (1976).

perform and a characteristic act of homosexuals, a proxy for homosexual identity. Janet E. Halley, Reasoning about Sodomy: Act and Identity In and After Bowers v. Hardwick, 79 Va. L. Rev. 1721 (1993). Arguing that same-sex sodomy does not involve a fundamental right, Justice White describes sodomy as an *act* that has been historically condemned. Explaining why the Georgia statute has a rational basis, he focuses on sodomy as a symbol or indicia of homosexual *identity:* he justifies the ban on sodomy as rationally related to public condemnation of homosexuality.

However, because the word "sodomy" has historically referred to many different kinds of acts, Halley argues, there can be no coherent history of moral attitudes toward sodomy based on acts alone. Justice White makes the history look coherent by associating sodomy (ahistorically) with moral disapproval of homosexual identity. The different kinds of sodomy can all be viewed as one because they are the kinds of acts performed by "homosexuals." Hence White's argument about acts really depends on unspoken assumptions about homosexual identity.

Conversely, Halley argues, because Georgia's sodomy statute does not distinguish between same-sex and opposite-sex sodomy, it is "frontally incoherent" to argue that its purpose is moral disapproval of a particular identity — homosexuality. Justice White can only make this argument look coherent by making us forget about what heterosexuals do in private, or in Halley's words, "confer[ring] invisibility and immunity" on opposite-sex sodomy. "By reasoning that the Georgia statute plausibly supports an anti-homosexual morality, the Justices engage in masking their own status as potential sodomites *even* if they never stray from the class of heterosexuals." Here White's argument about identity (homosexuality) disguises the fact that the statute concerns acts (sodomy).

As we shall see repeatedly in this chapter, this slippage between act and identity, or (as it is sometimes described) between conduct and status is not unique to *Bowers*. The association of homosexuals with sodomy is widespread, even in contexts having nothing to so with sexual activity; conversely, sodomy is often seen as the defining feature of homosexuality. By contrast, people do not normally associate heterosexuals primarily with their sexual activities, even if they engage in (among other things) sodomy, adultery, or fornication (sex between unmarried adults).

4. *Adultery and incest.* Does Justice Blackmun adequately address the state's putative power to prohibit adultery and incest? His dissent includes the following footnote:

> Although I do not think it necessary to decide today issues that are not even remotely before us, it does seem to me that a court could find simple, analytically sound distinctions between certain private, consensual sexual conduct, on the one hand, and adultery and incest (the only two vaguely specific "sexual crimes" to which the majority points), on the other. For example, marriage, in addition to its spiritual aspects, is a civil contract that entitles the contracting parties to a variety of governmentally provided benefits. A State might define the contractual commitment necessary to become eligible for these benefits to include a commitment of fidelity and then punish individuals for breaching that contract. Moreover, a State might conclude that adultery is likely to injure third persons, in particular, spouses and children of persons who engage in extramarital affairs. With respect to incest, a court might well agree with respondent that the nature of familial relationships renders true consent to incestuous activity sufficiently problematical that a blanket prohibition of such activity is warranted.

Even if adultery is conceptualized as a breach of the marriage contract, didn't the Court in Bailey v. Alabama, Chapter 4, supra, suggest that it violated the Constitution to criminalize breach of contract? What justifies the state's prohibition on a consensual incestuous relationship between adult siblings? Is it fear of lack of "real" consent? Fear of genetic abnormalities for offspring? (Does this justify prohibitions on incest for elderly siblings or for those who use contraceptives?) Or is the real basis the strong belief on the part of most members of the society that incest is simply wrong, even if consensual? Must supporters of constitutional rights for homosexuals embrace sexual libertarianism generally as a constitutional norm or, rather, can they simply say that same-sex conduct accords with the morality of enlightened persons in a way that, say, adulterous or incestuous conduct does not?

5. *Personhood, intimacy, and social construction.* Justice Blackmun's dissent argues that "sexual intimacy" is "central to . . . the development of personality," that "individuals define themselves in a significant way through their intimate sexual relationships with others," that "much of the richness of a relationship will come from the freedom an individual has to choose the form and nature of these intensely personal bonds" and hence that "individuals have a "fundamental interest in controlling the nature of their relationships with others." Jed Rubenfeld criticizes the claim that "homosexual sex should receive constitutional protection because it is so essential to an individual's self-definition — to his identity." Jed Rubenfeld, The Right of Privacy 102 Harv. L. Rev. 737 (1989). Arguing that homosexual sex should be protected because it is "expressive of innermost traits of being," Rubenfeld argues, is problematic because "[t]hose who engage in homosexual sex may or may not perceive themselves as bearing a 'homosexual identity.'" Moreover, the argument relies on a "sharply demarcated 'homosexual identity' to which a person is immediately consigned at the moment he seeks to engage in homosexual sex[,] strictly distinguished from the heterosexual," and defined in terms of that difference. This account, Rubenfeld explains, may actually reinforce the stigmatization of homosexuality and the hierarchical relation between heterosexuality and homosexuality. "To protect the rights of 'the homosexual' . . . because homosexuality is essential to a person's identity is no liberation, but simply the flip side of the same rigidification of sexual identities by which our society simultaneously inculcates sexual roles, normalizes sexual conduct, and vilifies 'faggots.'"[80] Drawing on the work of Michel Foucault, Rubenfeld argues that the real problem with restrictions on same-sex sexual practices is that they attempt to "define and inculcate social identities." "The proscription . . . against homosexual sex [produces] lives forced into relations with the opposite sex that substantially direct individuals' roles in society and a large part of their everyday existence."

---

80. Rubenfeld's argument against homosexual identity is connected to an ongoing debate between two different approaches, which might be called "gay-identity politics" and "queer politics." As Nancy Fraser explains, the gay-identity approach treats homosexuality as a more or less coherent culture or identity, much like the commonsense view of ethnicity or race. The queer politics approach, by contrast, views "homosexuality" as "the constructed and devalued correlate of heterosexuality," that is, it is what is not-heterosexual and therefore treated as abnormal in mainstream culture. The point of queer politics is not to defend or maintain a "gay identity" but to undermine the cultural opposition between heterosexuality and homosexuality in order to "destabilize all fixed sexual identities." Nancy Fraser, Justice Interruptus: Critical Reflections on the "Postsocialist" Condition 24 (1997). To what extent should this debate affect the arguments that litigators make in cases like *Bowers*?

The point of the right of privacy is not the protection of sexual intimacy, Rubenfeld argues. It is that

> childbearing, marriage, and the assumption of a specific sexual identity are undertakings that go on for years, define roles, direct activities, operate on or even create intense emotional relations, enlist the body, inform values, and in sum substantially shape the totality of a person's daily life and consciousness. Laws that force such undertakings on individuals may properly be called "totalitarian," and the right to privacy exists to protect against them.

What assumptions does Rubenfeld's argument make about the role and efficacy of law versus other forms of social structure and normalization that may push people towards heterosexuality, marriage, and childrearing? To what extent is law responsible for the maintenance of heterosexuality and the creation of a disfavored category called "homosexuals"? Rubenfeld objects to the normalization of sexual roles, behaviors, attitudes, and desires. Does his argument assume that there is an inherent sexual identity and/or form of desire that people possess outside of the processes of normalization? Does he claim that people are not subject to normalization and social construction when they are not subject to state coercion? Presumably he would at least claim that elimination of legal restraints on same-sex behavior would result in less "totalitarian" forms of normalization. Given the social construction of individuals in either case, what is the baseline against which to measure whether a form of normalization is good or bad, "totalitarian" or "anti-totalitarian"? Can one tell a coherent story about the protection of human freedom (and conversely, about its denial) if one takes the argument about social construction of desire and identity as far as someone like Foucault, say, would take it?

Is Rubenfeld's argument that sexual normalization by the state is prohibited by the Constitution but that sexual normalization by the "private" sphere of culture and commerce is not? What is the constitutional status of public education under this account?

6. *The problem of bisexuality.* An important element of Rubenfeld's critique is that people may engage in same-sex intercourse without understanding themselves as "homosexual." For example, some people may regard themselves as bisexual, or may not have the sense of a particular sexual orientation at all. Kenji Yoshino notes that the major studies about the numerical distribution of individuals across sexual orientations show that the number of bisexuals is comparable to or greater than the number of homosexuals in each study. Why, then, are homosexuals so much more politically visible than bisexuals? Yoshino argues that both straights and gays have different but overlapping interests in bisexual erasure. These include an interest in stabilizing straight and gay identity, an interest in retaining the importance of sex as a distinguishing attribute, and an interest in preserving a culture of monogamy. See Kenji Yoshino, The Epistemic Contract of Bisexual Erasure, 52 Stan. L. Rev. 353 (2000). Do all identity continuums get politically reduced to binaries through such a "both-ends-against-the-middle" dynamic? Why are multiracials erased while "the middle class" is not?

7. *The problem with "liberal toleration."* Michael Sandel points out that Justices Blackmun and Stevens argue for Hardwick's rights largely on the grounds that individuals should be free to choose how they will structure their intimate relationships and not on the ground that homosexual unions, like heterosexual ones,

realize important human goods. Michael Sandel, Moral Argument and Liberal Toleration: Abortion and Homosexuality, 77 Cal. L. Rev. 521 (1989). But this argument from toleration of individual choice begs the question whether the practices at issue are morally permissible. More importantly, "the analogy with Stanley [v. Georgia, which protected the right to view obscenity in the privacy of one's home] tolerates homosexuality at the risk of demeaning it; it puts homosexual intimacy on a par with obscenity — a base thing that should nonetheless be tolerated so long as it takes place in private." "[T]he interest at stake is bound to be reduced . . . to 'sexual gratification.'" The better analogy, Sandel suggests, should be to *Griswold,* and its protection of marital privacy, but that requires one to "articulate the human goods that homosexual intimacy may share with heterosexual unions." Does Sandel's argument mean that same-sex intercourse cannot be protected legally unless the Court is willing to state that homosexuality is just as good as heterosexuality? How likely is the Court to make such a claim? Are there good reasons to fight for liberal toleration even if one cannot achieve full acceptance?

8. *"Privacy" and the home: Four concepts of privacy.* Consider Justice Blackmun's reliance on the right of privacy in *Stanley v. Georgia.* There are at least four different concepts of privacy: locational (or zonal) privacy protects what one does in a particular space; relational privacy protects a relationship, such as marriage, from state interference; decisional privacy protects the right to make important choices (including intimate ones) and decide on a course of action free from state sanction; informational privacy concerns the right to control the flow of information about one's self.[81]

Which forms of privacy are involved in *Griswold's* protection of the "sacred precincts of marital bedrooms"? In *Eisenstadt's* protection of decisions "so fundamentally affecting a person as the decision whether to bear or beget a child"? Which are involved in *Bowers*? Do *Griswold* and *Eisenstadt* tend to promote confusion among these various categories because they involve more than one type of privacy?

9. *"Privacy" and the closet.* Another criticism of the dissent's conception of privacy is that it tends to reinforce the power of the closet. A right of privacy gives gays and lesbians the right to have same-sex relationships as long as they exist behind closed doors. On the other hand, if gays and lesbians make their orientation or their same-sex relationships public, or demand the right to engage in public displays of affection and intimacy, as heterosexuals routinely do, they may be accused of "flaunting." The closet conflates all four forms of privacy: decisional and relational privacy must be zonally private (behind closed doors) or informationally private (not salient to heterosexuals); it therefore uses the idea of privacy against gays and lesbians. (Compare Sandel's point that tolerance for closeted homosexuality offers very little respect for its positive attributes.)

10. *Justice Powell's acquaintances.* As John Jeffries explains, Justice Lewis Powell originally voted to join four other justices to strike down the law in Bowers, but later changed his mind and wrote a concurrence to what became the majority opinion as a result of his switch. See John C. Jeffries, Jr., Justice Lewis F. Powell, Jr.

---

81. Cf. Kendall Thomas, Beyond the Privacy Principle, 92 Colum. L. Rev. 1431-1443, 1448 (1992) (distinguishing between zonal, relational, and decisional privacy).

511-530 (1994). At the time Powell cast his decisive vote, he explained to one of his clerks that he had never met a homosexual. (Note that by 1986 Powell had been not only a Supreme Court Justice but a former president of the ABA and a public figure for many decades.) In fact, as Jeffries reports, the clerk he was addressing was gay, like many of Powell's prior clerks, but Powell was not aware of it.[82] Many scholars argue that the social pressures to stay in the closet are one reason why homosexuals are particularly disadvantaged in the political process. See the discussion infra on sexual orientation as a suspect classification. After his retirement from the Court, Justice Powell was quoted as saying that he regretted his concurrence in *Bowers*. He did not, however, attach much importance to the decision. "That case was not a major case," he explained, "and one of the reasons I voted the way I did was the case was a frivolous case" brought "just to see what the court would do." Powell considered the case "part of [his] past and not very important." Ex-Justice Powell Regrets Backing Law on Sodomy, Richmond Times Dispatch, Oct. 26, 1990, at 2.

11. *The Supreme Court and social movements.* One way of reading *Bowers* is that in 1986 the Supreme Court was not willing to get ahead of public opinion regarding homosexuality, or, to put it another way, that the social movement for gay rights had not yet sufficiently changed the attitudes of Americans so that the Court was comfortable in confirming this new understanding. Do you agree with this assessment? Even if you do, does this tell you what the proper role of the Court should have been with respect to the claims of this particular social movement? After all, a ruling in favor of Hardwick might have had significant effects in furthering the movement's goals, assuming you think those goals are just. On the other hand, analogous to Roe v. Wade, a ruling in Hardwick's favor might have stoked considerable reaction in the mid-1980s. To what extent, if any, should these prudential considerations matter in deciding the proper way to interpret the U.S. Constitution? Do you think any of them help explain (or, perhaps more importantly, justify) the Court's decision to overturn *Bowers* 17 years later in Lawrence v. Texas?

LAWRENCE v. TEXAS
539 U.S. 558 (2003)

Justice KENNEDY delivered the opinion of the Court.

Liberty protects the person from unwarranted government intrusions into a dwelling or other private places. In our tradition the State is not omnipresent in

---

82. As Jeffries tells the story:

Uncharacteristically, [just before oral argument] Powell had still not decided how he would vote. In great distress, the clerk debated whether to tell Powell of his sexual orientation. Perhaps if Powell could put a familiar face to these incomprehensible urges, they would seem less bizarre and threatening. He came to the edge of an outright declaration but ultimately drew back, settling for a "very emotional" speech urging Powell to support sexual freedom as a fundamental right. "The right to love the person of my choice," he argued, "would be far more important to me than the right to vote in elections." "That may be," Powell answered, "but that doesn't mean it's in the Constitution."

Id. at 1520-1521. What do you think the clerk should have done?
Eve Sedgwick gives a fictionalized account of the story, comparing it to the Biblical story in the book of Esther, in which Queen Esther reveals that she is a Jew to King Ahashuerus in order to save her people. Eve Kosofsky Sedgwick, Epistemology of the Closet 74-85 (1990).

the home. And there are other spheres of our lives and existence, outside the home, where the State should not be a dominant presence. Freedom extends beyond spatial bounds. Liberty presumes an autonomy of self that includes freedom of thought, belief, expression, and certain intimate conduct. The instant case involves liberty of the person both in its spatial and more transcendent dimensions.

I.

The question before the Court is the validity of a Texas statute making it a crime for two persons of the same sex to engage in certain intimate sexual conduct.

In Houston, Texas, officers of the Harris County Police Department were dispatched to a private residence in response to a reported weapons disturbance. They entered an apartment where one of the petitioners, John Geddes Lawrence, resided. The right of the police to enter does not seem to have been questioned. The officers observed Lawrence and another man, Tyron Garner, engaging in a sexual act. The two petitioners were arrested, held in custody over night, and charged and convicted before a Justice of the Peace.

The complaints described their crime as "deviate sexual intercourse, namely anal sex, with a member of the same sex (man)." The applicable state law is Tex. Penal Code Ann. §21.06(a) (2003). It provides: "A person commits an offense if he engages in deviate sexual intercourse with another individual of the same sex." The statute defines "[d]eviate sexual intercourse" as follows:

> (A) any contact between any part of the genitals of one person and the mouth or anus of another person; or
> (B) the penetration of the genitals or the anus of another person with an object.
> §21.01(1).

The petitioners . . . challenged the statute as a violation of the Equal Protection Clause of the Fourteenth Amendment and of a like provision of the Texas Constitution. Those contentions were rejected. The petitioners, having entered a plea of *nolo contendere,* were each fined $200 and assessed court costs of $141.25. App. to Pet. for Cert. 107a-110a. . . . The petitioners were adults at the time of the alleged offense. Their conduct was in private and consensual.

II.

We conclude the case should be resolved by determining whether the petitioners were free as adults to engage in the private conduct in the exercise of their liberty under the Due Process Clause of the Fourteenth Amendment to the Constitution. For this inquiry we deem it necessary to reconsider the Court's holding in *Bowers.* . . .

In *Griswold* the Court invalidated a state law prohibiting the use of drugs or devices of contraception and counseling or aiding and abetting the use of contraceptives. The Court described the protected interest as a right to privacy and placed emphasis on the marriage relation and the protected space of the marital bedroom.

After *Griswold* it was established that the right to make certain decisions regarding sexual conduct extends beyond the marital relationship. In Eisenstadt v. Baird, 405 U. S. 438 (1972), the Court invalidated a law prohibiting the distribution of contraceptives to unmarried persons. The case was decided under the Equal Protection Clause; but with respect to unmarried persons, the Court went on to state the fundamental proposition that the law impaired the exercise of their personal rights. It quoted from the statement of the Court of Appeals finding the law to be in conflict with fundamental human rights, and it followed with this statement of its own: "It is true that in *Griswold* the right of privacy in question inhered in the marital relationship. . . . If the right of privacy means anything, it is the right of the *individual,* married or single, to be free from unwarranted governmental intrusion into matters so fundamentally affecting a person as the decision whether to bear or beget a child."

The opinions in *Griswold* and *Eisenstadt* were part of the background for the decision in Roe v. Wade. *Roe* recognized the right of a woman to make certain fundamental decisions affecting her destiny and confirmed once more that the protection of liberty under the Due Process Clause has a substantive dimension of fundamental significance in defining the rights of the person.

In Carey v. Population Services Int'l, 431 U. S. 678 (1977), the Court confronted a New York law forbidding sale or distribution of contraceptive devices to persons under 16 years of age. Although there was no single opinion for the Court, the law was invalidated. Both *Eisenstadt* and *Carey,* as well as the holding and rationale in *Roe,* confirmed that the reasoning of *Griswold* could not be confined to the protection of rights of married adults. This was the state of the law with respect to some of the most relevant cases when the Court considered Bowers v. Hardwick.

The facts in *Bowers* had some similarities to the instant case. A police officer, whose right to enter seems not to have been in question, observed Hardwick, in his own bedroom, engaging in intimate sexual conduct with another adult male. The conduct was in violation of a Georgia statute making it a criminal offense to engage in sodomy. One difference between the two cases is that the Georgia statute prohibited the conduct whether or not the participants were of the same sex, while the Texas statute, as we have seen, applies only to participants of the same sex. Hardwick was not prosecuted, but he brought an action in federal court to declare the state statute invalid. He alleged he was a practicing homosexual and that the criminal prohibition violated rights guaranteed to him by the Constitution. The Court, in an opinion by Justice White, sustained the Georgia law. . . .

The Court began its substantive discussion in *Bowers* as follows: "The issue presented is whether the Federal Constitution confers a fundamental right upon homosexuals to engage in sodomy and hence invalidates the laws of the many States that still make such conduct illegal and have done so for a very long time." That statement, we now conclude, discloses the Court's own failure to appreciate the extent of the liberty at stake. To say that the issue in *Bowers* was simply the right to engage in certain sexual conduct demeans the claim the individual put forward, just as it would demean a married couple were it to be said marriage is simply about the right to have sexual intercourse. The laws involved in *Bowers* and here are, to be sure, statutes that purport to do no more than prohibit a particular sexual act. Their penalties and purposes, though, have more far-reaching consequences, touching upon the most private human conduct, sexual behavior, and in the most private of places, the home. The statutes do seek to control a personal relationship that, whether or not entitled to formal recognition in the law, is within the liberty of persons to choose without being punished as criminals.

This, as a general rule, should counsel against attempts by the State, or a court, to define the meaning of the relationship or to set its boundaries absent injury to a person or abuse of an institution the law protects. It suffices for us to acknowledge that adults may choose to enter upon this relationship in the confines of their homes and their own private lives and still retain their dignity as free persons. When sexuality finds overt expression in intimate conduct with another person, the conduct can be but one element in a personal bond that is more enduring. The liberty protected by the Constitution allows homosexual persons the right to make this choice.

Having misapprehended the claim of liberty there presented to it, and thus stating the claim to be whether there is a fundamental right to engage in consensual sodomy, the *Bowers* Court said: "Proscriptions against that conduct have ancient roots." In academic writings, and in many of the scholarly *amicus* briefs filed to assist the Court in this case, there are fundamental criticisms of the historical premises relied upon by the majority and concurring opinions in *Bowers*. We need not enter this debate in the attempt to reach a definitive historical judgment, but the following considerations counsel against adopting the definitive conclusions upon which *Bowers* placed such reliance.

At the outset it should be noted that there is no longstanding history in this country of laws directed at homosexual conduct as a distinct matter. Beginning in colonial times there were prohibitions of sodomy derived from the English criminal laws passed in the first instance by the Reformation Parliament of 1533. The English prohibition was understood to include relations between men and women as well as relations between men and men. Nineteenth-century commentators similarly read American sodomy, buggery, and crime-against-nature statutes as criminalizing certain relations between men and women and between men and men. The absence of legal prohibitions focusing on homosexual conduct may be explained in part by noting that according to some scholars the concept of the homosexual as a distinct category of person did not emerge until the late 19th century. Thus early American sodomy laws were not directed at homosexuals as such but instead sought to prohibit nonprocreative sexual activity more generally. This does not suggest approval of homosexual conduct. It does tend to show that this particular form of conduct was not thought of as a separate category from like conduct between heterosexual persons.

Laws prohibiting sodomy do not seem to have been enforced against consenting adults acting in private. A substantial number of sodomy prosecutions and convictions for which there are surviving records were for predatory acts against those who could not or did not consent, as in the case of a minor or the victim of an assault. As to these, one purpose for the prohibitions was to ensure there would be no lack of coverage if a predator committed a sexual assault that did not constitute rape as defined by the criminal law. . . . Instead of targeting relations between consenting adults in private, 19th-century sodomy prosecutions typically involved relations between men and minor girls or minor boys, relations between adults involving force, relations between adults implicating disparity in status, or relations between men and animals.

To the extent that there were any prosecutions for the acts in question, 19th-century evidence rules imposed a burden that would make a conviction more difficult to obtain even taking into account the problems always inherent in prosecuting consensual acts committed in private. Under then-prevailing standards, a man could not be convicted of sodomy based upon testimony of a consenting partner, because the partner was considered an accomplice. A partner's testimony, however, was admissible if he or she had not consented to the act or was a minor, and therefore incapable of consent. The rule may explain in part the infrequency of these prosecutions. In all events that infrequency makes it difficult to say that society approved of a rigorous and systematic punishment of the consensual acts committed in private and by adults. The longstanding criminal prohibition of homosexual sodomy upon which the *Bowers* decision placed such reliance is as consistent with a general condemnation of nonprocreative sex as it is with an established tradition of prosecuting acts because of their homosexual character.

The policy of punishing consenting adults for private acts was not much discussed in the early legal literature. We can infer that one reason for this was the very private nature of the conduct. Despite the absence of prosecutions, there may have been periods in which there was public criticism of homosexuals as such and an insistence that the criminal laws be enforced to discourage their practices. But far from possessing "ancient roots," American laws targeting same-sex couples did not develop until the last third of the 20th century. The reported decisions concerning the prosecution of consensual, homosexual sodomy between adults for the years 1880-1995 are not always clear in the details, but a significant number involved conduct in a public place.

It was not until the 1970's that any State singled out same-sex relations for criminal prosecution, and only nine States have done so. Post-*Bowers* even some of these States did not adhere to the policy of suppressing homosexual conduct. Over the course of the last decades, States with same-sex prohibitions have moved toward abolishing them.

In summary, the historical grounds relied upon in *Bowers* are more complex than the majority opinion and the concurring opinion by Chief Justice Burger indicate. Their historical premises are not without doubt and, at the very least, are overstated.

It must be acknowledged, of course, that the Court in *Bowers* was making the broader point that for centuries there have been powerful voices to condemn homosexual conduct as immoral. The condemnation has been shaped by religious beliefs, conceptions of right and acceptable behavior, and respect for the traditional family. For many persons these are not trivial concerns but profound and deep convictions accepted as ethical and moral principles to which they aspire and which thus determine the course of their lives. These considerations do not answer the question before us, however. The issue is whether the majority may use the power of the State to enforce these views on the whole society through operation of the criminal law. "Our obligation is to define the liberty of all, not to mandate our own moral code." Planned Parenthood of Southeastern Pa. v. Casey, 505 U. S. 833, 850 (1992).

Chief Justice Burger joined the opinion for the Court in *Bowers* and further explained his views as follows: "Decisions of individuals relating to homosexual conduct have been subject to state intervention throughout the history of Western civilization. Condemnation of those practices is firmly rooted in Judeao-Christian moral and ethical standards." As with Justice White's assumptions about history, scholarship casts some doubt on the sweeping nature of the statement by Chief

Justice Burger as it pertains to private homosexual conduct between consenting adults. In all events we think that our laws and traditions in the past half century are of most relevance here. These references show an emerging awareness that liberty gives substantial protection to adult persons in deciding how to conduct their private lives in matters pertaining to sex. "[H]istory and tradition are the starting point but not in all cases the ending point of the substantive due process inquiry."

This emerging recognition should have been apparent when *Bowers* was decided. In 1955 the American Law Institute promulgated the Model Penal Code and made clear that it did not recommend or provide for "criminal penalties for consensual sexual relations conducted in private." ALI, Model Penal Code §213.2, Comment 2, p. 372 (1980). It justified its decision on three grounds: (1) The prohibitions undermined respect for the law by penalizing conduct many people engaged in; (2) the statutes regulated private conduct not harmful to others; and (3) the laws were arbitrarily enforced and thus invited the danger of blackmail. ALI, Model Penal Code, Commentary 277-280 (Tent. Draft No. 4, 1955). In 1961 Illinois changed its laws to conform to the Model Penal Code. Other States soon followed.

In *Bowers* the Court referred to the fact that before 1961 all 50 States had outlawed sodomy, and that at the time of the Court's decision 24 States and the District of Columbia had sodomy laws. Justice Powell pointed out that these prohibitions often were being ignored, however. Georgia, for instance, had not sought to enforce its law for decades.

The sweeping references by Chief Justice Burger to the history of Western civilization and to Judeo-Christian moral and ethical standards did not take account of other authorities pointing in an opposite direction. A committee advising the British Parliament recommended in 1957 repeal of laws punishing homosexual conduct. Parliament enacted the substance of those recommendations 10 years later.

Of even more importance, almost five years before *Bowers* was decided the European Court of Human Rights . . . held that the laws proscribing [consensual homosexual] conduct were invalid under the European Convention on Human Rights. Dudgeon v. United Kingdom, 45 Eur. Ct. H. R. (1981). Authoritative in all countries that are members of the Council of Europe (21 nations then, 45 nations now), the decision is at odds with the premise in *Bowers* that the claim put forward was insubstantial in our Western civilization.

In our own constitutional system the deficiencies in *Bowers* became even more apparent in the years following its announcement. The 25 States with laws prohibiting the relevant conduct referenced in the *Bowers* decision are reduced now to 13, of which 4 enforce their laws only against homosexual conduct. In those States where sodomy is still proscribed, whether for same-sex or heterosexual conduct, there is a pattern of nonenforcement with respect to consenting adults acting in private. The State of Texas admitted in 1994 that as of that date it had not prosecuted anyone under those circumstances.

Two principal cases decided after *Bowers* cast its holding into even more doubt. In Planned Parenthood of Southeastern Pa. v. Casey, the Court reaffirmed the substantive force of the liberty protected by the Due Process Clause. The *Casey* decision again confirmed that our laws and tradition afford constitutional protection to personal decisions relating to marriage, procreation, contraception, family relationships, child rearing, and education. In explaining the respect the Constitution demands for the autonomy of the person in making these choices, we stated as follows:

These matters, involving the most intimate and personal choices a person may make
in a lifetime, choices central to personal dignity and autonomy, are central to the
liberty protected by the Fourteenth Amendment. At the heart of liberty is the right to
define one's own concept of existence, of meaning, of the universe, and of the mystery
of human life. Beliefs about these matters could not define the attributes of personhood were they formed under compulsion of the State.

Persons in a homosexual relationship may seek autonomy for these purposes, just
as heterosexual persons do. The decision in *Bowers* would deny them this right. . . .

Romer v. Evans . . . invalidated an amendment to Colorado's constitution which
named as a solitary class persons who were homosexuals, lesbians, or bisexual either
by "orientation, conduct, practices or relationships," and deprived them of protection under state antidiscrimination laws. We concluded that the provision was "born
of animosity toward the class of persons affected" and further that it had no rational
relation to a legitimate governmental purpose.

[C]ounsel for the petitioners and some *amici* contend that *Romer* provides the
basis for declaring the Texas statute invalid under the Equal Protection Clause.
That is a tenable argument, but we conclude the instant case requires us to address
whether *Bowers* itself has continuing validity. Were we to hold the statute invalid
under the Equal Protection Clause some might question whether a prohibition
would be valid if drawn differently, say, to prohibit the conduct both between same-
sex and different-sex participants.

Equality of treatment and the due process right to demand respect for conduct
protected by the substantive guarantee of liberty are linked in important respects,
and a decision on the latter point advances both interests. If protected conduct is
made criminal and the law which does so remains unexamined for its substantive
validity, its stigma might remain even if it were not enforceable as drawn for equal
protection reasons. When homosexual conduct is made criminal by the law of the
State, that declaration in and of itself is an invitation to subject homosexual persons
to discrimination both in the public and in the private spheres. The central holding
of *Bowers* has been brought in question by this case, and it should be addressed. Its
continuance as precedent demeans the lives of homosexual persons.

The stigma this criminal statute imposes, moreover, is not trivial. The offense, to
be sure, is but a class C misdemeanor, a minor offense in the Texas legal system. Still,
it remains a criminal offense with all that imports for the dignity of the persons
charged. The petitioners will bear on their record the history of their criminal convictions. Just this Term we rejected various challenges to state laws requiring the registration of sex offenders. We are advised that if Texas convicted an adult for private,
consensual homosexual conduct under the statute here in question the convicted
person would come within the registration laws of a least four States were he or she to
be subject to their jurisdiction. This underscores the consequential nature of the
punishment and the state-sponsored condemnation attendant to the criminal prohibition. Furthermore, the Texas criminal conviction carries with it the other collateral
consequences always following a conviction, such as notations on job application
forms, to mention but one example.

The foundations of *Bowers* have sustained serious erosion from our recent decisions in *Casey* and *Romer*. When our precedent has been thus weakened, criticism
from other sources is of greater significance. In the United States criticism of *Bowers*
has been substantial and continuing, disapproving of its reasoning in all respects,

not just as to its historical assumptions. The courts of five different States have declined to follow it in interpreting provisions in their own state constitutions parallel to the Due Process Clause of the Fourteenth Amendment.

To the extent *Bowers* relied on values we share with a wider civilization, it should be noted that the reasoning and holding in *Bowers* have been rejected elsewhere. The European Court of Human Rights has followed not *Bowers* but its own decision in Dudgeon v. United Kingdom. Other nations, too, have taken action consistent with an affirmation of the protected right of homosexual adults to engage in intimate, consensual conduct. The right the petitioners seek in this case has been accepted as an integral part of human freedom in many other countries. There has been no showing that in this country the governmental interest in circumscribing personal choice is somehow more legitimate or urgent.

The doctrine of *stare decisis* is essential to the respect accorded to the judgments of the Court and to the stability of the law. It is not, however, an inexorable command. In *Casey* we noted that when a Court is asked to overrule a precedent recognizing a constitutional liberty interest, individual or societal reliance on the existence of that liberty cautions with particular strength against reversing course. The holding in *Bowers*, however, has not induced detrimental reliance comparable to some instances where recognized individual rights are involved. Indeed, there has been no individual or societal reliance on *Bowers* of the sort that could counsel against overturning its holding once there are compelling reasons to do so. *Bowers* itself causes uncertainty, for the precedents before and after its issuance contradict its central holding.

The rationale of *Bowers* does not withstand careful analysis. In his dissenting opinion in *Bowers* Justice Stevens came to these conclusions:

> Our prior cases make two propositions abundantly clear. First, the fact that the governing majority in a State has traditionally viewed a particular practice as immoral is not a sufficient reason for upholding a law prohibiting the practice; neither history nor tradition could save a law prohibiting miscegenation from constitutional attack. Second, individual decisions by married persons, concerning the intimacies of their physical relationship, even when not intended to produce offspring, are a form of "liberty" protected by the Due Process Clause of the Fourteenth Amendment. Moreover, this protection extends to intimate choices by unmarried as well as married persons.

Justice Stevens' analysis, in our view, should have been controlling in *Bowers* and should control here.

Bowers was not correct when it was decided, and it is not correct today. It ought not to remain binding precedent. Bowers v. Hardwick should be and now is overruled.

The present case does not involve minors. It does not involve persons who might be injured or coerced or who are situated in relationships where consent might not easily be refused. It does not involve public conduct or prostitution. It does not involve whether the government must give formal recognition to any relationship that homosexual persons seek to enter. The case does involve two adults who, with full and mutual consent from each other, engaged in sexual practices common to a homosexual lifestyle. The petitioners are entitled to respect for their private lives. The State cannot demean their existence or control their destiny by making their private sexual conduct a crime. Their right to liberty under the Due Process Clause gives them the full right to engage in their conduct without intervention of the government. "It is a promise of the Constitution that there is a realm of personal liberty which the government may not enter." *Casey*. The Texas statute furthers no legitimate state interest which can justify its intrusion into the personal and private life of the individual.

Had those who drew and ratified the Due Process Clauses of the Fifth Amendment or the Fourteenth Amendment known the components of liberty in its manifold possibilities, they might have been more specific. They did not presume to have this insight. They knew times can blind us to certain truths and later generations can see that laws once thought necessary and proper in fact serve only to oppress. As the Constitution endures, persons in every generation can invoke its principles in their own search for greater freedom.

The judgment of the Court of Appeals for the Texas Fourteenth District is reversed, and the case is remanded for further proceedings not inconsistent with this opinion.

It is so ordered.

Justice O'CONNOR, concurring in the judgment.

The Court today overrules Bowers v. Hardwick, 478 U. S. 186 (1986). I joined *Bowers*, and do not join the Court in overruling it. Nevertheless, I agree with the Court that Texas' statute banning same-sex sodomy is unconstitutional. Rather than relying on the substantive component of the Fourteenth Amendment's Due Process Clause, as the Court does, I base my conclusion on the Fourteenth Amendment's Equal Protection Clause. . . .

We have consistently held, however, that some objectives, such as "a bare . . . desire to harm a politically unpopular group," are not legitimate state interests. When a law exhibits such a desire to harm a politically unpopular group, we have applied a more searching form of rational basis review to strike down such laws under the Equal Protection Clause, [especially] where, as here, the challenged legislation inhibits personal relationships. In Department of Agriculture v. Moreno, for example, we held that a law preventing those households containing an individual unrelated to any other member of the household from receiving food stamps violated equal protection because the purpose of the law was to "discriminate against hippies." . . . In Eisenstadt v. Baird, we refused to sanction a law that discriminated between married and unmarried persons by prohibiting the distribution of contraceptives to single persons. Likewise, in Cleburne v. Cleburne Living Center, supra, we held that it was irrational for a State to require a home for the mentally disabled to obtain a special use permit when other residences — like fraternity houses and apartment buildings — did not have to obtain such a permit. And in Romer v. Evans, we disallowed a state statute that "impos[ed] a broad and undifferentiated disability on a single named group" — specifically, homosexuals. The dissent apparently agrees that if these cases have *stare decisis* effect, Texas' sodomy law would not pass scrutiny under the Equal Protection Clause, regardless of the type of rational basis review that we apply.

[Texas] treats the same conduct differently based solely on the participants. Those harmed by this law are people who have a same-sex sexual orientation and thus are more likely to engage in behavior prohibited by §21.06. . . . The Texas statute makes homosexuals unequal in the eyes of the law by making particular conduct — and only that conduct — subject to criminal sanction. [Although] prosecutions . . . are rare, [t]his case shows, however, that [they] *do* occur. And while the penalty imposed on petitioners in this case was relatively minor, the consequences of conviction are not. [P]etitioners' convictions, if upheld, would disqualify them from or restrict their ability to engage in a variety of professions, including medicine, athletic training, and interior design. Indeed, were petitioners to move to one of four States, their convictions would require them to register as sex offenders to local law enforcement. . . . Texas' sodomy law brands all homosexuals as criminals, thereby making it more difficult for homosexuals to be treated in the same manner as everyone else. Indeed, Texas itself has previously acknowledged the collateral effects of the law, stipulating in a prior challenge to this action that the law "legally sanctions discrimination against [homosexuals] in a variety of ways unrelated to the criminal law," including in the areas of "employment, family issues, and housing." . . .

This case raises a different issue than *Bowers:* whether, under the Equal Protection Clause, moral disapproval is a legitimate state interest to justify by itself a statute that bans homosexual sodomy, but not heterosexual sodomy. It is not. Moral disapproval of this group, like a bare desire to harm the group, is an interest that is insufficient to satisfy rational basis review under the Equal Protection Clause. Indeed, we have never held that moral disapproval, without any other asserted state interest, is a sufficient rationale under the Equal Protection Clause to justify a law that discriminates among groups of persons.

Moral disapproval of a group cannot be a legitimate governmental interest under the Equal Protection Clause because legal classifications must not be "drawn for the purpose of disadvantaging the group burdened by the law." Texas' invocation of moral disapproval as a legitimate state interest proves nothing more than Texas' desire to criminalize homosexual sodomy. But the Equal Protection Clause prevents a State from creating "a classification of persons undertaken for its own sake." And because Texas so rarely enforces its sodomy law as applied to private, consensual acts, the law serves more as a statement of dislike and disapproval against homosexuals than as a tool to stop criminal behavior. The Texas sodomy law "raise[s] the inevitable inference that the disadvantage imposed is born of animosity toward the class of persons affected."

[T]he State maintains that the law discriminates only against homosexual conduct. While it is true that the law applies only to conduct, the conduct targeted by this law is conduct that is closely correlated with being homosexual. Under such circumstances, Texas' sodomy law is targeted at more than conduct. It is instead directed toward gay persons as a class. . . . When a State makes homosexual conduct criminal, and not "deviate sexual intercourse" committed by persons of different sexes, "that declaration in and of itself is an invitation to subject homosexual persons to discrimination both in the public and in the private spheres." . . .

In Romer v. Evans, we refused to sanction a law that singled out homosexuals "for disfavored legal status." The same is true here. The Equal Protection Clause "neither knows nor tolerates classes among citizens." Id. at 623 (quoting *Plessy*).

A State can of course assign certain consequences to a violation of its criminal law. But the State cannot single out one identifiable class of citizens for punishment that does not apply to everyone else, with moral disapproval as the only asserted state interest for the law. The Texas sodomy statute subjects homosexuals to "a lifelong penalty and stigma. A legislative classification that threatens the creation of an underclass . . . cannot be reconciled with" the Equal Protection Clause. Plyler v. Doe (Powell, J., concurring).

Whether a sodomy law that is neutral both in effect and application would violate the substantive component of the Due Process Clause is an issue that need not be decided today. I am confident, however, that so long as the Equal Protection Clause requires a sodomy law to apply equally to the private consensual conduct of homosexuals and heterosexuals alike, such a law would not long stand in our democratic society. In the words of Justice Jackson:

> The framers of the Constitution knew, and we should not forget today, that there is no more effective practical guaranty against arbitrary and unreasonable government than to require that the principles of law which officials would impose upon a minority be imposed generally. Conversely, nothing opens the door to arbitrary action so effectively as to allow those officials to pick and choose only a few to whom they will apply legislation and thus to escape the political retribution that might be visited upon them if larger numbers were affected. Railway Express Agency, Inc. v. New York, 336 U. S. 106, 112-113 (1949) (concurring opinion).

That this law as applied to private, consensual conduct is unconstitutional under the Equal Protection Clause does not mean that other laws distinguishing between heterosexuals and homosexuals would similarly fail under rational basis review. Texas cannot assert any legitimate state interest here, such as national security or preserving the traditional institution of marriage. Unlike the moral disapproval of same-sex relations — the asserted state interest in this case — other reasons exist to promote the institution of marriage beyond mere moral disapproval of an excluded group.

A law branding one class of persons as criminal solely based on the State's moral disapproval of that class and the conduct associated with that class runs contrary to the values of the Constitution and the Equal Protection Clause, under any standard of review. I therefore concur in the Court's judgment that Texas' sodomy law banning "deviate sexual intercourse" between consenting adults of the same sex, but not between consenting adults of different sexes, is unconstitutional.

Justice SCALIA, with whom the Chief Justice and Justice Thomas join, dissenting.

Most of . . . today's opinion has no relevance to its actual holding — that the Texas statute "furthers no legitimate state interest which can justify" its application to petitioners under rational-basis review. Though there is discussion of "fundamental proposition[s]," and "fundamental decisions," nowhere does the Court's opinion declare that homosexual sodomy is a "fundamental right" under the Due Process Clause; nor does it subject the Texas law to the standard of review that would be appropriate (strict scrutiny) if homosexual sodomy *were* a "fundamental right." Thus, while overruling the *outcome* of *Bowers,* the Court leaves strangely untouched its central legal conclusion: "[R]espondent would have us announce . . . a fundamental right to engage in homosexual sodomy. This we are quite unwilling to do." Instead the Court simply describes petitioners' conduct as "an exercise of their liberty" — which it undoubtedly is — and proceeds to apply an unheard-of form of rational-basis review that will have far-reaching implications beyond this case.

I.

I begin with the Court's surprising readiness to reconsider a decision rendered a mere 17 years ago in Bowers v. Hardwick. I do not myself believe in rigid adherence to *stare decisis* in constitutional cases; but I do believe that we should be consistent rather than manipulative in invoking the doctrine. Today's opinions in support of reversal do not bother to distinguish — or indeed, even bother to mention — the paean to *stare decisis* coauthored by three Members of today's majority in Planned Parenthood v. Casey. . . . Today, . . . the widespread opposition to *Bowers,* a decision resolving an issue as "intensely divisive" as the issue in *Roe,* is offered as a reason in favor of *overruling* it. Gone, too, is any "enquiry" (of the sort conducted in *Casey*) into whether the decision sought to be overruled has "proven 'unworkable.'"

Today's approach to *stare decisis* invites us to overrule an erroneously decided precedent (including an "intensely divisive" decision) *if:* (1) its foundations have been "eroded" by subsequent decisions; (2) it has been subject to "substantial and continuing" criticism; and (3) it has not induced "individual or societal reliance" that counsels against overturning. The problem is that *Roe* itself — which today's majority surely has no disposition to overrule — satisfies these conditions to at least the same degree as *Bowers.* . . .

(1) [I] do not quarrel with the Court's claim that Romer v. Evans, "eroded" the "foundations" of *Bowers'* rational-basis holding. But *Roe* and *Casey* have been equally "eroded" by Washington v. Glucksberg, which held that *only* fundamental rights which are "deeply rooted in this Nation's history and tradition" qualify for anything other than rational basis scrutiny under the doctrine of "substantive due process." *Roe* and *Casey,* of course, subjected the restriction of abortion to heightened scrutiny without even attempting to establish that the freedom to abort *was* rooted in this Nation's tradition.

(2) *Bowers,* the Court says, has been subject to "substantial and continuing [criticism], disapproving of its reasoning in all respects, not just as to its historical assumptions." . . . Of course, *Roe* too (and by extension *Casey*) had been (and still is) subject to unrelenting criticism, including criticism from the two commentators cited by the Court today.

(3) That leaves, to distinguish the rock-solid, unamendable disposition of *Roe* from the readily overrulable *Bowers,* only the third factor. "[T]here has been," the Court says, "no individual or societal reliance on *Bowers* of the sort that could counsel against overturning its holding. . . ." It seems to me that the "societal reliance" on the principles confirmed in *Bowers* and discarded today has been overwhelming. Countless judicial decisions and legislative enactments have relied on the ancient proposition that a governing majority's belief that certain sexual behavior is "immoral and unacceptable" constitutes a rational basis for regulation. . . . State laws against bigamy, same-sex marriage, adult incest, prostitution, masturbation, adultery, fornication, bestiality, and obscenity are likewise sustainable only in light of *Bowers'* validation of laws based on moral choices. Every single one of these laws is called into question by today's decision; the Court makes no effort to cabin the scope of its decision to exclude them from its holding. See ante, at [p. 1487] (noting "an emerging awareness that liberty gives substantial protection to adult persons in deciding how to conduct their private lives *in matters pertaining to sex*" (emphasis added)). The impossibility of distinguishing homosexuality from other traditional "morals" offenses is precisely why *Bowers* rejected the rational-basis challenge. "The law," it said, "is constantly based on notions of morality, and if all laws representing essentially moral choices are to be invalidated under the Due Process Clause, the courts will be very busy indeed."

What a massive disruption of the current social order, therefore, the overruling of *Bowers* entails. Not so the overruling of *Roe,* which would simply have restored the regime that existed for centuries before 1973, in which the permissibility of and restrictions upon abortion were determined legislatively State-by-State. . . . To tell the truth, it does not surprise me, and should surprise no one, that the Court has chosen today to revise the standards of *stare decisis* set forth in *Casey*. It has thereby exposed *Casey's* extraordinary deference to precedent for the result-oriented expedient that it is.

II.

[Texas] Penal Code Ann. §21.06(a) (2003) undoubtedly imposes constraints on liberty. So do laws prohibiting prostitution, recreational use of heroin, and, for that matter, working more than 60 hours per week in a bakery. But there is no right to "liberty" under the Due Process Clause, though today's opinion repeatedly makes that claim. The Fourteenth Amendment *expressly allows* States to deprive their citizens of "liberty," *so long as "due process of law" is provided:* "No state shall . . . deprive any person of life, liberty, or property, *without due process of law."* Amdt. 14 (emphasis added).

Our opinions applying the doctrine known as "substantive due process" hold that the Due Process Clause prohibits States from infringing *fundamental* liberty interests, unless the infringement is narrowly tailored to serve a compelling state interest. Washington v. Glucksberg. We have held repeatedly, in cases the Court today does not overrule, that *only* fundamental rights qualify for this so-called "heightened scrutiny" protection — that is, rights which are "deeply rooted in this Nation's history and tradition." . . . All other liberty interests may be abridged or abrogated pursuant to a validly enacted state law if that law is rationally related to a legitimate state interest. . . .

III.

The Court's description of "the state of the law" at the time of *Bowers* only confirms that *Bowers* was right. The Court points to Griswold v. Connecticut. But that case *expressly disclaimed* any reliance on the doctrine of "substantive due process," and grounded the so-called "right to privacy" in penumbras of constitutional provisions *other than* the Due Process Clause. Eisenstadt v. Baird likewise had nothing to do with "substantive due process"; it invalidated a Massachusetts law prohibiting the distribution of contraceptives to unmarried persons solely on the basis of the Equal Protection Clause. Of course *Eisenstadt* contains well known dictum relating to the "right to privacy," but this referred to the right recognized in *Griswold* — a right penumbral to the *specific* guarantees in the Bill of Rights, and not a "substantive due process" right.

Roe v. Wade recognized that the right to abort an unborn child was a "fundamental right" protected by the Due Process Clause. The *Roe* Court, however, made no attempt to establish that this right was "deeply rooted in this Nation's history and tradition" . . . We have since rejected *Roe's* holding that regulations of abortion must be narrowly tailored to serve a compelling state interest, see Planned Parenthood v. Casey, and thus, by logical implication, *Roe's* holding that the right to abort an unborn child is a "fundamental right."

After discussing the history of antisodomy laws, the Court proclaims that, "it should be noted that there is no longstanding history in this country of laws directed at homosexual conduct as a distinct matter." This observation in no way casts into doubt the "definitive [historical] conclusion," on which *Bowers* relied: that our Nation has a longstanding history of laws prohibiting *sodomy in general*— regardless of whether it was performed by same-sex or opposite-sex couples. . . .

It is (as *Bowers* recognized) entirely irrelevant whether the laws in our long national tradition criminalizing homosexual sodomy were "directed at homosexual conduct as a distinct matter." Whether homosexual sodomy was prohibited by a law targeted at same-sex sexual relations or by a more general law prohibiting both homosexual and heterosexual sodomy, the only relevant point is that it *was* criminalized — which suffices to establish that homosexual sodomy is not a right "deeply rooted in our Nation's history and tradition." The Court today agrees that homosexual sodomy was criminalized and thus does not dispute the facts on which *Bowers actually* relied.

Next the Court makes the claim, again unsupported by any citations, that "[l]aws prohibiting sodomy do not seem to have been enforced against consenting adults acting in private." The key qualifier here is "acting in private" — since the Court admits that sodomy laws *were* enforced against consenting adults (although the Court contends that prosecutions were "infrequent."). I do not know what "acting in private" means; surely consensual sodomy, like heterosexual intercourse, is rarely performed on stage. If all the Court means by "acting in private" is "on private premises, with the doors closed and windows covered," it is entirely unsurprising that evidence of enforcement would be hard to come by. (Imagine the circumstances that would enable a search warrant to be obtained for a residence on the ground that there was probable cause to believe that consensual sodomy was then and there occurring.) Surely that lack of evidence would not sustain the proposition that consensual sodomy on private premises with the doors closed and windows covered was regarded as a "fundamental right," even though all other consensual sodomy was criminalized. There are 203 prosecutions for consensual, adult homosexual sodomy reported in the West Reporting system and official state reporters from the years 1880-1995. There are also records of 20 sodomy prosecutions and 4 executions during the colonial period. *Bowers'* conclusion that homosexual sodomy is not a fundamental right "deeply rooted in this Nation's history and tradition" is utterly unassailable.

Realizing that fact, the Court instead says: "[W]e think that our laws and traditions in the past half century are of most relevance here. These references show *an emerging awareness* that liberty gives substantial protection to adult persons in deciding how to conduct their private lives *in matters pertaining to sex*." Apart from the fact that such an "emerging awareness" does not establish a "fundamental right," the statement is factually false. States continue to prosecute all sorts of crimes by adults "in matters pertaining to sex": prostitution, adult incest, adultery, obscenity, and child pornography. Sodomy laws, too, have been enforced "in the past half century," in which there have been 134 reported cases involving prosecutions for consensual, adult, homosexual sodomy. In relying, for evidence of an "emerging recognition," upon the American Law Institute's 1955 recommendation not to criminalize "consensual sexual relations conducted in private," the Court ignores the fact that this recommendation was "a point of resistance in most of the states that considered adopting the Model Penal Code."

In any event, an "emerging awareness" is by definition not "deeply rooted in this Nation's history and tradition[s]," as we have said "fundamental right" status requires.

Constitutional entitlements do not spring into existence because some States choose to lessen or eliminate criminal sanctions on certain behavior. Much less do they spring into existence, as the Court seems to believe, because *foreign nations* decriminalize conduct. . . . The Court's discussion of these foreign views (ignoring, of course, the many countries that have retained criminal prohibitions on sodomy) is therefore meaningless dicta. Dangerous dicta, however, since "this Court . . . should not impose foreign moods, fads, or fashions on Americans." Foster v. Florida, 537 U. S. 990, n. (2002) (Thomas, J., concurring in denial of certiorari).

IV.

[T]he Texas statute undeniably seeks to further the belief of its citizens that certain forms of sexual behavior are "immoral and unacceptable," — the same interest furthered by criminal laws against fornication, bigamy, adultery, adult incest, bestiality, and obscenity. *Bowers* held that this *was* a legitimate state interest. The Court today reaches the opposite conclusion. The Texas statute, it says, "furthers *no legitimate state interest* which can justify its intrusion into the personal and private life of the individual," (emphasis added). The Court embraces instead Justice Stevens' declaration in his *Bowers* dissent, that "the fact that the governing majority in a State has traditionally viewed a particular practice as immoral is not a sufficient reason for upholding a law prohibiting the practice." This effectively decrees the end of all morals legislation. If, as the Court asserts, the promotion of majoritarian sexual morality is not even a *legitimate* state interest, none of the above-mentioned laws can survive rational-basis review.

V.

Finally, I turn to petitioners' equal-protection challenge. . . . On its face §21.06(a) applies equally to all persons. Men and women, heterosexuals and homosexuals, are all subject to its prohibition of deviate sexual intercourse with someone of the same sex. To be sure, §21.06 does distinguish between the sexes insofar as concerns the partner with whom the sexual acts are performed: men can violate the law only with other men, and women only with other women. But this cannot itself be a denial of equal protection, since it is precisely the same distinction regarding partner that is drawn in state laws prohibiting marriage with someone of the same sex while permitting marriage with someone of the opposite sex.

Loving v. Virginia [does not apply]; we correctly applied heightened scrutiny . . . because the Virginia statute was "designed to maintain White Supremacy." A racially discriminatory purpose is always sufficient to subject a law to strict scrutiny, even a facially neutral law that makes no mention of race. See Washington v. Davis. No purpose to discriminate against men or women as a class can be gleaned from the Texas law, so rational-basis review applies. That review is readily satisfied here by the same rational basis that satisfied it in *Bowers* — society's belief that certain forms of sexual behavior are "immoral and unacceptable." This is the same justification that supports many other laws regulating sexual behavior that make a distinction based upon the identity of the partner — for example, laws against adultery, fornication, and adult incest, and laws refusing to recognize homosexual marriage.

Justice O'Connor argues that . . . "Texas' sodomy law is targeted at more than conduct. It is instead directed toward gay persons as a class." Of course the same could be said of any law. A law against public nudity targets "the conduct that is closely correlated with being a nudist," and hence "is targeted at more than conduct"; it is "directed toward nudists as a class." But be that as it may, even if the Texas law *does* deny equal protection to "homosexuals as a class," that denial *still* does not need to be justified by anything more than a rational basis, which our cases show is satisfied by the enforcement of traditional notions of sexual morality.

[T]he [rational basis] cases [Justice O'Connor] cites . . . reach their conclusions only after finding . . . that no conceivable legitimate state interest supports the classification at issue. [She argues] that laws exhibiting "a . . . desire to harm a politically unpopular group," are invalid *even though* there may be a conceivable rational basis to support them. This reasoning leaves on pretty shaky grounds state laws limiting marriage to opposite-sex couples. Justice O'Connor seeks to preserve them by the conclusory statement that "preserving the traditional institution of marriage" is a legitimate state interest. But "preserving the traditional institution of marriage" is just a kinder way of describing the State's *moral disapproval* of same-sex couples. Texas' interest in §21.06 could be recast in similarly euphemistic terms: "preserving the traditional sexual mores of our society." In the jurisprudence Justice O'Connor has seemingly created, judges can validate laws by characterizing them as "preserving the traditions of society" (good); or invalidate them by characterizing them as "expressing moral disapproval" (bad).

* * *

Today's opinion is the product of a Court, which is the product of a law-profession culture, that has largely signed on to the so-called homosexual agenda, by which I mean the agenda promoted by some homosexual activists directed at eliminating the moral opprobrium that has traditionally attached to homosexual conduct. . . .

One of the most revealing statements in today's opinion is the Court's grim warning that the criminalization of homosexual conduct is "an invitation to subject homosexual persons to discrimination both in the public and in the private spheres." It is clear from this that the Court has taken sides in the culture war, departing from its role of assuring, as neutral observer, that the democratic rules of engagement are observed. Many Americans do not want persons who openly engage in homosexual conduct as partners in their business, as scoutmasters for their children, as teachers in their children's schools, or as boarders in their home. They view this as protecting themselves and their families from a lifestyle that they believe to be immoral and destructive. The Court views it as "discrimination" which it is the function of our judgments to deter. So imbued is the Court with the law profession's anti-anti-homosexual culture, that it is seemingly unaware that the attitudes of that culture are not obviously "mainstream"; that in most States what the Court calls "discrimination" against those who engage in homosexual acts is perfectly legal; that proposals to ban such "discrimination" under Title VII have repeatedly been rejected by Congress; that in some cases such "discrimination" is *mandated* by federal statute, see 10 U. S. C. §654(b)(1) (mandating discharge from the armed forces of any service member who engages in or intends to engage in homosexual acts); and that in some cases such "discrimination" is a constitutional right, see Boy Scouts of America v. Dale, 530 U. S. 640 (2000).

Let me be clear that I have nothing against homosexuals, or any other group, promoting their agenda through normal democratic means. Social perceptions of sexual and other morality change over time, and every group has the right to persuade its fellow citizens that its view of such matters is the best. That homosexuals have achieved some success in that enterprise is attested to by the fact that Texas is one of the few remaining States that criminalize private, consensual homosexual acts. But persuading one's fellow citizens is one thing, and imposing one's views in absence of democratic majority will is something else. I would no more *require* a State to criminalize homosexual acts — or, for that matter, display *any* moral disapprobation of them — than I would *forbid* it to do so. What Texas has chosen to do is well within the range of traditional democratic action, and its hand should not be stayed through the invention of a brand-new "constitutional right" by a Court that is impatient of democratic change. It is indeed true that "later generations can see that laws once thought necessary and proper in fact serve only to oppress"; and when that happens, later generations can repeal those laws. But it is the premise of our system that those judgments are to be made by the people, and not imposed by a governing caste that knows best.

One of the benefits of leaving regulation of this matter to the people rather than to the courts is that the people, unlike judges, need not carry things to their logical conclusion. The people may feel that their disapprobation of homosexual conduct is strong enough to disallow homosexual marriage, but not strong enough to criminalize private homosexual acts — and may legislate accordingly. The Court today pretends that it possesses a similar freedom of action, so that that we need not fear judicial imposition of homosexual marriage, as has recently occurred in Canada. At the end of its opinion — after having laid waste the foundations of our rational-basis jurisprudence — the Court says that the present case "does not involve whether the government must give formal recognition to any relationship that homosexual persons seek to enter." Do not believe it. More illuminating than this bald, unreasoned disclaimer is the progression of thought displayed by an earlier passage in the Court's opinion, which notes the constitutional protections afforded to "personal decisions relating to *marriage*, procreation, contraception, family relationships, child rearing, and education," and then declares that "[p]ersons in a homosexual relationship may seek autonomy for these purposes, just as heterosexual persons do" (emphasis added). Today's opinion dismantles the structure of constitutional law that has permitted a distinction to be made between heterosexual and homosexual unions, insofar as formal recognition in marriage is concerned. If moral disapprobation of homosexual conduct is "no legitimate state interest" for purposes of proscribing that conduct; and if, as the Court coos (casting aside all pretense of neutrality), "[w]hen sexuality finds overt expression in intimate conduct with another person, the conduct can be but one element in a personal bond that is more enduring"; what justification could there possibly be for denying the benefits of marriage to homosexual couples exercising "[t]he liberty protected by the Constitution?" Surely not the encouragement of procreation, since the sterile and the elderly are allowed to marry. This case "does not involve" the issue of homosexual marriage only if one entertains the belief that principle and logic have nothing to do with the decisions of this Court. Many will hope that, as the Court comfortingly assures us, this is so.

The matters appropriate for this Court's resolution are only three: Texas' prohibition of sodomy neither infringes a "fundamental right" (which the Court does not dispute), nor is unsupported by a rational relation to what the Constitution considers a legitimate state interest, nor denies the equal protection of the laws. I dissent.

Justice THOMAS, dissenting.

I join Justice Scalia's dissenting opinion. I write separately to note that the law before the Court today "is . . . uncommonly silly." Griswold v. Connecticut, 381 U. S. 479, 527 (1965) (Stewart, J., dissenting). If I were a member of the Texas Legislature, I would vote to repeal it. Punishing someone for expressing his sexual preference through noncommercial consensual conduct with another adult does not appear to be a worthy way to expend valuable law enforcement resources.

Notwithstanding this, I recognize that as a member of this Court I am not empowered to help petitioners and others similarly situated. My duty, rather, is to "decide cases 'agreeably to the Constitution and laws of the United States.'" And, just like Justice Stewart, I "can find [neither in the Bill of Rights nor any other part of the Constitution a] general right of privacy," or as the Court terms it today, the "liberty of the person both in its spatial and more transcendent dimensions."

Discussion

1. *Anti-majoritarian or anti-federalism?* Lawrence continues a well-known tendency of the Court: It follows larger political and cultural trends, and declares a legal prohibition or practice unconstitutional only when most states have already repealed or greatly limited it. In 1960, for example, every state had an anti-sodomy law. By the time of the decision in *Lawrence,* these statutes had been repealed or overturned in 37 states. In *Lawrence* the Court eliminated sodomy laws in the remaining 13 jurisdictions, where the laws were only infrequently enforced in any case.

From this perspective, the Court is not necessarily bucking majority will. To be sure, it clearly overturns decisions by particular legislative majorities in states. But more important, it imposes a single national rule of minimal civil rights protection on the states that have contrary rules. This is a fairly characteristic effect of the Court's civil liberties and civil rights decisions. Much of the work of the Warren Court, for example, can be seen as imposing national standards for criminal procedure on recalcitrant states, particularly in the South, which had often cut corners where black defendants were concerned and violated their basic rights. It is probably more correct to say that *Lawrence* is more anti-federalism than anti-majoritarian. Thus, Justice Scalia's dissent argues that these issues should be left up to individual states to decide.

The federalism question is deeply connected to the original design of the Fourteenth Amendment, which assumed that there would be privileges or immunities of national citizenship that would be protected regardless of state laws to the contrary. The Privileges or Immunities Clause, of course, was effectively gutted by the *Slaughterhouse Cases,* and the Due Process Clause took its place as the basic guardian of fundamental rights as well as the site for incorporation of the Bill of Rights against the states. Nevertheless, the basic federalism issue still remains, simply in a different doctrinal guise: Should this extension of the right of intimate association be one of the basic privileges and immunities of citizens of the United States, regardless of state law?

2. *Does* Lawrence *recognize a fundamental right?* Justice Scalia argues that the majority does not specifically state that there is a fundamental right to same-sex conduct and that *Lawrence* is a rational basis decision. *Lawrence* is ambiguous on precisely this point. Justice Kennedy never uses the word "fundamental" to refer to the right in question; moreover, he argues that "[t]he Texas statute furthers no legitimate state

interest which can justify its intrusion into the personal and private life of the individual," which sounds like the test of rational basis. Does this mean that the Court will now apply heightened scrutiny, whether we call it undue burden or "rational basis with a bite" to certain nonfundamental rights? Under this theory, *Lawrence* is the due process/liberty analogue to equal protection cases like *Cleburne* (discussed in Chapter 7), Romer v. Evans (discussed infra) and Plyler v. Doe (discussed in Chapter 9). If that is the case, how do courts determine those specially protected nonfundamental rights and distinguish them from fundamental rights on the one hand, and from nonfundamental rights to which ordinary rational basis applies on the other?

At the same time, Justice Kennedy does not rule out the notion that *Lawrence* involved a fundamental right. For example, he argues that *Eisenstadt, Carey,* and *Roe* each extended the rights of intimate association and decisional privacy protected by *Griswold* beyond married adults. He then argues that homosexuals have similar rights to form intimate associations, which are more than mere sexual conduct. Finally, he endorses the reasoning of a portion of Justice Stevens's dissent in *Bowers*. All of this might suggest that *Lawrence* holds that the right to form same-sex intimate relations is part of a fundamental right of sexual privacy along with the rights protected in *Griswold, Carey,* and *Eisenstadt*.

Nevertheless, consider whether *Casey* undermines this conclusion because it does not apply strict scrutiny to regulations of abortion, but rather imposes a test of "undue burden." Hence one might argue that, after *Casey*, the right of intimate association, whether it is called privacy or sexual autonomy or something else, is not fundamental. Could one respond that *Casey* is based on the assumption that abortion must be treated differently from other aspects of the fundamental right of privacy because of the countervailing interest in potential human life that is not present in other contexts?

According to Justice Scalia, *Lawrence* holds that there is no fundamental right involved, but that Texas cannot criminalize same-sex sodomy unless the prohibition is rationally related to a legitimate state purpose, and mere moral disapproval of an activity cannot be a legitimate state purpose. Do you think the Court would uphold the statute if Texas repassed it arguing that same-sex relations are harmful to public health? Suppose that Texas argued that there is some evidence that homosexuality is a mental disorder (a position once taken but now long abandoned by the psychiatric profession) and that allowing same-sex sodomy might tend to exacerbate this mental disorder, while banning it would give marginal incentives for homosexuals to experiment with heterosexual relationships. Do you think this should have made a difference in the outcome? All this suggests that *Lawrence* is not, in fact, an application of the ordinary rational basis test.

Why, then, didn't Justice Kennedy simply say that there is a fundamental right to engage in same-sex sodomy? One possibility is that he objected to this characterization of the right, because it demeaned homosexuals by reducing their intimacy to a sex act in a way that would never be done to married heterosexual couples. The right to privacy, Justice Kennedy argues, is the right to form personal and intimate relationships of which sex is only a part. Justice Kennedy's view, in short, is that there is more to a relationship than just sex. Does it follow, then, that the State may regulate casual sex or commercial sex that is not part of an ongoing relationship?

3. *Deeply rooted in the nation's history and traditions?* Several lower courts have relied on Justice Scalia's dissent to argue that *Lawrence* does not recognize a

fundamental right of sexual privacy. For example, in Williams v. Attorney General of Alabama, 378 F. 3d 1232 (11th Cir. 2004), the Eleventh Circuit rejected a challenge based on *Lawrence* to uphold Alabama's Anti-Obscenity Enforcement Act, which prohibited the sale of "sex toys," defined as "any device designed or marketed as useful primarily for the stimulation of human genital organs for any thing of pecuniary value." The statute exempted sale of sexual devices for "for a bona fide medical, scientific, educational, legislative, judicial, or law enforcement purpose."

The court argued that there was no general constitutional right to privacy or autonomy; constitutional protection was afforded only to rights deeply rooted in the Nation's history or traditions, citing the historical test the Court used in Washington v. Glucksberg (discussed infra), which held that there was no fundamental right to physician-assisted suicide. "[T]he Supreme Court's substantive-due-process precedents [have never] recognized a free-standing 'right to sexual privacy,'" the court insisted, and "the [Supreme] Court has never indicated that the mere fact that an activity is sexual and private entitles it to protection as a fundamental right." In particular, the Eleventh Circuit rejected an argument based on *Lawrence,* maintaining that *Lawrence* did not involve recognition of a new fundamental right. "[W]e are not prepared to infer a new fundamental right from an opinion that never employed the usual *Glucksberg* analysis for identifying such rights. Nor are we prepared to assume that *Glucksberg*— a precedent that *Lawrence* never once mentions — is overruled by implication." Does this argument prove too much? If the right to privacy is not a coherent right but merely a collection of disparate rights whose contours are limited to those practices deeply rooted in the Nation's history or traditions, why is *Lawrence* even correct? Indeed, for that matter, why are *Griswold, Eisenstadt,* and *Carey?* These cases, decided in the early years of the sexual revolution, cannot reasonably be grounded in a long tradition of protecting the right to use contraception or the right to consensual sex between unmarried adults. Does *Lawrence* modify the "deeply rooted" test of *Glucksberg* sub silentio? Recall the debate between the Justices about how to characterize a tradition in Michael H. v. Gerald D. Has Justice Brennan's approach won out over Justice Scalia's?

4. *The reach of* Lawrence. Assuming for the moment that *Lawrence* does recognize a fundamental or quasi-fundamental right of same-sex intimate relations (or at the very least heightened scrutiny for regulations of the same), how far does that right extend? Do you agree with Justice Kennedy that the right should apply only to consensual acts between adults? If the right applies to consensual sexual relationships between adults, does it also protect the right to engage in polygamy, incest, adultery, and sadomasochism, where only consenting adults are involved? Does the answer turn on the degree of social acceptance that these practices have achieved, in contrast to homosexuality, which has become increasingly normalized in the United States by the beginning of the twenty-first century? If social acceptance is the key consideration, does this mean that *Bowers* might have been rightly decided in 1986 because the degree of social acceptance of homosexuality had not achieved its present state?

5. *Morality as a legitimate state interest.* Justice Kennedy quotes with approval Justice Stevens's statement in *Bowers* that "the fact that the governing majority in a State has traditionally viewed a particular practice as immoral is not a sufficient reason for upholding a law prohibiting the practice; neither history nor tradition could

save a law prohibiting miscegenation from constitutional attack." Kennedy also observes that the importance of intimate association "should counsel [as a general rule] against attempts by the State, or a court, to define the meaning of [a personal intimate] relationship or to set its boundaries absent injury to a person or abuse of an institution the law protects."

If *Lawrence* recognizes a fundamental right, then Kennedy is merely saying that moral objections by the community are not sufficient to overcome the exercise of a fundamental right. That would make sense of Kennedy's citation to Stevens's dissent in *Bowers*, which argues that laws against morality would be insufficient to uphold a law against miscegenation. Recall that in Loving v. Virginia the Court subjected the Virginia statute to strict, not rational basis, scrutiny on two separate grounds: First, the statute made an invidious racial classification, and second, it abridged the fundamental right to marry.

If Kennedy meant to say that morality is never, by itself, a sufficiently legitimate state interest to satisfy the rational basis test, the claim is far more novel. It might mean that the state was bound by some version of the harm principle. The state would have to show some "injury to a person or abuse of an institution which the law protects"; in other words, a harm that went beyond moral offense at the conduct involved.

Consider whether the question of harm can be so easily separated from moral offense, especially because moral objections can often be restated in terms of concerns about harm. For example, suppose legislatures believed that restricting same-sex relations would discourage people from adopting lifestyles and models of intimacy that the legislature believed would lead to more crime, more social disorder, more disease, and more collective and individual unhappiness in the long run. Even if one disagreed with these views on the merits, why wouldn't this pass the rational basis test of Williamson v. Lee Optical, which allows legislatures to presume all sorts of facts and causal connections? If one believes that these sorts of views should not pass constitutional scrutiny, does this suggest that we are dealing with something other than the garden-variety rational basis test?

Next, consider whether the question of what is a fundamental right (or a right whose regulation is subject to heightened scrutiny) can easily be separated from the question of what is immoral. Is *Lawrence*'s validation of the intimacy of homosexuals and its rejection of legal discrimination and stigma against homosexuals necessarily premised on the notion that people who think homosexuality is immoral are wrong?

Justice Scalia argues that a rule that harm must be shown in addition to moral offense would have wide-ranging (and undesirable) consequences: "State laws against bigamy, same-sex marriage, adult incest, prostitution, masturbation, adultery, fornication, bestiality, and obscenity are . . . sustainable only in light of *Bowers*' validation of laws based on moral choices." Do you agree that legislatures could not offer harm-based arguments in any of these cases? Do you agree with Justice Scalia's assumption that masturbation and fornication (sex between unmarried adults) had no constitutional protection after *Carey, Eisenstadt,* and *Roe*? Justice Scalia argues that the reasoning of *Lawrence* fatally undermines the constitutionality of laws that prohibit same-sex marriage. Is he correct? Could opponents argue that same-sex marriage would be "an abuse of an institution the law protects?" On the other hand, consider whether the real point is that *Lawrence* will lead to changes in social norms that will eventually lead courts to recognize same-sex marriage. Do you agree that a decision like *Lawrence* can have this effect?

6. *"Liberty" versus "privacy."* Justice Kennedy consistently uses the word "liberty," rather than "privacy," to describe the constitutional interest at stake. Indeed, the word "privacy" appears outside of a quotation only once in the majority opinion, and even then it is used only to describe the holding of *Griswold*. This is in marked contrast to *Roe* and *Eisenstadt*, which, like *Griswold*, expressly emphasized that the right at issue was the right of privacy. What explains this shift in language? Does the word "liberty" ground *Lawrence*'s holding more firmly in the text of the Fourteenth Amendment or better suggest the proper scope of the right at stake? Should advocates for gay rights who are concerned about the oppression caused by the closet strongly prefer "liberty" to "privacy"?

7. *Liberty versus equality.* In a case like *Lawrence,* the Court could have gone in several directions. First, the Supreme Court could have focused on expanding the liberty protected by the Due Process Clause, as it did in *Lawrence*. Second, it could have found that Texas's prohibition on same-sex but not opposite-sex sodomy violated the rational basis test. In that case, the laws of four jurisdictions would have been overturned, while nine states' laws, which prohibited both same-sex and opposite-sex sodomy, would have been preserved.

Why should Texas's law fail the rational basis test if the right of privacy does not apply to same-sex conduct? Is Justice O'Connor correct that prohibitions against same-sex sodomy are an attempt to punish homosexuals as a group, or that moral disapproval of same-sex sodomy is essentially anti-gay bias? Justice O'Connor is "confident . . . that so long as the Equal Protection Clause requires a sodomy law to apply equally to the private consensual conduct of homosexuals and heterosexuals alike, such a law would not long stand in our democratic society." She is suggesting that if the Court forced legislatures to pass even-handed laws, legislatures would not enact any prohibitions on sodomy. What explains the fact that 9 of the 13 jurisdictions that prohibited sodomy before *Lawrence* prohibited both same-sex and opposite-sex conduct?

Suppose that in those jurisdictions, facially neutral laws were not being enforced in an evenhanded way. Or suppose that the sodomy statutes were not being directly enforced at all, but used only against gays in other contexts, like custody determinations or employment decisions. Should the differential enforcement of those laws be subject to an equal protection challenge? At oral argument, Justice O'Connor asked Lawrence's attorney whether facially neutral laws prohibiting both same-sex and cross-sex sodomy might still violate the equal protection guarantee. Lawrence's attorney answered in the negative. Was that the best answer?

Third, the Court could have held that classifications based on sexual orientation are suspect and subject to heightened scrutiny, like those based on race or gender. By grounding gay rights in liberty rather than equality, the Court ensured that all of the remaining sodomy prohibitions in the country were declared invalid (something that O'Connor's rational basis approach did not necessarily do). At the same time, it did not have to hold that gays are a suspect class or that classifications based on sexual orientation are entitled to heightened scrutiny. And it also held off, for the time being, a decision about whether the failure to recognize same-sex marriage violates the Constitution.

8. *Liberty as equality.* Note that in a case like *Lawrence,* it is not always helpful to distinguish between considerations of liberty and equality. For example, a decision based on privacy grounds might still have significant consequences for equal protection. The Supreme Court will strictly scrutinize laws that place discriminatory burdens on the exercise of a fundamental right or fundamental interest. Because the right to form same-sex intimate relations is now a protected liberty under the Due Process Clause, some discrimination against same-sex conduct will be unconstitutional under both due process and equal protection. Does same-sex marriage fall into this category?

Note moreover, that *Lawrence* seems to merge liberty and equality considerations. Justice Kennedy's opinion is organized around themes of respect: It repeatedly discusses concerns of dignity, denigration, and status. Justice Kennedy states, for example, that when "homosexual conduct is made criminal by the law of the State, that declaration in and of itself is an invitation to subject homosexual persons to discrimination both in the public and in the private spheres," and goes on to observe that *Bowers'* "continuance as precedent demeans the lives of homosexual persons."

This suggests that *Lawrence* is a hybrid: a substantive due process opinion that is shaped by many of the same concerns that animate equal protection law. With this in mind, consider whether equality concerns also appear in some of the other substantive due process cases you have read up to this point, such as *Meyer, Pierce, Skinner, Griswold, Eisenstadt, Carey, Roe,* and *Casey.* How would you describe the groups whose equality is at stake in these various cases?

9. *Liberty versus equality: A queer perspective.* Basing *Lawrence* on liberty rather than equality has some advantages for sexual orientation minorities who do not wish courts to view all sexual orientation minorities as a single cohesive group. A holding grounded in equality would push sexual orientation minorities toward a civil rights paradigm: It would ascribe to all of them a common group identity, based on an analogy to blacks and women. Government could not discriminate against them on the basis of their identity as homosexuals. By contrast, a queer rights perspective would focus on the right of sexual orientation minorities to conduct their sexual lives as they see fit, free from government regulation, allowing them to experiment with different forms of attachment, different forms of sexuality, and different forms of sexual identity. A decision grounded in liberty rather than equality is more hospitable from this perspective.

10. *Anti-caste principle or mere tolerance?* Although some commentators have emphasized that Justice Kennedy's focus on dignity has equality overtones, see, e.g., Andrew Koppelman, Lawrence's Penumbra, 88 Minn. L. Rev. 1171, 1177 (2004) ("*Lawrence* is full of language that demonstrates the Court's concern with the subordination of gays as a group, rather than just the liberty of individuals."), others have been more skeptical, noting that *Lawrence* offers little more than tolerance for homosexuals. William N. Eskridge, Jr., Lawrence's Jurisprudence of Tolerance: Judicial Review to Lower the Stakes of Identity Politics, 88 Minn. L. Rev. 1021, 1025 (2004). ("*Lawrence* gives us nothing less than, but also nothing more than, a jurisprudence of tolerance.") Katherine M. Franke, The Domesticated Liberty of Lawrence v. Texas, 104 Colum. L. Rev. 1399, 1411. 1413 (2004) ("decriminalization does not necessarily mobilize any particular ethical projects, or for that matter, any ethics at all. . . . Without more, *Lawrence*-like decriminalization merely signals a public tolerance of the behavior, so long as it takes place in private and between

two consenting adults in a relationship."). Is *Lawrence*'s ambiguity a bit like *Brown*? Recall from Chapter 6 that decades of political struggles following the decision produced what *Brown* eventually came to mean. Is there any reason to think that *Lawrence* will prove different?

11. Lawrence, Casey, *and precedents for overturning precedents.* Recall that in *Casey,* the Joint Opinion outlined four "prudential and pragmatic considerations" that the Court should take into account in deciding whether to overrule a precedent: (1) workability, (2) reliance, (3) change in surrounding doctrines, and (4) changes in facts or changes in the perception of facts. This section of the *Casey* Joint Opinion commanded five votes. Does *Lawrence* adhere to these standards? If not, did it overrule or otherwise supersede the theory of stare decisis in *Casey*? What rules, if any, should the Court apply when it overturns a precedent that sets out rules for overturning precedents?

12. Lawrence *and foreign law.* Why precisely does Justice Kennedy cite the European Court of Human Rights opinion in Dudgeon v. United Kingdom, 45 Eur. Ct. H. R. (1981)? Does he regard the case as authoritative precedent, as persuasive authority (like a state Supreme Court decision construing a related provision in the state's own constitution), or merely as evidence of changing views in the West about the morality of homosexuality? Suppose it is merely the latter. Recall Justice Harlan's justification of looking to the evolving traditions of the American people in Poe v. Ullman. If substantive due process decisions are justified with reference to the evolving norms of Americans, why are the decisions of foreign courts relevant? Couldn't opponents of *Lawrence* point to a wide range of countries throughout the world that continue to regard homosexuality as sinful or immoral? And wouldn't some countries be inappropriate sources for guidance on basic human rights? What assumptions must a court make in deciding which foreign sources should count as persuasive, either as offering a plausible set of arguments about human rights or merely as evidence of changing norms among "civilized" nations? Are these assumptions uncontroversial? Are they legitimate?

B. Sexual Orientation and Equal Protection

ROMER v. EVANS
517 U.S. 620 (1996)

Justice KENNEDY delivered the opinion of the Court.

[In 1992 Colorado voters adopted "Amendment 2" by statewide referendum. The drive for Amendment 2 came after several Colorado municipalities — including Aspen, Boulder, and the City and County of Denver — passed ordinances banning discrimination based on sexual orientation in housing, employment, education, public accommodations, health and welfare services, and other transactions and activities. Amendment 2 provided:

No Protected Status Based on Homosexual, Lesbian, or Bisexual Orientation.
  Neither the State of Colorado, through any of its branches or departments, nor any of its agencies, political subdivisions, municipalities or school districts, shall enact, adopt or enforce any statute, regulation, ordinance or policy whereby

homosexual, lesbian or bisexual orientation, conduct, practices or relationships shall constitute or otherwise be the basis of or entitle any person or class of persons to have or claim any minority status, quota preferences, protected status or claim of discrimination. This Section of the Constitution shall be in all respects self-executing.]

I.

One century ago, the first Justice Harlan admonished this Court that the Constitution "neither knows nor tolerates classes among citizens." Plessy v. Ferguson, 163 U.S. 537, 559 (1896) (dissenting opinion). Unheeded then, those words now are understood to state a commitment to the law's neutrality where the rights of persons are at stake. The Equal Protection Clause enforces this principle and today requires us to hold invalid a provision of Colorado's Constitution. . . .

Amendment 2 . . . does more than repeal or rescind [local municipal anti-discrimination] provisions. It prohibits all legislative, executive or judicial action at any level of state or local government designed to protect the named class, a class we shall refer to as homosexual persons or gays and lesbians. . . .

[Although the Colorado Supreme Court held that Amendment 2] infringed the fundamental right of gays and lesbians to participate in the political process, [we] affirm the judgment . . . on a [different] rationale.

II.

The State's principal argument in defense of Amendment 2 is that it puts gays and lesbians in the same position as all other persons. So, the State says, the measure does no more than deny homosexuals special rights. This reading of the amendment's language is implausible. . . . Homosexuals, by state decree, are put in a solitary class with respect to transactions and relations in both the private and governmental spheres. The amendment withdraws from homosexuals, but no others, specific legal protection from the injuries caused by discrimination, and it forbids reinstatement of these laws and policies. . . .

Amendment 2 bars homosexuals from securing protection against [discrimination in] public[]accommodations[.] [I]n addition, [it] nullifies specific legal protections for this targeted class in all transactions in housing, sale of real estate, insurance, health and welfare services, private education, and employment. . . .

Amendment 2 also operates to repeal and forbid all laws or policies providing specific protection for gays or lesbians from discrimination by every level of Colorado government [including discrimination by state employers and state colleges]. . . .

Amendment 2's reach may not be limited to specific laws passed for the benefit of gays and lesbians. [It may deprive] gays and lesbians even of the protection of general laws and policies that prohibit arbitrary discrimination in governmental and private settings. . . . At some point in the systematic administration of these laws, an official must determine whether homosexuality is an arbitrary and thus forbidden basis for decision. Yet a decision to that effect would itself amount to a policy prohibiting discrimination on the basis of homosexuality [in violation of] Amendment 2. . . .

[E]ven if, as we doubt, homosexuals could find some safe harbor in laws of general application, we cannot accept the view that Amendment 2's prohibition on specific legal protections does no more than deprive homosexuals of special rights. To the contrary, the amendment imposes a special disability upon those persons alone. Homosexuals are forbidden the safeguards that others enjoy or may seek without constraint. They can obtain specific protection against discrimination only by enlisting the citizenry of Colorado to amend the state constitution or perhaps, on the State's view, by trying to pass helpful laws of general applicability. This is so no matter how local or discrete the harm, no matter how public and widespread the injury. We find nothing special in the protections Amendment 2 withholds. These are protections taken for granted by most people either because they already have them or do not need them; these are protections against exclusion from an almost limitless number of transactions and endeavors that constitute ordinary civic life in a free society. . . .

Amendment 2 fails, indeed defies, [the] conventional inquiry [into whether a law burdens a fundamental right or a suspect class]. First, the amendment has the peculiar property of imposing a broad and undifferentiated disability on a single named group, an exceptional and, as we shall explain, invalid form of legislation. Second, its sheer breadth is so discontinuous with the reasons offered for it that the amendment seems inexplicable by anything but animus toward the class that it affects; it lacks a rational relationship to legitimate state interests. . . .

By requiring that [a] classification bear a rational relationship to an independent and legitimate legislative end, we ensure that classifications are not drawn for the purpose of disadvantaging the group burdened by the law.

Amendment 2 confounds this normal process of judicial review. It is at once too narrow and too broad. It identifies persons by a single trait and then denies them protection across the board. The resulting disqualification of a class of persons from the right to seek specific protection from the law is unprecedented in our jurisprudence. . . .

It is not within our constitutional tradition to enact laws of this sort. Central both to the idea of the rule of law and to our own Constitution's guarantee of equal protection is the principle that government and each of its parts remain open on impartial terms to all who seek its assistance. . . . Respect for this principle explains why laws singling out a certain class of citizens for disfavored legal status or general hardships are rare. A law declaring that in general it shall be more difficult for one group of citizens than for all others to seek aid from the government is itself a denial of equal protection of the laws in the most literal sense. . . .

[L]aws of the kind now before us raise the inevitable inference that the disadvantage imposed is born of animosity toward the class of persons affected. "[I]f the constitutional conception of 'equal protection of the laws' means anything, it must at the very least mean that a bare . . . desire to harm a politically unpopular group cannot constitute a legitimate governmental interest." Department of Agriculture v. Moreno, 413 U.S. 528 (1973). Even laws enacted for broad and ambitious purposes often can be explained by reference to legitimate public policies which justify the incidental disadvantages they impose on certain persons. Amendment 2, however, in making a general announcement that gays and lesbians shall not have any particular protections from the law, inflicts on them immediate, continuing, and real injuries that outrun and belie any legitimate justifications that may be claimed for it. We conclude that, in addition to the far-reaching deficiencies of Amendment 2 that we have noted, the principles it offends, in another sense, are conventional and venerable; a law must bear a rational relationship to a legitimate governmental purpose, and Amendment 2 does not.

The primary rationale the State offers for Amendment 2 is respect for other citizens' freedom of association, and in particular the liberties of landlords or employers who have personal or religious objections to homosexuality. Colorado also cites its interest in conserving resources to fight discrimination against other groups. The breadth of the Amendment is so far removed from these particular justifications that we find it impossible to credit them. We cannot say that Amendment 2 is directed to any identifiable legitimate purpose or discrete objective. It is a status-based enactment divorced from any factual context from which we could discern a relationship to legitimate state interests; it is a classification of persons undertaken for its own sake, something the Equal Protection Clause does not permit. "[C]lass legislation . . . [is] obnoxious to the prohibitions of the Fourteenth Amendment. . . ." Civil Rights Cases, 109 U.S., at 24.

We must conclude that Amendment 2 classifies homosexuals not to further a proper legislative end but to make them unequal to everyone else. This Colorado cannot do. A State cannot so deem a class of persons a stranger to its laws. Amendment 2 violates the Equal Protection Clause, and the judgment of the Supreme Court of Colorado is affirmed.

It is so ordered.

Justice SCALIA, with whom the Chief Justice and Justice Thomas join, dissenting.

The Court has mistaken a Kulturkampf for a fit of spite. The constitutional amendment before us here is not the manifestation of a "bare . . . desire to harm" homosexuals, but is rather a modest attempt by seemingly tolerant Coloradans to preserve traditional sexual mores against the efforts of a politically powerful minority to revise those mores through use of the laws. . . .

In holding that homosexuality cannot be singled out for disfavorable treatment, the Court contradicts a decision, unchallenged here, pronounced only 10 years ago, see Bowers v. Hardwick, 478 U.S. 186 (1986), and places the prestige of this institution behind the proposition that opposition to homosexuality is as reprehensible as racial or religious bias. Whether it is or not is precisely the cultural debate that gave rise to the Colorado constitutional amendment (and to the preferential laws against which the amendment was directed). Since the Constitution of the United States says nothing about this subject, it is left to be resolved by normal democratic means, including the democratic adoption of provisions in state constitutions. This Court has no business imposing upon all Americans the resolution favored by the elite class from which the Members of this institution are selected, pronouncing that "animosity" toward homosexuality is evil. I vigorously dissent.

. . . The clear import of the Colorado court's conclusion [is] that "general laws and policies that prohibit arbitrary discrimination" would continue to prohibit discrimination on the basis of homosexual conduct as well. This analysis . . . lays to rest such horribles . . . as the prospect that assaults upon homosexuals could not be prosecuted. The amendment prohibits special treatment of homosexuals, and nothing more. It would not affect, for example, a requirement of state law that pensions be paid to all retiring state employees with a certain length of service; homosexual employees, as well as others, would be entitled to that benefit. But it would prevent the State or any municipality from making death-benefit payments to the "life partner" of a homosexual when it does not make such payments to the long-time roommate of a nonhomosexual employee. Or again, it does not affect the requirement of the State's general insurance laws that customers be afforded coverage without discrimination unrelated to anticipated risk. Thus, homosexuals could not be denied coverage, or charged a greater premium, with respect to auto collision insurance; but neither the State nor any municipality could require that distinctive health insurance risks associated with homosexuality (if there are any) be ignored.

Despite all of its hand-wringing about the potential effect of Amendment 2 on general antidiscrimination laws, the Court's opinion ultimately does not dispute all this, but assumes it to be true. The only denial of equal treatment it contends homosexuals have suffered is this: They may not obtain preferential treatment without amending the state constitution. That is to say, the principle underlying the Court's opinion is that one who is accorded equal treatment under the laws, but cannot as readily as others obtain preferential treatment under the laws, has been denied equal protection of the laws. If merely stating this alleged "equal protection" violation does not suffice to refute it, our constitutional jurisprudence has achieved terminal silliness.

The central thesis of the Court's reasoning is that any group is denied equal protection when, to obtain advantage (or, presumably, to avoid disadvantage), it must have recourse to a more general and hence more difficult level of political decisionmaking than others. The world has never heard of such a principle, which is why the Court's opinion is so long on emotive utterance and so short on relevant legal citation. And it seems to me most unlikely that any multilevel democracy can function under such a principle. . . . [C]onsider a state law prohibiting the award of municipal contracts to relatives of mayors or city councilmen. Once such a law is passed, the group composed of such relatives must, in order to get the benefit of city contracts, persuade the state legislature — unlike all other citizens, who need only persuade the municipality. It is ridiculous to consider this a denial of equal protection, which is why the Court's theory is unheard-of.

The Court might reply that the example I have given is not a denial of equal protection only because the same "rational basis" (avoidance of corruption) which renders constitutional the substantive discrimination against relatives (i.e., the fact that they alone cannot obtain city contracts) also automatically suffices to sustain what might be called the electoral-procedural discrimination against them (i.e., the fact that they must go to the state level to get this changed). . . . [A] law that is valid in its substance is automatically valid in its level of enactment. . . .

[But] there was a legitimate rational basis for . . . the prohibition of special protection for homosexuals. . . . If it is constitutionally permissible for a State to make homosexual conduct criminal, [under *Bowers*] surely it is constitutionally permissible for a State to enact other laws merely disfavoring homosexual conduct. . . . And a fortiori it is constitutionally permissible for a State to adopt a provision not even disfavoring homosexual conduct, but merely prohibiting all levels of state government from bestowing special protections upon homosexual conduct. . . .

[A]ssuming that, in Amendment 2, a person of homosexual "orientation" is someone who does not engage in homosexual conduct but merely has a tendency or desire to do so, *Bowers* still suffices to establish a rational basis for the provision. If it is rational to criminalize the conduct, surely it is rational to deny special favor and protection to those with a self-avowed tendency or desire to engage in the conduct. Indeed, where criminal sanctions are not involved, homosexual "orientation" is an acceptable stand-in for homosexual conduct. . . . Just as a policy barring the hiring of methadone users as transit employees does not violate equal protection simply because some methadone users pose no threat to passenger safety, see New York City Transit Authority v. Beazer, 440 U.S. 568 (1979), and just as a mandatory retirement age of 50 for police officers does not violate equal protection even though it prematurely ends the careers of many policemen over 50 who still have the capacity to do the job, see Massachusetts Bd. of Retirement v. Murgia, 427 U.S. 307 (1976) (per curiam), Amendment 2 is not constitutionally invalid simply because it could have been drawn more precisely so as to withdraw special antidiscrimination protections only from those of homosexual "orientation" who actually engage in homosexual conduct. . . .

The Court's opinion contains grim, disapproving hints that Coloradans have been guilty of "animus" or "animosity" toward homosexuality, as though that has been established as unAmerican. Of course it is our moral heritage that one should not hate any human being or class of human beings. But I had thought that one could consider certain conduct reprehensible — murder, for example, or polygamy, or cruelty to animals — and could exhibit even "animus" toward such conduct. Surely that is the only sort of "animus" at issue here: moral disapproval of homosexual conduct, the same sort of moral disapproval that produced the centuries-old criminal laws that we held constitutional in *Bowers*. The Colorado amendment does not, to speak entirely precisely, prohibit giving favored status to people who are homosexuals; they can be favored for many reasons — for example, because they are senior citizens or members of racial minorities. But it prohibits giving them favored status because of their homosexual conduct — that is, it prohibits favored status for homosexuality.

. . . Colorado not only is one of the 25 States that have repealed their antisodomy laws, but was among the first to do so [in 1971]. But the society that eliminates criminal punishment for homosexual acts does not necessarily abandon the view that homosexuality is morally wrong and socially harmful; often, abolition simply reflects the view that enforcement of such criminal laws involves unseemly intrusion into the intimate lives of citizens.

There is a problem, however, which arises when criminal sanction of homosexuality is eliminated but moral and social disapprobation of homosexuality is meant to be retained[; it] occasionally bubbles to the surface of the news, in heated political disputes over such matters as the introduction into local schools of books teaching that homosexuality is an optional and fully acceptable "alternate life style." . . . [B]ecause those who engage in homosexual conduct tend to reside in disproportionate numbers in certain communities, and of course care about homosexual-rights issues much more ardently than the public at large, they possess political power much greater than their numbers, both locally and statewide. Quite understandably, they devote this political power to achieving not merely a grudging social toleration, but full social acceptance, of homosexuality.

By the time Coloradans were asked to vote on Amendment 2, . . . [t]hree Colorado cities — Aspen, Boulder, and Denver — had enacted ordinances that listed "sexual orientation" as an impermissible ground for discrimination, equating the moral disapproval of homosexual conduct with racial and religious bigotry [and] the Governor of Colorado had signed an executive order [requiring non-discrimination on the basis of sexual orientation]. I do not mean to be critical of these legislative successes; homosexuals are as entitled to use the legal system for reinforcement of their moral sentiments as are the rest of society. But they are subject to being countered by lawful, democratic countermeasures as well.

Amendment 2 . . . sought to counter both the geographic concentration and the disproportionate political power of homosexuals by (1) resolving the controversy at the statewide level, and (2) making the election a single-issue contest for both sides. . . .

The constitutions of the States of Arizona, Idaho, New Mexico, Oklahoma, and Utah to this day contain provisions stating that polygamy is "forever prohibited." Polygamists, and those who have a polygamous "orientation," have been "singled out" by these provisions for much more severe treatment than merely denial of favored status; and that treatment can only be changed by achieving amendment of the state constitutions. The Court's disposition today suggests that these provisions are unconstitutional, and that polygamy must be permitted in these States on a state-legislated, or perhaps even local-option, basis — unless, of course, polygamists for some reason have fewer constitutional rights than homosexuals.

. . . I think it no business of the courts (as opposed to the political branches) to take sides in this culture war.

But the Court today has done so, not only by inventing a novel and extravagant constitutional doctrine to take the victory away from traditional forces, but even by verbally disparaging as bigotry adherence to traditional attitudes. To suggest, for example, that this constitutional amendment springs from nothing more than " 'a bare . . . desire to harm a politically unpopular group,' " is nothing short of insulting. (It is also nothing short of preposterous to call "politically unpopular" a group which enjoys enormous influence in American media and politics, and which, as the trial court here noted, though composing no more than 4% of the population had the support of 46% of the voters on Amendment 2.)

When the Court takes sides in the culture wars, it tends to be with the knights rather than the villains — and more specifically with the Templars, reflecting the views and values of the lawyer class from which the Court's Members are drawn. How that class feels about homosexuality will be evident to anyone who wishes to interview job applicants at virtually any of the Nation's law schools. The interviewer may refuse to offer a job because the applicant is a Republican; because he is an adulterer; because he went to the wrong prep school or belongs to the wrong country club; because he eats snails; because he is a womanizer; because she wears real-animal fur; or even because he hates the Chicago Cubs. But if the interviewer should wish not to be an associate or partner of an applicant because he disapproves of the applicant's homosexuality, then he will have violated the pledge which the Association of American Law Schools requires all its member-schools to exact from job interviewers: "assurance of the employer's willingness" to hire homosexuals. This law-school view of what "prejudices" must be stamped out may be contrasted with the more plebeian attitudes that apparently still prevail in the United States Congress, which has been unresponsive to repeated attempts to extend to homosexuals the protections of federal civil rights laws, and which took the pains to exclude them specifically from the Americans With Disabilities Act of 1990.

Today's opinion has no foundation in American constitutional law, and barely pretends to. The people of Colorado have adopted an entirely reasonable provision which does not even disfavor homosexuals in any substantive sense, but merely denies them preferential treatment. Amendment 2 is designed to prevent piecemeal deterioration of the sexual morality favored by a majority of Coloradans, and is not only an appropriate means to that legitimate end, but a means that Americans have employed before. Striking it down is an act, not of judicial judgment, but of political will. I dissent.

Discussion

1. *Class legislation?* Although Justice Scalia suggests that the court's decision in *Romer* is unprecedented, its logic does bear interesting similarities to at least some of the concerns of the framers of the Fourteenth Amendment.[83] Influenced by Jacksonianism and free soil theories, the framers of the Fourteenth Amendment were opposed to "class legislation" that denied equal privileges and protections to certain groups and treated them as social inferiors. When the Jacksonians spoke of "class legislation," they were more likely to be worried about special privileges for the rich and wealthy (like monopolies and corporate charters) that posed the danger of creating a new nobility or social elite. By the end of the Civil War, however, the framers of the Fourteenth Amendment understood the concept as involving the converse phenomenon: legislation that denigrated or demeaned a group of persons and held them as less equal than others.[84]

In his proposed joint resolution for drafting the Fourteenth Amendment, for example, Charles Sumner invoked the Jacksonian heritage when he claimed that the proposed Fourteenth Amendment should abolish "oligarchy, aristocracy, caste, or monopoly with particular privileges and powers."[85] Sumner spoke of monopoly and caste in the same breath, equating legislation that singles out groups for special treatment with legislation that demeans and stigmatizes groups as social inferiors. Likewise Senator Howard, the floor manager of the Fourteenth Amendment, offered an expanded interpretation of the Jacksonian principle. He argued that the amendment's goal was to "abolis[h] all class legislation . . . and [do] away with the injustice of subjecting one caste of persons to a code not applicable to another." Cong. Globe, 39th Cong. (1st Sess.) 2766 (1866).

From a modern standpoint, the notion of "class legislation" seems puzzling because all legislation divides groups into classes. Hence, modern constitutional law looks to whether a suspect classification is invoked or a fundamental right is abridged. However, the Fourteenth Amendment was enacted long before courts adopted the language of scrutiny. The concept of "class legislation" makes most sense in terms of social meaning, which would inquire whether the legislation treats a group as a whole as a sort of lower caste or social inferior. Did Colorado's Amendment 2 do this? Do Justice Scalia's remarks about the purpose of showing public disapproval for homosexuals and homosexuality shed any light on this

---

83. This discussion is drawn from J.M. Balkin, The Constitution of Status, 106 Yale L.J. 2313 (1997).

84. On the transformation of the Jacksonian idea of class legislation, see Eric Foner, Free Soil, Free Labor, Free Men 90-91 (1970); Mark G. Yudof, Equal Protection, Class Legislation, and Sex Discrimination: One Small Cheer for Mr. Herbert Spencer's Social Statics, 88 Mich. L. Rev. 1366, 1376-1379 (1990).

85. Cong. Globe, 39th Cong. (1st Sess.) 674 (1866). The joint resolution failed, but the debate affected the final language of the amendment. See Andrew Kull, The Color-Blind Constitution 74-75 (1992); see also Adamson v. California, 332 U.S. 46, 51 n.8 (1947) (quoting Sumner's resolution as evidence of meaning of Fourteenth Amendment).

question? Note that under the terms of Amendment 2 discrimination against *hetero-sexuals* could still be banned by any political subdivision in the State of Colorado. Does the fact that the Amendment directed itself at a class (sexual orientation minorities) rather than at a classification (sexual orientation) make the "class legislation" argument stronger?[86]

2. *Is* Romer *more like* Cleburne *or like* Reed? *Romer* purports to be an application of rational basis review. However, it seems importantly different from the approach the Court has taken in cases like Williamson v. Lee Optical or *Railway Express*. One possibility is that *Romer* belongs to a small group of cases like *Cleburne* in which the Court is convinced that irrational bias and prejudice are behind the legislation, but is unwilling to recognize the affected group as a suspect class. This, of course, begs the question why these particular groups get the benefit of an enhanced rational basis test or "rational basis with a bite" when so many other groups — for example, the poor, the elderly, and the homeless — do not.

Can *Romer* be justified on the grounds that Amendment 2 was clearly motivated by irrational prejudice against homosexuals? How does the Court know the motives of the persons who voted for it? What if some persons voted for Amendment 2 for prejudicial reasons, others voted for it because they felt that discrimination against homosexuals and bisexuals was not as morally reprehensible as discrimination against women and blacks, and still others voted for the Amendment because they felt that homosexuals and bisexuals were not in as much need of civil rights protections as women and blacks? Is the application of *Cleburne* here really a test not of what voters actually thought but what it appears they were thinking in voting for Amendment 2, i.e., the social meaning of Amendment 2? Recall Charles Lawrence's proposed "cultural meaning" test. Note that the cultural meaning of Amendment 2 was bitterly contested by Justice Scalia. Can the cultural meaning approach work without some measure of consensus about what things mean?

Another way of justifying the result in *Romer* is to argue that Amendment 2 had irrational results that did not preserve equal rights for homosexuals but instead created special and irrational burdens. Consider the following interpretation of Amendment 2: Under Amendment 2 police officers and other administrative officials would be free to discriminate against homosexuals and bisexuals at will, and other government agencies would be powerless to remedy this treatment if the stated reason for discrimination was that the person was homosexual or bisexual. Thus, if firemen wait to put out fires in the houses of homosexuals until the houses are completely destroyed, police officers fail to arrest gay bashers, or county clerks refuse to process parade permits for homosexuals because these persons are homosexual, they cannot be penalized because they acted out of anti-gay bias. Nor can any state agency create any policy that would prevent the exercise of anti-gay bias. There could only be a remedy if there were a general requirement of prosecuting all assaults, answering all fires promptly, and issuing parade permits on a first-come, first-served basis. Do you agree that this is the legal effect of Amendment 2? If it is, does it violate the rational basis test?

---

86. Along similar lines Akhil Amar has argued that Amendment 2 was an unconstitutional bill of attainder, see Akhil Reed Amar, Attainder and Amendment 2: Romer's Rightness, 95 Mich. L. Rev. 203, 218 (1996). Amar argues that the Bill of Attainder Clauses are designed to prevent governments from singling out and punishing identifiable social groups because of who they are.

A final possibility is that *Romer* is like Reed v. Reed, the 1971 sex discrimination case that struck down an Idaho statute favoring men over women as executors of estates. While *Reed* only applied rational basis review, it was soon followed by *Frontiero v. Richardson* in 1973 and *Craig v. Boren* in 1976, which ultimately established intermediate scrutiny for gender classifications. Under this view, *Romer* applied rational basis review while the Court is genuinely considering announcing a new suspect category of sexual orientation. In this sense, Justice Scalia's argument that *Romer* and *Bowers* are inconsistent might simply be another way of noting that one or the other case will have to go. As it turned out, the case that was jettisoned was *Bowers*.

3. Romer *and* Lawrence. Does the result in *Romer* make more sense in hindsight if states may not criminalize homosexual sexual relations? Couldn't Colorado respond, as Justice Scalia did, that even if homosexuals may not be punished for engaging in sodomy, the state may still express its moral disapproval of homosexuality?

One response to this argument is that Colorado may not single out a group and punish its members for exercising a fundamental right. For example, even though Colorado need not approve of abortion, it may not authorize discrimination against women who have abortions. Does this argument depend on whether *Lawrence* recognized a fundamental right, or merely held that the right to form same-sex intimate relations is a liberty protected by the Due Process Clause?

Assume for the moment that *Lawrence* did recognize a fundamental right to form same-sex relationships. Can Colorado respond that it is not punishing the exercise of that right, but rather disfavoring homosexual orientation regardless of whether homosexuals engage in homosexual sexual relations, i.e., that it is aiming at status, not conduct? Note that gay rights litigators before *Lawrence* sometimes endeavored to separate homosexual status from homosexual conduct so that they could avoid the implications of *Bowers*, arguing, for example, that celibate homosexuals should not be excluded from the Armed Forces. Now that *Bowers* has been overruled, this strategy may be less beneficial.

4. *Amendment 2 and status competition.* One way of understanding Amendment 2 is as an attempt by its proponents to preserve the superior moral meaning of heterosexuality over homosexuality at a time when public sympathies and attitudes about homosexuality are undergoing change. In other words, Amendment 2 was an example of *status competition*, in which social groups fight over the comparative social approval, respect, and esteem of their respective identities and distinctive styles of life. Status competition can be especially bitter because social status between such groups is, at least in the short run, a zero-sum good. High prestige is prestige over others and in distinction to others. Increased respect for lower status groups means a corresponding loss of respect for higher status groups because their identity has been constructed around their greater prestige and the greater propriety of their ways of living. Status competition is often phrased in terms of contrasting moral values; the struggle over Prohibition is perhaps the best example. The zero-sum nature of these struggles helps to explain why opponents of anti-discrimination measures for homosexuals see them as "special privileges":

Protecting homosexuals from discrimination is understood as a sign of increased social status mirrored in new legal protections. [T]his increase in status necessarily occurs at the expense of heterosexuals. From the perspective of the older baseline of social meanings, it appears that homosexuals are being given something new that is being taken away from heterosexuals. They are being given increased honor, respect, and esteem, hence "special treatment." . . . Every change in the semiotic status quo, no matter how unfair the previous baseline of social meanings, may be seen as sending the message of favoritism and special treatment. Any departure from a baseline that views homosexuality as deviant and immoral will be viewed by some members of the dominant status group eager to retain their status as a movement toward treating homosexuality as normal and morally appropriate.

In this zero-sum world, tolerance for homosexuals can be reconciled with their lower social status only so long as this tolerance is given grudgingly and without any social or moral approval of homosexuality. Tolerance that demands moral accept-ance of homosexuality, however, is in tension with the existing baseline of social meanings and hence will be viewed as deliberate approval or advocacy of gay lifestyles. This baseline of expectations explains the politics of the closet: Homosexuals who remain in the closet and act like heterosexuals will be treated equally as long as they do not make an issue of their homosexuality. To declare their homosexuality openly and then to demand equal rights appears to assert that it is wrong to discriminate against homosexuals because of their lifestyle, which in turn implies that perhaps homosexuality is not so immoral after all. Because such overt demands disturb the hierarchy of social meanings and the implicit moral superiority of heterosexuality, they are viewed as "flaunting," and thus as presenting demands for "special" treatment.[87]

Justice Scalia sees the controversy over Amendment 2 as a cultural struggle, or *Kulturkampf*. Hence, in his view, the Court confused a battle over whose vision of morality should prevail with "a fit of spite," i.e., invidious motivation. He argues that the Constitution has nothing to say about such cultural struggles,[88] and that they should be left to the political process. Do you agree? Consider the fact that virtually every successful social movement for equality in the United States has involved a similar *Kulturkampf*. Is Scalia saying that the Court should refuse to takes sides in battles by social movements for equality until the battle is over? Would this have been a wise idea in the case of the Civil Rights Movement? The Women's Movement? What, exactly, is the "neutral" position in a case like Brown v. Board of Education? Is Justice Scalia's view that the Court should defer to the political processes in ongoing cultural struggles consistent with his position in *Adarand* and *Croson*?

5. *Animus and adoption.* In Lofton v. Secretary of the Department of Children and Family Services, 358 F.3d 804 (11th Cir. 2004), the Eleventh Circuit upheld Florida's ban on adoption by "practicing homosexuals."[89] Fla. Stat. §63.042(3),

---

87. Balkin, The Constitution of Status, supra.

88. The original *Kulturkampf* was part of Otto von Bismarck's campaign for a unified sense of German nationhood. The expression "Kulturkampf" was coined in a March 1873 election appeal by Rudolf Virchow, who referred to the struggle against the Catholic Church as a struggle for culture. See E.J. Passant, A Short History of Germany 1815-1945, at 88-90 (1960). At Bismarck's instigation, the German government attempted to undermine the strength of the Catholic political party, the Zentrum, by assert-ing control over Church functions and appointments. The government arrested clergymen who resisted its initiatives, and left many parishes without priests. Do you think this is the sort of thing Justice Scalia had in mind when he said that the Court should stay out of *Kulturkampfs*?

passed in 1977, provides: "No person eligible to adopt under this statute may adopt if that person is a homosexual." Florida courts defined the term "homosexual" as being "limited to applicants who are known to engage in current, voluntary homosexual activity," drawing "a distinction between homosexual orientation and homosexual activity."

Judge Birch rejected arguments that the Florida statute was inconsistent with Lawrence v. Texas. He argued that *Lawrence* was premised on rational basis review and did not recognize a new fundamental right. In any case, *Lawrence* was distinguishable: "the involved actors are not only consenting adults, but minors as well. The relevant state action is not criminal prohibition, but grant of a statutory privilege. And the asserted liberty interest is not the negative right to engage in private conduct without facing criminal sanctions, but the affirmative right to receive official and public recognition."

The court then rejected the plaintiffs' equal protection claim, arguing that, "Florida clearly has a legitimate interest in encouraging a stable and nurturing environment for the education and socialization of its adopted children. [T]he state has a legitimate interest in encouraging [an] optimal family structure by seeking to place adoptive children in homes that have both a mother and father [because the legislature could rationally conclude that] the marital family structure is more stable than other household arrangements."

Applying rational basis scrutiny, the court rejected arguments that the ban on adoptions by homosexuals is irrational because Florida allows homosexuals to be foster parents, and that the ban was underinclusive because "Florida law permits adoption by unmarried individuals and that, among children coming out the Florida foster care system, 25% of adoptions are to parents who are currently single." Florida could have concluded that the criteria for foster care and permanent adoption are different, and it might also believe that single parents who are not homosexual are more likely to form traditional families at some point in the future. The court also rejected arguments that the statute is not well designed to further the best interests of children because it prevents placement of "over three thousand children who are currently in foster care . . . with permanent adoptive families" that might include homosexuals. "Florida's interest," the court explained, "is not simply to place children in a permanent home as quickly as possible, but, when placing them, to do so in an optimal home, i.e., one in which there is a heterosexual couple or the potential for one."

---

89. Currently Florida is the only state with a statutory ban on adoption by homosexual individuals. See Fla. Stat. §63.042(3) (2002). In several other states, however, courts have disfavored gays and lesbians in cases involving custody or adoption, often invoking notions of morality, proper role models, or the "natural" family. See, e.g., Ex parte J.M.F. 730 So.2d 1190, 1196 (Ala. 1998) ("The record contains evidence from which the trial court could have concluded that '[a] child raised by two women or two men is deprived of extremely valuable developmental experience and the opportunity for optimal individual growth and interpersonal development'. . . ."); Matter of Appeal in Pima County Juvenile Action B-10489, 727 P.2d 830, 831, 835 (Ariz. App. 1986) (affirming a juvenile court's order certifying a bisexual man as "nonacceptable to adopt children" and explaining that "[i]t would be anomalous for the state on the one hand to declare homosexual conduct unlawful and on the other create a parent after that proscribed model, in effect approving that standard, inimical to the natural family, as head of a state-created family"); Ex parte H.H., 830 So.2d 21, 26 (Ala. 2002) (Moore, C.J., concurring specially) ("[T]he homosexual conduct of a parent . . . creates a strong presumption of unfitness that alone is sufficient justification for denying that parent custody of his or her own children or prohibiting the adoption of the children of others.").

Appellants offered numerous scientific studies "show[ing] that the parenting skills of homosexual parents are at least equivalent to those of heterosexual parents and that children raised by homosexual parents suffer no adverse outcomes." Applying the rational basis standard, the court responded that Florida was under no obligation to credit these studies, and it might reasonably believe critiques of these studies. "Or the legislature might consider, and even credit, the research cited by appellants, but find it premature to rely on a very recent and still developing body of research, particularly in light of the absence of longitudinal studies following child subjects into adulthood and of studies of adopted, rather than natural, children of homosexual parents."

Finally, the court considered whether the ban on adoption violated *Romer:* "Unlike Colorado's Amendment 2, Florida's statute is not so 'sweeping and comprehensive' as to render Florida's rationales for the statute 'inexplicable by anything but animus' toward its homosexual residents. . . . Whereas Amendment 2's classification encompassed both conduct and status, Florida's adoption prohibition is limited to conduct. Thus, we conclude that *Romer's* unique factual situation and narrow holding are inapposite to this case."

A motion for rehearing in *Lofton* before the entire Eleventh Circuit was denied by a vote of 6-6. Lofton v. Secretary of the Department of Children and Family Services, 377 F.3d 1275 (11th Cir. 2004). Judge Barkett issued a vigorous dissent, arguing that the Florida statute should fall under the authority of *Moreno, Eisenstadt, Cleburne,* and *Romer:* "In all four cases, the Court concluded that the asserted justifications were not rationally related to the classification. Thus, the Court inferred that animus was the motivation behind the legislation and established that such a motivation could not constitute a legitimate state interest. . . . Here, there is no question that a politically unpopular group is being targeted, that the challenged legislation inhibits personal relationships, and that there is no legitimate rational relationship between Florida's proffered justifications and its sweeping categorical adoption ban against homosexuals. . . .

"Florida has explicitly tailored provisions to protect children placed in adoptive homes. Florida Statute § 63.092(3) (2003) requires a preliminary and thorough home study of prospective adoptive parents and the state uses its full power to screen all applicants and bar adoption by anyone not deemed to be a fit parent. The adoption statute accords everyone other than homosexuals the benefit of an individualized consideration that is directed toward the best interests of the child. Child abusers, terrorists, drug dealers, rapists and murderers are not categorically barred by the adoption statute from consideration for adoptive parenthood in Florida. On the other hand, individuals who take children into their care, including unwanted children, such as those who are HIV-positive, and who have raised them with loving care for years are categorically barred from adopting if they happen to be homosexual. In the context of adoption, this disparity of treatment on the face of the statute amounts to the purest form of irrationality. . . .

"The Florida statute was enacted after an organized and relentless anti-homosexual campaign led by Anita Bryant, a pop singer who sought to repeal a January 1977 ordinance of the Dade County Metropolitan Commission prohibiting discrimination against homosexuals in the areas of housing, public accommodations, and employment. Bryant organized a drive that collected the 10,000 signatures needed to force a public referendum on the ordinance. In the course of her campaign, which the Miami Herald described as creating a 'witch-hunting hysteria more appropriate to the 17th century than the 20th,' Bryant referred to homosexuals as 'human garbage.' She also promoted the insidious myth that schoolchildren were vulnerable to molestation at the hands of homosexual schoolteachers who would rely on the ordinance to avoid being dismissed from their positions. . . . The legislative history reveals the very close and utterly transparent connection between Bryant's campaign and the [anti-adoption statute]. Senator Don Chamberlin explicitly tied the Bryant campaign to the proposed ban on homosexual adoption, arguing that the latter would never have arisen without the ruckus over the Dade County antidiscrimination ordinance. The impetus for Florida's adoption ban exactly parallels the impetus for the state constitutional amendment struck down in *Romer*. See *Romer*, 517 U.S. at 623-24 ('The impetus for the amendment and the contentious campaign that preceded its adoption came in large part from [the campaigns against antidiscrimination] ordinances that had been passed in various Colorado municipalities.')."

"As the [Florida] House and Senate gave their final approval to the [legislation] on May 31, Senator Peterson stated that his bills were a message to homosexuals that '[w]e're really tired of you. We wish you would go back into the closet.' "

Judge Birch, concurring in the denial of rehearing responded: "As I understand the dissent's argument, once it is demonstrated that the motivation propelling a piece of legislation is animus, a different sort of analysis from a traditional 'any-existing-rational-basis-will-justify' approach must be employed, as putatively mandated by Supreme Court precedents in *Romer*, *Cleburne*, *Moreno* and *Eisenstadt*. Under this 'animus/analysis,' a court is required to examine whether the proffered reasons for the statute are pretextual. . . . The real point of disagreement [between my opinion and Judge Barkett's] is whether rational-basis review should always uphold a law as long as there exists some 'conceivable' rational basis — or whether there are certain instances that call for a 'more searching' form of rational-basis review that examines the actual motivations underlying the law."

Judge Barkett disagreed with this characterization of *Romer*, explaining that the proper test is that "when all the proffered rationales for a law are clearly and manifestly implausible, a reviewing court may infer that animus is the only explicable basis."

What exactly do Judges Birch and Barkett disagree about? Consider that whether one regards a state's justifications as "clearly and manifestly implausible" and therefore inexplicable except on grounds of animus may turn heavily on whether one thinks that the legislation was motivated by invidious prejudice, or instead by what Judge Birch describes as a desire to "plac[e] adoptive children in the *mainstream* of American family life" (emphasis in original).

C.   Sexual Orientation as a Suspect Classification

The Supreme Court has not yet decided whether classifications based on sexual orientation are suspect; however the issue has been debated by several lower courts. Most of these cases occurred before *Lawrence*, and thus assumed that states could constitutionally criminalize homosexual sodomy. As we have seen the Supreme Court avoided the issue in *Romer*. What effect does *Lawrence* have on this question? Consider four possibilities:

1. *Lawrence* makes no difference, because the doctrines of equal protection and substantive due process are analytically distinct and serve very different constitutional interests.

2. *Lawrence* will eventually lead to recognition of sexual orientation as a suspect or quasi-suspect classification (like gender). Due process and equal protection are deeply connected (recall, for example, Justice Warren's arguments in Bolling v. Sharpe, and recall how both *Casey* and *Lawrence* synthesize liberty and equality values). If same-sex sexual relations are constitutionally protected, it makes little sense to burden the status that is either correlated or constituted by that conduct. The same concerns that make it unconstitutional to criminalize same-sex sexual relations will develop into constitutional restrictions on laws that discriminatorily burden same-sex orientation. To be sure, one can distinguish homosexual orientation from homosexual sexual conduct. And there is much more to homosexual identity, culture, and conduct than same-sex sexual relations. Nevertheless the status–conduct distinction is tenuous at best where the question is the legality of state-supported discrimination. The Court will eventually recognize that homosexuals will never gain full social and legal equality until state-supported discrimination is treated as suspect.

3. *Lawrence* will indefinitely delay recognition of sexual orientation as a suspect or quasi-suspect classification. Having protected homosexuals and bisexuals through the Due Process Clause, the Court will find no need to give them the additional protection of the Equal Protection Clause. This might allow states to express their moral disapproval of homosexuality as long as they do not seriously burden the rights of homosexuals to form intimate relationships and express their sexuality privately. Under this scenario, *Lawrence* will justify a new legally sanctioned form of closeting, and delay full social acceptance of homosexuality.

4. *Lawrence* will delay recognition of sexual orientation as a suspect classification, but this is a good thing. Sexual orientation minorities need liberty more than equality. Creating a suspect classification for sexual orientation minorities adopts a civil rights paradigm that views them through the lens of African-Americans and tends to lump them all in a single category. This will ultimately be untrue to their experience, the distinctive forms of injustice they experience, and their political and legal aspirations.

WATKINS v. UNITED STATES ARMY, 847 F. 2d. 1349 (9th Cir. 1988): [The Ninth Circuit considered the constitutionality of Army regulations that excluded homosexuals and bisexuals from the Armed Forces. (These regulations were later superseded by the 1993 "Don't Ask Don't Tell" Policy, discussed infra.) The court considered whether sexual orientation should be considered a suspect classification.]

NORRIS, J.:

The first factor the Supreme Court generally considers is whether the group at issue has suffered a history of purposeful discrimination. See, e.g., Cleburne [v. Cleburne Living Center, 473 U.S. 432, 441 (1985)]; Massachusetts Bd. of Retirement v. Murgia, 427 U.S. 307, 313 (1976); *Frontiero* [v. Richardson], 411 U.S.

677, 1 684-85 (1973) (plurality). [I]t is indisputable that "homosexuals have historically been the object of pernicious and sustained hostility." . . . Homosexuals have been the frequent victims of violence and have been excluded from jobs, schools, housing, churches, and even families. In any case, the discrimination faced by homosexuals in our society is plainly no less pernicious or intense than the discrimination faced by other groups already treated as suspect classes, such as aliens or people of a particular national origin.

The second factor that the Supreme Court considers in suspect class analysis is difficult to capsulize and may in fact represent a cluster of factors grouped around a central idea — whether the discrimination embodies a gross unfairness that is sufficiently inconsistent with the ideals of equal protection to term it invidious. Considering this additional factor makes sense. After all, discrimination exists against some groups because the animus is warranted — no one could seriously argue that burglars form a suspect class. In giving content to this concept of gross unfairness, the Court has considered (1) whether the disadvantaged class is defined by a trait that "frequently bears no relation to ability to perform or contribute to society," *Frontiero*, 411 U.S. at 686; (2) whether the class has been saddled with unique disabilities because of prejudice or inaccurate stereotypes; and (3) whether the trait defining the class is immutable. See *Cleburne*, 473 U.S. at 440-44; *Murgia*, 427 U.S. at 313; *Frontiero*, 411 U.S. at 685-87. We consider these questions in turn.

Sexual orientation plainly has no relevance to a person's "ability to perform or contribute to society." . . . This irrelevance of sexual orientation to the quality of a person's contribution to society also suggests that classifications based on sexual orientation reflect prejudice and inaccurate stereotypes — the second indicia of a classification's gross unfairness. We agree with Justice Brennan that "discrimination against homosexuals is 'likely . . . to reflect deep-seated prejudice rather than . . . rationality.'" Rowland v. Mad River Local School Dist., 470 U.S. 1009, 1014 (1985) (Brennan, J., dissenting from denial of cert.). . . .

Finally, we turn to immutability as an indicator of gross unfairness. The Supreme Court has never held that only classes with immutable traits can be deemed suspect. We nonetheless consider immutability because the Supreme Court has often focused on immutability, and has sometimes described the recognized suspect classes as having immutable traits, see, e.g., Parham v. Hughes, 441 U.S. 347, 351 (1979) (plurality opinion) (describing race, national origin, alienage, illegitimacy, and gender as immutable).

. . . [B]y "immutability" the Court has never meant strict immutability in the sense that members of the class must be physically unable to change or mask the trait defining their class. People can have operations to change their sex. Aliens can ordinarily become naturalized citizens. The status of illegitimate children can be changed. People can frequently hide their national origin by changing their customs, their names, or their associations. Lighter skinned blacks can sometimes "pass" for White, as can Latinos for Anglos, and some people can even change their racial appearance with pigment injections. See J. Griffin, Black Like Me (1977). At a minimum, then, the Supreme Court is willing to treat a trait as effectively immutable if changing it would involve great difficulty, such as requiring a major physical change or a traumatic change of identity. Reading the case law in a more capacious manner, "immutability" may describe those traits that are so central to a person's identity that it would be abhorrent for government to penalize a person for refusing to change them, regardless of how easy that change might be physically. Racial discrimination, for example, would not suddenly become constitutional if medical science developed an easy, cheap, and painless method of changing one's skin pigment.

Under either formulation, we have no trouble concluding that sexual orientation is immutable for the purposes of equal protection doctrine. Although the causes of homosexuality are not fully understood, scientific research indicates that we have little control over our sexual orientation and that, once acquired, our sexual orientation is largely impervious to change. Scientific proof aside, it seems appropriate to ask whether heterosexuals feel capable of changing their sexual orientation. Would heterosexuals living in a city that passed an ordinance banning those who engaged in or desired to engage in sex with persons of the opposite sex find it easy not only to abstain from heterosexual activity but also to shift the object of their sexual desires to persons of the same sex? It may be that some heterosexuals and homosexuals can change their sexual orientation through extensive therapy, neurosurgery or shock treatment. But the possibility of such a difficult and traumatic change does not make sexual orientation "mutable" for equal protection purposes. To express the same idea under the alternative formulation, we conclude that allowing the government to penalize the failure to change such a central aspect of individual and group identity would be abhorrent to the values animating the constitutional ideal of equal protection of the laws.

The final factor the Supreme Court considers in suspect class analysis is whether the group burdened by official discrimination lacks the political power necessary to obtain redress from the political branches of government. Courts understandably have been more reluctant to extend heightened protection under equal protection doctrine to groups fully capable of securing their rights through the political process. In evaluating whether a class is politically underrepresented, the Supreme Court has focused on whether the class is a "discrete and insular minority;" see generally United States v. Carolene Products, 304 U.S. 144, 152-53 n.4 (1938).

The Court has held, for example, that old age does not define a discrete and insular group because "it marks a stage that each of us will reach if we live out our normal span." *Murgia.* By contrast, most of us are not likely to identify ourselves as homosexual at any time in our lives. Thus, many of us, including many elected officials, are likely to have difficulty understanding or empathizing with homosexuals. Most people have little exposure to gays, both because they rarely encounter gays and because the gays they do encounter may feel compelled to conceal their sexual orientation. In fact, the social, economic, and political pressures to conceal one's homosexuality commonly deter many gays from openly advocating pro-homosexual legislation, thus intensifying their inability to make effective use of the political process. "Because of the immediate and severe opprobrium often manifested against homosexuals once so identified publicly, members of this group are particularly powerless to pursue their rights openly in the political arena." *Rowland.* (Brennan, J., dissenting from denial of cert.).

Even when gays overcome this prejudice enough to participate openly in politics, the general animus towards homosexuality may render this participation wholly ineffective. Elected officials sensitive to public prejudice may refuse to support legislation that even appears to condone homosexuality. . . . These barriers to political power are underscored by the underrepresentation of avowed homosexuals in the decisionmaking bodies of government and the inability of homosexuals to prevent legislation hostile to their group interests. See *Frontiero,* 411 U.S. at

686 & n.17 (underrepresentation of women in government caused in part by history of discrimination); *Cleburne*, 473 U.S. at 445 (reasoning that the existence of legislation responsive to the needs of the mentally disabled belied the claim that they were politically powerless).

In sum, our analysis of the relevant factors in determining whether a given group should be considered a suspect class for the purposes of equal protection doctrine ineluctably leads us to the conclusion that homosexuals constitute such a suspect class. We find not only that our analysis of each of the relevant factors supports our conclusion, but also that the principles underlying equal protection doctrine — the principles that gave rise to these factors in the first place — compel us to conclude that homosexuals constitute a suspect class. . . .

Judge Reinhardt dissented. Although he criticized Bowers v. Hardwick severely, predicting "that history will view *Hardwick* much as it views Plessy v. Ferguson," he argued that it disposed of the question before the court: "When conduct that plays a central role in defining a group may be prohibited by the state, it cannot be asserted with any legitimacy that the group is specially protected by the Constitution."

The Ninth Circuit subsequently heard the case en banc and vacated the panel opinion. Watkins v. United States Army 875 F.2d 699 (9th Cir. 1989). In its opinion the court held that the Army was estopped from discharging Watkins because it had repeatedly allowed him to reenlist, knowing that he was gay.

A year later the Ninth Circuit reexamined the question of whether homosexuals constituted a suspect class.

HIGH TECH GAYS v. DEFENSE INDUSTRIAL SECURITY CLEARANCE OFFICE, 895 F.2d 563 (9th Cir. 1990), rehearing en banc denied, 909 F.2d 372 (9th Cir. 1990): [The Ninth Circuit upheld the Defense Department's policy of refusing to grant security clearances to known or suspected gay applicants. Judge Brunetti's opinion rejected the argument that discrimination against homosexuals and bisexuals should receive more than minimal scrutiny:]

BRUNETTI, J.:

[B]ecause homosexual conduct can . . . be criminalized, homosexuals cannot constitute a suspect or quasi-suspect class entitled to greater than rational basis review for equal protection purposes. . . .

To be a "suspect" or "quasi-suspect" class, homosexuals must 1) have suffered a history of discrimination; 2) exhibit obvious, immutable, or distinguishing characteristics that define them as a discrete group; and 3) show that they are a minority or politically powerless, or alternatively show that the statutory classification at issue burdens a fundamental right. . . .

While we do agree that homosexuals have suffered a history of discrimination, we do not believe that they meet the other criteria. Homosexuality is not an immutable characteristic; it is behavioral and hence is fundamentally different from traits such as race, gender, or alienage, which define already existing suspect and quasi-suspect classes. The behavior or conduct of such already recognized classes is irrelevant to their identification.

Moreover, legislatures have addressed and continue to address the discrimination suffered by homosexuals on account of their sexual orientation through the passage of anti-discrimination legislation. Thus, homosexuals are not without political power; they have the ability to and do "attract the attention of the lawmakers," as evidenced by such legislation.

[On denial for petition for rehearing en banc, Judge Canby, who was part of the original *Watkins* majority, dissented:]

CANBY, J., dissenting:

There is every reason to regard homosexuality as an immutable characteristic for equal protection purposes. It is not enough to say that the category is "behavioral." One can make "behavioral" classes out of persons who go to church on Saturday, persons who speak Spanish, or persons who walk with crutches. The question is, what causes the behavior? Does it arise from the kind of a characteristic that belongs peculiarly to a group that the equal protection clause should specially protect?

Homosexuals are physically attracted to members of their own sex. . . . Did they choose to be attracted by members of their own sex, rather than by members of the opposite sex? The answer, by the overwhelming weight of respectable authority, is "no." Sexual identity is established at a very early age; it is not a matter of conscious or controllable choice. Can homosexuals change their orientation? Again, from everything we now know, the answer is "no." At least they cannot change it without immense difficulty. As Judge Norris has asked, what would it take to get any one of us to change his or her sexual orientation?

For practical and constitutional purposes, then, homosexuality is an immutable characteristic. . . . When the government discriminates against homosexuals, it is discriminating against persons because of what they are, through no choice of their own, and what they are unable to change. . . .

The panel's opinion also concludes that homosexuals are not politically powerless[, arguing] that one state broadly bars employment discrimination against homosexuals, two other states more narrowly bar discrimination against homosexuals, and a few cities bar some types of discrimination. That showing is clearly insufficient to deprive homosexuals of the status of a suspect classification. Compare the situation with that of blacks, who clearly constitute a suspect category for equal protection purposes. Blacks are protected by three federal constitutional amendments, major federal Civil Rights Acts of 1866, 1870, 1871, 1875 (ill-fated though it was), 1957, 1960, 1964, 1965, and 1968, as well as by antidiscrimination laws in 48 of the states. By that comparison, and by absolute standards as well, homosexuals are politically powerless. They are so because of their numbers, which most estimates put at around 10 percent of the population, and by the fact that many of them keep their status secret to avoid discrimination. That secrecy inhibits organization of homosexuals as a pressure group. Certainly homosexuals as a class wield less political power than blacks, a suspect classification, or women, a quasi-suspect one. One can easily find examples of major political parties' openly tailoring their positions to appeal to black voters, and to female voters. One cannot find comparable examples of appeals to homosexual voters; homosexuals are regarded by the national parties as political pariahs. . . .

[I]t is not proper to assume generally that "homosexual conduct . . . can be criminalized." There are many varieties of conduct that might be characterized as homosexual, from hand-holding to sodomy. . . .

It is an error of massive proportions to define the entire class of homosexuals by sodomy. [H]omosexuals, in sexually expressing their affection for persons of their own sex, frequently engage in sodomy, as do heterosexuals sexually express-ing their affection for persons of the opposite sex. Homosexuals and heterosex-uals also engage in other affective conduct, criminalized nowhere. But homosexuality, like heterosexuality, is a status. As an amicus points out, one is a homosexual or a heterosexual while playing bridge just as much as while engag-ing in sexual activity. And the Department of Defense is discriminating against homosexuals for what they are, not what they do. The Department is not trying to send anyone to jail for sodomy. It is not asserting that acts of sodomy endan-ger national security. It is making the unsupported assumption that homosexu-als are more likely to betray their country than other classes of persons, and it is discriminating against them because of that assumption. That is the key to this case.

Discussion

1. *Deciding which classifications are suspect.* In *High Tech Gays* the Ninth Circuit uses a test for heightened scrutiny articulated by the Supreme Court in Bowen v. Gilliard, 483 U.S. 587, 602-603 (1987). To warrant suspect or quasi-suspect status, the class burdened by the challenged classification must (1) have been subjected to historical discrimination; (2) "exhibit obvious, immutable, or distinguishing char-acteristics that define them as a discrete group"; and (3) be "a minority or politi-cally powerless." Although the Supreme Court and lower courts have used other tests, most of them focus on similar factors. In the discussion that follows, ask your-self whether these tests get to the real reasons why courts should hold a classifica-tion suspect or subject it to ordinary rational basis review.

2. *A history of discrimination.* Asking whether a group has suffered a history of discrimination usually uses the history of other groups as benchmarks, particularly blacks. (Recall that the plurality opinion in Frontiero v. Richardson compares the history of discrimination suffered by women to the history of discrimination suffered by African-Americans.) Although few would deny that gays have suffered a history of discrimination, many commentators have argued that the analogy between gay oppression and African-American oppression should be approached with caution. For example, bell hooks has argued that "[w]hite people, gay and straight, could show greater understanding of the impact of racial oppression on people of color by not attempting to make these oppressions synonymous, but rather by showing the ways they are linked and yet differ."[90] Like African-Americans, gays have been discriminated against in employment and housing, and like blacks during the time of slavery, gays have been denied the right to marry and form their own families. Differences include the fact that African-Americans, unlike gays, were denied the right to vote and must struggle with economic disadvantage that has cumulated over generations. Conversely, gays, unlike African-Americans, have been subjected to the isolation of the closet. These differences might suggest that discrimination against gays is better analogized to religious persecution. See Kenji Yoshino, Suspect Symbols: The Literary Argument for Heightened Scrutiny for Gays, 96 Colum. L. Rev. 1753, 1783-1784 (1996) (arguing that Jews are a better analogy than blacks). For a general discussion of the problems of drawing analo-gies among the experiences of different groups, see Jane S. Schacter, The

---

90. bell hooks, Talking Back: Thinking Feminist, Thinking Black 125 (1989).

Civil-Rights Debate in the States: Decoding the Discourse of Equivalents, 29 Harv. C.R.-C.L. L. Rev. 283 (1994).

3. *Immutability and visibility.* In inquiring whether the class is marked by "obvious, immutable, or distinguishable characteristics," the Court focuses on two characteristics: immutability and visibility.

Immutability is often regarded as quite important to equal protection analysis. The usual arguments are that immutable characteristics make it more difficult for people to evade discrimination (because they cannot change their status) and make the discrimination less justifiable, because people should not be held responsible for attributes they did not choose. Nevertheless, immutability is neither necessary nor sufficient to justify heightened scrutiny. Sex, religion, and alienage, which are all arguably mutable traits, have all received some form of heightened scrutiny. Conversely, groups marked by immutable traits (such as individuals who are blind or who are below a certain height) have not received heightened scrutiny. To further complicate matters, although race and illegitimate status are usually thought of as immutable characteristics that justify heightened scrutiny, both can be altered by legal rules. For example, in 1896 Louisiana, Homer Plessy could have been transformed into a white person by changing Louisiana's one drop of blood rule, or, alternatively, if he crossed the state line into Mississippi, which defined race differently. Legal rules can also allow children to be legitimated after they are born.

Nonetheless, judges who deem orientation to be immutable are more likely to support heightened scrutiny for discrimination based on orientation. In this, judges are following public opinion: National polls suggest that many Americans would be more inclined to support legal protections for gays if shown that sexual orientation was immutable. However, scientific studies about the sources of homosexuality do not yield clear, uncomplicated conclusions. Moreover, even if a biological basis for homosexuality were found, it is hardly clear that this would make the trait "immutable" or worthy of constitutional protection. Advances in technology might lead to attempts to treat gays for a congenital defect, or to screen out and abort fetuses likely to grow up to be gay. Does this suggest that the factual question of whether an individual can change is less important than the normative question of whether he or she should have to do so?

Finally, as Janet Halley notes, treating sexual orientation as immutable may falsely represent the way many gay, lesbian, and bisexual people understand themselves and their sexuality. Some people may have experienced themselves as having made a choice about their identity and sexuality that they cannot now easily take back. Others may reject the notion of homosexuality as central to their identities "whether because they identify as bisexual, because they seek to de-emphasize the gender parameters of sexuality, because they are experimental about sexuality, or because they experience sexuality not as serious self-expressiveness but as play, drag, and ironic self-reflexivity."[91]

A group's visibility is a separate consideration in whether it deserves legal protection. The *Frontiero* plurality opinion discusses the "high visibility" of the sex

---

91. Janet E. Halley, Sexual Orientation and the Politics of Biology: A Critique of the Argument from Immutability, 46 Stan. L. Rev. 503, 520 (1994).

characteristic as one reason for applying heightened scrutiny to sex-based classifications. Frontiero v. Richardson, 411 U.S. 677, 686 (1973) (plurality opinion). The idea is that groups with highly salient attributes are more likely to be the targets of discrimination. After all, if an individual cannot discriminate between two individuals, he cannot discriminate against one of them.

Although visibility is an important means of facilitating discrimination and preserving social hierarchy, it is not always necessary. Members of different castes in India do not necessarily have visibly identifiable traits. Genocides have taken place against peoples not visibly different from those who persecuted them. And visibility and easily identifiable traits are not necessary as a doctrinal matter to receive heightened scrutiny. Religion, alienage, being born out of wedlock, and national origin are not generally easily identifiable, although in some religions believers dress or behave in ways that are readily identifiable, and immigrants may have accents that identify their national origin. Nevertheless, visibility is relevant to heightened scrutiny because it makes discrimination easier and facilitates the preservation of social hierarchy.

Unlike most blacks and women, gays can pass and remain invisible as gay. Although Jews can often pass, they may have Jewish family names and family connections. Gays, by contrast, are born into heterosexual families. Their ability to pass and reveal their orientation selectively might make them less deserving of protection. On the other hand, this apparent advantage is also a special source of disadvantage for homosexuals. The ability (and hence the pressure) to remain in the closet is an important device through which homosexuals are subordinated. Thus, Eve Sedgwick writes that "[t]he closet is the defining structure for gay oppression in this century."[92] The closet exacts considerable costs from gays as individuals, including isolation, fear of exposure and rebuke, and self-loathing, as well as requiring constant self-monitoring of what one says and does.[93] The closet also imposes considerable political costs in a democracy, as described next.

4. *Political powerlessness.* The Court has used a number of different proxies for measuring political powerlessness. The most famous formulation of political powerlessness (which sometimes stands by itself as the test for whether a group is worthy of judicial solicitude) is whether the group is a "discrete and insular minority." The phrase comes from footnote 4 of United States v. Carolene Products, 304 U.S. 144, 152 n.4 (1938). The basic idea is that judicial solicitude for minority rights is necessary for the integrity of the democratic process: Discrete and insular minorities deserve special protection because they cannot easily form coalitions to protect their interests. Hence democracies will systematically underrepresent their concerns and this will facilitate prejudice and injustices against them.

As Bruce Ackerman has pointed out, sometimes this logic may be backwards. Cohesive and easily identifiable groups are often able to form powerful lobbies because they can promise to deliver votes as a block. Bruce Ackerman, *Beyond Carolene Products*, 98 Harv. L. Rev. 713, 728, 742 (1985). By contrast, diffuse and anonymous groups are less likely to be protected by the political process because they will be unable or unlikely to assert their full strength in a concentrated fashion

---

92. Eve Kosofsky Sedgwick, Epistemology of the Closet 71 (1990).
93. See Kenji Yoshino, Assimilationist Bias in Equal Protection: The Visibility Presumption and the Case of "Don't Ask, Don't Tell," 108 Yale L.J. 485, 527-530, 535-536.

in pluralist bargaining. Ackerman argues that gays fall into this category because of their invisibility.[94]

Justice Scalia's *Romer* dissent disagrees that gays are relatively disempowered in the political process: "[B]ecause those who engage in homosexual conduct tend to reside in disproportionate numbers in certain communities, . . . and, of course, care about homosexual-rights issues much more ardently than the public at large, they possess political power much greater than their numbers, both locally and statewide." *Romer*, 517 U.S. 645-646 (Scalia, J., dissenting).

Consider how the closet imposes political costs on homosexuals. Although closeted homosexuals can vote through secret ballots, and can influence public debate about homosexuals in ways that do not reveal their sexual orientation, homosexuals face a collective action problem in political organization. The political influence of homosexuals as a group might increase if all homosexuals were not closeted. Nevertheless, closeted homosexuals may not be willing to risk revealing themselves to increase the political power of the group unless they are assured that others will also do so. In addition, homosexuals who remain closeted can ride on the political efforts of those who reveal their sexual orientation and openly organize for homosexual rights.

The closet also discourages heterosexuals from actively supporting homosexual rights or forming coalitions with homosexual advocacy groups. Heterosexuals may be concerned that if they actively identify themselves with the causes of homosexuals they will be assumed to be closeted homosexuals.

Finally, the closet affects the political and social influence of homosexuals because it allows heterosexuals to forget about the possible existence of homosexuals and homosexuality in many political and social situations. Being invisible means giving others the privilege to treat you as nonexistent. Put another way, the closet allows heterosexuals to accept homosexuals as long as they do not know that the latter are homosexual.[95]

Besides *Carolene Products*'s focus on discreteness and insularity, alternative formulations of political powerlessness include the "ability to attract the attention of the lawmakers," City of Cleburne v. Cleburne Living Ctr., 473 U.S. 432, 445 (1985), and the degree of representation in the "Nation's decisionmaking councils," *Frontiero*, 411 U.S. at 686 n.17. Is it realistic to believe that any one of these formulations can capture the various forms political powerlessness can take? If not, how should courts apply this consideration?

5. *Sexual orientation discrimination as sex discrimination.* So far we have discussed whether courts should employ heightened scrutiny for classifications based on

---

94. Along the same lines, William Eskridge points out that homosexuals are neither discrete nor insular: "Lesbians and gay men are a minority but are typically anonymous or closeted rather than discrete (you cannot tell by looking) and are often dispersed rather than insular (though there are gay ghettoes in most major cities)." However, Eskridge points out, discreteness and insularity cannot be a necessary requirement for political powerlessness or heightened scrutiny. Women are also "neither insular (everywhere you find men you find women) nor a minority (they are more than half the population)." William Eskridge, The Case for Same Sex Marriage 179 (1996).

In fact, many national origin groups protected by the Equal Protection Clause — for example, Irish-Americans and Polish-Americans — are not discrete and insular, although at certain points there may have been largely Irish or Polish neighborhoods in certain cities. Intermarriage between persons of different national origins is quite common. One can make a similar point about many religious groups: The intermarriage rate for Jews is estimated to be close to 50 percent.

95. Kenji Yoshino, Suspect Symbols, at 1789-1792.

sexual orientation by applying the doctrinal tests the Supreme Court has employed. A different approach would be sociological rather than doctrinal: It would consider the sociological basis of discrimination against homosexuals and ask whether this discrimination maintains or enforces an unjust social hierarchy that treats homosexuals as a disfavored or degraded caste. If it does, one would go on to ask whether this kind of subordination violates the principle of equal citizenship guaranteed by the Fourteenth Amendment.

Andrew Koppelman has argued that discrimination against homosexuals is actually a form of sex discrimination. Therefore it should be subject to intermediate scrutiny like other sex discrimination. Koppelman offers both a formal argument and a sociological argument. The formal argument is that when the law objects to the homosexual's choice of sex partner, it does so because of the homosexual's own sex (male or female). The law permits the same behavior if it came from a person of the opposite sex.[96] Thus, "[l]aws that discriminate against gays rest upon a normative stereotype: the bald conviction that certain behavior — for example, sex with women — is appropriate for members of one sex, but not for members of the other sex."[97] One might object that both sexes are treated equally because both are equally limited to members of the opposite sex. But Koppelman responds that this same kind of argument was rejected in Loving v. Virginia; the fact that blacks and whites were equally limited by the prohibition on miscegenation did not mean that the law did not discriminate on the basis of race. Indeed, the real purpose behind the miscegenation taboo was the preservation of a certain social order: white supremacy.

Behind Koppelman's formal argument is a sociological argument that the source and effects of the taboo against same-sex relations is the preservation of male supremacy:

> Much of the connection between sexism and the homosexuality taboo lies in social meanings that are accessible to everyone. It should be clear from ordinary experience that the stigmatization of the homosexual has something to do with the homosexual's supposed deviance from traditional sex roles. "Our society," Joseph Pleck observes, "uses the male heterosexual-homosexual dichotomy as a central symbol for all the rankings of masculinity, for the division on any grounds between males who are 'real men' and have power and males who are not. Any kind of powerlessness or refusal to compete becomes imbued with the imagery of homosexuality." Similarly, the denunciation of feminism as tantamount to lesbianism is depressingly familiar. The connection between sexism and the homosexuality taboo has been extensively documented by psychologists and historians. . . .
>
> Most Americans learn no later than high school that one of the nastier sanctions that one will suffer if one deviates from the behavior traditionally deemed appropriate for one's sex is the imputation of homosexuality. The two stigmas, sex-inappropriateness and homosexuality, are virtually interchangeable, and each is readily used as a metaphor for the other. There is nothing esoteric or sociologically abstract in the

---

96. Andrew Koppelman, Three Arguments for Gay Rights, 95 Mich. L. Rev. 1636, 1661 (1997) (citing Robert Wintemute, Sexual Orientation and Human Rights: The United States Constitution, the European Convention and the Canadian Charter 200 (1995)).

97. Andrew Koppelman, Why Discrimination Against Lesbians and Gay Men Is Sex Discrimination, 69 N.Y.U. L. Rev. 197, 219 (1994).

claim that the homosexuality taboo enforces traditional sex roles. Everyone knows that it is so. The recognition that in our society homosexuality is generally understood as a metaphor for failure to live up to the norms of one's gender resembles the recognition that segregation stigmatizes blacks, in that both are "matters of common notoriety, matters not so much for judicial notice as for the background knowledge of educated men who live in the world." . . .

Just as the hierarchy of whites over blacks is greatly strengthened by extreme differentiation of the races, so the hierarchy of males over females is greatly strengthened by extreme differentiation of the sexes. The element of both differentiations that promotes hierarchy is the idea that certain anatomical features necessarily entail certain social roles: one's status in society is obviously and unproblematically determined by the color of one's skin or the shape of one's reproductive organs. Blacks are supposed to defer to whites and obey whites' wishes because that is what blacks do. Women are supposed to defer to men and obey men's wishes because that is what women do. . . .

Overt homosexuality is . . . a greater danger to gender hierarchy in our society than it has been in other, more stable cultures. It threatens the hierarchy of the sexes because its existence suggests that even in a realm where a person's sex has been regarded as absolutely determinative, anatomy has less to do with destiny than one might have supposed. It is therefore unsurprising that [in the case of the miscegenation taboo and the same-sex taboo], the courts, which have enforced both of these putatively "natural" prohibitions, have struggled to conceal their socially constructed character.[98]

6. *Sexual orientation discrimination as gender subordination.* Koppelman's argument connects discrimination against homosexuals to the subordination of women. Does this mean that discrimination against homosexuals is wrong because it "keeps women in relationships in which men exert power over their lives"?[99] Jack Balkin argues that discrimination against homosexuals is about preserving heterosexual notions of gender, not sex.[100] He argues that discrimination against homosexuals is unjust because it is part of a "more general status hierarchy" based on dominant social meanings about gender that "define[] masculinity and femininity in heterosexual terms and bestow[] higher status on the former." These social meanings construct categories of "masculine" and "feminine" and subordinate the "feminine" and all things associated with it.

> This status hierarchy is unjust because it organizes social structure, distributes dignitary and material benefits, and shapes and justifies people's life chances through systematic privileging of things associated with being male over those associated with being female.

Society discriminates against homosexuals because they violate this set of social meanings about masculinity and femininity.

---

98. Id. at 234-235, 257-258 (1994).

99. Id. at 249.

100. J.M. Balkin, The Constitution of Status, at 2361-2363. See also Sylvia Law, Homosexuality and the Social Meaning of Gender, 1988 Wis. L. Rev. 187; Marc Fajer, Can Two Real Men Eat Quiche Together? Storytelling, Gender-Role Stereotypes, and Legal Protection for Lesbians and Gay Men, 46 U. Miami L. Rev. 511 (1992). The notion of "compulsory heterosexuality" originates with Adrienne Rich's 1980 essay "Compulsory Heterosexuality and Lesbian Existence," in A. Rich, Blood, Bread, and Poetry: Selected Prose 1979-1985, at 23-75 (1986).

Homosexuals transgress social meanings about gender that help constitute [heterosexual] gender identity. This system of meanings defines masculinity and femininity in terms of complementary traits and attraction to the opposite sex. Men are defined as people who are attracted to women; women are defined as people who are the object of sexual attraction by men. More importantly, this system of social meanings about gender is itself part of an unjust status hierarchy that privileges males and things associated with maleness over females and things associated with femaleness. Males and masculinity are defined not only in terms of their opposition to females and femininity, but in terms of their superiority.

Homosexuality, and especially male homosexuality, threatens this conceptual order because it undermines the clarity of traditional heterosexual male and female gender identities, and hence undermines what are judged to be appropriate male and female social roles, authority, and power. By failing to conform to the heterosexual definition of masculinity, gay men appear both to surrender their masculine privileges and to threaten the masculine privileges of other males. First, by being attracted to other men — a sign of femininity — they cheapen or ambiguate the masculinity and manliness of heterosexuals. Second, the mere presence of homosexual men causes heterosexual men to imagine that they could be objects of sexual desire by other men, which leads them to fear that they will be "feminized" and hence emasculated. This fear is particularly threatening precisely because the system of social meanings does not treat men and women equally: To play the role of "woman" is to be dominated and subordinate. In like fashion, lesbians threaten the conceptual order of male and female because they are attracted to women. They undermine the subordinate role of femininity because they refuse their roles as wives and mothers within a traditional heterosexual family.

This is a causal explanation of a social phenomenon of discrimination and not a claim about the inherent nature of either gender or homosexuality. This subordination is unjust on its own terms and not derivative from the subordination of women. . . . [D]iscrimination against homosexuals is [not] merely a "side effect" of discrimination against women. . . . [G]ender categories are general forms of social subordination that subordinate the feminine and all things associated with the feminine. Thus, this system subordinates not only women, but homosexuals, bisexuals, and effeminate men. . . . [This analysis] does not require clear-cut distinctions between homosexual and bisexual identity. Nor does it assume that sexual orientations and gender identities cannot exist along a continuum. A continuum also transgresses the dominant set of social meanings, which is essentially bivalent. . . . [Nor does it claim that] "gender" and gender identities are simply what heterosexuality defines them to be. Homosexuals and bisexuals may have their own views about gender and gender identity which may conflict with dominant views.

What threatens gender hierarchy is not so much what homosexuals do as the meaning of what they do. Because meaning matters, heterosexuals can deal with the threat of homosexuality in two different ways: They can pretend that it does not exist, or, if this is not possible, they can openly castigate it and declare it abnormal, immoral, and deviant. Each strategy helps preserve the traditional system of gender relations as normal, natural, and justified. Homosexuals who stay in the closet do not threaten the system of social meanings, because they do not appear as transgressors. However, if they do make an issue of their identity, it is important to demarcate them as outliers whose behavior is abnormal and immoral.

Koppelman's approach is designed to mesh with existing doctrines of sex discrimination. Does Balkin's approach fit into the existing categories, or does his emphasis on "unjust status hierarchies" require a different kind of doctrinal framework, one that returns to principles of equal citizenship and the prohibitions on caste embodied in the Fourteenth Amendment?

7. *Sexuality versus sexual orientation (and liberty versus equality).* Do Koppleman's or Balkin's accounts fail to capture important elements involved in discrimination against homosexuals? Consider Sylvia Law's argument that "[w]hile the desire to privilege and reward gender-differentiated family structures provides the primary impetus and justification for heterosexism, the perceived need to constrain sexuality is also important."[101] The anthropologist Gayle Rubin has argued that control of sexuality and sexual variety are independent elements behind the suppression of homosexuality. "Popular culture is permeated with ideas that erotic variety is dangerous, unhealthy, depraved, and a menace to everything from small children to national security." It features a system of "erotic stigma" that privileges controlled forms of sexuality and stigmatizes less controlled forms.[102] How could or should these elements of human sexuality be accommodated in constitutional doctrines of equality? If Rubin is correct, would constitutional protection of liberty be a more appropriate line of doctrinal development?

8. *Sexual orientation discrimination as a demand for covering.* A distinctive element of discrimination against gays is the demand that gays either be straight or behave like straights. Kenji Yoshino argues that the history of gay rights can be retold as a history of weakening demands for assimilation — the demand to convert, the demand to pass, and the demand to cover. The demand to convert was represented in the American Psychiatric Association's characterization of homosexuality as a psychopathology, which endured until 1973. Under this regime, gays were actively pressured to convert to heterosexuality. With the rise of gay activism, the demand to convert began to be replaced by the demand to pass — individuals were permitted to be gay so long as they were in the closet. The demand to pass is represented in the various forms of "Don't Ask, Don't Tell," ranging from the military's formal policy to the more subtle cultural forms of toleration for closeted homosexuals. At the turn of the millennium, the demand to pass is giving way to the demand to cover. "Covering" is the sociologist Erving Goffman's term for how individuals downplay known stigmatized identities. The demand for covering permits individuals to be gay and to be out, but it requires them to mute or "tone down" their gay identities in other ways. Yoshino identifies four different axes along which any group can cover: appearance, affiliation, activism, and association. For gays, covering can take the form of being "straight-acting" (appearance), minimizing one's allusions to gay culture (affiliation), eschewing political advocacy of gay causes (activism), and avoiding other gays (association).

Is same-sex marriage an act of covering or an act of flaunting? Yoshino argues that it is both. On the one hand, same-sex marriage is an act of covering one's affiliation with gay culture, insofar as marriage is culturally associated with heterosexuality. This is why "queers" like Michael Warner revile it, and "normals" like Andrew Sullivan celebrate it, as an act of assimilation. On the other hand, from the perspective of gay appearance, gay activism, or gay association, same-sex marriage is an act of flaunting.

---

101. Sylvia Law, Homosexuality and the Social Meaning of Gender, at 255.

102. Gayle S. Rubin, Thinking Sex: Notes for a Radical Theory of the Politics of Sexuality, in Pleasure and Danger: Exploring Female Sexuality (Carole Vance ed.) 14 (1984).

Yoshino argues that gays, because of their experience, have gotten a particularly clear view of the injustices of social and legal demands for assimilation, including demands for converting, passing, and covering. Indeed, he argues, this critique of assimilation is the signal contribution that gay rights might make to other civil rights groups. This is particularly true of covering. While racial minorities and women generally are not subjected to demands to convert or pass, they are systematically subjected to the demand to cover. Racial minorities, for instance, are pressured to "act white" by downplaying languages or grooming practices associated with their race. Women are likewise encouraged to "play like men" at work by eschewing stereotypically feminine traits or downplaying their status as primary caretakers of their children. Do you agree that the covering demand is a harm? If so, is it a harm that should have a constitutional remedy? See generally Kenji Yoshino, Covering: The Hidden Assault on Our Civil Rights (Random House, 2006).

Note: Freedom of Association and Other Constitutional Limits to Civil Rights Protections for Gays, Lesbians, and Bisexuals

Romer and other equal protection cases are concerned with whether the state may discriminate on the basis of sexual orientation. But suppose that the federal government or the states attempt to pass laws protecting homosexuals and bisexuals from discrimination by private citizens? Are there any constitutional limits on such laws? Morrison v. United States, 529 U.S. 598 (2000), discussed in Chapter 5, supra, suggests that the federal government may be limited in some respects. If the discrimination involves "noneconomic" activity, rather than discrimination in employment, for example, the federal government may not aggregate the effects of the discrimination to show a substantial effect on interstate commerce. This would be most relevant in the case of hate crimes legislation that imposes special criminal penalties for violence directed at gays, lesbians, and bisexuals.

One other possible limitation on anti-discrimination laws, which affects both the states and the federal government, arises from the First Amendment right to freedom of association. You may recall that one of Herbert Wechsler's concern about Brown v. Board of Education was that the right of blacks to integration conflicted with the interests of whites in not associating with them. (See supra p. 366). The Court effectively rejected that argument in *Brown*, holding that states could not protect freedom of association if it meant subordinating blacks.

Many states (and the federal government) have passed public accommodation laws, which prohibit places of public accommodation — like restaurants, hotels, stores, and certain clubs and businesses — from discriminating on the basis of race, sex, and other categories. About 15 states prohibit discrimination in public accommodations on the basis of sexual orientation. (The federal government does not include sexual orientation in its civil rights statutes.) Like employment discrimination and housing discrimination statutes, public accommodation statutes apply the anti-discrimination principle to selected areas of private conduct. And they apply anti-discrimination values on the basis of categories that are not necessarily suspect classifications for purposes of equal protection analysis.

In Boy Scouts of America v. Dale, 530 U.S. 640 (2000), the Court held in a 5-4 decision that New Jersey could not apply its public accommodations law to prevent the Boy Scouts from dismissing an assistant scoutmaster of a New Jersey troop because the Boy Scouts learned that he was an "an avowed homosexual and gay rights activist." Chief Justice Rehnquist's majority opinion was joined by Justices O'Connor, Scalia, Kennedy, and Thomas. The Court argued that the First Amendment protects the right of groups formed for purposes of "expressive association" to associate in order to promulgate their views. This right includes control over membership, because "[f]orcing a group to accept certain members may impair the ability of the group to express those views, and only those views, that it intends to express. . . . The forced inclusion of an unwanted person in a group infringes the group's freedom of expressive association if the presence of that person affects in a significant way the group's ability to advocate public or private viewpoints. But the freedom of expressive association, like many freedoms, is not absolute. We have held that the freedom could be overridden 'by regulations adopted to serve compelling state interests, unrelated to the suppression of ideas, that cannot be achieved through means significantly less restrictive of associational freedoms.'"

The Court held that the Boy Scouts engage in expressive activity because they seek to instill values in young people. Although the Boy Scout Oath and Law do not specifically mention sexuality or sexual orientation, "[t]he Boy Scouts asserts that it 'teach[es] that homosexual conduct is not morally straight,' and that it does 'not want to promote homosexual conduct as a legitimate form of behavior,'" It was irrelevant, the Court said, whether exclusion of homosexuals seemed "inconsistent with Boy Scouts' commitment to a diverse and 'representative' membership . . . it is not the role of the courts to reject a group's expressed values because they disagree with those values or find them internally inconsistent."

The Court then asked "whether Dale's presence as an assistant scoutmaster would significantly burden the Boy Scouts' desire to not 'promote homosexual conduct as a legitimate form of behavior.' As we give deference to an association's assertions regarding the nature of its expression, we must also give deference to an association's view of what would impair its expression. That is not to say that an expressive association can erect a shield against antidiscrimination laws simply by asserting that mere acceptance of a member from a particular group would impair its message. But here Dale, by his own admission, is one of a group of gay Scouts who have 'become leaders in their community and are open and honest about their sexual orientation.' Dale was the copresident of a gay and lesbian organization at college and remains a gay rights activist. Dale's presence in the Boy Scouts would, at the very least, force the organization to send a message, both to the youth members and the world, that the Boy Scouts accepts homosexual conduct as a legitimate form of behavior."

The Court rejected the New Jersey Supreme Court's contrary conclusion "that the Boy Scouts' ability to disseminate its message was not significantly affected by the forced inclusion of Dale as an assistant scoutmaster" because "Boy Scout members do not associate for the purpose of disseminating the belief that homosexuality is immoral." The Court responded that "associations do not have to associate for the 'purpose' of disseminating a certain message in order to be entitled to the protections of the First Amendment. An association must merely engage in expressive activity that could be impaired in order to be entitled to protection. . .

[Moreover], the First Amendment simply does not require that every member of a group agree on every issue in order for the group's policy to be 'expressive association.' The Boy Scouts takes an official position with respect to homosexual conduct, and that is sufficient for First Amendment purposes. . . ."

"We recognized in previous cases such as *Roberts* [v. United States Jaycees, 468 U.S. 609 (1984)] and [Board of Directors of Rotary Int'l v. Rotary Club of] *Duarte* [, 481 U.S. 537 (1987)] [involving exclusion of women by the Jaycees and the Rotary Club] that States have a compelling interest in eliminating discrimination against women in public accommodations. But in each of these cases . . . enforcement of these statutes would not materially interfere with the ideas that the organization sought to express. [Here we] have already concluded that a state requirement that the Boy Scouts retain Dale as an assistant scoutmaster would significantly burden the organization's right to oppose or disfavor homosexual conduct. The state interests embodied in New Jersey's public accommodations law do not justify such a severe intrusion on the Boy Scouts' rights to freedom of expressive association. That being the case, we hold that the First Amendment prohibits the State from imposing such a requirement through the application of its public accommodations law."

Justice Stevens dissented, joined by Justices Souter, Ginsburg, and Breyer. Justice Stevens argued that nothing in official Boy Scout publications mentioned anything about homosexuality, and that given the "BSA's self-proclaimed ecumenism, furthermore, it is even more difficult to discern any shared goals or common moral stance on homosexuality." The 1978 policy relied on by the majority "simply adopts an exclusionary membership policy." It appeared in an internal memorandum, and was never publicly expressed. "[S]imply adopting such a policy has never been considered sufficient, by itself, to prevail on a right to associate claim." The BSA, Stevens argued, failed to make its position clear and to connect its policy to its expressive activities, even after court decisions put it on notice that this would be required to establish a First Amendment associational claim. "[U]ntil today, we have never once found a claimed right to associate in the selection of members to prevail in the face of a State's antidiscrimination law. To the contrary, we have squarely held that a State's antidiscrimination law does not violate a group's right to associate simply because the law conflicts with that group's exclusionary membership policy." [*Roberts*]

"The relevant question is whether the mere inclusion of the person at issue would 'impose any serious burden,' 'affect in any significant way,' or be 'a substantial restraint upon' the organization's 'shared goals,' 'basic goals,' or 'collective effort to foster beliefs.' . . . The evidence before this Court makes it exceptionally clear that BSA has, at most, simply adopted an exclusionary membership policy and has no shared goal of disapproving of homosexuality.

"[An] organization can adopt the message of its choice, and it is not this Court's place to disagree with it. But we must inquire whether the group is, in fact, expressing a message (whatever it may be) and whether that message (if one is expressed) is significantly affected by a State's antidiscrimination law. More critically, that inquiry requires our independent analysis, rather than deference to a group's litigating posture. . . . If this Court were to defer to whatever position an organization is prepared to assert in its briefs, there would be no way to mark the proper boundary between genuine exercises of the right to associate, on the one hand, and sham claims that are simply attempts to insulate nonexpressive private discrimination, on the other hand. Shielding a litigant's claim from judicial scrutiny would, in turn, render civil rights legislation a nullity, and turn this important constitutional right into a farce.

"[Dale's] . . . participation [in the Boy Scouts] sends no cognizable message to the Scouts or to the world. . . . Dale did not carry a banner or a sign; he did not distribute any fact sheet; and he expressed no intent to send any message. . . . Though participating in the Scouts could itself conceivably send a message on some level, it is not the kind of act that we have recognized as speech. Indeed, if merely joining a group did constitute symbolic speech; and such speech were attributable to the group being joined; and that group has the right to exclude that speech (and hence, the right to exclude that person from joining), then the right of free speech effectively becomes a limitless right to exclude for every organization, whether or not it engages in any expressive activities. That cannot be, and never has been, the law.

"The only apparent explanation for the majority's holding, then, is that homosexuals are simply so different from the rest of society that their presence alone — unlike any other individual's — should be singled out for special First Amendment treatment. Under the majority's reasoning, an openly gay male is irreversibly affixed with the label 'homosexual.' That label, even though unseen, communicates a message that permits his exclusion wherever he goes. His openness is the sole and sufficient justification for his ostracism. Though unintended, reliance on such a justification is tantamount to a constitutionally prescribed symbol of inferiority. As counsel for the Boy Scouts remarked, Dale 'put a banner around his neck when he . . . got himself into the newspaper. . . . He created a reputation. . . . He can't take that banner off. He put it on himself and, indeed, he has continued to put it on himself.'"

Justice Souter also dissented.

Discussion

1. After *Dale,* what advice would you give an organization that wanted to avoid being bound by a public accommodations law? Is it enough to announce one's position for the first time during litigation? If not, what else is required? Does the Court's rule allow organizations like the Boy Scouts to have it both ways — because they do not have to take strong public stands against homosexuality except in litigation? On the other hand, does the Court's rule have a valuable "smoking out" effect — raising a First Amendment defense forces associations to state their biases publicly in litigation?

2. Note carefully Chief Justice Rehnquist's distinction of *Roberts* and *Duarte,* two earlier cases that rejected associational challenges made by the Jaycees and the Rotary Club; both organizations excluded women from membership in violation of public accommodations laws. Does Rehnquist's argument turn on the assumption (1) that preventing discrimination against homosexuals is not a compelling state interest, (2) that the public accommodations statute is not narrowly tailored to achieve that compelling interest, or (3) that even if the interest is compelling and the statute is narrowly tailored, the burden on the freedom of association of an organization like the Boy Scouts is simply too severe? If the latter, does this mean that the Boy Scouts could also exclude blacks? On the other hand, if a compelling

interest in preventing discrimination is sufficient to overcome an associational freedom claim, does this mean that the Boy Scouts have to admit women?

3. What is the reach of *Dale*'s holding? What if an organization opposes inter-faith relationships, or believes that women should not work outside the home? Does *Dale* allow an organization to exclude from membership anyone whose behavior conflicts with the organization's stated views? Does *Dale* shield only nonprofit organizations from the reach of antidiscrimination laws, or could businesses possess a constitutional right to refuse to accept customers or do business with persons if they believed this would conflict with their moral or political views and send the wrong message?

D.   Military Service

1.   The History of Homosexuals in the Military

As United States v. Watkins suggests, until 1993, the military took the official position that homosexuality was incompatible with military service. During the period prior to World War II, the military usually separated "sodomists" from service by using administrative discharge rather than court martials. Individuals who were suspected of homosexual acts were released under a "Section VIII" discharge for unsuitability. Some of these discharges were honorable, but if the discharge was for psychopathic behavior, it was regarded as less-than-honorable.

World War II brought considerable debate among the military about its policies regarding homosexuals.[103] Policies changed frequently during this period. By the end of the war, the term "homosexual" had replaced "sodomist" as the military's major focus of concern. Thus, a growing consensus emerged that even without a showing of same-sex sexual activity, homosexuals could be refused induction or separated from the service upon discovery of their orientation. By 1949, the Department of Defense (DoD) issued a memorandum that defined a unitary official policy. It stated that homosexuals should not be permitted to serve in any branch of the Armed Services in any capacity, and that prompt separation of known homosexuals from the Armed Forces should be made mandatory. The rate of discharges from the military increased tenfold during this period. Section VII.I of the 1959 DoD directive stated that "sexual perversion," which included homosexual acts and sodomy, was grounds for discharge for unfitness to serve.

In 1965, the military revised its regulations, permitting servicemembers facing a less-than-honorable discharge the chance to present their cases before administrative discharge boards and to be represented by counsel. Inconsistency in discharge policy and administrative procedures concerning homosexuals led to numerous court challenges; in response the Carter administration revised the policy regarding discharge once again, issuing a new DoD directive in January 1981, just before the Carter administration ended.

103. See generally Allan Berube, Coming Out Under Fire: The History of Gay Men and Women in World War Two (1990).

The 1981 directive removed the military's discretion to decide whether or not to remove an open or discovered homosexual; discharge was now made mandatory. The 1981 Department of Defense Regulations stated:

> Homosexuality is incompatible with military service. The presence in the military environment of persons who engage in homosexual conduct, or who, by their statements, demonstrate a propensity to engage in homosexual conduct, seriously impairs the accomplishment of the military mission. The presence of such members adversely affects the ability of the military services to maintain discipline, good order, and morale; to foster mutual trust and confidence among service-members; to ensure the integrity of the system of rank and command; to facilitate assignment and worldwide deployment of service members who frequently must live and work under close conditions affording minimal privacy; to recruit and retain members of the military services; to maintain the public acceptability of military service; and to prevent breaches of security.[104]

Under the new regulations, homosexuals could receive honorable discharges in the absence of other actions, such as violence. Between 1980 and 1991, according to a Government Accounting Office report, there were 16,919 discharges for homosexuality within the Armed Services, approximately 1.7 percent of all involuntary discharges.

2. The Constitutionality of "Don't Ask Don't Tell"

Shortly after President Clinton's election in 1992, he sought to fulfill a campaign promise to lift the ban on homosexuals serving in the military. This created a political uproar and led to highly publicized hearings on the military's policy, which led ultimately to a compromise, the "Don't Ask Don't Tell" Policy (DADT). DADT was incorporated in a new policy directive by the DoD in 1993, which, in turn was subsequently codified by Congress, Pub. L. No. 103-160, 107 Stat. 1679, now codified at 10 U.S.C.A. §654 (1998):

> §654. Policy concerning homosexuality in the armed forces
> (a) Findings. — Congress makes the following findings:
>   (6) Success in combat requires military units that are characterized by high morale, good order and discipline, and unit cohesion.
>   (7) One of the most critical elements in combat capability is unit cohesion, that is, the bonds of trust among individual service members that make the combat effectiveness of a military unit greater than the sum of the combat effectiveness of the individual unit members.
>   (8) Military life is fundamentally different from civilian life in that —
>
>   (A) the extraordinary responsibilities of the armed forces, the unique conditions of military service, and the critical role of unit cohesion, require that the military community, while subject to civilian control, exist as a specialized society; and

---

104. 32 C.F.R. pt 41, app. A (1982), at A.1.

(B) the military society is characterized by its own laws, rules, customs, and traditions, including numerous restrictions on personal behavior, that would not be acceptable in civilian society.

(9) The standards of conduct for members of the armed forces regulate a member's life for 24 hours each day beginning at the moment the member enters military status and not ending until that person is discharged or otherwise separated from the armed forces.

(10) Those standards of conduct, including the Uniform Code of Military Justice, apply to a member of the armed forces at all times that the member has a military status, whether the member is on base or off base, and whether the member is on duty or off duty.

(11) The pervasive application of the standards of conduct is necessary because members of the armed forces must be ready at all times for worldwide deployment to a combat environment.

(12) The worldwide deployment of United States military forces, the international responsibilities of the United States, and the potential for involvement of the armed forces in actual combat routinely make it necessary for members of the armed forces involuntarily to accept living conditions and working conditions that are often spartan, primitive, and characterized by forced intimacy with little or no privacy.

(13) The prohibition against homosexual conduct is a longstanding element of military law that continues to be necessary in the unique circumstances of military service.

(14) The armed forces must maintain personnel policies that exclude persons whose presence in the armed forces would create an unacceptable risk to the armed forces' high standards of morale, good order and discipline, and unit cohesion that are the essence of military capability.

(15) The presence in the armed forces of persons who demonstrate a propensity or intent to engage in homosexual acts would create an unacceptable risk to the high standards of morale, good order and discipline, and unit cohesion that are the essence of military capability.

(b) Policy. — A member of the armed forces shall be separated from the armed forces under regulations prescribed by the Secretary of Defense if one or more of the following findings is made and approved in accordance with procedures set forth in such regulations:

(1) That the member has engaged in, attempted to engage in, or solicited another to engage in a homosexual act or acts unless there are further findings, made and approved in accordance with procedures set forth in such regulations, that the member has demonstrated that —

(A) such conduct is a departure from the member's usual and customary behavior;
(B) such conduct, under all the circumstances, is unlikely to recur;
(C) such conduct was not accomplished by use of force, coercion, or intimidation;
(D) under the particular circumstances of the case, the member's continued presence in the armed forces is consistent with the interests of the armed forces in proper discipline, good order, and morale; and
(E) the member does not have a propensity or intent to engage in homosexual acts.

(2) That the member has stated that he or she is a homosexual or bisexual, or words to that effect, unless there is a further finding, made and approved in accordance with procedures set forth in the regulations, that the member has demonstrated

that he or she is not a person who engages in, attempts to engage in, has a propensity to engage in, or intends to engage in homosexual acts.

(3) That the member has married or attempted to marry a person known to be of the same biological sex.

(e) Rule of construction. — Nothing in subsection (b) shall be construed to require that a member of the armed forces be processed for separation from the armed forces when a determination is made in accordance with regulations prescribed by the Secretary of Defense that —

(1) the member engaged in conduct or made statements for the purpose of avoiding or terminating military service; and

(2) separation of the member would not be in the best interest of the armed forces.

(f) Definitions. — In this section:

(1) The term "homosexual" means a person, regardless of sex, who engages in, attempts to engage in, has a propensity to engage in, or intends to engage in homosexual acts, and includes the terms "gay" and "lesbian."

(2) The term "bisexual" means a person who engages in, attempts to engage in, has a propensity to engage in, or intends to engage in homosexual and heterosexual acts.

(3) The term "homosexual act" means —

(A) any bodily contact, actively undertaken or passively permitted, between members of the same sex for the purpose of satisfying sexual desires; and

(B) any bodily contact which a reasonable person would understand to demonstrate a propensity or intent to engage in an act described in subparagraph (A).

The DADT policy was immediately challenged in a number of courts. The following case gives a good sampling of the kinds of constitutional arguments that have been made for and against the policy.

THOMASSON v. PERRY, 80 F.3d 915 (4th Cir. 1996) (en banc): In December, 1993, the Department of Defense promulgated Directives implementing the DADT policy. One of these provides that an officer's statement that he or she is homosexual "creates a rebuttable presumption that the officer engages in homosexual acts or has a propensity or intent to do so." The officer is informed of this presumption and afforded an opportunity to rebut it by presenting appropriate evidence.

Former Navy Lieutenant Paul. G. Thomasson, after stating publicly that he was homosexual, challenged the constitutionality of the DADT policy and the accompanying DoD Directives. Applying rational basis scrutiny, the Fourth Circuit upheld the policy. Chief Judge Wilkinson noted that both Congress and the President had agreed on the DADT policy and that courts routinely defer to military judgments by the President and Congress as well as to the professional judgments of military officials. Noting that desegregation of the armed forces occurred by order of President Truman in 1948, Wilkinson argued that "the fact that the change emanates from the political branches minimizes both the likelihood of resistance in the military and the probability of prolonged societal division. In contrast, when courts impose military policy in the face of deep social division, the nation inherently runs the risk of long-term social discord because large segments of our population have been deprived of a democratic means of change. In the military context, such divisiveness could constitute an independent threat to national security."

Wilkinson rejected "Thomasson['s] claim[] that the stated justification for this statute — the protection of unit cohesion — is not a legitimate one because it is nothing more than a pretext for prejudice against homosexual service members." "Congress, after months of discussion, concluded that those who engage in or have a propensity to engage in homosexual acts impair military readiness. . . . These judgments reflect in turn Congress' view of military life, which can be, on a round-the-clock basis, 'spartan, primitive, and characterized by forced intimacy with little or no privacy.' 10 U.S.C. §654(a)(12). . . . In short, 'to win wars, we create cohesive teams of warriors who will bond so tightly that they are prepared to go into battle and give their lives if necessary for the accomplishment of the mission and for the cohesion of the group. . . . We cannot allow anything to happen which would disrupt that feeling of cohesion within the force.' Senate Hearings, at 708 (Statement of Chairman of the Joint Chiefs of Staff, General Colin L. Powell). Military leaders testified time and again how unit cohesion would be undermined: 'In my years of military service, I have experienced the fact that the introduction of an open homosexual into a small unit immediately polarizes that unit and destroys the very bonding that is so important for the unit's survival in time of war." S. Rep. No. 112, at 280 (Statement of General H. Norman Schwarzkopf).

"It was legitimate, therefore, for Congress to conclude that sexual tensions and attractions could play havoc with a military unit's discipline and solidarity. It was appropriate for Congress to believe that a military force should be as free as possible of sexual attachments and pressures as it prepared to do battle. Any argument that Congress was misguided in this view is one of legislative policy, not constitutional law. Courts have held that military authorities may discharge those who engage in homosexual acts. Given that it is legitimate for Congress to proscribe homosexual acts, it is also legitimate for the government to seek to forestall these same dangers by trying to prevent the commission of such acts. The statements provision, by discharging those with a propensity or intent to engage in homosexual acts, operates in this preventive way."

The court held that the DADT policy was rationally related to this legitimate government purpose: "The presumption that declared homosexuals have a propensity or intent to engage in homosexual acts certainly has a rational factual basis[,] perhaps the most sensible inference raised by a declaration of one's sexual orientation. As the Senate Committee noted: 'It would be irrational . . . to develop military personnel policies on the basis that all gays and lesbians will remain celibate.' Although Thomasson argues that some declared homosexuals have not engaged in or do not have a propensity or intent to engage in homosexual acts, 'courts are compelled . . . to accept a legislature's generalizations even when there is an imperfect fit between means and ends.' . . .

"Finally, the statute is not, as Thomasson maintains, irrational due to any purported distinction between declared and undeclared homosexuals. The policy instead rationally initiates discharge proceedings when service members, by declaring their homosexuality, thereby provide affirmative evidence to military officials of their propensity or intent to engage in homosexual acts.

"Thomasson apparently argues that the failure of military authorities to inquire into all service members' propensity to engage in homosexual acts somehow renders the policy unconstitutionally imprecise. But the decision to stop questioning new recruits about their sexual orientation reflects an allocation of military resources and a balance of competing interests, one that does not undermine the basic constitutionality of the Act [u]nder rational basis review. . . ."

Judge Luttig, concurring, argued that the presumption created by the DoD regulation was "in excess of [the DOD's] statutory authority" and asserted that Congress had the right to discharge anyone who merely said that he or she is homosexual. "I would sustain the policy that was actually enacted into law as a permissible exercise of Congress' constitutional authority 'to make Rules for the Government and Regulation' of the military. U.S. Const. Art. I, §8, cl. 14. . . . [I]t is well within the plenary authority of the Congress to exclude homosexuals from military service because of the deleterious effects that knowledge of their attraction for members of the same sex has on unit cohesion and military effectiveness."

The DADT policy is "a status-based policy, because it merely recognizes certain conduct as evidence of homosexuality; it does not exclude on the basis of that conduct itself. [It is not] status-based in the same way that an exclusion on the basis of an immutable characteristic would be. Rather [the] policy is based upon what is in fact a hybrid of status and conduct, namely, 'propensity.' 'Propensity' is different from a predetermined and immutable characteristic like race or sex. [I]t is a disposition toward certain conduct; but it is also different from conduct itself, or its likelihood, because it is neither itself action nor necessarily indicative of likely future action. It is, as commonly understood, merely an inclination, and it is that inclination, that propensity, not any likelihood of conduct, at which this particular policy is directed.

"The Solicitor General contends that there is a difference between a homosexual 'orientation' and a homosexual 'propensity' insofar as the likelihood that one will engage in homosexual acts is concerned, a difference the Administration has incorporated into its regulatory definition of 'orientation.' See DoD Directive No. 1332.30, Encl. 1, P 16 (March 4, 1994) (defining 'sexual orientation' as 'an abstract sexual preference for persons of a particular sex, as distinct from a propensity or intent to engage in sexual acts'). I do not know what homosexual orientation is, if it is not the propensity to commit homosexual acts; indeed, I do not understand how one even knows that he has a homosexual orientation except by realizing that he has a propensity toward the commission of homosexual acts." [Relocated footnote.]

Judge Hall dissented, noting Thomasson's "spotless" and "sparkling" military record. The DADT policy, Hall explained, "explicitly states that 'homosexual orientation is not a bar' to 'service entry or continued service.' Department of Defense Directive 1332.30 at 2-1 para. C (March 4, 1994)." Thomasson was dismissed not for any defect in his service record but "only because he has said [publicly] that he is homosexual." Citing City of Cleburne v. Cleburne Living Center, Judge Hall argued that the DADT policy failed the rational basis test because it was motivated by an impermissible purpose: "There is a great deal of evidence that the statute was motivated by a desire to accommodate prejudice against homosexuals. In announcing the policy, the President stated that 'those who oppose lifting the ban are clearly focused not on the conduct of individual gay service members, but on how nongay service members feel about gays in general and, in particular, those in the military service.' Assistant Secretary of Defense Edwin Dorn testified that 'much of the resistance to gays is grounded in fear and prejudice.' Retired Admiral Thomas Moorer, former Chairman of the Joint Chiefs of Staff, served on an advisory committee during development of the new policy. He was quite blunt about his views: homosexuals engage in 'a filthy, disease-ridden practice,' are 'inherently promiscuous,' and have no place in the military. He stated that many other 'military people' share his views. Finally, Lt. General John Otjen, who chaired the Military Working Group, stated that 'there's a collective sense in the military . . . that homosexuality is wrong.' Gen. Otjen believed that all members of the Military Working Group shared this 'collective sense.' Moreover, he conceded that, but for fear of and prejudice against homosexuals, the policy would be unnecessary. The evidence that prejudice against homosexuals is a purpose of 'don't ask, don't tell' is therefore quite strong."

Judge Hall also argued that the statute violated the First Amendment, because "it creates a classification among homosexuals based solely on speech." "The military has a broader power to control speech than a civilian government, Brown v. Glines, 444 U.S. 348 (1980), but even there the power is exceedingly narrow: speech may be suppressed only if it is likely to interfere with vital prerequisites to military effectiveness. The 'vital prerequisite' here is, I suppose, the accommodation of the prejudices of heterosexual servicemen. I very much doubt that such accommodation — never a legitimate legislative end — can ever be a 'vital prerequisite' to the military's mission. In any event, Lt. Thomasson has proved beyond any doubt that his speech had no deleterious impact at all, let alone to some 'vital prerequisite' to military effectiveness. If anything, the expulsion of a fine officer in retaliation for his speech will ultimately prove worse for the Navy."

Discussion

1. *The shower and the closet.* Kendall Thomas writes that "[i]n interview after interview" with straight servicemen, the fear of being looked at by gay soldiers in communal showers "has served as the chief conductor of the straight troop's deepest anxieties."[105] Nevertheless, Thomas notes, the matter is more complicated, because it is well known that gays have served and continue to serve in the military. These gay soldiers have, presumably, looked at hundreds of other men in showers before. Thomas notes the statement of an ex-Army Colonel who argued that the ban on homosexuals was what allowed them to serve so effectively in the Army: "The Colonel defended the ban because it had forced gay men and lesbians in the armed forces 'to be very, very discreet, to stay in the closet, so that no one knew [, so] that their conduct didn't become a matter of command attention or public attention.'" In short, Thomas, argues, the debate is "not so much a conflict over what can(not) be *seen,* as it is a controversy over what can(not) be *known.*"

The focus on the shower, Thomas contends, is not simply a fear of gay voyeurs but "a symptomatic sign of the independent, unacknowledged investment that straight militarists themselves have made in the epistemic structure that has come to be known as the closet." "[T]he presence of gay men in the military is something that 'we all know' and that 'no one knows.'" The straight male knows that he might be watched by a gay serviceman but does not know who is watching him. "For the straight troop, the image of the desiring gay glance is the source of a fear which is also a fascination." Thomas points out that this dual meaning is important to heterosexual identity in the military, which emphasizes male bonding and allows straight men to engage in homoerotic rituals that are part of male military culture without having to face the reality of homoeroticism directly.

The presence of "avowed" homosexuals in the military would strip the straight troop of his "privilege of unknowing," leaving him naked to confront the disavowal of

105. Kendall Thomas, Shower/Closet, 20 Assemblage, 80-81 (1993).

homosexual desire on which the homosocial apparatus of the military so crucially depends. . . . Given the homoerotic dimensions of male military culture, the straight troop might well be compelled to come to terms with the fragile and fluid nature of his own sexual and gender identities.

Does Thomas think that military performance will be improved if straight men are confronted with open homosexuals and forced to recognize the homoerotic elements of military service?

2. *Is DADT better than a categorical ban?* The DADT policy was touted by military and media voices as representing palpable progress for gays. See, e.g., Editorial, Don't Ask, Don't Give Up, Pittsburgh Post-Gazette, Dec. 27, 1993, at D2; Mark Thompson, Military Chiefs Tell Panel They Back Gay Policy, Philadelphia Inquirer, July 21, 1993, at A2. Yet Janet Halley has argued that DADT is "much, much worse" than its predecessor. Janet E. Halley, Don't: A Reader's Guide to the Military's Anti-Gay Policy 1 (1999). This counterintuitive claim is supported by statistics. In the years following implementation of the new policy, the number of yearly separations for homosexuality increased from fewer than 700 in 1993 to almost 1,300 in 2001. However, in accord with a historical pattern of reduced discharges for homosexuality during wartime, the number of servicemembers separated for homosexuality has dropped dramatically since the start of the wars in Afghanistan and Iraq. See Clarence Page, Military Gays Benefit from the War on Terror, Newsday, Apr. 26, 2004, at A38; Michelle Locke, New War Puts "Don't Ask, Don't Tell" Policy into Focus, Denver Post, Oct. 16, 2001, at A4; Office of the Under Secretary of Defense, Report to the Secretary of Defense: Review of the Effectiveness of the Application and Enforcement of the Department's Policy on Homosexual Conduct in the Military (1998).

Halley argues that the DADT policy is worse because it sounds better, making it easier to defend. Is this why the number of gay discharges rose after 1993? Or is it (also) that the debates over the policy about the unspeakability of homosexuality ironically made homosexuality in the military more visible than ever before? In this sense, was this policy a "performative contradiction" insofar as it "redoubles the term it seeks to restrain?" Judith Butler, Excitable Speech: A Politics of the Performative 104 (1997). Would there have been another way of drafting the statute that could have secured its stated ends without being self-defeating in this way?

3. *Promising it won't happen again.* Consider Thomas's point about the "privilege of unknowing" in light of §654(b)(1). Under this section, servicemembers can escape discharge even if they have engaged in homosexual conduct if they can demonstrate that this is not their normal behavior, that they are unlikely to engage in such conduct again, and do not have the propensity or intention to engage in homosexual acts; that is, that they are not a "homosexual" as defined in the act. How would a servicemember go about proving this? On the other hand, under §654 (b)(2), if a servicemember self-identifies as gay, this raises a presumption of homosexual conduct that — unless rebutted to the military's satisfaction — results in separation from military service. In addition, servicemembers who marry or who attempt to marry someone of the same sex will be categorically excluded. Does this balance of incentives and burdens of proof illuminate the animating purposes of DADT?

4. Romer *and DADT.* Thomasson was decided before the Supreme Court's decision in Romer v. Evans. In Able v. United States, 155 F.3d 628 (2d Cir. 1998),

plaintiff argued that under *Romer, Cleburne,* and Palmore v. Sidoti, 10 U.S.C. §654(b) "cannot survive even rational basis review because it is motivated by irrational fear and prejudice toward homosexuals." The Court rejected this argument:

> [P]laintiffs' reliance on *Romer, Cleburne Living Ctr.* and *Palmore* is misplaced. Those cases did not arise in the military setting. In the civilian context, the Court was willing to examine the benign reasons advanced by the government to consider whether they masked an impermissible underlying purpose. In the military setting, however, constitutionally-mandated deference to military assessments and judgments gives the judiciary far less scope to scrutinize the reasons, legitimate on their face, that the military has advanced to justify its actions.

5. Lawrence *and DADT.* Does Lawrence v. Texas undermine the military's DADT policy? Consider the following arguments:

1. *Lawrence* undermines the constitutionality of DADT because the military can no longer make homosexual sodomy a crime. Therefore the military cannot make propensity to commit homosexual sodomy a violation of military regulations. Hence it cannot discharge a serviceperson upon the revelation that he or she is a homosexual on the grounds that this presumptively establishes the propensity to commit homosexual sodomy. (Note that connecting homosexuality with sodomy in this way takes precisely the opposite strategy pursued by plaintiffs challenging the DADT policy before *Lawrence.*)
2. The DADT is premised on the need for unit cohesion, not morality. The goal is to separate persons who publicly state that they are homosexual, which means that they have a propensity to engage in homosexual conduct. Such homosexual conduct is not limited to sodomy, but may include kissing or handholding. In any case, it is irrelevant that same-sex sodomy cannot be criminalized in the civilian context; if the practice interferes with military efficiency it can be prohibited in the military context. See Rostker v. Goldberg, 453 U.S. 57 (1981). In this sense same-sex sodomy is no different than other sexual behavior that cannot be criminalized in civilian life but that undermines military efficiency and unit cohesion.

In United States v. Marcus, 60 M.J. 198 (C. M. A. 2004), a serviceman was charged with both forcible and non-forcible sodomy, and found guilty of non-forcible sodomy. Citing *Lawrence,* he challenged the constitutionality of Article 125 of the Uniform Code of Military Justice, which prohibits sodomy, defined as "unnatural carnal copulation with another person of the same or opposite sex or with an animal." The Court of Appeals for the Armed Forces noted that "The Supreme Court did not expressly state which test it used," and noted that different language in *Lawrence* might be consistent with recognition of a new fundamental right and with application of rational basis scrutiny. "Therefore, we will not presume the existence of such a fundamental right in the military environment when the Supreme Court declined in the civilian context to expressly identify such a fundamental right." Nevertheless, "*Lawrence* requires . . . searching constitutional inquiry" which "may require a court to go beyond a determination as to whether the activity at issue falls within column A — conduct of a nature to bring it within the liberty interest identified in *Lawrence,* or within column B — factors identified by the Supreme Court as outside its *Lawrence* analysis." "Thus, the door is held open for lower courts to address the scope and nature of the right identified in *Lawrence,* as well as its limitations, based on contexts and factors the Supreme Court may not have anticipated or chose not to address in *Lawrence.* In our view, this framework argues for contextual, as applied analysis, rather than facial review. This is particularly apparent in the military context."

The court noted that the appellant Marcus had sex with "a subordinate airman within Appellant's chain of command" and whom he "supervised and rated." Such a relationship was in violation of Air Force policy, and the sex was with "a person 'who might be coerced' or who was 'situated in [a] relationship[] where consent might not easily be refused.' [citing *Lawrence*] Thus, based on this factor, Appellant's conduct fell outside the liberty interest identified by the Supreme Court."

E.   Same-Sex Marriage

GOODRIDGE v. DEPARTMENT OF PUBLIC HEALTH
440 Mass. 309, 798 N.E.2d 941 (Mass. 2003)

MARSHALL, C.J.:

[Seven same-sex couples sued Massachusetts officials claiming that legal restrictions limiting marriage licenses to individuals of opposite sexes violated the Massachusetts state constitution.]

The Massachusetts Constitution requires, at a minimum, that the exercise of the State's regulatory authority not be "arbitrary or capricious." Under both the equality and liberty guarantees, regulatory authority must, at very least, serve "a legitimate purpose in a rational way"; a statute must "bear a reasonable relation to a permissible legislative objective." Any law failing to satisfy the basic standards of rationality is void. . . . For the reasons we explain below, we conclude that the marriage ban does not meet the rational basis test for either due process or equal protection. Because the statute does not survive rational basis review, we do not consider the plaintiffs' arguments that this case merits strict judicial scrutiny.

The department posits three legislative rationales for prohibiting same-sex couples from marrying: (1) providing a "favorable setting for procreation"; (2) ensuring the optimal setting for child rearing, which the department defines as "a two-parent family with one parent of each sex"; and (3) preserving scarce State and private financial resources. . . .

Our laws of civil marriage do not privilege procreative heterosexual intercourse between married people above every other form of adult intimacy and every other means of creating a family. General Laws c. 207 contains no requirement that the applicants for a marriage license attest to their ability or intention to conceive children by coitus. Fertility is not a condition of marriage, nor is it grounds for divorce. People who have never consummated their marriage, and never plan to, may be and stay married. While it is certainly true that many, perhaps most, married couples have children together (assisted or unassisted), it is the exclusive and permanent commitment of the marriage partners to one another, not the begetting of children, that is the sine qua non of civil marriage.

Moreover, the Commonwealth affirmatively facilitates bringing children into a family regardless of whether the intended parent is married or unmarried, whether the child is adopted or born into a family, whether assistive technology was used to conceive the child, and whether the parent or her partner is heterosexual, homosexual, or bisexual.[a] If procreation were a necessary component of civil marriage, our statutes would draw a tighter circle around the permissible bounds of nonmarital child bearing and the creation of families by noncoital means. . . . The "marriage is procreation" argument singles out the one unbridgeable difference between same-sex and opposite-sex couples, and transforms that difference into the essence of legal marriage. Like "Amendment 2" to the Constitution of Colorado, which effectively denied homosexual persons equality under the law and full access to the political process, the marriage restriction impermissibly "identifies persons by a single trait and then denies them protection across the board." *Romer v. Evans.* In so doing, the State's action confers an official stamp of approval on the destructive stereotype that same-sex relationships are inherently unstable and inferior to opposite-sex relationships and are not worthy of respect.

The department's first stated rationale, equating marriage with unassisted heterosexual procreation, shades imperceptibly into its second: that confining marriage to opposite-sex couples ensures that children are raised in the "optimal" setting. Protecting the welfare of children is a paramount State policy. Restricting marriage to opposite-sex couples, however, cannot plausibly further this policy. The demographic changes of the past century make it difficult to speak of an average American family. . . . Moreover, we have repudiated the common-law power of the State to provide varying levels of protection to children based on the circumstances of birth. The "best interests of the child" standard does not turn on a parent's sexual orientation or marital status.

The department has offered no evidence that forbidding marriage to people of the same sex will increase the number of couples choosing to enter into opposite-sex marriages in order to have and raise children. There is thus no rational relationship between the marriage statute and the Commonwealth's proffered goal of protecting the "optimal" child rearing unit. Moreover, the department readily concedes that people in same-sex couples may be "excellent" parents. These couples (including four of the plaintiff couples) have children for the reasons others do — to love them, to care for them, to nurture them. But the task of child rearing for same-sex couples is made infinitely harder by their status as outliers to the marriage laws. While establishing the parentage of children as soon as possible is crucial to the safety and welfare of children, same-sex couples must undergo the sometimes lengthy and intrusive process of second-parent adoption to establish their joint parentage. While the enhanced income provided by marital benefits is an important source of security and stability for married couples and their children, those benefits are denied to families headed by same-sex couples. While the laws of divorce provide clear and reasonably predictable guidelines for child support, child custody, and property division on dissolution of a marriage, same-sex couples who dissolve their relationships find themselves and their children in the highly unpredictable terrain of equity jurisdiction. Given the wide range of public benefits reserved only for married couples, we do not credit the department's contention that the absence of access to civil marriage amounts to little more than an inconvenience to same-sex couples and their children. Excluding same-sex

---

a. Adoption and certain insurance coverage for assisted reproductive technology are available to married couples, same-sex couples, and single individuals alike.

couples from civil marriage will not make children of opposite-sex marriages more secure, but it does prevent children of same-sex couples from enjoying the immeasurable advantages that flow from the assurance of "a stable family structure in which children will be reared, educated, and socialized." . . .

In this case, we are confronted with an entire, sizeable class of parents raising children who have absolutely no access to civil marriage and its protections because they are forbidden from procuring a marriage license. It cannot be rational under our laws, and indeed it is not permitted, to penalize children by depriving them of State benefits because the State disapproves of their parents' sexual orientation.

The third rationale advanced by the department is that limiting marriage to opposite-sex couples furthers the Legislature's interest in conserving scarce State and private financial resources. The marriage restriction is rational, it argues, because the General Court logically could assume that same-sex couples are more financially independent than married couples and thus less needy of public marital benefits, such as tax advantages, or private marital benefits, such as employer-financed health plans that include spouses in their coverage.

An absolute statutory ban on same-sex marriage bears no rational relationship to the goal of economy. First, the department's conclusory generalization — that same-sex couples are less financially dependent on each other than opposite-sex couples — ignores that many same-sex couples, such as many of the plaintiffs in this case, have children and other dependents (here, aged parents) in their care. The department does not contend, nor could it, that these dependents are less needy or deserving than the dependents of married couples. Second, Massachusetts marriage laws do not condition receipt of public and private financial benefits to married individuals on a demonstration of financial dependence on each other; the benefits are available to married couples regardless of whether they mingle their finances or actually depend on each other for support.

The department suggests additional rationales for prohibiting same-sex couples from marrying. . . . It argues that broadening civil marriage to include same-sex couples will trivialize or destroy the institution of marriage as it has historically been fashioned. Certainly our decision today marks a significant change in the definition of marriage as it has been inherited from the common law, and understood by many societies for centuries. But it does not disturb the fundamental value of marriage in our society.

Here, the plaintiffs seek only to be married, not to undermine the institution of civil marriage. They do not want marriage abolished. They do not attack the binary nature of marriage, the consanguinity provisions, or any of the other gate-keeping provisions of the marriage licensing law. Recognizing the right of an individual to marry a person of the same sex will not diminish the validity or dignity of opposite-sex marriage, any more than recognizing the right of an individual to marry a person of a different race devalues the marriage of a person who marries someone of her own race. If anything, extending civil marriage to same-sex couples reinforces the importance of marriage to individuals and communities. That same-sex couples are willing to embrace marriage's solemn obligations of exclusivity, mutual support, and commitment to one another is a testament to the enduring place of marriage in our laws and in the human spirit.

It has been argued that, due to the State's strong interest in the institution of marriage as a stabilizing social structure, only the Legislature can control and define its boundaries. Accordingly, our elected representatives legitimately may choose to exclude same-sex couples from civil marriage in order to assure all citizens of the Commonwealth that (1) the benefits of our marriage laws are available explicitly to create and support a family setting that is, in the Legislature's view, optimal for child rearing, and (2) the State does not endorse gay and lesbian parenthood as the equivalent of being raised by one's married biological parents. These arguments miss the point. The Massachusetts Constitution requires that legislation meet certain criteria and not extend beyond certain limits. It is the function of courts to determine whether these criteria are met and whether these limits are exceeded. In most instances, these limits are defined by whether a rational basis exists to conclude that legislation will bring about a rational result. The Legislature in the first instance, and the courts in the last instance, must ascertain whether such a rational basis exists. To label the court's role as usurping that of the Legislature is to misunderstand the nature and purpose of judicial review. We owe great deference to the Legislature to decide social and policy issues, but it is the traditional and settled role of courts to decide constitutional issues.

We also reject the argument suggested by the department, and elaborated by some amici, that expanding the institution of civil marriage in Massachusetts to include same-sex couples will lead to interstate conflict. We would not presume to dictate how another State should respond to today's decision. But neither should considerations of comity prevent us from according Massachusetts residents the full measure of protection available under the Massachusetts Constitution. The genius of our Federal system is that each State's Constitution has vitality specific to its own traditions, and that, subject to the minimum requirements of the Fourteenth Amendment, each State is free to address difficult issues of individual liberty in the manner its own Constitution demands.

Several amici suggest that prohibiting marriage by same-sex couples reflects community consensus that homosexual conduct is immoral. Yet Massachusetts has a strong affirmative policy of preventing discrimination on the basis of sexual orientation.

The department has had more than ample opportunity to articulate a constitutionally adequate justification for limiting civil marriage to opposite-sex unions. It has failed to do so. The department has offered purported justifications for the civil marriage restriction that are starkly at odds with the comprehensive network of vigorous, gender-neutral laws promoting stable families and the best interests of children. It has failed to identify any relevant characteristic that would justify shutting the door to civil marriage to a person who wishes to marry someone of the same sex.

The marriage ban works a deep and scarring hardship on a very real segment of the community for no rational reason. The absence of any reasonable relationship between, on the one hand, an absolute disqualification of same-sex couples who wish to enter into civil marriage and, on the other, protection of public health, safety, or general welfare, suggests that the marriage restriction is rooted in persistent prejudices against persons who are (or who are believed to be) homosexual.[b] . . .

b. It is not dispositive, for purposes of our constitutional analysis, whether the Legislature, at the time it incorporated the common-law definition of marriage into the first marriage laws nearly three centuries ago, did so with the intent of discriminating against or harming persons who wish to marry another of the same sex. We are not required to impute an invidious intent to the Legislature in determining that a statute of long standing has no applicability to present circumstances or violates the rights of individuals under the Massachusetts Constitution. That the Legislature may have intended what at the time of enactment was a perfectly reasonable form of discrimination — or a result not recognized as a form of discrimination — was not enough to salvage from later constitutional challenge laws burdening nonmarital children or denying women's equal partnership in marriage. We are concerned with the operation of challenged laws on the parties before us, and we do not inhibit our inquiry on the ground that a statute's original enactors had a benign or at the time constitutionally unassailable purpose.

Limiting the protections, benefits, and obligations of civil marriage to opposite-sex couples violates the basic premises of individual liberty and equality under law protected by the Massachusetts Constitution.

[N]o one argues that striking down the marriage laws is an appropriate form of relief. Eliminating civil marriage would be wholly inconsistent with the Legislature's deep commitment to fostering stable families and would dismantle a vital organizing principle of our society.[c] We face a problem similar to one that recently confronted the Court of Appeal for Ontario, the highest court of that Canadian province, when it considered the constitutionality of the same-sex marriage ban under Canada's Federal Constitution, the Charter of Rights and Freedoms (Charter). See Halpern v. Toronto (City), 172 O.A.C. 276 (2003). Canada, like the United States, adopted the common law of England that civil marriage is "the voluntary union for life of one man and one woman, to the exclusion of all others." Id. at par. (36), quoting Hyde v. Hyde, [1861-1873] All E.R. 175 (1866). In holding that the limitation of civil marriage to opposite-sex couples violated the Charter, the Court of Appeal refined the common-law meaning of marriage. We concur with this remedy, which is entirely consonant with established principles of jurisprudence empowering a court to refine a common-law principle in light of evolving constitutional standards.

We construe civil marriage to mean the voluntary union of two persons as spouses, to the exclusion of all others. This reformulation redresses the plaintiffs' constitutional injury and furthers the aim of marriage to promote stable, exclusive relationships. It advances the two legitimate State interests the department has identified: providing a stable setting for child rearing and conserving State resources. It leaves intact the Legislature's broad discretion to regulate marriage. . . . We remand this case to the Superior Court for entry of judgment consistent with this opinion. Entry of judgment shall be stayed for 180 days to permit the Legislature to take such action as it may deem appropriate in light of this opinion.

GREANEY, J., concurring.

I agree with the result reached by the court, the remedy ordered, and much of the reasoning in the court's opinion. In my view, however, the case is more directly resolved using traditional equal protection analysis.

. . . The right to marry is not a privilege conferred by the State, but a fundamental right that is protected against unwarranted State interference. *Zablocki* This right is essentially vitiated if one is denied the right to marry a person of one's choice.

Because our marriage statutes intend, and state, the ordinary understanding that marriage under our law consists only of a union between a man and a woman, they create a statutory classification based on the sex of the two people who wish to marry. That the classification is sex based is self-evident. The marriage statutes prohibit some applicants, such as the plaintiffs, from obtaining a marriage license, and that prohibition is based solely on the applicants' gender. As a factual matter, an individual's choice of marital partner is constrained because of his or her own

---

c. Similarly, no one argues that the restrictions on incestuous or polygamous marriages are so dependent on the marriage restriction that they too should fall if the marriage restriction falls. Nothing in our opinion today should be construed as relaxing or abrogating the consanguinity or polygamy prohibitions of our marriage laws. Rather, the statutory provisions concerning consanguinity or polygamous marriages shall be construed in a gender neutral manner.

sex. Stated in particular terms, Hillary Goodridge cannot marry Julie Goodridge because she (Hillary) is a woman. Likewise, Gary Chalmers cannot marry Richard Linnell because he (Gary) is a man. Only their gender prevents Hillary and Gary from marrying their chosen partners under the present law.

A classification may be gender based whether or not the challenged government action apportions benefits or burdens uniformly along gender lines. This is so because constitutional protections extend to individuals and not to categories of people. . . . I find it disingenuous, at best, to suggest that such an individual's right to marry has not been burdened at all, because he or she remains free to chose another partner, who is of the opposite sex.

The equal protection infirmity at work here is strikingly similar to (although, perhaps, more subtle than) the invidious discrimination perpetuated by Virginia's antimiscegenation laws [in] Loving v. Virginia. [T]he United States Supreme Court soundly rejected the proposition that the equal application of the ban (i.e., that it applied equally to whites and blacks) made unnecessary the strict scrutiny analysis traditionally required of statutes drawing classifications according to race. . . . That our marriage laws, unlike antimiscegenation laws, were not enacted purposely to discriminate in no way neutralizes their present discriminatory character.

With these two propositions established (the infringement on a fundamental right and a sex-based classification), the enforcement of the marriage statutes as they are currently understood is forbidden by our Constitution unless the State can present a compelling purpose furthered by the statutes that can be accomplished in no other reasonable manner. . . .

The rights of couples to have children, to adopt, and to be foster parents, regardless of sexual orientation and marital status, are firmly established. [T]he State's refusal to accord legal recognition to unions of same-sex couples has had the effect of creating a system in which children of same-sex couples are unable to partake of legal protections and social benefits taken for granted by children in families whose parents are of the opposite sex. The continued maintenance of this caste-like system is irreconcilable with, indeed, totally repugnant to, the State's strong interest in the welfare of all children and its primary focus, in the context of family law where children are concerned, on "the best interests of the child." The issue at stake is not one, as might ordinarily be the case, that can be unilaterally and totally deferred to the wisdom of the Legislature. "While the State retains wide latitude to decide the manner in which it will allocate benefits, it may not use criteria which discriminatorily burden the exercise of a fundamental right." Nor can the State's wish to conserve resources be accomplished by invidious distinctions between classes of citizens.

A comment is in order with respect to the insistence of some that marriage is, as a matter of definition, the legal union of a man and a woman. To define the institution of marriage by the characteristics of those to whom it always has been accessible, in order to justify the exclusion of those to whom it never has been accessible, is conclusory and bypasses the core question we are asked to decide. This case . . . requires that we confront ingrained assumptions with respect to historically accepted roles of men and women within the institution of marriage and requires that we reexamine these assumptions in light of the unequivocal language of [the constitutional guarantee of equality]. . . .

I do not doubt the sincerity of deeply held moral or religious beliefs that make inconceivable to some the notion that any change in the common-law definition of what constitutes a legal civil marriage is now, or ever would be, warranted. But, as matter of constitutional law, neither the mantra of tradition, nor individual conviction, can justify the perpetuation of a hierarchy in which couples of the same sex and their families are deemed less worthy of social and legal recognition than couples of the opposite sex and their families. . . . I am hopeful that our decision will be accepted by those thoughtful citizens who believe that same-sex unions should not be approved by the State. I am not referring here to acceptance in the sense of grudging acknowledgment of the court's authority to adjudicate the matter. My hope is more liberating. The plaintiffs are members of our community, our neighbors, our coworkers, our friends. As pointed out by the court, their professions include investment advisor, computer engineer, teacher, therapist, and lawyer. The plaintiffs volunteer in our schools, worship beside us in our religious houses, and have children who play with our children, to mention just a few ordinary daily contacts. We share a common humanity and participate together in the social contract that is the foundation of our Commonwealth. Simple principles of decency dictate that we extend to the plaintiffs, and to their new status, full acceptance, tolerance, and respect. We should do so because it is the right thing to do.

SPINA, J., dissenting, with whom Sosman and Cordy, JJ., join:

G.L. c. 207 does not unconstitutionally discriminate on the basis of gender. A claim of gender discrimination will lie where it is shown that differential treatment disadvantages one sex over the other. General Laws c. 207 enumerates certain qualifications for obtaining a marriage license. It creates no distinction between the sexes, but applies to men and women in precisely the same way. It does not create any disadvantage identified with gender, as both men and women are similarly limited to marrying a person of the opposite sex.

Similarly, the marriage statutes do not discriminate on the basis of sexual orientation. As the court correctly recognizes, constitutional protections are extended to individuals, not couples. The marriage statutes do not disqualify individuals on the basis of sexual orientation from entering into marriage. All individuals, with certain exceptions not relevant here, are free to marry. Whether an individual chooses not to marry because of sexual orientation or any other reason should be of no concern to the court.

The court concludes, however, that G.L. c. 207 unconstitutionally discriminates against the individual plaintiffs because it denies them the "right to marry the person of one's choice" where that person is of the same sex. To reach this result the court relies on Loving v. Virginia and transforms "choice" into the essential element of the institution of marriage. . . . The "choice" to which the Supreme Court referred [in *Loving*] was the "choice to marry," and it concluded that with respect to the institution of marriage, the State had no compelling interest in limiting the choice to marry along racial lines. The Supreme Court did not imply the existence of a right to marry a person of the same sex. . . . Unlike the *Loving* and *Sharp* cases, the Massachusetts Legislature has erected no barrier to marriage that intentionally discriminates against anyone. Within the institution of marriage, anyone is free to marry, with certain exceptions that are not challenged. In the absence of any discriminatory purpose, the State's marriage statutes do not violate principles of equal protection. This court should not have invoked even the most deferential standard of review within equal protection analysis because no individual was denied access to the institution of marriage.

[T]he marriage statutes do not impermissibly burden a right protected by our constitutional guarantee of due process. . . . There is no restriction on the right of any plaintiff to enter into marriage. Each is free to marry a willing person of the opposite sex. . . . .

Same-sex marriage, or the "right to marry the person of one's choice" as the court today defines that right, does not fall within the fundamental right to marry. Same-sex marriage is not "deeply rooted in this Nation's history," and the court does not suggest that it is. Except for the occasional isolated decision in recent years, same-sex marriage is not a right, fundamental or otherwise, recognized in this country. . . .

The court has extruded a new right from principles of substantive due process, and in doing so it has distorted the meaning and purpose of due process. The purpose of substantive due process is to protect existing rights, not to create new rights. Its aim is to thwart government intrusion, not invite it. . . . The statute in question does not seek to regulate intimate activity within an intimate relationship, but merely gives formal recognition to a particular marriage. The State has respected the private lives of the plaintiffs, and has done nothing to intrude in the relationships that each of the plaintiff couples enjoy. Ironically, by extending the marriage laws to same-sex couples the court has turned substantive due process on its head and used it to interject government into the plaintiffs' lives.

SOSMAN, J., dissenting, with whom Spina and Cordy, JJ., join:

. . . Reduced to its essence, the court's opinion concludes that, because same-sex couples are now raising children, and withholding the benefits of civil marriage from their union makes it harder for them to raise those children, the State must therefore provide the benefits of civil marriage to same-sex couples just as it does to opposite-sex couples. Of course, many people are raising children outside the confines of traditional marriage, and, by definition, those children are being deprived of the various benefits that would flow if they were being raised in a household with married parents. That does not mean that the Legislature must accord the full benefits of marital status on every household raising children. Rather, the Legislature need only have some rational basis for concluding that, at present, those alternate family structures have not yet been conclusively shown to be the equivalent of the marital family structure that has established itself as a successful one over a period of centuries. People are of course at liberty to raise their children in various family structures, as long as they are not literally harming their children by doing so. That does not mean that the State is required to provide identical forms of encouragement, endorsement, and support to all of the infinite variety of household structures that a free society permits.

. . .

Conspicuously absent from the court's opinion today is any acknowledgment that the attempts at scientific study of the ramifications of raising children in same-sex couple households are themselves in their infancy and have so far produced inconclusive and conflicting results. Notwithstanding our belief that gender and sexual orientation of parents should not matter to the success of the child rearing venture, studies to date reveal that there are still some observable differences between children raised by opposite-sex couples and children raised by same-sex couples. Interpretation of the data gathered by those studies then becomes clouded by the personal and political beliefs of the investigators, both as to whether the differences identified are positive or negative, and as to the untested explanations of what might account for those differences. (This is hardly the first time in history that the ostensible steel of the scientific method has melted and buckled under the intense heat of political and religious passions.) Even in the absence of bias or political agenda behind the various studies of children raised by same-sex couples, the most neutral and strict application of scientific principles to this field would be constrained by the limited period of observation that has been available. Gay and lesbian couples living together openly, and official recognition of them as their children's sole parents, comprise a very recent phenomenon, and the recency of that phenomenon has not yet permitted any study of how those children fare as adults and at best minimal study of how they fare during their adolescent years. The Legislature can rationally view the state of the scientific evidence as unsettled on the critical question it now faces: are families headed by same-sex parents equally successful in rearing children from infancy to adulthood as families headed by parents of opposite sexes? Our belief that children raised by same-sex couples *should* fare the same as children raised in traditional families is just that: a passionately held but utterly untested belief. The Legislature is not required to share that belief but may, as the creator of the institution of civil marriage, wish to see the proof before making a fundamental alteration to that institution.

Although ostensibly applying the rational basis test to the civil marriage statutes, it is abundantly apparent that the court is in fact applying some undefined stricter standard to assess the constitutionality of the marriage statutes' exclusion of same-sex couples. . . .

[T]he opinion ultimately opines that the Legislature is acting irrationally when it grants benefits to a proven successful family structure while denying the same benefits to a recent, perhaps promising, but essentially untested alternate family structure. Placed in a more neutral context, the court would never find any irrationality in such an approach. For example, if the issue were government subsidies and tax benefits promoting use of an established technology for energy efficient heating, the court would find no equal protection or due process violation in the Legislature's decision not to grant the same benefits to an inventor or manufacturer of some new, alternative technology who did not yet have sufficient data to prove that that new technology was just as good as the established technology. That the early results from preliminary testing of the new technology might look very promising, or that the theoretical underpinnings of the new technology might appear flawless, would not make it irrational for the Legislature to grant subsidies and tax breaks to the established technology and deny them to the still unproved newcomer in the field. While programs that affect families and children register higher on our emotional scale than programs affecting energy efficiency, our standards for what is or is not "rational" should not be bent by those emotional tugs. Where, as here, there is no ground for applying strict scrutiny, the emotionally compelling nature of the subject matter should not affect the manner in which we apply the rational basis test.

. . . In considering whether the Legislature has a rational reason for postponing a dramatic change to the definition of marriage, it is surely pertinent to the inquiry to recognize that this proffered change affects not just a load-bearing wall of our social structure but the very cornerstone of that structure. Before making a fundamental alteration to that cornerstone, it is eminently rational for the Legislature to require a high degree of certainty as to the precise consequences of that alteration, to make sure that it can be done safely, without either temporary or lasting damage to the structural integrity of the entire edifice. The court today blithely assumes that there are no such dangers and that it is safe to proceed, an assumption that is not supported by anything more than the court's blind faith that it is so.

More importantly, it is not our confidence in the lack of adverse consequences that is at issue, or even whether that confidence is justifiable. The issue is whether it is rational to reserve judgment on whether this change can be made at this time without damaging the institution of marriage or adversely affecting the critical role it has played in our society. Absent consensus on the issue (which obviously does not exist), or unanimity amongst scientists studying the issue (which also does not exist), or a more prolonged period of observation of this new family structure (which has not yet been possible), it is rational for the Legislature to postpone any redefinition of marriage that would include same-sex couples until such time as it is certain that that redefinition will not have unintended and undesirable social consequences. Through the political process, the people may decide when the benefits of extending civil marriage to same-sex couples have been shown to outweigh whatever risks — be they palpable or ephemeral — are involved. However minimal the risks of that redefinition of marriage may seem to us from our vantage point, it is not up to us to decide what risks society must run, and it is inappropriate for us to arrogate that power to ourselves merely because we are confident that "it is the right thing to do." (Greaney, J., concurring).

As a matter of social history, today's opinion may represent a great turning point that many will hail as a tremendous step toward a more just society. As a matter of constitutional jurisprudence, however, the case stands as an aberration. To reach the result it does, the court has tortured the rational basis test beyond recognition. I fully appreciate the strength of the temptation to find this particular law unconstitutional — there is much to be said for the argument that excluding gay and lesbian couples from the benefits of civil marriage is cruelly unfair and hopelessly outdated; the inability to marry has a profound impact on the personal lives of committed gay and lesbian couples (and their children) to whom we are personally close (our friends, neighbors, family members, classmates, and co-workers); and our resolution of this issue takes place under the intense glare of national and international publicity. Speaking metaphorically, these factors have combined to turn the case before us into a "perfect storm" of a constitutional question. In my view, however, such factors make it all the more imperative that we adhere precisely and scrupulously to the established guideposts of our constitutional jurisprudence, a jurisprudence that makes the rational basis test an extremely deferential one that focuses on the rationality, not the persuasiveness, of the potential justifications for the classifications in the legislative scheme. I trust that, once this particular "storm" clears, we will return to the rational basis test as it has always been understood and applied. Applying that deferential test in the manner it is customarily applied, the exclusion of gay and lesbian couples from the institution of civil marriage passes constitutional muster. I respectfully dissent.

CORDY, J., dissenting, with whom Spina and Sosman, JJ., join:
[T]he Massachusetts marriage statute does not impair the exercise of a recognized fundamental right, or discriminate on the basis of sex in violation of the equal rights amendment to the Massachusetts Constitution. Consequently, it is subject to review only to determine whether it satisfies the rational basis test.

Because a conceivable rational basis exists upon which the Legislature could conclude that the marriage statute furthers the legitimate State purpose of ensuring, promoting, and supporting an optimal social structure for the bearing and raising of children, it is a valid exercise of the State's police power.

Civil marriage is an institution created by the State. In Massachusetts, the marriage statutes are derived from English common law. They were enacted to secure public interests and not for religious purposes or to promote personal interests or aspirations. As the court notes in its opinion, the institution of marriage is "the legal union of a man and woman as husband and wife," and it has always been so under Massachusetts law, colonial or otherwise.

The plaintiffs contend that because the right to choose to marry is a "fundamental" right, the right to marry the person of one's choice, including a member of the same sex, must also be a "fundamental" right. While the court stops short of deciding that the right to marry someone of the same sex is "fundamental" such that strict scrutiny must be applied to any statute that impairs it, it nevertheless agrees with the plaintiffs that the right to choose to marry is of fundamental importance ("among the most basic" of every person's "liberty and due process rights") and would be "hollow" if an individual was foreclosed from "freely choosing the person with whom to share . . . the . . . institution of civil marriage." Hence, it concludes that a marriage license cannot be denied to an individual who wishes to marry someone of the same sex. In reaching this result the court has transmuted the "right" to marry into a right to change the institution of marriage itself. This feat of reasoning succeeds only if one accepts the proposition that the definition of the institution of marriage as a union between a man and a woman is merely "conclusory" rather than the basis on which the "right" to partake in it has been deemed to be of fundamental importance. In other words, only by assuming that "marriage" includes the union of two persons of the same sex does the court conclude that restricting marriage to opposite-sex couples infringes on the "right" of same-sex couples to "marry."[a]

Supreme Court cases that have described marriage or the right to marry as "fundamental" have focused primarily on the underlying interest of every individual in procreation, which, historically, could only legally occur within the construct of marriage because sexual intercourse outside of marriage was a criminal act. . . . Because same-sex couples are unable to procreate on their own, any right to marriage they may possess cannot be based on their interest in procreation, which has been essential to the Supreme Court's denomination of the right to marry as fundamental.

Supreme Court cases recognizing a right to privacy in intimate decision-making have also focused primarily on sexual relations and the decision whether or not to procreate, and have refused to recognize an "unlimited right" to privacy. . . .

The marriage statute, which regulates only the act of obtaining a marriage license, does not implicate privacy in the sense that it has found constitutional protection under Massachusetts and Federal law. It does not intrude on any right that the plaintiffs have to privacy in their choices regarding procreation, an

---

a. The same semantic sleight of hand could transform every other restriction on marriage into an infringement of a right of fundamental importance. For example, if one assumes that a group of mature, consenting, committed adults can form a "marriage," the prohibition on polygamy infringes on their "right" to "marry." In legal analysis as in mathematics, it is fundamentally erroneous to assume the truth of the very thing that is to be proved.

intimate partner or sexual relations. The plaintiffs' right to privacy in such matters does not require that the State officially endorse their choices in order for the right to be constitutionally vindicated.

Although some of the privacy cases also speak in terms of personal autonomy, no court has ever recognized such an open-ended right. "That many of the rights and liberties protected by the Due Process Clause sound in personal autonomy does not warrant the sweeping conclusion that any and all important, intimate, and personal decisions are so protected. . . " Washington v. Glucksberg. Such decisions are protected not because they are important, intimate, and personal, but because the right or liberty at stake is "so deeply rooted in our history and traditions, or so fundamental to our concept of constitutionally ordered liberty" that it is protected by due process. Id. Accordingly, the Supreme Court has concluded that while the decision to refuse unwanted medical treatment is fundamental, *Cruzan*, because it is deeply rooted in our nation's history and tradition, the equally personal and profound decision to commit suicide is not because of the absence of such roots. *Glucksberg*.

While the institution of marriage is deeply rooted in the history and traditions of our country and our State, the right to marry someone of the same sex is not. No matter how personal or intimate a decision to marry someone of the same sex might be, the right to make it is not guaranteed by the right of personal autonomy.

The protected right to freedom of association, in the sense of freedom of choice "to enter into and maintain certain intimate human relationships," Roberts v. United States Jaycees, 468 U.S. 609 (1984) (as an element of liberty or due process rather than free speech), is similarly limited and unimpaired by the marriage statute. As recognized by the Supreme Court, that right affords protection only to "certain kinds of highly personal relationships," such as those between husband and wife, parent and child, and among close relatives, that "have played a critical role in the culture and traditions of the Nation," and are "deeply rooted in this Nation's history and tradition." Unlike opposite-sex marriages, which have deep historic roots, or the parent-child relationship, which reflects a "strong tradition" founded on "the history and culture of Western civilization" and "is now established beyond debate as an enduring American tradition," or extended family relationships, which have been "honored throughout our history," Moore v. East Cleveland, same-sex relationships, although becoming more accepted, are certainly not so "deeply rooted in this Nation's history and tradition" as to warrant such enhanced constitutional protection. . . .

Finally, the constitutionally protected interest in child rearing is not implicated or infringed by the marriage statute here. The fact that the plaintiffs cannot marry has no bearing on their independently protected constitutional rights as parents which, as with opposite-sex parents, are limited only by their continued fitness and the best interests of their children.

Because the rights and interests discussed above do not afford the plaintiffs any fundamental right that would be impaired by a statute limiting marriage to members of the opposite sex, they have no fundamental right to be declared "married" by the State.

Insofar as the right to marry someone of the same sex is neither found in the unique historical context of our Constitution[b] nor compelled by the meaning

---

b. The statutes from which our current marriage laws derive were enacted prior to or shortly after the adoption of our Constitution in 1780, and "may well be considered . . . as affording some light in regard to the views and intentions of [the Constitution's] founders."

ascribed by this court to the liberty and due process protections contained within it, should the court nevertheless recognize it as a fundamental right? The consequences of deeming a right to be "fundamental" are profound, and this court, as well as the Supreme Court, has been very cautious in recognizing them. Such caution is required by separation of powers principles. If a right is found to be "fundamental," it is, to a great extent, removed from "the arena of public debate and legislative action"; utmost care must be taken when breaking new ground in this field "lest the liberty protected by the Due Process Clause be subtly transformed into the policy preferences of [judges]." *Glucksberg.*

This is not to say that a statute that has no rational basis must nevertheless be upheld as long as it is of ancient origin. However, "[t]he long history of a certain practice . . . and its acceptance as an uncontroversial part of our national and State tradition do suggest that [the court] should reflect carefully before striking it down." As this court has recognized, the "fact that a challenged practice 'is followed by a large number of states . . . is plainly worth considering in determining whether the practice offends some principle of justice so rooted in the traditions and conscience of our people as to be ranked as fundamental.' "

Although public attitudes toward marriage in general and same-sex marriage in particular have changed and are still evolving, "the asserted contemporary concept of marriage and societal interests for which [plaintiffs] contend" are "manifestly [less] deeply founded" than the "historic institution" of marriage. Indeed, it is not readily apparent to what extent contemporary values have embraced the concept of same-sex marriage. Perhaps the "clearest and most reliable objective evidence of contemporary values is the legislation enacted by the country's legislatures," Atkins v. Virginia, 536 U.S. 304 (1989). No State Legislature has enacted laws permitting same-sex marriages; and a large majority of States, as well as the United States Congress, have affirmatively prohibited the recognition of such marriages for any purpose. See P. Greenberg, State Laws Affecting Lesbians and Gays, National Conference of State Legislatures Legisbriefs at 1 (April/May 2001) (reporting that, as of May, 2001, thirty-six States had enacted "defense of marriage" statutes); 1 U.S.C. § 7 (2000); 28 U.S.C. § 1738C (2000) (Federal Defense of Marriage Act).

Given this history and the current state of public opinion, as reflected in the actions of the people's elected representatives, it cannot be said that "a right to same-sex marriage is so rooted in the traditions and collective conscience of our people that failure to recognize it would violate the fundamental principles of liberty and justice that lie at the base of all our civil and political institutions. Neither . . . [is] a right to same-sex marriage . . . implicit in the concept of ordered liberty, such that neither liberty nor justice would exist if it were sacrificed."

[I]n his concurrence, Justice Greaney contends that the marriage statute constitutes discrimination on the basis of sex in violation of art. 1 of the Declaration of Rights as amended by art. 106 of the Amendments to the Constitution of the Commonwealth, the Equal Rights Amendment (ERA). . . . The central purpose of the ERA was to eradicate discrimination against women and in favor of men or vice versa. Consistent with this purpose, we have construed the ERA to prohibit laws that advantage one sex at the expense of the other, but not laws that treat men and women equally. The Massachusetts marriage statute does not subject men to different treatment from women; each is equally prohibited from precisely the same conduct.

Of course, a statute that on its face treats protected groups equally may still harm, stigmatize, or advantage one over the other. Such was the circumstance in Loving v. Virginia, where the Supreme Court struck down a State statute that made interracial marriage a crime, as constituting invidious discrimination on the basis of race. While the statute purported to apply equally to whites and nonwhites, the Court found that it was intended and structured to favor one race (white) and disfavor all others (nonwhites). The statute's legislative history demonstrated that its purpose was not merely to punish interracial marriage, but to do so for the sole benefit of the white race. As the Supreme Court readily concluded, the Virginia law was "designed to maintain White Supremacy." Consequently, there was a fit between the class that the law was intended to discriminate against (nonwhite races) and the classification enjoying heightened protection (race).

By contrast, here there is no evidence that limiting marriage to opposite-sex couples was motivated by sexism in general or a desire to disadvantage men or women in particular. Moreover, no one has identified any harm, burden, disadvantage, or advantage accruing to either gender as a consequence of the Massachusetts marriage statute. In the absence of such effect, the statute limiting marriage to couples of the opposite sex does not violate the ERA's prohibition of sex discrimination.

This conclusion is buttressed by the legislative history of the ERA. . . . [A special state commission created by the legislature reporting on the likely effect of the proposed ERA on the laws of the Commonwealth stated that] "An equal rights amendment will have no effect upon the allowance or denial of homosexual marriages. The equal rights amendment is not concerned with the relationship of two persons of the same sex; it only addresses those laws or public-related actions which treat persons of opposite sexes differently." The views of the commission were reflected in the public debate surrounding the passage of the ERA that focused on gender equality. Claims that the ERA might be the basis for validating marriages between same-sex couples were labelled as "exaggerated" and "unfounded." For example, before the vote, the Boston Globe published an editorial discussing and urging favorable action on the ERA. In making its case, it noted that "[t]hose urging a no vote . . . argue that the amendment would . . . legitimize marriage between people of the same sex [and other changes]." In reality, the proposed amendment would require none of these things. Mass. ballot issues . . . 1 Equal Rights Amendment. Boston Globe, Nov. 1, 1976, at 29. . . . While the court, in interpreting a constitutional amendment, is not bound to accept either the views of a legislative commission studying and reporting on the amendment's likely effects, or of public commentary and debate contemporaneous with its passage, it ought to be wary of completely disregarding what appears to be the clear intent of the people recently recorded in our constitutional history. This is particularly so where the plain wording of the amendment does not require the result it would reach.

[T]he burden of demonstrating that a statute does not satisfy the rational basis standard rests on the plaintiffs. It is a weighty one. "[A] reviewing court will presume a statute's validity, and make all rational inferences in favor of it. . . . The Legislature is not required to justify its classifications, nor provide a record or finding in support of them." . . .

Paramount among its many important functions, the institution of marriage has systematically provided for the regulation of heterosexual behavior, brought order to the resulting procreation, and ensured a stable family structure in which children will be reared, educated, and socialized. Admittedly, heterosexual inter-course, procreation, and child care are not necessarily conjoined (particularly in the modern age of widespread effective contraception and supportive social welfare programs), but an orderly society requires some mechanism for coping with the fact that sexual intercourse commonly results in pregnancy and childbirth. The institution of marriage is that mechanism.

The institution of marriage provides the important legal and normative link between heterosexual intercourse and procreation on the one hand and family responsibilities on the other. The partners in a marriage are expected to engage in exclusive sexual relations, with children the probable result and paternity presumed. Whereas the relationship between mother and child is demonstratively and predictably created and recognizable through the biological process of preg-nancy and childbirth, there is no corresponding process for creating a relationship between father and child. Similarly, aside from an act of heterosexual intercourse nine months prior to childbirth, there is no process for creating a relationship between a man and a woman as the parents of a particular child. The institution of marriage fills this void by formally binding the husband-father to his wife and child, and imposing on him the responsibilities of fatherhood. The alternative, a society without the institution of marriage, in which heterosexual intercourse, procreation, and child care are largely disconnected processes, would be chaotic.

The marital family is also the foremost setting for the education and socializa-tion of children. Children learn about the world and their place in it primarily from those who raise them, and those children eventually grow up to exert some influ-ence, great or small, positive or negative, on society. The institution of marriage encourages parents to remain committed to each other and to their children as they grow, thereby encouraging a stable venue for the education and socialization of children. More macroscopically, construction of a family through marriage also formalizes the bonds between people in an ordered and institutional manner, thereby facilitating a foundation of interconnectedness and interdependency on which more intricate stabilizing social structures might be built. . . .

It is undeniably true that dramatic historical shifts in our cultural, political, and economic landscape have altered some of our traditional notions about marriage. . . . Nevertheless, the institution of marriage remains the principal weave of our social fabric. A family defined by heterosexual marriage continues to be the most prevalent social structure into which the vast majority of children are born, nurtured, and prepared for productive participation in civil society, see Children's Living Arrangements and Characteristics: March, 2002, United States Census Bureau Current Population Reports at 3 (June, 2003) (in 2002, 69% of children lived with two married parents, 23% lived with their mother, 5% lived with their father, and 4% lived in households with neither parent present).

It is difficult to imagine a State purpose more important and legitimate than ensuring, promoting, and supporting an optimal social structure within which to bear and raise children. At the very least, the marriage statute continues to serve this important State purpose.

[T]he question we must turn to next is whether the statute, construed as limiting marriage to couples of the opposite sex, remains a rational way to further that purpose. Stated differently, we ask whether a conceivable rational basis exists on which the Legislature could conclude that continuing to limit the institution of civil marriage to members of the opposite sex furthers the legitimate purpose of ensuring, promoting, and supporting an optimal social structure for the bearing and raising of children.

In considering whether such a rational basis exists, we defer to the decision-making process of the Legislature, and must make deferential assumptions about the information that it might consider and on which it may rely. We must assume that the Legislature (1) might conclude that the institution of civil marriage has successfully and continually provided this structure over several centuries; (2) might consider and credit studies that document negative consequences that too often follow children either born outside of marriage or raised in households lacking either a father or a mother figure, and scholarly commentary contending that children and families develop best when mothers and fathers are partners in their parenting; and (3) would be familiar with many recent studies that variously support the proposition that children raised in intact families headed by same-sex couples fare as well on many measures as children raised in similar families headed by opposite-sex couples; support the proposition that children of same-sex couples fare worse on some measures; or reveal notable differences between the two groups of children that warrant further study.

We must also assume that the Legislature would be aware of the critiques of the methodologies used in virtually all of the comparative studies of children raised in these different environments, cautioning that the sampling populations are not representative, that the observation periods are too limited in time, that the empirical data are unreliable, and that the hypotheses are too infused with political or agenda driven bias.

Taking all of this available information into account, the Legislature could rationally conclude that a family environment with married opposite-sex parents remains the optimal social structure in which to bear children, and that the raising of children by same-sex couples, who by definition cannot be the two sole biological parents of a child and cannot provide children with a parental authority figure of each gender, presents an alternative structure for child rearing that has not yet proved itself beyond reasonable scientific dispute to be as optimal as the biologically based marriage norm. Working from the assumption that a recognition of same-sex marriages will increase the number of children experiencing this alternative, the Legislature could conceivably conclude that declining to recognize same-sex marriages remains prudent until empirical questions about its impact on the upbringing of children are resolved.

The fact that the Commonwealth currently allows same-sex couples to adopt does not affect the rationality of this conclusion. The eligibility of a child for adoption presupposes that at least one of the child's biological parents is unable or unwilling, for some reason, to participate in raising the child. In that sense, society has "lost" the optimal setting in which to raise that child — it is simply not available. In these circumstances, the principal and overriding consideration is the "best interests of the child," considering his or her unique circumstances and the options that are available for that child. The objective is an individualized determination of the best environment for a particular child, where the normative social structure — a home with both the child's biological father and mother — is not an option. That such a focused determination may lead to the approval of a same-sex couple's adoption of a child does not mean that it would be irrational for a legislator, in fashioning statutory laws that cannot make such individualized determinations, to conclude generally that being raised by a same-sex couple has not yet been shown to be the absolute equivalent of being raised by one's married biological parents.

That the State does not preclude different types of families from raising children does not mean that it must view them all as equally optimal and equally deserving of State endorsement and support. For example, single persons are allowed to adopt children, but the fact that the Legislature permits single-parent adoption does not mean that it has endorsed single parenthood as an optimal setting in which to raise children or views it as the equivalent of being raised by both of one's biological parents. The same holds true with respect to same-sex couples — the fact that they may adopt children means only that the Legislature has concluded that they may provide an acceptable setting in which to raise children who cannot be raised by both of their biological parents. The Legislature may rationally permit adoption by same-sex couples yet harbor reservations as to whether parenthood by same-sex couples should be affirmatively encouraged to the same extent as parenthood by the heterosexual couple whose union produced the child.

In addition, the Legislature could conclude that redefining the institution of marriage to permit same-sex couples to marry would impair the State's interest in promoting and supporting heterosexual marriage as the social institution that it has determined best normalizes, stabilizes, and links the acts of procreation and child rearing. While the plaintiffs argue that they only want to take part in the same stabilizing institution, the Legislature conceivably could conclude that permitting their participation would have the unintended effect of undermining to some degree marriage's ability to serve its social purpose.

As long as marriage is limited to opposite-sex couples who can at least theoretically procreate, society is able to communicate a consistent message to its citizens that marriage is a (normatively) necessary part of their procreative endeavor; that if they are to procreate, then society has endorsed the institution of marriage as the environment for it and for the subsequent rearing of their children; and that benefits are available explicitly to create a supportive and conducive atmosphere for those purposes. If society proceeds similarly to recognize marriages between same-sex couples who cannot procreate, it could be perceived as an abandonment of this claim, and might result in the mistaken view that civil marriage has little to do with procreation: just as the potential of procreation would not be necessary for a marriage to be valid, marriage would not be necessary for optimal procreation and child rearing to occur.[c] In essence, the Legislature could conclude that the

---

c. The court contends that the exclusive and permanent commitment of the marriage partnership rather than the begetting of children is the sine qua non of civil marriage, and that "the 'marriage is procreation' argument singles out the one unbridgeable difference between same-sex and opposite-sex couples, and transforms that difference into the essence of legal marriage." The court has it backward. Civil marriage is the product of society's critical need to manage procreation as the inevitable consequence of intercourse between members of the opposite sex. Procreation has always been at the root of marriage and the reasons for its existence as a social institution. Its structure, one man and one woman committed for life, reflects society's judgment as how optimally to manage procreation and the resultant child rearing. The court, in attempting to divorce procreation from marriage, transforms the form of the structure into its purpose. In doing so, it turns history on its head.

The court compounds its error by likening the marriage statute to Colorado's "Amendment 2," which was struck by the United States Supreme Court in Romer v. Evans. That amendment repealed all Colorado laws and ordinances that barred discrimination against homosexuals, and prohibited any governmental entity from adopting similar statutes. The amendment withdrew from homosexuals, but no others, legal protection from a broad range of injuries caused by private and governmental discrimination, "imposing a broad and undifferentiated disability on a single named group." As the Court noted, its sheer breadth seems "inexplicable by anything but animus toward the class it affects." Id. The comparison to the Massachusetts marriage statute, which limits the institution of marriage (created to manage procreation) to opposite-sex couples who can theoretically procreate, is completely inapposite.

consequence of such a policy shift would be a diminution in society's ability to steer the acts of procreation and child rearing into their most optimal setting.[d]

The court recognizes this concern, but brushes it aside with the assumption that permitting same-sex couples to marry "will not diminish the validity or dignity of opposite-sex marriage, and that "we have no doubt that marriage will continue to be a vibrant and revered institution." Whether the court is correct in its assumption is irrelevant. What is relevant is that such predicting is not the business of the courts. A rational Legislature, given the evidence, could conceivably come to a different conclusion, or could at least harbor rational concerns about possible unintended consequences of a dramatic redefinition of marriage.[e]

There is no question that many same-sex couples are capable of being good parents, and should be (and are) permitted to be so. The policy question that a legislator must resolve is a different one, and turns on an assessment of whether the marriage structure proposed by the plaintiffs will, over time, if endorsed and supported by the State, prove to be as stable and successful a model as the one that has formed a cornerstone of our society since colonial times, or prove to be less than optimal, and result in consequences, perhaps now unforeseen, adverse to the State's legitimate interest in promoting and supporting the best possible social structure in which children should be born and raised. Given the critical importance of civil marriage as an organizing and stabilizing institution of society, it is eminently rational for the Legislature to postpone making fundamental changes to it until such time as there is unanimous scientific evidence, or popular consensus, or both, that such changes can safely be made.

There is no reason to believe that legislative processes are inadequate to effectuate legal changes in response to evolving evidence, social values, and views of fairness on the subject of same-sex relationships. Deliberate consideration of, and incremental responses to rapidly evolving scientific and social understanding is the norm of the political process — that it may seem painfully slow to those who are already persuaded by the arguments in favor of change is not a sufficient basis to conclude that the processes are constitutionally infirm. The advancement of the rights, privileges, and protections afforded to homosexual members of our community in the last three decades has been significant, and there is no reason to believe that that evolution will not continue. Changes of attitude in the civic, social, and professional communities have been even more profound. Thirty years ago, The Diagnostic and

---

d. Although the marriage statute is overinclusive because it comprehends within its scope infertile or voluntarily nonreproductive opposite-sex couples, this overinclusiveness does not make the statute constitutionally infirm. The overinclusiveness present here is constitutionally permissible because the Commonwealth has chosen, reasonably, not to test every prospective married couple for fertility and not to demand of fertile prospective married couples whether or not they will procreate. It is satisfied, rather, to allow every couple whose biological opposition makes procreation theoretically possible to join the institution.

e. Concerns about such unintended consequences cannot be dismissed as fanciful or far-fetched. Legislative actions taken in the 1950's and 1960's in areas as widely arrayed as domestic relations law and welfare legislation have had significant unintended adverse consequences in subsequent decades including the dramatic increase in children born out of wedlock, and the destabilization of the institution of marriage. See Nonmarital Childbearing in the United States 1940-99, National Center for Health Statistics, 48 Nat'l Vital Stat. Reps. at 2 (Oct. 2000) (nonmarital childbirths increased from 3.8% of annual births in 1940 to 33% in 1999); M.D. Bramlett, Cohabitation, Marriage, Divorce, and Remarriage in the United States, National Center for Health Statistics, Vital & Health Stat. at 4-5 (July 2002) (due to higher divorce rates and postponement of marriage, proportion of people's lives spent in marriage declined significantly during later half of Twentieth Century).

Statistical Manual, the seminal handbook of the American Psychiatric Association, still listed homosexuality as a mental disorder. Today, the Massachusetts Psychiatric Society, the American Psychoanalytic Association, and many other psychiatric, psychological, and social science organizations have joined in an amicus brief on behalf of the plaintiffs' cause. A body of experience and evidence has provided the basis for change, and that body continues to mount. The Legislature is the appropriate branch, both constitutionally and practically, to consider and respond to it. It is not enough that we as Justices might be personally of the view that we have learned enough to decide what is best. So long as the question is at all debatable, it must be the Legislature that decides. The marriage statute thus meets the requirements of the rational basis test. . . . While the courageous efforts of many have resulted in increased dignity, rights, and respect for gay and lesbian members of our community, the issue presented here is a profound one, deeply rooted in social policy, that must, for now, be the subject of legislative not judicial action.

Discussion

1. *Staying the mandate.* The Massachusetts Court stayed the mandate for 180 days, until May 17, 2004, the fiftieth anniversary of Brown v. Board of Education. The purpose of the stay was to give the Massachusetts legislature time to consider new legislation. The legislature asked the Supreme Judicial Court for an advisory opinion (permissible in the Massachusetts courts, unlike the federal courts) whether a ban on same-sex marriage coupled with a civil unions law granting all of the benefits of marriage would satisfy *Goodridge.* The Court held that it would not. Opinions of the Justices to the Senate, 440 Mass. 1201, 802 N.E.2d 565 (2004). In response, on March 29, 2004, the Massachusetts legislature passed a proposed a constitutional amendment to the same effect. Rick Klein, Vote Ties Unions to Gay-Marriage Ban. Boston Globe, March 30, 2004. Under the Massachusetts Constitution, the proposed amendment must be passed again during the 2005-2006 legislative session and approved in a statewide election in November 2006 to become law. A separate effort is underway to pass a state constitutional amendment that would ban gay marriage *without* creating civil unions; the earliest this proposal could appear on the ballot would be 2008. See Raphael Lewis, Romney Backs New Effort to Prohibit Gay Marriages, Boston Globe, June 17, 2005, at A1. In the meantime, on May 17, the *Goodridge* opinion went into effect and Massachusetts began marrying same-sex couples.

2. *Doing more by doing less? Vermont versus Massachusetts.* Compare *Goodridge* with Baker v. State, 744 A.2d 864 (Vt. 2000), in which the Supreme Court of Vermont held that denying same-sex couples the various benefits and protections that come from the right to marry violated the Common Benefits Clause of the Vermont state constitution. The court did not, however, order that the plaintiffs receive marriage licenses. Instead, it held that "[t]he effect of the [lower] Court's decision is suspended, and jurisdiction is retained in this Court, to permit the Legislature to consider and enact legislation consistent with the constitutional mandate described herein." The Vermont Legislature now had a "constitutional mandate" "to craft an appropriate means" of giving same-sex couples the "same benefits and protections afforded by Vermont law to married opposite-sex couples." The court noted that this might involve either the extension of marriage rights to same-sex couples or a "domestic partnership" with similar rights and benefits.

Justice Johnson, concurring in part and dissenting in part, criticized the majority's remedial approach: "[A]bsent 'compelling' reasons that dictate otherwise, it is not only the prerogative but the duty of courts to provide prompt relief for violations of individual civil rights. This basic principle is designed to assure that laws enacted through the will of the majority do not unconstitutionally infringe upon the rights of a disfavored minority. . . . During the civil rights movement of the 1960's, state and local governments defended segregation or gradual desegregation on the grounds that mixing the races would lead to interracial disturbances. The Supreme Court's 'compelling answer' to that contention was 'that constitutional rights may not be denied simply because of hostility to their assertion or exercise.' ". . . "While the laudatory goals of preserving institutional credibility and public confidence in our government may require elected bodies to wait for changing attitudes concerning public morals, those same goals require courts to act independently and decisively to protect civil rights guaranteed by our Constitution."

The majority responded: "We do not confront in this case the evil that was institutionalized racism . . . Plaintiffs have not demonstrated that the exclusion of same-sex couples from the definition of marriage was intended to discriminate against women or lesbians and gay men, as racial segregation was designed to maintain the pernicious doctrine of white supremacy. . . ."

Defending itself against Justice Johnson's charge that "our mandate represents an 'abdicat[ion]' of the constitutional duty to decide," the majority responded that "our opinion provides greater recognition of — and protection for — same sex relationships than has been recognized by any court of final jurisdiction in this country with the instructive exception of the Hawaii Supreme Court" in Baehr v. Lewin, 852 P.2d 44 (1993), which required same-sex marriage. That decision met with a political backlash and was superseded by a state constitutional amendment that gave the legislature the power "to reserve marriage to opposite-sex couples." The majority in *Baker* concluded that "[t]he concurring and dissenting opinion confuses decisiveness with wisdom and judicial authority with finality."

Following the court's December 20, 1999 decision in *Baker*, the Vermont Legislature passed a measure authorizing a new species of "civil unions." The bill establishing civil unions was signed into law by the Governor on April 26, 2000, and took effect on July 1, 2000. It allows any two adults of the same sex who are not closely related by blood to apply for a license for a civil union. Marriage is specifically reserved for opposite-sex couples, who may not enter into civil unions. Partners in civil unions enjoy virtually all of the same rights (and obligations) as married couples. In particular, partners in civil unions are protected by laws prohibiting discrimination based on marital status, have rights of inheritance, and have the right to make medical decisions for their partners. They must go to family court to dissolve their unions. Vermont civil unions are not, however, recognized by federal law and it is as yet unclear which, if any, states will recognize them. Thus, the benefits and obligations of civil unions may not be portable outside the state of Vermont.

3. *Backlash effects.* Do you agree more with the approach of the Vermont Supreme Court in *Baker* in 1999 or the Massachusetts Supreme Judicial Court in *Goodridge* in 2003? Was the Vermont Court simply very lucky that the Legislature produced a domestic partnership law so quickly? Would you have recommended the same strategy in a state much less liberal (or libertarian) than Vermont appears to have been

in 1999? Suppose that the Vermont legislature had produced a law that differed from marriage in important respects — for example with respect to support and custody issues, the right to inherit, or the right to make medical decisions for the other partner. Should the Vermont Supreme Court have struck the new law down and sent it back until it was substantially equal to Vermont's marriage laws? If so, what was the point of the original remand? Is it better that legislatures pass controversial laws, even with a "constitutional gun to their heads" as in *Baker,* than for controversial changes in the law to come wholly from courts, as in *Goodridge*?

Suppose that the Vermont Supreme Court had accepted Justice Johnson's position and simply ordered that the marriage laws henceforth be read to include same-sex couples. There is a danger — just as in the post-*Brown* South — that the political branches would have engaged in a series of measures to defeat the effect of the decision, arguing that it was the court's creation of new law out of whole cloth and an inappropriate form of "social engineering." (To this day, the Supreme Court's school prayer decisions from the 1960's onward are only fitfully enforced in parts of the country.)

Adopting the Supreme Judicial Court's strategy might also have larger, long-term backlash effects in American politics. Note that the Massachusetts legislature promptly began a process of amending the state constitution in response to *Goodridge,* and, as the court noted in Baker v. State, both Hawaii and Alaska passed constitutional amendments in response to judicial decisions legalizing same-sex marriage. Moreover, unlike Baker v. State, the *Goodridge* opinion quickly became a national cause celebre. Cultural conservatives within the Republican Party repeatedly employed *Goodridge* as a wedge issue to appeal to voters, while conservative candidates (including President Bush) in the 2004 elections ran against "activist judges" in Massachusetts who would destroy marriage and impose same-sex marriage on unwilling states. During the 2004 elections, 11 states passed amendments to their constitution prohibiting same-sex marriage. See Alan Cooperman, Same-Sex Bans Fuel Conservative Agenda, The Washington Post, Thursday, November 4, 2004, at p. A39. On the other hand, between February 2004 and March 2005, the percentage of Massachusetts voters who supported gay marriage increased from 35 percent to 56 percent. Deb Price, The Sky Didn't Fall in Mass, USA Today, May 17, 2005, at 13A. Was *Goodridge* on the whole a good thing for the cause of gay rights? Is it simply too soon to tell? Should any of this be relevant to how a court should decide a case like *Goodridge*?

Does the *Baker* court's approach — ordering the legislature to act — make it more difficult for the legislature (or politicians outside the state) to blame the court for same-sex marriage, or to engage in resistance or nonacquiesence? Couldn't legislators point out that the court was forcing them to legislate? Why couldn't the legislature simply refuse to act and force the court to issue a mandate, and then blame the court for issuing it?

Given that all of these scenarios are possible, the wisdom of the *Baker* court's decision seems to turn on how well it predicted what the Vermont legislature would do. Are courts particularly well suited to engage in this kind of political prediction? After all, if courts have no special political skills — and indeed, are supposed to be isolated from day-to-day political struggle — there is no reason to think that they are particularly well-suited to know when to push hard and when to back off, or when and under what conditions their restraint will be catalytic or synergistic. Put another way, if courts lack wisdom, why don't they also lack political savvy? If so, what precisely should courts do in cases like *Baker* or *Goodridge*?

4. *Rational basis.* Why did the Supreme Judicial Court decide *Goodridge* on rational basis grounds? Many state courts employ somewhat closer scrutiny for rational basis review than the U.S. Supreme Court. However, even taking this fact into account, is it clear that a distinction between same-sex and opposite-sex couples cannot pass rational basis review, especially if the court is permitted to assume *any* facts the legislature may have reasonably believed to be the case? Does the ban on same-sex marriage qualify as invidious discrimination designed to harm homosexuals, as in Romer v. Evans? Should the ban be scrutinized under the "more searching form of rational basis review" that Justice O'Connor advocated in her concurrence in *Lawrence*?

5. *Vanguardism: Courts versus the political branches.* In February 2004, the Mayor of San Francisco stated his opinion that Proposition 22, California's statutory ban on same-sex marriage, violated the California Constitution, and he instructed the city clerk to issue marriage licenses to same-sex couples beginning on February 14, 2004, Valentine's Day. This continued for 29 days until the California courts stayed the practice pending litigation of the constitutional issues. Several other state and municipal officials in various other jurisdictions, including Multnomah County, Oregon, adopted a similar strategy. In most cases, courts or other state officials halted further issuance of marriage licenses to same-sex couples.

State executive officials and state courts alike are sworn to uphold the law and their respective state constitutions. Is the decision of a mayor to begin issuing marriage licenses based on his or her interpretation of the state constitution more or less problematic than the decision of a court? On what grounds?

6. *DOMA.* In response to concerns that Hawaii might permit same-sex marriages, Congress passed and President Clinton signed into law the Defense of Marriage Act (DOMA) in 1996. Section 1 of DOMA forbids any federal recognition of same-sex marriages for purposes including income tax rules concerning marriage and Social Security benefits. Section 2 of DOMA relieves states from giving full faith and credit to "any public act, record, or judicial proceeding . . . respecting a relationship between persons of the same sex." (Presumably this refers to other forms of domestic partnership recognition short of marriage.) One constitutional issue raised by DOMA is whether the statute is consistent with Article IV §1, which provides that "Full Faith and Credit shall be given in each State to the public Acts, and Records, and judicial Proceedings of every other State."

Although the Supreme Court has held that divorces are "judgments" that must be recognized in all states, unless the state of divorce lacked subject matter jurisdiction, Williams v. North Carolina, 317 U.S. 287 (1942), it has never held the same for marriages. However, marriages are arguably "acts" or "records" for Full Faith and Credit purposes. If so, then one important question is whether the clause admits of no exceptions or whether, as some commentators have suggested, states may refuse to give recognition to marriages that violate their public policy.[106]

---

106. See generally Homer H. Clark, Jr., Law of Domestic Relations in the United States 85-88 (2d ed., student ed., 1988); Joseph W. Hovermill, A Conflict of Laws and Morals: The Choice of Law Implications of Hawaii's Recognition of Same-Sex Marriages, 53 Md. L. Rev. 450 (1994); Jennifer G. Brown, Competitive Federalism and the Legislative Incentives to Recognize Same-Sex Marriage, 68 S. Cal. L. Rev. 745 (1995); Andrew Koppelman, Dumb and DOMA: Why the Defense of Marriage Act is Unconstitutional, 83 Iowa L. Rev. 1, 22-23 (1997); Larry Kramer, Same-Sex Marriage, Conflict of Laws, and the Unconstitutional Public Policy Exception, 106 Yale L.J. 1965 (1997).

Another possibility is that DOMA is constitutional under Congress's powers under Article IV, §1, which states that "the Congress may by general Laws prescribe the Manner in which such Acts, Records, and Proceedings shall be proved, and the Effect thereof." Supporters of DOMA argue that Congress is merely refusing to give effect to same-sex marriages or other forms of domestic partnership. Could Congress do the same with respect to divorces?

7. *The proposed Federal Marriage Amendment.* The Federal Marriage Amendment (FMA) was introduced by Rep. Marilyn Musgrave (R-Colorado) in June 2003. President Bush endorsed it in February 2004. As initially proposed, the FMA provides: "Marriage in the United States shall consist only of the union of a man and a woman. Neither this Constitution, nor the constitution of any State, nor state or federal law, shall be construed to require that marriage or the legal incidents thereof be conferred upon any union other than the union of a man and a woman." Would this amendment permit federal or state executive officials to enforce civil unions laws passed by state legislatures? What if the words "nor state or federal law" are removed?

8. *The miscegenation analogy.* Justice Greaney's concurrence in *Goodridge* invokes Loving v. Virginia to argue that the ban on same-sex marriage discriminates on the basis of sex and violates the fundamental right to marry. Andrew Koppelman has made an elaborate comparison between the taboo against interracial marriage and the taboo against same-sex marriage as part of his larger claim, discussed earlier, that sexual orientation discrimination is a form of sex discrimination. Andrew Koppelman, Why Discrimination Against Lesbians and Gay Men Is Sex Discrimination, 69 N.Y.U. L. Rev. 197, 235-236 (1994). Both taboos against miscegenation and same-sex relations assume the hierarchical significance of sexual intercourse and the polluted and degraded status of the penetrated person. Miscegenation threatened white supremacy because it called into question the distinctive and superior status of being white; homosexuality threatens male supremacy because it calls into question the distinctive and superior status of being male. Gay men and lesbians, respectively, are guilty of one aspect of the dual crime of the miscegenating white woman: self-degradation and insubordination.

The *Loving* analogy is not without its flaws. Keeping whites and blacks from marrying presumably preserved White Supremacy by preventing racial mixing and preserving the purity of the white race, but also, and perhaps equally important, by establishing and preserving the notion blacks are not "good enough" to be social equals with whites. (Recall that intermarriage and social equality of blacks and whites became virtually synonymous in the South in the late nineteenth century.) Perhaps preventing same-sex unions preserves male supremacy because it preserves the (heterosexual) social meaning of gender, but it is not because we fear the mixing of offspring of men and men or because we think that men are not "good enough" to marry men (or for that matter, that women are not "good enough" to marry women).

In Chapter 7 we also noted arguments that intermediate scrutiny of sex classifications calls into question sex-differentiated roles in marriage. In traditional conceptions of marriage, one partner (the woman) is subordinated to and dependent upon another partner (the man). Gay and lesbian marriages violate these gender role expectations, and therefore undermine traditional notions of marriage as a site for female subordination and dependency. Nevertheless, when the state limits marriage to men and women, does it actually promote traditional notions of female dependence or gender stereotypes? Couldn't the state respond that it may limit marriage to opposite-sex couples without contributing to the subordination of women? What, precisely, is the causal connection between allowing same-sex marriages and improving the condition of women in heterosexual marriages?

9. *Sex discrimination or sexual orientation discrimination?* How do we know that Massachusetts's law involves sex discrimination rather than sexual orientation discrimination? If it is sex discrimination, why isn't the Don't Ask Don't Tell (DADT) policy also sex discrimination, because it defines homosexual acts and homosexuality in terms of same-sex conduct? Of course, if one accepts Koppelman's argument, the two forms of discrimination tend to collapse. Recall Balkin's argument that sexual orientation discrimination is not sex discrimination but a separate form of social inequality that comes from enforcing gender roles and gender definitions. Hence prohibitions on same-sex marriage are troublesome not because they help to oppress women, but because they demand that people abide by particular fixed gender roles (that also tend to privilege all things coded masculine over all things coded feminine).

The advantage of Greaney's and Koppelman's approach for gay rights advocates is that it employs existing doctrinal categories that already justify heightened scrutiny. But as Bill Eskridge points out, "[t]here is a transvestite quality to the argument. . . . It dresses a gay rights issue up in gender rights garb."[107] Even if there is a short-run advantage with this strategy, is there a long-term disadvantage? Eskridge argues that bans on same-sex marriage are both sex discrimination and sexual orientation discrimination. He claims that using both approaches together "in a two-pronged attack" creates "argumentative dilemmas" for states attempting to ban same-sex marriage:

> For example, if [the state] argues that the sexual orientation discrimination is justified by the state interest in procreation, the state is helping to prove the sex discrimination case, which posits that it is an unacceptable gender stereotype that women get married so that they can be baby producers. If the state argues that the sex discrimination is a benign classification not aimed against women . . . , it is helping to prove the sexual orientation discrimination case, which posits that the classification is targeted at gay and lesbian couples. The double-barrelled argument of sex and sexual orientation discrimination ought to be enough, standing alone, to shoot down the state's prohibition against same-sex marriages. When you add the constitutional arguments based on citizens' fundamental right to marry, the constitutional case becomes irrefutable.

Do you agree?

---

107. William N. Eskridge, Jr., The Case for Same-Sex Marriage: From Sexual Liberty to Civilized Commitment 172, 182 (1996).

VII. *Fundamental Rights in the Face of Death*

A.   The Right to Refuse Treatment

CRUZAN v. DIRECTOR, MISSOURI DEPARTMENT OF HEALTH
497 U.S. 261 (1990)

[Following severe injuries sustained during an automobile accident and unsuccessful efforts at rehabilitation, Nancy Cruzan was placed in a Missouri state hospital "in what is commonly referred to as a persistent vegetative state: generally, a condition in which a person exhibits motor reflexes but evinces no indications of significant cognitive function." She was kept alive as the result of use of artificial hydration and feeding equipment, paid for by the State of Missouri. Nancy's parents "sought a court order directing the withdrawal of their daughter's artificial feeding and hydration equipment after it became apparent that she had virtually no chance of recovering her cognitive faculties." Although the trial court granted the request, the Missouri Supreme Court reversed, holding that no one can decide that life-sustaining medical support should be withdrawn from a person "in the absence of the formalities required under Missouri's Living Will statutes or the clear and convincing, inherently reliable evidence" that the person would have desired the withdrawal. Nancy's parents appealed, claiming that Missouri's refusal to allow the withdrawal violated her constitutional right "to withdraw life-sustaining treatment from her under these circumstances."]

REHNQUIST, C.J., delivered the opinion of the Court.

[Chief Justice Rehnquist, in the course of analyzing the common law and statutory law of the states, noted that "the notion of bodily integrity has been embodied in the requirement that informed consent is generally required for medical treatment" and that "[t]he informed consent doctrine has become firmly entrenched in American tort law."]

The logical corollary of the doctrine of informed consent is that the patient generally possesses the right not to consent, that is, to refuse treatment. Until about 15 years ago and the seminal decision in In re Quinlan, 70 N.J. 10, 355 A.2d 647 (1976), the number of right-to-refuse-treatment decisions were relatively few. Most of the earlier cases involved patients who refused medical treatment forbidden by their religious beliefs, thus implicating First Amendment rights as well as common law rights of self-determination. More recently, however, with the advance of medical technology capable of sustaining life well past the point where natural forces would have brought certain death in earlier times, cases involving the right to refuse life-sustaining treatment have burgeoned. [T]he common-law doctrine of informed consent is viewed as generally encompassing the right of a competent individual to refuse medical treatment. . . .

In this Court, the question is simply and starkly whether the United States Constitution prohibits Missouri from choosing the rule of decision which it did. [The] principle that a competent person has a constitutionally protected liberty interest in refusing unwanted medical treatment may be inferred from our prior decisions. In Jacobson v. Massachusetts, 197 U.S. 11 (1905), for instance, the Court balanced an individual's liberty interest in declining an unwanted smallpox vaccine against the State's interest in preventing disease. . . .

Just this Term, in the course of holding that a State's procedures for administering antipsychotic medication to prisoners were sufficient to satisfy due process concerns, we recognized that prisoners possess "a significant liberty interest in avoiding the unwanted administration of antipsychotic drugs under the Due Process Clause of the Fourteenth Amendment." Washington v. Harper, 494 U.S. 210, (1990).

. . . [F]or purposes of this case, we assume that the United States Constitution would grant a competent person a constitutionally protected right to refuse lifesaving hydration and nutrition.

Petitioners go on to assert that an incompetent person should possess the same right [to refuse lifesaving treatment] as is possessed by a competent person. [The] difficulty with petitioners' claim is that in a sense it begs the question: an incompetent person is not able to make an informed and voluntary choice to exercise a hypothetical right to refuse treatment or any other right. Such a "right" must be exercised for her, if at all, by some sort of surrogate. Here, Missouri has in effect recognized that under certain circumstances a surrogate may act for the patient in electing to have hydration and nutrition withdrawn in such a way as to cause death, but it has established a procedural safeguard to assure that the action of the surrogate conforms as best it may to the wishes expressed by the patient while competent. Missouri requires that evidence of the incompetent's wishes as to the withdrawal of treatment be proved by clear and convincing evidence. The question, then, is whether the United States Constitution forbids the establishment of this procedural requirement by the State. We hold that it does not.

. . . Missouri relies on its interest in the protection and preservation of human life, and there can be no gainsaying this interest. [T]he majority of States in this country have laws imposing criminal penalties on one who assists another to commit suicide. We do not think a State is required to remain neutral in the face of an informed and voluntary decision by a physically-able adult to starve to death.

But in the context presented here, a State has more particular interests at stake. The choice between life and death is a deeply personal decision of obvious and overwhelming finality. We believe Missouri may legitimately seek to safeguard the personal element of this choice through the imposition of heightened evidentiary requirements. . . . Not all incompetent patients will have loved ones available to serve as surrogate decisionmakers. And even where family members are present, "[t]here will, of course, be some unfortunate situations in which family members will not act to protect a patient." A State is entitled to guard against potential abuses in such situations. Similarly, a State is entitled to consider that a judicial proceeding to make a determination regarding an incompetent's wishes may very well not be an adversarial one, with the added guarantee of accurate factfinding that the adversary process brings with it. Finally, we think a State may properly decline to make judgments about the "quality" of life that a particular individual may enjoy, and simply assert an unqualified interest in the preservation of human life to be weighed against the constitutionally protected interests of the individual.

In our view, Missouri has permissibly sought to advance these interests through the adoption of a "clear and convincing" standard of proof to govern such proceedings. [We] think it self-evident that the interests at stake in the instant proceedings are more substantial, both on an individual and societal level, than those in a run of the mill civil dispute. . . .

[T]he Missouri trial court . . . found that the evidence "suggest[ed]" Nancy Cruzan would not have desired to continue [hydration and nutrition], but . . . had not adopted the standard of "clear and convincing evidence" enunciated by the [Missouri] Supreme Court. The testimony adduced at trial consisted primarily of Nancy Cruzan's statement that she would not want to live should she face life as a "vegetable," and other observations to the same effect. The observations did not deal in terms [of] withdrawal of medical treatment or hydration and nutrition. We cannot say that the Supreme Court of Missouri committed constitutional error in reaching the conclusion that it did. . . .

No doubt is engendered by anything in this record but that Nancy Cruzan's mother and father are loving and caring parents. If the State were required by the United States Constitution to repose a right of "substituted judgment" with anyone, the Cruzans would surely qualify. But we do not think the Due Process Clause requires the State to repose judgment on these matters with anyone but the patient herself. Close family members may have a strong feeling — a feeling not at all ignoble or unworthy, but not entirely disinterested, either — that they do not wish to witness the continuation of the life of a loved one which they regard as hopeless, meaningless, and even degrading. But there is no automatic assurance that the view of close family members will necessarily be the same as the patient's would have been had she been confronted with the prospect of her situation while competent. All of the reasons previously discussed for allowing Missouri to require clear and convincing evidence of the patient's wishes lead us to conclude that the State may choose to defer only to those wishes, rather than confide the decision to close family members.

The judgment of the Supreme Court of Missouri is [a]ffirmed.

O'CONNOR, J., concurring.

I agree that a protected liberty interest in refusing unwanted medical treatment may be inferred from our prior decisions and that the refusal of artificially delivered food and water is encompassed within that liberty interest. I write separately to clarify why I believe this to be so.

As the Court notes, the liberty interest in refusing medical treatment flows from decisions involving the State's invasions into the body. Because our notions of liberty are inextricably entwined with our idea of physical freedom and self-determination, the Court has often deemed state incursions into the body repugnant to the interests protected by the Due Process Clause. The State's imposition of medical treatment on an unwilling competent adult necessarily involves some form of restraint and intrusion. A seriously ill or dying patient whose wishes are not honored may feel a captive of the machinery required for life-sustaining measures or other medical interventions. Such forced treatment may burden that individual's liberty interests as much as any state coercion.

The State's artificial provision of nutrition and hydration implicates identical concerns. Artificial feeding cannot readily be distinguished from other forms of medical treatment. Whether or not the techniques used to pass food and water into the patient's alimentary tract are termed "medical treatment," it is clear they all involve some degree of intrusion and restraint. Feeding a patient by means of a nasogastric tube requires a physician to pass a long flexible tube through the patient's nose, throat and esophagus and into the stomach. Because of the discomfort such a tube causes, "[m]any patients need to be restrained forcibly and their hands put into large mittens to prevent them from removing the tube." A gastrostomy tube (as was used to provide food and water to Nancy Cruzan) or jejunostomy tube must be surgically implanted into the stomach or small intestine. Requiring a competent adult to endure such procedures against her will burdens the patient's liberty, dignity, and freedom to determine the course of her own treatment. Accordingly, the liberty guaranteed by the Due Process Clause must protect, if it protects anything, an individual's deeply personal decision to reject medical treatment, including the artificial delivery of food and water.

Today's decision, holding only that the Constitution permits a State to require clear and convincing evidence of Nancy Cruzan's desire to have artificial hydration and nutrition withdrawn, does not preclude a future determination that the Constitution requires the States to implement the decisions of a patient's duly appointed surrogate. Nor does it prevent States from developing other approaches for protecting an incompetent individual's liberty interest in refusing medical treatment. As is evident from the Court's survey of state court decisions, no national consensus has yet emerged on the best solution for this difficult and sensitive problem. Today we decide only that one State's practice does not violate the Constitution; the more challenging task of crafting appropriate procedures for safeguarding incompetents' liberty interests is entrusted to the "laboratory" of the States in the first instance. . . .

SCALIA, J., concurring. . . .

While I agree with the Court's analysis today, and therefore join in its opinion, I would have preferred that we announce, clearly and promptly, that the federal courts have no business in this field; that American law has always accorded the State the power to prevent, by force if necessary, suicide — including suicide by refusing to take appropriate measures necessary to preserve one's life; that the point at which life becomes "worthless," and the point at which the means necessary to preserve it become "extraordinary" or "inappropriate," are neither set forth in the Constitution nor known to the nine Justices of this Court any better than they are known to nine people picked at random from the Kansas City telephone directory; and hence, that even when it is demonstrated by clear and convincing evidence that a patient no longer wishes certain measures to be taken to preserve her life, it is up to the citizens of Missouri to decide, through their elected representatives, whether that wish will be honored. It is quite impossible (because the Constitution says nothing about the matter) that those citizens will decide upon a line less lawful than the one we would choose; and it is unlikely (because we know no more about "life-and-death" than they do) that they will decide upon a line less reasonable.

The text of the Due Process Clause does not protect individuals against deprivations of liberty *simpliciter*. It protects them against deprivations of liberty "without due process of law." To determine that such a deprivation would not occur if Nancy Cruzan were forced to take nourishment against her will, it is unnecessary to reopen the historically recurrent debate over whether "due process" includes substantive restrictions. It is at least true that no "substantive due process" claim can be maintained unless the claimant demonstrates that the State has deprived him of a right historically and traditionally protected against State interference. That cannot possibly be established here.

At common law in England, a suicide — defined as one who "deliberately puts an end to his own existence, or commits any unlawful malicious act, the consequence of which is his own death," 4 W. Blackstone, Commentaries *189 — was criminally liable. [And] most States that did not explicitly prohibit assisted suicide in 1868 recognized, when the issue arose in the 50 years following the Fourteenth Amendment's ratification, that assisted and (in some cases) attempted suicide were unlawful. Thus, "there is no significant support for the claim that a right to suicide is so rooted in our tradition that it may be deemed 'fundamental' or 'implicit in the concept of ordered liberty.' "

Petitioners rely on three distinctions to separate Nancy Cruzan's case from ordinary suicide: (1) that she is permanently incapacitated and in pain; (2) that she would bring on her death not by any affirmative act but by merely declining treatment that provides nourishment; and (3) that preventing her from effectuating her presumed wish to die requires violation of her bodily integrity. None of these suffices. [Justice Scalia cites to Blackstone and state cases from the nineteenth century to show that the first distinction was not traditionally accepted.]

The second asserted distinction . . . relies on the dichotomy between action and inaction. . . . Even as a legislative matter . . . the intelligent line does not fall between action and inaction but between those forms of inaction that consist of abstaining from "ordinary" care and those that consist of abstaining from "excessive" or "heroic" measures. [But] that is not a line to be discerned by logic or legal analysis, and we should not pretend that it is. [Moreover] the action-inaction distinction [is irrelevant]. Starving oneself to death is no different from putting a gun to one's temple as far as the common-law definition of suicide is concerned. [The] third asserted basis of distinction — that frustrating Nancy Cruzan's wish to die in the present case requires interference with her bodily integrity — is likewise inadequate, because such interference is impermissible only if one begs the question whether her refusal to undergo the treatment on her own is suicide. It has always been lawful not only for the State, but even for private citizens, to interfere with bodily integrity to prevent a felony. That general rule has of course been applied to suicide. At common law, even a private person's use of force to prevent suicide was privileged. It is not even reasonable, much less required by the Constitution, to maintain that although the State has the right to prevent a person from slashing his wrists it does not have the power to apply physical force to prevent him from doing so, nor the power, should he succeed, to apply, coercively if necessary, medical measures to stop the flow of blood. The state-run hospital, I am certain, is not liable . . . for violation of constitutional rights, nor the private hospital liable under general tort law, if, in a State where suicide is unlawful, it pumps out the stomach of a person who has intentionally taken an overdose of barbiturates, despite that person's wishes to the contrary. . . .

What I have said above is not meant to suggest that I would think it desirable, if we were sure that Nancy Cruzan wanted to die, to keep her alive by the means at issue here. I assert only that the Constitution has nothing to say about the subject. To raise up a constitutional right here we would have to create out of nothing (for it exists neither in text nor tradition) some constitutional principle whereby, although the State may insist that an individual come in out of the cold and eat food, it may not insist that he take medicine; and although it may pump his stomach empty of poison he has ingested, it may not fill his stomach with food he has failed to ingest. Are there, then, no reasonable and humane limits that ought not to be exceeded in requiring an individual to preserve his own life? There obviously are, but they are not set forth in the Due Process Clause. What assures us that those limits will not be exceeded is the same constitutional guarantee that is the source of most of our protection — what protects us, for example, from being assessed a tax of 100% of our income above the subsistence level, from being forbidden to drive cars, or from being required to send our children to school for 10 hours a day, none of which horribles is categorically prohibited by the Constitution. Our salvation is the Equal Protection Clause, which requires the democratic majority to accept for themselves and their loved ones what they impose on you and me. This Court need not, and has no authority to, inject itself into every field of human activity where irrationality and oppression may theoretically occur, and if it tries to do so it will destroy itself.

BRENNAN, J., with whom Marshall and Blackmun JJ., join, dissenting.

[The] question before this Court is a relatively narrow one: whether the Due Process Clause allows Missouri to require a now-incompetent patient in an irreversible persistent vegetative state to remain on life-support absent rigorously clear and convincing evidence that avoiding the treatment represents the patient's prior, express choice. If a fundamental right is at issue, Missouri's rule of decision must be scrutinized under the standards this Court has always applied in such circumstances. As we said in Zablocki v. Redhail, 434 U.S. 374 (1978), if a requirement imposed by a State "significantly interferes with the exercise of a fundamental right, it cannot be upheld unless it is supported by sufficiently important state interests and is closely tailored to effectuate only those interests." . . . An evidentiary rule, just as a substantive prohibition, must meet these standards if it significantly burdens a fundamental liberty interest. . . .

The only state interest asserted here is a general interest in the preservation of life. But the State has no legitimate general interest in someone's life, completely abstracted from the interest of the person living that life, that could outweigh the person's choice to avoid medical treatment. [Thus,] the State's general interest in life must accede to Nancy Cruzan's particularized and intense interest in self-determination in her choice of medical treatment. There is simply nothing legitimately within the State's purview to be gained by superseding her decision.

This is not to say that the State has no legitimate interests to assert here. As the majority recognizes, Missouri has a *parens patriae* interest in providing Nancy Cruzan, now incompetent, with as accurate as possible a determination of how she would exercise her rights under these circumstances. Second, if and when it is determined that Nancy Cruzan would want to continue treatment, the State may legitimately assert an interest in providing that treatment. But *until* Nancy's wishes have been determined, the only state interest that may be asserted is an interest in safe-guarding the accuracy of that determination.

Accuracy, therefore, must be our touchstone. Missouri may constitutionally impose only those procedural requirements that serve to enhance the accuracy of a determination of Nancy Cruzan's wishes or are at least consistent with an accurate determination. The Missouri "safeguard" that the Court upholds today does not meet that standard. The determination needed in this context is whether the incompetent person would choose to live in a persistent vegetative state on life-support or to avoid this medical treatment. Missouri's rule of decision imposes a markedly asymmetrical evidentiary burden. Only evidence of specific statements of treatment choice made by the patient when competent is admissible to support a finding that the patient, now in a persistent vegetative state, would wish to avoid further medical treatment. Moreover, this evidence must be clear and convincing. No proof is required to support a finding that the incompetent person would wish to continue treatment.

[T]he majority explains that the State may constitutionally adopt this rule to govern determinations of an incompetent's wishes in order to advance the State's substantive interests, including its unqualified interest in the preservation of human life. [C]ourts have long erected clear and convincing evidence standards to place the greater risk of erroneous decisions on those bringing disfavored claims. [However], Missouri has no such power to disfavor a choice by Nancy Cruzan to avoid medical treatment, because Missouri has no legitimate interest in providing Nancy with treatment until it is established that this represents her choice. Just as a State may not override Nancy's choice directly, it may not do so indirectly through the imposition of a procedural rule.

. . . [A]ny concern[s] [about accuracy] would be better addressed by appointing a guardian ad litem, who could use the State's powers of discovery to gather and present evidence regarding the patient's wishes, [could] uncover any conflicts of interest and ensure that each party likely to have relevant evidence is consulted and brought forward — for example, other members of the family, friends, clergy, and doctors. Missouri's heightened evidentiary standard attempts to achieve balance by discounting evidence; the guardian ad litem technique achieves balance by probing for additional evidence. Where, as here, the family members, friends, doctors and guardian ad litem agree, it is not because the process has failed. . . . It is because there is no genuine dispute as to Nancy's preference.

STEVENS, J., dissenting. . . .

. . . An innocent person's constitutional right to be free from unwanted medical treatment is . . . categorically limited [by the Court] to those patients who had the foresight to make an unambiguous statement of their wishes while competent. The Court's decision affords no protection to children, to young people who are victims of unexpected accidents or illnesses, or to the countless thousands of elderly persons who either fail to decide, or fail to explain, how they want to be treated if they should experience a similar fate. Because Nancy Beth Cruzan did not have the foresight to preserve her constitutional right in a living will, or some comparable "clear and convincing" alternative, her right is gone forever and her fate is in the hands of the state legislature instead of in those of her family, her independent neutral guardian ad litem, and an impartial judge — all of whom agree on the course of action that is in her best interests. The Court's willingness to find a waiver of this constitutional right reveals a distressing misunderstanding of the importance of individual liberty.

. . . [D]eath is not life's simple opposite, or its necessary terminus, but rather its completion. . . . Nancy Beth Cruzan['s] interest in life, no less than that of any other person, includes an interest in how she will be thought of after her death by those whose opinions mattered to her. There can be no doubt that her life made her dear to her family, and to others. How she dies will affect how that life is remembered. The trial court's order authorizing Nancy's parents to cease their daughter's treatment would have permitted the family that cares for Nancy to bring to a close her tragedy and her death. Missouri's objection to that order subordinates Nancy's body, her family, and the lasting significance of her life to the State's own interests. The decision we review thereby interferes with constitutional interests of the highest order.

To be constitutionally permissible, Missouri's intrusion upon these fundamental liberties must, at a minimum, bear a reasonable relationship to a legitimate state end. Missouri asserts that its policy is related to a state interest in the protection of life. In my view, however, it is an effort to define life, rather than to protect it, that is the heart of Missouri's policy. Missouri insists, without regard to Nancy Cruzan's own interests, upon equating her life with the biological persistence of her bodily functions. Nancy Cruzan, it must be remembered, is not now simply incompetent. She is in a persistent vegetative state, and has been so for seven years. The trial court found, and no party contested, that Nancy has no possibility of recovery and no consciousness. . . .

In short, there is no reasonable ground for believing that Nancy Beth Cruzan has any personal interest in the perpetuation of what the State has decided is her life. [Moreover,] [i]t is not within the province of secular government to circumscribe the liberties of the people by regulations designed wholly for the purpose of establishing a sectarian definition of life. . . .

The Court suggests that Missouri's policy "results in a maintenance of the status quo," and is subject to reversal, while a decision to terminate treatment "is not susceptible of correction" because death is irreversible. Yet, this explanation begs the question, for it assumes either that the State's policy is consistent with Nancy Cruzan's own interests, or that no damage is done by ignoring her interests. The first assumption is without basis in the record of this case, and would obviate any need for the State to rely, as it does, upon its own interests rather than upon the patient's. The second assumption is unconscionable. Insofar as Nancy Cruzan has an interest in being remembered for how she lived rather than how she died, the damage done to those memories by the prolongation of her death is irreversible. Insofar as Nancy Cruzan has an interest in the cessation of any pain, the continuation of her pain is irreversible. Insofar as Nancy Cruzan has an interest in a closure to her life consistent with her own beliefs rather than those of the Missouri legislature, the State's imposition of its contrary view is irreversible. To deny the importance of these consequences is in effect to deny that Nancy Cruzan has interests at all, and thereby to deny her personhood in the name of preserving the sanctity of her life. . . .

[T]he Court's deference seems ultimately to derive from the premise that chronically incompetent persons have no constitutionally cognizable interests at all, and so are not persons within the meaning of the Constitution. Deference of this sort is patently unconstitutional. It is also dangerous in ways that may not be immediately apparent. Today the State of Missouri has announced its intent to spend several hundred thousand dollars in preserving the life of Nancy Beth Cruzan in order to vindicate its general policy favoring the preservation of human life. Tomorrow, another State equally eager to champion an interest in the "quality of life" might favor a policy designed to ensure quick and comfortable deaths by denying treatment to categories of marginally hopeless cases. . . .

However commendable may be the State's interest in human life, it cannot pursue this interest by appropriating Nancy Cruzan's life as a symbol for its own purposes. Lives do not exist in abstraction from persons, and to pretend otherwise is not to honor but to desecrate the State's responsibility for protecting life. A State that seeks to demonstrate its commitment to life may do so by aiding those who are actively struggling for life and health. In this endeavor, unfortunately, no State can lack for opportunities: there can be no need to make an example of tragic cases like that of Nancy Cruzan.

I respectfully dissent.

Discussion

1. *The aftermath of the* Cruzan *decision.* After the Supreme Court's decision, the State of Missouri, which had originally opposed removal of Cruzan's feeding tube, withdrew from the case. Missouri Attorney General William Webster declared that having received judicial confirmation of the constitutionality of the statute and its standard of proof, the state no longer possessed a legal interest in the litigation. Another Chapter in the Case of Nancy Cruzan; Missouri Seeks to Withdraw from Legal Case It Has Long Pursued The Washington Post, Oct. 16, 1990, at Z7; Malcolm, Judge Allows Feeding-Tube Removal, N.Y. Times, Dec. 15, 1990, at A10, col. 1. At this point no one in the case — including Cruzan's court-appointed guardian — was opposed to withdrawal of Cruzan's hydration and nutrition. Subsequently a state probate judge held a new hearing at the request of Cruzan's parents. On the basis of statements by three of Cruzan's former co-workers that they recalled hearing her say that she would not wish to "live like a vegetable" on medical life support machinery, the judge held that there was "clear" evidence that Cruzan's intent, "if mentally able, would be to withdraw nutrition and hydration," and ordered that nutrition and hydration cease on December 14, 1990. Cruzan died 12 days later, on December 26, 1990, almost eight years after she had lost consciousness and been intubated. Death Ends Cruzan Family's Ordeal, Newsday, Dec. 27, 1990, at 8, col. 1; Nancy Cruzan Dies, Outlived by a Debate Over the Right to Die, N.Y. Times, Dec. 27, 1990, A, at 1, col. 1. Consider the extent to which the State's withdrawal was crucial to this result. Does *Cruzan* stand only for the proposition that the States can keep citizens like Nancy Cruzan alive if they wish to expend sufficient legal and medical resources to do so?

2. *The persistence of substantive due process.* Robert Bork has written, "No [current member of the Supreme Court] renounces the power to override democratic majorities when the Constitution is silent." As the phrasing might indicate, Judge Bork vigorously opposes *any* reliance on "fundamental rights" by judges. Thus for him, the famous dissent by Justice Holmes in *Lochner*, supra Chapter 4, was "spoiled" by Holmes's "accept[ance of] substantive due process" in his acknowledgment that the courts could invalidate a law upon the finding "that a rational and fair man necessarily would admit that the statute proposed would infringe fundamental principles as they have been understood by the traditions of our people and our law." Turning to the recent Court, Judge Bork states:

> It may be that Scalia and Rehnquist are trying to come as close as they can get [to renouncing judicial authority to enforce fundamental albeit unwritten rights] by insisting on using the most specific tradition available. But even that assumes an illegitimate power, and the limitation will prove no restriction at all when there is only a general, unfocused tradition to be found. Seven Justices, in varying degrees, reject even that slight restriction on their powers. Nothing resembling an adequate justification has

ever been, is now, or ever will be offered for this taking by judges of a power that is not theirs.[108]

How does Judge Bork's description of the Justices comport with their positions in *Cruzan*?

3. Is Justice Scalia correct in stating that no principled distinction can be offered between upholding Nancy Cruzan's right to reject treatment and her "right to commit suicide"? Consider his example of a state-run hospital sued for violation of constitutional rights "if, in a State where suicide is unlawful, it pumps out the stomach of a person who has intentionally taken an overdose of barbiturates, despite that person's wishes to the contrary." Would your answer depend on your assessment of the "rationality" of the person's desire for death? Assume that the person had written an extensive note explaining her decision to die on the basis of having been informed that she has Alzheimer's disease. Now imagine a different person, a 30-year-old male, who offers an unhappy love affair and the decision by his beloved to break off relations as the rationale for "ending it all." Would you *ever* honor the choice of a 15-year-old to die?

4. Does Justice Scalia's conundrum apply with equal force to all of the other opinions? Most of the opinions rely on individual autonomy, but is Justice Stevens's approach less dependent on that concept than the other justices?

5. Justice O'Connor's relatively brief concurring opinion focuses primarily on the presence of a protected liberty interest in cases such as Cruzan's. She also addresses a problem not directly in front of the Court, though likely to arise at some point in the future: the designation by a competent person of a "surrogate" to make a decision as to when the termination of life support is appropriate.

> I also write separately to emphasize that the Court does not today decide the issue whether a State must also give effect to the decisions of a surrogate decisionmaker. In my view, such a duty may well be constitutionally required to protect the patient's liberty interest in refusing medical treatment. Few individuals provide explicit oral or written instructions regarding their intent to refuse medical treatment should they become incompetent. States which decline to consider any evidence other than such instructions may frequently fail to honor a patient's intent. Such failures might be avoided if the State considered an equally probative source of evidence: the patient's appointment of a proxy to make health care decisions on her behalf. Delegating the authority to make medical decisions to a family member or friend is becoming a common method of planning for the future. Several States have recognized the practical wisdom of such a procedure by enacting durable power of attorney statutes that specifically authorize an individual to appoint a surrogate to make medical treatment decisions. Some state courts have suggested that an agent appointed pursuant to a general durable power of attorney statute would also be empowered to make health care decisions on behalf of the patient. Other States allow an individual to designate a proxy to carry out the intent of a living will. These procedures for surrogate decision-making, which appear to be rapidly gaining in acceptance, may be a valuable additional safeguard of the patient's interest in directing his medical care. Moreover, as patients are likely to select a family member as a surrogate, giving effect to a proxy's decisions may also protect the "freedom of personal choice in matters of . . . family life."

108. Robert Bork, The Tempting of America: The Political Seduction of the Law 240, 245 (1989).

6. *Cruzan* deals with the withdrawal of what is sometimes described as "artificial" life support or the right to decline such support in the first place. More recently, a national debate has begun raging about the topic of "assisted suicide." The term is itself exceedingly complicated. At one extreme it could mean the physical infliction of death by a trained physician at the behest of the person wishing to die ("euthanasia"). At the other extreme, it could involve any act or omission that would help patients end their lives. The next two cases deal with a particular form of assistance, the provision by a doctor of fatal dosages of drugs to patients who have indicated a desire to have such drugs available in case they choose to commit suicide. The "assistance" here is the provision of the drugs, not, for example, participation by the doctor in the injection of the drugs, which would involve a more overt form of participation.

B. "Assisted Suicide"

WASHINGTON v. GLUCKSBERG
521 U.S. 702 (1997)

REHNQUIST, C.J., delivered the opinion of the Court.

The question presented in this case is whether Washington's prohibition against "caus[ing]" or "aid[ing]" a suicide offends the Fourteenth Amendment to the United States Constitution. We hold that it does not. . . .

Washington law provides: "A person is guilty of promoting a suicide attempt when he knowingly causes or aids another person to attempt suicide." "Promoting a suicide attempt" is a felony, punishable by up to five years' imprisonment and up to a $10,000 fine. At the same time, Washington's Natural Death Act, enacted in 1979, states that the "withholding or withdrawal of life-sustaining treatment" at a patient's direction "shall not, for any purpose, constitute a suicide." . . .

I.

We begin, as we do in all due-process cases, by examining our Nation's history, legal traditions, and practices. In almost every State — indeed, in almost every western democracy — it is a crime to assist a suicide. The States' assisted-suicide bans are not innovations. Rather, they are longstanding expressions of the States' commitment to the protection and preservation of all human life. Indeed, opposition to and condemnation of suicide — and, therefore, of assisting suicide — are consistent and enduring themes of our philosophical, legal, and cultural heritages. . . .

More specifically, for over 700 years, the Anglo-American common-law tradition has punished or otherwise disapproved of both suicide and assisting suicide. In the 13th century, Henry de Bracton, one of the first legal-treatise writers, observed that "[j]ust as a man may commit felony by slaying another so may he do so by slaying himself." The real and personal property of one who killed himself to avoid conviction and punishment for a crime were forfeit to the king; however, thought Bracton, "if a man slays himself in weariness of life or because he is unwilling to endure further bodily pain . . . [only] his movable goods [were] confiscated." Thus, "[t]he principle that suicide of a sane person, for whatever reason, was a punishable felony was . . . introduced into English common law." Centuries later, Sir

William Blackstone, whose Commentaries on the Laws of England not only provided a definitive summary of the common law but was also a primary legal authority for 18th and 19th century American lawyers, referred to suicide as "self-murder" and "the pretended heroism, but real cowardice, of the Stoic philosophers, who destroyed themselves to avoid those ills which they had not the fortitude to endure. . . ." Blackstone emphasized that "the law has . . . ranked [suicide] among the highest crimes," although, anticipating later developments, he conceded that the harsh and shameful punishments imposed for suicide "borde[r] a little upon severity."

For the most part, the early American colonies adopted the common-law approach. . . . Over time, however, the American colonies abolished these harsh common-law penalties. . . . [T]he movement away from the common law's harsh sanctions did not represent an acceptance of suicide; rather, . . . this change reflected the growing consensus that it was unfair to punish the suicide's family for his wrongdoing. Nonetheless, [t]hat suicide remained a grievous, though nonfelonious, wrong is confirmed by the fact that colonial and early state legislatures and courts did not retreat from prohibiting assisting suicide. . . .

Though deeply rooted, the States' assisted-suicide bans have in recent years been reexamined and, generally, reaffirmed. Because of advances in medicine and technology, Americans today are increasingly likely to die in institutions, from chronic illnesses. Public concern and democratic action are therefore sharply focused on how best to protect dignity and independence at the end of life, with the result that there have been many significant changes in state laws and in the attitudes these laws reflect. Many States, for example, now permit "living wills," surrogate health-care decisionmaking, and the withdrawal or refusal of life-sustaining medical treatment. At the same time, however, voters and legislators continue for the most part to reaffirm their States' prohibitions on assisting suicide.

The Washington statute at issue in this case was enacted in 1975 as part of a revision of that State's criminal code. Four years later, Washington passed its Natural Death Act, which specifically stated that the "withholding or withdrawal of life-sustaining treatment . . . shall not, for any purpose, constitute a suicide" and that "[n]othing in this chapter shall be construed to condone, authorize, or approve mercy killing. . . ." In 1991, Washington voters rejected a ballot initiative which, had it passed, would have permitted a form of physician-assisted suicide. Washington then added a provision to the Natural Death Act expressly excluding physician-assisted suicide.

II.

. . .

Our established method of substantive-due-process analysis has two primary features: First, we have regularly observed that the Due Process Clause specially protects those fundamental rights and liberties which are, objectively, "deeply rooted in this Nation's history and tradition" and "implicit in the concept of ordered liberty," such that "neither liberty nor justice would exist if they were sacrificed." Second, we have required in substantive-due-process cases a "careful description" of the asserted fundamental liberty interest. Our Nation's history, legal traditions, and practices thus provide the crucial "guideposts for responsible decisionmaking" that direct and restrain our exposition of the Due Process Clause. . . .

Justice Souter, relying on Justice Harlan's dissenting opinion in Poe v. Ullman, would largely abandon this restrained methodology, and instead ask "whether [Washington's] statute sets up one of those 'arbitrary impositions' or 'purposeless restraints' at odds with the Due Process Clause of the Fourteenth Amendment." In our view, however, the development of this Court's substantive-due-process jurisprudence, described briefly above, has been a process whereby the outlines of the "liberty" specially protected by the Fourteenth Amendment — never fully clarified, to be sure, and perhaps not capable of being fully clarified — have at least been carefully refined by concrete examples involving fundamental rights found to be deeply rooted in our legal tradition. This approach tends to rein in the subjective elements that are necessarily present in due-process judicial review. In addition, by establishing a threshold requirement — that a challenged state action implicate a fundamental right — before requiring more than a reasonable relation to a legitimate state interest to justify the action, it avoids the need for complex balancing of competing interests in every case. . . .

[W]e have a tradition of carefully formulating the interest at stake in substantive-due-process cases. For example, although *Cruzan* is often described as a "right to die" case, we were, in fact, more precise: we assumed that the Constitution granted competent persons a "constitutionally protected right to refuse lifesaving hydration and nutrition." The Washington statute at issue in this case prohibits "aid[ing] another person to attempt suicide," and, thus, the question before us is whether the "liberty" specially protected by the Due Process Clause includes a right to commit suicide which itself includes a right to assistance in doing so.

We now inquire whether this asserted right has any place in our Nation's traditions. Here, as discussed above, we are confronted with a consistent and almost universal tradition that has long rejected the asserted right, and continues explicitly to reject it today, even for terminally ill, mentally competent adults. To hold for respondents, we would have to reverse centuries of legal doctrine and practice, and strike down the considered policy choice of almost every State.

Respondents contend, however, that the liberty interest they assert is consistent with this Court's substantive-due-process line of cases, if not with this Nation's history and practice. Pointing to *Casey* and *Cruzan*, respondents read our jurisprudence in this area as reflecting a general tradition of "self-sovereignty," and as teaching that the "liberty" protected by the Due Process Clause includes "basic and intimate exercises of personal autonomy." According to respondents, our liberty jurisprudence, and the broad, individualistic principles it reflects, protects the "liberty of competent, terminally ill adults to make end-of-life decisions free of undue government interference." . . .

[The] right assumed in *Cruzan* . . . was not simply deduced from abstract concepts of personal autonomy. Given the common-law rule that forced medication was a battery, and the long legal tradition protecting the decision to refuse unwanted medical treatment, our assumption was entirely consistent with this Nation's history and constitutional traditions. The decision to commit suicide with the assistance of another may be just as personal and profound as the decision to refuse unwanted medical treatment, but it has never enjoyed similar legal protection. Indeed, the two acts are widely and reasonably regarded as quite distinct. . . .

Respondents also rely on *Casey*. [In reaffirming *Roe*,] the opinion moved from the recognition that liberty necessarily includes freedom of conscience and belief about ultimate considerations to the observation that "though the abortion decision may originate within the zone of conscience and belief, *it is more than a philosophic exercise.*" *Casey* (emphasis added). That many of the rights and liberties protected by the Due Process Clause sound in personal autonomy does not warrant the sweeping conclusion that any and all important, intimate, and personal decisions are so protected, and *Casey* did not suggest otherwise.

The history of the law's treatment of assisted suicide in this country has been and continues to be one of the rejection of nearly all efforts to permit it. That being the case, our decisions lead us to conclude that the asserted "right" to assistance in committing suicide is not a fundamental liberty interest protected by the Due Process Clause. The Constitution also requires, however, that Washington's assisted-suicide ban be rationally related to legitimate government interests. This requirement is unquestionably met here. As the court below recognized, Washington's assisted-suicide ban implicates a number of state interests.

First, Washington has an "unqualified interest in the preservation of human life." The State's prohibition on assisted suicide, like all homicide laws, both reflects and advances its commitment to this interest. This interest is symbolic and aspirational as well as practical. . . . The Court of Appeals . . . held that the "weight" of this interest depends on the "medical condition and the wishes of the person whose life is at stake." Washington, however, has rejected this sliding-scale approach and, through its assisted-suicide ban, insists that all persons' lives, from beginning to end, regardless of physical or mental condition, are under the full protection of the law. As we have previously affirmed, the States "may properly decline to make judgments about the 'quality' of life that a particular individual may enjoy." This remains true, as *Cruzan* makes clear, even for those who are near death.

Relatedly, all admit that suicide is a serious public-health problem, especially among persons in otherwise vulnerable groups. The State has an interest in preventing suicide, and in studying, identifying, and treating its causes. Those who attempt suicide — terminally ill or not — often suffer from depression or other mental disorders. [Research] indicates, however, that many people who request physician-assisted suicide withdraw that request if their depression and pain are treated. The New York Task Force, . . . , expressed its concern that, because depression is difficult to diagnose, physicians and medical professionals often fail to respond adequately to seriously ill patients' needs. Thus, legal physician-assisted suicide could make it more difficult for the State to protect depressed or mentally ill persons, or those who are suffering from untreated pain, from suicidal impulses.

The State also has an interest in protecting the integrity and ethics of the medical profession. [And] physician-assisted suicide could, it is argued, undermine the trust that is essential to the doctor-patient relationship by blurring the time-honored line between healing and harming.

Next, the State has an interest in protecting vulnerable groups — including the poor, the elderly, and disabled persons — from abuse, neglect, and mistakes. The Court of Appeals dismissed the State's concern that disadvantaged persons might be pressured into physician-assisted suicide as "ludicrous on its face." We have recognized, however, the real risk of subtle coercion and undue influence in end-of-life situations. Similarly, the New York Task Force warned that "[l]egalizing physician-assisted suicide would pose profound risks to many individuals who are ill and vulnerable. . . . The risk of harm is greatest for the many individuals in our society whose autonomy and well-being are already compromised by poverty, lack of access to good medical care, advanced age, or membership in a stigmatized social group."

If physician-assisted suicide were permitted, many might resort to it to spare their families the substantial financial burden of end-of-life health-care costs.

The State's interest here goes beyond protecting the vulnerable from coercion; it extends to protecting disabled and terminally ill people from prejudice, negative and inaccurate stereotypes, and "societal indifference." The State's assisted-suicide ban reflects and reinforces its policy that the lives of terminally ill, disabled, and elderly people must be no less valued than the lives of the young and healthy, and that a seriously disabled person's suicidal impulses should be interpreted and treated the same way as anyone else's.

Finally, the State may fear that permitting assisted suicide will start it down the path to voluntary and perhaps even involuntary euthanasia. [The Court of Appeals] noted, . . . that the "decision of a duly appointed surrogate decision maker is for all legal purposes the decision of the patient himself"; that "in some instances, the patient may be unable to self-administer the drugs and . . . administration by the physician . . . may be the only way the patient may be able to receive them"; and that not only physicians, but also family members and loved ones, will inevitably participate in assisting suicide. Thus, it turns out that what is couched as a limited right to physician-assisted suicide is likely, in effect, a much broader license, which could prove extremely difficult to police and contain. Washington's ban on assisting suicide prevents such erosion.

This concern is further supported by evidence about the practice of euthanasia in the Netherlands. The Dutch government's own study revealed that in 1990, there were 2,300 cases of voluntary euthanasia (defined as "the deliberate termination of another's life at his request"), 400 cases of assisted suicide, and more than 1,000 cases of euthanasia without an explicit request. In addition to these latter 1,000 cases, the study found an additional 4,941 cases where physicians administered lethal morphine overdoses without the patients' explicit consent. This study suggests that, despite the existence of various reporting procedures, euthanasia in the Netherlands has not been limited to competent, terminally ill adults who are enduring physical suffering, and that regulation of the practice may not have prevented abuses in cases involving vulnerable persons, including severely disabled neonates and elderly persons suffering from dementia. The New York Task Force, citing the Dutch experience, observed that "assisted suicide and euthanasia are closely linked" and concluded that the "risk of . . . abuse is neither speculative nor distant." Washington, like most other States, reasonably ensures against this risk by banning, rather than regulating, assisting suicide. We need not weigh exactingly the relative strengths of these various interests. They are unquestionably important and legitimate, and Washington's ban on assisted suicide is at least reasonably related to their promotion and protection. We therefore hold that Wash. Rev. Code §9A.36.060(1) (1994) does not violate the Fourteenth Amendment, either on its face or "as applied to competent, terminally ill adults who wish to hasten their deaths by obtaining medication prescribed by their doctors."

Throughout the Nation, Americans are engaged in an earnest and profound debate about the morality, legality, and practicality of physician-assisted suicide. Our holding permits this debate to continue, as it should in a democratic society. . . .

SOUTER, J., concurring in the judgment. . . .

My understanding of unenumerated rights in the wake of [Justice Harlan's] *Poe* dissent and subsequent cases avoids the absolutist failing of many older cases without embracing the opposite pole of equating reasonableness with past practice described at a very specific level. [This] approach calls for a court to assess the relative "weights" or dignities of the contending interests, and to this extent the judicial method is familiar to the common law. . . .

Just as results in substantive due process cases are tied to the selections of statements of the competing interests, the acceptability of the results is a function of the good reasons for the selections made. It is here that the value of common-law method becomes apparent, for the usual thinking of the common law is suspicious of the all-or-nothing analysis that tends to produce legal petrification instead of an evolving boundary between the domains of old principles. Common-law method tends to pay respect instead to detail, seeking to understand old principles afresh by new examples and new counterexamples. The "tradition is a living thing," albeit one that moves by moderate steps carefully taken. . . .

Th[e] liberty interest in bodily integrity was phrased in a general way by then-Judge Cardozo when he said, "[e]very human being of adult years and sound mind has a right to determine what shall be done with his own body" in relation to his medical needs. The familiar examples of this right derive from the common law of battery and include the right to be free from medical invasions into the body, *Cruzan,* as well as a right generally to resist enforced medication, see Washington v. Harper, 494 U.S. 210 (1990). Thus "[i]t is settled now . . . that the Constitution places limits on a State's right to interfere with a person's most basic decisions about . . . bodily integrity." *Casey.* Constitutional recognition of the right to bodily integrity underlies the assumed right, good against the State, to require physicians to terminate artificial life support, *Cruzan,* and the affirmative right to obtain medical intervention to cause abortion. . . .

The analogies between the abortion cases and this one are several. Even though the State has a legitimate interest in discouraging abortion, the Court recognized a woman's right to a physician's counsel and care. Like the decision to commit suicide, the decision to abort potential life can be made irresponsibly and under the influence of others, and yet the Court has held in the abortion cases that physicians are fit assistants. Without physician assistance in abortion, the woman's right would have too often amounted to nothing more than a right to self-mutilation, and without a physician to assist in the suicide of the dying, the patient's right will often be confined to crude methods of causing death, most shocking and painful to the decedent's survivors. . . .

The State has put forward several interests to justify the Washington law as applied to physicians treating terminally ill patients, even those competent to make responsible choices: protecting life generally, discouraging suicide even if knowing and voluntary, and protecting terminally ill patients from involuntary suicide and euthanasia, both voluntary and nonvoluntary.

It is not necessary to discuss the exact strengths of the first two claims of justification in the present circumstances, for the third is dispositive for me. That third justification is different from the first two, for it addresses specific features of respondents' claim, and it opposes that claim not with a moral judgment contrary to respondents', but with a recognized state interest in the protection of nonresponsible individuals and those who do not stand in relation either to death or to their physicians as do the patients whom respondents describe. The State claims interests in protecting patients from mistakenly and involuntarily deciding to end their lives, and in guarding against both voluntary and involuntary euthanasia. Leaving aside any difficulties in coming to a clear concept of imminent death, mistaken decisions may result from inadequate palliative care or a terminal prognosis that turns out to be error; coercion and abuse may stem from the large medical bills that family members cannot bear or unreimbursed hospitals decline to shoulder. Voluntary and involuntary euthanasia may result once doctors are authorized to prescribe lethal medication in the first instance, for they might find it pointless to distinguish between patients who administer their own fatal drugs and those who wish not to, and their compassion for those who suffer may obscure the distinction between those who ask for death and those who may be unable to request it. The argument is that a progression would occur, obscuring the line between the ill and the dying, and between the responsible and the unduly influenced, until ultimately doctors and perhaps others would abuse a limited freedom to aid suicides by yielding to the impulse to end another's suffering under conditions going beyond the narrow limits the respondents propose. The State thus argues, essentially, that respondents' claim is not as narrow as it sounds, simply because no recognition of the interest they assert could be limited to vindicating those interests and affecting no others. The State says that the claim, in practical effect, would entail consequences that the State could, without doubt, legitimately act to prevent.

The mere assertion that the terminally sick might be pressured into suicide decisions by close friends and family members would not alone be very telling. . . . [O]ne of the points of restricting any right of assistance to physicians, would be to condition the right on an exercise of judgment by someone qualified to assess the patient's responsible capacity and detect the influence of those outside the medical relationship.

The State, however, goes further, to argue that dependence on the vigilance of physicians will not be enough. First, the lines proposed here (particularly the requirement of a knowing and voluntary decision by the patient) would be more difficult to draw than the lines that have limited other recently recognized due process rights. Limiting a state from prosecuting use of artificial contraceptives by married couples posed no practical threat to the State's capacity to regulate contraceptives in other ways that were assumed at the time of *Poe* to be legitimate; the trimester measurements of *Roe* and the viability determination of *Casey* were easy to make with a real degree of certainty. But the knowing and responsible mind is harder to assess. Second, this difficulty could become the greater by combining with another fact within the realm of plausibility, that physicians simply would not be assiduous to preserve the line. They have compassion, and those who would be willing to assist in suicide at all might be the most susceptible to the wishes of a patient, whether the patient were technically quite responsible or not. Physicians, and their hospitals, have their own financial incentives, too, in this new age of managed care. Whether acting from compassion or under some other influence, a physician who would provide a drug for a patient to administer might well go the further step of administering the drug himself; so, the barrier between assisted suicide and euthanasia could become porous, and the line between voluntary and involuntary euthanasia as well. The case for the slippery slope is fairly made out here, not because recognizing one due process right would leave a court with no principled basis to avoid recognizing another, but because there is a plausible case that the right claimed would not be readily containable by reference to facts about the mind that are matters of difficult judgment, or by gatekeepers who are subject to temptation, noble or not.

Respondents propose an answer to all this, the answer of state regulation with teeth. Legislation proposed in several States, for example, would authorize physician-assisted suicide but require two qualified physicians to confirm the patient's diagnosis, prognosis, and competence; and would mandate that the patient make repeated requests witnessed by at least two others over a specified time span; and would impose reporting requirements and criminal penalties for various acts of coercion. But at least at this moment there are reasons for caution in predicting the effectiveness of the teeth proposed. Respondents' proposals, as it turns out, sound much like the guidelines now in place in the Netherlands, the only place where experience with physician-assisted suicide and euthanasia has yielded empirical evidence about how such regulations might affect actual practice.

Dutch physicians must engage in consultation before proceeding, and must decide whether the patient's decision is voluntary, well considered, and stable, whether the request to die is enduring and made more than once, and whether the patient's future will involve unacceptable suffering. There is, however, a substantial dispute today about what the Dutch experience shows. Some commentators marshall evidence that the Dutch guidelines have in practice failed to protect patients from involuntary euthanasia and have been violated with impunity. The day may come when we can say with some assurance which side is right, but for now it is the substantiality of the factual disagreement, and the alternatives for resolving it, that matter. They are, for me, dispositive of the due process claim at this time.

[The] experimentation that should be out of the question in constitutional adjudication displacing legislative judgments is entirely proper, as well as highly desirable, when the legislative power addresses an emerging issue like assisted suicide. The Court should accordingly stay its hand to allow reasonable legislative consideration. While I do not decide for all time that respondents' claim should not be recognized, I acknowledge the legislative institutional competence as the better one to deal with that claim at this time.

VACCO v. QUILL, 521 U.S. 793 (1997): [In this companion case to *Glucksberg*, the Court considered an equal protection challenge to New York's law prohibiting assisted suicide. Plaintiffs asserted the irrationality of New York's distinction between persons who wish to refuse or withdraw from lifesaving treatment and persons who wish assistance in committing suicide by receiving drugs that would hasten death. The Court, through Chief Justice Rehnquist, rejected the claim:]

REHNQUIST, C.J. . . .
This conclusion depends on the submission that ending or refusing lifesaving medical treatment "is nothing more nor less than assisted suicide." Unlike the Court of Appeals, we think the distinction between assisting suicide and withdrawing life-sustaining treatment, a distinction widely recognized and endorsed in the medical profession and in our legal traditions, is both important and logical; it is certainly rational.

The distinction comports with fundamental legal principles of causation and intent. First, when a patient refuses life-sustaining medical treatment, he dies from an underlying fatal disease or pathology; but if a patient ingests lethal medication prescribed by a physician, he is killed by that medication. . . .

The law has long used actors' intent or purpose to distinguish between two acts that may have the same result. Put differently, the law distinguishes actions taken "because of" a given end from actions taken "in spite of" their unintended but fore-seen consequences. . . .

[W]e disagree with respondents' claim that the distinction between refusing life-saving medical treatment and assisted suicide is "arbitrary" and "irrational." Granted, in some cases, the line between the two may not be clear, but certainty is not required, even were it possible. Logic and contemporary practice support New York's judgment that the two acts are different, and New York may therefore, consistent with the Constitution, treat them differently. By permitting everyone to refuse unwanted medical treatment while prohibiting anyone from assisting a suicide, New York law follows a longstanding and rational distinction.

New York's reasons for recognizing and acting on this distinction — including prohibiting intentional killing and preserving life; preventing suicide; maintaining physicians' role as their patients' healers; protecting vulnerable people from indifference, prejudice, and psychological and financial pressure to end their lives; and avoiding a possible slide towards euthanasia — are discussed in greater detail in our opinion in *Glucksberg*. These valid and important public interests easily satisfy the constitutional requirement that a legislative classification bear a rational relation to some legitimate end. . . .

[Justice Souter wrote a one-paragraph separate concurrence in *Vacco*. Four other Justices wrote or signed opinions applying to both cases.]

O'CONNOR, J., concurring. . . .

I join the Court's opinions because I agree that there is no generalized right to "commit suicide." But respondents urge us to address the narrower question whether a mentally competent person who is experiencing great suffering has a constitutionally cognizable interest in controlling the circumstances of his or her imminent death. I see no need to reach that question in the context of the facial challenges to the New York and Washington laws at issue here. The parties and amici agree that in these States a patient who is suffering from a terminal illness and who is experiencing great pain has no legal barriers to obtaining medication, from qualified physicians, to alleviate that suffering, even to the point of causing unconsciousness and hastening death. In this light, even assuming that we would recognize such an interest, I agree that the State's interests in protecting those who are not truly competent or facing imminent death, or those whose decisions to hasten death would not truly be voluntary, are sufficiently weighty to justify a prohibition against physician-assisted suicide.

Every one of us at some point may be affected by our own or a family member's terminal illness. There is no reason to think the democratic process will not strike the proper balance between the interests of terminally ill, mentally competent individuals who would seek to end their suffering and the State's interests in protecting those who might seek to end life mistakenly or under pressure. . . . [T]here is no need to address the question whether suffering patients have a constitutionally cognizable interest in obtaining relief from the suffering that they may experience in the last days of their lives. There is no dispute that dying patients in Washington and New York can obtain palliative care, even when doing so would hasten their deaths. The difficulty in defining terminal illness and the risk that a dying patient's request for assistance in ending his or her life might not be truly voluntary justifies the prohibitions on assisted suicide we uphold here.

STEVENS, J., concurring in the judgments. . . .

Today, the Court decides that Washington's statute prohibiting assisted suicide is not invalid "on its face," that is to say, in all or most cases in which it might be applied. That holding, however, does not foreclose the possibility that some applications of the statute might well be invalid. . . .

The state interests supporting a general rule banning the practice of physician-assisted suicide do not have the same force in all cases. First and foremost of these interests is the "unqualified interest in the preservation of human life," which is equated with "the sanctity of life." That interest not only justifies — it commands — maximum protection of every individual's interest in remaining alive, which in turn commands the same protection for decisions about whether to commence or to terminate life-support systems or to administer pain medication that may hasten death. Properly viewed, however, this interest is not a collective interest that should always outweigh the interests of a person who because of pain, incapacity, or sedation finds her life intolerable, but rather, an aspect of individual freedom.

Many terminally ill people find their lives meaningful even if filled with pain or dependence on others. Some find value in living through suffering; some have an abiding desire to witness particular events in their families' lives; many believe it a sin to hasten death. Individuals of different religious faiths make different judgments and choices about whether to live on under such circumstances. There are those who will want to continue aggressive treatment; those who would prefer terminal sedation; and those who will seek withdrawal from life-support systems and death by gradual starvation and dehydration. Although as a general matter the State's interest in the contributions each person may make to society outweighs the person's interest in ending her life, this interest does not have the same force for a terminally ill patient faced not with the choice of whether to live, only of how to die. Allowing the individual, rather than the State, to make judgments "about the 'quality' of life that a particular individual may enjoy" does not mean that the lives of terminally-ill, disabled people have less value than the lives of those who are healthy. Rather, it gives proper recognition to the individual's interest in choosing a final chapter that accords with her life story, rather than one that demeans her values and poisons memories of her.

Similarly, the State's legitimate interests in preventing suicide, protecting the vulnerable from coercion and abuse, and preventing euthanasia are less significant in this context. I agree that the State has a compelling interest in preventing persons from committing suicide because of depression, or coercion by third parties. But the State's legitimate interest in preventing abuse does not apply to an individual who is not victimized by abuse, who is not suffering from depression, and who makes a rational and voluntary decision to seek assistance in dying. . . .

[As to *Quill*,] I agree that the distinction between permitting death to ensue from an underlying fatal disease and causing it to occur by the administration of medication or other means provides a constitutionally sufficient basis for the State's classification. . . .

[But] [t]he illusory character of any differences in intent or causation is confirmed by the fact that the American Medical Association unequivocally endorses the practice of terminal sedation — the administration of sufficient dosages of pain-killing medication to terminally ill patients to protect them from excruciating pain even when it is clear that the time of death will be advanced. The purpose of terminal sedation is to ease the suffering of the patient and comply with her wishes, and the actual cause of death is the administration of heavy doses of lethal sedatives. This same intent and causation may exist when a doctor complies with a patient's request for lethal medication to hasten her death. Thus, although the differences the majority notes in causation and intent between terminating life-support and assisting in suicide support the Court's rejection of the respondents' facial challenge, these distinctions may be inapplicable to particular terminally ill patients and their doctors. . . .

GINSBURG, J., concurring in the judgments. . . .

I concur in the Court's judgments substantially for the reasons stated by Justice O'Connor in her concurring opinion.

BREYER, J., concurring in the judgments. . . .

I believe that Justice O'Connor's views, which I share, have greater legal significance than the Court's opinion suggests. I join her separate opinion, except insofar as it joins the majority. And I concur in the judgments. I shall briefly explain how I differ from the Court. . . .

. . . I agree with the Court in Vacco v. Quill that the articulated state interests justify the distinction drawn between physician-assisted suicide and withdrawal of life-support. I also agree with the Court that the critical question in both of the cases before us is whether "the 'liberty' specially protected by the Due Process Clause includes a right" of the sort that the respondents assert. I do not agree, however, with the Court's formulation of that claimed "liberty" interest. The Court describes it as a "right to commit suicide with another's assistance." But I would not reject the respondents' claim without considering a different formulation, for which our legal tradition may provide greater support. That formulation would use words roughly like a "right to die with dignity." But irrespective of the exact words used, at its core would lie personal control over the manner of death, professional medical assistance, and the avoidance of unnecessary and severe physical suffering — combined. . . .

I do not believe, however, that this Court need or now should decide whether or not such a right is "fundamental." That is because, in my view, the avoidance of severe physical pain (connected with death) would have to comprise an essential part of any successful claim and because, as Justice O'Connor points out, the laws before us do not force a dying person to undergo that kind of pain. . . .

Were the legal circumstances different — for example, were state law to prevent the provision of palliative care, including the administration of drugs as needed to avoid pain at the end of life — then the law's impact upon serious and otherwise unavoidable physical pain (accompanying death) would be more directly at issue. And as Justice O'Connor suggests, the Court might have to revisit its conclusions in these cases.

Discussion

1. *The Meaning of* Glucksberg *and Vacco v. Quill.* What, precisely, is the effective holding of the Court in these two cases? Do *Glucksberg* and *Vacco* mean that states in fact enjoy constitutional *carte blanche* to adopt whatever policies they wish with regard to the issue of "assisted suicide" or, rather, that, *for now,* the Court will allow "experimentation" in the states? This means in practice that some states, like Washington, will disallow any such assistance, with others, like Oregon,

adopting a complex machinery that allows certain kinds of assisted suicide. As you read these opinions, does the Court leave open the possibility of judicial intervention should a state prove unwilling to honor the wishes of someone who beyond any doubt is at the terminal stages of an illness that brings with it great suffering?

2. *Deeply rooted in our nation's traditions.* Note carefully Chief Justice Rehnquist's description of the Due Process test, and Justice Souter's objections to it. Is Rehnquist's test consistent with *Griswold, Eisenstadt, Roe,* or *Casey?* How likely is it that the Court would expand the scope of implied fundamental rights under this test? Note that Lawrence v. Texas, which struck down state sodomy laws, was decided only six years after *Glucksberg,* and makes no reference to it. What is the status of Rehnquist's test in light of *Lawrence?*

3. Roe *and* Glucksberg. Is *Glucksberg* an easier case for the discovery of implied fundamental rights than *Roe?* To what extent was the Court worried about its legitimacy in the face of the reaction to *Roe?*

In *Roe* and in *Bowers* we noted that the liberty claim also implicated an underlying equality principle for a particular group (women, homosexuals). We also noted the existence of social movements seeking the right (although in *Roe* the decision itself helped spur on a counter-social movement). Does the right to die implicate equality concerns? Are there any inherent limits on the organization of social movement politics on behalf of the terminally ill? Note that the promotion of their interests must largely be performed by their relatives and by members of the medical profession. In what ways is the interaction between popular opinion, social movements, legislatures, and courts different than the interaction that has occurred in the case of abortion and homosexual rights?

4. *Control over your body and civil commitment.* In Kansas v. Crane, 534 U.S. 407 (2002), the Supreme Court upheld a substantive due process challenge to the Kansas Sexually Violent Predatory Act, which establishes procedures for the civil commitment of persons who, due to a "mental abnormality" or a "personality disorder," are likely to engage in "predatory acts of sexual violence." Crane was a previously convicted sex offender who, according to at least one of the State's psychiatric witnesses, suffers from both exhibitionism and antisocial personality disorder. After a jury trial, the Kansas District Court ordered Crane's civil commitment.

The Court previously rejected a challenge to the statute in Kansas v. Hendricks, 521 U.S. 346 (1997), a case involving a pedophile. *Hendricks* distinguished criminal punishment from civil commitment, and held that substantive due process is satisfied if a civil commitment statute requires proof of dangerousness along with proof of some additional factor, such as a "mental illness" or "mental abnormality." In *Crane,* the question was what degree of dangerousness caused by the mental abnormality had to be shown. The Court argued that the state need not prove that the person committed by the state completely lacks the ability to control his or her behavior: "[I]n cases where lack of control is at issue, 'inability to control behavior' will not be demonstrable with mathematical precision. It is enough to say that there must be proof of serious difficulty in controlling behavior. And this, when viewed in light of such features of the case as the nature of the psychiatric diagnosis, and the severity of the mental abnormality itself, must be sufficient to distinguish the dangerous sexual offender whose serious mental illness, abnormality, or disorder subjects him to civil commitment from the dangerous but typical recidivist convicted in an ordinary criminal case." Without a showing of serious difficulty in controlling behavior, however, substantive due process prevented civil commitment. Justice Scalia, joined by Justice Thomas, would have applied a more relaxed standard. For them it would be sufficient "that the person previously convicted of one of the enumerated sexual offenses is suffering from a mental abnormality or personality disorder, and . . . that this condition renders him likely to commit future acts of sexual violence."

5. *Punitive damages:* Lochner *redux?* Is there any clear way to delimit the group of substantive due process rights? We close this chapter with what would seem to be a very different set of issues: punitive damage awards in tort suits. Despite the Court's general rejection of substantive due process challenges to economic regulation after 1937, the Supreme Court has recently begun to hold that the Due Process Clause imposes substantive limits on the size of punitive damage awards. In Browning-Ferris Industries v. Kelco Disposal, Inc., 492 U.S. 257 (1989), the Court held that the Eighth Amendment's excessive fines clause did not limit punitive damages in ordinary civil litigation between private parties. Two years later, however, in Pacific Mutual Life Insurance Company v. Haslip, 499 U.S. 1 (1991), the Court held that the Due Process Clause did limit punitive damage awards both procedurally and substantively. Procedurally, juries had to be properly instructed on the purposes for punitive damage awards and the proper methods of assessing them. In Honda Motor Co. v. Oberg, 512 U.S. 415 (1994) the Court invoked these procedural limits to punitive damages when it struck down, under the Due Process Clause, an amendment to the Oregon Constitution that prohibits judicial review of the amount of punitive damages awarded by a jury "unless the court can affirmatively say there is no evidence to support the verdict." In addition, as a substantive matter, the Court held in BMW of North America, Inc. v. Gore, 517 U.S. 559 (1996), that the actual awards themselves had to be reasonable and not disproportionate or "grossly excessive."

These doctrines inevitably led the Court into assessing what constituted a grossly excessive verdict. Compare *Gore* (striking down a $2 million punitive damages award which accompanied a $4,000 compensatory damages award) with TXO Production Corp. v. Alliance Resources Corp., 509 U.S. 443 (1993) (upholding a $10 million award that accompanied a $19,000 compensatory damages award).

In State Farm Mutual Automobile Insurance Co. v. Campbell, 538 U.S. 408 (2003), the Court, in a opinion by Justice Kennedy, struck down a $145 million punitive damage award arising out of an insurer's bad faith refusal to settle a claim, where the plaintiffs had been awarded $1 million in compensatory damages. Justice Kennedy explained that "courts must ensure that the measure of punishment is both reasonable and proportionate to the amount of harm to the plaintiff and to the general damages recovered." This means that "single-digit multipliers are more likely to comport with due process, while still achieving the State's goals of deterrence and retribution" than much larger ratios between punitive and compensatory damages. In addition Justice Kennedy's opinion suggested, "[w]hen compensatory damages are substantial, then a lesser ratio, perhaps only equal to compensatory damages, can reach the outermost limit of the due process guarantee."

Finally, the Court held that a punitive damage award cannot be used to punish a defendant's entire pattern of conduct when some of the conduct occurred within the state and some outside of it: "A State cannot punish a defendant for conduct that may have been lawful where it occurred, . . . [n]or, as a general rule, does a State have a legitimate concern in imposing punitive damages to punish a defendant for unlawful acts committed outside of the State's jurisdiction." Justices Scalia and Thomas dissented on the grounds that the Constitution imposes no substantive limits on punitive damage awards. Justice Ginsburg also dissented: "I remain of the view that this Court has no warrant to reform state law governing awards of punitive damages."

Chapter 9
The Constitution in the Modern Welfare State

Asa Briggs, writing on The Welfare State in Historical Perspective, defines the welfare state as one

> in which organized power is deliberately used (through politics and administration) in an effort to modify the play of market forces in at least three directions — first, by guaranteeing individuals and families a minimum income irrespective of the market value of their property; second, by narrowing the extent of insecurity by enabling individuals and families to meet certain "social contingencies" (for example, sickness, old age, and unemployment) which lead otherwise to individual and family crises; and third, by ensuring that all citizens without distinction of status or class are offered the best standards available in relation to a certain agreed range of social services.[1]

As Neil Gilbert explains:[2]

> Capitalism encourages competition and risk-taking behavior. Although success in the economic marketplace is often well rewarded, misfortune and failure can lead to harsh consequences. There are few market mechanisms to mitigate the consequences of accident, illness, age, and vicissitudes of industrial society. And these mechanisms, such as private insurance, provide the most protection to those who are relatively well off and least in need of it. The welfare state operates through a social market that provides a sort of communal safety net for the casualties of a market economy.

One should note that even most devotees of the "welfare state" have only limited notions of the citizen's "welfare" that is a proper concern of the state. Should, for example, the state be concerned with the religious salvation of its members? A tenet of the political liberalism identified with John Locke and his later American followers like Thomas Jefferson was that getting right with God was the responsibility of each individual, with the state having no role to play. Few contemporary adherents of a "welfare state" have been critical of this central aspect of political liberalism, even though proponents of a more traditional tutelary state might well argue that nothing could provide greater welfare to the citizenry than the state's firm guidance of the recalcitrant in the paths of eternal life or, at least, the avoidance of sin. Similarly, an Aristotelian might argue that the state should be concerned with the virtue of its members and act consciously so as to mold in them a sufficiently virtuous character. Although contemporary debates about the role of the state in, say, regulating pornography or sexual

---

1. Quoted in Evelyn Z. Brodkin and Dennis Young, Making Sense of Privatization: What Can We Learn from Economic and Policy Analysis?, in Privatization and the Welfare State (Kamerman & Kahn eds.) 140 (1989).
2. Neil Gilbert, Capitalism and the Welfare State 4-5 (1983). See also Amy Gutmann, ed., Democracy and the Welfare State (1988).

conduct or inculcating in the young the precepts of virtuous living are usually not couched as debates about the reach of the "welfare state," they could well merit that description under a broad conception of that term.

Most critics of the minimal state, however, especially those persons identified with the political left, have accepted the liberal notion of state neutrality in regard to basic questions about what counts as a life well lived. Critics have therefore focused on other questions, especially those involving the distributive justice of the allocation of economic resources found within a given society and the state's role, if any, in rectifying ostensible maldistributions.

At no point did American government adopt a posture of pure laissez-faire; regulation, occupational licensing, and subsidies for developing industries had existed since at least the eighteenth century.[3] And, as we have seen in earlier chapters, Congress was often more than willing to pass "disaster relief" legislation that, almost by definition, involves redistribution of resources to those rendered "have-nots" by the force of disaster, whether from cities burning down or the flooding of great rivers. Still, the magnitude of state intervention in the lives of individuals and enterprises increased enormously in the twentieth century, especially in the decades that followed the New Deal. These changes in the reach of government power were accompanied by shifts in a number of fundamental constitutional concepts.

We begin this chapter by asking whether the state is conceivably prohibited, as a constitutional matter, from the redistribution of goods and resources from the better off to the less-well-off that is the hallmark of any welfare state. We then move on to the opposite question, whether some kind of welfare state is constitutionally required. Then, given that most contemporary welfarist policy is neither prohibited nor required, the remainder of this chapter considers the constitutional constraints imposed on lawmakers who exercise their discretion to pass such legislation.

I.   Does the Constitution Prohibit a Welfare State?

Welfare benefits almost invariably involve some kind of taking (almost always of taxes) from A and giving either money or goods purchased with the tax revenues to a presumptively deserving B. Recall in this context Justice Miller's discussion in Loan Association v. Topeka, supra Chapter 4, not to mention Lochner v. New York and its warning against courts accepting too uncritically legislative proclamations that the public interest is served by a particular redistribution. In evaluating welfare legislation, only sometimes was a specific textual provision of the Constitution (such as the Takings Clause, applicable primarily to real property) pointed to; instead, reference was frequently made to basic principles ostensibly underlying the notion of constitutionalism, as in Calder v. Bull (1798), Chapter 2, supra. A fine example is Lucas County v. State of Ohio, 75 O.S. 131 (1906), which challenged an Ohio act providing relief "for worthy blind" persons:

> The care of the state for its dependent classes is considered by all enlightened
> people as a measure of its civilization and it is not doubted that the legislation under

3. See, e.g., William J. Novak, The People's Welfare: Law and Regulation in Nineteenth-Century America (1996).

consideration was inspired by beneficent if not enlightened motives. This state has provided institutions for the education of the blind; for feeble-minded youth; for honorably discharged soldiers, sailors and marines; a home for soldiers' and sailors' orphans; for the care and treatment of the insane; an asylum for epileptics and epileptic insane; a boys' industrial school; a girls' industrial home; for the establishment of homes of the friendless; a sanitarium for consumptives; and an institution for the treatment and education of deformed and crippled children.

The object of these institutions is sufficiently indicated by their designation, and may be stated to be, generally, to be provided places and means where their afflictions may be relieved, or where they may be taught and trained so that they may be self-supporting, or less likely to become a burden on the state, or where their physical wants may be supplied at the public expense. But it does not follow that it would be either wise or constitutional to select out a class, having some particular physical infirmity, and then confer a bounty upon individuals of that class. If a bounty may be conferred upon individuals of one class, then it may be upon individuals of another class, and if upon two, then upon all. And if upon those who have physical infirmities, then why not upon other classes who for various reasons may be unable to support themselves? And if these things may be done, why may not all property be distributed by the state?

The principal contention on the part of the auditor is that the law is unconstitutional, because the purpose for which the public funds are appropriated is not public. . . .

Section 2 of the [Ohio] Bill of Rights declares that all political power is inherent in the people. Government is instituted for their equal protection and benefit. And Section 1 declares that the right of acquiring, possessing and protecting property is one of the inalienable rights of all men. And section 19 provides that private property shall ever be held inviolate, but subservient to the public welfare. So that the power of the State to take the property of its citizens by a tax is not broader than the purposes for which the state is formed, and so is not wholly within the discretion of the Legislature, but . . . is subject to this inherent limitation that it may be exercised only for a public purpose.

. . . [I]t must be said that the act under consideration is without precedent in this state and that no provision is made in the act to insure the application of the money to the support of the individual, or to prevent him from becoming a public charge, or in any manner to control its use by him. . . . It is an indeterminate gratuitous annuity, a gift pure and simple, and, being so, the Legislature is without authority to make it from the public funds. . . .

It may be said that funds used for the care of the poor are used for a public purpose, and that money used under the provisions of this act will subserve a public purpose for the reason that they will enable many blind persons, aided by their own efforts or those of their friends, to support themselves, and thus to escape becoming a public charge. . . .

If the power of the Legislature to confer an annuity upon any class of needy citizens is admitted upon the ground that its tendency will be to prevent them from becoming a public charge, then innumerable classes may clamor for similar bounties, and if not upon equally meritorious grounds, still on ground that is valid in point of law, and it is doubted that any line could be drawn short of an equal distribution of property.

A few of the many cases more or less illustrative of the application of the rule may be noticed. . . . In State v. Switzler, 143 Mo. 287, an act was held invalid that provided for the payment of certain sums of money in monthly installments to certain students while attending the state university, who were dependent on their own efforts for an education, and financially unable to otherwise obtain the same.

Discussion

Note that the Ohio court accepts the legitimacy of the state's establishing a number of "homes" for the indigent, just as the *Lochner* majority had accepted the legitimacy of some regulation of the terms of employment. And some kinds of "poor relief" had been provided, usually at the local level, since colonial times. The question, then, is not whether the Constitution prevents *any* kind of welfare state, but, rather, whether the policies adopted in fact serve the public welfare. Many framers, after all, worried that the coercive mechanisms of the state, most certainly including the power to tax (and spend), might be captured by "factions" who would then pass legislation or issue executive orders that would serve only the "partial" interests of their political friends rather than the general "public" interest. The most famous statement of this view is surely Madison's Federalist Paper No. 10, though it is well reflected in such writings as Andrew Jackson's Veto of the bill renewing the Bank of the United States, supra Chapter 1, or the jurisprudence of Justice Field, supra Chapter 4.[4] The central issue, as a practical matter, is to what extent courts are charged with monitoring legislative judgments about the "public purpose" of any given decision allocating welfare benefits. Since 1937, of course, the Court has tended to give legislatures extremely wide berth, captured by the notion of "minimum rationality" as the sole question asked of a governmental policy. Consider the following, not atypical, case.

LYNG v. INTERNATIONAL UNION, UNITED AUTO WORKERS
485 US 360 (1988)

[The federal food stamp program provides an in-kind income supplement for the poor as well as a subsidy for the farmers producing the food. By 1988 the annual outlay for food stamps was $12.3 billion.[5] The program had earlier been the source of some constitutional litigation. In Department of Agriculture v. Moreno, 413 U.S. 528 (1973), the Court considered a 1971 amendment to the Food Stamp Act that excluded from participation in the food stamp program any member of a household whose members are not all related to each other. Although there is good reason to believe that Congress was attempting to prevent "hippie communes" from receiving any stamps, the plaintiffs in the case were not hippies. For example, one was a person with an acute hearing deficiency who, in order to live near a special school for the deaf, was sharing an apartment with someone on public assistance. Because they were not related, they became ineligible for the food stamps they would have received had they lived separately. Justice Brennan wrote for the Court invalidating the exclusion on the ground that it did not serve any valid legislative purpose and thus created an "irrational classification in violation of the equal protection component of the Due Process Clause of the Fifth Amendment." Justice Rehnquist, joined by Chief Justice Burger, dissented, arguing that the regulation was rationally related to assuring that a household exists for some purpose other than collecting federal food stamps.

---

4. See Howard Gillman, The Constitution Besieged: The Rise and Demise of Lochner Era Police Powers Jurisprudence (1993) for an excellent historical presentation of the differentiation, in late-nineteenth century thought, between "public"- and "class"-interest legislation. See also Cass R. Sunstein, The Partial Constitution (1993) for a vigorous defense of the continuing importance of "impartiality" as a bedrock aspect of the Constitution.

5. Budget of the United States Government, Fiscal Year 1990, at 9-40.

In 1981, Congress amended the Food Stamp Act to provide that no household shall become eligible to receive food stamps while any one of its members is on strike. If the household was already receiving food stamps, its allotment would not be increased by virtue of the striker's unemployment. A congressional committee report estimated that this measure would save a total of about $165 million in fiscal years 1982, 1983, and 1984. As the Court observed, "It would be difficult to deny that this statute works at least some discrimination against strikers and their households. For the duration of the strike, those households cannot increase their allotment of food stamps even though the loss of income occasioned by the strike may well be enough to qualify them for food stamps or to increase their allotment if the fact of the strike itself were ignored." The court below had declared the amendment unconstitutional on three different grounds. Two were based on the First Amendment: The amended act interfered with strikers' rights to associate with their families and unions as well as to express themselves freely about union matters by striking. The third was predicated on the "equal protection component of the Due Process Clause of the Fifth Amendment." The majority summarily dismissed the first two claims and focused on the third.]

WHITE, J.

III.

A

[W]e confine our consideration to whether the statutory classification "is rationally related to a legitimate governmental interest." The Government submits that this statute serves three objectives. Most obvious . . . is to cut federal expenditures. Second, the limited funds available were to be used where the need was likely to be greatest, an approach which Congress thought did not justify food stamps for strikers. Third was the concern that the food stamp program was being used to provide one-sided support for labor strikes; the Senate Report indicated that the amendment was intended to remove the basis for that perception and criticism.

We have little trouble in concluding that [the amendment] is rationally related to the legitimate governmental objective of avoiding undue favoritism to one side or the other in private labor disputes. . . .

Congress was in a difficult position when it sought to address the problems it had identified. Because a striking individual faces an immediate and often total drop in income during a strike, a single controversy pitting an employer against its employees can lead to a large number of claims for food stamps for as long as the controversy endures. It is the disbursement of food stamps in response to such a controversy that constitutes the sources of the concern, and of the dangers to the program, that Congress believed it was important to remedy. We are not free in this instance to reject Congress' views about "what constitutes wise economic or social policy." It is true that in terms of the scope and extent of their ineligibility for food stamps, [the amendment] is harder on strikers than on "voluntary quitters."[a]

---

a. For example, one who voluntarily quits a job is disqualified for food stamps for 90 days. Thereafter, he is eligible as long as he registers for work and cannot find a job. The striker, unless he quits his job, is disqualified for as long as he is on strike.

But the concern about neutrality in labor disputes does not arise with respect to those who, for one reason or another, simply quit their jobs. As we have stated in a related context, even if the statute "provides only 'rough justice,' its treatment . . . is far from irrational." Ohio Bureau of Employment Services v. Hodory, 431 U.S. 471 491 (1977).[6] . . . [W]e are not authorized to ignore Congress' considered efforts to avoid favoritism in labor disputes, which are evidenced also by the two significant provisos contained in the statute. The first proviso preserves eligibility for the program of any household that was eligible to receive stamps "immediately prior to such strike." The second proviso makes clear that the statutory ineligibility for food stamps does not apply [if a household member] "refuses to accept employment at a plant or site because of a strike or lockout." In light of all this, the statute is rationally related to the stated objective of maintaining neutrality in private labor disputes.

In view of the foregoing, we need not determine whether either of the other two proffered justifications for [the amendment] would alone suffice. . . .

Appellees contend and the District Court held that the legislative classification is irrational because of the "critical" fact that it "impermissibly strikes at the striker through his family." This, however, is nothing more than a description of how the food stamp program operates as a general matter. . . . Whenever an individual takes any action that hampers his or her ability to meet the program's eligibility requirements, such as quitting a job or failing to comply with the work-registration requirements, the entire household suffers accordingly. . . . That aspect of the program does not violate the Constitution. . . .

MARSHALL, J., joined by Justices Brennan and Blackmun, dissenting: . . .

I.

. . . The Court fails to note [that the rational basis] standard of review, although deferential, "is not a toothless one." Mathews v. De Castro, 429 U.S. 181, 185 (1976), quoting Mathews v. Lucas, 427 U.S. 495, 510 (1976). . . .

A

The Secretary's argument that the striker amendment will save money proves far too much. According to the Secretary's reasoning, the exclusion of any unpopular group from a public benefit program would survive rational basis scrutiny, because exclusion always would result in a decrease in governmental expenditures. . . . [T]his Court expressly has noted that "a concern for the preservation of resources standing alone can hardly justify the classification used in allocating those resources." We have insisted that such classifications themselves be rational rather than arbitrary. . . .

B

Perhaps recognizing this necessity, the Secretary defends the singling out of strikers and their households as rationally related to the goal of channeling resources to

6. An Ohio statute denied unemployment compensation benefits to workers thrown out of work because of a labor dispute, so long as they weren't "locked out" by employers. Hodory, a nonstriking employee of a parent company that shut down after a subsidiary went on strike, was denied unemployment compensation because of this statute. The Supreme Court upheld the denial, holding that it did not violate the equal protection clause.

those persons most "genuinely in need." As a threshold matter, however, house-holds denied food stamps because of the presence of a strike are as "needy" in terms of financial resources as households that qualify for food stamps: the former are denied food stamps despite the fact that they meet the financial eligibility requirements [of federal law], even after strike-fund payments are counted as household income. This point has particular poignancy for the infants and children of a striking worker. Their need for nourishment is in no logical way diminished by the striker's action. The denial to these children of what is often the only buffer between them and malnourishment and disease cannot be justified as a targeting of the most needy: they *are* the most needy. The record below bears witness to this point in a heartbreaking fashion.

The Secretary argues, however, that the striker amendment is related to need at least in the sense of willingness to work, if not in the strict sense of financial eligibility. Because the Food Stamp Act generally excludes persons unwilling to work — and their households — the Secretary argues that it is consistent to exclude strikers and their households as well, on the ground that strikers remain "unwilling to work," at least at the struck business, for the duration of the strike. In the Secretary's eyes, a striker is akin to an unemployed worker who day after day refuses to accept available work. One flaw in this argument is its false factual premise. It is simply not true, as the Secretary argues, that a striker always has a job that "remains available to him." Many strikes result in the complete cessation of a business's operations, so that the decision of an individual striker to return to work would be unavailing. Moreover, many of the businesses that continue to operate during a strike hire permanent replacements for the striking workers. In this situation as well, a striker no longer has the option of returning to work. In fact, the record in this case reveals that a number of appellees were denied food stamps even though they had been permanently replaced by their employers.

But even if it were true that strikers always can return to their jobs, the Secretary's "willingness to work" rationale falls apart in light of the glaring disparity between the treatment of strikers and the treatment of those who are unwilling to work for other reasons. People who voluntarily quit their jobs are not disqualified from receiving food stamps if, after notice and hearing, they can demonstrate that they quit with "good cause." Moreover, even if the state agency determines that the quit was without good cause, the voluntary quitter is disqualified only for a period of 90 days, and the quitter's household is disqualified only if the quitter was the "head of household." In contrast, a striker is given no opportunity to demonstrate that the strike was for "good cause," even though strikers frequently allege that unfair labor practices by their employer precipitated the strike. In addition, strikers and their entire households, no matter how minimal the striker's contribution to the household's income may have been, are disqualified for the duration of the strike, even if the striker is permanently replaced or business operations temporarily cease.

In a similar vein, the striker amendment expressly distinguishes between strikers and non-strikers in conditioning eligibility for food stamps on willingness to accept struck work. Unemployed workers may refuse to accept otherwise appropriate employment at a business involved in a strike or a lockout and still remain eligible to receive food stamps — as long as they are not themselves on strike. Only strikers, though they may be as "willing to work" in every salient respect, must give up their eligibility for food stamps if they refuse to cross a picket line. The Secretary's "willingness to work" argument provides no justification for this especially harsh treatment of strikers and their households.

C

Unable to explain completely the striker amendment by the "willingness to work" rationale, the Secretary relies most heavily on yet a third rationale: the promotion of governmental neutrality in labor disputes. Indeed, the Court relies solely on this explanation in rejecting appellees' Equal Protection challenge to the amendment. . . .

[T]he "neutrality" argument . . . is both deceptive and deeply flawed. Even on the most superficial level, the striker amendment does not treat the parties to a labor dispute evenhandedly: forepersons and other management employees who may become temporarily unemployed when a business ceases to operate during a strike remain eligible for food stamps. Management's burden during the course of the dispute is thus lessened by the receipt of public funds, whereas labor must struggle unaided. This disparity cannot be justified by the argument that the strike is labor's "fault," because strikes are often a direct response to illegal practices by management, such as failure to abide by the terms of a collective bargaining agreement or refusal to bargain in good faith.

On a deeper level, the "neutrality" argument reflects a profoundly inaccurate view of the relationship of the modern federal government to the various parties to a labor dispute. Both individuals and businesses are connected to the government by a complex web of supports and incentives. On the one hand, individuals may be eligible to receive a wide variety of health, education, and welfare-related benefits. On the other hand, businesses may be eligible to receive a myriad of tax subsidies through deductions, depreciation, and credits or direct subsidies in the form of government loans through the Small Business Administration (SBA). Businesses also may receive lucrative government contracts and invoke the protections of the Bankruptcy Act against their creditors. None of these governmental subsidies to businesses is made contingent on the businesses' abstention from labor disputes, even if a labor dispute is the direct cause of the claim to a subsidy. For example, a small business in need of financial support because of labor troubles may seek a loan from the SBA. And a business that claims a net operating loss as a result of a strike or a lockout presumably may carry the loss back three years and forward five years in order to maximize its tax advantage. In addition, it appears that businesses may be eligible for special tax credits for hiring replacement workers during a strike under the targeted Jobs Tax Credit program. When viewed against the network of governmental support of both labor and management, the withdrawal of the single support of food stamps — a support critical to the continued life and health of an individual worker and his or her family — cannot be seen as a "neutral" act. Altering the backdrop of governmental support in this one-sided and devastating way amounts to a penalty on strikers, not neutrality.

D

The successive failure of each of the Secretary's purported rationales for the striker amendment . . . suggests that the enactment at issue here rests on public animus toward strikers. . . . [S]upporters of the striker amendment likened strikers to "hippies" and "commune residents" — groups whose exclusion from the food stamp program this Court struck down fifteen years ago in Department of Agriculture v. Moreno. . . . Our warning in *Moreno* that "a bare congressional desire to harm a politically unpopular group cannot constitute a legitimate governmental interest," would seem directly applicable to the instant case. . . .

Note: On "Neutrality"

Throughout this chapter you will read cases that seem to agree both that neutrality is a meaningful term of analysis and that neutrality goes far toward upholding a policy challenged as unconstitutional. Do we, however, have theories that allow us to offer relatively uncontroversial examples of social arrangements as "neutral" or, if "non-neutral," otherwise clearly serving the public interest? Professor Sunstein, for example, suggests that we tend to identify as neutral those social practices that have sufficient longevity to be perceived as normal within the society.[7] Thus, throughout much of the nineteenth century, the ostensible norms of the common law were perceived to establish a baseline of vested rights in property holders that were protected against innovative legislation that redistributed the existing arrangements of legal rights. During the *Lochner* era, these arrangements were often treated as property or liberty interests protected by the Constitution. But, of course, a central tenet of much modern political analysis is that any given status quo may well represent little, if anything, more than the congealed social power of dominant social groups at a particular time. That is, there is nothing necessarily neutral about any existing assignment of legal rights or entitlements, for almost all can be understood historically as successful attempts to privilege one sector of society over another.

In *Lochner*, both Justices Peckham and Harlan, whatever their differences on the constitutional legitimacy of the New York law, appear to agree that legislation must genuinely serve public purposes and that courts can legitimately engage in some degree of monitoring to assure the presence of such purposes. Justice Holmes's famous dissent, however, is written from an entirely different point of view. As Sunstein writes, it "is a rejection of neutrality altogether" insofar as Holmes views the political process "as a kind of civil war, in which the powerful succeed," able to write their "naked preferences" into law. Indeed, Holmes had earlier written in The Common Law that "[t]he first requirement of a sound body of law is, that it should correspond with the actual feelings and demands of the community, whether right or wrong."[8] This underlies Holmes's injunction in *Lochner* that the Constitution should not be read to prevent "the natural outcome of a dominant opinion."

Assume for the moment that we can indeed distinguish the "neutral" from the "non-neutral." Is it the case that the Constitution requires those who control the apparatus of state power to constrain their partisanship when passing legislation or otherwise engaging in the business of governance? Does identifying a given policy as "non-neutral" necessarily call its constitutional bona fides into question?

---

7. See Cass Sunstein, Lochner's Legacy, 87 Colum. L. Rev. 873 (1987), a masterful synthesis of a critical tradition going back at least to some of the legal realists of the 1920s. All of the quotations below from Sunstein are taken from this article.

8. The Common Law 36 (Howe ed., 1963).

Which way, for example, does neutrality cut in *Lyng?* Is allowing strikers to receive food stamps partisan on their behalf, or does disallowance of benefits pit the state against strikers in a non-neutral manner by removing their eligibility for social welfare benefits that would otherwise be available? Is it any more helpful to ask if food stamps serve as "subsidies" to strikers or, in contrast, if the vindictive withdrawal of food stamp eligibility works as a "penalty" against those who strike?

Assume that Justice Marshall is correct that the amendment is rooted in anti-union animus, a "naked preference" that management be allowed to prevail over labor. (For that matter, food stamps for strikers might have been rooted in a similarly naked preference that union prevail over management.) So what? So long as the burdened group has not been accorded the status of a "suspect class" in equal protection analysis, do they merit any judicial protection against political animus?

Perhaps your answer depends on the extent to which you believe there is a constitutionally protected "right to strike," based, perhaps on the Thirteenth Amendment's prohibition of involuntary servitude. You might consider, though, Professor Pope's remark that "[d]uring the 1950s the Supreme Court all but withdrew constitutional protection from labor picketing and stood by while a host of lower courts resolved the 'momentous question' of the constitutional right to strike by summarily denying its existence."[9] One of President Reagan's first actions as President in 1981 was to fire several thousand members of the airline traffic controllers union for violating federal law by striking. If a legislature may prohibit public employees from striking, then what is the problem, especially given post-1937 views of congressional power under the Commerce Clause, with a law prohibiting strikes in the private sector? If the right to strike is not constitutionally protected, but merely a matter of legislative grace, why can't Congress, for whatever reason it wishes, hinder strikers by depriving them (and their families) of food stamps?

II. The Rise of the Modern Welfare State

Even if one concludes that a welfare state is not constitutionally required, it is beyond doubt that the United States in the twentieth century witnessed the development of at least a modified welfare state, as both state and national governments increasingly provide certain goods and services to members of society who are unable to purchase them on the private market.

The "welfare state" is distinct from the "regulatory state" whose emergence was traced in supra, Chapter 5. The regulatory state, characterized by statutory regulation of wages and hours, labor–management relations, the securities market, and the like, emerged in response to skepticism about the fairness of the unimpeded operations of the market. The government thus sought to redistribute power by conferring specific legal rights on more vulnerable groups to counter the private power of those who would prevail in the absence of regulation. Much of twentieth-century constitutional law, immediately following 1937, involved the validation of the regulatory state within the constraints of established constitutional doctrine.

---

9. James Gray Pope, Labor and the Constitution: From Abolition to Deindustrialization, 65 Tex. L. Rev. 1071 (1987). Professor Pope advocates the recognition of a constitutional right to strike, as did Archibald Cox, Strikes, Picketing and the Constitution, 4 Vand. L. Rev. 574 (1951).

Most of the New Deal legislation, however, required astonishingly little increase in the direct expenditures of state funds. Though the social goal may have been redistribution of income, legislators chose to effectuate this goal by simply rearranging the legal relations between private actors. The state, for example, did not itself finance higher wages or increased benefits for union members, but rather imposed the burden on private employers. The principal governmental expenditures of many of these statutory schemes were the quite modest costs of administration and enforcement. However important to the modern regulatory state the National Labor Relations Board or Securities and Exchange Commission may be, they do not make extraordinary demands on the federal budget.

A welfare state, in contrast to a regulatory state, plays a more active role in the redistribution of resources. Beyond merely shifting the boundaries of private legal relations, the welfare state directly allocates resources to a discrete group of individuals. Examples are legion, ranging from grants to college students to food stamps to subsidies to the blind. Laws of these kinds lead to significant increases in governmental budgets.

Although the origins of this transformation can be found in the New Deal and such programs as Social Security, the number of programs and level of expenditures increased dramatically in the 1960s. Between 1964 and 1966 alone Congress passed the Economic Opportunity Act, the Demonstration Cities and Metropolitan Development Act, the Older Americans Act, and the Food Stamp Act, and also established the basic medical coverage programs of Medicare and Medicaid. These initiatives, identified with President Lyndon Johnson's "Great Society," were substantially consolidated and in some instances expanded by the succeeding administration of President Richard Nixon. Even the comparatively minimalist welfare program of the Reagan Administration only slowed down, rather than reversed, the developments of the 1960s and 1970s.

Governmental expenditure figures provide vivid confirmation of the changing political reality. Between 1927 and 1932, when the consequences of the Great Depression ravaged the nation, "public welfare" expenditures at all levels of government — federal, state, and local — increased from only $161 million to $445 million. By 1936 they had climbed to nearly $1 billion. In 1960, the total expenditures were approximately $4.5 billion.[10] At the federal level, one can put the welfare budget, at the time of John Kennedy's "New Frontier" and Lyndon Johnson's "Great Society," in context by comparing it to the defense budget. Thus, in 1964, well before the peak of spending on the Vietnam War (which reached $80 billion in 1968), the United States gave the Defense Department $50 billion, while allocating only $5.7 billion to the "welfare state" departments of Health, Education, and Welfare (HEW, as it was then known) and Housing and Urban Development combined. By 1994, however, what was now the Department of Health and Human Services (HHS) alone was taking in more money than the Defense Department: $279 billion for HHS as compared to $268.6 billion for military defense. As a percentage of total outlays, HHS's 1994 funding accounted for a full 19 percent of all federal spending, exceeded only by outlays for the Social Security Administration (approximately 24 percent) and Treasury (approximately 21 percent). In 1962, by contrast, HEW outlays accounted for only 3.3 percent of total

10. See Series Y 533-566, Federal, State, and Local Government Expenditures, by Function: 1902 to 1970, Historical Statistics of the United States, Colonial Times to 1970, Part 2, 1120 (1975).

outlays.[11] The current HHS budgets account for less than half of the total "welfare department" outlays. If we add outlay percentages for the Department of Education (1.7 percent as of 1995), the Department of Housing and Urban Development (1.8 percent), and the Social Security Administration (23.7 percent), total welfare state outlays comprised over 46 percent of total federal expenditures in 1994, as compared to 18.3 percent in 1962.

Another way of expressing these developments is by looking at "constant dollar" expenditures (with 1987 dollars serving as the baseline), which therefore account for inflation. Whereas by this measure, the total federal welfare outlay in 1940 was $96.8 billion for a population of 132 million persons, with per capita spending therefore being $733 per person, by 1980 the outlays were $832.1 billion for a population of 228 million, with per capita expenditures of $3,650 per person. In 1994, $1140.3 billion was spent for 261 million persons, a per capita figure of $4,369. (This was less than the $4,424 per capita figure in 1990.) The rise in federal expenditures was mirrored at lower levels of government. Toward the end of the Great Depression, in 1940, all state and local governments in the United States spent approximately $11.8 billion (in constant 1987 dollars). By 1970 the amount had grown to $44.7 billion and then to $64.1 billion in 1980. The total nearly doubled once more by 1992, reaching $126.6 billion. In per capita terms, the total rose from $283 per person in 1980 to $497 in 1992.[12]

Even though Republicans took over Congress in 1995 and the presidency in 2001, the story told by the general figures remains perhaps surprisingly similar. Thus, even though defense and military expenditures leapt from $290 billion in 2001 to $437 billion in 2004, HHS expenditures went up from $426 billion in 2001 to $543 billion in 2004. Moreover, if one looks at estimates extending to 2010 issued by the Bush Administration in its proposed budget for Fiscal Year 2006 (which begins in October 2005), the 2010 defense and military expenditures are estimated at only $485 billion, whereas HHS is estimated to be spending $829 billion, reflecting, among other things, the anticipated costs of an expensive new drug program passed at the behest of the Bush Administration in 2004. If one looks at Social Security Administration expenditures, one discovers that total expenditures (both so-called "on-" and "off-budget") will rise from an actual total of $530 billion in 2004 to an estimated $714 billion in 2010.[13] Percentage distribution figures convey similar messages. Defense and military expenditures went from 15.6 percent of the budget in 2001 to 19.1 percent in 2004 (a higher percentage than any of the estimates for 2005-2010, which may rest on debatable assumptions about the pace of

11. See Budget of the United States Government: Fiscal Year 1996, Table 4.1 — Outlays by Agency: 1962-2000, Historical Tables, 58-62. This figure grew to 8.9 percent in 1970 and 14 percent in 1990. See Table 4.2 — Percentage Distribution of Outlays by Agency: 1962-2000, Historical Tables, 63-66.

12. All constant-dollar figures are expressed in terms of Fiscal Year 1987 dollars. Excerpted from Table 1.3 — Summary of Receipts, Outlays, and Surpluses or Deficits in Current Dollars, Constant (FY 1987) Dollars, and as Percentages of GDP: 1940-2000, Budget of the United States Government: Fiscal Year 1996, Historical Tables, 17 [Attachment #1]. Population data are from Table 173 — Government Employment and Population: 1962-1994, Historical Tables, 245; and Series A 6-8. Annual Population Estimates for the United States: 1790-1970, U.S. Bureau of the Census, Historical Statistics of the United States, Colonial Times to 1970, Part 1, 8 (1975).

13. All of these figures are taken from Table 4.1 — Outlays by Agency: 1962-2010, The Budget for Fiscal Year 2006: Historical Tables, available at *http://www.whitehouse.gov/omb/budget/fy2006/pdf/hist.pdf.*

U.S. withdrawal from Iraq and the lack of similar military operations in other areas of the world). But HHS also will see a rise from 22.9 percent of federal expenditures in 2001 to 23.7 percent in 2004 and then an anticipated 27.4 percent in 2010. Expenditures by the Social Security Administration will decline slightly, from 24.7 percent in 2001 to 23.1 percent in 2004 and an anticipated 23.6 percent in 2010.[14] And, to the consternation of some conservatives, federal spending on education went up during the Bush presidency from almost $38 billion (1.9 percent of the budget) in 2001 (which actually reflects the last budget prepared by the Clinton Administration in 2000) to $63 billion (2.7 percent) in 2004, reflecting, no doubt, one of the Bush Administration's most important legislative achievements, the No Child Left Behind Act passed in 2001.

It should be clear, then, that if one looks at federal spending in terms of function, welfare-state-related expenses now far exceed outlays for defense. As Harvard political scientist Paul Peterson points out, the most dramatic increases in spending by the national government have occurred in regard to what he calls "redistributive," as contrasted with "developmental," expenditures. For example, although federal expenditures on transportation went up, in constant dollars, from 1962 to 1982, the rise was relatively modest, and there was actually a decline from 1982 to 1992. Overall, Peterson's "developmental" expenditures (transportation, natural resources, safety, education, utilities, and miscellaneous) rose from 4.22 percent of the gross national product (GNP) in 1962 (approximately $100 billion in 1990 dollars) to 5.24 percent ($285.6 billion) in 1990, whereas "redistributive" spending (pensions and medical insurance, welfare, health and hospitals, and housing) went up from 4.78 percent of the GNP in 1962 ($114.3 million) to 10.26 percent ($560.7 billion) in 1990.[15] Peterson argues that this disparity between "developmental" and "redistributive" programs is not surprising for the following reason: State governments are, by and large, willing to finance much of their own "developmental" investment because they will be the primary beneficiaries of any improvements and, indeed, will gain some competitive advantage over states that fall behind in regard to transportation, and so on.

On the other hand, redistributive programs, by definition, involve shifts of resources from high taxpayers to low ones, and this, it is argued, can put high-benefit states at a competitive disadvantage. (Recall the earlier discussion, Chapter 4 supra, of the "prisoners' dilemma" and federalism.) Thus pro-redistribution states will try, as much as possible, to encourage national programs to eliminate the possibility of other states "competing" by offering lower welfare benefits and, therefore, lower tax rates. This is the basis of the so-called "race to the bottom" by states wishing to maximize their competitive advantage in regard to high-income taxpayers. Changes in federal welfare policy since 1996 that eliminate or otherwise cut back on certain federally financed programs will, among other things, serve as a natural experiment in regard to such arguments as Peterson's.

It can occasion little surprise, then, that the future of the American welfare state has become the most enduring contemporary domestic political issue, certainly contributing to the Republican takeover of Congress in 1994 and the passage by

---

14. See Table 4.2 — Percentage Distribution of Outlays by Agency: 1962-2010, id.

15. Paul Peterson, The Price of Federalism 66 (1995) (Table 3-2: Developmental and Redistributive Expenditures of National Government, by Category, Selected Years, 1962-1990).

Congress in 1996, and then signing by President Clinton, of so-called welfare reform. And President George W. Bush's attack on the traditional funding of Social Security has put that most venerable of all New Deal programs very much in the public spotlight. Still, no one seriously argues that the welfare state is truly being eliminated. Indeed, as noted earlier, President Bush strongly supported a 2004 bill expanding the federal funding of drugs for Medicare participants, expected to add at least $600 billion to the federal budget (or deficit) in the ensuing ten years. Moreover, inasmuch as the federal government does cut back the funding of some of its welfare programs, the burden often simply shifts to state governments to pick up the slack, assuming that the programs are at all popular. In any event, the problems examined in this chapter will most certainly survive into the twenty-first century. It may also be worth adding that Hurricane Katrina, which occurred as this book was going to press, will undoubtedly generate further debate about the federal duty (and ability) to engage in massive welfare expenditures, given that early estimates of the costs of the greatest natural disaster in American history range from $100 billion to $150 billion, amounts clearly beyond the capacity of the two major hurricane-stricken states, Louisiana and Mississippi, which are also among the poorest states in the Union.[16]

III.   Does the Constitution Affirmatively Guarantee Any Welfare Rights?

Lyng is clearly a "modern" case. That is, no one now challenges the premise that the state is permitted to operate redistributive programs; the debate is whether Congress faces any constraints when deciding who shall (or shall not) receive federally funded largesse. Might, however, the Constitution be legitimately read to *require* the state to engage in the supply of any goods or services to individuals who cannot afford to purchase them through the market?[17] One hint in this direction was contained in Chief Justice Hughes's opinion upholding a state-mandated minimum wage in the key New Deal case West Coast Hotel v. Parrish (1937), supra Chapter 5: "The exploitation of a class of workers who are in an unequal position with respect to bargaining power and are thus relatively defenseless against the denial of a living wage is not only detrimental to their health and well being but casts a direct burden for their support upon the community. What these workers lose in wages the taxpayers are called upon to pay. *The bare cost of living must be met*" (emphasis added). Hughes might have been simply referring to the sheer fact that states commonly would supply certain poor relief rather than making an otherwise unelaborated argument that the state had a duty to do so. In any event, several cases decided during the 1950s and 1960s suggested that there might indeed be some such duty by the state.

---

16. Louisiana and Mississippi, for example, ranked highest among the 50 states in the percentage of children under 18 living below poverty, at 26.3 percent and 26.7 percent, respectively (though 31.1 percent of the children in the District of Columbia live below poverty). See Percent of Children Under 18 Below Poverty, 2000 For All U.S. States, available at *http://oseda.missouri.edu/tables/youth_family/usst_pctpoorkids_2000.html*. In 1999, 19.6 percent of all Louisianans and 19.9 percent of all Mississippians were below poverty, as compared with an overall national percentage of 12.4 percent. See U.S. Census Bureau, State and County Quick Facts, available at *http://quickfacts.census.gov/qfd/*.

17. See, e.g., Sotorios Barber, Welfare and the Constitution (2003).

A.   The Rights of Indigents in the Criminal Justice System

The first cases arose within the system of criminal justice, involving the rights of indigents. Griffin v. Illinois, 351 U.S. 12 (1956), held that a state must provide a trial transcript or its equivalent to an indigent criminal defendant appealing his conviction based on trial errors, notwithstanding the state's general practice of conditioning appeals on appellants' furnishing transcripts at their own expense. Justice Black, writing for a plurality that included Chief Justice Warren and Justices Douglas and Clark, emphasized that

> [Our] constitutional guaranties of due process and equal protection both call for procedures in criminal trials which allow no invidious discriminations between persons and different groups of persons. . . .
>
> In criminal trials a State can no more discriminate on account of poverty than on account of religion, race, or color. Plainly the ability to pay costs in advance bears no rational relationship to a defendant's guilt or innocence and could not be used as an excuse to deprive a defendant of a fair trial. . . .
>
> It is true that a State is not required by the Federal Constitution to provide appellate courts or a right to appellate review at all. . . . But that is not to say that a State that does grant appellate review can do so in a way that discriminates against some convicted defendants on account of their poverty. Appellate review has now become an integral part of the Illinois trial system for finally adjudicating the guilt or innocence of a defendant. Consequently at all stages of the proceedings the Due Process and Equal Protection Clauses protect persons like petitioners from invidious discriminations. . . .
>
> Destitute defendants must be afforded as adequate appellate review as defendants who have money enough to buy transcripts.

Four Justices dissented. With respect to the petitioner's equal protection claim, Justice Harlan argued that "[a]ll that Illinois has done is to fail to alleviate the consequences of differences in economic circumstances that exist wholly apart from any state action. . . .The real issue in this case is not whether Illinois has discriminated [against the poor] but whether it has a duty to discriminate [in favor of the poor]." With respect to the due process claim, Justice Harlan argued that the state's practice was not arbitrary and did not deprive petitioner of a right "implicit in the concept of ordered liberty."[18]

In Gideon v. Wainwright, 372 U.S. 335 (1963), a unanimous Court held that the Constitution required that counsel be provided to all felony defendants at trial if they do not have the resources to hire private counsel. The Sixth Amendment states that "[i]n all criminal prosecutions, the accused shall enjoy the right . . . to have the Assistance of Counsel for his defence." Although for many years this was interpreted to mean only that the state could not deprive a criminal defendant of the right to representation by retained counsel, in the 1930s the Court began holding

---

18. A number of later decisions elaborated the circumstances under which indigent convicted criminals would be entitled to free transcripts. See, e.g., Lane v. Brown, 372 U.S. 477 (1963) (indigent must be afforded free transcript of a postconviction hearing where filing of the transcript in the reviewing court was necessary to confer appellate jurisdiction); Long v. District Court, 385 U.S. 192 (1966) (free transcript required on appeal from denial of postconviction relief even if its filing is not jursidictional); Roberts v. LaVallee, 389 U.S. 40 (1967) (entitlement to transcript of testimony of a major witness for the state at the preliminary hearing in order to aid prisoner in applying for postconviction relief).

that under certain circumstances, especially where there was a possibility of capital punishment, a criminal defendant who lacked the resources to retain a lawyer had the right to state-financed representation. See, e.g., Powell v. Alabama, 287 U.S. 45 (1932). As a matter of fact, Justice Black's majority opinion in *Gideon* made no real reference to the history or even the specific text of the Sixth Amendment. Instead he emphasized that "in our adversary system of criminal justice, any person haled into court, who is too poor to hire a lawyer, cannot be assured a fair trial unless counsel is provided for him. . . . That government hires lawyers to prosecute and defendants who have the money hire lawyers to defend are the strongest indications of the widespread belief that lawyers in criminal courts are necessities, not luxuries. The right of one charged with a crime to counsel may not be deemed fundamental and essential to fair trial in some countries, but it is in ours. . . ."

On the same day as it decided *Gideon*, a divided Court in Douglas v. California, 372 U.S. 353 (1963), invalidated California's procedure regulating the appointment of counsel for indigent defendants appealing criminal convictions. Under state procedure, the appellate court first made "an independent investigation of the record" in order to "determine whether it would be of advantage to the defendant or helpful to the appellate court to have counsel appointed." Appellants who retained private counsel were not required to submit to this prior scrutiny. In petitioner's case, the appellate court had concluded, based on the record, that "no good whatever could be served by appointment of counsel." Justice Douglas wrote that this violated the equal protection clause by drawing "an unconstitutional line . . . between rich and poor."

> [T]he discrimination is not between "possibly good and obviously bad cases," but between cases where the rich man can require the court to listen to argument of counsel before deciding on the merits, but a poor man cannot. There is lacking that equality demanded by the Fourteenth Amendment where the rich man, who appeals as of right, enjoys the benefit of counsel's examination into the record, research of the law, and marshalling of arguments on his behalf, while the indigent, already burdened by a preliminary determination that his case is without merit, is forced to shift for himself.

The most recent transcript case is M.L.B. v. S.L.J., 519 U.S. 102 (1996), in which a sharply divided Court, through Justice Ginsburg, ruled invalid Mississippi's requirement that a parent wishing to appeal a termination-of-parental-rights order must pay in advance — in this case $2,352.36 — for the preparation of the trial record. M.L.B.'s appeal was dismissed because of her inability to provide the record. The Court, relying substantially on *Griffin*, held that "Mississippi may not deny M.L.B., because of her poverty, appellate review of the sufficiency of the evidence on which the trial court found her unfit to remain a parent." Justice Ginsburg emphasized the "fundamental" importance of the state's decision to terminate the parental relationship. "The countervailing government interest . . . is financial. . . . But in the tightly circumscribed category of parental status termination cases, appeals are few, and not likely to impose an undue burden on the State." Justice Ginsburg thus dismissed the objection that the Court would "open floodgates if we do not rigidly restrict *Griffin* to cases typed 'criminal' " because of the special nature of parental status termination decrees, which set them apart "even from other domestic relations matters such as divorce, paternity, and child custody." Justice Kennedy concurred. Justice Thomas, joined by Chief Justice Rehnquist and Justice Scalia, dissented, calling for the overruling of *Griffin* or, in the alternative, limiting it rigorously to criminal cases. "[I]f all that is required to trigger the right to a free appellate transcript is that the interest at stake appear to us to be as fundamental as the interest of a convicted misdemeanant, several kinds of civil suits involving interests that seem fundamental enough leap to mind. Will the Court, for example, now extend the right to a free transcript to an indigent seeking to appeal the outcome of a paternity suit? To those who wish to appeal custody determinations? How about persons against whom divorce decrees are entered? Civil suits that arise out of challenges to zoning ordinances with an impact on families? Why not foreclosure actions — or at least foreclosure actions seeking to oust persons from their homes of many years?"

Again Justice Harlan dissented and insisted on distinguishing between due process and equal protection analysis. He suggested that if the holding were justified on equal protection grounds, rather than a conception of minimal requirements under the due process clause, then "the requirement of counsel on appeal is the right to the most skilled advocate who is theoretically at the call of the defendant of means."[19]

B.   The Creation of Fundamental Interests under the Equal Protection Clause

In 1966, the Court moved these doctrines out of the context of the criminal justice system. It created a new doctrinal structure, protecting certain "fundamental interests" under the guise of the Equal Protection Clause.

HARPER v. VIRGINIA BD. OF ELECTIONS, 383 U.S. 663 (1966): [The Court struck down a $1.50 annual poll tax levied by Virginia on all persons over 21, enforced by disfranchising those who did not pay. The Twenty-Fourth Amendment had invalidated poll taxes for federal elections in 1964; *Harper* concerned the constitutionality of poll taxes for state elections.]

DOUGLAS, J.:
[W]hile the right to vote in federal elections is conferred by Art. I, 2, of the Constitution, the right to vote in state elections is nowhere expressly mentioned. . . . We do not stop to canvass the relation between voting and [First Amendment rights of] political expression. For it is enough to say that once the franchise is granted to the electorate, lines may not be drawn which are inconsistent with the Equal Protection Clause of the Fourteenth Amendment. [In] Lassiter v. Northampton Election Board, 360 U.S. 45, [we upheld] a state literacy test . . . warning that the result would be different if a literacy test, fair on its face, were used to discriminate against a class. [U]nlike a poll tax, the "ability to read and write . . . has some relation to standards designed to promote intelligent use of the ballot."
    We conclude that a State violates the Equal Protection Clause of the Fourteenth Amendment whenever it makes the affluence of the voter or payment of any fee an electoral standard. Voter qualifications have no relation to wealth nor to paying or not paying this or any other tax. Our cases demonstrate that the Equal Protection Clause of the Fourteenth Amendment restrains the States from fixing voter qualifications which invidiously discriminate. . . . Thus without questioning the power of a State to impose reasonable residence restrictions on the availability of the ballot we held in Carrington v. Rash, 380 U.S. 89, that a State may not deny the opportunity to vote to a bona fide resident merely because he is a member of the armed services. . . . Previously we had said that neither homesite nor occupation "affords a permissible basis for distinguishing between qualified voters within the State."

---

19. See also Justice Harlan's concurring opinion in Williams v. Illinois, 399 U.S. 235 (1970), which invalidated an Illinois statute that required convicts unable to pay their fines or court costs to "work off" their obligations by remaining in jail at an imputed rate of $5 per day, even if this would result in incarceration for a term longer than the maximum statutory term. "If equal protection implications of the Court's opinion were to be fully realized," he wrote, "it would require that the consequences of punishment be comparable for all individuals," which he presumably assumed would be, if not fanciful, then at least not constitutionally required.

Gray v. Sanders, 372 U.S. 368. We think the same must be true of requirements of wealth or affluence or payment of a fee.

Long ago in Yick Wo v. Hopkins, 118 U.S. 356 (1886), the Court referred to "the political franchise of voting" as a "fundamental political right, because preservative of all rights." Recently in Reynolds v. Sims, 377 U.S. 533 (1964), we said, "Undoubtedly, the right of suffrage is a fundamental matter in a free and democratic society. Especially since the right to exercise the franchise in a free and unimpaired manner is preservative of other basic civil and political rights, any alleged infringement of the right of citizens to vote must be carefully and meticulously scrutinized." . . .

We say the same whether the citizen, otherwise qualified to vote, has $1.50 in his pocket or nothing at all, pays the fee or fails to pay it. The principle that denies the State the right to dilute a citizen's vote on account of his economic status or other such factors by analogy bars a system which excludes those unable to pay a fee to vote or who fail to pay.

It is argued that a State may exact fees from citizens for many different kinds of licenses; that if it can demand from all an equal fee for a driver's license, it can demand from all an equal poll tax for voting. But we must remember that the interest of the State, when it comes to voting, is limited to the power to fix qualifications. Wealth, like race, creed, or color, is not germane to one's ability to participate intelligently in the electoral process. Lines drawn on the basis of wealth or property, like those of race, are traditionally disfavored. See Edwards v. California, 314 U.S. 160 (Jackson, J., concurring); Griffin v. Illinois; Douglas v. California. To introduce wealth or payment of a fee as a measure of a voter's qualifications is to introduce a capricious or irrelevant factor. The degree of the discrimination is irrelevant. In this context — that is, as a condition of obtaining a ballot — the requirement of fee paying causes an "invidious" discrimination (Skinner v. Oklahoma) that runs afoul of the Equal Protection Clause. . . .

We agree, of course, with Mr. Justice Holmes that the Due Process Clause of the Fourteenth Amendment "does not enact Mr. Herbert Spencer's Social Statics" (Lochner v. New York). Likewise, the Equal Protection Clause is not shackled to the political theory of a particular era. In determining what lines are unconstitutionally discriminatory, we have never been confined to historic notions of equality, any more than we have restricted due process to a fixed catalogue of what was at a given time deemed to be the limits of fundamental rights. Notions of what constitutes equal treatment for purposes of the Equal Protection Clause do change. This Court in 1896 held that laws providing for separate public facilities for white and Negro citizens did not deprive the latter of the equal protection and treatment that the Fourteenth Amendment commands. Plessy v. Ferguson. Seven of the eight Justices then sitting subscribed to the Court's opinion, thus joining in expressions of what constituted unequal and discriminatory treatment that sound strange to a contemporary ear. When, in 1954 — more than a half-century later — we repudiated the "separate-but-equal" doctrine of Plessy as respects public education we stated: "In approaching this problem, we cannot turn the clock back to 1868 when the Amendment was adopted, or even to 1896 when Plessy v. Ferguson was written." Brown v. Board of Education.

In a recent searching re-examination of the Equal Protection Clause, we held, as already noted, that "the opportunity for equal participation by all voters in the election of state legislators" is required. Reynolds v. Sims. We decline to qualify that principle by sustaining this poll tax. Our conclusion, like that in Reynolds v. Sims, is founded not on what we think governmental policy should be, but on what the Equal Protection Clause requires.

We have long been mindful that where fundamental rights and liberties are asserted under the Equal Protection Clause, classifications which might invade or restrain them must be closely scrutinized and carefully confined. See, e.g., Skinner v. Oklahoma; Reynolds v. Sims; Carrington v. Rash.

Those principles apply here. For to repeat, wealth or fee paying has, in our view, no relation to voting qualifications; the right to vote is too precious, too fundamental to be so burdened or conditioned.

BLACK, J., dissenting:

[T]he Court's decision is to no extent based on a finding that the Virginia law as written or as applied is being used as a device or mechanism to deny Negro citizens of Virginia the right to vote on account of their color. . . . The mere fact that a law results in treating some groups differently from others does not, of course, automatically amount to a violation of the Equal Protection Clause. To bar a State from drawing any distinctions in the application of its laws would practically paralyze the regulatory power of legislative bodies. . . . All voting laws treat some persons differently from others in some respects. Some bar a person from voting who is under 21 years of age; others bar those under 18. Some bar convicted felons or the insane, and some have attached a freehold or other property qualification for voting. [T]his Court has refused to use the general language of the Equal Protection Clause as though it provided a handy instrument to strike down state laws which the Court feels are based on bad governmental policy. The equal protection cases carefully analyzed boil down to the principle that distinctions drawn and even discriminations imposed by state laws do not violate the Equal Protection Clause so long as these distinctions and discriminations are not "irrational," "irrelevant," "unreasonable," "arbitrary," or "invidious." [U]nder a proper interpretation of the Equal Protection Clause States are to have the broadest kind of leeway in areas where they have a general constitutional competence to act. State poll tax legislation can "reasonably," "rationally" and without an "invidious" or evil purpose to injure anyone be found to rest on a number of state policies including (1) the State's desire to collect its revenue, and (2) its belief that voters who pay a poll tax will be interested in furthering the State's welfare when they vote. Certainly it is rational to believe that people may be more likely to pay taxes if payment is a prerequisite to voting. . . . Property qualifications existed in the Colonies and were continued by many States after the Constitution was adopted. . . .

[T]he Court seems to be using the old "natural-law-due-process formula" to justify striking down state laws as violations of the Equal Protection Clause. I have heretofore had many occasions to express my strong belief that there is no constitutional support whatever for this Court to use the Due Process Clause as though it provided a blank check to alter the meaning of the Constitution as written so as to add to it substantive constitutional changes which a majority of the Court at any given time believes are needed to meet present-day problems. Nor is there in my opinion any more constitutional support for this Court to use the Equal Protection Clause, as it has today, to write into the Constitution its notions of what it thinks is good governmental policy. . . .

The Court's justification for consulting its own notions rather than following the original meaning of the Constitution, as I would, apparently is based on the belief of the majority of the Court that for this Court to be bound by the original meaning of the Constitution is an intolerable and debilitating evil; that our Constitution should not be "shackled to the political theory of a particular era," and that to save the country from the original Constitution the Court must have constant power to renew it and keep it abreast of this Court's more enlightened theories of what is best for our society. It seems to me that this is an attack not only on the great value of our Constitution itself but also on the concept of a written constitution which is to survive through the years as originally written unless changed through the amendment process which the Framers wisely provided. Moreover, when a "political theory" embodied in our Constitution becomes outdated, it seems to me that a majority of the nine members of this Court are not only without constitutional power but are far less qualified to choose a new constitutional political theory than the people of this country proceeding in the manner provided by Article V. . . . [Moreover,] Congress has the power under section 5 [of the Fourteenth Amendment] to pass legislation to abolish the poll tax in order to protect the citizens of this country if it believes that the poll tax is being used as a device to deny voters equal protection of the laws.

HARLAN, J., joined by Stewart, J., dissenting:

Property and poll-tax qualifications, very simply, are not in accord with current egalitarian notions of how a modern democracy should be organized. It is of course entirely fitting that legislatures should modify the law to reflect such changes in popular attitudes. However, it is all wrong, in my view, for the Court to adopt the political doctrines popularly accepted at a particular moment of our history and to declare all others to be irrational and invidious, barring them from the range of choice by reasonably minded people acting through the political process. It was not too long ago that Mr. Justice Holmes felt impelled to remind the Court that the Due Process Clause of the Fourteenth Amendment does not enact the laissez-faire theory of society, Lochner v. New York. The times have changed, and perhaps it is appropriate to observe that neither does the Equal Protection Clause of that Amendment rigidly impose upon America an ideology of unrestrained egalitarianism.

Discussion

1. *Harper* struck down the poll tax even as applied to persons who could clearly afford it, because, in effect, the state was charging the citizen in order to engage in a "fundamental" aspect of citizenship, voting.

2. The Court extended the "fundamental rights" wing of equal protection doctrine in Shapiro v. Thompson, 394 U.S. 618 (1969), holding that states could not deny welfare benefits to persons who had resided in the state less than a year. It held that this policy invidiously discriminated on the basis of the exercise of the fundamental right to travel. These "right to travel" cases are considered in more detail in section V infra.

3. *Fundamental rights versus fundamental interests.* Note carefully Justice Douglas's statement that "once the franchise is granted to the electorate, lines may not be drawn which are inconsistent with the Equal Protection Clause of the Fourteenth Amendment." His argument is that although the state does not have to extend the right to vote generally, once it does so it may not invidiously discriminate in how it provides the right. We might call such a guarantee a "fundamental interest" as opposed to a "fundamental right" like speech or the right to travel that the state

must guarantee to all of its citizens. Compare Chief Justice Warren's argument in *Brown v. Board of Education*: "In these days, it is doubtful that any child may reasonably be expected to succeed in life if he is denied the opportunity of an education. Such an opportunity, where the state has undertaken to provide it, is a right which must be made available to all on equal terms."

Why might it make sense for courts to label welfare state obligations like education as "fundamental interests" rather than "fundamental rights"? One reason is that this formula leaves up to legislatures the ultimate decision whether or not to provide the right (or the welfare benefit) at all if it proves too costly to offer it on an equal footing.

Note: Protecting the Poor Through the Fourteenth Amendment

The language of Justice Douglas's opinion in *Harper*, plus the earlier criminal procedure cases, led Harvard professor Frank Michelman, who had clerked for Justice Brennan, to write one of the most widely discussed articles of the 1960s, titled, fittingly enough, "On Protecting the Poor Through the Fourteenth Amendment." There he argued that the Constitution guaranteed some level of "minimum protection" against the effects of poverty.[20] Professor Michelman started from the premise that a pricing system is both constitutional and desirable: "We usually regard it as both the fairest and most efficient arrangement to require each consumer to pay the full market price of what he consumes, limiting his consumption to what his income permits." However, he notes that *Harper* held that a state may not charge a user fee for access to certain rights or privileges (in that case, access to the ballot). He placed *Harper* and other cases within the context of the ideas of political philosopher John Rawls and argued that even within a market economy that tolerates a measure of income and resource inequality, persons are both morally and constitutionally entitled to "minimum protection against economic hazard":

> As applied to economic hazards, a claim to "minimum protection" would mean that persons are entitled to have certain wants satisfied — certain existing needs filled — by government, free of any direct charge over and above the obligation to pay general taxes. . . .
>
> [It might be argued] that justice is satisfied as long as the prevailing social and economic institutions afford everyone a fair opportunity to derive an income sufficient over time to provide for whatever needs are considered "basic." [But] the argument of minimum protection as applied to specific needs and occasions . . . depend[s] on the proposition that justice requires more than a fair opportunity to realize an income which can cover these needs or insure against them — requires . . . absolute assurance that they will be met when and as felt, free of any remote[a] contingencies pertaining to effort, thrift or foresight.

---

20. See On Protecting the Poor Through the Fourteenth Amendment, 83 Harv. L. Rev. 7 (1969). For a response, see Ralph Winter, Poverty, Economic Equality, and the Equal Protection Clause, 1972 Sup. Ct. Rev. 41.

a. "Remote" is intended to save the possibility that a person might deliberately and effectively waive his claims by informed and proximate choice. Such choice could, conceivably, assume a variety of forms — monastic vows, perhaps, or deliberate waste of publicly provided food or shelter.

We might take our clue from Professor Rawls' idea of "justice as fairness." Rawls grants that social institutions and practices may be just, even though they produce unequal incomes and accumulations. Yet for an unequal system to be just, it must be the case that a rational person, hypothetically ignorant of what particular place in society awaits him, would find the inequalities acceptable. . . .

The identity of "just wants" would then be determined according to a judgment arrived at through the following process of reasoning. Assume that a man has no idea what his social and economic station in a predominantly competitive society is to be and that he fully recognizes the role of income incentives and free markets in maximizing social productivity. Will he nevertheless wish to have each person insured against the risk that certain needs will remain unfulfilled as and when they accrue — and what specific risks of that sort, if any, will he say should be insured against?[b] Might he, for example, say that insofar as the society provides for "democratic" political participation through such means as voting and standing for office, access to these activities should never be blocked by economic vicissitude? Or that persons must at all times be assured of effective access to some impartial and remedially competent forum for the peaceful settlement of bona fide legal disputes? Or that everyone at all times must be assured of facilities for a modicum of privacy, intimacy, confidentiality, self-expression? Or that each child must be guaranteed the means of developing his competence, self-knowledge, and tastes for living? . . .

If the relevant insight concerning payment requirements must be given a doctrinal form of statement, the appropriate construction would seem to be something like: "It is no justification for deprivation of a fundamental right (i.e., involuntary nonfulfillment of a just want) that the deprivation results from a general practice of requiring persons to pay for what they get." Such a construction focuses the inquiry on the crucial variable — the nature and quality of the deprivation — and thereby avoids the distractions, false stirring of hopes, and tunneling of vision which results from a rhetorical emphasis on acts of "discrimination" that consist of nothing more than charging a price.

Michelman indicates that the notion of "minimum protection" is more readily assimilated to the due process clause than to the equal protection clause, for it focuses not on relative but on absolute deprivation: " 'Minimum protection' radar scans, not for inequalities, but for instances in which persons have important needs or interests which they are prevented from satisfying because of traits or predicaments not adopted by free and proximate choice." But there are reasons why a court might choose to clothe a minimum protection decision "in the verbiage of

---

b. Here we may briefly note some possible reasons for insisting on such assurances, over and above insistence on a system of economic rewards and transfers which would tend generally to assure each household head of an income adequate to his household's important needs. Assurances may be desired against the risk that one — or the family head upon whom one is dependent — will not measure up to generally reasonable minimum standards of active participation in the economy, or against the risk that a generally fair system of judging the quality of one's participation, or the extenuating force of one's disabilities, will in a particular case miscarry.

More generally, assurance may be desired against the chance that the sincerest attempts to devise and maintain a generally fair system of rewards and transfers will nevertheless leave some persons on some occasions desperately unprovisioned. Most generally, flat assurances concerning just wants may upon reflection seem a desirable way of simplifying (and thus cheapening) the continuing task of adjustment of the reward/transfer system, either because this method obviates any need to place a dollar value from time to time on the whole catalogue of just wants (a composite we may call the just minimum) or because it assures society that transferred purchasing power will not be dissipated on other wants, leaving just wants unfulfilled and, accordingly, an unsatisfied claim still outstanding. The latter point, I suspect, will eventually turn out to be the key to the argument. It provides a reason why persons in a just system would agree to receive their guaranteed minimum in kind rather than in cash.

inequality and discrimination." The language of the due process clause requires that the state act to deprive a person of property, something not textually mandated by the equal protection clause. Moreover, an equal protection standard provides some guidance as to how much protection must be furnished by looking to the benefits enjoyed by others in society. Finally,

> it must be noted that while the idea of "just wants" or "severe deprivations" expresses an ethical precept distinct from that of "equality," detecting a failure to provide the required minimum may nonetheless depend in part upon the detection of inequalities; and elimination or reduction of inequality may be entailed in rectifying such a failure, insofar as the just minimum is understood to be a function (in part) of the existing maximum. Such an understanding could grow out of a residue of indissoluble interpenetration of the felt evils of relative deprivation and poignant hardship. Thus if the extent of society's obligation to tax itself for support of the needy depends in part upon its overall level of affluence, widening inequalities become increasingly suggestive of failure to furnish the just minimum. Or again, insofar as the components of the required (or "a decent") minimum are affected by what others have — by prevailing tastes and expectations, or by emulation — then extremity of inequality is suggestive. Standing on quite different ground is the relevance of what others have when the want in question is deemed specially significant — as education, for example, might be — because of its importance for success in competitive activities.

Several subsequent cases offered some reason to believe that the Court might be following a Michelmanian direction and moving toward some constitutionally mandated welfare state. One of them was Boddie v. Connecticut, 401 U.S. 371 (1971), which invalidated that state's requirement, as applied to an indigent person, that one must pay a filing fee of $45 and an average of $15 for service of process in order to commence divorce proceedings. Justice Harlan, writing for the majority, treated the case as raising due process (rather than equal protection) issues. In particular, he emphasized that *only* the state can grant a divorce, so that exclusion of the indigent from judicial process because of an inability to pay the requisite fees has the consequence of depriving them of something that only the state can provide. Moreover, wrote Justice Harlan, "[r]ecognition of this theoretical framework illuminates the precise issue presented in this case. As this Court on more than one occasion has recognized, marriage involves interests of basic importance in our society. See, e.g., Loving v. Virginia, 388 U.S. 1 (1967). . . . It is not surprising, then, that the States have seen fit to oversee many aspects of that institution. Without a prior judicial imprimatur, individuals may freely enter into and rescind commercial contracts, for example, but we are unaware of any jurisdiction where private citizens may . . . divorce and mutually liberate themselves from the constraints of legal obligations that go with marriage, and more fundamentally the prohibition against remarriage, without invoking the State's judicial machinery."

Justice Harlan concluded that "the State's refusal to admit these appellants to its courts, the sole means in Connecticut for obtaining a divorce, must be regarded as the equivalent of denying them an opportunity to be heard upon their claimed right to a dissolution of their marriages, and, in the absence of a sufficient countervailing justification for the State's action, a denial of due process."

Justice Douglas wrote a concurring opinion objecting to the reliance on the Due Process Clause and suggesting instead that the Equal Protection Clause, though "not definable with mathematical precision," offered the better rationale. "Here

the invidious discrimination is based on one of the guidelines: poverty. An invidious discrimination based on poverty is adequate for this case."

Justice Brennan also concurred only in the judgment, rejecting

> the Court's opinion insofar as today's holding is made to depend upon the factor that
> only the State can grant a divorce and that an indigent would be locked into a
> marriage if unable to pay the fees required to obtain a divorce. A State has an ulti-
> mate monopoly of all judicial process and attendant enforcement machinery. As a
> practical matter, if disputes cannot be successfully settled between the parties, the
> court system is usually "the only forum effectively empowered to settle their
> disputes. . . ." I see no constitutional distinction between appellants' attempt to
> enforce this state statutory right and an attempt to vindicate any other right arising
> under federal or state law. . . .
>
> The question that the Court treats exclusively as one of due process inevitably impli-
> cates considerations of both due process and equal protection. . . . The rationale of
> *Griffin* covers the present case. Courts are the central dispute-settling institutions in
> our society. They are bound to do equal justice under law, to rich and poor alike. They
> fail to perform their function in accordance with the Equal Protection Clause if they
> shut their doors to indigent plaintiffs altogether. Where money determines not merely
> "the kind of trial a man gets," but whether he gets into court at all, the great principle
> of equal protection becomes a mockery. . . .

Justice Black dissented, arguing that *Griffin* and its progeny were limited to criminal cases. In civil cases, "the government is not usually involved as a party, and there
is no deprivation of life, liberty, or property as punishment for crime. Our Federal
Constitution, therefore, does not place such private disputes on the same high level
as it places criminal trials and punishment."

C.   Minimum Needs Rejected

Whatever hopes (or, for Michelman's critics, fears) might have been raised by such
cases, they were rather quickly dashed.

DANDRIDGE v. WILLIAMS, 397 U.S. 471 (1970): [The year following Professor
Michelman's article, the Court in *Dandridge* upheld a provision of Maryland's
program of Aid to Families with Dependent Children that limited the monthly
grant to any one family to $250, regardless of its size or computed need. Justice
Stewart explained that "[l]ike every other State in the Union, Maryland participates
in the Federal Aid to Families With Dependent Children, which originated with the
Social Security Act of 1935 [and was repealed in the 1996 welfare legislation passed
by Congress and signed by President Clinton]. Under this jointly financed
program, a State computes the so-called 'standard of need' of each eligible family
unit within its borders. Some States provide that every family shall receive grants
sufficient to meet fully the determined standard of need. Other States provide that
each family unit shall receive a percentage of the determined need. Still others
provide grants to most families in full accord with the ascertained standard of need,
but impose an upper limit on the total amount of money any one family unit may
receive. Maryland, through administrative adoption of a 'maximum grant
regulation,' has followed this last course."

As a result, individual members of a large family received less per capita than the members of smaller families, and less per capita than the state itself recognized as the minimum required for subsistence. (One might note, though, that some states had chosen to fund everyone at below-minimum levels.). The Court upheld this scheme, 5-4.]

STEWART, J:

[A] State . . . may not, of course, impose a regime of invidious discrimination in violation of the Equal Protection Clause of the Fourteenth Amendment. Maryland says that its maximum grant regulation is wholly free of any invidiously discriminatory purpose or effect, and that the regulation is rationally supportable on at least four entirely valid grounds. The regulation can be clearly justified, Maryland argues, in terms of legitimate state interests in encouraging gainful employment, in maintaining an equitable balance in economic status as between welfare families and those supported by a wage-earner, in providing incentives for family planning, and in allocating available public funds in such a way as fully to meet the needs of the largest possible number of families. The District Court . . . nonetheless held that the regulation "is invalid on its face for overreaching," — that it violates the Equal Protection Clause "(b)ecause it cuts too broad a swath on an indiscriminate basis as applied to the entire group of AFDC eligibles to which it purports to apply, . . ."

If this were a case involving government action claimed to violate the First Amendment guarantee of free speech, a finding of "overreaching" would be significant and might be crucial. . . . But the concept of "overreaching" has no place in this case. For here we deal with state regulation in the social and economic field, not affecting freedoms guaranteed by the Bill of Rights, and claimed to violate the Fourteenth Amendment only because the regulation results in some disparity in grants of welfare payments to the largest AFDC families. For this Court to approve the invalidation of state economic or social regulation as "overreaching" would be far too reminiscent of an era when the Court thought the Fourteenth Amendment gave it power to strike down state laws "because they may be unwise, improvident, or out of harmony with a particular school of thought." Williamson v. Lee Optical. That era long ago passed into history. Ferguson v. Skrupa.

In the area of economics and social welfare, . . . [a] statutory discrimination will not be set aside if any state of facts reasonably may be conceived to justify it.

To be sure, the cases cited, and many others enunciating this fundamental standard under the Equal Protection Clause, have in the main involved state regulation of business or industry. The administration of public welfare assistance, by contrast, involves the most basic economic needs of impoverished human beings. We recognize the dramatically real factual differences between [those] cases and this one, but we can find no basis for applying a different constitutional standard. . . .

Under this long-established meaning of the Equal Protection Clause, it is clear that the Maryland maximum grant regulation is constitutionally valid. We need not explore all the reasons that the State advances in justification of the regulation. It is enough that a solid foundation for the regulation can be found in the State's legitimate interest in encouraging employment and in avoiding discrimination between welfare families and the families of the working poor. . . . [B]y keying the maximum family AFDC grants to the minimum wage a steadily employed head of a household receives, the State maintains some semblance of an equitable balance between families on welfare and those supported by an employed breadwinner.

It is true that in some AFDC families there may be no person who is employable. It is also true that with respect to AFDC families whose determined standard of need is below the regulatory maximum, and who therefore receive grants equal to the determined standard, the employment incentive is absent. But the Equal Protection Clause does not require that a State must choose between attacking every aspect of a problem or not attacking the problem at all. It is enough that the State's action be rationally based and free from invidious discrimination. The regulation before us meets that test.

[Justice Douglas dissented on statutory grounds.]

MARSHALL, J., joined by Brennan, J., dissenting:

[T]he Court's emasculat[es] . . . the Equal Protection Clause as a constitutional principle applicable to the area of social welfare administration. . . .

[T]he only distinction between those children with respect to whom assistance is granted and those children who are denied such assistance is the size of the family into which the child permits himself to be born. The class of individuals with respect to whom payments are actually made (the first four or five eligible dependent children in a family), is grossly underinclusive in terms of the class that the AFDC program was designed to assist, namely, all needy dependent children. Such underinclusiveness manifests "a prima facie violation of the equal protection requirement of reasonable classification," compelling the State to come forward with a persuasive justification for the classification.

The Court never undertakes to inquire for such a justification; rather it avoids the task by focusing upon the abstract dichotomy between two different approaches to equal protection problems that have been utilized by this Court. . . .

This case simply defies easy characterization in terms of [the "rational basis" versus "strict scrutiny" tests]. The cases relied on by the Court, in which a "mere rationality" test was actually used, e.g., Williamson v. Lee Optical, are most accurately described as involving the application of equal protection reasoning to the regulation of business interests. The extremes to which the Court has gone in dreaming up rational bases for state regulation in the area may in many instances be ascribed to a healthy revulsion from the Court's earlier excesses in using the Constitution to protect interests that have more than enough power to protect themselves in the legislative halls. This case, involving the literally vital interests of a powerless minority — poor families without breadwinners — is far removed from the area of business regulation, as the Court concedes. Why then is the standard used in those cases imposed here? We are told no more than that this case falls in "the area of economics and social welfare," with the implication that from there the answer is obvious.

In my view, equal protection analysis of this case is not appreciably advanced by the a priori definition of a "right," fundamental or otherwise. Rather, concentration must be placed upon the character of the classification in question, the relative importance to individuals in the class discriminated against of the governmental benefits that they do not receive, and the asserted state interests in support of the classification. . . .

[Justice Marshall examines the asserted state rationales:]

. . . Vital to the employment-incentive basis found by the Court to sustain the regulation is, of course, the supposition that an appreciable number of AFDC recipients are in fact employable. For it is perfectly obvious that limitations upon assistance cannot reasonably operate as a work incentive with regard to those who cannot work or who cannot be expected to work. . . . The State's position is . . . that the State may deprive certain needy children of assistance to which they would otherwise be entitled in order to provide an arguable work incentive for their parents. But the State may not wield its economic whip in this fashion when the effect is to cause a deprivation to needy dependent children in order to correct an arguable fault of their parents.

Even if the invitation of the State to focus upon the heads of AFDC families is accepted, the minimum rationality of the maximum grant regulation is hard to discern. The District Court found that of Maryland's more than 32,000 AFDC families, only about 116 could be classified as having employable members, and, of these, the number to which the maximum grant regulation was applicable is not disclosed by the record. . . . Thus . . . the total number of "employable" mothers is but a fraction of the total number of AFDC mothers. Furthermore, the record is silent as to what proportion of large families subject to the maximum have "employable" mothers. Indeed, one must assume that the presence of the mother in the homes can be less easily dispensed with in the case of large families, particularly where small children are involved and alternative provisions for their care are accordingly more difficult to arrange. In short, not only has the State failed to establish that there is a substantial or even a significant proportion of AFDC heads of households as to whom the maximum grant regulation arguably serves as a viable and logical work incentive, but it is also indisputable that the regulation at best is drastically overinclusive since it applies with equal vigor to a very substantial number of persons who like appellees are completely disabled from working.

Finally, it should be noted that, to the extent there is a legitimate state interest in encouraging heads of AFDC households to find employment, application of the maximum grant regulation is also grossly underinclusive because it singles out and affects only large families. No reason is suggested why this particular group should be carved out for the purpose of having unusually harsh "work incentives" imposed upon them. Not only has the State selected for special treatment a small group from among similarly situated families, but it has done so on a basis — family size — that bears no relation to the evil that the State claims the regulation was designed to correct. There is simply no indication whatever that heads of large families, as opposed to heads of small families, are particularly prone to refuse to seek or to maintain employment. . . .

In the final analysis, Maryland has set up an AFDC program structured to calculate and pay the minimum standard of need to dependent children. Having set up that program, however, the State denies some of those needy children the minimum subsistence standard of living, and it does so on the wholly arbitrary basis that they happen to be members of large families. One need not speculate too far on the actual reason for the regulation, for in the early stages of this litigation the State virtually conceded that it set out to limit the total cost of the program along the path of least resistance. . . .

[I]t cannot suffice merely to invoke the spectre of the past and to recite from . . . Williamson v. Lee Optical to decide the case. Appellees are not a gas company or an optical dispenser; they are needy dependent children and families who are discriminated against by the State. The basis of that discrimination — the classification of individuals into large and small families — is too arbitrary and too unconnected to the asserted rationale, the impact on those discriminated against — the denial of even a subsistence existence — too great, and the supposed interests served too contrived and attenuated to meet the requirements of the Constitution. In my view Maryland's maximum grant regulation is invalid under the Equal Protection Clause of the Fourteenth Amendment.

In Lindsey v. Normet, 405 U.S. 56 (1972), the Court rejected the claim that the "need for decent shelter" rose to the level of a fundamental interest that would call for heightened scrutiny of a summary "forcible entry and wrongful detainer" procedure for the eviction of tenants after alleged nonpayment of rent. Justice White, writing for the Court, stated:

> We do not denigrate the importance of decent, safe, and sanitary housing. But the Constitution does not provide judicial remedies for every social and economic ill. We are unable to perceive in that document any constitutional guarantee of access to dwellings of a particular quality. . . . Absent constitutional mandate, the assurance of adequate housing and the definition of landlord-tenant relationships are legislative, not judicial, functions.

As to criminal defendants, the Court also appeared to pull back from its earlier, more egalitarian, vision. Thus, in Ross v. Moffit, 417 U.S. 600 (1974), it declined to interpret *Gideon* as requiring the appointment of counsel for indigents seeking discretionary review in the Supreme Court. And in Murray v. Giarratano, 492 U.S. 1 (1989), the Court ruled against inmates of Virginia's death row who claimed a right to appointed counsel to challenge their convictions in collateral proceedings. Chief Justice Rehnquist, writing for a plurality including Justices White, O'Connor, and Scalia, found the case controlled by Pennsylvania v. Finley, 481 U.S. 551 (1987), which held that the Sixth Amendment does not require states to provide counsel in postconviction proceedings generally. In a concurring opinion, Justice O'Connor emphasized that "[a] postconviction proceeding is not part of the criminal process itself, but is instead a civil action designed to overturn a presumptively valid criminal judgment." Justice Stevens, in a dissent joined by Justices Brennan, Marshall, and Blackmun, argued that "even if it is permissible to leave an ordinary prisoner to his own resources in collateral proceedings, it is fundamentally unfair to require an indigent death row inmate to initiate collateral relief without counsel's guiding hand." He noted the presence of "significant evidence that in capital cases what is ordinarily considered direct review does not sufficiently safeguard against miscarriages of justice" to warrant the traditional presumption of finality. Thus, whereas "[f]ederal habeas courts granted relief in only 0.25% to 7% of noncapital cases in recent years, in striking contrast, the success rate in capital cases ranged from 60% to 70%. Such a high incidence of uncorrected error [at the ordinary appellate stage] demonstrates that the meaningful appellate review necessary in a capital case extends beyond the direct appellate process."

In Fuller v. Oregon, 417 U.S. 40 (1974), the Court held that a state may recoup legal expenses paid on behalf of a convicted defendant to the extent that he becomes able to repay and that it may condition a solvent defendant's probation on repayment. Against Fuller's argument that "a defendant's knowledge that he may remain under an obligation to repay the expenses incurred in providing him legal representation might impel him to decline the services of an appointed attorney and thus 'chill' his constitutional right to counsel," Justice Stewart responded:

> We live in a society where the distribution of legal assistance, like the distribution of all goods and services, is generally regulated by the dynamics of private enterprise. A defendant in a criminal case who is just above the line separating the indigent from the nonindigent must borrow money, sell off his meager assets, or call upon his family or friends in order to hire a lawyer. We cannot say that the Constitution requires that those only slightly poorer must remain forever immune from any obligation to shoulder the expenses of their legal defense, even when they are able to pay without hardship. . . .

Justice Marshall, joined by Justice Brennan, explicitly reserved judgment on the issue of "chilling effect" but dissented based on the state's different treatment of indigent criminal defendants and other judgment debtors.[21]

Almost a decade later, in Ake v. Oklahoma, 470 U.S. 68 (1985), the Court held that, in certain circumstances, a state must provide an indigent defendant with access to psychiatric assistance to make out a defense of insanity. In this case, the defendant Ake was sentenced to death, after his request for psychiatric evaluation at the state's expense was denied, for first-degree murder due to aggravating circumstances. With only Justice Rehnquist dissenting, the majority concluded that the denial of psychiatric assistance to Ake violated his due process rights to a fair trial. Justice Rehnquist dissented.[22]

Finally, with regard to filing fees in civil cases, the Court firmly limited the reach of *Boddie* two years later in U.S. v. Kras, 409 U.S. 434 (1973), which reviewed a decision granting a motion by an indigent petitioner in bankruptcy seeking a waiver of the usual $50 fees, which cover a portion of the referee's, trustee's, and clerk's costs. Justice Harry Blackmun, who wrote the opinion for the Court, emphasized that "[t]he appellants in *Boddie,* on the one hand, and Robert Kras, on the other, stand in materially different postures." First, Blackmun noted the different level of importance of the two relevant interests. The marital relationship and its potential dissolution involved interests of "fundamental importance . . . under our Constitution." By contrast, wrote Blackmun, "Kras' alleged interest in the elimination of his debt burden, and in obtaining his desired new start in life, although important and so recognized by the enactment of the Bankruptcy Act, does not rise to the same constitutional level. . . . We see no fundamental interest that is gained or lost depending on the availability of a discharge in bankruptcy. . . ."

A second variable concerned the degree of the government's monopoly over the relevant relief. "In contrast with divorce, bankruptcy is not the only method

---

21. James v. Strange, 407 U.S. 128 (1972), struck down a Kansas statute providing for the recoupment of all state expenditures for indigent defendants and depriving them of almost all of the usual exemptions and restrictions (e.g., limitations on wage garnishment, exemptions of personal clothing and food) afforded civil judgment debtors. The Court held that the equal protection clause required "more even treatment of indigent criminal defendants with other classes of indigents for self-sufficiency and self-respect." Rinaldi v. Yeager, 384 U.S. 305 (1966), struck down a New Jersey statute that required unsuccessful appellants confined to prisons to repay the state for the costs of transcripts, but did not exact repayment from defendants receiving suspended sentences, placed on probation, or penalized only by a fine.

22. See also M.L.B. v. S.L.J., 519 U.S. 102 (1996), discussed in n.10, supra.

available to a debtor for the adjustment of his legal relationship with his creditors. . . . However unrealistic the remedy may be in a particular situation, a debtor, in theory, and often in actuality, may adjust his debts by negotiated agreement with his creditors."

Thus, Blackmun concluded, "There is no constitutional right to obtain a discharge of one's debts in bankruptcy," and "[t]he rational basis for the fee requirement is readily apparent." Moreover, he suggested,

> If the $50 filing fees are paid in installments over six months as General Order No. 35(4) permits on a proper showing, the required average weekly payment is $1.92. If the payment period is extended for the additional three months as the Order permits, the average weekly payment is lowered to $1.28. This is a sum less than the payments Kras makes on his couch of negligible value in storage, and less than the price of a movie and little more than the cost of a pack or two of cigarettes. . . .[23]

Justice Stewart, joined by Douglas, Brennan, and Marshall, dissented: "The violation of due process seems to me [as] clear in the present case [as in *Boddie*]." In particular, he rejected the majority's view that the state enjoyed less of a monopoly in *Kras* than in *Boddie:*

> . . .[T]he debtor, like the married plaintiffs in *Boddie,* originally entered into his contract freely and voluntarily. But it is the government nevertheless that continues to enforce that obligation, and under our "legal system" that debt is effective only because the judicial machinery is there to collect it. The bankrupt is bankrupt precisely for the reason that the State stands ready to exact all of his debts through garnishment, attachment, and the panoply of other creditor remedies. The appellee can be pursued and harassed by his creditors since they hold his legally enforceable debts.
>
> And in the unique situation of the indigent bankrupt, the government provides the only effective means of his ever being free of these government-imposed obligations. As in *Boddie,* there are no "recognized, effective alternatives." While the creditors of a bankrupt with assets might well desire to reach a compromise settlement, that possibility is foreclosed to the truly indigent bankrupt. With no funds and not even a sufficient prospect of income to be able to promise the payment of a $50 fee in weekly installments of $1.28, the assetless bankrupt has absolutely nothing to offer his creditors. And his creditors have nothing to gain by allowing him to escape or reduce his debts; their only hope is that eventually he might make enough income for them to attach. Unless the government provides him access to the bankruptcy court, Kras will remain

---

23. Justice Marshall, who joined Justice Stewart's dissent, wrote separately to take the majority to task for its concluding comment:

> It may be easy for some people to think that weekly savings of less than $2 are no burden. But no one who has had close contact with poor people can fail to understand how close to the margin of survival many of them are. A sudden illness, for example, may destroy whatever savings they may have accumulated, and by eliminating a sense of security may destroy the incentive to save in the future. A pack or two of cigarettes may be, for them, not a routine purchase but a luxury indulged in only rarely. The desperately poor almost never go to see a movie, which the majority seems to believe is an almost weekly activity. They have more important things to do with what little money they have — like attempting to provide some comforts for a gravely ill child, as Kras must do.
>
> It is perfectly proper for judges to disagree about what the Constitution requires. But it is disgraceful for an interpretation of the Constitution to be premised upon unfounded assumptions about how people live. . . .

in the totally hopeless situation he now finds himself. The government has thus truly preempted the only means for the indigent bankrupt to get out from under a lifetime burden of debt. . . .

The Court today holds that Congress may say that some of the poor are too poor even to go bankrupt. I cannot agree.[24]

Discussion

1. As of 2005 the minimum filing fee for personal bankruptcies is $194. Even if filing fees were waived, one might well wonder about the capacity of indigent laypersons to navigate the legal shoals of the bankruptcy process. If you disagree with *Kras,* would you argue as well that the Constitution requires state-subsidized lawyers to help such people?

2. Reread very carefully Justice Stewart's dissent. Is it not true that *all* property rights have legal force if and only if the government puts its power behind the wishes of the property "owner" (as against the person who would otherwise like to use the good in question). Can't one say that the poor are poor only because the government will put them in jail if they try to make use of resources that are not recognized as belonging to them? Many of the cases in this chapter are unwilling to ascribe claimants' poverty to decisions of the state. Does Justice Stewart's dissent, if taken fully seriously, allow that response? (For further discussion of the state-action problem in the context of the modern welfare state, see pp. 1664-1667.)

By the middle 1970s the four Nixon appointees to the Supreme Court collectively signaled that they would put an end to the Court's experiment with securing affirmative welfare rights under the Constitution. The definitive statement came in a case litigating the right to one of the most important benefits provided by government, education.

D.   The Right To Education

Recall that the Supreme Court in Brown v. Board of Education said:

> Today, education is the very foundation of good citizenship . . . , a principal instrument in awakening the child to cultural values, in preparing him for later professional training, and in helping him to adjust normally to his environment. In these days, it is doubtful that any child may reasonably be expected to succeed in life if he is denied the opportunity of an education. Such an opportunity, where the state has undertaken to provide it, is a right which must be made available to all on equal terms.

In retrospect, *Brown* seems to have rested far less on the special status of education than on the illegitimacy of the criterion (i.e., race) on which the state

___

24. See also Ortwein v. Schwab, 410 U.S. 656 (1973), where the Court summarily upheld Oregon's $25 appellate court filing fee as applied to appeals by indigents from administrative decisions reducing welfare payments. "The purpose of the filing fee, as with the bankruptcy fees in *Kras,* is apparent. The Oregon court system incurs operating costs, and the fee produces some small revenue to assist in offsetting those expenses. . . . Appellants do not contend that the fee is disproportionate or that it is not an effective means to accomplish the State's goal. The requirement of rationality is met." Moreover, the Court noted, "[t]hese appellants have had hearings . . . , not conditioned on payments of any fee, through which appellants have been able to seek redress. . . . Under the facts of this case, appellants were not denied due process." Justices Douglas, Stewart, Brennan, and Marshall dissented.

separated children attending its public schools. Is education nonetheless so important or special an interest as to call for heightened scrutiny of nonracial laws that allocate educational benefits differentially? Is it so important, indeed, that the Constitution should require the state to provide at least a minimal level of education to everyone within its jurisdiction?

1.   *"Equal Provision" of Public Education*

SAN ANTONIO INDEPENDENT SCHOOL DISTRICT v. RODRIGUEZ
411 U.S. 1 (1973)

[Texas public school systems are financed through a combination of local property taxes and state funds. The state-funded "foundation program" tends to equalize disparities among district tax bases, but district expenditures nevertheless depend heavily on local property wealth. For example, in the 1967-1968 school year, the Edgewood Independent School District in San Antonio had an assessed property value per pupil of $5,960. By taxing itself at a rate of 1 percent and after paying its required share into the state program, it was able to raise $26 per pupil. State subventions brought its per pupil expenditure to $356. The Alamo Heights Independent School District, also located in San Antonio, had a tax base of $49,000 per pupil, and raised $333 locally by taxing itself at only .85 percent. State subventions brought its per pupil expenditure to $594. As Justice White noted in his dissent, "In order to equal the highest yield in any other Bexar County district, Alamo Heights would be required to tax at the rate of 68 cents per $100 of assessed valuation. Edgewood would be required to tax at the prohibitive rate of $5.76 per $100. But state law places a $1.50 per $100 ceiling on the maintenance tax rate, a limit that would surely be reached long before Edgewood attained an equal yield. Edgewood is thus precluded in law, as well as in fact, from achieving a yield even close to that of some other districts."

Appellees, the parents of children attending the Edgewood schools, brought this suit to invalidate the state school financing scheme on the ground that it violated the equal protection clause of the Fourteenth Amendment. On the state's appeal from the district court's judgment for appellees, the Supreme Court reversed.]

POWELL, J. . . .

I.

. . . We must decide, first, whether the Texas system of financing public education operates to the disadvantage of some suspect class or impinges upon a fundamental right explicitly or implicitly protected by the Constitution, thereby requiring strict judicial scrutiny. If so, the judgment of the District Court should be affirmed. If not, the Texas scheme must still be examined to determine whether it rationally furthers some legitimate, articulated state purpose and therefore does not constitute an invidious discrimination in violation of the Equal Protection Clause of the Fourteenth Amendment.

II.

. . . In concluding that strict judicial scrutiny was required [the District Court] relied on decisions dealing with the rights of indigents to equal treatment in the criminal trial and appellate processes, and on cases disapproving wealth restrictions on the right to vote. Those cases, the District Court concluded, established wealth as a suspect classification. Finding that the local property tax system discriminated on the basis of wealth, it regarded those precedents as controlling. It then reasoned, based on decisions of this Court affirming the undeniable importance of education, that there is a fundamental right to education and that, absent some compelling state justification, the Texas system could not stand.

We are unable to agree that this case, which in significant aspects is sui generis, may be so neatly fitted into the conventional mosaic of constitutional analysis under the Equal Protection Clause. Indeed, for the several reasons that follow, we find neither the suspect-classification nor the fundamental-interest analysis persuasive.

A

. . . The Texas system of school financing might be regarded as discriminating (1) against "poor" persons whose incomes fall below some identifiable level of poverty or who might be characterized as functionally "indigent," or (2) against those who are relatively poorer than others, or (3) against all those who, irrespective of their personal incomes, happen to reside in relatively poorer school districts. Our task must be to ascertain whether, in fact, the Texas system has been shown to discriminate on any of these possible bases and, if so, whether the resulting classification may be regarded as suspect.

The precedents of this Court provide the proper starting point. The individuals, or groups of individuals, who constituted the class discriminated against in our prior cases shared two distinguishing characteristics: because of their impecunity they were completely unable to pay for some desired benefit, and as a consequence, they sustained an absolute deprivation of a meaningful opportunity to enjoy that benefit. . . .

Only appellees' first possible basis for describing the class disadvantaged by the Texas school-financing system — discrimination against a class of definably "poor" persons — might arguably meet the criteria established in these prior cases. Even a cursory examination, however, demonstrates that neither of the two distinguishing characteristics of wealth classifications can be found here. First, in support of their charge that the system discriminates against the "poor," appellees have made no effort to demonstrate that it operates to the peculiar disadvantage of any class fairly definable as indigent, or as composed of persons whose incomes are beneath any designated poverty level. Indeed, there is reason to believe that the poorest families are not necessarily clustered in the poorest property districts. A recent and exhaustive study of school districts in Connecticut concluded . . . that the poor were clustered around commercial and industrial areas — those same areas that provide the most attractive sources of property tax income for school districts. Whether a similar pattern would be discovered in Texas is not known, but there is no basis on the record in this case for assuming that the poorest people — defined by reference to any level of absolute impecunity — are concentrated in the poorest districts.

Second, neither appellees nor the District Court addressed the fact that . . . lack of personal resources has not occasioned an absolute deprivation of the desired benefit. The argument here is not that the children in districts having relatively low assessable property values are receiving no public education; rather, it is that they are receiving a poorer quality education than that available to children in districts having more assessable wealth. Apart from the unsettled and disputed question whether the quality of education may be determined by the amount of money expended for it,[a] a sufficient answer to appellees' argument is that, at least where wealth is involved, the Equal Protection Clause does not require absolute equality or precisely equal advantages. . . .

For these two reasons — the absence of any evidence that the financing system discriminates against any definable category of "poor" people or that it results in the absolute deprivation of education — the disadvantaged class is not susceptible to identification in traditional terms.[b]

As suggested above, appellees and the District Court may have embraced a second or third approach, the second of which might be characterized as a theory of relative or comparative discrimination based on family income. Appellees sought to prove that a direct correlation exists between the wealth of families within each district and the expenditures therein for education. That is, along a continuum, the poorer the family the lower the dollar amount of education received by the family's children. . . .

If, in fact, [this correlation] could be sustained, . . . [a]ppellees' comparative-discrimination theory would still face serious unanswered questions, including whether a bare positive correlation or some higher degree of correlation is necessary to provide a basis for concluding that the financing system is designed to operate to the peculiar disadvantage of the comparatively poor, and whether a class of this size and diversity could ever claim the special protection accorded "suspect" classes. These questions need not be addressed in this case, however, since appellees' proof fails to support their allegations or the District Court's conclusions. . . .

This brings us, then, to the third way in which the classification scheme might be defined — district wealth discrimination. Since the only correlation indicated by the evidence is between district property wealth and expenditures, it may be argued that discrimination might be found without regard to the individual income characteristics of district residents. Assuming a perfect correlation between district property wealth and expenditures from top to bottom, the disadvantaged class might be viewed as encompassing every child in every district except the district that has the most assessable wealth and spends the most on education.

a. Each of appellees' possible theories of wealth discrimination is founded on the assumption that the quality of education varies directly with the amount of funds expended on it and that, therefore, the difference in quality between two schools can be determined simplistically by looking at the difference in per pupil expenditures. This is a matter of considerable dispute among educators and commentators. . . .

b. An educational financing system might be hypothesized, however, in which the analogy to the wealth discrimination cases would be considerably closer. If elementary and secondary education were made available by the State only to those able to pay a tuition assessed against each pupil, there would be a clearly defined class of "poor" people — definable in terms of their inability to pay the prescribed sum — who would be absolutely precluded from receiving an education. That case would present a far more compelling set of circumstances for judicial assistance than the case before us today. . . .

Alternatively, . . . the class might be defined more restrictively to include children in districts with assessable property which falls below the statewide average, or median, or below some other artificially defined level.

However described, it is clear that appellees' suit asks this Court to extend its most exacting scrutiny to review a system that allegedly discriminates against a large, diverse, and amorphous class, unified only by the common factor of residence in districts that happen to have less taxable wealth than other districts. The system of alleged discrimination and the class it defines have none of the traditional indicia of suspectness: the class is not saddled with such disabilities, or subjected to such a history of purposeful unequal treatment, or relegated to such a position of political powerlessness as to command extraordinary protection from the majoritarian political process.

We thus conclude that the Texas system does not operate to the peculiar disadvantage of any suspect class. But in recognition of the fact that this Court has never heretofore held that wealth discrimination alone provides an adequate basis for invoking strict scrutiny, appellees have not relied solely on this contention. They also assert that the State's system impermissibly interferes with the exercise of a "fundamental" right and that accordingly the prior decisions of this Court require the application of the strict standard of judicial review. . . .

B

In Brown v. Board of Education a unanimous Court recognized that "education is perhaps the most important function of state and local governments." . . .

Nothing this Court holds today in any way detracts from our historic dedication to public education. We are in complete agreement with the conclusion of the three-judge panel below that "the grave significance of education both to the individual and to our society" cannot be doubted. But the importance of a service performed by the State does not determine whether it must be regarded as fundamental for purposes of examination under the Equal Protection Clause. . . .

The lesson of [Lindsey v. Normet; Dandridge v. Williams; Jefferson v. Hackney, 406 U.S. 535 (1972); and Richardson v. Belcher, 404 U.S. 78 (1971)] in addressing the question now before the Court is plain. It is not the province of this Court to create substantive constitutional rights in the name of guaranteeing equal protection of the laws. Thus, the key to discovering whether education is "fundamental" is not to be found in comparisons of the relative societal significance of education as opposed to subsistence or housing. Nor is it to be found by weighing whether education is as important as the right to travel. Rather, the answer lies in assessing whether there is a right to education explicitly or implicitly guaranteed by the Constitution. Eisenstadt v. Baird, 405 U.S. 438 (1972); Dunn v. Blumstein;[c] Police

---

c. *Dunn* fully canvasses this Court's voting rights cases and explains that "this Court has made clear that a citizen has a constitutionally protected right to participate in elections on an equal basis with other citizens in the jurisdiction." Id. at 336 (emphasis supplied). The constitutional underpinnings of the right to equal treatment in the voting process can no longer be doubted even though, as the Court noted in Harper v. Virginia Bd. of Elections, . . . "the right to vote in state elections is nowhere expressly mentioned." . . .

Dept. of Chicago v. Mosley, 408 U.S. 92 (1972);[d] Skinner v. Oklahoma, 316 U.S. 535 (1942).[e]

Education, of course, is not among the rights afforded explicit protection under our Federal Constitution. Nor do we find any basis for saying it is implicitly so protected. As we have said, the undisputed importance of education will not alone cause this Court to depart from the usual standard for reviewing a State's social and economic legislation. It is appellees' contention, however, that education is distinguishable from other services and benefits provided by the State because it bears a peculiarly close relationship to other rights and liberties accorded protection under the Constitution. Specifically, they insist that education is itself a fundamental personal right because it is essential to the effective exercise of First Amendment freedoms and to intelligent utilization of the right to vote. In asserting a nexus between speech and education, appellees urge that the right to speak is meaningless unless the speaker is capable of articulating his thoughts intelligently and persuasively. The "marketplace of ideas" is an empty forum for those lacking basic communicative tools. . . . A similar line of reasoning is pursued with respect to the right to vote.[f] Exercise of the franchise, it is contended, cannot be divorced from the educational foundation of the voter.

We need not dispute any of these propositions. The Court has long afforded zealous protection against unjustifiable governmental interference with the individual's rights to speak and to vote. Yet we have never presumed to possess either the ability or the authority to guarantee to the citizenry the most effective speech or the most informed electoral choice. . . .

Whatever merit appellees' argument might have if a State's financing system occasioned an absolute denial of educational opportunities to any of its children, that argument provides no basis for finding an interference with fundamental rights where only relative differences in spending levels are involved and where — as is true in the present case — no charge fairly could be made that the system fails to provide each child with an opportunity to acquire the basic minimal skills necessary for the enjoyment of the rights of speech and of full participation in the political process.

Furthermore, the logical limitations on appellees' nexus theory are difficult to perceive. How, for instance, is education to be distinguished from the significant personal interests in the basics of decent food and shelter? Empirical examination might well buttress an assumption that the ill-fed, ill-clothed, and ill-housed are among the most ineffective participants in the political process, and that they derive the least enjoyment from the benefits of the First Amendment. If so,

d. In *Mosley,* the Court struck down a Chicago antipicketing ordinance that exempted labor picketing from its prohibitions. The ordinance was held invalid under the Equal Protection Clause after subjecting it to careful scrutiny and finding that the ordinance was not narrowly drawn. The stricter standard of review was appropriately applied since the ordinance was one "affecting First Amendment interests." . . .

e. *Skinner* applied the standard of close scrutiny to a state law permitting forced sterilization of "habitual criminals." Implicit in the Court's opinion is the recognition that the right of procreation is among the rights of personal privacy protected under the Constitution. See Roe v. Wade.

f. Since the right to vote, per se, is not a constitutionally protected right, we assume that appellees' references to that right are simply shorthand references to the protected right, implicit in our constitutional system, to participate in state elections on an equal basis with other qualified voters whenever the State has adopted an elective process for determining who will represent any segment of the State's population. See n.[c] supra.

appellees' thesis would cast serious doubt on the authority of Dandridge v. Williams and Lindsey v. Normet.

. . . In one further respect we find this a particularly inappropriate case in which to subject state action to strict judicial scrutiny. The present case, in another basic sense, is significantly different from any of the cases in which the Court has applied strict scrutiny to state or federal legislation touching upon constitutionally protected rights. Each of our prior cases involved legislation which "deprived," "infringed," or "interfered" with the free exercise of some such fundamental personal right or liberty. See Skinner v. Oklahoma; Shapiro v. Thompson; Dunn v. Blumstein. Every step leading to the establishment of the system Texas utilizes today — including the decisions permitting localities to tax and expend locally, and creating and continuously expanding state aid — was implemented in an effort to extend public education and to improve its quality. Of course, every reform that benefits some more than others may be criticized for what it fails to accomplish. But we think it plain that, in substance, the thrust of the Texas system is affirmative and reformatory and, therefore, should be scrutinized under judicial principles sensitive to the nature of the State's efforts and to the rights reserved to the States under the Constitution.

C

We need not rest our decision, however, solely on the inappropriateness of a strict-scrutiny test. A century of Supreme Court adjudication under the Equal Protection Clause affirmatively supports the application of the traditional standard of review, which requires only that the State's system be shown to bear some rational relationship to legitimate state purposes. . . .

While assuring a basic education for every child in the State, [the Texas system of school finance] permits and encourages a large measure of participation in and control of each district's schools at the local level. In an era that has witnessed a consistent trend toward centralization of the functions of government, local sharing of responsibility for public education has survived. . . . In part, local control means . . . the freedom to devote more money to the education of one's children. Equally important, however, is the opportunity it offers for participation in the decisionmaking process that determines how those local tax dollars will be spent. Each locality is free to tailor local programs to local needs. Pluralism also affords some opportunity for experimentation, innovation, and a healthy competition for educational excellence. . . .

Appellees suggest that local control could be preserved and promoted under other financing systems that resulted in more equality in educational expenditures. While it is no doubt true that reliance on local property taxation for school revenues provides less freedom of choice with respect to expenditures for some districts than for others, the existence of "some inequality" in the manner in which the State's rationale is achieved is not alone a sufficient basis for striking down the entire system. . . . Nor must the financing system fail because, as appellees suggest, other methods of satisfying the State's interest, which occasion "less drastic" disparities in expenditures, might be conceived. Only where state action impinges on the exercise of fundamental constitutional rights or liberties must it be found to have chosen the last restrictive alternative. It is also well to remember that even those districts that have reduced ability to make free decisions with respect to how much they spend on education still retain under the present system a large measure of authority as to how available funds will be allocated. They further enjoy the power to make numerous other decisions with respect to the operation of the schools. The people of Texas may be justified in believing that other systems of school financing, which place more of the financial responsibility in the hands of the State, will result in a comparable lessening of desired local autonomy. That is, they may believe that along with increased control of the purse strings at the state level will go increased control over local policies.

Appellees further urge that the Texas system is unconstitutionally arbitrary because it allows the availability of local taxable resources to turn on "happenstance." They see no justification for a system that allows, as they contend, the quality of education to fluctuate on the basis of the fortuitous positioning of the boundary lines of political subdivisions and the location of valuable commercial and industrial property. But any scheme of local taxation — indeed the very existence of identifiable local governmental units — requires the establishment of jurisdictional boundaries that are inevitably arbitrary. It is equally inevitable that some localities are going to be blessed with more taxable assets than others.[g] Nor is local wealth a static quantity. Changes in the level of taxable wealth within any district may result from any number of events, some of which local residents can and do influence. For instance, commercial and industrial enterprises may be encouraged to locate within a district by various actions — public and private.

Moreover, if local taxation for local expenditures were an unconstitutional method of providing for education then it might be an equally impermissible means of providing other necessary services customarily financed largely from local property taxes, including local police and fire protection, public health and hospitals, and public utility facilities of various kinds. . . .

In sum, to the extent that the Texas system of school financing results in unequal expenditures between children who happen to reside in different districts, we cannot say that such disparities are the product of a system that is so irrational as to be invidiously discriminatory. . . .

[A concurring opinion by Justice Stewart is omitted.]

WHITE, J., joined by Douglas and Brennan, JJ., dissenting. . . .

I cannot disagree with the proposition that local control and local decisionmaking play an important part in our democratic system of government. Much may be left to local option, and this case would be quite different if it were true that the Texas system, while insuring minimum educational expenditures in every district through state funding, extended a meaningful option to all local districts to increase their per-pupil expenditures and so to improve their children's education to the extent that increased funding would achieve that goal. The system would then arguably provide a rational and sensible method of achieving the stated aim of preserving an area for local initiative and decision.

The difficulty with the Texas system, however, is that it provides a meaningful option to Alamo Heights and like school districts but almost none to Edgewood and those other districts with a low per-pupil real estate tax base. In these latter districts, no matter how desirous parents are of supporting their schools with

---

g. This Court has never doubted the propriety of maintaining political subdivisions within the States and has never found in the Equal Protection Clause any per se rule of "territorial uniformity." . . .

greater revenues, it is impossible to do so through the use of the real estate property tax. In these districts, the Texas system utterly fails to extend a realistic choice to parents because the property tax, which is the only revenue-raising mechanism extended to school districts, is practically and legally unavailable. That this is the situation may be readily demonstrated. . . .

The Equal Protection Clause permits discriminations between classes but requires that the classification bear some rational relationship to a permissible object sought to be attained by the statute. It is not enough that the Texas system before us seeks to achieve the valid, rational purpose of maximizing local initiative; the means chosen by the State must also be rationally related to the end sought to be achieved. . . .

Neither Texas nor the majority heeds this rule. If the State aims at maximizing local initiative and local choice, by permitting school districts to resort to the real property tax if they choose to do so, it utterly fails in achieving its purpose in districts with property tax bases so low that there is little if any opportunity for interested parents, rich or poor, to augment school district revenues. Requiring the State to establish only that unequal treatment is in furtherance of a permissible goal, without also requiring the State to show that the means chosen to effectuate that goal are rationally related to its achievement, makes equal protection analysis no more than an empty gesture. In my view, the parents and children in Edgewood, and in like districts, suffer from an invidious discrimination violative of the Equal Protection Clause.

This does not, of course, mean that local control may not be a legitimate goal of a school financing system. Nor does it mean that the State must guarantee each district an equal per-pupil revenue from the state school-financing system. . . . On the contrary, it would merely mean that the State must fashion a financing scheme which provides a rational basis for the maximization of local control. . . .

MARSHALL, J., joined by Douglas, J., dissenting. . . .

I.

The Court acknowledges that "substantial interdistrict disparities in school expenditures" exist in Texas, and that these disparities are "largely attributable to differences in the amounts of money collected through local property taxation." But instead of closely examining the seriousness of these disparities and the invidiousness of the Texas financing scheme, the Court undertakes an elaborate exploration of the efforts Texas has purportedly made to close the gaps between its districts in terms of levels of district wealth and resulting educational funding. Yet, however praiseworthy Texas' equalizing efforts, the issue in this case is not whether Texas is doing its best to ameliorate the worst features of a discriminatory scheme but, rather, whether the scheme itself is in fact unconstitutionally discriminatory in the face of the Fourteenth Amendment's guarantee of equal protection of the laws. . . .

Certainly the Court has recognized that to demand precise equality of treatment is normally unrealistic, and thus minor differences inherent in any practical context usually will not make out a substantial equal protection claim. But . . . we are hardly presented here with some de minimis claim of discrimination resulting from the play necessary in any functioning system; to the contrary, it is clear that the Foundation Program utterly fails to ameliorate the seriously discriminatory effects of the local property tax.

Alternatively, . . . the majority may believe that the Equal Protection Clause cannot be offended by substantially unequal state treatment of persons who are similarly situated so long as the State provides everyone with some unspecified amount of education which evidently is "enough." The basis for such a novel view is far from clear. . . . [T]his Court has never suggested that because some "adequate" level of benefits is provided to all, discrimination in the provision of services is therefore constitutionally excusable. The Equal Protection Clause is not addressed to the minimal sufficiency but rather to the unjustifiable inequalities of state action. . . .

Despite the evident discriminatory effect of the Texas financing scheme, both the appellants and the majority raise substantial questions concerning the precise character of the disadvantaged class in this case.

I believe it is sufficient that the overarching form of discrimination in this case is between the schoolchildren of Texas on the basis of the taxable property wealth of the districts in which they happen to live. . . . In their complaint appellees asserted that the Constitution does not permit local district wealth to be determinative of educational opportunity. This is simply another way of saying, as the District Court concluded, that consistent with the guarantee of equal protection of the laws, "the quality of public education may not be a function of wealth, other than the wealth of the state as a whole." Under such a principle, the children of a district are excessively advantaged if that district has more taxable property per pupil than the average amount of taxable property per pupil considering the State as a whole. By contrast, the children of a district are disadvantaged if that district has less taxable property per pupil than the state average. The majority attempts to disparage such a definition of the disadvantaged class as the product of an "artificially defined level" of district wealth. But such is clearly not the case, for this is the definition unmistakably dictated by the constitutional principle for which appellees have argued throughout the course of this litigation. And I do not believe that a clearer definition of either the disadvantaged class of Texas schoolchildren or the allegedly unconstitutional discrimination suffered by the members of that class under the present Texas financing scheme could be asked for, much less needed. Whether this discrimination, against the schoolchildren of property-poor districts, inherent in the Texas financing scheme, is violative of the Equal Protection Clause is the question to which we must now turn.

II.

To avoid having the Texas financing scheme struck down because of the interdistrict variations in taxable property wealth, the District Court determined that . . . the discrimination inherent in the scheme had to be shown necessary to promote a "compelling state interest" in order to withstand constitutional scrutiny. The basis for this determination was twofold: first, the financing scheme divides citizens on a wealth basis, a classification which the District Court viewed as highly suspect; and second, the discriminatory scheme directly affects what it considered to be a "fundamental interest," namely, education. . . .

The majority today concludes, however, that the Texas scheme is not subject to such a strict standard of review under the Equal Protection Clause. Instead, in its view, the Texas scheme must be tested by nothing more than that lenient standard of rationality which we have traditionally applied to discriminatory state action in the context of economic and commercial matters. . . .

A

The Court apparently seeks to establish today that equal protection cases fall into one of two neat categories which dictate the appropriate standard of review — strict scrutiny or mere rationality. But this Court's decisions in the field of equal protection defy such easy categorization. A principled reading of what this Court has done reveals that it has applied a spectrum of standards in reviewing discrimination allegedly violative of the Equal Protection Clause. This spectrum clearly comprehends variations in the degree of care with which the Court will scrutinize particular classifications, depending, I believe, on the constitutional and societal importance of the interest adversely affected and the recognized invidiousness of the basis upon which the particular classification is drawn. . . .

I therefore cannot accept the majority's labored efforts to demonstrate that fundamental interests, which call for strict scrutiny of the challenged classification, encompass only established rights which we are somehow bound to recognize from the text of the Constitution itself. To be sure, some interests which the Court has deemed to be fundamental for purposes of equal protection analysis are themselves constitutionally protected rights. . . . See Police Dept. of Chicago v. Mosley . . . ; Shapiro v. Thompson. . . . But it will not do to suggest that the "answer" to whether an interest is fundamental for purposes of equal protection analysis is always determined by whether that interest "is a right . . . explicitly or implicitly guaranteed by the Constitution."[a] . . .

I would like to know where the Constitution guarantees the right to procreate, Skinner v. Oklahoma, or the right to vote in state elections, e.g., [Harper v. Virginia Bd. of Elections], or the right to an appeal from a criminal conviction, e.g., Griffin v. Illinois. These are instances in which, due to the importance of the interests at stake, the Court has displayed a strong concern with the existence of discriminatory state treatment. But the Court has never said or indicated that these are interests which independently enjoy full-blown constitutional protection.

Thus, in Buck v. Bell, 247 U.S. 200 (1927), the Court refused to recognize a substantive constitutional guarantee of the right to procreate. Nevertheless, in Skinner v. Oklahoma, . . . the Court, without impugning the continuing validity of Buck v. Bell, held that "strict scrutiny" of state discrimination affecting procreation "is essential," for "[m]arriage and procreation are fundamental to the very existence and survival of the race." . . .

Similarly, . . . "this Court has made clear that a citizen has a *constitutionally protected right* to participate in elections *on an equal basis with other citizens in the jurisdiction.*" Dunn v. Blumstein (emphasis added). The final source of such protection from inequality in the provision of the state franchise is, of course, the Equal Protection Clause. Yet it is clear that whatever degree of importance has been attached to the state electoral process when unequally distributed, the right to vote

a. Indeed, the Court's theory would render the established concept of fundamental interests in the context of equal protection analysis superfluous, for the substantive constitutional right itself requires that this Court strictly scrutinize any asserted state interest for restricting or denying access to any particular guaranteed right. . . .

in state elections has itself never been accorded the stature of an independent constitutional guarantee.[b] . . .

Finally, it is likewise "true that a State is not required by the Federal Constitution to provide appellate courts or a right to appellate review at all." Griffin v. Illinois. Nevertheless, discrimination adversely affecting access to an appellate process which a State has chosen to provide has been considered to require close judicial scrutiny. See, e.g., Griffin v. Illinois; Douglas v. California.[c]

The majority is, of course, correct when it suggests that the process of determining which interests are fundamental is a difficult one. But I do not think the problem is insurmountable. And I certainly do not accept the view that the process need necessarily degenerate into an unprincipled, subjective "picking-and-choosing" between various interests or that it must involve this Court in creating "substantive constitutional rights in the name of guaranteeing equal protection of the laws." Although not all fundamental interests are constitutionally guaranteed, the determination of which interests are fundamental should be firmly rooted in the text of the Constitution. The task in every case should be to determine the extent to which constitutionally guaranteed rights are dependent on interests not mentioned in the Constitution. As the nexus between the specific constitutional guarantee and the nonconstitutional interest draws closer, the nonconstitutional interest becomes more fundamental and the degree of judicial scrutiny applied when the interest is infringed on a discriminatory basis must be adjusted accordingly. Thus, it cannot be denied that interests such as procreation, the exercise of the state franchise, and access to criminal appellate processes are not fully guaranteed to the citizen by our Constitution. But these interests have nonetheless been afforded special judicial consideration in the face of discrimination because they are, to some extent, interrelated with constitutional guarantees. Procreation is now understood to be important because of its interaction with the established constitutional right of privacy. The exercise of the state franchise is closely tied to basic civil and political rights inherent in the First Amendment. And access to criminal appellate processes enhances the integrity of the range of rights implicit in the Fourteenth Amendment guarantee of due process of law. Only if we closely protect the related interests from state discrimination do we ultimately ensure the integrity of the constitutional guarantee itself. This is the real lesson that must be taken from our previous decisions involving interests deemed to be fundamental. . . . .

---

b. It is interesting that in its effort to reconcile the state voting rights cases with its theory of fundamentality the majority can muster nothing more than the contention that "[t]he constitutional underpinnings of the right to equal treatment in the voting process can no longer be doubted. . . ." (emphasis added). If, by this, the Court intends to recognize a substantive constitutional "right to equal treatment in the voting process" independent of the Equal Protection Clause, the source of such a right is certainly a mystery to me.

c. It is true that Griffin and Douglas also involved discrimination against indigents, that is, wealth discrimination. But, as the majority points out, the Court has never deemed wealth discrimination alone to be sufficient to require strict judicial scrutiny; rather, such review of wealth classifications has been applied only where the discrimination affects an important individual interest, see, e.g., Harper v. Virginia Bd. of Elections. Thus, I believe Griffin and Douglas can only be understood as premised on a recognition of the fundamental importance of the criminal appellate process.

B

It is true that this Court has never deemed the provision of free public education to be required by the Constitution. . . . Nevertheless, the fundamental importance of education is amply indicated by the prior decisions of this Court, by the unique status accorded public education by our society, and by the close relationship between education and some of our most basic constitutional values. . . . In large measure, the explanation for the special importance attached to education must rest . . . on the facts that "some degree of education is necessary to prepare citizens to participate effectively and intelligently in our open political system . . . ," and that "education prepares individuals to be self-reliant and self-sufficient participants in society." Both facets of this observation are suggestive of the substantial relationship which education bears to guarantees of our Constitution.

Education directly affects the ability of a child to exercise his First Amendment interests, both as a source and as a receiver of information and ideas, whatever interests he may pursue in life. . . . Education may instill the interest and provide the tools necessary for political discourse and debate. . . . But of most immediate and direct concern must be the demonstrated effect of education on the exercise of the franchise by the electorate. . . . Data from the Presidential Election of 1968 clearly demonstrates a direct relationship between participation in the electoral process and level of educational attainment; and, as this Court recognized in Gaston County v. United States, 395 U.S. 284, 296 (1969), the quality of education offered may influence a child's decision to "enter or remain in school." It is this very sort of intimate relationship between a particular personal interest and specific constitutional guarantees that has heretofore caused the Court to attach special significance, for purposes of equal protection analysis, to individual interests such as procreation and the exercise of the state franchise.[d]

While ultimately disputing little of this, the majority seeks refuge in the fact that the Court has "never presumed to possess either the ability or the authority to guarantee to the citizenry the most effective speech or the most informed electoral choice." . . . This serves only to blur what is in fact at stake. With due respect, the issue is neither provision of the most effective speech nor of the most informed vote. Appellees do not now seek the best education Texas might provide. They do seek, however, an end to state discrimination resulting from the unequal distribution of taxable district property wealth that directly impairs the ability of some districts to provide the same educational opportunity that other districts can provide with the same or even substantially less tax effort. The issue is, in other

d. I believe that the close nexus between education and our established constitutional values with respect to freedom of speech and participation in the political process makes this a different case from our prior decisions concerning discrimination affecting public welfare, see, e.g., Dandridge v. Williams, and housing, see, e.g., Lindsey v. Normet. There can be no question that, as the majority suggests, constitutional rights may be less meaningful for someone without enough to eat or without decent housing. But the crucial difference lies in the closeness of the relationship. Whatever the severity of the impact of insufficient food or inadequate housing on a person's life, they have never been considered to bear the same direct and immediate relationship to constitutional concerns for free speech and for our political processes as education has long been recognized to bear. Perhaps, the best evidence of this fact is the unique status which has been accorded public education as the single public service nearly unanimously guaranteed in the constitutions of our State. . . . Education, in terms of constitutional values, is much more analogous, in my judgment, to the right to vote in state elections than to public welfare or public housing. Indeed, it is not without significance that we have long recognized education as an essential step in providing the disadvantaged with the tools necessary to achieve economic self-sufficiency.

words, one of discrimination that affects the quality of the education which Texas has chosen to provide its children; and, the precise question here is what importance should attach to education for purposes of equal protection analysis of that discrimination. . . .

C

The District Court found that in discriminating between Texas schoolchildren on the basis of the amount of taxable property wealth located in the district in which they live, the Texas financing scheme created a form of wealth discrimination. . . . The majority, however, considers any wealth classification in this case to lack certain essential characteristics which it contends are common to the instances of wealth discrimination that this Court has heretofore recognized. We are told that in every prior case involving a wealth classification, the members of the disadvantaged class have "shared two distinguishing characteristics: because of their impecunity they were completely unable to pay for some desired benefit, and as a consequence, they sustained an absolute deprivation of a meaningful opportunity to enjoy that benefit." . . . I cannot agree. . . .

Under the first part of the theory announced by the majority, the disadvantaged class in *Harper*, in terms of a wealth analysis, should have consisted only of those too poor to afford the $1.50 necessary to vote. But the *Harper* Court did not see it that way. In its view, the Equal Protection Clause "bars a system which excludes [from the franchise] those unable to pay a fee to vote or who fail to pay." So far as the Court was concerned, the "degree of the discrimination [was] irrelevant." Thus, the Court struck down the poll tax in toto; it did not order merely that those too poor to pay the tax be exempted; complete impecunity clearly was not determinative of the limits of the disadvantaged class, nor was it essential to make an equal protection claim. . . .

[In Griffin v. Illinois and Douglas v. California] the right of appeal itself was not absolutely denied to those too poor to pay; but because of the cost of a transcript and of counsel, the appeal was a substantially less meaningful right for the poor than for the rich.[e] It was on these terms that the Court found a denial of equal protection, and those terms clearly encompassed degrees of discrimination on the basis of wealth which do not amount to outright denial of the affected right or interest.

This is not to say that the form of wealth classification in this case does not differ significantly from those recognized in the previous decisions of this Court. Our prior cases have dealt essentially with discrimination on the basis of personal wealth. Here, by contrast, the children of the disadvantaged Texas school districts are being discriminated against not necessarily because of their personal wealth or the wealth of their families, but because of the taxable property wealth of the residents of the district in which they happen to live. The appropriate question, then, is whether the same degree of judicial solicitude and scrutiny that has previously been afforded wealth classifications is warranted here.

---

e. This does not mean that the Court has demanded precise equality in the treatment of the indigent and the person of means in the criminal process. We have never suggested, for instance, that the Equal Protection Clause requires the best lawyer money can buy for the indigent. We are hardly equipped with the objective standards which such a judgment would require. But we have pursued the goal of substantial equality of treatment in the face of clear disparities in the nature of the appellate process afforded rich versus poor. . . .

As the Court points out, no previous decision has deemed the presence of just a wealth classification to be sufficient basis to call forth rigorous judicial scrutiny of allegedly discriminatory state action. . . . That wealth classifications alone have not necessarily been considered to bear the same high degree of suspectness as have classifications based on, for instance, race or alienage may be explainable on a number of grounds. The "poor" may not be seen as politically powerless as certain discrete and insular minority groups. Personal poverty may entail much the same social stigma as is historically attached to certain racial or ethnic groups. But personal poverty is not a permanent disability; its shackles may be escaped. Perhaps most importantly, though, personal wealth may not necessarily share the general irrelevance as a basis for legislative action that race or nationality is recognized to have. While the "poor" have frequently been a legally disadvantaged group, it cannot be ignored that social legislation must frequently take cognizance of the economic status of our citizens. Thus, we have generally gauged the invidiousness of wealth classifications with an awareness of the importance of the interests being affected and the relevance of personal wealth to those interests. See *Harper*.

When evaluated with these considerations in mind, it seems to me that discrimination on the basis of group wealth in this case likewise calls for careful judicial scrutiny. First, it must be recognized that while local district wealth may serve other interests, it bears no relationship whatsoever to the interest of Texas school children in the educational opportunity afforded them by the State of Texas. Given the importance of that interest, we must be particularly sensitive to the invidious characteristics of any form of discrimination that is not clearly intended to serve it, as opposed to some other distinct state interest. Discrimination on the basis of group wealth may not, to be sure, reflect the social stigma frequently attached to personal poverty. Nevertheless, insofar as group wealth discrimination involves wealth over which the disadvantaged individual has no significant control,[f] it represents in fact a more serious basis of discrimination than does personal wealth. For such discrimination is no reflection of the individual's characteristics or his abilities. And thus — particularly in the context of a disadvantaged class composed of children — we have previously treated discrimination on a basis which the individual cannot control as constitutionally disfavored. Cf. Weber v. Aetna Casualty & Surety Co., 406 U.S. 164 (1972); Levy v. Louisiana, 391 U.S. 68 (1968). . . .

Nor can we ignore the extent to which, in contrast to our prior decisions, the State is responsible for the wealth discrimination in this instance. *Griffin, Douglas, Williams, Tate,* and our other prior cases have dealt with discrimination on the basis of indigency which was attributable to the operation of the private sector. But we have no such simple de facto wealth discrimination here. The means for financing public education in Texas are selected and specified by the State. It is the State that has created local school districts, and tied educational funding to the local property tax and thereby to local district wealth. At the same time, governmentally imposed land use controls have undoubtedly encouraged and rigidified natural trends in the allocation of particular areas for residential or commercial use, and thus determined each district's amount of taxable property wealth. In short, this

---

f. True, a family may move to escape a property-poor school district, assuming it has the means to do so. But such a view would itself raise a serious constitutional question concerning an impermissible burdening of the right to travel, or, more precisely, the concomitant right to remain where one is. Cf. Shapiro v. Thompson.

case, in contrast to the Court's previous wealth discrimination decision, can only be seen as "unusual in the extent to which governmental action is the cause of the wealth classifications."

In the final analysis, then, the invidious characteristics of the group wealth classification present in this case merely serve to emphasize the need for careful judicial scrutiny of the State's justifications for the resulting interdistrict discrimination in the educational opportunity afforded to the schoolchildren of Texas.

D

The nature of our inquiry into the justifications for state discrimination is essentially the same in all equal protection cases: We must consider the substantiality of the state interests sought to be served, and we must scrutinize the reasonableness of the means by which the State has sought to advance its interests. Differences in the application of this test are, in my view, a function of the constitutional importance of the interests at stake and the invidiousness of the particular classification. In terms of the asserted state interests, the Court has indicated that it will require, for instance, a "compelling" or a "substantial" or "important" state interest to justify discrimination affecting individual interests of constitutional significance. Whatever the differences, if any, in these descriptions of the character of the state interest necessary to sustain such discrimination, basic to each is, I believe, a concern with the legitimacy and the reality of the asserted state interests. Thus, when interests of constitutional importance are at stake, the Court does not stand ready to credit the State's classification with any conceivable legitimate purpose, but demands a clear showing that there are legitimate state interests which the classification was in fact intended to serve. Beyond the question of the adequacy of the State's purpose for the classification, the Court traditionally has become increasingly sensitive to the means by which a State chooses to act as its action affects more directly interests of constitutional significance. Thus, by now, "less restrictive alternatives" analysis is firmly established in equal protection jurisprudence. It seems to me that the range of choice we are willing to accord the State in selecting the means by which it will act, and the care with which we scrutinize the effectiveness of the means which the State selects, also must reflect the constitutional importance of the interest affected and the invidiousness of the particular classification. Here both the nature of the interest and the classification dictate close judicial scutiny of the purposes which Texas seeks to serve with its present educational financing scheme and of the means it has selected to serve that purpose.

The only justification offered by appellants to sustain the discrimination in educational opportunity caused by the Texas financing scheme is local educational control. . . .

At the outset, I do not question that local control of public education, as an abstract matter, constitutes a very substantial state interest. . . . Consequently, true state dedication to local control would present, I think, a substantial justification to weigh against simply interdistrict variations in the treatment of a State's school children. But I need not now decide how I might ultimately strike the balance were we confronted with a situation where the State's sincere concern for local control inevitably produced educational inequality. For on this record, it is apparent that the State's purported concern with local control is offered primarily as an excuse rather than as a justification for interdistrict inequality.

In Texas, statewide laws regulate in fact the most minute details of local public education. . . . [But] even if we accept Texas' general dedication to local control in educational matters, it is difficult to find any evidence of such dedication with respect to fiscal matters. . . . If Texas had a system truly dedicated to local fiscal control, one would expect the quality of the educational opportunity provided in each district to vary with the decision of the voters in that district as to the level of sacrifice they wish to make for public education. In fact, the Texas scheme produces precisely the opposite result. Local school districts cannot choose to have the best education in the State by imposing the highest tax rate. Instead, the quality of the educational opportunity offered by any particular district is largely determined by the amount of taxable property located in the district — a factor over which local voters can exercise no control. . . .

In my judgment, any substantial degree of scrutiny of the operation of the Texas financing scheme reveals that the State has selected means wholly inappropriate to secure its purported interest in assuring its school districts local fiscal control.[g] At the same time, appellees have pointed out a variety of alternative financing schemes which may serve the State's purported interest in local control as well as, if not better than, the present scheme without the current impairment of the educational opportunity of vast numbers of Texas schoolchildren. I see no need, however, to explore the practical or constitutional merits of those suggested alternatives at this time for, whatever their positive or negative features, experience with the present financing scheme impugns any suggestion that it constitutes a serious effort to provide local fiscal control. . . .[h] [A dissenting opinion by Justice Brennan is omitted.]

g. My Brother White, in concluding that the Texas financing scheme runs afoul of the Equal Protection Clause, likewise finds on analysis that the means chosen by Texas — local property taxation dependent upon local taxable wealth — is completely unsuited in its present form to the achievement of the asserted goal of providing local fiscal control. Although my Brother White purports to reach this result by application of that lenient standard of mere rationality traditionally applied in the context of commercial interests, it seems to me that the care with which he scrutinizes the practical effectiveness of the present local property tax as a device for affording local fiscal control reflects the application of a more stringent standard of review, a standard which at the least is influenced by the constitutional significance of the process of public education.

h. . . . [E]ven centralized financing would not deprive local school districts of what has been considered to be the essence of local educational control. . . . Central financing would leave in local hands the entire gamut of local educational policymaking — teachers, curriculum, school sites, the whole process of allocating resources among alternative educational objectives. [Local fiscal control could be achieved under] the theory of district power equalization put forth by Professors Coons, Clune and Sugarman in their seminal work, Private Wealth and Public Education 201-242 (1970). Such a scheme would truly reflect a dedication to local fiscal control. Under their system, each school district would receive a fixed amount of revenue per pupil for any particular level of tax effort regardless of the level of local property tax base. Appellants criticize this scheme on the rather extraordinary ground that it would encourage poorer districts to overtax themselves in order to obtain substantial revenues for education. But under the present discriminatory scheme, it is the poor districts that are already taxing themselves at the highest rates, yet are receiving the lowest returns.

District wealth reapportionment is yet another alternative which would accomplish directly essentially what district power equalization would seek to do artificially. Appellants claim that the calculations concerning state property required by such a scheme would be impossible as a practical matter. Yet Texas is already making far more complex annual calculations — involving not only local property values but also local income and other economic factors — in conjunction with the Local Fund Assignment portion of the Minimum Foundation School Program. . . . [Another] possibility would be to remove commercial, industrial, and mineral property from local tax rolls, to tax this property on a statewide basis, and to return the resulting revenues to the local districts in a fashion that would compensate for remaining variations in the local tax bases. None of these particular alternatives are necessarily constitutionally compelled; rather, they indicate the breadth of choice which would remain to the State if the present interdistrict disparities were eliminated.

Discussion

1. *Comparative constitutional kinship.* Rank the following interests in terms of the firmness of their grounding in the text, structure, and original history of the Constitution: interstate mobility (protected in *Crandall* and *Shapiro*), privacy (protected in *Griswold* and Roe v. Wade), the franchise (protected in *Harper*), subsistence (denied protection in Dandridge v. Williams and Lindsey v. Normet), and education (denied protection in *Rodriguez*). Is Justice Powell persuasive that the Court has not picked and chosen among possible interests both in the creation of constitutional "rights" (e.g., privacy) and "fundamental interests" (e.g., political participation)? How persuasive is Justice Marshall's argument that education deserves special constitutional treatment because of its relationships with speech and the franchise? Assuming that some regulations concerning education do affect these interests, cf. Pierce v. Society of Sisters and Meyer v. Nebraska, supra, does the Texas school finance scheme affect them in a significant or in a constitutionally germane manner?

2. *The methodologies of due process and equal protection.* Is there a real difference between the methodologies of substantive due process — whether of the *Lochner* or Roe v. Wade variety — and "substantive equal protection"?[25] In Weber v. Aetna Casualty & Surety Co., 406 U.S. 164, 182 (1972) Justice Rehnquist argued that the two decisionmaking processes have the same defect:

> The relationship of the . . . "fundamental personal right" analysis to the constitutional guarantee of equal protection of the law is approximately the same as that of "freedom of contract" to the constitutional guarantee that no person shall be deprived of life, liberty, or property without due process of law. It is an invitation for judicial exegesis over and above the commands of the Constitution, in which values that cannot possibly have their source in that instrument are invoked to either validate or condemn the countless laws enacted by the various States.

3. *The nature of the interests protected.* Is there a difference between the kinds of interests that the Court has held to be constitutional "rights" independent of the equal protection clause and the interests that the Court has refused to deem "fundamental" under the equal protection clause? Is there a difference between the kinds of protection the Court has been asked to accord those interests? Recall the distinction between the "negative" state of classical liberalism and the "positive" welfare state. What are the likely implications of a decision that interests such as food, shelter, and education are independent constitutional rights?

4. *The standard of judicial review and the substantive requirements of the Equal Protection Clause.* In *Dandridge* and *Rodriguez,* Justice Marshall criticizes the Court for its binary or "two-tier"[26] approach to equal protection adjudication, under which a classification is subjected either to minimal or to very demanding scrutiny. He proposes, instead, a variable standard determined by the nature of the classifying trait and the interests affected. What are the rationales for the Court's and Justice Marshall's approaches?

---

25. See Kenneth Karst and Harold Horowitz, Reitman v. Mulkey: A Telophase of Substantive Equal Protection, 1967 Sup. Ct. Rev. 39.

26. See Gerald Gunther, In Search of Evolving Doctrine on a Changing Court: A Model for a Newer Equal Protection, 86 Harv. L. Rev. 1 (1972).

In a portion of *Rodriguez* not quoted above, Justice Powell asserts: "[I]f the degree of judicial scrutiny of state legislation fluctuated depending on the majority's view of the importance of the interest affected, we would have gone 'far toward making this Court a super-legislature.' We would, indeed, then be assuming a legislative role and one for which the Court lacks both authority and competence." Do *Dandridge* and *Rodriguez* reflect the Court's substantive position that the Equal Protection Clause demands nothing more than "minimum rationality" in the allocation of welfare and educational benefits or only an institutional reluctance to second-guess the legislature's application of a more demanding standard? What rationales support the two positions? Should we demand of legislators that they apply the imperatives of the Equal Protection Clause to their own decisions even in the absence of judicial monitoring?

5. *A "due process" minimum?* Does footnote b of Justice Powell's opinion suggest that the state can neither withdraw entirely from the educational marketplace nor bar children from public schools because of their or their families' inability to pay?[27]

6. *The importance of state constitutions.* As a matter of fact, *Rodriguez* by no means ended litigation about the fairness of state distribution of educational resources. Having lost on federal constitutional grounds, reform-oriented lawyers turned to state constitutions and, indeed, scored many successes in states ranging from New Jersey to Texas to California.[28]

2.   *Is There a Right to Some Minimal Provision of Educational Resources?*

PLYLER v. DOE
457 U.S. 202 (1982)

[In 1975, the Texas legislature revised its education laws (1) to withhold from local school districts any state funds to pay for the education of children not "legally admitted" into the United States; and (2) to authorize local school districts to deny enrollment to such children. A class action was filed challenging the Texas legislation.]

BRENNAN, J. . . .

II.

[Justice Brennan held that children of illegal aliens were "persons within [Texas's] jurisdiction" for purposes of the Fourteenth Amendment and that the Equal Protection Clause applied to them.]

---

27. By "public schools" we are referring to elementary and secondary schools. It is clear that public universities exclude qualified students because of their inability to pay the costs of their education, and this is not, at least currently, thought to present a constitutional problem.

28. See William E. Thro, To Render Them Safe: The Analysis of State Constitutional Provisions in School Finance Reform Litigation, 75 Va. L. Rev. 1639 (1989).

III.

...

A

Sheer incapability or lax enforcement of the laws barring entry into this country, coupled with the failure to establish an effective bar to the employment of undocumented aliens, has resulted in the creation of a substantial "shadow population" of illegal migrants — numbering in the millions — within our borders. This situation raises the specter of a permanent caste of undocumented resident aliens, encouraged by some to remain here as a source of cheap labor, but nevertheless denied the benefits that our society makes available to citizens and lawful residents. The existence of such an underclass presents most difficult problems for a Nation that prides itself on adherence to the principles of equality under law.

The children who are plaintiffs in these cases are special members of this underclass. Persuasive arguments support the view that a State may withhold its beneficence from those whose very presence within the United States is the product of their own unlawful conduct. These arguments do not apply with the same force to classifications imposing disabilities on the minor children of such illegal entrants. At the least, those who elect to enter our territory by stealth and in violation of our law should be prepared to bear the consequences, including, but not limited to, deportation. But the children of those illegal entrants are not comparably situated. Their "parents have the ability to conform their conduct to societal norms," and presumably the ability to remove themselves from the State's jurisdiction; but the children who are plaintiffs in these cases "can affect neither their parents' conduct nor their own status." Trimble v. Gordon, 430 U.S. 762, 770 (1977). Even if the State found it expedient to control the conduct of adults by acting against their children, legislation directing the onus of a parent's misconduct against his children does not comport with fundamental conceptions of justice. . . .

Public education is not a "right" granted to individuals by the Constitution. *Rodriguez*. But neither is it merely some governmental "benefit" indistinguishable from other forms of social welfare legislation. Both the importance of education in maintaining our basic institutions, and the lasting impact of its deprivation on the life of the child, mark the distinction. The "American people have always regarded education and the acquisition of knowledge as matters of supreme importance." Meyer v. Nebraska, 262 U.S. 390, 400 (1923). We have recognized "the public school as a most vital civic institution for the preservation of a democratic system of government" and as the primary vehicle for transmitting "the values on which our society rests." As noted early in our history, "some degree of education is necessary to prepare citizens to participate effectively and intelligently in our open political system if we are to preserve freedom and independence." And the historic "perceptions of the public schools as inculcating fundamental values necessary to the maintenance of a democratic political system have been confirmed by the observations of social scientists." In addition, education provides the basic tools by which individuals might lead economically productive lives to the benefit of us all. In sum, education has a fundamental role in maintaining the fabric of our society. We cannot ignore the significant social costs borne by our Nation when select groups are denied the means to absorb the values and skills upon which our social order rests.

In addition to the pivotal role of education in sustaining our political and cultural heritage, denial of education to some isolated group of children poses an affront to one of the goals of the Equal Protection Clause: the abolition of governmental barriers presenting unreasonable obstacles to advancement on the basis of individual merit. Paradoxically, by depriving the children of any disfavored group of an education, we foreclose the means by which that group might raise the level of esteem in which it is held by the majority. But more directly, "education prepares individuals to be self-reliant and self-sufficient participants in society." Illiteracy is an enduring disability. The inability to read and write will handicap the individual deprived of a basic education each and every day of his life. The inestimable toll of that deprivation on the social, economic, intellectual, and psychological well-being of the individual, and the obstacle it poses to individual achievement, makes it most difficult to reconcile the cost or the principle of a status-based denial of basic education within the framework of equality embodied in the Equal Protection Clause. . . .

B

These well-settled principles allow us to determine the proper level of deference to be afforded §21.031. Undocumented aliens cannot be treated as a suspect class because their presence in this country in violation of federal law is not a "constitutional irrelevancy." Nor is education a fundamental right; a State need not justify by compelling necessity every variation in the manner in which education is provided to its population. See *Rodriguez*. But more is involved in this case than the abstract question whether §21.031 discriminates against a suspect class, or whether education is a fundamental right. Section 21.031 imposes a lifetime hardship on a discrete class of children not accountable for their disabling status. The stigma of illiteracy will mark them for the rest of their lives. By denying these children a basic education, we deny them the ability to live within the structure of our civic institutions, and foreclose any realistic possibility that they will contribute in even the smallest way to the progress of our Nation. In determining the rationality of §21.031, we may appropriately take into account its costs to the Nation and to the innocent children who are its victims. In light of these countervailing costs, the discrimination contained in §21.031 can hardly be considered rational unless it furthers some substantial goal of the State.

IV.

Appellants argue that the classification at issue furthers interests in the "preservation of the state's limited resources for the education of its lawful residents." Of course, a concern for the preservation of resources standing alone can hardly justify the classification used in allocating those resources. The State must do more than justify its classification with a concise expression of an intention to discriminate. Apart from the asserted state prerogative to act against undocumented children solely on the basis of their undocumented status — an asserted prerogative that carries only minimal force in the circumstances of this case — we discern three colorable state interests that might support §21.031.

First, appellants appear to suggest that the State may seek to protect the State from an influx of illegal immigrants. While a State might have an interest in mitigating the potentially harsh economic effects of sudden shifts in population,

§21.031 hardly offers an effective method of dealing with an urgent demographic or economic problem. There is no evidence in the record suggesting that illegal entrants impose any significant burden on the State's economy. To the contrary, the available evidence suggests that illegal aliens under utilize public services, while contributing their labor to the local economy and tax money to the State fisc. The dominant incentive for illegal entry into the State of Texas is the availability of employment; few if any illegal immigrants come to this country, or presumably to the State of Texas, in order to avail themselves of a free education. Thus, even making the doubtful assumption that the net impact of illegal aliens on the economy of the State is negative, we think it clear that "[c]harging tuition to undocumented children constitutes a ludicrously ineffectual attempt to stem the tide of illegal immigration," at least when compared with the alternative of prohibiting the employment of illegal aliens.

Second, while it is apparent that a state may "not . . . reduce expenditures for education by barring [some arbitrarily chosen class of] children from its schools," appellants suggest that undocumented children are appropriately singled out for exclusion because of the special burdens they impose on the State's ability to provide high quality public education in the State. As the District Court noted, the State failed to offer any "credible supporting evidence that a proportionately small diminution of the funds spent on each child [which might result from devoting some State funds to the education of the excluded group] will have a grave impact on the quality of education." And, after reviewing the State's school financing mechanism, the District Court concluded that barring undocumented children from local schools would not necessarily improve the quality of education provided in these schools. Of course, even if improvement in the quality of education were a likely result of barring some number of children from the schools of the State, the State must support its selection of this group as the appropriate target for exclusion. In terms of educational cost and need, however, undocumented children are "basically indistinguishable" from legally resident alien children.

Finally, appellants suggest that undocumented children are appropriately singled out because their unlawful presence within the United States renders them less likely than other children to remain within the boundaries of the State, and to put their education to productive social or political use within the State. Even assuming that such an interest is legitimate, it is an interest that is most difficult to quantify. The State has no assurance that any child, citizen or not, will employ the education provided by the State within the confines of the State's borders. In any event, the record is clear that many of the undocumented children disabled by this classification will remain in this country indefinitely, and that some will become lawful residents or citizens of the United States. It is difficult to understand precisely what the State hopes to achieve by promoting the creation and perpetuation of a subclass of illiterates within our boundaries, surely adding to the problems and costs of unemployment, welfare, and crime. It is thus clear that whatever savings might be achieved by denying these children an education, they are wholly insubstantial in light of the costs involved to these children, the State, and the Nation.

V.

If the state is to deny a discrete group of innocent children the free public education that it offers to other children residing within its borders, that denial must be justified by a showing that it furthers some substantial state interest. No such showing was made here.

[Concurring opinions by Justices Blackmun and Powell have been omitted.]

BURGER, C.J., with whom White, Rehnquist, and O'Connor, JJ., join dissenting.

The dispositive issue in these cases, simply put, is whether, for purposes of allocating its finite resources, a State has a legitimate reason to differentiate between persons who are lawfully within the State and those who are unlawfully there. The distinction the State of Texas has drawn — based not only upon its own legitimate interests but on classifications established by the federal government in its immigration laws and policies — is not unconstitutional.

A

The Court acknowledges that except in those cases when state classifications disadvantage a "suspect class" or impinge upon a "fundamental right," the Equal Protection Clause permits a State "substantial latitude" in distinguishing between different groups of persons. Moreover, the Court expressly — and correctly — rejects any suggestion that illegal aliens are a suspect class, or that education is a fundamental right. Yet by patching together bits and pieces of what might be termed quasi-suspect-class and quasi-fundamental-rights analysis, the Court spins out a theory custom-tailored to the facts of these cases. In the end, we are told little more than that the level of scrutiny employed to strike down the Texas law applies only when illegal alien children are deprived of a public education. If ever a court was guilty of an unabashedly result-oriented approach, this case is a prime example.

1

The Court first suggests that these illegal alien children, although not a suspect class, are entitled to special solicitude under the Equal Protection Clause because they lack "control" over or "responsibility" for their unlawful entry into this country. Similarly, the Court appears to take the position that §21.031 is presumptively "irrational" because it has the effect of imposing "penalties" on "innocent" children. However, the Equal Protection Clause does not preclude legislators from classifying among persons on the basis of factors and characteristics over which individuals may be said to lack "control." Indeed, in some circumstances persons generally, and children in particular, may have little control over or responsibility for such things as their ill-health, need for public assistance, or place of residence. Yet a state legislature is not barred from considering, for example, relevant differences between the mentally healthy and the mentally ill, or between the residents of different counties, simply because these may be factors unrelated to individual choice or to any "wrongdoing." The Equal Protection Clause protects against arbitrary and irrational classifications, and against invidious discrimination stemming from prejudice and hostility; it is not an all-encompassing "equalizer" designed to eradicate every distinction for which persons are not "responsible."

The Court does not presume to suggest that appellees' purported lack of culpability for their illegal status prevents them from being deported or otherwise "penalized" under federal law. Yet would deportation be any less a "penalty" than denial of privileges provided to legal residents? Illegality of presence in the United States does not — and need not — depend on some amorphous concept of "guilt" or "innocence" concerning an alien's entry. Similarly, a State's use of federal immigration status as a basis for legislative classification is not necessarily rendered suspect for its failure to take such factors into account.

The Court's analogy to cases involving discrimination against illegitimate children is grossly misleading. The State has not thrust any disabilities upon appellees due to their "status of birth." Cf. Weber v. Aetna Casualty & Surety Co., 406 U.S. 164, 176 (1972). Rather, appellees' status is predicated upon the circumstances of their concededly illegal presence in this country, and is a direct result of Congress' obviously valid exercise of its "broad constitutional powers" in the field of immigration and naturalization. U.S. Const., Art. I, §8, cl. 4. This Court has recognized that in allocating governmental benefits to a given class of aliens, one "may take into account the character of the relationship between the alien and this country." Mathews v. Diaz. When that "relationship" is a federally-prohibited one, there can, of course, be no presumption that a State has a constitutional duty to include illegal aliens among the recipients of its governmental benefits.

2

The second strand of the Court's analysis rests on the premise that, although public education is not a constitutionally-guaranteed right, "neither is it merely some governmental 'benefit' indistinguishable from other forms of social welfare legislation." Whatever meaning or relevance this opaque observation might have in some or other contexts, it simply has no bearing on the issues at hand. Indeed, it is never made clear what the Court's opinion means on this score. The importance of education is beyond dispute. Yet we have held repeatedly that the importance of a governmental service does not elevate it to the status of a "fundamental right" for purposes of equal protection analysis. In *Rodriguez*, supra, Justice Powell, speaking for the Court, expressly rejected the proposition that state laws dealing with public education are subject to special scrutiny under the Equal Protection Clause. Moreover, the Court points to no meaningful way to distinguish between education and other governmental benefits in this context. Is the Court suggesting that education is more "fundamental" than food, shelter, or medical care? . . .

B

Once it is conceded — as the Court does — that illegal aliens are not a suspect class, and that education is not a fundamental right, our inquiry should focus on and be limited to whether the legislative classification at issue bears a rational relationship to a legitimate state purpose.

The State contends primarily that §21.031 serves to prevent undue depletion of its limited revenues available for education, and to preserve the fiscal integrity of the State's school financing system against an ever-increasing flood of illegal aliens — aliens over whose entry or continued presence it has no control. Of course such fiscal concerns alone could not justify discrimination against a group of persons. Yet I assume no member of this Court would argue that prudent conservation of finite state revenues is per se an illegitimate goal. Indeed, the numerous classifications this Court has sustained in social welfare legislation were invariably related to the limited amount of revenues available to spend on any given program or set of programs. See, e.g., Jefferson v. Hackney, 406 U.S. 535, 549-51

(1972); Dandridge v. Williams. The significant question here is whether the requirement of tuition from illegal aliens who attend the public schools — as well as from residents of other States, for example — is a rational and reasonable means of furthering the State's legitimate fiscal ends.

Without laboring what will undoubtedly seem obvious to many, it simply is not "irrational" for a State to conclude that it does not have the same responsibility to provide benefits for persons whose very presence in the State and this country is illegal as it does to provide for persons lawfully present. By definition, illegal aliens have no right whatever to be here, and the State may reasonably, and constitutionally, elect not to provide them with governmental services at the expense of those who are lawfully in the State. In DeCanas v. Bica, 424 U.S. 351, 357 (1976), we held that a State may protect its "fiscal interests and lawfully resident labor force from the deleterious effects on its economy resulting from the employment of illegal aliens." And only recently this Court made clear that a State has a legitimate interest in protecting and preserving the quality of its schools and "the right of its own *bona fide* residents to attend such institutions on a preferential tuition basis." Vlandis v. Kline, 412 U.S. 441, 452-453 (1973) (emphasis added). The Court has failed to offer even a plausible explanation why illegality of residence in this country is not a factor that may legitimately bear upon the bona fides of state residence and entitlement to the benefits of lawful residence.

Discussion

1. What is the value of education? Both Marshall's dissenting opinion in *Rodriguez* and Brennan's opinion in *Plyler* assume that education is an extremely important, indeed constitutionally protected, interest. What is it about education that makes it so important, however? Consider two possibilities:

a) Some education is necessary in order to make one a functioning citizen of a republican political order; i.e., one must know to read and to analyze political arguments. It is also a good idea to have a sense of the history of the American nation and an appreciation of American culture in order to become a functioning member of that order. This vision is captured by Amy Gutmann's comment that "[a] democratic state . . . must take the steps that it can to avoid those inequalities in educational attainment that deprive children of an intellectual ability adequate to enable them to participate in the democratic political processes that socially structure individual choices."[29]

b) An education is important because it provides the knowledge and skill base with which to get a job and support oneself in a market-oriented society. From this perspective, the most important courses are not, say, American history, literature, or civics, but, rather, computer science and statistics. Ideally, a student should take both kinds of courses, but if choices have to made with regard to funding, required courses, and the like, they should always be made in terms of what will best prepare a student for gainful appointment (and thus to minimize the probability that the students will later turn out to make claims for public assistance).

Which of these two visions seems to feature in the Marshall and Brennan opinions? Is one more entrenched in the Constitution than the other?

---

29. Amy Gutmann, Public Education in a Democracy, in Democracy and the Welfare State (Gutmann ed.) 112 (1988). See also Amy Gutmann, Democratic Education (2d ed. 1998).

Note: On The Enforceability of "Positive Rights"

One might object to constitutional rights to minimum levels of assistance on the grounds that they are contrary to the constitutional text or to existing precedents. Professor Frank Cross argues that the best case against judicial recognition of positive rights "does not rest upon moral philosophy [or doctrinal analysis] but relies upon a pragmatic understanding of the operation of government, particularly the judicial system."[30]

[There are] two significant problems with relying on the courts to enforce positive rights and to promote the interests of the poor. The first problem involves the economics of rights enforcement. . . . The second problem is the politics of rights enforcement. While we espouse an independent judiciary in this nation, the reality is that courts are loathe to displease the elected branches or to tread upon their constitutional turf. An order requiring those branches to fund and to offer economic assistance to the poor is the sort of action that the judiciary is unlikely to make or to enforce.

. . . Rights enforcement requires resources. The mere introduction of a positive right into the Constitution may not have much effect unless and until it is fleshed out through litigation. The ability to litigate "depends on ample purses and effective mobilization of legal services, which vary greatly among different classes, groups, and sections of the country." Poor individuals and, to a degree, groups representing the poor may lack the resources to advance effectively the right. . . .

Research supports doubts about the ability of the poor to advance their interests in court. . . . Poor individuals clearly are the least successful litigants before the Court, which bodes ill for their ability to achieve positive rights. . . . [P]ositive rights cases will pit poor individuals against the government. When poor individuals are matched against the federal government in litigation . . . , their prospects of success are minimal.

. . . To some, positive rights are a "horror," because their enforcement raises the spectre of "the courts running everything — raising taxes and deciding how the money should be spent." [But] both the critics and the proponents often misconceive the likely consequences of positive rights recognition, namely that positive rights would not be aggressively enforced.

It is futile to rely on the judiciary to provide basic welfare for the disadvantaged, if the political branches are unwilling to do so. . . . The interaction of the judiciary with the political branches makes the courts reluctant to countermand aggressively the preferences of the legislature and the executive. They may fear that the cooperation of those branches could "be jeopardized by excessively controversial or far-reaching policy decisions." . . .

Although Cross's principal argument is that "recognition of positive rights is likely to be practically trivial, if not meaningless," he also suggests that the consequences of "aggressive enforcement" of positive rights "are highly uncertain. Indeed, there is a high probability that judicial involvement will only make things worse for the beneficiaries of the positive rights," largely because of the complexity of required judgments and the lack of any particular reason to believe that judges will be skilled in making such judgments.

Suppose an impoverished plaintiff appears before the Court and demands his or her right to government support. How would the Court decide if the individual were impoverished enough to qualify to invoke the right? Should it be an absolute or a

---

30. Frank Cross, The Error of Positive Rights, 48 UCLA L. Rev. 857 (2001).

relative standard? At what quantitative level should the standard be set? If the plaintiff qualifies under that standard, should the Court enter an order simply directing that this individual (and presumably all others similarly situated) be paid a certain amount of cash monthly or should in-kind services (such as food stamps or housing vouchers) be ordered? Should assistance be nationally uniform or geographically variable? Might the Court consider defenses to the government's constitutional obligations? What if the federal budget were strapped, and a court order would necessitate higher taxes or that money be taken from other programs, such as defense or environmental protection? Would alternative uses of the money be relevant? Could the Court consider the possibility that the plaintiff bore some responsibility for his impoverished status? What if he had gambled away a considerable sum of money? What if he had lost his job due to misfeasance? All of these questions are potentially answerable, but they illustrate the complexity of enforcing a positive right. . . . Given these complexities, it is unclear that the judiciary is the best branch for making wise decisions about positive rights. . . .

Cross also notes that there is no guarantee that the judges trusted with enforcing positive rights will be sympathetic to these rights as ways of improving the condition of the poor.

> Conservative Justices are unlikely to take positive rights to minimal subsistence and interpret them to compel greater government redistribution of income to the poor. . . . [In fact] [a]n activist conservative Court might use that positive right of minimal substance to dismantle the very programs that advocates of positive rights seek to expand. . . .
>
> Ultimately, a defense of positive rights can only come down to a comparative institutional analysis of courts and other branches of government. Because courts could actually make the problem worse, they are not merely a backstop to legislative protection. For positive constitutional rights to make sense, the advocates have to explain why courts would do a better job of providing minimally adequate welfare support than would the legislative and executive branches. The historical record does not offer much support for this position. The Court has been "indifferen[t] to economic inequality" in society. . . .
>
> While one can certainly argue with the sufficiency of prevailing levels of statutory assistance to the poor, the various government entitlement programs in 1996 did provide $700 billion in assistance to various groups deemed deserving. Between 1965 and 1990, social security funding rose from $17 billion to $250 billion, medicare and medicaid spending grew from zero to $150 billion, and programs such as food stamps and AFDC grew from $3 billion to $40 billion. . . .
>
> Proponents of positive rights might still complain that the record of statutory assistance to the poor is insufficient. Perhaps so, but the real issue regarding positive rights is one of institutional comparison. The legislative and executive branches have done a lot more for the poor than have the courts.

Discussion

1. *Polycentric problems.* Are there significant differences in judicial enforcement of positive rights and negative rights? Consider the following argument:

> Generally speaking, it is easier for courts to supervise the regulatory state — the state's creation of crimes, administrative regulations, civil fines and penalties, and civil causes of action — than to supervise the welfare state. Supervising the regulatory state is easier because fewer variables are involved and enforcement generally runs

through the courts. Thus courts can protect constitutional rights simply by striking down laws that they believe violate the Constitution and refusing to enforce them thereafter.

Imposing constitutional requirements on the welfare state is usually considerably more difficult, particularly if courts require government officials to spend money to achieve a certain goal such as equal educational opportunity, adequate housing, or minimum levels of subsistence. Achieving these goals requires many complicated tradeoffs. It is often difficult to define or prove when a particular affirmative goal has been met. Government compliance may be hard to monitor, and government officials may have many different ways of dragging their heels and evading a court's constitutional demands. Often different groups of government actors with different political agendas may have to cooperate over long periods of time to make genuine progress, and securing their continuing collective cooperation may prove quite difficult. Reforms may require significant expenditures that cut into the government's budget and drain money away from other valuable government projects and services. Government officials may be unwilling or unable to raise additional revenues and may plead that they lack the funds necessary to carry out the reforms.[31]

Is this distinction necessarily clear-cut? Consider, for example, that the right to vote, the right against self-incrimination and coerced confessions, the right against custodial mistreatment and/or torture, and the Establishment Clause's prohibitions on school prayer also may require the cooperation of public officials; indeed these constitutional norms may be effectively unenforceable without cooperation from the political branches. In addition, many negative rights, for example the right to use public forums for speech, and the right to vote, are actually positive rights to the extent that they require governments to spend money to make them possible. Finally, consider the extent to which almost every negative liberty requires some expenditure of money or cooperation by political officials to be effectively vindicated. Does this suggest that the distinctions between positive and negative liberties are matters of degree rather than kind? Even if so, does it demonstrate that they are equally enforceable by courts?

2. *Statutory versus constitutional entitlements.* Professor Cross notes that statutes often contain positive entitlements. Thus he notes "[t]here is an indisputable statutory right to receive payments under the Earned Income Tax Credit, for example, assuming one meets the statutory conditions and at least until its statutory authority is revoked." If so, what distinguishes the ability of courts to enforce statutory versus constitutional entitlements, at least if one's concerns are principally those set out by Cross?

3. *Aspirational provisions and underenforced constitutional norms.* Suppose one is persuaded by Cross's argument that one ought not to look to judges to enforce positive rights. Nevertheless, one might still argue that the Constitution should be interpreted or amended to include such rights as "aspirations" to goad legislators and executives as to their "constitutional duties" to help the poor, even if that duty is not in fact subject to judicial enforcement in the absence of statutory entitlements. Professor Larry Sager famously suggested that judicial protections for the poor were part of the underenforced norms of the Due Process and Equal Protection Clauses,

31. Jack M. Balkin, What Brown Teaches Us About Constitutional Theory, 90 Va. L. Rev. 1537, 1568-1569 (2004).

which it was the job of legislatures to enforce.[32] And several constitutions, including those of Ireland and India, have social rights provisions that operate only as aspirations — or directives to legislators — insofar as they explicitly prohibit judicial enforcement of these provisions. What are the strengths and weaknesses of such an approach? Does it depend on whether legislatures take their constitutional obligations seriously? Does it let legislatures off the hook too easily, or, to the contrary, does it give them incentives to reason and talk directly about constitutional values when they consider the questions of poverty and social welfare?

Professor Cass Sunstein has recently suggested the passage of a "Second Bill of Rights" of the following form:

Section 1. Every citizen has the right to a good education.

Section 2. Every citizen has the right to adequate protection in the event of extreme need stemming from illness, accident, old age, or unemployment.

Section 3. Every citizen has the right of access to adequate food, shelter, clothing, and health care.

Section 4. Every citizen has the right to a chance at remunerative employment.

Section 5. Every citizen has the right to freedom from unfair competition and domination by monopolies at home or abroad.

Section 6. Congress and state governments must take reasonable legislative and other measures, within available resources, to achieve the realization of these rights.[33]

Such an amendment would serve, Sunstein argues, as at least a "constitutive commitment" binding upon legislators who, after all, take an oath of constitutional fidelity, even if one concludes, as may be suggested by Section 6, that there should be little or no judicial enforcement.

Would you support the passage of an amendment of this sort, knowing it to be aspirational? Would it alter the way that courts and legislatures approached other constitutional provisions? Would this be a good or a bad thing?

4. The South African constitution is probably the most notable example in the world today of a constitution with ostensibly strong guarantees of positive rights that are judicially enforceable. Consider only the following sections from that Constitution:

26. (1) Everyone has the right to have access to adequate housing.

(2) The state must take reasonable legislative and other measures, within its available resources, to achieve the progressive realisation of this right. . . .

27. (1) Everyone has the right to have access to —

a. health care services, including reproductive health care;

b. sufficient food and water; and

c. social security, including, if they are unable to support themselves and their dependents, appropriate social assistance.

---

32. Lawrence Gene Sager, Fair Measure: The Legal Status of Underenforced Constitutional Norms, 91 Harv. L. Rev. 1212 (1978). See also Charles L. Black, Jr., Further Reflections on the Constitutional Justice of Livelihood, 86 Colum. L. Rev. 1103 (1986) (arguing that Congress has constitutional duty to provide for "the common defence" and "promote the general welfare").

33. Cass R. Sunstein, The Second Bill of Rights, FDR's Unfinished Revolution and Why We Need It More Than Ever 183 (2004).

(2) The state must take reasonable legislative and other measures, within its available resources, to achieve the progressive realisation of each of these rights.

(3) No one may be refused emergency medical treatment.

28. (1) Every child has the right —

c. . . . to basic nutrition, shelter, basic health care services, and social services . . .

29. (1) Everyone has the right —

a. to a basic education, including adult basic education; and

b. to further education, which the state must take reasonable measures to make progressively available and accessible. . . .

One might wonder how the now ten-year history of implementation of the South African constitution accords with Cross's deep skepticism about positive rights. An interesting example is Government of the Republic of South Africa v. Grootboom, 11 BCLA 1169 (CC) (2000), a case brought under section 26, in which plaintiffs invoked the right to housing. The Constitutional Court held that the government had indeed been derelict in its constitutional duties, but held that the appropriate remedy was simply that the government had an obligation to "establish a coherent public housing programme directed towards the progressive realisation of the right of access to adequate housing within the State's available means". The South African Constitutional Court did not hold that the government would have to provide a "minimum core" level of housing, nor did it require that any specific amount be appropriated for housing in the government's budget. It simply stated that "a reasonable part of the national housing budget [must] be devoted to [providing housing to those in desperate need], but the precise allocation is for national government to decide in the first instance." As a result of this holding, the actual plaintiffs in *Grootboom* received no specific remedy addressing their individual lack of adequate housing. Might courts play a useful role in forcing certain issues on the legislative agenda even if, as a matter of prudence, they decline to order specific remedies?[34]

It is worth comparing the result in *Grootboom* with the U.S. Supreme Court's response in *Brown* II, which did not give the individual plaintiffs relief but simply ordered Southern school districts to desegregate "with all deliberate speed." Indeed, there are striking analogies between the history of desegregation efforts in the United States and the problem of positive rights, in part because the point of desegregation suits was to secure greater educational equality for African-American students. If one thinks that the history of school desegregation following *Brown* was a mixed success, are there reasons to think that judicial enforcement of positive rights would be significantly more successful?

E.   Does the State Have a "Duty to Rescue"?

Perhaps the two most dramatic recent cases rejecting claims of affirmative welfare rights have occurred within the context of failures of state agencies — in one instance a child welfare department, in the other a local police force — to provide protection to persons clearly within their domain.

---

34. For a discussion, see Cass R. Sunstein, Social and Economic Rights: Lessons from South Africa, 11 Forum Constitutionnel 123-132 (2000/2001).

DESHANEY v. WINNEBAGO COUNTY DEPARTMENT
OF SOCIAL SERVICES
489 U.S. 189 (1989)

[Joshua DeShaney, born in 1979, had been placed in the custody of his father, Randy, following the divorce of Joshua's parents. In January 1982, the Winnebago (Wisconsin) County Department of Social Services (DSS) was notified by Joshua's stepmother, who at the time sought a divorce from Randy, that Randy had abused Joshua. The DSS interviewed Randy, who denied the accusations. In January 1983, Joshua was admitted to a hospital; his multiple bruises and abrasions led the examining physician to notify the DSS of potential child abuse. At the insistence of the DSS, a Wisconsin juvenile court placed Joshua in the temporary custody of the hospital. A "Child Protection Team" then considered Joshua's situation and decided that there was insufficient evidence of abuse to justify retaining custody over Joshua. It did, however, recommend, among other things, that Randy receive counseling. A month later Joshua was again taken to a hospital emergency room with "suspicious" injuries, but the DSS caseworker decided that there was no cause for further action. Over the next six months the caseworker made monthly visits to the DeShaney home, during which "she observed a number of suspicious injuries on Joshua's head." "The caseworker dutifully recorded . . . her continuing suspicion that someone in the DeShaney household was physically abusing Joshua, but she did nothing more." In November 1983, Joshua was treated yet again for injuries believed to be the result of child abuse. "On the caseworker's next two visits to the DeShaney home, she was told that Joshua was too ill to see her. Still DSS took no action."

Five months later, in March 1984, "Randy DeShaney beat . . . Joshua so severely that he fell into a life-threatening coma." He "did not die, but he suffered brain damage so severe that he is expected to spend the rest of his life confined to an institution for the profoundly retarded." Randy was subsequently tried and convicted of child abuse.

Joshua, through his mother, claimed that the DSS had deprived him of his Fourteenth Amendment rights to liberty by its failure to protect him "against a risk of violence at his father's hands of which they knew or should have known."]

REHNQUIST, C.J. . . .

[P]etitioners do not claim that the State denied Joshua protection without according him appropriate procedural safeguards, but that it was categorically obligated to protect him in these circumstances.

But nothing in the language of the Due Process Clause itself requires the State to protect the life, liberty, and property of its citizens against invasion by private actors. The Clause is phrased as a limitation on the State's power to act, not as a guarantee of certain minimal levels of safety and security. . . . Its purpose was to protect the people from the State, not to ensure that the State protected them from each other. The Framers were content to leave the extent of governmental obligation in the latter area to the democratic political processes.

Consistent with these principles, our cases have recognized that the Due Process Clauses generally confer no affirmative right to governmental aid, even where such aid may be necessary to secure life, liberty, or property interests of which the government itself may not deprive the individual. See, e.g., Harris v. McRae, 448 U.S. 297 (1980) (no obligation to fund abortions or other medical services) (discussing Due Process Clause of Fifth Amendment); Lindsey v. Normet (no obligation to provide adequate housing) (discussing Due Process Clause of Fourteenth Amendment); see also Youngsberg v. Romeo, 457 U.S. 307, 317 (1982) ("As a general matter, a State is under no constitutional duty to provide substantive services for those within its border"). As we said in Harris v. McRae, "[a]lthough the liberty protected by the Due Process Clause affords protection against unwarranted government interference, . . . it does not confer an entitlement to such [governmental aid] as may be necessary to realize all the advantages of that freedom." If the Due Process Clause does not require the State to provide its citizens with particular protective services, it follows that the State cannot be held liable under the Clause for injuries that could have been averted had it chosen to provide them.[a] As a general matter, then, we conclude that a State's failure to protect an individual against private violence simply does not constitute a violation of the Due Process Clause.

[The Court also rejected the argument that the State had in effect created a "special relationship" with Joshua through such services as the DSS did in fact provide. It distinguished earlier cases that had found the State obligated to provide certain services to incarcerated prisoners or involuntarily committed mental patients on the ground that] they stand only for the proposition that when the State takes a person into its custody and holds him there against his will, the Constitution imposes upon it a corresponding duty to assume some responsibility for his safety and general well-being. The rationale for this principle is simple enough: when the State by the affirmative exercise of its power so restrains an individual's liberty that it renders him unable to care for himself, and at the same time fails to provide for his basic human needs — e.g., food, clothing, shelter, medical care, and reasonable safety — it transgresses the substantive limits on state action set by the Eighth Amendment and the Due Process Clause. See Estelle v. Gamble, 429 U.S. 97 (1976); Youngberg v. Romeo. The affirmative duty to protect arises not from the State's knowledge of the individual's predicament or from its expressions of intent to help him, but from the limitation which it has imposed on his freedom to act on his own behalf. In the substantive due process analysis, it is the State's affirmative act of restraining the individual's freedom to act on his own behalf — through incarceration, institutionalization, or other similar restraint of personal liberty — which is the "deprivation of liberty" triggering the protections of the Due Process Clause, not its failure to act to protect his liberty interests against harms inflicted by other means.

The *Estelle-Youngberg* analysis simply has no applicability in the present case. Petitioners concede that the harms Joshua suffered did not occur while he was in the State's custody, but while he was in the custody of his natural father, who was in no sense a state actor. While the State may have been aware of the dangers that Joshua faced in the free world, it played no part in their creation, nor did it do anything to render him any more vulnerable to them. That the State once took temporary custody of Joshua does not alter the analysis, for when it returned him to his father's custody, it placed him in no worse position than that in which he would have been had it not acted at all; the State does not become the permanent guarantor of an individual's safety by having once offered him shelter. Under these circumstances, the State had no constitutional duty to protect Joshua. . . .

a. The State may not, of course, selectively deny its protective services to certain disfavored minorities without violating the Equal Protection Clause. But no such argument has been made here.

BRENNAN, J., joined by Marshall and Blackmun, JJ., dissenting.

. . . It may well be . . . that the Due Process Clause as construed by our prior cases creates no general right to basic government services. That, however, is not the question presented here. . . .

The Court's baseline is the absence of positive rights in the Constitution and a concomitant suspicion of any claim that seems to depend on such rights. From this perspective, the DeShaneys' claim is first and foremost about inaction (the failure, here, of respondents to take steps to protect Joshua), and only tangentially about action (the establishment of a state program specifically designed to help children like Joshua). And from this perspective, holding these Wisconsin officials liable — where the only difference between this case and one involving a general claim to protective services is Wisconsin's establishment and operation of a program to protect children — would seem to punish an effort that we should seek to promote.

I would begin from the opposite direction. I would focus first on the action that Wisconsin has taken with respect to Joshua and children like him, rather than on the action that the State failed to take. Such a method is not new to this Court. Both *Estelle* and *Youngberg* began by emphasizing that the States had confined J.W. Gamble to prison and Nicholas Romeo to a psychiatric hospital. This initial action rendered these people helpless to help themselves or to seek help from persons unconnected to the government. Cases from the lower courts also recognize that a State's actions can be decisive in assessing the constitutional significance of subsequent inaction. . . .

Because of the Court's initial fixation on the general principle that the Constitution does not establish positive rights, it is unable to appreciate our recognition in *Estelle* and *Youngberg* that this principle does not hold true in all circumstances. . . . In addition, the Court's exclusive attention to State-imposed restraints of "the individual's freedom to act on his own behalf" suggests that it was the State that rendered Romeo unable to care for himself, whereas in fact — with an I.Q. of between 8 and 10, and the mental capacity of an 18-month-old child — he had been quite incapable of taking care of himself long before the State stepped into his life. Thus, the fact of hospitalization was critical in *Youngberg* not because it rendered Romeo helpless to help himself, but because it separated him from other sources of aid that, we held, the State was obligated to replace. Unlike the Court, therefore, I am unable to see in *Youngberg* a neat and decisive divide between action and inaction.

. . . Thus, I would read *Youngberg* and *Estelle* to stand for the much more generous proposition that, if a State cuts off private sources of aid and then refuses aid itself, it cannot wash its hands of the harm that results from its inaction. . . .

[After discussing the complex structure established by Wisconsin in regard to child abuse, Justice Brennan wrote:] In these circumstances, a private person, or even a person working in a government agency other than DSS, would doubtless feel that her job was done as soon as she had reported her suspicions of child abuse to DSS. Through its child-welfare program, in other words, the State of Wisconsin has relieved ordinary citizens and governmental bodies other than the Department of any sense of obligation to do anything more than report their suspicions of child abuse to DSS. If DSS ignores or dismisses these suspicions, no one will step in to fill the gap. . . . Conceivably, then, children like Joshua are made worse off by the existence of this program when the persons and entities charged with carrying it out fail to do their jobs.

It simply belies reality, therefore, to contend that the State "stood by and did nothing" with respect to Joshua. Through its child-protection program, the State actively intervened in Joshua's life and, by virtue of this intervention, acquired ever more certain knowledge that Joshua was in grave danger. . . .

My disagreement with the Court arises from its failure to see that inaction can be every bit as abusive of power as action, that oppression can result when a State undertakes a vital duty and then ignores it. Today's opinion construes the Due Process Clause to permit a State to displace private sources of protection and then, at the critical moment, to shrug its shoulders and turn away from the harm that it has promised to try to prevent. Because I cannot agree that our Constitution is indifferent to such indifference, I respectfully dissent.

BLACKMUN, J., dissenting:

. . . The Court fails to recognize [the state's "fundamental duty to aid the boy" once it "learned of the severe danger to which he was exposed"] because it attempts to draw a sharp and rigid line between action and inaction. But such formalistic reasoning has no place in the interpretation of the broad and stirring Clauses of the Fourteenth Amendment. Indeed, I submit that these Clauses were designed, at least in part, to undo the formalistic legal reasoning that infected antebellum jurisprudence, which the late Professor Robert Cover analyzed so effectively in his significant work entitled Justice Accused (1975). Like the antebellum judges who denied relief to fugitive slaves, the Court today claims that its decision, however harsh, is compelled by existing legal doctrine. On the contrary, the question presented by this case is an open one, and our Fourteenth Amendment precedents may be read more broadly or narrowly depending upon how one chooses to read them. Faced with the choice, I would adopt a "sympathetic" reading, one which comports with dictates of fundamental justice and recognizes that compassion need not be exiled from the province of judging. Cf. A. Stone, Law, Psychiatry, and Morality 262 (1984) ("We will make mistakes if we go forward, but doing nothing can be the worst mistake. What is required of us is moral ambition. Until our composite sketch becomes a true portrait of humanity we must live with our uncertainty; we will grope, we will struggle, and our compassion may be our only guide and comfort").

Poor Joshua! Victim of repeated attacks by an irresponsible, bullying, cowardly, and intemperate father, and abandoned by respondents who placed him in a dangerous predicament and who knew or learned what was going on, and yet did essentially nothing except, as the Court revealingly observes, "dutifully recorded these incidents in [their] files." It is a sad commentary upon American life, and constitutional principles — so full of late of patriotic fervor and proud proclamations about "liberty and justice for all" — that this child, Joshua DeShaney, now is assigned to live out the remainder of his life profoundly retarded. Joshua and his mother, as petitioners here, deserve — but now are denied by this Court — the opportunity to have the facts of their case considered in the light of the constitutional protection that §42 U.S.C. 1983 is meant to provide.

Discussion

1. A report released by UNICEF, "Child Poverty in Rich Countries, 2005," indicated that the child poverty rate in the United States based on 2000 figures was 21.9 percent, a rate exceeded among the 26 countries surveyed only by Mexico. UNICEF defined "poverty" in "relative" terms as family income of less than 50 percent of the

nation's median income. The lowest rates (2.4 percent-4.2 percent) were found in the Scandinavian countries. The next highest rate behind the United States was Italy, with 16.6 percent.[35] Although there may be legitimate controversy about how to measure poverty — and, therefore, the precise numbers of children who can be said to live in poverty — there is little doubt that these children face an increased risk of suffering from ills ranging from malnutrition to learning disabilities. How is the situation of these children, who might claim that their lives are blighted by a lack of social services beyond what the state is willing to provide, different from Joshua's situation, in terms of the state's duty to rescue a child from the threat of irreparable harm?

2. Consider the following provisions from the Universal Declaration of Human Rights, adopted by the General Assembly of the United Nations on December 10, 1948:[36]

Article 23
1. Everyone has the right to work, to free choice of employment, [and] to just and favourable conditions of work. . . .
3. Everyone who works has the right to just and favourable remuneration ensuring for himself and his family an existence worthy of human dignity, and supplemented, if necessary, by other means of social protection. . . .

Article 25
1. Everyone has the right to a standard of living adequate for the health and well-being of himself and of his family, including food, clothing, housing and medical care and necessary social services, and the right to security in the event of unemployment, sickness, disability, widowhood, old age or other lack of livelihood in circumstances beyond his control.
2. Motherhood and childhood are entitled to special care and assistance. All children, whether born in or out of wedlock, shall enjoy the same social protection.

Article 26
Everyone has the right to education. . . .

If they were a part of our Constitution, would they compel a ruling in Joshua's favor?

3. Justice Blackmun's "poor Joshua" opinion has become famous (or notorious) for its invocation of "compassion" as a standard for interpreting the Constitution. And recall the earlier discussion, Chapter 2, supra, of Robert Cover's model of judging within the context of cases involving slavery. To what degree should judges rely on their compassion for the plaintiffs (or for defendants) in deciding what the Constitution means? Recall Justice Frankfurter's impassioned memorandum to his colleagues, at the time of the *Quirin* case during World War II, Chapter 5 supra, that invoked the likely response of soldiers fighting against "the Japs" in the Pacific. Would such paragraphs be appropriate in a judicial opinion involving, say, presidential power during time of war?

---

35. See also *http://www.census.gov/prod/2005pubs/p60-227.pdf*, Alternative Poverty Estimates in the United States: 2003 (issued June 2005), which indicates a lower rate (17.6 percent) for persons under 18. As should be readily obvious, the measurement of a concept like "poverty" involves highly technical issues, not to mention the political implications of any given definition.

36. See Human Rights: A Compilation of International Instruments 1-3 (1983).

4. *Slavery, childhood, and Joshua DeShaney. DeShaney* is, doctrinally speaking, a Fourteenth Amendment case. However, Professors Akhil Reed Amar and Daniel Widawsky, in A Thirteenth Amendment Response to *DeShaney,* 105 Harv. L. Rev. 1359 (1992), have suggested that *DeShaney* should have been argued under the Thirteenth Amendment and, as such, decided in DeShaney's favor. "Indisputably, the amendment was designed to end slavery in America — of children as well as adults." Amar and Widawsky point out that no one doubted that "[a] mulatto slave child sired by a white slaveowner" was freed by the amendment. "Nor did the amendment protect only those slaves with some biological roots in America, for it abolished the enslavement of all persons, whatever their race or national origin." As the Court wrote in the Slaughterhouse Cases, "while negro slavery alone was in the mind of the Congress which proposed the thirteenth article, it forbids any other kind of slavery, now or hereafter." Thus, the Court indicated that "Mexican peonage" or "the Chinese coolie labor system" would be made equally "void" under the amendment. "Finally," they write, "the amendment guaranteed personal freedom in all respects, not only freedom from forced labor for the master's economic enrichment: The amendment speaks to the enslavement of a person, whether the ultimate motive for such domination is greed or sadism or power lust." Thus, they conclude, the amendment "extends its affirmative protection to a slave even if (1) the slave is a child, (2) the slave child is the offspring of the master, (3) the slave child has no African roots, and (4) the slave child is not used to maximize the master's financial profit. One such slave child was Joshua DeShaney."

One question posed by Amar's and Widawsky's analysis, of course, is precisely what constitutes "involuntary servitude." The answer, they suggest, is the "unconstrained power" of one person over another, so that one cannot meaningfully find "consent" to be present in any given relationship. For the state to fail to intervene in a situation where a parent is known to be abusing a child is, they argue, to place the child in a condition of just such "involuntary servitude" relative to the parent.

One virtue of a Thirteenth Amendment analysis, according to Amar and Widawsky, is that it answers the slippery-slope fears expressed by the majority about the possibility of crime victims suing the government for inadequate police protection or of persons mired in poverty claiming that the state must supply adequate social services to rectify the situation. "Under the Thirteenth Amendment, a State has an obligation only in cases of slavery or involuntary servitude rather than in every case of interpersonal violence." There is no reason to believe that the current members of the Supreme Court would be receptive to such an analysis. Should they?

CASTLE ROCK v. GONZALES, 125 S.Ct. 2796 (2005): [According to what Justice Scalia termed "[t]he horrible facts of this case" Jessica Gonzales obtained a restraining order against her husband in May 1999, which commanded him not to "molest or disturb the peace of [respondent] or of any child," and to remain at least 100 yards from the family home at all times. Violation of the order constituted a criminal offense. The form served on Gonzales included a "Notice to Law Enforcement Officials," which read in part:

YOU SHALL USE EVERY REASONABLE MEANS TO ENFORCE THIS RESTRAIN-ING ORDER. YOU SHALL ARREST, OR, IF AN ARREST WOULD BE IMPRACTICAL UNDER THE CIRCUMSTANCES, SEEK A WARRANT FOR THE ARREST OF THE RESTRAINED PERSON WHEN YOU HAVE INFORMATION AMOUNTING TO PROBABLE CAUSE THAT THE RESTRAINED PERSON HAS VIOLATED OR

ATTEMPTED TO VIOLATE ANY PROVISION OF THIS ORDER AND THE RESTRAINED PERSON HAS BEEN PROPERLY SERVED WITH A COPY OF THIS ORDER OR HAS RECEIVED ACTUAL NOTICE OF THE EXISTENCE OF THIS ORDER.

The state court in June modified the terms of the restraining order to give Mr. Gonzales limited rights to spend time with his three daughters and made the order permanent. According to Ms. Gonzales's complaint, on June 22, 1999, her husband took the three daughters without warning. She called the Castle Rock Police Department and showed them a copy of the restraining order, requesting that it be enforced and that her children be returned to her immediately. The officers said there was nothing they could do and suggested that she call the Police Department again at 10:00 P.M. if the three children did not return. At 8:30 P.M. her husband called stating that he "had the children [at an] amusement park in Denver." She called police again requesting that they arrest her husband but she was rebuffed and once again told to call back at 10:00 P.M. At 10:00 P.M. she was told to call back at midnight. At midnight she was told to wait for an officer to arrive; when no one arrived she went to the police station at 12:50 A.M. and submitted an incident report. The officer who took the report "made no reasonable effort to enforce the TRO or locate the three children. Instead he went to dinner." At approximately 3:20 A.M., the respondent's husband arrived at the police station and opened fire with a semiautomatic handgun he had purchased earlier that evening. Police shot back, killing him. Inside the cab of his pickup truck, they found the bodies of all three daughters, whom he had already murdered.

Gonzales sued, alleging that the town violated the Due Process Clause because its police department had "an official policy or custom of failing to respond properly to complaints of restraining order violations" and "tolerate[d] the non-enforcement of restraining orders by its police officers." The complaint also alleged that the town's actions "were taken either willfully, recklessly or with such gross negligence as to indicate wanton disregard and deliberate indifference to" respondent's civil rights.]

Scalia, J.:

Respondent claims that . . . she had a property interest in police enforcement of the restraining order against her husband; and that the town deprived her of this property without due process by having a policy that tolerated nonenforcement of restraining orders. . . . We noted [in *Deshaney* that we had not considered whether] state "child protection services" gave [Joshua Deshaney] an "entitlement" to receive protective services in accordance with the terms of the statute, and entitlement which would enjoy due process protection.

The procedural component of the Due Process Clause does not protect everything that might be described as a "benefit": "To have a property interest in a benefit, a person clearly must have more than an abstract need or desire" and "more than a unilateral expectation of it. He must, instead, have a legitimate claim of entitlement to it." Board of Regents of State Colleges v. Roth, 408 U.S. 564, 577 (1972). Such entitlements are " 'of course, . . . not created by the Constitution. Rather, they are created and their dimensions are defined by existing rules or understandings that stem from an independent source such as state law.' "

Our cases recognize that a benefit is not a protected entitlement if government officials may grant or deny it in their discretion. . . .

The critical language in the restraining order came . . . from the preprinted notice to law-enforcement personnel that appeared on the back of the order. That notice effectively restated the statutory provision describing "peace officers' duties" related to the crime of violation of a restraining order. At the time of the conduct at issue in this case, that provision read as follows:

> (a) Whenever a restraining order is issued, the protected person shall be provided with a copy of such order. *A peace officer shall use every reasonable means to enforce a restraining order.*
>
> (b) *A peace officer shall arrest, or, if an arrest would be impractical under the circumstances, seek a warrant for the arrest of a restrained person* when the peace officer has information amounting to probable cause [that the restrained person has violated an order that he or she has properly been served with].
>
> (c) . . . *A peace officer shall enforce a valid restraining order whether or not there is a record of the restraining order in the registry.*

. . . We do not believe that these provisions of Colorado law truly made enforcement of restraining orders *mandatory.* Whatever mandatory language might exist as to arresting those who violate a restraining order, "[a] well established tradition of police discretion has long coexisted with apparently mandatory arrest statutes." . . .

Against that backdrop, a true mandate of police action would require some stronger indication from the Colorado Legislature than "shall use every reasonable means to enforce a restraining order" (or even "shall arrest . . . or . . . seek a warrant"). . . . It is hard to imagine that a Colorado peace officer would not have some discretion to determine that — despite probable cause to believe a restraining order has been violated — the circumstances of the violation or the competing duties of that officer or his agency counsel decisively against enforcement in a particular instance. The practical necessity for discretion is particularly apparent in a case such as this one, where the suspected violator is not actually present and his whereabouts are unknown.

Colorado's restraining-order statute appears to contemplate . . . that when arrest is "impractical" — which was likely the case when the whereabouts of respondent's husband were unknown — the officers' statutory duty is to "seek a warrant" rather than "arrest."

Respondent does not specify the precise means of enforcement that the Colorado restraining-order statute assertedly mandated — whether her interest lay in having police arrest her husband, having them seek a warrant for his arrest, or having them "use every reasonable means, up to and including arrest, to enforce the order's terms." Such indeterminacy is not the hallmark of a duty that is mandatory. Nor can someone be safely deemed "entitled" to something when the identity of the alleged entitlement is vague. The dissent, after suggesting various formulations of the entitlement in question, ultimately contends that the obligations under the statute were quite precise: either make an arrest or (if that is impractical) seek an arrest warrant. The problem with this is that the seeking of an arrest warrant would be an entitlement to nothing but procedure. . . . After the warrant is sought, it remains within the discretion of a judge whether to grant it, and after it is granted, it remains within the discretion of the police whether and when to execute it. Respondent would have been assured nothing but the seeking of a warrant. This is not the sort of "entitlement" out of which a property interest is created.

Even if the statute could be said to have made enforcement of restraining orders "mandatory" because of the domestic-violence context of the underlying statute, that would not necessarily mean that state law gave *respondent* an entitlement to *enforcement* of the mandate. Making the actions of government employees obligatory can serve various legitimate ends other than the conferral of a benefit on a specific class of people. The serving of public rather than private ends is the normal course of the criminal law because criminal acts, "besides the injury [they do] to individuals, . . . strike at the very being of society; which cannot possibly subsist, where actions of this sort are suffered to escape with impunity."

. . . [I]t is by no means clear that an individual entitlement to enforcement of a restraining order could constitute a "property" interest for purposes of the Due Process Clause. Such a right would not, of course, resemble any traditional conception of property. . . . [T]he right to have a restraining order enforced does not "have some ascertainable monetary value . . . Perhaps most radically, the alleged property interest here arises *incidentally*, not out of some new species of government benefit or service, but out of a function that government actors have always performed — to wit, arresting people who they have probable cause to believe have committed a criminal offense."

. . . We conclude, therefore, that respondent did not, for purposes of the Due Process Clause, have a property interest in police enforcement of the restraining order against her husband. It is accordingly unnecessary to address the Court of Appeals' determination that the town's custom or policy prevented the police from giving her due process when they deprived her of that alleged interest.

In light of today's decision and that in *DeShaney*, the benefit that a third party may receive from having someone else arrested for a crime generally does not trigger protections under the Due Process Clause, neither in its procedural nor in its "substantive" manifestations. This result reflects our continuing reluctance to treat the Fourteenth Amendment as " 'a font of tort law,' " but it does not mean States are powerless to provide victims with personally enforceable remedies. . . .

SOUTER, J., joined by Breyer, J., concurring:

The Due Process Clause extends procedural protection to guard against unfair deprivation by state officials of substantive state-law property rights or entitlements; the federal process protects the property created by state law. But Gonzales claims a property interest in a state-mandated process in and of itself. This argument is at odds with the rule that "[p]rocess is not an end in itself. Its constitutional purpose is to protect a substantive interest to which the individual has a legitimate claim of entitlement." . . . Just as a State cannot diminish a property right, once conferred, by attaching less than generous procedure to its deprivation, neither does a State create a property right merely by ordaining beneficial procedure unconnected to some articulable substantive guarantee. . . .

There is no articulable distinction between the object of Gonzales's asserted entitlement and the process she desires in order to protect her entitlement; both amount to certain steps to be taken by the police to protect her family and herself. Gonzales's claim would thus take us beyond *Roth* or any other recognized theory of Fourteenth Amendment due process, by collapsing the distinction between property protected and the process that protects it, and would federalize every mandatory state-law direction to executive officers whose performance on the job can be vitally significant to individuals affected.

STEVENS, J., joined by Ginsburg, J., dissenting:

[Although] neither the Federal Constitution itself, nor any federal statute, granted respondent or her children any individual entitlement to police protection

[*DeShaney*], federal law imposes no impediment to the creation of such an entitlement by Colorado law. Respondent certainly could have entered into a contract with a private security firm, obligating the firm to provide protection to respondent's family; respondent's interest in such a contract would unquestionably constitute "property" within the meaning of the Due Process Clause. If a Colorado statute enacted for her benefit, or a valid order entered by a Colorado judge, created the functional equivalent of such a private contract by granting respondent an entitlement to mandatory individual protection by the local police force, that state-created right would also qualify as "property" entitled to constitutional protection.

    . . . The central question in this case is therefore whether, as a matter of Colorado law, respondent had a right to police assistance comparable to the right she would have possessed to any other service the government or a private firm might have undertaken to provide.

    . . . [Justice Stevens criticizes the majority for failing to defer to the 10th Circuit's construction of Colorado state law and argues that this failure conflicts with past practice of the Court. Even if the failure to defer were proper, he would have had the Supreme Court "certify the question to the Colorado Supreme Court" for an authoritative resolution.]

    [Justice Stevens offers his own construction of Colorado law, concluding that it does indeed establish a substantive right of protection for the beneficiaries of domestic restraining order.] [T]he Court gives short shrift to the unique case of "mandatory arrest" statutes in the domestic violence context; States passed a wave of these statutes in the 1980's and 1990's with the unmistakable goal of eliminating police discretion in this area. . . . [T]he Colorado statute at issue in this case was enacted for the benefit of the narrow class of persons who are beneficiaries of domestic restraining orders, and that the order at issue in this case was specifically intended to provide protection to respondent and her children. . . . [T]he Court is simply wrong to assert that a citizen's interest in the government's commitment to provide police enforcement in certain defined circumstances does not resemble any "traditional conception of property." In fact, a citizen's property interest in such a commitment is just as concrete and worthy of protection as her interest in any other important service the government or a private firm has undertaken to provide.

    In 1994, the Colorado General Assembly passed omnibus legislation targeting domestic violence. The part of the legislation at issue in this case mandates enforcement of a domestic restraining order upon probable cause of a violation, §18-6-803.5(3), while another part directs that police officers "shall, without undue delay, arrest" a suspect upon "probable cause to believe that a crime or offense of domestic violence has been committed," §18-6-803.6(1). [W]hen Colorado passed its statute in 1994, it joined the ranks of 15 States that mandated arrest for domestic violence offenses and 19 States that mandated arrest for domestic restraining order violations. . . .

    Given the specific purpose of these statutes, there can be no doubt that the Colorado Legislature used the term "shall" advisedly in its domestic restraining order statute. While "shall" is probably best read to mean "may" in other Colorado statutes that seemingly mandate enforcement, . . . , it is clear that the elimination of police discretion was integral to Colorado and its fellow States' solution to the problem of underenforcement in domestic violence cases. Since the text of Colorado's statute perfectly captures this legislative purpose, it is hard to imagine what the Court has in mind when it insists on "some stronger indication from the Colorado Legislature." . . .

[T]he Court glosses over the dispositive question — whether the police enjoyed discretion to deny enforcement — and focuses on a different question — which "precise means of enforcement" were called for in this case. But . . . [t]he statute directs that, upon probable cause of a violation, "a peace officer shall arrest, or, if an arrest would be impractical under the circumstances, seek a warrant for the arrest of a restrained person." [T]he crucial point is that, under the statute, the police were *required* to provide enforcement; *they lacked the discretion to do nothing.* . . . Our cases have never required the object of an entitlement to be some mechanistic, unitary thing. Suppose a State entitled every citizen whose income was under a certain level to receive health care at a state clinic. The provision of health care is not a unitary thing — doctors and administrators must decide what tests are called for and what procedures are required, and these decisions often involve difficult applications of judgment. But it could not credibly be said that a citizen lacks an entitlement to health care simply because the content of that entitlement is not the same in every given situation. Similarly, the enforcement of a restraining order is not some amorphous, indeterminate thing. Under the statute, if the police have probable cause that a violation has occurred, enforcement consists of either making an immediate arrest or seeking a warrant and then executing an arrest — traditional, well-defined tasks that law enforcement officers perform every day.

Police enforcement of a restraining order is a government service that is no less concrete and no less valuable than other government services, such as education. . . . In this case, Colorado law *guaranteed* the provision of a certain service, in certain defined circumstances, to a certain class of beneficiaries, and respondent reasonably relied on that guarantee. . . . Surely, if respondent had contracted with a private security firm to provide her and her daughters with protection from her husband, it would be apparent that she possessed a property interest in such a contract. Here, Colorado undertook a comparable obligation, and respondent — with restraining order in hand — justifiably relied on that undertaking. Respondent's claim of entitlement to this promised service is no less legitimate than the other claims our cases have upheld, and no less concrete than a hypothetical agreement with a private firm. The fact that it is based on a statutory enactment and a judicial order entered for her special protection, rather than on a formal contract, does not provide a principled basis for refusing to consider it "property" worthy of constitutional protection. . . .

Discussion

Does *Castle Rock* follow from *DeShaney* or does it represent a significant expansion of the view that the Constitution guarantees no affirmative right to be protected by the state against private violence? Many observers have noted the increasing numbers of "private security guards" in the United States. Thus a September 12, 2005 story in the Houston Chronicle was headlined "Business Booming for Private Security," discussing the aftermath of Hurricane Katrina. More than 1 million persons were employed as private guards in 2002,[37] and one can be confident that the number is larger today, especially given concerns about terrorism. Does *Castle Rock* suggest that citizens should expect to spend more of their

---

37. See United States Department of Labor, Bureau of Labor Statistics, Security Guards and Gambling Surveillance Officers, available at *http://www.bls.gov/oco/ocos159.htm.*

income on private security inasmuch as they can no longer rely on the premise that
the State is under a duty to protect them?

Note: State Action in the Age of the Welfare State

One might paraphrase Chief Justice Rehnquist's analysis in *DeShaney* as follows:
The Constitution prohibits the state from depriving individuals, without due
process of law, of whatever preexisting rights to life, liberty, or property they might
have; but it does not require the State to provide anyone with resources, save for
such "special circumstances" as where it confines individuals in a way that prevents
them from being responsible for their own welfare. That is, "state action" must be
present. Justice Brennan in effect found such state action in the consequences for
others of the existence of the Wisconsin child welfare agency. Thus, he suggests,
the state agency's intervention in situations like Joshua's may obviate others'
concern for his welfare that would otherwise exist.

Moreover, we saw the suggestion, intended or not, in Justice Stewart's dissenting
opinion in *Kras,* that one's economic status is in fact a function of state action
insofar as it is the state's passage of laws criminalizing theft or requiring the repayment of debts that accounts for the level of one's resources in the world. (Recall
our earlier discussion, in Chapter 6, supra, of Shelley v. Kraemer and the invalidation of judicial enforcement of racially restrictive covenants.) Not surprisingly, the
modern welfare state has brought with it a spate of state action cases especially
insofar as that state includes, very often, the payment or reimbursement for services provided to individuals covered by welfare programs. Under what circumstances does the receipt of such funds bind a putatively private entity to
constitutional constraints? In Rendell-Baker v. Kohn, 457 U.S. 830 (1982), teachers
employed by a private school claimed that its director violated the Due Process
Clause when he dismissed them without a hearing. Ninety percent of the school's
funds came from the state's payment of tuition for students referred to the school
by local school boards or from other state and federal agencies. Similarly, in Blum v.
Yaretsky, 457 U.S. 991 (1982), a patient in a New York nursing home funded under
Medicaid complained about the procedures by which he was determined to require
a lower level of medical services than he desired. The Supreme Court refused to
find state action in either case.

In *Rendell-Baker,* Chief Justice Burger, for a six-Justice majority, rejected the argument that the level of dependence on state funds subjected the school to the First
and Fourteenth Amendments. "The school, like the nursing homes [in *Blum,*] is
not fundamentally different from many private corporations whose business
depends primarily on contracts to build roads, bridges, dams, ships, or submarines
for the government. Acts of such private contractors do not become acts of their
government by reason of their significant or even total engagement in performing
public contracts." The Court went on to cite Polk County v. Dodson, 454 U.S. 312
(1981), which had declined to hold that a state public defender's activities vis-à-vis
her client implicated the state. Justice Marshall, joined by Justice Brennan,
dissented.

The Justices' lineup was identical in *Blum*; they focused here on the private
decisionmakers' independence from state coercion: "[O]ur precedents indicate
that a State normally can be held responsible for a private decision only when it has

exercised coercive power or has provided such significant encouragement, either overt or covert, that the choice must in law be deemed to be that of the State." Although New York did require physicians to classify patients based on a computed "score" of their need for services, the physicians retained the ultimate judgment to authorize nursing home care even if the patient had a "low score": "These decisions ultimately turn on medical judgments made by private parties according to professional standards that are not established by the State."

More recently, the Court addressed similar issues in American Manufactures Mutual Insurance Company v. Sullivan, 526 U.S. 40 (1999), which involved the administration of Pennsylvania's system of workers' compensation. Generally speaking, once a work-related injury is claimed to have occurred, the employer or its ensurer is obligated to pay for all "reasonable" and "necessary" medical treatment within 30 days of receiving a bill. In 1993 Pennsylvania amended its system to create a "utilization review" procedure by which the reasonableness and necessity of an employee's medical treatment, whether past, ongoing, or prospective, could be reviewed prior to payment. Should an insurer wish to dispute "the reasonableness or necessity of the treatment provided," it may, within 30 days, request utilization review by filing with the Pennsylvania Workers' Compensation Bureau a notice to that effect.

The only function of the Bureau is to determine whether the form is "properly completed — i.e., that all information required by the form is provided." Once the request has been properly filed, the insurer is allowed to withhold payments to health care providers for the particular services being challenged. In the meantime, the Bureau notifies the relevant parties that utilization review has been requested and forwards the request to a randomly selected "utilization review organization" (URO), a private organization composed of health care providers who are "licensed in the same profession and hav[e] the same or similar specialty as that of the provider of the treatment under review." The URO determines "whether the treatment under review is reasonable or necessary for the medical condition of the employee" in light of "generally accepted treatment protocols." A number of affected employees and organizations representing them claimed that the procedures denied them due process of law. The first question, of course, was whether the relevant organizations implicated the state sufficiently to trigger any constitutional guarantees. Chief Justice Rehnquist, writing for a unanimous court (on this point), held that no such state action was present:

> [I]n cases involving extensive state regulation of private activity, we have consistently held that "[t]he mere fact that a business is subject to state regulation does not by itself convert its action into that of the State for purposes of the Fourteenth Amendment." Faithful application of the state-action requirement in these cases ensures that the prerogative of regulating private business remains with the States and the representative branches, not the courts. Thus, the private insurers in this case will not be held to constitutional standards unless "there is a sufficiently close nexus between the State and the challenged action of the regulated entity so that the latter may be fairly treated as that of the State itself." Whether such a "close nexus" exists, our cases state, depends on whether the State "has exercised coercive power or has provided such significant encouragement, either overt or covert, that the choice must in law be deemed to be that of the State." Action taken by private entities with the mere approval or acquiescence of the State is not state action.
>
> Here, respondents do not assert that the decision to invoke utilization review should be attributed to the State because the State compels or is directly involved in

that decision. Obviously the State is not so involved. It authorizes, but does not require, insurers to withhold payments for disputed medical treatment. The decision to withhold payment, like the decision to transfer Medicaid patients to a lower level of care in *Blum,* is made by concededly private parties, and "turns on . . . judgments made by private parties" without "standards . . . established by the State." Respondents do assert, however, that the decision to withhold payment to providers may be fairly attributable to the State because the State has "authorized" and "encouraged" it. Respondents' primary argument in this regard is that, in amending the Act to provide for utilization review and to grant insurers an option they previously did not have, the State purposely "encouraged" insurers to withhold payments for disputed medical treatment. This argument reads too much into the State's reform, and in any event cannot be squared with our cases.

We do not doubt that the State's decision to provide insurers the option of deferring payment for unnecessary and unreasonable treatment pending review can in some sense be seen as encouraging them to do just that. But, as petitioners note, this kind of subtle encouragement is no more significant than that which inheres in the State's creation or modification of any legal remedy. . . .

The State's decision to allow insurers to withhold payments pending review can just as easily be seen as state inaction, or more accurately, a legislative decision not to intervene in a dispute between an insurer and an employee over whether a particular treatment is reasonable and necessary. Before the 1993 amendments, Pennsylvania restricted the ability of an insurer (after liability had been established, of course) to defer workers' compensation medical benefits, including payment for unreasonable and unnecessary treatment, beyond 30 days of receipt of the bill. The 1993 amendments, in effect, restored to insurers the narrow option, historically exercised by employers and insurers before the adoption of Pennsylvania's workers' compensation law, to defer payment of a bill until it is substantiated. The most that can be said of the statutory scheme, therefore, is that whereas it previously prohibited insurers from withholding payment for disputed medical services, it no longer does so. Such permission of a private choice cannot support a finding of state action. . . .

Nor does the State's role in creating, supervising, and setting standards for the URO process differ in any meaningful sense from the creation and administration of any forum for resolving disputes. While the decision of a URO, like that of any judicial official, may properly be considered state action, a private party's mere use of the State's dispute resolution machinery, without the "overt, significant assistance of state officials," cannot. The State, in the course of administering a many-faceted remedial system, has shifted one facet from favoring the employees to favoring the employer. This sort of decision occurs regularly in legislative review of such systems. But it cannot be said that such a change "encourages" or "authorizes" the insurer's actions as those terms are used in our state-action jurisprudence.

We also reject the notion, relied upon by the Court of Appeals, that the challenged decisions are state action because insurers must first obtain "authorization" or "permission" from the Bureau before withholding payment. . . . [T]he Bureau's participation is limited to requiring insurers to file "a form prescribed by the Bureau," processing the request for technical compliance, and then forwarding the matter to a URO and informing the parties that utilization review has been requested. In *Blum,* we rejected the notion that the State, "by requiring completion of a form," is responsible for the private party's decision. The additional "paper shuffling" performed by the Bureau here in response to an insurers' request does not alter that conclusion.

Respondents next contend that state action is present because the State has delegated to insurers "powers traditionally exclusively reserved to the State." Their argument here is twofold. Relying on West v. Atkins, 487 U.S. 42 (1988), respondents first argue that workers' compensation benefits are state-mandated "public benefits," and that the State has delegated the provision of these "public benefits" to private insurers. They also contend that the State has delegated to insurers the traditionally exclusive government function of determining whether and under what circumstances an injured worker's medical benefits may be suspended. The Court of Appeals apparently agreed on both points, stating that insurers "providing public benefits which honor State entitlements . . . become an arm of the State, fulfilling a uniquely governmental obligation," and that "[t]he right to invoke the supersedeas, or to stop payments, is a power that traditionally was held in the hands of the State."

We think neither argument has merit. *West* is readily distinguishable: there the State was constitutionally obligated to provide medical treatment to injured inmates, and the delegation of that traditionally exclusive public function to a private physician gave rise to a finding of state action. Here, on the other hand, nothing in Pennsylvania's constitution or statutory scheme obligates the State to provide either medical treatment or workers' compensation benefits to injured workers. Instead, the State's workers' compensation law imposes that obligation on employers. . . .

Even if one believes that state action doctrine is, as Charles Black once said, "a conceptual disaster area," it is clear that the Court remains strongly committed to the concept and that, as a practical matter, it seems unwilling to find state action where the government makes use of private agencies to administer its welfare programs.

IV. *The Procedural Due Process Protection of Entitlements and Other Nontraditional Property and Liberty Interests: The Basic Doctrine*

A.   What Procedural Safeguards Are Due?

The Constitution provides that a person may not be deprived of "liberty" or "property" without due process of law, or, put another way, that government may not punish you or take your property until after a hearing at which it has been determined that, as a matter of fact and law, the deprivation is authorized by an applicable statute or regulation.

What implications does this requirement have for constitutional doctrine in the welfare state? In a seminal 1964 article, Charles Reich argued that the subsidies and licenses characteristic of the welfare state constituted "the new property" and deserved some of the constitutional protections granted to traditional property. Reich wrote that "[r]egulation of [traditional] property has been limited, not because society had no interest in property, but because it was in the interest of society that property be free."[38] Private property, according to Reich, provided the individual some space for a private life away from, and sometimes in opposition to, the desires of the state. Those dependent on the "new property," he argued, require constitutional protection lest their dependence on governmental largesse leave them at the mercy of the state.

---

38. Charles A. Reich, The New Property, 73 Yale L.J. 733, 779 (1964).

GOLDBERG v. KELLY, 397 U.S. 254 (1970): [*Goldberg* involved the administration of New York's public assistance program and its policy of terminating welfare payments prior to the holding of a hearing. (A posttermination hearing was available, however.) The Court held that New York's program violated the Due Process Clause and it required that the state provide a pretermination hearing.]

BRENNAN, J.:

The constitutional challenge cannot be answered by an argument that public assistance benefits are "a 'privilege' and not a 'right.'" Relevant constitutional restraints apply as much to the withdrawal of public assistance benefits as to disqualification for unemployment compensation, Sherbert v. Verner, 374 U.S. 398 (1963); or to denial of a tax exemption, Speiser v. Randall, 357 U.S. 513 (1958); or to discharge from public employment, Slochower v. Board of Higher Education, 350 U.S. 551 (1956). The extent to which procedural due process must be afforded the recipient is influenced by the extent to which he may be "condemned to suffer grievous loss," Joint Anti-Fascist Refugee Committee v. McGrath, 341 U.S. 123, 168 (1951) (Frankfurter, J., concurring), and depends upon whether the recipient's interest in avoiding that loss outweighs the governmental interest in summary adjudication. . . .

It is true, of course, that some governmental benefits may be administratively terminated without affording the recipient a pre-termination evidentiary hearing. But we agree with the District Court that when welfare is discontinued, only a pre-termination evidentiary hearing provides the recipient with procedural due process. For qualified recipients, welfare provides the means to obtain essential food, clothing, housing, and medical care. Thus the crucial factor in this context — a factor not present in the case of the blacklisted government contractor, the discharged government employee, the taxpayer denied a tax exemption, or virtually anyone else whose governmental entitlements are ended — is that termination of aid pending resolution of a controversy over eligibility may deprive an eligible recipient of the very means by which to live while he waits. Since he lacks independent resources, his situation becomes immediately desperate. His need to concentrate upon finding the means for daily subsistence, in turn, adversely affects his ability to seek redress from the welfare bureaucracy. . . . The same governmental interests that counsel the provision of welfare, counsel as well its uninterrupted provision to those eligible to receive it; pre-termination evidentiary hearings are indispensable to that end.

Appellant does not challenge the force of these considerations but argues that they are outweighed by countervailing governmental interests in conserving fiscal and administrative resources. These interests, the argument goes, justify the delay of any evidentiary hearing until after discontinuance of the grants. Summary adjudication protects the public fisc by stopping payments promptly upon discovery of reason to believe that a recipient is no longer eligible. Since most terminations are accepted without challenge, summary adjudication also conserves both the fisc and administrative time and energy by reducing the number of evidentiary hearings actually held.

We agree with the District Court, however, that these governmental interests are not overriding in the welfare context. The requirement of a prior hearing doubtless involves some greater expense, and the benefits paid to ineligible recipients pending decision at the hearing probably cannot be recouped, since these recipients are likely to be judgment-proof. But the State is not without weapons to minimize these increased costs. Much of the drain on fiscal and administrative resources can be reduced by developing procedures for prompt pre-termination hearings and by skillful use of personnel and facilities. . . .

[The pre-termination hearings] need not take the form of a judicial or quasi-judicial trial. [Their only function is] to produce an initial determination of the validity of the welfare department's grounds for discontinuance of payments in order to protect a recipient against an erroneous termination of his benefits. Thus, a complete record and a comprehensive opinion, which would serve primarily to facilitate judicial review and to guide future decisions, need not be provided at the pre-termination stage. We recognize, too, that both welfare authorities and recipients have an interest in relatively speedy resolution of questions of eligibility, that they are used to dealing with one another informally, and that some welfare departments have very burdensome caseloads. These considerations justify the limitation of the pre-termination hearing to minimum procedural safeguards, adapted to the particular characteristics of welfare recipients, and to the limited nature of the controversies to be resolved. . . .

In the present context these principles require that a recipient have timely and adequate notice detailing the reasons for a proposed termination, and an effective opportunity to defend by confronting any adverse witnesses and by presenting his own arguments and evidence orally. These rights are important in cases such as those before us, where recipients have challenged proposed terminations as resting on incorrect or misleading factual premises or on misapplication of rules or policies to the facts of particular cases. . . .

"The right to be heard would be, in many cases, of little avail if it did not comprehend the right to be heard by counsel." Powell v. Alabama, 287 U.S. 45, 68-69 (1932). We do not say that counsel must be provided at the pre-termination hearing, but only that the recipient must be allowed to retain an attorney if he so desires. Counsel can help delineate the issues, present the factual contentions in an orderly manner, conduct cross-examination, and generally safeguard the interests of the recipient. We do not anticipate that this assistance will unduly prolong or otherwise encumber the hearing. . . .

Finally, the decisionmaker's conclusion as to a recipient's eligibility must rest solely on the legal rules and evidence adduced at the hearing. To demonstrate compliance with this elementary requirement, the decisionmaker should state the reasons for his determination and indicate the evidence he relied on, though his statement need not amount to a full opinion or even formal findings of fact and conclusions of law. And, of course, an impartial decisionmaker is essential. We agree with the District Court that prior involvement in some aspects of a case will not necessarily bar a welfare official from acting as a decisionmaker. He should not, however, have participated in making the determination under review.

BLACK, J., dissenting:

[Justice Black argued that the Court's decision would, in effect, guarantee the provision of welfare assistance to given individuals who do not in fact meet the legal requirements, at least until the pretermination hearing can be provided. (A post-termination hearing, of course, would run the opposite risk, in which individuals who would be found to have been wrongfully deprived of their payments would, nonetheless, have had to bear the burden of being without them until the hearing restored them.)]

The Court holds that the government is helpless and must continue, until after an evidentiary hearing, to pay money that it does not owe, never has owed, and never could owe.

. . . It somewhat strains credulity to say that the government's promise of charity to an individual is property belonging to that individual when the government denies that the individual is honestly entitled to receive such a payment. . . . Once the verbiage is pared away it is obvious that this Court today adopts the views of the District Court "that to cut off a welfare recipient in the face of . . . 'brutal need' without a prior hearing of some sort is unconscionable," and therefore, says the Court, unconstitutional. . . .

I know of no situation in our legal system in which the person alleged to owe money to another is required by law to continue making payments to a judgment-proof claimant without the benefit of any security or bond to insure that these payments can be recovered if he wins his legal argument. Yet today's decision in no way obligates the welfare recipient to pay back any benefits wrongfully received during the pretermination evidentiary hearings or post any bond, and in all "fairness" it could not do so. These recipients are by definition too poor to post a bond or to repay the benefits that, as the majority assumes, must be spent as received to insure survival.

The Court apparently feels that this decision will benefit the poor and needy. In my judgment the eventual result will be just the opposite. While today's decision requires only an administrative, evidentiary hearing, the inevitable logic of the approach taken will lead to constitutionally imposed, time-consuming delays of a full adversary process of administrative and review. . . . [T]he inevitable result of such a constitutionally imposed burden will be that the government will not put a claimant on the rolls initially until it has made an exhaustive investigation to determine his eligibility. While this Court will perhaps have insured that no needy person will be taken off the rolls without a full "due process" proceeding, it will also have insured that many will never get on the rolls, or at least that they will remain destitute during the lengthy proceedings followed to determine initial eligibility.

For the foregoing reasons I dissent from the Court's holding. The operation of a welfare state is a new experiment for our Nation. For this reason, among others, I feel that new experiments in carrying out a welfare program should not be frozen into our constitutional structure. They should be left, as are other legislative determinations, to the Congress and the legislatures that the people elect to make our laws.[39]

Discussion

Recall Dandridge v. Williams, which upheld the right of Maryland to impose a "cap" on family welfare benefits. There was, obviously, no individualized determination by the state that the family's per capita needs were in fact diminished by the birth of a new child (and common sense would suggest that any such diminution is extraordinarily unlikely). Six justices — Black, Burger, Stewart, Brennan, Marshall, and Douglas — would have decided *Dandridge* and *Goldberg* "the same way," i.e., either granted the welfare recipient or the state victory in both cases. Only

39. Dissenting opinions by Chief Justice Burger and Justice Stewart are omitted.

three justices — Harlan, White, and Blackmun — believed they were analytically distinguishable. Because the first six in fact split 3-3 on the direction they would have gone, the "middle three" controlled the decisions. Were the six other justices correct that the cases were decided inconsistently, or were Harlan, White, and Blackmun correct that the issues raised by *Dandridge* or *Goldberg* were sufficiently different to justify the varying outcomes?

The promise (or threat) articulated in *Goldberg* was considerably diminished five years later in Mathews v. Eldridge, 424 U.S. 319 (1976), where the Court distinguished *Goldberg* while holding that a recipient of disability benefits under the Social Security Act was not entitled to a hearing prior to termination. The Act requires a state agency to make a continuing assessment, based on information from the recipient and his sources of medical treatment, that he remains medically disabled from engaging in substantial gainful activity. Before the agency makes a final determination, the recipient is entitled to review his file and to submit additional evidence and respond to the proposed determination of noneligibility. A final determination of noneligibility is reviewed, and typically accepted, by the Social Security Agency Bureau of Disability Insurance, which notifies the recipient of the reasons for termination and of his right to de novo reconsideration by the state agency; benefits are terminated two months after the month in which medical recovery is found to have occurred. If the recipient seeks reconsideration by the state agency and the determination is adverse and accepted by the SSA, the recipient is entitled to an evidentiary hearing before an SSA administrative law judge.

Justice Powell articulated the factors to be balanced in determining the administrative procedures required by the due process clause. The Court must consider "first, the private interest that will be affected by the official action; second, the risk of an erroneous deprivation of such interest through the procedures used and the probable value, if any, of additional or substitute procedural safeguards; and finally, the Government's interest, including the function involved and the fiscal and administrative burdens that the addition or substitute procedural requisites would entail." Turning to the facts of *Eldridge*, Justice Powell wrote: "In view of the torpidity of this administrative review process [which typically takes more than a year], and the typically modest resources of the family unit of the physically disabled worker, the hardship imposed on the erroneously terminated disability recipient may be significant. Still, the disabled worker's need is likely to be less than that of a welfare recipient. In addition to the possibility of access to private resources, other forms of government assistance will become available where the termination of disability benefits places a worker or his family below the subsistence level." Moreover, the medical assessment requisite to termination "is a more sharply focused and easily documented decision than the typical determination of welfare entitlement." Fairness was further assured by the recipient's access to his file and opportunity to respond and produce additional evidence. Justices Brennan and Marshall dissented.

Governments make individualized determinations adverse to citizens in a broad variety of situations. Schoolteachers grade examinations and punish students by making them stay after class or by suspending them; agencies grant or refuse licenses to drive, practice dentistry, operate bars, and construct buildings; wardens grant or deny prisoners "good time" and put them in solitary confinement; parole boards grant, deny, and revoke parole. Each situation may present the questions of what procedural safeguards are due and, more fundamentally, whether any process is due at all.

What is the consequence of a determination that a person does not deserve the disability benefits that he/she is receiving? One obvious answer, given by the Court itself, is that the person in question loses the money in question, and it suggests that any decisionmaking calculus as to pre- or posttermination hearings must take into account the value of these monies and, of course, the probability of inaccurate decisions by the state. Consider, though, the comment of Yale professor of law Jerry Mashaw that "more [is] at stake in disability claims than temporary loss of income." "The major cash income-support programs," he writes,

> determine eligibility, not only on the basis of simple insufficiency of income, but also, or exclusively, on the basis of a series of excuses for partial or total nonparticipation in the work force: agedness, childhood, family responsibility, injury, disability. A grant under any of these programs is an official, if sometimes grudging, stamp of approval of the claimant's status as a partially disabled worker or nonworker. It proclaims, in effect, that those who obtain it have encountered one of the politically legitimate hazards to self-sufficiency in a market economy. The recipients, therefore, are entitled to society's support. Conversely, the denial of an income-maintenance claim implies that the claim is socially illegitimate, and the claimant, however impecunious, is not excused from normal work force status.

Thus Mashaw argues that the Court, "in distinguishing *Goldberg* largely on the ground that terminated welfare recipients were more desperate financially than terminated disability recipients . . . ignored a very substantial similarity" insofar as the "potential for feelings of demoralization, rejection, or simple righteous indignation seems essentially the same in both types of cases."[40]

Indeed, a finding of non-entitlement inevitably raises questions that one has tried to "cheat" the government (and, therefore, the public) not only of the money payments, but also of the participation in the labor force that we expect of "abled" persons in our society. Even if the posttermination hearing determines that benefits were illegitimately terminated, the individual in question has had to bear not only the loss of money income, but also the stigma attached to being thought a de facto cheat. Should this be weighed in determining whether hearings should be pre- or posttermination?

Note: To What Extent Does Goldberg Rest on Legal Formality?

Consider Congress's declaration, in 1977 legislation involving the federal food stamp program, that each determination of a particular household's or person's eligibility for the program expired at the end of three months. According to the statute, "[I]f such household is found to be ineligible or to be eligible for a smaller allotment during the new certification period it shall not continue to participate and receive benefits on the basis authorized for the preceding certification period

---

40. Jerry Mashaw, The Supreme Court's Due Process Calculus — Three Factors in Search of a Theory, 441 U. Chi. L. Rev. 28 (1976).

even if it makes a timely request for a hearing." Thus, as Shep Melnick points out in Between the Lines: Interpreting Welfare Rights 225 (1994):

> This means, in effect, that recipients do not receive the pretermination hearing mandated for welfare recipients by the Supreme Court in Goldberg v. Kelly. . . . The food stamp program was no longer[, according to the Committee Report of the Committee on Agriculture of the House of Representatives,] "a program of permanent or continuing eligibility subject to periodic review" but "a program of distinct and separate entitlements known as certification periods." The end of the certification period, the report added, is "the definite cut-off of the right to participate in the absence of recertification." This procedure reinforces the limited nature of the property interest conferred by certification — an entitlement for one certification period and one certification period only.

Federal courts upheld the constitutionality of this process, and the Supreme Court denied certiorari.

Does the Constitution preclude defining any welfare eligibility by reference to limited periods of time, with automatic loss of benefits at the end of the period unless one is affirmatively deemed eligible, upon reapplication, for renewed benefits? Does such program design assure that any (time-limited) grant of benefits escapes the designation of "property" for the purpose of the Due Process Clause?

V.   *The Welfare State and Burdens on Interstate Mobility*

We last encountered the constitutional protection of interstate mobility in Crandall v. Nevada, 73 U.S. (6 Wall.) 35 (1868), Chapter 3, supra, in which the Court, reasoning from the structure of the federal union, invalidated a $1 Nevada departure tax. The only significant decision between *Crandall* and Shapiro v. Thompson was Edwards v. California, 314 U.S. 160 (1941), in which the Court unanimously struck down a California law that forbade bringing indigents into the state. The Court, in an opinion by Justice Byrnes, relied on the commerce clause, asserting that the subject was one demanding uniformity under the *Cooley* standard. Justice Byrnes responded to the state's citation of Miln v. New York, Chapter 3, supra, and its proposition that persons could not be items of commerce: "Whatever may have been the notion then prevailing, we do not think that it will now be seriously contended that because a person is without employment and without funds he constitutes a 'moral pestilence.'" Justice Douglas, joined by Justices Black and Murphy, concurred on the ground that "the right to move freely from State to State is an incident of national citizenship protected by the privileges or immunities clause of the Fourteenth Amendment against state interference." Justice Jackson also based his concurrence on the privileges and immunities clause, but while Douglas did not reach the commerce clause issue, Jackson explicitly rejected the Court's reasoning: "[T]he migrations of a human being, of whom it is charged that he possesses nothing that can be sold and has no wherewithal to buy, do not fit easily into my notions as to what is commerce. To hold that the measure of his rights is the commerce clause is likely to result eventually either in distorting the commercial law or in denaturing human rights."

A.   The Right to Travel as a Fundamental Right

SHAPIRO v. THOMPSON[41]
394 U.S. 618 (1969)

BRENNAN, J. . . . :

Each [of these cases] is an appeal from a decision of a three-judge District Court holding unconstitutional a State or District of Columbia statutory provision which denies welfare assistance to residents of the State or District who have not resided within their jurisdictions for at least one year immediately preceding their applications for such assistance. We affirm the judgments of the District Courts in the three cases. . . .

II.

There is no dispute that the effect of the waiting-period requirement in each case is to create two classes of needy resident families indistinguishable from each other except that one is composed of residents who have resided a year or more, and the second of residents who have resided less than a year, in the jurisdiction. [T]he second class is denied welfare aid upon which may depend the ability of the families to obtain the very means to subsist — food, shelter, and other necessities of life. . . . [A]ppellees [contend that this] creates a classification which constitutes an invidious discrimination denying them equal protection of the laws. We agree. The interests which appellants assert are promoted by the classification either may not constitutionally be promoted by government or are not compelling governmental interests.

III.

Primarily, appellants justify the waiting-period requirement as a protective device to preserve the fiscal integrity of state public assistance programs. It is asserted that people who require welfare assistance during their first year of residence in a State are likely to become continuing burdens on state welfare programs. Therefore, the argument runs, if such people can be deterred from entering the jurisdiction by denying them welfare benefits during the first year, state programs to assist long-time residents will not be impaired by a substantial influx of indigent newcomers. . . .

We do not doubt that the one-year waiting-period device is well suited to discourage the influx of poor families in need of assistance. An indigent who desires to migrate, resettle, find a new job, and start a new life will doubtless hesitate if he knows that he must risk making the move without the possibility of falling back on state welfare assistance during his first year of residence, when his need may be most acute. But the purpose of inhibiting migration by needy persons into the State is constitutionally impermissible.

---

41. Together with Washington v. Legrant, on appeal from the United States District Court for the District of Columbia, and Reynolds v. Smith, on appeal from the United States District Court for the Eastern District of Pennsylvania.

This Court long ago recognized that the nature of our Federal Union and our constitutional concepts of personal liberty unite to require that all citizens be free to travel throughout the length and breadth of our land uninhibited by statutes, rules, or regulations which unreasonably burden or restrict this movement. That proposition was early stated by Chief Justice Taney in the Passenger Cases, 7 How. 283, 492 (1849). . . .

We have no occasion to ascribe the source of this right to travel interstate to a particular constitutional provision.[a] It suffices that, as Mr. Justice Stewart said for the Court in United States v. Guest, 383 U.S. 745, 757-58 (1966): "The constitutional right to travel from one State to another . . . occupies a position fundamental to the concept of our Federal Union. It is a right that has been firmly established and repeatedly recognized. . . ."

Thus, the purpose of deterring the in-migration of indigents cannot serve as justification for the classification created by the one-year waiting period, since that purpose is constitutionally impermissible. If a law has "no other purpose . . . than to chill the assertion of constitutional rights by penalizing those who choose to exercise them, then it [is] patently unconstitutional." Alternatively, appellants argue that even if it is impermissible for a State to attempt to deter the entry of all indigents, the challenged classification may be justified as a permissible state attempt to discourage those indigents who would enter the State solely to obtain larger benefits. We observe first that none of the statutes before us is tailored to serve that objective. . . .

More fundamentally, a State may no more try to fence out those indigents who seek higher welfare benefits than it may try to fence out indigents generally. Implicit in any such distinction is the notion that indigents who enter a State with the hope of securing higher welfare benefits are somehow less deserving than indigents who do not take this consideration into account. But we do not perceive why a mother who is seeking to make a new life for herself and her children should be regarded as less deserving because she considers, among other factors, the level of a State's public assistance. Surely such a mother is no less deserving than a mother who moves into a particular State in order to take advantage of its better educational facilities.

Appellants argue further that the challenged classification may be sustained as an attempt to distinguish between new and old residents on the basis of the contribution they have made to the community through the payment of taxes. . . . Appellants' reasoning would logically permit the State to bar new residents from schools, parks, and libraries or deprive them of police and fire protection. Indeed it would permit the State to apportion all benefits and services according to the

---

a. In Corfield v. Coryell, 6 F. Cas. 546, 552 (No. 3230) (C.C.E.D. Pa. 1825), Paul v. Virginia, 8 Wall. 168, 180 (1869), and Ward v. Maryland, 12 Wall. 418, 430 (1871), the right to travel interstate was grounded upon the Privileges and Immunities Clauses of Art. IV, §2. See also Slaughterhouse Cases, 16 Wall. 36, 79 (1873); Twining v. New Jersey, 211 U.S. 78, 97 (1908). In Edwards v. California, 314 U.S. 160, 181, 183-185 (1941) (Douglas and Jackson, JJ., concurring), and Twining v. New Jersey, supra, reliance was placed on the Privileges and Immunities Clause of the Fourteenth Amendment. See also Crandall v. Nevada, 6 Wall. 35 (1868). In Edwards v. California, supra, and the Passenger Cases, 7 How. 283 (1849), a Commerce Clause approach was employed.

See also Kent v. Dulles, 357 U.S. 116, 125 (1958); Aptheker v. Secretary of State, 378 U.S. 500, 505-506 (1964); Zemel v. Rusk, 381 U.S. 1, 14 (1965), where the freedom of Americans to travel outside the country was grounded upon the Due Process Clause of the Fifth Amendment.

past tax contributions of its citizens. The Equal Protection Clause prohibits such an apportionment of state services.[b]

We recognize that a State has a valid interest in preserving the fiscal integrity of its programs. It may legitimately attempt to limit its expenditures, whether for public assistance, public education, or any other program. But a State may not accomplish such a purpose by invidious distinctions between classes of its citizens. It could not, for example, reduce expenditures for education by barring indigent children from its schools. Similarly, in the cases before us, appellants must do more than show that denying welfare benefits to new residents saves money. The saving of welfare costs cannot justify an otherwise invidious classification. In sum, neither deterrence of indigents from migrating to the State nor limitation of welfare benefits to those regarded as contributing to the State is a constitutionally permissible state objective.

IV.

Appellants next advance as justification certain administrative and related governmental objectives allegedly served by the waiting-period requirement. They argue that the requirement (1) facilitates the planning of the welfare budget; (2) provides an objective test of residency; (3) minimizes the opportunity for recipients fraudulently to receive payments from more than one jurisdiction; and (4) encourages early entry of new residents into the labor force.

At the outset, we reject appellants' argument that a mere showing of a rational relationship between the waiting period and these four admittedly permissible state objectives will suffice to justify the classification. The waiting-period provision denies welfare benefits to otherwise eligible applicants solely because they have recently moved into the jurisdiction. But in moving from State to State or to the District of Columbia appellees were exercising a constitutional right, and any classification which serves to penalize the exercise of that right, unless shown to be necessary to promote a compelling governmental interest, is unconstitutional.

[The Court concludes that the states did not in fact use the residency requirement to further (1) or (2) above; that the states could accomplish (3) by less drastic means; and that (4) does not justify treating old and new residents differently.] We conclude therefore that appellants in these cases do not use and have no need to use the one-year requirement for the governmental purposes suggested. Thus, even under traditional equal protection tests a classification of welfare applicants according to whether they have lived in the State for one year would seem irrational and unconstitutional. But, of course, the traditional criteria do not apply in these cases. Since the classification here touches on the fundamental right of interstate movement, its constitutionality must be judged by the stricter standard of whether it promotes a compelling state interest. Under this standard, the waiting-period requirement clearly violates the Equal Protection Clause.

---

b. We are not dealing here with state insurance programs which may legitimately tie the amount of benefits to the individual's contributions.

V.

[The Court considers and rejects appellants' argument that Congress expressly approved the one-year waiting period and concludes that "even if we were to assume, arguendo, that Congress did approve the imposition of a one-year waiting period, . . . the provision . . . would be unconstitutional. Congress may not authorize the states to violate the Equal Protection Clause."][42]

WARREN, C.J., joined by Black, J., dissenting. . . .: Congress has imposed a residence requirement in the District of Columbia and authorized the States to impose similar requirements. The issue before us must therefore be framed in terms of whether Congress may create minimal residence requirements, not whether the States, acting alone, may do so. Appellees insist that a congressionally mandated residence requirement would violate their right to travel. The import of their contention is that Congress, even under its "plenary" power to control interstate commerce, is constitutionally prohibited from imposing residence requirements. I reach a contrary conclusion for I am convinced that the extent of the burden on interstate travel when compared with the justification for its imposition requires the Court to uphold this exertion of federal power.

Congress, pursuant to its commerce power, has enacted a variety of restrictions upon interstate travel. It has taxed air and rail fares and the gasoline needed to power cars and trucks which move interstate. Many of the federal safety regulations of common carriers which cross state lines burden the right to travel. And Congress has prohibited by criminal statute interstate travel for certain purposes. E.g., 18 U.S.C. §1952. Although these restrictions operate as a limitation upon free interstate movement of persons, their constitutionality appears well settled. . . .

The Court's right-to-travel cases lend little support to the view that congressional action is invalid merely because it burdens the right to travel. Most of our cases fall into two categories: those in which *state*-imposed restrictions were involved, see, e.g., Edwards v. California; Crandall v. Nevada, [Chapter 3], and those concerning congressional decisions to remove impediments to interstate movement, see, e.g., United States v. Guest, 383 U.S. 745 (1966). Since the focus of our inquiry must be whether Congress would exceed permissible bounds by imposing residence requirements, neither group of cases offers controlling principles. . . .

[R]esidence requirements do not create a flat prohibition [on travel], for potential welfare recipients may move from State to State and establish residence wherever they please. Nor is any claim made by appellees that residence requirements compel them to choose between the right to travel and another constitutional right. . . . Any burden inheres solely in the fact that a potential welfare recipient might take into consideration the loss of welfare benefits for a limited period of time if he changes his residence. Not only is this burden of uncertain degree, but appellees themselves assert there is evidence that few welfare recipients have in fact been deterred by residence requirements. . . .

Congress belie[ved] that a program of cooperative federalism combining federal aid with enhanced state participation would [allay] the apprehensions of many States that an increase in benefits without minimal residence requirements would result in an inability to provide an adequate welfare system. . . . Our cases require

42. The scope of congressional authority to determine what are and are not violations of the Equal Protection Clause was treated in Chapter 5, supra.

only that Congress have a rational basis for finding that a chosen regulatory scheme is necessary to the furtherance of interstate commerce. Certainly, a congressional finding that residence requirements allowed each State to concentrate its resources upon new and increased programs of rehabilitation ultimately resulting in an enhanced flow of commerce as the economic condition of welfare recipients progressively improved is rational and would justify imposition of residence requirements under the Commerce Clause. And Congress could have also determined that residence requirements fostered personal mobility. An individual no longer dependent upon welfare would be presented with an unfettered range of choices so that a decision to migrate could be made without regard to considerations of possible economic dislocation. . . .

HARLAN, J., dissenting.
. . . [I]n upholding the equal protection argument, the Court has applied an equal protection doctrine of relatively recent vintage: the rule that statutory classifications which . . . affect "fundamental rights" will be held to deny equal protection unless justified by a "compelling" governmental interest.

The "compelling interest" doctrine, which today is articulated more explicitly than ever before, constitutes an increasingly significant exception to the long-established rule that a statute does not deny equal protection if it is rationally related to a legitimate governmental objective. The "compelling interest" doctrine has two branches. The branch which requires that classifications based upon "suspect" criteria be supported by a compelling interest apparently had its genesis in cases involving racial classifications, which have, at least since Korematsu v. United States, 323 U.S. 214, 216 (1944), been regarded as inherently "suspect." . . . Today the list [of suspect classifications] apparently has been further enlarged to include classifications based upon recent interstate movement, and perhaps those based upon the exercise of *any* constitutional right. . . .

I think that this branch of the "compelling interest" doctrine is sound when applied to racial classifications, for historically the Equal Protection Clause was largely a product of the desire to eradicate legal distinctions founded upon race. However, I believe that the more recent extensions have been unwise. . . . And when, as in . . . the present case, a classification is based upon the exercise of rights guaranteed against state infringement by the Federal Constitution, then there is no need for any resort to the Equal Protection Clause; in such instances, this Court may properly and straightforwardly invalidate any undue burden upon those rights under the Fourteenth Amendment's Due Process Clause.

The second branch of the "compelling interest" principle is even more troublesome. For it has been held that a statutory classification is subject to the "compelling interest" test if the result of the classification may be to affect a "fundamental right," regardless of the basis of the classification. . . .[a] [The notion] has reappeared today in the Court's cryptic suggestion that the "compelling interest"

---

a. Analysis is complicated when the statutory classification is grounded upon the exercise of a "fundamental" right. For then the statute may come within the first branch of the "compelling interest" doctrine because exercise of the right is deemed a "suspect" criterion and also within the second because the statute is considered to affect the right by deterring its exercise. . . . The present case is [an] instance, insofar as welfare residence statutes both deter interstate movement and distinguish among welfare applicants on the basis of such movement. Consequently, I have not attempted to specify the branch of the doctrine upon which these decisions rest.

test is applicable merely because the result of the classification may be to deny the appellees "food, shelter, and other necessities of life," as well as in the Court's statement that "[s]ince the classification here touches on the fundamental right of interstate movement, its constitutionality must be judged by the stricter standard of whether it promotes a *compelling* state interest."

I think this branch of the "compelling interest" doctrine particularly unfortunate and unnecessary. . . . When the right affected is one assured by the Federal Constitution, any infringement can be dealt with under the Due Process Clause. But when a statute affects only matters not mentioned in the Federal Constitution and is not arbitrary or irrational, I must reiterate that I know of nothing which entitles this Court to pick out particular human activities, characterize them as "fundamental," and give them added protection under an unusually stringent equal protection test. . . .

[In his concurring opinion, Justice Stewart rejected Justice Harlan's charge that the Court was simply "pick[ing] out particular human activities" and responded that "the Court simply recognizes, as it must, an established constitutional right, and gives to that right no less protection than the Constitution itself demands." "The constitutional right to travel from one State to another . . . has been firmly established and repeatedly recognized.". . . .]

III.

The next issue . . . is whether a one-year welfare residence requirement amounts to an undue burden upon the right of interstate travel [which I conclude] is a "fundamental" right which, for present purposes, should be regarded as having its source in the Due Process Clause of the Fifth Amendment.

. . . The number or proportion of persons who are actually deterred from changing residence by the existence of [the one-year waiting period] is unknown. If one accepts evidence put forward by the appellees, to the effect that there would be only a minuscule increase in the number of welfare applicants were existing residence requirements to be done away with, it follows that the requirements do not deter an appreciable number of persons from moving interstate.

[T]he States, and of Congress with respect to the District of Columbia, [have four sets of interests] in imposing residence conditions[:] deny[ing] welfare benefits to persons who moved into the jurisdiction primarily in order to collect those benefits[;] . . . the prevention of fraud[;] . . . help[ing] predict[] the budgetary amount which will be needed for public assistance in the future[;] . . . [and] restrict[ing] welfare payments financed in part by state tax funds to persons who have recently made some contribution to the State's economy, through having been employed, having paid taxes, or having spent money in the State. . . .

[T]he decisive [question is] whether the governmental interests served by residence requirements outweigh the burden imposed upon the right to travel. In my view, a number of considerations militate in favor of constitutionality. First, as just shown, four separate, legitimate governmental interests are furthered by residence requirements. Second, the impact of the requirements upon the freedom of individuals to travel interstate is indirect and, according to evidence put forward by the appellees themselves, insubstantial. Third, these are not cases in which a State or States, acting alone, have attempted to interfere with the right of citizens to travel, but one in which the States have acted within the terms of a limited authorization by the National Government, and in which Congress itself has laid down a like rule for the District of Columbia. Fourth, the legislatures which enacted these statutes have been fully exposed to the arguments of the appellees as to why these residence requirements are unwise, and have rejected them. This is not, therefore, an instance in which legislatures have acted without mature deliberation.

Fifth, and of longer-range importance, the field of welfare assistance is one in which there is a widely recognized need for fresh solutions and consequently for experimentation. Invalidation of welfare residence requirements have the unfortunate consequence of discouraging the Federal and State Governments from establishing unusually generous welfare programs in particular areas on an experimental basis, because of fears that the program would cause an influx of persons seeking higher welfare payments. Sixth and finally, a strong presumption of constitutionality attaches to statutes of the types now before us. . . .

Taking all of these competing considerations into account, I believe that the balance definitely favors constitutionality. In reaching that conclusion, I do not minimize the importance of the right to travel interstate. However, the impact of residence conditions upon that right is indirect and apparently quite insubstantial. On the other hand, the governmental purposes served by the requirements are legitimate and real, and the residence requirements are clearly suited to their accomplishment. . . .

B. The Right to Relocate

Although couched in terms of a "right to travel," *Shapiro* might better be conceptualized as concerning the "right to relocate." After all, the plaintiffs were not simply passing through the states on the way to somewhere else; instead, they claimed to be (and were recognized as) legal residents of their new states, and the issue was whether the mere status as a legal resident, without more, established eligibility for the welfare benefits. Not surprisingly, so-called "durational residency requirements" became a topic of a great deal of litigation following *Shapiro.*

In Dunn v. Blumstein, 405 U.S. 330 (1972), the Court struck down Tennessee's one-year residence requirement for voting in state elections, under the Equal Protection Clause, despite Tennessee's claim that the requirement protected against double registration and other forms of fraud and that it also assured that voters would be knowledgeable of state and community affairs. The Court subjected the requirement to strict equal protection scrutiny both because it affected the franchise and because it "penalized" the right of interstate mobility. On the latter issue, Justice Marshall wrote that "[d]urational residence laws impermissibly condition and penalize the right to travel by imposing their prohibitions on only those persons who have recently exercised that right. In the present case, such laws force a person who wishes to travel and change residences to choose between travel and the basic right to vote. Absent a compelling state interest, a State may not burden the right to travel in this way."

In Memorial Hospital v. Maricopa County, 415 U.S. 250 (1974), the Court held that an Arizona statute requiring one year's residence in a county as a condition for an indigent's receiving nonemergency medical care at the county's expense violated the equal protection clause. Justice Marshall wrote for the majority:

> Whatever the ultimate parameters of the *Shapiro* penalty analysis, it is at least clear that medical care is as much "a basic necessity of life" to an indigent as welfare assistance. And, governmental privileges or benefits necessary to basic sustenance have often been viewed as being of greater constitutional significance than less essential forms of governmental entitlements. It would be odd, indeed, to find that the State of Arizona was required to afford [appellant] Evaro welfare assistance to keep him from the discomfort of inadequate housing or the pangs of hunger but could deny him the medical care necessary to relieve him from the wheezing and gasping for breath that attend his illness.

Justice Douglas concurred in a separate opinion; Chief Justice Burger and Justice Blackmun concurred in the result. Justice Rehnquist dissented:

> The solicitude which the Court has shown in cases involving the right to vote, and the virtual denial of entry inherent in denial of welfare benefits . . . ought not be so casually extended to the alleged deprivation here. Rather the Court should examine, as it has done in the past, whether the challenged requirement erects a real and purposeful barrier to movement, or the threat of such a barrier, or whether the effects on travel, viewed realistically, are merely incidental and remote. . . . [T]he barrier here is hardly a counterpart to the barriers condemned in earlier cases. That being so, the Court should observe its traditional respect for the State's allocation of its limited financial resources rather than unjustifiedly imposing its own preferences.

In Sosna v. Iowa, 419 U.S. 393 (1975), however, the Court upheld Iowa's requirement that a party reside in the state for one year before bringing a divorce action against a nonresident. Justice Rehnquist wrote for the majority:

> Appellant was not irretrievably foreclosed from obtaining some part of what she sought, as was the case with the welfare recipients in *Shapiro,* the voters in *Dunn,* or the indigent patient in *Maricopa County.* She would eventually qualify for the same sort of adjudication which she demanded virtually upon her arrival in the State. . . . A decree of divorce is not a matter in which the only interested parties are the State as a sort of "grantor," and a plaintiff such as appellant in the role of "grantee." Both spouses are obviously interested in the proceedings, since it will affect their marital status and very likely their property rights. Where a married couple has minor children, a decree of divorce would usually include provisions for their custody and support. With consequences of such moment riding on a divorce decree issued by its courts, Iowa may insist that one seeking to initiate such a proceeding have the modicum of attachment to the State required here. . . .

Justice Marshall, joined by Justice Brennan, dissented, criticizing the Court's failure to inquire "whether the right to obtain a divorce is of sufficient importance that its denial to recent interstate immigrants constitutes a penalty on interstate travel" and its refusal to apply a "compelling interest" test.

In addition to *Sosna,* the Supreme Court has upheld requirements, like those found in Texas and other states, that persons live in the state a full year (as nonstudents) before becoming eligible for reduced university tuition available only to residents. In Starns v. Maklerson, 401 U.S. 985 (1971), the Court affirmed, without opinion, such a Minnesota state law. The district court below had noted the lack of "any dire effects" on the students in question, in presumed contrast to the welfare recipients who were the subject of *Shapiro*. This obviously underscores the point that something more than a simple "right to travel" is at stake. See also Martinez v. Bynum, 461 U.S. 321 (1983) (upholding a bona fide residency requirement for attending a state's public schools), discussed below.

Note that the Court has considered residency requirements outside the Equal Protection Clause context. Cf. Supreme Court of New Hampshire v. Piper, 470 U.S. 274 (1985) (bona fide residency requirement for admission to the state bar violates the Privileges and Immunities Clause of Article V, §2); Vlandis v. Kline, 412 U.S. 441 (1973) (striking down as unconstitutional under the Due Process Clause an irrebuttable presumption of nonresidency for state university students whose legal addresses were outside of the State before they applied for admission).

C.   Can the State Give More Welfare to Long-Time Residents Than to Newcomers?

Shapiro holds that a state may not use a durational residency requirement to deny welfare benefits to new residents. But may the state award benefits on a sliding scale based on duration, where the newcomer receives something, but long-timers receive even more? In Zobel v. Williams, 457 U.S. 55 (1982), the Alaska legislature had passed a bill distributing some of the vast income from the development of North Slope oil directly to Alaska citizens. The amount received was a function of length of residence. "Dividend units" would be apportioned at the rate of one unit per year of residence since 1959, the first year of statehood. Each unit was worth $50 in 1979, although the State estimated that it would be worth four times as much by 1985. The Court, by an 8 to 1 vote, declared the Alaska scheme unconstitutional. Chief Justice Burger, writing for the majority, found the statute in violation of the Equal Protection Clause, unable to pass even a test of minimal rationality.

The State could not justify the program to "creat[e] financial incentive[s] for individuals to establish and maintain residence in Alaska" because it applied to persons who were already residents at the time the program was established. The program did not "encourage . . . prudent management of the Permanent Fund." Finally, the Court held that "reward[ing] citizens for past contributions" was "not a legitimate state purpose. A similar 'past contributions' argument was made and rejected in Shapiro v. Thompson."

Justice Brennan concurred, joined by Justices Marshall, Blackmun, and Powell. His opinion emphasized "what has come to be called the 'right to travel' . . . , or, more precisely, the federal interest in free interstate migration." The "threat to free interstate migration" presented by the Alaska law "provides an independent rationale for holding that law unconstitutional." "[I]f each State were free to reward its citizens incrementally for their years of residence, so that a citizen leaving one State would thereby forfeit his accrued seniority, only to have to begin building such seniority again in his new State of residence, then the mobility so essential to the economic progress of our Nation, and so commonly accepted as a fundamental aspect of our social order would not long survive."

Justice O'Connor concurred only in the judgment. She rejected the majority's equal protection analysis, stating that the Fourteenth Amendment does not render illegitimate the objective of rewarding citizens for past contributions: "[A] generalized desire to reward citizens for past endurance, particularly in a State where years of hardship only recently have produced prosperity, is not innately improper." Yet the differentiation in treatment between shorter and longer term citizens "conflicts with the constitutional purpose of maintaining a Union rather than a mere 'league of States.' The Court's task, therefore, should be (1) to articulate this constitutional principle, explaining its textual sources, and (2) to test the strength of Alaska's objective against the constitutional imperative." Justice O'Connor's analysis emphasized the Privileges and Immunities Clause of Article IV.

Justice Rehnquist dissented, finding the Alaska program rational and thus passing muster under the Equal Protection Clause.

Discussion

In his article Equal Treatment for Newcomers: The Core Meaning of National and State Citizenship, 1 Constitutional Commentary 9 (1984), Professor Cohen suggests that the conceptual "disarray" generated by *Shapiro* and successor cases, including *Zobel,* can be alleviated if one adopts, in place of "right to travel" analysis, a constitutional principle of "equal state citizenship." "Under the fourteenth amendment, any United States citizen becomes a full-fledged member of the state community immediately upon establishing residence there." That principle, in turn, "demands that newcomers be treated as full members of the state community. . . . [D]urational residency requirements for state benefits and services are permissible only to the extent they respond to a reasonable concern for proof of domiciliary intent." As an example of a case which asks the correct question under his equal-citizenship analysis, Professor Cohen offers Martinez v. Bynum, 461 U.S. 321 (1983), where the Court upheld the constitutionality of a Texas law denying tuition-free admission to the public schools by a minor living apart from a "parent, guardian, or other person having lawful control of him under an order of a court" if the minor's presence in the school district is "for the primary purpose of attending the public free schools." Roberto Morales, a U.S. citizen by birth, left his parents' home in Reynosa, Mexico, in order to reside with his sister, Oralia Martinez, in McAllen, Texas. Finding that the move was motivated primarily by the desire to attend the local schools, the McAllen Independent School District denied Morales tuition-free admission. A class action suit was filed challenging the Texas statute on its face. Both the District and Fifth Circuit courts upheld the statute against facial attack, and the Supreme Court, in an 8 to 1 vote, affirmed, with only Justice Marshall dissenting.

Still, despite Professor Cohen's analysis, the question of defining "equality" remains. Although Dunn v. Blumstein prohibited Tennessee from imposing a durational residency requirement for the franchise, Justice Brennan readily acknowledges New Hampshire's power to prohibit newcomers from running for governor until they have lived in the state for seven years. One can vote immediately, but the newcomer must wait before running for governor. Is this not a sliding scale of eligibility for participation in state politics?

D. Congressional Consent

Federal law punishes interstate travel under certain circumstances. See 18 U.S.C. §1073 (flight to avoid prosecution or giving testimony), 18 U.S.C. §1952 (travel in aid of racketeering), 18 U.S.C. §1201 (transportation of kidnapping victim), 18 U.S.C. §2101 (travel to incite riot), 18 U.S.C. §2421 (transportation for prosecution). The Court has not suggested that these provisions are constitutionally problematic.

Recall that the majority in Edwards v. California relied on the commerce clause to invalidate California's attempt to bar the entry of indigents during the Great Depression. In view of Congress's general power to impede or authorize the states to impede interstate commerce, could Congress prohibit indigents from crossing state lines or authorize the states to deny them admission? Your answer may depend on the source of the right to travel — whether it is derived from the relationship of the states to one another, or is based on a citizen's relationship to the federal government, or is a fundamental personal right of the individual.

Perhaps the Court decided to base *Shapiro* on the Equal Protection Clause in order to insulate the holding against a congressional "overruling." (Recall the consideration of Congress's power to disagree with, and in effect overrule, judicial interpretations of the Fourteenth Amendment in Chapter 5.) If heightened equal protection scrutiny in *Shapiro* is based on the unequal treatment of persons because they exercised a constitutional "right," isn't the source of that right relevant to the question whether Congress can in effect overrule the decision?

E.   The Court Reconsiders (and Reconceptualizes) *Shapiro*

SAENZ v. ROE, 526 U.S. 489 (1999): [California limited welfare benefits, for the first 12 months of the residency of a new citizen of the state, to the level enjoyed by the person in his or her state of origin. This approach was approved by the Department of Health and Human Services; it was also authorized by Congress's subsequent passage of the 1996 welfare reform act, the Personal Responsibility and Work Opportunity Reconciliation Act of 1996 (PRWORA). California argued that the statute would save approximately $10.9 million in annual welfare costs out of its annual expenditures of $2.9 billion for the entire program. The Court held that California's limitation of welfare benefits was unconstitutional.]

STEVENS, J. . . . .: The "right to travel" . . . embraces at least three different components. It protects the right of a citizen of one State to enter and to leave another State, the right to be treated as a welcome visitor rather than an unfriendly alien when temporarily present in the second State, and, for those travelers who elect to become permanent residents, the right to be treated like other citizens of that State. . . .

What is at issue in this case . . . is [the] third aspect of the right to travel — the right of the newly arrived citizen to the same privileges and immunities enjoyed by other citizens of the same State. That right is protected not only by the new arrival's status as a state citizen, but also by her status as a citizen of the United States. That additional source of protection is plainly identified in the opening words of the Fourteenth Amendment. . . . : "All persons born or naturalized in the United States, and subject to the jurisdiction thereof, are citizens of the United States and of the State wherein they reside. No State shall make or enforce any law which shall abridge the privileges or immunities of citizens of the United States."

. . . [I]t has always been common ground that this Clause protects the third component of the right to travel. Writing for the majority [in the Slaughterhouse Cases], Justice Miller explained that one of the privileges conferred by this Clause "is that a citizen of the United States can, of his own volition, become a citizen of any State of the Union by a bona-fide residence therein, with the same rights as other citizens of that State."

. . . [N]either mere rationality nor some intermediate standard of review should be used to judge the constitutionality of a state rule that discriminates against some of its citizens because they have been domiciled in the State for less than a year. . . .

Because this case involves discrimination against citizens who have completed their interstate travel, the State's argument that its welfare scheme affects the right to travel only "incidentally" is beside the point. Were we concerned solely with actual deterrence to migration, we might be persuaded that a partial withholding of benefits constitutes a lesser incursion on the right to travel than an outright denial of all benefits. But since the right to travel embraces the citizen's right to be treated equally in her new State of residence, the discriminatory classification is itself a penalty. . . .

We . . . have no occasion to consider what weight might be given to a citizen's length of residence if the bona fides of her claim to state citizenship were questioned. Moreover, because whatever benefits they receive will be consumed while they remain in California, there is no danger that recognition of their claim will encourage citizens of other States to establish residency for just long enough to acquire some readily portable benefit, such as a divorce or a college education, that will be enjoyed after they return to their original domicile. See, e.g., Sosna v. Iowa (1975); Vlandis v. Kline (1973).

[California favors] all eligible California citizens who have resided there for at least one year, plus those new arrivals who last resided in another country or in a State that provides benefits at least as generous as California's. . . . [W]ithin the broad sub-category of new arrivals who are treated less favorably, there are many smaller classes whose benefit levels are determined by the law of the States from whence they came. . . . California must therefore explain not only why it is sound fiscal policy to discriminate against those who have been citizens for less than a year, but also why it is permissible to apply such a variety of rules within that class. . . .

Disavowing any desire to fence out the indigent, California has instead advanced an entirely fiscal justification[; that] the State approximately $10.9 million a year. [But] [a]n evenhanded, across-the-board reduction of about 72 cents per month for every beneficiary would produce the same result. [T]he Citizenship Clause of the Fourteenth Amendment expressly equates citizenship with residence: "That Clause does not provide for, and does not allow for, degrees of citizenship based on length of residence." *Zobel.* It is equally clear that the Clause does not tolerate a hierarchy of 45 subclasses of similarly situated citizens based on the location of their prior residence. . . . Neither the duration of respondents' California residence, nor the identity of their prior States of residence, has any relevance to their need for benefits. Nor do those factors bear any relationship to the State's interest in making an equitable allocation of the funds to be distributed among its needy citizens. As in *Shapiro,* we reject any contributory rationale for the denial of benefits to new residents. . . . In short, the State's legitimate interest in saving money provides no justification for its decision to discriminate among equally eligible citizens.

The question that remains is whether congressional approval of durational residency requirements in the 1996 amendment to the Social Security Act somehow resuscitates the constitutionality of §11450.03. That question is readily answered, for we have consistently held that Congress may not authorize the States to violate the Fourteenth Amendment. Moreover, the protection afforded to the citizen by the Citizenship Clause of that Amendment is a limitation on the powers of the National Government as well as the States. . . .

REHNQUIST, C.J., joined by Thomas, J., dissenting:

. . . [I] cannot see how the right to become a citizen of another State is a necessary "component" of the right to travel. . . . A person is no longer "traveling" in any sense of the word when he finishes his journey to a State which he plans to make his home. . . . [T]he Court ignores a State's need to assure that only persons who establish a bona fide residence receive the benefits provided to current residents of the State. . . . [T]he Court has consistently recognized that while new citizens must have the same opportunity to enjoy the privileges of being a citizen of a State, the States retain the ability to use bona fide residence requirements to ferret out those who intend to take the privileges and run. . . .

While the physical presence element of a bona fide residence is easy to police, the subjective intent element is not. It is simply unworkable and futile to require States to inquire into each new resident's subjective intent to remain. Hence, States employ objective criteria such as durational residence requirements to test a new resident's resolve to remain before these new citizens can enjoy certain in-state benefits. . . .

If States can require individuals to reside in-state for a year before exercising the right to educational benefits, the right to terminate a marriage, or the right to vote in primary elections that all other state citizens enjoy, then States may surely do the same for welfare benefits. . . . Durational residence requirements were upheld when used to regulate the provision of higher education subsidies, and the same deference should be given in the case of welfare payments.

. . . In one respect, the State has a greater need to require a durational residence for welfare benefits than for college eligibility. The impact of a large number of new residents who immediately seek welfare payments will have a far greater impact on a State's operating budget than the impact of new residents seeking to attend a state university. In the case of the welfare recipients, a modest durational residence requirement to allow for the completion of an annual legislative budget cycle gives the State time to decide how to finance the increased obligations.

The Court tries to distinguish education and divorce benefits by contending that the welfare payment here will be consumed in California, while a college education or a divorce produces benefits that are "portable" and can be enjoyed after individuals return to their original domicile. But this "you can't take it with you" distinction is more apparent than real, and offers little guidance to lower courts who must apply this rationale in the future. Welfare payments are a form of insurance, giving impoverished individuals and their families the means to meet the demands of daily life while they receive the necessary training, education, and time to look for a job. The cash itself will no doubt be spent in California, but the benefits from receiving this income and having the opportunity to become employed or employable will stick with the welfare recipient if they stay in California or go back to their true domicile. Similarly, tuition subsidies are "consumed" in-state but the recipient takes the benefits of a college education with him wherever he goes. A welfare subsidy is

thus as much an investment in human capital as is a tuition subsidy, and their attendant benefits are just as "portable." . . .

THOMAS, J., joined by Rehnquist, C.J., dissenting:
. . . Because I believe that the demise of the Privileges or Immunities Clause has
contributed in no small part to the current disarray of our Fourteenth Amendment
jurisprudence, I would be open to reevaluating its meaning in an appropriate case.
Before invoking the Clause, however, we should endeavor to understand what the
framers of the Fourteenth Amendment thought that it meant. We should also
consider whether the Clause should displace, rather than augment, portions of our
equal protection and substantive due process jurisprudence. The majority's failure
to consider these important questions raises the specter that the Privileges or
Immunities Clause will become yet another convenient tool for inventing new
rights, limited solely by the "predilections of those who happen at the time to be
Members of this Court."

Discussion
1. How successful is the switch to the Privileges or Immunities Clause as a replacement for the Equal Protection Clause as the foundation of the Court's analysis? And
what does the Privileges or Immunities Clause add to the Citizenship Clause
(perhaps combined with the Equal Protection Clause) in the Court's analysis?
2. Assume that California passes a law requiring that resident aliens moving from
another state to California receive, for the first year, only the level of benefits of
their original state. Is the resident alien covered by the *Saenz* doctrine, which
focuses on the privileges and immunities of national citizenship? Would some
combination of the Equal Protection Clause of the Fourteenth Amendment and
the Due Process Clause of the Fifth Amendment adequately protect the resident
alien against congressional authorization of the California law?
3. Why doesn't *Saenz* invalidate the differential-tuition practices of several states
that take duration of residence into account? Consider that Texas charges out-of-
state tuition rates to persons who, under *Dunn,* have become voting citizens of the
state. If Texas may require a year of residence to test the residential bona fides of
the claimant for state resources, why shouldn't it be able to impose a yearlong wait
to become a member of the voting polity? (Instead, according to *Dunn* and subsequent cases, one is entitled to the suffrage after a month's residency.) Is the relevant difference, when all is said and done, that eligibility for residential tuition
involves a significant economic subsidy, whereas the right to vote is effectively "free"
in economic terms?
4. California also requires a year of residence for eligibility for in-state tuition,
but, unlike Texas, it does not require that one be a nonstudent during the year.
Therefore second-year students at the University of California law schools, for
example, pay in-state rates (assuming they have declared themselves to be
Californians), whereas University of Texas Law School students must continue to
pay nonresident tuition for the entirety of their stay at the University. Does the
Texas rule survive *Saenz*? Or can Texas argue that it still can't be sure that the
purported "Texans" won't simply leave upon graduation?
5. The Court makes much of the distinction between "portable" and "non-
portable" benefits. How successful do you find this distinction? Could the state,
upon reading Chief Justice Rehnquist's opinion, require a year's residency before

eligibility for state-funded job training programs even if it had to give, say, food stamps immediately?

VI.   *Conditioning Spending in the Welfare State — The Problem of Unconstitutional Conditions*

A.   Introduction: Rights, Waivers, and Inducements to Change Behavior

We now arrive at what is perhaps the most important — and certainly the most labyrinthine — question of contemporary constitutional analysis: what conditions can the state can place on the welfare state goods and benefits it bestows on the public?

We normally think of constitutional rights as protected from government abridgement even when the abridgement is "evenhanded" and does not discriminate among persons. For example, the First Amendment prohibits the government from censoring newspapers for criticizing the president, even if it censors all newspapers equally and even if it affords a full hearing to an editor who complains that the censor has erred in believing that an editorial criticizes the president. One need not believe that the First Amendment offers "absolute protection"; we have already seen — see Chapter 4 — that this is not the case, but the point is that the state must offer a substantive "compelling interest" in order to justify suppression of speech. Similarly, one is entitled to a jury trial upon being charged with a crime, as per the Sixth Amendment, even if the state or national government believes that it is a waste of public funds to provide it (as against a bench trial, for example).

Even so, it should also be obvious that individuals *can* consciously choose to waive their rights. Whatever the formal guarantee set out in the Constitution to a jury trial, the overwhelming number of convictions in the United States occur through the submission of guilty pleas, in which defendants choose to forgo their constitutional rights, usually in return for a "plea bargain" with the state by which the prosecutor reduces the charge or expresses a willingness to recommend a significantly lighter sentence than might otherwise be the case.[43] Of course, even those defendants who choose to exercise their right to a jury trial with some frequency waive their Fifth Amendment right to remain silent by taking the stand in their own defense.

A classical topic of political theory is whether there indeed exist, as suggested by the Declaration of Independence, any truly "inalienable rights," that is, rights not subject to waiver. The standard example of such an "inalienable right" is the illegitimacy of a contract by which one sells oneself into slavery, on the ground that one cannot waive one's right to enjoy at least some degree of personal autonomy. As suggested above, rights are often consciously waived to gain something: In exchange for a guilty plea, the criminal defendant receives probation rather than a jail sentence, just as persons agree in the private market to waive their rights to

---

43. See George Fisher, Plea Bargaining's Triumph: A History of Plea Bargaining in America (2003).

"liberty" by agreeing to the terms of an employment contract. The central question then becomes whether government induces the waiver of otherwise protected constitutional rights by granting benefits — e.g., employment, housing, education, and welfare — only on the condition that the recipients waive their constitutional rights. (Although we focus on government, it should be clear that similar questions arise in the private marketplace. Standard contract law, for example, relies on an image of more-or-less equal bargainers and explicitly invalidates contracts entered into under "duress.")

Most classical rights cases involve what might be termed governmental "intrusion" into a protected realm of private life. The state insists on searching a home, preventing speech, or prohibiting an abortion. The cases in the rest of this chapter do not fit so easily into this model inasmuch as they all deal with the modern welfare state that, as noted earlier, offers many benefits to citizens that they in fact wish to have. That is, the typical citizen in a welfare state has no desire to be completely left alone; instead, he or she wishes to enjoy the benefits of state-provided education, medical care, grants to create art, etc. The contemporary state is involved in supplying an almost infinite set of these and other welfare benefits, at least if one defines "welfare" simply as the provision of goods or services at below-market costs to individuals or institutions.

Consider a public zoo. This is certainly a "welfare benefit" provided to the citizenry. Must the city distribute the benefit to all without any conditions being attached? The answer is certainly no. The city can, for starters, charge an entrance fee. Although, as seen earlier in this chapter, the state may not be able to charge user fees where certain "fundamental rights" or "interests" are involved, no such argument would be available with regard to the zoo. No one's constitutional rights would be affected if San Antonio simply decided to eliminate the zoo, whether as a cost-cutting measure or as an endorsement of animal rights. Yet it should also be clear that most equal protection and procedural due process rights above would be meaningless if the state could attach just *any* condition it wished on entrance to the zoo. A state could avoid the racial desegregation decisions simply by making waiver of the right not to be segregated a part of the contract of admission to public zoos. Nor could a state open the zoo only to registered Republicans, or provide discounts for the entrance fee to persons who sign a loyalty oath or who pledge to refrain from using contraceptives for a month.

To be sure, courts on occasion have asserted that the induced waiver of substantive constitutional rights presents no difficulties at all. For example, Justice Holmes, writing for the Supreme Judicial Court of Massachusetts in McAuliffe v. Mayor of New Bedford, 155 Mass. 216, 29 N.E. 517 (1892), dismissed the petition of a policeman who was fired for violating a departmental regulation against political activities with the quip: "The petitioner may have a constitutional right to talk politics, but he has no constitutional right to be a policeman. . . . [H]e takes the employment on the terms which are offered him." Almost 80 years later Justice Blackmun wrote for the Court in Wyman v. James, 400 U.S. 309 (1971), that a state did not violate the Fourth Amendment by conditioning Aid for Dependent Children benefits on the recipient family's acquiescence to occasional "home visits" by a welfare caseworker: "[T]he visitation in itself is not forced or compelled, and . . . the beneficiary's denial of permission is not a criminal act. If consent to the visitation is withheld, no visitation takes place. The aid then never begins or merely ceases, as the case may be."

A classic argument against this view was forcefully presented in Frost & Frost Trucking Co. v. Railroad Commission, 271 U.S. 583 (1926). In this case, California attempted to condition the right of a trucking company to use the public roads on its agreement to follow certain limitations on charges to its customers. Justice Sutherland wrote:

> It would be a palpable incongruity to strike down an act of state legislation which, by words of express divestment, seeks to strip the citizen of rights guaranteed by the federal Constitution, but to uphold an act by which the same result is accomplished under the guise of a surrender of a right in exchange for a valuable privilege which the state threatens otherwise to withhold. . . . If the state may compel the surrender of one constitutional right as a condition of its favor, it may, in a like manner, compel a surrender of all. It is inconceivable that guarantees embedded in the Constitution of the United States may thus be manipulated out of existence.

The particular right that Justice Sutherland was protecting from coerced waiver was based on the doctrine of substantive economic rights, which, of course, was significantly undercut by the New Deal repudiation of *Lochner*-era cases. However, the concern about so-called unconstitutional conditions is not limited to any particular substantive constitutional doctrine. Consider, for example, Justice Douglas's dissent in *Wyman,* where he condemned the willingness of the majority to acquiesce in the "invasion of the privacy of Barbara James" by viewing the state's demand for her waiver of privacy as a constitutionally tolerable predicate for the benefits given her by the state: "[T]he central question is whether the government by force of its largesse has the power to 'buy up' rights guaranteed by the Constitution. But for the assertion of her constitutional right [protected by the Fourth Amendment], Barbara James in this case would have received the welfare benefit."

Justice Douglas cited a number of cases forbidding the requirement of waivers in order to receive government benefits. For example, "[w]hile second-class mail rates may be granted or withheld by the Government, we would not allow them to be granted 'on condition that certain economic or political ideas not be disseminated.' Hannegan v. Esquire, Inc., 327 U.S. 146 (1946)." The state also cannot condition public employment on waiver of the privilege against self-incrimination with respect to alleged misconduct connected with the activities. Lefkowitz v. Turley, 414 U.S. 70 (1973); Gardner v. Broderick, 392 U.S. 273 (1968).

Perhaps the central issue of the modern welfare state is whether one can devise a plausible comprehensive theory that explains when the imposition of a given condition should be ruled unconstitutional and when, on the contrary, it is a perfectly acceptable demand by the state, even if we view it as the government "buy[ing] up" rights guaranteed by the Constitution." Many law professors have attempted to create a coherent doctrine of "unconstitutional conditions," see e.g., Richard Epstein, The Supreme Court, 1987 Term, Foreword: Unconstitutional Conditions, State Power, and the Limits of Consent, 102 Harv. L. Rev. 4 (1988); Seth Kreimer, Allocational Sanctions: The Problem of Negative Rights in a Positive State, 132 U. Pa. L. Rev. 1293 (1984); Kathleen Sullivan, Unconstitutional Conditions, 102 Harv. L. Rev. 1413 (1989); Mitchell N. Berman, Coercion Without Baselines: Unconstitutional Conditions in Three Dimensions, 90 Georgetown L. Rev. 1 (2001). None of these scholars, however, has produced a solution that has stilled the debate. Indeed, other scholars have suggested abandoning the quest for a unified theory of unconstitutional conditions. See, e.g., Cass R. Sunstein, Is There an Unconstitutional Conditions Doctrine?, 26 San Diego L. Rev. 337 (1989); Cass R. Sunstein, Why the Unconstitutional Conditions Doctrine is an Anachronism (With Particular Reference to Religion, Speech, and Abortion), 70 Boston U. L. Rev. 593 (1990); Frederick Schauer, Too Hard: Unconstitutional Conditions and the Chimera of Constitutional Consistency, 72 Denver U. L. Rev. 989 (1995). As you consider the following cases, then, you need not expect to find them to cohere into a standard-model doctrine. The conundrum of unconstitutional conditions presents such challenging puzzles that it is unrealistic to expect more than a trace of consistency, if that, among the cases.

Most cases challenging conditional spending as unconstitutional conditions on a right can be viewed as equality claims. For example, providing driver's licenses only to persons who waive their Fourth Amendment rights with respect to police searches of their vehicles treats those who will and those who will not consent to waive their rights differently. But not all equality claims are claims of unconstitutional conditions. When the government makes classifications based on an immutable characteristic, we do not assume that the government is conditioning the benefit on a person's decision to "be" white or black, male or female. On the other hand, cases where the government conditions a benefit on behavior forbidden by one's religion usually do present a problem of unconstitutional conditions (although on balance the particular government policy may ultimately be judged constitutional). That is because the hallmark of the unconstitutional conditions case is the attempt — whether successful or not — to alter behavior by creating incentives and disincentives. The unconstitutional conditions claim is that the government is trying to shape behavior in ways that unfairly or improperly induce people to exercise fundamental rights (or not exercise them) in ways the government prefers.

Government, of course, is always trying to shape behavior, and if all such attempts were unconstitutional conditions, the power to govern would be very limited indeed. Thus, when governments create public libraries and stock only what are deemed "worthwhile" books or when they give subsidies to students who study particular subjects (for example, Arabic or biology) they encourage people to exercise their First Amendment rights in particular ways, which is presumably what the government prefers; but few would regard these particular programs as unconstitutional conditions. On the other hand, if the government offered its citizens $500 to sign a loyalty oath, to register with a particular political party, or to refrain for a year from making speeches critical of the government on public property, it also induces its citizens to exercise their First Amendment rights in particular ways, but here the policies seem far more problematic. The question is what best explains these intuitions.

Several standard theories have been offered to explain when government is putting people to an unconstitutional choice. The most familiar asks whether the government is making an offer that makes a person better off as opposed to a threat that would leave the person worse off. The distinction between threats and offers, however, requires a baseline of justified expectations. Is the appropriate baseline receiving the government benefit without the condition attached (in which case the government is threatening to remove it and punish the individual), or receiving no benefit at all (in which case the government is merely making an offer subject to the condition that makes the target no worse off if he or she refuses it).

To determine that baseline, one can ask whether the benefit in question is of the sort that is broadly given to many people, with only a small carve-out for a disfavored few. Another possible inquiry is whether the government would likely have given the benefit anyway even if it could not have imposed the condition. (If it would have, then one might regard the recipient's acquiescence to the state's desire for a waiver of rights as an illegitimate "windfall," as against a situation where a refusal to waive would indeed have served as a "deal breaker" leading the legislature to refuse to pass the legislation at all. One can, of course, ask how we can ascertain what description best fits the legislation in question.) Still another test is whether there is a sufficiently close nexus between the condition demanded by the government and the purpose for establishing the benefit in the first place. If the condition is unrelated to the purpose for the program it is more likely to be improper. As you will see in the materials that follow, although each of these inquiries is of some help, none is conclusive in every case.

Consider, then, a state's decision to offer impoverished pregnant women medical expenses if they carry the child to term but provide no aid at all if the woman wishes to exercise her constitutionally protected right to abort the fetus. Is this an offer of financial support for women who wish to have children, or is it a threat, an attempt to coerce women to forego their right to an abortion? Note that government generally has wide discretion with regard to funding given for medical procedures. The state can choose to pay for heart transplants but not for kidney dialysis, or vice versa. (Is it conceivable that the state by paying for *some* medical care must pay for *all* conceivable medical care that someone might need?) Whatever else one might say about distinguishing between dialysis and heart transplants, it would surely be bizarre to say that Congress is trying to "encourage" people to develop the funded disease or to waive their right to develop the disfavored one. Is it equally bizarre, though, to say that with regard to abortion funding, the state *is* attempting to generate a certain *choice* by the woman as to her future conduct?

B. The Abortion Funding Cases

MAHER v. ROE
432 U.S. 464 (1977)

POWELL, J. . . . .

I.

A regulation of the Connecticut Welfare Department limits state Medicaid benefits for first trimester abortions to those that are "medically necessary," a term defined to include psychiatric necessity. Connecticut enforces this limitation through a system of prior authorization from its Department of Social Services. In order to obtain authorization for a first trimester abortion, the hospital or clinic where the abortion is to be performed must submit, other things, a certificate from the patient's attending physician stating that the abortion is medically necessary. This attack on the validity of the Connecticut regulation was brought against appellant Maher, the Commissioner of Social Services, by appellees Poe and Roe, two indigent women who were unable to obtain a physician's certificate of medical necessity.[a] [A three-judge district court held the statute unconstitutional.]

II.

The Constitution imposes no obligation on the States to pay the pregnancy-related medical expenses of indigent women, or indeed to pay any of the medical expenses of indigents. But when a State decides to alleviate some of the hardships of poverty by providing medical care, the manner in which it dispenses benefits is subject to constitutional limitations. Appellees' claim is that Connecticut must accord equal treatment to both abortion and childbirth, and may not evidence a policy preference by funding only the medical expenses incident to childbirth. This challenge to the classifications established by the Connecticut regulation presents a question arising under the Equal Protection Clause of the Fourteenth Amendment. The basic framework of analysis of such a claim is well settled: "We must decide, first, whether [state legislation] operates to the disadvantage of some suspect class or impinges upon a fundamental right explicitly or implicitly protected by the Constitution, thereby requiring strict judicial scrutiny. . . . If not, the [legislative] scheme must still be examined to determine whether it rationally furthers some legitimate, articulated state purpose and therefore does not constitute an invidious discrimination. . . ." Applying this analysis here, we think the District Court erred in holding that the Connecticut regulation violated the Equal Protection Clause of the Fourteenth Amendment.

A

This case involves no discrimination against a suspect class. An indigent woman desiring an abortion does not come within the limited category of disadvantaged classes so recognized by our cases. Nor does the fact that the impact of the regulation falls upon those who cannot pay lead to a different conclusion. In a sense, every denial of welfare to an indigent creates a wealth classification as compared to nonindigents who are able to pay for the desired goods or services. But this Court has never held that financial need alone identifies a suspect class for purposes of equal protection analysis.[b] Accordingly, the central question in this case is whether the regulation "impinges upon a fundamental right explicitly or implicitly protected by the Constitution." The District Court read our decisions in Roe v. Wade, 410 U.S. 113 (1973), and the subsequent cases applying it, as establishing a

---

a. At the time this action was filed, Mary Poe, a 16-year-old high school junior, had already obtained an abortion at a Connecticut hospital. Apparently because of Poe's inability to obtain a certificate of medical necessity, the hospital was denied reimbursement by the Department of Social Services. As a result, Poe was being pressed to pay the hospital bill of $244. Susan Roe, an unwed mother of three children, was unable to obtain an abortion because of her physician's refusal to certify that the procedure was medically necessary. . . .

b. In cases such as Griffin v. Illinois and Douglas v. California, the Court held that the Equal Protection Clause requires States that allow appellate review of criminal convictions to provide indigent defendants with trial transcripts and appellate counsel. These cases are grounded in the criminal justice system, a governmental monopoly in which participation is compelled. Our subsequent decisions have made it clear that the principles underlying *Griffin* and *Douglas* do not extend to legislative classifications generally.

fundamental right to abortion and therefore concluded that nothing less than a compelling state interest would justify Connecticut's different treatment of abortion and childbirth. We think the District Court misconceived the nature and scope of the fundamental right recognized in *Roe.*

B

Roe did not declare an unqualified "constitutional right to an abortion," as the District Court seemed to think. Rather, the right protects the woman from unduly burdensome interference with her freedom to decide whether to terminate her pregnancy. It implies no limitation on the authority of a State to make a value judgment favoring childbirth over abortion, and to implement that judgment by the allocation of public funds.

. . . The Connecticut regulation places no obstacles — absolute or otherwise — in the pregnant woman's path to an abortion. An indigent woman who desires an abortion suffers no disadvantage as a consequence of Connecticut's decision to fund childbirth; she continues as before to be dependent on private sources for the service she desires. The State may have made childbirth a more attractive alternative, thereby influencing the woman's decision, but it has imposed no restriction on access to abortions that was not already there. The indigency that may make it difficult — and in some cases, perhaps, impossible — for some women to have abortions is neither created nor in any way affected by the Connecticut regulation. We conclude that the Connecticut regulation does not impinge upon the fundamental right recognized in *Roe.* . . .

D

The question remains whether Connecticut's regulation can be sustained under the less demanding test of rationality that applies in the absence of a suspect classification or the impingement of a fundamental right. This test requires that the distinction drawn between childbirth and nontherapeutic abortion by the regulation be "rationally related" to a "constitutionally permissible" purpose. We hold that the Connecticut funding scheme satisfies this standard.

Roe itself explicitly acknowledged the State's strong interest in protecting the potential life of the fetus. That interest exists throughout the pregnancy, "grow[ing] in substantiality as the woman approaches term." Because the pregnant woman carries a potential human being, she "cannot be isolated in her privacy. . . . [Her] privacy is no longer sole and any right of privacy she possesses must be measured accordingly." The State unquestionably has a "strong and legitimate interest in encouraging normal childbirth," an interest honored over the centuries.[c] Nor can there be any question that the Connecticut regulation rationally furthers that interest. The medical costs associated with childbirth are substantial, and have increased significantly in recent years. As recognized by the District Court in this

---

c. In addition to the direct interest in protecting the fetus, a State may have legitimate demographic concerns about its rate of population growth. Such concerns are basic to the future of the State and in some circumstances could constitute a substantial reason for departure from a position of neutrality between abortion and childbirth. [Query: Could "demographic concerns" offer a "substantial reason" to criminalize the sale of contraceptives?]

case, such costs are significantly greater than those normally associated with elective abortions during the first trimester. The subsidizing of costs incident to childbirth is a rational means of encouraging childbirth. . . .

BRENNAN, J., joined by Marshall and Blackmun, JJ., dissenting. . . .:

The stark reality for too many, not just "some," indigent pregnant women is that indigency makes access to competent licensed physicians not merely "difficult" but "impossible." As a practical matter, many indigent women will feel they have no choice but to carry their pregnancies to term because the State will pay for the associated medical services, even though they would have chosen to have abortions if the State had also provided funds for that procedure, or indeed if the State had provided funds for neither procedure. This disparity in funding by the State clearly operates to coerce indigent pregnant women to bear children they would not otherwise choose to have, and just as clearly, this coercion can only operate upon the poor, who are uniquely the victims of this form of financial pressure. . . .

[C]ases involving other fundamental rights also make clear that the Court's concept of what constitutes an impermissible infringement upon the fundamental right of a pregnant woman to choose to have an abortion makes new law. We have repeatedly found that infringements of fundamental rights are not limited to outright denials of those rights. First Amendment decisions have consistently held in a wide variety of contexts that the compelling-state-interest test is applicable not only to outright denials but also to restraints that make exercise of those rights more difficult. See, e.g., Sherbert v. Verner (free exercise of religion). . . . Similarly, cases involving the right to travel have consistently held that statutes penalizing the fundamental right to travel must pass muster under the compelling-state-interest test, irrespective of whether the statutes actually deter travel. *Maricopa County*: Dunn v. Blumstein; *Shapiro*. And indigents asserting a fundamental right of access to the courts have been excused payment of entry costs without being required first to show that their indigency was an absolute bar to access. *Griffin*; Douglas v. California; *Boddie*.

. . . The fact that the Connecticut scheme may not operate as an absolute bar preventing all indigent women from having abortions is not critical. What is critical is that the State has inhibited their fundamental right to make that choice free from state interference.

Nor does the manner in which Connecticut has burdened the right freely to choose to have an abortion save its Medicaid program. The Connecticut scheme cannot be distinguished from other grants and withholdings of financial benefits that we have held unconstitutionally burdened a fundamental right. Sherbert v. Verner struck down a South Carolina statute that denied unemployment compensation to a woman who for religious reasons could not work on Saturday, but that would have provided such compensation if her unemployment had stemmed from a number of other nonreligious causes. Even though there was no proof of indigency in that case, *Sherbert* held that "the pressure upon her to forgo [her religious] practice [was] unmistakable," and therefore held that the effect was the same as a fine imposed for Saturday worship. Here, though the burden is upon the right to privacy derived from the Due Process Clause and not upon freedom of religion under the Free Exercise Clause of the First Amendment, the governing principle is the same, for Connecticut grants and withholds financial benefits in a manner that discourages significantly the exercise of a fundamental constitutional right. Indeed, the case for application of the principle actually is stronger than in *Verner* since appellees are all indigents and therefore even more vulnerable to the financial pressures imposed by the Connecticut regulation. . . .

Although appellant does not argue it as justification, the Court concludes that the State's interest "in protecting the potential life of the fetus" suffices.[a] Since only the first trimester of pregnancy is involved in this case, that justification is totally foreclosed if the Court is not overruling the holding of Roe v. Wade that "[w]ith respect to the State's important and legitimate interest in potential life, the 'compelling' point is at viability," occurring at about the end of the second trimester. The appellant also argues a further justification not relied upon by the Court, namely, that the State needs "to control the amount of its limited public funds which will be allocated to its public welfare budget." The District Court correctly held, however, that the asserted interest was "wholly chimerical" because the "state's assertion that it saves money when it declines to pay the cost of a welfare mother's abortion is simply contrary to undisputed facts."

HARRIS v. McRAE, 448 U.S. 297 (1980): [The Court relied on Maher v. Roe to sustain the Hyde Amendment to the Medicaid program established in Title XIX of the Social Security Act. The Medicaid program provides federal financial assistance to states that assist indigents in meeting certain medical costs (including costs incurred in connection with pregnancy). The Hyde Amendment prohibits the use of federal funds "to perform abortions except where the life of the mother would be endangered if the fetus were carried to term; or except for such medical procedures necessary for the victims of rape or incest . . . ," thereby forbidding the funding of abortions necessary to the mother's health in situations where her life is not threatened.]

STEWART, J. . . . :

[T]he Court in *Wade* emphasized the fact that the woman's decision carries with it significant personal health implications — both physical and psychological. . . . Because even the compelling interest of the State in protecting potential life after fetal viability was held to be insufficient to outweigh a woman's decision to protect her life or health, it could be argued that the freedom of a woman to decide whether to terminate her pregnancy for health reasons does in fact lie at the core of the constitutional liberty identified in *Wade*.

But, regardless of whether the freedom of a woman to choose to terminate her pregnancy for health reasons lies at the core or the periphery of the due process liberty recognized in *Wade,* it simply does not follow that a woman's freedom of choice carries with it a constitutional entitlement to the financial resources to avail herself of the full range of protected choices. . . . Although Congress has opted to subsidize medically necessary services generally, but not certain medically necessary abortions, the fact remains that the Hyde Amendment leaves an indigent woman with at least the same range of choice in deciding whether to obtain a medically necessary abortion as she would have had if Congress had chosen to subsidize no health care costs at all. We are thus not persuaded that the Hyde Amendment impinges on the constitutionally protected freedom of choice recognized in *Wade*.

---

a. The Court also suggests that a "State may have legitimate demographic concerns about its rate of population growth" which might justify a choice to favor live births over abortions. While it is conceivable that under some circumstances this might be an appropriate factor to be considered as part of a State's "compelling" interest, no one contends that this is the case here, or indeed that Connecticut has any demographic concerns at all about the rate of its population growth.

. . . Whether freedom of choice that is constitutionally protected warrants federal subsidization is a question for Congress to answer, not a matter of constitutional entitlement. Accordingly, we conclude that the Hyde Amendment does not impinge on the due process liberty recognized in *Wade*. [The Court went on to add that the Hyde Amendment did not violate the establishment clause of the First Amendment.]

Justice Brennan, joined by Justices Marshall and Blackmun, dissented for essentially the reasons given in his dissent in *Maher*. Justice Marshall wrote a separate dissent arguing that this case was distinguishable from *Maher:*

> . . . The result in *Maher* turned on the fact that the legislation there under consideration discouraged only nontherapeutic, or medically unnecessary, abortions. In the Court's view, denial of Medicaid funding for nontherapeutic abortions was not a denial of equal protection because Medicaid funds were available only for medically necessary procedures. Thus the plaintiffs were seeking benefits which were not available to others similarly situated. . . . [Respondents in this case] are protesting their exclusion from a benefit that is available to all others similarly situated. This, it need hardly be said, is a crucial difference for equal protection purposes.

Justice Stevens made a similar point, adding as well that the

> Court focuses exclusively on the "legitimate interest in protecting the potential life of the fetus." It concludes that since the *Hyde* amendments further that interest, the exclusion they create is rational and therefore constitutional. But it is misleading to speak of the Government's legitimate interest in the fetus without reference to the context in which that interest was held to be legitimate. For Roe v. Wade squarely held that the States may not protect that interest when a conflict with the interest in a pregnant woman's health exists.

Discussion

1. Justice Blackmun described the right protected in Roe v. Wade in terms of the pregnant woman's choice between childbirth and abortion — her right to make a "decision whether or not to terminate her pregnancy." Would this right be interfered with in the following situations?

a. If Connecticut did not provide any medical assistance to indigent people?

b. If (leaving aside claims of gender discrimination) Connecticut provided medical assistance to the poor for many purposes but excluded both childbirth and abortion?

c. If the preamble to the Connecticut statute in *Maher* provided: "Whereas it is the public policy of the State to discourage abortions . . ."? How does this hypothetical statute differ constitutionally from the practices described in parts a and b of this question?

2. Assume that Missouri, as part of its efforts to maintain families in times of stress, offers free marriage counseling services to any couple with children that is contemplating divorce. It does not, however, offer "divorce counseling," in which efforts are made to minimize the well-documented stress attached to the process of divorce. Even if one assumes that the right to dissolve a marriage is constitutionally protected, see Boddie v. Connecticut, would there be anything unconstitutional about Missouri's policy and its decision to place public funds behind one vision of life, maintaining intact families, rather than another, aiding unhappy individuals in dissolving their marriages? Cf. *Michael H.*, Chapter 8.

C.   Abortions and Public Hospital Facilities

Maher and *Harris* deal with direct state payment either to a woman or her doctor to subsidize an abortion. The Court has relied on these decisions in dealing with policies prohibiting abortions in public hospitals even when the woman seeks no other state aid and is willing to pay the full cost of the hospital services. Thus, in Poelker v. Doe, 432 U.S. 519 (1977), the Court sustained St. Louis's policy of refusing to permit abortions in public hospitals unless there was a threat of great physiological injury or death. "For the reasons stated in *Maher,* the Constitution does not forbid a State or city, pursuant to democratic processes, from expressing a preference for normal childbirth."

The Court returned to the issue in Webster v. Reproductive Health Services, 492 U.S. 490 (1989), where Missouri law made it "unlawful for any public facility to be used for the purpose of performing or assisting an abortion not necessary to save the life of the mother." Chief Justice Rehnquist wrote:

> Missouri's refusal to allow . . . abortions in public hospitals leaves a pregnant woman with the same choices as if the State had chosen not to operate any public hospitals at all. The challenged provisions only restrict a woman's ability to obtain an abortion to the extent that she chooses to use a physician affiliated with a public hospital. The circumstance is more easily remedied, and thus considerably less burdensome, than indigency. . . . Having held that the State's refusal to fund abortions does not violate Roe v. Wade, it strains logic to reach a contrary result for the use of public facilities and employees. If the State may "make a value judgment favoring childbirth over abortion and . . . implement that judgment by the allocation of public funds," *Maher,* surely it may do so through the allocation of other public resources, such as hospitals and medical staff.
>
> The Court of Appeals sought to distinguish our cases on the additional ground that "[t]he evidence here showed that all of the public facility's costs in providing abortion services are recouped when the patient pays." "Absent any expenditure of publics costs in providing abortion services are recouped when the patient pays." Absent any expenditure of public funds, the court thought that Missouri was "expressing" more than "its preference for childbirth over abortions," but rather was creating an "obstacle to exercise of the right to choose an abortion [that could not] stand absent a compelling state interest." We disagree.
>
> . . . Nothing in the Constitution requires States to enter or remain in the business of performing abortions. Nor, as appellees suggest, do private physicians and their patients have some kind of constitutional right of access to public facilities for the performance of abortions. Indeed, if the State does recoup all of its costs in performing abortions, and no state subsidy, direct or indirect, is available, it is difficult to see how any procreational choice is burdened by the State's ban on the use of its facilities or employees for performing abortions.
>
> *Maher, Poelker,* and *McRae* all support the view that the State need not commit any resources to facilitating abortions, even if it can turn a profit by doing so.

Justice O'Connor, though concurring in this part of Chief Justice Rehnquist's opinion, noted that Missouri broadly defined a "public facility" as "any public institution, public facility, public equipment, or any physical asset owned, leased, or controlled by this state or any agency or political subdivisions thereof." She thought that "there may be conceivable applications of the ban on the use of public facilities that would be unconstitutional. . . . [For example,] the State could try to enforce the ban against private hospitals using public water and sewage lines, or against private hospitals leasing state-owned equipment or state land." Justice O'Connor believed that the issues need not be decided in *Webster*. In his dissent Justice Blackmun similarly emphasized the "sweeping scope" of Missouri's definition of "public facilities," and would have struck down the Missouri law on its face.[44]

Discussion

At the end of the penultimate paragraph quoted above from *Webster*, Chief Justice Rehnquist drops the following footnote: "A different analysis might apply if a particular State had socialized medicine and all of its hospitals and physicians were publicly funded. This case might also be different if the State barred doctors who performed abortions in private facilities from the use of public facilities for any purpose." With respect to the first sentence, why would the state become obligated to provide a service if it legally monopolizes an enterprise, but not if the enterprise is left to the market? Suppose that state monopolization occurs not by force of law — i.e., competitors are prohibited — but as a consequence of market conditions — e.g., the malpractice insurance rate for abortions is prohibitively high? Suppose that all of the private hospitals in a state are operated by the Roman Catholic Church, which has a strong policy against performing abortions, even when the life of the mother is at stake?

Note: Further Reflections on the State's Control over Public Property

One might analyze the abortion-and-public-hospital cases by reference to the prerogatives of ownership. But does the state have the same rights to control "its" property as do owners of private property? The answer is clearly no. Even if the owners of private property can, in the absence of statutory regulation, engage in racial discrimination in granting access to the property, it is clearly the case that the state cannot.

In Commonwealth v. Davis, 162 Mass. 510 (1895), aff'd, 167 U.S. 53 (1897), Justice Holmes, then on the Supreme Judicial Court of Massachusetts, sustained a preacher's conviction for making a public address on the Boston Common without first securing a permit from the mayor. Holmes held that the state had the same control over "its" property that private owners have over theirs: "For the legislature absolutely or conditionally to forbid speaking in a highway or public part is no more of an infringement of the rights of a member of the public than for the owner of a private house to forbid it in his house." In affirming the decision for a unanimous Supreme Court, Justice Edward White rejected the notion of a citizen's right "to use public property in defiance of the constitution and laws of the State. . . . The right to absolutely exclude all right to use, necessarily includes the authority to determine under what circumstances such use may be availed of, as the greater power contains the lesser." Forty-two years later, however, Justice Roberts sent the

---

44. Justice Blackmun noted that "in 1985, 97 percent of all Missouri hospital abortions at 16 weeks or later were performed" at the Truman Medical Center in Kansas City, "a private hospital, staffed by private doctors, and administered by a private corporation[, but] located on ground leased from a political subdivision of the State" and therefore possibly "public" under the Missouri statute.

Court in a decidedly different direction, when he wrote, for a plurality in Hague v. CIO, 307 U.S. 495 (1939):

> Wherever the title of streets and parks may rest, they have immemorially been held in trust for the use of the public and, time out of mind, have been used for purposes of assembly, communicating thoughts between citizens, and discussing public questions. Such use of the streets and public places has, from ancient times, been a part of the privileges, immunities, rights and liberties of citizens.

Hague held that access to such public property could be subject to reasonable regulation, "but it must not, in the guise of regulation, be abridged or denied." Subsequent case law over many years, see, e.g., Schneider v. State, 308 U.S. 1147 (1939); Grayned v. City of Rockford, 408 U.S. 104 (1972); and Lamb's Chapel v. Center Moriches Union Free School District, 508 U.S. 384 (1993), may be broadly summarized as standing for the following proposition: The state holds public property in trust for the public at large, and any limitation of access to it must be shown to serve the public interest. That is, the state cannot claim the (relatively) plenary discretion of a private owner to control access to her property on whatever basis she chooses, even one that would strike most observers as "unreasonable." This has the consequence of requiring the state, in effect, to subsidize some of the costs of free expression. For example, *Schneider* involved a prohibition on public handbilling because of the ostensible costs involved in picking up the inevitable litter. That cost was held irrelevant, as was the fact that the leaflets could presumably have been handed out at other places. Similarly, local governments must incur expenses to provide police protection for groups using the public streets or parks for political expression.[45]

Lamb's Chapel involved a less "public" venue than a street or a park; it concerned a New York school board's refusal of permission to Lamb's Chapel, an evangelical church in the community of Center Moriches, to use public school facilities, otherwise available, after school, to the public for certain uses, to "show a six-part film series containing lectures" on the family and arguing the necessity of "returning to traditional Christian family values instilled at an early stage." The board was applying a rule prohibiting use of public school property for "religious purposes." The Court ruled unconstitutional the Board's action because it violated the principle "that the First Amendment forbids the government to regulate speech in ways that favor some viewpoints or ideas at the expense of others."

Similarly, in Arkansas Educational Television Commission v. Forbes, 523 U.S. 666 (1998), the Court held that the First Amendment constrained "a state-owned public television broadcaster [that] sponsored a candidate debate from which it excluded an independent candidate with little popular support." As it happened, the Court held that the criteria by which the candidate was excluded were reasonable, which

---

45. After *DeShaney*, could the state simply refuse to provide special protection even where violence might be anticipated? Could the state, in any event, require demonstrators to post bonds adequate to cover any costs beyond those "normally budgeted" (whatever this might mean) for police services? See, e.g., Collin v. Smith, 447 F. Supp. 676, 578 F.2d. 1197 (7th Cir. 1978), which involved the attempted prohibition by Skokie, Illinois, of a planned march by Nazis. The town required, among other things, that the demonstrators obtain $3 million in public liability insurance and $50,000 in property damage insurance. The Court of Appeals struck down the insurance requirement as applied, saying that "we do not need to determine now that no insurance requirement could be imposed in any circumstances, which would be a close question."

provoked dissent, but the central point is that the managers of the state-operated station were viewed as possessing less independence than, say, the editors of privately owned newspaper or television stations.

Return now to the cases involving abortions in public hospitals. Recall that *Webster* said that "the State need not commit any resources to facilitating abortions, even if it can turn a profit by doing so. . . . Nothing in the Constitution requires States to enter or remain in the business of performing abortions. Nor, as appellees suggest, do private physicians and their patients have some kind of constitutional right of access to public facilities for the performance of abortions." Can you square this assertion with the free-speech cases discussed above? As long as Roe v. Wade remains the law, isn't a woman's constitutional right to choose to have an abortion as "fundamental" as that of freedom of speech? (If not, what procedure or criteria do you use for ranking constitutional rights?) If, after *Schneider*, the state cannot prohibit handbilling on public sidewalks just because one could distribute hand-bills in other public or private places, or the Center Moriches school board can't take refuge in the argument that Lamb's Chapel could always rent a privately owned auditorium, why can Missouri prohibit abortions in public hospitals just because they remain available in private hospitals?

The First Amendment cases indicate that access to public property may be limited where the intended use would be inappropriate. In view of the uses to which the property has been dedicated, can one plausibly assert that a hospital is not an appropriate place in which to perform an abortion? What governmental interest other than animosity regarding the exercise of the woman's constitution-ally protected right to an abortion can justify the Missouri ordinance, which applies even if the woman is willing to pay the full costs incurred by the state?

Michael McConnell addresses this issue in The Selective Funding Problem: Abortions and Religious Schools, 104 Harv. L. Rev. 989, 1031-1033 (1991). He notes both that "[t]here are at least a dozen cases in the Supreme Court alone upholding the right of religious groups and speakers to carry on their activities on public prop-erty on terms equal to those imposed on other groups" and that "the Court has reached the opposite conclusion" with regard to access and abortion. "It is," he says, "difficult to see how the Court could reach such a conclusion in the face of cases . . . which prohibit direct funding of religion but require equal access to public facilities."

> Providing access to public property is different from direct funding, for precisely the reason that differentiates penalties from mere refusals to subsidize. A religious group or an abortionist who uses public property for purposes compatible with its ordinary use does not impose any additional costs on the public. In *Webster*, for example, the evidence showed that the patient paid "all of the public facility's costs in providing [the] abortion."
>
> However, if the public property had been off limits, the patient's cost would have exceeded the cost of the abortion itself (because of the need to travel and related complications, which could far exceed the cost of the abortion alone). Therefore, under the analysis [offered earlier in the article, which defends the refusal-to-fund cases], a ban from access to public facilities is unconstitutional because it is more than a mere refusal to fund.
>
> Moreover, it is not true, as the Court assumed in *Webster*, that the refusal to allow abortions in public facilities "leaves a pregnant woman with the same choices as if the State had chosen not to operate any public hospitals at all." If the state had so chosen,

there would be more private hospitals at which abortions might be more readily available. By the same token, if the state had chosen not to operate any public schools, there would surely be more private schools, including more religious schools. In the extreme case, if all hospitals were public, the ban on abortions in public facilities would be equivalent to a ban of all abortions that must be performed in a hospital. The *Webster* Court conceded that "[a] different analysis might apply if a particular State had socialized medicine and all of its hospitals and physicians were publicly funded," but it failed to recognize that partially socialized medicine has a similar, if less extreme, effect.

D. Freedom of Speech in the Welfare State

1. Can Congress Condition Tax Deductibility on Foregoing the Constitutional Right to Lobby?

REGAN v. TAXATION WITH REPRESENTATION OF WASHINGTON
461 U.S. 540 (1983)

REHNQUIST, J.

Appellee Taxation With Representation of Washington (TWR) is a nonprofit corporation organized to promote what it conceives to be the "public interest" in the area of federal taxation. It proposes to advocate its point of view before Congress, the Executive Branch, and the Judiciary. This case began when TWR applied for tax-exempt status under §501(c)(3) of the Internal Revenue Code. The Internal Revenue Service denied the application because it appeared that a substantial part of TWR's activities would consist of attempting to influence legislation, which is not permitted by §501(c)(3)....

TWR was formed to take over the operations of two other nonprofit corporations. One . . . was organized to promote TWR's goals by publishing a journal and engaging in litigation; it had tax-exempt status under §501(c)(3). The other . . . attempted to promote the same goals by influencing legislation; it had tax-exempt status under §501(c)(4). Neither predecessor organization was required to pay federal income taxes. For purposes of our analysis, there are two principal differences between §501(c)(3) organizations and §501(c)(4) organizations. Taxpayers who contribute to [the former] are permitted . . . to deduct the amount of their contributions on their federal income tax returns, while contributions to [the latter] are not deductible....

In these cases, TWR is attacking the prohibition against substantial lobbying in §501(c)(3) because it wants to use tax-deductible contributions to support substantial lobbying activities. To evaluate TWR's claims, it is necessary to understand the effect of the tax-exemption system enacted by Congress.

Both tax exemptions and tax deductibility are a form of subsidy that is administered through the tax system. A tax exemption has much the same effect as a cash grant to the organization of the amount of tax it would have to pay on its income. Deductible contributions are similar to cash grants of the amount of a portion of the individual's contributions. The system Congress has enacted provides this kind of subsidy to nonprofit civic welfare organizations that do not engage in substantial lobbying. In short, Congress chose not to subsidize lobbying as extensively as it chose to subsidize other activities. . . .

TWR contends that Congress' decision not to subsidize its lobbying . . . imposes an "unconstitutional condition" on the receipt of tax-deductible contributions. [TWR relied on Speiser v. Randall, 357 U.S. 513 (1958), in which] California established a rule requiring anyone who sought to take advantage of a property tax exemption to sign a declaration stating that he did not advocate the forcible overthrow of the Government of the United States. This Court stated that "[t]o deny an exemption to claimants who engage in certain forms of speech is in effect to penalize them for such speech [and thus violates the First Amendment]."

TWR is certainly correct when it states that we have held that the government may not deny a benefit to a person because he exercises a constitutional right. See Perry v. Sindermann. But TWR is just as certainly incorrect when it claims that this case fits the *Speiser-Perry* model. The Code does not deny TWR the right to receive tax deductible contributions to support its non-lobbying activity, nor does it deny TWR any independent benefit on account of its intention to lobby. Congress has merely refused to pay for the lobbying out of public moneys. This Court has never held that Congress must grant a benefit such as TWR claims here to a person who wishes to exercise a constitutional right.

This aspect of these cases is controlled by Cammarano v. United States, 358 U.S. 498 (1959), in which we upheld a Treasury Regulation that denied business expense deductions for lobbying activities. . . .

TWR also contends that the equal protection component of the Fifth Amendment renders the prohibition against substantial lobbying invalid. [The Internal Revenue Code] permits taxpayers to deduct contributions to veterans' organizations[, which are permitted by the Code] to lobby as much as they want in furtherance of their exempt purposes. TWR argues that because Congress has chosen to subsidize the substantial lobbying activities of veterans' organizations, it must also subsidize the lobbying of §501(c)(3) organizations. . . .

Legislatures have especially broad latitude in creating classifications and distinctions in tax statutes. . . .

The case would be different if Congress were to discriminate invidiously in its subsidies in such a way as to "ai[m] at the suppression of dangerous ideas." *Speiser,* 357 U.S. at 519. But the veterans' organizations . . . are entitled to receive tax-deductible contributions regardless of the content of any speech they may use, including lobbying. We find no indication that the statute was intended to suppress any ideas or any demonstration that it has had that effect. . . .

We have held in several contexts that a legislature's decision not to subsidize the exercise of a fundamental right does not infringe the right, and thus is not subject to strict scrutiny. . . .

It is not irrational for Congress to decide that tax-exempt charities such as TWR should not further benefit at the expense of taxpayers at large by obtaining a further subsidy for lobbying.

It is also not irrational for Congress to decide that, even though it will not subsidize substantial lobbying by charities generally, it will subsidize lobbying by veterans' organizations. . . . Our country has a longstanding policy of compensating veterans for their past contributions by providing them with numerous advantages. This policy has "always been deemed to be legitimate." . . .

[Justice Blackmun, joined by Justices Brennan and Marshall, concurred in the opinion, but wrote separately to emphasize TWR's ability to return to its old organizational structure and thus gain the advantage of §501(c)(3) for its nonlobbying component. "A §501(c)(3) organization's right to speak is not infringed, because it is free to make known its views on legislation through its §501(c)(4) affiliate without losing tax benefits for its nonlobbying activities." Without this possibility, Justice Blackmun would regard the prohibition imposed on §501(c)(3) organizations as raising a significant constitutional question.]

Discussion

Justice Rehnquist suggests that any subsidy of veterans' speech is content-neutral inasmuch as it suppresses no ideas or, presumably, encourages any particular ideas. What if empirical evidence demonstrates that most (though certainly not all) lobbying by veterans' groups involves pleading for ever greater (redistributive) welfare benefits from non-veterans to veterans, whereas those who oppose such expenditures, or simply treat other groups, such as uninsured children, as more worthy, are discouraged from engaging in direct lobbying by the taxation rules?

2.   *Can Congress Impose Restrictions on What Can Be Said by Radio Stations Accepting Federal Subsidies?*

FCC v. LEAGUE OF WOMEN VOTERS OF CALIFORNIA
468 U.S. 364 (1984)

[The Public Broadcasting Act of 1967 establishing the Corporation for Public Broadcasting included a section that, as amended in 1981, forbids any "noncommercial educational broadcasting station which receives a grant from the Corporation" to "engage in editorializing." 47 U.S.C. §399. The Pacifica Foundation, the principal appellee, operates several noncommercial educational stations in five major metropolitan areas and receives federal grants from the Corporation. The Foundation challenged §399 in 1979 as a limitation on its First Amendment rights and sought a declaratory judgment that it was unconstitutional.[a]

The District Court granted summary judgment in favor of Pacifica, finding that the ban on editorializing violated the First Amendment. The United States appealed directly to the Supreme Court, which, through Justice Brennan, affirmed. "Were a similar ban on editorializing applied to newspapers and magazines, we would not hesitate to strike it down as violative of the First Amendment." However,

---

a. The Department of Justice informed both Houses of the Congress that it had decided not to defend the constitutionality of the statute. Attorney General Civiletti stated that the "Department of Justice is, of course, fully mindful of its duty to support the laws enacted by Congress. Here, however, the Department has determined, after careful study and deliberation, that reasonable arguments cannot be advanced to defend the challenged statute." The suit was dismissed on the grounds that there was no justiciable controversy because the Government had decided not to enforce the statute.

Pacifica appealed; while the appeal was pending in the Ninth Circuit, the Justice Department, under the leadership of a new Attorney General appointed by Ronald Reagan, announced that it would defend the statute, and the case was remanded to the District Court. Moreover, Congress amended §399 by adding a section prohibiting all noncommercial stations from making political endorsements, regardless of whether they received federal funds. The plaintiffs, however, ultimately chose to challenge only the ban on editorializing and dropped an attack on the prohibition of political endorsements.

the case involved the electronic media, where, because of the scarcity of the spectrum, the Court has "never gone so far as to demand that . . . regulations serve 'compelling' governmental interests." As a result, "the broadcasting industry plainly operates under restraints not imposed upon other media." Such restraints are legitimate, though, only if the Court is "satisfied that the restriction is narrowly tailored to further a substantial governmental interest, such as ensuring adequate and balanced coverage of public issues."][46]

BRENNAN, J.

III.

A

First, the restriction imposed by §399 is specifically directed at a form of speech — namely, the expression of editorial opinion — that lies at the heart of First Amendment protection. . . .

Second, the scope of §399's ban is defined solely on the basis of the content of the suppressed speech. . . . Section 399 . . . singles out noncommercial broadcasters and denies them the right to address their chosen audience on matters of public importance. Thus, in enacting §399 Congress appears to have sought . . . to limit discussion of controversial topics and thus to shape the agenda for public debate. . . .

B

. . . [T]he Government urges that the statute was aimed at preventing two principal threats to the overall success of the Public Broadcasting Act of 1967. According to the argument, the ban was necessary, first, to protect noncommercial educational broadcasting stations from being coerced, as result of federal financing, into becoming vehicles for governmental propagandizing or the objects of governmental influence; and second, to keep these stations from becoming convenient targets for capture by private interest groups wishing to express their own partisan viewpoints. By seeking to safeguard the public's right to a balanced presentation of public issues through the prevention of either governmental or private bias, these objectives are, of course, broadly consistent with the goals identified in our earlier broadcast regulation cases[, where the Court had upheld the power of the Federal Communications Commission to impose certain "fairness" standards on electronic media]. But, in sharp contrast to the restrictions upheld in [those cases,] which left room for editorial discretion and simply required broadcast edition to grant others access to the microphone, §399 directly prohibits the broadcaster from speaking out on public issues even in a balanced and fair manner. The Government insists, however, that the hazards posed in the "special" circumstances of noncommercial educational broadcasting are so great that §399 is an indispensable means of preserving the public's First Amendment interests. We disagree.

---

46. This distinction between print and electronic media is extremely controversial, though space constraints prohibit us from going into the debate in this casebook. See, e.g., Lucas Powe, American Broadcasting and the First Amendment (1987); Thomas Krattenmaker and Lucas Powe, Regulating Broadcast Programming (1994).

... [A]n examination of both the overall legislative scheme established by the 1967 Act and the character of public broadcasting demonstrates that the interest asserted by the Government is not substantially advanced by §399. First, to the extent that federal financial support creates a risk that stations will lose their independence through the bewitching power of governmental largesse, the elaborate structure established by the Public Broadcasting Act already operates to insulate local stations from governmental interference. . . .

Even if these statutory protections were thought insufficient to the task, however, suppressing the particular category of speech restricted by §399 is simply not likely, given the character of the public broadcasting system, to reduce substantially the risk that the Federal Government will seek to influence or put pressure on local stations. . . . [W]hat is far more likely than local station editorials to pose the kinds of dangers hypothesized by the Government are the wide variety of programs addressing controversial issues produced, often with substantial CPB funding, for national distribution to local stations. Such programs truly have the potential to reach a large audience and, because of the critical commentary they contain, to have the kind of genuine national impact that might trigger a congressional response or kindle governmental resentment. The ban imposed by §399, however, is plainly not directed at the potentially controversial content of such programs; it is, instead, leveled solely at the expression of editorial opinion by local station management, a form of expression that is far more likely to be aimed at a smaller local audience, to have less national impact, and to be confined to local issues. . . .

Furthermore, the manifest imprecision of the ban imposed by §399 reveals that its proscription is not sufficiently tailored to the harm it seeks to prevent to justify its substantial interference with broadcasters' speech. . . . Indeed, the breadth of editorial commentary is as wide as human imagination permits. But the Government never explains how, say, an editorial by local station management urging improvements in a town's parks or museums will so infuriate Congress or other Federal officials that the future of public broadcasting will be imperiled unless such editorials are suppressed. . . .

The Government appears to recognize these flaws in §399, because it focuses instead on the suggestion that the source of governmental influence may well be state and local governments, many of which have established public broadcasting commissions that own and operate local noncommercial educational stations. . . . The Government's argument, however, proves too much. First, §399's ban applies to the many private noncommercial community organizations that own and operate stations that are not in any way controlled by state or local government. Second, the legislative history of the Public Broadcasting Act clearly indicates that Congress was concerned with "assur[ing] complete freedom from any Federal Government influence." Consistently with the concern, Congress refused to create any federally owned stations and it expressly forbid the CPB to own or operate any television or radio stations. By contrast, although Congress was clearly aware in 1967 that many noncommercial educational stations were owned by state and local governments, it did not hesitate to extend Federal assistance to such stations, it imposed no special requirements to restrict state or local control over these stations, and, indeed, it ensured through the structure of the Act that these stations would be as insulated from Federal interference as the wholly private stations.

Finally, although the Government certainly has a substantial interest in ensuring that the audiences of noncommercial stations will not be led to think that the broadcaster's editorials reflect the official view of the government, this interest can be fully satisfied by less restrictive means that are readily available[, including the requirement that stations] broadcast a disclaimer every time they editorialize which would state that the editorial represents only the view of the station's management and does not in any way represent the views of the Federal Government or any of the station's other sources of funding. . . .

2

Assuming that the Government's second asserted interest in preventing noncommercial stations from becoming a "privileged outlet for the political and ideological opinions of station owners and management" is legitimate, the substantiality of this asserted interest is dubious. . . .

IV.

[The Government also tried] to justify §399 on the basis of Congress' Spending Power. [T]he Government argues that by prohibiting noncommercial educational stations that receive CPB grants from editorializing, Congress has, in the proper exercise of its Spending Power, simply determined that it "will not subsidize public broadcasting station editorials." In *Taxation with Representation*, the Court found that Congress could, in the exercise of its Spending Power, reasonably refuse to subsidize the lobbying activities of tax-exempt charitable organizations by prohibiting such organizations from using tax-deductible contributions to support their lobbying efforts. In so holding, however, we explained that such organizations remained free "to receive tax-deductible contributions to support non-lobbying activit[ies]." . . .

In this case, however . . . , a noncommercial educational station that receives only 1 percent of its overall income from CPB grants is barred absolutely from all editorializing. . . . The station has no way of limiting the use of its Federal funds to all non-editorializing activities, and, more importantly, it is barred from using even wholly private funds to finance its editorial activity. . . .

REHNQUIST, J., joined by Chief Justice Burger and Justice White, dissenting. . . .:

Pacifica, well aware of §399's condition on its receipt of public money, nonetheless accepted the public money and now seeks to avoid the conditions which Congress legitimately has attached to receipt of that funding. . . .

The Court's . . . discussion of why §399, repeatedly reexamined and retained by Congress, violates the First Amendment is to me utterly unpersuasive. Congress has rationally determined that the bulk of the taxpayers whose monies provide the funds for grants by the CPB would prefer not to see the management of local educational stations promulgate its own private views on the air at taxpayers' expense. Accordingly Congress simply has decided not to subsidize stations which engage in that activity. . . .

This is not to say that the government may attach any condition to its largess; it is only to say that when the government is simply exercising its power to allocate its own public funds, we need only find that the condition imposed has a rational relationship to Congress' purpose in providing the subsidy and that it is not primarily "aimed at the suppression of dangerous ideas." In this case Congress' prohibition is directly related to its purpose in providing subsidies for public broadcasting, and it is plainly rational for Congress to have determined that taxpayer monies should not be used to subsidize management's views or to pay for management's exercise of partisan politics. Indeed, it is entirely rational for Congress to have wished to avoid the appearance of government sponsorship of a particular view or a particular political candidate. Furthermore, Congress' prohibition is strictly neutral. In no sense can it be said that Congress has prohibited only editorial views of one particular ideological bent. Nor has it prevented public stations from airing programs, documentaries, interviews, etc. dealing with controversial subjects, so long as management itself does not expressly endorse a particular viewpoint. And Congress has not prevented station management from communicating its own views on those subjects through any medium other than subsidized public broadcasting. . . .

WHITE, J.:

Believing that the editorializing and candidate endorsement proscription stand or fall together and being confident that Congress may condition use of its funds on abstaining from political endorsements, I join Justice Rehnquist's dissenting opinion.[47]

3.   Can the State Prohibit Disclosing Information About Abortion as a Condition of Accepting Governmental Funding?

RUST v. SULLIVAN
500 U.S. 173 (1991)

REHNQUIST, C.J.

These cases concern a facial challenge to Department of Health and Human Services (HHS) regulations which limit the ability of Title X fund recipients to engage in abortion-related activities. . . .

I.

A

In 1970, Congress enacted Title X of the Public Health Service Act (Act), which provides federal funding for family planning services. The Act authorizes the Secretary to "make grants to and enter into contracts with public or nonprofit private entities to assist in the establishment and operation of voluntary family planning projects which shall offer a broad range of acceptable and effective family planning methods and services." Grants and contracts under Title X must "be made in accordance with such regulations as the Secretary may promulgate." [A section] of the Act, however, provides that "[n]one of the funds appropriated under this subchapter shall be used in programs where abortion is a method of family planning.". . .

---

47. A dissenting opinion by Justice Stevens is omitted.

In 1988, the Secretary promulgated new regulations designed to provide " 'clear and operational guidance' to grantees about how to preserve the distinction between Title X programs and abortion as a method of family planning." 53 Fed. Reg. 2923-2924 (1988). The regulations clarify, through the definition of the term "family planning," that Congress intended Title X funds "to be used only to support preventive family planning services." Accordingly, Title X services are limited to "preconceptual counseling, education, and general reproductive health care," and expressly exclude "pregnancy care (including obstetric or prenatal care)." . . .

The regulations attach three principal conditions on the grant of federal funds for Title X projects. First, the regulations specify that a "Title X project may not provide counseling concerning the use of abortion as a method of family planning or provide referral for abortion as a method of family planning." Because Title X is limited to preconceptional services, the program does not furnish services related to childbirth. Only in the context of a referral out of the Title X program is a pregnant woman given transitional information. Title X projects must refer every pregnant client "for appropriate prenatal and/or social services by furnishing a list of available providers that promote the welfare of the mother and the unborn child." The list may not be used indirectly to encourage or promote abortion, "such as by weighing the list of referrals in favor of health care providers which perform abortions, by including on the list of referral providers health care providers whose principal business is the provision of abortions, by excluding available providers who do not provide abortions, or by 'steering' clients to providers who offer abortion as a method of family planning." The Title X project is expressly prohibited from referring a pregnant woman to an abortion provider, even upon specific request. One permissible response to such an inquiry is that "the project does not consider abortion an appropriate method of family planning and therefore does not counsel or refer for abortion." §59.8(b)(5).

Second, the regulations broadly prohibit a Title X project from engaging in activities that "encourage, promote or advocate abortion as a method of family planning." Forbidden activities include lobbying for legislation that would increase the availability of abortion as a method of family planning, developing or disseminating materials advocating abortion as a method of family planning, providing speakers to promote abortion as a method of family planning, using legal action to make abortion available in any way as a method of family planning, and paying dues to any group that advocates abortion as a method of family planning as a substantial part of its activities.

Third, the regulations require that Title X projects be organized so that they are "physically and financially separate" from prohibited abortion activities. To be deemed physically and financially separate, "a Title X project must have an objective integrity and independence from prohibited activities. Mere bookkeeping separation of Title X funds from other monies is not sufficient." . . .

B

Petitioners are Title X grantees and doctors who supervise Title X funds. . . . Petitioners challenged the regulations on the grounds that they were not authorized by Title X and that they violate the First and Fifth Amendment rights of Title X clients and the First Amendment rights of Title X health providers. . . .

II.

... [The Court first found the regulations to be authorized by the congressional statute.]

III.

Petitioners contend that the regulations violate the First Amendment by impermissibly discriminating based on viewpoint because they prohibit "all discussion about abortion as a lawful option — including counseling, referral, and the provision of neutral and accurate information about ending a pregnancy — while compelling the clinic or counselor to provide information that promotes continuing a pregnancy to term." They assert that the regulations violate the "free speech rights of private health care organizations that receive Title X funds, of their staff, and of their patients" by impermissibly imposing "viewpoint-discriminatory conditions on government subsidies" and thus penaliz[e] speech funded with non-Title X monies." . . . Relying on Regan v. Taxation With Representation of Wash., and Arkansas Writers Project, Inc. v. Ragland, 481 U.S. 221, 234 (1987), petitioners also assert that while the Government may place certain conditions on the receipt of federal subsidies, it may not "discriminate invidiously in its subsidies in such a way as to 'ai[m]' at the suppression of dangerous ideas.'"

There is no question but that the statutory prohibition . . . is constitutional. . . . The Government can, without violating the Constitution, selectively fund a program to encourage certain activities it believes to be in the public interest, without at the same time funding an alternate program which seeks to deal with the problem in another way. . . .

The challenged regulations . . . are designed to ensure that the limits of the federal program are observed. The Title X program is designed not for prenatal care, but to encourage family planning. A doctor who wished to offer prenatal care to a project patient who became pregnant could properly be prohibited from doing so because such service is outside the scope of the federally funded program. The regulations prohibiting abortion counseling and referral are of the same ilk. . . . This is not a case of the Government "suppressing a dangerous idea," but of a prohibition on a project grantee or its employees from engaging in activities outside of its scope.

To hold that the Government unconstitutionally discriminates on the basis of viewpoint when it chooses to fund a program dedicated to advance certain permissible goals, because the program in advancing those goals necessarily discourages alternate goals, would render numerous government programs constitutionally suspect. When Congress established a National Endowment for Democracy to encourage other countries to adopt democratic principles, it was not constitutionally required to fund a program to encourage competing lines of political philosophy such as Communism and Fascism. Petitioners' assertions ultimately boil down to the position that if the government chooses to subsidize one protected right, it must subsidize analogous counterpart rights. But the Court has soundly rejected that proposition. . . .

Petitioners rely heavily on their claim that the regulations would not, in the circumstance of a medical emergency, permit a Title X project to refer a woman whose pregnancy places her life in imminent peril to a provider of abortions or abortion-related services. This case, of course, involves only a facial challenge to the regulations, and we do not have before us any application by the Secretary to a specific fact situation. On their face, we do not read the regulations to bar abortion referral or counseling in such circumstances. Abortion counseling as a "method of family planning" is prohibited, and it does not seem that a medically necessitated abortion in such circumstances would be the equivalent of its use as a "method of family planning." . . . Moreover, the regulations themselves contemplate that a Title X project would be permitted to engage in otherwise prohibited abortion-related activity in such circumstances. . . . Section 59.8(a)(2) provides a specific exemption for emergency care and requires Title X recipients "to refer the client immediately to an appropriate provider of emergency medical services." Section 59.5(b)(1) also requires Title X projects to provide "necessary referral to other medical facilities when medically indicated."

Petitioners also contend that the restrictions on the subsidization of abortion-related speech contained in the regulations are impermissible because they condition the receipt of a benefit, in this case Title X funding, on the relinquishment of a constitutional right, the right to engage in abortion advocacy and counseling. . . . Relying on Perry v. Sindermann, and FCC v. League of Women Voters of Cal., petitioners argue that "even though the government may deny [a] . . . benefit for any number of reasons, there are some reasons upon which the government may not rely. It may not deny a benefit to a person on a basis that infringes his constitutionally protected interests — especially, his interest in freedom of speech."

Petitioners' reliance on these cases is unavailing, however, because here the government is not denying a benefit to anyone, but is instead simply insisting that public funds be spent for the purposes for which they were authorized. The Secretary's regulations do not force the Title X grantee to give up abortion-related speech; they merely require that the grantee keep such activities separate and distinct from Title X activities. Title X expressly distinguishes between a Title X grantee and a Title X project. The grantee, which normally is a health care organization, may receive funds from a variety of sources for a variety of purposes. The grantee receives Title X funds, however, for the specific and limited purpose of establishing and operating a Title X project. The regulations govern the scope of the Title X project's activities, and leave the grantee unfettered in its other activities. The Title X grantee can continue to perform abortions, provide abortion-related services, and engage in abortion advocacy; it simply is required to conduct those activities through programs that are separate and independent from the project that receives Title X funds.

In contrast, our "unconstitutional conditions" cases involve situations in which the government has placed a condition on the recipient of the subsidy rather than on a particular program or service, thus effectively prohibiting the recipient from engaging in the protected conduct outside the scope of the federally funded program. In *League of Women Voters,* we invalidated a federal law providing that noncommercial television and radio stations that receive federal grants may not "engage in editorializing." Under that law, a recipient of federal funds was "barred absolutely from all editorializing" because it "is not able to segregate its activities according to the source of its funding" and thus "has no way of limiting the use of its federal funds to all noneditorializing activities." The effect of the law was that "a noncommercial educational station that receives only 1% of its overall income from [federal] grants is barred absolutely from all editorializing" and "barred from using even wholly private funds to finance its editorial activity." . . .

Similarly, in *Regan* we held that Congress could, in the exercise of its spending power, reasonably refuse to subsidize the lobbying activities of tax-exempt charitable organizations by prohibiting such organizations from using tax-deductible contributions to support their lobbying efforts. In so holding, we explained that such organizations remained free "to receive deductible contributions to support . . . nonlobbying activit[ies]." . . .

By requiring that the Title X grantee [and their employees] engage in abortion-related activity separately from activity receiving federal funding, Congress has . . . not denied [them] the right to engage in abortion-related activities. Congress has merely refused to fund such activities out of the public fisc, and the Secretary has simply required a certain degree of separation from the Title X project in order to ensure the integrity of the federally funded program. . . .

This is not to suggest that funding by the Government, even when coupled with the freedom of the fund recipients to speak outside the scope of the Government-funded project, is invariably sufficient to justify government control over the content of expression. For example, this Court has recognized that the existence of a Government "subsidy," in the form of Government-owned property, does not justify the restriction of speech in areas that have "been traditionally open to the public for expressive activity," or have been "expressly dedicated to speech activity." Similarly, we have recognized that the university is a traditional sphere of free expression so fundamental to the functioning of our society that the Government's ability to control speech within that sphere by means of conditions attached to the expenditure of Government funds is restricted by the vagueness and overbreadth doctrines of the First Amendment.

It could be argued by analogy that traditional relationships such as that between doctor and patient should enjoy protection under the First Amendment from government regulation, even when subsidized by the Government. We need not resolve that question here, however, because the Title X program regulations do not significantly impinge upon the doctor-patient relationship. Nothing in them requires a doctor to represent as his own any opinion that he does not in fact hold. Nor is the doctor-patient relationship established by the Title X program sufficiently all-encompassing so as to justify an expectation on the part of the patient of comprehensive medical advice. The program does not provide postconception medical care, and therefore a doctor's silence with regard to abortion cannot reasonably be thought to mislead a client into thinking that the doctor does not consider abortion an appropriate option for her. The doctor is always free to make clear that advice regarding abortion is simply beyond the scope of the program. In these circumstances, the general rule that the Government may choose not to subsidize speech applies with full force.

IV.

[The Court also rejects] petitioners' argument that the regulations violate a woman's Fifth Amendment right to choose whether to terminate her pregnancy. . . .

The difficulty that a woman encounters when a Title X project does not provide abortion counseling or referral leaves her in no different position than she would have been if the government had not enacted Title X. . . .

In [earlier cases,] we invalidated a city ordinance requiring all physicians to make specified statements to the patient prior to performing an abortion in order to ensure that the woman's consent was "truly informed." Similarly, . . . we struck down a state statute mandating that a list of agencies offering alternatives to abortion and a description of fetal development be provided to every woman considering terminating her pregnancy through an abortion. Critical to our decisions . . . was the fact that the laws in both cases required all doctors within their respective jurisdictions to provide all pregnant patients contemplating an abortion a litany of information, regardless of whether the patient sought the information or whether the doctor thought the information necessary to the patient's decision. Under the Secretary's regulations, however, a doctor's ability to provide, and a woman's right to receive, information concerning abortion and abortion-related services outside the context of the Title X project remains unfettered. It would undoubtedly be easier for a woman seeking an abortion if she could receive information about abortion from a Title X project, but the Constitution does not require that the Government distort the scope of its mandated program in order to provide that information.

Petitioners contend, however, that most Title X clients are effectively precluded by indigency and poverty from seeing a health care provider who will provide abortion-related services. But once again, even these Title X clients are in no worse position than if Congress had never enacted Title X. . . .

BLACKMUN, J., with whom Justice Marshall joins, with whom Justice Stevens joins as to Parts II and III, and with whom Justice O'Connor joins as to Part I, dissenting. . . .:

[The first section of the opinion argues that the underlying legislation did not authorize the regulation in question, especially if one adheres to the principle of statutory construction that "[f]ederal statutes are to be so construed as to avoid serious doubt of their constitutionality." Machinists v. Street, 367 U.S. 740, 749 (1961). . . .]

II.

I also strongly disagree with the majority's disposition of petitioners' constitutional claims. . . .

A

. . . It cannot seriously be disputed that the counseling and referral provisions at issue in the present cases constitute content-based regulation of speech. Title X grantees may provide counseling and referral regarding any of a wide range of family planning and other topics, save abortion. . . .

The Regulations are also clearly viewpoint-based. While suppressing speech favorable to abortion with one hand, the Secretary compels anti-abortion speech with the other. For example, the Department of Health and Human Services' own description of the Regulations makes plain that "Title X projects are required to facilitate access to prenatal care and social services, including adoption services, that might be needed by the pregnant client to promote her well-being and that of her child, while making it abundantly clear that the project is not permitted to promote abortion by facilitating access to abortion through the referral process."

Moreover, the Regulations command that a project refer for prenatal care each woman diagnosed as pregnant, irrespective of the woman's expressed desire to continue or terminate her pregnancy. If a client asks directly about abortion, a Title X physician or counselor is required to say, in essence, that the project does not consider abortion to be an appropriate method of family planning. §59.8(b)(4). Both requirements are antithetical to the First Amendment.

The Regulations pertaining to "advocacy" are even more explicitly viewpoint-based. These provide: "A Title X project may not encourage, promote or advocate abortion as a method of family planning." . . . The Regulations do not, however, proscribe or even regulate anti-abortion advocacy. These are clearly restrictions aimed at the suppression of "dangerous ideas." Remarkably, the majority concludes that "the Government has not discriminated on the basis of viewpoint; it has merely chosen to fund one activity to the exclusion of another." But the majority's claim that the Regulations merely limit a Title X project's speech to preventive or precon-ceptional services rings hollow in light of the broad range of non-preventive serv-ices that the Regulations authorize Title X projects to provide.[a] By refusing to fund those family-planning projects that advocate abortion because they advocate abor-tion, the Government plainly has targeted a particular viewpoint. . . .

[I]n addition to their impermissible focus upon the viewpoint of regulated speech, the provisions intrude upon a wide range of communicative conduct, including the very words spoken to a woman by her physician. By manipulating the content of the doctor/patient dialogue, the Regulations upheld today force each of the petitioners "to be an instrument for fostering public adherence to an ideo-logical point of view [he or she] finds unacceptable." This type of intrusive, ideo-logically based regulation of speech . . . cannot be justified simply because it is a condition upon the receipt of a governmental benefit.[b]

B

The Court concludes that the challenged Regulations do not violate the First Amendment rights of Title X staff members because any limitation of the employ-ees' freedom of expression is simply a consequence of their decision to accept employment at a federally funded project. But it has never been sufficient to justify an otherwise unconstitutional condition upon public employment that the employee may escape the condition by relinquishing his or her job. . . .

a. In addition to requiring referral for prenatal care and adoption services, the Regulations permit general health services such as physical examinations, screening for breast cancer, treatment of gyneco-logical problems, and treatment for sexually transmitted diseases. 53 Fed. Reg. 2927 (1988). None of the latter are strictly preventative, preconceptional services.

b. The majority attempts to obscure the breadth of its decision through its curious contention that "the Title X program regulations do not significantly impinge upon the doctor-patient relationship." That the doctor-patient relationship is substantially burdened by a rule prohibiting the dissemination by the physician of pertinent medical information is beyond serious dispute. This burden is undiminished by the fact that the relationship at issue here is not an "all-encompassing" one. A woman seeking the services of a Title X clinic has every reason to expect, as do we all, that her physician will not withhold relevant information regarding the very purpose of her visit. To suggest otherwise is to engage in unin-formed fantasy. Further, to hold that the doctor-patient relationship is somehow incomplete where a patient lacks the resources to seek comprehensive health care from a single provider is to ignore the situation of a vast number of Americans. As Justice Marshall has noted in a different context: "It is perfectly proper for judges to disagree about what the Constitution requires. But it is disgraceful for an interpretation of the Constitution to be premised upon unfounded assumptions about how people live." United States v. Kras, 409 U.S. 434, 460 (1973) (dissenting opinion).

The majority attempts to circumvent this principle by emphasizing that Title X physicians and counselors "remain free . . . to pursue abortion-related activities when they are not acting under the auspices of the Title X project." . . . Under the majority's reasoning, the First Amendment could be read to tolerate any governmental restriction upon an employee's speech so long as that restriction is limited to the funded workplace. This is a dangerous proposition. . . .

In the cases at bar, the speaker's interest in the communication is both clear and vital. In addressing the family planning needs of their clients, the physicians and counselors who staff Title X projects seek to provide them with the full range of information and options regarding their health and reproductive freedom. Indeed, the legitimate expectations of the patient and the ethical responsibilities of the medical profession demand no less. . . . The Government's articulated interest in distorting the doctor/patient dialogue — ensuring that federal funds are not spent for a purpose outside the scope of the program — falls far short of that necessary to justify the suppression of truthful information and professional medical opinion regarding constitutionally protected conduct. Moreover, the offending Regulation is not narrowly tailored to serve this interest. For example, the governmental interest at stake could be served by imposing rigorous bookkeeping standards to ensure financial separation or adopting content-neutral rules for the balanced dissemination of family-planning and health information. By failing to balance or even to consider the free speech interests claimed by Title X physicians against the Government's asserted interest in suppressing the speech, the Court falters in its duty to implement the protection that the First Amendment clearly provides for this important message.

C

Finally, it is of no small significance that the speech the Secretary would suppress is truthful information regarding constitutionally protected conduct of vital importance to the listener. . . .

III.

. . . Roe v. Wade, and its progeny are not so much about a medical procedure as they are about a woman's fundamental right to self-determination. Those cases serve to vindicate the idea that "liberty," if it means anything, must entail freedom from governmental domination in making the most intimate and personal of decisions. By suppressing medically pertinent information and injecting a restrictive ideological message unrelated to considerations of maternal health the Government places formidable obstacles in the path of Title X clients' freedom of choice and thereby violates their Fifth Amendment rights. . . .

As recounted above, the Regulations require Title X physicians and counselors to provide information pertaining only to childbirth, to refer a pregnant woman for prenatal care irrespective of her medical situation, and, upon direct inquiry, to respond that abortion is not an "appropriate method" of family planning.

The undeniable message conveyed by this forced speech, and the one that the Title X client will draw from it, is that abortion nearly always is an improper medical option. . . .

The substantial obstacles to bodily self-determination that the Regulations impose are doubly offensive because they are effected by manipulating the very words spoken by physicians and counselors to their patients. In our society, the doctor/patient dialogue embodies a unique relationship of trust. . . . One seeks a physician's aid not only for medication or diagnosis, but also for guidance, professional judgment, and vital emotional support. . . .

4.   Public Forums and Funding

ROSENBERGER v. RECTOR AND VISITORS OF
THE UNIVERSITY OF VIRGINIA
515 U.S. 819 (1995)

[The University of Virginia denied on application for funds to cover the printing costs of a student-run journal published by Wide Awake Productions (WAP), a recognized student organization formed in 1990, "[t]o publish a magazine of philosophical and religious expression," "[t]o facilitate discussion which fosters an atmosphere of sensitivity to and tolerance of Christian viewpoints," and "[t]o provide a unifying focus for Christians of multicultural backgrounds."

WAP publishes Wide Awake: A Christian Perspective at the University of Virginia. The editors committed the paper to a two-fold mission: "to challenge Christians to live, in word and deed, according to the faith they proclaim and to encourage students to consider what a personal relationship with Jesus Christ means." . . .

The University did not deny funding to WAP as a "religious organization" — defined as "an organization whose purpose is to practice a devotion to an acknowledged ultimate reality or deity." Instead, the University of Virginia Student Council denied the funding, given to a host of student organizations to cover similar printing costs and available to the Council in the first place through the payment of a $14 fee by each student, "on the ground that Wide Awake was a 'religious activity' within the meaning of the Guidelines, i.e., that the newspaper 'promote[d] or manifest[ed] a particular belie[f] in or about a deity or an ultimate reality.' It made its determination after examining the first issue." The U.S. Court of Appeals for the Fourth Circuit agreed with WAP that the University's guidelines discriminated on the basis of content, but it went on to find that the University's policy was justified by the "compelling interest in maintaining strict separation of church and state." The Supreme Court reversed, in a sharply divided 5-4 decision.]

KENNEDY, J:

We conclude . . . that here, as in *Lamb's Chapel*, viewpoint discrimination is the proper way to interpret the University's objections to Wide Awake. By the very terms of the S[tudent] A[ctivities] F[und] prohibition, the University does not exclude religion as a subject matter but selects for disfavored treatment those student journalistic efforts with religious editorial viewpoints. Religion may be a vast area of inquiry, but it also provides, as it did here, a specific premise, a perspective, a standpoint from which a variety of subjects may be discussed and considered. The prohibited perspective, not the general subject matter, resulted in the refusal to make third-party payments [to the printers of Wide Awake], for the subjects discussed were otherwise within the approved category of publications [that the SAF was willing to subsidize].

. . . The University tries to escape the consequences of our holding in *Lamb's Chapel* by urging that this case involves the provision of funds rather than access to facilities. The University begins with the unremarkable proposition that the State must have substantial discretion in determining how to allocate scarce resources to accomplish its educational mission. Citing our decisions in Rust v. Sullivan, Regan v. Taxation with Representation of Wash., and Widmar v. Vincent, 454 U.S. 263 (1981), the University argues that content-based funding decisions are both inevitable and lawful. Were the reasoning of *Lamb's Chapel* to apply to funding decisions as well as to those involving access to facilities, it is urged, its holding "would become a judicial juggernaut, constitutionalizing the ubiquitous content-based decisions that schools, colleges, and other government entities routinely make in the allocation of public funds."

To this end the University relies on our assurance in Widmar v. Vincent. There, in the course of striking down a public university's exclusion of religious groups from use of school facilities made available to all other student groups, we stated: "Nor do we question the right of the University to make academic judgments as to how best to allocate scarce resources." The quoted language in *Widmar* was but a proper recognition of the principle that when the State is the speaker, it may make content-based choices. When the University determines the content of the education it provides, it is the University speaking, and we have permitted the government to regulate the content of what is or is not expressed when it is the speaker or when it enlists private entities to convey its own message. [A similar analysis is offered of *Rust*.] It does not follow, however, . . . that viewpoint-based restrictions are proper when the University does not itself speak or subsidize transmittal of a message it favors but instead expends funds to encourage a diversity of views from private speakers. . . .

Having offered to pay the third-party contractors on behalf of private speakers who convey their own messages, the University may not silence the expression of selected viewpoints.

The University urges that, from a constitutional standpoint, funding of speech differs from provision of access to facilities because money is scarce and physical facilities are not. Beyond the fact that in any given case this proposition might not be true as an empirical matter, the underlying premise that the University could discriminate based on viewpoint if demand for space exceeded its availability is wrong as well. The government cannot justify viewpoint discrimination among private speakers on the economic fact of scarcity. Had the meeting rooms in *Lamb's Chapel* been scarce, had the demand been greater than the supply, our decision would have been no different. It would have been incumbent on the State, of course, to ration or allocate the scarce resources on some acceptable neutral principle; but nothing in our decision indicated that scarcity would give the State the right to exercise viewpoint discrimination that is otherwise impermissible.

Vital First Amendment speech principles are at stake here. The first danger to liberty lies in granting the State the power to examine publications to determine whether or not they are based on some ultimate idea and if so for the State to classify them. The second, and corollary, danger is to speech from the chilling of individual thought and expression. That danger is especially real in the University setting, where the State acts against a background and tradition of thought and experiment that is at the center of our intellectual and philosophic tradition. . . .

The Guideline invoked by the University to deny third-party contractor payments on behalf of WAP effects a sweeping restriction on student thought and student inquiry in the context of University sponsored publications. The prohibition on funding on behalf of publications that "primarily promot[e] or manifes[t] a particular belie[f] in or about a deity or an ultimate reality," in its ordinary and commonsense meaning, has a vast potential reach. The term "promotes" as used here would comprehend any writing advocating a philosophic position that rests upon a belief in a deity or ultimate reality. And the term "manifests" would bring within the scope of the prohibition any writing that is explicable as resting upon a premise which presupposes the existence of a deity or ultimate reality. Were the prohibition applied with much vigor at all, it would bar funding of essays by hypothetical student contributors named Plato, Spinoza, and Descartes. And if the regulation covers, as the University says it does, those student journalistic efforts which primarily manifest or promote a belief that there is no deity and no ultimate reality, then undergraduates named Karl Marx, Bertrand Russell, and Jean-Paul Sartre would likewise have some of their major essays excluded from student publications. If any manifestation of beliefs in first principles disqualifies the writing, as seems to be the case, it is indeed difficult to name renowned thinkers whose writings would be accepted, save perhaps for articles disclaiming all connection to their ultimate philosophy. . . .

Based on the principles we have discussed, we hold that the regulation invoked to deny SAF support, both in its terms and in its application to these petitioners, is a denial of their right of free speech guaranteed by the First Amendment. It remains to be considered whether the violation following from the University's action is excused by the necessity of complying with the Constitution's prohibition against state establishment of religion. . . .

[The Court goes on to hold that because WAP would be funded as part of a "neutral" scheme of subsidization of diverse student organizations, it does not constitute an establishment of religion.]

There is no suggestion that the University created it to advance religion or adopted some ingenious device with the purpose of aiding a religious cause. The object of the SAF is to open a forum for speech and to support various student enterprises, including the publication of newspapers, in recognition of the diversity and creativity of student life. The University's SAF Guidelines have a separate classi- fication for, and do not make third-party payments on behalf of, "religious organi- zations," which are those "whose purpose is to practice a devotion to an acknowledged ultimate reality or deity." The category of support here is for "student news, information, opinion, entertainment, or academic communications media groups," of which Wide Awake was 1 of 15 in the 1990 school year. WAP did not seek a subsidy because of its Christian editorial viewpoint; it sought funding as a student journal, which it was.

The neutrality of the program distinguishes the student fees from a tax levied for the direct support of a church or group of churches. A tax of that sort, of course, would run contrary to Establishment Clause concerns dating from the earliest days of the Republic. The apprehensions of our predecessors involved the levying of taxes upon the public for the sole and exclusive purpose of establishing and supporting specific sects. The exaction here, by contrast, is a student activity fee designed to reflect the reality that student life in its many dimensions includes the necessity of wide-ranging speech and inquiry and that student expression is an integral part of the University's educational mission. The fee is mandatory, and we do not have before us the question whether an objecting student has the First Amendment right to demand a pro rata return to the extent the fee is expended for speech to which he or she does not subscribe. We must treat it, then, as an exaction upon the students. But the $14 paid each semester by the students is not a general tax designed to raise revenue for the University. The SAF cannot be used for unlimited purposes, much less the illegitimate purpose of supporting one religion. . . . [T]he money goes to a special fund from which any group of students with [approved] status can draw for purposes consistent with the University's educational mission; and to the extent the student is interested in speech, withdrawal is permitted to cover the whole spectrum of speech, whether it manifests a religious view, an antireligious view, or neither. Our decision, then, cannot be read as addressing an expenditure from a general tax fund. Here, the disbursements from the fund go to private contractors for the cost of printing that which is protected under the Speech Clause of the First Amendment. This is a far cry from a general public assessment designed and effected to provide financial support for a church. . . .

It does not violate the Establishment Clause for a public university to grant access to its facilities on a religion-neutral basis to a wide spectrum of student groups, including groups which use meeting rooms for sectarian activities, accompanied by some devotional exercises. This is so even where the upkeep, maintenance, and repair of the facilities attributed to those uses is paid from a student activities fund to which students are required to contribute. The government usually acts by spending money. Even the provision of a meeting room, as in *Widmar*, involved governmental expenditure, if only in the form of electricity and heating or cooling costs. The error made by the Court of Appeals, as well as by the dissent, lies in focusing on the money that is undoubtedly expended by the government, rather than on the nature of the benefit received by the recipient. If the expenditure of governmental funds is prohibited whenever those funds pay for a service that is, pursuant to a religion-neutral program, used by a group for sectarian purposes, then *Widmar* . . . and *Lamb's Chapel* would have to be overruled. Given our holdings in these cases, it follows that a public university may maintain its own computer facility and give student groups access to that facility, including the use of the printers, on a religion neutral, say first-come-first-served, basis. If a religious student organization obtained access on that religion-neutral basis and used a computer to compose or a printer or copy machine to print speech with a religious content or viewpoint, the State's action in providing the group with access would no more violate the Establishment Clause than would giving those groups access to an assembly hall. . . .

[Justices O'Connor and Thomas wrote separate concurring opinions. O'Connor's opinion was noteworthy primarily because of its description of the case as lying "at the intersection of the principle of government neutrality and the prohibition of state funding of religious activities" and her comment that the issue "does not admit of categorical answers, nor should any be inferred from the Court's decision today." Justice Thomas devoted his opinion to an attack on the historical analysis of the First Amendment set out in Justice Souter's dissenting opinion.]

SOUTER, J, joined by Stevens, Breyer, and Ginsburg JJ, dissenting: [T]he University's refusal to support petitioners' religious activities is compelled by the Establishment Clause. [The Court's argument] that providing religion with economically valuable services is permissible on the theory that services are economically indistinguishable from religious access to governmental speech forums, which sometimes is permissible, [would] commit the Court to approving direct religious aid beyond anything justifiable for the sake of access to speaking forums....The majority makes the novel assumption that only direct aid financed with tax revenue is barred, and draws the erroneous conclusion that the involuntary Student Activities Fee is not a tax....The resulting decision is in unmistakable tension with the accepted law that the Court continues to avow.

A

The Court's difficulties will be all the more clear after a closer look at Wide Awake than the majority opinion affords. . . .

This writing is not merely descriptive examination of religious doctrine or even of ideal Christian practice in confronting life's social and personal problems. Nor is it merely the expression of editorial opinion that incidentally coincides with Christian ethics and reflects a Christian view of human obligation. It is straightforward exhortation to enter into a relationship with God as revealed in Jesus Christ, and to satisfy a series of moral obligations derived from the teachings of Jesus Christ. These are not the words of "student news, information, opinion, entertainment, or academic communicatio[n] . . ." (in the language of the University's funding criterion), but the words of "challenge [to] Christians to live, in word and deed, according to the faith they proclaim and . . . to consider what a personal relationship with Jesus Christ means" (in the language of Wide Awake's founder). The subject is not the discourse of the scholar's study or the seminar room, but of the evangelist's mission station and the pulpit. It is nothing other than the preaching of the word, which (along with the sacraments) is what most branches of Christianity offer those called to the religious life.

Using public funds for the direct subsidization of preaching the word is categorically forbidden under the Establishment Clause, and if the Clause was meant to accomplish nothing else, it was meant to bar this use of public money. [At this point, Justice Souter offers extensive analysis of the historical background of the Establishment Clause, focusing particularly on the thought of James Madison.]

The principle against direct funding with public money is patently violated by the contested use of today's student activity fee. . . . The University exercises the power of the State to compel a student to pay it, and the use of any part of it for the direct support of religious activity thus strikes at what we have repeatedly held to be the heart of the prohibition on establishment. . . .

B

Why does the Court not apply this clear law to these clear facts and conclude, as I do, that the funding scheme here is a clear constitutional violation? The answer must be in part that the Court fails to confront the evidence set out in the preceding section. Throughout its opinion, the Court refers uninformatively to Wide Awake's "Christian viewpoint," or its "religious perspective," and in distinguishing funding of Wide Awake from the funding of a church, the Court maintains that "[Wide Awake] is not a religious institution, at least in the usual sense." The Court does not quote the magazine's adoption of Saint Paul's exhortation to awaken to the nearness of salvation, or any of its articles enjoining readers to accept Jesus Christ, or the religious verses, or the religious textual analyses, or the suggested prayers. And so it is easy for the Court to lose sight of what the University students and the Court of Appeals found so obvious, and to blanch the patently and frankly evangelistic character of the magazine by unrevealing allusions to religious points of view.

Nevertheless, even without the encumbrance of detail from Wide Awake's actual pages, the Court finds something sufficiently religious about the magazine to require examination under the Establishment Clause, and one may therefore ask why the unequivocal prohibition on direct funding does not lead the Court to conclude that funding would be unconstitutional. The answer is that the Court focuses on a subsidiary body of law, which it correctly states but ultimately misapplies. That subsidiary body of law accounts for the Court's substantial attention to the fact that the University's funding scheme is "neutral," in the formal sense that it makes funds available on an evenhanded basis to secular and sectarian applicants alike. While this is indeed true and relevant under our cases, it does not alone satisfy the requirements of the Establishment Clause, as the Court recognizes when it says that evenhandedness is only a "significant factor" in certain Establishment Clause analysis, not a dispositive one. This recognition reflects the Court's appreciation of two general rules: that whenever affirmative government aid ultimately benefits religion, the Establishment Clause requires some justification beyond evenhandedness on the government's part; and that direct public funding of core sectarian activities, even if accomplished pursuant to an evenhanded program, would be entirely inconsistent with the Establishment Clause and would strike at the very heart of the Clause's protection. . . .

2

[Justice Souter turns to the] assumption that a public university may give a religious group the use of any of its equipment or facilities so long as secular groups are likewise eligible. . . . The common factual thread running through *Widmar, Mergens,* and *Lamb's Chapel* is that a governmental institution created a limited forum for the use of students in a school or college, or for the public at large, but sought to exclude speakers with religious messages. In each case the restriction was struck down either as an impermissible attempt to regulate the content of speech in an open forum (as in *Widmar* and *Mergens*) or to suppress a particular religious viewpoint (as in *Lamb's Chapel*). In each case, to be sure, the religious speaker's use of the room passed muster as an incident of a plan to facilitate speech generally for a secular purpose, entailing neither secular entanglement with religion nor risk that the religious speech would be taken to be the speech of the government or that the government's endorsement of a religious message would be inferred. But each case drew ultimately on unexceptionable Speech Clause doctrine treating the evangelist, the Salvation Army, the millennialist or the Hare Krishna like any other speaker in a public forum. It was the preservation of free speech on the model of the street corner that supplied the justification going beyond the requirement of evenhandedness.

The Court's claim of support from these forum-access cases is ruled out by the very scope of their holdings. While they do indeed allow a limited benefit to religious speakers, they rest on the recognition that all speakers are entitled to use the street corner (even though the State paves the roads and provides police protection to everyone on the street) and on the analogy between the public street corner and open classroom space.

Thus, the Court found it significant that the classroom speakers would engage in traditional speech activities in these forums, too, even though the rooms (like street corners) require some incidental state spending to maintain them. The analogy breaks down entirely, however, if the cases are read more broadly than the Court wrote them, to cover more than forums for literal speaking. There is no traditional street corner printing provided by the government on equal terms to all comers, and the forum cases cannot be lifted to a higher plane of generalization without admitting that new economic benefits are being extended directly to religion in clear violation of the principle barring direct aid. The argument from economic equivalence thus breaks down on recognizing that the direct state aid it would support is not mitigated by the street corner analogy in the service of free speech. Absent that, the rule against direct aid stands as a bar to printing services as well as printers.

³

. . . The opinion of the Court concludes . . . that the activity fee is not a tax, and then proceeds to find the aid permissible on the legal assumption that the bar against direct aid applies only to aid derived from tax revenue. . . . [I]t is fanciful to treat the fee as anything but a tax. [Justice Souter had noted earlier in the opinion that the litigating parties had stipulated that "The University of Virginia has charged at all times relevant herein and currently charges each full-time student a compulsory student activity fee of $14.00 per semester. There is no procedural or other mechanism by which a student may decline to pay the fee."] The novelty of the assumption that the direct aid bar only extends to aid derived from taxation, however, requires some response.

Although it was a taxation scheme that moved Madison to write in the first instance, the Court has never held that government resources obtained without taxation could be used for direct religious support, and our cases on direct government aid have frequently spoken in terms in no way limited to tax revenues.

Allowing non-tax funds to be spent on religion would, in fact, fly in the face of clear principle. . . . [A]ny such use of them would ignore one the dual objectives of the Establishment Clause, which was meant not only to protect individuals and their republics from the destructive consequences of mixing government and religion, but to protect religion from a corrupting dependence on support from the Government. Since the corrupting effect of government support does not turn on whether the Government's own money comes from taxation or gift or the sale of public lands, the Establishment Clause could hardly relax its vigilance simply because tax revenue was not implicated. Accordingly, in the absence of a forthright disavowal, one can only assume that the Court does not mean to eliminate one half of the Establishment Clause's justification. . . .

Discussion

1. Can you distinguish between the compulsory University of Virginia student fee and a "tax"?

2. Assume that a state university offers to fund all student publications that a committee of faculty decides "serve the educational purposes of the University." The Committee explicitly refuses any publications that endorse in any way astrology or religious belief "because of our considered judgment that well-educated persons will recognize the lack of foundation underlying such views." Does this present constitutional problems? Consider the following exchange, from an e-mail discussion group, between Michael McConnell, then a professor at the University of Utah (and now a member of the Tenth Circuit Court of Appeals) and Rodney Smith, then at the Capitol University Law School:

McConnell: If the University limited funding to publications deemed to be of educational value, it would be very difficult for a religious publication like Wide Awake, let alone the astrology journal, to prevail. This would be like schemes that give out money to artists on the basis of artistic merit. Obviously, these lines are thin and are subject to abuse, but nonetheless I think such programs would be sustained, and the government would receive great deference with regard to its decisions. The scheme in *Rosenberger* was not of this sort, and there was no suggestion that the content of Wide Awake failed to live up to some educational standard.

Smith: I am puzzled by the fact that Michael is so quick to conclude that religious publications would not satisfy an 'educational value' standard. Religion and religious/theological matter is, to my mind, clearly educational, speaking as it does in two powerful epistemological senses — to the spirit (heart) and the mind. The exclusion of religion would, to my mind, have to be based on some grounds other than the fact that it lacked educational merit.

Assume that you agree with Professor Smith (and, for that matter, then-Professor McConnell, who as a matter of fact personally agrees that religious publications have great "educational value"), but that the university is controlled by persons who see no "educational value" in religious discourse. Would you be entitled, as a judge, to substitute your notion of "educational value" for that of the university officials? Consider a university that funds, among a broad variety of journals, one journal published by student members of the university's biology department who publish articles predicated on Darwinian theories of evolution. Could the university deny funding to a competing journal committed to presenting "intelligent design" as an alternative to Darwinian evolution, on the ground that "intelligent design" is an idea wholly without scientific merit and thus undeserving of the university's funds?

Note: Subsidized Speech and Public Discourse

Congress created the National Endowment for the Arts (NEA) in 1965 "to develop and promote a broadly conceived national policy of support for the . . . arts in the United States." The NEA is authorized to award grants to "individuals of exceptional talent engaged in or concerned with the arts." By statute, applications for grants must be submitted "in accordance with regulations issued and procedures established" by the NEA Chair. Although the NEA attempted to insulate these procedures "from partisan political considerations" by ceding de facto authority to

"panels of experts, usually peers of the applicant consisting of museum professionals or artists involved in the same discipline," the work of artists subsidized by the
NEA came under severe ideological attack in the late 1980s and early 1990s, especially by members of the Republican Party, who regarded them as unfairly tilted to
the left, elitist, obscene, and blasphemous.

As a result of these controversies, Congress qualified the NEA's granting authority. 20 U.S.C. §954(d)(1) directs that although "artistic excellence and artistic merit
are the criteria by which applications are judged," when judging the artistic merit
of grant applications, the NEA should also "tak[e] into consideration general standards of decency and respect for the diverse beliefs and values of the American
public." In 1992 this qualification was challenged by four individual performance
artists, as well as by the National Association of Artists' Organizations. A federal
district court declared the " 'decency' clause . . . void for vagueness under the Fifth
Amendment and . . . overbroad under the First Amendment."

In National Endowment for the Arts v. Finley, 524 U.S. 569 (1998), the Court,
through Justice O'Connor, upheld 20 U.S.C. §954(d)(1). The Court argued that
"the text of §954(d)(1) imposes no categorical" duty to reject any given proposals.
"The advisory language stands in sharp contrast to congressional efforts to prohibit
the funding of certain classes of speech. When Congress has in fact intended to
affirmatively constrain the NEA's grant-making authority, it has done so in no
uncertain terms. See §954(d)(2) ('[O]bscenity is without artistic merit, is not
protected speech, and shall not be funded')." Thus, according to the majority,
Congress in effect "admonishes the NEA merely to take 'decency and respect' into
consideration. . . . [T]he legislation was aimed at reforming procedures rather than
precluding speech," which "undercut[s] respondents' argument that the provision
inevitably will be utilized as a tool for invidious viewpoint discrimination. . . ." This
was enough to save the statute from the "facial" challenge mounted by Finley and
the other plaintiffs. Justice O'Connor emphasized that

> we have no occasion here to address an as-applied challenge in a situation where the
> denial of a grant may be shown to be the product of invidious viewpoint discrimina-
> tion. If the NEA were to leverage its power to award subsidies on the basis of subjective
> criteria into a penalty on disfavored viewpoints, then we would confront a different
> case. We have stated that, even in the provision of subsidies, the Government may not
> "ai[m] at the suppression of dangerous ideas," and if a subsidy were "manipulated" to
> have a "coercive effect," then relief could be appropriate. In addition, as the NEA itself
> concedes, a more pressing constitutional question would arise if government funding
> resulted in the imposition of a disproportionate burden calculated to drive "certain
> ideas or viewpoints from the marketplace." Unless and until §954(d)(1) is applied in a
> manner that raises concern about the suppression of disfavored viewpoints, however,
> we uphold the constitutionality of the provision.

Justices Scalia and Thomas, concurring, and Justice Souter, dissenting, all took
issue with the majority's interpretation of the statute. As Justice Souter put it, the
statute "obviously means that art that disrespects the ideology, opinions, or convictions of a significant segment of the American public is to be disfavored, whereas
art that reinforces those values is not." This is, patently, a viewpoint discrimination.
For Scalia and Thomas this was no problem, whereas for Souter this made the
statute unconstitutional.

For Scalia and Thomas, the crux of the matter was that

Congress did not abridge the speech of those who disdain the beliefs and values of the American public, nor did it abridge indecent speech. Those who wish to create inde-cent and disrespectful art are as unconstrained now as they were before the enactment of this statute. Avant-garde artists such as respondents remain entirely free to epater les bourgeois; they are merely deprived of the additional satisfaction of having the bourgeoisie taxed to pay for it. It is preposterous to equate the denial of taxpayer subsidy with measures "aimed at the suppression of dangerous ideas."

Justice Souter, on the other hand, protested in dissent that "the Government has wholly failed to explain why the statute should be afforded an exemption from the fundamental rule of the First Amendment that viewpoint discrimination in the exercise of public authority over expressive activity is unconstitutional." He noted, for example, that the Court, in Reno v. American Civil Liberties Union, 521 U.S. 844 (1997), invalidated on its face a federal statute regulating "indecency" on the Internet. "[R]estrictions turning on decency, especially those couched in terms of 'general standards of decency,' are quintessentially viewpoint based: they require discrimination on the basis of conformity with mainstream mores."

The Government calls attention to the roles of government-as-speaker and govern-ment-as-buyer, in which the government is of course entitled to engage in viewpoint discrimination: if the Food and Drug Administration launches an advertising campaign on the subject of smoking, it may condemn the habit without also having to show a cowboy taking a puff on the opposite page; and if the Secretary of Defense wishes to buy a portrait to decorate the Pentagon, he is free to prefer George Washington over George the Third.

The Government freely admits, however, that it neither speaks through the expres-sion subsidized by the NEA, nor buys anything for itself with its NEA grants. On the contrary, believing that "[t]he arts . . . reflect the high place accorded by the American people to the nation's rich cultural heritage," §951(6), and that "[i]t is vital to a democracy . . . to provide financial assistance to its artists and the organizations that support their work," §951(10), the Government acts as a patron, financially underwrit-ing the production of art by private artists and impresarios for independent consump-tion. Accordingly, the Government would have us liberate government-as-patron from First Amendment strictures not by placing it squarely within the categories of govern-ment-as-buyer or government-as-speaker, but by recognizing a new category by analogy to those accepted ones. The analogy is, however, a very poor fit, and this patronage falls embarrassingly on the wrong side of the line between government-as-buyer or -speaker and government-as-regulator-of-private-speech.

Note: Robert Post on "Subsidized Speech"

In his article Subsidized Speech, 106 Yale L.J. 151 (1996), Professor Robert C. Post argues that courts and commentators wrongly focus on whether speech is a subsidy or a penalty, and whether the government is engaged in viewpoint discrimi-nation. The crucial questions, Post argues, involve the "social characterization" of the speech. He offers a set of distinctions to help decide how and under what condi-tions subsidized speech can be regulated by the government.

1. *Regulation of "public discourse" versus regulation of the managerial domain.* Post argues that it is quite important whether we characterize speech as part of a domain of public discourse or part of a domain of government management. According to

Post, "First Amendment doctrine envisions a distinct realm of citizen speech, called 'public discourse,'" in which people are assumed to be "independent and autonomous. . . . Within the democratic domain of public discourse, persons must be given the freedom to determine their own collective identity and ends." The mere fact that government subsidizes speech does not mean that it falls outside of the realm of public discourse. Such speech should be protected just like unsubsidized speech in the public sphere.

> The public forum cases provide the most obvious illustration of how persons can receive government benefits and nevertheless remain within public discourse. These cases hold that speech occurring on certain kinds of government property, like streets and parks, will be "subject to the highest scrutiny." . . . Publications that receive the "subsidy" extended by the United States to second-class mail provide another example of subsidized speech that receives significant First Amendment protection. Receipt of the subsidy does not remove such publications from the safeguards otherwise accorded public discourse. . . .
>
> It follows from this that (then) Justice Rehnquist could not have been correct when he observed in *Regan* that "a legislature's decision not to subsidize the exercise of a fundamental right does not infringe the right." [C]onsider, for example, the fatal constitutional difficulties that would arise if a state were to exclude speech about nuclear power or abortion from a public forum, or if Congress were to withhold second-class mailing subsidies from magazines that discuss these issues.

Post also points to *Rosenberger* as a case that demonstrates that "speech may be subsidized and yet remain within public discourse." Similarly, Justice Brennan's opinion in FCC v. League of Women Voters turned on the characterization of public broadcasters "as independent contributors to public discourse; like the press generally, they were to be regarded as possessing the self-determining agency of private citizens." Nevertheless, Post contends, not all speech falls in the realm of public discourse:

> Public discourse must be distinguished from [speech that occurs in] "managerial" [domains, where], the state organizes its resources so as to achieve specified ends. The constitutional value of managerial domains is that of instrumental rationality, a value that conceptualizes persons as means to an end rather than as autonomous agents. Within managerial domains, therefore, ends may be imposed upon persons. . . .
>
> First Amendment doctrine within managerial domains differs fundamentally from First Amendment doctrine within public discourse. The state must be able to regulate speech within managerial domains so as to achieve explicit governmental objectives. Thus the state can regulate speech within public educational institutions so as to achieve the purposes of education; it can regulate speech within the judicial system so as to attain the ends of justice; it can regulate speech within the military so as to preserve the national defense; it can regulate the speech of government employees so as to promote "the efficiency of the public services [the government] performs through its employees"; and so forth.

While the government may not discriminate against speech in the public domain based on its viewpoint, such discrimination is permissible and quite common in speech that falls into the managerial domain:

> [T]he president may fire cabinet officials who publicly challenge rather than support Administration policies; the military may discipline officers who publicly attack rather

than uphold the principle of civilian control over the armed forces; public defenders who prosecute instead of defend their clients may be sanctioned; prison guards who encourage instead of condemn drug use may be chastised. Viewpoint discrimination occurs within managerial domains whenever the attainment of legitimate managerial objectives requires it. . . .

[Within universities,] speech is necessarily and routinely constrained on the basis of both its content and its viewpoint. Academic evaluations of students and faculty are regularly based upon viewpoint. Historians who deny the Holocaust are not likely to receive appointments to reputable departments; students who deny the legitimacy of the taxing power of the federal government are not likely to receive high grades in law schools. The same principles apply to university decisions concerning the subsidization of speech. So, for example, no First Amendment issue would be raised if a graduate student who proposed to study the mythical combustive element phlogiston were to be refused a research grant by the chemistry department of a public university, however much the student were to complain about discrimination against her view of the causes of chemical reactions. The constitutionality of the refusal would instead turn on whether the chemistry department's criteria for awarding grants were related to its legitimate educational mission. That the department had both the purpose and effect of discriminating against the student's particular viewpoint would properly be deemed immaterial. . . .

Post thus argues that characterization of the realm in which speech falls is crucial to any First Amendment analysis.

In cases of subsidized speech, . . . the provision of a benefit can sometimes convert a citizen into a public functionary and thereby alter the nature of the relevant First Amendment rights and analysis. The abstract principles underlying the unconstitutional conditions doctrine simply do not address this possibility.

The question of characterization, Post insists, is normative as well as merely descriptive. It rests on how we want to understand a particular class of speech and why:

Ultimately, speech will be assigned to public discourse on the basis of normative and ascriptive judgments as to whether particular speakers in particular contexts should constitutionally be regarded as autonomous participants in the ongoing process of democratic self-governance. Whether explicitly addressed or not, such judgments are essential predicates to all cases of subsidized speech.

How would this distinction between public discourse and managerial speech apply to Rust v. Sullivan? Post notes that

[I]t is highly questionable whether the speech of the Title X clinics and their employees could also be classified as public discourse. It is in fact superficially plausible to locate that speech instead within a managerial domain established by Title X. [One could argue that] Congress enacted Title X to accomplish certain purposes, that these purposes are legitimate, and that the HHS regulations function within this managerial domain to regulate speech so as to achieve these purposes.

Nevertheless, Post argues, there are other reasons to avoid assigning the speech at issue to the managerial domain.

[T]he HHS regulations . . . prohibit physicians from offering advice or referrals about abortion in the course of their consultations with their patients, even when, in the medical judgment of the physician, it would be appropriate to do so.

Physicians are . . . professionals, and . . . professionals do not fit well into the instrumental rationality of organizations. [P]rofessionals must always qualify their loyalty and commitment to the vertical hierarchy of an organization by their horizontal commitment to general professional norms and standards.

Thus, Post argues, physicians' special roles do not allow "organizational logic . . . to override the necessary exercise of independent professional judgment." Similarly, because "physicians routinely exercise independent judgment, patients come to expect and rely upon that judgment." Except in the most unusual of circumstances, patients expect the independent judgment of their physicians to trump inconsistent managerial demands.

[V]iewpoint discriminatory regulations that prohibit the dissemination of information are ordinarily justified by a showing that the foreclosed information will lead to some harm that the government has a right to prevent. Thus if the government were to prohibit doctors subsidized by the Veterans Administration from discussing a certain drug, the constitutionality of the prohibition would normally turn on some showing that the drug was harmful and that the provision of information would increase the likelihood of harm. But this whole class of justifications seems unavailable to the government in *Rust*, because they would require that the government characterize abortion as a positive harm. The right to choose abortion is constitutionally protected, however, on the grounds that its exercise is "central to personal dignity and autonomy." Surely the solecism of characterizing the exercise of such a right as a harm is both obvious and fatal.

Is this argument in any way undermined by the Court's decision in *Casey*, which held that the government may actively discourage abortion as long as the regulation does not create an "undue burden"?

2. *Decision rules versus conduct rules.* Post offers a second distinction for deciding subsidized speech cases. The question is not what social domain the speech falls into, but "whether conditions on government subsidies should be classified as regulations imposed upon persons, or whether they should instead be classified as internal directives guiding the conduct of state institutions." Borrowing vocabulary from Professor Meir Dan-Cohen, Post distinguishes between "conduct rules" in which the government tries to regulate the conduct of its citizens, and "decision rules" where the government is merely trying to give internal direction to government officials or government functionaries. If a rule that affects public discourse is classified as a conduct rule, it is treated like any other attempt to regulate public discourse, but if it is characterized as a decision rule, it is within the government's power to direct its own internal affairs even if it has incidental effects on public discourse.

[A] statute barring indecent magazines from second-class mailing subsidies [should be considered] a direct regulation of public discourse rather than as an internal guideline of the Post Office. . . . [M]agazines are so completely dependent on the operation of the mail that the statute would as a practical matter function to disable magazines branded as indecent. In such a case we might even go so far as to agree with Owen Fiss's observation that "the effect of a denial" of a subsidy "is roughly equivalent to that of a criminal prosecution." But this equivalence, if it exists, is practical, not theoretical. It derives from the particular way in which subsidies for second-class mailing privileges have infiltrated their social environment. We can easily imagine counter examples. [T]he federal government subsidizes [the Kennedy Center] to "present classical and contemporary music, opera, drama, dance, and other performing arts." These criteria . . . exclude political and academic speech. Such speech is of course public discourse, yet its dependence upon the Center is so slight that we would not be tempted to read the effects of the government's exclusions as "roughly equivalent to that of a criminal prosecution." We would interpret the exclusions instead as decision rules for the internal direction of the Center's administrators. The exclusions would be constitutionally characterized as instrumental regulations confined to a managerial domain, rather than as general regulations of public discourse. . . .

Cases of subsidized speech thus typically raise two independent issues of constitutional characterization. The first refers to the characterization of speech, and it requires us to determine whether subsidized speech is within public discourse or whether it is within some other constitutional domain. The second refers to the characterization of government action, and it requires us to determine whether standards allocating state subsidies should be regarded as conduct rules or as decision rules. . . .

Post uses the conduct/decision rule distinction to analyze the controversy in *Finley:*

> In *Finley* . . . the artistic work supported by NEA grants may for the most part unproblematically be regarded as part of public discourse. But . . . the decency clause . . . [might] be understood as a direct regulation of the speech of NEA grantees, or instead as a rule directed at the internal operation of the NEA. . . . We must decide, therefore, how the NEA "decency clause" should be characterized: as a conduct rule directly regulating public discourse or instead as a decision rule directing NEA officials to intervene in public discourse to achieve a distinct objective.
>
> The problem with characterizing the clause as a conduct rule is that it would also render unconstitutional not merely the clause itself, but also the larger criterion of "artistic excellence." It would be flatly unconstitutional for the state to regulate public discourse in a way that penalizes art deemed insufficiently excellent.

On the other hand, if the NEA decency clause is merely "an internal policy guideline directing the NEA to intervene into public discourse to encourage and facilitate excellent art that is also decent" it should be permissible, even though "the government could not directly regulate public discourse to achieve that purpose." Thus

> viewpoint discrimination alone will never be a sufficient ground for striking down decision rules. Whenever the state acts to support a particular conception of community identity, it will engage in viewpoint discrimination with respect to that conception. So, for example, if the NEA allocates grants to support artistic excellence, it must adopt a perspective about the meaning of that value; if the value is contested, the NEA's perspective will necessarily be viewpoint discriminatory from the standpoint of those who hold a different interpretation of the value.

A different case would be presented if "Congress were to enact a statute requiring the NEA to distribute grants only to art supportive of the party in control of

Congress." Yet if this statute is unconstitutional, it is not because "the goal and effect of the statute is to shape the content of public discourse" but because of "specific views about the distinct realm of partisan politics." By contrast, "a congressionally authorized prize to be awarded annually to the best 'patriotic' work of art" is not obviously unconstitutional.

> A decision rule allocating government subsidies to patriotic art, even though supportive of the political status quo, is in every material respect analogous to a decision rule allocating government subsidies to excellent art. Both artistic excellence and patriotism transcend the specifically political, because neither can be said to be disputable in a manner framed for decision; both embody shared values, not preferences; and neither would violate fundamental norms of political fairness. If the NEA decency clause were measured by these standards, I suspect that it would easily pass muster. . . . [T]he NEA decency clause does not appear to constitute the kind of rare and exceptional case that would or should be found unconstitutional. . . .
>
> [The NEA controversy presents] a conflict between two constitutional values: that of democratic self-governance and that of community self-definition. . . . To characterize the decency clause as a decision rule or as a conduct rule is, in effect, to fix the boundary between two constitutional values. Where we set that boundary will depend in part upon the manner in which the decency clause affects the production of art within the public discourse enveloping the NEA. We would be more likely to classify the clause as a conduct rule, and hence to subject it to the constraints of a constitutional regime of democratic self-governance, if we were to regard the clause as imposing community norms on public discourse. Conversely, we would be more likely to classify the clause as a decision rule — and hence to be constitutionally legitimized, if we were to view the clause as merely encouraging a shared and important community value.

Discussion

1. *Reasoning by domains.* Post argues that the question of subsidy versus penalty and viewpoint based versus viewpoint neutral are conclusory terms. Is his analysis, which decides cases by characterizing which domain they fit into, or what kind of government action is involved, less conclusory? Is it clear to you whether the NEA rule is a (prohibited) attempt to shape public discourse or a (permissible) promotion of shared community values? Note that opponents of the congressional restrictions have argued that NEA funding often encourages other donors to support controversial artists; withdrawing funding may lead to artists receiving little or no funding at all from the private sector. Does this mean that the NEA rule was "really" a conduct rule? On the other hand, the Court in *Finley* argued that the decency provision was merely advice from Congress about how to assess competing applications. Does this mean that it was "really" a decision rule?

Does Post's argument assume that the NEA rule must be either a decision rule or a conduct rule, or could it be both at the same time? Similarly, could a particular form of speech be both part of the domain of public discourse and part of governmental management? If so, what analysis should apply? One possibility suggested by Post is that we must simply ascribe a practice to one domain or another, even if descriptively it could fall into either domain. But if so, how do we decide? The next two sections consider this question in the contexts first of public libraries and then of governmentally funded lawyers who work for the Legal Services Corporation or other similar agencies.

5.   Conceptualizing the Public Library

In 2000, there were more than 9,000 public libraries in the United States.[48] One might, of course, easily analogize them to public schools with regard to their having a specific mission to educate the public (including, of course, adult users of public libraries). Libraries increasingly offer their patrons access to computers (and, therefore, the Internet), which means, as a practical matter, access to sexually explicit and, indeed, pornographic materials. Responding to this reality, Congress enacted the Children's Internet Protection Act (CIPA), which forbids public libraries from receiving federal assistance for Internet access — discounted rates under the E-rate program and grants under the Library Services and Technology Act (LSTA) — unless libraries install software to block obscene or pornographic images and to prevent minors from accessing material harmful to them. In United States v. American Library Association, 539 U.S. 194 (2003), the Court upheld CIPA, though there was no majority opinion. The plurality opinion was written by Chief Justice Rehnquist, joined by Justices O'Connor, Scalia, and Thomas. Justice Kennedy and Justice Breyer filed opinions concurring only in the judgment.

Chief Justice Rehnquist noted that libraries have never sought to provide

"universal coverage." Instead, public libraries seek to provide materials that would be of the greatest direct benefit or interest to the commuity. To this end, libraries collect only those materials deemed to have "requisite and appropriate quality."

We have held in two analogous contexts that the government has broad discretion to make content-based judgments in deciding what private speech to make available to the public. In Arkansas Ed. Television Comm'n v. Forbes, 523 U.S. 666 (1998), we held that public forum principles do not generally apply to a public television station's editorial judgments regarding the private speech it presents to its viewers. "[B]road rights of access for outside speakers would be antithetical, as a general rule, to the discretion that stations and their editorial staff must exercise to fulfill their journalistic purpose and statutory obligations." Recognizing a broad right of public access "would [also] risk implicating the courts in judgments that should be left to the exercise of journalistic discretion."

Similarly, in National Endowment for Arts v. Finley, 524 U.S. 569 (1998), we upheld an art funding program that required the National Endowment for the Arts (NEA) to use content-based criteria in making funding decisions. We explained that "[a]ny content-based considerations that may be taken into account in the grant-making process are a consequence of the nature of arts funding." In particular, "[t]he very assumption of the NEA is that grants will be awarded according to the 'artistic worth of competing applicants,' and absolute neutrality is simply inconceivable." We expressly declined to apply forum analysis, reasoning that it would conflict with "NEA's mandate . . . to make esthetic judgments, and the inherently content-based 'excellence' threshold for NEA support."

The principles underlying Forbes and Finley also apply to a public library's exercise of judgment in selecting the material it provides to its patrons. . . . Public library staffs necessarily consider content in making collection decisions and enjoy broad discretion in making them.

---

48. See 4 Education Statistics Quarterly, Issue 3, Public Libraries in the United States: Fiscal Year 2000, available at *http://nces.ed.gov/programs/quarterly/vol_4/4_3/5_1.asp#H2.*

But, of course, the program in question in effect took discretion away from professional librarians and instead required them, should they wish the government funds in question, to accept the government's conditions with regard to access to the Internet on the part of their patrons. Thus

> Appellees urge us to affirm the District Court's judgment [striking down CIPA on the ground that it] imposes an unconstitutional condition on libraries that receive E-rate and LSTA subsidies by requiring them, as a condition on their receipt of federal funds, to surrender their First Amendment right to provide the public with access to constitutionally protected speech. The Government counters that this claim fails because Government entities do not have First Amendment rights.

As one might expect from reading Chief Justice Rehnquist's earlier opinions, he rejected this argument on the grounds that the government is providing subsidies to libraries and therefore can "define the limits" of the given program, which does not include funding unimpeded access to sexually explicit materials.

> The E-rate and LSTA programs were intended to help public libraries fulfill their traditional role of obtaining material of requisite and appropriate quality for educational and informational purposes. Congress may certainly insist that these "public funds be spent for the purposes for which they were authorized." Especially because public libraries have traditionally excluded pornographic material from their other collections, Congress could reasonably impose a parallel limitation on its Internet assistance programs. As the use of filtering software helps to carry out these programs, it is a permissible condition under *Rust*.
>
> Justice STEVENS asserts the premise that "[a] federal statute penalizing a library for failing to install filtering software on every one of its Internet-accessible computers would unquestionably violate [the First] Amendment." But — assuming . . . that public libraries have First Amendment rights — CIPA does not "penalize" libraries that choose not to install such software, or deny them the right to provide their patrons with unfiltered Internet access. Rather, CIPA simply reflects Congress' decision not to subsidize their doing so. To the extent that libraries wish to offer unfiltered access, they are free to do so without federal assistance.

Justice Kennedy concurred in the judgment in large part because "[i]f, on the request of an adult user, a librarian will unblock filtered material or disable the Internet software filter without significant delay, there is little to this case. The Government represents this is indeed the fact." Should a given library not have the capacity to unblock asked-for Web sites or should it be "shown that an adult user's election to view constitutionally protected Internet material is burdened in some other substantial way, that would be the subject for an as-applied challenge, not the facial challenge made in this case." Given what Justice Kennedy labeled the "substantial" and perhaps even "compelling" governmental interest in preventing minors from gaining access to pornographic materials, coupled with "the failure to show that the ability of adult library users to have access to the material is burdened in any significant degree, the statute is not unconstitutional on its face. For these reasons, I concur in the judgment of the Court."

Justice Breyer also wrote a separate opinion concurring in the judgment, which focused primarily on the standard of scrutiny the Court should apply to legislation like CIPA. (The answer, for Justice Breyer, was "heightened, but not 'strict,' scrutiny — where, for example, complex, competing constitutional interests are potentially at issue or speech-related harm is potentially justified by unusually strong governmental interests.") CIPA easily passed muster under these standards. Breyer noted that certain "software filters both 'overblock,' screening out some perfectly legitimate material, and 'underblock,' allowing some obscene material to escape detection by the filter. But no one has presented any clearly superior or better fitting alternatives."

Moreover, Breyer, like Justice Kennedy, emphasized the relatively minor burden placed on a patron who would like access to the site in question: "[I]t is difficult to see how that burden (or any delay associated with compliance) could prove more onerous than traditional library practices associated with segregating library materials in, say, closed stacks, or with interlibrary lending practices that require patrons to make requests that are not anonymous and to wait while the librarian obtains the desired materials from elsewhere."

Justice Stevens dissented:

> . . . I agree with the plurality that it is neither inappropriate nor unconstitutional for a local library to experiment with filtering software as a means of curtailing children's access to Internet Web sites displaying sexually explicit images. I also agree with the plurality that the 7% of public libraries that decided to use such software on *all* of their Internet terminals in 2000 did not act unlawfully. Whether it is constitutional for the Congress of the United States to impose that requirement on the other 93%, however, raises a vastly different question. Rather than allowing local decisionmakers to tailor their responses to local problems, the Children's Internet Protection Act (CIPA) operates as a blunt nationwide restraint on adult access to "an enormous amount of valuable information" that individual librarians cannot possibly review. Most of that information is constitutionally protected speech. In my view, this restraint is unconstitutional.

Justice Stevens focused on "fundamental defects in the filtering software" that lead to the "underblocking" and, more seriously, "overblocking" noted by Justice Breyer.

> The effect of the overblocking is the functional equivalent of a host of individual decisions excluding hundreds of thousands of individual constitutionally protected messages from Internet terminals located in public libraries throughout the Nation. Neither the interest in suppressing unlawful speech nor the interest in protecting children from access to harmful materials justifies this overly broad restriction on adult access to protected speech. "The Government may not suppress lawful speech as the means to suppress unlawful speech." Ashcroft v. Free Speech Coalition, 535 U.S. 234 (2002).
>
> [L]ess restrictive alternatives exist that further the government's legitimate interest in preventing the dissemination of obscenity, child pornography, and material harmful to minors, and in preventing patrons from being unwillingly exposed to patently offensive, sexually explicit content. To prevent patrons from accessing visual depictions that are obscene and child pornography, public libraries may enforce Internet use policies that make clear to patrons that the library's Internet terminals may not be used to access illegal speech. Libraries may then impose penalties on patrons who violate these policies, ranging from a warning to notification of law enforcement, in the appropriate case. Less restrictive alternatives to filtering that further libraries' interest in preventing minors from exposure to visual depictions that are harmful to minors include requiring parental consent to or presence during unfiltered access, or restricting minors' unfiltered access to terminals within view of library staff. Finally, optional

filtering, privacy screens, recessed monitors, and placement of unfiltered Internet terminals outside of sight-lines provide less restrictive alternatives for libraries to prevent patrons from being unwillingly exposed to sexually explicit content on the Internet.

. . . Unless we assume that the statute is a mere symbolic gesture, we must conclude that it will create a significant prior restraint on adult access to protected speech. A law that prohibits reading without official consent, like a law that prohibits speaking without consent, "constitutes a dramatic departure from our national heritage and constitutional tradition."

Justice Stevens thus found that CIPA acted as an unconstitutional condition. A librarian's discretion over what is to be offered patrons "is comparable," he argued,

to the "business of a university . . . to determine for itself on academic grounds who may teach, what may be taught, how it shall be taught, and who may be admitted to study." . . . Given our Nation's deep commitment "to safeguarding academic freedom" and to the "robust exchange of ideas," a library's exercise of judgment with respect to its collection is entitled to First Amendment protection.

A federal statute penalizing a library for failing to install filtering software on every one of its Internet-accessible computers would unquestionably violate that Amendment. I think it equally clear that the First Amendment protects libraries from being denied funds for refusing to comply with an identical rule. An abridgment of speech by means of a threatened denial of benefits can be just as pernicious as an abridgment by means of a threatened penalty.

Rust [*v. Sullivan*] only involved and only applies to instances of governmental speech — that is, situations in which the government seeks to communicate a specific message. The discounts under the E-rate program and funding under the Library Services and Technology Act (LSTA) program involved in this case do not subsidize any message favored by the Government. As Congress made clear, these programs were designed "[t]o help public libraries provide their patrons with Internet access," which in turn "provide[s] patrons with a vast amount of valuable information." These programs thus are designed to provide access, particularly for individuals in low-income communities, to a vast amount and wide variety of private speech. They are not designed to foster or transmit any particular governmental message.

The plurality's reliance on [*Finley*] is also misplaced. . . . Unlike this case, the Federal Government was not seeking to impose restrictions on the administration of a nonfederal program. . . . Further, like a library, the NEA experts in *Finley* had a great deal of discretion to make judgments as to what projects to fund. But unlike this case, *Finley* did not involve a challenge by the NEA to a governmental restriction on its ability to award grants. Instead, the respondents were performance artists who had applied for NEA grants but were denied funding. If this were a case in which library patrons had challenged a library's decision to install and use filtering software, it would be in the same posture as *Finley*. Because it is not, *Finley* does not control this case.

Also unlike *Finley*, the Government does not merely seek to control a library's discretion with respect to computers purchased with Government funds or those computers with Government-discounted Internet access. CIPA requires libraries to install filtering software on *every* computer with Internet access if the library receives *any* discount from the E-rate program or *any* funds from the LSTA program.[a] If a

---

a. Thus, respondents are not merely challenging a "refusal to fund protected activity, without more," as in Harris v. McRae, or a "decision not to subsidize the exercise of a fundamental right," as in Regan v. Taxation With Representation of Wash. They are challenging a restriction that applies to property that they acquired without federal assistance.

library has 10 computers paid for by nonfederal funds and has Internet service for those computers also paid for by nonfederal funds, the library may choose not to put filtering software on any of those 10 computers. Or a library may decide to put filtering software on the 5 computers in its children's section. Or a library in an elementary school might choose to put filters on every single one of its 10 computers. But under this statute, if a library attempts to provide Internet service for even *one* computer through an E-rate discount, that library must put filtering software on *all* of its computers with Internet access, not just the one computer with E-rate discount. . . .

Justice Souter, though "agree[ing] in the main with Justice Stevens," wrote a separate dissent, joined by Justice Ginsburg. Justice Souter explicitly took issue with the assumption that the burden placed on adult users of the computers in question was minor. He also argued that "the restrictions on adult Internet access have no justification in the object of protecting children" inasmuch as "[c]hildren could be restricted to blocked terminals, leaving other unblocked terminals in areas restricted to adults and screened from casual glances."

> The question for me, then, is whether a local library could itself constitutionally impose these restrictions on the content otherwise available to an adult patron through an Internet connection, at a library terminal provided for public use. The answer is no. A library that chose to block an adult's Internet access to material harmful to children (and whatever else the undiscriminating filter might interrupt) would be imposing a content-based restriction on communication of material in the library's control that an adult could otherwise lawfully see. This would simply be censorship. True, the censorship would not necessarily extend to every adult, for an intending Internet user might convince a librarian that he was a true researcher or had a "lawful purpose" to obtain everything the library's terminal could provide. But as to those who did not qualify for discretionary unblocking, the censorship would be complete and, like all censorship by an agency of the Government, presumptively invalid owing to strict scrutiny in implementing the Free Speech Clause of the First Amendment. "The policy of the First Amendment favors dissemination of information and opinion, and the guarantees of freedom of speech and press were not designed to prevent the censorship of the press merely, but any action of the government by means of which it might prevent such free and general discussion of public matters as seems absolutely essential."

Justice Souter distinguished between libraries' need to be selective, because of constraints of both money and shelf space, in what libraries "acquire to place in their stacks," and the new realities of the Internet.

> At every significant point, however, the Internet blocking here defies comparison to the process of acquisition. Whereas traditional scarcity of money and space require a library to make choices about what to acquire, and the choice to be made is whether or not to spend the money to acquire something, blocking is the subject of a choice made after the money for Internet access has been spent or committed. Since it makes no difference to the cost of Internet access whether an adult calls up material harmful for children or the Articles of Confederation, blocking (on facts like these) is not necessitated by scarcity of either money or space. In the instance of the Internet, what the library acquires is electronic access, and the choice to block is a choice to limit access that has already been acquired. Thus, deciding against buying a book means there is no book (unless a loan can be obtained), but blocking the Internet is merely blocking access purchased in its entirety and subject to unblocking if the librarian

agrees. The proper analogy therefore is not to passing up a book that might have been bought; it is either to buying a book and then keeping it from adults lacking an acceptable "purpose," or to buying an encyclopedia and then cutting out pages with anything thought to be unsuitable for all adults.

The plurality claims to find support for its conclusions in the "traditional missio[n]" of the public library. The plurality thus argues, in effect, that the traditional responsibility of public libraries has called for denying adult access to certain books, or bowdlerizing the content of what the libraries let adults see. But, in fact, the plurality's conception of a public library's mission has been rejected by the libraries themselves. And no library that chose to block adult access in the way mandated by the Act could claim that the history of public library practice in this country furnished an implicit gloss on First Amendment standards, allowing for blocking out anything unsuitable for adults.

Institutional history of public libraries in America discloses an evolution toward a general rule, now firmly rooted, that any adult entitled to use the library has access to any of its holdings. [B]y the end of the 1930s, librarians' "basic position in opposition to censorship [had] emerged."

Thus, there is no preacquisition scarcity rationale to save library Internet blocking from treatment as censorship, and no support for it in the historical development of library practice. To these two reasons to treat blocking differently from a decision declining to buy a book, a third must be added. Quite simply, we can smell a rat when a library blocks material already in its control, just as we do when a library removes books from its shelves for reasons having nothing to do with wear and tear, obsolescence, or lack of demand. Content-based blocking and removal tell us something that mere absence from the shelves does not.

. . . [T]he Act's blocking requirement in its current breadth calls for unconstitutional action by a library recipient, and is itself unconstitutional.

Discussion

1. *Asking politely.* The result in *American Library Association* seems to turn on the ease with which adult patrons can get access to unfiltered Internet access. Does this mean that any future "as applied" challenges will rely on very specific facts concerning ease of access? At what point would you find "normal delay" turning into an "unconstitutional burden" on a library patron's presumptive First Amendment right of access?

2. *Refusal to fund or penalty?* What response can the plurality give to Justice Stevens's point that funding is withdrawn even if some of the computers hooked up to the Internet were not purchased by the government, and do not make use of subsidized Internet access? Is it enough to answer that it would not violate the First Amendment for the federal government to mandate directly that all libraries install filtering software? (Note the possible federalism problems under *Printz.*)

In a footnote, Chief Justice Rehnquist notes various cases holding that government may not "reduce the adult population . . . to reading only what is fit for children," but argues that "these cases are inapposite because they addressed Congress' direct regulation of private conduct, not exercises of its Spending Power." Why should that be?

3. *Content-based censorship or interference with professional judgment?* The dissenters acknowledge that librarians inevitably make selective judgments in what books to include in their collections, and their judgments may include issues of quality as well as cost and upkeep. If a library can make restrictions based on subject matter (for example, a music library), why can't it also exclude pornographic materials

using a filtering program? And if it can do so constitutionally, why can't the government choose to provide subsidized computer and Internet services only to libraries that make these sorts of exclusions in Internet access?

Is the answer that when the federal government does so, it is impinging on First Amendment rights of public librarians that are akin to the academic freedom enjoyed by public universities? Under this line of reasoning, the issue is not federalism but *professionalism:* Even federal public libraries would have some degree of freedom from Congressional attempts to dictate how they organize their collections or provide information. Frederick Schauer, in Comment: Principles, Institutions, and the First Amendment, 112 Harv. L. Rev. 84 (1998), emphasized the importance of what he terms an "institution-specific" analysis of the speech-related interests involved in the operation of public institutions (like public television, public libraries, and the National Endowment for the Arts or Humanities) and a concomitant deference to trained professionals that he sees as a theme in both *Finley* and the Arkansas public television case. Are we in fact more comfortable with judgments about the "worth" or "value" of certain speech being made by professional librarians, artists, or journalists, than by nonprofessional members of the public, including politicians? Note, however, that the majority in *Rust* was quite unsympathetic to the value of protecting the professional judgment of physicians if that would permit the physician to mention even the possibility of abortion to his or her patient. By contrast, the next section considers constitutional challenges to conditions placed on professional lawyers, paid by the government, when representing their clients. Why does the professionalism argument succeed in one case but not the other? When do you think it *should* succeed?

6.   Speech by Government Lawyers

Almost everyone agrees that a state cannot condition the provision of funds to public defenders or court-appointed criminal defense lawyers on their agreement not to inform their clients that the Fifth Amendment gives them the right to refuse to talk to the police or testify at trial. But why, precisely, is this so? What response do you think Professor Post would give? What, however, if the state required only that state-subsidized criminal defense lawyers, after informing their clients of their Fifth Amendment rights, go on to say to them that "refusing to tell the authorities what you know about the crime is considered an antisocial act by most right-thinking people, and confessing one's misdeeds is the first step toward rehabilitation"? Would this be unconstitutional under Post's approach? Should it? Would your answer depend on the empirical truth or falsity of the information given?

Consider the following limitations passed by Congress and signed by President Clinton in 1996 as part of the Omnibus Consolidated Recission and Appropriations Act of 1996.

Sec. 504: (a) None of the funds appropriated in this Act to the Legal Services Corporation may be used to provide financial assistance to any person or entity . . .

(1) that makes available any funds, personnel, or equipment for use in advocating or opposing any plan or proposal, or represents any party or participates in any other way in litigation, that is intended to or has the effect of altering, revising, or reapportioning a legislative, judicial, or elective district at any level of government, including influencing the timing or manner of the taking of a census; . . .

(4) that attempts to influence the passage or defeat of any legislation, constitutional amendment, referendum, initiative, or any similar procedure of the Congress or a State or local legislative body; . . .

(7) that initiates or participates in a class action suit; . . .

(14) that participates in any litigation with respect to abortion;

(15) that participates in any litigation on behalf of a person incarcerated in a Federal, State, or local prison;

(16) that initiates legal representation or participates in any other way, in litigation, lobbying, or rulemaking, involving an effort to reform a Federal or State welfare system, except that this paragraph shall not be construed to preclude a recipient from representing an individual eligible client who is seeking specific relief from a welfare agency if such relief does not involve an effort to amend or otherwise challenge existing law in effect on the date of the initiation of the representation;

(17) that defends a person in a proceeding to evict the person from a public housing project if — (A) the person has been charged with the illegal sale or distribution of a controlled substance; and (B) the eviction proceeding is brought by a public housing agency because the illegal drug activity of the person threatens the health or safety of another tenant residing in the public housing project or employee of the public housing agency. . . .

Clause 16 of this section was struck down by the Supreme Court in *Legal Services Corporation v. Velazquez*, 531 U.S. 533 (2001). Justice Kennedy wrote the majority opinion, joined by Justices Stevens, Souter, Ginsburg, and Breyer. As one might imagine, the Court's holding in *Rust* was much discussed. Admitting that the Court's opinion in that case "did not place explicit reliance on the rationale that the counseling activities of the doctors under Title X amounted to governmental speech," Justice Kennedy said that

when interpreting the holding in later cases, however, we have explained *Rust* on this understanding. . . . The latitude which may exist for restrictions on speech where the government's own message is being delivered flows in part from our observation that, "when the government speaks, for instance to promote its own policies or to advance a particular idea, it is, in the end, accountable to the electorate and the political process for its advocacy. If the citizenry objects, newly elected officials later could espouse some different or contrary position." Board of Regents of Univ. of Wis. System v. Southworth, 529 U.S. 217 (2000).

An attorney representing a private party, even if financed by the government, does not, however "promote a governmental message. . . . [A]n LSC-funded attorney speaks on the behalf of the client in a claim against the government for welfare benefits. The lawyer is not the government's speaker." To allow the government to control the attorney's presentation to the court would "distort [the] usual functioning" of the adversary system.

Restricting LSC attorneys in advising their clients and in presenting arguments and analyses to the courts distorts the legal system by altering the traditional role of the attorneys in much the same way broadcast systems [in FCC v. League of Women Voters] or student publication networks [in *Rosenberger*] were changed. . . . Just as government in those cases could not elect to use a broadcasting network or a college publication structure in a regime which prohibits speech necessary to the proper functioning of those systems . . . it may not design a subsidy to effect this serious and fundamental restriction on advocacy of attorneys and the functioning of the judiciary. . . . LSC has advised us, furthermore, that upon determining a question of statutory validity is present in any anticipated or pending case or controversy, the

LSC-funded attorney must cease the representation at once. This is true whether the validity issue becomes apparent during initial attorney-client consultations or in the midst of litigation proceedings. . . . It is well understood that when there are two reasonable constructions for a statute, yet one raises a constitutional question, the Court should prefer the interpretation which avoids the constitutional issue. . . . Yet, as the LSC advised the Court, if, during litigation, a judge were to ask an LSC attorney whether there was a constitutional concern, the LSC attorney simply could not answer.

. . . The restriction imposed by the statute here threatens severe impairment of the judicial function. . . . If the restriction on speech and legal advice were to stand, the result would be two tiers of cases. In cases where LSC counsel were attorneys of record, there would be lingering doubt whether the truncated representation had resulted in complete analysis of the case, full advice to the client, and proper presentation to the court. The courts and the public would come to question the adequacy and fairness of professional representations when the attorney, either consciously to comply with this statute or unconsciously to continue the representation despite the statute, avoided all reference to questions of statutory validity and constitutional authority. A scheme so inconsistent with accepted separation-of-powers principles is an insufficient basis to sustain or uphold the restriction on speech.

It is no answer to say the restriction on speech is harmless because, under LSC's interpretation of the Act, its attorneys can withdraw. This misses the point. The statute is an attempt to draw lines around the LSC program to exclude from litigation those arguments and theories Congress finds unacceptable but which by their nature are within the province of the courts to consider.

The restriction on speech is even more problematic because in cases where the attorney withdraws from a representation, the client is unlikely to find other counsel. The explicit premise for providing LSC attorneys is the necessity to make available representation "to persons financially unable to afford legal assistance." 42 U.S.C. §2996(a)(3). There often will be no alternative source for the client to receive vital information respecting constitutional and statutory rights bearing upon claimed benefits. Thus, with respect to the litigation services Congress has funded, there is no alternative channel for expression of the advocacy Congress seeks to restrict. This is in stark contrast to *Rust*. There, a patient could receive the approved Title X family planning counseling funded by the Government and later could consult an affiliate or independent organization to receive abortion counseling. Unlike indigent clients who seek LSC representation, the patient in *Rust* was not required to forfeit the Government-funded advice when she also received abortion counseling through alternative channels. Because LSC attorneys must withdraw whenever a question of a welfare statute's validity arises, an individual could not obtain joint representation so that the constitutional challenge would be presented by a non-LSC attorney, and other, permitted, arguments advanced by LSC counsel.

Finally, LSC and the Government maintain that §504(a)(16) is necessary to . . . ensure[] funds can be spent for those cases most immediate to congressional concern[:] [providing] limited congressional funds for the provision of simple suits for benefits [and] removing from the program complex challenges to existing welfare laws. The effect of the restriction, however, is to prohibit advice or argumentation that existing welfare laws are unconstitutional or unlawful. Congress cannot recast a condition on funding as a mere definition of its program in every case, lest the First Amendment be reduced to a simple semantic exercise. . . . We must be vigilant when Congress imposes rules and conditions which in effect insulate its own laws from legitimate judicial challenge. Where private speech is involved, even Congress' antecedent funding decision cannot be aimed at the suppression of ideas thought inimical to the Government's own interest.

Justice Scalia dissented, joined by Chief Justice Rehnquist and Justices O'Connor and Thomas. For them, "[t]he LSC Act is a federal subsidy program, not a federal regulatory program," which, as such, gave the government wide latitude in conditioning the dispensation and spending of its funds. [S]imply denying a subsidy "does not 'coerce' belief" or otherwise threaten "to drive certain ideas or viewpoints from the marketplace," the government may therefore "allocate . . . funding according to criteria that would be impermissible were direct regulation of speech or a criminal penalty at stake."

> §504(a)(16) [does not] discriminate on the basis of viewpoint, since it funds neither challenges to nor defenses of existing welfare law. The provision simply declines to subsidize a certain class of litigation, and under *Rust* that decision "does not infringe the right" to bring such litigation. . . .
>
> The Court contends that *Rust* is different because the program at issue subsidized government speech, while the LSC funds private speech. . . . If the private doctors' confidential advice to their patients at issue in *Rust* constituted "government speech," it is hard to imagine what subsidized speech would not be government speech. Moreover, the majority's contention that the subsidized speech in these cases is not government speech because the lawyers have a professional obligation to represent the interests of their clients founders on the reality that the doctors in *Rust* had a professional obligation to serve the interests of their patients. . . .
>
> [T]here is utterly no precedent for the novel and facially implausible proposition that the First Amendment has anything to do with government funding that — though it does not actually abridge anyone's speech — "distorts an existing medium of expression." . . . The Court's "nondistortion" principle is also wrong on the facts, since there is no basis for believing that §504(a)(16), by causing "cases [to] be presented by LSC attorneys who cannot advise the courts of serious questions of statutory validity," will distort the operation of the courts. It may well be that the bar of §504(a)(16) will cause LSC-funded attorneys to decline or to withdraw from cases that involve statutory validity. But that means at most that fewer statutory challenges to welfare laws will be presented to the courts because of the unavailability of free legal services for that purpose. So what? The same result would ensue from excluding LSC-funded lawyers from welfare litigation entirely. It is not the mandated, nondistortable function of the courts to inquire into all "serious questions of statutory validity" in all cases. Courts must consider only those questions of statutory validity that are presented by litigants, and if the Government chooses not to subsidize the presentation of some such questions, that in no way "distorts" the courts' role. . . . Nor will the judicial opinions produced by LSC cases systematically distort the interpretation of welfare laws. Judicial decisions do not stand as binding "precedent" for points that were not raised, not argued, and hence not analyzed. The statutory validity that courts assume in LSC cases will remain open for full determination in later cases.
>
> Finally, the Court is troubled "because in cases where the attorney withdraws from a representation, the client is unlikely to find other counsel." That is surely irrelevant, since it leaves the welfare recipient in no worse condition than he would have been in had the LSC program never been enacted. . . .

Justice Scalia argued that if the provision was held unconstitutional, the statute providing funding for indigent litigants in welfare cases should be struck down as a whole. "The severability question here is, essentially, whether, without the restriction that the Court today invalidates, the permission for conducting welfare litigation would have been accorded. As far as appears from the best evidence (which is the structure of the statute), I think the answer must be no."

Discussion

Is *Velazquez* a case about protecting the rights of indigents or protecting the rights of lawyers and judges? Is it a case about an attempt to regulate the public domain of speech or rather a case about an attempt to skew the adversarial system in the government's favor? Justice Kennedy argues that when courts decide cases without the benefit of counsel who can make all relevant arguments, the legal system is distorted and both justice and the perception of justice suffer. Why does this concern not also apply to indigent criminal defendants represented by harried and underprepared counsel who are appointed to defend them?

Recall the earlier discussion of potential "inconsistency" in the Court's decisions because of the fact that it is a multimember institution with the so-called "median" justices dictating the outcome in close cases. For example, it is entirely possible that eight of the nine justices believe that *Rust* and *Velazquez* should be decided the same way. However, because they split 4-4 on what the right outcome should be, Justice Kennedy's possibly idiosyncratic view that they are distinguishable controls (and generates a precedent for future justices — not to mention law students and their professors — to contend with).

E.   Religion in the Modern Welfare State

Cases like *Rosenberger* have already suggested how religious belief and practice intersect with the demands of the modern welfare state. In this section we look at a number of cases that consider whether the state can condition aid on the willingness of recipients to forego what they believe to be the "free exercise" of their religion.

1.   Unemployment Compensation and Religious Commitments

THOMAS v. REVIEW BOARD OF THE INDIANA EMPLOYMENT SECURITY DIVISION
450 U.S. 707 (1981)

BURGER, C.J., delivered the opinion of the Court.

[Thomas, a Jehovah's Witness, lost his job upon his refusal to participate in what, from his perspective, was the production of armaments, conduct he viewed as barred by his religious beliefs. Indiana thereupon refused to grant him unemployment compensation benefits because Thomas had left his job without "good cause," as required by Indiana law. After several intermediate appeals, the Indiana Supreme Court upheld the denial of benefits on the grounds that Thomas quit voluntarily and "for personal reasons." According to the Court, "A personal philosophical choice rather than a religious choice does not rise to the level of a First Amendment claim." The Court went on to hold, moreover, that even if Thomas's quitting was ascribable to religious reasons, he would still not be entitled to benefits, for Indiana law did not recognize a termination motivated by religion as work-related "good cause." The Court also held that granting unemployment benefits to persons who quit voluntarily for religious reasons, but not to persons who leave their jobs for personal but nonreligious reasons, would violate the Establishment Clause of the First Amendment.]

The judgment under review must be examined in light of our prior decisions, particularly Sherbert v. Verner, 374 U.S. 398 (1963).

II.

Only beliefs rooted in religion are protected by the Free Exercise Clause. . . . [The Court goes on to hold that Thomas's action was indeed rooted in religious beliefs. In deciding otherwise,] the Indiana court seems to have placed considerable reliance on the facts that Thomas was "struggling" with his beliefs and that he was not able to "articulate" his belief precisely. It noted, for example, that Thomas admitted before the referee that he would not object to "working for United States Steel or Inland Steel . . . produc[ing] the raw product necessary for the production of any kind of tank . . . [because I] would not be a direct party to whoever they shipped it to [and] would not be . . . chargeable in . . . conscience. . . ." The court found this position inconsistent with Thomas' stated opposition to participation in the production of armaments. But Thomas' statements reveal no more than that he found work in the roll foundry sufficiently insulated from producing weapons of war. We see, therefore, that Thomas drew a line, and it is not for us to say that the line he drew was an unreasonable one. Courts should not undertake to dissect religious beliefs because the believer admits that he is "struggling" with his position or because his beliefs are not articulated with the clarity and precision that a more sophisticated person might employ.

The Indiana court also appears to have given significant weight to the fact that another Jehovah's Witness had no scruples about working on tank turrets; for that other Witness, at least, such work was "scripturally" acceptable. Intrafaith differences of that kind are not uncommon among followers of a particular creed, and the judicial process is singularly ill equipped to resolve such differences in relation to the Religion Clauses. One can, of course, imagine an asserted claim so bizarre, so clearly nonreligious in motivation, as not to be entitled to protection under the Free Exercise Clause; but that is not the case here, and the guarantee of free exercise is not limited to beliefs which are shared by all of the members of a religious sect. Particularly in this sensitive area, it is not within the judicial function and judicial competence to inquire whether the petitioner or his fellow worker more correctly perceived the commands of their common faith. Courts are not arbiters of scriptural interpretation. . . .

III.

A

More than 30 years ago, the Court held that a person may not be compelled to choose between the exercise of a First Amendment right and participation in an otherwise available public program. . . . Everson v. Board of Education, 330 U.S. 1, 16 (1947).

Later, in *Sherbert,* the Court examined South Carolina's attempt to deny unemployment compensation benefits to a Sabbatarian who declined to work on Saturday. In sustaining her right to receive benefits, the Court held: "The ruling [disqualifying Mrs. Sherbert from benefits because of her refusal to work on Saturday in violation of her faith] forces her to choose between following the precepts of her religion and forfeiting benefits, on the one hand, and abandoning one of the precepts of her religion in order to accept work, on the other hand. Governmental imposition of such a choice puts the same kind of burden upon the free exercise of religion as would a fine imposed against [her] for her Saturday worship." . . . Here, as in *Sherbert,* the employee was put to a choice between fidelity to religious belief or cessation of work; the coercive impact on Thomas is indistinguishable from *Sherbert,* where the Court held: "[N]ot only is it apparent that appellant's declared ineligibility for benefits derives solely from the practice of her religion, but the pressure upon her to forego that practice is unmistakable." Where the state conditions receipt of an important benefit upon conduct proscribed by a religious faith, or where it denies such a benefit because of conduct mandated by religious belief, thereby putting substantial pressure on an adherent to modify his behavior and to violate his beliefs, a burden upon religion exists. While the compulsion may be indirect, the infringement upon free exercise is nonetheless substantial. . . .

B

The mere fact that the petitioner's religious practice is burdened by a governmental program does not mean that an exemption accommodating his practice must be granted. The state may justify an inroad on religious liberty by showing that it is the least restrictive means of achieving some compelling state interest. . . .

The purposes urged to sustain the disqualifying provision of the Indiana unemployment compensation scheme are twofold: (1) to avoid the widespread unemployment and the consequent burden on the fund resulting if people were permitted to leave jobs for "personal" reasons; and (2) to avoid a detailed probing by employers into job applicants' religious beliefs. These are by no means unimportant considerations. When the focus of the inquiry is properly narrowed, however, we must conclude that the interests advanced by the State do not justify the burden placed on free exercise of religion.

There is no evidence in the record to indicate that the number of people who find themselves in the predicament of choosing between benefits and religious beliefs is large enough to create "widespread unemployment," or even to seriously affect unemployment — and no such claim was advanced by the Review Board. Similarly, although detailed inquiry by employers into applicants' religious beliefs is undesirable, there is no evidence in the record to indicate that such inquiries will occur in Indiana, or that they have occurred in any of the states that extend benefits to people in the petitioner's position. Nor is there any reason to believe that the number of people terminating employment for religious reasons will be so great as to motivate employers to make such inquiries. . . .

IV.

The respondents contend that to compel benefit payments to Thomas involves the State in fostering a religious faith. There is, in a sense, a "benefit" to Thomas deriving from his religious beliefs, but this manifests no more than the tension between the two Religious Clauses which the Court resolved in *Sherbert:*

> In holding as we do, plainly we are not fostering the "establishment" of the Seventh-
> day Adventist religion in South Carolina, for the extension of unemployment benefits

to Sabbatarians in common with Sunday worshippers reflects nothing more than the governmental obligation of neutrality in the face of religious differences, and does not represent that involvement of religious with secular institutions which it is the object of the Establishment Clause to forestall.

REHNQUIST, J., dissenting . . . :

I.

The Court correctly acknowledges that there is a "tension" between the Free Exercise and Establishment Clauses of the First Amendment of the United States Constitution. Although the relationship of the two Clauses has been the subject of much commentary, the "tension" is a fairly recent vintage, unknown at the time of the framing and adoption of the First Amendment. The causes of the tension, it seems to me, are threefold. First, the growth of social welfare legislation during the latter part of the 20th century has greatly magnified the potential for conflict between the two Clauses, since such legislation touches the individual at so many points in his life. Second, the decision by this Court that the First Amendment was "incorporated" into the Fourteenth Amendment and thereby made applicable against the States similarly multiplied the number of instances in which the "tension" might arise. The third, and perhaps most important, cause of the tension is our overly expansive interpretation of both Clauses. By broadly construing both Clauses, the Court has constantly narrowed the channel between the Scylla and Charybdis through which any state or federal action must pass in order to survive constitutional scrutiny.

None of these developments could have been foreseen by those who framed and adopted the First Amendment. . . .

II.

. . . Just as it did in Sherbert v. Verner, the Court today reads the Free Exercise Clause more broadly than is warranted. As to the proper interpretation of the Free Exercise Clause, I would accept the decision of Braunfeld v. Brown, 366 U.S. 599 (1961), and the dissent in *Sherbert*. In *Braunfeld*, we held that Sunday closing laws do not violate the First Amendment rights of Sabbatarians. Chief Justice Warren explained that the statute did not make unlawful any religious practices of appellants; it simply made the practice of their religious beliefs more expensive. We concluded that "[t]o strike down, without the most critical scrutiny, legislation which imposes only an indirect burden on the exercise of religion, i.e., legislation which does not make unlawful the religious practice itself, would radically restrict the operating latitude of the legislature." Likewise in this case, it cannot be said that the State discriminated against Thomas on the basis of his religious beliefs or that he was denied benefits because he was a Jehovah's Witness. Where, as here, a State has enacted a general statute, the purpose and effect of which is to advance the State's secular goals, the Free Exercise Clause does not in my view require the State to conform that statute to the dictates of religious conscience of any group. As Justice Harlan recognized in his dissent in Sherbert v. Verner: "Those situations in which the Constitution may require special treatment on account of religion are . . . few and far between." Like him I believe that although a State could choose to grant exemptions to religious persons from state unemployment regulations, a State is not constitutionally compelled to do so.

The Court's treatment of the Establishment Clause issue is equally unsatisfying. . . . I would agree that the Establishment Clause, properly interpreted, would not be violated if Indiana voluntarily chose to grant unemployment benefits to those persons who left their jobs for religious reasons. But I also believe that the decision below is inconsistent with many of our prior Establishment Clause cases. . . .

Justice Stewart noted this point in his concurring opinion in *Sherbert*. He observed that decisions like *Sherbert*, and the one rendered today, squarely conflict with the more extreme language of many of our prior Establishment Clause cases. In Everson v. Board of Education, 330 U.S. 1 (1947), the Court stated that the Establishment Clause bespeaks a "government . . . stripped of all power . . . to support, or otherwise to assist any or all religions . . . ," and no State "can pass laws which aid one religion . . . [or] all religions." In Torcaso v. Watkins, 367 U.S. 488, 495 (1961), the Court asserted that the government cannot "constitutionally pass laws or impose requirements which aid all religions as against non-believers." . . .

In recent years the Court has moved away from the mechanistic "no-aid-to-religion" approach to the Establishment Clause and has stated a three-part test to determine the constitutionality of governmental aid to religion. See Lemon v. Kurtzman, 403 U.S. 602 (1971). . . . First, the statute must serve a secular legislative purpose. Second, it must have a "primary effect" that neither advances nor inhibits religion. And third, the State and its administration must avoid excessive entanglement with religion.

It is not surprising that the Court today makes no attempt to apply those principles to the facts of this case. If Indiana were to legislate what the Court today requires — an unemployment compensation law which permitted benefits to be granted to those persons who quit their jobs for religious reasons — the statute would "plainly" violate the Establishment Clause as interpreted in such cases. . . . First . . . , the proviso would . . . grant financial benefits for the sole purpose of accommodating religious beliefs. Second, there can be little doubt that the primary effect of the proviso would be to "advance" religion by facilitating the exercise of religious belief. Third, any statute including such a proviso would surely "entangle" the State in religion far more than the mere grant of tax exemptions . . . or the award of tuition grants and tax credits. . . . By granting financial benefits to persons solely on the basis of their religious beliefs, the State must necessarily inquire whether the claimant's belief is "religious" and whether it is sincerely held. . . . It is unclear from the Court's opinion whether it has temporarily retreated from its expansive view of the Establishment Clause, or wholly abandoned it. . . .

Discussion

In Hobbie v. Unemployment Appeals Commission of Florida, 480 U.S. 136 (1987), the Court overturned the refusal of Florida to award unemployment benefits after Hobbie, who had been employed by a jeweler for two and a half years, informed her immediate supervisor that she was to be baptized into the Seventh-Day Adventist Church and that, for religious reasons, she would no longer be able to work on her Sabbath, from sundown on Friday to sundown on Saturday. Although the supervisor devised an arrangement with Hobbie that accommodated her new beliefs, the general manager of the jewelry store, upon learning of the arrangement, informed Hobbie that she could either work her scheduled shifts or submit her resignation to the company. When Hobbie refused to do either, she was discharged.

However, in a case involving the administration of Oregon's unemployment compensation system, the Court in effect held that a drug counselor was discharged "for cause" after using peyote as part of a centuries-old religious ceremony of Native Americans. See Employment Division, Department of Human Resources of Oregon v. Smith, 494 U.S. 872 (1990). The difference was based on the legitimacy of Oregon's criminalizing all use of such drugs, regardless of the circumstances. Justice Scalia, for the Court, rejected a Free Exercise challenge and held that the Oregon law was neutrally applied to the religious and nonreligious alike and that, therefore, only a "rational basis" was necessary in order to sustain it. Justice Scalia's opinion explicitly distinguished the earlier compensation cases by noting that the state conducts individual inquiries before granting compensation. But, of course, the key question is whether the reason "I left my job because of my religious views" must be treated differently by the hearing examiner than the reason "I left my job because I had to take care of my sick child." The *Sherbert* line of cases presumably requires different treatment (at least if the latter reason is not treated as legitimate by the state).

2.   Can Aid to Schools (or Parents) Be Conditioned on Offering (or Having Their Children Receive) Only a Secular Education?

The funding of education is clearly one of the most important "public welfare programs" carried out by state and national government alike. A pervasive issue, both political and constitutional, is the legitimacy of granting aid to private schools on condition that they are non-religious. One argument is that the Establishment Clause of the First Amendment itself requires that the state not in any way fund religious schools. In response, some analysts read either the Free Exercise Clause or the Equal Protection Clause as disallowing the distinction between secular and religious private schools. It is obvious, incidentally, that quite different doctrinal arguments can be (and are) made in this area. We present them as part of the materials dealing with "unconstitutional conditions" not because it is the only appropriate area of this casebook, but, rather, because we think it most useful to treat the cases involving religion together. You might ask yourself, though, if most equal protection cases could be "translated" into "unconstitutional conditions" cases and, concomitantly, if most "unconstitutional conditions" cases could also be stated as equal protection claims. If, in fact, this is the case, then the obvious question is: which way of conceptualizing the issue casts most light on the underlying dilemmas of state power and individual (or group) rights?

3.   The "No-Aid" Paradigm in the Warren and Early Burger Courts

We do not in this casebook come close to a full survey of the immensely complicated, indeed many would say garbled and incoherent, law of the establishment clause over the past generation, or even of the particular application of that clause to the problem of state aid to religious schools. Rather, our purpose is to introduce the problem and provide a basic literacy that students can draw on in further courses on the First Amendment or on religion and the Constitution.

We first present a case that served as the paradigm, for at least a quarter-century, of how best to analyze the problem of state aid to religious schools.

COMMITTEE FOR PUBLIC EDUCATION & LIBERTY v. NYQUIST
413 U.S. 756 (1973)

[In 1972, New York established three financial aid programs for nonpublic elementary and secondary schools. Under the first, the state would give direct money grants to "qualifying" schools to be used for the "maintenance and repair of . . . school facilities and equipment to ensure the health, welfare and safety of enrolled pupils." "Qualifying" schools were those that "serv[ed] a high concentration of pupils from low-income families. . . ." This section of the legislation is prefaced by an assertion that the State "has a primary responsibility to ensure the health, welfare and safety of children attending . . . nonpublic schools" and a finding that the "fiscal crisis in nonpublic education . . . has caused a diminution of proper maintenance and repair programs, threatening the health, welfare and safety of nonpublic school children" in low-income urban areas.

The other two aspects of the legislation consist of tuition grants and a tax benefit program. Parents having annual taxable income under $5,000 (which is equivalent to approximately $23,250 in 2005 dollars[49]) could receive limited reimbursement ($50 and $100 for each child attending elementary and high school, respectively) for tuition payments to private schools. The legislature had found that the ability to choose among alternative educational programs "is diminished or even denied to children of lower-income families, whose parents, of all groups, have the least options in determining where their children are to be educated." Furthermore, the legislature found that any "precipitious decline in the number of nonpublic school pupils would cause a massive increase in public school enrollment and costs," which would "aggravate an already serious fiscal crisis in public education" and would "seriously jeopardize quality education for all children."

Finally, parents who cannot qualify for tuition reimbursement are provided some state tax relief by allowing them to deduct part of the money expended in private school tuition from their gross income. Taxpayers with less than $9,000 gross income can deduct $1,000 for each of up to three dependents. The deduction diminishes as one goes up the income scale — for example, a taxpayer with $15,000 gross income can deduct only $400 per dependent — and is eliminated at the $25,000 level.

Plaintiff-petitioners challenged the legislation on the ground that religious schools were included among "qualifying" schools. Approximately 20 percent of the New York school population attended nonpublic schools, of which 85 percent were church affiliated, most of these being Roman Catholic, with some Jewish, Lutheran, Episcopal, and Seventh-Day Adventist schools as well. The Supreme Court declared all three programs unconstitutional.]

POWELL, J. . . . :

49. See *http://www.bls.gov/cpi/home.htm* for an inflation calculator.

II.

The history of the Establishment Clause has been recounted frequently and need not be repeated here. See Everson v. Board of Education, 330 U.S. 1 (1947); McCollum v. Board of Education, 333 U.S. 203, 212 (1948) (separate opinion of Frankfurter, J.); McGowan v. Maryland, 366 U.S. 420 (1961); Engel v. Vitale, 370 U.S. 421 (1962). It is enough to note that it is now firmly established that a law may be one "respecting an establishment of religion" even though its consequence is not to promote a "state religion," Lemon v. Kurtzman, 403 U.S. 602, 612 (1971), and even though it does not aid one religion more than another but merely benefits all religions alike. It is equally well established, however, that not every law that confers an "indirect," "remote," or "incidental" benefit upon religious institutions is, for that reason alone, constitutionally invalid. What our cases require is careful examination of any law challenged on establishment grounds with a view to ascertaining whether it furthers any of the evils against which that Clause protects. Primary among those evils have been "sponsorship, financial support, and active involvement of the sovereign in religious activity." Walz v. Tax Commissioner, 397 U.S. 664, 668 (1970) [upholding tax exemptions granted to religious institutions].

. . . [A] now well-defined three-part test . . . has emerged from our decisions. . . . [T]o pass muster under the Establishment Clause the law in question, first, must reflect a clearly secular legislative purpose, second, must have a primary effect that neither advances nor inhibits religions, and third, must avoid excessive government entanglement with religion.

In applying these criteria to the three distinct forms of aid involved in this case, we need touch only briefly on the requirement of a "secular legislative purpose." . . . [E]ach measure is adequately supported by legitimate, nonsectarian state interests. We do not question the propriety, and fully secular content, of New York's interest in preserving a healthy and safe educational environment for all of its schoolchildren. And we do not doubt . . . the validity of the State's interests in promoting pluralism and diversity among its public and nonpublic schools. Nor do we hesitate to acknowledge the reality of its concern for an already overburdened public school system that might suffer in the event that a significant percentage of children presently attending nonpublic schools should abandon those schools in favor of the public schools. . . .

A

The "maintenance and repair" provisions . . . authorize direct payments to nonpublic schools, virtually all of which are Roman Catholic schools in low-income areas. The grants, totaling $30 or $40 per pupil depending on the age of the institution, are given largely without restriction on usage. . . . No attempt is made to restrict payments to those expenditures related to the upkeep of facilities used exclusively for secular purposes, nor do we think it possible within the context of these religion-oriented institutions to impose such restrictions. Nothing in the statute, for instance, bars a qualifying school from paying out of state funds the salaries of employees who maintain the school chapel, or the cost of renovating classrooms in which religion is taught, or the cost of heating and lighting those same facilities. Absent appropriate restrictions on expenditures for these and similar purposes, it simply cannot be denied that this section has a primary effect that advances religion in that it subsidizes directly the religious activities of sectarian elementary and secondary schools.

The state officials nevertheless argue that these expenditures for "maintenance and repair" are similar to other financial expenditures approved by this Court. Primarily they rely on Everson v. Board of Education, supra; Board of Education v. Allen, 392 U.S. 236 (1968); and Tilton v. Richardson, 403 U.S. 672 (1971). In each of those cases it is true that the Court approved a form of financial assistance which conferred undeniable benefits upon private, sectarian schools. But a close examination of those cases illuminates their distinguishing characteristics. In *Everson,* the Court, in a five to-four decision, approved a program of reimbursements to parents of public as well as parochial schoolchildren for bus fares paid in connection with transportation to and from school, a program which the Court characterized as approaching the "verge" of impermissible state aid. In *Allen,* decided some 20 years later, the Court upheld a New York law authorizing the provision of secular textbooks for all children in grades seven through 12 attending public and nonpublic schools. Finally, in *Tilton,* the Court upheld federal grants of funds for the construction of facilities to be used for clearly secular purposes by public and nonpublic institutions of higher learning.

. . . *Tilton* draws the line most clearly. While a bare majority was there persuaded . . . that carefully limited construction grants to colleges and universities could be sustained, the Court was unanimous in its rejection of one clause of the federal statute in question. Under that clause, the Government was entitled to recover a portion of its grant to a sectarian institution in the event that the constructed facility was used to advance religion by, for instance, converting the building to a chapel or otherwise allowing it to be "used to promote religious interests." But because the statute provided that the condition would expire at the end of 20 years, the facilities would thereafter be available for use by the institution for any sectarian purpose. [The Court struck down the expiration provision.] If tax-raised funds may not be granted to institutions of higher learning where the possibility exists that those funds will be used to construct a facility utilized for sectarian activities 20 years hence, a fortiori they may not be distributed to elementary and secondary sectarian schools for the maintenance and repair of facilities without any limitations on their use. If the State may not erect buildings in which religious activities are to take place, it may not maintain such buildings or renovate them when they fall into disrepair. . . .

New York's maintenance and repair provisions violate the Establishment Clause because their effect, inevitably, is to subsidize and advance the religious mission of sectarian schools. . . .

B

New York's tuition reimbursement program also fails the "effect" test, for much the same reasons that govern its maintenance and repair grants. . . .

There can be no question that these grants could not, consistently with the Establishment Clause, be given directly to sectarian schools. . . . The controlling question here, then, is whether the fact that the grants are delivered to parents rather than schools is of such significance as to compel a contrary result. The State and intervenor-appellees rely on *Everson* and *Allen* for their claim that grants to parents, unlike grants to institutions, respect the "wall of separation" required by the Constitution. It is true that in those cases the Court upheld laws that provided benefits to children attending religious schools and to their parents. . . . But . . . the fact that aid is disbursed to parents rather than to the schools is only one among many factors to be considered.

In *Everson*, the Court found the bus fare program analogous to the provision of services such as police and fire protection, sewage disposal, highways, and sidewalks for parochial schools. Such services, provided in common to all citizens, are "so separate and so indisputably marked off from the religious function" that they may fairly be viewed as reflections of a neutral posture toward religious institutions. *Allen* is founded upon a similar principle. The Court there repeatedly emphasized that upon the record in that case there was no indication that textbooks would be provided for anything other than purely secular courses. . . .[a]

The tuition grants here are subject to no such restrictions. There has been no endeavor "to guarantee the separation between secular and religious educational functions and to ensure that State financial aid supports only the former." Indeed, it is precisely the function of New York's law to provide assistance to private schools, the great majority of which are sectarian. By reimbursing parents for a portion of their tuition bill, the State seeks to relieve their financial burdens sufficiently to assure that they continue to have the option to send their children to religion-oriented schools. And while the other purposes for that aid — to perpetuate a pluralistic educational environment and to protect the fiscal integrity of overburdened public schools — are certainly unexceptionable, the effect of the aid is unmistakably to provide desired financial support for nonpublic, sectarian institutions. . . .

[W]e will address briefly the subsidiary arguments made by the state officials and intervenors in [defense of the tuition grant program].

First, it has been suggested that it is of controlling significance that New York's program calls for reimbursement for tuition already paid rather than for direct contributions which are merely routed through the parents to the schools, in advance of or in lieu of payment by the parents. The parent is not a mere conduit, we are told, but is absolutely free to spend the money he receives in any manner he chooses. . . .

[However,] if the grants are offered as an incentive to parents to send their children to sectarian schools by making unrestricted cash payments to them, the Establishment Clause is violated whether or not the actual dollars given eventually find their way into the sectarian institutions. Whether the grant is labeled a reimbursement, a reward, or a subsidy, its substantive impact is still the same. . . .

Second, [it is argued] that it is significant here that the tuition reimbursement grants pay only a portion of the tuition bill, and an even smaller portion of the

---

a. *Allen* and *Everson* differ from the present litigation in a second important respect. In both cases the class of beneficiaries included all schoolchildren, those in public as well as those in private schools. . . . We do not agree with the suggestion in the dissent of [Chief Justice Burger] that tuition grants are an analogous endeavor to provide comparable benefits to all parents of schoolchildren whether enrolled in public or nonpublic schools. The grants to parents of private schoolchildren are given in addition to the right that they have to send their children to public schools "totally at state expense." And in any event, the argument proves too much, for it would also provide a basis for approving through tuition grants the complete subsidization of all religious schools on the ground that such action is necessary if the State is fully to equalize the position of parents who elect such schools — a result wholly at variance with the Establishment Clause. . . .

religious school's total expenses. The New York statute limits reimbursement to 50% of any parent's actual outlay. Additionally, intervenor estimates that only 30% of the total cost of nonpublic education is covered by tuition payments, with the remaining coming from "voluntary contribution, endowments and the like." On the basis of these two statistics, appellees reason that the "maximum tuition reimbursement by the State is thus only 15% of educational costs in the nonpublic schools." And, since the compulsory education laws of the State, by necessity require significantly more than 15% of school time to be devoted to teaching secular courses, the New York statute provides "a statistical guarantee of neutrality." . . . Our cases, however, have long since foreclosed the notion that mere statistical assurances will suffice to sail between the Scylla and Charybdis of "effect" and "entanglement."

Finally, the State argues that its program of tuition grants should survive scrutiny because it is designed to promote the free exercise of religion. The State notes that only "low-income parents" are aided by this law, and without state assistance their right to have their children educated in a religious environment "is diminished or even denied." It is true, of course, that this Court has long recognized and maintained the right to choose nonpublic over public education. Pierce v. Society of Sisters, 268 U.S. 510 (1925). It is also true that a state law interfering with a parent's right to have his child educated in a sectarian school would run afoul of the Free Exercise Clause. But this Court repeatedly has recognized that tension inevitably exists between the Free Exercise and the Establishment Clauses and that it may often not be possible to promote the former without offending the latter. As a result of this tension, our cases require the State to maintain an attitude of "neutrality," neither "advancing" nor "inhibiting" religion. In its attempt to enhance the opportunities of the poor to choose between public and nonpublic education, the State has taken a step which can only be regarded as one "advancing" religion. However great our sympathy for the burdens experienced by those who must pay public school taxes at the same time that they support other schools because of the constraints of "conscience and discipline," and notwithstanding the "high social importance" of the State's purposes, neither may justify an eroding of the limitations of the Establishment Clause now firmly emplanted.

C

[The final provisions of the New York legislation] establish a system for providing income tax benefits to parents of children attending New York's nonpublic schools. . . .

In practical terms there would appear to be little difference, for purposes of determining whether such aid has the effect of advancing religion, between the tax benefit allowed here and the tuition grant [invalidated in the previous section of the opinion]. . . .

[A]ppellees place their strongest reliance on Walz v. Tax Commission, in which New York's property tax exemption for religious organizations was upheld. We think that *Walz* provides no support for appellees' position. Indeed, its rationale plainly compels the conclusion that New York's tax package violates the Establishment Clause.

Tax exemptions for church property enjoyed an apparently universal approval in this country both before and after the adoption of the First Amendment. . . . We know of no historical precedent for New York's recently promulgated tax relief program. Indeed, it seems clear that tax benefits for parents whose children attend parochial schools are a recent innovation, occasioned by the growing financial plight of nonpublic institutions. . . .

But historical acceptance without more would not alone have sufficed, as "no one acquires a vested or protected right in violation of the Constitution by long use." It was the reason underlying that long history of tolerance of tax exemptions for religion that proved controlling. A proper respect for both the Free Exercise and the Establishment Clauses compels the State to pursue a course of "neutrality" toward religion. . . . Special tax benefits . . . cannot be squared with the principle of neutrality established by the decisions of this Court. To the contrary, insofar as such benefits render assistance to parents who send their children to sectarian schools, their purpose and inevitable effect are to aid and advance those religious institutions.

Apart from its historical foundations, *Walz* is a product of the same dilemma and inherent tension found in most government-aid-to-religion controversies. To be sure, the exemption of church property from taxation conferred a benefit, albeit a direct and incidental one. Yet that "aid" was a product not of any purpose to support or to subsidize, but of a fiscal relationship designed to minimize involvement and entanglement between Church and State. "The exemption," the Court emphasized, "tends to complement and reinforce the desired separation insulating each from the other." Furthermore, "[e]limination of the exemption would tend to expand the involvement of government by giving rise to tax valuation of church property, tax liens, tax foreclosures, and the direct confrontations and conflicts that follow in the train of those legal processes." The granting of the tax benefits under the New York statute, unlike the extension of an exemption, would tend to increase rather than limit the involvement between Church and State.

One further difference between tax exemptions for church property and tax benefits for parents should be noted. The exemption challenged in *Walz* was not restricted to a class composed exclusively or even predominantly of religious institutions. Instead, the exemption covered all property devoted to religious, educational, or charitable purposes. As the parties here must concede, tax reductions authorized by this law flow primarily to the parents of children attending sectarian, nonpublic schools. . . . [I]t should be apparent that in terms of the potential divisiveness of any legislative measure the narrowness of the benefited class would be an important factor. . . .

III.

Because we have found that the challenged sections have the impermissible effect of advancing religion, we need not consider whether such aid would result in entanglement of the State with religion in the sense of "[a] comprehensive, discriminating, and continuing state surveillance." Lemon v. Kurtzman, 403 U.S., at 619. But the importance of the competing societal interests implicated here prompts us to make the further observation that, apart from any specific entanglement of the State in particular religious programs, assistance of the sort here involved carries grave potential for entanglement in the broader sense of continuing political strife over aid to religion. . . .

One factor of recurring significance . . . is the potentially divisive political effect of an aid program. . . .

In this situation, where the underlying issue is the deeply emotional one of Church-State relationships, the potential for seriously divisive political consequences needs no elaboration. And while the prospect of such divisiveness may not alone warrant the invalidation of state laws that otherwise survive the careful scrutiny required by the decisions of this Court, it is certainly a "warning signal" not to be ignored. . . .

BURGER, C.J., joined in part by Justice White and joined by Justice Rehnquist, concurring in part and dissenting in part.

[The Chief Justice agreed that the "maintenance and repair" provision was unconstitutional "because it is a direct aid to religion," but he would have upheld the other two aspects of the program under precedents such as *Everson, Allen,* and *Walz.*]

The tuition grant and tax relief programs now before us are, in my view, indistinguishable in principle, purpose, and effect from the statutes in *Everson* and *Allen.* . . . [T]he States have merely attempted to equalize the costs incurred by parents in obtaining an education for their children. The only discernible difference between the programs in *Everson* and *Allen* and these cases is in the method of the distribution of benefits: here the particular benefits . . . are given only to parents of private school children, while in *Everson* and *Allen* the statutory benefits were made available to parents of both public and private school children. But to regard that difference as constitutionally meaningful is to exalt form over substance. . . . [New York's statute] is no more than simple equity to grant partial relief to parents who support the public schools they do not use. . . .

However sincere our collective protestations of the debt owed by the public generally to the parochial school systems, the wholesome diversity they engender will not survive on expressions of goodwill.

[Justice White joined this opinion only as it related to the tuition grant and tax relief statute.]

REHNQUIST, C.J., and Justice White, dissenting in part.

[Justice Rehnquist dissented from the invalidation of the tuition reimbursement and tax benefit provisions:]

Here the effect of the tax benefit is trebly attenuated as compared with the outright exemption considered in *Walz.* There the result was a complete forgiveness of taxes, while here the result is merely a reduction in taxes. There the ultimate benefit was available to an actual house of worship, while here even the ultimate benefit redounds only to a religiously sponsored school. There the churches themselves received the direct reduction in the tax bill, while here it is only the parents of the children who are sent to religiously sponsored schools who receive the direct benefit. . . .

[Justice Rehnquist also emphasized the similarity of New York's plan to those upheld in *Everson* and *Allen* and justified them as similar exercises in "benevolent neutrality."]

The reimbursement and tax benefit plans today struck down, no less than the plans in *Everson* and *Allen,* are consistent with the principle of neutrality. New York has recognized that parents who are sending their children to nonpublic schools are rendering the State a service by decreasing the costs of public education and by physically relieving an already overburdened public school system. Such parents are nonetheless compelled to support public school services unused by them and to pay for their own children's education. Rather than offering "an incentive to parents to send their children to sectarian schools," as the majority suggests, New York is effectuating the secular purpose of the equalization of the cost of educating New York children that are borne by parents who send their children to nonpublic schools. . . .

WHITE, J., joined in part by the Chief Justice and Justice Rehnquist, dissenting.

[Justice White would have upheld the New York statute in its entirety.] About 10% of the Nation's children, approximately 5.2 million students, . . . are not being educated in public schools at public expense. [Elsewhere in his opinion, Justice White notes that of these 5.2 million, approximately 4.4 million (83 percent of the total) were enrolled in Roman Catholic schools at the time of the decision. As of 2001, there were a total of 47,204,000 students enrolled in public elementary and secondary schools.[50] As of the 1999-2000 school year, the number of students in private schools was almost exactly the same number as in 1972, 5.26 million, which also continued to represent almost exactly 10% of the total population attending schools. Of the 5.26 million students attending private schools, approximately half, 2,550,000, attended Catholic schools, and approximately 1,870,000 went to "other religious" schools; only 842,000 were enrolled in "nonsectarian" private schools.[51]] Under state law these children have a right to a free public education and it would not appear unreasonable if the State, relieved of the expense of educating a child in the public school, contributed to the expense of his education elsewhere. The parents of such children pay taxes, including school taxes. They could receive in return a free education in the public schools. They prefer to send their children, as they have the right to do, to nonpublic schools that furnish the satisfactory equivalent of a public school education but also offer subjects or other assumed advantages not available in public schools. Constitutional considerations aside, it would be understandable if a State gave such parents a call on the public treasury up to the amount it would have cost the State to educate the child in public school, or, to put it another way, up to the amount the parents save the State by not sending their children to public school.

In light of the Free Exercise Clause of the First Amendment, this would seem particularly the case where the parent desires his child to attend a school that offers not only secular subjects but religious training as well. A State should put no unnecessary obstacles in the way of religious training for the young. . . .

[Justice White also notes a declining enrollment in nonpublic schools as of 1973, in part because of severe financial pressures.] Whatever the reasons, there has been, and there probably will continue to be, a movement to the public schools, with the prospect of substantial increases in public school budgets that are already under intense attack and with the States and cities that are primarily involved already facing severe financial crises. It is this prospect that has prompted some of

---

50. National Center for Education Statistics, Digest of Education Statistics, 2003. Chapter 2, Elementary and Secondary Education. Table 36. Historical summary of public elementary and secondary school statistics: Selected years, 1869-70 to 2000-01. Available at *http://nces.ed.gov/programs/ digest/d03/tables/dt036.asp.*

51. Id. Table 60. Private elementary and secondary enrollment and schools, by level, orientation of school, and amount of tuition: 1999-2000, available at *http://nces.ed.gov/programs/digest/d03/ tables/dt060.asp.*

these States to attempt, by a variety of devices, to save, or slow the demise of, the nonpublic school system, an educational resource that could deliver quality education at a cost to the public substantially below the per-pupil cost of the public schools.

. . . No one contends that he can discern from the sparse language of the Establishment Clause that a State is forbidden to aid religion in any manner whatsoever or, if it does not mean that, what kind of or how much aid is permissible. And one cannot seriously believe that the history of the First Amendment furnishes unequivocal answers to many of the fundamental issues of church-state relations. In the end, the courts have fashioned answers to these questions as best they can, the language of the Constitution and its history having left them a wide range of choice among many alternatives. But decision has been unavoidable; and, in choosing, the courts necessarily have carved out what they deemed to be the most desirable national policy governing various aspects of church-state relationships.

. . . I . . . have little difficulty in accepting the New York maintenance grant, which does not and could not, by its terms, approach the actual repair and maintenance cost incurred in connection with the secular education services performed for the State in parochial schools. . . .

At the very least I would not strike down these statutes on their face. The Court's opinion emphasizes a particular kind of parochial school, one restricted to students of particular religious beliefs and conditioning attendance on religious study. Concededly, there are many parochial schools that do not impose such restrictions. Where they do not, it is even more difficult for me to understand why the primary effect of these statutes is to advance religion. . . .

Discussion

Assume that Justice White's view had prevailed. Consider the fact that the National Center for Education Statistics reported in July 2004 that approximately 1.1 million children were being home-schooled as of 2003, which it estimated as 2.2% of the entire school-age population.[52] It is safe to say that home-schooling accounted for an absolutely negligible number of students in 1972. Would home-schooling parents have a plausible claim to state aid if every student enrolled in a formal school received such aid? Would it matter if the home-schooling was being done because of religious reasons? Or could the state legitimately restrict aid to formal educational institutions on the ground that it believed that an important part of "education" was learning to work with others and that it was highly unlikely that home-schooled students would develop such skills as well as institutionally schooled ones (not to mention that supervision of schools with regard to state-mandated curricula is far easier than supervision of individual home-schoolers)?

Note: The Unsuccessful Search for Coherence Following Nyquist

Nyquist was scarcely the last word on the issue. By 1986, a spate of laws — and cases — had followed, generating results and analyses that mystified many commentators. We saw earlier in this chapter one possible explanation for such

---

52. See NCES, Issue Brief, July 2004, available at *http://nces.ed.gov/pubs2004/2004115.pdf*.

confusion, which is simply the phenomenon of decisionmaking by individual justices on multimember courts. There might well have been majorities in each and every subsequent decision who would have agreed that the given case "made little sense"; the problem, of course, is that there was nothing near majoritarian agreement on what particular solution was the intellectually attractive one. Such a situation, by definition, gives significant power to the "median" justice at the halfway point between two more ideologically coherent, but strongly divided, blocs of justices.

LAYCOCK, A SURVEY OF RELIGIOUS LIBERTY IN THE UNITED STATES, 47 OHIO ST. L.J. 409, 443-449 (1986): [In 1986 University of Texas law professor Douglas Laycock assayed the range of cases and theories in Establishment Clause jurisprudence. He discerned "[a]t least six inconsistent theories" that were endorsed by at least one justice in the years since *Nyquist*, which generated "a series of inconsistent and almost inexplicable decisions."]

1. THE POSSIBLE THEORIES

The no-aid theory. One plausible view is the no-aid theory: that any state money paid to a religious school or its students expands the school's budget and thereby aids religion. Even if the state's money is used to buy math books, that frees some of the school's money to spend on religion, or it enables the school to lower tuition and make it easier for children to attend a religious school. . . .

The purchase-of-services theory. A second plausible view is the purchase-of-services theory: that state money paid to a religious school is simply a purchase of educational services. The state is obligated [by its constitution] to provide a free education for all its children; it can do so directly or through independent contractors. As long as the state does not pay more than the costs of the secular education provided, it is simply paying for services rendered and not subsidizing religion. . . .

The equal-treatment theory. A third plausible view is the equal-treatment theory. In its strong form, it holds that the government is obligated to pay for the secular aspects of education in religious schools; in its weak form, it holds that government is free to make such payments if it wishes.

Children have a constitutional right to attend religious schools. If they do not exercise that right and attend public schools, the state will be required to spend substantial sums on their education. If they do exercise their constitutional right, they forfeit the state subsidy of their education. This can plausibly be viewed as a penalty on the exercise of their constitutional right. . . .

The equal-treatment theory relies on the principle that government cannot discriminate against religion, which is as basic as the principle that the government cannot support religion. . . .

The child-benefit theory. A fourth plausible view of the school aid issue is the child-benefit theory: that the state can provide educational benefits directly to children or their parents, even if the benefits are used at or in connection with a religious school. But the state cannot provide the same aid directly to the school. . . .

Proponents of the no-aid theory note that aid to a school and aid to the students in that school are economically equivalent: either makes it less expensive for students to attend the school. But others have found it symbolically important that the aid goes to the child rather than to the school. Directing the aid to the child may be seen as a symbolic affirmation of the purchase-of-services or equal-treatment theory, emphasizing that these programs provide education as well as religion. . . .

The tracing theory. A fifth view of the school aid issue has attracted the Court, but it is only superficially plausible. Under the tracing theory the Court tries to divide all the activities of a religious school into components that are wholly secular and components that are, or might be, affected by religion. Then it tries to trace each dollar of government money to see what the school spent it on. The Court approves aid if, and only if, the money can be traced to a wholly secular expenditure. . . . [T]his approach cannot be applied consistently. The task of dividing school activities into secular and religious components is conceptually impossible; the whole purpose of such schools is to integrate secular and religious education. . . .

The little-bit theory. The Court occasionally alludes to a sixth theory, which may explain more of the Court's results than the theories it relies on more often. This is the theory that a little bit of aid to religious schools is permissible, but it must be structured in a way that keeps it from becoming too much. . . .

2. The Court's Results

It is hardly a surprise that this mix of theories has not produced coherent results. The variety of theories and the attempt to distinguish the indistinguishables in the tracing theory have produced distinctions that do not commend themselves to common sense.

For example, bus transportation to and from school is permitted, but bus transportation on field trips is forbidden[, Wolman v. Walter, 433 U.S. 229 (1977)]. Why? Because the teacher might discuss religion on the field trip. Thus, under the tracing theory, the bus ride to school is wholly secular, but the field trip might not be.

The state can loan secular textbooks to students in religious schools [*Allen*,] but it cannot loan maps, projectors, or other instructional materials [*Wolman*]. The child-benefit theory might have reconciled these holdings, because each child needs his own textbook but only the school needs maps and projectors. But that is not what the Court said. Rather, it decided the first textbook cases on a combination of child-benefit and tracing theories; then it decided the instructional materials case on the theory that any aid to the school helps religion. The Court noted that its approach to books was inconsistent with its approach to other instructional materials, but it declined to reconcile the cases. Even more strange, in the very opinion [*Wolman*] in which it adopted the no-aid theory for instructional materials, it used the tracing theory to allow state-administered tests in religious schools.

The Court also used the tracing theory to hold that guidance counseling, remedial instruction, and other therapeutic services are permissible if provided by public school teachers away from the religious school campus [*Wolman*] but not if provided by public school teachers on the religious school campus [Aguilar v. Felton, 473 U.S. 402 (1985), overruled in Agostini v. Felton, 521 U.S. 203 (1997); Grand Rapids School District v. Ball, 473 U.S. (1985)]. Why? Because the public school teachers might be influenced by the religious environment and inadvertently discuss religion with their students; that danger is insubstantial away from the religious school. However, diagnostic services are permissible even on the religious school campus because the diagnostician will not spend enough time with any one student to develop a relationship. Without a relationship he is unlikely to talk religion [*Wolman*]. . . .

The tracing theory also produced paradoxical results with respect to teacher salaries and testing expenses. The state cannot pay fifteen percent of the salary of teachers who teach secular subjects in religious schools[, *Lemon*]. It cannot pay religious schools for the cost of conducting state-mandated testing if the religious school teachers design and grade the test [Levitt v. Committee for Public Educ. and Religious Liberty, 413 U.S. 472 (1973)]. In neither case could the money be traced to wholly secular uses, because the teachers might include religious material in their classes or on the exams, even in secular subjects. But the state is permitted to administer required tests to religious school students and grade the tests itself [*Wolman*]. State designed and administered tests present no danger of religious content; they are wholly secular.

Does it follow that the state can pay the school to administer objective secular tests designed by the state? The Court said yes [Committee for Public Education & Religious Liberty v. Regan, 444 U.S. 646 (1980)]. There was no risk of testing religious content, and paying the school to administer the tests was no more a subsidy than having the state administer the tests directly. Either approach relieved the school of the expenses. On the same rationale, the state could require religious schools to take attendance and pay for the expense of doing so. In each case the expense consisted of part of the teachers' time; the state paid as much as 5.4% of faculty payroll under this program. So, it turns out that, with enough red tape, the state can pay part of the salaries of teachers after all. The state need only identify wholly secular job components and the time required to perform them, and pay the school for that time. This carried the tracing theory to its fictional extreme. And this decision came after the Court rejected the tracing theory with respect to instructional materials.

In 1983, Mueller v. Allen[, 463 U.S. 388 (1983),] held that state income tax deductions for the expenses of sending children to religious schools are permissible. But ten years earlier, Committee for Public Education and Religious Liberty v. Nyquist [, 413 U.S. 756 (1973),] held that state income tax credits for the expenses of sending children to religious schools are forbidden. What is the difference? The Court said that the tax credits in *Nyquist* were dovetailed with a scholarship program for low income students, making it clear that the tax credits were themselves a thinly disguised scholarship. In addition, the credit applied to private school tuition only. The tax deduction in *Mueller* also applied to transportation and supply expenses, which could be claimed by parents of public school children, and to tuition payments by the handful of children attending public schools outside their own district.

Those were real differences, but they were not very significant. Again, a theory shift was more important. *Nyquist* was written on the tracing theory, or perhaps on the no-aid theory. Scholarships and tax credits were invalid under either theory because once the students paid the money to the school it went into general revenues and could not be traced. But in *Mueller* the Court emphasized the child-benefit theory and the equal-treatment theory. The Court thought it important that the tax savings went to parents instead of religious schools, and that parents decided independently whether to send their children to public or private schools. The state was not required to discriminate against religion by denying a deduction available to parents of public school children. It was irrelevant that ninety-six percent of the deductions were in fact claimed by parents of children in Catholic and Lutheran schools. This was a break with earlier cases in which the Court had thought it significant that most private schools were religious[, Meek v. Pittenger, 421 U.S. 349 (1975)]. . . .

Whatever the Court said, a comparison of tax deductions and tax credits suggests consistent application of the little-bit theory. There is no structural limit on a tax credit; a state could allow a credit for 100% of private school tuition. But a deduction can never be worth more than the private school's tuition multiplied by the state's marginal tax rate; and most state income tax rates are quite low. . . .

These tax deduction and tax credit cases also highlight an inconsistency in public perception of the issues, and probably in judicial perception as well. Tax deductions for tuition paid to religious schools are widely perceived as a form of aid that at least raise serious questions under the establishment clause. Yet tax deductions for gifts to the same schools, or to churches themselves for purely religious purposes, are widely perceived as raising no problem. It is hard to believe that both perceptions can be correct. The breadth of the charitable deduction offers weak ground for distinction, because a tuition tax deduction is always a small part of a state's efforts to finance, encourage, and subsidize education. The long-standing familiarity of the charitable contribution deduction, and the novelty of tuition deductions, explain but do not justify the differences in constitutional perception.

Many commentators thought that *Mueller's* approval of tuition tax deductions indicated a substantial shift in direction. . . . But in 1985, in Grand Rapids v. Ball and Aguilar v. Felton, the Court returned to the tracing theory to strike down supplemental courses in religious schools. The political context highlights the majority's [including "liberals" like Justices Brennan and Marshall] aversion to substantial aid: *Aguilar* struck down federally funded remedial instruction for impoverished children. The Court again thought it significant that most private schools receiving the aid were religious schools. . . .

4.   *The Court Moves Toward a New Paradigm*

Five new members of the Court arrived in the six years following Laycock's 1986 article, three appointed by Republican Presidents Reagan (Kennedy) and George H. W. Bush (Souter and Thomas), and two by Democratic President Bill Clinton (Breyer and Ginsburg). (Reagan had earlier appointed O'Connor and Scalia, and Justices Rehnquist and Stevens had been appointed by Presidents Nixon and Ford, respectively). Perhaps most important from the standpoint of the direction of future cases were the replacements of Lewis Powell by Justice Kennedy and Thurgood Marshall by Justice Thomas.

In 1986 the Court held, in Witters v. Washington Department of Services for the Blind, 474 U.S. 481 (1986), that the Constitution allowed a blind student to use vocational rehabilitation funds for payment to a Christian college that would prepare him for a career as a minister. According to the majority, through Justice Marshall, it was "central" that the payments were made "directly to the student, who transmits [the money] to the educational institution of his or her choice." Even though the Christian college obviously receives aid, that is "only as a result of the genuinely independent and private choices of aid recipients." The state "creates no financial incentive for students to undertake sectarian education" by, for example, "provid[ing] greater or broader benefits for recipients who apply their aid to religious education." Although this language seemingly supports a great deal of aid to parochial schools, Justice Marshall went on to state that

> no more than a miniscule amount of the aid awarded under the program is likely to flow to religious education. . . . Aid recipients' choices are made among a huge variety of possible careers, of which only a small handful are sectarian. Further, and importantly, nothing in the record indicates that . . . any significant portion of the aid expended under the Washington program as a whole will end up flowing to religious education. The function of the Washington program is hardly "to provide desired financial support for nonpublic, sectarian institutions" [quoting *Nyquist*].[53]

The Court proved similarly tolerant of a state aid to religion in Zobrest v. Catalina Foothills Schools District, 509 U.S. 1 (1993). James Zobrest, deaf since birth, had been enrolled by his parents, "[f]or religious reasons" in Salpointe High School, which is Roman Catholic. While earlier attending an Arizona public school, James had been supplied with a sign-language interpreter. However, when Zobrest claimed a right, under the federal Individuals with Disabilities Education Act (IDEA) and its Arizona counterpart, to have an interpreter supplied at Salpointe, the Arizona Attorney General maintained that providing an interpreter would violate the Establishment Clause.

The Ninth Circuit Court of Appeals agreed, and the Supreme Court, through Chief Justice Rehnquist, reversed, describing the program at issue as one "that neutrally provides benefits to a broad class of citizens defined without reference to religion." The concept of "neutrality" soon moved to center state in the Court's analysis. (Recall the role of the concept of neutrality in Lyng v. UAW, at the beginning of this chapter.)

---

53. The Washington State Supreme Court, on remand, held that the provision of aid to Witters violated the no-establishment clause of the State constitution, Witters v. State Commission for the Blind, 771 P.2d 1119 (1989), cert. denied, 493 U.S. 850 (1989). The state court also rejected Witters's claim of a free exercise right to use his scholarship at a seminary on the ground that Witters was not required by the tenets of his faith to be a minister. The view that free exercise protects only what is required is frequently asserted in free exercise litigation. Consider the following response: "This position implies a wholly negative view of religion. It assumes that religions lay down certain binding rules, and that the exercise of religion consists only of obeying the rules. It is as though all of religious experience were reduced to the Book of Leviticus." Douglas Laycock, The Remnants of Free Exercise, 1990 Sup. Ct. Rev. 1, 24.

The aftermath of the U.S. Supreme Court decision reinforces the importance of taking into account state constitutions (and courts) in much contemporary litigation involving the issues raised in this chapter.

Thus, in Mitchell v. Helms, 530 U.S. 793 (2000), the Court upheld a program ("Chapter 2") involving the distribution of federal funds and education-related materials including computer hardware and software, first to state and local educa-tion agencies and finally to public and private elementary and secondary schools charged with implementing "secular, neutral, and nonideological" programs. The suit involved Jeffferson Parish, Louisiana, in which approximately 30 percent of the relevant funds were allocated for private schools, most of which are Catholic or otherwise religiously affiliated.

Although there was no majority opinion, six Justices agreed that Chapter 2, as applied in Jefferson Parish, did not violate the Establishment Clause. The same six justices also agreed that Meek v. Pittenger, 421 U.S. 349 (1975), and Wolman v. Walter, 433 U.S. 229 (1977) — which struck down programs that loaned instruc-tional materials to religious schools — should be overruled as inconsistent with recent cases. The plurality opinion was written by Justice Thomas, joined by Chief Justice Rehnquist, Justice Scalia, and Justice Kennedy. Thomas offered a concep-tion of permissible government aid to religion based on the idea of neturality:

> [T]he question whether governmental aid to religious schools results in governmental indoctrination is ultimately a question whether any religious indoctrination that occurs in those schools could reasonably be attributed to governmental action. . . . In distin-guishing between indoctrination that is attributable to the State and indoctrination that is not, we have consistently turned to the principle of neutrality, upholding aid that is offered to a broad range of groups or persons without regard to their religion. If the religious, irreligious, and areligious are all alike eligible for governmental aid, no one would conclude that any indoctrination that any particular recipient conducts has been done at the behest of the government. For attribution of indoctrination is a relative question. If the government is offering assistance to recipients who provide, so to speak, a broad range of indoctrination, the government itself is not thought responsible for any particular indoctrination. To put the point differently, if the government, seeking to further some legitimate secular purpose, offers aid on the same terms, without regard to religion, to all who adequately further that purpose, then it is fair to say that any aid going to a religious recipient only has the effect of furthering that secular purpose. The government, in grafting such an aid program, has had to conclude that a given level of aid is necessary to further that purpose among secular recipients and has provided no more than that same level to religious recipients.
>
> As a way of assuring neutrality, we have repeatedly considered whether any govern-mental aid that goes to a religious institution does so "only as a result of the genuinely independent and private choices of individuals.". . . For if numerous private choices, rather than the single choice of a government, determine the distribution of aid pursuant to neutral eligibility criteria, then a government cannot, or at least cannot easily, grant special favors that might lead to a religious establishment. Private choice also helps guarantee neutrality by mitigating the preference for pre-existing recipients that is arguably inherent in any governmental aid program, and that could lead to a program inadvertently favoring one religion or favoring religious private schools in general over nonreligious ones.

In offering this analysis, the plurality specifically rejected two principles offered by respondents: first, "that 'direct, nonincidental' aid to the primary educational mission of religious schools is always impermissible," and second "that provision to religious schools of aid that is divertible to religious use is similarly impermissible." The "formalistic line [between direct and indirect aid] breaks down in the application to real-world programs." The plurality added, "[o]f course, we have seen 'special Establishment Clause dangers,' when money is given to religious schools or entities directly rather than, as in *Witters* and *Mueller*, indirectly. But direct payments of money are not at issue in this case, and we refuse to allow a 'special' case to create a rule for all cases."

Finally, the plurality also specifically rejected the notion that Establishment Clause analysis should turn on

whether a school that receives aid (or whose students receive aid) is pervasively sectarian. The dissent is correct that there was a period when this factor mattered, particularly if the pervasively sectarian school was a primary or secondary school. But that period is one that the Court should regret, and it is thankfully long past. . . .

[T]he religious nature of a recipient should not matter to the constitutional analysis, so long as the recipient adequately furthers the government's secular purpose. If a program offers permissible aid to the religious (including the pervasively sectarian), the areligious, and the irreligious, it is a mystery which view of religion the government has established, and thus a mystery what the constitutional violation would be. The pervasively sectarian recipient has not received any special favor, and it is most bizarre that the Court would, as the dissent seemingly does, reserve special hostility for those who take their religion seriously, who think that their religion should affect the whole of their lives, or who make the mistake of being effective in transmitting their views to children.

[T]he inquiry into the recipient's religious views required by a focus on whether a school is pervasively sectarian is not only unnecessary but also offensive. It is well established, in numerous other contexts, that courts should refrain from trolling through a person's or institution's religious beliefs. . . . In addition, and related, the application of the "pervasively sectarian" factor collides with our decisions that have prohibited governments from discriminating in the distribution of public benefits based upon religious status or sincerity.

Finally, hostility to aid to pervasively sectarian schools has a shameful pedigree that we do not hesitate to disavow. . . . Opposition to aid to "sectarian" schools acquired prominence in the 1870's with Congress's consideration (and near passage) of the Blaine Amendment, which would have amended the Constitution to bar any aid to sectarian institutions. Consideration of the amendment arose at a time of pervasive hostility to the Catholic Church and to Catholics in general, and it was an open secret that "sectarian" was code for "Catholic." . . . In short, nothing in the Establishment Clause requires the exclusion of pervasively sectarian schools from otherwise permissible aid programs, and other doctrines of this Court bar it. This doctrine, born of bigotry, should be buried now.

Justice O'Connor concurred in the judgment (joined by Justice Breyer). Justice Souter dissented, joined by Justices Stevens and Ginsburg. *Mitchell's* version of a theory of neutrality was soon eclipsed by a decision that commanded a majority of the Court.

ZELMAN v. SIMMONS-HARRIS
536 U.S. 639 (2002)

Chief Justice REHNQUIST delivered the opinion of the Court.

The State of Ohio has established a pilot program designed to provide educational choices to families with children who reside in the Cleveland City School

District. The question presented is whether this program offends the Establishment Clause of the United States Constitution. We hold that it does not.

There are more than 75,000 children enrolled in the Cleveland City School District. The majority of these children are from low-income and minority families. Few of these families enjoy the means to send their children to any school other than an inner-city public school. For more than a generation, however, Cleveland's public schools have been among the worst performing public schools in the Nation. In 1995, a Federal District Court declared a "crisis of magnitude" and placed the entire Cleveland school district under state control. Shortly thereafter, the state auditor found that Cleveland's public schools were in the midst of a "crisis that is perhaps unprecedented in the history of American education." The district had failed to meet any of the 18 state standards for minimal acceptable performance. Only 1 in 10 ninth graders could pass a basic proficiency examination, and students at all levels performed at a dismal rate compared with students in other Ohio public schools. More than two-thirds of high school students either dropped or failed out before graduation. Of those students who managed to reach their senior year, one of every four still failed to graduate. Of those students who did graduate, few could read, write, or compute at levels comparable to their counterparts in other cities.

It is against this backdrop that Ohio enacted, among other initiatives, its Pilot Project Scholarship Program. The program provides financial assistance to families in any Ohio school district that is or has been "under federal court order requiring supervision and operational management of the district by the state superintendent." Cleveland is the only Ohio school district to fall within that category.

The program provides two basic kinds of assistance to parents of children in a covered district. First, the program provides tuition aid for students in kindergarten through third grade, expanding each year through eighth grade, to attend a participating public or private school of their parent's choosing. Second, the program provides tutorial aid for students who choose to remain enrolled in public school.

The tuition aid portion of the program is designed to provide educational choices to parents who reside in a covered district. Any private school, whether religious or nonreligious, may participate in the program and accept program students so long as the school is located within the boundaries of a covered district and meets statewide educational standards. Participating private schools must agree not to discriminate on the basis of race, religion, or ethnic background, or to "advocate or foster unlawful behavior or teach hatred of any person or group on the basis of race, ethnicity, national origin, or religion." Any public school located in a school district adjacent to the covered district may also participate in the program. Adjacent public schools are eligible to receive a $2,250 tuition grant for each program student accepted in addition to the full amount of per-pupil state funding attributable to each additional student. . . .

Tuition aid is distributed to parents according to financial need. Families with incomes below 200% of the poverty line are given priority and are eligible to receive 90% of private school tuition up to $2,250. For these lowest-income families, participating private schools may not charge a parental co-payment greater than $250. For all other families, the program pays 75% of tuition costs, up to $1,875, with no co-payment cap. These families receive tuition aid only if the number of available

scholarships exceeds the number of low-income children who choose to participate. Where tuition aid is spent depends solely upon where parents who receive
tuition aid choose to enroll their child. If parents choose a private school, checks
are made payable to the parents who then endorse the checks over to the chosen
school.

The tutorial aid portion of the program provides tutorial assistance through
grants to any student in a covered district who chooses to remain in public school.
Parents arrange for registered tutors to provide assistance to their children and then
submit bills for those services to the State for payment. Students from low-income
families receive 90% of the amount charged for such assistance up to $360. All other
students receive 75% of that amount. The number of tutorial assistance grants
offered to students in a covered district must equal the number of tuition aid scholarships provided to students enrolled at participating private or adjacent public
schools.

The program has been in operation within the Cleveland City School District
since the 1996–1997 school year. In the 1999–2000 school year, 56 private schools
participated in the program, 46 (or 82%) of which had a religious affiliation. None
of the public schools in districts adjacent to Cleveland have elected to participate.
More than 3,700 students participated in the scholarship program, most of whom
(96%) enrolled in religiously affiliated schools. Sixty percent of these students were
from families at or below the poverty line. In the 1998–1999 school year, approximately 1,400 Cleveland public school students received tutorial aid. This number
was expected to double during the 1999–2000 school year.

The program is part of a broader undertaking by the State to enhance the
educational options of Cleveland's schoolchildren in response to the 1995
takeover. That undertaking includes programs governing community and
magnet schools. Community schools are funded under state law but are run by
their own school boards, not by local school districts. These schools enjoy
academic independence to hire their own teachers and to determine their own
curriculum. They can have no religious affiliation and are required to accept
students by lottery. During the 1999–2000 school year, there were 10 start-up
community schools in the Cleveland City School District with more than 1,900
students enrolled. For each child enrolled in a community school, the school
receives state funding of $4,518, twice the funding a participating program
school may receive.

Magnet schools are public schools operated by a local school board that emphasize a particular subject area, teaching method, or service to students. For each
student enrolled in a magnet school, the school district receives $7,746, including
state funding of $4,167, the same amount received per student enrolled at a tradi-
tional public school. As of 1999, parents in Cleveland were able to choose from
among 23 magnet schools, which together enrolled more than 13,000 students in
kindergarten through eighth grade. These schools provide specialized teaching
methods, such as Montessori, or a particularized curriculum focus, such as foreign
language, computers, or the arts.

[Federal district and circuit courts below had held that the program violated the
Establishment Clause of the First Amendment on the ground that they had a
"primary effect" of furthering religion.]

The Establishment Clause of the First Amendment, applied to the States
through the Fourteenth Amendment, prevents a State from enacting laws that

have the "purpose" or "effect" of advancing or inhibiting religion. There is no dispute that the program challenged here was enacted for the valid secular purpose of providing educational assistance to poor children in a demonstrably failing public school system. Thus, the question presented is whether the Ohio program nonetheless has the forbidden "effect" of advancing or inhibiting religion.

To answer that question, our decisions have drawn a consistent distinction between government programs that provide aid directly to religious schools and programs of true private choice, in which government aid reaches religious schools only as a result of the genuine and independent choices of private individuals, *Mueller* v. *Allen, Witters* v. *Washington Dept. of Servs. for Blind, Zobrest* v. *Catalina Foothills School Dist.* While our jurisprudence with respect to the constitutionality of direct aid programs has "changed significantly" over the past two decades, our jurisprudence with respect to true private choice programs has remained consistent and unbroken. Three times we have confronted Establishment Clause challenges to neutral government programs that provide aid directly to a broad class of individuals, who, in turn, direct the aid to religious schools or institutions of their own choosing. Three times we have rejected such challenges.

[The Court's discussion of *Mueller, Witters,* and *Zobrest* is omitted.]

Mueller, Witters, and *Zobrest* thus make clear that where a government aid program is neutral with respect to religion, and provides assistance directly to a broad class of citizens who, in turn, direct government aid to religious schools wholly as a result of their own genuine and independent private choice, the program is not readily subject to challenge under the Establishment Clause. A program that shares these features permits government aid to reach religious institutions only by way of the deliberate choices of numerous individual recipients. The incidental advancement of a religious mission, or the perceived endorsement of a religious message, is reasonably attributable to the individual recipient, not to the government, whose role ends with the disbursement of benefits. . . . It is precisely for these reasons that we have never found a program of true private choice to offend the Establishment Clause.

We believe that the program challenged here is a program of true private choice, consistent with *Mueller, Witters,* and *Zobrest,* and thus constitutional. As was true in those cases, the Ohio program is neutral in all respects toward religion. It is part of a general and multifaceted undertaking by the State of Ohio to provide educational opportunities to the children of a failed school district. It confers educational assistance directly to a broad class of individuals defined without reference to religion, *i.e.,* any parent of a school-age child who resides in the Cleveland City School District. The program permits the participation of *all* schools within the district, religious or nonreligious. Adjacent public schools also may participate and have a financial incentive to do so. Program benefits are available to participating families on neutral terms, with no reference to religion. The only preference stated anywhere in the program is a preference for low-income families, who receive greater assistance and are given priority for admission at participating schools.

There are no "financial incentive[s]" that "ske[w]" the program toward religious schools. Such incentives "[are] not present . . . where the aid is allocated on the basis of neutral, secular criteria that neither favor nor disfavor religion, and is made available to both religious and secular beneficiaries on a nondiscriminatory basis." The program here in fact creates financial *dis*incentives for religious schools, with private schools receiving only half the government assistance given to community schools and one-third the assistance given to magnet schools. Adjacent public schools, should any choose to accept program students, are also eligible to receive two to three times the state funding of a private religious school. Families too have a financial disincentive to choose a private religious school over other schools. Parents that choose to participate in the scholarship program and then to enroll their children in a private school (religious or nonreligious) must copay a portion of the school's tuition. Families that choose a community school, magnet school, or traditional public school pay nothing. Although such features of the program are not necessary to its constitutionality, they clearly dispel the claim that the program "creates . . . financial incentive[s] for parents to choose a sectarian school."

Respondents suggest that even without a financial incentive for parents to choose a religious school, the program creates a "public perception that the State is endorsing religious practices and beliefs." But we have repeatedly recognized that no reasonable observer would think a neutral program of private choice, where state aid reaches religious schools solely as a result of the numerous independent decisions of private individuals, carries with it the *imprimatur* of government endorsement. . . . The argument is particularly misplaced here since "the reasonable observer in the endorsement inquiry must be deemed aware" of the "history and context" underlying a challenged program. Any objective observer familiar with the full history and context of the Ohio program would reasonably view it as one aspect of a broader undertaking to assist poor children in failed schools, not as an endorsement of religious schooling in general.

. . . Cleveland schoolchildren enjoy a range of educational choices. . . . That 46 of the 56 private schools now participating in the program are religious schools does not condemn it as a violation of the Establishment Clause. The Establishment Clause question is whether Ohio is coercing parents into sending their children to religious schools, and that question must be answered by evaluating *all* options Ohio provides Cleveland schoolchildren, only one of which is to obtain a program scholarship and then choose a religious school.

. . . Respondents and Justice Souter claim that even if we do not focus on the number of participating schools that are religious schools, we should attach constitutional significance to the fact that 96% of scholarship recipients have enrolled in religious schools. They claim that this alone proves parents lack genuine choice, even if no parent has ever said so. We need not consider this argument in detail, since it was flatly rejected in *Mueller,* where we found it irrelevant that 96% of parents taking deductions for tuition expenses paid tuition at religious schools. Indeed, we have recently found it irrelevant even to the constitutionality of a direct aid program that a vast majority of program benefits went to religious schools. [*Mitchell.*] The constitutionality of a neutral educational aid program simply does not turn on whether and why, in a particular area, at a particular time, most private schools are run by religious organizations, or most recipients choose to use the aid at a religious school. . . .

This point is aptly illustrated here. The 96% figure upon which respondents and Justice Souter rely discounts entirely (1) the more than 1,900 Cleveland children enrolled in alternative community schools, (2) the more than 13,000 children enrolled in alternative magnet schools, and (3) the more than 1,400 children enrolled in traditional public schools with tutorial assistance. . . .

Respondents finally claim that we should look to Committee for Public Ed. & Religious Liberty v. Nyquist to decide these cases. We disagree for two reasons. First, the program in *Nyquist* was quite different from the program challenged here. *Nyquist* involved a New York program that gave a package of benefits exclusively to private schools and the parents of private school enrollees. Although the program was enacted for ostensibly secular purposes, we found that its "function" was "*unmistakably* to provide desired financial support for nonpublic, sectarian institutions" (emphasis added). Its genesis, we said, was that private religious schools faced "increasingly grave fiscal problems." The program thus provided direct money grants to religious schools. It provided tax benefits "unrelated to the amount of money actually expended by any parent on tuition," ensuring a windfall to parents of children in religious schools. It similarly provided tuition reimbursements designed explicitly to "offe[r] . . . an incentive to parents to send their children to sectarian schools." Indeed, the program flatly prohibited the participation of any public school, or parent of any public school enrollee. Ohio's program shares none of these features.

Second, were there any doubt that the program challenged in *Nyquist* is far removed from the program challenged here, we expressly reserved judgment with respect to "a case involving some form of public assistance (*e.g.*, scholarships) made available generally without regard to the sectarian-nonsectarian, or public-nonpublic nature of the institution benefited." That, of course, is the very question now before us, and it has since been answered [in *Mueller, Witters,* and *Zobrest*]. To the extent the scope of *Nyquist* has remained an open question in light of these later decisions, we now hold that *Nyquist* does not govern neutral educational assistance programs that, like the program here, offer aid directly to a broad class of individual recipients defined without regard to religion.

In sum, the Ohio program is entirely neutral with respect to religion. It provides benefits directly to a wide spectrum of individuals, defined only by financial need and residence in a particular school district. It permits such individuals to exercise genuine choice among options public and private, secular and religious. The program is therefore a program of true private choice. In keeping with an unbroken line of decisions rejecting challenges to similar programs, we hold that the program does not offend the Establishment Clause.

Justice O'CONNOR, concurring:

. . . While I join the Court's opinion, I write separately for two reasons. First, although the Court takes an important step, I do not believe that today's decision, when considered in light of other longstanding government programs that impact religious organizations and our prior Establishment Clause jurisprudence, marks a dramatic break from the past. Second, given the emphasis the Court places on verifying that parents of voucher students in religious schools have exercised "true private choice," I think it is worth elaborating on the Court's conclusion that this inquiry should consider all reasonable educational alternatives to religious schools that are available to parents. To do otherwise is to ignore how the educational system in Cleveland actually functions.

I.

. . . The share of public resources that reach religious schools is not, however, as significant as respondents suggest. Data from the 1999–2000 school year indicate that 82 percent of schools participating in the voucher program were religious and that 96 percent of participating students enrolled in religious schools, but these data are incomplete. These statistics do not take into account all of the reasonable educational choices that may be available to students in Cleveland public schools. When one considers the option to attend community schools, the percentage of students enrolled in religious schools falls to 62.1 percent. If magnet schools are included in the mix, this percentage falls to 16.5 percent. See J. Greene, The Racial, Economic, and Religious Context of Parental Choice in Cleveland 11, Table 4 (Oct. 8, 1999), App. 217a (reporting 2,087 students in community schools and 16,184 students in magnet schools).

Even these numbers do not paint a complete picture. The Cleveland program provides voucher applicants from low-income families with up to $2,250 in tuition assistance and provides the remaining applicants with up to $1,875 in tuition assistance. In contrast, the State provides community schools $4,518 per pupil and magnet schools, on average, $7,097 per pupil. Even if one assumes that all voucher students came from low-income families and that each voucher student used up the entire $2,250 voucher, at most $8.2 million of public funds flowed to religious schools under the voucher program in 1999–2000. Although just over one-half as many students attended community schools as religious private schools on the state fisc, the State spent over $1 million more — $9.4 million — on students in community schools than on students in religious private schools because per-pupil aid to community schools is more than double the per-pupil aid to private schools under the voucher program. Moreover, the amount spent on religious private schools is minor compared to the $114.8 million the State spent on students in the Cleveland magnet schools.

Although $8.2 million is no small sum, it pales in comparison to the amount of funds that federal, state, and local governments already provide religious institutions. [Justice O'Connor discusses the amounts involved in such programs as exemptions from a wide variety of taxes.] The state property tax exemptions for religious institutions alone amount to very large sums annually. For example, available data suggest that Colorado's exemption lowers that State's tax revenues by more than $40 million annually; Maryland's exemption lowers revenues by more than $60 million; Wisconsin's exemption lowers revenues by approximately $122 million; and Louisiana's exemption, looking just at the city of New Orleans, lowers revenues by over $36 million. As for the Federal Government, the tax deduction for charitable contributions reduces federal tax revenues by nearly $25 billion annually. . . . These tax exemptions, which have "much the same effect as [cash grants] . . . of the amount of tax [avoided]," Regan v. Taxation With Representation of Washington, are just part of the picture. Federal dollars also reach religiously affiliated organizations through [many programs]. These programs are well-established parts of our social welfare system and can be quite substantial. . . . For example, it has been reported that religious hospitals, which account for 18 percent of all hospital beds nationwide, rely on Medicare funds for 36 percent of their revenue. Moreover, taking into account both Medicare and Medicaid, religious hospitals received nearly $45 billion from the federal fisc in 1998. Federal aid to religious schools is also substantial. Although data for all States is not available, data from Minnesota, for example, suggest that a substantial share of Pell Grant and other federal funds for college tuition reach religious schools. Roughly one-third or $27.1 million of the federal tuition dollars spent on students at schools in Minnesota were used at private 4-year colleges. The vast majority of these funds — $23.5 million — flowed to religiously affiliated institutions.

Against this background, the support that the Cleveland voucher program provides religious institutions is neither substantial nor atypical of existing government programs. While this observation is not intended to justify the Cleveland voucher program under the Establishment Clause, it places in broader perspective alarmist claims about implications of the Cleveland program and the Court's decision in these cases. . . .

III.

There is little question in my mind that the Cleveland voucher program is neutral as between religious schools and nonreligious schools. . . .

I find the Court's answer to the question whether parents of students eligible for vouchers have a genuine choice between religious and nonreligious schools persuasive. In looking at the voucher program, all the choices available to potential beneficiaries of the government program should be considered. In these cases, parents who were eligible to apply for a voucher also had the option, at a minimum, to send their children to community schools. . . .

Justice THOMAS, concurring:

Frederick Douglass once said that "[e]ducation . . . means emancipation. It means light and liberty. It means the uplifting of the soul of man into the glorious light of truth, the light by which men can only be made free." Today many of our inner-city public schools deny emancipation to urban minority students. . . . [U]rban children have been forced into a system that continually fails them. . . .

To determine whether a federal program survives scrutiny under the Establishment Clause, we have considered whether it has a secular purpose and whether it has the primary effect of advancing or inhibiting religion. I agree with the Court that Ohio's program easily passes muster under our stringent test, but, as a matter of first principles, I question whether this test should be applied to the States.

[Justice Thomas's critique of the incorporation of the Establishment Clause against the States is omitted.]

. . . Although one of the purposes of public schools was to promote democracy and a more egalitarian culture, failing urban public schools disproportionately affect minority children most in need of educational opportunity. . . . Just as blacks supported public education during Reconstruction, many blacks and other minorities now support school choice programs because they provide the greatest educational opportunities for their children in struggling communities. Opponents of the program raise formalistic concerns about the Establishment Clause but ignore the core purposes of the Fourteenth Amendment.

While the romanticized ideal of universal public education resonates with the cognoscenti who oppose vouchers, poor urban families just want the best education for their children, who will certainly need it to function in our high-tech and advanced society. . . . An individual's life prospects increase dramatically with each successfully completed phase of education. For instance, a black high school dropout earns just over $13,500, but with a high school degree the average income is almost $21,000. Blacks with a bachelor's degree have an average annual income of about $37,500, and $75,500 with a professional degree. Staying in school and earning a degree generates real and tangible financial benefits, whereas failure to obtain even a high school degree essentially relegates students to a life of poverty and, all too often, of crime. The failure to provide education to poor urban children perpetuates a vicious cycle of poverty, dependence, criminality, and alienation that continues for the remainder of their lives. If society cannot end racial discrimination, at least it can arm minorities with the education to defend themselves from some of discrimination's effects. . . .

Ten States have enacted some form of publicly funded private school choice as one means of raising the quality of education provided to underprivileged urban children. These programs address the root of the problem with failing urban public schools that disproportionately affect minority students. . . . [S]chool choice programs that involve religious schools appear unconstitutional only to those who would twist the Fourteenth Amendment against itself by expansively incorporating the Establishment Clause. Converting the Fourteenth Amendment from a guarantee of opportunity to an obstacle against education reform distorts our constitutional values and disserves those in the greatest need. . . .

Justice STEVENS, dissenting:

. . . First, the severe educational crisis that confronted the Cleveland City School District when Ohio enacted its voucher program is not a matter that should affect our appraisal of its constitutionality. In the 1999-2000 school year, that program provided relief to less than five percent of the students enrolled in the district's schools. The solution to the disastrous conditions that prevented over 90 percent of the student body from meeting basic proficiency standards obviously required massive improvements unrelated to the voucher program. Of course, the emergency may have given some families a powerful motivation to leave the public school system and accept religious indoctrination that they would otherwise have avoided, but that is not a valid reason for upholding the program.

Second, the wide range of choices that have been made available to students *within the public school system* has no bearing on the question whether the State may pay the tuition for students who wish to reject public education entirely and attend private schools that will provide them with a sectarian education. The fact that the vast majority of the voucher recipients who have entirely rejected public education receive religious indoctrination at state expense does, however, support the claim that the law is one "respecting an establishment of religion." The State may choose to divide up its public schools into a dozen different options and label them magnet schools, community schools, or whatever else it decides to call them, but the State is still required to provide a public education and it is the State's decision to fund private school education over and above its traditional obligation that is at issue in these cases.

Third, the voluntary character of the private choice to prefer a parochial education over an education in the public school system seems to me quite irrelevant to the question whether the government's choice to pay for religious indoctrination is constitutionally permissible. Today, however, the Court seems to have decided that the mere fact that a family that cannot afford a private education wants its children educated in a parochial school is a sufficient justification for this use of public funds.

For the reasons stated by Justice Souter and Justice Breyer, I am convinced that the Court's decision is profoundly misguided. Admittedly, in reaching that conclusion I have been influenced by my understanding of the impact of religious strife on the decisions of our forbears to migrate to this continent, and on the decisions of neighbors in the Balkans, Northern Ireland, and the Middle East to mistrust one another. Whenever we remove a brick from the wall that was designed to separate religion and government, we increase the risk of religious strife and weaken the foundation of our democracy.

Justice SOUTER, with whom Justice Stevens, Justice Ginsburg, and Justice Breyer join, dissenting:

. . . . If there were an excuse for giving short shrift to the Establishment Clause, it would probably apply here. But there is no excuse. Constitutional limitations are placed on government to preserve constitutional values in hard cases, like these. . . .

The applicability of the Establishment Clause to public funding of benefits to religious schools was settled in Everson v. Board of Ed. of Ewing, 330 U.S. 1 (1947), which inaugurated the modern era of establishment doctrine. The Court stated the principle in words from which there was no dissent:

"No tax in any amount, large or small, can be levied to support any religious activities or institutions, whatever they may be called, or whatever form they may adopt to teach or practice religion." The Court has never in so many words repudiated this statement, let alone, in so many words, overruled Everson.

Today, however, the majority holds that the Establishment Clause is not offended by Ohio's Pilot Project Scholarship Program, under which students may be eligible to receive as much as $2,250 in the form of tuition vouchers transferable to religious schools. In the city of Cleveland the overwhelming proportion of large appropriations for voucher money must be spent on religious schools if it is to be spent at all, and will be spent in amounts that cover almost all of tuition. The money will thus pay for eligible students' instruction not only in secular subjects but in religion as well, in schools that can fairly be characterized as founded to teach religious doctrine and to imbue teaching in all subjects with a religious dimension. Public tax money will pay at a systemic level for teaching the covenant with Israel and Mosaic law in Jewish schools, the primacy of the Apostle Peter and the Papacy in Catholic schools, the truth of reformed Christianity in Protestant schools, and the revelation to the Prophet in Muslim schools, to speak only of major religious groupings in the Republic.

How can a Court consistently leave Everson on the books and approve the Ohio vouchers? . . . .

[Justice Souter's review of the caselaw is omitted.]

Although it has taken half a century since Everson to reach the majority's twin standards of neutrality and free choice, the facts show that, in the majority's hands, even these criteria cannot convincingly legitimize the Ohio scheme.

A

[T]he majority employs the neutrality criterion in a way that renders it impossible to understand.

Neutrality in this sense refers, of course, to evenhandedness in setting eligibility as between potential religious and secular recipients of public money. Thus, for example, the aid scheme in *Witters* provided an eligible recipient with a scholarship to be used at any institution within a practically unlimited universe of schools; it did not tend to provide more or less aid depending on which one the scholarship recipient chose, and there was no indication that the maximum scholarship amount would be insufficient at secular schools. Neither did any condition of Zobrest's interpreter's subsidy favor religious education. In order to apply the neutrality test, then, it makes sense to focus on a category of aid that may be directed to religious as well as secular schools, and ask whether the scheme favors a religious direction. Here, one would ask whether the voucher provisions, allowing for as much as $2,250 toward private school tuition (or a grant to a public school in an adjacent district), were written in a way that skewed the scheme toward benefiting religious schools.

This, however, is not what the majority asks. The majority looks not to the provisions for tuition vouchers, but to every provision for educational opportunity: "The program permits the participation of *all* schools within the district, [as well as public schools in adjacent districts], religious or nonreligious." The majority then finds confirmation that "participation of *all* schools" satisfies neutrality by noting that the better part of total state educational expenditure goes to public schools, thus showing there is no favor of religion.

The illogic is patent. If regular, public schools (which can get no voucher payments) "participate" in a voucher scheme with schools that can, and public expenditure is still predominantly on public schools, then the majority's reasoning would find neutrality in a scheme of vouchers available for private tuition in districts with no secular private schools at all. "Neutrality" as the majority employs the term is, literally, verbal and nothing more. . . .

B

. . . The majority's view that all educational choices are comparable for purposes of choice . . . ignores the whole point of the choice test. . . . The question is whether the private hand is genuinely free to send the money in either a secular direction or a religious one. The majority now has transformed this question about private choice in channeling aid into a question about selecting from examples of state spending (on education) including direct spending on magnet and community public schools that goes through no private hands and could never reach a religious school under any circumstance. When the choice test is transformed from where to spend the money to where to go to school, it is cut loose from its very purpose.

. . . If "choice" is present whenever there is any educational alternative to the religious school to which vouchers can be endorsed, then there will always be a choice and the voucher can always be constitutional, even in a system in which there is not a single private secular school as an alternative to the religious school. And because it is unlikely that any participating private religious school will enroll more pupils than the generally available public system, it will be easy to generate numbers suggesting that aid to religion is not the significant intent or effect of the voucher scheme.

That is, in fact, just the kind of rhetorical argument that the majority accepts in these cases. . . .

Although leaving the selection of alternatives for choice wide open, as the majority would, virtually guarantees the availability of a "choice" that will satisfy the criterion, limiting the choices to spending choices will not guarantee a negative result in every case. There may, after all, be cases in which a voucher recipient will have a real choice, with enough secular private school desks in relation to the number of religious ones, and a voucher amount high enough to meet secular private school tuition levels. But, even to the extent that choice-to-spend does tend to limit the number of religious funding options that pass muster, the choice criterion has to be understood this way in order, as I have said, for it to function as a limiting principle. Otherwise there is surely no point in requiring the choice to be a true or real or genuine one. . . .

If, contrary to the majority, we ask the right question about genuine choice to use the vouchers, the answer shows that something is influencing choices in a way that aims the money in a religious direction: of 56 private schools in the district participating in the voucher program (only 53 of which accepted voucher students in 1999–2000), 46 of them are religious; 96.6% of all voucher recipients go to religious schools, only 3.4% to nonreligious ones. Unfortunately for the majority position, there is no explanation for this that suggests the religious direction results simply from free choices by parents. One answer to these statistics, for example, which would be consistent with the genuine choice claimed to be operating, might be that 96.6% of families choosing to avail themselves of vouchers choose to educate their children in schools of their own religion. This would not, in my view, render the scheme constitutional, but it would speak to the majority's choice criterion. Evidence shows, however, that almost two out of three families using vouchers to send their children to religious schools did not embrace the religion of those schools. The families made it clear they had not chosen the schools because they wished their children to be proselytized in a religion not their own, or in any religion, but because of educational opportunity.

Even so, the fact that some 2,270 students chose to apply their vouchers to schools of other religions might be consistent with true choice if the students "chose" their religious schools over a wide array of private nonreligious options, or if it could be shown generally that Ohio's program had no effect on educational choices and thus no impermissible effect of advancing religious education. But both possibilities are contrary to fact. First, even if all existing nonreligious private schools in Cleveland were willing to accept large numbers of voucher students, only a few more than the 129 currently enrolled in such schools would be able to attend, as the total enrollment at all nonreligious private schools in Cleveland for kindergarten through eighth grade is only 510 children, and there is no indication that these schools have many open seats. Second, the $2,500 cap that the program places on tuition for participating low-income pupils has the effect of curtailing the participation of nonreligious schools: "nonreligious schools with higher tuition (about $4,000) stated that they could afford to accommodate just a few voucher students." By comparison, the average tuition at participating Catholic schools in Cleveland in 1999–2000 was $1,592, almost $1,000 below the cap.

Of course, the obvious fix would be to increase the value of vouchers so that existing nonreligious private and non-Catholic religious schools would be able to enroll more voucher students, and to provide incentives for educators to create new such schools given that few presently exist. Private choice, if as robust as that available to the seminarian in *Witters,* would then be "true private choice" under the majority's criterion. But it is simply unrealistic to presume that parents of elementary and middle schoolchildren in Cleveland will have a range of secular and religious choices even arguably comparable to the statewide program for vocational and higher education in *Witters.* And to get to that hypothetical point would require that such massive financial support be made available to religion as to disserve every objective of the Establishment Clause even more than the present scheme does.

There is, in any case, no way to interpret the 96.6% of current voucher money going to religious schools as reflecting a free and genuine choice by the families that apply for vouchers. The 96.6% reflects, instead, the fact that too few nonreligious school desks are available and few but religious schools can afford to accept more than a handful of voucher students....

III.

...

A

The scale of the aid to religious schools approved today is unprecedented, both in the number of dollars and in the proportion of systemic school expenditure supported....

B

It is virtually superfluous to point out that every objective underlying the prohibition of religious establishment is betrayed by this scheme, but something has to be said about the enormity of the violation. . . . [These objectives are, first,] respect for freedom of conscience. Jefferson described it as the idea that no one "shall be compelled to . . . support any religious worship, place, or ministry whatsoever."

As for the second objective, to save religion from its own corruption, Madison wrote of the " 'experience . . . that ecclesiastical establishments, instead of maintaining the purity and efficacy of Religion, have had a contrary operation.' " . . .

The risk is already being realized. In Ohio, for example, a condition of receiving government money under the program is that participating religious schools may not "discriminate on the basis of . . . religion," which means the school may not give admission preferences to children who are members of the patron faith; children of a parish are generally consigned to the same admission lotteries as non-believers. . . . Indeed, a separate condition that "[t]he school . . . not . . . teach hatred of any person or group on the basis of . . . religion," could be understood (or subsequently broadened) to prohibit religions from teaching traditionally legitimate articles of faith as to the error, sinfulness, or ignorance of others, if they want government money for their schools. . . .

When government aid goes up, so does reliance on it; the only thing likely to go down is independence.

As appropriations for religious subsidy rise, competition for the money will tap sectarian religion's capacity for discord. . . . [I]t is enough to say that the intensity of the expectable friction can be gauged by realizing that the scramble for money will energize not only contending sectarians, but taxpayers who take their liberty of conscience seriously. Religious teaching at taxpayer expense simply cannot be cordoned from taxpayer politics, and every major religion currently espouses social positions that provoke intense opposition. Not all taxpaying Protestant citizens, for example, will be content to underwrite the teaching of the Roman Catholic Church condemning the death penalty. Nor will all of America's Muslims acquiesce in paying for the endorsement of the religious Zionism taught in many religious Jewish schools, which combines "a nationalistic sentiment" in support of Israel with a "deeply religious" element. Nor will every secular taxpayer be content to support Muslim views on differential treatment of the sexes, or, for that matter, to fund the espousal of a wife's obligation of obedience to her husband, presumably taught in any schools adopting the articles of faith of the Southern Baptist Convention. Views like these, and innumerable others, have been safe in the sectarian pulpits and classrooms of this Nation not only because the Free Exercise Clause protects them directly, but because the ban on supporting religious establishment has protected free exercise, by keeping it relatively private. With the arrival of vouchers in religious schools, that privacy will go, and along with it will go confidence that religious disagreement will stay moderate.

Justice BREYER, with whom Justice Stevens and Justice Souter join, dissenting:

I join Justice Souter's opinion, and I agree substantially with Justice Stevens. I write separately, however, to emphasize the risk that publicly financed voucher programs pose in terms of religiously based social conflict. . . .

I.

The First Amendment begins with a prohibition, that "Congress shall make no law respecting an establishment of religion," and a guarantee, that the government shall not prohibit "the free exercise thereof." These Clauses . . . reflect the Framers' vision of an American Nation free of the religious strife that had long plagued the nations of Europe. . . .

[Justice Breyer's discussion of caselaw is omitted.]

The upshot is the development of constitutional doctrine that reads the Establishment Clause as avoiding religious strife, *not* by providing every religion with an *equal opportunity* (say, to secure state funding or to pray in the public schools), but by drawing fairly clear lines of *separation* between church and state — at least where the heartland of religious belief, such as primary religious education, is at issue.

II.

. . . The principle underlying these cases — avoiding religiously based social conflict — remains of great concern. As religiously diverse as America had become when the Court decided its major 20th century Establishment Clause cases, we are exponentially more diverse today. America boasts more than 55 different religious groups and subgroups with a significant number of members. Major religions include, among others, Protestants, Catholics, Jews, Muslims, Buddhists, Hindus, and Sikhs. And several of these major religions contain different subsidiary sects with different religious beliefs. Newer Christian immigrant groups are "expressing their Christianity in languages, customs, and independent churches that are barely recognizable, and often controversial, for European-ancestry". . . .

Under these modern-day circumstances, how is the "equal opportunity" principle to work — without risking the "struggle of sect against sect" against which Justice Rutledge warned? School voucher programs finance the religious education of the young. And, if widely adopted, they may well provide billions of dollars that will do so. Why will different religions not become concerned about, and seek to influence, the criteria used to channel this money to religious schools? Why will they not want to examine the implementation of the programs that provide this money — to determine, for example, whether implementation has biased a program toward or against particular sects, or whether recipient religious schools are adequately fulfilling a program's criteria? If so, just how is the State to resolve the resulting controversies without provoking legitimate fears of the kinds of religious favoritism that, in so religiously diverse a Nation, threaten social dissension?

. . . I recognize that other nations, for example Great Britain and France, have in the past reconciled religious school funding and religious freedom without creating serious strife. Yet British and French societies are religiously more homogeneous — and it bears noting that recent waves of immigration have begun to create problems of social division there as well.

In a society as religiously diverse as ours, the Court has recognized that we must rely on the Religion Clauses of the First Amendment to protect against religious strife, particularly when what is at issue is an area as central to religious belief as the shaping, through primary education, of the next generation's minds and spirits.

III.

I concede that the Establishment Clause currently permits States to channel various forms of assistance to religious schools, for example, transportation costs for students, computers, and secular texts. Yet the consequence has not been great turmoil. . . .

School voucher programs differ, however, in both *kind* and *degree* from aid programs upheld in the past. They differ in kind because they direct financing to a core function of the church: the teaching of religious truths to young children. For that reason the constitutional demand for "separation" is of particular constitutional concern.

Private schools that participate in Ohio's program, for example, recognize the importance of primary religious education, for they pronounce that their goals are to "communicate the gospel," "provide opportunities to . . . experience a faith community," "provide . . . for growth in prayer," and "provide instruction in religious truths and values." History suggests, not that such private school teaching of religion is undesirable, but that *government funding* of this kind of religious endeavor is far more contentious than providing funding for secular textbooks, computers, vocational training, or even funding for adults who wish to obtain a college education at a religious university. Contrary to Justice O'Connor's opinion, history also shows that government involvement in religious primary education is far more divisive than state property tax exemptions for religious institutions or tax deductions for charitable contributions, both of which come far closer to exemplifying the neutrality that distinguishes, for example, fire protection on the one hand from direct monetary assistance on the other. Federal aid to religiously based hospitals, is even further removed from education, which lies at the heartland of religious belief.

Vouchers also differ in *degree*. The aid programs recently upheld by the Court involved limited amounts of aid to religion. But the majority's analysis here appears to permit a considerable shift of taxpayer dollars from public secular schools to private religious schools. That fact, combined with the use to which these dollars will be put, exacerbates the conflict problem. . . .

IV.

I do not believe that the "parental choice" aspect of the voucher program sufficiently offsets the concerns I have mentioned. Parental choice cannot help the taxpayer who does not want to finance the religious education of children. It will not always help the parent who may see little real choice between inadequate nonsectarian public education and adequate education at a school whose religious teachings are contrary to his own. It will not satisfy religious minorities unable to participate because they are too few in number to support the creation of their own private schools. It will not satisfy groups whose religious beliefs preclude them from participating in a government-sponsored program, and who may well feel ignored as government funds primarily support the education of children in the doctrines of the dominant religions.

Discussion

1. *The Supreme Court and social movements.* Like many of the other examples encountered in this book, *Zelman* is the result of social movement politics, in particular, years of social activism and political organization by various conservative and religious groups attempting to change the Constitution's treatment of religion. By the turn of the twenty-first century they had found a friendly audience in the five-person conservative majority on the Supreme Court. Four of those five Justices had been appointed by Presidents Reagan and Bush, who actively sought the support of religious conservatives. Social movement activism is not enough to effect significant constitutional change; it is also important to install jurists who will listen to what social movements have to say.

Note that the majority and concurring opinions spend very little time justifying the result in terms of original intention; indeed, it is the dissenters who invoke the lessons of history and the wisdom of the framers. One reason for this is that by the time *Zelman* had been decided, the majority had a series of doctrinal precedents like *Zobrest, Mitchell,* and *Agostini* to draw from — which had limited or overruled many earlier cases — while the dissenters were largely fighting a rearguard action.

2. *Neutrality and choice.* Like *Mitchell, Zobrest,* and *Agostini, Zelman* represents the emerging approach in Establishment Clause cases, which focuses on whether government benefits are bestowed without regard to religion and on whether the benefits to religion arise from what the majority calls "true private choice." In determining whether a government program is neutral, and whether it offers genuine choice, one must consider the appropriate baseline of expectations. Is the appropriate baseline of comparison the schools that are most likely to benefit from the voucher program or all of the schools that parents may send their children to? (The majority picks the latter, the dissent the former.) Is true private choice the formal opportunity to send a child to a religious or sectarian school, or must one also take economic incentives into account if they will push large numbers of parents toward religious schools? Does a "true private choice" require secular and

religious educational alternatives that are equally affordable for all parents or does it take economic inequalities as an inevitable component of choice?

3. *Blaine amendments.* Although the Supreme Court has held that the Establishment Clause presents no constitutional barriers to voucher programs like the one in *Zelman,* state constitutional provisions may still stand in the way. Many state constitutions feature so-called Blaine amendments, which forbid public monies to be used to finance religious schools or religious education. The amendments are named for James G. Blaine, a nineteenth-century Speaker of the House who championed the idea in a proposed amendment to the U.S. Constitution. Although the federal amendment failed, its substance was adopted in many state constitutions; according to one count as many as 37 states have some form of restriction.[54] Many of the Blaine amendments responded to anti-Catholic and anti-immigrant sentiments among the Protestant majority in the nineteenth century.

How do these amendments interact with *Zelman?* Even if the amendments were passed for the wrong reasons in the nineteenth century, would they be constitutional if enacted today? If so, is there any problem with enforcing the amendments already in the text of state constitutions? See Locke v. Davey, infra.

4. *Multiculturalism and the Constitution.* One way of understanding the purpose of the Religion Clauses is that they offer a settlement between various religious groups who must all live together in a democracy. Justice Breyer argues that the separation principle is best suited to prevent religious strife and cultural conflict, and he argues that as the United States becomes more diverse, separation becomes even more essential. Do you agree? Couldn't one argue in precisely the opposite direction — that as America becomes more multicultural, it is less and less likely that one group will dominate the others — as Protestants dominated Catholics in the nineteenth century — and that religious groups will find a common interest in working for an equitable share of government funding? Or is the danger that in the twenty-first century, Protestants, Catholics, Jews, and Mormons will tend to dominate the process to the exclusion of Muslims, Hindus, Buddhists, Scientologists, and relatively small and politically powerless religions? Do you agree that as a result of the Court's new doctrines, religious groups will ask for and receive an increasingly larger portion of government funding? What, if anything, would be wrong with this result?

5. *"Divisiveness" and the Constitution.* The central focus of Justice Breyer's dissent is the threat of a religion-based politics, which, he suggests, may ultimately threaten the social order. Consider the majority's response:

> Justice Breyer would raise the invisible specters of "divisiveness" and "religious strife" to find the program unconstitutional. It is unclear exactly what sort of principle Justice Breyer has in mind, considering that the program has ignited no "divisiveness" or "strife" other than this litigation. Nor is it clear where Justice Breyer would locate this presumed authority to deprive Cleveland residents of a program that they have chosen but that we subjectively find "divisive." We quite rightly have rejected the claim that some speculative potential for divisiveness bears on the constitutionality of educational aid programs.

Assume that one shares Justice Breyer's concern about "divisive" politics. Does religion present *unique* challenges to a polity, or is it simply fortuitous, given Justice

54. See Laurie Goodstein, In States, Hurdles Loom, New York Times, June 30, 2002.

Breyer's worries, that the Establishment Clause, at least as interpreted by four Justices, selects religion out for special treatment? Consider, for example, fears expressed about the destabilizing impact of race- or ethnic-based politics, or about the politics of "class conflict." Would concerns about the former, for example, justify reading the Fourteenth Amendment to prohibit all race-based classifications, on the grounds that any tolerance of their use, as in affirmative action programs, would generate an unaffordable "divisiveness" in American politics?

5.   *The Welfare State and the Boundary Between Establishment and Free Exercise: What a State May Do Versus What It Must Do*

As with *West Coast Hotel* two generations earlier, *Zelman* can be read to "liberate" states to pass legislation that includes funding of religious schools. Does it do more, however, and *require* such funding, or are states still free to adopt programs that treat religious institutions differently from secular ones?

LOCKE v. DAVEY, 540 U.S. 712 (2004): [The State of Washington established the Promise Scholarship Program to assist needy students with their college expenses. Recipients of Promise Scholarships are allowed to use their funds in any college located within the state, including religious colleges, so long, however, as they are not majoring in "theology." One rationale for this limitation is found in the Washington State constitution, Art. I, §11, which states, in relevant part, "No public money or property shall be appropriated for or applied to any religious worship, exercise or instruction, or the support of any religious establishment."

The statute establishing the Program, in stating that "No aid shall be awarded to any student who is pursuing a degree in theology," does not define "theology," but there was agreement among the litigants that the statute simply codifies the State's constitutional prohibition on providing funds to students to pursue degrees that are "devotional in nature or designed to induce religious faith."

Joshua Davey chose to use his Promise Scholarship at Northwest College, a private Christian college affiliated with the Assemblies of God. Given his long-time desire to become a pastoral minister, he attempted to pursue a double major in pastoral ministries and business management/administration. "There is no dispute," according to the Supreme Court, "that the pastoral ministries degree is devotional and therefore excluded under the Promise Scholarship Program." Davey was therefore informed at the beginning of the 1999-2000 academic year that he could not use his Promise Scholarship to major in the pastoral ministries program. Indeed, a condition of his receiving the scholarship funds was his certification in writing that he was not pursuing such a degree as part of his studies at Northwest. Upon his failure to sign the form, he was denied the scholarship funds to which he would otherwise have been entitled.

Davey sued and prevailed in the Ninth Circuit Court of Appeals. The Supreme Court, in an opinion by Chief Justice Rehnquist, reversed.]

REHNQUIST, C.J.:

[T]he Establishment Clause and the Free Exercise Clause, are frequently in tension. Yet we have long said that "there is room for play in the joints" between them. In other words, there are some state actions permitted by the Establishment Clause but not required by the Free Exercise Clause.

This case involves that "play in the joints" described above. Under our Establishment Clause precedent, the link between government funds and religious training is broken by the independent and private choice of recipients. See Zelman v. Simmons-Harris. As such, there is no doubt that the State could, consistent with the Federal Constitution, permit Promise Scholars to pursue a degree in devotional theology, see *Witters.* The question before us, however, is whether Washington, pursuant to its own constitution, which has been authoritatively interpreted as prohibiting even indirectly funding religious instruction that will prepare students for the ministry, can deny them such funding without violating the Free Exercise Clause.

Davey . . . contends that under the rule we enunciated in Church of Lukumi Babalu Aye, Inc. v. Hialeah, 508 U.S. 520 (1993), the program is presumptively unconstitutional because it is not facially neutral with respect to religion. . . . In *Lukumi,* the city of Hialeah made it a crime to engage in certain kinds of animal slaughter. We found that the law sought to suppress ritualistic animal sacrifices of the Santeria religion. In the present case, the State's disfavor of religion (if it can be called that) is of a far milder kind. It imposes neither criminal nor civil sanctions on any type of religious service or rite. It does not deny to ministers the right to participate in the political affairs of the community. And it does not require students to choose between their religious beliefs and receiving a government benefit. The State has merely chosen not to fund a distinct category of instruction.

Justice Scalia argues, however, that generally available benefits are part of the "baseline against which burdens on religion are measured." Because the Promise Scholarship Program funds training for all secular professions, Justice Scalia contends the State must also fund training for religious professions. But training for religious professions and training for secular professions are not fungible. Training someone to lead a congregation is an essentially religious endeavor. Indeed, majoring in devotional theology is akin to a religious calling as well as an academic pursuit. And the subject of religion is one in which both the United States and state constitutions embody distinct views — in favor of free exercise, but opposed to establishment — that find no counterpart with respect to other callings or professions. That a State would deal differently with religious education for the ministry than with education for other callings is a product of these views, not evidence of hostility toward religion.

Even though the differently worded Washington Constitution draws a more stringent line than that drawn by the United States Constitution, the interest it seeks to further is scarcely novel. In fact, we can think of few areas in which a State's antiestablishment interests come more into play. Since the founding of our country, there have been popular uprisings against procuring taxpayer funds to support church leaders, which was one of the hallmarks of an "established" religion.

Most States that sought to avoid an establishment of religion around the time of the founding placed in their constitutions formal prohibitions against using tax funds to support the ministry. The plain text of these constitutional provisions prohibited *any* tax dollars from supporting the clergy. We have found nothing to indicate, as Justice Scalia contends, that these provisions would not have applied so long as the State equally supported other professions or if the amount at stake was *de minimis.* That early state constitutions saw no problem in explicitly excluding *only* the ministry from receiving state dollars reinforces our conclusion that religious instruction is of a different ilk.[a]

Far from evincing the hostility toward religion which was manifest in *Lukumi*, we believe that the entirety of the Promise Scholarship Program goes a long way toward including religion in its benefits. The program permits students to attend pervasively religious schools, so long as they are accredited. . . . And under the Promise Scholarship Program's current guidelines, students are still eligible to take devotional theology courses. Davey notes all students at Northwest are required to take at least four devotional courses, "Exploring the Bible," "Principles of Spiritual Development," "Evangelism in the Christian Life," and "Christian Doctrine," and some students may have additional religious requirements as part of their majors.

In short, we find neither in the history or text of Article I, §11 of the Washington Constitution, nor in the operation of the Promise Scholarship Program, anything that suggests animus towards religion. Given the historic and substantial state interest at issue, we therefore cannot conclude that the denial of funding for vocational religious instruction alone is inherently constitutionally suspect.

Without a presumption of unconstitutionality, Davey's claim must fail. The State's interest in not funding the pursuit of devotional degrees is substantial and the exclusion of such funding places a relatively minor burden on Promise Scholars. If any room exists between the two Religion Clauses, it must be here. We need not venture further into this difficult area in order to uphold the Promise Scholarship Program as currently operated by the State of Washington.

Justice SCALIA, with whom Justice Thomas joins, dissenting:

I.

. . . When the State makes a public benefit generally available, that benefit becomes part of the baseline against which burdens on religion are measured; and when the State withholds that benefit from some individuals solely on the basis of religion, it violates the Free Exercise Clause no less than if it had imposed a special tax.

That is precisely what the State of Washington has done here. It has created a generally available public benefit, whose receipt is conditioned only on academic performance, income, and attendance at an accredited school. It has then carved out a solitary course of study for exclusion: theology. No field of study but religion is singled out for disfavor in this fashion. Davey is not asking for a special benefit to which others are not entitled. He seeks only *equal* treatment — the right to direct his scholarship to his chosen course of study, a right every other Promise Scholar enjoys.

---

a. The *amici* contend that Washington's Constitution was born of religious bigotry because it contains a so-called "Blaine Amendment," which has been linked with anti-Catholicism. As the State notes and Davey does not dispute, however, the provision in question is not a Blaine Amendment. The enabling Act of 1889, which authorized the drafting of the Washington Constitution, required the state constitution to include a provision "for the establishment and maintenance of systems of public schools, which shall be . . . free from sectarian control." This provision was included in Article IX, §4, of the Washington Constitution ("All schools maintained and supported wholly or in part by the public funds shall be forever free from sectarian control or influence"), and is not at issue in this case. Neither Davey nor *amici* have established a credible connection between the Blaine Amendment and Article I, §11, the relevant constitutional provision. Accordingly, the Blaine Amendment's history is simply not before us.

The Court's reference to historical "popular uprisings against procuring taxpayer funds to support church leaders" is therefore quite misplaced. That history involved not the inclusion of religious ministers in public benefits programs like the one at issue here, but laws that singled them out for financial aid. For example, the Virginia bill at which Madison's Remonstrance was directed provided: "[F]or the support of Christian teachers . . . [a] sum payable for tax on the property within this Commonwealth, is hereby assessed. . . ." A Bill Establishing a Provision for Teachers of the Christian Religion (1784). Laws supporting the clergy in other States operated in a similar fashion. One can concede the Framers' hostility to funding the clergy *specifically,* but that says nothing about whether the clergy had to be excluded from benefits the State made available to all. No one would seriously contend, for example, that the Framers would have barred ministers from using public roads on their way to church.[a]

The Court does not dispute that the Free Exercise Clause places some constraints on public benefits programs, but finds none here, based on a principle of " 'play in the joints.' " I use the term "principle" loosely, for that is not so much a legal principle as a refusal to apply *any* principle when faced with competing constitutional directives. There is nothing anomalous about constitutional commands that abut. A municipality hiring public contractors may not discriminate *against* blacks or *in favor of* them; it cannot discriminate a little bit each way and then plead "play in the joints" when haled into court. If the Religion Clauses demand neutrality, we must enforce them, in hard cases as well as easy ones.

Even if "play in the joints" were a valid legal principle, surely it would apply only when it was a close call whether complying with one of the Religion Clauses would violate the other. But that is not the case here. It is not just that "the State could, consistent with the Federal Constitution, permit Promise Scholars to pursue a degree in devotional theology." The establishment question *would not even be close,* as is evident from the fact that this Court's decision in *Witters* was unanimous. Perhaps some formally neutral public benefits programs are so gerrymandered and devoid of plausible secular purpose that they might raise specters of state aid to religion, but an evenhanded Promise Scholarship Program is not among them.

In any case, the State already has all the play in the joints it needs. There are any number of ways it could respect both its unusually sensitive concern for the conscience of its taxpayers *and* the Federal Free Exercise Clause. It could make the scholarships redeemable only at public universities (where it sets the curriculum), or only for select courses of study. Either option would replace a program that facially discriminates against religion with one that just happens not to subsidize it. The State could also simply abandon the scholarship program altogether. If that seems a dear price to pay for freedom of conscience, it is only because the State has

---

a. Equally misplaced is the Court's reliance on founding-era state constitutional provisions that prohibited the use of tax funds to support the ministry. There is no doubt what these provisions were directed against: measures of the sort discussed earlier in text, singling out the clergy for public support. The Court offers no historical support for the proposition that they were meant to exclude clergymen from general benefits available to all citizens. In choosing to interpret them in that fashion, the Court needlessly gives them a meaning that not only is contrary to our Religion Clause jurisprudence, but has no logical stopping-point short of the absurd. No State with such a constitutional provision has, so far as I know, ever prohibited the hiring of public employees who use their salary to conduct ministries, or excluded ministers from generally available disability or unemployment benefits. . . .

defined that freedom so broadly that it would be offended by a program with such an incidental, indirect religious effect.

What is the nature of the State's asserted interest here? It cannot be protecting the pocketbooks of its citizens; given the tiny fraction of Promise Scholars who would pursue theology degrees, the amount of any citizen's tax bill at stake is *de minimis*. It cannot be preventing mistaken appearance of endorsement; where a State merely declines to penalize students for selecting a religious major, "[n]o reasonable observer is likely to draw . . . an inference that the State itself is endorsing a religious practice or belief." Nor can Washington's exclusion be defended as a means of assuring that the State will neither favor nor disfavor Davey in his religious calling. Davey will throughout his life contribute to the public fisc through sales taxes on personal purchases, property taxes on his home, and so on; and nothing in the Court's opinion turns on whether Davey winds up a net winner or loser in the State's tax-and-spend scheme.

No, the interest to which the Court defers is not fear of a conceivable Establishment Clause violation, budget constraints, avoidance of endorsement, or substantive neutrality — none of these. It is a pure philosophical preference: the State's opinion that it would violate taxpayers' freedom of conscience *not* to discriminate against candidates for the ministry. This sort of protection of "freedom of conscience" has no logical limit and can justify the singling out of religion for exclusion from public programs in virtually any context. The Court never says whether it deems this interest compelling (the opinion is devoid of any mention of standard of review) but, self-evidently, it is not.[b]

II.

The Court makes no serious attempt to defend the program's neutrality, and instead identifies two features thought to render its discrimination less offensive. The first is the lightness of Davey's burden. The Court offers no authority for approving facial discrimination against religion simply because its material consequences are not severe. The indignity of being singled out for special burdens on the basis of one's religious calling is so profound that the concrete harm produced can never be dismissed as insubstantial. The Court has not required proof of "substantial" concrete harm with other forms of discrimination, see, *e.g.,* Brown v. Board of Education, 347 U.S. 483 (1954); cf. Craig v. Boren, 429 U.S. 190 (1976), and it should not do so here.

b. The Court argues that those pursuing theology majors are not comparable to other Promise Scholars because "training for religious professions and training for secular professions are not fungible." That may well be, but all it proves is that the State has a *rational basis* for treating religion differently. If that is all the Court requires, its holding is contrary not only to precedent, but to common sense. If religious discrimination required only a rational basis, the Free Exercise Clause would impose no constraints other than those the Constitution already imposes on all government action. The question is not whether theology majors are different, but whether the differences are substantial enough to justify a discriminatory financial penalty that the State inflicts on no other major. Plainly they are not.

Equally unpersuasive is the Court's argument that the State may discriminate against theology majors in distributing public benefits because the Establishment Clause and its state counterparts are themselves discriminatory. The Court's premise is true at some level of abstraction — the Establishment Clause discriminates against religion by singling it out as the one thing a State may not establish. All this proves is that a State has a compelling interest in not committing *actual* Establishment Clause violations. We have never inferred from this principle that a State has a constitutionally sufficient interest in discriminating against religion in whatever other context it pleases, so long as it claims some connection, however attenuated, to establishment concerns.

Even if there were some threshold quantum-of-harm requirement, surely Davey has satisfied it. The First Amendment, after all, guarantees *free* exercise of religion, and when the State exacts a financial penalty of almost $3,000 for religious exercise — whether by tax or by forfeiture of an otherwise available benefit — religious practice is anything *but* free. The Court's only response is that "Promise Scholars may still use their scholarship to pursue a secular degree at a different institution from where they are studying devotional theology." But part of what makes a Promise Scholarship attractive is that the recipient can apply it to his *preferred* course of study at his *preferred* accredited institution. That is part of the "benefit" the State confers. The Court distinguishes our precedents only by swapping the benefit to which Davey was actually entitled (a scholarship for his chosen course of study) with another, less valuable one (a scholarship for any course of study *but* his chosen one). On such reasoning, any facially discriminatory benefits program can be redeemed simply by redefining what it guarantees.

The other reason the Court thinks this particular facial discrimination less offensive is that the scholarship program was not motivated by animus toward religion. The Court does not explain why the legislature's motive matters, and I fail to see why it should. If a State deprives a citizen of trial by jury or passes an *ex post facto* law, we do not pause to investigate whether it was actually trying to accomplish the evil the Constitution prohibits. It is sufficient that the citizen's rights have been infringed. "[It does not] matter that a legislature consists entirely of the pure-hearted, if the law it enacts in fact singles out a religious practice for special burdens."

The Court has not approached other forms of discrimination this way. When we declared racial segregation unconstitutional, we did not ask whether the State had originally adopted the regime, not out of "animus" against blacks, but because of a well-meaning but misguided belief that the races would be better off apart. It was sufficient to note the current effect of segregation on racial minorities. Similarly, the Court does not excuse statutes that facially discriminate against women just because they are the vestigial product of a well-intentioned view of women's appropriate social role. We do sometimes look to legislative intent to smoke out more subtle instances of discrimination, but we do so as a *supplement* to the core guarantee of facially equal treatment, not as a replacement for it.

There is no need to rely on analogies, however, because we have rejected the Court's methodology in this very context. In McDaniel v. Paty, 435 U.S. 618 (1978), we considered a Tennessee statute that disqualified clergy from participation in the state constitutional convention. That statute, like the one here, was based upon a state constitutional provision — a clause in the 1796 Tennessee Constitution that disqualified clergy from sitting in the legislature. The State defended the statute as an attempt to be faithful to its constitutional separation of church and state, and we accepted that claimed benevolent purpose as bona fide. Nonetheless, because it did not justify facial discrimination against religion, we invalidated the restriction.

It may be that Washington's original purpose in excluding the clergy from public benefits was benign, and the same might be true of its purpose in maintaining the exclusion today. But those singled out for disfavor can be forgiven for suspecting more invidious forces at work. Let there be no doubt: This case is about discrimination against a religious minority. Most citizens of this country identify themselves as professing some religious belief, but the State's policy poses no obstacle to practitioners of only a tepid, civic version of faith. Those the statutory exclusion actually affects — those whose belief in their religion is so strong that they dedicate their study and their lives to its ministry — are a far narrower set. One need not delve too far into modern popular culture to perceive a trendy disdain for deep religious conviction. In an era when the Court is so quick to come to the aid of other disfavored groups, see, *e.g.,* Romer v. Evans, its indifference in this case, which involves a form of discrimination to which the Constitution actually speaks, is exceptional.

Discussion

1. *Vouchers for private schools.* After Zelman v. Simmons-Harris, a key question was no longer whether states could include sectarian schools in voucher programs, but whether they could exclude sectarian schools from voucher programs if they included secular private schools, or if they allowed formation of privately run charter schools. Does Locke v. Davey help to answer that question? Note Justice Scalia's assumption that Washington "could make the [Promise] scholarships redeemable only at public universities." What if the scholarships could not be used in religiously affiliated private schools? Pervasively religious private schools?

2. Recall Justice Brennan's vigorous dissent in Harris v. McRae, which upheld the federal government's refusal to fund abortions except in very limited situations. Many political liberals sympathized with Brennan's argument that the state had a duty to fund abortions if it, for example, also funded childbirth. Yet we have also seen Justice Brennan consistently vote with majorities, such as those in *Nyquist,* that strike down the distribution of governmental funds to religious schools. Is there a tension — indeed, a contradiction — here? Consider then-Professor Michael McConnell's "revised" version of Justice Brennan's dissent in *Harris,* in which McConnell changes the issue in *Harris* from abortion funding to the provision of funds to parents who wish to exercise their constitutional right, see Pierce v. Society of Sisters, to send their children to religious schools.[55]

> A poor woman [with school-age children] confronts two alternatives: she may elect either to [send them to secular schools] or to [send them to religious schools]. In the abstract, of course, the choice is hers alone, and the Court rightly observes that [*Lemon*] "places no governmental obstacle in the path of a woman who chooses to [send her children to religious school]." But the reality of the situation is that [the Supreme Court in its decisions] has effectively removed this choice from the indigent woman's hands. By funding all of the expenses associated with [secular education] and none of the expenses incurred in [religious education,] the Government literally makes an offer that the indigent woman cannot afford to refuse. It matters not that in this instance the Government has used the carrot rather than the stick. What is critical is the realization that as a practical matter, many poverty-stricken women will choose to [send their children to secular schools] simply because the Government provides funds for [this,] even though these same women would have chosen [religious schools] if the Government had also paid for that option, or indeed if the Government had stayed out of the picture altogether and had defrayed the costs of neither.

Consider also the implications of Justice Brennan's dissent in *DeShaney,* in which he emphasized the consequences of state decisions for private decisionmaking. Does not the burden of state taxation to fund public education make it difficult

55. Michael W. McConnell, The Selective Funding Problem: Abortions and Religious Schools, 104 Harv. L. Rev. 989, 990 (1991).

even for nonindigent families to afford private secular and parochial education? If
you think this is constitutionally relevant, would you agree as well that the burdens
of state education taxes also make it more difficult to purchase health care or any
other goods of life or make it less likely that other people will have enough dispos-
able income to contribute to scholarship funds or charities that look after the indigent? Is the state responsible, after all, for the plight of those without sufficient
material resources to purchase necessary services?

6. Administering the Welfare State Through Religious Organizations

BOWEN v. KENDRICK
487 U.S. 589 (1988)

REHNQUIST, C.J., delivered the opinion of the Court.

This litigation involves a challenge to a federal grant program that provides
funding for services relating to adolescent sexuality and pregnancy. Considering
the federal statute both "on its face" and "as applied," the District Court ruled that
the statute violated the Establishment Clause of the First Amendment insofar as it
provided for the involvement of religious organizations in the federally funded
programs. We conclude, however, that the statute is not unconstitutional on its face,
and that a determination of whether any of the grants made pursuant to the statute
violate the Establishment Clause requires further proceedings in the District Court.

I.

The Adolescent Family Life Act (AFLA or Act) was passed by Congress in 1981 in
response to the "severe adverse health, social, and economic consequences" that often
follow pregnancy and childbirth among unmarried adolescents. Like its predecessor,
the Adolescent Health Services and Pregnancy Prevention and Care Act of 1978, the
AFLA is essentially a scheme for providing grants to public or nonprofit private organizations or agencies "for services and research in the area of premarital adolescent
sexual relations and pregnancy." These grants are intended to serve several purposes,
including the promotion of "self discipline and other prudent approaches to the
problem of adolescent premarital sexual relations," the promotion of adoption as an
alternative for adolescent parents, the establishment of new approaches to the delivery of care services for pregnant adolescents, and the support of research and demonstration projects "concerning the societal causes and consequences of adolescent
premarital sexual relations, contraceptive use, pregnancy, and child rearing."

. . . In drawing up the AFLA and determining what services to provide under
the Act, Congress was well aware that "the problems of adolescent premarital
sexual relations, pregnancy, and parenthood are multiple and complex." . . .
Accordingly, the AFLA expressly states that federally provided services in this area
should promote the involvement of parents, and should "emphasize the provision of support by other family members, religious and charitable organizations,
voluntary associations, and other groups." . . . The AFLA implements this goal by
providing . . . that demonstration projects funded by the government "shall use
such methods as will strengthen the capacity of families to deal with the sexual

behavior, pregnancy, or parenthood of adolescents and to make use of support systems such as other family members, friends, religious and charitable organizations, and voluntary associations."

In addition, AFLA requires grant applicants, among other things, to describe how they will, "as appropriate in the provision of services[,] involve families of adolescents[, and] involve religious and charitable organizations, voluntary associations, and other groups in the private sector as well as services provided by publicly sponsored initiatives."

. . . Since 1981, when the AFLA was adopted, the Secretary has received 1,088 grant applications and awarded 141 grants. Funding has gone to a wide variety of recipients, including state and local health agencies, private hospitals, community health associations, privately operated health care centers, and community and charitable organizations. It is undisputed that a number of grantees or subgrantees were organizations with institutional ties to religious denominations. . . .

II.

. . . [W]e turn to consider whether the District Court was correct in concluding that the AFLA was unconstitutional on its face. As in previous cases involving facial challenges on Establishment Clause grounds, we assess the constitutionality of an enactment by reference to the three factors first articulated in Lemon v. Kurtzman, 403 U.S. 602 (1971). Under the *Lemon* standard, which guides "[t]he general nature of our inquiry in this area," a court may invalidate a statute only if it is motivated wholly by an impermissible purpose, if its primary effect is the advancement of religion, or if it requires excessive entanglement between church and state. We consider each of these factors in turn.

. . . AFLA was motivated primarily, if not entirely, by a legitimate secular purpose — the elimination or reduction of social and economic problems caused by teenage sexuality, pregnancy, and parenthood. . . . As usual in Establishment Clause cases, the more difficult question is whether the primary effect of the challenged statute is impermissible. Before we address this question, however, it is useful to review again just what the AFLA sets out to do. Simply stated, it authorizes grants to institutions that are capable of providing certain care and prevention services to adolescents. Because of the complexity of the problems that Congress sought to remedy, potential grantees are required to describe how they will involve other organizations, including religious organizations, in the programs funded by the federal grants. . . .

The services to be provided under the AFLA are not religious in character, nor has there been any suggestion that religious institutions or organizations with religious ties are uniquely well qualified to carry out those services. Certainly it is true that a substantial part of the services listed as "necessary services" under the Act involve some sort of education or counseling, but there is nothing inherently religious about these activities and appellees do not contend that, by themselves, the AFLA's "necessary services" somehow have the primary effect of advancing religion. Finally, it is clear that the AFLA takes a particular approach toward dealing with adolescent sexuality and pregnancy — for example, two of its stated purposes are to "promote self discipline and other prudent approaches to the problem of adolescent premarital sexual relations," and to "promote adoption as an alternative" — but again, that approach is not inherently religious, although it may coincide with the approach taken by certain religions.

Given this statutory framework, there are two ways in which the statute, considered "on its face," might be said to have the impermissible primary effect of advancing religion. First, it can be argued that the AFLA advances religion by expressly recognizing that "religious organizations have a role to play" in addressing the problems associated with teenage sexuality. In this view, even if no religious institution receives aid or funding pursuant to the AFLA, the statute is invalid under the Establishment Clause because, among other things, it expressly enlists the involvement of religiously affiliated organizations in the federally subsidized programs, it endorses religious solutions to the problems addressed by the Act, or it creates symbolic ties between church and state. Secondly, it can be argued that the AFLA is invalid on its face because it allows religiously affiliated organizations to participate as grantees or subgrantees in AFLA programs. From this standpoint, the Act is invalid because it authorizes direct federal funding of religious organizations which, given the AFLA's educational function and the fact that the AFLA's "viewpoint" may coincide with the grantee's "viewpoint" on sexual matters, will result unavoidably in the impermissible "inculcation" of religious beliefs in the context of a federally funded program.

We consider the former objection first. As noted previously, the AFLA expressly mentions the role of religious organizations in four places. It states (1) that the problems of teenage sexuality are "best approached through a variety of integrated and essential services provided to adolescents and their families by[, among others,] religious and charitable organizations," (2) that federally subsidized services "should emphasize the provision of support by[, among others,] religious organizations," that AFLA programs "shall use such methods as will strengthen the capacity of families . . . to make use of support systems such as . . . religious . . . organizations," and (4) that grant applicants shall describe how they will involve religious organizations, among other groups, in the provision of services under the Act.

Putting aside for the moment the possible role of religious organizations as grantees, these provisions of the statute reflect at most Congress' considered judgment that religious organizations can help solve the problems to which the AFLA is addressed. Nothing in our previous cases prevents Congress from making such a judgment or from recognizing the important part that religion or religious organizations may play in resolving certain secular problems. . . . In addition, although the AFLA does require potential grantees to describe how they will involve religious organizations in the provision of services under the Act, it also requires grantees to describe the involvement of "charitable organizations, voluntary associations, and other groups in the private sector."

In our view, this reflects the statute's successful maintenance of "a course of neutrality among religions, and between religion and non-religion." This brings us to the second ground for objecting to the AFLA: the fact that it allows religious institutions to participate as recipients of federal funds. . . . [A] fairly wide spectrum of organizations is eligible to apply for and receive funding under the Act, and nothing on the face of the Act suggests it is anything but neutral with respect to the grantee's status as a sectarian or purely secular institution. In this regard, then, the AFLA is similar to other statutes that this Court has upheld against Establishment Clause challenges in the past. In Roemer v. Maryland Board of Public Works, 426 U.S. 736 (1976), for example, we upheld a Maryland statute that provided annual subsidies directly to qualifying colleges and universities in the State, including religiously affiliated institutions. As the plurality stated, "religious institutions need not be quarantined from public benefits that are neutrally available to all." . . . In other cases involving indirect grants of state aid to religious institutions, we have found it important that the aid is made available regardless of whether it will ultimately flow to a secular or sectarian institution.

We note in addition that this Court has never held that religious institutions are disabled by the First Amendment from participating in publicly sponsored social welfare programs. To the contrary, in Bradfield v. Roberts, 175 U.S. 291 (1899), the Court upheld an agreement between the Commissioners of the District of Columbia and a religiously affiliated hospital whereby the Federal Government would pay for the construction of a new building on the grounds of the hospital. In effect, the Court refused to hold that the mere fact that the hospital was "conducted under the auspices of the Roman Catholic Church" was sufficient to alter the purely secular legal character of the corporation, particularly in the absence of any allegation that the hospital discriminated on the basis of religion or operated in any way inconsistent with its secular charter. In the Court's view, the giving of federal aid to the hospital was entirely consistent with the Establishment Clause, and the fact that the hospital was religiously affiliated was "wholly immaterial." The propriety of this holding, and the long history of cooperation and interdependency between governments and charitable or religious organizations is reflected in the legislative history of the AFLA.

Of course, even when the challenged statute appears to be neutral on its face, we have always been careful to ensure that direct government aid to religiously affiliated institutions does not have the primary effect of advancing religion. One way in which direct government aid might have that effect is if the aid flows to institutions that are "pervasively sectarian." . . . [A] relevant factor in deciding whether a particular statute on its face can be said to have the improper effect of advancing religion is the determination of whether, and to what extent, the statute directs government aid to pervasively sectarian institutions. . . . In this lawsuit, nothing on the face of the AFLA indicates that a significant proportion of the federal funds will be disbursed to "pervasively sectarian" institutions. Indeed, the contention that there is a substantial risk of such institutions receiving direct aid is undercut by the AFLA's facially neutral grant requirements, the wide spectrum of public and private organizations which are capable of meeting the AFLA's requirements, and the fact that, of the eligible religious institutions, many will not deserve the label of "pervasively sectarian." . . . [W]e do not think the possibility that AFLA grants may go to religious institutions that can be considered "pervasively sectarian" is sufficient to conclude that no grants whatsoever can be given under the statute to religious organizations. We think that the District Court was wrong in concluding otherwise.

Nor do we agree with the District Court that the AFLA necessarily has the effect of advancing religion because the religiously affiliated AFLA grantees will be providing educational and counseling services to adolescents. Of course, we have said that the Establishment Clause does "prohibit government-financed or government-sponsored indoctrination into the beliefs of a particular religious faith," and we have accordingly struck down programs that entail an unacceptable risk that government funding would be used to "advance the religious mission" of the religious institution receiving aid. But nothing in our prior cases warrants the presumption adopted by the District Court that religiously affiliated AFLA grantees are not capable of carrying out their functions under the AFLA in a lawful, secular manner. Only in the context of aid to "pervasively sectarian" institutions have we invalidated an aid program on the grounds that there was a "substantial" risk that aid to these religious institutions would, knowingly or unknowingly, result in religious indoctrination. In contrast, when the aid is to flow to religiously affiliated institutions that were not pervasively sectarian, . . . we refused to presume that it would be used in a way that would have the primary effect of advancing religion. We think that the type of presumption that the District Court applied in this case is simply unwarranted. . . .

We also disagree with the District Court's conclusion that the AFLA is invalid because it authorizes "teaching" by religious grant recipients on "matters [that] are fundamental elements of religious doctrine," such as the harm of premarital sex and the reasons for choosing adoption over abortion. On an issue as sensitive and important as teenage sexuality, it is not surprising that the Government's secular concerns would either coincide or conflict with those of religious institutions. But the possibility or even the likelihood that some of the religious institutions who receive AFLA funding will agree with the message that Congress intended to deliver to adolescents through the AFLA is insufficient to warrant a finding that the statute on its face has the primary effect of advancing religion.

Nor does the alignment of the statute and the religious views of the grantees run afoul of our proscription against "fund[ing] a specifically religious activity in an otherwise substantially secular setting." The facially neutral projects authorized by the AFLA — including pregnancy testing, adoption counseling and referral services, prenatal and postnatal care, educational services, residential care, child care, consumer education, etc. — are not themselves "specifically religious activities," and they are not converted into such activities by the fact that they are carried out by organizations with religious affiliations.

As yet another reason for invalidating parts of the AFLA, the District Court found that the involvement of religious organizations in the Act has the impermissible effect of creating a "crucial symbolic link" between government and religion. If we were to adopt the District Court's reasoning, it could be argued that any time a government aid program provides funding to religious organizations in an area in which the organization also has an interest, an impermissible "symbolic link" could be created, no matter whether the aid was to be used solely for secular purposes. This would jeopardize government aid to religiously affiliated hospitals, for example, on the ground that patients would perceive a "symbolic link" between the hospital — part of whose "religious mission" might be to save lives — and whatever government entity is subsidizing the purely secular medical services provided to the patient. We decline to adopt the District Court's reasoning and conclude that, in this litigation, whatever "symbolic link" might in fact be created by the AFLA's disbursement of funds to religious institutions is not sufficient to justify striking down the statute on its face.

. . . This, of course, brings us to the third prong of the Lemon Establishment Clause "test" — the question whether the AFLA leads to "an excessive government entanglement with religion." There is no doubt that the monitoring of AFLA grants is necessary if the Secretary is to ensure that public money is to be spent in the way that Congress intended and in a way that comports with the Establishment Clause. Accordingly, this litigation presents us with yet another "Catch-22" argument: the very supervision of the aid to assure that it does not further religion renders the statute invalid. For this and other reasons, the "entanglement" prong of the Lemon test has been much criticized over the years. Most of the cases in which the Court has divided over the "entanglement" part of the *Lemon* test have involved aid to parochial schools. . . .

Here, by contrast, there is no reason to assume that the religious organizations which may receive grants are "pervasively sectarian" in the same sense as the Court has held parochial schools to be. There is accordingly no reason to fear that the less intensive monitoring involved here will cause the Government to intrude unduly in the day-to-day operation of the religiously affiliated AFLA grantees. Unquestionably, the Secretary will review the programs set up and run by the AFLA grantees, and undoubtedly this will involve a review of, for example, the educational materials that a grantee proposes to use. The Secretary may also wish to have Government employees visit the clinics or offices where AFLA programs are being carried out to see whether they are in fact being administered in accordance with statutory and constitutional requirements. But in our view, this type of grant monitoring does not amount to "excessive entanglement," at least in the context of a statute authorizing grants to religiously affiliated organizations that are not necessarily "pervasively sectarian." In sum, . . . we have concluded that the statute has a valid secular purpose, does not have the primary effect of advancing religion, and does not create an excessive entanglement of church and state. . . . [W]e conclude that the AFLA does not violate the Establishment Clause "on its face."

III.

We turn now to consider whether the District Court correctly ruled that the AFLA was unconstitutional as applied. . . . On the merits of the "as applied" challenge, it seems to us that the District Court did not follow the proper approach in assessing appellees' claim that the Secretary is making grants under the Act that violate the Establishment Clause of the First Amendment. Although the District Court stated several times that AFLA aid had been given to religious organizations that were "pervasively sectarian," it did not identify which grantees it was referring to, nor did it discuss with any particularity the aspects of those organizations which in its view warranted classification as "pervasively sectarian." The District Court did identify certain instances in which it felt AFLA funds were used for constitutionally improper purposes, but in our view the court did not adequately design its remedy to address the specific problems it found in the Secretary's administration of the statute. Accordingly, although there is no dispute that the record contains evidence of specific incidents of impermissible behavior by AFLA grantees, we feel that this lawsuit should be remanded to the District Court for consideration of the evidence presented by appellees insofar as it sheds light on the manner in which the statute is presently being administered. . . .

[Concurring opinions by Justice O'Connor and by Justice Kennedy, joined by Justice Scalia, are omitted.]

BLACKMUN, J., with whom Brennan, Marshall, and Stevens, JJ., join, dissenting:

. . . It is unclear whether Congress ever envisioned that public funds would pay for a program during a session of which parents and teenagers would be instructed:

> "You want to know the church teachings on sexuality. . . . You are the church. You people sitting here are the body of Christ. The teachings of you and the things you value are, in fact, the values of the Catholic Church."

Or of curricula that taught:

> "The Church has always taught that the marriage act, or intercourse, seals the union of husband and wife (and is a representation of their union on all levels). Christ commits Himself to us when we come to ask for the sacrament of marriage. We ask Him to be active in our life. God is love. We ask Him to share His love in ours, and God procreates with us, He enters into our physical union with Him, and we begin new life."

Or the teaching of a method of family planning described on the grant application as "not only a method of birth regulation but also a philosophy of procreation," and promoted as helping "spouses who are striving . . . to transform their married life into testimony[,] . . . to cultivate their matrimonial spirituality[, and] to make themselves better instruments in God's plan," and as "facilitat[ing] the evangelization of homes."

Whatever Congress had in mind, however, it enacted a statute that facilitated and, indeed, encouraged the use of public funds for such instruction, by giving religious groups a central pedagogical and counseling role without imposing any restraints on the sectarian quality of the participation. As the record developed thus far in this litigation makes all too clear, federal tax dollars appropriated for AFLA purposes have been used, with Government approval, to support religious teaching. Today the majority upholds the facial validity of this statute and remands the action to the District Court for further proceedings concerning appellees' challenge to the manner in which the statute has been applied. Because I am firmly convinced that our cases require invalidating this statutory scheme, I dissent.

I.

. . . By designating appellees' broad attack on the statute as a "facial" challenge, the majority justifies divorcing its analysis from the extensive record developed in the District Court, and thereby strips the challenge of much of its force and renders the evaluation of the *Lemon* "effects" prong particularly sterile and meaningless. By characterizing appellees' objections to the real-world operation of the AFLA an "as-applied" challenge, the Court risks misdirecting the litigants and the lower courts toward piecemeal litigation continuing indefinitely throughout the life of the AFLA. In my view, a more effective way to review Establishment Clause challenges is to look to the type of relief prayed for by the plaintiffs, and the force of the arguments and supporting evidence they marshal. Whether we denominate a challenge that focuses on the systematically unconstitutional operation of a statute a "facial" challenge — because it goes to the statute as a whole — or an "as-applied" challenge — because we rely on real-world events — the Court should not blind itself to the facts revealed by the undisputed record.

. . . [T]his law suit has been litigated primarily as a broad challenge to the statutory scheme as a whole, not just to the awarding of grants to a few individual applicants.

The thousands of pages of depositions, affidavits, and documentary evidence were not intended to demonstrate merely that particular grantees should not receive further funding. Indeed, because of the 5-year grant cycle, some of the original grantees are no longer AFLA participants. This record was designed to show that the AFLA had been interpreted and implemented by the Government in a manner that was clearly unconstitutional, and appellees sought declaratory and injunctive relief as to the entire statute. . . .

II.

Before proceeding to apply *Lemon's* three-part analysis to the AFLA, I pause to note a particular flaw in the majority's method. A central premise of the majority opinion seems to be that the primary means of ascertaining whether a statute that appears to be neutral on its face in fact has the effect of advancing religion is to determine whether aid flows to "pervasively sectarian" institutions. . . .

"Pervasively sectarian," a vaguely defined term of art, has its roots in this Court's recognition that government must not engage in detailed supervision of the inner workings of religious institutions, and the Court's sensible distaste for the "picture of state inspectors prowling the halls of parochial schools and auditing classroom instruction." Under the "effects" prong of the *Lemon* test, the Court has used one variant or another of the pervasively sectarian concept to explain why any but the most indirect forms of government aid to such institutions would necessarily have the effect of advancing religion. For example, in *Meek*, the Court explained: .

> "[I]t would simply ignore reality to attempt to separate secular educational functions from the predominantly religious role performed by many of Pennsylvania's church-related elementary and secondary schools and to then characterize Act 195 as channeling aid to the secular without providing direct aid to the sectarian."

The majority first skews the Establishment Clause analysis by adopting a cramped view of what constitutes a pervasively sectarian institution. Perhaps because most of the Court's decisions in this area have come in the context of aid to parochial schools, which traditionally have been characterized as pervasively sectarian, the majority seems to equate the characterization with the institution. In support of that, the majority relies heavily on three cases in which the Court has upheld direct government funding to liberal arts colleges with some religious affiliation, noting that such colleges were not "pervasively sectarian." But the happenstance that the few cases in which direct-aid statutes have been upheld have concerned religiously affiliated liberal arts colleges no more suggests that only parochial schools should be considered "pervasively sectarian," than it suggests that the only religiously affiliated institutions that may ever receive direct government funding are private liberal arts colleges. In fact, the cases on which the majority relies have stressed that the institutions' "predominant higher education mission is to provide their students with a secular education." In sharp contrast, the District Court here concluded that AFLA grantees and participants included "organizations with institutional ties to religious denominations and corporate requirements that the organizations abide by and not contradict religious doctrines. In addition, other recipients of AFLA funds, while not explicitly affiliated with a religious denomination, are religiously inspired and dedicated to teaching the dogma that inspired them." On a continuum of "sectarianism" running from parochial schools at one end to the colleges funded by the statutes [that have been] upheld . . . at the other, the AFLA grantees described by the District Court clearly are much closer to the former than to the latter.

More importantly, the majority also errs in suggesting that the inapplicability of the label is generally dispositive. While a plurality of the Court has framed the inquiry as "whether an institution is so 'pervasively sectarian' that it may receive no direct state aid of any kind," Roemer v. Maryland Public Works Board, the Court never has treated the absence of such a finding as a license to disregard the potential for impermissible fostering of religion. The characterization of an institution as "pervasively sectarian" allows us to eschew further inquiry into the use that will be made of direct government aid. In that sense, it is a sufficient, but not a necessary, basis for a finding that a challenged program creates an unacceptable Establishment Clause risk. The label thus serves in some cases as a proxy for a more detailed analysis of the institution, the nature of the aid, and the manner in which the aid may be used.

The voluminous record compiled by the parties and reviewed by the District Court illustrates the manner in which the AFLA has been interpreted and implemented by the agency responsible for the aid program, and eliminates whatever need there might be to speculate about what kind of institutions might receive funds and how they might be selected; the record explains the nature of the activities funded with Government money, as well as the content of the educational programs and materials developed and disseminated. There is no basis for ignoring the volumes of depositions, pleadings, and undisputed facts reviewed by the District Court simply because the recipients of the Government funds may not in every sense resemble parochial schools.

III.

As is often the case, it is the effect of the statute, rather than its purpose, that creates Establishment Clause problems. Because I have no meaningful disagreement with the majority's discussion of the AFLA's essentially secular purpose, and because I find the statute's effect of advancing religion dispositive, I turn to that issue directly.

A. . . .

(1)

. . . The AFLA, unlike any statute this Court has upheld, pays for teachers and counselors, employed by and subject to the direction of religious authorities, to educate impressionable young minds on issues of religious moment. Time and again we have recognized the difficulties inherent in asking even the best-intentioned individuals in such positions to make "a total separation between secular teaching and religious doctrine." Where the targeted audience is composed of children, of course, the Court's insistence on adequate safeguards has always been greatest. In those cases in which funding of colleges with religious affiliations has been upheld, the Court has relied on the assumption that "college students are less impressionable and less susceptible to religious indoctrination. . . . The skepticism of the college student is not an inconsiderable barrier to any attempt or tendency to subvert the congressional objectives and limitations."

(2)

By observing that the alignment of the statute and the religious views of the grantees do not render the AFLA a statute which funds "specifically religious activity," the majority makes light of the religious significance in the counseling provided by some grantees. Yet this is a dimension that Congress specifically sought to capture by enlisting the aid of religious organizations in battling the problems associated with teenage pregnancy. Whereas there may be secular values promoted by the AFLA, including the encouragement of adoption and premarital chastity and the discouragement of abortion, it can hardly be doubted that when promoted in theological terms by religious figures, those values take on a religious nature. Not surprisingly, the record is replete with observations to that effect. It should be undeniable by now that religious dogma may not be employed by government even to accomplish laudable secular purposes such as "the promotion of moral values, the contradiction to the materialistic trends of our times, the perpetuation of our institutions and the teaching of literature." . . .

There is a very real and important difference between running a soup kitchen or a hospital, and counseling pregnant teenagers on how to make the difficult decisions facing them. The risk of advancing religion at public expense, and of creating an appearance that the government is endorsing the medium and the message, is much greater when the religious organization is directly engaged in pedagogy, with the express intent of shaping belief and changing behavior, than where it is neutrally dispensing medication, food, or shelter. . . .

B

. . . [Justice Blackmun criticizes the statute for failing specifically to limit the ways that federal funds can be spent.]

IV.

. . . [T]he unconstitutionality of the statute becomes even more apparent when we consider the unprecedented degree of entanglement between Church and State required to prevent subsidizing the advancement of religion with AFLA funds. . . .

To determine whether a statute fosters excessive entanglement, a court must look at three factors: (1) the character and purpose of the institutions benefited; (2) the nature of the aid; and (3) the nature of the relationship between the government and the religious organization. Thus, in *Lemon*, it was not solely the fact that teachers performed their duties within the four walls of the parochial school that rendered monitoring difficult and, in the end, unconstitutional. It seems inherent in the pedagogical function that there will be disagreements about what is or is not "religious" and which will require an intolerable degree of government intrusion and censorship. . . . As the majority readily acknowledges, the Secretary will have to "review the programs set up and run by the AFLA grantees [, including] a review of, for example, the educational materials that a grantee proposes to use." And, as the majority intimates, monitoring the use of AFLA funds will undoubtedly require more than the "minimal" inspection "necessary to ascertain that the facilities are devoted to secular education." Since teachers and counselors, unlike buildings, "are not necessarily religiously neutral, greater governmental surveillance would be required to guarantee that state salary aid would not in fact subsidize religious instruction." . . .

Discussion

Section 104 of the Personal Responsibility and Work Opportunity Reconciliation Act of 1996 includes the following language:

(1) STATE OPTIONS A state may

(A) administer and provide services under the programs described [in the Act] through contracts with charitable, religious, or private organizations; and

(B) provide beneficiaries of assistance under the programs described [in the Act] with certificates, vouchers, or other forms of disbursement which are redeemable with such organizations. . . .

(b) RELIGIOUS ORGANIZATIONS The purpose of this section is to allow States to contract with religious organizations, or to allow religious organizations to accept certificates, vouchers, or other forms of disbursement under any program described [earlier], on the same basis as any other nongovernmental provider without impairing the religious character of such organization, and without diminishing the religious freedom of beneficiaries of assistance funded under such program.

(c) NONDISCRIMINATION AGAINST RELIGIOUS ORGANIZATIONS . . . [R]eligious organizations are eligible, on the same basis as any other private organization, as contractors to provide assistance, or to accept certificates, vouchers, or other forms of disbursement, under any program described [earlier] so long as the programs are implemented consistent with the Establishment Clause of the United States Constitution. . . .

(d) RELIGIOUS CHARACTER AND FREEDOM

(1) RELIGIOUS ORGANIZATIONS A religious organization with a contract described [above] . . . shall retain its independence from Federal, State, and local governments, including such organization's control over the definition, development, practice, and expression of its religious beliefs.

(2) ADDITIONAL SAFEGUARDS Neither the Federal Government nor a State shall require a religious organization to

(A) alter its form of internal governance; or

(B) (B) remove religious art, icons, scripture, or other symbols; in order to be eligible [for federal funds]. . . .

(e) RIGHTS OF BENEFICIARIES OF ASSISTANCE

(1) IN GENERAL If an individual . . . has an objection to the religious character of the organization or institution from which the individual receives, or would receive, assistance . . . , the State in which the individual resides shall provide such individual . . . within a reasonable period of time after the date of such objection with assistance from an alternative provider that is accessible to the individual and the value of which is not less than the value of the assistance which the individual would have received from such organization.

By 2000, both candidates supported the use of "faith-based institutions" to implement the welfare state; indeed, incorporation of such institutions into governmental programs has been a motif of President George W. Bush's administration. Many constitutional issues are presented by such programs, most of them beyond the limited scope of this casebook. Consider for now only the following, based on the language of §104:

a) A young person seeking treatment for the use of drugs is assigned to a religiously sponsored program that meets in a room that prominently features the religious symbols of the particular religion. Assume as well that, upon registering an objection, the youngster is told that there are no other programs currently available. He sues. What result?

b) A state inspector, charged with the task of making sure that the beneficiaries of state funds do not use them for illegitimate purposes, discovers that religious symbols, as well as religious literature, are prominently displayed (with large signs in front of the stand containing the religious literature saying "TAKE SOME") in the waiting room immediately outside the room in which the program meets, where every participant usually spends 10 to 15 minutes before moving into the room next door (which does not contain any religious symbols at all). The inspector demands that the literature be moved to a less prominent place. As the lawyer to the religious institution, what would you advise?

Note: A Concluding Conundrum — Disaster Relief, the Welfare State, and the Establishment Clause

As noted earlier, the origins of the welfare state can be said to lie in the provision by the state to victims of disasters. An important agency of the contemporary national government is the Federal Emergency Management Administration (FEMA), which immediately responds to disasters, whether natural (e.g., a hurricane) or otherwise (e.g., the 1995 Oklahoma City bombing). FEMA commonly offers low-interest loans or outright grants to victims, including owners of damaged buildings, for purposes of repairing property that has been damaged. Can (or must) FEMA limit disaster relief to buildings that serve only "secular purposes," or should aid be available, for example, to rebuild the apse of a church or replace the shattered Ark of the Covenant in which Torah scrolls are placed in synagogues?

Consider in this context a September 25, 2002, memorandum signed by Jay Bybee, then the head of the Office of Legal Counsel (OLC) within the Justice Department, to the General Counsel of FEMA analyzing "whether [FEMA] may . . . provide disaster assistance to the Seattle Hebrew Academy," which, "like other Seattle institutions, sustained severe damage as a result of" an earthquake the previous year. The OLC is responsible for issuing authoritative opinions, upon request of the president or any given executive-branch agency, as to the meaning of federal statutes and their legitimacy under the Constitution. OLC opinions guide the executive branch interpretation of the Constitution until overruled by judicial decision, and hence determine the Constitution's practical effect in a wide variety of situations.

FEMA had earlier denied the Academy's application for assistance on the ground that "the Academy's building was not a 'private nonprofit facility'" within the meaning of the relevant statute "because it was not open to 'the general public.'" The FEMA official had "determined that a religiously affiliated educational facility is not open to 'the general public' if it only admits students of a particular faith." The OLC ruled that this was not a proper interpretation of the relevant congressional statutes. That did not conclude the inquiry, because the next question, of course, was whether such aid was permissible under the Establishment Clause.

. . . Although there is no precedent that directly controls this specific issue, we conclude that the Establishment Clause does not pose a barrier to FEMA's provision of a disaster assistance grant to the Academy. The aid that is authorized by federal law is made available on the basis of neutral criteria to an unusually broad class of beneficiaries defined without reference to religion and including not only educational institutions but a host of other public and private institutions as well. Moreover, the program's design is not characterized by the sort of administrative discretion that can readily be used to favor religion, and the evidence demonstrates that FEMA has exercised its discretion in a neutral manner. Thus, we believe that provision of disaster assistance to the Academy cannot be materially distinguished from aid programs that are constitutional under longstanding Supreme Court precedent establishing that religious institutions are fully entitled to receive generally available government benefits and services, such as fire and police protection.

[T]he FEMA grants in question are made available not only to public and private schools, but to "private nonprofit . . . utility, irrigation, emergency, medical, rehabilitational, and temporary or permanent custodial care facilities (including those for the aged and disabled), other private nonprofit facilities which provide essential services of a governmental nature to the general public, and facilities on Indian reservations as defined by the President." 42 U.S.C.A. §5122(9). Accordingly, we think that the "circumference" of this program can fairly be said to " 'encircle[] a class so broad that it can be fairly concluded that religious institutions could be thought to fall within the natural perimeter.' " Texas Monthly, Inc. v. Bullock, 489 U.S. 1, 17 (1989) (plurality opinion) (quoting Walz v. Tax Commn., 397 U.S. 664, 696 (1970) (Harlan, J.)). As the Court stated in Widmar v. Vincent, 454 U.S. 263, 274 (1981), "[t]he provision of benefits to so broad a spectrum of groups is an important index of secular effect." Accord Texas Monthly, 489 U.S. at 14-15 (plurality opinion) ("[i]nsofar as [a] subsidy is conferred upon a wide array of nonsectarian groups as well as religious organizations in pursuit of some legitimate secular end, the fact that religious groups benefit incidentally does not deprive the subsidy of the secular purpose and primary effect mandated by the Establishment Clause" (footnote omitted)). . . . We cannot say, however, that there are no arguments to the contrary. Most important, there is an argument that providing FEMA disaster relief to repair a school used for religious instruction would run afoul of Supreme Court precedent restricting the use of "direct" aid that can be put to specifically religious uses. In particular, one might argue that insofar as the grant used to rebuild the Academy's building would ultimately support the building's use for secular *and* religious purposes — *i.e.*, both secular and religious teaching — such aid is unlawful under Supreme Court decisions from the 1970s holding that public construction grants for educational institutions may not be applied toward buildings used for religious purposes. . . .

The argument that direct aid to education unlawfully advances the mission of religious schools applies with the greatest force where such schools constitute a substantial percentage of those that receive aid. That argument is much harder to make where the aid is provided to a range of nonprofit institutions of which schools are but one part. The broad class of beneficiaries that are eligible for aid under the statute here . . . confirms that, in contrast to the education-specific aid at issue in the foregoing cases, the disaster relief provided by FEMA serves goals entirely unrelated to education — namely, rehabilitation of a community that has suffered great loss from a natural disaster by helping to rebuild institutions that perform quasi-public functions and are (by virtue of their nonprofit status) most in need of assistance.

We find further support for our decision in the fact that [the 1970s cases] are in considerable tension with a long and growing line of cases holding that the Free Speech Clause does not permit the government to deny religious groups equal access to *the government's own property*, even where such groups seek to use the property " 'for purposes of religious worship or religious teaching.' " Widmar v. Vincent, 454 U.S. 263, 265 (1981). See *Lamb's Chapel*. Providing religious groups with access to property is a form of direct aid — albeit not financial aid — and allowing such groups to conduct worship services plainly "advances" their religious mission. The Court, however, has consistently refused to *permit* (let alone require) state officials to deny churches equal access to public school property "on the ground that to permit its property to be used for religious purposes would be an establishment of religion." Indeed, the Court has gone so far as to extend the reasoning of these cases to require equal *funding* of religious student expression, reasoning that "[e]ven the provision of a meeting room . . . involve[s] governmental expenditure" for "upkeep, maintenance, and repair of the facilities." See *Rosenberger.*

As in *Rosenberger,* the issue here "lies at the intersection of the principle of government neutrality and the prohibition on state funding of religious activities." In such a case, "[r]eliance on categorical platitudes," such as an absolute "no direct aid" principle, "is unavailing.". . . . Accordingly, we conclude that the FEMA assistance here is more analogous to the police and fire services discussed in *Everson* than to the educational assistance at issue in [the 1970s cases].

For similar reasons, we do not believe that a reasonable observer would perceive an endorsement of religion in the government's evenhanded provision of aid to a religious school damaged by an earthquake. . . . Our conclusion is strongly supported by the evidence regarding FEMA's application of the criteria for receiving funds under the Act. Apart from the Academy, of the 268 Nisqually Earthquake applications on which FEMA has ruled, 267 applicants–all but *one*–were declared eligible for funding. It thus appears that there is little exercise of discretion regarding religion in the distribution of grant funds — indeed, in this instance, funding was virtually automatic — and the diverse makeup of those that have received funds confirms that the program's administration is not "skewed towards religion." This largely (if not entirely) eliminates any "special risks" that direct aid "will have the effect of advancing religion (or, even more, a purpose of doing so)." . . . Of the funded institutions, 245 are public facilities, while only 22 are private nonprofit facilities. The public facilities include, among other things, schools and school districts (of which there are 63), fire stations, libraries, prisons, utilities, and buildings that provide public social services. The private facilities likewise include a broad array of institutions — hospitals and other health facilities, low income housing centers, social services organizations, and even a "maritime discovery center." Judging from the names of the private organizations, moreover, it appears that only a handful have religious affiliations. In sum, we see no basis for concern that FEMA administrators have discretion to favor religious applicants, or that those administrators have exercised what little discretion they do have in a manner that favors religion.

Discussion

The OLC memo clearly gives the executive branch *permission* to award funds to religious institutions, as does a later memorandum, issued on April 30, 2003, concerning historic preservation grants to help restore still-operating churches of historical significance, such as the Old North Church in Boston from which Paul Revere received the signal to begin his famous ride.[56] This latter opinion reverses an earlier 1995 memorandum, written by then-Assistant Attorney General for OLC Walter Dellinger (see *http://www.usdoj.gov/olc/doi.24.htm*), that held such grants unconstitutional.[57]

The Seattle earthquake was of minor significance compared to the devastation wrought by Hurricane Katrina in 2005. No doubt many churches and synagogues were destroyed along with thousands upon thousands of homes and businesses. So what should FEMA's response be when religious institutions ask for the same

56. See Memorandum from M. Edward Whelan III, to the Solicitor, Department of the Interior: Authority of the Department of the Interior to Provide Historic Preservation Grants to Historic Religious Properties such as The Old North Church, available at *http://www.usdoj.gov/olc/OldNorthChurch.htm.*

57. See Ira C. Lupu and Robert Tuttle, Historic Preservation Grants to Houses of Worship: A Case Study in the Survival of Separationism, 43 Boston College L. Rev. 1139 (2002).

degree of aid as will undoubtedly be available to homeowners and businesses? Does the OLC memorandum — or *Rosenberger*—mean that FEMA or other agencies might be under a *duty* to award funds to religious institutions if they are, in effect, among the few (or only) institutions excluded from participation in a wide-ranging program of the modern welfare state. Does Locke v. Davey shed light on this question? If you were assisting a member of Congress charged with drafting post-Katrina disaster-relief legislation, what would you advise?

Table of Justices

Year	President	Chief (1)	2	3	4	5	6	7	8	9
1789	George Washington (1789-1797)	John Jay (1789-1795)	John Rutledge (1789-1791)	William Cushing (1789-1810)	James Wilson (1789-1798)	John Blair (1789-1795)				
1790							James Iredell (1790-1799)			
• • • •			Thomas Johnson (1791-1793)							
			William Paterson (1793-1806)							
1795	John Adams (1797-1801)	John Rutledge (1795) Oliver Ellsworth (1796-1800)			Bushrod Washington (1798-1829)	Samuel Chase (1796-1811)	Alfred Moore (1799-1804)			
• • • • •										
1800										

Year	President	Chief (1)	2	3	4	5	6	7	8	9
	Thomas Jefferson (1801-1809)	John Marshall (1801-1835) (appointed by Adams)								
1805										
			H. Brockholst Livingston (1806-1823)				William Johnson (1804-1834)	Thomas Todd (1807-1826)		
	James Madison (1809-1817)									
1810										
				Joseph Story (1811-1845)		Gabriel Duvall (1811-1835)				
1815										

Year	President	Chief (1)	2	3	4	5	6	7	8	9
•	James Monroe (1817-1825)									
•										
1820										
•										
•										
•			Smith Thompson (1823-1843)							
•										
1825	John Quincy Adams (1825-1829)									
•								Robert Trimble (1826-1828)		
•										
•	Andrew Jackson (1829-1837)							John McLean (1829-1861)		
1830					Henry Baldwin (1830-1844)					
•										
•										

Year	President	Chief (1)	2	3	4	5	6	7	8	9
· · 1835 · · · · 1840 · · · · 1845 ·	Martin Van Buren (1837-1841) William Henry Harrison (1841) John Tyler (1841-1845) James K. Polk (1845-1849)	Roger B. Taney (1836-1864)	Samuel Nelson (1845-1872) (appointed by Tyler)	Levi Woodbury (1845-1851)	Robert C. Grier (1846-1870)	Philip P. Barbour (1836-1841) Peter V. Daniel 1841-1860 (appointed by Van Buren)	James M. Wayne (1835-1867)		John Catron (1837-1865)	John McKinley (1837-1852)

Year	President	Chief (1)	2	3	4	5	6	7	8	9
	Zachary Taylor (1849-1850)									
	Millard Fillmore (1850-1853)									
1850										
				Benjamin R. Curtis (1851-1857)						
	Franklin Pierce (1853-1857)									John A. Campbell (1853-1861)
	James Buchanan (1857-1861)									
1855										
				Nathan Clifford (1858-1881)						
1860	Abraham Lincoln (1861-1865)									

Year	President	Chief (1)	2	3	4	5	6	7	8	9
						Samuel F. Miller (1862-1890)		Noah H. Swayne (1862-1881)	Stephen J. Field[1] (1863-1897) (held tenth seat)	David Davis (1862-1877)
		Salmon P. Chase (1864-1873)								
1865	Andrew Johnson (1865-1869)									
[2]										
	Ulysses S. Grant (1869-1877)				William Strong (1870-1880)	Joseph P. Bradley (1870-1892)				
1870			Ward Hunt (1872-1882)							

1 Congress established a tenth seat in 1863, to which Stephen J. Field was appointed.

2 Congress reduced the size of the Court to six justices in 1866. As a result, the seats of Justices Catron and Wayne remained unfilled after their deaths in 1865 and 1867. Congress restored the Court to nine seats in 1869.

Year	President	Chief (1)	2	3	4	5	6	7	8	9
		Morrison Waite (1874-1888)								John Marshall Harlan (1877-1911)
1875	Rutherford B. Hayes (1877-1881)									
1880	James A. Garfield (1881) Chester A. Arthur (1881-1885)		Samuel Blatchford (1882-1893)	Horace Gray (1881-1902) (appointed by Arthur)	William B. Woods (1880-1887)			Stanley Matthews (1881-1889) (appointed by Garfield)		

Year	President	Chief (1)	2	3	4	5	6	7	8	9
1885	Grover Cleveland (1885-1889)									
		Melville W. Fuller (1888-1910)			Lucius Q.C. Lamar (1888-1893)					
	Benjamin Harrison (1889-1893)							David J. Brewer (1889-1910)		
1890						Henry B. Brown (1890-1906)				
							George Shiras (1892-1903)			
	Grover Cleveland (1893-1897)				Howell E. Jackson (1893-1895) (appointed by Harrison)					
			Edward D. White (1894-1910)							
1895					Rufus W. Peckham (1895-1909)					

Year	President	Chief (1)	2	3	4	5	6	7	8	9
•										
•	William McKinley (1897-1901)									
1900										
•										
•	Theodore Roosevelt (1901-1909)			Oliver Wendell Holmes (1902-1932)						
•							William R. Day (1903-1922)			
•						William H. Moody (1906-1910)				
1905									Joseph McKenna (1898-1925)	
•										
•										
•	William Howard Taft (1909-1913)				Horace H. Lurton (1909-1914)					
•										

Year	President	Chief (1)	2	3	4	5	6	7	8	9
1910		Edward D. White (1910-1921)	Willis Van Devanter (1910-1937)			Joseph R. Lamar (1910-1916)		Charles E. Hughes (1910-1916)		Mahlon Pitney (1912-1922)
	Woodrow Wilson (1913-1921)				James C. McReynolds (1914-1941)					
1915						Louis D. Brandeis (1916-1939)		John H. Clarke (1916-1922)		
1920	Warren G. Harding (1921-1923)	William Howard Taft (1921-1930)					Pierce Butler (1922-1939)	George Sutherland (1922-1938)		

Year	President	Chief (1)	2	3	4	5	6	7	8	9
	Calvin Coolidge (1923-1929)									Edward T. Sanford (1923-1930) (appointed by Harding)
1925									Harlan F. Stone (1925-1941)	
	Herbert Hoover (1929-1933)									
1930		Charles E. Hughes (1930-1941)								Owen J. Roberts (1930-1945)
				Benjamin N. Cardozo (1932-1938)						
	Franklin D. Roosevelt (1933-1945)									
1935			Hugo L. Black (1937-1971)							

Year	President	Chief (1)	2	3	4	5	6	7	8	9
				Felix Frankfurter (1939-1962)		William O. Douglas (1939-1975)		Stanley F. Reed (1938-1957)		
1940							Frank Murphy (1940-1949)			
		Harlan F. Stone (1941-1946)			James F. Byrnes (1941-1942)				Robert H. Jackson (1941-1954)	
					Wiley B. Rutledge (1943-1949)					
1945	Harry S. Truman (1945-1953)									Harold H. Burton (1945-1958)
		Fred M. Vinson (1946-1953)								
					Sherman Minton (1949-1956)		Tom C. Clark (1949-1967)			
1950										

Year	President	Chief (1)	2	3	4	5	6	7	8	9
		Earl Warren (1953-1969)								
1955									John Marshall Harlan (1955-1971)	
					William J. Brennan, Jr. (1956-1990)			Charles E. Whittaker (1957-1962)		Potter Stewart (1958-1981)
1960										
	John F. Kennedy (1961-1963)			Arthur J. Goldberg (1962-1965)				Byron R. White (1962-1993)		
	Lyndon B. Johnson (1963-1969)			Abe Fortas (1965-1969)						
1965										

Year	President	Chief (1)	2	3	4	5	6	7	8	9
	Richard M. Nixon (1969-1974)	Warren E. Burger (1969-1986)	Lewis F. Powell, Jr. (1972-1987)	Harry A. Blackmun (1970-1994)		John Paul Stevens (1975-)	Thurgood Marshall (1967-1991)		William H. Rehnquist (1972-1986)	
1970										
1975	Gerald Ford (1974-1977)									
1980	Jimmy Carter (1977-1981)									

Year	President	Chief (1)	2	3	4	5	6	7	8	9
	Ronald Reagan (1981-1989)	William H. Rehnquist (1986-2005)	Anthony M. Kennedy (1988-)	Stephen G. Breyer (1994-)	David H. Souter (1990-)		Clarence Thomas (1991-)	Ruth Bader Ginsburg (1993-)	Antonin Scalia (1986-)	Sandra Day O'Connor (1981-2006)
1985										
	George Bush (1989-1993)									
1990										
	William J. Clinton (1993-2001)									

Year	President	Chief (1)	2	3	4	5	6	7	8	9
1995 • • • • • •										
2000 • • • • •	George W. Bush (2001-2009)									
2005 •		John G. Roberts (2005-)								Samuel A. Alito, Jr. (2006-)

Table of Cases

Index